The Sports Encyclopedia: Pro Basketball

Other Books Authored by Sports Products Inc.

PRO FOOTBALL: THE EARLY YEARS
THE SPORTS ENCYCLOPEDIA: BASEBALL
THE SPORTS ENCYCLOPEDIA: PRO FOOTBALL
THE SCRAPBOOK HISTORY OF BASEBALL
THE SCRAPBOOK HISTORY OF PRO FOOTBALL
THE ALL-SPORTS WORLD RECORD BOOK
THE WORLD SERIES
THE WORLD BOOK OF ODDS
MONDAY MORNING QUARTERBACK
THE COMPLETE ALL-TIME BASEBALL REGISTER
THE COMPLETE ALL-TIME PRO FOOTBALL REGISTER
THE UNIVERSITY OF MICHIGAN FOOTBALL SCRAPBOOK
THE NOTRE DAME FOOTBALL SCRAPBOOK
THE OHIO STATE FOOTBALL SCRAPBOOK
PRO FOOTBALL WEEKLY'S 1980 ALMANAC
PRO FOOTBALL WEEKLY'S 1981 ALMANAC
BEAT THE SPREAD 1982
THE PRO FOOTBALL BETTOR'S COMPANION

The Sports Encyclopedia: Pro Basketball

3rd Edition

David S. Neft & Richard M. Cohen

Revised and updated with assistance from John Hogrogian and Bob Gill

St. Martin's Press
New York

 For information, address St. Martin's Press, 175 Fifth Avenue, New York, N.Y. 10010.

Library of Congress Cataloging-in-Publication Data

Neft, David S.

The sports encyclopedia. Pro basketball, 1891–1990 / David S. Neft & Richard M. Cohen.—3rd ed.

p. cm.

Rev. ed. of: The Sports encyclopedia. Pro basketball. c1975.

ISBN 0-312-05162-X

1. Basketball—History. 2. Basketball—Records. 3. Basketball—United States—History. I. Cohen, Richard M., 1938– II. Sports encyclopedia. Pro basketball. III. Title.

GV885.5.N44 1990

796.323'64'0973—dc20 90-37267 CIP

Third Edition

10 9 8 7 6 5 4 3 2

CONTENTS

1976-77 through 1989-90

New Teams, New Players, More TV, More Money

PREFACE

The Sports Encyclopedia: Pro Basketball (3rd edition) is the third reference book in a continuing series of major sports encyclopedias. The two other books in the series, *The Sports Encyclopedia: Baseball and The Sports Encyclopedia: Pro Football,* were first published in 1974 with the latest updates in 1990.

The book presents the most complete statistical record of professional basketball. It also provides an historical summary of professional basketball as it was played from its infancy to the game as it is played today.

As with the other books in this series, the authors have arranged the material into various periods. The first period, 1937-1946, covers the National Basketball League. The second period, 1946-1954 includes the N.B.L., the Basketball Association of America (1946-1949), and the National Basketball Association, which was formed when the N.B.L. and the B.A.A. merged for the start of the 1949-1950 season. The third major period runs from 1954-1967, starting with the revolutionary 24-second rule in 1954. The next major period starts in 1967, when the American Basketball Association was formed, and the last period begins in 1976-1977, marking the demise of A.B.A. and expansion into the N.B.A.

Needless to say, the task of assembling the amount of demographic, statistical, and historical data contained in this book could not have been accomplished by the two authors alone. In order to make this book a reality the cooperation and efforts of many individuals and institutions were needed. The authors would like to take this opportunity to acknowledge all those who contributed so much of their time and energy to help shape the most complete encyclopedia of professional basketball.

Manuscript Preparation Chiefs —
- Roland T. Johnson
- Jordan A. Deutsch

Chief consultants in the preparation of the written manuscript—
- John G. Hogrogian
- Bob Gill

Basketball Hall of Fame —
- Joseph O'Brien, Executive Director
- Wayne Patterson, Research Specialist
- James Chute, Hall of Fame Intern
- Tom Trudell, Hall of Fame Intern

American Basketball Association —
- Jim Bukata, Public Relations Director

National Basketball Association

Continental Basketball Association

Independent Contributors —
- Jimmy Carter
- John Duxbury
- Richard A. Gill
- Stan Grosshandler
- Bill Himmelman
- George Mashin, Detroit Pistons
- Bill Mokray
- Patrick K. Petree, Goodyear International Corp.
- Gordon Sears, Dow Chemical
- Mark Swayne
- Bob Troyer, Firestone Tire & Rubber Co.

Former Players and Coaches —
- Benny Borgmann
- Ernie Calverly
- Al Cervi
- Ray Corley
- Bob Douglas
- Marty Friedman
- George Glamack
- Eddie Gottlieb
- Nick Grunzweig
- Nat Holman
- Fuzzy Levane
- Mike Novak
- Elmer Ripley

Sports Information Directors (at the time) —
- Jerry Kissel, University of Cincinnati
- Sidney Fox, University of Detroit
- Russell Rice, University of Kentucky
- Otis Dypwick, University of Minnesota
- Roger Valdiserri, University of Notre Dame
- Ted Haracz, Purdue University
- Father Leonard Piotrowski, S.J.Marquette University

Libraries —
- Buffalo and Erie County Historical Society, Buffalo, N.Y..
- Dayton & Montgomery County Public Library, Dayton, Ohio
- Hammond Public Library, Hammond, Ind.
- Illinois State Historical Society, Springfield, Ill.
- Indiana State Library, Indianapolis, Ind.
- Michigan State University Library, Lansing, Mich.
- Newington Public Library, Newington, Conn.
  - Gertrude Hollings, Librarian
- Ohio State Historical Society, Columbus, Ohio
- State Historical Society of Wisconsin, Madison, Wisc.
- University of Northern Iowa Library, Cedar Falls, Iowa
- University of Wisconsin at Oshkosh, Oshkosh, Wisc.

St. Martin's Press —
- George Witte, Editor

Computer Data and Type —
- Land Systems: (Ridgefield, CT)
  - David M. Land
  - Carrie W. Gordon
  - Sarah Thornburg

The author's wives (whose faith and cooperation continue): Naomi Neft and Nancy Cohen.

A book of this magnitude will include some errors (we hope very few), therefore the authors would appreciate, for the purpose of keeping future editions as accurate and complete as possible, if readers would send any corrections and additions to:

SPORTS PRODUCTS, INC.
P.O. Box 458
Ridgefield, CT 06877

Codes and Explanations

In each section of the book there are certain abbreviations and other markings that may not be familiar to the reader. The following, by section, is an explanation of this matter:

Yearly Sections

Age — The age shown for each player is as of January 1st of that year

Traded Players — The records of men who played with two or more teams in the same league in one season are shown in two ways:

1 — The player is listed with each of the teams he played for and his statistics are shown separately for each team. This method has been used wherever the data were available; for all the years of the National Basketball League and the American Basketball Association and the National Basketball Association since 1964-65.

2 — The player is shown only on the last team he played for during the season with his entire season record.

Bold Facing — Indicates league leaders. When team playoff statistics are shown, the league leading team in any category is designated on a per game basis.

Team Name Line — Shown alongside the name of each team is the team Won-Lost record and the head coaches.

Career Interruptions — Whenever a symbol appears in parentheses after a player's name, it indicates a career interruption of 30 days or more duration, or a career end due to injury, illness, or some other reason. These symbols are explained under the Career Interruption Codes on this page

Playoff Game Scores — The letter "H" in front of the score indicates a home game.

Register Sections

Players have been assigned to the various register sections according to the time period in which they played the most, starting with 1937-38. The register sections are broken down into five periods: 1937-38 through 1945-56, 1946-47 through 1953-54, 1954-55 through 1966-67, 1967-68 through 1975-76, and 1976-77 through the present.

Each player is shown with one or two lines of statistical information. The first line represents lifetime regular season statistics. The second line represents lifetime playoff statistics. If any statistic appears in bold face, it means that the data were not available for the player's entire career.

Year Codes — Alongside each player's name are the years and teams for which he played. Only the last two digits of the year are given so that "55" means 1955. Also, even though each season spanned two years, only the second year is indicated so that "55" refers to the 1954-1955 season.

League Codes — Following the year and team played for is the code for the league. "N" indicates the N.B.L. and "A" indicates the A.B.A. If a player played in the N.B.A. or the B.A.A., the league is not shown, only the team

HC — Indicates that the individual was a non-playing head coach.

PC — Indicates that the individual was a player coach.

Weight — Player's average weight for his career.

Career Interruption Codes

If a player missed a year of had a career end due to any of the following reasons, it would be shown after the year using the following codes (or as an interruption during the season):

AA — Injured in automobile accident
AJ — Arm injury
AL — Alcohol problem
BA — Broken arm
BB — Left before end of season to report for baseball spring training
BC — Broken or dislocated collarbone
BE — Broken bone in elbow
BF — Broken bone in foot
BG — Broken finger
BH — Broken bone in hand
BJ — Broken jaw
BK — Broken bone in knee
BL — Broken leg
BN — Broken ankle
BP — Broken hip bone
BR — Broken rib or ribs
BS — Broken bone in shoulder
BT — Broken toe
BW — Broken wrist
BX — Broken spine
BY — Broken cheek bone
BZ — Broken nose
CC — Missed some games because of duties as college coach
CJ — Face injury
CN — Concussion
CO — Missed some games attending college
CP — Blood poisoning
CT — Court order prohibiting player from playing with new team after switching leagues.
DD — Died during the season or the following off-season
DE — Declared ineligible by commissioner
DL — Declared inelgible for life by commissioner
DR — Drug problem
EJ — Elbow injury
FB — Reported late from playing professional football
FJ — Foot of heel injury
FR — Badly burned
FS — Fractured skull
GJ — Groin injury
GW — Gunshot wounds
HJ — Hand injury
HO — Holdout
IF — Didn't play in order to be with a family member who was ill
IJ — Eye injury
IL — Illness
JJ — Injury or on disable list — type of injury unknown
KJ — Knee injury
LJ — Leg or thigh injury — including Achilles tendon
MD — Missed some games attending medical school or interning
MS — Military service
NJ — Ankle injury
PJ — Hip injury
QJ — Brain injury
RB — Retired to play baseball
RC — Retired to coach
RJ — Finger injury
SJ — Shoulder injury
SL — Suspended by commissioner or league president
SR — Sat out for religious reasons
ST — Suspended by team
TJ — Chest injury
UJ — Side injury
VJ — Rib injury
VR — Voluntarily retired
WJ — Wrist injury
WW — Voluntarily retired or played only part time while working for the government or in plants producing war material
XJ — Back injury
YJ — Head injury
ZJ — Neck injury

1891-1931

A Game to Break the Winter Boredom

I

The cold early winter of December, 1891 underlined a flaw in the curriculum to James Naismith, a thirty-year-old physical education instructor at the International YMCA Training School in Springfield, Massachusetts. Naismith's gym class enthusiastically followed the fall program of football and other outdoor games, but his students found the indoor program of calisthenics and gymnastic activities a crashing bore. Faced with fading interest in his class, Naismith put his mind to developing a new game for the indoor winter season.

After sifting various elements through his mind, he had wooden peach baskets nailed onto the balcony railings at the two ends of the gym, divided his 18-man class into two nine-man teams, gave the players a soccer ball, and provided a loose set of rules which made throwing the ball into the baskets the idea of the game. Thus did Naismith hecome the father of basketball and Springfield its birthplace.

Naismith's game, however, bore little resemblance to today's fast-paced sport. Many rules of the game were tested on a trial-and-error basis, with local variations in the rules becoming common as basketball's popularity spread. For instance, no limit was placed on the number of players in the game; one early outdoor contest at Cornell University had 50 men on each side. The early players also experimented with a foul rule. At first, fouls led to a temporary suspension, much like the penalty box in ice hockey, and only after several years did foul shots become standard.

But even with the confusion over some of the rules, the new game of basketball quickly caught on in the YMCA and in colleges, among both men and women. The YMCA held regional tournaments in the 1890's, while intercollegiate play began in a strictly sectional fashion.

By 1900, basketball was being played throughout the United States and had taken a shape that would be recognizable to a modern basketball fan. Five men made up a team, field goals were worth two points and foul shots one point, and tailormade basketballs and rims were in use. With some exceptions, the rules were the same as today's.

Perhaps the major difference in the rules was the extended use of the center jump. Not only at the start of each period but also after every basket, the referee threw the ball up for grabs at center court. Not until 1937 did the ball automatically go to the team scored against. Fouls and foul-shooting also differed from the modern rules. Until 1923, one man on each team shot all the fouls for his club, a sort of designated free throw man.

Another 1923 rules change demoted from fouls to violations such infractions as walking and double-dribbling. Dribbling has undergone several changes since 1900. Before 1916, a player could not legally shoot the ball after taking a dribble. Into the 1940's, amateur and professional rules had different dribbling codes. The amateur rules were identical with today's rules, while the professional rules allowed two-hand dribbling and discontinued dribbling. Missing from the 1900 rules were the three-second and ten-second rules, with no restriction put on the foul lane or backcourt until 1932.

In addition to the rules, the equipment used in 1900 was somewhat different from that used in modern basketball. Backboards were an optional device well into the 1920's; some places favored wooden backboards, some used wire backings, and some simply connected the hoop without any backing to a long pole. In some areas, the court was surrounded by a rope net cage. This cage, which lasted into the 1920's in some parts ofthe East, kept the ball in bounds at all times and gave the players another surface besides the floor to use for bounce passes. The ball itself was larger than the modern ball until rules changes in the 1930's shrunk it several times .

The tactics of the early game emphasized defense, and produced games in which 20 points was often good enough to win. All shooting was done with the two-hand set shot and the layup, with the jump shot considered a completely unsound tactic. Defense was all man-to-man, very physical, and prone to excessive fouling. In fact, one reason against the use of the jump shot was that it left the shooter open to a mid-air slugging which as often as not went unpunished by the referees. Players regularly played through both 20-minute halves, with substitutions an uncommon occurence. This early game was physical and slow, with centers rarely standing over 6'3"; the contrast with today's baskethall hardly needs underlining

II

This new game of basketball was fun to play and fun to watch, and it became standard fare in many colleges and YMCA's before the turn of the century. Even before 1900, however, the YMCA became disenchanted with the game, seeing gyms monopolized by a comparatively small number of players whose games often showed a most un-Christian roughness and drew crowds whose enthusiasm seemed rather unrespectable. So the YMCA dropped basketball from its program, orphaning hundreds of enthusiastic players.

Thrown out of the only gyms at their disposal, these devoted players decided to rent armories and dance halls in which they could continue playing. But since the rental for these buildings exceeded whatever the men could afford to pay, they decided to admit those same crowds that had gathered at the YMCA and to charge them an admission fee. Any money left over after the rent was paid was split among the players. These first professionals thus turned pro not to make money, but simply to keep on playing their game. Although there is no incontestable evidence, a group of YMCA players in Trenton, New Jersey, in 1896 are generally honored as the first professionals.

Promoters soon came into the game, combining a love of basketball with a desire for profits. Promoters would hire players on a per-game basis and arrange contests against local outfits who might bring in a crowd on the basis of local rivalry or reputation. These early team owners used promotions other than basketball to bring in a crowd. Many promoters offered dancing before and after games; a band might play from 6:00 to 8:00 for dancing, then the floor would be cleared for the basketball game, and the music and dancing would resume. Of course, playing in the dance halls presented some problems for the players, with sudden stops and starts next to impossible on the slippery dance surface.

Pro basketball games, with and without dancing, drew respectable crowds in many places, including New York City, Philadelphia, parts of New Jersey, and in the coal mining districts of northern and central Pennsylvania. Most of the crowds were well behaved, but some arenas won reputations for their fanatical fans. Spectators in Brooklyn's Prospect Hall often threw things onto the playing floor, sometimes even heaving the chairs they were sitting on at their chosen villain among the players. In the Pennsylvania coal mining country, a visiting player who fell into the spectators' seats might get a quick working over from the fans before returning to the court. Referees particularly felt the heat of crowd pressure.

Another kind of pressure, but one more constructive, was the desire to have professional leagues. The first known pro league was the National Basketball League, formed in 1898 with teams from the Philadelphia area. This league broke up in 1903, leading a typical existence for a pre-World War I professional basketball circuit. Leagues formed on a regional basis, flourished for a few years, and broke up when one team grew too strong for the competition. After the National Basketball League, other strong circuits coming to life included the Philadelphia League, New England League, Central League, Hudson Valley League, Eastern League, New York State League, Tri-County League, Pennsylvania State League, and Inter-State League.

The teams in these leagues hired players on a game-to-game basis, with the better clubs having several local players and two or three imported stars. Ex-college players rarely played the rougher professional brand of ball, hampered also by the difference in dribbling rules between the amateur and pro rules. The professional stars of the prewar era could make a good living playing for several clubs at a time, since competing leagues often scheduled their games on different nights. A good player might play for a team in the Eastern League on Mondays and Thursdays, for a team in the Hudson Valley League on Tuesdays and Fridays, and then pick up some extra money by playing in exhibition games over the weekend.

This era of loose leagues and loose contracts produced great teams whose fame rarely spread past the local area and whose accomplishments have come down to us shrouded in myth and lore. Nevertheless, statistics and the eyewitness accounts of oldtime players and fans have pointed out the outstanding performers of the period.

The Trenton and New York outfits in the original National Basketball League were renowned YMCA teams that continued winning championships after being forced into the professional ranks. Pennsylvania produced many strong pro clubs in the prewar period, both in the Philadelphia area and in the coal mining districts. The Conshohocken team which won the Philadelphia League title in 1904-05 fielded a lineup which featured defensive ace Charles Bossert and 6' center Bill Keenan, both considered by their contemporaries as among the best players of the time.

The Central League, operating in western Pennsylvania, collared the strongest players available, turning out a powerhouse team in McKeesport, which won the league title in 1909-10 and 1910-11, and in Johnstown, the 1911-12 league champion. The strongest outfit turned out by the Eastern League was the 1912-13 champion Reading squad, led by 5'11" guard Andy Sears, another of the era's superstars.

Perhaps the most famous club of the era in Pennsylvania was the 1914-15 Carbondale club, champions of the Tri-County League and the winners of 35 straight games during the season. Defensive star Marty Friedman and 5'4" Barney Sedran, a speedster with an elusive dribble and accurate set shot, led this Carbondale squad and also found time to play a full schedule with the Utica team in the New York State League that same year.

It was also during this period that two of pro basketball's legendary teams came into being. One of these teams was the Buffalo Germans, which started in 1895 as a YMCA team of fourteen-year-olds. Building teamwork as they played through the years, the Germans won the amateur championship of the country in 1904 and shortly thereafter turned pro. Never a member of any league, the Germans thrived as a barnstorming team, compiling a lll-game winning streak between 1908 and 1911. Allie Heerdt starred on this squad and coached later editions of the club which competed up until 1929.

Probably the greatest team of the prewar era was the Trojans of Troy, New York. Most of the players had played together on teams in Schenectady and Gloversville before coming to Troy, so they brought with them a strong foundation of teamwork. The Trojans won the Hudson River League crown in 1909-10 and 1910-11, jumped to the New York State League and won the next three championships, and then went on a barnstorming tour through the South and West in early 1915 during which they won all 38 games played. Through their intelligent teamwork, the Trojans pioneered the use of bounce passes and the fast break. The stars of the club included Ed Wachter, the best center of the era and later the coach at Harvard University; guard Jack Inglis, who some witnesses claim could handle the ball in a manner just as dazzling as did Bob Cousy in the 1950's; and guard Andy Suils, a marvelous defensive player who rarely even bothered to come up into the forecourt when the Trojans had the ball. The Trojans disbanded after their triumphant tour of 1915, just as war was raging in Europe .

III

The American entry into the Great War put an end to pro basketball, the players were getting drafted and the armories were no longer available for games. But after the war ended, pro leagues again formed in the East. The Metropolitan League, organized by John O'Brien in 1921, grew into the strongest circuit, taking in popular teams in New York City, New Jersey, and the Hudson Valley.

A new class of powerhouse teams, league members as well as independents, flourished in the 1920's. The Kingston Colonials won the New York State League title in 1923 and claimed the "world's championship" on the basis of taking three out of five games during the winter and spring from the original Celtics of New York City. Coached by Frank Morgenweck, known as the "Connie Mack" of pro basketball, and sparked by scoring ace Benny Borgmann, the entire Kingston club also doubled as the Paterson Crescents in the Metropolitan League and won the second-half race in that league. Several ethnic teams fielded strong clubs and developed sizeable followings, with the Philadelphia Sphas (South Philadelphia Hebrew Association) fielding an all-Jewish team, the New York Rens an all-black team, and the Brooklyn Visitations an all-Irish team. Out in the Midwest, the Cleveland Rosenblums were strong enough to compete with the eastern powers.

But the best and most famous team of the 1920's was the Celtics of New York. Begun as a settlement house team before the war with Pete Barry and Johnny Whitty the star players, the Celtics broke up during the war, but were reorganized in 1918 by promoter Jim Furey. Officially known as the Original Celtics because the earlier sponsor of the team refused to relinquish rights to the name "New York Celtics," the team played well with Barry, Whitty, and Ernie Reich at the core. In the 1920-21 season, however, the Celtics joined the ranks of the leading pro teams with the addition of Johnny Beckman, Dutch Dehnert, and Swede Grimstead. Beckman was the premier offensive player of the 1920's, a great shooter and driver, and a first-rate box office draw. Dehnert excelled as a defensive player and passer, becoming a master feeder on the pivot play. Grimstead was a tough veteran center. With this new talent, the Celtics won a large following among New York basketball fans.

The Celtics shared the market, however, with the New York Whirlwinds, another popular local team. In addition to veteran stars Marty Friedman and Barney Sedran, the Whirlwinds featured Nat Holman, a top shooter, ball-handler, and defender who also boosted the attendance, and Chris Leonard, a tough defensive player who jumped center and could also play guard.

In the spring of 1921, the Celtics and Whirlwinds met in a series which generated a lot of interest in New York. A record crowd of 11,000 filled the 71st Regiment Armory to see the Whirlwinds win, 40-27. The Celtics took the second game, 26-24, but the rubber match was never played, for reasons unclear to this day. One explanation was that the team owners had problems contracting for an armory in which to play the third game, but another school of thought believes that Whirlwind stars Holman and Leonard signed with the Celtics during the series and refused to play the third game, thus forcing the Whirlwinds out of the series. At any rate, when the 1921-22 season began, Holman and Leonard were playing with the Celtics, and the Whirlwinds were out of business.

This was the start of the Celtics' golden age. Owner Furey signed his entire team to exclusive contracts, forbidding them from playing with any other club during the season. No other team had ever made such an arrangement. Holman and Beckman ranked among the best paid players of the era, and the other Celtics also drew good salaries. To cover costs, the team barnstormed endlessly, and the players developed a close relationship on and off the court. The Celtic attack relied on quick and fluid passing, always hitting the open man, and the team pioneered the give-and-go, the pivot play, and switching on defense .

In the 1921-22 season, the Celtic lineup had 6'4" Horse Haggerty at center, Holman and Beckman at forward, and Dehnert and Leonard at guard, with Barry and Whitty on the bench. Ernie Reich, the team captain, played the early part of the season, but became ill and died in February 1922. In 1922-23, this unit put together a 193-11 barnstorming record. Joe Lapchick, a towering 6'5" center, replaced Haggerty for the 1923-24 season, when the club went 89-10.

The Celtic lineup remained unchanged until 1926-27, when the team signed shooter Davey Banks and sold Johnnny Beckman's contract to Baltimore. Other men to play with the Celtics during these seasons included Eddie Burke, a reserve guard; Elmer Ripley, who joined the team as playmaker whenever Holman's duties as coach at City College of New York kept him away; Benny Borgmann, who was brought in as Beckman's heir apparent in 1925-26 but left the team after only one season; and center Shang Chadwick, who filled in when Lapchick's knee put him out of action for part of the 1925-26 campaign.

The Celtics were basketball's top attraction, using the new Madison Square Garden for their home games after 1925, and scheduling games almost every night of the week. Nevertheless, owner Furey had problems making money, since he had so many high-priced players. In 1926, he was indicted for the embezzlement of $187,000 from the Arnold Constable clothing store, of which he was the head cashier. He pleaded guilty to charges of grand larceny and forgery, drawing a sentence of five years in Sing-Sing. The players continued to run the team for two years, but the club broke up after the 1927-28 season. Furey was released from jail in 1929 and attempted to start the team up again, but he went broke after only two months of play, and the team again scattered.

IV

Oddly enough, although the Celtics were the best of a growing number of strong teams scattered over the East and Midwest, they did not choose to join the first major league when it was created in 1925. With Joe Carr, also the N.F.L. president, as its chief executive, the American Basketball League began operations with strong clubs in Boston, Brooklyn, Washington, Rochester, Buffalo, Ft. Wayne, Cleveland, Detroit, and Chicago. Six of these cities had "big-league" images because of major league baseball teams, and the A.B.L. gave off enough of a big-time glow to even win a place for itself in the sports pages of newspapers in major cities. But even with this support, the A.B.L. was light years away from baseball's popularity, and succeeded mostly in opening the way for college stars to turn pro by adopting the one-hand dribble rule, the rule used by the colleges but supplanted by the two-hand dribble among Eastern professional teams.

The competition was dominated by the Celtics, who joined the circuit in 1926 and won two championships in as many seasons before breaking up, and the Cleveland Rosenblums, who rose to their greatest heights after snapping up several Celtic players after the demise of that team. The league never made much money for its team owners and had to be reorganized in 1928 by John O'Brien, but the Depression which fell upon the nation in 1929 dried up the main pockets of support for the teams. With money in scarce supply, pro basketball could not support a major league structure, and the collapse of the A.B.L. in 1931 marked the return of pro basketball to local leagues and barnstorming teams.

1925-26 A.B.L.

Embarrassment and Success

In the favorable climate of the Roaring 1920's, pro basketball made its first attempt to go big league. The American Basketball League extended from the Atlantic coast to Chicago, the first circuit to go beyond a strict regional operation. At the head of the league was President Joe Carr, a man well versed in sports administration. In addition to running the fledgling basketball league, Carr was also the president of the National Football League and a minor league baseball executive.

To stock the new league, Carr brought together nine successful pro teams in the East and Midwest, including most of the top clubs in the nation. The opening lineup for the league included the Cleveland Rosenblums, sponsored by department store owner Max Rosenblum and coached by old pro Marty Friedman; the Washington Palace Five, owned by laundry tycoon and later pro football magnate George Preston Marshall; the Brooklyn Arcadians, bankrolled by baseball star Harry Heilmann and coached by veteran Gary Schmeelk; the Buffalo Bisons, coached by original German Allie Heerdt; and the Chicago Bruins, owned by George Halas of the Chicago Bears. Other clubs in the loop were the Rochester Centrals, Ft. Wayne Caseys, Detroit Pulaski Post Five, and Boston Whirlwinds.

With clubs from different sections of the country, the league had to decide on a uniform set of rules fair to all. The two-hand dribble was ruled out, since the midwestern teams were accustomed to only the one-hand dribble. All league games had to be played with backboards and most were played without cages. Each team had to sign its players to an exclusive contract, and the schedule was divided into first and second half races, with separate champions for each. Each team had to play an average of two games a week, with no restrictions on the booking of exhibitions on open dates.

Oddly enough, it was these exhibition games which gave the league its first embarrassment. The Original Celtics, based in New York, had scorned an invitation to join the new league, preferring instead to continue as a free-lance barnstorming team. The A.B.L. clubs eagerly signed up matches with the famous Celtics, and the New Yorkers habitually showed up the league clubs by beating them handily.

But except for the Celtics, the country's top pro teams answered the league's starting bell in November. The first half of the season was marked by a big trade between Brooklyn and Washington and a tight three-way pennant race. Early in the season, Brooklyn sent Rusty Saunders and George Glasco, two good shooters, to Washington in exchange for Rody Cooney and Red Conaty, a pair of small quick players.

The trade helped both clubs, as the Brooklyn Arcadians and the Washington Palace Five both battled the Cleveland Rosenblums for the first-half title. Brooklyn featured Cooney, Conaty, and Elmer Ripley, a top defensive guard who later became a famous college coach, but the team lacked a good center. Washington blended Saunders and Glasco with Ray Kennedy, a very tough defensive player who also led the league in scoring average, and playmaker Ted Keams. The Cleveland Rosenblums fielded a top-notch young offensive player in Nat Hickey, three solid veteran players in Honey Russell, Carl Husta, and Dave Kerr, and an adequate center in Rich Deighan. Coach Friedman, a longtime great defensive guard, rarely played because of a bad knee. As expected, all three clubs came to the wire with a chance for firsthalf honors. When the smoke cleared on the scant 16-game schedule, Brooklyn emerged the winner by one game over Washington and two over Cleveland.

Only eight clubs competed in the second-half race, as the Boston Whirlwinds were expelled after the first half because of certain problems with player contracts. Cleveland quickly sewed up the spring pennant hy running offeight straight wins out of the starting gate. Washington again ran second, while Brooklyn slipped to fourth despite picking Up centers Horse Haggerty, a Celtic veteran, from Washington and Tilly Voss, a pro football player, from Rochester.

Brooklyn's slump continued into the championship playoffs against the Cleveland Rosenblums. The Arcadians blew an eight-point lead in the second half of the opening game and dropped a 35-33 decision. The Rosenblums then took the next two games to sweep the series and cop the first A.B.L. championship.

The attendance figures for the playoffs offered hope to the owners. The first two games, played in Cleveland, averaged about 10,000, while the third game in New York drew only 2,000 because of the Arcadians' hopeless 0-2 situation. Although no one grew rich from this first season, most of the team owners were confident that pro basketball had successfully survived its inaugural year.

Standing

First Half

	W	L	PCT	GB
Brooklyn	12	4	.750	—
Washington	11	5	.688	1
Cleveland	10	6	.625	2
Rochester	9	7	.563	3
Ft. Wayne	7	9	.438	5
Boston	6	10	.375	6
Chicago	6	10	.375	6
Detroit	6	10	.375	6
Buffalo	5	11	.313	7

Second Half

	W	L	PCT	GB
Cleveland	13	1	.929	—
Washington	11	3	.786	2
Rochester	9	5	.643	4
Brooklyn	7	7	.500	6
Ft. Wayne	6	8	.429	7
Buffalo	5	9	.357	8
Chicago	3	11	.214	10
Detroit	2	12	.143	11

Playoffs — Cleveland beat Brooklyn 3 games to 0
Note: Boston dropped out after first half

Scoring Leaders

	G	FG	FT	PTS	PPG
Rusty Saunders, Bkn-Was	34	73	92	238	7.0
Ray Kennedy, Was	27	66	84	216	8.0
Nat Hickey, Cle	30	68	80	216	7.2
Honey Russell, Cle	30	68	80	216	7.2
Elmer Ripley, Bkn	30	59	96	214	7.1
George Glasco, Bkn-Was	35	64	70	198	5.7
Marty Barry, Roch	27	50	81	181	6.7
Carl Husta, Cle	30	50	68	168	5.6
Red Conaty, Was-Bkn	28	55	52	162	5.8

1926-27 A.B.L.

The One and Only Original Celtics

The American Basketball League shuffled its franchises both before and during the season and came up with a stronger array of teams. All of the last year's members, except the Buffalo Bisons, returned for the start of this season, and the Philadelphia Warriors and Baltimore Orioles were added to the circuit to bring the opening day register up to nine clubs.

After a few weeks of action, Cleveland, Washington, and Philadelphia emerged as the league powers. The Cleveland Rosenblums had added Ohio State center Cookie Cunningham to their 1925-26 championship squad, while the Washington Palace Five strengthened their team by signing veterans Elmer Ripley and Tillie Voss away from the Brooklyn team. The newborn Warriors replaced the defunct Sphas as Philadelphia's top pro outfit; Spha coach Eddie Gottlieb handled the reins for the Warriors, bringing with him 6'7" Stretch Meehan, Chick Passon, tough Tommy Barlow, and Lou Schneiderman.

At the other end of the standings, the Detroit and Brooklyn clubs fielded the weakest entries. Detroit had not improved since its last place standing the previous year, while Brooklyn lost all its Cleveland top players to other league and non-league clubs. By mid-December, Detroit was 0-6, Brooklyn was 0-5, and neither team was drawing any paying fans. By New Year's Day, both clubs dropped out of the league.

A.B.L. President Joe Carr simply nullified all of Detroit's games and struck them from the standings. To fill the other vacant spot, the league convinced the New York Celtics to take over as the Brooklyn A.B.L. team .

By bringing in the Celtics, the league obtained pro basketball's most famous team. The Celtics had traveled throughout the East and Midwest on their barnstorming tours, beating the overwhelming majority of their opponents. Snappy passing made the club's attack colorful and attractive, and the team's roster included some of the game's best players and top gate draws. Nat Holman, the handsome 5'11" guard who starred as a ballhandler, shooter, and defender, had pro basketball's biggest reputation (and salary), and veteran Johnny Beckman, a top offensive player, was known as"the Babe Ruth of basketball." The other Celtic players were 6'5" center Joe Lapchick, taller than every A.B.L. player except Stretch Meehan; Dutch Dehnert, a superb passer and defensive players; 5'8" Davey Banks, a young shooting whiz picked up from last year's Philadelphia Sphas; and tough veterans Chris Leonard and Pete Barry.

The Celtics assumed the previous Brooklyn club's mark of 0-5, and a 13-3 record the rest of the first half could not make up for the lost ground. Cleveland and Washington battled down to the wire for the top spot, with the Rosenblums finally clinching it by beating tbe Palace Five twice in early January.

At the start of the second half, the Celtics made a surprising personnel move which wound up helping the club. The Celts sold Johnny Beckman to the pitiful Baltimore team, where he would be player coach. By dropping a high-salaried player who was slowing up, the Celtics made room for young Davey Banks in the starting lineup. Although his defense left much to be desired, Banks blended in with Holman as the team's offensive spearhead.

With a fresh start in the second half, the Celtics roared out to nine straight wins, lost a game to Cleveland, and then won 10 more games before dropping their last regular season game. The Rosenblums fell off badly after star player Honey Russell had a personal falling-out with team owner Max Rosenblum and was sold to the Chicago Bruins. Four straight losses on the road took the wind out of Washington's sails, and the surprising Ft. Wayne Hoosiers sneaked into second place behind the Celtics. The Hoosiers had strengthened themselves late in the first half of the season when they signed 5'8" Benny Borgmann, a deadly set-shooter who was one of the game's top offensive threats.

At the end of the regular season, the Rosenblums and their fans relished the prospect of beating the Celtics in the playoffs and winning their second A.B.L. crown. The loss of Russell, however, had weakened the Rosenblums too much. Despite good play by Cleveland's Nat Hickey and Carl Husta, the Celtics swept three straight games and took the championship.

Standings
First Half

	W	L	PCT	GB
Cleveland	17	4	.810	—
Washington	16	5	.762	1
Philadelphia	14	7	.667	3
Brooklyn	13	8	.619	4
Ft. Wayne	8	13	.381	9
Rochester	8	13	.381	9
Chicago	7	14	.333	10
Baltimore	1	20	.048	16

Second Half

	W	L	PCT	GB
Brooklyn	19	2	.905	—
Flt. Wayne	15	6	.714	4
Washington	14	7	.667	5
Philadelphia	10	11	.476	9
Cleveland	9	12	.429	10
Chicago	6	15	.286	13
Rochester	6	15	.286	13
Baltimore	5	16	.238	14

Playoffs—Brooklyn beat Cleveland 3 games to 0
Note: Detroit dropped out in middle of first half with 0-5 record; games struck from standings
Brooklyn Arcadians dropped out during the first half with 0-5 record; Celtics then assumed record and continued as Brooklyn representative

Scoring Leaders

	G	FG	FT	PTS	PPG
Rusty Saunders, Was	42	119	161	399	9.5
Benny Borgmann, FtW	34	87	206	380	11.2
Chick Passon, Phi	41	93	181	367	9.0
Nat Hickey, Cle	41	103	137	343	8.4
Carl Husta, Cle	41	84	162	330	8.0
Johnny Beckman, Bkn-BAL	37	91	141	323	8.7
Ray Kennedy, Was	40	68	172	308	7.7
Nat Holman	34	82	135	299	8.8
Honey Russell, Cle-Chi	40	61	134	256	6.4
Harry Topel, Roch	37	81	91	253	6.8

1927-28 A.B.L.

Too Many Celtics, Not Enough Fans

With the shift to divisional play this season, the league placed one colossus of power in each section. The Celtics, now representing New York instead of Brooklyn and playing some of their home games in the new Madison Square Garden, lived up to all expectations by waltzing through their schedule and handily winning the Eastern Division crown by 11 games. The veteran Celtic squad of Nat Holman, Joe Lapchick, Dutch Dehnert, Davey Banks, Pete Barry, and Chris Leonard used a sharp passing attack and tenacious defense to string together 15 straight victories in December and January to pull away from the second-place Philadelphia Warriors.

In the Western Division, the preseason favorite was Cleveland, the finalist in last year's playoffs. The team had suffered in the second half of the last season after selling Honey Russell to Chicago, but owner Max Rosenblum brought his squad back to full strength by signing Vic Hanson, 3-time All-American from Syracuse University, and by promoting Dave Kerr to player coach to replace the retiring Marty Friedman.

The Rosenblums lived up to their promise in the early going, winning their first eight games and running out to a substantial lead in the Western Division. Nat Hickey, Carl Husta, Hanson, and Kerr filled the forward and guard spots solidly, and Rich Deighan and Cookie Cunningham held down the center position in workmanlike fashion. By early January, the Rosenblums were coasting along with a 15-7 record.

But then Hanson quit the team, citing his contract problems and disappointment with the rougher professional brand of basketball. After the rookie left in a storm of publicity, the Rosenblums went into a nose dive. Further hurt by injuries to Hickey, Husta, and Kerr, the Rosenblums stumbled to a 7-22 mark after early January.

Cashing in on the Cleveland slump were the Ft. Wayne Hoosiers, who sneaked into first place late in the season. Frank Morgenweck, who had been organizing and coaching professional teams since the turn of the century, handled the coaching reins on the team. Benny Borgmann, one of Morgenweck's sandlot discoveries in the early 1920's, did most of the shooting for the club until Rusty Saunders, the league's leading scorer the last two years, was purchased in January from the new Brooklyn team. The supporting cast on the Hoosiers included Shang Chadwick, Ralph Miller, Frank Shimek, Bill McElwain, and Pip Koehler.

The Western Division had shrunk to three teams with the collapse of the Detroit Cardinals at the beginning of the new year. Despite the presence of aging superstar Johnny Beckman, the Cardinals folded from a lack of paying customers, and Beckman wound up the season on George Halas' Chicago Bruins.

An Eastern Division franchise also folded in early January, as the Washington Palace Five gave up the ghost. Owner George Preston Marshall had traded shooter George Glasco and playmaker Ted Kearns to Philadelphia in the off-season for 6'7" center Stretch Meehan, scorer Chick Passon, and guard Harry Riconda, but the deal immediately turned sour when Meehan and Riconda signed with independent teams. Without Meehan, Washington lacked a good center, and the considerable talents of Rusty Saunders, Elmer Ripley, Ray Kennedy, and Red Conaty went to waste without a strong big man. When the club lost its first eight games, it also lost most of its following, and with a 7-16 record, owner Marshall sold his franchise and players to the Brooklyn Visitations, who had been playing in the Metropolitan League.

The Visitations had two good little men in Rody Cooney and Willie Scrill, and they added one of the game's best set-shooters in Joe Brennan. Of the old Washington players, Kennedy and Conaty stayed on with Brooklyn while Saunders was sent to Ft. Wayne and Ripley to Cleveland. Over the rest of the schedule, the Visitations built a strong 18-10 record.

Saddled with Washington's previous losses, however, the Visitations couldn't make the playoffs. Under the new divisional format, the first two teams in each division would play a three-game series, with the winners meeting for the championship. Both first-round matches were one-sided, with the Celtics easily handling the Warriors in two games, while the Hoosiers eliminated the fading Rosenblums with two quick wins.

The Ft. Wayne club came into the championship series a definite underdog, and its chances got slimmer when Benny Borgmann hurt his knee six minutes into the opening contest of the five-game series. Although the Celtics easily took the first match, 30-21, the Hoosiers fought back to take the second game 28-21, holding the fabled New York club without a field goal in the entire second half. The Celtics reasserted themselves in the next two games, however, and wrapped up their second championship with 35-18 and 27-26 victories

All was not well with the Celtics and the league, however. Attendance at the Madison Square Garden for Celtic games was poor, and the owners of the arena debated about evicting the team. Club owner Jim Furey had been in prison for two years on an embezzlement charge, and the players were running the team as a sort of cooperative venture, with Johnny Whitty handling the paperwork and coaching duties in addition to playing at times. But with no wealthy owner backing the club, the players were not making as much money as they had under straight salary.

The Celtic domination on the court also hurt the league, with attendance slumping off as the New York club made a shambles of the championship race. The style of play in the league also alienated some fans, as roughness and frequent fouling drove some spectators to prefer the more open and cleaner college game. The league had tried to deal with the excessive fouling by putting in a foul-out rule, with players disqualified once they compiled five fouls, but this rule was not enough to offset pro basketball's "wrestling" image. As a result of these factors, along with the folding of two clubs during the season, the league found itself in deep trouble as the campaign came to a close.

Standings

Eastern Division

	W	L	PCT	GB
New York	40	9	.816	—
Philadelphia	30	21	.588	11
Washington-Brooklyn	25	26	.490	16
Rochester	24	28	.462	17.5

Western Division

	W	L	PCT	GB
Ft..Wayne	27	24	.529	—
Cleveland	22	29	.431	5
Detroit	5	13	.278	5.5
Chicago	13	36	.265	13

Playoffs — Ft. Wayne beat Cleveland 2 games to 0
New York beat Philadelphia 2 games to 0
New York beat Ft. Wayne 3 games to 1
Note: Detroit faranchise disbanded on January 3
Washington franchise shifted to Brooklyn on January 3
Washington record was 7-16

Scoring Leaders

	G	FG	FT	PTS	PPG
Harry Topel, Roch	52	171	96	438	8.4
Davey Banks, NY	49	170	72	412	8.4
Benny Borgmann, Roch	51	128	143	399	7.8
Nat Hickey, Cle	47	155	69	379	8.1
Honey Russell, Chi	49	137	85	359	7.3
Al Kellett, Phi	43	132	82	346	8.0
Tom Barlow, Phi	48	142	51	335	7.0
Rusty Saunders, Bkn-FtW	50	127	76	330	6.6
Red Conaty, Was-Bkn	47	148	28	324	6.9
Carl Husta, Cle	41	115	89	319	7.8

1928-29 A.B.L.

A Different Champion, But the Same Faces

With the defending champion Celtics no longer around to bully the opposition, the league took on a new look this season. The great Celtic club had lost its fight for survival. Poor attendance and the continued imprisonment of owner Jim Furey were the major causes of the team's demise. The league as a whole shed few tears, since Celtic players would be distributed among the other teams.

Other departures from the league this year included the Philadelphia Warriors and President Joe Carr. With the demise of the Warriors, Philadelphia coach Eddie Gottlieb spent the season promoting games in the City of Brotherly Love. Carr resigned his league presidency to concentrate on his executive positions in professional football and baseball.

With no league president and only five teams returning from last season, the A.B.L. built itself back up to full strength by absorbing two teams from the Metropolitan League, a strong circuit operating in the New York City area. John O'Brien, president of the local league, took over as the chief executive of the A.B.L. The two clubs he brought from his old circuit were the Trenton Bengals and Paterson Whirlwinds. The New York Hakoahs, a Jewish club organized by ex-Celtic players Nat Holman and Davey Banks, also joined the returning Cleveland Rosenblums, Ft. Wayne Hoosiers, Chicago Bruins, Rochester Centrals, and Brooklyn Visitations to form the A.B.L.'s field of eight. Last year's divisional arrangement was scrapped, and the split-season format was brought back.

As the schedule began, no club stood out as an overwhelming favorite, although the Ft. Wayne Hoosiers seemed the strongest team on paper. The Hoosiers, led by scorers Benny Borgmann and Rusty Saunders, fielded the same squad as last year, with ex-Philadelphia forward George Glasco coming over to strengthen the team. The Brooklyn Visitations, with a lineup of shooters Joe Brennan and Red Conaty, guards Willie Scrill and Rody Cooney and bruising center Pat Herlihy, ranked close consideration after the Hoosiers.

But another club suddenly became a powerhouse one week into the campaign. After losing their first two games, the Cleveland Rosenblums signed up ex-Celtic players Joe Lapchick, Dutch Dehnert, and Pete Barry. Lapchick excelled at getting the center tap, Dehnert passed the ball on the pivot play better than anyone else, and all three men played a very tough defense. Combined with Nat Hickey and Carl Husta in the Cleveland lineup, these players gave the Rosenblums a definite Celtic-like look. Mindful of the dangers of one-club domination, the league forced owner Max Rosenblum to sell Hickey to Chicago in December, but the team still fielded a very powerful squad.

The Rosenblums, relying on the league's best defense, edged out the Ft. Wayne team for the first-half pennant, with the Brooklyn and Chicago entries tied for third. George Halas' Bruins surprised everyone by finishing high; the addition of Hickey and ex-Brooklyn guard Ray Kennedy helped the club immeasurably. The Hakoahs, despite the presence of Holman and Banks, came in fifth, while Trenton, with many of last year's Philadelphia players, and Rochester, strengthened by veteran scorer Johnny Beckman, also fielded second-division clubs. Paterson, coached by Frank Morgenweck, had the weakest entry in the league.

Cleveland, Ft. Wayne, and Brooklyn again fought it out for the top spot in the second half of the season, with the Hoosiers clinching the race by beating Brooklyn 30-29 on March 18, right at the closing wire. The Rosenblums finished a close second. More important, they had traded with Rochester for Johnny Beckman in mid-February.

With ex-Celtics Lapchick, Dehnert, Barry, and Beckman in the lineup with Carl Husta, the Rosenblums headed into their playoff meeting with the Ft. Wayne Hoosiers in fine order. In the first game, Dutch Dehnert's 11 points paced Cleveland to a 2~17 victory. Joe Lapchick's 11 points led the way to a 28 23 win in the second game. The third game developed into a tough defensive battle, but a long set shot by substitute Red Skurnick with one minute left gave Cleveland a 19-18 triumph. Beckman and Husta scored in double figures in the final game to give the Rosenblums a 30-22 win and a four-game sweep of the series. For the Hoosiers, Benny Borgmann poured in 40 points in the four games. It was a great showing, but not enough to prevent the Celtic alumni from bringing Cleveland their second title in four years.

Standings

First Half

	W	L	PCT	GB
Cleveland	19	9	.679	—
Ft. Wayne	18	10	.643	1
Brooklyn	15	12	.556	3.5
Chicago	15	12	.556	3.5
New York	13	16	.448	6.5
Trenton	12	16	.429	7
Rochester	11	15	.423	7
Paterson	6	19	.240	11.5

Second Half

	W	L	PCT	GB
Ft. Wayne	11	3	.786	—
Brooklyn	10	4	.714	1
Cleveland	10	4	.714	1
Rochester	7	7	.500	4
NewYork	5	9	.357	6
Trenton	4	8	.333	6
Chicago	4	10	.286	7
Paterson	3	9	.250	7

Playoffs — Cleveland beat Ft. Wayne 4 games to 0

Scoring Leaders

	G	FG	FT	PTS	PPG
Benny Borgmann, FtW	42	100	125	325	7.7
Nat Hickey, Cle-Chi	46	124	74	322	7.0
Carl Husta, Cle	42	101	83	285	6.8
Lou Rabin, Roch	40	110	54	274	6.9
Tom Barlow, Trenton	38	120	34	274	7.2
Johnny Beckman, Roch-Cle	38	101	67	269	7.1
Rusty Saunders, FtW	42	104	50	258	6.1
Red Conaty, Bkn	39	107	37	251	6.4
Davey Banks, NY	42	98	48	244	5.8
Al Kellett, Trenton-Chi	38	79	79	237	6.2

1929-30 A.B.L.
The Continuation of Rosenblum and Co.

The stock market crash on October 29, 1929, ushered in the Great Depression, and pro basketball teams found fewer fans willing and able to spend money on tickets. Most of the team owners, however, expected the Depression to be only a temporary setback, so the American Basketball League headed into the season with a full slate of eight clubs. Trenton and the New York Hakoahs had dropped out, but the Syracuse All-Americans and New York Celtics came in to take their places.

The new Syracuse club hired two veteran pros, Tom Barlow and Ted Kearns, and filled the rest of the roster with former college players from Eastern schools. The college men, with Ed Wineapple of Providence at the head, had developed big reputations as undergraduates, and the Syracuse management hoped they could transfer their talents to the professional game.

Relying on old pros rather than former college players, the reorganized Celtics came back into the league after a year's inactivity, looking to regain the A.B.L. crown they had twice won. Owner Jim Furey had been paroled from Sing Sing after serving three years for embezzlement, and he immediately signed Nat Holman, Davey Banks, and Johnny Beckman to play for the new team. Joe Lapchick, Dutch Dehnert, and Pete Barry were still under contract to the Cleveland Rosenblums, so Furey filled out his team with 6'7" center Stretch Meehan, veteran guard Harry Riconda, and younger guard Bill McElwain.

As the season progressed, all could see that these Celtics didn't come close to the quality of the earlier teams. Beckman had slowed down noticeably, Meehan was no ball of fire despite his height, and Holman had to miss most Saturday games because he was coaching the City College of New York team.

But even more serious, owner Furey quickly ran out of money. The reduced number of customers who came to Celtic games both on Long Island and at Madison Square Garden could not support the high salaries Furey was paying to Holman and Beckman, both of whom were making close to $10,000. In early December, Furey sold Beckman to Cleveland, Banks to Ft. Wayne, and Holman and Meehan to Syracuse. He then stocked his club with younger, less expensive talent, but the team finally folded after playing only two games with the new men. The team's five wins and five losses were stricken from the standings, and the league went on with seven teams.

The Syracuse Club, however, also found the going rockier than expected. The college men failed to pan out as professional players, so the All-Americans brought in veterans Nat Holman, Stretch Meehan, and Marty Barry to turn the team around. The team kept losing, however, and the fans stayed away, so the club called it quits, on January 6, two weeks from the end of the first half.

When the All-Americans disbanded with four games remaining they had a 4-16 record. League President John O'Brien ordered the four games forfeited to the scheduled opponents, a ruling which vitally affected the pennant race.

The Brooklyn Visitations and Cleveland Rosenblums were battling for the first half title, with both clubs tied at 13-7. Two of the unplayed Syracuse games were with the Visitations, so Brooklyn suddenly found itself with a 15-7 record and a clear shot at the pennant. The Rosenblums, unblessed with any forfeits, tied up the race by beating Rochester and Ft. Wayne. They then squared off with the Visitations in a showdown battle on January 11 at Cleveland. The Rosenblums took a tough 17-15 decision, and then went on to clinch the title by beating Chicago while the disappointed Visitations lost to Paterson.

The second-half race began with only six clubs, each measurably strengthened by absorbing the former Syracuse and New York players. Rochester, coached by Frank Morgenweck, won the title behind the good playing of little men Lou Rabin, Manny Hirsch and Lloyd Kintzing, and big men Gaza Chizmadia and Tiny Hearn, a towering 6'9" rookie center from Georgia Tech. The Rosenblums ran a close second, hurt by center Joe Lapchick s recurring knee problems.

Coming in third were the surprising Chicago Bruins, helped by the signing of Nat Holman for the second-half race. The Visitations finished a disappointing fourth, due in part to Joe Brennan's staying behind on road trips because of his job in a New York bank. The Ft. Wayne team failed to make a run at the top despite picking up scorers Davey Banks from the Celtics and Johnny Beckman from Cleveland. Paterson, too, failed to improve, despite picking up scoring champ Benny Borgmann, a local product, from Ft. Wayne when Banks joined the Hoosiers.

As the playoffs got underway, Cleveland found itself on the short end of a 20-16 score to Rochester, who had edged out the Rosenblums by one game for second-half honors. But in the second game, coach Dave Kerr made a key switch. He moved Lapchick, who was slowed down by bad knees, to a forward's position, and he stuck 6'3" Cookie Cunningham, who also played football for the Chicago Bears, at center opposite 6'9" Tiny Hearn. From that point on, the Rosenblums moved more smoothly, and they won four straight games: 18-17, 23-16, 18-13, 21-15. Thus, they wrapped up their second straight title in a league whose life was quickly waning.

Standings
First Half

	W	L	PCT	GB
Cleveland	17	7	.738	—
Brooklyn	15	9	.625	2
Rochester	14	10	.583	3
Ft. Wayne	12	12	.500	5
Chicago	12	12	.500	5
Paterson	10	14	.417	7
Syracuse	4	20	.167	13

Second Half

	W	L	PCT	GB
Rochester	19	11	.633	—
Cleveland	18	12	.600	1
Chicago	17	13	.567	2
Brooklyn	15	15	.500	4
Ft. Wayne	13	17	.433	6
Paterson	8	22	.267	11

Playoffs—Cleveland beat Rochester 4 games to 1
Note: New York dropped out on December 10 with a record of 5-5; all games stricken from records
Syracuse dropped out on January 6; forfeited 4 remaining first-half games

Scoring Leaders

	G	FG	FT	PTS	PPG
Benny Borgmann, FtW-Pat	50	149	118	416	8.3
Gaza Chizmadia, Roch	55	113	117	343	6.2
Carl Husta, Cle	56	135	61	331	5.9
Nat Hickey, Chi	53	133	51	317	6.0
Davey Banks, NY-FtW	50	122	63	307	6.1
Joe Brennan, Bkn	43	108	61	277	6.4
Red Conaty, Bkn	54	109	40	258	4.8
Pat Herlihy, Bkn	53	101	37	239	4.5
Lloyd Kintzing, Roch	52	100	32	232	4.5
Nat Holman, NY-Syr-Chi	47	88	51	227	4.8

1930-31 A.B.L.
A Futile Transfusion

The Great Depression was here and millions of people were out of work, but the American Basketball League looked for other reasons to explain its drastic drop in attendance. League President John O'Brien theorized that the fans were tired of seeing the same players year after year, so he instituted a rule which made the clubs take on two rookies, either college players or local semipros. Forced into signing young players, the league recruited some talented collegians, among them high-scoring Branch McCracken of Indiana, Loll Spindell of C.C.N.Y. and Charley Murphy from Loyola of Chicago. McCracken signed with Ft. Wayne, Spindell with Cleveland, and Murphy with Chicago.

With the teams having to assign two roster spots to rookies, many old pros were left out in the cold. Former bright lights, such as Nat Holman, Johnny Beckman, Gaza Chizmadia, Stretch Meehan, Ted Kearns, Dave Kerr, George Glasco, Tom Barlow, Tillie Voss, Bill McElwain, and Harry Riconda no longer appeared in A.B.L. boxscores.

The league also instituted a rule forbidding a player from holding the ball in the foul lane for more than three seconds. This new rule especially hurt the Cleveland Rosenblums, who had built their offense around Dutch Dehnert's pivot play from inside the key.

Through the early going, the Rosenblums played dull basketball and slipped back into the pack, which had increased to seven teams with the addition of the Toledo Redmen. While the Brooklyn Visitations built up an early lead, the Rosenblums treaded water at the .500 mark until owner Max Rosenblum shocked the league by folding up his team on December 8 because of poor attendance. All of his players became free agents; Joe Lapchick, Dutch Dehnert, Pete Barry, and Lou Spindell all signed with Toledo, while Carl Husta joined the Ft. Wayne club.

Three weeks later, on December 30, the Paterson Crescents pulled out of the league. Despite an improved team featuring Benny Borgmann, Honey Russell, and Red Conaty, the Crescents simply could not make enough money to run a big-league operation. The team released all its expensive players and continued to play local ball in the New Jersey area.

With the loss of two teams in a month many people believed that the league was about to fold. President O'Brien kept the circuit going, however, and no more clubs dropped out before the end of the season.

Of the five clubs which finished the first half, the Brooklyn Visitations wound up in first place. The Visitations had two veteran little men in Willie Scrill and Rody Cooney, a veteran shooter in Joe Brennan, a newly-acquired center in 6'3" Al Kellett, and two helpful rookies in Frank Conaty and Happy Reilly. The team lost three straight road games in January, but they had built up such a lead in the early going that the Ft. Wayne Hoosiers could not catch them.

In the second half, the Visitations were hurt when Joe Brennan quit the team to concentrate on his career in banking, and the team finished third. Ft. Wayne, with a good center in Shang Chadwick and four good scorers in Carl Husta, Rusty Saunders, Frank Shimek, and Branch McCracken, took a piece of the crown by tying Chicago with a 11-5 record. The Bruins had finished last in the first half, but had built themselves up by picking up Benny Borgmann, Lloyd Kintzing, and Ralph Miller for the second half.

Finishing in last place were the Toledo Redmen, despite the four ex-Celtics on their roster. Davey Banks still scored points as quickly as anyone in the game, but Lapchick, Dehnert, and Barry were all getting on in years. Bad knees also contributed to Lapchick's slowing down.

With the ex-Celtics out of the playoffs for the first time since the 1926-27 season, new faces filled the limelight for the A.B.L. championship. First, the Hoosiers and Bruins had to break their second-half tie, and Ft. Wayne beat the Bruins 20-16 in a one-game showdown; the Bruins had to play the game without high-scoring Nat Hickey, who was laid up with a bad ankle.

After getting past Chicago, the Hoosiers were then favored to beat the Visitations for the title. The Brooklyn team, however, surprised the Hoosiers by winning the series four games to two. In all four of their victories, the Visitations held the Ft. Wayne crew to under 20 points with a tough, switching defense.

But it soon became clear that the Visitations would never defend their title. During the summer, A.B.L. President O'Brien looked over the disasterous financial records of the last two seasons and recommended that the league suspend operations during the next season.

The league in fact stayed inactive for two seasons, and O'Brien reorganized it in 1933-34. In its second incarnation, however, the A.B.L. was strictly an East Coast league, with all its teams bunched around the Philadelphia-New York-Hudson Valley region that had fostered many local leagues in the years before the A.B.L. After 1933, the A.B.L. had no pretensions about national big-league status, and it was soon eclipsed in importance and quality of play by the National Basketball League, a midwestern circuit created in 1937.

Although the A.B.L. lost its major league status after 1931, it had succeeded in providing the first national professional basketball league as well as implementing important rule changes—the one-handed dribble, foul disqualification, and the three-second foul lane violation—all factors which helped shape the modern game of basketball. The A.B.L.'s one drawback may have been that it was simply premature.

Standings

First Half

	W	L	PCT	GB
Brooklyn	14	7	.667	—
Ft. Wayne	13	9	.591	1.5
Rochester	10	9	.526	3
Paterson	9	9	.500	3.5
Cleveland	6	6	.500	3.5
Toledo	8	13	.381	6
Chicago	7	14	.333	7

Second Half

	W	L	PCT	GB
Ft. Wayne	11	5	.688	—
Chicago	11	5	.688	—
Brooklyn	8	8	.500	3
Rochester	5	10	.333	5
Toledo	4	11	.274	6.5

Ft. Wayne beat Chicago 2 games to 0 for 2nd Half Championship

Playoffs — Brooklyn beat Ft. Wayne 4 games to 2

Note: Cleveland dropped out on December 8

Paterson dropped out on December 30

Scoring Leaders

	G	FG	FT	PTS	PPG
Benny Borgmann, Pat-Chi	33	111	68	290	8.8
Davey Banks, Tol	34	94	66	254	7.5
Manny Hirsch, Roch	28	81	49	211	7.6
Willie Scrill, Bkn	37	87	29	203	5.5
Frank Shimek, FtW	37	78	47	203	5.5
Al Kellett, Bkn	36	59	55	173	4.8
Carl Husta, Cle-FtW	35	64	42	170	4.9
Rusty Saunders, FtW	38	66	34	166	4.4
Cookie Cunningham, Tol	35	53	44	150	4.5
Lou Spindell, Cle-Tol	35	58	28	144	4.1

1931-1937

Reseeding the Professional Soil

Amateur basketball found the 1930's a fertile period for growth despite the Depression that gripped the nation's collective wallet. College basketball broke into the big time after Ned Irish began promoting intersectional double-headers at Madison Square Garden. With several strong New York schools as regular attractions and a steady flow of the nation's best undergraduate teams as guest attractions, the college doubleheaders at the Garden grew into popular events and dependable money-makers.

The success of intersectional college basketball in New York spurred similar programs in other large arenas throughout the country, and the undergrads blossomed into the game's most glamorous and best known players. In the Midwest, amateur industrial teams drew a large following of enthusiastic fans. Players who starred on college teams often continued their playing careers with industrial teams while also starting their business careers. The dual offer of a secure job plus a chance to continue playing ball was a lot more than the shaky world of pro basketball could offer these college men.

Pro ball had enjoyed a brief period of major league status in the late 1920's, when the American Basketball League linked strong clubs in large cities together in a top-flight circuit. But the A.B.L. never really got off the ground as a profit-making venture, and the Depression drove it out of business in 1931. The concept of big-league pro basketball went into mothballs, and the fragmented structure of earlier years was all that was left of the pro game. Regional circuits operated both in the East and in the Midwest, cutting expenses by limiting team membership to a certain geographic area.

Of the several leagues operating during this period, the strongest was the reborn A.B.L., which was reorganized by President John O'Brien in 1933. In its second life, the A.B.L. included only Eastern teams, played out its schedule in small gymnasiums and armories, and had a hard time trying to get any press publicity away from the blossoming college game. Although it featured several of the stronger pro clubs of the decade, the A.B.L. lacked the organizational strength and popular recognition to rate as a major league.

But even with only limited league play, several teams survived and prospered with some mixture of league and free-lance competition. The original Celtics, the kingpins of the 1920's, regrouped in 1931 and again toured the country in tireless barnstorming activity. Veteran Celtics Joe Lapchick, Dutch Dehnert, Pete Barry, and Davey Banks joined with experienced pros Pat Herlihy, Nat Hickey, and Carl Husta on a strong squad which again ranked with the best in the country in the early part of the decade. But age was catching up with the veteran players, and the Celtics never regained their stature as the best in the field. However, the Celtics remained a powerful gate draw and added younger talent, such as Bobby McDermott and Paul Birch. But the club lived out its life as a reminder of its glory years until it finally died in 1940. Another old-time club that continued strong into the 1930's were the Brooklyn Visitations, who won the A.B.L. title in 1935 but soon lapsed into weakness and decay.

Some newer teams won a measure of recognition for their strong performances. The New York Jewels built a squad around graduates from the powerful St. John's University team of the late 1920's and were a major force in the rebuilt A.B.L. The Oshkosh All-Stars were formed in 1931 by Lon Darling and fielded a topnotch club which bested most competition in the Midwest. Another team originating in the Midwest were the Harlem Globetrotters, whose home base was Chicago despite their name. Started in 1927 by Abe Saperstein, the Trotters had no homecourt and played a full barnstorming schedule. Even in the 1930's, this all-black squad was developing its comedy routines which would later make it famous. But it could also play a brand of serious basketball which could beat many of the best clubs.

The best teams of the 1930's were the Philadelphia Sphas and the New York Rens. Named after their sponsor, the South Philadelphia Hebrew Association, the Sphas had been a strong club in the 1920's but came into full blossom in the Depression decade. Coach Eddie Gottlieb's all-Jewish roster included stars Inky Lautman, Red Wolfe, Shikey Gotthoffer, Moe Goldman, and Harry Litwak. Using products of both college and sandlot ball, the Sphas dominated the A.B.L. in the 1930's and also met the best of the nation's free-lance teams.

Probably the best pro club of the 1930's, independent or league, were the New York Rens, who took their name from their homecourt, the Renaissance Ballroom. Started in 1922 by Bob Douglas, the all-black Rens hit their peak during the four seasons from 1932 to 1936, during which their record was a staggering 473-49. Douglas chose carefully from the untapped pool of black players and came up with seven players who formed the core of this free-lance club. Fats Jenkins was the captain and speedy 5'6" backcourt ace, in addition to starring as an outfielder in the black baseball leagues. The club had two superb centers in 6'3" Tarzan Cooper, a master at the pivot play, and 6'6" Wee Willie Smith. The best long shooters on the team were veteran Pappy Ricks and Eyre Saitch, who was also a prominent pro tennis player. Concentrating on defense were Casey Holt and Bill Yancey, who was also a stand-out shortstop in the black baseball leagues. The Rens made frequent tours of the South and Midwest, traveling in a bus fully equipped for sleeping. The Rens' most remarkable feat was an 88-game winning streak beginning January 1, 1933 and ending March 27, 1933 with a 39-32 loss to the Celtics. After the 1935-36 campaign, Douglas began rebuilding the Rens with younger talent, and his team won the 1939 World Professional Tournament with a completely new squad.

The Rens, the Sphas, and the A.B.L. were the prominent landmarks in pro basketball in the East in the 1930's, and all three persisted until after the Second World War, when the creation of the B.A.A. sealed their doom. In the Midwest, the birth of the National Basketball League in 1937 brought order to pro play in that section and would prove a surprisingly hardy link to the new major league image of pro ball, which first began to grow in stature after the war.

1937-38 through 1945-46

Courting the Big Time

1937-38 N.B.L.

A Flawed Beginning

The National Basketball League, one of the forerunners of today's N.B.A., was born when three large corporations decided to enter the field of pro basketball. Firestone and Goodyear, both of Akron, Ohio, and General Electric, of Ft. Wayne, Indiana, had fielded strong amateur entries in the Midwest Basketball Conference, and decided to run their teams against professional competition in the 1937-38 season. These three teams then joined forces with 10 independent professional teams in the Midwest to form the N.B.L.

The eastern-most franchises were the Buffalo Bisons, the Pittsburgh Pirates, and the Warren Penns. Ohio had four clubs: the Columbus Athletic Supply, the Akron Firestone NonSkids, the Akron Goodyear Wingfoots, and the Dayton Metros. In Indiana were the Whiting Ciesar All-Americans, the Ft. Wayne General Electrics, the Indianapolis Kautskys, and the Richmond King Clothiers. The western fringe of the league was made up of the Kankakee Gallagher Trojans from Illinois and the Oshkosh AllStars from Wisconsin.

These clubs were among the best, but the league organization during this first season left much to be desired. The league, under the direction of Commissioner Hubert Johnson of Detroit, never mapped out a uniform schedule, but left the arranging of games up to each individual team. As a result, the teams didn't play the same number of games, and several clubs played their full league schedules against only three or four opponents. All the teams played many exhibition games during the season, and some games against other N.B.L. teams were billed as exhibitions and left out of the league records.

On the subject of playing rules, the league could not agree on a uniform policy concerning the center jump. College ball this season had taken the revolutionary step of abolishing the center jump after every basket, automatically giving the ball to the team scored against. League meetings heatedly thrashed out the issue without ever reaching a decision. As a compromise, the decision to use the center jump rule was left to the home team.

The teams themselves were made up primarily of veteran players from each club's local area. None of the teams had much success in signing graduating college stars. Guard Ed Campion from DePaul, who was signed by Whiting, was the biggest name among the league's rookies. The Firestone, Goodyear, and General Electric teams had been able to recruit players from schools all over the country by offering athletes a career management position with the corporation. The old-line pro teams had to settle for local college and sandlot products, signing men who had regular jobs during the day. Many of the players had positions coaching high school or college teams; Johnny Wooden, for instance, was starting his illustrious coaching career with a high school team while playing with the Whiting team.

League play began in November. The set shot was still the most common way of scoring and the defense was still a rough, bruising struggle much like football. In the Eastern Division, the Firestone and Goodyear teams ran ahead of the rest of the pack in a struggle for first place. The Firestone team, coached by company athletic director Paul Sheeks, excelled at moving the ball and passing it to the open man for the clean shot. The stars of the team were 6'1" guard Jack Ozburn, who often took his man into the pivot despite his slender build, and Soup Cable, a solid all-around forward from the University of Akron. The Goodyear team, the archrival of Firestone and the 1937 champion of the Midwest Conference, fielded a well-rounded team which got most of its scoring from the guards career employee Chuck Bloedorn, and sandlot product Charley Shipp.

The General Electric team surged to the front in the Western Division, but met stiff opposition from the Oshkosh and Whiting teams. The General Electrics had three good scorers in Scotty Armstrong, Bart Quinn, and Jim Hilgemann, but Oshkosh and Whiting each had one shining star as the hub of the team. Leroy (Cowboy) Edwards, a 6'4" center who had played one brilliant year at the University of Kentucky before turning pro with Indianapolis in 1935, almost single-handedly kept the All-Stars near the top of the standings with his scoring. Armed with a deadly hook shot with either hand, Edwards scored an amazing 30 points in one game against Kankakee and averaged a league-leading 16.2 points per game. The All-Stars, coached since the team's birth in 1929 by Lon Darling, recruited Edwards' supporting cast from midwestern colleges. The Whiting Ciesar All-Americans found their star in guard Johnny Wooden, a great scorer at Purdue from 1929 to 1932. Combining his high school coaching job in Indiana with playing pro ball, Wooden used his speed and great set shot to lead the Whiting team with a scoring average of 11 points per game .

As the season headed toward the closing date of February 16, several of the league's also-rans forfeited their meaningless last games by not bothering to show up. The Richmond franchise ran into rough financial waters and moved to Cincinnati before the season was out. The strong teams, however, battled to the end for league playoff berths. A late-season slump by Goodyear gave first place to Firestone, but both clubs qualified for the playoffs in the Eastern Division. In the Western Division, Oshkosh and Whiting won playoff spots, just barely edging out Ft. Wayne.

In the battle of the Akron teams, Goodyear used a balanced attack to upset Firestone in two straight games, 26-21 and 37-31. In the best-of-three Western playoff, Oshkosh took the first game from Whiting 40-33 in Hammond, Indiana, where the Ciesars were playing their late-season home games; Johnny Wooden's 17 points for the losers topped Leroy Edwards' high of 16 for the victors. The All-Stars wrapped up the series with a 41-38 second-game triumph in which Wooden's 16 and Edwards' 15 points led both teams.

The championship series opened up in Oshkosh with a 29-28 Goodyear victory despite Edwards' 13 points. The All-Stars evened the series in Akron, with Edwards' 16 points leading the way in a 39-31 triumph. In the final game, however, Goodyear center Wes Bennett held Edwards to nine points, and Goodyear captured the first N.B.L. crown with a 35-27 victory.

Team	W	L	Pct.	GB	vs. playoff teams W	L	Pct.	vs.non-playoff teams W	L	Pct.	HOME W	L	Pct.	ROAD W	L	Pct.	Average Points G	For	Agnst.	Diff.	PLAYOFFS Average Points G	For	Agnst.	Diff.
1937/38 N.B.L. STANDINGS																								
EASTERN DIVISION																								
Akron Firestone	**14**	4	.778	—	2	2	.500	11	2	.846	8	1	.889	**5**	3	.625	17	40.1	34.0	+6.1	2	26.0	31.5	-5.5
Akron Goodyear	13	5	.722	1.0	1	3	.250	**12**	2	.857	8	1	.889	**5**	4	.556	18	35.8	**27.7**	+8.1	5	31.6	**29.2**	**+2.4**
Pittsburgh	8	5	.615	3.5	1	3	.250	7	2	.778	5	1	.667	3	4	.429	13	37.3	33.4	+3.9				
Buffalo	3	6	.333	6.5	0	4	.000	3	2	.600	2	2	.500	1	4	.200	9	29.1	30.6	-1.5				
Warren	3	9	.250	8.0	0	4	.000	3	5	.375	2	3	.400	1	6	.143	12	26.5	38.6	-12.1				
Columbus	1	**12**	.091	10.5	0	3	.000	1	7	.125	1	3	.250	0	**7**	.000	11	25.6	38.7	-13.1				
WESTERN DIVISION																								
Oshkosh	12	2	**.857**	—	0	2	.000	11	0	**1.000**	**9**	1	.900	2	1	**.667**	13	49.1	35.2	**+13.9**	5	35.0	33.2	+1.8
Whiting	12	3	.800	0.5	**5**	1	**.833**	7	2	.778	7	0	**1.000**	**5**	3	.625	15	41.3	37.3	+4.0	2	**35.5**	40.5	-5.0
Fort Wayne	13	7	.650	2.0	3	5	.375	8	2	.800	**9**	1	.900	2	6	.250	18	40.4	31.6	+8.8				
Indianapolis	4	9	.308	7.5	1	6	.143	3	2	.600	4	2	.667	0	6	.000	12	36.3	37.7	-1.4				
Cincinnati	3	7	.300	7.0	0	4	.000	3	2	.600	3	1	.750	0	5	.000	9	29.1	37.6	-8.5				
Kankakee	3	11	.214	9.0	0	**8**	.000	1	3	.250	1	**4**	.200	0	**7**	.000	12	33.3	53.3	-20.0				
Dayton	2	11	.154	9.5	1	4	.200	1	5	.167	2	**4**	.333	0	5	.000	11	31.5	37.6	-6.1				

Use Name	Pos.	Hgt.	Wgt.	Age	REGULAR SEASON G	FG	FT	Points	PPG	PLAYOFFS G	FG	FT	Points	PPG	Results
1937/38 N.B.L. — EASTERN DIVISION															
AKRON FIRESTONE NON-SKIDS	**14-4 .778**				**PAUL SHEEKS (record includes 1 forfeit win)**										
Warren Whitlinger	F	5'9	170	23	13	17	25	59	4.5	2	2	0	4	2.0	lost to Akron Goodyear 0-2;
Soup Cable	F-C	6'3	200	24	15	42	**45**	129	8.6	2	6	10	22	11.0	Road 21-26,
Duck Dowell	C-F	6'3	200	25	14	15	19	49	3.5	2	1	0	2	1.0	Home 31-37,
Al Bonniwell	G-F	6'2	185	26	15	36	19	91	6.1	2	0	1	1	0.5	
Jack Ozburn	G-F	6'1	170	23	15	59	26	144	9.6	2	6	3	15	7.5	
Paul Tobin	G	5'9	170	—	14	20	22	62	4.4	2	0	3	3	1.5	
Slim Shoun	C	6'11	200	33	13	15	11	41	3.2	2	2	0	4	2.0	
MallyJohnson	F	5'9	—	23	11	15	6	36	3.3	2	0	1	1	0.5	
Jack Shaffer	F-C	6'3	190	—	6	16	2	34	5.7						
Sew Leeka	G	6'1	185	30	9	9	4	22	2.4	1	0	0	0	0.0	
Bill Reeves	G	5'10	165	33	8	5	4	14	1.8	1	0	0	0	0.0	
AKRON GOODYEAR WINGFOOTS	**13-5 .722**				**LEFTY BYERS**										
Ray Morstadt (ankle injury)	F	6'2	220	24	9	25	23	73	8.1						defeated Akron Firestone 2-0;
Wes Bennett	F-C	6'3	175	24	15	28	31	87	5.8	5	10	5	25	5.0	Home 26-21,
Bob Cope	C-F	6'4	190	26	15	26	19	71	4.7	5	7	4	18	3.6	Road 37-31,
Charley Shipp	G	6'1	190	24	16	38	14	90	5.6	5	5	7	17	3.4	
Chuck Bloedorn	G	6'	180	25	18	58	16	132	7.3	5	14	5	33	6.6	
Russ Ochsenhirt	F	6'3	195	25	17	24	21	69	4.1	5	9	8	26	5.2	defeated Oshkosh 2-1;
Chelso Tamagno	G-F	5'10	—	24	17	17	4	38	2.2	5	2	1	5	1.0	Road 29-28,
Dean Mealy	C	6'4	195	22	8	6	16	28	3.5	3	2	5	9	3.0	Home 31-39,
Wilson Fitts	F	6'2	165	22	12	8	6	22	1.8	5	2	6	10	2.0	Road 35 37,
Mel Rush	F	6'	170	28	7	6	6	18	2.6	4	4	3	11	2.8	
Johnny McAdams	G	5'10	147	22	6	6	1	13	2.2	3	2	0	4	1.3	
Leroy Lins	G	6'1	175	24	8	1	2	4	0.5						
PITTSURGH PIRATES	**8-5 .615**				**DUDEY MOORE**										
Herb Bonn	F	6'	195	23	8	24	10	58	7.3						
Walt Miller	F	6'2	190	22	9	18	10	46	5.1						
Eddie Wisbar	C	6'6	200	21	13	27	22	76	5.8						
Ted Rigg	G	6'	175	24	11	18	11	47	4.3						
Hymie Ginsburg	G	5'9	170	23	13	36	20	92	7.1						
Don Smith	G	6'	170	27	13	16	21	53	4.1						
Bill Jesko	F	5'10	170	22	10	14	14	42	4.2						
Tim Lawry	F	5'10	155	26	9	9	8	26	2.9						
Dudey Moore	G-F	5'9	180	27	8	10	5	25	3.1						
Ed Kweller	C	6'7	225	22	8	4	5	13	1.6						
Marty Reiter	G	5'7	160	26	1	3	1	7	7.0						

Use Name	Pos	Hgt	Wgt	Age	REGULAR SEASON G	FG	FT	Points	PPG	PLAYOFFS G	FG	FT	Points	PPG	Results
1937/38 N.B.L. — EASTERN DIVISION (continued)															
BUFFALO BISONS	**3-6 .333**				**ALLIE HEERDT**										
Bello Snyder	F	5'9	185	25	8	18	10	46	5.8						
Neil O'Donnell	F-C	6'5	220	23	9	14	7	35	3.9						
Eddie Malanowicz	C	6'3	220	27	5	14	8	36	7.2						
Al Cervi	G	5'11	170	20	9	19	6	44	4.9						
Paul Coleman	G	6'2	160	22	6	12	1	25	4.2						
Dan Carnevale	G	6'	185	19	9	10	6	26	2.9						
Stan Raiman	G-F	5'9	140	23	9	10	2	22	2.4						
Stan Jackson	F	—	—	—	7	8	2	18	2.6						
Jim O'Donnell	F-C	6'1	180	25	8	3	4	10	1.3						
Johnny Lenhart	F	6'4	180	22	3	0	0	0	0.0						
WARREN PENNS	**3-9 .250**				**GERRY ARCHIBALD**										
Johnny Pawk	F	6'2	210	27	12	22	10	54	4.5						
Walt Stankey	F-C	6'3	200	26	9	21	17	59	6.6						
Jack Sterling	C	6'5	—	20	6	13	10	36	6.0						
Red Malackany	G	5'9	165	24	11	13	8	34	3.1						
Frank Maury	G	5'5	155	27	12	31	13	75	6.3						
Steve Pawk	C-F	6'4	175	23	6	8	5	21	3.5						
Emmett Morrison	F-G	6'3	180	22	11	5	9	19	1.7						
Bill Holland	C-F	6'5	210	23	2	3	1	7	3.5						
Stub Jacobson	C	6'6	—	—	4	2	2	6	1.5						
Gerry Archibald	G	6'	170	29	7	2	1	5	0.7						
Bob Lytle	F	6'4	180	21	1	1	0	2	2.0						
COLUMBUS ATHLETIC SUPPLY	**1-12 .077**				**COOKIE CUNNINGHAM**					(record includes 2 forfeit losses)					
Herbie Hutchison	F-G	—	—	—	7	25	6	56	8.0						
Cookie Cunningham	F-C	6'3	210	32	11	27	27	81	7.4						
Sam Loucks	C-F	6'4	195	22	9	15	7	37	4.1						
Woody Pitzer	G-F	6'	160	27	11	20	10	50	4.5						
Denny Elliott	G	5'9	150	23	9	10	5	25	2.8						
Clyde Anton	G	—	—	—	7	4	2	10	1.4						
Norm Wagner*	C	6'5	200	25	3	3	3	9	3.0	*(from & to & from Cin, to Day)					
McConnell	G-F	—	—	—	5	2	1	5	1.0						
Jack Sullivan	F	6'1	182	21	2	1	1	3	1.5						
Pete Basich	G	5'9	145	20	1	1	1	3	3.0						
Gene Scholz	F	5'8	160	20	3	1	0	2	0.7						
Beanie Berens	C	6'5	190	24	1	0	1	1	1.0						
Buck Lamme	G	6'2	—	32	1	0	0	0	0.0						
Miller	F	—	—	—	1	0	0	0	0.0						
1937/38 N.B.L — WESTERN DIVISION															
OSHKOSH ALL-STARS	**12-2 .857**				**GEORGE HOTCHKISS**					(record includes 1 forfeit win)					
Pete Preboski	F	6'1	195	23	11	25	13	63	5.7	5	10	11	31	6.2	defeated Whiting 2-0;
Augie Vander Meulen (HC)	F	6'4	175	28	10	29	19	77	7.7	5	6	12	24	4.8	Road 40-33,
Leroy Edwards	C	6'4	200	23	13	**83**	44	**210**	**16.2**	5	**24**	**21**	**69**	13.8	Home 41-38
Herm Witasek	G	6'2	210	24	13	29	11	69	5.3	5	4	1	9	1.8	
Frank Linskey	G	6'2	180	24	11	16	15	47	4.3	4	2	1	5	1.3	
Ray Adams	F	6'2	185	23	12	26	10	62	5.2	5	5	7	17	3.4	lost to Akron Goodyear 1-2;
Ray Hamann (HC)	G-F	6'4	205	26	11	22	5	49	4.5	3	6	0	12	4.0	Home 28-29,
George Svendsen (FB)	C-F	6'4	230	24	11	18	9	45	4.1	1	0	0	0	0.0	Road 39-31,
Ed Mullen	G	6'3	185	24	9	8	0	16	1.8	5	1	6	8	1.6	Home 27-35
Ed Stege	F	6'6	220	24	2	0	0	0	0.0						
WHITING CIESAR ALL-AMERICANS	**12-3 .800**				**WHITEY WICKHORST**										
Ken Gunning	F	—	—	23	15	37	31	105	7.0	2	3	5	11	5.5	lost to Oshkosh 0-2;
Bill Haarlow	F	6'1	170	24	10	26	14	66	6.6	1	2	3	7	7.0	Home 33-40,
Vince McGowan	C	6'6	200	24	15	57	30	144	9.6	2	5	1	11	5.5	Road 38-41
Ed Campion	G	6'2	190	22	15	19	4	42	2.8	2	1	0	2	1.0	
Johnny Wooden	G	5'10	183	27	13	52	39	143	11.0	2	8	17	33	**16.5**	
Joe Stack	G-F	5'10	185	24	14	23	14	60	4.3	2	0	0	0	0.0	
Bill Perigo	F	6'	180	26	15	22	11	55	3.7	1	0	0	0	0.0	
Joe Sotak	F-C	6'2	210	23	5	2	1	5	1.0	2	1	2	4	2.0	
Fred Arndt	F	—	—	—	—	—	—	—	—	2	1	0	2	1.0	
Marty Cullen	G-F	—	—	—	—	—	—	—	—	2	0	1	1	0.5	
Willie Young	C	—	—	—	—	—	—	—	—	2	0	0	0	0.0	

Use Name	Pos	Hgt	Wgt	Age	REGULAR SEASON G	FG	FT	Points	PPG	PLAYOFFS G	FG	FT	Points	PPG	Results

1937/38 N.B.L. — WESTERN DIVISION (continued)

Use Name	Pos	Hgt	Wgt	Age	G	FG	FT	Points	PPG	G	FG	FT	Points	PPG	Results
FORT WAYNE GENERAL ELECTRICS	**13-7 .650**				**BYRON EVARD** (record includes 2 forfeit wins)										
Bart Quinn	F	6'2	210	—	18	71	28	170	9.4						
Scotty Armstrong	F-C	6'4	190	23	17	56	35	147	8.6						
Pres Slack	C	6'2	180	26	16	38	10	86	5.4						
Jim Hilgemann	G	6'	170	21	17	50	30	130	7.6						
Bud Lindberg	G	6'	175	26	18	30	20	80	4.4						
Willie Adams	F	5'11	160	—	16	21	16	58	3.6						
Ife Holmes	G	5'6	150	30	15	17	7	41	2.7						
Byron Evard	G	5'8	155	—	10	7	2	16	1.6						
INDIANAPOLIS KAUTSKYS	**4-9 .308**				**FRANK KAUTSKY** (record includes 1 forfeit loss)										
Bob Kessler	F	6'	165	23	10	36	31	103	10.3						
Cy Proffitt	F	6'3	190	26	12	19	13	51	4.3						
George Chestnut	C-F	6'5	210	23	12	15	23	53	4.4						
Leo Crowe	G	5'11	170	25	12	30	14	74	6.2						
Harlan Wilson	G	5'11	160	23	11	24	24	72	6.5						
Frank Baird	G-F	5'11	160	25	12	21	8	50	4.2						
Bill Schrader	C	6'7	210	26	8	6	2	14	1.8						
Everett Swank	G	5'11	165	24	4	4	2	10	2.5						
Fred Fechtman	C	6'8	210	27	3	4	1	9	3.0						
CINCINNATI COMELLOS	**3-7 .300**				**BOB McCONACHIE (1-4 .200), JOHN WIETHE (2-3 .400) (record includes 1 forfeit loss)**										
Richmond, Ind. King Clothiers until January 5, 1938, 1-2 .333)															
Ken Jordan	F	6'2	180	25	8	14	10	38	4.8						
Carl Austing	F-C	6'4	180	27	5	16	5	37	7.4						
Norm Wagner*	C	6'5	200	25	4	9	2	20	5.0						*(to & from & to Col, to Day)
John Wiethe	G-F	6'	205	25	6	10	12	32	5.3						
Leo Sack	G	5'8	145	23	6	20	3	43	7.2						
Stan Arnzen	F	—	—	—	5	10	3	23	4.6						
Joe Kruse	G	6'2	200	23	6	8	4	20	3.3						
Gene Mechling	G	6'1	215	28	3	8	2	18	6.0						
Frank Shamel	F	6'	200	25	3	5	0	10	3.3						
Harold Bower	G	5'10	165	25	2	4	1	9	4.5						
Earle Thomas	C	6'4	205	22	3	4	0	8	2.7						
Loren Wright	F	—	—	—	4	2	0	4	1.0						
Junior Saffer	F	—	—	20	1	0	0	0	0.0						
KANKAKEE GALLAGHER TROJANS	**3-11 .214**				**DON BETOURNE**										
Don Betourne	F	6'1	200	22	12	30	16	76	6.3						
Louie Sauer	F-C	6'6	235	22	12	31	17	78	6.5						
Johnny Hoekstra	C	6'5	—	—	12	27	16	70	5.8						
Warren Hair	G	—	—	—	11	15	16	46	4.2						
Fred Grafft	G	5'9	—	22	10	33	20	86	8.6						
Big Moose Meyer	F-C	6'7	—	—	9	14	2	30	3.3						
Little Moose Meyer	G	6'	—	21	3	3	1	7	2.3						
Don Walsh	F	—	—	—	4	2	0	4	1.0						
Bob DeWeese	G	5'11	160	22	2	1	0	2	1.0						
Tarzan Woltzen	G-F	—	—	—	8	0	0	0	0.0						
DAYTON METROS	**2-11 .154**				**BILL HOSKET**										
Bobby Colburn	F	5'10	190	26	11	32	16	80	7.3						
Glen Roberts	F-C	6'5	200	25	8	14	11	39	4.9						
Bill Hosket	C	6'5	—	26	10	11	12	34	3.4						
Bud Moodler	C	6'3	215	26	7	4	9	17	2.4						
Lou Rutter	G	6'2	180	23	8	30	20	80	10.0						
Clovis Stark	F	6'4	175	23	9	14	10	38	4.2						
Howard Stammler	G-F	5'10	155	26	4	9	2	20	5.0						
Curt McMahon	G	6'	150	22	10	8	3	19	1.9						
Glenn Schlechty	F	6'6	185	25	4	3	1	7	1.8						
Wyman Roberts	F	5'11	160	21	2	2	2	6	3.0						
Norm Wagner (from Cin & Col)	C	6'5	200	25	1	2	1	5	5.0						
Beryl Drummond	G	6'1	185	19	2	1	0	2	1.0						

1938-39 N.B.L.

Losing One Rule, Two Plums, and Five Teams

With a glamorous group of college stars graduating in the class of 1938, N.B.L. teams this season made more of an effort to sign these young players. The league couldn't land Hank Luisetti, the famous one-hand shooting whiz from Stanford, who chose to play A.A.U. ball. Nor could they sign Mike Bloom, the star centerfrom N.I.T.-champion Temple, who signed with the Philadelphia Sphas of the American Basketball League. But a good number of popular players did bring their reputations directly from college into the league.

The Akron Firestones added three top frontcourt stars in Paul Nowak and Johnny Moir of Notre Dame and Jerry Bush from St. John's. The Indianapolis Kautskys began rebuilding their team by signing Jewell Young and Johnny Sines, two scoring aces from Purdue, while the Akron Goodyears strengthened their championship squad by adding bruising center Floyd Ebaugh from Nebraska. The Warren Penns picked up forward Bill Laughlin and guard Buddy Jeannette out of Washington & Jefferson, and the Hammond Ciesar All-Americans signed Johnny Townsend, an All-American forward from Michigan, and guard Lou Boudreau, the future Major league baseball star who had been declared ineligible to compete in sports at the University of Illinois.

These professional rookies found their way into a smaller, tighter N.B.L. The league had shrunk from 13 teams to 8, with the Buffalo, Columbus, Ft. Wayne, Cincinnati, Kankakee, and Dayton franchises dropped. The Whiting team shifted to nearby Hammond, and the Sheboygan Redskins, formerly a semipro outfit in Wisconsin, was added to the circuit. A regular schedule, with all teams playing 28 games, was drawn up, and the center jump rule was abolished.

Once tbe playing season started, the Firestone team quickly established itself at the head of the circuit. Veterans Soup Cable and Jack Ozburn held down the backcourt slots, with rookies Bush, Moir, and Nowak playing up front. Bush and Moir both played solid all-around games in the forward slots, while 6'6" center Nowak concentrated on rebounding and setting picks. Using a lot of screens, picks, and sharp passing, Firestone wrapped up the Eastern Division title by mid-February by winning their first 17 games. Only a shoulder injury to Nowak slowed the team down enough to lose three games the rest of the season.

The rest of the Eastern clubs had to settle for table scraps. Goodyear fielded essentially the same team that won last year's championship, but the rest of the league had improved enough to demote them to also-ran status. The Warren club received a big boost from rookies Laughlin, a good shooting forward, and Jeannette, a tough, smart guard who would have a long professional career, but financial problems forced a franchise shift to Cleveland late in the season. Pittsburgh helped itself by signing Paul Birch, a star forward at Duquesne who had played for the Celtics, but a lack of height killed any chances of a challenge for first place.

In the Western Division, the race was tighter, with Indianapolis, Oshkosh, and Sheboygan all in the running into late January. The Oshkosh club put together a hot February and won the title, with center Leroy Edwards again winning the league scoring championship. Edwards' average fell off from 16.2 to 11.9 but the All-Stars got strong supporting performances from defensive star Herm Witasek and from Scotty Armstrong, a solid all-around forward who joined the team from the defunct Ft. Wayne club.

Oshkosh's Wisconsin rivals, the Sheboygan Redskins, slumped in February and fell into third place, a very creditable showing for a club which had been playing local semipro ball last year. Forwards Rube Lautenschlager and Paul Sokody led the Redskins in scoring, but center Ed Dancker was the hub of the team. The 6'7" Dancker came to the Redskins without any college training, but with a definite talent for rebounding and defense. In early March, after the close of the college season and near the end of the N.B.L. slate, the Redskins signed two Marquette seniors, guard Dave Quabius and center Moose Graf. This signing college seniors in March soon became a common practice for pro teams throughout the country.

The two remaining Western clubs, Hammond and Indianapolis, never lived up to their high preseason hopes. The Hammond club, which had made last year's playoffs, began the season with star veteran Johnny Wooden and two rookie stars, Townsend and Boudreau. However, Townsend's position as assistant coach at Michigan forced him to the sidelines soon after the start of the season because the Big Ten passed a rule forbidding any of its coaches or officials to participate in pro ball. Without Townsend, the team fell apart, and Wooden was sold to Indianapolis in December with the team deep in the cellar. The Kautskys, owned by florist Frank Kautsky, had only two men back from last year and fielded a trio of good scorers in Wooden, Jewell Young, and Johnny Sines.

At the end of the regular season, the Akron Firestones and Oshkosh All-Stars squared off in the league's five-game championship playoff. Firestone center Nowak was still out of action, but coach Paul Sheeks successfully plugged the gap with 6'2" Johnny Moir and 6'11" Slim Shoun. The Firestones and All-Stars split the first two games in Akron and headed up to Oshkosh to play the final three matches. Firestone easily won the third game 40-29, but Leroy Edwards' 25 points led Oshkosh to a 49-37 fourth game triumph. With the title on the line, the Firestones held Edwards to nine points by constantly double-teaming him, and won the deciding game 37-30.

But even after the championship playoff ended, the season wasn't over for Sheboygan and Oshkosh. These two clubs participated in the first annual World Tournament, an invitational tournament for pro teams staged in Chicago by the *Chicago Herald American*. Besides Oshkosh and Sheboygan, the field of 11 included the original Celtics and the nation's two top black teams, the New York Rens and the Harlem Globetrotters. Both N.B.L. teams lasted into the late rounds, with Sheboygan losing the consolation game to the Trotters 36-33, while Oshkosh lost the championship game to the Rens 34-25. Oshkosh's Leroy Edwards led all scorers and won All-Star center honors.

Team	W	L	Pct.	GB	vs. playoff teams W	vs. playoff teams L	vs. playoff teams Pct.	vs.non-playoff teams W	vs.non-playoff teams L	vs.non-playoff teams Pct.	HOME W	HOME L	HOME Pct.	ROAD W	ROAD L	ROAD Pct.	Average Points G	Average Points For	Average Points Agnst.	Average Points Diff.	PLAYOFFS Average Points G	PLAYOFFS For	PLAYOFFS Agnst.	PLAYOFFS Diff.
1938/39 N.B.L.STANDINGS																								
EASTERN DIVISION																								
Akron Firestone	24	3	.889		3	1	.750	21	2	.913	11	2	.846	13	1	.929	27	44.6	35.9	+8.7	5	40.0	36.8	+3.2
Akron Goodyear	14	14	.500	10.5	2	6	.250	12	8	.600	7	7	.500	7	7	.500	28	34.1	35.5	-1.4				
Cleveland	14	14	.500	10.5	4	4	.500	9	10	.474	9	5	.643	7	7	.500	27	38.1	39.6	-1.5				
Pittsburgh	13	14	.481	11	1	7	.125	12	7	.632	9	5	.643	4	9	.308	27	36.9	39.3	-2.4				
WESTERN DIVISION																								
Oshkosh	17	11	.607		1	3	.250	16	8	.667	10	4	.714	7	7	.500	28	41.2	36.1	+5.1	5	36.8	40.0	-3.2
Indianapolis	13	13	.500	3	2	5	.286	11	8	.579	9	4	.692	4	9	.308	26	43.3	43.6	-0.3				
Sheboygan	11	17	.393	6	0	8	.000	11	9	.550	7	7	.500	4	10	.286	28	35.6	37.5	-1.9				
Hammond	4	24	.143	13	1	7	.125	3	16	.158	4	9	.308	0	14	.000	27	36.0	42.1	-6.1				

Use Name	Pos.	Hgt.	Wgt.	Age	REGULAR SEASON G	FG	FT	Points	PPG	PLAYOFFS G	FG	FT	Points	PPG	Results
1938/39 N.B.L.—EASTERN DIVISION															
AKRON FIRESTONE NON-SKIDS	**24-3 .889**				**PAUL SHEEKS**										
Jerry Bush	F	6'3	200	24	24	50	26	126	5.3	5	8	14	30	6.0	defeated Oshkosh 3-2;
Johnny Moir	F-C	6'2	184	21	23	78	26	182	7.9	5	18	8	44	8.8	Home 50-38,
Paul Nowak (shoulder injury)	C	6'6	205	24	15	33	14	80	5.3						Home 36-38,
Soup Cabie	G-F	6'3	200	25	24	99	64	262	10.9	5	12	17	41	8.2	Road 40-29,
Jack Ozburn	G	6'1	170	24	19	75	34	184	9.7	5	18	11	47	9.4	Road 37-49
Al Bonniwell	G-F	6'2	185	27	24	49	8	106	4.4	5	5	3	13	2.6	
Rip Terjesen	F-C	6'3	195	23	25	38	23	99	4.0	5	5	3	13	2.6	
Paul Tobin	G	5'9	170	—	15	21	6	48	3.2	5	2	3	7	1.4	
Glen Roberts	C-F	6'5	200	26	15	20	6	46	3.1	2	0	1	1	0.5	
Slim Shoun	C	6'11	200	34	6	13	12	38	6.3	2	2	0	4	2.0	
Ted Migdal	F	5'9	140	20	2	8	2	18	9.0	1	0	0	0	0.0	
Mally Johnson	F-G	5'9	—	29	12	5	2	12	1.0	1	0	0	0	0.0	
Don Smith	G	6'	170	28	1	1	0	2	2.0						
AKRON GOODYEAR WINGFOOTS	**14-14 .500**				**LEFTY BYERS**										
George Hesik	F	6'2	195	25	23	24	21	69	3.0						
Russ Ochsenhirt	F	6'3	195	26	24	40	23	103	4.3						
Wes Bennett	C-F	6'3	175	25	22	36	37	109	5.0						
Charley Shipp	G	6'1	190	25	24	59	24	142	5.9						
Chuck Bloedorn	G	6'	180	26	25	79	46	204	8.2						
Ray Morstadt	F	6'2	220	25	23	21	12	54	2.3						
Nick Frascella	F	6'2	185	24	18	24	5	53	2.9						
Dean Mealy	C	6'4	195	23	10	15	14	44	4.4						
Mike McMichael	G	6'2	195	23	11	17	9	43	3.9						
Wilson Fitts	G	6'2	165	23	19	16	7	39	2.1						
Floyd Ebaugh	C	6'7	230	24	22	13	12	38	1.7						
Bob Parsons	F-G	6'1	175	23	11	11	4	26	2.4						
Chelso Tamagno	G	5'10	—	25	11	6	3	15	1.4						
Bob Johnson	G	6'2	170	21	4	6	3	15	3.8						
CLEVELAND WHITE HORSES	**14-14 .500**				**GERRY ARCHIBALD(record includes 1 forfeit win)**										
(Warren Penns until February 10,1939, 9-10 .474)															
Bill Laughlin	F	6'2	185	23	27	92	48	232	8.6						
Walt Stankey	F-C	6'3	205	27	27	97	25	219	8.1						
Bill Holland	C	6'5	210	24	27	73	34	180	6.7						
Buddy Jeannette	G	5'11	175	21	26	54	65	173	6.7						
Frank Maury	G	5'5	155	28	27	49	14	112	4.1						
Reno Strand	G-F	6'	195	29	15	17	8	42	2.8						
Art Hyatt	G	6'2	190	25	7	14	9	37	5.3						
Joe Leson	F	6'2	210	26	17	9	11	29	1.7						
Johnny Pawk	F	6'2	210	28	2	1	2	4	2.0						
Gerry Archibald	G	6'	170	30	2	0	0	0	0.0						
PITTSBURGH PIRATES	**13-14 .481**				**DUDEY MOORE**										
Paul Birch	F-C	6'1	190	27	22	85	51	221	10.0						
Walt Miller	F-C	6'2	190	23	19	52	44	148	7.8						
Emie Fortney	C	6'4	220	24	11	16	11	43	3.9						
Bill Jesko	G-F	5'10	170	23	24	66	19	151	6.3						
Hymie Ginsburg	G	5'9	170	24	23	46	17	109	4.7						
Marty Reiter	G	5'7	160	27	17	30	19	79	4.6						
Squint Phares	G-F	5'10	—	23	7	18	12	48	6.9						
Dudey Moore	G	5'9	180	28	13	20	7	47	3.6						
Ed Kweller	C	6'7	225	23	13	14	14	42	3.2						
Gene Rosenthal	F	5'11	175	24	9	13	4	30	3.3						
Herb Bonn	F	6'	195	24	7	12	4	28	4.0						
Chub Watson	C	6'2	—	22	1	8	0	16	16.0						
Ed Spotovich	F-C	6'2	190	22	3	6	1	13	4.3						
Red Malackany	G	5'9	165	25	4	3	2	8	2.0						
Joe Fabel	F	6'1	190	21	1	3	0	6	6.0						
Joe Kinney	C	6'6	—	—	2	1	1	3	1.5						
Jack Sterling	C	6'5	—	21	12	1	1	3	1.5						

1938/39 N.B.L. — WESTERN DIVISION

Use Name	Pos	Hgt	Wgt	Age	REGULAR SEASON G	FG	FT	Points	PPG	PLAYOFFS G	FG	FT	Points	PPG	Results
OSHKOSH ALL-STARS	**17-11 .607**				**GEORGE HOTCHKISS**										
Pete Preboski	F	6'1	195	24	27	76	36	188	7.0	5	4	11	19	3.8	lost to Akron Firestone 2-3;
Scotty Armstrong	F-C	6'4	190	25	27	65	36	166	6.1	5	10	5	25	5.0	Road 38-50,
Leroy Edwards	C	6'4	210	24	28	**124**	**86**	**334**	**11.9**	5	**23**	**24**	**70**	**14.0**	Road 38-36,
Herm Witasek	G	6'2	210	25	28	56	29	141	5.0	5	15	5	35	7.0	Home 29-40,
Frank Linskey	G	6'2	180	25	24	22	17	61	2.5	4	5	2	12	3.0	Home 49-37,
															Home 30-37
Ray Adams	F	6'2	185	24	24	42	26	110	4.6	5	3	3	9	1.8	
Ed Mullen	G	6'3	185	25	26	25	11	61	2.3	5	0	3	3	0.6	
Ray Hamann (HC)	G-F	6'4	205	27	18	27	6	60	3.3	4	1	1	3	0.8	
Augie Vander Meulen (HC)	F-C	6'4	175	29	7	10	8	28	4.0	3	2	4	8	2.7	
Byron Bell	C	6'3	180	24	1	1	2	4	4.0						
Dave Dupee	F	6'3	185	22	1	0	1	1	1.0						
Bob Weigandt	G	5'10	190	24	1	0	0	0	0.0						
Emmet Birk	F	6'1	185	24	1	0	0	0	0.0						
INDIANAPOLIS KAUTSKYS	**13-13 .500**				**BOB NIPPER**										
Johnny Sines	F	6'1	190	24	23	86	43	215	9.3						
Jim Birr	F-C	6'3	215	22	24	77	28	182	7.6						
Herm Schuessler	C	6'8	210	24	19	28	14	70	3.7						
Jewell Young	G-F	6'	160	25	26	96	72	264	10.2						
Frank Baird (HC)	G	5'11	160	26	23	81	19	181	7.9						
Glynn Downey (HC)	G	6'	180	23	15	27	19	73	4.9						
Dave Williams	C-F	6'3	210	24	18	24	10	58	3.2						
Johnny Wooden (from Ham) (HC)	G	5'10	183	28	5	14	11	39	7.8						
Vern Huffman (FB)	F	6'2	215	24	3	7	6	20	6.7						
Everett Swank	G-F	5'11	165	25	9	3	4	10	1.1						
Lorvin Proctor	F	—	—	—	3	4	0	8	2.7						
Rex Rudicel	G	5'6	150	26	3	2	0	4	1.3						
Earle Thomas	C	6'4	205	23	6	0	1	1	0.2						
Carl Anderson	G	6'3	215	25	3	0	0	0	0.0						
Merle Alexander (illness)	C-F	6'6	185	31	2	0	0	0	0.0						
Bob Phillips	G	—	—	22	1	0	0	0	0.0						
SHEBOYGAN REDSKINS	**11-17 .393**				**DOC SCHUTTE**										
Paul Sokody	F	6'2	185	24	28	88	47	223	8.0						
Rube Lautenschlager	F	6'3	190	23	27	83	38	204	7.6						
Ed Dancker	C	6'7	200	24	28	63	36	162	5.8						
Otto Kolar	G	6'3	180	27	26	57	22	136	5.2						
Johnny Posewitz	G	6'	185	32	24	25	6	56	2.3						
Scoop Posewitz	G	5'11	180	30	22	15	13	43	2.0						
Les Kuplic	F	6'3	200	26	26	14	6	34	1.3						
Stan Zadel	C-F	6'5	215	22	10	9	13	31	3.1						
Carl Roth (VR)	G-F	6'2	200	29	14	14	1	29	2.1						
Slim Lonsdorf	F-C	6'3	185	33	17	5	10	20	1.2						
Kenny Suesens	G	6'1	175	22	10	4	7	15	1.5						
Pres Slack	C-F	6'2	180	27	7	5	2	12	1.7						
Kiernan Crowley	G	5'8	155	22	5	3	4	10	2.0						
Moose Graf	C	6'3	200	21	1	3	3	9	9.0						
Sparky Adams	F	6'1	185	21	1	3	2	8	8.0						
Eddie Kolar	G	5'10	170	29	1	1	2	4	4.0						
Dave Quabius	G	6'	185	22	1	0	0	0	0.0						
Walter Grauman	G	6'2	200	23	1	0	0	0	0.0						
HAMMOND CIESAR ALL-AMERICANS	**4-24 .143**				**WHITEY WICKHORST** (record includes 1 forfeit loss)										
Johnny Townsend* (VR)	F	6'4	205	22	5	14	15	43	8.6	*(forced to quit to retain post as assistant basketball coach at					
Nick Yost	F-C	6'4	220	23	9	36	9	81	9.0						U. of Michigan)
Vince McGowan	C	6'6	210	25	24	48	45	141	5.9						
Lou Boudreau (BB)	G-F	5'11	170	21	23	78	33	189	8.2						
Johnny Wooden (to Ind) (HC)	G	5'10	183	28	5	10	12	32	6.4						
Joe Sotak	F-C	6'2	210	24	23	47	48	142	6.2						
Ed Campion	G	6'2	190	23	23	40	15	95	4.1						
Joe Stack	F-G	5'10	185	25	15	26	22	74	4.9						
Tommy Nisbet	G	5'10	165	21	5	16	4	36	7.2						
Nich Hashu	G	6'1	195	21	15	10	8	28	1.9						
Bob Kessler	F	6'	165	24	4	9	4	22	5.5						
James	F	—	—	—	4	6	9	21	5.3						
Bill Wendt	F	6'3	180	23	8	8	4	20	2.5						
Pick Dehner	F-C	6'5	190	24	1	7	1	15	15.0						
Bob McElliott	C-F	—	—	23	5	5	1	11	2.2						
Bill Perigo	F	6'	180	27	4	2	6	10	2.5						
Boris	F	—	—	—	1	2	2	6	6.0						
Vince Oliver	G	5'10	185	23	5	1	0	2	0.4						
Thornton	F	—	—	—	1	1	0	2	2.0						
Brown	G	—	—	—	1	1	0	2	2.0						
Willett	F	—	—	—	2	0	0	0	0.0						
Steve Fowdy	F	6'2	180	23	1	0	0	0	0.0						
Sicky	G	—	—	—	1	0	0	0	0.0						

1939-40 N.B.L.

Firestoning the Opposition

The two new franchises in the N.B.L. this season led the way in signing fresh talent from the crop of graduating college seniors. The Detroit Eagles took over last year's Cleveland franchise, but kept only five men from that squad. Coach Gerry Archibald was held over from last year, and he used only two ex-Cleveland players, Buddy Jeannette and Bill Holland, in prominent roles. The Eagles built practically an entire new team by signing four of the nation's best college players. From N.C.A.A.-champion Oregon came forward Laddie Gale and 6'8" center Slim Wintermute. Long Island University, the N.I.T. champion, contributed forward Irv Torgoff. Guard Bernie Opper signed from the University of Kentucky. The Eagles also added guard Nat Frankel, a noncollege man who had been playing in the American Basetball League.

The Chicago Bruins also joined the league, replacing the disbanded Pittsburgh Pirates. Owned by George Halas of the Chicago Bears, the Bruins signed a few marginal veterans from other N.B.L. teams and even used Bears' end George Wilson and halfback Bob MacLeod as reserve forwards. Two rookies from Loyola of Chicago, however, formed the heart of the new team. Guard Wibs Kautz, and 6'9" center Mike Novak had led Loyola to the N.I.T. finals before losing their first game of the year. Kautz and Novak formed the league's best one-two punch and scored 566 of the Bruins' 1030 points.

Some of the older N.B.L. teams were also successful in signing rookie talent. The Indianapolis Kautskys landed a prize in All-American guard Ernie Andres out of Indiana, and the Sheboygan Redskins signed Marquette guard Dave Quabius, who had turned pro late last season. The Hammond Ciesar All-Americans signed a pair of blue-chip prospects in forwards Bobby Neu of DePaul and Chuck Chuckovits of Toledo. Looking to completely rebuild their team, the Akron Goodyears signed seven rookies, the best being guard Ben Stephens of Iowa.

One team that had signed no rookies, the Akron Firestones, showed no ill effects in their battle with the Detroit Eagles for first place in the Eastern Division. The Firestone lineup of veteran backcourtmen Soup Cable and Jack Ozburn and sophomore frontcourtmen Johnny Moir, Jerry Bush, and Paul Nowak continued last year's championship form of crisp passing and getting the ball to the open man. The Firestones just edged out the young Detroit team for first place, moving past the slumping Eagles at the tail end of the season.

The Goodyear team finished a distant third in a rebuilding year. The old club, which had won the league title in 1937-38, was dismantled, with star guard Chuck Bloedorn demoted to the bench and his backcourt partner Charley Shipp released to join the Oshkosh All-Stars. Of the many newcomers, Stephens, the quick 6' guard, took the leadership role on the team with his fine scoring. The Indianapolis team finished in last place. Despite three good scorers in Jewell Young, Johnny Sines, and rookie Ernie Andres, the Kautskys suffered from a lack of size and from Johnny Wooden's retirement.

In the Western Division, Oshkosh, Sheboygan, and Chicago all stayed near the top of the standings for the entire season, with the two Wisconsin teams winding up in a dead heat for first place, one game ahead of Chicago. Leroy Edwards, although the smallest center in the league at 6'4", used his strength and great hook shot to lead Oshkosh and the league in scoring for the third straight season. General Manager Lon Darling built his strongest squad yet around Edwards and holdover guard Herm Witasek, the team's defensive leader. Charley Shipp came over from the Goodyear club to quarterback the All-Stars from the backcourt, and coach Darling added two burly forwards to his squad in Connie Mack Berry and Lou Barle, both football players in the N.F.L. The Sheboygan Redskins also fielded a bulky team, with center Ed Dancker, guard Otto Kolar, and forward Rube Lautenschlager among the league's best defensive players.

The third-place Chicago Bruin team got top seasons from star rookies Novak, a big center who could both rebound and shoot from the corners, and Kautz, a quick-shooting guard. The last-place Hammond club got a good rookie season out of Bobby Neu and a sorely diasappointing one from Chuck Chuckovits, who retired before the end of the season.

In March, the league began its playoffs, which were expanded to two rounds. In the Eastern semifinals, the Firestones eliminated the Detroit club, who played without injured center Wintermute, two games to one. In the West, Oshkosh also needed three games to eliminate Sheboygan. The finals shaped up as a rematch between Firestone and Oshkosh. In the first two games at Oshkosh, the All-Stars ran roughshod over the defending champs, beating them 47-37 and 60-46. The two teams then traveled to Akron, where the Firestones took the first game 35-32. In the fourth game of the series, the Firestone passing attack kept hitting the open man as the Akron team evened the series with a 41-40 squeeker.

The final game, played in the Kent State University gym, seesawed back and forth between the two tired, but determined teams. The halftime score stood at 39-39, and Oshkosh took a 48-46 lead in the third quarter. Firestone coach Paul Sheeks then put little-used sub Tommy O'Brien into the game. He quickly threw in two long set shots to put the Firestones in front 50-48. From that point on, the Akron team never lost the lead. They won the game 61-60 and thus earned their second straight N.B.L. crown .

Disappointed in their second try for the title, the Oshkosh club hoped to do well in the second annual World Tournament in Chicago. Sheboygan and Chicago also entered the field from the N.B.L., and while Oshkosh and Sheboygan lost in the quarterfinals, the hometown Bruins stayed alive until the very end, losing the championship game to the Harlem Globetrotters 31-29. Two N.B.L. players, center Leroy Edwards and guard Wibs Kautz, won berths in this year's All-Tournament team.

Team	W	L	Pct.	GB	vs. playoff teams W	L	Pct.	vs.non-playoff teams W	L	Pct.	HOME W	L	Pct.	ROAD W	L	Pct.	Average Points G	For	Agnst.	Diff.	PLAYOFFS Average Points G	For	Agnst.	Diff.
1939/40 N.B.L. STANDINGS																								
EASTERN DIVISION																								
Akron Firestone	**18**	9	**.667**	—	7	4	**.636**	11	5	.688	10	3	.769	**8**	**6**	**.571**	27	**44.2**	40.8	**+3.4**	8	43.9	44.8	-0.9
Detroit	17	10	.630	1	5	6	.455	**12**	4	.750	**12**	2	**.857**	5	8	.385	27	39.8	36.6	+3.2	3	39.7	43.7	-4.0
Akron Goodyear	14	14	.500	4.5	4	**12**	.250	10	2	**.833**	8	6	.571	6	8	.429	28	37.4	37.0	+0.4				
Indianapolis	9	**19**	.321	9.5	5	11	.313	4	**8**	.333	6	**8**	.429	3	11	.214	28	41.5	45.6	-4.1				
WESTERN DIVISION																								
Oshkosh	15	13	.536	—	6	6	.500	9	7	.563	**12**	2	**.857**	3	11	.214	28	42.7	40.2	+2.5	8	**44.1**	39.5	**+4.6**
Sheboygan	15	13	.536	—	4	8	.333	10	6	.625	11	3	.786	4	10	.286	28	36.7	38.3	-1.6	3	32.0	**38.0**	-6.0
Chicago	14	14	.500	1	**8**	8	.500	6	6	.500	10	4	.714	4	10	.286	28	36.8	**36.4**	0.4				
Hammond	9	**19**	.321	6	5	11	.313	4	**8**	.333	7	7	.500	2	**12**	.143	28	36.9	40.8	-3.9				

1939/40 N.B.L. — EASTERN DIVISION

Use Name	Pos.	Hgt.	Wgt.	Age	G	FG	FT	Points	PPG	G	FG	FT	Points	PPG	Results
AKRON FIRESTONE NON-SKIDS	**18-9 .667**			**PAUL SHEEKS**											
Johnny Moir	F-C	6'2	184	22	27	59	47	165	6.1	7	31	16	78	11.1	defeated Detroit 2-1
Jerry Bush	F-C	6'3	200	25	27	63	36	162	6.0	8	13	5	31	3.9	Home 48-35,
Paul Nowak	C	6'6	210	25	26	45	34	124	4.8	8	13	8	34	4.3	Road 37-49,
Soup Cable	G-F	6'3	200	26	25	77	60	214	8.6	8	11	20	42	5.3	Home 46 35
Jack Ozburn	G	6'1	170	25	26	102	60	264	10.2	8	30	20	80	10.0	
															defeated Oshkosh 3-2
Rip Terjesen	F	6'3	195	24	26	31	19	81	3.1	7	2	1	5	0.7	Road 37-47,
Bob Hassmiller	G	6'1	185	—	23	32	8	72	3.1	4	9	1	19	4.8	Road 46-60,
Tom Wukovits	G	6'	165	24	22	18	15	51	2.3	8	14	5	33	4.1	Home 35-32,
Harry Sorensen	C-F	6'4	200	26	17	11	8	30	1.8	5	1	3	5	1.0	Home 41-40,
Tommy O'Brien	F-G	—	—	23	13	9	3	21	1.6	6	11	2	24	4.0	Home 61-60
Paul Tobin	G	5'9	170	—	13	4	1	9	0.7	2	0	0	0	0.0	
DETROIT EAGLES	**17-10 .630**														
Nat Frankel	F-G	6'3	197	26	27	73	55	201	7.4	3	10	4	24	8.0	lost to Akron Firestone 1-2;
Irv Torgoff	F	6'2	192	22	26	64	43	171	6.6	3	10	7	27	9.0	Road 35-48,
Slim Wintermute	C	6'8	200	22	25	65	50	180	7.2	2	3	0	6	3.0	Home 49-37
Bernie Opper	G	6'	185	24	27	42	20	104	3.9	3	6	3	15	5.0	Road 35 46
Buddy Jeannette	G	5'11	175	22	25	45	52	142	5.7	3	6	8	20	6.7	
Bill Holland	F-C	6'5	210	25	27	36	35	107	4.0	3	1	1	3	1.0	
Laddie Gale	F	6'4	195	23	8	22	16	60	7.5	3	6	5	17	5.7	
Walt Stankey (to Osh)	F	6'3	205	28	16	24	6	54	3.4						
Art Hyatt (knee injury)	G	6'2	190	26	16	13	6	32	2.0						
Bud Moodler	G	6'3	215	28	11	4	12	20	1.8						
Ed Parry	F	6'2	175	21	3	1	0	2	0.7	3	3	1	7	2.3	
Lou Jagnow	G	6'1	180	29	1	0	1	1	1.0	1	0	0	0	0.0	
AKRON GOODYEAR WINGFOOTS	**14-14 .500**			**RAY DETRICK**											
Jim Montgomery	F	6'3	190	22	26	41	35	117	4.5						
Ray Morstadt	F-C	6'2	220	26	25	29	17	75	3.0						
Floyd Ebaugh	C	6'7	230	25	28	45	37	127	4.5						
Ben Stephens	G	6'	190	22	28	91	113	295	10.5						
Howard Vocke	G	6'	190	24	27	49	42	140	5.2						
Gene Anderson	G-F	6'2	190	22	25	47	14	108	4.3						
Jake Nagode	F	6'3	175	24	25	33	12	78	3.1						
Bill Lloyd	G F	6'2	180	24	17	18	11	47	2.8						
Chuck Bloedorn	G	6'	180	27	11	9	2	20	1.8						
Nick Frascella	F	6'2	185	25	13	6	3	15	1.2						
Wilbur Fox	F-C	6'5	185	22	11	3	5	11	1.0						
Joel Hitt	C-F	6'2	180	23	13	3	3	9	0.7						
Johnny McAdams	G	5'10	147	24	2	2	0	4	2.0						
INDIANAPOLIS KAUTSKYS	**9-19 .321**			**BOB NIPPER**											
Johnny Sines	F	6'1	190	25	16	34	33	101	6.3						
Homer Thompson	F-C	6'4	215	23	24	27	52	106	4.4						
George Chestnut	C-F	6'5	210	25	21	38	53	129	6.1						
Ernie Andres	G-F	6'1	200	21	27	130	32	292	10.8						
Jewell Young	G-F	6'	160	26	28	95	70	260	9.3						
Scotty Armstrong	C-F	6'4	190	26	28	42	29	113	4.0						
Frank Baird (shoulder injury)	G	5'11	160	27	16	28	16	72	4.5						
Eddie Sadowski	G	5'10	175	24	12	17	4	38	3.2						
Jim Birr	F	6'3	215	23	3	10	1	21	7.0						
Sally Suddith	G	6'1	170	29	6	5	4	14	2.3						
Dave Williams	C-F	6'3	—	—	7	3	4	10	1.4						
Ward Myers	C	6'1	185	31	2	1	2	4	2.0						
Marvin Stout	G	5'11	155	24	1	1	0	2	2.0						
Rube Reiswerg	G	5'8	175	27	4	0	1	1	0.3						
Garmon Lewis	F	—	—	—	1	0	0	0	0.0						
Bill Cramer	C	—	—	—	1	0	0	0	0.0						

1939/40 N.B.L. — WESTERN DIVISION

Use Name	Pos	Hgt	Wgt	Age	REGULAR SEASON G	FG	FT	Points	PPG	PLAYOFFS G	FG	FT	Points	PPG	Results
OSHKOSH ALL-STARS	**15-13 .536**				**LON DARLING**										
Lou Barle (FB)	F	6'1	200	23	27	54	40	148	5.5	8	17	14	48	6.0	defeated Sheboygan 2-1;
Connie Mack Berry (FB)	F-C	6'4	200	24	26	65	49	179	6.9	8	28	10	66	8.3	Home 41-24,
Leroy Edwards	C	6'4	220	25	28	111	139	361	12.9	8	33	27	93	11.6	Road 42-43,
Herm Witasek	G	6'2	210	25	28	62	38	162	5.8	8	16	12	44	5.5	Road 31-29
Charley Shipp	G	6'1	195	23	28	74	26	174	6.2	8	13	12	38	4.8	
Pete Pederson	F-C	6'4	—	27	26	33	12	78	3.0	8	15	9	39	4.9	lost to Akron Firestone 2-3;
Walt Stankey (from Det)	F	6'3	205	28	11	12	1	25	2.3	8	6	3	15	1.9	Home 47-37,
Buck Batterman	F-C	6'3	195	21	17	6	8	20	1.2	2	0	1	1	0.5	Home 60-46,
Tex Mueller	G	6'1	175	23	20	6	7	19	1.0	2	2	0	4	2.0	Road 32-35,
Scoop Putnam	G	6'	175	25	8	6	2	14	1.8	5	2	1	5	1.0	Road 40-41,
Ed Mullen	G	6'3	185	26	7	1	2	4	0.6						Road 60-61
Sonny Olson	F	6'	165	22	2	1	2	4	2.0						
Ray Adams (HC)	F	6'2	185	25	1	1	1	3	3.0						
Buzz Knoblauch	F	6'1	170	23	3	1	0	2	0.7						
Carl Lillage	F-G	—	—	—	3	0	2	2	0.7						
Dean Mealy	C	6'4	195	24	1	0	0	0	0.0						
SHEBOYGAN REDSKINS	**15-13 .536**				**FRANK ZUMMACH**										
Paul Sokody	F	6'2	170	25	28	51	31	133	4.8	3	6	6	18	6.0	lost to Oshkosh 1-2;
Rube Lautenschlager	F-C	6'3	190	24	28	76	32	184	6.6	3	5	6	16	5.3	Road 24-41,
Ed Dancker	C	6'7	200	25	24	31	24	86	3.6	3	2	3	7	2.3	Home 43-42,
Otto Kolar	G	6'3	180	28	27	SS	36	146	5.4	3	4	1	9	3.0	Home 29 -31
Dave Quabius	G	6'	185	23	27	42	31	115	4.3	3	4	8	16	5.3	
Sparky Adams	F	6'1	185	22	26	43	33	119	4.6	3	2	1	5	1.7	
George Hesik	F-C	6'2	195	26	26	31	49	111	4.3	3	2	5	9	3.0	
Kenny Suesens	G	6'1	175	23	28	19	28	66	2.4	3	5	5	15	5.0	
Johnny Posewitz	G	6'	185	33	12	15	4	34	2.8						
Les Kuplic	F	6'3	200	27	13	6	1	13	1.0	1	0	0	0	0.0	
George Swanson	G-F	—	—	—	11	4	5	13	1.2	1	0	1	1	1.0	
Marv Colen (from Chi)	G	6'	170	24	5	3	0	6	1.2	1	0	0	0	0.0	
Scoop Posewitz	G	5'11	180	31	5	0	2	2	0.4						
Moose Graf-injured															
CHICAGO BRUINS	**14-14 .500**				**SAM LIFSCHULZ**										
Stan Zadel	F	6'5	215	23	18	42	24	108	6.0						
Elmer Johnson	F-C	6'4	190	29	28	32	39	103	3.7						
Mike Novak	C	6'9	212	24	28	114	65	293	10.5						
Wibs Kautz	G-F	6'	180	24	28	105	63	273	9.8						
Frank Linskey	G	6'2	180	26	27	38	21	97	3.6						
Eddie Oram	F-G	6'3	175	25	18	18	17	53	2.9						
Willie Phillips	G	5'8	175	24	28	16	17	49	1.8						
George Hogan (to Ham)	F-G	6'1	170	22	13	7	6	20	1.5						
George Wilson	F	6'1	190	25	16	5	8	18	1.1						
Bob MacLeod	F	6'	190	22	9	4	3	11	1.2						
Ray Hayes	G-F	—	180	33	4	1	1	3	0.8						
Dembo	G	—	—	—	2	1	0	2	1.0						
Marv Colen (to Sheb)	G	—	170	24	1	0	0	0	0.0						
Tony Carp	F	6'7	215	28	1	0	0	0	0.0						
Riskind	G	—	—	—	1	0	0	0	0.0						
HAMMOND CIESAR ALL-AMERICANS	**9-19 .321**				**LOU BOUDREAU (1-4 .200), EDDIE CIESAR (0-2 .000), LEO BEREOLOS (8-13 .381)**										
Bobby Neu (broken foot)	F-G	6'1	175	22	24	44	71	159	6.6						
Pim Goff	F-C	6'4	190	26	26	68	12	148	5.7						
Dar Hutchins	C-F	6'5	195	24	24	59	38	156	6.5						
Jim Currie	G-F	6'2	185	23	27	38	29	105	3.9						
Glynn Downey	G	6'	180	24	22	37	41	115	5.2						
Chuck Chuckovits (VR)	F-G	6'1	175	27	14	30	30	90	6.4						
Vince McGowan	C	6'6	210	26	17	29	24	82	4.8						
Joe Sotak	F	6'2	210	25	23	21	19	61	2.7						
Nick Yost (broken arm)	F	6'4	220	24	8	18	7	43	5.4						
George Hogan (from Chi)	G-F	6'1	170	22	13	17	7	41	3.2						
Tommyrlisbet (suspended by team)	G	5'10	165	22	5	4	8	16	3.2						
Dale Hamilton	G	6'1	180	21	7	5	1	11	1.6						
Gordon McComb	G	5'10	160	22	2	1	1	3	1.5						
Spudich	F	—	—	—	2	1	0	2	1.0						
Hale Swanson	G-F	6'3	200	25	2	0	0	0	0.0						

1940-41 N.B.L.

One Division, Two Champions

The N.B.L. lost a member when the Indianapolis Kautskys pulled out to become an independent club. The league then closed ranks by pooling the remaining seven teams into one group without any divisions. At the start of the season, the Akron Firestones and the Oshkosh All-Stars were the popular favorites; the Firestones had won the Eastern Division title last year and had beaten Oshkosh for the league crown. For the third and fourth playoff spots experts figured on a dogfight among the Detroit Eagles, Sheboygan Redskins, Akron Goodyears, Chicago Bruins, and Hammond Ciesar All-Americans.

Once the starting bell for the regular season rang, the Oshkosh club bounded away to a strong start. General Manager Lon Darling had the same club as last year, featuring hook shot ace Leroy Edwards and playmaker Charley Shipp, and he added valuable reserve strength in rookie Bob Carpenter, a 6'5" forward-center from East Texas State. By mid-January, the All-Stars were 10-1 and had practically locked up a playoff-spot. The Firestones, on the other hand, had signed no prominent rookies and suffered when injuries took center Paul Nowak and guard Soup Cable out of the lineup.

The other five teams lived up to expectations by battling for the remaining playoff berths. Sheboygan, whose only rookie addition was forward Bill McDonald of Marquette, held down second place halfway through January with an 8-6 mark, while the Goodyears were close in third place with an 8-7 record. The Goodyears continued their rebuilding process by signing two of the best college big men, Jake Pelkington of Manhattan and Marv Huffman of N.C.A.A.-champion Indiana. Second-year pro Ben Stephens scored enough points from the backcourt to dethrone Oshkosh's Leroy Edwards as scoring champion.

The remaining four teams all had losing records by January 17, but were still in the running for a playoff spot. Hammond, sparked by second-year man Bobby Neu and rookie shooter Ralph Vaughn from Southern California, had a surprisingly good 5-7 record. The Chicago Bruins were 4-7 despite signing two local rookie favorites, forward Bill Hapac from Illinois and guard Stan Szukala from DePaul, to go with second-year stars Wibs Kautz and Mike Novak.

Tied with the Bruins were the Detroit Eagles, a team almost completely rebuilt since last season. Center Slim Wintermute and forward Laddie Gale had quit the team to play in a local league in Oregon, and forward Irv Torgoff and guard Nat Frankel jumped to the American Basketball League. To further decimate last year's playoff squad, a leg injury laid up guard Bernie Opper for a good part of the season. With only guard Buddy Jeannette back from last year's top players, coach Dutch Dehnert built his club back up by signing bruising center Ed Sadowski out of Seton Hall and forward Bob Calihan out of Detroit, and adding forward Ed Parry and guard Jim Brown. In mid-season, he brought in longtime pro Rusty Saunders and American League guard Jake Ahearn. Treading water in last place at 4-9 were the injury-plagued Firestones.

After January 19, however, the pennant race suddenly reversed its field. Oshkosh kept on winning, but Sheboygan, Goodyear, and Hammond went into tailspins. The bottom fell out of the Hammond club. The team lost 11 of its final 12 games and fell out of contention. Goodyear went 3-6 to fall under .500 for the season, while Sheboygan's 5-5 record put the club's playoff hopes in jeopardy. Chicago never made a strong rally, despite buying Ralph Vaughn from Hammond late in the campaign. A fatal flaw in the Bruin offense was that rookie forward Bill Hapac could play only a pivot position, forcing 6'9" center Novak, a good outside shooter, to operate away from the basket. While half the league slumbered, the Detroit and Firestone clubs came roaring out of the second division. With Detroit putting together an 8-5 mark and Firestone a 9-2 mark after January 19, these two clubs sneaked into the top four by the end of the season and won playoff berths along with Oshkosh and Sheboygan.

In the opening round of the playoffs, Detroit faced Sheboygan while Oshkosh squared off with the Firestones. Detroit beat Sheboygan 43-32 in their opening game, with substitute Jim Brown hitting five straight baskets to put the Eagles ahead for keeps in the third period. The defense-minded Redskins reasserted themselves in the next two games, however, and clinched the series with 22-19 and 54-40 victories.

In the other series, Firestone took a 16-9 lead over Oshkosh in the opening game, when coach George Hotchkiss unleashed the All-Stars' new weapon. Hotchkiss used 6'5" Bob Carpenter and 6'4' center Leroy Edwards in a double pivot offense. The All-Stars snapped back and won the first game 30-28 on a shot by Carpenter with less than a minute left. The second game went into overtime when Firestone's Rip Terjesen hit a long set shot with seconds left on the clock, but when center Paul Nowak fouled out in the extra period, Edwards hit three baskets for Oshkosh to lead his mates to a 47-41 triumph. In the championship series between Oshkosh and Sheboygan, the All-Stars cracked the Redskin defense and took the title with three straight wins, 53-38, 49-38, and 54-36.

After winning their first N.B.L. crown after three years of playoff losses, the All-Stars went off to celebrate by playing in the annual World Tournament in Chicago. Sheboygan, Chicago, and Detroit also joined the 16-team field, and the championship game turned out to be a showdown between two N.B.L. clubs, Detroit and Oshkosh. The Eagles, who had beaten the Harlem Globetrotters and New York Rens to get to the finals, upset the All-Stars by taking the championship with a 39-37 win. Three N.B.L. players, Ed Sadowski and Buddy Jeannette of Detroit, and Bob Carpenter of Oshkosh, won places on the All-Tournament team.

Team	W	L	Pct.	GB	vs. playoff teams W	L	Pct.	vs.non-playoff teams W	L	Pct.	HOME W	L	Pct.	ROAD W	L	Pct.	Average Points G	For	Agnst.	Diff.	PLAYOFFS Average Points G	For	Agnst.	Diff.
1940/41 N.B.L. STANDINGS																								
Oshkosh	**18**	6	**.750**	—	**9**	3	**.750**	**9**	3	**.750**	**11**	1	**.917**	**7**	5	**.583**	24	42.2	37.1	**+5.1**	5	**45.6**	36.2	**+9.4**
Sheboygan	13	11	.542	5	5	7	.417	8	4	.667	7	5	.583	6	6	.500	24	36.1	**34.7**	+1.4	6	36.7	42.2	-5.5
Akron Firestone	13	11	.542	5	6	6	.500	7	5	.583	7	5	.583	6	6	.500	24	**42.3**	40.4	+1.9	2	34.5	38.5	-4.0
Detroit	12	12	.500	6	4	8	.333	8	4	.667	8	4	.667	4	8	.333	24	40.5	43.7	-3.2	3	34.0	**36.0**	-2.0
Chicago	11	13	.458	7	7	9	.438	4	4	.500	8	4	.667	3	9	.250	24	38	37.2	0.8				
Akron Goodyear	11	13	.458	7	5	11	.313	6	2	**.750**	6	**6**	.500	5	7	.417	24	38.6	38.8	-0.2				
Hammond	6	18	.250	12	4	**12**	.250	2	**6**	.250	6	**6**	.500	0	**12**	.000	24	38.6	44.4	-5.8				

Use Name	Pos.	Hgt.	Wgt.	Age	REGULAR SEASON G	FG	FT	Points	PPG	PLAYOFFS G	FG	FT	Points	PPG	Results
							1940/41 N.B.L.								
OSHKOSH ALL-STARS		**18-6 .750**					**GEORGE HOTCHKISS**								
Lou Barle	F	6'1	200	24	24	45	28	118	4.9	5	4	4	12	2.4	defeated Akron Firestone 2-0;
Bob Carpenter	F-C	6'5	200	23	24	40	41	121	5.0	5	15	**25**	55	11.0	Road 30-28,
Leroy Edwards	C	6'4	225	26	23	57	**76**	190	8.3	5	**23**	**25**	**71**	**14.2**	Home 47-41, (OT)
Herm Witasek	G-F	6'2	215	27	24	54	28	136	5.7	5	11	6	28	5.6	
Charley Shipp	G	6'1	195	27	22	46	21	113	5.1	5	7	6	20	4.0	
															defeated Sheboygan 3-0
Scoop Putnam	F-G	6'	175	26	22	40	17	97	4.4	3	5	0	10	3.3	Home 53-38,
Connie Mack Berry (FB)	F	6'4	210	25	23	40	14	94	4.1	5	5	2	12	2.4	Home 54-36
Erv Prasse	G-F	6'2	190	23	24	25	27	77	3.2	5	2	6	10	2.0	
Tommy Nisbet	G	5'10	165	23	24	21	16	58	2.4	5	3	4	10	2.0	
Tex Mueller	G	6'1	175	24	7	4	0	8	1.1	1	0	0	0	0.0	
Pete Hecomovich	G	6'4	205	—	1	0	0	0	0.0						
SHEBOYGAN REDSKINS		**13-11 .542**					**FRANK ZUMMACH**								
Paul Sokody	F	6'2	185	26	24	43	28	114	4.8	6	10	5	25	4.2	defeated Detroit 2-1;
Rube Lautenschlager	F	6'3	190	25	23	31	26	88	3.8	6	5	6	16	2.7	Road 32-43,
Ed Dancker	C	6'7	205	26	23	39	27	105	4.6	5	8	9	25	5.0	Home 22-19,
Otto Kolar	G-C	6'3	180	29	24	53	32	138	5.8	6	17	7	41	6.8	Home 54-40
Dave Quabius	G	6'	185	24	24	56	40	152	6.3	6	13	6	32	5.3	
															lost to Oshkosh 0-3;
Bill McDonald	F-G	6'3	190	24	24	31	26	88	3.7	6	12	5	29	4.8	Home 38-53,
George Hesik	F-C	6'2	195	27	23	24	32	80	3.5	6	9	10	28	4.7	Road 38-44,
Kenny Suesens	G	6'1	175	24	24	18	41	77	3.2	6	3	8	14	2.3	Road 36-54
Ralph Amsden	C	6'4	200	23	11	6	12	24	2.2	5	2	6	10	2.0	
Dick Evans (FB, to Ham)	C	6'3	200	20	1	0	0	0	0.0						
Moose Graf (injured)															
AKRON FIRESTONE NON-SKIDS		**13-11 .542**					**PAUL SHEEKS**								
Johnny Moir	F	6'2	184	23	24	59	35	153	6.4	2	5	2	12	6.0	lost to Oshkosh 0-2;
Soup Cable (injury)	F	6'3	200	27	15	30	34	94	6.3	2	7	8	22	11.0	Home 28-30,
Jack Jennings	C-F	6'6	195	22	19	41	12	94	4.9	2	2	0	4	2.0	Road 41-47 (OT)
Jack Ozburn	G-F	6'1	170	26	24	88	35	211	8.8	2	1	1	3	1.5	
Tom Wukovits	G	6'	165	25	24	54	45	153	6.4	2	3	3	9	4.5	
Bob Hassmiller	G	6'1	185	—	24	52	10	114	4.8	2	1	0	2	1.0	
Jerry Bush	F-C	6'3	200	26	22	29	33	91	4.1	2	1	2	4	2.0	
Paul Nowak (injury)	C	6'6	210	26	18	13	19	45	2.5	2	1	5	7	3.5	
Tommy O'Brien	GF	—	—	24	15	13	8	34	2.3	1	1	0	2	2.0	
Rip Terjesen	F	6'3	195	25	11	6	3	15	1.4	1	2	0	4	4.0	
Harry Sonensen	C	6'4	200	27	7	3	1	7	1.0						
Fred Beretta	G	—	—	23	9	1	0	2	0.2						
Paul DuCharme	G	5'11	160	23	3	0	1	1	0.3						

1940/41 N.B.L. (continued)

Use Name	Pos	Hgt	Wgt	Age	G	FG	FT	Points	PPG	G	FG	FT	Points	PPG	Results
					REGULAR SEASON					PLAYOFFS					
DETROIT EAGLES	**12-12 .500**				**DUTCH DEHNERT**										
Ed Parry	F	6'2	175	22	24	34	37	105	4.4	3	4	4	12	4.0	lost to Sheboygan 1-2;
Bob Calihan	F	6'3	200	22	23	69	43	181	7.9	3	10	1	21	7.0	Home 43-32,
Ed Sadowski	C	6'5	223	23	24	95	66	256	10.7	3	7	9	23	7.7	Road 19-22,
Jake Ahearn	G	6'2	185	23	15	32	15	79	5.3	3	3	2	8	2.7	Road 40-54
Buddy Jeannette	G	5'11	175	23	23	75	54	204	8.9	3	8	5	21	7.0	
Jim Brown	G-F	6'1	190	28	22	42	19	103	4.7	3	7	1	15	5.0	
Rusty Saunders	F-C	6'2	210	34	14	6	9	21	1.5						
Al Benson (from Ham)	C	6'6	220	26	8	7	2	16	2.0	2	1	0	2	1.0	
Bernie Opper (leg injury)	G	6'	185	25	5	3	0	6	1.2						
Bill Lane	F-C	6'4	220	24	3	0	0	0	0.0						
Jack Piana	F	6'2	190	22	2	0	0	0	0.0	1	0	0	0	0.0	
Adam Filipczak	G	5'10	170	24	2	0	0	0	0.0						
Page	G	—	—	—	1	0	0	0	0.0						
CHICAGO BRUINS	**11-13 .458**				**FRANK LINSKEY**										
Bill Hapac	F	6'2	188	22	24	80	67	227	9.5						
Ray Adams	F-C	6'2	185	26	20	23	14	60	3.0						
Mike Novak	C	6'9	220	25	23	56	34	146	6.3						
Wibs Kautz	G	6'	180	25	21	94	39	227	10.8						
Stan Szukala	G	6'	175	22	24	45	12	102	4.3						
George Hogan	G	6'1	170	23	22	19	11	49	2.2						
Vince McGowan	C-F	6'6	210	27	17	10	10	30	1.8						
Frank Linskey	G	6'2	180	27	15	8	5	21	1.4						
Bill O'Brien	F	6'4	185	22	19	5	10	20	1.1						
Ralph Vaughn (from Ham)	F	6'1	175	22	3	5	6	16	5.3						
Elmer Johnson	F	6'4	190	30	13	4	4	12	0.9						
Ball	F-G	—	—	—	6	1	1	3	0.5						
AKRON GOODYEAR WINGFOOTS	**11-13 .458**				**RAY DETRICK**										
Marv Huffman	F	6'2	185	23	22	47	19	113	5.1						
Gene Anderson	F	6'3	190	23	23	43	28	114	5.0						
Jake Pelkington	C	6'6	220	24	24	57	70	184	7.7						
Ben Stephens	G-F	6'	175	23	24	**98**	69	**265**	**11.0**						
Howard Vocke	G	6'3	190	25	24	48	17	113	4.5						
Julie Rivlin	G	5'11	160	23	21	20	11	51	2.4						
Jake Nagode	F-G	6'3	170	25	18	19	9	47	2.6						
Jim Montgomery	F-C	6'3	190	23	15	3	13	19	1.3						
Art Anderson	C	6'6	190	24	12	2	4	8	0.7						
Steve Sitko	G	6'	185	23	8	3	0	6	0.8						
John Wiggers	C	6'9	200	23	5	1	1	3	0.6						
Bill	G	6'2	180	25	2	1	1	3	1.5						
Nick Frascella	F	6'2	185	26	1	0	0	0	0.0						
Floyd Ebaugh, Bob Parsons-injured															
HAMMOND CIESAR ALL-AMERICANS	**6-18 .250**				**CARL ANDERSON**										
Ralph Vaughn (to Chi)	F-G	6'1	175	22	20	64	51	179	9.0						
Splinter Johnson	F-C	6'3	190	20	23	35	23	93	4.0						
Dar Hutchins	C	6'5	195	25	24	70	28	168	7.0						
Bobby Neu	G-F	6'1	175	23	22	66	63	195	8.9						
Clem Ruh	G	5'10	165	25	21	26	25	77	3.7						
Bill Behr	G	6'2	190	21	20	28	14	70	3.5						
Pim Goff	F-C	6'4	190	27	12	18	4	40	3.3						
Chet Tollstam	F-C	6'2	180	22	11	13	6	32	2.9						
Bob Dille	F	6'3	190	23	3	8	3	19	6.3						
Joe Sotak	F	6'2	210	26	4	8	1	17	4.3						
Dick Evans (from Sheb)	C	6'3	200	20	4	4	4	12	3.0						
Art Bowman	G	—	—	—	8	4	1	9	1.1						
Paul Price	F	—	—	26	1	3	0	6	6.0						
Danko	G	—	—	—	1	2	0	4	4.0						
Teddy Falda	G	6'	180	20	3	1	0	2	0.7						
Bill Summers	G	—	—	—	1	1	0	2	2.0						
Jim Higgins	C	6'8	—	—	1	0	1	1	1.0						
Carl Anderson	G	6'3	215	27	2	0	0	0	0.0						
Al Benson (to Det)	C	6'6	220	26	2	0	0	0	0.0						
Tom O'Toole	C	—	—	—	1	0	0	0	0.0						

1941-42 N.B.L.

Finally, a Clean Sweep

Two weeks after the N.B.L. season began, the Japanese attacked Pearl Harbor and brought the United States into the Second World War. The next several years would see hordes of athletes entering military service, but this season the N.B.L. felt only a slight twinge from manpower losses to the war effort. Of the front-line players in the league, only Bob Carpenter and Herm Witasek of Oshkosh, Bob Calihan of Ft. Wayne, Bill Hapac and Stan Szukala of Chicago, Ernie Andres and Bob Dietz of Indianapolis, and Jack Ozburn of Toledo missed all or most of the season because of military service.

Indeed, the league shuffled franchises this season more than it shuffled players. The Firestone corporation decided to drop pro basketball from its large-scale promotions, so the league lost its only two-time champion. The Hammond Ciesar All-Americans folded after two miserable seasons, and the Detroit Eagles, surprise winners of last year's World Tournament, bolted the N.B.L. to become an independent club. The Eagles kept players Buddy Jeannette, Bernie Opper, Ed Parry, and Jake Ahearn, signed forward Jerry Bush from the defunct Firestone outfit, sold forward Bob Calihan to the Ft. Wayne Zollner Pistons, and lost center Ed Sadowski to the Wilmington Blue Bombers of the American Basketball League.

To replace the three lost clubs, the N.B.L. brought in three clubs that operated as independents last season. The Indianapolis Kautskys rejoined the league after a year on their own, bringing scoring ace Jewell Young back into the circuit. New additions to the squad included forward Bob Dietz of Butler and Michigan's Johnny Townsend, who was now free to play pro ball after the Big Ten had forced him to sit out the 1938-39 season. The Toledo Jim White Chevrolets also came into the N.B.L., built entirely around high-scoring Chuck Chuckovits of the University of Toledo. Although he had flopped as a rookie with the Hammond Ciesar All-Americans in 1939-40, this year Chuckovits drove and shot his way to the league scoring championship with a record 18.5 points per game, hitting a high mark of 33 points in a game against Sheboygan on February 12. The rest of the Toledo team was pitiful, however, with a total of 22 other players, including several ex-Firestone men, coming and going during the season. The team wound up last with a 3-21 record. And one of the three victories was a forfeit.

The third newcomer to the league was the Ft. Wayne Zollner Pistons, owned by industrialist Fred Zollner. The Pistons had played a few games last season as a small-time, independent operation, but Zollner put together a first-rate club by signing rookies Herm Schaefer and Curly Armstrong of Indiana, Blackie Towery of Western Kentucky, and Elmer Gainer of DePaul, and by signing veteran guard Bobby McDermott, one of the game's best longrange set shooters, from the original Celtics.

Once the season got under way, a group of familiar faces rode atop the league standings. The Oshkosh All-Stars ran out to a quick lead and insured a fifth straight first-place finish; the starting lineup of Leroy Edwards, Connie Mack Berry, Lou Barle, Charley Shipp, and Herm Witasek had jelled into a peerless combination. Forward Bob Carpenter was now in the Navy but coach Lon Darling replenished his cupboard with three sterling rookies, high-jumping center Gene Englund of Wisconsin, forward Bill Komenich of Marquette, and guard Eddie Riska of Notre Dame. When Witasek left for the military in February, rookie Riska filled his backcourt spot without a hitch.

Behind the All-Stars, the same three clubs held the remaining playoff berths practically the whole season. The Goodyear team had a veteran backcourt star in Ben Stephens and a rookie frontcourt ace in George Glamack. Billed at North Carolina as the "Blind Bomber," Glamack overcame acute nearsightedness to develop one of the game's most accurate hook shots . Rivals often said that he shot strictly from memory. Tying the Goodyears for second place were the Zollner Pistons, helped down the stretch by the late acquisition of veteran forward Paul Birch. The Indianapolis club held on to the fourth playoff spot right through to the end of the season. Finishing out of the playoffs were the Sheboygan Redskins, who had one of the league's toughest defenses but lacked an ace scorer; the Chicago Bruins, who lost Bill Hapac and Stan Szukala to the service, finished sixth despite having stars Wibs Kautz, Mike Novak, and Ralph Vaughn.

At the start of the playoffs, the experts labeled Oshkosh as the easy favorite over Indianapolis, while the Goodyear-Ft. Wayne series was rated an even match. Both predictions came true. The Oshkosh All-Stars quickly eliminated Indianapolis with 40-33 and 64-48 victories, while the Goodyears and Pistons battled on practically even terms. Goodyear captured the first game 46-30 on its own home court, but the Pistons bounced back to squeeze out a 51-48 triumph in the second game at Ft. Wayne. The Pistons moved into the championship round by beating the Goodyears 49-43 in the deciding game held in the Ft. Wayne gym.

The homecourt advantage held up in the finals as the Pistons took the first game 61-43 in Ft. Wayne; Bobby McDermott connected for 20 points, but Oshkosh's Leroy Edwards led all scorers with 22 points. The scene then shifted to Oshkosh for the final two games, and the All-Stars took charge. Edwards went on a binge in the second game, canning 35 points in leading Oshkosh to a 68-60 win to even the series. In the final game, the Pistons decided to stop Edwards at any cost, and they succeeded. Edwards scored only one point, but his Oshkosh mates found enough open shots to score a 52-46 victory and wrap up the team's second straight N.B.L. crown. As icing on the cake, the All-Stars then won the World Tournament in Chicago, beating the Harlem Globetrotters in the semifinals and the Detroit Eagles in the championship game .

Team	W	L	Pct.	GB	vs. playoff teams W	vs. playoff teams L	vs. playoff teams Pct.	vs.non-playoff teams W	vs.non-playoff teams L	vs.non-playoff teams Pct.	HOME W	HOME L	HOME Pct.	ROAD W	ROAD L	ROAD Pct.	Average Points G	Average Points For	Average Points Agnst.	Average Points Diff.	PLAYOFFS Average Points G	PLAYOFFS Average Points For	PLAYOFFS Average Points Agnst.	PLAYOFFS Average Points Diff.
1941/42 N.B.L. STANDINGS																								
Oshkosh	**20**	4	**.833**	—	**8**	4	**.667**	**12**	0	**1.000**	**13**	1	**.929**	**7**	3	**.700**	24	**49.3**	**40.7**	**+8.6**	5	**53.4**	49.6	**+3.8**
Fort Wayne	15	9	.625	5	5	7	.417	10	2	.833	11	3	.786	4	6	.400	24	47.0	44.4	+2.6	6	49.5	50.0	-0.5
Akron Goodyear	15	9	.625	5	7	5	.583	8	4	.667	11	2	.846	4	7	.364	24	45.4	40.8	+4.6	3	45.7	**43.3**	+2.4
Indianapolis	12	11	.522	7.5	4	8	.333	8	3	.727	10	1	.909	2	10	.167	23	41.5	41.2	+0.3	2	40.5	52.0	-11.5
Sheboygan	10	14	.417	10	5	11	.313	5	3	.625	8	5	.615	2	9	.182	24	39.3	42.4	-3.1				
Chicago	8	15	.348	11.5	3	12	.200	4	2	.667	4	**6**	.400	3	8	.273	21	41.8	44.6	-2.8				
Toledo	3	21	.125	17	1	**15**	.063	1	**5**	.167	2	4	.333	0	**16**	.000	22	39.7	51.2	-11.5				

Use Name	Pos.	Hgt.	Wgt.	Age	REGULAR SEASON G	REGULAR SEASON FG	REGULAR SEASON FT	REGULAR SEASON Points	REGULAR SEASON PPG	PLAYOFFS G	PLAYOFFS FG	PLAYOFFS FT	PLAYOFFS Points	PLAYOFFS PPG	Results
					1941/42 N.B.L.										
OSHKOSH ALL-STARS	**20-4 .833**				**LON DARLING**										
Lou Barle	F	6'1	200	25	24	55	13	123	5.1	5	15	3	33	6.6	defeated Indianapolis 2-0;
Connie Mack Berry (FB)	F	6'4	210	26	24	53	18	124	5.2	5	5	5	15	3.0	Road 40-33,
Leroy Edwards	C	6'4	225	27	24	85	92	262	10.9	5	**30**	**23**	**83**	16.6	Home 64-48,
Herm Witasek (military service)	G-F	6'2	215	28	21	25	20	70	3.3						
Charley Shipp	G	6'1	200	28	24	70	38	178	7.4	4	5	6	16	4.0	defeated Fort Wayne 2-1;
															Road 43-61,
Gene Englund	C-F	6'5	205	24	22	61	42	164	7.5	4	11	7	29	7.3	Home 68-60,
Bill Komenich	F	6'3	210	23	24	31	18	80	3.3	5	7	11	25	5.0	Home 52-46,
Tommy Nisbet	G	5'10	165	24	24	24	28	76	3.2	5	11	9	31	6.2	
Eddie Riska (leg injury)	G	6'	175	22	16	24	15	63	3.9	5	3	12	18	3.6	
Warner Engdahl (leg injury)	G	6'1	210	23	19	10	16	36	1.9	4	2	0	4	1.0	
Erv Prasse	F	6'2	190	24	5	3	1	7	1.4	5	4	5	13	2.6	
Bob Carpenter—military service															
FORT WAYNE ZOLLNER PISTONS	**15-9 .625**				**CARL BENNETT**										
Curly Armstrong	F-G	5'11	170	23	24	69	60	198	8.3	6	25	21	71	11.8	defeated Akron Goodyear 2
Paul Birch	F	6'1	195	31	8	16	10	42	5.3	6	15	7	37	6.2	Road 30-46
Blackie Towery	C-F	6'4	210	21	24	64	35	163	6.8	6	17	13	47	7.8	Home 51-48,
Herm Schaefer	G	6'	175	22	24	85	37	207	8.6	6	13	5	31	5.2	Home 49 43
Bobby McDermott	G	6'	185	27	21	115	47	277	13.2	6	28	16	72	12.0	
Elmer Gainer	C	6'6	195	22	24	36	28	100	4.2	6	1	10	12	2.0	lost to Oshkosh 1-2;
Jack Keller	F	6'2	185	21	18	18	16	52	2.9	4	1	4	6	1.5	Home 61-43,
Red Oberbruner	F-G	5'11	175	23	19	17	8	42	2.2	6	4	4	12	2.0	Road 60-68,
Dale Hamilton	F-G	6' 1	185	23	16	10	16	36	2.3	5	2	3	7	1.4	Road 46-52,
Don Beery	G	6'	180	21	11	3	2	8	0.7	2	1	0	2	1.0	
Jim Hilgemann	G	6'	170	25	4	1	0	2	0.5						
Bob Calihan—military service															
AKRON GOOOYEAR WINGFOOTS	**15-9 .625**				**RAY DETRICK**										
Gene Anderson	F	6'3	190	24	23	45	18	108	4.7	3	8	1	17	5.7	lost to Fort Wayne 1-2;
George Glamack	F-C	6'8	225	22	24	87	82	256	10.7	3	11	15	37	12.3	Home 46-30,
Floyd Ebaugh	C	6'7	230	27	23	61	20	142	6.2	3	3	6	12	4.0	Road 48-51,
Ben Stephens	G-F	6'	175	24	24	81	60	222	9.3	3	13	13	39	13.0	Road 43-49,
Rudy Debnar	G	5'11	160	25	24	56	29	141	5.9	3	0	0	0	0.0	
Howard Vocke	G-F	6'3	190	26	24	34	13	81	3.4	3	5	3	13	4.3	
Lee Huber (military service)	G	6'1	—	22	11	32	6	70	6.4						
Bob Parsons	F	6'1	175	26	15	12	4	28	1.9	3	1	2	4	1.3	
John O'Brien	G	6'1	180	25	7	5	7	17	2.4	3	2	7	11	3.7	
Harold Hull	F	6'4	190	21	12	3	8	14	1.2	2	0	4	4	2.0	
Ken Griffith	G	6'2	195	23	6	4	1	9	1.5	1	0	0	0	0.0	
Elch	F	—	—	—	1	1	0	2	2.0						

Use Name	Pos	Hgt	Wgt	Age	REGULAR SEASON G	FG	FT	Points	PPG	PLAYOFFS G	FG	FT	Points	PPG	Results

1941/42 N.B.L. (continued)

Use Name	Pos	Hgt	Wgt	Age	G	FG	FT	Points	PPG	G	FG	FT	Points	PPG	Results
INDIANAPOLIS KAUTSKYS	**12-11 .522**				**FRANK KAUTSKY**										
Bob Dietz (military service)	F-G	6'1	160	24	15	45	7	97	6.5						lost to Oshkosh 0-2;
Scotty Armstrong	F	6'4	190	28	22	32	27	91	4.1						Home 33-40,
Johnny Townsend	C-F	6'4	210	25	22	53	63	169	7.7	2	6	11	23	11.5	Road 48-64
Jewell Young	G	6'	160	28	23	93	77	263	11.4	2	12	11	35	**17.5**	
Eddie Sadowski	G	5'11	175	26	22	52	23	127	5.8	2	2	1	5	2.5	
Mark Ertel	C-F	6'4	196	22	20	20	26	66	3.3	2	1	1	3	1.5	
Bob Dro	G-F	6'	190	23	15	20	6	46	3.1						
Woody Norris	F-G	6'1	170	22	7	20	3	43	6.1	2	2	5	9	4.5	
Johnny Sines	F	6'1	190	27	10	14	9	37	3.7						
Frank Baird	G	5'11	160	29	11	7	1	15	1.4	2	0	0	0	0.0	
Hugh Carter	G	—	—	—	—	—	—	—	—	2	2	1	5	2.5	
Cleary	F	—	—	—	—	—	—	—	—	2	0	1	1	0.5	
Ernie Andres - military service															
SHEBOYGAN REDSKINS	**10-14 .417**				**FRANK ZUMMACH**										
Paul Sokody	F	6'2	185	27	24	52	22	126	5.3						
Rube Lautenschlager	F-C	6'3	195	26	24	67	21	155	6.5						
Ed Dancker	C	6'7	210	27	24	98	47	243	10.1						
Bill McDonald	G	6'3	190	25	24	39	25	103	4.3						
Kenny Suesens	G	6'1	175	25	24	30	19	79	3.3						
George Hesik	F-C	6'2	195	28	18	20	18	58	3.2						
George Blacklidge	F	6'3	185	21	11	17	17	51	4.6						
Charlie Epperson	F-G	6'2	195	22	9	20	9	49	5.4						
Babe Ziegenhorn	G-F	6'	185	23	15	17	6	40	2.7						
Paul Maki	G	6'1	175	23	8	13	9	35	4.4						
Jack Thornton	C	6'5	200	27	2	0	3	3	1.5						
Ralph Amsden-military service															
Moose Graf-injured															
CHICAGO BRUINS	**8-15 .348**				**JACK TIERNEY (record includes 1 forfeit win and 1 forfeit loss)**										
Wibs Kautz	F	6'	180	26	20	85	40	210	10.5						
Dick Evans (FB)	F-C	6'3	200	21	18	17	20	54	3.0						
Mike Novak	C	6'9	220	26	19	58	31	147	7.7						
George Hogan	G	6'1	170	24	20	43	18	104	5.2						
Ralph Vaughn	G	6'1	175	23	21	72	46	190	9.0						
Otto Kolar	G-F	6'3	180	30	18	27	14	68	3.8						
George Ratkovicz	C	6'6	210	19	13	9	14	32	2.5						
John Drish	F	—	—	24	8	10	3	23	2.9						
Ed Sachs	G	6'2	175	23	8	8	4	20	2.5						
Vince McGowan	F-C	6'6	210	28	6	4	5	13	2.2						
Stan Szukala (military service)	G	6'	175	23	6	5	0	10	1.7						
Lou Possner	F-C	6'3	180	24	4	2	1	5	1.3						
Morris	C	—	—	—	1	0	0	0	0.0						
Ted Strain	G	6'	155	24	1	0	0	0	0.0						
George Morse	F-G	—	—	22	2	0	2	2	1.0						
Bill Hapac - military service															
TOLEDO JIM WHITE CHEVROLETS	**3-21 .125**				**TOMMY EDWARDS (record includes 1 forfeit win and 1 forfeit loss)**										
Chuck Chuckovits	F	6'1	175	29	22	**143**	**120**	**406**	**18.5**						
Soup Cable	F-C	6'3	200	28	5	10	9	29	5.8						
Pete Pederson	C	6'4	—	29	9	12	8	32	3.6						
Scoop Putnam	G-F	6'	175	27	20	36	11	83	4.2						
George Nelmark	G	6'1	180	24	21	40	32	112	5.3						
Bill Thompson	G-F	6'4	—	—	16	25	9	59	3.7						
Ed Erban	C-F	6'4	—	20	15	8	12	28	1.9						
Don Elser	F-C	6'4	220	28	6	10	7	27	4.5						
Dave Williams	C	6'3	—	—	7	9	6	24	3.4						
Al Alvarez	G	6'	160	29	4	8	5	21	5.3						
Jack Ozburn (military service)	G	6'1	170	27	3	7	1	15	5.0						
Bill Brownell	C	6'6	235	—	4	3	4	10	2.5						
Jim Rae	C	6'4	200	24	3	5	0	10	3.3						
Glen Edwards	G	—	—	—	3	2	1	5	1.7						
Bob Hassmiller	G	6'1	185	—	2	2	1	5	2.5						
Tom Wukovits	G	6'	165	26	3	2	0	4	1.3						
Glenn Roberts	C	6'5	200	25	1	1	0	2	2.0						
Benny Schall	G	5'11	170	24	2	0	1	1	0.5						
Tommy Edwards	F	5'10	170	30	1	0	1	1	1.0						
Paul Nowak	C	6'6	210	27	1	0	0	0	0.0						
Pat Hintz	G	6'	175	27	1	0	0	0	0.0						
Abe Yourist	C	6'2	210	30	1	0	0	0	0.0						
Paul Wallace	G	—	—	—	1	0	0	0	0.0						

1942-43 N.B.L.
And Then There Were Four

Like the rest of the home front, the N.B.L. this year had to improvise as players and teams suddenly became scarce commodities. The military was grabbing more and more players, and the supply of teams also was shrinking. The Indianapolis Kautskys suspended operations for the duration of the war and the Goodyear corporation decided to drop professional basketball in favor of an amateur program . George Halas, owner of the Chicago Bruins, also decided to fold his team, but the league was still able to field a Chicago franchise thanks to the local Studebaker plant.

The Studebaker factory had been converted to war-industry production, so the workers there were exempt from the draft. When quite a few pro basketball players got jobs at the plant, the United Auto Workers union picked up the N.B.L. Chicago franchise and sponsored a team. Working in the plant were Mike Novak and Dick Evans of the Bruins, Paul Sokody of Sheboygan, and a host of Harlem Globetrotters led by stars Sonny Boswell, Duke Cumberland, and Bernie Price. Thus the N.B.L. had its first racially integrated club, one that shaped up as among the strongest in the five-team field.

The Oshkosh club began the season on the wrong foot, losing the College All-Star Game, an annual exhibition in Chicago between the winner of last spring's World Toumament and a team of newly-graduated college players. Oshkosh continued to play sluggish ball into the regular season, with an extreme thinness at forward sapping much of the club's strength. Bob Carpenter and Lou Barle both were in the service, Connie Mack Berry could take little time off from work to play basketball, Gene Englund and Don Smith missed a total of 16 games due to their high school coaching duties and Bill Komenich quit pro ball on February 2nd. Despite the acquisition of high-scoring guard Ralph Vaughn from Chicago, the All-Stars slumped off to their first sub-.500 season.

In the battle to replace Oshkosh at the head of the standings, Toledo quickly fell by the wayside. Star scorer Chuck Chuckovits had gone into the service, but the Chevys rebuilt their squad around rookie center Bob Gerber, an All-American from the University of Toledo, and veteran guard Jewell Young. Young was recovering from an operation at the start of the season, however, and although Gerber scored 22 points on opening day, he then marched off into the military. After four straight losses, the Chevys gave up and left the league. With four clubs, the N.B.L. had just enough to fill all the playoff berths.

The Chicago Studebakers also ran into heavy sledding, with the club breaking up into hostile camps of white and black players. Charges of racial and financial discrimination shot back and forth between the two groups, and the club which started the season in very promising fashion ended up a dismal loser.

With Chicago hurt by racial strife and Oshkosh by military losses, Ft. Wayne and Sheboygan were left in the top two spots. The Zollner Pistons added to last year's strong squad a bulky center in ex-Goodyear Jake Pelkington, a veteran forward in Jerry Bush from the independent Detroit Eagles, and a solid rookie guard in Gus Doerner of Evansville. Doerner missed most of the season with injuries, but the first seven of Pelkington, Bush, Bobby McDermott, Blackie Towery, Paul Birch, Curly Armstrong, and Herm Schaefer was too much for the war-weakened opposition. The Zollner outfit cruised to a 17-6 regular season mark, easily the best in the league.

The Sheboygan Redskins, relatively free from military losses and bolstered by rookie forward Ken Buehler of Wisconsin-Milwaukee, hung back around the .500 mark until they signed Buddy Jeannette away from the independent Detroit Eagles in February. A crafty leader and floor general, Jeannette took over a backcourt spot and led the Redskins on a hot streak as the regular season ended.

All four surviving N.B.L. teams started over again on an even footing as the playoffs began, with Ft. Wayne beating Chicago and Sheboygan beating Oshkosh. The championship series opened in Ft. Wayne, and although the Pistons held a 27-21 halftime lead in the first game, the Redskins came back to take a 55-50 upset victory. In the second game, played at Sheboygan, a long shot by Jeannette knotted the score at 44-44 just seconds before the final buzzer. The Pistons, however, got two field goals from Armstrong and one from Towery in overtime to take a 50-45 win and even the series. With the homecourt advantage meaningless so far in the series, the Redskins and Pistons squared off in Ft. Wayne for the N.B.L. championship. Both clubs battled tooth and nail, and when the smoke cleared, the visiting Redskins held a 30-29 victory and their first title.

					HOME			ROAD			Average Points				PLAYOFFS Average Points			
Team	W	L	Pct.	GB	W	L	PCT.	W	L	Pct.	G	For	Agnst.	Diff.	G	For	Agnst.	Diff.
1942/43 N.B.L. STANDINGS																		
Fort Wayne Zollner Pistons	**17**	6	**.739**	—	**10**	2	**.833**	**7**	4	**.636**	23	**51.1**	46.4	**+4.5**	6	42.3	**40.7**	+1.6
Sheboygan Redskins	12	11	.522	5	9	4	.692	3	7	.300	23	43.2	43.7	-0.5	5	**47.2**	42.8	**+4.4**
Oshkosh All-Stars	11	12	.478	6	7	5	.583	4	7	.364	23	44.4	44.2	+0.2	2	42.5	53.0	-10.5
Chicago Studebakers	8	15	.348	9	5	**6**	.455	3	**9**	.250	23	48.2	50.8	-2.6	3	38.0	41.7	-3.7
Toledo Jim White Chevrolets	0	4	.000	7.5	—	—	—	0	4	.000	4	38.8	48	-9.2				

Use Name	Pos	Hgt	Wgt	Age	REGULAR SEASON G	FG	FT	Points	PPG	PLAYOFFS G	FG	FT	Points	PPG	Results
1942/43 N.B.L.															
FORT WAYNE ZOLLNER PISTONS	**17-6 .739**				**CARL BENNETT**										
Jerry Bush	F	6'3	205	28	23	39	32	110	4.8	6	14	6	34	5.7	defeated Chicago 2-1;
Blackie Towery	F-C	6'4	210	22	23	53	33	139	6.0	6	9	7	25	4.2	Home 49-37,
Jake Pelkington	C	6'6	220	25	23	83	70	236	10.3	6	12	15	39	6.5	Road 32-45,
Curly Armstrong	G-F	5'11	170	24	23	67	49	183	8.0	6	20	**19**	59	9.8	Home 44-32
Bobby McDermott	G	6'	185	28	23	**132**	52	**316**	**13.7**	6	**29**	16	**74**	**12.3**	
															lost to Sheboygan 1-2;
Herm Schaefer	G-F	6'	175	23	21	36	12	84	4.0	5	6	3	15	3.0	Home 50-55,
Paul Birch	F-G	6'1	195	32	23	29	20	78	3.4	6	3	2	8	1.3	Road 50-45(OT),
Dale Hamilton	F-G	6'	185	23	18	8	1	17	0.9	1	0	0	0	0.0	Home 29-30
Gus Doerner (BN)	F	6'2	195	20	4	4	1	9	2.3						
Jack Keller	F-G	6'2	185	22	9	1	1	3	0.3	1	0	0	0	0.0	
military service - Bob Calihan															
SHEBOYGAN REDSKINS	**12-11 .522**				**CARL ROTH**										
Rube Lautenschlager	F	6'3	195	27	23	88	36	212	9.2	5	22	12	56	11.2	defeated Oshkosh 2-0;
Ken Buehler (military service)	F-C	6'2	180	23	22	62	41	165	7.5						Home 50-38,
Ed Dancker	C	6'7	215	28	22	96	48	240	10.9	5	22	13	57	11.4	Road 56-47
Kenny Suesens	G	6'1	180	25	23	32	21	85	3.7	5	9	5	23	4.6	
Buddy Jeannette	G	5'11	175	26	4	24	14	62	15.5	5	16	17	49	9.8	defeated Fort Wayne 2-1
															Road 55-50,
Bob Schwartz (military service)	F	6'3	—	—	13	32	9	73	5.6	4	6	0	12	3.0	Home 45-50(OT),
Bill McDonald	G	6'3	190	26	22	20	25	65	3.0	5	5	6	16	3.2	Road 30-29
Eddie Sadowski (from Tol)	G	5'10	175	27	8	16	11	43	5.4	2	1	1	3	1.5	
Bob Regh	G-F	6'2	—	—	11	10	4	24	2.2	4	2	0	4	1.0	
George Jablonsky	C	6'7	215	23	11	7	5	19	1.7	5	3	7	13	2.6	
Moose Graf	F	6'3	200	25	5	2	0	4	0.8						
Warren Schrage	F-C	6'5	190	22	10	1	0	2	0.2	1	1	1	3	3.0	
Dick Schulz	F	6'2	192	25	1	0	0	0	0.0	1	0	0	0	0.0	
Joel Mason (FB)	G	6'	195	30	1	0	0	0	0.0						
Pete Lalich	F	6'2	190	22	1	0	0	0	0.0						
military service - Charlie Epperson, George Hesik, Paul Maki, Babe Ziegenhorn															
OSHKOSH ALL-STARS	**11-12 .478**				**LON DARLING**										
Don Smith (HC)	F	6'2	190	22	13	22	15	59	4.5	2	1	2	4	2.0	lost to Sheboygan 0-2;
Gene Englund (HC)	F-C	6'5	205	25	17	41	48	130	7.6	2	7	8	22	11.0	Road 38-50,
Leroy Edwards	C-F	6'4	225	28	23	74	72	220	9.6	2	8	8	24	12.0	Home 47-56
Charley Shipp	G	6'1	200	29	23	52	36	140	6.1	2	4	2	10	5.0	
Ralph Vaughn	G	6'1	175	24	22	86	50	222	10.1	2	7	0	14	7.0	
Bill Komenich (WW)	F	6'3	210	24	17	23	18	64	3.8						
Dave Quabius	G	6'	185	26	13	15	9	39	3.0	1	1	0	2	2.0	
Tommy Nisbet	G	5'10	165	25	9	7	8	22	2.4	2	3	3	9	4.5	
Bob Alwin	G	5'10	145	22	4	7	7	21	5.3						
Johnny Townsend (from Tol) (IL-MS)	C-F	6'4	210	26	5	4	10	18	3.6						
Gene Lorendo	F	6'3	215	21	9	7	3	17	1.9						
Connie Mack Berry (FB)	F-C	6'4	210	27	5	5	5	15	3.0						
Bob Kramer	G-F	6'3	—	21	5	6	0	12	2.4	2	0	0	0	0.0	
Fred Nimz (military service)	C-F	6'3	200	28	5	4	3	11	2.2						
Neal Adams (FB)	F-C	6'3	195	23	13	4	1	9	0.7						
Lou Barle (military service)	F	6'1	200	26	4	3	2	8	2.0						
Jewell Young (from Tol - illness)	G-F	6'	160	29	3	3	1	7	2.3						
Ray Krzoska	G	6'2	190	24	2	3	0	6	3.0						
Warner Engdahl (military service)	G	6'1	210	24	1	0	1	1	1.0						
Tex Mueller	G	6'1	175	26	1	0	0	0	0.0						
military service - Bob Carpenter, Erv Prasse, Eddie Riska, Herm Witasek															
CHICAGO STUDEBAKER FLYERS	**8-15 .348**				**JOHNNY JORDAN**										
Duke Cumberland	F	6'3	195	23	22	53	45	151	6.9	3	8	3	19	6.3	lost to Fort Wayne 1-2;
Bernie Price	F-C	6'3	180	27	22	60	**77**	197	9.0	3	7	9	23	7.7	Road 37-49,
Mike Novak	C	6'9	220	27	18	50	35	135	7.5	3	3	7	13	4.3	Home 45-32,
Sonny Boswell	G	6'1	180	27	22	88	53	229	10.4	3	13	4	30	10.0	Road 32-44
Roosie Hudson	G	6'	160	27	21	50	27	127	6.0	2	0	3	3	1.5	
Hillery Brown	G-F	6'3	190	30	23	36	22	94	4.1	3	2	2	6	2.0	
Johnny Orr	G	5'11	180	—	20	26	5	57	2.9						
Tony Peyton (broken leg)	F-G	6'2	200	21	18	17	9	43	2.4						
Ted Strong	F-C	6'3	220	26	10	13	10	36	3.6	3	2	4	8	2.7	
Paul Sokody	F	6'2	185	28	14	10	6	26	1.9						
Dick Evans (FB)	C-F	6'3	205	22	9	3	6	12	1.3						
Al Johnson	F	6'3	210	29	1	1	0	2	2.0	2	0	0	0	0.0	
Babe Pressley	G	6'2	195	26	—	—	—	—	—	3	4	4	12	4.0	
military service - Bill Hapac, George Hogan, Wibs Kautz, Stan Szukala, George Ratkovicz, Vince McGowan															
TOLEDO JIM WHITE CHEVROLETS	**0-4 .000**				**SID GOLDBERG**										(disbanded December 14, 1942 for remainder of World War II)
Billy Jones	F	—	—	25	4	11	0	22	5.5						
Cortez Gray	F-C	6'5	185	26	4	7	4	18	4.5						
Bob Gerber (military service)	C	6'5	210	28	1	9	4	22	22.0						
Pat Hintz	G	6'	175	28	4	18	4	40	10.0						
Eddie Sadowski (to Sheb)	G	5'9	175	27	2	4	0	8	4.0						
Johnny Townsend (to Osh)	C	6'4	210	26	2	6	4	16	8.0						
Shannie Barnett	F-C	6'3	175	23	4	5	4	14	3.5						
Al Price	G	6'	180	25	3	3	2	8	2.7						
Casey Jones	G	6'2	175	27	3	3	1	7	2.3						
Zane Wast	F	6'2	175	26	1	0	0	0	0.0						
military service - Jack Ozburn, Benny Schall, Chuck Chuckovits															

1943-44 N.B.L.

Unity Among the Ruins

The N.B.L. went on its annual scavenger hunt during the summer and came up with just enough teams to stay alive. When the Chicago Studebaker franchise folded, the league managed to get the Chase Brass Company of Cleveland to sponsor the fourth N.B.L. franchise. With only four clubs in the circuit, each member had to make the playoffs, but the regular season still provided entertaining basketball for the people of the upper Midwest. Some doubleheaders were scheduled during the regular season, with all four N.B.L. teams playing on one night.

Fans who saw these doubleheaders had to admit that the Ft. Wayne Zollner Pistons were tops in the league. The Pistons had lost Curly Armstrong, Herm Schaefer, and Gus Doerner to the military since last season, but the club brought itself back up to strength by signing guards Buddy Jeannette away from Sheboygan and Chick Reiser away from the Brooklyn team in the American Basketball League. The addition of these two backcourtmen helped the defending champion Pistons to compile an even better record than last season.

The heart of the Pistons was the backcourt, where Jeannette and Bobby McDermott were the starters. Jeannette could drive, pass, and defend with any guard in the league, and he gave the Pistons an aggressive leader on the floor. McDermott was the best outside shooter in the game, a threat from anywhere inside halfcourt to sink a two-hand set shot. A veteran pro from New York City with no college experience, McDermott led the Pistons in scoring and ranked second in the league with a 13.9 average.

At center, Jake Pelkington controlled the boards and used his 6'6", 220-pound frame to set broad picks for McDermott and Jeannette. Both forwards, Jerry Bush and Blackie Towery, were complete players who helped out with the rebounding and played tough defense. The Piston bench was thin but talented. Reiser, the newcomer from the A.B.L., had developed into an all-around guard during years of professional play on the East Coast. Veteran Paul Birch spelled the forwards, using his long experience to best advantage. The only other man on the squad, guard Dale Hamilton, played very little. So although the Pistons were essentially a seven-man team, close teamwork more than overcame the short roster.

Just as last year, the Sheboygan Redskins finished second behind the Pistons in the regular season. The Redskins had lost Jeannette to the Pistons and Ken Buehler to the military, but coach Carl Roth came up with some of the finest players available. He added 6'9" Mike Novak from the defunct Chicago team, signed 6'6" veteran Elmer Gainer, and added a rookie backup center in 6'9" Kleggie Hermsen from Minnesota. Combined with 6'7" veteran Ed Dancker, these newcomers made the Redskins the tallest team in the league. Coach Roth had three good returning smaller men in Rube Lautenschlager, Bill McDonald, and Ken Suesens, and he added two more in youngsters Tony Kelly and Dick Schulz. The Redskins relied on a deliberate offense and tough defense to put together their 14-8 regular season record, and they hoped to again take all the marbles in the playoffs.

Coming in third were the Oshkosh All-Stars, a shadow of their great team of two years ago. Gene Englund, Don Smith, Ralph Vaughn, and Bill Komenich were lost to the war effort, as were several key men who had left the team the year before. Coach Lon Darling signed forward Clint Wager, a pro football player with the Chicago Cardinals, but this wasn't enough to offset the losses to Uncle Sam. The club got off to a bad start from which it never recovered, and morale fell when star center Leroy Edwards was suspended for three games in December because of an uncooperative attitude. Edwards wound up the season with a 7.8 scoring average, his lowest mark ever as a pro.

Winding up a distant fourth was the new Cleveland team. Built around Mel Reibe, a 5'11" pivot man with a great hook shot, the Chase Brass team found itself completely outclassed by the other three teams. Despite Reibe's great scoring ability, the club lost 12 of its first 13 games. Wee Willie Smith, the veteran center of the New York Rens, joined the team in February and helped the club to two wins in its final five games. With Smith at center and Reibe at forward, Cleveland had some hope for the playoffs.

Those hopes were quickly dashed by the Ft. Wayne Pistons, who began one of the greatest playoff campaigns in history. The Pistons kayoed the Chase Brass outfit with 64-37 and 42-31 romps in the opening round, while Sheboygan eliminated Oshkosh in three games in a rough battle between two physical teams. In the finals, the Pistons took the first game at Sheboygan, 55-53, on a long bomb by Bobby McDermott with only seconds left in the game. In the second game, also at Sheboygan, the Pistons again triumphed, winning by a comfortable 36-26 score. The Zollner crew then wrapped up the league title with a 48-38 victory before their hometown fans. Thus, with five straight wins in the playoffs, four of them by comfortable margins, the Pistons won their first N.B.L. crown after two years of disappointing playoff failures

The Pistons did not stop there, however, and went on to the World Tournament in Chicago along with the other three N.B.L. teams. With attendance ranging from 7,200 to 14,226 for the five-day, 14-team meet, the Pistons repeated their playoff performance, sweeping the tournament with three straight victories. After swamping the Dayton Aviators 59-34 in their first game, the Pistons edged past the New York Rens 42-38 in the semifinals while the Brooklyn Eagles, behind Bob Tough's 32 points, captured the other spot in the finals by whipping the Harlem Globetrotters 63-41. The Pistons then beat the Eagles 50-33 for the title.

Team	W	L	Pct.	GB	HOME W	HOME L	HOME PCT.	ROAD W	ROAD L	ROAD Pct.	Average Points G	For	Agnst.	Diff.	PLAYOFFS Average Points G	For	Agnst.	Diff.
1943/44 N.B.L. STANDINGS																		
Fort Wayne Zollner Pistons	**18**	4	**.818**	—	**9**	2	**.818**	**9**	2	**.818**	22	**47.2**	41.2	**+6.0**	5	**49.0**	37.0	**+12.0**
Sheboygan Redskins	14	8	.636	4	8	3	.727	6	5	.545	22	41.5	**40.9**	+0.6	6	36.8	38.5	-1.7
Oshkosh All-Stars	7	**15**	.318	11	6	5	.545	1	**10**	.091	22	42.1	43.5	-1.4	3	30.7	**34.7**	-4.0
Cleveland Chase Brass	3	**15**	.167	13	3	**6**	.333	0	9	.000	18	42.1	48.4	-6.3	2	34	53.0	-19.0

Use Name	Pos.	Hgt.	Wgt.	Age	REGULAR SEASON G	FG	FT	Points	PPG	PLAYOFFS G	FG	FT	Points	PPG	Results
						1943/44 N.B.L.									
FORT WAYNE ZOLLNER PISTONS 18-4 .818						**BOBBY McDERMOTT**									
Jerry Bush	F	6'3	210	29	22	55	22	132	6.0	5	12	7	31	6.2	defeated Cleveland2-0;
Blackie Towery	F-C	6'4	210	23	22	48	33	129	5.9	5	14	3	31	6.2	Home 64-37,
Jake Pelkington	C	6'6	220	26	20	46	40	132	6.6	5	11	10	32	6.4	Road 42-31,
Buddy Jeannette	G	5'11	175	26	22	68	48	184	8.4	5	12	10	34	6.8	
Bobby McDermott	G	6'	185	29	22	**123**	60	306	13.9	5	**27**	13	**67**	**13.4**	defeated Sheboygan 3-0;
															Road 55-53,
Chick Reiser	G-F	5'11	165	29	22	28	25	81	3.7	5	13	8	34	6.8	Road 36-26,
Paul Birch	F-G	6'1	195	33	22	27	17	71	3.2	5	7	2	16	3.2	Home 48-38,
Dale Hamilton	F-G	6'	185	24	11	2	0	4	0.4	5	0	0	0	0.0	
military service—Curly Armstrong, Bob Calihan, Gus Doerner, Herm Schaefer															
SHEBOYGAN REDSKINS 14-8 .636						**CARL ROTH**									
Rube Lautenschlager	F	6'3	200	28	21	68	28	164	7.8	4	3	2	8	2.0	defeated Oshkosh 2-1;
Ed Dancker	F-C	6'7	215	29	22	70	52	192	8.7	6	16	**15**	47	7.8	Home 32-31,
Mike Novak	C	6'9	220	28	22	39	14	92	4.2	6	6	4	16	2.7	Road 32-34,
Bill McDonald	G	6'3	190	27	20	43	34	120	6.0	6	8	12	28	4.7	Home 40-27,
Kenny Suesens	G	6'1	180	26	21	34	32	100	4.8	6	6	12	24	4.0	
															lost to Fort Wayne 0 3;
Tony Kelly	G	6'1	165	23	19	40	30	110	5.8	6	13	8	34	5.7	Home 53 55,
Elmer Gainer	F	6'6	195	24	22	15	20	50	2.3	6	2	3	7	1.2	Home 26 36,
Dick Shulz	F	6'2	192	26	20	18	10	46	2.3	5	17	14	48	9.6	Road 38 48,
Johnny Orr	G	5'11	180	—	19	10	8	28	1.6	5	1	2	4	0.8	
Kleggie Hermsen	C-F	6'9	225	20	12	3	5	11	0.9						
Bob Regh	G	6' 2	—	—	1	0	0	0	0.0						
George Jablonsky	C	6'7	215	24	—	—	—	—	—	2	1	3	5	2.5	
military service—Ken Buehler, Charlie Epperson George Hesik, Paul Mahi, Warren Schrage, Bob Schwartz, Babe Ziegenhorn															
OSHKOSH ALL-STARS 7-15 .318						**LON DARLING**									
Ed Erban	F	6'4	—	22	22	19	20	58	2.6	3	2	2	6	2.0	lost to Sheboygan 1-2;
Clint Wager (FB)	F-C	6'6	220	23	22	79	72	230	10.5	3	8	5	21	7.0	Road 31-32,
Leroy Edwards (ST)	C-F	6'4	225	29	19	48	52	148	7.8	3	6	5	17	5.7	Home 3432,
Charley Shipp	G	6'1	200	30	20	57	36	150	7.5	3	3	7	13	4.3	Road 27-40,
Frank Sachse (FB)	G	6'	197	26	22	42	12	96	4.4	3	2	2	6	2.0	
Ed Scheiwe	G	5'11	170	25	16	28	16	72	4.5	3	1	1	3	1.0	
Ray Terzynski	F	6'1	180	24	19	23	18	64	3.4	3	1	3	5	1.7	
Connie Mack Berry (FB)	F-C	6'4	212	28	11	16	7	39	3.5	3	6	3	15	5.0	
Gene Englund (military service)	C-F	6'5	205	26	2	9	5	23	11.5						
Eric Plahna	G-F	—	—	22	9	7	0	14	1.6	3	2	2	6	2.0	
Bob Sullivan (military service)	G-F	6'	180	22	3	6	1	13	4.3						
Ed Glancy	G-F	6'3	180	25	5	3	3	9	1.8						
Harold Dahl	F	5'9	190	20	5	1	2	4	0 8						
Gordon Flick	F	6'3	200	22	3	2	0	4	13						
Leo Osiewalski	F	6'4	190	22	4	1	0	2	0.5						
Bill Komenich—war plant work															
military service—Lou Barle, Bob Carpenter, Warner Engdahl, Bob Kramer, Fred Nimz, Erv Prasse, Eddie Riska, Don Smith, Ralph Vaughn, Herm Witasek															
CLEVELAND CHASE BRASS 3-15 .167						**VITO KUBILUS (2-10), NICK RADLICK (1-5)**									
Mel Riebe	F-C	5'11	180	27	18	113	**97**	**323**	**17.9**	2	8	9	25	12.5	lost to Fort Wayne O-2;
Pete Lalich	F	6'2	190	23	17	44	21	109	6.4	2	1	2	4	2.0	Road 37-64,
Willie Smith	C	6'6	230	32	4	9	6	24	6.0	2	5	7	17	8.5	Home 31-42
Ned Endress	G-F	6'2	200	25	16	25	15	65	4.1	2	1	1	3	1.5	
Bill Riebe	G	5'11	175	26	18	44	23	111	6.2	2	3	5	11	5.5	
Willard Swihart	F-C	6'3	190	29	15	14	11	39	2.6	2	0	1	1	0.5	
Vito Kubilus	G	6'1	180	29	16	11	10	32	2.0	1	1	0	2	2.0	
John Poncar	C-F	6'3	190	30	18	11	8	30	1.7	2	0	1	1	0.5	
Frank Garcia	G-F	6'	175	25	7	8	7	23	3.3	2	2	0	4	2.0	
Hal Cihlar	F-C	6'5	210	29	4	0	1	1	0.3						
Bill Brownell	C	6'6	235	—	1	0	0	0	0.3						

1944-45 N.B.L.

The Pride of Fort Wayne

With the end of the war now in sight, the N.B.L. began a return to full strength after years of extreme belt-tightening. Although some players still were being drafted, most of the eligible men had already joined the service. With the manpower situation stabilized, enough players were collected in Chicago and Pittsburgh to stock new clubs in those cities. With league membership now up to six teams, the N.B.L. reinstated divisional play for the first time since 1939-40. The increased membership also meant that the regular season would eliminate two clubs from the playoffs, a definite improvement over the makeshift practice of letting all the league teams into the "second season."

The defending champion Ft. Wayne Zollner Pistons served notice right from the start of the season that they were not going to be one of the teams eliminated. After losing the College All-Star exhibition in Chicago, the Pistons opened their N.B.L. schedule with two wins before losing to Oshkosh on December 9. From that point, the Pistons ran off 14 straight victories until dropping a 52-50 decision in Chicago on January 27. That one burst locked up first place in the Eastern Division for the Zollner outfit, despite the team's loss of starting forward Blackie Towery to the military. Coach Carl Bennett plugged the gap in the starting lineup by shifting Buddy Jeannette from guard to forward and promoting Chick Reiser to a starting backcourt spot. Bennett then replenished his bench by signing forward Bob Synnott and by getting veteran guard Charley Shipp from Oshkosh. Bobby McDermott again paced the club in scoring, averaging 20.1 points per game with a high game of 36 points in a contest against Cleveland.

The only man to put together a scoring average higher than McDermott's was Mel Reibe of Cleveland, who hit for 20.2 points per game from his pivot position. Reibe's team, now sponsored by the Allmen Transfer Company, finished a distant second to the Pistons in the East, but was markedly improved by the addition of Mike Bytzura and Tom Wukovits, a veteran of the Firestone team which had won N.B.L. titles in 1939 and 1940. Finishing last in the division were the Pittsburgh Raiders. The Raiders put together a team primarily of local players, but poor defense and disorganization saddled the team with the league's worst record.

In the Western Division, the Sheboygan Redskins used their height, deliberate offense, and physical defense to capture first place with a 19-11 record. Coach Dutch Dehnert had lost Kenny Suesens, Bill McDonald, Elmer Gainer, and Kleggie Hermsen since last season, but he still had 6'7" Ed Dancker and 6'9" Mike Novak as pillars for his front line. To bolster the backcourt and the bench, he signed three players from Eastern schools, Bobby Holm of Seton Hall, Al Lucas of Fordham, and Al Moschetti of St. John's. Veteran swingmen Rube Lautenschlager and Dick Schulz helped keep the Redskin machine well-oiled and running smoothly in the drive to first place.

The new Chicago club compiled a creditable 14-16 record, finishing five games behind Sheboygan and capturing a playoff spot. Sponsored by the American Gear Company, the new team built its attack around a pair of rookies from local schools, forward Stan Patrick from Illinois and guard Dick Triptow from DePaul. Both rookies were fine shooters, with Patrick setting a league record of 38 points in the season's final game against Pittsburgh. The veterans in the starting lineup, center Vince McGowan, forward Elmer Gainer, and guard Bill McDonald, concentrated mostly on defense.

Two games behind the Gears were the Oshkosh All-Stars, the team which had lost 12 men to the military. Coach Lon Darling pared two veterans from the roster by selling guard Charley Shipp to Ft. Wayne and forward Connie Mack Berry to Chicago, and he came up with a useful young forward in Pete Pasko out of tiny East Stroudsburg State. Although finishing out of the playoffs for the first time in N.B.L. history, the All-Stars improved on their 1943-44 record, thanks largely to center Leroy Edwards. Coming off his worst pro campaign, the 30-year-old Edwards brought his scoring average back up to 13.6, fourth best in the league. Late in the season, the All-Stars signed Green Bay Packer fullback Ted Fritsch as a guard; the burly Fritsch had starred in the 1944 N.F.L. championship game, but as a basketball player his team would not even make it into the playoffs.

The opening round of the playoffs pitted Sheboygan against Chicago in the West, while Ft. Wayne and Cleveland met in the East. The strong Pistons received a boost for the playoffs by signing 6'5", 245 Ib. center Ed Sadowski fresh from the Army. The Pistons didn't need any additional help in getting past the Cleveland team, using a balanced attack to offset Mel Reibe's 19- and 22-point games to take 78-50 and 58-51 victories. In the Western semifinals, Chicago upset Sheboygan 50-49 in the opening game, infuriating the Wisconsin fans by freezing the ball for the last two minutes. The Redskins had their revenge in the next game at Chicago by taking an easy 49-36 decision. In the deciding game at Sheboygan, the Redskins destroyed the Gears, limiting them to six points in the second half in carving out a 57-27 win.

The Pistons were expected to sweep through the finals as they did last year, but the Redskins ended those hopes by winning the first two games of the series in Sheboygan by scores of 65-53 and 50-47. With their backs up against the wall, the Pistons reacted with the poise of experienced champions. With Bobby McDermott leading a well-distributed attack, the Pistons came right back to take three games in Ft. Wayne, winning by scores of 58-47, 58-41, and 59-49.

To go with their second straight N.B.L. title, the Pistons then captured their second straight World Tournament championship. All the N.B.L. teams except Sheboygan entered the 14-team field with the hometown favorites, the Gears, beating the New York Rens 63-45 for third place while the Pistons dismantled the Dayton Acmes 78-52 in the final before a crowd of 15,119.

Team	W	L	Pct.	GB	vs. playoff teams W	L	Pct.	vs.non-playoff teams W	L	Pct.	HOME W	L	Pct.	ROAD W	L	Pct.	Average Points G	For	Agnst.	Diff.	PLAYOFFS Average Points G	For	Agnst.	Diff.
1944 /45 N.B.L. STANDINGS																								
EASTERN DIVISION																								
Fort Wayne	**25**	5	**.833**	—	**13**	5	**.722**	**12**	0	**1.000**	**14**	1	**.933**	**11**	4	**.733**	30	**56.9**	50.2	**+6.7**	7	**58.7**	50.4	**+8.3**
Cleveland	13	17	.433	12	7	11	.389	6	**6**	.500	8	7	.533	5	10	.333	30	51.0	51.0	—	2	50.5	68.0	-17.5
Pittsburgh	7	**23**	.233	18	4	**20**	.167	3	3	.500	5	**9**	.357	2	**14**	.125	30	48.7	55.5	-6.8				
WESTERN DIVISION																								
Sheboygan	19	11	.633	—	10	8	.556	9	3	.750	12	3	.800	7	8	.467	30	49.8	**46.0**	+3.8	8	50.9	**48.5**	+2.4
Chicago	14	16	.467	5	5	13	.278	9	3	.750	11	4	.733	3	12	.200	30	51.6	53.9	-23.0	3	37.7	51.7	-14.0
Oshkosh	12	18	.400	7	9	15	.375	3	3	.500	10	6	.625	2	12	.143	30	46.9	48.2	-13.0				

1944/45 N.B.L. — EASTERN DIVISION

Use Name	Pos.	Hgt.	Wgt.	Age	REGULAR SEASON G	FG	FT	Points	PPG	PLAYOFFS G	FG	FT	Points	PPG	Results
FORT WAYNE ZOLLNER PISTONS 25-5 .833 BOBBY MCDERMOTT															
Buddy Jeannette	F	5'11	175	27	27	85	82	252	9.3	7	22	23	67	9.6	defeated Cleveland 2-0;
Jerry Bush	F	6'3	210	30	28	62	30	154	5.5	7	14	10	38	5.4	Home 78-50
Jake Pelkington	C	6'6	220	27	30	85	76	246	8.2	7	19	18	56	8	Road 58-51
Chick Reiser	G	5'11	165	30	30	82	53	217	7.2	7	23	12	58	8.3	
Bobby McDermott	G	6'	185	30	30	**258**	87	603	20.1	7	**45**	15	105	15.0	
															defeated Sheboygan 3-2;
Charley Shipp	G	6'1	205	31	30	31	16	78	2.6	7	4	5	13	1.9	Road 47-50
Bob Synnott	F-C	6'3	190	32	30	32	11	75	2.5	6	7	5	19	3.2	Home 58-47,
Paul Birch	F-G	6'1	200	34	28	29	7	65	2.3	3	2	3	7	2.3	Home 58-41
Ed Sadowski (military service)	C	6'5	245	27	1	4	2	10	10.0	7	17	11	45	6.4	Home 59-49
Jim Glass	C	6'8	210	23	14	2	3	7	0.5	2	1	1	3	1.5	
Blackie Towery (military service)	F	6'4	210	24	1	0	1	1	1.0						
Dale Hamilton	F	6'	190	25	2	0	0	0	0.0						
military service—Curly Armstrong, Bob Calihan, Gus Doerner, Herm Schaefer															
CLEVELAND ALLMEN TRANSFERS 13-17 .433 JEFF CARLIN															
Mike Bytzura	F	6'1	170	22	30	113	35	261	8.7	2	4	3	11	5.5	lost to Fort Wayne 0-2;
Ned Endress	F-C	6'2	200	26	29	62	46	170	5.9	2	4	2	10	5.0	Road 50-78,
John Mills	C	6'8	210	25	29	29	42	100	3.4	2	3	6	12	6.0	Home 51-58
Mel Riebe	G-F	5'11	195	28	30	223	**161**	**607**	**20.2**	2	15	11	41	20.5	
Tom Wukovits	G	6'	175	28	26	85	74	244	9.4	2	5	12	22	11.0	
Bill Riebe	G	5'11	175	27	24	24	22	70	2.9	2	0	5	5	2.5	
Frank Garcia	G-F	6'	175	26	25	16	8	40	1.6	2	0	0	0	0.0	
Don Warnke (knee injury)	C	6'10	200	23	20	10	9	29	1.5						
Johnny Malokas (military service)	G	5'11	195	28	1	2	1	5	5.0						
Herm Weiss (hand injury)	G	6'	180	28	3	2	0	4	1.3						
Paul Kessy (to Pit)	F-C	6'3	170	27	4	0	0	0	0.0						
Steve Sitko	G	6'	200	27	1	0	0	0	0.0						
Tom Becker	F	6'1	180	21	1	0	0	0	0.0						
PITTSBURGH RAIDERS 7-23 .233 JOE URSO															
Matt Vaniel	F	6'3	170	25	24	78	23	179	7.5						
Hank Evans	F-C	6'3	195	29	28	97	44	238	8.5						
Huck Hartman	C	6'7	205	23	30	127	73	327	10.9						
Freddie Crum	G-F	6'	170	32	29	69	30	168	5.8						
Joe Urso	G	5'10	170	28	29	81	40	202	7.0						
George Haines	F-G	5'10	160	23	26	56	33	145	5.6						
Ralph Churchfield	G-F	6'5	220	26	20	26	15	67	3.4						
Irv Brenner	F-C	6'4	200	31	14	28	8	64	4.6						
Pete Lalich	F	6'2	190	24	9	8	4	20	2.2						
Sid Levine	G	5'7	185	26	18	4	1	9	0.5						
Nat Hickey	G	5'11	190	42	2	3	2	8	4.0						
Jack Scarry	F-C	6'3	195	27	6	3	1	7	1.2						
Al Schrecker	F	6'1	160	27	1	3	1	7	7.0						
Joe Proska	G	6'1	185	30	1	2	3	7	7.0						
John Stephens	G	5'6	—	—	1	2	0	4	4.0						
John Novotny	G	5'10	165	26	1	2	0	4	4.0						
Paul Kessy (from Cle)	F	6'3	170	27	2	1	1	3	1.5						
Bobby Neu	F	6'1	180	27	3	0	1	1	0.3						
Frank Vukosic	G-F	—	—	—	4	0	0	0	0.0						

1944/45 N.B.L. — WESTERN DIVISION

Use Name	Pos	Hgt	Wgt	Age	REGULAR SEASON G	FG	FT	Points	PPG	PLAYOFFS G	FG	FT	Points	PPG	Results
SHEBOYGAN REDSKINS	**19-11 .633**				**DUTCH DEHNERT**										
Dick Schulz	F-G	6'2	192	27	29	86	71	243	8.4	8	22	32	76	9.5	defeated Chicago 2-1;
Mike Novak	F-C	6'9	220	29	27	88	57	233	8.6	8	24	16	64	8.0	Home 49-50,
Ed Dancker	C-F	6'7	220	30	30	111	61	283	9.4	8	41	27	109	13.6	Road 49-36,
Rube Lautenschlager	G-F	6'3	200	29	30	83	28	194	6.5	8	16	13	45	5.6	Home 57-27
Bobby Holm	G	6'	210	25	30	57	50	164	5.5	8	16	13	45	5.6	lost to Fort Wayne 2-3;
Al Lucas	F-G	6'3	195	22	26	57	36	150	5.8	8	13	8	34	4.3	Home 65-53,
Al Moschetti	F	6'1	180	24	24	43	35	121	5.0	2	2	1	5	2.5	Home 50-47,
Tony Kelly	G	6'1	165	24	28	35	35	105	3.8	8	10	9	29	3.6	Road 47-58,
Bill Durkin (military service)	G	6'1	160	22	1	1	0	2	2.0						Road 41-58,
Johnny Posewitz	G	6'	185	38	1	0	0	0	0.0						Road 49-59
Hal Tidrick	G	6'1	190	29	1	0	0	0	0.0						

military service - Ken Buehler, Charlie Epperson, George Hesik, Paul Maki, Warren Schrage, Bob Schwartz, Kenny Suesens, Babe Ziegenhorn

Use Name	Pos	Hgt	Wgt	Age	REGULAR SEASON G	FG	FT	Points	PPG	PLAYOFFS G	FG	FT	Points	PPG	Results
CHICAGO AMERICAN GEARS	**14-16 .467**				**JACK TIERNEY**										
Stan Patrick	F	6'3	215	22	28	187	84	458	16.4	3	7	5	19	6.3	lost to Sheboygan 1-2;
Elmer Gainer	F-C	6'6	195	25	29	44	38	126	4.3	3	10	2	22	7.3	Road 50-49,
Vince McGowan	C	6'6	210	31	27	54	45	153	5.7	3	1	7	9	3.0	Home 36-49,
Dick Triptow	G-F	6'	170	22	30	113	73	299	10.0	3	11	6	28	9.3	Road 27-57
Bill McDonald	G	6'3	190	28	30	83	73	239	8.0	3	1	9	11	3.7	
Ray Krzoska	G	6'2	190	26	21	30	21	81	3.9	3	4	5	13	4.3	
Swede Roos	G-F	6'1	180	31	22	24	22	70	3.2						
Connie Mack Berry (FB)	C-F	6'4	212	29	18	11	6	28	1.6	3	0	0	0	0.0	
Johnny Orr	G	5'11	180	—	18	11	2	24	1.3	3	1	0	2	0.7	
John Styler	F-C	6'6	225	28	16	10	2	22	1.4	1	0	0	0	0.0	
Joe Stampf	C-F	6'4	210	25	7	8	5	21	3.0						
Ed Scheiwe	G-F	5'11	170	26	16	6	4	16	1.0	2	0	1	1	0.5	
Nick Hashu	F-C	—	—	—	2	4	2	10	5.0	3	4	0	8	2.7	
Frank Otway (military service)	F	6'4	205	21	1	0	0	0	0.0						
Chet Strumillo (military service)	F	5'11	175	20	1	0	0	0	0.0						

military service - George Hogan, Stan Szukala, George Ratkovicz

Use Name	Pos	Hgt	Wgt	Age	REGULAR SEASON G	FG	FT	Points	PPG	PLAYOFFS G	FG	FT	Points	PPG	Results
OSHKOSH ALL-STARS	**12-18 .400**				**LON DARLING**										
Pete Pasco	F	6'3	190	21	26	89	50	228	8.8						
Clint Wager (FB)	F-C	6'6	220	24	27	70	28	168	6.2						
Leroy Edwards	C	6'4	225	30	30	125	##	407	13.6						
Homer Fuller	G-F	6'3	220	24	28	66	17	149	5.3						
Chuck Shanklin	G	—	—	—	30	42	13	97	3.2						
Ray Terzynski	F	6'1	180	25	29	41	45	127	4.4						
Howie Hoffman	G-F	—	—	24	18	44	17	105	5.8						
Bill Komenich	G	6'3	210	26	24	16	13	45	1.9						
Frank Sachse (FB)	G	6'	197	27	8	16	7	39	4.9						
Ed Erban	F	6'4	—	23	15	13	10	36	2.4						
Ted Fritsch (FB)	G	5'10	210	24	9	1	3	5	0.6						

military service - Lou Barle, Bob Carpenter, Warner Engdahl, Gene Englund, Bob Kramer, Fred Nimz, Erv Prasse, Eddie Riska, Don Smith, Bob Sullivan, Ralph Vaughn, Herm Witasek.

1945-46 N. B. L.

Chicago's Late $60,000 Surprise

A record crowd of 23,912, the largest audience yet to see a basketball game, saw the Ft. Wayne Pistons beat a team of freshly-graduated college players in the annual College All-Star game held in November in Chicago. The success of this exhibition underlined the new vigor of pro basketball now that World War II had ended. Pro players, as well as former collegiate stars, were returning to civilian life. Looking to cash in on the postwar economic boom, the N.B.L. hired famous Purdue coach Piggy Lambert as commissioner and took in the Rochester Royals and Indianapolis Kautskys as the seventh and eighth members.

The defending champion Zollner Pistons, with two straight championships under their belt, stood head and shoulders over the competition as preseason favorites. In addition to their last year's players, the Pistons added veteran guard Herm Schaefer, just out of the service, and center Bob Kinney, a star at Rice University before the war. As if that weren't enough, the Pistons signed guard Bob Tough away from the American Basketball League in February and got veteran Curly Armstrong back from Uncle Sam just in time for the playoffs.

But the new Rochester Royals, owned and coached by Les Harrison, stayed right on Ft. Wayne's heels all season. Harrison built a surprisingly strong club, mostly from discharged former college stars. He signed forward George Glamack, hook shot ace from North Carolina; Bob Davies, fancy-Dan dribbler and passer from Seton Hall; 6'8" center John Mahnken from Georgetown; guard Red Holzman, a smart, good-shooting backcourtman from C.C.N.Y.; Northwestern's Otto Graham, whose pro football career with the Cleveland Browns would later completely overshadow his fine basketball talents; and Fuzzy Levane, who had captained St. John's to the N.I.T. championship in 1943. To add leadership to his backcourt, Harrison signed Al Cervi, a tough guard with no college experience but plenty of professional and service ball playing to his credit. Two lesser lights on the Rochester roster were Chuck Connors, who would find fame as a television actor in the 1950's, and Del Rice, who was also a catcher for the St. Louis Cardinals baseball team. The Royals started slowly, with Davies in the service for the first month of the season and with Mahnken and forward Al Negratti able to play only on weekends until their discharge from the Navy in February. By playoff time, however, the Royals were in full swing and ready to face the Pistons. The two other Eastern Division clubs, the Youngstown Bears (transplanted from Pittsburgh) and Cleveland Allmen Transfers, finished far out of the playoffs.

In the Western Division, the two Wisconsin rivals, the Sheboygan Redskins and Oshkosh All-Stars, battled for first place all through the winter. The Redskins, who eventually finished on top, had essentially the same club as last year, with big men Ed Dancker and Mike Novak the key players. Oshkosh coach Lon Darling had his forward corps return to top strength when Bob Carpenter, and Gene Englund were discharged from the service. The sharpshooting Carpenter led the league in scoring and hit for a record 40 points in one game against Cleveland. Two pro rookies started at guard, Santa Clara's Bob Feerick, who used a Hank Luisetti-style one-hand shot, and Wisconsin's Fred Rehm. At center, veteran Leroy Edwards scored at a 10.8 clip, his last season in double figures. Finishing out of the money were the Chicago American Gears and Indianapolis Kautskys.

While Sheboygan eliminated Oshkosh in five games in the first round of the playoffs, most attention focused on the Eastern Division showdown between Ft. Wayne and Rochester. The Pistons took the first game on their home court, 54-44, with Big Ed Sadowski throwing in a game-high 21 points. The Royals, however, then evened the score with a 58-52 upset win in the Ft. Wayne gym. The series resumed in Rochester, with the homecourt advantage now held by the Royals. With George Glamack hooking in 14 points and Al Cervi popping in 12, the Royals took the third game of the series 58-52 and forced the Pistons to the wall. The Zollner team had come from behind to beat Sheboygan in last year's finals, but the Royals were not about to let the Pistons off the hook. With Glamack hitting for 23, Davies for 23, and Red Holzman for 11, the Royals knocked the crown from the Pistons' head with a resounding 70-54 triumph. In the finals, the Royals swept three straight games from the bigger, slower Sheboygan Redskins, using a sharp passing attack to take 60-50, 61-54, and 66-48 decisions. Four Royals, Glamack, Davies, Holzman, and Cervi, averaged at least 10 points per game in the playoffs, a tribute to the team's balanced attack.

The Royals did not compete in the annual World Tournament, but Ft. Wayne, Oshkosh, Sheboygan, Chicago, Cleveland, and Indianapolis did join the 14-team field. The biggest news of the tournament was the pro debut of 6'10" George Mikan with the Chicago American Gears. Mikan, who had starred at DePaul for the past three seasons, was the first big man to regularly score 20 points a game. The Gears inked this most famous college player in the country to a $60,000, five-year contract and put him into uniform as soon as his college season ended. Mikan didn't appear in any N. B. L. league games, but he did play in a few exhibitions with the Gears in preparation for the World Tournament.

The Gears beat Pittsburgh 69-58 in the first round and squeezed past the Sheboygan Redskins 52-51 in the second round. In the semifinals, however, veteran Leroy Edwards scored 24 points and gave Mikan a lesson in center play as Oshkosh knocked off the Gears 72-66. The Ft. Wayne Pistons eventually beat Oshkosh in the finals to capture their third straight World Tournament title, but Mikan was the talk of the crowd after the action had ended. He led the Gears to a pair of smashing victories over the A.B.L. Baltimore Bullets in the consolation round, scored 100 points in five games, and won first team All-Tournament honors as well as the MVP award.

Team	W	L	Pct.	GB	vs. playoff teams W	vs. playoff teams L	vs. playoff teams PCT.	vs. non-playoff teams W	vs. non-playoff teams L	vs. non-playoff teams Pct.	HOME W	HOME L	HOME Pct.	ROAD W	ROAD L	ROAD Pct.	Average Points G	Average Points FT%	Average Points For	Average Points Agnst.	Average Points Diff.	PLAYOFFS Average Points G	PLAYOFFS FT%	PLAYOFFS For	PLAYOFFS Agnst.	PLAYOFFS Diff.
1945/46 N.B.L. STANDINGS																										
EASTERN DIVISION																										
Fort Wayne	**26**	8	**.765**	—	**9**	5	**.643**	17	3	**.850**	**14**	3	**.824**	**12**	5	**.706**	34	**70**	**58.7**	51.0	**+7.7**	**4**	68	53.0	57.5	-4.5
Rochester	24	10	.706	2	8	6	.571	16	4	.800	**14**	3	**.824**	10	7	.588	34	64	56.8	50.8	+6.0	7	72	**59.6**	52.0	**+7.6**
Youngstown	13	20	.394	12.5	5	15	.250	8	5	.615	9	8	.529	4	12	.250	33	64	46.6	50.5	-3.9					
Cleveland	**4**	**29**	.121	21.5	0	**20**	.000	4	**9**	.308	4	**11**	.267	0	**18**	.000	33	62	46.1	56.4	10.3					
WESTERN DIVISION																										
Sheboygan	21	13	.618	—	6	8	.429	15	5	.750	12	6	.667	9	7	.563	34	61	51.0	**48.2**	+2.8	8	63	50.5	56.4	-5.9
Oshkosh	19	15	.559	2	5	9	.357	14	6	.700	13	5	.722	6	10	.375	34	66	53.4	49.2	+4.2	5	**72**	52.8	**50.4**	+2.4
Chicago	17	17	.500	4	8	12	.400	9	5	.643	10	7	588	7	10	.412	34	60	48.4	51.6	-3.2					
Indianapolis	10	22	.313	10	5	15	.250	5	7	.417	4	**11**	267	6	11	.353	32	58	46.4	49.8	-3.4					

1945/46 N.B.L. — EASTERN DIVISION

FORT WAYNE ZOLLNER PISTONS **26-8 .765** **CARL BENNETT** lost to Rochester 1-3; H54-44, H52-58, 52-58,54-70

Use Name	Pos.	Hgt.	Wgt.	Age	REGULAR SEASON G	FG	FT	FTA	Pct.	Points	PPG	PLAYOFFS G	FG	FT	FTA	Pct.	Point	PPG
Buddy Jeannette	F-G	5'11	175	28	34	99	105	136	77	303	8.9	4	7	5	6	83	19	4.8
Jerry Bush	F	6'3	210	31	34	61	31	43	72	153	4.5	4	3	7	12	58	13	3.3
Ed Sadowski	C	6'5	245	28	34	122	82	120	68	326	9.6	4	20	17	23	74	57	**14.3**
Chick Reiser	G	5'11	165	31	34	90	53	80	66	233	6.9	4	15	4	8	50	34	8.5
Bobby McDermott	G	6'	185	31	34	184	90	119	76	458	13.5	4	7	10	12	83	24	6
Jake Pelkington	C-F	6'6	220	28	33	94	76	104	73	264	8.0	4	8	5	5	100	21	5.3
Charley Shipp	G-F	6'1	205	32	34	42	14	24	58	98	2.9	4	0	0	1	0	0	0.0
Bob Synnott	F	6'3	195	33	24	24	0	—	—	48	2.0							
Bob Kinney (BW)	C-F	6'6	215	25	13	16	2	—	—	34	2.6	3	5	1	2	50	11	3.7
Bob Tough (military service)	F-G	6'	185	25	5	12	5	—	—	29	5.8	4	9	4	8	50	22	5.5
Herm Schaefer	G-F	6'	175	26	15	10	3	—	—	23	1.5							
Gus Doerner	F	6'2	195	23	11	8	5	—	—	21	1.9							
Curly Armstrong(military service)	G	5'11	170	27	6	3	1	—	—	7	1.2	3	5	1	2	50	11	3.7
military service — Blackie Towery																		

ROCHESTER ROYALS **24-10 .706** **ED MALANOWICZ** defeated Fort Wayne 3-1; 44-54,58-52, H58-52, H70-54
defeated Sheboygan 3-0; H60-50, H61-54, 66-48

Use Name	Pos.	Hgt.	Wgt.	Age	REGULAR SEASON G	FG	FT	FTA	Pct.	Points	PPG	PLAYOFFS G	FG	FT	FTA	Pct.	Point	PPG
Bob Davies (military service)	F-G	6'1	175	25	27	86	70	103	68	242	9.0	7	28	**30**	**41**	73	86	12.3
George Glamack	F-C	6'6	225	26	34	151	115	184	63	417	12.3	7	**34**	20	27	74	**88**	12.6
John Mahnken (military service)	C	6'8	220	23	16	50	23	39	59	123	7.7	7	19	8	9	89	46	6.7
Al Cervi (IL)	G	5'11	185	28	28	112	76	108	70	300	10.7	7	23	24	30	80	70	10.0
Red Holzman	G	5'10	175	25	34	143	77	115	67	363	10.7	7	30	21	31	68	81	11.6
Otto Graham	F-G	6'1	190	24	32	59	47	73	64	165	5.2	5	3	0	0	—	6	1.2
Fuzzy Levane (military service)	F-G	6'2	190	25	22	52	8	19	42	112	5.1	3	0	2	2	100	2	0.7
Al Negratti (military service)	F-C	6'4	220	24	16	19	10	—	—	48	3.0	7	9	7	14	50	25	3.6
Tommy Rich	F	6'4	185	29	17	18	8	—	—	44	2.6							
Dutch Garfinkel (military service)	G	6'	190	27	18	14	6	—	—	34	1.9	6	1	1	2	50	3	0.5
Bob Fitzgerald	C-F	6'5	195	22	10	9	15	—	—	33	3.3	6	2	6	10	60	10	1.7
Chuck Connors (military service)	C-F	6'5	190	24	14	11	6	—	—	28	2.0							
Del Rice (BB)	F	6'2	190	23	11	8	6	—	—	22	2.0							
Bernie Voorheis	G	5'10	150	23	8	0	0	—	—	0	0.0	1	0	0	0	—	0	0.0
Buddy O'Grady	G	5'11	160	25	1	0	0	—	—	0	0.0							

Use Name	Pos	Hgt	Wgt	Age	REGULAR SEASON G	FG	FT	FTA	Pct.	Points	PPG	PLAYOFFS G	FG	FT	FTA	Pct.	Points	PPG
1945/46 N.B.L — EASTERN DIVISION (continued)																		
YOUNGSTOWN BEARS	13-20 .394				PAUL BIRCH													
Moe Becker	F	6'1	185	28	30	115	40	69	58	270	9.0							
Leo Mogus (military service)	F-C	6'4	205	24	16	61	66	98	67	188	11.8							
Huck Hartman	C	6'7	215	24	26	63	71	91	78	197	7.6							
Press Maravich	G	6'	185	25	32	72	34	51	67	178	5.6							
Frankie Baumholtz (BB)	G	5'10	175	26	26	99	76	107	71	274	10.5							
Rudy Debnar	G	5'11	160	29	31	51	60	78	77	162	5.2							
Paul Birch (SL)	F	6'1	200	35	31	35	26	—	—	96	3.1							
Irv Brenner	C-F	6'4	200	32	22	26	15	—	—	67	3.0							
Joe Urso	G	5'10	170	29	15	16	11	—	—	43	2.9							
Walt Miller (military service)	F	6'2	190	30	10	4	5	—	—	13	1.3							
John Wright	G	6'1	—	—	2	3	5	—	—	11	5.5							
Pete Lalich	F	6'2	190	25	11	2	3	—	—	7	0.6							
Nick Lalich	G	6'2	220	29	4	3	1	—	—	7	1.8							
Bob Hanshew	F	6'	180	26	3	1	1	—	—	3	1.0							
Stan Noszka	G	6'1	185	25	2	0	1	—	—	1	0.5							
Ray Bellingham	C	6'8	200	29	1	0	1	—	—	1	1.0							
Ernie Fortney	C	6'4	220	31	3	0	0	—	—	0	0.0							
Bob Shaw (from Cle)	C	6'4	225	24	1	0	0	—	—	0	0.0							
Larry Kenney	C	—	—	27	1	0	0	—	—	0	0.0							
Bob Armstrong	F	6'1	180	25	1	0	0	—	—	0	0.0							
Don Wamke	C	6'10	220	24	1	0	0	—	—	0	0.0							
Carl Baer	C	6'5	—	—	1	0	0	—	—	0	0.0							
CLEVELAND ALLMEN TRANSFERS	4-29 .121				JEFF CARLIN													
Mel Riebe (military service)	F	5'11	180	29	5	23	26	—	—	72	14.4							
Mike Bytzura	F	6'3	175	23	33	78	35	65	54	191	5.8							
Bob Shaw (to You) (FB)	C	6'4	225	24	12	43	36	—	—	122	10.2							
Herm Fuetsch	G	6'	170	27	27	82	61	75	81	225	8.3							
Tom Wukovits	G	6'	170	29	33	76	79	124	64	231	7.0							
Ned Endress	F-C	6'2	200	27	22	58	36	74	49	152	6.9							
Paul Widowitz	F	6'1	170	28	16	52	10	19	53	114	7.1							
Howie McCarty	F-C	6'2	190	26	13	40	13	—	—	93	7.2							
Johnny Moir	F	6'2	184	28	13	27	8	—	—	62	4.8							
John Mills	C	6'8	210	26	19	13	25	—	—	51	2.7							
Bill Riebe (dislocated shoulder)	G	5'11	175	28	22	13	16	—	—	42	1.9							
Joe Scott	C-F	—	—	27	15	14	9	—	—	37	2.5							
Paul McCall	F	6'2	195	25	6	15	7	—	—	37	6.2							
Marshall Brown	F	6'3	170	27	10	12	12	—	—	36	3.6							
Frank Garcia	G	6'	175	27	7	7	1	—	—	15	2.1							
George Rung (to Ind)	G	6'	185	29	10	4	4	—	—	12	1.2							
Jack Oberst	F	5'11	175	27	9	2	6	—	—	10	1.1							
Bruce Boehler	G	5'11	195	28	5	4	0	—	—	8	1.6							
Johnny Malokas (military service)	G	5'11	195	29	8	2	0	—	—	4	0.5							
1945/46 N.B.L. — WESTERN DIVISION																		
SHEBOYGAN REDSKINS	21-13 .618				DUTCH DEHNERT				defeated Oshkosh 3-2; H46-45, H41-53, 58-52, 42-68, H65-46 lost to Rochester 0-3; 50-60, 54-61, H48-66									
Dick Schulz	F	6'2	192	28	29	56	66	94	70	178	6.1	8	12	23	30	77	47	5.9
Mike Novak	F-C	6'9	220	30	34	111	88	144	61	310	9.1	8	22	21	34	62	65	8.1
Ed Dancker	C-F	6'7	220	31	33	162	69	153	45	393	11.9	7	33	18	30	60	84	12.0
Al Lucas	G-F	6'3	195	23	32	75	24	38	63	174	5.4	3	3	1	2	50	7	2.3
Bobby Holm	G	6'	210	26	33	70	42	55	76	182	5.5	8	21	7	13	54	49	6.1
Al Grenert	F	6'	190	26	31	64	46	66	70	174	5.6	4	6	2	4	50	14	3.5
Tony Kelly	G	6'1	165	25	29	26	29	—	—	81	2.8	8	11	7	9	78	29	3.6
John Kotz (military serice)	F	6'3	200	26	11	26	22	—	—	74	6.7	3	3	1	1	100	7	2.3
Kleggie Hermsen	C-F	6'9	225	22	21	19	17	—	—	55	2.6	5	4	5	8	63	13	2.6
Steve Sharkey	G-F	6'	190	27	22	18	14	—	—	50	2.3	7	20	11	16	69	51	7.3
Mickey Rottner	G	5'10	185	26	5	10	0	—	—	20	4.0	8	10	4	9	44	24	3.0
Rube Lautenschlager (military service)	F	6'3	205	30	3	8	1	—	—	17	5.7							
Ken Buehler (military service)	F	6'2	180	26	3	7	2	—	—	16	5.3							
Babe Ziegenhorn	G	6'	185	27	7	2	1	—	—	5	0.7							
Kenny Suesens (military service)	G	6'1	185	28	4	1	1	—	—	3	0.8	5	5	2	5	40	12	2.4
Pop Goodwin	F	6'2	203	25	2	1	1	—	—	3	1.5							
Don Harvey	G-F	5'11	180	25	1	0	0	—	—	0	0.0	1	1	0	0	—	2	2.0
Charlie Epperson (military service)	F	6'2	185	26	1	0	0	—	—	0	0.0							

military service - Paul Maki, Jack Stanton

1945/46 N.B.L. — WESTERN DIVISION (continued)

Use Name	Pos	Hgt	Wgt	Age	REGULAR SEASON G	FG	FT	FTA	Pct.	Points	PPG	PLAYOFFS G	FG	FT	FTA	Pct.	Points	PPG
OSHKOSH ALL-STARS	**19-15 .559**			**LON DARLING**			lost to Sheboygan 2-3; 45-46, 53-41, H52-58, H62-48, 46-65											
Bob Carpenter	F	6'5	200	28	34	186	101	144	70	473	13.9	5	18	17	21	81	53	10.6
Gene Englund	F-C	6'5	205	28	33	78	64	102	63	220	6.7	5	14	6	15	40	34	6.8
Leroy Edwards	C	6'4	225	31	34	120	119	200	60	359	10.6	5	15	14	21	67	44	8.8
Bob Feerick (military service)	G	6'3	190	25	21	81	36	44	82	198	9.4	5	16	10	11	91	42	8.4
Fred Rehm	G	6'3	195	24	32	36	18	—	—	90	2.8	5	9	2	2	100	20	4.0
Clint Wager (FB)	F-C	6'6	220	25	34	68	31	48	65	167	4.9	5	13	6	7	86	32	6.4
Eddie Riska	G	6'	180	26	32	38	47	69	68	123	3.8	5	4	4	5	80	12	2.4
Bob Sullivan	G-F	6'	180	24	30	34	34	50	68	102	3.4	5	5	7	9	78	17	3.4
Pete Pasco	F	6'3	190	22	17	12	9	—	—	33	1.9							
Warner Engdahl	G	6'1	210	27	21	10	11	—	—	31	1.5	4	0	1	2	50	1	0.3
Erv Prasse (military service)	G	6'2	190	28	9	2	5	—	—	9	1.0	5	1	3	4	75	5	1.0
Don Smith	F	6'2	190	25	9	1	6	—	—	8	0.9							
Dick Lange	F	—	—	—	4	1	0	—	—	2	0.5							
Ed Erban (military service)	F	6'4	—	24	1	0	0	—	—	0	0.0	3	2	0	0	—	4	1.3
Ray Terzynski	F	6'1	180	26	4	0	0	—	—	0	0.0							
military service - Bob Kramer, Ralph Vaughn																		
CHICAGO AMERICAN GEARS	**17-17 .500**			**SWEDE ROOS**														
Stan Patrick	F	6'3	215	23	33	123	66	100	66	312	9.5							
Bob Calihan	F-C	6'3	200	27	31	109	52	77	68	270	8.7							
George Ratkovicz	C	6'7	225	23	33	80	66	113	58	226	6.8							
Bobby Neu	G	6'1	180	28	31	61	56	83	67	178	5.7							
Dick Triptow	G	6'	170	23	34	68	85	127	67	221	6.5							
Stan Szukala (military service)	G	6'	185	27	19	52	17	33	52	121	6.4							
Bill Hapac	F	6'2	195	27	19	35	35	61	57	105	5.5							
Dick Klein	C-F	6'3	215	25	15	30	13	—	—	73	4.9							
Johnny Orr	G	5'11	180	—	22	13	10	—	—	36	1.6							
Jim Olsen	C-F	6'6	205	24	9	9	8	—	—	26	2.9							
Charlie Butler	F-G	6'2	165	24	10	8	7	—	—	23	2.3							
Nick Hashu	G	6'1	195	28	6	8	2	—	—	18	3.0							
Bob Rensberger	F	6'2	170	24	16	6	3	—	—	15	0.9							
Ed Lewinski	F	6'4	210	25	6	2	4	—	—	8	1.3							
Elmer Gainer	F	6'6	195	26	5	2	2	—	—	6	1.2							
George Hogan	G	6'1	175	28	3	2	0	—	—	4	1.3							
Bud O'Rourke	F	6'4	170	26	6	1	0	—	—	2	0.3							
Connie Mack Berry (FB)	F	6'4	218	30	6	1	0	—	—	2	0.3							
military service - Bill McDonald																		
INDIANAPOLIS KAUTSKYS	**10-22 .313**			**NAT HICKEY**														
Roy Hurley	F-G	6'2	170	23	30	76	24	38	63	176	5.9							
Woody Norris (military service)	F	6'1	170	26	21	83	22	29	76	188	9.0							
Arnie Risen (CO)	C	6'9	200	21	18	77	65	110	59	219	12.2							
Ernie Andres*	G	6'1	200	27	3	20	8	—	—	48	16.0							
Jerry Steiner	G	5'7	160	27	30	106	58	94	62	270	9.0							
Bob Gerber (military service)	C-F	6'5	220	29	29	74	49	82	60	197	6.8							
Bob Dietz (military service)	G	6'1	165	28	20	66	22	38	58	154	7.7							
Nat Hickey	G	5'11	190	43	13	30	13	—	—	73	5.6							
George Fields	F-C	5'11	170	24	20	20	8	—	—	48	2.4							
Jake Weber	C	6'6	225	27	5	7	4	—	—	18	3.6							
Bob Baker	G	—	—	—	6	6	3	—	—	15	2.5							
John Styler	F-C	6'6	225	29	4	5	2	—	—	12	3.0							
Oren Nichols	G	6'3	185	22	5	4	3	—	—	11	2.2							
Wilbur Schumacher	F	—	—	25	5	4	2	—	—	10	2.0							
Jewell Young	G	6'	160	32	8	3	3	—	—	9	1.1							
George Rung (from Cle)	G	6'	185	29	3	4	0	—	—	8	2.7							
Jim Birr (military service)	F	6'3	215	29	3	3	0	—	—	6	2.0							
Bob Brown	F-C	6'7	—	22	3	1	3	—	—	5	1.7							
Dave Strack	G	5'11	—	22	2	2	1	—	—	5	2.5							
George Sobek	G	6'	180	25	1	2	1	—	—	5	5.0							
Rusty Saunders	F	6'2	215	39	5	0	3	—	—	3	0.6							
Chet Francis	F	6'2	180	27	3	1	0	—	—	2	0.7							
Eddie Sadowski	G	5'10	175	30	1	1	0	—	—	2	2.0							
Ken Gunning (military service)	G	—		31	1	0	0	—	—	0	0.0							

* (quit at request of Boston Red Sox to concentrate on baseball)
Scott Armstrong - military service

Use Name-Nickname	Team by Year	Birth Year	Hgt	Wgt	Pos.	College	# Yr	G	Field Goals FG	Att.	%	Free Throws FT	Att.	%	Reb	Ass	PF	DQ	Pts	Per Game Min.	Reb	Ass	Pts
Neal Adams	43OshN	1919	6'3	195	F-C	Arkansas	1	13	4			1							9				0.7
42-44 played in N.F.L., 46-47 played in A.A.F.C.																							
Ray Adams	38-40OshN, 41 ChiN	1914	6'2	185	F-C	DePaul	4	57	92			51							235				4.1
	38-39						2	10	8			10							26				2.6
Sparky Adams	39-40ShebN	1917	6'1	185	F	Marquette	2	27	46			35							127				4.7
	40						1	3	2			1							5				1.7
Willie Adams	38FtWN		5'11	165	F		1	16	21			16							58				3.6
Jake Ahearn	41DetN	1917	6'2	185	G	St. John's (NY)	1	15	32			15							79				5.3
	41						1	3	3			2							8				2.7
Merle Alexander	39IndN	1907	6'6	185	C-F	none	1	2	0			0							0				0.0
Al Alvarez	42TolN	1912	6'0	160	G	Toledo	1	4	8			5							21				5.3
Bob Alwin	43OshN	1920	5'10	145	G	Wisconsin	1	4	7			7							21				5.3
Ralph Amsden	41ShebN	1917	6'4	200	C	Marquette	1	11	6			12							24				2.2
	41						1	5	2			6							10				2.0
Art Anderson	41AG-N	1916	6'6	190	C	Augustana (IL)	1	12	2			4							8				0.7
Carl Anderson (Buttercup)	39Ind PC41HamN	1913	6'3	215	G	Southern Cal.	2	5	0			0							0				0.0
Gene Anderson	40-42AG-N	1917	6'3	190	F	Purdue	3	71	135			60							330				4.6
	42						1	3	8			1							17				5.7
Clyde Anton	38ColN				G		1	7	4			2							10				1.4
Gerry Archibald	PC38WarN PCCleN HC40DetN	1908	6'	170	G	none	2	9	2			1							5				0.6
Bob Armstrong	46YouN	1920	6'1	180	F	Glenville State	1	1	0			0							0				0.0
Scotty Armstrong	38FtWN 39OshN 40,42 IndN	1913	6'4	190	F-C	Butler	4	94	195			127							517				5.5
	39						1	5	10			5							25				5.0
Fred Arndt	playoffs only - 38WhiN				F		1	2	1			0							2				1.0
Stan Arnzen	38CinN				F		1	5	10			3							23				4.6
Carl Austing	38CinN	1910	6'4	180	F-C	Cincinnati	1	5	16			5							37				7.4
Carl Baer	46YouN		6'5		C		1	1	0			0							0				0.0
Frank Baird	38-40, 42IndN	1912	5'11	160	G-F	Butler	4	62	137			44							318				5.1
	42						1	2	0			0							0				0.0
Bob Baker	46IndN				G		1	6	6			3							15				2.5
Ball	41ChiN				F-G		1	6	1			1							3				0.5
Lou Barle	40-43OshN 44-45MS	1916	6'1	200	F	Minn.-Duluth	4	79	157			83							397				5.0
38-39 played in N.F.L.	40-42						3	18	36			21							93				5.2
Shannie Barnett	43TolN	1919	6'3	175	F-C	none	1	4	5			4							14				3.5
Pete Basich	38ColN	1917	5'9	145	G	Michigan St.	1	1	1			1							3				3.0
Buck Batterman	40OshN	1918	6'3	195	F	Wis. St.-Oshkosh	1	17	6			8							20				1.2
	40						1	2	0			1							1				0.5
Moe Becker	45Cle 46YouN 47Pit 47Bos	1917	6'1	185	G-F	Duquesne	3	74	185	358	20	62	113	55			30	96	432			0.7	5.8
47Det																							
Don Beery	42FtWN	1920	6'	180	G	none	1	11	3			2							8				0.7
	42						1	2	1			0							2				1.0
Bill Behr	41HamN	1919	6'2	190	G	none	1	20	28			14							70				3.5
Byron Bell	39OshN	1914	6'3	180	C	Wisconsin	1	1	1			2							4				4.0
Ray Bellingham	46YouN	1916	6'8	200	C	Westminster, PA	1	1	0			1							1				1.0
Carl Bennett	HC42-43, 46-48FtWN	1915	6'2	195		none																	
HC49FtW																							
Wes Bennett	38-39AG-N	1913	6'3	175	C-F	Westminster, PA	2	37	64			68							196				5.3
	38						1	5	10			5							25				5.0
Al Benson	41HamN 41DetN	1914	6'6	220	C	none	1	10	7			2							16				2.3
	41						1	2	1			0							2				1.0
Beanie Berens	38ColN	1913	6'5	190	C	Ohio U.	1	1	0			1							1				1.0
Leo Bereolos	HC40HamN	1910	6'2	180		Indiana																	
Fred Beretta	41AF-N	1917			G	Purdue	1	9	1			0							2				0.2
Connie Mack Berry	40-44OshN 45-46ChiN	1915	6'4	210	F-C	N.C. State	7	113	191			99							481				4.3
39-40, 42-46 played in	40-42, 44-45						5	24	44			20							108				4.5
N.F.L., 47 played in A.A.F.C.																							
Don Betourne	PC38KankN	1915	6'1	200	F	St. Viator	1	12	30			16							76				6.3
Paul Birch (Polly)	39PitN 42-45FtWN 46YouN	1910	6'1	196	F-G-C	Duquesne	6	134	221			131							573				4.3
HC47Pt HC52-54FtWN	42-45						4	20	27			14							68				3.4
Emmet Birk	39OshN	1914	6'1	185	F	North Dakota	1	1	0			0							0				0.0
Jim Birr (Crash)	39-40, 46IndN	1916	6'3	215	F-C	Indiana	3	30	90			29							209				7.0
Thermon Blacklidge	42ShebN	1920	6'3	185	F	Delta State	1	11	17			17							51				4.6
Chuck Bloedorn	38-40AG-N	1912	6'	180	G	Bowling Green, Baldwin-Wallace	3	54	146			64							356				6.6
Bruce Boehler	46CleN	1917	5'11	195	G	Akron, Ky.	1	5	4			0							8				1.6
Herb Bonn	38-39PitN	1914	6'	195	F	Duquesne	2	15	36			14							86				5.7
Al Bonniwell	38-39AF-N	1911	6'2	185	G-F	Dartmouth	2	39	85			27							197				5.1
	38-39						2	7	5			4							14				2.0
Boris	39HamN				F		1	1	2			2							6				6.0

Use Name-Nickname	Team by Year	Birth Year	Hgt	Wgt	Pos.	College	# Yr	G	Field Goals			Free Throws			Reb.	Ass.	PF	DQ	Points	Per Game			
									FG	Att.	%	FT	Att.	%						Min.	Reb	Ass	Pts
Sonny Boswell	43ChiN	1915	6'1	180	G	none	1	22	88			53							229				10.4
	43						1	3	13			4							30				10.0
Lou Boudreau	39, HC40HamN	1917	5'11	170	G-F	Illinois	1	23	78			33							189				8.2
38-52 played major league baseball																							
42-50, 52-57, 60 managed major league baseball																							
Harold Bowers	38CinN	1912	5'10	165	G	Earlham	1	2	4			1							9				4.5
Art Bowman	41HamN				G	St. Joseph's(IN)	1	8	4			1							9				1.1
Irv Brenner	45PitN 46-47YouN	1913	6'4	200	C-F	Duquesne	3	37	55			23							133				3.6
Brown	39HamN				G		1	1	1			0							2				2.0
Bob Brown	46IndN	1923	6'7		F-C	Oklahoma	1	3	1			3							5				1.7
Hillery Brown	43ChiN	1912	6'3	190	F-G	none	1	23	36			22							94				4.1
	43						1	3	2			2							6				2.0
Jim Brown	41DetN	1912	6'1	190	G-F	Temple	1	22	42			19							103				4.7
	41						1	3	7			1							15				5.0
Marshall Brown	46CleN	1918	6'3	170	F	Texas Tech	1	10	12			12							36				3.6
Bill Brownell	42TolN 44CleN		6'6	235	C		2	5	3			4							11				2.2
Ken Buehler	43ShebB 44-45MS	1919	6'2	180	F-C	Wisc.-Milwauk.	3	33	73			46	10	30					192				5.8
46ShebN 47FtWN																							
Jerry Bush	39-41AF-N 43-47FtWN	1914	6'3	206	F-C	St. John's (NY)	9	238	449			249	102	69					1147				4.8
47AndN 48TolN	39-41, 43-46						7	37	65			51	12	58					181				4.9
Lefty Byers	HC38-39AG-N	1905	6'	165		Kansas State																	
Mike Bytzura	45-46Cle 47Pit	1922	6'3	175	F	Duquesne,	3	123	278	356	24	106	137	52		31	108		662			0.5	5.4
	45					Long Island U.	1	2	4			3							11				5.5
Soup Cable	38-41AF-N 42TolN	1913	6'3	200	F-G-C	Akron	5	84	258			212							728				8.7
	38-41						4	17	36			55							127				7.5
Ed Campion	38WhiN 39HamN	1915	6'2	190	G	DePaul	2	38	59			19							137				3.6
	38						1	2	1			0							2				1.0
Jeff Carlin	HC45-46CleN	1904	6'	195		Wash. & Jeff.																	
Dan Carnevale	38BufN	1918	6'	185	G	Canisius	1	9	10			6							26				2.9
Tony Carp	40ChiN	1911	6'7	215	F	none	1	1	0			0							0				0.0
Hugh Carter	playoffs only - 42IndN				G		1	2	2			1							5				2.5
George Chestnut	38, 40IndN	1914	6'5	210	C-F	Indiana State	2	33	53			76							182				5.5
Chuck Chuckovits	40HamN 42TolN 43-45MS	1912	6'1	175	F-G	Toledo	2	36	173			150							496				13.8
Ralph Churchfield	45PitN	1918	6'5	220	G-F	Wash. & Jeff.	1	20	26			15							67				3.4
Eddie Ciesar	HC40HamN	1910	5'11	170		Northwestern																	
Hal Cihlar	44CleN	1914	6'5	210	F-C	Case Reserve	1	4	0			1							1				0.3
Don Cleary	playoffs only - 42IndN				F		1	2	0			1							1				0.5
Bobby Colburn	38DayN	1911	5'10	190	F	Ohio State	1	11	32			16							80				7.3
Pual Coleman	38BufN	1915	6'2	160	G	Buffalo St.	1	6	12			1							25				4.2
Marv Colen	40ChiN 40ShebN	1915	6'	170	G	Loyola (Chic.)	1	6	3			0							6				1.0
	40						1	1	0			0							0				0.0
Bob Cope	38AG-N	1911	6'4	190	C-F	Mt. Union	1	15	26			19							71				4.7
	38						1	5	7			4							18				3.6
Bill Cramer	40IndN				C		1	1	0			0							0				0.0
Leo Crowe	38IndN	1912	5'11	170	G	Notre Dame	1	12	30			14							74				6.2
Kiernan Crowley	39ShebN	1916	5'8	155	G	DePaul	1	5	3			4							10				2.0
Freddie Crum	45PitN	1912	6'0	170	G-F	none	1	29	69			30							168				5.8
Marty Cullen	playoffs only - 38WhiN				G-F		1	2	0			1							1				0.5
Duke Cumberland	43ChiN	1919	6'3	195	F	Knoxville	1	22	53			45							151				6.9
	43						1	3	8			3							19				6.3
Cookie Cunningham	PC38ColN	1905	6'3	210	F-C	Ohio State	1	11	27			27							81				7.4
27, 29, 31, played in N.F.L.																							
Jim Currie	40HamN	1916	6'2	185	G-F	Northwestern	1	27	38			29							105				3.9
Harold Dahl	44OshN	1923	5'9	190	F	Miami (FL),	1	5	1			2							4				0.8
						Wisconsin																	
Ed Dancker	39-48ShebN 49OshN	1914	6'7	214	C-F	none	11	321	955			580	516	55					2490				7.8
	40-41, 43-47						7	39	136			96	48	60					368				9.4
Danko	41HamN				G		1	1	2			0							4				4.0
Lon Darling	HC42-49OshN	1902	6'3	195		Ripon																	
Rudy Debnar	42AG-N 46YouN	1916	5'11	160	G	Duquesne	2	55	107			89	78	77					303				5.5
	42						1	3	0			0							0				0.0
Pick Dehner	39HamN	1914	6'5	190	F-C	Illinois	1	1	7			1							15				15.0
Dutch Dehnert	HC41DetN HC45-46ShebN	1898	6'1	195		none																	
HC47Cle																							
Dembo	40ChiN				G		1	2	1			0							2				1.0
Ray Detrick	HC40-42AG-N	1899				Wittenberg																	
Bob DeWeese	38KankN	1915	5'11	160	G	Gallagher Bus.	1	2	1			0							2				1.0
Gus Doerner	43FtWN 44-45MS 46FtWN	1922	6'2	195	F	Evansville	3	60	106			52	82	56					264				4.4
47IndN	47						1	5	23			13	22	59					59				11.8
Duck Dowell	38AF-N	1912	6'3	200	C-F	NW Mo. State	1	14	15			19							49				3.5
	38						1	2	1			0							2				1.0

Use Name-Nickname	Team by Year	Birth Year	Hgt	Wgt	Pos.	College	# Yr	G	Field Goals FG	Att.	%	Free Throws FT	Att.	%	Reb.	Ass.	PF	DQ	Pts	Per Game Min.	Reb	Ass	Pts
Glynn Downey	39IndN 40HamN	1915	6'0	180	G	Purdue	2	37	64			60							188				5.1
John Drish	42ChiN	1917			F	Illinois	1	8	10			3							23				2.9
Bob Dro	42IndN	1918	6'	190	G-F	Indiana	1	15	20			6							46				3.1
Beryl Drummond	38DayN	1918	6'1	185	G	none	1	2	1			0							2				1.0
	47ToIN						1	1	0			0	0						0				0.0
Paul DuCharme	41AF-N	1917	5'11	160	G	Notre Dame	1	3	0			1							1				0.3
Dave Dupee	39OshN	1916	6'3	185	F	Wisconsin	1	1	0			1							1				1.0
Bill Durkin	45ShebN	1922	6'1	160	G	Loyola (Chic.)	1	1	1			0							2				2.0
Floyd Ebaugh	39-40, 42AG-N	1914	6'7	230	C	Nebraska	3	73	119			69							307				4.2
	42						1	3	3			6							12				4.0
Glen Edwards	42ToIN				G		1	3	2			1							5				1.7
Leroy Edwards (Cowboy)	38-49OshN	1914	6'4	222	C-F	Kentucky	12	322	1045			1131	647	64					3221				10.0
	38-44, 46-49						11	57	189			170	69	52					548				9.6
Tommy Edwards	PC42ToIN	1911	5'10	170	F	Ohio U.	1	1	0			1							1				1.0
Eich	42AG-N				F		1	1	1			0							2				2.0
Denny Elliot	38CoIN	1914	5'9	150	G	Otterbein	1	9	10			5							25				2.8
Don Elser	42ToIN	1913	6'4	220	F-C	Notre Dame	1	6	10			7							27				4.5
Ned Endress	44-46CleN 47Cle	1918	6'2	200	F-G-C	Akron	4	83	148	25	12	105	89	49		4	13		401			0.3	4.8
	44-45						2	4	5			3							13				3.3
Warner Engdahl (Bud)	42-43OshN 44-45MS 46OshN	1916	6'1	210	G	Wisc.-Superior	3	41	20			28							68				1.7
	42, 46						2	8	2			1	2	50					5				0.6
Charlie Epperson	42ShebN 43-45MS 46ShebN	1919	6'2	180	F-G	Wisonsin	2	10	20			9							49				4.9
Ed Erban	42ToIN 44-46OshN 47SyrN	1921	6'4		F-C	Marquette	5	58	40			43							123				2.1
	44, 46						2	6	4			2							10				1.7
Mark Ertel	42IndN	1919	6'4	196	C-F	Notre Dame	1	20	20			26							66				3.3
	42						1	2	1			1							3				1.5
Dick Evans 40-43 played in N.F.L.	41ShebN 41HamN 42-43ChiN	1920	6'3	204	F-C	Iowa	3	32	24			30							78				2.4
Hank Evans	45PitN	1915	6'3	195	F-C	none	1	28	97			44							238				8.5
Byron Evard (Boob)	PC38FtWN	1908	5'8	155	G	St. Viator	1	10	7			2							16				1.6
Teddy Falda	41HamN	1920	6'	180	G	Indiana State	1	3	1			0							2				0.7
Fred Fechtman	38IndN	1910	6'8	210	C	Indiana	1	3	4			1							9				3.0
Herm Fuetsch (Dutch)	46CleN 48Bal	1918	6'0	170	G	U.C.L.A	2	69	124	140	30	86	115	75		17	39		334			0.4	4.8
							1	9	3	8	38	6	8	75		0	10		12			0.0	1.3
George Fields	46IndN	1921	5'11	170	F-C	Purdue	1	20	20			8							48				2.4
Adam Filipczak	41DetN	1916	5'10	170	G	Wayne St (MI)	1	2	0			0							0				0.0
Wilson Fitts	38-39AG-N	1915	6'2	165	G-F	Akron	2	31	24			13							61				2.0
	38						1	5	2			6							10				2.0
Gordon Flick	44OshN 49WatN	1921	6'3	200	F-C	Drake	2	5	4			0							8				1.6
Ernie Fortney	39PitN 46YouN	1914	6'4	220	C	Duquesne	2	14	16			11							43				3.1
Steve Fowdy	39HamN	1915	6'2	180	F	North Dakota	1	1	0			0							0				0.0
Wilbur Fox	40AG-N	1917	6'5	185	F-C	Akron	1	11	3			5							11				1.0
Francis	46IndN	1918			F	Indiana	1	3	1			0							2				0.7
Nat Frankel	40DetN 47Pit	1913	6'3	197	F-G	St. John's (NY)	2	33	77	27	15	63	12	67		3	6		217			0.5	6.6
	40						1	3	10			4							24				8.0
Nick Frascella	39-41AG-N	1914	6'2	185	F	Wooster	3	32	30			8							68				2.1
Homer Fuller	45OshN	1920	6'3	220	G-F	East Texas St.	1	28	66			17							149				5.3
Elmer Gainer 47AndN 48Bal 49WatN50Wat	42FtWN 44ShebN 45-46ChiN	1919	6'6	198	F-C	DePaul	8	179	217	44	23	186	132	74		10	36		620			0.5	3.5
	42, 44-45						3	15	13			15							41				2.7
Laddie Gale	40DetN	1916	6'4	195	F	Oregon	1	8	22			16							60				2.7
	40						1	3	6			5							17				5.7
Frank Garcia	44-46CleN	1918	6'	175	G-F	none	3	39	31			16							78				2.0
	44-45						2	4	2			0							4				1.0
Hymie Ginsburg	38-39PitN	1914	5'9	170	G	Geneva	2	36	82			37							201				5.6
Ed Glancy	44OshN	1918	6'3	180	G-F	Manhattan	1	5	3			3							9				1.8
Jim Glass	45FtWN	1921	6'8	210	C	Toledo,	1	14	2			3							7				0.5
	45					Marshall	1	2	1			1							3				1.5
Pim Goff	40-41HamN	1913	6'4	190	F-C	Illinois State	2	38	86			16							188				4.9
Sid Goldberg	HC43ToIN	1912	6'	160		Toledo, Ohio St.																	
Moose Graf	39, 43ShebB	1917	6'3	200	F-C	Marquette	2	6	5			3							13				2.6
Fred Grafft	38KankN	1915	5'9		G	Gallagher Bus.	1	10	33			20							86				8.6
Otto Graham 46-49 played in A.A.F.C. 50-55 played in N.F.L., 66-68 head coach in N.F.L.	46RochN	1921	6'1	190	F-G	Northwestern,	1	32	59			47	73	64					165				5.2
	46					Colgate	1	5	3			0	0						6				1.2
Walter Grauman (Boney)	39ShebN	1915	6'2	200	G	none	1	1	0			0							0				0.0
Cortez Gray	43ToIN	1916	6'5	185	F-C	Toledo	1	4	7			4							18				4.5
Ken Griffith	42AG-N	1918	6'2	195	G	Alderson-	1	6	4			1							9				1.5
	42					Broaddus	1	1	0			0							0				0.0
Ken Gunning	38WhiN 46IndN	1914			F-G	Indiana	2	16	37			31							105				2.8
							1	2	3			5							11				5.5

Use Name-Nickname	Team by Year	Birth Year	Hgt	Wgt	Pos.	College	# Yr	G	Field Goals FG	Att.	%	Free Throws FT	Att.	%	Reb.	Ass.	PF	DQ	Pts	Per Game Min.	Reb	Ass	Pts
Bill Haarlow	38WhiN	1913	6'1	170	F	Chicago	1	10	26			14							66				6.6
	38						1	1	2			3							7				7.0
George Haines	45PitN	1921	5'10	160	F-G	Bucknell	1	26	56			33							145				5.6
Warren Hair	38KankN				G	Gallagher Bus.	1	11	15			16							46				4.2
Ray Hamann	38-39OshN	1911	6'4	205	G-F	Wisconsin	2	29	49			11							109				3.8
	38-39						2	8	3			2							8				2.9
Dale Hamilton	40HamN 42-45FtWN	1919	6'	190	G-F	Franklin (Ind.)	9	227	318	33	24	250	462	50		17			886			1.2	3.9
47-48TolN 49WatN	42-44, 47						4	15	8			10	20	35					26				1.7
50Wat																							
Bob Hanshaw	46YouN	1919	6'	180	F	none	1	3	1			1							3				1.0
Bill Hapac	41ChiN 42-45MS 46ChiN	1918	6'2	196	F-G	Illinois	4	131	286			267	314	64					839				6.4
47AndN 48OshN	48						1	4	6			11	16	69					23				5.8
Huck Hartman	45PitN 46YouN	1921	6'7	210	C	Wash. & Jeff.	2	56	190			144	91	78					524				9.4
Don Harvey	46ShebN	1920	5'11	180	G-F	Missouri	1	1	0			0							0				0.0
	46						1	1	1			0	0						2				2.0
Nick Hashu	39HamN 45-46ChiN	1917	6'1	195	G	Valparaiso, Michigan St.	3	23	22			12							56				2.4
	45						1	3	4			0							8				2.7
Bob Hassmiller	40-41AF-N 42TolN		6'1	185	G	Fordham	3	49	86			19							191				2.2
	40-41						2	6	10			1							21				3.5
Ray Hayes	40ChiN	1906	6'	180	G-F	Chicago	1	4	1			1							3				0.8
Pete Hecomovich	41OshN		6'4	205	G		1	1	0			0							0				0.0
Allie Heerdt	HC38BufN	1881				none																	
George Hesik	39AG-N 40-42ShebN	1913	6'2	195	F-C	Marquette	4	90	99			120							318				3.5
43-45MS	40-41						2	9	11			15							37				4.1
Nat Hickey	45PitN PC47-48TC-N	1902	5'11	190	G	none	5	27	43			22	13	54					108				4.0
PC48Prov																							
Jim Higgins	41HamN		6'8		C	none	1	1	0			1							1				1.0
Jim Hilgemann	38, 42FtWN	1916	6'	170	G	Toledo	2	21	51			30							132				6.3
Pat Hintz	42-43TolN	1914	6'	175	G	Toledo	2	5	18			4							40				8.0
Joel Hitt	40AG-N	1916	6'2	180	C-F	Miss. College	1	13	3			3							9				0.7
Johnny Hoekstra	38KankN		6'5		C	Gallagher Bus.	1	12	27			16							70				5.8
Howie Hoffman	45OshN 47AndN	1920			G-F	Purdue	2	23	49			20	6	50					118				5.1
George Hogan	40ChiN 40HamN 41-42ChiN	1917	6'1	171	G-F	Loyola (Chic.)	4	71	88			42							218				3.1
43-45MS 46ChiN																							
Bill Holland	38WarN 39CleN 40DetN	1914	6'5	210	C-F	Edinboro State	3	56	112			70							294				5.3
	40						1	3	1			1							3				1.0
Bobby Holm	45-47ShebB 49HamN	1919	6'0	210	G	Seton Hall	4	125	228			198	190	78					654				5.2
	45-47						3	21	47			22	15	60					116				5.5
Ife Holmes	38FtWN	1907	5'6	150	G	DePauw	1	15	17			7							41				2.7
Bill Hosket	PC38DayN	1911	6'5		C	Ohio State	1	10	11			12							34				3.4
George Hotchkiss	HC38-41OshN	1906	5'11			Wisconsin																	
Lee Huber	42AG-N 43-45MS	1919	6'1		G	Kentucky	1	11	32			6							70				6.4
Roosie Hudson	43ChiN	1915	6'	160	G	Morris-Brown	1	21	50			27							127				6.0
	43						1	2	0			3							3				1.5
Marv Huffman	41AG-N	1917	6'2	185	F	Indiana	1	22	47			19							113				5.1
Vern Huffman	39IndN	1914	6'2	215	F	Indiana	1	3	7			6							20				6.7
37-38 played in N.F.L.																							
Harold Hull	42AG-N	1920	6'4	190	F	NW Missouri St.	1	12	3			8							14				1.2
	42						1	2	0			4							4				2.0
Dar Hutchins	40-41HamN	1915	6'6	195	C-F	Bradley	2	48	129			66							324				6.8
Herbie Hutchinson (Reindeer)	38ColN				F-G		1	7	25			6							56				8.0
Art Hyatt	39CleN 40DetN	1913	6'2	190	G	none	2	23	27			15							69				3.0
George Jablonsky (Jabbo)	43ShebN	1919	6'7	215	C	Wisc.-Milwauk.	1	11	7			5							19				1.7
	43, 44ShebN						2	7	4			10							18				2.6
Stan Jackson	38BufN				F	Syracuse	1	7	8			2							18				2.6
Stub Jacobson	38WarN		6'6		C		1	4	2			2							6				1.5
Lou Jagnow	40DetN	1910	6'1	180	G	Carnegie-Mellon	1	1	0			1							1				1.0
	40						1	1	0			0							0				0.0
James	39HamN				F		1	4	6			9							21				5.3
Buddy Jeannette	39Cle 40-41DetN 43ShebN	1917	5'11	175	G	Wash. & Jeff.	10	300	715	777	34	887	734	78		287	386		2317			2.1	7.7
44-46FtWN	40-41, 43-46, 48-49						8	41	103	74	43	109	52	88		17	56		315			1.2	7.7
PC48-50Bal HC51, 65, 67Bal HC70PitA																							
Jack Jennings	41AF-N	1918	6'6	195	C-F	Washington St.	1	19	41			12							94				4.9
	41						1	2	2			0							4				2.0
Bill Jesko	38-39PitN	1915	5'10	170	G-F	Pittsburgh	2	34	80			33							193				5.7
Al Johnson (Big Train)	43ChiN	1913	6'3	210	F	Illinois	1	1	1			0							2				2.0
	43						1	2	0			0							0				0.0
Bob Johnson	39AG-N	1917	6'2	170	G	Pittsburgh	1	4	6			3							15				3.8
Elmer Johnson	40-41ChiN	1910	6'4	190	F-C	Northwestern	2	41	36			43							115				2.8
Mally Johnson (Swede)	38-39AF-N	1909	5'9		F-G	N.C. State	2	23	20			8							48				2.1
							2	3	0			1							1				0.3
Splinter Johnson	41HamN	1920	6'3	190	F-C	Purdue	1	23	35			23							93				4.0
Billy Jones	43TolN	1920			F	Toledo	1	4	11			0							22				5.5

Use Name-Nickname	Team by Year	Birth Year	Hgt	Wgt	Pos.	College	# Yr	G	Field Goals FG	Att.	%	Free Throws FT	Att.	%	Reb	Ass.	PF	DQ	Pts	Per Game Min.	Reb	Ass	Pts
Johnny Jordan	HC43ChiN	1910	5'11	170		Notre Dame																	
Ken Jordan	38CinN	1912	6'2	180	F	Xavier (OH)	1	8	14			10							38				4.8
Frank Kautsky	HC38IndN	1888				none																	
Wibs Kautz	40-42ChiN 43-46MS 47Chi	1915	6'	185	G-F	Loyola (Chic.)	4	119	391	420	25	181	73	53		37	114		963			0.7	8.1
	47						1	9	10	45	22	2	6	33		0	14		22			0.0	2.4
Jack Keller	42-43FtWN	1920	6'2	185	F-G	none	2	27	19			17							55				2.0
	42-43						2	5	1			4							6				1.2
Tony Kelly	44-46ShebN	1920	6'1	175	G	DePaul	3	76	101			94							296				3.9
	44-46						3	22	34			24	9	78					92				4.2
Larry Kenney	46YouN	1918			C	St. Joseph's	1	1	0			0							0				0.0
Bob Kessler	38IndN 39HamN	1914	6'	165	F	Purdue	2	14	45			35							125				8.9
Paul Kessy	45CleN 45PitN	1917	6'3	170	F-C	Wisc.-Milwauk.	1	6	1			1							3				0.5
Joe Kinney	39PitN		6'6		C	W.V. Wesleyan	1	2	1			1							3				1.5
Dick Klein	46ChiN	1920	6'3	215	C-F	Northwestern	1	15	30			13							73				4.9
Buzz Knoblauch	40OshN	1916	6'1	170	F	Carroll (Wis.)	1	3	1			0							2				0.7
Eddie Kolar	39ShebN	1909	5'10	170	G	none	1	1	1			2							4				4.0
Otto Kolar	39-41ShebN 42ChiN	1911	6'3	180	G-F-C	Wisc.-Oshkosh	4	95	192			104							488				5.1
	40-41						2	9	21			8							50				5.6
Bill Komenich	42-43OshN 44WW 45OshN	1918	6'3	210	F-G	Marquette	3	65	70			49							189				2.7
	42						1	5	7			11							25				5.0
John Kotz	46ShebN	1919	6'3	200	F	Wisconsin	1	11	26			22							74			6.7	
	46						1	3	3			1	1	100					7				2.3
Bob Kramer 47YouN	43OshN 44-46MS 47OshN	1921	6'3		G-F	North Carolina	2	7	7			2	3	67					16				2.3
	43						1	2	0			0							0				0.0
Joe Kruse	38CinN	1914	6'2	200	G	Xavier (Ohio)	1	6	8			4							20				3.3
Ray Krzoska	43OshN 44MS 45ChiN	1918	6'2	190	G	Wisc.-Milwauk.	2	23	33			21							87				3.8
	45						1	3	4			5							13				4.3
Vito Kubilus	PC44CleN	1914	6'1	180	G	Ohio College	1	16	11			10							32				2.0
	44					of Chiropody	1	1	1			0							2				2.0
Lee Kublic	39-40ShebN	1912	6'3	200	F	Beloit	2	39	20			7							47				1.2
	40						1	1	0			0							0				0.0
Ed Kweller	38-39PitN	1915	6'5	225	C	Duquesne	2	21	18			19							55				2.6
Nick Lalich	46Youn	1916	6'2	220	G	Ohio U.	1	4	3			1							7				1.8
Pete Lalich 46YouN 47Cle	43ShebN 44CleN 45PitN	1920	6'2	190	F	Ohio U.	5	45	54			28							136				3.0
	44						1	2	1			2							4				2.0
Buck Lamme	38ColN	1905	6'2		G	Ohio Wesleyan	1	1	0			0							0				0.0
Bill Lane	41DetN	1916	6'4	220	F-C	Michigan	1	3	0			0							0				0.0
Dick Lange	46OshN				F		1	4	1			0							2				0.5
Bill Laughlin	39CleN	1915	6'2	185	F	Wash. & Jeff.	1	27	92			48							232				8.6
Rube Lautenschleger	39-47ShebN	1915	6'3	197	F-G-C	Wisc.-Oshkosh	9	222	598			246							1442				6.5
	40-41, 43-45, 47						6	31	62			51							175				5.6
Tim Lawry	38PitN	1911	5'10	155	F	Pittsburgh	1	9	9			8							26				2.9
Sew Leeka	38AF-N	1907	6'1	185	G	Iowa,	1	9	9			4							22				2.4
	38					N. Carolina St.	1	1	0			0							0				0.0
Johnny Lenhart	38BufN	1915	6'6	180	F	Colgate	1	3	0			0							0				0.0
Joe Leson	39CleN	1912	6'2	210	F	Edinboro State	1	17	9			11							29				1.7
Sid Levine	45PitN	1918	5'7	185	G	none	1	18	4			1							9				0.5
Garmon Lewis	40IndN				F		1	1	0			0							0				0.0
Sam Lifschulz	HC40ChiN																						
Carl Lillage	40OshN				F-G		1	3	0			2							2				0.7
Bud Lindberg	38FtWN	1911	6'	175	G	none	1	18	30			20							80				4.4
Leroy Lins	38AG-N	1913	6'1	175	G	Rutgers	1	8	1			2							4				0.5
Frank Linskey	38-39OshN 40, PC41ChiN	1913	6'2	180	G	DePaul	4	77	84			58							226				2.9
	38-39						2	8	7			3							17				2.1
Bill Lloyd	40-41AG-N	1915	6'2	180	G-F	St. John's (NY)	2	19	19			12							50				2.6
Slim Lonsdorf	39ShebN	1905	6'3	175	F-C	Marquette	1	17	5			10							20				1.2
Gene Lorendo	43OshN	1921	6'3	215	F	Georgia	1	9	7			3							17				1.9
Sam Loucks	38ColN	1915	6'4	195	C-F	Otterbein	1	9	15			7							37				4.1
Bob Lytle	38WarN	1916	6'4	180	F	Endinboro St.	1	1	1			0							2				2.0
Bob MacLeod 39 played in N.F.L.	40ChiN	1917	6'	190	F	Dartmouth	1	9	4			3							11				1.2
Paul Maki	42ShebN 43-46MS 47FJ	1918	6'1	185	G	Minnesota	1	8	13			9							35				4.4
Red Malackany	38WarN 39PitN	1913	5'9	165	G	Duquesne	2	15	16			10							42				2.8
Eddie Malanowicz	38BufN HC47-48RochN	1910	6'3	220	C	Buffalo	1	5	14			8							36				7.2
Johnny Malokas	45-46CleN	1916	5'11	195	G	Ohio U.	2	9	4			1							9				1.0
Joel Mason 39-42, 45 played in N.F.L.	43ShebN HC47DetN	1912	6'	195	G	Western Mich., Texas	1	1	0			0							0				0.0
Frank Maury (X)	38WarN 39CleN	1910	5'5	155	G	none	2	39	80			27							187				4.8

Use Name-Nickname	Team by Year	Birth Year	Hgt	Wgt	Pos.	College	# Yr	G.	Field Goals FG	Att.	%	Free Throws FT	Att.	%	Reb.	Ass.	PF	DQ	Pts	Per Game Min.	Reb	Ass	Pts
Johnny McAdams	38, 40AG-N	1915	5'10	147	G	Ohio Wesleyan	2	8	8			1							17				2.1
	38						1	3	2			0							14				1.3
Paul McCall	46CleN	1920	6'2	195	F	Bradley	1	6	15			7							37				6.2
Gordon McComb	40HamN	1917	5'10	160	G	Tenn.-Chatt.	1	2	1			1							3				1.5
Bob McConachie	HC38CinN	1905																					
McConnell	38ColN				G-F	S. Illinois, Ill.	1	5	2			1							5				1.0
Bobby McDermott	42-43, PC44-45, 46,	1914	6'	185	G	none	8	287	1465			653	556	73					3583				12.5
PC47FtWN 48ShebN	42-49						8	45	195			104	50	88					494				11.0
PC48-49TC-N 49HamN																							
Bill McDonald	41-44ShebN 45ChiN 46MS	1916	6'3	190	G-F	Marquette	7	172	246			216	52	63					708				4.1
47ChiN 47-48OshN	41, 43-45, 47						5	27	36			40	9	89					112				4.1
Bob McElliott	39HamN	1915			C-F		1	5	5			1							11				2.2
Vince McGowan	38WhiN 39-40HamN	1913	6'6	208	C-F	DePaul	6	106	202			159							563				5.3
41-42ChiN 43MS 45ChiN	38, 45						2	5	6			8							20				4.0
Curt McMahon	38DayN	1915	6'	150	G	none	1	10	8			3							19				1.9
Mike McMichael	39AG-N	1915	6'2	195	G	Northwestern	1	11	17			9							43				3.9
Dean Mealy	38-39AG-N 40OshN	1915	6'4	195	C	Muskingum	3	19	21			30							72				3.8
	38						1	3	2			5							9				3.0
Gene Mechling	38CinN	1909	6'1	215	G	Capital	1	3	8			2							18				6.0
Big Moose Meyer	38KankN		6'7		F-C	Gallagher Bus.	1	9	14			2							30				3.3
Little Moose Meyer	38KankN	1916	6'		G	Gallagher Bus.	1	3	3			1							7				2.3
Ward Meyers	40IndN	1908	6'1	185	C	none	1	2	1			2							4				2.0
Ted Migdal	39AF-N	1918	5'9	140	F	Miami (OH)	1	2	8			2							18				9.0
	39						1	1	0			0							0				0.0
Miller	38ColN				F		1	1	0			0							0				0.0
Walt Miller	38-39PitN 46YounN 47Pit	1915	6'2	190	F	Duquesne	4	50	81	21	33	68	18	50		6	16		230			0.5	4.6
John Mills	45-46CleN 47Pit	1920	6'8	203	C-F	Western Ky.	3	95	97	187	29	138	129	55		9	94		332			0.2	3.5
	45						1	2	3			6							12				6.0
Johnny Moir	39-41AF-N 46CleN	1915	6'2	184	F-C	Notre Dame	4	87	223			116							562				6.5
	39-41						3	14	54			26							134				9.6
Jim Montgomery	40-41AG-N	1917	6'3	190	F-C	Villanove	2	41	44			48							136				3.3
Doxie Moore	HC47-48ShebN HC50And	1911	5'10	180		Purdue																	
HC52Mil																							
Bud Moodler	38DayN 40DetN	1911	6'3	215	G	Defiance	2	18	8			21							37				2.1
Dudey Moore	PC38-39PitN	1910	5'9	180	G	Duquesne	2	21	30			12							72				3.4
Morris	42ChiN				C-F		1	1	0			0							0				0.0
Emmett Morrison	38WarN	1915	6'3	180	F-G	Pittsburgh	1	11	5			9							19				1.7
George Morse	42ChiN	1919			F-G	Marquette	1	2	0			2							2				1.0
Ray Morstadt	38-40AG-N	1913	6'2	220	F-C	Marquette	3	57	75			52							202				3.5
Al Moschetti	45ShebN	1920	6'1	180	F	St. John's (NY)	1	24	43			35							121				5.0
	45						1	2	2			1							5				2.5
Tex Mueller	40-41, 43OshN	1916	6'1	175	G	Western State	3	28	10			7							27				1.0
	40-41						2	3	2			0							4				1.3
Ed Mullen	38-40OshN	1913	6'3	185	G	Marquette	3	42	34			13							81				1.9
	38-39						2	10	1			9							11				1.1
Jake Nagode	40-41AG-N	1915	6'2	170	F-G	Northwestern	2	43	52			21							125				2.9
Bobby Neu	40-41HamN 45PitN 46ChiN	1917	6'1	178	G-F	DePaul	4	80	171			191	83	67					533				6.7
Oren Nichols	46IndN	1923	6'3	185	G	none	1	5	4			3							11				2.2
Fred Nimz	43OshN 44-45MS	1914	6'3	200	C-F	Wisconsin-Stevens Pt.	1	5	4			3							11				2.2
Bob Nipper	HC39-40IndN	1903	5'10	170		Butler																	
Tommy Nisbet	39-40HamN 41-43OshN	1917	5'10	165	G	Illinois	5	67	72			64							208				3.1
	41-43						3	12	17			16							50				4.2
Woody Norris	42IndN 43-45MS 46-48IndN	1919	6'1	170	F-G	Butler	4	76	154			50	76	62					358				4.7
	42, 47						2	5	3			5	0	—					11				2.2
Mike Novak	40-43ChiN 44-47ShebN	1915	6'9	219	C-F	Loyola (Chic.)	12	392	1041	519	31	619	664	59	2	175	336	0	2701	5	0.4	1.4	6.9
47-48SyrN	43-49						7	36	96	22	27	66	61	64		10	13		258			2.5	7.2
49-50Roch 50Phi 54Syr																							
John Novotny	45PitN	1918	5'10	165	G	Appalachian St.	1	1	2			0							4				4.0
Paul Nowalk (Butch, Giz)	39-41AF-N 42TolN	1914	6'6	209	C	Notre Dame	4	60	91			67							249				4.2
	40-41						2	10	14			13							41				4.1
Red Oberbruner	42FtWN	1918	5'11	175	F-G	Notre Dame	1	19	17			8							42				2.2
	42						1	6	4			4							12				2.0
Jack Oberst	46CleN	1918	5'11	175	F	Bald.-Wallace	1	9	2			6							10				1.1
Bill O'Brien	41ChiN	1918	6'4	185	F	Loyola (Chic.)	1	9	5			10							20				2.2
Jack O'Brien	42AG-N	1916	6'1	180		Columbia	1	7	5			7							17				2.4
	42						1	3	2			7							11				3.7
Tommy O'Brien	40-41AF-N	1916			G-F	G. Washington	2	28	22			11							55				2.0
	40-42						2	7	12			2							26				3.7
Russ Ochsenhirt	38-39AG-N	1912	6'3	195	F	Pittsburgh	2	41	64			44							172				4.2
	38						1	5	9			8							26				5.2
Jim O'Donnell	38BufN	1912	6'1	180	F-C	Canisius	1	8	3			4							10				1.3
Neil O'Donnell	38BufN	1914	6'5	210	F-C	Canisius	1	9	14			7							35				3.9
Vince Oliver	39HamN	1915	5'10	185	G	Indiana	1	5	1			0							2				0.4
Jim Olsen	46ChiN	1921	6'6	205	C-F	Dartmouth	1	9	9			8							26				2.9
Sonny Olson	40OshN	1917	6'	165	F	Carleton	1	2	1			2							4				2.0

Use Name-Nickname	Team by Year	Birth Year	Hgt	Wgt	Pos.	College	# Yr	G.	Field Goals FG	Att.	%	Free Throws FT	Att.	%	Reb.	Ass.	PF	DQ	Pts	Per Game Min.	Reb	Ass	Pts
Bernie Opper	40-41DetN	1915	6'	185	G	Kentucky	2	32	45			20							110				3.4
	40						1	3	6			3							15				5.0
Bud O'Rourke	46ChiN	1919	6'4	170	F	DePaul	1	6	1			0							2				0.3
Johnny Orr	43ChiN 44ShebN 45-46ChiN		5'11	180	G	St. Benedict's	4	79	60			25							145				1.8
	44-45						2	8	2			2							6				0.8
Leo Osiewalski	44OshN	1921	6'4	190	F	none	1	4	1			0							2				0.5
Tom O'Toole	41HamN				C		1	1	0			0							0				0.0
Frank Otway	45ChiN	1923	6'4	205	F	Chicago, Rider, L.I.U.	1	2	0			0							0				0.0
Jack Ozburn	38-41AF-N 42TolN 43-45MS	1914	6'2	170	G-F	Monmouth (IL)	5	87	331			156							818				9.4
	38-41						4	17	55			35							145				8.5
Page	41DetN				G		1	1	0			0							0				0.0
Ed Parry	40-41, 47DetN	1918	6'2	178	F	none	3	61	116			110	113	65					342				5.6
	40-41						2	6	7			5							19				3.2
Bob Parsons	39, 42,AG-N	1915	6'1	175	F-G	Nebraska	2	26	23			8							54				2.1
Pete Pasco	45-46OshN	1923	6'3	190	F	E. Stroudsburg	2	43	101			59							261				6.1
Johnny Pawk	38WarN 39CleN	1910	6'2	210	F	Westmin., (Pa.)	2	14	23			12							58				4.1
Steve Pawk	38WarN	1914	6'4	175	C-F	none	1	6	8			5							21				3.5
Pete Pederson	40OshN 42TolN	1912	6'4		F-C	Western State	2	35	45			20							110				3.1
	40						1	8	15			9							39				4.9
Jake Pelkington	41AG-N 43-48FtWN 49FtW	1917	6'6	220	C-F	Manhatten	8	280	861	469	41	824	751	76		131	216		2546			2.4	9.1
49Bal	43-49						7	37	95	33	39	100	78	73		3	13		290			1.0	7.8
Bill Perigo	38WhiN 39HamN	1911	6'	180	F	Western Mich.	2	19	24			17							65				2.7
	38						1	1	0			0							0				0.0
Tony Peyton	43ChiN	1921	6'2	200	F-G	Mich., Ala. St., Toledo	1	18	17			9							43				2.4
Squint Phares	39PitN	1915	5'10		G-F	West Virginia	1	7	18			12							48				6.9
Bob Phillips	39IndN	1916			G		1	1	0			0							0				0.0
Willie Phillips	40ChiN	1915	5'8	175	G	DePaul	1	28	16			17							49				1.8
Jack Piana	41DetN	1918	6'2	190	F	Detroit	1	2	0			0							0				0.0
	41						1	1	0			0							0				0.0
Woody Pitzer	38ColN	1910	6'	160	G-F	Wittenberg	1	11	20			10							50				4.5
Eric Plahna	44OshN	1921			G-F	Wisconsin-Milwaukee	1	9	7			0							14				1.6
	44						1	3	2			2							6				2.0
John Poncar	44CleN	1913	6'3	190	C-F	none	1	18	11			8							30				1.7
	44						1	2	0			1							1				0.5
Johnny Posewitz	39-40, 45ShebN	1906	6'	185	G	none	3	35	40			10							90				2.6
Scoop Posewitz	39-40ShebN	1908	5'11	180	G	none	2	29	15			15							45				1.6
Lou Possner	42ChiN 47SyrN	1917	6'3	180	F-C	DePaul	2	7	6			2	2	50					14				2.0
Erv Prasse	41-42OshN 43-45MS 46OshN	1917	6'2	190	G-F	Iowa	3	38	30			33							93				2.4
	41-42, 46						3	15	7			14	4	75					28				1.9
Pete Preboski	38-39OshN	1914	6'1	195	F	Wisonsin	2	38	101			49							251				6.6
	38-39						2	10	14			22							50				5.0
Babe Pressley	playoffs only - 43ChiN	1916	6'2	195	G	Xavier of La.	1	3	4			4							12				4.0
Al Price	43TolN	1917	6'	180	G	Toledo	1	3	3			2							8				2.7
Bernie Price	43ChiN	1915	6'4	210	F-C	none	1	22	60			77							197				9.0
	43						1	3	7			9							23				7.7
Paul Price	41HamN	1914			F	Notre Dame	1	1	3			0							6				6.0
Lorvin Proctor	39IndN				F	none	1	3	4			0							8				2.7
Cy Proffitt	38IndN	1911	6'3	190	F	Butler, Indiana State	1	12	19			13							51				4.3
Proska	45PitN				G		1	1	2			3							7				7.0
Scoop Putnam	40-41OshN 42TolN	1914	6'	175	G-F	Tennessee	3	50	82			30							194				3.9
	40-41						2	8	7			1							15				1.9
Dave Quabius	39-41ShebN 43OshN	1916	6'	185	G	Marquette	4	65	113			80							306				4.7
	40-41, 43						3	10	18			14							50				5.0
Bert Quinn	38FtWN	1917	6'2	210	F	Toledo	1	18	71			28							170				9.4
Nick Radlick	HC44CleN	1911	6'	180		Case Reserve																	
Jim Rae	42TolN	1917	6'4	200	C	Michigan	1	3	5			0							10				3.3
Stan Raiman	38BufN	1914	5'9	140	G-F	Canisius, Buffalo St.	1	9	10			2							22				2.4
Bill Reeves	38AF-N	1904	5'10	165	G	Central Normal	1	8	5			4							14				1.8
	38						1	1	0			0							0				0.0
Bob Regh	43-44ShebN		6'2		G-F		2	12	10			4							24				2.0
	43						1	4	2			0							4				1.0
Marty Reiter	38-39PitN	1911	5'7	160	G	Duquesne	2	18	33			20							86				4.8
Rob Rensberger	46ChiN 47Chi	1921	6'2	170	F	Notre Dame	2	19	6			3							15				0.8
Del Rice	46RochN	1922	6'2	190	F	none	1	11	8			6							22				2.0
45-61played major league baseball																							
72 managed in major league baseball																							
Tommy Rich	46RochN	1916	6'4	185	F	Cornell	1	17	18			8							44				2.6
Bill Reibe	44-46CleN	1917	5'11	175	G	none	3	64	81			61							223				3.5
	44-45						2	4	3			10							16				4.0
Ted Rigg	38PitN	1913	6'	175	G	Carn.-Mellon	1	11	18			11							47				4.3

Use Name-Nickname	Team by Year	Birth Year	Hgt	Wgt	Pos.	College	# Yr	G.	Field Goals FG	Att.	%	Free Throws FT	Att	%	Reb.	Ass.	PF	DQ	Pts	Per Game Min.	Reb	Ass	Pts
Rube Reiswerg	40IndN	1912	5'8	175	G	none	1	4	0			1							1				0.3
Riskind	40ChiN				G		1	1	0			0							0				0.0
Glenn Roberts	38DayN 39AF-N 42TolN	1912	6'5	200	C-F	Emory & Henry	3	24	35			17							87				3.6
	39						1	2	0			1							1				0.5
Wyman Roberts	38DayN	1916	5'11	160	F	none	1	2	2			2							6				3.0
Swede Roos	45, HC46ChiN	1913	6'1	180	G-F	none	1	22	24			22							70				3.2
Gene Rosenthal	39PitN	1914	5'11	175	F	Car.-Mellon	1	9	13			4							30				3.3
Carl Roth (toughy)	39, HC43-44ShebN	1909	6'2	200	G-F	Wisconsin	1	14	14			1							29				2.1
Rex Rudicel	39IndN	1912	5'6	150	G	Ball State	1	3	2			0							4				1.3
Clem Ruh	41HamN	1915	5'10	165	G	Southern Cal.	1	21	26			25							77				3.7
George Rung	46CleN 46IndN	1916	6'	185	G	Miami (OH)	1	13	8			4							20				1.5
Mal Rush	38AG-N	1909	6'	170	F	Bethany	1	7	6			6							18				2.6
	38						1	4	4			3							11				2.8
Lou Rutter	38DayN	1914	6'2	180	G	Otterbein	1	8	30			20							80				10.0
Leo Sack	38CinN	1914	5'8	145	G	Xavier (Ohio)	1	6	20			3							43				7.2
Ed Sachs	42CinN	1918	6'2	175	G	DePaul	1	8	8			4							20				2.5
Frank Sachse	44-45OshN	1917	6'	197	G	Texas Tech	2	30	58			19							135				4.5
43-45 played in N.F.L.	44						1	3	2			2							6				2.0
Eddie Sadowski	40, 42IndN 43TolN	1915	5'10	175	G	Notre Dame	4	45	90			38							218				4.8
43ShebN 46IndN	42-43						2	4	3			2							8				2.0
Junior Saffer	38CinN	1917			F	none	1	1	0			0							0				0.0
Louie Sauer (Whitey)	38KankN	1915	6'6	235	F-C	Valparaiso	1	12	31			17							79				6.6
Rusty Saunders 27 played major league basball	41DetN 46IndN	1906	6'2	212	F-C	none	2	19	6			12							24				1.3
Jack Scarry	45PitN	1917	6'3	195	F-C	Duquesne	1	6	3			1							7				1.2
Ed Scheiwe	44OshN 45ChiN	1918	5'11	170	G-F	Wisconsin	2	32	34			20							88				2.8
	44-45						2	5	1			2							4				0.8
Glenn Schlechty	38DayN	1912	6'6	185	F	Findlay, Stoddard	1	4	3			1							7				1.8
Bill Schrader	38IndN	1911	6'7	210	C	Notre Dame	1	8	6			2							14				1.8
Warren Schrage (Doc)	43ShebN 44-45MS	1920	6'5	190	F-C	Wisconsin	1	10	1			0							2				0.2
Al Schrecker	45PitN	1917	6'1	160	F	none	1	1	3			1							7				7.0
Gene Scholz	38ColN	1917	5'8	160	F	Capital, Marietta	1	3	1			0							2				0.7
Wilbur Schumacher	46IndN	1920			F	Butler	1	5	4			2							10				2.0
Herm Schuessler	39IndN	1914	6'8	210	C	none	1	19	28			14							70				3.7
Doc Schutte	HC39ShebN	1906	5'11	195		Marquette																	
Bob Schwartz	43ShebN 44-45MS		6'3		F	Wisconsin	1	13	32			9							73				5.6
	43						1	4	6			0							12				3.0
Joe Scott	46CleN	1918			C-F	Case Reserve	1	15	14			9							37				2.5
Jack Schaffer	38AF-N		6'3	190	F-C	Nebraska	1	6	16			2							34				5.7
Frank Shamel	38CinN	1912	6'	200	F	Earlham	1	3	5			0							10				3.3
Chuck Shanklin	45OshN				G		1	30	42			13							97				3.2
Bob Shaw 45-46, 49-50 played in N.F.L.	46CleN 46YouN 47TolN	1921	6'4	225	C-F	Ohio State	2	21	49			43	10	70					141				6.7
Paul Sheeks 21-22 played in N.F.L.	HC38-41AF-N	1889	5'8	175		Dak. Wesleyan, South Dakota																	
Charley Shipp	38-39AG-N 40-44OshN	1914	6'1	200	G-F	none	13	399	800	137	26	442	343	67		46	46		2042			2.0	5.1
45-47FtWN 47-48AndN PC49WatN PC50Wat	38, 40-46, 48						9	40	43			48	5	60					134				3.4
Slim Shoun (Bud)	38-39AF-N	1904	6'11	200	C	Carson-Newman	2	19	28			23							79				4.2
	38-39						2	4	4			0							8				2.0
Johnny Sines	39-40, 42IndN	1914	6'1	190	F	Purdue	3	49	134			85							353				7.2
Steve Sitko	41AG-N 45CleN	1917	6'	193	G	Notre Dame	2	9	3			0							6				0.7
Pres Slack	38FtWN 39ShebN	1911	6'2	180	C-F	none	2	23	43			12							98				4.3
Don Smith	38PitN 39AF-N	1910	6'0	170	G	Pittsburgh	2	14	17			21							55				3.9
Bello Snyder	38BufN	1912	5'9	185	F	none	1	8	18			10							46				5.8
Paul Sokody	39-42ShebN 43ChiN	1914	6'2	185	F	Marquette	5	118	244			134							622				5.3
	40-41						2	9	16			11							43				4.8
Harry Sorensen	40-41AF-N	1914	6'4	200	C-F	Nebraska	2	24	14			9							37				1.5
	40						1	5	1			3							5				1.0
Joe Sotak (Bull)	38WhiN 39-41HamN	1914	6'2	210	F-C	none	4	55	78			69							225				4.1
	38						1	2	1			2							4				2.0
Ed Spovich	39PitN	1916	6'2	190	F-C	Pittsburgh	1	3	6			1							13				4.3
Spudich	40HamN				F		1	2	1			0							2				1.0
Joe Stack	38WhiN 39HamN	1913	5'10	185	G-F	none	2	29	49			36							134				4.6
	38						1	2	0			0							0				0.0
Howard Stammier	38DayN	1911	5'10	155	G-F	Ohio Wesleyan	1	4	9			2							20				5.0
Joe Stampf	45ChiN	1919	6'4	210	C-F	Chicago	1	7	8			5							21				3.0

Use Name-Nickname	Team by Year	Birth Year	Hgt	Wgt	Pos.	College	# Yr	G.	Field Goals FG	Att	%	Free Throws FT	Att	%	Reb	Ass	PF	DQ	Points	Per Game Min.	Pts	Ass	Pts
Walt Stankey (Deacon) 40OshN	38WarN 39CleN 40DenN	1911	6'3	203	F-C	none	3	63	154			49							357				5.7
	40						1	8	6			3							15				1.9
Clovis Stark	38DayN	1914	6'4	175	F	Ohio Wesleyan	1	9	14			10							38				4.2
Ed Stege	38OshN	1913	6'6	220	F	Wisconsin	1	2	0			0							0				0.0
Jerry Steiner	46IndN 47FtWN	1918	5'7	160	G	Butler	2	46	118			63	103	61					299				6.5
	47						1	4	1			1	4	25					3				0.8
Ben Stephens	40-42AG-N	1917	6'0	175	G-F	Iowa	3	76	270			242							782				10.3
	42						1	3	13			13							39				13.0
John Stephans	45PitN		5'6		G	none	1	1	2			0							4				4.0
Jack Sterling	38WarN 39PitN	1917	6'5		C	Geneva	2	8	14			11							39				4.9
Marvin Stout	40IndN	1915	5'11	155	G	Ball State	1	1	1			0							2				2.0
Dave Strack	46IndN	1923	5'11		G	Michigan	1	2	2			1							5				2.5
Ted Strain	42ChiN	1917	6'	155	G	Wisconsin	1	1	0			0							0				0.0
Reno Strand	39CleN	1909	6'	195	G-F	none	1	15	17			8							42				2.8
Ted Strong	43ChiN	1916	6'3	220	F-C	none	1	10	13			10							36				3.1
	43						1	3	2			4							8				2.7
Chet Strumillo	45ChiN	1924	5'11	175	F	Northwestern, Illinois	1	1	0			0							0				0.0
John Styler	45ChiN 46IndN	1916	6'6	225	F-C	none	2	20	15			4							34				1.7
	45						1	1	0			0							0				0.0
Sally Suddith	40IndN	1910	6'1	170	G	Indiana	1	6	5			4							14				2.3
Kenny Suesens 46-48, PC49ShebN HC50Sheb	39-44ShebN 45MS	1916	6'1	180	G	Iowa	10	208	158			198	106	46					514				2.5
	40-41, 43-44, 46-47						6	29	29			33	8	38					91				3.1
Bob Sullivan	44OshN 45MS 46-48OshN	1921	6'	180	G-F	Wisconsin	4	87	89			87	115	75					265				2.3
	46-47						2	10	8			7	11	64					23				2.3
Jack Sullivan	38ColN	1916	6'1	182	F	Notre Dame	1	2	1			1							3				1.5
Bill Summers	41HamN				G		1	1	1			0							2				2.0
George Svendsen 35-37, 40-41 played in N.F.L.	38OshN	1913	6'4	230	C-F	Minnesota	1	11	18			9							45				4.1
	38						1	1	0			0							0				0.0
Everett Swank	38-39IndN	1913	5'11	165	G-F	Indiana Central	2	13	7			6							20				1.5
George Swanson	40ShebN				G-F	Toledo	1	11	4			5							13				1.2
	40						1	1	0			1							1				1.0
Hale Swanson	40HamN	1914	6'3	200	G-F	Illinois	1	2	0			0							0				0.0
Willard Swihart	44CleN	1914	6'3	190	F-C	Toledo	1	15	14			11							39				2.6
	44						1	2	0			1							1				0.5
Bob Synott	45-46FtWN 47SyrN 47ChiN	1912	6'3	195	F-C	none	3	59	62			15	6	67					139				2.4
	45						1	6	7			5							19				3.2
Stan Szukala 46-47ChiN	41-42ChiN 43-45MS	1918	6'	180	G	DePaul	4	87	158			46	60	58					362				4.2
	47						1	7	2			4	5	80					8				1.1
Rip Terjesen (Swede)	39-41AF-N	1915	6'3	195	F-C	N.Y.U.	3	62	75			45							195				3.1
	39-41						3	13	9			4							22				1.7
Ray Terzynski	44-46OshN	1919	6'1	180	F	Wisconsin-Stevens Pt.	3	52	64			63							191				3.7
	44						1	3	1			3							5				1.7
Earle Thomas	38CinN 39IndN	1915	6'4	205	C	Ohio State	2	9	4			1							9				1.0
Bill Thompson	42ToIN		6'4		G-F	St. John's (OH)	1	16	25			9							59				3.7
Homer Thompson (Tarzan)	40, 47IndN 47ShebN	1916	6'4	215	F-C	Kentucky	2	28	30			54							114				4.1
Thornton	39HamN						1	1	1			0							2				2.0
Jack Thornton	42ShebN	1914	6'5	200	C-F	Tex. Wesleyan	1	2	0			3							3				1.5
Jack Tierney	HC42, 45ChiN		5'9	165		none																	
Paul Tobin (Toby)	38-40AF-N		5'9	170	G	Akron	3	42	45			29							119				2.8
	38-40						3	9	2			6							10				1.1
Chet Tollstam	41HamN	1918	6'2	180	F-C	DePaul	1	11	13			6							32				2.9
Chelso Tamagno	38-39AG-N	1913			G-F	Michigan	2	28	23			7							53				1.9
	38						1	5	2			1							5				1.0
Johnny Townsend (Houdini of the Hardwood) 42IndN 43ToIN 43OshN 44-45MS	39HamN 40-41VR 41-42ChiN	1916	6'4	208	C-F	Michigan	3	34	77			92							246				7.2
	42						1	2	6			11							23				11.5
Joe Urso	PC45PitN 46YouN	1916	5'10	170	G	Duquesne, Pitts.	2	44	97			51							245				5.6
Augie Vander Meulen	38-39OshN	1909	6'4	175	F-C	Carroll (Wis.)	2	17	39			27							105				6.2
	38-39						2	8	8			16							32				4.0
Matt Vaniel	45PitN	1919	6'3	170	F	none	1	24	78			23							179				7.5
Ralph Vaughn 44-46MS 47OshN	41HamN 41-42ChiN 43OshN	1918	6'1	175	G-F	Southern Cal.	4	101	303			202	64	77					808				8.0
	43, 47						2	8	32			11	16	69					75				8.3
Howard Vocke	40-42AG-N	1915	6'3	190	G	St. John's (NY)	3	75	131			72							334				4.5
	42						1	3	5			3							13				4.3
Bernie Voorheis	46RochN	1922	5'10	150	G	Cornell	1	8	0			0							0				0.0
	46						1	1	0			0	0	—					0				0.0
Frank Vukosic	45PitN				G-F	none	1	4	0			0							0				0.0
Norm Wagner 38ColN 38DayN	38CinN 38ColN 38CinN	1912	6'5	200	C	Missouri	1	8	14			6							34				4.3
Paul Wallace	42ToIN				G	Toledo	1	1	0			0							0				0.0
Don Walsh	38KankN				F	Gallagher Bus.	1	4	2			0							4				1.0
Don Warnke	45CleN 46YouN	1921	6'10	200	C	Valparaiso	2	21	10			9							29				1.4
Zeno West	43ToIN	1916	6'2	175	F	Toledo	1	1	0			0							0				0.0

Use Name-Nickname	Team by Year	Birth Year	Hgt	Wgt	Pos.	College	# Yr	G.	Field Goals FG	Att	%	Free Throws FT	Att	%	Reb	Ass	PF	DQ	Points	Per Game Min.	Pts	Ass	Pts
Chub Watson	39PitN	1916	6'2		C	Marshall	1	1	8			0							16				16.0
Bob Weigandt	39OshN	1914	5'10	190	G	Wisconsin	1	1	0			0							0				0.0
Herm Weiss	45CleN	1916	6'	180	G	Case Reserve	1	3	2			0							4				1.3
Bill Wendt	39HamN	1915	6'3	180	F	DePaul	1	8	8			4							20				2.5
Warren Whitlinger	38AF-N	1914	5'9	170	F	Ohio State	1	13	17			25							59				4.5
	38						1	2	2			0							4				2.0
Whitey Wickhorst	HC38WhiN HC39HamN	1904	5'10	150		none																	
Paul Widowitz	46CleN	1917	6'1	170	F	Duquesne	1	16	52			10	19	53					114				7.1
John Wiethe 39-42 played in N.F.L.	PC38CinN	1912	6'	205	G-F	Xavier (Ohio)	1	6	10			12							32				5.3
John Wiggers	41AG-N	1917	6'9	200	C	Morehead State, Kentucky	1	5	1			1							3				0.6
Willett	39HamN				F		1	2	0			0							0				0.0
Dave Williams	39-40IndN 42TolN		6'3		C-F	Central Normal	3	32	36			20							92				2.9
George Wilson 37-46 played in N.F.L., 57-64 head coach in N.F.L., 66-69 head coach in A.F.L.	40ChiN	1914	6'1	190	F	Northwestern	1	16	5			8							18				1.1
Harlan Wilson	38IndN	1914	5'11	160	G	Central Normal	1	11	24			24							72				6.5
Slim Wintermute	40DetN	1917	6'8	200	C	Oregon	1	25	65			50							180				7.2
	40						1	2	3			0							6				3.0
Eddie Wisbar	38PitN	1916	6'6	200	C	none	1	13	27			22							76				5.8
Herm Witasek	38-42OshN 43-45MS	1913	6'2	211	G-F	North Dakota	5	114	226			126							578				5.1
	38-41						4	23	46			24							116				5.0
Tarzan Woltzen	38KankN	1918			G-F		1	8	0			0							0				0.0
Johnny Wooden	38WhiN 39HamN 39IndN	1910	5'10	183	G	Purdue	2	23	76			62							214				9.3
*	38						1	2	8			17							33				16.5
John Wright	46YouN		6'1		G	G.. Washington	1	2	3			5							11				5.5
Loren Wright	38CinN				G		1	4	2			0							4				1.0
Tom Wukovits	40-41AF-N 42TolN 45-46CleN	1916	6'	167	G	Notre Dame	5	108	235			213	124	64					683				6.3
	40-41, 45						3	12	22			20							64				5.3
Nick Yost	39-40HamN	1915	6'4	220	F-C	DePaul	2	17	54			16							124				7.3
Jewell Young 43OshN 46IndN	39-40, 42IndN 34TolN	1913	6'	160	G-F	Purdue	5	88	290			223							803				9.1
	42						1	2	12			11							35				17.5
Willie Young	playoffs only - 38WhiN				C	Wisconsin	1	2	0			0							0				0.0
Abe Yourist	42TolN	1911	6'2	210	C	Heidelberg	1	1	0			0							0				0.0
Stan Zadel	39ShebN 40ChiN	1916	6'5	215	F-C	none	2	28	51			37							139				5.0
Babe Ziegenhorn	42ShebN 43-45MS 46ShebN	1918	6'	185	G-F	Notre Dame	2	22	19			7							45				2.0
Frank Zummach	HC40-42ShebN	1911	5'10	165		Marquette																	

1946-1947 through 1953-54

Merging the Old into the New

1946-47 N.B.L.
Nearly Losing the Most Vital Gear

The N.B.L. added five new teams this season, but the biggest addition to the league was rookie center George Mikan of the Chicago American Gears. Although Mikan had joined the team in time to play in last year's World Tournament, this was his first season of regular league play. The most famous college player since Hank Luisetti, Mikan had starred at DePaul by using his great strength and 6'10" frame to score repeatedly on hook shots and tap-ins. Famous for his thick eyeglasses and whirling elbows, Mikan rounded out his game with fine passing from the pivot, very tough defense, and superb rebounding.

But before the season was a month old, Mikan had quit his Chicago team, claiming that the financially-troubled Gears had tried to cut his salary below the $12,000 specified in his contract. For six weeks, Mikan stayed at home and let his lawyers handle the court work; during those six weeks, the Gears fell below the .500 level and dropped to fifth place in the Western Division. When Mikan finally rejoined the team, things looked up for the Gears. At the same time, the Gears purchased veteran guard Bobby McDermott from Ft. Wayne; this move gave the Gears an outside scoring threat to go along with Mikan's devastating inside game. Guard Bruce Hale and forwards Bob Calihan and Price Brookfield filled out a talented starting five. With McDermott running the club as player coach, the Gears took 17 of their last 23 games to edge the Anderson Packers out of a playoff spot. Joining the Gears in the playoffs from the West were the Oshkosh AllStars, who survived the loss of playmaker Bob Feerick to the new Basketball Association of America; the Indianapolis Kautskys, a young team built around rookie forward Leo Klier and sophomore center Arnie Risen; and the Sheboygan Redskins, strengthened by rookie set-shooter Fred Lewis

In the Eastern Division, the defending champion Rochester Royals easily captured first place. The Royals lost center John Mahnken to the B A A, but they replaced him by moving George Glamack to center and adding Dolly King, a veteran of several black teams, and strong rookie Arnie Johnson. The heart of the Royals, however, was still the little men, Bob Davies, Al Cervi, and Red Holzman.

The rival Ft. Wayne Zollner Pistons came in second despite severe personnel losses. Buddy Jeanette left the team to hecome player coach of the Baltimore Bullets of the American Basketball League, and Ed Sadowski jumped to the new B.A.A. In addition, Bobby McDermott, Charley Shipp, and rookie Milo Komenich had a run-in with owner Fred Zollner and were suspended on December 19. Komenich was eventually reinstated, but McDermott was sold to Chicago and Shipp to Anderson.

Finishing behind the Pistons, but in the playoffs, were the new Syracuse Nationals, coached by old pro Benny Borgmann and led on the floor by rookie guard Jerry Rizzo and veteran center Mike Novak. The Toledo Jeeps, another new team, came in fourth. This team was built around freshman pros Hal Tidrick and George Sobek.

Once the regular season closed, the playoffs began with the spectre of the red-hot Chicago American Gears looming tall over the field. The Gears met the quick Indianapolis team in the opening round and went the full route of five games before eliminating them; the Kautskys had the edge in speed, but center Arnie Risen was too frail to handle Mikan. In the other Western quarter-final, Oshkosh kept its late-season hot hand by beating Sheboygan three games to two. The opening-round Eastern matches held no surprises, as the Royals kayoed Syracuse in four games and the Pistons took Toledo in five.

The semifinal matches were close and exciting. Oshkosh forwards Bob Carpenter and Gene Englund helped center Leroy Edwards defend against Mikan, but the Gears still took two straight victories, 60-54 and 61-60. The Royals and Pistons split the first two games in the East, but the Royals walloped the Pistons 76-47 in Rochester to win a chance at defending their title against the Gears.

The playoff finals pitted the inside-oriented Gears against the outside-oriented Royals, with the series opening in Rochester. Dolly King and George Glamack held Mikan to 14 points in the first game, and Bob Davies' 23 points led the Royals to a 71-65 win. In the second game, however, Mikan bulled his way to 27 points as the Gears evened the score with a 67-63 triumph. The scene then shifted to Chicago, where the Gears immediately gained the upper hand with a 78-70 victory; Mikan scored 23 points, and teammate Bob Calihan added 22 to the pot. The Royals managed to hold Mikan to 14 points in the fourth game, but Calihan's 11 baskets paced the Gears to a 79-68 win and the N.B.L. title.

					vs. playoff teams			vs. non-playoff teams			HOME			ROAD			Average Points					Average Points				
Team	W	L	Pct.	GB	W	L	PCT.	W	L	Pct.	W	L	Pct.	W	L	Pct.	G	FT%	For	Agnst.	Diff.	G	FT%	For	Agnst.	Diff.
1946/47 N.B.L. STANDINGS																										
EASTERN DIVISION																										
Rochester	31	13	.705		18	10	.643	13	3	.813	19	3	.864	12	10	.545	44	67	62.9	56.5	+6.4	11	72	63.5	61.3	+2.2
Fort Wayne	25	19	.568	6	12	16	.429	13	3	.813	17	5	.773	8	14	.364	44	66	58.3	55.6	-2.7	8	67	54.3	51.8	+2.5
Toledo	21	23	.477	10	11	17	.393	10	6	.625	13	9	.591	8	14	.364	44	65	57.3	56.0	+1.3	5	60	45.8	56.4	-10.6
Syracuse	21	23	.477	10	10	18	.357	11	5	.688	14	8	.636	7	15	.318	44	65	55.8	55.5	+0.3	4	67	58.3	60.8	-2.5
Tri-Cities	19	25	.432	12	12	20	.375	7	5	.583	12	10	.545	7	15	.318	44	62	49.1	51.8	-2.7					
Youngstown	12	32	.273	19	6	26	.188	6	6	.500	10	12	.455	2	20	.091	44	62	53.5	60.1	6.6					
Western Division																										
Oshkosh	28	16	.636	—	16	12	.571	12	4	.750	19	3	.864	9	13	.409	44	69	58.0	55.3	+2.7	7	58	50.3	50.1	+0.2
Indianapolis	27	17	.614	1	17	11	.607	10	6	.625	19	3	.864	8	14	.364	44	64	56.9	53.1	+3.8	5	72	63.6	68.0	-4.4
Chicago	26	18	.591	2	14	14	.500	12	4	.750	15	7	.682	11	11	.500	44	67	58.4	54.3	+4.1	11	72	68.2	64.0	+4.3
SHeboygan	26	18	.591	2	14	14	.500	12	4	.750	20	2	.909	6	16	.273	44	67	54.5	53.0	+1.5	5	56	46.0	47.6	-1.6
Anderson	24	20	.545	4	14	18	.438	10	2	.833	16	6	.727	8	14	.364	44	66	59.7	58.5	+1.2					
Detroit	4	40	.091	24	3	29	.094	1	11	.083	4	18	.182	0	22	.000	44	58	47.6	63.0	-14.4					

Use Name	Pos	Hgt	Wgt	Age	REGULAR SEASON G	FG	FT	FTA	Pct.	Points	PPG	PLAYOFFS G	FG	FT	FTA	Pct.	Points	PPG
1946/47 N.B.L. — EASTERN DIVISION																		
ROCHESTER ROYALS	31-13 .705				EDDIE MALANOWICZ													
defeated Syracuse 3-1; H66-64, 61-64, H54-48, 62-57																		
defeated Fort Wayne 2-1; H58-49, 49-56, H76-47																		
lost to Chicago 1-3; H71-65, H63-67, 70-78, 68-79																		
Bob Davies (CC)	F-G	6'1	175	26	32	166	130	166	78	462	14.4	11	54	43	63	68	151	13.7
Arnie Johnson (Brohen foot)	F-C	6'5	225	26	32	68	68	98	69	204	6.4							
George Glamack	C-F	6'8	230	27	44	141	90	135	67	372	8.5	10	35	28	33	85	98	9.8
Al Cervi	G	5'11	185	29	44	228	176	236	75	**632**	14.4	11	49	50	68	74	148	13.5
Red Holzman	G	5'10	175	26	44	227	74	139	53	528	12.0	11	42	22	29	76	106	9.6
Fuzzy Levane (Broken nose)	F-G	6'2	190	26	39	133	49	87	56	315	8.1	11	37	18	27	67	92	8.4
Dolly King	C-F	6'4	217	29	41	52	60	97	62	164	4.0	11	30	31	43	72	91	8.3
Al Negratti (from Was BAA)	F	6'4	220	25	33	15	14	24	58	44	1.3	11	3	4	7	57	10	0.9
Bill Coven	F-C	6'7	220	26	13	10	4	8	50	24	1.8	5	0	0	0	—	0	0.0
Dutch Garfinkel (to Bos BAA)	G	6'	190	28	10	5	3	6	50	13	1.3							
Bob Gauchat (from TC)	G	6'	180	25	6	1	2	2	100	4	0.7	2	0	0	0	—	0	0.0
Jim Cominsky (VR)	G	6'2	185	26	5	2	0	0	—	4	0.8							
Frank Beaty	F	6'3	205	24	6	0	1	4	25	1	0.2	2	1	0	2	0	2	1.0
Jim Quinlan	F	6'4	205	24	3	0	1	2	50	1	0.3							
FORT WAYNE ZOLLNER PISTONS	25-19 .568				BOBBY McDERMOTT (7-7 .500), CARL BENNETT (17-12 .586), PAUL ARMSTRONG (1-0 1.000)													
defeated Toledo 3-2; H65-38, H54-31, 46-56, 53-58, H64-46																		
lost to Rochester 1-2; 49-58, H56-49, 47-76																		
Curly Armstrong	F-G	5'11	170	28	44	127	134	195	69	388	8.8	8	24	23	31	74	71	8.9
Blackie Towery	F	6'4	210	26	41	100	80	134	60	280	6.8	8	15	7	15	47	37	4.6
Jake Pelkington (SL)	C	6'6	220	29	42	129	125	166	75	383	9.1	8	18	19	25	76	55	6.9
Chick Reiser	G	5'11	165	32	44	153	104	139	75	410	9.3	8	26	20	29	69	72	9.0
Bobby McDermott (to Chi, ST)	G	6'	185	32	14	59	41	60	68	159	11.4							
Bob Tough	G	6'	185	26	44	124	55	81	68	303	6.9	8	17	16	19	84	50	6.3
Bob Kinney	C	6'6	215	26	44	102	42	84	50	246	5.6	8	18	17	22	77	53	6.6
Milo Komenich (suspended by team)	F-C	6'7	212	26	36	50	23	50	46	123	3.4	8	15	6	14	43	36	4.5
Richie Niemiera (CC)	F-G	6'1	165	25	13	28	17	23	74	73	5.6	6	11	5	8	63	27	4.5
Jerry Bush (to And)	F	6'3	210	32	21	26	14	21	67	66	3.1							
Frank Gates (from And)	G	6'	167	25	16	20	9	16	56	49	3.1	7	10	9	17	53	29	4.1
Charley Shipp (to And, ST)	G	6'1	205	33	14	12	11	16	69	35	2.5							
Jerry Steiner (HC)	G	5'7	160	28	16	12	5	9	56	29	1.8	4	1	1	4	25	3	0.8
Whitey Dienelt	G	6'	185	25	13	4	3	4	75	11	0.8	1	0	1	2	50	1	1.0
Ken Buehler (CO, leg injury)	F	6'2	180	27	8	4	3	10	30	11	1.4							
Ben Gardner (from And, VR)	F	6'3	190	25	1	0	0	0	—	0	0.0							
Lyle Neat (HC)	G	6'	180	30	1	0	0	0	—	0	0.0							
TOLEDO JEEPS	21-23 .477				JULIE RIVLIN	lost to Ft. Wayne 2-3; 38-65, 31-54, H56-46, H58-53, 46-64												
Hal Tidrick	F-G	6'1	190	31	44	**232**	115	165	70	579	13.2	5	19	13	21	62	51	10.2
George Sobek	F	6'	180	26	42	186	**179**	248	72	551	13.1	5	14	19	26	73	47	9.4
Bob Gerber	C-F	6'5	220	30	41	151	72	127	57	374	9.1	3	4	6	11	55	14	4.7
Dale Hamilton	G-F	6'	195	27	44	114	67	131	51	295	6.7	4	6	7	20	35	19	4.8
Julie Rivlin	G	5'11	180	29	44	105	70	90	78	280	6.4	5	8	11	13	85	27	5.4
Johnny Schick	C-F	6'6	230	30	42	86	37	69	54	209	5.0	5	2	2	6	33	6	1.2
Paul Seymour	G-F	6'2	180	18	33	41	17	30	57	99	3.0	5	2	6	10	60	10	2.0
Joe Patanelli	F	6'3	205	27	35	29	29	40	73	87	2.5	5	4	10	21	48	18	3.6
Bernie Mehen (from You)	F	6'4	185	28	4	10	4	7	57	24	6.0	5	11	11	14	79	33	6.6
Bob Shaw (FB)	F-C	6'4	225	25	8	6	7	10	70	19	2.4							
Johnny Bianco	C	6'4	195	24	10	4	2	6	33	10	1.0							
Frankie Gilhooley	G	5'11	180	22	8	3	1	6	17	7	0.9	3	1	2	2	100	4	1.3
Ed Costain	G	6'	170	23	3	2	0	0	—	4	1.3							
Benny Schall	F	5'11	170	29	5	1	0	0	—	2	0.4							
Jim Gibbs	C	6'5	195	27	1	0	0	0	—	0	0.0							
Beryl Drummond	G-F	6'1	185	28	1	0	0	0	—	0	0	2	0	0	0	—	0	0.0
Jim Glass-injured																		
BENNY BORGMANN (13-17 .433), GEORGE MINGIN (2-0 1.000), JERRY RIZZO (6-6 .500)																		
SYRACUSE NATIONALS	21-23 .477								lost to Rochester 1-3; 64-66, H64-61, 48-54, H57-62									
Chick Meehan (eye injury)	F-G	6'1	195	29	29	83	43	63	68	209	7.2							
John Chaney	F-C	6'3	190	26	42	138	86	119	72	362	8.6	4	12	2	6	33	26	6.5
Mike Novak (from Sheb)	C	6'9	220	31	33	150	69	129	53	369	11.2	4	26	13	21	62	65	16.3
George Nelmark	G	6'1	185	29	37	107	51	92	55	265	7.2	4	13	5	7	71	31	7.8
Jerry Rizzo	G-F	5'8	150	28	44	155	169	238	71	479	10.9	4	16	19	26	73	51	12.8
Steve Sharkey (from Sheb)	F-G	6'	190	28	37	99	39	52	75	237	6.4	4	15	10	12	83	40	10.0
Johnny Gee (HC)	C-F	6'9	225	31	24	59	38	60	63	156	6.5	3	1	1	4	25	3	1.0
Bob Nugent	G	5'11	170	31	31	39	31	45	69	109	3.5	4	6	5	6	83	17	4.3
Bill McCahan (BB)	G-F	5'11	200	25	27	35	24	46	52	94	3.5							
Les Rothman (to Chi, Leg injury)	F	6'1	195	20	13	24	15	21	71	63	4.8							
Jack Dugger (FB)	F-C	6'3	225	23	21	13	10	19	53	36	1.7							
Ken Exel (from Osh)	G	6'1	178	26	10	8	7	11	64	23	2.3	1	0	0	0	—	0	0.0
John Moiseichik	G	5'11	180	26	9	6	4	9	44	16	1.8							
Bob Synnott (to Chi)	F	6'3	200	34	4	6	4	6	67	16	4.0							
Lou Possner	F	6'3	180	29	3	4	1	2	50	9	3.0							
Charlie Butler (to You)	F	6'2	165	25	3	2	1	1	100	5	1.7							
Jim Zeravich	C	6'7	—	25	2	1	3	5	60	5	2.5							
Mort Hill	G	6'1	175	—	3	1	0	0	—	2	0.7							
Ed Erban	F	6'4	—	25	5	0	1	2	50	1	0.2							
Sam Lieberman	C	6'8	—	—	2	0	1	2	50	1	0.5							
Bob Shaddock	G	6'1	160	26	2	0	0	0	—	0	0.0							

Use Name	Pos	Hgt	Wgt	Age	REGULAR SEASON G	FG	FT	FTA	Pct.	Points	PPG	PLAYOFFS G	FG	FT	FTA	Pct.	Points	PPG
1946/47 N.B.L — EASTERN DIVISION (continued)																		
TRI-CITIES BLACKHAWKS	**19-25 .432**			**NAT HICKEY**														
(Buffalo Bisons until December 27, 1946, 5-8 .385)																		
Pop Gates	F	6'2	205	29	41	125	60	115	52	310	7.6							
Ed Lewinski (from And)	F	6'4	210	26	18	60	15	29	52	135	7.5							
Don Otten	C	7'	245	25	44	200	169	261	65	569	12.9							
Billy Hassett (CO)	G	6'1	180	25	27	73	66	101	65	212	7.9							
Stan Waxman (knee injury)	G	5'11	180	24	18	59	10	17	59	128	7.1							
Al Grenert (from Sheb)	F	6'	190	27	30	85	28	42	67	198	6.6							
Howie Rader	G-F	6'1	190	25	41	76	43	64	67	195	4.8							
Nick Grunzweig	F-C	6'5	215	28	43	39	42	70	60	120	2.8							
Mel Thurston	G	6'	175	27	39	39	36	59	61	114	2.9							
Len Rader (broken hand)	G	6'2	185	25	20	27	15	30	50	69	3.5							
Bob Sims (to Sheb) (broken finger)	C-F	6'6	220	31	10	10	11	14	79	31	3.1							
Wilbur Schu (from You)	F	6'3	190	24	22	8	10	17	59	26	1.2							
Nat Hickey	G	5'11	190	44	8	9	6	12	50	24	3.0							
Dick Starzyk	G	5'10	180	25	9	4	4	5	80	12	1.3							
Vic Siegel	G	5'10	160	26	8	3	5	5	100	11	1.4							
Rooney (from Det)	G	6'3	—	20	5	2	0	0	—	4	0.8							
Bob Gauchat (ST, to Roch)	G	6'	180	25	4	0	2	5	40	2	0.5							
Ed Moeller (from & to You)	G	6'	175	27	3	0	0	0	—	0	0.0							
Paul Anthony	C	6'5	195	22	1	0	0	0	—	0	0.0							
YOUNGSTOWN BEARS	**12-32 .273**			**FRANK SHANNON**														
Milt Ticco (BB)	F	6'3	205	24	36	180	46	63	73	406	11.3							
Bernie Mehen (to Tol)	F	6'4	185	28	36	140	65	91	71	345	9.6							
Bill Farrow	C	6'4	198	28	32	65	52	106	49	182	5.7							
Charlie Joachim (toe injury)	G-F	6'2	184	26	33	125	102	143	71	352	10.7							
Paul Herman	G	6'1	175	25	44	109	45	77	58	263	6.0							
Charlie Butler(from Syr)	F	6'2	165	25	32	85	88	144	61	258	8.1							
Bill Sattler	C	6'8	197	30	42	85	50	105	48	220	5.2							
Frank Shannon	G	5'11	178	29	29	55	14	20	70	124	4.3							
Red Mihalik (from Pit BAA)	G	6'	180	30	31	41	12	29	41	94	3.0							
Ed Moeller (to ~ from TC)	G	6'	175	27	19	13	13	14	93	39	2.1							
John Bosak	G-C	6'3	185	24	10	11	2	5	40	24	2.4							
Wilbur Schu (to TC)	F	6'3	190	24	11	7	6	9	67	20	1.8							
Jack Mills	F-C	6'4	210	28	8	5	8	10	80	18	2.3							
Bob Kramer (from Osh)	F	6'3	—	25	2	2	2	3	67	4	3.0							
Sotnik	F-G	—	—	—	4	1	0	0	—	2	0.5							
Irv Brenner	C	6'4	200	33	1	1	0	0	—	2	2.0							
1946/47 N.B.L. — WESTERN DIVISION																		
OSHKOSH ALL-STARS	**28-16 .636**			**LON DARLING**					defeated Sheboygan 3-2; 48-54, 35-40, H53-44, H53-45, H49-47 lost to Chicago 0-2; H60, H60-61									
Bob Carpenter	F	6'5	200	29	44	199	115	169	68	513	11.7	7	17	7	21	33	41	5.9
Gene Englund	F-C	6'5	205	29	43	187	105	151	70	479	11.1	7	36	26	49	53	98	14.0
Leroy Edwards	C	6'4	225	32	44	135	144	222	65	414	9.4	6	7	3	14	21	17	2.8
Eddie Riska	G	6'	180	27	44	81	71	102	70	233	5.3	7	16	22	27	81	54	7.7
Ralph Vaughn (VR)	G-F	6'1	180	28	35	76	49	64	77	201	5.7	7	25	11	16	69	61	8.7
Jack Maddox	F-G	6'3	190	25	43	102	33	39	85	237	5.5	7	3	1	2	50	7	1.0
Clint Wager	C-F	6'6	230	26	44	68	50	69	72	186	4.2	7	15	10	12	83	40	5.7
Bob Sullivan	G-F	6'	180	25	41	45	48	60	80	138	3.4	5	3	0	2	0	6	1.2
Bill McDonald (from Chi)	G	6'3	190	30	21	18	20	26	77	56	2.7	7	10	8	9	89	28	4.0
Billy Reed (VR)	G	5'11	185	—	17	20	5	18	28	45	2.6							
Ken Exel (to Syr)	G	6'1	178	26	17	10	9	24	38	29	1.7							
Don Smith (to Ind) (leg injury)	F	6'2	190	26	10	4	4	6	67	12	1.2							
Ted Fritsch (FB)	G	5'10	210	26	10	5	1	2	50	11	1.1	3	0	0	0	—	0	0.0
Bob Kramer(to You)	G	6'3	—	25	1	0	0	0	—	0	0.0							
INDIANAPOLIS KAUTSKYS	**27-17 .614**			**ERNIE ANDRES (20-13 .606) BOB DIETZ & HERM SCHAEFER (7-4 .636)**								lost to Chicago 2-3; H72-74, H61-69, 68-67, 55-54, 62-76						
Leo Klier	F	6'2	170	23	44	162	93	128	73	417	9.5	5	16	9	12	75	41	8.2
Gus Doerner	F	6'2	195	24	43	94	46	82	56	234	5.4	5	23	13	22	59	59	11.8
Arnie Risen	C	6'9	200	22	44	204	174	276	63	582	13.2	5	32	31	40	78	95	19.0
Ernie Andres	G	6'1	200	28	44	140	66	88	75	346	7.9	5	14	5	6	83	33	6.6
Herm Schaefer	G	6'	175	27	44	147	65	90	72	359	8.2	5	22	14	18	78	58	11.6
Bill Closs	F-C	6'6	195	24	44	119	34	63	54	272	6.2	4	10	3	6	50	23	5.8
Bob Dietz	G	6'1	165	29	39	56	28	42	67	140	3.6	4	1	0	1	0	2	0.5
Woody Norris	F-G	6'1	170	27	38	42	18	36	50	102	2.7	3	1	0	0	—	2	0.7
Lowell Galloway	F-C	6'4	210	25	31	14	18	34	53	46	1.5	3	2	1	1	100	5	1.7
Don Smith (from Osh)	G	6'2	190	26	2	1	1	2	50	3	1.5							
Homer Thompson (to Sheb)	C	6'4	215	30	1	1	0	1	0	2	2.0							

Use Name	Pos	Hgt	Wgt	Age	REGULAR SEASON G	FG	FT	FTA	Pct.	Points	PPG	PLAYOFFS G	FG	FT	FTA	Pct.	Points	PPG
1946/47 N.B.L. - WESTERN DIVISION (continued)																		
CHICAGO AMERICAN GEARS	**26-18 .591**				**DAVEY BANKS (3-3 .500), HARRY FOOTE (1-1 .500), BOBBY McDERMOTT (19-8 .704) HARRY FOOTE & BRUCE HALE (3-6 .333)**							defeated Indianapolis 3-2; 74-72, 69-61, H67-68, H54-55, H76-62; defeated Oshkosh 2-0, H60-54, 61-60; defeated Rochester 3-1; 65-71, 67-63, H78-70, H79-68						
Price Brookfield	F-G	6'4	200	26	42	82	24	33	73	188	4.5	11	29	3	7	43	61	5.5
Bob Calihan	F-C	6'3	200	28	44	196	92	132	70	484	11.0	11	57	21	37	57	135	12.3
George Mikan (contract dispute)	C	6'10	235	22	25	147	119	164	73	413	**16.5**	11	**72**	**73**	**96**	76	**217**	**19.7**
Bruce Hale	G-F	6'1	170	28	41	156	116	141	**82**	428	10.4	11	35	24	30	80	94	8.5
Bobby McDermott (from FtW,SL)	G	6'	185	32	27	123	58	81	72	304	11.3	9	26	22	24	**92**	74	8.2
Stan Patrick	F-G	6'3	215	24	42	72	36	67	54	180	4.3	11	30	10	15	67	70	6.4
Dick Triptow	G	6'	170	24	44	59	60	90	67	178	4.0	11	19	15	22	68	53	4.8
Stan Szukala	G	6'	185	28	38	56	17	27	63	129	3.4	7	2	4	5	80	8	1.1
Max Morris (FB)	F-C	6'2	195	21	33	44	33	63	52	121	3.7	10	8	2	6	33	18	1.8
George Ratkovicz	C	6'7	225	24	37	43	26	58	45	112	3.0	10	6	8	9	89	20	2.0
Art Stoefen	C-F	6'7	215	31	18	8	8	19	42	24	1.3	2	0	0	1	0	0	0.0
Bob Cotton	F-C-G	6'7	205	24	4	1	3	6	50	5	1.3							
Bill McDonald (to Osh)(MS)	G	6'3	190	30	5	0	2	3	67	2	0.4							
Irv Noren	F	6'	180	22	3	0	1	2	50	1	0.3							
Bob Synnott (from Syr)	F	6'3	200	34	1	0	0	0	—	0	0.0							
Les Rothman (from Syr)	F	6'1	195	20	1	0	0	0	—	0	0.0							
SHEBOYGAN REDSKINS	**26-18 .591**				**DOXIE MOORE**							lost to Oshkosh 2-3; H54-48, H40-35, 44-53, 45-53, 47-49						
Luther Harris	F-G	6'3	195	23	44	170	127	179	71	467	10.6	5	11	5	14	36	27	5.4
Fred Lewis	F	6'2	195	25	44	230	125	170	74	585	13.3	5	23	9	15	60	55	11.0
Ed Dancker	C	6'7	220	32	44	160	131	187	70	451	10.3	5	14	11	18	61	39	7.8
Rube Lautenschlager	G-F	6'3	205	31	43	94	36	65	55	224	5.2	5	11	12	21	57	34	6.8
Bobby Holm	G	6'	210	27	44	63	78	101	77	204	4.6	5	10	2	2	100	22	4.4
Al Lucas	F-G	6'3	195	24	42	87	32	60	53	206	4.9	5	15	6	7	86	36	7.2
Al Grenert (to TC)	F	6'	190	27	13	27	10	15	67	64	4.9							
Kenny Suesens	G	6'1	185	30	37	14	34	73	47	62	1.7	4	1	1	3	33	3	0.8
Bob Dykstra (from Det)	C	6'9	230	24	18	10	15	28	54	35	1.9	4	3	2	5	40	8	2.0
Dean White	F	6'7	220	23	5	7	7	9	78	21	4.2	1	1	0	0	—	2	2.0
Jim Dawson	C-F	6'7	210	24	10	8	4	7	57	20	2.0							
Bob Sims (from TC)	C-F	6'6	220	31	13	4	7	11	64	15	1.2	1	1	0	0	—	2	2.0
Pete Mount	F	6'4	185	21	10	6	3	5	60	15	1.5							
Bill Schroeder (FB)	G-F	6'	190	23	9	5	5	8	63	15	1.7							
Mike Novak (to Syr)	C	6'9	220	31	3	3	4	7	57	10	3.3							
HomerThompson (from Ind)	C	6'4	215	30	3	2	2	3	67	6	2.0							
Steve Sharkey (to Syr)	G	6'	190	28	1	0	0	0	—	0	0.0							
Max Biggs	F-C	6'	190	20	—	—	—	—	—	—	—	4	1	0	0	—	2	0.5
Paul Maki - foot injury																		
ANDERSON DUFFEY PACKERS	**24-20 .545**				**MURRAY MENDENHALL (23-19 .548), IKE DUFFEY (1-1 .500)**													
Bill Hapac	F	6'2	200	28	41	93	91	134	68	277	6.8							
Ed Stanczak	F	6'3	205	25	44	142	118	201	59	402	9.1							
Howie Schultz (BB)	C	6'7	200	24	41	155	147	213	69	457	11.1							
Charley Shipp (from FtW)	G	6'1	205	33	30	77	47	67	70	201	6.7							
Rollie Seltz	G	5'10	170	22	41	123	104	143	73	350	8.5							
Elmer Gainer	C-F	6'6	200	27	43	77	59	79	75	213	5.0							
Ed Lewinski (to TC)	F-C	6'4	210	26	27	82	25	48	52	189	7.0							
Bob Bolyard	G-F	6'	185	26	38	73	38	50	76	184	4.8							
Frank Gates (to FtW)	G	6'	167	25	16	48	21	36	58	117	7.3							
Jerry Bush (from FtW)	F	6'3	210	32	15	39	10	19	53	88	5.9							
Dale Morey	G-F	6'	180	28	24	32	13	18	72	77	3.2							
Dick Furey	F	6'3	195	21	11	11	8	10	80	30	2.7							
Jack Stanton	G	6'	175	25	7	10	2	7	29	22	3.1							
Howie Hoffman	G	—	—	26	5	5	3	6	50	13	2.6							
Russ Wilkins	F-G	6'1	190	—	5	2	1	2	50	5	1.0							
Ben Gardner (to FtW)	C	6'3	190	25	6	0	3	8	38	3	0.5							
DETROIT GEMS	**4-40 .091**				**JOEL MASON (3-13 .188), FRED CAMPBELL (1-27 .D36)**													
Del Loranger (HC)	F	6'3	175	26	27	94	45	71	63	233	8.6							
Tom Meyer	F-C	6'4	214	—	24	77	34	53	64	188	7.8							
Dave Latter	C	6'6	210	24	41	123	75	132	57	321	7.8							
Paul Juntunen	G-F	6'1	180	25	43	76	26	38	68	178	4.1							
Fred Campbell	G	5'11	175	26	39	105	58	81	72	268	6.9							
Ed Parry	F	6'2	185	28	34	81	73	113	65	235	6.9							
Connie O'Connor	F	6'1	—	22	36	82	32	78	41	196	5.4							
Herb Scheffler	C-F	6'4	220	29	33	43	40	67	60	126	3.8							
Howie McCarty (to Det BAA)	G	6'2	190	27	16	46	29	75	39	121	7.6							
Willie King	G	5'7	—	—	14	42	31	49	63	115	8.2							
Bob Dykstra (to Sheb)	C	6'9	230	24	14	19	20	30	67	58	4.1							
Vaughn Waddell	G	6'1	190	36	8	10	5	8	63	25	3.1							
Chuck Hawley	G-F	6'3	195	31	12	6	5	6	83	17	1.4							
Frank Sabo	G	6'1	190	24	3	7	2	3	67	16	5.3							
Perry	G	—	—	—	5	4	7	14	50	15	3.0							
Pat Rooney (to TC)	F	6'3	—	20	5	4	3	7	43	11	2.2							
Frank Mekules	F	6'4	218	27	3	3	0	1	0	6	2.0							
Walt Czarnecki	F	6'5	215	30	4	2	1	7	14	5	1.3							
Curt Henderson	G	5'8	150	29	4	1	2	3	67	4	1.0							

1946-47 B.A.A.

Filling the Empty Seats With a New League

With the end of World War II, the operators of the country's largest sports arenas realized that pro basketball could be a fine attraction to fill their arenas on dates not taken by pro hockey and college basketball games. As a result, these executives, led hy Walter Brown of Boston, founded the Basketball Association of America in the summer of 1946.

Charter members of the new league were Boston, Toronto, Providence, New York, Philadelphia, Washington, Pittsburgh, Cleveland, Detroit, Chicago, and St. Louis; all the franchise owners knew each other through the Arena Managers Association of America and through their teams in the National and American Hockey Leagues. For a chief executive, the members chose Maurice Podoloff, the colorful 5'2" president of the A.H.L.

The new league had the advantage of playing in large arenas in large cities, but its players were generally inferior to those in the National Basketball League, the established league operating chiefly in smaller cities in the Midwest. Only a handful of N.B.L. players jumped to the B.A.A., but the new league did pick up the prime talent of the American Basketball League, the primary circuit in the East till the formation of the B.A.A. To go with these established pros, the teams went all out to sign college stars who had built their reputations in the very arenas the B.A.A. teams were moving into. Although none of the three best graduating centers, George Mikan, Bob Kurland, or Don Otten, signed with the new league, many college stars from the war years joined the new teams.

Once the bell rang for the start of the regular season, the Washington Capitols quickly proved themselves the class of the circuit. Coached by Red Auerbach, a brash 29-year-old high school coach, the Caps ran off a 17-game winning streak early in the season to jump out to a large lead in the East. The leader of this experienced squad was guard Bob Feerick, a superb floor general who jumped over from the N.B.L. Joining Feerick in the backcourt was Freddie Scolari, a top shooter. In the forecourt were ex-Rochester center John Mahnken, forward Johnny Norlander, and 27-year-old rookie Bones McKinney, who had just completed his war-interrupted career at North Carolina. Able to play both a running and ball-control game, the Caps finished 14 games in front in the East.

Taking second place behind the Caps were the Philadelphia Warriors, coached by Eddie Gottlieb of Sphas fame. Gottlieb had two solid all-around players in Howie Dallmar and Angelo Musi, but his prize possession was the league's first superstar, forward Joe Fulks. A star at tiny Murray State before joining the Marines during the war, Fulks set the league on its ear with a machine gun jump shot that baffled conventional defenses. Gottlieb had the Warriors feed Fulks as much as possible, and the slender gunner led the B.A.A with an eye-opening 23.2 scoring average, hitting a high game of 41 points against Toronto on January 14. Fulks, more than anyone else, drew the public s attention to the new B.A.A. this season.

The New York Knickerbockers grabbed the third and final playoff spot in the East. Although run by Ned Irish, the Knicks played only six home games in Madison Square Garden; the crowded schedule of hockey and college basketball games in the prestigious Garden forced them into the 69th Regiment Armory. Former A.B.L. players formed the heart of the Knicks, led by guards Sonny Hertzberg md Stan Stutz. Finishing out of the playoffs were the Providence Steamrollers, led by local favorite Ernie Calverly; the Toronto Huskies, who went through a stack of players and four coaches, ending the season under the direction of baseball great Red Rolfe; and the Boston Celtics, coached by old pro Honey Russell.

In the Western Division, the Chicago Stags and St. Louis Bombers wound up in a dead heat for first place, with the Stags winning a one-game tie-breaker at the end of the regular season. Chicago coach Ole Olsen built a quick fast break around rebounding center Chick Halbert, feeder Mickey Rottner, and set-shooter Max Zaslofsky. St. Louis coach Ken Loeffler also organized a running team, with all-around guard Johnny Logan the ace of the club.

The Cleveland Rebels captured the third playoff spot despite some personnel changes in midseason; coach Dutch Dehnert was replaced by Roy Clifford, and three veteran players were shipped to Toronto for center Ed Sadowski, whose hook shot was still potent after years of pro play. The Rebel guards were Frankie Baumholtz, a future major league baseball player, and rookie Kenny Sailors, a fine playmaker with an accurate jump shot. Coming in fourth were the Detroit Falcons, who had a strong center in bulky Stan Miasek. In last place were the Pittsburgh Ironmen coached by old Celtic Paul Birch.

The playoff system devised by the league fathers pitted the first-place teams, second-place teams, and the third-place teams against each other in the opening round. The basic flaw in this setup was that one of the first-place teams would be knocked off right at tne start. But with this fact overlooked, Washington and Chicago squared off in a seven-game series to begin the playoffs. The Stags shocked the heavily-favored Caps by beating them 81-65 and 69-53 in the first two games at Washington, where the Caps had won 29 of 30 games during the season. The Stags finished off the Caps in six games and waited for the other matches to provide them with an opponent for the championship.

Philadelphia bested St. Louis in a three-game showdown of second-place finishers, while New York topped Cleveland in three games in the third bracket. The Warriors than beat the Knicks 82-70 and 72-53 to move into the finals with the Stags.

The championship series opened in Philadelphia before a crowd of 7,918 who saw Joe Fulks score 37 points in leading the Warriors to an 84-71 victory. The Warriors got only 13 points from Fulks in the second game, but center Art Hillhouse sparked a late rally which gave the Warriors an 85 74 win and a commanding 2-0 lead in the series. The Chicago club expected to turn things around on their home floor, but the Warriors took the third game behind Fulks' 26 points, and it was all over but the shouting. The Stags won the fourth game, but the Warriors won the title before 8,221 hometown fans with an 83-80 victory which saw "Jumpin Joe" Fulks throw in 34 points and Howie Dallmar put in the winning basket to break an 80-80 tie with only one minute left in the game.

1946/47 B.B.A. — EASTERN DIVISION

					TOTAL										PER GAME			PLAYOFFS										
Use Name	Pos	Hgt	Wgt	Age	G	FG	FGA	%	FT	FTA	%	Ass.	PF	Pts	Ass.	PF	Pts.	G	FG	FGA	%	FT	FTA	%	Ass	PF	Pts	PPG
WASHINGTON CAPITOLS	**49-11 .817**	**RED AUERBACH**	lost to Chicago 2-4; H65-81, H53-69, 55-67, H76-69, 67-55, 61-66																									
Johnny Norlander	F	6'3	180	25	60	223	698	32	180	276	65	50	122	626	0.8	2.0	10.4	6	14	50	28	13	17	76	2	11	41	6.8
Bones McKinney	F-C	6'6	187	27	58	275	987	28	145	210	69	69	162	695	1.2	2.8	12.0	6	18	85	21	22	34	65	3	17	58	9.7
John Mahnken	C	6'8	220	24	60	223	876	25	111	163	68	60	181	557	1.0	3.0	9.3	6	23	96	24	16	19	84	1	25	62	10.3
Bob Feerick	G-F	6'3	190	26	55	364	908	**40**	198	260	76	69	142	926	1.3	2.6	16.8	6	35	110	32	20	27	74	6	22	90	15.0
Freddie Scolari	G	5'11	180	24	58	291	989	29	146	180	**81**	58	159	728	1.0	2.7	12.6	6	22	95	23	27	34	79	5	17	71	11.8
Irv Torgoff	F-G	6'2	192	29	58	187	684	27	116	159	73	30	173	490	0.5	3.0	8.4	6	13	81	16	13	19	68	5	23	39	6.5
Buddy O'Grady	G	5'11	160	26	55	55	231	24	38	53	72	20	60	148	0.4	1.1	2.7	6	2	20	10	5	5	100	0	5	9	1.5
Marty Passaglia	G	6'1	170	27	43	51	221	23	18	32	56	9	44	120	0.2	1.0	2.8	6	2	14	14	1	3	33	0	10	5	0.8
Bob Gantt	F-C	6'4	205	24	23	29	89	33	13	28	46	5	45	71	0.2	2.0	3.1	2	1	3	33	0	1	0	0	0	2	1.0
Al Negratti (to Roch NBL)	F-C	6'4	220	25	11	13	69	19	5	8	63	5	20	31	0.5	1.8	2.8											
Gene Gillette	F	6'2	205	25	14	1	11	9	6	9	67	2	13	8	0.1	0.9	0.6											
Al Lujack	F	6'3	220	25	5	1	8	13	2	5	40	0	6	4	0.0	1.2	0.8											
Ben Goldfaden	F	6'3	185	33	2	0	2	0	2	4	50	0	3	2	0.0	1.5	1.0											
PHILADELPHIA WARRIORS	**35-25 .583**	**EDDIE GOTTLIEB**	defeated St. Louis 2-1; H73-68, 51-73, 75-59 defeated New York 2-0; H82-70, 72-53, defeated Chicago 4-1; H84-71, H85-74, 75-72, 73-74, H83-80																									
Howie Dallmar	F	6'4	202	24	60	199	710	28	130	203	64	104	141	528	1.7	2.4	8.8	10	26	104	25	30	40	75	**16**	28	82	8.2
Joe Fulks	F-C	6'5	190	25	60	**475**	**1557**	31	**439**	**601**	73	25	199	**1389**	0.4	3.3	**23.2**	10	**74**	**257**	29	**74**	**94**	79	3	32	**222**	22.2
Art Hillhouse	C	6'7	230	30	60	120	412	29	120	166	72	41	139	360	0.7	2.3	6.0	10	24	91	26	39	46	85	8	41	87	8.7
George Senesky	G	6'2	175	24	58	142	531	27	82	124	66	34	83	366	0.6	1.4	6.3	10	44	139	32	21	26	81	8	15	109	10.9
Angelo Musi	G	5'9	145	28	60	230	818	28	102	123	83	26	120	562	0.4	2.0	9.4	10	48	160	30	21	29	72	5	27	117	11.7
Ralph Kaplowicz (27g. NY)	F-G	6'2	170	27	57	146	523	28	111	151	74	38	122	403	0.7	2.1	7.1	10	22	98	22	22	27	81	6	25	66	6.6
Jerry Fleishman	F	6'2	190	24	59	97	372	26	69	127	54	40	101	263	0.7	1.7	4.5	9	22	70	31	13	18	72	3	20	57	6.3
Petey Rosenberg	G	5'10	165	28	51	60	287	21	30	49	61	27	64	150	0.5	1.3	2.9	9	1	12	8	0	3	0	3	4	2	0.2
Jerry Rullo	G	5'10	165	23	50	52	174	30	23	47	49	20	61	127	0.4	1.2	2.5	7	3	13	23	1	1	100	0	1	7	1.0
Matt Guokas	F	6'3	195	31	47	28	104	27	26	47	55	9	70	82	0.2	1.5	1.7	8	1	9	11	2	5	40	0	11	4	0.5
Fred Sheffield (CO)	F	6'2	165	23	22	29	146	20	16	26	62	4	34	74	0.2	1.5	3.4											
John Murphy (9g. NY)	F	6'2	185	22	20	11	40	28	10	15	67	0	8	32	0.0	0.4	1.6											
NEW YORK KNICKERBOCKERS	**33-27 .550**	**NEIL COHALAN**	defeated Cleveland 2-1; 51-77, H86-74, H93-71 lost to Philadelphia 0-2; 70-82, H53-72																									
Tommy Byrnes	F	6'3	175	23	60	175	583	30	103	160	64	35	90	453	0.6	1.5	7.6	5	11	46	24	2	11	18	0	2	24	4.8
Bud Palmer	F-C	6'4	180	25	42	160	521	31	81	121	67	34	110	401	0.8	2.6	9.5	5	33	94	35	12	20	60	4	8	78	15.6
Lee Knorek (CO)	C	6'7	215	25	22	62	219	28	47	72	65	21	64	171	1.0	2.9	7.8	5	21	58	36	11	19	58	8	22	53	10.6
Ossie Schectman (stomach injury)	G	6'	175	27	54	162	588	28	111	179	62	109	115	435	2.0	2.1	8.1	(injury)										
Sonny Hertzberg	G	5'10	175	24	59	201	695	29	113	149	76	37	109	515	0.6	1.8	8.7	5	15	69	22	6	8	75	5	14	36	7.2
Stan Stutz	G-F	5'10	175	26	60	172	641	27	133	170	78	49	127	477	0.8	2.1	8.0	5	28	101	28	28	32	**88**	7	13	84	16.8
Leo Gottlieb	G	5'11	180	26	57	149	494	30	36	55	65	24	71	334	0.4	1.2	5.9	4	10	39	26	4	6	67	1	6	24	6.0
Bob Cluggish	C	6'10	235	29	54	93	356	26	52	91	57	22	113	238	0.4	2.1	4.4	5	4	27	15	0	2	0	0	12	8	1.6
Bob Fitzgerald (31g. Tor)	F-C	6'5	195	23	50	70	362	19	81	130	62	35	153	221	0.7	3.1	4.4	5	1	9	11	3	4	75	1	3	5	1.0
Frido Frey	F	6'2	195	25	23	28	97	29	32	56	57	14	37	88	0.6	1.6	3.8	5	3	19	16	4	11	36	7	11	10	2.0
Aud Brindley	F	6'4	180	23	12	14	49	29	6	7	86	1	16	34	0.1	1.3	2.8	3	3	6	50	4	6	67	0	4	10	3.3
Butch Van Breda Kolff	F-G	6'3	185	24	16	7	34	21	11	17	65	6	10	25	0.4	0.6	1.6	5	7	32	22	7	13	54	4	5	21	4.2
Frank Mangiapane	G	5'10	195	21	6	2	13	15	1	3	33	0	6	5	0.0	1.0	0.8											
PROVIDENCE STEAMROLLERS	**28-32 .467**	**BOB MORRIS**																										
Earl Shannon	F-G	5'11	170	23	57	245	722	34	197	348	57	84	169	687	1.5	3.0	12.1											
George Mearns	F	6'3	175	24	57	128	478	27	126	175	72	35	137	382	0.6	2.4	6.7											
Hank Beenders	C-F	6'6	185	30	58	266	1016	26	181	257	70	37	196	713	0.6	3.4	12.3											
Earnie Calverly	G	5'10	155	22	59	323	1102	29	199	283	70	**202**	191	845	**3.4**	3.2	14.3											
Dino Martin	G	5'8	160	26	60	311	1022	30	111	168	66	59	98	733	1.0	1.6	12.2											
Hank Rosenstein (31g. NY)	F	6'4	185	26	60	119	390	31	144	225	64	36	172	382	0.6	2.9	6.4											
Pop Goodwin	F-C	6'2	203	26	55	98	348	28	60	75	80	15	94	256	0.3	1.7	4.7											
Jake Weber (11g. NY)	C	6'6	225	28	50	59	202	29	55	79	70	4	111	173	0.1	2.2	3.5											
George Pastushok	G	6'1	195	24	39	48	183	26	25	46	54	15	42	121	0.4	1.1	3.1											
Bob Shea	F	6'2	194	22	43	37	153	24	19	33	58	6	42	93	0.1	1.0	2.2											
Woody Grimshaw	G	6'1	185	27	21	20	56	36	21	44	48	1	25	61	0.0	1.2	2.9											
Ken Keller (25g. Was)	G	6'1	180	24	28	10	30	33	2	5	40	1	15	22	0.0	0.5	0.8											
Tom Callahan	G	6'1	180	25	13	6	29	21	5	12	42	4	9	17	0.3	0.7	1.3											
Elmore Morgenthaler	C	7'1	235	24	11	4	13	31	7	12	58	3	3	15	0.3	0.3	1.4											
Bob Dehnert	F	6'3	178	22	10	6	15	40	2	6	33	0	8	14	0.0	0.8	1.4											
Armand Cure	F	6'1	198	27	12	4	15	27	2	3	67	0	5	10	0.0	0.4	0.8											
Lou Spicer	F	6'2	195	23	4	0	7	0	1	2	50	0	3	1	0.0	0.8	0.3											

1946/47 B.A.A. — EASTERN DIVISION (continued)

TORONTO HUSKIES 22-38 .367 ED SADOWSKI (3-9 .250), LEW HAYMAN (0-1 .000) DICK FITZGERALD (2-1 .667), RED ROLFE (17-27 .386)

Use Name	Pos	Hgt	Wgt	Age	TOTAL G	FG	FGA	%	FT	FTA	%	Ass.	PF	Pts	PER GAME Ass.	PF	Pts.	PLAYOFFS G	FG	FGA	%	FT	FTA	%	Ass	PF	Pts	PPG
Dick Schultz (16g. Cle)	F	6'2	192	29	57	130	548	24	94	138	68	56	123	354	1.0	2.2	6.2											
Leo Mogus (17g. Cle)	F	6'4	205	25	58	259	879	29	235	325	72	84	176	753	1.4	3.0	13.0											
Kleggie Hermsen (11g. Cle)	C	6'9	235	23	32	113	394	29	71	112	63	25	86	297	0.8	2.7	9.3											
Red Wallace (24g. Bos)	G	6'1	185	28	61	225	809	28	106	196	54	58	167	556	1.0	2.7	9.1											
Mike McCarron	G	5'11	180	24	60	236	838	28	177	288	61	59	184	649	1.0	3.1	10.8											
Bob Mullens (26g. NY)	G	6'1	175	24	54	125	445	28	62	104	60	54	94	314	1.0	1.7	5.8											
Dick Fitzgerald	F	6'2	175	25	60	118	495	24	41	60	68	40	89	277	0.7	1.5	4.6											
Nat Militzok (36g. NY)	F	6'3	195	23	56	90	343	26	64	112	57	42	120	244	0.8	2.1	4.4											
Roy Hurley	F-G	6'2	170	24	46	100	447	22	39	64	61	34	85	239	0.7	1.8	5.2											
Harry Miller	C-F	6'4	220	23	53	58	260	22	36	82	44	42	119	152	0.8	2.2	2.9											
Frank Fucarino	F	6'2	175	26	28	53	198	27	34	60	57	7	38	140	0.3	1.4	5.0											
Ralph Siewert (7g. StL)	C	7'1	230	23	21	6	44	14	8	15	53	4	18	20	0.2	0.9	1.0											
Ed Kasid	G	5'11	185	23	8	6	21	29	0	6	0	6	8	12	0.8	1.0	1.5											
Gino Sovran	F-G	6'2	175	22	6	5	15	33	1	2	50	1	5	11	0.2	0.8	1.8											
Hank Biasatti	G	6'	175	21	6	2	5	40	2	4	50	0	3	6	0.0	0.5	1.0											

BOSTON CELTICS 22-38 .367 HONEY RUSSELL

Use Name	Pos	Hgt	Wgt	Age	TOTAL G	FG	FGA	%	FT	FTA	%	Ass.	PF	Pts	PER GAME Ass.	PF	Pts.	PLAYOFFS G	FG	FGA	%	FT	FTA	%	Ass	PF	Pts	PPG
Al Brightman	F	6'2	195	23	58	223	870	26	121	193	63	60	115	567	1.0	2.0	9.8											
Art Spector	F	6'4	200	29	55	123	460	27	83	150	55	46	130	329	0.8	2.4	6.0											
Connie Simmons	C	6'7	210	21	60	246	768	32	128	189	68	62	130	620	1.0	2.2	10.3											
Wyndol Gray	G-F	6'1	175	24	55	139	476	29	72	124	58	47	105	350	0.9	1.9	6.4											
Chuck Hoefer (23g. Tor)	G	5'9	158	29	58	130	514	25	91	139	65	33	142	351	0.6	2.4	6.1											
Tony Kappen (41g. Pit)	G	5'10	175	27	59	128	537	24	128	161	80	28	78	384	0.5	1.3	6.5											
Johnny Simmons	G	6'2	184	22	60	120	429	28	78	127	61	29	78	318	0.5	1.3	5.3											
Jerry Kelly	F	6'3	185	28	43	91	313	29	74	111	67	21	128	256	0.5	3.0	6.0											
Chuck Connors	F-C	6'5	190	25	49	94	380	25	39	84	46	40	129	227	0.8	2.6	4.6											
Dutch Garfinkle (from Roch N.B.L.)	G	6'	190	28	40	81	304	27	17	28	61	58	62	179	1.5	1.6	4.5											
Harold Kottman	C	6'8	220	24	53	59	188	31	47	101	47	17	58	165	0.3	1.1	3.1											
Warren Fenley	F	6'3	190	24	33	31	138	22	23	45	51	16	59	85	0.5	1.8	2.6											
Virgil Vaughn	F	6'4	205	28	17	15	78	19	15	28	54	10	18	45	0.6	1.1	2.6											
Dick Murphy (24g. NY)	G	6'1	180	25	31	15	75	20	4	9	44	8	15	34	0.3	0.5	1.1											
Bob Duffy (11g. Chi)	F	6'4	175	24	17	7	32	22	5	7	71	0	17	19	0.0	1.0	1.1											
Mel Hirsch	G	5'6	165	25	13	9	45	20	1	2	50	10	18	19	0.8	1.4	1.5											
Hal Crisler (FB)	F	6'4	215	23	4	2	6	33	2	2	100	0	6	6	0.0	1.5	1.5											
Don Eliason (FB)	F	6'2	210	28	1	0	1	0	0	0	—	0	1	0	0.0	1.0	0.0											

1946/47 B .A.A. — WESTERN DIVISION

CHICAGO STAGS 39-22 .639 OLE OLSEN defeated Washington 4-2; 81-65, 69-53, H67-55, 69-76, H55-67, H66-61 lost to Philadelphia 1-4; 71-84, 74-85, H72-75, H74-73, 80-83

Use Name	Pos	Hgt	Wgt	Age	TOTAL G	FG	FGA	%	FT	FTA	%	Ass.	PF	Pts	PER GAME Ass.	PF	Pts.	PLAYOFFS G	FG	FGA	%	FT	FTA	%	Ass	PF	Pts	PPG
Jim Seminoff	F	6'2	200	24	60	184	586	31	71	130	55	63	155	439	1.1	2.6	7.3	11	31	132	23	13	19	68	8	27	75	6.8
Tony Jaros	F	6'3	185	26	59	177	613	29	128	181	71	28	156	482	0.5	2.6	8.2	11	40	151	26	22	31	71	4	32	102	9.3
Chick Halbert	C	6'9	225	27	61	280	915	31	213	356	60	46	161	773	0.8	2.6	12.7	11	50	198	25	55	91	60	3	32	155	14.1
Max Zaslofsky	G-F	6'2	170	21	61	336	1020	33	205	278	74	40	121	877	0.7	2.0	14.4	11	60	199	30	29	44	66	4	26	149	13.5
Swede Carlson	G	6'	170	25	59	272	845	32	86	159	54	59	182	630	1.0	3.1	10.7	11	54	200	27	27	44	61	6	31	135	12.3
Mickey Rottner	G	5'10	185	27	56	190	655	29	43	79	54	93	109	423	1.7	1.9	7.6	10	5	43	12	1	4	25	3	10	11	1.1
Doyle Parrack	F-G	6'	165	25	58	110	413	27	52	80	65	20	77	272	0.3	1.3	4.7	7	0	9	0	3	3	100	1	3	3	0.4
Chet Carlisle	F-C	6'5	195	30	51	100	373	27	56	92	61	17	136	256	0.3	2.7	5.0	10	20	88	23	16	28	57	2	33	56	5.6
Wibs Kautz	G	6'	180	31	50	107	420	25	39	73	53	37	114	253	0.7	2.3	5.1	9	10	45	22	2	6	33	0	14	22	2.4
Chuck Gilmur	C-F	6'4	225	24	51	76	253	30	26	66	39	21	139	178	0.4	2.7	3.5	11	29	114	25	6	13	46	1	**45**	64	5.8
Bill Davis	F	6'3	215	25	47	35	146	24	14	41	34	11	92	84	0.2	2.0	1.8	7	2	14	14	2	5	40	0	10	6	0.9
Buck Sydnor	G	5'10	175	25	15	5	26	19	5	10	50	0	6	15	0.0	0.4	1.0											
Garland O'Sheilds	G	6'1	195	25	9	2	11	18	0	2	0	1	8	4	0.1	0.9	0.4											
Norm Baker	G	6'2	180	23	4	0	1	0	0	0	—	0	0	0	0.0	0.0	0.0											
Bob Rensberger	F	6'2	170	25	3	0	7	0	0	0	—	0	4	0	0.0	1.3	0.0											

1946/47 B.B.A. — WESTERN DIVISION (continued)

Use Name	Pos	Hgt	Wgt	Age	TOTAL G	FG	FGA	%	FT	FTA	%	Ass.	PF	Pts	PER GAME Ass.	PF	Pts.	PLAYOFFS G	FG	FGA	%	FT	FTA	%	Ass	PF	Pts	PPG
ST. LOUIS BOMBERS	38-23 .623				**KEN LOEFFLER**													lost to Philadelphia 1-2; 68-73, H73-51, H59-75										
Belus Smawley	F	6'1	195	28	22	113	352	32	36	47	77	10	37	262	0.5	1.7	11.9	3	23	71	32	6	11	55	1	12	52	17.3
Bob Doll	F-C	6'5	195	27	60	194	768	25	134	206	65	22	167	522	0.4	2.8	8.7	3	6	39	15	8	12	67	0	11	20	6.7
Giff Roux	C-F	6'5	195	23	60	142	478	30	70	160	44	17	95	354	0.3	1.6	5.9	3	11	29	38	0	2	0	0	6	22	7.3
Johnny Logan	G	6'2	175	25	61	290	1043	28	190	254	75	78	136	770	1.3	2.2	12.6	3	10	45	22	11	15	73	3	7	31	10.3
George Munroe	G	5'11	180	24	59	164	623	26	86	133	65	17	91	414	0.3	1.5	7.0	3	15	31	**48**	4	7	57	0	8	34	11.3
Don Putman	G	6'1	170	24	58	156	635	25	68	105	65	30	106	380	0.5	1.8	6.6	3	7	24	29	1	4	25	1	7	15	5.0
Cecil Hankins	G	6'1	175	24	55	117	391	30	90	150	60	14	49	324	0.3	0.9	5.9	2	2	7	29	1	2	50	0	1	5	2.5
John Barr	F	6'3	205	28	58	124	438	28	47	79	59	54	164	295	0.9	2.8	5.1											
Aubrey Davis	G-F	6'2	175	25	59	107	381	28	73	115	63	14	136	287	0.2	2.3	4.9	3	2	6	33	3	3	100	0	3	7	2.3
Don Martin	C	6'7	210	26	54	89	304	29	13	31	42	9	75	191	0.2	1.4	3.5	3	4	36	11	2	2	100	1	10	10	3.3
Herschel Baltimore	F	6'4	195	25	58	53	263	20	32	69	46	16	98	138	0.3	1.7	2.4	3	2	10	20	0	1	0	0	3	4	1.3
Deb Smith	F	6'3	180	26	48	32	119	27	9	21	43	6	47	73	0.1	1.0	1.5	1	0	0	—	0	1	0	0	1	0	0.0
Fred Jacobs	F	6'3	175	24	18	19	69	28	12	25	48	5	25	50	0.3	1.4	2.8											
CLEVELAND REBELS	30-30 .500				**DUTCH DEHNERT (17-20 .459), ROY CLIFFORD (13-10 .565)**													lost to New York 1-2; H77-51, 74-86, 71-93										
Mel Riebe	F-G	5'11	190	30	55	276	898	31	111	173	64	67	169	663	1.2	3.1	12.1	3	9	37	24	3	6	50	2	3	21	7.0
Bob Faught	F	6'5	185	25	51	141	478	29	61	106	58	33	97	343	0.6	1.9	6.7	3	11	32	34	3	3	100	1	10	25	8.3
Ed Sadowski (10g. Tor, ST)	C	6'5	255	29	53	329	891	37	219	328	67	46	194	877	0.9	3.7	16.5	3	22	56	39	27	34	79	5	10	71	**23.7**
Frankie Baumholtz (BB)	G	5'10	175	27	45	255	856	30	121	156	78	54	93	631	1.2	2.1	14.0											
Kenny Sailors	G	5'10	176	24	58	229	741	31	119	200	60	134	177	577	2.3	3.1	9.9	2	6	16	38	3	4	75	4	8	15	7.5
George Nostrand (13g. Tor)	C-F	6'8	197	22	61	192	656	29	98	210	47	31	145	482	0.5	2.4	7.9	3	14	40	35	5	7	71	3	10	33	11.0
Nick Shaback	G	5'11	182	28	53	102	385	26	38	53	72	29	75	242	0.5	1.4	4.6	3	6	22	27	3	5	60	0	6	15	5.0
Ray Wertis (18g. Tor)	G	5'11	175	24	61	79	366	22	56	91	62	39	82	214	0.6	1.3	3.5	3	6	26	23	4	5	80	6	6	16	5.3
Ben Schamus	F	6'2	173	28	51	33	165	20	37	59	63	19	83	103	0.4	1.6	2.0	3	6	21	29	5	9	56	2	10	17	5.7
Irv Rothenberg	C	6'8	215	25	29	36	167	22	30	54	56	15	62	102	0.5	2.1	3.5											
Hank Lefkowitz	F	6'2	190	23	24	22	114	19	7	13	54	4	35	51	0.2	1.5	2.1	3	4	18	22	1	1	100	0	4	9	3.0
Ned Endress	F	6'2	200	28	16	3	25	12	8	15	53	4	13	14	0.3	0.8	0.9											
Leon Brown	F	6'3	190	27	5	0	3	0	0	0	—	0	2	0	0.0	0.4	0.0											
Pete Lalich	F	6'2	190	26	1	0	1	0	0	0	—	0	1	0	0.0	1.0	0.0											
Ken Corley	C	6'5	210	—	3	0	0	—	0	0	—	0	0	0	0.0	0.0	0.0											
DETROIT FALCONS	20-40 .333				**GLENN CURTIS (12-23 .343), CINCY SACHS (8-17 .320)**																							
John Janisch	F	6'3	200	26	60	283	983	29	131	198	66	49	132	697	0.8	2.2	11.6											
Ariel Maughan	F	6'4	190	23	59	224	929	24	84	114	74	57	180	532	1.0	3.1	9.0											
Stan Miasek	C-F	6'5	210	22	60	331	1154	29	233	385	61	93	**208**	895	1.6	3.5	14.9											
Hal Brown	G	6'	155	23	54	95	383	25	74	117	63	39	122	264	0.7	2.3	4.9											
Tom King	G	6'	165	22	58	97	410	24	101	160	63	32	102	295	0.6	1.8	5.1											
Bob Dille	F	6'3	200	29	57	111	563	20	74	111	67	40	92	296	0.7	1.6	5.2											
Grady Lewis	F-C	6'7	215	29	60	106	520	20	75	138	54	54	166	287	0.9	2.8	4.8											
Moe Becker (17g. Pit. 6g. Bos)	G	6'1	185	29	43	70	358	20	22	44	50	30	98	162	0.7	2.3	3.8											
Milt Schoon (CO)	C	6'9	230	24	41	43	199	22	34	80	43	12	75	120	0.3	1.8	2.9											
Art Stolkey	G	6'1	180	26	23	36	164	22	30	44	68	38	72	102	1.7	3.1	4.4											
George Pearcy	G	6'1	165	27	37	31	130	24	32	44	73	13	68	94	0.4	1.8	2.5											
Henry Pearcy	G	6'1	170	24	29	24	108	22	25	34	74	7	20	73	0.2	0.7	2.5											
Chet Aubuchon	G	5'10	145	30	30	23	91	25	19	35	54	20	46	65	0.7	1.5	2.2											
Howie McCarty (from Det NBL)	F	6'2	190	27	19	10	82	12	1	10	10	2	22	21	0.1	1.2	1.1											
Harold Johnson (injury)	C	6'6	240	26	27	4	20	20	7	14	50	11	13	15	0.4	0.5	0.6											
PITTSBURGH IRONMEN	15-45 .250				**PAUL BIRCH**																							
Brooms Abramovic	F	6'3	196	27	47	202	834	24	123	178	69	35	161	527	0.7	3.4	11.2											
Colby Gunther	F	6'4	190	22	52	254	756	34	226	351	64	32	117	734	0.6	2.3	14.1											
Harry Zeller	C-F	6'4	210	27	48	120	382	31	122	177	69	31	177	362	0.6	**3.7**	7.5											
Stan Noszka	G	6'1	185	26	58	199	693	29	109	157	69	39	163	507	0.7	2.8	8.7											
Ed Milkovich	G	5'9	170	30	57	99	376	26	83	127	65	37	150	281	0.6	2.6	4.9											
Press Maravich	G	6'	185	26	51	102	375	27	30	58	52	6	102	234	0.1	2.0	4.6											
Mike Bytzura	F	6'3	175	24	60	87	356	24	36	72	50	31	108	210	0.5	1.8	3.5											
John Mills	C	6'8	210	26	47	55	187	29	71	129	55	9	94	181	0.2	2.0	3.9											
Noble Jorgensen	C	6'9	220	21	15	25	112	22	16	25	64	4	40	66	0.3	2.7	4.4											
Joe Fabel	F-G	6'1	190	29	30	25	96	26	13	26	50	2	64	63	0.1	2.1	2.1											
Roger Jorgensen	C-F	6'5	200	26	28	14	54	26	13	19	68	1	36	41	0.0	1.3	1.5											
Walt Miller	F	6'2	190	31	12	7	21	33	9	18	50	6	16	23	0.5	1.3	1.9											
Nat Frankel	F	6'3	197	33	6	4	27	15	8	12	67	3	6	16	0.5	1.0	2.7											
Red Mihalik (to You NBL)	G	6'	180	30	7	3	9	33	0	0	—	0	10	6	0.0	1.4	0.9											
Gorham Getchell	C	6'6	215	26	16	0	8	0	5	5	100	0	5	5	0.0	0.3	0.3											

1946/47 B.A.A. TEAM STATISTICS

Team	Regular Season G	FG	FGA	%	FT	FTA	%	Ass.	Average Points For	Agnst.	Diff.	Playoffs G	FG	FGA	%	FT	FTA	%	Ass.	Average Points For	Agnst.	Diff.
EASTERN DIVISION																						
Washington	60	1723	5794	30	982	1391	71	378	73.8	**63.9**	**+9.9**	6	130	554	23	117	159	74	22	62.8	67.8	-5.0
Philadelphia	60	1510	5384	28	**1098**	1596	69	343	68.6	65.2	+3.4	10	265	953	28	**223**	**289**	**77**	52	75.3	69.4	**+5.9**
New York	60	1465	5255	28	951	1438	66	457	64.7	64.0	+0.7	5	136	500	27	81	132	61	37	70.6	75.2	-4.6
Providence	60	1629	5582	29	1092	**1666**	66	481	72.5	74.2	-1.7											
Toronto	60	1515	5672	27	966	1552	62	463	66.6	71.0	-4.4											
Boston	60	1397	5133	27	811	1375	59	470	60.1	65.0	-4.9											
WESTERN DIVISION																						
Chicago	61	**1879**	**6309**	**30**	939	1550	61	436	**77.0**	73.3	+3.7	11	301	**1193**	25	176	288	61	32	70.7	70.6	+0.1
St. Louis	61	1601	5877	27	862	1400	62	292	66.6	64.1	+2.5	3	82	298	28	36	60	60	6	66.7	**66.3**	+0.4
Cleveland	60	1674	5699	29	903	1428	63	494	70.9	71.8	-0.9	3	**84**	268	**31**	54	74	73	**23**	74.0	76.7	-2.7
Detroit	60	1437	5843	25	923	1494	62	482	63.3	65.3	-2.0											
Pittsburgh	60	1345	4961	27	984	1507	65	272	61.2	676	-6.4											

1946/47 B.A.A. STANDINGS

Team	W	L	Pct.	GB	Record against playoff teams W	L	Pct.	Record against non - playoff teams W	L	Pct.	Home W	L	Pct.	Road W	L	Pct.
EASTERN DIVISION																
Washington Capitols	**49**	11	**.817**	—	**23**	7	**.767**	**26**	4	**.867**	**29**	1	**.967**	**20**	10	**.667**
Philadelphia Warriors	35	25	.583	14	12	18	.400	23	7	.767	23	7	.767	12	18	.400
New York Knickerbockers	33	27	.550	16	13	17	.433	20	10	.667	18	12	.600	15	15	.500
Providence Steamrollers	28	32	.467	21	13	23	.361	15	9	.625	19	11	.633	9	21	.300
Toronto Huskies	22	38	.367	27	11	25	.306	11	13	.458	15	15	.500	7	23	.233
Boston Celtics	22	38	.367	27	9	27	.250	13	11	.542	14	16	.467	8	22	.267
WESTERN DIVISION																
Chicago Stags	39	22	.639	—	17	14	.548	22	8	.733	22	9	.710	17	13	.567
St. Louis Bombers	38	23	.623	1	16	15	.516	22	8	.733	22	8	.733	16	15	.516
Cleveland Rebels	30	30	.500	8.5	10	20	.333	20	10	.667	17	13	.567	13	17	.433
Detroit Falcons	20	40	.333	18.5	9	27	.250	11	13	.458	12	18	.400	8	22	.267
Pittsburgh Ironmen	15	**45**	.250	23.5	5	31	.139	10	**14**	.417	11	**19**	.367	4	**26**	.133

1946/47 B.A.A. INDIVIDUAL LEADERS

SCORING
(Minimum 40 Games Played)

Name	Team	G	FG	FT	Pts.	Avg.
Fulks	Phi	60	475	439	1389	23.2
Sadowski	Tor-Cle	53	329	219	877	16.5
Feerick	Was	55	364	198	926	16.3
Miasek	Det	60	331	233	895	14.9
Zaslofsky	Chi	61	336	205	877	14.4
Calverly	Prov	59	323	199	845	14.3
Gunther	Pit	52	254	226	734	14.1
Baumholtz	Cle	45	255	121	631	14.0
Mogus	Cle-Tor	58	259	235	753	13.0
Halbert	Chi	61	280	213	773	12.7

FIELD GOAL PERCENTAGE
(Minimum 200 Field Goals)

Name	Team	FG	FGA	Pct.
Feerick	Was	364	908	.401
Sadowski	Tor-Cle	329	891	.369
Shannon	Prov	245	722	.339
Gunther	Pit	254	756	.336
Zaslofsky	Chi	336	1020	.329
Carlson	Chi	272	845	.322
C. Simmons	Bos	246	768	.320
Norlander	Was	223	698	.319
Sailors	Cle	229	741	.309
Riebe	Cle	276	898	.307

FREE THROW PERCENTAGE
(Minimum 125 Free Throws)

Name	Team	FT	FTA	Pct.
Scolari	Was	146	180	.811
Kappen	Pit-Bos	128	161	.795
Stutz	NY	133	170	.782
Feerick	Was	198	260	.762
Logan	StL	190	254	.748
Zaslofsky	Chi	205	278	.737
Fulks	Phi	439	601	.730
Mogus	Cle-Tor	235	325	.723
Mearns	Prov	126	175	.720
Janos	Chi	128	181	.707

PERSONAL FOULS

Name	Team	PF
Miasek	Det	208
Fulks	Phi	199
Beenders	Prov	196
Sadowski	Tor-Cle	194
Calverly	Prov	191

ASSISTS PER GAME
(Minimum 40 Games Played)

Name	Team	G	Ass.	Avg.
Calverly	Prov	59	202	3.4
Sailors	Cle	58	134	2.3
Schectman	NY	54	109	2.0
Dallmar	Phi	60	104	1.7
Rottner	Chi	56	93	1.7
Miasek	Det	60	93	1.6
Shannon	Prov	57	84	1.5
Garfinkle	Bos	40	58	1.5
Mogus	Cle-Tor	58	84	1.4
Logan	StL	61	78	13

1947-48 N. B. L.

Jumping into Oblivion

The N.B.L. started the season without a defending champion; the Chicago American Gears had jumped over to the Professional Basketball League of America, this year's new circuit. With the Gears, Youngstown, and Detroit no longer in the league, the N.B.L. added new clubs in Flint and Minneapolis, and resigned itself to the loss of George Mikan and the other Gear players.

Before a month was out, however, Mikan and his mates were back in the N.B.L. The P.B.L.A., a loose circuit of 24 clubs, collapsed two weeks into its season, and the better players from that loop found themselves parcelled out among the N.B.L. teams through a special draft. Ex-Chicago players went to several teams: Flint got Bob Calihan and Stan Patrick, Sheboygan got aging star Bobby McDermott, Rochester got George Ratkovicz, Anderson got Price Brookfield, Tri-Cities got Dick Triptow, and Minneapolis got the plum, George Mikan.

The newborn Lakers already had a prize in Jim Pollard, a superbly graceful all-around forward who had been playing A.A.U. ball since graduating from Stanford in 1942. With the addition of Mikan, the Minneapolis front line was the tops in the league, and ex-Indianapolis guard Herm Schaefer concentrated on feeding the ball in to the big men. Coached by Johnny Kundla of the University of Minnesota, the Lakers easily took first place in the Western Division. The Tri-Cities Blackhawks, Oshkosh All-Stars, and Indianapolis Kautskys captured the remaining playoff berths, with the aging Sheboygan Redskins left out in the cold.

Three clubs in the Eastern Division played up to the level of the Lakers. The Rochester Royals still had little men Bob Davies, Al Cervi, and Red Holzman at the heart of the team, but owner Les Harrison added rookie help in forward Andy Duncan and guard Bobby Wanzer. Harrison's biggest coup, however, came in January, when he purchased 6'9" center Arnie Risen from the financially-troubled Indianapolis team. The slim but mobile Risen gave the Royals their first blue-chip center. Finishing two games back in second place were the Anderson Duffey Packers, a team vastly improved over last season. The Packers were lacking in height, but rookies Frankie Brian and John Hargis triggered an all-out fast break which wore down opposing clubs. Two games behind the Packers came the Ft. Wayne Zollner Pistons. Even after losing several key men in recent years, the Pistons' remaining veterans played smart enough basketball for a .667 season record. Far behind in the final playoff spot were the Syracuse Nationals, while the Toledo Jeeps and Flint Dow A.C.'s finished out of the money. The Dow A.C.'s, who started the season in Flint, Michigan, were crippled when 6'7" star Ted Bokina came down with pleurisy after the final exhibition game and never played in a regular season pro game.

The playoffs shaped up as a tight battle, with Rochester and Minneapolis the favorites and Anderson and Ft. Wayne long shots. Anderson drew the easiest match in the opening round, downing Syracuse in three straight games. The other Eastern series pitted Rochester against Ft. Wayne, and the Royals beat the scrappy Pistons three games to one. In the West, the Lakers did away with Oshkosh in four games, while Tri-Cities eliminated Indianapolis in four games; without the traded Risen, the Kautskys had no one to pit against the Blackhawks' 7' Don Otten.

The Lakers, however, had a match for Otten in Mikan, and the Minneapolis team made short order of the Blackhawks with two straight wins in their semifinal match. The Eastern showdown between Rochester and Anderson featured two running, passing teams with slight, mobile centers. The two clubs split their first two meetings and put everything on the line in game three in Rochester. Red Holzman had missed the second game with a bad leg, but he returned in this vital match to play a solid game at guard. The Royal passing attack clicked perfectly to bring the Rochester crew a smashing 74-48 triumph. The victory was a costly one, however, as a well-placed elbow fractured Arnie Risen's jaw and put him out of service for the finals. The Royals would have to face Mikan and the other Lakers without their top center.

The injury list went on past Risen's name as the Royals prepared for the best-of-five championship series. Holzman's leg still bothered him, a bad knee made Al Cervi a stationary guard, and Fuzzy Levane was ill and playing below par. The Lakers, all healthy, were the almost universal choice to take the crown. With bulky George Ratovicz guarding him, Mikan threw in 26 points in game one to lead the Lakers to an 80-72 victory. Cervi, Holzman, and Levane made only token appearances, and rookie guard Bobby Wanzer led the Royals with 16 points. The Royals did only a slightly better job on Mikan in the second game, as he scored 25 to lead the Lakers to another win, 82-67. Cervi had joined Risen on the totally unavailable list, while Holzman and Levane played briefly. With two wins on their home floor, the Lakers headed to Rochester needing only one more win to wrap up the title. Big George elbowed and hooked his way to 32 points before the Rochester crowd, but the Royals nevertheless scratched out a 74-60 victory to break the ice. Levane, Cervi, and Risen were now counted out, but Holzman played well in the backcourt; the balanced Rochester attack featured 18 points from Andy Duncan and 16 points from playmaker Bob Davies. The Lakers could be held off no longer, however, taking the fourth game behind Mikan's 27 points and Jim Pollard's 19. The Lakers then returned home as N.B.L. champions in their first season on the circuit.

Just before the final round with the Royals, the Lakers had joined four other N.B.L. clubs in the final World Tournament in Chicago. Besides the N.B.L. entries of Minneapolis, Anderson, Indianapolis, Tri-Cities, and Ft. Wayne, the Tournament included the New York Rens, Bridgeport Newfield Steelers, and Wilkes-Barre Barons to make a field of eight. The Rens lacked the strength of their earlier squads, but they still made it to the finals against the Lakers. In the championship game, Mikan poured in 40 points against Sweetwater Clifton and the rest of the Rens as the Lakers won 75-71. As things turned out, the Lakers' victory proved to be the last in this competition as the World Toumament was never held again.

Team	W	L	Pct.	GB	vs. playoff teams W	L	PCT.	vs. non-playoff teams W	L	Pct.	HOME W	L	Pct.	ROAD W	L	Pct.	Average Points G	FT%	For	Agnst.	Diff.	PLAYOFFS Average Points G	FT%	For	Agnst.	Diff.
1947/48 N.B.L. STANDINGS																										
EASTERN DIVISION																										
Rochester	**44**	16	**.733**	—	**28**	14	**.667**	**16**	2	**.889**	26	4	.867	**17**	11	**.607**	60	69	64.6	58.2	+6.4	11	72	68.7	65.5	+3.2
Anderson	42	18	.700	2	27	15	.643	15	3	.931	**27**	2	**.931**	13	15	.464	60	63	**65.0**	59.4	+5.6	6	61	69.0	**65.3**	+3.7
Fort Wayne	40	20	.667	4	25	17	.595	15	3	.889	24	3	.889	14	16	.467	60	68	59.9	56.9	+3.0	4	56	58.3	66.0	-7.7
Syracuse	24	36	.400	20	12	30	.286	12	6	.517	15	14	.517	7	19	.269	60	66	59.3	62.5	+3.2	3	71	59.3	74.0	-15.4
Toledo	22	37	.373	21.5	17	30	.362	5	7	.536	15	13	.536	6	22	.214	59	**70**	55.8	57.1	-1.3					
Flint	8	**52**	.133	36	5	**43**	.104	3	**9**	.241	7	**22**	.241	1	**26**	.037	60	65	58.4	69.4	-11.0					
WESTERN DIVISION																										
Minneapolis	43	17	.717	—	**28**	14	**.667**	15	3	.821	23	5	.821	15	11	.577	60	69	64.1	**56.6**	**+7.5**	10	69	**75.8**	67.3	**+8.5**
Tri-Cities	30	30	.500	13	18	24	.429	12	6	.654	17	9	.654	11	19	.367	60	65	60.9	61.1	-0.2	6	66	71.5	76.2	-4.7
Oshkosh	29	31	.483	14	18	24	.429	11	7	.714	20	8	.714	8	20	.286	60	67	59.7	59.6	+0.1	4	**76**	64.3	70.0	-5.7
Indianapolis	24	35	.407	18.5	12	30	.286	12	5	.630	17	10	.630	5	25	.167	59	66	60.2	63.2	-3.0	4	70	69.0	72.8	-3.8
Sheboygan	23	37	.383	20	13	25	.342	10	2	.481	13	14	.481	8	21	.276	60	64	56.8	60.9	-4.1					

1947/48 N.B.L. — EASTERN DIVISION

Use Name	Pos.	Hgt.	Wgt.	Age	REGULAR SEASON G	FG	FT	FTA	Pct.	Points	PPG	PLAYOFFS G	FG	FT	FTA	Pct.	Point	PPG
ROCHESTER ROYALS — 44-16 .733 — EDDIE MALANOWICZ (40-12 .769), LES HARRISON (4-4 .500)												defeated Fort Wayne 3-1; 65-68, H64-47, H71-62; defeated Anderson 2-1; 71-66, H69-76,H74-48; lost to Minneapolis 1-3; 72-80 67-82, H74-60, H65-75						
Bob Davies (KJ, ankle injury)	F-G	6'1	175	27	48	176	120	160	75	472	9.8	11	56	49	64	77	161	14.6
Andy Duncan	F-C	6'6	195	24	60	200	119	199	60	519	8.7	11	39	23	34	68	101	9.2
Arnie Risen (from Ind, broken jaw)	C	6'9	200	23	28	145	117	161	73	407	14.5	7	35	30	44	68	100	14.3
Al Cervi (SL, KJ, flu)	G-F	5'11	185	30	49	234	187	242	77	655	13.4	6	18	14	19	74	50	8.3
Red Holzman	G	5'10	175	27	60	246	117	182	64	609	10.1	10	35	10	15	67	80	8
Fuzzy Levane (foot injury)	F-G	6'2	190	27	54	147	45	62	73	339	6.3	9	20	2	3	67	42	4.7
Arnie Johnson	C-F	6'5	230	27	57	101	97	147	66	299	5.2	11	23	20	24	83	66	6
George Ratkovicz	C	6'7	225	23	53	79	76	119	64	234	4.4	11	22	16	28	57	60	5.5
Bobby Wanzer (ST)	G-F	6'	172	26	40	55	57	69	83	167	4.2	11	21	24	28	**86**	66	6
Bill Calhoun (ST)	F-G	6'3	180	20	42	31	18	34	53	80	1.9	8	11	2	3	67	24	3
John Mandic	F-C	6'4	205	28	33	32	13	23	57	77	2.3	5	2	2	4	50	6	1.2
Leroy King	C	6'7	200	26	12	3	6	8	75	12	1							
Joe Lord	G	6'1	175	23	4	3	0	1	0	6	1.5							
Ocie Richie	F	6'3	195	26	1	0	1	1	100	1	1							
ANDERSON DUFFY PACKERS — 42-18 .700 — MURRAY MENDENHALL												defeated Syracuse 3-0; H73-56, H72-54, 79-68; lost to Rochester 1-2; H66-71, 76-69, 48-74						
John Hargis	F-G	6'2	180	27	59	235	172	329	52	642	10.9	6	30	25	38	66	85	14.2
Charlie Black	F-C	6'5	200	26	58	148	149	249	60	445	7.7	6	28	10	22	45	66	11
Howie Schultz (BB)	C-F	6'7	200	25	60	213	179	258	69	605	10.1	6	23	9	18	50	55	9.2
Frankie Brian	G	6'1	180	24	69	248	155	210	74	651	11	6	18	11	16	68	47	7.8
Rollie Seltz	G-F	5'10	170	23	59	118	90	119	76	326	5.5	6	11	4	4	100	26	4.3
Milo Komenich (from FtW)	C-F	6'7	220	27	43	120	43	88	49	283	6.6	6	10	7	14	50	27	4.5
Charley Shipp	G	6'1	205	34	55	103	63	95	65	269	4.9	2	2	3	4	75	7	3.5
Ed Stanczak	F-C	6'3	205	26	55	73	61	102	60	207	3.8	6	7	11	18	61	25	4.2
Boag Johnson	G-F	5'11	170	26	57	84	31	53	58	199	3.5	6	15	3	5	60	33	5.5
Price Brookfield	F-G	6'4	200	27	49	82	27	40	68	191	3.9	6	17	9	12	75	43	7.2
Slats Borrevik (to Fli & TC)	C	6'7	215	26	15	13	12	25	48	38	2.5							
Dick Furey (to Fli & TC)	G	6'3	195	22	12	10	5	7	71	25	2.1							
Jim Springer (to Ind)	C	6'9	235	22	6	4	9	14	64	17	2.8							
FORT WAYNE ZOLLNER PISTONS — 40-20 .667 — CARL BENNETT												lost to Rochester 1-3; H56-65. H68-64, 67-64, 62-71						
Ralph Hamilton (leg injury)	F-G	6'1	188	26	49	143	101	135	75	387	7.9	2	1	2	4	50	4	2
Blackie Towery	F-C	6'4	210	27	59	139	129	187	69	407	6.9	4	7	5	10	50	19	4.8
Jake Pelkington (broken nose)	C	6'6	220	30	54	174	156	214	73	504	9.3	4	14	6	13	46	34	8.5
Curly Armstrong (broken finger)	G-F	5'11	170	29	53	148	139	206	67	435	8.2	4	13	11	16	69	37	9.3
Bob Tough	G	6'	185	27	60	129	48	71	68	306	5.1	4	9	3	3	100	21	5.3
Bob Kinney	C-F	6'6	215	25	58	149	92	147	63	390	6.7	4	20	3	8	38	43	10.8
Richie Niemiera	G-F	6'1	165	26	59	118	97	135	72	333	5.6	4	10	7	8	88	27	6.8
Jack Smiley	F-G	6'3	190	25	60	105	90	135	67	300	5	4	7	6	8	75	20	5
Dick Triptow (from TC)	G-F	6'	170	25	48	74	75	119	63	223	4.6	4	9	1	3	33	19	4.8
Walt Kirk (leg injury)	F	6'3	173	23	45	62	44	90	49	168	3.7	3	3	1	6	17	7	2.3
Ken Menke	G	6'	168	25	44	39	45	57	79	123	2.8	1	1	0	0	—	2	2
Milo Komenich (to And)	F-C	6'7	220	27	7	7	1	7	14	15	2.1							

Use Name	Pos	Hgt	Wgt	Age	REGULAR SEASON G	FG	FT	FTA	Pct.	Points	PPG	PLAYOFFS G	FG	FT	FTA	Pct.	Points	PPG
					1947/48 N.B.L. — EASTERN DIVISION (continued)													
SYRACUSE NATIONALS	**24-36 .400**				**BENNY BORGMANN (21-34 .382), EMIL BARBONI (0-1 .000), DAN BIASONE (3-1 .750)**													
									lost to Anderson 0-3; 56 73, 54-72, H68-79									
John Chaney (broken hand)	F	6'3	190	27	40	107	78	103	76	292	7.3	3	6	5	11	45	17	5.7
Jim Homer	F-C	6'5	220	24	56	250	198	324	61	698	12.5	3	11	14	18	78	36	12.0
Mike Novak	C	6'9	220	32	60	211	124	201	62	546	9.1	3	9	4	5	80	22	7.3
Paul Seymour (from Bal BAA)	G	6'2	180	19	30	79	47	64	73	205	6.8	3	12	5	7	71	29	9.7
Jerry Rizzo	G	5'8	165	29	60	160	217	303	72	537	9.0	3	6	16	18	89	28	9.3
Steve Sharkey	G-F	6'	190	29	60	108	64	110	58	280	4.7	3	4	2	3	67	10	3.3
Bob Kitterman	G-F	6'	180	22	54	117	38	53	72	272	5.0	3	5	2	2	100	12	4.0
George Nelmark (rib injury)	G	6'1	185	30	52	76	51	85	60	203	3.9	3	1	0	1	0	2	0.7
Brooms Abramovic (from StL-Bal BAA)	F-C	6'3	196	28	35	72	42	54	78	186	5.3	3	5	2	3	67	12	4.0
Eddie Oram	F	6'3	175	33	24	39	29	44	66	107	4.5							
Bob O'Shaughnessy	G	6'	175	26	25	41	19	31	61	101	4.0							
Virgil Vaughn	F-C	6'4	205	—	11	29	5	9	56	63	5.7	3	2	6	11	55	10	3.3
Chick Meehan	F	6'1	195	30	22	16	10	16	63	42	1.9							
Bill DeVenzio	G	6'	185	22	6	2	7	9	78	11	1.8							
Garland O'Shields	F	6'1	195	26	5	3	3	4	75	9	1.8							
Roy Hurley (from TC)	G	6'2	170	25	4	1	4	5	80	6	1.5							
Bob Fitzgerald	F	6'5	195	26	1	0	0	1	0	0	0.0							
Ken Walters	G	6'	170	25	1	0	0	0	—	0	0.0							
Johnny Sebastian	G	6'1	185	26	1	0	0	0	—	0	0.0							
TOLEDO JEEPS	**22-37 .373**				**JULIE RIVLIN**													
Hal Tidrick	F	6'1	190	32	59	267	189	243	78	723	12.3							
Dick Mehen	F-C	6'6	195	25	57	151	85	125	68	387	6.8							
Hany Boykoff	C	6'10	235	25	59	225	124	161	77	574	9.7							
George Sobek (illness)	G-F	6'	180	27	48	118	124	170	73	360	7.5							
Fran Curran	G	6'	175	25	58	129	119	156	76	377	6.5							
Bernie Mehen	F	6'4	195	29	55	118	46	72	64	282	5.1							
Dale Hamilton	G-F	6'	198	28	53	93	62	133	47	248	4.7							
Johnny Schick	F-C	6'6	230	31	55	64	23	37	62	151	2.7							
Julie Rivlin (leg injury)	G	5'11	180	30	40	28	16	25	64	72	1.8							
Jerry Bush (CC)	F	6'3	210	31	22	25	15	19	79	65	3.0							
Jackie Goldsmith	G	5'7	160	25	12	20	6	9	67	46	3.8							
Wyndol Gray (KJ)	G	—	—	—	2	2	2	4	50	6	3.0							
FLINT DOW A.C.'s (started season in Midland, Mich.)	**8-52 .133**				**JIMMY WALSH (0-2 .000), MATT ZUNIC (8-50 .138)**													
Ray Patterson	F	6'2	195	24	56	147	72	117	62	366	6.5							
Bob Calihan	F	6'3	200	29	56	273	260	371	70	806	14.4							
Milt Schoon	C	6'9	230	25	55	114	120	214	56	348	6.3							
Stan Patrick	G-F	6'3	215	26	48	149	90	144	63	388	8.1							
Hal Gensichen (from Ind) (Illness)	G	5'11	170	26	4	18	7	13	54	43	10.8							
Matt Zunic (leg injury)	G	6'3	195	28	57	123	85	128	66	331	5.8							
Jim Gibbs	C-F	6'5	195	28	55	107	92	147	63	306	5.6							
Danny Wagner (FJ)	G	6'	170	24	50	96	59	92	64	251	5.0							
Milt Ticco (to Ind & Sheb)	F-G	6'3	205	26	30	74	25	35	71	173	5.8							
Keith Carey	G	6'3	190	27	37	33	45	64	70	111	3.0							
John Janish (from Bos & Prov BAA)	F-G	6'3	200	27	36	36	21	28	75	93	2.6							
Danny Smick	F-C	6'5	215	29	35	26	24	43	56	76	2.2							
Charlie Joachim	G	6'2	184	27	15	19	27	37	73	65	4.3							
Fred Rehm (to Osh)	G	6'3	195	26	14	19	23	30	77	61	4.4							
Bill Sattler	C	6'8	197	31	7	15	15	25	60	45	6.4							
Slats Borrevik (from And, to TC)	C	6'8	215	26	5	6	2	7	29	14	2.8							
Hal Korovin	C-G	6'5	205	22	3	4	3	5	60	11	3.7							
Frank Carswell	G	6'	185	28	4	4	2	2	100	10	2.5							
Paul Herman	G	6'1	175	26	2	1	1	3	33	3	1.5							
Dick Furey (from And, to TC)	F	6'3	195	22	1	1	0	2	0	2	2.0							
John Gibbs	G	6'6	190	32	2	0	0	0	—	0	0.0							
					1947/48 N.B.L. — WESTERN DIVISION													
MINNEAPOLIS LAKERS	**43-17 .717**				**JONNNY KUNDLA**				defeated Oshkosh 3-1; H80-68, H88-65, 51-69, 61-55									
									defeated Tri-Cities 2-0; 98-79, H83-59									
									defeated Rochester 3-1; H80-12, H82-67, 60-74, 75-65									
Jack Owan (broken wrist)	F-G	6'4	200	26	55	128	50	73	68	306	5.6	10	27	5	9	56	59	5.9
Jim Pollard	F-C	6'5	190	25	59	310	140	207	68	760	12.9	10	48	27	41	66	123	12.3
George Mikan	C	6'10	245	23	56	**406**	**383**	**509**	75	**1195**	**21.3**	10	**88**	**68**	**96**	71	**244**	**24.4**
Swede Carlson (KJ)	G-F	6'	170	27	58	205	65	109	60	475	8.2	9	17	4	10	40	38	4.2
Herm Schaefer (from Ind)	G	6'	175	28	54	108	72	90	80	288	5.3	10	51	31	38	82	133	13.3
Tony Janos	F-G	6'3	185	27	58	95	83	114	73	273	4.7	10	29	22	33	67	80	8.0
Don Smith	G-F	6'2	190	27	57	69	62	94	66	200	3.5	10	13	9	12	75	35	3.5
Paul Napolitano	F-G	6'2	185	25	52	72	11	21	52	155	3.0	9	8	4	5	80	20	2.2
Johnny Jorgensen (from Chi & Bal BAA)	F-G	6'2	185	26	38	37	27	49	55	101	2.7	10	11	4	8	50	26	2.6
Bill Durkee	G-F	6'3	205	26	23	15	11	24	46	41	1.8							
Bob Gerber (to TC)	F-C	6'5	220	31	15	13	10	22	45	36	2.4							
Jack Rocker (to Phi BAA)	F-C	6'5	186	25	5	2	0	0	—	4	0.8							
Ken Exel	G	6'1	178	27	5	1	2	6	33	4	0.8							
Joe Patanelli (hip injury)	F	6'3	205	28	5	1	2	5	40	4	0.8							
Warren Ajax	F-C	6'2	170	26	3	0	1	2	50	1	0.3							
Ted Cook (FB)	G-C	6'	160	26	2	0	0	0	—	0	0.0							

Use Name	Pos.	Hgt.	Wgt.	Age	REGULAR SEASON G	FG	FT	FTA	Pct.	Points	PPG	PLAYOFFS G	FG	FT	FTA	Pct.	Points	PPG
					1947/48 N.B.L. — WESTERN DIVISION (continued)													
TRI-CITIES BLACKHAWKS	30-30 .500		NAT HICKEY (9-12 .429), BILLY HASSETT (1-0 1.000) BOBBY McDERMOTT (20-18 .526)									defeated Indianapolis 3-1- 77-67, 70-89, H70-59, H74-61 lost to Minneapolis 0-2; H79-98, 59-83						
Whitey Von Nieda	F-G	6'1	175	25	60	276	174	287	61	726	12.1	6	41	15	28	54	97	16.2
Joe Camic	F-C	6'5	210	25	60	129	75	113	66	333	5.6	6	11	9	12	75	31	5.2
Don Otten	C	7'	245	26	60	282	260	392	66	824	13.7	6	34	30	38	79	98	16.3
Billy Hassett	G	6'	180	26	56	199	203	269	75	601	10.7	6	18	17	26	65	53	8.8
Bobby McDermott (from Sheb)	G	5'11	185	33	37	191	67	93	72	449	12.1	6	26	7	9	78	59	9.8
Ed Lewinski	F-G	6'4	210	27	48	59	39	67	58	157	3.3	6	13	1	3	33	27	4.5
Howie Rader (SL)	G-F	6'1	190	26	45	44	29	54	54	117	2.6	6	8	6	12	50	22	3.7
Mel Thurston (to Prov BAA)	G	6'	175	28	34	36	38	61	62	110	3.2							
Luther Harris (from Sheb)	F	6'3	195	24	23	26	33	55	60	85	3.7	6	7	9	14	64	23	3.8
Bob Hubbard (to Prov BAA)	F-C	6'6	215	25	20	27	22	26	85	76	3.8							
Dick Triptow (to FtW)	G	6'	170	25	9	18	12	19	63	48	5.3							
Roy Hurley (to Syr)	F-G	6'2	170	25	12	18	9	16	56	45	3.8							
Slats Borrevik (from And & Fli)	C	6'8	215	26	30	14	8	23	35	36	1.2	5	4	5	7	71	13	2.6
Johnny Ezersky (to Prov BAA)	F	6'3	175	26	5	9	5	8	63	23	4.6							
Bob Skarda	G-F	6'3	190	22	8	5	0	1	0	10	1.3	6	1	1	2	50	3	0.5
Bob Gerber (from Min)	F-C	6'5	220	31	7	3	0	5	0	6	0.9							
Al Grenert (SL)	F-G	6'	190	28	3	2	0	0	—	4	1.3	6	1	1	2	50	3	0.5
Nat Hickey (to Prov BAA)	G-F	5'11	190	45	3	1	1	1	100	3	1.0							
Dick Furey (from And & Fli)	G	6'3	195	22	1	1	0	0	—	0	0.0							
Jimmy Joyce	F-G	6'5	195	23	4	0	1	1	100	1	0.3							
Ray Ramsey (FB,broken collarbone)	G-F	6'2	166	26	2	0	0	0	—	0	0.0							
Paul Anthony	F-G	6'5	195	23	1	0	0	0	—	0	0.0							
OSHKOSH ALL-STARS	29-31 .483		LON DARLING									lost to Minneapolis 1-3; 68-80, 65-88, H69-51, H55-61						
Bob Carpenter	F	6'5	200	30	60	211	160	213	75	582	9.7	4	7	12	14	86	26	6.5
Gene Englund	F-C	6'5	205	30	58	246	242	333	73	734	12.7	4	20	11	14	79	51	12.8
Leroy Edwards (ST)	C-F	6'4	230	33	46	76	142	205	69	294	6.4	4	13	15	23	65	41	10.3
Glen Selbo	G-F	6'3	195	21	59	157	62	100	62	376	6.4	4	5	5	5	100	15	3.8
Walt Lautenbach	G	6'2	190	25	60	159	36	60	60	354	5.9	4	14	5	6	83	33	8.3
Jack Maddox	F	6'3	190	26	60	146	59	90	66	351	5.9	4	4	1	1	100	9	2.3
Clint Wager	F-C	6'6	230	27	59	90	56	93	60	236	4.0	3	2	0	2	0	4	1.3
Floyd Volker	F-C	6'4	205	25	57	102	31	66	47	235	4.1	4	12	4	5	80	28	7.0
Bill Hapac (ankle injury)	G-F	6'2	200	29	47	78	74	119	62	230	4.9	4	6	11	16	69	23	5.8
Fred Rehm (from Fli)	G	6'3	195	26	26	21	30	42	71	72	2.8	4	4	9	10	90	17	4.3
Eddie Riska (elbow injury)	G-F	6'	180	28	18	21	15	24	63	57	3.2	4	1	8	10	80	10	2.5
Bill McDonald (VR)	G	6'3	190	31	26	12	11	21	52	35	1.3							
Bob Sullivan	F	6'	180	26	13	4	4	5	80	12	0.9							
Abel Rodrigues	G	6'	175	25	8	4	1	2	50	9	1.1							
Ted Scalissi (FB)	G	5'8	160	26	7	1	3	3	100	5	0.7							
INDIANAPOLIS KAUTSKYS	24-35 .407		GLENN CURTIS (2-2 .500), LEO KLIER (1-2 .333), BRUCE HALE (21-31 .404)									lost to Tri-Cities 1-3; H67-77, H89-70, 59-70, 61-74						
Leo Klier	F	6'2	170	24	56	227	152	223	68	606	10.8	4	16	17	23	74	49	12.3
Bill Closs	F-C	6'6	195	25	55	162	72	123	59	396	7.2	4	15	7	13	54	37	9.3
Arnie Risen (to Roch)	C	6'9	200	23	33	137	124	191	65	398	12.1							
Bruce Hale	G-F	6'1	170	29	48	196	155	215	72	547	11.4	4	21	20	25	80	62	15.5
Fred Lewis (from Sheb)	G	6'2	195	26	17	66	35	50	70	167	9.8	4	18	5	8	63	41	10.3
George Glamack	C-F	6'8	240	29	57	215	162	244	66	592	10.4	4	24	20	28	71	68	17.0
Ernie Andres	G	6'1	200	29	47	106	47	75	63	259	5.5	4	1	3	3	100	5	1.3
Hal Gensichen (to Fli)	G	5'11	170	25	32	69	58	88	66	196	6.1							
Fritz Nagy	F-G	6'2	185	23	39	42	42	63	67	126	3.2	4	1	6	8	75	8	2.0
Bob Dietz	G-F	6'1	165	30	37	48	25	45	56	121	3.3	4	3	0	1	0	6	1.5
Jim Springer (from And)	C-F	6'9	235	22	19	8	16	26	62	32	1.7	3	0	0	2	0	0	0.0
Ed Bogdanski	F	6'4	220	26	19	15	2	11	18	32	1.7							
Don Grate	F-G	6'2	185	25	11	14	3	6	50	31	2.8							
Woody Norris	F-G	6'1	170	28	10	9	7	11	64	25	2.5							
Herm Schaefer (to Minn)	G	6'	175	28	3	2	6	6	100	10	3.3							
Milt Ticco (from Fli, to Sheb)	F	6'3	205	26	10	3	3	3	100	9	0.9							
Roy Pugh	F-C	6'6	210	24	4	1	2	4	50	4	1.0							
Jack Forestieri (to Sheb)	G-F	—	—	19	1	1	2	4	50	4	4.0							
Del Loranger	F	6'3	180	27	1	0	0	0	—	0	0.0							
SHEBOYGAN REDSKINS	23-37 .383		BOBBY MCDERMOTT (4-5 .444), DOXIE MOORE (19-32 .373)															
Max Morris (FB)	F	6'2	195	22	39	132	132	215	61	396	10.2							
Mike Todorovich	F-C	6'5	230	24	60	277	223	343	65	777	13.0							
Ed Dancker	C	6'7	220	33	58	109	78	155	50	296	5.1							
Paul Cloyd	G-F	6'2	180	25	60	213	129	181	71	555	9.3							
Fred Lewis (to Ind) (SL)	G	6'2	195	26	27	103	66	87	76	272	10.1							
Les Deaton	F-C	6'4	210	24	51	83	71	119	60	237	4.6							
Al Lucas	G-F	6'3	195	25	58	98	39	56	70	235	4.1							
Bob Bolyard	G	6'	185	27	56	72	50	73	68	194	3.5							
Bobby McDermott (to TC)	G	6'	185	33	16	54	30	39	77	138	8.6							
Luther Harris (ST, to TC)	F	6'3	195	24	24	50	37	61	61	137	5.7							
Milt Ticco (from Fli & Ind)	G	6'3	205	26	20	35	12	13	92	82	4.1							
Bob Dykstra	C	6'9	230	25	51	19	26	52	50	64	1.3							
Kenny Suesens	G	6'1	185	31	11	3	5	15	33	11	1.0							
Fred Gantt	F-G	6'3	170	25	6	4	3	3	100	11	1.8							
Jack Forestieri (from Ind)	G-F	—	—	19	4	0	1	1	100	1	0.3							
Cecil Hankins (from Bos BAA)	G	6'1	175	25	1	0	1	1	100	1	1.0							

1947-48 B.A.A.

A Dull and Nameless Champion

The B.A.A. came out of last season on shaky legs. Attendance and press coverage of league games fell far short of expectations, and the franchises in Cleveland, Detroit, Pittsburgh, and Toronto folded over the summer. With three-fifths of the Western Division gone and league enrollment down to seven clubs, league president Maurice Podoloff acted to get the circuit back into working order. He talked the Baltimore Bullets into jumping over from the American Basketball League, the old East Coast circuit which was living out its last few seasons in minor-league fashion. With only eight teams instead of eleven, Podoloff pared down the schedule from 60 to 48 games, and put Washington and Baltimore in the Western Division with Chicago and St. Louis.

But even with the shaky condition of the league, the B.A.A. clubs generally strengthened themselves with a tonic of fresh talent. Players from the disbanded clubs helped some of the teams; Boston got veterans Ed Sadowski and Mel Reibe, Baltimore signed ex-N.B.L. players Kleggie Hermsen and Dick Schulz, Providence wound up with guard Kenny Sailors after he made quick stops in Chicago and Philadelphia, and Chicago picked up Stan Miasek, last season's all-league center. After getting Miasek, the Stags then dealt their center, Chick Halbert, to the Philadelphia Warriors, who needed a big man.

Several rookies also brightened the B.A.A. scene. The New York Knicks signed guard Sid Tannenbaum, a popular player from N.Y.U. and forward Carl Braun from Colgate. Chicago added Andy Phillip and Gene Vance, two of the Illinois Whiz Kids who led their school to Big Ten championships during the War. St. Louis signed center Red Rocha from Oregon State, and Baltimore inked forward Paul Hoffman of Purdue. Although none of these rookies were as famous as George Mikan, they nevertheless had reputations which added to the big-league image of the B.A.A. Another key addition to the league was New York coach Joe Lapchick, a representative of the best of old-time pro ball, and more recently the popular coach at St. John's.

The best news for the league's survival was a torrid first-place battle in both divisions. All four Western teams fought down to the wire in a pack, with St. Louis finishing at 29-19 and Baltimore, Chicago, and Washington all at 28-20. The Bombers now had a top center in rookie Rocha to go along with backcourt aces Johnny Logan and Belus Smawley. The Stags got important help from newcomers Miasek, Phillip, and Vance, but holdover guard Max Zaslofsky led the team in scoring with a 21.0 average. The Washington Caps, transplanted to the Western Division, fielded essentially the same team as last year's first-place entry, headed by guard Bob Feerick. Baltimore, the new club on the block, had a veteran squad which played methodical, ball-control basketball. Player coach Buddy Jeannette brought in N.B.L. veterans Kleggie Hermsen, Dick Schulz, and Chick Reiser, traded for centers Connie Simmons and Grady Lewis during the season, and had a poised rookie in Paul Hoffman.

The Eastern Division race came down to a struggle between Philadelphia and New York. The Warriors, last year's playoff champs, added a strong center in Chick Halbert to complement forwards Joe Fulks and Howie Dallmar; Fulks led the B.A.A. with a 22.1 scoring average although he trailed Max Zaslofsky in total points scored. The Knicks finished one game back with a quartet of talented young players: Carl Braun, Bud Palmer, Dick Holub, and Sid Tannenbaum. The 20-year-old Braun used his deadly one-handed shot to score 47 points against Providence on December 6, and he soon added to his arsenal a jump shot which he learned from Palmer, a handsome forward from Princeton. Tannenbaum, from N.Y.U. and Holub, from L.I.U., both had lots of past exposure in Madison Square Garden.

The two New England clubs fared the worst in the league. The Boston Celtics had the all-league center in Ed Sadowski but little else, while the Providence Steamrollers had a stable of fine guards with no one of note up front. The Celtics captured the final playoff spot with a 20-28 record, while Providence was the league punching bag at 6-42.

The regular season eliminated only Providence from the playoffs, since three Western clubs were in a deadlock for the final two playoff spots. A round robin was set up, with Chicago beating Washington and Baltimore beating Chicago. The Caps were thus shut out of the playoffs despite a record only one game below the best in the league.

The playoff procedure was the same as last year, with first, second, and third place finishers meeting each other in the opening round. The first-place Bombers and Warriors split the first six games of their series before the ailing St. Louis squad went down to a crushing 85-46 defeat in the final game at Philadelphia. In the second place matchup, New York and Baltimore split their first two games and met in the rubber game in Baltimore; the Knicks held a three-point lead with less than two minutes to play, but the Bullets fired back to surge out to an 84-77 victory. The third place series also went the full route of three games, with the Chicago Stags eliminating Boston.

Baltimore and Chicago met to decide an opponent for Philadelphia in the finals, and the old pro Bullets proved a match for the fast-breaking Stags. With Connie Simmons continuing to show the hot hand he showed late in the regular season after coming over from Boston, the Bullets took 73-67 and 89-72 victories to head into the championship round.

The defending champion Warriors confirmed their status as favorites by whipping the Bullets 71-60 in the opening game before 7,201 fans in Philadelphia. The Warriors evidently began relishing their victory too soon when they led 41-20 at halftime in the second game; the Bullets came on in the last half to win a 66-63 decision to even the series. The Bullets then ran off 72-70 and 78-75 victories in Baltimore to take full.charge of the series. The Warriors took the next game in Philadelphia by a score of 91-82, but the Bullets ended it with an 88-73 win on their own home floor. With the Bullets, a dull club to watch and one without any big-name players, as reigning champs, the B.A.A. couldn't honestly hold up its champion as the best pro basketball had to offer. But better things were on the way, starting next year.

1947/48 B.A.A. — EASTERN DIVISION

PHILADELPHIA WARRIORS 27-21 .563 **EDDIE GOTTLIEB** defeated St. Louis 4-3; 58-60, 65-64, H84-56, 51-56, 62-69, H84-61, 85-46
lost to Baltimore 2-4; H71-60, H63-66, 70-72, 75-78, H91-82, 73-88

Use Name	Pos	Hgt	Wgt	Age	TOTAL G	FG	FGA	%	FT	FTA	%	Ass.	PF	Pts	PER GAME Ass.	PF	Pts.	PLAYOFFS G	FG	FGA	%	FT	FTA	%	Ass	PF	Pts	PPG
Howie Dallmar	F	6'4	202	25	48	215	781	28	157	211	74	**120**	141	587	2.5	2.9	12.2	13	38	178	21	30	48	63	**37**	**55**	106	8.2
Joe Fulks	F	6'5	190	26	43	326	**1258**	26	**297**	309	96	26	162	949	0.6	3.8	**22.1**	13	**92**	**380**	24	**98**	**121**	81	3	**55**	**282**	**21.7**
Chick Halbert (6g. Chi)	C	6'9	225	28	46	156	605	26	140	220	64	32	126	452	0.7	2.7	9.8	13	49	185	26	51	84	61	4	45	149	11.5
George Senesky	G	6'2	180	25	47	158	570	28	98	147	67	52	90	414	1.1	1.9	8.8	13	50	159	31	29	45	64	10	33	129	9.9
Angelo Musi	G	5'9	145	29	43	134	485	28	51	73	70	10	56	319	0.2	1.3	7.4	13	26	129	20	21	28	75	11	30	73	5.6
Jerry Fleishman	F-G	6'2	190	25	46	119	501	24	95	138	69	43	122	333	0.9	2.7	7.2	7	5	29	17	6	8	75	2	7	16	2.3
Hank Beenders (21g. Prov)	C	6'6	185	31	45	76	269	28	51	82	62	13	99	203	0.3	2.2	4.5	12	8	35	23	7	13	54	4	15	23	1.9
Ralph Kaplowitz	G	6'2	170	28	48	71	292	24	47	60	78	19	100	189	0.4	2.1	3.9	13	32	93	34	22	29	76	7	22	86	6.6
Chink Crossin	G	6'1	165	24	39	29	121	24	13	23	57	20	28	71	0.5	0.7	1.8	10	16	49	33	8	9	89	10	18	40	4.0
Art Hillhouse (VR)	C	6'7	230	31	11	14	71	20	30	37	81	3	30	58	0.3	2.7	5.3											
Stan Brown	F	6'3	200	18	19	19	71	27	12	19	63	1	16	50	0.1	0.8	2.6											
Bob O'Brien	F	6'4	190	20	22	17	81	21	15	26	58	1	40	49	0.0	1.8	2.2	9	9	38	24	10	15	67	3	13	28	3.1
Jack Rocker (from Min NBL)	C	6'5	186	25	9	8	22	36	1	1	100	3	2	17	0.3	0.2	1.9											

Matt Guokas-leg amputated after auto accident in June 1947

NEW YORK KNICKERBOCKERS 26-22 .542 **JOE LAPCHICK** lost to Baltimore 1-2; 81-85, H79-60, 77-84

Use Name	Pos	Hgt	Wgt	Age	TOTAL G	FG	FGA	%	FT	FTA	%	Ass.	PF	Pts	PER GAME Ass.	PF	Pts.	PLAYOFFS G	FG	FGA	%	FT	FTA	%	Ass	PF	Pts	PPG
Carl Braun	F	6'5	180	20	47	276	854	32	119	183	65	61	102	671	1.3	2.2	14.3	3	12	41	29	6	10	60	2	6	30	10.0
Bud Palmer	F	6'4	180	26	48	224	710	32	174	234	74	45	149	622	0.9	3.1	13.0	3	16	38	42	10	13	77	0	17	42	14.0
Dick Holub	C	6'6	205	26	48	195	662	29	114	180	63	37	159	504	0.8	3.3	10.5	3	9	36	25	8	14	57	0	12	26	8.7
Sid Tannenbaum	G	6'	160	22	24	90	360	25	62	74	84	37	33	242	1.5	1.4	10.1	3	11	33	33	8	11	73	4	8	30	10.0
Stan Stutz	G	5'10	175	27	47	109	501	22	113	135	**84**	57	121	331	1.2	2.6	7.0	3	3	11	27	9	11	82	1	9	15	5.0
Tommy Byrnes	G-F	6'3	175	24	47	117	410	29	65	103	63	17	56	299	0.4	1.2	6.4	3	11	27	41	4	12	33	2	7	26	8.7
Lee Knorek	C	6'7	215	26	48	99	369	27	61	120	51	50	171	259	1.0	3.6	5.4	3	14	34	41	10	13	77	5	10	38	12.7
Ray Kuka	F	6'3	200	25	44	89	273	33	50	84	60	27	117	228	0.6	2.7	5.2	3	3	10	30	2	2	100	0	12	8	2.7
Butch Van Breda Kolff	G	6'3	185	25	44	53	192	28	74	120	62	29	81	180	0.7	1.8	4.1	3	6	16	38	10	14	71	2	8	22	7.3
Leo Gottlieb	G	5'11	180	27	27	59	288	20	13	21	62	12	36	131	0.4	1.3	4.9											
Paul Noel	F	6'4	185	23	29	40	138	29	19	30	63	3	41	99	0.1	1.4	3.4	3	0	7	0	0	1	0	0	4	0	0.0
Wat Misaka	G	5'7	150	24	3	3	13	23	1	3	33	0	7	7	0.0	2.3	2.3											

BOSTON CELTICS 20-28 .417 **HONEY RUSSELL** lost to Chicago 1-2; H72-79, H81-77, H74-81

Use Name	Pos	Hgt	Wgt	Age	TOTAL G	FG	FGA	%	FT	FTA	%	Ass.	PF	Pts	PER GAME Ass.	PF	Pts.	PLAYOFFS G	FG	FGA	%	FT	FTA	%	Ass	PF	Pts	PPG
Eddie Ehlers	F	6'3	198	24	40	104	417	25	78	144	54	44	92	286	1.1	2.3	7.2	(injury)										
Mike Bloom (34g. Bal)	F-C	6'6	190	32	48	174	640	27	160	229	70	38	116	508	0.8	2.4	10.6	3	11	42	26	14	19	74	2	10	36	12.0
Ed Sadowski	C	6'5	255	30	47	308	953	32	294	**422**	70	74	182	910	1.6	3.9	19.4	3	19	55	35	23	38	61	6	17	61	20.3
Mel Riebe	G-F	5'11	190	31	48	202	653	31	85	137	62	41	137	489	0.9	2.9	10.2	3	14	43	33	14	20	70	3	10	42	14.0
Saul Mariaschin	G	5'11	165	23	43	125	463	27	83	117	71	60	121	333	1.4	2.8	7.7	3	10	42	24	9	14	64	1	12	29	9.7
Dutch Garfinkle	G	6'	200	29	43	114	380	30	35	46	76	59	78	263	1.4	1.8	6.1	3	7	23	30	8	10	80	7	15	22	7.3
Art Spector	F	6'4	200	30	48	67	243	28	60	92	65	17	106	194	0.4	2.2	4.0	3	2	9	22	2	4	50	0	9	6	2.0
Gene Stump	F	6'2	185	24	43	59	247	24	24	38	63	18	66	142	0.4	1.5	3.3	3	1	3	33	0	0	—	0	2	2	0.7
Stan Noszka	G	6'1	185	27	22	27	97	28	24	35	69	4	52	78	0.2	2.4	3.5	3	10	30	33	5	8	63	2	11	25	8.3
George Munroe	G	5'11	180	25	21	27	91	30	17	26	65	3	20	71	0.1	1.0	3.4	3	1	5	20	2	2	100	1	2	4	1.3
Cecil Hankins (to Sheb NBL)	G	6'1	175	25	25	23	116	20	24	35	69	8	28	70	0.3	1.1	2.8											
Jack Hewson	F-C	6'6	195	23	24	22	89	25	21	30	70	1	9	65	0.0	0.4	2.7											
Chuck Connors	F	6'5	190	26	4	5	13	38	2	3	67	1	5	12	0.3	1.3	3.0											
Chuck Hoefer	G	5'9	158	30	7	3	19	16	4	8	50	3	17	10	0.4	2.4	1.4											

PROVIDENCE STEAMROLLERS 6-42 .125 **HANK SOAR (2-17 .105), NAT HICKEY (4-25 .138)**

Use Name	Pos	Hgt	Wgt	Age	TOTAL G	FG	FGA	%	FT	FTA	%	Ass.	PF	Pts	PER GAME Ass.	PF	Pts.
Johnny Ezersky (from TC NBL)	F	6'3	175	26	25	95	376	25	63	104	61	16	62	253	0.6	2.5	10.1
Lee Robbins	F	6'3	175	24	31	72	260	28	51	93	55	7	93	195	0.2	3.0	6.3
George Nostrand	C	6'8	197	23	45	196	660	30	129	239	54	30	148	521	0.7	3.3	11.6
Kenny Sailors (1g. Chi, 2g. Phi)	G	5'10	176	25	44	207	689	30	110	159	69	59	162	524	1.3	3.7	11.9
Ernie Calverly	G	5'10	155	23	47	226	835	27	107	161	66	119	168	559	**2.5**	3.6	11.9
Earl Shannon	G-F	5'11	170	26	45	123	469	26	116	183	63	49	106	362	1.1	2.4	8.0
Jack Toomay (9g. Chi)	C	6'6	215	25	23	61	191	32	60	91	66	7	71	182	0.3	3.1	7.9
Bob Hubbard (from TC NBL)	C-F	6'6	215	25	28	58	199	29	36	52	69	11	34	152	0.4	1.2	5.4
Dino Martin	G	5'8	160	27	32	46	193	24	9	20	45	14	17	101	0.4	0.5	3.2
Pop Goodwin	F	6'2	203	27	24	36	155	23	19	27	70	7	36	91	0.3	1.5	3.8
Mel Thurston (from TC NBL)	G	6'	175	28	14	32	113	28	14	28	50	4	42	78	0.3	3.0	5.6
George Mearns	F	6'3	175	25	24	23	115	20	15	31	48	10	65	61	0.4	2.7	2.5
John Janisch (3g. Bos, to Fli NBL)	F	6'3	200	27	10	14	50	28	9	16	56	2	5	37	0.2	0.5	3.7
Ray Wertis	G	5'11	175	25	7	13	72	18	6	14	43	6	13	32	0.9	1.9	4.6
Jerry Kelly	F	6'3	185	29	3	3	10	30	0	1	0	0	3	6	0.0	1.0	2.0
Nat Hickey (from TC NBL)	G	5'11	190	45	1	0	3	0	0	0	—	0	1	0	0.0	1.0	0.0
Dick Fitzgerald	F	6'2	175	26	1	0	3	0	0	0	—	0	1	0	0.0	1.0	0.0
Bill Downey	C	6'6	210	24	3	0	2	0	0	0	—	0	0	0	0.0	0.0	0.0

1947/48 B.A.A. — WESTERN DIVISION

Use Name	Pos	Hgt	Wgt	Age	TOTAL G	FG	FGA	%	FT	FTA	%	Ass.	PF	Pts	PER GAME Ass.	PF	Pts.	PLAYOFFS G	FG	FGA	%	FT	FTA	%	Ass	PF	Pts	PPG
ST. LOUIS BOMBERS	**29-19 .604**	**KEN LOEFFLER**	lost to Philedelphia 3-4; H60-58, H64-65, 56-84, 56-51, H69-62, 61-84, H85-46																									
Ariel Maughan (14g Prov)	F	6'4	190	24	42	76	256	30	32	53	60	6	89	184	0.1	2.1	4.4	7	32	122	26	16	23	70	1	22	80	11.4
Bob Doll	F	6'5	195	28	42	174	658	26	98	148	66	26	107	446	0.6	2.5	10.6	7	18	91	20	14	26	54	5	18	50	7.1
Red Rocha	C-F	6'9	185	24	48	232	740	31	147	213	69	39	209	611	0.8	4.4	12.7	7	29	118	25	22	30	73	6	30	80	11.4
Belus Smawley	G-F	6'1	195	29	48	212	688	31	111	150	74	18	88	535	0.4	1.8	11.1	6	26	86	30	14	18	78	2	15	66	11.0
Johnny Logan	G	6'2	175	26	48	221	734	30	202	272	74	62	141	644	1.3	2.9	13.4	5	17	55	31	22	28	79	8	19	56	11.2
Irv Rothenberg (11g Was, 14g. Bal)	C	6'8	215	26	49	103	364	28	87	150	58	7	115	293	0.1	2.3	6.0	5	5	34	15	4	7	57	0	9	14	2.8
Don Putman	G	6'1	170	25	42	174	658	26	57	84	68	25	95	267	0.6	2.3	6.4	7	8	44	18	7	12	58	5	15	23	3.3
Giff Roux	F	6'5	195	24	46	68	258	26	40	68	59	12	60	176	0.3	1.3	3.8	5	2	24	8	3	7	43	0	3	7	1.4
Buddy O'Grady	G	5'11	160	27	44	67	257	26	36	54	67	9	61	170	0.2	1.4	3.9	7	11	33	33	3	3	100	0	5	25	3.6
Don Martin	F-C	6'7	210	27	39	35	150	23	15	33	45	2	61	85	0.1	1.6	2.2	5	5	20	25	1	1	100	1	6	11	2.2
Wyndol Gray (1g Prov)	G	6'1	175	25	12	6	37	16	1	4	25	3	16	13	0.3	1.3	1.1											
BALTIMORE BULLETS	**28-20 .583**	**BUDDY JEANNETTE**	defeated Chicago 75-72 at Chicago in playoff for second place; defeated New York 2-1; H85-81, 69-79, H84-77; defeated Chicago 2-0; 73-67, H89-72; defeated Philadelphia 4-2; 60-71, 66-63, H72-70, H78-75, 82-91, H88-73																									
Paul Hoffman (injury)	F	6'2	205	22	37	142	408	35	104	157	66	23	123	388	0.6	3.3	10.5	11	44	141	31	41	62	66	7	39	129	11.7
Dick Schulz	F	6'2	192	30	48	133	469	28	117	160	73	28	116	383	0.6	2.4	8.0	11	22	114	19	38	51	75	7	30	82	7.5
Kleggie Hermsen	C	6'9	235	24	48	212	765	28	151	227	67	48	154	575	1.0	3.2	12.0	11	38	151	25	45	63	71	12	45	121	11.0
Chick Reiser	G	5'11	165	33	47	202	628	32	137	185	74	40	175	541	0.9	3.7	11.5	11	36	139	26	31	42	74	7	46	103	9.4
Buddy Jeannette	G	5'11	175	30	46	150	430	**35**	191	251	76	70	147	491	1.5	3.2	10.7	11	30	61	**49**	37	42	**88**	12	45	97	8.8
Connie Simmons (32g Bos)	C-F	6'7	210	22	45	162	545	30	62	108	57	24	122	386	0.5	2.7	8.6	11	65	175	37	58	78	74	11	42	188	17.1
Grady Lewis (24g StL)	F-C	6'7	215	30	45	114	425	27	87	135	64	41	151	315	0.9	3.4	7.0	11	23	109	21	22	29	76	9	49	68	6.2
Carl Meinhold	G-F	6'2	185	21	48	108	356	30	37	60	62	16	64	253	0.3	1.3	5.3	11	17	67	25	6	13	46	0	6	40	3.6
Herm Fuetsch	G	6'	170	29	42	42	140	30	25	40	63	17	39	109	0.4	0.9	2.6	9	3	8	38	6	8	75	0	10	12	1.3
Paul Seymour (to SyrNBL)	F	6'2	180	19	22	27	101	27	22	37	59	6	34	76	0.3	1.5	3.5											
Herm Klotz	G	5'7	150	26	11	7	31	23	1	3	33	7	3	15	0.6	0.3	1.4	6	2	9	22	2	3	67	1	3	6	1.0
Johnny Jorgensen (1g Chi, to MinNBL)	F	6'2	185	26	3	4	9	44	1	1	100	0	2	9	0.0	0.7	3.0											
Elmer Gainer	F	6'6	200	28	5	1	9	11	3	6	50	3	8	5	0.6	1.6	1.0											
Brooms Abramovic (4g StL, to SyrNBL)	F	6'3	196	28	9	1	21	5	4	7	57	2	10	6	0.2	1.1	0.7											
Chet McNabb	F	6'2	200	26	2	0	1	0	0	0	—	0	1	0	0.0	0.5	0.0											
Jerry Rullo	G	5'10	165	24	2	0	4	0	0	0	—	0	1	0	0.0	0.5	0.0											
CHICAGO STAGS	**28-20 .583**	**OLE OLSEN (28-19 .596)**; **JIM SEMINOFF (0-1.000)**	defeated Washington 74-70 at home and lost to Baltimore 72-75 at home in playoff for second place.; defeated Boston 2-1; 79-72, 77-81, 81-74; lost to Baltimore 0-2; H67-73, 72-89																									
Gene Vance	F	6'3	196	24	48	163	617	26	76	126	60	49	193	402	1.0	4.0	8.4	5	17	66	26	13	17	76	1	15	47	9.4
Chuck Gilmur	F-C	6'4	225	25	48	181	597	30	97	148	66	77	**231**	459	1.6	**4.8**	9.6	5	13	65	20	18	23	78	10	27	44	8.8
Stan Miasek	C	6'5	210	23	48	263	867	30	190	310	61	31	192	716	0.6	4.0	14.9	5	28	76	37	17	30	57	3	27	73	14.6
Max Zaslofsky	G-F	6'2	170	22	48	**373**	1156	32	261	333	78	29	125	**1007**	0.6	2.6	21.0	5	30	88	34	37	47	79	0	17	97	19.4
Andy Phillip	G	6'3	195	25	32	143	425	34	60	103	58	74	75	346	2.3	2.3	10.8	5	13	46	28	10	14	71	4	11	36	7.2
Jim Seminoff	G-F	6'2	200	25	48	113	381	30	73	105	70	89	105	299	1.9	2.2	6.2	5	16	62	26	17	26	65	8	21	49	9.8
Paul Huston	F	6'3	185	22	46	51	215	24	62	89	70	27	82	164	0.6	1.8	3.6	5	3	19	16	7	13	54	2	14	13	2.6
Mickey Rottner	G	5'10	185	28	44	53	184	29	11	34	32	46	49	117	1.0	1.1	2.7	4	3	15	20	1	3	33	2	13	7	1.8
Ben Schadler	F	6'2	185	23	37	23	116	20	10	13	77	6	40	56	0.2	1.1	1.5	4	5	23	22	0	2	0	1	4	10	2.5
Gene Rock	G	5'9	155	26	11	4	18	22	2	4	50	0	8	10	0.0	0.7	0.9	2	0	0	—	0	1	0	0	0	0	0.0
WASHINGTON CAPITOLS	**28-20 .583**	**RED AUERBACH**	lost to Chicago 70-74 at Chicago in playoff for second place																									
Johnny Norlander	F	6'3	180	26	48	167	543	31	135	182	74	44	102	469	0.9	2.1	9.8											
Bones McKinney	F-C	6'6	187	28	43	182	680	27	121	188	64	36	176	485	0.8	4.1	11.3											
John Mahnken	C	6'8	220	25	48	131	526	25	54	88	61	31	151	316	0.6	3.1	6.6											
Bob Feerick	G-F	6'3	190	27	48	293	861	34	189	240	79	56	139	775	1.2	2.9	16.1											
Freddie Scolari	G	5'11	180	25	47	229	780	29	131	179	73	58	153	589	1.2	3.3	12.5											
Irv Torgoff	F-G	6'2	192	30	47	111	541	21	117	144	81	32	153	339	0.7	3.3	7.2											
Sonny Hertzberg (4g NY)	G	5'10	175	25	41	110	414	27	58	73	79	23	61	278	0.6	1.5	6.8											
Dick O'Keefe	G	6'2	175	24	37	63	257	25	30	59	51	18	85	156	0.5	2.3	4.2											
Jack Tingle	F	6'4	205	22	37	36	137	26	17	33	52	7	45	89	0.2	1.2	2.4											

1947/48 B.A.A. TEAM STATISTICS

Team	Regular Season G	FG	FGA	%	FT	FTA	%	Ass.	Average Points For	Agnst.	Diff.	Playoffs G	FG	FGA	%	FT	FTA	%	Ass.	Average Points For	Agnst.	Diff.
EASTERN DIVISION																						
Philadelphia	48	1279	**4875**	26	963	1349	71	335	73.4	72.1	+1.3	13	325	**1275**	25	282	400	71	91	71.7	**66.0**	**+5.7**
New York	48	1355	4724	29	868	1291	67	376	74.5	71.4	+3.1	3	**85**	253	**34**	67	101	66	16	**79.0**	79.3	-0.3
Boston	48	1241	4323	29	821	1246	66	364	68.8	72.7	-3.9	3	75	252	30	77	**115**	67	**22**	75.7	79.0	-3.3
Providence	48	1268	4630	27	782	1275	61	347	69.1	80.7	-11.6											
WESTERN DIVISION																						
St Louis	48	1297	4551	28	838	1244	67	218	71.5	**69.5**	+2.0	7	153	627	24	106	155	68	28	58.9	69.9	-11.0
Baltimore	48	1288	4283	**30**	**994**	**1443**	69	320	74.4	70.5	**+3.9**	11	280	974	29	**286**	391	**73**	66	76.9	74.5	+ 2.4
Chicago	48	**1390**	4683	30	860	1305	66	**432**	**75.8**	73.2	+2.6	5	128	460	27	120	176	68	31	75.2	77.8	-2.6
Washington	48	1336	4785	28	865	1203	**72**	305	73.7	71.1	+2.6											

1947/48 B.A.A. STANDINGS

Team	W	L	Pct.	GB	Record against playoff teams W	L	Pct.	Record against non - playoff teams W	L	Pct.	Home W	L	Pct.	Road W	L	Pct.
EASTERN DIVISION																
Philadelphia Warriors	27	21	.563	—	17	17	.500	**10**	4	.714	14	10	.583	13	11	.542
New York Knickerbockers	26	22	.542	1	16	18	.471	**10**	4	.714	12	12	.500	**14**	10	**.583**
Boston Celtics	20	28	.417	7	11	23	.324	9	5	.643	11	13	.458	9	15	.375
Providence Steamrollers	6	**42**	.125	21	5	**37**	.119	1	5	.167	3	**21**	.125	3	**21**	.1
WESTERN DIVISION																
St. Louis Bombers	**29**	19	**.604**	—	19	15	.559	**10**	4	.714	17	7	.708	12	12	.500
Baltimore Bullets	28	20	.583	1	20	14	**.588**	8	**6**	.571	17	7	.708	11	13	.458
Chicago Stags	28	20	.583	1	19	15	.559	9	5	.643	14	10	.583	**14**	10	**.583**
Washington Capitols	28	20	.583	1	**23**	19	.548	5	1	**.833**	**19**	5	**.792**	9	15	.375

1947/48 B.A.A. INDIVIDUAL LEADERS

SCORING
(Minimum 32 Games Played)

Name	Team	G	FG	FT	Pts.	Avg.
Fulks	Phi	43	326	297	949	22.1
Zaslofsky	Chi	48	373	261	1007	21.0
Sadowski	Bos	47	308	294	910	19.4
Feerick	Was	48	293	189	775	16.1
Miasek	Chi	48	263	190	716	14.9
Braun	NY	47	276	119	671	14.3
Logan	StL	48	221	202	644	13.4
Palmer	NY	48	224	174	622	13.0
Rocha	StL	48	232	147	611	12.7
Scolari	Was	47	229	131	589	12.5

FIELD GOAL PERCENTAGE
(Minimum 150 Field Goals)

Name	Team	FG	FGA	Pct.
Jeanrette	Bal	150	430	.349
Feerick	Was	293	861	.340
Sadowski	Bos	308	953	.323
Braun	NY	276	854	.323
Zaslofsky	Chi	373	1156	.323
Reiser	Bal	202	628	.322
Palmer	NY	224	710	.315
Rocha	StL	232	740	.314
Riebe	Bos	202	653	.309
Smawley	StL	212	688	.308

FREE THROW PERCENTAGE
(Minimum 100 Free Throws)

Name	Team	FT	FTA	Pct.
Stutz	NY	113	135	.837
Torgoff	Was	117	144	.813
Feerick	Was	189	240	.788
Zaslofsky	Chi	261	333	.784
Fulks	Phi	297	390	.762
Jeanrette	Bal	191	252	.758
Palmer	NY	174	234	.744
Dallmar	Phi	157	211	.743
Logan	StL	202	272	.742
Norlander	Was	135	182	.742

PERSONAL FOULS

Name	Team	PF
Gilmur	Chi	231
Rocha	StL	209
Vance	Chi	193
Miasek	Chi	192
Sadowski	Bos	182

ASSISTS PER GAME
(Minimum 32 Games Played)

Name	Team	G	Ass.	Avg.
Calverly	Prov	47	119	2.5
Dallmar	Phi	48	120	2.5
Phillip	Chi	32	74	2.3
Seminoff	Chi	48	89	1.8
Gilmur	Chi	48	77	1.6
Sadowski	Bos	47	74	1.6
Jeannette	Bal	46	70	1.5
Mariaschin	Bos	43	60	1.4
Garfinkle	Bos	43	59	1.4
Sailors	Chi-Phi-Prov	44	59	1.3

1948-49 N.B.L.

Dying but Determined

The heart had been cut out of the N.B.L. during the summer when the Minneapolis Lakers, Rochester Royals, Ft. Wayne Pistons, and Indianapolis Kautskys jumped over to the rival B.A.A. Lured away by the prospect of playing teams in larger cities, these clubs took with them such top players as George Mikan, Jim Pollard, Bob Davies, and Arnie Risen. To add to the N.B.L.'s troubles, the Toledo and Flint franchises folded, and Commissioner Piggy Lambert resigned because of ill health.

Rather than disband, the league pulled itself together under a new commissioner, Doxie Moore, and staged an interesting season of basketball. To go with the five returning franchises—Anderson, Syracuse, Tri-Cities, Sheboygan, and Oshkosh—the N.B.L. added new franchises in Hammond, Detroit, Waterloo (Iowa), and Denver. There were enough fans in these smaller cities to keep the N. B.L. alive despite the loss of four of its better clubs.

As the regular season unfolded, the five returning clubs all put together winning records. The Anderson Duffey Packers had the third best record in the league last season, but now that Minneapolis and Rochester were gone from the league, they prospered. The Packers, led by popular guard Frankie Brian, were a running team, but they had been hurt in the past by big clubs. Now, there was no Mikan or Risen to bully 6'6" center Howie Schultz, who relied more on his quickness than his size. Schultz did get some help on the boards from ex-Piston Milo Komenich and rookie Bill Closs from Rice. The Packers ran their way to a 49-15 record, 8.5 games better than anyone else in the league.

Trailing the Packers in second place in the Eastern Division were the Syracuse Nationals. Although they had a weak 24-36 last season, the Nats had an entire new starting five, featuring Al Cervi and Dolph Schayes. Cervi had been the captain and floor leader of the Rochester Royals since 1945, but an argument with Royal owner Les Harrison led to the tough veteran switching to Syracuse as player coach. One of coach Cervi's pupils this season was Schayes, a 6'7" rookie forward out of N.Y.U. Schayes had a deadeye set shot and developed a fine inside game. The Nats' mark of 40-23 stood second only to Anderson's in the entire N.B.L.

The three veteran clubs in the Western Division, Oshkosh, Tri-Cities, and Sheboygan, all finished within two games of each other at the top of the standings. For Oshkosh, it was a season of profound change. Veteran center Leroy Edwards, the first star in the N.B.L., was now only a bench warmer. Only center Gene Englund was a familiar Oshkosh face, with the rest of the squad filled with rookies like 6'7" Alex Hannum, Marshall Hawkins, Jack Burmaster, and Gene Berce. Forward Bob Carpenter returned to the club in mid-season after getting canned as Hammond's player coach, and he joined Englund and Hawkins in a tough front line. With all the changes, the traditional Oshkosh style of physical basketball kept the All-Stars in the running.

The Tri-Cities Blackhawks also had a tough front line, thanks mostly to center Don Otten. With Mikan and Risen no longer around, the 7' Otten was in a class by himself at center, leading the league in scoring with a 14.0 average. Veteran guard Bobby McDermott led the club as player coach through most of the campaign, but he was sent to Hammond in February with his best playing days behind him.

The Sheboygan Redskins came in a close third, playing their traditionally physical game with a whole new cast of players. Former coach Doxie Moore was now league commissioner, and center Ed Dancker, a pillar of the team for many seasons, was no longer on the squad. Veteran guard Kenny Suesens took over as coach, and the new front line of Mike Todorovich, Bob Brannum, and Noble Jorgensen showed plenty of muscle.

While the five holdover clubs were compiling winning records, the four new clubs were losing more than winning. Waterloo and Denver finished out of the playoffs in the West; Waterloo was coached by Charley Shipp and got good seasons from ex-Toledo players Harry Boykoff and Dick Mehen, while Denver fielded practically the same squad that had been an A.A.U. power up until last season. In the East, Hammond pieced together a veteran squad and won the third playoff spot with a limp 21-41 record. The Detroit Vagabond Kings lasted until mid-December, when they folded with a 2-17 record; to replace them, the league brought in the powerful black New York Rens. A much weakened outfit playing their final season, the Rens came into the N.B.L. representing Dayton but playing very few home games. They were led by player coach Pop Gates, Hank DeZonie and future baseball star George Crowe. Despite a lack of size, too many players being over the hill, a thin bench, and DeZonie's illness which caused him to miss the last 17 games, this only all-black franchise in the history of major league sports built a competitive 14-26 record over the rest of the season.

In the playoffs, the first-place teams got a bye while the second-place and third-place teams battled it out in the opening round. Syracuse easily disposed of the weaker Hammond squad with two straight wins, while Tri-Cities surprisingly took two straight easy decisions from Sheboygan. In the divisional finals the Anderson fast break overcame the steady Syracuse attack to take their series three games to one and Oshkosh veteran Gene Englund and Bob Carpenter led the All-Stars past the Blackhawks in four games. The championship series came down to the fast Anderson Packers against the physical Oshkosh All-Stars. Speed won, as the Packers took three straight games, the final one an easy 88-64 romp at Anderson.

With this season in the books, the N.B.L. made plans for its 1949-50 campaign. It scored a major triumph by getting the graduating starters of the glamorous University of Kentucky team, N.C.A.A. champions and members of the 1948 Olympic squad, to turn pro as the Indianapolis Olympians. This master stroke was the final blow in the war between the B.A.A. and the N.B.L., for the B.A.A. decided to immediately move for a merger.

Team	W	L	Pct.	GB	vs. playoff teams W	L	PCT.	vs. non-playoff teams W	L	Pct.	HOME W	L	Pct.	ROAD W	L	Pct.	Average Points G	FT%	For	Agnst.	Diff.	PLAYOFFS Average Points G	FT%	For	Agnst.	Diff.
1948/49 N.B.L. STANDINGS																										
EASTERN DIVISION																										
Anderson	49	15	.766	—	**28**	12	**.700**	**21**	3	**.875**	**32**	2	**.941**	**17**	13	**.567**	64	68	**72.1**	63.1	**+9.0**	7	68	**78.6**	71.6	**+7.0**
Syracuse	40	23	.635	8.5	23	17	.575	17	6	.739	27	4	.871	7	19	.269	63	**69**	66.5	63.8	+2.7	6	73	74.8	75.3	-0.5
Hammond	21	41	.339	17	11	29	.275	10	**12**	.455	15	**16**	.484	5	25	.167	62	69	61.0	64.9	-3.9	2	63	67.5	76.0	-8.5
Dayton	14	26	.350	30.5	9	22	.290	5	4	.556	4	5	.444	9	18	.333	40	61	56.7	61.7	-5.0					
Detroit	2	17	.105		0	14	.000	2	3	.400	1	4	.200	0	12	.000	19	64	61.1	75.2	-14.1					
WESTERN DIVISION																										
Oshkosh	37	27	.578	—	19	21	.475	18	6	.750	27	8	.771	9	18	.333	64	65	60.9	**59.0**	+1.9	7	70	68.6	71.1	-2.5
Tri-Cities	36	28	.563	1	20	20	.500	16	8	.667	25	10	.714	10	17	.307	64	67	65.1	62.4	+2.7	6	71	66.3	**64.3**	+2.0
Sheboygan	35	29	.547	2	19	21	.475	16	8	.667	24	7	.774	10	21	.323	64	68	62.0	61.7	+.3	2	**76**	55.5	67.0	11.5
Waterloo	30	32	.484	6	21	27	.438	9	5	.643	23	6	.793	7	22	.241	62	68	58.9	59.2	-0.3					
Denver	18	**44**	.290	18	13	**35**	.271	5	9	.357	15	15	.500	3	**28**	.097	62	64	58.9	64.1	-5.9					

Use Name	Pos.	Hgt.	Wgt.	Age	REGULAR SEASON G	FG	FT	FTA	Pct.	Points	PPG	PLAYOFFS G	FG	FT	FTA	Pct.	Point	PPG

1948/49 N.B.L. — EASTERN DIVISION

ANDERSON DUFFEY PACKERS **49-15 .766** **MURRAY MENDENHALL**

defeated Syracuse 3-1; 89-74, 62-80, H76-59, H90-84
defeated Oshkosh 3-0; 74-70, 72-70, H88-64

Use Name	Pos.	Hgt.	Wgt.	Age	G	FG	FT	FTA	Pct.	Points	PPG	G	FG	FT	FTA	Pct.	Point	PPG
Ed Stanczak	F	6'3	210	27	64	191	202	275	73	584	9.1	7	10	16	27	59	36	5.1
Milo Komenich	F-C	6'7	230	28	64	243	124	217	57	610	9.5	7	25	26	41	63	76	10.9
Howie Schultz	C	6'7	210	26	64	176	186	256	73	538	8.4	7	13	38	52	73	64	9.1
Frankie Brian	G	6'1	180	25	64	216	201	129	**79**	633	9.9	7	26	27	32	**84**	79	11.3
Boag Johnson	G	5'11	170	27	64	218	85		67	521	8.1	7	**34**	18	23	78	86	12.3
Bill Closs	F-C	6'6	195	26	64	203	110	166	66	516	8.1	7	25	35	47	74	85	12.1
John Hargis	G-F	6'2	180	28	57	169	106	173	61	444	7.8	7	22	28	43	65	72	10.3
Frank Gates	G	6'	160	27	64	150	78	123	63	378	5.9	7	13	5	11	45	31	4.4
Dillard Crocker (from FtW BAA, Det)	F	6'4	205	23	43	70	68	93	73	208	4.8	6	5	3	8	38	13	2.2
Bud Mendenhall	G	5'10	155	23	60	64	40	70	57	168	2.8	7	3	3	7	43	9	1.3
Jack Walton	F	6'2	192	25	8	5	4	5	80	14	1.8							

SYRACUSE NATIONALS **40-23 .635** **AL CERVI**

defeated Hammond 2-0; 80-69, H72-66
lost to Anderson 1-3; H74-89, H80-62, 59-76, 84-90

Use Name	Pos.	Hgt.	Wgt.	Age	G	FG	FT	FTA	Pct.	Points	PPG	G	FG	FT	FTA	Pct.	Point	PPG
Johnny Macknowski	F-G	6'1	185	25	62	146	128	178	72	420	6.8	6	3	7	9	78	13	2.2
Dolph Schayes	F-C	6'7	205	20	63	271	267	370	72	809	12.8	6	27	32	41	78	86	14.3
Ed Peterson	C	6'9	230	23	63	165	104	177	59	434	6.9	6	14	16	28	57	44	7.3
Al Cervi	G	5'11	185	31	57	204	287	382	75	695	12.2	6	12	22	30	73	46	7.7
Billy Gabor	G	5'11	170	26	58	115	125	169	74	355	6.1	6	12	12	15	80	36	6.0
Jim Homer	F-C	6'5	220	25	59	141	104	164	63	386	6.5	6	13	6	14	43	32	5.3
Paul Seymour	G-F	6'2	180	20	63	120	70	106	66	310	4.9	6	21	9	10	90	51	8.5
Jerry Rizzo (SL)	G	5'8	165	30	45	67	106	150	71	240	5.3	6	13	18	22	82	44	7.3
Hank O'Keeffe	F	6'3	195	25	56	94	52	90	58	240	4.3	5	2	2	2	100	6	1.2
John Chaney	F	6'3	190	28	59	82	59	88	67	223	3.8	6	13	6	8	75	32	5.3
Bob Calihan (CC)	F	6'3	200	30	11	28	13	21	62	69	6.3	6	21	17	23	74	59	9.8
Paul Yesawich	F	6'2	190	25	5	2	4	5	80	8	1.6							

HAMMOND CALUMET BUCCANEERS **21-41 .399** **BOB CARPENTER(11-16 .407), GEORGE SOBEK(10-25 .286)** lost to Syracuse 0-2; H69-80, 66-72

Use Name	Pos.	Hgt.	Wgt.	Age	G	FG	FT	FTA	Pct.	Points	PPG	G	FG	FT	FTA	Pct.	Point	PPG
Bob Carpenter (FJ, to Osh)	F	6'5	200	31	23	87	67	91	74	241	10.5							
Jake Carter	F-C	6'5	195	24	62	133	188	267	70	454	7.3	2	7	5	13	38	19	9.5
George Glamack (from Ind BAA)	C	6'8	245	29	43	169	163	216	75	501	11.7	2	5	5	8	63	15	7.5
George Sobek	G-F	6'	180	28	57	143	232	322	72	518	9.1	2	4	1	1	100	9	4.5
Bobby McDermott (from TC)	G	6'	185	34	18	56	37	51	73	149	8.3	2	7	5	5	100	19	9.5
Stan Patrick	F-G	6'3	215	26	61	150	127	192	66	427	7.0	2	2	1	2	50	5	2.5
Clint Wager	C	6'6	230	28	61	125	82	146	56	332	5.4	2	3	3	7	43	9	4.5
Johnny Sebastian (from Det)	G	6'1	185	27	42	99	64	105	61	262	6.2	2	6	3	4	75	15	7.5
Ollie Shoaff (from Det)	G	5'10	165	25	42	103	49	66	74	255	6.1	2	9	2	3	67	20	10.0
Joe Camic (from TC)	F	6'5	200	26	31	71	60	97	62	202	6.6	2	7	5	5	100	19	9.5
Bobby Holm	G	6'	210	29	18	38	28	34	82	104	5.8							
Carl Loyd	G	6'	172	23	29	43	11	23	48	97	3.3							
Jack Maddox (to Ind BAA)	F	6'3	190	27	17	39	18	29	62	96	5.6							
Ken Campbell	F	6'4	198	22	14	29	12	18	67	70	5.0							
Len Rader	G	6'2	185	27	14	15	23	34	68	53	3.8	2	2	1	1	100	5	2.5
Hal Devoll (from Det)	F	6'6	210	25	9	4	3	5	60	11	1.2							
Aubrey Davis	G-F	6'2	175	27	8	3	3	7	43	9	1.1							
Ted Cook (from Sheb)	G	6'	160	27	5	0	1	2	50	1	0.2							
Art Grove	G	6'1	185	25	1	0	0	0	—	0	0.0							

Use Name	Pos	Hgt	Wgt	Age	REGULAR SEASON G	FG	FT	FTA	Pct.	Points	PPG	PLAYOFFS G	FG	FT	FTA	Pct.	Points	PPG
1948/49 N.B.L. — EASTERN DIVISION (continued)																		
DAYTON-DETROIT	16-43 .271		(Detroit Vagabond Kings until December 17, 1948 when the team ceased to operate and was disbanded, Franchise awarded to Dayton, Ohio. New York Rens played as the Dayton Rens, assuming Detroit's 2-17 record.)															
DETROIT VAGABOND KINGS	2-17 .105		DEL LORANGER															
Ben Schadler (to Wat)	F	6'2	185	24	13	58	20	28	71	136	10.5							
Dillard Crocker (from Ft W BAA, to And)	F	6'4	205	23	8	31	27	38	71	89	11.1							
Dave Latter	C-F	6'6	210	26	13	26	38	66	58	90	6.9							
Johnny Sebastian (to Ham)	G	6'1	185	27	19	86	62	101	61	234	12.3							
Ollie Shoaff (to Ham)	G	5'10	165	25	19	108	44	59	75	260	13.7							
Hal Devoll (to Ham)	F-C	6'6	210	25	18	46	22	32	69	114	6.3							
Del Loranger	F-G	6'3	180	28	16	20	24	35	69	64	4.0							
Art Bakeraitis	F-C	6'4	210	23	13	18	24	37	65	60	4.6							
Tony Kaseta	C	6'8	220	25	17	16	20	32	63	52	3.1							
Doyle Cofer	F	6'4	—	24	8	9	9	23	39	27	3.4							
Fred Campbell	G	5'11	175	28	10	5	8	11	73	18	1.8							
Dick Shrider (to NY BAA)	G	6'2	190	25	3	3	3	6	50	9	3.0							
Paul Juntunen	G	6'1	180	27	4	4	0	1	0	8	2.0							
DAYTON RENS	14-26 .350		POP GATES															
George Crowe	F-C	6'2	210	25	40	164	109	159	69	437	10.9							
Jim Usry	F-C	6'4	225	26	36	129	71	134	53	329	9.1							
Hank DeZonie (illness)	C-F	6'6	215	26	18	90	44	59	75	224	12.4							
Pop Gates	G-F	6'2	205	31	40	161	126	220	57	448	11.2							
Sonny Wood	G	5'11	195	25	40	105	56	98	57	266	6.7							
Tom Sealy	G	6'2	190	27	40	100	60	92	65	260	6.5							
Willie Smith	C	6'6	230	37	32	45	37	49	76	127	4.0							
Johnny Isaacs	G	6'3	190	33	8	18	22	34	65	58	7.3							
Rookie Brown	F-C	6'4	190	23	10	19	10	20	50	48	4.8							
Robert Powell	F-C	6'5	—	—	6	11	8	13	62	30	5.0							
Leroy Pryor	F-G	6'3	180	25	10	6	0	3	0	12	1.2							
Dolly King	F	6'4	217	31	1	3	5	7	71	11	11.0							
Len Ford (FB)	C-F	6'4	230	22	6	2	2	8	25	6	1.0							
Vic Krafft	G	6'3	195	29	3	3	0	1	0	6	2.0							
Bill Farrow	C	6'4	198	30	3	1	3	3	100	5	1.7							
Eddie Wollen	F	—	—	—	1	0	0	0	—	0	0.0							
1948/49 N.B.L. — WESTERN DIVISION																		
OSHKOSH ALL-STARS	37-27.578		LON DARLING (34-26 .567), GENE ENGLUND & EDDIE RISKA(3-1 .750)								defeated Tri-Cities 3-1; H68-66, H73-59, 64-70, 70-69 lost to Anderson 0-3; H70-74, H70-72, 64-68							
Marshall Hawkins	F	6'3	205	24	64	200	116	160	73	516	8.1	7	25	20	26	77	70	10.0
FJob Carpenter (from Ham)	F	6'5	200	31	24	73	64	89	72	210	8.8	7	25	30	42	71	80	11.4
Gene Englund	C-F	6'5	205	31	63	284	282	393	72	850	13.5	7	32	31	37	84	95	13.6
Jack Burmaster	G	6'3	190	22	64	140	80	128	63	360	5.6	7	14	16	24	67	44	6.3
Gene Berce	G	5'11	175	22	58	120	101	153	66	341	5.9	7	8	32	39	82	48	6.9
Floyd Volker	F	6'4	205	27	64	166	78	134	58	410	6.4	7	22	9	17	53	53	7.6
Alex Hannum	C	6'7	210	25	64	126	113	191	59	365	5.7	7	12	16	26	62	40	5.7
Glen Selbo (BB)	G	6'3	195	22	60	119	77	114	68	315	5.3							
Walt Lautenbach	F-G	6'2	190	26	61	104	26	45	58	234	3.8	7	12	6	15	40	30	4.3
Eddie Riska	G	6'	180	29	42	42	61	93	66	145	3.5							
Ed Dancker	C	6'7	225	34	13	16	7	21	33	39	3.0							
Bill Brown (to Wat)	F	6'3	—	—	10	13	10	17	59	36	3.6							
Bob Mulvihill	G	6'1	185	24	34	8	14	24	58	30	0.9	3	0	0	0	—	0	0.0
Ed Mills	C	6'8	225	26	8	8	7	12	58	23	2.9							
Leroy Edwards (VR)	C	6'4	230	34	10	7	8	20	40	22	2.2	6	7	5	11	45	19	3.2

1948/49 N.B.L — WESTERN DIVISION (continued)

Use Name	Pos	Hgt	Wgt	Age	G	FG	FT	FTA	Pct.	Points	PPG	G	FG	FT	FTA	Pct.	Points	PPG
					REGULAR SEASON							PLAYOFFS						
TRI-CITIES BLACK HAWKS	**36-28 .563**				**BOBBY McDERMOTT (25-20 .556), ROGER POTTER (11-8 .579)**							defeated Sheboygan 2-0; H75-60, 59-51; lost to Oshkosh 1-3; 66-68, 59-13, H70-64, H69-70						
Ward Gibson (from Den)	F	6'5	210	27	20	77	47	73	64	201	10.1	6	9	6	9	67	24	4.0
Don Ray (broken hand)	F-C	6'6	200	27	46	123	80	117	68	326	7.1	6	16	17	21	81	49	8.2
Don Otten	C	7'	245	27	64	**301**	**297**	**424**	70	**899**	**14.0**	6	24	**43**	**55**	78	91	**15.2**
Whitey Von Nieda	G-F	6'1	175	26	64	247	147	226	65	641	10.0	6	20	13	24	54	53	8.8
Bobby McDermott (to Ham)	G	6'	185	34	45	170	84	113	74	424	9.4							
Billy Hassett	G	6'1	180	27	64	125	106	156	68	356	5.6	5	11	17	21	81	39	7.8
Luther Harris	F-G	6'3	208	25	63	118	102	152	67	338	5.4	6	3	2	5	40	8	1.3
Geone Ratkovicz	C-F	6'7	225	26	64	109	106	175	61	324	5.1	6	11	16	22	73	38	6.3
Dee Gibson	G-F	5'11	175	25	64	94	113	177	64	301	4.7	6	19	19	30	63	57	9.5
Murray Wier	G	5'9	155	22	60	80	79	113	70	239	4.0	6	13	9	13	69	35	5.8
Joe Camic (to Ham)	F	6'5	210	26	31	32	27	47	57	91	2.9							
Bobby Lowther (from Wat)	F-C	6'5	190	25	15	8	2	4	50	18	1.2	4	1	2	2	100	4	1.0
Earl Hawkins	F	6'4	225	27	2	2	1	1	100	5	2.5							
Ed Lewinski	F	6'4	210	28	3	1	0	0	—	2	0.7							
SHEBOYGAN REDSKINS	**35-29 .547**				**KENNY SUESENS**				lost to Tri-Cities 0-2; 60-75, H51-59									
Mike Todorovich	F	6'5	230	25	60	239	170	281	60	648	10.8							
Bob Brannum	F-C	6'6	215	23	64	169	169	261	65	507	7.9	2	7	2	3	67	16	8.0
Noble Jorgensen	C	6'9	230	23	63	218	194	255	76	630	10.0	2	11	7	8	88	29	14.5
Danny Wagner	G	6'	170	26	62	111	109	146	75	331	5.3	2	3	1	1	100	7	3.5
Bobby Cook	G	5'10	155	25	64	172	98	136	72	442	6.9	2	5	9	10	90	19	9.5
Paul Cloyd	F-G	6'2	180	28	56	119	98	137	72	336	6.0	2	3	2	3	67	8	4.0
Bob Bolyard	G	6'	185	27	64	98	112	150	75	308	4.8	2	2	5	6	83	9	4.5
Milt Schoon	C	6'9	230	26	57	81	109	184	59	271	4.8	2	2	2	5	40	6	3.0
Boody Gilbertson	G-F	6'3	205	26	64	87	74	115	64	248	3.9	2	1	5	7	71	7	3.5
Max Morris (FB)	F	6'2	195	23	41	70	68	104	65	208	5.1	2	4	2	3	67	10	5.0
Kenny Suesens	G	6'1	190	32	26	3	10	18	56	16	0.6							
Les Deaton (to Wat)	C-F	6'4	210	25	6	5	3	5	60	13	2.2							
Ted Cook (KJ, FB, to Ham)	G	6'	160	27	4	1	4	4	100	6	1.5							
Jack Watkins	G	6'2	180	25	7	1	3	4	75	5	0.7							
WATERLOO HAWKS	**30-32 .484**				**CHARLEY SHIPP**													
Ben Schadler (from Det)	F	6'2	185	24	40	92	38	61	62	222	5.6							
Dick Mehen	F-C	6'6	195	26	62	315	211	304	69	841	13.6							
Harry Boykoff	C	6'10	235	26	61	293	191	265	72	777	12.7							
Rollie Sertz	G	5'10	170	24	62	188	127	174	73	503	8.1							
Leo Kubiak	G	5'11	170	22	62	177	108	142	76	462	7.5							
Charley Shipp	G-F	6'1	205	35	56	104	59	90	66	267	4.8							
Dale Hamilton	G-F	6'1	198	29	62	78	94	179	53	250	4.0							
Bill Brown (from Osh)	F	6'3	—	—	43	41	31	48	65	113	2.6							
Elmer Gainer	C-F	6'6	200	29	36	33	30	39	77	96	2.7							
Les Deaton (from Sheb)	C-F	6'4	210	25	26	18	19	33	58	55	2.1							
Bobby Lowther (to TC)	F-C	6'5	190	25	9	11	5	7	71	27	3.0							
Ray Ellefson (from Min BAA)	C	6'8	230	26	7	4	8	11	73	16	2.3							
Jack Spencer	F	6'3	160	25	11	6	4	4	100	16	1.5							
Gordon Flick	F	6'3	200	27	2	2	0	0	—	4	2.0							
Dave Wareham	G	6'1	185	24	4	1	1	3	33	3	0.8							
DENVER NUGGETS	**18-44 .290**				**RALPH BISHOP**													
Morris Udall	F	6'5	200	26	57	125	121	171	71	371	6.5							
Ward Gibson (to TC)	F-C	6'5	210	27	42	214	176	261	67	604	14.4							
Ace Gruenig	C	6'8	230	35	49	194	170	260	65	558	11.4							
Al Guokas	G-F	6'5	200	23	60	146	81	129	63	373	6.2							
Jimmy Darden	G	6'1	170	26	57	197	193	259	75	587	10.3							
Hal Hutcheson	F-G	6'5	190	28	59	106	53	78	68	265	4.5							
Jack Cotton	C-F	6'7	205	24	57	71	67	121	55	209	3.7							
Chink Alterman	G	6'3	185	26	50	67	62	100	62	196	3.9							
Gene Lalley	G	5'9	160	26	60	77	27	70	39	181	3.0							
Guy Mitchell	F-G	6'3	190	24	57	67	37	75	49	171	3.0							
Bob Doll (to Bos BAA)	F	6'5	195	29	9	15	13	28	46	43	4.8							
Kayo Wnorowski	G	6'	215	27	19	14	3	8	38	31	1.6							
Ralph Bishop	F	6'4	190	33	12	10	2	3	67	22	1.8							

1948-49 B.A.A.

Podoloff's Grand Coup

It was an ingenious move. It didn't insure survival, but it gave the B.A.A. a strong upper hand in the war between the leagues. B.A.A. President Maurice Podoloff convinced the Minneapolis Lakers. Rochester Royals, Ft. Wayne Zollner Pistons, and Indianapolis Kautskys to leave the N.B.L. and cast their lots with the newer league. Podoloff had the big arenas and big cities to offer these clubs, and they had the first-rate players that the B.A.A. needed to draw customers into those arenas. With George Mikan and Bob Davies and their teammates now in the circuit, the B.A.A. was certainly the best professional league in the country.

All eight B.A.A. clubs from last season returned for this campaign, giving Podoloff a lineup of twelve teams. Baltimore and Washington joined New York, Philadelphia, Boston, and Providence in the Eastern Division, while the four new members combined with Chicago and St. Louis to form the Western Division. Ft. Wayne and Indianapolis caused a mild surprise by finishing at the bottom of standings in the West. The Pistons had been a winning club in the tough N.B.L. last season, but age was cutting into the squad. The Indianapolis team, renamed the Jets, also was declining into ineptitude. The other two newcomers, however, went right to the head of the class.

The Lakers and Royals had met in last year's N.B.L. championship series, and their rivalry resumed in the regular campaign in the B.A.A. The Lakers had George Mikan, the man the entire league was talking about. A famous college player at DePaul and a fabulously successful pro in two seasons in the N.B.L., Mikan had the biggest name in the world of basketball. In the realm of college ball, only Alex Groza and Ralph Beard of the University of Kentucky could rival Mikan's reputation. Now Mikan was coming into cities like New York, Philadelphia, and Boston as a pro, and crowds were filling the arenas there to see him play. Indeed, the Madison Square Garden marquee advertised an upcoming event as "Tonite: George Mikan vs. Knicks." Big George rarely disappointed the customers, averaging 28.3 and hitting over 45 points six times.

But the Lakers had more than just the high-scoring Mikan. Jim Pollard at forward relied on grace as much as Mikan did on strength. A tremendous leaper with a soft shooting touch, Pollard would score when opponents double-teamed and triple-teamed Mikan. Just as easily, he could shoot passes into Mikan when the big man was free to score. Herm Schaefer and Swede Carlson were the guards who fed the ball to Mikan and Pollard, and the other forward was Arnie Ferrin, who had led Utah to the N.C.A.A. championship in 1944 and the N.I.T. title in 1947.

The Rochester Royals, however, conceded nothing to the Lakers and actually finished one game ahead of them in the West. The Royals had in Arnie Risen a center who was not as strong as Mikan but who was much more mobile. Risen ranked fourth in league scoring with a 16.6 average and he led the league in field goal percentage. The Royals lacked the Lakers' strength up front, but they clearly outclassed them in the backcourt. Even without Al Cervi, who left the team to join the N.B.L. Syracuse Nats, the Royals had Bob Davies, Red Holzman, and Bobby Wanzer. Davies was the B.A.A.'s top driving guard and a master at triggering the fast break.

Behind these two titans and ahead of Ft. Wayne and Indianapolis came the Chicago Stags and St. Louis Bombers, oldline B.A.A. clubs. The Stags had two top guards in set-shooter Max Zaslofsky and playmaker Andy Phillip and a very competent center in rookie Ed Mikan, George's baby brother, but they put together an ordinary 31-20 record until coach Ole Olsen was canned. Under Phil Brownstein, the Stags streaked to a 7-2 mark down the stretch. The Bombers fell under .500 despite continued good play from guards Johnnny Logan and Belus Smawley.

The Eastern Division had only old-line B.A.A. clubs. The Washington Capitols took first place with a 38-22 record, the same mark that earned Chicago third place in the West. Coach Red Auerbach still had Freddie Scolari, Bob Feerick and Bones McKinney in his starting lineup, but he got Kleggie Hermsen from Baltimore to take over the center job. Six games back in second place came the New York Knicks. Forwards Carl Braun and Bud Palmer did most of the scoring in the early going, with rookie Ray Lumpp helping out after coming over from Indianapolis in a mid-season deal. Rookie Harry Gallatin joined the team after the first eight games of the season, and played in every single contest until he retired in 1958, a career of 746 consecutive games.

The other Eastern teams all finished below the .500 mark. The defending champion Bullets were getting old and had to work some new blood into the lineup. Philadelphia got good scoring from Joe Fulks and Ed Sadowski, but an injury to Howie Dallmar severely hurt the team. The Boston Celtics had a new coach in Doggie Julian, a blue-chip rookie in George Kaftan, and lots of new faces via trades; the result, unfortunately, was a 25-35 record and no playoff berth. The Providence Steamrollers had the worst record in the league despite the fine play of guards Kenny Sailors and Ernie Calverly.

Eight teams made it to the playoffs, with an entirely new playoff schedule. The first two rounds would decide divisional representatives for the finals, so that the two first-place clubs theoretically could meet in the championship series. The opening round saw Washington down Philadelphia and New York eliminate defending champion Baltimore in the East. In the West, Rochester knocked off St. Louis, and Minneapolis beat Chicago. Washington then bested New York two games to one while the basketball universe paid most of its attention to the Rochester-Minneapolis showdown. The Lakers took an 80-79 decision in Rochester, then beat the Royals 67-55 in St. Paul after trailing 52-49 after three periods. The finals, then, came down to Minneapolis versus Washington.

The Lakers ran off three quick victories in the best-of-seven set, with Mikan scoring 42, 10, and 35 points. In the fourth game, Mikan netted 27, but the Caps broke his wrist and won the game 83-71. George sported a cast for the fifth game and scored 22 points while the Caps won 74-65. Ahead by only a 3-2 margin, the Lakers wrapped up the B.A.A. title with a 77-56 victory in St. Paul.

Use Name	Pos	Hgt	Wgt	Age	TOTAL G	FG	FGA	%	FT	FTA	%	Ass.	PF	Pts	PER GAME Ass.	PF	Pts.	PLAYOFFS G	FG	FGA	%	FT	FTA	%	Ass	PF	Pts	PPG
1948/49 B.A.A. - EASTERN DIVISION																												
WASHINGTON CAPITOLS	**38-22 .633**				**RED AUERBACH**										defeated Philadelphia 2-0; 92-70, H80-78; defeated New York 2-1; H77-71, 84-86(OT), H84-76; lost to Minneapolis 2-4; 84-88, 62-76, H74-94, H83-71, H74-65, 56-77													
Bob Feerick (knee injury)	F-G	6'3	190	28	58	248	708	35	256	298	**86**	188	171	752	3.2	2.9	13.0	1	0	0	—	2	2	100	1	1	2	2.0
Bones McKinney	F	6'6	187	29	57	263	801	33	197	279	71	114	216	723	2.0	3.8	12.7	10	45	127	35	38	52	73	9	36	128	12.8
Kleggie Hermson	C	6'9	235	25	60	248	794	31	212	311	68	99	257	708	1.7	4.3	11.8	11	40	149	27	55	83	66	12	**53**	135	12.3
Freddie Scolari (broken finger)	G	5'11	180	26	48	196	633	31	146	183	80	100	150	538	2.1	3.1	11.2	9	27	100	27	28	40	70	16	24	82	9.1
Sonny Hertzburg	G	5'10	175	26	60	154	541	28	134	164	82	114	140	442	1.9	2.3	7.4	11	39	112	35	40	47	85	27	33	118	10.7
Johnny Norlander	F	6'3	180	27	60	164	454	36	116	171	68	86	124	444	1.4	2.1	7.4	11	25	73	34	20	26	77	7	27	70	6.4
Jack Nichols	C-F	6'7	215	22	34	153	392	39	92	126	73	56	118	398	1.6	3.5	11.7	11	62	152	41	34	51	67	27	44	158	14.4
Matt Zunic	G-F	6'3	195	29	56	98	323	30	77	109	71	50	182	273	0.9	3.3	4.9	9	7	39	18	12	19	63	6	26	26	2.9
Leo Katkaveck	G	6'	185	25	53	84	253	33	53	71	75	68	110	221	1.3	2.1	4.2	9	7	29	24	6	8	75	10	13	20	2.2
Dick Schulz	F-G	6'2	192	30	50	65	278	23	65	91	71	53	107	195	1.1	2.1	3.9	11	17	74	23	20	35	57	27	36	54	4.9
Dick O'Keefe	G	6'2	185	25	50	70	274	26	51	99	52	43	119	191	0.9	2.4	3.8	11	22	60	37	13	20	65	11	37	57	5.2
NEW YORK KNICKERBOCKERS	**32-28 .533**				**JOE LAPCHICK (28—24 .539)** **RAY KUKA (4—4 .500)**										defeated Baltimore 2-1; 81-82, H84-74, H103-99(OT); lost to Washington 1-2; 71-77, H86-84(OT), 76-84													
Carl Braun	F-G	6'5	180	21	57	299	906	33	212	279	76	173	144	810	3.0	2.5	14.2	6	33	102	32	50	62	81	19	22	116	19.3
Bud Palmer	F	6'4	180	27	58	240	685	35	234	307	76	108	206	714	1.9	3.6	12.3	6	27	64	42	27	35	77	10	31	81	13.5
Lee Knorek	C	6'7	215	27	60	156	457	34	131	183	72	135	258	443	2.3	4.3	7.4	6	15	37	41	9	16	56	10	25	39	6.5
Butch Van Breda Kolff	G	6'3	185	26	59	127	401	32	161	240	67	143	148	415	2.4	2.5	7.0	6	15	40	38	19	23	83	7	14	49	8.2
Ray Lumpp (37g. Ind)	G	6'1	178	24	61	279	800	35	219	283	77	158	173	777	2.6	2.8	12.7	6	21	73	29	27	35	77	11	26	69	11.5
Harry Gallatin	C-F	6'6	215	21	52	157	479	33	120	169	71	63	127	434	1.2	2.4	8.3	6	20	56	36	32	39	82	10	31	72	12.0
Tex Ritter	G-F	6'2	185	24	55	123	353	35	91	146	62	57	71	337	1.0	1.3	6.1	5	10	33	30	11	20	55	2	15	31	6.2
Irv Rothenberg	C	6'8	215	26	53	101	367	28	112	174	64	68	174	314	1.3	3.3	5.9	6	4	19	21	2	10	20	2	12	10	1.7
Paul Noel	F	6'4	185	24	47	70	277	25	37	60	62	33	84	177	0.7	1.8	3.8	3	5	12	42	4	5	80	2	12	14	4.7
Mel McGaha	G-F	6'1	190	22	51	62	195	32	52	88	59	51	104	175	1.0	2.0	3.4	2	0	3	0	1	2	50	2	6	1	0.5
Joe Colone	F	6'5	210	22	15	35	113	31	13	19	68	9	25	83	0.6	1.7	5.5	4	7	30	23	3	6	50	3	13	17	4.3
Gene James	F	6'4	180	23	11	18	48	38	6	12	50	5	20	42	0.5	1.8	3.8	3	0	6	0	2	4	50	2	6	2	0.7
Ray Kuka (back injury)	F	6'3	200	26	8	10	36	28	5	9	56	11	16	25	1.4	2.0	3.1	(back injury)										
Dick Shrider (from Det NBL)	G	6'2	190	25	4	0	0	—	1	3	33	2	2	1	0.5	0.5	0.3											
BALTIMORE BULLETS	**29-31 .483**				**BUDDY JEANNETTE**										lost to New York 1-2; H82-81, 74-84, 99-103(OT)													
Fred Lewis (8g. Ind)	F-G	6'2	195	27	61	272	834	33	138	181	76	107	167	682	1.8	2.7	11.2	3	15	35	43	7	10	70	3	13	37	12.3
Walt Budko	F	6'5	220	23	60	224	644	35	244	309	79	99	201	692	1.7	3.4	11.5	3	11	26	42	15	19	79	4	16	37	12.3
Connie Simmons	C	6'8	220	23	60	299	794	38	181	265	68	116	215	779	1.9	3.6	13.0	3	13	37	35	22	29	76	7	12	48	16.0
Sid Tannenbaum (32g. NY, HO, IL)	G	6'	160	23	46	146	501	29	99	120	83	125	74	391	2.7	1.6	8.5	3	6	29	21	5	5	100	10	5	17	5.7
Chick Reiser	G	5'11	165	32	57	219	653	34	188	257	73	132	202	626	2.3	3.5	11.0	3	6	25	24	18	20	**90**	8	15	30	10.0
Jake PeLkington (14g. FtW)	C-F	6'6	220	31	54	193	469	41	211	267	79	131	216	597	2.4	4.0	11.1	3	13	33	39	27	35	77	3	13	53	17.7
Hal Tidrick (8g. Ind)	G-F	6'1	190	29	61	194	616	31	164	205	80	101	191	552	1.7	3.1	9.0	3	5	19	26	3	5	60	1	16	13	4.3
Stan Stutz	G	5'11	175	28	59	121	431	28	131	159	82	82	149	373	1.4	2.5	6.3	3	1	5	20	3	6	50	0	9	5	1.7
Johnny Ezersky (11g. Prov, 18g. Bos)	F	6'3	175	27	56	128	407	31	109	160	68	67	98	365	1.2	1.8	6.5											
Buddy Jeannette	G	5'11	175	31	56	73	199	37	167	213	78	124	157	313	2.2	2.8	5.6	3	2	13	15	4	4	100	5	11	8	2.7
Don Martin (37g. StL)	C-G	6'7	210	28	44	52	170	31	30	47	64	25	115	134	0.6	2.6	3.0											
Jack Toomay (13g. Was)	F-C	6'6	215	24	36	32	84	38	36	53	68	12	65	100	0.3	1.8	2.8	1	1	5	20	5	7	71	0	6	7	7.0
Dan Kraus	G	6'	195	25	13	5	35	14	11	24	46	7	24	21	0.5	1.8	1.6											
Howie Rader	G	6'1	190	25	13	7	45	16	3	10	30	14	25	17	1.1	1.9	1.3											
Doug Holcomb	F	6'4	200	25	3	3	12	25	9	14	64	5	5	15	1.7	1.7	5.0											
Herb Krautblatt	G	6'1	190	22	10	4	18	22	5	11	45	4	14	13	0.4	1.4	1.3											
Darrell Brown	F	6'2	175	25	3	2	6	33	0	2	0	0	3	4	0.0	1.0	1.3											
Ray Ramsey (FB)	G	6'2	166	27	2	0	1	0	2	2	100	0	0	2	0.0	0.0	1.0											
Paul Hoffman-heart condition, voluntarily retired																												
PHILADELPHIA WARRIORS	**28-32 .467**				**EDDIE GOTTLIEB**										lost to Washington 0-2; 70-92, H78-80													
Howie Dallmar (injury, CC)	F	6'4	202	26	38	105	342	31	83	116	72	116	104	293	3.1	2.7	7.7	2	4	18	22	5	7	71	4	9	13	6.5
Joe Fulks	F	6'5	190	27	60	529	**1689**	31	502	638	79	74	262	1560	1.2	4.4	26.0	1	0	0	—	0	0	—	0	1	0	0.0
Ed Sadowski	C	6'5	260	31	60	340	839	41	240	350	69	160	**273**	920	2.7	4.6	15.3	2	6	28	21	8	13	62	3	6	20	10.0
George Senesky	G	6'2	180	26	60	138	516	27	111	152	73	233	133	387	3.9	2.2	6.5	2	3	22	14	6	8	75	4	6	12	6.0
Angelo Musi	G	5'9	145	30	58	194	618	31	90	119	76	81	108	478	1.4	1.9	8.2	2	3	17	18	2	2	100	0	1	8	4.0
Gale Bishop	F	6'3	195	26	56	170	523	33	127	195	65	92	137	467	1.6	2.4	8.3	2	7	26	27	4	8	50	2	3	18	9.0
Jerry Fleishman	G-F	6'2	190	26	59	123	424	29	77	118	65	120	137	323	2.0	2.3	5.5	2	7	26	27	6	9	67	4	5	20	10.0
Chink Crossin	G	6'1	165	25	44	74	212	35	26	42	62	55	53	174	1.3	1.2	4.0	2	13	31	42	5	7	71	3	3	31	15.5
Irv Torgoff (29g. Bal, ST)	F-G	6'2	192	31	42	59	226	26	50	64	78	44	110	168	1.0	2.6	4.0	2	0	3	0	0	0	—	2	2	0	0.0
Jerry Rullo	G	5'10	165	25	39	53	183	29	31	45	69	48	71	137	1.2	1.8	3.5	2	2	8	25	2	2	100	1	9	6	3.0
Jake Bornheimer	C-F	6'5	205	21	15	34	109	31	20	29	69	13	47	88	0.9	3.1	5.9	2	7	17	41	6	9	67	2	11	20	10.0
Elmore Morgenthaler	C	7'	235	24	20	15	39	38	12	18	67	7	18	42	0.4	0.9	2.1											
Roy Pugh (4g. FtW, 6g. Ind)	C	6'6	210	25	23	13	51	25	6	19	32	9	17	32	0.4	0.7	1.4											

					TOTAL										PER GAME			PLAYOFFS										
Use Name	Pos	Hgt	Wgt	Age	G	FG	FGA	%	FT	FTA	%	Ass.	PF	Pts	Ass.	PF	Pts.	G	FG	FGA	%	FT	FTA	%	Ass	PF	Pts	PPG
1948/49 B.A.A. — EASTERN DIVISION (continued)																												
BOSTON CELTICS	25-35 .417				**DOGGIE JULIAN**																							
George Kaftan (CO)	F	6'3	190	20	21	116	315	37	72	115	63	61	28	304	2.9	1.3	14.5											
Bob Doll (from Den NBL)	F	6'5	195	29	47	145	438	33	80	117	68	117	118	370	2.5	2.5	7.9											
George Nostrand (33g. Prov)	C	6'8	197	24	60	212	651	33	165	284	58	94	164	589	1.6	2.7	9.8											
Dermie Connell (CO)	G	6'	174	20	21	87	315	28	30	56	54	65	40	204	3.1	1.9	9.7											
Jim Seminoff	G	6'2	210	26	58	153	487	31	151	219	69	229	195	457	3.9	3.4	7.9											
Eddie Ehlers	G-F	6'3	198	25	59	182	583	31	150	225	67	133	119	514	2.3	2.0	8.7											
Gene Stump	F	6'2	185	25	56	193	580	33	92	129	71	56	102	478	1.0	1.8	8.5											
Bob Kinnney (37g. FtW)	C	6'6	215	26	58	161	495	33	136	234	58	77	224	458	1.3	3.9	7.9											
Art Spector	F	6'4	200	31	59	130	434	30	64	116	55	77	111	324	1.3	1.9	5.5											
Tom Kelly	G	6'2	172	24	27	73	218	33	45	73	62	38	73	191	1.4	2.7	7.1											
Phil Farbman (27g. Phi)	F	6'4	185	24	48	50	163	31	55	81	68	36	86	155	0.8	1.8	3.2											
Johnny Bach	F-G	6'2	180	24	34	34	119	29	51	75	68	25	24	119	0.7	0.7	3.5											
Earl Shannon (27g. Prov)	G	5'11	170	25	32	34	127	27	39	58	67	44	33	107	1.4	1.0	3.3											
Stan Noszka (VR)	G	6'1	185	28	30	30	123	24	15	30	50	25	56	75	0.8	1.9	2.5											
Dutch Garfinkle	G	6'	205	30	9	12	70	17	10	14	71	17	19	34	1.9	2.1	3.8											
Hank Beeders	C	6'6	185	32	8	6	28	21	7	9	78	3	9	19	0.4	1.1	2.4											
John Hazen	G	6'2	172	21	6	6	17	35	6	7	86	3	10	18	0.5	1.7	3.0											
Al Lucas	F	6'3	195	26	2	1	3	33	0	0	—	2	0	2	1.0	0.0	1.0											
PROVIDENCE STEAMROLLERS	12-48 .200				**KEN LOEFFLER (11-41 .212), KENNY SAILORS & ERNIE CALVERLY (0-2 .000), JOE FAY (1-5 .167)**																							
Howie Shannon (IL)	F	6'2	175	25	55	292	802	36	152	189	80	125	154	736	2.3	2.8	13.4											
Brady Walker	F	6'6	205	27	59	202	556	36	87	155	56	68	100	491	1.2	1.7	8.3											
Chick Halbert (33g. Bos)	C	6'9	225	29	60	202	647	31	214	345	62	113	175	618	1.9	2.9	10.3											
Kenny Sailors	G	5'10	176	26	57	309	906	34	281	367	77	209	239	899	3.7	4.2	15.8											
Ernie Calverly	G	5'10	155	24	59	218	696	31	121	160	76	251	183	557	4.3	3.1	9.4											
Les Pugh	C-F	6'7	195	25	60	168	556	30	125	167	75	59	168	461	1.0	2.8	7.7											
Mel Riebe (33g. Bos)	G	5'11	195	32	43	172	589	29	79	133	59	104	110	423	2.4	2.6	9.8											
Carl Meinhold (15g. Chi)	G	6'2	185	22	50	101	306	33	61	96	64	47	60	263	0.9	1.2	5.3											
Buddy O'Grady (30g. StL)	G-F	5'11	160	28	47	85	293	29	49	71	69	68	57	219	1.4	1.2	4.7											
Bob Brown	F	6'4	205	25	20	37	111	33	34	47	72	14	67	108	0.7	3.4	5.4											
Giff Roux (19g. , sprained foot, StL)	F	6'5	195	25	45	29	118	25	29	44	66	20	30	87	0.4	0.7	1.9											
Bob Hubbard	C	6'6	215	26	34	25	135	19	22	34	65	18	39	72	0.5	1.1	2.1											
Andy Tonkovich (KJ)	G	6'1	185	26	17	19	71	27	6	9	67	10	12	44	0.6	0.7	2.6											
Lee Robbins	F	6'3	175	25	16	9	25	36	11	17	65	12	24	29	0.8	1.5	1.8											
Fred Paine	F	6'5	210	23	3	3	19	16	1	5	20	1	3	7	0.3	1.0	2.3											
Ben Scharnus	F	6'2	173	30	1	0	1	0	0	1	0	0	0	0	0.0	0.0	0.0											
Colb Gunther-VR, to St. Louis																												
1948/49 B.A.A. — WESTERN DIVISION																												
ROCHESTER ROYALS	45-15 .750				**EDDIE MALANOWICZ**									defeated St Louis 2-0; H93-64, 66-64 lost to Minneapolis 0-2; H79-80, 55-67														
Bill Calhoun (broken nose)	F	6'3	180	21	56	146	408	36	75	131	57	125	97	367	2.2	1.7	6.6	4	13	30	43	13	18	72	14	6	39	9.8
Arnie Johnson	F	6'5	240	28	60	156	375	42	199	284	70	80	247	511	1.3	4.1	8.5	4	11	41	27	16	22	73	7	16	38	9.5
Arnie Risen	C	6'9	200	24	60	345	816	**42**	305	462	66	100	216	995	1.7	3.6	16.6	4	22	53	42	22	33	67	10	16	66	16.5
Bob Davies	G-F	6'1	175	28	60	317	871	36	270	348	78	**321**	197	904	5.4	3.3	15.1	4	19	51	37	10	13	77	13	12	48	12.0
Bobby Wanzer	G	6'	172	27	60	202	533	38	209	254	82	186	132	613	3.1	2.2	10.2	4	13	41	32	12	17	71	9	9	38	9.5
Red Holzman	G	5'10	175	28	60	225	691	33	96	157	61	149	93	546	2.5	1.6	9.1	4	18	40	45	5	6	83	13	3	41	10.3
Andy Duncan	F	6'6	195	25	55	162	391	41	83	135	61	51	179	407	0.9	3.3	7.4	4	3	13	23	0	1	0	2	5	6	1.5
Mike Novak	C	6'9	220	33	60	124	363	34	72	124	58	112	188	320	1.9	3.1	5.3	4	6	22	27	1	1	100	10	13	13	3.3
Lionel Malamed (35g. Ind)	G	5'9	180	24	44	97	290	33	64	77	83	61	53	258	1.4	1.2	5.9											
Fran Curran (CT)	G	6'	175	26	57	61	168	36	85	126	67	78	118	207	1.4	2.1	3.6	4	1	5	20	2	2	100	3	3	4	1.0
Fuzzy Levane	F	6'2	190	28	36	55	193	28	13	21	62	39	37	123	1.1	1.0	3.4											
Bob Fitzgerald	F	6'5	195	25	18	6	29	21	7	10	70	12	26	19	0.7	1.4	1.1	1	0	1	0	0	0	—	0	1	0	0.0
MINNEAPOLIS LAKERS	44-16 .733				**JOHNNY KUNDLA**									defeated Chicago 2-0; H84-77, 101-85 defeated Rochester 2-0; 80-79, H67-55 defeated Washington 4-2; H88-84, H76-62, 94-74, 71-83, 65-74, H77-56														
Arnie Ferrin	F	6'4	180	23	47	130	378	34	85	128	66	76	142	508	1.6	3.0	10.8	10	26	77	34	30	45	67	21	41	82	8.2
Jim Pollard (leg injury)	F-C	6'5	190	26	53	314	792	40	156	227	69	142	144	784	2.7	2.7	14.8	10	43	147	29	44	62	71	**39**	31	130	13.0
George Mikan	C	6'10	245	24	60	**583**	1403	42	**532**	**689**	77	218	260	**1698**	3.6	4.3	**28.3**	10	**103**	**227**	45	**97**	**121**	80	21	44	**303**	**30.3**
Swede Carlson (ankle injury)	G	6'	170	28	55	211	632	33	86	130	66	170	180	508	3.1	3.3	9.2	10	23	95	24	14	25	56	28	30	60	6.0
Herm Schaefer	G	6'	175	30	58	214	572	37	174	213	82	185	121	602	3.2	2.1	10.4	10	48	104	**46**	28	32	88	31	22	124	12.4
Tony Jaros	F	6'3	185	28	59	132	385	34	79	110	72	58	114	343	1.0	1.9	5.8	10	20	56	36	18	23	78	11	28	58	5.8
Jack Dwan	F	6'4	200	27	60	121	380	32	34	69	49	129	157	276	2.2	2.6	4.6	10	7	29	24	4	9	44	9	22	18	1.8
Donnie Forman	G	5'10	175	22	44	68	231	29	43	67	64	74	94	179	1.7	2.1	4.1	9	3	20	15	7	11	64	7	15	13	1.4
Whitely Kachan (33g. Chi)	G	6'2	175	23	52	38	142	27	36	56	64	37	81	112	0.7	1.6	2.2	8	2	5	40	0	0	—	2	3	4	0.5
Johnny Jorgensen	G	6'2	185	27	48	41	114	36	24	33	73	33	68	106	0.7	1.4	2.2	6	3	7	43	1	1	100	0	4	7	1.2
Earl Gardner	F	6'3	200	22	50	38	101	38	13	28	46	19	50	89	0.4	1.0	1.8	7	1	9	11	2	4	50	1	3	4	0.6
Don Smith (ST)	F	6'2	190	28	8	2	13	15	2	3	67	2	6	6	0.3	0.8	0.8											
Jack Tingle	F	6'4	205	23	2	1	6	17	0	0	—	1	2	2	0.5	1.0	1.0											
Ray Ellerson (to Wat NBL)	C	6'8	230	26	3	1	5	20	0	0	—	0	2	2	0.0	0.7	0.7											

1948/49 B.A.A. - WESTERN DIVISION (continued)

Use Name	Pos	Hgt	Wgt	Age	G	FG	FGA	%	FT	FTA	%	Ass.	PF	Pts.	Ass.	PF	Pts.	G	FG	FGA	%	FT	FTA	%	Ass	PF	Pts.	PPG
					TOTAL										PER GAME			PLAYOFFS										
CHICAGO STAGS	**38-22 .633**				**OLE OLSEN (31-20 .608), PHIL BROWNSTEIN (7-2 .778)**													lost to Minneapolis 0-2; 77-84, H85-101										
Gene Vance	F-G	6'3	196	25	56	222	657	34	131	181	72	167	217	575	3.0	3.9	10.3	2	8	35	23	5	6	83	7	11	21	10.5
Odie Spears	F	6'5	205	23	57	200	631	32	131	197	66	97	200	531	1.7	3.5	9.3	2	7	26	27	4	7	57	2	9	18	9.0
Ed Mikan	C	6'8	230	23	60	229	729	31	136	183	74	62	191	594	1.0	3.2	9.9	2	8	38	21	0	3	0	1	6	16	8.0
Andy Phillip	G	6'3	195	26	60	285	818	35	148	219	68	319	205	718	5.3	3.4	12.0	2	14	36	39	11	11	100	12	9	39	19.5
Max Zaslofsky	G	6'2	170	23	58	425	1216	35	347	413	84	149	156	1197	2.6	2.7	20.6	2	15	49	31	14	18	78	6	3	44	22.0
Stan Miasek	F-C	6'5	210	24	58	169	488	35	113	216	52	57	208	451	1.0	3.6	7.8	2	6	16	38	7	11	64	1	9	19	9.5
Kenny Rollins	G	6'	168	25	59	144	520	28	77	104	74	167	150	365	2.8	2.5	6.2	2	0	6	0	0	0	—	2	2	0	0.0
Chuck Gilmur	F	6'4	225	26	56	110	281	39	66	121	55	125	194	286	2.2	3.5	5.1	2	1	3	33	1	3	33	3	8	3	1.5
Mike Bloom (24g. Min)	C-F	6'6	190	33	45	35	181	19	56	74	76	32	53	126	0.7	1.2	2.8	1	0	0	—	0	0	—	0	1	0	0.0
Joe Graboski	C	6'7	195	18	45	54	157	34	19	47	35	18	86	125	0.4	1.9	2.8	1	0	6	0	0	0	—	0	1	0	0.0
Jim Browne	C	6'10	235	18	4	1	2	50	1	2	50	0	4	3	0.0	1.0	0.8											
ST LOUIS BOMBERS	**29-31 .483**				**GRADY LEWIS**													lost to Rochester 0-2; 64-93, H64-66										
Easy Parham	F-G	6'3	200	27	60	124	404	31	96	172	56	151	134	344	2.5	2.2	5.7	2	5	13	38	0	0	—	6	6	10	5.0
Ariel Maughan	F-G	6'4	190	25	55	206	650	32	184	285	65	99	134	596	1.8	2.4	10.8	2	0	6	0	2	3	67	3	3	2	1.0
Red Rocha	C-F	6'9	185	25	58	223	574	39	162	211	77	157	251	608	2.7	4.3	10.5	2	16	36	44	4	5	80	6	6	36	18.0
Belus Smawley	G-F	6'1	195	30	59	352	946	37	210	281	75	183	145	914	3.1	2.5	15.5	2	5	12	42	0	0	—	0	4	10	5.0
Johnny Logan	G-F	6'2	175	27	57	282	816	35	239	302	79	276	191	803	4.8	3.4	14.1	2	7	23	30	6	9	67	8	10	20	10.0
Otto Schnellbacher (23g. KJ, Prov-FB)	F-G	6'5	185	25	43	93	280	33	89	133	67	64	109	275	1.5	2.5	6.4	2	6	20	30	6	12	50	6	9	18	9.0
Don Putman	G-F	6'1	170	26	59	98	330	30	52	97	54	140	132	248	2.4	2.2	4.2	2	2	11	18	0	3	0	4	6	4	2.0
Bill Roberts (2g. Chi, 26g. Bos)	C	6'9	210	23	50	89	267	33	44	63	70	41	113	22	0.8	2.3	0.4	2	10	29	34	2	5	40	2	10	22	11.0
Colby Gunther (from Prov-VR)	F	6'4	190	24	32	57	181	31	45	71	63	33	64	159	1.0	2.0	5.0	1	0	1	0	0	0	—	0	0	0	0.0
Grady Lewis	C	6'7	215	31	34	53	137	39	42	70	60	37	104	148	1.1	3.1	4.4											
Bill Miller (14g. Chi)	F	6'3	190	24	28	21	72	29	11	20	55	20	32	53	0.7	1.1	1.9	1	0	0	—	0	2	0	0	0	0	0.0
D.C. Wilcutt	G	6'2	165	25	22	18	51	35	15	18	83	31	9	51	1.4	0.4	2.3	2	3	7	43	0	0	—	4	2	6	3.0
Bob O'Brien (16g. Phi)	F	6'4	190	25	24	10	50	20	12	32	38	9	32	32	0.4	1.3	1.3											
Lonnie Eggleston	G	6'	170	30	2	1	4	25	2	3	67	1	3	4	0.5	1.5	2.0											
FORT WAYNE PISTONS	**22-38 .367**				**CARL BENNETT (0-6 .000), CURLY ARMSTRONG (22-32 .407)**																							
Jack Smiley	F-G	6'3	190	26	59	141	571	25	112	164	68	138	202	394	2.3	3.4	6.7											
Charlie Black (41g. Ind)	F-C	6'5	200	27	58	203	691	29	161	291	55	140	247	567	2.4	4.3	9.8											
John Mahnken (7g. Bal, 13g. Ind)	C	6'8	220	26	57	215	830	26	104	167	62	125	215	534	2.2	3.8	9.4											
Brule Hale	G-F	6'1	170	30	52	187	585	32	172	228	75	156	112	546	3.0	2.2	10.5											
Bob Tough (KJ)	G-F	6'	185	26	53	183	661	28	100	138	72	99	101	466	1.9	1.9	8.8											
Curly Armstrong	G	5'11	170	30	52	131	428	31	118	169	70	105	152	380	2.0	2.9	7.3											
Richie Niemiera	G-F	6'1	165	27	55	115	331	35	132	165	80	96	115	362	1.7	2.1	6.6											
Leo Klier (leg and chest injuries)	F	6'2	170	25	47	125	492	25	97	137	71	56	124	347	1.2	2.6	7.4											
Dick Triptow	G	6'	170	26	55	116	417	28	102	141	72	96	107	334	1.7	1.9	6.1											
Bill Henry	C	6'9	220	24	32	96	300	32	125	203	62	55	110	317	1.7	3.4	9.9											
Ward Williams	F-C	6'4	195	25	53	61	257	24	93	124	75	82	158	215	1.5	3.0	4.1											
Dillard Crocker (to And NBL)	F	6'4	205	23	2	1	4	25	4	6	67	0	3	6	0.0	1.5	3.0											
INDIANAPOLIS JETS	**18-42 .300**				**BRUCE HALE (3-13 .188), BURL FRIDDLE (15-29 .341)**																							
Price Brookfield	F-G	6'4	200	28	54	176	638	28	90	125	72	136	145	442	2.5	2.7	8.2											
Leo Mogus (13g. Bal, 20g. FtW)	F-C	6'4	205	27	52	172	509	34	177	243	73	104	170	521	2.0	3.3	10.0											
Blackie Towery (22g. FtW)	C-F	6'4	210	28	60	203	771	26	195	263	74	171	243	601	2.9	4.1	10.0											
Tommy Byrnes (35g. NY)	G-F	6'3	175	25	57	160	525	30	92	149	62	102	84	412	1.8	1.5	7.2											
Walt Kirk (14g. FtW)	G	6'3	180	24	49	140	406	34	167	231	72	118	127	447	2.4	2.6	9.1											
Ralph Hamilton (10g. FtW)	G	6'1	188	27	48	114	447	26	61	91	67	83	67	289	1.7	1.4	6.0											
John Mandic	F	6'4	205	29	56	97	302	32	75	115	65	80	151	269	1.4	2.7	4.8											
Fritz Nagy	G-F	6'2	185	24	50	94	271	35	65	97	67	68	84	253	1.4	1.7	5.1											
Andy Kostecka (ST)	F-G	6'3	203	27	21	46	110	42	43	70	61	14	48	135	0.7	2.3	6.4											
George Glamack (to Ham NBL)	C	6'8	245	29	11	30	121	25	42	55	76	19	28	102	1.7	2.5	9.3											
Jack Eskridge (3g. Chi)	C-F	6'5	200	24	23	25	69	36	14	20	70	14	25	64	0.6	1.1	2.8											
Marty Passaglia	G-F	6'1	170	29	10	14	57	25	3	4	75	17	17	31	1.7	1.7	3.1											
Dick Wehr	F-G	6'4	180	23	9	5	21	24	2	6	33	3	12	12	0.3	1.3	1.3											
Jim Spruill (FB)	F-G	6'2	225	25	1	1	3	33	0	0	—	0	3	2	0.0	3.0	2.0											
Jim Springer	C	6'9	235	23	2	0	0	—	1	1	100	0	0	1	0.0	0.0	0.5											
Jack Maddox (from Ham NBL)	F-G	6'3	190	27	1	0	0	—	0	0	—	1	0	0	1.0	0.0	0.0											
Paul Napolitano	G	6'2	185	25	1	0	0	—	0	0	—	0	0	0	0.0	0.0	0.0											

Ken Menke - voluntarily retired

1948/49 B.A.A. TEAM STATISTICS

Team	REGULAR SEASON								AVERAGE POINTS			PLAYOFFS								AVERAGE POINTS		
	G	FG	FGA	%	FT	FTA	%	Ass.	For	Agnst.	Diff.	G	FG	FGA	%	FT	FTA	%	Ass.	For	Agnst.	Diff.
EASTERN DIVISION																						
Washington	60	1751	5472	32	1408	1914	74	972	81.8	79.4	+2.4	11	291	915	32	268	383	70	153	77.3	77.5	-0.2
New York	60	1688	5237	32	1376	1959	70	1017	79.2	77.7	+1.5	6	157	476	33	187	257	73	80	83.5	83.3	+0.2
Baltimore	60	1736	5162	34	**1545**	2053	**75**	1000	83.6	82.2	+1.4	3	73	227	32	**109**	**140**	78	41	**85.0**	89.3	-4.3
Philadelphia	60	1831	5695	32	1360	1897	72	1043	83.7	83.4	+0.3	2	52	196	27	44	65	68	25	74.0	86.0	-12.0
Boston	60	1706	5483	31	1181	1856	64	1135	76.6	79.5	-2.9											
Providence	60	1750	5427	32	1207	1742	69	1026	78.5	87.6	-9.1											
WESTERN DIVISION																						
Rochester	60	1811	4869	**37**	1420	**2060**	69	1259	**84.0**	77.4	+6.6	4	106	297	36	81	113	72	**81**	73.3	68.8	+4.5
Minneapolis	60	1885	5146	37	1272	1759	72	1134	**84.0**	**76.7**	**+7.3**	10	279	776	**36**	245	333	**74**	170	80.3	**72.9**	**+7.4**
Chicago	60	**1905**	**5750**	33	1228	1775	69	1220	84.0	80.0	+4.0	2	**59**	**215**	27	44	61	72	34	81.0	92.5	-11.5
St. Louis	60	1659	4858	34	1229	1770	69	**1269**	75.8	79.4	-3.6	2	54	158	34	20	39	61	39	64.0	79.5	-15.5
Fort Wayne	60	1536	5370	29	1385	1979	70	1082	74.3	77.5	-3.2											
Indianapolis	60	1621	5367	30	1240	1798	69	1225	74.7	79.4	-4.7											

1948/49 B.A.A. STANDINGS

Team	W	L	Pct.	GB	Record against playoff teams			Record against non - playoff teams			HOME			ROAD			NEUTRAL		
					W	L	Pct.	W	L	Pct.	W	L	Pct.	W	L	Pct.	W	L	Pct.
EASTERN DIVISION																			
Washington Capitols	38	22	.633	—	21	17	.553	17	5	.773	22	7	.759	15	14	.517	1	1	.500
New York Knickerbockers	32	28	.533	6	16	22	.421	16	6	.727	18	11	.621	12	17	.414	2	0	**1.000**
Baltimore Bullets	29	31	.483	9	14	24	.368	15	7	.682	17	12	.586	11	17	.393	1	2	.333
Philadelphia Warriors	28	32	.467	10	15	23	.395	13	9	.591	19	10	.655	9	21	.300	0	1	.000
Boston Celtics	25	35	.417	13	15	29	.341	10	6	.625	17	12	.586	7	20	.259	1	3	.250
Providence Steamrollers	12	**48**	.200	26	7	**37**	.159	5	**11**	.313	7	**23**	.233	5	23	.179	0	2	.000
WESTERN DIVISION																			
Rochester Royals	**45**	15	**.750**	—	**27**	11	**.711**	18	4	.818	24	5	.828	**20**	10	**.667**	1	0	**1.000**
Minneapolis Lakers	44	16	.733	1	26	12	.684	18	4	.818	**26**	3	**.897**	16	13	.552	2	0	**1.000**
Chicago Stags	38	22	.633	7	19	19	.500	**19**	3	**.864**	16	8	.667	18	14	.563	4	0	**1.000**
St. Louis Bombers	29	31	.483	16	14	24	.368	15	7	.682	17	12	.586	10	18	.357	2	1	.667
Fort Wayne Pistons	22	38	.367	23	14	30	.318	8	8	.500	15	14	.517	5	**23**	.179	2	1	.000
Indianapolis Jets	18	42	.300	27	9	35	.205	9	7	.563	14	15	.483	4	22	.154	0	**5**	.000

1948/49 B.A.A. INDIVIDUAL LEADERS

SCORING
(Minimum 40 Games Played)

Name	Team	G	FG	FT	Pts.	Avg.
Mikan	Min	60	583	532	1698	28.3
Fulks	Phi	60	529	502	1560	26.0
Zaslofsky	Chi	58	425	347	1197	20.6
Risen	Roch	60	345	305	995	16.6
Sailors	Prov	57	309	281	899	15.8
Smawley	StL	59	352	210	914	15.5
Sadowski	Phi	60	340	240	920	15.3
Davies	Roch	60	317	270	904	15.1
Pollard	Min	53	314	156	784	14.8
Braun	NY	57	299	212	810	14.2

FIELD GOAL PERCENTAGE
(Minimum 200 Field Goals)

Name	Team	FG	FGA	Pct.
Risen	Roch	345	816	.423
Mikan	Min	583	1403	.416
Sadowski	Phi	340	839	.405
Pollard	Min	314	792	.396
Rocha	StL	223	573	.389
Wamer	Roch	202	533	.379
Simmons	Bal	299	794	.377
Schaefer	Min	214	572	.374
Smawley	StL	352	946	.372
Shannon	Prov	292	802	.364

FREE THROW PERCENTAGE
(Minimum 150 Free Throws)

Name	Team	FT	FTA	Pct.
Feerik	Was	256	298	.859
Zaslofsky	Chi	347	413	.840
Wanzer	Roch	209	254	.823
Schaefer	Min	174	213	.817
Shannon	Prov	152	189	.804
Tidrick	Ind-Bal	164	205	.800
Logan	StL	239	302	.791
Pelkington	FtW-Bal	211	267	.790
Budko	Bal	244	309	.790
Fulks	Phi	502	638	.787

PERSONAL FOULS

Name	Team	PF
Sadowski	Phi	273
Fulks	Phi	262
Mikan	Min	260
Knorek	NY	258
Hermsen	Was	257

ASSISTS PER GAME
(Minimum 40 Games Played)

Name	Team	G	Ass.	Avg.
Davies	Roch	60	321	5.4
Phillip	Chi	60	319	5.3
Logan	StL	57	276	4.8
Calverly	Prov	59	251	4.3
Seminoff	Bos	58	229	3.9
Senesky	Phi	60	233	3.9
Sailors	Prov	57	209	3.7
Mikan	Min	60	218	3.6
Feerick	Was	58	188	3.2
Schaefer	Min	58	185	3.2

1949-50 N.B.A.

An Overflowing Consolidation

Three years of financial warfare ended with the merger of the B.A.A. and the N.B.L., giving birth to a far-flung hodgepodge called the National Basketball Association. From last year's B.A.A. came New York, Boston, Philadelphia, Washington, Baltimore, Rochester, Minneapolis, Chicago, St. Louis, and Ft. Wayne. From the N.B.L. came Syracuse, Anderson, Tri-Cities Waterloo, Sheboygan, and Denver. Debuting in the pro ranks were the Indianapolis Olympians, composed mostly of graduated University of Kentucky stars. The seventeen clubs stretched from Boston to Denver as the merger weeded out only five teams. The B.A.A. clubs of Providence and Indianapolis and the N.B.L. entries of Hammond, Oshkosh, and Dayton fell by the wayside.

League Commissioner Maurice Podoloff faced tremendous scheduling problems. He put the new Indianapolis club and five N.B.L. teams into the Western Division, kept the B.A.A's western wing together as the Central Division, and put Syracuse, the strongest of the N.B.L. clubs, in with the B.A.A.'s eastern clubs. The demands of travel, especially in an era before flying was common, led to an unbalanced schedule, with Eastern and Central teams slated for 68 games and Western teams for 62 games. To add to the confusion, Syracuse was a member of the Eastern Division but played a Western schedule of 62 games.

But as chaotic as it seemed, this league admittedly had the nation's top pro teams (with the possible exception of the Globetrotters) The two best teams battled it out at the top of the Central Division. The Minneapolis Lakers had George Mikan at center, and he was at the peak of his game; he led the circuit with a 27.4 scoring average, hit for a high game of 51 points in one contest, and was brutally effective as a rebounder and defender. Forward Jim Pollard headed up the supporting cast that included three top rookies: 6'7" rebounder Vern Mikkelsen, 5'10" playmaker Slater Martin, and 6'3" reserve forward Bud Grant, a future great football coach. As strong as the Lakers were, the Rochester Royals tied them for first place with a late-season winning streak of 15 games. Relying on mobility and ball-handling, the Royal attack centered on veteran guards Bob Davies and Bobby Wanzer and on center Arnie Risen. Both the Lakers and Royals finished at 51-17.

Tied for third were the Ft. Wayne Pistons, with a hot rookie in forward Fred Schaus, and the Chicago Stags, with guards Max Zaslofsky and Andy Phillip still the heart of the team. The St. Louis Bombers signed rookie Ed Macauley, a weak-rebounding but high-scoring center from the University of St. Louis, but the Bombers nevertheless finished last.

In the West, only Indianapolis and Anderson finished above .500. The Olympians had two of the best known college players of the postwar years: center Alex Groza and guard Ralph Beard. Both reacted splendidly to their new pro surroundings. Groza finished second to Mikan with a 23.4 scoring average, three times going over 40 points in one game. The Anderson Packers had won the final N.B.L. championship, and led by guard Frankie Brian, they made their only season in the N.B.A. a winning one. The Tri-Cities Blackhawks came in third despite owner Ben Kerner hiring Red Auerbach as coach after he was fired by Washington. Sheboygan won the fourth playoff spot with a 22-40 record, while Waterloo and Denver finished out of sight in the depths of the West.

Playing a heavy schedule against the weaker Western teams, the Syracuse Nats put together the best record in the league, a sparkling 51-13 mark. The schedule didn't explain how the Nats won nine of ten games against Eastern teams and seven of ten from Central teams; their talent did that. Old pro Al Cervi was the backcourt leader and coach, and Dolph Schayes, Now a rugged star who could score both with long set shots and with inside muscle, was the ace scorer. Other key men on this scrappy squad included strong center George Ratkovicz, forward Alex Hannum, and guards Billy Gabor and Paul Seymour.

The New York Knicks finished a strong second in the East, with coach Joe Lapchick putting together a deep squad which excelled at running and team basketball. Bud Palmer had quit to concentrate on a broadcasting career, but shooter Carl Braun and rebounder Harry Gallatin returned from last year's team. Center Connie Simmons came over from Baltimore, and rookies Vince Boryla, Dick McGuire, and Ernie Vandeweghe added their college reputations and solid talent. The stocky Boryla had just finished setting scoring records at the University of Denver with his hook shot, McGuire came from St. John's with a poor shot but great playmaking ability, and Colgate's Vandeweghe added forward strength whenever he could get away from his medical studies. The Washington Capitols, without coach Auerbach but with lots of veteran players, finished third. Philadelphia barely managed to take the fourth playoff spot abead of Baltimore and Boston as Joe Fulks had a poor season.

After Minneapolis beat Rochester and Ft. Wayne beat Chicago in one-game tie-breakers in the Central Division, the opening round of the playoffs began. Six clubs bit the dust in that round, and the second round left Syracuse Minneapolis, and Anderson as the divisional champs. The Lakers then polished off the Packers in two straight games and readied themselves for the Nats in the title series.

The Lakers took the first game in Syracuse 68-66 on a last-second heave by Bob Harrison. The Nats won the second game 91-85, but the Lakers were happy to come away with a split on enemy territory. Back in Minnesota, the Lakers drilled out 91-77 and 77-69 victories, using their superior strength to beat down the well-coordinated Nats. The scene for the sixth game shifted to Syracuse, and the Nats used new tactics to combat the Lakers. Coach Cervi put tough Paul Seymour on Jim Pollard as a watchdog, and he sent his big men into the game in relays to physically work George Mikan over. The strategy worked, as the Nats held a 21-point lead with only six minutes left and coasted to an 83-76 triumph. But once the teams got back to Minneapolis, the Lakers took the upper hand; with Mikan muscling his way to 40 points, and with several fights enlivening the proceedings, the Lakers pounded out a 110-95 victory that brought them the first N.B.A. championship.

1949/50 N.B.A. - CENTRAL DIVISION

MINNEAPOLIS LAKERS 51-17 .750 **JOHNNY KUNDLA**

defeated Rochester 78-76 at Rochester in playoff for first place
defeated Chicago 2-0; H85-75, 75-67
defeated Fort Wayne 2-0; H93-79, 89-82
defeated Anderson 2-0; H75-50, 90-71
defeated Syracuse 4-2; 68-66, 85-92, H91-77, H77-69, 76-83, H110-95

Use Name	Pos	Hgt	Wgt	Age	TOTAL G	FG	FGA	%	FT	FTA	%	Ass.	PF	Pts.	PER GAME Ass.	PF	Pts.	PLAYOFFS G	FG	FGA	%	FT	FTA	%	Ass	PF	Pts	PPG
Jim Pollard	F	6'5	190	27	66	394	1140	35	185	242	76	252	143	973	3.8	2.2	14.7	12	50	175	29	44	62	71	**56**	36	144	12.0
Vern Mikkelsen	F-C	6'7	230	21	68	288	722	40	215	286	75	123	222	791	1.8	3.3	11.6	12	55	149	37	46	60	77	18	**52**	156	13.0
George Mikan	C	6'10	245	25	68	**649**	**1595**	41	**567**	**728**	78	197	**297**	**1865**	2.9	4.4	**27.4**	12	**121**	**316**	38	**134**	**170**	79	36	47	**376**	**31.3**
Herm Schaefer	G	6'	175	31	65	122	314	39	86	101	85	203	104	330	3.1	1.6	5.1	12	16	42	38	19	22	86	16	12	51	4.3
Slater Martin	G	5'10	170	24	67	106	302	35	59	93	63	148	162	271	2.2	2.4	4.0	12	21	50	42	14	24	58	25	35	56	4.7
Arnie Ferrin	F-G	6'4	180	24	63	132	396	33	76	109	70	95	147	340	1.5	2.3	5.4	12	33	97	34	16	29	55	30	51	82	6.8
Bob Harrison	G	6'2	190	22	66	125	348	36	50	74	68	131	175	300	2.0	2.7	4.5	12	16	37	43	10	14	71	12	34	42	3.5
Billy Hassett (18g. TC)	G	5'11	180	28	60	84	302	28	104	161	65	137	136	272	2.3	2.3	4.5	7	3	12	25	3	10	30	4	8	9	1.3
Swede Carlson	G	6'	170	29	57	99	290	34	69	95	73	76	126	267	1.3	2.2	4.7	10	21	37	57	12	15	80	11	19	54	5.4
Tony Jaros	F	6'3	185	29	61	84	289	29	72	96	75	60	106	240	1.0	1.7	3.9	2	0	3	0	1	2	50	0	2	1	0.5
Bud Grant	F	6'3	195	22	35	42	115	37	7	17	41	19	36	91	0.5	1.0	2.6	11	18	45	40	7	14	50	7	25	43	3.9
Normie Glick	F	6'7	195	22	1	1	1	100	0	0	—	1	2	2	1.0	2.0	2.0											

ROCHESTER ROYALS 51-17 .750 **LES HARRISON**

lost to Minneapolis 76-78 at home in playoff for first place
lost to Fort Wayne 0-2; H84-90, 78-79(OT)

Use Name	Pos	Hgt	Wgt	Age	TOTAL G	FG	FGA	%	FT	FTA	%	Ass.	PF	Pts.	PER GAME Ass.	PF	Pts.	PLAYOFFS G	FG	FGA	%	FT	FTA	%	Ass	PF	Pts	PPG
Arnie Johnson	F	6'5	240	29	68	149	376	40	200	294	68	141	260	498	2.1	3.8	7.3	2	6	12	50	8	12	67	5	11	20	10.0
Jack Coleman	F-C	6'7	195	25	68	250	663	38	90	121	74	153	223	590	2.3	3.3	8.7	2	7	20	35	1	1	100	4	8	15	7.5
Arnie Risen (KJ)	C	6'9	205	25	62	206	598	34	213	321	66	92	228	625	1.5	3.7	10.1	2	7	19	37	9	15	60	4	7	23	11.5
Bob Davies (ankle injury)	G	6'1	175	29	64	317	887	36	261	347	75	294	187	895	4.6	2.9	14.0	2	4	17	24	7	8	88	9	11	15	7.5
Bobby Wanzer	G	6'	172	28	67	254	614	41	283	351	81	214	102	791	3.2	1.5	11.8	2	8	17	47	11	13	85	4	7	27	13.5
Bill Calhoun	F	6'3	180	22	62	207	549	38	146	203	72	115	100	560	1.9	1.6	9.0	(injured)										
Red Holzman	G	5'10	175	29	68	206	625	33	144	210	69	200	67	556	2.9	1.0	8.2	2	3	9	33	1	2	50	0	3	7	3.5
Fran Curran	G	6'	175	24	66	98	235	42	199	241	83	71	113	395	1.1	1.7	6.0	2	2	7	29	1	1	100	0	0	5	2.5
Andy Duncan	F	6'6	195	27	67	125	289	43	60	108	56	42	160	310	0.6	2.4	4.6	2	2	3	67	2	2	100	1	5	6	3.0
Ed Mikan (21g. Chi)	C-F	6'8	230	24	65	89	321	28	92	120	77	42	143	270	0.6	2.2	4.2	2	8	24	33	10	11	91	2	8	26	13.0
Pep Saul	G	6'2	185	25	49	74	183	40	34	47	72	28	33	182	0.6	0.7	3.7	2	7	13	54	4	5	80	4	8	18	9.0
Price Brookfield	F	6'4	200	29	7	11	23	48	12	13	92	1	7	34	0.1	1.0	4.9											

FORT WAYNE PISTONS 40-28 .588 **MURRAY MENDENHALL**

Use Name	Pos	Hgt	Wgt	Age	TOTAL G	FG	FGA	%	FT	FTA	%	Ass.	PF	Pts.	PER GAME Ass.	PF	Pts.	PLAYOFFS G	FG	FGA	%	FT	FTA	%	Ass	PF	Pts	PPG
Fred Schaus	F	6'5	195	24	68	351	996	35	270	330	82	176	232	972	2.6	3.4	14.3	4	24	66	36	26	31	84	11	9	74	18.5
Bob Carpenter	F	6'5	200	32	66	212	617	34	190	256	74	92	168	614	1.4	2.5	9.3	4	11	30	37	10	14	71	2	6	32	8.0
Howie Shultz (35g. And)	C-F	6'6	220	27	67	179	771	23	196	282	70	169	244	554	2.5	3.6	8.3	4	15	61	25	13	17	76	4	15	37	9.3
Curly Armstrong	G	5'11	170	31	63	144	516	28	170	241	71	170	217	458	2.7	3.4	7.3	3	4	22	18	1	4	25	6	6	9	3.0
Boag Johnson (35g. And)	G	5'11	170	28	67	243	779	31	104	129	81	171	207	590	2.6	3.1	8.8	4	8	32	25	12	16	75	8	13	28	7.0
Jack Kerris (4g. TC)	F-C	6'6	215	24	68	157	481	33	169	260	65	119	175	483	1.8	2.6	7.1	4	12	30	40	13	22	59	5	17	37	9.3
Bob Harris	F	6'7	195	22	62	168	465	36	140	223	63	129	190	476	2.1	3.1	7.7	4	9	32	28	12	20	60	11	15	30	7.5
Duane Klueh (33g. Den)	G-F	6'3	175	23	52	159	414	38	157	222	71	91	111	475	1.8	2.1	9.1	2	2	10	20	5	5	100	3	8	9	4.5
Leo Klier	G	6'2	170	26	66	157	516	30	141	190	74	121	177	455	1.8	2.7	6.9	2	0	3	0	1	1	100	3	1	1	0.5
Johnny OLdham	G	6'3	175	26	59	127	426	30	103	145	71	99	192	357	1.7	3.3	6.1											
Clint Wager	C-G	6'6	230	29	63	57	203	28	29	47	62	90	175	143	1.4	2.8	2.3	4	11	25	44	8	10	80	8	22	30	7.5
Jerry Nagel	G	6'	190	21	14	6	28	21	1	4	25	18	11	13	1.3	0.8	0.9											
Gene Englund-(VR)(to Boston)																												

CHICAGO STAGS 40-28 .588 **PHIL BROWNSTEIN**

lost to Fort Wayne 69-86 at Fort Wayne in playoff for third place
lost Minneapolis 0-2; 75-85, H67-75

Use Name	Pos	Hgt	Wgt	Age	TOTAL G	FG	FGA	%	FT	FTA	%	Ass.	PF	Pts.	PER GAME Ass.	PF	Pts.	PLAYOFFS G	FG	FGA	%	FT	FTA	%	Ass	PF	Pts	PPG
Leo Barnhorst	F	6'4	190	25	67	174	499	35	90	129	70	140	192	438	2.1	2.9	6.5	2	8	25	32	6	6	100	4	10	22	11.0
Odie Spears	F	6'5	205	24	68	277	775	36	158	230	69	159	250	712	2.3	3.7	10.5	2	9	22	41	5	10	50	1	11	23	11.5
Kleggie Hermsen	C	6'9	235	26	67	196	615	32	153	247	62	98	267	545	1.5	4.0	8.1	2	7	24	29	4	5	80	5	12	18	9.0
Andy Phillip	G	6'3	195	27	65	284	814	35	190	270	70	377	210	758	**5.8**	3.2	11.7	2	7	27	26	10	13	77	12	8	24	12.0
Max Zaslofsky	G-F	6'2	170	24	68	397	1132	35	321	381	**84**	155	185	1115	2.3	2.7	16.4	2	15	32	47	15	18	83	6	7	45	22.5
Stan Miasek	F-C	6'5	210	25	68	176	462	38	146	221	66	75	264	498	1.1	3.9	7.3	1	2	4	50	1	1	100	0	2	5	5.0
Frank Kudelka	G-F	6'2	193	24	65	172	528	33	89	140	64	132	198	433	2.0	3.0	6.7	2	2	10	20	1	2	50	4	4	5	2.5
Kenny Rollins	G	6'	168	26	66	144	421	34	66	89	74	131	129	354	2.0	2.0	5.4	2	0	3	0	0	0	—	0	4	0	0.0
George Nostrand (18g. Bos, 1g. TC)	C	6'8	197	25	55	78	255	31	56	99	57	29	118	212	0.5	2.1	3.9											
Joe Graboski	C-F	6'8	200	19	57	75	247	30	53	89	60	37	95	203	0.6	1.7	3.6	1	0	0	—	0	0	—	0	0	0	0.0
Joe Bradley	G	6'3	175	21	46	36	134	27	15	38	39	36	51	87	0.8	1.1	1.9											
Bob Hahn	C	6'10	240	24	10	4	13	31	2	7	29	1	17	10	0.1	1.7	1.0											
Gene Vance - VR, to T-C																												

ST. LOUIS BOMBERS 26-42 .382 **GRADY LEWIS (23-38 .377), JOHNNY LOGAN (3-4 .333)**

Use Name	Pos	Hgt	Wgt	Age	TOTAL G	FG	FGA	%	FT	FTA	%	Ass.	PF	Pts.	PER GAME Ass.	PF	Pts.	PLAYOFFS G	FG	FGA	%	FT	FTA	%	Ass	PF	Pts	PPG
Ariel Maughan	F	6'4	190	26	68	160	574	28	157	205	77	101	174	477	1.5	2.6	7.0											
Red Rocha	F	6'9	185	26	65	275	679	41	220	313	70	155	257	770	2.4	4.0	11.8											
Ed Macauley	C	6'8	190	21	67	351	882	40	379	528	72	200	221	1081	3.0	3.3	16.1											
Belus Smawley	G	6'1	195	31	61	287	832	34	260	314	83	215	160	834	3.5	2.6	13.7											
Johnny Logan	G	6'2	175	28	62	251	759	33	253	323	78	240	206	755	3.9	3.3	12.2											
Easy Parham	F-G	6'3	200	28	66	137	421	33	88	178	49	132	158	362	2.0	2.4	5.5											
Dermie O'Connell (37g. Bos)	G	6'	174	21	61	111	425	26	47	89	53	91	91	269	1.5	1.5	4.4											
Bill Roberts	C	6'9	210	24	67	77	222	35	28	39	72	24	90	182	0.4	1.3	2.7											
Mac Otten (12g. TC)	F-C	6'7	220	23	59	51	155	33	40	81	49	36	119	142	0.6	2.0	2.4											
Don Putman	G	6'1	170	27	57	51	200	26	33	52	63	90	116	135	1.6	2.0	2.4											
D.C. Wilcutt	G	6'2	165	26	37	24	73	33	29	42	69	49	27	77	1.3	0.7	2.1											
Mike McCarron (3g. Bal)	G	5'11	180	27	8	3	15	20	3	5	60	3	5	9	0.4	0.6	1.1											

Use Name	Pos	Hgt	Wgt	Age	TOTAL G	FG	FGA	%	FT	FTA	%	Ass.	PF	Pts	PER GAME Ass.	PF	Pts.	PLAYOFFS G	FG	FGA	%	FT	FTA	%	Ass	PF	Pts	PPG
1949/50 N.B.A. — EASTERN DIVISION																												
SYRACUSE NATIONALS 51-13 .797 **AL CERVI** — defeated Philadelphia 2-0; H93-76, 59-53; defeated New York 2-1; H91-83(OT), 76-80, H91-80; lost to Minneapolis 2-4; H66-68, H91-85, 77-91, 69-77, H83-76, 95-110																												
Alex Hannum	F	6'7	225	26	64	177	488	36	128	186	69	129	264	482	2.0	4.1	7.5	11	38	86	44	17	34	50	10	50	93	8.5
Dolph Schayes	F	6'7	215	21	64	348	903	39	376	486	77	259	225	1072	4.0	3.5	16.8	11	57	148	39	74	101	73	28	43	188	17.1
George Ratkovicz	C	6'7	225	27	62	162	439	37	211	348	61	124	201	535	2.0	3.2	8.6	11	47	121	39	50	73	68	21	45	144	13.1
Al Cervi	G	5'11	185	32	56	143	431	33	287	346	83	264	223	573	4.7	4.0	10.2	11	23	68	34	38	46	83	52	36	84	7.6
Billy Gabor	G	5'11	170	27	56	226	671	34	157	228	69	108	198	609	1.9	3.5	10.9	10	25	97	26	26	31	84	25	27	76	7.6
Paul Seymour	G-F	6'2	180	21	62	175	524	33	126	176	72	189	157	476	3.0	2.5	7.7	11	27	93	29	24	28	86	32	34	78	7.1
Ed Peterson	C	6'9	230	24	62	167	390	43	111	185	60	33	198	445	0.5	3.2	7.2	11	18	43	42	8	14	57	1	33	44	4.0
Johnny Macknowski	G	6'1	185	26	59	154	463	33	131	178	74	65	128	439	1.1	2.2	7.4	11	39	100	39	39	51	76	21	18	117	10.6
Fuzzy Levane	F-G	6'2	190	29	60	139	418	33	54	85	64	156	106	332	2.6	1.8	5.5	9	13	37	35	5	5	100	13	11	31	3.4
Ray Corley	G	6'	180	21	60	117	370	32	75	122	61	109	81	309	1.8	1.4	5.2	6	6	36	17	5	11	45	10	5	17	2.8
Leroy Chollet	F	6'2	190	24	49	61	179	34	35	56	63	37	52	157	0.8	1.1	3.2	8	7	26	27	5	13	38	4	11	19	2.4
NEW YORK KNICKERBOCKERS 40-28 .588 **JOE LAPCHICK (39-27 .591)** **BUTCH VAN BREDA KOLFF (1-1 .500)** — defeated Washington 2-0; 90-87, H103-83; lost to Syracuse 1-2; 83-91(OT), H80-76, 80-91																												
Vince Boryla	F	6'5	210	22	59	204	600	34	204	267	76	95	203	612	1.6	3.4	10.4	5	23	52	44	29	32	91	7	25	75	15.0
Harry Gallatin	F-C	6'6	215	22	68	263	664	40	277	366	76	56	215	803	0.8	3.2	11.8	5	20	52	38	25	32	78	6	23	65	13.0
Connie Simmons (back injury)	C	6'8	225	24	60	241	729	33	198	299	66	102	203	680	1.7	3.4	11.3	5	11	40	28	20	21	**95**	7	21	42	8.4
Carl Braun	C-F	6'5	180	22	67	373	1024	36	285	374	76	247	188	1031	3.7	2.8	15.4	5	28	68	41	29	38	76	19	21	85	17.0
Dick McGuire	G	6'	180	23	68	190	563	34	204	313	65	**386**	160	584	5.7	2.4	8.6	5	22	52	42	19	26	73	27	21	63	12.6
Ernie Vandeweghe (MD)	F-G	6'3	195	23	42	164	390	42	93	140	66	78	126	421	1.9	3.0	10.0	4	9	26	35	14	16	88	3	16	32	8.0
Tex Ritter	G	6'2	185	25	62	100	297	34	125	176	71	51	101	325	0.8	1.6	5.2	5	10	33	30	25	28	89	8	22	45	9.0
Ray Lumpp	G	6'1	178	25	58	91	283	32	86	108	80	90	117	268	1.6	2.0	4.6	5	10	18	56	2	3	67	3	10	22	4.4
Harry Donovan	G	6'2	180	23	45	90	275	33	73	106	69	38	107	253	0.8	2.4	5.6	3	0	4	0	2	2	100	0	4	2	0.7
Paul Noel	F	6'4	185	25	65	98	291	34	53	87	61	67	132	249	1.0	2.0	3.8	5	1	7	14	1	3	33	1	8	3	0.6
Butch Van Breda Kolff	G	6'3	185	27	56	55	167	33	96	134	72	78	111	206	1.4	2.0	3.7	1	0	0	—	0	0	—	0	2	0	0.0
Ed Bartels (13g. Den)	F	6'5	195	24	15	22	86	26	19	33	58	20	29	63	1.3	1.9	4.2											
Gene James	F	6'4	180	24	29	19	64	30	14	31	45	20	53	52	0.7	1.8	1.8	1	1	3	33	0	0	—	0	0	2	2.0
WASHINGTON CAPITOLS 32-36 .471 **BOB FEERICK** — lost to New York 0-2; H87-90, 83-103																												
Bob Feerick	F-G	6'3	190	29	60	172	500	34	139	174	80	127	140	483	2.1	2.3	8.1	2	3	12	25	3	4	75	6	10	9	4.5
Bones McKinney (hand injury)	F	6'6	187	30	53	187	631	30	118	152	78	88	185	492	1.7	3.5	9.3	2	6	22	27	4	5	80	3	11	16	8.0
Don Otten (46g. TC)	C	7'	245	28	64	242	648	37	341	463	74	91	246	825	1.4	3.8	12.9	2	10	25	40	21	26	81	6	7	41	20.5
Chick Reiser	G	5'11	165	35	67	197	646	30	212	254	83	174	223	606	2.6	3.3	9.0	2	7	27	26	9	11	82	5	11	23	11.5
Freddie Scolari	G	5'11	185	27	66	312	910	34	236	287	82	175	181	860	2.7	2.7	13.0	2	13	27	48	11	11	100	3	6	37	18.5
Dick O'Keefe	G-F	6'2	185	26	68	162	529	31	150	203	74	74	217	474	1.1	3.2	7.0	2	4	13	31	7	8	88	5	10	15	7.5
Chuck Gilmur (11g. Chi)	F	6'4	225	27	68	127	379	34	164	241	68	108	275	418	1.6	4.0	6.1	(injury)										
Chick Halbert	C	6'9	225	30	68	108	284	38	112	175	64	89	136	328	1.3	2.0	4.8	2	7	16	44	5	9	56	3	7	19	9.5
Johnny Norlander (leg injury)	F	6'3	180	28	40	99	293	34	53	85	62	33	71	251	0.8	1.8	6.3											
Leo Katkavek (3g. Bal)	G	6'	185	26	54	101	330	31	34	56	61	68	102	236	1.3	1.9	4.4	2	2	13	15	2	3	67	3	7	6	3.0
Hooks Dillon	F	6'3	180	25	22	10	55	18	16	22	73	5	19	36	0.2	0.9	1.6	1	1	1	100	2	2	100	0	2	4	4.0
PHILADELPHIA WARRIORS 26-42 .382 **EDDIE GOTTLIEB**																												
Leo Mogus	F	6'4	205	28	64	172	434	40	218	300	73	99	169	562	1.5	2.6	8.8	2	3	18	17	4	7	57	7	10	10	5.0
Joe Fulks	F	6'5	190	28	68	336	1209	28	293	421	70	56	240	965	0.8	3.5	14.2	2	5	26	19	5	10	50	2	10	15	7.5
Vern Gardner	C-F	6'5	200	24	63	313	916	34	227	296	77	119	236	853	1.9	3.7	13.5	2	15	44	34	6	9	67	2	11	36	18.0
George Senesky	G	6'2	180	27	68	227	709	32	157	223	70	264	164	611	3.9	2.4	9.0	2	6	16	38	2	4	50	3	2	14	7.0
Chink Crossin	G	6'1	165	26	64	185	574	32	79	101	78	148	139	449	2.3	2.2	7.0	2	9	27	33	8	9	89	4	3	26	13.0
Ron Livingstone (16g. Bal)	C	6'10	220	24	54	163	579	28	122	177	69	141	260	448	2.6	4.8	8.3	2	6	16	38	4	7	57	5	12	16	8.0
Jerry Fleishman	G	6'2	190	27	65	102	353	29	93	151	62	118	129	297	1.8	2.0	4.6	2	1	3	33	0	1	0	3	6	2	1.0
Jake Bornheimer	F	6'5	205	22	60	88	305	29	78	117	67	40	111	254	0.7	1.9	4.2	2	1	3	33	0	0	—	0	2	2	1.0
Nelson Bobb	G	6'	170	25	57	80	248	32	82	131	63	46	97	242	0.8	1.7	4.2	2	1	3	33	0	0	—	1	3	2	1.0
Al Guokas (41g. Den)	F-G	6'5	200	24	57	93	299	31	28	50	56	95	143	214	1.7	2.5	3.8	2	2	4	50	2	6	33	5	3	6	3.0
Fred Lewis (18g. Bal)	F	6'2	195	28	34	46	184	25	25	32	78	25	40	117	0.7	1.2	3.4											
Mike Novak (5g. Roch, ST)	C	6'9	220	34	60	37	149	25	25	47	53	61	139	99	1.0	2.3	1.7											
Charlie Parsley	G	6'2	175	23	9	8	31	26	6	7	86	8	7	22	0.9	0.8	2.4											
Jim Nolan	C	6'8	210	22	5	4	21	19	0	0	—	4	14	8	0.8	2.8	1.6											
Jerry Rullo	G	5'10	165	26	4	3	9	33	1	1	100	2	2	7	0.5	0.5	1.8											

					TOTAL										PER GAME			PLAYOFFS										
Use Name	Pos	Hgt	Wgt	Age	G	FG	FGA	%	FT	FTA	%	Ass.	PF	Pts.	Ass.	PF	Pts.	G	FG	FGA	%	FT	FTA	%	Ass	PF	Pts.	PPG
1949/50 N.B.A. — EASTERN DIVISION (continued)																												
BALTIMORE BULLETS	**25-43 .368**				**BUDDY JEANNETTE**																							
Blackie Towery	F	6'4	210	29	68	222	678	33	153	202	76	142	244	597	2.1	3.6	8.8											
Walt Budko	F	6'5	220	24	66	198	652	30	199	263	76	146	259	595	2.2	3.9	9.0											
Ed Sadowski (17g. Phi)	C	6'5	265	32	69	299	922	32	274	373	73	136	244	872	2.0	3.5	12.6											
Paul Hoffman	G	6'2	205	24	60	312	914	34	242	364	66	161	234	866	2.7	3.9	14.4											
Joe Dolhon	G	6'	175	22	64	143	458	31	157	214	73	155	193	443	2.4	3.0	6.9											
Tommy Byrnes (ankle injury)	F	6'3	175	26	53	120	397	30	87	124	70	88	76	327	1.7	1.4	6.2											
Whitney Von Nieda	G	6'1	175	27	59	120	336	36	73	115	63	143	127	313	2.4	2.2	5.3											
Les Pugh	C	6'8	190	26	56	68	273	25	115	136	85	16	118	251	0.3	2.1	4.5											
Buddy Jeannette (KJ)	G	5'11	175	32	37	42	148	28	109	133	82	93	82	193	2.5	2.2	5.2											
Marv Schatzman	F	6'5	200	22	34	43	174	25	29	50	58	38	49	115	1.1	1.4	3.4											
Andy O'Donnell	G	6'1	180	24	25	38	108	35	14	18	78	17	32	90	0.7	1.3	3.6											
John Mandic (22g. Wash)	F	6'4	205	30	25	22	75	29	22	32	69	8	54	66	0.3	2.2	2.6											
George Feigenbaum	G	6'1	185	20	12	14	57	25	8	18	44	10	15	36	0.8	1.3	3.0											
Howie Janotta	F	6'3	185	25	9	9	30	30	13	16	81	4	10	31	0.4	1.1	3.4											
Paul Gordon	F	6'3	190	22	4	0	6	0	3	5	60	3	3	3	0.8	0.8	0.8											
Dick Triptow	G	6'	170	27	4	0	5	0	2	2	100	1	5	2	0.3	1.3	0.5											
Lee Knorek (VR)	C	6'7	215	28	1	0	2	0	0	0	—	0	4	0	0.0	4.0	0.0											
BOSTON CELTICS	**22-46 .324**				**DOGGIE JULIAN**																							
Ed Leede	F	6'3	185	22	64	174	507	34	223	316	71	130	167	571	2.0	2.6	8.9											
George Kaftan	F	6'3	190	21	55	199	535	37	136	208	65	145	92	534	2.6	1.7	9.7											
Bob Kinney	C	6'6	215	29	60	233	621	38	201	320	63	101	251	667	1.7	4.2	11.1											
Howie Shannon	G	6'3	185	26	67	222	646	34	143	182	79	174	148	587	2.6	2.2	8.8											
Sonny Hertzberg	G	5'10	175	27	68	275	865	32	143	191	75	200	153	693	2.9	2.3	10.2											
Brady Walker	C-F	6'6	205	28	68	218	583	37	72	114	63	109	100	508	1.6	1.5	7.5											
Tony Lavelli	F	6'3	185	23	56	162	436	37	168	197	85	40	107	492	0.7	1.9	8.8											
Johnny Ezersky (38g. Bal)	G-F	6'3	175	28	54	143	487	29	127	183	69	86	139	413	1.6	2.6	7.6											
John Mahnken (2g. FtW, 36. TC)	C	6'8	230	27	62	132	495	27	77	115	67	108	231	341	1.7	3.7	5.5											
Bob Doll	F	6'5	195	30	47	120	347	35	75	114	66	108	117	315	2.3	2.5	6.7											
Jim Seminoff	G	6'2	210	27	65	85	283	30	142	188	76	249	154	312	3.8	2.4	4.8											
Joe Mullaney	G	6'	165	24	37	9	70	13	12	15	80	52	30	30	1.4	0.8	0.8											
Art Spector	F	6'4	200	32	7	2	12	17	1	4	25	3	4	5	0.4	0.6	0.7											
1949/50 N.B.A. — WESTERN DIVISION																												
INDIANAPOLIS OLYMPIANS	**39-25 .609**				**CLIFF BARKER**													defeated Sheboygan 2-1; H86-85, 85-95, H91-84 lost to Anderson 1-2; H77-74, 67-84, H65-67										
Joe Holland	F	6'4	185	24	64	145	453	32	98	142	69	130	220	388	2.0	3.4	6.1	6	21	61	34	6	15	40	15	29	48	8.0
Wah Wah Jones	F	6'4	225	23	60	264	706	37	223	297	75	194	241	751	3.2	4.0	12.5	5	22	73	30	29	34	85	22	26	73	14.6
Alex Groza	C	6'7	218	23	64	521	1090	**48**	454	623	73	162	221	1496	2.5	3.5	23.4	6	44	74	**59**	49	59	83	12	21	137	22.8
Bruce Hale	G	6'1	170	31	64	217	614	35	223	285	78	226	143	657	3.5	2.2	10.3	6	14	40	35	15	17	88	17	11	43	7.2
Ralph Beard	G	5'10	175	22	60	340	936	36	215	282	76	233	132	895	3.9	2.2	14.9	5	22	70	31	22	28	79	22	11	66	13.2
Mal Mcmullan	C-F	6'5	210	22	58	123	380	32	77	141	55	87	212	323	1.5	3.7	5.6	6	4	21	19	6	9	67	9	19	14	2.3
Paul Walther (22g. Min)	G-F	6'2	160	22	53	114	290	39	63	109	58	56	123	291	1.1	2.3	5.5	6	12	41	29	9	19	47	8	17	33	5.5
Cliff Barker	G	6'2	185	28	49	102	274	37	75	106	71	109	99	279	2.2	2.0	5.7	6	12	31	39	10	15	67	13	10	34	5.7
Marshall Hawkins (injury)	F	6'3	205	25	39	55	195	28	42	61	69	51	87	152	1.3	2.2	3.9	2	0	1	0	0	0	—	0	1	0	0.0
Carl Shaeffer	F	6'3	185	25	43	59	160	37	32	57	56	40	103	150	0.9	2.4	3.5	6	7	21	33	7	14	50	7	20	21	3.5
Bob Evans	G	6'2	175	24	47	56	200	28	30	44	68	55	99	142	1.2	2.1	3.0	2	1	4	25	0	0	—	0	3	2	1.0
Jack Parkinson	G	6'	174	25	4	1	12	8	1	1	100	2	3	3	0.5	0.8	0.8											
ANDERSON DUFFY PACKERS	**37-27 .578**				**HOWIE SHULTZ (21-14 .600), IKE DUFFEY (1-2 .333), DOXIE MOORE (15-11 .577)**													defeated Tri-Cities 2-1; H89-77, 75-76, H94-71 defeated Indianapolis 2-1; 74-77, H84-67, 67-65 lost to Minneapolis 0-2; 50-75, H71										
Charlie Black (36g. FtW)	F	6'5	200	28	65	226	813	28	209	321	65	163	273	661	2.5	4.2	10.2	8	18	61	30	21	29	72	17	38	57	7.1
Bill Closs	F-C	6'5	200	27	64	283	898	32	186	259	72	160	190	752	2.5	3.0	11.8	8	33	109	30	25	30	83	14	27	91	11.4
Milo Komenich	C-F	6'7	230	29	64	244	861	28	146	250	58	124	246	634	1.9	3.8	9.9	8	26	107	24	16	28	57	14	36	68	8.5
John Hargis	G	6'2	180	29	60	223	550	41	197	277	71	102	170	643	1.7	2.8	10.7	8	32	89	36	37	45	82	13	26	99	12.4
Frankie Brian	G	6'1	180	26	64	368	1156	32	402	488	82	189	192	1138	3.0	3.0	17.8	8	26	96	27	43	48	90	19	24	95	11.9
Ed Stanczak	F	6'3	210	28	57	159	456	35	203	270	75	67	166	521	1.2	2.9	9.1	8	14	48	29	23	30	77	10	26	51	6.4
Richie Niemiera (31g. FtW)	G	6'1	165	28	60	110	350	31	104	139	75	116	77	324	1.9	1.3	5.4	8	11	27	41	6	8	75	8	10	28	3.5
Frank Gates	G	6'	167	28	64	113	402	28	61	98	62	91	147	287	1.4	2.3	4.5	7	9	37	24	7	10	70	9	15	25	3.6
Rollie Seltz (injury)	G	5'10	170	25	34	93	309	30	80	104	77	64	72	266	1.9	2.1	7.8	(injured)										
Jim Owens (26g. TC)	F-G	6'3	185	24	61	86	288	30	68	101	67	73	152	240	1.2	2.5	3.9	8	26	89	29	28	41	68	19	37	80	10.0
Jake Carter (13g. Den)	F	6'5	195	25	24	23	75	31	36	53	68	24	59	82	1.0	2.5	3.4	8	3	21	14	4	6	67	3	12	10	1.3
Murray Mitchell	C	6'6	—	26	2	1	3	33	0	0	—	2	1	2	1.0	0.5	1.0											

1949/50 N.B.A. — WESTERN DIVISION (continued)

Use Name	Pos	Hgt	Wgt	Age	TOTAL G	FG	FGA	%	FT	FTA	%	Ass.	PF	Pts.	PER GAME Ass.	PF	Pts.	PLAYOFFS G	FG	FGA	%	FT	FTA	%	Ass	PF	Pts.	PPG
TRI-CITIES BLACKHAWKS	29-35 .453				ROGER POTTER (1-6 .143), RED AUERBACH (28-29 .491)													lost to Anderson 1-2; 77-89, H76-75, 71-94										
Dick Eddleman	F-G	6'3	189	27	64	332	906	37	162	260	62	142	254	826	2.2	4.0	12.9	3	17	45	38	15	25	60	7	17	49	16.3
Mike Todorovich (14g. StL)	F	6'5	230	26	65	263	852	31	266	370	72	207	230	792	3.2	3.5	12.2	3	6	31	19	19	24	79	8	14	31	10.3
Jack Nichols (49g. Was)	C	6'7	215	23	67	310	848	37	259	344	75	142	179	879	2.1	2.7	13.1	3	18	60	30	23	31	74	11	11	59	19.7
Gene Vance (from Chi, VR)	G	6'3	196	26	35	110	325	34	86	120	72	121	145	306	3.5	4.1	8.7	3	7	31	23	5	10	50	9	17	19	6.3
Murray Wier	G	5'9	155	23	56	157	480	33	115	166	69	107	141	429	1.9	2.5	7.7	3	3	9	33	4	8	50	0	4	10	3.3
Warren Perkins	G	6'3	190	25	60	128	422	30	115	195	59	114	260	371	1.9	4.3	6.2	2	1	1	100	2	2	100	0	2	4	2.0
Don Ray	F-C	6'6	215	28	61	130	403	32	104	149	70	60	147	364	1.0	2.4	6.0	3	4	13	31	10	11	91	0	7	18	6.0
Gene Englund (VR, FtW, 24g. Bos)	F	6'5	205	32	46	104	274	38	152	192	79	41	167	360	0.9	3.6	7.8	2	1	5	20	9	11	82	1	6	11	5.5
Walt Kirk (26g. And)	G-F	6'3	180	25	58	97	361	27	155	216	72	103	155	349	1.8	2.7	6.0	3	2	7	29	1	6	17	1	8	5	1.7
Bill Henry (44g. FtW)	C	6'9	220	25	63	89	278	32	118	176	67	48	122	296	0.8	1.9	4.7	3	2	17	12	5	9	56	5	14	9	3.0
Dee Gibson	G-F	5'11	175	26	44	77	245	31	127	177	72	126	113	281	2.9	2.6	6.4	3	4	11	36	3	5	60	2	11	11	3.7
Gene Berce	G	5'11	175	23	3	5	16	31	0	5	0	0	6	10	0.0	2.0	3.3											
SHEBOYGAN REDSKINS	22-40 .355				KENNY SUESENS													lost to Indianapolis 1-2; 85-86, H95-85, 84-91										
Max Morris	F	6'2	195	24	62	252	694	36	277	415	67	194	172	781	3.1	2.8	12.6	3	14	40	35	15	26	58	14	8	43	14.3
Bob Brannum	F	6'6	215	24	59	234	718	33	245	355	69	205	279	713	3.5	4.7	12.1	3	15	43	35	13	20	65	11	16	43	14.3
Noble Jorgensen (injury)	C	6'9	230	24	54	218	618	35	268	350	77	90	201	704	1.7	3.7	13.0	3	17	44	39	18	30	60	8	15	52	17.3
Jack Burmaster	G	6'3	190	23	61	237	711	33	124	182	68	179	237	598	2.9	3.9	9.8	3	16	31	52	4	4	100	8	7	36	12.0
Bobby Cook (FJ)	G	5'10	155	26	51	222	620	36	143	181	79	158	114	587	3.1	2.2	11.5	3	3	10	30	3	6	50	6	3	9	3.0
Milt Schoon	C	6'9	230	27	62	150	366	41	196	300	65	84	190	496	1.4	3.1	8.0	3	5	17	29	7	10	70	3	6	17	5.7
George Sobek	G	6'	180	29	60	95	251	38	156	205	76	95	158	346	1.6	2.6	5.8	3	10	20	50	12	16	75	3	15	32	10.7
Stan Patrick (34g. Wat)	F-G	6'3	215	28	53	116	294	39	89	147	61	74	76	321	1.4	1.4	6.1	3	4	7	57	2	3	67	1	2	10	3.3
Walt Lautenbach	F-G	6'2	190	27	55	100	332	30	38	55	69	73	122	238	1.3	2.2	4.3											
Jack Phelan (15g. Wat)	F	6'5	240	24	55	87	268	32	52	90	58	57	151	226	1.0	2.7	4.1	3	4	10	40	2	3	67	3	10	10	3.3
Dick Schultz (13g. Was, 8g. TC)	G	6'2	192	32	50	63	212	30	83	110	75	66	106	209	1.3	2.1	4.2	3	1	9	11	10	10	100	2	12	12	4.0
Matt Mazza	F	6'3	210	26	26	33	110	30	32	45	71	27	34	98	1.0	1.3	3.8											
John Chaney (6g. TC)	F	6'3	190	29	16	25	86	29	20	29	69	20	23	70	1.3	1.4	4.4											
Danny Wagner	G	6'	170	27	11	19	54	35	31	35	89	18	22	69	1.6	2.0	6.3											
Glen Selbo	F	6'3	195	23	13	10	51	20	22	29	76	23	15	42	1.8	1.2	3.2											
Bob Wood	G	5'10	—	28	6	3	14	21	1	2	50	1	6	7	0.2	1.0	1.2											
Don Grate	G	6'2	185	25	2	1	6	17	2	2	100	3	3	4	1.5	1.5	2.0											
WATERLOO HAWKS	19-43 .306				CHARLEY SHIPP (8-27 .229), JACK SMILEY (11-16 .407)																							
Don Boven	F	6'4	210	24	62	208	558	37	240	349	69	137	255	656	2.2	4.1	10.6											
Dick Mehen	F	6'6	195	27	62	347	826	42	198	281	70	191	203	892	3.1	3.3	14.4											
Harry Boykoff	C	6'10	250	27	61	288	698	41	203	262	77	149	229	779	2.4	3.8	12.8											
Jack Smiley (12g. And)	G-F	6'3	190	27	59	98	364	27	136	201	68	161	193	332	2.7	3.3	5.6											
Leo Kubiak	G	5'11	170	23	62	259	794	33	192	236	81	201	250	710	3.2	4.0	11.5											
Wayne See	G	6'3	190	26	61	113	303	37	94	135	70	143	147	320	2.3	2.4	5.2											
Johnny Payak (17g. Phi)	F	6'4	185	23	52	98	331	30	121	173	70	86	113	317	1.7	2.2	6.1											
Ward Gibson (2g. Bos, ST)	C-F	6'5	210	28	32	67	195	34	42	64	66	37	106	176	1.2	3.3	5.5											
Gene Stump (23g. Min)	G-F	6'2	185	26	49	63	213	30	37	54	69	44	59	163	0.9	1.2	3.3											
Bob Tough (8g. Bal)	G	6'	185	27	29	43	153	28	37	40	93	38	40	123	1.3	1.4	4.2											
Charley Shipp	G	6'1	205	36	23	35	137	26	37	51	73	46	46	107	2.0	2.0	4.7											
Johnny Orr (21g. StL)	F	6'3	195	22	34	40	118	34	12	14	86	20	34	92	0.6	1.0	2.7											
Gene Ollrich	G	5'11	160	27	14	17	72	24	10	14	71	24	34	44	1.7	2.4	3.1											
Al Miksis	C	6'7	210	21	8	5	21	24	17	21	81	4	22	27	0.5	2.8	3.4											
Dale Hamilton	G	6'1	198	30	14	8	33	24	9	19	47	17	30	25	1.2	2.1	1.8											
Elmer Gainer	C-F	6'6	205	30	15	9	35	26	6	8	75	7	28	24	0.5	1.9	1.6											
John Pritchard	C	6'9	220	22	7	9	29	31	4	11	36	8	14	22	1.1	2.0	3.1											
Paul Cloyd (3g. Bal)	G	6'2	180	29	7	7	26	27	5	8	63	2	5	19	0.3	0.7	2.7											
Ken Menke (HC)	G	6'1	168	27	6	6	17	35	3	8	38	7	7	15	1.2	1.2	2.5											
DENVER NUGGETS	11-51 .178				JIMMY DARDEN																							
Bob Brown	F	6'4	205	26	62	276	764	36	172	252	68	101	269	724	1.6	4.3	11.7											
Dillard Crocker	F	6'4	205	24	53	245	840	29	233	317	74	85	223	723	1.6	4.2	13.6											
Jack Toomay	C	6'6	215	27	62	204	514	40	186	264	70	94	213	594	1.5	3.4	9.6											
Jimmy Darden (injury)	G	6'1	170	27	26	78	243	32	55	80	69	67	67	211	2.6	2.6	8.1											
Kenny Sailors	G	5'10	176	27	57	329	944	35	329	456	72	229	242	987	4.0	4.2	17.3											
Floyd Volker (17g. Ind)	F	6'4	205	28	54	163	527	31	71	129	55	112	169	397	2.1	3.1	7.4											
Jack Cotton	F-C	6'7	205	25	54	97	332	29	82	161	51	65	184	276	1.2	3.4	5.1											
Bob Royer	G	5'10	155	22	42	78	231	34	41	58	71	85	72	197	2.0	1.7	4.7											
Bill Herman	G	6'3	170	25	13	25	65	38	6	11	55	15	13	56	1.2	1.0	4.3											
Jim Browne	C	6'10	235	19	31	17	48	35	13	27	48	8	16	47	0.3	0.5	1.5											
Earl Dodd	F	6'5	175	25	9	6	27	22	3	5	60	6	13	15	0.7	1.4	1.7											

1949/50 B.A.A. TEAM STATISTICS

Team	REGULAR SEASON G	FG	FGA	%	FT	FTA	%	Ass.	AVERAGE POINTS For	Agnst.	Diff.	PLAYOFFS G	FG	FGA	%	FT	FTA	%	Ass.	AVERAGE POINTS For	Agnst.	Diff.
EASTERN DIVISION																						
Syracuse	64	1869	5276	35	1691	2396	71	**1473**	84.8	76.7	+8.1	11	300	855	35	291	407	71	219	81.0	79.9	+1.1
New York	68	1889	5351	35	**1710**	**2404**	71	1308	80.7	78.6	+2.1	5	135	355	38	**166**	201	**83**	81	87.2	85.6	+1.6
Washington	68	1813	5493	33	1575	2111	75	1057	76.5	77.4	-0.9	2	53	156	34	64	79	81	34	85.0	96.5	-11.5
Philadelphia	68	1779	5711	31	1425	2037	70	1142	73.3	76.4	-3.1	2	49	160	31	31	53	58	32	64.5	76.0	-11.5
Baltimore	68	1712	5516	31	1549	2123	73	1189	73.1	78.7	-5.6											
Boston	68	1945	5756	34	1530	2163	71	**1473**	79.7	82.2	-2.5											
CENTRAL DIVISION																						
Minneapolis	68	**2139**	5832	37	1439	1943	74	1406	84.1	75.7	+8.4	12	354	963	37	306	422	73	215	84.5	**75.4**	**+9.1**
Rochester	68	1956	5247	37	1690	2319	73	1383	82.4	**74.6**	+7.8	2	54	141	38	54	70	77	33	81.0	84.5	-3.5
hrtWayne	68	1878	5901	32	1634	2331	70	1364	79.3	77.9	+1.4	4	108	338	32	114	157	73	69	82.5	86 .0	-3.5
Chicago	68	2003	5892	34	1346	1934	70	1366	78.7	77.1	+1.6	2	50	147	34	42	55	76	32	71.0	80.0	-9.0
St. Louis	68	1741	5086	34	1528	2149	71	1285	73.7	76.5	-2.8											
WESTERN DIVISION																						
Indianapolis	64	1982	5283	**38**	1529	2145	71	1342	85.8	82.1	+3.7	6	159	437	36	153	210	73	**125**	78.5	81.5	-3.0
Anderson	64	1943	**6254**	31	1703	2343	73	1240	**87.3**	83.6	+3.7	8	198	**684**	29	208	277	75	126	75.5	74.8	+0.7
Tri-Cities	64	1818	5515	33	1677	2308	73	1330	83.0	83.6	-0.6	3	65	230	28	94	**140**	67	45	74.7	86.0	-11.3
Sheboygan	62	1727	5022	34	1654	2338	71	1279	82.4	87.8	-5.4	3	**89**	231	**39**	86	128	67	59	**88.0**	87.3	+0.7
Waterloo	62	1746	4904	36	1429	2002	71	1324	79.4	84.9	-5.5											
Denver	62	1731	5182	33	1355	1999	68	1044	77.7	89.1	-11.4											

1949/50 N.B.A. STANDINGS

Team	W	L	Pct.	GB	Record against playoff teams W	L	Pct.	Record against non-playoff teams W	L	Pct.	HOME W	L	Pct.	ROAD W	L	Pct.	NEUTRAL W	L	Pct.
EASTERN DIVISION																			
Syracuse Nationals	**51**	13	**.797**	—	34	10	.773	17	3	.850	31	1	.969	15	12	**.556**	5	0	**1.000**
New York Knickeroockers	40	28	.588	13	22	24	.478	18	4	.818	19	10	.655	**18**	16	.529	3	2	.600
Washington Capitols	32	36	.471	21	20	30	.400	12	6	.667	21	13	.618	10	20	.333	1	3	.250
Philadelphia Warriors	26	42	.382	27	10	32	.238	16	10	.615	15	**15**	.500	8	23	.258	3	4	.429
Baltimore Bullets	25	43	.368	28	18	34	.346	7	9	.438	16	**15**	.516	8	25	.242	1	3	.250
Boston Celtics	22	46	.324	31	14	38	.269	8	8	.500	12	14	.462	5	**28**	.152	5	4	.556
CENTRAL DIVISION																			
Minneapolis Lakers	**51**	17	.750	—	32	14	.696	19	3	.864	30	1	.968	**18**	16	.529	3	0	**1.000**
Rochester Royals	**51**	17	.750	—	33	13	.717	18	4	.818	**33**	1	**.971**	17	16	.515	I	0	**1.000**
Fort Wayne Zollner Pistons	40	28	.588	11	25	21	.543	15	7	.682	28	6	.824	12	22	.353	0	0	—
Chicago Stags	40	28	.588	11	20	26	.435	**20**	2	**.900**	18	6	.750	14	21	.400	**8**	1	.889
St. Louis Bombers	26	42	.382	25	16	36	.308	10	6	.625	17	14	.548	7	26	.212	2	2	.500
WESTERN DIVISION																			
Indianapolis Olympians	39	25	.609	—	24	20	.545	15	5	.750	23	5	.821	13	18	.419	3	2	.600
Anderson Duffey Packers	37	27	.578	2	23	21	.523	14	6	.700	23	9	.719	11	18	.379	3	0	**1.000**
Tri-Cities Blackhawks	29	35	.453	10	14	30	.318	15	5	.750	22	13	.629	4	20	.167	3	2	.600
Sheboygan Redskins	22	40	.355	16	13	29	.310	9	**11**	.450	17	14	.548	5	22	.185	0	4	.000
Waterloo Hawks	19	43	.306	19	11	38	.224	8	5	.615	17	**15**	.531	1	22	.043	1	6	.143
Denver Nuggets	11	**51**	.177	27	7	**42**	.143	4	9	.308	9	**15**	.375	1	26	.037	1	**10**	.091

1949/50 N.B.A. INDIVIDUAL LEADERS

SCORING
(Minimum 46 Games Played)

Name	Team	G	FG	FT	Pts.	Avg.
Mikan	Min	68	649	567	1865	27.4
Groza	Ind	64	521	454	1496	23.4
Brian	And	64	368	402	1138	17.8
Sailors	Den	57	329	329	987	17.3
Schayes	Syr	64	348	276	1072	16.8
Zaslofsky	Chi	68	397	321	1115	16.4
Macauley	StL	67	351	379	1081	16.1
Braun	NY	67	373	285	1031	15.4
Beard	Ind	60	340	215	895	14.9
Pollard	Min	66	394	185	973	14.7

FIELD GOAL PERCENTAGE
(Minimum 200 Field Goals)

Name	Team	FG	FGA	Pct.
Groza	Ind	521	1090	.478
Mehen	Wat	347	826	.420
Wanzer	Roch	254	614	.414
Boykoff	Wat	288	698	.413
Mikan	Min	649	1595	.407
Hargis	And	223	550	.405
Rocha	StL	275	679	.405
Mikkelsen	Min	288	722	.399
Macauley	StL	351	882	.398
Toomay	Den	204	514	.397

FREE THROW PERCENTAGE
(Minimum 170 Free Throws)

Name	Team	FT	FTA	Pct.
Zaslofsky	Chi	321	381	.843
Reiser	Was	212	254	.835
Cervi	Syr	287	346	.829
Smawley	StL	260	314	.828
Brian	And	402	488	.824
Scolari	Was	236	287	.822
Schaus	FtW	270	330	.818
Kubiak	Wat	192	236	.814
Wanzer	Roch	283	351	.806
Logan	StL	253	323	.783

PERSONAL FOULS

Name	Team	PF
Mikan	Min	297
Brannum	Sheb	279
Gilmur	Chi-Was	275
Black	FtW-And	273
Brown	Den	269

ASSISTS PER GAME
(Minimum 46 Games Played)

Name	Team	G	Ass.	Avg.
Phillip	Chi	65	377	5.8
McGuire	NY	68	386	5.7
Cervi	Syr	56	264	4.7
Davies	Roch	64	294	4.6
Schayes	Syr	64	259	4.0
Sailors	Den	57	229	4.0
Beard	Ind	60	233	3.9
Senesky	Phi	68	264	3.9
Logan	StL	62	240	3.9
Seminoff	Bos	65	249	3.8

1950-51 N.B.A.

New York: The Scandals and the Near Miracle

The shock waves rippled throughout college basketball: Manhattan College star Junius Kellogg reported in January that he had been offered a bribe from gamblers to shave points in a game in Madison Square Garden. District Attorney Frank Hogan followed up with an investigation that shocked the basketball world. College games at the Garden, it turned out, had often been fixed, and several New York powerhouses were directly implicated. Practically the entire C.C.N.Y. squad, winners of both the N.I.T. and N.C.A.A. crowns last spring, confessed to point shaving; players from L.I.U. and N.Y.U. were also involved, and St. John's squad was mentioned but never indicted. With the college basketball world recoiling in horror, pro ball now had its first opportunity to capture some of the hoop spotlight in New York, the media capital of the nation.

The N.B.A., which offered an alternative to college ball, had consolidated into ten teams by early 1951; Chicago, St. Louis, Anderson, Sheboygan, Waterloo, and Denver had all dropped out after last season, and the Washington Capitols folded on January 9 after compiling a 10-25 record in relative privacy. The ten remaining clubs snapped up the top players from these defunct teams, making the league a much tougher circuit. Black players were admitted into the league this year, with Boston's Chuck Cooper and New York's Sweetwater Clifton the trailblazers at the start of the season. There was now even an All-Star game, a March affair in Boston won by the East, 111-94.

But although the West lost the exhibition, the two strongest clubs were still in that division. The Minneapolis Lakers had the All-Star front line of George Mikan, Jim Pollard, and Vern Mikkelsen, plus a backcourt ace in Slater Martin. The Rochester Royals had a smart, veteran club featuring Bob Davies, Bobby Wanzer, and Arnie Risen. As usual, these two clubs finished first and second in their division, with the Lakers this season taking first place by three games.

The next two playoff spots went to the Ft. Wayne Pistons, who were helped by 6'9" rookie center Larry Foust, and the Indianapolis Olympians, with Alex Groza and Ralph Beard among the top ten scorers in the league. Tri-Cities, a surprise survivor of the league consolidation, got backcourt star Frankie Brian out of the wreckage of the folded teams in a very complicated fashion. After Anderson folded, the Chicago Stags picked up Brian's contract; the Stags then sent Brian to Tri-Cities for an unproven rookie named Bob Cousy.

A star at Holy Cross, Cousy found himself passed around like a bad check before he had even played a game. After the Boston Celtics had passed over the local star, Tri-Cities signed him and sent him to Chicago; then Chicago folded, leaving Cousy without a team. Three guards from the Chicago roster went into a pot, with New York, Philadelphia, and Boston drawing their names out of a hat. The Knicks took Max Zaslofsky, a top shooter and the prize of the bunch. The Warriors picked next and came up with Andy Phillip, a great playmaker. The Celtics were stuck with Cousy, a popular New England player but one that new coach Red Auerbach figured as an unlikely pro.

The 6'1" Cousy proved Auerbach wrong and made a winning coach out of him in the process. Cousy immediately set the league on its ear with his fancy-Dan passes, rocketing the ball from behind his back to open teammates, shoveling it blind to waiting Celtics. His dribbling also delighted spectators, as he could put the ball behind his back or between his legs without losing a step. That he could score was evident in his 15.6 average.

Easy Ed Macauley came to the Celtics in a special draft of the players from the disbanded St. Louis team. This draft was held after commissioner Podoloff refused to allow the Knicks to buy the Bombers franchise to obtain Macauley. With these two new aces and with Auerbach's fast break philosophy, the Celtics broke the .500 barrier for the first time and finished a strong second behind the Philadelphia Warriors. The Warriors also came back from a poor campaign last season. A return to form by Joe Fulks, the playmaking of newcomer Andy Phillip, and the scoring of star rookie Paul Arizin, a jump shooter with a line drive shot and the ability to hang at the top of his jump, made the Warriors practically a new club.

The Knicks finished third in the East despite the loss of Carl Braun to the Army. Coach Joe Lapchick replaced Braun with Max Zaslofsky and added rebounding help by purchasing Sweetwater Clifton from the Harlem Globetrotters. Clifton was short for a center at 6'6", but he was very strong and had years of experience with the Globetrotters and New York Rens. Glueing the Knicks together was the playmaking of guard Dick McGuire. Syracuse slumped to fourth place; Dolph Schayes was now an established star at forward, but Al Cervi was playing less at guard. The weak Baltimore Bullets finished fifth, and the Washington club didn't finish at all.

The playoffs began with Minneapolis and Rochester winning their opening matches in the West as expected, and with New York and Syracuse upsetting Philadelphia and Boston in the East. The Lakers began the Western finals with a 76-73 victory at home, but the Royals then outmaneuvered the larger Lakers for three straight victories and a trip to the finals. In the East, the Syracuse-New York series came down to a decisive fifth game; the Nats led by a 70-58 count with 10 minutes left, but the Knicks then caught fire and took an 83-81 victory to put themselves into the title round.

With the Knicks in their first championship series, New York City fans were excited about their professional team. That enthusiasm took a severe beating when the Royals captured the first three games, but the Knicks at least saved a little face by winning game four 79-73 with a late rally in front of the hometown fans. Back in Rochester, Connie Simmons' 26 points led the Knicks to a 92-89 win and brought the series back to New York. Game six went to the Knicks, 80-73, and the series was suddenly tied at three games all. The championship now came down to a seventh-game showdown. The two teams battled on an even basis all game, with the score knotted at 75-75 with 40 seconds left. Bob Davies then got two foul shots on a blocking foul against McGuire, and he canned both to put the Royals ahead 77-75. The rules called for a jump ball after successful free throws in the final three minutes of a game, and the Royals grabbed the jump, held on to the ball, and scored at the buzzer for a 79-75 triumph over the gallant New York squad.

Use Name	Pos	Hgt	Wgt	Age	G	Min	FG	FGA	%	FT	FTA	%	Reb	Ass	PF	DQ	Points	Min	Reb	Ass	PF	Points
					TOTAL													PER GAME				

1950/51 N.B.A. — EASTERN DIVISION

Use Name	Pos	Hgt	Wgt	Age	G	Min	FG	FGA	%	FT	FTA	%	Reb	Ass	PF	DQ	Points	Min	Reb	Ass	PF	Points
PHILADELPHIA WARRIORS	40-26 .606				EDDIE GOTTLIEB																	
Paul Arizin	F	6'4	190	22	65	—	352	864	41	417	526	79	640	138	284	18	1121	—	9.8	2.1	4.4	17.2
Joe Fulks	F	6'5	190	29	66	—	429	1358	32	378	442	86	523	117	247	8	1236	—	7.9	1.8	3.7	18.7
Bill Closs	C-F	6'6	205	28	65	—	202	631	32	166	223	74	401	110	156	4	570	—	6.2	1.7	2.4	8.8
Andy Phillip	G	6'3	195	28	66	—	275	690	40	190	253	75	446	414	221	8	740	—	6.8	6.3	3.3	11.2
George Senesky	G	6'2	180	28	65	—	249	703	35	181	238	76	326	342	144	1	679	—	5.0	5.3	2.2	10.4
Ed Mikan (from Roch, Was)	C	6'8	230	25	61	—	193	556	35	137	189	72	344	63	194	6	523	—	5.6	1.0	3.2	8.6
Vern Gardner (ankle injury)	F	6'5	205	25	61	—	129	383	34	69	97	71	237	89	149	6	327	—	3.9	1.5	2.4	5.4
Ron Livingstone	C	6'10	220	25	63	—	104	353	29	76	109	70	297	76	220	10	284	—	4.7	1.2	3.5	4.5
Nelson Bobb	G	6'	170	26	53	—	52	158	33	44	79	56	101	82	83	1	148	—	1.9	1.5	1.6	2.8
Leo Mogus	F	6'4	205	29	57	—	43	122	35	53	86	62	102	32	60	0	139	—	1.8	0.6	1.1	2.4
Ike Borsavage	C-F	6'8	220	26	24	—	26	74	35	12	18	67	24	4	34	1	64	—	1.0	0.2	1.4	2.7
Easy Parham	F	6'3	200	29	7	—	3	7	43	4	9	44	12	3	5	0	10	—	1.7	0.4	0.7	1.4
BOSTON CELTICS	39-30 .565				RED AUERBACH (38-29 .567), WALTER BROWN (1-1 .5000)																	
Bob Donham	F-G	6'2	190	24	68	—	151	298	51	114	229	50	235	139	179	3	416	—	3.5	2.0	2.6	6.1
Chuck Cooper	F	6'5	205	24	66	—	207	601	34	201	267	75	562	174	219	7	615	—	8.5	2.6	3.3	9.3
Ed Macauley	C-F	6'8	190	22	68	—	459	985	47	466	614	76	616	252	205	4	1384	—	9.1	3.7	3.0	20.4
Bob Cousy	G	6'1	175	22	69	—	401	1138	35	276	365	76	474	341	185	2	1078	—	6.9	4.9	2.7	15.6
Sonny Hertzberg	G	5'10	175	28	65	—	206	651	32	223	270	83	260	244	156	4	635	—	4.0	3.8	2.4	9.8
Kleggie Hermsen (from TC)	C	6'9	235	27	71	—	189	644	29	155	237	65	448	92	261	8	533	—	6.3	1.3	3.7	7.5
Frank Kudelka (from Was)	G	6'2	193	25	62	—	179	518	35	83	119	70	158	105	211	8	441	—	2.5	1.7	3.4	7.1
Ed Leede	G-F	6'3	185	23	57	—	119	370	32	140	189	74	118	95	144	3	378	—	2.1	1.7	2.5	6.6
Bob Harris (from FtW, KJ)	F	6'7	195	23	56	—	98	295	33	86	127	68	291	64	157	4	282	—	5.2	1.1	2.8	5.0
Bones McKinney(from Was)	F	6'6	187	31	44	—	102	327	31	58	81	72	198	85	136	6	262	—	4.5	1.9	3.1	6.0
Ed Stanczak	F	6'3	210	29	17	—	11	48	23	35	43	81	34	6	6	0	57	—	2.0	0.4	0.4	3.4
Andy Duncan (KJ, broken leg)	F	6'6	195	28	14	—	7	40	18	15	22	68	30	8	27	0	29	—	2.1	0.6	1.9	2.1
NEW YORK KNICKERBOCKERS	36-30 .545				JOE LAPCHICK																	
Vince Bolyla	F	6'5	210	23	66	—	352	867	41	278	332	84	249	182	244	6	982	—	3.8	2.8	3.7	14.9
Harry Gallatin	F-C	6'6	215	23	66	—	293	705	42	259	354	73	800	180	244	4	845	—	12.1	2.7	3.7	12.8
Sweetwater Clifton	C-F	6'6	210	28	65	—	211	656	32	140	263	53	491	162	269	13	562	—	7.6	2.5	4.1	8.6
Max Zaslofsky	G	6'2	170	25	66	—	302	853	35	231	298	78	228	136	150	3	835	—	3.5	2.1	2.3	12.7
Dick McGuire	G	6'	180	24	64	—	179	482	37	179	276	65	334	400	154	2	537	—	5.2	6.3	2.4	8.4
Connie Simmons	C-F	6'8	225	25	66	—	229	613	37	146	208	70	426	117	222	8	604	—	6.5	1.8	3.4	9.2
Ray Lumpp	G	6'1	178	26	64	—	153	379	40	124	160	78	125	115	160	2	430	—	2.0	1.8	2.5	6.7
Ernie Vanderweghe (MD)	G-F	6'3	195	24	44	—	135	336	40	68	97	70	195	121	144	6	338	—	4.4	2.8	3.3	7.7
George Kaftan	F	6'3	190	22	61	—	111	286	39	78	125	62	153	74	102	1	300	—	2.5	1.2	1.7	4.9
Tex Ritter	G	6'2	185	26	34	—	39	103	38	49	71	69	65	37	52	1	127	—	1.9	1.1	1.5	3.7
Tony Lavelli (from Bos-HO)	F	6'3	185	24	30	—	32	93	34	35	41	85	59	23	56	1	99	—	2.0	0.8	1.9	3.3
Ray Ellefson	C	6'8	230	28	3	—	0	4	0	4	4	100	8	0	6	0	4	—	2.7	0.0	2.0	1.3
Carl Braun - military service																						
SYRACUSE NATIONALS	32-34 .485				AL CERVI																	
Alex Hannum	F	6'7	225	27	63	—	182	494	37	107	197	54	301	119	271	16	471	—	4.8	1.9	4.3	7.5
Dolph Schayes	F	6'8	220	22	66	—	332	930	36	457	608	75	1080	251	271	9	1121	—	16.4	3.8	4.1	17.0
Noble Jorgensen (from TC)	C	6'9	230	25	63	—	223	600	37	182	265	69	338	91	237	8	628	—	5.4	1.4	3.8	10.0
Freddie Scolari (from Was)	G	5'11	185	28	66	—	302	923	33	279	331	84	218	255	183	1	883	—	3.3	3.9	2.8	13.4
Billy Gabor (back injury)	G	5'11	170	28	61	—	255	745	34	179	242	74	150	125	213	7	689	—	2.5	2.0	3.5	11.3
George Ratkovicz	C-F	6'7	225	28	66	—	264	636	42	321	439	73	547	193	256	11	849	—	8.3	2.9	3.9	12.9
Al Cervi (hand injury)	G	5'11	185	33	53	—	132	346	38	194	237	82	152	208	180	9	458	—	2.9	3.9	3.4	8.6
Johnny Macknowski (leg injury)	G	6'1	185	27	58	—	131	435	30	122	170	72	110	69	134	3	384	—	1.9	1.2	2.3	6.6
Paul Seymour (IL)	G-F	6'2	180	22	51	—	125	385	32	117	159	74	194	187	138	0	367	—	3.8	3.7	2.7	7.2
Gerry Calabrese	G	6'1	175	25	46	—	70	197	36	61	88	69	65	65	80	0	201	—	1.4	1.4	1.7	4.4
Leroy Chollet	F	6'2	190	25	14	—	6	51	12	12	19	63	15	12	29	0	24	—	1.1	0.9	2.1	1.7
Earl Lloyd (from Was, military service)																						
BALTIMORE BULLETS	24-42 .364				BUDDY JEANETTE (14-23 .378), WALT BUDKO (10-19 .345)																	
Walt Budko	F	6'5	220	25	64	—	165	464	36	166	223	74	452	135	203	7	496	—	7.1	2.1	3.2	7.8
Red Rocha	F-C	6'9	185	27	64	—	297	843	35	242	299	81	511	147	242	9	836	—	8.0	2.3	3.8	13.1
Chick Halbert (from Was)	C	6'9	225	31	68	—	164	449	37	172	248	69	539	158	216	7	500	—	7.9	2.3	3.2	7.4
Paul Hoffman (back injury, ST)	G	6'2	205	25	41	—	127	399	32	105	156	67	202	111	135	2	359	—	4.9	2.7	3.3	8.8
Belus Smawley (from Syr, ankle injury)	G	6'1	195	32	60	—	252	663	38	227	267	85	178	161	145	4	731	—	3.0	2.7	2.4	12.2
Kenny Sailors (from Bos)	G	5'10	176	28	60	—	181	533	34	131	180	73	120	150	196	8	493	—	2.0	2.5	3.3	8.2
Don Rehfeldt	F	6'6	210	23	59	—	164	426	38	103	139	74	251	68	146	4	431	—	4.3	1.2	2.5	7.3
Brady Walker (from Bos)	F	6'6	205	29	66	—	164	416	39	72	103	70	354	111	82	2	400	—	5.4	1.7	1.2	6.1
Gene James (from NY)	F	6'4	180	25	48	—	79	235	34	44	71	62	141	70	118	2	202	—	2.9	1.5	2.5	4.2
Billy Hassett (injury)	G	5'11	180	29	31	—	45	160	28	43	63	68	35	47	72	1	133	—	1.1	1.5	2.3	4.3
Norm Mager	F	6'5	185	24	24	—	40	142	28	44	56	79	47	22	68	3	124	—	2.0	1.0	2.8	5.2
Joe Dolhon (KJ)	G	6'	175	23	13	—	17	56	30	17	23	74	18	19	32	1	51	—	1.4	1.5	2.5	3.9

					TOTAL													PER GAME				
Use Name	Pos	Hgt	Wgt	Age	G	Min	FG	FGA	%	FT	FTA	%	Reb	Ass	PF	DQ	Points	Min	Reb	Ass	PF	Points
					1950/51 N.B.A. — WESTERN DIVISION																	
MINNEAPOLIS LAKERS	44-24 .647				JONNNY KUNDLA (43-24 .642), HERM SCHAEFER (1-0 1.000)																	
Jim Polland (IL, broken cheekbone)	F	6'5	190	28	54	—	256	728	35	117	156	75	484	184	157	4	629	—	9.0	3.4	2.9	11.6
Vern Mikkelsen	F-C	6'7	230	22	64	—	359	893	40	186	275	68	655	181	260	13	904	—	10.2	2.8	4.1	14.1
George Mikan	C	6'10	245	26	68	—	**678**	**1564**	43	**576**	**717**	80	958	208	**308**	14	1932	—	14.1	3.1	**4.5**	**28.4**
Bob Harrison	G	6'2	190	23	68	—	150	432	35	101	128	79	172	195	218	5	401	—	2.5	2.9	3.2	5.9
Slater Martin	G	5'10	170	25	68	—	227	627	36	121	177	68	246	235	199	3	575	—	3.6	3.5	2.9	8.5
Arnie Ferrin	F	6'4	180	25	68	—	119	373	32	114	164	70	271	107	220	8	352	—	4.0	1.6	3.2	5.2
Kevin O'Shea	G	6'2	175	25	63	—	87	267	33	97	134	72	125	100	99	1	271	—	2.0	1.6	1.6	4.3
Tony Jaros	F-G	6'3	185	30	63	—	88	287	31	65	103	63	131	72	131	0	241	—	2.1	1.1	2.1	3.8
Bud Grant	F	6'3	195	23	61	—	53	184	29	52	83	63	115	71	106	0	158	—	1.9	1.2	1.7	2.6
Joe Hutton	G	6'1	170	22	60	—	59	180	33	29	43	67	102	53	89	1	147	—	1.7	0.9	1.5	2.5
Dick Schnittker (from Was)-military service																						
ROCHESTER ROYALS	41-27 .603				LES HARRISON																	
Arnie Johnson	F	6'5	240	30	68	—	185	403	46	269	371	73	449	175	290	11	639	—	6.6	2.6	4.3	9.4
Jack Coleman	F-C	6'7	210	26	67	—	315	749	42	134	172	78	584	197	193	4	764	—	8.7	2.9	2.9	11.4
Arnie Risen	C	6'9	210	26	66	—	377	940	40	323	440	73	795	158	278	9	1077	—	12.0	2.4	4.2	16.3
Bob Davies	G	6'1	175	30	63	—	326	877	37	303	381	80	197	287	208	7	955	—	3.1	4.6	3.3	15.2
Bobby Wanzer	G	6'	172	29	68	—	252	628	40	232	273	85	232	181	129	0	736	—	3.4	2.7	1.9	10.8
Bill Calhoun	F	6'3	180	23	66	—	175	506	35	161	228	71	199	99	87	1	511	—	3.0	1.5	1.3	7.7
Red Holzman	G	5'10	175	30	68	—	183	561	33	130	179	73	152	147	94	0	496	—	2.2	2.2	1.4	7.3
Pep Saul	G	6'2	185	26	65	—	105	310	34	72	105	69	84	68	85	0	282	—	1.3	1.0	1.3	4.3
Paul Noel	F	6'4	185	26	52	—	49	174	28	32	45	71	81	34	61	1	130	—	1.6	0.7	1.2	2.5
Joe McNamee	C-F	6'6	210	24	60	—	48	167	29	27	42	64	101	18	88	2	123	—	1.7	0.3	1.5	2.1
FORT WAYNE PISTONS	32-36 .471				MURRAY MENDENHALL																	
Fred Schaus	F	6'5	200	25	68	—	312	918	34	404	484	83	495	184	240	11	1028	—	7.3	2.7	3.5	15.1
Jack Kerris	F-C	6'6	215	25	68	—	255	689	37	201	295	68	477	181	253	12	711	—	7.0	2.7	3.7	10.5
Larry Foust	C-F	6'9	200	22	68	—	327	944	35	261	396	66	681	90	247	6	915	—	10.0	1.3	3.6	13.5
Ken Murray (from Bal)	G	6'2	195	22	66	—	301	887	34	248	332	75	355	202	164	7	850	—	5.4	3.1	2.5	12.9
Boag Johnson	G	5'11	170	29	68	—	235	737	32	114	162	70	275	183	247	11	584	—	4.0	2.7	3.6	8.6
Don Otten (from Was, Bal)	C	7'	245	29	67	—	162	479	34	246	308	80	404	62	255	15	570	—	6.0	0.9	3.8	8.5
Johnny Oldham	G	6'3	175	27	68	—	199	597	33	171	292	59	242	127	242	15	569	—	3.6	1.9	3.6	8.4
Dick Mehen (from Bal, Bos)	F	6'6	195	28	66	—	192	532	36	90	123	73	223	188	149	4	474	—	3.4	2.8	2.3	7.2
Duane Klueh	G	6'3	175	24	61	—	157	458	34	135	184	73	183	82	143	5	449	—	3.0	1.3	2.3	7.4
Curly Armstrong (KJ)	G	5'11	170	32	38	—	72	232	31	58	90	64	89	77	97	2	202	—	2.3	2.0	2.6	5.3
Jim Riffey	F	6'4	200	27	35	—	65	185	35	20	26	77	61	16	54	0	150	—	1.7	0.5	1.5	4.3
Art Burris	F	6'5	220	26	33	—	28	113	25	21	36	58	106	27	51	0	77	—	3.2	0.8	1.5	2.3
Chuck Share-(CT)																						
Bill Sharman (from Was)-(VR)																						
INDIANAPOLIS OLYMPIANS	31-37 .456				CLIFF BARKER (24-32 .429), WAH WAH JONES (7-5 .563)																	
Leo Barnhorst	F-G	6'4	190	26	68	—	232	671	35	82	119	69	296	218	197	1	546	—	4.4	3.2	2.9	8.0
Wah Wah Jones (knee injury)	F	6'4	225	24	22	—	93	237	39	61	77	79	125	85	74	4	247	—	5.7	3.9	3.4	11.2
Alex Groza	C	6'7	218	24	66	—	492	1046	**47**	445	566	79	709	156	237	8	1429	—	10.7	2.4	3.6	21.7
Paul Walther	G	6'2	160	23	63	—	213	634	34	145	209	69	226	225	201	8	571	—	3.6	3.6	3.2	9.1
Ralph Beard	G	5'10	176	23	66	—	409	1110	37	293	378	78	251	318	96	0	1111	—	3.8	**4.8**	1.5	16.8
Bob Lavoy	F-C	6'7	185	24	63	—	221	619	36	84	133	63	310	76	190	2	526	—	4.9	1.2	3.0	8.3
Joe Hollend	F	6'4	185	25	67	—	196	594	33	78	137	57	344	150	228	8	470	—	5.1	2.2	3.4	7.0
John Mahnken (from Bos)	C	6'8	240	28	58	—	111	351	32	45	70	64	219	77	164	6	267	—	3.8	1.3	2.8	4.6
Don Lofgran (from Syr)	F	6'6	200	22	61	—	79	270	29	79	127	62	157	36	132	4	237	—	2.6	0.6	2.2	3.9
Mal McMullan	F	6'5	210	23	51	—	78	277	28	48	82	59	128	33	109	2	204	—	2.5	0.6	2.1	4.0
Cliff Barker	G	6'2	185	29	56	—	51	202	25	50	77	65	100	115	98	0	152	—	1.8	2.1	1.8	2.7
Bruce Hale (IL)	G	6'1	170	32	26	—	40	135	30	14	23	61	49	42	30	0	94	—	1.9	1.6	1.2	3.6
Chuck Mrazovich	F	6'5	185	26	23	—	24	73	33	28	46	61	33	12	48	1	76	—	1.4	0.5	2.1	3.3
Carl Shaeffer	G-F	6'3	185	26	10	—	6	22	27	3	3	100	10	6	15	0	15	—	1.0	0.6	1.5	1.5
Leon Blevins	G	6'2	160	24	3	—	1	4	25	0	1	0	2	1	3	0	2	—	0.7	0.3	1.0	0.7
Marshall Hawkins-(VR)																						
TRI-CITIES BLACKHAWKS	25-43 .368				DAVE MCMILLAN (9-14 .391), JONNNY LOGAN (2-1 .667), MIKE TODOROVICH (14-28 .333)																	
Dike Eddleman	F-G	6'3	189	28	68	—	398	1120	36	244	349	70	410	170	231	5	1040	—	6.0	2.5	3.4	15.3
Mike Todorovich	F	6'5	230	27	66	—	221	715	31	211	301	70	455	179	197	5	653	—	6.9	2.7	3.0	9.9
Jack Nichols (MS, KJ)	C	6'7	215	24	5	—	18	48	38	10	13	77	52	14	18	0	46	—	10.4	2.8	3.6	9.2
Johnny Logan(MS)	G	6'2	175	29	29	—	81	257	32	62	83	75	134	127	66	2	224	—	4.6	4.4	2.3	7.7
Frankie Brian	G	6'1	180	27	68	—	363	1127	32	418	508	82	244	266	215	4	1144	—	3.6	3.9	3.2	16.8
Ed Peterson (from Syr, IL)	C	6'9	230	25	53	—	130	384	34	99	150	66	288	66	188	9	359	—	5.4	1.2	3.5	6.8
Cal Christensen	F	6'5	210	23	67	—	134	445	30	175	245	71	523	161	266	**19**	443	—	7.8	2.4	4.0	6.6
Warren Perkins	G-F	6'3	190	26	66	—	135	428	32	126	195	65	319	143	232	13	396	—	4.8	2.2	3.5	6.0
Harry Boykoff (from Bos) (KJ)	C	6'10	265	28	48	—	126	336	38	74	100	74	220	60	197	12	326	—	4.6	1.3	4.1	6.8
Bob Carpenter (from FtW)	F	6'5	200	33	56	—	109	355	31	105	128	82	229	79	115	2	323	—	4.1	1.4	2.1	5.8
Tommy Byrnes (from Bal, Was)	G	6'3	180	27	48	—	83	275	30	55	84	65	72	69	86	0	221	—	1.5	1.4	1.8	4.6
Gene Vance (MS, nose injury)	G	6'3	196	27	28	—	44	110	40	43	61	70	88	53	91	0	131	—	3.1	1.9	3.3	4.7
Ray Corley (from Bal)	G	6'	180	22	18	—	29	85	34	16	29	55	43	38	26	0	74	—	2.4	2.1	1.4	4.1
Herb Scherer	C	6'9	212	21	20	—	24	84	29	20	35	57	50	17	56	1	68	—	2.5	0.9	2.8	3.4
John Hargis (from FtW)	G	6'2	180	30	14	—	25	66	38	17	24	71	30	9	26	0	67	—	2.1	0.6	1.9	4.8
Ed Gayda	G-F	6'4	210	23	14	—	18	42	43	18	23	78	38	13	32	0	54	—	2.7	0.9	2.3	3.9
Ed Beach (from Min)	F	6'3	200	21	12	—	8	38	21	6	9	67	25	3	14	0	22	—	2.1	0.3	1.2	1.8
Hank DeZonie	F	6'6	215	—	5	—	6	25	24	5	7	71	18	9	6	0	17	—	3.6	1.8	1.2	3.4
Walt Kirk-military service, Bill Henry, Alan Sawyer (from Was)-VR																						

1950/51 N.B.A. — EASTERN DIVISION (continued)

Use Name	Pos	Hgt	Wgt	Age	G	Min	FG	FGA	%	FT	FTA	%	Reb	Ass	PF	DQ	Points	Min	Reb	Ass	PF	Points
					TOTAL													PER GAME				
WASHINGTON CAPITOLS	10-25 .286				**BONES McKINNEY**		Capitols disbanded January 9,1951.															
Bones McKinney	F	6'6	187	31	(See Boston)																	
Dick Schnittker (BY) (to Min-MS)	F	6'5	205	22	29	—	85	219	39	123	139	88	153	42	76	0	293	—	5.3	1.4	2.6	10.1
Don Otten	C	7'	245	29	(See Fort Wayne)																	
Bill Sharman (to FtW-VR)	G	6'1	175	24	31	—	141	361	39	96	108	89	96	39	86	3	378	—	3.1	1.3	2.8	12.2
Freddie Scolari	G	5'11	185	28	(See Syracuse)																	
Ariel Maughan	F	6'4	190	27	35	—	78	250	31	101	120	84	141	48	91	2	257	—	4.0	1.4	2.6	7.3
Alan Sawyer (to TC-VR)	F	6'5	195	22	33	—	87	215	40	43	54	80	125	25	75	1	217	—	3.8	0.8	2.3	6.6
Ed Bartels	F	6'5	195	25	17	—	24	97	25	24	46	52	84	12	54	0	72	—	4.9	0.7	3.2	4.2
Dick O'Keefe	G	6'2	185	27	17	—	21	102	21	25	39	64	37	25	48	0	67	—	2.2	1.5	2.8	3.9
Chuck Gilmur (injury)	F	6'4	225	28	16	—	17	61	28	17	32	53	75	17	57	3	51	—	4.7	1.1	3.6	3.2
Earl Lloyd (to Syr-MS)	C-F	6'6	210	22	7	—	16	35	46	11	13	85	47	11	26	0	43	—	6.7	1.6	3.7	6.1
Swede Carlson (from Bal)	G	6'	170	29	9	—	17	46	37	8	16	50	15	19	23	0	42	—	1.7	2.1	2.6	4.7
Tommy O'Keefe (from Bal)	G	6'2	185	24	6	—	10	28	36	3	4	75	7	10	5	0	23	—	1.2	1.7	0.8	3.8
Johnny Noriander	F	6'3	180	29	9	—	6	19	32	9	14	64	9	5	14	0	21	—	1.0	0.6	1.6	2.3

1950/51 N.B.A. — PLAYOFFS

ROCHESTER ROYALS — **LES HARRISON**

defeated Fort Wayne 2-1; H110-81, 78-83, H97-78
defeated Minneapolis 3-1; 73-76, 70-66, H83-70, H80-75
defeated New York 4-3; H92-65, H99-84, 78-77, 73-79, H89-92, 73-80, H79-75

Use Name	Pos	Hgt	Wgt	Age	G	Min	FG	FGA	%	FT	FTA	%	Reb	Ass	PF	DQ	Points	Min	Reb	Ass	PF	Points
Arnie Johnson	F	6'5	240	30	14	—	48	107	45	61	78	78	126	40	**68**	2	157	—	9.0	2.9	4.9	11.2
Jack Coleman	F-C	6'7	210	26	14	—	55	139	40	30	41	73	179	66	49	0	140	—	12.8	4.7	3.5	10.0
Arnie Risen	C	6'9	210	26	14	—	**93**	**239**	39	**87**	**135**	64	**196**	33	59	2	**273**	—	14.0	2.4	4.2	19.5
Bob Davies	G	6'1	175	30	14	—	79	234	34	64	80	80	43	75	45	1	222	—	3.1	5.4	3.2	15.9
Bobby Wanzer	G	6'	172	29	14	—	57	121	47	61	67	91	71	59	45	1	175	—	5.1	4.2	3.2	12.5
Red Holzman	G	5'10	175	30	14	—	31	76	41	23	34	68	19	20	14	0	85	—	1.4	1.4	1.0	6.1
Bill Calhoun	F	6'3	180	23	14	—	20	48	42	21	28	75	41	20	19	0	61	—	2.9	1.4	1.4	4.4
Joe McNamee	C-F	6'6	210	24	13	—	12	41	29	9	12	75	35	9	26	0	33	—	2.7	0.7	2.0	2.5
Paul Noel	F	6'4	185	26	9	—	7	18	39	5	7	71	9	1	11	0	19	—	1.0	0.1	1.2	2.1
Pep Saul	G	6'2	185	26	9	—	4	12	33	1	2	50	3	6	2	0	9	—	0.3	0.7	0.2	1.0

NEW YORK KNICKERBOCKERS — **JOE LAPCHICK**

defeated Boston 2-0; 83-69, H92-78
defeated Syracuse 3-2; H103-92, 80-102, H97-75, 83-90, H83-81
lost to Rochester 3-4; 65-92, 84-99, H77-78, H79-73 92-89, H80-73, 75-79

Use Name	Pos	Hgt	Wgt	Age	G	Min	FG	FGA	%	FT	FTA	%	Reb	Ass	PF	DQ	Points	Min	Reb	Ass	PF	Points
Vince Boryla	F	6'5	210	23	14	—	83	193	43	51	56	**91**	52	37	42	1	217	—	3.7	2.6	3.0	15.5
Harry Gallatin	F-C	6'6	215	23	14	—	49	140	35	67	87	77	163	26	57	3	165	—	11.6	1.9	4.1	11.8
Sweetwater Clifton	C-F	6'6	210	28	14	—	41	118	35	18	46	39	137	46	62	**4**	100	—	9.8	3.3	4.4	7.1
Max Zaslofsky	G	6'2	170	25	14	—	88	217	41	74	100	74	58	38	43	2	250	—	4.1	2.7	3.1	17.9
Dick McGuire	F	6'	180	24	14	—	25	80	31	24	53	45	83	**78**	50	1	74	—	5.9	5.6	3.6	5.3
Connie Simmons	C-F	6'8	225	25	14	—	55	151	36	42	68	62	94	24	61	1	152	—	6.7	1.7	4.4	10.9
Ernie Vandeweghe	G-F	6'3	195	24	14	—	37	91	41	27	37	73	66	34	55	**4**	101	—	4.7	2.4	3.9	7.2
Ray Lumpp	G	6'1	178	26	13	—	24	67	36	20	23	87	20	23	40	3	68	—	1.5	1.8	3.1	5.2
George Kaftan	F	6'3	190	22	8	—	6	18	33	1	3	33	6	2	7	0	13	—	0.8	0.3	0.9	1.6
Tony Lavelli	F	6'3	185	24	2	—	1	5	20	2	2	100	1	1	2	0	4	—	0.5	0.5	1.0	2.0
Tex Riner	G	6'2	185	26	3	—	1	5	20	1	1	100	2	0	5	0	3	—	0.7	0.0	1.7	1.0
Carl Braun - military service																						

SYRACUSE NATIONALS — **AL CERVI**

defeated Philadelphia 2-0; 91-89(OT), H90-78
lost to New York 2-3; 92-103, H102-80, 75-97, H90-83, 81-83

Use Name	Pos	Hgt	Wgt	Age	G	Min	FG	FGA	%	FT	FTA	%	Reb	Ass	PF	DQ	Points	Min	Reb	Ass	PF	Points
Alex Hannum	F	6'7	225	27	7	—	17	39	44	8	10	80	47	17	37	3	42	—	6.7	2.4	5.3	6.0
Dolph Schayes	F	6'8	220	22	7	—	47	105	45	49	64	77	102	20	28	2	143	—	**14.6**	2.9	4.0	20.4
Noble Jorgensen	C	6'9	230	25	7	—	18	43	42	14	22	64	21	7	19	0	50	—	3.0	1.0	2.7	7.1
Freddie Scolari	G	5'11	185	28	7	—	33	93	35	22	27	81	41	16	23	1	88	—	5.9	2.3	3.3	12.6
Al Cervi	G	5'11	185	33	7	—	17	56	30	44	50	88	33	38	31	1	78	—	4.7	5.4	4.4	11.1
George Ratkovicz	C-F	6'7	225	28	7	—	28	59	47	41	55	75	63	14	33	0	97	—	9.0	2.0	4.7	13.9
Billy Gabor	G	5'11	170	28	7	—	27	72	38	9	14	64	20	18	24	1	63	—	2.9	2.6	3.4	9.0
Paul Seymour	G-F	6'2	180	22	7	—	10	48	21	14	21	67	26	25	22	1	34	—	3.7	3.6	3.1	4.9
Johnny Macknowski	G	6'1	185	27	2	—	6	13	46	1	3	33	7	4	5	0	13	—	3.5	2.0	2.5	6.5
Leroy Chollet	F	6'2	190	25	7	—	4	23	17	5	8	63	16	9	16	1	13	—	2.3	1.3	2.3	1.9
Gerry Calabrese - injury																						
Earl Lloyd-military service																						

MINNEAPOLIS LAKERS — **JONNNY KUNDLA**

defeated Indianapolis 2-1; H95-81, 88-108, H85-80
lost to Rochester 1-3; H76-73, H66-70, 70-83, 75-80

Use Name	Pos	Hgt	Wgt	Age	G	Min	FG	FGA	%	FT	FTA	%	Reb	Ass	PF	DQ	Points	Min	Reb	Ass	PF	Points
Jim Pollard	F	6'5	190	28	7	—	35	108	32	25	30	83	62	27	27	1	95	—	8.9	3.9	3.9	13.6
Vern Mikkelsen	F-C	6'7	230	22	7	—	39	96	41	31	47	66	67	17	35	3	109	—	9.6	2.4	5.0	15.6
George Mikan	C	6'10	245	26	7	—	62	152	41	44	55	80	74	9	25	1	168	—	10.6	1.3	3.6	24.0
Bob Harrison	G	6'2	190	23	7	—	24	52	46	6	8	75	27	19	30	3	54	—	3.9	2.7	4.3	7.7
Slater Martin	G	5'10	170	25	7	—	18	51	35	14	27	52	42	25	20	0	50	—	6.0	3.6	2.9	7.1
Arnie Ferrin	F	6'4	185	25	7	—	12	36	33	17	18	94	33	16	21	1	41	—	4.7	2.3	3.0	5.9
Tony Jaros	F-G	6'3	185	30	7	—	6	20	30	8	11	73	7	6	11	0	20	—	1.0	0.9	1.6	2.9
Bud Grant	F	6'3	195	23	6	—	4	11	36	3	3	100	5	0	12	0	11	—	0.8	0.0	2.0	1.8
Kevin O'Shea	G	6'2	175	25	5	—	1	7	14	3	4	75	5	1	8	0	5	—	1.0	0.2	1.6	1.0
Joe Hutton	G	6'1	170	22	7	—	0	3	0	2	4	50	3	1	5	0	2	—	0.4	0.1	0.7	0.3
Dick Schnittker-military service																						

1950/51 N.B.A. — PLAYOFFS (continued)

Use Name	Pos	Hgt	Wgt	Age	G	Min	FG	FGA	%	FT	FTA	%	Reb	Ass	PF	DQ	Points	Min	Reb	Ass	PF	Points
					TOTAL													PER GAME				
INDIANAPOLIS OLYMPIANS	**WAH WAH JONES**				lost to Minneapolis 1-2; 81-95; H108-88, 80-85																	
Leo Barnhorst	F-G	6'4	190	26	3	—	13	35	37	8	10	80	9	12	7	0	34	—	3.0	4.0	2.3	11.3
Joe Holland	F	6'4	185	25	3	—	17	36	47	1	4	25	12	11	10	0	35	—	4.0	3.7	3.3	11.7
Alel Groza	C	6'7	218	24	3	—	36	73	49	25	33	76	42	2	14	0	97	—	14.0	0.7	4.7	**32.3**
Cliff Barkerr	G	6'2	185	29	3	—	4	19	21	0	3	0	15	10	10	0	8	—	5.0	3.3	3.3	2.7
Ralph Beard	G	5'10	176	23	3	—	27	61	44	12	17	71	12	13	6	0	66	—	4.0	4.3	2.0	22.0
Paul Walther	G	6'2	160	23	3	—	3	7	43	11	15	73	5	9	6	0	17	—	1.7	3.0	2.0	5.7
Don Lofgran	F	6'6	200	22	1	—	2	6	33	1	1	100	1	0	3	0	5	—	1.0	0.0	3.0	5.0
John Mahnken	C	6'8	240	28	3	—	2	15	13	0	0	—	11	9	11	1	4	—	3.7	3.0	3.7	1.3
Bob Lavoy	F	6'7	185	24	3	—	0	7	0	3	5	60	6	4	6	0	3	—	2.0	1.3	2.0	1.0
Bruce Hale	G	6'1	170	32	1	—	0	0	—	0	0	—	0	0	0	0	0	—	0.0	0.0	0.0	0.0
Wah Wah Jones - knee injury																						
FORT WAYNE PISTONS	**MURRAY MENDENHALL**				lost to Rochester 1-2; 81-110, H83-78, 78-97																	
Fred Schaus	F	6'5	200	25	3	—	17	44	39	9	11	82	16	10	10	0	43	—	5.3	3.3	3.3	14.3
Dick Mehen	F	6'6	195	28	3	—	12	29	41	2	4	50	14	3	9	0	26	—	4.7	1.0	3.0	8.7
Don Otten	C	7'	245	29	3	—	8	26	31	13	16	81	19	8	15	1	29	—	6.3	2.7	5.0	9.7
Ken Murray	G	6'2	195	22	3	—	11	48	23	4	5	80	14	10	7	0	26	—	4.7	3.3	2.3	8.7
Boag Johnson	G	5'11	170	29	3	—	12	32	38	1	2	50	7	7	17	2	25	—	2.3	2.3	**5.7**	8.3
Larry Foust	C-F	6'9	200	22	3	—	14	45	31	8	10	80	37	5	5	0	36	—	12.3	1.7	1.7	12.0
Jack Kerris	F	6'6	215	25	3	—	9	26	35	5	10	50	20	10	15	1	23	—	6.7	3.3	5.0	7.7
Johnny Oldham	G	6'3	175	27	3	—	6	16	38	5	10	50	5	5	13	0	17	—	1.7	1.7	4.3	5.7
Curly Armstrong	G	5'11	170	32	3	—	7	19	37	1	1	100	7	5	8	0	15	—	2.3	1.7	2.7	5.0
Duane Klueh	G	6 3	175	24	2	—	1	6	17	0	0	—	3	3	3	0	2	—	1.5	1.5	1.5	1.0
PHILADELPHIA WARRIORS	**EDDIE GOTTLIEB**				lost to Syracuse 0-2; H89-91(OT), 78-90																	
Paul Arizin	F	6'4	190	22	2	—	14	27	**52**	13	16	81	20	3	10	1	52	—	10.0	1.5	5.0	26.0
Joe Fulks	F	6'5	190	29	2	—	16	49	33	20	27	74	16	1	9	0	41	—	8.0	0.5	4.5	20.5
Ed Mikan	C	6'8	230	25	2	—	6	26	23	10	11	91	21	3	6	0	22	—	10.5	1.5	3.0	11.0
Andy Phillip	G	6'3	195	28	2	—	6	15	40	3	6	50	15	14	9	0	15	—	7.5	7.0	4.5	7.5
George Senesky	G	6'2	180	28	2	—	4	22	18	7	9	78	7	15	6	0	15	—	3.5	**7.5**	3.0	7.5
Vern Gandner	F	6'5	205	25	2	—	4	8	50	3	3	100	4	0	8	1	11	—	2.0	0.0	4.0	5.5
Bill Closs	F-C	6'6	205	28	2	—	2	8	25	3	5	60	8	5	5	0	7	—	4.0	2.5	2.5	3.5
Ron Livingstone	C	6'10	220	25	2	—	2	3	67	0	0	—	2	0	1	0	4	—	1.0	0.0	0.5	2.0
Nelson Bobb	G	6'	170	26	1	—	0	0	—	0	0	—	0	2	2	0	0	—	0.0	2.0	2.0	0.0
Leo Mogus	F	6'4	205	29	1	—	0	0	—	0	0	—	0	0	0	0	0	—	0.0	0.0	0.0	0.0
BOSTON CELTICS	**RED AUERBACH**				lost to New York 0-2; H69-83, 78-92																	
Bones McKinney	F	6'6	187	31	2	—	11	25	44	4	5	80	10	8	9	0	26	—	5.0	4.0	4.5	13.0
Chuck Cooper	F	6'5	205	24	2	—	4	12	33	2	5	40	13	3	8	0	10	—	6.5	1.5	4.0	5.0
Ed Macauley	C	6'8	190	22	2	—	17	36	47	10	16	63	18	8	4	0	44	—	9.0	4.0	2.0	22.0
Bob Cousy	G	6'1	175	22	2	—	9	42	21	10	12	83	15	12	8	0	28	—	7.5	6.0	4.0	14.0
Sonny Hertzben	G	5'10	175	28	2	—	3	13	23	4	5	80	2	3	8	0	10	—	1.0	1.5	4.0	5.0
Bob Donham	F-G	6'2	190	24	2	—	4	9	44	5	12	42	8	2	9	1	13	—	4.0	1.0	4.5	6.5
Bob Harris	F	6'7	195	23	2	—	1	10	10	5	7	71	4	2	4	0	7	—	2.0	1.0	2.0	3.5
Frank Kudelka	G	6'2	193	25	1	—	2	4	50	0	3	0	5	2	3	0	4	—	5.0	2.0	3.0	4.0
Ed Leede	G-F	6'3	185	23	2	—	1	7	14	1	1	100	0	2	3	0	3	—	0.0	1.0	1.5	1.5
Kleggie Hermsen	C	6'9	235	27	2	—	1	6	17	0	0	—	3	0	6	0	2	—	1.5	0.0	3.0	1.0

1950/51 N.B.A. TEAM STATISTICS

Team	Regular Season G	FG	FGA	%	FT	FTA	%	Reb.	Ass.	Average Points For	Agnst.	Diff.	Playoffs G	FG	FGA	%	FT	FTA	%	Reb.	Ass.	Average Points For	Agnst.	Diff.
EASTERN DIVISION																								
Philadelphia	66	1985	5665	35	1664	2181	**76**	3586	1432	85.4	81.6	+3.8	2	54	158	34	59	77	**77**	99	43	83.5	90.5	-7.0
Boston	69	2065	5607	37	1751	2415	73	3499	**1579**	85.2	85.5	-0.3	2	53	164	32	41	66	62	89	42	73.5	87.5	-14.0
New York	66	2037	5380	**38**	1592	2231	71	3421	1551	85.8	85.4	+0.4	14	410	1085	38	327	476	69	743	309	81.9	83.6	-1.7
Syracuse	66	1884	5365	35	**1912**	**2634**	73	3259	1493	**86.1**	85.5	+0.6	7	207	551	38	**207**	**274**	76	**410**	**168**	88.7	84.7	+4.0
Baltimore	66	1955	5542	35	1504	2020	74	3044	1345	82.0	84.3	-2.3												
Washington	35	967	2893	33	910	1244	73	1567	584	81.3	86.0	-4.7												
WESTERN DIVISION																								
Minneapolis	68	2084	5590	37	1464	1989	74	3409	1408	82.8	**77.4**	**+5.4**	7	201	536	38	153	207	74	325	121	79.3	82.1	-2.8
Rochester	68	2032	5377	38	1692	2248	75	3015	1368	84.6	81.7	+2.9	14	406	1035	39	362	484	75	753	329	83.9	**76.8**	**+7.1**
Fort Wayne	68	2002	5927	34	1718	2387	72	**3725**	1142	84.1	86	-1.9	3	97	**291**	33	48	69	70	150	66	80.7	95.0	-14.3
Indianapolis	68	**2096**	5779	36	1363	1902	72	2779	1455	81.7	84.1	-2.4	3	**104**	259	**40**	61	88	69	113	70	**89.7**	89.3	+0.4
Tri Cities	68	1988	**6041**	33	1754	2425	72	3715	1476	84.3	88.1	-3.8												

1950/51 N.B.A STANDINGS

Team	W	L	Pct.	GB	Record against playoff teams W	L	Pct.	Record against non-playoff teams W	L	Pct.	HOME W	L	Pct.	ROAD W	L	Pct.	NEUTRAL W	L	Pct.
EASTERN DIVISION																			
Philadelphia Warriors	40	26	.606	—	27	21	**.563**	13	5	.722	**29**	3	**.906**	10	22	.313	1	1	.500
Boston Celtics	39	30	.565	2.5	25	22	.532	14	8	.636	26	6	.813	9	22	.290	**4**	2	.667
New York Knickerbockers	36	30	.545	4	25	25	.500	11	5	.688	22	5	.815	10	25	.286	**4**	0	**1.000**
Syracuse Nationals	32	34	.485	8	22	28	.440	10	6	.625	24	9	.727	8	25	.242	0	0	—
Baltimore Bullets	24	42	.364	16	20	37	.351	4	5	.444	21	11	.656	3	25	.107	0	**6**	.000
Washington Capitols	10	25	.286	14.5	7	23	.233	3	2	.600	6	11	.353	4	13	.235	0	1	.000
WESTERN DIVISION																			
Minneapolis Lakers	**44**	24	**.647**	—	**28**	22	.560	**16**	2	**.889**	**29**	3	**.906**	**12**	21	**.364**	3	0	**1.000**
Rochester Royals	41	27	.603	3	26	23	.531	15	4	.789	29	5	.853	**12**	22	.353	0	0	—
Fort Wayne Pistons	32	36	.471	12	22	26	.458	10	**10**	.500	27	7	.794	5	27	.156	0	2	.000
Indianapolis Olympians	31	37	.456	13	21	29	.420	10	8	.556	19	12	.613	10	24	.294	2	1	.667
Tri-Cities Blackhawks	25	**43**	.368	19	21	**39**	.350	4	4	.500	22	**13**	.629	2	**28**	.067	1	2	.333

1950/51 N.B.A. INDIVIDUAL LEADERS

SCORING
(Minimum 46 Games Played)

Name	Team	G	FG	FT	Pts.	Avg.
Mikan	Min	68	678	576	1932	28.4
Groza	Ind	66	492	445	1429	21.7
Macauley	Bos	68	459	466	1384	20.4
Fulks	Phi	66	429	378	1236	18.7
Arizin	Phi	65	352	417	1121	17.2
Schayes	Syr	66	332	457	1121	17.0
Beard	Ind	66	409	293	1111	16.8
Brian	TC	68	363	418	1144	16.8
Risen	Roch	66	377	323	1077	16.3
Cousy	Bos	69	401	276	1078	15.6

FIELD GOAL PERCENTAGE
(Minimum 200 Field Goals)

Name	Team	FG	FGA	Pct.
Groza	Ind	492	1046	.470
Macauley	Bos	459	985	.466
Mikan	Min	678	1584	.428
Coleman	Roch	315	749	.421
Gallatin	NY	293	705	.416
Ratkovicz	Syr	264	636	.415
Arizin	Phi	352	864	.407
Boryla	NY	352	867	.406
Mikkelsen	Min	359	893	.402
Wanzer	Roch	252	628	.401

FREE THROW PERCENTAGE
(Minimum 190 Free Throws)

Name	Team	FT	FTA	Pct.
Fulks	Phi	378	442	.855
Smawley	Syr-Bal	227	267	.850
Wanzer	Roch	232	273	.850
Scolari	Was-Syr	279	331	.843
Boryla	NY	278	332	.837
Schaus	FtW	404	484	.835
Hertzoerg	Bos	223	270	.826
Brian	TC	418	508	.823
Cervi	Syr	194	237	.819
Rocha	Bal	242	299	.809

PERSONAL FOULS

Name	Team	PF
Mikan	Min	308
Johnson	Roch	290
Arizin	Phi	284
Risen	Roch	278
Hannum	Syr	271
Schayes	Syr	271

GAMES DISQUALIFIED

Name	Team	PF
Christensen	TC	19
Arizin	Phi	18
Hannum	Syr	16
Otten	Was-Bal-FtW	15
Oldham	FtW	15

REBOUNDS PER GAME
(Minimum 46 Games Played)

Name	Team	G	Ass.	Avg.
Schayes	Syr	66	1080	16.4
Mikan	Min	68	958	14.1
Gallatin	NY	66	800	12.1
Risen	Roch	66	795	12.0
Groza	Ind	66	709	10.7
Mikkelsen	Min	64	655	10.2
Foust	FtW	68	681	10.0
Arizin	Phi	65	640	9.8
Macauley	Bos	68	616	9.1
Pollard	Min	54	484	9.0

ASSISTS PER GAME
(Minimum 46 Games Played)

Name	Team	G	Ass.	Avg.
Phillip	Phi	66	414	6.3
McGuire	NY	64	400	6.3
Senesky	Phi	65	342	5.3
Cousy	Bos	69	341	4.9
Beard	Ind	66	318	4.8
Davies	Roch	63	287	4.6
Cervi	Syr	53	208	3.9
Brian	TC	68	266	3.9
Scolari	Was-Syr	66	255	3.9
Schayes	Syr	66	251	6.6

1951-52 N.B.A.

Benefiting from the College Scandals

The stink of scandal now hung heavy over all of big-time college basketball. New York's Madison Square Garden had been disgraced by last year's disclosures of widespread fixing of games between large local schools, but the stain had spread far beyond New York when new revelations were made over the summer. Players on prominent teams all over the country had been shaving points while on the take from professional gamblers. The two most spectacular discoveries were that Bradley and Kentucky had been doing business with the gamblers. Coach Adolph Rupp of Kentucky had said that gamblers, "couldn't touch my boys with a ten-foot pole," but stars Alex Groza and Ralph Beard were found to have been rigging games after returning from their triumphs in the 1948 Olympics. A series of hearings and trials brought the sordid details out into the open, and basketball fans, betting or otherwise, thought twice when faced with a college match.

With new audiences now available, the N.B.A. offered a tight ten-team circuit which had stepped up in class with the transfer of the Tri-Cities Blackhawks to Milwaukee. The still glamorous Madison Square Garden hosted most New York home games, and most of the top college players of recent seasons displayed their polished skills in this professional setting. Although Groza and Beard were banned because of their college improprieties, no taint of scandal had touched the N.B.A.

So with more eyes watching than ever before, both divisions staged blistering battles for first place. The Rochester Royals and Minneapolis Lakers as usual slugged it out for the top spot in the West. Bob Davies, Bobby Wanzer, and Arnie Risen led the Royals to a 41-25 record, tops in the league and one game better than the Lakers. Minneapolis still had the All-Star front line of George Mikan, Jim Pollard, and Vern Mikkelsen. To negate Mikan's brute strength, the league this year widened the foul lane from six feet to twelve feet; Big George kept wheeling in, however, and averaged 23.8 points per game, with a high-water mark of 61 against the Royals on January 20. Although the Lakers finished second, both clubs expected to meet again in a showdown in the playoffs.

The rest of the Western teams trailed the Royals and Lakers by a big margin. Indianapolis had lost their top players and gate attractions with the disgrace of Groza and Beard, but the club pulled itself together and actually improved on last season's record. The Ft. Wayne Pistons picked up star guard Frankie Brian from Milwaukee in a deal, but the good play of Brian, Larry Foust, and Fred Schaus could not lift the Pistons up to the .500 level. The Milwaukee Hawks came in a dismal fifth just as they did last year in Tri-Cities, but the club got a warm reception from the Wisconsin fans who had supported strong clubs in Sheboygan and Oshkosh for years.

The Eastern Division produced a dogfight just as fierce as the Royals-Lakers battle. Syracuse and Boston finished one game apart in the standings after five months of regular season play. Just like the Royals and Lakers, the Nats and Celtics played two different styles of ball. Syracuse coach Al Cervi schooled his men in a tough, scrappy brand of defense and a ball-control offense which worked the ball around until someone got open for a shot. Forward Dolph Schayes led the Nats in scoring and rebounding, and he typified the battling spirit ofthe team. Center Red Rocha came over from Baltimore to help Schayes in the forecourt, while rookie George King joined Paul Seymour in a top-flight defensive backcourt.

While the Nats played a tight team-oriented game, the Celtics relied on three stars for most of the scoring. Bob Cousy, now in his second season, upped his scoring average to 21.7 while continuing to dazzle opponents and audiences with his passing and dribbling. Ed Macauley scored at a 19.2 pace at center, while guard Bill Sharman, a superb outside shooter, signed with Boston after spending part of last season with the defunct Washington team. Coach Red Auerbach had all his theories of fast-break basketball in good order, but the Celtics lacked the good rebounder to make it work at peak efficiency.

Finishing a close third were the New York Knicks; with essentially the same squad as last season, the New Yorkers hoped to win a return trip to the playoff finals. The Philadelphia Warriors fell off from their 1950-51 form but still captured a playoff spot behind Paul Arizin's league-leading 25.4 scoring and Andy Phillip's league-leading 539 assists. The Baltimore Bullets limped home a weak fifth.

When the top eight teams started the season all over again in the playoffs, there was only one minor surprise in the opening round; the Knicks upset the Celtics, taking the deciding match of the three-game series with an 88-87 double overtime win. The Lakers, Royals, and Nats all marched to expected victories. The Royals had whipped the Lakers in last year's playoffs, but the Lakers turned the tables this year, taking three straight games after losing the first game. The Syracuse-New York series excited fans in both cities. The Knicks took the first game 87-85 in Syracuse, with Max Zaslofsky and Connie Simmons leading the way back from a 16-point halftime deficit. The Nats won game two by a 102-92 margin, but the Knicks then captured hard-fought 99-92 and 100-93 decisions in New York to move into the finals against the Lakers.

In the opening game, the Knicks lost two points in the early going when the referees called a foul on the Lakers but did not see Al McGuire's shot go in; McGuire missed both foul shots, and the Knicks went on to lose, 83-79, in overtime. The Knicks surprisingly took game two in St. Paul 80-72, and headed back to New York with a split. With the Garden tied up with the circus, the Knicks played in the 69th Regiment Armory and lost game three, 82-73, but fought back to even the series with a 90-89 win in overtime. The Lakers took game five in St. Paul, 102-89, with Mikan and Pollard both notching 32 points, but the Knicks took game six in New York, 76-68. With all the marbles riding on one game, the Lakers hosted the Knicks on April 25; their hospitality was hardly warm, as the Minneapolis team rolled to an 82-65 victory and their second N.B.A. title in three seasons.

1951/52 N.B.A. — EASTERN DIVISION

Use Name	Pos	Hgt	Wgt	Age	TOTAL G	Min	FG	FGA	%	FT	FTA	%	Reb	Ass	PF	DQ	Points	PER GAME Min	Reb	Ass	PF	Points
SYRACUSE NATIONALS	**40-26 .606**				**AL CERVI**																	
Wally Osterkorn	F	6'5	210	23	66	1721	145	413	35	199	335	59	444	117	226	8	489	26	6.7	1.8	3.4	7.4
Dolph Schayes	F	6'8	220	23	63	2004	263	740	36	342	424	81	773	182	213	5	868	32	12.3	2.9	3.4	13.8
Red Rocha	C-F	6'9	190	28	66	2543	300	749	40	254	330	77	549	128	249	4	854	39	8.3	1.9	3.8	12.9
Paul Seymour	G-F	6'2	185	23	66	2209	206	615	33	186	245	76	225	220	165	4	598	33	3.4	3.3	2.5	9.1
George King	G	6'	180	23	66	1889	235	579	41	188	264	71	274	244	199	6	658	29	4.2	3.7	3.0	10.0
George Ratkovicz	F-C	6'7	225	29	66	1356	165	473	35	163	242	67	328	90	235	8	493	21	5.0	1.4	3.6	7.5
Noble Jorgensen	C	6'9	230	26	66	1318	190	460	41	149	187	80	288	63	190	2	529	20	4.4	1.0	2.9	8.0
Bilb Gabor	G	5'11	180	29	57	1085	173	538	32	142	183	78	93	86	188	5	488	19	1.6	1.5	3.3	8.6
Gerry Calabrese	G	6'1	175	26	58	937	109	317	34	73	103	71	84	83	107	0	291	16	1.4	1.4	1.8	5.0
Al Cervi	G	5'11	185	34	55	850	99	280	35	219	248	88	87	148	176	7	417	15	1.6	2.7	3.2	7.6
Don Savage	F	6'3	205	23	12	118	9	43	21	18	28	64	24	12	22	0	36	10	2.0	1.0	1.8	3.0
Earl Lloyd - military service																						
BOSTON CELTICS	**39-27 .591**				**RED AUERBACH**																	
Chuck Cooper	F	6'5	205	25	66	1976	197	545	36	149	201	74	502	134	219	8	543	30	7.6	2.0	3.3	8.2
Bob Harris	F	6'7	195	24	66	1899	190	463	41	134	209	64	531	120	194	5	514	29	8.0	1.8	2.9	7.8
Ed Macauley	C	6'8	190	23	66	2631	384	888	43	496	621	80	529	232	174	0	1264	40	8.0	3.5	2.6	19.2
Bob Donham	G	6'2	197	25	66	1980	201	413	49	149	293	51	330	228	223	9	551	30	5.0	3.5	3.4	8.3
Bob Cousy	G	6'1	175	23	66	2681	512	1388	37	409	506	81	421	441	190	5	1433	41	6.4	6.7	2.9	21.7
Bill Sharman	G	6'1	175	25	63	1389	244	628	39	183	213	86	221	151	181	3	671	22	3.5	2.4	2.9	10.7
Bob Brannum	F	6'6	220	26	66	1324	149	404	37	107	171	63	406	76	235	9	405	20	6.2	1.2	3.6	6.1
Bones McKinney	F	6'6	187	32	63	1083	136	418	33	65	80	81	175	111	148	4	337	17	2.8	1.8	2.3	5.3
John Mahnken	C	6'8	230	29	60	581	78	227	34	26	43	60	132	63	91	2	182	10	2.2	1.1	1.5	3.0
Dick Dickey	G	6'1	175	25	45	440	40	136	29	47	69	68	81	50	79	2	127	10	1.8	1.1	1.8	2.8
NEW YORK KNICKERBOCKERS	**37-29 .561**				**JOE LAPCHICK**																	
Vince Boryla (knee injury)	F	6'5	210	24	42	1440	202	522	39	96	115	83	219	90	121	2	500	34	5.2	2.1	2.9	11.9
Harry Gallatin	F-C	6'6	220	24	66	1931	233	527	44	275	341	81	661	115	223	5	741	29	10.0	1.7	3.4	11.2
Connie Simmons	C	6'8	225	26	66	1558	227	600	38	175	254	69	471	121	214	8	629	24	7.1	1.8	3.2	9.5
Max Zaslofsky	G	6'2	170	26	66	2113	322	958	34	287	380	76	194	156	183	5	931	32	2.9	2.4	2.8	14.1
Dick McGuire	G	6'	180	25	64	2018	204	474	43	183	290	63	332	388	181	4	591	32	5.2	6.1	2.8	9.2
Sweetwater Clifton	C-F	6'6	220	29	62	2101	244	729	33	170	256	66	731	209	227	8	658	34	11.8	3.4	3.7	10.6
Ernie Vandeweghe	F-G	6'3	195	25	57	1507	200	457	44	124	160	78	264	164	188	3	524	26	4.6	2.9	3.3	9.2
Ray Lumpp	G	6'1	182	27	62	1317	184	476	39	90	119	76	125	123	165	4	458	21	2.0	2.0	2.7	7.4
George Kaftan	F	6'3	195	23	52	955	115	307	37	92	134	69	196	88	107	0	322	18	3.8	1.7	2.1	6.2
Al McGuire	G	6'2	180	23	59	788	72	167	43	64	122	52	121	107	136	8	208	13	2.1	1.8	2.3	3.5
Herb Scherer	C	6'9	212	22	12	167	19	65	29	9	14	64	26	6	25	0	47	14	2.2	0.5	2.1	3.9
Tom Smith	G	6'1	165	22	1	3	0	0	—	0	0	—	0	0	0	0	0	3	0.0	0.0	0.0	0.0
Carl Braun - military service																						
PHILADELPHIA WARRIORS	**33-33 .561**				**EDDIE GOTTLIEB**																	
Paul Arizin	F	6'4	195	23	66	**2939**	**548**	1222	**45**	**578**	**707**	82	745	170	250	5	**1674**	**45**	11.3	2.6	3.8	**25.4**
Joe Fulks	F	6'5	190	30	61	1904	336	1078	31	250	303	83	368	123	255	13	922	31	6.0	2.0	4.2	15.1
Ed Mikan	C	6'8	230	26	66	1781	202	571	35	116	148	78	492	87	252	7	520	27	7.5	1.3	3.8	7.9
Andy Phillip	G	6'3	195	29	66	2933	279	762	37	232	308	75	434	**539**	218	6	790	44	6.6	**8.2**	3.3	12.0
George Senesky	G	6'2	180	29	57	1925	164	454	36	146	194	75	232	280	123	0	474	34	4.1	4.9	2.2	8.3
Nelson Bobb	G	6'	175	27	62	1192	110	306	36	99	167	59	147	168	182	9	319	19	2.4	2.7	2.9	5.1
Walt Budko	F-C	6'5	220	26	63	1126	97	240	40	60	89	67	232	91	196	10	254	18	3.7	1.4	3.1	4.0
Neil Johnston	C	6'8	215	22	64	993	141	299	47	100	151	66	342	39	154	5	382	16	5.3	0.6	2.4	6.0
Vern Gardner (broken hand)	C-F	6'5	205	26	27	507	72	194	37	15	23	65	112	37	60	2	159	19	4.1	1.4	2.2	5.9
Mel Payton	G-F	6'4	185	25	45	471	54	140	39	21	28	75	83	45	68	2	129	10	1.8	1.0	1.5	2.9
Stan Brown	F	6'3	200	22	15	141	22	63	35	10	18	56	17	9	32	0	54	9	1.1	0.6	2.1	3.6
Ed Dahler	F	6'5	190	25	14	112	14	38	37	7	7	##	22	5	16	0	35	8	1.6	0.4	1.1	2.5
BALTIMORE BULLETS	**20-46 .303**				**FREDDIE SCOLARI (12-27 .308), CHICK REISER (8-19 .296)**																	
Bill Calhoun	F	6'3	180	24	55	1594	129	409	32	125	183	68	252	117	84	0	383	29	4.6	2.1	1.5	7.0
Don Barksdale	F	6'6	200	28	62	2014	272	804	34	237	343	69	601	137	230	13	781	32	9.7	2.2	3.7	12.6
Stan Miasek	C	6'5	215	27	66	2174	258	707	36	263	372	71	639	140	257	12	779	33	9.7	2.1	3.9	11.8
Kevin O'Shea (from Mil)	G	6'2	185	26	65	1725	153	466	33	144	210	69	201	171	175	7	450	27	3.1	2.6	2.7	6.9
Freddie Scolari	G	5'11	185	29	64	2242	290	867	33	353	423	83	214	303	213	6	933	35	3.3	4.7	3.3	14.6
Frank Kudelka	G	6'2	193	26	65	1583	204	614	33	198	258	77	275	183	220	11	606	24	4.2	2.8	3.4	9.3
Dave Minor	F-G	6'2	185	29	57	1558	185	522	35	101	132	77	275	160	161	2	471	27	4.8	2.8	2.8	8.3
Brady Walker	C-F	6'6	205	30	35	699	89	217	41	26	34	76	195	40	38	0	204	20	5.6	1.1	1.1	5.8
Joe McNamee (from Roch)	F-G	6'6	210	25	58	695	68	222	31	30	50	60	137	40	108	4	166	12	2.4	0.7	1.9	2.9
Jim Slaughter	C	6'11	212	23	28	525	53	165	32	41	68	60	148	25	91	0	147	19	5.3	0.9	3.3	5.3
Belus Smawley	G	6'1	195	33	11	—	13	63	21	14	17	82	18	8	9	—	40	—	1.6	0.7	0.8	3.6
Paul Hoffman - voluntarily retired																						

Use Name	Pos	Hgt	Wgt	Age	TOTAL													PER GAME				
					G	Min	FG	FGA	%	FT	FTA	%	Reb	Ass	PF	DQ	Points	Min	Reb	Ass	PF	Points
1951/52 N.B.A. — WESTERN DIVISION																						
ROCHESTER ROYALS	41-25 .621				LES HARRISON																	
Arnie Johnson	F	6'5	240	31	66	2158	178	411	43	301	387	78	404	182	259	9	657	33	6.1	2.8	3.9	10.0
Jack Coleman	F-C	6'7	225	27	66	2606	308	742	42	120	169	71	692	208	218	7	736	39	10.5	3.2	3.3	11.2
Arnie Risen	C	6'9	210	27	66	2396	365	926	39	302	431	70	841	150	258	3	1032	36	12.7	2.3	3.9	15.6
Bob Davies	G	6'1	175	31	65	2394	379	990	38	294	379	78	189	390	269	10	1052	37	2.9	6.0	4.1	16.2
Bobby Wanzer	G	6'	172	30	66	2498	328	772	42	377	417	**90**	333	262	201	5	1033	38	5.0	4.0	3.0	15.7
Odie Spears	F-G	6'5	205	26	66	1673	225	570	39	116	152	76	303	163	225	8	566	25	4.6	2.5	3.4	8.6
Alex Hannum (from Bal)	F-C	6'7	225	28	66	1508	170	462	37	98	137	72	336	133	271	16	438	23	5.1	2.0	4.1	6.6
Red Holzman	G	5'10	175	31	65	1065	104	372	28	61	85	72	106	115	95	1	269	16	1.6	1.8	1.5	4.1
Ray Ragelis	F	6'4	205	23	51	337	25	96	26	18	29	62	76	31	62	1	68	7	1.5	0.6	1.2	1.3
Sam Ranzino	G	6'1	185	24	39	234	30	90	33	26	37	70	39	25	63	2	86	6	1.0	0.6	1.6	2.2
Paul Noel	F	6'4	185	27	8	32	2	9	22	2	3	67	4	3	6	0	6	4	0.5	0.4	0.8	0.8
MINNEAPOLIS LAKERS	40-26 .606				JOHNNY KUNDLA																	
Jim Pollard	F	6'5	190	29	65	2545	411	1155	36	183	260	70	593	234	199	4	1005	39	9.1	3.6	3.1	15.5
Vern Mikkelsen	F-C	6'7	240	23	66	2345	363	866	42	283	372	76	681	180	282	16	1009	36	10.3	2.7	4.3	15.3
George Mikan	C	6'10	250	27	64	2572	545	**1414**	39	433	555	78	866	194	**286**	14	1523	40	**13.5**	3.0	**4.5**	23.8
Whitey Skoog (knee injury)	G	5'11	180	25	35	988	102	296	34	30	38	79	122	60	94	4	234	28	3.5	1.7	2.7	6.7
Slater Martin	G	5'10	170	26	66	2480	237	632	38	142	190	75	228	249	226	9	616	38	3.5	3.8	3.4	9.3
Bob Harrison	G	6'2	190	24	65	1712	156	487	32	89	124	72	160	188	203	9	401	26	2.5	2.9	3.1	6.2
Pep Saul (from Bal)	G	6'2	185	27	64	1479	157	436	36	119	153	78	165	147	120	3	433	23	2.6	2.3	1.9	6.8
Howie Schultz	F-C	6'7	220	29	66	1301	89	315	28	90	119	76	246	102	197	13	268	20	3.7	1.5	3.0	4.1
Lew Hitch	F-C	6'8	200	22	61	849	77	215	36	63	94	67	243	50	89	3	217	14	4.0	0.8	1.5	3.6
Joe Hutton	G	6'1	170	23	60	723	53	158	34	49	70	70	85	62	110	1	155	12	1.4	1.0	1.8	2.6
John Pilch	F	6'4	185	25	9	41	1	10	10	3	6	50	9	2	10	0	5	5	1.0	0.2	1.1	0.6
Dick Schnittker - military service																						
INDIANAPOLIS OLYMPIANS	34-32 .515				HERM SCHAEFER																	
Leo Barnhorst	F-G	6'4	195	27	66	2344	349	897	39	122	187	65	430	255	196	3	820	36	6.5	3.9	3.0	12.4
Bob Lavoy	F-C	6'7	185	25	63	1829	240	604	40	168	223	75	479	107	210	5	648	29	7.6	1.7	3.3	10.3
Joe Graboski	C	6'8	210	21	66	2439	320	827	39	264	396	67	655	130	254	10	904	37	9.9	2.0	3.8	13.7
Paul Walther	G	6'2	160	24	55	1903	220	549	40	231	308	75	246	137	171	6	671	35	4.5	2.5	3.1	12.2
Bill Tosheff	G	6'1	175	25	65	2055	213	651	33	181	221	82	216	222	204	7	608	32	3.3	3.4	3.1	9.4
Ralph O'Brien	G	5'9	160	23	64	1577	228	613	37	122	149	82	122	124	115	0	578	25	1.9	1.9	1.8	9.0
Wah Wah Jones	F	6'4	225	25	58	1320	164	524	31	102	136	75	283	150	137	3	430	23	4.9	2.6	2.4	7.4
Don Lofgran	F-C	6'6	200	23	63	1254	149	417	36	156	219	71	257	48	147	3	454	20	4.1	0.8	2.3	7.2
Joe Holland	F	6'4	185	26	55	737	93	265	35	40	69	58	166	47	90	0	226	13	3.0	0.9	1.6	4.1
Cliff Barker	G	6'2	185	30	44	494	48	161	30	30	51	59	81	70	56	0	126	11	1.8	1.6	1.3	2.9
Ralph Beard and Alex Groza - declared ineligible for life																						
FORT WAYNE PISTONS	29-37 .439				PAUL BIRCH																	
Fred Schaus	F	6'5	210	26	62	2581	281	778	36	310	372	83	434	247	221	7	872	42	7.0	4.0	3.6	14.1
Jack Kerris	F	6'6	215	26	66	2148	186	480	39	217	325	67	514	212	265	16	589	33	7.8	3.2	4.0	8.9
Larry Foust	C-F	6'9	215	23	66	2615	390	989	39	267	394	68	**880**	200	245	10	1047	40	13.3	3.0	3.7	15.9
Frankie Brian	G	6'1	180	28	66	2672	342	972	35	367	433	85	232	233	220	6	1051	40	3.5	3.5	3.3	15.9
Boag Johnson	G	5'11	170	30	66	2265	211	592	36	101	140	72	222	210	243	6	523	34	3.4	3.2	3.7	7.9
Dike Eddleman (from Mil)	F-G	6'3	189	29	65	1893	269	809	33	202	329	61	267	134	249	9	740	29	4.1	2.1	3.8	11.4
Bill Closs	F	6'6	205	29	57	1120	120	389	31	107	157	68	204	76	125	2	347	20	3.6	1.3	2.2	6.1
Chuck Share	C	6'11	235	24	63	882	76	236	32	96	155	62	331	66	141	9	248	14	5.3	1.0	2.2	3.9
Jake Fendley	G	6'1	180	22	58	651	54	170	32	75	95	79	80	58	118	3	183	11	1.4	1.0	2.0	3.2
Jack Kiley	G	6'1	170	21	47	477	44	193	23	30	54	56	49	62	54	2	118	10	1.0	1.3	1.1	2.5
Zeke Sinicola (MS)	G	5'10	165	22	3	15	1	4	25	0	2	0	1	0	2	0	2	5	0.3	0.0	0.7	0.7
Ken Murray - military service																						
MILWAUKEE HAWKS	17-49 .258				DOXIE MOORE																	
Dick Mehen	F-G	6'6	195	29	65	2294	293	824	36	117	167	70	282	171	209	10	703	35	4.3	2.6	3.2	10.8
Mel Hutchins	F-C	6'6	205	23	66	2618	231	633	36	145	225	64	**880**	190	192	5	607	40	13.3	2.9	2.9	9.2
Don Otten (from FtW)	C	7'	245	30	64	1789	222	636	35	323	418	77	435	123	218	11	767	28	6.8	1.9	3.4	12.0
Don Boven	G-F	6'4	210	26	66	1982	200	668	30	256	350	73	336	177	271	**18**	656	30	5.1	2.7	4.1	9.9
Walt Kirk (MS)	G	6'3	180	27	11	396	28	101	28	55	78	71	44	28	47	3	111	36	4.0	2.5	4.3	10.1
Bob Wilson	G	6'4	195	25	63	1308	79	264	30	78	135	58	210	108	172	8	236	21	3.3	1.7	2.7	3.7
Don Rehfeldt (from Bal)	F	6'6	210	24	39	788	99	285	35	63	80	79	243	50	102	2	261	20	6.2	1.3	2.6	6.7
Dillard Crocker (from Ind)	F-G	6'4	205	26	38	783	98	279	35	97	145	67	111	57	132	7	293	21	2.9	1.5	3.5	7.7
Jim Owens (from Bal)	G	6'3	185	26	29	626	83	252	33	64	114	56	102	64	92	5	230	22	3.5	2.2	3.2	7.9
Art Burris (from FtW)	F	6'5	220	27	41	514	42	156	27	26	39	67	99	27	49	3	110	13	2.4	0.7	1.2	2.7
Cal Christensen	C-F	6'5	230	24	24	374	29	96	30	30	57	53	82	34	47	2	88	16	3.4	1.4	2.0	3.7
Nate DeLong	C	6'6	220	25	17	132	20	42	48	24	35	69	31	14	47	3	64	8	1.8	0.8	2.8	3.8
Gene Vance	G	6'3	196	28	7	118	7	26	27	9	14	64	15	9	18	0	23	17	2.1	1.3	2.6	3.3
Charlie Black	F-C	6'5	200	30	13	117	6	31	19	5	12	42	31	9	31	2	17	9	2.4	0.7	2.4	1.3
John McConathy	F	6'5	195	21	11	106	4	29	14	6	14	43	20	8	7	0	14	10	1.8	0.7	0.6	1.3
Elmer Behnke	C	6'7	210	22	4	55	6	22	27	4	7	57	17	4	13	1	16	14	4.3	1.0	3.3	4.0
John Rennicke	G	6'2	195	22	6	54	4	18	22	3	9	33	9	1	7	0	11	9	1.5	0.2	1.2	1.8
Jerry Fowler	C	6'8	236	24	6	41	4	13	31	1	4	25	10	2	9	0	9	7	1.7	0.3	1.5	1.5
Jack Nichols-military service																						

1951/52 N.B.A. — PLAYOFFS

MINNEAPOLIS LAKERS — **JOHNNY KUNDLA**

defeated Indianapolis 2-0; H78-70, 94-87
defeated Rochester 3-1; 78-88, 83-78, H77-67, H82-80
defeated New York 4-3; H83-79(OT), H72-80, 82-77, 89-90(OT), H102-89, 68-76, H82-65

Use Name	Pos	Hgt	Wgt	Age	G	Min	FG	FGA	%	FT	FTA	%	Reb	Ass	PF	DQ	Points	Min	Reb	Ass	PF	Points
					TOTAL													PER GAME				
Jim Polland	F	6'5	190	29	11	469	70	173	40	37	50	74	71	33	34	1	177	43	6.5	3.0	3.1	16.1
Vern Mikkelsen	F	6'7	240	23	13	495	60	139	43	53	64	83	110	20	66	**4**	173	38	8.5	1.5	5.1	13.3
Geoge Mikan	C	6'10	250	27	13	**553**	**99**	**261**	38	**109**	**138**	79	**207**	36	63	3	**307**	43	**15.9**	2.8	4.8	23.6
Pep Saul	G-F	6'2	185	27	13	530	56	121	46	35	48	73	36	45	42	1	147	41	2.8	3.5	3.2	11.3
Slater Martin	G	5'10	170	26	13	523	38	110	35	41	56	73	37	56	64	**4**	117	40	2.8	4.3	4.9	9.0
Bob Harrison	G	6'2	190	24	12	235	30	68	44	14	17	82	20	24	39	2	74	20	1.7	2.0	3.3	6.2
Lew Hitch	F-C	6'8	200	22	13	152	9	25	36	6	21	29	44	9	16	0	24	12	3.4	0.7	1.2	1.8
Joe Hurton	G	6'1	170	23	12	139	12	29	41	9	14	64	13	12	17	0	33	12	1.1	1.0	1.4	2.8
Howie Schultz	F-C	6'7	220	29	12	99	6	18	33	6	10	60	19	5	18	1	18	8	1.6	0.4	1.5	1.5

Whitey Skoog - knee injury, Dick Schnittker - military service

NEW YORK KNICKERBOCKERS — **JOE LAPCHICK**

defeated Boston 2-1; 94-105, H101-97, 88-87(2OT)
defeated Syracuse 3-1; 87-85, 92-102, H99-92, H100-93
lost to Minneapolis 1-3; 79-83(OT), 80-72, H77-82, H90-89(OT), 89-102, H76-68, 65-82

Use Name	Pos	Hgt	Wgt	Age	G	Min	FG	FGA	%	FT	FTA	%	Reb	Ass	PF	DQ	Points	Min	Reb	Ass	PF	Points
Ernie Vandeweghe	F	6'3	195	25	14	414	51	118	43	49	60	82	69	27	58	1	151	30	4.9	1.9	4.1	10.8
Harry Gallatin	F-C	6'6	220	24	14	471	50	122	41	51	66	77	134	19	45	1	151	34	9.6	1.4	3.2	10.8
Connie Simmons	C	6'8	225	26	14	427	77	166	46	68	89	76	108	12	55	3	222	31	7.7	0.9	3.9	15.9
Max Zaslofsky	G	6'2	170	26	14	506	69	185	37	89	110	81	44	23	51	1	227	36	3.1	1.6	3.6	16.2
Dick McGuire	G	6'	180	24	14	546	48	107	45	49	86	57	71	**90**	46	1	145	39	5.1	6.4	3.3	10.4
Sweetwater Clifton	F-C	6'6	220	29	14	462	39	133	29	54	76	71	133	34	**67**	**4**	132	33	9.5	2.4	4.8	9.4
George Kaftan	F	6'3	195	23	13	232	26	66	39	28	42	67	30	22	41	3	80	18	2.3	1.7	3.2	6.2
Al McGuire	G-F	6'2	180	23	13	208	20	51	39	20	27	74	17	14	34	1	60	16	1.3	1.1	2.6	4.6
Ray Lumpp	G	6'1	182	27	12	194	13	53	25	23	25	92	19	15	35	1	49	16	1.6	1.3	2.9	4.1

Vince Boryla - knee injury, Carl Braun - military service

ROCHESTER ROYALS — **LES HARRISON**

defeated Fort Wayne 2-0; H95-78, 92-86
lost to Minneapolis 1-3; H88-78, H78-83, 67-77, 80-82

Use Name	Pos	Hgt	Wgt	Age	G	Min	FG	FGA	%	FT	FTA	%	Reb	Ass	PF	DQ	Points	Min	Reb	Ass	PF	Points
Arnie Johnson	F	6'5	240	31	6	166	8	27	30	23	32	72	31	24	27	0	39	28	5.2	4.0	4.5	6.5
Jack Coleman	F-C	6'7	225	27	6	247	24	59	41	11	18	61	73	35	25	1	59	41	12.2	5.8	4.2	9.8
Arnie Risen	C	6'9	210	27	6	229	33	81	41	28	40	70	75	9	24	0	94	38	12.5	1.5	4.0	15.7
Bob Davies	G	6'1	175	31	6	233	37	92	40	45	55	82	13	28	18	0	119	39	2.2	4.7	3.0	19.8
Bobby Wanzer	G	6'	172	30	6	249	33	77	43	47	49	**96**	38	19	23	2	113	42	6.3	3.2	3.8	18.8
Alex Hannum	F-C	6'7	225	28	6	146	16	42	38	8	13	62	26	8	30	3	40	24	4.3	1.3	5.0	6.7
Odie Spears	F-G	6'5	205	26	6	123	10	33	30	9	16	56	21	9	18	0	29	21	3.5	1.5	3.0	4.8
Red Holzman	G	5'10	175	31	6	65	3	15	20	1	6	17	6	2	3	0	7	11	1.0	0.3	0.5	1.2
Ray Ragelis	F	6'4	205	23	3	7	0	1	0	0	0	—	1	1	0	0	0	2	0.3	0.3	0.0	0.0

SYRACUSE NATIONALS — **AL CERVI**

defeated Philadelphia 2-1; H102-83, 95-100, H84-73
lost to New York 1-3; H85-87, H102-92, 92-99, 93-100

Use Name	Pos	Hgt	Wgt	Age	G	Min	FG	FGA	%	FT	FTA	%	Reb	Ass	PF	DQ	Points	Min	Reb	Ass	PF	Points
Wally Osterkorn	F	6'5	210	23	7	249	23	67	34	28	47	60	57	20	32	1	74	36	8.1	2.9	4.6	10.6
Dolph Schayes	F	6'8	220	23	7	248	41	91	45	60	78	77	90	15	34	2	142	35	12.9	2.1	4.9	20.3
Noble Jorgensen	C	6'9	230	26	7	150	19	52	37	23	31	74	27	5	30	2	61	21	3.9	0.7	4.3	8.7
Paul Seymour	G-F	6'2	185	23	7	270	25	60	42	35	43	81	26	25	33	1	85	39	3.7	3.6	4.7	12.1
George King	G	6'	180	23	6	207	19	54	35	19	28	68	29	21	17	0	57	35	4.8	3.5	2.8	9.5
Red Rocha	C-F	6'9	190	28	7	276	41	95	43	37	51	73	48	10	36	3	119	39	6.9	1.4	5.1	17.0
Al Cervi	G	5'11	185	34	7	88	7	30	23	22	23	96	10	15	23	1	36	13	1.4	2.1	3.3	5.1
Billy Gabor	G	5'11	180	29	7	80	11	33	33	12	16	75	6	10	16	0	34	11	0.9	1.4	2.3	4.9
George Ratkovicz	F-C	6'7	225	29	6	59	5	15	33	8	20	40	22	3	16	0	18	10	3.7	0.5	2.7	3.0
Gerry Calabrese	G	6'1	175	26	6	53	10	24	42	4	4	100	8	4	18	0	24	9	1.3	0.7	3.0	4.0

BOSTON CELTICS — **RED AUERBACH**

lost to New York 1-2; H105-94, 97-101, H87-88(2OT)

Use Name	Pos	Hgt	Wgt	Age	G	Min	FG	FGA	%	FT	FTA	%	Reb	Ass	PF	DQ	Points	Min	Reb	Ass	PF	Points
Chuck Cooper	F	6'5	205	25	3	128	8	25	32	17	19	89	16	4	17	2	33	43	5.3	1.3	**5.7**	11.0
Bob Harris	F	6'7	195	24	3	87	9	21	43	5	5	100	25	4	16	1	23	29	8.3	1.3	5.3	7.7
Ed Macauley	C-F	6'8	190	23	3	129	27	49	**55**	16	19	84	33	11	11	1	70	43	11.0	3.7	3.7	23.3
Bob Donham	G	6'2	197	25	3	112	9	19	47	9	18	50	13	17	16	1	27	37	4.3	5.7	5.3	9.0
Bob Cousy	G	6'1	175	23	3	138	26	65	40	41	44	93	12	19	13	1	93	46	4.0	6.3	4.3	**31.0**
John Mahnken	C	6'8	230	29	3	50	2	7	29	3	6	50	10	3	11	1	7	17	3.3	1.0	3.7	2.3
Bob Brannum	F	6'6	220	26	3	48	4	12	33	1	6	17	10	3	16	2	9	16	3.3	1.0	5.3	3.0
Dick Dickey	G	6'1	175	25	3	31	1	8	13	6	7	86	3	5	7	0	8	10	1.0	1.7	2.3	2.7
Bill Sharman	G	6'1	175	25	1	27	7	12	58	1	1	100	3	7	4	0	15	27	3.0	7.0	4.0	15.0
Bones McKinney	F	6'6	187	32	3	20	2	9	22	0	0	—	6	2	9	0	4	7	2.0	0.7	3.0	1.3

PHILADELPHIA WARRIORS — **EDDIE GOTTLIEB**

lost to Syracuse 1-2; 83-102, H100-95, 73-84

Use Name	Pos	Hgt	Wgt	Age	G	Min	FG	FGA	%	FT	FTA	%	Reb	Ass	PF	DQ	Points	Min	Reb	Ass	PF	Points
Paul Arizin	F	6'4	195	23	3	120	24	53	45	29	33	88	38	8	17	2	77	40	12.7	2.7	**5.7**	25.7
Joe Fulks	F	6'5	190	30	3	70	5	33	15	7	9	78	12	2	13	1	17	23	4.0	0.7	4.3	5.7
Ed Mikan	C	6'8	230	26	3	74	7	22	32	6	7	86	20	2	15	0	20	25	6.7	0.7	5.0	6.7
Andy Phillip	G	6'3	195	29	3	122	8	19	42	19	24	79	14	22	16	1	35	41	4.7	**7.3**	5.3	11.7
George Senesky	G	6'2	180	29	3	120	18	33	55	7	11	64	12	11	9	0	43	40	4.0	3.7	3.0	14.3
Vern Gardner	F-C	6'5	205	26	3	77	7	19	37	10	11	91	14	3	14	0	24	26	4.7	1.0	4.7	8.0
Walt Budko	F	6'5	220	26	3	58	6	14	43	4	7	57	12	5	11	0	16	19	4.0	1.7	3.7	5.3
Neil Johnston	C	6'8	215	22	3	32	5	10	50	6	8	75	10	1	8	0	16	11	3.3	0.3	2.7	5.3
Nelson Bobb	G	6'	175	27	3	29	1	3	33	2	5	40	2	1	4	0	4	10	0.7	0.3	1.3	1.3
Mel Payton	G	6'4	185	25	3	18	1	2	50	2	2	100	3	1	6	0	4	6	1.0	0.3	2.0	1.3

Use Name	Pos.	Hgt.	Wgt.	Age	G	Min.	FG	FGA	%	FT	FTA	%	Reb.	Ass.	PF	Disq.	Points	Min.	Reb.	Ass.	PF	Points
					TOTAL													PER GAME				
1951/52 N.B.A. PLAYOFFS (continued)																						
INDIANAPOLIS OLYMPIANS		**HERM SCHAEFER**			lost to Minneapolis 0-2, 70-78, H87-94																	
Leo Barnhorst	F	6'4	195	27	2	85	14	34	41	3	7	43	9	8	7	0	31	43	4.5	4.0	3.5	15.5
Bob Lavoy	F	6'7	185	25	2	78	9	27	33	6	8	75	20	4	8	1	24	39	10.0	2.0	4.0	12.0
Joe Graboski	C	6'8	210	21	2	96	19	48	40	8	15	53	23	3	7	0	46	**48**	11.5	1.5	3.5	23.0
Paul Walther	G-F	6'2	160	24	2	85	8	16	50	16	18	89	7	6	8	0	32	43	3.5	3.0	4.0	16.0
Bill Tosheff	G	6'1	175	25	2	68	2	18	11	3	3	100	6	7	9	0	7	34	3.0	3.5	4.5	3.5
Ralph O'Brien	G	5'9	160	23	2	49	5	11	45	5	5	100	3	3	1	0	15	25	1.5	1.5	0.5	7.5
Don Lofgran	F	6'6	200	23	2	10	0	3	0	0	0	—	0	0	3	0	0	5	0.0	0.0	1.5	0.0
Wah Wah Jones	F	6'4	225	25	1	8	1	3	33	0	0	—	0	0	2	0	2	8	0.0	0.0	2.0	2.0
Joe Holland	F	6'4	185	26	1	1	0	0	—	0	0	—	0	0	0	0	0	1	0.0	0.0	0.0	0.0
Ralph Beard and Alex Groza—declared ineligible for life																						
FORT WAYNE PISTONS		**PAUL BIRCH**			lost to Rochester 0-2; 78-95, H86-92																	
Fred Schaus	F	6'5	210	26	2	90	12	35	34	7	8	88	15	14	9	0	31	45	7.5	7.0	4.5	15.5
Jack Kerris	F	6'6	215	26	2	63	7	20	35	11	20	55	18	9	11	1	25	32	9.0	4.5	5.5	12.5
Larry Foust	C-F	6'9	215	23	2	77	12	23	52	6	7	86	30	5	8	1	30	39	15.0	2.5	4.0	15.0
Frankie Brian	G	6'1	180	28	2	81	6	24	25	5	6	83	6	9	10	0	17	41	3.0	4.5	5.0	8.5
Boag Johnson	G	5'11	170	30	2	70	8	23	35	1	1	100	6	7	11	1	17	35	3.0	3.5	5.5	8.5
Dike Eddleman	G-F	6'3	189	29	2	37	6	16	38	4	7	57	7	4	9	1	16	19	3.5	2.0	4.5	8.0
Chuck Share	C	6'11	235	24	2	35	8	11	73	3	5	60	10	3	8	0	19	18	5.0	1.5	4.0	9.5
Bill Closs	F	6'6	205	29	1	21	1	6	17	3	3	100	8	4	0	0	5	21	8.0	4.0	0.0	5.0
Jake Fendley	G	6'1	180	22	1	4	1	4	25	0	0	—	1	1	2	0	2	4	1.0	1.0	2.0	2.0
Jack Kiley	G	6'1	170	21	1	2	1	3	33	0	0	—	0	1	0	0	2	2	0.0	1.0	0.0	2.0
Ken Murray and Zeke Sinicola—military service																						

Team	G	FG	FGA	%	FT	FTA	%	Reb.	Ass.	For	Agnst.	Diff.	G	FG	FGA	%	FT	FTA	%	Reb.	Ass.	For	Agnst.	Diff.
	REGULAR SEASON									AVERAGE POINTS			PLAYOFFS									AVERAGE POINTS		
1951/52 N.B.A. TEAM STATISTICS																								
EASTERN DIVISION																								
Syracuse	66	1894	5207	36	**1933**	**2589**	75	3603	1373	86.7	82.2	+4.5	7	201	521	39	**248**	**341**	73	377	128	93.3	90.6	+2.7
Boston	66	**2131**	5510	39	1765	2406	73	3750	**1606**	**91.3**	87.3	+4.0	3	**95**	227	**42**	99	125	**79**	158	75	**96.3**	94.3	+2.0
New York	66	2022	5282	38	1565	2185	72	**3834**	1567	85.0	84.2	+0.8	14	393	1001	39	431	581	74	711	256	86.9	88.5	-1.6
Philadelphia	66	2039	5367	38	1634	2143	76	3647	1593	86.5	87.8	-1.3	3	82	208	39	92	117	79	150	56	85.3	93.7	-8.4
Baltimore	66	1882	5495	34	1614	2211	73	3780	1417	81.5	89.0	-7.5												
WESTERN DIVISION																								
Rochester	66	2014	5172	**39**	1661	2150	**77**	3373	1590	86.2	82.9	+3.3	6	164	427	38	172	229	75	292	135	83.3	80.7	+2.6
Minneapolis	66	2106	**5733**	37	1436	1921	75	3543	1389	85.6	**79.5**	**+6.1**	13	380	944	40	310	418	74	597	240	82.3	**78.9**	**+3.4**
Indianapolis	66	2026	5513	37	1422	1965	72	3288	1290	82.9	82.8	+0.1	2	58	**160**	36	41	56	73	77	31	78.5	86.0	-7.5
Fort Wayne	66	1771	5013	35	1609	2194	73	3619	1403	78.0	80.1	-2.1	2	65	162	38	40	57	70	**110**	**57**	82.0	93.5	-11.5
Milwaukee	66	1674	5055	33	1485	2177	68	3540	1229	73.2	81.2	-8.0												

Team	W	L	Pct.	GB	W	L	Pct.	W	L	Pct.	W	L	Pct.	W	L	Pct.	W	L	Pct.
					Record against playoff teams			Record against non-playoff teams			HOME			ROAD			NEUTRAL		
1951/52 N.B.A. STANDINGS																			
EASTERN DIVISION																			
Syracuse Nationals	40	26	.606	—	**30**	21	**.588**	10	5	.667	26	7	.788	12	18	.400	2	1	.667
Boston Celtics	39	27	.591	1	26	25	.510	13	2	.867	22	7	.759	10	19	.345	**7**	1	**.875**
New York Knicherbockers	37	29	.561	3	26	25	.510	11	4	.733	21	4	.840	12	22	.353	4	3	.571
Philadelphia Warriors	33	33	.500	7	23	28	.451	10	5	.667	24	7	.774	6	**25**	.194	3	1	.750
Baltimore Bullets	20	46	.303	20	16	44	.267	4	2	.667	17	**15**	.531	2	22	.083	1	9	.100
WESTERN DIVISION																			
Rochester Royals	**41**	25	**.621**	—	29	22	.569	12	3	.800	**28**	5	**.848**	12	18	.400	1	2	.333
Minneapolis Lakers	40	26	.606	1	26	25	.510	**14**	1	**.933**	21	5	.808	**13**	19	**.406**	6	2	.750
Indianapolis Olympians	34	32	.515	7	23	28	.451	11	4	.733	25	6	.806	4	24	.143	5	2	.714
Fort Wayne Pistons	29	37	.439	12	21	30	.412	8	**7**	.533	22	11	.667	6	24	.200	1	2	.333
Milwaukee Hawks	17	**49**	.258	24	15	**45**	.250	2	4	.333	7	13	.350	3	22	.120	**7**	**14**	.333

1951/52 N.B.A. INDIVIDUAL LEADERS

SCORING
(Minimum 44 Games Played)

Name	Team	G	FG	FT	Pts.	Avg.
Arizin	Phi	66	548	578	1674	25.4
Mikan	Min	64	545	433	1523	23.8
Cousy	Bos	66	512	409	1433	21.7
Macauley	Bos	66	384	496	1264	19.2
Davies	Roch	65	379	294	1052	16.2
Brian	FtW	66	342	367	1051	15.9
Foust	FtW	66	390	267	1047	15.9
Wanzer	Roch	66	328	377	1033	16.7
Risen	Roch	66	365	302	1032	15.6
Pollard	Min	65	411	183	1005	15.5

FIELD GOAL PERCENTAGE
(Minimum 210 Field Goals)

Name	Team	FG	FGA	Pct.
Arizin	Phi	548	1222	.448
Gallatin	NY	233	527	.442
Macauley	Bos	384	888	.432
Wanzer	Roch	328	772	.425
Mikkelsen	Min	363	866	.419
Coleman	Roch	308	742	.415
King	Syr	235	579	.406
Walther	Ind	220	549	.401
Rocha	Syr	300	749	.401
Lavoy	Ind	240	604	.397

FREE THROW PERCENTAGE
(Minimum 180 Free Throws)

Name	Team	FT	FTA	Pct.
Wanzer	Roch	377	417	.904
Cervi	Syr	219	248	.883
Sharman	Bos	183	213	.859
Brian	FtW	367	433	.848
Scolari	Bal	353	423	.835
Schaus	FtW	310	372	.833
Fulks	Phi	250	303	.825
Tosheff	Ind	182	221	.824
Arizin	Phi	578	707	.818
Cousy	Bos	409	506	.808

PERSONAL FOULS

Name	Team	PF
Mikan	Min	286
Mikkelsen	Min	282
Boven	Mil	271
Davies	Roch	269
Kerris	FtW	265

GAMES DISQUALIFIED

Name	Team	Disq
Boven	Mil	18
Hannum	Bal-Roch	16
Kerris	FtW	16
Mikkelsen	Min	16
Mikan	Min	14

REBOUNDS PER GAME
(Minimum 44 Games Played)

Name	Team	G	Reb.	Avg.
Mikan	Min	64	866	13.5
Foust	FtW	66	880	13.3
Hutchins	Mil	66	880	13.3
Risen	Roch	66	841	12.7
Schayes	Syr	63	773	12.3

ASSISTS PER GAME
(Minimum 44 Games Played)

Name	Team	G	Ass.	Avg.
Phillip	Phi	66	539	8.2
Cousy	Bos	66	441	6.7
D. McGuire	NY	64	388	6.1
Davies	Roch	65	390	6.0
Senesky	Phi	57	280	4.9

1952-53 N.B.A.

Freezing the Climax

The N.B.A. was slowly carving a permanent place in America's winter sports menu. The league had ten stable franchises, all returning from last season, and while smaller cities like Ft. Wayne, Rochester, Syracuse, and Indianapolis were still on the circuit, the large outposts of New York, Boston, and Philadelphia created a"big-league" aura in the public's eyes. And although television was still in its infancy, it was bringing N.B.A. games to many fans who had never seen a pro basketball game before. Most important, however, the N.B.A. had escaped the scandals which had seriously discredited college ball; word did come out that an official had taken bribes to affect games in 1950, but immediate dismissal of the official nipped the affair in the bud. Star players gave almost every team gate appeal, with Laker center George Mikan and Celtic guard Bob Cousy the premier attractions in the league.

But offsetting these assets in large measure was the unattractive style of play in the N.B.A. The widening of the foul lane from six feet to twelve feet opened the game up a bit, but roughhouse tactics were still the order of the day close to the basket. Action ground to a virtual halt toward the end of many games, when tension should have been at its highest. Strategic fouling and seemingly endless trips to the foul line gummed up the final minutes of games, and freezing the ball frequently ended the day's scoring with quite a bit of time left on the clock. Reforms were needed in the playing rules, but these were not to come for several seasons.

Regardless of the problems in playing style, the N.B.A. could still boast of five top-flight teams with distinct images. The Minneapolis Lakers relied on their frontcourt muscle, with George Mikan, Vern Mikkelsen, and Jim Pollard combining bulk with talent. Little Slater Martin, a mere 5'10" tall, handled the ball in the backcourt and did most of the running for the Western Division champion Lakers. Short on size but long on guile, the smart Rochester Royals finished a close second in the West. Key veterans Bob Davies, Bobby Wanzer, and Arnie Risen had been together since the days of the N.B.L., and the savvy of the squad showed up in reserves Jack McMahon, Alex Hannum, and Red Holzman, all future N.B.A. coaches.

The Eastern Division counted three superior clubs in its ranks. The New York Knicks blended a horde of talented players together into a tight unit. Coach Joe Lapchick got shooter Carl Braun back from the Army, and the ex-Colgate star moved right into a starting post at guard. Harry Gallatin, Sweetwater Clifton, Connie Simmons, Ernie Vandeweghe, Max Zaslofsky, Dick McGuire, Vince Boryla, and Al McGuire formed the rest of the Knick chassis. After a blazing start, the team cooled off toward the end of the season after Zaslofsky broke his arm in January and various other, less serious, injuries dogged other players.

Another club relying on teamwork, good passing, and tough defense was the Syracuse Nats. Dolph Schayes and Paul Seymour epitomized the Syracuse team, both being able scorers and rough characters in their floor play. The Boston Celtics finished practically even with New York and Syracuse despite channeling most of the scoring to three men. Bob Cousy, Bill Sharman, and Ed Macauley all placed in the top six scorers in the league, thus offsetting the Boston weaknesses in defense and rebounding.

The league's five lesser franchises offered less to the general fan. The Ft. Wayne Pistons captured third place in the West with a transfusion of healthy new blood. Rookie Monk Meineke of Dayton added muscle to the frontcourt, while newcomers Freddie Scolari, Andy Phillip, and Dick Groat bolstered the guard positions. Trades brought Scolari from Baltimore and Phillip from Philadelphia, and these two combined with Frankie Brian in furnishing experience in the backcourt. Groat, a high-scoring All-American from Duke, played well in the first half of the season before going into the service; after his discharge, he gave up basketball for a career as shortstop for the Pittsburgh Pirates. With center Larry Foust leading the scoring, the Pistons took a playoff spot with a 36-33 record. The final Western playoff position went to the Indianapolis Olympians, struggling along without the scandal-disgraced Alex Groza and Ralph Beard. One game back in fifth place came the Milwaukee Hawks, whose defense was nearly invisible.

The Eastern Division fielded the two weakest entries in the league—the Baltimore Bullets and Philadelphia Warriors— with the Bullets winning a playoff berth practically by default. Clair Bee, longtime coach at L.I.U., took over the management of the Bullets but could do little with this mediocre squad. The Philadelphia team won only 12 of 69 contests, a mighty fall from the first-place finish of 1951. Scoring champion Paul Arizin marched off into the service, but coach Eddie Gottlieb came up with another scoring champion in second-year center Neil Johnston. With his teammates feeding him the ball steadily, the hook-shooting Johnston put together a 22.3 scoring average, tops in the circuit. Joe Fulks, meanwhile, had slowed down to 11.9 in his final season as a regular.

At the start of the playoffs, the Knicks and Lakers swept to easy victories over the Bullets and Olympians. Ft. Wayne, meanwhile, upset Rochester by taking the deciding third game by a score of 67-65 on the enemy's court. In the remaining first round series, Boston downed Syracuse with straight wins, the second one a drawn out 111-105 victory in four overtimes. The Celtics couldn't survive the next round, however, bowing to the Knicks in four games. The Pistons extended the Lakers to their fullest but came up short in the deciding fifth game, dropping a 74-58 decision to Mikan and Co.

The championship series then shaped up as a rematch of last year's New York-Minneapolis tilt. The series opened in Minneapolis with a surprising 96-88 Knick victory, as Connie Simmons and Sweetwater Clifton did a good job controlling Mikan. The Lakers took game two 73-71, with fouling slowing the game practically to a walk for the final eight minutes. With a split on the road, the Knicks hoped to make hay at home instead, the Lakers plowed them under. The three contests in New York all were hard fought, close games, but the Lakers came out on top in all three of them. For the third straight season, the Knicks had lost in the finals. And for the third time in four N.B.A. seasons, George Mikan and the Lakers had won the crown.

Use Name	Pos	Hgt	Wgt	Age	TOTAL G	Min	FG	FGA	%	FT	FTA	%	Reb	Ass	PF	DQ	Points	PER GAME Min	Reb	Ass	PF	Points
1952/53 N.B.A. — EASTERN DIVISION																						
NEW YORK KNICKERBOCKERS	**47-23 .671**				**JOE LAPCHICK**																	
Vince Boryla	F	6'5	210	25	66	2200	254	686	37	165	201	82	233	166	226	8	673	33	3.5	2.5	3.4	10.2
Harry Gallatin	F-C	6'6	220	25	70	2333	282	635	44	301	430	70	916	126	224	6	865	33	13.1	1.8	3.2	12.4
Sweetwater Clifton	C-F	6'6	220	30	70	2496	272	794	34	200	343	58	761	231	274	6	744	36	10.9	3.3	3.9	10.6
Carl Braun	G	6'5	185	25	70	2316	323	807	40	331	401	83	233	243	287	14	977	33	3.3	3.5	4.1	14.0
Dick McGuire	G	6'	180	26	61	1783	142	373	38	153	269	57	280	296	172	3	437	29	4.6	4.9	2.8	7.2
Ernie Vandeweghe (MD)	F-G	6'3	195	24	61	1745	272	625	44	187	244	77	342	144	242	11	731	29	5.6	2.4	4.0	12.0
Connie Simmons	C	6'8	225	27	65	1707	240	637	38	249	340	73	458	127	252	9	729	26	7.0	2.0	3.9	11.2
Al McGuire	G	6'2	180	24	58	1231	112	287	39	128	201	64	167	145	206	8	352	21	2.9	2.5	3.6	6.1
Jerry Fleishman (from Phi)	G	6'2	190	30	33	882	100	303	33	96	140	69	152	108	118	7	296	27	4.6	3.3	3.6	9.0
Max Zaslofsky (broken arm)	G	6'2	175	27	29	722	123	320	38	98	142	69	75	55	81	1	344	25	2.6	1.9	2.8	11.9
Dick Surhoff	F	6'4	210	22	26	187	13	61	21	19	30	63	25	9	36	1	45	7	1.0	0.3	1.4	1.7
Sherwin Raiken	G	6'2	185	24	6	63	3	21	14	3	8	38	8	6	10	0	9	11	1.3	1.0	1.7	1.5
SYRACUSE NATIONALS	**47-24 .662**				**AL CERVI**																	
Earl Lloyd	F	6'6	215	24	64	1806	156	453	34	160	231	69	444	64	241	6	472	28	6.9	1.0	3.8	7.4
Dolph Schayes	F-C	6'8	220	24	71	2668	375	1022	37	512	619	83	920	227	271	9	1262	38	13.0	3.2	3.8	17.8
Red Rocha	C-F	6'9	190	29	69	2454	268	690	39	234	310	75	510	137	257	5	770	36	7.4	2.0	3.7	11.2
Paul Seymour	G-F	6'2	185	24	67	2684	306	798	38	340	416	82	246	294	210	3	952	40	3.7	4.4	3.1	14.2
George King	G	6'	180	24	71	2519	255	635	40	284	442	64	281	364	244	2	794	35	4.0	5.1	3.4	11.2
Noble Jorgensen	C	6'9	230	27	70	1355	145	436	33	146	199	73	236	76	247	7	436	19	3.4	1.1	3.5	6.2
Billy Gabor	G	5'11	180	30	69	1337	215	614	35	217	284	76	104	134	262	11	647	19	1.5	1.9	3.8	9.4
Wally Osterkorn	F	6'5	210	24	49	1016	85	262	32	106	168	63	217	61	129	2	276	21	4.4	1.2	2.6	5.6
Bob Lochmueller	F	6'5	185	25	62	802	79	245	32	74	122	61	162	47	143	1	232	13	2.6	0.8	2.3	3.7
Al Cervi	G	5'11	185	35	38	301	31	71	44	81	100	81	22	28	90	2	143	8	0.6	0.7	2.4	3.8
BOSTON CELTICS	**46-25 .648**				**RED AUERBACH**																	
Chuck Cooper	F	6'5	210	26	70	1994	157	466	34	144	190	76	439	112	258	11	458	28	6.3	1.6	3.7	6.5
Bob Harris	F	6'7	195	25	70	1971	192	459	42	133	226	59	485	95	238	6	517	28	6.9	1.4	3.4	7.4
Ed Macauley	C-F	6'8	190	24	69	2902	451	997	45	500	667	75	629	280	188	0	1402	42	9.1	4.1	2.7	20.3
Bill Sharman	G	6'1	180	26	71	2333	403	925	44	341	401	**85**	288	191	240	7	1147	33	4.1	2.7	3.4	16.2
Bob Cousy	G	6'1	175	24	71	2945	464	**1320**	35	479	587	82	449	**547**	227	4	1407	41	6.3	7.7	3.2	19.8
Bob Brannum	F	6'6	225	27	71	1900	188	541	35	110	185	59	537	147	287	17	486	27	7.6	2.1	4.0	6.8
Bob Donham	G-F	6'2	197	26	71	1435	169	353	48	113	240	47	239	153	213	8	451	20	3.4	2.2	3.0	6.4
John Mahnken	C	6'8	230	30	69	771	76	252	30	39	56	70	182	75	110	1	191	11	2.6	1.1	1.6	2.8
Gene Conley	C-F	6'8	225	22	39	461	35	108	32	18	31	58	171	19	74	1	88	12	4.4	0.5	1.9	2.3
Kenny Rollins	G	6'	168	29	43	426	38	115	33	22	27	81	45	46	63	1	98	10	1.0	1.1	1.5	2.3
Mo Mahoney	F	6'2	205	25	6	34	4	10	40	4	5	80	7	1	7	0	12	6	1.2	0.2	1.2	2.0
BALTIMORE BULLETS	**16-54 .229**				**CHICK REISER (0-3 .000), CLAIR BEE (16-51 .239)**																	
Don Barksdale	F-C	6'6	200	29	65	2298	321	829	39	257	401	64	597	166	273	13	899	35	9.2	2.6	4.2	13.8
Don Henriksen	F-C	6'7	225	23	68	2263	199	475	42	176	281	63	506	129	242	12	574	33	7.4	1.9	3.6	8.4
Eddie Miller (from Mil)	C-F	6'8	225	21	70	2018	273	781	35	187	287	65	669	115	252	12	733	29	9.6	1.6	3.6	10.5
Jim Baechtold	G-F	6'4	205	25	64	1893	242	621	39	177	240	74	219	154	203	8	661	30	3.4	2.4	3.2	10.3
Paul Hoffman	G	6'2	205	27	69	1955	240	656	37	224	342	65	317	237	282	13	704	28	4.6	3.4	4.1	10.2
Jack Kerris (from FtW)	F-C	6'6	215	27	69	1424	93	256	36	88	140	63	295	156	165	7	274	21	4.3	2.3	2.4	4.0
Ray Lumpp (from NY)	G	6'1	182	29	55	1422	188	506	37	153	206	74	141	168	178	5	529	26	2.6	3.1	3.2	9.6
Ralph O'Brien (from Ind)	G	5'9	160	24	55	758	96	286	34	78	92	85	70	56	74	0	270	14	1.3	1.0	1.3	4.9
Kevin O'Shea	G	6'2	185	27	46	643	71	189	38	48	81	59	76	87	82	1	190	14	1.7	1.9	1.8	4.1
George Kaftan	F	6'3	195	24	23	380	45	142	32	44	67	66	75	31	59	2	134	17	3.3	1.3	2.6	5.8
Dick Bunt (from NY)	G	6'	172	22	26	271	29	107	27	34	48	71	28	17	40	0	92	10	1.1	0.7	1.5	3.5
Bob Priddy	F	6'3	190	22	16	149	14	38	37	8	14	57	36	7	36	3	36	9	2.3	0.4	2.3	2.3
George McLeod	F	6'5	200	21	10	85	2	16	13	8	15	53	21	4	16	0	12	9	2.1	0.4	1.6	1.2
Blaine Denning	G	6'2	175	22	1	9	2	5	40	1	1	100	4	0	3	0	5	9	4.0	0.0	3.0	5.0
PHILADELPHIA WARRIORS	**12-57 .174**				**EDDIE GOTTLIEB**																	
Joe Fulks	F	6'5	195	31	70	2085	332	960	35	168	231	73	387	138	319	20	832	30	5.5	2.0	4.6	11.9
Don Lofgran	F	6'6	200	24	64	1788	173	525	33	126	173	73	339	106	178	6	472	28	5.3	1.7	2.8	7.4
Neil Johnston	C	6'8	215	23	70	**3166**	**504**	1114	**45**	**556**	**794**	70	976	197	248	6	**1564**	**45**	13.9	2.8	3.5	22.3
George Senesky	G	6'2	180	30	69	2336	160	485	33	93	146	64	254	264	166	1	413	34	3.7	3.8	2.4	6.0
Danny Finn	G	6'1	185	24	31	1015	135	409	33	99	182	54	175	146	124	9	369	33	5.6	4.7	4.0	11.9
Nelson Bobb	G	6'	175	28	55	1286	119	318	37	105	162	65	157	192	161	7	343	23	2.9	3.5	2.9	6.2
Mark Workman (from Mil)	F-C	6'9	217	22	65	1030	130	408	32	70	113	62	193	37	166	5	330	16	3.0	0.6	2.6	5.1
Ralph Polson (from NY)	F-C	6'7	205	22	49	810	65	179	36	61	96	64	211	24	102	5	191	17	4.3	0.5	2.1	3.9
Bill Mlkvy	F	6'4	190	21	31	608	75	246	30	31	48	65	101	62	54	1	181	20	3.3	2.0	1.7	5.8
Frank Kudelka (from Bal)	G	6'2	193	27	36	567	59	193	31	44	68	65	88	70	109	2	162	16	2.4	1.9	3.0	4.5
Jim Mooney (from Bal)(MS)	F	6'5	215	22	18	529	54	148	36	27	40	68	70	35	50	1	135	29	3.9	1.9	2.8	7.5
Claude Overton	G	6'2	195	25	15	182	19	75	25	20	30	67	25	15	25	0	58	12	1.7	1.0	1.7	3.9
Moe Radovich	G	6'	160	23	4	33	5	13	38	4	4	100	1	8	5	0	14	8	0.3	2.0	1.3	3.5
Jack McCloskey	G	6'2	192	26	1	16	3	9	33	0	0	—	3	1	2	0	6	16	3.0	1.0	2.0	6.0

Paul Arizin-military service

Use Name	Pos	Hgt	Wgt	Age	G	Min	FG	FGA	%	FT	FTA	%	Reb	Ass	PF	DQ	Points	Min	Reb	Ass	PF	Points
					TOTAL													PER GAME				

1952/53 N.B.A. — WESTERN DIVISION

Use Name	Pos	Hgt	Wgt	Age	G	Min	FG	FGA	%	FT	FTA	%	Reb	Ass	PF	DQ	Points	Min	Reb	Ass	PF	Points
MINNEAPOLIS LAKERS	**48-22 .686**				**JOHNNY KUNDLA**																	
Jim Pollard	F	6'5	190	30	66	2403	333	933	36	193	251	77	452	231	194	3	859	36	6.8	3.5	2.9	13.0
Vern Mikkelsen	F-C	6'7	230	24	70	2465	378	868	44	291	387	75	654	148	289	14	1047	35	9.3	2.1	4.1	15.0
George Mikan	C	6'10	250	28	70	2651	500	1252	40	442	567	78	**1007**	201	290	12	1442	38	**14.4**	2.9	4.1	20.6
Pep Saul	G	6'2	185	28	70	1796	187	471	40	142	200	71	141	110	174	3	516	26	2.0	1.6	2.5	7.4
Slater Martin	G	5'10	170	27	70	2556	260	634	41	224	287	78	186	250	246	4	744	37	2.7	3.6	3.5	10.6
Bob Harrison	G	6'2	190	25	70	1643	195	518	38	107	165	65	153	160	264	16	497	23	2.2	2.3	3.8	7.1
Lew Hitch	F-C	6'8	200	23	70	1027	89	255	35	83	136	61	275	66	122	2	261	15	3.9	0.9	1.7	3.7
Whitey Skoog	G	5'11	180	26	68	996	102	264	39	46	61	75	121	82	137	2	250	15	1.8	1.2	2.0	3.7
Jim Holstein	F	6'3	170	22	66	989	98	274	36	70	105	67	173	74	128	1	266	15	2.6	1.1	1.9	4.0
Howie Schultz	F-C	6'7	220	30	40	474	24	90	27	43	62	69	80	29	73	1	91	12	2.0	0.7	1.8	2.3
Dick Schnittker - military service																						
ROCHESTER ROYALS	**44-26 .629**				**LES HARRISON**																	
Arnie Johnson	F	6'5	240	32	70	1984	140	369	38	303	405	75	419	153	282	14	583	28	6.0	2.2	4.0	8.3
Jack Coleman	F-C	6'7	230	28	70	2625	314	748	42	135	208	65	774	231	245	12	763	38	11.1	3.3	3.5	10.9
Arnie Risen	C	6'9	210	28	68	2288	295	802	37	294	429	69	745	135	274	10	884	34	11.0	2.0	4.0	13.0
Bob Davies	G	6'1	175	32	66	2216	339	880	39	351	466	75	195	280	261	7	1029	34	3.0	4.2	4.0	15.6
Bobby Wanzer	G	6'	178	31	70	2577	318	866	37	384	473	81	351	252	206	7	1020	37	5.0	3.6	2.9	14.6
Jack McMahon	G	6'1	185	24	70	1665	176	534	33	155	236	66	183	186	253	16	507	24	2.6	2.7	3.6	7.2
Odie Spears	F	6'5	205	27	62	1414	198	494	40	199	243	82	251	113	227	15	595	23	4.0	1.8	3.7	9.6
Alex Hannum	F-C	6'7	225	29	68	1288	129	360	36	88	133	66	279	81	258	18	346	19	4.1	1.2	3.8	5.1
Cal Christensen	F	6'5	230	25	59	777	72	230	31	68	114	60	199	54	148	6	212	13	3.4	0.9	2.5	3.6
Red Holzman	G	5'10	180	32	46	392	38	149	26	27	38	71	40	35	56	2	103	9	0.9	0.8	1.2	2.2
FORT WAYNE PISTONS	**36-33 .522**				**PAUL BIRCH**																	
Fred Schaus	F	6'5	210	27	69	2541	240	719	33	243	296	82	413	245	261	11	723	37	6.0	3.6	3.8	10.5
Monk Meineke	F-C	6'7	205	22	68	2250	245	630	39	245	313	78	466	148	**334**	**26**	735	33	6.9	2.2	**4.9**	10.8
Larry Foust	C	6'9	225	24	67	2303	311	865	36	336	465	72	769	151	267	16	958	34	11.5	2.3	4.0	14.3
Andy Phillip (from Phi)	G	6'3	195	30	70	2690	250	629	40	222	301	74	364	397	229	9	722	38	5.2	5.7	3.3	10.3
Freddie Scolari (from Bal)	G	5'11	185	30	62	2123	277	809	34	276	327	84	209	233	212	4	830	34	3.4	3.8	3.4	13.4
Frankie Brian	G	6'1	180	29	68	1910	245	699	35	236	297	79	133	142	205	8	726	28	2.0	2.1	3.0	10.7
Dike Eddleman	F-G	6'3	189	30	69	1571	241	687	35	134	237	57	236	104	220	5	616	23	3.4	1.5	3.2	8.9
Don Boven (from Mil)	F-G	6'4	210	27	67	1373	153	427	36	145	209	69	217	79	227	13	451	20	3.2	1.2	3.4	6.7
Chuck Share	C	6'11	235	25	67	1044	91	254	36	172	234	74	373	74	213	13	354	16	5.6	1.1	3.2	5.3
Dick Groat (MS)	G	6'1	185	22	26	663	100	272	37	109	138	79	86	69	90	7	309	26	3.3	2.7	3.5	11.9
Jake Fendley	G	6'1	180	23	45	380	32	80	40	40	60	67	46	36	82	3	104	8	1.0	0.8	1.8	2.3
Ray Corley	G	6'	180	24	8	65	3	24	13	5	6	83	5	5	18	0	11	8	0.6	0.6	2.3	1.4
Boag Johnson	G	5'11	170	31	3	30	3	9	33	2	3	67	1	5	6	0	8	10	0.3	1.7	2.0	2.7
Jack Kiley	G	6'1	170	22	6	27	2	10	20	2	2	100	2	3	7	0	6	5	0.3	0.5	1.2	1.0
Ken Murray - military service																						
Zeke Sinicola - military service																						
INDIANAPOLIS OLYMPIANS	**28-43 .394**				**HERM SCHAEFER**																	
Leo Barnhorst	F-G	6'4	195	28	71	2871	402	1034	39	163	259	63	483	277	245	8	967	40	6.8	3.9	3.5	13.6
Bob Lavoy	F	6'7	185	26	70	2327	225	560	40	168	242	69	528	130	274	18	618	33	7.5	1.9	3.9	8.8
Joe Graboski	C	6'8	210	22	69	2769	272	799	34	350	513	68	687	156	303	18	894	40	10.0	2.3	4.4	13.0
Paul Walther	G	6'2	160	25	67	2468	227	645	35	264	354	75	284	205	260	7	718	37	4.2	3.1	3.9	10.7
Bill Tosheff	G	6'1	180	26	67	2459	253	783	32	253	314	81	229	243	243	5	759	37	3.4	3.6	3.6	11.3
Mel Payton	F	6'4	185	26	66	1424	173	485	36	120	161	75	313	81	118	0	466	22	4.7	1.2	1.8	7.1
Gene Rhodes	G	6'1	170	25	65	1162	109	342	32	119	169	70	98	91	78	2	337	18	1.5	1.4	1.2	5.2
Ed Mikan (from Phi)	C	6'8	230	27	62	927	78	292	27	79	98	81	237	39	124	0	235	15	3.8	0.6	2.0	3.8
Zeke Zawoluk (KJ)	F-C	6'7	215	22	41	622	55	150	37	77	116	66	146	31	83	1	187	15	3.6	0.8	2.0	4.6
Oon Hanrahan	F	6'7	200	23	18	121	11	32	34	11	15	73	30	11	24	1	33	7	1.7	0.6	1.3	1.8
Kleggie Hermsen (from Bos)	C	6'9	235	29	10	62	4	31	13	3	5	60	19	4	18	0	11	6	1.9	0.4	1.8	1.1
Bob Naber	F	6'3	185	23	4	11	0	4	0	1	2	50	5	1	6	0	1	3	1.3	0.3	1.5	0.3
MILWAUKEE HAWKS	**27-44 .380**				**FUZZY LEVANE**																	
Mel Hutchins	F	6'6	205	24	71	2891	319	842	38	193	295	65	793	227	214	5	831	41	11.2	3.2	3.0	11.7
George Ratkovicz (from Bal)	F-C	6'7	225	30	71	2235	208	619	34	262	373	70	522	217	287	16	678	31	7.4	3.1	4.0	9.5
Jack Nichols	C	6'7	225	26	69	2626	425	1170	36	240	339	71	533	196	237	9	1090	38	7.7	2.8	3.4	15.8
Bill Calhoun (from Syr)	G-F	6'3	180	25	62	2148	180	534	34	211	292	72	277	156	136	4	571	35	4.5	2.5	2.2	9.2
Dave Minor(from Bal)	G-F	6'2	185	30	59	1610	154	420	37	98	132	74	252	128	211	11	406	27	4.3	2.2	3.6	6.9
Al Masino	G	5'10	174	24	72	1773	134	400	34	128	204	63	177	160	252	12	396	25	2.5	2.2	3.5	5.5
Stan Miasek (from Bal)	F-C	6'5	215	28	65	1584	178	488	36	156	248	63	360	122	229	13	512	24	5.5	1.9	3.5	7.9
Johnny Payak	G	6'4	174	26	68	1470	128	373	34	180	248	73	114	140	194	7	436	22	1.7	2.1	2.9	6.4
Dillard Crocker	F-G	6'4	205	27	61	776	100	284	35	130	189	69	104	63	199	11	330	13	1.7	1.0	3.3	5.4
Don Otten	C	7'	245	31	24	384	34	87	39	64	91	70	89	21	68	4	132	16	3.7	0.9	2.8	5.5
Jim Brasco (from Syr)	G	6'1	170	21	30	359	36	142	25	38	48	79	39	33	48	3	110	12	1.3	1.1	1.6	3.7
Bucky McConnell	G	5'10	170	24	14	297	27	71	38	14	29	48	34	41	39	0	68	21	2.4	2.9	2.8	4.9
John O'Boyle	G	6'2	186	24	5	97	18	26	31	5	7	71	10	5	20	1	21	19	2.0	1.0	4.0	4.2
Pete Darcey	C	6'7	225	22	12	90	3	18	17	5	9	56	10	2	29	2	11	8	0.8	0.2	2.4	0.9
George Feigenbaum	G	6'1	185	23	5	79	4	22	18	8	15	53	7	9	14	1	16	16	1.4	1.8	2.8	3.2
Fuzzy Levane	G	6'2	190	32	7	68	3	24	13	2	3	67	9	9	15	0	8	10	1.3	1.3	2.1	1.1
Mike O'Neil	F	6'3	210	25	4	50	4	17	24	4	4	100	9	3	10	1	12	13	2.3	0.8	2.5	3.0

1952/53 N.B.A. — PLAYOFFS

Use Name	Pos	Hgt	Wgt	Age	G	Min	FG	FGA	%	FT	FTA	%	Reb	Ass	PF	DQ	Points	Min	Reb	Ass	PF	Points
					TOTAL													PER GAME				
MINNEAPOLIS LAKERS	**JOHNNY KUNDLA**	defeated Indianapolis 2-0; H85-69, 81-79																				
		defeated Fort Wayne 3-2; H83-73, H82-75, 95-98, 82-85, H74-58																				
		defeated New York 4-1; H88-96, H73-71, 90-75, 71-69, 91-84																				
Jim Pollard	F	6'5	190	30	12	455	62	167	37	48	62	77	86	49	37	2	172	38	7.2	4.1	3.1	14.3
Vern Mikkelsen	F	6'7	230	24	12	400	44	133	33	56	66	85	104	24	**59**	3	144	33	8.7	2.0	4.9	12.0
George Mikan	C	6'10	250	28	12	**463**	**78**	**213**	37	**82**	**112**	73	**185**	23	56	**5**	**238**	39	15.4	1.9	4.7	19.8
Pep Saul	G	6'2	185	28	12	297	31	74	42	24	33	73	28	18	40	1	86	25	2.3	1.5	3.3	7.2
Slater Martin	G	5'10	170	27	12	453	41	103	40	39	51	76	31	43	49	1	121	38	2.6	3.6	4.1	10.1
Bob Harrison	G	6'2	190	25	12	204	25	65	38	10	20	50	22	14	32	1	60	17	1.8	1.2	2.7	5.0
Whitey Skoog	G	5'11	180	26	11	198	24	56	43	16	20	80	23	13	29	1	64	18	2.1	1.2	2.6	5.8
Jim Holstein	F	6'3	170	22	12	192	20	42	48	12	23	52	30	11	30	0	52	16	2.5	0.9	2.5	4.3
Lew Hitch	C-F	6'8	200	23	12	189	16	46	35	17	32	53	64	11	32	1	49	16	5.3	0.9	2.7	4.1
Dick Schnittker	F	6'5	205	24	7	29	1	8	13	7	11	64	4	0	8	0	9	4	0.6	0.0	1.1	1.3
NEW YORK KNICKERBOCKERS	**JOE LAPCHICK**	defeated Baltimore 2-0; H80-62, 90-81																				
		defeated Boston 3-1; H95-91, 70-86, H101-82, 82-75																				
		lost to Minneapolis 1-4; 96-88, 71-73, H75-90, H69-71, H84-91																				
Vince Boryla	F	6'5	210	25	11	397	44	116	38	29	34	85	35	20	35	2	117	36	3.2	1.8	3.2	10.6
Sweetwater Clifton	F-C	6'6	220	30	11	405	51	129	40	30	47	64	140	39	48	1	132	37	12.7	3.5	4.4	12.0
Connie Simmons	C	6'8	225	27	11	341	47	128	37	51	70	73	82	25	48	1	145	31	7.5	2.3	4.4	13.2
Carl Braun	G	6'5	185	25	11	374	47	145	32	54	67	81	44	31	46	2	148	34	4.0	2.8	4.2	13.5
Dick McGuire	G	6'	180	26	11	360	24	59	41	35	55	64	63	**70**	25	0	83	33	5.7	**6.4**	2.3	7.5
Ernie Vandeweghe	G-F	6'3	195	26	11	340	49	112	44	46	61	75	64	27	50	0	144	31	5.8	2.5	4.5	13.1
Harry Gallatin	F-C	6'6	220	25	11	303	36	86	42	44	59	75	120	15	29	0	116	28	10.9	1.4	2.6	10.5
Al McGuire	G	6'2	180	24	7	62	3	14	21	0	7	0	7	9	11	0	6	9	1.0	1.3	1.6	0.9
Jerry Fleishman	G	6'2	190	30	2	26	2	3	67	6	13	46	5	7	7	1	10	13	2.5	3.5	3.5	5.0
Sherwin Raiken	G	6'2	185	24	4	19	4	5	80	0	1	0	1	2	3	0	8	5	0.3	0.5	0.8	2.0
Dick Surhoff	F	6'4	210	22	4	13	2	4	50	0	0	—	2	2	2	0	4	3	0.5	0.5	0.5	1.0
Max Zaslofsky - injury																						
FORT WAYNE PISTONS	**PAUL BIRCH**	defeated Rochester 2-1; 84-77, H71-83, 67-65																				
		lost to Minneapolis 2-3; 73-83, 75-82, H98-95, H85-82, 58-74																				
Fred Schaus	F	6'5	210	27	8	244	18	60	30	35	46	76	42	12	40	2	71	31	5.3	1.5	5.0	8.9
Monk Meineke	F	6'7	205	22	8	227	15	40	38	30	44	68	26	10	37	4	60	28	3.3	1.3	4.6	7.5
Chuck Share	C	6'11	235	25	8	198	11	27	41	26	39	67	52	12	45	**5**	48	25	6.5	1.5	5.6	6.0
Andy Phillip	G	6'3	195	30	8	329	24	71	34	34	51	67	32	30	23	1	82	41	4.0	3.8	2.9	10.3
Freddie Scolari	G	5'11	185	30	8	268	29	90	32	49	61	80	25	21	31	0	107	34	3.1	2.6	3.9	13.4
Larry Foust	C-F	6'9	225	24	8	332	48	121	40	57	68	84	111	6	34	2	153	42	13.9	0.8	4.3	19.1
Frankie Brian	G	6'1	180	29	8	146	13	42	31	19	25	76	9	11	23	1	45	18	1.1	1.4	2.9	5.6
Don Boven	F	6'4	210	27	8	111	7	28	25	9	16	56	16	2	22	0	23	14	2.0	0.3	2.8	2.9
Dike Eddleman	F-G	6'3	189	30	7	63	9	23	39	4	15	27	5	2	19	1	22	9	0.7	0.3	2.7	3.1
Jake Fendley	G	6'1	180	23	1	2	0	0	—	0	0	—	1	0	1	0	0	2	1.0	0.0	1.0	0.0
Dick Groat, Ken Murray, Zeke Sinicola-military service																						
BOSTON CELTICS	**RED AUERBACH**	defeated Syracuse 2-0; 87-81, H111-105(4OT)																				
		lost to New York 1-3; 91-95 H86-70, 82-101, H75-82																				
Chuck Cooper	F	6'5	210	26	6	195	19	48	40	22	27	81	39	14	27	2	60	33	6.5	2.3	4.5	10.0
Bob Harris	F	6'7	195	25	6	193	16	35	46	18	24	75	56	12	28	3	50	32	9.3	2.0	4.7	8.3
Ed Macauley	C-F	6'8	190	24	6	278	31	71	44	39	54	72	58	21	23	2	101	46	9.7	3.5	3.8	16.8
Bill Sharman	G	6'1	180	26	6	201	20	60	33	30	32	**94**	15	15	26	1	70	34	2.5	2.5	4.3	11.7
Bob Cousy	G	6'1	175	24	6	270	46	120	38	61	73	84	25	37	21	0	153	45	4.2	6.2	3.5	**25.5**
Bob Donham	G-F	6'2	197	26	6	138	11	38	29	11	27	41	21	13	24	3	33	23	3.5	2.2	4.0	5.5
Bob Brannum	F	6'6	225	27	6	83	12	23	52	7	11	64	21	10	23	2	31	14	3.5	1.7	3.8	5.2
John Mahnken	C	6'8	230	30	6	72	0	10	0	5	5	100	19	6	16	0	5	12	3.2	1.0	2.7	0.8
Kenny Rollins	G	6'	168	29	6	65	6	15	40	8	8	100	8	7	14	0	20	11	1.3	1.2	2.3	3.3
Mo Mahoney	F	6'2	205	25	4	45	3	14	21	3	5	60	7	2	14	0	9	11	1.8	0.5	3.5	2.3
ROCHESTER ROYALS	**LES HARRISON**	lost to Fort Wayne 1-2; H77-84, 83-71, H65-67																				
Arnie Johnson	F	6'5	240	32	3	87	4	14	29	16	21	76	18	6	15	1	24	29	6.0	2.0	5.0	8.0
Jack Coleman	F-C	6'7	230	28	3	110	7	24	29	8	10	80	40	7	13	0	22	37	13.3	2.3	4.3	7.3
Arnie Risen	C	6'9	210	28	3	109	11	38	29	17	24	71	35	2	16	1	39	36	11.7	0.7	5.3	13.0
Bob Davies	G	6'1	175	32	3	91	6	29	21	14	20	70	4	14	11	0	26	30	1.3	4.7	3.7	8.7
Bobby Wanzer	G	6'	178	31	3	116	14	37	38	23	27	85	21	9	13	0	51	39	7.0	3.0	4.3	17.0
Jack McMahon	G	6'1	18S	24	3	66	8	20	40	10	14	71	5	6	14	2	26	22	1.7	2.0	4.7	8.7
Odie Spears	F	6'5	205	27	3	62	8	19	42	4	5	80	12	0	12	1	20	21	4.0	0.0	4.0	6.7
Alex Hannum	F-C	6'7	225	29	3	52	4	10	40	3	8	38	4	2	16	1	11	17	1.3	0.7	5.3	3.7
Red Holzman	G	5'10	180	32	2	14	1	5	20	1	4	25	1	1	4	0	3	7	0.5	0.5	2.0	1.5
Cal Christensen	F	6'5	230	25	2	13	0	3	0	3	4	75	4	1	5	0	3	7	2.0	0.5	2.5	1.5
SYRACUSE NATIONALS	**AL CERVI**	lost to Boston 0-2; H81-87, 105-111(4OT)																				
Earl Lloyd	F	6'6	215	24	2	73	4	17	24	7	10	70	9	5	10	0	15	37	4.5	2.5	5.0	7.5
Dolph Schayes	F	6'8	220	24	2	58	4	16	25	10	13	77	17	1	7	0	18	29	8.5	0.5	3.5	9.0
Red Rocha	C-F	6'9	190	29	2	107	10	26	38	11	14	79	17	7	11	1	31	54	8.5	3.5	5.5	15.5
Paul Seymour	G	6'2	185	24	2	112	9	24	38	18	19	95	10	8	11	1	36	**56**	5.0	4.0	5.5	18.0
George King	G	6'	180	24	2	67	6	13	46	10	12	83	5	9	12	2	22	34	2.5	4.5	**6.0**	11.0
Noble Jorgensen	C	6'9	230	27	2	44	5	9	56	4	6	67	10	3	11	1	14	22	5.0	1.5	5.5	7.0
Wally Osterkorn	F	6'5	210	24	2	42	4	9	44	1	3	33	4	2	11	1	9	21	2.0	1.0	5.5	4.5
Billy Gabor	G	5'11	180	30	2	28	5	12	42	8	13	62	3	2	12	2	18	14	1.5	1.0	**6.0**	9.0
Al Cervi	G	5'11	185	35	2	28	3	5	60	12	15	80	0	1	12	1	18	14	0.0	0.5	**6.0**	9.0
Bob Lochmueller	F	6'5	185	25	2	21	2	10	20	1	4	25	5	2	12	2	5	11	2.5	1.0	**6.0**	2.5

1952/53 N.B.A. PLAYOFFS (continued)

Use Name	Pos.	Hgt.	Wgt.	Age	G	Min.	FG	FGA	%	FT	FTA	%	Reb.	Ass.	PF	Disq.	Points	Min.	Reb.	Ass.	PF	Points
					TOTAL													PER GAME				
INDIANAPOLIS OLYMPIANS	**HERM SCHAEFER**				lost to Minneapolis 0-2; 69-85, H79-81																	
Leo Barnhorst	F	6'4	195	28	2	79	12	33	36	6	9	67	22	5	10	0	30	40	11.0	2.5	5.0	15.0
Bob Lavoy	F	6'7	185	26	2	47	4	16	25	2	5	40	10	2	10	1	10	24	5.0	1.0	5.0	5.0
Joe Graboski	C-F	6'8	210	22	2	76	14	28	50	6	8	75	16	0	5	0	34	38	8.0	0.0	2.5	17.0
Paul Walther	G	6'2	160	25	2	75	5	20	25	16	17	94	8	4	8	1	26	38	4.0	2.0	4.0	13.0
Bill Tosheff	G	6'1	180	26	2	66	1	16	6	7	7	100	5	4	5	0	9	33	2.5	2.0	2.5	4.5
Gene Rhodes	G	6'1	170	25	2	51	4	14	29	1	4	25	7	5	5	0	9	26	3.5	2.5	2.5	4.5
Mel Payton	F	6'4	185	26	2	36	7	17	41	7	8	88	6	0	7	0	21	18	3.0	0.0	3.5	10.5
Ed Mikan	C	6'8	230	27	2	32	2	10	20	3	3	100	7	0	1	0	7	16	3.5	0.0	0.5	3.5
Zeke Zawoluk	F	6'7	215	22	2	18	1	6	17	0	2	0	2	0	5	0	2	9	1.0	0.0	2.5	1.0
BALTIMORE BULLETS	**CLAIR BEE**				lost to New York 0-2; 62-80, H81-90																	
Jim Baechtold	F-G	6'4	205	25	2	86	16	30	**53**	6	11	55	8	11	9	0	38	43	4.0	5.5	4.5	19.0
Don Henricksen	F-C	6'7	225	23	2	94	10	15	67	5	9	56	24	8	11	1	25	47	12.0	4.0	5.5	12.5
Eddie Miller	C	6'8	225	21	2	93	13	34	38	7	16	44	36	5	9	0	33	47	**18.0**	2.5	4.5	16.5
Paul Hoffman	G	6'2	205	30	2	81	5	28	18	7	12	58	7	11	10	1	17	41	3.5	5.5	5.0	8.5
Ray Lumpp	G	6'1	182	29	2	75	7	33	21	7	10	70	8	5	8	0	21	38	4.0	2.5	4.0	10.5
Jack Kerris	F	6'6	215	27	2	31	2	10	20	3	3	100	2	0	4	0	7	16	1.0	0.0	2.0	3.5
Ralph O'Brien	G	5'9	160	24	1	18	0	2	0	2	2	100	1	0	2	0	2	18	1.0	0.0	2.0	2.0
Bob Priddy	F	6'3	190	22	1	1	0	0	—	0	0	—	0	0	1	0	0	1	0.0	0.0	1.0	0.0
Dick Bunt	G	6'	172	22	1	1	0	0	—	0	0	—	0	0	0	0	0	1	0.0	1.0	0.0	0.0
Don Barksdale—injury																						

1952/53 N.B.A. TEAM STATISTICS

Team	G	FG	FGA	%	FT	FTA	%	Reb.	Ass.	For	Agnst.	Diff.	G	FG	FGA	%	FT	FTA	%	Reb.	Ass.	For	Agnst.	Diff.
	REGULAR SEASON									AVERAGE POINTS			PLAYOFFS									AVERAGE POINTS		
EASTERN DIVISION																								
New York	70	2059	5339	39	1867	2652	70	**4007**	1575	85.5	80.3	+5.2	11	309	801	**39**	295	414	71	**640**	247	83.0	80.9	+2.1
Syracuse	71	1942	5329	36	**2197**	**2950**	**74**	3472	1459	85.6	81.3	+4.3	2	52	141	37	**82**	**109**	75	87	40	**93.0**	99.0	-6.0
Boston	71	**2177**	5555	**39**	1904	2617	73	3865	**1666**	**88.1**	85.8	+2.3	6	164	434	38	204	266	**77**	300	**137**	88.7	89.0	-0.3
Baltimore	70	2083	**5615**	37	1745	2542	69	3727	1514	84.4	90.9	-6.5	2	53	152	35	37	63	59	103	41	71.5	85.0	-13.5
Philadelphia	69	1987	5546	36	1560	2298	68	3763	1513	80.2	88.9	-8.7												
WESTERN DIVISION																								
Minneapolis	70	2166	5559	39	1641	2221	74	3406	1351	85.3	79.2	**+6.1**	12	**342**	907	38	311	430	72	636	206	82.9	**77.8**	**+5.1**
Rochester	70	2019	5432	37	2005	2747	73	3625	1520	86.3	83.5	+2.8	3	63	199	32	99	137	72	155	48	75.0	74.0	+1.0
Fort Wayne	69	1876	5230	36	1839	2491	74	3548	1438	81.0	81.1	-0.1	8	174	502	35	263	365	72	342	106	76.4	80.1	-3.7
Indinapolis	71	1829	5204	35	1637	2277	72	3326	1281	74.6	**77.4**	-2.8	2	50	**160**	31	48	63	76	88	20	74.0	83.0	-9.0
Milwaukee	71	1873	5320	35	1643	2400	68	3429	1427	75.9	78.8	-2.9												

1952/53 N.B.A. STANDINGS

Team	W	L	Pct.	GB	W	L	Pct.	W	L	Pct.	W	L	Pct.	W	L	Pct.	W	L	Pct.
					Record against playoff teams			Record against non - playoff teams			HOME			ROAD			NEUTRAL		
EASTERN DIVISION																			
New York Knickerbockers	47	23	.671	—	32	22	.593	**15**	1	**.938**	21	4	.840	15	14	**.517**	11	5	.688
Syracuse Nationals	47	24	.662	0.5	**36**	19	**.655**	11	5	.688	32	2	**.941**	10	19	.345	5	3	.625
Boston Celtics	46	25	.648	1.5	32	23	.582	14	2	.875	21	3	.875	11	18	.379	**14**	4	**.778**
Baltimore Bullets	16	54	.299	31	7	47	.130	9	**7**	.563	11	**20**	.355	1	19	.050	4	15	.211
Philadelphia Warriors	12	**57**	.174	34.5	10	**53**	.159	2	4	.235	4	13	.235	1	**28**	.034	7	**16**	.304
WESTERN DIVISION																			
Minneapolis Lakers	**48**	22	**.686**	—	35	19	.648	13	3	.813	24	2	.923	**16**	15	.516	8	5	.615
Rochester Royals	44	26	.629	4	33	21	.611	11	5	.688	24	8	.750	13	16	.448	7	2	**.778**
Fort Wayne Pistons	36	33	.522	11.5	24	30	.444	12	3	.800	25	9	.735	8	19	.296	3	5	.375
Indianapolis Olympians	28	43	.394	20.5	18	36	.333	10	7	.588	19	14	.576	4	23	.148	5	6	.455
Milwaukee Hawks	27	44	.380	21.5	23	42	.354	4	2	.667	14	8	.636	4	24	.143	9	12	.429

1952/53 N.B.A. INDIVIDUAL LEADERS

SCORING
(Minimum 48 Games Played)

Name	Team	G	FG	FT	Pts.	Avg.
Johnston	Phi	70	504	556	1564	22.3
Mikan	Min	70	500	442	1442	20.6
Cousy	Bos	69	451	500	1402	20.3
Macauley	Bos	71	464	479	1407	19.8
Schayes	Syr	71	375	512	1262	17.8
Sharman	Bos	71	403	341	1147	16.2
Nichols	Mil	69	425	240	1090	15.8
Davies	Roch	66	339	351	1029	15.6
Mikkelsen	Min	70	378	291	1047	15.0
Wanzer	Roch	70	318	384	1020	14.6

FIELD GOAL PERCENTAGE
(Minimum 210 Field Goals)

Name	Team	FG	FGA	Pct.
Johnston	Phi	504	1114	.452
Macauley	Bos	451	997	.452
Gallatin	NY	282	635	.444
Sharman	Bos	403	925	.436
Mikkelsen	Min	378	868	.435
Vandeweghe	NY	272	625	.435
Coleman	Roch	314	748	.420
Martin	Min	260	634	.410
Lavoy	Ind	255	635	.402
King	Syr	225	560	.402

FREE THROW PERCENTAGE
(Minimum 180 Free Throws)

Name	Team	FT	FTA	Pct.
Sharman	Bos	341	401	.850
Scolari	FtW	276	327	.844
Schayes	Syr	512	619	.827
Braun	NY	331	401	.825
Schaus	FtW	243	296	.821
Spears	Roch	199	243	.819
Seymour	Syr	340	416	.817
Cousy	Bos	479	587	.816
Wanzer	Roch	384	473	.812
Tosheff	Ind	253	314	.806

PERSONAL FOULS

Name	Team	PF
Meineke	FtW	334
Fulks	Phi	319
Graboski	Ind	303
Mikan	Min	290
Mikkelsen	Min	289

GAMES DISQUALIFIED

Name	Team	Disq
Meineke	FtW	26
Fulks	Phi	20
Hannum	Roch	18
Lavoy	Ind	18
Graboski	Ind	18

REBOUNDS PER GAME
(Minimum 48 Games Played)

Name	Team	G	Reb.	Avg.
Mikan	Min	70	1007	14.4
Johnston	Phi	70	976	13.9
Gallatin	NY	70	916	13.1
Schayes	Syr	71	920	13.0
Foust	FtW	67	769	11.5

ASSISTS PER GAME
(Minimum 48 Games Played)

Name	Team	G	Ass.	Avg.
Cousy	Bos	71	547	7.7
Phillip	Phi-FtW	70	397	5.7
King	Syr	71	364	5.1
D. McGuire	NY	61	296	4.9
Seymour	Syr	67	294	4.4

1953-54 N.B.A.

Too Much Mikan, Not Enough Action

Things looked brighter for the N.B.A. at the start of this season than at any other time in its short history. The National Broadcasting Company thought enough of the product to start a modest program of national telecasts. With the weak Indianapolis franchise dropped from the league, there were now nine teams to show to the country. Veteran pro players stocked these nine clubs with deep benches, and a slew of new talent came into the league from several sources . Rookies Ray Felix of L.I.U., Jack Molinas of Columbia, Bob Houbregs of Washington, and Ernie Beck of Pennsylvania turned pro after prominent college careers. In addition, former All-Americans Clyde Lovellette, George Yardley, Ernie Barrett, Don Sunderlage, and Walt Davis came into the league after playing A.A.U. ball. With plenty of talent compressed into nine teams, and with a television program to spark interest, how could this help but be the N.B.A.'s most profitable campaign?

Simply stated, the season was a flop because the game itself was degenerating into a pushing and shoving match reminiscent of the notorious days of pro ball before the growth of stable leagues. The area under the basket was no-man's-land, with guards rarely daring to drive in close to the hoop. Hot-handed shooters were often cooled off with heavy-handed policing. Officials tried to keep order by calling fouls, but a steady succession of charity throws reduced action to a yawn. Indeed, coaches found it best to have their players repeatedly foul the enemy in the final minutes of a contest, giving up a probable one point in return for a chance at two. Add an occasional policy of sitting on a lead in the fourth quarter, and the N.B.A.'s product was wasted in a boring match of technicalities.

Another problem which sent a shudder through the circuit involved rookie Jack Molinas of Ft. Wayne. A talented forward, Molinas enjoyed gambling, and a story broke in December about his betting on games. Molinas admitted that he had bet small sums on the Pistons to win in several games, and although there was no question of his throwing a game, Commissioner Podoloff banned him from the N.B.A. Several years later Molinas was convicted of being a "fixer" in a new round of college basketball scandals, and was sent to prison.

But even with all the problems that turned many fans off, the N.B.A. played through its fifth season. With the Western Division down to four teams, the league governers allotted only three playoff spots to each division this year. Minneapolis, Rochester, and Ft. Wayne took those berths in the West, leaving Milwaukee far behind in the dust. Bothered by bad knees, George Mikan fell to an 18.1 scoring average, fourth best in the league; he still ranked second in the league in rebounding, however, and his strength made driving on the Lakers a risky proposition. The Rochester Royals, too, were starting to creak with age but they still finished a strong second behind their longtime rivals from Minnesota. With Bobby Wanzer, Bob Davies, and Arnie Risen all starting to slow down, the Royals were to slip into mediocrity after this season.

Ft. Wayne, on the other hand, looked like a team on the way up. Despite losing an outstanding young talent in Molinas, the Pistons added George Yardley, an explosive jump-shooter, to the holdover forward corps of Mel Hutchins and Monk Meineke. Larry Foust gave the team a high-scoring center, and veteran guards Max Zaslofsky and Leo Barnhorst came over in mid-season to help old hands Andy Phillip, Freddie Scolari, and Frankie Brian in the backcourt. Although only third-place finishers this year, the Pistons were good bets to pass the Royals next season. The last-place Hawks were a team easily forgotten, with Red Holzman's coaching debut the squad's only claim to fame.

New York, Boston, and Syracuse captured the Eastern playoff spots with little trouble from Baltimore and Philadelphia. After three straight flops in the playoff finals, the Knicks were itching for another shot at the title. Even with Max Zaslofsky traded away and Ernie Vandeweghe rarely able to get away from his medical studies, the Knicks captured first place with a blend of different talents, ranging from Carl Braun's hot shooting to Harry Gallatin's league-leading rebounding. The Celtics and Nats tied for second place on the strength of hot offenses. Boston fans were now accustomed to the fine shooting of Bob Cousy, Bill Sharman, and Ed Macauley and to the lack of defense and rebounding muscle on the squad. The Nats had one of pro ball's best offensive weapons in forward Dolph Schayes, and they had a tough defense led by guard Paul Seymour. The problem with the Nats was that they didn't have a legitimate starting center. The also-ran Bullets and Warriors each had a high-scoring center; Baltimore rookie Ray Felix scored at a 17.6 clip, while Warrior veteran Neil Johnston retained his scoring championship with a 24.4 average.

With only three teams in the playoffs from each division, the league set up a round robin to whittle the field down to two clubs in each sector. After this confusing first round was over, the Knicks and Pistons had been eliminated. That left Syracuse and Boston in the East, with the Nats then winning a place in the championship series with two straight victories. The Lakers and Royals squared off in what was to be the last of their classic battles in the West. The Lakers took game one, 89-76, the Royals won game two, 74-73, and the Lakers captured the deciding game by an 82-72 score.

The championship series between Syracuse and Minneapolis involved so-called "minor league" cities but definitely major league teams. The Lakers used their size in a 79-68 first game triumph, but the Nats came back to take game two, 62-60, on a bucket by Paul Seymour with seven seconds left. Mikan's 30 points led the Lakers to an 81-67 win in game three, with the Nats coming back with an 80-69 triumph in the fourth game. When the Lakers took game five, 84-73, in Syracuse and headed back to Minneapolis for the final two contests with a one-game edge, the series was all but over. The scrappy Nats then battled the Lakers to a standstill in the sixth game and won, 65-63, on a Jim Neal basket with four seconds left in the game. But the Lakers' superior size came out in the rubber game, with an 87-80 triumph bringing Minneapolis its third straight N.B.A. championship. It was a fitting way for George Mikan to go out, as the big man would announce his retirement before the next season. And it was the end of an era in another way, as the 24-second rule was about to change the entire complexion of the game.

se Name	Pos	Hgt	Wgt	Age	TOTAL G	Min	FG	FGA	%	FT	FTA	%	Reb	Ass	PF	DQ	Points	PER GAME Min	Reb	Ass	PF	Points
1953/54 N.B.A. — EASTERN DIVISION																						
EW YORK KNICKERBOCKERS	**44-28 .611**				**JOE LAPCHICK**																	
ince Boryla (back injury)	F	6'5	212	26	52	1522	175	525	33	70	81	86	130	77	128	0	420	29	2.5	1.5	2.5	8.1
arry Gallatin	F-C	6'6	220	26	72	2690	258	639	40	433	552	78	**1098**	153	208	2	949	37	**15.3**	2.1	2.9	13.2
weetwater Clifton	C-F	6'6	220	31	72	2179	257	699	37	174	277	63	528	176	215	0	688	30	7.3	2.4	3.0	9.6
arl Braun	G	6'5	187	26	72	2373	354	884	40	354	429	83	246	209	259	6	1062	33	3.4	2.9	3.6	14.8
ich McGuire	G	6'	180	27	68	2343	201	493	41	220	345	64	310	354	190	3	622	34	4.6	5.2	2.8	9.1
onnie Simmons	C-F	6'8	225	28	72	2006	255	713	36	210	305	69	484	128	234	1	720	28	6.7	1.8	3.3	10.0
m Baechtold	G-F	6'4	205	26	70	1627	170	465	37	134	177	76	183	117	195	5	474	23	2.6	1.7	2.8	6.8
red Schaus (from FtW)	F	6'5	210	28	67	1515	161	415	39	153	195	78	267	109	176	3	475	23	4.0	1.6	2.6	7.1
l McGuire	G	6'2	185	25	64	849	58	177	33	58	133	44	121	103	144	2	174	13	1.9	1.5	2.3	2.7
mie Vandeweghe (MD-KJ)	G	6'3	195	27	15	271	37	103	36	25	31	81	29	29	38	1	99	18	1.9	1.9	2.5	6.6
uddy Ackerman	G	6'1	183	23	28	220	14	63	22	15	28	54	15	23	43	0	43	8	0.5	0.8	1.5	1.5
d Smith (broken wrist)	F	6'6	210	24	11	104	11	45	24	6	10	60	26	9	15	0	28	10	2.4	0.8	1.4	2.5
OSTON CELTICS	**42-30 .583**				**RED AUERBACH**																	
ob Harris	F	6'7	195	26	71	1898	156	409	38	108	172	63	517	94	224	8	420	27	7.3	1.3	3.2	5.9
ob Brannum	F	6'6	230	28	71	1729	140	453	31	129	206	63	509	144	280	10	409	24	7.2	2.0	3.9	5.8
d Macauley	C	6'8	190	25	71	2792	462	950	**49**	420	554	76	571	271	168	1	1344	39	8.0	3.8	2.4	18.9
ill Sharman	G	6'1	185	27	72	2467	412	915	45	331	392	**84**	255	229	211	4	1155	34	3.5	3.2	2.9	16.0
ob Cousy	G	6'1	175	25	72	2857	486	1262	39	411	522	79	394	**518**	201	3	1383	40	5.5	7.2	2.8	19.2
ack Nichols (from Mil)	F-C	6'7	225	27	75	1607	163	528	31	113	152	74	363	104	187	2	439	21	4.8	1.4	2.5	5.9
ob Donham	G	6'2	197	27	68	1451	141	315	45	118	213	55	267	186	235	11	400	21	3.9	2.7	3.5	5.9
on Barksdale	F	6'6	200	30	63	1358	156	415	38	149	225	66	345	117	213	4	461	22	5.5	1.9	3.4	7.3
huck Cooper	F	6'5	215	27	70	1101	78	261	30	78	116	67	304	74	150	1	234	16	4.3	1.1	2.1	3.3
mie Barrett	F-G	6'3	180	24	59	641	60	191	31	14	25	56	100	55	116	2	134	11	1.7	0.9	2.0	2.3
d Mikan	C	6'8	230	28	9	71	8	24	33	5	9	56	20	3	15	0	21	8	2.2	0.3	1.7	2.3
Gene Conley - retired to play baseball																						
YRACUSE NATIONALS	**42-30 .583**				**AL CERVI**																	
/ally Osterkorn	F	6'5	215	25	70	2164	203	586	35	209	361	58	487	151	209	1	615	31	7.0	2.2	3.0	8.8
arl Lloyd	F-C	6'6	220	25	72	2206	249	666	37	156	209	75	529	115	**303**	**12**	654	31	7.3	1.6	**4.2**	9.1
olph Schayes	C-F	6'8	220	25	72	2655	370	973	38	488	590	83	870	214	232	4	1228	37	12.1	3.0	3.2	17.1
aul Seymour	G	6'2	185	25	71	2727	316	838	38	299	368	81	291	364	187	2	931	38	4.1	5.1	2.6	13.1
eorge King	G	6'	185	25	72	2370	280	744	38	257	410	63	262	272	179	2	817	33	3.6	3.8	2.5	11.3
illy Kenville	F-G	6'2	185	23	72	1405	149	388	38	136	182	75	247	122	138	0	434	20	3.4	1.7	1.9	6.0
ob Lavoy (from Mil)	F	6'7	190	27	68	1277	135	356	38	94	129	73	317	78	215	2	364	19	4.7	1.1	3.2	5.4
illy Gabor	G	5'11	180	31	61	1211	204	551	37	139	194	72	96	162	183	4	547	20	1.6	2.7	3.0	9.0
im Neal	C	6'11	235	23	67	899	117	369	32	78	132	59	257	24	139	0	312	13	3.8	0.4	2.1	4.7
ato Govedarica	G	5'11	185	25	23	258	25	79	32	25	37	68	18	24	44	1	75	11	0.8	1.0	1.9	3.3
l Masino (from Roch)	G	5'10	178	25	27	181	26	62	42	30	49	61	28	22	44	0	82	7	1.0	0.8	1.6	3.0
ick Knostman	C	6'6	215	22	5	47	3	10	30	7	11	64	17	6	9	0	13	9	3.4	1.2	1.8	2.6
like Novak	C	6'9	220	38	5	24	0	7	0	1	2	50	2	2	9	0	1	5	0.4	0.4	1.8	0.2
d Earle	F	6'3	190	26	2	12	1	2	50	2	4	50	2	0	0	0	4	6	1.0	0.0	0.0	2.0
Red Rocha - voluntarily retired																						
HILADELPHIA WARRIORS	**29-43 .403**				**EDDIE GOTTLIEB**																	
eke Zawoluk	F	6'7	215	23	71	1795	203	540	38	186	230	81	330	99	220	6	592	25	4.6	1.4	3.1	8.3
oe Graboski	F	6'8	210	23	71	2759	354	1000	35	236	350	67	670	163	223	4	944	39	9.4	2.3	3.1	13.3
ed Johnston	C	6'8	215	24	72	**3296**	**591**	**1317**	45	**577**	**772**	75	797	203	259	7	**1759**	**46**	11.1	2.8	3.6	**24.4**
ack George	G	6'3	190	25	71	2648	259	736	35	157	266	59	386	312	210	4	675	37	5.4	4.4	3.0	9.5
aul Walther	G	6'2	160	26	64	2067	138	392	35	145	206	70	257	220	199	5	421	32	4.0	3.4	3.1	6.6
/alt Davis	F-C	6'8	205	22	68	1568	167	455	37	65	101	64	435	58	207	9	399	23	6.4	0.9	3.0	5.9
anny Finn	G	6'1	185	25	68	1562	170	495	34	126	196	64	216	265	215	7	466	23	3.2	3.9	3.2	6.9
eorge Senesky	G	6'2	180	31	58	771	41	119	34	29	53	55	66	84	79	0	111	13	1.1	1.4	1.4	1.9
oe Fulks	F	6'5	195	32	61	501	61	229	27	28	49	57	101	28	90	0	150	8	1.7	0.5	1.5	2.5
mie Beck (MS)	F	6'4	190	22	15	422	39	142	27	34	43	79	50	34	29	0	112	28	3.3	2.3	1.9	7.5
im Phelan	G	6'1	175	24	4	33	0	6	0	3	6	50	5	2	9	0	3	8	1.3	0.5	2.3	0.8
orm Grekin	F	6'5	180	23	1	1	0	0	—	0	0	—	0	0	1	0	0	1	0.0	0.0	1.0	0.0
Paul Arizin and Jim Mooney - military service																						
BALTIMORE BULLETS	**16-56 .222**				**CLAIR BEE**																	
Eddie Miller	F-C	6'8	225	22	72	1657	244	600	41	231	317	73	537	95	194	0	719	23	7.5	1.3	2.7	10.0
Bob Houbregs (from Mil)	F-C	6'8	230	21	70	1970	209	562	37	190	266	71	375	123	209	2	608	28	5.4	1.8	3.0	8.7
Ray Felix	C	6'11	220	23	72	2672	410	983	42	449	704	64	958	82	253	5	1269	37	13.3	1.1	3.5	17.6
Paul Hoffman	G-F	6'2	205	28	72	2505	253	761	33	217	303	72	486	285	271	10	723	35	6.8	4.0	3.8	10.0
Al Roges	G	6'4	200	23	67	1937	220	614	36	130	179	73	213	160	177	1	570	29	3.2	2.4	2.6	8.5
Rollen Hans	G	6'2	210	23	67	1556	191	515	37	101	180	56	160	181	172	1	483	23	2.4	2.7	2.6	7.2
Jim Fritsche (from Min)	F	6'8	210	22	68	1221	116	379	31	49	68	72	217	73	103	0	281	18	3.2	1.1	1.5	4.1
Joe Smyth (from NY)	F	6'6	215	24	40	495	48	138	35	35	65	54	98	49	53	0	131	12	2.5	1.2	1.3	3.3
Jim Luisi	G	6'2	180	25	31	367	31	95	33	27	41	66	25	35	45	0	89	12	0.8	1.1	1.5	2.9
Hal Uplinger	G	6'4	185	24	23	268	33	94	35	20	22	91	31	26	42	0	86	12	1.3	1.1	1.8	3.7
Bill Bolger	F	6'5	205	22	20	202	24	59	41	8	13	62	36	11	27	0	56	10	1.8	0.6	1.4	2.8
Connie Rea	G-F	6'3	175	18	20	154	9	43	21	5	16	31	31	16	13	0	23	8	1.6	0.8	0.7	1.2
Mark Workman	C-F	6'9	217	23	14	151	25	60	42	6	10	60	37	7	31	0	56	11	2.6	0.5	2.2	4.0
Don Asmonga	G	6'2	185	25	7	46	2	15	13	1	1	100	1	5	12	1	5	7	0.1	0.7	1.7	0.7
Mo Mahoney	F	6'2	205	26	2	11	0	2	0	0	0	—	2	1	0	0	0	6	1.0	0.5	0.0	0.0
Paul Nolen	C	6'10	215	24	1	2	0	1	0	0	0	—	1	0	1	0	0	2	1.0	0.0	1.0	0.0
Don Henriksen-voluntarily retired																						

Use Name	Pos	Hgt	Wgt	Age	G	Min	FG	FGA	%	FT	FTA	%	Reb	Ass	PF	DQ	Points	Min	Reb	Ass	PF	Points
					TOTAL													PER GAME				

1953/54 N.B.A. — WESTERN DIVISION

Use Name	Pos	Hgt	Wgt	Age	G	Min	FG	FGA	%	FT	FTA	%	Reb	Ass	PF	DQ	Points	Min	Reb	Ass	PF	Points
MINNEAPOLIS LAKERS	**46-26 .639**				**JOHNNY KUNDLA**																	
Jim Pollard	F	6'5	195	31	71	2483	326	882	37	179	230	78	500	214	161	0	831	35	7.0	3.0	2.3	11.7
Vern Mikkelsen	F	6'7	230	25	72	2247	288	771	37	221	298	74	615	119	264	7	797	31	8.5	1.7	3.7	11.1
George Mikan	C	6'10	255	29	72	2362	441	1160	38	424	546	78	1028	174	268	4	1306	33	14.3	2.4	3.7	18.1
Whitey Skoog	G	5'11	180	27	71	1877	212	530	40	72	97	74	224	179	234	5	496	26	3.2	2.5	3.3	7.0
Slater Martin	G	5'10	170	28	69	2472	254	654	39	176	243	72	166	253	198	3	684	36	2.4	3.7	2.9	9.9
Pep Saul	G	6'2	185	29	71	1805	162	467	35	128	170	75	159	139	149	3	452	25	2.2	2.0	2.1	6.4
Clyde Lovellette	C-F	6'9	250	24	72	1255	237	560	42	114	164	70	419	51	210	2	588	17	5.8	0.7	2.9	8.2
Jim Holstein	F-G	6'3	180	23	70	1155	88	288	31	64	112	57	204	79	140	0	240	17	2.9	1.1	2.0	3.4
Dick Schnittker	F	6'5	205	25	71	1040	122	307	40	86	132	65	178	59	178	3	330	15	2.6	0.8	2.5	4.6
ROCHESTER ROYALS	**44-28 .611**				**LES HARRISON**																	
Cal Christensen	F	6'5	230	26	70	1654	137	395	35	138	261	53	395	107	196	1	412	24	5.6	1.5	2.8	5.9
Jack Coleman	F-C	6'7	230	29	71	2377	289	714	40	108	181	60	589	158	201	3	686	33	8.3	2.2	2.8	9.7
Arnie Risen	C	6'9	210	29	72	2385	321	872	37	307	430	71	728	120	284	9	949	33	10.1	1.7	3.9	13.2
Bob Davies	G	6'1	180	33	72	2137	288	777	37	311	433	72	194	323	224	4	887	30	2.7	4.5	3.1	12.3
Bobby Wanzer	G	6'	185	32	72	2538	322	835	39	314	428	73	392	254	171	2	958	35	5.4	3.5	2.4	13.3
Jack McMahon	G	6'1	188	25	71	1891	250	691	36	211	303	70	211	238	221	6	711	27	3.0	3.4	3.1	10.0
Alex Hannum	F-C	6'7	225	30	72	1707	175	503	35	102	164	62	350	105	279	11	452	24	4.9	1.5	3.9	6.3
Odie Spears	F-G	6'5	205	28	72	1633	184	505	36	183	238	77	310	109	211	5	551	23	4.3	1.5	2.9	7.7
Norm Swanson	F	6'6	212	23	63	611	31	137	23	38	64	59	110	33	91	3	100	10	1.7	0.5	1.4	1.6
Frank Reddout	F	6'5	195	22	7	18	5	6	83	3	4	75	9	0	6	0	13	3	1.3	0.0	0.9	1.9
FORT WAYNE PISTONS	**40-32 .556**				**PAUL BIRCH**																	
Jack Molinas (DL)	F	6'6	210	21	29	993	108	278	39	134	176	76	209	47	74	2	350	34	7.2	1.6	2.6	12.1
Mel Hutchins	F	6'6	205	25	72	2934	295	736	40	151	223	68	695	210	229	4	741	41	9.7	2.9	3.2	10.3
Larry Foust	C	6'9	240	25	72	2693	376	919	41	338	475	71	967	161	258	4	1090	37	13.4	2.2	3.6	15.1
Andy Phillip	G	6'3	195	31	71	2705	255	680	38	241	330	73	265	449	204	4	751	38	3.7	6.3	2.9	10.6
Max Zaslofsky (from Bal, Mil)	G	6'2	180	28	65	1881	278	756	37	255	357	71	160	154	142	1	811	29	2.5	2.4	2.2	12.5
Leo Barnhorst (from Bal)	G-F	6'4	195	29	72	2064	199	588	34	63	88	72	297	226	203	4	461	29	4.1	3.1	2.8	6.4
Freddie Scolari	G	5'11	185	31	64	1589	159	491	32	144	180	80	139	131	155	1	462	25	2.2	2.0	2.4	7.2
George Yardley	F	6'5	190	25	63	1489	209	492	42	146	205	71	407	99	166	3	564	24	6.5	1.6	2.6	9.0
Monk Meineke	F-C	6'7	205	23	71	1466	135	393	34	136	169	80	372	81	214	6	406	21	5.2	1.1	3.0	5.7
Frankie Brian	G	6'1	185	30	64	973	132	352	38	137	182	75	79	92	100	2	401	15	1.2	1.4	1.6	6.3
Ken Murray	G	6'2	195	25	49	528	53	195	27	43	60	72	65	56	60	0	149	11	1.3	1.1	1.2	3.0
Zeke Sinicola	G	5'10	165	24	9	53	4	16	25	3	6	50	1	3	8	0	11	6	0.1	0.3	0.9	1.2
Dick Groat - military service																						
MILWAUKEE HAWKS	**21-51 .292**				**FUZZY LEVANE (11-53 .239), RED HOLZMAN (10-16 .385)**																	
Lew Hitch	F-C	6'8	200	24	72	2452	221	603	37	133	208	64	691	141	176	3	575	34	9.6	2.0	2.4	8.0
George Ratkovicz	F-C	6'7	225	31	69	2170	197	501	39	176	273	64	523	154	255	11	570	31	7.6	2.2	3.7	8.3
Chuck Share (from FtW)	C	6'11	235	26	68	1576	188	493	38	188	275	68	555	80	210	8	564	23	8.2	1.2	3.1	8.3
Bill Calhoun	G-F	6'3	190	26	72	2370	190	545	35	214	292	73	274	189	151	3	594	33	3.8	2.6	2.1	8.3
Don Sunderlage	G	6'1	180	24	68	2232	254	748	34	252	337	75	225	187	263	8	760	33	3.3	2.8	3.9	11.2
Bill Tosheff	G	6'1	195	27	71	1825	168	578	29	156	210	74	163	196	207	3	492	26	2.3	2.8	2.9	6.9
Irv Bemoras	F	6'3	187	23	69	1496	185	505	37	139	208	67	214	79	152	2	509	22	3.1	1.1	2.2	7.4
Bob Harrison (from Min)	G	6'2	190	26	64	1443	144	449	32	94	158	59	130	139	218	9	382	23	2.0	2.2	3.4	6.0
Red Holzman	G	5'10	185	33	51	649	74	224	33	48	73	66	46	75	73	1	196	13	0.9	1.5	1.4	3.8
Don Lofgran	F	6'6	200	25	21	380	35	112	31	32	49	65	64	26	34	0	102	18	3.0	1.2	1.6	4.9
Dick Surhoff	F	6'4	210	23	32	358	43	129	33	47	62	76	69	23	53	0	133	11	2.2	0.7	1.7	4.2
Gene Dyker	F	6'6	225	23	11	91	6	26	23	4	8	60	16	5	21	0	16	8	1.5	0.5	1.9	1.5
Bob Peterson (from Bal)	F	6'5	210	21	8	60	3	10	30	9	11	82	12	3	15	1	15	8	1.5	0.4	1.9	1.9
Rabbit Walthour	G	5'11	163	25	4	30	1	6	17	0	0	—	1	2	6	0	2	8	0.3	0.5	1.5	0.5

Use Name	Pos	Hgt	Wgt	Age	G	Min	FG	FGA	%	FT	FTA	%	Reb	Ass	PF	DQ	Points	Min	Reb	Ass	PF	Points
					TOTAL													PER GAME				

1953/54 N.B.A.—PLAYOFFS

MINNEAPOLIS LAKERS — **JOHNNY KUNDLA**
defeated Fort Wayne 2-0; 90-85, H78-73
defeated Rochester 3-1; H109-88, H89-76, 73-74, H82-72
defeated Syracuse 4-3; H79-68, H60-62, 81-67 69-80, 84-73, H63-65, H87-80

Use Name	Pos	Hgt	Wgt	Age	G	Min	FG	FGA	%	FT	FTA	%	Reb	Ass	PF	DQ	Points	Min	Reb	Ass	PF	Points
Jim Pollard	F	6'5	195	31	13	543	56	155	36	48	60	80	110	41	27	0	160	42	8.5	3.2	2.1	12.3
Vern Mikkelsen	F	6'7	230	25	13	375	51	111	46	31	36	86	73	17	52	0	133	29	5.6	1.3	4.0	10.2
Geone Mikan	C	6'10	255	29	13	424	**87**	**190**	46	78	96	81	**171**	25	56	1	**252**	33	13.2	1.9	4.3	19.4
Whitey Skoog	G	5'11	180	27	13	402	42	107	39	12	21	57	47	23	**60**	3	96	31	3.6	1.8	4.6	7.4
Slater Martin	G	5'10	170	28	13	533	37	112	33	52	70	74	29	**60**	52	3	126	41	2.2	4.6	4.0	9.7
Clyde Lovellette	C-F	6'9	250	24	13	265	54	120	45	28	58	48	126	7	37	0	136	20	9.7	0.5	2.8	10.5
Pep Saul	G	6'2	185	29	13	227	18	51	35	25	34	74	27	14	27	0	61	17	2.1	1.1	2.1	4.7
Jim Holstein	F-G	6'3	180	23	13	188	15	49	31	16	23	70	35	11	28	0	46	14	2.7	0.8	2.2	3.5
Dick Schnittker	F	6'5	205	25	13	163	11	32	34	12	20	60	21	5	32	0	34	13	1.6	0.4	2.5	2.6

SYRACUSE NATIONALS — **AL CERVI**
defeated New York 2-0; H75-68,103-99
defeated Boston 4-0; 96-95(OT), H98-85, H109-94, 83-76
lost to Minneapolis 3-4; 68-79, 62-60, H67-81, H80-69, H73-84, 65-63, 80-87

Use Name	Pos	Hgt	Wgt	Age	G	Min	FG	FGA	%	FT	FTA	%	Reb	Ass	PF	DQ	Points	Min	Reb	Ass	PF	Points
Wally Osterkorn	F	6'5	215	25	13	542	45	122	37	50	90	56	125	37	40	1	140	42	9.6	2.8	3.1	10.8
Bob Lavoy	F	6'7	190	27	13	358	37	95	39	44	55	80	85	20	50	0	118	28	6.5	1.5	3.8	9.1
Dolph Schayes	C-F	6'8	220	25	13	374	64	140	46	**80**	**108**	74	136	24	40	1	208	29	10.5	1.8	3.1	16.0
Paul Seymour	G	6'2	185	25	13	**559**	59	143	41	76	94	81	34	**60**	39	1	194	43	2.6	4.6	3.0	14.9
George King	G	6'	185	25	10	286	25	62	40	38	63	60	22	21	30	1	88	29	2.2	2.1	3.0	8.8
Billy Kenville	F-G	6'2	185	23	13	374	36	74	49	44	62	71	48	25	46	1	116	29	3.7	1.9	3.5	8.9
Earl Lloyd	C-F	6'6	220	25	10	260	25	73	34	17	26	65	57	20	34	0	67	26	5.7	2.0	3.4	6.7
Billy Gabor	G	5'11	180	31	10	196	24	83	29	28	40	70	28	19	36	1	76	20	2.8	1.9	3.6	7.6
Jim Neal	C	6'11	235	23	11	100	13	35	37	5	13	38	27	2	14	0	31	9	2.5	0.2	1.3	2.8
Al Masino	G	5'10	178	25	13	96	7	20	35	7	15	47	6	7	23	0	21	7	0.5	0.5	1.8	1.6

Red Rocha - voluntarily retired

ROCHESTER ROYALS — **LES HARRISON**
defeated Fort Wayne 2-0; H82-75, 89-71
lost to Minneapolis 1-3; 88-109, 76-89, H74-73, 72-82

Use Name	Pos	Hgt	Wgt	Age	G	Min	FG	FGA	%	FT	FTA	%	Reb	Ass	PF	DQ	Points	Min	Reb	Ass	PF	Points
Cal Christensen	F	6'5	230	26	6	137	10	28	36	12	22	55	35	15	16	0	32	23	5.8	2.5	2.7	5.3
Jack Coleman	F-C	6'7	230	29	6	238	27	54	50	16	18	89	74	12	17	1	70	40	12.3	2.0	2.8	11.7
Arnie Risen	C	6'9	210	29	6	200	28	67	42	33	44	75	54	4	25	0	89	33	9.0	0.7	4.2	14.8
Jack McMahon	G	6'1	188	25	6	197	27	69	39	14	25	56	24	24	15	0	68	33	4.0	4.0	2.5	11.3
Bobby Wanzer	G	6'	185	32	6	245	30	74	41	36	44	82	35	26	18	0	96	41	5.8	4.3	3.0	16.0
Bob Davies	G-F	6'1	180	33	6	172	17	52	33	17	23	74	12	14	16	0	51	29	2.0	2.3	2.7	8.5
Odie Spears	F	6'5	205	28	6	121	8	28	29	12	14	86	13	8	17	1	28	20	2.2	1.3	2.8	4.7
Alex Hannum	F-C	6'7	225	30	6	107	12	29	41	15	24	63	22	5	28	3	39	18	3.7	0.8	4.7	6.5
Norm Swanson	F	6'6	212	23	6	23	3	7	43	2	3	67	5	0	5	0	8	4	0.8	0.0	0.8	1.3

BOSTON CELTICS — **RED AUERBACH**
defeated New York 2-0; 93-71, H79 78
lost to Syracuse 0-4; H95-96(0T), 85-98, 94-109, H76-83

Use Name	Pos	Hgt	Wgt	Age	G	Min	FG	FGA	%	FT	FTA	%	Reb	Ass	PF	DQ	Points	Min	Reb	Ass	PF	Points
Bob Harris	F	6'7	195	26	6	150	16	25	**64**	16	23	70	35	3	25	1	48	25	5.8	0.5	4.2	8.0
Bob Brannum	F	6'6	230	28	6	136	11	38	29	6	11	55	45	10	29	2	28	23	7.5	1.7	4.8	4.7
Jack Nichols	C-F	6'7	225	27	6	211	35	72	49	30	38	79	62	31	24	0	100	35	10.3	5.2	4.0	16.7
Bill Sharman	G	6'1	185	27	6	206	35	81	43	43	50	86	25	10	29	2	113	34	4.2	1.7	4.8	18.8
Bob Cousy	G	6'1	175	25	6	260	33	116	28	60	75	80	32	38	20	0	126	**43**	5.3	**6.3**	3.3	**21.0**
Ed Macauley	C	6'8	190	25	5	127	8	22	36	9	13	69	21	21	14	0	25	25	4.2	4.2	2.8	5.0
Chuck Cooper	F	6'5	215	27	6	108	8	16	50	8	11	73	31	4	21	1	24	18	5.2	0.7	3.5	4.0
Don Barksdale	F	6'6	200	30	6	106	11	36	31	8	11	73	27	7	23	2	30	18	4.5	1.2	3.8	5.0
Bob Donham	G	6'2	197	27	6	98	7	15	47	6	19	32	12	6	32	**4**	20	16	2.0	1.0	5.3	3.3
Ernie Barrett	F-G	6'3	180	24	6	63	3	20	15	2	2	100	6	4	14	0	8	11	1.0	0.7	2.3	1.3

Gene Conley-retired to play baseball

NEW YORK KNICKERBOCKERS — **JOE LAPCHICK**
lost to Boston 0-2; H71-93, 78-79
lost to Syracuse 0-2; 68-75, H99-103

Use Name	Pos	Hgt	Wgt	Age	G	Min	FG	FGA	%	FT	FTA	%	Reb	Ass	PF	DQ	Points	Min	Reb	Ass	PF	Points
Fred Schaus	F	6'5	210	28	4	119	7	25	28	14	15	93	12	8	18	2	28	30	3.0	2.0	4.5	7.0
Harry Gallatin	F-C	6'6	220	26	4	151	16	35	46	22	31	71	61	6	12	0	54	38	**15.3**	1.5	3.0	13.5
Sweetwater Clifton	C-F	6'6	220	31	4	125	8	27	30	9	17	53	39	6	15	0	25	31	9.8	1.5	3.8	6.3
Jim Baechtold	G	6'4	205	26	4	106	12	29	41	11	13	85	10	11	19	1	35	27	2.5	2.8	4.8	8.8
Carl Braun	G	6'5	187	26	4	125	18	52	35	35	40	**88**	12	9	22	2	71	31	3.0	2.3	**5.5**	17.8
Connie Simmons	C-F	6'8	225	28	4	111	10	31	32	25	36	69	33	10	17	1	45	28	8.3	2.5	4.3	11.3
Al McGuire	G	6'2	185	25	4	69	8	18	44	2	9	22	4	7	15	2	18	17	1.0	1.8	3.8	4.5
Dick McGuire	G	6'	180	27	4	68	4	16	25	3	5	60	4	5	12	0	11	17	1.0	1.3	3.0	2.8
Vince Boryla	F	6'5	212	26	3	66	8	14	57	11	13	85	2	1	12	1	27	22	0.7	0.3	4.0	9.0
Buddy Ackerman	G	6'1	183	23	4	20	1	3	33	0	0	—	4	1	7	0	2	5	1.0	0.3	1.8	0.5

Ernie Vandeweghe - voluntarily retired

FORT WAYNE PISTONS — **PAUL BIRCH**
lost to Rochester 0-2; 75-82, H71-89
lost to Minneapolis 0-2; H85-90, 73-78

Use Name	Pos	Hgt	Wgt	Age	G	Min	FG	FGA	%	FT	FTA	%	Reb	Ass	PF	DQ	Points	Min	Reb	Ass	PF	Points
George Yardley	F	6'5	190	25	4	107	16	33	48	10	12	83	24	3	10	0	42	27	6.0	0.8	2.5	10.5
Mel Hutchins	F	6'6	205	25	4	162	15	46	33	12	17	71	37	6	18	1	42	41	9.3	1.5	4.5	10.5
Larry Foust	C	6'9	240	25	4	129	11	41	27	19	25	76	38	7	21	2	41	32	9.5	1.8	5.3	10.3
Andy Phillip	G-F	6'3	195	31	4	136	13	38	34	9	12	75	12	17	9	0	35	34	3.0	4.3	2.3	8.8
Frankie Brian	G	6'1	185	30	4	106	15	36	42	11	16	69	12	10	7	0	41	27	3.0	2.5	1.8	10.3
Max Zaslofsky	G	6'2	180	28	4	98	11	36	31	13	15	87	3	6	7	0	35	25	0.8	1.5	1.8	8.8
Monk Meineke	C-F	6'7	205	23	4	87	6	23	26	7	11	64	15	6	11	1	19	22	3.8	1.5	2.8	4.8
Leo Barnhorst	F	6'4	195	29	4	60	10	19	53	3	5	60	5	6	10	0	23	15	1.3	1.5	2.5	5.8
Freddie Scolari	G	5'11	185	31	4	60	6	24	25	0	0	—	7	6	8	0	12	15	1.8	1.5	2.0	3.0
Ken Murray	F-G	6'2	195	25	3	15	6	10	60	2	2	100	0	0	6	0	14	5	0.0	0.0	2.0	4.7

Jack Molinas - declared ineligible for life, Dick Groat - military service

1953/54 N.B.A. TEAM STATISTICS

Team	G	FG	FGA	%	FT	FTA	%	Reb.	Ass.	For	Agnst.	Diff.	G	FG	FGA	%	FT	FTA	%	Reb.	Ass.	For	Agnst.	Diff.
	REGULAR SEASON									AVERAGE POINTS			PLAYOFFS									AVERAGE POINTS		
EASTERN DIVISION																								
New York	72	1934	5177	37	1820	2525	72	3830	1469	79.0	79.1	-0.1	4	92	250	37	**132**	**179**	74	200	64	79.0	87.5	-8.5
Boston	72	2232	5580	**40**	1851	2550	73	**3867**	**1773**	**87.7**	85.4	+2.3	6	167	**441**	38	188	253	74	**312**	**134**	**87.0**	89.2	-2.2
Syracuse	72	2054	5579	37	**1905**	**2650**	72	3652	1541	83.5	78.6	**+4.9**	13	335	847	40	389	566	69	591	235	81.5	80.0	+1.5
Philadelphia	72	2023	5431	37	1586	2272	70	3589	1468	78.2	80.4	-2.2												
Baltimore	72	2036	5539	37	1566	2312	68	3816	1385	78.3	85.1	-6.8												
WESTERN DIVISION																								
Minneapolis	72	2184	**5803**	38	1512	2067	73	3752	1323	81.7	78.3	+3.4	13	**371**	927	**40**	302	418	72	648	203	80.3	**74.1**	**+6.2**
Rochester	72	2010	5451	37	1722	2518	68	3494	1454	79.8	77.3	+2.5	6	162	408	40	157	217	72	278	108	80.2	83.2	-3.0
Fort Wayne	72	1952	5187	38	1689	2315	73	3785	1474	77.0	76.1	+0.9	4	109	306	36	86	115	**75**	165	67	76.0	84.8	-8.8
Milwaukee	72	1757	5087	35	1524	2202	69	3202	1298	70.0	**75.3**	-5.3												

1953/54 N.B.A. STANDINGS

Team	W	L	Pct.	GB	Record against playoff teams W	L	Pct.	Record against non-playoff teams W	L	Pct.	HOME W	L	Pct.	ROAD W	L	Pct.	NEUTRAL W	L	Pct.
EASTERN DIVISION																			
New York Knickerbockers	44	28	.611	—	25	19	.568	19	9	.679	18	8	.692	**15**	13	.536	11	7	.611
Boston Celtics	42	30	.583	2	21	23	.477	21	7	.750	16	6	.727	11	19	.367	**15**	5	.750
Syracuse Nationals	42	30	.583	2	24	20	.545	18	10	.643	**27**	5	.844	10	19	.345	5	6	.455
Philadelphia Warriors	29	43	.403	15	18	36	.333	11	7	.611	10	9	.526	6	16	.273	13	18	.419
Baltimore Bullets	16	56	.222	28	10	**44**	.185	6	**12**	.333	12	**20**	.375	0	**20**	.000	4	16	.200
WESTERN DIVISION																			
Minneapolis Lakers	46	26	.639	—	**26**	19	.578	20	7	.741	21	4	.840	13	15	.464	12	7	.632
Rochester Royals	44	28	.611	2	21	25	.457	**23**	3	.885	18	10	.643	12	15	.444	14	3	.824
Fort Wayne Pistons	40	32	.556	6	17	28	.378	**23**	4	.852	19	8	.704	11	17	.393	10	7	.588
Milwaukee Hawks	21	51	.292	25	12	**44**	.214	9	7	.563	10	14	.417	6	17	.261	5	**20**	.200

1953/54 N.B.A. INDIVIDUAL LEADERS

SCORING
(Minimum 48 Games Played)

Name	Team	G	FG	FT	Pts.	Avg.
Johnston	Phi	72	591	577	1759	24.4
Cousy	Bos	72	486	411	1383	19.2
Macauley	Bos	71	462	420	1344	18.9
Mikan	Min	72	441	424	1306	18.1
Felix	Bal	72	410	449	1269	17.6
Schayes	Syr	72	370	488	1228	17.1
Sharman	Bos	72	412	331	1155	16.0
Foust	FtW	72	376	338	1090	15.1
Braun	NY	72	354	354	1062	14.8
Wanzer	Roch	72	322	314	958	13.3

FIELD GOAL PERCENTAGE
(Minimum 210 Field Goals)

Name	Team	FG	FGA	Pct.
Macauley	Bos	462	950	.486
Sharman	Bos	412	915	.450
Johnston	Phi	591	1317	.449
Lovellette	Min	237	560	.423
Felix	Bal	410	983	.417
Foust	FtW	376	919	.409
Miller	Bal	244	600	.407
Coleman	Roch	289	714	.405
Gallatin	NY	258	639	.404
Hutchins	FtW	295	736	.401

FREE THROW PERCENTAGE
(Minimum 180 Free Throws)

Name	Team	FT	FTA	Pct.
Sharman	Bos	331	392	.844
Schayes	Syr	488	590	.827
Braun	NY	354	429	.825
Seymour	Syr	299	368	.813
Zawoluk	Phi	186	230	.809
Cousy	Bos	411	522	.787
Gallatin	NY	433	552	.784
Mikan	Min	424	546	.777
Spears	Roch	183	238	.769
Macauley	Bos	420	554	.758

PERSONAL FOULS

Name	Team	PF
Lloyd	Syr	303
Risen	Roch	284
Brannum	Bos	280
Hannum	Roch	279
Hoffman	Bal	271

GAMES DISQUALIFIED

Name	Team	Disq.
Lloyd	Syr	12
Donham	Bos	11
Hannum	Roch	11
Ratkovicz	Mil	11
Brannum	Bos	10
Hoffman	Bal	10

REBOUNDS PER GAME
(Minimum 48 Games Played)

Name	Team	G	Reb.	Avg.
Gallatin	NY	72	1098	15.3
Mikan	Min	72	1028	14.3
Foust	FtW	72	967	13.4
Felix	Bal	72	958	13.3
Schayes	Syr	72	870	12.1
Johnston	Phi	72	797	11.1
Risen	Roch	72	728	10.1
Hutchins	FtW	72	695	9.7
Hitch	Mil	72	691	9.6
Graboski	Phi	71	670	9.4

ASSISTS PER GAME
(Minimum 48 Games Played)

Name	Team	G	Ass.	Avg.
Cousy	Bos	72	518	7.2
Phillip	FtW	71	449	6.3
D. McGuire	NY	68	354	5.2
Seymour	Syr	71	364	5.1
Davies	Roch	72	323	4.5
George	Phi	71	312	4.4
Honman	Bal	72	285	4.0
Finn	Phi	68	265	3.9
Macauley	Bos	71	271	3.8
King	Syr	72	272	3.8

MINUTES PLAYED

Name	Team	Min.
Johnston	Phi	3296
Hutchins	FtW	2934
Cousy	Bos	2857
Macauley	Bos	2857
Graboski	Phi	2759

Use Name-Nickname	Team by Year	Birth Year	Hgt.	Wgt	Pos.	College	# Yr	G	Field Goals FG	Att.	%	Free Throws FT	Att.	%	Reb.	Ass.	PF	DQ	Pts	Per Game Min.	Reb	Ass	Pts
Brooms Abramovic	47Pit 48StL 48Bal 48SyrN	1919	6'3	196	F	Salem (W.Va.)	2	91	275	856	24	169	239	71		37	171		719			0.7	7.9
	48						1	3	5			2	3	67					12				4.0
Buddy Ackerman	54NY	1930	6'	183	G	Long Island U.	1	28	14	63	22	15	28	54	15	23	43	0	43	8	0.5	0.8	1.5
	54						1	4	1	3	33	0	0		4	1	7	0	2	5	1.0	0.3	0.5
Warren Ajax	48MinN	1921	6'2	170	F	Minnesota	1	3	0			1	2	50					1				0.3
Chink Alterman	49DenN	1922	6'3	185	G	Denver	1	50	67			62	100	62					196				3.9
Ernie Andres (Junie)	40IndN 42-45MS 46, PC47, 48IndN	1918	6'1	200	G-F	Indiana	4	121	396			153	163	94					945				7.8
46 played major league basball	47-48						2	9	15			8	9	89					38				4.2
Paul Anthony	47-48TC-N	1924	6'5	195	C-F	Wash. & Jeff.	2	2	0			0	0	—					0				0.0
Curly Armstrong	42-43FtWN 44-45MS	1918	5'11	170	G-F	Indiana	8	303	761	1176	30	729	901	69	89	352	464	2	2251		2.3	2.3	7.4
46, PC47, 48FtWN PC49, 50-51FtW	42-43, 46-48, 50-51						7	33	98	41	27	77	54	69	7	11	14	0	273		2.3	1.8	8.3
Don Asmonga	54Bal	1928	6'2	185	G	Alliance, Cal. St.	1	7	2	15	13	1	1	100	1	5	12	1	5	7	0.1	0.7	0.7
Chet Aubuchon	47Det	1916	5'10	137	G	Mich. State	1	30	23	91	25	19	35	54		20	46		65			0.7	2.2
Johnny Bach	49Bos HC80, 84-86GS	1925	6'2	180	F-G	Rochester, Fordham	1	34	34	119	29	51	75	68		25	24		119			0.7	3.5
Norm Baker	47Chi	1923	6'2	180	G	Brown	1	4	0	1	0	0	0	—		0	0		0			0.0	0.0
Art Bakeraitis	49DetN	1925	6'4	210	F-C	Bay City Jr.	1	13	18			24	37	65					60				4.6
Herschel Baltimore	47StL	1921	6'4	195	F	Penn State	1	58	53	263	20	32	69	46		6	47		138			0.1	2.4
	47						1	3	2	10	20	0	1	0		0	3		4			0.0	1.3
Davey Banks	HC47ChiN	1901	5'8	160		none																	
Emil Barboni	HC48 SyrN																						
Cliff Barker	PC50-51, 52Ind	1921	6'2	185	G	Kentucky	3	149	201	637	32	155	234	66	181	294	253	0	557	11	1.8	2.0	3.7
	50-51						2	9	16	50	32	10	18	56	15	23	20	0	42		5.0	2.6	4.7
Leo Barnhorst	50Chi 51-53Ind 54Bal 54FtW	1924	6'4	193	F-G	Notre Dame	5	344	1356	3689	37	520	782	66	1506	1116	1033	16	3232	35	5.4	3.2	9.4
	50-54						5	13	57	146	39	26	37	70	45	35	44	0	140	28	4.1	2.7	10.8
John Barr	47StL	1918	6'3	205	F	Penn State	1	58	124	438	28	47	79	59		54	164		295			0.9	5.1
Ed Bartels	50Den 50NY 51Was	1925	6'5	195	F	N.C. State	2	32	46	183	25	43	79	54	84	32	83	0	135		4.9	1.0	4.2
Frankie Baumholtz 47-57 played major league basball	46YouN 47Cle	1919	5'10	175	G	Ohio U.	2	71	354	856	30	197	263	75		54	93		905			1.2	12.7
Ed Beach	51Min 51TC	1929	6'3	200	F	West Virginia	1	12	8	38	21	6	9	67	25	3	14	0	22		2.1	0.3	1.8
Ralph Beard	50-51Ind 52DL	1927	5'10	176	G	Kentucky	2	126	749	2046	37	508	660	77	251	551	228	0	2006		3.8	4.4	15.9
	50-51						2	8	49	131	37	34	45	76	12	35	17	0	132		4.0	4.4	16.5
Frank Beaty	47RochN	1922	6'3	205	F	Rochester Tech	1	6	0			1	4	25					1				0.2
	47						1	2	1			0	2	0					2				1.0
Hank Beenders	47-48Prov 48Phi 49Bos	1916	6'6	185	C-F	Long Island U.	3	111	348	1313	27	239	348	69		53	304		935			0.5	8.4
	48						1	12	8	35	23	7	13	54		4	15		23			0.3	1.9
Elmer Behnke	52Mil	1929	6'7	210	C	Bradley	1	4	6	22	27	4	7	57	17	4	13	1	16	14	4.3	1.0	4.0
Irv Bemoras	54Mil 55-56MS 57StL	1930	6'3	191	F-G	Illinois	2	131	309	890	35	209	311	67	341	125	228	2	827	19	2.6	1.0	6.3
	57						1	3	3	8	38	3	3	100	6	1	4	0	9	7	2.0	0.3	3.0
Gene Bearce	49OshN 50TC	1926	5'11	175	G	Marquette, Cornell	2	61	125	16	31	101	158	64		0	6		351			0.0	5.8
	49						1	7	8			32	39	82					48				6.9
Johnny Bianco	47TolN	1922	6'4	195	C	St. John's (NY)	1	10	4			2	6	33					10				1.0
Hank Biasatti 49 played major league baseball	47Tor	1925	5'11	175	G	Assumption	1	6	2	5	40	2	4	50		0	3		6			0.0	1.0
Danny Biasone	HC48 SyrN																						
Max Biggs	playoffs only - 47ShebN	1926	6'	190	F-C	Purdue	1	4	1			0	0	—					2				0.5
Gale Bishop	49Phi	1922	6'3	195	F	Washington St.	1	56	170	523	33	127	195	65		92	137		467			1.6	8.3
	49						1	2	7	26	27	4	8	50		2	3		18			1.0	9.0
Ralph Bishop	PC49DenN	1915	6'4	190	F	Washington	1	12	10			2	3	67					22				1.8
Charlie Black	48AndN 49Ind 49-50FtW 50And	1921	6'5	200	F-C	Kansas	4	194	583	1535	28	524	873	60	31	312	551	2	1690	9	2.4	2.3	8.7
52Mil	48, 50						2	14	46	61	30	31	51	61		17	38		123		2.1		8.8
Leon Blevins	51Ind	1926	6'2	160	G	Arizona	1	3	1	4	25	0	1	0	2	1	3	0	2		0.7	0.3	0.7
Mike Bloom	48Bal 48Bos 49Min 49Chi	1915	6'6	190	F-C	Temple	2	93	209	821	25	216	303	71		70	169		634			0.8	6.8
	48-49						2	4	11	48	23	16	21	76		2	10		38			0.5	9.5
Nelson Bobb	50-53Phi	1924	6'0	173	G	Temple	4	227	361	1030	35	330	539	61	405	486	523	17	1052	21	2.4	2.1	4.6
	50-52						3	6	2	6	33	2	5	40	2	4	9	0	6	10	0.5	0.7	1.0
Ed Bogdanski	48IndN	1921	6'4	230	F	De Paul, Loyola (Chic.)	1	19	15			2	11	18					32				1.7
Bill Bolger	54Bal	1931	6'5	205	F	Georgetown	1	20	24	59	41	8	13	62	36	11	27	0	56	10	1.8	0.6	2.8
Bob Bolyard	47AndN 48-49ShebN	1920	6'0	185	G-F	Toledo	3	158	243			200	273	73					686				4.3
	49						1	2	2			5	6	83					9				4.5
Benny Borgmann	HC47-48SyrN	1898	5'8	165		none																	
Jake Bornheimer	49-50Phi	1927	6'5	205	F-C	Muhlenberg	2	81	122	414	29	98	146	67		53			342			0.7	4.2
	49-50						2	4	8	20	40	6	9	67		2			22			0.5	5.5
Slats Borrevik	48AndN 48FliN 48TC-N	1921	6'8	215	C-F	Oregon	1	50	33			22	55	40					88				1.8
	48						1	6	4			5	7	71					13				2.2
Ike Borsavage	51Phi	1924	6'8	220	C-F	Temple	1	24	26	74	35	12	18	67	24	4	34	1	64		1.0	0.2	2.7
Vince Boryla (Moose)	50-54, HC56-58NY	1927	6'5	210	F	Notre Dame, Denver	5	285	1187	3200	37	813	996	82	831	610	922	16	3187	32	3.7	2.1	11.2
	50-51, 53-54						4	33	158	375	42	120	135	89	89	65	114	4	436	33	3.2	2.0	13.2
John Bosak	47YouN	1922	6'3	185	G	none	1	10	11			2	5	40					24				2.4
Don Boven	50Wat 52-53Mil 53FtW	1925	6'4	210	F-G-C	Western Mich.	3	195	561	1653	34	641	908	71	553	393	753	31	1763	25	4.2	2.0	9.0
	53						1	8	7	28	25	9	16	56	16	2	22	0	23	14	2.0	0.3	2.9
Harry Boykoff 51Bos 51TC	48TolN 49WatN 50Wat	1922	6'10	246	C	St. John's (NY)	4	229	932	1034	40	592	788	75	220	209	426	12	2456		4.6	1.9	10.7
Joe Bradley	50Chi	1928	6'3	175	G	Oklahoma St.	1	46	36	134	27	15	38	39		36	51		87			0.8	1.9
Bob Brannum (The Tank)	49ShebN 50Sheb 52-55Bos	1925	6'6	224	F-C	Kentucky, Michigan State	6	402	1056	2581	34	850	1305	65	1944	699	1313	42	2962	24	7.0	2.1	7.4
	49-50, 52-55						6	27	75	177	38	40	70	57	155	47	116	8	190	22	7.0	2.0	7.0

Use Name-Nickname	Team by Year	Birth Year	Hgt	Wgt	Pos.	College	# Yrs	Games	Field Goals FG	Att.	%	Free Throws FT	Att.	%	Reb.	Ass.	PF	DQ	Pts	Per Game Min.	Reb	Ass	Pts
Jim Brasco	53Syr 53Mil	1931	6'1	170	G	N.Y.U.	1	30	36	142	25	38	48	79	39	33	48	3	110	12	1.3	1.1	3.7
Frankie Brian	48-49AndN 50And 51TC	1923	6'1	181	G	L.S.U.	9	561	2229	5192	34	2205	2717	81	903	1138	1127	20	6663	26	2.4	2.6	11.9
52-56FtW	48-50, 52-56						8	56	178	386	35	164	202	81	61	93	105	1	520	22	1.7	2.2	9.3
Al Brightman	47Bos HC68AnaA	1923	6'2	195	F	Morris Harvey, Long Beach State	1	58	223	870	26	121	193	63		60	115		567			1.0	9.8
Aud Brindley	47NY	1923	6'4	175	F	Dartmouth	1	12	14	49	29	6	7	86		1	16		34			0.1	2.8
	47						1	3	3	6	50	4	6	67		0	4		10			0.0	3.3
Price Brookfield	47ChiN 48AndN 49Ind 50Roch	1920	6'4	185	F-G	West Texas State, Iowa State	4	152	351	681	28	153	211	73		137	152		855			2.2	5.6
	47-48						2	17	46			12	19	63					104				6.1
Bill Brown	49OshN 49WatN		6'3		F	Maryland	1	53	54			41	65	63					149				2.8
Bob Brown	49Prov 50Den	1923	6'4	205	F	Miami (Ohio)	2	82	313	875	36	206	301	68		115	336		832			1.4	10.1
Darrell Brown	49Bal	1923	6'2	175	F	Humboldt State, College of the Pacific	1	3	2	6	33	0	2	0		0	3		4			0.0	1.3
Harold Brown	47Det	1923	6'	155	G	Evansville	1	54	95	383	25	74	117	63		39	122		264			0.7	4.9
Leon Brown (Stretch)	47Cle	1919	6'3	190	F	Wyoming	1	5	0	3	0	0	0			0	2		0			0.0	0.0
Rookie Brown	49DayN	1925	6'4	190	F-C	Howard, Va.Union	1	10	19			10	20	50					48				4.8
Stan Brown	48, 52Phi	1929	6'3	200	F	none	2	34	41	134	31	22	37	59	17	10	48	0	104	9	1.1	0.3	3.1
Walter Brown	HC51Bos	1905				none																	
Jim Browne	49Chi 50Den	1930	6'10	235	C	none	2	35	18	50	36	14	29	48		8	20		50			0.2	1.4
Phil Brownstein	HC49-50Chi	1906	5'8	175		Illinois																	
Walt Budko	49-50, PC51Bal 52Phi	1925	6'5	220	F-C	Columbia	4	253	684	2000	34	669	884	76	684	471	859	17	2037	18	5.4	1.9	8.1
	49, 52						2	6	17	40	43	19	26	73	12	9	27	0	53	19	4.0	1.5	8.8
Dick Bunt	53NY 53Bal	1930	6'	172	G	N.Y.U.	1	26	29	107	27	34	48	71	28	17	40	0	92	10	1.1	0.7	3.5
	53						1	1	0	0		0	0		0	1	0	0	0	1	0.0	1.0	0.0
Jack Burmaster	49OshN 50Sheb	1926	6'3	190	G	Illinois	2	125	377	711	33	204	310	66		179	237		958			2.9	7.7
	49-50						2	10	30	31	52	20	28	71		8	7		80			2.7	8.0
Art Burris	51-52FtW 52Mil	1924	6'5	220	F	Tennessee	2	74	70	269	26	47	75	63	205	54	100	3	187	13	2.8	0.7	2.5
Charlie Butler	46ChiN 47SyrN 47YouN	1921	6'2	165	F-G	Notre Dame	2	45	95			96	145	61					286				6.4
Tommy Byrnes	47-49NY 49Ind 50-51Bal 51TC	1923	6'3	176	F-G	Seton Hall	5	265	655	2190	30	402	620	65	72	311	392	0	1712		1.5	1.2	6.5
	47-48						2	8	22	73	30	6	18	33		2	9		50			0.3	6.3
Gerry Calabrese	51-52Syr	1925	6'1	175	G	St. John's (NY)	2	104	179	514	35	134	191	70	149	148	187	0	492	16	1.4	1.4	4.7
	52						1	6	10	24	42	4	4	100	8	4	18	0	24	9	1.3	0.7	4.0
Bill Calhoun	48RochN 49-51Roch 52Bal	1927	6'3	183	F-G	S. Francisco City	8	484	1202	3431	34	1116	1599	70	1292	1036	836	12	3520	32	4.0	2.3	7.3
53Syr 53-55Mil	48-49, 51						3	26	44	78	42	36	49	73	41	34	25	0	124		2.6	1.9	4.8
Bob Calihan	41DetN 42-45MS 46-47ChiN	1918	6'3	200	F-C	Detroit	5	165	675			460	601	69					1810				11.0
48FliN 49SyrN	41, 47, 49						3	20	88			39	60	63					215				10.8
Tom Callahan	47Prov	1921	6'1	180	G	Notre Dame, Rockhurst	1	13	6	29	21	5	12	42		4	9		17			0.3	1.3
Ernie Calverly	47-PC49Prov	1924	5'10	155	G	Rhode Island	3	165	767	2633	29	427	604	71		572	542		1961			3.5	11.9
Joe Camic	48-49TC-N 49HamN	1922	6'5	210	F-C	Duquesne	2	122	232			162	257	63					626				5.1
	48						1	6	11			9	12	75					31				5.2
Fred Campbell	PC47, 49DetN	1920	5'11	175	G	So. Illinois	2	49	110			66	92	72					286				5.8
Ken Campbell (Dutch)	49HamN	1926	6'4	198	F	Kentucky	1	14	29			12	18	67					70				5.0
Keith Carey	48FliN	1920	6'3	190	G	Alma	1	37	33			45	64	70					111				3.0
Chet Carlisle	47Chi	1916	6'5	195	F-C	California	1	51	100	373	27	56	92	61		17	136		256			0.3	5.0
	47						1	10	20	88	23	16	28	57		2	33		56			0.2	5.6
Swede Carlson	47Chi 48MinN 49-50Min	1921	6'	170	G-F	Minnesota	5	238	804	1813	33	314	509	62		324	511		1922			1.8	8.1
51Was	47-50						4	40	115	332	30	57	94	61		45	80		287			1.5	7.2
Bob Carpenter	41OshN 42-45MS 46-48OshN	1917	6'5	200	F-C	East Texas State	7	331	1117	972	33	843	1090	74	229	171	283	2	3077		4.1	1.4	9.3
PC49HamN 49OshN 50FtW 51TC	41, 46-50						6	32	93	30	37	101	112	68		2	6		287			0.5	9.0
Frank Carswell	48FliN	1919	6'	185	G	Rice	1	4	4			2	2	100					10				2.5
53 played major league baseball																							
Jake Carter	49HamN 50Den 50And	1924	6'5	195	F-C	East Texas State	2	86	156	75	31	224	320	70		24	59		536			1.0	6.2
	50						1	8	3	21	14	4	6	67		3	12		10			0.4	1.3
Al Cervi	38BufN 46-48RochN PC49SyrN	1917	5'11	170	G	none	9	389	1202	1128	36	1513	1899	79	261	648	669	16	3917	12	1.8	3.2	10.1
PC50-53Syr	46-53						8	57	152	159	31	226	281	80	43	106	102	3	530	13	2.7	3.9	9.3
HC54-57Syr HC59Phi																							
John Chaney	47-49SyrN 50TC 59Sheb	1920	6'3	190	F-C	L.S.U.	4	157	352	86	29	243	339	72		20	23		947			1.3	6.0
	47-49						3	13	31			13	25	52					75				5.8
Leroy Chollet	50-51Syr	1925	6'2	190	F	Canisius, Loyola (La.)	2	63	67	230	29	47	75	63	15	49	81	0	181		0.2	0.8	2.9
	50-51						2	15	11	49	22	10	21	48	16	13	27	1	32		2.3	0.9	2.1
Cal Christensen	51TC 52Mil 53-55Roch	1927	6'5	226	F-C	Toledo	5	291	486	1471	33	535	883	61	1587	460	831	30	1507	18	5.5	1.6	5.2
	53-55						3	11	12	39	31	18	32	56	45	16	22	0	42	16	4.1	1.5	3.8
Roy Clifford	HC47Cle	1900	5'9	165		Western Michigan																	
Bill Closs	47-48IndN 49AndN 50And	1922	6'6	199	F-C	Rice	6	349	1089	1918	32	675	991	68	605	346	471	6	2853	20	5.0	1.9	8.2
51Phi 52FtW	47-52						6	26	86	123	29	76	104	73	16	23	32	0	248	21	5.3	2.1	9.5
Paul Cloyd	48-49ShebN 50Bal 50Wat	1920	6'2	180	G-F	Wisconsin	3	123	339			232	326	71					910				7.4
	49						1	2	3			2	3	67					8				4.0
Bob Cluggish	47NY	1917	6'10	235	C	Kentucky	1	54	93	356	26	52	91	57		22	113		238			0.4	4.4
	47						1	5	4	27	15	0	2	0		0	12		8			0.0	1.6
Doyle Cofer	49DetN	1924	6'4		F	Indiana State	1	8	9			9	23	39					27				3.4
Neil Cohalan	HC47NY	1906	5'10	170		Manhattan																	
Jack Coleman	50-56Roch 56-58StL	1924	6'7	223	F-C	Louisville	9	633	2813	6763	42	1095	1575	70	5186	1749	1927	37	6721	33	9.2	2.8	10.6
	50-58						9	63	249	646	39	133	206	65	621	216	224	4	631	33	10.2	3.4	10.0
Joe Colone	49NY	1926	6'5	210	F	Bloomsburg St.	1	15	35	113	31	13	19	68		9	25		83			0.6	5.5
	49						1	4	7	30	23	3	6	50		3	13		17			0.8	4.3
Jim Cominsky	47RochN	1920	6'2	185	G	DePaul	1	5	2			0	0						4				0.8

Use Name-Nickname	Team by Year	Birth Year	Hgt	Wgt	Pos.	College	# Yr	G	Field Goals FG	Att.	%	Free Throws FT	Att.	%	Reb.	Ass.	PF	DQ	Pts	Per Game Min.	Reb	Ass	Pts
Chuck Connors	46RochN 47-48Bos	1921	6'5	190	F-C	Seton Hall	3	67	110	393	25	47	87	47		41	134		267			0.8	4.0
49, 51 played major league baseball																							
Bobby Cook	49ShebN 50Sheb	1923	5'10	155	G	Wisconsin	2	115	394	620	36	241	317	76		158	114		1029			3.1	8.9
	49-50						2	5	8	10	30	12	16	75		6	3		28			2.0	5.6
Ted Cook	48MinN 49ShebN 49HamN	1921	6'	160	G	Tennessee	2	11	1			5	6	83					7				0.6
47-50 played in N.F.L.																							
Chuck Cooper	51-54Bos 55Mil 56StL 56FtW	1926	6'5	210	F	Duquesne	6	409	933	2750	34	589	1156	51	2431	734	1196	35	2725	23	5.9	1.8	6.7
	51-54, 56						5	26	44	127	35	51	65	78	116	27	78	5	139	20	4.5	1.0	5.3
Ken Corley	47Cle		6'5	210	C	Oklahoma State	1	3	0	0		0	0			0	0		0			0.0	0.0
Ray Corley	50Syr 51Bal 51TC 53FtW	1928	6'	180	G	Georgetown,	3	86	149	479	31	96	157	61	48	152	125	0	394	8	1.8	1.8	4.6
	50					Notre Dame	1	6	6	36	17	5	11	45		10	5		17			1.7	2.8
Ed Costain	47ToIN	1923	6'	170	G	none	1	3	2			0	0						4				1.3
Bob Cotton	47ChiN						1	4	1			3	6	50					5				1.3
Jack Cotton	49DenN 50Den	1924	6'7	205	F-C	Wyoming	2	111	168	332	29	149	282	53		65	184		485			0.6	4.4
Bill Coven	47RochN	1920	6'7	220	F-C	Bald.-Wallace	1	13	10			4	8	50					24				1.8
						Toledo, N. Carolina																	
Hal Crisler	47Bos	1923	6'3	215	F	Iowa St.,	1	4	2	6	33	2	2	100		0	6		6			0.0	1.5
46-50 played in N.F.L.						San Jose St.																	
Dillard Crocker	49FtW 49DetN 49AndN 50Den	1925	6'4	205	F-G	Western Mich.	4	205	545	1307	34	559	788	71	215	205	567	18	1649	16	2.2	1.3	8.0
52Ind 52-53Mil	49						1	6	5			3	8	38					13				2.2
Chink Crossin	48-50Phi	1924	6'1	165	G	Pennsylvania	3	147	288	907	32	118	166	71		223	220		694			1.5	4.7
	48-50						3	14	38	107	36	21	25	84		17	24		97			1.2	6.9
George Crowe	49DayN	1923	6'2	210	F-C	Indiana Central	1	40	164			109	159	69					437				10.9
52-53, 55-61 played major league baseball																							
Armand Cure	47Prov	1919	6'	198	F	Rhode Island	1	12	4	15	27	2	3	67		0	5		10			0.0	0.8
47 played in A.A.F.C.																							
Fran Curran	48ToIN 49-50Roch	1925	6'	175	G	Notre Dame	3	181	288	403	40	403	523	77		149	231		979			0.8	5.4
	49-50						2	6	3	12	25	3	3	100		3	3		9			0.5	1.5
Glenn Curtis	HC47Det	1894				Indiana State																	
Walt Czarnecki	47DetN	1916	6'5	215	F	none	1	4	2			1	7	14					5				1.3
Ed Dahler	52Phi	1926	6'5	190	F	Duquesne	1	14	14	38	37	7	7	100	22	5	16	0	35	8	1.6	0.4	2.5
Howie Dallmar	47-49Phi	1922	6'4	202	F	Stanford,	3	146	519	1833	28	370	530	70		340	386		1408			2.3	9.6
	47-49					Pennsylvania	3	25	68	300	23	65	95	68		57	92		201			2.3	8.0
Pete Darcey	53Mil	1930	6'9	217	C	Oklahoma State	1	12	3	18	17	5	9	56	10	2	29	2	11	8	0.8	0.2	0.9
Jimmy Darden	49DenN PC50Den	1922	6'1	170	G	Wyoming, Denver	2	83	275	243	32	248	339	73		67	67		798			2.6	9.6
Bob Davies	46-48RochN 49-55Roch	1920	6'1	176	G-F	Seton Hall,	10	569	2720	6067	68	2330	3076	76	960	2250	1501	30	7770	31	2.9	4.9	13.7
(The Harrisburg Houdini)	46-55					F & M	10	67	311	508	34	282	371	76	78	162	124	1	904	32	2.4	4.3	13.5
Aubrey Davis	47StL 49HamN	1921	6'2	175	G-F	Oklahoma Baptist	2	67	110	381	28	76	122	62		14	136		296			0.2	4.4
	47						1	3	2	6	33	3	3	100		0	3		7			0.0	2.3
Bill Davis	47Chi	1921	6'3	215	F	Notre Dame	1	47	35	146	24	14	41	34		11	92		84			0.2	1.8
	47						1	7	2	14	14	2	5	40		0	10		6			0.0	0.9
Jim Dawson	47ShebN	1922	6'7	210	C-F	Texas A&M	1	10	8			4	7	57					20				2.0
Les Deaton	48-49ShebN 49WatN	1923	6'4	210	F-C	Simpson, Denison	2	83	106			93	157	59					305				3.7
Red Dehnert	47Prov	1924	6'3	178	F	Columbia	1	10	6	15	40	2	6	33		0	8		14			0.0	1.4
Nate DeLong	52Mil	1926	6'6	220	C	Wis. St.-River Falls	1	17	20	42	48	24	35	69	31	14	47	3	64	8	1.8	0.8	3.8
Blaine Denning	53Bal	1930	6'2	175	G	Lawrence Tech	1	1	2	5	40	1	1	100	4	0	3	0	5	9	4.0	0.0	5.0
Bill DeVenzio	48SyrN	1925	6'	185	G	Geneva,	1	6	2			7	9	78					11				1.8
						Eastern Kentucky																	
Hal Devoll	49DetN 49HamN	1923	6'6	210	F-C	Lawrence Tech,	1	27	50			25	37	68					125				4.6
						Michigan State																	
Hank DeZonie	49DayN 51TC	1922	6'6	215	C-F	Clark (GA.)	2	23	96	25	24	49	66	74	18	9	6	0	241		3.6	1.8	10.5
Dick Dickey	52Bos	1926	6'1	175	G	N. Carolina State,	1	45	40	136	29	47	69	68	81	50	79	2	127	10	1.8	1.1	2.8
	52					DePauw	1	3	1	8	13	6	7	86	3	5	7	0	8	10	1.0	1.7	2.7
Whitey Dienelt	47FtWN	1921	6'	185	G	Indiana	1	13	4			3	4	75					11				0.8
	47						1	1	0			1	2	50					1				1.0
Bob Dietz	42IndN 43-45MS	1917	6'1	164	G-F	Butler,	4	111	215			82	125	60					512				4.6
46, PC47,48IndN	47-48					North Carolina	2	8	4			0	2	0					8				1.0
Bob Dille	41HamN 47Det	1917	6'3	195	F	Valparaiso	2	60	119	583	20	77	111	67		40	92		315			0.7	5.3
Hooks Dillon	50Wash	1924	6'3	180	F	Kentucky,	1	22	10	55	18	16	22	73		5	19		36			0.2	1.6
	50					North Carolina	1	1	1	1	100	2	2	100		0	2		4			0.0	4.0
Earl Dodd	50Den	1924	6'5	175	F	NE Missouri State	1	9	6	27	22	3	5	60		6	13		15			0.7	1.7
Joe Dolhon	50-51Bal	1928	6'	175	G	N.Y.U.	2	75	158	508	31	166	227	73	15	170	221	1	482		1.4	2.3	6.4
Bob Doll	47-48StL 49DenN 49-50Bos	1919	6'5	195	F-C	Colorado	4	205	648	2211	29	400	613	65		273	509		1696			1.4	8.3
	47-48						2	10	24	130	18	22	38	58		5	29		70			0.5	7.0
Bob Donham	51-54Bos	1926	6'2	195	G-F	Ohio State	4	273	662	1379	48	494	975	51	1071	706	850	31	1818	24	3.9	2.6	6.7
	51-54						4	17	31	81	38	31	76	41	54	38	81	9	93	23	3.2	2.2	5.5
Harry Donovan	50NY	1926	6'2	180	G	Muhlenberg	1	45	90	275	33	73	106	69		38	107		253			0.8	5.6
	50						1	3	0	4	0	2	2	100		0	4		2			0.0	0.7
Bill Downey	48Prov	1923	6'6	210	C	Marquette	1	3	0	2	0	0	0			0	0		0			0.0	0.0
Ike Duffey	HC47, 50And	1906	6'1	250		none																	
Bob Duffy	47Chi 47Bos	1922	6'4	175	F	Tulane	1	17	7	32	22	5	7	71		0	17		19			0.0	1.1
Jack Dugger	47SyrN	1923	6'3	225	F-C	Ohio State	1	21	13			10	19	53					36				1.7
46 played in A.A.F.C., 47-49 played in N.F.L.																							
Andy Duncan	48RochN 49-50Roch 51Bos	1922	6'6	195	F-C	William & Mary,	4	196	494	720	41	277	464	60		101	366		1265			0.7	6.5
	48-50					Kentucky	3	17	44	16	31	25	37	68		3	10		113			0.5	6.6
Bill Durkee	48MinN	1921	6'3	205	G-F	California	1	23	15			11	24	46					41				1.8
Jack Dwan	48MinN 49Min	1921	6'4	200	F	Loyola (Chic.)	2	115	249	380	32	84	142	59		129	157		582			2.2	5.1
	48-49						2	20	34	29	24	9	18	50		9	22		77			0.9	3.9

Use Name-Nickname	Team by Year	Birth Year	Hgt	Wgt	Pos.	College	# Yr	G	Field Goals FG	Att.	%	Free Throws FT	Att.	%	Reb.	Ass.	PF	DQ	Pts	Per Game Min.	Reb	Ass	Pts
Gene Dyker	54M	1930	6'6	225	F	DePaul	1	11	6	26	23	4	8	50	16	5	21	0	16	8	1.5	0.5	1.5
Bob Dykstra	47DetN 47-48ShebN		6'9	230	C	Simpson	2	83	48			61	110	55					157				1.9
	47						1	4	3			2	5	40					8				2.0
Ed Earle	54Syr	1927	6'3	190	F	Loyola (Chic.)	1	2	1	2	50	2	4	50	2	0	0	0	4	6	1.0	0.0	2.0
Dike Eddleman	50-51TC 52Mil 52-53FtW	1922	6'3	189	F-G	Illinois	4	266	1240	3522	35	742	1175	63	913	550	954	19	3222	28	4.5	2.1	12.1
	50, 52-53						3	12	32	84	38	23	47	49	12	13	45	2	87	11	1.3	1.1	7.3
Lonnie Eggleston	49StL	1918	6'	170	G	Oklahoma State	1	2	1	4	25	2	3	67		1	3		4				2.0
Eddie Ehlers (Bulbs)	48-49Bos	1923	6'3	198	F-G	Purdue	2	99	286	1000	29	228	369	62		177	211		800			1.8	8.1
Don Eliason	47Bos	1918	6'2	210	F	Hamline	1	1	0	1	0	0	0			0	1		0				0.0
42, 46 played in N.F.L.																							
Ray Ellefson	49Min 49WatN 51NY 51Bal	1922	6'8	230	C	Oklahoma St., Colorado, West Texas St.	2	13	5	9	11	12	15	80	8	0	8	0	22		2.7	0.0	1.7
Gene Englund	42-44OshN 45MS 46-48, PC49OshN 50Bos 50TC	1917	6'5	205	F-C	Wisconsin	8	284	1010	274	38	940	1171	72		41	167		2960			0.9	10.4
	42-43, 46-50						7	31	121	5	20	98	126	66		1	6		340			0.5	11.0
Jack Eskridge	49Chi 49Ind	1924	6'5	200	C-F	Kansas	1	23	25	69	36	14	20	70		14	25		64			0.6	2.8
Bob Evans	50Ind	1925	6'2	175	G	Butler, Indiana	1	47	56	200	28	30	44	68		55	99		142			1.2	3.0
	50						1	2	1	4	25	0	0			0	3		2			0.0	1.0
Ken Exel	47OshN 47SyrN 48MinN	1920	6'1	178	G	Minnesota	2	32	19			18	41	44					56				1.8
Johnny Ezersky	48TC-N 48-49Prov 49Bos 49-50Bal 50Bos	1921	6'3	175	F-G	Rhode Island	3	140	375	1270	29	304	455	67		169	299		1054			1.3	7.5
Joe Fabel	39PitN 47Pit	1917	6'1	190	F-G	Pittsburgh	2	31	28	96	26	13	26	50		2	64		69			0.1	2.2
Phil Farbman	49Phi 49Bos	1924	6'4	185	F	C.C.N.Y., Brooklyn	1	48	50	163	31	55	81	68		36	86		155			0.8	3.2
Bill Farrow	47YouN 49DayN	1918	6'4	198	C	Ky. State	2	35	66			55	109	50					187				5.3
Bob Faught	47Cle	1921	6'5	185	F	Notre Dame	1	51	141	478	29	61	106	58		33	97		343			0.6	6.7
	47						1	3	11	32	34	3	3	100		1	10		25			0.3	8.3
Joe Fay	HC49Prov																						
Bob Feerick	46OshN 47-50Was HC62SF	1920	6'3	190	F-G	Santa Clara	5	242	1158	2979	36	818	1016	81		440			3134			2.0	13.0
	46-47, 49-50						4	14	54	122	31	35	44	80		13			143			1.6	10.2
George Feigenbaum	50Bal 53Mil	1929	6'1	185	G	Long Island U., Kentucky	2	17	18	79	23	16	33	48	7	19	29	1	52	16	1.4	1.1	3.1
Jake Fendley	52-53FtW	1929	6'	180	G	Northwestern	2	103	86	250	34	115	155	74	126	94	200	6	287	10	1.2	0.9	2.8
	52-53						2	2	1	4	25	0	0		2	1	3	0	2	3	1.0	0.5	1.0
Bill Fenley	47Bos	1922	6'3	190	F	Manhattan	1	33	31	138	23	23	45	51		16	59		85			0.5	2.7
Arnie Ferrin	49-51Min	1925	6'4	180	F-G	Utah	3	178	381	1147	33	275	401	69	271	278	509	8	1037		4.0	1.6	5.8
	49-51						3	29	71	210	34	63	92	68	33	67	113	1	205		4.7	2.3	7.1
Danny Finn	53-55Phi	1928	6'1	185	G	St. John's (NY)	3	142	382	1169	33	278	464	60	548	566	453	19	1042	24	3.9	4.0	7.3
Bob Fitzgerald	46RochN 47Tor 47NY 48SyrN 49Roch	1923	6'5	195	F-C	Fordham	4	79	85	391	19	103	141	62		47	179		273			0.7	3.5
	46-47, 49						3	12	3	10	10	9	14	64		1	4		15			0.2	1.3
Dick Fitzgerald	HC47Tor 48Prov	1921	6'2	175	F	Seton Hall	2	61	118	498	24	41	60	68		40	90		277			0.7	4.5
Jerry Fleishman	47-50, 53Phi 53NY	1922	6'2	190	G-F	N.Y.U., Long Island U.	5	262	541	1953	28	430	674	64	152	429	607	7	1512	27	4.6	1.6	5.8
	47-50, 53						5	22	37	131	28	31	49	63	5	19	45	1	105	13	2.5	0.9	4.8
Harry Foote	HC47ChiN																						
Len Ford	49DayN	1926	6'4	230	C-F	Michigan	1	6	2			2	8	25					6				1.0
48-49 played in A.A.F.C, 50-58 played in N.F.L.																							
Jack Forestieri	48IndN 48ShebB	1928			G-F	none	1	5	1			3	5	60					5				1.0
Donnie Forman	49Min	1926	6'1	175	G	N.Y.U.	1	44	68	231	29	43	67	64		74	94		179			1.7	4.1
	49						1	9	3	20	15	7	11	64		7	15		13			0.8	1.4
Jerry Fowler	52Mil	1927	6'8	236	C	Missouri	1	6	4	13	31	1	4	25	10	2	9	0	9	7	1.7	0.3	1.5
Frido Frey	47NY	1921	6'2	195	F	Long Island U., St. John's (NY)	1	23	28	97	29	32	56	57		14	37		88			1.6	3.8
	47						1	5	3	19	16	4	11	36		7	11		10			1.4	2.0
Burl Friddle	HC49Ind	1900				Franklin																	
Ted Fritsch	45, 47OshN	1920	5'10	210	G	Wis.-Stevens Pt., Wisconsin	2	19	6			4	2	50					16				0.8
42-50 played in N.F.L.	47						1	3	0			0	0						0				0.0
Jim Fritsche	54Bal 55FtW	1931	6'8	210	F-C	Hamline	2	84	132	427	31	62	84	74	249	77	131	0	326	16	3.0	0.9	3.9
Frank Fucarino	47Tor	1920	6'2	175	F	Long Island U.	1	28	53	198	27	34	60	57		7	8		140			0.3	5.0
Joe Fulks (Jumpin' Joe)	47-54Phi	1921	6'5	191	F-C	Murray State, Millsaps	8	489	2824	9338	30	2355	3075	77	1379	587	1774	41	8003	23	5.3	1.2	16.4
	47-52						6	31	192	745	26	204	261	78	28	11	120	1	588	23	5.6	0.4	19.0
Dick Furey	47-48AndN 48FliN 48TC-N	1925	6'3	195	F-G	St. Thomas	2	25	23			13	19	68					59				2.6
Billy Gabor (Bullet Bill) (The Human Projectile)	49SyrN 50-55Syr	1922	5'11	176	G	Syracuse	7	365	1195	3141	34	962	1305	74	448	626	1050	27	3352	19	1.8	2.0	9.2
	49-54						6	42	104	297	31	95	129	74	57	74	115	4	303	16	2.2	2.1	7.2
Harry Gallatin (The Horse)	50-57NY 58Det HC63-65StL HC65-66NY	1927	6'6	218	F-C	NE Missouri St.	10	682	2810	7057	40	3223	4167	77	6684	1208	2086	34	8843	32	11.9	1.8	13.0
	49-55, 58						8	64	242	620	39	284	373	76	592	100	235	4	768	31	11.2	1.6	12.0
Lowell Galloway	47IndN	1921	6'4	210	F-C	Evansville	1	31	14			18	34	53					46				1.5
	47						1	3	2			1	1	100					5				1.7
Bob Gantt	47Was	1922	6'4	205	F-C	Duke	1	23	29	89	33	13	28	46		5	45		71			0.2	3.1
Fred Gantt	48ShebN	1922	6'3	170	F-G	Richmond	1	6	4			3	3	100					11				1.8
Ben Gardner	47AndN 47FtWN	1921	6'3	190	C-F	Sam Houston St.	1	7	0			3	8	38					3				0.4
Earl Gardner	49Min	1923	6'3	200	F	DePauw, Wabash	1	50	38	101	38	13	28	46		19	50		89			0.4	1.8
	49						1	7	1	9	11	2	4	50		1	3		4			0.1	0.6
Vern Gardner	50-52Phi	1925	6'5	203	F-C	Utah, Wyoming	3	151	514	1493	34	311	416	75	349	245	445	8	1339	19	4.0	1.6	8.9
	50-52						3	7	26	71	37	19	23	83	18	5	33	1	71	26	3.6	0.7	10.1
Dutch Garfinkle	46-47RochN 47-49Bos	1918	6'	196	G	St. John's (NY)	4	120	226	754	27	71	94	69		134	159		523			1.5	4.4
	46, 48						2	9	8	23	30	9	12	75		7	15		25			2.3	2.8
Frank Gates (Needle)	47AndN 47FtWN 49AndN 50And	1921	6'	162	G	Sam Houston St.	3	160	331	402	28	169	273	62		91	147		831			1.4	5.2
	47, 49-50						3	21	32	37	24	21	38	55		9	15		85			1.3	4.0
Pop Gates	47TC-N PC49DayN	1917	6'2	205	F-G	Clark	2	81	286			186	335	56					758				9.4

Use Name-Nickname	Team by Year	Birth Year	Hgt	Wgt	Pos.	College	# Yr	G	Field Goals FG	Att.	%	Free Throws FT	Att.	%	Reb.	Ass.	PF	DQ	Pts	Per Game Min.	Reb	Ass	Pts
Bob Gauchat	47TC-N 47RochN	1921	6'	180	G	Canisius,	1	10	1			4	7	57					6				0.6
	47					Buffalo	1	2	0			0	0						0				0.0
Ed Gayda	51TC	1927	6'4	210	G-F	Washington St.	1	14	18	42	43	18	23	78	38	13	32	0	54		2.7	0.9	3.9
Johnny Gee	47SyrN	1915	6'9	225	C-F	Michigan	1	24	59			38	60	63					156				6.5
43-46 played major league baseball	47						1	3	1			1	4	25					3				1.0
Hal Gensichen	48IndN 48FliN	1921	5'11	170	G	Western Michigan	1	36	87			65	101	64					239				6.6
Bob Gerber	43ToIN 44-45MS 46IndN	1916	6'5	218	C-F	Toledo	4	93	250			135	236	56					635				6.8
47ToIN 48MinN 48TC-N	47						1	3	4			6	11	55					14				4.7
Gorham Getchell	47Pit	1920	6'6	215	C	Temple	1	16	0	8	0	5	5	100		0	5		5			0.0	0.3
47 played in A.A.F.C.																							
Jim Gibbs	47ToIN 48FliN	1919	6'5	195	C-F	Cent. Missouri St.	2	56	107			92	147	63					306				5.5
John Gibbs	48FliN	1915	6'6	190	G	Cent. Missouri St., Oklahoma St.	1	2	0			0	0						0				0.0
Dee Gibson	49TC-N 50TC	1923	5'11	175	F-G	Western Kentucky	2	108	171	245	31	240	354	68		126	113		582			1.2	5.4
	49-50						2	9	23	11	36	22	35	63		2	11		68			0.2	7.6
Ward Gibson (Hoot)	49DenN 49TC-N 50Wat	1921	6'5	210	F-C	Creighton	2	94	358	195	34	265	398	67		37	106		981			1.2	10.4
	49						1	6	9			6	9	67					24				4.0
Boody Gilbertson	49ShebN	1922	6'3	205	G-F	Washigton	1	64	87			74	115	64					248				3.9
	49						1	2	1			5	7	71					7				3.5
Frankie Gilhooley	47ToIN	1924	5'11	180	G	Notre Dame	1	8	3			1	6	17					7				0.9
	47						1	3	1			2	2	100					4				1.3
Gene Gillette	47Was	1921	6'2	205	F	St. Mary's	1	14	1	11	9	6	9	67		2	13		8			0.1	0.6
Chuck Gilmur	47-50Chi 50-51Was	1922	6'4	225	F-C	Washington	5	239	511	1571	33	370	604	61		348	896		1392			1.5	5.8
	47-49						3	18	43	182	24	25	39	64		14	80		111			0.8	6.2
George Glamack	42AG-N 43-45MS	1919	6'8	233	C-F	North Carolina	5	213	793			654	834	69					2240				10.5
(The Blind Bomber)	42, 46-48						4	24	104			83	88	77					291				12.1
46-47RochN 48IndN 49Ind 49HamN																							
Normie Glick	50Min	1927	6'7	195	F	Loyola (LA)	1	1	1	1	100	0	0			1	2		2			1.0	2.0
Ben Godfaden	47Was	1913	6'3	185	F	GW	1	2	0	2	0	2	4	50		0	3		2			0.0	1.0
Jackie Goldsmith	48ToIN	1922	5'7	150	G	Long Island U.	1	12	20			6	9	67					46				3.8
Pop Goodwin	46ShebN 47-48Prov	1920	6'2	203	F-C	none	3	81	135	503	27	80	102	77		22	130		350			0.3	4.3
Paul Gordon	50Bal	1927	6'3	185	F	Notre Dame, Baltimore City	1	4	0	6	0	3	5	60		3	3		3			0.8	0.8
Eddie Gottlieb	HC47-55Phi	1898	5'8	195		Penn. School of Pedagogy																	
Leo Gottlieb	47-48NY	1920	5'11	180	G	none	2	84	208	782	27	49	76	64		36	107		465			0.4	5.5
	47						1	4	10	39	26	4	6	67		1	6		24			0.3	6.0
Bato Govedarica	54Syr	1928	5'11	185	G	DePaul	1	23	25	79	32	25	37	68	18	24	44	1	75	11	0.8	1.0	3.3
Bud Grant	50-51Min	1927	6'3	195	F	Minnesota	2	96	95	299	32	59	100	59	115	90	142	0	249		1.9	0.9	2.6
51-52 played in N.F.L.	50-51						2	17	22	56	39	10	17	59	5	7	37	0	54		0.8	0.4	3.2
67-74 head coach in N.F.L.																							
Don Grate	48IndN 50Sheb	1924	6'2	185	F-G	Ohio State	2	13	15			5	8	63					35				2.7
45-46 played major league baseball																							
Wyndol Gray	47Bos 48ToIN 48Prov 48StL	1922	6'1	175	G-F	Bowling Green, Harvard	2	69	147	513	28	75	132	57		50	125		369				5.3
Norm Grekin	54Phi	1930	6'5	180	F	LaSalle	1	1	0	0		0	0		0	0	1	0	0	1	0.0	0.0	0.0
Al Grenert	46-47ShebN 47-48TC-N	1919	6'	190	F-G	N.Y.U.,	3	77	178			84	123	68					440				5.7
	46, 48					Yale	2	10	7			3	6	50					17				1.7
Woody Grimshaw	47Prov	1919	6'1	185	G	Brown	1	21	20	56	36	21	44	48		1	25		61				2.9
Dick Groat	53FtW 54-55MS 56RB	1930	6'1	185	G	Duke	1	26	100	272	37	109	138	79	86	69	90	7	309	26	3.3	2.7	11.9
52, 55-67 played major league baseball																							
Art Grove	49HamN	1923	6'1	185	C	Toledo	1	1	0			0	0						0				0.0
Alex Groza	50-51Ind 52DL HC71KyA	1926	6'7	218	C	Kentucky	2	130	1013	2136	47	899	1189	76	709	318	458	8	2925		10.7	2.4	22.5
HC75SD-A	50-51						2	9	80	147	54	74	92	80	42	14	35	0	234		14.0	1.6	26.0
Ace Gruenig	49DenN	1913	6'8	230	C	none	1	49	194			170	260	65					588				11.4
Nick Grunzweig	47TC-N	1918	6'5	215	F-C	Niagara	1	43	39			42	70	60					120				2.8
Coulby Gunther	47Pit 49StL	1924	6'4	190	F	St. John's (NY)	2	84	311	937	33	271	422	64		65	181		893			0.8	10.6
	49						1	1	0	1	0	0	0			0	0		0			0.0	0.0
Al Guokas	49DenN 50Den 50Phi	1925	6'5	200	F-G	St. Joseph's	2	117	239	299	31	109	179	61		95	143		587			1.7	5.0
	50						1	2	2	4	50	2	6	33		5	3		6			2.5	3.0
Matt Guokas	47Phi	1915	6'3	195	F	St. Joseph's	1	47	28	104	27	26	47	55		9	70		82			0.2	1.7
	47						1	8	1	9	11	2	5	40		0	11		4			0.0	0.5
Bob Hahn	50Chi	1925	6'10	240	C	N.Carolina St.	1	10	4	13	31	2	7	29		1	17		10			0.1	1.0
Chick Halbert	47-48Chi 48Phi 49Bos 49Prov	1919	6'9	225	C	West Texas St.	5	303	910	2900	31	851	1344	63	539	438	814	7	2671		7.9	1.4	8.8
50-51Was 51Bal	47-48, 50						3	26	106	399	27	11	184	60		10	84		323			0.4	12.4
Bruce Hale	PC47ChiN PC48IndN PC49Ind	1918	6'1	170	G-F	Santa Clara	5	231	796	1334	33	680	892	76		424	285		2272			3.0	9.8
49FtW 50-51Ind	47-48, 50-51						4	22	70	40	35	59	72	82		17	11		199			2.4	9.0
HC68OakA																							
Ralph Hamilton	48IndN 49FtW 49Ind	1921	6'1	188	G-F	Indiana	2	97	257	447	26	162	26	72		83	67		676			1.7	7.0
	48						1	2	1			2	4	50					4				2.0
Cecil Hankins	47StL 48Bos 48ShebN	1922	6'1	175	G	Oklahoma State	3	81	140	407	34	115	186	62		22	77		395			0.3	4.9
												1	2	50					5				2.5
Alex Hannum	49OshN 50-51Syr 52Bal	1923	6'7	224	F-C	Southern Cal.	9	580	1308	3341	35	827	1325	62	2013	857	1955	82	3443	20	4.5	1.7	5.9
52-54Roch55Mil 56StL	49-54, 56-57						8	50	120	274	39	86	150	57	128	52	199	13	326	19	4.0	1.2	6.5
57FtW PC57, HC58StL HC61-63Syr HC64-66SF																							
HC67-68Phi HC69OakA HC70-71SD-A HC72-74DenA																							
Don Hanrahan	53Ind	1929	6'7	200	F	Loyola (Chic.)	1	18	11	32	34	11	15	73	30	11	24	1	33	7	1.7	0.6	1.8
Rollen Hans	54-55Bal	1930	6'2	210	G	Long Island U.	2	80	221	582	38	114	205	56	176	207	192	1	556	22	2.2	2.6	7.0
John Hargis (Shotgun)	48-49AndN 50And 51FtW 51TC	1920	6'2	180	G-F	Texas	4	190	652	616	40	492	803	61		111	196		1796			1.5	9.5
	48-50						3	21	84	89	36	88	128	69		13	26		256			1.6	12.2

Use Name-Nickname	Team by Year	Birth Year	Hgt	Wgt	Pos.	College	# Yr	G	Field Goals FG	Att.	%	Free Throws FT	Att.	%	Reb.	Ass.	PF	DQ	Pts	Per Game Min.	Reb	Ass	Pts
Bob Harris	50-51FtW 51-54Bos	1927	6'7	195	F	Oklahoma State,	5	325	804	2091	38	601	957	63	1824	502	1003	23	2209	28	6.9	1.5	6.8
	50-54					Murray St. (OK)	5	21	51	123	41	56	79	71	120	32	88	5	158	29	7.1	1.5	7.5
Luther Harris	47-48ShebN 48-49TC-N	1923	6'3	195	F-G		3	154	364			299	447	67					1027				6.7
	47-49						3	17	21			16	33	48					58				3.4
Bob Harrison	50-54Min 54-55Mil 56-57StL	1927	6'2	190	G	Michigan	9	615	1782	5067	35	854	1232	69	1358	1672	2035	65	4418	27	2.5	2.7	7.2
57-58Syr	50-53, 56-58						7	59	138	358	39	62	90	69	113	118	189	8	338	22	2.4	2.0	5.7
Les Harrison	HC48RochN HC50-55Roch	1904	5'11	165		none																	
Billy Hassett	47-PC48TC-N 50TC 50Min	1921	6'1	180	G	Notre Dame,	5	237	526	458	28	519	747	69		183	204		1571			2.0	6.6
51Bal	48-50					Georgetown	3	18	32	12	25	37	57	65		4	8		101			0.6	5.6
Earl Hawkins	49TC-N	1921	6'4	225	F	Auburn	1	2	2			1	1	100					5				2.5
Marshall Hawkins	49OshN 50Ind	1924	6'3	205	F	Tennessee	2	103	255	196	28	158	221	71		51	87		666			1.3	6.5
	49-50						2	9	25			20	26	77					70				7.8
Chuck Hawley	47DetN	1915	6'3	195	G-F	none	1	12	6			5	6	83					17				1.4
Lew Hayman	HC47Tor	1908				Syracuse																	
John Hazen	49Bos	1927	6'2	172	G	Indiana State	1	6	6	17	35	6	7	86		3	10		18			0.5	3.0
Curt Henderson	47DetN	1917	5'8	150	G	Sparks	1	4	1			2	3	67					4				1.0
Don Henrikson	53, 55Bal 55Roch	1929	6'7	225	F-C	California	2	138	338	881	38	313	576	66	990	240	432	14	989	26	7.2	1.7	7.2
	53, 55						2	5	13	27	48	12	19	63	40	11	16	1	38	33	8.0	2.2	7.6
Bill Henry (Big Bill)	49-50FtW 50TC	1924	6'9	220	C	Rice	2	95	185	578	32	243	379	64		103	232		613			1.1	6.5
	50						1	3	2	17	12	5	9	56		5	14		9			1.7	3.0
Bill Herman	50Den	1924	6'3	170	G	Mt. Union	1	13	25	65	38	6	11	55		15	13		56			1.2	4.3
Paul Herman	47YouN 48FliN	1921	6'1	175	G	Tennessee	2	46	110			46	80	58					266				5.8
Kleggie Hermsen	44, 46ShebN 47Cle 47Tor	1923	6'9	233	C-F	Minnesota	8	321	984	3243	30	767	1139	65	457	366	1043	8	2735		5.8	1.3	8.5
48Bal 49Was 50Chi	46, 48-51						5	31	90	330	26	109	159	69	3	29	116	0	289		1.5	1.1	9.3
51TC 51, 53Bos 53Ind																							
Sonny Hertzberg	47-48NY 48-49Was 50-51Bos	1922	5'10	175	G	C.C.N.Y.	5	293	946	3166	30	671	847	79	260	618	619	4	2563		4.0	2.1	8.7
	47, 49, 51						3	18	57	194	29	50	60	83	2	35	56	0	164		1.0	1.9	9.1
Jack Hewson	48Bos	1924	6'6	195	F-C	Temple	1	24	22	89	25	21	30	70		1	9		65			0.0	2.7
						Bucknell																	
Mort Hill	47SyrN	1921	6'1	175	G	Calif- S. Barbara	1	3	1			0	0						2				0.7
Art Hillhouse	47-48Phi	1916	6'7	230	C	Long Island U.,	2	71	134	483	28	150	203	74		44	169		418			0.6	5.9
	47					Rutgers	1	10	24	91	26	39	46	85		8	41		87			0.8	8.7
Mel Hirsch	47Bos	1921	5'8	165	G	Brooklyn	1	13	9	45	20	1	2	50		10	18		19			0.8	1.5
Lew Hitch	52-53Min 54-55Mil 55-56Min	1929	6'8	205	F-C	Kansas State	6	414	759	2021	38	557	827	67	2183	499	685	8	2075	20	5.3	1.2	5.0
57Roch 57Phi	52-3, 55-57						5	37	45	115	39	55	94	59	167	32	64	1	145	14	4.5	0.9	3.9
Dutch Hoefer	47Tor 47-48Bos	1917	5'9	158	G	Queens	2	65	133	533	25	95	147	65		36	159		361			0.6	5.6
Paul Hoffman (The Body)	48Bal 49VR 50-51Bal 52VR	1925	6'2	205	G-F	Purdue	6	317	1139	3354	34	956	1415	68	1129	911	1138	25	3234	29	3.6	2.9	10.2
54-55Bal 55NY 55Phi	48, 53						2	13	49	169	29	48	74	65	7	18	49	1	146	41	0.5	1.4	11.2
Doug Holcomb	49Bal	1925	6'4	200	F	Wisconsin	1	3	3	12	25	9	14	64		5	5		15			1.7	5.0
Joe Holland	50-52Ind	1925	6'4	185	F	Kentucky,	3	186	434	1312	33	216	348	62	510	327	538	8	1084	13	4.2	1.8	5.8
	50-52					Berea, Iowa	3	10	38	97	39	7	19	37	12	26	39	0	83		3.0	2.6	8.3
Jim Holstein	53-55Min 56FtW	1930	6'3	180	F-G	Cincinnati	4	225	317	981	32	225	348	65	659	249	426	2	859	15	2.9	1.1	3.8
	53-55						3	32	51	129	40	36	55	65	95	28	66	0	138	16	3.0	0.9	4.3
Dick Holub	48NY	1921	6'6	205	C	Long Island U.	1	48	195	662	29	114	180	63		37	159		504			0.8	10.5
	48						1	3	9	36	25	8	14	57		0	12		26			0.0	8.7
Red Holzman	46-48RochN 49-53Roch	1920	5'10	177	G	C.C.N.Y.,	9	496	1446	2622	32	774	1178	66	344	721	478	4	3666	13	1.5	2.0	7.4
PC54, HC55Mil	46-53					Baltimore	8	56	163	145	39	84	127	66	26	36	27	0	410	10	1.2	1.3	7.3
HC56-57StL HC68-75NY																							
Jim Homer	48-49SyrN	1923	6'5	220	F-C	Alabama	2	115	391			302	488	62					1084				9.4
	48-49						2	9	24			20	32	63					68				7.6
Bob Hubbard	48TC-N 48-49Prov	1922	6'6	215	C-F	Springfield	2	82	110	334	25	80	112	71		29	73		300			0.5	3.7
Roy Hurley	46IndN 47Tor 48TC-N 48SyrN	1922	6'2	170	F-G	Murray State,	3	92	195	447	22	76	123	62		34	86		466			0.7	5.1
						Indiana																	
Paul Huston	48Chi	1925	6'3	175	F	Ohio State	1	46	51	215	24	62	89	70		27	82		164			0.6	3.6
	48						1	5	3	19	16	7	13	54		2	14		13			0.4	2.6
Harold Hutcheson	49DenN	1920	6'5	190	G-F	NW Missouri St.	1	59	106			53	78	68					265				4.5
Joe Hutton	51-52Min	1928	6'1	170	G	Hamline	2	120	112	338	33	78	113	69	187	115	199	2	302	12	1.6	1.0	2.5
	51-52						2	19	12	32	38	11	18	61	16	13	22	0	35	12	0.8	0.7	1.8
Johnny Isaacs	49DayN	1915	6'3	190	G	none	1	8	18			22	34	65					58				7.3
Fred Jacobs	47StL	1922	6'3	175	F	Denver	1	18	19	69	28	12	25	48		5	25		50			0.3	2.8
Gene James	49-51NY 51Bal	1925	6'4	180	F	Marshall	3	88	116	347	33	64	114	56	141	95	191	2	296		2.9	1.1	3.4
	49-50						2	3	1	9	11	2	4	50		2	6		4			0.7	1.3
John Janisch	47Det 48FliN 48Bos 48Prov	1920	6'3	200	F-G	Valparaiso	3	106	333	1033	29	161	242	67		51	137		827			0.7	7.8
Howie Janotta	50Bal	1924	6'3	185	F	Seton Hall	1	9	9	30	30	13	16	81		4	10		31			0.4	3.4
Tony Jaros	47Chi 48MinN 49-51Min	1920	6'3	185	F-G	Minnesota	5	300	576	1574	31	427	604	71	131	218	507	0	1579		2.1	0.9	5.3
	47-51						5	40	95	230	29	71	100	71	7	21	73	0	261		1.0	0.7	6.5
Charlie Joachim (Pappy)	47YouN 46FliN	1920	6'2	184	G-F	Mt. Union	2	48	144			129	180	72					417				8.7
Arnie Johnson	47-48RochN 49-53Roch	1920	6'5	236	F-C	Bemidji State	7	421	977	1934	42	1437	1986	72	1272	731	1336	34	3391	30	6.2	2.2	8.1
	48-53						6	40	100	201	38	144	189	76	175	82	137	3	334	28	7.6	2.8	8.6
Boag Johnson	48-49AndN 50And 50-53FtW	1921	5'11	170	G	Huntington	6	325	994	2117	33	437	616	71	498	569	703	17	2425	33	3.6	2.8	7.5
	48-52						5	22	77	87	32	35	47	74	13	22	41	3	189	35	2.6	2.4	8.6
Harold Johnson	47Det	1920	6'6	240	C	Indiana State	1	27	4	20	20	7	14	50		11	13		15			0.4	0.6
Wah Wah Jones	50, PC51, 52Ind	1926	6'4	225	F	Kentucky	3	140	521	1467	36	386	510	76	408	429	452	7	1428	23	5.1	3.1	10.2
	50, 52						2	6	23	76	30	29	34	85		22	28		75			3.7	12.5

Use Name-Nickname	Team by Year	Birth Year	Hgt	Wgt	Pos.	College	# Yr	G	Field Goals			Free Throws			Reb.	Ass.	PF	DQ	Pts	Per Game			
									FG	Att.	%	FT	Att.	%						Min.	Reb	Ass	Pts
Johnny Jorgensen	48Chi 48Bal 48MinN 49Min	1921	6'2	185	G-F	DePaul	2	89	82	123	37	52	83	63		33	70		216			0.6	2.4
	48-49						2	16	14	7	43	5	9	56		0	4		33			0.0	2.1
Noble Jorgensen	47Pit 49ShebN 50Sheb 51TC	1925	6'9	228	C	Westminster (PA),	6	331	1019	2226	36	955	1281	75	862	324	915	17	2993	20	4.3	1.2	9.0
51-53Syr	49-53					Iowa	5	21	70	148	40	66	97	68	58	23	75	3	206	22	3.6	1.2	9.8
Roger Jorgensen	47Pit	1920	6'5	200	C-F	Ohio State, Pittsburgh	1	28	14	54	26	13	19	68		1	36		41			0.0	1.5
Jimmy Joyce	48TC-N	1924	6'5	195	F	Temple	1	4	0			1	1	100					1				0.3
Doggie Julian	HC49-50Bos	1901	5'9	185		Bucknell																	
Paul Juntunen	47, 49DetN	1921	6'1	180	G-F	Wayne State	2	47	80			26	39	67					186				4.0
Whitey Kachan	49Chi49 49Min	1925	6'2	175	G	DePaul	1	52	38	142	27	36	56	64		37	81		112			0.7	2.2
	49						1	8	2	5	40	0	0			2	3		4			0.3	0.5
George Kaftan	49-50Bos 51-52NY 53Bal	1928	6'3	192	F	Holy Cross	5	212	586	1585	37	422	649	65	424	399	388	3	1594	18	3.1	1.9	7.5
(The Golden Greek)	51-52						2	21	32	84	38	29	45	64	36	24	48	3	93	18	1.7	1.1	4.4
Ralph Kaplowitz	47NY 47-48Phi	1919	6'2	170	G-F	N.Y.U.	2	105	217	815	27	158	211	75		57	222		592			0.5	5.6
	47-48						2	23	54	191	28	44	56	79		13	47		152			0.6	6.6
Tony Kappen	47Pit 47Bos	1919	5'10	175	G	none	1	59	128	537	24	128	161	80		28	78		384			0.5	6.5
Tony Kaseta	49DetN	1923	6'8	220	C	none	1	17	16			20	32	63					52				3.1
Ed Kasid	47Tor	1923	5'11	185	G	none	1	8	6	21	29	0	6	0		6	8		12			0.8	1.5
Leo Katkaveck	49-50Was	1923	6'	185	G	N.Carolina St.	2	107	185	583	32	87	127	69		136	212		457			1.3	4.3
	49-50						2	11	9	42	21	8	11	73		13	20		26			1.2	2.4
Ken Keller	47Was 47Prov	1922	6'1	180	G	St. John's (NY), Vermont	1	28	10	30	33	2	5	40		1	15		22			0.0	0.8
Jerry Kelly	47Bos 48Prov	1918	6'3	185	F	John Marshall	2	46	94	323	29	74	112	66		21	131		262			0.5	5.7
Tom Kelly	49Bos	1924	6'	172	G	N.Y.U.	1	27	73	218	33	45	73	62		38	73		191			1.4	7.1
Jack Kerris	50TC 50-53FtW 53Bal	1925	6'6	215	F-C	Loyola (Chic.)	4	271	691	1906	36	675	1020	66	1286	668	85	35	2057	26	6.3	2.5	7.6
	50-53						4	11	30	86	35	32	55	58	40	24	47	2	92	24	5.7	2.2	8.4
Jack Kiley	52-53FtW	1930	6'1	170	G	Syracuse	2	53	46	203	23	32	56	57	51	65	61	2	124	10	1.0	1.2	2.3
	52						1	1	1	3	33	0	0		0	1	0	0	2	2	0.0	1.0	2.0
Dolly King	47RochN 49DayN	1917	6'4	217	C-F	Long Island U.	2	42	55			65	104	63					175				4.2
	47						1	11	30			31	43	72					91				8.3
George King	52-56Syr 57VR 58Cin	1928	6'	180	G	Morris Harvey	6	411	1517	3971	38	1185	1847	64	1606	1958	1044	12	4219	33	3.9	4.8	10.3
	52-56, 58						6	39	142	382	37	144	212	68	149	180	113	3	428	34	3.8	4.6	11.0
LeRoy King	48RochN	1921	6'7	200	C	Monmouth (Ill) Northwestern	1	12	3			6	8	75					12				1.0
Tom King	47Det	1924	6'	165	G	Michigan	1	58	97	410	24	101	160	63		32	102		295			0.6	5.1
Willie King	47DetN		5'7		G		1	14	42			31	49	63					115				8.2
Bob Kinney	46-48FtWN 49FtW 49-50Bos	1920	6'6	215	C-F	Rice	5	233	661	1116	35	473	785	60		177	475		1795			1.5	7.7
	46-48						3	15	43			21	32	66					107				7.1
Walt Kirk (Junior)	48FtWN 49FtW 49Ind 50And	1924	6'3	178	G-F	Illinois	4	163	327	868	31	421	615	68	44	249	329	3	1075	36	4.0	2.1	6.6
50TC 52Mil	48, 50						2	6	5	7	29	2	12	17		1	8		12			0.3	2.0
Bob Kitterman	48SyrN	1925	6'	180	G-F		1	54	117			38	53	72					272				5.0
	48						1	3	5			2	2	100					12				4.0
Leo Klier (Crystal)	47, 48PCIndN 49-50FtW	1923	6'2	170	F-G	Notre Dame	4	213	671	1008	28	483	678	71		177	301		1825			1.6	8.6
	47-48, 50						3	11	32			27	36	75		3	1		91			1.5	8.3
Herm Klotz (Red)	48Bal	1921	5'7	150	G	Villanova	1	11	7	31	23	1	3	33		7	3		15			0.6	1.4
	48						1	6	2	9	22	2	3	67		1	3		6			0.2	1.0
Duane Klueh	50Den 50-51FtW	1926	6'3	175	G	Indiana State	2	113	316	962	33	292	406	72	183	173	254	5	924		3.0	1.5	8.2
	50-51						2	4	3	16	19	5	5	100	3	6	11	0	11		1.5	1.5	2.8
Lee Knorek	47-49NY 50Bal	1921	6'7	215	C	Denison,	4	131	317	1047	30	239	375	64		206	497		873			1.5	6.7
	47-49					Detroit	3	14	50	129	39	30	48	63		23	57		130			1.6	9.3
Dick Knostman	54Syr	1931	6'6	215	C	Kansas State	1	5	3	10	30	7	11	64	17	6	9	0	13	9	3.4	1.2	2.6
Milo Komenich	47-48FtWN 48-49AndN 50And	1920	6'7	223	F-C	Wyoming	4	214	664	861	28	337	612	55		124	246		1665			1.9	7.8
	47-50						4	29	75	107	24	55	97	57		14	36		207			1.8	7.1
Hal Korovin	48FliN	1925	6'5	205	C	C.C.N.Y.	1	3	4			3	5	60					11				3.7
Andy Kostecka	49Ind	1921	6'3	203	F	Georgetown	1	21	46	110	42	43	70	61		14	48		135			0.7	6.4
Harold Kottman	47Bos	1922	6'8	220	C	Culver-Stockton	1	53	59	188	31	47	101	47		17	58		165			0.3	3.1
Vic Krafft	49DayN	1919	6'3	195	G	none	1	3	3			0	1	0					6				2.0
Dan Kraus	49Bal	1923	6'	195	G	Georgetown	1	13	5	35	14	11	24	46		7	24		21			0.5	1.6
Herb Krautblatt	49Bal	1926	6'1	190	G	Rider	1	10	4	18	22	5	11	45		4	14		13			0.4	1.3
Leo Kubiak	49WatN 50Wat	1927	5'11	160	G	Bowling Green	2	124	436	794	33	300	378	79		210	250		1172			3.2	9.5
Frank Kudelka (Apples)	50Chi 51Was 51Bos 52-53Bal	1925	6'2	193	G-F	St. Mary's	4	228	614	1853	33	414	585	71	521	490	738	21	1642		3.2	2.1	7.2
53Phi	50-51						2	3	4	14	29	1	5	20	5	6	7	0	9		5.0	2.0	3.0
Ray Kuka	48-PC49NY	1922	6'3	200	F	Notre Dame,	2	52	99	309	32	55	93	59		38	133		253			0.7	4.9
	48					Montana State	1	3	3	10	30	2	2	100		0	12		8			0.0	2.7
Johnny Kundla	HC48MinN HC49-59Min	1916	6'2	180		Minnesota																	
Gene Lalley	49DenN	1922	5'9	160	G	Crieghton	1	60	77			27	70	39					181				3.0
Joe Lapchick	HC48-56NY	1900	6'5	185		none																	
Dave Latter	47, 49DetN	1922	6'6	210	C-F	none	2	54	149			113	198	57					411				7.6
Walt Lautenbach	48-49OshN 50Sheb	1922	6'2	190	G-F	Wisconsin	3	176	363	332	30	100	160	63		73	122		826			1.3	4.7
	48-49						2	11	26			11	21	52					63				5.7
Tony Lavelli	50Bos 51NY	1926	6'3	185	F	Yale	2	86	194	529	37	203	238	85	59	63	163	1	591		2.0	0.7	6.9
	51						1	2	1	5	20	2	2	100	1	1	2	0	4		0.5	0.5	2.0

		Birth					#		Field Goals			Free Throws								Per Game			
Use Name-Nickname	Team by Year	Year	Hgt	Wgt	Pos.	College	Yr	G	FG	Att.	%	FT	Att.	%	Reb.	Ass.	PF	DQ	Pts	Min.	Reb	Ass	Pts
Bob Lavoy	51-53Ind 54Syr	1926	6'7	186	F-C	Western Ky	4	264	821	2139	38	514	727	71	1634	391	889	27	2156	27	6.2	1.5	8.2
	51-54						4	20	50	145	34	55	73	75	121	30	74	2	155	28	6.1	1.5	7.8
Ed Leede	50-51Bos	1927	6'3	185	F-G	Dartmouth	2	121	293	877	33	363	505	71	118	225	311	3	949		2.1	1.9	7.8
	51						1	2	1	7	14	1	1	100	0	2	3	0	3		0.0	1.0	1.5
Hank Lefkowitz	47Cle	1923	6'2	190	F	Case Reserve	1	24	22	114	19	7	13	54		4	35		51			0.2	2.1
	47						1	3	4	18	22	1	1	100		0	4		9			0.0	3.0
Fuzzy Levane	46-48RochN 49Roch 50Syr	1920	6'2	190	F-G	St. John's (NY)	6	218	529	635	31	171	277	62		204	158		1229			2.0	5.6
PC53, HC54Mil	46-48, 50						4	32	70	37	35	27	37	73		13	11		167			1.4	5.2
HC59-60NY HC62StL																							
Ed Lewinski (Gooch)	46ChiN 47AndN 47-49TC-N	1920	6'4	210	F	Chicago	4	102	204			83	144	55					491				4.8
	48						1	6	13			1	3	33					27				4.5
Fred Lewis	47-48ShebN 48IndN 49Ind	1921	6'2	195	F-G	Eastern Ky,	4	183	717	1018	31	389	520	75		132	207		1823			1.4	10.0
49-50Bal 50Phi	47-49					Long Island U.	3	12	56	35	43	21	33	64		3	13		133			1.0	11.1
Grady Lewis	47Det 48StL 48Bal	1917	6'7	215	F-C	SW Okla. State,	3	139	273	1082	25	204	343	59		132	421		750			0.9	5.4
PC49, HC50StL	48					Oklahoma	1	11	23	109	21	22	29	76		9	49		68			0.8	6.2
Sam Lieberman	47SyrN		6'8		C	Lawrence Tech	1	2	0			1	2	50					1				0.5
Ron Livingstone	50Bal 50-51Phi	1925	6'10	220	C	Wyoming,	2	117	267	932	29	198	286	69	297	217	480	10	732		4.7	1.9	6.3
	50-51					St. Mary's	2	4	8	19	42	4	7	57	2	5	13	0	20		1.0	1.3	5.0
Bob Lochmueller	53Syr	1927	6'5	185	F	Louisville	1	62	79	245	32	74	122	61	162	47	143	1	232	13	2.6	0.8	3.7
	53						1	2	2	10	20	1	4	25	5	2	12	2	5	11	2.5	1.0	2.5
Ken Loeffler	HC47-48StL HC49Prov	1902	5'11	205		Penn State																	
Don Lofgran	51Syr 51-52Ind 53Phi 54Mil	1928	6'6	200	F-C	San Fransisco	4	209	436	1324	33	393	568	69	817	216	491	13	1265	23	3.9	1.0	6.1
	51-52						2	3	2	9	22	1	1	100	1	0	6	0	5	5	0.3	0.0	1.7
Johnny Logan	47-PC50StL PC51TC	1921	6'2	175	G	Indiana	5	257	1125	3609	31	946	1234	77		783	740		3196			3.0	12.4
	47-49						3	10	34	123	28	39	52	75		19	36		107			1.9	10.7
Del Loranger	47DetN 48IndN PC49DetN	1920	6'3	178	F-G	Western Mich.	3	44	114			69	106	65					297				6.8
Joe Lord	48RochN	1924	6'1	175	G	Villanova	1	4	3			0	1	0					6				1.5
Bobby Lowther	49WatN 49TC-N	1923	6'5	190	F-C	Louisianna State	1	24	19			7	11	64					45				1.9
	49						1	4	1			2	2	100					4				1.0
Carl Loyd	49HamN	1925	6'0	172	G	Notre Dame	1	29	43			11	23	48					97				3.3
Al Lucas	45-48ShebB 49Bos	1922	6'3	195	F-G	Fordham	5	160	318			131	154	62					767				4.8
	45-47						3	16	31			15	9	78					77				4.8
Jim Luisi	54Bal	1928	6'2	180	G	St. Francis (NY)	1	31	31	95	33	27	41	66	25	35	45	0	89	11	0.8	1.1	2.9
Al Lujack	47Was	1921	6'3	220	F	Georgetown	1	5	1	8	13	2	5	40		0	6		4			0.0	0.8
Ray Lumpp	49Ind 49-53NY 53Bal	1923	6'1	180	G	N.Y.U.	5	300	895	2444	37	672	876	77	391	654	793	11	2462	23	2.2	2.2	8.2
	49-53						5	38	75	244	31	79	96	82	47	57	119	4	229	19	1.7	1.5	6.0
Ed Macauley (Easy Ed)	50StL 51-56Bos	1928	6'8	192	C-F	St. Louis	10	641	3742	8589	44	3750	4929	76	4325	2079	1667	12	11234	36	7.5	3.2	17.5
57-58, PC59, HC60StL	51-58						8	48	218	499	44	212	291	73	321	138	141	6	648	31	6.7	2.9	13.5
Johnny Macknowski	49SyrN 50-51Syr	1923	6'1	185	G-F	Seton Hall	3	179	431	898	32	381	526	72	110	134	262	3	1243		1.9	1.1	6.9
(Whitey)	49-51						3	19	48	113	40	47	63	75	7	26	23	0	143		3.5	1.9	7.5
Jack Maddox	47-48OshN 49HamN 49Ind	1921	6'3	190	F	W. Texas State	3	121	287			110	158	70					684				5.7
	47-48						2	11	7			2	3	67					16				1.5
Norm Mager	51Bal	1926	6'5	185	F	C.C.N.Y.,	1	22	32	126	25	37	48	77	44	22	56	3	101		2.0	1.0	4.6
						St. John's (NY)																	
John Mahnken	46RochN 47-48Was 49Bal 49Ind	1922	6'8	226	C	Georgetown	8	430	1016	3557	27	479	741	65	533	539	1143	9	2511		2.9	1.3	5.8
49-50FtW 50TC	46-47, 51-53						5	25	46	128	21	32	39	82	40	19	63	2	124		3.3	1.1	5.0
50-51Bos 51Ind 52-53Bos																							
Mo Mahoney	53Bos 54Bal	1927	6'2	205	F	Brown	2	8	4	12	33	4	5	80	9	2	7	0	12	6	1.1	0.3	1.5
	53						1	4	3	14	21	3	5	60	7	2	14	0	9	11	1.8	0.5	2.3
Lionel Malamed	49Ind 49Roch	1924	5'9	150	G	C.C.N.Y.	1	44	97	290	33	64	77	83		61	53		258			1.4	5.9
John Mandic	48RochN 49Ind 50Was 50Bal	1919	6'4	205	F-C	Oregon State	3	114	151	377	32	110	170	65		88	206		412		1.1	2.5	3.6
	48						1	5	2			2	4	50					6				1.2
Frank Mangiapane	47NY	1925	5'10	195	G	N.Y.U.	1	6	2	13	15	1	3	33		0	6		5			0.0	0.8
Press Maravich	46YouN 47Pit	1920	6'0	185	G	Davis & Elkins	2	83	174	375	27	64	109	59		6	102		412			0.1	5.0
Saul Mariaschin	48Bos	1924	5'11	165	G	Harvard,	1	43	125	463	27	83	117	71		60	121		333			1.4	7.7
	48					Syracuse	1	3	10	42	24	9	14	64		1	12		29			0.3	9.7
Dino Martin	47-48Prov	1920	5'8	160	G	Georgetown	2	92	357	1215	29	120	188	64		73	115		834			0.8	9.1
Don Martin	47-49StL 49Bal	1920	6'7	210	C-F	Cent. Missouri St.	3	137	176	624	28	58	111	52		36	251		410			0.3	3.0
	47-48						2	8	9	56	16	3	3	100		2	16		21			0.3	2.6
Al Masino	53Mil 54Syr	1928	5'10	176	G	Canisius	2	99	160	462	35	158	253	62	205	182	296	12	478	20	2.1	1.8	4.8
	54						1	13	7	20	35	7	15	47	6	7	23	0	21	7	0.5	0.5	1.6
Ariel Maughan (Ace)	47Det 48Prov 48-50StL 51Was	1923	6'4	190	F	Utah State	5	259	744	2659	28	558	777	72		311	668		2046			1.2	7.9
	48-49						2	9	32	128	25	18	26	69		4	25		82			0.4	9.1
Matt Mazza	50Sheb	1923	6'3	210	F	Michigan State,	1	26	33	110	30	32	45	71		27	34		98			1.0	3.8
						Canisius																	
Bill McCahan	47SyrN	1921	5'11	200	G	Duke	1	27	35			24	46	52					94				3.5
46-49 played major league baseball																							
Mike McCarron	47Tor 50Bal 50StL	1922	5'11	180	G	Seton Hall	2	68	239	853	28	180	293	61		62	189		658			0.9	9.7
Howie McCarty	46CleN 47DetN 47Det	1919	6'2	190	F-G-C	Wayne State	3	48	96			43	85	35					235				4.9
Jack McCloskey	53Phi HC73-74Port	1926	6'2	192	G	Pennsylvania	1	1	3	9	33	0	0		3	1	2	0	6	16	3.0	1.0	6.0
John McConathy	52Mil	1930	6'5	195	F	Northwest St.-La.	1	11	4	29	14	6	14	43	20	8	7	0	14	10	1.8	0.7	1.3
Bucky McConnell	53Mil	1928	5'10	170	G	John Marshall	1	14	27	71	38	14	29	48	34	41	39	0	68	21	2.4	2.9	4.9
Mel McGaha	49NY	1926	6'1	190	G	Arkansas	1	51	62	195	32	52	88	59		51	104		176			1.0	3.5
62, 64-65 managed in	49						1	2	0	3	0	1	2	50		2	6		1			1.0	0.5
major league baseball																							
Al McGuire	52-54NY 55Bal	1928	6'2	183	G-F	St. John's (NY)	4	191	251	663	38	255	463	55	418	363	501	18	757	16	2.2	1.9	4.0
	52-54						3	24	31	83	37	22	43	51	28	30	60	3	84	14	1.2	1.3	3.5

Use Name-Nickname	Team by Year	Birth Year	Hgt	Wgt	Pos.	College	# Yr	G	Field Goals			Free Throws			Reb.	Ass.	PF	DQ	Pts	Per Game			
									FG	Att.	%	FT	Att.	%						Min.	Reb	Ass	Pts
Bones McKinney	47-50, PC51Was 51-52Bos	1919	6'6	187	F-C	North Carolina,	6	318	1145	3844	30	704	990	71	373	503	1023	10	2994		3.5	1.6	9.4
HC70-71CarA	47, 49-52					N. Carolina St.	5	23	82	268	31	68	96	71	16	26	82	0	232		3.2	1.1	10.1
George McLeod	53Bal	1931	6'5	200	F	T.C.U.	1	10	2	16	13	8	15	53	21	4	16	0	12	9	2.1	0.4	1.2
Dave McMillan	HC51TC	1897				Idaho, Oberlin																	
Mal McMullen	50-51Ind	1927	6'5	210	F-C	Kentucky,	2	109	201	657	31	125	223	56	128	120	321	2	527		2.5	1.1	4.8
	50					Xavier (Ohio)	1	6	4	21	19	6	9	67		9	19		14			1.5	2.3
Chet McNabb	48Bal	1921	6'2	200	F	W. Texas St., Arizona State	1	2	0	1	0	0	0	—		0	1		0			0.0	0.0
Joe McNamee	51-52Roch 52Bal	1926	6'6	210	F-C-G	San Fransisco	2	118	116	389	30	57	92	62	238	58	196	6	289	12	2.0	0.5	2.4
	51						1	13	12	41	29	9	12	75	35	9	26	0	33		2.7	0.7	2.5
George Mearns	47-48Prov	1922	6'3	175	F	Rhode Island	2	81	151	593	25	141	206	68		45	202		443			0.6	5.5
Chick Meehan	47-48SyrN	1917	6'1	195	F-G	Syracuse	2	51	99			53	79	67					251				4.9
Bernie Mehen	47YouN 47-48TolN	1918	6'4	190	F-C	Tennessee	2	95	268			115	170	68					651				6.9
	47						1	5	11			11	14	79					33				6.6
Dick Mehen	48TolN 49WatN 50Wat 51Bal	1922	6'6	195	F-C-G	Tennessee	5	312	1298	2182	38	701	1000	70	505	550	561	14	3297	35	3.9	2.8	10.6
51Bos 51FtW 52Mil	51						1	3	12	29	41	2	4	50	14	3	9	0	26		4.7	1.0	8.7
Carl Meinhold	48Bal 49Chi 49Prov	1926	6'2	185	G-F	Long Island U.	2	98	209	662	32	98	156	63		63	124		516			0.6	5.3
	48						1	11	17	67	25	6	13	46		0	6		40			0.0	3.6
Frank Mekules	47DetN	1919	6'4	218	F	Michigan St.	1	3	3			0	1	0					6				2.0
Bud Mendenhall	49AndN	1925	5'10	155	G	Indiana, Rice	1	60	64			40	70	57					168				2.8
	49						1	7	3			3	7	43					9				1.3
Murray Mendenhall (Ike)	HC47-49AndN HC50-51FtW	1899				DePauw, Butler																	
Ken Menke	48FtWN 50Wat	1922	6'	168	G	Illinois	2	50	45			48	65	74					138				2.8
	48						1	1	1			0	0						2				2.0
Tom Meyer	47DetN		6'4	214	F-C	Detroit	1	24	77			34	53	64					188				7.8
Stan Miasek	47Det 48-50Chi 52-53Bal	1924	6'5	212	C-F	none	6	365	1375	4166	33	1101	1752	63	999	518	1358	25	3851	29	7.6	1.4	10.6
53Mil	48-50						3	8	36	96	38	25	42	60		4	38		97			0.5	12.1
Red Mihalik	47Pit 47YouN	1916	6'	180	G	none	1	38	44			12	29	41					100				2.6
Ed Mikan	49-50Chi 50-51Roch 51Was	1925	6'8	230	C-F	DePaul	6	323	799	2493	32	565	747	76	1093	296	919	13	2163	20	5.5	0.9	6.7
51-53Phi 52Ind 54Bos	49-53						5	11	31	120	26	29	35	83	48	8	36	0	91	21	6.9	0.7	8.3
George Mikan	47ChiN 48MinN 49-54Min	1924	6'10	248	C	DePaul	9	520	4097	8783	40	3570	4597	78	4167	1245	1862	50	11764	34	13.4	2.8	22.6
55VR 56, HC58Min	47-54, 56						9	91	723	1394	40	695	897	77	655	155	306	10	2141	37	13.6	2.2	23.5
Al Miksis	50Wat	1928	6'7	210	C	Eastern Illinois, Western Illinois St.	1	8	5	21	24	17	21	81		4	22		27			0.5	3.4
Nat Militzok	47NY 47Tor	1923	6'3	195	F	C.C.N.Y., Hofstra, Cornell	1	56	90	343	26	64	112	57		42	120		244			0.8	4.4
Ed Milkovich	47Pit	1916	5'9	170	G	Duquesne	1	57	99	376	26	83	127	65		37	150		281			0.6	4.9
Bill Miller	49Chi 49StL	1924	6'3	190	F	North Carolina	1	28	21	72	29	11	20	55		20	32		53			0.7	1.9
	49						1	1	0	0		0	2	0		0	0		0			0.0	0.0
Eddie Miller	53Mil 53-54Bal 55ST	1931	6'8	225	C-F	Syracuse	2	142	517	1381	37	418	604	69	1206	210	444	12	1452	26	8.5	1.5	10.2
	53						1	2	13	34	38	7	16	44	36	5	9	0	33	47	18.0	2.5	16.5
Harry Miller	47Tor	1923	6'4	230	C-F	North Carolina, Seton Hall	1	53	58	260	22	36	82	44		42	119		152			0.8	2.9
Ed Mills	49OshN	1922	6'8	225	C	Wisconsin	1	8	8			7	12	58					23				2.9
Jack Mills	47YouN	1918	6'4	210	F-C	Mt. Union	1	8	5			8	10	80					18				2.3
Dave Minor	52-53Bal 53Mil	1922	6'2	185	G-F	Toledo, U.C.L.A.	2	116	339	942	36	199	264	75	527	288	372	13	877	27	4.5	2.5	7.6
Wat Misaka	48NY	1923	5'7	150	G	Utah	1	3	3	13	23	1	3	33		0	7		7			0.0	2.3
Guy Mitchell	49DenN	1924	6'3	190	F-G	Pittsburgh St., Denver	1	57	67			37	75	49					171				3.0
Murray Mitchell	50And	1923	6'6		C	S. Houston St.	1	2	1	3	33	0	0			2	1		2			1.8	1.0
Bill Mlkvy (The Owl Without a Vowel)	53Phi	1931	6'4	190	F	Temple	1	31	75	246	30	31	48	65	101	62	54	1	181	20	3.3	2.0	5.8
Ed Moeller	47YouN 47TC-N 47YouN	1919	6'	175	G	Ohio State	1	22	13			13	14	93					39				1.8
Leo Mogus	46YouN 47Cle 47Tor 49Bal	1921	6'4	205	F-C	Youngstown	5	247	707	1944	33	749	1052	71	102	319	575	0	2163		1.8	1.4	8.8
49FtW 49Ind 50-51Phi	50-51						2	3	3	18	17	4	7	57	0	7	10	0	10		0.0	2.3	3.3
John Moiseichik	47SyrN	1920	5'11	180	G	Cortland St., Hobart	1	9	6			4	9	44					16				1.8
Jack Molinas	54FtW	1932	6'6	210	F	Columbia	1	29	108	278	39	134	176	76	209	47	74	2	350	34	7.2	1.6	12.1
Jim Mooney	53Bal 53Phi	1930	6'5	215	F	Villanova	1	18	54	148	36	27	40	68	70	35	50	1	135	29	3.9	1.9	7.5
Dale Morey	47AndN	1916	6'1	180	G	Louisiana State	1	24	32			13	18	72					77				3.2
Elmore Morganthaler	47Prov 49Phi	1922	7'1	230	C	Boston Coll., New Mexico Mines	2	31	19	52	37	19	30	63		10	21		57			0.3	1.8
Bob Morris	HC47Prov	1902	6'	170		East Stroudsburg State																	
Max Morris	47Chi 48-49ShebN 50Sheb	1925	6'2	195	F-C	Illinois,	4	175	498	694	36	510	797	64		194	172		1506			3.1	8.6
46-48 played in A.A.F.C.	47, 49-50					Northwestern	3	15	26	40	35	19	35	54		14	8		71			4.7	4.7
Pete Mount	47ShebN	1925	6'4	185	F	none	1	10	6			3	5	60					15				1.5
Chuck Mrazovich	51Ind	1924	6'5	185	F	Eastern Ky.	1	23	24	73	33	28	46	61	33	12	48	1	76		1.4	0.5	3.3
Joe Mullaney HC72-73KyA HC74UtahA HC75MemA	50Bos HC70-71LA	1925	6'	165	G	Holy Cross	1	37	9	70	13	12	15	80		52	30		30			1.4	0.8
Bob Mullens	47NY 47Tor	1922	6'1	175	G	Fordham	1	54	125	445	28	64	102	63		54	94		314			1.0	5.8
Bob Mulvihill	49OshN	1924	6'1	185	G	Fordham,	1	34	8			14	24	58					30				0.9
	49					Rochester	1	3	0			0	0						0				0.0
George Munroe	47StL 48Bos	1922	5'11	180	G	Dartmouth,	2	80	191	714	27	103	159	65		20	111		485			0.3	6.1
	47-48					Columbia	2	6	16	36	44	6	9	67		1	10		38			0.2	6.3
Dick Murphy	47NY 47Bos	1921	6'1	180	G	Manhattan, John Marshall	1	31	15	75	20	4	9	44		8	15		34			0.3	1.1
John Murphy	47NY 47Phi	1924	6'2	185	F	none	1	20	11	40	28	10	15	67		0	8					0.0	1.6

Use Name-Nicknam	Team by Year	Birth Year	Hgt	Wgt	Pos	College	# Yr	G	Field Goals FG	Att.	%	Free Throws FT	Att.	%	Reb.	Ass.	PF	DQ	Pts	Per Game Min.	Reb	Ass	Pts
Ken Murray	51Bal 51FtW 52-53MS 54FtW	1928	6'2	195	G-F	St. Bonaventure	3	181	541	1617	33	389	512	76	599	482	350	8	1471	18	3.3	2.7	8.1
55Bal 55Phi	51, 54						2	6	17	58	29	6	7	86	14	10	13	0	40	5	2.3	1.7	6.7
Angelo Musi (Tony)	47-49Phi	1918	5'9	145	G	Temple	3	161	558	1921	29	243	315	77		117	284		1359			0.7	8.4
	48-49						3	25	77	306	25	44	59	75		16	58		198			0.6	7.9
Bob Naber	53Ind	1929	6'3	185	F	Louisville	1	4	0	4	0	1	2	50	5	1	6	0	1	3	1.3	0.3	0.3
Jerry Nagel	50FtW	1928	6'	190	G	Loyola (Chic.)	1.	4	6	28	21	1	4	25		18	11		13			1.3	0.9
Fritz Nagy	48IndN 49Ind	1924	6'2	185	G-F	Akron, N. Carolina	2	89	136	**271**	**35**	107	160	67		**68**	**84**		379			**1.4**	4.3
	48						1	4	1			6	8	75					8				2.0
Paul Napolitano	48MinN 49Ind	1923	6'2	185	F-G	San Francisco	2	53	72			11	21	52					155				2.9
	48						1	9	8			4	5	80					20				2.2
Jim Neal	54Syr 55Bal	1930	6'11	235	C	Wofford	2	80	129	428	30	93	154	60	304	33	166	0	351	14	2.8	0.4	4.4
	54						1	11	13	35	37	5	13	38	27	2	14	0	31	9	2.5	0.2	2.8
Al Negratti	46RochN 47Was 47RochN	1921	6'4	220	F-C	Seton Hall	2	60	47	**69**	**19**	29	**32**	**59**		**5**	**20**		123			**0.5**	2.1
	46-47						2	18	12			11	21	52					35				1.9
George Nelmark	42ToIN 43-46MA 47-48SyrN	1917	6'1	183	G	Cal.-Santa Barbara,	3	110	223			134	**177**	**58**					580				5.3
						NE Missouri St.	2	7	14			5	8	63					33				4.7
Jack Nichols	49-50Was 50-51TC 52MS	1926	6'7	222	C-F	Washington,	9	504	2013	5462	37	1219	1620	75	**2782**	964	**##**	**33**	5245	**27**	**6.9**	1.9	10.4
53-54Mil	49-50, 54-58					Southern Cal.	7	51	200	514	39	119	161	74	**209**	117	164	**2**	519	**22**	**5.6**	2.3	10.2
54-58Bos																							
Richie Niemiera	47-48FtWN 49-50FtW 50And	1921	6'1	165	G-F	Notre Dame	4	187	371	**681**	**33**	350	462	76		212	192		1092			**1.8**	5.8
	47-48, 50						3	18	32	**27**	41	8	24	75		8	10		82			**0.4**	4.6
Paul Noel	48-50NY 51-52Roch	1924	6'4	185	F	Kentucky	5	201	259	889	29	143	225	64	**86**	140	324	1	661		**1.4**	0.7	3.3
	48-51						4	20	13	44	30	10	16	63		4	35	**0**	36			0.2	1.8
Jim Nolan	50Phi	1927	6'8	210	C	Georgia Tech	1	5	4	21	19	0	0			4	14		8			0.8	1.6
Paul Nolen	54Bal	1929	6'10	215	C	Texas Tech	1	1	0	1	0	0	0		1	0	1	0	0	2	1.0	0.0	0.0
Irv Noren	47ChiN	1924	6'	180	F	Pasadena City	1	3	0			1	2	50					1				0.3
50-60 played major league baseball																							
Johnny Norlander	47-51Was	1921	6'3	180	F	Hamline	5	217	659	2007	33	493	728	68		218	433		1811			1.0	8.3
	47, 49						2	17	39	123	32	33	43	77		9	38		111			0.5	6.5
George Nostrand	47Tor 47Cle 48-49Prov	1924	6'8	197	C-F	Wyoming,	4	221	678	2222	31	448	832	54		184	575		1804			0.8	8.2
49-50Bos 50TC	47					High Point	1	3	14	40	35	5	7	71		3	10		33			1.0	11.0
50Chi																							
Stan Noszka	46YouN 47Pit 48-49Bos	1920	6'1	185	G	Duquesne	4	112	256	**913**	**28**	149	**222**	**67**		**68**	271		661			**0.6**	5.9
	48						1	3	10	30	33	5	8	63		2	11		25			0.7	8.3
Bob Nugent	47SyrN	1915	5'11	170	G	none	1	31	39			31	45	69					109				3.5
	47						1	4	6			5	6	83					17				4.3
John O'Boyle	53Mil	1928	6'2	186	G	Colorado State	1	5	8	26	31	5	7	71	10	5	20	1	21	19	2.0	1.0	4.2
Bob O'Brien	48-49Phi 49StL	1927	6'4	190	F	Pepperdine,	2	46	27	131	21	27	58	47		10	72		81			0.2	1.8
	48					Kansas	1	9	9	38	24	10	15	67		3	13		28			0.3	3.1
Ralph O'Brien	52-53Ind 53Bal	1928	5'9	160	G	Butler	2	119	324	899	36	200	241	83	192	180	189	0	848	20	1.6	1.5	7.1
	52-53						2	3	5	13	38	7	7	100	4	3	3	0	17	22	1.3	1.0	5.7
Dermie O'Connell	49-50Bos 50StL	1928	6'	174	G	Holy Cross	2	82	198	740	27	77	145	53		156	131		473			1.9	5.8
Connie O'Connor	47DetN	1924	6'1		F	South Dakota	1	36	82			32	78	41					196				5.4
Andy O'Donnell	50Bal	1925	6'1	180	G	Loyola (Balt.)	1	25	38	108	35	14	18	78		17	32		90			0.7	3.6
Buddy O'Grady	46RochN 47Was 48-49StL	1920	5'11	160	G	Georgetown	4	147	207	**781**	**27**	123	**178**	**69**		**97**	**178**		537			0.7	3.7
49Prov	47-48						2	13	13	53	25	8	8	100		0	10		34			0.0	2.6
Dick O'Keefe	48-51Was	1923	6'2	185	G-F	Santa Clara	4	173															
	49-50						2	13															
Tommy O'Keefe	51Bal 51Was	1926	6'2	185	G	Georgetown,	1	6	10	28	36	3	4	75	7	10	5	0	23		1.2	1.7	3.3
						Notre Dame																	
Hank O'Keeffe	49SyrN	1923	6'3	195	F	Canisius	1	56	94			52	90	58					240				4.3
	49						1	5	2			2	2	100					6				1.2
Johnny Oldham	50-51FtW	1923	6'3	175	G	Western Kentucky	2	127	326	1023	32	274	437	63	**242**	226	434	**15**	926		**3.6**	1.8	7.3
	50-51						2	7	18	43	42	18	27	67	**5**	9	28	0	54		1.7	1.3	7.7
Gene Olrich	50Wat	1922	5'11	160	G	Drake	1	14	17	72	24	10	14	71		24	34		44			1.7	3.1
Ole Olsen	HC47-49Chi	1895				Wisconsin																	
Mike O'Neil	53Mil	1927	6'3	210	F	California	1	4	4	17	24	4	4	100	9	3	10	1	12	13	2.3	0.8	3.0
Eddie Oram	40ChiN 48SyrN	1914	6'3	175	F-G	Southern California	2	42	57			46	**44**	66					160				3.8
Johnny Orr	50StL 50Wat	1927	6'3		F	Illinois, Beloit	1	34	40	118	34	12	14	86		20	34		92			0.6	2.7
Bob O'Shaughnessy	48SyrN	1921	6'	175	G	Nevada-Reno	1	25	41			19	31	61					101				4.0
Kevin O'Shea	51-52Min 52-53Bal	1925	6'2	182	G	Notre Dame	3	174	311	922	34	289	425	68	402	358	356	9	911	**21**	2.3	2.1	5.2
	51						1	5	1	7	14	3	4	75	5	1	8	0	5		1.0	0.2	1.0
Garland O'Shields	47Chi 48SyrN	1921	6'1	195	G-F	Tennessee	2	14	5	11	**18**	3	6	50		1	**8**		13			**0.1**	0.9
Wally Osterkorn	52-55Syr	1928	6'5	215	F	Illinois	4	204	453	1358	33	530	896	59	1218	346	596	11	1436	25	6.0	1.7	7.0
	52-55						4	33	83	232	36	92	157	59	207	70	97	3	258	28	6.3	2.1	7.8
Don Otten	47-49TC-N 50TC 50-51Was	1921	7'	245	C	Bowling Green	7	387	1443	**1850**	**36**	1700	2357	72	**928**	**297**	**787**	**30**	4586	**25**	**6.0**	**1.4**	11.9
51Bal 51-52FtW	48-51						4	17	76	**51**	**35**	107	135	79	**19**	14	**22**	1	259		**6.3**	**2.8**	15.2
52-53Mil																							
Mac Otten	50TC 50StL	1925	6'7	220	F-C	Bowling Green	1	59	51	155	33	40	81	49		36	119		142			0.6	2.4
Claude Overton	53Phi	1927	6'2	195	G	E. Central Okla. St.	1	15	19	75	25	20	30	67	25	15	25	0	58	12	1.7	1.0	3.9
Jim Owens	50TC 50And 52Bal 52Mil	1925	6'3	185	G-F	Baylor	2	90	169	540	31	132	215	61	102	137	244	**5**	470	**22**	**3.5**	1.5	5.2
	50						1	8	26	89	29	28	41	68		19	37		80			2.4	10.0
Fred Paine	49Prov	1925	6'5	210	F	Westminster (PA)	1	3	3	19	16	1	5	20		1	3		7			0.3	2.3
Bud Palmer	47-49NY	1921	6'4	180	F-C	Princeton	3	148	624	1916	33	489	662	74		187	465		1737			1.3	11.7
	47-49						3	14	76	196	39	49	68	72		14	56		201			1.0	14.4
Easy Parham	49-50StL 51Phi	1921	6'3	200	F-G	Texas Wesleyan	3	133	264	832	32	188	358	53		286	297		716			2.2	5.4
	49						1	2	5	13	38	0	0			6	6		10			3.0	5.0

Use Name-Nickname	Team by Year	Birth Year	Hgt	Wgt	Pos.	College	# Yr	G	Field Goals FG	Att.	%	Free Throws FT	Att.	%	Reb.	Ass.	PF	DQ	Pts	Per Game Min	Reb	Ass	Pts
Jack Parkinson	50Ind	1924	6'	175	G	Kentucky	1	4	1	12	8	1	1	100		2	3		3			0.5	0.8
Doyle Parrack	47Chi	1921	6'	165	F-G	Oklahoma St.	1	58	110	413	27	52	80	65		20	77		272			0.3	4.7
	47						1	7	0	9	0	3	3	100		1	3		3			0.1	0.4
Charlie Parsley	50Phi		6'2	175	G	Western Ky.	1	9	8	31	26	6	7	86		8	7		22			0.9	2.4
Marty Passaglia	47Was 49Ind	1919	6'1	170	G	Santa Clara	2	53	65	278	23	21	36	58		26	61		151			0.5	2.8
	47						1	6	2	14	14	1	3	33		0	10		5			0.0	0.8
George Pastushok	47Prov	1922	6'1	195	G	Manhattan, St. John's (NY)	1	39	48	183	26	25	46	54		15	42		121			0.4	3.1
Joe Patanelli (Pat)	47TolN 48MinN	1919	6'3	205	F	none	2	40	30			31	45	69					91				2.3
	47						1	5	4			10	21	48					18				3.6
Stan Patrick 50Wat 50Sheb	45-47ChiN 48FliN 49HamN	1922	6'3	215	F-G	Illinois, Santa Clara	6	265	797	294	39	492	660	63		74	76		2086			1.4	7.9
	45, 47, 50						3	17	41	7	57	17	18	67		3	10		99			1.0	5.8
Ray Patterson	48FliN	1923	6'2	195	F	Wisconsin	1	56	147			72	117	62					366				6.5
Johnny Payak	50Phi 50Wat 53Mil	1926	6'4	174	G-F	Bowling Green	2	120	226	704	32	301	421	71	114	226	307	7	753	22	1.7	1.9	6.3
Mel Payton	52Phi 53Ind	1926	6'4	185	F-G	Tulane	2	111	227	625	36	141	189	75	396	126	186	2	595	17	3.6	1.1	5.4
	52-53						2	5	8	19	42	9	10	90	9	1	13	0	25	11	1.8	0.2	5.0
George Pearcy	47Det	1919	6'1	165	G	Indiana State	1	37	31	130	24	32	44	73		13	68		94			0.4	2.5
Henry Pearcy	47Det	1922	6'1	170	G	Indiana State	1	29	24	108	22	25	34	74		7	20		73			0.2	2.5
Warren Perkins	50-51TC	1924	6'3	190	G-F	Tulane	2	126	263	850	31	241	390	62	319	257	492	13	767		4.8	2.0	6.1
	50						1	2	1	1	100	0	0			1	4		2			0.5	1.0
Perry	47DetN				G		1	5	4			7	14	50					15				3.0
Ed Peterson	49SyrN 50-51Syr 51TC	1925	6'9	230	C	Cornell	3	178	462	774	38	314	512	61	288	99	386	9	1238		5.4	0.9	7.0
	49-50						2	17	32	43	42	24	42	57		1	33		88			0.1	5.2
Jack Phelan	50WatN 50Sheb	1925	6'5	240	F	DePaul	1	55	87	268	32	52	90	58		57	151		226			1.0	4.1
	50						1	3	4	10	40	2	3	67		3	10		10			1.0	3.3
Jim Phelan	54Phi	1929	6'1	175	G	LaSalle	1	4	0	6	0	3	6	50	5	2	9	0	3	8	1.3	0.5	0.8
Andy Phillip 53-56FtW 57-58Bos HC59StL	48-50Chi 51-53Phi	1922	6'3	195	G-F	Illinois	11	701	2323	6318	37	1736	2499	70	2396	3759	1925	31	6384	32	4.4	5.4	9.1
	48-58						11	67	137	415	33	154	220	70	193	248	176	2	428	25	3.3	3.7	6.4
John Pilch	52Min	1925	6'3	185	F	Wyoming	1	9	1	10	10	3	6	50	9	2	10	0	5	5	1.0	0.2	0.6
Jim Polland (The Kangaroo Kid) HC61Bal HC68MinA HC69-70MiaA	48MinN 49-55 HC59Min	1922	6'5	191	F-C-G	Stanford	8	497	2609	6379	36	1304	1759	74	2487	1417	1146	14	6522	35	7.8	3.2	13.1
	48-55						8	82	397	1029	34	306	413	74	407	259	205	4	1100	40	8.1	3.6	13.4
Ralph Polson	53NY 53Phi	1930	6'7	205	F-C	Whitworth	1	49	65	179	36	61	96	64	211	24	102	5	191	17	4.3	0.5	3.9
Roger Potter	HC49TC-N HC50TC	1907	6'1	200		Illinois																	
Robert Powell	49DayN		6'5		F-C		1	6	11			8	13	62					30				5.0
Bob Priddy	53Bal	1930	6'3	190	F	N. Mexico St.	1	16	14	38	37	8	14	57	36	7	36	3	36	9	2.3	0.4	2.3
	53						1	1	0	0		0	0		0	0	1	0	0	1	0.0	0.0	0.0
John Pritchard	53Bal	1927	6'9	220	C	Drake	1	7	9	29	31	4	11	36		8	14		22			1.1	3.1
Leroy Pryor (Red)	49DayN	1923	6'3	180	F-G	DePaul	1	10	6			0	3	0					12				1.2
Lee Pugh	49Prov 50Bal	1923	6'6	190	C-F	Ohio State	2	116	236	829	28	240	303	79		75	286		712			0.7	6.1
Roy Pugh	48IndN 49FtW 49Ind 49Phi	1923	6'6	210	C-F	S.M.U.	2	27	14	51	25	8	23	35		9	17		36			0.4	1.3
Don Putman	47-50StL	1922	6'1	170	G	Colorado, Denver	4	216	410	1564	26	210	338	62		285	449		1030			1.3	4.8
	47-49						3	12	17	79	22	8	19	42		10	28		42			0.8	3.5
Jim Quinlan	47RochN	1922	6'5	205	F	Canisius	1	3	0			1	2	50					1				0.3
Howie Rader	47-48TC-N 49Bal	1921	6'1	190	G-F	Long Island U.	3	99	127			75	128	59					329				3.3
	48						1	6	8			6	12	50					22				3.7
Len Rader	47TC-N 49HamN	1921	6'2	185	G	Long Island U.	2	34	42			38	64	59					122				3.6
Moe Radovich	53Phi	1929	6'	160	G	Wyoming	1	4	5	13	38	4	4	100	1	8	5	0	14	8	0.3	2.0	3.5
Ray Ragelis	52Roch	1928	6'4	205	F	Northwestern	1	51	25	96	26	18	29	62	76	31	62	1	68	7	1.5	0.6	1.3
	52						1	3	0	1	0	0	0		1	1	0	0	0	2	0.3	0.3	0.0
Sherwin Raiken	53NY	1928	6'2	185	G	Villanova	1	6	3	21	14	3	8	38	8	6	10	0	9	11	1.3	1.0	1.5
	53						1	4	4	5	80	0	1	0	1	2	3	0	8	5	0.3	0.5	2.0
Ray Ramsey 47-49 played in A.A.F.C.	48TC-N 49Bal	1921	6'2	166	G-F	Bradley	2	4	0			2	2	100					2				0.5
Sam Ranzino	52Roch	1927	6'1	185	G	N. C. State	1	39	30	90	33	26	37	70	39	25	63	2	86	6	1.0	0.6	2.2
George Ratkovicz 48RochN 49TC-N 50-52Syr 53Bal 53-55Mil	42ChiN 43-45MS 46-47ChiN	1922	6'7	224	C-F	none	11	543	1319	2687	37	1431	2163	66	1937	791	1249	46	4069	27	6.9	2.3	7.5
	47-52						6	51	119	195	41	139	207	67	85	38	94	0	377	10	6.5	1.8	7.4
Don Ray	49TC-N 50TC	1921	6'6	215	F-C	Western Ky.	2	107	253	403	32	184	266	69		60	147		690			1.0	6.4
	49-50						2	9	20	13	31	27	32	84		0	7		67			0.0	7.4
Connie Rea	54Bal	1935	6'3	175	G-F	Centenary, Vanderbilt	1	20	9	43	21	5	16	31	31	16	13	0	23	8	1.6	0.8	1.2
Frank Reddout	54Roch	1931	6'5	195	F	Syracuse	1	7	5	6	83	3	4	75	9	0	6	0	13	3	1.3	0.0	1.9
Billy Reed	47OshN		5'11	185	F	Notre Dame, Ripon	1	17	20			5	18	28					45				2.6
Dod Rehfeldt	51-52Bal 52Mil	1927	6'6	210	F	DePaul, Wisconsin	2	98	263	711	37	166	219	76	494	118	248	6	692	20	5.0	1.2	7.1
Fred Rehm	46OshN 49FliN 48OshN	1921	6'3	195	G	Wisconsin	2	72	76			71	72	74					223				3.1
	46, 48						2	9	13			11	12	92					37				4.1
Chick Reiser 50Was HC52-53Bal	44-47FtWN 48-49Bal	1914	5'11	165	G-F	N.Y.U., Pratt	7	301	971	1927	32	772	915	76		346	600		2714			2.0	9.0
	44-50						7	40	126	191	26	102	110	75		20	72		354			0.5	8.9
John Rennicke	52Mil	1929	6'2	185	G	Drake	1	6	4	18	22	3	9	33	9	1	7	0	11	9	1.5	0.2	1.8
Gene Rhodes	53Ind HC70-71KyA	1927	6'1	170	G	Western Ky.	1	65	109	342	32	119	169	70	98	91	78	2	337	18	1.5	1.4	5.2
	53						1	2	4	14	29	1	4	25	7	5	5	0	9	26	3.5	2.5	4.5
Ocie Richie	48RochN	1921	6'3	195	F	NW La. State, Arkansas	1	1	0			1	1	100					1				1.0

Use Name-Nickname	Team by Year	Birth Year	Hgt.	Wgt	Pos	College	# Yr	G	Field Goals FG	Att.	%	Free Throws FT	Att.	%	Reb.	Ass.	PF	DQ	Pts	Per Game Min	Reb	Ass	Pts
Mel Riebe (Mouse)	44-46CleN 47Cle 48-49Bos	1916	5'11	180	G-F	none	6	199	1009	2140	30	559	443	62		212	416		2577			1.5	12.9
49Prov	44-45, 47-48						4	10	46	80	29	37	26	65		5	13		129			0.8	12.9
Jim Riffey	51FtW	1923	6'4	200	F	Tulane	1	35	65	185	35	20	26	77	61	16	54	0	150		1.7	0.5	4.3
Arnie Risen	46-48IndN 48RochN 49-55Roch	1924	6'9	207	C-F	Ohio State,	13	760	3173	6850	38	2893	4189	69	5011	1058	3449	67	9239	28	9.7	1.7	12.2
56-58Bos	47-58					Kentucky St.	12	73	330	684	38	325	474	69	561	86	256	9	985	25	10.2	1.4	13.5
Eddie Riska	42OshN 43-45MS	1919	6'	179	G	Notre Dame	5	152	206			209	288	67					621				4.1
46-48PC, 49OshN	42, 46-48						4	21	24			46	42	81					94				4.5
Tex Ritter	49-51NY	1924	6'2	185	G-F	Eastern Ky	3	151	262	753	35	265	393	67	65	145	224	1	789		1.9	1.0	5.2
	49-51						3	13	21	71	30	37	49	76	2	10	42	0	79		0.2	0.8	6.1
Julie Rivlin	41AG-N 43-45MS PC47-48TolN	1917	5'11	173	G	Marshall	3	105	153			97	115	75					403				3.8
	47						1	5	8			11	13	85					27				5.4
Jerry Rizzo	PC47, 48-49SyrN	1918	5'8	160	G	Fordham	3	149	382			492	691	71					1256				8.4
	47-49						3	13	35			53	66	80					123				9.5
Lee Robbins	48-49Prov	1923	6'3	175	F	Colorado	2	47	81	285	28	62	110	56		19	117		224			0.4	4.8
Bill Roberts	49Chi 49Bos 49-50StL	1925	6'9	210	C	Wyoming	2	117	166	489	34	72	102	71		65	203		404			0.6	3.5
	49						1	2	10	29	34	2	5	40		2	10		22			1.0	11.0
Red Rocha (The Thin Man)	48-50StL 51Bal 52-53Syr	1923	6'9	195	C-F	Oregon State,	9	586	2276	6158	37	1810	2385	76	2747	1153	2113	30	6362	30	6.6	2.0	10.9
54VR 55-56Syr	48-49, 52-53, 55-57					Hawaii	7	39	165	458	36	144	190	76	197	58	167	8	474	32	6.6	1.5	12.2
57FtW HC58-60Det																							
Gene Rock	48Chi	1921	5'9	155	G	Southern Cal.	1	11	4	18	22	2	4	50		0	8		10			0.0	0.9
	48						1	2	0	0		0	1	0		0	0		0			0.0	0.0
Jack Rocker	48MinN 48Phi	1922	6'5	186	C-F	California	1	14	10	22	36	1	1	100		3	2		21			0.3	1.5
Abel Rodrigues	48OshN	1922	6'	175	G	San Francisco, Occidental	1	8	4			1	2	50					9				1.1
Al Roges	54-55Bal 55FtW	1930	6'4	200	G-F	Long Island U.	2	84	243	675	36	145	193	75	237	179	197	1	631	25	2.8	2.1	7.5
Red Rolfe	HC47Tor	1908				Dartmouth																	
31, 34-42 played major league baseball																							
49-52 managed in major league baseball																							
Kenny Rollins	49-50Chi 51-52MS 53Bos	1923	6'	168	G	Kentucky	3	168	326	1056	31	165	220	75		344	342		817			2.0	4.9
	49-50, 53						3	10	6	24	25	8	8	100		9	20		20			0.9	2.0
Paul Rooney	47DetN 47TC-N	1926	6'3		F-G		1	10	6			3	7	43					15				1.5
Petey Rosenberg	47Phi	1918	5'10	165	G	St. Joseph's	1	51	60	287	21	30	49	61		27	64		150			0.5	2.9
	47						1	9	1	12	8	0	3	0		3	4		2			0.3	0.2
Hank Rosenstein	47NY 47Prov	1920	6'4	185	F	C.C.N.Y.	1	60	119	390	31	144	225	64		36	172		382			0.6	6.4
Irv Rothenberg	47Cle 48Was 48Bal 48StL 49NY	1921	6'8	215	C	Long Island U.	3	131	240	898	27	229	378	61		90	351		709			0.7	5.4
	48-49						2	11	9	53	17	6	17	35		2	21		24			0.2	2.2
Lee Rothman	47SyrN 47ChiN	1926	6'1	195	F-G	Long Island U.	1	14	24			15	21	71					63				4.5
Mickey Rottner	46ShebN 47-48Chi	1919	5'10	185	G	Loyola (Chic.)	3	105	253	839	29	54	113	48		139	158		560			1.4	5.3
	46-48						3	22	18	58	14	6	16	38		5	23		42			0.4	1.9
Giff Roux	47-49StL 49Prov	1923	6'5	195	F-C	Kansas	3	151	239	854	28	139	272	51		49	185		617			0.3	4.1
	47-48						2	8	13	53	25	3	9	33		0	9		29			0.0	3.6
Bob Royer	50Den	1927	5'10	155	G	Indiana State	1	42	78	231	34	41	58	71		85	72		197			2.0	4.7
Jerry Rullo	47Phi 48Bal 49-50Phi	1923	5'10	165	G	Temple	4	95	108	370	29	55	93	59		70	135		271			0.7	2.9
	47, 49						2	9	5	21	24	3	3	100		1	10		13			0.1	1.4
Honey Russell	HC47-48Bos	1902	6'1	185		Savage School, Seton Hall																	
Frank Sabo	47DetN	1922	6'1	190	G	Wayne State	1	3	7			2	3	67					16				5.3
Cincy Sachs	HC 47 Det	1902				Xavier (Ohio)																	
Ed Sadowski (Big Ed)	41DetN 43-44MS 45-46FtWN	1917	6'5	250	C	Seton Hall	7	288	1497	3605	35	1177	1593	70		416	893		4171			1.8	14.5
PC47Tor 47Cle 48Bos	41, 45-49						6	22	91	139	34	95	108	69		14	33		277			1.8	12.6
49-50Phi 50Bal																							
Kenny Sailors	47Cle 48Chi 48Phi 48, PC49Prov	1922	5'10	176	G	Wyoming	5	276	1255	3813	33	970	1362	71		781	1016		3480			2.8	12.6
50Den 51Bos 51Bal	47						1	2	6	16	38	3	4	75		4	8		15			2.0	7.5
Bill Sattler (Slats)	47YouN 48FliN	1916	6'8	197	C	Ohio State	2	49	100			65	130	50					265				5.4
Pep Saul	50-51Roch 52Bal 52-54Min	1924	6'2	185	G-F	Seton Hall	6	384	781	2170	36	590	798	74	683	596	687	9	2152	23	2.0	1.6	5.6
55Mil	50-54						5	49	116	271	43	89	122	73	94	87	119	2	321	28	2.0	1.8	6.6
Don Savage	52, 57Syr	1928	6'3	205	F-G	LeMoyne	2	17	15	62	24	24	35	69	31	14	29	0	54	10	1.8	0.8	3.2
Alan Sawyer	51Was	1928	6'5	195	F	U.C.L.A.	1	33	87	215	40	43	54	80	125	25	75	1	217		3.8	0.8	6.6
Ted Scalissi	48OshN	1921	5'8	160	G	Ripon	1	7	1			3	3	100					5				0.7
47-played in A.A.F.C.																							
Ben Schadler	48Chi 49DetN 49WatN	1924	6'2	185	F	Northwestern	2	90	173	116	20	68	102	67		6	40		414			0.2	4.6
	48						1	4	5	23	22	0	2	0		1	4		10			0.3	2.5
Herm Schaefer	42-43FtWN 44-45MS 46FtWN	1919	6'	175	G-F	Indiana	7	284	724	886	38	455	500	81		388	225		1903			3.2	6.7
PC47, 48IndN 48MinN	42-43, 47-50						6	48	156	146	44	100	110	84		47	34		412			2.1	8.6
49-50Min HC51 Min HC52-53Ind																							
Carl Schaeffer	50-51Ind	1924	6'3	185	F-G	Alabama	2	53	65	182	36	35	60	58		46	118		165			0.9	3.1
	50						1	6	7	21	33	7	14	50		7	20		21			1.2	3.5
Benny Schall	42, 47TolN	1917	5'11	170	F	Toledo	2	7	1			1							3				0.4
Ben Schamus (Whitey)	47Cle 49Prov	1918	6'2	173	F	Seton Hall	2	52	33	166	20	37	60	62		19	83		103			0.4	2.0
	47						1	3	6	21	29	5	9	56		2	10		17			0.7	5.7
Marv Schatzman	50Bal	1927	6'5	200	F	St. Louis	1	34	43	174	25	29	50	58		38	49		115			1.1	3.4
Fred Schaus	50-54FtW 54NY HC61-67LA	1925	6'5	205	F	West Virginia	5	334	1345	3826	35	1380	1677	82	1609	961	1130	32	4070	34	6.0	2.9	12.2
	50-54						5	21	78	230	34	91	111	82	86	55	86	4	247	32	5.0	2.6	11.8
	47NY	1919	6'	175	G	Long Island U.	1	54	162	588	28	111	179	62		109	115		435			2.0	8.1
Herb Scheffler	47DetN	1917	6'4	220	C-F	Oklahoma, Nwn. Illinois	1	33	43			40	67	60					126				3.8
Herb Scherer	51TC 52NY	1929	6'9	212	C	Long Island U.	2	32	43	149	29	29	49	59	76	23	81	1	115	14	2.4	0.7	3.6
Johnny Schick	47-48TolN	1916	6'6	230	C-F	Ohio State	2	97	150			60	106	57					360				3.7
	47						1	5	2			2	6	33					6				1.2
Otto Schnellbacher (The Claw)	49Prov 49StL	1923	6'5	185	F-G	Kansas	1	43	93	280	33	89	133	67		64	109		275			1.5	6.4
48-49 played in A.A.F.C.,	49						1	2	6	20	30	6	12	50		6	9		18			3.0	9.0
50-53 played in N.F.L.																							

Use Name-Nickname	Team by Year	Birth Year	Hgt	Wgt	Pos.	College	# Yr	G	Field Goals FG	Att.	%	Free Throws FT	Att.	%	Reb.	Ass.	PF	DQ	Pts	Per Game Min.	Reb	Ass	Pts
Milt Schoon	47Det 48FliN 49ShebN	1922	6'9	230	C	Valparaiso	4	215	388	565	34	459	778	59		96	265		1235			0.9	5.7
50Sheb	49-50						2	5	7	17	29	9	15	60		3	6		23			1.0	4.6
Bill Schroeder	47ShebN	1923	6'	190	G	Wisconsin	1	9	5			5	8	63					15				1.7
46-47 played in A.A.F.C.																							
Wilbur Schu	47YouN 47TC-N	1922	6'3	190	F-G	Kentucky	1	33	15			16	26	62					46				1.4
Howie Schultz (Stretch)	47-49AndN PC50And	1922	6'7	212	C-F	Hamline	6	338	836	1176	25	841	1190	71	326	300	514	14	2513	15	3.1	1.7	7.4
50FtW 52-53Min	48-50, 52						4	29	57	79	27	66	97	68	19	13	36	1	180	8	1.6	0.8	6.2
43-48 played major league baseball																							
Dick Schultz	43-46ShebN 47Cle 47Tor	1917	6'2	192	F-G	Wisconsin	8	284	551	1507	26	506	593	72		203	452		1608			1.0	5.7
48Bal 49-50Was	43-46, 48-50						7	47	91	197	20	137	126	72		36	78		319			1.4	6.8
50TC 50Sheb																							
Freddie Scolari (Fat Freddie)	47-51Was 51Syr	1922	5'11	183	G	San Fransisco	9	534	2132	6651	32	1750	2139	82	857	1406	1482	12	6014	26	2.7	2.6	11.3
PC52, 53Bal 53-54FtW	47, 49-51, 53-55						7	41	134	444	30	141	178	79	78	70	116	1	409	21	3.3	1.7	10.0
55Bos																							
Tom Sealy	49DayN	1921	6'1	190	G	Brooklyn	1	40	100			60	92	65					260				6.5
Johnny Sebastian	48SyrN 49DetN 49HamN	1921	6'1	185	G	Southern Illinois	2	62	185			126	206	61					496				8.0
Wayne See	50Wat	1923	6'3	190	G	Arizona State-Flagstaff	1	61	113	303	37	94	135	70		143	147		320			2.3	5.2
Glen Selbo	48-49OshN 50Sheb	1926	6'3	195	G-F	Wisconsin	3	132	286			161	243	66					733				5.6
	48						1	4	5			5	5	100					15				3.8
Rollie Seltz	47-48AndN 49WatN 50And	1924	5'10	170	G	Hamline	4	196	522	309	30	401	540	74		64	72		1445			1.9	7.4
	48						1	6	11			4	4	100					26				4.3
Jim Seminoff	47, PC48Chi 49-50Bos	1922	6'2	200	G-F	Southern Cal.	4	231	535	1737	31	437	642	68		630	609		1507			2.7	6.5
	47-48						2	16	47	194	24	30	45	67		16	48		124			1.0	7.8
George Senesky	47-54, HC56-58Phi	1922	6'2	179	G	St. Joseph's	8	482	1279	4087	31	897	1277	70	878	1553	982	2	3455	27	3.5	2.0	7.2
	47-52						6	32	125	391	32	72	101	71	19	51	71	0	322	40	3.8	1.6	10.1
Paul Seymour	47TolN 48Bal 48-49SyrN	1928	6'2	183	G-F	Toledo	14	748	2279	5826	35	1892	2419	78	1694	2341	1363	10	6450	30	3.1	3.8	8.6
50-60Syr	47-58						12	80	243	632	33	254	311	82	164	257	185	4	740	34	3.0	3.9	9.3
HC61-62StL HC66Bal-HC69Det																							
Nick Shaback	47Cle	1918	5'11	182	G	none	1	53	102	385	26	38	53	72		29	75		242			0.5	4.6
	47						1	3	6	22	27	3	5	60		0	6		15			0.0	5.0
Bob Shaddock	47SyrN	1920	6'1	160	G	Syracuse	1	2	0			0	0						0				0.0
Earl Shannon	47-49Prov 49Bos	1921	5'11	170	G-F	Rhode Island	3	134	402	1318	31	352	589	60		177	308		1156			1.3	8.6
Frank Shannon	PC47YouN	1917	5'11	178	G	Wittenberg	1	29	55			14	20	70					124				4.3
Howie Shannon	49Prov 50Bos	1923	6'3	175	G-F	North Texas St., Kansas State	2	122	514	1448	35	295	371	80		299	302		1323			2.5	10.8
Steve Sharkey	46-47ShebN 47-48SyrN	1918	6'	190	G-F	none	3	120	225			117	162	64					567				4.7
	46-48						3	14	39			23	31	74					101				7.2
Bob Shea	47Prov	1924	6'2	194	F	Rhode Island	1	43	37	153	24	19	33	58		6	42		93			0.1	2.2
Fred Sheffield	47Phi	1923	6'2	165	F	Utah	1	22	29	146	20	16	26	62		4	34		74			0.2	3.4
Ollie Shoaff	49DetN 49HamN	1923	5'10	165	G	Illinois, Southern Illinois	1	61	211			93	125	74					515				8.4
Dick Schrider	49DetN 49NY	1923	6'2	190	G	Ohio U.	1	7	3			4	9	44		2	2		10			0.5	1.4
Vic Siegel	47TC-N	1920	5'10	160	G	Iowa	1	8	3			5	5	100					11				1.4
Ralph Siewert (Sky)	47StL 47Tor	1923	7'1	230	C	Dakota Wesleyan	1	21	6	44	14	8	15	53		4	18		20			0.2	1.0
Connie Simmons	47-48Bos 48-49Bal	1925	6'8	222	C-F	none	10	598	2180	6211	35	1499	2211	68	2294	940	1843	30	5859	23	6.2	1.6	9.8
50-54NY 55Bal	48-54						7	62	278	728	38	286	391	73	317	96	256	6	842	30	7.4	1.5	13.6
55Syr 56Roch																							
Johnny Simmons	47Bos	1924	6'2	184	G	N.Y.U.	1	60	120	429	28	78	127	61		29	78		318			0.5	5.3
49 played major league baseball																							
Bob Sims	47TC-N ShebN	1915	6'6	220	C-F	Western Mich., Michigan	1	23	14			18	25	72					46				2.0
	47						1	1	1			0	0						2				2.0
Zeke Sinicola	52FtW 53MS 54FtW	1929	5'10	165	G	Niagara	2	12	5	20	25	3	8	38	2	3	10	0	13	6	0.4	0.6	1.1
Bob Skarda	48TC-N	1925	6'3	190	G-F	Tufts	1	8	5			0	1	0					10				1.3
	48						1	6	1			1	2	50					3				0.5
Jim Slaughter	52Bal	1928	6'11	212	C	South Carolina	1	28	53	165	32	41	68	60	148	25	81	0	147	19	5.3	0.9	5.3
Belus Smawley	47-50StL 51Syr 51Bal	1918	6'1	195	G-F	Appalachian State	5	250	1216	3418	35	844	1059	80	178	587	575	4	3276		3.0	2.3	13.1
	47-49						3	11	54	169	32	20	29	69		3	31		128			0.3	11.6
Danny Smick	48FliN	1918	6'5	215	F-C	Michigan	1	35	26			24	43	56					76				2.2
Jack Smiley	48FtWN 49FtW 50And	1922	6'3	190	F-G	Illinois	3	178	344	935	26	338	500	67		299	395		1026			2.5	5.8
PC50Wat	48						1	4	7			6	8	75					20				5.0
Deb Smith	47StL	1920	6'3	180	F	Utah	1	48	32	119	27	9	21	43		6	47		73			0.1	1.5
	47						1	1	0	0		0	1	0		0	1		0			0.0	0.0
Don Smith	43OshN 44-45MS	1920	6'2	190	G-F	Minnesota	5	99	99			90	105	66					288				2.9
46-47OshN 47IndN	43, 48						2	12	14			11	12	75					39				3.3
48MinN 49Min																							
Ed Smith	54NY	1929	6'6	210	F	Harvard	1	11	11	45	24	6	10	60	26	9	15	0	28	9	2.4	0.8	2.5
Tom Smith	52NY	1929	6'1	165	G	St. Peter's	1	1	0	0		0	0		0	0	0	0	0	3	0.0	0.0	0.0
Willie Smith (Wee Willie)	44CleN 49DayN	1911	6'6	230	C	none	2	36	54			43	49	76					151				4.2
	44						1	2	5			7							17				8.5
Joe Smyth	54Bal	1929	6'3	215	F	Niagara	1	40	48	138	35	35	65	54	98	49	53	0	131	12	2.5	1.2	3.3
Hank Soar	HC48Prov	1914	6'2	210		Providence																	
37-44, 46 played in N.F.L.																							
George Sobek (Chips)	46IndN 47-48TolN PC49HamN	1920	6'	180	G-F	Notre Dame	5	208	544	251	38	692	945	73		95	158		1780			1.8	8.6
50Sheb	47, 50						2	8	24	20	50	31	42	74		3	15		79			1.0	9.9
Sotnik	47YouN				F		1	4	1			0	0						2				0.5
Gino Sovran	47Tor	1924	6'2	175	F-G	Assumpt'n (Ont.), Detroit	1	6	5	15	33	1	2	50		1	5		11			0.2	1.8
Odie Spears	49-50Chi 52-55Roch	1925	6'5	205	F-G	Western Ky.	8	479	1486	4066	37	1185	1554	76	1409	917	1580	36	4161	23	4.0	1.9	8.7
56-57FtW 57StL	49-50, 52-56						7	32	74	208	36	58	91	64	89	44	114	3	206	20	3.2	1.4	6.4
Art Spector	47-50Bos	1920	6'4	200	F	Villanova	4	169	322	1149	28	208	362	57		143	351		852			0.8	5.0
	48						1	3	2	9	22	2	4	50		0	9		6			0.0	2.0
Jack Spencer	49WatN	1923	6'3	160	F	Iowa	1	11	6			4	4	100					16				1.5

Use Name-Nickname	Team by Year	Birth Year	Hgt	Wgt	Pos.	College	# Yr	G	Field Goals FG	Att.	%	Free Throws FT	Att.	%	Reb.	Ass.	PF	DQ	Pts	Per Game Min.	Reb	Ass	Pts
Lou Spicer	47Prov	1923	6'2	195	F	Syracuse	1	4	0	7	0	1	2	50		0	3		1			0.0	0.3
Jim Springer	48AndN 48IndN 49Ind	1925	6'9	235	C	Canterbury	2	27	12			26	41	63					50				1.9
	48						1	3	0			0	2	0					0				0.0
Jim Spruill	49Ind	1923	6'2	225	G	Rice	1	1	1	3	33	0	0			0	3		2			0.0	2.0
48, 49 played in A.A.F.C.																							
Ed Stanczak	47-49AndN 50And 51Bos	1921	6'3	208	F	none	5	237	576	504	34	619	891	69		71	172		1771			1.0	7.5
	48-50						3	21	31	48	29	50	75	67		10	26		112			1.3	5.3
Jack Stanton	47AndN	1921	6'	175	G	Loyola (Chic.)	1	7	10			2	7	29					22				3.1
Dick Starzyk	47TC-N	1921	5'10	180	G	DePaul	1	9	4			4	5	80					12				1.3
Art Stoefen	47ChiN	1915	6'7	215	C-F	Stanford	1	18	8			8	19	42					24				1.3
	47						1	2	0			0	1	0					0				0.0
Art Stolkey	47Det	1920	6'1	180	G	Detroit	1	23	36	164	22	30	44	68		38	72		102				4.4
Gene Stump	48-49Bos 50Min 50Wat	1923	6'2	185	F-G	DePaul	3	148	315	1040	30	153	221	69		118	227		783				5.3
	48						1	3	1	3	33	0	0	—		0	2		2				0.7
Stan Stutz	47-48NY 49Bal	1920	5'10	175	G-F	Rhode Island	3	166	402	1573	26	377	564	67		188	397		1181			1.1	7.1
(born Stan Modzelewski)							3	11	32	117	27	40	49	82		8	31		104			0.7	9.5
Don Sunderlage	54Mil 55Min	1929	6'1	180	G	Illinois	2	113	287	881	33	300	410	73	281	224	320	8	874	23	2.5	2.0	7.7
Dick Surhoff	53NY 54Mil	1930	6'4	210	F	Long Island U.,	2	58	56	190	29	66	92	72	94	32	89	1	178	9	1.6	0.6	3.1
	53					John Marshall	1	4	2	4	50	0	0		2	2	2	0	4	3	0.5	0.5	1.0
Norm Swanson	54Roch	1930	6'6	212	F	Detroit	1	63	31	137	23	38	64	59	110	33	91	3	100	10	1.7	0.5	1.6
	54						1	6	3	7	43	2	3	67	5	0	5	0	8	4	0.8	0.0	1.3
Buck Sydor	47Chi	1921	5'10	175	G	Western Ky	1	15	5	26	19	5	10	50		0	6		15			0.0	1.0
Sid Tannenbaum	48-49NY 49Bal	1925	6'	160	G	N.Y.U.	2	70	236	961	25	161	194	83		162	107		633			2.3	9.0
	48-49						2	6	17	62	27	13	16	81		14	13		47			2.3	7.8
Mel Thurston	47-48TC-N 48Prov	1919	6'	175	G	Canisius	2	87	107	113	28	88	148	59		4	42		302			0.3	3.5
Milt Ticco	47YouN 48FliN 48IndN	1922	6'3	205	F-G	Kentucky	2	96	292			86	114	75					670				7.0
478ShebN																							
Hal Tidrick	45ShebN 47-48TolN 49Ind	1915	6'1	190	F-G	Wash. & Jefferson	4	165	693	616	31	468	613	76		101	191		1854			1.7	11.2
49Bal	47, 46						2	8	24	19	26	16	26	62		1	16		64			0.3	8.0
Jack Tingle	48Was 49Min	1925	6'4	205	F	Kentucky	2	39	37	143	26	17	33	52		8	47		91			0.2	2.3
Mike Todorovich	48-49ShebN 50StL 50	1923	6'5	230	F-C	Washington-StL,	4	251	1000	1567	31	870	1295	67	455	366	427	5	2870		6.9	2.9	11.4
HC51TC	50					Notre Dame, Wyo.	1	3	6	31	19	19	24	79		8	14		31			2.7	10.3
Andy Tonkovich	49Prov	1922	6'1	185	G	Marshall	1	17	19	71	27	6	9	67		10	12		44			0.6	2.6
Jack Toomay	48Chi 48Prov 49Was 49Bal 49Phi	1922	6'6	215	C-F	U. of the Pacific	3	121	297	789	38	282	408	69		113	349		876			0.9	7.2
	49						1	1	1	5	20	5	7	71		0	6		7			0	7
Irv Torgoff	40DetN 47-48Was 49Bal	1917	6'2	192	F	Long Island U.	4	173	421	1451	25	326	367	77		106	436		1168			0.7	6.8
49Phi	40, 47, 49						3	11	23	84	15	20	19	68		7	25		66			0.9	6.0
Bill Tosheff	52-53Ind 54Mil	1926	6'1	183	G	Indiana	3	203	634	2012	32	591	745	79	608	661	654	15	1859	31	3.0	3.3	9.2
	52-53						2	4	3	34	8.8	10	10	100	11	11	14	0	16	34	2.8	2.8	4.0
Bob Tough	46-48FtW 49FtW 50Bal	1920	6'	185	G-F	St. John's (N.Y.)	5	191	491	814	28	245	330	73		137	141		227			1.7	1.2
50Wat	46-48						3	16	35			23	31	74					93				5.8
Blackie Towery	42-45FtWN 46MS	1920	6'4	210	F-C	Western Ky	8	298	829	1449	29	659	786	71		313	487		2317			2.4	7.8
47-48FtWN 49FtW	42-44, 47-48						5	29	62			35	25	48					159				5.5
49Ind 50Bal																							
Dick Triptow	45-47ChiN 48TC-N 48FtWN	1922	6'	170	G-F	DePaul	6	224	448	422	27	409	496	67		97	112		1305			1.6	5.8
49FtW 50Bal	45, 47-48						3	18	39			22	25	64					100				5.6
Morris Udall (Moe)	49DenN	1922	6'5	200	F	Arizona	1	57	125			121	171	71					371				6.5
Hal Uplinger	54Bal	1929	6'4	185	G	Long Island U.	1	23	33	94	35	20	22	91	31	26	42	0	86	12	1.3	1.1	3.7
Jim Usry	49DayN	1922	6'4	225	F-C	Lincoln (Mo.)	1	36	129			71	134	53					329				9.1
Butch Van Breda Kolff	47-PC50NY HC68-69LA	1922	6'3	185	G-F	Princeton,	4	175	242	794	30	342	511	67		254	350		826			1.5	4.7
HC70-72Det	47-50					N.Y.U.	4	15	28	88	32	36	50	72		13	29		92			0.9	6.1
HC73Phoe HC74MemA HC75-77NO																							
Gene Vance	48-49Chi 50-51TC 52Mil	1923	6'3	196	G-F	Illinois	5	174	546	1735	31	345	502	69	103	399	664	0	1437		2.9	2.3	8.3
	48-50						3	10	32	132	24	23	33	70		17	43		87			1.7	8.7
Ernie Vandeweghe (Doc)	50-54NY 55VR 56NY	1928	6'3	195	F-G	Colgate	6	224	818	1942	42	499	674	74	843	548	753	21	2135	26	4.6	2.4	9.5
	50-53						4	43	146	347	42	136	174	78	199	91	179	5	428	30	5.1	2.1	10.0
Virgil Vaughn	47Bos 48SyrN		6'4	205	F-C	Ky Wesleyan	2	28	44	78	19	20	37	54					108				3.9
	48						1	3	2			6	11	55					10				3.3
Floyd Volker	48-49SohN 50Ind 50Den	1921	6'4	205	F_C	Wyoming	3	175	431	527	31	180	329	55		112	169		1042			2.1	6.0
	48-49						2	11	34			13	22	59					81				7.4
Whitey Von Nieda	48-49TC-N 50Bal	1922	6'1	175	G-F	Penn State	3	183	643	336	36	394	628	63		143	127		1680			2.4	9.2
	48-49						2	12	61			28	52	54					150				12.5
Vaughn Waddell	47DetN	1910	6'1	190	G	none	1	8	10			5	8	63					25				3.1
Clint Wager	44-48OshN 49Ham 50FtW	1920	6'6	226	C-F	St. Mary's (Minn.)	7	310	557	203	28	348	403	62		90	175		1462			1.4	4.7
42-45 played in N.F.L.	44, 46-48, 50						5	22	49	25	44	29	31	77		8	22		127			2.0	5.8
Danny Wagner	48FliN 49ShebN 50Sheb	1922	6'	170	G	Texas	3	123	226	54	35	199	273	73		18	22		651			1.6	5.3
	49						1	2	3			1	1	100					7				3.5
Brady Walker	49Prov 50-51Bos 51-52Bal	1921	6'6	205	F-C	Brigham Young	4	228	673	1772	38	257	406	63	549	328	320	2	1603		5.4	1.4	7.0
Red Wallace	47Bos 47Tor	1918	6'1	185	G	Scranton	1	61	225	809	28	106	196	54		58	167		556			1.0	9.1
Jimmy Walsh	HC48FliN	1914	5'6	140		Eastern Michigan																	
Ken Walters	48SyrN	1922	6'	170	G	Ohio Univ.	1	1	0			0	0						0				0.0
Paul Walther	50Min 50-53Ind 54Phi	1927	6'2	160	G-F	Tennessee	6	370	968	2671	36	902	1274	71	1168	974	1069	27	2838	29	3.7	2.6	7.7
55FtW	50-53, 55						5	23	40	106	38	63	87	72	40	35	59	1	143	18	2.4	1.5	6.2
Rabbit Walthour	54Mil	1928	5'11	175	G	none	1	4	1	6	17	0	0		1	2	6	0	2	8	0.3	0.5	0.5

Use Name-Nickname	Team by Year	Birth Year	Hgt	Wgt	Pos.	College	# Yr	G	Field Goals FG	Att.	%	Free Throws FT	Att.	%	Reb.	Ass.	PF	DQ	Pts	Per Game Min.	Reb	Ass	Pts
Jack Walton	49AndN	1923	6'2	192	F	Oklahoma State	1	8	5			4	5	80					14				1.8
Bobby Wanzer	48RochN 49-55	1921	6'	178	G	Colgate,	10	608	2323	5766	39	2445	3045	80	1979	1830	1275	16	7091	33	4.5	3.2	11.7
PC56-57Roch	48-55					Seton Hall	8	49	192	402	43	236	269	88	196	134	123	3	620	39	5.8	3.5	12.7
HC58-59Cin																							
Dave Wareham	49WatN	1924	6'1	185	G	Loras	1	4	1			1	3	33					3				0.8
Jack Watkins	49ShebN	1923	6'2	180	G	Oklahoma	1	7	1			3	4	75					5				0.7
Stan Waxman	47TC-N	1922	5'11	180	G	Long Island U.	1	18	59			10	17	59					128				7.1
Jake Weber	46IndN 47NY 47Prov	1918	6'6	225	C	Purdue	2	55	66	202	29	59	79	70		4	111		191			0.1	3.5
Dick Wehr	49Ind	1925	6'4	180	F	Rice, Indiana	1	9	5	21	24	2	6	33		3	12		12			0.3	1.3
Ray Wertis	47Tor 47Cle 48Prov	1922	5'11	175	G	St. John's (N.Y.)	2	68	92	438	21	62	105	59		45	95		246			0.7	3.6
	47						1	3	6	26	23	4	5	80		6	6		16			2.0	5.3
Dean White (Donk)	474ShebN	1923	6'7	220	F	Valparaiso	1	5	7			7	9	78					21				4.2
	47						1	1	1			0	0	—					2				2.0
Murray Wier	49TC-N 50TC	1926	5'9	155	G	Iowa	2	116	237	480	33	194	279	70		107	141		668			1.9	5.8
	49-50						2	9	16	9	33	13	21	62		0	4		45			0.0	5.0
D. C. Wilcutt	49-50StL	1923	6'2	165	G	St. Louis	2	59	42	124	34	44	60	73		80	36		128			1.4	2.2
	49						1	2	3	7	43	0	0	—		4	2		6			2.0	3.0
Russ Wilkins	47AndN		6'1	190	F-G	none	1	5	2			1	2	50					5				1.0
Ward Williams	49FtW	1923	6'4	195	F	Indiana	1	53	61	257	24	93	124	75		82	158		215			1.5	4.1
Bob Wilson	52Mil	1926	6'4	185	G	W. Virginia St.	1	63	79	264	30	78	135	58	210	108	172	8	236	21	3.3	1.7	3.7
Kayo Wnorowski	49DenN	1921	6'	215	G	Sienna, Denver	1	19	14			3	8	38					31				1.6
Eddie Wollen (Mo)	49DayN				F	none	1	1	0			0	0	—					0				0.0
Sonny Wood	49DayN	1923	5'11	195	G	none	1	40	105			56	98	57					266				6.7
Bob Woods	50Sheb	1921	5'10		G	Northern Illinois	1	6	3	14	21	1	1	100		1	6		7			0.2	1.2
Mark Workman	53Phi 54Bal	1930	6'9	217	F-C	West Virginia	2	79	155	468	33	76	123	62	230	44	197	5	386	15	2.9	0.6	4.9
Paul Yesawich	49SyrN	1923	6'2	190	F	Niagara	1	5	2			4	5	80					8				1.6
MAx Zaslofsky	47-50Chi 51-53NY 54Bal	1925	6'2	174	G-F	St. John's (N.Y.),	10	540	2854	8313	34	2282	2969	77	864	1093	1291	11	7990	28	2.8	2.0	14.8
54Mil54-56FtW	47-52, 54-55					Chicago	8	63	306	850	36	287	372	77	121	101	174	3	899	25	2.8	1.6	14.3
HC68NJ-A HC69NY-A																							
Zeke Zawoluk	53Ind 54-55Phi	1930	6'7	215	F-C	St. John's (N.Y.)	3	179	396	1065	37	418	545	77	732	217	450	10	1210	20	4.1	1.2	6.8
	53						1	2	1	6	17	0	2	0	2	0	5	0	2	9	1.0	0.0	1.0
Harry Zeller	47Pit	1919	6'4	210	C-F	Wash. & Jeff., Pittsburgh	1	48	120	382	31	122	177	69		31	177		362			0.6	7.5
Jim Zeravich	47SyrN		6'7		C	Wash. & Jeff.	1	2	1			3	5	60					5				2.5
Matt Zunic (Mad Matt)	PC48FliN 49Was	1919	6'3	195	G-F	G. Washington	2	113	221	323	30	162	237	68		50	182		604			0.9	5.3
							1	9	7	39	18	12	19	63		6	26		26			0.7	2.9

1954-55 through 1966-67

Twenty-four Seconds to Recognition

1954-55 N.B.A.

A Whole New Ball Game

Two changes in the rules this season streamlined the N.B.A.'s play and turned the standings practically upside down. The new 24-second clock kept teams from stalling by forcing them to shoot within 24 seconds of gaining possession of the ball. The league also cut down on intentional fouling by limiting each team to five infractions in each period; when a team notched its sixth foul of the period, the opponent would receive a penalty shot on all free throw situations. Thus, N.B.A. games crammed a lot more action into their 48 minutes than ever before.

This change in playing style brought on a shift in power in the league. The Minneapolis Lakers, champions for the last three years, suffered from the 24-second rule as well as from the retirement of George Mikan. Moving upstairs as general manager, Mikan left a large gap at center into which Clyde Lovellette was thrown; the young center scored frequently enough, but could not approach Mikan's value as a rebounder or defender. Vern Mikkelsen and Slater Martin kept pace with the quicker play demanded by the new rules, but Jim Pollard endured a sub-par season before retiring. The Lakers adapted well enough to finish eight games over .500 and only three games out of first place in the West, but the defending champs no longer were the intimidating powerhouse of old. The Rochester Royals fell a lot farther and a lot more quickly. Although age had been slowly catching up with key men Arnie Risen, Bob Davies, and Bobby Wanzer, the 24-second clock made the Royals' lack of speed a painful liability. The Royals thudded to a 29-43 mark and barely grabbed off the third Western playoff spot ahead of the Milwaukee Hawks.

With Minneapolis and Rochester coming down from the twin peaks they had held for years, Syracuse and Ft. Wayne became the new N.B.A. powers. New York and Boston remained close contenders, and Philadelphia, Milwaukee, and Baltimore continued in the also-ran category. Baltimore had a blue-chip rookie in Furman's Frank Selvy, the collegiate scoring champion who had poured in 100 points in a single undergraduate contest. The Bullets, however, drew few paying customers and were in full financial retreat until the club finally called it quits on November 27 with a 3-11 record. A draft parcelled the players to the other clubs, with Selvy going to Milwaukee. The Hawks had another rookie forward who would become one of the N.B.A.'s superstars Bob Pettit, a slim 6'9" graduate of Louisiana State, went uncompromisingly to the boards on rebounds and used a fine-tuned jump shot to accumulate points at a rapid rate; the Hawks were still a cellar team, but Pettit was the cornerstone around which owner Ben Kerner would build a champion. The Philadelphia Warriors got jump-shooter Paul Arizin back from the military and paired him with center Neil Johnston in a potent one-two scoring punch. The Warriors had too many holes to make the playoffs this year, but like the Hawks, they were very close to a championship season.

The Knicks and Celtics, meanwhile, made the playoffs despite some pressing problems. The Knicks were rebuilding; Connie Simmons and Al McGuire were traded, while Vince Boryla, Freddie Schaus, and Ernie Vandeweghe retired. Coach Joe Lapchick still got scoring from Carl Braun and rebounding from Harry Gallatin, and he brought in new help in the persons of center Ray Felix from Baltimore and guard Gene Shue from Philadelphia. Up in Boston, Celtic coach Red Auerbach had the guns to run a fast-break attack in Bob Cousy, Bill Sharman, and Ed Macauley, but a persistent weakness on the boards and on defense kept the Celts a .500 club. Auerbach did uncover one fine rookie in swingman Frank Ramsey, the first of the high-scoring "sixth men" that are standard equipment in the N.B.A. today.

The two clubs that rose to the top in the new setup were the Syracuse Nationals and the Ft. Wayne Pistons. The Nats had finished second in the East last season and had made it to the finals in the playoffs before losing to the Lakers. This year, they finished first in the East by five games over New York. Dolph Schayes supplied the big offensive spark from his forward position, and guard Paul Seymour spearheaded the N.B.A.'s most hard-nosed defense. Coach Al Cervi counted his riches when he came up with two competent centers; veteran Red Rocha returned after a season in retirement, and rookie Johnny Kerr brought mobility and fine passing skill to the pivot position.

The Ft. Wayne club matched Syracuse by taking first place in the West. Owner Fred Zollner hired referee Charlie Eckman to run the Pistons. Lacking any coaching experience, Eckman kept his men loose with fast-flowing stories and good-humored profanity, leaving most of the basketball strategy up to the good sense of his veteran squad. Larry Foust, George Yardley, Mel Hutchins, Max Zaslofsky, Andy Phillip, and Frankie Brian had all demonstrated All-Star skills in the past, and the weakening of the Lakers and Royals gave them a chance to bring Ft. Wayne to the top for the first time in the Western Division.

The playoffs produced exciting, attractive basketball games, testaments to the good sense of the new rules changes. The Celtics edged the Knicks two-to-one in a series of high-scoring contests in the Eastern semifinal, while the Lakers also had to go the limit to eliminate old rival Rochester in the West. Then the first-place clubs stepped into the picture, with the Nats beating Boston and the Pistons beating Minneapolis in four games each. The two division winners, then, got ready for the final.

The Pistons were saddled with a heavy disadvantage when their home court was unavailable, forcing them into a smaller gym in Indianapolis for their home games. The first two games were played in Syracuse, with both going to the Nats in close finishes. Back in Indiana, the veteran Pistons relaxed and copped three straight games, putting themselves in the driver's seat. Back in Syracuse for the sixth game, Dolph Schayes' 28 points led the Nats to a 109-104 victory. The final game came down to the wire tied up at 91-all; with 12 seconds left, George King sank a free throw to put Syracuse up 92-91. The Nats promptly stole the ball back and had their first (and only) N.B.A. championship in their hip pocket.

1954/55 N.B.A. — EASTERN DIVISION

Use Name	Pos	Hgt	Wgt	Age	TOTAL G	Min	FG	FGA	%	FT	FTA	%	Reb	Ass	PF	DQ	Points	PER GAME Min	Reb	Ass	PF	Points
SYRACUSE NATIONALS	**43-29 .597**				**AL CERVI**																	
Earl Lloyd	F	6'6	220	26	72	2212	286	784	36	159	212	75	553	151	283	4	731	31	7.7	2.1	3.9	10.2
Dolph Schayes	F	6'8	220	26	72	2526	422	1103	38	489	587	83	887	213	247	6	1333	35	12.3	3.0	3.4	18.5
Red Rocha	C-F	6'9	205	31	72	2473	295	801	37	222	284	78	489	178	242	5	812	34	6.8	2.5	3.4	11.3
Paul Seymour	G-F	6'2	185	26	72	2950	375	1036	36	300	370	81	309	483	137	0	1050	41	4.3	6.7	1.9	14.6
George King	G	6'	180	26	67	2015	228	605	38	140	229	61	227	331	148	0	596	30	3.4	4.9	2.2	8.9
Johnny Kerr	C	6'9	230	22	72	1529	301	718	42	152	223	68	474	80	165	2	754	21	6.6	1.1	2.3	10.5
Billy Kenville	G-F	6'2	185	24	70	1380	172	482	36	154	201	77	247	150	132	1	498	20	3.5	2.1	1.9	7.1
Dick Farley	G-F	6'4	190	22	69	1113	136	353	39	136	201	68	167	111	145	1	408	16	2.4	1.6	2.1	5.9
Connie Simmons (14g. Bal)	C-F	6'8	225	29	36	862	137	384	36	72	114	63	220	61	109	2	346	24	6.1	1.7	3.0	9.6
Jim Tucker	F	6'7	185	22	20	287	39	116	34	27	38	71	97	12	50	0	105	14	4.9	0.6	2.5	5.3
Wally Osterkorn (injury)	F	6'5	215	26	19	286	20	97	21	16	32	50	70	17	32	0	56	15	3.7	0.9	1.7	2.9
Billy Gabor (IL, VR)	G	5'11	180	32	3	47	7	22	32	3	5	60	5	11	6	0	17	16	1.7	3.7	2.0	5.7
NEW YORK KNICKERBOCKERS	**38-34 .528**				**JOE LAPCHICK**																	
Sweetwater Clifton	F-C	6'6	225	32	72	2390	360	932	39	224	328	68	612	198	221	2	944	33	8.5	2.8	3.1	13.1
Harry Gallatin	F-C	6'6	220	27	72	2548	330	859	38	393	483	81	995	176	206	5	1053	35	13.8	2.4	2.9	14.6
Ray Felix	C	6'11	220	24	72	2024	364	832	44	310	498	62	818	67	286	11	1038	28	11.4	0.9	4.0	14.4
Carl Braun	G	6'5	187	27	71	2479	400	1032	39	274	342	80	295	274	208	3	1074	35	4.2	3.9	2.9	15.1
Dick McGuire	G	6'	180	28	71	2310	226	581	39	195	303	64	322	542	143	0	647	33	4.5	7.6	2.0	9.1
Jim Baechtold	F-G	6'4	205	27	72	2536	362	898	40	279	339	82	307	218	202	0	1003	35	4.3	3.0	2.8	13.9
Gene Shue (6g. Phi)	G	6'2	175	23	62	947	100	289	35	59	78	76	154	89	64	0	259	15	2.5	1.4	1.0	4.2
Jack Turner	F-G	6'4	170	24	65	922	111	308	36	60	76	79	154	77	76	0	282	14	2.4	1.2	1.2	4.3
Bob Peterson (MS)	F	6'5	210	22	37	503	62	169	37	30	45	67	154	31	80	2	154	14	4.2	0.8	2.2	4.2
Bert Cook (FJ)	G-F	6'3	186	25	37	424	42	133	32	34	50	68	72	33	39	0	118	11	1.9	0.9	1.1	3.2
Fred Christ	G	6'4	210	24	6	48	5	18	28	10	11	91	8	7	3	0	20	8	1.3	1.2	0.5	3.3
Chuck Grigsby	G	6'5	190	26	7	45	7	19	37	2	8	25	11	7	9	0	16	6	1.6	1.0	1.3	2.3
Bob Knight	G	6'2	185	23	2	29	3	7	43	1	1	100	1	8	6	0	7	15	0.5	4.0	3.0	3.5
Herm Hederick (from Bal-MS)	G	6'5	170	24	5	23	2	9	22	0	1	0	4	2	3	0	4	5	0.8	0.4	0.6	0.8
Don Anielak	F	6'7	192	24	1	10	0	4	0	3	4	75	2	0	0	0	3	10	2.0	0.0	0.0	3.0
Ernie Vandeweghe-injury, voluntarily retired																						
BOSTON CELTICS	**36-36 .500**				**RED AUERBACH**																	
Don Barksdale	F	6'6	210	31	72	1790	267	699	38	220	338	65	545	129	225	7	754	25	7.6	1.8	3.1	10.5
Jack Nichols	F-C	6'7	230	28	64	1910	249	656	38	138	177	78	533	144	238	10	636	30	8.3	2.3	3.7	9.9
Ed Macauley	C-F	6'8	190	26	71	2706	403	951	42	442	558	79	600	275	171	0	1248	38	8.5	3.9	2.4	17.6
Bill Sharman	G	6'1	185	28	68	2453	453	1062	43	347	387	**90**	302	280	212	2	1253	36	4.4	4.1	3.1	18.4
Bob Cousy	G	6'1	175	26	71	2747	522	1316	40	460	570	81	424	**557**	165	1	1504	39	6.0	**7.8**	2.3	21.2
Frank Ramsey (injury)	F-G	6'3	190	23	64	1754	236	592	40	243	322	75	402	185	250	11	715	27	6.3	2.9	3.9	11.2
Bob Brannum	F	6'6	240	29	71	1623	176	465	38	90	127	71	492	127	232	6	442	23	6.9	1.8	3.3	6.2
Red Morrison	C-F	6'8	225	22	71	1227	120	284	42	72	115	63	451	82	222	10	312	17	6.4	1.2	3.1	4.4
Freddie Scolari	G	5'11	185	32	59	619	76	249	31	39	49	80	77	93	76	0	191	10	1.3	1.6	1.3	3.2
Togo Palazzi	G-F	6'4	205	22	53	504	101	253	40	45	60	75	146	30	60	1	247	10	2.8	0.6	1.1	4.7
Skippy Whitaker	G	6'1	185	24	3	15	1	6	17	0	0	—	1	1	4	0	2	5	0.3	0.3	1.3	0.7
Gene Conley - retired to play baseball																						
Eddie Miller (from Bal)-voluntarily retired																						
PHILADELPHIA WARRIORS	**33-39 .458**				**EDDIE GOTTLIEB**																	
Paul Arizin	F-G	6'4	200	26	72	**2953**	**529**	**1325**	40	454	585	78	675	210	270	5	1512	**41**	9.4	2.9	3.8	21.0
Joe Graboski	F	6'8	215	24	70	2515	373	1096	34	208	303	69	636	182	259	8	954	36	9.1	2.6	3.7	13.6
Neil Johnston	C	6'8	215	25	72	2917	521	1184	44	**589**	**769**	77	**1085**	215	255	4	**1631**	41	**15.1**	3.0	3.5	**22.7**
George Dempsey (MS)	G	6'3	192	25	48	1387	127	360	35	98	141	70	236	174	141	1	352	29	4.9	3.6	2.9	7.3
Jack George	G	6'3	190	26	68	2480	291	756	38	192	291	66	302	359	191	2	774	36	4.4	5.3	2.8	11.4
Ken Murray (14g. Bal)	G	6'2	195	26	66	1590	187	535	35	98	129	76	179	224	126	1	472	24	2.7	3.4	1.9	7.2
Zeke Zawoluk	F	6'7	215	24	67	1117	138	375	37	155	199	78	256	87	147	3	431	17	3.8	1.3	2.2	6.4
Danny Finn	G	6'1	185	26	43	820	77	265	29	53	86	62	157	155	114	3	207	19	3.7	3.6	2.7	4.8
Walt Davis	C-F	6'8	205	23	61	766	70	182	38	35	48	73	206	36	100	0	175	13	3.4	0.6	1.6	2.9
Paul Hoffman (13g. Bal, 16g. NY)	G-F	6'2	205	29	38	670	65	216	30	64	93	69	124	94	93	0	194	18	3.3	2.5	2.4	5.1
Larry Costello (MS)	G	6'1	175	23	19	463	46	139	33	26	32	81	49	78	37	0	118	24	2.6	4.1	1.9	6.2
Jackie Moore (1g. Syr, 1g. Mil)	F	6'5	182	22	23	376	44	115	38	22	47	47	105	20	62	2	110	16	4.6	0.9	2.7	4.8
Tom Brennan	F	6'5	200	24	11	52	5	11	45	0	0	—	5	2	5	0	10	5	0.5	0.2	0.5	0.9
Ted Kearns	G	6'4	185	25	6	25	0	5	0	1	4	25	3	5	1	0	1	4	0.5	0.8	0.2	0.2
Ernie Beck - military service																						
Jim Mooney - military service																						
BALTIMORE BULLETS	**3-11 .214**				**CLAIR BEE (1-4 .200), AL BARTHELME (2-7 .222)**																	

Bullets disbanded November 27,1954.

The Bullets' games and team statistics and the statistics of opposing players and teams in games played against the Bullets were not included in the official N.B.A. records. The statistics of the Bullets players were included in the official records, except that the 7 Bullets who went to other teams had some of their Bullets' statistics not counted so that they could only have a maximum of 72 scheduled games. The number of Bullets games shown here for these 7 men is the number they actually played, but their data are the official statistics

Use Name	Pos	Hgt	Wgt	Age	G	Min	FG	FGA	%	FT	FTA	%	Reb	Ass	PF	DQ	Points	Min	Reb	Ass	PF	Points
Jim Neal	C	6'11	235	24	13	194	12	59	20	14	21	67	47	9	22	0	38	15	3.6	0.7	1.7	2.9
Rollen Hans	G	6'2	210	24	12	178	27	67	40	14	26	54	16	26	19	0	68	15	1.3	2.2	1.6	5.7
Dan King	F	6'6	220	23	10	103	6	22	27	4	10	40	25	3	5	0	16	10	2.5	0.3	0.5	1.6
Al McGuire (leg injury)	G	6'2	185	26	9	98	6	32	19	3	7	43	9	8	14	0	15	11	1.0	0.9	1.6	1.7
Eddie Miller-suspended by team																						

Use Name	Pos	Hgt	Wgt	Age	TOTAL G	Min	FG	FGA	%	FT	FTA	%	Reb	Ast	PF	DQ	Points	PER GAME Min	Reb	Ast	PF	Points
1954/55 N.B.A. — WESTERN DIVISION																						
FORT WAYNE PISTONS	**43-29 .597**				**CHARLIE ECKMAN**																	
George Yardley (injury)	F	6'5	195	26	60	2150	363	869	42	310	416	75	594	126	205	7	1036	36	9.9	2.1	3.4	17.3
Mel Hutchins	F	6'6	205	26	72	2860	341	903	38	182	257	71	665	247	232	0	864	40	9.2	3.4	3.2	12.0
Larry Foust	C	6'9	240	26	70	2264	398	818	**49**	393	513	77	700	118	264	9	1189	32	10.0	1.7	3.8	17.0
Andy Phillip	G	6'3	195	32	64	2332	202	545	37	213	308	69	290	491	166	1	617	36	4.5	7.7	2.6	9.6
Max Zaslofsky	G	6'2	180	29	70	1862	269	821	33	247	352	70	191	203	130	0	785	27	2.7	2.9	1.9	11.2
Dick Rosenthal	F-G	6'5	205	21	67	1406	197	523	38	130	181	72	300	153	179	2	524	21	4.5	2.3	2.7	7.8
Frankie Brian	G	6'1	185	31	71	1381	237	623	38	217	255	85	127	142	133	0	691	19	1.8	2.0	1.9	9.7
Bob Houbregs(13g. Bal, 2g. Bos)	C-F	6'8	230	22	64	1326	148	386	38	129	182	71	297	86	180	5	425	21	4.6	1.3	2.8	6.6
Monk Meineke	F-C	6'7	210	24	68	1026	136	366	37	119	170	70	246	64	153	1	391	15	3.6	0.9	2.3	5.8
Paul Walther	G	6'2	160	27	68	820	56	161	35	54	88	61	155	131	115	1	166	12	2.3	1.9	1.7	2.4
Al Roges (13g. Bal)	F	6'4	200	24	17	201	23	61	38	15	24	63	24	19	20	0	61	12	1.4	1.1	1.2	3.6
Jim Fritsche	C-F	6'8	210	23	16	151	16	48	33	13	16	81	32	4	28	0	45	9	2.0	0.3	1.8	2.8
Dick Groat - military service																						
Bob Harris-voluntarily retired																						
MINNEAPOLIS LAKERS	**40-32 .556**				**JOHNNY KUNDLA**																	
Jim Pollard	F-G	6'5	195	32	63	1960	265	749	35	151	186	81	458	160	147	3	681	31	7.3	2.5	2.3	10.8
Vern Mikkelsen	F	6'7	230	26	72	2559	440	1043	42	447	598	75	722	145	**319**	14	1327	36	10.0	2.0	**4.4**	18.4
Clyde Lovellette	C	6'9	250	25	70	2361	519	1192	44	273	398	69	802	100	262	6	1311	34	11.5	1.4	3.7	18.7
Whitey Skoog	G	5'11	180	28	72	2365	330	836	39	126	155	81	303	251	265	10	785	33	4.2	3.5	3.7	10.9
Slater Martin	G	5'10	170	29	72	2784	350	919	38	276	359	77	260	427	221	7	976	39	3.6	5.9	3.1	13.6
Dick Schnittker	F	6'5	205	26	72	1798	226	583	39	298	362	82	349	114	231	7	750	25	4.8	1.6	3.2	10.4
Lew Hitch (57g. Mil)	F-C	6'8	200	25	74	1774	167	417	40	115	169	68	438	125	110	0	449	24	5.9	1.7	1.5	6.1
Ed Kalafat	C-F	6'6	245	22	72	1102	118	375	31	111	168	66	317	75	205	9	347	15	4.4	1.0	2.8	4.8
Jim Holstein	F-G	6'3	180	24	62	980	107	330	32	67	94	71	206	38	107	0	281	16	3.3	0.6	1.7	4.5
Don Sunderlage	G	6'1	180	25	45	404	33	133	25	48	73	66	56	37	57	0	114	9	1.2	0.8	1.3	2.5
Bob Carney	G	6'3	172	22	19	244	24	64	38	21	40	53	45	16	36	0	69	13	2.4	0.8	1.9	3.6
George Mikan - voluntarily retired																						
ROCHESTER ROYALS	**29-43 .403**				**LES HARRISON**																	
Odie Spears	F-G	6'5	205	29	71	1888	226	585	39	220	271	81	299	148	252	6	672	27	4.2	2.1	3.5	9.5
Jack Coleman	F	6'7	230	30	72	2482	400	866	46	124	183	68	729	232	201	1	924	34	10.1	3.2	2.8	12.8
Amie Risen	C	6'9	210	30	69	1970	259	699	37	279	375	74	703	112	253	10	797	29	10.2	1.6	3.7	11.6
Bob Davies	G	6'1	180	34	72	1870	326	785	42	220	293	75	205	355	155	2	872	26	2.8	4.9	2.2	12.1
Bobby Wanzer	G	6'	185	33	72	2376	324	820	40	294	374	79	374	247	163	2	942	33	5.2	3.4	2.3	13.1
Jack McMahon	G	6'1	188	26	72	1807	251	721	35	143	225	64	211	246	179	1	645	25	2.9	3.4	2.5	9.0
Don Henriksen (14g. Bal)	F-C	6'7	225	25	70	1664	139	406	34	137	195	70	484	111	190	2	415	24	6.9	1.6	2.7	5.9
Tom Marshall	F-G	6'4	215	23	72	1337	223	505	44	131	194	68	256	111	99	.0	577	19	3.6	1.5	1.4	8.0
Cal Christensen	F	6'5	230	27	71	1204	114	305	37	124	206	60	388	104	174	2	352	17	5.5	1.5	2.5	5.0
Art Spoelstra	C	6'9	220	22	70	1127	159	399	40	108	156	69	285	58	170	2	426	16	4.1	0.8	2.4	6.1
Boris Nachamkin	F	6'6	210	21	6	59	6	20	30	8	13	62	19	3	6	0	20	10	3.2	0.5	1.0	3.3
MILWAUKEE HAWKS	**26-46 .361**				**RED HOLZMAN**																	
Frank Selvy (14g. Bal)	F-G	6'3	180	22	71	2668	452	1195	38	444	610	73	394	245	230	3	1348	38	5.5	3.5	3.2	19.0
Bob Pettit	F-C	6'9	210	22	72	2659	520	1279	41	426	567	75	994	229	258	5	1466	37	13.8	3.2	3.6	20.4
Chuck Share	C	6'11	240	27	69	1685	235	577	41	351	492	71	684	84	273	**17**	821	24	9.9	1.2	4.0	11.9
Bill Calhoun	G-F	6'3	190	27	69	2109	144	480	30	166	236	70	290	235	181	4	454	31	4.2	3.4	2.6	6.6
Bob Harrison	G	6'2	190	27	72	2300	299	875	34	126	185	68	226	252	291	14	724	32	3.1	3.5	4.0	10.1
Chuck Cooper	F	6'5	215	28	70	1749	193	569	34	187	249	75	385	151	210	8	573	25	5.5	2.2	3.0	8.2
Pep Saul (KJ)	G	6'2	185	30	65	1139	96	303	32	95	123	77	134	104	126	0	287	18	2.1	1.6	1.9	4.4
Alex Hannum	F	6'7	225	31	53	1088	126	358	35	61	107	57	245	105	206	9	313	21	4.6	2.0	3.9	5.9
Bobby Watson (from Min)	G	6'	162	24	63	702	72	223	32	31	45	69	87	79	67	0	175	11	1.4	1.3	1.1	2.8
Ken McBride	G-F	6'3	190	23	12	249	48	147	33	21	29	72	31	14	31	0	117	21	2.6	1.2	2.6	9.8
George Ratkovicz	F	6'7	225	32	9	102	3	19	16	10	23	43	17	13	15	0	16	11	1.9	1.4	1.7	1.8
Fred Diute	G	6'3	210	25	7	72	2	21	11	7	12	58	13	4	12	0	11	10	1.9	0.6	1.7	1.6
Ronnie MacGilvray	G	6'2	185	24	6	57	2	12	17	4	7	57	9	11	5	0	8	10	1.5	1.8	0.8	1.3
Phil Martin	G	6'3	190	26	7	47	5	19	26	2	2	100	10	6	7	0	12	7	1.4	0.9	1.0	1.7
Carl McNulty	G	6'3	185	24	1	14	1	6	17	0	0	—	0	0	1	0	2	14	0.0	0.0	1.0	2.0
Iru Bemoras-military service																						

1954/55 N.B.A. — PLAYOFFS

e Name	Pos	Hgt	Wgt	Age	G	Min	FG	FGA	%	FT	FTA	%	Reb	Ass	PF	DQ	Points	Min	Reb	Ass	PF	Points
					TOTAL													PER GAME				
'RACUSE NATIONALS	**AL CERVI**				defeated Boston 3-1; H110-100, H116-100, 97-100(OT), 110-94; defeated Fort Wayne 4-3; H86-82, H87-84, 89-96,102-109, 71-74, H109-104, H92-91																	
rl Lloyd	F	6'6	220	26	11	355	44	122	36	39	52	75	89	35	41	0	127	32	8.1	3.2	3.7	11.5
olph Schayes	F	6'8	220	26	11	363	**60**	**167**	36	**89**	**106**	84	**141**	40	**48**	3	**209**	33	12.8	3.6	4.4	19.0
hnny Kerr	C	6'9	230	22	11	363	59	151	39	34	61	56	118	13	27	0	152	33	10.7	1.2	2.5	13.8
ul Seymour	G	6'2	185	26	11	410	46	149	31	45	50	90	43	75	21	0	137	37	3.9	6.8	1.9	12.5
orge King	G	6'	180	26	11	371	46	117	39	35	55	64	41	62	33	0	127	34	3.7	5.6	3.0	11.5
d Rocha	F-C	6'9	205	31	11	371	46	110	42	44	58	76	74	14	45	1	136	34	6.7	1.3	4.1	12.4
ck Farley	G	6'4	190	22	11	168	19	56	34	14	25	56	13	20	29	0	52	15	1.2	1.8	2.6	4.7
ly Kenville	G-F	6'2	185	24	11	130	17	48	35	36	49	73	31	11	23	1	70	12	2.8	1.0	2.1	6.4
ally Osterkorn	F	6'5	215	26	11	75	11	34	32	13	17	76	21	11	14	0	35	7	1.9	1.0	1.3	3.2
n Tucker	F	6'7	185	22	9	59	8	27	30	8	9	89	15	1	13	0	24	7	1.7	0.1	1.4	2.7
)RT WAYNE PISTONS	**CHARLIE ECKMAN**				defeated Minneapolis 3-1; H(Elkhart) 96-79, H(Indianapolis) 98-97(OT), 91-99(OT), 105-96; lost to Syracuse 3-4 (H at Indianapolis); 82-86, 84-87, H96-89, H109-102, H74-71, 104-109, 91-92																	
eorge Yardley	F	6'5	195	26	11	420	57	143	40	60	79	76	99	36	37	2	174	38	9.0	3.3	3.4	15.8
el Hutchins	F	6'6	205	26	11	417	**60**	144	42	38	56	68	89	31	47	3	158	38	8.1	2.8	4.3	14.4
rry Foust	C	6'9	240	26	11	331	**60**	152	39	52	73	71	107	26	43	0	172	30	9.7	2.4	3.9	15.6
dy Phillip	G	6'3	195	32	11	**445**	30	93	32	34	40	85	60	**78**	37	0	94	40	5.5	7.1	3.4	8.5
ankie Brian	G	6'1	185	31	11	269	48	120	40	31	38	82	22	27	26	0	127	24	2.0	2.5	2.4	11.5
ob Houbregs	C	6'8	230	22	11	213	24	63	38	29	37	78	62	19	31	0	77	19	5.6	1.7	2.8	7.0
ck Rosenthal	G-F	6'5	205	21	11	209	27	84	32	28	39	72	48	26	39	1	82	19	4.4	2.4	3.5	7.5
onk Meineke	F	6'7	210	24	11	162	18	40	45	23	25	92	48	9	22	0	59	15	4.4	0.8	2.0	5.4
ax Zaslofsky	G	6'2	180	29	11	129	18	44	41	16	20	80	16	18	20	0	52	12	1.5	1.6	1.8	4.7
ul Walther	G	6'2	160	27	10	95	12	22	55	11	18	61	20	8	20	0	35	10	2.0	0.8	2.0	3.5
Dick Groat - military service																						
INNEAPOLIS LAKERS	**JOHNNY KUNDLA**				defeated Rochester 2-1 (H at St. Paul); H82-78, 92-94, HI19-110; lost to Fort Wayne 1-3; 79-96, 97-98(OT), H99-91(OT), H96-105																	
n Pollard	F	6'5	195	32	7	257	33	104	32	33	46	72	78	14	13	0	99	37	11.1	2.0	1.9	14.1
rn Mikkelsen	F	6'7	230	26	7	209	30	85	35	36	46	78	78	13	36	**4**	96	30	11.1	1.9	**5.1**	13.7
yde Lovellette	C	6'9	250	25	7	197	44	98	45	29	40	73	64	3	32	1	117	28	9.1	0.4	4.6	16.7
hitey Skoog	G	5'11	180	28	7	241	36	92	39	19	21	90	37	16	30	1	91	34	5.3	2.3	4.3	13.0
ater Martin	G	5'10	170	29	7	315	28	94	30	40	49	82	28	31	23	0	96	**45**	4.0	4.4	3.3	13.7
ck Schnittker	F	6'5	205	26	7	140	14	51	27	25	36	69	31	7	23	1	53	20	4.4	1.0	3.3	7.6
w Hitch	C-F	6'8	200	25	7	137	16	40	40	23	29	79	42	10	9	0	55	20	6.0	1.4	1.3	7.9
n Holstein	G-F	6'3	180	24	7	117	16	38	42	8	9	89	30	6	8	0	40	17	4.3	0.9	1.1	5.7
l Kalafat	C	6'6	245	22	7	76	2	22	9	3	10	30	18	0	16	1	7	11	2.6	0.0	2.3	1.0
ob Carney	G	6'3	172	22	7	41	1	8	13	8	9	89	5	3	7	0	10	6	0.7	0.4	1.0	1.4
George Mikan - voluntarily retired																						
OSTON CELTICS	**RED AUERBACH**				defeated New York 2-1; H122-101, 95-102, 116-109; lost to Syracuse 1-3; 100-110, 110-116, H100-97(OT), H94-110																	
ob Brannum	F	6'6	240	29	7	225	26	61	27	11	19	58	79	13	32	2	63	32	11.3	1.9	4.6	9.0
ck Nichols	F-C	6'7	230	28	7	231	30	81	37	13	16	81	49	23	28	1	73	33	7.0	3.3	4.0	10.4
l Macauley	C	6'8	190	26	7	283	43	93	46	41	54	76	52	32	21	0	127	40	7.4	4.6	3.0	18.1
ll Sharman	G	6'1	185	28	7	290	55	110	50	35	38	92	38	38	24	1	145	41	5.4	5.4	3.3	20.7
ob Cousy	G	6'1	175	26	7	299	53	139	38	46	48	**96**	43	65	26	0	152	43	6.1	**9.3**	3.7	**21.7**
ank Ramsey	F-G	6'3	190	23	7	154	28	54	**52**	19	26	73	35	16	27	0	75	22	5.0	2.3	3.9	10.7
on Barksdale	F	6'6	210	31	7	122	18	40	45	18	21	86	35	10	17	1	54	17	5.0	1.4	2.4	7.7
d Morrison	C-F	6'8	225	22	7	42	3	8	38	1	3	33	14	1	22	1	7	6	2.0	0.1	3.1	1.0
go Palazzi	F	6'4	205	22	5	30	12	24	50	5	10	50	14	1	7	0	29	6	2.8	0.2	1.4	5.8
eddie Scolari	G	5'11	185	32	5	29	4	15	27	4	5	80	5	3	7	0	12	6	1.0	0.6	1.4	2.4
Gene Conley - retired to play baseball																						
OCHESTER ROYALS	**LES HARRISON**				lost to Minneapolis 1-2; 78-82, H94-92, 110-119																	
die Spears	F	6'5	205	29	3	90	12	45	27	11	16	69	14	10	14	1	35	30	4.7	3.3	4.7	11.7
ck Coleman	F	6'7	230	30	3	91	11	36	31	2	9	22	28	8	11	0	24	30	9.3	2.7	3.7	8.0
nie Risen	C	6'9	210	30	3	77	17	38	45	14	19	74	37	5	13	0	48	26	12.3	1.7	4.3	16.0
obby Wanzer	G	6'	185	33	3	100	16	35	46	22	24	92	21	8	8	0	54	33	7.0	2.7	2.7	18.0
ack McMahon	G	6'1	188	26	3	109	17	42	40	18	28	64	17	15	7	0	52	36	5.7	5.0	2.3	17.3
ob Davies	G	6'1	180	34	3	75	11	33	33	3	4	75	6	9	11	0	25	25	2.0	3.0	3.7	8.3
on Henriksen	C-F	6'7	225	25	3	70	3	12	25	7	10	70	16	3	5	0	13	23	5.3	1.0	1.7	4.3
m Marshall	F-G	6'4	215	23	3	50	3	20	15	3	5	60	17	2	1	0	9	17	5.7	0.7	0.3	3.0
al Christensen	F	6'5	230	27	3	30	2	8	25	3	6	50	6	0	1	0	7	10	2.0	0.0	0.3	2.3
t Spoelstra	C	6'9	220	22	3	28	7	14	50	1	1	100	9	0	11	0	15	9	3.0	0.0	3.7	5.0
EW YORK KNICKERBOCKERS	**JOE LAPCHICK**				lost to Boston 1-2; 101-122, H102-95, H109-116																	
m Baechtold	F-G	6'4	205	27	3	115	17	45	38	14	15	93	14	14	13	0	48	38	4.7	4.7	4.3	16.0
weetwater Clifton	F-C	6'6	225	32	3	110	20	52	38	19	24	79	23	13	12	0	59	37	7.7	4.3	4.0	19.7
arry Gallatin	C-F	6'6	220	27	3	108	19	42	45	17	22	77	44	7	11	0	55	36	**14.7**	2.3	3.7	18.3
arl Braun	G	6'5	187	27	3	103	18	44	41	18	20	90	14	16	11	0	54	34	4.7	5.3	3.7	18.0
ck McGuire	G	6'	180	28	3	75	6	19	32	8	12	67	9	12	7	0	20	25	3.0	4.0	2.3	6.7
ob Peterson	F	6'5	210	22	3	71	7	15	47	10	11	91	16	5	3	0	24	24	5.3	1.7	1.0	8.0
ay Felix	C	6'11	220	24	3	63	2	16	13	13	21	61	12	1	6	0	17	21	4.0	0.3	2.0	5.7
ene Shue	G	6'2	175	23	3	49	8	17	47	6	7	86	12	4	5	0	22	16	4.0	1.3	1.7	7.3
ert Cook	G	6'3	186	25	1	20	4	6	67	0	2	0	0	2	3	0	8	20	0.0	2.0	3.0	8.0
ack Turner	F	6'4	170	24	2	16	2	6	33	1	3	33	4	2	1	0	5	8	2.0	1.0	0.5	2.5
Ernie Vandeweghe - voluntarily retired																						

1954/55 N.B.A. TEAM STATISTICS

Team	REGULAR SEASON G	FG	FGA	%	FT	FTA	%	Reb.	Ass.	AVERAGE POINTS For	Agnst.	Diff.	PLAYOFFS G	FG	FGA	%	FT	FTA	%	Reb.	Ass.	AVERAGE POINTS For	Agnst.	Diff.
EASTERN DIVISION																								
Syracuse	72	2360	6343	37	1837	2450	75	3933	1778	91.1	**89.7**	+1.4	11	356	981	36	357	482	74	611	282	97.2	94.9	**+2.3**
New York	72	2392	6149	39	1887	2593	73	**4379**	1744	92.7	92.6	+0.1	3	103	262	39	**106**	**137**	77	177	76	104.0	111.0	-7.0
Boston	72	**2604**	**6533**	**40**	**2097**	2704	**78**	4293	**1905**	**101.4**	101.5	-0.1	7	**272**	625	**44**	193	240	**80**	398	**202**	**105.3**	106.4	-1.1
Philadelphia	72	2392	6234	38	1928	2625	73	4238	1744	93.2	93.5	-0.3												
WESTERN DIVISION																								
Fort Wayne	72	2333	5980	39	1986	**2710**	73	3826	1737	92.4	90.0	**+2.4**	11	354	905	39	322	425	76	581	278	93.7	**91.5**	+2.2
Minneapolis	72	2506	6465	39	1873	2517	74	3865	1458	95.6	94.5	+1.1	7	220	**632**	35	224	295	76	**411**	103	94.9	96.0	-1.1
Rochester	72	2399	6020	40	1737	2420	72	3904	1695	90.8	92.4	-1.6	3	99	263	38	84	122	69	171	60	94.0	97.7	-3.7
Milwaukee	72	2187	6041	36	1917	2672	72	3854	1544	87.4	90.4	-3.0												

1954/55 N.B.A. STANDINGS

Team	W	L	Pct.	GB	Record against playoff teams W	L	Pct.	Record against non-playoff teams W	L	Pct.	HOME W	L	Pct.	ROAD W	L	Pct.	NEUTRAL W	L	Pct.
EASTERN DIVISION																			
Syracuse Nationals	**43**	29	**.597**	—	**31**	20	**.608**	12	9	.571	**25**	7	.781	**10**	16	.385	8	6	.571
New York Knickerbockers	38	34	.528	5	27	24	.529	11	10	.524	17	8	.680	8	19	.296	13	7	**.650**
Boston Celtics	36	36	.500	7	23	28	.451	13	8	.619	20	5	**.800**	5	**22**	.185	11	9	.550
Philadelphia Warriors	33	39	.458	10	28	35	.444	5	4	.556	16	5	.762	4	19	.174	13	15	.464
WESTERN DIVISION																			
Fort Wayne Pistons	**43**	29	**.597**	—	26	25	.510	**17**	4	**.810**	20	6	.769	9	14	.391	**14**	9	.609
Minneapolis Lakers	40	32	.556	3	27	24	.529	13	8	.619	18	6	.750	**10**	14	**.417**	12	12	.500
Rochester Royals	29	43	.403	14	19	32	.373	10	**11**	.476	17	**11**	.607	4	19	.174	8	13	.381
Milwaukee Hawks	26	**46**	.361	17	22	**41**	.349	4	5	.444	6	**11**	.353	9	16	.360	11	**19**	.367

1954/55 INDIVIDUAL LEADERS

SCORING
(Minimum 48 Games Played)

Name	Team	G	FG	FT	Pts.	Avg.
Johnston	Phi	72	521	589	1631	22.7
Cousy	Bos	71	522	460	1504	21.2
Anzin	Phi	72	529	454	1512	21.0
Pettit	Mil	72	520	426	1466	20.4
Selvy	Bal-Mil	71	452	444	1348	19.0
Mikkelsen	Min	70	519	273	1311	18.7
Schayes	Syr	72	422	489	1333	18.5
Lovellette	Min	72	440	447	1327	18.4
Sharman	Bos	68	453	347	1253	18.4
Macauley	Bos	71	403	442	1248	17.6

FIELD GOAL PERCENTAGE
(Minimum 210 Field Goals)

Name	Team	FG	FGA	Pct.
Foust	FtW	398	818	.487
Coleman	Roch	400	866	.462
Johnston	Phi	521	1184	.440
Felix	NY	364	832	.438
Lovellette	Min	519	1192	.435
Sharman	Bos	453	1062	.427
Macauley	Bos	403	951	.424
Mikkelsen	Min	440	1043	.422
Kerr	Syr	301	718	.419
Yardley	FtW	363	869	.418

FREE THROW PERCENTAGE
(Minimum 180 Free Throws)

Name	Team	FT	FTA	Pct.
Sharman	Bos	347	387	.897
Brian	FtW	217	255	.851
Schayes	Syr	489	587	.833
Schnittker	Min	298	362	.823
Baechtold	NY	279	339	.823
Gallatin	NY	393	483	.814
Spears	Roch	220	271	.812
Seymour	Syr	300	370	.811
Cousy	Bos	460	560	.821
Braun	NY	274	342	.801

PERSONAL FOULS

Name	Team	PF
Mikkelsen	Min	319
Harrison	Mil	291
Felix	NY	286
Lloyd	Syr	283
Share	Mil	273

GAMES DISQUALIFIED

Name	Team	Disq
Share	Mil	17
Harrison	Mil	14
Mikkelsen	Min	14
Ramsey	Bos	11
Felix	NY	11

MINUTES PLAYED

Name	Team	Min.
Arzin	Phi	2953
Seymour	Syr	2950
Johnston	Phi	2917
Hutchins	FtW	2860
Martin	Min	2794

REBOUNDS PER GAME
(Minimum 48 Games Played)

Name	Team	G	Reb.	Avg.
Johnston	Phi	72	1085	15.1
Gallatin	NY	72	995	13.8
Pettit	Mil	72	994	13.8
Schayes	Syr	72	887	12.3
Lovellette	Min	70	802	11.5
Felix	NY	72	818	11.4
Risen	Roch	69	703	10.2
Coleman	Roch	72	729	10.1
Mikkelsen	Min	72	722	10.0
Foust	FtW	70	700	10.0

ASSISTS PER GAME
(Minimum 48 Games Played)

Name	Team	G	Ass.	Avg.
Cousey	Bos	71	557	7.8
Phillip	FtW	64	491	7.7
McGuire	NY	71	542	7.6
Seymour	Syr	72	483	6.7
Martin	Min	72	427	5.9
George	Phi	68	359	5.3
King	Syr	67	331	4.9
Davies	Roch	72	335	4.0
Sharman	Bos	68	280	4.1
Macauley	Bos	71	275	3.9

1955-56 N.B.A.

Way Up From the Basement

With a minimum of personnel changes, the Philadelphia Warriors soared from last place to the top of the Eastern Division this season. The first champions of the B.A.A. back in 1947, the Warriors had recently fallen on hard times and finished at the bottom of the East last year with a 33-39 mark. Owner-coach Eddie Gottlieb began the rebuilding process by turning over the coaching reins to George Senesky, a long-time player under Gottlieb with the old Sphas and with the Warriors. A second step in building the Warriors back up to a position of strength was the signing of rookie Tom Gola. Acclaimed as one of the best all-around players in collegiate history, Gola led LaSalle to the N.I.T. championship in 1952 and to the N.C.A.A. finals in 1955 before losing to San Francisco and Bill Russell. Reserve forward Ernie Beck also returned to the club from the military, but no other key personnel changes were made.

The Warriors had a lot of talented players who suddenly started pulling together under Senesky's direction. Paul Arizin and Neil Johnston finished two-three in the league scoring tables, giving the Warriors an unmatched outside-inside scoring tandem. Arizin popped in enough jump shots from his forward slot to average 24.2 despite an asthma condition which often set him coughing and wheezing while running up and down court. Johnston, a tough 6'8" center, used a hook shot to average over 20 points per game for the fourth straight season. These two scorers were the established stars on the club. The supporting cast, however, surprised the league with its solid play. Veteran forward Joe Graboski furnished muscle to the forecourt, and guard Jack George blossomed into a first-rate playmaker in his third pro season. Gola helped the Warriors immensely as the other starting guard; a 6'6" forward in college, he smoothly converted to the backcourt, giving the Warriors the N.B.A.'s biggest guard and giving the league's other clubs a sizeable problem on defense. With the bench making occasional contributions, with the offense as potent as ever, and with the defense tightened up considerably, the Warriors leapfrogged all the way to first place with a 45-27 record, the best in the league.

The Boston Celtics trailed the Warriors by six games, still missing the rebounding muscle and defense to make its fast-break offense pay top dividends. Bob Cousy, Bill Sharman, and Ed Macauley all finished in the top ten in scoring, but the Celtics had to wait for a first-class center before they could reach championship status. Nevertheless, coach Red Auerbach continued adding serviceable bodies to his squad by signing rookie forward Jim Loscutoff, a rugged rebounder who soon became known around the league as a"hatchet man."

Falling under the .500 level were the New York Knicks, who were in the midst of a rebuilding program that would show scant results until the late 1960's. Rookie forward Kenny Sears, a pencil-thin shooter, and center Walter Dukes, a refugee from the Harlem Globetrotters, were this year's key additions to the aging squad. The biggest loss to the New York squad was coach Joe Lapchick, a very popular figure with the press and the public; having lost the confidence of team President Ned Irish, Lapchick resigned in February, and Vince Boryla took over as the new coach. The Knicks finished in a tie for third with the Syracuse Nats who slumped badly from last season's championship form. With the final playoff spot at stake, the Nats beat the Knicks in a one-game showdown at the end of the regular season, thus shutting the New Yorkers out of the playoffs for the first time ever.

While the Eastern Division was thoroughly shaking up its standings, the Western clubs finished in practically the same order as last season. The Ft. Wayne Pistons won six less games than they did last season, but they still captured first place with a 37-35 record. Forward George Yardley and center Larry Foust continued to pace the team's scoring, but coach Charlie Eckman rebuilt his backcourt by releasing Max Zaslofsky, benching Frankie Brian, and replacing these two veterans with rookies Chuck Noble and Corky Devlin.

Finishing four games back in a tie for the remaining playoff berths were the Minneapolis Lakers and the St. Louis Hawks. The Lakers slipped under .500 for the first time despite fine scoring from center Clyde Lovellette and fine playmaking from guard Slater Martin. Jim Pollard had retired, but when the Lakers began to panic in mid-season, they prevailed upon George Mikan to come out of retirement to play center. Mikan was overweight and rusty at first, but he played himself back into shape by the time the playoffs began; he could not, however, again be the dominant force he had been, since his age and the 24-second clock worked against him.

Tying the Lakers for second place were the Hawks, transplanted to St. Louis by owner Ben Kerner in a move which paid off at the box office. The improving Hawks got help from former Royals Jack Coleman and Jack McMahon, but the major force on the club was the vastly improving Bob Pettit. A glowing competitor and hard worker, Pettit led the N. B.A. both in scoring and rebounding, and he led the Hawks into the playoffs for the first time since 1950, when the club was still in Tri-Cities.

The Royals tumbled into last place and out of the playoffs for the first time in the club's history. Veteran guard Bob Davies quit, and center Arnie Risen was dispatched to Boston; coach Les Harrison installed three rookies in his starting lineup: forwards Maurice Stokes and Jack Twyman and guard Ed Fleming. A product of tiny St. Francis (Pa.), Stokes gave the Royals a top-notch strong forward, while Twyman brought polished shooting skills from his career at the University of Cincinnati. But the fans were showing up in smaller numbers at Royal games, and Harrison was already thinking of greener pastures elsewhere.

The early matches in the playoffs all went the limit. Syracuse beat Boston and St. Louis beat Minneapolis in three-game series, and Philadelphia beat Syracuse and Ft. Wayne beat St. Louis in five-game series. With the 24-second clock now filling all the games with basketball action, the N.B.A. expected an exciting seven-game championship series between the Warriors and Pistons. It didn't happen, however, as the Warriors upended the Pistons in five games to easily take their first N.B.A. title. Starting next year, though, a new champion would take the crown and prove very difficult to dislodge from the throne.

Use Name	Pos	Hgt	Wgt	Age	TOTAL G	Min	FG	FGA	%	FT	FTA	%	Reb	Ass	PF	DQ	Points	PER GAME Min	Reb	Ass	PF	Points
1955/56 N.B.A. — EASTERN DIVISION																						
PHILADELPHIA WARRIORS	**45-27 .625**				**GEORGE SENESKY**																	
Paul Arizin	F	6'4	200	27	72	2724	617	1378	45	507	626	81	539	189	282	11	1741	38	7.5	2.6	3.9	24.2
Joe Graboski	F	6'8	225	25	72	2375	397	1075	37	240	340	71	642	190	272	5	1034	33	8.9	2.6	3.8	14.4
Neil Johnston	C	6'8	215	26	70	2594	499	1092	**46**	549	685	80	872	225	251	8	1547	37	12.5	3.2	3.6	22.1
Tom Gola	G-F	6'6	205	22	68	2346	244	592	41	244	333	73	616	404	272	11	732	35	9.1	5.9	4.0	10.8
Jack George	F	6'3	195	27	72	**2840**	352	940	37	296	391	76	313	457	202	1	1000	**39**	4.3	6.3	2.8	13.9
George Dempsey	G	6'3	195	26	72	1444	126	265	48	88	139	63	264	205	146	7	340	20	3.7	2.8	2.0	4.7
Walt Davis	C-F	6'8	210	24	70	1097	123	333	37	77	112	69	276	56	230	7	323	16	3.9	0.8	3.3	4.6
Ernie Beck	F	6'4	195	24	67	1007	136	351	39	76	106	72	196	79	86	0	348	15	2.9	1.2	1.3	5.2
Larry Hennessy	G	6'3	185	26	53	444	85	247	34	26	32	81	49	46	37	0	196	8	0.9	0.9	0.7	3.7
Jackie Moore	F	6'5	195	23	54	402	50	129	39	32	53	60	117	26	80	1	132	7	2.2	0.5	1.5	2.4
Larry Costello - military service																						
BOSTON CELTICS	**39-33 .542**				**RED AUERBACH**																	
Jim Loscutoff	F	6'5	230	25	71	1582	226	628	36	139	207	67	622	65	213	4	591	22	8.8	0.9	3.0	8.3
Jack Nichols	F	6'7	230	29	60	1964	330	799	41	200	253	79	625	160	228	7	860	33	10.4	2.7	3.8	14.3
Ed Macauley	C-F	6'8	190	27	71	2354	420	995	42	400	504	79	422	211	158	2	1240	33	5.9	3.0	2.2	17.5
Bill Sharman	G	6'1	185	29	72	2698	538	1229	44	358	413	**87**	259	339	197	1	1434	37	3.6	4.7	2.7	19.9
Bob Cousy	G	6'1	175	27	72	2767	440	1223	36	476	564	84	492	**642**	206	2	1356	38	6.8	**8.9**	2.9	18.8
Arnie Risen	C	6'9	210	31	68	1597	189	493	38	170	240	71	553	88	300	**17**	548	23	8.1	1.3	4.4	8.1
Ernie Barrett	G	6'3	180	26	72	1451	207	533	39	93	118	79	243	174	184	4	507	20	3.4	2.4	2.6	7.0
Dick Hemric	F	6'6	220	22	71	1329	161	400	40	177	273	65	399	60	142	2	499	19	5.6	0.8	2.0	7.0
Red Morrison	F-C	6'8	225	23	71	910	89	240	37	44	89	49	345	53	159	5	222	13	4.9	0.7	2.2	3.1
Togo Palazzi	F-G	6'4	205	23	63	703	145	373	39	85	124	69	182	42	87	0	375	11	2.9	0.7	1.4	6.0
Gene Conley - retired to play baseball																						
Frank Ramsey - military service																						
SYRACUSE NATIONALS	**35-37 .486**				**AL CERVI**	defeated New York 82-77 at home in playoff for third place.																
Earl Lloyd	F	6'6	220	27	72	1837	213	636	33	186	241	77	492	116	267	6	612	26	6.8	1.6	3.7	8.5
Dolph Schayes	F	6'8	220	27	72	2517	465	1202	39	542	632	86	891	200	251	9	1472	35	12.4	2.8	3.5	20.4
Johnny Kerr	C	6'9	230	23	72	2114	377	935	40	207	316	66	607	84	168	3	961	29	8.4	1.2	2.3	13.3
Paul Seymour (injury)	G	6'2	185	27	57	1826	227	670	34	188	233	81	152	276	130	1	642	32	2.7	4.8	2.3	11.3
George King	G	6'	180	27	72	2343	284	763	37	176	275	64	250	410	150	2	744	33	3.5	5.7	2.1	10.3
Red Rocha	C-F	6'9	215	32	72	1883	250	692	36	220	281	78	416	131	244	6	720	26	5.8	1.8	3.4	10.0
Dick Farley	G	6'4	190	23	72	1429	168	451	37	143	207	69	165	151	154	2	479	20	2.3	2.1	2.1	6.7
Ed Conlin	F	6'6	200	22	66	1423	211	574	37	121	178	68	326	145	121	1	543	22	4.9	2.2	1.8	8.2
Billy Kenville	G	6'2	185	25	72	1278	170	448	38	195	257	76	215	159	132	0	535	18	3.0	2.2	1.8	7.4
Jim Tucker	F	6'7	185	23	70	895	101	290	35	66	83	80	232	38	166	2	268	13	3.3	0.5	2.4	3.8
NEW YORK KNICKERBOCKERS	**35-37 .486**				**JOE LAPCHICK (26-25 .510), VINCE BORYLA (9-12 .429)**	lost to Syracuse 77-82 at Syracuse in playoff for third place.																
Kenny Sears	F	6'9	195	22	70	2069	319	728	44	258	324	80	616	114	201	4	896	30	8.8	1.6	2.9	12.8
Harry Gallatin	F	6'6	220	28	72	2378	322	834	39	358	455	79	740	168	220	6	1002	33	10.3	2.3	3.1	13.9
Ray Felix	C	6'11	220	25	72	1702	277	668	41	331	469	71	623	47	293	13	885	24	8.7	0.7	4.1	12.3
Carl Braun	G	6'5	187	28	72	2316	396	1064	37	320	382	84	259	298	215	3	1112	32	3.6	4.1	3.0	15.4
Dick McGuire	G	6'	180	29	62	1685	152	438	35	121	193	63	220	362	146	0	425	27	3.5	5.8	2.4	6.9
Gene Shue	G	6'2	175	24	72	1750	240	625	38	181	237	76	212	179	111	0	661	24	2.9	2.5	1.5	9.2
Jim Baechtold	F-G	6'4	207	28	70	1738	268	695	39	233	291	80	220	163	156	2	769	25	3.1	2.3	2.2	11.0
Sweetwater Clifton	F-C	6'6	225	33	64	1537	213	541	39	135	191	71	386	151	189	4	561	24	6.0	2.4	3.0	8.8
Walter Dukes	C	7'	220	25	60	1290	149	370	40	167	236	71	443	39	211	11	465	22	7.4	0.7	3.5	7.8
Bob Peterson	F	6'5	210	23	58	779	121	303	40	68	104	65	223	44	123	0	310	13	3.8	0.8	2.1	5.3
Dick Atha	G	6'2	190	25	25	288	36	88	41	21	27	78	42	32	39	0	93	12	1.7	1.3	1.6	3.7
Ernie Vandeweghe (VR)	G	6'3	195	29	5	77	10	31	32	2	2	100	13	12	15	0	22	15	2.6	2.4	3.0	4.4
Bob Santini	F	6'5	190	20	4	23	5	10	50	1	2	50	3	1	4	0	11	6	0.8	0.3	1.0	2.8

ee Name	Pos	Hgt	Wgt	Age	TOTAL G	Min	FG	FGA	%	FT	FTA	%	Reb	Ass	PF	DQ	Points	PER GAME Min	Reb	Ass	PF	Points

1955/56 N.B.A. — WESTERN DIVISION

ee Name	Pos	Hgt	Wgt	Age	G	Min	FG	FGA	%	FT	FTA	%	Reb	Ass	PF	DQ	Points	Min	Reb	Ass	PF	Points
ORT WAYNE PISTONS	**37-35 .514**				**CHARLIE ECKMAN**																	
eoge Yardley	F	6'5	195	27	71	2353	434	1067	41	365	492	74	686	159	212	2	1233	33	9.7	2.2	3.0	17.4
el Hutchins	F	6'6	205	27	66	2240	325	764	43	142	221	64	496	180	166	1	792	34	7.5	2.7	2.5	12.0
arry Foust	C	6'9	240	27	72	2024	367	821	45	432	555	78	648	127	263	7	1166	28	9.0	1.8	3.7	16.2
huck Noble	G	6'4	195	24	72	2013	270	767	35	146	195	75	261	282	253	3	686	28	3.6	3.9	3.5	9.5
ndy Phillip	G	6'3	195	33	70	2078	148	405	37	112	199	56	257	410	155	2	408	30	3.7	5.9	2.2	5.8
orky Devlin	G	6'5	195	24	69	1535	200	541	37	146	192	76	171	138	119	0	546	22	2.5	2.0	1.7	7.9
ob Houbregs	C-F	6'8	225	23	70	1535	247	575	43	283	383	74	414	159	147	0	777	22	5.9	2.3	2.1	11.1
die Spears	F-G	6'5	205	30	72	1378	166	468	35	159	201	79	231	121	191	2	491	19	3.2	1.7	2.7	6.8
huck Cooper (35g. StL)	F	6'5	215	29	67	1140	101	308	33	100	133	75	239	89	140	0	302	17	3.6	1.3	2.1	4.5
rankie Brian	G	6'1	185	32	37	680	78	263	30	72	88	82	88	74	62	0	228	18	2.4	2.0	1.7	6.2
esse Arnelle	F	6'5	220	22	31	409	52	164	32	43	69	62	170	18	60	0	147	13	5.5	0.6	1.9	4.7
lax Zaslofsky	G	6'2	180	30	9	182	29	81	36	30	35	86	16	16	18	1	88	20	1.8	1.8	2.0	9.8
m Holstein	F-G	6'3	190	25	27	352	24	89	27	24	37	65	76	38	51	1	72	13	2.8	1.4	1.9	2.7
on Bielke	C	6'8	240	—	7	38	5	9	56	4	7	57	9	1	9	0	14	5	1.3	0.1	1.3	2.0
Dick Groat - retired to play baseball																						
Dick Rosenthal - military service																						
INNEAPOLIS LAKERS	**33-39 .458**				**JOHNNY KUNDLA**					defeated St Louis 103-97 at St. Louis in playoff for second place.												
ick Schnittker	F	6'5	205	27	72	1930	254	647	39	304	355	86	296	142	253	4	812	27	4.1	2.0	3.5	11.3
ern Mikkelsen	F	6'7	230	27	72	2100	317	821	39	328	408	80	608	173	**319**	**17**	962	29	8.4	2.4	**4.4**	13.4
lyde Lovellette	C-F	6'9	245	26	71	2518	594	1370	43	338	469	72	992	164	245	5	1526	35	14.0	2.3	3.5	21.5
hitey Skoog	G	5'11	185	29	72	2311	340	854	40	155	193	80	291	255	232	5	835	32	4.0	3.5	3.2	11.6
later Martin	G	5'10	170	30	72	2838	309	863	36	329	395	83	260	445	202	2	947	39	3.6	6.2	2.8	13.2
d Kalafat	C-F	6'6	245	23	72	1639	194	540	36	186	252	74	440	130	236	2	574	23	6.1	1.8	3.3	8.0
ew Hitch	F-C	6'8	210	26	69	1129	94	235	40	100	132	76	283	77	85	0	288	16	4.1	1.1	1.2	4.2
huch Mencel	G	6'	173	22	69	973	120	375	32	78	96	81	110	132	74	1	318	14	1.6	1.9	1.1	4.6
ick Garmaker	G-F	6'3	205	23	68	870	138	373	37	112	139	81	132	104	127	0	388	13	1.9	1.5	1.9	5.7
eorge Mihan (VR)	C	6'10	260	31	37	765	148	375	39	94	122	77	308	53	153	6	390	21	8.3	1.4	4.1	10.5
ob Williams	F	6'6	230	24	20	173	21	46	46	24	45	53	54	7	36	1	66	9	2.7	0.4	1.8	3.3
ohnny Horan (7g. FtW)	F	6'8	190	23	19	93	12	42	29	10	11	91	10	2	21	0	34	5	0.5	0.1	1.1	1.8
on Feiereisel	G	6'3	185	24	10	59	8	28	29	14	16	88	6	6	9	0	30	6	0.6	0.6	0.9	3.0
T LOUIS HAWKS	**33-39 .458**				**RED HOLZMAN**					lost to Minneapolis 97-103 at home in playoff for second place.												
ack Coleman (34g. Roch)	F-C	6'7	230	31	75	2738	390	946	41	177	249	71	688	294	242	2	957	37	9.2	3.9	3.2	12.8
ob Pettit	F-C	6'9	210	23	72	2794	**646**	**1507**	43	**557**	**757**	74	**1164**	189	202	1	**1849**	39	16.2	2.6	2.8	**25.7**
huck Share	C	6'11	240	28	72	1975	315	733	43	346	498	69	774	131	318	13	976	27	10.8	1.8	4.4	13.6
ack Stephens	G-F	6'3	185	22	72	2219	248	643	39	247	357	69	377	207	144	6	743	31	5.2	2.9	2.0	10.3
ob Harrison	G	6'2	190	28	72	2219	260	725	36	97	146	66	195	277	246	6	617	31	2.7	3.8	3.4	8.6
ack McMahon (34g. Roch)	G	6'1	188	27	70	1713	202	615	33	110	185	59	180	222	170	1	514	24	2.6	3.2	2.4	7.3
l Ferrari	G-F	6'4	190	22	68	1611	191	534	36	164	236	69	186	163	192	3	546	24	2.7	2.4	2.8	8.0
lex Hannum	F-C	6'7	225	32	71	1480	146	453	32	93	154	60	344	157	271	10	385	21	4.8	2.2	3.8	5.4
ob Schafer (12g. Phi)	G	6'3	195	22	54	578	81	270	30	62	81	77	71	53	75	0	224	11	1.3	1.0	1.4	4.1
rank Selvy (MS)	G	6'3	185	23	17	444	67	183	37	53	71	75	54	35	38	1	187	26	3.2	2.1	2.2	11.0
led Park	F	6'2	205	22	40	424	53	152	35	44	70	63	94	40	64	0	150	11	2.4	1.0	1.6	3.8
Irv Bemoras - military service																						
OCHESTER ROYALS	**31-41 .431**				**BOBBY WANZER**																	
ack Twyman	F-G	6'6	210	21	72	2186	417	987	42	204	298	68	466	171	239	4	1038	30	6.5	2.4	3.3	14.4
laurice Stokes	F	6'7	230	22	67	2323	403	1137	35	319	447	71	1094	328	276	11	1125	35	**16.3**	4.9	4.1	16.8
rt Spoelstra	C	6'9	220	23	72	1640	226	576	39	163	238	68	436	95	248	11	615	23	6.1	1.3	3.4	8.5
d Fleming	G	6'3	185	22	71	2028	306	824	37	277	372	74	489	197	178	1	889	29	6.9	2.8	2.5	12.5
obby Wanzer	G	6'	185	34	72	1980	245	651	38	259	360	72	272	225	151	0	749	28	3.8	3.1	2.1	10.4
ick Richetts (29g. StL)	F	6'7	205	22	68	1943	235	752	31	138	195	71	490	206	287	14	608	29	7.2	3.0	4.2	8.9
ichie Regan	G	6'2	180	25	72	1746	240	681	35	85	133	64	174	222	179	4	565	24	2.4	3.1	2.5	7.8
lonk Meineke	F-C	6'7	210	25	69	1248	154	414	37	181	232	78	316	102	191	4	489	18	4.6	1.5	2.8	7.1
onnie Simmons	C	6'8	225	30	68	903	144	428	34	78	129	60	235	82	142	2	366	13	3.5	1.2	2.1	5.4
hris Harris (15g. StL)	G	6'3	190	22	41	420	37	149	25	27	45	60	44	44	43	0	101	10	1.1	1.1	1.0	2.5
im Davis	C	6'7	220	23	3	16	0	6	0	2	2	100	4	1	2	0	2	5	1.3	0.3	0.7	0.7
Tom Marshall - military service																						

1955/56 N.B.A. — PLAYOFFS

Use Name	Pos	Hgt	Wgt	Age	G	Min	FG	FGA	%	FT	FTA	%	Reb	Ass	PF	DQ	Points	Min	Reb	Ass	PF	Point
					TOTAL													PER GAME				
PHILADELPHIA WARRIORS	**GEORGE SENESKY**				defeated Syracuse 3-2; H109-87, 118-122, H119-96, 104-108, H109-104 defeated Fort Wayne 4-1; H98-94, 83-84, H100-96, 107-105, H99-88																	
Paul Arizin	F	6'4	200	27	10	**409**	**103**	**229**	45	**83**	**99**	84	84	29	31	1	**289**	41	8.4	2.9	3.1	**28.**
Joe Graboski	F-C	6'8	225	25	10	313	53	154	34	26	35	74	94	27	37	2	132	31	9.4	2.7	3.7	13.
Neil Johnston	C	6'8	215	26	10	397	69	169	41	65	92	71	**143**	51	41	0	203	40	14.3	5.1	4.1	20.
Tom Gola	G-F	6'6	205	22	10	360	38	107	36	47	60	78	101	58	**47**	2	123	36	10.1	5.8	4.7	12.
Jack George	G	6'3	195	27	10	405	46	118	39	44	59	75	47	52	37	2	136	41	4.7	5.2	3.7	13.
Ernie Beck	G-F	6'4	195	24	10	250	31	72	43	22	31	71	51	22	32	1	84	25	5.1	2.2	3.2	8
George Dempsey	G	6'3	195	26	10	134	12	30	40	14	20	70	25	13	11	0	38	13	2.5	1.3	1.1	3.
Walt Davis	C	6'8	210	24	10	69	10	22	45	3	6	50	28	3	21	0	23	7	2.8	0.3	2.1	2.
Jackie Moore	F	6'5	195	23	8	52	8	20	40	2	6	33	17	2	14	0	18	7	2.1	0.3	1.8	2.
Larry Hennessy	G	6'3	185	26	3	11	0	9	0	0	0	—	1	2	1	0	0	4	0.3	0.7	0.3	0.
Larry Costello - military service																						
FORT WAYNE PISTONS	**CHARLIE ECKMAN**				defeated St. Louis 3-2; H85-86, 74-84, H107-84, 93-84, H102-97 lost to Philadelphia 1-4; 94-98, H84-83, 96-100, H105-107, 88-99																	
George Yardley	F	6'5	195	27	10	406	77	183	42	76	98	78	139	26	25	0	230	41	13.9	2.6	2.5	23.
Mel Hutchins	F	6'6	205	27	10	377	34	112	30	25	41	61	88	23	27	1	93	38	8.8	2.3	2.7	9.
Larry Foust	C	6'9	240	27	10	289	49	130	38	70	89	79	127	14	38	2	168	29	12.7	1.4	3.8	16.
Corky Devlin	G	6'5	195	24	10	275	41	101	41	15	25	60	21	23	21	0	97	28	2.1	2.3	2.1	9.
Chuck Noble	G	6'4	195	24	10	261	29	92	32	16	17	94	30	41	30	1	74	26	3.0	4.1	3.0	7.
Bob Houbregs	C-F	6'8	225	23	10	217	36	78	46	31	44	70	67	14	21	1	103	22	6.7	1.4	2.1	10.
Odie Spears	F-G	6'5	205	30	10	177	20	62	32	13	23	57	29	14	33	0	53	18	2.9	1.4	3.3	5.
Andy Phillip	G	6'3	195	33	10	173	9	27	33	11	25	44	26	35	16	0	29	17	2.6	3.5	1.6	2.
Frankie Brian	G	6'1	185	32	10	166	26	68	38	17	21	81	12	17	15	0	69	17	1.2	1.7	1.5	6.
Chuck Cooper	F	6'5	215	29	9	59	5	26	19	2	3	67	17	2	5	0	12	7	1.9	0.2	0.6	1.
Dick Groat - retired to play baseball, Dick Rosenthal - military service																						
SYRACUSE NATIONALS	**AL CERVI**				defeated Boston 2-1; 93-110, H101-98, 102-97 lost to Philadelphia 2-3; 87-109, H122-118, 96-119, H108-104,104-109																	
Ed Conlin	F	6'6	200	22	8	197	31	85	36	22	38	58	47	9	14	0	84	25	5.9	1.1	1.8	10.
Dolph Schayes	F	6'8	220	27	8	310	52	142	37	73	83	88	111	27	27	0	177	39	13.9	3.4	3.4	22.
Johnny Kerr	C	6'9	230	23	8	213	37	77	48	15	33	45	68	10	23	0	89	27	8.5	1.3	2.9	11.
Dick Farley	G	6'4	190	23	8	169	34	72	47	19	31	61	21	28	31	2	87	21	2.6	3.5	3.9	10.
George King	G	6'	180	27	8	317	39	108	36	38	48	79	47	**60**	16	0	116	40	5.9	7.5	2.0	14.
Red Rocha	C-F	6'9	215	32	8	189	23	68	34	22	26	85	52	15	37	3	68	24	6.5	1.9	4.6	8.
Earl Lloyd	F	6'6	220	27	8	172	26	81	32	13	14	93	43	7	37	1	65	22	5.4	0.9	4.6	8.
Paul Seymour	G	6'2	185	27	7	153	16	55	29	15	20	75	11	18	11	0	47	22	1.6	2.6	1.6	6.
Billy Kenville	G	6'2	185	25	8	128	16	45	36	16	23	70	17	14	21	0	48	16	2.1	1.8	2.6	6.
Jim Tucker	F	6'7	185	23	6	72	13	34	38	6	8	75	25	2	15	0	32	12	4.2	0.3	2.5	5.
ST. LOUIS HAWKS	**RED HOLZMAN**				defeated Minneapolis 2-1; H116-115, 75-133, 116-115 lost to Fort Wayne 2-3; 86-85, H84-74, 84-107, H84-93, 97-102																	
Jack Coleman	F	6'7	230	31	8	331	44	112	39	22	35	63	79	32	31	0	110	**41**	9.9	4.0	3.9	13.
Bob Pettit	F-C	6'9	210	23	8	274	47	128	37	59	70	84	84	18	20	0	153	34	10.5	2.3	2.5	19.
Chuck Share	C	6'11	240	28	8	231	36	73	49	31	48	65	73	13	41	**4**	103	29	9.1	1.6	**5.1**	12.
Al Ferrari	G	6'4	190	22	8	264	32	85	38	54	70	77	33	24	28	0	118	33	4.1	3.0	3.5	14.
Bob Harrison	G	6'2	190	28	8	256	27	75	36	12	19	63	24	29	27	1	66	32	3.0	3.6	3.4	8.
Jack McMahon	G	6'1	188	27	8	162	19	55	35	5	11	45	9	15	18	0	43	20	1.1	1.9	2.3	5.
Alex Hannum	F-C	6'7	225	32	8	159	21	66	32	19	35	54	29	10	36	3	61	20	3.6	1.3	4.5	7.
Jack Stephens	F-G	6'3	185	22	7	116	12	41	29	15	25	60	23	9	9	0	39	17	3.3	1.3	1.2	5.6
Med Park	F	6'2	205	22	6	88	7	30	23	24	33	73	17	11	19	1	38	15	2.8	1.8	3.2	6.3
Bob Schafer	G	6'3	195	22	4	39	3	20	15	5	6	83	9	1	8	1	11	10	2.3	0.3	2.0	2.8
Irv Bemoras and Frank Selvy - military service																						
MINNEAPOLIS LAKERS	**JOHNNY KUNDLA**				lost to St. Louis 1-2; 115-116, H133-75, H115-116																	
Dick Schnittker	F	6'5	205	27	3	87	13	23	**57**	17	20	85	15	5	14	2	43	29	5.0	1.7	4.7	14.3
Vern Mikkelsen	F	6'7	230	27	3	90	11	26	42	18	20	90	17	2	14	2	40	30	5.7	0.7	4.7	13.3
George Mikan	C	6'10	260	31	3	60	13	35	37	10	13	77	28	5	14	0	36	20	9.3	1.7	4.7	12.0
Whitey Skoog	G	5'11	185	29	3	90	13	31	42	3	11	27	18	18	11	0	29	30	6.0	6.0	3.7	9.7
Slater Martin	G	5'10	170	30	3	121	17	37	46	20	24	83	7	15	9	0	54	40	2.3	5.0	3.0	18.0
Clyde Lovellette	C-F	6'9	245	26	3	69	19	39	49	19	32	59	25	6	13	1	57	23	8.3	2.0	4.3	19.0
Ed Kalafat	C-F	6'6	245	23	3	55	9	21	43	15	19	79	21	2	13	1	33	18	7.0	0.7	4.3	11.0
Lew Hitch	F	6'8	210	26	3	54	4	13	31	7	10	70	15	2	7	0	15	18	5.0	0.7	2.3	5.0
Chuck Mencel	G	6'	173	22	3	52	10	19	53	6	7	86	5	8	4	0	26	17	1.7	2.7	1.3	8.7
Dick Garmaker	G-F	6'3	205	23	3	42	7	19	37	16	17	94	8	11	8	0	30	14	2.7	3.7	2.7	10.0
BOSTON CELTICS	**RED AUERBACH**				lost to Syracuse 1-2; H110-93, 98-101, H97-102																	
Jim Loscutoff	F	6'5	230	25	3	89	11	31	35	7	9	78	26	4	8	0	29	30	8.7	1.3	2.7	9.7
Jack Nichols	F	6'7	230	29	3	100	16	43	37	9	10	90	36	10	13	0	41	33	12.0	3.3	4.3	13.7
Arne Risen	C	6'9	210	31	3	88	12	34	35	13	18	72	44	2	15	0	37	29	**14.7**	0.7	5.0	12.3
Bill Sharman	G	6'1	185	29	3	119	18	46	39	16	17	94	7	12	7	0	52	40	2.3	4.0	2.3	17.3
Bob Cousy	G	6'1	175	27	3	124	28	56	50	23	25	**92**	24	26	4	0	79	41	8.0	**8.7**	1.3	26.3
Ed Macauley	C-F	6'8	190	27	3	73	12	30	40	7	11	64	15	5	6	0	31	24	5.0	1.7	2.0	10.3
Dick Hemric	F	6'6	220	22	3	54	5	24	21	9	16	56	22	1	7	0	19	18	7.3	0.3	2.3	6.3
Ernie Barrett	G	6'3	180	26	3	43	4	13	31	3	3	100	7	4	7	0	11	14	2.3	1.3	2.3	3.7
Red Morrison	F-C	6'8	225	23	3	23	2	7	29	0	4	0	11	0	5	0	4	8	3.7	0.0	1.7	1.3
Togo Palazzi	F-G	6'4	205	23	2	7	1	5	20	0	0	-	2	0	1	0	2	4	1.0	0.0	0.5	1.0
Gene Conley-retired to play baseball, Frank Ramsey-military service																						

1955/56 N.B.A. TEAM STATISTICS

Team	REGULAR SEASON									AVERAGE POINTS			PLAYOFFS									AVERAGE POINTS		
	G	FG	FGA	%	FT	FTA	%	Reb	Ass	For	Agnst.	Diff.	G	FG	FGA	%	FT	FTA	%	Reb.	Ass.	For	Agnst.	Diff.
EASTERN DIVISION																								
Philadelphia	72	2641	6437	**41**	2142	2829	76	4362	**1886**	103.1	98.8	**+4.3**	10	370	930	40	306	408	75	644	**259**	104.6	98.4	+6.3
Boston	72	**2745**	**6913**	40	2142	2785	77	**4583**	1834	**106.0**	105.3	+0.7	3	109	**289**	38	87	113	**77**	**205**	64	101.7	98.7	+3.4
Syracuse	72	2466	6661	37	2044	2703	76	4060	1710	96.9	96.9	—	8	287	767	37	239	324	74	486	190	101.6	108.0	-6.4
New York	72	2508	6395	39	**2196**	**2913**	75	4562	1610	100.2	100.6	-0.4												
WESTERN DIVISION																								
Fort Wayne	72	2396	6174	39	2002	2729	73	3974	1752	94.4	**93.7**	+0.7	10	326	879	37	276	386	72	609	209	92.8	**92.2**	+0.6
Minneapolis	72	2541	6543	39	2066	2627	**79**	4133	1689	99.3	100.2	-0.9	3	**116**	263	**44**	**131**	**173**	76	175	7	**121.0**	102.3	**+18.7**
St. Louis	72	2506	6628	38	1941	2761	70	4493	1748	96.6	98.0	-1.4	8	248	685	36	246	352	70	423	162	92.8	103.0	+10.2
Rochester	72	2551	6890	37	1798	2567	70	4449	1747	95.8	98.7	-2.9												

1955/56 N.B.A. STANDINGS

Team	W	L	Pct.	GB	Record against playoff teams W	L	Pct.	Record against non-playoff teams W	L	Pct.	HOME W	L	Pct.	ROAD W	L	Pct.	NEUTRAL W	L	Pct.
EASTERN DIVISION																			
Philadelphia Warriors	**45**	27	**.625**	—	33	18	**.647**	**12**	9	.571	21	7	**.750**	11	17	.393	13	3	**.813**
Boston Celtics	39	33	.542	6	29	22	.569	10	**11**	.476	20	7	.741	12	15	.444	7	11	.389
Syracuse Nationals	35	37	.486	10	23	28	.451	**12**	9	.571	14	**14**	.500	**15**	14	**.517**	6	9	.400
New York Knickerbockers	35	37	.486	10	29	34	.460	6	3	**.667**	**23**	8	.742	9	19	.321	3	10	.231
WESTERN DIVISION																			
Fort Wayne Pistons	37	35	.514	—	25	26	.490	**12**	9	.571	19	8	.704	10	17	.370	8	10	.444
Minneapolis Lakers	33	39	.458	4	21	30	.412	**12**	9	.571	13	12	.520	6	**21**	.222	**14**	6	.700
St. Louis Hawks	33	39	.458	4	22	29	.431	11	10	.524	16	10	.615	10	17	.370	7	12	.368
Rochester Royals	31	**41**	.431	6	28	**35**	.444	3	6	.333	15	**14**	.517	7	**21**	.250	9	6	.600

1955 N.B.A. INDIVIDUAL LEADERS

SCORING
(Minimum 48 Games Played)

Name	Team	G	FG	FT	Pts.	Avg.
Pettit	StL	72	646	557	1849	25.7
Arizin	Phi	72	617	507	1741	24.2
Johnston	Phi	70	499	549	1547	22.1
Lovellette	Min	71	594	338	1526	21.5
Schayes	Syr	72	465	542	1472	20.4
Sharman	Bos	72	538	352	1434	19.9
Cousy	Bos	72	440	476	1356	18.8
Macauley	Bos	71	420	400	1240	17.5
Yardley	FtW	71	434	365	1233	17.4
Stokes	Roch	67	403	319	1125	16.8

FIELD GOAL PERCENTAGE
(Minimum 230 Field Goals)

Name	Team	FG	FGA	Pct.
Johnston	Phi	499	1092	.457
Arizin	Phi	617	1378	.448
Foust	FtW	367	821	.447
Sears	NY	319	728	.438
Sharman	Bos	538	1229	.438
Lovellette	Min	594	1370	.434
Share	StL	315	733	.430
Houbregs	FtW	247	575	.430
Pettit	StL	646	1507	.429
Hutchins	FtW	325	764	.425

FREE THROW PERCENTAGE
(Minimum 190 Free Throws)

Name	Team	FT	FTA	Pct.
Sharman	Bos	358	413	.867
Schayes	Syr	542	632	.858
Schnittker	Min	304	355	.856
Cousy	Bos	476	564	.844
Braun	NY	320	382	.838
Martin	Min	329	395	.833
Arizin	Phi	507	626	.810
Mikkelsen	Min	328	408	.804
Johnston	Phi	549	685	.801
Baechtold	NY	233	291	.801

PERSONAL FOULS

Name	Team	PF
Mikkelsen	Min	319
Share	StL	318
Risen	Bos	300
Felix	NY	293
Ricketts	StL-Roch	287

GAMES DISQUALIFIED

Name	Team	Disq
Risen	Bos	17
Mikkelsen	Min	17
Ricketts	StL-Roch	14
Felix	NY	13
Share	StL	13

REBOUNDS PER GAME
(Minimum 48 Games Played)

Name	Team	G	Reb.	Avg.
Stokes	Roch	67	1094	16.3
Pettit	StL	72	1164	16.2
Lovellette	Min	71	992	14.0
Johnston	Phi	70	872	12.5
Schayes	Syr	72	891	12.4
Share	StL	72	774	10.8
Nichols	Bos	60	625	10.4
Gallatin	NY	72	740	10.3
Yardley	FtW	71	686	9.7
Coleman	Roch-StL	75	688	9.2

ASSISTS PER GAME
(Minimum 48 Games Played)

Name	Team	G	Ass.	Avg.
Cousy	Bos	72	642	8.9
George	Phi	72	457	6.3
Martin	Min	72	445	6.2
Phillip	FtW	70	410	5.9
McGuire	NY	62	362	5.8
King	Syr	72	410	5.7
Stokes	Roch	67	328	4.9
Seymour	Syr	57	276	4.8
Sharman	Bos	72	339	4.7
Braun	NY	72	298	4.1

MINUTES PLAYED

Name	Team	Min.
George	Phi	2840
Martin	Min	2838
Pettit	StL	2794
Cousy	Bos	2767
Coleman	Roch-StL	2738

1956-57 N.B.A.

Auerbach's Defensive Dream

The Boston Celtics had long had a full stable of hot shooters, but had lacked a strong rebounder to get the ball for the gunners. This season, coach Red Auerbach found his man in 6'9" Bill Russell, a lean center who had just led the University of San Francisco to 55 straight wins and two N.C.A.A. championships. A master at gaining position for rebounds and a magician at blocking shots, Russell seemed so much an answer to Aurebach's dreams that the Boston coach sent veteran center Ed Macauley and rookie forward Cliff Hagan to St. Louis for the Hawks' number two pick in the first round of the draft. After the Royals passed him by, the Celtics picked Russell and outbid the Harlem Globetrotters to sign him to a lucrative contract. The only problem was that Russell planned to play in the Olympic Games in Melbourne, which would keep him out of the pro ranks until mid-December.

Thus Auerbach had to wait for his rookie star; he had other new help to tide the team over until then. Veteran guard Andy Phillip came from Ft. Wayne to provide wisdom to the bench, and rookie Tom Heinsohn won a starting forward position. Called "Ack-Ack" because of his love of shooting the ball, the 6'7" Heinsohn excited Boston fans with his offense the way Russell would with his defense. With the incomparable Bob Cousy quarterbacking the club, Bill Sharman throwing in long-range jumpers with automatic accuracy, and Jim Loscutoff muscling his way to rebounds, the Celtics caught fire in the early going and ran off a 10-game winning streak with Heinsohn in the pivot. The Celtics cooled off to a 16-8 mark by December 22, the day that Bill Russell joined the team.

After getting settled with the Celtics, Russell went on to revolutionize pro basketball with his rebounding, defense, and shot-blocking. He made the foul lane posted territory for opposing drivers, and his rebounds on the defensive boards usually triggered the fabled Celtic fast-break, led by Cousy. The starting five of Russell, Heinsohn, Loscutoff, Cousy, and Sharman was the class unit of pro ball, and swingman Frank Ramsey added zip to the shock troops after his discharge from the service in January. An eight-game win streak in January put the Celtics out of reach in the East.

The Syracuse Nats came on strong near the end of the season to finish second behind Boston. A slow start had driven coach Al Cervi to resign, but veteran guard Paul Seymour stabilized the club after taking over as the new mentor. On the floor, Syracuse's biggest asset still was Dolph Schayes, third in the N.B.A. in both scoring and rebounding. The Philadelphia Warriors slumped to 37-35 this season and barely squeaked into the playoffs; Paul Arizin and Neil Johnston still scored at prolific rates, but the loss of Tom Gola to the military hurt the backcourt. The Knicks finished last and out of the money despite a respectable 36-36 record; two key additions to the roster were guard Richie Guerin, a rookie from Iona by route of the military service, and forward Willie Naulls, a rookie from U.C.L.A. picked up from the St. Louis Hawks in a trade for Slater Martin.

Over in the Western Division, all four clubs finished below the .500 level that had eamed New York last place in the East. Three clubs deadlocked for first place with mediocre 34-38 marks. The Ft. Wayne Pistons managed to hold on to a share of first place despite a continued slide in the win column. George Yardley was the only consistent scoring threat, and coach Charlie Eckman continued to revise his backcourt by sending Andy Phillip to Boston and picking up Gene Shue from New York. The Minneapolis Lakers also grabbed a portion of first place while unloading veteran players. George Mikan retired for good, and guard Slater Martin had been traded to New York before the season started for center Walt Dukes. Clyde Lovellette and Dick Garmaker led the Laker offense by placing in the N.B.A.'s top ten scoring leaders.

The third co-leader, the St. Louis Hawks, added lots of new talent, but got off to a very disappointing start. The Russell trade with Boston brought Ed Macauley, a popular figure from his college days at the University of St. Louis, and Cliff Hagan, a muscular 6'4" forward just discharged from the Army. Slater Martin came over in mid-season after a short stint in New York, and he immediately filled the bill of feeding Bob Pettit and the other Hawk frontcourt men. Pettit finished second in the N.B.A. scoring race to Paul Arizin, an imposing fact when one considers that a broken wrist forced Pettit to wear a cast on his hand after mid-February. The Hawks went through three coaches this season, beginning under Red Holzman, playing eight games under Slater Martin before he decided to concentrate on playing, and finishing the campaign under the direction of reserve forward Alex Hannum, who had been picked up on waivers earlier in the year. Under Hannum, the Hawks jelled late in the season and entered the playoffs in fine condition. The last-place Rochester Royals enjoyed good seasons by Jack Twyman and Maurice Stokes, but the club was on shaky legs both on the court and at the box office.

Unlike last season, the playoffs produced lopsided early matches, with the Celtics and Hawks finally emerging as the contestants in the championship round. Neither club had won an N.B.A. crown before, and the Celtics were heavily favored to break the ice. Large crowds filled the houses in both Boston and St. Louis and gave this series a large jolt of electricity. The Hawks surprised the Celtics with a 125-123, double overtime win in Boston in game one, with the Celtics evening the series the next night. In St. Louis, the Hawks took game three only to drop the next two contests to the Celtics. The sixth game went to the Hawks when Bob Cousy missed a free throw with 12 seconds left; the Hawks came downcourt, Bob Pettit missed a shot, and Cliff Hagan tapped it in at the buzzer for a 96-94 triumph. The final game of the series was a seesaw affair, with two Pettit foul shots tying the game at 103-all at the end of regulation time. Jack Coleman's shot with nine seconds left tied the score again at 113, and sent the game into a second overtime period. Tension mounted as the clubs battled into this extra period. With the Celtics up 125-123 with two seconds left the Hawks heaved the ball inbounds at the backboard, and Pettit soared up to tap it in; it rolled around the rim and dropped out. The Celtics were champs for the first time.

1956/57 N.B.A. — EASTERN DIVISION

Use Name	Pos	Hgt	Wgt	Age	TOTAL													PER GAME				
					G	Min	FG	FGA	%	FT	FTA	%	Reb	Ass	PF	DQ	Points	Min	Reb	Ass	PF	Points
BOSTON CELTICS	**44-28 .611**				**RED AUERBACH**																	
Jim Loscutoff	F	6'5	230	26	70	2220	306	888	34	132	187	71	730	89	244	5	744	32	10.4	1.3	3.5	10.6
Tom Heinsohn	F-C	6'7	218	22	72	2150	446	1123	40	271	343	79	705	117	304	12	1163	30	9.8	1.6	4.2	16.2
Bill Russell (Olympics)	C	6'10	220	22	48	1695	277	649	43	152	309	49	943	88	143	2	706	35	**19.6**	1.8	3.0	14.7
Bill Sharman	G	6'1	190	30	67	2403	516	1241	42	381	421	**90**	286	236	188	1	1413	36	4.3	3.5	2.8	21.1
Bob Cousy	G	6'1	175	28	64	2364	478	1264	38	363	442	82	309	**478**	134	0	1319	37	4.8	**7.5**	2.1	20.6
Andy Phillip	G	6'3	195	34	67	1476	105	277	38	88	137	64	181	168	121	1	298	22	2.7	2.5	1.8	4.4
Jack Nichols	C-F	6'7	230	30	61	1372	195	537	36	108	136	79	374	85	185	4	498	22	6.1	1.4	3.0	8.2
Dick Hemric	F	6'6	230	23	67	1055	109	317	34	146	210	70	304	42	98	0	364	16	4.5	0.6	1.5	5.4
Arnie Risen (brohen wrist)	C	6'9	210	32	43	935	119	307	39	106	156	68	286	53	163	4	344	22	6.7	1.2	3.8	8.0
Frank Ramsey (MS)	G-F	6'3	200	25	35	807	137	349	39	144	182	79	178	67	113	3	418	23	5.1	1.9	3.2	11.9
Lou Tsioropoulos	F	6'5	210	26	52	670	79	256	31	69	89	78	207	33	135	6	227	13	4.0	0.6	2.6	4.4
Gene Conley - retired to play baseball																						
SYRACUSE NATIONALS	**38-34 .528**				**AL CERVI (4-8 .333), PAUL SEYMOUR (34-26 .567)**																	
Earl Lloyd	F	6'6	220	28	72	1965	256	687	37	134	179	75	435	114	282	10	646	27	6.0	1.6	3.9	9.0
Dolph Schayes	F-C	6'8	220	28	72	**2851**	496	1308	38	**625**	691	90	1008	229	219	5	1617	**40**	14.0	3.2	3.0	22.5
Johnny Kerr	C	6'9	230	24	72	2191	333	827	40	225	313	72	807	90	190	3	891	30	11.2	1.3	2.6	12.4
Ed Conlin	G-F	6'6	200	23	71	2250	335	896	37	283	368	77	430	205	170	0	953	32	6.1	2.9	2.4	13.4
Bob Harrison (10g. StL)	G	6'2	190	29	66	1810	243	629	39	93	130	72	156	161	220	5	579	27	2.4	2.4	3.3	8.8
Al Bianchi	G	6'3	185	24	68	1577	199	567	35	165	239	69	227	106	198	5	563	23	3.3	1.6	2.9	8.3
Joe Holup	F	6'6	215	22	71	1284	160	487	33	204	253	81	279	84	177	5	524	18	3.9	1.2	2.5	7.4
Paul Seymour	G	6'2	185	28	65	1235	143	442	32	101	123	82	130	193	91	0	387	19	2.0	3.0	1.4	6.0
Togo Palazzi (21g. Bos)	F-G	6'4	205	24	63	1013	210	571	37	136	175	78	262	49	117	1	556	16	4.2	0.8	1.9	8.8
Bob Hophins	C	6'8	205	22	62	764	130	343	38	94	126	75	233	22	106	0	354	12	3.8	0.4	1.7	5.7
Larry Hennessy	G	6'3	185	27	21	373	56	175	32	23	32	72	45	27	28	0	135	18	2.1	1.3	1.3	6.4
Bob Schafer	G	6'3	200	23	11	167	19	66	29	11	13	85	11	15	16	0	49	15	1.0	1.4	1.5	4.5
Jim Tucker	F	6'7	185	24	9	119	17	44	39	0	1	0	20	2	26	0	34	13	2.2	0.2	2.9	3.8
Don Savage	F-G	6'3	205	28	5	55	6	19	32	6	7	86	7	2	7	0	18	11	1.4	0.4	1.4	3.6
Jim Ray	G	6'1	180	22	4	43	2	11	18	3	5	60	5	3	4	0	7	11	1.3	0.8	1.0	1.8
Forest Able	G	6'3	180	24	1	1	0	2	0	0	0	—	1	1	1	0	0	1	1.0	1.0	1.0	0.0
Dick Farley - military service																						
George King - voluntarily retired																						
PHILADELPHIA WARRIORS	**37-35 .514**				**GEORGE SENESKY**																	
Paul Arizin	F	6'4	200	28	71	2767	**613**	1451	42	591	**713**	83	561	150	274	13	**1817**	39	7.9	2.1	3.9	**25.6**
Joe Graboski	F	6'8	225	26	72	2501	390	1118	35	252	322	78	614	140	244	5	1032	35	8.5	1.9	3.4	14.3
Neil Johnston	C	6'8	215	27	69	2531	520	1163	**45**	535	648	83	855	203	231	2	1575	37	12.4	2.9	3.3	22.8
Jack George	G	6'3	195	28	67	2229	253	750	34	200	293	68	318	307	165	3	706	33	4.7	4.6	2.5	10.5
Larry Costello	G	6'1	180	25	72	2111	186	497	37	175	222	79	323	236	182	2	547	29	4.5	3.3	2.5	7.6
Ernie Beck	G-F	6'4	195	25	72	1743	195	508	38	111	157	71	312	190	155	1	501	24	4.3	2.6	2.2	7.0
Walt Davis	C-F	6'8	210	25	65	1250	178	437	41	74	106	70	306	52	235	9	430	19	4.7	0.8	3.6	6.6
George Dempsey	G	6'3	195	27	71	1147	134	302	44	55	102	54	251	136	107	0	323	16	3.5	1.9	1.5	4.5
Lew Hitch (30g. Roch)	F-C	6'8	220	27	68	1133	111	296	38	63	88	72	253	40	103	0	285	17	3.7	0.6	1.5	4.2
Jackie Moore	F	6'5	205	24	57	400	43	106	41	37	46	80	116	21	75	1	123	7	2.0	0.4	1.3	2.2
Bob Armstrong	C-F	6'8	220	23	19	110	11	37	30	6	12	50	39	3	13	0	28	6	2.1	0.2	0.7	1.5
Hal Lear	G	6'	165	21	3	14	2	6	33	0	0	—	1	1	3	0	4	5	0.3	0.3	1.0	1.3
Tom Gola - military service																						
NEW YORK KNICKERBOCKERS	**36-36 .500**				**VINCE BORYLA**																	
Kenny Sears	F	6'9	195	23	72	2516	343	821	42	383	485	79	614	101	226	2	1069	35	8.5	1.4	3.1	14.8
Harry Gallatin	F-C	6'6	220	29	72	1943	332	817	41	415	519	80	725	85	202	1	1079	27	10.1	1.2	2.8	15.0
Sweetwater Clifton	C-F	6'6	225	34	71	2231	308	818	38	146	217	67	557	164	243	5	762	31	7.8	2.3	3.4	10.7
Richie Guerin	G	6'4	195	24	72	1793	257	699	37	181	292	62	334	182	186	3	695	25	4.6	2.5	2.6	9.7
Carl Braun	G	6'5	185	29	72	2345	378	993	38	245	303	81	259	256	195	1	1001	33	3.6	3.6	2.7	13.9
Willie Naulls (l9g. StL)	F	6'6	225	22	71	1778	293	820	36	132	195	68	617	84	186	1	718	25	8.7	1.2	2.6	10.1
Ray Felix	C	6'11	220	26	72	1622	295	709	42	277	371	75	587	36	284	8	867	23	8.2	0.5	3.9	12.0
Ron Sobie	G	6'3	195	23	71	1378	166	442	38	152	199	76	326	129	158	0	484	19	4.6	1.8	2.2	6.8
Dick McGuire	G	6'	180	30	72	1191	140	366	38	105	163	64	146	222	103	0	385	17	2.0	3.1	1.4	5.3
Jim Baechtold	F-G	6'4	207	29	45	462	75	197	38	66	88	75	80	33	39	0	216	10	1.8	0.7	0.9	4.8
Phil Jordon	C	6'10	205	23	9	91	18	49	37	8	12	67	34	2	15	0	44	10	3.8	0.2	1.7	4.9
Ron Shavlik	F	6'8	200	23	7	72	4	22	18	2	5	40	22	0	12	0	10	10	3.1	0.0	1.7	1.4
Gary Bergen	C	6'8	212	24	6	40	3	11	27	2	2	100	8	1	4	0	8	7	1.3	0.2	0.7	1.3

1956/57 N.B.A. — WESTERN DIVISION

Use Name	Pos	Hgt	Wgt	Age	G	Min	FG	FGA	%	FT	FTA	%	Reb	Ass	PF	DQ	Points	Min	Reb	Ass	PF	Points
					TOTAL													PER GAME				
ST. LOUIS HAWKS	34-38 .472				**RED HOLZMAN (14-19 .424), SLATER MARTIN (5-3 .625), ALEX HANNUM (15-16 .484),** defeated Fort Wayne 115-103 at home and Minneapolis 114-111(OT) at home in playoff for first place.																	
Ed Macauley	F	6'8	195	28	72	2582	414	987	42	359	479	75	440	202	206	2	1187	36	6.1	2.8	2.9	16.5
Jack Coleman	F	6'7	230	32	72	2145	316	775	41	123	161	76	645	159	235	7	755	30	9.0	2.2	3.3	10.5
Bob Pettit	C-F	6'9	210	24	71	2491	**613**	**1477**	42	529	684	77	1037	133	181	1	1755	35	14.6	1.9	2.5	24.7
Jack McMahon	G	6'1	188	28	72	2344	239	725	33	142	225	63	222	367	213	2	620	33	3.1	5.1	3.0	8.6
Slater Martin (13g. NY)	G	5'10	170	31	66	2401	244	736	33	230	291	79	288	269	193	1	718	36	4.4	4.1	2.9	10.9
Chuck Share	C	6'11	240	29	72	1673	235	535	44	269	393	68	642	79	269	15	739	23	8.9	1.1	3.7	10.3
Med Park	G-F	6'2	205	23	66	1130	118	324	36	108	146	74	200	94	137	2	344	17	3.0	1.4	2.1	5.2
Irv Bemoras	G-F	6'3	195	26	62	983	124	385	32	70	103	68	127	46	76	0	318	16	2.0	0.7	1.2	5.1
Cliff Hagan	F-G	6'4	210	25	67	971	134	371	36	100	145	69	247	86	165	3	368	14	3.7	1.3	2.5	5.5
Alex Hannum (22g. FtW)	F-C	6'7	225	33	59	642	77	223	35	37	56	66	158	28	135	2	191	11	2.7	0.5	2.3	3.2
Odie Spears (4g. FtW)	F-G	6'5	205	31	11	118	12	38	32	19	22	86	15	7	24	0	43	10	1.4	0.6	2.2	3.9
Norm Stewart	F	6'5	205	21	5	37	4	15	27	2	6	33	5	2	9	0	10	7	1.0	0.4	1.8	2.0
John Barber	F	6'6	210	29	5	19	2	8	25	3	6	50	6	0	4	0	7	4	1.2	0.0	0.8	1.4
Al Ferrari, Jack Stephens, Frank Selvy - military service																						
MINNEAPOLIS LAKERS	34-38 .472				**JOHNNY KUNDLA** lost to St. Louis 111-114(OT) at St. Louis in playoff for first place.																	
Vern Mikkelsen	F	6'7	230	28	72	2198	322	854	38	342	424	81	630	121	**312**	**18**	986	31	8.8	1.7	**4.3**	13.7
Clyde Lovellette	F-C	6'9	245	27	69	2492	574	1348	43	286	399	72	932	139	251	4	1434	36	13.5	2.0	3.6	20.8
Walter Dukes	C	7'	220	26	71	1866	228	626	36	264	383	69	794	54	273	10	720	26	11.2	0.8	3.8	10.1
Dick Garmaker	G	6'3	205	24	72	2406	406	1015	40	365	435	84	336	190	199	1	1177	33	4.7	2.6	2.8	16.3
Whitey Skoog (back injury)	G	5'11	185	30	23	656	78	220	35	44	47	94	72	76	65	1	200	29	3.1	3.3	2.8	8.7
Bob Leonard	G	6'3	185	24	72	1943	303	867	35	186	241	77	220	169	140	0	792	27	3.1	2.3	1.9	11.0
Chuck Mencel	G	6'	185	23	72	1848	243	688	35	179	240	75	237	201	95	0	665	26	3.3	2.8	1.3	9.2
Ed Kalafat	C-F	6'6	245	24	65	1617	178	507	35	197	298	66	425	105	243	9	553	25	6.5	1.6	3.7	8.5
Jim Paxson	F	6'6	205	24	71	1274	138	485	28	170	236	72	266	86	163	3	446	18	3.7	1.2	2.3	6.3
Dick Schnittker	F	6'5	205	28	70	997	113	353	32	160	193	83	185	52	144	3	386	14	2.6	0.7	2.1	5.5
Bob Williams	F	6'6	230	25	4	20	1	4	25	2	3	67	5	0	2	0	4	5	1.3	0.0	0.5	1.0
FORT WAYNE PISTONS	34-38 .472				**CHARLIE ECKMAN** lost to St. Louis 103-115 at St. Louis in playoff for first place.																	
George Yardley	F	6'5	195	28	72	2691	522	1273	41	503	639	79	755	147	231	2	1547	37	10.5	2.0	3.2	21.5
Mel Hutchins	F	6'6	205	28	72	2647	369	953	39	152	206	74	571	210	182	0	890	37	7.9	2.9	2.5	12.4
Larry Foust (injury)	C	6'9	245	28	61	1533	243	617	39	273	380	72	555	71	221	7	759	25	9.1	1.2	3.6	12.4
Billy Kenville	G	6'2	185	26	71	1701	204	608	34	174	218	80	324	172	169	3	582	24	4.6	2.4	2.4	8.2
Gene Shue	G	6'2	175	25	72	2470	273	710	38	241	316	76	421	238	137	0	787	34	5.8	3.3	1.9	10.9
Bob Houbregs	C-F	6'8	225	24	60	1592	253	585	43	167	234	71	401	113	118	2	673	27	6.7	1.9	2.0	11.2
Chuck Noble (injury)	G	6'4	195	25	54	1260	200	556	36	76	102	75	135	180	161	2	476	23	2.5	3.3	3.0	8.8
Corky Devlin	G	6'5	195	25	71	1242	190	502	38	97	143	68	146	141	114	0	477	17	2.1	2.0	1.6	6.7
Red Rocha	C-F	6'9	215	33	72	1154	136	390	35	109	144	76	272	81	162	1	381	16	3.8	1.1	2.3	5.3
Bill Thieben	F-C	6'7	215	21	58	633	90	256	35	57	87	66	207	17	78	0	237	11	3.6	0.3	1.3	4.1
Dick Rosenthal	G	6'5	205	23	18	188	21	79	27	9	17	53	52	17	22	0	51	10	2.9	0.9	1.2	2.8
ROCHESTER ROYALS	31-41 .431				**BOBBY WANZER**																	
Dave Piontek	F-C	6'6	230	22	71	1759	257	637	40	122	183	67	351	108	141	1	636	25	4.9	1.5	2.0	9.0
Maurice Stokes	F-C	6'7	230	23	72	2761	434	1249	35	256	385	66	**1256**	331	287	12	1124	38	17.4	4.6	4.0	15.6
Dick Ricketts	C-F	6'7	220	23	72	2114	299	869	34	206	297	69	437	127	307	12	804	29	6.1	1.8	4.3	11.2
Jack Twyman	G-F	6'6	210	22	72	2338	449	1023	44	276	363	76	354	123	251	4	1174	32	4.9	1.7	3.5	16.3
Richie Regan	G	6'2	180	26	71	2100	257	780	33	182	235	77	205	222	179	1	696	30	2.9	3.1	2.5	9.8
Johnny McCarthy	G	6'1	185	22	72	1560	173	460	38	130	193	67	201	107	130	4	476	22	2.8	1.5	1.8	6.6
Art Spoelstra	C	6'9	220	24	69	1176	217	559	39	88	120	73	220	56	168	5	522	17	3.2	0.8	2.4	7.6
Bob Burrow	C-F	6'7	225	22	67	1028	137	366	37	130	211	62	293	41	165	2	404	15	4.4	0.6	2.5	6.0
Ed Fleming	G	6'3	190	23	51	927	109	364	30	139	191	73	183	81	94	0	357	18	3.6	1.6	1.8	7.0
Tom Marshall (MS)	F-G	6'4	215	25	40	460	56	163	34	47	58	81	83	31	33	0	159	12	2.1	0.8	0.8	4.0
Si Green (MS)	G	6'2	185	22	13	423	50	143	35	49	69	71	67	47	36	1	149	33	5.2	3.6	2.8	11.5
Bobby Wanzer	G	6'	185	35	21	159	23	49	47	36	46	78	25	9	20	0	82	8	1.2	0.4	1.0	3.9

1956/57 N.B.A. - PLAYOFFS

BOSTON CELTICS — **RED AUERBACH**

defeated Syracuse 3-0; H108-90,120-105, H83-80
defeated St. Louis 4-3; H123-125 (2OT), H119-99, 98-100,123-118, H124-109, 94-96, H125-123 (2OT)

se Name	Pos	Hgt	Wgt	Age	G	Min	FG	FGA	%	FT	FTA	%	Reb	Ass	PF	DQ	Points	Min	Reb	Ass	PF	Points
					TOTAL													PER GAME				
im Loscutoff	F	6'5	230	26	10	259	31	109	28	18	28	64	83	5	46	2	80	26	8.3	0.5	4.6	8.0
om Heinsohn	F	6'7	218	22	10	370	90	231	39	46	69	67	117	20	40	1	229	37	11.7	2.0	4.0	22.9
Bill Russell	C	6'10	220	22	10	409	54	148	36	31	61	51	**244**	32	41	1	139	41	**24.4**	3.2	4.1	13.9
Bill Sharman	G	6'1	190	30	10	377	75	197	38	61	64	**95**	35	29	23	1	211	38	3.5	2.9	2.3	21.1
Bob Cousy	G	6'1	175	28	10	**440**	67	207	32	68	71	75	61	**93**	27	0	202	44	6.1	**9.3**	2.7	20.2
rank Ramsey	F-G	6'3	200	25	10	229	38	82	46	46	59	78	43	17	36	1	122	23	4.3	1.7	3.6	12.2
Arnie Risen	C-F	6'9	210	32	10	152	28	63	44	19	29	66	58	8	**48**	**5**	75	15	5.8	0.8	4.8	7.5
Andy Phillip	G	6'3	195	34	10	128	8	22	36	6	15	40	20	17	18	0	22	13	2.0	1.7	1.8	2.2
Jack Nichols	F	6'7	230	30	10	117	16	40	40	3	5	60	17	7	23	0	35	12	1.7	0.7	2.3	3.5
Dick Hemric	F	6'6	230	23	2	19	1	7	14	0	0	—	9	1	1	0	2	10	4.5	0.5	0.5	1.0

Gene Conley - retired to play baseball

ST. LOUIS HAWKS — **ALEX HANNUM**

defeated Minneapolis 3-0; H118-109, H106-104, 143-135 (2OT)
lost to Boston 3-4; 125-123 (2OT), 99-119, H100-98, H118-123,109-124, H96-94,123-125 (2OT)

Name	Pos	Hgt	Wgt	Age	G	Min	FG	FGA	%	FT	FTA	%	Reb	Ass	PF	DQ	Points	Min	Reb	Ass	PF	Points
Ed Macauley	F	6'8	195	28	10	297	44	109	40	54	74	73	62	22	39	3	142	30	6.2	2.2	3.9	14.2
Jack Coleman	F	6'7	230	32	10	313	36	113	32	20	34	59	88	33	32	1	92	31	8.8	3.3	3.2	9.2
Bob Pettit	C-F	6'9	210	24	10	430	**98**	**237**	41	102	133	77	168	25	33	0	**298**	43	16.8	2.5	3.3	**29.8**
Jack McMahon	G	6'1	188	28	10	375	52	137	38	20	36	56	38	57	**48**	4	124	38	3.8	5.7	4.8	12.4
Slater Martin	G	5'10	170	31	10	439	55	155	35	56	74	76	42	49	39	2	166	44	4.2	4.9	3.9	16.6
Cliff Hagan	F-G	6'4	210	25	10	319	62	143	43	46	63	73	112	28	47	3	170	32	11.2	2.8	4.7	17.0
Med Park	G-F	6'2	205	23	10	183	14	49	29	16	22	73	33	12	18	0	44	18	3.3	1.2	1.8	4.4
Chuck Share	C	6'11	240	29	10	168	31	72	43	30	50	60	63	6	39	2	92	17	6.3	0.6	3.9	9.2
rv Bemoras	G-F	6'3	195	26	3	20	3	8	38	3	3	100	6	1	4	0	9	7	2.0	0.3	1.3	3.0
Alex Hannum	F	6'7	225	33	2	6	0	2	0	0	0	—	0	0	2	0	0	3	0.0	0.0	1.0	0.0

Al Ferrari, Jack Stephens, Frank Selvy - military service

SYRACUSE NATIONALS — **PAUL SEYMOUR**

defeated Philadelphia 2-0; 103-96, H91-80
lost to Boston 0-3, 90-108, H105-120, 80-83

Name	Pos	Hgt	Wgt	Age	G	Min	FG	FGA	%	FT	FTA	%	Reb	Ass	PF	DQ	Points	Min	Reb	Ass	PF	Points
Joe Holup	F	6'6	215	22	5	88	6	28	21	8	12	67	20	1	3	0	20	18	4.0	0.2	0.6	4.0
Dolph Schayes	F-C	6'8	220	28	5	215	29	95	31	49	55	89	90	14	18	0	107	43	18.0	2.8	3.6	21.4
Johnny Kerr	C	6'9	230	24	5	162	28	65	43	20	29	69	69	6	7	0	76	32	13.8	1.2	1.4	15.2
Ed Conlin	G-F	6'6	200	23	5	164	28	71	39	21	27	78	17	15	11	0	77	33	3.4	3.0	2.2	15.4
Bob Harrison	G	6'2	190	29	5	133	12	45	27	8	9	89	13	15	21	1	32	27	2.6	3.0	4.2	6.4
Paul Seymour	G	6'2	185	28	5	98	8	37	22	5	6	83	10	8	11	0	21	20	2.0	1.6	2.2	4.2
Al Bianchi	G	6'3	185	24	5	97	12	38	32	8	12	67	15	8	16	1	32	19	3.0	1.6	3.2	6.4
Togo Palazzi	F	6'4	205	24	5	87	19	49	39	7	9	78	18	5	11	0	45	17	3.6	1.0	2.2	9.0
Earl Lloyd	F	6'6	220	28	5	83	12	30	40	7	11	64	21	5	18	0	31	17	4.2	1.0	3.6	6.2
Bob Hopkins	C	6'8	205	22	5	73	9	25	36	10	15	67	19	2	4	1	28	15	3.8	0.4	0.8	5.6

Dick Farley - military service, George King - voluntarily retired

MINNEAPOLIS LAKERS — **JOHNNY KUNDLA**

defeated Fort Wayne 2-0; H131-127, 110-108
lost to St. Louis 0-3; 109-118, 104-106, H135-143 (2OT)

Name	Pos	Hgt	Wgt	Age	G	Min	FG	FGA	%	FT	FTA	%	Reb	Ass	PF	DQ	Points	Min	Reb	Ass	PF	Points
Vern Mikkelsen	F	6'7	230	28	5	162	33	83	40	22	34	65	43	17	29	4	88	32	8.6	3.4	**5.8**	17.6
Clyde Lovellette	F	6'9	245	27	5	181	51	118	43	19	26	73	47	11	21	1	121	36	9.4	2.2	4.2	24.2
Walter Dukes	C	7'	220	26	5	177	24	57	42	20	27	74	74	5	26	2	68	35	14.8	1.0	5.2	13.6
Dick Garmaker	G	6'3	205	24	5	187	19	69	28	27	32	84	35	17	19	1	65	37	7.0	3.4	3.8	13.0
Bob Leonard	G	6'3	185	24	5	204	42	100	42	23	26	88	30	38	15	0	107	41	6.0	7.6	3.0	21.4
Ed Kalafat	C-F	6'6	245	24	5	104	21	36	**58**	21	31	68	24	9	20	1	63	21	4.8	1.8	4.0	12.6
Chuck Mencel	G	6'	185	23	5	98	9	36	25	7	9	78	13	6	7	0	25	20	2.6	1.2	1.4	5.0
Dick Schnittker	F	6'5	205	28	5	83	6	21	29	15	17	88	12	8	6	0	27	17	2.4	1.6	1.2	5.4
Jim Paxson	F-G	6'6	205	24	5	54	9	27	33	7	14	50	14	3	4	0	25	11	2.8	0.6	0.8	5.0

Whitey Skoog - back injury

FORT WAYNE PISTONS — **CHARLIE ECKMAN**

lost to Minneapolis 0-2; 127-131, H108-110

Name	Pos	Hgt	Wgt	Age	G	Min	FG	FGA	%	FT	FTA	%	Reb	Ass	PF	DQ	Points	Min	Reb	Ass	PF	Points
George Yardley	F-G	6'5	195	28	2	85	24	53	45	9	11	82	19	8	7	0	57	43	9.5	4.0	3.5	28.5
Mel Hutchins	F	6'6	205	28	2	68	9	30	30	5	7	71	23	10	8	0	23	34	11.5	5.0	4.0	11.5
Larry Foust	C	6'9	245	28	2	64	13	23	57	19	23	83	25	6	10	0	45	32	12.5	3.0	5.0	22.5
Chuck Noble	G	6'4	195	25	2	45	10	26	38	1	2	50	3	4	5	0	21	23	1.5	2.0	2.5	10.5
Gene Shue	G	6'2	175	25	2	79	14	27	52	4	4	100	7	8	3	0	32	40	3.5	4.0	1.5	16.0
Bob Houbregs	C-F	6'8	225	24	2	38	7	17	41	8	11	73	6	3	3	0	22	19	3.0	1.5	1.5	11.0
Billy Kenville	G	6'2	185	26	2	30	2	13	15	0	1	0	1	5	1	0	4	15	0.5	2.5	0.5	2.0
Bill Thieben	F	6'7	215	21	2	28	6	7	86	2	6	33	6	3	5	0	14	14	3.0	1.5	2.5	7.0
Corky Devlin	G	6'5	195	25	1	25	6	8	75	1	1	100	5	5	5	0	13	25	5.0	5.0	5.0	13.0
Red Rocha	C-F	6'9	215	33	2	18	0	5	0	4	6	67	6	0	4	0	4	9	3.0	0.0	2.0	2.0

PHILADELPHIA WARRIORS — **GEORGE SENESKY**

lost to Syracuse 0-2, H96-103, 80-91

Name	Pos	Hgt	Wgt	Age	G	Min	FG	FGA	%	FT	FTA	%	Reb	Ass	PF	DQ	Points	Min	Reb	Ass	PF	Points
Ernie Beck	F-G	6'4	195	25	2	89	14	38	37	3	3	100	10	5	4	0	31	45	5.0	2.5	2.0	15.5
Joe Graboski	F	6'8	225	26	2	91	13	40	33	9	11	82	22	4	7	0	35	**46**	11.0	2.0	3.5	17.5
Neil Johnston	C	6'8	215	27	2	84	17	53	32	4	6	67	35	9	9	0	38	42	17.5	4.5	4.5	19.0
George Dempsey	G	6'3	195	27	2	74	9	21	43	7	16	44	15	12	5	0	25	37	7.5	6.0	2.5	12.5
Jack George	G	6'3	195	28	2	63	7	15	47	4	6	67	7	6	5	0	18	32	3.5	3.0	2.5	9.0
Walt Davis	F-C	6'8	210	25	2	37	4	13	31	4	4	100	14	1	8	0	12	19	7.0	0.5	4.0	6.0
Paul Arizin	F	6'4	200	28	2	22	3	8	38	3	5	60	8	1	3	0	9	11	4.0	0.5	1.5	4.5
Larry Costello	G	6'1	180	25	2	16	3	8	38	0	1	0	5	2	3	0	6	8	2.5	1.0	1.5	3.0
Lew Hitch	F	6'8	220	27	2	3	0	1	0	2	2	100	2	0	0	0	1	2	1.0	0.0	0.0	1.0
Jackie Moore	F	6'5	205	24	1	1	0	0	—	0	0	—	0	0	0	0	0	1	0.0	0.0	0.0	0.0

Tom Gola - military service

1956/57 N.B.A. TEAM STATISTICS

Team	REGULAR SEASON G	FG	FGA	%	FT	FTA	%	Reb.	Ass.	AVERAGE POINTS For	Agnst.	Diff.	PLAYOFFS G	FG	FGA	%	FT	FTA	%	Reb.	Ass.	AVERAGE POINTS For	Agnst.	Diff.
EASTERN DIVISION																								
Boston	72	**2808**	**7326**	38	1983	2644	75	**4963**	1464	**105.5**	100.2	**+5.3**	10	408	**1106**	37	301	421	71	**729**	229	11.7	104.5	+7.2
Syracuse	72	2550	6915	37	2075	2613	**79**	4350	1282	99.7	101.1	-1.4	5	163	483	34	143	185	77	311	79	93.8	97.4	-3.6
Philadelphia	72	2584	6533	**40**	2062	2658	78	4305	**1467**	100.4	98.8	+1.6	2	70	197	36	36	54	67	133	40	88.0	**97.0**	-9.0
New York	72	2569	6645	39	2117	2844	74	4723	1312	100.8	100.9	-0.1												
WESTERN DIVISION																								
St. Louis	72	2557	6669	38	1977	2710	73	4566	1454	98.5	98.6	-0.1	10	395	1025	39	**347**	**489**	71	673	233	113.7	115.4	-1.7
Minneapolis	72	2584	6965	37	**2195**	**2899**	76	4581	1195	102.3	103.1	-0.8	5	214	547	39	161	216	75	334	114	**117.8**	120.4	-2.6
Fort Wayne	72	2532	6612	38	1874	2510	75	4289	1398	96.4	98.7	-2.3	2	**91**	209	**44**	53	72	74	113	**52**	117.5	120.5	-3.0
Rochester	72	2515	6807	37	1698	2402	71	4171	1298	93.4	**95.6**	-2.2												

1956/57 N.B.A. STANDINGS

Team	W	L	Pct.	GB	Record against playoff teams W	L	Pct.	Record against non-playoff teams W	L	Pct.	HOME W	L	Pct.	ROAD W	L	Pct.	NEUTRAL W	L	Pct.
EASTERN DIVISION																			
Boston Celtics	**44**	28	**.611**	—	**31**	20	**.608**	**13**	8	**.619**	**27**	4	**.871**	**12**	19	**.387**	5	5	.500
Syracuse Nationals	38	34	.528	6	27	24	.529	11	10	.524	22	9	.710	**12**	19	**.387**	4	6	.400
Philadelphia Warriors	37	35	.514	7	25	26	.490	12	9	.571	26	5	.839	5	**26**	.161	6	4	.600
New York Knickerbockers	36	36	.500	8	31	32	.492	5	4	.556	19	12	.613	11	20	.355	6	4	.600
WESTERN DIVISION																			
St. Louis Hawks	34	38	.472	—	25	26	.490	9	**12**	.429	18	**13**	.581	11	20	.355	5	5	.500
Minneapolis Lakers	34	38	.472	—	22	29	.431	12	9	.571	18	**13**	.581	9	22	.290	7	3	**.700**
Fort Wayne Pistons	34	38	.472	—	23	28	.451	11	10	.524	23	8	.742	7	24	.226	4	6	.400
Rochester Royals	31	41	.431	3	27	**36**	.429	4	5	.444	19	12	.613	9	22	.290	3	7	.300

1956/57 N.B.A. INDIVIDUAL LEADERS

SCORING
(Minimum 48 Games Played)

Name	Team	G	FG	FT	Pts.	Avg.
Arizin	Phi	71	613	591	1817	25.6
Pettit	StL	71	613	529	1755	24.7
Johnston	Phi	69	520	535	1575	22.8
Schayes	Syr	72	496	625	1617	22.5
Yardley	FtW	72	522	503	1547	21.5
Sharman	Bos	67	516	381	1413	21.1
Lovellette	Min	69	574	286	1434	20.8
Cousy	Bos	64	478	363	1319	20.6
Macauley	StL	72	414	359	1187	16.5
Garmaker	Min	72	406	365	1177	16.3

FIELD GOAL PERCENTAGE
(Minimum 230 Field Goals)

Name	Team	FG	FGA	Pct.
Johnston	Phi	520	1163	.447
Share	StL	235	535	.439
Twyman	Roch	449	1023	.439
Houbregs	FtW	253	585	.432
Russell	Bos	277	649	.427
Lovellette	Min	574	1348	.426
Arizin	Phi	613	1451	.422
Macauley	StL	414	987	.419
Sears	NY	343	821	.418
Felix	NY	295	709	.416

FREE THROW PERCENTAGE
(Minimum 190 Free Throws)

Name	Team	FT	FTA	Pct.
Sharman	Bos	381	421	.905
Schayes	Syr	625	691	.904
Garmaker	Min	365	435	.839
Arizin	Phi	591	713	.829
Johnston	Phi	535	648	.826
Cousy	Bos	363	442	.821
Braun	NY	245	303	.808
Mikkelsen	Min	342	424	.807
Holup	Syr	204	253	.806
Gallatin	NY	415	519	.800

PERSONAL FOULS

Name	Team	PF
Mikkelsen	Min	312
Ricketts	Roch	307
Heinsohn	Bos	304
Stokes	Roch	287
Felix	NY	284

GAMES DISQUALIFIED

Name	Team	Disq
Mikkelsen	Min	18
Share	StL	15
Arizin	Phi	13
Richetts	Roch	12
Heinsohn	Bos	12
Stokes	Roch	12

REBOUNDS PER GAME
(Minimum 55 Games Played)

Name	Team	G	Reb.	Avg.
Russell	Bos	48	943	19.6
Stokes	Roch	72	1256	17.4
Pettit	StL	71	1037	14.6
Schayes	Syr	72	1008	14.0
Lovellette	Min	69	932	13.5
Johnston	Phi	69	855	12.4
Kerr	Syr	72	807	11.2
Dukes	Min	71	794	11.2
Yardley	FtW	72	755	10.5
Loscutoff	Bos	70	730	10.4

ASSISTS PER GAME
(Minimum 48 Games Played)

Name	Team	G	Ass.	Avg.
Cousy	Bos	64	478	7.5
McMahon	StL	72	367	5.1
Stokes	Roch	72	331	4.6
George	Phi	67	307	4.6
Marrin	NY-StL	66	269	4.1
Braun	NY	72	256	3.6
Sharman	Bos	67	236	3.5
Noble	FtW	54	180	3.3
Shue	FtW	72	238	3.3
Costello	Phi	72	236	3.3

MINUTES PLAYED

Name	Team	Min.
Schayes	Syr	2851
Arizin	Phi	2767
Stokes	Roch	2761
Yardley	FtW	2691
Hutchins	FtW	2647

1957-58 N.B.A.

Russell's Ankle and Pettit's Fifty

Like a caterpillar changing into a butterfly, the N.B.A. was slowly shedding its small-time image and changing into a big-league operation. Ft. Wayne and Rochester, two traditional basketball towns that had come into the N.B.A. from the old N.B.L., were replaced on the circuit by Detroit and Cincinnati, a pair of larger cities that had long held big-league status through the exploits of their baseball teams. Owner Fred Zollner moved his Pistons to Detroit and Les Harrison took the Royals to Cincinnati, both men hoping to expand their profits with a larger population base. Another old-line franchise, the Minneapolis Lakers, was sold to Bob Short, who felt no obligation to stay in Minnesota if attendance did not pick up. So the compact, eight-team N.B.A. was moving into the big cities, with Minneapolis and Syracuse the smallest outposts still in operation.

This growing big-league image was further nourished by the glamour of the Boston Celtics, the defending champions. Coach Red Auerbach had fine tuned his club to excellence, with a firehouse fast break offense and a tenacious, pressing defense. Bob Cousy fueled his national reputation by making outrageously spectacular passes and drives as the middle man in the fast break, while Bill Sharman and Tom Heinsohn kept the attack in high gear with their long-range shooting. Center Bill Russell started the fast break moving with his rebounds and quick outlet passes to Cousy, and his unmatched shot-blocking ability freed the Celtic guards to press on defense, confident that anyone who got through the middle would be stopped by Russell. The key subs were veteran players, but rookie guard Sam Jones, a superb shooter from North Carolina College, caught on as the tenth man and as a diamond in the rough for the future. With Russell around for the entire season, the Celtics improved to a 49-23 record, the best in the league.

The rest of the Eastern teams entertained little hope of catching the Celtics during the regular season. Syracuse came closest, finishing eight games back in second place. Dolph Schayes was still the heart and soul of the Nats, but he got strong supporting performances from Johnny Kerr, Ed Conlin, and Larry Costello, a set-shooter picked up from the Philadelphia Warriors. The Warriors still had two hot scorers in Paul Arizin and Neil Johnston, and they got Tom Gola back from the military in mid-season, but they barely edged out New York for the third playoff spot. The Knicks sent veterans Harry Gallatin, Sweetwater Clifton, and Dick McGuire to Detroit in a general housecleaning which saw the team finish out of the playoffs for the third straight year.

Out on the banks of the Mississippi, the St. Louis Hawks made the playoffs with a talented, experienced club. After coming of age in the playoff finals against Boston last spring, the Hawks soared to a 41-31 record and an easy first-place finish in the Western Division. Coach Alex Hannum had the deepest frontcourt in the N.B.A. Bob Pettit led the Hawks by example, ranking second in the N.B.A. in rebounding and third in scoring with a 24.6 clip. Cliff Hagan took over the other forward spot and scored at a 19.9 pace. Ed Macauley added offensive skills to the front line while Chuck Share concentrated on defense and rebounding. Guards Slater Martin and Jack McMahon limited themselves to feeding the ball inside to the big men and playing tough defense on enemy guards. In contrast to the Celtics, the Hawks played a pattern, control offense which relied on the inside scoring of the forwards.

Behind the Hawks, the transplanted Pistons and Royals tied for the remaining playoff spots. The Pistons made lots of changes but still wound up at 33-39: coach Charlie Eckman was canned in favor of Red Rocha; Mel Hutchins was sent to New York for Harry Gallatin, Sweetwater Clifton, and Dick McGuire; and Larry Foust and Corky Devlin were traded to Minneapolis for Walt Dukes. The high note of the campaign was George Yardley's winning the N.B.A. scoring crown with a 27.8 average and setting a league record with 2001 points.

The Royals, too, were of little note on the court. Clyde Lovellette came from Minneapolis to join Maurice Stokes and Jack Twyman in a first-rate frontcourt, but the Royals still needed to build themselves back up from their collapse in the last few seasons in Rochester. The Lakers, meanwhile, hit bottom, tumbling into the basement with a chaotic 19-53 season. Owner Short made George Mikan coach of the Lakers, but the club fell apart under the great center's tutelage. John Kundla came out of the front offfice to resume the coaching duties in the second half of the campaign, but the talent-poor club could not make a comeback. The team's leading scorer was forward Vern Mikkelsen, the last remaining veteran of the championship squads of the early 1950's.

With the Lakers out of the playoffs for the first time in N.B.A. history, the Celtics and Hawks started out as favorites to meet again in the championship series. The semifinal rounds had to be played first, with the Warriors upsetting the Nats in the East and the Pistons downing the Royals in the West. The Royals lost more than the series, however; they lost star forward Maurice Stokes. Although he struck his head on the floor during the last game of the regular season, Stokes was able to play in the first game of the playoffs. However, he went into a coma the next day. At first the diagnosis was encephalitis, but later it was found that his coma and subsequent paralysis were caused by his head injury. Stokes never recovered, and the Royals would search in vain for a replacement in the years to come.

In the divisional finals, the Celtics and Hawks both swept into the finals by soundly beating the contending Warriors and Pistons.

The rematch between the Celtics and Hawks sparked a heated interest in the championship series. The Hawks edged out a 104-102 victory in game one, while the Celtics easily took game two, 136-112. In game three, disaster hit the Celtics as Bill Russell injured his ankle, opening the way for a 111-108 Hawk win. Using subs Arnie Risen and Jack Nichols, the Celtics pulled even with a 109-98 fourth game victory, but the Hawks again pulled ahead with a 102-100 squeaker in game five. With their backs to the wall, the Celtics called on Russell for 20 minutes of action in game six; his ankle, however, stripped him of all mobility and forced coach Auerbach to lift him from the lineup. Pettit, meanwhile, scored a playoff record 50 points and led his mates to the title with a 110-109 victory. The Celtics had been dethroned after only one year on top, but they would be back.

1957/58 N.B.A.— EASTERN DIVISION

Use Name	Pos	Hgt	Wgt	Age	TOTAL													PER GAME				
					G	Min	FG	FGA	%	FT	FTA	%	Reb	Ass	PF	DQ	Points	Min	Reb	Ass	PF	Points
BOSTON CELTICS	**49-23 .681**				**RED AUERBACH**																	
Lou Tsioropoulos	F	6'5	205	27	70	1819	198	624	32	142	207	69	434	112	242	8	538	26	6.2	1.6	3.5	7.7
Tom Heinsohn	F	6'7	218	23	69	2206	468	1226	38	294	394	75	705	125	274	6	1230	32	10.2	1.8	4.0	17.8
Bill Russell	C	6'10	220	23	69	2640	456	1032	44	230	443	52	**1564**	202	181	2	1142	38	**22.7**	2.9	2.6	16.6
Bill Sharman	G	6'1	190	31	63	2214	550	1297	42	302	338	89	295	167	156	3	1402	35	4.7	2.7	2.5	22.3
Bob Cousy	G	6'1	178	29	65	2222	445	1262	35	277	326	85	322	**463**	136	1	1167	34	5.0	**7.1**	2.1	18.0
Frank Ramsey	G-F	6'3	195	26	69	2047	377	900	42	383	472	81	504	167	245	8	1137	30	7.3	2.4	3.6	16.5
Jack Nichols	F	6'7	230	31	69	1224	170	484	35	59	80	74	302	63	123	1	399	18	4.4	0.9	1.8	5.8
Andy Phillip	G	6'3	195	35	70	1164	97	273	36	42	71	59	158	121	121	0	236	17	2.3	1.7	1.7	3.4
Arnie Risen	C-F	6'9	210	33	63	1119	134	397	34	114	167	68	360	50	195	5	382	18	5.7	0.8	3.1	6.1
Sam Jones	F	6'4	205	24	56	594	100	233	43	60	84	71	160	37	42	0	260	11	2.9	0.7	0.8	4.6
Jim Loscutoff (illness)	F	6'5	230	27	5	56	11	31	35	1	3	33	20	1	8	0	23	11	4.0	0.2	1.6	4.6
Gene Conley - retired to play baseball																						
SYRACUSE NATIONALS	**41-31 .569**				**PAUL SEYMOUR**																	
Ed Conlin	F-G	6'5	200	24	60	1871	343	877	39	215	270	80	436	133	168	2	901	31	7.3	2.2	2.8	15.0
Dolph Schayes	F	6'8	220	29	72	**2918**	581	1458	40	629	696	**90**	1022	224	244	6	1791	**41**	14.2	3.1	3.4	24.9
Johnny Kerr	C	6'9	230	25	72	2384	407	1020	40	280	422	66	963	88	197	4	1094	33	13.4	1.2	2.7	15.2
Bob Harrison	G	6'2	190	30	72	1799	210	604	35	97	122	80	166	169	200	1	517	25	2.3	2.3	2.8	7.2
Larry Costello	G	6'1	188	26	72	2746	378	888	43	320	378	85	378	317	246	3	1076	38	5.3	4.4	3.4	14.9
Al Bianchi	G	6'3	185	25	69	1421	215	625	34	140	205	68	221	114	188	4	570	21	3.2	1.7	2.7	8.3
Bob Hopkins	C-F	6'8	215	23	69	1224	221	554	40	123	161	76	392	45	162	5	565	18	5.7	0.7	2.3	8.2
Earl Lloyd	F	6'6	220	29	61	1045	119	359	33	79	106	75	287	60	179	3	317	17	4.7	1.0	2.9	5.2
Togo Palazzi	F	6'4	205	25	67	1001	228	579	39	123	171	72	243	42	125	0	579	15	3.6	0.6	1.9	8.6
Paul Seymour	G	6'2	185	29	64	763	107	315	34	53	63	84	107	93	88	0	267	12	1.7	1.5	1.4	4.2
Dick Farley - military service																						
PHILADELPHIA WARRIORS	**37-35 .514**				**GEORGE SENESKY**																	
Paul Arizin	F	6'4	200	29	68	2377	483	1229	39	440	544	81	503	135	235	7	1406	35	7.4	2.0	3.5	20.7
Woody Sauldsberry	F	6'7	220	23	71	2377	389	1082	36	134	218	61	729	58	245	3	912	33	10.3	0.8	3.5	12.8
Neil Johnston	C	6'8	225	28	71	2408	473	1102	43	442	540	82	790	166	233	4	1388	34	11.1	2.3	3.3	19.5
Tom Gola (MS)	G-F	6'6	205	24	59	2126	295	711	41	223	299	75	639	327	225	11	813	36	10.8	5.5	3.8	13.8
Ernie Beck	G	6'4	195	26	71	1974	272	683	40	170	203	84	307	190	173	2	714	28	4.3	2.7	2.4	10.1
Joe Graboski	C-F	6'8	230	27	72	2077	341	1017	34	227	303	75	570	125	249	3	909	29	7.9	1.7	3.5	12.6
Jack George	G	6'3	195	29	72	1910	232	627	37	178	242	74	288	234	140	1	642	27	4.0	3.3	1.9	8.9
George Dempsey	G	6'3	195	28	67	1048	112	311	36	70	105	67	214	128	113	0	294	16	3.2	1.9	1.7	4.4
Lennie Rosenbluth	F	6'5	200	24	53	373	91	265	34	53	84	63	91	23	39	0	235	7	1.7	0.4	0.7	4.4
Pat Dunn	G	6'2	170	26	28	206	28	90	31	14	17	82	31	28	20	0	70	7	1.1	1.0	0.7	2.5
Jim Walsh	F	6'4	195	26	10	72	5	27	19	10	17	59	15	8	9	0	20	7	1.5	0.8	0.9	2.0
Ray Radziszewski	F	6'5	210	22	1	6	0	3	0	0	0	-	2	1	1	0	0	6	2.0	1.0	1.0	0.0
NEW YORK KNICKERBOCKERS	**35-37 .486**				**VINCE BORYLA**																	
Kenny Sears	F	6'9	195	24	72	2685	445	1014	44	452	550	82	785	126	251	7	1342	37	10.9	1.8	3.5	18.6
Willie Naulls	F	6'6	225	23	68	2369	472	1189	40	284	344	83	799	97	220	4	1228	35	11.8	1.4	3.2	18.1
Ray Felix	C	6'11	225	27	72	1709	304	688	44	271	389	70	747	52	283	12	879	24	10.4	0.7	3.9	12.2
Richie Guerin	G	6'4	195	25	63	2368	344	973	35	353	511	69	489	317	202	3	1041	38	7.8	5.0	3.2	16.5
Carl Braun	G	6'5	185	30	71	2475	426	1018	42	321	378	85	330	393	183	2	1173	35	4.6	5.5	2.6	16.5
Guy Sparrow	F	6'6	218	25	72	1661	318	838	38	165	257	64	461	69	232	6	801	23	6.4	1.0	3.2	11.1
Ron Sobie (foot injury)	G	6'3	195	24	55	1399	217	539	40	196	239	82	263	125	147	3	630	25	4.8	2.3	2.7	11.5
Art Spoelstra (50g. Min)	C	6'9	220	25	67	1305	161	419	38	127	187	68	332	57	225	11	449	19	5.0	0.9	3.4	6.7
Charlie Tyra	C	6'8	235	22	68	1182	175	490	36	150	224	67	480	34	175	3	500	17	7.1	0.5	2.6	7.4
Larry Friend	G-F	6'4	186	22	44	569	74	226	33	27	41	66	106	47	54	0	175	13	2.4	1.1	1.2	4.0
Mel Hutchins (back injury)	F	6'6	205	29	18	384	51	131	39	24	43	56	86	34	31	0	126	21	4.8	1.9	1.7	7.0
Brendan McCann	G	6'2	178	22	36	295	22	100	22	25	37	68	45	54	34	0	69	8	1.3	1.5	0.9	1.9
Ron Shavlik	F	6'8	200	24	1	2	0	1	0	0	0	-	1	0	0	0	0	2	1.0	0.0	0.0	0.0

1957/58 N.B.A. — WESTERN DIVISION

Use Name	Pos	Hgt	Wgt	Age	TOTAL G	Min	FG	FGA	%	FT	FTA	%	Reb	Ass	PF	DQ	Points	PER GAME Min	Reb	Ass	PF	Points
ST. LOUIS HAWKS	**41-31 .569**				**ALEX HANNUM**																	
Cliff Hagan	F	6'4	210	26	70	2190	503	1135	44	385	501	77	707	175	267	9	1391	31	10.1	2.5	3.8	19.9
Ed Macauley	F	6'8	195	29	72	1908	376	879	43	267	369	72	478	143	156	2	1019	27	6.6	2.0	2.2	14.2
Bob Pettit	C-F	6'9	215	25	70	2528	581	1418	41	557	744	75	1216	157	222	6	1719	36	17.4	2.2	3.2	24.6
Jack McMahon	G	6'1	188	29	72	2239	216	719	30	134	221	61	195	333	184	2	566	31	2.7	4.6	2.6	7.9
Slater Martin	G	5'10	170	32	60	2098	258	768	34	206	276	75	228	218	187	0	722	35	3.8	3.6	3.1	12.0
Chuck Share	C	6'11	240	30	72	1824	216	545	40	190	293	65	749	130	279	15	622	25	10.4	1.8	3.9	8.6
Jack Coleman	F	6'7	230	33	72	1506	231	560	41	84	131	64	485	117	169	3	546	21	6.7	1.6	2.3	7.6
Win Wilfong	G	6'2	185	25	71	1360	196	543	36	163	238	68	290	163	199	3	555	19	4.1	2.3	2.8	7.8
Med Park	G	6'2	205	24	71	1103	133	363	37	118	162	73	184	76	106	0	384	16	2.6	1.1	1.5	5.4
Walt Davis (35g. Phi)	F-C	6'8	210	26	61	663	85	244	35	61	82	74	174	29	143	0	231	11	2.9	0.5	2.3	3.8
Red Morrison	F-C	6'8	225	25	13	79	9	26	35	3	4	75	26	0	12	0	21	6	2.0	0.0	0.9	1.6
Worthy Patterson	G	6'2	175	26	4	13	3	8	38	1	2	50	2	2	3	0	7	3	0.5	0.5	0.8	1.8
Al Ferrari and Jack Stephens - military service																						
DETROIT PISTONS	**33-39 .458**				**CHARLIE ECKMAN (9-16 .360), RED ROCHA (24-23 .511)**																	
George Yardley	F	6'5	195	29	72	2843	673	**1624**	41	**655**	**808**	81	768	97	226	3	**2001**	39	10.7	1.3	3.1	**27.8**
Harry Gallatin	F	6'6	220	30	72	1900	340	898	38	392	498	79	749	86	217	5	1072	26	10.4	1.2	3.0	14.9
Walter Dukes	C	7'	220	27	72	2184	278	796	35	247	366	67	954	52	**311**	17	803	30	13.3	0.7	**4.3**	11.2
Gene Shue	G	6'2	175	26	63	2333	353	919	38	276	327	84	333	172	150	1	982	37	5.3	2.7	2.4	15.6
Dick McGuire	G	6'	180	31	69	2311	203	544	37	150	225	67	291	454	178	0	556	33	4.2	6.6	2.6	8.1
Sweetwater Clifton	F-C	6'6	225	35	68	1435	217	597	36	91	146	62	403	76	202	3	525	21	5.9	1.1	3.0	7.7
Chuch Noble	G	6'4	195	26	61	1363	199	601	33	56	77	73	140	153	166	0	454	22	2.3	2.5	2.7	7.4
Phil Jordon (12g. NY)	C	6'10	205	24	58	898	193	467	41	64	93	69	301	37	108	1	450	17	5.2	0.6	1.9	7.8
Joe Holup (16g. Syr)	F	6'6	215	23	53	740	91	278	33	71	94	76	221	36	99	2	253	14	4.2	0.7	1.9	4.8
Billy Kenville	G	6'2	190	27	35	649	106	280	38	46	75	61	102	66	68	0	258	19	2.9	1.9	1.9	7.4
Bob Houbregs (XJ)	C-F	6'8	225	25	17	302	49	137	36	30	43	70	65	19	36	0	128	18	3.8	1.1	2.1	7.5
Bill Thieben	F	6'7	220	22	27	243	42	143	29	16	27	59	65	7	44	0	100	9	2.4	0.3	1.6	3.7
Dick Atha	G	6'2	195	27	18	160	17	47	36	10	12	83	24	19	24	0	44	9	1.3	1.1	1.3	2.4
Bill Ebben	G	6'4	190	22	8	50	6	28	21	3	4	75	8	4	5	0	15	6	1.0	0.5	0.6	1.9
Doug Bolstorff	G	6'4	195	26	3	21	2	5	40	0	0	—	0	0	1	0	4	7	0.0	0.0	1.0	1.3
CINCINNATI ROYALS	**33-39 .458**				**BOBBY WANZER**																	
Jack Twyman	F-G	6'6	210	23	72	2178	465	1028	**45**	307	396	78	464	110	224	3	1237	30	6.4	1.5	3.1	17.2
Maurice Stokes	F	6'7	235	24	63	2460	414	1181	35	238	333	71	1142	403	226	9	1066	39	18.1	6.4	3.6	16.9
Clyde Lovellette	C	6'9	245	28	71	2589	**679**	1540	44	301	405	74	862	134	236	3	1659	36	12.1	1.9	3.3	23.4
Jim Paxson	G	6'6	200	25	67	1795	225	639	35	209	285	73	350	139	183	2	659	27	5.2	2.1	2.7	9.8
George King	G	6'	185	29	63	2272	235	645	36	140	227	62	306	337	124	0	610	36	4.9	5.3	2.0	9.7
Richie Regan	G	6'2	180	27	72	1648	202	569	36	120	172	70	175	185	174	0	524	23	2.4	2.6	2.4	7.3
Dick Ricketts	F-C	6'7	220	24	72	1620	215	664	32	132	196	67	410	114	277	8	562	23	5.7	1.6	3.8	7.8
Dave Piontek	F	6'6	230	23	71	1032	150	397	38	95	151	63	254	52	134	2	395	15	3.6	0.7	1.9	5.6
Monk Meineke	C	6'7	210	27	67	792	125	351	36	77	119	65	226	38	155	3	327	12	3.4	0.6	2.3	4.9
Tom Marshall (9g. Det)	F	6'4	215	26	38	518	52	166	31	48	63	76	101	19	43	0	152	14	2.7	0.5	1.1	4.0
Dick Duckett	G	6'1	185	24	34	424	54	158	34	24	27	89	56	47	60	0	132	12	1.6	1.4	1.8	3.9
Jerry Paulson	G	6'2	187	22	6	68	8	23	35	4	6	67	10	4	5	0	20	11	1.7	0.7	0.8	3.3
Si Green, Johnny McCarthy - military service																						
MINNEAPOLIS LAKERS	**19-53 .264**				**GEORGE MIKAN (9-30 .231), JONNNY KUNDLA (10-23 .303)**																	
Ed Fleming	F-G	6'3	190	24	72	1686	226	655	35	181	255	71	492	139	222	5	633	23	6.8	1.9	3.1	8.8
Vern Mikkelsen	F	6'7	230	29	72	2390	439	1070	41	370	471	79	805	166	299	**20**	1248	33	11.2	2.3	4.2	17.3
Larry Foust	C	6'9	250	29	72	2200	391	982	40	428	566	76	876	108	299	11	1210	31	12.2	1.5	4.2	16.8
Dick Garmaker	G	6'3	205	25	68	2216	390	988	39	314	411	76	365	183	190	2	1094	33	5.4	2.7	2.8	16.1
Bob Leonard	G	6'3	185	25	66	2074	266	794	34	205	268	76	237	218	145	0	737	31	3.6	3.3	2.2	11.2
Jim Krebs	F-C	6'8	230	22	68	1259	199	527	38	135	176	77	502	27	182	4	533	19	7.4	0.4	2.7	7.8
Corky Devlin	G	6'5	195	26	70	1248	170	489	35	133	172	77	132	167	104	1	473	18	1.9	2.4	1.5	6.8
Rod Hundley	G	6'4	185	23	65	1154	174	548	32	104	162	64	186	121	99	0	452	18	2.9	1.9	1.5	7.0
Dick Schnittker	F	6'5	205	29	50	979	128	357	36	201	237	82	211	71	126	5	457	20	4.2	1.4	2.5	9.1
Frank Selvy (MS)	F	6'3	185	25	38	426	44	167	26	47	77	61	88	35	44	0	135	11	2.3	0.9	1.2	3.6
Bo Erias	F	6'3	220	25	18	401	59	170	35	30	47	64	83	26	52	1	148	22	4.6	1.4	2.9	8.2
McCoy Ingram	F	6'	210	26	24	267	27	103	26	13	28	46	116	20	44	1	67	11	4.8	0.8	1.8	2.8
Bob Burrow	C-F	6'7	230	23	14	171	22	70	31	11	33	33	64	6	15	0	55	12	4.6	0.4	1.1	3.9
George Brown	F	6'6	190	22	1	6	0	2	0	1	2	50	1	0	1	0	1	6	1.0	0.0	1.0	1.0

1957/58 N.B.A. — PLAYOFFS

Use Name	Pos	Hgt	Wgt	Age	G	Min	FG	FGA	%	FT	FTA	%	Reb	Ass	PF	DQ	Points	Min	Reb	Ass	PF	Points
					TOTAL													PER GAME				
ST. LOUIS HAWKS	**ALEX HANNUM**				defeated Detroit 4-1; H114-111, 99-96, H89-109, 145-101, H120-96																	
					defeated Boston 4-2; 104-102,112-136, H111-107, H98-109, 102-100, H11O-109																	
Cliff Hagan	F	6'4	210	26	11	418	**111**	221	**50**	83	99	84	115	37	48	3	**305**	38	10.5	3.4	4.4	**27.7**
Jack Coleman	F	6'7	230	33	11	243	38	89	43	23	40	58	60	19	38	1	99	22	5.5	1.7	3.5	9.0
Bob Pettit	C-F	6'9	215	25	11	430	90	**230**	39	**86**	**118**	73	181	20	31	0	266	39	16.5	1.8	2.8	24.2
Jach McMahon	G	6'1	188	29	11	332	36	88	41	14	26	54	37	51	36	0	86	30	3.4	4.6	3.3	7.8
Slater Martin	G	5'10	170	32	11	416	44	137	32	39	63	62	48	40	40	1	127	38	4.4	3.6	3.6	11.5
Ed Macauley	F	6'8	195	29	11	227	36	89	40	36	50	72	62	18	23	0	108	21	5.6	1.6	2.1	9.8
Chuck Share	C	6'11	240	30	11	199	24	61	39	25	38	66	68	11	49	**4**	73	18	6.2	1.0	4.5	6.6
Win Wilfong	G	6'2	185	25	11	162	19	69	28	23	33	70	41	25	24	0	61	15	3.7	2.3	2.2	5.5
Med Park	G	6'2	205	24	10	147	17	42	40	13	22	59	24	12	24	0	47	15	2.4	1.2	2.4	4.7
Walt Davis	F-C	6'8	210	26	9	66	11	29	38	10	12	83	27	3	22	0	32	7	3.0	0.3	2.4	3.6
Al Ferrari and Jack Stephens - military service																						
BOSTON CELTICS	**RED AUERBACH**				defeated Philadelphia 4-1; H107-98, 109-87, H106-92, 97-111, H93-88																	
					lost to St. Louis 4-2; H102-104, H136-112, 107-111, 109-98, H100-102, 109-110																	
Lou Tsioropoulos	F	6'5	205	27	11	239	25	85	29	19	29	66	64	14	40	**4**	69	22	5.8	1.3	3.6	6.3
Tom Heinsohn	F	6'7	218	23	11	349	68	194	35	56	72	78	119	18	**52**	3	192	32	10.8	1.6	4.7	17.5
Bill Russell	C	6'10	220	23	9	355	48	133	36	40	66	61	**221**	24	24	0	136	39	**24.6**	2.7	2.7	15.1
Bill Sharman	G	6'1	190	31	11	406	90	221	41	52	56	93	54	25	28	0	232	37	4.9	2.3	2.5	21.1
Bob Cousy	G	6'1	178	29	11	**457**	67	196	34	64	75	85	71	**82**	20	0	198	42	6.5	**7.5**	1.8	18.0
Frank Ramsey	F-G	6'3	195	26	11	352	74	174	43	54	59	92	90	16	50	3	202	32	8.2	1.5	4.5	18.4
Arnie Risen	C-F	6'9	210	33	10	168	12	52	23	22	33	67	62	9	32	1	46	17	6.2	0.9	3.2	4.6
Jack Nichols	F-C	6'7	230	31	11	148	23	66	35	7	10	70	45	8	21	1	53	13	4.1	0.7	1.9	4.8
Andy Phillip	G	6'3	195	35	10	91	5	21	24	7	9	78	14	7	20	0	17	9	1.4	0.7	2.0	1.7
Sam Jones	F	6'4	205	24	8	75	10	22	45	11	16	69	24	4	7	0	31	9	3.0	0.5	0.9	3.9
Jim Loscutoff - illness, Gene Conley - retired to play baseball																						
DETROIT PISTONS	**RED ROCHA**				defeated Cincinnati 2-0; H100-93, 124-104																	
					lost to St. Louis 1-4; 111-114, H96-99, 109-89, H101-145, 96-120																	
George Yardley	F	6'5	195	29	7	254	52	127	41	60	67	90	72	17	26	0	164	36	10.3	2.4	3.7	23.4
Harry Gallatin	F	6'6	220	30	7	182	32	87	37	26	37	70	70	11	27	1	90	26	10.0	1.6	3.9	12.9
Walter Dukes	C	7'	220	27	7	286	37	101	37	37	56	66	97	4	38	3	111	41	13.9	0.6	**5.4**	15.9
Gene Shue	G	6'2	175	26	7	281	45	123	37	40	43	**93**	46	33	15	0	130	40	6.6	4.7	2.1	18.6
Dick McGuire	G	6'	180	31	7	236	25	60	42	17	24	71	33	40	13	0	67	34	4.7	5.7	1.9	9.6
Joe Holup	F	6'6	215	23	7	134	15	43	35	12	16	75	36	3	20	0	42	19	5.1	0.4	2.9	6.0
Billy Kenville	G-F	6'2	190	27	7	99	18	44	41	10	18	56	19	5	12	0	46	14	2.7	0.7	1.7	6.6
Sweetwater Clifton	F	6'6	225	35	7	74	11	30	37	6	8	75	23	4	11	0	28	11	3.3	0.6	1.6	4.0
Chuck Noble	G	6'4	195	26	7	72	8	38	21	4	8	50	13	6	9	0	20	10	1.9	0.9	1.3	2.9
Phil Jordon	C-F	6'10	205	24	6	62	12	30	40	15	20	75	12	2	15	0	39	10	2.0	0.3	2.5	6.5
Bob Houbregs - back injury																						
PHILADELPHIA WARRIORS	**GEORGE SENESKY**				defeated Syracuse 2-1; 82-86, H95-93, 101-88																	
					lost to Boston 1-4; 98-107, H87-109, 92-106, H111-97, 88-93																	
Paul Arizin	F	6'4	200	29	8	309	66	169	39	56	72	78	62	16	26	1	188	39	7.8	2.0	3.3	23.5
Woody Sauldsberry	F	6'7	220	23	8	290	45	131	34	13	23	57	87	6	27	0	103	36	10.9	0.8	3.4	12.9
Joe Graboski	C-F	6'8	230	27	8	252	40	138	29	18	23	78	82	30	21	0	98	32	10.3	3.8	2.6	12.3
Tom Gola	G-F	6'6	205	24	8	327	36	109	33	38	51	75	84	32	24	0	110	41	10.5	4.0	3.0	13.8
Jack George	G	6'3	195	29	8	277	30	81	37	16	20	80	38	31	14	0	76	35	4.8	3.9	1.8	9.5
Neil Johnston	C	6'8	225	28	8	189	30	78	38	27	33	82	69	14	18	0	87	24	8.6	1.8	2.3	10.9
Ernie Beck	G	6'4	195	26	8	156	23	61	38	6	9	67	32	13	16	0	52	20	4.0	1.6	2.0	6.5
George Dempsey	G	6'3	195	28	8	101	14	28	50	5	9	56	18	6	11	0	33	13	2.3	0.8	1.4	4.1
Lennie Rosenbluth	F	6'5	200	24	4	11	3	9	33	2	3	67	3	0	0	0	8	3	0.8	0.0	0.0	2.0
Pat Dunn	G	6'2	170	26	3	8	0	4	0	0	0	—	1	1	1	0	0	3	0.3	0.3	0.3	0.0
SYRACUSE NATIONALS	**PAUL SEYMOUR**				lost to Philadelphia 1-2; H86-82, 93-95, H88-101																	
Ed Conlin	F-G	6'5	200	24	3	113	14	45	31	5	7	71	21	4	10	0	33	38	7.0	1.3	3.3	11.0
Dolph Schayes	F	6'8	220	29	3	131	25	64	39	30	36	83	45	6	10	0	80	44	15.0	2.0	3.3	26.7
Johnny Kerr	C	6'9	230	25	3	116	18	55	33	14	18	78	61	3	5	0	50	39	20.3	1.0	1.7	16.7
Paul Seymour	G	6'2	185	29	3	50	8	23	35	2	3	67	4	4	5	0	18	17	1.3	1.3	1.7	6.0
Larry Costello	G	6'1	188	26	3	134	10	34	29	14	14	100	25	12	6	0	34	**45**	8.3	4.0	2.0	11.3
Bob Harrison	G	6'2	190	30	3	43	4	16	25	2	3	67	7	5	6	0	10	14	2.3	1.7	2.0	3.3
Bob Hopkins	C-F	6'8	215	23	3	39	4	16	25	4	6	67	14	0	7	0	12	13	4.7	0.0	2.3	4.0
Al Bianchi	G	6'3	185	25	2	37	4	12	33	3	8	38	7	2	4	0	11	19	3.5	1.0	2.0	5.5
Earl Lloyd	F	6'6	220	29	3	32	5	14	36	0	0	—	8	0	8	0	10	11	2.7	0.0	2.7	3.3
Togo Palazzi	F	6'4	205	25	3	25	3	14	21	3	6	50	4	0	4	0	9	8	1.3	0.0	1.3	3.0
Dick Farley - military service																						
CINCINNATI ROYALS	**BOBBY WANZER**				lost to Detroit 0-2; 93-100, H104-124																	
Jack Twyman	F-G	6'6	210	23	2	74	15	45	33	7	12	58	22	1	6	0	37	37	11.0	0.5	3.0	18.5
Maurice Stokes	F	6'7	237	24	1	39	3	12	25	6	7	86	15	2	3	0	12	39	15.0	2.0	3.0	12.0
Clyde Lovellette	C	6'9	245	28	2	72	12	31	39	9	14	64	21	1	9	0	33	36	10.5	0.5	4.5	16.5
Richie Regan	G	6'2	180	27	2	63	12	26	46	0	1	0	9	3	5	0	24	32	4.5	1.5	2.5	12.0
George King	G	6'	185	29	2	79	7	28	25	4	6	67	5	7	5	0	18	40	2.5	3.5	2.5	9.0
Tom Marshall	F	6'4	215	26	2	33	7	17	41	4	5	80	16	2	1	0	18	17	8.0	1.0	0.5	9.0
Monk Meineke	C-F	6'7	210	27	2	32	1	11	9	6	8	75	11	1	3	0	8	16	5.5	0.5	1.5	4.0
Dick Ricketts	F	6'7	220	24	2	31	5	15	33	5	5	100	10	2	9	0	15	16	5.0	1.0	4.5	7.5
Jim Paxson	G	6'6	200	25	2	30	3	20	15	6	8	75	8	5	7	0	12	15	4.0	2.5	3.5	6.0
Dave Piontek	F	6'6	230	23	2	27	4	10	40	2	5	40	10	0	7	1	10	14	5.0	0.0	3.5	5.0
Si Green and Johnny McCarthy - military service																						

1957/58 N.B.A. TEAM STATISTICS

Team	REGULAR SEASON G	FG	FGA	%	FT	FTA	%	Reb.	Ass.	AVERAGE POINTS For	Agnst.	Diff.	PLAYOFFS G	FG	FGA	%	FT	FTA	%	Reb.	Ass.	AVERAGE POINTS For	Agnst.	Diff.
EASTERN DIVISION																								
Boston	72	**3006**	**7759**	39	1904	2585	74	5402	1508	109.9	104.4	**+5.5**	11	422	1164	36	332	425	**78**	**855**	207	106.9	101.3	**+5.6**
Syracuse	72	2823	7336	38	2075	2617	**79**	4895	1298	107.2	105.1	+2.1	3	95	293	32	77	101	76	220	36	89.0	**92.7**	-3.7
Philadelphia	72	2765	7276	38	1977	2596	76	4836	1441	104.3	104.4	-0.1	8	287	808	36	181	243	74	548	149	94.4	97.4	-3.0
New York	72	2884	7307	**39**	**2300**	**3056**	75	5385	1359	112.1	110.8	+1.3												
WESTERN DIVISION																								
St. Louis	72	2779	7162	39	2180	3047	72	**5445**	1541	107.5	106.2	+1.3	11	**426**	1055	**40**	352	501	70	787	**236**	**109.5**	107.0	+2.5
Detroit	72	2746	7295	38	2093	2774	75	5168	1264	105.3	107.7	-2.4	7	255	683	37	**227**	297	76	505	125	105.3	107.7	-2.4
Cincinnati	72	2817	7339	38	1688	2372	71	4959	**1578**	101.7	**103.1**	-1.4	2	69	**215**	32	49	71	69	151	24	93.5	112.0	-18.5
Minneapolis	72	2660	7192	37	2246	3007	75	5189	1322	105.1	111.5	-6.4												

1957/58 N.B.A. STANDINGS

Team	W	L	Pct.	GB	Record against playoff teams W	L	Pct.	Record against non-playoff teams W	L	Pct.	HOME W	L	Pct.	ROAD W	L	Pct.	NEUTRAL W	L	Pct.
EASTERN DIVISION																			
Boston Celtics	**49**	23	**.681**	—	**33**	18	**.647**	**16**	5	.762	25	4	**.862**	**17**	13	**.567**	7	6	.538
Syracuse Nationals	41	31	.569	8	27	24	.529	14	7	.667	**26**	5	.839	9	21	.300	6	5	.545
Philadelphia Warriors	37	35	.514	12	23	28	.451	14	7	.667	16	12	.571	12	19	.387	**9**	4	**.692**
New York Knickerbockers	35	37	.486	14	27	36	.429	8	1	**.889**	16	13	.552	11	19	.367	8	5	.615
WESTERN DIVISION																			
St. Louis Hawks	41	31	.569	—	26	25	.510	15	6	.714	23	8	.742	9	19	.321	**9**	4	**.692**
Detroit Pistons	33	39	.458	8	23	28	.451	10	**11**	.476	14	14	.500	13	18	.419	6	7	.462
Cincinnati Royals	33	39	.458	8	21	30	.412	12	9	.571	17	12	.586	10	19	.345	6	8	.429
Minneapolis Lakers	19	**53**	.264	22	18	**45**	.286	1	8	.111	13	**17**	.433	4	**22**	.154	2	**14**	.125

1957/58 INDIVIDUAL LEADERS

SCORING
(Minimum 55 Games Played)

Name	Team	G	FG	FT	Pts.	Avg.
Yardley	Det	72	673	655	2001	27.8
Schayes	Syr	72	581	629	1791	24.9
Pettit	StL	70	581	557	1719	24.6
Lovellette	Cin	71	679	301	1659	23.4
Sharman	Bos	63	550	302	1402	22.3
Arizin	Phi	68	483	440	1406	20.7
Hagan	StL	70	503	385	1391	19.9
Johnston	Phi	71	473	442	1388	19.5
Sears	NY	72	445	452	1342	18.6
Naulls	NY	68	472	284	1228	18.1

FIELD GOAL PERCENTAGE
(Minimum 230 Field Goals)

Name	Team	FG	FGA	Pct.
Twyman	Cin	465	1028	.452
Hagan	StL	503	1135	.443
Russell	Bos	456	1032	.442
Felix	NY	304	688	.442
Lovellette	Cin	679	1540	.441
Sears	NY	445	1014	.439
Johnston	Phi	473	1102	.429
Macauley	StL	376	879	.428
Costello	Syr	378	888	.426
Sharman	Bos	550	1297	.424

FREE THROW PERCENTAGE
(Minimum 190 Free Throws)

Name	Team	FT	FTA	Pct.
Schayes	Syr	629	696	.904
Sharman	Bos	302	338	.893
Cousy	Bos	277	326	.850
Braun	NY	321	378	.849
Schnittker	Min	201	237	.848
Costello	Syr	320	378	.847
Shue	Det	276	327	.844
Naulls	NY	284	344	.826
Sears	NY	452	550	.822
Sobie	NY	196	239	.820

PERSONAL FOULS

Name	Team	PF
Dukes	Det	311
Foust	Min	299
Mikkelsen	Min	299
Felix	NY	283
Share	StL	279

GAMES DISQUALIFIED

Name	Team	Disq
Mikkelsen	Min	20
Dukes	Det	17
Share	StL	15
Felix	NY	12
Spoelstra	Min-NY	11
Gola	Phi	11
Foust	Min	11

REBOUNDS PER GAME
(Minimum 55 Games Played)

Name	Team	G	Reb.	Avg.
Russell	Bos	69	1564	22.7
Stokes	Cin	63	1142	18.1
Pettit	StL	70	1216	17.4
Schayes	Syr	72	1022	14.2
Kerr	Syr	72	963	13.4
Dukes	Det	72	954	13.3
Foust	Min	72	876	12.2
Lovellette	Cin	71	872	12.3
Naulls	NY	68	799	11.8
Mikkelsen	Min	72	805	11.2

ASSISTS PER GAME
(Minimum 55 Games Played)

Name	Team	G	Ass.	Avg.
Cousy	Bos	65	463	7.1
McGuire	Det	69	454	6.6
Stokes	Cin	63	403	6.4
Gola	Phi	59	327	5.5
Braun	NY	71	393	5.5
King	Cin	63	337	5.3
Guerin	NY	63	317	5.0
McMahon	StL	72	333	4.6
Costello	Syr	72	317	4.4
Martin	StL	60	218	3.6

MINUTES PLAYED

Name	Team	Min.
Schayes	Syr	2918
Yardley	Det	2843
Costello	Syr	2746
Sears	NY	2685
Russell	Bos	2640

1958-59 N.B.A.

Baylor's Debut and Boston's Sweeping Return

Elgin Baylor arrived on the pro basketball scene with a spark that lit a new fire of interest in the sporting public. A strong 6'5" forward out of the University of Seattle, Baylor stepped into the Minneapolis Laker's lineup and displayed a set of moves unknown to most basketball fans. A tough rebounder and sound ballhandler, Baylor shone most brightly when putting the ball in the hoop. He tapped in rebounds, he sank long jumpers, and he seemed to soar and float in his ad lib drives to the basket. The rookie scored at a 24.9 clip, fourth best in the N.B.A., and drew curious crowds in all the league cities. In fact, the N.B.A. enjoyed its highest attendance yet as it played its tenth season.

One of the clubs enjoying the attendance boom was the New York Knicks, who drew a record 18,496 fans to one of their games in Madison Square Garden. With Fuzzy Levane the new coach, the Knicks spurred fan interest by winning 10 of their first 11 games to take an early lead in the Eastern Division. But the rebuilt Knick squad, headed by guard Richie Guerin and forwards Kenny Sears and Willie Naulls, could not hold off the Boston Celtics for long. With Bill Russell, Bob Cousy, and Bill Sharman all first-team All-Stars, and with Jim Loscutoff back after an illness and K.C. Jones joining the club as a rookie guard after an Army stint, the Celtics had more assets in hand than ever. The Boston club caught up with the slumping Knicks in mid-season and ran away to a 12-game lead by the end of the regular season.

The third-place Syracuse Nationals added rookie Hal Greer to the backcourt and strengthened the forecourt by trading Ed Conlin to Detroit for George Yardley, last season's scoring champ. This deal made the Nats a club to contend with in the playoffs. Philadelphia finished last, hurt most by the loss of center Neil Johnston for most of the schedule because of a knee injury. For assets, the Warriors counted the continued high scoring of Paul Arizin, the poised play of rookie guard Guy Rodgers, and the future draft rights to Wilt Chamberlain, who quit the University of Kansas this season to tour with the Harlem Globetrotters. But the Warriors played this season without a big-league center.

The St. Louis Hawks captured a playoff spot and first place in the West despite a case of rotating coaches. Owner Ben Kerner found coach Alex Hannum too strong-willed for his liking, so he fired him despite last season's championship banner. Kerner hired Andy Phillip as the new coach but tired of him 10 games into the season. Ed Macauley then got the job; the easy-going Macauley was a popular local favorite who was at the end of his playing career. The chaotic coaching situation did not spoil the talent on the floor. Bob Pettit and Cliff Hagan handled the bulk of the scoring and rebounding from the forward positions, with Pettit scoring a record 2105 points. Clyde Lovellette was obtained from Cincinnati to split the center duties with Chuck Share. Guards Slater Martin and Jack McMahon confined most of their attention to feeding the forwards and playing defense. This blend of talents ran away with the Western crown.

The Lakers improved to 33-39 and a second-place finish, strengthened tremendously by the rookie Baylor. The Pistons took the third playoff spot practically by default, with Detroit's 28-44 record outdone in futility by Cincinnati's 19-53 log. The Royals suffered tremendously from the loss of star forward Maurice Stokes, who was still paralyzed.

A local group purchased the Royals from Les Harrison, and the new owners canned coach Bobby Wanzer early in the campaign and replaced him with Tom Marshall, a young player in his fifth pro season. The only true bright spot in the Royals' season was Jack Twyman, the sharpshooting forward who blossomed into one of the N.B.A.'s hottest scorers; only Bob Pettit finished ahead of Twyman in the N.B.A. scoring race.

Pettit and his Hawks enjoyed a bye in the opening round of the playoffs while the Lakers and Pistons squared off in the Western semifinal. The Pistons had no one to match young Baylor, and the Lakers eliminated the Pistons two games to one. The rejuvenated Lakers then took on the first-place Hawks in what many fans mistakenly wrote off as a mismatch. The unheralded Lakers had two solid veterans in center Larry Foust and forward Vern Mikkelsen, whose career bridged the Mikan and Baylor eras. Minneapolis guards Dick Garmaker and Hot Rod Hundley also scored more than their St. Louis counterparts. The Hawks nevertheless were favored to reach the finals for a third straight season. The Hawks seemed in control when they captured two out of the first three games, but then the Lakers came storming back. With Baylor's hot hand leading the way, the Lakers took three straight victories to send the defending champion Hawks home and to head on into the championship round against the Celtics.

While all this activity had been going on in the West, the Eastern rounds played off in routine fashion. Syracuse appeared stronger for the playoffs than they had been during the season, and they confirmed this appraisal by knocking off the Knicks in two quick decisions. The Nats stood second in talent only behind the Celtics. Dolph Schayes, George Yardley, Hal Greer, and Larry Costello all could score from the outside, and Schayes and Johnny Kerr hit the boards effectively. Most important, the Nats played a selfless brand of team ball, flowing on offense and tenacious on defense. The Nats pressed the Celtics to their limit in the Eastern finals, but the Celtics emerged from game seven with a 130-125 victory that sent them into the championship round.

The Lakers had made it to this series by upsetting the Hawks, but the deep Boston team was too much for the rebuilt Lakers to handle. The Celtics had beaten the Lakers 18 straight times heading into the playoffs, and the pattern held true as the Celtics took four consecutive victories and swept into the throne room. After a year as bridesmaid, the Celtics again held the center spotlight and would not give it up until they had built one of the greatest dynasties of sports history.

Use Name	Pos	Hgt	Wgt	Age	TOTAL													PER GAME				
					G	Min	FG	FGA	%	FT	FTA	%	Reb	Ass	PF	DQ	Points	Min	Reb	Ass	PF	Points
1958/59 N.BA. — EASTERN DIVISION																						
BOSTON CELTICS	**52-20 .722**				**RED AUERBACH**																	
Jim Loscutoff	F	6'5	230	28	66	1680	242	686	35	62	84	74	460	60	285	15	546	25	7.0	0.9	4.3	8.3
Tom Heinsohn	F	6'7	220	24	66	2089	465	1192	39	312	391	80	638	164	271	11	1242	32	9.7	2.5	4.1	18.8
Bill Russell	C	6'10	220	24	70	2979	456	997	46	256	428	60	**1612**	222	161	3	1168	**43**	**23.0**	3.2	2.3	16.7
Bill Sharman	G	6'1	190	32	72	2382	562	1377	41	342	367	**93**	292	179	173	1	1466	33	4.1	2.5	2.4	20.4
Bob Cousy	G	6'1	178	30	65	2403	484	1260	38	329	385	85	355	**557**	135	0	1297	37	5.5	**8.6**	2.1	20.0
Frank Ramsey	F-G	6'3	195	27	72	2013	383	1013	38	341	436	78	491	147	266	11	1107	28	6.8	2.0	3.7	15.4
Sam Jones	G-F	6'4	205	25	71	1466	305	703	43	151	196	77	428	101	102	0	761	21	6.0	1.4	1.4	10.7
Bennie Swain	F	6'8	222	25	58	708	99	244	41	67	110	61	262	29	127	3	265	12	4.5	0.5	2.2	4.6
Gene Conley	C-F	6'8	225	28	50	663	86	262	33	37	64	58	276	19	117	2	209	13	5.5	0.4	2.3	4.2
K. C. Jones	G	6'1	202	26	49	609	65	192	34	41	68	60	127	70	58	0	171	12	2.6	1.4	1.2	3.5
Lou Tsioropoulos	F	6'5	210	28	35	488	60	190	32	25	33	76	110	20	74	0	145	14	3.1	0.6	2.1	4.1
NEW YORK KNICKERBOCKERS	**40-32 .556**				**FUZZY LEVANE**																	
Kenny Sears	F	6'9	195	25	71	2498	491	1002	**49**	506	588	86	658	136	237	6	1488	35	9.3	1.9	3.3	21.0
Willie Naulls	F-C	6'6	225	24	68	2061	405	1072	38	258	311	83	723	102	233	8	1068	30	10.6	1.5	3.4	15.7
Ray Felix	C	6'11	225	28	72	1588	260	700	37	229	321	71	569	49	275	9	749	22	7.9	0.7	3.8	10.4
Richie Guerin	G	6'4	195	26	71	2558	443	1046	42	405	505	80	518	364	255	1	1291	36	7.3	5.1	3.6	18.2
Carl Braun	G	6'5	185	31	72	1959	287	684	42	180	218	83	251	349	178	3	754	27	3.5	4.8	2.5	10.5
Jack George (46g. Phi)	G	6'3	195	30	71	1881	233	674	35	153	203	75	293	221	149	0	619	26	4.1	3.1	2.1	8.7
Charlie Tyra	C	6'8	235	23	69	1586	240	606	40	129	190	68	485	33	180	2	609	23	7.0	0.5	2.6	8.8
Mike Farmer	F	6'7	210	22	72	1545	176	498	35	83	99	84	315	66	152	1	435	21	4.4	0.9	2.1	6.0
Frank Selvy	F-G	6'3	185	26	68	1448	233	605	39	201	262	77	248	96	113	1	667	21	3.6	1.4	1.7	9.8
Ron Sobie (foot injury)	G	6'3	195	25	50	857	144	400	36	112	133	84	154	78	84	0	400	17	3.1	1.6	1.7	8.0
Pete Brennan	F	6'6	205	22	16	136	13	43	30	14	25	56	31	6	15	0	40	9	1.9	0.4	0.9	2.5
Jerry Bird	F	6'6	220	23	11	45	12	32	38	1	1	100	12	4	7	0	25	4	1.1	0.4	0.6	2.3
Brendan McCann	G	6'2	178	23	1	7	0	3	0	0	0	—	1	1	1	0	0	7	1.0	1.0	1.0	0.0
SYRACUSE NATIONALS	**35-37 .486**				**PAUL SEYMOUR**																	
George Yardley (46g. Det)	F	6'5	195	30	61	1839	446	1042	43	317	407	78	431	65	159	2	1209	30	7.1	1.1	2.6	19.8
Dolph Schayes	F	6'8	220	30	72	2645	504	1304	39	526	609	86	962	178	280	9	1534	37	13.4	2.5	3.9	21.3
Johnny Kerr	C	6'9	230	26	72	2671	502	1139	44	281	367	77	1008	142	183	1	1285	37	14.0	2.0	2.5	17.8
Al Bianchi	G	6'3	185	26	72	1779	285	756	38	149	206	72	199	159	260	8	719	25	2.8	2.2	3.6	10.0
Larry Costello	G	6'1	188	27	70	2750	414	948	44	280	349	80	365	379	263	7	1108	39	5.2	5.4	3.8	15.8
Hal Greer	G	6'3	176	22	68	1625	308	679	45	137	176	78	196	101	189	1	753	24	2.9	1.5	2.8	11.1
Bob Hopkins	F-C	6'8	225	24	67	1518	246	611	40	176	234	75	436	67	181	5	668	23	6.5	1.0	2.7	10.0
Togo Palazzi	F	6'4	205	26	71	1053	240	612	39	115	158	73	266	67	174	5	595	15	3.7	0.9	2.5	8.4
Connie Dierking	C	6'9	222	22	64	726	105	290	36	83	140	59	233	34	148	2	293	11	3.6	0.5	2.3	4.6
George Dempsey (23g. Phi)	G	6'3	195	29	57	694	92	215	43	81	106	76	160	68	95	0	265	12	2.8	1.2	1.7	4.6
Paul Seymour	G	6'2	185	30	21	266	32	98	33	26	29	90	39	36	25	0	90	13	1.9	1.7	1.2	4.3
Tommy Kearns	G	5'11	185	22	1	7	1	1	100	0	0	—	2	0	2	0	2	7	2.0	0.0	2.0	2.0
PHILADELPHIA WARRIORS	**32-40 .444**				**AL CERVI**																	
Paul Arizin	F	6'4	200	30	70	2799	632	1466	43	587	722	81	637	119	264	7	1851	40	9.1	1.7	3.8	26.4
Woody Sauldsberry	F-C	6'7	220	24	72	2743	501	1380	36	110	176	63	826	71	276	12	1112	38	11.5	1.0	3.8	15.4
Joe Graboski	C	6'8	230	28	72	2482	394	1116	35	270	360	75	751	148	249	5	1058	34	10.4	2.1	3.5	14.7
Tom Gola	G-F	6'6	205	25	64	2333	310	773	40	281	357	79	710	269	243	7	901	36	11.1	4.2	3.8	14.1
Guy Rodgers (MS)	G	6'	185	23	45	1565	211	535	39	61	112	54	281	261	132	1	483	35	6.2	5.8	2.9	10.7
Andy Johnson	F	6'5	215	27	67	1158	174	466	37	115	191	60	212	90	176	4	463	17	3.2	1.3	2.6	6.9
Vern Hatton (24g. Cin)	G	6'3	195	22	64	1109	149	418	36	77	105	73	178	70	111	0	375	17	2.8	1.1	1.7	5.9
Ernie Beck	G	6'4	195	27	70	1017	163	418	39	43	65	66	176	89	124	0	369	15	2.5	1.3	1.8	5.3
Guy Sparrow (44g. NY)	F	6'6	218	26	67	842	129	406	32	78	138	57	244	67	158	3	336	13	3.6	1.0	2.4	5.0
Neil Johnston (knee injury)	C	6'8	225	29	28	393	54	164	33	69	88	78	139	21	50	0	177	14	5.0	0.8	1.8	6.3
Lennie Rosenbluth	F	6'5	200	25	29	205	43	145	30	21	29	72	54	6	20	0	107	7	1.9	0.2	0.7	3.7

1958/59 N.B.A. — WESTERN DIVISION

					TOTAL													PER GAME				
Use Name	Pos	Hgt	Wgt	Age	G	Min	FG	FGA	%	FT	FTA	%	Reb	Ass	PF	DQ	Points	Min	Reb	Ass	PF	Points
ST. LOUIS HAWKS	**49-23 .681**				**ANDY PHILLIP (6-4 .600), ED MACAULEY (43-19 .694)**																	
Cliff Hagan	F	6'4	210	27	72	2702	646	1417	46	415	536	77	783	245	275	10	1707	38	10.9	3.4	3.8	23.7
Bob Pettit	F-C	6'9	215	26	72	**2873**	**719**	1640	44	**667**	**879**	76	1182	221	200	3	**2105**	40	16.4	3.1	2.8	**29.2**
Chuck Share	C	6'11	240	31	72	1713	147	381	39	139	184	76	657	103	261	6	433	24	9.1	1.4	3.6	6.0
Jack McMahon	G	6'1	188	30	72	2235	248	692	36	96	156	62	164	298	221	2	592	31	2.3	4.1	3.1	8.2
Slater Martin	G	5'10	170	33	71	2504	245	706	35	197	254	78	253	336	230	8	687	35	3.6	4.7	3.2	9.7
Clyde Lovellette	F-C	6'9	240	29	70	1599	402	885	45	205	250	82	605	91	216	1	1009	23	8.6	1.3	3.1	14.4
Al Ferrari	G	6'4	195	25	72	1189	134	385	35	145	199	73	142	122	155	1	413	17	2.0	1.7	2.2	5.7
Si Green (20g. Cin)(CN)	G-F	6'2	185	24	46	1109	146	415	35	104	160	65	252	113	127	1	396	24	5.5	2.5	2.8	8.6
Hub Reed	F	6'9	215	22	65	950	136	317	43	53	71	75	317	32	171	2	325	15	4.9	0.5	2.6	5.0
Win Wilfong	G-F	6'2	185	26	63	741	99	285	35	62	82	76	121	50	102	0	260	12	1.9	0.8	1.6	4.1
Ed Macauley	F	6'8	195	30	14	196	22	75	29	21	35	60	40	13	20	1	65	14	2.9	0.9	1.4	4.6
Dave Gambee	F	6'6	215	21	2	7	1	1	100	0	0	—	0	0	1	0	2	4	0.0	0.0	0.5	1.0
MINNEAPOLIS LAKERS	**33-39 .458**				**JOHNNY KUNDLA**																	
Elgin Baylor	F	6'5	225	24	70	2855	605	1482	41	532	685	78	1050	287	270	4	1742	41	15.0	4.1	3.9	24.9
Vern Mikkelsen	F-C	6'7	230	30	72	2139	353	904	39	286	355	81	570	159	246	8	992	30	7.9	2.2	3.4	13.8
Larry Foust	C	6'9	250	30	72	1933	301	771	39	280	366	77	627	91	233	5	882	27	8.7	1.3	3.4	13.8
Dick Garmaker	G	6'3	205	26	72	2493	350	885	40	284	368	77	325	211	226	3	984	35	4.5	2.9	3.1	13.7
Bob Leonard (injury)	G	6'3	185	26	58	1598	206	552	37	120	160	75	178	186	119	0	532	28	3.1	3.2	2.1	9.2
Rod Hundley	G	6'4	185	24	71	1664	259	719	36	164	218	75	250	205	139	0	682	23	3.5	2.9	2.0	9.6
Jim Krebs	C	6'8	230	23	72	1578	271	679	40	92	123	75	491	50	212	4	634	22	6.8	0.7	2.9	8.8
Boo Ellis	F	6'5	185	22	72	1202	163	379	43	102	144	71	380	59	137	0	428	17	5.3	0.8	1.9	5.9
Ed Fleming	G	6'3	190	25	71	1132	162	419	39	137	190	72	281	89	148	1	461	16	4.0	1.3	2.1	6.5
Steve Hamilton	F	6'7	190	25	67	847	109	294	37	74	109	68	220	36	144	2	292	13	3.3	0.5	2.1	4.4
DETROIT PISTONS	**28-44 .389**				**RED ROCHA**																	
Ed Conlin (57g. Syr)	F-G	6'5	200	25	72	1955	329	891	37	197	274	72	394	132	188	6	855	27	5.5	1.8	2.6	11.9
Earl Lloyd	F	6'6	220	30	72	1796	234	670	35	137	182	75	500	90	291	15	605	25	6.9	1.3	4.0	8.4
Walter Dukes	C	7'	220	28	72	2338	318	904	35	297	452	66	958	64	**332**	**22**	933	32	13.3	0.9	**4.6**	13.0
Gene Shue	G	6'2	175	27	72	2745	464	1197	39	338	421	80	335	231	129	1	1266	38	4.7	3.2	1.8	17.6
Dick McGuire	G	6'	180	32	71	2063	232	543	43	191	258	74	285	443	147	1	655	29	4.0	6.2	2.1	9.2
Phil Jordon	C-F	6'10	205	25	72	2058	399	967	41	231	303	76	594	83	193	1	1029	29	8.3	1.2	2.7	14.3
Joe Holup	F	6'6	215	24	68	1502	209	580	36	152	200	76	352	73	239	12	570	22	5.2	1.1	3.5	8.4
Dick Farley	G-F	6'4	195	26	70	1280	177	448	40	137	186	74	195	124	130	2	491	18	2.8	1.8	1.9	7.0
Chuck Noble	G	6'4	195	27	65	939	189	560	34	83	113	73	115	114	126	0	461	14	1.8	1.8	1.9	7.1
Shellie McMillon	F	6'5	205	22	48	700	127	289	44	55	104	53	285	26	110	2	309	15	5.9	0.5	2.3	6.4
Barney Cable	F	6'7	200	22	31	271	43	126	34	23	29	79	88	12	30	0	109	9	2.8	0.4	1.0	3.5
CINCINNATI ROYALS	**19-53 .264**				**BOBBY WANZER (3-35 .167), TOM MARSHALL (16-38 .296)**																	
Jack Twyman	F-G	6'6	210	24	72	2713	710	**1691**	42	437	558	78	653	209	277	6	1857	38	9.1	2.9	3.8	25.8
Dave Piontek	F	6'6	230	24	72	1674	305	813	38	156	227	69	385	124	162	3	766	23	5.3	1.7	2.3	10.6
Wayne Embry	C	6'8	240	21	66	1590	272	702	39	206	314	66	597	96	232	9	750	24	9.0	1.5	3.5	11.4
Arlen Bockhorn	G	6'4	200	25	71	2251	294	771	38	138	196	70	460	206	215	6	726	32	6.5	2.9	3.0	10.2
Johnny McCarthy (MS)	G	6'1	185	24	47	1827	245	657	37	116	174	67	227	225	158	4	606	39	4.8	4.8	3.4	12.9
Jim Palmer	C-F	6'8	224	25	67	1624	256	633	40	178	246	72	472	65	211	7	690	24	7.0	1.0	3.1	10.3
Archie Dees	F	6'8	205	22	68	1252	200	562	36	159	204	78	339	56	114	0	559	18	5.0	0.8	1.7	8.2
Med Park (29g. StL)	G	6'2	205	25	62	1126	145	361	40	115	150	77	188	108	93	0	405	18	3.0	1.7	1.5	6.5
Jack Parr	C	6'9	222	22	66	1037	109	307	36	44	73	60	278	51	138	1	262	16	4.2	0.8	2.1	4.0
Phil Rollins (23g. Phi)	G	6'2	190	24	44	691	83	231	36	63	90	70	118	102	49	0	229	16	2.7	2.3	1.1	5.2
Larry Staverman	F	6'7	205	22	57	681	101	215	47	45	59	76	218	54	103	0	247	12	3.8	0.9	1.8	4.3
Tom Marshall	F	6'4	215	27	18	272	23	79	29	18	29	62	52	27	22	0	64	15	2.9	1.5	1.2	3.6

Dick Ricketts - retired to play baseball

Maurice Stokes - illness

1958/59 N.B.A. — PLAYOFFS

Use Name	Pos	Hgt	Wgt	Age	TOTAL G	Min	FG	FGA	%	FT	FTA	%	Reb	Ass	PF	DQ	Points	PER GAME Min	Reb	Ass	PF	Points
BOSTON CELTICS	**RED AUERBACH**	defeated Syracuse 4-3; H131-109, 118-120, H133-111, 107-119, H129-108, 121-133, H130-125 defeated Minneapolis 4-0; H118-115, H128-108, 123-120, 118-113																				
Jim Loscutoff	F	6'5	230	28	11	260	39	113	35	11	21	52	73	13	49	1	89	24	6.6	1.2	4.5	8.1
Tom Heinsohn	F	6'7	220	24	11	348	91	220	41	37	56	66	98	32	41	0	219	32	8.9	2.9	3.7	19.9
Bill Russell	C	6'10	220	24	11	496	65	159	41	41	67	61	**305**	40	28	1	171	**45**	**27.7**	3.6	2.5	15.5
Bill Sharman	G	6'1	190	32	11	322	82	193	42	57	59	**97**	36	28	35	0	221	29	3.3	2.5	3.2	20.1
Bob Cousy	G	6'1	178	30	11	460	72	221	33	70	94	74	76	**119**	28	0	214	42	6.9	**10.8**	2.5	19.5
Frank Ramsey	F-G	6'3	195	27	11	303	95	192	49	65	81	80	68	20	52	4	255	28	6.2	1.8	4.7	23.2
Sam Jones	G-F	6'4	205	25	11	192	40	108	37	33	39	85	63	17	14	0	113	17	5.7	1.5	1.3	10.3
Gene Conley	F-C	6'8	225	28	11	157	24	66	36	6	13	46	75	7	40	2	54	14	6.8	0.6	3.6	4.9
K. C. Jones	G	6'1	202	26	8	75	5	20	25	5	5	100	12	10	8	0	15	9	1.5	1.3	1.0	1.9
Bennie Swain	F	6'8	222	25	5	27	2	6	33	1	2	50	14	1	4	0	5	5	2.8	0.2	0.8	1.0
MINNEAPOLIS LAKERS	**JOHNNY KUNDLA**	defeated Detroit 2-1; H92-89, 103-117, H129-102 defeated St. Louis 4-2; 90-124, H106-98, 97-127, H108-98, 98-97(OT), H106-104 lost to Boston 0-4, 115-118, 108-128, H120-123, H113-118																				
Elgin Baylor	F	6'5	225	24	13	**556**	**122**	**303**	40	87	**113**	77	156	43	52	0	**331**	43	12.0	3.3	4.0	25.5
Vern Mikkelsen	F-C	6'7	230	30	13	371	73	177	41	56	73	77	93	24	**54**	3	202	29	7.2	1.8	4.2	15.5
Larry Foust	C	6'9	250	30	13	404	56	134	42	41	50	82	136	12	47	2	153	31	10.5	0.9	3.6	11.8
Dick Garmaker	G	6'3	205	26	13	439	70	165	42	49	63	78	55	39	44	1	189	34	4.2	3.0	3.4	14.5
Bob Leonard	G	6'3	185	26	13	467	63	173	36	32	40	80	44	70	38	0	158	36	3.4	5.4	2.9	12.2
Boo Ellis	F	6'5	185	22	13	255	35	80	44	18	31	58	93	16	34	0	88	20	7.2	1.2	2.6	6.8
Jim Krebs	C	6'8	230	23	13	213	36	103	35	22	23	96	77	5	36	1	94	16	5.9	0.4	2.8	7.2
Ed Fleming	G	6'3	190	25	13	178	27	77	35	22	25	88	39	18	32	0	76	14	3.0	1.4	2.5	5.8
Rod Hundley	G	6'4	185	24	13	175	20	58	34	12	14	86	23	20	15	0	52	13	1.8	1.5	1.2	4.0
Steve Hamilton	F	6'7	190	24	10	87	12	43	28	8	10	80	35	5	14	0	32	9	3.5	0.5	1.4	3.2
SYRACUSE NATIONALS	**PAUL SEYMOUR**	defeated New York 2-0; 129-123, H131-115 lost to Boston 3-4; 109-131, H120-118, 111-133, H119-107, 108-129, H133-121, 125-130																				
George Yardley	F	6'5	195	30	9	333	83	189	44	60	70	86	87	21	29	0	226	37	9.7	2.3	3.2	25.1
Dolph Schayes	F	6'8	220	30	9	351	78	195	40	**98**	107	92	117	41	36	0	254	39	13.0	4.6	4.0	28.2
Johnny Kerr	C	6'9	230	26	9	312	50	142	35	30	33	91	108	24	20	0	130	35	12.0	2.7	2.2	14.4
Hal Greer	G	6'3	176	22	9	278	39	93	42	26	32	81	47	20	35	2	104	31	5.2	2.2	3.9	11.6
Larry Costello	G	6'1	188	27	9	361	54	121	45	51	61	84	53	54	40	2	159	40	5.9	6.0	4.4	17.7
Bob Hopkins	F-C	6'8	225	24	9	203	23	68	34	28	34	82	60	9	33	1	74	23	6.7	1.0	3.7	8.2
Al Bianchi	G	6'3	185	26	9	192	34	74	46	14	22	64	29	25	41	**4**	82	21	3.2	2.8	4.6	9.1
Togo Palazzi	F	6'4	205	26	8	67	13	44	30	10	14	71	21	6	10	0	36	8	2.6	0.8	1.3	4.5
Connie Dierking	C	6'9	222	22	4	34	2	12	17	7	9	78	17	2	5	0	11	9	4.3	0.5	1.3	2.8
George Dempsey	G	6'3	195	29	5	29	3	8	38	3	4	75	6	4	8	0	9	6	1.2	0.8	1.6	1.8
ST. LOUIS HAWKS	**ED MACAULEY**	lost to Minneapolis 2-4; H124-90, 98-106, H127-97, 98-108, H97-98(OT), 104-106																				
Cliff Hagan	F	6'4	210	27	6	259	63	123	51	45	54	83	72	16	21	0	171	43	12.0	2.7	3.5	**28.5**
Bob Pettit	F-C	6'9	215	26	6	257	58	137	42	51	65	78	75	14	20	0	167	43	12.5	2.3	3.3	27.8
Clyde Lovellette	C	6'9	240	29	6	161	35	70	50	22	28	79	59	8	23	1	92	27	9.8	1.3	3.8	15.3
Al Ferrari	G	6'4	195	25	6	173	14	40	35	20	25	80	15	15	25	1	48	29	2.5	2.5	4.2	8.0
Jack McMahon	G	6'1	188	30	6	250	30	90	33	10	19	53	18	32	20	1	70	42	3.0	5.3	3.3	11.7
Si Green	G-F	6'2	185	24	6	131	12	25	48	12	24	50	23	14	20	1	36	22	3.8	2.3	3.3	6.0
Chuck Share	C	6'11	240	31	6	122	8	27	30	10	14	71	52	9	16	1	26	20	8.7	1.5	2.7	4.3
Hub Reed	F	6'9	215	22	4	48	4	11	36	3	6	50	17	1	7	0	11	12	4.3	0.3	1.8	2.8
Win Wilfong	G-F	6'2	185	26	5	46	7	19	37	5	6	83	6	3	7	0	19	9	1.2	0.6	1.4	3.8
Slater Martin	G	5'10	170	33	1	18	4	5	80	0	0	—	3	2	2	0	8	18	3.0	2.0	2.0	8.0
DETROIT PISTONS	**RED ROCHA**	lost to Minneapolis 1-2; 89-92, H117-103, 102-129																				
Earl Lloyd	F	6'6	220	30	3	87	9	28	32	8	8	100	18	7	12	0	26	29	6.0	2.3	4.0	8.7
Phil Jordon	F-C	6'10	205	25	3	99	15	45	33	15	18	83	24	5	9	0	45	33	8.0	1.7	3.0	15.0
Walter Dukes	C	7'	220	28	3	113	15	30	50	13	17	76	40	3	15	1	43	38	13.3	1.0	5.0	14.3
Gene Shue	G	6'2	175	27	3	118	28	60	47	27	33	82	14	10	7	0	83	39	4.7	3.3	2.3	27.7
Dick McGuire	G	6'	180	32	3	109	20	32	**63**	7	11	64	17	19	10	0	47	36	5.7	6.3	3.3	15.7
Shellie McMillon	F	6'5	205	22	3	54	7	23	30	5	6	83	14	0	16	1	19	18	4.7	0.0	5.3	6.3
Ed Conlin	F-G	6'5	200	25	3	43	4	16	25	2	4	50	7	4	5	0	10	14	2.3	1.3	1.7	3.3
Joe Holup	F	6'6	215	24	3	36	3	14	21	6	7	86	8	3	7	0	12	12	2.7	1.0	2.3	4.0
Dick Farley	G-F	6'4	195	26	3	33	5	12	42	1	1	100	6	3	6	0	11	11	2.0	1.0	2.0	3.7
Chuck Noble	G	6'4	195	27	3	28	5	17	29	2	2	100	0	1	3	0	12	9	0.0	0.3	1.0	4.0
NEW YORK KNICKERBOCKERS	**FUZZY LEVANE**	lost to Syracuse 0-2; H123-129, 115-131																				
Kenny Sears	F	6'9	195	25	2	64	10	27	37	13	15	87	17	6	6	0	33	32	8.5	3.0	3.0	16.5
Willie Naulls	F	6'6	225	24	2	63	14	42	33	6	8	75	21	3	11	1	34	32	10.5	1.5	**5.5**	17.0
Charlie Tyra	C	6'8	235	23	2	55	12	28	43	6	9	67	31	1	5	0	30	28	15.5	0.5	2.5	15.0
Richie Guerin	G	6'4	195	26	2	77	9	35	26	12	14	86	18	15	11	1	30	39	9.0	7.5	**5.5**	15.0
Carl Braun	G	6'5	185	31	2	62	12	32	38	8	9	89	4	10	4	0	32	31	2.0	5.0	2.0	16.0
Ray Felix	C	6'11	225	28	2	45	12	28	43	2	4	50	23	2	12	2	26	23	11.5	1.0	6.0	13.0
Frank Selvy	G-F	6'3	185	26	2	43	10	20	50	9	11	82	4	3	6	0	29	22	2.0	1.5	3.0	14.5
Mike Farmer	F	6'7	210	22	2	34	5	17	29	2	5	40	10	0	7	0	12	17	5.0	0.0	3.5	6.0
Jack George	G	6'3	195	30	2	31	4	12	33	0	0	—	4	3	4	0	8	16	2.0	1.5	2.0	4.0
Pete Brennan	F	6'6	205	22	2	6	2	7	29	0	1	0	5	0	4	0	4	3	2.5	0.0	2.0	2.0

Ron Sobie - foot injury

1958/59 N.B.A. TEAM STATISTICS

Team	REGULAR SEASON G	FG	FGA	%	FT	FTA	%	Reb.	Ass.	AVERAGE POINTS For	Agnst.	Diff.	PLAYOFFS G	FG	FGA	%	FT	FTA	%	Reb	Ass.	AVERAGE POINTS For	Agnst.	Diff.
EASTERN DIVISION																								
Boston	72	**3208**	**8116**	40	1963	2563	77	**5601**	**1568**	**116.4**	109.9	**+6.5**	11	**515**	1298	40	326	437	75	**909**	**287**	**123.3**	115.5	**+7.8**
New York	72	2863	7170	40	**2217**	**2802**	**79**	4991	1383	110.3	110.1	-0.2	2	90	**248**	36	58	76	76	155	43	119.0	130.0	-11.0
Syracuse	72	3050	7490	41	2046	2642	77	4900	1340	113.1	109.1	+4.0	9	379	946	40	**327**	**386**	**85**	639	206	120.6	123.0	-2.4
Philadelphia	72	2826	7423	38	1783	2425	74	4910	1375	103.3	106.3	-3.0												
WESTERN DIVISION																								
St. Louis	72	2879	7015	**41**	2072	2757	75	5045	1567	108.8	**105.1**	+3.7	6	235	547	**43**	178	241	74	391	14	108.0	**100.8**	**+7.2**
Minneapolis	72	2779	7084	39	2071	2718	76	5149	1373	106.0	107.3	-1.3	13	514	1313	39	347	442	79	837	252	105.8	111.0	-5.2
Detroit	72	2811	7305	38	1943	2627	74	4860	1317	105.1	106.6	-1.4	3	111	277	40	86	107	80	180	55	102.7	108.0	-5.3
Cincinnati	72	2854	7340	39	1713	2375	72	4887	1369	103.1	112.0	-8.9												

1958/59 N.B.A. STANDINGS

Team	W	L	Pct.	GB	Record against playoff teams W	L	Pct.	Record against non - playoff teams W	L	Pct.	HOME W	L	Pct.	ROAD W	L	Pct.	NEUTRAL W	L	Pct.
EASTERN DIVISION																			
Boston Celtics	52	20	.722	-	**35**	16	**.686**	17	4	.810	26	4	.867	13	15	.464	13	1	.929
New York Knickerbockers	40	32	.556	12	29	22	.569	11	10	.524	21	9	.700	15	15	.500	4	8	.333
Syracuse Nationals	35	37	.486	17	21	30	.412	14	7	.667	19	12	.613	12	17	.414	4	8	.333
Philadelphia Warriors	32	40	.444	20	25	38	.397	7	2	.778	17	9	.654	7	24	.226	8	7	.533
WESTERN DIVISION																			
St. Louis Hawks	49	23	.681	-	33	18	.647	16	5	.762	28	3	.903	14	15	.483	7	5	.583
Minneapolis Lakers	33	39	.458	16	21	30	.412	12	9	.571	15	7	.682	9	17	.346	9	15	.375
Detroit Pistons	28	44	.389	21	14	37	.275	14	7	.667	13	17	.433	8	20	.286	7	7	.500
Cincinnati Royals	19	53	.264	30	17	46	.270	2	7	.222	9	19	.321	2	25	.074	8	9	.471

1958/59 N.B.A. INDIVIDUAL LEADERS

SCORING
(Minimum 55 Games Played)

Name	Team	G	FG	FT	Pts.	Avg.
Pettit	StL	72	719	667	2105	29.2
Arizin	Phi	70	632	587	1851	26.4
Twyman	Cin	72	710	437	1857	25.8
Baylor	Min	70	605	532	1742	24.9
Hagan	StL	72	646	415	1707	23.7
Schayes	Syr	72	504	526	1534	21.3
Sears	NY	71	491	506	1488	21.0
Sharman	Bos	72	562	342	1466	20.4
Cousy	Bos	65	484	329	1297	20.0
Yardley	Det-Syr	61	446	317	1209	19.8

FIELD GOAL PERCENTAGE
(Minimum 230 Field Goals)

Name	Team	FG	FGA	Pct.
Sears	NY	491	1002	.490
Russell	Bos	456	997	.457
Hagan	StL	646	1417	.456
Lovellette	StL	402	885	.454
Greer	Syr	308	679	.454
Kerr	Syr	502	1139	.441
Penit	StL	719	1640	.438
Costello	Syr	414	948	.437
S. Jones	Bos	305	703	.434
Arizin	Phi	632	1466	.431

FREE THROW PERCENTAGE
(Minimum 190 Free Throws)

Name	Team	FT	FTA	Pct.
Sharman	Bos	342	367	.932
Schayes	Syr	526	609	.864
Sears	NY	506	588	.861
Cousy	Bos	329	385	.855
Naulls	NY	258	311	.830
Lovellette	StL	205	250	.820
Arizin	Phi	587	722	.813
Mikkelsen	Min	286	355	.806
Shue	Det	338	421	.803
Costello	Syr	280	349	.802

PERSONAL FOULS

Name	Team	PF
Dukes	Det	332
Lloyd	Det	291
Loscutoff	Bos	285
Schayes	Syr	280
Twyman	Cin	277

GAMES DISQUALIFIED

Name	Team	Disq
Dukes	Det	22
Loscutoff	Bos	15
Lloyd	Det	15
Holup	Det	12
Sauldsberry	Phi	12

REBOUNDS PER GAME
(Minimum 55 Games Played)

Name	Team	G	Reb.	Avg.
Russell	Bos	70	1612	23.0
Pettit	StL	72	1182	16.4
Baylor	Min	70	1050	15.0
Kerr	Syr	72	1008	14.0
Schayes	Syr	72	962	13.4
Dukes	Det	72	958	13.3
Sauldsberry	Phi	72	826	11.5
Gola	Phi	64	710	11.1
Hagan	StL	72	783	10.9
Naulls	NY	68	723	10.6

ASSISTS PER GAME
(Minimum 55 Games Played)

Name	Team	G	Ass.	Avg.
Cousy	Bos	65	557	8.6
McGuire	Det	71	443	6.2
Costello	Syr	70	379	5.4
Guerin	NY	71	364	5.1
Braun	NY	72	349	4.8
Martin	StL	71	336	4.7
Gola	Phi	64	269	4.2
McMahon	StL	72	298	4.1
Baylor	Min	70	287	4.1
Sharman	Bos	72	292	4.1

MINUTES PLAYED

Name	Team	Min.
Pettit	StL	2873
Baylor	Min	2855
Arizin	Phi	2799
Costello	Syr	2750
Shue	Det	2745

1959-60 N.B.A.

The Tallest Warrior of Them All

Pro basketball fans had never seen anyone like Wilt Chamberlain, the rookie center of the Philadelphia Warriors. Standing 7'1" with awesome strength, Wilt had signed with the Warriors for a reported $65,000, a sum previously unheard-of in the sport. Warrior owner Eddie Gottlieb spent his money wisely, for Chamberlain not only would be a massive asset on the court, but he also would draw crowds eager to see the giant they had heard so much about. A native of Philadelphia, Chamberlain had played two well-publicized seasons at the University of Kansas, then had passed up his senior year to travel with the Harlem Globetrotters. Now that he was bringing his reputation into the league, the N.B.A. owners were gleefully anticipating greater attendance.

On the playing floor, Chamberlain provided just the show that the curiosity seekers were looking for. Very quick in addition to very big, Wilt averaged a record 37.6 points per game. He tapped in offensive rebounds in bunches, he sank fall-away jumpers with surprising accuracy, and he made the dunk shot famous, soaring above the basket and slamming the ball down through the hoop with backboard-rattling force. He went over 50 points in six games, and also led the N.B.A. in rebounding. He played almost every minute of every game and never fouled out, intimidating enemy drivers without having to foul them. Wilt did have some clashes with coach Neil Johnston, whose job as center had been usurped by the rookie, but his effectiveness on the floor for the Warriors was obvious to anyone. With Wilt the hub of the team, and with a solid supporting cast of Paul Arizin, Tom Gola, Guy Rodgers, and Woody Sauldsberry, the Warriors jumped to an impressive 49-26 mark.

But the Boston Celtics, with Bill Russell, put together an even more impressive 59-16 record to take first place in the East for the fourth straight year. Russell starred on defense as spectacularly as Wilt did on offense; he blocked shots and rebounded with an enthusiastic flair. The scoring for Boston was left mostly to long range gunners like Tom Heinsohn, Bob Cousy, Bill Sharman, and Frank Ramsey. The Celtic bench shuttled fresh help into the breach whenever needed, with young guards Sam Jones and K.C. Jones and forward Gene Conley (a major league baseball pitcher in the summer) the important shock troops. At one point during the season, the Celtics ran off a 17-game winning streak, and their ten-game final margin over Philadelphia underlined the team's class.

Finishing just behind the Warriors in third place in the East were the Syracuse Nationals, whose 45-30 record was only one game worse than the first-place record in the West. Rookie guard Dick Barnett, a fine shooter, strengthened the Syracuse bench, while veteran Dolph Schayes led the club in scoring as usual and sank his 15,000th career point during the campaign. Finishing far out of the playoffs were the New York Knicks, whose disappointing play after a promising showing last season cost coach Fuzzy Levane his job. Veteran player Carl Braun took over as coach in mid-season but he could not put the disjointed Knicks back together again.

While the Knicks were rebuilding at the bottom of the East, the St. Louis Hawks were doing some minor refurbishing at the top of the West. The Hawks had been knocked off by the Lakers in the Western finals of last season's playoffs, and owner Ben Kerner and coach Ed Macauley acted to prevent further decay from setting in. The starting front line of Bob Pettit, Cliff Hagan, and Clyde Lovellette needed no alteration, but backup help was obtained in the persons of veterans Larry Foust and Dave Piontek. Slater Martin continued to quarterback the Hawks, but the other guard spot was filled by younger men, Johnny McCarthy and Si Green. Although the Hawks seemed no stronger than three of the Eastern clubs, they easily captured first place in the West with a 16-game margin over Detroit. The Pistons hadn't had a winning season since moving to Detroit, and coach Red Rocha paid with his job, replaced in mid-season by veteran guard Dick McGuire; nevertheless, the team's 30-45 record was good enough for second place in the weak Western Division. Guard Gene Shue led the Pistons in scoring and won a place on the first team All-League squad. The Lakers captured third place despite a relapse into the chaotic situation of two years ago. Elgin Baylor upped his scoring average to 29.6, but the rest of the squad fell apart under the coaching reins of John Castellani, who had coached Baylor at the University of Seattle. Old favorite Jim Pollard replaced Castellani mid-way through the schedule, but a combination of trades and rookie help could not stop a skid to a 25-50 record and a continued lethargy at the ticket window. The punchless Cincinnati Royals finished far back in last place despite Jack Twyman's 31.2 scoring average, second only to Chamberlain in the N.B.A.

The Western Division semifinal playoff series between Detroit and Minneapolis was a battle of losers, with the Lakers getting past the Pistons in two straight games largely on the back of Elgin Baylor. The Eastern semifinal pitted Philadelphia and Syracuse against each other, with the Warriors triumphing in three games. The divisional finals then matched the Boston Celtics against the Warriors and Wilt Chamberlain, while the St. Louis Hawks took on the Lakers and Elgin Baylor. The Celtics could not keep Chamberlain from scoring, but they did play a better team game than the Warriors; the defending champs thus eliminated the Warriors four games to two. The Hawks had more trouble with the upstart Lakers; playing their final series as a representative of Minneapolis, the Lakers took a three-to-two edge in games before the veteran Hawks came back to take the final two games.

In the championship round, the Celtics clearly seemed to be the better team, but the Hawks pushed the series to a decisive seventh game in Boston. A second period Boston blitz, outscoring the Hawks 41-23, broke the game wide open and made the second half a futile basket-trading affair. Now it was three titles in four years for the Celtics, and the first repeat at the top since the Lakers of George Mikan.

Use Name	Pos	Hgt	Wgt	Age	TOTAL G	Min	FG	FGA	%	FT	FTA	%	Reb	Ass	PF	DQ	Points	PER GAME Min	Reb	Ass	PF	Points

1959/60 N.B.A. — EASTERN DIVISION

Use Name	Pos	Hgt	Wgt	Age	G	Min	FG	FGA	%	FT	FTA	%	Reb	Ass	PF	DQ	Points	Min	Reb	Ass	PF	Points
BOSTON CELTICS	**59-16 .787**				**RED AUERBACH**																	
Frank Ramsey	F-G	6'3	195	28	73	2009	422	1062	40	273	347	79	506	137	251	10	1117	28	6.9	1.9	3.4	15.3
Tom Heinsohn	F	6'7	220	25	75	2420	673	1590	42	283	386	73	794	171	275	8	1629	32	10.6	2.3	3.7	21.7
Bill Russell	C	6'10	220	25	74	3146	555	1189	47	240	392	61	1778	277	210	0	1350	43	24.0	3.7	2.8	18.2
Bill Sharman	G	6'1	190	33	71	1916	559	1225	46	252	291	87	262	114	154	2	1370	27	3.7	1.6	2.2	19.3
Bob Cousy	G	6'1	178	31	75	2588	568	1481	38	319	403	79	352	**715**	146	2	1455	35	4.7	**9.5**	1.9	19.4
Sam Jones	G-F	6'4	205	26	74	1512	355	782	45	168	220	76	375	125	101	1	878	20	5.1	1.7	1.4	11.9
Gene Conley	F-C	6'8	225	29	71	1330	201	539	37	76	114	67	590	32	270	10	478	19	8.3	0.5	3.8	6.7
K. C. Jones	G	6'1	202	27	74	1274	169	414	41	128	170	75	199	189	109	1	466	17	2.7	2.6	1.5	6.3
John Richter	F	6'9	225	22	66	808	113	332	34	59	117	50	312	27	158	1	285	12	4.7	0.4	2.4	4.3
Jim Loscutoff (back injury)	F	6'5	230	29	28	536	66	205	32	22	36	61	108	12	108	6	154	19	3.9	0.4	3.9	5.5
Gene Guarilia	F	6'5	220	22	48	423	58	154	38	29	41	71	85	18	57	1	145	9	1.8	0.4	1.2	3.0
Maury King	G	6'3	195	24	1	19	5	8	63	0	1	0	4	2	3	0	10	19	4.0	2.0	3.0	10.0
PHILADELPHIA WARRIORS	**49-26 .653**				**NEIL JOHNSTON**																	
Paul Arizin	F	6'4	200	31	72	2618	593	1400	42	420	526	80	621	165	263	6	1606	36	8.6	2.3	3.7	22.3
Woody Sauldsberry	F	6'7	220	25	71	1848	325	974	33	55	103	53	447	112	203	2	705	26	6.3	1.6	2.9	9.9
Wilt Chamberlain	C	7'1	250	23	72	**3338**	**1065**	**2311**	46	577	**991**	58	**1941**	168	150	0	**2707**	**46**	**27.0**	2.3	2.1	**37.6**
Tom Gola	G-F	6'6	205	26	75	2870	426	983	43	270	340	79	779	409	**311**	9	1122	38	10.4	5.5	4.1	15.0
Guy Rodgers	G	6'	185	24	68	2483	338	870	39	111	181	61	391	482	196	3	787	37	5.8	7.1	2.9	11.6
Andy Johnson	F-G	6'5	215	28	75	1421	245	648	38	125	208	60	282	152	196	5	615	19	3.8	2.0	2.6	8.2
Joe Graboski	F-C	6'8	230	29	73	1269	217	583	37	131	174	75	358	111	147	1	565	17	4.9	1.5	2.0	7.7
Vern Hatton	G	6'3	195	23	67	1049	127	356	36	53	87	61	159	82	61	0	307	16	2.4	1.2	0.9	4.6
Ernie Beck	G	6'4	195	28	66	809	114	294	39	27	32	84	127	72	90	0	255	12	1.9	1.1	1.4	3.9
Joe Ruklick	F	6'9	220	21	39	384	85	214	40	26	36	72	137	24	70	0	196	10	3.5	0.6	1.8	5.0
Guy Sparrow	F	6'6	218	27	11	80	14	45	31	2	8	25	23	6	20	0	30	7	2.1	0.5	1.8	2.7
SYRACUSE NATIONALS	**45-30 .600**				**PAUL SEYMOUR**																	
George Yardley	F	6'5	195	31	73	2402	546	1205	45	381	467	82	579	122	227	3	1473	33	7.9	1.7	3.1	20.2
Dolph Schayes	F	6'8	220	31	75	2741	578	1440	40	533	597	**89**	959	256	263	10	1689	37	12.8	3.4	3.5	22.5
Johnny Kerr	C	6'9	230	27	75	2372	436	1111	39	233	310	75	913	167	207	4	1105	32	12.2	2.2	2.8	14.7
Hal Greer	G	6'3	176	23	70	1979	388	815	48	148	189	78	303	188	208	4	924	28	4.3	2.7	3.0	13.2
Larry Costello	G	6'1	188	28	71	2469	372	822	45	249	289	86	388	449	234	4	993	35	5.5	6.3	3.3	14.0
Bob Hopkins	F-C	6'8	230	25	75	1616	257	660	39	136	174	78	465	55	193	4	650	22	6.2	0.7	2.6	8.7
Al Bianchi	G	6'3	185	27	69	1256	211	576	37	109	155	70	179	169	231	5	531	18	2.6	2.4	3.3	7.7
Dick Barnett (MS)	G	6'4	190	23	57	1235	289	701	41	128	180	71	155	160	98	0	706	22	2.7	2.8	1.7	12.4
Connie Dierking	C	6'9	222	23	71	1119	192	526	37	108	188	57	456	54	168	4	492	16	6.4	0.8	2.4	6.9
Barney Cable (7g. Det)	F	6'7	200	23	57	715	109	290	38	44	67	66	225	39	93	1	262	13	3.9	0.7	1.6	4.6
Togo Palazzi	F	6'4	205	27	7	70	13	41	32	4	8	50	14	3	7	0	30	10	2.0	0.4	1.0	4.3
Jim Ray	G	6'1	180	25	4	21	1	6	17	0	0	—	0	2	3	0	2	5	0.0	0.5	0.8	0.5
Paul Seymour	G	6'2	185	31	4	7	0	4	0	0	0	—	1	0	1	0	0	2	0.3	0.0	0.3	0.0
NEW YORK KNICKERBOCKERS	**27-48 .360**				**FUZZY LEVANE (8-19 .296), CARL BRAUN (19-29 .396)**																	
Kenny Sears (knee injury)	F	6'9	200	26	64	2099	412	863	**48**	363	418	87	876	127	191	2	1187	33	13.7	2.0	3.0	18.5
Willie Naulls	F	6'6	225	25	65	2250	551	1286	43	286	342	84	921	138	214	4	1388	35	14.2	2.1	3.3	21.4
Charlie Tyra	C	6'8	235	24	74	2023	406	942	43	133	189	70	598	80	258	8	945	27	8.1	1.1	3.5	12.8
Richie Guerin	G	6'4	195	27	74	2420	579	1379	42	457	591	77	505	468	242	3	1615	33	6.8	6.3	3.3	21.8
Carl Braun (back injury)	G	6'5	185	32	54	1514	285	659	43	129	154	84	168	270	127	2	699	28	3.1	5.0	2.4	12.9
Dick Garmaker (44g. Min)	G	6'3	205	27	70	1932	323	815	40	203	263	77	313	206	186	4	849	28	4.5	2.9	2.7	12.1
Jack George (leg injury)	G	6'3	195	31	69	1604	250	650	38	155	202	77	197	240	148	1	655	23	2.9	3.5	2.1	9.5
Mike Farmer	F	6'7	210	23	67	1536	212	568	37	70	83	84	385	57	130	1	494	23	5.7	0.9	1.9	7.4
Jim Palmer (20g. Cin)	F-C	6'8	224	26	74	1482	246	574	43	119	174	68	389	70	224	6	611	20	5.3	0.9	3.0	8.3
Johnny Green	C	6'5	200	26	69	1232	209	468	45	63	155	41	539	52	195	3	481	18	7.8	0.8	2.8	7.0
Whitey Bell	G	6'	181	27	31	449	70	185	38	28	43	65	87	55	59	0	168	14	2.8	1.8	1.9	5.4
Bob Anderegg	F-G	6'3	200	22	33	373	55	143	38	23	42	55	69	29	32	0	133	11	2.1	0.9	1.0	4.0
Cal Ramsey (4g. StL)	F	6'4	200	22	11	195	39	96	41	19	33	58	66	9	25	1	97	18	6.0	0.8	2.3	8.8
Brendan McCann	G	6'2	178	24	4	29	1	12	8	4	4	100	7	9	3	0	6	7	1.8	2.3	0.8	1.5

Use Name	Pos	Hgt	Wgt	Age	TOTAL G	Min	FG	FGA	%	FT	FTA	%	Reb	Ass	PF	DQ	Points	PER GAME Min	Reb	Ass	PF	Points
1959/60 N.B.A. — WESTERN DIVISION																						
ST. LOUIS HAWKS	**46-29 .613**				**ED MACAULEY**																	
Cliff Hagan	F	6'4	210	28	75	2798	719	1549	46	421	524	80	803	299	270	4	1859	37	10.7	4.0	3.6	24.8
Bob Pettit	F-C	6'9	220	27	72	2896	669	1526	44	544	722	75	1221	257	204	0	1882	40	17.0	3.6	2.8	26.1
Clyde Lovellette	C-F	6'9	240	30	68	1953	550	1174	47	316	385	82	721	127	248	6	1416	29	10.6	1.9	3.6	20.8
Johnny McCarthy	G	6'1	185	25	75	2383	240	730	33	149	226	66	301	328	233	3	629	32	4.0	4.4	3.1	8.4
Slater Martin	G	5'10	170	34	64	1756	142	383	37	113	155	73	187	330	174	2	397	27	2.9	5.2	2.7	6.2
Larry Foust (47g. Min)	C	6'9	250	31	72	1964	312	766	41	253	320	79	621	96	241	7	877	27	8.6	1.3	3.3	12.2
Dave Piontek (52g. Cin)	F	6'6	230	25	77	1833	292	728	40	129	202	64	461	118	211	5	713	24	6.0	1.5	2.7	9.3
Al Ferrari	G	6'4	200	26	71	1567	216	523	41	176	225	78	162	188	205	7	608	22	2.3	2.6	2.9	8.6
Si Green	G-F	6'2	195	25	70	1354	159	427	37	111	175	63	257	133	150	3	429	19	3.7	1.9	2.1	6.1
Bob Ferry	F-C	6'8	230	22	62	875	144	338	43	76	119	64	223	40	132	2	364	14	3.6	0.6	2.1	5.9
Jack McMahon	G	6'1	195	31	25	334	33	93	35	16	29	55	24	49	42	1	82	13	1.0	2.0	1.7	3.3
DETROIT PISTONS	**30-45 .400**				**RED ROCHA (13-21 .382), DICK McGUIRE (17-24 .415)**																	
Earl Lloyd	F	6'6	220	31	68	1610	237	665	36	128	160	80	322	89	226	1	602	24	4.7	1.3	3.3	8.9
Bailey Howell	F	6'7	210	22	75	2346	510	1119	46	312	422	74	790	63	282	13	1332	31	10.5	0.8	3.8	17.8
Walter Dukes	C	7'	220	29	66	2140	314	871	36	376	508	74	883	80	310	**20**	1004	32	13.4	1.2	**4.7**	15.2
Chuck Noble (broken ribs)	G	6'4	195	28	58	1621	276	774	36	101	138	73	201	265	172	2	653	28	3.5	4.6	3.0	11.3
Gene Shue	G	6'2	175	28	75	**3338**	620	1501	41	472	541	87	409	295	146	2	1712	45	5.5	3.9	1.9	22.8
Ed Conlin	F-G	6'5	200	26	70	1636	300	831	36	181	238	76	346	126	158	2	781	23	4.9	1.8	2.3	11.2
Dick McGuire	G	6'	180	33	68	1466	179	402	45	124	201	62	264	358	112	0	482	22	3.9	5.3	1.6	7.1
Shellie McMillon	F	6'5	205	23	75	1416	267	627	43	132	199	66	431	49	198	3	666	19	5.7	0.7	2.6	8.9
Archie Dees	C-F	6'8	205	23	73	1244	271	617	44	165	204	81	397	43	188	3	707	17	5.4	0.6	2.6	9.7
Gary Alcorn	C	6'9	225	23	58	670	91	312	29	48	84	57	279	22	123	4	230	12	4.8	0.4	2.1	4.0
Billy Kenville	G	6'2	190	29	25	365	47	131	36	33	41	80	71	46	31	0	127	15	2.8	1.8	1.2	5.1
Tony Windis	G	6'1	160	26	9	193	16	60	27	4	6	67	47	32	20	0	36	21	5.2	3.6	2.2	4.0
MINNEAPOLIS LAKERS	**25-50 .333**				**JOHN CASTELLANI (11-25 .306), JIM POLLARD (14-25 .359)**																	
Elgin Baylor	F	6'5	225	25	70	2873	755	1781	42	564	770	73	1150	243	234	2	2074	41	16.4	3.5	3.3	29.6
Rudy LaRusso	F	6'7	220	22	71	2092	355	913	39	265	357	74	679	83	222	8	975	29	9.6	1.2	3.1	13.7
Jim Krebs	C	6'8	230	24	75	1269	237	605	39	98	136	72	327	38	210	2	572	17	4.4	0.5	2.8	7.6
Rod Hundley	G	6'4	190	25	73	2279	365	1019	36	203	273	74	390	338	194	0	933	31	5.3	4.6	2.7	12.8
Bob Leonard	G	6'3	185	27	73	2074	231	717	32	136	193	70	245	252	171	3	598	28	3.4	3.5	2.3	8.2
Tom Hawkins	F	6'5	210	23	69	1467	220	579	38	106	164	65	428	54	188	3	546	21	6.2	0.8	2.7	7.9
Frank Selvy (19g. Syr)	G	6'3	185	27	62	1308	205	521	39	153	208	74	175	111	101 I		563	21	2.8	1.8	1.6	9.1
Ray Felix (16g. NY)	C	6'11	225	29	47	883	136	355	38	70	112	63	338	23	177	5	342	19	7.2	0.5	3.8	7.3
Boo Ellis	F	6'5	200	23	46	671	64	185	35	51	76	67	236	27	64	2	179	15	5.1	0.6	1.4	3.9
Chuck Share (38g. StL)	C	6'11	245	32	41	651	59	151	39	53	80	66	221	62	142	9	171	16	5.4	1.5	3.5	4.2
Ed Fleming	G-F	6'3	190	26	27	413	59	141	42	53	69	77	83	38	46	0	171	15	3.1	1.4	1.7	6.3
Steve Hamilton	C	6'7	200	26	15	247	29	77	38	18	23	78	58	7	39	1	76	16	3.9	0.5	2.6	5.1
Ron Sobie (l5g. NY, KJ)	G	6'3	195	26	16	234	37	108	34	31	37	84	48	21	32	0	105	15	3.0	1.3	2.0	6.6
Bobby Smith	G	6'4	190	22	10	130	13	54	24	11	16	69	33	14	10	0	37	13	3.3	1.4	1.0	3.7
Nick Mantis	G	6'3	190	24	10	71	10	39	26	1	2	50	6	9	8	0	21	7	0.6	0.9	0.8	2.1
CINCINNATI ROYALS	**19-56 .253**				**TOM MARSHALL**																	
Jack Twyman	F	6'6	210	25	75	3023	870	2063	42	**598**	762	78	664	260	275	10	2338	40	8.9	3.5	3.7	31.2
Hub Reed (2g. StL)	F-C	6'9	230	23	71	1820	270	601	45	134	184	73	614	69	230	6	674	26	8.6	1.0	3.2	9.5
Phil Jordon	C-F	6'10	205	26	75	2066	381	970	39	242	338	72	624	207	227	7	1004	28	8.3	2.8	3.0	13.4
Arlen Bockhorn	G	6'4	200	26	75	2103	323	812	40	145	194	75	382	256	249	8	791	28	5.1	3.4	3.3	10.5
Win Wilfong	G	6'2	185	27	72	1992	283	764	37	161	207	78	352	265	229	1	727	28	4.9	3.7	3.2	10.1
Med Park	G	6'2	205	26	74	1849	226	582	39	189	260	73	301	214	180	2	641	25	4.1	2.9	2.4	8.7
Wayne Embry	C	6'8	240	22	73	1594	303	690	44	167	325	51	692	83	226	1	773	22	9.5	1.1	3.1	10.6
Phil Rollins	G	6'2	190	25	72	1235	158	386	41	77	127	61	180	233	150	1	393	17	2.5	3.2	2.1	5.5
Dave Gambee (42g. StL)	F	6'6	215	22	61	656	117	291	40	69	106	65	229	38	83	1	303	11	3.8	0.6	1.4	5.0
Larry Staverman	F	6'7	205	23	49	479	70	149	47	47	64	73	180	36	98	0	187	10	3.7	0.7	2.0	3.8
Wayne Stevens	F	6'3	185	23	8	49	3	19	16	7	10	70	16	4	4	0	13	6	2.0	0.5	0.5	1.6

1959/60 N.B.A. — PLAYOFFS

Use Name	Pos	Hgt	Wgt	Age	G	Min	FG	FGA	%	FT	FTA	%	Reb	Ass	PF	DQ	Points	Min	Reb	Ass	PF	Points
					TOTAL													PER GAME				
BOSTON CELTICS	**RED AUERBACH**				defeated Philadelphia 4-2; H111-105, 110-115, H120-90, 112-104, H107-128, 119-117																	
					defeated St. Louis 4-3; H140-122, H103-113, 102-86, 96-106, H127-102, 102-105, H122-103																	
Frank Ramsey	F	6'3	195	28	13	459	81	196	41	55	63	87	100	27	51	1	217	35	7.7	2.1	3.9	16.7
Tom Heinsohn	F	6'7	220	25	13	423	112	267	42	60	80	75	126	27	53	2	284	33	9.7	2.1	4.1	21.8
Bill Russell	C	6'10	220	25	13	572	94	206	46	53	75	71	**336**	38	38	1	241	44	**25.8**	2.9	2.9	18.5
Bill Sharman	G	6'1	190	33	13	364	88	209	42	43	53	81	45	20	22	1	219	28	3.5	1.5	1.7	16.8
Bob Cousy	G	6'1	178	31	13	468	80	262	31	39	51	76	48	**116**	27	0	199	36	3.7	**8.9**	2.1	15.3
Gene Conley	F-C	6'8	225	29	13	269	34	88	39	16	22	73	116	3	**59**	2	84	21	8.9	0.2	4.5	6.5
K. C. Jones	G	6'1	202	27	13	232	27	80	34	17	22	77	45	14	28	0	71	18	3.5	1.1	2.2	5.5
Sam Jones	G-F	6'4	205	26	13	197	45	117	38	17	21	81	41	18	17	0	107	15	3.2	1.4	1.3	8.2
John Richter	F	6'9	225	22	8	95	15	38	39	5	14	36	29	2	18	1	35	12	3.6	0.3	2.3	4.4
Gene Guarilia	F	6'5	220	22	7	41	4	18	22	6	6	100	19	3	4	0	14	6	2.7	0.4	0.6	2.0
Jim Loscutoff - back injury																						
ST. LOUIS HAWKS	**ED MACAULEY**				defeated Minneapolis 4-3; H112-99, H113-120, 93-89, 101-103, H110-117(OT), 117-96, H97-86																	
					lost to Boston 3-4; 122-140, 113-103, H86-102, H106-96, 102-127, H105-102, 103-122																	
Cliff Hagan	F	6'4	210	28	14	544	125	**296**	42	89	109	82	138	54	54	1	339	39	9.9	3.9	3.9	24.2
Bob Pettit	F	6'9	220	27	14	**576**	**129**	292	44	**107**	**142**	75	221	52	43	1	**365**	41	15.8	3.7	3.1	26.1
Clyde Lovellette	C	6'9	240	30	14	426	95	242	39	56	68	82	151	39	53	0	246	30	10.8	2.8	3.8	17.6
Si Green	G	6'2	195	25	14	565	81	171	47	35	58	60	121	88	50	1	197	40	8.6	6.2	3.6	14.1
Johnny McCarthy	G	6'1	185	25	14	566	43	106	41	27	36	75	64	98	49	0	113	40	4.6	7.0	3.5	8.1
Dave Piontek	F	6'6	230	25	14	220	27	79	34	18	25	72	41	18	28	0	72	16	2.9	1.2	2.0	5.1
Larry Foust	C	6'9	250	31	12	205	29	74	39	20	25	80	68	11	36	0	78	17	5.7	0.9	3.0	6.5
Al Ferrari	G	6'4	200	26	9	142	15	38	39	10	18	56	9	15	13	0	40	16	1.0	1.7	1.4	4.4
Slater Martin	G	5'10	170	34	3	58	1	13	8	1	4	25	3	8	9	0	3	19	1.0	2.7	3.0	1.0
Bob Ferry	C-F	6'8	230	22	11	56	10	19	53	4	7	57	15	0	10	0	24	5	1.4	0.0	0.9	2.2
Jack McMahon	G	6'1	195	31	2	27	2	4	50	0	4	0	1	3	5	0	4	14	0.5	1.5	2.5	2.0
MINNEAPOLIS LAKERS	**JIM POLLARD**				defeated Detroit 2-0; 113-112, H114-99																	
					lost to St. Louis 3-4; 99-112, 120-113, H89-93, H103-101, 117-110 (OT), H96-117, 86-97																	
Elgin Baylor	F	6'5	225	25	9	408	111	234	47	79	94	84	128	31	38	0	301	45	14.2	3.4	4.2	**33.4**
Rudy LaRusso	F-C	6'7	220	22	9	321	56	132	42	27	35	77	70	22	34	1	139	36	7.8	2.4	3.8	15.4
Jim Krebs	C	6'8	230	24	9	157	23	55	42	5	10	50	47	8	31	0	51	17	5.2	0.9	3.4	5.7
Rod Hundley	G	6'4	190	25	9	337	41	122	34	24	37	65	61	55	18	0	106	37	6.8	6.1	2.0	11.8
Frank Selvy	G	6'3	185	27	9	330	55	153	36	31	44	70	55	29	21	0	141	37	6.1	3.2	2.3	15.7
Bob Leonard	G	6'3	185	27	9	207	20	67	30	18	28	64	10	45	17	0	58	23	1.1	5.0	1.9	6.4
Ray Felix	C	6'11	225	29	8	147	17	41	41	18	25	72	53	9	34	1	52	18	6.6	1.1	4.3	6.5
Chuck Share	C	6'11	245	32	9	123	6	14	43	10	11	91	34	5	26	1	22	14	3.8	0.6	2.9	2.4
Tom Hawkins	F	6'5	210	23	8	119	22	45	49	15	18	83	21	3	24	0	59	15	2.6	0.4	3.0	7.4
Boo Ellis	F	6'5	200	23	3	36	2	10	20	4	8	50	12	2	3	0	8	12	4.0	0.7	1.0	2.7
PHILADELPHIA WARRIORS	**NEIL JOHNSTON**				defeated Syracuse 2-1; H115-92, 119-125, H132-112																	
					lost to Boston 2-4; 105-111, H115-110, 90-120, H104-112, 128-107, H117-119																	
Paul Arizin	F	6'4	200	31	9	371	84	195	43	69	79	87	86	33	29	0	237	41	9.6	3.7	3.2	26.3
Woody Sauldsberry	F	6'7	220	25	9	298	54	159	34	8	14	57	64	12	40	**3**	116	33	7.1	1.3	4.4	12.9
Wilt Chamberlain	C	7'1	250	23	9	415	125	252	50	49	110	45	232	19	17	0	299	**46**	25.8	2.1	1.9	33.2
Tom Gola	G-F	6'6	205	26	9	340	42	102	41	29	36	81	95	50	41	**3**	113	38	10.6	5.6	4.6	12.6
Guy Rodgers	G	6'	185	24	9	370	49	136	36	20	36	56	77	54	39	**3**	118	41	8.6	6.0	4.3	13.1
Andy Johnson	G-F	6'5	215	28	9	183	28	67	42	24	47	51	45	21	26	1	80	20	5.0	2.3	2.9	8.9
Joe Graboski	F-C	6'8	230	29	9	129	17	58	29	7	9	78	30	9	23	0	41	14	3.3	1.0	2.6	4.6
Ernie Beck	G	6'4	195	28	4	22	4	9	44	0	1	0	6	3	1	0	8	6	1.5	0.8	0.3	2.0
Vern Hatton	G	6'3	195	23	6	17	4	13	31	1	3	33	3	1	3	0	9	3	0.5	0.2	0.5	1.5
Joe Ruklick	F	5'9	220	21	4	15	2	9	22	0	0	—	5	0	3	0	4	4	1.3	0.0	0.8	1.0
SYRACUSE NATIONALS	**PAUL SEYMOUR**				lost to Philadelphia 1-2; 92-115, H125-119, 112-132																	
George Yardley	F	6'5	195	31	3	88	15	39	38	10	12	83	17	1	9	0	40	29	5.7	0.3	3.0	13.3
Dolph Schayes	F	6'8	220	31	3	126	30	66	45	28	30	**93**	48	8	10	0	88	42	16.0	2.7	3.3	29.3
Johnny Kerr	C	6'9	230	27	3	104	15	51	29	11	12	92	25	9	9	0	41	35	8.3	3.0	3.0	13.7
Hal Greer	G	6'3	176	23	3	84	22	43	51	3	4	75	14	10	5	0	47	28	4.7	3.3	1.7	15.7
Larry Costello	G	6'1	188	28	3	122	20	47	43	10	12	83	14	20	15	1	50	41	4.7	6.7	5.0	16.7
Dick Barnett	G	6'4	190	23	3	64	12	38	32	6	7	86	14	4	4	0	30	21	4.7	1.3	1.3	10.0
Barney Cable	F	6'7	200	23	3	63	5	14	36	4	8	50	28	1	12	0	14	21	9.3	0.3	4.0	4.7
Connie Dierking	C	6'9	222	23	3	32	6	20	30	0	1	0	15	1	6	0	12	11	5.0	0.3	2.0	4.0
Bob Hopkins	F-C	6'8	230	25	1	19	2	8	25	3	3	100	6	0	3	0	7	19	6.0	0.0	3.0	7.0
Al Bianchi	G	6'3	185	27	2	18	0	8	0	0	0	—	3	3	2	0	0	9	1.5	1.5	1.0	0.0
DETROIT PISTONS	**DICK McGUIRE**				lost to Minneapolis 0-2; H112-113, 99-114																	
Earl Lloyd	F	6'6	220	31	2	53	6	24	25	5	8	63	9	3	11	1	17	27	4.5	1.5	**5.5**	8.5
Bailey Howell	F	6'7	210	22	2	72	14	41	34	6	8	75	17	3	8	0	34	36	8.5	1.5	4.0	17.0
Walter Dukes	C	7'	220	29	2	78	16	31	**52**	16	22	73	33	2	9	1	48	39	16.5	1.0	4.5	24.0
Chuck Noble	G	6'4	195	28	2	61	7	26	27	0	0	—	9	13	6	0	14	31	4.5	6.5	3.0	7.0
Gene Shue	G	6'2	175	28	2	89	15	38	39	18	20	90	12	6	5	0	48	45	6.0	3.0	2.5	24.0
Shellie McMillon	F	6'5	205	23	2	47	8	21	38	4	5	80	16	2	5	0	20	24	8.0	1.0	2.5	10.0
Dick McGuire	G	6'	180	33	2	42	5	12	42	1	3	33	4	9	3	0	11	21	2.0	4.5	1.5	5.5
Ed Conlin	F	6'5	200	26	2	20	3	10	30	2	2	100	4	0	2	0	8	10	2.0	0.0	1.0	4.0
Archie Dees	C	6'8	205	23	2	18	4	12	33	3	3	100	4	2	2	0	11	9	2.0	1.0	1.0	5.5

1959/60 N.B.A. TEAM STATISTICS

Team	REGULAR SEASON G	FG	FGA	%	FT	FTA	%	Reb.	Ass.	AVERAGE POINTS For	Agnst.	Diff.	PLAYOFFS G	FG	FGA	%	FT	FTA	%	Reb.	Ass.	AVERAGE POINTS For	Agnst.	Diff.
EASTERN DIVISION																								
Boston	75	3744	8971	42	1849	2519	73	6014	1849	124.5	116.2	+8.3	13	580	1481	39	311	407	76	1003	268	113.1	108.4	+4.7
Philadelphia	75	3549	8678	41	1797	2686	67	5916	1796	118.6	116.4	+2.2	9	409	1000	41	207	335	62	700	202	113.9	112.0	+1.9
Syracuse	75	3406	8232	41	2105	2662	79	5406	1676	118.9	116.4	+2.5	3	127	334	38	75	89	84	210	57	109.7	122.0	-12.3
New York	75	3429	8253	42	1942	2539	76	5251	1667	117.3	119.6	-2.3												
WESTERN DIVISION																								
St. Louis	75	3179	7580	42	2148	2885	74	5343	1881	113.4	110.7	+2.7	14	557	1334	42	366	496	74	943	386	105.7	107.3	-1.6
Detroit	75	3146	7920	40	2075	2847	73	5491	1472	111.6	115.0	-3.4	2	78	215	36	55	71	77	149	40	105.5	113.5	-8.0
Minneapolis	75	3040	7884	39	1965	2691	73	5432	1447	107.3	111.4	-4.1	9	353	873	40	231	310	75	578	209	104.1	106.0	-1.9
Cincinnati	75	3210	7786	41	1913	2672	72	5251	1747	111.1	117.4	-6.3												

1959/60 N.B.A. STANDINGS

Team	W	L	Pct.	GB	Record against playoff teams W	L	Pct.	Record against non-playoff teams W	L	Pct.	HOME W	L	Pct.	ROAD W	L	Pct.	NEUTRAL W	L	Pct.
EASTERN DIVISION																			
Boston Celtics	59	16	.787	—	39	14	.736	20	2	.909	25	2	.926	23	9	.719	11	5	.688
Philadelphia Warriors	49	26	.653	10	31	22	.585	18	4	.818	22	6	.786	12	19	.387	15	1	.938
Syracuse Nationals	45	30	.600	14	27	26	.509	18	4	.818	26	4	.867	11	19	.367	8	7	.533
New York Knickerbockers	27	48	.360	32	20	46	.303	7	2	.778	13	18	.419	9	19	.321	5	11	.313
WESTERN DIVISION																			
St. Louis Hawks	46	29	.613	—	31	22	.585	15	7	.682	28	5	.848	12	20	.375	6	4	.600
Detroit Pistons	30	45	.400	16	18	35	.340	12	10	.545	17	14	.548	6	21	.222	7	10	.412
Minneapolis Lakers	25	50	.333	21	13	40	.245	12	10	.545	9	13	.409	9	22	.290	7	15	.318
Cincinnati Royals	19	56	.253	27	17	49	.258	2	7	.222	9	22	.290	2	20	.091	8	14	.364

1959/60 N.B.A. INDIVIDUAL LEADERS

SCORING
(Minimum 60 Games Played)

Name	Team	G	FG	FT	Pts.	Avg.
Chamberlain	Phi	72	1065	577	2707	37.6
Twyman	Cin	75	870	598	2338	31.2
Baylor	Min	70	755	564	2074	29.6
Pettit	StL	72	669	544	1882	26.1
Hagan	StL	75	719	421	1859	24.8
Shue	Det	75	620	472	1712	22.8
Schayes	Syr	75	578	533	1689	22.5
Arizin	Phi	72	593	420	1606	22.3
Guerin	NY	74	579	457	1615	21.8
Heinsohn	Bos	75	673	283	1629	21.7

FIELD GOAL PERCENTAGE
(Minimum 190 Field Goals)

Name	Team	FG	FGA	Pct.
Sears	NY	412	863	.477
Greer	Syr	388	815	.476
Lovellette	StL	550	1174	.468
Russell	Bos	555	1189	.467
Hagan	StL	719	1549	.464
Chamberlain	Phi	1065	2311	.461
Sharman	Bos	559	1225	.456
Howell	Det	510	1119	.456
S. Jones	Bos	355	782	.454
Yardley	Syr	546	1205	.453

FREE THROW PERCENTAGE
(Minimum 185 Free Throws)

Name	Team	FT	FTA	Pct.
Schayes	Syr	533	597	.893
Shue	Det	472	541	.872
Sears	NY	363	418	.868
Sharman	Bos	252	291	.866
Costello	Syr	249	290	.859
Naulls	NY	286	342	.836
Lovellette	StL	316	385	.821
Yardley	Syr	381	467	.816
Hagan	StL	421	524	.803
Arizin	Phi	420	526	.798

PERSONAL FOULS

Name	Team	PF
Gola	Phi	311
Dukes	Det	310
Howell	Det	282
Heinsohn	Bos	275
Twyman	Cin	275

GAMES DISQUALIFIED

Name	Team	Disq
Dukes	Det	20
Howell	Det	13
Conley	Bos	10
Ramsey	Bos	10
Schayes	Syr	10
Twyman	Cin	10

REBOUNDS PER GAME
(Minimum 60 Games Played)

Name	Team	G	Reb.	Avg.
Chamberlain	Phi	72	1941	27.0
Russell	Bos	74	1778	24.0
Pettit	StL	72	1221	17.0
Baylor	Min	70	1150	16.4
Naulls	NY	65	921	14.2
Sears	NY	64	876	13.7
Dukes	Det	66	883	13.4
Schayes	Syr	75	959	12.8
Kerr	Syr	75	913	12.2
Hagan	StL	75	803	10.7

ASSISTS PER GAME
(Minimum 60 Games Played)

Name	Team	G	Ass.	Avg.
Cousy	Bos	75	715	9.5
Rodgers	Phi	68	482	7.1
Guerin	NY	74	468	6.3
Costello	Syr	71	449	6.3
Gola	Phi	75	409	5.5
McGuire	Det	68	358	5.3
Martin	StL	64	330	5.2
Hundley	Min	73	338	4.6
McCarthy	StL	75	328	4.4
Hagan	StL	75	299	4.0

MINUTES PLAYED

Name	Team	Min.
Chamberlain	Phi	3338
Shue	Det	3338
Russell	Bos	3146
Twyman	Cin	3023
Pettit	StL	2896

1960-61 N.B.A.

Too Much Smoke

For the first time, the N.B.A. stretched from coast to coast, joining major league baseball and pro football in California. Just as baseball had moved two tradition-steeped clubs, the Brooklyn Dodgers and New York Giants, to the virgin territory, the N.B.A. sent the Minneapolis Lakers to open up the West Coast for pro basketball. The Lakers had been going nowhere on the floor and downhill at the ticket window since George Mikan retired, and owner Bob Short decided to take his club to Los Angeles, where the baseball Dodgers and football Rams had struck it rich. The Lakers, too, would prosper here, and the entire N.B.A. reaped the benefits of high attendance and publicity in one of the nation's most glamorous cities.

But Los Angeles was not the only new asset in the N.B.A. this season; two new superstars turned pro after superb college careers. The Cincinnati Royals made Oscar Robertson the number one pick in the college draft, taking the product of the University of Cincinnati both for his local gate appeal and his playing ability. A 6'5" guard, the Big 0 combined more skills than any other player ever in the public eye. His outside shot rang up points in a steady flow, his passes threaded the tightest of openings between defenders, his ball-handling created opportunities both for himself and his teammates, and he could rebound as well as many forwards. As a rookie, Oscar scored at a 30.5 clip, third best in the league, and he made the first-team All-League squad. As an overall player, only Elgin Baylor of the Lakers approached Robertson.

Baylor was the Lakers' biggest asset, scoring a record 71 points in one game. But he had a worthy partner this season in Jerry West, a rookie guard out of the University of West Virginia. West was not as big as Robertson, but his shooting, ball-handling, and competitive drive were just as keen. West got off to a slow start, acclimating himself to the rigors of play and travel in the N.B.A., but by the end of the regular season, he and Baylor gave the Lakers an unmatched inside-outside scoring punch, a duo that would carry the Lakers for years.

But while one new city and two new stars changed the N.B.A. scene, the same clubs remained dominant in each division, the Boston Celtics in the East and the St. Louis Hawks in the West. The Celtics took first place by nine games over the Warriors, compiling the league's best record with a 57-22 mark. The Celtics by now were a public institution, known even by non-fans as the paragon of basketball excellence. Some fans celebrated guard Bob Cousy as the key element in the dynasty, pointing to his passing and ball-handling on the fast break as the indispensible ingredient. Other fans pointed out that the Celtics had never won a title until center Bill Russell arrived; with his rebounding and defensive prowess in the pivot, the Celtics had never finished out of first place.

The remaining Celtics held less of the limelight but nevertheless had definite identities in the eyes of pro basketball fans. Tom Heinsohn and Bill Sharman were the scorers, the shooters the Celtics went to in a pinch. Frank Ramsey hustled and shot from the other forward spot. With Sharman's playing time cut down by injuries, Sam Jones and K.C. Jones got more playing time this season. Sam was a pure shooter, with a classic jump shot; K.C. rarely shot, but played some of the tightest defense in the league. Veterans Jim Loscutoff and Gene Conley furnished reserve muscle to the forward wall, and rookie forward Satch Sanders began earning his reputation as a tough defender and rebounder. Orchestrating all this talent was coach Red Auerbach, considered by some fans to be the biggest star of all. His frequent storming at referees riled fans up all over the circuit, and his victory cigar, lit when the Celtics had the game in hand, became a symbol of Celtic supremacy .

The St. Louis Hawks had no coach as distinctive as Auerbach; in fact, owner Ben Kerner fired his coaches quite frequently. Paul Seymour was this year's new coach, put in charge of a talented squad which repeated as Western champion. The front line of Bob Pettit, Cliff Hagan, and Clyde Lovellette averaged 72 points per game, and veteran guards Si Green and Johnny McCarthy were joined by rookie Lenny Wilkens, a top-flight ball-handler from Providence College. The Hawk reserves were veteran performers who rarely captured the public's attention. The spotlight on the Hawks fell on Pettit, third in the N.B.A. in rebounding and fourth in scoring. The Hawks finished first in the Western Division race, and first in the N.B.A. in attendance. They even seemed capable of upending the Celtics in the playoffs.

The other N.B.A. clubs took a backseat to the Celtics and Hawks both on the court and in the newspapers. The Philadelphia Warriors were the only other club to finish over .500, capturing second place in the East with a 46-33 record; Wilt Chamberlain upped his scoring average to 38.4 in taking his second scoring crown in two pro seasons. Syracuse had a new coach in Alex Hannum, got a good season out of old standby Dolph Schayes, lost George Yardley to retirement, and took the last Eastern playoff berth with a 38-1 record. The New York Knicks finished a distant last again as their first draft choice, center Darrall Imhoff, was a sore disappointment.

In the Western Division, the Lakers took second place with a 36-43 mark, unveiling the combination of Baylor and West to their new Los Angeles fans. The Detroit Pistons, led by veterans Gene Shue and Bailey Howell, edged out the Cincinnati Royals, led by young Robertson, for the final playoff berth.

The first round of the playoffs produced one upset and one near upset. Syracuse minimized the damage Wilt Chamberlain could do by closely pressing the rest of the Philadelphia players, and the Nats took three straight games to win the series. The Pistons took the Lakers to a decisive fifth game before bowing out in the West. In the divisional finals, the Celtics and Hawks won, the Celtics handily and the Hawks barely.

Fans watched to see if the Hawks could knock the Celtics off in the title round, but 129-95 and 116-108 Boston victories in the first two games served notice that the crown was staying in Boston for another year. The Hawks won game three, but the Celtics stood for no more nonsense as Red Auerbach enjoyed a good smoke toward the end of the fourth and fifth games and counted his fourth championship in the last five years.

Use Name	Pos	Hgt	Wgt	Age	G	Min	FG	FGA	%	FT	FTA	%	Reb	Ass	PF	DQ	Points	Min	Reb	Ass	PF	Points
					TOTAL													PER GAME				

1960/61 N.B.A — EASTERN DIVISION

Use Name	Pos	Hgt	Wgt	Age	G	Min	FG	FGA	%	FT	FTA	%	Reb	Ass	PF	DQ	Points	Min	Reb	Ass	PF	Points
BOSTON CELTICS	**57-22 .722**				**RED AUERBACH**																	
Frank Ramsey	F	6'3	205	29	79	2019	448	1100	41	295	354	83	431	146	284	14	1191	26	5.5	1.8	3.6	15.1
Tom Heinsohn	F	6'7	220	26	74	2256	627	1566	40	325	424	77	732	141	260	7	1579	30	9.9	1.9	3.5	21.3
Bill Russell	C	6'10	220	26	78	3458	532	1250	43	258	469	55	1868	268	155	0	1322	44	23.9	3.4	2.0	16.9
Sam Jones	G	6'4	205	27	78	2028	480	1069	45	211	268	79	421	217	148	1	1171	26	5.4	2.8	1.9	15.0
Bob Cousy	G	6'1	180	32	76	2464	513	1382	37	352	452	78	331	587	196	0	1378	32	4.4	7.7	2.6	18.1
K. C. Jones	G	6'1	202	28	78	1605	203	601	34	186	280	66	279	253	190	3	592	21	3.6	3.2	2.4	7.6
Bill Sharman	G	6'1	190	34	61	1538	383	908	42	210	228	92	223	146	127	0	976	25	3.7	2.4	2.1	16.0
Gene Conley	F-C	6'8	235	30	75	1242	183	495	37	106	153	69	550	40	275	15	472	17	7.3	0.5	3.7	6.3
Jim Loscutoff	F	6'5	230	30	76	1154	144	478	30	49	76	64	291	25	238	5	337	15	3.8	0.3	3.1	4.4
Satch Sanders	F	6'6	210	22	68	1084	148	352	42	67	100	67	385	44	131	1	363	16	5.7	0.6	1.9	5.3
Gene Guarilia	F	6'5	220	23	25	209	38	94	40	3	10	30	71	5	28	0	79	8	2.8	0.2	1.1	3.2
PHILADELPHIA WARRIORS	**46-33 .582**				**NEIL JOHNSTON**																	
Andy Johnson	F-G	6'5	217	29	79	2000	299	834	36	157	275	57	345	205	249	3	755	25	4.4	2.6	3.2	9.6
Paul Arizin	F	6'4	200	32	79	2905	650	1529	43	532	639	83	681	188	**335**	11	1832	37	8.6	2.4	4.2	23.2
Wilt Chamberlain	C	7'1	250	24	79	**3773**	**1251**	**2457**	**51**	531	**1054**	50	**2149**	148	130	0	**3033**	48	**27.2**	1.9	1.6	**38.4**
Tom Gola	G-F	6'6	208	27	74	2712	420	940	45	210	281	75	692	292	321	13	1050	37	9.4	3.9	**4.3**	14.2
Guy Rodgers	G	6'	185	25	78	2905	397	1029	39	206	300	69	509	677	262	3	1000	37	6.5	8.7	3.4	12.8
Al Attles	G	6'2	175	24	77	1544	222	543	41	97	162	60	214	174	235	5	541	20	2.8	2.3	3.1	7.0
Ed Conlin	F-G	6'5	200	27	77	1294	216	599	36	104	139	75	262	123	153	1	536	17	3.4	1.6	2.0	7.0
Joe Graboski	F-C	6'8	230	30	68	1011	169	507	33	127	183	69	262	74	148	2	465	15	3.9	1.1	2.2	6.8
Vern Hatton	G	6'3	195	24	54	609	97	304	32	46	56	82	92	59	59	0	240	11	1.7	1.1	1.1	4.4
Joe Ruklick	F	6'9	220	22	29	223	43	120	36	8	13	62	62	10	38	0	94	8	2.1	0.3	1.3	3.2
Pickles Kennedy	G	5'11	180	22	7	52	4	21	19	4	6	67	8	9	6	0	12	7	1.1	1.3	0.9	1.7
SYRACUSE NATIONALS	**38-41 .481**				**ALEX HANNUM**																	
Dave Gambee	F	6'6	225	23	79	2090	397	947	42	291	352	83	581	101	276	6	1085	26	7.4	1.3	3.5	13.7
Dolph Schayes	F	6'8	220	32	79	3007	594	1595	37	**680**	783	87	960	296	296	9	1868	38	12.2	3.7	3.7	23.6
Johnny Kerr	C	6'9	230	28	79	2676	419	1056	40	218	299	73	951	199	230	4	1056	34	12.0	2.5	2.9	13.4
Hal Greer	G	6'3	176	24	79	2763	623	1381	45	305	394	77	455	302	242	0	1551	35	5.8	3.8	3.1	19.6
Larry Costello	G	6'1	188	29	75	2167	407	844	48	270	338	80	292	413	286	9	1084	29	3.9	5.5	3.8	14.5
Dick Barnett	G	6'4	190	24	78	2070	540	1194	45	240	337	71	283	218	169	0	1320	27	3.6	2.8	2.2	16.9
Barney Cable	F	6'7	205	24	75	1642	266	574	46	73	108	68	469	85	246	1	605	22	6.3	1.1	3.3	8.1
Swede Halbrook	C	7'3	245	27	79	1131	155	463	33	76	140	54	550	31	262	9	386	14	7.0	0.4	3.3	4.9
Joe Roberts	F	6'6	214	24	68	800	130	351	37	62	104	60	243	43	125	0	322	12	3.6	0.6	1.8	4.7
Al Bianchi (injury)	G	6'3	185	28	52	667	118	342	35	60	87	69	105	93	137	5	296	13	2.0	1.8	2.6	5.7
Ernie Beck (7g. StL)	G	6'4	195	29	10	82	10	29	34	6	7	86	23	15	10	0	26	8	0.8	1.5	1.0	2.6
Cal Ramsey	F	6'4	200	23	2	27	2	11	18	2	4	50	7	3	7	0	6	14	3.5	1.5	3.5	3.0
Bob Hopkins - knee injury																						
NEW YORK KNICKERBOCKERS	**21-58 .266**				**CARL BRAUN**																	
Kenny Sears (injury)	F	6'9	200	27	52	1396	241	596	40	268	325	82	293	102	165	6	750	27	5.6	2.0	3.2	14.4
Willie Naulls	F	6'6	225	26	79	2976	737	1723	43	372	456	82	1055	191	268	5	1846	38	13.4	2.4	3.4	23.4
Phil Jordon (48g. Cin)	C	6'10	215	27	79	2064	360	932	39	208	297	70	674	181	273	5	928	26	8.5	2.3	3.5	11.7
Richie Guerin	G	6'4	195	28	79	3023	612	1545	40	496	626	79	628	503	310	3	1720	38	7.9	6.4	3.9	21.8
Dick Garmaker	G	6'3	205	28	71	2238	415	943	44	275	358	77	277	220	240	2	1105	32	3.9	3.1	3.4	15.6
Johnny Green	F-G	6'5	200	27	78	1784	326	758	43	145	278	52	838	97	194	3	797	23	10.7	1.2	2.5	10.2
Bob McNeill	G	6'1	180	22	75	1387	166	427	39	105	126	83	123	238	148	2	437	18	1.6	3.2	2.0	5.8
Charlie Tyra	C	6'8	235	25	59	1384	199	549	36	120	173	69	394	82	164	7	518	23	6.7	1.4	2.8	8.8
Dave Budd	F	6'6	210	22	61	1075	156	361	43	87	134	65	297	45	171	2	399	18	4.9	0.7	2.8	6.5
Darrall Imhoff	C	6'10	220	22	62	994	122	310	39	49	96	51	296	51	143	2	293	16	4.8	0.8	2.3	4.7
Phil Rollins (14g. Cin, 7g. StL)	G	6'2	190	26	60	816	109	293	37	58	88	66	97	123	121	1	276	14	1.6	2.1	2.0	4.6
Jim Palmer	F	6'8	225	27	55	688	125	310	40	44	65	68	179	30	128	0	294	13	3.3	0.5	2.3	5.3
Jack George	G	6'3	195	32	16	268	31	93	33	20	30	67	32	39	37	0	82	17	2.0	2.4	2.3	5.1
Carl Braun (back injury)	G	6'5	185	33	15	218	37	79	47	11	14	79	31	48	29	0	85	15	2.1	3.2	1.9	5.7
Whitey Bell	G	6'	181	28	5	45	7	18	39	1	3	33	7	1	7	0	15	9	1.4	0.2	1.4	3.0

Use Name	Pos	Hgt	Wgt	Age	TOTAL													PER GAME				
					G	Min	FG	FGA	%	FT	FTA	%	Reb	Ass	PF	DQ	Points	Min	Reb	Ass	PF	Points
1960/61 N.B.A. — WESTERN DIVISION																						
ST. LOUIS HAWKS	**51-28 .646**				**PAUL SEYMOUR**																	
Cliff Hagan	F	6'4	210	29	77	2701	661	1490	44	383	467	82	715	381	286	9	1705	35	9.3	4.9	3.7	22.1
Bob Pettit	F-C	6'9	220	28	76	3027	769	1720	45	582	804	72	1540	262	217	1	2120	40	20.3	3.4	2.9	27.9
Clyde Lovellette	C-F	6'9	240	31	67	2111	599	1321	45	273	329	83	677	172	248	4	1471	32	10.1	2.6	3.7	22.0
Si Green	G	6'2	190	26	76	1968	263	718	37	174	247	70	380	258	234	2	700	26	5.0	3.4	3.1	9.2
Johnny McCarthy	G	6'1	185	26	79	2519	266	746	36	122	226	54	325	430	272	8	654	32	4.1	5.4	3.4	8.3
Lenny Wilkens	G	6'1	185	23	75	1898	333	783	43	214	300	71	335	212	215	5	880	25	4.5	2.8	2.9	11.7
Woody Sauldsberry	F	6'7	220	26	69	1491	230	768	30	56	100	56	491	74	197	3	516	22	7.1	1.1	2.9	7.5
Larry Foust	C	6'9	250	32	68	1208	194	489	40	164	208	79	389	77	185	0	552	18	5.7	1.1	2.7	8.1
Al Ferrari	G	6'4	200	27	63	1031	117	328	36	95	116	82	115	143	157	4	329	16	1.8	2.3	2.5	5.2
Fred LaCour	F-G	6'5	210	22	55	722	123	295	42	63	84	75	178	84	73	0	309	13	3.2	1.5	1.3	5.6
Dave Piontek	F	6'6	240	26	29	254	47	96	49	16	31	52	68	19	31	0	110	9	2.3	0.7	1.1	3.8
LOS ANGELES LAKERS	**36-43 .456**				**FRED SCHAUS**																	
Elgin Baylor	F	6'5	225	26	73	3135	931	2166	43	676	863	78	1447	371	279	3	2538	43	19.8	5.1	3.8	34.8
Rudy LaRusso	F-C	6'7	220	23	79	2593	416	992	42	323	409	79	781	135	280	8	1155	33	9.9	1.7	3.5	14.6
Jim Krebs	C	6'8	230	25	75	1655	271	692	39	75	93	81	456	68	223	2	617	22	6.1	0.9	3.0	8.2
Jerry West	G	6'3	175	22	79	2797	529	1264	42	331	497	67	611	333	213	1	1389	35	7.7	4.2	2.7	17.6
Rod Hundley	G	6'4	190	26	79	2172	323	921	35	223	296	75	289	350	144	0	869	27	3.7	4.4	1.8	11.0
Frank Selvy	G-F	6'3	185	28	77	2153	311	767	41	210	279	75	299	246	219	3	832	28	3.9	3.2	2.8	10.8
Tom Hawkins	F	6'5	210	24	78	1846	310	719	43	140	235	60	479	88	209	2	760	24	6.1	1.1	2.7	9.7
Ray Felix	C	6'11	225	30	78	1510	189	508	37	135	193	70	539	37	302	12	513	19	6.9	0.5	3.9	6.6
Bob Leonard	G	6'3	185	28	55	600	61	207	29	71	100	71	70	81	70	0	193	11	1.3	1.5	1.3	3.5
Howie Jolliff	C	6'7	218	22	46	352	46	141	33	11	23	48	141	16	53	0	103	8	3.1	0.3	1.2	2.2
Gary Alcorn	C	6'9	225	24	20	174	12	40	30	7	8	88	50	2	47	1	31	9	2.5	0.1	2.4	1.6
Ron Johnson (4g. Det)	F	6'8	215	22	14	92	13	43	30	11	17	65	29	2	10	0	37	7	2.1	0.1	0.7	2.6
DETROIT PISTONS	**34-45 .430**				**DICK McGUIRE**																	
George Lee	F	6'4	200	24	74	1735	310	776	40	276	394	70	490	89	158	1	896	23	6.6	1.2	2.1	12.1
Bailey Howell	F	6'7	215	23	77	2952	607	1293	47	601	798	75	1111	196	297	10	1815	38	14.4	2.5	3.9	23.6
Walter Dukes	C	7'	220	30	73	2047	286	706	41	281	400	70	1028	139	313	**16**	853	28	14.1	1.9	4.3	11.7
Don Ohl	G	6'3	190	24	79	2173	427	1085	39	200	278	72	256	265	224	3	1054	28	3.2	3.4	2.8	13.3
Gene Shue	G	6'2	175	29	78	3361	650	1545	42	465	543	86	334	530	207	1	1765	43	4.3	6.8	2.7	22.6
Chuck Noble	G	6'4	195	29	75	1665	196	566	35	82	115	71	180	287	195	4	474	22	2.4	3.8	2.6	6.3
Bob Ferry	C	6'8	230	23	79	1657	350	776	45	189	255	74	500	129	205	1	889	21	6.3	1.6	2.6	11.3
Shellie McMillon	F	6'5	210	24	78	1639	322	752	43	140	201	70	487	98	238	6	784	21	6.2	1.3	3.1	10.1
Jackie Moneland	F	6'7	215	22	64	1003	191	477	40	86	132	65	315	52	174	3	468	16	4.9	0.8	2.7	7.3
Willie Jones	G	6'3	185	24	35	452	216	448	48	40	63	63	94	63	90	2	196	13	2.7	1.8	2.6	5.6
Archie Dees	F-C	6'8	210	24	28	308	135	308	44	39	47	83	94	17	50	0	145	11	3.4	0.6	1.8	5.2
CINCINNATI ROYALS	**33-46 .418**				**CHARLIE WOLF**																	
Jack Twyman	F	6'6	210	26	79	2920	796	1632	49	405	554	73	672	225	279	5	1997	37	8.5	2.8	3.5	25.3
Mike Farmer (2g. NY)	F	6'7	210	24	59	1301	180	461	39	69	94	73	380	81	130	1	429	22	6.4	1.4	2.2	7.3
Wayne Embry	C	6'8	240	23	79	2233	458	1015	45	221	331	67	864	127	286	7	1137	28	10.9	1.6	3.6	14.4
Oscar Robertson	G	6'5	205	22	71	3012	756	1600	47	653	794	82	716	**690**	219	3	2165	42	10.1	**9.7**	3.1	30.5
Arlen Bockhorn	G	6'4	200	27	79	2669	420	1059	40	152	208	73	434	338	282	9	992	34	5.5	4.3	3.6	12.6
Bob Boozer	F	6'8	215	23	79	1573	250	603	41	166	247	67	488	109	193	1	666	20	6.2	1.4	2.4	8.4
Hub Reed	F-C	6'9	230	24	75	1216	156	364	43	85	122	70	367	69	199	7	397	16	4.9	0.9	2.7	5.3
Ralph Davis	G	6'4	180	22	73	1210	181	451	40	34	52	65	86	177	127	1	396	17	1.2	2.4	1.7	5.4
Larry Staverman	F	6'7	215	24	66	944	111	249	45	79	93	85	287	86	164	4	301	14	4.3	1.3	2.5	4.6
Win Wilfong	G-F	6'2	190	28	62	717	106	305	35	72	89	81	147	87	119	1	284	12	2.4	1.4	1.9	4.6

Use Name	Pos	Hgt	Wgt	Age	TOTAL G	Min	FG	FGA	%	FT	FTA	%	Reb	Ass	PF	DQ	Points	PER GAME Min	Reb	Ass	PF	Points

1960/61 N.B.A. - PLAYOFFS

BOSTON CELTICS — **RED AUERBACH**

defeated Syracuse 4-1; H128-115, 98-115, H133-110, 120-107, H123-101
defeated St. Louis 4-1; H129-95, H116-108, 120-124, 119-104, H121-112

Use Name	Pos	Hgt	Wgt	Age	G	Min	FG	FGA	%	FT	FTA	%	Reb	Ass	PF	DQ	Points	Min	Reb	Ass	PF	Points
Frank Ramsey	F	6'3	205	29	10	300	55	136	40	61	75	81	64	23	40	0	171	30	6.4	2.3	4.0	17.1
Tom Heinsohn	F	6'7	220	26	10	291	82	201	41	33	43	77	99	20	36	1	197	29	9.9	2.0	3.6	19.7
Bill Russell	C	6'10	220	26	10	462	73	171	43	45	86	52	**299**	48	24	0	191	46	**29.9**	4.8	2.4	19.1
Bill Sharman	G	6'1	190	34	10	261	68	133	**51**	32	36	89	27	17	22	0	168	26	2.7	1.7	2.2	16.8
Bob Cousy	G	6'1	180	32	10	337	50	147	34	67	88	76	43	**91**	33	1	167	34	4.3	**9.1**	3.3	16.7
Sam Jones	G	6'4	205	27	10	258	50	112	45	31	35	89	54	22	24	0	131	26	5.4	2.2	2.4	13.1
Satch Sanders	F	6'6	210	22	10	216	37	75	49	15	24	63	84	7	42	2	89	22	8.4	0.7	4.2	8.9
Jim Loscutoff	F	6'5	230	30	10	116	15	54	28	7	9	78	35	3	34	0	37	12	3.5	0.3	3.4	3.7
K. C. Jones	G	6'1	202	28	9	103	9	30	30	7	14	50	19	15	17	0	25	11	2.1	1.7	1.9	2.8
Gene Conley	F-C	6'8	235	30	9	56	12	33	36	7	12	58	31	1	20	0	31	6	3.4	0.1	2.2	3.4

ST. LOUIS HAWKS — **PAUL SEYMOUR**

defeated Los Angeles 4-3; H118-122, H121-106, 112-118, 118-117, H112-121, 114-113(OT), H105-103
lost to Boston 1-4; 95-129, 108-116, H124-120, H104-119, 112-121

Use Name	Pos	Hgt	Wgt	Age	G	Min	FG	FGA	%	FT	FTA	%	Reb	Ass	PF	DQ	Points	Min	Reb	Ass	PF	Points
Cliff Hagan	F	6'4	210	29	12	455	104	235	44	56	69	81	118	54	45	1	264	38	9.8	4.5	3.8	22.0
Woody Sauldsberry	F	6'7	220	26	12	407	75	206	36	14	25	56	108	34	51	1	164	34	9.0	2.8	4.3	13.7
Bob Pettit	C-F	6'9	220	28	12	526	117	284	41	109	**144**	76	211	38	42	0	343	44	17.6	3.2	3.5	28.6
Si Green	G	6'2	190	26	12	350	56	148	38	25	37	68	71	48	38	1	137	29	5.9	4.0	3.2	11.4
Lenny Wilkens	G	6'1	185	23	12	437	63	166	38	44	58	76	72	42	51	**4**	170	36	6.0	3.5	4.3	14.2
Johnny McCarthy	G	6'1	185	26	12	236	19	55	35	6	9	67	31	33	29	0	44	20	2.6	2.8	2.4	3.7
Clyde Lovellette	C	6'9	240	31	8	191	46	114	40	31	47	66	52	11	23	0	123	24	6.5	1.4	2.9	15.4
Al Ferrari	G	6'4	200	27	10	157	20	44	45	10	17	59	22	21	31	1	50	16	2.2	2.1	3.1	5.0
Larry Foust	C	6'9	250	32	8	89	9	20	45	8	14	57	28	2	13	0	26	11	3.5	0.3	1.6	3.3
Fred LaCour	F	6'5	210	22	5	47	7	21	33	6	7	86	6	4	6	0	20	9	1.2	0.8	1.2	4.0
Dave Piontek	F	6'6	240	26	1	10	1	7	14	0	0	—	3	1	2	0	2	10	3.0	1.0	2.0	2.0

LOS ANGELES LAKERS — **FRED SCHAUS**

defeated Detroit 3-2; H120-102, H120-118, 113-124, 114-123, H137-120
lost to St. Louis 3-4; 122-118, 106-121, H118-112, H117-118, 121-112, H113-114(OT), 103-105

Use Name	Pos	Hgt	Wgt	Age	G	Min	FG	FGA	%	FT	FTA	%	Reb	Ass	PF	DQ	Points	Min	Reb	Ass	PF	Points
Elgin Baylor	F	6'5	225	26	12	**540**	**170**	**352**	48	**117**	142	82	183	55	44	1	**457**	45	15.3	4.6	3.7	**38.1**
Rudy LaRusso	F-C	6'7	220	23	12	360	57	144	40	32	48	67	96	24	43	1	146	30	8.0	2.0	3.6	12.2
Ray Felix	C	6'11	225	30	12	339	46	109	42	30	39	77	125	10	**52**	2	122	28	10.4	0.8	4.3	10.2
Jerry West	G	6'3	175	22	12	461	99	202	49	77	106	73	104	66	39	0	275	38	8.7	5.5	3.3	22.9
Frank Selvy	G	6'3	185	28	12	371	43	111	39	37	48	77	44	50	42	1	123	31	3.7	4.2	3.5	10.3
Rod Hundley	G	6'4	190	26	12	287	30	101	30	20	29	69	41	45	19	0	80	24	3.4	3.8	1.6	6.7
Tom Hawkins	F	6'5	210	24	12	283	54	116	47	31	47	66	76	13	43	0	139	24	6.3	1.1	3.6	11.6
Jim Krebs	C	6'8	230	25	12	183	16	47	34	14	18	78	60	9	37	3	46	15	5.0	0.8	3.1	3.8
Bob Leonard	G	6'3	185	28	7	46	5	24	21	1	4	25	6	12	7	0	11	7	0.9	1.7	1.0	1.6
Howie Jolliff	C	6'7	218	22	4	35	6	13	46	0	0	—	25	8	4	0	12	9	6.3	2.0	1.0	3.0

SYRACUSE NATIONALS — **ALEX HANNUM**

defeated Philadelphia 3-0; 115-107, H115-114, 106-103
lost to Boston 1-4; 115-128, H98-115, 110-133, H107-120, 101-123

Use Name	Pos	Hgt	Wgt	Age	G	Min	FG	FGA	%	FT	FTA	%	Reb	Ass	PF	DQ	Points	Min	Reb	Ass	PF	Points
Dave Gambee	F	6'6	225	23	8	208	34	95	36	32	41	78	55	12	33	0	100	26	6.9	1.5	4.1	12.5
Dolph Schayes	F	6'8	220	32	8	308	51	152	34	63	70	**90**	91	21	32	2	165	39	11.4	2.6	4.0	20.6
Johnny Kerr	C	6'9	230	28	8	210	30	88	34	16	23	70	99	20	18	0	76	26	12.4	2.5	2.3	9.5
Hal Greer	G	6'3	176	24	8	232	41	106	39	33	40	83	33	19	32	1	115	29	4.1	2.4	4.0	14.4
Larry Costello	G	6'1	188	29	8	269	42	103	41	47	55	85	35	52	39	3	131	34	4.4	6.5	4.9	16.4
Dick Barnett	G-F	6'4	190	24	8	226	49	112	44	26	36	72	36	12	25	0	124	28	4.5	1.5	3.1	15.5
Barney Cable	F	6'7	205	24	8	185	26	65	40	10	17	59	61	7	29	1	62	23	7.6	0.9	3.6	7.8
Swede Halbrook	C	7'3	245	27	8	172	24	72	33	14	20	70	83	12	21	0	62	22	10.4	1.5	2.6	7.8
Al Bianchi	G	6'3	185	28	7	90	17	46	37	8	9	89	7	5	20	1	42	13	1.0	0.7	2.9	6.0
Joe Roberts	F	6'6	214	24	5	20	3	10	30	0	0	—	4	0	3	0	6	4	0.8	0.0	0.6	1.2
Bob Hopkins-knee injury																						

DETROIT PISTONS — **DICK McGUIRE**

lost to Los Angeles 2-3; 102-120, 118-120, H124-113, H123-114, 120-137

Use Name	Pos	Hgt	Wgt	Age	G	Min	FG	FGA	%	FT	FTA	%	Reb	Ass	PF	DQ	Points	Min	Reb	Ass	PF	Points
George Lee	F	6'4	200	24	5	135	29	70	41	20	27	74	34	14	11	0	78	27	6.8	2.8	2.2	15.6
Bailey Howell	F	6'7	215	23	5	154	20	57	35	16	23	70	46	22	22	1	56	31	9.2	4.4	4.4	11.2
Walter Dukes	C	7'	220	30	5	152	20	53	38	10	18	56	49	11	25	2	50	30	9.8	2.2	5.0	10.0
Don Ohl	G	6'3	190	24	5	130	25	78	32	13	19	68	19	14	13	0	63	26	3.8	2.8	2.6	12.6
Gene Shue	G	6'2	175	29	5	186	35	72	49	23	29	79	12	22	11	0	93	37	2.4	4.4	2.2	18.6
Bob Ferry	C-F	6'8	230	23	5	167	30	74	41	41	49	84	63	11	12	0	101	33	12.6	2.2	2.4	20.2
Chuck Noble	F	6'4	195	29	5	124	20	45	44	5	7	71	8	21	18	1	45	25	1.6	4.2	3.6	9.0
Shellie McMillon	F	6'5	210	24	4	67	13	27	48	13	18	72	9	7	16	2	39	17	2.3	1.8	4.0	9.8
Jackie Moreland	F	6'7	215	22	3	45	14	31	45	4	5	80	18	3	10	0	32	15	6.0	1.0	3.3	10.7
Willie Jones	G	6'3	185	24	3	40	12	29	41	6	7	86	7	6	6	0	30	13	2.3	2.0	2.0	10.0

PHILADELPHIA WARRIORS — **NEIL JOHNSTON**

lost to Syracuse 0-3; H107-115, 114-115, H103-106

Use Name	Pos	Hgt	Wgt	Age	G	Min	FG	FGA	%	FT	FTA	%	Reb	Ass	PF	DQ	Points	Min	Reb	Ass	PF	Points
Tom Gola	F-G	6'6	208	27	3	127	7	34	21	15	20	75	37	15	14	1	29	42	12.3	5.0	4.7	9.7
Paul Arizin	F	6'4	200	32	3	125	22	67	33	23	33	70	26	12	17	2	67	42	8.7	4.0	5.7	22.3
Wilt Chamberlain	C	7'1	250	24	3	144	45	96	47	21	38	55	69	6	10	0	111	**48**	23.0	2.0	3.3	37.0
Al Attles	G	6'2	175	24	3	110	12	26	46	5	14	36	12	9	14	0	29	37	4.0	3.0	4.7	9.7
Guy Rodgers	G	6'	185	25	3	121	21	57	37	11	20	55	21	15	16	2	53	40	7.0	5.0	5.3	17.7
Andy Johnson	F	6'5	217	29	3	50	7	22	32	6	9	67	10	1	11	0	20	17	3.3	0.3	3.7	6.7
Ed Conlin	F	6'5	200	27	3	42	5	17	29	5	5	100	4	4	4	0	15	14	1.3	1.3	1.3	5.0
Joe Graboski	F	6'8	230	30	1	1	0	0	—	0	0	—	0	0	0	0	0	1	0.0	0.0	0.0	0.0

1960/61 N.B.A. TEAM STATISTICS

Team	REGULAR SEASON									AVERAGE POINTS			PLAYOFFS									AVERAGE POINTS		
	G	FG	FGA	%	FT	FTA	%	Reb.	Ass.	For	Agnst.	Diff.	G	FG	FGA	%	FT	FTA	%	Reb.	Ass.	For	Agnst.	Diff.
EASTERN DIVISION																								
Boston	79	3699	**9295**	40	2062	2804	74	**6131**	1872	119.7	114.1	+5.6	10	**451**	**1092**	41	305	422	72	**821**	247	**120.7**	**109.1**	**+11.6**
Philadelphia	79	**3768**	8883	42	2022	3108	65	5938	1959	121.0	120.1	+0.9	3	119	319	37	86	**139**	62	210	62	108.0	112.0	-4.0
Syracuse	79	3654	8746	41	2278	2948	77	5726	1786	**121.3**	119.2	+2.1	8	317	855	37	**250**	313	**80**	604	160	110.5	118.2	-7.7
New York	79	3422	8347	41	2135	2838	**75**	5315	1822	113.7	120.1	-6.4												
WESTERN DIVISION																								
St. Louis	79	3618	8795	41	2147	2921	74	5994	**2136**	118.8	116.5	+2.3	12	517	1300	40	309	427	72	815	288	111.9	117.1	-6.2
Los Angeles	79	3401	8430	40	2204	2999	73	5816	1728	114.0	**114.1**	-0.1	12	526	1224	**43**	359	481	75	876	28	117.6	115.6	+2.0
Detroit	79	3481	8357	42	**2408**	**3240**	74	5813	1866	118.6	121.0	-2.4	5	218	536	41	151	202	75	327	**131**	117.4	122.2	-4.8
Cincinnati	79	3626	8281	**44**	2060	2761	75	5581	2107	117.9	121.3	-3.4												

1960/61 N.B.A. STANDINGS

Team	W	L	Pct.	GB	Record against playoff teams W	L	Pct.	Record against non - playoff teams W	L	Pct.	HOME W	L	Pct.	ROAD W	L	Pct.	NEUTRAL W	L	Pct.
EASTERN DIVISION																			
Boston Celtics	57	22	.722	—	40	16	.714	17	6	.739	21	7	.750	24	11	.686	12	4	.750
Philadelphia Warriors	46	33	.582	11	27	29	.482	19	4	.826	23	6	.793	12	21	.364	11	6	.647
Syracuse Nationals	38	41	.481	19	22	32	.407	16	9	.640	19	9	.679	8	21	.276	11	11	.500
New York Knickerbockers	21	58	.266	36	19	50	.275	2	8	.200	10	22	.313	7	25	.219	4	11	.267
WESTERN DIVISION																			
St. Louis Hawks	51	28	.646	—	35	21	.625	16	7	.696	29	5	.853	15	20	.429	7	3	.700
Los Angeles Lakers	36	43	.456	15	24	32	.429	12	11	.522	16	12	.571	8	20	.286	12	11	.522
Detroit Pistons	34	45	.430	17	18	38	.321	16	7	.696	20	11	.645	3	19	.136	11	15	.423
Cincinnatti Royals	33	46	.418	18	25	44	.362	8	2	.800	18	13	.581	8	19	.296	7	14	.333

1960/61 N.B.A. INDIVIDUAL LEADERS

SCORING
(Minimum 55 Games Played)

Name	Team	G	FG	FT	Pts.	Avg.
Chamberlain	Phi	79	1251	531	3033	38.4
Baylor	LA	73	931	676	2538	34.8
Robertson	Cin	71	756	653	2165	30.5
Pettit	StL	76	769	482	2120	27.9
Twyman	Cin	79	796	405	1997	25.3
Schayes	Syr	79	594	680	1868	23.6
Howell	Det	77	607	601	1815	23.6
Naulls	NY	79	737	372	1846	23.4
Arizin	Phi	79	650	532	1832	23.2
Shue	Det	78	650	465	1765	22.6

FIELD GOAL PERCENTAGE
(Minimum 230 Field Goals)

Name	Team	FG	FGA	Pct.
Chamberlain	Phi	1251	2457	.509
Twyman	Cin	796	1632	.488
Costello	Syr	407	844	.482
Robertson	Cin	756	1600	.473
Cable	Syr	266	564	.472
Howell	Det	607	1293	.469
Lovellette	StL	599	1321	.453
Barnett	Syr	540	1194	.452
Embry	Cin	458	1015	.451
Greer	Syr	623	1381	.451

FREE THROW PERCENTAGE
(Minimum 190 Free Throws)

Name	Team	FT	FTA	Pct.
Sharman	Bos	210	228	.921
Schayes	Syr	680	783	.868
Shue	Det	465	543	.856
Ramsey	Bos	295	354	.833
Arizin	Phi	532	639	.833
Lovellette	StL	273	329	.830
Gambee	Syr	291	352	.827
Sears	NY	268	325	.825
Robertson	Cin	653	794	.822
Hagan	StL	383	467	.820

PERSONAL FOULS

Name	Team	PF
Arizin	Phi	335
Gola	Phi	321
Dukes	Det	313
Guerin	NY	310
Felix	LA	302

GAMES DISQUALIFIED

Name	Team	Disq
Dukes	Det	16
Conley	Bos	15
Ramsey	Bos	14
Gola	Phi	13
Felix	LA	12

REBOUNDS PER GAME
(Minimum 55 Games Played)

Name	Team	G	Reb.	Avg.
Chamberlain	Phi	79	2149	27.2
Russell	Bos	78	1868	23.9
Pettit	StL	76	1540	20.3
Baylor	LA	73	1447	19.8
Howell	Det	77	1111	14.4
Dukes	Det	73	1028	14.1
Naulls	NY	79	1055	13.4
Schayes	Syr	79	960	12.2
Kerr	Syr	79	951	12.0
Embry	Cin	79	864	10.9

ASSISTS PER GAME
(Minimum 55 Games Played)

Name	Team	G	Ass.	Avg.
Robertson	Cin	71	690	9.7
Rodgers	Phi	78	677	8.7
Cousy	Bos	76	587	7.7
Shue	Det	78	530	6.8
Guerin	NY	79	503	6.4
Costello	Syr	75	413	5.5
McCarthy	StL	79	430	5.4
Baylor	LA	73	371	5.1
Hagan	StL	78	381	4.9
Hundley	LA	79	350	4.4

MINUTES PLAYED

Name	Team	Min.
Chamberlain	Phi	3773
Russell	Bos	3458
Shue	Det	3361
Baylor	LA	3135
Pettit	StL	3027

1961-62 N.B.A.

Chamberlain 100, Boston 4

It was a year of expansion, new competition, a scoring explosion, military activation, a fading power, a rising power, and a continuing power. The expansion brought the Chicago Packers into the league, the first new franchise in the N.B.A.'s history. Star rookie Walt Bellamy and a bunch of castoff veterans stocked the Packers, who finished a distant last in the Western Division. The poor showing disappointed the Packers' fans, and the league itself found the low attendance figures most disappointing. Chicago had never warmed up to the Stags, who competed in the N.B.A. until 1950, and pro basketball again seemed to be failing in the nation's second largest city.

But the Packers were not the only new team on the pro basketball scene this season. Abe Saperstein, the owner of the Harlem Globetrotters, organized and presided over the new American Basketball League. Los Angeles, Chicago, Hawaii, Kansas City, Pittsburgh, Washington, Cleveland, and San Francisco fielded teams for the A.B.L.'s inaugural season and scrounged for players to put on the floor. Only a handful of N.B.A. players jumped over to the A.B.L., the most prominent of which were Dick Barnett and Ken Sears; Bill Sharman ended his career with the Boston Celtics to coach the Los Angeles franchise.

Most of the A.B.L. players were N.B.A. rejects, older players past their peak, and several players whom the N.B.A. had barred because of some connection with the college betting scandals of 1960. In fact, the A.B.L.'s leading scorer and most exciting player was Connie Hawkins of Pittsburgh, who had been barred by the N.B.A. and the University of Iowa for not reporting a bribe offer. The Western Division champs turned out to be the Kansas City Steers, who featured rookies Bill Bridges and Gene Tormohlen and veteran Larry Staverman, while the Eastern crown plus the playoff championship went to the Cleveland Pipers, who had Dick Barnett, Larry Siegfried, Connie Dierking, Ben Warley, and John Barnhill.

The A.B.L. broke ice on two fronts. It employed a black coach, John McLendon of Cleveland. It also made all baskets from more than 25 feet out worth three points. But the players in the A. B.L. were in no way comparable to those in the N.B.A., and by the end of the season, Los Angeles had folded, Washington had moved to New York, and the entire A.B.L. was treading water in a sea of red ink.

While the A.B.L. was going through its faceless season, the N.B.A. was raking in publicity over the unprecedented scoring feats of Wilt Chamberlain. Frank McGuire, the new coach of the Philadelphia Warriors, wanted big Wilt to go to the basket as much as possible, and the Big Dipper responded by averaging 50.4 points a game. No one could stop Wilt near the basket, and the giant center demonstrated his full offensive might against the New York Knicks on March 2 at Hershey, Pennsylvania. With the Knicks helpless to stop him, Wilt hit for 36 field goals and 28 of 32 free throws to score 100 points in a 169-147 Warrior triumph. Newspapers devoted much space to the event, and basketball fans throughout the country had either good or bad things to say about Wilt; very few ignored him. Some fans believed that his overwhelming size was ruining the game, but it was a fact that even stars of a smaller size were scoring at paces unheard of years ago. Elgin Baylor, Walt Bellamy, Bob Pettit, Oscar Robertson, and Jerry West all topped the 30 points per game mark, a plateau broken for the first time only two seasons ago.

Baylor compiled a 38.3 average, second in the league, while playing only on weekends after mid-season. The activation of military reserve units for the Berlin crisis had called Baylor away into uniform and only on weekend passes could he get back into his basketball outfit. The N.B.A., however, made out better than either baseball or football in the call-up; aside from Bavlor, the only other star player to be activated was guard Lenny Wilkins of St. Louis.

The loss of Wilkins triggered the collapse of the Hawks, who had finished first in the West for the past five years. The backcourt had no other first-rate playmaker besides Wilkins, and the frontcourt suffered after Clyde Lovellette went out in mid-season with a heel injury. To add to the chaos, owner Ben Kerner kept the coaching situation in disarray; he canned Paul Seymour early in the campaign, replaced him with Fuzzy Levane, and then replaced Levane with six games to go by putting Bob Pettit in charge on an interim basis. Pettit and Cliff Hagan still performed at All-Star levels at the forward positions, but the Hawks finished out of the playoffs with a 29-51 mark.

The Los Angeles Lakers filled the power vacuum left by the fall of the Hawks. Elgin Baylor and Jerry West spearheaded the Laker offense, and the Laker club had enough supporting strength to keep on winning even when Baylor was away. Rudy LaRusso, Frank Selvy, and Jim Krebs filled the other Los Angeles starting slots, while Tom Hawkins, Hot Rod Hundley, and Ray Felix came off the bench to provide a lift when needed. Enjoying life at the top, the Lakers would be at or near the head of the West for years to come. For this season, the Cincinnati Royals and Detroit Pistons joined them in the playoffs, while the Hawks and the newborn Packers finished out of the money.

In the East, the Boston Celtics kept right on rolling along. Despite the defection of Bill Sharman to the A.B.L., the Celtics finished in first place for the sixth straight year. Bill Russell, Bob Cousy, and Tom Heinsohn were at the peak of their games, and Sam Jones, K.C. Jones and Satch Sanders were distinguishing themselves with more playing time. The Celtics' 60-20 record was the best in the N.B.A. and topped the Philadelphia Warriors by 11 games in the East. The Syracuse Nats, with Dolph Schayes slowing down, took the third playoff spot, ahead of the New York Knicks.

The two most interesting playoff series involved the Celtics. In the Eastern finals, the Warriors and Celtics battled into a decisive seventh game, which the Celtics won 109-107 when the Warriors failed in a last-second play to Chamberlain. In the championship series, the Lakers and Celtics also went into a seventh game. In a match of sizzling competition, the clubs battled to a 100-all deadlock after regulation time, with L.A.'s Selvy missing a short jumper at the buzzer. That was the closest the Lakers came to dethroning the Celtics; the defending champs outscored the challengers 10-7 in the overtime period to take the title game 110-107. Despite their close call, when Selvy's last-second shot slid off the rim, the Celtics still wore the crown for the fourth straight year.

1961/62 N.B.A. - EASTERN DIVISION

Use Name	Pos	Hgt	Wgt	Age	TOTAL G	Min	FG	FGA	%	FT	FTA	%	Reb	Ass	PF	DQ	Points	PER GAME Min	Reb	Ass	PF	Points
BOSTON CELTICS	**60-20 .750**				**RED AUERBACH**																	
Satch Sanders	F	6'6	210	23	80	2325	350	804	44	197	263	75	762	74	279	9	897	29	9.5	0.9	3.5	11.2
Tom Heinsohn	F-C	6'7	220	27	79	2383	692	1613	43	358	437	82	747	165	280	2	1742	30	9.5	2.1	3.5	22.1
Bill Russell	C	6'10	220	27	76	3433	575	1258	46	286	481	59	1790	341	207	3	1436	45	23.6	4.5	2.7	18.9
Sam Jones	G	6'4	205	28	78	2390	596	1284	46	243	297	82	458	232	149	0	1435	31	5.9	3.0	1.9	18.4
Bob Cousy	G	6'1	180	33	75	2116	462	1181	39	251	333	75	261	584	135	0	1175	28	3.5	7.8	1.8	15.7
K. C. Jones	G	6'1	202	29	80	2056	294	724	41	147	232	63	298	343	206	1	735	26	3.7	4.3	2.6	9.2
Frank Ramsey	F-G	6'3	205	30	79	1913	436	1019	43	334	405	82	387	109	245	10	1206	24	4.9	1.4	3.1	15.3
Jim Loscutoff	F	6'5	230	31	79	1146	188	519	36	45	84	54	329	51	185	3	421	15	4.2	0.6	2.3	5.3
Gary Phillips	G	6'3	189	22	67	693	110	310	35	50	86	58	107	64	109	0	270	10	1.6	1.0	1.6	4.0
Carl Braun	G	6'5	185	34	48	414	78	207	38	20	27	74	50	71	49	0	176	9	1.0	1.5	1.0	3.7
Gene Guarilia	F	6'5	220	24	45	367	61	161	38	41	64	64	124	11	56	0	163	8	2.8	0.2	1.2	3.6
PHILADELPHIA WARRIORS	**49-31 .613**				**FRANK McGUIRE**																	
Paul Arizin	F	6'4	200	33	78	2785	611	1490	41	484	601	81	527	201	307	18	1706	36	6.8	2.6	3.9	21.9
Tom Meschery	F	6'6	215	23	80	2509	375	929	40	216	262	82	729	145	**330**	15	966	31	9.1	1.8	4.1	12.1
Wilt Chamberlain	C	7'1	260	25	80	**3882**	**1597**	**3159**	51	**835**	**1363**	61	**2052**	192	123	0	4029	**49**	**25.7**	2.4	1.5	50.4
Tom Gola (wrist injury)	G-F	6'6	208	28	60	2462	322	765	42	176	230	77	587	295	267	16	820	41	9.8	4.9	**4.5**	13.7
Guy Rodgers	G	6'	185	26	80	2648	267	749	36	121	182	66	348	643	312	12	655	33	4.4	8.0	3.9	8.2
Al Attles	G	6'2	175	25	75	2468	343	724	47	158	267	59	355	333	279	8	844	33	4.7	4.4	3.7	11.3
Ed Conlin	F	6'5	200	28	70	963	128	371	35	66	89	74	155	85	118	1	322	14	2.2	1.2	1.7	4.6
Yorh Larese (8g. Chi)	G	6'4	183	23	59	703	122	327	37	58	72	81	77	94	104	0	302	12	1.3	1.6	1.8	5.1
Ted Luckenbill	F	6'6	205	22	67	396	43	120	36	49	76	64	110	27	67	0	135	6	1.6	0.4	1.0	2.0
Joe Ruklick	F-C	6'9	220	23	46	302	48	147	33	12	26	46	87	14	56	1	108	7	1.9	0.3	1.2	2.3
Frank Radovich	F	6'8	235	23	37	175	37	93	40	13	26	50	51	4	27	0	87	5	1.4	0.1	0.7	2.4
SYRACUSE NATIONALS	**41-39 .513**				**ALEX HANNUM**																	
Dave Gambee	F	6'6	225	24	80	2314	477	1126	42	384	470	82	631	114	275	10	1338	29	7.9	1.4	3.4	16.7
Dolph Schayes (broken jaw)	F	6'8	220	33	56	1480	268	751	36	286	319	**90**	439	120	167	4	822	26	7.8	2.1	3.0	14.7
Johnny Kerr	C	6'9	230	29	80	2767	541	1220	44	222	302	74	1176	243	272	7	1304	35	14.7	3.0	3.4	16.3
Hal Greer	G	6'3	176	25	71	2676	644	1442	45	331	404	82	526	313	252	2	1619	38	7.4	4.4	3.5	22.8
Larry Costello	G	6'1	188	30	63	1854	310	726	43	247	295	84	245	359	220	5	867	29	3.9	5.7	3.5	13.8
Lee Shaffer	F	6'7	220	22	75	2093	514	1180	44	239	310	77	511	99	266	6	1267	28	6.8	1.3	3.5	16.9
Al Bianchi	G	6'3	185	29	80	1925	336	847	40	154	221	70	281	263	232	5	826	24	3.5	3.3	2.9	10.3
Joe Roberts	F	6'6	215	25	80	1642	243	619	39	129	194	66	538	50	230	4	615	21	6.7	0.6	2.9	7.7
Paul Neumann	G	6'1	175	23	79	1365	172	401	43	133	172	77	194	176	203	3	477	17	2.5	2.2	2.6	6.0
Swede Halbrook (injury)	C	7'3	245	28	64	908	152	422	36	96	151	64	399	33	179	7	400	14	6.2	0.5	2.8	6.3
Joe Graboski (3g. StL, 12g. Chi)	F-C	6'8	230	31	38	468	77	221	35	39	65	60	154	28	62	0	193	12	4.1	0.7	1.6	5.1
Chuck Osborne	F	6'6	210	22	4	21	1	8	13	3	4	75	9	1	3	0	5	5	2.3	0.3	0.8	1.3
NEW YORK KNICKERBOCKERS	**29-51 .363**				**EDDIE DONOVAN**																	
Willie Naulls	F	6'6	225	27	75	2978	747	1798	42	383	455	84	867	192	260	6	1877	40	11.6	2.6	3.5	25.0
Johnny Green	F	6'5	200	28	80	2789	507	1164	44	261	434	60	1066	191	265	4	1275	35	13.3	2.4	3.3	15.9
Phil Jordon	C	6'10	215	28	76	2195	403	1028	39	96	168	57	482	156	258	7	902	29	6.3	2.1	3.4	11.9
Richie Guerin	G	6'4	195	29	78	3346	839	1897	44	625	762	82	501	539	299	3	2303	43	6.4	6.9	3.8	29.5
Al Butler (5g. Bos)	G	6'2	175	23	59	2016	349	754	46	129	182	71	337	205	156	0	827	34	5.7	3.5	2.6	14.0
Darrall Imhoff	C	6'10	220	23	76	1501	186	482	39	80	139	58	470	82	230	10	452	20	6.2	1.1	3.0	5.9
Dave Budd	F	6'6	210	23	79	1370	188	431	44	138	231	60	345	86	162	4	514	17	4.4	1.1	2.1	6.5
Whitey Martin	G	6'2	185	22	66	1018	95	292	33	37	55	67	158	115	158	4	227	15	2.4	1.7	2.4	3.4
Cleveland Buckner	F-C	6'9	210	23	62	696	158	367	43	83	133	62	236	39	114	1	399	11	3.8	0.6	1.8	6.4
Donnie Butcher	G	6'3	200	25	47	479	48	155	31	42	69	61	79	51	63	0	138	10	1.7	1.1	1.3	2.9
Sam Stith	G	6'2	185	24	32	440	59	162	36	23	38	61	51	60	55	0	141	14	1.6	1.9	1.7	4.4
George Blaney	G	6'1	175	22	36	363	54	142	38	9	17	53	36	45	34	0	117	10	1.0	1.3	0.9	3.3
Bill Smith	G-F	6'5	190	22	9	83	8	33	24	7	8	88	16	7	6	0	23	9	1.8	0.8	0.7	2.6
Ed Burton	F	6'6	225	22	8	28	7	14	50	1	4	25	5	1	3	0	15	4	0.6	0.1	0.4	1.9
Doug Kistler	F	6'9	210	23	5	13	3	6	50	2	4	50	1	0	2	0	8	3	0.2	0.0	0.4	1.6

1961/62 N.B.A. — WESTERN DIVISION

Use Name	Pos	Hgt	Wgt	Age	G	Min	FG	FGA	%	FT	FTA	%	Reb	Ass	PF	DQ	Points	Min	Reb	Ass	PF	Points
					TOTAL													PER GAME				
OS ANGELES LAKERS	54-26 .675				FRED SCHAUS																	
lgin Baylor(MS)	F	6'5	225	27	48	2129	680	1588	43	476	631	75	892	222	155	1	1836	44	18.6	4.6	3.2	38.3
udy LaRusso	F	6'7	220	24	80	2754	516	1108	47	342	448	76	828	179	255	5	1374	34	10.4	2.2	3.2	17.2
im Krebs	C	6'8	230	26	78	2012	312	701	45	156	208	75	616	110	290	9	780	26	7.9	1.4	3.7	10.0
erry West	G	6'3	175	23	75	3087	799	1795	45	712	926	77	591	402	173	4	2310	41	7.9	5.4	2.3	30.8
rank Selvy	G	6'3	185	29	79	2806	433	1032	42	298	404	74	412	381	232	0	1164	36	5.2	4.8	2.9	14.7
om Hawkins	F	6'5	210	25	79	1903	289	704	41	143	222	64	514	95	244	7	721	24	6.5	1.2	3.1	9.1
od Hundley	G	6'4	190	27	78	1492	173	509	34	83	127	65	199	290	129	1	429	19	2.6	3.7	1.7	5.5
ay Felix	C	6'11	225	31	80	1478	171	398	43	90	130	69	473	55	266	6	432	18	5.9	0.7	3.3	5.4
owie Jolliff	F-C	6'7	218	23	64	1094	104	253	41	41	78	53	383	76	175	4	249	17	6.0	1.2	2.7	3.9
ob McNeill (21g. Phi)	G	6'1	180	23	50	441	56	136	41	26	34	76	56	89	56	0	138	9	1.1	1.8	1.1	2.8
Vayne Yates	C	6'8	235	24	37	263	31	105	30	10	22	45	94	16	72	1	72	7	2.5	0.4	1.9	1.9
obby Smith	G	6'4	190	24	3	7	0	1	0	0	0	—	0	0	1	0	0	2	0.0	0.0	0.3	0.0
INCINNATI ROYALS	43-37 .538				CHARLIE WOLF																	
ack Twyman	F	6'6	210	27	80	2991	739	1542	48	353	435	81	638	215	323	5	1831	37	8.0	2.7	4.0	22.9
ob Boozer	F	6'8	215	24	79	2488	410	936	44	263	372	71	804	130	275	3	1083	31	10.2	1.6	3.5	13.7
Vayne Embry	C	6'8	245	24	75	2623	564	1210	47	356	516	69	977	182	286	6	1484	35	13.0	2.4	3.8	19.8
Oscar Robertson	G-F	6'5	205	23	79	3503	866	1810	48	700	872	80	985	**899**	258	1	2432	44	12.5	**11.4**	3.3	30.8
rlen Bockhorn	G	6'4	200	28	80	3062	531	1234	43	198	251	79	376	366	280	5	1260	38	4.7	4.6	3.5	15.8
drian Smith	G	6'1	180	25	80	1462	202	499	40	172	222	77	151	167	101	0	576	18	1.9	2.1	1.3	7.2
ub Reed	C-F	6'9	230	25	80	1446	203	460	44	60	82	73	440	53	267	9	466	18	5.5	0.7	3.3	5.8
oe Buckhalter	F	6'7	210	24	63	728	153	334	46	67	108	62	262	43	123	1	373	12	4.2	0.7	2.0	5.9
evo Nordmann	C	6'10	262	22	58	344	51	126	40	29	57	51	128	18	81	1	131	6	2.2	0.3	1.4	2.3
ob Wiesenhahn	F	6'4	215	23	60	326	51	161	32	17	30	57	112	23	50	0	119	5	1.9	0.4	0.8	2.0
Dave Zeller	G	6'1	175	22	61	278	36	102	35	18	24	75	27	58	37	0	90	5	0.4	1.0	0.6	1.5
DETROIT PISTONS	37-43 .463				DICK McGUIRE																	
ailey Howell	F	6'7	215	24	79	2857	553	1193	46	470	612	77	996	186	317	10	1576	36	12.6	2.4	4.0	19.9
ay Scott	F-C	6'9	215	23	75	2087	370	956	39	255	388	66	865	132	232	6	995	28	11.5	1.8	3.1	13.3
Valter Dukes	C	7'	220	31	77	1896	256	647	40	208	291	71	803	125	327	**20**	720	25	10.4	1.6	4.2	9.4
Don Ohl	G	6'3	190	25	77	2526	555	1250	44	201	280	72	267	244	173	2	1311	33	3.5	3.2	2.2	17.0
Gene Shue	G	6'2	175	30	80	3143	580	1422	41	362	447	81	372	465	192	1	1522	39	4.7	5.8	2.4	19.0
Bob Ferry	C-F	6'8	230	24	80	1918	411	939	44	286	422	68	503	145	199	2	1108	24	6.3	1.8	2.5	13.9
George Lee	F	6'4	200	25	75	1351	179	500	36	213	280	76	349	64	128	1	571	18	4.7	0.9	1.7	7.6
ackie Moreland	F	6'7	215	23	74	1219	205	487	42	139	186	75	427	76	179	2	549	16	5.8	1.0	2.4	7.4
Villie Jones	G	6'3	185	25	69	1006	177	475	37	64	101	63	177	115	137	1	418	15	2.6	1.7	2.0	6.1
Johnny Egan	G	5'11	180	22	58	696	128	301	43	64	84	76	86	102	64	0	320	12	1.5	1.8	1.1	5.5
Chuck Noble	G	6'4	195	30	26	361	32	113	28	8	15	53	43	63	55	1	72	14	1.7	2.4	2.1	2.8
ST. LOUIS HAWKS	29-51 .363				PAUL SEYMOUR (5-9 .357), FUZZY LEVANE (20-40 .333), BOB PETTIT (4-2 .667)																	
Cliff Hagan	F	6'4	210	30	77	2784	701	1490	47	362	439	82	633	370	282	8	1764	36	8.2	4.8	3.7	22.9
Clyde Lovellette (FJ)	F-C	6'9	240	32	40	1192	341	724	47	155	187	83	350	68	136	4	837	30	8.8	1.7	3.4	20.9
Bob Pettit	C-F	6'9	220	29	78	3282	867	1928	45	695	901	77	1459	289	296	4	2429	42	18.7	3.7	3.8	31.1
Al Ferrari	G	6'4	200	28	79	2046	208	582	36	175	219	80	213	313	278	9	591	26	2.7	4.0	3.5	7.5
enny Wilkens (MS)	G	6'1	185	24	20	870	140	364	38	84	110	76	131	116	63	0	364	44	6.6	5.8	3.2	18.2
Barney Cable (l5g. Chi)	F	6'7	205	25	67	1861	305	749	41	118	181	65	563	115	211	4	728	28	8.4	1.7	3.1	10.9
Fred LaCour	G	6'5	210	23	73	1507	230	536	43	106	130	82	272	166	168	3	566	21	3.7	2.3	2.3	7.8
Bob Sims (l9g. LA)	G-F	6'5	220	23	65	1345	193	491	39	123	216	57	183	154	187	4	509	21	2.8	2.4	2.9	7.8
Shellie McMillon (14g. Det)	F	6'5	210	25	62	1225	265	591	45	108	182	59	368	59	202	10	638	20	5.9	1.0	3.3	10.3
Cleo Hill	G	6'1	185	23	58	1150	107	309	35	106	137	77	178	114	98	1	320	20	3.1	2.0	1.7	5.5
arry Foust	C	6'9	250	33	57	1143	204	433	47	145	178	81	328	78	186	3	553	20	5.8	1.4	3.3	9.7
Vern Hanon (l5g. Chi)	G	6'3	195	25	40	898	112	331	34	98	125	78	102	99	63	0	322	22	2.6	2.5	1.6	8.1
Johnny McCarthy (KJ)	G	6'1	185	27	15	333	18	73	25	12	27	44	56	70	50	1	48	22	3.7	4.7	3.3	3.2
Archie Dees (13g. Chi)	F	6'8	210	25	21	288	51	115	44	35	46	76	77	16	33	0	137	14	3.7	0.8	1.6	6.5
Stacey Arceneaux	F	6'4	210	25	7	110	22	56	39	6	13	46	32	4	10	0	50	16	4.6	0.6	1.4	7.1
Jimmy Darrow	G	5'10	175	24	5	34	3	15	20	6	7	86	7	6	9	0	12	7	1.4	1.2	1.8	2.4
Ron Horn	F	6'7	225	23	3	25	1	12	8	1	2	50	6	1	4	0	3	8	2.0	0.3	1.3	1.0
Dick Eichhorst	G	6'3	200	28	1	10	1	2	50	0	0	—	1	3	1	0	2	10	1.0	3.0	1.0	2.0
CHICAGO PACKERS	1 -62 .225				JIM POLLARD																	
Andy Johnson	F-G	6'5	217	30	71	2193	365	814	45	284	452	63	351	228	247	5	1014	31	4.9	3.2	3.5	14.3
Woody Sauldsberry (14g. StL)	F	6'7	220	27	63	1765	298	869	34	79	123	64	536	90	179	5	675	28	8.5	1.4	2.8	10.7
Walt Bellamy	C	6'11	225	22	79	3344	973	1875	**52**	549	853	64	1500	210	281	6	2495	42	19.0	2.7	3.6	31.6
Si Green (14g. StL)	G	6'2	190	27	71	2388	341	905	38	218	311	70	399	318	226	3	900	34	5.6	4.5	3.2	12.7
Bob Leonard	G	6'3	185	29	70	2464	423	1128	38	279	371	75	199	378	186	0	1125	35	2.8	5.4	2.7	16.1
Ralph Davis	G	6'4	180	23	77	1992	364	881	41	71	103	69	162	247	187	1	799	26	2.1	3.2	2.4	10.4
Charlie Tyra	F-C	6'8	235	26	78	1606	193	534	36	133	214	62	610	86	210	7	519	21	7.8	1.1	2.7	6.7
Horace Walker	F	6'3	210	23	65	1331	149	439	34	140	193	73	466	69	194	2	438	20	7.2	1.1	3.0	6.7
Dave Piontek	F	6'6	240	27	45	614	83	225	37	39	59	66	155	31	89	1	205	14	3.4	0.7	2.0	4.6
Jack Turner	G-F	6'5	200	22	42	567	84	221	38	32	42	76	85	44	51	0	200	14	2.0	1.0	1.2	4.8
Howie Carl	G	5'9	160	23	31	382	67	201	33	36	51	71	39	57	41	1	170	12	1.3	1.8	1.3	5.5
George BonSalle	F	6'8	230	26	3	9	2	8	25	0	0	—	2	0	0	0	4	3	0.7	0.0	0.0	1.3

1961/62 N.B.A. — PLAYOFFS

Use Name	Pos	Hgt	Wgt	Age	G	Min	FG	FGA	%	FT	FTA	%	Reb	Ass	PF	DQ	Points	Min	Reb	Ass	PF	Points
					TOTAL													PER GAME				
BOSTON CELTICS	**RED AUERBACH**				defeated Philadelphia 4-3; H117-89, 106-113, H129-114, 106-110, H119-104, 99-109, H109-107																	
					defeated Los Angeles 4-3; H122-108, H122-129, 115-117, 115-103, H121-126, 119-105, H110-107(OT)																	
Satch Sanders	F	6'6	210	23	14	439	56	130	43	29	36	81	115	14	**65**	4	141	31	8.2	1.0	4.6	10.1
Tom Heinsohn	F-C	6'5	220	27	14	445	116	291	40	58	76	76	115	34	58	4	290	32	8.2	2.4	4.1	20.7
Bill Russell	C	6'10	220	27	14	**672**	116	253	46	82	113	73	**370**	70	49	0	314	**48**	26.4	5.0	3.5	22.4
Sam Jones	G-F	6'4	205	28	14	504	123	277	44	42	60	70	101	44	30	0	288	36	7.2	3.1	2.1	20.6
Bob Cousy	G	6'1	180	33	14	474	86	241	36	52	76	68	64	**123**	43	0	224	34	4.6	8.8	3.1	16.0
K. C. Jones	G	6'1	202	29	14	329	44	102	43	38	53	72	56	55	50	1	126	24	4.0	3.9	3.6	9.0
Jim Loscutoff	F	6'5	230	31	14	212	31	86	36	4	10	40	59	6	59	**5**	66	15	4.2	0.4	4.2	4.7
Frank Ramsey	F-G	6'3	205	30	13	210	39	104	38	41	45	**91**	38	10	38	3	119	16	2.9	0.8	2.9	9.2
Carl Braun	G	6'5	185	34	6	42	11	28	39	3	4	75	7	2	3	0	25	7	1.2	0.3	0.5	4.2
Gary Phillips	G	6'3	189	22	6	32	1	16	6	8	11	73	3	1	6	0	10	5	0.5	0.2	1.0	1.7
Gene Guarilia	F	6'5	220	24	5	26	2	8	25	2	5	40	4	1	6	0	6	5	0.8	0.2	1.2	1.2
LOS ANGELES LAKERS	**FRED SCHAUS**				defeated Detroit 4-2; H132-108, H127-112, 111-106, 117-118, H125-132, 123-117																	
					lost to Boston 3-4; 108-122, 129-122, H117-115, H103-115, 126-121, H105-119, 107-110(OT)																	
Rudy LaRusso	F	6'7	220	24	13	461	57	156	37	69	91	76	118	22	51	3	183	35	9.1	1.7	3.9	14.1
Elgin Baylor	F	6'5	225	27	13	571	**186**	**425**	44	**130**	**168**	77	230	47	45	1	**502**	44	17.7	3.6	3.5	**38.6**
Jim Krebs	C	6'8	230	26	11	327	30	90	33	22	26	85	102	21	50	4	82	30	9.3	1.9	4.5	7.5
Jerry West	G	6'3	175	23	13	557	144	310	46	121	150	81	88	57	38	0	409	43	6.8	4.4	2.9	31.5
Frank Selvy	G	6'3	185	29	13	478	66	152	43	33	39	85	73	65	34	0	165	37	5.6	5.0	2.6	12.7
Ray Felix	C	6'11	225	31	13	242	29	59	49	26	38	68	77	7	39	1	84	19	5.9	0.5	3.0	6.5
Tom Hawkins	F	6'5	210	25	13	203	22	61	36	10	24	42	66	19	34	0	54	16	5.1	1.5	2.6	4.2
Rod Hundley	G	6'4	190	27	12	187	7	25	28	9	12	75	18	32	27	0	23	16	1.5	2.7	2.3	1.9
Howie Jolliff	C-F	6'7	218	23	9	77	2	9	22	8	8	100	28	7	17	1	12	9	3.1	0.8	1.9	1.3
Bob McNeill	G	6'1	180	23	5	20	4	7	57	1	2	50	6	5	6	0	9	4	1.2	1.0	1.2	1.8
Wayne Yates	C	6'8	235	24	4	12	3	8	38	1	2	50	5	1	2	0	7	3	1.3	0.3	0.5	1.8
PHILADELPHIA WARRIORS	**FRANK McGUIRE**				defeated Syracuse 3-2; H110-103, 97-82, H100-101, 99-106, H121-104																	
					lost to Boston 3-4; 89-117, H113-106, 114-129, H110-106, 104-119, H109-99, 107-109																	
Paul Arizin	F	6'4	200	33	12	459	95	253	38	88	102	86	80	26	44	1	278	38	6.7	2.2	3.7	23.2
Tom Meschery	F	6'6	215	23	12	508	89	224	40	63	73	86	138	32	48	2	241	42	11.5	2.7	4.0	20.1
Wilt Chamberlain	C	7'1	260	25	12	576	162	347	47	96	151	64	319	37	27	0	420	**48**	**26.6**	3.1	2.3	35.0
Tom Gola	G-F	6'6	208	28	9	316	19	70	27	19	25	76	74	24	38	2	57	35	8.2	2.7	4.2	6.3
Guy Rodgers	G	6'	185	26	12	482	52	145	36	35	55	64	71	88	57	3	139	40	5.9	7.3	4.8	11.6
Al Attles	G	6'2	175	25	12	338	28	76	37	17	31	55	55	27	54	4	73	28	4.6	2.3	4.5	6.1
Ed Conlin	C	6'5	200	28	11	86	9	45	20	8	13	62	20	3	14	0	26	8	1.8	0.3	1.3	2.4
York Larese	G	6'4	183	23	9	78	11	35	31	8	12	67	19	5	14	0	30	9	2.1	0.6	1.6	3.3
Ted Luckenbill	F	6'6	205	22	4	17	0	5	0	2	5	40	3	1	3	0	2	4	0.8	0.3	0.8	0.5
Frank Radovich	F	6'8	235	23	2	12	1	6	17	2	4	50	3	0	2	0	4	6	1.5	0.0	1.0	2.0
Joe Ruklick	F	6'9	220	23	2	8	1	4	25	1	2	50	4	0	2	0	3	4	2.0	0.0	1.0	1.5
DETROIT PISTONS	**DICK McGUIRE**				defeated Cincinnati 3-1; H123-122, 107-129, H118-107, 112-111																	
					lost to Los Angeles 2-4; 108-132, 112-127, H106-111, H118-117, 132-125, H117-123																	
Bailey Howell	F	6'7	215	24	10	378	69	163	42	62	75	83	96	23	48	3	200	38	9.6	2.3	4.8	20.0
Ray Scott	F-C	6'9	215	23	10	400	69	170	41	35	67	52	145	43	39	2	173	40	14.5	4.3	3.9	17.3
Walter Dukes	C	7'	220	31	10	342	39	91	43	46	61	75	138	24	52	**5**	124	34	13.8	2.4	**5.2**	12.4
Oon Ohl	G	6'3	190	25	8	317	71	171	42	22	27	81	27	25	22	0	164	40	3.4	3.1	2.8	20.5
Gene Shue	G	6'2	175	30	10	363	62	151	41	37	48	77	30	49	29	0	161	36	3.0	4.9	2.9	16.1
Willie Jones	G	6'3	185	25	9	180	43	101	43	13	14	93	23	31	27	2	99	20	2.6	3.4	3.0	11.0
Bob Ferry	C-F	6'8	230	24	9	156	37	81	46	26	43	60	41	13	20	0	100	17	4.6	1.4	2.2	11.1
Johnny Egan	G	5'11	180	22	5	106	29	62	47	10	10	100	9	16	8	0	68	21	1.8	3.2	1.6	13.6
Jackie Moreland	F	6'7	215	23	7	96	17	33	52	4	7	57	24	7	22	0	38	14	3.4	1.0	3.1	5.4
George Lee	F	6'4	200	25	6	50	10	20	50	6	7	86	8	1	6	0	26	8	1.3	0.2	1.0	4.3
SYRACUSE NATIONALS	**ALEX HANNUM**				lost to Philadelphia 2-3; 103-110, H82-97, 101-100, H106-99, 104-121																	
Dave Gambee	F	6'6	225	24	5	170	17	54	31	22	25	88	45	4	22	1	56	34	9.0	0.8	4.4	11.2
Lee Shaffer	F	6'7	220	22	5	174	35	99	35	24	31	77	55	7	17	0	94	35	11.0	1.4	3.4	18.8
Johnny Kerr	C	6'9	230	29	5	193	41	109	38	6	8	75	80	10	15	0	88	39	16.0	2.0	3.0	17.6
Al Bianchi	G	6'3	185	29	5	184	27	69	39	17	20	85	26	18	17	0	71	37	5.2	3.6	3.4	14.2
Larry Costello	G	6'1	188	30	5	167	22	51	43	29	33	88	16	28	21	0	73	33	3.2	5.6	4.2	14.6
Paul Neumann	G	6'1	175	23	5	124	12	29	41	4	6	67	17	14	13	0	28	25	3.4	2.8	2.6	5.6
Dolph Schayes	F-C	6'8	220	33	5	95	24	66	36	9	13	69	35	5	21	0	57	19	7.0	1.0	4.2	11.4
Joe Roberts	F	6'6	215	25	4	64	8	22	36	10	14	71	28	0	9	0	26	16	7.0	0.0	2.3	6.5
Joe Graboski	F-C	6'8	230	31	4	24	1	7	14	1	1	100	4	0	3	0	3	6	1.0	0.0	0.8	0.8
Hal Greer	G	6'3	176	25	1	5	0	0	—	0	0	—	0	0	1	0	0	5	0.0	0.0	1.0	0.0
Swede Holbrook-injury																						
CINCINNATI ROYALS	**CHARLIE WOLF**				lost to Detroit 1-3; 122-123, H129-107, 107-118, H111-112																	
Jack Twyman	F	6'6	210	27	4	149	34	78	44	8	8	100	29	12	18	0	76	37	7.3	3.0	4.5	19.0
Bob Boozer	F	6'8	215	24	4	143	32	57	56	9	12	75	42	3	16	0	73	36	10.5	0.8	4.0	18.3
Wayne Embry	C	6'8	245	24	4	128	14	30	47	28	36	78	45	8	17	0	56	32	11.3	2.0	4.3	14.0
Oscar Robertson	G-F	6'5	205	23	4	185	42	81	52	31	39	79	44	44	18	1	115	46	11.0	**11.0**	4.5	28.8
Arlen Bockhorn	G	6'4	200	28	4	157	27	62	44	14	16	88	19	20	11	0	68	39	4.8	5.0	2.8	17.0
Hub Reed	C-F	6'9	230	25	4	69	9	21	43	3	4	75	20	5	9	0	21	17	5.0	1.3	2.3	5.3
Joe Buckhalter	F	6'7	210	24	4	60	16	38	42	2	3	67	22	4	14	0	34	15	5.5	1.0	3.5	8.5
Adrian Smith	G	6'1	180	25	4	53	8	19	42	5	5	100	5	3	2	0	21	13	1.3	0.8	0.5	5.3
Bob Wiesenhahn	F	6'4	215	23	2	6	1	4	25	1	1	100	2	0	0	0	3	3	1.0	0.0	0.0	1.5
Dave Zeller	G	6'1	175	22	2	5	1	2	50	0	0	—	1	1	0	0	2	3	0.5	0.5	0.0	1.0
Bevo Nordmann	C	6'10	262	22	2	5	0	1	0	0	0	—	2	0	1	0	0	3	1.0	1.0	0.5	0.0

1961/62 N.B.A. TEAM STATISTICS

Team	Regular Season									Average Points			Playoffs									Average Points		
	G	FG	FGA	%	FT	FTA	%	Reb.	Ass.	For	Agnst.	Diff.	G	FG	FGA	%	FT	FTA	%	Reb.	Ass.	For	Agnst.	Diff.
EASTERN DIVISION																								
Boston	80	3855	**9109**	42	1977	2715	73	**6080**	2049	121.1	**111.9**	**+9.2**	14	625	**1536**	41	359	489	73	934	**360**	114.9	110.1	**+4.8**
Philadelphia	80	**3917**	8929	44	2201	3207	69	5939	2073	**125.4**	122.7	+2.7	12	467	1211	39	339	473	72	883	243	106.1	106.8	-0.7
Syracuse	80	3706	8875	42	2246	2880	**78**	5764	1791	120.7	118.4	+2.3	5	187	506	37	122	151	81	347	86	99.2	**105.4**	-6.2
New York	80	3638	8696	42	1911	2693	71	5440	1765	114.8	119.7	-4.9												
WESTERN DIVISION																								
Los Angeles	80	3552	8315	43	2378	**3240**	73	5600	1878	118.5	116.3	+2.2	13	550	1302	42	**430**	**560**	77	**914**	283	117.7	116.7	+1.0
Cincinnati	80	3806	8414	**45**	2233	2969	75	5665	**2154**	123.1	121.3	+1.8	4	**184**	393	**47**	101	124	**81**	254	100	117.3	115.0	+2.3
Detroit	80	3472	8366	42	2290	3142	73	5823	1723	115.4	117.1	-1.7	10	446	1043	43	261	359	73	635	232	115.3	120.4	-5.1
St. Louis	80	3641	8461	43	2226	2939	76	5557	1996	118.9	122.1	-3.2												
Chicago	80	3461	8405	41	1952	2901	67	5547	1802	110.9	119.4	-8.5												

1961/62 N.B.A. STANDINGS

Team	W	L	Pct.	GB	Record against playoff teams W	L	Pct.	Record against non - playoff teams W	L	Pct.	HOME W	L	Pct.	ROAD W	L	Pct.	NEUTRAL W	L	Pct.
EASTERN DIVISION																			
Boston Celtics	**60**	20	**.750**	—	**36**	13	**.735**	**24**	7	.774	23	5	.821	**26**	12	**.684**	11	3	.786
Philadelphia Warriors	49	31	.613	11	25	24	.510	**24**	7	.774	18	11	.621	18	19	.486	**13**	1	**.929**
Syracuse Nationals	41	39	.513	19	19	31	.380	22	8	.733	18	10	.643	11	19	.367	12	10	.545
New York Knickerbockers	29	51	.363	31	21	41	.339	8	10	.444	19	14	.576	2	23	.080	8	14	.364
WESTERN DIVISION																			
Los Angeles Lakers	54	26	.675	—	30	20	.600	24	6	**.800**	**26**	5	**.839**	18	13	.581	10	8	.556
Cincinnati Royals	43	37	.538	11	20	29	.408	23	8	.742	18	13	.581	14	16	.467	11	8	.579
Detroit Pistons	37	43	.463	17	18	31	.367	19	**12**	.613	16	14	.533	8	17	.320	13	12	.520
St. Louis Hawks	29	51	.363	25	19	43	.306	10	8	.556	19	16	.543	7	**27**	.259	3	8	.273
Chicago Packers	18	**62**	.225	36	8	**52**	.133	10	10	.500	9	19	.321	3	20	.130	6	**23**	.207

1961/62 INDIVIDUAL LEADERS

SCORING
(Minimum 65 Games Played)

Name	Team	G	FG	FT	Pts.	Avg.
Chamberlain	Phi	80	1597	835	4029	50.4
Bellamy	Chi	79	973	549	2495	31.6
Pettit	StL	78	867	695	2429	31.1
West	LA	75	799	712	2310	30.8
Robertson	Cin	79	866	700	2432	30.8
Guerin	NY	78	839	625	2303	29.5
Naulls	NY	75	747	383	1877	25.0
Hagan	StL	77	701	362	1764	22.9
Twyman	Cin	80	739	353	1831	22.9
Greer	Syr	71	644	331	1619	22.8

FIELD GOAL PERCENTAGE
(Minimum 200 Field Goals)

Name	Team	FG	FGA	Pct.
Bellamy	Chi	973	1875	.519
Chamberlain	Phi	1597	3159	.506
Twyman	Cin	739	1542	.479
Robertson	Cin	860	1810	.478
Attles	Phi	343	724	.474
Foust	StL	204	433	.471
Lovellette	StL	341	724	.471
Hagan	StL	701	1490	.470
Embry	Cin	564	1210	.466
LaRusso	LA	516	1108	.466

FREE THROW PERCENTAGE
(Minimum 200 Free Throws)

Name	Team	FT	FTA	Pct.
Schayes	Syr	286	319	.897
Naulls	NY	383	455	.842
Costello	Syr	247	295	.837
Ramsey	Bos	334	405	.825
Hagan	StL	362	439	.825
Meschery	Phi	216	262	.824
Guerin	NY	625	762	.820
Greer	Syr	331	404	.819
Heinsohn	Bos	358	437	.819
S. Jones	Bos	243	297	.818

PERSONAL FOULS

Name	Team	PF
Meschery	Phi	330
Dukes	Det	327
Twyman	Cin	323
Howell	Det	317
Rodgers	Phi	312

GAMES DISQUALIFIED

Name	Team	Disq
Dukes	Det	20
Arizin	Phi	18
Gola	Phi	16
Meschery	Phi	15
Rodgers	Phi	12

REBOUNDS PER GAME
(Minimum 65 Games Played)

Name	Team	G	Reb.	Avg.
Chamberlain	Phi	80	2052	25.7
Russell	Bos	76	1790	23.6
Bellamy	Chi	79	1500	19.0
Pettit	StL	78	1459	18.7
Kerr	Syr	80	1176	14.7
Green	NY	80	1066	13.3
Embry	Cin	75	977	13.0
Howell	Det	79	996	12.6
Robertson	Cin	79	985	12.5
Naulls	NY	75	867	11.6

ASSISTS PER GAME
(Minimum 65 Games Played)

Name	Team	G	Ass.	Avg.
Robertson	Cin	79	899	11.4
Rodgers	Phi	80	643	8.0
Cousy	Bos	75	584	7.8
Guerin	NY	78	539	6.9
Shue	Det	80	465	5.8
Leonard	Chi	70	378	5.4
West	LA	75	402	5.4
Selvy	LA	79	381	4.8
Hagan	StL	77	370	4.8
Bockhorn	Cin	80	366	4.6

MINUTES PLAYED

Name	Team	Min.
Chamberlain	Phi	3882
Robertson	Cin	3503
Russell	Bos	3433
Guerin	NY	3346
Bellamy	Chi	3344

1962-63 N.B.A.

Goodbye Philadelphia

Pro basketball had flourished in Philadelphia long before the N.B.A. was born. Strong leagues had operated in the area before World War I, and the Philadelphia Sphas had won respect as one of the strongest pro teams in the years between the World Wars. The Philadelphia Warriors joined the B.A.A. at its start in 1946, and had competed in the N.B.A. ever since its creation in 1949. The Warriors had produced Joe Fulks, Paul Arizin, and Wilt Chamberlain and two championships—one in 1947 and another in 1956. But now the Warriors were leaving, and Philadelphia no longer had a professional basketball team. Owner Eddie Gottlieb, who had run the Sphas before starting the Warriors, sold his club to a San Francisco group who moved it to that city. So now pro basketball had joined baseball and pro football in posting bases in both Los Angeles and San Francisco. The Warriors now lined up in the Western Division, with Cincinnati shifting over to take their place in the East.

While the Warriors headed West, the rival leagues, the A.B.L., headed toward oblivion. After stumbling through a debt-ridden first year, the A.B.L. began its new season with only six clubs; many of the better players had left to sign with N.B.A. teams . The only bright spot for the A.B.L. was the signing of All-American forward Jerry Lucas of Ohio State by the Cleveland Pipers, but even that turned to dust as the Pipers were financially unable to get a team on the floor. Lucas sat out the entire basketball season, and the rest of the A.B.L. joined him on the sidelines on New Year's Eve, when the league gave up the fight and collapsed, a failure at challenging the N.B.A. for a portion of the pro basketball dollar. Although some of the players caught on with N.B.A. clubs, most of them returned to minor league ball or civilian pursuits.

Dick Barnett, who had played in the A.B.L. last year, helped keep the Los Angeles Lakers atop the Western Division. Barnett's keen jump shot complemented the offensive power of Elgin Baylor and Jerry West, and became even more important when West missed time with injuries. The Lakers were strong everywhere but at center, where veteran Jim Krebs and rookies Leroy Ellis and Gene Wiley acted as stopgaps. But even without the sort of imposing center who could rival Bill Russell and Wilt Chamberlain, the Lakers repeated as the first-place finisher in the West.

The St. Louis Hawks regrouped from last year's disastrous campaign and finished second to the Lakers, five games back. New coach Harry Gallatin retained only Bob Pettit and Cliff Hagan from the squad that finished the 1961-62 campaign. Rookie Zelmo Beaty and veteran Phil Jordon, picked up from New York, filled the center spot left vacant with Clyde Lovellette's sale to Boston. Lenny Wilkins returned from military service to quarterback the club from the backcourt, and A.B.L. expatriot John Barnhill and rookie Chico Vaughn filled the other guard spot. Gallatin brought in three new forwards in veteran Woody Sauldsberry, who came over from the Chicago club in a mid-season trade, and Mike Farmer and Bill Bridges, both of whom came from the A.B.L. Another A.B.L. product, center Gene Tormohlen, joined the Hawks near the end of the season. But with all the personnel changes, Pettit was still the ace, the leading scorer and rebounder.

After the Hawks, the other three Western clubs finished under .500. The Detroit Pistons captured third place with a big team. Bailey Howell, Bob Ferry, and Ray Scott gave the Pistons a lot of beef up front and forced rookie Dave DeBusschere, a natural forward, to spend some of his court time playing guard alongside Don Ohl. A local favorite from the University of Detroit, DeBusschere also drew a salary as a pitcher with the Chicago White Sox.

Behind the Pistons, in fourth place, were the disappointing Warriors . Although Wilt Chamberlain again led the N.B.A. with a 44.8 average, opposing teams found success in stopping Wilt's teammates. Paul Arizin had retired rather than go to San Francisco, and Tom Gola was traded to New York early in the season for Willie Naulls and Ken Sears. But trades could not shore up the Warriors, and they fell out of the playoffs with a 31-49 record, an inauspicious start on the West Coast. The Chicago Zephyrs, with a new nickname but few new fans, had two high scorers in Walt Bellamy and rookie Terry Dischinger, but again finished in last place.

Although the Warriors suffered through a bad season, the Boston Celtics had viewed their move to the West as the removal of their strongest rival. But regardless of the Warriors the Celtics were stronger than ever, stocking perhaps their best squad in history. Boston's one dim note was Bob Cousy. Cousy, the N.B.A.'s most popular player through the years, announced that this would be his last season. Although he played less than usual, Cousy's floor play stood up to the highest standards of his career and when the aging star was not playing, shooter Sam Jones and ball-hawk K.C. Jones kept the Boston backcourt in fine shape. Bill Russell was still the unsurpassed master at defense and clutch rebounding at center, and he had backup help from veteran Clyde Lovellette, who had been picked up from St. Louis. At forward, Tom Heinsohn was the offensive ace, Satch Sanders the defensive star, and Jim Loscutoff furnished muscle when needed from the bench. For swingmen, the Celtics had the game's best in veteran Frank Ramsey and rookie John Havlicek. Both played guard and forward, and both could shoot and run.

Behind the Celtics came the Syracuse Nats, a club which on appearances had no right to finish at 48-32. Veteran star Dolph Schayes, at 34, was on his last legs as a player and the team lacked size. But the Nats hustled their way into the playoffs, followed in the third spot by the Cincinnati Royals. The New York Knicks, as usual, finished fourth and out of the playoffs.

In the playoffs, the Celtics and Lakers went through a seven-game divisional series, with the Celtics downing Cincinnati and the Lakers beating back the Hawks. The Lakers had come within one shot of dethroning the Celtics last season, but this year's title was never in doubt. The Celtics defeated the Lakers in six games to win their fifth straight championship, the sixth in the last seven years.

Use Name	Pos	Hgt	Wgt	Age	TOTAL													PER GAME				
					G	Min	FG	FGA	%	FT	FTA	%	Reb	Ass	PF	DQ	Points	Min	Reb	Ass	PF	Points
1962/63 N.B.A. - EASTERN DIVISION																						
BOSTON CELTICS	**58-22 .725**				**RED AUERBACH**																	
Tom Heinsohn	F	6'7	220	28	76	2004	550	1300	42	340	407	84	569	95	270	4	1440	26	7.5	1.3	3.6	18.9
Satch Sanders	F	6'6	210	24	80	2148	339	744	46	186	252	74	576	95	262	5	864	27	7.2	1.2	3.3	10.8
Bill Russell	C	6'10	220	28	78	3500	511	1182	43	287	517	56	1843	348	189	1	1309	45	23.6	4.5	2.4	16.8
Sam Jones	G	6'4	205	29	76	2323	621	1305	48	257	324	79	396	241	162	1	1499	31	5.2	3.2	2.1	19.7
Bob Cousy	G	6'1	180	34	76	1975	392	988	40	219	298	73	193	515	175	0	1003	26	2.5	6.8	2.3	13.2
John Havlicek	F-G	6'5	205	22	80	2200	483	1085	45	174	239	73	534	179	189	2	1140	28	6.7	2.2	2.4	14.3
K. C. Jones	G	6'1	202	30	79	1945	230	591	39	112	177	63	263	317	221	3	572	25	3.3	4.0	2.8	7.2
Frank Ramsey	F-G	6'3	205	31	77	1541	284	743	38	271	332	82	288	95	259	13	839	20	3.7	1.2	3.4	10.9
Jim Loscutoff	F	6'5	230	32	63	607	94	251	37	22	42	52	157	25	126	1	210	10	2.5	0.4	2.0	3.3
Clyde Lovellette	C-F	6'9	240	33	61	568	161	376	43	73	98	74	177	27	137	0	395	9	2.9	0.4	2.2	6.5
Dan Swartz	F	6'4	215	28	39	335	57	150	38	61	72	85	88	21	92	0	175	9	2.3	0.5	2.4	4.5
Gene Guarilia	F	6'5	220	25	11	83	11	38	29	4	11	36	14	2	5	0	26	8	1.3	0.2	0.5	2.4
SYRACUSE NATIONALS	**48-32 .600**				**ALEX HANNUM**																	
Chet Walker	F	6'6	200	22	78	1992	352	751	47	253	362	70	561	83	220	3	957	26	7.2	1.1	2.8	12.3
Lee Shaffer	F	6'7	220	23	80	2392	597	1393	43	294	375	78	524	97	249	5	1488	30	6.6	1.2	3.1	18.6
Johnny Kerr	C	6'9	230	30	80	2561	507	1069	47	241	320	75	1039	214	208	3	1255	32	13.0	2.7	2.6	15.7
Hal Greer	G	6'3	176	26	80	2631	600	1293	46	362	434	83	457	275	286	4	1562	33	5.7	3.4	3.6	19.5
Larry Costello	G	6'1	188	31	78	2066	285	660	43	288	327	88	237	334	263	4	858	26	3.0	4.3	3.4	11.0
Paul Neumann	G	6'1	175	24	80	1581	237	503	47	181	222	82	200	227	221	5	655	20	2.5	2.8	2.8	8.2
Dolph Schayes (knee injury)	F-C	6'8	220	34	66	1438	223	575	39	181	206	88	375	175	177	2	627	22	5.7	2.7	2.7	9.5
Len Chappell	C	6'8	240	21	80	1241	281	604	47	148	238	62	461	56	171	1	710	16	5.8	0.7	2.1	8.9
Dave Gambee (broken foot)	F	6'6	225	25	60	1234	235	537	44	199	238	84	289	48	190	2	669	21	4.8	0.8	3.2	11.2
Al Bianchi (broken hand)	G	6'3	185	30	61	1159	202	476	42	120	164	73	134	170	165	2	524	19	2.2	2.8	2.7	8.6
Joe Roberts	F	6'6	215	26	33	466	73	196	37	35	51	69	155	16	66	1	181	14	4.7	0.5	2.0	5.5
Porter Meriwether	G	6'2	180	22	31	268	48	122	39	23	33	70	29	43	19	0	119	9	0.9	1.4	0.6	3.8
Ben Warley	F	6'5	200	26	26	206	50	111	45	25	35	71	86	4	42	1	125	8	3.3	0.2	1.6	4.8
Connie Dierking-voluntarily retired																						
CINCINNATI ROYALS	**42-38 .525**				**CHARLIE WOLF**																	
Jack Twyman	F	6'6	215	28	80	2623	641	1335	48	304	375	81	598	214	286	7	1586	33	7.5	2.7	3.6	19.8
Bob Boozer	F	6'8	215	25	79	2488	440	992	44	252	353	71	878	102	299	8	1132	31	11.1	1.3	3.8	14.3
Wayne Embry	C	6'8	250	25	76	2511	534	1165	46	343	514	67	936	177	286	7	1411	33	12.3	2.3	3.8	18.6
Oscar Robertson	G-F	6'5	205	24	80	3521	825	1593	52	614	758	81	835	758	293	1	2264	44	10.4	9.5	3.7	28.3
Arlen Bockhorn	G	6'4	200	29	80	2612	375	954	39	183	242	76	322	261	260	6	933	33	4.0	3.3	3.3	11.7
Tom Hawkins	F	6'5	210	26	79	1721	299	635	47	147	241	61	543	100	197	2	745	22	6.9	1.3	2.5	9.4
Adrian Smith	G	6'1	180	26	79	1522	241	544	44	223	275	81	174	141	157	1	705	19	2.2	1.8	2.0	8.9
Hub Reed	C	6'9	230	26	80	1299	199	427	47	74	98	76	398	83	261	7	472	16	5.0	1.0	3.3	5.9
Dave Piontek	F	6'6	240	28	48	457	60	158	38	10	16	63	96	26	67	0	130	10	2.0	0.5	1.4	2.7
Bud Olsen	F	6'8	220	22	52	373	43	133	32	27	39	69	105	42	78	0	113	7	2.0	0.8	1.5	2.2
Dan Tieman	G	6'	185	22	29	176	15	57	26	4	10	40	22	27	18	0	34	6	0.8	0.9	0.6	1.2
Joe Buckhalter	F	6'7	210	25	2	12	0	5	0	2	2	100	3	0	1	0	2	6	1.5	0.0	0.5	1.0
NEW YORK KNICKERBOCKERS	**21-59 .263**				**EDDIE DONOVAN**																	
Tom Gola (21g. SF)	F-G	6'6	208	29	73	2670	363	791	46	170	219	78	517	298	295	9	896	37	7.1	4.1	4.0	12.3
Johnny Green	F-C	6'5	200	29	80	2553	582	1261	46	280	439	64	964	152	243	5	1444	32	12.1	1.9	3.0	18.1
Gene Conley (broken finger)	C	6'8	255	32	70	1544	254	651	39	122	186	66	469	70	263	10	630	22	6.7	1.0	3.8	9.0
Richie Guerin	G	6'4	195	30	79	2712	596	1380	43	509	600	85	331	348	228	2	1701	34	4.2	4.4	2.9	21.5
Gene Shue	G	6'2	175	31	78	2288	354	894	40	208	302	69	191	259	171	0	916	29	2.4	3.3	2.2	11.7
Dave Budd	F	6'6	210	24	78	1725	294	596	49	151	202	75	395	87	204	3	739	22	5.1	1.1	2.6	9.5
Al Butler	G	6'2	175	24	74	1488	297	676	44	144	187	77	170	156	145	3	738	20	2.3	2.1	2.0	10.0
Paul Hogue (illness)	C	6'9	240	22	50	1340	152	419	36	79	174	45	430	42	220	12	383	27	8.6	0.8	4.4	7.7
Donnie Butcher	G	6'3	200	26	68	1193	172	424	41	131	194	68	180	138	164	1	475	18	2.6	2.0	2.4	7.0
Bevo Nordmann (27g. StL)	C	6'10	255	23	53	1000	156	319	49	59	122	48	316	47	156	6	371	19	6.0	0.9	2.9	7.0
John Rudometkin	F	6'6	205	22	56	572	108	307	35	73	95	77	149	30	58	0	289	10	2.7	0.5	1.0	5.2
Tom Stith	F	6'5	210	23	25	209	37	110	34	3	10	30	39	18	23	0	77	8	1.6	0.7	0.9	3.1
Jack Foley (5g. Bos, MS)	F	6'5	185	23	11	83	20	51	39	13	15	87	16	5	8	0	53	8	1.5	0.5	0.7	4.8
Cleveland Buckner	F	6'9	210	24	6	27	5	10	50	2	4	50	4	5	6	0	12	5	0.7	0.8	1.0	2.0

Use Name	Pos	Hgt	Wgt	Age	TOTAL G	Min	FG	FGA	%	FT	FTA	%	Reb	Ass	PF	DQ	Points	PER GAME Min	Reb	Ass	PF	Points

1962/63 N.B.A. — WESTERN DIVISION

Use Name	Pos	Hgt	Wgt	Age	G	Min	FG	FGA	%	FT	FTA	%	Reb	Ass	PF	DQ	Points	Min	Reb	Ass	PF	Points
LOS ANGELES LAKERS	53-27 .663				FRED SCHAUS																	
Elgin Baylor	F	6'5	225	28	80	3370	1029	2273	45	661	790	84	1146	386	226	1	2719	42	14.3	4.8	2.8	34.0
Rudy LaRusso	F	6'7	220	25	75	2505	321	761	42	282	393	72	747	187	255	5	924	33	10.0	2.5	3.4	12.3
Jim Krebs	C	6'8	230	27	79	1913	272	627	43	115	154	75	502	87	256	2	659	24	6.4	1.1	3.2	8.3
Dick Barnett	G	6'4	190	26	80	2544	547	1162	47	343	421	81	242	224	189	3	1437	32	3.0	2.8	2.4	18.0
Jerry West (leg injury)	G	6'3	175	24	55	2163	559	1213	46	371	477	78	384	307	150	1	1489	39	7.0	5.6	2.7	27.1
Frank Selvy	G	6'3	185	30	80	2369	317	747	42	192	269	71	289	281	149	0	826	30	3.6	3.5	1.9	10.3
Leroy Ellis	F-C	6'10	210	22	80	1628	222	530	42	133	202	66	518	46	194	1	577	20	6.5	0.6	2.4	7.2
Gene Wiley	C	6'10	210	25	75	1488	109	236	46	23	68	34	504	40	180	4	241	20	6.7	0.5	2.4	3.2
Rod Hundley	G	6'4	190	28	65	785	88	262	34	84	119	71	106	151	81	0	260	12	1.6	2.3	1.2	4.0
Howie Jolliff	F	6'7	218	24	28	293	15	55	27	6	9	67	62	20	49	1	36	10	2.2	0.7	1.8	1.3
Ron Horn	F	6'7	225	24	28	289	27	82	33	20	29	69	71	10	46	0	74	10	2.5	0.4	1.6	2.6
ST. LOUIS HAWKS	48-32 .600				HARRY GALLATIN																	
Woody Sauldsberry (54g. Chi, ST)	F	6'7	220	28	77	2034	366	966	38	107	163	66	447	78	241	4	839	26	5.8	1.0	3.1	10.9
Bob Pettit	F	6'9	220	30	79	3090	778	1746	45	**685**	885	77	1191	245	282	8	2241	39	15.1	3.1	3.6	28.4
Zelmo Beaty	C	6'9	235	23	80	1922	297	677	44	220	307	72	665	85	**312**	12	814	24	8.3	1.1	3.9	10.2
John Barnhill	G	6'1	180	24	77	2694	360	838	43	181	255	71	359	322	168	0	901	35	4.7	4.2	2.2	11.7
Lenny Wilkens	G	6'1	185	25	75	2569	333	834	40	222	319	70	403	381	256	6	888	34	5.4	5.1	3.4	11.8
Chico Vaughn	G	6'3	215	22	77	1845	295	708	42	188	261	72	258	252	201	3	778	24	3.4	3.3	2.6	10.1
Mike Farmer	F	6'7	215	26	80	1724	239	562	43	117	139	84	369	143	155	0	595	22	4.6	1.8	1.9	7.4
Cliff Hagan	F	6'4	210	31	79	1716	491	1055	47	244	305	80	341	193	211	2	1226	22	4.3	2.4	2.7	15.5
Phil Jordon	C	6'10	215	29	73	1420	211	527	40	56	101	55	319	103	172	3	478	19	4.4	1.4	2.4	6.5
Bob Duffy	G	6'3	185	22	42	435	66	174	38	22	39	56	39	83	42	0	154	10	0.9	2.0	1.0	3.7
Bill Bridges	F	6'6	228	23	27	374	66	160	41	32	51	63	144	23	58	0	164	14	5.3	0.9	2.1	6.1
Gene Tormohlen	C	6'9	235	25	7	47	5	10	50	2	10	20	15	5	11	0	12	7	2.1	0.7	1.6	1.7
Johnny McCarthy—knee injury, voluntarily retired																						
DETROIT PISTONS	34-46 .425				DICK McGUIRE																	
Bailey Howell	F	6'7	215	25	79	2971	637	1235	52	519	650	80	910	232	300	9	1793	38	11.5	2.9	3.8	22.7
Ray Scott	F	6'9	215	24	76	2538	460	1110	41	308	457	67	772	191	263	9	1228	33	10.2	2.5	3.5	16.2
Bob Ferry	C	6'8	230	25	79	2479	426	984	43	220	339	65	537	170	246	1	1072	31	6.8	2.2	3.1	13.6
Don Ohl	G	6'3	190	26	80	2961	636	1450	44	275	380	72	239	325	234	3	1547	37	3.0	4.1	2.9	19.3
Willie Jones	G	6'3	185	26	79	1470	305	730	42	118	164	72	233	188	207	4	728	19	2.9	2.4	2.6	9.2
Dave DeBusschere	F-G	6'6	220	22	80	2352	406	944	43	206	287	72	694	207	247	2	1018	29	8.7	2.6	3.1	12.7
Jackie Moreland	F-G	6'7	215	24	78	1516	271	622	44	145	214	68	449	114	226	5	687	19	5.8	1.5	2.9	8.8
Walter Dukes	C	7'	220	32	62	913	83	255	33	101	137	74	360	55	183	5	267	15	5.8	0.9	3.0	4.3
Kevin Loughery	G	6'3	190	22	57	845	146	397	37	71	100	71	109	104	135	1	363	15	1.9	1.8	2.4	6.4
Johnny Egan	G	5'11	180	23	46	752	110	296	37	53	69	77	59	114	70	0	273	16	1.3	2.5	1.5	5.9
Darrall Imhoff	C	6'10	220	24	45	458	48	153	31	24	50	48	155	28	66	1	120	10	3.4	0.6	1.5	2.7
Danny Doyle	F	6'8	215	22	4	25	6	12	50	4	5	80	8	3	4	0	16	6	2.0	0.8	1.0	4.0
SAN FRANCISCO WARRIORS	31-49 .388				BOB FEERICK																	
Willie Naulls (23g. NY)	F	6'6	225	28	70	1901	370	887	42	166	207	80	515	102	205	3	906	27	7.4	1.5	2.9	12.9
Tom Meschery (broken arm, MS)	F	6'6	215	24	64	2245	397	935	42	228	313	73	624	104	249	11	1022	35	9.8	1.6	3.9	16.0
Wilt Chamberlain	C	7'1	265	26	80	**3806**	**1463**	**2770**	**53**	660	**1113**	59	**1946**	275	136	0	**3586**	**48**	**24.3**	3.4	1.7	**44.8**
Al Attles	G	6'2	175	26	71	1878	301	630	48	133	206	65	205	184	253	7	735	26	2.9	2.6	3.6	10.4
Guy Rodgers	G	6'	185	27	79	3249	445	1150	39	208	286	73	394	**825**	296	7	1098	41	5.0	**10.4**	3.7	13.9
Gary Phillips	G	6'3	189	23	75	1801	256	643	40	97	152	64	225	137	185	7	609	24	3.0	1.8	2.5	8.1
Wayne Hightower	F-C	6'9	192	22	66	1387	192	543	35	105	157	67	354	51	181	5	489	21	5.4	0.8	2.7	7.4
George Lee (BROKEN FINGER)	F	6'4	200	26	64	1192	149	394	38	152	193	79	217	64	113	0	450	19	3.4	1.0	1.8	7.0
Kenny Sears (23g. NY)	F	6'9	200	29	77	1141	161	304	53	131	168	78	206	95	128	0	453	15	2.7	1.2	1.7	5.9
Howie Montgomery	F	6'5	220	22	20	364	65	153	42	14	23	61	69	21	35	1	144	18	3.5	1.1	1.8	7.2
Hubie White	G	6'4	205	22	29	271	40	111	36	12	18	67	35	28	47	0	92	9	1.2	1.0	1.6	3.2
Tom Luckenbill	F	6'6	205	23	20	201	26	68	38	9	20	45	56	8	34	0	61	10	2.8	0.4	1.7	3.1
Fred LaCour	G	6'5	210	24	16	171	28	73	38	9	16	56	24	19	27	0	65	11	1.5	1.2	1.7	4.1
Dave Fedor	F	6'6	192	22	7	27	3	10	30	0	1	0	6	1	4	0	6	4	0.9	0.1	0.6	0.9
Dave Gunther	F	6'7	220	25	1	5	1	2	50	0	0	—	3	3	1	0	2	5	3.0	3.0	1.0	2.0
CHICAGO ZEPHYRS	25-55 .313				JACK McMAHON (12-26 .316), BOB LEONARD (13-29 .310)																	
Terry Dischinger (CO)	F-G	6'7	189	22	57	2294	525	1026	51	402	522	77	458	175	188	2	1452	40	8.0	3.1	3.3	25.5
Charlie Hardnett	F-C	6'8	225	24	78	1657	301	683	44	225	349	64	602	74	225	4	827	21	7.7	0.9	2.9	10.6
Walt Bellamy	C	6'11	230	23	80	3306	840	1595	53	553	821	67	1309	233	283	7	2233	41	16.4	2.9	3.5	27.9
Johnny Cox	G	6'4	180	26	73	1685	239	568	42	95	135	70	280	142	149	4	573	23	3.8	1.9	2.0	7.8
Si Green	G	6'2	190	28	73	2648	322	783	41	209	306	68	335	422	274	5	853	36	4.6	5.8	3.8	11.7
Barney Cable (29g. StL)	F	6'7	205	26	61	1200	173	380	46	62	96	65	242	82	136	0	408	20	4.0	1.3	2.2	6.7
Don Nelson	F	6'6	210	22	62	1071	129	293	44	161	221	73	279	72	136	3	419	17	4.5	1.2	2.2	6.8
Maury King	G	6'3	195	27	37	954	94	241	39	28	34	82	102	142	87	0	216	26	2.8	3.8	2.4	5.8
Bob Leonard (shoulder injury)	G	6'3	185	30	32	879	84	245	34	59	85	69	68	143	84	1	227	27	2.1	4.5	2.6	7.1
Nick Mantis (9g. StL)	G	6'3	190	27	32	684	94	244	39	27	49	55	85	83	94	0	215	21	2.7	2.6	2.9	6.7
Bill McGill	C	6'9	225	23	60	590	181	353	51	80	119	67	161	38	118	1	442	10	2.7	0.6	2.0	7.4
Mel Nowell	G	6'2	174	23	39	589	92	237	39	48	66	73	67	84	86	0	232	15	1.7	2.2	2.2	5.9
Larry Staverman	F	6'7	215	26	33	602	94	194	48	49	62	79	158	43	94	3	237	18	4.8	1.3	2.8	7.2
Al Ferrari (knee injury)	G	6'4	200	29	18	138	12	37	32	14	17	82	12	14	21	0	38	8	0.7	0.8	1.2	2.1
Ralph Wells	G	6'1	180	22	3	48	1	7	14	0	7	0	6	7	6	0	2	16	2.0	2.3	2.0	0.7
Jeff Slade	F	6'6	220	21	3	20	2	5	40	0	1	0	7	0	3	0	4	7	2.3	0.0	1.0	1.3

1962/63 N.B.A. — PLAYOFFS

BOSTON CELTICS — RED AUERBACH

defeated Cincinnati 4-3; H132-135, 125-102, H116-121, 128-110, H125-120, 99-109, H142-131
defeated Los Angeles 4-2; H117-114, H113-106, 99-119, 108-105, H119-126, 112-109

Use Name	Pos	Hgt	Wgt	Age	G	Min	FG	FGA	%	FT	FTA	%	Reb	Ass	PF	DQ	Points	Min	Reb	Ass	PF	Points
					TOTAL													PER GAME				
Tom Heinsohn	F	6'7	220	28	13	413	123	270	46	75	98	77	116	15	55	2	321	32	8.9	1.2	4.2	24.7
Satch Sanders	F	6'6	210	24	13	387	52	119	44	24	31	77	96	19	**61**	**4**	128	30	7.4	1.5	4.7	9.8
Bill Russell	C	6'9	220	28	13	**617**	96	212	45	72	109	66	**326**	66	36	0	264	47	**25.1**	5.1	2.8	20.3
Sam Jones	G	6'4	205	29	13	450	120	248	48	69	83	83	81	32	42	1	309	35	6.2	2.5	3.2	23.8
Bob Cousy	G	6'1	180	34	13	398	72	204	35	39	47	83	32	**116**	44	2	183	31	2.5	8.9	3.4	14.1
John Havlicek	F-G	6'5	205	22	11	254	56	125	45	18	27	67	53	17	28	1	130	23	4.8	1.5	2.5	11.8
Frank Ramsey	F-G	6'3	205	31	13	251	37	104	36	34	47	72	35	12	43	1	108	19	2.7	0.9	3.3	8.3
K. C. Jones	G	6'1	202	30	13	250	19	64	30	21	30	70	36	37	42	1	59	19	2.8	2.8	3.2	4.5
Jim Loscutoff	F	6'5	230	32	9	56	7	25	28	1	2	50	21	1	20	0	15	6	2.3	0.1	2.2	1.7
Clyde Lovellette	F-C	6'9	240	33	6	40	7	26	27	4	6	67	5	1	13	0	18	7	0.8	0.2	2.2	3.0
Dan Swartz	F	6'4	215	28	1	4	0	0	—	0	0	—	0	0	0	0	0	4	0.0	0.0	0.0	0.0

LOS ANGELES LAKERS — FRED SCHAUS

defeated St. Louis 4-3; H112-104, H101-99, 112-125, 114-124, H123-100, 113-121, H115-100
lost to Boston 2-4; 114-117, 106-113, H119-99, H105-108, 126-119, H109-112

Use Name	Pos	Hgt	Wgt	Age	G	Min	FG	FGA	%	FT	FTA	%	Reb	Ass	PF	DQ	Points	Min	Reb	Ass	PF	Points
Elgin Baylor	F	6'5	225	28	13	562	**160**	**362**	44	104	126	83	177	58	48	0	**424**	43	13.6	4.5	3.7	**32.6**
Rudy LaRusso	F	6'7	220	25	13	465	65	154	42	57	75	76	127	28	58	2	187	36	9.8	2.2	4.5	14.4
Gene Wiley (broken hand)	C	6'10	210	25	9	278	14	35	40	2	15	13	97	11	29	1	30	31	10.8	1.2	3.2	3.3
Dick Barnett	G-F	6'4	190	26	13	370	71	151	47	77	97	79	38	21	35	0	219	28	2.9	1.6	2.7	16.8
Jerry West	G	6'3	175	24	13	538	144	286	50	74	100	74	106	61	34	0	362	41	8.2	4.7	2.6	27.8
Frank Selvy	G	6'3	185	30	13	317	32	81	40	39	48	81	45	36	36	0	103	24	3.5	2.8	2.8	7.9
Leroy Ellis	F-C	6'10	210	22	13	302	27	53	**51**	27	33	82	85	13	35	0	81	23	6.5	1.0	2.7	6.2
Jim Krebs	C	6'8	230	27	13	199	16	47	34	10	15	67	40	4	49	**4**	42	15	3.1	0.3	3.8	3.2
Ron Horn	F	6'7	225	24	7	55	4	12	33	4	5	80	11	2	13	0	12	8	1.6	0.3	1.9	1.7
Rod Hundley	G	6'4	190	28	7	34	3	10	30	3	3	100	6	5	1	0	9	5	0.9	0.7	0.1	1.3

ST. LOUIS HAWKS — HARRY GALLATIN

defeated Detroit 3-1; H118-99, H122-108, 103-107, 104-100
lost to Los Angeles 3-4; 104-112, 99-101, H125-112, H124-114, 100-123, H121-113, 100-115

Use Name	Pos	Hgt	Wgt	Age	G	Min	FG	FGA	%	FT	FTA	%	Reb	Ass	PF	DQ	Points	Min	Reb	Ass	PF	Points
Cliff Hagan	F	6'4	210	31	11	255	83	179	46	37	53	70	55	34	42	**4**	203	23	5.0	3.1	3.8	18.5
Bob Pettit	F-C	6'9	220	30	11	463	119	259	46	112	144	78	166	33	34	0	350	42	15.1	3.0	3.1	31.8
Zelmo Beaty	C	6'9	235	23	11	307	43	97	44	27	36	75	84	11	47	3	113	28	7.6	1.0	4.3	10.3
John Barnhill	G	6'1	180	24	11	314	31	77	40	15	22	68	27	36	28	0	77	29	2.5	3.3	2.5	7.0
Lenny Wilkens	G	6'1	185	25	11	400	57	154	37	37	49	76	69	69	51	2	151	36	6.3	6.3	4.6	13.7
Chico Vaughn	G	6'3	215	22	11	314	46	96	48	18	27	67	31	31	46	2	110	29	2.8	2.8	4.2	10.0
Mike Farmer	F	6'7	215	26	11	262	27	74	36	13	17	76	52	27	27	0	67	24	4.7	2.5	2.5	6.1
Bill Bridges	F	6'6	228	23	11	204	41	96	43	20	27	74	86	9	31	0	102	19	7.8	0.8	2.8	9.3
Phil Jordan	C	6'10	215	29	7	82	9	24	38	3	4	75	15	7	10	0	21	12	2.1	1.0	1.4	3.0
Bob Duffy	G	6'3	185	22	5	24	6	15	40	2	2	100	3	3	3	0	14	5	0.6	0.6	0.6	2.8
Gene Tormohlen	C	6'9	235	25	5	15	4	10	40	0	0	—	5	3	6	0	8	3	1.0	0.6	1.2	1.6

Woody Sauldsberry-suspended by team   Johnny McCarthy-voluntarily retired

CINCINNATI ROYALS — CHARLIE WOLF

defeated Syracuse 3-2; 120-123, H133-115, 117-121, H125-118, 131-127(OT)
lost to Boston 3-4;135-132, H102-125, 121-116, H110-128, 120-125, H109-99, 131-142

Use Name	Pos	Hgt	Wgt	Age	G	Min	FG	FGA	%	FT	FTA	%	Reb	Ass	PF	DQ	Points	Min	Reb	Ass	PF	Points
Jack Twyman	F	6'6	215	28	12	410	92	205	45	65	77	84	98	30	47	1	249	34	8.2	2.5	3.9	20.8
Bob Boozer	F	6'8	215	25	12	381	57	138	41	45	63	71	96	18	44	0	159	32	8.0	1.5	3.7	13.3
Wayne Embry	C	6'8	250	25	12	394	76	169	45	49	74	66	162	16	55	2	201	33	13.5	1.3	4.6	16.8
Oscar Robertson	G-F	6'5	205	24	12	570	124	264	47	**133**	**154**	86	156	108	41	0	381	**48**	13.0	**9.0**	3.4	31.8
Arlen Bockhorn	G	6'4	200	29	12	407	56	135	41	23	31	74	45	39	44	1	135	34	3.8	3.3	3.7	11.3
Tom Hawkins	F	6'5	210	26	12	261	46	91	51	34	47	72	81	23	45	2	126	22	6.8	1.9	3.8	10.5
Adrian Smith	G	6'1	180	26	12	200	33	82	40	31	44	70	16	28	19	0	97	17	1.3	2.3	1.6	8.1
Hub Reed	C	6'9	230	26	12	187	28	70	40	15	18	83	64	10	38	0	71	16	5.3	0.8	3.2	5.9
Dave Piontek	F	6'6	240	28	8	68	8	17	47	4	7	57	16	1	7	0	20	9	2.0	0.1	0.9	2.5
Bud Olsen	F	6'8	220	22	5	21	7	9	78	1	5	20	10	3	4	0	15	4	2.0	0.6	0.8	3.0

SYRACUSE NATIONALS — ALEX HANNUM

lost to Cincinnati 2-3; H123-120, 115-133, H121-117, 118-125, H127-131(OT)

Use Name	Pos	Hgt	Wgt	Age	G	Min	FG	FGA	%	FT	FTA	%	Reb	Ass	PF	DQ	Points	Min	Reb	Ass	PF	Points
Chet Walker	F	6'6	200	22	5	130	27	53	**51**	22	30	73	47	9	8	0	76	26	9.4	1.8	1.6	15.2
Lee Shaffer	F	6'7	220	23	5	173	56	117	48	24	30	80	23	6	19	0	136	35	4.6	1.2	3.8	27.2
Johnny Kerr	C	6'9	230	30	5	187	26	60	43	16	21	76	75	9	12	0	68	37	15.0	1.8	2.4	13.6
Hal Greer	G	6'3	176	26	5	214	44	87	51	29	35	83	27	21	21	1	117	43	5.4	4.2	4.2	23.4
Larry Costello	G	6'1	188	31	5	134	16	37	43	19	23	83	4	23	27	2	51	27	0.8	4.6	**5.4**	10.2
Dolph Schayes	F-C	6'8	220	34	5	108	20	44	45	11	12	92	28	7	17	0	51	22	5.6	1.4	3.4	10.2
Al Bianchi	G	6'3	185	30	5	77	15	34	44	4	7	57	8	2	17	0	34	15	1.6	0.4	3.4	6.8
Dave Gambee	F	6'6	225	25	5	75	10	34	29	12	13	92	16	0	14	0	32	15	3.2	0.0	2.8	6.4
Paul Neumann	G	6'1	175	24	4	65	8	18	44	0	1	0	14	9	11	0	16	16	3.5	2.3	2.8	4.0
Len Chappell	C	6'8	240	21	4	53	4	21	19	13	16	81	18	3	7	0	21	13	4.5	0.8	1.8	5.3
Ben Warley	F	6'5	200	26	2	9	0	4	0	2	4	50	3	0	2	0	2	5	1.5	0.0	1.0	1.0

Connie Dierking-voluntarily retired

DETROIT PISTONS — DICK McGUIRE

lost to St. Louis 1-3; 99-118, 108-122, H107-103, H100-104

Use Name	Pos	Hgt	Wgt	Age	G	Min	FG	FGA	%	FT	FTA	%	Reb	Ass	PF	DQ	Points	Min	Reb	Ass	PF	Points
Bailey Howell	F	6'7	215	25	4	163	24	64	38	23	27	85	42	11	19	1	71	41	10.5	2.8	4.8	17.8
Ray Scott	F-C	6'9	215	24	4	155	27	77	35	9	13	69	48	9	19	0	63	39	12.0	2.3	4.8	15.8
Bob Ferry	C	6'8	230	25	4	143	20	45	44	8	24	33	35	11	10	0	48	36	8.8	2.8	2.5	12.0
Don Ohl	G	6'3	190	26	4	155	33	83	40	19	22	86	12	19	18	0	85	39	3.0	4.8	4.5	21.3
Willie Jones	G	6'3	185	26	4	67	11	28	39	6	8	75	7	6	10	0	28	17	1.8	1.5	2.5	7.0
Dave DeBusschere	F-G	6'6	220	22	4	159	25	59	42	30	44	68	63	6	14	1	80	40	15.8	1.5	3.5	20.0
Jackie Moreland	G-F	6'7	215	24	4	82	13	26	50	7	10	70	20	6	18	1	33	21	5.0	1.5	4.5	8.3
Kevin Loughery	G	6'3	190	22	2	26	1	10	10	1	1	100	0	4	3	0	3	13	0.0	2.0	1.5	1.5
Walter Dukes	C	7'	220	32	3	8	0	0	—	3	3	100	1	2	3	0	3	3	0.3	0.7	1.0	1.0
Darrall Imhoff	C	6'10	220	24	1	2	0	0	—	0	0	—	1	0	0	0	0	2	1.0	0.0	0.0	0.0

1962/63 N.B.A. TEAM STATISTICS

	REGULAR SEASON									AVERAGE POINTS			PLAYOFFS									AVERAGE POINTS		
Team	G	FG	FGA	%	FT	FTA	%	Reb.	Ass.	For	Agnst.	Diff.	G	FG	FGA	%	FT	FTA	%	Reb.	Ass.	For	Agnst.	Diff.
EASTERN DIVISION																								
Boston	80	3746	8779	43	2012	2777	72	5818	1960	118.8	111.6	+7.2	13	589	1397	42	357	480	74	893	31	118.1	115.9	+2.2
Syracuse	80	3690	8290	45	2350	3005	78	5516	1742	121.6	117.8	+3.8	5	226	509	44	152	192	79	296	89	120.8	125.2	-4.4
Cincinnati	80	3672	7998	46	2183	2923	75	5561	1931	119.0	117.8	+1.2	12	527	1180	45	400	520	77	815	276	121.2	122.6	-1.4
New York	80	3433	8007	43	1971	2778	71	4952	1658	110.5	117.7	-7.2												
WESTERN DIVISION																								
Los Angeles	80	3506	7948	44	2230	2931	76	5282	1739	115.5	112.4	+3.1	13	536	1191	45	396	517	77	833	239	113.0	110.5	+2.5
St. Louis	80	3355	7780	43	2056	2820	73	5096	1902	109.6	107.8	+1.8	11	466	1081	43	284	381	75	692	263	110.5	109.5	+1.0
Detroit	80	3534	8188	43	2044	2852	72	5315	1731	113.9	117.6	-3.7	4	154	392	39	106	152	70	269	74	103.5	111.8	-8.3
San Francisco	80	3805	8449	45	1870	2797	67	5359	1906	118.5	120.6	-2.1												
Chicago	80	3371	7448	45	2053	2944	70	5145	1773	109 9	113 9	-4.0												

1962/63 N.B.A. STANDINGS

					Record against playoff teams			Record against non - playoff teams			HOME			ROAD			NEUTRAL		
Team	W	L	Pct.	GB	W	L	Pct.	W	L	Pct.	W	L	Pct.	W	L	Pct.	W	L	Pct.
EASTERN DIVISION																			
Boston Celtics	58	22	.725	—	32	17	.653	26	5	.839	25	5	.833	21	16	.568	12	1	.923
Syracuse Nationals	48	32	.600	10	25	25	.500	23	7	.767	23	5	.821	13	19	.406	12	8	.600
Cincinnati Royals	42	38	.525	16	20	29	.408	22	9	.710	23	10	.697	15	19	.441	4	9	.308
New Yorh Knickerbockers	21	59	.263	37	13	49	.210	8	10	.444	12	22	.353	5	28	.152	4	9	.308
WESTERN DIVISION																			
Los Angeles Lakers	53	27	.663	—	33	17	.660	20	10	.667	27	7	.794	20	17	.541	6	3	.667
St. Louis Hawks	48	32	.600	5	26	23	.531	22	9	.710	30	7	.811	13	18	.419	5	7	.417
Detroit Pistons	34	46	.425	19	12	37	.245	22	9	.710	14	16	.467	8	19	.296	12	11	.522
San Francisco Warriors	31	49	.388	22	19	43	.306	12	6	.667	13	20	.394	11	25	.306	7	4	.636
Chicago Zephyrs	25	55	.313	28	17	43	.283	8	12	.400	17	17	.500	3	23	.115	5	15	.250

1962/63 N.B.A. INDIVIDUAL LEADERS

SCORING
(Minimum 65 Games Played)

Name	Team	G	FG	FT	Pts.	Avg.
Chamberlain	SF	80	1463	660	3586	44.8
Baylor	LA	80	1029	661	2719	34.0
Pettit	StL	79	778	685	2241	28.4
Robertson	Cin	80	825	614	2264	28.3
Bellamy	Chi	80	840	553	2233	27.9
Howell	Det	79	637	519	1793	22.7
Guerin	NY	79	596	509	1701	21.5
Twyman	Cin	80	641	304	1586	19.8
S. Jones	Bos	76	621	257	1499	19.7
Greer	Syr	80	600	362	1562	19.5

FIELD GOAL PERCENTAGE
(Minimum 210 Field Goals)

Name	Team	FG	FGA	Pct.
Chamberlain	SF	1463	2770	.528
Bellamy	Chi	840	1595	.527
Robertson	Cin	825	1593	.518
Howell	Det	637	1235	.516
Dischinger	Chi	525	1026	.512
Budd	NY	294	596	.493
Twyman	Cin	641	1335	.480
Attles	SF	301	630	.478
S. Jones	Bos	621	1305	.476
Kerr	Syr	507	1069	.474

FREE THROW PERCENTAGE
(Minimum 210 Free Throws)

Name	Team	FT	FTA	Pct.
Costello	Syr	288	327	.881
Guerin	NY	509	600	.848
Baylor	LA	661	790	.837
Heinsohn	Bos	340	407	.835
Greer	Syr	362	434	.834
Ramsey	Bos	271	332	.816
Barnett	LA	343	421	.815
Smith	Cin	223	275	.811
Twyman	Cin	304	375	.811
Robertson	Cin	614	758	.810

PERSONAL FOULS

Name	Team	PF
Beaty	StL	312
Howell	Det	300
Boozer	Cin	299
Rodgers	SF	296
Gola	SF-NY	295

GAMES DISQUALIFIED

Name	Team	Disq
Ramsey	Bos	13
Beaty	StL	12
Hogue	NY	12
Meschery	SF	11
Conley	NY	10

REBOUNDS PER GAME
(Minimum 65 Games Played)

Name	Team	G	Reb.	Avg.
Chamberlain	SF	80	1946	24.3
Russell	Bos	78	1843	23.6
Bellamy	Chi	80	1309	16.4
Pettit	StL	79	1191	15.1
Baylor	LA	80	1146	14.3
Kerr	Syr	80	1039	13.0
Embry	Cin	76	936	12.3
Green	NY	80	964	12.1
Howell	Det	79	910	11.5
Boozer	Cin	79	878	11.1

ASSISTS PER GAME
(Minimum 65 Games Played)

Name	Team	G	Ass.	Avg.
Rodgers	SF	79	825	10.4
Robertson	Cin	80	758	9.5
Cousy	Bos	76	515	6.8
Green	Chi	73	422	5.8
Wilkens	StL	75	381	5.1
Baylor	LA	80	386	4.8
Russell	Bos	78	348	4.5
Guerin	NY	79	348	4.4
Costello	Syr	78	334	4.3
Barnhill	StL	77	322	4.2

MINUTES PLAYED

Name	Team	Min.
Chamberlain	SF	3806
Robertson	Cin	3521
Russell	Bos	3500
Baylor	LA	3370
Bellamy	Chi	3306

1963-64 N.B.A.

Russell's Defensive Answer

Three familiar institutions were gone from the N.B.A. picture this season: Commissioner Maurice Podoloff, the Syracuse Nationals, and Bob Cousy. Podoloff had reached age 73 and retired as the N.B.A.'s chief executive. He had been president of the B.A.A. at its founding in 1946, and had presided over the N.B.A. since its creation in 1949. Through the lean years of the 1940's and 1950's, the colorful Podoloff had kept the league going through compromise and improvisation, and was now leaving behind a solid circuit which had just set a new attendance record.

The man the owners chose for a new commissioner was Walter Kennedy, the B.A.A.'s original publicity director and since then the mayor of Stamford, Connecticut—a background which helped him overcome a threatened strike at the All-Star game when the players demanded that a pension plan be instituted. Kennedy talked the players into going through with the game, and then he arranged a modest pension plan after the season. Attendance kept climbing under Kennedy's reign, passing the 2,500,000 mark this season.

Another departure this season was the move of the Syracuse Nationals to Philadelphia, where they became known as the 76ers. The Nats had come into the N.B.A. from the N.B.L. in the 1949 merger, and they had won the league crown in 1955. Never a physically big club, the Nats had one star in Dolph Schayes and had always shown an inexhaustible supply of hustle. But Schayes was at the end of the line as a player, and the small base of Syracuse was off the main travel routes and the area was too small to compete with the large cities on the circuit. So owner Danny Biasone sold the club to a Philadelphia group, who moved the club in as a replacement for the departed Warriors. Dolph Schayes went along as player coach.

The missing face most talked about by fans however, was that of Bob Cousy. As the dynasty of the Boston Celtics extended, even non-basketball fans knew about Cousy. His fancy dribbling and razor-sharp passes brought fans to their feet and his leading of the firehouse Boston fast break made him the most noticeable element in the Celtic machine. Some fans figured that the Celtic string of championships had to end now that Cousy was gone, but others claimed that the dynasty would go on, because the key element was not Cousy but the defensive-minded Bill Russell.

The Celtics again came in first place and thus partially answered the question. The Celtic fast break kept rolling without Cousy, and the pressing defense even improved. Sam Jones and K.C. Jones started in the backcourt, the perfect blend of an offensive and a defensive star. Tom Heinsohn and Satch Sanders were the same combination of offense and defense at forward, and Russell held all the pieces together with his rebounding, his shotblocking, and his unnoticed 15 points per game scoring. The leading scorer on the club didn't even start; John Havlicek came off the bench, played both forward and guard, never shied away from a shot, and ran up and down the court without a sign of exhaustion. His performance won him the title of the N.B.A.'s best sixth man, an honor taken away from teammate Frank Ramsey, who was still a dangerous man in stretches. Willie Naulls came from the San Francisco Warriors to provide backup strength at forward, and Clyde Lovellette and Jim Loscutoff were still available for spot duty.

But even with all of coach Red Auerbach's talented squad, the Celtics got a chase from the Cincinnati Royals, who finished only four games back with a 55-25 mark. Oscar Robertson shot, passed, dribbled, and rebounded as well or better than any other guard in the N.B.A. In the frontcourt, Jerry Lucas signed with the Royals after sitting out a season. He ranked third in the N.B.A. in rebounding, behind only Chamberlain and Russell. In addition to his rebounding talent, Lucas had a fine outside shot and averaged 17.7 points per game in his pro debut. With bulky Wayne Embry setting picks and boxing out at center, with Jack Twyman and Tom Hawkins playing forward opposite Lucas, and with Adrian Smith and Arlen Bockhorn in the backcourt with Oscar, the Royals stayed hot on the Celtics' heels all season.

The Philadelphia 76ers, hurt by a foot injury to Larry Costello, a knee injury to Lee Shaffer, and Dave Gambee's broken foot, fell to a 3446 mark in their first season in Philadelphia, yet still beat out the New York Knicks for the final playoff spot. The Knicks added Len Chappell, Bob Boozer, Johnny Egan, and Bill McGill in trades and had the first-picked rookie in Art Heyman, but they still finished with the worst record in the league 22-58.

Over in the Western Division, the San Francisco Warriors joined the Lakers and Hawks as the major powers in the division. The Warriors came in first under new coach Alex Hannum, who installed a deliberate style into the team's offense and affirmed a new concentration on defense. Hannum convinced Wilt Chamberlain to concentrate on blocking shots, a la Bill Russell, and passing the ball off more often; Wilt's scoring average thus "fell" to 36.9, still the best in the league, while his value as a defender and playmaker from the pivot increased. The Warriors controlled the boards against most teams, with 6'11" rookie Nate Thurmond joining veterans Tom Meschery and Wayne Hightower in the forward corps which grabbed off any loose rebounds Chamberlain didn't get. Guy Rodgers, Al Attles, and Gary Phillips handled the backcourt chores.

Two games back of the Warriors came the St. Louis Hawks, who added ex-Knick Richie Guerin to the backcourt and used rebounder Bill Bridges more extensively at forward. Bob Pettit still paced the club in scoring and rebounding, with Cliff Hagan, Lenny Wilkens, and Zelmo Beaty key contributors. The Lakers finished a strong third, with a weakness at center partially offsetting the scoring feats of Elgin Baylor and Jerry West. Finishing fourth were the Baltimore Bullets, who had moved from Chicago, and fifth were the Detroit Pistons, who lost Dave DeBusschere to the military.

The playoffs further answered the question as to whether Cousy or Russell was the key factor in the Celtic dynasty. Both Boston and San Francisco made it to the title senes, with Russell and Chamberlain facing each other for the crown. Chamberlain outscored Russell, but Russell's defense and rebounding combined with the other talent on the Boston roster to blow the Warriors out in five games.

Use Name	Pos	Hgt	Wgt	Age	G	Min	FG	FGA	%	FT	FTA	%	Reb	Ass	PF	DQ	Points	Min	Reb	Ass	PF	Points
					TOTAL													PER GAME				
1963/64 N.B.A. — EASTERN DIVISION																						
BOSTON CELTICS	**59-21 .738**				**RED AUERBACH**																	
Tom Heinsohn	F	6'7	220	29	76	2040	487	1223	40	283	342	83	460	183	268	3	1257	27	6.1	2.4	3.5	16.5
Satch Sanders	F	6'6	210	25	80	2370	349	836	42	213	280	76	667	102	277	6	911	30	8.3	1.3	3.5	11.4
Bill Russell	C	6'10	220	29	78	3482	466	1077	43	236	429	55	**1930**	370	190	0	1168	45	**24.7**	4.7	2.4	15.0
Sam Jones	G	6'4	205	30	76	2381	612	1359	45	249	318	78	349	202	192	1	1473	31	4.6	2.7	2.5	19.4
K. C. Jones	G	6'1	202	31	80	2424	283	722	39	88	168	52	372	407	253	0	654	30	4.7	5.1	3.2	8.2
John Havlicek	G-F	6'5	205	23	80	2587	640	1535	42	315	422	75	428	238	227	1	1595	32	5.4	3.0	2.8	19.9
Willie Naulls	F	6'6	225	29	78	1409	321	769	42	125	157	80	356	64	208	0	767	18	4.6	0.8	2.7	9.8
Frank Ramsey	F-G	6'3	205	32	75	1227	226	604	37	196	233	84	223	81	245	7	648	16	3.0	1.1	3.3	8.6
Jim Loscutoff	F	6'5	230	33	53	451	56	182	31	18	31	58	131	25	90	1	130	9	2.5	0.5	1.7	2.5
Clyde Lovellette	C-F	6'9	240	34	45	437	128	305	42	45	57	79	126	24	100	0	301	10	2.8	0.5	2.2	6.7
Larry Siegfried	G	6'3	192	24	31	261	35	110	32	31	39	79	51	40	33	0	101	8	1.6	1.3	1.1	3.3
Johnny McCarthy	G	6'1	185	29	28	206	16	48	33	5	13	38	35	24	42	0	37	7	1.3	0.9	1.5	1.3
CINCINNATI ROYALS	**55-25 .688**				**JACK McMAHON**																	
Jack Twyman (broken hand)	F	6'6	215	29	68	1996	447	993	45	189	228	83	364	137	267	7	1083	29	5.4	2.0	3.9	15.9
Jerry Lucas	F-C	6'8	230	23	79	3273	545	1035	**53**	310	398	78	1375	204	300	6	1400	41	17.4	2.6	3.8	17.7
Wayne Embry	C	6'8	250	26	80	2915	556	1213	46	271	417	65	925	113	**325**	7	1383	36	11.6	1.4	4.1	17.3
Oscar Robertson	G	6'5	205	25	79	3559	840	1740	48	**800**	938	**85**	783	**868**	280	3	2480	45	9.9	11.0	3.5	31.4
Arlen Bockhorn	G	6 4	200	30	70	1670	242	587	41	96	126	76	205	173	227	4	580	24	2.9	2.5	3.2	8.3
Tom Hawkins	F	6'5	210	27	73	1770	256	580	44	113	188	60	435	74	198	4	625	24	6.0	1.0	2.7	8.6
Adrian Smith	G	6'1	180	27	66	1524	234	576	41	154	197	78	147	145	164	1	622	23	2.2	2.2	2.5	9.4
L. Staverman (6g. Bal, 20g. Det)	F	6'7	220	27	60	674	98	212	46	69	90	77	176	32	118	3	265	11	2.9	0.5	2.0	4.4
Bud Olsen	F	6'8	220	23	49	513	85	210	40	32	57	56	149	29	78	0	202	10	3.0	0.6	1.6	4.1
Jay Arnette	G	6'2	175	25	48	501	71	196	36	42	54	78	54	71	105	2	184	10	1.1	1.5	2.2	3.8
Tom Thacher (MS)	G	6'2	170	22	48	457	53	181	29	26	53	49	115	51	51	0	132	10	2.4	1.1	1.1	2.8
PHILADELPHIA 76ers	**34-46 .425**				**DOLPH SCHAYES, (33-46 .418), AL BIANCHI (1-0 1.000)**																	
Chet Walker	F	6'6	200	23	76	2775	492	1118	44	330	464	71	784	124	232	3	1314	37	10.3	1.6	3.1	17.3
Lee Shaffer (knee injury)	F	6'7	220	24	41	1013	217	587	37	102	133	77	205	36	116	1	536	25	5.0	0.9	2.8	13.1
Johnny Kerr	C	6'9	230	31	80	2938	536	1250	43	268	357	75	1017	275	187	2	1340	37	12.7	3.4	2.3	16.8
Hal Greer	G	6'3	176	27	80	3157	715	1611	44	435	525	83	484	374	291	6	1865	39	6.1	4.7	3.6	23.3
Larry Costello (foot injury)	G	6'1	188	32	45	1137	191	408	47	147	170	86	105	167	150	3	529	25	2.3	3.7	3.3	11.8
Paul Neumann	G	6'1	175	25	74	1973	324	732	44	210	266	79	246	291	211	1	858	27	3.3	3.9	2.9	11.6
Ben Warley	F	6'5	200	27	79	1740	215	494	44	220	305	72	619	71	274	5	650	22	7.8	0.9	3.5	8.2
Al Bianchi	G	6'3	185	31	78	1437	257	684	38	109	141	77	147	149	248	6	623	18	1.9	1.9	3.2	8.0
Connie Dierking	C-F	6'9	222	27	76	1286	191	514	37	114	169	67	422	50	221	3	496	17	5.6	0.7	2.9	6.5
Dave Gambee (broken foot)	F	6'6	225	26	41	927	149	378	39	151	185	82	256	35	161	6	449	23	6.2	0.9	3.9	11.0
Dolph Schayes	F	6'8	220	35	24	350	44	143	31	46	57	81	110	48	76	3	134	15	4.6	2.0	3.2	5.6
Jerry Greenspan	F	6'5	195	22	20	280	32	90	36	34	50	68	72	11	54	0	98	14	3.6	0.6	2.7	4.9
Hubie White	G	6'4	205	23	23	196	31	105	30	17	28	61	42	12	28	0	79	9	1.8	0.5	1.2	3.4
NEW YORK KNICKERBOCKERS	**22-58 .275**				**EDDIE DONOVAN**																	
Bob Boozer (32g. Cin)	F	6'8	215	26	81	2379	468	1096	43	272	376	72	596	96	231	1	1208	29	7.4	1.2	2.9	14.9
Len Chappell (1g. Phi)	F-C	6'8	240	22	79	2505	531	1185	45	288	403	71	771	83	214	1	1350	32	9.8	1.1	2.7	17.1
Bill McGill (6g. Bal)	C	6'9	225	24	74	1784	456	937	49	204	282	72	414	121	217	7	1116	24	5.6	1.6	2.9	15.1
Art Heyman	G	6'5	205	22	75	2236	432	1003	43	289	422	68	298	256	229	2	1153	30	4.0	3.4	3.1	15.4
Johnny Egan (24g. Det)	G	5'11	180	24	66	2325	334	758	44	193	243	79	191	358	181	3	861	35	2.9	5.4	2.7	13.0
Tom Gola	G-F	6'6	208	30	74	2156	258	602	43	154	212	73	469	257	278	7	670	29	6.3	3.5	3.8	9.1
Johnny Green	F	6'5	200	30	80	2134	482	1026	47	195	392	50	799	157	246	4	1159	27	10.0	2.0	3.1	14.5
Al Butler	G	6'2	175	25	76	1379	260	616	42	138	187	74	168	157	167	3	658	18	2.2	2.1	2.2	8.7
Dave Budd	F	6'6	210	25	73	1031	128	297	43	84	115	73	276	57	130	1	340	14	3.8	0.8	1.8	4.7
Tom Hoover	C	6'10	240	22	59	988	102	247	41	81	132	61	331	36	185	4	285	17	5.6	0.6	3.1	4.8
John Rudometkin	F	6'6	205	23	52	696	154	326	47	87	116	75	164	26	86	0	395	13	3.2	0.5	1.7	7.6
Gene Conley	C	6'8	255	33	46	551	74	189	39	44	65	68	156	21	124	2	192	12	3.4	0.5	2.7	4.2
Jerry Harkness	G	6'2	175	23	5	59	13	30	43	3	8	38	6	6	4	0	29	12	1.2	1.2	0.8	5.8

1963/64 N.B.A. — WESTERN DIVISION

Use Name	Pos	Hgt	Wgt	Age	G	Min	FG	FGA	%	FT	FTA	%	Reb	Ass	PF	DQ	Points	Min	Reb	Ass	PF	Points
					TOTAL													PER GAME				
SAN FRANCISCO WARRIORS	**48-32 .600**				**ALEX HANNUM**																	
Tom Meschery	F	6'6	215	25	80	2422	436	951	46	207	295	70	612	149	288	6	1079	30	7.7	1.9	3.6	13.5
Wayne Hightower	F	6'9	210	23	79	2536	393	1022	38	260	329	79	566	133	269	7	1046	32	7.2	1.7	3.4	13.2
Wilt Chamberlain	C	7'1	275	27	80	**3689**	**1204**	**2298**	52	540	**1016**	53	1787	403	182	0	**2948**	**46**	22.3	5.0	2.3	**36.9**
Gary Phillips (broken ankle)	G	6'3	190	24	66	2010	256	691	37	146	218	67	248	203	245	8	658	30	3.8	3.1	3.7	10.0
Guy Rodgers	G	6'	185	28	79	2695	337	923	37	198	280	71	328	556	245	4	872	34	4.2	7.0	3.1	11.0
Nate Thurmond	F-C	6'11	225	22	76	1966	219	554	40	95	173	55	790	86	184	2	533	26	10.4	1.1	2.4	7.0
Al Attles	G	6'2	180	27	70	1883	289	640	45	185	275	67	236	197	249	4	763	27	3.4	2.8	3.6	10.9
Gary Hill	G	6'4	185	22	67	1015	146	384	38	51	77	66	114	103	165	2	343	15	1.7	1.5	2.5	5.1
George Lee	F-G	6'4	200	27	54	522	64	169	38	47	71	66	97	25	67	0	175	10	1.8	0.5	1.2	3.2
Kenny Sears	F	6'9	200	30	51	519	53	120	44	64	79	81	94	42	71	0	170	10	1.8	0.8	1.4	3.3
John Windsor	F	6'8	215	23	11	68	10	27	37	7	8	88	26	2	13	0	27	6	2.4	0.2	1.2	2.5
ST. LOUIS HAWKS	**46-34 .575**				**HARRY GALLATIN**																	
Cliff Hagan	F	6'4	210	32	77	2279	572	1280	45	269	331	81	377	193	273	4	1413	30	4.9	2.5	3.5	18.4
Bob Pettit	F-C	6'9	220	31	80	3296	791	1708	46	608	771	79	1224	259	300	3	2190	41	15.3	3.2	3.8	27.4
Zelmo Beaty (knee injury)	C	6'9	235	24	59	1922	287	647	44	200	270	74	633	79	262	**11**	774	33	10.7	1.3	**4.4**	13.1
Richie Guerin (2g. Nn	G	6'4	200	31	80	2366	351	846	41	347	424	82	256	375	276	4	1049	30	3.2	4.7	3.5	13.1
Lenny Wilkens	G	6'1	185	26	78	2526	334	808	41	270	365	74	335	359	287	7	938	32	4.3	4.6	3.7	12.0
Bill Bridges	F-C	6'6	235	24	80	1949	268	675	40	146	224	65	680	181	269	6	682	24	8.5	2.3	3.4	8.5
John Barnhill	G	6'1	180	25	74	1367	208	505	41	70	115	61	157	145	107	0	486	18	2.1	2.0	1.4	6.6
Mike Farmer	F	6'7	215	27	76	1361	178	438	41	68	83	82	225	109	140	0	424	18	3.0	1.4	1.8	5.6
Chico Vaughn	G	6'3	215	23	68	1340	238	538	44	107	148	72	126	129	166	0	583	20	1.9	1.9	2.4	8.6
Gene Tormohlen	C	6'9	235	26	51	640	94	250	38	22	46	48	216	50	128	3	210	13	4.2	1.0	2.5	4.1
Bevo Nordmann (7g. NY)	C	6'10	255	24	19	259	27	66	41	9	19	47	65	5	51	1	63	14	3.4	0.3	2.7	3.3
Gerry Ward	G	6'4	200	22	24	139	16	53	30	11	17	65	21	21	26	0	43	6	0.9	0.9	1.1	1.8
Ken Rohloff	G	6'	195	24	2	7	0	1	0	0	0	—	0	1	4	0	0	4	0.0	0.5	2.0	0.0
LOS ANGELES LAKERS	**42-38 .525**				**FRED SCHAUS**																	
Elgin Baylor	F	6'5	225	29	78	3164	756	1778	43	471	586	80	936	347	235	1	1983	41	12.0	4.4	3.0	25.4
Rudv LaRusso	F	6'7	220	26	79	2746	337	776	43	298	397	75	800	190	268	5	972	35	10.1	2.4	3.4	12.3
Gene Wiley	C	6'10	210	26	78	1510	146	273	53	45	75	60	510	44	225	4	337	19	6.5	0.6	2.9	4.3
Dich Barnett	G	6'4	190	27	78	2620	541	1197	45	351	454	77	250	238	233	3	1433	34	3.2	3.1	3.0	18.4
Jerry West	G	6'3	175	25	72	2906	740	1529	48	584	702	83	433	403	200	2	2064	40	6.0	5.6	2.8	28.7
Leroy Ellis	C-F	6'10	210	23	78	1459	200	473	42	112	170	66	498	41	192	3	512	19	6.4	0.5	2.5	6.6
Don Nelson	F	6'6	210	23	80	1406	135	323	42	149	201	74	323	76	181	1	419	18	4.0	1.0	2.3	5.2
Frank Selvy	G	6'3	185	31	73	1286	160	423	38	78	122	64	139	149	115	1	398	18	1.9	2.0	1.6	5.5
Jim Krebs	C	6'8	230	28	68	975	134	357	38	65	85	76	283	49	166	6	333	14	4.2	0.7	2.4	4.9
Jim King	G	6'2	175	22	60	762	84	198	42	66	101	65	113	110	99	0	234	13	1.9	1.8	1.7	3.9
Hub Reed	C-F	6'9	230	27	46	386	33	91	36	10	15	67	107	23	73	0	76	8	2.3	0.5	1.6	1.7
Mel Gibson	G	6'3	180	23	9	53	6	20	30	1	2	50	4	6	10	0	13	6	0.4	0.7	1.1	1.4
BALTIMORE BULLETS	**31-49 .388**				**BOB LEONARD**																	
Terry Dischinger	F-G	6'7	189	23	80	2816	604	1217	50	454	585	78	667	157	321	10	1662	35	8.3	2.0	4.0	20.8
Gus Johnson	F	6'6	235	25	78	2847	571	1329	43	210	319	66	1064	169	321	**11**	1352	37	13.6	2.2	4.1	17.3
Walt Bellamy	C	6'11	230	24	80	3394	811	1582	51	537	825	65	1361	126	300	7	2159	42	17.0	1.6	3.8	27.0
Rod Thorn	G	6'4	195	22	75	2594	411	1015	40	258	353	73	360	281	187	3	1080	35	4.8	3.7	2.5	14.4
Si Green	G	6'2	190	29	75	2070	287	691	42	198	290	68	282	215	224	5	772	28	3.8	2.9	3.0	10.3
Kevin Loughery (1g. Det)	G	6'3	190	23	66	1463	236	631	37	126	177	71	138	182	175	2	598	22	2.1	2.8	2.7	9.1
Don Kojis	F	6'4	215	24	78	1148	203	484	42	82	146	56	309	57	123	0	488	15	4.0	0.7	1.6	6.3
Barney Cable	F	6'7	205	27	71	1125	116	290	40	28	42	67	301	47	166	3	260	16	4.2	0.7	2.3	3.7
Gene Shue	G	6'2	175	32	47	963	81	276	29	36	61	59	94	150	98	2	198	20	2.0	3.2	2.1	4.2
Charlie Hardnett	F-C	6'8	225	25	66	617	107	260	41	84	125	67	251	27	114	1	298	9	3.8	0.4	1.7	4.5
Paul Hogue (6g. NY)	C	6'9	240	23	15	147	12	30	40	2	7	29	31	6	35	1	26	10	2.1	0.4	2.3	1.7
Larry Comley	G	6'5	210	24	11	88	8	37	22	9	16	56	19	12	11	0	25	8	1.7	1.1	1.0	2.3
Roger Strickland	F	6'5	200	23	1	4	1	3	33	0	0	—	0	0	1	0	2	4	0.0	0.0	1.0	2.0
Mel Peterson	G	6'4	185	25	2	3	1	1	100	0	0	—	1	0	2	0	2	2	0.5	0.0	1.0	1.0
DETROIT PISTONS	**23-57 .288**				**CHARLIE WOLF**																	
Bailey Howell	F	6'7	220	26	77	2700	598	1267	47	470	581	81	776	205	290	9	1666	35	10.1	2.7	3.8	21.6
Ray Scott	F-C	6'9	215	25	80	2964	539	1307	41	328	456	72	1078	244	296	7	1406	37	13.5	3.1	3.7	17.6
Reggie Harding	C	7'	245	21	39	1158	184	460	40	61	98	62	410	52	119	1	429	30	10.5	1.3	3.1	11.0
Donnie Butcher (26g. NY)	G	6'3	200	27	78	1971	202	507	40	159	256	62	329	244	249	4	563	25	4.2	3.1	3.2	7.2
Don Ohl	G	6'3	190	27	71	2366	500	1224	41	225	331	68	180	225	219	3	1225	33	2.5	3.2	3.1	17.3
Jackie Moreland	F-G	6'7	215	25	78	1780	272	639	43	164	210	78	405	121	268	9	708	23	5.2	1.6	3.4	9.1
Willie Jones	G	6'3	185	27	77	1539	265	680	39	100	141	71	253	172	211	5	630	20	3.3	2.2	2.7	8.2
Bob Ferry	C-F	6'8	230	26	74	1522	298	670	44	186	279	67	428	94	174	2	782	21	5.8	1.3	2.4	10.6
Darrall Imhoff	C	6'10	220	25	58	871	104	251	41	69	114	61	283	56	167	5	277	15	4.9	1.0	2.9	4.8
Eddie Miles	G	6'4	196	23	60	811	131	371	35	62	87	71	95	58	92	0	324	14	1.6	1.0	1.5	5.4
Bob Duffy (2g. StL, 4g. NY)	G	6'3	185	23	48	662	94	229	41	44	65	68	61	79	48	0	232	14	1.3	1.6	1.0	4.8
Dave DeBusschere (broken leg, MS)	F	6'6	220	23	15	304	52	133	39	25	43	58	105	23	32	1	129	20	7.0	1.5	2.1	8.6

1963/64 N.B.A. — PLAYOFFS

Use Name	Pos	Hgt	Wgt	Age	G	Min	FG	FGA	%	FT	FTA	%	Reb	Ass	PF	DQ	Points	Min	Reb	Ass	PF	Points
					TOTAL													PER GAME				
BOSTON CELTICS	**RED AUERBACH**				defeated Cincinnati 4-1; H103-87, H101-90, 102-92, 93-102, H109-95; defeated San Francisco 4-1; H108-96, H124-101, 91-115, 98-95, H105-99																	
Tom Heinsohn	F	6'7	220	29	10	308	70	170	41	34	42	81	80	26	36	0	174	31	8.0	2.6	3.6	17.4
Satch Sanders	F	6'6	210	25	10	302	34	94	36	23	34	68	71	6	45	5	91	30	7.1	0.6	4.5	9.1
Bill Russell	C	6'10	220	29	10	451	47	132	36	37	67	55	272	44	23	0	131	45	**27.2**	4.4	2.3	13.1
Sam Jones	G	6'4	205	30	10	356	91	181	50	50	68	74	47	23	24	0	232	36	4.7	2.3	2.4	23.2
K. C. Jones	G	6'1	202	31	10	312	25	72	35	13	25	52	37	68	40	0	63	31	3.7	6.8	4.0	6.3
John Havlicek	G-F	6'5	205	23	10	289	61	159	38	35	44	80	43	32	26	0	157	29	4.3	3.2	2.6	15.7
Willie Naulls	F	6'6	225	29	10	167	37	95	39	17	23	74	46	8	31	1	91	17	4.6	0.8	3.1	9.1
Frank Ramsey	F-G	6'3	205	32	10	138	22	63	35	18	21	86	21	10	25	0	62	14	2.1	1.0	2.5	6.2
Clyde Lovellette	C-F	6'9	240	34	5	40	8	34	24	4	4	100	7	2	8	0	20	8	1.4	0.4	1.6	4.0
Larry Siegfried	G	6'3	192	24	4	24	2	6	33	3	6	50	4	1	4	0	7	6	1.0	0.3	1.0	1.8
Johnny McCarthy	G	6'1	185	29	1	8	1	1	100	0	0	—	1	1	0	0	2	8	1.0	1.0	0.0	2.0
Jim Loscutoff	F	6'5	230	33	1	5	2	2	100	0	0	—	2	0	3	0	4	5	2.0	0.0	3.0	4.0
SAN FRANCISCO WARRIORS	**ALEX HANNUM**				defeated St. Louis 4-3; H111-116, H120-85, 109-113, 111-109, H121-97, 95-123, H105-95; lost to Boston 1-4; 96-108, 101-124, H115-91, H95-98, 99-105																	
Tom Meschery	F	6'6	215	25	12	405	80	181	44	42	54	78	87	21	37	0	202	34	7.3	1.8	3.1	16.8
Nate Thurmond	F-C	6'11	225	22	12	410	42	96	44	36	53	68	148	10	46	0	120	34	12.3	0.8	3.8	10.0
Wilt Chamberlain	C	7'1	275	27	12	**558**	**175**	**322**	**54**	66	**139**	47	**302**	39	27	0	**416**	47	25.2	3.3	2.3	**34.7**
Al Attles	G	6'2	180	27	12	386	58	144	40	30	56	54	37	30	54	**5**	146	32	3.1	2.5	4.5	12.2
Guy Rodgers	G	6'	185	28	12	419	57	173	33	33	47	70	58	**90**	46	1	147	35	4.8	7.5	3.8	12.3
Wayne Hightower	F	6'9	210	23	12	286	29	112	26	23	33	70	50	18	42	1	81	24	4.2	1.5	3.5	6.8
Gary Phillips	G	6'3	190	24	11	256	35	97	36	26	40	65	24	20	36	2	96	23	2.2	1.8	3.3	8.7
Gary Hill	G	6'4	185	22	9	69	12	24	50	4	13	31	6	8	13	0	28	8	0.7	0.9	1.4	3.1
George Lee	F-G	6'4	200	27	10	67	9	20	45	12	20	60	16	4	15	0	30	7	1.6	0.4	1.5	3.0
Kenny Sears	F	6'9	200	30	7	24	6	10	60	0	0	—	12	3	4	0	12	3	1.7	0.4	0.6	1.7
ST. LOUIS HAWKS	**HARRY GALLATIN**				defeated Los Angeles 3-2; H115-104, H106-90, 105-107, 88-97, H121-108; lost to San Francisco 3-4; 116-111, 85-120, H113-109, H109-111, 97-121, H123-95, 95-105																	
Cliff Hagan	F	6'4	210	32	12	392	75	175	43	45	54	83	74	57	34	0	195	33	6.2	4.8	2.8	16.3
Bob Pettit	F-C	6'9	220	31	12	494	93	226	41	66	79	84	174	33	44	0	252	41	14.5	2.8	3.7	21.0
Zelmo Beaty	C	6'9	235	24	12	436	63	121	52	46	77	60	114	12	**56**	1	172	36	9.5	1.0	**4.7**	14.3
Richie Guerin	G-F	6'4	200	31	12	428	75	169	44	67	85	79	50	49	54	1	217	36	4.2	4.1	4.5	18.1
Lenny Wilkens	G	6'1	185	26	12	413	64	143	45	44	58	76	60	64	42	0	172	34	5.0	5.3	3.5	14.3
Chico Vaughn	G	6'3	215	23	12	242	43	101	43	19	26	73	25	21	31	0	105	20	2.1	1.8	2.6	8.8
Bill Bridges	F	6'6	235	24	12	240	26	83	31	12	19	63	84	24	46	0	64	20	7.0	2.0	3.8	5.3
Mike Farmer	F	6'7	215	27	11	119	19	34	56	8	10	80	16	9	10	0	46	11	1.5	0.8	0.9	4.2
John Barnhill	G	6'1	180	25	5	61	12	23	52	2	5	40	5	5	8	0	26	12	1.0	1.0	1.6	5.2
Gene Tormohlen	C	6'9	235	26	6	39	5	13	38	3	5	60	14	9	12	0	13	7	2.3	1.5	2.0	2.2
Gerry Ward	G	6'4	200	22	6	16	5	10	50	1	1	100	0	2	5	0	11	3	0.0	0.3	0.8	1.8
CINCINNATI ROYALS	**JACK McMAHON**				defeated Philadelphia 3-2; H127-102 ,114-122, H101-89, 120-129, H130-124; lost to Boston 1-4; 87-103, 90 101, H92-102, H102-93, 95 109																	
Jack Twyman	F	6'6	215	29	10	354	83	176	47	39	49	80	87	16	41	1	205	35	8.7	1.6	4.1	20.5
Jerry Lucas	F-C	6'8	230	23	10	370	48	123	39	26	37	70	125	34	37	1	122	37	12.5	3.4	3.7	12.2
Wayne Embry	C	6'8	250	26	10	363	53	139	38	28	45	62	124	21	46	3	134	36	12.4	2.1	4.6	13.4
Oscar Robertson	G	6'5	205	25	10	471	92	202	46	**109**	127	86	89	84	30	0	293	**47**	8.9	**8.4**	3.0	29.3
Arlen Bockhorn	G	6'4	200	30	10	301	41	108	38	15	20	75	39	39	40	1	97	30	3.9	3.9	4.0	9.7
Tom Hawkins	F	6'5	210	27	10	273	43	97	44	15	22	68	93	11	38	2	101	27	9.3	1.1	3.8	10.1
Jay Arnette	G	6'2	175	25	8	79	11	31	35	7	8	88	10	9	21	1	29	10	1.3	1.1	2.6	3.6
Larry Staverman	F	6'7	220	27	7	70	11	23	48	15	19	79	26	5	16	0	37	10	3.7	0.7	2.3	5.3
Adrian Smith	G	6'1	180	27	7	66	8	26	31	5	7	71	9	4	8	0	21	9	1.3	0.6	1.1	3.0
Tom Thacker	G	6'2	170	24	6	43	6	23	26	1	4	25	13	3	4	0	13	7	2.2	0.5	0.7	2.2
Bud Olsen	F	6'8	220	23	2	10	3	6	50	0	0	—	4	1	2	0	6	5	2.0	0.5	1.0	3.0
PHILADELPHIA 76ers	**DOLPH SCHAYES**				lost to Cincinnati 2-3; 102-127, H122-114, 89-101, H129-120, 124-130																	
Chet Walker	F	6'6	200	23	5	190	30	77	39	34	46	74	52	13	15	0	94	38	10.4	2.6	3.0	18.8
Dave Gambee	F	6'6	225	26	5	149	24	60	40	21	27	78	29	8	23	1	69	30	5.8	1.6	4.6	13.8
Johnny Kerr	C	6'9	230	31	5	185	40	83	48	15	20	75	69	16	12	0	95	37	13.8	3.2	2.4	19.0
Hal Greer	G	6'3	176	27	5	211	37	95	39	33	39	85	28	30	19	1	107	42	5.6	6.0	3.8	21.4
Paul Neumann	G	6'1	175	25	5	165	27	59	46	26	31	84	13	25	13	0	80	33	2.6	5.0	2.6	16.0
Ben Warley	F	6'5	200	27	4	85	9	23	39	10	15	67	33	2	11	0	28	21	8.3	0.5	2.8	7.0
Connie Dierking	C-F	6'9	222	27	5	71	14	33	42	5	9	56	30	5	10	0	33	14	6.0	1.0	2.0	6.6
Al Bianchi	G	6'3	185	31	5	68	12	29	41	3	4	75	4	4	12	0	27	14	0.8	0.8	2.4	5.4
Lee Shaffer	F	6'7	220	24	3	40	8	22	36	1	2	50	4	2	5	0	17	13	1.3	0.7	1.7	5.7
Larry Costello	G	6'1	188	32	5	36	3	14	21	10	10	100	3	4	14	1	16	7	0.6	0.8	2.8	3.2
LOS ANGELES LAKERS	**FRED SCHAUS**				lost to St. Louis 2-3, 104-115, 90-106, H107-105, H97-88, 108-121																	
Elgin Baylor	F	6'5	225	29	5	221	45	119	38	31	40	78	58	28	17	0	121	44	11.6	5.6	3.4	24.2
Rudy LaRusso	F	6'7	220	26	5	189	13	33	39	19	22	**86**	30	11	23	2	45	38	6.0	2.2	4.6	9.0
Leroy Ellis	C-F	6'10	210	23	5	144	8	27	30	11	15	73	50	4	11	0	27	29	10.0	0.8	2.2	5.4
Dick Barnett	G	6'4	190	27	5	154	21	52	40	27	32	84	8	17	16	0	69	31	1.6	3.4	3.2	13.8
Jerry West	G	6'3	175	25	5	206	57	115	50	42	53	79	36	17	20	0	156	41	7.2	3.4	4.0	31.2
Frank Selvy	G	6'3	185	31	3	69	13	27	48	2	2	100	5	6	8	0	28	23	1.7	2.0	2.7	9.3
Don Nelson	F	6'6	210	23	5	56	7	13	54	3	3	100	13	2	11	1	17	11	2.6	0.4	2.2	3.4
Jim King	G	6'2	175	22	4	51	4	10	40	4	4	100	4	6	2	0	12	13	1.0	1.5	0.5	3.0
Jim Krebs	C	6'8	230	28	4	50	6	9	67	2	4	50	22	6	8	0	14	13	5.5	1.5	2.0	3.5
Gene Wiley	C	6'10	210	26	5	48	5	8	63	3	3	100	16	0	9	1	13	10	3.2	0.0	1.8	2.6
Hub Reed	C	6'9	230	27	1	12	2	4	50	0	2	0	2	0	2	0	4	12	2.0	0.0	2.0	4.0

1963/64 N.B.A. TEAM STATISTICS

Team	Regular Season G	FG	FGA	%	FT	FTA	%	Reb.	Ass.	Average Points For	Agnst.	Diff.	Playoffs G	FG	FGA	%	FT	FTA	%	Reb.	Ass.	Average Points For	Agnst.	Diff.
EASTERN DIVISION																								
Boston	80	3619	8770	41	1804	2489	72	5736	1760	113.0	105.1	+7.9	10	400	918	44	234	334	70	736	221	103.4	97.2+	6.2
Cincinnati	80	3516	7761	45	2146	2828	76	5400	1916	114.7	109.7	+5.0	10	399	954	42	260	338	77	684	227	105.8	107.4	-1.6
Philadelphia	80	3394	8116	42	2184	2851	77	5132	1643	112.2	116.5	-4.3	5	204	495	41	158	203	78	289	109	113.2	118.4	-5.2
New York	80	3512	7888	45	1952	2852	68	5067	1563	112.2	119.6	-7.4												
WESTERN DIVISION																								
San Francisco	80	3407	7779	44	1800	2821	64	5499	1899	107.7	102.6	+5.1	12	503	1171	43	272	455	60	736	245	106.5	105.3	+1.2
St. Louis	80	3341	7776	43	2115	2795	76	4959	1901	110.0	108.4	+1.6	12	480	1098	44	313	409	77	709	281	106.1	106.5	-0.4
Los Angeles	80	3272	7438	44	2230	2910	77	5025	1676	109.7	108.7	+1.0	5	181	417	43	144	180	77	270	97	101.2	107.0	-5.8
Baltimore	80	3456	7862	44	2036	2958	69	5460	1423	111.9	113.6	-1.7												
Detroit	80	3346	7943	42	1928	2685	72	5145	1633	107.8	115.5	-7.7												

1963/64 N.B.A. STANDINGS

Team	W	L	Pct.	GB	Record against playoff teams W	L	Pct.	Record against non-playoff teams W	L	Pct.	Home W	L	Pct.	Road W	L	Pct.	Neutral W	L	Pct.
EASTERN DIVISION																			
Boston Celtics	59	21	.738	—	33	17	.660	26	4	.867	26	4	.867	21	17	.553	12	0	1.000
Cincinnati Royals	55	25	.688	4	29	20	.592	26	5	.839	26	7	.788	18	18	.500	11	0	1.000
Philadelphia 76ers	34	46	.425	25	16	34	.320	18	12	.600	18	12	.600	12	22	.353	4	12	.250
New York KnickerBockers	22	58	.275	37	14	47	.230	8	11	.421	10	25	.286	8	27	.229	4	6	.400
WESTERN DIVISION																			
San Francisco Warriors	48	32	.600	—	24	25	.490	24	7	.774	25	14	.641	21	15	.583	2	3	.400
St. Louis Hawks	46	34	.575	2	25	25	.500	21	9	.700	27	12	.692	17	19	.472	2	3	.400
Los Angeles Lakers	42	38	.525	6	22	28	.440	20	10	.667	24	12	.667	15	21	.417	3	5	.375
Baltimore Bullets	31	49	.388	17	17	43	.283	14	6	.700	20	19	.513	8	21	.276	3	9	.250
Detroit Pistons	23	57	.288	25	16	45	.262	7	12	.368	9	21	.300	6	25	.194	8	11	.421

1963/64 N.B.A. INDIVIDUAL LEADERS

SCORING
(Minimum 65 Games Played)

Name	Team	G	FG	FT	Pts.	Avg.
Chamberlain	SF	80	1204	540	2948	36.9
Robertson	Cin	79	840	800	2480	31.4
West	LA	72	740	584	2064	28.7
Pettit	StL	80	791	608	2190	27.4
Bellamy	Bal	80	811	537	2159	27.0
Baylor	LA	78	756	471	1983	25.4
Greer	Phi	80	715	435	1865	23.3
Howell	Det	77	598	470	1666	21.6
Dischinger	Bal	80	604	454	1662	20.8
Havlicek	Bos	80	640	315	1595	19.9

FIELD GOAL PERCENTAGE
(Minimum 210 Field Goals)

Name	Team	FG	FGA	Pct.
Lucas	Cin	545	1035	.527
Chamberlain	SF	1204	2298	.524
Bellamy	Bal	811	1582	.513
Dischinger	Bal	604	1217	.496
McGill	NY	456	937	.487
West	LA	740	1529	.484
Robertson	Cin	840	1740	.483
Howell	Det	598	1267	.472
Green	NY	482	1026	.470
Pettit	StL	791	1708	.463

FREE THROW PERCENTAGE
(Minimum 210 Free Throws)

Name	Team	FT	FTA	Pct.
Robertson	Cin	800	938	.853
West	LA	584	702	.832
Gneer	Phi	435	525	.829
Heinsohn	Bos	283	342	.827
Guerin	NY-StL	347	424	.818
Hagan	StL	269	331	.813
Howell	Det	470	581	.809
Baylor	LA	471	586	.804
Hightower	SF	260	329	.790
Neumann	Phi	210	266	.789

PERSONAL FOULS

Name	Team	PF
Embry	Cin	325
Dischinger	Bal	321
Johnson	Bal	321
Bellamy	Bal	300
Lucas	Cin	300
Pettit	StL	300

GAMES DISQUALIFIED

Name	Team	Disq.
Beaty	StL	11
Johnson	Bal	11
Dischinger	Bal	10
Howell	Det	9
Moreland	Det	9

REBOUNDS PER GAME
(Minimum 65 Games Played)

Name	Team	G	Reb.	Avg.
Russell	Bos	78	1930	24.7
Chamberlain	SF	80	1787	22.3
Lucas	Cin	79	1375	17.4
Bellamy	Bal	80	1361	17.0
Pettit	StL	80	1224	15.3
Johnson	Bal	78	1064	13.6
Scott	Det	80	1078	13.5
Kerr	Phi	80	1017	12.7
Baylor	LA	78	936	12.0
Embry	Cin	80	925	11.6

ASSISTS PER GAME
(Minimum 65 Games Played)

Name	Team	G	Ass.	Avg.
Robertson	Cin	79	868	11.0
Rogers	SF	79	556	7.0
West	LA	72	403	5.6
Egan	Det-NY	66	358	5.4
K.C. Jones	Bos	80	407	5.1
Chamberlain	SF	80	403	5.0
Russell	Bos	78	370	4.7
Guerin	NY-StL	80	375	4.7
Greer	Phi	80	374	4.7
Wilkens	StL	78	359	4.6

MINUTES PLAYED

Name	Team	Min.
Chamberlain	SF	3689
Robertson	Cin	3559
Russell	Bos	3482
Bellamy	Bal	3394
Pettit	StL	3296

1964-65 N.B.A.

From Frisco to Philly to Beantown

The East beat the West 124-123 in the annual All-Star game on January 13, but newspapers the next morning gave headline coverage to another basketball story; Wilt Chamberlain had been traded. The greatest scorer in basketball history, Wilt was averaging 38.9 points per game for the San Francisco Warriors. The Warriors, however, decided that they could do better by unloading Wilt. After winning the Western Division last season, the team dropped 16 of its first 21 games of this season to drop far back in the standings.

The Warriors couldn't put their winning formula back together after that, and they had practically fallen out of the running for a playoff berth by the All-Star break. Nate Thurmond, a potentially great center, was playing out of position at forward for the Warriors and would cover the team's needs at center. And finally, the Warriors had drawn only moderate crowds on the West Coast so far, with fans failing to warm up to Chamberlain; if Wilt's high salary were dropped and he were sold for a lot of money, perhaps the Warriors would have sufflcient capital to build an attractive squad.

Within hours after the All-Star game, the Warriors traded Wilt to the Philadelphia 76ers. The Warriors got a lot of money plus three players, guard Paul Neumann, center Connie Dierking, and forward Lee Shaffer. (Shaffer was a holdout with the 76ers, he did not sign with the Warriors, and he never played again in the N.B.A.) Wilt went back to his hometown, with the team that had been known as the Syracuse Nats until two years ago. He again had an admiring public, and was playing on a team that had always emphasized teamwork and defense but had lacked a big man at center. Hal Greer, Larry Costello, Chet Walker, Dave Gambee, Al Bianchi and Johnny Kerr all came out of the Syracuse tradition, as did head coach Dolph Schayes, and now Chamberlain and rookie Luke Jackson would give the club the rebounding stength it had never had. The rest of the regular season would be taken up by working Wilt into the 76er system, but the club posed a new threat to the Boston Celtics in the playoffs.

The Celtics had sewn up their ninth straight Eastern Division first-place finish by winning their first 11 games and slowing up very little after that. It was a season of transition for the Celtics, as team owner and founder Walter Brown died and veteran players Frank Ramsey, Jim Loscutoff, and Clyde Lovellette retired. Tom Heinsohn missed 13 games because of injuries, and Larry Siegfried started to see considerable action as a backup guard. But the core of the Celtics remained the same, with Bill Russell, Satch Sanders, and K.C. Jones the defensive stars and Sam Jones, John Havlicek, and Heinsohn the offensive aces. Coach Red Auerbach lit his victory cigar 62 times during the season, going without his smoke only 18 times.

The Cincinnati Royals finished a distant second at 48-32; playmaker-scorer Oscar Robertson and rebounder-scorer Jerry Lucas made the Royals a dangerous club, but they were unable to press the Celtics as closely as they did last season. The 76ers finished third at 40-40, biding their time until the playoffs. The Knicks finished fourth again, but found hope for the future in rookies Willis Reed, Jim Barnes, Howie Komives, and Em Bryant.

While the Celtics wrapped up their division early, the Los Angeles Lakers did the same in the West by winning 15 of their first 21 games. With Elgin Baylor and Jerry West good for 58.1 points per game, the Lakers built up a 49-31 record for the regular season. The St. Louis Hawks got off to a slow start, due largely to a knee injury to Bob Pettit and a leg injury to Richie Guerin. With the team's record at 17-16, owner Ben Kerner fired coach Harry Gallatin and made Guerin a player coach; the Hawks played better the rest of the way and made an unsuccessfill run on first place late in the season.

The surprise winner of the third playoff spot was the Baltimore Bullets, only two years removed from their Chicago origins. Coached by Buddy Jeannette, who had taken an earlier version of the Bullets to the B.A.A. championship in 1948, the Baltimore club made a key trade by sending Terry Dischinger and Rod Thorn to the Detroit Pistons in exchange for Bailey Howell, Don Ohl, and Bob Ferry. Howell and Ohl fit into a high-scoring starting lineup which included holdovers Walt Bellamy, Gus Johnson, and Kevin Loughery. With Johnson developing into one of the N.B.A.'s best forwards, and with the veteran firepower picked up from Detroit, the Bullets immediately became a club to contend with. The trade worked out less well for the Pistons, who finished six games behind the Bullets in fourth place. Dischinger helped the club with his shooting, but the key addition was Dave DeBusschere, who returned after missing most of last season because of military service. The trade with Baltimore opened up room for him in the frontcourt, where his rebounding skill blossomed, and his leadership qualities were called upon when owner Fred Zollner fired coach Charlie Wolf and made DeBusschere a mere 24 years old, the player coach of the team . With his added basketball duties, DeBusschere decided to end his burgeoning career as a pitcher with the Chicago White Sox. Finishing far back in last place were the Warriors. For the Pistons and Warriors, there were no playoffs this season.

Again this year, the most publicized playoff series involved the Celtics. In the Eastern finals, the 76ers had every hope of ending the Celtic domination. The Celtics took the first game at Boston, 108-98, with the 76ers taking the second at Philly, 109-103. The pattern repeated in the next two games, with each club winning on its home court. The fifth and sixth games also went to the home teams, bringing the clubs together for a seventh game in Boston.

The Celtics streaked out to a 30-12 lead in the first period, but the 76ers slowly came back. With five seconds left in the game, Boston led 110-109 and had the ball out of bounds. In trying to throw the ball into play, Bill Russell hit a wire supporting the backboard, and the 76ers got the ball. The 76ers now had a final shot at a victory, but the inbounds pass from Hal Greer was deflected by John Havlicek. With the 76ers disposed of, the rest was easy for the Celtics. Their opponent in the championship series was the Lakers, who had lost Elgin Baylor to a knee injury. Although Jerry West played heroically, averaging 40 points per game, the Lakers went down in five games, victims of the Celtics' seventh straight title.

1964/65 N.B.A. — EASTERN DIVISION

					TOTAL													PER GAME				
Use Name	Pos	Hgt	Wgt	Age	G	Min	FG	FGA	%	FT	FTA	%	Reb	Ass	PF	DQ	Points	Min	Reb	Ass	PF	Points
BOSTON CELTICS	**62-18 .775**				**RED AUERBACH**																	
Tom Heinsohn (leg injury)	F	6'7	220	30	67	1706	365	954	38	182	229	79	399	157	252	5	912	25	6.0	2.3	3.8	13.6
Satch Sanders	F	6'6	210	26	80	2459	374	871	43	193	259	75	661	92	318	**15**	941	31	8.3	1.2	4.0	11.8
Bill Russell	C	6'10	220	30	78	**3466**	429	980	44	244	426	57	**1878**	410	204	1	1102	44	**24.1**	5.3	2.6	14.1
Sam Jones	G	6'4	205	31	80	2885	821	1818	45	428	522	82	411	223	176	0	2070	36	5.1	2.8	2.2	25.9
K. C. Jones	G	6'1	202	32	78	2434	253	639	40	143	227	63	318	437	263	5	649	31	4.1	5.6	3.4	8.3
John Havlicek	G-F	6'5	205	24	75	2169	570	1420	40	235	316	74	371	199	200	2	1375	29	4.9	2.7	2.7	18.3
Willie Naulls	F	6'6	225	30	71	1465	302	786	38	143	176	81	336	72	225	5	747	21	4.7	1.0	3.2	10.5
Larry Siegfried	G	6'3	192	25	72	996	173	417	41	109	140	78	134	119	108	1	455	14	1.9	1.7	1.5	6.3
John Thompson	F	6'10	230	23	64	699	84	209	40	62	105	59	230	16	141	1	230	11	3.6	0.3	2.2	3.6
Mel Counts	C-F	7'	230	23	54	572	100	272	37	58	74	78	265	19	134	1	258	11	4.9	0.4	2.5	4.8
Ron Bonham	F	6'5	200	22	37	369	91	220	41	92	112	82	78	19	33	0	274	10	2.1	0.5	0.9	7.4
Gerry Ward	G	6'4	200	23	3	30	2	18	11	1	1	100	5	6	6	0	5	10	1.7	2.0	2.0	1.7
Bevo Nordmann	C	6'10	255	25	3	25	3	5	60	0	0	—	8	3	5	0	6	8	2.7	1.0	1.7	2.0
CINCINNATI ROYALS	**48-32 .600**				**JACK MCMAHON**																	
Jack Twyman	F	6'6	215	JA	80	2236	479	1081	44	198	239	83	383	137	239	4	1156	28	4.8	1.7	3.0	14.5
Jerry Lucas (rib injury)	F-C	6'8	230	30	66	2864	558	1121	50	298	366	81	1321	157	214	1	1414	43	20.0	2.4	3.2	21.4
Wayne Embry	C	6'8	250	24	74	2243	352	772	46	239	271	88	741	92	297	10	943	30	10.0	1.2	4.0	12.7
Oscar Robertson	G	6'5	205	27	75	3421	807	1681	48	**665**	793	84	674	**861**	205	2	2279	**46**	9.0	**11.5**	2.7	30.4
Ardrian Smith	G	6'1	180	26	80	2745	463	1016	46	284	342	83	220	240	199	2	1210	34	2.8	3.0	2.5	15.1
Tom Hawkins	F	6'5	210	28	79	1864	220	538	41	116	204	57	475	80	240	4	556	24	6.0	1.0	3.0	7.0
Bud Olsen	F	6'8	220	24	79	1372	224	512	44	144	195	74	333	84	203	5	592	17	4.2	1.1	2.6	7.5
Happy Hairston	F	6'7	225	22	61	736	131	351	37	110	165	67	293	27	95	0	372	12	4.8	0.4	1.6	6.1
Jay Arnette	G	6'2	175	26	63	662	91	245	37	56	75	75	62	68	125	1	238	11	1.0	1.1	2.0	3.8
Tom Thacker	G	6'2	170	23	55	470	56	168	33	23	47	49	127	41	64	0	135	9	2.3	0.7	1.2	2.5
Arlen Bockhorn (knee injury)	G	6'4	200	31	19	424	60	157	38	28	39	72	55	45	52	1	148	22	2.9	2.4	2.7	7.8
George Wilson	C	6'8	215	22	39	288	41	155	26	9	30	30	102	11	59	0	91	7	2.6	0.3	1.5	2.3
PHILADELPHIA 76ers	**40-40 .500**				**DOLPH SCHAYES**																	
Chet Walker	F	6'6	200	24	79	2187	377	936	40	288	388	74	528	132	200	2	1.042	28	6.7	1.7	2.5	13.2
Luke Jackson	F-C	6'9	240	23	76	2590	419	1013	41	288	404	71	980	93	251	4	1126	34	12.9	1.2	3.3	14.8
Wilt Chamberlain (from SF)	C	7'1	275	28	35	1558	**427**	**808**	**53**	200	**380**	53	780	133	70	0	**1054**	45	22.3	3.8	2.0	**30.1**
Hal Greer	G	6'3	176	28	70	2600	539	1245	43	335	413	81	355	313	254	7	1413	37	5.1	4.5	3.6	20.2
Larry Costello (leg injury)	G	6'1	188	33	64	1967	309	695	44	243	277	**88**	169	275	242	10	861	31	2.6	4.3	3.8	13.5
Dave Gambee	F	6'6	220	27	80	1993	356	864	41	299	368	81	468	113	277	7	1011	25	5.9	1.4	3.5	12.6
Johnny Kerr	C-F	6'9	230	32	80	1810	264	714	37	126	181	70	551	197	132	1	654	23	6.9	2.5	1.7	8.2
Al Bianchi	G	6'3	185	32	60	1116	175	486	36	54	76	71	95	140	178	10	404	19	1.6	2.3	3.0	6.7
Paul Neumann (to SF)	G	6'1	175	26	40	1100	213	434	49	148	184	80	102	139	119	1	574	28	2.6	3.5	3.0	14.4
Ben Warley	F-G	6'5	200	28	65	900	94	253	37	124	176	70	277	53	170	6	312	14	4.3	0.8	2.6	4.8
Connie Dierking (to SF)	C-F	6'9	222	28	38	729	121	311	39	54	83	65	239	42	101	3	296	19	6.3	1.1	2.7	7.8
Larry Jones	G	6'2	180	23	23	359	47	153	31	37	52	71	57	40	46	2	131	16	2.5	1.7	2.0	5.7
Steve Courtin	G	6'1	188	22	24	317	42	103	41	17	21	81	22	22	44	0	101	13	0.9	0.9	1.8	4.2
Jerry Greenspan	F	6'5	195	23	5	49	8	13	62	8	8	100	11	0	12	0	24	10	2.2	0.0	2.4	4.8
Lee Shaffer (to SF) - holdout																						
NEW YORK KNICKERBOCKERS	**31-49 .388**				**EDDIE DONOVAN (12-26 .316), HARRY GALLATIN (19-23 .442)**																	
Bob Boozer	F	6'8	215	27	80	2139	424	963	44	288	375	77	604	108	183	0	1136	27	7.6	1.4	2.3	14.2
Jim Barnes	F-C	6'8	240	23	75	2586	454	1070	42	251	379	66	729	93	312	8	1159	34	9.7	1.2	4.2	15.5
Willis Reed	C	6'9	235	22	80	3042	629	1457	43	302	407	74	1175	133	339	14	1560	38	14.7	1.7	4.2	19.5
Tom Gola	G	6'6	208	31	77	1727	204	455	45	133	180	74	319	220	269	8	541	22	4.1	2.9	3.5	7.0
Howie Komives	G	6'1	185	23	80	2376	381	1020	37	212	254	83	195	265	246	2	974	30	2.4	3.3	3.1	12.2
Johnny Green	F	6'5	200	31	78	1720	346	737	47	165	301	55	545	129	194	3	857	22	7.0	1.7	2.5	11.0
Johnny Egan	G	5'11	180	25	74	1664	258	529	49	162	199	81	143	252	139	0	678	22	1.9	3.4	1.9	9.2
Em Bryant	G	6'1	175	26	77	1332	145	436	33	87	133	65	167	167	212	3	377	17	2.2	2.2	2.8	4.9
Dave Budd	F	6'6	210	26	62	1188	196	407	48	121	170	71	310	62	147	1	513	19	5.0	1.0	2.4	8.3
Art Heyman	G	6'5	205	23	55	663	114	267	43	88	132	67	99	79	96	0	316	12	1.8	1.4	1.7	5.7
Len Chappell (broken foot)	C-F	6'8	240	23	43	655	145	367	40	68	100	68	140	15	73	0	358	15	3.3	0.3	1.7	8.3
Barry Kramer (from SF)	F-G	6'4	200	22	19	231	27	86	31	30	40	75	41	15	31	1	81	12	2.2	0.8	1.6	4.3
Tom Hoover	C	6'10	240	23	24	151	13	32	41	8	14	57	58	12	37	0	34	6	2.4	0.5	1.5	1.4
John Rudometkin (to SF) (IL)	F	6'6	205	24	1	22	3	8	38	0	0	—	7	0	5	0	6	22	7.0	0.0	5.0	6.0

Use Name	Pos	Hgt	Wgt	Age	TOTAL													PER GAME				
					G	Min	FG	FGA	%	FT	FTA	%	Reb	Ass	PF	DQ	Points	Min	Reb	Ass	PF	Points
1964/65 N.B.A. — WESTERN DIVISION																						
LOS ANGELES LAKERS	**49-31 .613**				**FRED SCHAUS**																	
Elgin Baylor	F	6'5	225	30	74	3056	763	1903	40	483	610	79	950	280	235	0	2009	41	12.8	3.8	3.2	27.1
Rudy LaRusso	F	6'7	220	27	78	2588	381	827	46	321	415	77	725	198	258	3	1083	33	9.3	2.5	3.3	13.9
Gene Wiley	C	6'10	210	27	80	2002	175	376	47	56	111	50	690	105	235	11	406	25	8.6	1.3	2.9	5.1
Dick Barnett	G	6'4	190	28	74	2026	375	908	41	270	338	80	200	159	209	1	1020	27	2.7	2.1	2.8	13.8
Jerry West	G	6'3	175	26	74	3066	822	1655	50	648	789	82	447	364	221	2	2292	41	6.0	4.9	3.0	31.0
Leroy Ellis	F-C	6'10	210	24	80	2026	311	700	44	198	284	70	652	49	196	1	820	25	8.2	0.6	2.5	10.3
Jim King	G	6'2	175	23	77	1671	184	469	39	118	151	78	214	178	193	2	486	22	2.8	2.3	2.5	6.3
Darrall Imhoff	C	6'10	220	26	76	1521	145	311	47	88	154	57	500	87	238	7	378	20	6.6	1.1	3.1	5.0
Walt Hazzard	G	6'2	190	22	66	919	117	306	38	46	71	65	111	140	132	0	280	14	1.7	2.1	2.0	4.2
Don Nelson	F	6'6	210	24	39	238	36	85	42	20	26	77	73	24	40	1	92	6	1.9	0.6	1.0	2.4
Cotton Nash (to SF)	F	6'6	225	22	25	167	14	57	25	25	32	78	35	10	30	0	53	7	1.4	0.4	1.2	2.1
Jerry Grote	G	6'4	216	24	11	33	6	11	55	2	2	100	4	4	5	0	14	3	0.4	0.4	0.5	1.3
Bill McGill (from StL)	C	6'9	225	25	8	37	7	20	35	1	1	100	12	3	6	0	15	5	1.5	0.4	0.8	1.9
ST. LOUIS HAWKS	**45-35 .563**				**HARRY GALLATIN (17-16 .395), RICHIE GUERIN (28-19 .595)**																	
Bill Bridges	F-C	6'6	235	25	79	2362	362	938	39	186	275	68	853	187	276	3	910	30	10.8	2.4	3.5	11.5
Bob Pettit (knee injury)	F-C	6'9	220	32	50	1754	396	923	43	332	405	82	621	128	167	0	1124	35	12.4	2.6	3.3	22.5
Zèlmo Beaty	C	6'9	235	25	80	2916	505	1047	48	341	477	71	966	111	328	11	1351	36	12.1	1.4	4.1	16.9
Richie Guerin (leg injury)	G	6'4	200	32	57	1678	295	662	45	231	301	77	149	271	193	1	821	29	2.6	4.8	3.4	14.4
Lenny Wilkens	G	6'1	185	27	78	2854	434	1048	41	416	558	75	365	431	283	7	1284	37	4.7	5.5	3.6	16.5
Chico Vaughn	G	6'3	215	24	75	1965	344	811	42	182	242	75	173	157	192	2	870	26	2.3	2.1	2.6	11.6
Cliff Hagan	F	6'4	210	33	77	1739	393	901	44	214	268	80	276	136	182	0	1000	23	3.6	1.8	2.4	13.0
Mike Farmer	F	6'7	215	28	60	1272	167	408	41	75	94	80	258	88	123	0	409	21	4.3	1.5	2.1	6.8
Paul Silas	F	6'7	235	21	79	1243	140	375	37	83	164	51	576	48	161	1	363	16	7.3	0.6	2.0	4.6
John Barnhill (leg injury)	G	6'1	180	26	41	777	121	312	39	45	70	64	91	76	56	0	287	19	2.2	1.9	1.4	7.0
Jeff Mullins	G-F	6'4	190	22	44	492	87	209	42	41	61	67	102	44	60	0	215	11	2.3	1.0	1.4	4.9
Bill McGill (to LA)	C	6'9	225	25	16	96	14	45	31	12	16	75	24	6	26	1	40	6	1.5	0.4	1.6	2.5
Ed Burton	F	6'6	225	25	7	42	7	20	35	4	7	57	13	2	13	0	18	6	1.9	0.3	1.9	2.6
John Tresvant	F	6'7	215	25	4	35	4	11	36	6	9	67	18	6	9	0	14	9	4.5	1.5	2.3	3.5
BAUIMORE BULLETS	**37-43 .463**				**BUDDY JEANNETTE**																	
Gus Johnson	F	6'6	235	26	76	2899	577	1379	42	261	386	68	988	270	258	4	1415	38	13.0	3.6	3.4	18.6
Bailey Howell	F	6'7	225	27	80	2975	515	1040	50	504	629	80	869	208	**345**	10	1534	37	10.9	2.6	**4.3**	19.2
Walt Bellamy	C	6'11	235	25	80	3301	733	1441	51	515	752	68	1166	191	260	2	1981	41	14.6	2.4	3.3	24.8
Don Ohl	G	6'3	190	28	77	2821	568	1297	44	284	388	73	336	250	274	7	1420	37	4.4	3.2	3.6	18.4
Kevin Loughery	G	6'3	190	24	80	2417	406	957	42	212	281	75	235	296	320	13	1024	30	2.9	3.7	4.0	12.8
Bob Ferry	F-C	6'8	230	27	77	1280	143	338	42	122	199	61	355	60	156	2	408	17	4.6	0.8	2.0	5.3
Wally Jones	G	6'2	180	22	77	1250	154	411	37	99	136	73	140	200	196	1	407	16	1.8	2.6	2.5	5.3
Si Green	G	6'2	190	30	70	1086	152	368	41	101	161	63	169	140	134	1	405	16	2.4	2.0	1.9	5.8
Wayne Hightower (from SF)	F	6'9	210	24	27	510	60	174	34	62	81	77	173	16	61	1	182	19	6.4	0.6	2.3	6.7
Gary Bradds	F	6'8	210	22	41	335	46	111	41	45	63	71	84	19	36	0	137	8	2.0	0.5	0.9	3.3
Charlie Hardnett	F	6'8	225	26	20	200	25	80	31	23	39	59	77	2	37	0	73	10	3.9	0.1	1.9	3.7
Al Butler	G	6'2	175	26	25	172	24	73	33	11	15	73	21	12	25	0	59	7	0.8	0.5	1.0	2.4
Les Hunter	F	6'7	212	22	24	114	18	64	28	6	14	43	50	11	16	0	42	5	2.1	0.5	0.7	1.8
Gary Hill (from SF)	G	6'4	185	23	3	15	0	1	0	0	0	—	1	1	1	0	0	5	0.3	0.3	0.3	0.0
DETROIT PISTONS	**31-49 .388**				**CHARLIE WOLF (2-9 .181), DAVE DeBUSSCHERE (29-40 .420)**																	
Dave DeBusschere	F	6'6	220	24	79	2769	508	1196	42	306	437	70	874	253	242	5	1322	35	11.1	3.2	3.1	16.7
Ray Scott	F-C	6'9	215	26	66	2167	402	1092	37	220	314	70	634	239	209	5	1024	33	9.6	3.6	3.2	15.5
Reggie Harding	C	7'	245	22	78	2699	405	987	41	128	209	61	906	179	258	5	938	35	11.6	2.3	3.3	12.0
Terry Dischinger	G-F	6'7	189	24	80	2698	568	1153	49	320	424	75	479	198	253	5	1456	34	6.0	2.5	3.2	18.2
Eddie Miles	G	6'4	196	24	76	2074	439	994	44	166	223	74	258	157	201	1	1044	27	3.4	2.1	2.6	13.7
Rod Thorn	G	6'4	195	23	74	1770	320	750	43	176	243	72	266	161	122	0	816	24	3.6	2.2	1.6	11.0
Joe Caldwell	F-G	6'5	195	23	66	1543	290	776	37	129	210	61	441	118	171	3	709	23	6.7	1.8	2.6	10.7
Donnie Butcher	G	6'3	200	28	71	1157	143	353	41	126	204	62	200	122	183	4	412	16	2.8	1.7	2.6	5.8
Don Kojis	F	6'4	215	25	65	836	180	416	43	62	98	63	243	63	115	1	422	13	3.7	1.0	1.8	6.5
Hub Reed	C	6'9	230	28	62	753	84	221	38	40	58	69	206	38	136	2	208	12	3.3	0.6	2.2	3.4
Jackie Moreland	F	6'5	215	26	54	732	103	296	35	66	104	63	183	69	151	4	272	14	3.4	1.3	2.8	5.0
Willie Jones	G	6'3	185	28	12	101	21	52	40	2	6	33	10	7	13	0	44	8	0.8	0.6	1.1	3.7
Bob Duffy	G	6'3	185	24	4	26	4	11	36	6	7	86	4	5	4	0	14	7	1.0	1.3	1.0	3.5
SAN FRANCISCO WARRIORS	**17-63 .213**				**ALEX HANNUM**																	
Tom Meschery	F	6'6	215	26	79	2408	361	917	39	278	370	75	655	106	279	6	1000	30	8.3	1.3	3.5	12.7
McCoy McLemore	F	6'7	230	22	78	1731	244	725	34	157	220	71	488	81	224	6	645	22	6.3	1.0	2.9	8.3
Nate Thurmond	C-F	6'11	225	23	77	3173	519	1240	42	235	357	66	1395	157	232	3	1273	41	18.1	2.0	3.0	16.5
Paul Neumann (from Phi)	G	6'1	175	26	36	934	152	338	45	86	119	72	96	94	99	2	390	26	2.7	2.6	2.8	10.8
Guy Rodgers	G	6'	185	29	79	2699	465	1225	38	223	325	69	323	565	256	4	1153	34	4.1	7.2	3.2	14.6
Wilt Chamberlain (to Phi)	C	7'1	275	28	38	1743	**636**	**1275**	50	208	**500**	42	893	117	76	0	**1480**	46	23.5	3.1	2.0	**38.9**
Al Attles	G	6'2	180	28	73	1733	254	662	38	171	274	62	239	205	242	7	679	24	3.3	2.8	3.3	9.3
Gary Phillips	G	6'3	190	25	73	1541	198	553	36	120	199	60	189	148	184	3	516	21	2.6	2.0	2.5	7.1
Wayne Hightower (to Bal)	F	6'9	210	24	48	1037	136	396	34	133	173	77	247	38	143	1	405	22	5.1	0.8	3.0	8.4
Bud Koper	G	6'6	210	22	56	631	106	241	44	35	42	83	61	43	59	1	247	11	1.1	0.8	1.1	4.4
Connie Dierking (from Phi)	C-F	6'9	222	28	30	565	97	227	43	46	85	54	196	30	64	1	240	19	6.5	1.0	2.1	8.0
John Rudometkin (from NY) (IL)	F	6'6	205	24	22	354	49	146	34	34	50	68	92	16	49	0	132	16	4.2	0.7	2.2	6.0
Barry Kramer (to NY)	F-G	6'4	200	22	33	276	36	100	36	30	44	68	59	26	36	0	102	8	1.8	0.8	1.1	3.1
George Lee	F	6'4	200	28	19	247	27	77	35	38	52	73	55	12	22	0	92	13	2.9	0.6	1.2	4.8
Cotton Nash (from LA)	F	6'6	225	22	20	190	33	88	38	18	20	90	48	9	27	0	84	10	2.4	0.5	1.4	4.2
Gary Hill (to Bal)	F	6'4	185	23	9	88	10	35	29	7	14	50	15	6	10	0	27	10	1.7	0.7	1.1	3.0
Lee Shuffer (from Phi) — holdout																						

Use Name	Pos	Hgt	Wgt	Age	TOTAL G	Min	FG	FGA	%	FT	FTA	%	Reb	Ass	PF	DQ	Points	PER GAME Min	Reb	Ass	PF	Points
1964/65 N B.A. — PLAYOFFS																						
BOSTON CELTICS	**RED AUERBACH**	defeated Philadelphia 4-3; H108-98, 103-109, H112-94, 131-134(OT), H114-108, 106-112, H110-109 defeated Los Angeles 4-1; H142-110, H129-123, 105-126, 112-99, H129-96																				
Tom Heinsohn	F	6'7	220	30	12	276	66	181	36	20	32	63	84	23	46	1	152	23	7.0	1.9	3.8	12.7
Satch Sanders	F	6'6	210	26	12	365	64	152	42	31	43	72	102	19	**58**	**4**	159	30	8.5	1.6	4.8	13.3
Bill Russell	C	6'10	220	30	12	**561**	79	150	53	40	76	53	**302**	**76**	43	2	198	47	25.2	6.3	3.6	16.5
Sam Jones	G	6'4	205	31	12	495	135	294	46	73	84	87	55	30	39	1	343	41	4.6	2.5	3.3	28.6
K. C. Jones	G	6'1	202	32	12	396	43	104	41	35	45	78	39	74	49	1	121	33	3.3	6.2	4.1	10.1
John Havlicek	F-G	6'5	205	24	12	405	88	250	35	46	55	84	88	29	44	1	222	34	7.3	2.4	3.7	18.5
Willie Naulls	F	6'6	225	30	12	180	39	95	41	10	15	67	51	9	27	0	88	15	4.3	0.8	2.3	7.3
Larry Siegfried	G	6'3	192	25	12	163	30	79	38	24	28	86	25	21	25	0	84	14	2.1	1.8	2.1	7.0
Mel Counts	C-F	7'	230	23	4	30	4	15	27	1	1	100	11	1	10	0	9	8	2.8	0.3	2.5	2.3
John Thompson	F	6'10	230	23	3	21	2	7	29	7	7	100	12	1	2	0	11	7	4.0	0.3	0.7	3.7
Ron Bonham	F	6'5	200	22	4	13	5	12	42	4	5	80	1	0	1	0	14	3	0.3	0.0	0.3	3.5
LOS ANGELES LAKERS	**FRED SCHAUS**	defeated Baltimore 4-2; H121-115, H118-115, 115-122, 114-112, H112-120, 117-115 lost to Boston 1-4; 110-142, 123-129, H126-105, H99-112, 96-129																				
Rudy LaRusso	F	6'7	220	27	11	395	56	137	41	53	74	72	89	29	52	**4**	165	36	8.1	2.6	4.7	15.0
Leroy Ellis	F-C	6'10	210	24	11	405	57	145	39	44	65	68	133	7	37	0	158	37	12.1	0.6	3.4	14.4
Gene Wiley	C	6'10	210	27	11	379	33	59	56	11	19	58	158	23	41	0	77	34	14.4	2.1	3.7	7.0
Dick Barnett	G	6'4	190	28	10	287	72	150	48	31	39	79	30	33	25	0	175	29	3.0	3.3	2.5	17.5
Jerry West	G	6'3	175	26	11	470	**155**	**351**	44	**137**	**154**	89	63	58	37	0	**447**	43	5.7	5.3	3.4	**40.6**
Don Nelson	F	6'6	210	24	11	212	24	53	45	19	25	76	59	19	31	0	67	19	5.4	1.7	2.8	6.1
Jim King	G	6'2	175	23	11	184	28	63	44	15	17	88	36	24	29	1	71	17	3.3	2.2	2.6	6.5
Darrall Imhoff	C	6'10	220	26	11	151	13	24	**54**	7	12	58	43	13	26	0	33	14	3.9	1.2	2.4	3.0
Walt Hazzard	G	6'2	190	22	7	118	19	57	33	15	20	75	18	30	18	0	53	17	2.6	4.3	2.6	7.6
Bill McGill	C-F	6'9	225	25	5	34	5	9	56	1	1	100	9	2	9	1	11	7	1.8	0.4	1.8	2.2
Elgin Baylor (KJ)	F	6'5	225	30	1	5	0	2	0	0	0	—	0	1	0	0	0	5	0.0	1.0	0.0	0.0
PHILADELPHIA 76ers	**DOLPH SCHAYES**	defeated Cincinnati 3-1; 119-117(OT), H120-121, 108-94, H119-112 lost to Boston 3-4; 98-108, H109-103, 94-112, H134-131(OT), 108-114, H112-106, 109-110																				
Chet Walker	F-G	6'6	200	24	11	469	83	173	48	57	75	76	79	18	38	0	223	43	7.2	1.6	3.5	20.3
Luke Jackson	F	6'9	240	23	11	321	44	130	34	25	32	78	79	24	31	0	113	29	7.2	2.2	2.8	10.3
Wilt Chamberlain	C	7'1	275	28	11	536	123	232	53	76	136	56	299	48	29	0	322	49	**27.2**	4.4	2.6	29.3
Hal Greer	G	6'3	176	28	11	505	101	222	45	69	87	79	81	55	45	2	271	46	7.4	5.0	4.1	24.6
Larry Costello	G	6'1	188	33	10	207	22	53	42	11	16	69	12	20	43	2	55	21	1.2	2.0	4.3	5.5
Al Bianchi	G	6'3	185	32	11	308	45	118	38	14	21	67	16	30	45	2	104	28	1.5	2.7	4.1	9.5
Johnny Kerr	F-C	6'9	230	32	11	181	24	67	36	15	21	71	38	28	20	0	63	16	3.5	2.5	1.8	5.7
Dave Gambee	F	6'6	220	27	10	132	16	48	33	30	34	88	23	6	31	1	62	13	2.3	0.6	3.1	6.2
Larry Jones	G	6'2	180	23	5	25	5	12	42	7	11	64	4	2	5	0	17	5	0.8	0.4	1.0	3.4
Ben Warley	F-G	6'5	200	28	2	6	0	1	0	0	0	—	1	1	1	0	0	3	0.5	0.5	0.5	0.0
BALTIMORE BULLETS	**BUDDY JEANNETTE**	defeated St. Louis 3-1; 108-105, 105-129, H131-99, H109-103 lost to Los Angeles 2-4; 115-121, 115-118, H122-115, H112-114, 120-112, H115-117																				
Gus Johnson	F	6'6	235	26	10	377	62	173	36	34	46	74	111	34	38	1	158	38	11.1	3.4	3.8	15.8
Bailey Howell	F	6'7	225	27	9	350	67	130	52	53	70	76	105	19	38	3	187	39	11.7	2.1	4.2	20.8
Walt Bellamy	C	6'11	235	25	10	427	74	158	47	61	92	66	151	34	38	0	209	43	15.1	3.4	3.8	20.9
Don Ohl	G	6'3	190	28	10	432	100	208	48	61	78	78	64	27	46	1	261	43	6.4	2.7	4.6	26.1
Kevin Loughery	G	6'3	190	24	10	297	53	137	39	34	38	89	34	30	36	0	140	30	3.4	3.0	3.6	14.0
Wayne Hightower	F	6'9	210	24	10	196	27	64	42	14	22	64	57	8	25	0	68	20	5.7	0.8	2.5	6.8
Wally Jones	G	6'2	180	22	10	162	29	63	46	15	20	75	20	18	28	1	73	16	2.0	1.8	2.8	7.3
Bob Ferry	C-F	6'8	230	27	10	67	7	16	44	2	9	22	19	8	8	0	16	7	1.9	0.8	0.8	1.6
Si Green	G	6'2	190	30	9	65	7	16	44	4	5	80	7	15	13	0	18	7	0.8	1.7	1.4	2.0
Charlie Hardnett	F	6'8	225	26	5	22	4	10	40	2	5	40	6	2	2	0	10	4	1.2	0.4	0.4	2.0
Gary Bradds	F	6'8	210	22	1	5	2	3	67	2	2	100	2	0	0	0	6	5	2.0	0.0	0.0	6.0
ST. LOUIS HAWKS	**RICHIE GUERIN**	lost to Baltimore 1-3; H105-108, H129-105, 99-131, 103-109																				
Bill Bridges	F	6'6	235	25	4	145	21	59	36	10	15	67	67	9	19	1	52	36	16.8	2.3	4.8	13.0
Bob Pettit	F-C	6'9	220	32	4	95	15	41	37	16	20	80	24	8	10	0	46	24	6.0	2.0	2.5	11.5
Zelmo Beaty	C	6'9	235	25	4	154	29	59	49	19	25	76	55	1	19	1	77	39	13.8	0.3	4.8	19.3
Richie Guerin	G	6'4	200	32	4	125	25	65	38	19	25	76	8	21	14	0	69	31	2.0	5.3	3.5	17.3
Lenny Wilkens	G	6'1	185	27	4	147	20	57	35	24	29	83	12	15	14	0	64	37	3.0	3.8	3.5	16.0
Cliff Hagan	F	6'4	210	33	4	123	34	75	45	6	12	50	26	7	14	0	74	31	6.5	1.8	3.5	18.5
Chico Vaughn	G	6'3	215	24	4	75	9	29	31	7	8	88	6	10	14	0	25	19	1.5	2.5	3.5	6.3
Paul Silas	F	6'7	235	21	4	42	4	10	40	3	4	75	18	1	6	0	11	11	4.5	0.3	1.5	2.8
John Barnhill	G	6'1	180	26	4	36	2	11	18	2	4	50	7	2	3	0	6	9	1.8	0.5	0.8	1.5
Jeff Mullins	F	6'4	190	22	2	11	4	8	50	0	0	—	6	1	0	0	8	6	3.0	0.5	0.0	4.0
Mike Farmer	F	6'7	215	28	1	7	2	4	50	0	0	—	1	0	1	0	4	7	1.0	0.0	1.0	4.0
CINCINNATI ROYALS	**JACK McMAHON**	lost to Philadelphia 1-3; H117-119(OT), 121-120, H94-108, 112-119																				
Jack Twyman	F	6'6	215	30	4	97	19	48	40	11	11	100	17	3	16	0	49	24	4.3	0.8	4.0	12.3
Jerry Lucas	F-C	6'8	230	24	4	195	38	75	51	17	22	77	84	9	12	0	93	**49**	21.0	2.3	3.0	23.3
Wayne Embry	C	6'8	250	27	4	123	21	48	44	9	11	82	25	8	20	1	51	31	6.3	2.0	**5.0**	12.8
Oscar Robertson	G	6'5	205	26	4	195	38	89	43	36	39	92	19	48	14	0	112	**49**	4.8	**12.0**	3.5	28.0
Adrian Smith	G	6'1	180	28	4	150	18	48	38	21	22	**95**	11	21	11	0	57	38	2.8	5.3	2.8	14.3
Tom Hawkins	F	6'5	210	28	4	95	17	33	52	4	5	80	28	1	13	0	38	24	7.0	0.3	3.3	9.5
Tom Thacker	G	6'2	170	23	4	47	5	13	38	3	4	75	12	3	8	0	13	12	3.0	0.8	2.0	3.3
Happy Hairston	F	6'7	225	22	3	39	5	18	28	2	3	67	20	3	2	0	12	13	6.7	1.0	0.7	4.0
Bud Olsen	F	6'8	220	24	4	39	7	17	41	3	5	60	9	1	8	0	17	10	2.3	0.3	2.0	4.3
George Wilson	C	6'8	215	22	2	3	1	1	100	0	0	—	2	1	1	0	2	2	1.0	0.5	0.5	1.0
Jay Arnette	G	6'2	175	26	1	2	0	1	0	0	0	—	0	1	1	0	0	2	0.0	1.0	1.0	0.0

1964/65 N.B.A. TEAM STATISTICS

Team	REGULAR SEASON G	FG	FGA	%	FT	FTA	%	Reb.	Ass.	AVERAGE POINTS For	Agnst.	Diff.
EASTERN DIVISION												
Boston	80	3567	8609	41	1890	2587	73	5748	1772	112.8	104.5	+8.3
Cincinnati	80	3482	7797	45	2170	2866	76	5387	1843	114.2	111.9	+2.3
Philadelphia	80	3391	8028	42	2221	3011	74	5246	1692	112.5	112.7	-0.2
New York	80	3339	7834	43	1915	2684	71	5206	1550	107.4	111.1	-3.7
WESTERN DIVISION												
Los Angeles	80	3336	7628	44	2276	2984	76	5231	1601	111.9	109.9	+2.0
St. Louis	80	3269	7710	42	2168	2947	74	5208	1691	108.8	105.8	+3.0
Baltimore	80	3421	7734	44	2245	3144	71	5298	1676	113.6	115.8	-2.2
Detroit	80	3467	8297	42	1747	2537	69	5394	1609	108.5	111.9	-3.4
San Francisco	80	3323	8245	40	1819	2844	64	5715	1653	105.8	112.0	-6.2

Team	PLAYOFFS G	FG	FGA	%	FT	FTA	%	Reb.	Ass.	AVERAGE POINTS For	Agnst.	Diff.
EASTERN DIVISION												
Boston	12	555	1339	41	291	391	74	867	283	116.8	109.8	+7.0
Cincinnati	4	169	391	43	106	122	87	255	99	111.0	116.5	-5.5
Philadelphia	11	463	1056	44	304	433	70	707	232	111.8	111.7	+0.1
WESTERN DIVISION												
Los Angeles	11	462	1050	44	333	427	78	724	239	114.3	119.1	-4.8
St. Louis	4	165	418	39	106	142	75	265	75	109.0	113.3	-4.3
Baltimore	10	432	978	44	282	387	73	648	195	114.6	113.9	+0.7

1964/65 N.B.A. STANDINGS

Team	W	L	Pct.	GB	Record against playoff teams W	L	Pct.	Record against non - playoff teams W	L	Pct.	HOME W	L	Pct.	ROAD W	L	Pct.	NEUTRAL W	L	Pct.
EASTERN DIVISION																			
Boston Celtics	**62**	18	**.775**	—	**36**	14	**.720**	**26**	4	**.867**	**27**	3	**.900**	**27**	11	.711	8	4	.667
Cincinnati Royals	48	32	.600	14	26	24	.520	22	8	.733	25	7	.781	17	21	.447	6	4	.600
Philadelphia 76ers	40	40	.500	22	23	27	.460	17	13	.567	13	12	.520	10	21	.323	**17**	7	**.708**
New York Knickerbockers	31	49	.388	31	19	41	.317	12	8	.600	16	19	.457	9	22	.290	6	8	.429
WESTERN DIVISION																			
Los Angeles Lakers	49	31	.613	—	24	26	.480	25	5	.833	25	13	.658	21	16	.568	3	2	.600
St. Louis Hawks	45	35	.563	4	19	31	.380	**26**	4	**.867**	26	14	.650	15	17	.469	4	4	.500
Baltimore Bullets	37	43	.463	12	22	28	.440	15	**15**	.500	23	14	.622	13	19	.406	1	10	.090
Detroit Pistons	31	49	.388	18	18	42	.300	13	7	.650	13	17	.433	11	20	.355	7	**12**	.368
San Francisco Warriors	17	**63**	.213	32	12	**48**	.200	5	**15**	.250	10	**29**	.256	5	**31**	.139	2	3	.400

1964/65 N.B.A. INDIVIDUAL LEADERS

SCORING
(Minimum 65 Games Played)

Name	Team	G	FG	FT	Pts.	Avg.
Chamberlain	SF-Phi	73	1063	408	2534	34.7
West	LA	74	822	648	2292	31.0
Robertson	Cin	75	807	665	2279	30.4
Baylor	LA	74	763	483	2009	27.1
S. Jones	Bos	80	821	428	2070	25.9
Bellamy	Bal	80	733	515	1981	24.8
Lucas	Cin	66	558	298	1414	21.4
Greer	Phi	70	539	335	1413	20.2
Reed	NY	80	629	302	1560	19.5
Howell	Bal	80	515	504	1534	19.2

FIELD GOAL PERCENTAGE
(Minimum 220 Field Goals)

Name	Team	FG	FGA	Pct.
Chamberlain	SF-Phi	1063	2083	.510
Bellamy	Bal	733	1441	.509
Lucas	Cin	558	1121	.498
West	LA	822	1655	.497
Howell	Bal	515	1040	.495
Dischinger	Det	568	1153	.493
Egan	NY	258	529	.488
Beaty	StL	505	1047	.482
Robertson	Cin	807	1681	.480
Neumann	Phi-SF	365	772	.473

FREE THROW PERCENTAGE
(Minimum 210 Free Throws)

Name	Team	FT	FTA	Pct.
Costello	Phi	243	277	.877
Robertson	Cin	665	793	.839
Komives	NY	212	254	.835
Smith	Cin	284	342	.830
West	LA	648	789	.821
S. Jones	Bos	428	522	.820
Pettit	StL	332	405	.820
Lucas	Cin	298	366	.814
Gambee	Phi	299	368	.813
Greer	Phi	335	413	.811

PERSONAL FOULS

Name	Team	PF
Howell	Bal	345
Reed	NY	339
Beaty	StL	328
Loughery	Bal	320
Sanders	Bos	318

GAMES DISQUALIFIED

Name	Team	Disq.
Sanders	Bos	15
Reed	NY	14
Loughery	Bal	13
Beaty	StL	11
Wiley	LA	11

REBOUNDS PER GAME
(Minimum 65 Games Played)

Name	Team	G	Reb.	Avg.
Russell	Bos	78	1878	24.1
Chamberlain	SF-Phi	73	1673	22.9
Lucas	Cin	66	1321	20.0
Thurmond	SF	77	1395	18.1
Reed	NY	80	1175	14.7
Bellamy	Bal	80	1166	14.6
Johnson	Bal	76	988	13.0
Jackson	Phi	76	980	12.9
Baylor	LA	74	950	12.8
Beaty	StL	80	966	12.1

ASSISTS PER GAME
(Minimum 65 Games Played)

Name	Team	G	Ass.	Avg.
Robertson	Cin	75	861	11.5
Rodgers	SF	79	565	7.2
K. C. Jones	Bos	78	437	5.6
Wilkens	StL	78	431	5.5
Russell	Bos	78	410	5.3
West	LA	74	364	4.9
Greer	Phi	70	313	4.5
Costello	Phi	64	275	4.3
Baylor	LA	74	280	3.8
Loughery	Bal	80	296	3.7

MINUTES PLAYED

Name	Team	Min.
Russell	Bos	3466
Robertson	Cin	3421
Bellamy	Bal	3301
Chamberlain	SF-Phi	3301
Thurmond	SF	3173

1965-66 N.B.A.

Humbled, but Unbeaten

The Philadelphia 76ers had come within one shot of beating the Boston Celtics in last spring's playoffs, and they started this season with high hopes of ending the Celtics' long string of N.B.A. championships. Wilt Chamberlain had a half season of experience in the 76er system, and he eagerly anticipated answering those critics who said that he lacked the competitive zeal of rival center Bill Russell of the long-successful Celtics. Around Wilt's scoring, rebounding, and defense in the pivot, coach Dolph Schayes had offensive aces in Hal Greer, Chet Walker, rookie Billy Cunningham, and newcomer Wally Jones, obtained from Baltimore. He had a strong rebounder in Luke Jackson, and two experienced reserves in Syracuse veterans Al Bianchi and Dave Gambee. Chamberlain began to change his style, going to the basket less frequently, passing off more often to his sharp-shooting teammates, and concentrating on defense and blocking shots. He still managed to lead the league in scoring as well as rebounding and field goal percentage, and finished seventh in the N.B.A. in assists.

Bill Russell was still the shot-blocker without equal, but he and the Celtics started to feel the inevitable creep of time. Tom Heinsohn retired, and coach Red Auerbach replaced him at forward by starting veteran Willie Naulls and using super-sub John Havlicek more often at that position. Further forward help came from Don Nelson, who blossomed into a key reserve after Auerbach picked him up from Los Angeles on waivers. The other starters were familiar figures, with Russell, Sam Jones, K.C. Jones, and Satch Sanders identified in the public's mind with the excellence of the Celtic dynasty. Various injuries kept several of these veterans out of the lineup for stretches of time and made the Celtics' task of repeating that much harder.

But they did look like they were on the way to another first place finish in the East when they held a four-game lead over the 76ers on New Year's Day. On February 12, the Celtics met their rivals from Philly head-on in Syracuse and beat them 85-83; this victory put the Celtics five up in the win column and three up in the loss column. But then the tide turned, as the Celtics dropped three straight games while the 76ers won three straight. Now Boston's record stood at 42-22 and Philadelphia's at 40-22. On March 5 and 6, the two rivals squared off in a home-and-away series which swung the balance of power; the 76ers won 102-85 at home and 113-110 in Boston. The 76ers then swept their last eight games, and not even a sweep of their last six games could save the Celtics from finishing one game behind the 76ers. For the first time since 1956, the Celtics were in second place.

The Cincinnati Royals, led as usual by Oscar Robertson and Jerry Lucas, took the third Eastern playoff berth with a 45-35 record, which would have been good enough for first place in the West. The fourth place team, as always, was the New York Knicks, who slowly but surely were building back into respectability. First draft pick Bill Bradley, the All-American forward from Princeton, turned down pro ball to accept a Rhodes scholarship to Oxford, but the Knicks did come up with a pair of solid rookie forwards in Dick Van Arsdale and Dave Stallworth. In addition. trades brought in new offensive power in center Walt Bellamy and guard Dick Barnett, although the acquisition of Bellamy forced talented second-year man Willis Reed to play an unfamiliar forward spot.

There was nothing unfamiliar about the Los Angeles Lakers taking first place in the West for the fourth time in five years. Bad knees kept Elgin Baylor out of the lineup for a long stretch and cut his effectiveness far below normal when he did play. But Jerry West kept scoring at a 31.3 level, and the supporting cast of Rudy LaRusso, Walt Hazzard, Leroy Ellis, and Bob Boozer picked up some of the slack left by Baylor's injuries.

The four other Western teams all finished under the .500 mark. The Baltimore Bullets came in second with a 38-42 record, Gus Johnson's bad knees kept him on the shelf for half the season and forced the team to trade center Walt Bellamy to New York for forward Jim Barnes, who turned out to be less helpful than expected. Veteran Johnny Kerr took over at center, and he finally missed a game early in the campaign after playing 917 consecutive regular season and playoff games. Behind Baltimore came the St. Louis Hawks, who dearly felt the absence of retired star Bob Pettit. The San Francisco Warriors just missed the playoffs in fourth place, but unveiled a new scoring star in rookie forward Rick Barry, a thin 6'7" shooting ace from the University of Miami. The Detroit Pistons had picked center Bill Buntin as their first draft choice, and his poor season helped the team reserve another high draft place by finishing last with a 22-58 record.

But with the end of the regular season, attention focused on the playoff situation in the East. The Celtics, humbled by their second place finish, had to compete in the opening round for the first time in ten years. Paired with the Royals, the defending champions dropped two of the first three games before winning the fourth and fifth games to take the series. Now the stage was set for the rematch of Russell and Chamberlain, of Boston and Philadelphia. The 76ers had enjoyed the first-round bye given to the divisional champion, and the two weeks of inactivity seemed to dull the sharp edge developed in their closing spurt of 18 out of 21 games and the last 11 in a row. The Celtics, however, got their house in order in the Cincinnati series and came roaring into the confrontation. The defending champs knocked the 76ers off 114-93 in the opening game in Philly, and then took a commanding edge with a 114-93 win in Boston. The 76ers then won game three at home, but a 114-110 overtime win for the Celtics in game four foretold the final outcome. Game five at Philly went to the Celtics, and the 76ers went home for the summer with the taste of victory still unrealized. The Celtics, meanwhile, headed into the championship series for the tenth straight year, and captured their eighth straight title with a seven-game triumph over the Lakers.

During the series, Red Auerbach announced that he was stepping down as coach next season, to concentrate on his duties as general manager, with Bill Russell succeeding him as player coach. After running off an incredible string of nine titles in ten years, Auerbach's victory cigar would no longer glow from the Boston bench.

					TOTAL													PER GAME				
Use Name	Pos	Hgt	Wgt	Age	G	Min	FG	FGA	%	FT	FTA	%	Reb	Ass	PF	DQ	Points	Min	Reb	Ass	PF	Points
1965/66 N.B.A. — EASTERN DIVISION																						
PHILADELPHIA 76ers	**55-25 .688**				**DOLPH SCHAYES**																	
Chet Walker	F	6'6	205	25	80	2603	443	982	45	335	468	72	636	201	238	3	1221	33	8.0	2.5	3.0	15.3
Billy Cunningham	F	6'7	220	22	80	2134	431	1011	43	281	443	63	599	207	301	12	1143	27	7.5	2.6	3.8	14.3
Wilt Chamberlain	C	7'1	275	29	79	**3737**	**1074**	**1990**	**54**	501	976	51	**1943**	414	171	0	**2649**	**47**	**24.6**	5.2	2.2	**33.5**
Hal Greer	G	6'3	176	29	80	3326	703	1580	44	413	514	80	473	384	315	6	1819	42	5.9	4.8	3.9	22.7
Wally Jones	G	6'2	180	23	80	2196	296	799	37	128	172	74	169	273	250	6	720	27	2.1	3.4	3.1	9.0
Luke Jackson	F-C	6'9	240	24	79	1966	246	614	40	158	214	74	676	132	216	2	650	25	8.6	1.7	2.7	8.2
Al Bianchi	G	6'3	185	33	78	1312	214	560	38	66	98	67	134	134	232	4	494	17	1.7	1.7	3.0	6.3
Dave Gambee	F	6'6	220	28	72	1068	168	437	38	159	187	85	273	71	189	3	495	15	3.8	1.0	2.6	6.9
Gerry Ward	G	6'4	190	24	66	838	67	189	35	39	60	65	89	80	163	3	173	13	1.3	1.2	2.5	2.6
Bob Weiss	G	6'2	180	23	7	30	3	9	33	0	0	—	7	4	10	0	6	4	1.0	0.6	1.4	0.9
Art Heyman (from Cin)	G	6'5	205	24	6	20	3	9	33	4	5	80	4	4	4	0	10	3	0.7	0.7	0.7	1.7
Jesse Branson	F	6'7	200	23	5	14	1	6	17	3	4	75	9	1	4	0	5	3	1.8	0.2	0.8	1.0
Ben Warley (to Bal)	F	6'5	200	29	1	6	1	3	33	0	0	—	2	0	1	0	2	6	2.0	0.0	1.0	2.0
BOSTON CELTICS	**54-26 .675**				**RED AUERBACH**																	
John Havlicek	F-G	6'5	205	25	71	2175	530	1328	40	274	349	79	423	210	158	1	1334	31	6.0	3.0	2.2	18.8
Satch Sanders	F	6'6	210	27	72	1896	349	816	43	211	276	76	508	90	317	**19**	909	26	7.1	1.3	**4.4**	12.6
Bill Russell	C	6'10	220	31	78	3386	391	943	41	223	405	55	1779	371	221	4	1005	43	22.8	4.8	2.8	12.9
Sam Jones (injury)	G	6'4	205	32	68	2155	626	1335	47	325	407	80	347	216	170	0	1577	32	5.1	3.2	2.5	23.2
K. C. Jones	G	6'1	202	33	80	2710	240	619	39	209	303	69	304	503	243	4	689	34	3.8	6.3	3.0	8.6
Don Nelson	F	6'6	210	25	75	1765	271	618	44	223	326	68	403	79	187	1	765	24	5.4	1.1	2.5	10.2
Larry Siegfried	G	6'3	192	26	71	1675	349	825	42	274	311	**88**	196	165	157	1	972	24	2.8	2.3	2.2	13.7
Willie Naulls	F	6'6	225	31	71	1433	328	815	40	104	131	79	319	72	197	4	760	20	4.5	1.0	2.8	10.7
Mel Counts	F-C	7'	230	24	67	1021	221	549	40	120	145	83	432	50	207	5	562	15	6.4	0.7	3.1	8.4
Woody Sauldsberry	F	6'7	220	31	39	530	80	249	32	11	22	50	142	15	94	0	171	14	3.6	0.4	2.4	4.4
Ron Bonham	F	6'5	200	23	39	312	76	207	37	52	61	85	35	11	29	0	204	8	0.9	0.3	0.7	5.2
Si Green	G	6'2	190	31	10	92	12	31	39	8	16	50	11	9	16	0	32	9	1.1	0.9	1.6	3.2
John Thompson	F	6'10	230	24	10	72	14	30	47	4	6	67	30	3	15	0	32	7	3.0	0.3	1.5	3.2
Ron Watts	F	6'6	210	22	1	3	1	2	50	0	0	—	1	1	1	0	2	3	1.0	1.0	1.0	2.0
CINCINNATI ROYALS	**45-35 .563**				**JACK McMAHON**																	
Tom Hawkins	F	6'5	210	29	79	2126	273	604	45	116	209	56	575	99	274	4	662	27	7.3	1.3	3.5	8.4
Jerry Lucas	F-C	6'8	230	25	79	3517	690	1523	45	317	403	79	1668	213	274	5	1697	45	21.1	2.7	3.5	21.5
Wayne Embry	C	6'8	260	28	80	1882	232	564	41	141	234	60	525	81	287	9	605	24	6.6	1.0	3.6	7.6
Oscar Robertson	G	6'5	210	27	76	3493	818	1723	47	742	881	84	586	**847**	227	1	2378	46	7.7	**11.1**	3.0	31.3
Adrian Smith	G	6'1	185	29	80	2982	531	1310	41	408	480	85	287	256	276	1	1470	37	3.6	3.2	3.5	18.4
Happy Hairston	F	6'7	225	23	72	1794	398	814	49	220	321	69	546	44	216	3	1016	25	7.6	0.6	3.0	14.1
Jack Twyman	F	6'6	220	31	73	943	224	498	45	95	117	81	168	60	122	1	543	13	2.3	0.8	1.7	7.4
Jon McGlocklin	G-F	6'5	205	22	72	852	153	363	42	62	79	78	133	88	77	0	368	12	1.8	1.2	1.1	5.1
Connie Dierking	C	6'9	230	29	57	782	134	322	42	50	82	61	245	43	113	0	318	14	4.3	0.8	2.0	5.6
Tom Thacker	G	6'2	170	24	50	478	84	207	41	15	38	39	119	61	85	0	183	10	2.4	1.2	1.7	3.7
George Wilson	C	6'8	215	23	47	276	54	138	39	27	42	64	98	17	56	0	135	6	2.1	0.4	1.2	2.9
Art Heyman (to Phi)	G	6'5	205	24	11	100	15	43	35	10	17	59	13	7	19	0	40	9	1.2	0.6	1.7	3.6
Bud Olsen (to SF)	C-F	6'8	220	25	4	36	3	8	38	1	3	33	13	2	4	0	7	9	3.3	0.5	1.0	1.8
Jay Arnette	G	6'2	175	27	4	14	1	6	17	0	0	—	0	0	3	0	2	4	0.0	0.0	0.8	0.5
NEW YORK KNICKERBOCKERS	**30-50 .375**				**HARRY GALLATIN (6-15 .286), DICK McGUIRE (24-35 .407)**																	
Dick Van Arsdale	F-G	6'5	210	22	79	2289	359	838	43	251	351	72	376	184	235	5	969	29	4.8	2.3	3.0	12.3
Willis Reed	F-C	6'9	235	23	76	2537	438	1009	43	302	390	77	883	91	323	13	1178	33	11.6	1.2	4.3	15.5
Walt Bellamy (from Bal)	C	6'11	240	26	72	3084	639	1249	51	399	622	64	1152	217	262	7	1668	43	16.0	3.0	3.6	23.2
Dick Barnett	G	6'4	190	29	75	2589	631	1344	47	467	605	77	310	259	235	6	1729	35	4.1	3.5	3.1	23.1
Howie Komives	G	6'1	185	24	80	2612	436	1116	39	241	280	86	281	425	278	5	1113	33	3.5	5.3	3.5	13.9
Dave Stallworth	F	6'7	200	24	80	1893	373	820	45	258	376	69	492	186	237	4	1004	24	6.2	2.3	3.0	12.6
Em Bryant	G	6'1	175	27	71	1193	212	449	47	74	101	73	170	216	215	4	498	17	2.4	3.0	3.0	7.0
Tom Gola	G	6'6	208	32	74	1127	122	271	45	82	105	78	289	191	207	3	326	15	3.9	2.6	2.8	4.4
Barry Clemens	F	6'7	210	23	70	877	161	391	41	54	78	69	183	67	113	0	376	13	2.6	1.0	1.6	5.4
Len Chappell	F-C	6'8	240	24	46	545	100	238	42	46	78	59	127	26	64	1	246	12	2.8	0.6	1.4	5.3
Jim Barnes (to Bal)	F-C	6'8	240	24	7	263	40	90	44	30	42	71	72	9	33	0	110	38	10.3	1.3	4.7	15.7
Johnny Green (to Bal)	F	6'5	200	32	7	208	43	79	54	15	31	48	74	11	21	0	101	30	10.6	1.6	3.0	14.4
Johnny Egan (to Bal)	G	5'11	180	26	7	58	5	16	31	7	10	70	2	14	4	0	17	8	0.3	2.0	0.6	2.4

Use Name	Pos	Hgt	Wgt	Age	TOTAL G	Min	FG	FGA	%	FT	FTA	%	Reb	Ass	PF	DQ	Points	PER GAME Min	Reb	Ass	PF	Points
1965/66 N.B.A. — WESTERN DIVISION																						
LOS ANGELES LAKERS	**45-35 .563**				**FRED SCHAUS**																	
Elgin Baylor (knee injury)	F	6'5	225	31	65	1975	415	1034	40	249	337	74	631	224	157	0	1079	30	9.7	3.4	2.4	16.6
Rudv LaRusso	F	6'7	200	28	77	2316	410	897	46	350	445	79	660	165	261	9	1170	30	8.6	2.1	3.4	15.2
Darrall Imhoff	C	6'10	220	27	77	1413	151	337	45	77	136	57	509	113	234	7	379	18	6.6	1.5	3.0	4.9
Jerry West	G-F	6'3	175	27	79	3218	818	1731	47	**840**	**977**	86	562	480	243	1	2476	41	7.1	6.1	3.1	31.3
Walt Hazzard	G	6'2	190	23	80	2198	458	1003	46	182	257	71	219	393	224	0	1098	27	2.7	4.9	2.8	13.7
Leroy Ellis	F-C	6'10	210	25	80	2219	393	927	42	186	256	73	735	74	232	3	972	28	9.2	0.9	2.9	12.2
Bob Boozer	F	6'8	215	28	78	1847	365	754	48	225	289	78	548	87	196	0	955	24	7.0	1.1	2.5	12.2
Jim King	G	6'2	175	24	76	1499	238	545	44	94	115	82	204	223	181	1	570	20	2.7	2.9	2.4	7.5
Gene Wiley	C	6'10	210	28	67	1386	123	289	43	43	76	57	490	63	171	3	289	21	7.3	0.9	2.6	4.3
Gail Goodrich	G	6'1	170	22	65	1008	203	503	40	103	149	69	130	103	103	1	509	16	2.0	1.6	1.6	7.8
John Fairchild	F	6'8	205	22	30	171	23	89	26	14	20	70	45	11	33	0	60	6	1.5	0.4	1.1	2.0
BALTIMORE BULLETS	**38-42 .475**				**PAUL SEYMOUR**																	
Gus Johnson (knee injury)	F	6'6	235	27	42	1284	273	661	41	131	178	74	546	114	136	3	677	31	13.0	2.7	3.2	16.1
Bailey Howell	F	6'7	230	28	79	2328	481	986	49	402	551	73	773	155	306	12	1364	29	9.8	2.0	3.9	17.3
Johnny Kerr	C	6'9	230	33	71	1770	286	692	41	209	272	77	586	225	148	0	781	25	8.3	3.2	2.1	11.0
Kevin Loughery	G	6'3	190	25	74	2455	526	1264	42	297	358	83	227	356	273	8	1349	33	3.1	4.8	3.7	18.2
Don Ohl	G	6'3	190	29	73	2645	593	1334	44	316	430	73	280	290	208	1	1502	36	3.8	4.0	2.8	20.6
Jim Bames (from NY)	F-C	6'8	240	24	66	1928	308	728	42	182	268	68	683	85	250	10	798	29	10.3	1.3	3.8	12.1
Johnny Egan (from NY)	G	5'11	180	26	69	1586	254	558	46	166	217	76	181	259	163	1	674	23	2.6	3.8	2.4	9.8
Johnny Green (from NY)	F	6'5	200	32	72	1437	315	589	53	187	357	52	571	96	162	3	817	20	7.9	1.3	2.3	11.3
Bob Ferry	C	6'8	230	28	66	1229	188	457	41	105	157	67	334	111	134	1	481	19	5.1	1.7	2.0	7.3
Jerry Sloan	G-F	6'6	195	23	59	952	120	289	42	98	139	71	230	110	176	7	338	16	3.9	1.9	3.0	5.7
Ben Warley (from Phi)	F	6'5	200	29	56	767	115	281	41	64	97	66	215	25	128	2	294	14	3.8	0.4	2.3	5.3
Wayne Hightower	F	6'9	210	25	24	460	63	186	34	57	78	73	131	35	61	2	183	19	5.5	1.5	2.5	7.6
Walt Bellamy (to NY)	C	6'11	240	26	8	268	56	124	45	40	67	60	102	18	32	2	152	34	12.8	2.3	4.0	19.0
Willie Somerset	G	5'10	180	23	8	98	18	43	42	9	11	82	15	9	21	0	45	12	1.9	1.1	2.6	5.6
Thales McReynolds	G	6'3	185	22	5	28	1	12	8	1	2	50	6	1	0	0	3	6	1.2	0.2	0.0	0.6
Gary Bradds	F	6'8	210	23	3	15	2	6	33	3	4	75	8	1	1	0	7	5	2.7	0.3	0.3	2.3
ST. LOUIS HAWKS	**36-44 .450**				**RICHIE GUERIN**																	
Cliff Hagan	F	6'4	215	34	74	1851	419	942	44	176	206	85	234	164	177	1	1014	25	3.2	2.2	2.4	13.7
Bill Bridges	F	6'6	235	26	78	2677	377	927	41	257	364	71	951	208	333	11	1011	34	12.2	2.7	4.3	13.0
Zelmo Beaty	C	6'9	240	26	80	3072	616	1301	47	424	559	76	1086	125	**344**	15	1656	38	13.6	1.6	4.3	20.7
Richie Guerin	G	6'4	210	33	80	2363	414	998	41	362	446	81	314	388	256	4	1190	30	3.9	4.9	3.2	14.9
Lenny Wilkens	G	6'1	185	28	69	2692	411	954	43	422	532	79	322	429	248	4	1244	39	4.7	6.2	3.6	18.0
Joe Caldwell (from Det)	F	6'5	195	24	46	1141	268	600	45	119	166	72	246	61	140	3	655	25	5.3	1.3	3.0	14.2
Jim Washington	F	6'7	215	22	65	1104	158	393	40	68	120	57	353	43	176	4	384	17	5.4	0.7	2.7	5.9
Rod Thorn (from Det)	G	6'4	195	24	46	924	163	385	42	78	113	69	109	81	77	0	404	20	2.4	1.8	1.7	8.8
Gene Tormohlen	C	6'9	245	28	71	775	144	324	44	54	82	66	314	60	138	3	342	11	4.4	0.8	1.9	4.8
John Barnhill (to Det)	G	6'1	180	27	31	691	104	243	43	54	86	63	91	83	58	0	262	22	2.9	2.7	1.9	8.5
Jeff Mullins	G	6'4	200	23	44	587	113	296	38	29	36	81	69	66	68	1	255	13	1.6	1.5	1.5	5.8
Paul Silas	F	6'7	235	22	46	586	70	173	40	35	61	57	236	22	72	0	175	13	5.1	0.5	1.6	3.8
Chico Vaughn (to Det)	G	6'3	205	25	19	445	72	192	38	46	62	74	46	36	39	1	190	23	2.4	1.9	2.1	10.0
John Tresvant (to Det)	F	6'7	220	26	15	213	37	78	47	27	32	84	85	10	43	0	101	14	5.7	0.7	2.9	6.7
Mike Farmer	F	6'7	215	29	9	79	13	30	43	4	5	80	18	6	10	0	30	9	2.0	0.7	1.1	3.3
SAN FRANCISCO WARRIORS	**35-45 .438**				**ALEX HANNUM**																	
Tom Meschery	F	6'6	215	27	80	2383	401	895	45	224	293	76	716	81	285	7	1026	30	9.0	1.0	3.6	12.8
Rick Barry	F	6'7	205	21	80	2990	745	1698	44	569	660	86	850	173	297	2	2059	37	10.6	2.2	3.7	25.7
Nate Thurmond	C	6'11	225	24	73	2891	454	1119	41	280	428	65	1312	111	223	7	1188	40	18.0	1.5	3.1	16.3
Paul Neumann	G	6'1	175	27	66	1729	343	817	42	265	317	84	208	184	174	0	951	26	3.2	2.8	2.6	14.4
Guy Rodgers	G	6'	185	30	79	2902	586	1571	37	296	407	73	421	846	241	6	1468	37	5.3	10.7	3.1	18.6
Al Attles	G	6'2	180	29	79	2053	364	724	50	154	252	61	322	225	265	7	882	26	4.1	2.8	3.4	11.2
McCoy McLemore	F	6'7	230	23	80	1467	225	528	43	142	191	74	488	55	197	4	592	18	6.1	0.7	2.5	7.4
Gary Phillips	G	6'3	190	26	67	867	106	303	35	54	87	62	134	113	97	0	266	13	2.0	1.7	1.4	4.0
Fred Hetzel	C-F	6'8	230	23	56	722	160	401	40	63	92	68	290	27	121	2	383	13	5.2	0.5	2.2	6.8
Keith Erickson	F-G	6'5	195	21	64	646	95	267	36	43	65	66	162	38	91	1	233	10	2.5	0.6	1.4	3.6
Bud Olsen (from Cin)	C-F	6'8	220	25	55	566	78	185	42	38	85	45	179	18	77	1	194	10	3.3	0.3	1.4	3.5
Wilbert Frazier	F	6'7	210	23	2	9	0	4	0	1	2	50	5	1	1	0	1	5	2.5	0.5	0.5	0.5
DETROIT PISTONS	**22-58 .275**				**DAVE DeBUSSCHERE**																	
Dave DeBusschere	F	6'6	220	25	79	2696	524	1284	41	249	378	66	916	209	252	5	1297	34	11.6	2.6	3.2	16.4
Ray Scott	F-C	6'9	215	27	70	2652	544	1309	42	323	435	74	755	238	209	1	1411	38	10.8	3.4	3.0	20.2
Joe Strawder	C	6'10	235	25	79	2180	250	613	41	176	256	69	820	78	305	10	676	28	10.4	1.0	3.9	8.6
Tom Van Arsdale	G	6'5	215	22	79	2041	312	834	37	209	290	72	309	205	251	1	833	26	3.9	2.6	3.2	10.5
Eddie Miles	G	6'4	196	25	80	2788	634	1418	45	298	402	74	302	221	203	2	1566	35	3.8	2.8	2.5	19.6
Ron Reed (BB)	F	6'6	215	23	57	997	186	524	35	54	100	54	339	92	133	1	426	17	5.9	1.6	2.3	7.5
John Barnhill (from StL)	G	6'1	180	27	45	926	139	363	38	59	98	60	112	113	76	0	337	21	2.5	2.5	1.7	7.5
Rod Thorn (to StL)	G	6'4	195	24	27	815	143	343	42	90	123	73	101	64	67	0	376	30	3.7	2.4	2.5	13.9
Don Kojis	F	6'4	215	26	60	783	182	439	41	76	141	54	260	42	94	0	440	13	4.3	0.7	1.6	7.3
Chico Vaughn (from StL)	G	6'3	205	25	37	774	110	282	39	60	82	73	63	104	60	0	280	21	1.7	2.8	1.6	7.6
John Tresvant (from StL)	F	6'7	220	26	46	756	134	322	42	115	158	73	728	62	136	2	383	16	15.8	1.3	3.0	8.3
Joe Caldwell (to StL)	F	6'5	195	24	33	716	143	338	42	60	88	68	190	65	63	0	346	22	5.8	2.0	1.9	10.5
Bill Buntin	C-F	6'7	250	23	42	713	118	299	39	88	143	62	252	36	119	4	324	17	6.0	0.9	2.8	7.7
Donnie Butcher	G	6'3	200	29	15	285	45	96	47	18	34	53	33	30	40	1	108	19	2.2	2.0	2.7	7.2
Bob Warlick	G-F	6'5	205	24	10	78	11	38	29	2	6	33	16	10	8	0	24	8	1.6	1.0	0.8	2.4
Terry Dischinger - military service																						
Reggie Harding - (SL)																						

1965/66 N.B.A. — PLAYOFFS

Use Name	Pos	Hgt	Wgt	Age	G	Min	FG	FGA	%	FT	FTA	%	Reb	Ass	PF	DQ	Points	Min	Reb	Ass	PF	Points
					TOTAL													PER GAME				
BOSTON CELTICS	**RED AUERBACH**	defeated Cincinnati 3-2; H103-107, 132-125, H107-113, 120-103, H112-103 defeated Philadelphia 4-1; 115-96, H114-93, 105-111, H114-110(OT), 120-112 defeated Los Angeles 4-3; H129-133(OT), H129-109, 120-106,122-117, H117-121, 115-123, H95-93																				
John Havlicek	F-G	6'5	205	25	17	719	153	**374**	41	95	113	84	154	70	69	**2**	401	42	9.1	4.1	4.1	23.6
Satch Sanders	F	6'6	210	27	17	500	97	201	48	36	48	75	110	27	**70**	**2**	230	29	6.5	1.6	4.1	13.5
Bill Russell	C	6'10	220	31	17	**814**	124	261	48	76	123	62	**428**	**85**	60	0	324	48	25.2	5.0	3.5	19.1
Sam Jones	G	6'4	205	32	17	602	154	343	45	**114**	**136**	84	86	53	65	1	422	35	5.1	3.1	3.8	24.8
K. C. Jones	G	6'1	202	33	17	543	45	109	41	39	57	68	52	75	65	0	129	32	3.1	4.4	3.8	7.6
Larry Siegfried	G	6'3	192	26	17	452	81	193	42	62	75	83	42	41	52	0	224	27	2.5	2.4	3.1	13.2
Don Nelson	F	6'6	210	25	17	316	50	118	42	42	52	81	85	13	50	0	142	19	5.0	0.8	2.9	8.4
Mel Counts	F-C	7'	230	24	10	82	14	39	36	15	17	88	40	3	26	0	43	8	4.0	0.3	2.6	4.3
Willie Naulls	F	6'6	225	31	11	75	9	35	26	17	21	81	16	1	23	0	35	7	1.5	0.1	2.1	3.2
Ron Bonham	F	6'5	200	23	5	16	7	11	64	3	9	33	3	0	2	0	17	3	0.6	0.0	0.4	3.4
John Thompson	F	6'10	230	24	3	11	1	7	14	0	0	—	4	0	2	0	2	4	1.3	0.0	0.7	0.7
LOS ANGELES LAKERS	**FRED SCHAUS**	defeated St. Louis 4-3; H129-106, H125-116, 113-120, 107-95, H100-112, 127-131, H130-121 lost to Boston 3-4; 133-129(OT), 109-129, H106-120, H117-122, 121-117, H123-115, 93-95																				
Elgin Baylor	F	6'5	225	31	14	586	145	328	44	85	105	81	197	52	38	0	375	42	14.1	3.7	2.7	26.8
Rudy LaRusso	F	6'7	200	28	14	397	57	124	46	53	67	79	99	26	47	0	167	28	7.1	1.9	3.4	11.9
Leroy Ellis	C-F	6'10	210	25	14	426	56	138	41	25	39	64	133	8	52	1	137	30	9.5	0.6	3.7	9.8
Jerry West	G-F	6'3	175	27	14	619	**185**	357	52	109	125	87	88	79	40	0	**479**	44	6.3	5.6	2.9	**34.2**
Walt Hazzard	G	6'2	190	23	14	340	70	142	49	26	42	62	41	44	40	0	166	24	2.9	3.1	2.9	11.9
Gail Goodrich	G	6'1	170	22	11	290	43	92	47	29	43	67	42	33	35	0	115	26	3.8	3.0	3.2	10.5
Jim King	G	6'2	175	24	13	287	35	84	42	12	17	71	33	31	40	1	82	22	2.5	2.4	3.1	6.3
Darrall Imhoff	C	6'10	220	27	14	243	14	40	35	13	18	72	81	30	42	1	41	17	5.8	2.1	3.0	2.9
Bob Boozer	F	6'8	215	28	10	181	26	65	40	15	20	75	50	7	20	0	67	18	5.0	0.7	2.0	6.7
Tom Hoover	C	6'10	240	24	4	11	2	3	67	0	0	—	3	1	3	0	4	3	0.8	0.3	0.8	1.0
Gene Wiley	C	6'10	210	28	2	5	0	1	0	0	0	—	1	0	1	0	0	3	0.5	0.0	0.5	0.0
ST. LOUIS HAWKS	**RICHIE GUERIN**	defeated Baltimore 3-0; 113-111, 105-100, H121-112 lost to Los Angeles 3-4; 106-129, 116-125, H120-113, H95-107, 112-100, H131-127, 121-130																				
Joe Caldwell	F-G	6'5	195	24	10	315	78	169	46	31	49	63	55	16	29	0	187	32	5.5	1.6	2.9	18.7
Bill Bridges	F	6'6	235	26	10	421	86	170	51	31	43	72	149	28	47	2	203	42	14.9	2.8	**4.7**	20.3
Zelmo Beaty	C	6'9	240	26	10	418	73	148	49	44	58	76	131	22	38	1	190	42	13.1	2.2	3.8	19.0
Richie Guerin	G	6'4	210	33	10	399	72	159	45	62	76	82	37	79	41	0	206	40	3.7	**7.9**	4.1	20.6
Lenny Wilkens	G	6'1	185	28	10	391	57	143	40	57	83	69	54	70	43	0	171	39	5.4	7.0	4.3	17.1
Cliff Hagan	F	6'4	215	34	10	200	44	97	45	25	27	93	34	18	15	0	113	20	3.4	1.8	1.5	11.3
Rod Thorn	G	6'4	195	24	10	119	12	39	31	14	18	78	17	10	9	0	38	12	1.7	1.0	0.9	3.8
Paul Silas	F-C	6'7	235	22	7	80	5	18	28	8	11	73	34	2	11	0	18	11	4.9	0.3	1.6	2.6
Gene Tormohlen	C	6'9	245	28	6	38	2	10	20	3	4	75	18	6	7	0	7	6	3.0	1.0	1.2	1.2
Jeff Mullins	G	6'4	200	23	4	13	1	9	11	1	2	50	4	0	5	0	3	3	1.0	0.0	1.3	0.8
Jim Washington	F	6'7	215	22	4	6	2	4	50	0	0	—	3	0	2	0	4	2	0.8	0.0	0.5	1.0
PHILADELPHIA 76ers	**DOLPH SCHAYES**	lost to Boston 1-4; H96-115, 93-114, H111-105, 110-114(OT), H112-120																				
Chet Walker	F	6'6	205	25	5	181	24	64	38	25	31	81	37	15	18	0	73	36	7.4	3.0	3.6	14.6
Luke Jackson	F-C	6'9	240	24	5	163	21	49	43	18	22	82	44	8	21	**2**	60	33	8.8	1.6	4.2	12.0
Wilt Chamberlain	C	7'1	275	29	5	240	56	110	51	28	68	41	151	15	10	0	140	**48**	**30.2**	3.0	2.0	28.0
Hal Greer	G	6'3	176	29	5	226	32	91	35	18	23	78	36	21	21	0	82	45	7.2	4.2	4.2	16.4
Wally Jones	G	6'2	180	23	5	156	25	77	32	15	22	68	15	18	18	0	65	31	3.0	3.6	3.6	13.0
Dave Gambee	F	6'6	220	28	5	82	11	29	38	8	11	73	14	4	14	0	30	16	2.8	0.8	2.8	6.0
Billy Cunningham	F	6'7	220	22	4	69	5	31	16	11	13	85	18	10	11	0	21	17	4.5	2.5	2.8	5.3
Al Bianchi	G	6'3	185	33	5	64	18	43	42	9	12	75	10	4	19	1	45	13	2.0	0.8	3.8	9.0
Gerry Ward	G	6'4	190	24	5	44	2	8	25	0	1	0	5	1	11	0	4	9	1.0	0.2	2.2	0.8
CINCINNATI ROYALS	**JACK McMAHON**	lost to Boston 2-3; 107-103, H125-132, 113-107, H103-120, 103-112																				
Happy Hairston	F	6'7	225	23	5	150	25	62	40	27	38	71	37	0	20	1	77	30	7.4	0.0	4.0	15.4
Jerry Lucas	F-C	6'8	230	25	5	231	40	85	47	27	35	77	101	14	14	0	107	46	20.2	2.8	2.8	21.4
Wayne Embry	C	6'8	260	28	5	139	16	38	42	7	12	58	34	2	23	2	39	28	6.8	0.4	4.6	7.8
Oscar Robertson	G	6'5	210	27	5	224	49	120	41	61	68	90	38	39	20	1	159	45	7.6	7.8	4.0	31.8
Adrian Smith	G	6'1	185	29	5	157	22	59	37	21	22	**95**	12	13	12	0	65	31	2.4	2.6	2.4	13.0
Tom Hawkins	F	6'5	210	29	5	109	11	24	46	1	6	17	22	1	16	0	23	22	4.4	0.2	3.2	4.6
Jon McGlocklin	G-F	6'5	205	22	4	66	14	29	48	2	2	100	8	4	11	0	30	17	2.0	1.0	2.8	7.5
Connie Dierking	C	6'9	230	29	4	64	9	18	50	9	10	90	15	1	11	0	27	16	3.8	0.3	2.8	6.8
Tom Thacker	G	6'2	170	24	4	46	7	22	32	3	4	75	9	5	11	0	17	12	2.3	1.3	2.8	4.3
Jack Twyman	F	6'6	220	31	2	11	2	4	50	1	2	50	2	0	3	0	5	6	1.0	0.0	1.5	2.5
George Wilson	C	6'8	215	23	1	3	1	1	100	0	0	—	1	0	1	0	2	3	1.0	0.0	1.0	2.0
BALTIMORE BULLETS	**PAUL SEYMOUR**	lost to St. Louis 0-3; H111-113, H100-105, 112-121																				
Johnny Green	F	6'5	200	32	3	96	20	34	**59**	1	8	13	27	4	9	0	41	32	9.0	1.3	3.0	13.7
Bailey Howell	F	6'7	230	28	3	94	23	50	46	8	11	73	30	2	13	1	54	31	10.0	0.7	4.3	18.0
Bob Ferry	C	6'8	230	28	3	82	11	20	55	9	13	69	25	3	10	0	31	27	8.3	1.0	3.3	10.3
Don Ohl	G	6'3	190	29	3	111	34	67	51	12	16	75	14	8	13	1	80	37	4.7	2.7	4.3	26.7
Johnny Egan	G	5'11	180	26	3	117	19	47	40	10	16	63	9	23	14	1	48	39	3.0	7.7	4.7	16.0
Jim Barnes	F-C	6'8	240	24	3	93	16	32	50	7	13	54	28	3	15	2	39	31	9.3	1.0	5.0	13.0
Johnny Kerr	C	6'9	230	33	3	49	2	11	18	1	2	50	17	4	5	0	5	16	5.7	1.3	1.7	1.7
Jerry Sloan	G	6'6	195	23	2	34	5	12	42	3	4	75	16	6	6	1	13	17	8.0	3.0	3.0	6.5
Kevin Loughery	G	6'3	190	25	3	27	3	7	43	3	6	50	1	1	4	0	9	9	0.3	0.3	1.3	3.0
Ben Warley	F	6'5	200	29	2	9	0	4	0	1	1	100	2	0	2	0	1	5	1.0	0.0	1.0	0.5
Gus Johnson	F	6'6	235	27	1	8	1	4	25	0	0	—	0	0	1	0	2	8	0.0	0.0	1.0	2.0

Team	REGULAR SEASON G	FG	FGA	%	FT	FTA	%	Reb.	Ass.	AVERAGE POINTS For	Agnst.	Diff.	PLAYOFFS G	FG	FGA	%	FT	FTA	%	Reb.	Ass.	AVERAGE POINTS For	Agnst.	Diff.
1958/59 N.B.A. TEAM STATISTICS																								
EASTERN DIVISION																								
Philadelphia	80	3650	8189	45	2087	3141	66	5652	1905	117.3	112.7	+4.6	5	194	502	39	132	203	65	361	96	104.0	113.6	-9.6
Boston	80	3488	8367	42	2038	2758	74	5591	1795	112.7	107.8	+4.9	17	735	1691	43	499	651	77	1153	368	115.8	110.2	+5.6
Cincinnati	80	3610	8123	44	2204	2906	76	5559	1818	117.8	116.6	+1.2	5	196	462	42	159	199	80	314	7	110.2	114.8	-4.6
New York	80	3559	7910	45	2217	3078	72	5119	1896	116.7	119.3	-2.6												
WESTERN DIVISION																								
Los Angeles	80	3597	8109	44	2363	3057	77	5334	1936	119.5	116.4	+3.1	14	633	1363	46	367	476	77	768	311	116.6	116.3	+0.3
Baltimore	80	3599	8210	44	2267	3186	71	5542	1890	118.3	119.5	-1.2	3	134	288	47	55	90	61	188	54	107.7	113.0	-5.3
St. Louis	80	3379	7836	43	2155	2870	75	5167	1782	111.4	112.0	-0.6	10	432	966	45	276	371	74	597	251	114.0	115.4	-1.4
San Francisco	80	3557	8612	42	2129	2879	73	5727	1872	115.5	118.2	-2.7												
Detroit	80	3475	8502	41	1877	2734	69	5427	1569	110.3	117.2	-6.9												

Team	W	L	Pct.	GB	Record against playoff teams W	L	Pct.	Record against non - playoff teams W	L	Pct.	HOME W	L	Pct.	ROAD W	L	Pct.	NEUTRAL W	L	Pct.
1965/66 N.B.A. STANDINGS																			
EASTERN DIVISION																			
Philadelphia 76ers	55	25	.688	—	32	18	.640	23	7	.767	22	3	.880	20	17	.541	13	5	.722
Boston Celtics	54	26	.675	1	30	20	.600	24	6	.800	26	5	.839	19	18	.514	9	3	.750
Cincinnati Royals	45	35	.563	10	25	25	.500	20	10	.667	25	6	.806	11	23	.324	9	6	.600
New York Knickerbockers	30	50	.375	25	17	43	.283	13	7	.650	20	14	.588	4	30	.188	6	6	.500
WESTERN DIVISION																			
Los Angeles Lakers	45	35	.563	—	25	25	.500	20	10	.667	28	11	.718	13	21	.382	4	3	.571
Baltimore Bullets	38	42	.475	7	22	28	.440	16	14	.533	29	9	.763	4	25	.138	5	8	.385
St. Louis Hawks	36	44	.450	9	16	34	.320	20	10	.667	22	10	.688	6	22	.214	8	12	.400
San Francisco Warriors	35	45	.438	10	22	38	.367	13	7	.650	12	14	.462	8	19	.296	15	12	.555
Detroit Pistons	22	58	.275	23	18	42	.300	4	16	.200	13	17	.433	4	22	.154	5	19	.208

1965/66 N.B.A. INDIVIDUAL LEADERS

SCORING
(Minimum 65 Games Played)

Name	Team	G	FG	FT	Pts.	Avg.
Chamberlain	Phi	79	1074	501	2649	33.5
West	LA	79	818	840	2476	31.3
Robertson	Cin	76	818	742	2378	31.3
Barry	SF	80	745	569	2059	25.7
S. Jones	Bos	68	626	325	1577	23.2
Barnett	NY	75	631	467	1729	23.1
Bellamy	Bal-NY	80	695	430	1820	22.8
Greer	Phi	80	703	413	1819	22.7
Lucas	Cin	79	690	317	1697	21.5
Beaty	StL	80	616	424	1656	20.7

FIELD GOAL PERCENTAGE
(Minimum 210 Field Goals)

Name	Team	FG	FGA	Pct.
Chamberlain	Phi	1074	1990	.540
Green	NY-Bal	358	668	.536
Bellamy	Bal-NY	695	1373	.506
Attles	SF	364	724	.503
Hairston	Cin	398	814	.489
Howell	Bal	481	986	.488
Boozer	LA	365	754	.484
Robertson	Cin	818	1723	.475
Beaty	StL	616	1301	.473
West	LA	818	1731	.473

FREE THROW PERCENTAGE
(Minimum 210 Free Throws)

Name	Team	FT	FTA	Pct.
Siegfried	Bos	274	311	.881
Barry	SF	569	660	.862
Komives	NY	241	280	.861
West	LA	840	977	.860
Smith	Cin	408	480	.850
Robertson	Cin	742	881	.842
Neumann	SF	265	317	.836
Loughery	Bal	297	358	.830
Guerin	StL	362	446	.812
Greer	Phi	413	514	.804

PERSONAL FOULS

Name	Team	PF
Beaty	StL	344
Bridges	StL	333
Gola	NY	326
Reed	NY	323
Sanders	Bos	317

GAMES DISQUALIFIED

Name	Team	Disq
Sanders	Bos	19
Beaty	StL	15
Reed	NY	13
Cunningham	Phi	12
Howell	Bal	12

REBOUNDS PER GAME
(Minimum 65 Games Played)

Name	Team	G	Reb.	Avg.
Chamberlain	Phi	79	1943	24.6
Russell	Bos	78	1779	22.8
Lucas	Cin	79	1668	21.1
Thurmond	SF	73	1312	18.0
Bellamy	Bal-NY	80	1254	15.7
Beaty	StL	80	1086	13.6
Bridges	StL	78	951	12.2
Reed	NY	76	883	11.6
DeBusschere	Det	79	916	11.6
Barry	SF	80	850	10.6

ASSISTS PER GAME
(Minimum 65 Games Played)

Name	Team	G	Ass.	Avg.
Robertson	Cin	76	847	11.1
Rodgers	SF	79	846	10.7
K. C. Jones	Bos	80	503	6.3
Wilkens	StL	69	429	6.2
West	LA	79	480	6.1
Komives	NY	80	425	5.3
Chamberlain	Phi	79	414	5.2
Hazzard	LA	80	393	4.9
Guerin	StL	80	388	4.9
Greer	Phi	80	384	4.8

MINUTES PLAYED

Name	Team	Min.
Chamberlain	Phi	3737
Lucas	Cin	3517
Robertson	Cin	3493
Russell	Bos	3386
Bellamy	Bal-NY	3352

1966-67 N.B.A.

Finally, a Philadelphia Story

After two unsuccessful attempts to put the nation's second largest city on the N.B.A. circuit, the league once, again took a chance at securing a foothold in the Windy City. The first failure for the N.B.A. came in 1950 when the Chicago Stags went out of business. The second attempt came when the Packers, who changed their name to the Zephyrs in 1962, picked up and moved to Baltimore for the start of the 1963-64 season.

In order to accommodate this third attempt, the N.B.A. expanded its ranks to ten members, the newest one named the Chicago Bulls. With Johnny Kerr as head coach, the Bulls got off to a fast start and wound up winning a playoff berth in the Western Division, in addition to winning a paying clientele among Chicago sports fans. The addition of this tenth member forced some changes in the league, namely, the shift of Baltimore from the West to the East, and the revision of the playoff system to include the first four finishers in each division.

So while the N.B.A. was taking another shot at Chicago, the Philadelphia 76ers were ready to take another shot at the Boston Celtics. The 76ers had taken first place in the East away from the Celtics last season, only to collapse in the playoffs. Coach Dolph Schayes was fired as a result of that disappointment, with Alex Hannum taking over as the new coach. Hannum had taken the San Francisco Warriors to the playoff finals several years before, with Wilt Chamberlain playing a large role in passing the ball and on defense. Hannum again had Wilt pass the ball off more often than shoot, with Chamberlain dipping to a 24.1 scoring average, the lowest in his career and the first not to win him the N.B.A. scoring crown. But Wilt ranked first in shooting percentage, first in rebounds, and third in assists, and his accumulation of blocked shots rivaled that of Boston's Bill Russell. The forward corps had two offensive aces in Chet Walker and Billy Cunningham, plus a tough rebounder in Luke Jackson. Hal Greer spearheaded the backcourt with his playmaking and precision jump-shooting. The other guard was Wally Jones, and the reserves were rookies Matt Guokas and Billy Melchionni, and veteran Larry Costello, who came out of retirement only to injure his knee midway through the campaign. Coach Hannum welded this crew into a tight unit, but the 76ers still had to deal with the champion Celtics.

Although Boston had lost first place last year, they had still won the championship in the playoffs, and the addition of veterans Bailey Howell and Wayne Embry more than offset the retirement of Willie Naulls and the trade of Mel Counts. The big question mark for the Celtics was Bill Russell, not as a player but as the coach. Red Auerbach had retired to the sanctuary of the general manager's office, and the public wondered if the Celtics would continue as champions under Russell, the first black coach in major league sports.

The Celtics actually improved under Russell, moving up to a 60-21 record, but they couldn't come close to keeping the amazing pace set by the 76ers. With Wilt clogging up the middle on defense, clearing the boards, and passing the ball to Greer, Walker, and Cunningham, the 76ers flattened all the regular season competition, winning 45 of their first 49 and cruising to a 68-13 season's tally. The 76ers were the most powerful team in pro basketball, and the Celtics would have to muster all their guile to upset them again in the playoffs.

The Cincinnati Royals, still paced by Oscar Robertson and Jerry Lucas, and the New York Knicks, in the playoffs for the first time since 1959, also qualified for the post-season tournament, but had no hope of upsetting either Philadelphia or Boston. Baltimore, the second-place finisher in the West last season, fell apart and finished last in the East this season.

The first-place finisher in the West last season, the Los Angeles Lakers, also slipped, falling under the .500 level and finishing a distant third. Although Elgin Baylor had recovered from his knee troubles to rejoin Jerry West in a superb one-two offensive punch, the Lakers suffered at center, where the trade of Leroy Ellis left the position in Darrall Imhoff's hands, and at forward, where Audy LaRusso retired after being traded to Detroit in mid-season.

Replacing the Lakers at the top of the heap were the San Francisco Warriors, coached by ex-Celtic Bill Sharman. Nate Thurmond gave the Warriors strength at center to fight Russell and Chamberlain, and forward Rick Barry shot often and straight enough to win the scoring championship, the first man to unseat Chamberlain since Wilt came into the league. A supporting cast of tried veterans and untested youngsters meshed into a solid outfit behind the two stars.

The St. Louis Hawks finished second, with rookie shooter Lou Hudson replacing the retired Cliff Hagan. The fledgling Bulls took the fourth playoff spot with a scrappy club led by veterans Guy Rodgers and Bob Boozer and by second-year pro Jerry Sloan, rescued from the Baltimore bench in the expansion draft. The Pistons had a fine rookie guard in Dave Bing and a fine veteran forward in Dave DeBusschere, who turned over the coaching reins to assistant Donnie Butcher late in the season to concentrate on playing, but the club nevertheless missed the playoffs for the fourth straight year.

The Western playoffs took the expected shape, with the Warriors emerging as the divisional representative in the championship series. In the East, all eyes focused on the Philadelphia-Boston series; the physically overwhelming 76ers versus the poised Celtics. The first game in Philly opened some eyes, as Chamberlain outscored Russell 32-15 and the 76ers swamped the Celtics 127-113. The Celtics took an early lead in game two at Boston, but the 76ers wore the champions down and won, 107-102. With their backs to the wall, the Celtics started super-subs John Havlicek and Larry Siegfried and sprinted out to a 24-15 lead in the first nine minutes of game three. But Chamberlain's rebounding and clutch shooting by Greer and Wally Jones brought the 76ers all the way back to a 115-104 win. The handwriting was on the wall for the Celtics, their string of eight championships was about to end. The outgoing champs won game four 121-117 in Boston, but the 76ers simply overpowered the Celtics in game five; the final buzzer ended the 140-116 76er victory and also the Celtic reign. It seemed strange not to have the Celtics in the title round, but Chamberlain and his 76ers had decisively proven the better team. And they continued proving it to the end by dispensing with the Warriors in six games. Now, after years of scoring titles, Wilt Chamberlain was able to enjoy his first N.B.A. championshlp.

Use Name	Pos	Hgt	Wgt	Age	TOTAL G	Min	FG	FGA	%	FT	FTA	%	Reb	Ass	PF	DQ	Points	PER GAME Min	Reb	Ass	PF	Points

1966/67 N.B.A. — EASTERN DIVISION

Use Name	Pos	Hgt	Wgt	Age	G	Min	FG	FGA	%	FT	FTA	%	Reb	Ass	PF	DQ	Points	Min	Reb	Ass	PF	Points
PHILADELPHIA 76ers	**68-13 .840**				**ALEX HANNUM**																	
Chet Walker	F	6'6	210	26	81	2691	561	1150	49	445	581	77	660	188	232	4	1567	33	8.1	2.3	2.9	19.3
Luke Jackson	F-C	6'9	240	25	81	2377	386	882	44	198	261	76	724	114	276	6	970	29	8.9	1.4	3.4	12.0
Wilt Chamberlain	C	7'1	275	30	81	**3682**	785	1150	**68**	386	**875**	44	**1957**	630	143	0	1956	**45**	**24.2**	7.8	1.8	24.1
Hal Greer	G	6'3	176	30	80	3086	699	1524	46	367	466	79	422	303	302	5	1765	39	5.3	3.8	3.8	22.1
Wally Jones	G	6'2	180	24	81	2249	423	982	43	223	266	84	265	303	246	6	1069	28	3.3	3.7	3.0	13.2
Billy Cunningham	F	6'7	220	23	81	2168	556	1211	46	383	558	69	589	205	260	2	1495	27	7.3	2.5	3.2	18.5
Larry Costello (knee injury)	G	6'1	188	35	49	976	130	293	44	120	133	90	103	140	141	2	380	20	2.1	2.9	2.9	7.8
Matt Guokas	G	6'5	175	22	69	808	79	203	39	49	81	60	83	105	82	0	207	12	1.2	1.5	1.2	3.0
Dave Gambee	F	6'6	220	29	63	757	150	345	43	107	125	86	197	42	143	5	407	12	3.1	0.7	2.3	6.5
Bill Melchionni	G	6'1	165	22	73	692	138	353	39	39	60	65	98	98	73	0	315	9	1.3	1.3	1.0	4.3
Bob Weiss	G	6'2	180	24	6	29	5	10	50	2	5	40	3	10	8	0	12	5	0.5	1.7	1.3	2.0
BOSTON CELTICS	**60-21 .741**				**BILL RUSSELL**																	
John Havlicek	F-G	6'5	205	26	81	2602	684	1540	44	365	441	83	532	278	210	0	1733	32	6.6	3.4	2.6	21.4
Bailey Howell	F	6'7	220	29	81	2503	636	1242	51	349	471	74	677	103	296	4	1621	31	8.4	1.3	3.7	20.0
Bill Russell	C	6'10	220	32	81	3297	395	870	45	285	467	61	1700	472	258	4	1075	41	21.0	5.8	3.2	13.3
Sam Jones	G	6'4	205	33	72	2325	638	1406	45	318	371	86	338	217	191	1	1594	32	4.7	3.0	2.7	22.1
K. C. Jones	G	6'1	202	34	78	2446	182	459	40	119	189	63	239	389	273	7	483	31	3.1	5.0	3.5	6.2
Satch Sanders	F	6'6	210	28	81	1926	323	755	43	178	218	82	439	91	304	6	824	24	5.4	1.1	3.8	10.2
Larry Siegfried	G	6'3	192	27	73	1891	368	833	44	294	347	85	228	250	207	1	1030	26	3.1	3.4	2.8	14.1
Don Nelson	F	6'6	210	26	79	1202	227	509	45	141	190	74	295	65	143	0	595	15	3.7	0.8	1.8	7.5
Wayne Embry	C-F	6'8	255	29	72	729	147	359	41	82	144	57	294	42	137	0	376	10	4.1	0.6	1.9	5.2
Jim Barnett	G	6'4	180	22	48	383	78	211	37	42	62	68	53	41	61	0	198	8	1.1	0.9	1.3	4.1
Toby Kimball	F	6'8	220	24	38	222	35	97	36	27	40	68	146	13	42	0	97	6	3.8	0.3	1.1	2.6
Ron Watts (KJ)	F	6'6	210	23	27	89	11	44	25	16	23	70	38	1	16	0	38	3	1.4	0.0	0.6	1.4
CINCINNATI ROYALS	**39-42 .481**				**JACK McMANON**																	
Happy Hairston	F	6'7	225	24	79	2442	461	962	48	252	382	66	631	62	273	5	1174	31	8.0	0.8	3.5	14.9
Jerry Lucas	F-C	6'8	230	26	81	3558	577	1257	46	284	359	79	1547	268	280	2	1438	44	19.1	3.3	3.5	17.8
Connie Dierking	C	6'9	235	30	77	1905	291	729	40	134	180	74	603	158	251	7	716	25	7.8	2.1	3.3	9.3
Oscar Robertson	G	6'5	210	28	79	3468	838	1699	49	736	843	87	486	845	226	2	2412	44	6.2	10.7	2.9	30.5
Adrian Smith	G	6'1	185	30	81	2636	502	1147	44	343	380	**90**	205	187	272	0	1347	33	2.5	2.3	3.4	16.6
Jon McGlocklin	F-G	6'5	205	23	60	1194	217	493	44	74	104	71	164	93	84	0	508	20	2.7	1.6	1.4	8.5
Flynn Robinson	G	6'1	190	25	76	1140	274	599	46	120	154	78	133	110	197	3	668	15	1.8	1.4	2.6	8.8
Bob Love	F	6'8	215	24	66	1074	173	403	43	93	147	63	257	49	153	3	439	16	3.9	0.7	2.3	6.7
Walt Wesley	C	6'11	220	21	64	909	131	333	39	52	123	42	329	19	161	2	314	14	5.1	0.3	2.5	4.9
Len Chappell (from Chi)	C-F	6'8	240	25	54	529	92	224	41	39	60	65	151	21	73	0	223	10	2.8	0.4	1.4	4.1
Freddie Lewis	G	6'	180	23	32	334	60	153	39	29	41	71	44	40	49	1	149	10	1.4	1.3	1.5	4.7
Jim Ware	F	6'7	210	22	33	201	30	97	31	10	17	59	69	6	35	0	70	6	2.1	0.2	1.1	2.1
George Wilson (to Chi)	C	6'8	225	24	12	125	8	41	20	13	16	81	43	0	19	0	29	10	3.6	0.0	1.6	2.4
NEW YORK KNICKERBOCKERS	**36-45 .444**				**DICK McGUIRE**																	
Dick Van Arsdale	F-G	6'5	210	23	79	2892	410	913	45	371	509	73	555	247	264	3	1191	37	7.0	3.1	3.3	15.1
Willis Reed	F-C	6'9	235	24	78	2824	635	1298	49	358	487	74	1136	126	293	9	1628	36	14.6	1.6	3.8	20.9
Walt Bellamy	C	6'11	245	27	79	3010	565	1084	52	369	580	64	1064	206	275	5	1499	38	13.5	2.6	3.5	19.0
Dick Barnett	G	6'4	190	30	67	1969	454	949	48	231	295	78	226	161	185	2	1139	29	3.4	2.4	2.8	17.0
Howie Komives	G	6'1	185	25	65	2282	402	995	40	217	253	86	183	401	213	1	1021	35	2.8	6.2	3.3	15.7
Dave Stallworth (IL)	F	6'7	210	25	76	1889	380	816	47	229	320	72	472	144	226	4	989	25	6.2	1.9	3.0	13.0
Cazzie Russell	G-F	6'5	218	22	77	1696	344	789	44	179	228	79	251	187	174	1	867	22	3.3	2.4	2.3	11.3
Em Bryant	G	6'1	175	28	63	1593	236	577	41	74	114	65	273	218	231	4	546	25	4.3	3.5	3.7	8.7
Henry Akin	F-C	6'10	225	22	50	453	83	230	36	26	37	70	120	25	82	0	192	9	2.4	0.5	1.6	3.8
Neil Johnson	F	6'7	220	23	51	522	59	171	35	57	86	66	167	38	102	0	175	10	3.3	0.7	2.0	3.4
Freddie Crawford	G	6'4	190	25	19	192	44	116	38	24	38	63	48	12	39	0	112	10	2.5	0.6	2.1	5.9
Wayne Molis	F	6'8	230	23	13	75	19	51	37	7	13	54	22	2	9	0	45	6	1.7	0.2	0.7	3.5
Dave Deutsch	G	6'1	170	21	19	93	6	36	17	9	20	45	21	15	17	0	21	5	1.1	0.8	0.9	1.1
BALTIMORE BULLETS	**20-61 .247**				**MIKE FARMER (1-8 .111), BUDDY JEANNETTE (3-13 .186), GENE SHUE (16-40 .286)**																	
Jack Marin	F	6'7	200	22	74	1323	283	632	45	145	187	78	313	75	199	6	711	18	4.2	1.0	2.7	9.6
Gus Johnson	F	6'6	235	28	73	2626	620	1377	45	271	383	71	855	194	281	7	1511	36	11.7	2.7	3.8	20.7
Leroy Ellis	C-F	6'10	210	26	81	2938	496	1166	43	211	286	74	970	170	258	3	1203	36	12.0	2.1	3.2	14.9
Kevin Loughery	G	6'3	190	26	76	2577	520	1306	40	340	412	83	349	288	294	10	1380	34	4.6	3.8	3.9	18.2
Don Ohl (knee injury)	G	6'3	190	30	58	2024	452	1002	45	276	354	78	189	168	153	1	1180	35	3.3	2.9	2.6	20.3
Johnny Egan	G	5'11	180	27	71	1743	267	624	43	185	219	84	180	275	190	3	719	25	2.5	3.9	2.7	10.1
John Barnhill	G	6'1	180	28	53	1214	187	447	42	66	103	64	157	136	80	0	440	23	3.0	2.6	1.5	8.3
Ben Warley	F-G	6'5	200	30	62	1037	125	312	40	134	170	79	325	51	176	6	384	17	5.2	0.8	2.8	6.2
Bob Ferry	C	6'8	235	29	51	991	132	315	42	70	110	64	258	92	97	0	334	19	5.1	1.8	1.9	6.5
Ray Scott (from Det)	C-F	6'9	220	28	27	969	206	463	44	100	160	63	356	76	83	1	512	36	13.2	2.8	3.1	19.0
Johnny Green	F	6'5	200	33	61	948	203	437	46	96	207	46	394	57	139	7	502	16	6.5	0.9	2.3	8.2
Wayne Hightower (to Det)	F	6'9	210	26	44	746	103	308	33	89	124	72	241	36	110	5	295	17	5.5	0.8	2.5	6.7
Mel Counts (to LA)	C-F	7'	230	25	25	343	65	167	39	29	40	73	155	30	81	2	159	14	6.2	1.2	3.2	6.4
Johnny Austin	G	6'	175	22	4	61	5	22	23	13	16	81	7	4	12	0	23	15	1.8	1.0	3.0	5.8

Use Name	Pos	Hgt	Wgt	Age	TOTAL G	Min	FG	FGA	%	FT	FTA	%	Reb	Ass	PF	DQ	Points	PER GAME Min	Reb	Ass	PF	Points
1966/67 N.B.A. — WESTERN DIVISION																						
SAN FRANCISCO WARRIORS	**44-37 .543**				**BILL SHARMAN**																	
Rick Barry	F	6'7	205	22	78	3175	**1011**	**2240**	45	**753**	852	88	714	282	258	1	**2775**	41	9.2	3.6	3.3	**35.6**
Fred Hetzel	F	6'8	230	24	77	2123	373	932	40	192	237	81	639	111	228	3	938	28	8.3	1.4	3.0	12.2
Nate Thurmond (broken hand)	C	6'11	225	25	65	2755	467	1068	44	280	445	63	1382	166	183	3	1214	42	21.3	2.6	2.8	18.7
Jeff Mullins	G	6'4	200	24	77	1835	421	919	46	150	214	70	388	226	195	5	992	24	5.0	2.9	2.5	12.9
Paul Neumann	G	6'1	175	28	78	2421	386	911	42	312	390	80	272	342	266	4	1084	31	3.5	4.4	3.4	13.9
Tom Meschery (broken nose)	F	6'6	215	28	72	1846	293	706	42	175	244	72	549	94	264	8	761	26	7.6	1.3	3.7	10.6
Al Attles	G	6'2	180	30	70	1764	212	467	45	88	151	58	321	269	265	13	512	25	4.6	3.8	3.8	7.3
Jim King	G	6'2	175	25	67	1667	286	685	42	174	221	79	319	240	193	5	746	25	4.8	3.6	2.9	11.1
Clyde Lee	C-F	6'10	205	22	74	1247	205	503	41	105	166	63	551	77	168	5	515	17	7.4	1.0	2.3	7.0
Bud Olsen	C-F	6'8	220	26	40	348	75	167	45	23	58	40	103	32	51	1	173	9	2.6	0.8	1.3	4.3
Joe Ellis	F-G	6'6	175	22	41	333	67	164	41	19	25	76	112	27	45	0	153	8	2.7	0.7	1.1	3.7
Bob Warlick	F-G	6'5	205	25	12	65	15	52	29	6	11	55	20	10	4	0	36	5	1.7	0.8	0.3	3.0
George Lee	F	6'4	200	30	1	5	3	4	75	6	7	86	0	0	0	0	12	5	0.0	0.0	0.0	12.0
ST. LOUIS HAWKS	**39-42 .481**				**RICHIE GUERIN**																	
Joe Caldwell	F	6'5	195	25	81	2256	458	1076	43	200	308	65	442	166	230	4	1116	28	5.5	2.0	2.8	13.8
Bill Bridges	F	6'6	235	27	79	3130	503	1106	45	367	523	70	1190	222	325	12	1373	40	15.1	2.8	4.1	17.4
Zelmo Beaty (knee injury)	C	6'9	240	27	48	1661	328	694	47	197	260	76	515	60	189	3	853	35	10.7	1.3	3.9	17.8
Richie Guerin	G	6'4	210	34	79	2275	394	904	44	304	416	73	192	345	247	2	1092	29	2.4	4.4	3.1	13.8
Lenny Wilkens	G	6'1	185	29	78	2974	448	1036	43	459	583	79	412	442	280	6	1355	38	5.3	5.7	3.6	17.4
Lou Hudson	F-G	6'5	220	22	80	2446	620	1328	47	231	327	71	435	95	277	3	1471	31	5.4	1.2	3.5	18.4
Paul Silas	C-F	6'7	240	23	77	1570	207	482	43	113	213	53	669	74	208	4	527	20	8.7	1.0	2.7	6.8
Rod Thorn	G	6'4	195	25	67	1166	233	524	44	125	172	73	160	118	88	0	591	17	2.4	1.8	1.3	8.8
Gene Tormohlen	C	6'9	245	29	63	1036	172	403	43	50	84	60	347	73	177	4	394	16	5.5	1.2	2.8	6.3
Dick Snyder (MS)	G	6'5	210	22	55	676	144	333	43	46	61	75	91	59	82	1	334	12	1.7	1.1	1.5	6.1
Tommy Kron (MS)	G	6'5	200	23	33	221	27	87	31	13	19	68	36	46	35	0	67	7	1.1	1.4	1.1	2.0
Tom Hoover	C	6'10	240	25	17	129	13	31	42	5	13	38	36	8	35	1	31	8	2.1	0.5	2.1	1.8
LOS ANGELES LAKERS	**36-45 .444**				**FRED SCHAUS**																	
Elgin Baylor (injury)	F	6'5	225	32	70	2706	711	1658	43	440	541	81	898	215	211	1	1862	39	12.8	3.1	3.0	26.6
Rudy LaRusso (to Det)	F	6'7	220	29	45	1292	211	509	41	156	224	70	351	78	149	6	578	29	7.8	1.7	3.3	12.8
Darrall Imhoff	C	6'10	220	28	81	2725	370	780	47	127	207	61	1080	222	281	7	867	34	13.3	2.7	3.5	10.7
Jerry West (injury)	G	6'3	175	28	66	2676	645	1389	46	602	686	88	392	447	160	1	1892	41	5.9	6.8	2.4	28.7
Gail Goodrich	G	6'1	170	23	77	1780	352	776	45	253	337	75	251	210	294	3	957	23	3.3	2.7	3.8	12.4
Tom Hawkins	F	6'5	210	30	76	1798	275	572	48	82	173	47	434	83	207	1	632	24	5.7	1.1	2.7	8.3
Archie Clark	G	6'2	175	25	76	1763	331	732	45	136	192	71	218	205	193	1	798	23	2.9	2.7	2.5	10.5
Walt Hazzard	G	6'2	190	24	79	1642	301	706	43	129	177	73	231	323	203	1	731	21	2.9	4.1	2.6	9.3
Jim Barnes	C-F	6'8	240	25	80	1398	217	497	44	128	187	68	450	47	266	5	562	17	5.6	0.6	3.3	7.0
Jerry Chambers	F	6'5	186	23	69	1015	224	496	45	68	93	73	208	44	143	0	516	15	3.0	0.6	2.1	7.5
Mel Counts (from Bal)	C-F	7'	230	25	31	517	112	252	44	40	54	74	189	22	102	4	264	17	6.1	0.7	3.3	8.5
John Block	F	6'10	207	22	22	118	20	52	38	24	34	71	45	5	20	0	64	5	2.0	0.2	0.9	2.9
Henry Finkel	C	7'	240	24	27	141	17	47	36	7	12	58	64	5	39	1	41	5	2.4	0.2	1.4	1.5
Gene Wiley - voluntarily retired John Wetzel - broken wrist																						
CHICAGO BULLS	**33-48 .407**				**JOHNNY KERR**																	
Don Kojis	F	6'4	215	27	78	1655	329	773	43	134	222	60	479	70	204	3	792	21	6.1	0.9	2.6	10.2
Bob Boozer	F	6'8	215	29	80	2451	538	1104	49	360	461	78	679	90	212	0	1436	31	8.5	1.1	2.7	18.0
Erwin Mueller	C	6'8	230	22	80	2136	422	957	44	171	260	66	497	131	223	2	1015	27	6.2	1.6	2.8	12.7
Jerry Sloan	G	6'6	195	24	80	2942	525	1214	43	340	427	80	726	170	293	7	1390	37	9.1	2.1	3.7	17.4
Guy Rodgers	G	6'	185	31	81	3063	538	1377	39	383	475	81	346	**908**	243	1	1459	38	4.3	**11.2**	3.0	18.0
Jim Washington	F	6'7	215	23	77	1475	252	604	42	88	159	55	468	56	181	1	592	19	6.1	0.7	2.4	7.7
Keith Erickson	F-G	6'5	195	22	76	1454	235	641	37	117	159	74	339	119	199	2	587	19	4.5	1.6	2.6	7.7
McCoy McLemore	C-F	6'7	230	24	79	1382	258	670	39	210	272	77	374	62	189	2	726	17	4.7	0.8	2.4	9.2
Gerry Ward	G	6'4	190	25	76	1042	117	307	38	87	138	63	179	130	169	2	321	14	2.4	1.7	2.2	4.2
Barry Clemens	F	6'7	210	24	60	986	186	444	42	68	90	76	201	39	143	1	440	16	3.4	0.7	2.4	7.3
George Wilson (from Cin)	C	6'8	225	24	43	448	77	193	40	45	70	64	163	15	73	0	199	10	3.8	0.3	1.7	4.6
Dave Schellhase	G	6'3	205	22	31	212	40	111	36	14	22	64	29	23	27	0	94	7	0.9	0.7	0.9	3.0
Len Chappell (to Cin)	C-F	6'8	240	25	19	179	40	89	45	14	21	67	38	12	31	0	94	9	2.0	0.6	1.6	4.9
Nate Bowman (broken leg)	C	6'10	230	23	9	65	8	21	38	6	8	75	28	2	18	0	22	7	3.1	0.2	2.0	2.4
Ron Bonham - voluntarily retired																						
DETROIT PISTONS	**30-51.370**				**DAVE DeBUSSCHERE (28-45 .384), DONNIE BUTCHER (2-6 .250)**																	
Dave DeBusschere	F	6'6	220	26	78	2897	531	1278	42	361	512	71	924	216	297	7	1423	37	11.8	2.8	3.8	18.2
John Tresvant	F	6'7	220	27	68	1553	256	585	44	164	234	70	483	88	246	8	676	23	7.1	1.3	3.6	9.9
Joe Strawder	C	6'10	235	26	79	2156	281	660	43	188	262	72	791	82	**344**	**19**	750	27	10.0	1.0	**4.4**	9.5
Eddie Miles	G	6'4	196	26	81	2419	582	1363	43	261	338	77	298	181	216	2	1425	30	3.7	2.2	2.7	17.6
Dave Bing	G	6'3	180	23	80	2762	664	1522	44	273	370	74	359	330	217	2	1601	35	4.5	4.1	2.7	20.0
Tom Van Arsdale	G-F	6'5	215	23	79	2134	347	887	39	272	347	78	341	193	241	3	966	27	4.3	2.4	3.1	12.2
Ray Scott (to Bal)	C-F	6'9	220	28	45	1477	252	681	37	156	206	76	404	84	132	1	660	33	9.0	1.9	2.9	14.7
Reggie Harding	C	7'	250	24	74	1367	172	383	45	63	103	61	455	94	164	2	407	18	6.1	1.3	2.2	5.5
Ron Reed (BB)	F	6'6	215	24	62	1248	223	600	37	79	133	59	423	81	145	2	525	20	6.8	1.3	2.3	8.5
Chico Vaughn	G	6'3	200	26	51	680	85	226	38	50	74	68	67	75	54	0	220	13	1.3	1.5	1.1	4.3
Wayne Hightower (from Bal)	F	6'9	210	26	29	564	92	259	36	64	86	74	164	28	80	1	248	19	5.7	1.0	2.8	8.6
Dorie Murrey	F	6'8	215	23	35	311	33	82	40	32	54	59	102	12	57	2	98	9	2.9	0.3	1.6	2.8
Bob Hogsett	F	6'7	230	25	7	22	5	16	31	6	6	100	3	1	5	0	16	3	0.4	0.1	0.7	2.3
Bill Buntin - illness																						
Terry Dischinger - military service																						
Rudy LaRusso (from LA) - refused to report																						

1966/1967 N.B.A. — PLAYOFFS

PHILADELPHIA 76ers — **ALEX HANNUM**

defeated Cincinnati 3-1; H116-120, 123-102, H121-106, 112-94
defeated Boston 4 -1; H127-113, 107-102, H115-104, 117-121, H140-116
defeated San Francisco 4-2; H141-135 (OT), H126-95, 124-130, 122-108, H109-117, 125-122

Use Name	Pos	Hgt	Wgt	Age	TOTAL G	Min	FG	FGA	%	FT	FTA	%	Reb	Ass	PF	DQ	Points	PER GAME Min	Reb	Ass	PF	Points
Chet Walker	F	6'6	210	26	15	551	115	246	47	96	119	81	114	32	44	0	326	37	7.6	2.1	2.9	21.7
Luke Jackson	F-C	6'9	240	25	15	543	64	161	40	37	51	73	176	30	47	1	165	36	11.7	2.0	3.1	11.0
WiltChamberlain	C	7'1	275	30	15	**718**	132	228	58	62	**160**	39	**437**	**135**	37	0	326	**48**	**29.1**	9.0	2.5	21.7
Hal Greer	G	6'3	176	30	15	688	161	375	43	94	118	80	88	79	55	1	416	46	5.9	5.3	3.7	27.7
Wally Jones	G	6'2	180	24	15	476	109	244	45	45	58	78	42	61	58	0	263	32	2.8	4.1	3.9	17.5
Billy Cunningham	F	6'7	220	23	15	339	83	221	38	59	90	66	93	33	53	1	225	23	6.2	2.2	3.5	15.0
Matt Goukas	G	6'5	175	22	15	252	26	64	41	13	17	76	30	23	33	0	65	17	2.0	1.5	2.2	4.3
Larry Costello	G	6'1	188	35	2	25	6	8	75	5	5	100	4	3	2	0	17	13	2.0	1.5	1.0	8.5
Dave Gambee	F	6'6	220	29	5	24	6	11	55	6	6	100	6	2	6	0	18	5	1.2	0.4	1.2	3.6
Bill Melchionni	G	6'1	165	22	1	5	0	2	0	0	2	0	3	1	0	0	0	5	3.0	1.0	0.0	0.0
Bob Weiss	G	6'2	180	24	1	4	2	3	67	0	0	—	2	2	1	0	4	4	2.0	2.0	1.0	4.0

SAN FRANCISCO WARRIORS — **BILL SHARMAN**

defeated Los Angeles 3-0; H124-108, 113-102, H122-115
defeated St. Louis 4-2; H117-115, H143-136, 109-115, 104-109, H123-102, 112-107
lost to Philadelphia 2-4; 135-141(OT), 95-126, H130-124, H108-122, 117-109, H122-125

Use Name	Pos	Hgt	Wgt	Age	TOTAL G	Min	FG	FGA	%	FT	FTA	%	Reb	Ass	PF	DQ	Points	PER GAME Min	Reb	Ass	PF	Points
Rick Barry	F	6'7	205	22	15	614	**197**	**489**	40	**127**	157	81	113	58	49	0	**521**	41	7.5	3.9	3.3	**34.7**
Tom Meschery	F	6'6	215	28	15	408	79	175	45	35	46	76	119	25	**68**	**5**	193	27	7.9	1.7	4.5	12.9
Nate Thurmond	C	6'11	225	25	15	690	93	215	43	52	91	57	346	47	52	1	238	46	**23.1**	3.1	3.5	15.9
Jeff Mullins	G	6'4	200	24	15	498	109	242	45	47	59	80	91	58	53	3	265	33	6.1	3.9	3.5	17.7
Jim King	G	6'2	175	25	15	458	102	216	47	40	58	69	101	50	59	2	244	31	6.7	3.3	3.9	16.3
Fred Hetzel	F	6'8	230	24	13	308	51	133	38	22	28	79	93	23	36	1	124	24	7.2	1.8	2.8	9.5
Paul Neumann	G	6'1	175	28	15	254	29	88	33	35	47	74	17	34	50	0	93	17	1.1	2.3	3.3	6.2
Al Attles	G	6'2	180	30	15	237	20	46	43	6	16	38	62	38	45	1	46	16	4.1	2.5	3.0	3.1
Clyde Lee	F-C	6'10	205	22	11	130	19	57	33	2	10	20	54	8	20	0	40	12	4.9	0.7	1.8	3.6
Bud Olsen	F	6'8	220	26	4	14	4	13	31	0	2	0	9	1	2	0	8	4	2.3	0.3	0.5	2.0
Joe Ellis	F-G	6'6	175	22	3	6	1	4	25	0	0	—	1	2	2	0	2	2	0.3	0.7	0.7	0.7
Bob Warlick	F-G	6'5	205	25	2	8	0	2	0	0	0	—	0	1	0	0	0	4	0.0	0.5	0.0	0.0

ST. LOUIS HAWKS — **RICHIE GUERIN**

defeated Chicago 3-0; H114-100, 113-107, H119-106
lost to San Francisco 2-4; 115-117, 136-143, H115-109, H109-104, 102-123, H107-112

Use Name	Pos	Hgt	Wgt	Age	TOTAL G	Min	FG	FGA	%	FT	FTA	%	Reb	Ass	PF	DQ	Points	PER GAME Min	Reb	Ass	PF	Points
Joe Caldwell	F	6'5	195	25	9	217	42	105	40	26	39	67	39	13	27	1	110	24	4.3	1.4	3.0	12.2
Bill Bridges	F	6'6	235	27	9	369	48	128	38	45	67	67	169	22	36	2	141	41	18.8	2.4	4.0	15.7
Zelmo Beaty	C	6'9	240	27	9	318	46	104	44	51	65	78	89	12	34	0	143	35	9.9	1.3	3.8	15.9
Richie Guerin	G	6'4	210	34	9	228	36	86	42	24	30	80	23	39	26	0	96	25	2.6	4.3	2.9	10.7
Lenny Wilkens	G	6'1	185	29	9	378	58	145	40	77	90	86	68	65	34	0	193	42	7.6	7.2	3.8	21.4
Lou Hudson	F-G	6'5	220	22	9	317	77	179	43	49	68	72	48	15	35	1	203	35	5.3	1.7	3.9	22.6
Rod Thorn	G	6'4	195	25	9	156	33	77	43	25	27	93	28	11	13	0	91	17	3.1	1.2	1.4	10.1
Paul Silas	C-F	6'7	240	23	8	122	9	36	25	11	18	61	52	6	17	0	29	15	6.5	0.8	2.1	3.6
Gene Tormohlen	C	6'9	245	29	6	52	11	21	52	2	5	40	22	2	11	0	24	9	3.7	0.3	1.8	4.0
Dick Snyder	G	6'5	210	22	1	2	0	0	—	0	0	—	0	0	0	0	0	2	0.0	0.0	0.0	0.0
Tommy Kron	G	6'5	200	23	1	1	0	1	0	0	0	—	0	0	1	0	0	1	0.0	0.0	1.0	0.0

BOSTON CELTICS — **BILL RUSSELL**

defeated New York 3-1; H140-110, 115-108, H112-123, 118-109
lost to Philadelphia 4-1; 113-127, H102-107, 104-115, H121-117, 116-140

Use Name	Pos	Hgt	Wgt	Age	TOTAL G	Min	FG	FGA	%	FT	FTA	%	Reb	Ass	PF	DQ	Points	PER GAME Min	Reb	Ass	PF	Points
John Havlicek	F	6'5	205	26	9	330	95	212	45	57	71	80	73	28	30	0	247	37	8.1	3.1	3.3	27.4
Bailey Howell	F	6'7	220	29	9	241	59	122	48	20	30	67	66	5	35	2	138	27	7.3	0.6	3.9	15.3
Bill Russell	C	6'10	220	32	9	390	31	86	36	33	52	63	198	50	32	1	95	43	22.0	5.6	3.6	10.6
Sam Jones	G	6'4	205	33	9	326	95	207	46	50	58	86	46	28	30	1	240	36	5.1	3.1	3.3	26.7
K.C. Jones	G	6'1	202	34	9	254	24	75	32	11	18	61	24	48	36	1	59	28	2.7	5.3	4.0	6.6
Larry Siegfried	G	6'3	192	27	9	260	38	102	37	35	43	81	40	44	33	1	111	29	4.4	4.9	3.7	12.3
Satch Sanders	F	6'6	210	28	9	144	21	61	34	2	5	40	43	5	31	1	44	16	4.8	0.6	3.4	**4.9**
Don Nelson	F	6'6	210	26	9	142	27	59	46	10	17	59	42	9	12	0	64	16	4.7	1.0	1.3	7.1
Wayne Embry	C	6'8	255	29	5	38	12	31	39	2	4	50	13	3	9	0	26	8	2.6	0.6	1.8	5.2
Jim Barnett	G	6'4	180	22	5	26	6	21	29	2	2	100	4	1	5	0	14	5	0.8	0.2	1.0	2.8
Ron Watts	F	6'6	210	23	1	5	1	6	17	1	2	50	2	0	3	0	3	5	2.0	0.0	3.0	3.0
Toby Kimball	C	6'8	220	24	1	4	0	2	0	0	0	—	3	0	1	0	0	4	3.0	0.0	1.0	0.0

Use Name	Pos	Hgt	Wgt	Age	TOTAL G	Min	FG	FGA	%	FT	FTA	%	Reb	Ass	PF	DQ	Points	PER GAME Min	Reb	Ass	PF	Points
1966/67 N.B.A. — PLAYOFFS (continued)																						
NEW YORK KNICKERBOCKERS	**DICK McGUIRE**				lost to Boston 1-3; 110-140, H108-115, 123-112, H109-118																	
Dick Van Arsdale	F-G	6'5	210	23	4	153	15	47	32	16	22	73	25	14	16	1	46	38	6.3	3.5	4.0	11.5
Willis Reed	F-C	6'9	235	24	4	148	43	80	54	24	25	96	55	7	19	1	110	37	13.8	1.8	4.8	27.5
Walt Bellamy	C	6'11	245	27	4	157	28	54	52	17	29	59	66	12	15	0	73	39	16.5	3.0	3.8	18.3
Freddie Crawford	G	6'4	190	25	4	112	31	73	42	6	12	50	24	16	16	1	68	28	6.0	4.0	4.0	17.0
Howie Komives	G	6'1	185	25	4	128	16	59	27	10	13	77	11	15	13	0	42	32	2.8	3.8	3.3	10.5
Cazzie Russell	G-F	6'5	218	22	4	89	26	66	39	10	13	77	19	11	16	1	62	22	4.8	2.8	4.0	15.5
Em Bryant	G	6'1	175	28	4	76	5	21	24	11	11	100	9	9	16	0	21	19	2.3	2.3	4.0	5.3
Neil Johnson	F	6'7	220	23	4	64	8	27	30	7	8	88	23	5	8	0	23	16	5.8	1.3	2.0	5.8
Henry Akin	F-C	6'10	225	22	2	16	1	7	14	1	2	50	8	0	3	0	3	8	4.0	0.0	1.5	1.5
Wayne Molis	F	6'8	230	23	1	10	0	2	0	0	0	—	1	1	1	0	0	10	1.0	1.0	1.0	0.0
Dave Deutsch	G	6'1	170	21	1	7	1	5	20	0	0	—	3	1	0	0	2	7	3.0	1.0	0.0	2.0
Dave Stallworth - ilness																						
CINCINNATI ROYALS	**JACK McMAHON**				lost to Philadelphia 1-3; 120-116, H102-123, 106-121, H94-112																	
Happy Hairston	F	6'7	225	24	4	140	28	54	52	8	15	53	27	6	15	0	64	35	6.8	1.5	3.8	16.0
Jerry Lucas	F	6'8	230	26	4	183	24	55	44	2	2	100	77	8	15	0	50	46	19.3	2.0	3.8	12.5
Connie Dierking	C	6'9	235	30	4	151	32	75	43	6	6	100	52	14	13	0	70	38	13.0	3.5	3.3	17.5
Oscar Robertson	G	6'5	210	28	4	183	33	64	52	33	37	89	16	45	9	0	99	46	4.0	11.3	2.3	24.8
Adrian Smith	G	6'1	185	30	4	120	18	48	38	9	12	75	8	11	8	0	45	30	2.0	2.8	2.0	11.3
Flynn Robinson	G	6'1	190	25	4	72	24	47	51	2	4	50	7	8	8	0	50	18	1.8	2.0	2.0	12.5
Len Chappell	F-C	6'8	240	25	4	66	10	27	37	2	4	50	13	9	14	0	22	17	3.3	2.3	3.5	5.5
Walt Wesley	C	6'11	220	21	3	23	2	10	20	0	0	—	9	0	7	0	4	8	3.0	0.0	2.3	1.3
Jim Ware	F	6'7	210	22	3	13	5	13	38	0	0	—	2	0	1	0	10	4	0.7	0.0	0.3	3.3
Freddie Lewis	G	6'	180	23	3	9	4	9	44	0	0	—	4	0	1	0	8	3	1.3	0.0	0.3	2.7
CHICAGO BULLS	**JOHNNY KERR**				lost to St. Louis 0-3; 100-114, H107-113, 106-119																	
Don Kojis	F-G	6'4	215	27	3	104	23	48	48	5	8	63	30	4	10	0	51	35	10.0	1.3	3.3	17.0
Bob Boozer	F	6'8	215	29	3	105	24	38	63	11	14	79	35	1	8	0	59	35	11.7	0.3	2.7	19.7
Erwin Mueller	C	6'8	230	22	3	84	8	26	31	10	14	71	14	9	7	0	26	28	4.7	3.0	2.3	8.7
Jerry Sloan	G	6'6	195	24	3	71	12	31	39	6	9	67	10	1	7	0	30	24	3.3	0.3	2.3	10.0
Guy Rodgers	G	6'	185	31	3	97	15	40	38	4	5	80	6	18	11	0	34	32	2.0	6.0	3.7	11.3
Keith Erickson	G	6'5	195	22	3	68	12	27	44	0	0	—	11	4	12	1	24	23	3.7	1.3	4.0	8.0
Jim Washington	F	6'7	215	23	3	58	6	16	38	2	4	50	5	8	11	0	14	19	1.7	2.7	3.7	4.7
McCoy McLemore	C-F	6'7	230	24	3	45	12	30	40	13	15	87	9	4	5	0	37	15	3.0	1.3	1.7	12.3
Gerry Ward	G	6'4	190	25	3	38	10	22	45	4	5	80	10	2	7	0	24	13	3.3	0.7	2.3	8.0
George Wilson	C	6'8	225	24	2	27	2	9	22	3	6	50	9	0	5	0	7	14	4.5	0.0	2.5	3.5
Barry Clemens	F	6'7	210	24	3	20	0	4	0	6	7	86	3	2	3	0	6	7	1.0	0.7	1.0	2.0
Dave Schellhase	G	6'3	205	22	2	3	0	2	0	1	2	50	1	0	0	0	1	2	0.5	0.0	0.0	0.5
Nate Bowman - broken leg																						
Ron Bonham - voluntarily retired																						
LOS ANGELES LAKERS	**FRED SCHAUS**				lost to San Francisco 0-3, 108-124, H102-113, 115-122																	
Tom Hawkins	F	6'5	210	30	3	95	13	31	42	4	8	50	20	10	12	1	30	32	6.7	3.3	4.0	10.0
Elgin Baylor	F	6'5	225	32	3	121	28	76	37	15	20	75	39	9	6	0	71	40	13.0	3.0	2.0	23.7
Darrall Imhoff	C	6'10	220	28	3	86	13	24	54	4	5	80	37	5	8	0	30	29	12.3	1.7	2.7	10.0
Archie Clark	G-F	6'2	175	25	3	125	32	62	52	13	17	76	13	15	11	1	77	42	4.3	5.0	3.7	25.7
Gail Goodrich	G	6'1	170	23	3	81	11	31	35	11	18	61	9	10	5	0	33	27	3.0	3.3	1.7	11.0
Walt Hazzard	G	6'2	190	24	3	86	6	25	24	8	10	80	8	16	11	0	20	29	2.7	5.3	3.7	6.7
Jim Barnes	C-F	6'8	240	25	3	50	7	19	37	5	5	100	12	2	7	0	19	17	4.0	0.7	2.3	6.3
Jerry Chambers	F	6'5	186	23	3	44	12	23	52	7	7	100	8	1	7	0	31	15	2.7	0.3	2.3	10.3
Mel Counts	C-F	7'	230	25	3	29	5	19	26	4	4	100	8	0	6	0	14	10	2.7	0.0	2.0	4.7
John Block	F	6'10	207	22	1	1	0	0	—	0	0	—	0	0	0	0	0	1	0.0	0.0	0.0	0.0
Henry Finkel	C	7'	240	24	1	1	0	0	—	0	0	—	0	0	0	0	0	1	0.0	0.0	0.0	0.0
Jerry West (injury)	G	6'3	175	28	1	1	0	0	—	0	0	—	1	0	0	0	0	1	1.0	0.0	0.0	0.0
John Wetzel - broken wrist																						
Gene Wiley - Voluntarily retired																						

1966/67 N.B.A. TEAM STATISTICS

Team	REGULAR SEASON G	FG	FGA	%	FT	FTA	%	Reb.	Ass.	AVERAGE POINTS For	Agnst.	Diff.	PLAYOFFS G	FG	FGA	%	FT	FTA	%	Reb.	Ass.	AVERAGE POINTS For	Agnst.	Diff.
EASTERN DIVISION																								
Philadelphia	81	3912	8103	48	2319	3411	68	5701	2138	125.2	115.8	+9.4	15	704	1563	45	417	626	67	1115	401	121.7	112.3	+ 9.4
Boston	81	3724	8325	45	2216	2963	75	5703	1962	119.3	111.3	+8.0	9	409	984	42	223	302	74	642	221	115.7	116.2	-0.5
Cincinnati	81	3654	8137	45	2179	2806	78	5198	1858	117.1	117.4	-0.3	4	180	402	45	62	80	78	237	10	105.5	118.0	+12.5
New York	81	3637	8025	45	2151	2980	72	5178	1782	116.4	119.4	-3.0	4	174	441	39	102	135	76	288	91	112.5	121.3	-8.8
Baltimore	81	3664	8578	43	2025	2771	73	5342	1652	115.5	122.0	-7.5												
WESTERN DIVISION																								
San Francisco	81	3814	8818	43	2283	3021	76	5974	1876	122.4	119.5	+2.9	15	704	1680	42	366	514	71	1134	345	118.3	117.1	+1.2
St. Louis	81	3547	8004	44	2110	2979	71	5219	1708	113.6	115.2	-1.6	9	360	882	41	310	409	76	638	185	114.4	113.4	+1.0
Los Angeles	81	3786	8466	45	2192	2917	75	5415	1906	120.5	120.2	+0.3	3	127	310	41	71	94	76	185	68	108.3	119.7	-11.4
Chicago	81	3565	8505	42	2037	2784	73	5295	1827	113.2	116.9	-3.7	3	124	293	42	65	89	73	167	53	104.3	115.3	-11.0
Detroit	81	3523	8542	41	1969	2725	72	5511	1465	111.3	116.8	-5.5												

1966/67 N.B.A. STANDINGS

Team	W	L	Pct.	GB	Record against playoff teams W	L	Pct.	Record against non-playoff teams W	L	Pct.	HOME W	L	Pct.	ROAD W	L	Pct.	NEUTRAL W	L	Pct.
EASTERN DIVISION																			
Philadelphia 76ers	68	13	.840	—	51	12	.810	17	1	.944	28	2	.933	26	8	.765	14	3	.824
Boston Celtics	60	21	.741	8	46	17	.730	14	4	.778	27	4	.871	25	11	.694	8	6	.571
Cincinnati Royals	39	42	.481	29	26	37	.413	13	5	.722	20	11	.645	12	24	.333	7	7	.500
New York Knickerbockers	36	45	.444	32	24	39	.381	12	6	.667	20	15	.571	9	24	.273	7	6	.538
Baltimore Bullets	20	61	.247	48	18	54	.250	2	7	.222	12	20	.375	3	30	.091	5	11	.313
WESTERN DIVISION																			
San Francisco Warriors	44	37	.543	—	30	33	.476	14	4	.778	18	10	.643	11	19	.367	15	8	.652
St. Louis Hawks	39	42	.481	5	27	36	.429	12	6	.667	18	11	.621	12	21	.364	9	10	.474
Los Angeles Lakers	36	45	.444	8	25	38	.397	11	7	.611	21	18	.538	12	20	.375	3	7	.300
Chicago Bulls	33	48	.407	11	23	40	.365	10	8	.556	17	19	.472	9	17	.346	7	12	.368
Detroit Pistons	30	51	.370	14	23	49	.319	7	2	.777	12	18	.400	9	19	.321	9	14	.391

1966/67 N.B.A. INDIVIDUAL LEADERS

SCORING
(Minimum 65 Games Played)

Name	Team	G	FG	FT	Pts.	Avg.
Barry	SF	78	1011	753	2775	35.6
Robertson	Cin	79	838	736	2412	30.5
West	LA	66	645	602	1892	28.7
Baylor	LA	70	711	440	1862	26.6
Chamberlain	Phi	81	785	386	1956	24.1
S. Jones	Bos	72	638	318	1594	22.1
Greer	Phi	80	699	367	1765	22.1
Havlicek	Bos	81	684	365	1733	21.4
Reed	NY	78	635	358	1628	20.9
Johnson	Bal	73	520	271	1511	20.7

FIELD GOAL PERCENTAGE
(Minimum 220 Field Goals)

Name	Team	FG	FGA	Pct.
Chamberlain	Phi	785	1150	.683
Bellamy	NY	565	1084	.521
Howell	Bos	636	1242	.512
Robertson	Cin	838	1699	.493
Reed	NY	635	1298	.490
Walker	Phi	561	1150	.488
Boozer	Chi	538	1104	.487
Hawkins	LA	275	572	.481
Hairston	Cin	461	962	.479
Barnett	NY	454	949	.478

FREE THROW PERCENTAGE
(Minimum 220 Free Throws)

Name	Team	FT	FTA	Pct.
Smith	Cin	343	380	.903
Barry	SF	753	852	.884
West	LA	602	686	.878
Robertson	Cin	736	843	.873
S. Jones	Bos	318	371	.857
Siegfried	Bos	294	347	.847
Jones	Phi	223	266	.838
Havlicek	Bos	365	441	.828
Loughery	Bal	340	412	.825
Baylor	LA	440	541	.813

PERSONAL FOULS

Name	Team	PF
Strawder	Det	344
Bridges	StL	325
Greer	Phi	302
DeBusschere	Det	297
Howell	Bos	296

GAMES DISQUALIFIED

Name	Team	Disq
Strawder	Det	19
Attles	SF	13
Bridges	StL	12
Loughery	Bal	10
Reed	NY	9

REBOUNDS PER GAME
(Minimum 65 Games Played)

Name	Team	G	Reb.	Avg.
Chamberlain	Phi	81	1957	24.2
Thurmond	SF	65	1382	21.3
Russell	Bos	81	1700	21.0
Lucas	Cin	81	1547	19.1
Bridges	StL	79	1190	15.1
Reed	NY	78	1136	14.6
Bellamy	NY	79	1064	13.5
Imhoff	LA	81	1080	13.3
Ellis	Bal	81	970	12.0
DeBusschere	Det	78	924	11.8

ASSISTS PER GAME
(Minimum 65 Games Played)

Name	Team	G	Ass.	Avg.
Rodgers	Chi	81	908	11.2
Robertson	Cin	79	845	10.7
Chamberlain	Phi	81	630	7.8
West	LA	66	447	6.8
Komives	NY	65	401	6.2
Russell	Bos	81	472	5.8
Wilkens	StL	78	442	5.7
K. C. Jones	Bos	78	389	5.0
Neumann	SF	78	342	4.4
Guerin	StL	79	345	4.4

MINUTES PLAYED

Name	Team	Min.
Chamberlain	Phi	3682
Lucas	Cin	3558
Robertson	Cin	3468
Russell	Bos	3297
Barry	SF	3175

Use Name-Nickname	Team by Year	Birth Yr	Hgt	Wgt	Pos	College	# Yr	G	Field Goals FG	Att.	%	3 pt. FG FG	Att	%	Free Throws FT	Att.	%	Reb.	Ass	PF	DQ	Pts	Per game Min	Reb	Ass	Pt
Forest Able	57Syr	1932	6'3	180	G	Western Ky., Louisville	1	1	0	2	0				0	0	—	1	1	1	0	0	1	1.0	1.0	0.
Gary Alcorn	60Det 61LA	1936	6'9	225	C	Fresno State	2	78	103	352	29				55	92	60	329	24	170	5	261	11	4.2	0.3	3.
Bob Anderegg	60NY	1937	6'3	200	F-G	Michigan State	1	33	55	143	38				23	42	55	69	29	32	0	133	11	2.1	0.9	4.
Don Anielak	55NY	1930	6'7	192	F	SW Missouri St.	1	1	0	4	0				3	4	75	2	0	0	0	3	10	2.0	0.0	3.
Stacey Arceneaux	62StL	1936	6'4	210	F	Iowa State	1	7	22	56	39				6	13	46	32	4	10	0	50	16	4.6	0.6	7.
Paul Arizin	51-52 Phi 53-54MS	1928	6'4	198	F-G	Villanova	10	713	5628	13354	42				5010	6189	81	6129	1665	2764	101	16266	38	8.6	2.3	22.
55-62Phi	51-52, 56-58, 60-62						8	49	411	1001	41				364	439	83	404	128	177	8	1186	39	8.2	2.6	24
Bob Armstrong	57Phi	1933	6'8	230	C-F	Michigan State	1	19	11	37	30				6	12	50	39	3	13	0	28	6	2.1	0.2	1.
Jesse Arnelle	56FtW	1933	6'5	220	F	Penn State	1	31	52	164	32				43	69	62	170	18	60	0	147	13	5.5	0.6	4.
Jay Arnette	64-66Cin	1936	6'2	175	G	Texas	3	114	163	447	36				98	129	76	116	139	233	3	424	10	1.0	1.2	3.
	65-66						2	9	11	32	34				7	8	88	10	10	22	1	29	9	1.1	1.1	3
Dick Atha	56NY 58Det	1931	6'2	193	G	Indiana State	2	43	53	135	39				31	39	79	66	51	63	0	137	10	1.5	1.2	3.
Al Attles	61-62Phi	1936	6'2	180	G	N. C. A&T	11	712	2499	5543	45				1330	2106	63	2463	2483	2417	65	6328	25	3.5	3.5	8.
63-69, PC70-71SF	61-62, 64-67, 69, 71						7	62	154	382	40				86	158	54	245	206	246	12	394	24	4.0	3.3	6.
HC72-83GS																										
Red Auerbach	HC47-49Was HC50TC	1917				G. Washington																				
HC51-66Bos																										
Jim Baechtold	53Bal 54-57NY	1927	6'4	206	F-G	Eastern Ky.	5	321	1117	2876	39				889	1135	78	1009	685	795	15	3123	26	3.1	2.1	9.
	53-55						3	9	45	104	43				31	39	79	32	36	41	1	121	34	3.6	4.0	13.
John Barber	57StL	1927	6'6	210	F	L.A. State	1	5	2	8	25				3	6	50	6	0	4	0	7	4	1.2	0.0	1.
Don Barksdale	52-53Bal 54-55Bos	1923	6'6	203	F-C	U.C.L.A.	4	262	1011	2747	37				863	1307	66	2086	549	941	37	2895	28	8.0	2.1	11.
	54-55						2	13	29	76	38				26	32	81	62	17	40	3	84	18	4.8	1.3	6.
Dick Barnett	60-61Syr 63-65LA	1936	6'4	190	G-F	Tennessee St.	14	971	6034	13227	46				3290	4324	76	2812	2729	2514	24	15358	30	2.9	2.8	15.
66-74NY	60-61, 63-65, 68-73						11	102	603	1317	46				333	445	75	273	247	282	1	1539	30	2.7	2.4	15.
John Barnhill (Rabbit)	63-66StL 66Det 67Bal	1938	6'1	181	G	Tennessee St.	10	589	2024	4990	41	107	454	24	930	1413	66	1501	1693	1069	3	5085	24	2.5	2.9	8.
68SD 69Bal	63-65, 69-70						5	35	74	201	37	8	35	23	40	72	56	74	69	83	0	196	21	2.1	2.0	5.
70-71IndA 71DenA 72IndA																										
Ernie Barrett	54, 56Bos	1929	6'3	180	G-F	Kansas State	2	131	267	724	37				107	143	75	343	229	300	6	641	16	2.6	1.7	4.
	54, 56						2	9	7	33	21				5	5	100	13	8	21	0	19	12	1.4	0.9	2.
Al Barthelme	HC55Bal					Loyola (Md.)																				
Elgin Baylor	59-60Min 61-72LA HC75	1934	6'5	225	F	Coll. of Idaho,	14	846	8693	20171	43				5763	7391	78	11463	3650	2596	14	23149	40	13.5	4.3	27
HC75, 77-79NO	59, 70					Seattle	12	134	1388	3161	44				847	1101	77	1725	541	435	3	3623	41	12.9	4.0	27.
Ernie Beck	54Phi 55MS 56-60Phi	1931	6'4	194	G-F	Pennsylvania	7	371	929	2425	38				467	613	76	1191	669	667	3	2325	19	3.2	1.8	6.
61StL 61Syr	56-58, 60						4	24	72	180	40				31	44	70	99	43	53	1	175	22	4.1	1.8	7.
Clair Bee	HC53-55Bal	1900				Waynesburg																				
Whitey Bell	60-61NY	1932	6'	181	G	N. C. State	2	36	77	203	38				29	46	63	94	56	66	0	183	14	2.6	1.6	5.
Gary Bergen	57NY	1932	6'8	212	C	Kansas State Utah	1	6	3	11	27				2	2	100	8	1	4	0	8	7	1.3	0.2	1.
Al Bianchi	57-63Syr PC64, 65-66Phi	1932	6'3	185	G	Bowling Green	10	687	2212	5919	37				1126	1592	71	1722	1487	2069	54	5550	20	2.5	2.2	8.
HC68-69Sea	57-66						10	56	194	471	41				80	115	70	125	101	193	9	448	20	2.2	1.8	8
HC70WasA HC71-76VaA																										
Don Bielke	56FtW		6'8	240	C	Valparaiso	1	7	5	9	56				4	7	57	9	1	9	0	14	5	1.3	0.1	2
Jerry Brid	59NY	1935	6'6	220	F	Kentucky	1	11	12	32	38				1	1	100	12	4	7	0	25	4	1.1	0.4	2
George Blaney	62NY	1939	6'1	175	G	Holy Cross	1	36	54	142	38				9	17	53	36	45	34	0	117	10	1.0	1.3	3
Arlen Bockhorn (Bucky)	59-66Cin	1933	6'4	200	G	Dayton	7	474	2245	5574	40				940	1256	75	2234	1645	1565	39	5430	31	4.7	3.5	11
	62-64						3	26	124	305	41				52	67	78	103	98	95	2	300	33	4.0	3.8	11
Doug Bolstorff	58Det	1931	6'4	195	G	Minnesota	1	3	2	5	40				0	0	—	0	0	1	0	4	7	0.0	0.0	1
Ron Bonham	65-66Bos 67VR 68IndA	1942	6'5	200	F	Cincinnati	3	118	247	637	39	0	2	0	229	278	82	170	44	98	0	723	9	1.4	0.4	6
	65-66, 68						3	12	16	38	42	0	0	—	12	20	60	10	3	7	0	44	5	0.8	0.3	3
George Bon Salle	62Chi	1935	6'8	220	F	Illinois	1	3	2	8	25				0	0	—	2	0	0	0	4	3	0.7	0.0	1
Bob Boozer	61-64Cin 64-65NY 66LA	1937	6'8	219	F	Kansas State	11	874	4961	10738	46				3042	3998	76	7119	1237	2789	18	12964	29	8.1	1.4	14
67-69Chi 70Sea	62-63, 66-68, 71						6	48	213	456	47				130	176	74	341	58	136	0	556	27	7.1	1.2	11
71Mil																										
Carl Braun	48-50NY 51-52MS	1927	6'5	184	G-F	Colgate	13	788	3912	10211	38				2801	3484	80	2122	2892	2164	34	10625	30	2.7	3.7	13
53-59, PC60-61NY	48-50, 53-55, 59, 62						8	40	179	512	35				203	250	81	81	108	135	4	561	27	2.0	2.7	14
62Bos																										
Pete Brennan	59NY	1936	6'6	205	F	N. Carolina	1	16	13	43	30				14	25	56	31	6	15	0	40	9	1.9	0.4	2
	59						1	2	2	7	29				0	1	0	5	0	4	0	4	3	2.5	0.0	2
Tom Brennan	55Phi	1930	6'5	200	F	Villanova	1	11	5	11	45				0	0	—	5	2	5	0	10	5	0.5	0.2	0
George Brown	58Min	1935	6'6	190	F	Wayne State	1	1	0	2	0				1	2	50	1	0	1	0	1	6	1.0	0.0	1
Joe Buckhalter	62-63Cin	1937	6'7	210	F	Tennessee St.	2	65	153	339	45				69	110	63	265	43	124	1	375	11	4.1	0.7	5
	62						1	4	16	38	42				2	3	67	22	4	14	0	34	15	5.5	1.0	8
Cleveland Buckner	62-63NY	1938	6'9	210	F-C	Jackson State	2	68	163	377	43				85	137	62	240	44	120	1	411	11	3.5	0.6	6
Dave Budd	61-65NY	1938	6'6	210	F	Wake Forest	5	353	962	2092	46				581	852	68	1623	337	814	11	2505	18	4.6	1.0	7
Bill Buntin	66Det 67IL	1942	6'7	250	C-F	Michigan	1	42	118	299	39				88	143	62	252	36	119	4	324	17	6.0	0.9	7
Bob Burrow	57Roch 58Min	1934	6'7	228	C-F	Kentucky	2	81	159	436	36				141	244	58	357	47	180	2	459	15	4.4	0.6	5
Ed Burton	62NY 65StL	1939	6'6	225	F	Michigan State	2	15	14	34	41				5	11	45	18	3	16	0	33	5	1.2	0.2	2
Donnie Butcher	62-64NY 64-66 HC67-69Det	1936	6'3	200	G	Pikeville	5	279	610	1535	40				476	757	63	821	585	699	10	1696	18	2.9	2.1	6
Al Butler	62Bos 62-64NY 65Bal	1938	6'2	175	G	Niagara	4	234	930	2119	44				422	571	74	696	530	493	6	2282	22	3.0	2.3	9
Barney Cable	59-60Det 60-61Syr 62Chi	1935	6'7	203	F	Bradley	6	362	1012	2409	42				348	523	67	1686	380	882	9	2372	19	5.2	1.0	6
62-63StL 63Chi	60-61						2	11	31	79	39				14	25	56	89	8	41	1	76	23	8.1	0.7	6
64Bal																										
Howie Carl	62Chi	1936	5'9	160	G	DePaul, Ill.	1	31	67	201	33				36	51	71	39	57	41	1	170	12	1.3	1.8	5
Bob Carney	55Min	1932	6'3	172	G	Bradley	1	19	24	64	38				21	40	53	45	16	36	0	69	13	2.4	0.8	3
	55						1	7	1	8	13				8	9	89	5	3	7	0	10	6	0.7	0.4	1.
John Castellani	HC60Min					Notre Dame																				

Use Name-Nickname	Team by Year	Birth Yr	Hgt	Wgt	Pos	College	# Yr	G	Field Goals FG	Att.	%	3 pt. FG FG	Att	%	Free Throws FT	Att.	%	Reb.	Ass.	PF	DQ	Pts	Per Game Min	Reb	Ass	Pts
Wilt Chamberlain	60-62Phi 63-65SF 65-68Phi	1936	7'1	270	C	Kansas	14	1045	12681	23497	54				6057	11862	51	23924	4643	2075	0	31419	46	23.9	4.4	30.1
(Wilt the Stilt,	60-62, 64-73						13	160	1425	2728	52				757	1627	47	3913	673	402	0	3607	47	24.5	4.2	22.5
The Big Dipper)																										
69-73LA HC74SD-A																										
Fred Christ	55NY	1930	6'4	210	G	Fordham	1	6	5	18	28				10	11	91	8	7	3	0	20	8	1.3	1.2	3.3
Sweetwater Clifton	51-57NY 58Det	1922	6'6	221	C-F	Xavier (La.)	8	544	2082	5766	36				1280	2021	63	4469	1367	1840	41	5444	30	8.2	2.5	10.0
(Sweets)	51-55, 58						6	53	170	489	35				136	218	62	495	142	215	9	476	30	9.3	2.7	9.0
Larry Comley	64Bal	1939	6'5	210	G	Kansas St.	1	11	8	37	22				9	16	56	19	12	11	0	25	8	1.7	1.1	2.3
Gene Conley	53Bos 54-58RB	1930	6'8	237	C-F	Wash. St.	6	351	833	2234	37				403	613	66	2212	201	1123	40	2069	16	6.3	0.6	5.9
59-61Bos 63-64NY	59-61						3	33	70	187	37				29	47	62	222	11	119	4	169	15	6.7	0.3	5.1
52, 54-63 played major league baseball																										
Ed Conlin	56-59Syr 59-60Det 61-62Phi	1933	6'5	200	F-G	Fordham	7	486	1862	5039	37				1167	1556	75	2349	949	1076	13	4891	23	4.8	2.0	10.1
	56-62						7	35	94	289	33				65	96	68	120	39	60	0	253	19	3.4	1.1	7.2
Bert Cook	55NY	1929	6'3	186	G-F	Utah State	1	37	42	133	32				34	50	68	72	33	39	0	118	11	1.9	0.9	3.2
	55						1	1	4	6	67				0	2	0	0	2	3	0	8	20	0.0	2.0	8.0
Larry Costello	55Phi 56MS 57Phi 58-63Syr	1931	6'1	186	G	Niagara	12	706	3095	7068	44				2432	2891	84	2705	3215	2326	49	8622	31	3.8	4.6	12.2
64-65Phi 66VR	55, 57-65, 67						10	52	198	476	42				196	230	85	171	218	210	11	592	28	3.3	4.2	11.4
67-68Phi HC69-77Mil HC79Chi																										
Steve Courtin	65Phi	1942	6'1	188	G	St. Joseph's	1	24	42	103	41				17	21	81	22	22	44	0	101	13	0.9	0.9	4.2
Bob Cousy	51-63Bos PC70, HC71-72Cin	1928	6'1	177	G	Holy Cross	14	924	6168	16468	37				4624	5756	80	4786	6955	2242	20	16960	35	5.2	7.5	18.4
HC73-74KCO	51-63						13	109	689	2016	34				640	799	80	546	937	314	4	2018	39	5.0	8.6	18.5
Johnny Cox	63Chi	1936	6'4	180	G	Kentucky	1	73	239	568	42				95	135	70	280	142	149	4	573	23	3.8	1.9	7.8
Jimmy Darrow	62StL	1937	5'10	175	G	Bowling Grn	1	5	3	15	20				6	7	86	7	6	9	0	12	7	1.4	1.2	2.4
Jim Davis (Red)	56Roch	1932	6'7	230	C	St. John's	1	3	0	6	0				2	2	100	4	1	2	0	2	5	1.3	0.3	0.7
Ralph Davis	61Cin 62Chi	1938	6'4	180	G	Cincinnati	2	149	545	1332	41				105	145	72	248	424	314	2	1195	21	1.7	2.8	8.0
Walt Davis	54-58Phi 58StL	1931	6'8	208	C-F	Texas A&M	5	325	623	1651	38				312	449	69	1397	231	915	25	1558	16	4.3	0.7	4.8
	56-58						3	21	25	64	39				17	22	77	69	7	51	0	67	8	3.3	0.3	3.2
Archie Dees	59Cin 60-61Det 62Chi 62StL	1936	6'8	208	F-C	Indiana	4	200	575	1429	40				398	501	79	907	132	385	3	1548	15	4.5	0.7	7.7
	60						1	2	4	12	33				3	3	100	4	2	2	0	11	9	2.0	1.0	5.5
George Dempsey	55-59Phi 59Syr	1929	6'3	194	G	King's (Del)	5	315	591	1453	41				392	593	66	1125	711	602	8	1574	18	3.6	2.3	5.0
	56-59						4	25	38	87	44				29	49	59	64	35	35	0	105	14	2.6	1.4	4.2
Dave Deutsch	67NY	1945	6'1	170	G	Rochester	1	19	6	36	17				9	20	45	21	15	17	0	21	5	1.1	0.8	1.1
	67						1	1	1	5	20				0	0	—	3	1	0	0	2	7	3.0	1.0	2.0
Corky Devlin	56-57FtW 58Min	1931	6'5	195	G	George Washington	3	210	560	1532	37				376	507	74	449	446	337	1	1496	19	2.1	2.1	7.1
	56-57						2	11	47	109	43				16	26	62	26	28	26	0	110	27	2.4	2.5	10.0
Connie Dierking	59-60Syr 63VR 64-65Phi	1936	6'9	229	C-F	Cincinnati	10	706	2867	6880	42				1360	1951	70	4757	1053	2075	43	7094	22	6.7	1.5	10.0
65SF 66-71Cin 71Phi	59-60, 64, 66-67						5	20	63	158	40				27	35	77	129	23	45	0	153	18	6.5	1.2	7.7
Fred Diute	55Mil	1929	6'3	210	G	St. Bonavent.	1	7	2	21	9.5				7	12	58	13	4	12	0	11	10	1.9	0.6	1.6
Eddie Donovan	HC62-65NY	1923				St. Bonavent.																				
Danny Doyle	63Det	1940	6'8	215	F	Belmont Abb.	1	4	6	12	50				4	5	80	8	3	4	0	16	6	2.0	0.8	4.0
Dick Duckett	58Cin	1933	6'1	185	G	St. John's	1	34	54	158	34				24	27	89	56	47	60	0	132	12	1.6	1.4	3.9
Bob Duffy	63-64StL 64NY 64-65Det	1940	6'3	185	G	Colgate	3	94	164	414	40				72	111	65	104	167	94	0	400	12	1.1	1.8	4.3
	63						1	5	6	15	40				2	2	100	3	3	3	0	14	5	0.6	0.6	2.8
Walter Dukes	56NY 57Min 58-63Det	1930	7'	220	C	Seton Hall	8	553	1912	5175	37				1941	2773	70	6193	608	2260	121	5765	27	11.2	1.1	10.4
	57-63						7	35	151	363	42				145	204	71	393	63	161	13	447	33	11.2	1.8	12.8
Pat Dunn	58Phi	1931	6'2	170	G	Utah State	1	28	28	90	31				14	17	82	31	28	20	0	70	7	1.1	1.0	2.5
	58						1	3	0	4	0				0	0	—	1	1	1	0	0	3	0.3	0.3	0.0
Bill Ebben	58Det	1935	6'4	190	G	Detroit	1	8	6	28	21				3	4	75	8	4	5	0	15	6	1.0	0.5	1.9
Charlie Eckman	HC55-57FtW HC58Det	1921	5'9	170		none																				
Johnny Egan	62-64Det 64-66NY 66-68Bal	1939	5'11	180	G	Providence	11	712	2089	4867	43				1343	1668	81	1294	2102	1441	10	5521	20	1.8	3.0	7.8
69-70LA 71Cle	65, 66, 69-70						4	42	165	369	45				93	117	79	67	131	97	1	423	23	1.6	3.1	10.1
71SD 72, HC73-75Hou																										
Dick Eichhorst	62StL	1933	6'3	200	G	SE Mo. St.	1	1	1	2	50				0	0		1	3	1	0	2	10	1.0	3.0	2.0
Boo Ellis	59-60Min	1936	6'5	193	F	Niagara	2	118	227	564	40				153	220	70	616	86	201	2	607	16	5.2	0.7	5.1
	59-60						2	16	37	90	41				22	39	56	105	18	37	0	96	18	6.6	1.1	6.0
Wayne Embry	59-66Cin 67-68Bos 69Mil	1937	6'8	249	C-F	Miami (Ohio)	11	831	3993	9067	44				2394	3741	64	7544	1194	2838	65	10380	26	9.1	1.4	12.5
	62-68						7	56	215	514	42				136	211	64	448	64	206	8	566	24	8.0	1.1	10.1
Bo Erias	58Min	1932	6'3	220	F	Niagara	1	18	59	170	35				30	47	64	83	26	52	1	148	22	4.6	1.4	8.2
Dick Farley	55-56Det 57-58MS 59Det	1932	6'4	190	G-F	Indiana	3	211	481	1252	38				416	594	70	527	386	429	5	1378	18	2.5	1.8	6.5
	55-56, 59						3	22	58	140	41				34	57	60	40	51	66	2	150	17	1.8	2.3	6.8
Mike Farmer	59-61NY 61Cin 63-66StL	1936	6'7	213	F	S. Fransisco	7	423	1165	2965	39				486	597	81	1950	550	840	3	2816	21	4.6	1.3	6.7
HC67Bal	59, 63-65						4	25	53	129	41				23	32	72	79	36	45	0	129	17	3.2	1.4	5.2
Dave Fedor	63SF	1940	6'6	192	F	Florida St.	1	7	3	10	30				0	1	0	6	1	4	0	6	4	0.9	0.1	0.9
Ron Feiereisel	56Min	1931	6'3	185	G	DePaul	1	10	8	28	29				14	16	88	6	6	9	0	30	6	0.6	0.6	3.0
Ray Felix	54Bal 55-60NY 60Min	1930	6'11	223	C	L.I.U.	9	637	2406	5841	41				2162	3187	68	5652	448	2419	81	6974	24	8.9	0.7	10.9
61-62LA	55-56, 60-62						5	38	106	253	42				89	127	70	290	29	143	6	301	22	7.6	0.8	7.9
Al Ferrari	56StL 57-58MS 59-62StL	1933	6'4	198	G-F	Mich. State	6	371	878	2389	37				769	1012	76	830	943	1006	24	2525	20	2.2	2.5	6.8
63Chi	56, 59-61						4	33	81	207	39				94	130	72	79	75	97	2	256	22	2.4	2.3	7.8
Bob Ferry	60StL 61-64Det 65-69Bal	1937	6'8	232	C-F	St. Louis	10	634	2225	5142	43				1330	2003	66	3343	906	1438	11	5780	20	5.3	1.4	9.1
	60-63, 65-66						6	42	115	255	45				90	145	62	185	40	64	0	320	16	4.4	1.0	7.6
Ed Fleming	56-57Roch 58-60Min	1933	6'3	189	G-F	Niagara	5	292	862	2403	36				787	1077	73	1532	544	688	7	2511	21	5.2	1.9	8.6
	59						1	13	27	77	35				22	25	88	39	18	32	0	76	14	3.0	1.4	5.8
Jack Foley (The Shot)	63Bos 63NY	1939	6'5	185	F	Holy Cross	1	11	20	51	39				13	15	87	16	5	8	0	53	8	1.5	0.5	4.8
Larry Foust	51-57FtW 58-60Min 60-62StL	1928	6'9	238	C-F	LaSalle	12	817	3814	9414	41				3570	4816	74	8041	1368	2909	85	11198	29	9.8	1.7	13.7
	51-57, 59-61						10	73	301	763	39				300	384	78	707	94	255	9	902	27	9.7	1.3	12.4
Larry Friend	58NY	1935	6'4	186	G-F	California	1	44	74	226	33				27	41	66	106	47	54	0	175	13	2.4	1.1	4.0

Use Name-Nickname	Team by Year	Birth Yr	Hgt	Wgt	Pos	College	# Yr	G	Field Goals FG	Att.	%	3 pt. FG FG	Att	%	Free Throws FT	Att.	%	Reb.	Ass	PF	DQ	Pts	Per Game Min	Reb	Ass	Pts
Dave Gambee	59-60StL 60Cin 61-63Syr	1937	6'6	221	F	Oregon State	12	750	2820	6708	42				2295	2791	82	3891	757	2180	49	7935	20	5.2	1.0	10.6
64-67Phi 68SD	61-67						7	43	118	331	36				131	157	83	188	36	143	3	367	20	4.4	0.8	8.5
69Mil 69Det																										
Dick Garmaker	56-60Min 60-61NY	1932	6'3	205	G-F	Minnesota	6	421	2022	5019	40				1553	1974	79	1748	1114	1168	12	5597	29	4.2	2.6	13.3
	56-57, 59						3	21	96	253	38				92	112	82	98	67	71	2	284	32	4.7	3.2	13.5
Jack George	54-59Phi 59-61NY	1928	6'3	194	G	LaSalle,	8	506	1901	5226	36				1351	1918	70	2129	2169	1242	12	5153	31	4.2	4.3	10.2
	56-59					Notre Dame	4	22	87	226	38				64	85	75	96	92	60	2	238	35	4.4	4.2	10.8
Mel Gibson	64LA	1940	6'3	180	G	W. Carolina	1	9	6	20	30				1	2	50	4	6	10	0	13	6	0.4	0.7	1.4
Tom Gola	56Phi 57MS 58-62Phi 63SF	1933	6'6	207	G-F	LaSalle	10	698	2964	6883	43				1943	2556	76	5617	2962	2688	94	7871	32	8.0	4.2	11.3
63-66NY	56, 58, 60-62						5	39	142	422	34				148	192	77	391	179	164	8	432	38	10.0	4.6	11.1
Joe Grabowski	49-50Chi 52-53Ind 54-61Phi	1930	6'8	218	F-C	none	13	845	3433	9763	35				2414	3447	70	5999	1502	2591	61	9280	31	8.0	1.8	11.0
62StL 62Chi 62Syr	49-50, 52-53, 56-58, 60-62						10	40	157	473	33				75	102	74	271	73	108	2	389	26	7.1	1.8	9.7
Johnny Green	60-66NY 66-67Bal 68SD	1933	6'5	202	F-C	Mich. State	14	1057	4973	10091	49				2335	4226	55	9083	1459	2856	60	12281	23	8.6	1.4	11.6
68-69Phi 70-72Cin	66, 68-69						3	20	67	115	58				26	60	43	107	13	40	1	160	18	5.4	0.7	8.0
73KCO																										
Si Green	57Roch 58MS 59Cin	1934	6'2	189	G-F	Duquesne	9	504	1732	4481	39				1172	1735	68	2152	1655	1421	21	4636	26	4.3	3.3	9.2
59-62StL 62-63Chi	59-61, 65						4	41	156	360	43				76	124	61	222	165	121	3	388	27	5.4	4.0	9.5
64-65Bal 66Bos																										
Jerry Greenspan	64-65Phi	1941	6'5	195	F	Maryland	2	25	40	103	39				42	58	72	83	11	66	0	122	13	3.3	0.4	4.9
Hal Greer	59-63Syr 64-73Phi	1936	6'3	176	G-F	Marshall	15	1122	8504	18821	45				4578	5717	80	5665	4540	3855	72	21586	35	5.0	4.0	19.2
	59-71						13	92	705	1657	43				466	574	81	505	393	357	13	1876	40	5.5	4.3	20.4
Chuck Grigsby	55NY	1928	6'5	190	G	Dayton	1	7	7	19	37				2	8	25	11	7	9	0	16	6	1.6	1.0	2.3
Jerry Grote	65LA	1940	6'4	216	G	Loyola (L.A.)	1	11	6	11	55				2	2	100	4	4	5	0	14	3	0.4	0.4	1.
Gene Guarilia	60-63Bos	1937	6'5	220	F	G. Washington,	4	129	168	447	38				77	126	61	294	36	146	1	413	8	2.3	0.3	3.2
	60, 62					Potomac St.	2	12	6	27	22				8	11	73	23	4	10	0	20	6	1.9	0.3	1.7
Richie Guerin	57-63NY 64, PC65-67 HC68StL	1932	6'4	201	G	Iona	13	847	5174	12451	42				4328	5549	78	4278	4211	2769	29	14676	32	5.1	5.0	17.3
PC69-70, HC71-73Atl	59, 64-67, 69-70						7	42	231	539	43				192	239	80	149	214	157	2	654	32	3.5	5.1	15.6
Dave Gunther	63SF	1937	6'7	220	F	Iowa	1	1	1	2	50				0	0	—	3	3	1	0	2	5	3.0	3.0	2.0
Cliff Hagan (Li'l Abner)	57-66StL PC68-70DalA	1931	6'4	212	F-G	Kentucky	13	839	5750	12661	45	0	5	0	3370	4219	80	5555	2646	2665	58	14870	29	6.6	3.2	17.7
	57-61, 63-66, 68-69						11	95	720	1595	45	0	0	—	449	563	80	763	328	336	13	1889	32	8.0	3.5	19.
Swede Halbrook	61-62Syr	1933	7'3	255	C	Oregon State	2	143	307	885	35				172	291	59	949	64	441	16	786	14	6.6	0.4	5.
	61						1	8	24	72	33				14	20	70	83	12	21	0	62	22	10.4	1.5	7.
Steve Hamilton	59-60Min	1933	6'7	195	F-C	Morehead St.	2	82	136	371	37				92	132	70	278	43	174	3	368	13	3.4	0.5	4.
61-72 played major	59						1	10	12	43	28				8	10	80	35	5	14	0	32	9	3.5	0.5	3.2
league baseball																										
Reggie Harding	64-65Det 66SL 67Det 68Chi	1942	7'	249	C	none	5	230	927	2215	42	0	1	0	321	533	60	2199	396	635	8	2175	28	9.6	1.7	9.
68IndA																										
Charlie Hardnett	63Chi 64-65Bal	1938	6'8	225	F-C	Grambling	2	165	433	1023	42				332	513	65	930	103	376	5	1198	15	5.6	0.6	7.3
	65						1	5	4	10	40				2	5	40	6	2	2	0	10	4	1.2	0.4	2.
Chris Harris	56StL 56Roch	1933	6'3	190	G	Dayton	1	41	37	149	25				27	45	60	44	44	43	0	101	10	1.1	1.1	2.5
Vern Hatton	59Cin 59-61Phi 62Chi 62StL	1936	6'3	195	G	Kentucky	4	225	485	1409	34				274	373	73	531	310	294	0	1244	16	2.4	1.4	5.5
	60						1	6	4	13	31				1	3	33	3	1	3	0	9	3	0.5	0.2	1.
Tom Hawkins	60Min 61-62LA 63-66Cin	1936	6'5	210	F	Notre Dame	10	764	2761	6171	45				1150	2016	57	4607	871	2214	35	6672	24	6.0	1.1	8.7
67-69LA	60-69						10	96	311	677	46				145	235	62	537	106	310	7	767	22	5.6	1.1	8.
Herm Heddrick	55NY	1930	6'5	170	G	Canisius	1	5	2	9	22				0	1	0	4	2	3	0	4	5	0.8	0.4	0.
Tom Heinsohn (Ack-Ack)	57-65, HC70-78Bos	1934	6'7	220	F-C	Holy Cross	9	654	4773	11787	40				2647	3353	79	5749	1318	2454	58	12194	29	8.8	2.0	18.
	57-65						9	104	818	2025	40				422	568	74	954	215	417	14	2058	31	9.2	2.1	19.
Dick Hemric	56-57Bos	1933	6'6	225	F	Wake Forest	2	138	270	717	38				323	483	67	703	102	240	2	863	17	5.1	0.7	6.3
	56-57						2	5	6	31	19				9	16	56	31	2	8	0	21	15	6.2	0.4	4.2
Larry Hennessy	56Phi 57Syr	1929	6'3	185	G	Villanova	2	74	141	422	33				49	64	77	94	73	65	0	331	11	1.3	1.0	4.5
	56						1	3	0	9	0				0	0	—	1	2	1	0	0	4	0.3	0.7	0.0
Cleo Hill	62StL	1936	6'1	185	G	Winst.-Salem	1	58	107	309	35				106	137	77	178	114	98	1	320	20	3.1	2.0	5.5
Gary Hill	64-65SF 65Bal	1941	6'4	185	G	Okla. City	2	79	156	420	37				58	91	64	130	110	176	2	370	14	1.6	1.4	4.7
	64						1	9	12	24	50				4	13	31	6	8	13	0	28	8	0.7	0.9	3.1
Paul Hogue (Duke)	63-64NY 64Bal	1940	6'9	240	C	Cincinnati	2	65	164	449	37				81	181	45	461	48	255	13	409	23	7.1	0.7	6.3
Joe Holup	57-58Syr 58-59Det	1934	6'6	215	F	G. Washington	3	192	460	1345	34				427	547	78	852	193	515	19	1347	18	4.4	1.0	7.
	57-59						3	15	24	85	28				26	35	74	64	7	30	0	74	17	4.3	0.5	4.
Tom Hoover	64-65NY 67StL 68DenA	1941	6'10	244	C	Villanova	5	223	480	1075	45	4	12	33	347	554	63	1368	237	748	26	1311	19	6.2	1.1	5.9
69HouA 69MinA	66LA, 68						2	6	6	10	60	0	0	—	5	7	71	7	2	9	0	17	5	1.2	0.3	2.
Bob Hopkins	57-60Syr HC78Sea	1934	6'8	219	C-F	Grambling	4	273	854	2168	39				529	695	76	1526	189	642	14	2237	19	5.6	0.7	8.2
	57-60						4	18	38	117	32				45	58	78	99	11	57	2	121	19	5.5	0.6	6.7
Johnny Horan	56Min	1932	6'8	190	F	Dayton	1	19	12	42	29				10	11	91	10	2	21	0	34	5	0.5	0.1	1.
(The Vertical Hyphen)																										
Ron Horn	62StL 63LA 68DenA	1938	6'7	225	F	Indiana	3	32	28	96	29	0	0	—	23	33	70	78	11	50	0	79	10	2.4	0.3	2.5
	63						1	7	4	12	33				4	5	80	11	2	13	0	12	8	1.6	0.3	1.7
Bob Houbregs	54Mil 54-55Bal 55Bos	1932	6'8	227	C-F	Washington	5	281	906	2245	40				799	1108	72	1552	500	690	9	2611	24	5.5	1.8	9.
55-57FtW 58Det	55-57						3	23	67	158	42				68	92	74	135	36	55	1	202	20	5.9	1.6	8.8
Bailey Howell	60-64Det 65-66Bal	1937	6'7	219	F	Miss. State	12	951	6515	13585	48				4740	6224	76	9383	1853	3498	90	17770	32	9.9	1.9	18.7
67-70Bos 71Phi	60-63, 65-69, 71						10	86	542	1165	47				317	433	73	697	130	372	21	1401	32	8.1	1.5	16.3
Rod Hundley (Hot Rod)	58-60Min 61-63LA	1934	6'4	188	G	West Virginia	6	431	1382	3978	35				861	1195	72	1420	1455	786	1	3625	22	3.3	3.4	8.4
	59-63						5	53	101	316	32				68	95	72	149	157	80	0	270	19	2.8	3.0	5.1
Mel Hutchins	52-53Mil 54-57FtW 58NY	1928	6'6	205	F-C	B.Y.U.	7	437	1931	4962	39				989	1470	67	4186	1298	1246	15	4851	38	9.6	3.0	11.1
	54-57						4	27	118	332	36				80	121	66	237	70	100	5	316	38	8.8	2.6	11.7
Darrell Imhoff (Big D)	61-62NY 63-64Det 65-68LA	1938	6'10	223	C	California	12	801	2299	5016	46				1161	1954	59	6099	1405	2435	68	5759	22	7.6	1.8	7.2
69-70Phi 71-72Cin	63, 65-70						7	54	139	291	48				76	131	58	442	101	179	2	354	23	8.2	1.9	6.6
72Port																										
McCoy Ingram	58Min	1931	6'	210	F	Jackson State	1	24	27	103	26				13	28	46	116	20	44	1	67	11	4.8	0.8	2.
Andy Johnson	59-61Phi 62Chi	1931	6'5	216	F-G	Portland	4	292	1083	2762	39				681	1126	60	1190	675	868	17	2847	23	4.1	2.3	9.
	60-61						2	12	35	89	39				30	56	54	55	22	37	1	100	19	4.6	1.8	8.
Ron Johnson	61Det 61LA	1938	6'8	215	F	Minnesota	1	14	13	43	30				11	17	65	29	2	10	0	37	7	2.1	0.1	2.

se Name-Nickname	Team by Year	Birth Yr	Hgt	Wgt	Pos	College	# Yr	G	Field Goals FG	Att.	%	3 Pt FG FG	Att	%	Free Throws FT	Att.	%	Reb.	Pts	PF	DQ	Pts	Per Game Min	Reb	Ass	Pts
eil Johnston (Gabby)	52-59, HC60-61Phi	1929	6'8	218	C	Ohio St.	8	516	3303	7435	44				3417	4447	77	5865	1269	1681	36	10023	35	11.4	2.5	19.4
	52, 56-58						4	23	121	310	39				102	139	73	257	75	76	0	344	31	11.2	3.3	15.0
owie Joliff	61-63LA	1936	6'7	218	F-C	Ohio U.	3	138	165	449	37				58	110	53	586	112	277	5	388	13	4.2	0.8	2.8
	61-62						2	13	8	22	36				8	8	100	53	15	21	1	24	9	4.1	1.2	1.8
. C. Jones	59-67Bos HC73SD-A	1932	6'1	202	G	S. Fransisco	9	676	1919	4961	39				1173	1814	65	2399	2908	1816	24	5011	26	3.5	4.3	7.4
HC74Cap HC75-76Was	59-67						9	105	241	656	37				186	269	69	320	396	335	4	668	24	3.0	3.8	6.4
HC84-88Bos																										
am Jones	58-69Bos	1933	6'4	205	G-F	N.C. Central	12	872	6271	13745	46				2869	3572	80	4305	2209	1735	5	15411	28	4.9	2.5	17.7
	58-69						12	154	1149	2572	45				611	753	81	720	358	395	5	2909	30	4.7	2.3	18.9
illie Jones	61-65Det	1936	6'3	185	G	Northwestern	4	272	846	2153	39				324	475	68	767	545	658	12	2016	17	2.8	2.0	7.4
	61-63						3	16	66	158	42				25	29	86	37	43	43	2	157	18	2.3	2.7	9.8
hil Jordon	57-58NY 58-59Det 60-61Cin	1933	6'10	209	C-F	Whitworth	7	442	1965	4940	40				905	1312	69	3028	769	1246	24	4835	24	6.9	1.7	10.9
61-62NY 63StL	58-59, 63						3	16	36	99	36				33	42	79	51	14	34	0	105	15	3.2	0.9	6.6
d Kalafat	55-57Min	1932	6'6	245	C-F	Minnesota	3	209	490	1422	34				494	718	69	1182	310	684	20	1474	21	5.7	1.5	7.1
	55-57						3	15	32	79	41				39	60	65	63	11	49	3	103	16	4.2	0.7	6.9
ed Kearns	55Phi		6'4	185	G	Princeton	1	6	0	5	0				1	4	25	3	5	1	0	1	4	0.5	0.8	0.2
ommy Kearns	59Syr	1936	5'11	185	G	N. Carolina	1	1	1	1	100				0	0	—	0	0	1	0	2	7	0.0	0.0	2.0
ickles Kennedy	61Phi	1938	5'11	180	G	Temple	1	7	4	21	19				4	6	67	8	9	6	0	12	7	1.1	1.3	1.7
illy Kenville	54-56Syr 57FtW 58, 60Det	1930	6'2	187	G-F	St. Bonavent.	6	345	848	2337	36				738	974	76	1206	715	670	4	2434	19	3.5	2.1	7.1
	54-58						5	41	89	224	40				106	153	69	116	60	103	2	284	19	2.8	1.5	6.9
ohnny Kerr (Red)	53-63Syr 64-65Phi 66Bal	1932	6'9	230	C-F	Illinois	12	905	4909	11751	42				2662	3682	72	10092	2004	2287	34	12480	31	11.2	2.2	13.8
HC67-68Chi	55-56						12	76	370	959	39				193	281	69	827	152	173	0	933	30	10.9	2.0	12.3
HC69-70Phoe																										
an King	55Bal	1931	6'6	220	F	W. Kentucky	1	12	7	22	32				5	10	50	25	3	5	0	19	9	2.1	0.3	1.6
aury King	60Bos 63Chi	1935	6'3	195	G	Kansas	2	38	99	249	40				28	35	80	106	144	90	0	226	26	2.8	3.8	5.9
oug Kistler	62NY	1938	6'9	210	F	Duke	1	5	3	6	50				2	4	50	1	0	2	0	8	3	0.2	0.0	1.6
ob Knight	55NY	1931	6'2	185	G	none	1	2	3	7	43				1	1	100	1	8	6	0	7	15	0.5	4.0	3.5
ud Koper	65SF	1942	6'6	210	G	Okla. City	1	56	106	241	44				35	42	83	61	43	59	1	247	11	1.1	0.8	4.4
arry Kramer	65SF 65NY 70NY-A	1942	6'4	200	F-G	N.Y.U.	2	59	73	217	34	0	1	0	67	92	73	113	44	77	1	213	10	1.9	0.7	3.6
m Krebs (Red)	58-60Min 61-64LA	1935	6'8	230	C-F	S.M.U.	7	515	1696	4186	40				736	975	75	3177	429	1539	29	4128	21	6.2	0.8	8.0
	59-64						6	62	127	351	36				75	96	78	348	53	211	12	329	18	5.6	0.9	5.3
red LaCour	61-62StL 63SF	1938	6'5	210	G-F	S. Fransisco	3	144	381	904	42				178	230	77	474	269	269	3	940	17	3.3	1.9	6.5
	61						1	5	7	21	33				6	7	86	6	4	6	0	20	9	1.2	0.8	4.0
ork Larese	62Chi 62Phi HC70NY-A	1938	6'4	183	G	N. Carolina	1	59	122	327	37				58	72	81	77	94	104	0	302	12	1.3	1.6	5.1
	62						1	9	11	35	31				8	12	67	19	5	14	0	30	9	2.1	0.6	3.3
udy LaRusso	60Min 61-67LA HO67	1937	6'7	220	F-C	Dartmouth	10	738	4102	9521	43				3303	4308	77	6936	1556	2553	72	11507	33	9.4	2.1	15.6
Det 68-69SF	60-66, 68-69						9	93	467	1152	41				410	546	75	779	194	366	13	1344	34	8.4	2.1	14.5
al Lear	57Phi	1935	6'	165	G	Temple	1	3	2	6	33				0	0		1	1	3	0	4	5	0.3	0.3	1.3
eorge Lee	61-62Det	1936	6'4	200	F-G	Michigan	7	297	740	1955	38				749	1021	73	1235	258	504	2	2229	17	4.2	0.9	7.5
63-65, 67-68, HC63-64SF	61-62, 64						3	21	48	110	44				38	54	70	58	19	32	0	134	12	2.8	0.9	6.4
ob Leonard (Slick)	57-60Min 61LA 62-63Chi	1932	6'3	185	G	Indiana	7	426	1574	4510	35				1056	1418	74	1217	1427	915	4	4204	27	2.9	3.3	9.9
HC63-64Bal HC69-76IndA	57, 59-61						4	34	130	364	36				74	98	76	90	165	77	0	334	27	2.6	4.9	9.8
HC77Ind																										
arl Lloyd	51Was 52MS 53-58Syr	1928	6'6	218	F-C	W. Virginia St.	9	560	1766	4955	36				1150	1533	75	3609	810	2098	57	4682	26	6.4	1.4	8.4
59-60, HC72-73Det	53-60						8	44	131	389	34				96	129	74	254	82	171	2	358	25	5.8	1.9	8.1
m Loscutoff (Jungle Jim)	56-64Bos	1930	6'5	230	F	Oregon	9	511	1333	3868	34				490	750	65	2848	353	1497	40	3156	18	5.6	0.7	6.2
	56-57, 59, 61-64						7	58	136	420	32				48	79	61	299	32	219	8	320	17	5.2	0.6	5.5
lyde Lovellette	54-57Min 58Cin 59-62StL	1929	6'9	243	C-F	Kansas	11	704	4784	10795	44				2379	3141	76	6663	1097	2289	35	11947	27	9.5	1.6	17.0
63-64Bos	54-61, 63-64						10	69	371	892	42				221	323	68	557	89	232	4	963	24	8.1	1.3	14.0
ed Luckenbill	62Phi 63SF	1939	6'6	205	F	Houston	2	87	69	188	37				58	96	60	166	35	101	0	196	7	1.9	0.4	2.3
	62						1	4	0	5	0				2	5	40	3	1	3	0	2	4	0.8	0.3	0.5
onnie MacGilvray	55Mil	1930	6'2	185	G	St. John's (NY)	1	6	2	12	17				4	7	57	9	11	5	0	8	10	1.5	1.8	1.3
ick Mantis	60Min 63StL 63Chi	1935	6'3	190	G	Northwestern	2	42	104	283	37				28	51	55	91	92	102	0	236	18	2.2	2.2	5.6
om Marshall	55Roch 56MS 57Roch	1931	6'4	215	F-G	Wn. Kentucky	4	168	354	913	39				244	344	71	492	188	197	0	952	15	2.9	1.1	5.7
58Det 58, PC59, HC60Cin	55, 58						2	5	10	37	27				7	10	70	33	4	2	0	27	17	6.6	0.8	5.4
hil Martin	55Mil	1928	6'3	190	G	Toledo	1	7	5	19	26				2	2	100	10	6	7	0	12	7	1.4	0.9	1.7
later Martin (Dugie)	50-56Min 57NY PC57	1925	5'10	170	G	Texas	11	745	2632	7224	36				2073	2720	76	2302	3160	2238	39	7337	36	3.1	4.2	9.8
58-60StL HC68-69HouA	50-60						11	92	304	867	35				316	442	71	270	354	342	11	924	39	2.9	3.8	10.0
hitey Martin	62NY	1939	6'2	185	G	St. Bonavent.	1	66	95	292	33				37	55	67	158	115	158	4	227	15	2.4	1.7	3.4
en McBride	55Mil	1931	6'3	190	G-F	Md. En. Shore	1	12	48	147	33				21	29	72	31	14	31	0	117	21	2.6	1.2	9.8
rendan McCann	58-60NY	1935	6'2	178	G	St. Bonavent.	3	41	23	115	20				29	41	71	53	64	38	0	75	8	1.3	1.6	1.8
ohnny McCarthy	57Roch 58MS 59Cin 60-62StL	1934	6'1	185	G	Canisius	6	316	958	2714	35				534	859	62	1145	1184	885	16	2450	28	3.6	3.7	7.8
64Bos HC72Buf	60-61, 64						3	27	63	162	39				33	45	73	96	132	78	0	159	30	3.6	4.9	5.9
ill McGill (The Hill)	63Chi 64Bal 64NY 65StL 65LA	1939	6'9	225	C-F	Utah	5	295	1270	2469	51	0	0	—	554	790	70	1444	373	895	24	3094	17	4.9	1.3	10.5
69DenA 70LA-A	65, 69						2	12	24	48	50	0	0	—	10	11	91	32	8	35	3	58	11	2.7	0.7	4.8
70PitA 70DalA																										
ick McGuire (Tricky Dick)	50-57NY 58-59, PC60Det	1926	6'	180	G	Dartmouth,	11	738	2048	5259	39				1825	2836	64	2784	4205	1686	13	5921	28	3.8	5.7	8.0
HC61-63Det HC66-68NY	50-55, 58-60					St. John's (NY)	9	63	179	437	41				163	275	59	284	350	187	2	521	33	4.5	5.6	8.3
rank McGuire	HC62Phi	1911				St. John's, N.Y.U.																				
ack McMahon	53-56Roch 56-60StL	1928	6'1	188	G	St. John's (NY)	8	524	1615	4790	34				1007	1580	64	1390	1939	1483	31	4237	27	2.7	3.7	8.1
HC63Bal HC64-67Cin	53-60						8	49	191	505	38				91	163	56	149	203	163	7	473	31	3.0	4.1	9.7
HC68-70SD-A HC71-72PitA																										
hellie McMillon	59-62Det 62StL	1936	6'5	208	F	Bradley	4	263	981	2259	43				435	686	63	1571	232	748	21	2397	19	6.0	0.9	9.1
	59-61						3	9	28	71	39				22	29	76	39	9	37	3	78	19	4.3	1.0	8.7
ob McNeill	61NY 62Phi 62LA	1938	6'1	180	G	St. Joseph's	2	125	222	563	39				131	160	82	179	327	204	2	575	15	1.4	2.6	4.6
	62						1	5	4	7	57				1	2	50	6	5	6	0	9	4	1.2	1.0	1.8
arl McNulty	55Mil	1930	6'3	185	G	Purdue	1	1	1	6	17				0	0		0	0	1	0	2	14	0.0	0.0	2.0

		Birth					#		Field Goals			3 pt. FG			Free Throws								Per Game			
Use Name-Nickname	Team by Year	Year	Hgt	Wgt	Pos	College	Yr	G	FG	Att.	%	FG	Att	%	FT	Att.	%	Reb.	Ass	PF	DQ	Pts	Min	Reb	Ass	Pts
Thales McReynolds	66Bal	1943	6'3	185	G	Miles	1	5	1	12	8				1	2	50	6	1	0	0	3	6	1.2	0.2	0.6
Monk Meineke	53-55FtW 56Roch 58Cin	1930	6'7	208	F-C	Dayton	5	343	795	2154	37				758	1003	76	1626	433	1047	40	2348	22	4.7	1.3	6.8
	53-55, 58						4	25	40	114	35				66	88	75	100	26	73	5	146	20	4.0	1.0	5.8
Chuck Mencel	56-57Min	1933	6'	179	G	Minnesota	2	141	363	1063	34				257	336	76	347	333	169	1	983	20	2.5	2.4	7.0
	56-57						2	8	19	55	35				13	16	81	18	14	11	0	51	19	2.3	1.8	6.4
Porter Meriweather	63Syr	1940	6'2	180	G	Tennessee St.	1	31	48	122	39				23	33	70	29	43	19	0	119	9	0.9	1.4	3.8
Tom Meschery	62Phi 63-67SF 68-71Sea	1938	6'6	217	F	St. Mary's	10	778	3877	8793	44				2150	2885	75	6698	1331	2841	89	9904	30	8.6	1.7	12.7
HC72CarA	62, 64, 67						3	39	248	580	43				140	173	81	344	78	153	7	636	34	8.8	2.0	16.3
Vern Mikkelsen	50-59Min HC69MinA	1928	6'7	231	F-C	Hamline	10	700	3547	8812	40				2969	3874	77	5940	1515	2812	127	10063	32	8.5	2.2	14.4
	50-57, 59						9	85	396	999	40				349	446	78	585	152	397	24	1141	32	6.9	1.8	13.4
Howie Montgomery	63SF	1940	6'5	220	F	Pan American	1	20	65	153	42				14	23	61	69	21	35	1	144	18	3.5	1.1	7.2
Jackie Moore	55Syr 55Mil 55-57Phi	1932	6'5	194	F	LaSalle	3	134	137	350	39				91	146	62	338	67	217	4	365	9	2.5	0.5	2.7
	56-57						2	9	8	20	40				2	6	33	17	2	14	0	18	6	1.9	0.2	2.0
Jackie Moreland	61-65Det 68-70NO-A 71IL	1938	6'7	215	F-G	La. Tech,	7	582	2286	5446	42	6	20	30	1152	1589	72	3417	937	1847	55	5730	23	5.9	1.6	9.8
died of cancer-12/19/71	61-63, 68-69					N.C. State	5	42	187	432	43	0	2	0	76	114	67	255	86	173	5	450	25	6.1	2.0	10.7
Red Morrison	55-56Bos 58StL	1932	6'8	225	F-C	Idaho	3	155	218	550	40				119	208	57	822	135	393	15	555	14	5.3	0.9	3.6
	55-56						2	10	5	15	33				1	7	14	25	1	27	1	11	7	2.5	0.1	1.1
Boris Nachamkin	55Roch	1933	6'6	210	F	N.Y.U.	1	6	6	20	30				8	13	62	19	3	6	0	20	10	3.2	0.5	3.3
Willie Naulls	57StL 57-63NY 63SF	1934	6'6	225	F-C	U.C.L.A.	10	716	4526	11145	41				2253	2774	81	6508	1114	2216	40	11305	29	9.1	1.6	15.8
64-66Bos	59, 64-66						4	35	99	267	37				50	67	75	134	21	92	2	248	14	3.8	0.6	7.1
Paul Neumann	62-63Syr 64-65Phi 65-67SF	1938	6'1	175	G	Stanford	6	453	1827	4136	44				1335	1670	80	1318	1453	1293	16	4989	25	2.9	3.2	11.0
	62-64, 67						4	29	76	194	39				65	85	76	61	82	87	0	217	21	2.1	2.8	7.5
Chuck Noble	56-57FtW 58-62Det	1931	6'4	195	G	Louisville	7	411	1362	3937	35				552	755	73	1075	1344	1128	12	3276	22	2.6	3.3	8.0
	56-61						6	29	79	244	32				28	38	74	63	86	71	2	186	20	2.2	3.0	6.4
Bevo Nordmann	62Cin 63StL 63-64NY 64StL	1939	6'10	257	C	St. Louis	4	133	237	516	46				97	198	49	517	73	293	8	571	12	3.9	0.5	4.3
65Bos	62						1	2	0	1	0				0	0	—	2	0	1	0	0	3	1.0	0.0	0.0
Don Ohl	61-64Det 65-68Bal 68StL	1936	6'3	190	G	Illinois	10	737	4685	10806	43				2179	2975	73	2163	2243	2014	27	11549	30	2.9	3.0	15.7
69-70Atl	61-63, 65-66, 68-69						7	47	320	749	43				155	206	75	161	130	154	3	795	32	3.4	2.8	16.9
Bud Olsen	63-66Cin 66-67SF 68Sea	1940	6'8	220	F-C	Louisville	8	453	811	1872	43	1	4	25	312	590	53	1485	542	875	13	1935	12	3.3	1.2	4.3
69Bos 69Det 70KyA	63-65, 67, 70						5	27	39	88	44	0	1	0	5	19	26	32	6	16	0	83	11	2.1	0.4	3.1
Chuck Osborne	62Syr	1939	6'6	210	F	Western Ky.	1	4	1	8	13				3	4	75	9	1	3	0	5	5	2.3	0.3	1.3
Togo Palazzi	55-57Bos 57-60Syr	1932	6'4	205	F-G	Holy Cross	6	324	937	2429	39				508	696	73	1113	233	570	7	2382	13	3.4	0.7	7.4
	55-59						5	23	48	136	35				25	39	64	59	12	33	0	121	9	2.6	0.5	5.3
Jim Palmer	59-60Cin 60-61NY	1933	6'8	224	F-C	Dayton	3	196	627	1517	41				341	485	70	1040	165	563	13	1595	19	5.3	0.8	8.1
Med Park	56-59StL 59-60Cin	1933	6'2	205	G-F	Missouri	5	313	675	1782	38				584	788	74	967	532	580	4	1924	18	3.1	1.7	6.1
	56-58						3	26	38	121	31				53	77	69	74	35	61	1	129	16	2.8	1.3	5.0
Jack Parr	59Cin	1936	6'9	222	C	Kansas St.	1	66	109	307	36				44	73	60	278	51	138	1	262	16	4.2	0.8	4.0
Worthy Patterson	58StL	1931	6'2	175	G	Connecticut	1	4	3	8	38				1	2	50	2	2	3	0	7	3	0.5	0.5	1.8
Jerry Paulson	58Cin	1935	6'2	187	G	Manhattan	1	6	8	23	35				4	6	67	10	4	5	0	20	10	1.7	0.7	3.3
Jim Paxson	57Min 58Cin	1932	6'6	203	F-G	Dayton	2	138	363	1124	32				379	521	73	616	225	346	5	1105	22	4.5	1.6	8.0
	57-58						2	7	12	47	26				13	22	59	22	8	11	0	37	12	3.1	1.1	5.3
Bob Peterson	54Bal 54Mil 55-56NY	1932	6'5	210	F	Oregon	3	103	186	482	39				107	160	67	389	78	218	3	479	13	3.8	0.8	4.7
	55						1	3	7	15	47				10	11	91	16	5	3	0	24	24	5.3	1.7	8.0
Bob Pettit	55Mil 56-61, PC62, 63-65StL	1932	6'9	216	F-C	L.S.U.	11	792	7349	16872	44				6182	8119	76	12849	2369	2529	32	20880	39	16.2	3.0	26.4
	56-61, 63-65						9	88	766	1834	42				708	915	77	1304	241	277	1	2240	40	14.8	2.7	25.5
Gary Phillips	62Bos 63-66SF	1939	6'3	190	G	Houston	5	348	926	2500	37				467	742	63	903	665	820	18	2319	20	2.6	1.9	6.7
	62, 64						2	17	36	113	32				34	51	67	27	21	42	2	106	17	1.6	1.2	6.2
Dave Piontek	57Roch 58-60Cin 60-61StL	1934	6'6	234	F-C	Xavier (Ohio)	7	413	1194	3054	39				567	869	65	1770	478	835	12	2955	18	4.3	1.2	7.2
62Chi 63Cin	58, 60-61, 63						4	25	40	115	35				24	37	65	70	20	44	1	104	13	2.8	0.8	4.2
Frank Radovich	62Phi	1938	6'8	235	F	Indiana	1	37	37	93	40				13	26	50	51	4	27	0	87	5	1.4	0.1	2.4
	62						1	2	1	6	17				2	4	50	3	0	2	0	4	6	1.5	0.0	2.0
Ray Radziszewski	58Phi	1935	6'5	210	F	St. Joseph's	1	1	0	3	0				0	0	—	2	1	1	0	0	6	2.0	1.0	0.0
Cal Ramsey	60StL 60NY 61Syr	1937	6'4	200	F	N.Y.U.	2	13	41	107	38				21	37	57	73	12	32	1	103	17	5.6	0.9	7.9
Frank Ramsey	55Bos 56MS 57-64Bos	1931	6'3	199	F-G	Kentucky	9	623	2949	7382	40				2480	3083	80	3410	1134	2158	87	8378	25	5.5	1.8	13.4
HC71KyA	55, 57-64						9	98	469	1105	42				393	476	83	494	151	362	13	1331	24	5.0	1.5	13.6
Jim Ray	57, 60Syr	1934	6'1	180	G	Toledo	2	8	3	17	18				3	5	60	5	5	7	0	9	8	0.6	0.6	1.1
Hub Reed	59-60StL 60-63Cin 64LA	1936	6'9	228	C-F	Okla. City	7	479	1081	2481	44				456	630	72	2440	367	1337	33	2618	16	5.1	0.8	5.5
65Det	59, 62-64						4	21	43	106	41				21	30	70	103	16	56	0	107	15	4.9	0.8	5.1
Ron Reed	66-67Det 68RB	1942	6'6	215	F	Notre Dame	2	119	409	1124	36				133	233	57	762	173	278	3	951	19	6.4	1.5	8.0
66-75 played major league baseball																										
Richie Regan	56-57Roch 58Cin	1930	6'2	180	G	Seton Hall	3	215	699	2030	34				387	540	72	554	629	532	5	1785	26	2.6	2.9	8.3
	58						1	2	12	26	46				0	1	0	9	3	5	0	24	32	4.5	1.5	12.0
John Richter	60Bos	1937	6'9	225	F	N.C. State	1	66	113	332	34				59	117	50	312	27	158	1	285	12	4.7	0.4	4.3
	60						1	8	15	38	39				5	14	36	29	2	18	1	35	12	3.6	0.3	4.4
Dick Ricketts	56StL 56-57Roch 58Cin 59RB	1933	6'7	215	F-C	Duquesne	3	212	749	2285	33				476	688	69	1337	447	871	34	1974	27	6.3	2.1	9.3
59 played	58						1	2	5	15	33				5	5	100	10	2	9	0	15	16	5.0	1.0	7.5
major league baseball																										
Joe Roberts	61-63Syr 68KyA	1936	6'6	215	F	Ohio State	4	218	500	1312	38	1	3	33	254	399	64	1075	123	485	6	1255	16	4.9	0.6	5.8
	61-62, 68						3	14	16	47	34	0	0	—	12	20	60	47	1	25	0	44	11	3.4	0.1	3.1
Guy Rodgers	59-62Phi 63-66SF 67-68Chi	1935	6'	186	G	Temple	12	892	4125	10908	38				2165	3003	72	3791	6917	2630	45	10415	32	4.3	7.8	11.7
68Cin 69-70Mil	60-62, 64, 67, 70						6	46	198	565	35				112	175	64	237	286	176	9	508	34	5.2	6.2	11.0
Ken Rohloff	64StL	1939	6'	195	G	N.C. State	1	2	0	1	0				0	0	—	0	1	4	0	0	4	0.0	0.5	0.0
Phil Rollins	59Phi 59-61Cin 61StL 61NY	1934	6'2	190	G	Louisville	3	196	350	910	38				198	305	65	390	458	320	2	898	14	2.0	2.3	4.6
Lennie Rosenbluth	58-59Phi	1933	6'5	200	F	N. Carolina	2	82	134	410	33				74	113	65	145	29	59	0	342	7	1.8	0.4	4.2
	58						1	4	3	9	33				2	3	67	3	0	0	0	8	3	0.8	0.0	2.0

Use Name-Nickname	Team by Year	Birth				College	#		Field Goals			3 Pt. FG			Free Throws								Per Game			
		Yr	Hgt.	Wgt	Pos		Yr	G	FG	Att.	%	FG	Att	%	FT	Att.	%	Reb.	Ass	PF	DQ	Pts	Min	Reb	Ass	Pts
Dick Rosenthal	55FtW 56MS 57FtW	1933	6'5	205	F-G	Notre Dame	2	85	218	602	36				139	198	70	352	170	201	2	575	19	4.1	2.0	6.8
	55						1	11	27	84	32				28	39	72	48	26	39	1	82	19	4.4	2.4	7.5
John Rudometkin	63-65NY 65SF	1940	6'6	205	F	Southern Cal.	3	131	314	787	40				194	261	74	412	72	198	0	822	13	3.1	0.5	6.3
Joe Ruklick	60-62Phi	1938	6'9	220	F-C	Northwestern	3	114	176	481	37				46	75	61	286	47	164	1	398	8	2.5	0.4	3.5
	60, 62						2	6	3	13	23				1	2	50	9	0	5	0	7	4	1.5	0.0	1.2
Bill Russell	57-66, PC67-69Bos	1934	6'10	220	C	San Francisco	13	963	5687	12930	44				3148	5614	56	21620	4100	2592	24	14522	42	22.5	4.3	15.1
HC74-77Sea HC88Sac	57-69						13	165	1003	2335	43				667	1106	60	4104	770	536	8	2673	45	24.9	4.7	16.2
Satch Sanders	61-73, HC78-79Bos	1938	6'6	210	F	N.Y.U.	13	916	3416	7984	43				1934	2520	77	5798	1026	3044	94	8766	24	6.3	1.1	9.6
	61-69, 72-73						11	130	465	1066	44				212	297	71	763	127	508	26	1142	33	5.9	1.0	8.8
Bob Santini	56NY	1935	6'5	190	F	Iona	1	4	5	10	50				1	2	50	3	1	4	0	11	6	0.8	0.3	2.8
Woody Sauldsberry	58-60Phi 61-62StL 62-63Chi	1934	6'7	220	F-C	Texas Southn	7	462	2189	6288	35				552	905	61	3618	498	1435	29	4930	28	7.8	1.1	10.7
63StL 66Bos	58, 60-61, 63ST						3	29	174	496	35				35	62	56	259	52	118	4	383	34	8.9	1.8	13.2
Bob Schafer	56Phi 56StL 57Syr	1933	6'3	198	G	Villanova	2	65	100	336	30				73	94	78	82	68	71	0	273	11	1.3	1.0	4.2
	56						1	4	3	20	15				5	6	83	9	1	8	1	11	10	2.3	0.3	2.8
Dolph Schayes	49SyrN 50-63Syr	1928	6'8	219	F-C	N.Y.U.	16	1059	6134	15447	38				6979	8274	84	11256	3072	3432	90	19247	34	12.1	3.1	18.2
PC64, HC65-66Phi	49-63						15	103	609	1491	39				755	917	82	1051	257	371	10	1973	34	12.2	2.6	19.2
HC71-72Buf																										
Dick Schnittker	51Was 52-53MS 54-58Min	1928	6'5	205	F	Ohio State	6	364	928	2464	38				1172	1418	83	1372	480	1008	22	3028	20	3.8	1.3	8.3
	53Min 54-57						5	35	45	135	33				76	104	73	83	25	83	3	166	14	2.4	0.7	4.7
Ray Scott	62-67Det 67-70Bal 71-72VaA	1938	6'9	219	F-C	Portland	11	811	4489	10967	41	3	5	60	2648	3643	73	7979	1781	2315	33	11629	29	9.8	2.2	14.3
HC73-76Det	62-63, 69-72						6	48	262	595	44	0	0	—	136	196	69	382	98	150	2	660	26	8.0	2.0	13.8
Kenny Sears	56-61, 63NY 63-64SF	1933	6'9	198	F	Santa Clara	8	529	2465	5420	45				2425	2937	83	4142	843	1470	27	7335	28	7.8	1.6	13.9
	59, 64						2	9	16	37	43				13	15	87	29	9	10	0	45	10	3.2	1.0	5.0
Frank Selvy	55Bal 55Mil 56StL 57MS	1932	6'3	184	G-F	Furman	9	565	2222	5640	39				1676	2302	73	2098	1579	1241	10	6120	26	3.7	2.8	10.8
58StL 58Min 59NY	59-64						6	52	219	544	40				151	192	79	226	189	147	1	589	31	4.3	3.6	11.3
60Syr 60Min 61-64LA																										
Lee Shaffer	62-63Syr 64Phi 65HO	1939	6'7	220	F	N. Carolina	3	196	1328	3160	42				635	818	78	1240	232	631	12	3291	28	6.3	1.2	16.8
	62-64						3	13	99	238	42				49	63	78	82	15	41	0	247	30	6.3	1.2	19.0
Chuck Share	52-54FtW 54-55Mil 56-60StL	1927	6'11	239	C	Bowling Green	9	596	1562	3905	40				1804	2604	69	4986	809	2106	105	4928	22	8.4	1.4	8.3
60Min	52-53, 56-60						7	54	124	285	44				135	205	66	352	59	224	17	383	20	6.5	1.1	7.1
Bill Sharman	51Was 52-61Bos HC67-68SF	1926	6'1	185	G	Southern Cal.	11	711	4761	1168	408				3143	3559	88	2779	2101	1925	27	12665	32	3.9	3.0	17.8
HC69-70LA-A	52-61						10	78	538	1262	43				370	406	91	285	201	220	6	1446	33	3.7	2.6	18.5
HC71UtahA HC72-76LA																										
Ron Shavlik	57-58NY	1933	6'8	200	F	N. C. State	2	8	4	23	17				2	5	40	23	0	12	0	10	10	2.9	0.0	1.3
Gene Shue	55Phi 55-56NY 57FtW	1931	6'2	175	G	Maryland	10	699	3715	9378	40				2638	3273	81	2855	2608	1405	8	10068	33	4.1	3.7	14.4
58-62Det 63NY	55, 57-62						7	32	207	488	42				155	184	84	133	132	75	0	569	36	4.2	4.1	17.8
64, HC67-73Bal HC74-78Phi																										
HC79-80SD HC81-86Was HC88-89LAC																										
Bob Sims	62LA 62StL 68AnaA	1938	6'5	220	G-F	Pepperdine	2	67	195	498	39	0	0	—	127	222	57	184	156	193	5	517	20	2.7	2.3	7.7
Whitey Skoog	52-57Min	1926	5'11	182	G	Minnesota	6	341	1164	3000	39				472	591	80	1133	903	1027	27	2800	27	3.3	2.6	8.2
	53-56						4	34	115	286	40				50	73	68	125	70	130	5	280	27	3.7	2.1	8.2
Jeff Slade	63Chi	1941	6'6	220	F	Kenyon	1	3	2	5	40				0	1	0	7	0	3	0	4	7	2.3	0.0	1.3
Adrian Smith (Odie)	62-70Cin 70-71SF 72VaA	1936	6'1	185	G	Kentucky	11	772	3174	7389	43	2	11	18	2400	2865	84	1626	1730	1829	12	8750	25	2.1	2.2	11.3
	62-67, 72						7	47	153	381	40	1	5	20	124	149	83	80	97	88	0	431	22	1.7	2.1	9.2
Bill Smith	62NY	1939	6'5	190	G-F	St. Peter's	1	9	8	33	24				7	8	88	16	7	6	0	23	9	1.8	0.8	2.6
Bobby Smith	60Min 62LA	1937	6'4	190	G	West Virginia	2	13	13	55	24				11	16	69	33	14	11	0	37	11	2.5	1.1	2.8
Ron Sobie	57-60NY 60Min	1934	6'3	195	G	DePaul	4	192	564	1489	38				491	608	81	791	353	421	3	1619	20	4.1	1.8	8.4
(born Sobieszczyk)																										
Guy Sparrow	58-59NY 59-60Phi	1932	6'6	218	F	Detroit	3	150	461	1289	36				245	403	61	728	142	410	9	1167	17	4.9	0.9	7.8
Art Spoelstra	55-57Roch 58Min 58NY	1932	6'9	220	C	Western	4	278	763	1953	39				486	701	69	1273	266	811	29	2012	19	4.6	1.0	7.2
	55					Kentucky	1	3	7	14	50				1	1	100	9	0	11	0	15	9	3.0	0.0	5.0
Larry Staverman	59-61Cin 63Chi 64Bal	1936	6'7	212	F	Thomas More	5	265	474	1019	47				289	373	77	1019	251	577	10	1237	13	3.8	0.9	4.7
64Det 64Cin	64						1	7	11	23	48				15	19	79	26	5	16	0	37	10	3.7	0.7	5.3
HC68-69IndA HC78KC																										
Jack Stephens (Junior)	56StL/57-58MS	1933	6'3	185	G-F	Notre Dame	1	72	248	643	39				247	357	69	377	207	144	6	743	31	5.2	2.9	10.3
	56						1	7	12	41	29				15	25	60	23	9	9	0	39	17	3.3	1.3	5.6
Wayne Stevens	60Cin	1936	6'3	185	F	Cincinnati	1	8	3	19	16				7	10	70	16	4	4	0	13	6	2.0	0.5	1.6
Norm Stewart	57StL	1935	6'5	205	F	Missouri	1	5	4	15	27				2	6	33	5	2	9	0	10	7	1.0	0.4	2.0
Sam Stith	62NY	1937	6'2	185	G	St. Bonavent.	1	32	59	162	36				23	38	61	51	60	55	0	141	14	1.6	1.9	4.4
Tom Stith	63NY	1939	6'5	210	F	St. Bonavent.	1	25	37	110	34				3	10	30	39	18	23	0	77	8	1.6	0.7	3.1
Maurice Stokes	56-57Roch 58Cin 59IL	1933	6'7	232	F-C	St. Francis	3	202	1251	3567	35				813	1165	70	3492	1062	789	32	3315	37	17.3	5.3	16.4
became ill after head	58						1	1	3	12	25				6	7	86	15	2	3	0	12	39	15.0	2.0	12.0
injury, March 16, 1958																										
Joe Strawder	66-68Det	1940	6'10	235	C	Bradley	3	231	737	1729	43				503	733	69	2296	245	961	47	1977	28	9.9	1.1	8.6
	68						1	6	14	42	33				14	22	64	65	9	27	1	42	30	10.8	1.5	7.0
Roger Strickland (The Rifle)	64Bal	1940	6'5	200	F	Jacksonville	1	1	1	3	33				0	0	—	0	0	1	0	2	4	0.0	0.0	2.0
Bennie Swain	59Bos	1933	6'8	222	F	Texas Southn	1	58	99	244	41				67	110	61	262	29	127	3	265	12	4.5	0.5	4.6
	59						1	5	2	6	33				1	2	50	14	1	4	0	5	5	2.8	0.2	1.0
Dan Swartz (Dogpatch)	63Bos	1934	6'4	215	F	Morehead St.,	1	39	57	150	38				61	72	85	88	21	92	0	175	9	2.3	0.5	4.5
	63					Kentucky	1	1	0	0	—				0	0	—	0	0	0	0	0	4	0.0	0.0	0.0
Bill Thieben .	57FtW 58Det	1935	6'7	218	F-C	Hofstra	2	85	132	399	33				73	114	64	272	24	122	0	337	10	3.2	0.3	4.0
	57						1	2	6	7	86				2	6	33	6	3	5	0	14	14	3.0	1.5	7.0
John Thompson	65-66Bos	1941	6'10	230	F	Providence	2	74	98	239	41				66	111	59	260	19	156	1	262	10	3.5	0.3	3.5
	65-66						2	6	3	14	21				7	7	100	16	1	4	0	13	5	2.7	0.2	2.2
Rod Thorn	64Bal 65-66Det	1941	6'4	196	G	West Virginia	8	466	1939	4479	43				1134	1569	72	1463	1214	784	4	5012	22	3.1	2.6	10.8
66-67StL 68-71Sea	66-67						2	19	45	166	27				39	45	87	45	21	22	0	129	14	2.4	1.1	6.8
HC76StLA HC82Chi																										
Dan Tieman	63Cin	1940	6'	185	G	Thomas More	1	29	15	57	26				4	10	40	22	27	18	0	34	6	0.8	0.9	1.2
Gene Tormohlen (Bumper)	63-64, 66-68StL 70Atl	1937	6'9	242	C-F	Tennessee	6	271	515	1253	41				161	278	58	1122	257	551	10	1191	12	4.1	0.9	4.4
HC76Atl	63-64, 66-68						5	26	24	60	40				11	18	61	65	25	40	0	59	7	2.5	1.0	2.3
Lou Tsioropoulos	57-59Bos	1930	6'5	208	F	Kentucky	3	157	337	1070	31				236	329	72	751	165	451	14	910	19	4.8	1.1	5.8
	58						1	11	25	85	29				19	29	66	64	14	40	4	69	22	5.8	1.3	6.3

		Birth					#		Field Goals			3 pt. FG			Free Throws								Per Game			
Use Name-Nickname	Team by Year	Yr	Hgt	Wgt	Pos	College	Yr	G	FG	Att.	%	FG	Att	%	FT	Att.	%	Reb.	Ass	PF	DQ	Pts	Min	Reb	Ass	Pts
Jim Tucker	55-57Syr	1932	6'7	185	F	Duquesne	3	99	175	450	39				93	122	76	349	52	242	2	407	13	3.5	0.5	4.1
	55-56						2	15	21	61	34				14	17	82	40	3	28	0	56	9	2.7	0.2	3.7
Jack Turner	55NY	1930	6'4	170	F-G	Western Ky.	1	65	111	308	36				60	76	79	154	77	76	0	282	14	2.4	1.2	4.3
	55						1	2	2	5	40				1	3	33	4	2	1	0	5	8	2.0	1.0	2.5
Jack Turner	62Chi	1939	6'5	200	G-F	Louisville	1	42	84	221	38				32	42	76	85	44	51	0	200	14	2.0	1.0	4.8
Jack Twyman	56-57Roch 58-66Cin	1934	6'6	212	F-G	Cincinnati	11	823	6237	13873	45				3366	4325	78	5424	1861	2782	56	15840	32	6.6	2.3	19.2
	58, 62-66						6	34	245	556	44				131	159	82	255	62	137	2	621	32	7.5	1.8	18.3
Charlie Tyra	58-61NY 62Chi	1935	6'8	235	C-F	Louisville	5	348	1213	3121	39				665	990	67	2567	315	987	27	3091	22	7.4	0.9	8.9
	59						1	2	12	28	43				6	9	67	31	1	5	0	30	28	15.5	0.5	15.0
Chico Vaughn	63-66StL 66-67Det 69PitA	1940	6'3	204	G	Southern Ill.	8	491	2137	5457	39	306	1015	30	1242	1684	74	1224	1027	1146	8	5822	26	2.5	2.1	11.9
69MinA 70PitA	63-65, 68-69						5	47	199	519	38	30	114	26	112	146	77	121	107	149	3	540	27	2.6	2.3	11.5
Horace Walker	62Chi	1936	6'3	210	F	Michigan St.	1	65	149	439	34				140	193	73	466	69	194	2	438	20	7.2	1.1	6.7
Jim Walsh	58Phi	1931	6'4	195	F	Stanford	1	10	5	27	19				10	17	59	15	8	9	0	20	7	1.5	0.8	2.0
Gerry Ward	64StL 65Bos 66Phi 67Chi	1941	6'4	195	G	Boston Coll.	4	169	202	567	36				138	216	64	294	237	364	5	542	12	1.7	1.4	3.2
	64, 66-67						3	14	17	40	43				5	7	71	15	5	23	0	39	7	1.1	0.4	2.8
Ben Warley	63Syr 64-66Phi 66-67Bal	1936	6'5	200	F-G	Tenn. State	8	437	1267	3032	42	98	345	28	1054	1403	75	2436	356	1292	38	3686	19	5.6	0.8	8.4
68AnaA 69LA-A 70DenA	63-66, 70						5	20	25	70	36	7	16	44	19	30	63	68	14	43	1	76	12	3.4	0.7	3.8
Bobby Watson	55Mil	1930	6'	162	G	Kentucky	1	63	72	223	32				31	45	69	87	79	67	0	175	11	1.4	1.3	2.8
Ron Watts	66-67Bos	1943	6'6	210	F	Wake Forest	2	28	12	46	26				16	23	70	39	2	17	0	40	3	1.4	0.1	1.4
	67						1	1	1	6	17				1	2	50	2	0	3	0	3	5	2.0	0.0	3.0
Ralph Wells	63Chi	1940	6'1	180	G	Northwestern	1	3	1	7	14				0	7	0	6	7	6	0	2	16	2.0	2.3	0.7
Skippy Whitaker	55Bos	1930	6'1	185	G	Kentucky	1	3	1	6	17				0	0	—	1	1	4	0	2	5	0.3	0.3	0.7
Bob Wiesenhahn	62Cin	1936	6'4	215	F	Cincinnati	1	60	51	161	32				17	30	57	112	23	50	0	119	5	1.9	0.4	2.0
	62						1	2	1	4	25				1	1	100	2	0	0	0	3	3	1.0	0.0	1.5
Gene Wiley	63-66LA 67VR 68Oak 68DalA	1937	6'10	214	C	Wichita State	5	309	560	1194	47	0	0	—	171	338	51	2214	254	821	22	1291	21	7.2	0.8	4.2
	63-66						4	27	52	103	50				16	37	43	272	34	80	2	120	26	10.1	1.3	4.4
Win Wilfong	58-59StL 60-61Cin	1932	6'2	186	G-F	Missouri,	4	268	684	1897	36				458	616	74	910	565	649	5	1826	18	3.4	2.1	6.8
	58-59					Memphis St.	2	16	23	80	29				26	39	67	58	26	31	0	72	13	3.6	1.6	4.5
Bob Williams	56-57Min	1931	6'6	230	F	Florida A & M	2	24	22	50	44				26	48	54	59	7	28	1	70	8	2.5	0.3	2.9
Tony Windis	60Det	1933	6'1	160	G	Wyoming	1	9	16	60	27				4	6	67	47	32	20	0	36	21	5.2	3.6	4.0
John Windsor	64SF	1940	6'8	215	F	Stanford	1	11	10	27	37				7	8	88	26	2	13	0	27	6	2.4	0.2	2.5
Charlie Wolf	HC61-63Cin HC64-65Det	1926				Notre Dame, Thomas More, Xavier (OH)																				
George Yardley	54-57FtW 58-59et 59-60Syr	1928	6'5	194	F-G	Stanford	7	472	3193	7572	42				2677	3434	78	4220	815	1426	22	9063	33	8.9	1.7	19.2
	54-60						7	46	324	767	42				285	349	82	457	112	143	2	933	37	9.9	2.4	20.3
Wayne Yates	62LA	1937	6'8	235	C	Memphis State	1	37	31	105	30				10	22	45	94	16	72	1	72	7	2.5	0.4	1.9
	62						1	4	3	8	38				1	2	50	5	1	2	0	7	3	1.3	0.3	1.8
Dave Zeller	62Cin	1939	6'1	175	G	Miami (Ohio)	1	61	36	102	35				18	24	75	27	58	37	0	90	5	0.4	1.0	1.5
	62						1	2	1	2	50				0	0	—	1	1	0	0	2	3	0.5	0.5	1.0

1967-68 through 1975-76
Expanding the Competition

1967-68 N.B.A.

Boston's Incredible Brinkmanship

The N.B.A. had two new teams this season, with the addition of the Seattle Supersonics and San Diego Rockets, two expansion teams created mostly from castoffs from other clubs. The N.B.A. also had two new arenas to play in; the Forum in Los Angeles and the new Madison Square Garden in New York opened their doors in mid-season. And the N.B.A. had new competition, as the American Basketball Association began play with eleven new clubs.

The A.B.A. made no dent in the N.B.A.'s attendance figures, but the new league did spirit away Rick Barry, the established league's scoring champion. Barry jumped the San Francisco Warriors to sign a lucrative contract with the new Oakland Oaks (coached by Bruce Hale, Barry's father-in-law), but the Warriors took Barry to court to force him to play under the reserve clause of his San Francisco contract. The court ruled that Barry could sit out the season and join the Oaks next year, and Barry spent the campaign broadcasting the Oaks' games. But no other major players jumped to the A.B.A., leaving the balance of power relatively undisturbed .

Wielding the most power in the N.B.A. were the Philadelphia 76ers, the defending champions. With Wilt Chamberlain leading the league in rebounds, assists, and field goal percentage, and with Hal Greer, Chet Walker, Billy Cunningham, Wally Jones, and Luke Jackson working tightly around Wilt, the 76ers still were the class of the league. They couldn't keep the torrid pace of last season, but 24 wins in their last 29 games made the 76ers easy winners of the Eastern Division.

The 76ers were simply too strong for the aging Boston Celtics over an 82-game schedule. K.C. Jones had retired to become a college coach, and Bill Russell and Sam Jones were feeling the pains of injury and age. But even if they were no longer the invincible champions, the Celtics still had plenty of talent and cohesion, and they finished second with a 54-28 record.

The New York Knicks captured third place on the strength of their first .500 season since 1958-59. The addition of rookies Walt Frazier and Phil Jackson, plus the signing of Princeton great Bill Bradley after two years in England as a Rhodes scholar plus a short Air Force hitch, gave the Knicks a very deep squad which somehow got off to a poor start under coach Dick McGuire. Red Holzman took over as coach on December 27, and his constant stress on defense and team-oriented offense paid immediate dividends. Under Holzman, the Knicks compiled a 28-17 record.

The Detroit Pistons, shifted to the Eastern Division to make room for Seattle and San Diego, also improved markedly, as their 40-42 record was their best since 1955-56. Rookie guard Jimmy Walker and veteran Terry Dischinger, back from two years of military service, joined scoring champ Dave Bing and Dave DeBusschere as key men on this fourth-place club. Finishing out of the playoffs were the Cincinnati Royals, who missed Oscar Robertson when he sat out with a thigh injury, and the Baltimore Bullets, who lost forward Gus Johnson to injuries. The Royals lost first draft pick Mel Daniels to the A.B.A., but the Bullets had an ace rookie in flashy guard Earl (The Pearl) Monroe.

The St. Louis Hawks almost lost Lou Hudson to the A.B.A., but the high scorer changed his mind about jumping shortly after announcing that he would change leagues. As it turned out, Hudson played only a part of the season before getting called into the Army. The Hawks didn't let Hudson's status upset the team, as they used a tough pressing defense to lead the West with a 56-26 record. Coach Richie Guerin had retired as a player, leaving the backcourt chores to Lenny Wilkens, Don Ohl, and Dick Snyder. Zelmo Beaty, Bill Bridges, and Paul Silas hit the boards with a lot of muscle for the Hawks. The Los Angeles Lakers couldn't match the Hawks for strength up front, but the combination of Elgin Baylor and Jerry West spurred them home in second place; young guard Archie Clark developed into an offensive threat while West missed 31 games with an injury.

Without Rick Barry, the Warriors finished a distant third, helped not at all by an injury which sidelined center Nate Thurmond for the second half of the season. The Chicago Bulls captured the last playoff spot with a 29-53 mark, while the expansion teams in Seattle and San Diego, as expected, lost plenty of games; San Diego, in fact, had the worst record of any team since 1950.

The playoffs this year had two clear favorites in the 76ers and the Hawks, with the Celtics and Lakers outside shots. The Celtics came back from a 2-1 deficit to beat the Pistons in six games in their Eastern semifinals, while the 76ers ran into trouble with the upstart Knicks. The two clubs split the first four games, with Billy Cunningham going out with a fractured arm and Walt Frazier with an injured leg. The 76ers won games five and six, but the loss of Cunningham robbed the club of any punch its bench had. The Western semifinals saw a major upset when the Warriors bumped off the Hawks in six games, while the Lakers, as expected, easily eliminated the Bulls. The Lakers then beat the Warriors to head into the title series against the Eastern representative, Philadelphia or Boston.

The Eastern showdown between the 76ers and Celtics had the air of a rematch for the heavyweight championship of the world; the Celtics had beat the 76ers two years ago; the 76ers had won last year. The opening game, one day after the assassination of Dr. Martin Luther King, saw the Celtics use long-range shooting to take a 127-118 victory. But then the 76ers settled down to their power game and took three straight from the Celtics. With their backs to the wall, the Celtics staved off elimination with a 122-104 win in Philly. Then, back in Boston, they evened the series at three games all with a 114-106 win. With the series riding now on a seventh game, it came down to the 76er muscle vs. the Celtic savvy. Chamberlain concentrated on feeding his teammates, who had a collective off-night in the shooting department. The Celtics stayed right with the stronger 76ers and led 97-95 with 34 seconds left on the clock. Russell then sank a foul shot, blocked a shot by Chet Walker, grabbed a rebound of Hal Greer's shot, and got the ball out to Sam Jones, who sunk a final basket for a 100-96 victory. The Celtic dynasty was back in business, and Russell and company were not about to let a championship slip away; they knocked off the Lakers in six games and savored their return to the top of the hill.

Use Name	Pos	Hgt	Wgt	Age	G (TOTAL)	Min	FG	FGA	%	FT	FTA	%	Reb	Ass	PF	DQ	Points	Min (PER GAME)	Reb	Ass	PF	Points
1967/68 N.B.A. — EASTERN DIVISION																						
PHILADELPHIA 76ers	62-20 .756				**ALEX HANNUM**																	
Chet Walker	F	6'6	210	27	82	2623	539	1172	46	387	533	73	607	157	252	3	1465	32	7.4	1.9	3.1	17.9
Luke Jackson	F-C	6'9	240	26	82	2570	401	927	43	166	231	72	872	139	287	6	968	31	10.6	1.7	3.5	11.8
Wilt Chamberlain	C	7'1	275	31	82	**3836**	819	1377	**59**	354	**932**	38	**1952**	**702**	160	0	1992	**47**	**23.8**	8.6	2.0	24.3
Hal Greer	G	6'3	176	31	82	3263	777	1626	48	422	549	77	444	372	289	6	1976	40	5.4	4.5	3.5	24.1
Wally Jones	G	6'2	180	25	77	2058	413	1040	40	159	202	79	219	245	225	5	985	27	2.8	3.2	2.9	12.8
Billy Cunningham	F	6'7	220	24	74	2076	516	1178	44	368	509	72	562	187	260	3	1400	28	7.6	2.5	3.5	18.9
Matt Guokas	G-F	6'5	190	23	82	1612	190	393	48	118	152	78	185	191	172	0	498	20	2.3	2.3	2.1	6.1
Bill Melchionni	G	6'1	165	23	71	758	146	336	43	33	47	70	104	105	75	0	325	11	1.5	1.5	1.1	4.6
Larry Costello (foot injury)	G	6'1	188	36	28	492	67	148	45	67	81	83	51	68	62	0	201	18	1.8	2.4	2.2	7.2
Johnny Green (from SD)	F	6'5	200	34	35	367	69	150	46	39	83	47	122	21	51	0	177	10	3.5	0.6	1.5	5.1
Ron Filipek	F	6'5	210	23	19	73	18	47	38	7	14	50	25	7	12	0	43	4	1.3	0.4	0.6	2.3
Jim Reid	F	6'6	210	22	6	52	10	20	50	1	5	20	11	3	6	0	21	9	1.8	0.5	1.0	3.5
BOSTON CELTICS	54-28 .659				**BILL RUSSELL**																	
Satch Sanders	F	6'6	210	29	78	1981	296	691	43	200	255	78	454	100	300	12	792	23	5.8	1.3	3.8	10.2
Bailey Howell	F	6'7	220	30	82	2801	643	1336	48	335	461	73	805	133	285	4	1621	34	9.8	1.6	3.5	19.8
Bill Russell	C	6'10	220	33	78	2953	365	858	43	247	460	54	1451	357	242	2	977	38	18.6	4.6	3.1	12.5
John Havlicek	G-F	6'5	205	27	82	2921	666	1551	43	368	453	81	546	384	237	2	1700	36	6.7	4.7	2.9	20.7
Sam Jones (injury)	G	6'4	205	34	73	2408	621	1348	46	311	376	83	357	216	181	0	1553	33	4.9	3.0	2.5	21.3
Larry Seigfried (XJ)	G	6'3	192	28	62	1937	261	629	41	236	272	87	215	289	194	2	758	31	3.5	4.7	3.1	12.2
Don Nelson	F	6'6	210	27	82	1498	312	632	49	195	268	73	431	103	178	1	819	18	5.3	1.3	2.2	10.0
Wayne Embry	C-F	6'8	255	30	78	1088	193	483	40	109	185	59	321	52	174	1	495	14	4.1	0.7	2.2	6.3
Mal Graham (MS)	G	6'1	185	22	78	786	117	272	43	56	88	64	94	61	123	0	290	16	2.0	1.3	2.6	6.0
Tom Thacker	G-F	6'2	190	28	65	782	114	272	42	43	84	51	161	69	165	2	271	12	2.5	1.1	2.5	4.2
Johnny Jones	F	6'7	210	24	51	475	86	253	34	42	68	62	114	26	60	0	214	9	2.2	0.5	1.2	4.2
Rick Weitzman	G	6'2	185	21	25	75	12	46	26	9	13	69	10	8	8	0	33	3	0.4	0.3	0.3	1.3
NEW YORK KNICKERBOCKERS	43-39 .524				**DICK MCGUIRE (15-22 .405), RED HOLZMAN (28-17 .622)**																	
Cazzie Russell	F	6'5	218	23	82	2296	551	1192	46	282	349	81	374	195	223	2	1384	28	4.6	2.4	2.7	16.9
Willis Reed	F-C	6'9	235	25	81	2879	659	1346	49	367	509	72	1073	159	343	12	1685	36	13.2	2.0	4.2	20.8
Walt Bellamy	C	6'11	245	28	82	2695	511	944	54	350	529	66	961	164	259	3	1372	33	11.7	2.0	3.2	16.7
Dick Barnett	G	6'4	190	31	81	2488	559	1159	48	343	440	78	238	242	222	0	1461	31	2.9	3.0	2.7	18.0
Walt Frazier	G	6'4	202	22	74	1588	256	568	45	154	235	66	313	305	199	2	666	21	4.2	4.1	2.7	9.0
Dick Van Arsdale	F-G	6'5	210	24	78	2348	316	725	44	227	339	67	424	230	225	0	859	30	5.4	2.9	2.9	11.0
Howie Komives	G	6'1	185	26	78	1660	233	631	37	132	161	82	168	246	170	1	598	21	2.2	3.2	2.2	7.7
Phil Jackson	F-C	6'8	220	22	75	1093	182	455	40	99	168	59	338	55	212	3	463	15	4.5	0.7	2.8	6.2
Em Bryant	G	6'1	175	29	77	968	112	291	38	59	86	69	133	134	173	0	283	13	1.7	1.7	2.2	3.7
Bill Bradley (MS)	G	6'5	205	24	45	874	142	341	42	76	104	73	113	137	138	2	360	19	2.5	3.0	3.1	8.0
Freddie Crawford (to LA)	G	6'4	190	26	31	426	65	177	37	37	59	63	83	46	67	0	167	14	2.7	1.5	2.2	5.4
Neil Johnson	F	6'7	220	24	43	286	44	106	42	23	48	48	75	33	63	0	111	7	1.7	0.8	1.5	2.6
Nate Bowman	C	6'10	230	24	42	272	52	134	39	10	15	67	113	20	69	0	114	6	2.7	0.5	1.6	2.7
Jim Caldwell (to NJ-A)	C	6'10	240	24	2	7	0	1	0	0	0	—	1	1	1	0	0	4	0.5	0.5	0.5	0.0
Dave Stallworth - illness																						
DETROIT PISTONS	40-42 .488				**DONNIE BUTCHER**																	
Dave DeBusschere	F	6'6	225	27	80	3125	573	1295	44	289	435	66	1081	181	304	3	1435	39	13.5	2.3	3.8	17.9
Happy Hairston (from Cin)	F	6'7	225	25	26	892	164	357	46	162	226	72	262	37	72	0	490	34	10.1	1.4	2.8	18.8
Joe Strawder (ST)	C	6'10	235	27	73	2029	206	456	45	139	215	65	685	85	312	**18**	551	28	9.4	1.2	4.3	7.5
Eddie Miles	G	6'4	196	27	76	2303	561	1180	48	282	369	76	264	215	200	3	1404	30	3.5	2.8	2.6	18.5
Dave Bing	G	6'3	180	24	79	3209	**835**	**1893**	44	472	668	71	373	509	254	2	**2142**	41	4.7	6.4	3.2	27.1
Terry Dischinger	F	6'7	208	27	78	1936	394	797	49	237	311	76	483	114	247	6	1025	25	6.2	1.5	3.2	13.1
John Tresvant (to Cin)	F-C	6'7	220	28	55	1671	275	597	46	183	278	66	540	114	239	15	733	30	9.8	2.1	4.3	13.3
Jimmy Walker	G	6'3	205	23	81	1585	289	733	39	134	175	77	135	226	204	1	712	20	1.7	2.8	2.5	8.8
Len Chappell (from Cin)	C-F	6'8	240	26	57	999	220	428	51	130	184	71	346	48	113	1	570	18	6.1	0.8	2.0	10.0
Tom Van Arsdale (to Cin)	G-F	6'5	215	24	50	832	114	307	37	101	136	74	132	79	119	3	329	17	2.6	1.6	2.4	6.6
George Patterson	C-F	6'8	240	28	59	559	44	133	33	32	38	84	159	51	85	0	120	9	2.7	0.9	1.4	2.0
Jim Fox (from Cin)	C	6'10	230	24	24	380	34	82	41	30	52	58	135	17	51	0	98	16	5.6	0.7	2.1	4.1
Sonny Dove	F	6'8	198	22	28	162	22	75	29	12	26	46	52	11	27	0	56	6	1.9	0.4	1.0	2.0
Paul Long	G	6'2	180	23	16	93	23	51	45	11	15	73	15	12	13	0	57	6	0.9	0.8	0.8	3.6
George Carter (MS)	F	6'5	218	23	1	5	1	2	50	1	1	100	0	1	0	0	3	5	0.0	1.0	0.0	3.0
CINCINNATI ROYALS	39-43 .476				**ED JUCKER**																	
John Tresvant (from Det)	F-C	6'7	220	28	30	802	121	270	45	67	106	63	169	46	105	3	309	27	5.6	1.5	3.5	10.3
Jerry Lucas	F-C	6'8	235	27	82	3619	707	1361	52	346	445	78	1560	251	243	3	1760	44	19.0	3.1	3.0	21.5
Connie Dierking	C	6'9	235	31	81	2637	544	1164	47	237	310	76	766	191	315	6	1325	33	9.5	2.4	3.9	16.4
Oscar Robertson (thigh injury)	G	6'5	218	29	65	2765	660	1321	50	**576**	660	**87**	391	633	199	2	1896	43	6.0	**9.7**	3.1	**29.2**
Adrian Smith	G	6'1	185	31	82	2783	480	1035	46	320	386	83	185	272	259	6	1280	34	2.3	3.3	3.2	15.6
Happy Hairston (from Det)	F	6'7	225	25	48	1625	317	630	50	203	296	69	355	58	127	1	837	34	7.4	1.2	2.6	17.4
Guy Rodgers (from Chi)	G	6'	190	32	75	1417	132	372	35	98	122	80	136	352	156	1	362	19	1.8	4.7	2.1	4.8
Bob Love	F	6'8	215	25	72	1068	193	455	42	78	114	68	209	55	141	1	464	15	2.9	0.8	2.0	6.4
Walt Wesley (ankle injury)	C	6'11	220	22	66	918	188	404	47	76	152	50	281	34	168	2	452	14	4.3	0.5	2.5	6.8
Bill Dinwiddie	F	6'7	220	24	67	871	141	358	39	62	102	61	237	31	122	2	344	13	3.5	0.5	1.8	5.1
Tom Van Arsdale (from Det)	G-F	6'5	215	24	27	682	97	238	41	87	116	75	93	76	83	2	281	25	3.4	2.8	3.1	10.4
Gary Gray	G	6'1	185	22	44	276	49	134	37	7	10	70	23	26	48	0	105	6	0.5	0.6	1.1	2.4
Jim Fox (to Det)	C	6'10	230	24	31	244	32	79	41	36	56	64	95	12	34	0	100	8	3.1	0.4	1.1	3.2
Len Chappell (To Det)	C-F	6'8	240	26	10	65	15	30	50	8	10	80	15	5	6	0	38	7	1.5	0.5	0.6	3.8
Al Jackson	G	6'1	185	24	2	17	0	3	0	0	0	—	0	1	6	0	0	9	0.0	0.5	3.0	0.0
Flynn Robinson (to Chi)	G	6'1	190	26	2	16	3	10	30	3	7	43	4	5	4	0	9	8	2.0	2.5	2.0	4.5

Use Name	Pos	Hgt	Wgt	Age	TOTAL													PER GAME				
					G	Min	FG	FGA	%	FT	FTA	%	Reb	Ass	PF	DQ	Points	Min	Reb	Ass	PF	Points
1967/68 N.B.A. — EASTERN DIVISION (continued)																						
BALTIMORE BULLETS	**36-46 .439**				**GENE SHUE**																	
Gus Johnson (broken finger)	F	6'6	235	29	60	2271	482	1033	47	180	270	67	782	159	223	7	1144	38	13.0	2.7	3.7	19.1
Ray Scott	F-C	6'9	220	29	81	2924	490	1189	41	348	447	78	1111	167	252	2	1328	36	13.7	2.1	3.1	16.4
Leroy Ellis	C	6'10	218	27	78	2719	380	800	48	207	286	72	862	158	256	5	967	35	11.1	2.0	3.3	12.4
Kevin Loughery	G	6'3	190	27	77	2297	458	1127	41	305	392	78	247	256	301	13	1221	30	3.2	3.3	3.9	15.9
Earl Monroe	G	6'3	180	23	82	3012	742	1637	45	507	649	78	465	349	282	3	1991	37	5.7	4.3	3.4	24.3
Jack Marin	F	6'7	200	23	82	2037	429	932	46	250	314	80	473	110	246	4	1108	25	5.8	1.3	3.0	13.5
Don Ohl (to StL)	G	6'3	190	31	39	1096	232	536	43	114	148	77	113	84	91	0	578	28	2.9	2.2	2.3	14.8
Ed Manning	F	6'7	215	24	71	951	112	259	43	60	99	61	375	32	153	3	284	13	5.3	0.5	2.2	4.0
Johnny Egan	G	5'11	180	28	67	930	163	415	39	142	183	78	112	134	127	0	468	14	1.7	2.0	1.9	7.0
Bob Ferry	C	6'8	235	30	59	841	128	311	41	73	117	62	186	61	92	0	329	14	3.2	1.0	1.6	5.6
Stan McKensie	F-G	6'5	210	23	50	653	73	182	40	58	88	66	121	24	98	1	204	13	2.4	0.5	2.0	4.1
Roland West	G	6'4	178	23	4	14	2	5	40	0	0	—	5	0	3	0	4	4	1.3	0.0	0.8	1.0
Tom Workman (from StL)	F	6'7	230	23	1	10	0	2	0	1	1	100	1	0	3	0	1	10	1.0	0.0	3.0	1.0
1967/68 - WESTERN DIVISION																						
ST. LOUIS HAWKS	**56-26 .683**				**RICHIE GUERIN**																	
Bill Bridges	F	6'6	235	28	82	3197	466	1009	46	347	484	72	1102	253	**366**	12	1279	39	13.4	3.1	**4.5**	15.6
Paul Silas	F	6'7	235	24	82	2652	399	871	46	299	424	71	958	162	243	4	1097	32	11.7	2.0	3.0	13.4
Zelmo Beaty	C	6'9	240	28	82	3068	639	1310	49	455	573	79	959	174	295	6	1733	37	11.7	2.1	3.6	21.1
Don Ohl (from Bal)	G	6'3	190	31	31	823	161	355	45	83	106	78	62	73	93	1	405	27	2.0	2.4	3.0	13.1
Lenny Wilkens	G	6'1	185	30	82	3169	546	1246	44	546	711	77	438	679	255	3	1638	39	5.3	8.3	3.1	20.0
Joe Caldwell	F-G	6'5	200	26	79	2641	564	1219	46	165	290	57	338	240	208	1	1293	33	4.3	3.0	2.6	16.4
Dick Snyder	G	6'5	210	23	75	1622	257	613	42	129	167	77	194	164	215	5	643	22	2.6	2.2	2.9	8.6
Lou Hudson (MS)	F-G	6'5	220	23	46	966	227	500	45	120	164	73	193	65	113	2	574	21	4.2	1.4	2.5	12.5
Gene Tormohlen	F-C	6'9	245	30	77	714	98	262	37	33	56	59	226	68	94	0	229	9	2.9	0.9	1.2	3.0
George Lehmann	G	6'3	190	25	55	497	59	172	34	35	43	81	44	93	54	0	153	9	0.8	1.7	1.0	2.8
Jim Davis	C	6'9	235	26	50	394	61	139	44	25	64	39	123	13	85	2	147	8	2.5	0.3	1.7	2.9
Tom Workman (to Bal)	F	6'7	230	23	19	85	19	38	50	17	22	77	24	3	14	0	55	4	1.3	0.2	0.7	2.9
Jay Miller (MS, ankle injury)	F	6'5	210	24	8	52	8	31	26	4	7	57	7	1	11	0	20	7	0.9	0.1	1.4	2.5
LOS ANGELES LAKERS	**52-30 .634**				**BUTCH VAN BREDA KOLFF**																	
Tom Hawkins	F	6'5	210	31	78	2463	389	779	50	125	229	55	458	117	289	7	903	32	5.9	1.5	3.7	11.6
Elgin Baylor	F	6'5	225	33	77	3029	757	1709	44	488	621	79	941	355	232	0	2002	39	12.2	4.6	3.0	26.0
Darral Imhoff	C	6'10	220	29	82	2271	293	613	48	177	286	62	893	206	264	3	763	28	10.9	2.5	3.2	9.3
Jerry West (injury)	G	6'3	180	29	51	1919	476	926	51	391	482	81	294	310	152	1	1343	38	5.8	6.1	3.0	26.3
Archie Clark	G	6'2	175	26	81	3039	628	1309	48	356	481	74	342	353	235	3	1612	38	4.2	4.4	2.9	19.9
Gail Goodrich	G	6'1	178	24	79	2057	395	812	49	302	392	77	199	205	228	2	1092	26	2.5	2.6	2.9	13.8
Mel Counts	F-C	7'	230	26	82	1739	384	808	48	190	254	75	732	139	309	6	958	21	8.9	1.7	3.8	11.7
Erwin Mueller (from Chi)	C	6'8	235	23	39	973	132	254	52	61	103	59	222	78	86	2	325	25	5.7	2.0	2.2	8.3
Freddie Crawford (from NY)	G	6'4	190	26	38	756	159	330	48	74	120	62	112	95	104	1	392	20	2.9	2.5	2.7	10.3
Jim Barnes (to Chi)	F-C	6'8	240	26	42	713	101	235	43	59	88	67	211	27	134	4	261	17	5.0	0.6	3.2	6.2
John Wetzel (MS)	F-G	6'5	185	23	38	434	52	119	44	35	46	76	84	51	55	0	139	11	2.2	1.3	1.4	3.7
Dennis Hamilton	F	6'8	210	23	44	378	54	108	50	13	13	100	72	30	46	0	121	9	1.6	0.7	1.0	2.8
Cliff Anderson	G-F	6'4	200	23	18	94	7	29	24	12	28	43	11	17	18	1	26	5	0.6	0.9	1.0	1.4
Jerry Chambers - military service																						
SAN FRANCISCO WARRIORS	**43-39 .524**				**BILL SHARMAN**																	
Rudy LaRusso	F	6'7	220	30	79	2819	602	1389	43	522	661	79	741	182	337	14	1726	36	9.4	2.3	4.3	21.8
Fred Hetzel	F	6'8	230	25	77	2394	533	1287	41	395	474	83	546	131	262	7	1461	31	7.1	1.7	3.4	19.0
Nate Thurmond (knee injury)	C	6'11	225	26	51	2222	382	989	39	282	438	64	1121	215	137	1	1046	44	22.0	4.2	2.7	20.5
Jeff Mullins	G	6'4	200	25	79	2805	610	1391	44	273	344	79	447	351	271	2	1493	36	5.7	4.4	3.4	18.9
Jim King (groin injury)	G	6'2	175	26	54	1743	340	800	43	217	268	81	243	226	172	1	897	32	4.5	4.2	3.2	16.6
Clyde Lee	C-F	6'10	205	23	82	2699	373	894	42	229	335	68	1141	135	331	10	975	33	13.9	1.6	4.0	11.9
Al Attles	G	6'2	180	31	67	1992	252	540	47	150	216	69	276	390	284	9	654	30	4.1	5.8	4.2	9.8
Bob Warlick	G-F	6'5	205	26	69	1320	257	610	42	97	171	57	264	159	164	1	611	19	3.8	2.3	2.4	8.9
Joe Ellis	F	6'6	175	23	51	624	111	302	37	32	50	64	195	37	83	2	254	12	3.8	0.7	1.6	5.0
Bill Turner	F	6'7	220	23	42	482	68	157	43	36	60	60	155	16	74	1	172	11	3.7	0.4	1.8	4.1
Bobby Lewis	G	6'3	185	22	41	342	59	151	39	61	79	77	56	41	40	0	179	8	1.4	1.0	1.0	4.4
Dave Lattin	F	6'7	230	24	44	257	37	102	36	23	33	70	104	14	94	4	97	6	2.4	0.3	2.1	2.2
George Lee	F	6'4	200	31	10	106	8	35	23	17	24	71	27	4	16	0	33	11	2.7	0.4	1.6	3.3
CHICAGO BULLS	**29-53 .354**				**JOHNNY KERR**																	
Jim Washington	F	6'7	215	24	82	2525	418	915	46	187	274	68	825	113	233	1	1023	31	10.1	1.4	2.8	12.5
Bob Boozer	F	6'8	225	30	77	2988	622	1265	49	411	535	77	756	121	229	1	1655	39	9.8	1.6	3.0	21.5
McCoy McLemore	C	6'7	230	25	76	2100	374	940	40	215	276	78	430	130	219	4	963	28	5.7	1.7	2.9	12.7
Keith Erickson	G	6'5	195	23	78	2257	377	940	40	194	257	75	423	267	276	15	948	29	5.4	3.4	3.5	12.2
Flynn Robinson (from Cin)	G	6'1	190	26	73	2030	441	1000	44	285	344	83	268	214	180	1	1167	28	3.7	2.9	2.5	16.0
Jerry Sloan	G-F	6'6	200	25	77	2454	369	959	38	289	386	75	591	229	291	11	1027	32	7.7	3.0	3.8	13.3
Barry Clemens	F	6'7	210	25	78	1631	301	670	45	123	170	72	375	98	223	4	725	21	4.8	1.3	2.9	9.3
Clem Haskins	G	6'3	195	23	76	1477	273	650	42	133	202	66	227	165	175	1	679	19	3.0	2.2	2.3	8.9
Erwin Mueller	C	6'8	235	23	35	815	91	235	39	46	82	56	167	76	78	1	228	23	4.8	2.2	2.2	6.5
Jim Barnes (from LA)	C-F	6'8	240	26	37	712	120	264	45	74	103	72	204	28	128	3	314	19	5.5	0.8	3.5	8.5
Reggie Harding (to IndA)	C	7'	255	25	14	305	24	71	34	17	33	52	94	18	35	0	65	22	6.7	1.3	2.5	4.6
Dave Schellhase	G	6'3	205	23	42	301	47	138	34	20	38	53	47	37	43	0	114	7	1.1	0.9	1.0	2.7
Guy Rodgers (to Cin)	G	6'	190	32	4	129	16	54	30	9	11	82	14	28	11	0	41	32	3.5	7.0	2.8	10.3
Craig Spitzer	C	7'	230	22	10	44	8	21	38	2	3	67	24	0	4	0	18	4	2.4	0.0	0.4	1.8
Ken Wilburn	F	6'6	205	23	3	26	5	9	56	1	4	25	10	2	4	0	11	9	3.3	0.7	1.3	3.7
Jim Burns (to DalA)	G	6'3	195	22	3	11	2	7	29	0	0	—	2	1	1	0	4	4	0.7	0.3	0.3	1.3

1967/68 N.B.A. — WESTERN DIVISION (continued)

Use Name	Pos	Hgt	Wgt	Age	G	Min	FG	FGA	%	FT	FTA	%	Reb	Ass	PF	DQ	Points	Min	Reb	Ass	PF	Points
					TOTAL													PER GAME				
SEATTLE SUPERSONICS	**23-59 .280**				**AL BIANCHI**																	
Tom Meschery	F	6'6	215	29	82	2857	473	1008	47	244	345	71	840	193	323	14	1190	35	10.2	2.4	3.9	14.5
Al Tucker	F	6'8	190	24	81	2368	437	989	44	186	263	71	605	111	262	6	1060	29	7.5	1.4	3.2	13.1
Bob Rule	C	6'9	235	23	82	2424	568	1162	49	348	529	66	776	99	316	10	1484	30	9.5	1.2	3.9	18.1
Tommy Kron	G	6'5	200	24	76	1794	277	699	40	184	233	79	355	281	231	4	738	24	4.7	3.7	3.0	9.7
Walt Hazzard	G	6'2	190	25	79	2666	733	1662	44	428	553	77	332	493	246	3	1894	34	4.2	6.2	3.1	24.0
Rod Thorn	G	6'4	195	26	66	1668	377	835	45	252	342	74	265	230	117	1	1006	25	4.0	3.5	1.8	15.2
Bob Weiss	G	6'2	180	25	82	1614	295	686	43	213	254	84	150	342	137	0	803	20	1.8	4.2	1.7	9.8
Dorie Murrey	F	6'8	215	24	81	1494	211	484	44	168	244	69	600	68	273	7	590	18	7.4	0.8	3.4	7.3
George Wilson	C	6'8	235	25	77	1236	179	498	36	109	155	70	470	56	218	1	467	16	6.1	0.7	2.8	6.1
Bud Olsen	F	6'8	220	27	73	897	130	285	46	17	62	27	204	75	136	1	277	12	2.8	1.0	1.9	3.8
Plummer Lott	F-G	6'5	210	22	44	478	46	148	31	19	31	61	93	36	65	1	111	11	2.1	0.8	1.5	2.5
Henry Akin	C	6'10	235	23	36	259	46	137	34	20	31	65	57	14	48	1	112	7	1.6	0.4	1.3	3.1
SAN DIEGO ROCKETS	**15-67 .183**				**JACK McMAHON**																	
Don Kojis	F	6'4	215	28	69	2548	530	1189	45	300	413	73	710	176	259	5	1360	37	10.3	2.6	3.8	19.7
Dave Gambee	F	6'6	220	30	80	1755	375	853	44	321	379	85	464	93	253	5	1071	22	5.8	1.2	3.2	13.4
John Block (broken hand)	C	6'10	210	23	52	1805	366	865	42	316	394	80	571	71	189	3	1048	35	11.0	1.4	3.6	20.2
Jon McGlocklin	G	6'5	205	24	65	1876	316	757	42	156	180	87	199	178	117	0	788	29	3.1	2.7	1.8	12.1
John Barnhill	G	6'1	180	29	75	1883	295	700	42	154	234	66	173	259	143	1	744	25	2.3	3.5	1.9	9.9
Toby Kimball	F-C	6'8	220	25	81	2519	354	894	40	181	306	59	947	147	273	3	889	31	11.7	1.8	3.4	11.0
Hambone Williams	G	6'2	180	28	79	1739	265	718	37	113	165	68	286	391	204	0	643	22	3.6	4.9	2.6	8.1
Pat Riley	G-F	6'4	208	22	80	1263	250	660	38	128	202	63	177	138	205	1	628	16	2.2	1.7	2.6	7.9
Henry Finkel	C	7'	240	25	53	1116	242	492	49	131	191	69	375	72	175	5	615	21	7.1	1.4	3.3	11.6
Johnny Green (to Phi)	F	6'5	200	34	42	1073	241	526	46	100	212	47	423	59	112	3	582	26	10.1	1.4	2.7	13.9
Jim Barnett (KJ)	G	6'4	180	23	47	1068	179	456	39	84	118	71	155	134	101	0	442	23	3.3	2.9	2.1	9.4
Nick Jones (MS)	G	6'2	190	22	42	603	86	232	37	55	69	80	67	89	84	0	227	14	1.6	2.1	2.0	5.4
Jim Ware (MS)	F	6'7	210	23	30	228	25	97	26	23	34	68	77	7	28	1	73	8	2.6	0.2	0.9	2.4
Bud Acton	F	6'6	210	25	23	195	29	74	39	19	29	66	47	11	35	0	77	8	2.0	0.5	1.5	3.3
Tyrone Britt	G	6'4	190	23	11	84	13	34	38	2	3	67	15	12	10	0	28	8	1.4	1.1	0.9	2.5

1967/68 N.B.A. - PLAYOFFS

BOSTON CELTICS **BILL RUSSELL**

defeated Detroit 4-2; H123-116, 116-126,H98-109, 135-110, H110-96, 111-103
defeated Philadelphia 4-3; 127-118, H106-115, 114-122, H105-110, 122-104, H114-106,100-96
defeated Los Angeles 4-2; H107-101, H113-123, 127-119, 105-119, H120-117 (OT), 124-109

Use Name	Pos	Hgt	Wgt	Age	G	Min	FG	FGA	%	FT	FTA	%	Reb	Ass	PF	DQ	Points	Min	Reb	Ass	PF	Points
Satch Sanders	F	6'6	210	29	14	289	50	99	51	16	21	76	63	12	53	4	116	21	4.5	0.9	3.8	8.3
Bailey Howell	F	6'7	220	30	19	597	135	264	51	74	107	69	146	22	**84**	**6**	344	31	7.7	1.2	4.4	18.1
Bill Russell	C	6'10	220	33	19	**869**	99	242	41	76	130	58	**434**	99	73	1	274	46	22.8	5.2	3.8	14.4
John Havlicek	G-F	6'5	205	27	19	862	**184**	**407**	45	125	151	83	164	**142**	67	1	**493**	45	8.6	7.5	3.5	25.9
Sam Jones	G	6'4	205	34	19	685	162	367	44	66	84	79	64	50	58	0	390	36	3.4	2.6	3.1	20.5
Larry Siegfried	G	6'3	192	28	19	535	78	201	39	77	85	**91**	50	56	75	3	233	28	2.6	2.9	3.9	12.3
Don Nelson	F	6'6	210	27	19	468	91	175	52	55	74	74	143	32	49	0	237	25	7.5	1.7	2.6	12.5
Wayne Embry	F-C	6'8	255	30	16	162	23	59	39	13	29	45	45	6	36	0	59	10	2.8	0.4	2.3	3.7
Tom Thacker	G	6'2	190	28	17	81	7	24	29	2	7	29	17	8	23	0	16	5	1.0	0.5	1.4	0.9
Mal Graham	G	6'1	185	22	5	22	2	5	40	1	3	33	4	1	3	0	5	4	0.8	0.2	0.6	1.0
Johnny Jones	F	6'7	210	24	5	10	3	6	50	0	0	—	4	0	2	0	6	2	0.8	0.0	0.4	1.2
Rick Weitzman	G	6'2	185	21	3	5	2	3	67	0	0	—	1	1	0	0	4	2	0.3	0.3	0.0	1.3

LOS ANGELES LAKERS **B. VAN BREDA KOLFF**

defeated Chicago 4-1; H109-101, H111-106, 98-104, 93-87, H122-99
defeated San Francisco 4-0; H133-105, H115-112, 128-124, 106-100
lost to Boston 2-4; 101-107, 123-113, H119-127, H119-105, 117-120 (OT), H109-124

Use Name	Pos	Hgt	Wgt	Age	G	Min	FG	FGA	%	FT	FTA	%	Reb	Ass	PF	DQ	Points	Min	Reb	Ass	PF	Points
Tom Hawkins	F	6'5	210	31	15	478	59	129	46	24	40	60	90	18	53	2	142	32	6.0	1.2	3.5	9.5
Elgin Baylor	F	6'5	225	33	15	633	176	376	47	76	112	68	218	60	41	0	428	42	14.5	4.0	2.7	28.5
Darrall Imhoff	C	6'10	20	29	15	440	44	89	49	26	51	51	163	30	56	0	114	29	10.9	2.0	3.7	7.6
Jerry West	G	6'3	180	29	15	622	165	313	53	**132**	**169**	78	81	82	47	0	462	41	5.4	5.5	3.1	**30.8**
Archie Clark	G	6'2	175	26	15	528	88	206	43	53	69	77	47	60	42	0	229	35	3.1	4.0	2.8	15.3
Mel Counts	F-C	7'	230	26	15	306	54	101	53	21	31	68	133	24	52	1	129	20	8.9	1.6	3.5	8.6
Freddie Crawford	G-F	6'4	190	26	15	257	36	83	43	19	35	54	35	16	41	0	91	17	2.3	1.1	2.7	6.1
Erwin Mueller	C	6'8	235	23	14	250	20	59	34	5	14	36	54	18	32	0	45	18	3.9	1.3	2.3	3.2
Gail Goodrich	G	6'1	178	24	10	100	23	47	49	14	18	78	14	14	10	0	60	10	1.4	1.4	1.0	6.0
Dennis Hamilton	F	6'8	210	23	2	11	1	3	33	0	0	—	2	1	0	0	2	6	1.0	0.5	0.0	1.0

PHILADELPHIA 76ers **ALEX HANNUM**

defeated New York 4-2; H118-110, 117-128, H138-132 (2OT), 98-107, H123-107, 113-97
lost to Boston 3-4; H118-127, 115-106, H122-114, 110-105, H104-122, 106-114, H96-100

Use Name	Pos	Hgt	Wgt	Age	G	Min	FG	FGA	%	FT	FTA	%	Reb	Ass	PF	DQ	Points	Min	Reb	Ass	PF	Points
Chet Walker	F	6'6	210	27	13	485	86	210	41	76	112	68	96	24	44	1	248	37	7.4	1.8	3.4	19.1
Luke Jackson	F-C	6'9	240	26	13	432	62	158	39	24	35	69	115	16	59	3	148	33	8.8	1.2	4.5	11.4
Wilt Chamberlain	C	7'1	275	31	13	631	124	232	53	60	158	38	321	85	29	0	308	**49**	**24.7**	6.5	2.2	23.7
Hal Greer	G	6'3	176	31	13	553	120	278	43	95	111	86	79	55	49	1	335	43	6.1	4.2	3.8	25.8
Wally Jones	G	6'2	180	25	13	387	69	193	36	45	57	79	31	39	48	2	183	30	2.4	3.0	3.7	14.1
Matt Guokas	G-F	6'5	190	23	13	327	30	79	38	20	27	74	43	30	39	0	80	25	3.3	2.3	3.0	6.2
Johnny Green	F	6'5	200	34	12	219	38	65	58	20	43	47	66	8	19	0	96	18	5.5	0.7	1.6	8.0
Billy Cunningham (arm injury)	F	6'7	220	24	3	86	24	43	56	14	17	82	22	10	16	1	62	29	7.3	3.3	5.3	20.7
Bill Melchionni	G	6'1	165	23	9	50	8	24	33	2	4	50	4	10	4	0	18	6	0.4	1.1	0.4	2.0

1967/68 N.B.A. — PLAYOFFS (continued)

SAN FRANCISCO WARRIORS — **BILL SHARMAN** — defeated St. Louis 4-2; 111-106, 103-111, H124-109, H108-107, 103-129, H111-106
lost to Los Angeles 0-4, 105-133, 112-115, H124-128, H100-106

Use Name	Pos	Hgt	Wgt	Age	G	Min	FG	FGA	%	FT	FTA	%	Reb	Ast	PF	DQ	Points	Min	Reb	Ast	PF	Points
					TOTAL													PER GAME				
Rudy LaRusso	F	6'7	220	30	10	385	72	182	40	59	81	73	99	17	35	0	203	39	9.9	1.7	3.5	20.3
Fred Hetzel	F-C	6'8	230	25	10	321	69	150	46	50	61	82	66	16	44	2	188	32	6.6	1.6	4.4	18.8
Clyde Lee	C	6'10	205	23	10	405	48	117	41	18	36	50	132	22	38	2	114	41	13.2	2.2	3.8	11.4
Jeff Mullins	G	6'4	200	25	10	390	110	211	52	31	43	72	44	49	36	2	251	39	4.4	4.9	3.6	25.1
Al Attles	G	6'2	180	31	10	277	25	62	40	23	30	77	53	70	49	2	73	28	5.3	7.0	4.9	7.3
Bob Warlick	G-F	6'5	205	26	10	226	55	118	47	28	37	76	53	24	26	2	138	23	5.3	2.4	2.6	13.8
Bill Turner	F	6'7	220	23	9	148	19	40	48	9	12	75	29	10	30	2	47	16	3.2	1.1	3.3	5.2
Jim King	G	6'2	175	26	9	113	16	38	42	12	19	63	19	20	15	0	44	13	2.1	2.2	1.7	4.9
Joe Ellis	F	6'6	175	23	9	104	13	44	30	6	7	86	19	7	16	0	32	12	2.1	0.8	1.8	3.6
Dave Lattin	C	6'7	230	24	5	27	1	5	20	5	6	83	5	1	9	0	7	5	1.0	0.2	1.8	1.4
Bobby Lewis	G	6'3	185	22	1	4	2	3	67	0	0	—	0	0	0	0	4	4	0.0	0.0	0.0	4.0

ST. LOUIS HAWKS — **RICHIE GUERIN** — lost to San Francisco 2-4; H106-111, H111-103, 109-124, 107-108, H129-103, 106-111

Use Name	Pos	Hgt	Wgt	Age	G	Min	FG	FGA	%	FT	FTA	%	Reb	Ast	PF	DQ	Points	Min	Reb	Ast	PF	Points
Bill Bridges	F	6'6	235	28	6	216	38	75	51	18	25	72	77	14	23	0	94	36	12.8	2.3	3.8	15.7
Paul Silas	F-C	6'7	235	24	6	178	22	51	43	27	38	71	57	21	17	0	71	30	9.5	3.5	2.8	11.8
Zelmo Beaty	C	6'9	240	28	6	239	43	92	47	43	55	78	81	15	26	1	129	40	13.5	2.5	4.3	21.5
Don Ohl	G	6'3	190	31	6	143	27	56	48	15	22	68	12	21	17	1	69	24	2.0	3.5	2.8	11.5
Lenny Wilkens	G	6'1	185	30	6	237	40	91	44	30	40	75	38	47	23	1	110	40	6.3	7.8	3.8	18.3
Lou Hudson	F-G	6'5	220	23	6	181	44	99	44	42	47	89	43	14	21	0	130	30	7.2	2.3	3.5	21.7
Joe Caldwell	F-G	6'5	200	26	6	148	15	46	33	2	15	13	21	15	10	0	32	25	3.5	2.5	1.7	5.3
Dick Snyder	G	6'5	210	23	4	62	10	22	45	4	5	80	5	4	6	0	24	16	1.3	1.0	1.5	6.0
Gene Tormohlen	C	6'9	245	30	3	25	2	6	33	3	4	75	6	5	4	0	7	8	2.0	1.7	1.3	2.3
Jim Davis	C	6'9	235	26	2	9	1	3	33	0	0	—	3	0	2	0	2	5	1.5	0.0	1.0	1.0
George Lehmann	G	6'3	190	25	1	2	0	1	0	0	0	—	0	2	1	0	0	2	0.0	2.0	1.0	0.0

NEW YORK KNICKERBOCKERS — **RED HOLZMAN** — lost to Philadelphia 2-4, 110-118, H128-117, 132-138(2OT), H107-98, 107-123, H97-113

Use Name	Pos	Hgt	Wgt	Age	G	Min	FG	FGA	%	FT	FTA	%	Reb	Ast	PF	DQ	Points	Min	Reb	Ast	PF	Points
Cazzie Russell	F	6'5	218	23	6	209	55	98	56	20	24	83	23	10	16	0	130	35	3.8	1.7	2.7	21.7
Willis Reed	F-C	6'9	235	25	6	210	53	98	54	22	30	73	62	11	24	1	128	35	10.3	1.8	4.0	21.3
Walt Bellamy	C	6'11	245	28	6	277	45	107	42	30	48	63	96	21	22	0	120	46	16.0	3.5	3.7	20.0
Dick Barnett	G	6'4	190	31	6	211	61	117	52	21	29	72	27	21	24	1	143	35	4.5	3.5	4.0	23.8
Walt Frazier (leg injury)	G	6'4	202	22	4	119	12	33	36	14	18	78	22	25	12	0	38	30	5.5	6.3	3.0	9.5
Howie Komives	G	6'1	185	26	6	135	15	44	34	4	6	67	14	23	22	1	34	23	2.3	3.8	3.7	5.7
Phil Jackson	F-C	6'8	220	22	6	90	10	35	29	4	5	80	25	2	23	0	24	15	4.2	0.3	3.8	4.0
Dick Van Arsdale	F-G	6'5	210	24	4	88	5	22	23	3	4	75	16	13	9	0	13	22	4.0	3.3	2.3	3.3
Em Bryant	G	6'1	175	29	5	75	4	13	31	4	5	80	14	7	13	0	12	15	2.8	1.4	2.6	2.4
Bill Bradley	G-F	6'5	205	24	6	64	12	28	43	9	13	69	6	2	7	0	33	11	1.0	0.3	1.2	5.5
Neil Johnson	F	6'7	220	24	2	6	2	4	50	0	0	—	3	0	1	0	4	3	1.5	0.0	0.5	2.0
Nate Bowman	C	6'10	230	24	1	6	0	4	0	0	0	—	3	0	1	0	0	6	3.0	0.0	1.0	0.0

DETROIT PISTONS — **DONNIE BUTCHER** — lost to Boston 2-4; 116-123, H126-116, 109-98, H110-135, 96-110, H103-111

Use Name	Pos	Hgt	Wgt	Age	G	Min	FG	FGA	%	FT	FTA	%	Reb	Ast	PF	DQ	Points	Min	Reb	Ast	PF	Points
Dave DeBusschere	F	6'6	225	27	6	263	45	106	42	26	56	46	97	13	23	0	116	44	16.2	2.2	3.8	19.3
Happy Hairston	F	6'7	225	25	6	149	29	71	41	12	20	60	37	7	22	1	70	25	6.2	1.2	3.7	11.7
Joe Strawder	C	6'10	235	27	6	177	14	42	33	14	22	64	65	9	27	1	42	30	10.8	1.5	4.5	7.0
Eddie Miles	G	6'4	196	27	6	197	39	95	41	9	12	75	22	15	16	0	87	33	3.7	2.5	2.7	14.5
Dave Bing	G	6'3	180	24	6	254	68	166	41	33	45	73	24	29	21	0	169	42	4.0	4.8	3.5	28.2
Terry Dischinger	F	6'7	208	27	6	154	21	56	38	14	19	74	29	9	19	0	56	26	4.8	1.5	3.2	9.3
Jimmy Walker	G	6'3	205	23	6	121	31	67	46	14	17	82	9	9	17	1	76	20	1.5	1.5	2.8	12.7
Jim Fox	C	6'10	230	24	6	90	6	19	32	15	19	79	37	3	11	1	27	15	6.2	0.5	1.8	4.5
Len Chappell	C-F	6'8	240	26	5	21	2	7	29	3	6	50	12	0	3	0	7	4	2.4	0.0	0.6	1.4
Sonny Dove	F	6'8	198	22	2	6	2	4	50	0	0	—	2	0	0	0	4	3	1.0	0.0	0.0	2.0
Paul Long	G	6'2	180	23	1	4	3	3	100	0	0	—	0	1	1	0	6	4	0.0	1.0	1.0	6.0
George Patterson	C	6'8	240	28	1	4	0	0	—	0	0	—	1	1	0	0	0	4	1.0	1.0	0.0	0.0

CHICAGO BULLS — **JOHNNY KERR** — lost to Los Angeles 1-4; 101-109, 106-111, H104-98, H87-93, 99-122

Use Name	Pos	Hgt	Wgt	Age	G	Min	FG	FGA	%	FT	FTA	%	Reb	Ast	PF	DQ	Points	Min	Reb	Ast	PF	Points
Bob Boozer	F	6'8	225	30	5	190	33	73	45	28	38	74	44	12	13	0	94	38	8.8	2.4	2.6	18.8
Jim Washington	F-C	6'7	215	24	5	205	38	85	45	10	15	67	75	10	15	0	86	41	15.0	2.0	3.0	17.2
McCoy McLemore	C	6'7	230	25	5	142	19	49	39	16	21	76	24	5	18	1	54	28	4.8	1.0	3.6	10.8
Keith Erickson	G	6'5	195	23	5	183	25	65	38	15	17	88	41	11	19	0	65	37	8.2	2.2	3.8	13.0
Flynn Robinson	G	6'1	190	26	5	180	42	98	43	17	24	71	10	13	14	0	101	36	2.0	2.6	2.8	20.2
Jerry Sloan	F-G	6'6	200	25	5	137	12	37	32	19	25	76	32	12	19	0	43	27	6.4	2.4	3.8	8.6
Jim Barnes	C	6'8	240	26	5	57	3	12	25	0	0	—	21	1	13	0	6	11	4.2	0.2	2.6	1.2
Clem Haskins	G	6'3	195	23	5	53	11	28	39	4	6	67	9	7	5	0	26	11	1.8	1.4	1.0	5.2
Barry Clemens	F	6'7	210	25	4	45	8	16	50	4	4	100	2	5	6	0	20	11	0.5	1.3	1.5	5.0
Dave Schellhase	G	6'3	205	23	1	5	1	3	33	0	0	—	0	0	0	0	2	5	0.0	0.0	0.0	2.0
Craig Spitzer	C	7'	230	22	1	3	0	3	0	0	0	—	3	1	0	0	0	3	3.0	1.0	0.0	0.0

1967/68 N.B.A. TEAM STATISTICS

Team	REGULAR SEASON									AVERAGE POINTS			PLAYOFFS									AVERAGE POINTS		
	G	FG	FGA	%	FT	FTA	%	Reb.	Ass.	For	Agnst.	Diff.	G	FG	FGA	%	FT	FTA	%	Reb.	Ass.	For	Agnst.	Diff.
EASTERN DIVISION																								
Philadelphia	82	**3965**	8414	47	2121	**3338**	64	5914	2197	**122.6**	114.0	**+8.6**	13	561	1282	44	356	**564**	63	890	277	113.7	112.8	+0.9
Boston	82	3686	8371	44	2151	2983	72	5666	1798	116.1	112.0	+4.1	19	836	1852	45	505	691	73	**1301**	429	**114.6**	111.5	+3.1
New York	82	3682	8070	46	2159	3042	71	5122	1967	116.1	114.3	+1.8	6	**274**	603	45	131	182	72	363	135	113.2	117.8	-4.6
Detroit	82	3755	8386	45	2215	3129	71	5452	1700	118.6	120.6	-2.0	6	260	**636**	41	140	205	68	405	96	110.0	115.5	-5.5
Cincinnati	82	3679	7864	47	2204	2892	**76**	5129	2048	116.6	117.4	-0.8												
Baltimore	82	3691	8428	44	2245	2994	75	5431	1534	117.4	117.8	-0.4												
WESTERN DIVISION																								
St. Louis	82	3504	7765	45	2258	3111	73	5325	1988	113.0	**110.3**	+2.7	6	242	542	45	**184**	251	73	397	**158**	111.3	110.0	+1.3
Los Angeles	82	3827	8031	**48**	2283	3143	73	5225	1983	121.2	115.6	+5.6	15	666	1406	**47**	370	539	69	962	323	113.5	108.9	**+4.6**
San Francisco	82	3632	8587	42	**2334**	3153	74	**6029**	1901	117.0	117.6	-0.6	10	430	970	44	241	332	73	585	236	110.1	115.1	-4.9
Chicago	82	3488	8138	43	2006	2718	74	5117	1527	109.5	113.5	-4.0	5	192	469	41	113	150	**75**	307	77	99.4	**106.6**	-7.2
Seattle	82	3772	**8593**	44	2188	3042	72	5338	1998	118.7	125.1	-6.4												
San Diego	82	3466	8547	42	2083	2929	71	5418	1837	112.4	121.0	-8.6												

1967/68 N.B.A. STANDINGS

Team	W	L	Pct.	GB	Record against playoff teams			Record against non - playoff teams			HOME			ROAD			NEUTRAL		
					W	L	Pct.	W	L	Pct.	W	L	Pct.	W	L	Pct.	W	L	Pct.
EASTERN DIVISION																			
Philadelphia 76ers	**62**	20	**.756**	—	**36**	16	**.692**	**26**	4	**.867**	27	8	.771	**25**	12	**.676**	**10**	0	**1.000**
Boston Celtics	54	28	.659	8	33	19	.635	21	9	.667	28	9	.757	20	16	.556	6	3	.667
New York Knickerbockers	43	39	.524	19	23	29	.442	20	10	.667	20	17	.541	21	16	.568	2	6	.250
Detroit Pistons	40	42	.488	22	21	31	.404	19	11	.633	21	11	.656	12	23	.343	7	8	.467
Cincinnati Royals	39	43	.476	23	23	37	.383	16	6	.727	18	12	.600	13	23	.361	8	8	.500
Baltimore Bullets	36	46	.439	26	19	41	.317	17	5	.773	17	19	.472	12	23	.343	7	4	.636
WESTERN DIVISION																			
St. Louis Hawks	56	26	.683	—	30	22	.577	**26**	4	**.867**	25	7	.781	22	13	.629	9	6	.600
Los Angeles Lakers	52	30	.634	4	31	21	.596	21	9	.700	30	11	.732	18	19	.486	4	0	**1.000**
San Francisco Warriors	43	39	.524	13	22	30	.440	21	9	.700	27	14	.659	16	23	.410	0	2	.000
Chicago Bulls	29	53	.354	27	12	40	.231	17	13	.567	11	22	.333	12	23	.343	6	8	.429
Seattle Supersonics	23	59	.280	33	15	45	.250	8	14	.364	9	19	.321	7	24	.226	7	**16**	.304
San Diego Rockets	15	**67**	.183	41	12	**48**	.200	3	**19**	.136	8	33	.195	4	**26**	.133	3	8	.273

1967/68 N.B.A. INDIVIDUAL LEADERS

SCORING
(Minimum 65 Games Played)

Name	Team	G	FG	FT	Pts.	Avg.
Robertson	Cin	65	660	576	1896	29.2
Bing	Det	79	835	472	2142	27.1
Baylor	LA	77	757	488	2002	26.0
Chamberlain	Phi	82	819	354	1992	24.3
Monroe	Bal	82	742	507	1991	24.3
Greer	Phi	82	777	422	1976	24.1
Hazzard	Sea	79	733	428	1894	23.9
LaRusso	SF	79	602	522	1726	21.8
Boozer	Chi	77	622	411	1655	21.5
Lucas	Cm	82	707	346	1760	21.4

FIELD GOAL PERCENTAGE
(Minimum 220 Field Goals)

Name	Team	FG	FGA	Pct.
Chamberlain	Phi	819	1377	.595
Bellamy	NY	511	944	.541
Lucas	Cin	707	1361	.519
West	LA	476	926	.514
Chappell	Cin-Det	235	458	.513
Robertson	Cin	660	1321	.500
Hawkins	LA	389	779	.499
Dischinger	Det	394	797	.494
Nelson	Bos	312	632	.494
Finkel	SD	242	492	.492

FREE THROW PERCENTAGE
(Minimum 220 Free Throws)

Name	Team	FT	FTA	Pct.
Robertson	Cin	576	660	.873
Siegfried	Bos	236	272	.868
Gambee	SD	321	379	.847
Hetzel	SF	395	474	.833
Smith	Cin	320	386	.829
Jones	Bos	311	376	.827
Robinson	Cin-Chi	288	352	.818
Havlicek	Bos	368	453	.812
West	LA	391	482	.811
Russell	NY	282	349	.808

PERSONAL FOULS

Name	Team	PF
Bridges	StL	366
Reed	NY	343
LaRusso	SF	337
Lee	SF	331
Meschery	Sea	323

GAMES DISQUALIFIED

Name	Team	Disq
Strawder	Det	18
Tresvant	Det-Cin	18
Erickson	Chi	15
LaRusso	SF	14
Meschery	Sea	14

REBOUNDS PER GAME
(Minimum 65 Games Played)

Name	Team	G	Reb.	Avg.
Chamberlain	Pni	82	1952	23.8
Lucas	Cin	82	1560	19.0
Russell	Bos	78	1451	18.6
Lee	SF	82	1141	13.9
Scott	Bal	81	1111	13.7
DeBusschere	Det	80	1081	13.5
Bridges	StL	82	1102	13.4
Reed	NY	81	1073	13.2
Baylor	LA	77	941	12.2
Bellamy	NY	82	961	11.7

ASSISTS PER GAME
(Minimum 65 Games Played)

Name	Team	G	Ass.	Avg.
Robertson	Cin	65	633	9.7
Chamberlain	Phi	82	702	8.6
Wilkens	StL	82	679	8.3
Bing	Det	79	509	6.4
Hazzard	Sea	79	493	6.2
Attles	SF	67	390	5.8
Williams	SD	79	391	4.9
Rodgers	Chi-Cin	78	380	4.9
Havlicek	Bos	82	384	4.7
Russell	Bos	78	357	4.6

MINUTES PLAYED

Name	Team	Min.
Chamberlain	Pni	3836
Lucas	Cin	3619
Greer	Phi	3263
Bing	Det	3209
Wilkens	StL	3199

1967-68 A.B.A.

Hardly an Auspicious Beginning

The American Basketball Association began its life with a big-name commisssioner and mostly lesser-name players. Organized by a group of California promoters led by Gary Davidson, the A.B.A. entered battle with the established and hostile N.B.A. with George Mikan as the league's chief executive. Although Mikan had been the dominant figure in the N.B.A. during his playing days with the Minneapolis Lakers, the players he now presided over were by and large rejects from the older circuit. The Oakland Oaks did sign Rick Barry, the N.B.A.'s leading scorer, but a court order forced him to sit out the season to fulfill the reserve clause of his contract with the San Francisco Warriors. Rookies Mel Daniels and Randy Mahaffey had been picked on the first round of the N.B.A. draft but chose instead to sign with A.B.A. clubs, and guards Louie Dampier, Bob Verga, and Bob Lloyd all were fresh out of college with All-American credentials.

But aside from these blue-chip athletes, the A.B.A. clubs came up with whatever players were available to stock their rosters for this maiden campaign. There were old-time N.B.A. veterans like Cliff Hagan, and marginal N.B.A. journeymen like Ben Warley and Wayne Hightower. Men who had had a cup of coffee in the N.B.A. now had another shot a pro basketball; this class of players included Larry Jones, Freddie Lewis, and Les Hunter, among many others. Other candidates for jobs had starred in college several years ago but had not broken into the N.B.A.; Donnie Freeman, Walt Simon, Ollie Darden, Jim Hadnot, Willie Somerset, and Levern Tart ranked among those seeking to recall the glories of their undergraduate careers. Some rookies without big reputations but sizable talent also made the new squads, with Bob Netolicky, Trooper Washington, Jimmy Jones, Stew Johnson, and Byron Beck foremost among these. Connie Hawkins, Doug Moe, Roger Brown, and Tony Jackson were signed despite their peripheral involvement with the 1961 scandals which led the N.B.A. to ban them. A handful of players came from industrial A.A.U. teams and some came from the minor pro leagues, including several men who had played in the A.B.L. which folded in 1963.

With this hodge-podge of players, the A.B.A. opened its inaugural season with clubs in Pittsburgh, Minnesota, New Jersey, Indiana, Kentucky, New Orleans, Houston, Dallas, Denver, Anaheim, and Oakland; the Minnesota team played in Minneapolis, Indiana in Indianapolis, Kentucky in Louisville, and New Jersey in Teaneck, a suburb of New York City. Some of the head coaches had reputations as star players in the N.B.A.; others were relatively unknown out of the college ranks.

Three innovations made the A.B.A. games look very different from N.B.A. conntests. Just as in the A.B.L. of 1961-62, field goals from beyond 25 feet away counted three points, and a 30-second clock gave the league clubs six extra seconds to work the ball around. Perhaps the most distinctive feature of the game was the red, white, and blue ball the A.B.A. used, a stark contrast to the traditional brown hall.

Play started without a television contract, and attendance was sparse in most league cities, but the eleven teams headed into a championship race which was almost impossible to handicap ahead of time. The Western Division had three strong clubs in the New Orleans Buccaneers, Dallas Chapparals, and Denver Rockets, and three weak teams in the Houston Mavericks, Anaheim Amigos, and Oakland Oaks. The New Orleans squad was coached by Babe McCarthy and featured a hustling lineup of Doug Moe, Jackie Moreland, Red Robbins, 5'9" Larry Brown, and Jimmy Jones, with Jesse Branson and George Govan among the better subs in the league. Cliff Hagan came out of a year's retirement to coach and play forward for the Dallas Chaps, and he teamed with youngsters Cincy Powell and John Beasley in a high-scoring front line; rookie Bob Verga gave the Chaps a high-scoring guard until the Army snatched him away in mid-season. The Denver Rockets had the A.B.A.'s best all-around guard in N.B.A.-castoff Larry Jones, with veteran Wayne Hightower and young Willie Murrell the stars up front.

These three clubs battled for first place most of the season with the final 1-2-3 standings showing New Orleans, Dallas, and Denver. Houston took fourth place under the direction of old N.B.A. star Slater Martin. Out of the playoffs were the Anaheim Amigos, whose Les Selvage led the league in three-point tries, and the Oakland Oaks, who were owned by singer Pat Boone and used Rick Barry up in the broadcasting booth.

First place in the East went to the Pittsburgh Pipers, whose Connie Hawkins was the star of the league. A gifted one-on-one player who had played in the old A.B.L. and with the Globetrotters after being banned by the N.B.A. for not reporting a bribe offer while at the University of Iowa, "Hawk" started the season at forward, moved to center in mid-season, and led the A.B.A. with a 26.8 scoring average. His mates in the starting lineup included forwards Trooper Washington and Art Heyman and guards Chico Vaughn and Charlie Williams, both good long-range shots. The Minnesota Muskies finished a close second with a strong nucleus made up of center Mel Daniels, forward Les Hunter, and guard Donnie Freeman.

The Indiana Pacers faded after a good start but hung on to third place, while Kentucky and New Jersey tied for the fourth and final playoff spot. These two clubs were scheduled to break their tie with a one-game playoff at Teaneck, but the Armory there was unavailable. The game was then set up in an arena in Commack, Long Island, but when the players showed up for the game, they found floor boards missing and bolts protruding from the floor; the Kentucky squad won the playoff berth by forfeit.

This incident cast the playoffs in a somewhat bush-league light, and crowds like the 661 who attended one opening round game in Minneapolis gave the players an embarrassing sense of privacy. The first two rounds went according to expectations, with Pittsburgh and New Orleans the contestants in the first A.B.A. championship series. The Buccaneers had the tighter team and the stronger bench, but the Pipers had Connie Hawkins. New Orleans took a 3-2 lead in the series, but the Hawk led his mates to 118-112 and 122-113 victories in games six and seven to bring the first A.B.A. crown to Pittsburgh, a city not long destined to be in the A.B.A. circuit.

Use Name	Pos	Hgt	Wgt	Age	TOTAL													PER GAME				
					G	Min	FG	FGA	%	FT	FTA	%	Reb	Ass	PF	DQ	Points	Min	Reb	Ass	PF	Points
1967/1968 A.B.A. — EASTERN DIVISION																						
PITTSBURGH PIPERS	**54-24 .692**				**VINCE CAZETTA**																	
Art Heyman (from NJ)	F	6'5	210	26	54	2116	360	806	45	335	446	75	426	239	153	0	1087	39	7.9	4.4	2.8	20.1
Connie Hawkins	F-C	6'8	215	25	70	3146	635	1223	52	**603**	**789**	76	945	320	248	2	1875	**45**	13.5	4.6	3.5	**26.8**
Craig Dill	C	6'11	215	23	65	1354	187	488	38	71	106	67	378	31	164	3	445	21	5.8	0.5	2.5	6.8
Chico Vaughn	G	6'3	195	27	74	2858	512	1350	38	308	416	74	298	142	203	0	1469	39	4.0	1.9	2.7	19.9
Charlie Williams	G	6'	165	24	78	3042	642	1573	41	290	429	68	377	173	295	6	1625	39	4.8	2.2	3.8	20.8
Trooper Washington	F	6'7	225	23	63	1844	312	596	**52**	106	186	57	672	102	189	4	732	29	10.7	1.6	3.0	11.6
Ira Harge (to Oak)	C	6'9	225	26	52	1652	176	441	40	119	184	65	593	38	194	6	471	32	11.4	0.7	3.7	9.1
Jim Jarvis	G	6'1	175	24	63	818	132	343	38	53	64	83	106	72	103	0	329	13	1.7	1.1	1.6	5.2
Barry Liebowitz (to NJ-Oak)	G	6'2	185	24	23	447	83	207	40	52	60	87	40	52	44	0	220	19	1.7	2.3	1.9	9.6
Rich Parks	F	6'7	235	24	40	374	59	133	44	12	21	57	116	14	68	3	131	9	2.9	0.4	1.7	3.3
Leroy Wright	F	6'9	215	29	17	331	24	60	40	9	22	41	108	14	49	1	57	19	6.4	0.8	2.9	3.4
Willie Porter (from Oak)	F	6'7	205	25	13	171	26	74	35	32	48	67	69	9	28	0	84	13	5.3	0.7	2.2	6.5
Arvesta Kelly	G	6'3	190	22	16	146	26	76	34	8	13	62	33	13	34	0	63	9	2.1	0.8	2.1	3.9
Bob Hogsett	F	6'7	230	26	13	119	7	20	35	7	17	41	23	1	11	0	21	9	1.8	0.1	0.8	1.6
Steve Vacendak	G	6'1	185	23	9	73	13	35	37	10	15	67	15	8	14	0	36	8	1.7	0.9	1.6	4.0
Tom Kerwin	F	6'7	210	23	13	68	7	22	32	0	2	0	20	1	5	0	14	5	1.5	0.1	0.4	1.1
Dexter Westbrook (from NJ)	F	6'8	210	24	5	68	7	20	35	3	5	60	14	3	14	0	17	14	2.8	0.6	2.8	3.4
Herschell Turner (to Ana)	G	6'2	195	29	9	65	6	21	29	3	6	50	6	5	10	0	16	7	0.7	0.6	1.1	1.8
Cal Graham	G	6'2	195	23	8	52	4	14	29	5	8	63	10	0	12	0	13	7	1.3	0.0	1.5	1.6
Bill Meyer	G	6'3	195	24	7	45	10	22	45	2	2	100	5	1	7	0	22	6	0.7	0.1	1.0	3.1
John Postley	F	6'5	220	23	1	6	1	3	33	0	0	—	6	1	1	0	2	6	6.0	1.0	1.0	2.0
MINNESOTA MUSKIES	**50-28 .641**				**JIM POLLARD**																	
Sam Smith	F	6'7	230	23	77	2175	284	750	38	185	280	66	586	81	171	1	755	28	7.6	1.1	2.2	9.8
Les Hunter	F	6'7	235	25	75	2552	513	1207	43	290	468	62	738	116	297	7	1318	34	9.8	1.5	4.0	17.6
Mel Daniels	C	6'9	220	23	78	2938	**669**	**1640**	41	390	678	58	**1213**	109	268	11	1729	38	**15.6**	1.4	3.4	22.2
Donnie Freeman (injury)	G	6'3	185	23	69	2431	414	1013	41	296	414	71	326	190	185	5	1124	35	4.7	2.8	2.7	16.3
Ron Perry (MS)	G	6'3	190	24	67	2125	339	878	39	118	179	66	223	139	151	2	858	32	3.3	2.1	2.3	12.8
Erv Inniger	G	6'4	190	22	75	1993	345	790	44	99	137	72	325	115	201	2	794	27	4.3	1.5	2.7	10.6
Gary Keller	F-C	6'9	220	23	69	1211	184	483	38	139	214	65	383	39	168	7	507	18	5.6	0.6	2.4	7.3
Skip Thoren	F-C	6'10	230	24	63	1203	206	475	43	102	164	62	436	59	124	3	514	19	6.9	0.9	2.0	8.2
Errol Palmer	F	6'5	195	22	63	1191	165	453	36	170	253	67	471	91	169	2	500	19	7.5	1.4	2.7	7.9
Terry Kunze	G-F	6'4	210	24	46	662	83	245	34	59	102	58	75	47	77	0	230	14	1.6	1.0	1.7	5.0
Dick Clark	G	6'4	195	23	26	414	46	150	31	48	79	61	52	33	49	0	140	16	2.0	1.3	1.9	5.4
INDIANA PACERS	**38-40 .487**				**LARRY STAVERMAN**																	
Roger Brown	F-G	6'5	207	25	76	2974	544	1286	42	390	517	75	647	327	296	10	1492	39	8.5	4.3	3.9	19.6
Ollie Darden	F	6'7	240	23	77	2045	371	831	45	180	270	67	527	69	277	2	922	27	6.8	0.9	3.6	12.0
Reggie Harding (from Chi-NBA, ST)	C	7'	255	25	25	840	142	314	45	52	90	58	334	53	59	0	336	34	13.4	2.1	2.4	13.4
Jimmy Rayl	G	6'2	170	26	74	2193	317	819	39	195	243	80	238	210	197	1	886	30	3.2	2.8	2.7	12.0
Freddie Lewis	G	6'	180	24	76	2921	542	1287	42	465	583	80	440	183	217	2	1565	38	5.8	2.4	2.9	20.6
Bob Netolicky	C-F	6'9	225	25	71	2385	468	928	50	220	369	60	819	69	162	0	1156	34	11.5	1.0	2.3	16.3
Bobby Edmonds	F	6'6	220	26	72	1338	213	488	44	150	229	66	374	29	183	4	577	19	5.2	0.4	2.5	8.0
Jerry Harkness	G	6'2	175	27	71	1241	172	394	44	152	223	68	193	129	109	1	497	17	2.7	1.8	1.5	7.0
George Peeples	C	6'8	205	24	65	1203	138	339	41	115	188	61	378	29	136	1	391	19	5.8	0.4	2.1	6.0
Matt Aitch	F	6'7	238	23	45	637	100	247	40	52	77	68	160	18	69	1	252	14	3.6	0.4	1.5	5.6
Ron Bonham	F	6'5	200	25	42	426	80	210	38	85	105	81	57	14	36	0	245	10	1.4	0.3	0.9	5.8
Ron Kozlicki	F	6'7	215	23	37	354	41	121	34	21	34	62	69	14	31	0	109	10	1.9	0.4	0.8	2.9
Jimmy Dawson (MS)	G	6'	175	22	21	288	46	133	35	25	43	58	21	32	16	0	118	14	1.0	1.5	0.8	5.6
KENTUCKY COLONELS	**37-42 .468**				**JOHN GIVENS (5-12 .294), GENE RHODES (32-30 .516)**																	
Randy Mahaffey	F	6'7	210	22	75	2325	373	875	43	281	411	68	684	129	278	**15**	1027	31	9.1	1.7	3.7	13.7
Goose Ligon	F-C	6'7	215	23	78	2801	428	942	45	405	595	68	929	143	307	6	1262	36	11.9	1.8	3.9	16.2
Jim Caldwell (from NY-NBA, NJ)	C	6'10	240	24	58	1582	200	469	43	89	144	62	543	136	205	9	490	27	9.4	2.3	3.5	8.4
Darel Carrier	G	6'3	185	27	77	3192	643	1545	42	395	479	82	352	172	263	7	1765	41	4.6	2.2	3.4	22.9
Louie Dampier (MS)	G	6'	170	23	72	2961	620	1473	42	209	254	82	333	256	143	0	1487	41	4.6	3.6	2.0	20.7
Bobby Rascoe	F-G	6'4	205	27	77	1606	245	563	44	190	249	76	284	102	158	2	680	21	3.7	1.3	2.1	8.8
Howard Bayne	F	6'6	235	25	69	1181	130	361	36	77	143	54	456	71	199	6	338	17	6.6	1.0	2.9	4.9
Cotton Nash (BB)	F	6'6	225	25	39	786	106	305	35	121	162	75	190	46	63	0	333	20	4.9	1.2	1.6	8.5
Joe Roberts	F	6'6	215	31	37	564	54	146	37	28	50	56	139	14	64	1	137	15	3.8	0.4	1.7	3.7
Kendall Rhine	C	6'10	240	24	52	552	50	158	32	27	56	48	235	31	120	2	127	11	4.5	0.6	2.3	2.4
Bill Bradley	G	5'11	167	26	58	521	82	258	32	51	56	91	47	54	40	0	218	9	0.8	0.9	0.7	3.8
Stew Johnson (to NJ)	F	6'9	225	23	17	279	55	162	34	14	25	56	88	5	19	0	133	16	5.2	0.3	1.1	7.8
Tommy Woods	F	6'7	215	24	18	184	14	43	33	14	16	88	55	4	25	0	42	10	3.1	0.2	1.4	2.3
Rubin Russell (from Dal)	G	6'2	180	23	10	112	29	78	37	16	23	70	29	1	22	0	76	11	2.9	0.1	2.2	7.6
Orb Bowling	C	6'10	215	28	11	90	9	28	32	3	12	25	29	1	16	0	21	8	2.6	0.1	1.5	1.9
Dave Gaines	G	6'1	170	25	3	36	4	16	25	1	2	50	10	0	4	0	10	12	3.3	0.0	1.3	3.3
Larry Conley (MS)	G	6'3	175	23	1	18	1	4	25	0	0	—	0	0	0	0	2	18	0.0	0.0	0.0	2.0
George Sutor	C	6'8	240	24	1	5	0	0	—	0	0	—	1	0	2	0	0	5	1.0	0.0	2.0	0.0

Use Name	Pos	Hgt	Wgt	Age	TOTAL													PER GAME				
					G	Min	FG	FGA	%	FT	FTA	%	Reb	Ass	PF	DQ	Points	Min	Reb	Ass	PF	Points
1967/1968 A.B.A. — EASTERN DIVISION (continued)																						
NEW JERSEY AMERICANS	36-43 .456				MAX ZASLOFSKY																	
Tony Jackson	F-G	6'4	200	27	74	2638	449	1171	38	450	543	83	500	140	184	1	1439	36	6.8	1.9	2.5	19.4
Hank Whitney	F-C	6'7	235	28	37	1159	217	552	39	157	220	71	477	56	158	3	591	31	12.9	1.5	4.3	16.0
Dan Anderson	C	6'10	230	24	78	2626	463	938	49	223	320	70	856	92	**329**	10	1149	34	11.0	1.2	4.2	14.7
Levern Tart (from Oak)	G-F	6'3	195	25	31	1085	212	517	41	165	199	83	120	102	89	0	589	35	3.9	3.3	2.9	19.0
Walt Simon	G-F	6'6	200	28	78	2518	433	955	45	169	266	64	524	212	272	8	1036	32	6.7	2.7	3.5	13.3
Bruce Spraggins	F	6'5	188	27	70	1590	306	686	45	238	336	71	329	66	173	2	852	23	4.7	0.9	2.5	12.2
Mel Nowell	G	6'2	180	28	76	1555	273	679	40	176	213	83	193	155	188	1	731	20	2.5	2.0	2.5	9.6
Stew Johnson (from KY)	C-F	6'9	225	23	55	1196	200	581	34	55	88	63	327	44	128	2	471	22	5.9	0.8	2.3	8.6
Bobby Lloyd	G	6'2	185	21	58	995	147	349	42	170	199	85	108	93	114	1	467	17	1.9	1.6	2.0	8.1
Barry Liebowitz (from Pit, to Oak)	G	6'2	185	24	24	707	98	287	34	77	96	80	72	93	68	0	273	29	3.0	3.9	2.8	11.4
Johnny Austin	G	6'	175	23	41	692	108	279	39	101	140	72	64	58	110	0	317	17	1.6	1.4	2.7	7.7
Johnny Mathis	F	6'6	220	24	51	656	69	186	37	35	55	64	194	28	102	3	173	13	3.8	0.5	2.0	3.4
Bob McIntyre (leg injury)	F	6'7	220	23	21	451	70	187	37	34	58	59	101	11	27	0	174	21	4.8	0.5	1.3	8.3
Art Heyman (to Pit)	G-F	6'5	210	26	19	439	97	252	38	65	101	64	70	37	35	0	262	23	3.7	1.9	1.8	13.8
Jim Caldwell (from NY-NBA, to KY)	C	6'10	240	24	12	261	23	66	35	10	22	45	85	11	29	1	56	22	7.1	0.9	2.4	4.7
Al Beard	C	6'9	200	25	12	118	12	23	52	6	11	55	46	0	39	1	30	10	3.8	0.0	3.3	2.5
DexterWestbrook (to Pit)	F	6'8	210	24	7	59	12	19	63	7	9	78	9	2	16	0	31	8	1.3	0.3	2.3	4.4
1967/68 A.B.A. — WESTERN DIVISION																						
NEW ORLEANS BUCCANEERS	48-30 .615				BABE McCARTHY																	
Doug Moe	F-G	6'5	220	29	78	3113	665	1610	41	551	693	80	795	202	282	4	**1884**	40	10.2	2.6	3.6	24.2
Jackie Moreland	F	6'7	220	29	76	2332	459	1051	44	192	263	73	619	138	289	13	1112	31	8.1	1.8	3.8	14.6
Red Robbins	C-F	6'8	200	23	73	2159	448	918	49	245	308	80	894	73	157	0	1143	30	12.2	1.0	2.2	15.7
Jimmy Jones	G	6'4	188	22	78	**3255**	551	1181	47	360	508	71	443	179	243	6	1464	42	5.7	2.3	3.1	18.8
Larry Brown	G	5'9	160	27	78	2807	330	901	37	366	450	81	249	**506**	220	1	1045	36	3.2	**6.5**	2.8	13.4
Jess Branson	F	6'7	200	25	78	1892	376	877	43	332	473	70	541	67	248	3	1086	24	6.9	0.9	3.2	13.9
Gerald Govan	C	6'10	220	25	78	1587	156	390	40	79	131	60	596	95	156	2	392	20	7.6	1.2	2.0	5.0
Leland Mitchell	G	6'4	210	26	78	1091	122	350	35	56	85	66	182	73	159	1	321	14	2.3	0.9	2.0	4.1
John Comeaux	F	6'5	193	24	23	189	27	63	43	23	32	72	28	11	27	0	77	8	1.2	0.5	1.2	3.3
Ron Widby	F	6'4	210	22	20	137	27	70	39	4	7	57	45	4	18	0	58	7	2.3	0.2	0.9	2.9
Marl Pradd	G	6'3	170	23	29	125	27	60	45	20	27	74	26	3	22	0	74	4	0.9	0.1	0.8	2.6
John Dickson	C	6'10	240	22	21	100	14	39	36	8	13	62	33	3	11	0	36	5	1.6	0.1	0.5	1.7
Red Stroud	G	6'1	160	26	7	33	5	11	45	9	10	90	2	1	7	0	20	5	0.3	0.1	1.0	2.9
DALLAS CHAPARRALS	46-32 .590				CLIFF HAGAN																	
Cliff Hagan	F	6'4	215	36	56	1737	371	759	49	277	351	79	334	276	202	6	1019	31	6.0	4.9	3.6	18.2
Cincy Powell	F	6'7	227	25	77	2524	533	1089	49	343	496	69	694	106	254	7	1410	33	9.0	1.4	3.3	18.3
Jonh Beasley	C-F	6'9	225	23	77	2840	622	1264	49	271	322	84	982	112	245	3	1515	37	12.8	1.5	3.2	19.7
Charlie Beasley	G	6'5	190	22	78	2969	374	758	49	285	327	**87**	295	290	202	3	1036	38	3.8	3.7	2.6	13.3
Bob Verga (military service)	G	6'1	190	22	31	1285	280	633	44	162	218	74	138	74	93	1	735	41	4.5	2.4	3.0	23.7
Maurice McHartley	G	6'3	200	25	58	2175	330	825	40	225	324	69	273	230	216	5	888	38	4.7	4.0	3.7	15.3
Bobby Wilson	F	6'8	215	23	69	1562	226	581	39	163	265	62	450	55	209	8	616	23	6.5	0.8	3.0	8.9
Riney Lochmann	F	6'6	215	23	63	808	108	285	38	49	79	62	166	44	113	2	266	13	2.6	0.7	1.8	4.2
Rich Peek	C	6'11	230	24	51	759	101	209	48	35	65	54	197	22	94	1	237	15	3.9	0.4	1.8	4.6
Carroll Hooser	F	6'7	230	23	56	720	128	297	43	59	83	71	216	29	139	6	316	13	3.9	0.5	2.5	5.6
Denny Holman	G	6'3	175	22	46	554	55	153	36	62	103	60	78	73	85	1	176	12	1.7	1.6	1.8	3.8
Jim Burns (from Chi-NBA)	G	6'3	195	22	33	392	52	137	38	51	89	57	60	24	52	0	155	12	1.8	0.7	1.6	4.7
Elton McGriff	C	6'9	225	25	20	369	49	89	55	33	62	53	114	2	65	3	131	18	5.7	0.1	3.3	6.6
Rubin Russell (to KY)	G	6'2	180	23	16	157	27	80	34	9	18	50	23	6	18	0	65	10	1.4	0.4	1.1	4.1
Mike Dabich (from Oak)	C	7'	255	25	3	23	4	7	57	2	5	40	7	1	7	0	10	8	2.3	0.3	2.3	3.3
Gene Wiley (from Oak)	C	6'10	230	30	1	21	0	1	0	1	3	33	3	0	3	0	1	21	3.0	0.0	3.0	1.0
DENVER ROCKETS	45-33 .577				BOB BASS																	
Willie Murrell	F	6'6	225	26	71	2495	498	1069	47	166	236	70	637	64	200	1	1165	35	9.0	0.9	2.8	16.4
Wayne Hightower	F	6'9	210	27	74	2459	431	1126	38	420	543	77	536	143	237	5	1282	33	7.2	1.9	3.2	17.3
Byron Beck	C	6'9	240	22	71	1623	275	570	48	119	159	75	559	38	219	6	669	23	7.9	0.5	3.1	9.4
Larry Jones	G-F	6'2	180	26	76	3085	602	1409	43	530	683	78	599	270	268	4	1742	41	7.9	3.6	3.5	22.9
Grant Simmons	G	6'3	190	24	78	2264	292	688	42	208	295	71	240	182	236	3	793	29	3.1	2.3	3.0	10.2
Tom Hoover	C	6'10	250	26	70	1588	161	357	45	128	206	62	491	64	268	8	454	23	7.0	0.9	3.8	6.5
Julie Hammond	F	6'5	205	24	74	1364	224	458	49	143	209	68	327	62	112	0	591	18	4.4	0.8	1.5	8.0
Tom Bowens	F-C	6'8	220	27	67	1287	177	453	39	55	90	61	374	41	159	3	410	19	5.6	0.6	2.4	6.1
Lonnie Wright (FB)	G	6'2	205	23	38	896	146	346	42	79	121	65	96	68	96	0	373	24	2.5	1.8	2.5	9.8
Willis Thomas (to Ana)	G	6'3	185	30	24	542	136	305	45	22	32	69	58	25	45	1	294	23	2.4	1.0	1.9	12.3
Chuck Gardner	F	6'8	205	23	42	487	71	175	41	55	79	70	136	13	74	1	197	12	3.2	0.3	1.8	4.7
Jeff Congdon (from Ana)	G	6'1	190	24	41	398	67	191	35	20	25	80	34	59	37	0	159	10	0.8	1.4	0.9	3.9
Richie Moore	G	6'2	190	22	18	211	24	71	34	21	28	75	19	8	16	0	69	12	1.1	0.4	0.9	3.8
John Morrison	G	6'2	190	22	9	76	10	34	29	6	9	67	9	7	15	0	27	8	1.0	0.8	1.7	3.0
R. B. Lynam	G	6'1	200	23	7	39	5	17	29	7	8	88	5	0	10	0	17	6	0.7	0.0	1.4	2.4
Ron Horn	F	6'7	225	29	1	6	0	2	0	2	2	100	1	0	0	0	2	6	1.0	0.0	0.0	2.0

Use Name	Pos	Hgt	Wgt	Age	G	Min	FG	FGA	%	FT	FTA	%	Reb	Ass	PF	DQ	Points	Min	Reb	Ass	PF	Points
					TOTAL													PER GAME				
					1967/68 A.B.A. — WESTERN DIVISION (continued)																	
HOUSTON MAVERICKS	**29-49 .372**				**SLATER MARTIN**																	
Leary Lentz	F	6'6	200	22	78	2504	343	845	41	147	221	67	648	89	175	0	833	32	8.3	1.1	2.2	10.7
Art Becker	F	6'8	210	25	76	2689	563	1204	47	297	362	82	713	95	321	12	1427	35	9.4	1.3	4.2	18.8
Wilbert Frazier	C-F	6'7	235	25	76	2125	358	870	41	228	376	61	666	104	219	3	945	28	8.8	1.4	2.9	12.4
Joe Hamood	G	6'	180	24	76	1839	274	819	33	186	252	74	217	227	200	2	750	24	2.9	3.0	2.6	9.9
Willie Somerset (CT)	G	5'10	170	25	61	2334	467	1042	45	359	460	78	305	225	211	5	1326	38	5.0	3.7	3.5	21.7
DeWitt Menyard	C	6'10	210	23	71	1756	256	692	37	131	197	66	551	84	218	5	643	25	7.8	1.2	3.1	9.1
Hal Hale	G	6'1	180	22	72	1706	133	408	33	60	89	67	206	144	143	1	361	24	2.9	2.0	2.0	5.0
Jerry Pettway	G-F	6'3	185	23	76	1572	289	838	34	119	183	65	274	103	132	2	713	21	3.6	1.4	1.7	9.4
Guy Manning	F	6'6	205	23	59	1107	206	502	41	115	199	58	311	37	151	4	529	19	5.3	0.6	2.6	9.0
Wayne Molis (from Oak)	F	6'8	235	24	41	489	91	212	43	37	57	65	160	36	46	1	221	12	3.9	0.9	1.1	5.4
Bob Riedy	F	6'6	215	22	23	331	45	129	35	41	67	61	68	5	27	0	131	14	3.0	0.2	1.2	5.7
Roger Schurig	G	6'3	195	25	21	252	35	94	37	27	36	75	29	18	38	0	100	12	1.4	0.9	1.8	4.8
Darrell Hardy	F	6'7	220	23	17	172	32	74	43	25	35	71	56	8	23	0	89	10	3.3	0.5	1.4	5.2
Gary Turner	F	6'7	200	22	2	21	2	2	100	2	3	67	3	0	2	0	6	11	1.5	0.0	1.0	3.0
ANAHEIM AMIGOS	**25-53 .321**				**AL BRIGHTMAN (12-24 .333), HARRY DINNEL (13-29 .310)**																	
Ben Warley	F	6'5	200	31	71	2297	435	985	44	313	389	80	608	96	276	12	1235	32	8.6	1.4	3.9	17.4
Warren Davis	F	6'6	215	22	54	1816	343	758	45	229	353	65	566	75	193	3	916	34	10.5	1.4	3.6	17.0
Larry Bunce	C	7'	245	22	71	2266	300	716	42	256	352	73	589	75	189	8	856	32	8.3	1.1	2.7	12.1
Steve Chubin	G	6'2	200	23	77	2441	439	1057	42	518	639	81	433	364	292	10	1398	32	5.6	4.7	3.8	18.2
Les Selvage	G	6'1	175	24	78	2432	371	1044	36	206	278	74	217	247	239	3	1095	31	2.8	3.2	3.1	14.0
Bob Bedell	F	6'8	205	23	76	1492	325	736	44	142	190	75	506	79	203	5	792	20	6.7	1.0	2.7	10.4
John Fairchild	F	6'8	205	24	62	1311	271	620	44	135	200	68	332	63	155	0	678	21	5.4	1.0	2.5	10.9
Steve Kramer	G-F	6'5	200	22	50	1140	218	497	44	129	165	78	173	85	149	3	566	23	3.5	1.7	3.0	11.3
Bill Allen	C-F	6'8	205	22	38	857	120	280	43	58	99	59	269	23	121	5	300	23	7.1	0.6	3.2	7.9
Jeff Congdon (to Den)	G	6'1	190	24	23	622	83	213	39	29	39	74	72	74	47	1	203	27	3.1	3.2	2.0	8.8
Willis Thomas (from Den)	G	6'3	185	30	38	525	107	245	44	47	61	77	56	30	62	0	261	14	1.5	0.8	1.6	6.9
Bill Garner	C	6'10	220	27	53	514	28	103	27	25	50	50	119	24	101	4	81	10	2.2	0.5	1.9	1.5
Herschell Turner (from Pit)	G	6'2	195	29	32	435	45	138	33	20	41	49	68	40	62	1	115	14	2.1	1.3	1.9	3.6
Randy Stoll	C	6'7	235	22	25	403	66	138	48	10	25	40	91	12	42	0	142	16	3.6	0.5	1.7	5.7
Harry Dinnel (knee injury)	F	6'4	200	26	11	87	6	19	32	7	8	88	23	5	14	0	19	8	2.1	0.5	1.3	1.7
Larry Moore	F	6'7	215	24	12	78	8	33	24	11	13	85	16	1	17	0	27	7	1.3	0.1	1.4	2.3
Paul Scranton	F	6'5	230	23	5	41	4	9	44	1	4	25	16	1	5	0	9	8	3.2	0.2	1.0	1.8
Bob Sims	F	6'5	220	29	2	19	2	7	29	4	6	67	1	2	6	1	8	10	0.5	1.0	3.0	4.0
Bill Crow	G	6'1	180	27	1	16	1	8	13	1	4	25	2	0	0	0	3	16	2.0	0.0	0.0	3.0
Dick Lee	F	—	—	—	2	2	0	0	—	0	0	—	1	1	0	0	0	1	0.5	0.5	0.0	0.0
OAKLAND OAKS	**22-56 .282**				**BRUCE HALE**																	
Steve Jones	F	6'5	205	25	76	1950	278	665	42	186	233	80	343	111	239	7	765	26	4.5	1.5	3.1	10.1
Ron Franz	F	6'7	207	22	74	2080	354	903	39	197	285	69	469	129	249	11	930	28	6.3	1.7	3.4	12.6
Jim Hadnot	C-F	6'10	237	27	77	3004	488	1045	47	368	551	67	936	135	279	9	1344	39	12.2	1.8	3.6	17.5
Levern Tart (CT, to NJ)	G	6'3	195	25	42	1768	421	983	43	286	367	78	274	147	123	0	1129	42	6.5	3.5	2.9	26.9
Andy Anderson	G	6'2	185	22	77	1894	279	756	37	163	225	72	167	118	190	1	730	25	2.2	1.5	2.5	9.5
Barry Liebowitz (from Pit-NJ)	G	6'2	185	24	35	1014	139	379	37	119	152	78	58	156	96	1	401	29	1.7	4.5	2.7	11.5
Mel Peterson	G	6'4	190	29	77	1589	323	756	43	76	93	82	451	104	161	1	731	21	5.9	1.4	2.1	9.5
Wes Bialosuknia	G	6'2	185	22	70	1224	238	570	42	103	132	78	89	57	101	1	608	17	1.3	0.8	1.4	8.7
Willie Porter (to Pit)	F	6'7	205	25	43	1123	199	472	42	167	246	68	380	50	162	11	565	26	8.8	1.2	3.8	13.1
Gary Bradds	F	6'8	215	25	49	1052	199	440	45	221	283	78	289	51	131	1	619	21	5.9	1.0	2.7	12.6
Ira Harge (from Pit)	C	6'9	225	26	30	1047	135	340	40	83	114	73	445	61	100	1	353	35	14.8	2.0	3.3	11.8
Dave Lee	F	6'7	225	25	54	753	125	276	45	120	140	86	184	20	83	2	372	14	3.4	0.4	1.5	6.9
Al Salvadori	F	6'9	220	22	17	186	21	58	36	11	16	69	46	4	28	0	54	11	2.7	0.2	1.6	3.2
Gene Wiley (to Dal)	C	6'10	230	30	8	64	7	19	37	3	5	60	17	2	7	0	17	8	2.1	0.3	0.9	2.1
Wayne Molis (to Hou)	F	6'8	235	24	5	46	5	13	38	4	4	100	10	3	3	0	14	9	2.0	0.6	0.6	2.8
Mike Dabich (to Dal)	C	7'	255	25	7	26	4	5	80	2	4	50	6	1	5	0	10	4	0.9	0.1	0.7	1.4
Rick Barry - (CT)																						

Use Name	Pos	Hgt	Wgt	Age	TOTAL													PER GAME				
					G	Min	FG	FGA	%	FT	FTA	%	Reb	Ass	PF	DQ	Points	Min	Reb	Ass	PF	Points

1967/68 A.B.A.—PLAYOFFS

PITTSBURGH PIPERS — **VINCE CAZETTA**

defeated Indiana 3-0; 146-127, 121-108, 133-114
defeated Minnesota 4-1; 125-117, 123-137, 107-99, 117-108, 114-105
defeated New Orleans 4-3; 120-112, 100-109, 101-109, 106-105, 108-111, 118-112, 122-113

Use Name	Pos	Hgt	Wgt	Age	G	Min	FG	FGA	%	FT	FTA	%	Reb	Ass	PF	DQ	Points	Min	Reb	Ass	PF	Points
Art Heyman	F-G	6'5	210	26	15	564	94	194	48	94	139	68	107	58	44	0	296	38	7.1	3.9	2.9	19.7
Trooper Washington	F	6'7	225	23	15	610	95	179	53	28	57	49	261	42	60	3	218	41	**17.4**	2.8	4.0	14.5
Connie Hawkins	C	6'8	215	25	14	616	**145**	244	**59**	**129**	**177**	73	172	64	58	**4**	**419**	44	12.3	4.6	4.1	**29.9**
Chico Vaughn	G	6'3	195	27	15	576	90	256	35	62	78	79	53	44	53	1	266	38	3.5	2.9	3.5	17.7
Charlie Williams	G	6'	165	24	15	626	**145**	**336**	43	60	82	73	64	37	61	3	356	42	4.3	2.5	4.1	23.7
Jim Jarvis	G	6'1	175	24	15	211	39	89	44	16	20	80	21	15	29	0	94	14	1.4	1.0	1.9	6.3
Leroy Wright	F-C	6'9	215	29	13	190	9	28	32	8	22	36	73	8	30	2	26	15	5.6	0.6	2.3	2.0
Willie Porter	F	6'7	205	25	14	167	19	43	44	20	29	69	69	6	43	0	58	12	4.9	0.4	3.1	4.1
Arvesta Kelly	G	6'3	190	22	8	27	5	14	36	4	5	80	5	0	8	0	16	3	0.6	0.0	1.0	2.0
Steve Vacendak	G	6'1	185	23	7	16	2	7	28	0	0	—	3	2	2	0	4	2	0.4	0.3	0.3	0.6
Craig Dill	C	6'11	215	23	6	15	3	8	38	1	1	100	6	2	5	0	7	3	1.0	0.3	0.8	1.2
Rich Parks	F	6'7	235	24	5	7	0	2	0	1	4	25	2	0	3	0	1	1	0.4	0.0	0.6	0.2

NEW ORLEANS BUCCANEERS — **BABE McCARTHY**

defeated Denver 3-2; 130-104, 105-93, 98-105, 100-108, 102-97
defeated Dallas 4-1; 104-99, 109-112, 110-107, 119-103, 108-107
lost to Pittsburgh 3-4; 112-120, 109-100, 109-101, 105-106, 111-108, 112-118, 113-122

Use Name	Pos	Hgt	Wgt	Age	G	Min	FG	FGA	%	FT	FTA	%	Reb	Ass	PF	DQ	Points	Min	Reb	Ass	PF	Points
Doug Moe	F-G	6'5	220	29	17	715	144	346	42	107	149	72	169	40	71	2	399	42	9.9	2.4	4.2	23.5
Jackie Moreland	F	6'7	220	29	17	487	84	193	44	40	59	68	114	43	**74**	1	208	29	6.7	2.5	4.4	12.2
Red Robbins	C-F	6'8	200	23	17	621	115	252	46	66	93	71	**234**	28	45	0	296	37	13.8	1.6	2.6	17.4
Jimmy Jones	G	6'4	188	22	17	**785**	144	315	46	87	118	74	117	56	56	2	375	**46**	6.9	3.3	3.3	22.1
Larry Brown	G	5'9	160	27	17	696	90	212	42	100	122	82	59	**129**	58	0	284	41	3.5	**7.6**	3.4	16.7
Jess Branson	F	6'7	200	25	17	402	61	155	39	71	87	82	102	20	62	0	193	24	6.0	1.2	3.6	11.4
Gerald Govan	C	6'10	220	25	17	290	24	77	31	20	32	63	116	23	46	1	68	17	6.8	1.4	2.7	4.0
Leland Mitchell	G	6'4	210	26	7	57	1	9	11	1	2	50	3	3	8	0	3	8	0.4	0.4	1.1	0.4
Ron Widby	F	6'4	210	22	6	31	8	19	42	0	2	0	17	1	5	0	18	5	2.8	0.2	0.8	3.0
Marl Praad	G	6'3	170	23	6	18	3	9	33	6	11	55	5	0	3	0	12	3	0.8	0.0	0.5	2.0
John Dickson	C	6'10	240	22	1	3	0	4	0	0	0	—	2	0	0	0	0	3	2.0	0.0	0.0	0.0

DALLAS CHAPARRALS — **CLIFF HAGAN**

defeated Houston 3-0; 111-110, 115-97, 116-103
lost to New Orleans 1-4; 99-104, 112-109, 107-110, 103-119, 107-108

Use Name	Pos	Hgt	Wgt	Age	G	Min	FG	FGA	%	FT	FTA	%	Reb	Ass	PF	DQ	Points	Min	Reb	Ass	PF	Points
Cincy Powell	F	6'7	227	25	8	334	63	144	44	61	73	84	87	17	30	0	187	42	10.9	2.1	3.8	23.4
John Beasley	F-C	6'9	225	22	8	332	63	133	47	43	51	84	101	10	21	0	170	42	12.6	1.3	2.6	21.3
Elton McGriff	C	6'9	225	25	8	206	30	69	43	20	38	53	72	6	32	1	80	26	9.0	0.8	4.0	10.0
Charlie Beasley	G	6'5	190	22	8	345	55	115	48	36	43	84	20	28	27	0	146	43	2.5	3.5	3.4	18.3
Maurice McHartley	G	6'3	200	25	8	279	59	139	42	28	38	74	45	28	40	2	146	35	5.6	3.5	**5.0**	18.3
Rich Peek	C	6'11	230	24	8	137	18	37	49	7	15	47	42	3	17	1	43	17	5.3	0.4	2.1	5.4
Denny Holman	G	6'3	175	22	8	128	9	31	29	12	12	100	16	15	19	0	31	16	2.0	1.9	2.4	3.9
Cliff Hagan	F	6'4	215	36	3	70	14	37	38	9	13	69	13	9	11	1	37	23	4.3	3.0	3.7	12.3
Bobby Wilson	F	6'8	215	23	6	50	7	25	28	6	13	46	26	2	12	1	21	8	4.3	0.3	2.0	3.5
Riney Lochmann	F-G	6'6	215	23	5	33	2	6	33	3	3	100	3	0	5	0	7	7	0.6	0.0	1.0	1.4
Carroll Hooser	F	6'7	230	23	3	6	1	2	50	0	0	—	2	0	3	0	2	2	0.7	0.0	1.0	0.7
Bob Verga - military service																						

MINNESOTA MUSKIES — **JIM POLLARD**

defeated Kentucky 3-2; 115-102, 95-100, 116-107, 86-94, 114-108
lost to Pittsburgh 1-4; 117-125, 137-123, 99-107, 108-117, 105-114

Use Name	Pos	Hgt	Wgt	Age	G	Min	FG	FGA	%	FT	FTA	%	Reb	Ass	PF	DQ	Points	Min	Reb	Ass	PF	Points
Sam Smith	F	6'7	230	23	10	374	56	142	39	35	51	69	81	12	39	0	147	37	8.1	1.2	3.9	14.7
Les Hunter	F	6'7	235	25	10	388	76	188	40	62	98	63	110	24	48	3	214	39	11.0	2.4	4.8	21.4
Mel Daniels	C	6'9	220	23	10	409	98	226	43	57	94	61	161	19	35	1	253	41	16.1	1.9	3.5	25.3
Erv Inniger	G	6'4	190	22	10	364	55	140	39	26	32	81	57	35	36	0	136	36	5.7	3.5	3.6	13.8
Donnie Freeman	G	6'3	185	23	10	365	56	134	42	46	63	73	50	56	46	**4**	158	37	5.0	5.6	4.6	15.8
Dick Clark	G	6'4	195	23	10	231	17	65	26	21	28	75	33	13	18	0	56	23	3.3	1.3	1.8	5.6
Gary Keller	F-C	6'9	220	23	10	142	25	67	37	13	23	57	50	8	27	0	63	14	5.0	0.8	2.7	6.3
Errol Palmer	F	6'5	195	22	6	75	10	25	40	8	10	80	27	7	17	0	28	13	4.5	1.2	2.8	4.7
Skip Thoren	C	6'10	230	24	2	52	14	28	50	7	12	58	27	4	5	0	35	26	13.5	2.0	2.5	17.5
Ron Perry - military service																						

1967/68 A.B.A. — PLAYOFFS (continued)

Use Name	Pos	Hgt	Wgt	Age	G	Min	FG	FGA	%	FT	FTA	%	Reb	Ass	PF	DQ	Points	Min	Reb	Ass	PF	Points
					TOTAL													PER GAME				
KENTUCKY COLONELS	**GENE RHODES**				lost to Minnesota 2-3; 102-115, 100-95, 107-116, 94-86, 108-114																	
Randy Mahaffey	F	6'7	210	22	5	147	24	53	45	17	24	71	23	3	16	1	65	29	4.6	0.6	3.2	13.0
Goose Ligon	F-C	6'7	215	23	5	173	20	46	43	32	42	76	58	7	25	1	72	35	11.6	1.4	**5.0**	14.4
Jim Caldwell	C	6'10	240	24	5	175	22	51	43	14	20	70	59	14	25	0	58	35	11.8	2.8	**5.0**	11.6
Darel Carrier	G	6'3	185	27	5	211	38	100	38	31	36	86	25	13	15	0	115	42	5.0	2.6	3.0	23.0
Louie Dampier	G	6'	170	23	5	224	46	104	44	26	31	84	24	23	9	0	133	45	4.8	4.6	1.8	26.6
Howard Bayne	F	6'6	235	25	5	85	3	19	16	6	11	55	23	5	12	0	12	17	4.6	1.0	2.4	2.4
Joe Roberts	F	6'6	215	31	5	63	5	15	33	2	6	33	15	1	13	0	12	13	3.0	0.2	2.6	2.4
Kendall Rhine	C	6'10	240	24	5	62	5	17	29	0	7	0	15	4	16	0	10	12	3.0	0.8	3.2	2.0
Bobby Rascoe	G-F	6'4	205	27	5	51	12	27	44	4	4	100	5	3	7	0	28	10	1.0	0.6	1.4	5.6
Bill Bradley	G	5'11	167	26	2	9	2	2	100	2	2	100	1	1	3	0	6	5	0.5	0.5	1.5	3.0
DENVER ROCKETS	**BOB BASS**				lost to New Orleans 2-3; 104-130, 93-105, 105-98, 108-100, 97-102																	
Willie Murrell	F	6'6	225	26	5	198	45	88	51	22	26	85	47	7	24	1	112	40	9.4	1.4	4.8	22.4
Wayne Hightower	F	6'9	210	27	5	209	35	100	35	43	54	80	44	11	25	2	113	42	8.8	2.2	**5.0**	22.6
Byron Bech	C	6'9	240	22	5	160	23	50	46	11	15	73	55	5	21	1	57	32	11.0	1.0	4.2	11.4
Grant Simmons	G	6'3	190	24	5	145	13	36	36	12	16	75	22	15	20	1	38	29	4.4	3.0	4.0	7.6
Lonnie Wright	G	6'2	205	23	5	149	13	50	26	9	14	64	13	10	9	0	36	30	2.6	2.0	1.8	7.2
Julie Hammond	G-F	6'5	205	24	5	153	22	38	58	16	24	67	28	8	17	1	60	31	5.6	1.6	3.4	12.0
Tom Bowens	C-F	6'8	220	27	5	94	14	31	45	2	2	100	25	5	17	1	30	19	5.0	1.0	3.4	6.0
Larry Jones	G	6'2	180	26	1	41	12	20	60	5	8	63	4	4	5	0	29	41	4.0	4.0	5.0	29.0
Jeff Congdon	G	6'1	190	24	3	35	7	21	33	3	7	43	4	5	5	0	19	12	1.3	1.7	1.7	6.3
Tom Hoover	C	6'10	250	26	2	16	4	7	57	5	7	71	4	1	6	0	13	8	2.0	0.5	3.0	6.5
HOUSTON MAVERICKS	**SLATER MARTIN**				lost to Dallas 0-3; 110-111, 97-115, 103-116																	
Leary Lentz	F	6'6	200	22	3	73	12	26	46	1	3	33	19	3	6	0	25	24	6.3	1.0	2.0	8.3
Art Becker	F	6'8	210	25	3	94	18	43	42	15	18	83	16	5	10	0	51	31	5.3	1.7	3.3	17.0
Wilbert Frazier	C-F	6'7	235	25	3	85	13	29	45	3	7	43	12	4	11	0	29	28	4.0	1.3	3.7	9.7
Hal Hale	G	6'1	180	22	3	103	6	16	38	7	7	100	8	3	10	0	22	34	2.7	1.0	3.3	7.3
Willie Somerset	G	5'10	170	25	3	131	30	73	41	27	34	79	25	9	11	0	91	44	8.3	3.0	3.7	30.3
Guy Manning	F	6'6	205	23	3	66	15	34	44	11	19	58	19	2	11	0	41	22	6.3	0.7	3.7	13.7
DeWitt Menyard	C	6'10	210	23	3	64	7	18	39	1	3	33	11	0	8	0	15	21	3.7	0.0	2.7	5.0
Jerry Pettway	F-G	6'3	185	23	3	62	12	29	41	4	5	80	14	5	5	0	29	21	4.7	1.7	1.7	9.7
Joe Hamood	G	6'	180	24	3	42	3	17	18	1	2	50	5	2	8	0	7	14	1.7	0.7	2.7	2.3
INDIANA PACERS	**LARRY STAVERMAN**				lost to Pittsburgh 0-3, 127-146, 108-121, 114-133																	
Roger Brown	F-G	6'5	207	25	3	129	26	57	46	13	21	62	31	20	14	2	65	43	10.3	6.7	4.7	21.7
Ollie Darden	F	6'7	240	23	3	60	16	28	57	3	5	60	27	4	13	0	35	20	9.0	1.3	4.3	11.7
Bob Netolicky	C-F	6'9	225	25	3	117	29	51	57	9	16	56	22	6	10	0	67	39	7.3	2.0	3.3	22.3
Jimmy Rayl	G	6'2	170	26	3	118	15	42	36	5	7	71	10	14	14	0	39	39	3.3	4.7	4.7	13.0
Freddie Lewis	G	6'	180	24	3	116	21	49	43	28	29	**97**	19	7	10	0	70	39	6.3	2.3	3.3	23.3
George Peoples	C	6'8	205	24	3	62	12	21	57	2	3	67	31	4	9	1	26	21	10.3	1.3	3.0	8.7
Bobby Edmonds	F	6'6	220	26	3	47	6	14	43	7	9	78	18	2	12	1	20	16	6.0	0.7	4.0	6.7
Jerry Harkness	G	6'2	175	27	3	32	4	12	33	2	2	100	5	5	6	0	10	11	1.7	1.7	2.0	3.3
Ron Bonham	F	6'5	200	25	3	30	4	15	27	5	6	83	6	3	4	0	13	10	2.0	1.0	1.3	4.3
Ron Kozlicki	F	6'7	215	23	2	5	0	2	0	0	0	-	1	0	1	0	0	3	0.5	0.0	0.5	0.0
Matt Aitch	F	6'7	238	23	2	4	2	4	50	0	0	-	0	0	0	0	4	2	0.0	0.0	0.0	2.0
Reggie Harding - (ST)																						

Team	W	L	Pct.	GB	Record against playoff teams W	L	Pct.	Record against non-playoff teams W	L	Pct.	HOME W	L	Pct.	ROAD W	L	Pct.	NEUTRAL W	L	Pct.
EASTERN DIVISION																			
Pinsburgh Pipers	**54**	24	**.692**	—	**35**	20	**.636**	**19**	4	**.826**	31	6	**.838**	**20**	16	**.566**	3	2	.600
Minnesota Muskies	50	28	.641	4	33	23	.589	17	5	.773	**32**	7	.821	15	21	.417	3	0	**1.000**
Indiana Pacers	38	40	.487	16	24	32	.429	14	8	.636	24	8	.750	10	26	.278	4	6	.400
Kentucky Colonels	37	42	.468	17.5	23	32	.418	13	10	.565	25	14	.641	10	26	.278	1	2	.330
New Jersey Americans	36	43	.456	18.5	27	39	.409	9	3	.750	26	13	.667	9	26	.257	1	3	.250
WESTERN DIVISION																			
New Orleans Buccaneers	48	30	.615	—	32	22	.593	16	8	.667	23	6	.793	14	20	.412	**11**	4	.733
Dallas Chaparrals	46	32	.590	2	28	25	.528	18	7	.720	29	10	.744	17	20	.459	0	2	.000
Denver Rockets	45	33	.577	3	26	26	.500	**19**	7	.731	31	8	.795	13	22	.371	1	3	.250
Houston Mavericks	29	49	.372	19	16	37	.302	13	**12**	.520	23	16	.590	6	**32**	.158	0	1	.000
Anaheim Amigos	25	53	.321	23	17	**45**	.274	8	8	.500	12	**19**	.387	7	27	.206	6	7	.462
Oakland Oaks	22	**56**	.282	26	17	**45**	.274	5	11	.313	12	18	.400	4	**32**	.111	6	6	.500

1967/68 A.B.A. INDIVIDUAL LEADERS

SCORING
(Minimum 70 Games Played)

Name	Team	G	FG	FT	Pts.	Avg.
Hawkins	Pit	70	635	603	1875	26.8
Moe	NO	78	665	551	1884	24.2
Tart	Oak-NJ	73	633	451	1718	23.5
Carrier	KY	77	643	395	1765	22.9
Jones	Den	76	602	530	1742	22.9
Daniels	Min	78	669	390	1729	22.2
Williams	Pit	78	642	290	1625	20.8
Dampier	KY	72	620	209	1487	20.7
Lewis	Ind	76	542	465	1565	20.6
Vaughn	Pit	74	512	308	1469	19.9

FIELD GOAL PERCENTAGE
(Minimum 560 Attempts)

Name	Team	FG	FGA	Pct.
Washington	Pit	312	596	.523
Hawkins	Pit	635	1223	.519
Netolicky	Ind	468	928	.504
Anderson	NJ	463	938	.494
C. Beasley	Dal	374	758	.493
J. Beasley	Dal	622	1264	.492
Powell	Dal	533	1089	.489
Hagan	Dal	371	759	.489
Robbins	NO	448	918	.489
Beck	Den	275	570	.482

3-POINT FIELD GOAL PERCENTAGE
(Minimum 20 Made)

Name	Team	FG	FTA	Pct.
Jones	Oak	23	54	.426
Bialosuknia	Oak	29	73	.397
Carrier	KY	84	235	.357
Perry	Min	62	178	.348
Vaughn	Pit	137	410	.334
Rayl	Ind	57	175	.326
Selvage	Ana	147	461	.320
Johnson	KY-NJ	25	79	.316
Warley	Ana	52	166	.313
Hale	Hou	35	112	.313

FREE THROW PERCENTAGE
(Minimum 160 Attempts)

Name	Team	FT	FTA	Pct.
C. Beasley	Dal	285	327	.872
Lloyd	NJ	170	199	.854
J. Beasley	Dal	271	322	.842
Jackson	NJ	450	543	.829
Nowell	NJ	176	213	.826
Carrier	KY	395	479	.825
Dampier	KY	209	254	.823
Becker	Hou	297	362	.820
Brown	NO	366	450	.813
Chubin	Ana	518	639	.811

REBOUNDS PER GAME
(Minimum 70 Games Played)

Name	Team	G	Reb.	Avg.
Daniels	Min	78	1213	15.6
Hawkins	Pit	70	945	13.5
J. Beasley	Dal	77	982	12.8
Harge	Pit-Oak	82	1038	12.7
Robbins	NO	73	894	12.2
Hadnot	Oak	77	936	12.2
Ligon	KY	78	929	11.9
Netolicky	Ind	71	819	11.5
Anderson	NJ	78	856	11.0
Moe	NO	78	795	10.2

ASSISTS PER GAME
(Minimum 70 Games Played)

Name	Team	G	Ass.	Avg.
Brown	NO	78	506	6.5
Chubin	Ana	77	364	4.7
Hawkins	Pit	70	320	4.6
Brown	Ind	76	327	4.3
Heyman	NJ-Pit	73	276	3.8
C. Beasley	Dal	78	290	3.7
Leibowitz	Pit-NJ-Oak	82	301	3.7
Dampier	KY	72	256	3.6
Jones	Den	76	270	3.6
Tart	Oak-NJ	73	249	3.4

MINUTES PLAYED

Name	Team	Min.
Jones	NO	3255
Carner	KY	3192
Hawkins	Pit	3146
Moe	NO	3113
Jones	Den	3085

PERSONAL FOULS

Name	Team	PF
Anderson	NJ	329
Becker	Hou	321
Ligon	KY	307
Hunter	Min	297
Brown	Ind	296

GAMES DISQUALIFIED

Name	Team	Disq.
Mahaffey	KY	15
Moreland	NO	13
Becker	Hou	12
Warley	Ana	12
Daniels	Min	11
Franz	Oak	11
Porter	Oak-Pit	11

TEAM STATISTICS

EASTERN DIVISION

Team		REGULAR SEASON												PLAYOFFS											
		G	FG	FGA	%	FT	FTA	%	Reb.	Ass.	PF	Points	PPG	G	FG	FGA	%	FT	FTA	%	Reb.	Ass.	PF	Points	PPG
Pittsburgh	**Off.**	78	3230	7528	43	2028	2839	71	4260	1239	1846	**8731**	**111.9**	15	646	1400	**46**	423	614	69	836	278	396	1761	**117.4**
	Def.	78	3233	7543	43	1928	2711	71	4619	1357	1886	8479	108.7	15	642	1517	42	389	555	70	895	314	416	1686	112.4
	Diff.		-3	-15	—	+100	+128	-1	-359	-118	+40	+252	+3.2		+4	-117	**+4**	+34	+59	-1	-59	-36	+20	+75	+5.0
Minnesota	**Off.**	78	3248	**8084**	40	1896	2968	64	**4828**	1019	1860	8469	108.6	10	407	**1015**	40	275	411	67	**596**	178	271	1092	109.2
	Def.	78	3019	7334	41	1989	2779	72	**3910**	1134	2012	8163	104.7	10	385	875	44	286	400	72	508	158	275	1097	109.7
	Diff.		+229	**+750**	-1	-93	+189	-8	**+918**	-115	+152	+306	+3.9		**+22**	+140	-4	-11	+11	-5	**+88**	+20	+4	-5	-0.5
Indiana	**Off.**	78	3174	7397	43	2102	2971	71	4257	1176	**1788**	8546	109.6	3	**135**	295	46	74	98	**76**	170	**65**	93	349	116.3
	Def.	78	3311	7844	42	**1767**	**2473**	71	4131	1257	2013	8530	109.4	3	149	289	52	93	140	**66**	164	67	79	400	133.3
	Diff.		-137	-447	+1	**+335**	**+498**	—	+126	-81	**+225**	+16	+0.2		-14	+6	-6	-19	-42	**+9**	+6	-2	-14	-51	-17.0
Kentucky	**Off.**	78	3044	7427	41	1921	2677	72	4404	1165	1928	8150	104.5	5	177	434	41	134	183	73	248	74	140	511	102.2
	Def.	78	2997	7236	41	2112	2890	73	4262	1043	1880	8207	105.2	5	193	487	**40**	139	207	67	282	**77**	127	526	**105.2**
	Diff.		+47	+191	—	-191	-213	-1	+142	+122	-48	-57	-0.7		-16	-53	+1	-5	-24	+6	-34	-3	-13	-15	-3.0
New Jersey	**Off.**	78	3189	7727	41	2138	2876	74	4075	1200	2051	8641	110.8												
	Def.	78	3285	7659	43	2086	2955	71	4406	1095	1952	8768	112.4												
	Diff.		-96	+68	-2	+52	-79	**+3**	-331	+105	-99	-127	-1.6												

WESTERN DIVISION

Team		G	FG	FGA	%	FT	FTA	%	Reb.	Ass.	PF	Points	PPG	G	FG	FGA	%	FT	FTA	%	Reb.	Ass.	PF	Points	PPG
New Orleans	**Off.**	78	3207	7521	43	**2245**	**3000**	75	4453	**1355**	1839	8712	111.7	17	674	1591	42	**498**	675	74	938	343	**428**	1856	109.2
	Def.	78	3144	7784	40	1951	2699	72	4328	1084	**2043**	8334	106.8	17	678	1598	42	**432**	**606**	71	929	267	**476**	1810	106.5
	Diff.		+63	-263	+3	+294	+301	+3	+125	**+271**	+204	**+378**	+4.9		-4	-7	—	**+66**	**+69**	+3	**+9**	**+76**	**+48**	+46	+2.7
Dallas	**Off.**	78	**3260**	7167	45	2027	2810	72	4030	1344	1997	8576	109.9	8	321	738	43	225	299	75	427	118	217	870	108.8
	Def.	78	3092	7492	41	2153	2954	73	3973	1277	1887	8470	108.6	8	313	768	41	222	303	73	423	132	207	860	107.5
	Diff.		+168	-325	+4	-126	-144	-1	+57	+67	-110	+106	+1.3		+8	-30	+2	+3	-4	+2	+4	-14	-10	+10	+1.3
Denver	**Off.**	78	3119	7271	43	1981	2725	73	4121	1044	1992	8244	105.7	5	188	441	43	128	173	74	246	71	149	507	101.4
	Def.	78	**2853**	**7133**	40	2092	2916	72	3933	**993**	1903	**7914**	**101.5**	5	**184**	**414**	44	167	217	77	**233**	96	122	535	107.0
	Diff.		**+266**	+138	+3	-111	-191	+1	+188	+51	-89	+330	+4.2		+4	+27	-1	-39	-44	-3	+13	-25	-27	-28	-5.6
Houston	**Off.**	78	3094	7731	40	1774	2537	70	4207	1175	1906	8074	103.5	3	116	285	41	70	98	71	129	33	80	310	103.3
	Def.	78	3118	7261	43	2066	2798	74	4448	1252	1839	8407	107.8	3	120	251	48	99	123	80	156	49	72	342	114.0
	Diff.		-24	+470	-3	-292	-261	-4	-241	-77	-67	-333	-4.3		-4	+34	-7	-29	-25	-9	-27	-16	-8	-32	-10.7
Anaheim	**Off.**	78	3172	7606	42	2141	2916	73	4158	1297	2174	8704	111.6												
	Def.	78	3388	7768	44	2182	3100	70	4449	1308	1977	9057	116.1												
	Diff.		-216	-162	-2	-41	-184	+3	-291	-11	-197	-353	-4.5												
Oakland	**Off.**	78	3215	7680	42	2109	2850	74	4164	1149	1957	8642	110.8												
	Def.	78	3512	8085	43	2036	2804	73	4498	1363	1946	9160	117.4												
	Diff.		-297	-405	-1	+73	+46	+1	-334	-214	-11	-518	-6.6												

1968-69 N.B.A.

The Seven Foot, One-Inch Bridesmaid

The Boston Celtics came into this season as the defending champions, but one deal during the summer had established the Los Angeles Lakers as the odds-on favorite to take the N.B.A. title this year; they traded for Wilt Chamberlain. After the Philadelphia 76ers had lost to Boston in the playoffs last spring, coach Alex Hannum jumped to the Oakland Oaks of the A B.A. and general manager Jack Ramsay took over as coach. He wanted to turn the 76ers into a running club, and his first move was to send Chamberlain to Los Angeles for guard Archie Clark, center Darrall Imhoff, and forward Jerry Chambers, plus cash. With Chamberlain, Elgin Baylor, and Jerry West on the same club, the league and the fans immediately classified the Lakers as the new superteam of the N.B.A. After all, Baylor and West had regularly led the Lakers into the playoff finals without winning the title, so the addition of the most powerful center in basketball filled the only weak spot on the team.

The N.B.A. not only had a new glamour team, but it had two new franchises and a transplanted old team. The Milwaukee Bucks and Phoenix Suns came into the league as expansion clubs, and the St. Louis Hawks moved to Atlanta, as owner Ben Kemer sold the club after helping found it in 1946 and then moving it from Buffalo to Tri-Cities to Milwaukee to St. Louis. The rival A.B.A. also moved a few franchises, but the new league failed to make much of a dent on the N.B.A. in terms of playing personnel. Coaches Alex Hannum of Philadelphia and Bill Sharman of San Francisco moved over to the A.B.A., but centers Elvin Hayes and Wes Unseld, the cream of the rookie class, signed with N.B.A. teams after enjoying a bidding war which drove pro basketball contracts to new heights.

Chamberlain, too, used the new league to boost his bargaining power, signing a four-year contract worth one million dollars. As the season progressed, Wilt's rebounding and defense made the Lakers a very tough club, but they were not the powerhouse that fans had expected. It took time for the other Lakers to get used to Wilt, Jerry West lost some time to injuries, and coach Butch Van Breda Kolff and Wilt had cool personal relations right from the start. The Lakers nevertheless logged a 55-27 record and easily copped the Western Division title.

The transplanted Hawks finished second in the West, seven games behind the Lakers. The return of Lou Hudson from military service bolstered the Hawks, but a salary dispute forced the trade of Lenny Wilkens to Seattle for Walt Hazzard, a deal which hurt the Hawks in the leadership department. The San Francisco Warriors came in a distant third, and the surprising San Diego Rockets took the final playoff spot with a respectable 37-45 record, thanks mostly to the league-leading 28.4 scoring of rookie Elvin Hayes.

The Chicago Bulls came in fifth and out of the playoffs, but started putting together the elements of a contending club; Dick Motta was the new coach, Tom Boerwinkle was the rookie center, and subs Bob Love and Bob Weiss came from Milwaukee in a minor deal. Seattle finished sixth despite Wilkens, and the new Phoenix club finished last despite solid seasons from Gale Goodrich and Dick Van Arsdale.

Last season's cellar club in the East, the Baltimore Bullets, shocked the league by shooting to the top of the division with a 57-25 record, the best in the N.B.A. The Bullets already had shooters in Earl (The Pearl) Monroe, Kevin Loughery, and Jack Marin, and Wes Unseld's rebounding and quick outlet passes instantly turned the Bullets into a dangerous fast-breaking team. Unseld won both the MVP and Rookie of the Year awards, and the Bullets became the first major league pro team to rocket from last to first place in one season.

The Philadelphia 76ers finished a close second, getting along fine without Chamberlain in their new wide open format. Billy Cunningham and Hal Greer handled the burden of the scoring, and not even a leg injury to Luke Jackson, who had succeeded Chamberlain at center, seriously disrupted the new pattern. Close behind in third place were the New York Knicks, who enjoyed a great second half of the season after getting Dave DeBusschere in December from the Detroit Pistons for Walt Bellamy and Howie Komives. The trade gave the Knicks one of the game's best all-around forwards, enabled Willis Reed to move back to his normal center position, and made room for Walt Frazier in the starting lineup. After the trade, the Knicks went 36-11 despite injuries which sidelined Cazzie Russell and Phil Jackson and reduced the bench to a skeleton crew.

Back in fourth place came the Boston Celtics, one year older and apparently no longer a power to be contended with; Bill Russell suffered from a bad knee, Sam Jones sat out a few games with a pulled groin muscle, and only the insertion of John Havlicek into the starting lineup late in the season pumped some semblance of the old spark back into the Celtics. The Cincinnati Royals and Detroit Pistons both had severe weaknesses up front and finished out of the playoffs along with the fledgling Milwaukee Bucks.

The playoffs went according to schedule in the West, with the Lakers emerging as divisional representatives in the championship series. The East, however, produced plenty of surprises, starting with the Baltimore-New York series. with starters Willis Reed, Dave DeBusschere, Bill Bradley, Walt Frazier, and Dick Barnett forced to play most of the game because of injuries to Russell and Jackson, the Knicks blitzed the Bullets with a pressing defense and sharp passing attack and eliminated the startled Baltimore squad with four straight wins. The Celtics, meanwhile, exercised some of their old-time playoff magic by kayoing Philadelphia in five games. The Eastern final matched the rising powers from New York against the experienced but aging powers from Boston. It went against logic, but somehow seemed normal, when the Celtics forced the Knicks into making errors, won the first two games to take command of the series, and closed it out in six .

For the second straight season, the Celtics finished out of first place in the East, yet made it to the championship final. So now the Celtics and Russell faced another crucial showdown with Wilt Chamberlain, this time in a Los Angeles uniform. The Lakers captured the first two games to move comfortably out in front, but the old pros from Boston took game three to stay in contention. The fourth game came down to two seconds left, with the Lakers leading 88-87; but at the buzzer, Sam Jones hit on an off-balance jumper to give the Celtics an 89-88 win.

The two clubs split the next two games, and the showdown seventh game shaped up as perhaps the final hurrah of the Boston dynasty. The Celtic old men ran from the opening whistle on, and while the Lakers made a move to catch up in the fourth period Wilt hurt his leg and left the game with five minutes left. Without the big man in the game, the Laker drive fell short, and the Celtics came away with a 108-106 win. This was it for the Celtic dynasty, the final championship for the dominant team of the sixties; Bill Russell and Sam Jones retired at this point, going out as unparalleled winners.

Use Name	Pos	Hgt	Wgt	Age	TOTAL G	Min	FG	FGA	%	FT	FTA	%	Reb	Ass	PF	DQ	Points	PER GAME Min	Reb	Ass	PF	Points
1968/69 N. B.A. — EASTERN DIVISION																						
BALTIMORE BULLETS	**57-25 .695**				**GENE SHUE**																	
Jack Marin	F-G	6'7	210	24	82	2710	505	1109	46	292	352	83	608	231	275	4	1302	33	7.4	2.8	3.4	15.9
Gus Johnson (knee injury)	F	6'6	235	30	49	1671	359	782	46	160	223	72	568	97	176	1	878	34	11.6	2.0	3.6	17.9
Wes Unseld	C	6'7	245	22	82	2970	427	897	48	277	458	60	1491	213	276	4	1131	36	18.2	2.6	3.4	13.8
Kevin Loughery	G	6'3	190	28	80	3135	717	1636	44	372	463	80	266	384	299	3	1806	39	3.3	4.8	3.7	22.6
Earl Monnoe	G	6'3	190	24	80	3075	809	1837	44	447	582	77	280	392	261	1	2065	38	3.5	4.9	3.3	25.8
Ray Scott	F-C	6'9	225	30	82	2168	386	929	42	195	257	76	722	133	212	1	967	26	8.8	1.6	2.6	11.8
Leroy Ellis	F	6'10	225	28	80	1603	229	527	43	117	155	75	510	73	168	0	575	20	6.4	0.9	2.1	7.2
Barry Orms	G	6'3	190	22	64	916	76	246	31	29	60	48	158	49	155	3	181	14	2.5	0.8	2.4	2.8
Ed Manning	F	6'7	215	24	63	727	129	288	45	35	54	65	246	21	120	0	293	12	3.9	0.3	1.9	4.7
John Barnhill	G	6'1	180	25	30	504	76	175	43	39	65	60	53	71	63	0	191	17	1.8	2.4	2.1	6.4
Bob Quick (MS)	G	6'5	215	22	28	154	30	73	41	27	44	61	25	12	14	0	87	6	0.9	0.4	0.5	3.1
Tom Workman	F	6'7	230	24	21	86	22	54	41	9	15	60	27	2	16	0	53	4	1.3	0.1	0.8	2.5
Bob Ferry	C	6'8	235	31	7	36	5	14	36	3	6	50	9	4	3	0	13	5	1.3	0.6	0.4	1.9
PHILADELPHIA 76ers	**55—27 .671**				**JACK RAMSAY**																	
Chet Waiker	F	6'6	215	28	82	2752	554	1145	48	369	459	80	640	144	244	0	1477	34	7.8	1.8	3.0	18.0
Bilh Cunningham	F	6'7	220	25	82	3345	739	1736	43	556	754	74	1050	287	329	10	2034	41	12.8	3.5	4.0	24.8
Luke Jackson (leg injury)	C	6'9	240	27	25	840	145	332	44	69	97	71	286	54	102	3	359	34	11.4	2.2	4.1	14.4
Hal Greer	G	6'3	176	32	82	3311	732	1595	46	432	543	80	435	414	294	8	1896	40	5.3	5.0	3.6	23.1
Wally Jones	G	6'2	180	26	81	2340	432	1005	43	207	256	81	251	292	280	5	1071	29	3.1	3.6	3.5	13.2
Darrall Imhoff	C	6'10	220	30	82	2360	279	593	47	194	325	60	792	218	310	12	752	29	9.7	2.7	3.8	9.2
Archie Clark	G	6'2	175	27	82	2144	444	928	48	219	314	70	265	296	188	1	1107	26	3.2	3.6	2.3	13.5
Matt Guokas	F-G	6'5	200	24	72	838	92	216	43	54	81	67	94	104	121	1	238	12	1.3	1.4	1.7	3.3
Johnny Green	F	6'5	200	35	74	795	146	282	52	57	125	46	330	47	110	1	349	11	4.5	0.6	1.5	4.7
George Wiison (from Fnoe)	C	6'8	240	26	38	552	81	182	45	60	84	71	216	32	87	1	222	15	5.7	0.8	2.3	5.8
Shaler Halimon	F	6'6	200	23	50	350	88	196	45	10	32	31	86	18	34	0	186	7	1.7	0.4	0.7	3.7
Craig Raymond	C	6'11	235	23	27	177	22	64	34	11	17	65	68	8	46	2	55	7	2.5	0.3	1.7	2.0
Jerry Chambers - military service																						
NEW YORK KNICKERBOCKERS	**54-28 .659**				**RED HOLZMAN**																	
Bill Bradley	F-G	6'5	205	25	82	2413	407	948	43	206	253	81	350	302	295	4	1020	29	4.3	3.7	3.6	12.4
Dave DeBusschere (from Det)	F	6'6	230	28	47	1851	317	717	44	135	198	68	535	128	179	5	769	39	11.4	2.7	3.8	16.4
Willis Reed	C-F	6'9	238	26	82	3108	704	1351	52	325	435	75	1191	190	314	7	1733	38	14.5	2.3	3.8	21.1
Dick Barnett	G	6'4	190	32	82	2953	565	1220	46	312	403	77	251	291	239	4	1442	36	3.1	3.5	2.9	17.6
Walt Fraaier	G	6'4	202	23	80	2949	531	1052	50	341	457	75	499	635	245	2	1403	37	6.2	7.9	3.1	17.5
Cazzie Russell (BN)	F-G	6'5	218	24	50	1645	362	804	45	191	240	80	209	115	140	1	915	33	4.2	2.3	2.8	18.3
Walt Bellamy (to Det)	C	6'11	245	29	35	1136	204	402	51	125	202	62	385	77	123	1	533	32	11.0	2.2	3.5	15.2
Phil Jackson (back injury)	F	6'8	220	23	47	924	126	294	43	80	119	67	246	43	168	6	332	20	5.2	0.9	3.6	7.1
Howie Komives (to Det)	G	6'1	185	27	32	836	107	309	35	73	86	85	95	137	96	0	287	26	3.0	4.3	3.0	9.0
Nate Bowman	C	6'10	230	25	67	607	82	226	36	29	61	48	220	53	142	4	193	9	3.3	0.8	2.1	2.9
Don May	F	6'4	220	22	48	560	81	223	36	42	58	72	114	35	64	0	204	12	2.4	0.7	1.3	4.3
Mike Riordan	G	6'4	200	23	54	397	49	144	34	28	42	67	57	46	93	1	126	7	1.1	0.9	1.7	2.3
Bill Hosket	F	6'8	225	22	50	351	53	123	43	24	42	57	94	19	77	0	130	7	1.9	0.4	1.5	2.6
Dave Stallworth - illness																						
BOSTON CELTICS	**48-34 .585**				**BILL RUSSELL**																	
Satch Sanders	F	6'6	210	30	82	2184	364	847	43	187	255	73	574	110	293	9	915	27	7.0	1.3	3.6	11.2
Bailey Howell	F	6'7	220	31	78	2527	612	1257	49	313	426	73	685	137	285	3	1537	32	8.8	1.8	3.7	19.7
Bill Russell (KJ)	C	6'10	220	34	77	3291	279	645	43	204	388	53	1484	374	231	2	762	43	19.3	4.9	3.0	9.9
John Havlicek	G-F	6'5	205	28	82	3174	692	1709	40	387	496	78	570	441	247	0	1771	39	7.0	5.4	3.0	21.6
Larry Siegfried	G	6'3	192	29	79	2560	392	1031	38	336	389	86	282	370	222	0	1120	32	3.6	4.7	2.8	14.2
Sam Jones (injury)	G	6'4	205	35	70	1820	496	1103	45	148	189	78	265	182	121	0	1140	26	3.8	2.6	1.7	16.3
Don Nelson	F	6'6	210	28	82	1773	374	771	49	201	259	78	458	92	198	2	949	22	5.6	1.1	2.4	11.6
Em Bryant	G	6'1	175	30	80	1388	197	488	40	65	100	65	192	176	264	9	459	17	2.4	2.2	3.3	5.7
Jim Barnes (from Chi)	C-F	6'8	240	27	49	595	92	202	46	65	92	71	194	27	107	2	249	12	4.0	0.6	2.2	5.1
Don Chaney (MS)	G	6'5	210	22	20	209	36	113	32	8	20	40	46	19	32	0	80	10	2.3	1.0	1.6	4.0
Rich Johnson	C	6'9	210	22	31	163	29	76	38	11	23	48	52	7	40	0	69	5	1.7	0.2	1.3	2.2
Mal Graham (IL)	G	6'1	185	23	22	103	13	55	24	11	14	79	24	14	27	0	37	5	1.1	0.6	1.2	1.7
Bud Olsen (to Det)	F	6'8	220	28	7	43	7	19	37	0	6	0	14	4	6	0	14	6	2.0	0.6	0.9	2.0

Use Name	Pos	Hgt	Wgt	Age	TOTAL G	Min	FG	FGA	%	FT	FTA	%	Reb	Ass	PF	DQ	Points	PER GAME Min	Reb	Ass	PF	Points
1968/69 N.B.A. - EASTERN DIVISION (continued)																						
CINCINNATI ROYALS	**41-41 .500**				**ED JUCKER**																	
Fred Hetzel (from Mil)	F	6'8	230	26	31	685	140	287	49	88	105	84	140	29	94	3	368	22	4.5	0.9	3.0	11.9
Jerry Lucas	F	6'8	235	28	74	3075	555	1007	55	247	327	76	1360	306	206	0	1357	42	18.4	4.1	2.8	18.3
Connie Dierking	C	6'9	235	32	82	2540	546	1232	44	243	319	76	739	222	305	9	1335	31	9.0	2.7	3.7	16.3
Tom Van Arsdale	G-F	6'5	215	25	77	3059	547	1233	44	398	533	75	356	208	300	6	1492	40	4.6	2.7	3.9	19.4
Oscar Robertson	G	6'5	220	30	79	3461	656	1351	49	**643**	767	84	502	**772**	231	2	1955	44	6.4	**9.8**	2.9	24.7
John Tresvant (to Sea)	F	6'7	220	29	51	1681	239	531	45	130	223	58	419	103	193	5	608	33	8.2	2.0	3.8	11.9
Adrian Smith	G	6'1	185	32	73	1336	243	562	43	217	269	81	105	127	166	1	703	18	1.4	1.7	2.3	9.6
Walt Wesley	C	6'11	220	23	82	1334	245	534	46	134	207	65	403	47	191	0	624	16	4.9	0.6	2.3	7.6
Bill Dinwiddie	F	6'7	220	25	69	1028	124	352	35	45	87	52	242	55	146	0	293	15	3.5	0.8	2.1	4.2
Al Tucker (from Sea)	F	6'8	190	25	28	626	126	265	48	49	73	67	122	19	75	2	301	22	4.4	0.7	2.7	10.8
Fred Foster	F	6'5	210	22	56	497	74	193	38	43	66	65	61	36	49	0	191	9	1.1	0.6	0.9	3.4
Pat Frmk	G	6'4	195	23	48	363	50	147	34	23	29	79	41	55	54	1	123	8	0.9	1.1	1.1	2.6
Don Smith (to Mil)	F-C	6'9	235	22	20	108	18	43	42	2	7	29	31	4	17	0	38	5	1.6	0.2	0.9	1.9
Doug Sims	F	6'7	195	25	4	12	2	5	40	0	0	—	4	0	4	0	4	3	1.0	0.0	1.0	1.0
DETROIT PISTONS	**32-50 .390**				**DONNIE BUTCHER (10-12 .455), PAUL SEYMOUR (22-38 .367)**																	
Happy Hairston	F	6'7	225	26	81	2889	530	1131	47	404	553	73	959	109	255	3	1464	36	11.8	1.3	3.1	18.1
McCoy McLemore (from Phoe)	F	6'7	235	26	50	910	141	356	40	84	104	81	236	44	113	3	366	18	4.7	0.9	2.3	7.3
Walt Bellamy (from NY)	C	6'11	245	29	53	2023	359	701	51	276	416	66	716	99	197	4	994	38	13.5	1.9	3.7	18.8
Dave Bing	G	6'3	180	25	77	3039	678	1594	43	444	623	71	382	546	256	3	1800	39	5.0	7.1	3.3	23.4
Howie Komives (from NYJ	G	6'1	185	27	53	1726	272	665	41	138	178	78	204	266	178	1	682	33	3.8	5.0	3.4	12.9
Eddie Miles	G-F	6'4	196	28	80	2252	441	983	45	182	273	67	283	180	201	0	1064	28	3.5	2.3	2.5	13.3
Jimmy Walker	G	6'3	205	24	69	1639	312	670	47	182	229	79	157	221	172	1	806	24	2.3	3.2	2.5	11.7
Otto Moore	C-F	6'11	205	22	74	1605	241	544	44	88	.168	52	524	68	182	2	570	22	7.1	0.9	2.5	7.7
Terry Dischinger	F	6'7	208	28	75	1456	264	513	51	130	178	73	323	93	230	5	658	19	4.3	1.2	3.1	8.8
Dave DeBusschere (to NY)	F	6'6	230	28	29	1092	189	423	45	94	130	72	353	63	111	1	472	38	12.2	2.2	3.8	16.3
Jim Fox (to Phoe)	C	6'10	230	25	25	375	45	96	47	34	53	64	139	23	56	1	124	15	5.6	0.9	2.2	5.0
Dave Gambee (from Mil)	F	6'6	220	31	25	302	60	142	42	49	62	79	78	15	60	0	169	12	3.1	0.6	2.4	6.8
Sonny Dove	F	6'8	198	23	29	236	47	100	47	24	36	67	62	12	49	0	118	8	2.1	0.4	1.7	4.1
Rich Niemann (to Mil)	C	7'	245	22	16	123	20	47	43	8	10	80	41	9	30	0	48	8	2.6	0.6	1.9	3.0
Bud Olsen (from Bos)	F	6'8	220	28	10	70	8	23	35	4	12	33	11	7	8	0	20	7	1.1	0.7	0.8	2.0
Cliff Williams	G	6'3	180	23	3	18	2	9	22	0	0	—	3	2	7	0	4	6	1.0	0.7	2.3	1.3
George Carter - military service																						
MILWAUKEE BUCKS	**27-55 .329**				**LARRY COSTELLO**																	
Greg Smith	F	6'5	195	21	79	2207	276	613	45	91	155	59	804	137	264	12	643	28	10.2	1.7	3.3	8.1
Ien Chappell	F	6'8	240	27	80	2207	459	1011	45	250	339	74	637	95	247	3	1168	28	8.0	1.2	3.1	14.6
Wayne Embry	C	6'8	255	31	78	2355	382	894	43	259	390	66	672	149	302	8	1023	30	8.6	1.9	3.9	13.1
Jon McGlocklin	G	6'5	205	25	80	2888	662	1358	49	246	292	84	343	312	186	1	1570	36	4.3	3.9	2.3	19.6
Flynn Robinson (from Chi)	G	6'1	185	27	65	2066	501	1149	44	317	377	84	237	320	209	6	1319	32	3.6	4.9	3.2	20.3
Guy Rodgers	G	6'	190	33	81	2157	325	862	38	184	232	79	226	561	207	2	834	27	2.8	6.9	2.6	10.3
Fred Hetzel (to Cin)	F	6'8	230	26	53	1591	316	760	42	211	252	84	473	83	193	6	843	30	8.9	1.6	3.6	15.9
Dick Cunningham	C	6'10	240	22	77	1236	141	332	42	69	106	65	438	58	166	2	351	16	5.7	0.8	2.2	4.6
Don Smith (from Cin)	F-C	6'9	235	22	29	837	126	347	36	68	106	64	378	33	98	3	320	29	13.0	1.1	3.4	11.0
Sam Williams	G	6'3	180	23	55	628	78	228	34	72	134	54	109	61	106	1	228	11	2.0	1.1	1.9	4.1
Dave Gambee (to Det)	F	6'6	220	31	34	624	150	323	46	110	133	83	179	32	99	4	410	18	5.3	0.9	2.9	12.1
Bob Weiss (to Chi)	G	6'2	180	26	15	242	36	114	32	27	34	79	27	27	24	1	99	16	1.8	1.8	1.6	6.6
Bob Love (to Chi)	F	6'8	215	26	14	227	39	106	37	29	38	76	64	3	22	0	107	16	4.6	0.2	1.6	7.6
Charlie Paulk (MS)	F	6'8	220	24	17	217	19	84	23	13	23	57	78	3	26	0	51	13	4.6	0.2	1.5	3.0
Rich Neimann (from Det)	C	7'	245	22	18	149	24	59	41	11	15	73	59	7	31	1	59	8	3.3	0.4	1.7	3.3
Jay Miller(to LA-A)	F	6'5	210	25	3	27	2	10	20	5	7	71	2	0	4	0	9	9	0.7	0.0	1.3	3.0
Bob Warlick (to Phoe)	G	6'5	205	27	3	22	1	8	13	4	5	80	1	1	3	0	6	7	0.3	0.3	1.0	2.0
1968/69 N.B.A. - WESTERN DIVISION																						
LOS ANGELES LAKERS	**55-27 .671**				**BUTCH VAN BREDA KOLFF**																	
Elgin Baylor	F	6'5	225	34	76	3064	730	1632	45	421	567	74	805	408	204	0	1881	40	10.6	5.4	2.7	24.8
Mel Counts	F-C	7'	230	27	77	1866	390	867	45	178	221	81	600	109	223	5	958	24	7.8	1.4	2.9	12.4
Wilt Chamberlain	C	7'1	275	32	81	3669	641	1099	**58**	382	**857**	45	**1712**	366	142	0	1664	**45**	**21.1**	4.5	1.8	20.5
Jerry West (injury)	G	6'3	180	30	61	2394	545	1156	47	490	597	82	262	423	156	1	1580	39	4.3	6.9	2.6	25.9
Johnny Egan	G	5'11	180	29	82	1805	246	597	41	204	240	85	147	215	206	1	696	22	1.8	2.6	2.5	8.5
Keith Erickson	G-F	6'5	200	24	77	1974	264	629	42	120	175	69	308	194	222	6	648	26	4.0	2.5	2.9	8.4
Freddie Crawford	G	6'4	190	27	81	1690	211	454	46	83	154	54	215	154	224	1	505	21	2.7	1.9	2.8	6.2
Tom Hawkins	F	6'5	210	32	74	1507	230	461	50	62	151	41	266	81	168	1	522	20	3.6	1.1	2.3	7.1
Bill Hewitt	F	6'7	210	24	75	1455	239	528	45	61	106	58	332	76	139	1	539	19	4.4	1.0	1.9	7.2
Cliff Anderson	G	6'4	200	24	35	289	44	108	41	47	82	57	44	31	58	0	135	8	1.3	0.9	1.7	3.9
Jay Carty	F	6'8	230	27	28	192	34	89	38	8	11	73	58	11	31	0	76	7	2.1	0.4	1.1	2.7

1968/69 N.B.A. — WESTERN DIVISION (continued)

Use Name	Pos	Hgt	Wgt	Age	G	Min	FG	FGA	%	FT	FTA	%	Reb	Ass	PF	DQ	Points	Min	Reb	Ass	PF	Points
					TOTAL													PER GAME				
ATLANTA HAWKS	**48-34 .585**				**RICHIE GUERIN**																	
Lou Hudson	F-G	6'5	220	24	81	2869	716	1455	49	338	435	78	533	216	248	0	1770	35	6.6	2.7	3.1	21.9
Bill Bridges	F	6'6	235	29	80	2930	351	775	45	239	353	68	1132	298	290	3	941	37	14.2	3.7	3.6	11.8
Zelmo Beaty	C	6'9	240	29	72	2578	588	1251	47	370	506	73	798	131	272	7	1546	36	11.1	1.8	3.8	21.5
Joe Caldwell	G-F	6'5	205	27	81	2720	561	1106	51	159	296	54	303	320	231	1	1281	34	3.7	4.0	2.9	15.8
Walt Hazzard	G	6'2	190	26	80	2420	345	869	40	208	294	71	266	474	264	6	898	30	3.3	5.9	3.3	11.2
Don Ohl	G	6'3	190	32	76	1995	385	901	43	147	208	71	170	221	232	5	917	26	2.2	2.9	3.1	12.1
Paul Silas	F	6'7	235	25	79	1853	241	575	42	204	333	61	745	140	166	0	686	23	9.4	1.8	2.1	8.7
Jim Davis	C	6'9	235	27	78	1367	265	568	47	154	231	67	529	97	239	6	684	18	6.8	1.2	3.1	8.8
Richie Guerin	G	6'4	210	36	27	472	47	111	42	57	74	77	59	99	66	0	151	17	2.2	3.7	2.4	5.6
Skip Harlicka (MS)	G	6'1	185	22	26	218	41	90	46	24	31	77	16	37	29	0	106	8	0.6	1.4	1.1	4.1
Dennis Hamilton	F	6'8	210	24	25	141	37	67	55	2	5	40	29	8	19	0	76	6	1.2	0.3	0.8	3.0
George Lehmann (to LA-A)	G	6'3	190	26	11	138	26	67	39	8	12	67	9	27	18	0	60	13	0.8	2.5	1.6	5.5
Dwight Waller	F	6'7	230	23	11	29	2	9	22	3	7	43	10	1	8	0	7	3	0.9	0.1	0.7	0.6
SAN FRANCISCO WARRIORS	**41-41 .500**				**GEORGE LEE**																	
Rudy LaRusso	F	6'7	230	31	75	2782	553	1349	41	444	559	79	624	159	268	9	1550	37	8.3	2.1	3.6	20.7
Clyde Lee (ankle injury)	F-C	6'10	205	24	65	2237	268	674	40	160	256	63	897	82	225	1	696	34	13.8	1.3	3.5	10.7
Nate Thurmond	C	6'11	235	27	71	3208	571	1394	41	382	621	62	1402	253	171	0	1524	45	19.7	3.6	2.4	21.5
Jeff Mullins	G	6'4	200	26	78	2916	697	1517	46	381	452	84	460	339	251	4	1775	37	5.9	4.3	3.2	22.8
Al Attles	G	6'2	180	32	51	1516	162	359	45	95	149	64	181	306	183	3	419	30	3.5	6.0	3.6	8.2
Joe Ellis	F-G	6'6	175	24	74	1731	371	939	40	147	201	73	481	130	258	13	889	23	6.5	1.8	3.5	12.0
Bill Turner	F	6'7	220	24	79	1486	222	535	41	175	230	76	380	67	231	6	619	19	4.8	0.8	2.9	7.8
Ron Williams	G	6'3	190	24	75	1472	238	567	42	109	142	77	178	247	176	3	585	20	2.4	3.3	2.3	7.8
Jim King (groin injury)	G	6'2	175	27	46	1010	137	394	35	78	108	72	120	123	99	1	352	22	2.6	2.7	2.2	7.7
Bobby Lewis	G	6'3	185	23	62	756	113	290	39	83	113	73	114	76	117	0	309	12	1.8	1.2	1.9	5.0
Dale Schlueter	C	6'10	226	23	31	559	68	157	43	45	82	55	216	30	81	3	181	18	7.0	1.0	2.6	5.8
Bob Allen	F	6'9	205	22	27	232	14	43	33	20	36	56	56	10	27	0	48	9	2.1	0.4	1.0	1.8
SAN DIEGO ROCKETS	**37-45 .451**				**JACK McMAHON**																	
Don Kojis	F	6'4	215	29	81	3130	687	1582	43	446	596	75	776	214	303	6	1820	39	9.6	2.6	3.7	22.5
John Block	F	6'10	218	24	78	2489	448	1061	42	299	400	75	703	141	249	0	1195	32	9.0	1.8	3.2	15.3
Elvin Hayes	C	6'9	235	23	82	**3695**	**930**	**2082**	45	467	746	63	1406	113	266	2	**2327**	45	17.1	1.4	3.2	**28.4**
Jim Barnett	G	6'4	180	24	80	2346	465	1093	43	233	310	75	362	339	240	2	1163	29	4.5	4.2	3.0	14.5
Hambone Williams	G	6'2	185	29	79	1987	227	592	38	105	149	70	364	524	238	0	559	25	4.6	6.6	3.0	7.1
Toby Kimball	F	6'8	220	26	76	1680	239	537	45	117	250	47	669	90	216	6	595	22	8.8	1.2	2.8	7.8
Rick Adelman	G	6'1	178	22	77	1448	177	449	39	131	204	64	216	238	158	1	485	19	2.8	3.1	2.1	6.3
Stu Lantz	G	6'3	175	22	73	1378	220	482	46	129	167	77	236	99	178	0	569	19	3.2	1.4	2.4	7.8
Pat Riley (injury)	G-F	6'4	208	23	56	1027	202	498	41	90	134	67	112	136	146	1	494	18	2.0	2.4	2.6	8.8
Henry Finkel	C	7'	240	26	35	332	49	111	44	31	41	76	107	21	53	1	129	9	3.1	0.6	1.5	3.7
John Trapp	F	6'7	215	23	25	142	29	80	36	19	29	66	49	5	38	0	77	6	2.0	0.2	1.5	3.1
Harry Barnes	F	6'3	205	23	22	126	18	64	28	7	13	54	26	5	25	0	43	6	1.2	0.2	1.1	2.0
CHICAGO BULLS	**33-49 .402**				**DICK MOTTA**																	
Jim Washington	F	6'7	215	25	80	2705	440	1023	43	241	356	68	847	104	226	0	1121	34	10.6	1.3	2.8	14.0
Bob Boozer	F	6'8	225	31	79	2872	661	1375	48	394	489	81	614	156	218	2	1716	36	7.8	2.0	2.8	21.7
Tom Boerwinkle	C	7'	265	23	80	2365	318	831	38	145	222	65	889	178	317	11	781	30	11.1	2.2	4.0	9.8
Jerry Sloan	G	6'6	200	26	78	2939	488	1170	42	333	447	74	619	276	313	6	1309	38	7.9	3.5	4.0	16.8
Clem Haskins	G	6'3	195	24	79	2874	537	1275	42	282	361	78	359	306	230	0	1356	36	4.5	3.9	2.9	17.2
Barry Clemens	F	6'7	210	26	75	1444	235	628	37	82	125	66	318	125	163	1	552	19	4.2	1.7	2.2	7.4
Bob Weiss (from Mil)	G	6'2	180	26	62	1236	153	385	40	101	126	80	135	172	150	0	407	20	2.2	2.8	2.4	6.6
Dave Newmark	C	7'	240	22	81	1159	185	475	39	86	139	62	347	58	205	7	456	14	4.3	0.7	2.5	5.6
Erwin Mueller (to Sea)	F-C	6'8	240	24	52	872	75	224	33	46	90	51	193	124	98	1	196	17	3.7	2.4	1.9	3.8
Flynn Robinson (to Mil)	G	6'1	185	27	18	550	124	293	42	95	114	83	69	57	52	1	343	31	3.8	3.2	2.9	19.1
Bob Love (from Mil)	F	6'8	215	26	35	315	69	166	42	42	58	72	86	14	37	0	180	9	2.5	0.4	1.1	5.1
Loy Petersen	G	6'5	205	23	38	299	44	109	40	19	27	70	41	25	39	0	107	8	1.1	0.7	1.0	2.8
Jim Barnes (to Bos)	F-C	6'8	240	27	10	111	23	59	39	10	19	53	30	1	15	0	56	11	3.0	0.1	1.5	5.6
Ken Wilburn (to MinA)	F	6'6	205	24	4	14	3	8	38	1	4	25	3	1	1	0	7	4	0.8	0.3	0.3	1.8

Use Name	Pos	Hgt	Wgt	Age	G	Min	FG	FGA	%	FT	FTA	%	Reb	Ass	PF	DQ	Points	Min	Reb	Ass	PF	Points
					TOTAL													PER GAME				
1968/69 N.B.A. — WESTERN DIVISION (continued)																						
SEATTLE SUPERSONICS	**30-52 .366**				**AL BIANCHI**																	
Tom Meschery	F	6'6	215	30	82	2673	462	1019	45	220	299	74	822	194	304	7	1144	33	10.0	2.4	3.7	14.0
John Tresvant (from Cin)	F	6'7	220	29	26	801	141	289	49	72	107	67	267	63	107	4	354	31	10.3	2.4	4.1	13.6
Bob Rule	C	6'9	250	24	82	3104	776	1655	47	413	606	68	941	141	322	8	1965	38	11.5	1.7	3.9	24.0
Art Harris	G	6'4	186	21	80	2556	416	1054	39	161	251	64	301	258	326	**14**	993	32	3.8	3.2	**4.1**	12.4
Lenny Wilkens	G	6'1	185	31	82	3463	644	1462	44	547	710	77	511	674	294	8	1835	42	6.2	8.2	3.6	22.4
Bob Kauffman	C-F	6'8	240	22	82	1660	219	496	44	203	289	70	484	83	252	8	641	20	5.9	1.0	3.1	7.8
Al Tucker (to Cin)	F	6'8	190	25	56	1259	235	544	43	109	171	64	317	55	111	0	579	22	5.7	1.0	2.0	10.3
Joe Kennedy	F	6'6	210	21	72	1241	174	411	42	98	124	79	241	60	158	2	446	17	3.3	0.8	2.2	6.2
Tommy Kron	G	6'5	200	25	76	1124	146	372	39	96	137	70	212	191	179	2	388	15	2.8	2.5	2.4	5.1
Rod Thorn (knee injury)	G	6'4	195	27	29	567	131	283	46	71	97	73	83	80	58	0	333	20	2.9	2.8	2.0	11.5
Erwin Mueller (from Chi)	F-C	6'8	240	24	26	483	69	160	43	43	72	60	104	62	45	0	181	19	4.0	2.4	1.7	7.0
Dorie Murrey (shoulder injury)	F	6'8	220	25	38	465	75	194	39	62	97	64	149	21	81	1	212	12	3.9	0.6	2.1	5.6
Al Hairston	G	6'1	170	23	39	274	38	114	33	8	14	57	36	38	35	0	84	7	0.9	1.0	0.9	2.2
Plummer Lott	F	6'5	210	23	23	160	17	66	26	2	5	40	30	7	9	0	36	7	1.3	0.3	0.4	1.6
PNOENIX SUNS	**16-66 .195**				**JONNNY KERR**																	
Dick Van Arsdale	F-G	6'5	210	25	80	3388	612	1386	44	454	644	70	548	385	245	2	1678	42	6.9	4.8	3.1	21.0
Gary Gregor	F	6'7	235	23	80	2182	400	963	42	85	131	65	711	96	249	2	885	27	8.9	1.2	3.1	11.1
Jim Fox (from Det)	C	6~1(	230	25	51	1979	273	581	47	157	214	73	679	143	210	5	703	39	13.3	2.8	4.1	13.8
Dick Snyder	G-F	6'5	210	24	81	2108	399	846	47	185	255	73	328	211	213	2	983	26	4.0	2.6	2.6	12.1
Gail Goodrich	G	6'1	175	25	81	3236	718	1746	41	495	663	75	437	518	253	3	1931	40	5.4	6.4	3.1	23.8
Stan McKenzie	F	6'5	210	24	80	1569	264	618	43	219	287	76	251	123	191	3	747	20	3.1	1.5	2.4	9.3
Neil Johnson	F-C	6'7	225	25	80	1319	177	368	48	110	177	62	396	134	214	3	464	16	5.0	1.7	2.7	5.8
George Wilson (ankle injury, to Phi)	C	6'8	240	26	41	1294	191	481	40	93	151	62	505	76	145	4	475	32	12.3	1.9	3.5	11.6
Dave Lattin (broken hand)	C-F	6'7	230	25	68	987	150	366	41	109	172	63	323	48	163	5	409	15	4.8	0.7	2.4	6.0
Bob Warlick (from Mil)	G	6'5	205	27	63	975	212	501	42	83	137	61	151	131	119	0	507	15	2.4	2.1	1.9	8.0
McCoy McLemore (to Det	F	6'7	235	26	31	710	141	366	39	85	110	77	168	50	73	1	367	23	5.4	1.6	2.4	11.8
Rod Knowles (to NY-A)	C	6'9	215	22	8	40	4	14	29	1	3	33	9	0	10	0	9	5	1.1	0.0	1.3	1.1
Ed Biedenbach	G	6'1	175	23	7	18	0	6	0	4	6	67	2	3	1	0	4	3	0.3	0.4	0.1	0.6
John Wetzel - military service																						
Bill Melchionni - holdout																						
1968/69 N.B.A. - PLAYOFFS																						
BOSTON CELTICS	**BILL RUSSELL**						defeated Philadelphia 4-1; 114-100, H134-103, 125-118, H116-119, 93-90															
							defeated New York 4-2; 108-100, H112-97, 91-101, H97-96, 104-112, H106-105															
							defeated Los Angeles 4-3, 118-120, 112-118, H111-105, H89-88, 104-117, H99-90, 108-106															
John Havlicek	F-G	6'5	205	28	18	**850**	170	382	45	118	138	**86**	179	100	58	2	458	**47**	9.9	5.6	3.2	25.4
Bailey Howell	F	6'7	220	31	18	551	112	229	49	46	64	72	118	19	**84**	**3**	270	31	6.6	1.1	4.7	15.0
Bill Russell	C	6'10	220	34	18	829	77	182	42	41	81	51	369	98	65	1	195	46	20.5	5.4	3.6	10.8
Sam Jones	G	6'4	205	35	18	514	124	296	42	55	69	80	58	37	45	1	303	29	3.2	2.1	2.5	16.8
Em Bryant	G	6'1	175	30	18	607	79	193	41	40	53	75	88	54	75	0	198	34	4.9	3.0	4.2	11.0
Larry Siegfried	G	6'3	192	29	18	392	72	172	42	55	70	79	38	46	60	1	199	22	2.1	2.6	3.3	11.1
Don Nelson	F	6'6	210	28	18	348	87	168	52	50	60	83	83	21	51	0	224	19	4.6	1.2	2.8	12.4
Satch Sanders	F	6'6	210	30	15	197	32	73	44	23	31	74	48	7	40	0	87	13	3.2	0.5	2.7	5.8
Don Chaney	G	6'5	210	22	7	25	1	6	17	3	4	75	4	0	7	0	5	4	0.6	0.0	1.0	0.7
Rich Johnson	C	6'9	210	22	2	4	1	1	100	0	0	—	2	0	0	0	2	2	1.0	0.0	0.0	1.0
Mal Graham (IL)	G	6'1	185	23	2	3	0	2	0	0	0	—	0	1	0	0	0	2	0.0	0.5	0.0	0.0
LOS ANGELES LAKERS	**B. VAN BREDA KOLFF**						defeated San Francisco 4-2; H94-99, H101-107, 115-98, 103-88, H103-98, 118-78															
							defeated Atlanta 4-1; H95-93, H104-102, 86-99, 100-85, H104-96															
							lost to Boston 3-4; H120-118, H118-112, 105-111, 88-89, H117-104, 90-99, H106-108															
Elgin Baylor	F	6'5	225	34	18	640	107	278	38	63	100	63	166	74	56	0	277	36	9.2	4.1	3.1	15.4
Mel Counts	F-C	7'	230	27	18	442	74	192	39	54	71	76	143	26	67	1	202	25	7.9	1.4	3.7	11.2
WiltChamberlain	C	7'1	275	32	18	832	96	176	**55**	58	148	39	**444**	46	46	0	250	46	**24.7**	2.6	2.6	13.9
Jerry West	G	6'3	180	30	18	757	**196**	**423**	46	**164**	**204**	80	71	**135**	52	1	**556**	42	3.9	7.5	2.9	**30.9**
Johnny Egan	G	5'11	180	29	18	571	94	217	43	63	80	79	44	70	55	0	251	32	2.4	3.9	3.1	13.9
Keith Erickson	G-F	6'5	200	24	18	446	56	142	39	15	25	60	86	40	64	2	127	25	4.8	2.2	3.6	7.1
Bill Hewitt	F	6'7	210	24	15	412	61	151	40	18	29	62	78	17	40	0	140	27	5.2	1.1	2.7	9.3
Tom Hawkins	F	6'5	210	32	14	180	24	50	48	7	18	39	40	7	32	0	55	13	2.9	0.5	2.3	3.9
Freddie Crawford	G	6'4	190	27	5	20	2	4	50	0	1	0	3	3	4	0	4	4	0.6	0.6	0.8	0.8
Cliff Anderson	G	6'4	200	24	3	10	2	5	40	0	0	—	1	0	1	0	4	3	0.3	0.0	0.3	1.3
Jay Carry	F	6'8	230	27	3	10	0	2	0	1	3	33	2	1	3	0	1	3	0.7	0.3	1.0	0.3
NEW YORK KNICKERBOCKERS	**RED HOLZMAN**						defeated Baltimore 4-0; 113-101, H107-91, 119-116, H115-108															
							lost to Boston 2-4; H100-108, 97-112, H101-91, 96-97, H112-104, 105-106															
Bill Bradley	F-G	6'5	205	25	10	419	65	141	46	30	39	77	73	40	38	1	160	42	7.3	4.0	3.8	16.0
Dave DeBusschere	F	6'6	230	28	10	419	61	174	35	41	50	82	148	33	43	0	163	42	14.8	3.3	4.3	16.3
Willis Reed	C-F	6'9	238	26	10	429	101	198	51	55	70	79	141	19	40	1	257	43	14.1	1.9	4.0	25.7
Dick Barnett	G	6'4	190	32	10	402	65	163	40	37	54	69	35	27	32	0	167	40	3.5	2.7	3.2	16.7
Walt Frazier	G	6'4	202	23	10	415	89	177	50	34	57	60	74	91	30	0	212	42	7.4	**9.1**	3.0	21.2
Mike Riordan	G	6'4	200	23	10	108	20	39	51	12	16	75	17	3	27	0	52	11	1.7	0.3	2.7	5.2
Don May	F	6'4	220	22	9	88	9	30	30	7	9	78	23	8	7	0	25	10	2.6	0.9	0.8	2.8
Nate Bowman	C	6'10	230	25	10	62	4	15	27	3	3	100	32	3	16	0	11	6	3.2	0.3	1.6	1.1
Cazzie Russell	F-G	6'5	218	24	5	36	5	21	24	2	2	100	5	1	4	0	12	7	1.0	0.2	0.8	2.4
Bill Hosket	F	6'8	225	22	4	22	3	6	50	0	1	0	7	2	3	0	6	6	1.8	0.5	0.8	1.5
Dave Stallworth - illness Phil Jackson - back injury																						

1968/69 N.B.A. - PLAYOFFS (continued)

Use Name	Pos	Hgt	Wgt	Age	G	Min	FG	FGA	%	FT	FTA	%	Reb	Ass	PF	DQ	Points	Min (per game)	Reb (per game)	Ass (per game)	PF (per game)	Points (per game)
ATLANTA HAWKS	**RICHIE GUERIN**				defeated San Diego 4-2; H107-98, H116-114, 97-104, 112-114, H112-101, 108-106																	
					lost to Los Angeles 1-4; 93-95, 102-104, H99-86, H85-100, 96-104																	
Joe Caldwell	F-G	6'5	205	27	11	404	65	134	49	32	69	46	55	37	40	1	162	37	5.0	3.4	3.6	14.7
Bill Bridges	F	6'6	235	29	11	442	69	156	44	34	48	71	178	37	48	2	172	40	16.2	3.4	4.4	15.6
Zelmo Beaty	C	6'9	240	29	11	473	102	236	43	43	64	67	142	25	47	0	247	43	12.9	2.3	4.3	22.5
Lou Hudson	G-F	6'5	220	24	11	424	101	216	47	40	52	77	59	32	43	1	242	39	5.4	2.9	3.9	22.0
Walt Hazzard	G	6'2	190	26	11	360	53	135	39	48	61	79	33	43	38	0	154	33	3.0	3.9	3.5	14.0
Paul Silas	F-C	6'7	235	25	11	258	21	58	36	19	37	51	92	21	32	0	61	23	8.4	1.9	2.9	5.5
Don Ohl	G	6'3	190	32	11	194	30	86	35	13	22	59	13	16	25	0	73	18	1.2	1.5	2.3	6.6
Jim Davis	C	6'9	235	27	8	52	4	15	27	5	8	63	17	1	7	0	13	7	2.1	0.1	0.9	1.6
Richie Guerin	G	6'4	210	36	3	32	1	4	25	1	2	50	5	7	8	0	3	11	1.7	2.3	2.7	1.0
Skip Harlicka	G	6'1	185	22	1	1	0	0	—	0	0	—	0	0	1	0	0	1	0.0	0.0	1.0	0.0
SAN DIEGO ROCKETS	**JACK McMAHON**				lost to Atlanta 2-4; 98-107, 114-116, H104-97, H114-112, 101-112, H106-108																	
Don Kojis	F	6'4	215	29	6	232	48	109	44	25	31	81	51	21	22	1	121	39	8.5	3.5	3.7	20.2
Toby Kimball	F	6'8	220	26	6	197	23	53	43	13	25	52	74	4	17	0	59	33	12.3	0.7	2.8	9.8
Elvin Hayes	C-F	6'9	235	23	6	278	60	114	53	35	53	66	83	5	21	0	155	46	13.8	0.8	3.5	25.8
Stu Lantz	G	6'3	175	22	6	208	30	69	43	21	27	78	21	10	22	0	81	35	3.5	1.7	3.7	13.5
Rick Adelman	G	6'1	178	22	6	187	24	53	45	22	37	59	15	29	18	0	70	31	2.5	4.8	3.0	11.7
Hambone Williams	G	6'2	185	29	6	102	12	25	48	3	7	43	17	32	15	0	27	17	2.8	5.3	2.5	4.5
John Block (broken wrist)	F	6'10	218	24	5	97	24	45	53	14	18	78	14	3	18	0	62	19	2.8	0.6	3.6	12.4
Pat Riley	F-G	6'4	208	23	5	76	16	37	43	5	6	83	11	2	13	0	37	15	2.2	0.4	2.6	7.4
Jim Barnett	G	6'4	180	24	6	51	9	23	39	7	8	88	3	7	5	0	25	9	0.5	1.2	0.8	4.2
Henry Finkel	C	7'	240	26	2	12	0	3	0	0	0	—	7	0	3	0	0	6	3.5	0.0	1.5	0.0
SAN FRANCISCO WARRIORS	**GEORGE LEE**				lost to Los Angeles 2-4; 99-94, 107-101, H98-115, H88-103, 98-103, H78-118																	
Rudy LaRusso	F	6'7	230	31	6	215	34	90	38	41	53	77	51	15	23	0	109	36	8.5	2.5	3.8	18.2
Clyde Lee	F	6'10	205	24	6	129	9	33	27	9	11	82	43	5	14	0	27	22	7.2	0.8	2.3	4.5
Nate Thurmond	C	6'11	235	27	6	263	40	102	39	20	34	59	117	28	18	0	100	44	19.5	4.7	3.0	16.7
Jeff Mullins	G	6'4	200	26	6	180	39	96	41	8	11	73	18	23	16	0	86	30	3.0	3.8	2.7	14.3
Jim King	G	6'2	175	27	6	142	29	78	37	14	18	78	25	17	10	0	72	24	4.2	2.8	1.7	12.0
Joe Ellis	F-G	6'6	175	24	6	161	23	79	29	16	25	64	51	3	22	0	62	27	8.5	0.5	3.7	10.3
Al Attles	G	6'2	180	32	6	109	7	21	33	1	4	25	18	21	17	0	15	18	3.0	3.5	2.8	2.5
Bill Turner	F	6'7	220	24	6	96	13	35	37	7	11	64	25	7	14	0	33	16	4.2	1.2	2.3	5.5
Bobby Lewis	G	6'3	185	23	5	59	11	28	39	1	3	33	5	6	12	0	23	12	1.0	1.2	2.4	4.6
Ron Williams	G	6'3	190	24	4	42	10	26	38	4	4	100	4	3	4	0	24	11	1.0	0.8	1.0	6.0
Dale Schlueter	C	6'10	226	23	3	25	3	9	33	7	15	47	22	1	4	0	13	8	7.3	0.3	1.3	4.3
Bob Allen	F	6'9	205	22	3	19	0	4	0	4	7	57	6	0	2	0	4	6	2.0	0.0	0.7	1.3
PHILADELPHIA 76ers	**JACK RAMSAY**				lost to Boston 1-4; H100-114, 103-134, H118-125, 119-116, H90-93																	
Chet Walker	F	6'6	215	28	4	109	23	43	53	8	12	67	23	8	5	0	54	27	5.8	2.0	1.3	13.5
Billy Cunningham	F	6'7	220	25	5	217	49	117	42	24	38	63	63	12	24	1	122	43	12.6	2.4	4.8	24.4
Darrall Imhoff	C	6'10	220	30	5	191	33	66	50	25	38	66	82	12	24	1	91	38	16.4	2.4	4.8	18.2
Hal Greer	G-F	6'3	176	32	5	204	26	81	32	28	36	78	30	23	23	0	80	41	6.0	4.6	4.6	16.0
Archie Clark	G	6'2	175	27	5	185	40	77	52	17	19	89	19	22	17	0	97	37	3.8	4.4	3.4	19.4
Wally Jones	G	6'2	180	26	5	103	12	45	27	8	10	80	16	9	17	1	32	21	3.2	1.8	3.4	6.4
Matt Goukas	F	6'5	200	24	5	100	11	27	41	4	5	80	12	8	12	0	26	20	2.4	1.6	2.4	5.2
George Wilson	C	6'8	240	26	5	45	0	7	0	3	4	75	18	8	9	0	3	9	3.6	1.6	1.8	0.6
Johnny Green	F	6'5	200	35	5	44	9	16	56	5	9	56	14	1	12	1	23	9	2.8	0.2	2.4	4.6
Shaler Halimon	F	6'6	200	23	1	2	1	2	50	0	0	—	0	0	0	0	2	2	0.0	0.0	0.0	2.0
Luke Jackson - leg injury Jerry Chambers - military service																						
BALTIMORE BULLETS	**GENE SHUE**				lost to New York 0-4; H101-113, 91-107, H116-119, 108-115																	
Jack Marin	F-G	6'7	210	24	4	153	24	51	47	7	11	64	18	12	13	0	55	38	4.5	3.0	3.3	13.8
Ray Scott	F-C	6'9	225	30	4	137	23	52	44	7	8	88	32	4	16	0	53	34	8.0	1.0	4.0	13.3
Wes Unseld	C	6'7	245	22	4	165	30	57	53	15	19	79	74	5	14	0	75	41	18.5	1.3	3.5	18.8
Kevin Loughery	G	6'3	190	28	4	173	29	79	37	23	35	66	18	21	16	0	81	43	4.5	5.3	4.0	20.3
Earl Monroe	G	6'3	190	24	4	171	44	114	39	25	31	81	21	16	10	0	113	43	5.3	4.0	2.5	28.3
Leroy Ellis	F	6'10	225	28	4	67	8	16	50	3	5	60	18	2	8	0	19	17	4.5	0.5	2.0	4.8
Ed Manning	F	6'7	215	24	4	63	7	18	39	0	0	—	23	1	11	0	14	16	5.8	0.3	2.8	3.5
Barry Orms	G	6'3	190	22	3	10	0	0	—	0	0	—	1	0	2	0	0	3	0.3	0.0	0.7	0.0
John Barnhill	G	6'1	180	30	1	10	1	2	50	0	0	—	2	1	3	0	2	10	2.0	1.0	3.0	2.0
Bob Quick	G	6'5	215	22	2	9	2	3	67	0	2	—	1	0	1	0	4	5	0.5	0.0	0.5	2.0
Tom Workman	F	6'7	230	24	1	2	0	1	0	0	0	—	1	0	0	0	0	2	1.0	0.0	0.0	0.0
Gus Johnson - knee injury																						

1968/69 N.B.A. TEAM STATISTICS

Team	G	FG	FGA	%	FT	FTA	%	Reb.	Ass.	For	Agnst.	Diff.
	REGULAR SEASON									AVERAGE POINTS		
EASTERN DIVISION												
Baltimore	82	3770	8567	44	2002	2734	73	4963	1682	116.4	112.1	+4.3
Philadelphia	82	3754	8274	45	2238	3087	72	4513	1914	118.9	113.8	+5.1
New York	82	3588	7813	46	1911	2596	74	4246	2071	110.8	105.2	+5.6
Boston	82	3583	8316	43	1936	2657	73	4840	1953	111.0	105.4	+5.6
Cincinnati	82	3565	7742	46	2262	3012	75	4525	1983	114.5	115.6	-1.1
Detroit	82	3609	7997	45	2141	3025	71	4471	1757	114.1	117.3	-3.2
Milwaukee	82	3537	8258	43	1966	2638	75	4727	1882	110.2	115.4	-5.2
WESTERN DIVISION												
Los Angeles	82	3574	7620	47	2056	3161	65	4749	2068	112.2	108.1	+4.1
Atlanta	82	3605	7844	46	1913	2785	69	4599	2069	111.3	109.4	+1.9
San Francisco	82	3414	8218	42	2119	2949	72	5109	1822	109.1	110.7	-1.6
San Diego	82	3691	8631	43	2074	3039	68	5026	1925	115.3	115.5	-0.2
Chicago	82	3355	8021	42	1877	2577	73	4550	1597	104.7	106.9	-2.2
Seattle	82	3543	8149	43	2105	2979	71	4498	1927	112.1	116.6	-4.5
Phoenix	82	3541	8242	43	2080	2950	71	4508	1918	111.7	120.5	-8.8

Team	G	FG	FGA	%	FT	FTA	%	Reb.	Ass.	For	Agnst.	Diff.
	PLAYOFFS									AVERAGE POINTS		
EASTERN DIVISION												
Baltimore	4	168	393	43	80	111	72	209	62	104.0	113.5	-8.5
Philadelphia	5	204	481	42	122	171	71	277	103	106.0	116.4	-10.4
New York	10	422	964	44	221	301	73	555	227	106.5	103.4	+3.1
Boston	18	755	1704	44	431	570	76	987	383	107.8	104.7	+3.1
WESTERN DIVISION												
Los Angeles	18	712	1640	43	443	679	65	1078	419	103.7	99.1	+4.6
Atlanta	11	446	1040	43	235	363	65	594	219	102.5	102.4	+0.1
San Francisco	6	218	601	36	132	196	67	385	129	94.7	105.7	-11.0
San Diego	6	246	531	46	145	212	68	296	113	106.2	108.7	-2.5

1968/69 N.B.A. STANDINGS

Team	W	L	Pct.	GB	Record against playoff teams W	L	Pct.	Record against non-playoff teams W	L	Pct.	HOME W	L	Pct.	ROAD W	L	Pct.	NEUTRAL W	L	Pct.
EASTERN DIVISION																			
Baltimore Bullets	57	25	.695	—	25	19	.568	32	6	.842	29	9	.763	24	15	.615	4	1	.800
Philadelphia 76ers	55	27	.671	2	25	19	.568	30	8	.789	26	8	.765	24	16	.600	5	3	.625
New York Knickerbockers	54	28	.659	3	27	18	.600	27	10	.730	30	7	.811	19	20	.487	5	I	.833
Boston Celtics	48	34	.585	9	20	25	.444	28	9	.757	24	12	.667	21	19	.525	3	3	.500
Cincinnati Royals	41	41	.500	16	21	30	.412	20	11	.645	15	13	.536	15	21	.417	11	7	.611
Detroit Pistons	32	50	.390	25	15	36	.254	17	14	.548	21	17	.553	7	30	.189	4	3	.571
Milwaukee Bucks	27	55	.329	30	12	36	.250	15	19	.441	15	19	.441	8	27	.229	4	9	.308
WESTERN DIVISION																			
Los Angeles Lakers	55	27	.671	—	28	17	.622	27	10	.730	32	9	.780	21	18	.538	2	0	1.000
Atlanta Hawks	48	34	.585	7	18	27	.400	30	7	.811	28	12	.700	18	21	.462	2	1	.667
San Francisco Warriors	41	41	.500	14	20	24	.455	21	17	.553	22	19	.537	18	21	.462	1	1	.500
San Diego Rockets	37	45	.451	18	15	29	.341	22	16	.579	25	16	.610	8	25	.242	4	4	.500
Chicago Bulls	33	49	.402	22	16	35	.314	17	14	.548	19	21	.475	12	25	.324	2	3	.400
Seattle Supersonics	30	52	.366	25	14	35	.286	16	17	.485	18	18	.500	6	29	.171	6	5	.545
Phoenix Suns	16	66	.195	39	5	45	.100	11	21	.344	11	26	.297	4	27	.129	1	13	.071

1968/69 N.B.A. INDIVIDUAL LEADERS

SCORING
(Minimum 65 Games Played)

Name	Team	G	FG	FT	Pts.	Avg.
Hayes	SD	82	930	467	2327	28.4
Monroe	Bal	80	809	447	2065	25.8
Cunningham	Phi	82	739	556	2034	24.8
Baylor	LA	76	730	421	1881	24.8
Robertson	Cin	79	656	643	1955	24.7
Rule	Sea	82	776	413	1965	24.0
Goodrich	Phoe	81	718	495	1931	23.8
Greer	Phi	82	732	432	1896	23.1
Mullins	SF	78	697	381	1775	22.8
Loughery	Bal	80	717	372	1806	22.6

FIELD GOAL PERCENTAGE
(Minimum 230 Field Goals)

Name	Team	FG	FGA	Pct.
Chamberlain	LA	641	1099	.583
Lucas	Cin	555	1007	.551
Reed	NY	704	1351	.521
Dischinger	Det	264	513	.515
Bellamy	NY-Det	563	1103	.510
Caldwell	Atl	561	1106	.507
Frazier	NY	531	1052	.505
Hawkins	LA	230	461	.499
Hudson	Atl	716	1455	.492
McGlocklin	Mil	622	1358	.487

FREE THROW PERCENTAGE
(Minimum 230 Free Throws)

Name	Team	FT	FTA	Pct.
Siegfried	Bos	336	389	.864
Mullins	SF	381	452	.843
McGlocklin	Mil	246	292	.842
Robinson	Chi-Mil	412	491	.839
Robertson	Cin	643	767	.838
Hetzel	Mil-Cin	299	357	.838
Marin	Bal	292	352	.830
West	LA	490	597	.821
Boozer	Chi	394	489	.806
Walker	Phi	369	459	.804

PERSONAL FOULS

Name	Team	PF
Cunningham	Phi	329
Harris	Sea	326
Rule	Sea	322
Bellamy	NY-Det	320
Boerwmkle	Chi	317

GAMES DISQUALIFIED

Name	Team	Disq
Hanis	Sea	14
Ellis	SF	13
Imhoff	Phi	12
G. Smith	Mil	12
Boerwinkle	Chi	11

REBOUNDS PER GAME
(Minimum 65 Games Played)

Name	Team	G	Reb.	Avg.
Chamberlain	LA	81	1712	21.1
Thurmond	SF	71	1402	19.7
Russell	Bos	77	1484	19.3
Lucas	Cin	74	1360	18.4
Unseld	Bal	82	1491	18.2
Hayes	SD	82	1406	17.1
Reed	NY	82	1191	14.5
Bridges	Atl	80	1132	14.2
Lee	SF	65	897	13.8
Cunningham	Phi	82	1050	12.8

ASSISTS PER GAME
(Minimum 65 Games Played)

Name	Team	G	Ass.	Avg.
Robertson	Cin	79	772	9.8
Wilkens	Sea	82	674	8.2
Frazier	NY	80	635	7.9
Bing	Det	77	546	7.1
Rodgers	Mil	81	561	6.9
Williams	SD	79	524	6.6
Goodrich	Phoe	81	518	6.4
Hazzard	Atl	80	474	5.9
Havlicek	Bos	82	441	5.4
Baylor	LA	76	408	5.4

MINUTES PLAYED

Name	Team	Min.
Hayes	SD	3695
Chamberlain	LA	3669
Wilkens	Sea	3463
Robertson	Cin	3461
D. Van Arsdale	Phoe	3388

1968-69 A.B.A

Still Running a Distant Second

Poor attendance last year sent the league's weaker links looking for new lands to settle. The Anaheim team packed its bags for the big city of Los Angeles, a very unlikely challenger for the Los Angeles Lakers. The Minnesota Muskies fled to the warmer climes of Miami, and the champion Pittsburgh Pipers left town to move into Minneapolis, oblivious to the debt-ridden season of the Muskies.

The New Jersey Americans were reborn as the New York Nets, playing in an arena in Commack, Long Island which had been ruled unfit for play in last season's tie-breaker for a playoff spot. Opening day this season didn't go much better, as the hockey ice over which the floor was laid began to melt and seep up through the boards during the pre-game drills, treating the crowd of 1,848 to the spectacle of players skidding and sliding all over the court. The heat in the building was turned off, the ice stopped melting, and the game started an hour late, with Kentucky winning the match, 99-92. In this damp, cold arena with sparse crowds, the Nets reminded no one of the New York Knicks and Madison Square Garden.

The A.B.A.'s attendance wasn't much better this season, rising from last year's average of 2,804 for regular season games to only 2,981. The new Miami team could pay off its outstanding debts in Minnesota only by selling All-Star center Mel Daniels to the Indiana Pacers for cash plus two insignificant players. The Houston club went broke early in the season, and Commissioner George Mikan kept the team going with league funds. One reason for the lack of enthusiasm over the A.B.A. was its failure to sign any prominent rookies, with Elvin Hayes of Houston and Wes Unseld of Louisville spurning large offers from hometown A.B.A. clubs to sign with the established league. Bill Sharman and Alex Hannum, two of the N.B.A.'s more famous coaches, joined A.B.A. teams this year, but their press value was small. The major publicity event for the A.B.A. was the debut of Rick Barry, who wore the uniform of the Oakland Oaks after sitting out his option year. Barry and Connie Hawkins of Minnesota were the big A.B.A. stars, but both of them went out of action in mid-season with knee injuries.

Before hurting his knee, however, Barry got the Oakland club off to a flying start. Under the direction of Alex Hannum, who had made the Philadelphia 76ers the scourge of the N.B.A., the Oaks won 15 of their first 17 games and later strung together a 16-game winning streak to quickly amass an insurmountable lead in the Western Division. Barry had lots of help from the supporting cast. Forward Doug Moe and guard Larry Brown came in a trade from New Orleans to considerably strengthen the club, and rookies Warren Armstrong, Henry Logan, and Jim Eakins joined with holdovers Ira Harge and Gary Bradds in making the Oaks the class of the league. Even after Barry took his 34.0 scoring average with him to the infirmary, the Oaks kept on winning.

The New Orleans Bucs held second place, relying more on Jimmy Jones and Red Robbins in the absence of Moe and Brown. The Denver Rockets stood fast in third place, and the Dallas Chaps captured fourth place, with Cliff Hagan playing less frequently and with rookies Ron Boone and Glen Combs making strong contributions. Bill Sharman coached the new Los Angeles Stars, who fielded a rookie-laden squad and finished out of the playoffs in fifth place. The Houston Rockets came in last, with players coming and going in chaotic fashion while the front office affairs of the club approached the same state.

By contrast, the Indiana Pacers were one of the A.B.A.'s showcase franchises. Attendance reached acceptable levels, and the team was much strengthened by the addition of center Mel Daniels from the Miami franchise. A slow start of 2-7 cost coach Larry Staverman his job, but Bob Leonard came in and got the Pacers moving to a 42-27 clip. One game behind the first-place Pacers came the Miami Floridians, who remained a strong outfit despite the forced sale of Daniels. Coach Jim Pollard strung together a close-knit unit whose star was guard Donnie Freeman.

The Kentucky Colonels captured third place with a strong 42-36 record, relying on guards Louie Dampier and Darrel Carrier for the bulk of the team's scoring. In the midst of a controversy over whether women should be hired as professional jockeys, the Colonels won some press coverage by signing woman jockey Penny Ann Early to a player's contract. Miss Early threw the ball into play on an out-of-bounds play in a game against the Los Angeles Stars; the Colonels immediately called time out and took her out of the lineup forever.

The champion Pipers weren't enjoying any jokes in their new home in Minnesota. In addition to losing Connie Hawkins in mid-campaign with a knee injury, the Pipers had a most incompatible new coach in Jim Harding, a strict disciplinarian who freely yelled at his players and officials. He was so hot tempered that during the All-Star break, he punched team owner Gabe Rubin. After this, Vern Mikkelsen and then Gus Young handled the coaching duties, bringing the Pipers home a weak fourth. In last place were the New York Nets, who used a revolving door more for the players than the fans.

For the playoffs, Connie Hawkins was back in action for Minnesota while Rick Barry was still out for Oakland. Notwithstanding Hawk's presence, the Pipers lost in the opening round, while the Oaks joined Indiana, Miami, and New Orleans in moving into the second round. Both divisional finals were one-sided, with Indiana beating Miami in five games and Oakland taking four straight from New Orleans. The Pacers had two hot hands in Roger Brown and Freddie Lewis, plus two good big men in Mel Daniels and Bob Netolicky; the Oaks seemed weaker on paper without Barry. But rookie Warren Armstrong picked up the scoring slack left by Barry, averaging 28.8 for the playoffs, and the Oaks had a surprisingly easy time downing the Pacers in five games, including an exciting 134-126 overtime win in game three. But in the shadow of the Celtics dramatic championship in the N.B.A., the A.B.A. crown went almost completely unnoticed.

1968/69 A.B.A. — EASTERN DIVISION

Use Name	Pos	Hgt	Wgt	Age	G	Min	FG	FGA	%	FT	FTA	%	Reb	Ass	PF	DQ	Points	Min	Reb	Ass	PF	Points
					TOTAL													PER GAME				
INDIANA PACERS	44-34 .564				LARRY STAVERMAN (2-7 .222), BOB LEONARD (42-27 .609)																	
Roger Brown	F-G	6'5	207	26	75	2658	563	1169	48	442	563	79	510	345	281	11	1573	35	6.8	4.6	3.7	21.0
Bob Netolicky	F	6'9	225	26	78	2721	583	1145	51	306	491	62	798	87	231	4	1472	35	10.2	1.1	3.0	18.9
Mel Daniels	C	6'9	220	24	76	2934	712	1496	48	400	662	60	**1256**	116	276	8	1824	39	**16.5**	1.5	3.6	24.0
Ron Perry (from Mia-NY)	G	6'3	190	25	27	865	137	336	41	58	70	83	73	97	108	3	365	32	2.7	3.6	4.0	13.5
Freddie Lewis	G	6'	180	25	78	3055	572	1300	44	419	510	82	374	346	289	5	1585	39	4.8	4.4	3.7	20.3
George Peeples	F-C	6'8	205	25	64	1111	122	278	44	101	142	71	358	33	137	2	345	17	5.6	0.5	2.1	5.4
Don Dee	F	6'8	210	25	58	989	138	387	36	56	75	75	292	33	179	9	332	17	5.0	0.6	3.1	5.7
Bobby Hooper	G	6'	180	22	54	955	112	271	41	43	59	73	109	142	91	0	271	18	2.0	2.6	1.7	5.0
S. Chubin (Fnom LA-Min, to NY)	G	6'2	200	24	24	725	101	245	41	129	162	80	95	125	104	1	332	30	4.0	5.2	4.3	13.8
John Fairchild (From Den)	F	6'8	205	25	52	582	101	260	39	73	103	71	111	28	90	0	285	11	2.1	0.5	1.7	5.5
Jimmy Rayl	G	6'2	180	27	27	567	72	202	36	61	68	90	67	63	80	2	239	21	2.5	2.3	3.0	8.9
Jay Miller (from Mil-NBA-LA)	F	6'5	210	25	41	494	103	229	45	77	112	69	81	20	65	2	283	12	2.0	0.5	1.6	6.9
Mike Lewis (to Min)	C	6'8	225	22	24	457	75	163	46	47	68	69	181	29	68	1	197	19	7.5	1.2	2.8	8.2
Tom Thacker	G	6'2	190	29	18	346	40	117	34	18	31	58	67	52	51	0	98	19	3.7	2.9	2.8	5.4
Jerry Harkness	G	6'2	175	28	10	272	31	67	46	30	47	64	34	21	17	0	92	27	3.4	2.1	1.7	9.2
Phil Wagner	G	6'2	190	23	12	180	11	41	27	13	17	77	23	14	28	0	36	15	1.9	1.2	2.3	3.0
Butch Joyner	F	6' 5	200	23	2	5	0	0	—	0	0	—	1	0	1	0	0	3	0.5	0.0	0.5	0.0
Jack Thompson (injury)	G	6'1	185	23	2	4	1	3	33	0	0	—	1	2	0	0	2	2	0.5	1.0	0.0	1.0
MIAMI FLORIDIANS	43-35 .551				JIM POLLARD																	
Willie Murrell	F	6'6	225	27	75	2493	476	1019	47	191	269	71	566	103	239	5	1147	33	7.5	1.4	3.2	15.3
Les Hunter	F	6'7	235	26	77	2537	476	1073	44	335	448	75	743	127	311	14	1287	33	9.6	1.6	4.0	16.7
Skip Thoren	C	6'10	230	25	78	2645	532	1100	48	241	392	61	1046	195	324	11	1305	34	13.4	2.5	4.2	16.7
Maurice McHartley (from NY)	G	6'3	200	26	52	1503	283	696	41	180	224	80	135	193	165	4	752	29	2.6	3.7	3.2	14.5
Donnie Freeman	G	6'3	185	24	78	2874	651	1346	48	420	534	79	285	501	229	7	1724	37	3.7	6.4	2.9	22.1
Don Sidle	F-C	6'9	215	22	77	1984	305	656	46	321	450	71	551	73	212	3	931	26	7.2	0.9	2.8	12.1
Dan Sparks	F	6'8	200	23	64	1138	153	396	39	113	165	68	287	43	171	5	419	18	4.5	0.7	2.7	6.5
Dallas Thornton	G	6'4	190	22	45	756	108	249	43	79	125	63	119	63	92	1	297	17	2.6	1.4	2.0	6.6
Andy Anderson (from Oak, MS)	G	6'2	185	23	33	718	118	263	45	96	120	80	101	42	71	1	332	22	3.1	1.3	2.2	10.1
Ron Perry (to NY-Ind)	G	6'3	190	25	24	708	100	299	33	62	91	68	73	62	66	0	274	30	3.0	2.6	2.8	11.4
Willie Iverson	G	6'	180	23	28	531	50	146	34	36	60	60	46	80	47	0	136	19	1.6	2.9	1.7	4.9
Gary Keller (injury)	C	6'9	220	24	53	503	78	192	41	72	120	60	167	8	102	2	228	9	3.2	0.2	1.9	4.3
Erv Inniger	G	6'4	190	23	34	484	73	182	40	21	25	84	60	41	59	0	170	14	1.8	1.2	1.7	5.0
Nick Jones (from Dal)	G	6'2	190	23	3	21	3	8	38	0	0	-	3	1	4	0	6	7	1.0	0.3	1.3	2.0
KENTUCKY COLONELS	42-36 .538				GENE RHODES																	
Goose Ligon	F	6'7	215	24	75	2815	391	879	44	337	510	66	819	172	312	6	1120	38	10.9	2.3	4.2	14.9
Ollie Darden (from NY)	F	6'7	240	24	47	1221	185	435	43	100	130	77	380	62	167	4	471	26	8.1	1.3	3.6	10.0
Gene Moore	C-F	6'9	240	23	76	2026	417	920	45	204	290	70	817	90	311	18	1038	27	10.8	1.2	4.1	13.7
Darel Carrier	G	6'3	185	28	73	2858	559	1376	41	447	545	82	283	214	227	1	1690	39	3.9	2.9	3.1	23.2
Louie Dampier	G	6'	170	24	78	**3326**	713	**1696**	42	308	380	81	299	456	156	1	1933	**43**	3.8	5.8	2.0	24.8
Sam Smith	F	6'7	230	24	62	1421	173	437	40	114	172	66	390	64	143	0	461	23	6.3	1.0	2.3	7.4
Bobby Rascoe	G	6'4	205	28	78	1247	201	477	42	129	167	77	150	105	131	1	534	16	1.9	1.3	1.7	6.8
Jim Caldwell (ankle injury)	C	6'10	240	25	65	1235	167	381	44	87	129	67	423	130	211	3	422	19	6.5	2.0	3.2	6.5
Randy Mahaffey (to NY)	F	6'7	210	23	31	759	102	251	41	68	101	67	184	35	99	4	272	24	5.9	1.1	3.2	8.8
Manny Leaks (to NY-Dal)	C	6'8	235	23	31	674	88	238	37	46	67	69	234	32	103	3	222	22	7.5	1.0	3.3	7.2
Wayne Chapman (injury)	F	6'6	190	23	48	458	68	202	34	54	72	75	74	38	95	0	194	10	1.5	0.8	2.0	4.0
Johnny Jones	F	6'7	210	25	29	449	81	213	38	41	71	58	117	34	53	0	203	15	4.0	1.2	1.8	7.0
Elton McGriff (fnom Dal-NO)	C	6'9	225	26	9	107	7	20	35	15	20	75	30	2	20	1	29	12	3.3	0.2	2.2	3.2
Dan Anderson (from NY, to Min)	C	6'10	230	25	8	94	7	22	32	6	8	75	25	6	19	1	20	12	3.1	0.8	2.4	2.5
Paul Long	G	6'2	180	24	9	82	9	40	23	17	21	81	9	12	21	0	35	9	1.0	1.3	2.3	3.9
Reggie Lacefield	F	6'5	230	23	8	48	11	22	50	2	4	50	11	0	9	0	24	6	1.4	0.0	1.1	3.0
Henry Akin	C	6'10	235	24	2	25	1	4	25	2	3	67	4	1	0	0	4	13	2.0	0.5	0.0	2.0
Penny Ann Early (arm injuries)	G	5'3	115	—	1	1	0	0	—	0	0	—	0	0	0	0	0	1	0.0	0.0	0.0	0.0
MINNESOTA PIPERS	36-42 .462				JIM HARDING (20-12 .625), VERN MIKKELSEN (6-7 .462), GUS YOUNG (10-23 .303)																	
Art Heyman	F-G	6'5	210	27	71	2362	350	832	42	285	409	70	494	217	195	2	1022	33	7.0	3.1	2.7	14.4
Trooper Washington	F	6'7	225	24	69	2625	421	839	50	190	316	60	868	178	239	2	1032	38	12.6	2.6	3.5	15.0
Connie Hawkins (knee injury)	C-F	6'8	215	26	47	1852	496	971	51	425	554	77	534	184	166	3	1420	39	11.4	3.9	3.5	30.2
Chico Vaughn	G	6'3	195	28	69	2301	415	1170	35	253	329	77	165	107	178	1	1228	33	2.4	1.6	2.6	17.8
Charlie Williams	G	6'	165	25	66	2282	484	1298	37	203	286	71	246	163	222	6	1237	35	3.7	2.5	3.4	18.7
Frank Card	F	6'7	195	24	76	1596	222	537	41	146	244	60	419	81	155	2	591	21	5.5	1.1	2.0	7.8
Steve Vacendak	G	6'1	185	24	60	1589	288	716	40	167	215	78	210	166	158	1	745	26	3.5	2.8	2.6	12.4
Mike Lewis (from Ind)	C-F	6'8	225	22	52	1160	172	405	42	106	167	63	451	78	178	7	450	22	8.7	1.5	3.4	8.7
Arvesta Kelly	G	6'3	190	23	68	1066	155	425	36	63	103	61	157	61	141	0	398	16	2.3	0.9	2.1	5.9
George Sutor	C	6'8	240	25	64	886	139	397	35	71	114	62	348	27	170	8	349	14	5.4	0.4	2.7	5.5
Dan Anderson (from NY-KY)	C	6'10	230	25	29	628	112	228	49	37	50	74	218	26	72	1	261	22	7.5	0.9	2.5	9.0
Willie Porter(to Hou)	F	6'7	205	26	11	137	25	45	56	13	27	48	48	6	23	0	63	12	4.4	0.5	2.1	5.7
Jim Jarvis (to LA)	G	6'1	175	25	11	134	14	45	31	10	12	83	14	15	24	0	40	12	1.3	1.4	2.2	3.6
Leroy Wright	F	6'9	215	30	10	95	4	13	31	0	5	0	30	1	15	0	8	10	3.0	0.1	1.5	0.8
Tom Hoover (from Hou, to NY)	C	6'10	250	27	9	83	12	26	46	10	21	48	31	6	21	1	34	9	3.4	0.7	2.3	3.8
S. Chubin (from LA, to Ind-NY)	G	6'2	200	24	8	54	6	21	29	6	6	100	12	12	17	0	18	7	1.5	1.5	2.1	2.3
Ken Wilburn (to NY-Den)	F	6'6	205	24	6	34	2	9	22	2	5	40	18	2	6	0	6	6	3.0	0.3	1.0	1.0
Jim Kissane	F	6'7	210	22	2	15	2	6	33	2	2	100	3	0	3	0	6	8	1.5	0.0	1.5	3.0
Tom Kondla (to Hou)	C	6'8	225	22	2	11	1	2	50	2	3	67	1	0	3	0	4	6	0.5	0.0	1.5	2.0
Tony Jackson (from NY to Hou)	G	6'4	200	28	1	10	0	2	0	0	0	—	1	1	2	0	0	10	1.0	1.0	2.0	0.0

Use Name	Pos	Hgt	Wgt	Age	G	Min	FG	FGA	%	FT	FTA	%	Reb	Ass	PF	DQ	Points	Min	Reb	Ass	PF	Points
					TOTAL													PER GAME				
1968/69 A.B.A. — EASTERN DIVISION (continued)																						
NEW YORK NETS	**17-61 .218**				**MAX ZASLOFSKY**																	
Walt Simon	F-G	6'6	200	29	68	2750	570	1296	44	290	417	70	554	234	289	5	1436	40	8.1	3.4	4.3	21.1
Randy Mahaffey (from KY)	F	6'7	210	23	48	1594	249	577	43	164	228	72	387	64	162	4	662	33	8.1	1.3	3.4	13.8
Tom Hoover (from Hou-Min)	C	6'10	250	27	40	1256	165	354	47	110	162	68	411	106	187	11	440	31	10.3	2.7	4.7	11.0
S. Chubin (from LA-Min-Ind)	G	6'2	200	24	28	828	153	394	39	138	169	82	103	139	109	3	445	30	3.7	5.0	3.9	15.9
Willie Somerset (from Hou)	G	5'10	195	26	31	1325	282	657	43	164	200	82	135	106	103	1	747	43	4.4	3.4	3.3	24.1
Tom Bowens	F	6'8	220	28	76	1550	186	453	41	83	128	65	455	52	236	6	455	20	6.0	0.7	3.1	6.0
Wilbert Frazier	C-F	6'7	235	26	75	1370	217	512	42	120	194	62	416	66	200	1	554	18	5.5	0.9	2.7	7.4
Bobby Lloyd	G	6'2	185	22	67	1358	215	541	40	218	246	89	112	136	176	1	660	20	1.7	2.0	2.6	9.9
Levern Tart (to Hou-Den)	G	6'2	195	26	35	920	190	427	44	133	170	78	128	87	85	1	513	26	3.7	2.5	2.4	14.7
Ron Perry (from Mia, to Ind)	G	6'3	190	25	23	812	165	425	39	92	131	70	95	85	81	5	444	35	4.1	3.7	3.5	19.3
Ollie Darden (to KY)	F	6'7	240	24	30	726	133	279	48	78	110	71	214	42	107	1	344	24	7.1	1.4	3.6	11.5
Manny Leaks (from KY, to Dal)	C	6'8	235	23	20	713	96	289	33	58	81	72	283	40	62	0	250	36	14.2	2.0	3.1	12.5
Dan Anderson (to KY-Min)	C	6'10	230	25	25	677	101	233	43	75	91	82	217	34	83	7	277	27	8.7	1.4	3.3	11.1
Maurice McHartley (to Mia)	G	6'3	200	26	24	645	107	266	40	83	107	78	76	76	86	1	297	27	3.2	3.2	3.6	12.4
Hank Whitney (to Hou)	F	6'7	235	29	31	643	104	248	42	60	82	73	181	38	90	1	268	21	5.8	1.2	2.9	8.6
Bob Verga (from Den, to Hou)	G	6'1	190	23	24	521	99	273	36	103	144	72	68	41	68	1	306	22	2.8	1.7	2.8	12.8
Willie Worsley	G	5'9	175	23	24	460	36	123	29	63	84	75	35	39	48	0	145	19	1.5	1.6	2.0	6.0
Leary Lentz (from Hou)	F	6'6	200	23	26	442	48	126	38	33	43	77	107	9	46	1	129	17	4.1	0.3	1.8	5.0
Stew Johnson (to Hou)	F-C	6'8	225	24	9	205	28	72	39	16	17	94	44	9	24	1	74	23	4.9	1.0	2.7	8.2
Tony Koski	F	6'8	215	22	5	30	2	7	29	2	2	100	7	4	9	0	6	6	1.4	0.8	1.8	1.2
Ken Wilburn (from Min, to Den)	F	6'6	205	24	4	22	2	8	25	6	9	67	4	2	6	0	10	6	1.0	0.5	1.5	2.5
Tony Jackson (to Min-Hou)	F	6'4	200	28	3	20	0	3	0	1	1	100	3	0	2	0	1	7	1.0	0.0	0.7	0.3
Rod Knowles (from Phoe-NBA)	C	6'9	215	22	1	3	0	0	—	0	0	—	0	0	1	0	0	3	0.0	0.0	1.0	0.0
1968/69 A.B.A. — WESTERN DIVISION																						
OAKLAND OAKS	**60-18 .769**				**ALEX HANNUM**																	
Doug Moe	F	6'5	220	30	75	2528	529	1227	43	360	444	81	614	151	266	9	1423	34	8.2	2.0	3.5	19.0
Rich Barry (knee injury)	F	6'7	215	24	35	1361	392	767	51	403	454	**89**	329	136	124	1	1190	39	9.4	3.9	3.5	34.0
Ira Harge	C	6'9	225	27	78	2095	269	578	47	123	200	62	816	96	245	1	661	27	10.5	1.2	3.1	8.5
Warren Armstrong (SL)	G	6'2	200	22	71	2545	573	1276	45	373	545	68	688	252	263	4	1530	36	9.7	3.5	3.7	21.5
Larry Brown	G	5'9	160	28	77	2381	308	706	44	301	379	79	235	**544**	230	6	925	31	3.1	**7.1**	3.0	12.0
Gary Bradds	F	6'8	215	26	75	2249	517	1041	50	364	444	82	577	88	244	6	1399	30	7.7	1.2	3.3	18.7
Henry Logan	G	6'	180	22	76	1751	339	694	49	268	382	70	287	185	226	4	947	23	3.8	2.4	3.0	12.5
Jim Eakins	C	6'11	215	22	78	1671	351	646	54	309	430	72	563	53	234	4	1011	21	7.2	0.7	3.0	13.0
John Clawson	F	6'4	200	24	70	1067	147	309	48	37	54	69	195	51	187	1	331	15	2.8	0.7	2.7	4.7
Mel Peterson	G-F	6'4	190	30	51	709	132	263	50	12	15	80	170	55	61	0	276	14	3.3	1.1	1.2	5.4
Rusty Critchfield	G	5'10	150	22	47	439	53	147	36	55	84	65	29	54	41	0	161	9	0.6	1.1	0.9	3.4
Andy Anderson (to Mia, MS)	G	6'2	185	23	3	24	5	9	56	2	3	67	4	3	5	0	12	8	1.3	1.0	1.7	4.0
NEW ORLEANS BUCCANEERS	**46-32 .590**				**BABE McCARTHY**																	
Ron Franz	F	6'7	207	23	73	2195	381	850	45	286	388	74	518	189	233	5	1059	30	7.1	2.6	3.2	14.5
Jackie Moreland	F	6'7	220	30	78	2714	468	1109	42	221	313	71	633	207	310	11	1159	35	8.1	2.7	4.0	14.9
Gerald Govan	C	6'10	220	26	77	1902	211	537	39	134	208	64	701	150	238	4	557	25	9.1	1.9	3.1	7.2
Steve Jones	G-F	6'5	205	26	78	3024	576	1372	42	348	437	80	393	226	280	4	1552	39	5.0	2.9	3.6	19.9
Jimmy Jones	G	6'4	188	23	77	3188	**764**	1429	53	521	647	81	441	437	225	4	2050	41	5.7	5.7	2.9	26.6
Red Robbins	F-C	6'8	200	24	76	2736	456	1035	44	291	361	81	1024	142	200	1	1210	36	13.5	1.9	2.6	15.9
Mike Butler	G	6'2	170	22	77	1315	207	528	39	112	133	84	115	171	130	0	576	17	1.5	2.2	1.7	7.5
Jasper Wilson (finger injury)	F	6'6	200	21	66	756	128	339	38	82	127	65	173	43	127	1	343	11	2.6	0.7	1.9	5.2
Lee Davis	C	6'8	240	23	65	570	88	227	39	45	90	50	202	18	87	1	222	9	3.1	0.3	1.3	3.4
Marl Pradd	G	6'3	170	24	50	323	81	186	44	93	119	78	50	23	60	0	258	6	1.0	0.4	1.2	5.2
Glynn Saulters	G	6'2	175	23	22	120	22	70	31	15	22	68	19	11	25	0	59	5	0.9	0.5	1.1	2.7
Dave Lee	F	6'7	225	26	4	16	1	9	11	0	0	—	3	0	0	0	2	4	0.8	0.0	0.0	0.5
Elton McGriff (from Dal, to KY)	C	6'9	225	26	3	11	2	5	40	0	0	—	4	0	2	0	4	4	1.3	0.0	0.7	1.3
DENVER ROCKETS	**44-34 .564**				**BOB BASS**																	
Julie Hammond	F	6'5	205	25	78	2335	329	601	55	165	253	65	600	124	213	3	823	30	7.7	1.6	2.7	10.6
Wayne Hightower (finger injury)	F	6'9	210	28	67	2318	311	762	41	311	426	73	641	203	241	5	933	35	9.6	3.0	3.6	13.9
Byron Beck	C	6'9	240	23	71	2289	423	843	50	182	238	76	779	77	248	9	1030	32	11.0	1.1	3.5	14.5
Lonnie Wright (eye injury)	G	6'2	205	24	69	2538	453	1089	42	205	276	74	290	175	250	2	1130	37	4.2	2.5	3.6	16.4
Larry Jones	G	6'2	180	27	75	3042	759	1631	47	**591**	**760**	78	493	258	273	3	**2133**	41	6.6	3.4	3.6	**28.4**
Walt Piatkowski	F	6'8	220	23	77	1819	399	956	42	117	151	77	363	46	226	2	942	24	4.7	0.6	2.9	12.2
Bill McGill	C-F	6'9	225	29	78	1760	411	745	**55**	180	264	68	460	102	289	13	1002	23	5.9	1.3	3.7	12.8
Jeff Congdon (broken hand)	G	6'1	190	25	59	979	107	277	39	69	85	81	93	135	104	1	288	17	1.6	2.3	1.8	4.9
Ken Wilburn (from Min-NY)	F	6'6	205	24	37	409	72	181	40	30	57	53	177	22	56	1	174	11	4.8	0.6	1.5	4.7
Levern Tart (from NY-Hou)	G	6'2	195	26	20	345	56	159	35	42	56	75	51	44	40	1	154	17	2.6	2.2	2.0	7.7
Willie Rogers	G-F	6'3	185	23	40	294	27	80	34	31	52	60	47	16	51	1	85	7	1.2	0.4	1.3	2.1
Grant Simmons	G	6'3	190	25	17	252	22	59	37	20	29	69	26	15	42	2	65	15	1.5	0.9	2.5	3.8
Larry Bunce (from Dal to Hou)	C	7'	245	23	23	225	22	59	37	49	70	70	58	2	44	1	93	10	2.5	0.1	1.9	4.0
Bob Verga (to NY-Hou)	G	6'1	190	23	6	150	24	77	31	18	28	64	21	11	16	0	67	25	3.5	1.8	2.7	11.2
John Fairchild (to Ind)	F	6'8	205	25	11	135	12	34	35	16	24	67	18	9	8	1	40	12	1.6	0.8	0.7	3.6
Charley Parks	F	6'5	210	22	2	5	0	1	0	0	0	—	0	0	1	0	0	3	0.0	0.0	0.5	0.0

1968/69 A.B.A. — WESTERN DIVISION (continued)

Use Name	Pos	Hgt	Wgt	Age	G	Min	FG	FGA	%	FT	FTA	%	Reb	Ass	PF	DQ	Points	Min	Reb	Ass	PF	Points
					TOTAL													PER GAME				
DALLAS CHAPARRALS	41-37 .526				**CLIFF HAGAN**																	
Cincy Powell	F	6'7	227	26	75	2573	555	1179	47	342	470	73	671	173	275	5	1454	34	8.9	2.3	3.7	19.
John Beasley	F-C	6'9	225	24	78	3050	585	1200	49	332	402	83	830	110	259	5	1505	39	10.6	1.4	3.3	19.
John Smith	C	7'	235	24	77	2172	246	623	39	116	214	54	809	58	**328**	**19**	608	28	10.5	0.8	4.3	7.
Ron Boone	G	6'2	200	22	78	2682	520	1197	43	436	537	81	394	279	303	8	1478	34	5.1	3.6	3.9	18.
Glen Combs	G	6'2	185	22	72	2241	364	868	42	300	394	76	195	165	218	3	1112	31	2.7	2.3	3.0	15.
Charlie Beasley	G	6'5	190	23	75	1719	220	506	43	161	192	84	158	208	158	0	602	23	2.1	2.8	2.1	8.
Riney Lochmann	F	6'6	215	24	60	950	115	279	41	60	97	62	204	59	138	4	291	16	3.4	1.0	2.3	4.
Spider Bennett (to Hou)	G	6'3	190	25	46	823	116	311	37	118	179	66	114	69	125	8	352	18	2.5	1.5	2.7	7.
Manny Leaks (from KY-NY)	C	6'8	235	23	27	702	115	229	50	56	81	69	246	20	88	1	286	26	9.1	0.7	3.3	10.
Cliff Hagan	F	6'4	215	37	35	579	132	259	51	123	144	85	102	122	73	2	387	17	2.9	3.5	2.1	11.
Bob Bedell	F	6'8	205	24	42	479	92	221	42	48	84	57	116	30	76	1	232	11	2.8	0.7	1.8	5.
Larry Bunce (to Den-Hou)	C	7'	245	23	24	423	50	113	44	55	76	72	127	15	62	2	155	18	5.3	0.6	2.6	6.
Elton McGriff (to NO-KY)	C	6'9	225	26	24	377	66	146	45	42	70	60	110	6	63	0	174	16	4.6	0.3	2.6	7.
Nick Jones (to Mia)	G	6'2	190	23	4	60	6	20	30	2	6	33	5	5	10	0	14	15	1.3	1.3	2.5	3.
Jim Ware	F	6'7	210	24	1	15	3	4	75	1	2	50	7	1	4	0	7	15	7.0	1.0	4.0	7.
LOS ANGELES STARS	33-45 .423				**BILL SHARMAN**																	
Larry Miller	F-G	6'4	210	22	78	2871	473	1162	41	340	475	72	599	177	193	0	1328	37	7.7	2.3	2.5	17.
George Stone	F	6'7	195	22	74	2199	437	964	45	261	337	77	504	57	254	8	1163	30	6.8	0.8	3.4	15.
Ed Johnson (broken arm)	C	6'9	205	24	58	1662	263	548	48	156	303	51	539	58	281	18	682	29	9.3	1.0	4.8	11.
George Lehmann (from Atl-NBA)	G	6'3	190	26	32	937	212	511	41	132	164	80	73	159	96	1	604	29	2.3	5.0	3.0	18.
Merv Jackson (toe injury)	G	6'3	175	22	71	2314	423	1000	42	249	302	82	299	237	262	9	1114	33	4.2	3.3	3.7	15.
Warren Davis	F-C	6'6	220	25	78	2406	356	711	50	282	433	65	777	129	269	3	994	31	10.0	1.7	3.4	12.
Bobby Warren	G	6'5	190	22	76	2045	285	645	44	297	385	77	349	155	252	6	898	27	4.6	2.0	3.3	11.
Dennis Grey	C	6'8	215	21	58	1317	184	439	42	157	292	54	320	52	196	11	525	23	5.5	0.9	3.4	9.
Ben Warley	F	6'5	200	32	35	876	172	423	41	116	155	75	194	26	127	6	491	25	5.5	0.7	3.6	14.
Jim Jarvis (from Min)	G	6'1	175	25	51	777	133	357	37	76	97	78	115	65	113	1	359	15	2.3	1.3	2.2	7.
Edgar Lacy	F	6'6	190	24	46	609	98	219	45	38	67	57	180	30	92	1	234	13	3.9	0.7	2.0	5.
Steve Chubin (to Min-Ind-NY)	G	6'2	200	24	17	490	84	215	39	113	135	84	81	78	57	2	282	29	4.8	4.6	3.4	16.
Jay Miller (from Mil-NBA, to Ind)	F	6'5	210	25	11	248	44	127	35	50	64	78	32	9	38	0	138	23	2.9	0.8	3.5	12.
Elvin Ivory	F	6'8	215	20	20	188	38	87	44	11	17	65	166	9	38	0	88	9	8.3	0.5	1.9	4.
Brian Brunkhorst	F	6'6	210	23	3	56	6	11	55	13	17	76	13	3	8	0	25	19	4.3	1.0	2.7	8.
HOUSTON MAVERICKS	23-55 .295				**SLATER MARTIN (3-9 .250), JIM WEAVER (20-46 .303)**																	
Art Becker	F	6'8	210	26	78	2429	423	888	48	200	240	83	597	103	304	9	1046	31	7.7	1.3	3.9	13.
Keith Swagerty	F	6'7	235	23	77	2447	362	883	41	256	421	61	822	92	238	5	980	32	10.7	1.2	3.1	12.
Kendall Rhine	C	6'10	240	25	73	2116	255	629	41	149	265	56	804	150	321	16	659	29	11.0	2.1	**4.4**	9.
Steve Kramer	G	6'5	200	23	23	701	113	281	40	95	117	81	85	112	96	4	321	30	3.7	4.9	4.2	14.
Bob Verga (from Den-NY)	G	6'1	190	23	33	1133	293	656	45	215	282	76	144	136	116	0	814	34	4.4	4.1	3.5	24.
Stew Johnson (from NY)	F-C	6'8	225	24	69	2279	588	1372	43	183	236	78	560	133	154	0	1421	33	8.1	1.9	2.2	20.
Willie Somerset (to NY)	G	5'10	170	26	43	1793	337	853	40	320	383	84	197	174	158	3	1011	42	4.6	4.0	3.7	23.
Don Carlos	G-F	6'5	210	24	56	1527	207	505	41	214	283	76	279	159	231	10	628	27	5.0	2.8	4.1	11.
Tony Jackson (from NY-Min)	G	6'4	200	28	60	1423	210	583	36	298	336	89	237	138	143	2	750	24	4.0	2.3	2.4	12.
Dick Clark	G	6'4	195	24	32	723	64	222	29	89	124	72	88	68	99	0	218	23	2.8	2.1	3.1	6.
Leary Lentz (to NY)	F	6'6	200	23	44	687	87	208	42	43	74	58	164	22	57	0	217	16	3.7	0.5	1.3	4.
Tom Kondla (from Min)	C	6'8	225	22	40	342	57	143	40	20	43	47	124	13	53	0	134	9	3.1	0.3	1.3	3.
Jerry Pettway	G	6'3	185	24	11	264	37	123	30	5	7	71	29	17	19	0	79	24	2.6	1.5	1.7	7.
Hank Whitney (from NY)	F	6'7	235	29	18	249	27	81	33	29	48	60	73	18	54	0	83	14	4.1	1.0	3.0	4.
Spider Bennett (from Dal)	G	6'3	190	25	13	170	31	74	42	22	37	59	33	15	40	1	88	13	2.5	1.2	3.1	6.
Guy Manning	F	6'6	205	24	14	167	27	95	28	21	37	57	42	2	20	0	75	12	3.0	0.1	1.4	5.
Larry Bunce (from Dal-Den)	C	7'	245	23	11	156	14	31	45	10	19	53	47	2	22	0	38	14	4.3	0.2	2.0	3.
Levern Tart (from NY, to Den)	G	6'2	195	26	6	138	28	63	44	18	29	62	16	12	16	0	74	23	2.7	2.0	2.7	12.
Tom Hoover (SJ, to Min-NY)	C	6'10	250	27	4	80	14	28	50	5	6	83	30	5	15	1	33	20	7.5	1.3	3.8	8.
Willie Porter (from Min)	F	6'7	205	26	2	11	3	7	43	4	4	100	7	0	0	0	10	6	3.5	0.0	0.0	5.
Rich Dumas	G	6'3	170	23	1	5	1	5	20	0	0	—	1	0	1	0	2	5	1.0	0.0	1.0	2.
Bill Gaines	G	6'4	185	22	1	5	1	2	50	0	0	—	1	0	0	0	2	5	1.0	0.0	0.0	2.

1968/69 A.B.A.—PLAYOFFS

AKLAND OAKS — **ALEX HANNUM**

defeated Denver 4-3; 129-99, H119-122, H121-99, 108-109, H128-118, 115-126, H115-102
defeated New Orleans 4-0; H128-118, H135-124, 113-107, 128-114
defeated Indiana 4-1; H123-114, H122-150, 134-126(OT), 144-117, H135-131(OT)

se Name	Pos	Hgt	Wgt	Age	TOTAL G	Min	FG	FGA	%	FT	FTA	%	Reb	Ass	PF	DQ	Points	PER GAME Min	Reb	Ass	PF	Points
oug Moe	F	6'5	220	30	16	593	115	284	40	87	111	78	124	31	67	1	317	37	7.8	1.9	4.2	19.8
ary Bradds	F-C	6'8	215	26	16	517	121	253	48	86	103	83	162	15	66	1	328	32	10.1	0.9	4.1	20.5
a Harge	C	6'9	225	27	16	445	45	108	42	24	39	62	192	20	50	1	114	28	12.0	1.3	3.1	7.1
Varren Armstrong	G-F	6'2	200	22	16	662	161	**350**	46	**135**	**202**	67	207	46	56	1	**460**	41	12.9	2.9	3.5	28.8
arry Brown	G	5'9	160	28	16	534	74	173	43	76	90	84	52	**87**	49	0	24	33	3.3	**5.4**	3.1	1.5
enry Logan	G	6'	180	22	16	380	75	176	43	67	99	68	40	34	50	3	217	24	2.5	2.1	3.1	13.6
m Eakins	C	6'11	215	22	16	329	65	121	54	59	83	71	102	15	52	0	189	21	6.4	0.9	3.3	11.8
ohn Clawson	F	6'4	200	24	16	313	42	95	44	15	24	63	54	14	60	2	100	20	3.4	0.9	3.8	6.3
lel Peterson	F-G	6'4	190	30	14	98	18	30	60	7	12	58	28	4	11	0	44	7	2.0	0.3	0.8	3.1
usty Critchfield	G	5'10	150	22	5	19	1	6	17	2	6	33	2	7	6	0	4	4	0.4	1.4	1.2	0.8
Rick Barry (knee injury)																						

IDIANA PACERS — **BOB LEONARD**

defeated Kentucky 4-2; H118-128, H120-115, 111-130, 104-114(OT), H116-97, 107-89, H120-111
defeated Miami 4-1; H126-110, H131-116, 119-105, 110-114, H127-105
lost to Oakland 1-4; 114-123, 150-122, H126-134(OT), H117-144, 131-135(OT)

se Name	Pos	Hgt	Wgt	Age	TOTAL G	Min	FG	FGA	%	FT	FTA	%	Reb	Ass	PF	DQ	Points	PER GAME Min	Reb	Ass	PF	Points
oger Brown	F-G	6'5	207	26	17	668	**169**	329	51	120	155	77	143	57	**86**	**6**	459	39	8.4	3.4	5.1	27.0
ob Netolicky	F	6'9	225	26	17	702	161	303	53	61	97	63	214	17	55	2	383	41	12.6	1.0	3.2	22.5
lel Daniels	C	6'9	220	24	17	570	127	301	42	79	130	61	**237**	22	75	1	333	34	13.9	1.3	4.4	19.6
om Thacker	G	6'2	190	29	16	391	36	117	31	28	47	60	77	59	53	1	100	24	4.8	3.7	3.3	6.3
reddie Lewis	G	6'	180	25	17	**727**	144	327	44	116	133	87	70	79	68	2	409	43	4.1	4.6	4.0	24.1
eorge Peeples	C-F	6'8	205	25	17	419	32	81	40	38	57	67	116	11	41	0	102	25	6.8	0.6	2.4	6.0
ob Hooper	G	6'	180	22	16	288	25	74	34	22	26	85	38	45	41	0	76	18	2.4	2.8	2.6	4.8
on Perry	G	6'3	190	25	17	202	34	114	30	18	27	67	21	18	33	0	97	12	1.2	1.1	1.9	5.7
ohn Fairchild	F	6'8	205	25	9	85	19	44	43	4	6	67	21	3	13	0	46	9	2.3	0.3	1.4	5.1
ay Miller	F	6'5	210	25	11	62	15	33	45	4	10	40	21	2	14	0	34	6	1.9	0.2	1.3	3.1
on Dee	F	6'8	210	25	12	41	4	13	31	0	0	-	10	1	10	0	8	3	0.8	0.1	0.8	0.7

IAMI FLORIDIANS — **JIM POLLARD**

defeated Minnesota 4-3; H119-110, H99-106, 93-109, 116-109, H122-107, 100-105, 137-128
lost to Indiana 1-4; 110-126, 116-131, H105-119, H114-110, 105-127

se Name	Pos	Hgt	Wgt	Age	TOTAL G	Min	FG	FGA	%	FT	FTA	%	Reb	Ass	PF	DQ	Points	PER GAME Min	Reb	Ass	PF	Points
Villie Murrell	F	6'6	225	27	12	456	82	179	46	32	38	84	101	21	38	0	197	38	8.4	1.8	3.2	16.4
es Hunter	F	6'7	235	26	10	209	42	116	36	31	42	74	88	13	39	2	117	21	8.8	1.3	3.9	11.7
lUp Tnoren	C	6'10	230	25	12	402	61	129	47	35	61	57	155	17	48	3	157	34	12.9	1.4	4.0	13.1
laurice McHartley	G	6'3	200	26	12	369	60	173	35	54	66	82	42	50	48	1	174	31	3.5	4.2	4.0	14.5
onnie Freeman	G	6'3	185	24	12	434	98	214	46	61	75	81	48	50	28	0	257	36	4.0	4.2	2.3	21.4
on Sidle	F-C	6'9	215	22	12	340	60	117	51	43	60	72	100	16	35	1	163	28	8.3	1.3	2.9	13.6
an Sparks	F	6'8	200	23	12	251	29	65	45	19	30	63	57	8	35	0	77	21	4.8	0.7	2.9	6.4
ndy Anderson	G	6'2	184	23	12	244	35	81	43	26	35	74	23	16	21	0	97	20	1.9	1.3	1.8	8.1
allas Thornton	G-F	6'4	190	22	7	118	23	59	39	21	34	62	23	6	9	0	67	17	3.3	0.9	1.3	9.6
ary Keller	C	6'9	220	24	6	57	12	21	57	6	10	60	23	3	12	0	30	10	3.8	0.5	2.0	5.0

EW ORLEANS BUCCANEERS — **BABE McCARTHY**

defeated Dallas 4-3; H129-106, H122-108, 106-130, 114-107, H112-123, 118-136, H101-95
lost to Oakland 0-4; 118-128,124-135, H107-113, H114-128

se Name	Pos	Hgt	Wgt	Age	TOTAL G	Min	FG	FGA	%	FT	FTA	%	Reb	Ass	PF	DQ	Points	PER GAME Min	Reb	Ass	PF	Points
on Frantz	F	6'7	205	23	11	261	38	112	34	25	37	68	47	18	28	0	102	24	4.3	1.6	2.5	9.3
ackie Moreland	F	6'7	220	30	11	342	59	149	40	21	33	64	79	27	49	3	139	31	7.2	2.5	4.5	12.6
erald Govan	C	6'10	220	26	11	317	51	114	45	20	27	74	108	28	40	1	123	29	9.8	2.5	3.6	11.2
teve Jones	G-F	6'5	205	26	11	428	72	174	41	37	50	74	54	18	44	0	185	39	4.9	1.6	4.0	16.8
mmy Jones	G	6'4	188	23	11	445	123	223	**55**	86	113	76	58	59	35	0	332	40	5.3	5.4	3.2	**30.2**
ed Robbins	F-C	6'8	200	24	11	410	71	146	49	41	53	77	175	17	32	0	185	37	**15.9**	1.5	2.9	16.8
like Butler	G	6'2	170	22	11	237	30	107	28	26	29	90	29	17	26	0	100	22	2.6	1.5	2.4	9.1
asper Wilson	F	6'6	200	21	10	92	11	42	26	17	23	74	26	2	20	0	39	9	2.6	0.2	2.0	3.9
ee Davis	C	6'8	240	23	9	69	13	33	39	6	11	55	32	6	13	0	32	8	3.6	0.7	1.4	3.6

Use Name	Pos	Hgt	Wgt	Age	TOTAL G	Min	FG	FGA	%	FT	FTA	%	Reb	Ass	PF	DQ	Points	PER GAME Min	Reb	Ass	PF	Point

1968/69 A.B.A. — PLAYOFFS (continued)

Use Name	Pos	Hgt	Wgt	Age	G	Min	FG	FGA	%	FT	FTA	%	Reb	Ass	PF	DQ	Points	Min	Reb	Ass	PF	Point
DALLAS CHAPARRALS	**CLIFF HAGAN**				lost to New Orleans 3-4; 106-129, 108-122, H130-106, H107-114, 123-112, H136-118, 95-101																	
Cincy Powell	F	6'7	227	26	7	227	51	114	45	37	43	86	68	10	21	0	140	32	9.7	1.4	3.0	20
John Beasley	F-C	6'9	225	24	7	240	46	94	49	30	34	88	73	8	27	0	122	34	10.4	1.1	3.9	17
Manny Leaks	C	6'8	235	23	7	199	28	69	41	15	18	83	63	8	25	0	71	28	9.0	1.1	3.6	10
Ron Boone	G	6'2	200	22	7	196	38	85	45	21	25	84	22	27	25	1	97	28	3.1	3.9	3.6	13
Glen Combs	G	6'2	185	22	7	278	55	138	40	41	48	85	17	17	18	0	156	40	2.4	2.4	2.6	22
Charlie Beasley	G	6'5	190	23	7	198	22	53	42	17	23	74	13	24	13	0	62	28	1.9	3.4	1.9	8
Bob Bedell	F	6'8	205	24	7	148	38	70	54	18	23	78	49	6	25	1	94	21	7.0	0.9	3.6	13
John Smith	C	7'	235	24	7	131	16	31	52	7	13	54	42	8	19	0	39	19	6.0	1.1	2.7	5
Cliff Hagan	F	6'4	215	37	2	45	5	14	36	8	10	80	6	14	5	0	18	23	3.0	7.0	2.5	9
Riney Lochmann	F	6'6	215	24	3	18	3	8	38	0	0	—	4	1	2	0	6	6	1.3	0.3	0.7	2
MINNESOTA PIPERS	**GUS YOUNG**				lost to Miami 3-4; 110-119, 106-99, H109-93, H109-116, 107-122, H105-100, H128-137																	
Art Heyman	F-G	6'5	210	27	7	264	41	92	45	32	41	78	51	20	24	1	121	38	7.3	2.9	3.4	17
Trooper Washington	F	6'7	225	24	6	230	26	62	42	15	21	71	79	14	17	0	67	38	13.2	2.3	2.8	11.
Connie Hawkins	C-F	6'8	215	26	7	320	65	172	38	40	62	65	86	27	25	0	174	46	12.3	3.9	3.6	24
Steve Vacendak	G	6'1	185	24	7	214	39	85	46	37	41	90	17	12	24	0	115	31	2.4	1.7	3.4	16
Charlie Williams	G	6'	165	25	7	255	41	112	37	27	39	69	24	14	28	1	120	36	3.4	2.0	4.0	17.
Mike Lewis	C-F	6'8	225	22	7	131	20	52	38	10	19	53	47	11	28	2	50	19	6.7	1.6	4.0	7.
Frank Card	F	6'7	195	24	6	113	23	41	56	8	13	62	28	6	17	0	54	19	4.7	1.0	2.8	9.
Chico Vaughn	G	6'3	195	28	5	57	11	37	30	6	7	86	6	1	5	0	34	11	1.2	0.2	1.0	6
Arvesta Kelly	G	6'3	190	23	5	50	8	22	36	3	3	100	11	5	14	0	24	10	2.2	1.0	2.8	4.
Dan Anderson	C	6'10	230	25	5	38	6	13	46	3	4	75	10	5	8	0	15	8	2.0	1.0	1.6	3.
Leroy Wright	F	6'9	215	30	1	5	0	3	0	0	0	—	0	0	2	0	0	5	0.0	0.0	2.0	0
George Sutor	C	6'8	240	25	1	3	0	1	0	0	1	0	0	0	2	0	0	3	0.0	0.0	2.0	0.
KENTUCKY COLONELS	**GENE RHODES**				lost to Indiana 2-4; 128-118, 115-120, H130-111, H105-104(OT), 97-116, H89-107, 111-120																	
Ollie Darden	F	6'7	240	24	7	102	26	49	53	10	15	67	31	6	19	0	63	15	4.4	0.9	2.7	9.
Goose Ligon	F-C	6'7	215	24	7	260	34	78	44	30	41	73	89	8	25	0	98	37	12.7	1.1	3.6	14.
Gene Moore	C	6'9	240	23	7	204	44	100	44	26	34	76	101	15	37	2	114	29	14.4	2.1	5.3	16.
Darel Carrier	G	6'3	185	28	7	303	51	117	44	52	64	81	21	19	28	1	168	43	3.0	2.7	4.0	24.
Louie Dampier	G	6'	170	24	7	326	50	140	36	40	46	87	30	28	17	0	156	47	4.3	4.0	2.4	22
Bobby Rascoe	F-G	6'4	205	28	7	200	30	63	48	30	32	94	20	10	25	0	90	29	2.9	1.4	3.6	12.
Sam Smith	F	6'7	230	24	7	157	19	57	33	7	16	44	42	9	24	0	45	22	6.0	1.3	3.4	6
Jim Caldwell	C	6'10	240	25	7	63	4	15	27	3	7	43	21	5	11	0	11	9	3.0	0.7	1.6	1.
Elton McGriff	C	6'9	225	26	5	61	8	22	36	7	10	70	27	2	17	2	23	12	5.4	0.4	3.4	4.
Wayne Chapman	F	6'6	190	23	5	29	3	8	38	1	2	50	4	2	13	0	7	6	0.8	0.4	2.6	1.
DENVER ROCKETS	**BOB BASS**				lost to Oakland 3-4; H99-129, 122-119, 99-121, H109-108, 118-128, H126 -115, 102-115																	
Julie Hammond	F	6'5	205	25	7	191	33	64	52	25	33	76	50	4	26	1	91	27	7.1	0.6	3.7	13.
Wayne Hightower	F	6'9	210	28	7	187	25	63	40	34	45	76	47	12	22	1	84	27	6.7	1.7	3.1	12.
Byron Beck	C	6'9	240	23	7	214	48	95	51	14	17	82	63	9	23	0	110	31	9.0	1.3	3.3	15.
Lonnie Wright	G	6'2	205	24	7	224	31	86	36	20	28	71	37	14	24	0	84	32	5.3	2.0	3.4	12.
Larry Jones	G	6'2	180	27	7	282	48	134	36	55	76	72	54	32	21	0	154	40	7.7	4.6	3.0	22.
Walt Piatkowski	F-C	6'8	220	23	7	201	48	111	43	10	11	91	29	6	32	1	107	29	4.1	0.9	4.6	15.
Jeff Congdon	G	6'1	190	25	7	183	20	42	48	22	22	100	16	34	21	0	62	26	2.3	4.9	3.0	8.
Bill McGill	C	6'9	225	29	7	96	19	39	49	9	10	90	23	6	26	2	47	14	3.3	0.9	3.7	6.
Ken Wilburn	F	6'6	205	24	7	93	16	33	48	4	16	25	32	5	21	0	36	13	4.6	0.7	3.0	5.
Grant Simmons	G	6'3	190	25	2	9	0	1	0	0	0	—	0	0	1	0	0	5	0.0	0.0	0.5	0.

Team	W	L	Pct.	GB	Record against playoff teams			Record against non - playoff teams			HOME			ROAD			NEUTRAL		
					W	L	Pct.	W	L	Pct.	W	L	Pct.	W	L	Pct.	W	L	Pct.
EASTERN DIVISION																			
Indiana Pacers	44	34	.564	—	25	30	.455	19	4	.826	29	11	.725	15	23	.395	0	0	—
Miami Floridians	43	35	.551	1	26	29	.473	17	6	.739									
Kentucky Colonels	42	36	.538	2	27	29	.482	15	7	.682	25	14	.641	17	22	.436	0	0	—
Minnesota Pipers	36	42	.462	8	22	34	.393	14	8	.636									
New York Nets	17	61	.218	27	12	**54**	.182	5	7	.417	12	**28**	.300	5	**33**	.132	0	0	—
WESTERN DIVISION																			
Oakland Oaks	**60**	18	**.769**	—	**39**	13	**.750**	21	5	.808	31	8	.795	**28**	10	**.737**	1	0	1
New Orleans Buccaneers	46	32	.590	14	24	28	.462	**22**	4	**.846**	29	11	.725	17	21	.447	0	0	—
Denver Rockets	44	34	.564	16	27	25	.519	17	**9**	.654	**32**	7	**.821**	12	27	.308	0	0	—
Dallas Chaparrals	41	37	.526	19	26	28	.481	15	**9**	.625	25	14	.641	16	22	.421	0	1	0
Los Angeles Stars	33	45	.423	27	24	39	.381	9	6	.600	22	16	.579	11	29	.275	0	0	—
Houston Mavericks	23	55	.295	37	16	47	.254	7	8	.467	15	23	.395	8	32	.200	0	0	—

1968/69 A.B.A. INDIVIDUAL LEADERS

SCORING
(Minimum 70 Games Played)

Name	Team	G	FG	FT	Pts.	Avg.
Jones	Den	75	759	591	2133	28.4
J.Jones	NO	77	764	521	2050	26.6
Dampier	KY	78	713	308	1933	24.8
Daniels	Ind	76	712	400	1824	24.0
Somerset	Hou-NY	74	619	484	1758	23.8
Carrier	KY	73	559	447	1690	23.2
Freeman	Mia	78	651	420	1724	22.1
Armstrong	Oah	71	573	373	1530	21.5
Brown	Ind	75	563	442	1573	21.0
Lewis	Ind	78	572	419	1585	20.3

FIELD GOAL PERCENTAGE
(Minimum 560 Field Goals)

Name	Team	FG	FGA	Pct.
McGill	Den	411	745	.552
Hammond	Den	329	601	.547
Eakins	Oak	351	646	.543
J.Jones	NO	764	1429	.535
Barry	Oak	392	767	.511
Hawkins	Min	496	971	.511
Netolicky	Ind	583	1145	.509
Beck	Den	423	843	.502
Washington	Min	421	839	.502
Davis	LA	356	711	.501

3-POINT FIELD GOAL PERCENTAGE
(Minimum 20 Made)

Name	Team	FG	FTA	Pct.
Carrier	KY	125	330	.379
Stone	LA	28	74	.378
Rayl	Ind	34	92	.370
Combs	Dal	84	233	.361
Dampier	KY	199	552	.361
Lehmann	LA	48	137	.350
Johnson	NY-Hou	64	183	.350
Perry	Mia-NY-Ind	67	192	.349
Warren	LA	31	89	.348
S.Jones	ND	52	151	.344

FREE THROW PERCENTAGE
(Minimum 160 Attempts)

Name	Team	FT	FTA	Pct.
Barry	Oak	403	454	.888
Jackson	NY-Min-Hou	299	337	.887
Lloyd	NY	218	246	.886
C. Beasley	Dal	161	192	.839
Becker	Hou	200	240	.833
Somerset	Hou-NY	484	583	.830
J. Beasley	Dal	332	402	.826
Jackson	LA	249	302	.825
Lewis	Ind	419	510	.822
Carrier	KY	447	545	.820

REBOUNDS PER GAME
(Minimum 70 Games Played)

Name	Team	G	Reb.	Avg.
Daniels	Ind	76	1256	16.5
Robbins	NO	76	1024	13.5
Thoren	Mia	78	1046	13.4
Rhine	Hou	73	804	11.0
Beck	Den	71	779	11.0
Ligon	KY	75	819	10.9
Moore	KY	76	817	10.8
Swagerty	Hou	77	822	10.7
J. Beasley	Dal	78	830	10.6
Smith	Dal	77	809	10.5

ASSISTS PER GAME
(Minimum 70 Games Played)

Name	Team	G	Ass.	Avg.
Brown	Oak	77	544	7.1
Freeman	Mia	78	501	6.4
Dampier	NY	78	456	5.8
J.Jones	NO	77	437	5.7
Brown	Ind	75	345	4.6
Chubin	LA-Min-Ind-NY	77	354	4.6
Lewis	Ind	78	346	4.4
Somerset	Hou-NY	74	280	3.8
Boone	Dal	78	279	3.6
Armstrong	Oak	71	252	3.6

MINUTES PLAYED

Name	Team	Min.
Dampier	KY	3326
J.Jones	NO	3188
Somerset	Hou-NY	3118
Lewis	Ind	3055
J. eeasley	Dal	3050

PERSONAL FOULS

Name	Team	PF
Smith	Dal	328
Thoren	Mia	324
Rhine	Hou	321
Ligon	KY	312
Hunter	Mia	311
Moore	KY	311

GAMES DISQUALIFIED

Name	Team	Disq.
Smith	Dal	19
Johnson	LA	18
Moore	KY	18
Rhine	Hou	16
Hunter	Mia	14

Team		REGULAR SEASON												PLAYOFFS											
		G	FG	FGA	%	FT	FTA	%	Reb.	Ass.	PF	Points	PPG	G	FG	FGA	%	FT	FTA	%	Reb.	Ass.	PF	Points	PPG
TEAM STATISTICS																									
EASTERN DIVISION																									
Indiana	Off.	78	3474	7709	45	2273	3180	71	4431	1553	2106	9331	119.6	17	**766**	**1736**	44	490	688	71	968	**324**	489	2047	120.4
	Def.	78	3356	7829	43	2157	2939	73	4288	1469	2172	9010	115.5	17	720	1661	43	508	681	75	950	288	504	1983	116.6
	Diff.		+118	-120	+2	+116	+241	-2	+143	+84	+66	+321	+4.1		**+46**	**+75**	+1	-18	+7	-4	+18	**+36**	+15	+64	+3.8
Miami	Off.	78	3406	7625	45	2167	3023	72	4182	1532	2092	9008	115.5	12	502	1154	44	328	451	73	660	200	313	1336	111.3
	Def.	78	3316	7610	44	2170	2934	74	**3895**	1628	2156	8975	115.1	12	511	1190	43	327	449	73	**635**	237	325	1387	115.6
	Diff.		+90	+15	+1	-3	+89	-2	+287	-96	+64	+33	+.4		-9	-36	+1	+1	+2	—	+25	-37	+12	-51	-4.3
Kentucky	Off.	78	3180	7613	42	1977	2690	73	4249	1453	2077	8672	111.2	7	269	649	41	206	267	77	386	104	216	775	110.7
	Def.	78	3162	7467	42	2210	3051	72	4424	1458	2017	**8659**	**111.0**	7	**295**	679	43	197	289	68	390	117	207	796	113.7
	Diff.		+18	+146	—	-233	-361	+1	-175	-5	-60	+13	+.2		-26	-30	-2	+9	-22	**+9**	-4	-13	-9	-21	-3.0
Minnesota	Off.	78	3320	**7985**	42	1991	2868	69	4268	1331	1988	8914	114.3	7	280	692	40	181	251	72	359	115	194	774	110.6
	Def.	78	3353	7566	44	2069	2793	74	4259	1344	1975	8904	114.2	7	296	664	45	192	272	71	383	116	175	786	112.3
	Diff.		-33	**+419**	-2	-78	+75	-5	+9	-13	-13	+10	+.1		-16	+28	-5	-11	-21	+1	-24	-1	-19	-12	-1.7
New York	Off.	78	3148	7563	42	2090	2816	74	4035	1409	2260	8463	108.5												
	Def.	78	3324	**7396**	45	2369	3273	72	4401	1489	1962	9143	117.2												
	Diff.		-176	+167	-3	-279	-457	+2	-366	-80	-298	-680	-8.7												
WESTERN DIVISION																									
Oakland	Off.	78	3615	7663	47	**2607**	**3434**	76	**4507**	**1668**	2126	**9866**	**126.5**	16	717	1596	45	**558**	**769**	73	**963**	273	467	1997	**124.8**
	Def.	78	3491	8159	43	2058	2822	73	4016	1403	2327	9211	118.1	16	703	1637	43	444	605	73	868	272	**490**	1876	117.3
	Diff.		+124	-496	**+4**	**+549**	**+612**	**+3**	**+491**	**+265**	**+201**	**+655**	**+8.4**		+14	-41	+2	**+114**	**+164**	—	**+95**	+1	**+23**	+121	**+7.5**
New Orleans	Off.	78	3386	7697	44	2148	2845	76	4276	1617	1917	9053	116.1	11	478	1122	43	283	383	74	612	193	294	1265	115.0
	Def.	78	3307	7708	43	2042	2766	74	4347	1520	2050	8787	112.7	11	479	1084	44	343	436	79	610	**180**	293	1309	119.0
	Diff.		+79	-11	+1	+106	+79	+2	-71	+97	+133	+266	+3.4		-1	+38	-1	-60	-53	-5	+2	+13	-1	-44	-4.0
Denver	Off.	78	3427	7554	45	2026	2769	73	4117	1239	2102	8959	114.9	7	288	668	43	193	258	75	351	122	217	775	110.7
	Def.	78	3269	7438	44	2132	3036	70	4171	**1193**	2045	8842	113.4	7	**295**	**666**	44	243	335	73	412	116	204	835	119.3
	Diff.		+158	+116	+1	-106	-267	+3	-54	+46	-57	+117	+1.5		-7	+2	-1	-50	-77	+2	-61	+6	-13	-60	-8.6
Dallas	Off.	78	3185	7155	45	2192	2948	74	4088	1320	2180	8657	111.0	7	302	676	45	194	237	82	357	123	**180**	805	115.0
	Def.	78	3189	7559	42	2193	3035	72	4146	1271	2114	8710	111.7	7	303	712	43	**179**	**237**	76	397	128	172	802	114.6
	Diff.		-4	-404	+3	-1	-87	+2	-58	+49	-66	-53	-.7		-1	-36	**+2**	+15		+6	-40	-5	-8	+3	+.4
Los Angeles	Off.	78	3208	7419	43	2291	3243	71	4141	1244	2276	8925	114.4												
	Def.	78	3407	7416	46	2247	3042	74	4209	1452	**2366**	9163	117.5												
	Diff.		-199	+3	-3	+44	+201	-3	-68	-208	+90	-238	-3.1												
Houston	Off.	78	3179	7732	41	2196	2991	73	4380	1371	2157	8683	111.3												
	Def.	78	3355	7567	44	2311	3116	74	4518	1510	2097	9127	117.0												
	Diff.		-176	+165	-3	-115	-125	-1	-138	-139	-60	-444	-5.7												

1969-70 N.B.A.

Limping to a First Championship

The Celtics had won the playoffs as aged underdogs the last two seasons and now the Boston dynasty crashed to the end with the retirement of Bill Russell and Sam Jones. Russell had played on 11 championship squads in his 13 seasons, and Jones had played on 10 of them . The Celtics could in no way make up for their defense, rebounding, shooting, experience, and class. Tommy Heinsohn took over as coach, but with Henry Finkel at center, the Celtics collapsed to a 34-48 record, a fall to sixth place in the East.

But a new club embodied the fine precision of the Celtic machine in its heyday. The New York Knicks, with a deep squad built around center Willis Reed, forward Dave DeBusschere, and guard Walt Frazier, came roaring out of the gate to take an early lead which held up all season. The New Yorkers won their first game, then dropped one to San Francisco, and then proceeded to run off a record 18 straight victories. The Knick calling card was a pressing defense which stayed well-oiled with frequent substitutions, and the team's offensive slogan was, "Hit the open man," a capsule summary of the selfless passing game which kept the ball constantly moving.

And if the Knicks were acting like a new version of the Celtics, the league had a new Bill Russell in Lew Alcindor, the 7'3" center out of U.C.L.A. Combining the defensive awareness of Russell with the offensive power of Wilt Chamberlain, Alcindor signed a five year, $1.2 million contract with the Milwaukee Bucks, who had won a coin toss with the Phoenix Suns for the first draft pick and rights to Alcindor. Big Lew immediately proved that he was worth every penny, changing the Bucks overnight from a cellar dwelling expansion club into an instant title contender. With some help from fellow rookie Bob Dandridge, Alcindor sparked the Bucks to a 56-26 season, with a strong finish that brought them home only four games behind New York. The Baltimore Bullets and Philadelphia 76ers took the third and fourth playoff spots in the East.

Fifth place in the East went to the Cincinnati Royals, coached by Russell's old teammate on the Celtics, Bob Cousy. The former star guard actually played in a few games, but his main concern was to change the Royals into a running team in the image of the old Celtics. Rookie guards Norm Van Lier and Herm Gilliam fit right into this new style, but veterans Jerry Lucas and Oscar Robertson, long-time Cincinnati stars, felt more at home in the old pattern offense. Cousy dealt Lucas off early in the season to San Francisco for the surprisingly cheap price of Jim King and Bill Turner. He then tried to send Robertson to Baltimore for Gus Johnson, only to have the Big 0 exercise a contractual right to veto the deal. Finishing behind the Royals were the Celtics, out of the playoffs for the first time since 1950, and the pereniially-weak Detroit Pistons.

While ex-teammate Cousy spent a tumultuous season rebuilding the Royals, Russell's long-time rival Wilt Chamberlain spent a restless season on the sidelines. In the Los Angeles Lakers' ninth game of the year, Chamberlain hurt his knee and underwent surgery. Elgin Baylor also had problems with his knees, so the Lakers were often down to one superstar, Jerry West. Winning his first scoring title with a 31.2 average, West often carried the team single-handedly, and the Lakers finished second in the Western Division with a 46-36 record.

The Atlanta Hawks finished in first place despite some personnel problems. Center Zelmo Beaty signed with the A.B.A. and sat out his option season, leaving sub Jim Davis to hold down the pivot position until Walt Bellamy came down from Detroit in a late-season trade. Another trade hurt the Hawks, as the Phoenix Suns took rebounder Paul Silas off their hands for the less-talented Gary Gregor.

The Chicago Bulls and Phoenix Suns took the third and fourth playoff spots with identical 39-43 records. Coach Dick Motta had his Bulls playing a physical, ball-control style of play, and a major portion of the team's offensive power came from the new forward combination of Chet Walker and Bob Love. Walker came to Chicago from Philadelphia in a swap for Jim Washington, and Love was promoted to a starting role after three years of benchsitting for the Royals, Bucks, and Bulls; the pair scored an average of 42.5 points per game.

The Suns got off to a slow start, which cost coach Johnny Kerr his job, but they came on strong late in the season with their completely revamped front wall. First draft pick Neal Walk shared the center job with veteran Jim Fox, Paul Silas held down one forward spot, and the famous Connie Hawkins filled the other forward spot. The N.B.A. admitted Hawkins into the league as part of an out-of-court settlement to his damage suits, eight years after he was barred for not reporting a bribe offer while a freshman at the University of Iowa. Long celebrated as the best of the one-on-one players, "the Hawk" broke into the N.B.A. with a 24.6 scoring average and a first-team All-Star berth, proving himself a star in this league as he had in the A.B.A. for the past two seasons. Seattle, San Francisco, and San Diego all had new coaches either at the start of the season or during the campaign, and all of them finished out of the playoffs.

The first round of the playoffs went according to the expected line, with the Knicks, Bucks, Hawks, and Lakers emerging victorious. The young Bucks relied entirely on Alcindor in the middle, but the Knicks used a well-balanced team performance to kayo them in five games in the Eastern final. In the West, the Lakers had Chamberlain and Baylor back in working order for the playoffs and disposed of the Hawks in four straight games. The title series would be between the team-oriented Knicks and the star-oriented Lakers.

The Knicks ran away with a 124-112 win in the opening game in a packed Madison Square Garden, as Willis Reed hit for 37 points against Chamberlain. Jerry West's 34 points three days later helped the Lakers even the series with a 105-103 win. The third game, in California, was knotted at 100-all until Dave DeBusschere put New York ahead with a bucket with three seconds left. Chamberlain then threw the ball in to West, and the star guard heaved it from deep in the backcourt, 55 feet away, into the basket to tie the score at the buzzer. Undaunted, the Knicks took a 111-108 win in overtime. The fourth game also went into overtime, with little-used sub John Tresvant sparking the Lakers in the extra period to a 121-115 win.

Game five in New York started well for the Knicks, but then Willis Reed collapsed with a torn thigh muscle; down by 13 points at the half, coach Red Holzman used a no-center lineup in the second half, with DeBusschere and Dave Stallworth covering Chamberlain. It worked, as a pressing defense and pinpoint shooting led the Knicks back to a rousing 107-100 win. Reed sat out game six, and Chamberlain jammed home 45 points against the helpless Knicks in a 135-113 Laker victory. Back in New York for the seventh game, the Knicks took the floor without Reed, but he limped onto the floor to a thunderous ovation. Reed couldn't move, but he leaned on Chamberlain and kept him away from the basket; he also hit the first basket of the day, a jumper from the head of the key. The rest of the Knicks, inspired bv Reed and cheered on by their fans, clicked with their pressing defense and outside shooting. They pulled away from the Lakers and never stopped running on the way to a 113-99 victory which brought New York its first N.B.A. title.

Use Name	Pos	Hgt	Wgt	Age	TOTAL G	Min	FG	FGA	%	FT	FTA	%	Reb	Ass	PF	DQ	Points	PER GAME Min	Reb	Ass	PF	Points
1969/70 N.B.A. — EASTERN DIVISION																						
NEW YORK KNICKERBOCKERS	**60-22 .732**				**RED HOLZMAN**																	
Bill Bradley	F-G	6'5	205	26	67	2098	413	897	46	145	176	82	239	268	219	0	971	31	3.6	4.0	3.3	14.5
Dave DeBusschere	F	6'6	235	29	79	2627	488	1082	45	176	256	69	790	194	244	2	1152	33	10.0	2.5	3.1	14.6
Willis Reed	C	6'9	238	27	81	3089	702	1385	51	351	464	76	1126	161	287	2	1755	38	13.9	2.0	3.5	21.7
Dick Barnett	G	6'4	190	33	82	2772	494	1039	48	232	325	71	221	298	220	0	1220	34	2.7	3.6	2.7	14.9
Walt Frazier	G	6'4	202	24	77	3040	600	1158	52	409	547	75	465	629	203	1	1609	39	6.0	8.2	2.6	20.9
Mike Riordan	G	6'4	200	24	81	1677	255	549	46	114	165	69	194	201	192	1	624	21	2.4	2.5	2.4	7.7
Cazzie Russell	F	6'5	218	25	78	1563	385	773	50	124	160	78	236	135	137	0	894	20	3.0	1.7	1.8	11.5
Dave Stallworth	F	6'7	210	28	82	1375	239	557	43	161	225	72	323	139	194	2	639	17	3.9	1.7	2.4	7.8
Nate Bowman	C	6'10	230	26	81	744	98	235	42	41	79	52	257	46	189	2	237	9	3.2	0.6	2.3	2.9
Johnny Warren	G	6'3	180	22	44	272	44	108	41	24	35	69	40	30	53	0	112	6	0.9	0.7	1.2	2.5
Don May	F	6'4	220	23	37	238	39	101	39	18	19	95	52	17	42	0	96	6	1.4	0.5	1.1	2.6
Bill Hosket	F-C	6'8	225	23	36	235	46	91	51	26	33	79	63	17	36	0	118	7	1.8	0.5	1.0	3.3
Phil Jackson (back injury)																						
MILWAUKEE BUCKS	**56-26 .683**				**LARRY COSTELLO**																	
Greg Smith	F	6'5	200	22	82	2368	339	664	51	125	174	72	712	156	304	8	803	29	8.7	1.9	3.7	9.8
Bob Dandridge	F	6'6	195	22	81	2461	434	895	48	199	264	75	625	292	279	1	1067	30	7.7	3.6	3.4	13.2
Lew Alcindor	C	7'2	225	22	82	3534	938	1810	52	485	743	65	1190	337	283	8	**2361**	43	14.5	4.1	3.5	28.8
Jon McGlocklin	G	6'5	205	26	82	2966	639	1206	53	169	198	85	252	303	164	0	1447	36	3.1	3.7	2.0	17.6
Flynn Robinson	G	6'1	185	28	81	2762	663	1391	48	439	489	**90**	263	449	254	5	1765	34	3.2	5.5	3.1	21.8
Don Smith	F	6'9	235	23	80	1637	237	546	43	119	185	64	603	62	167	2	593	20	7.5	0.8	2.1	7.4
Freddie Crawford	G	6'4	200	28	77	1331	243	506	48	101	148	68	184	225	181	1	587	17	2.4	2.9	2.4	7.6
Len Chappell	F	6'8	240	28	75	1134	243	523	46	135	211	64	276	56	127	1	621	15	3.7	0.7	1.7	8.3
Guy Rodgers	G	6'	190	34	64	749	68	191	36	67	90	74	74	213	73	1	203	12	1.2	3.3	1.1	3.2
Dick Cunningham	C	6'10	255	23	60	416	52	141	37	22	33	67	160	28	70	0	126	7	2.7	0.5	1.2	2.1
Bob Greacen (MS, ankle injury)	F	6'7	205	22	41	292	44	109	40	18	28	64	59	27	49	0	106	7	1.4	0.7	1.2	2.6
John Arthurs	G	6'4	185	22	11	86	12	35	34	11	15	73	14	17	15	0	35	8	1.3	1.5	1.4	3.2
Sam Williams	G	6'3	195	24	11	44	11	24	46	5	11	45	7	3	5	0	27	4	0.6	0.3	0.5	2.5
Charlie Paulk - military service																						
BALTIMORE BULLETS	**50-32 .610**				**GENE SHUE**																	
Jack Marin	F-G	6'7	210	25	82	2947	666	1363	49	286	339	84	537	217	248	6	1618	36	6.5	2.6	3.0	19.7
Gus Johnson	F	6'6	235	31	78	2919	578	1282	45	197	272	72	1086	264	269	6	1353	37	13.9	3.4	3.4	17.3
Wes Unseld	C	6'7	250	23	82	3234	526	1015	52	273	428	64	1370	291	250	2	1325	39	16.7	3.5	3.0	16.2
Kevin Loughery (rib injury)	G	6'3	190	29	55	2037	477	1082	44	253	298	85	168	292	183	3	1207	37	3.1	5.3	3.3	21.9
Earl Monroe	G	6'3	190	25	82	3051	695	1557	45	532	641	83	257	402	258	3	1922	37	3.1	4.9	3.1	23.4
Ray Scott	C-F	6'9	225	31	73	1393	257	605	42	139	173	80	457	114	147	0	653	19	6.3	1.6	2.0	8.9
Mike Davis (broken wrist)	G	6'3	185	23	56	1330	260	586	44	149	192	78	128	111	174	1	669	24	2.3	2.0	3.1	11.9
Fred Carter	G	6'3	185	24	76	1219	157	439	36	80	116	69	192	121	137	0	394	16	2.5	1.6	1.8	5.2
Leroy Ellis	F	6'10	225	29	72	1163	194	414	47	86	116	74	376	47	129	0	474	16	5.2	0.7	1.8	6.6
Al Tucker (from Chi)	F	6'8	190	26	28	262	49	96	51	33	42	79	53	7	34	0	131	9	1.9	0.3	1.2	4.7
Ed Manning (to Chi)	F	6'7	215	26	29	161	32	66	48	5	8	63	35	2	33	0	69	6	1.2	0.1	1.1	2.4
Brian Heaney	G	6'2	180	23	14	70	13	24	54	2	4	50	4	6	17	0	28	5	0.3	0.4	1.2	2.0
Bob Quick (to Det)	F	6'5	215	23	15	67	14	28	50	12	18	67	12	3	9	0	40	4	0.8	0.2	0.6	2.7
Eddie Miles (from Det) (KJ)	F-G	6'4	196	29	3	52	7	10	70	3	5	60	4	4	8	0	17	17	1.3	1.3	2.7	5.7
PHILADELPHIA 76ers	**42-40 .512**				**JACK RAMSAY**																	
Jim Washington	F	6'7	215	26	79	2459	401	842	48	204	273	75	734	104	262	5	1006	31	9.3	1.3	3.3	12.7
Billy Cunningham	F	6'7	220	26	81	3194	802	1710	47	510	700	73	1101	352	331	15	2114	39	13.6	4.3	4.1	26.1
Darrall Imhoff	C	6'10	225	31	79	2474	430	796	54	215	331	65	754	211	294	7	1075	31	9.5	2.7	3.7	13.6
Hal Greer	G	6'3	176	33	80	3024	705	1551	45	352	432	81	376	405	300	8	1762	38	4.7	5.1	3.8	22.0
Archie Clark	G	6'2	175	28	76	2772	594	1198	50	311	396	79	301	380	201	2	1499	36	4.0	5.0	2.6	19.7
WallyJones	G	6'2	185	27	78	1740	366	851	43	190	226	84	173	276	210	2	922	22	2.2	3.5	2.7	11.8
Matt Guokas	F-G	6'6	195	25	80	1558	189	416	45	106	149	71	216	222	201	0	484	19	2.7	2.8	2.5	6.1
George Wilson	C	6'8	230	27	67	836	118	304	39	122	172	71	317	52	145	3	358	12	4.7	0.8	2.2	5.3
Fred Hetzel	F	6'8	230	27	63	757	156	323	48	71	85	84	207	44	110	3	383	12	3.3	0.7	1.7	6.1
Luke Jackson (broken foot)	C	6'9	250	28	37	583	71	181	39	60	81	74	198	50	80	0	202	16	5.4	1.4	2.2	5.5
Bud Ogden	F	6'6	215	23	47	357	82	172	48	27	39	69	86	31	62	2	191	8	1.8	0.7	1.3	4.1
Dave Scholz	F	6'8	220	21	1	1	1	1	100	0	0	—	0	0	0	0	2	1	0.0	0.0	0.0	2.0
CINCINNATI ROYALS	**36-46 .439**				**BOB COUSY**																	
Tom Van Arsdale	F-G	6'5	215	26	71	2544	620	1376	45	381	492	77	463	155	247	3	1621	36	6.5	2.2	3.5	22.8
Johnny Green	F	6'5	200	36	78	2278	481	860	**56**	254	429	59	841	112	268	6	1216	29	10.8	1.4	3.4	15.6
Connie Dierking	C	6'9	235	33	76	2448	521	1243	42	230	306	75	624	169	275	7	1272	32	8.2	2.2	3.6	16.7
Oscar Robertson	G	6'5	220	31	69	2865	647	1267	51	454	561	81	422	558	175	1	1748	42	6.1	8.1	2.5	25.3
Norm Van Lier	G	6'1	175	22	81	2895	302	749	40	166	224	74	409	500	329	**18**	770	36	5.0	6.2	4.1	9.5
Fred Foster	F	6'5	210	23	74	2077	461	1026	45	176	243	72	310	107	209	2	1098	28	4.2	1.4	2.8	14.8
Luther Rackley	C	6'10	220	23	66	1256	190	423	45	124	195	64	378	56	204	5	504	19	5.7	0.8	3.1	7.6
Herm Gilliam	G	6'3	190	23	57	1161	179	441	41	68	91	75	215	178	163	6	426	20	3.8	3.1	2.9	7.5
Bill Turner (from SF)	F	6'7	220	25	69	1095	188	451	42	118	157	75	290	42	187	3	494	16	4.2	0.6	2.7	7.2
Adrian Smith (to SF)	G	6'1	190	33	32	453	60	148	41	52	60	87	33	45	56	0	172	14	1.0	1.4	1.8	5.4
Wally Anderzunas	C-F	6'7	220	23	44	370	65	166	39	29	46	63	82	9	47	1	159	8	1.9	0.2	1.1	3.6
Jim King (from SF, broken leg)	G	6'2	175	28	31	286	34	83	41	22	27	81	46	42	39	0	90	9	1.5	1.4	1.3	2.9
Bob Cousy	G	6'1	185	41	7	34	1	3	33	3	3	100	5	10	11	0	5	5	0.7	1.4	1.6	0.7
Jerry Lucas (to SF)	F	6'8	235	29	4	118	18	35	51	5	7	71	45	9	5	0	41	30	11.3	2.3	1.3	10.3
Bill Dinwiddie (knee injury, to Bos)																						

Use Name	Pos	Hgt	Wgt	Age	TOTAL G	Min	FG	FGA	%	FT	FTA	%	Reb	Ass	PF	DQ	Points	PER GAME Min	Reb	Ass	PF	Points
1969/70 N.B.A.—EASTERN DIVISION (continued)																						
BOSTON CELTICS	**34-48 .415**				**TOM HEINSOHN**																	
Satch Sanders (knee injury)	F	6'6	210	31	57	1616	246	555	44	161	183	88	314	92	199	5	653	28	5.5	1.6	3.5	11.5
Don Nelson	F	6'6	210	29	82	2224	461	920	50	337	435	77	601	148	238	3	1259	27	7.3	1.8	2.9	15.4
Henry Finkel	C	7'	240	27	80	1866	310	683	45	156	233	67	613	103	292	13	776	23	7.7	1.3	3.7	9.7
John Havlicek	G-F	6'5	205	29	81	3369	736	1585	46	488	578	84	635	550	211	1	1960	42	7.8	6.8	2.6	24.2
Larry Siegfried	G	6'3	192	30	78	2081	382	902	42	220	257	86	212	299	187	2	984	27	2.7	3.8	2.4	12.6
Bailey Howell	F	6'7	220	32	82	2078	399	931	43	235	308	76	550	120	261	4	1033	25	6.7	1.5	3.2	12.6
Em Bryant	G	6'1	175	31	71	1617	210	520	40	135	181	75	269	231	201	5	555	23	3.8	3.3	2.8	7.8
Jo Jo White (MS)	G	6'3	190	23	60	1328	309	684	45	111	135	82	169	145	132	1	729	22	2.8	2.4	2.2	12.2
Jim Barnes	C	6'8	240	28	77	1049	178	434	41	95	128	74	350	52	229	4	451	14	4.5	0.7	3.0	5.9
Rich Johnson	C	6'9	215	23	65	898	167	361	46	46	70	66	208	32	155	3	380	14	3.2	0.5	2.4	5.8
Don Chaney	G	6'5	210	23	63	839	115	320	36	82	109	75	152	72	118	0	312	13	2.4	1.1	1.9	5.0
Steve Kuberski	F-C	6'8	215	22	51	797	130	335	39	64	92	70	257	29	87	0	324	16	5.0	0.6	1.7	6.4
Rich Nieman (to CarA)	C	7'	252	23	6	18	2	5	40	2	2	100	6	2	10	0	6	3	1.0	0.3	1.7	1.0
Bill Dinwiddie (from Cin, knee injury)																						
Mal Graham (illness)																						
DETROIT PISTONS	**31-51 .378**				**BUTCH VAN BREDA KOLFF**																	
Terry Dischinger	F	6'7	208	29	75	1754	342	650	53	174	241	72	369	106	213	5	858	23	4.9	1.4	2.8	11.4
Erwin Mueller (from Sea)	F-C	6'8	230	25	74	2284	287	614	47	185	254	73	469	199	186	1	759	31	6.3	2.7	2.5	10.3
Otto Moore	C-F	6'11	220	23	81	2523	383	805	48	194	305	64	900	104	232	3	960	31	11.1	1.3	2.9	11.9
Jimmy Walker	G	6'3	205	25	81	2869	666	1394	48	355	440	81	242	248	203	4	1687	35	3.0	3.1	2.5	20.8
Dave Bing (injury)	G	6'3	185	26	70	2334	575	1295	44	454	580	78	299	478	196	0	1604	33	4.3	6.8	2.8	22.9
Howie Komives	G	6'1	185	28	82	2418	363	878	41	190	234	81	193	312	247	2	916	29	2.4	3.8	3.0	11.2
McCoy McLemore	F	6'7	235	27	73	1421	233	500	47	119	145	82	336	83	159	3	585	19	4.6	1.1	2.2	8.0
Eddie Miles (to Bal) (KJ)	F-G	6'4	196	29	44	1243	231	531	44	130	170	76	173	82	99	0	592	28	3.9	1.9	2.3	13.5
Walt Bellamy (to Atl)	C	6'11	245	30	56	1173	210	384	55	140	249	56	397	55	163	3	560	21	7.1	1.0	2.9	10.0
Bill Hewitt (from LA)	F	6'7	210	25	45	801	85	210	40	38	63	60	213	36	91	1	208	18	4.7	0.8	2.0	4.6
Bob Quick (from Bal)	F	6'5	215	23	19	297	49	111	44	37	53	70	63	11	41	0	135	16	3.3	0.6	2.2	7.1
Happy Hairston (to LA)	F	6'7	225	27	15	282	57	103	55	45	63	71	88	11	36	0	159	19	5.9	0.7	2.4	10.6
Steve Mix (military service)	F	6'7	215	22	18	276	48	100	48	23	39	59	64	15	31	0	119	15	3.6	0.8	1.7	6.6
Paul Long	G	6'2	180	25	25	130	28	62	45	27	38	71	11	17	22	0	83	5	0.4	0.7	0.9	3.3
George Reynolds	G	6'4	198	22	10	44	8	19	42	5	7	71	14	12	10	0	21	4	1.4	1.2	1.0	2.1
Tom Workman (to LA-A)	F	6'7	230	25	2	6	0	1	0	0	0	—	0	0	1	0	0	3	0.0	0.0	0.5	0.0
1969/70 N.B.A. - WESTERN DIVISION																						
ATLANTA HAWKS	**48-34 .585**				**RICHIE GUERIN**																	
Joe Caldwell	F-G	6'5	205	28	82	2857	674	1329	51	379	551	69	407	287	255	3	1727	35	5.0	3.5	3.1	21.1
Bill Bridges	F	6'6	235	30	82	3269	443	932	48	331	451	73	1181	345	292	6	1217	40	14.4	4.2	3.6	14.8
Jim Davis	C-F	6'9	235	28	82	2623	438	943	46	240	318	75	796	238	335	5	1116	32	9.7	2.9	4.1	13.6
Lou Hudson	G	6'5	220	25	80	3091	830	1564	53	371	450	82	373	276	225	1	2031	39	4.7	3.5	2.8	25.4
Walt Hazzard	G	6'2	190	27	82	2757	493	1056	47	267	330	81	329	561	264	3	1253	34	4.0	6.8	3.2	15.3
Gary Gregor	F	6'7	235	24	81	1603	286	661	43	88	113	78	397	63	159	5	660	20	4.9	0.8	2.0	8.1
Don Ohl	G	6'3	190	33	66	984	176	372	47	58	72	81	71	98	113	1	410	15	1.1	1.5	1.7	6.2
Butch Beard	G	6'3	185	22	72	941	183	392	47	135	163	83	140	121	124	0	501	13	1.9	1.7	1.7	7.0
Walt Bellamy (from Det)	C	6'11	245	30	23	855	141	287	49	75	124	60	310	88	97	2	357	37	13.5	3.8	4.2	15.5
Dave Newmark	C	7'	260	23	64	612	127	296	43	59	77	77	174	42	128	3	313	10	2.7	0.7	2.0	4.9
Grady O'Malley	F	6'5	205	21	24	113	21	60	35	8	19	42	26	10	12	0	50	5	1.1	0.4	0.5	2.1
Richie Guerin	G	6'4	210	37	8	64	3	11	27	1	1	100	2	12	9	0	7	8	0.3	1.5	1.1	0.9
Gene Tormohlen	F	6'9	245	32	2	11	2	4	50	0	0	—	4	1	3	0	4	6	2.0	0.5	1.5	2.0
Skip Harlicka - military service																						
LOS ANGELES LAKERS	**46-36 .561**				**JOE MULLANEY**																	
Elgin Baylor (knee injury)	F	6'5	225	35	54	2213	511	1051	49	276	357	77	559	292	132	1	1298	41	10.4	5.4	2.4	24.0
Happy Hairston (from Det)	F	6'7	225	27	56	2145	426	870	49	281	350	80	687	110	194	9	1133	38	12.3	2.0	3.5	20.2
Wilt Chamberlain (knee injury)	C	7'1	275	33	12	505	129	227	57	70	157	45	221	49	31	0	328	42	18.4	4.1	2.6	27.3
Jerry West	G	6'3	180	31	74	3106	831	1673	50	647	785	82	338	554	160	3	2309	42	4.6	7.5	2.2	31.2
Dick Garrett	G	6'3	185	22	73	2318	354	816	43	138	162	85	235	180	236	5	846	32	3.2	2.5	3.2	11.6
Mel Counts	C-F	7'	230	28	81	2193	434	1017	43	156	201	78	683	160	304	7	1024	27	8.4	2.0	3.8	12.6
Rick Roberson (injury)	C	6'9	230	22	74	2005	262	586	45	120	212	57	672	92	256	7	644	27	9.1	1.2	3.5	8.7
Keith Erickson (ankle injury)	F-G	6'5	200	25	68	1755	258	563	46	91	122	75	304	209	175	3	607	26	4.5	3.1	2.6	8.9
Johnny Egan (injury)	G	5'11	180	30	72	1627	215	491	44	99	121	82	104	216	171	2	529	23	1.4	3.0	2.4	7.3
Willie McCarter (ankle injury)	G	6'3	175	23	40	861	132	349	38	43	60	72	83	93	71	0	307	22	2.1	2.3	1.8	7.7
Bill Hewitt (to Det)	F	6'7	210	25	20	478	25	88	28	16	31	52	141	28	39	0	66	24	7.1	1.4	2.0	3.3
Mike Lynn	F	6'7	215	24	44	403	44	133	33	31	48	65	64	30	87	4	119	9	1.5	0.7	2.0	2.7
John Tresvant (from Sea)	F	6'7	220	30	20	221	47	88	53	23	35	66	63	17	40	0	117	11	3.2	0.9	2.0	5.9

1969/70 N.B.A.—WESTERN DIVISION (continued)

					TOTAL													PER GAME				
Use Name	Pos	Hgt	Wgt	Age	G	Min	FG	FGA	%	FT	FTA	%	Reb	Ass	PF	DQ	Points	Min	Reb	Ass	PF	Points
CHICAGO BULLS	**39-43 .476**				**DICK MOTTA**																	
Chet Walker	F	6'6	215	29	78	2726	596	1249	48	483	568	85	604	192	203	1	1675	35	7.7	2.5	2.6	21.5
Bob Love	F	6'8	215	27	82	3123	640	1373	47	422	525	80	712	148	260	2	1722	38	8.7	1.8	3.2	21.0
Tom Boerwinkle	C	7'	270	24	81	2335	348	775	45	150	226	66	1016	229	255	4	846	29	12.5	2.8	3.1	10.4
Clem Haskins	G	6'3	195	25	82	3214	668	1486	45	332	424	78	378	624	237	0	1668	39	4.6	7.6	2.9	20.3
Bob Weiss	G	6'2	185	27	82	2544	365	855	43	213	253	84	227	474	206	0	943	31	2.8	5.8	2.5	11.5
Jerry Sloan (injury)	F-G	6'6	200	27	53	1822	310	737	42	207	318	65	372	165	179	3	827	34	7.0	3.1	3.4	15.6
Walt Wesley	C	6'11	220	24	72	1407	270	648	42	145	219	66	455	68	184	1	685	20	6.3	0.9	2.6	9.5
Bob Kauftman	F-C	6'8	240	23	64	775	94	221	43	88	123	72	211	76	117	1	276	12	3.3	1.2	1.8	4.3
Ed Manning (from Bal)	F	6'7	215	26	39	616	87	255	34	37	48	77	197	34	89	1	211	16	5.1	0.9	2.3	5.4
Al Tucker (to Bal)	F	6'8	190	26	33	557	97	189	51	37	45	82	113	31	52	0	231	17	3.4	0.9	1.6	7.0
Shaler Halimon (MS)	G	6'6	200	24	38	517	96	244	39	49	73	67	68	69	58	0	241	14	1.8	1.8	1.5	6.3
Loy Petersen	G	6'5	205	24	31	231	33	90	37	26	39	67	26	23	22	0	92	7	0.8	0.7	0.7	3.0
Johnny Baum (MS)	F	6'5	200	23	3	13	3	11	27	0	0	—	4	0	1	0	6	4	1.3	0.0	0.3	2.0
PHOENIX SUNS	**39-43 .476**				**JOHNNY KERR (15-23 .395), JERRY COLANGELO (24-20 .545)**																	
Paul Silas	F	6'7	225	26	78	2836	373	804	46	250	412	61	916	214	266	5	996	36	11.7	2.7	3.4	12.8
Connie Hawkins	F-C	6'8	220	27	81	3312	709	1447	49	577	741	78	846	391	287	4	1995	41	10.4	4.8	3.5	24.6
Jim Fox	C	6'10	230	26	81	2041	413	788	52	218	283	77	570	93	261	7	1044	25	7.0	1.1	3.2	12.9
Dick Van Arsdale	G	6'5	210	26	77	2966	592	1166	51	459	575	80	264	338	282	5	1643	39	3.4	4.4	3.7	21.3
Gail Goodrich	G	6'1	175	26	81	3234	568	1251	45	488	604	81	340	605	251	3	1624	40	4.2	7.5	3.1	20.0
Neal Walk	C	6'10	250	21	82	1394	257	547	47	155	242	64	455	80	225	2	669	17	5.5	1.0	2.7	8.2
Art Harris (from Sea)	G	6'4	186	22	76	1375	257	650	40	82	125	66	142	211	209	0	596	18	1.9	2.8	2.8	7.8
Jerry Chambers	F	6'5	190	26	79	1139	283	658	43	91	125	73	219	54	162	3	657	14	2.8	0.7	2.1	8.3
Lamar Green	F	6'7	220	22	58	700	101	234	43	41	70	59	276	17	115	2	243	12	4.8	0.3	2.0	4.2
Stan McKenzie	F-G	6'5	210	25	58	525	81	206	39	1	73	1	93	52	67	1	220	9	1.6	0.9	1.2	3.8
Dick Snyder (to Sea)	G	6'5	210	25	6	147	22	45	49	7	8	88	15	9	20	1	51	25	2.5	1.5	3.3	8.5
Neil Johnson	F	6'7	225	26	28	136	20	60	33	8	12	67	47	12	38	0	48	5	1.7	0.4	1.4	1.7
John Wetzel - military service																						
SEATTLE SUPERSONICS	**36-46 .439**				**LENNY WILKENS**																	
Tom Meschery	F	6'6	225	31	80	2294	394	818	48	196	248	79	666	157	317	13	984	29	8.3	2.0	4.0	12.3
Bob Boozer	F	6'8	225	32	82	2549	493	1005	49	263	320	82	717	110	237	2	1249	31	8.7	1.3	2.9	15.2
Bob Rule	C	6'9	235	25	80	2959	789	1705	46	387	542	71	825	144	278	6	1965	37	10.3	1.8	3.5	24.6
Dick Snyder (from Phoe)	G	6'5	210	25	76	2290	434	818	53	162	200	81	308	333	257	7	1030	30	4.1	4.4	3.4	13.6
Lenny Wilkens	G	6'1	185	32	75	2802	448	1066	42	438	556	79	378	**683**	212	5	1334	37	5.0	**9.1**	2.8	17.8
Lucius Allen	G	6'2	175	22	81	1817	306	692	44	182	249	73	211	342	201	0	794	22	2.6	4.2	2.5	9.8
Barry Clemens	F	6'7	210	27	78	1487	270	595	45	111	140	79	316	116	188	1	651	19	4.1	1.5	2.4	8.3
John Tresvant (to LA)	F	6'7	220	30	49	1278	217	507	43	183	249	73	362	95	164	4	617	26	7.4	1.9	3.3	12.6
Dorie Murrey	C-F	6'8	220	26	81	1079	153	343	45	136	186	73	357	76	191	4	442	13	4.4	0.9	2.4	5.5
Lee Winfield	G	6'2	175	22	64	771	138	288	48	87	116	75	98	102	95	0	363	12	1.5	1.6	1.5	5.7
Art Harris (to Phoe)	G	6'4	186	22	5	178	28	73	38	4	9	44	19	20	11	0	60	36	3.8	4.0	2.2	12.0
Rod Thorn (knee injury)	G	6'4	200	28	19	105	20	45	44	15	24	63	16	17	8	0	55	6	0.8	0.9	0.4	2.9
Joe Kennedy	F	6'6	210	22	14	82	3	34	9	2	2	100	20	7	7	0	8	6	1.4	0.5	0.5	0.6
Erwin Mueller (to Det)	F-C	6'8	230	25	4	69	13	32	41	4	9	44	14	6	6	0	30	17	3.5	1.5	1.5	7.5
Al Hairston	G	6'1	170	24	3	20	3	8	38	1	1	100	5	6	3	0	7	7	1.7	2.0	1.0	2.3
SAN FRANCISCO WARRIORS	**30-52 .366**				**GEORGE LEE (22-30 .423), AL ATTLES (8-22 .267)**																	
Joe Ellis (hand injury)	F	6'6	175	25	76	2380	501	1223	41	200	270	74	594	139	281	13	1202	31	7.8	1.8	3.7	15.8
Jerry Lucas (from Cin, broken hand)	F	6'8	235	29	63	2302	387	764	51	195	248	79	906	166	159	2	969	37	14.4	2.6	2.5	15.4
Nate Thurmond (knee injury)	C	6'11	235	28	43	1919	341	824	41	261	346	75	762	150	110	l	943	45	17.7	3.5	2.6	21.9
Jeff Mullins	G	6'4	200	27	74	2861	656	1426	46	320	378	85	382	360	240	4	1632	39	5.2	4.9	3.2	22.1
Ron Williams	G	6'3	190	25	80	2435	452	1046	43	277	337	82	190	424	287	7	1181	30	2.4	5.3	3.6	14.8
Clyde Lee	C-F	6'10	210	25	82	2641	362	822	44	178	300	59	929	80	263	5	902	32	11.3	1.0	3.2	11.0
Bobby Lewis	G	6'3	185	24	73	1353	213	557	38	100	152	66	157	194	170	0	526	19	2.2	2.7	2.3	7.2
Dave Gambee	F	6'6	220	32	73	951	185	464	40	156	186	84	244	55	172	0	526	13	3.3	0.8	2.4	7.2
Bob Portman	F	6'5	200	22	60	813	177	398	44	66	85	78	224	28	77	0	420	14	3.7	0.5	1.3	7.0
Dale Schlueter	C	6'10	226	24	63	685	82	167	49	60	97	62	231	25	108	0	224	11	3.7	0.4	1.7	3.6
Al Attles (broken hand)	G	6'2	180	33	45	676	78	202	39	75	113	66	74	142	103	0	231	15	1.6	3.2	2.3	5.1
Adrian Smith (from Cin)	G	6'1	190	33	45	634	93	268	35	100	110	91	49	87	66	0	286	14	1.1	1.9	1.5	6.4
Jim King (to Cin)	G	6'2	175	28	3	105	19	46	41	11	14	79	16	10	8	0	49	35	5.3	3.3	2.7	16.3
Bill Turner (to Cin)	F	6'7	220	25	3	75	9	17	53	5	10	50	14	1	7	0	23	25	4.7	0.3	2.3	7.7

1969/70 N.B.A.—WESTERN DIVISION (continued)

se Name	Pos	Hgt	Wgt	Age	G	Min	FG	FGA	%	FT	FTA	%	Reb	Ass	PF	DQ	Points	Min	Reb	Ass	PF	Points
					TOTAL													PER GAME				
AN DIEGO ROCKETS	**27-55 .329**	**JACK McMAHON (9-17 .346), ALEX HANNUM (18-38 .391)**																				
on Kojis (ankle injury)	F	6'5	215	30	56	1578	338	756	45	181	241	75	388	78	135	1	857	28	6.9	1.4	2.4	15.3
ohn Block	F	6'10	218	25	82	2152	453	1025	44	287	367	78	609	137	275	2	1193	26	7.4	1.7	3.4	14.5
vin Hayes	C	6'9	235	24	82	**3665**	914	**2020**	45	428	622	69	**1386**	162	270	5	2256	**45**	**16.9**	2.0	3.3	27.5
m Barnett	G-F	6'4	180	25	80	2105	450	998	45	289	366	79	305	287	222	3	1189	26	3.8	3.6	2.8	14.9
tu Lantz	G	6'3	175	23	82	2471	455	1027	44	278	361	77	255	287	238	2	1188	30	3.1	3.5	2.9	14.5
oby Kimball	F	6'8	225	27	77	1622	218	508	43	107	185	58	621	95	187	1	543	21	8.1	1.2	2.4	7.1
ambone Williams	G	6'2	185	30	80	1545	189	464	41	88	118	75	292	503	168	0	466	19	3.7	6.3	2.1	5.8
emie Williams	G	6'3	175	24	72	1228	251	641	39	98	122	80	155	165	124	0	598	17	2.2	2.3	1.7	8.3
obby Smith	F	6'5	212	23	75	1198	242	567	43	66	96	69	328	75	119	0	550	16	4.4	1.0	1.6	7.3
ohn Trapp	F	6'7	215	24	70	1025	185	434	43	72	104	69	309	49	200	3	442	15	4.4	0.7	2.9	6.3
ick Adelman (injury)	G	6'1	178	23	35	717	96	247	39	68	91	75	81	113	90	0	260	20	2.3	3.2	2.6	7.4
at Riley (injury)	F	6'4	208	24	36	474	75	180	42	40	55	73	57	85	68	0	190	13	1.6	2.4	1.9	5.3

1969/70 N.B.A. — PLAYOFFS

se Name	Pos	Hgt	Wgt	Age	G	Min	FG	FGA	%	FT	FTA	%	Reb	Ass	PF	DQ	Points	Min	Reb	Ass	PF	Points
EW YORK KNICKERBOCKERS	**RED HOLZMAN**	defeated Baltimore 4-3; H120-117 (2OT), 106-99, H113-127, 92-102, H101-80, 87-96, H127-114 defeated Milwaukee 4-1; H110-102, H112-111, 96-101, 117-105, H132-96 defeated Los Angeles 4-3; H124-112, H103-105, 111-108(OT), 115-121(OT), H107-100, 113-135, H113-99																				
ill Bradley	F	6'5	205	26	19	616	100	233	43	35	43	81	72	60	59	1	235	32	3.8	3.2	3.1	12.4
ave DeBusschere	F-C	6'6	235	29	19	701	130	309	42	45	68	66	220	46	63	1	305	37	11.6	2.4	3.3	16.1
Villis Reed	C	6'9	238	27	18	732	178	378	47	70	95	74	248	51	60	0	426	41	13.8	2.8	3.3	23.7
ick Barnett	G	6'4	190	33	19	714	131	280	47	59	76	78	39	64	64	0	321	38	2.1	3.4	3.4	16.9
Valt Frazier	G	6'4	202	24	19	834	118	247	48	68	89	76	149	156	53	0	304	44	7.8	8.2	2.8	16.0
azzie Russell	F	6'5	218	25	19	306	80	165	48	18	19	95	47	16	31	0	178	16	2.5	0.8	1.6	9.4
like Riordan	G	6'4	200	24	19	296	53	109	49	25	35	71	46	27	33	0	131	16	2.4	1.4	1.7	6.9
ave Stallworth	F-C	6'7	210	28	19	275	61	133	46	15	16	94	77	20	35	0	137	14	4.1	1.1	1.8	7.2
late Bowman	C	6'10	230	26	18	128	18	47	38	7	10	70	44	6	34	0	43	7	2.4	0.3	1.9	2.4
ill Hosket	C	6'8	225	23	5	29	4	10	40	3	4	75	5	2	6	0	11	6	1.0	0.4	1.2	2.2
ohnny Warren	G	6'3	180	22	10	22	2	5	40	0	0	—	3	2	6	0	4	2	0.3	0.2	0.6	0.4
on May	F	6'4	220	23	2	7	2	3	67	0	0	—	0	0	2	0	4	4	0.0	0.0	1.0	2.0
Phil Jackson (back injury)																						
OS ANGELES LAKERS	**JOE MULLANEY**	defeated Phoenix 4-3; H128-112, H101-114, 98-112, 102-112, H138-121, 104-93, H129-94 defeated Atlanta 4-0; 119-115, 105-94, H115-114(OT), H133-114 lost to New York 3-4; 112-124, 105-103, H108-111(OT), H121-115(OT), 100-107, H135-113, 99-113																				
lgin Baylor	F	6'5	225	35	18	667	138	296	47	60	81	74	173	83	50	1	336	37	9.6	4.6	2.8	18.7
lappy Hairston	F	6'7	225	27	16	296	47	108	44	24	35	69	76	20	31	0	118	19	4.8	1.3	1.9	7.4
Vilt Chamberlain	C	7'1	275	33	18	**851**	158	288	55	82	202	41	**399**	81	42	0	398	**47**	22.2	4.5	2.3	22.1
erry West	G	6'3	180	31	18	830	**196**	**418**	47	**170**	**212**	80	66	151	55	1	**562**	46	3.7	**8.4**	3.1	31.2
ick Garrett	G	6'3	185	22	18	595	101	198	51	28	32	88	52	39	**68**	**2**	230	33	2.9	2.2	3.8	12.8
eith Erickson	F-G	6'5	200	25	17	553	71	153	46	27	35	77	77	74	44	0	169	33	4.5	4.4	2.6	9.9
lel Counts	F	7'	230	28	14	212	37	88	42	11	13	85	74	16	48	**2**	85	15	5.3	1.1	3.4	6.1
ohnny Egan	G	5'11	180	30	16	162	23	43	53	10	11	91	5	22	20	0	56	10	0.3	1.4	1.3	3.5
ohn Tresvant	F	6'7	220	30	11	148	23	51	45	19	23	83	38	16	22	1	65	13	3.5	1.5	2.0	5.9
ick Roberson	F-C	6'9	230	22	9	61	8	18	44	6	10	60	16	0	13	0	22	7	1.8	0.0	1.4	2.4
Villie McCarter	G	6'3	175	23	5	14	3	7	43	1	1	100	3	3	2	0	7	3	0.6	0.6	0.4	1.4
like Lynn	F	6'7	215	24	3	6	2	3	67	0	0	—	2	1	1	0	4	2	0.7	0.3	0.3	1.3
ILWAUKEE BUCKS	**LARRY COSTELLO**	defeated Philadelphia 4-1; H125-118, H105-112, 156-120, 118-111, H115-106 lost to New York 1-4; 102-110, 111-112, H101-96, H105-117, 96-132																				
ireg Smith	F	6'5	200	22	10	329	47	94	50	13	22	59	85	22	34	1	107	33	8.5	2.2	3.4	10.7
ob Dandridge	F	6'6	195	22	10	399	72	142	51	19	29	66	87	57	39	1	163	40	8.7	5.7	3.9	16.3
ew Alcindor	C	7'2	225	22	10	435	139	245	**57**	74	101	73	168	41	25	1	352	44	16.8	4.1	2.5	35.2
lon McGlocklin	G	6'5	205	26	10	377	62	144	43	25	31	81	36	21	22	0	149	38	3.6	2.1	2.2	14.9
lynn Robinson	G	6'1	185	28	10	300	42	129	33	44	50	**88**	23	50	22	0	128	30	2.3	5.0	2.2	12.8
reddie Crawford	G-F	6'4	200	28	10	208	34	88	39	20	24	83	35	37	27	1	88	21	3.5	3.7	2.7	8.8
en Chappell	F	6'8	240	28	9	133	28	50	56	13	19	68	26	5	10	0	69	15	2.9	0.6	1.1	7.7
on Smith	F	6'9	235	23	7	82	11	19	58	8	10	80	26	4	5	0	30	12	3.7	0.6	0.7	4.3
uy Rodgers	G	6'	190	34	7	68	4	14	29	9	12	75	4	21	7	0	17	10	0.6	3.0	1.0	2.4
ick Cunningham	C	6'10	255	23	8	45	10	18	56	1	2	50	12	2	6	0	21	6	1.5	0.3	0.8	2.6
am Williams	G	6'3	195	24	2	16	4	7	57	0	2	0	4	1	5	0	8	8	2.0	0.5	2.5	4.0
ob Greacen	F	6'7	205	22	1	8	1	4	25	0	1	0	2	3	0	0	2	8	2.0	3.0	0.0	2.0
Charlie Paulk (MS)																						

1969/70 N.B.A. - PLAYOFFS (continued)

ATLANTA HAWKS — RICHIE GUERIN

defeated Chicago 4-1; H129-111, H124-104, 106-101, 120-131, H113-107
lost to Los Angeles 0-4; H115-119, H94-105, 114-115(OT), 114-133

Use Name	Pos	Hgt	Wgt	Age	G	Min	FG	FGA	%	FT	FTA	%	Reb	Ass	PF	DQ	Points	Min	Reb	Ass	PF	Points
					TOTAL													PER GAME				
Joe Caldwell	F-G	6'5	205	28	9	393	93	198	47	39	60	65	45	38	34	1	225	44	5.0	4.2	3.8	25.
Bill Bridges	F	6'6	235	30	9	381	44	110	40	16	27	59	154	29	37	1	104	42	17.1	3.2	4.1	11.
Walt Bellamy	C	6'11	245	30	9	368	59	126	47	33	46	72	140	35	32	0	151	41	15.6	3.9	3.6	16.
Lou Hudson	G	6'5	220	25	9	360	78	187	42	41	50	82	40	33	34	2	197	40	4.4	3.7	3.8	21
Walt Hazzard	G	6'2	190	27	7	255	65	130	50	20	32	63	24	54	23	0	150	36	3.4	7.7	3.3	21.
Butch Beard	G	6'3	185	22	9	146	31	65	48	19	26	73	26	8	19	0	81	16	2.9	0.9	2.1	9
Jim Davis	F-C	6'9	235	28	9	117	14	37	38	10	17	59	30	6	24	1	38	13	3.3	0.7	2.7	4.
Gary Gregor	F	6'7	235	24	7	67	6	21	29	4	6	67	17	2	14	0	16	10	2.4	0.3	2.0	2.
Richie Guerin	G	6'4	210	37	2	56	13	21	62	7	7	100	8	4	6	0	33	28	4.0	2.0	3.0	16.
Dave Newmark	C	7'	260	23	6	42	15	33	45	4	4	100	12	2	8	0	34	7	2.0	0.3	1.3	5.
Skip Harlicka - military service																						

BALTIMORE BULLETS — GENE SHUE

lost to New York 3-4; 117-120(2OT), H99-106, 127-113, H102-92, 80-101, H96-87, 114-127

Use Name	Pos	Hgt	Wgt	Age	G	Min	FG	FGA	%	FT	FTA	%	Reb	Ass	PF	DQ	Points	Min	Reb	Ass	PF	Points
Jack Marin	F	6'7	210	25	7	265	48	114	42	29	34	85	47	22	27	1	125	38	6.7	3.1	3.9	17.
Gus Johnson	F	6'6	235	31	7	298	51	111	46	27	34	79	80	9	20	0	129	43	11.4	1.3	2.9	18.
Wes Unseld	C	6'7	250	23	7	289	29	70	41	15	19	79	165	24	25	1	73	41	**23.6**	3.4	3.6	10.
Fred Carter	F-G	6'3	185	24	7	253	41	107	38	17	28	61	31	24	27	0	99	36	4.4	3.4	3.9	14.
Earl Monore	G	6'3	190	25	7	299	74	154	48	48	60	80	23	28	23	0	196	43	3.3	4.0	3.3	28.
Kevin Loughery	G	6'3	190	29	7	153	26	77	34	15	21	71	16	8	24	0	67	22	2.3	1.1	3.4	9.
Ray Scott	C-F	6'9	225	31	7	90	11	34	32	10	14	71	21	4	8	0	32	13	3.0	0.6	1.1	4.
Eddie Miles	F	6'4	196	29	5	63	4	10	40	0	0	—	5	0	5	0	8	13	1.0	0.0	1.0	1.
Leroy Ellis	F	6'10	225	29	3	8	0	4	0	2	2	100	3	0	0	0	2	3	1.0	0.0	0.0	0.
Brian Heaney	G	6'2	180	23	6	7	0	2	0	0	0	—	1	1	0	0	0	1	0.2	0.2	0.0	0.
Al Tucker	F	6'8	190	26	4	5	2	2	100	0	0	—	0	0	0	0	4	1	0.0	0.0	0.0	1.
Mike Davis (broken wrist)																						

PHOENIX SUNS — JERRY COLANGELO

lost to Los Angeles 3-4; 112-128, 114-101, H112-98, H112-102, 121-138, H93-104, 94-129

Use Name	Pos	Hgt	Wgt	Age	G	Min	FG	FGA	%	FT	FTA	%	Reb	Ass	PF	DQ	Points	Min	Reb	Ass	PF	Points
Paul Silas	F	6'7	225	26	7	286	46	109	42	21	32	66	111	30	29	1	113	41	15.9	4.3	4.1	16.1
Connie Hawkins	F-C	6'8	220	27	7	328	62	150	41	54	66	82	97	41	22	0	178	47	13.9	5.9	3.1	25.4
Jim Fox	C	6'10	230	26	6	174	25	69	36	17	24	71	64	8	20	0	67	29	10.7	1.3	3.3	11.2
Tom Van Arsdale	G	6'5	210	26	7	255	43	100	43	29	33	88	18	29	23	0	115	36	2.6	4.1	3.3	16.4
Gail Goodrich	G	6'1	175	26	7	265	56	118	47	30	35	86	32	38	21	0	142	38	4.6	5.4	3.0	20.3
Art Harris	G	6'4	186	22	7	89	15	42	36	0	2	0	13	12	13	0	30	13	1.9	1.7	1.9	4.3
Jerry Chambers	F	6'5	190	26	7	73	14	37	38	5	8	63	17	7	6	0	33	10	2.4	1.0	0.9	4.7
Stan McKenzie	G-F	6'5	210	25	7	71	8	29	28	4	5	80	9	3	14	0	16	10	1.3	0.4	2.0	2.3
Lamar Green	F	6'7	220	22	6	69	8	28	29	2	5	40	23	5	8	0	18	12	3.8	0.8	1.3	3.0
Neal Walk	C	6'10	250	21	5	63	17	43	40	6	8	75	35	2	13	0	40	13	7.0	0.4	2.6	8.0
Neil Johnson	F	6'7	225	26	2	7	1	3	33	0	0	—	4	0	4	0	2	4	2.0	0.0	2.0	1.0
John Wetzel - military service																						

CHICAGO BULLS — DICK MOTTA

lost to Atlanta 1-4; 111-129, 104-124, H101-106, H131-120, 107-113

Use Name	Pos	Hgt	Wgt	Age	G	Min	FG	FGA	%	FT	FTA	%	Reb	Ass	PF	DQ	Points	Min	Reb	Ass	PF	Points
Chet Walker	F	6'6	215	29	5	178	35	83	42	27	33	82	42	11	14	0	97	36	8.4	2.2	2.8	19.4
Bob Love	F	6'8	215	27	5	172	20	52	38	19	24	79	46	4	12	0	59	34	9.2	0.8	2.4	11.8
Tom Boerwinkle	C	7'	270	24	5	177	40	79	51	8	13	62	72	16	19	0	88	35	14.4	3.2	3.8	17.6
Jerry Sloan	G-F	6'6	200	27	5	190	29	74	39	16	25	64	39	11	18	0	74	38	7.8	2.2	3.6	14.8
Clem Haskins	G	6'3	195	25	5	154	32	68	47	17	19	89	16	25	13	0	81	31	3.2	5.0	2.6	16.2
Bob Weiss	G	6'2	185	27	5	121	25	59	42	8	10	80	6	24	11	0	58	24	1.2	4.8	2.2	11.6
Shaler Halimon	G	6'6	200	24	5	106	21	61	34	2	3	67	20	18	13	0	44	21	4.0	3.6	2.6	8.8
Walt Wesley	C	6'11	220	24	4	59	16	31	52	6	12	50	19	2	9	0	38	15	4.8	0.5	2.3	9.5
Ed Manning	F	6'7	215	26	2	29	5	10	50	1	2	50	9	3	2	0	11	15	4.5	1.5	1.0	5.5
Bob Kauffman	F-C	6'8	240	23	3	14	1	3	33	2	3	67	6	4	2	0	4	5	2.0	1.3	0.7	1.3
John Baum - military service																						

PHILADELPHIA 76ers — JACK RAMSAY

lost to Milwaukee 1-4; 118-125, 112-105, H120-156, H111-118, 106-115

Use Name	Pos	Hgt	Wgt	Age	G	Min	FG	FGA	%	FT	FTA	%	Reb	Ass	PF	DQ	Points	Min	Reb	Ass	PF	Points
Jim Washington	F	6'7	215	26	5	167	25	57	44	13	23	57	49	9	18	0	63	33	9.8	1.8	3.6	12.6
Billy Cunningham	F	6'7	220	26	5	205	61	123	50	24	36	67	52	20	19	0	146	41	10.4	4.0	3.8	29.2
Darrall Imhoff	C	6'10	225	31	5	138	22	48	46	1	7	14	35	11	23	0	45	28	7.0	2.2	**4.6**	9.0
Hal Greer	G	6'3	176	33	5	178	33	74	45	11	13	85	17	27	16	0	77	36	3.4	5.4	3.2	15.4
Archie Clark	G	6'2	175	28	5	146	26	60	43	16	22	73	14	18	10	0	68	29	2.8	3.6	2.0	13.6
Wally Jones	G	6'2	185	27	5	160	34	65	52	11	14	79	11	24	16	0	79	32	2.2	4.8	3.2	15.8
Fred Hetzel	F	6'8	230	27	5	75	13	25	52	9	11	82	18	3	10	0	35	15	3.6	0.6	2.0	7.0
Luke Jackson	C	6'9	250	28	5	73	9	19	47	2	2	100	33	3	11	1	20	15	6.6	0.6	2.2	4.0
Matt Guokas	F	6'6	195	25	2	23	6	8	75	1	1	100	3	1	1	0	13	12	1.5	0.5	0.5	6.5
George Wilson	C	6'8	230	27	2	23	4	13	31	1	1	100	12	1	4	0	9	12	6.0	0.5	2.0	4.5
Bud Ogden	F	6'6	215	23	1	12	5	9	56	2	4	50	1	6	0	0	12	12	1.0	6.0	0.0	12.0

1969/70 N.B.A. TEAM STATISTICS

Team	REGULAR SEASON G	FG	FGA	%	FT	FTA	%	Reb.	Ass.	AVERAGE POINTS For	Agnst.	Diff.	PLAYOFFS G	FG	FGA	%	FT	FTA	%	Reb.	Ass.	AVERAGE POINTS For	Agnst.	Diff.
EASTERN DIVISION																								
New York	82	3803	7975	48	1821	2484	73	4006	2135	115.0	**105.9**	**+9.1**	19	877	1919	46	345	455	76	950	450	110.5	106.8	+3.7
Milwaukee	82	3923	8041	**49**	1895	2589	73	4419	2168	118.8	114.2	+4.6	10	454	954	48	226	303	75	506	264	113.4	113.4	—
Baltimore	82	**3925**	8567	46	2050	2652	77	4679	1881	120.7	118.6	+2.1	7	286	685	42	163	212	77	392	120	105.0	**106.6**	-1.6
Philadelphia	82	3915	8345	47	2168	2884	75	4463	2127	**121.9**	118.5	+3.4	5	**238**	501	48	91	134	68	245	123	113.4	123.8	-10.4
Cincinnati	82	3767	8271	46	2082	2841	73	4163	1992	117.3	120.2	-2.9												
Boston	82	3645	8235	44	2132	2711	**79**	4336	1875	114.9	116.8	-1.9												
Detroit	82	3565	7657	47	2116	2881	73	3831	1709	112.8	116.1	-3.3												
WESTERN DIVISION																								
Atlanta	82	3817	7907	48	2012	2669	75	4210	2142	117.6	117.2	+0.4	9	418	928	45	193	275	70	496	211	**114.3**	114.0	+0.3
Los Angeles	82	3668	7952	46	1991	2641	75	4154	2030	113.7	111.8	+1.9	18	807	1671	**48**	**438**	**655**	67	981	**506**	114.0	110.1	**+3.9**
Chicago	82	3607	8133	44	2209	2861	77	4383	2133	114.9	116.7	-1.8	5	224	**520**	43	106	144	74	275	118	110.8	118.4	-7.6
Phoenix	82	3676	7856	47	**2434**	**3270**	74	4183	2076	119.3	121.1	-1.8	7	295	**728**	41	168	218	**77**	**423**	175	108.3	114.3	-6.0
Seattle	82	3709	8029	46	2171	2851	76	4312	**2214**	116.9	119.5	-2.6												
San Francisco	82	3555	8224	43	2004	2646	76	4772	1861	111.1	115.6	-4.5												
San Diego	82	2866	**8867**	44	2000	2728	73	**4786**	2036	118.7	121.8	-3.1												

1969/70 N.B.A. STANDINGS

Team	W	L	Pct.	GB	Record against playoff teams W	L	Pct.	Record against non-playoff teams W	L	Pct.	HOME W	L	Pct.	ROAD W	L	Pct.	NEUTRAL W	L	Pct.
EASTERN DIVISION																			
New York Knickerbockers	**60**	22	**.732**	—	**32**	11	**.744**	28	11	.718	**30**	11	**.732**	**27**	10	**.730**	3	1	.750
Milwaukee Bucks	56	26	.683	4	24	19	.558	**32**	7	**.821**	27	11	.711	24	14	.632	5	1	.833
Baltimore Bullets	50	32	.610	10	23	20	.535	27	12	.692	25	12	.676	19	18	.514	6	2	.750
Philadelphia 76ers	42	40	.512	18	20	25	.444	22	15	.595	22	16	.579	16	22	.421	4	2	.667
Cincinnati Royals	36	46	.439	24	22	30	.423	14	16	.467	19	13	.594	14	25	.359	3	**8**	.273
Boston Celtics	34	48	.415	26	16	35	.314	18	13	.581	16	**21**	.432	13	27	.325	5	0	**1.000**
Detroit Pistons	31	51	.378	29	17	34	.333	14	17	.452	18	20	.474	10	25	.286	3	6	.333
WESTERN DIVISION																			
Atlanta Hawks	48	34	.585	—	23	21	.523	25	13	.658	25	13	.658	18	16	.529	5	5	.500
Los Angeles Lakers	46	36	.561	2	19	25	.432	27	11	.711	27	14	.659	17	21	.447	2	1	.667
Chicago Bulls	39	43	.476	9	19	25	.432	20	**18**	.526	23	10	.697	9	25	.265	7	**8**	.467
Phoenix Suns	39	43	.476	9	15	29	.341	24	14	.632	22	15	.595	12	25	.324	5	3	.625
Seattle Supersonics	36	46	.439	12	21	30	.412	15	16	.484	22	14	.611	10	26	.278	4	6	.400
San Francisco Warriors	30	52	.366	18	14	36	.280	16	16	.500	16	20	.444	14	26	.350	0	6	.000
San Diego Rockets	27	**55**	.329	21	11	**40**	.216	16	15	.516	21	17	.553	4	**33**	.108	2	5	.286

1969/70 INDIVIDUAL LEADERS

SCORING
(Minimum 70 Games Played)

Name	Team	G	FG	FT	Pts.	Avg.
West	LA	74	831	647	2309	31.2
Alcindor	Mil	82	938	485	2361	28.8
Hayes	SD	82	914	428	2256	27.5
Cunningham	Phi	81	802	510	2114	26.1
Hudson	Atl	80	830	371	2031	25.4
Hawkins	Phoe	81	709	577	1995	24.6
Rule	Sea	80	789	387	1965	24.6
Havlicek	Bos	81	736	488	1960	24.2
Monroe	Bal	82	695	532	1922	23.4
Bing	Det	70	575	454	1604	22.9

FIELD GOAL PERCENTAGE
(Minimum 700 Attempts, 70 Games Played)

Name	Team	FG	FGA	Pct.
Green	Cin	481	860	.559
Imhoff	Phi	430	796	.540
Hudson	Atl	830	1564	.531
McGlocklin	Mil	639	1206	.530
Snyder	Sea	456	863	.528
Fox	Phoe	413	788	.524
Alcindor	Mil	938	1810	.518
Unseld	Bal	526	1015	.518
Frazier	NY	600	1158	.518
Van Arsdale	Phoe	592	1166	.508

FREE THROW PERCENTAGE
(Minimum 350 Attempts, 70 Games Played)

Name	Team	FT	FTA	Pct.
Robinson	Mil	439	489	.898
Walker	Chi	483	568	.850
Mullins	SF	320	378	.847
Havlicek	Bos	488	578	.844
Love'	Chi	442	525	.842
Monroe	Bal	532	641	.830
Hudson	Atl	371	450	.824
West	LA	647	785	.824
Greer	Phi	352	432	.815
Walker	Det	355	440	.807

PERSONAL FOULS

Name	Team	PF
Davis	Atl	335
Cunningham	Phi	331
Van Lier	Cin	329
Meschery	Sea	317
Counts	LA	304
G. Smith	Mil	304

GAMES DISQUALIFIED

Name	Team	Disq
Van Lier	Cin	18
Cunningham	Phi	15
Ellis	SF	13
Finkel	Bos	13
Meschery	Sea	13

REBOUNDS PER GAME
(Minimum 70 Games Played)

Name	Team	G	Reb.	Avg.
Hayes	SD	82	1386	16.9
Unseld	Bal	82	1370	16.7
Alcindor	Mil	82	1190	14.5
Bridges	Atl	82	1181	14.4
Johnson	Bal	78	1086	13.9
Reed	NY	81	1126	13.9
Cunningham	Phi	81	1101	13.6
Boerwinkle	Chi	81	1016	12.5
Silas	Phoe	78	916	11.7
Lee	SF	82	929	11.3

ASSISTS PER GAME
(Minimum 70 Games Played)

Name	Team	G	Ass.	Avg.
Wilkens	Sea	75	683	9.1
Frazier	NY	77	629	8.2
Haskins	Chi	82	624	7.6
West	LA	74	554	7.5
Goodrich	Phoe	81	605	7.5
Hauard	Atl	82	561	6.8
Havlicek	Bos	81	550	6.8
H. Williams	SD	80	503	6.3
Van Lier	Cin	81	500	6.2
Bing	Det	70	418	6

MINUTES PLAYED

Name	Team	Min.
Hayes	SD	3665
Alcindor	Mil	3534
Havlicek	Bos	3369
Hawkins	Phoe	3312
Bridges	Atl	3269

1969-70 A.B.A.

Picking the Plum Before the Harvest

The A.B.A.'s third season turned out to be a mixed bag of comings and goings. At the very top, Commissioner George Mikan was ousted by the team owners, who wanted a more aggressive leader to handle the growing "war" with the N.B.A. Mikan resigned under pressure on July 14, and Jim Gardner, the owner of the new Carolina franchise, moved in as temporary commissioner until a suitable occupant for the position could be found. Gardner took a more aggressive stand toward the established circuit, and actually lured away four of its top referees. In October, Jack Dolph won appointment to the commissioner's chair. A former executive at the Columbia Broadcasting System, Dolph wielded enough clout to get the A.B.A. All-Star Game on C.B.S. in prime time.

The shuffling in the league offce was matched by the shuffling of franchises. For the second straight year, the defending A.B.A. champion pulled up roots and moved to a new city, with the Oakland Oaks this year becoming the Washington Capitols. The Minnesota Pipers, who had won the league title the first year in Pittsburgh, returned to that city this year after a dismal one-year sojourn in the far North. The Houston Mavericks had never won any championships, and had trouble winning an occasional game, but they joined these two former champs in the moving game, shifting headquarters to the cities of Charlotte, Raleigh, and Greensboro and adopting the name of the Carolina Cougars.

In the personnel department, both of the A.B.A.'s superstars jumped to the N.B.A. Connie Hawkins jumped after the N.B.A., in order to settle Hawkins suit against the league, voted to rescind the ban it had imposed on him for his involvement in the college betting scandals of 1961. While Hawkins joined the Phoenix N.B.A. club, Rick Barry had no desire to accompany the Oakland club to its new home in Washington, and he decided to jump back to the San Francisco Warriors, whom he had left two years ago after leading the N.B.A. in scoring. But Earl Foreman, the new owner of the transplanted franchise, went to court and got an order forcing Barry to play out his multi-year A.B.A. contract.

But beyond these two, the flow of incoming N.B.A. and college personnel was encouraging for the league's survival. Zelmo Beaty of the Atlanta Hawks signed a contract with the Los Angeles Stars and sat out this option season, while Billy Cunningham of the Philadelphia 76ers inked a lucrative pact with the Carolina Cougars which would take effect in three years, and the Detroit Pistons' Dave Bing signed a contract with the Washington Caps, for the next season. Yet as things turned out for Bing, the failure of the team to stay in Washington nullified the pact before he ever suited up in an A.B.A. game. But these signings of three N.B.A. stars buoyed the spirits of the younger league, as did the agreement of Lou Carnesecca, respected coach at St. John's University, to take charge of the New York Nets starting next year. The league also signed two first-round N.B.A. draft picks in Larry Cannon and Simmie Hill, neither of whom, unfortunately, lived up to his advance billings.

The real prize among freshman pros came from the hardship category, which was the A.B.A.'s rationale for signing college undergraduates before the N.B.A. could pluck them off at graduation. Spencer Haywood had starred in the 1968 Olympics and had won All-American honors at the University of Detroit in his sole season of varsity play; his signing with the Denver Rockets after his sophomore year put the A.B.A. back into the sports headlines.

Haywood was an immediate hit with his rebounding and scoring, but the Denver club nevertheless got off to a disorganized start under coach John McLendon. With the team record at 9-19, McLendon was canned and replaced by former referee Joe Belmont. Under the new coach's reins, the Rockets pulled an immediate about-face and won 17 of their first 19 contests. Haywood paced the A.B.A. in both scoring and rebounding, while Larry Jones headed up the Denver backcourt. With Haywood leading the way, the Rockets stormed back from their limp start to win first place in the West with a 51-33 record.

The steady Dallas Chaparalls came in second with a 45-39 record. Chap coach Cliff Hagan decided to confine himself to the bench after two seasons as a playing coach, but the management seemingly found him less of an asset as a bench coach and fired him with the team record standing at 22-21. The Washington Caps, nee Oakland Oaks, slumped to third place in the West; both Rick Barry and Warren Armstrong suffered knee injuries, which took the starch out of new coach Al Bianchi's club.

Bill Sharman's Los Angeles Stars took fourth place, bolstered by rookies Mack Calvin and Willie Wise and by mid-season acquisitions Craig Raymond and Trooper Washington. The New Orleans Buccaneers started the year with a rush, winning 12 of their first 13 matches, but a knee injury to Jimmy Jones in December started the club on a skid which carried it out of the playoffs despite a final 42-42 record.

A 42-42 mark was good enough for third place in the East, with the new Carolina Cougars achieving that level. The Cougars stocked their club mostly with local talent, relying on familiar faces from college ball to win a following among the fans. The Indiana Pacers, meanwhile, won a secure following among their fans with a deep squad that put together a 59-25 record, the best in the league. Center Mel Daniels, forwards Bob Netolicky and Roger Brown, and guard Freddie Lewis all were carry-overs from the A.B.A.'s first year of existence, and they still ranked among the best at their positions. Veteran John Barnhill filled the fifth spot on the fioor early in the season, with popular rookie Bill Keller coming on strong towards the end of the regular campaign.

The Kentucky Colonels finished a distant second, relying as usual on guards Louie Dampier and Darrel Carrier to carry the team's offense. After the third-place Carolina team came the New York Nets, who had their third home in as many years in an arena in Hempstead, Long Island. On the floor, the biggest improvement came in the backcourt, where N.B.A. veteran Bill Melchionni teamed with A.B.A. traveler Levern Tart to put some punch into the New York attack. The Pittsburgh and Miami clubs, which had been strong franchises in the A.B.A.'s initial season, collapsed in a heap at the bottom of the East and of the league.

The playoffs matched the strong Pacers against the unheralded Los Angeles Stars in the championship series. The Pacers had run through their Eastern competitors as expected, but the Stars surprised even their fans by beating the Dallas Chaps in the first round and then by decisively upsetting the Denver Rockets in five games. The A.B.A.'s first Cinderella team couldn't make it to midnight, however, bowing to the Goliath-like Pacers in six games.

1969/70 A.B.A. — EASTERN DIVISION

Use Name	Pos	Hgt	Wgt	Age	G	Min	FG	FGA	%	FT	FTA	%	Reb	Ass	PF	DQ	Points	Min	Reb	Ass	PF	Points
					TOTAL													PER GAME				
INDIANA PACERS	59-25 .702				BOB LEONARD																	
Roger Brown	F-G	6'5	207	27	84	3495	719	1444	50	457	562	81	620	392	308	3	1935	42	7.4	4.7	3.7	23.0
Bob Netolicky	F-C	6'9	225	27	82	3222	673	1393	48	343	502	68	876	123	206	2	1691	39	10.7	1.5	2.5	20.6
Mel Daniels	C	6'9	220	25	83	3039	613	1295	47	330	489	67	1462	131	309	7	1556	37	17.6	1.6	3.7	18.7
John Barnhill	G	6'1	183	31	77	2374	325	824	39	158	238	66	173	312	196	2	879	31	2.2	4.1	2.5	11.4
Freddie Lewis	G	6'	180	26	81	2877	448	1065	42	383	485	79	277	289	294	5	1326	36	3.4	3.6	3.6	16.4
Art Becker	F	6'8	210	27	82	1504	309	593	52	111	137	81	379	45	249	8	729	18	4.6	0.5	3.0	8.9
Bill Keller	G	5'10	180	22	82	1482	252	634	40	164	193	85	174	235	153	0	710	18	2.1	2.9	1.9	8.7
Tom Thacker	G	6'2	190	30	70	1016	70	212	33	38	69	55	211	185	177	2	188	15	3.0	2.6	2.5	2.7
Jay Miller	F	6'5	210	26	52	415	75	167	45	41	57	72	80	16	72	2	191	8	1.5	0.3	1.4	3.7
S. Chubin (from NY-Pit, to KY)	G	6'2	200	25	32	381	41	93	44	50	60	83	41	69	73	1	134	12	1.3	2.2	2.3	4.2
Ollie Darden (from KY)	F-C	6'7	240	25	26	288	47	121	39	16	23	70	90	13	48	0	111	11	3.5	0.5	1.8	4.3
Barry Orms (to Pit)	G	6'3	190	23	9	143	17	40	43	17	26	65	37	13	30	1	51	16	4.1	1.4	3.3	5.7
John Fairchild (to KY)	F	6'8	205	26	3	26	1	6	17	1	2	50	9	2	8	0	3	9	3.0	0.7	2.7	1.0
Bobby Edmonds	F	6'6	220	28	3	12	1	5	20	1	3	33	4	0	1	0	3	4	1.3	0.0	0.3	1.0
Dick Grubar (knee injury)	G	6'4	184	22	2	8	2	3	67	0	0	—	0	1	1	0	4	4	0.0	0.5	0.5	2.0
Jerry McKee	G	6'3	190	23	1	3	0	1	0	0	0	—	0	0	0	0	0	3	0.0	0.0	0.0	0.0
KENTUCKY COLONELS	45-39 .536				GENE RHODES																	
Goose Ligon	F	6'7	215	25	84	3130	507	1000	51	287	445	64	1094	190	360	13	1301	37	13.0	2.3	4.3	15.5
Sam Smith	F	6'7	230	25	81	2405	307	724	42	163	249	65	719	109	202	4	778	30	8.9	1.3	2.5	9.6
Gene Moore	C	6'9	240	24	83	2613	630	1390	45	209	311	67	1002	188	**382**	**25**	1471	31	12.1	2.3	**4.6**	17.7
Darel Carrier	G	6'3	185	29	77	2805	608	1458	42	454	509	**89**	249	212	268	8	1775	36	3.2	2.8	3.5	23.1
Louie Dampier	G	6'	175	25	82	3353	743	1864	40	447	538	83	310	447	235	2	2131	41	3.8	5.5	2.9	26.0
Wayne Chapman	G-F	6'6	190	24	82	1519	261	654	40	134	204	66	252	139	250	7	664	19	3.1	1.7	3.0	8.1
George Tinsley (from Was)	F	6'5	205	23	77	1419	173	400	43	159	214	74	321	76	189	3	506	18	4.2	1.0	2.5	6.6
Bud Olsen	C	6'8	220	29	84	1375	158	330	48	26	73	36	374	249	234	5	343	16	4.5	3.0	2.8	4.1
Ollie Darden (to Ind)	F	6'7	240	25	43	531	79	206	38	41	64	64	170	33	94	1	199	12	4.0	0.8	2.2	4.6
Tommy Kron (CT)	G	6'5	200	26	40	493	55	147	37	41	46	89	69	87	80	1	158	12	1.7	2.2	2.0	4.0
Willie Murrell (from Mia)	F	6'6	225	28	35	438	48	118	41	18	28	64	141	10	68	0	118	13	4.0	0.3	1.9	3.4
S. Chubin (from NY-Pit-Ind)	G	6'2	200	25	15	139	10	34	29	27	33	82	13	17	24	0	47	9	0.9	1.1	1.6	3.1
John Fairchild (from Ind)	F	6'8	205	26	7	52	6	17	35	4	8	50	8	2	10	0	19	7	1.1	0.3	1.4	2.7
Bobby Rascoe	G	6'4	205	29	4	34	4	21	19	6	7	86	4	1	3	0	14	9	1.0	0.3	0.8	3.5
Keith Swagerty	F	6'7	235	24	3	30	2	9	22	3	3	100	6	3	4	0	7	10	2.0	1.0	1.3	2.3
Sam Little	G	6'	180	22	3	11	2	4	50	1	1	100	1	2	4	0	5	4	0.3	0.7	1.3	1.7
Gene Williams	F	6'7	235	22	1	8	0	1	0	0	0	—	0	0	2	0	0	8	0.0	0.0	2.0	0.0
Bobby Washington	G	6'	175	22	2	5	0	1	0	0	0	—	0	0	0	0	0	3	0.0	0.0	0.0	0.0
CAROLINA COUGARS	42-42 .500				BONES McKINNEY																	
Doug Moe	F	6'5	220	31	80	2671	535	1254	43	304	399	76	437	425	282	8	1382	33	5.5	5.3	3.5	17.3
Randy Mahaffey	F	6'7	210	24	84	2558	367	821	45	194	283	69	681	164	275	7	928	30	8.1	2.0	3.3	11.0
George Peeples	C	6'8	205	26	83	2220	279	682	41	209	315	66	685	123	232	0	767	27	8.3	1.5	2.8	9.2
Bob Verga	G	6'1	190	24	82	3411	867	1984	44	458	565	81	430	290	268	3	2258	42	5.2	3.5	3.3	27.5
Gene Littles	G	6'1	165	26	82	2832	414	817	51	197	254	78	415	282	255	0	1025	35	5.1	3.4	3.1	12.5
Rich Niemann (from Bos-NBA)	C	7'	245	23	63	1466	285	601	47	141	192	73	563	87	219	7	711	23	8.9	1.4	3.5	11.3
Larry Miller (from LA)	F-G	6'4	205	23	59	1383	223	510	44	127	197	64	267	100	117	0	579	23	4.5	1.7	2.0	9.8
Cal Fowler	G	6'	175	29	78	1234	131	288	45	74	119	62	170	126	156	2	343	16	2.2	1.6	2.0	4.4
Hank Whitney	F	6'7	235	30	59	981	170	403	42	57	88	65	371	56	200	4	397	17	6.3	0.9	3.4	6.7
Bill Bunting	F-C	6'8	200	22	57	701	96	248	39	79	106	75	169	34	106	3	271	12	3.0	0.6	1.9	4.8
Steve Kramer	G-F	6'5	200	24	51	447	49	107	46	63	86	73	52	39	70	0	161	9	1.0	0.8	1.4	3.2
Ron Perry (ST, to NO)	G	6'3	190	26	19	221	42	103	41	32	43	74	18	18	34	1	118	12	0.9	0.9	1.8	6.2
George Sutor (to Mia)	C	6'8	240	26	11	135	12	41	29	7	15	47	51	2	29	0	31	12	4.6	0.2	2.6	2.8
NEW YORK NETS	39-45 .464				YORK LARESE																	
Walt Simon	F-G	6'6	200	30	81	2696	454	1030	44	253	338	75	474	294	296	5	1162	33	5.9	3.6	3.7	14.3
Les Hunter	F-C	6'7	235	27	79	2859	486	1122	43	317	432	73	673	215	335	15	1295	36	8.5	2.7	4.2	16.4
Ed Johnson	C	6'9	205	25	74	2486	405	848	48	226	404	56	879	88	305	18	1037	34	11.9	1.2	4.1	14.0
Lavern Tart	G	6'2	195	27	80	3210	756	1528	49	412	526	78	546	264	268	4	1935	40	6.8	3.3	3.4	24.2
Bill Melchionni	G	6'1	165	25	80	3157	479	1030	47	255	311	82	230	457	282	7	1218	39	2.9	5.7	3.5	15.2
Sonny Dove	F	6'8	208	24	80	2284	456	987	46	240	379	63	543	107	295	12	1154	29	6.8	1.3	3.7	14.4
Ron Taylor (from Was)	C	7'1	265	23	72	873	153	318	48	54	97	56	286	64	207	11	360	12	4.0	0.9	2.9	5.0
Luther Green	F	6'7	190	23	59	739	114	303	38	55	97	57	263	27	117	2	283	13	4.5	0.5	2.0	4.8
G. Lehmann (from LA, to Mia)	G	6'3	190	27	46	679	111	300	37	81	94	86	39	104	80	0	344	15	0.8	2.3	1.7	7.5
Billy Evans	G	6'	170	22	53	602	32	87	37	38	70	54	39	100	89	1	102	11	0.7	1.9	1.7	1.9
Steve Chubin (to Pit-Ind-KY)	G	6'2	200	25	11	232	40	118	34	37	42	88	35	26	29	0	119	21	3.2	2.4	2.6	10.8
John Smith (from Dal-Pit)	C	7'	235	25	16	165	9	40	23	5	7	71	60	3	30	0	23	10	3.8	0.2	1.9	1.4
Bob Arnzen	F	6'6	215	22	13	98	19	48	40	2	6	33	22	5	11	0	40	8	1.7	0.4	0.8	3.1
Bob McIntyre	F	6'6	220	25	7	94	12	32	38	0	1	0	20	5	8	0	25	13	2.9	0.7	1.1	3.6
Dennis Grey	F	6'8	215	22	4	74	6	24	25	6	12	50	25	0	15	1	18	19	6.3	0.0	3.8	4.5
Barry Kramer	F	6'4	200	27	7	56	10	31	32	7	8	88	13	3	10	0	27	8	1.9	0.4	1.4	3.9
Jack Gillespie	F	6'9	220	22	2	27	0	5	0	2	2	100	7	0	3	0	2	14	3.5	0.0	1.5	1.0
Bob Christian (from Dal)	C	7'	260	25	1	4	1	3	33	0	0		2	0	1	0	2	4	2.0	0.0	1.0	2.0

Use Name	Pos	Hgt	Wgt	Age	G	Min	FG	FGA	%	FT	FTA	%	Reb	Ass	PF	DQ	Points	Min	Reb	Ass	PF	Points
					TOTAL													PER GAME				
1969/70 A.B.A. — EASTERN DIVISION (continued)																						
PITTSBURGH PIPERS	**29-55 .345**				**JOHN CLARK (14-25 .359), BUDDY JEANNETTE (15-30 .333)**																	
John Brisker	F-G	6'5	210	22	77	2173	627	1361	46	329	398	83	441	133	236	4	1617	28	5.7	1.7	3.1	21.0
Stew Johnson	F-C	6'8	225	25	81	2347	544	1337	41	137	176	78	547	120	210	2	1240	29	6.8	1.5	2.6	15.3
Mike Lewis	C	6'8	225	23	78	2698	499	1006	50	269	356	76	1054	268	306	7	1267	35	13.5	3.4	3.9	16.2
Arvesta Kelly (neck injury)	G	6'3	190	24	70	2391	384	778	49	168	257	65	267	226	195	4	957	34	3.8	3.2	2.8	13.7
Charlie Williams (knee injury)	G	6'	165	26	26	925	193	537	36	104	135	77	78	94	80	1	506	36	3.0	3.6	3.1	19.5
Barry Orms (from Ind)	G	6'3	190	23	68	1948	255	655	39	135	250	54	310	119	185	2	650	29	4.6	1.8	2.7	9.6
Dennis Hamilton	F	6'8	210	25	72	1331	190	375	51	86	100	86	340	73	144	0	456	18	4.7	1.0	2.0	6.3
Trooper Washington (to LA)	F	6'7	225	25	44	1249	165	308	**54**	89	141	63	444	116	141	3	422	28	10.1	2.6	3.2	9.6
Warren Davis (from LA)	F	6'6	215	27	34	1145	151	301	50	125	186	67	407	139	125	2	427	34	12.0	4.1	3.7	12.6
George Thompson (toe injury)	G	6'2	210	22	54	1017	259	587	44	176	260	68	94	73	109	0	701	19	1.7	1.4	2.0	13.0
Craig Raymond (to LA)	C	6'11	235	24	34	789	100	229	44	52	98	53	256	55	100	2	252	23	7.5	1.6	2.9	7.4
Lonnie Lynn (from Den)	F	6'7	215	26	40	639	92	229	40	28	62	45	208	39	102	1	212	16	5.2	1.0	2.6	5.3
Chico Vaughn	G	6'3	195	29	21	401	66	180	37	48	70	69	28	22	53	1	204	19	1.3	1.0	2.5	9.7
M. McHartley (from Mia, to Dal)	G	6'3	200	27	17	380	57	132	43	40	52	77	39	55	48	1	156	22	2.3	3.2	2.8	9.2
S. Chubin (from NY, to Ind-KY)	G	6'2	200	25	14	306	36	107	34	56	64	88	48	5	48	2	129	22	3.4	0.4	3.4	9.2
Larry Bergh	F	6'8	215	24	20	255	49	120	41	23	33	70	85	18	52	2	121	13	4.3	0.9	2.6	6.1
Bill McGill (from LA, to Dal)	C	6'9	225	30	8	157	40	76	53	14	21	67	39	13	20	0	94	20	4.9	1.6	2.5	11.8
John Smith (from Dal, to NY)	C	7'	235	25	6	59	4	12	33	3	9	33	15	3	6	0	11	10	2.5	0.5	1.0	1.8
Justus Thigpen	G	6'1	170	22	3	58	5	19	26	1	3	33	8	4	14	1	11	19	2.7	1.3	4.7	3.7
Steve Vacendak (to Mia)	G	6'1	185	25	2	36	2	13	15	2	2	100	1	3	4	0	6	18	0.5	1.5	2.0	3.0
Wilbur Kirkland	F	6'7	190	22	2	27	3	7	43	0	0	—	11	1	5	0	6	14	5.5	0.5	2.5	3.0
Art Heyman (to Mia)	F	6'5	210	28	1	4	0	1	0	0	0	—	0	0	1	0	0	4	0.0	0.0	1.0	0.0
MIAMI FLORIDIANS	**23-61 .274**				**JIM POLLARD (5-15 .250), HAL BLITMAN (18-46 .281)**																	
Simmie Hill (from LA)	F	6'7	235	23	47	1458	289	684	42	123	164	75	389	46	194	10	706	31	8.3	1.0	4.1	15.0
Don Sidle	F-C	6'9	215	23	84	3493	639	1320	48	469	634	74	1082	129	272	3	1748	42	12.9	1.5	3.2	20.8
Skip Thoren (knee injury)	C	6'10	230	26	29	1020	164	364	45	92	155	59	393	75	112	2	420	35	13.6	2.6	3.9	14.5
Larry Cannon (MS)	G	6'5	195	22	57	1503	253	660	38	158	232	68	141	153	133	2	672	26	2.5	2.7	2.3	11.8
Donnie Freeman	G	6'3	185	25	79	3164	766	1684	45	**626**	**762**	82	400	291	253	5	2163	40	5.1	3.7	3.2	27.4
Wilben Jones	F	6'8	205	22	74	1697	243	616	39	118	162	73	565	48	207	5	606	23	7.6	0.6	2.8	8.2
Willie Murrell (to KY)	F	6'6	225	28	47	1321	228	478	48	99	126	79	311	56	133	2	558	28	6.6	1.2	2.8	11.9
Al Cueto	C	6'8	230	23	78	1265	182	449	41	102	144	71	452	58	257	12	471	16	5.8	0.7	3.3	6.0
George Lehmann (from LA-NY)	G	6'3	190	27	25	1078	168	415	40	66	81	81	70	124	83	0	448	43	2.8	5.0	3.3	17.9
Erv Staggs	F-G	6'6	195	21	53	1058	189	474	40	73	114	64	122	76	155	7	453	20	2.3	1.4	2.9	8.5
Hubie White	G	6'4	205	29	54	824	146	363	40	62	84	74	155	56	147	2	361	15	2.9	1.0	2.7	6.7
Andy Anderson (to LA)	G	6'2	185	24	32	617	109	253	43	89	113	79	56	39	74	0	307	19	1.8	1.2	2.3	9.6
M. McHartley (to Pit-Dal)	G	6'3	200	27	11	319	42	118	36	27	37	73	32	45	51	1	111	29	2.9	4.1	4.6	10.1
Art Heyman (XJ, from Pit)	F	6'5	210	28	18	300	47	105	45	46	65	71	57	20	31	1	140	17	3.2	1.1	1.7	7.8
Bob Woollard	C	6'10	225	29	19	234	32	82	39	20	25	80	69	6	42	1	84	12	3.6	0.3	2.2	4.4
Butch Booker (knee injury)	C	6'10	230	24	12	221	30	61	49	10	18	56	91	6	23	0	70	18	7.6	0.5	1.9	5.8
Lynn Shackelford	F	6'5	195	22	22	183	22	72	31	10	13	77	27	11	34	0	58	8	1.2	0.5	1.5	2.6
Steve Vacendak (fnom Pit)	G	6'1	185	25	12	137	13	46	28	11	20	55	12	17	18	0	37	11	1.0	1.4	1.5	3.1
Dallas Thomton	G	6'4	190	23	5	114	15	35	43	14	17	82	22	11	14	0	44	23	4.4	2.2	2.8	8.8
Walt Byrd	F	6'7	205	27	22	109	14	43	33	5	17	29	25	6	22	0	33	5	1.1	0.3	1.0	1.5
Dan Sparks	F	6'8	200	24	3	52	7	18	39	5	6	83	16	2	7	0	19	17	5.3	0.7	2.3	6.3
George Sutor (from Car)	C	6'8	240	26	3	12	0	5	0	0	2	0	4	1	2	0	0	4	1.3	0.3	0.7	0.0
1969/70 A.B.A.—WESTERN DIVISION																						
DENVER ROCKETS	**51-33 .607**				**JOHN McLENDON (9-19 .321), JOE BELMONT (42-14 .750)**																	
Julie Hammond (injury)	F	6'5	210	26	69	1847	329	660	50	169	243	70	471	109	183	2	827	27	6.8	1.6	2.7	12.0
Spencer Haywood	F	6'8	225	20	84	**3808**	**986**	**1998**	49	547	705	78	**1637**	190	221	1	**2519**	**45**	**19.5**	2.3	2.6	**30.0**
Byron Beck	C	6'9	240	24	79	2454	440	841	52	137	174	79	764	112	293	12	1017	31	9.7	1.4	3.7	12.9
Lonnie Wright	G	6'2	205	25	79	2237	393	952	41	121	175	69	216	149	278	7	961	28	2.7	1.9	3.5	12.2
Larry Jones	G	6'2	180	28	75	3027	625	1441	43	579	732	79	391	426	228	1	1870	40	5.2	5.7	3.0	24.9
Jeff Congdon	G	6'1	190	26	83	2461	299	775	39	151	192	79	233	446	205	3	812	30	2.8	5.4	2.5	9.8
Julius Keye	C-F	6'10	225	23	77	1641	245	618	40	116	193	60	530	47	209	2	606	21	6.9	0.6	2.7	7.9
Walt Piatkowski	F	6'8	225	24	74	1302	215	535	40	76	99	77	252	41	180	1	517	18	3.4	0.6	2.4	7.0
Ben Warley	F	6'5	200	33	42	475	60	170	35	58	76	76	110	30	98	0	193	11	2.6	0.7	2.3	4.6
Greg Wittman	F	6'8	210	22	50	453	80	204	39	32	59	54	98	15	87	2	196	9	2.0	0.3	1.7	3.9
Floyd Theard	G	6'1	170	25	25	406	39	113	35	18	28	64	51	44	49	1	96	16	2.0	1.8	2.0	3.8
Lonnie Lynn (to Pit)	F	6'7	215	26	12	140	20	46	43	8	12	67	50	4	18	0	48	12	4.2	0.3	1.5	4.0
Dwight Waller	F	6'7	230	24	7	87	10	24	42	9	19	47	38	4	12	0	29	12	5.4	0.6	1.7	4.1
Cliff Anderson	F	6'4	200	25	3	22	2	4	50	2	6	33	4	4	3	0	6	7	1.3	1.3	1.0	2.0

Use Name	Pos	Hgt	Wgt	Age	TOTAL G	Min	FG	FGA	%	FT	FTA	%	Reb	Ass	PF	DQ	Points	PER GAME Min	Reb	Ass	PF	Points
1969/70 A.B.A. — WESTERN DIVISION (continued)																						
DALLAS CHAPARRALS	**45-39 .536**				**CLIFF HAGAN (22-21 .512), MAX WILLIAMS (23-18 .561)**																	
Cincy Powell	F	6'7	227	27	76	2624	562	1200	47	402	519	77	682	192	250	6	1528	35	9.0	2.5	3.3	20.1
John Beasley	F	6'9	225	25	84	3066	626	1254	50	284	347	82	1006	132	278	4	1539	37	12.0	1.6	3.3	18.3
Manny Leaks	C-F	6'8	235	24	84	3086	636	1287	49	305	428	71	1047	100	283	11	1577	37	12.5	1.2	3.4	18.8
Ron Boone	G	6'2	200	23	84	2340	423	980	43	300	382	79	366	272	265	5	1163	28	4.4	3.2	3.2	13.8
Glen Combs	G	6'2	185	23	84	3260	640	1474	43	458	548	84	289	342	265	2	1868	39	3.4	4.1	3.2	22.2
Charlie Beasley	G	6'5	190	24	80	2150	292	667	44	231	262	88	205	280	222	2	834	27	2.6	3.5	2.8	10.4
Bob Bedell	F	6'8	205	25	80	1536	285	677	42	207	246	84	454	126	192	3	779	19	5.7	1.6	2.4	9.7
John Smith (to Pit-NY)	C	7'	235	25	48	966	92	232	40	48	78	62	329	52	149	5	232	20	6.9	1.1	3.1	4.8
Riney Lochmann	F	6'6	215	25	47	447	73	166	44	25	45	56	96	40	61	0	174	10	2.0	0.9	1.3	3.7
M. McHartley (from Mia-Pit)	G-F	6'3	200	27	27	293	56	138	41	31	41	76	44	42	59	1	147	11	1.6	1.6	2.2	5.4
Tom Hagan (MS, NJ)	G	6'4	185	22	24	226	37	81	46	22	29	76	30	29	42	0	103	9	1.3	1.2	1.8	4.3
Bill McGill (from LA-Pit)	C	6'9	225	30	24	181	30	61	49	15	24	63	57	17	41	0	75	8	2.4	0.7	1.7	3.1
Willie Scott	F	6'5	210	22	8	51	6	15	40	1	6	17	4	2	16	0	13	6	0.5	0.3	2.0	1.6
Rich Jones	F	6'8	230	23	2	50	9	20	45	10	11	91	23	1	11	1	28	25	11.5	0.5	5.5	14.0
Cliff Hagan	F	6'4	215	38	3	27	8	13	62	1	2	50	3	6	2	0	17	9	1.0	2.0	0.7	5.7
Bob Christian (to NY)	C	7'	260	25	1	7	0	0	—	0	0	—	1	0	2	0	0	7	1.0	0.0	2.0	0.0
WASHINGTON CAPITOLS	**44-40 .524**				**AL BIANCHI**																	
W. Armstrong (knee injury)	F-G	6'2	200	23	40	1510	342	768	45	210	293	72	416	173	143	5	913	38	10.4	4.3	3.6	22.8
Rick Barry (knee injury)	F	6'7	215	25	52	1849	517	1036	50	400	463	86	363	178	174	1	1442	36	7.0	3.4	3.3	27.7
Ira Harge	C	6'9	225	28	84	2991	415	886	47	196	289	68	1177	200	328	8	1026	36	14.0	2.4	3.9	12.2
Mike Barrett	G	6'2	160	26	84	2262	479	1126	43	232	305	76	296	259	243	2	1252	27	3.5	3.1	2.9	14.9
Larry Brown	G	5'9	160	29	82	2766	376	854	44	362	439	82	246	580	257	4	1124	34	3.0	7.1	3.1	13.7
Fatty Taylor	G	6'	175	23	83	1994	243	520	47	178	264	67	377	201	285	4	665	24	4.5	2.4	3.4	8.0
George Carter (knee injury)	F	6'5	218	25	67	1848	397	871	46	167	216	77	425	94	203	1	968	28	6.3	1.4	3.0	14.4
Frank Card	F	6'7	195	25	74	1820	351	666	53	178	286	62	480	92	216	3	881	25	6.5	1.2	2.9	11.9
Gary Bradds	F	6'8	220	27	60	1239	292	608	48	217	262	83	336	54	181	1	801	21	5.6	0.9	3.0	13.4
Jim Eakins	C	6'11	215	23	82	1214	181	364	50	166	224	74	412	71	184	0	528	15	5.0	0.9	2.2	6.4
Henry Logan (knee injury)	G	6'	185	23	32	659	110	269	41	91	127	72	89	59	93	3	311	21	2.8	1.8	2.9	9.7
Ron Taylor (to NY)	C	7'1	265	23	3	37	3	9	33	3	5	60	7	0	11	0	9	12	2.3	0.0	3.7	3.0
George Tinsley (to KY)	F	6'5	205	23	5	27	2	7	29	3	4	75	4	0	3	0	7	5	0.8	0.0	0.6	1.4
Hal Jeter	G	6'4	190	24	5	19	1	4	25	0	0	—	1	0	8	0	2	4	0.2	0.0	1.6	0.4
LOS ANGELES STARS	**43-41 .512**				**BILL SHARMAN**																	
Willie Wise	F	6'6	215	22	82	2709	483	1014	48	278	427	65	952	204	301	8	1248	33	11.6	2.5	3.7	15.2
George Stone	F	6'7	195	23	83	2639	512	1194	43	239	306	78	551	145	280	4	1328	32	6.6	1.7	3.4	16.0
Craig Raymond (from Pit)	C	6'11	235	24	46	1567	286	583	49	138	206	67	540	99	174	6	710	34	11.7	2.2	3.8	15.4
Andy Anderson (from Mia)	G	6'2	185	24	49	1533	292	677	43	115	155	74	199	125	122	1	700	31	4.1	2.6	2.5	14.3
Mack Calvin	G	6'	165	22	84	2955	441	1047	42	529	642	82	294	478	289	6	1414	35	3.5	5.7	3.4	16.8
Bobby Warren (ankle injury)	G	6'5	190	23	72	1672	266	647	41	176	238	74	277	141	190	1	733	23	3.8	2.0	2.6	10.2
Warren Davis (to Pit)	F	6'6	215	26	46	1502	277	560	49	179	232	77	500	105	175	3	734	33	10.9	2.3	3.8	16.0
Merv Jackson (knee injury)	G	6'3	175	23	52	1118	169	475	36	92	114	81	138	114	145	4	446	22	2.7	2.2	2.8	8.6
Trooper Washington (from Pit)	F-C	6'7	225	25	37	1104	155	274	57	66	99	67	378	80	144	5	377	30	10.2	2.2	3.9	10.2
Wayne Hightower	C	6'9	210	29	27	961	180	403	45	129	170	76	255	71	101	4	489	36	9.4	2.6	3.7	18.1
Bob Warlick	F-G	6'5	205	28	29	711	112	309	36	65	96	68	114	76	70	0	289	25	3.9	2.6	2.4	10.0
Larry Miller (to Car)	F-G	6'4	205	23	21	654	94	248	38	96	134	72	147	47	56	0	293	31	7.0	2.2	2.7	14.0
Bill McGill (to Pit, Dal)	C	6'9	225	30	27	492	131	232	56	48	63	76	119	30	79	1	310	18	4.4	1.1	2.9	11.5
Tom Workman (from Det-NBA)	C	6'7	230	25	26	445	116	251	46	77	98	79	94	22	69	0	310	17	3.6	0.8	2.7	11.9
George Lehmann (to NY-Mia)	G	6'3	190	27	10	237	39	132	30	33	36	92	12	28	26	0	116	24	1.2	2.8	2.6	11.6
Mel Peterson	G	6'4	190	—	4	53	10	35	29	3	3	100	13	1	4	0	23	13	3.3	0.3	1.0	5.8
Simmie Hill (to Mia)	F	6'7	235	23	6	41	8	25	32	3	3	100	12	1	7	0	19	7	2.0	0.2	1.2	3.2
Les Selvage	G	6'1	175	26	4	17	4	14	29	0	0	—	2	5	2	0	8	4	0.5	1.3	0.5	2.0
Zelmo Beaty - court order (sat out option with Atl-NBA)																						
NEW ORLEANS BUCCANEERS	**42-42.500**				**BABE McCARTHY**																	
Jackie Moreland	F	6'7	215	31	80	2321	317	765	41	139	176	79	386	160	250	8	775	29	4.8	2.0	3.1	9.7
Gerald Govan	F-C	6'10	220	27	84	3701	422	1044	40	208	285	73	1217	385	273	5	1053	44	14.5	4.6	3.3	12.5
Red Robbins	C	6'8	200	25	82	3266	525	1091	48	285	366	78	1332	182	251	1	1342	40	16.2	2.2	3.1	16.4
Steve Jones	G-F	6'5	205	27	84	3116	689	1558	44	412	495	83	388	195	290	3	1805	37	4.6	2.3	3.5	21.5
Jimmy Jones (knee injury)	G	6'4	188	24	70	2513	533	1072	50	380	469	81	315	340	238	5	1448	36	4.5	4.9	3.4	20.7
Mike Butler	G	6'2	175	23	83	1728	298	800	37	135	161	84	119	134	193	1	818	21	1.4	1.6	2.3	9.9
Ron Franz (military service)	F	6'7	207	24	55	1305	231	547	42	163	259	63	287	91	139	3	632	24	5.2	1.7	2.5	11.5
Skeeter Swift (knee injury)	G	6'3	210	23	66	1089	215	546	39	139	168	83	100	77	208	4	607	17	1.5	1.2	3.2	9.2
Tom Bowens	F	6'8	220	29	68	753	110	251	44	47	62	76	178	41	147	2	267	11	2.6	0.6	2.2	3.9
Ron Perry (from Car)	G	6'3	190	26	27	301	62	169	37	37	54	69	35	19	44	0	169	11	1.3	0.7	1.6	6.3
Jerry Rook	F	6'5	220	26	28	155	37	82	45	11	13	85	31	10	21	0	85	6	1.1	0.4	0.8	3.0
Lee Davis	C	6'8	240	24	16	128	16	36	44	8	15	53	40	2	31	0	40	8	2.5	0.1	1.9	2.5
Jasper Wilson	F	6'6	200	22	4	59	8	21	38	6	8	75	14	2	6	0	23	15	3.5	0.5	1.5	5.8

1969/70 A.B.A. — PLAYOFFS

INDIANA PACERS — **BOB LEONARD**

defeated Carolina 4-0; H123-105, H103-98, 115-106,110-106
defeated Kentucky 4-1; H110-114, H121-110, 114-110, 111-103, H117-103
defeated Los Angeles 4-2; H109-93, H114-111, 106-109,142-120, H113-117, 111-107

Use Name	Pos	Hgt	Wgt	Age	TOTAL G	Min	FG	FGA	%	FT	FTA	%	Reb	Ass	PF	DQ	Points	PER GAME Min	Reb	Ass	PF	Points
Roger Brown	F	6'5	207	27	15	693	151	318	47	108	131	82	151	84	58	—	428	46	10.1	5.6	—	28.5
Bob Netolicky	F-C	6'9	225	27	15	603	124	249	50	56	82	68	194	20	43	—	304	40	12.9	1.3	—	20.3
Mel Daniels	C	6'9	220	25	15	533	108	243	44	74	111	67	**265**	15	62	—	290	36	17.7	1.0	—	19.3
Freddie Lewis	G	6'	180	26	14	532	89	234	38	97	116	84	57	54	50	—	285	38	4.1	3.9	—	20.4
Bill Keller	G	5'10	180	22	15	527	75	177	42	42	46	**91**	51	68	41	—	195	35	3.4	4.5	—	13.0
John Barnhill	G	6'1	183	31	14	317	28	88	32	21	41	51	33	25	41	—	85	23	2.4	1.8	—	6.1
Art Becker	F	6'8	210	27	15	227	36	69	52	21	24	88	58	5	36	—	93	15	3.9	0.3	—	6.2
Tom Thacker	G-F	6'2	190	30	14	187	12	38	32	6	11	55	48	36	37	—	33	13	3.4	2.6	—	2.4
Ollie Darden	F	6'7	240	25	8	21	2	6	33	0	0	—	4	2	3	—	4	3	0.5	0.3	—	0.5
Jay Miller	F	6'5	210	26	3	10	1	5	20	0	0	—	4	0	4	—	2	3	1.3	0.0	—	0.7

LOS ANGELES STARS — **BILL SHARMAN**

defeated Dallas 4-2; 115-103, 121-129, H104-116, H144-138, 146-139, H124-123
defeated Denver 4-1; 113-123(OT), 114-105, H119-113, H114-110, 109-107
lost to Indiana 2-4; 93-109, 111-114, H109-106, H120-142, 117-113, H107-111

Use Name	Pos	Hgt	Wgt	Age	TOTAL G	Min	FG	FGA	%	FT	FTA	%	Reb	Ass	PF	DQ	Points	PER GAME Min	Reb	Ass	PF	Points
Willie Wise	F	6'6	215	22	12	237	50	97	52	15	31	48	64	23	—	—	115	20	5.3	1.9	—	9.6
George Stone	F	6'7	195	23	17	**724**	165	**388**	43	58	77	75	158	42	—	—	402	43	9.3	2.5	—	23.6
Craig Raymond	C	6'11	235	24	17	664	113	240	47	70	91	77	254	41	—	—	296	39	14.9	2.4	—	17.4
Merv Jackson	G	6'3	175	23	17	526	102	229	45	39	48	81	74	53	—	—	252	31	4.4	3.1	—	14.8
Mack Calvin	G	6'	165	22	17	593	133	294	45	**122**	**156**	78	63	**101**	—	—	392	35	3.7	5.9	—	23.1
Bobby Warren	F-G	6'5	190	23	17	576	96	223	43	49	64	77	127	67	—	—	256	34	7.5	3.9	—	15.1
Trooper Washington	F-C	6'7	225	25	17	471	58	93	**62**	10	25	40	188	45	—	—	126	28	11.1	2.6	—	7.4
Andy Anderson	G	6'2	185	24	16	307	50	134	37	28	31	90	37	—	—	—	128	19	2.3	—	—	8.0
Mel Peterson	G	6'4	190	31	4	22	3	6	50	1	2	50	—	—	—	—	7	6	—	—	—	1.8
Tom Workman	C	6'7	230	25	3	9	3	7	43	0	0	—	3	0	—	—	6	3	1.0	0.0	—	2.0
Les Salvage	G	6'1	175	26	1	1	0	0	—	0	0	—	—	—	—	—	0	1	—	—	—	0.0
Zelmo Beaty - (CT)																						

DENVER ROCKETS — **JOE BELMONT**

defeated Washington 4-3; H130-111, H143-133, 120-125, 114-131, H132-110, 111-116, H143-119
lost to Los Angeles 1-4; H123-113(OT), H105-114, 113-119, 110-114, H107-109

Use Name	Pos	Hgt	Wgt	Age	TOTAL G	Min	FG	FGA	%	FT	FTA	%	Reb	Ass	PF	DQ	Points	PER GAME Min	Reb	Ass	PF	Points
Julie Hammond	F	6'5	210	26	12	395	85	170	50	22	36	61	79	34	49	1	192	33	6.6	2.8	4.1	16.0
Spencer Haywood	F	6'8	225	20	12	568	**185**	362	51	69	83	83	237	39	31	0	**440**	**47**	**19.8**	3.3	1.6	36.7
Byron Beck	C	6'9	240	24	12	439	77	176	44	36	47	77	144	19	41	0	191	37	12.0	1.6	3.4	15.9
Lonnie Wright	G-F	6'2	205	25	11	334	32	109	29	18	23	78	32	44	33	0	84	30	2.9	4.0	3.0	7.6
Larry Jones	G	6'2	180	28	12	535	113	207	55	88	101	87	64	76	41	0	319	45	5.3	6.3	3.4	26.6
Jeff Congdon	G	6'1	190	26	12	313	43	118	36	24	32	75	33	68	41	0	126	26	2.8	5.7	3.4	10.5
Julius Keye	C	6'10	225	23	7	138	10	42	24	3	6	50	29	6	16	0	23	20	4.1	0.9	2.3	3.3
Ben Warley	F	6'5	200	33	10	129	16	38	42	6	10	60	29	11	27	1	45	13	2.9	1.1	2.7	4.5
Walt Piatkowski	F-C	6'8	225	24	6	50	12	24	50	2	4	50	11	4	9	0	27	8	1.8	0.7	1.5	4.5
Greg Wittman	F	6'8	210	22	2	4	1	2	50	1	3	33	0	0	2	0	4	2	0.0	0.0	1.0	2.0

KENTUCKY COLONELS — **GENE RHODES**

defeated New York 4-3; H118-122(OT), H113-111, 99-107, 128-101, H112-127, 116-113, H112-101
lost to Indiana 4-1; 114-110, 110-121, H110-111, H103-111, 103-117

Use Name	Pos	Hgt	Wgt	Age	TOTAL G	Min	FG	FGA	%	FT	FTA	%	Reb	Ass	PF	DQ	Points	PER GAME Min	Reb	Ass	PF	Points
Goose Ligon	F	6'7	215	25	12	475	73	134	54	66	99	67	141	26	—	—	212	40	11.8	2.2	—	17.7
Sam Smith	F-C	6'7	230	25	12	354	54	99	55	28	38	74	96	12	—	—	136	30	8.0	1.0	—	11.3
Gene Moore	C	6'9	240	24	12	369	97	202	48	35	49	71	150	26	—	—	229	31	12.5	2.2	—	19.1
Darel Carrier	G	6'3	185	29	12	487	87	228	38	70	79	89	46	29	—	—	258	41	3.8	2.4	—	21.5
Louie Dampier	G	6'	175	25	12	526	73	198	37	41	53	77	45	81	—	—	212	44	3.8	6.8	—	17.7
George Tinsley	F	6'5	205	23	12	270	41	91	45	32	44	73	64	16	—	—	116	23	5.3	1.3	—	9.7
Bud Olsen	C	6'8	220	29	12	211	18	43	42	1	7	14	—	—	—	—	37	18	—	—	—	3.1
Wayne Chapman	G-F	6'6	190	24	10	148	37	75	49	27	36	75	22	12	—	—	102	15	2.2	1.2	—	10.2
Steve Chubin	G	6'2	200	25	11	55	8	17	47	12	14	86	—	—	—	—	28	5	—	—	—	2.5
Willie Murrell	F	6'6	225	28	7	35	3	11	27	2	5	40	11	1	—	—	8	5	1.6	0.1	—	1.1

1969/70 A.B.A. — PLAYOFFS (continued)

					TOTAL													PER GAME				
Use Name	Pos	Hgt	Wgt	Age	G	Min	FG	FGA	%	FT	FTA	%	Reb	Ass	PF	DQ	Points	Min	Reb	Ass	PF	Points
NEW YORK NETS	**YORK LARESE**						lost to Kentucky 3-4; 122-118 (OT), 111-113, H107-99, H101-128, 127-112, H113-116, 101-112															
Walt Simon	F-G	6'6	200	30	7	222	39	78	50	23	28	82	53	21	—	—	101	32	7.6	3.0	—	14.4
Sonny Dove	F	6'8	208	24	7	281	48	97	49	26	39	67	71	9	—	—	123	40	10.1	1.3	—	17.6
Ed Johnson	C	6'9	205	25	7	216	32	69	46	30	52	58	67	5	—	—	94	31	9.6	0.7	—	13.4
Levern Tart	G	6'2	195	27	7	313	70	143	49	45	52	87	30	36	—	—	187	45	4.3	5.1	—	26.7
Bill Melchionni	G	6'1	165	25	7	316	48	104	46	31	38	82	22	33	—	—	128	45	3.1	4.7	—	18.3
Les Hunter	F-C	6'7	235	27	7	233	45	100	45	20	29	69	42	11	—	—	113	33	6.0	1.6	—	16.1
Luther Green	F	6'7	190	23	7	82	11	29	38	10	15	67	28	3	—	—	33	12	4.0	0.4	—	4.7
Billy Evans	G	6'	170	22	6	27	1	2	50	1	3	33	—	—	—	—	3	5	—	—	—	0.5
John Smith	C	7'	235	25	2	10	0	3	0	0	0	—	2	—	—	—	0	5	1.0	—	—	0.0
Ron Taylor	C	7'	265	23	2	5	0	4	0	0	1	0	2	—	—	—	0	3	1.0	—	—	0.0
WISHINGTON CAPITOLS	**AL BIANCHI**						lost to Denver 3-4; 111-130, 133-143, H125-120, H131-114, 110-132, H116-111, 119-143															
Frank Card	F	6'7	195	25	7	197	37	61	61	13	27	48	49	13	—	—	87	28	7.0	1.9	—	12.4
Rick Barry	F	6'7	215	25	7	302	108	203	53	62	68	91	70	23	—	—	281	43	10.0	3.3	—	40.1
Ira Harge	C	6'9	225	28	7	267	30	67	45	11	18	61	95	19	—	—	71	38	13.6	2.7	—	10.1
Mike Barrett	G	6'2	160	26	7	270	73	150	49	28	33	85	23	19	—	—	185	39	3.3	2.7	—	26.4
Larry Brown	G	5'9	160	29	7	269	33	73	45	30	34	88	35	68	—	—	97	38	5.0	9.7	—	13.9
Fatty Taylor	G	6'	175	23	7	129	5	11	45	0	0	—	22	19	—	—	10	18	3.1	2.7	—	1.4
Gary Bradds	F-C	6'8	220	27	6	116	25	61	41	6	12	50	17	3	—	—	57	19	2.8	0.5	—	9.5
Jim Eakins	C	6'11	215	23	7	65	14	24	58	3	3	100	14	5	—	—	31	9	2.0	0.7	—	4.4
George Carter	F	6'5	218	25	3	65	11	21	52	4	5	80	18	2	—	—	26	22	6.0	0.7	—	8.7
Warren Armstrong - knee injury																						
DALLAS CHIPARRALS	**MAX WILLIAMS**						lost to Los Angeles 2-4; H103-115, H129-121, 116-104, 138-144, H139-146, 123-124															
Cincy Powell	F	6'7	227	27	6	219	51	108	47	29	41	71	81	29	—	—	131	37	13.5	4.8	—	21.8
John Beasley	F-C	6'9	225	25	6	219	50	86	58	8	9	89	64	19	—	—	108	37	10.7	3.2	—	18.0
Manny Leaks	C	6'8	235	24	6	237	48	98	49	25	35	71	86	9	—	—	121	40	14.3	1.5	—	20.2
Ron Boone	G	6'2	200	23	6	193	46	97	47	15	21	71	49	54	—	—	110	32	8.2	9.0	—	18.3
Glen Combs	G	6'2	185	23	6	251	56	124	45	24	31	77	23	31	—	—	146	42	3.8	5.2	—	24.3
Charlie Beasley	G	6'5	190	24	5	110	18	36	50	8	9	89	10	23	—	—	45	22	2.0	4.6	—	9.0
Rich Jones	F-C	6'8	230	23	6	91	16	40	40	4	8	50	23	5	—	—	36	15	3.8	0.8	—	6.0
Bob Bedell	F	6'8	205	25	6	69	10	27	37	5	6	83	18	4	—	—	25	12	3.0	0.7	—	4.2
Maurice McHartley	G-F	6'3	200	27	5	51	8	25	32	8	10	80	—	—	—	—	26	10	—	—	—	5.2
CAROLINA COUGARS	**BONES McKINNEY**						lost to Indiana 0-4; 105-123, 98-103, H106-115, H106-110															
Doug Moe	F	6'5	220	31	4	168	25	76	33	12	16	75	26	25	—	—	62	42	6.5	6.3	—	15.5
Randy Mahaffey	F	6'7	210	24	4	91	19	38	50	10	14	71	27	8	—	—	48	23	6.8	2.0	—	12.0
George Peeples	C	6'8	205	26	4	126	15	42	36	9	13	69	54	4	—	—	39	32	13.5	1.0	—	9.8
Bob Verga	G	6'1	190	24	4	156	48	102	47	8	11	73	11	10	—	—	108	39	2.8	2.5	—	27.0
Gene Littles	G	6'1	165	26	4	133	18	33	55	6	9	67	18	14	—	—	42	33	4.5	3.5	—	10.5
Larry Miller	F-G	6'4	205	23	4	79	11	33	33	13	17	76	10	13	—	—	37	20	2.5	3.3	—	9.3
Cal Fowler	G	6'	175	29	4	76	6	14	43	7	10	70	—	—	—	—	19	19	—	—	—	4.8
Hank Whitney	F-C	6'7	235	30	4	60	17	33	52	4	9	44	21	—	—	—	38	15	5.3	—	—	9.5
Rich Niemann	C	7'	245	23	4	51	6	16	38	3	3	100	12	—	—	—	15	13	3.0	—	—	3.8
Steve Kramer	G-F	6'5	200	24	2	20	2	5	40	3	3	100	—	—	—	—	7	10	—	—	—	3.5

Team	W	L	Pct.	GB	Record against playoff teams W	L	Pct.	Record against non-playoff teams W	L	Pct.	HOME W	L	Pct.	ROAD W	L	Pct.	NEUTRAL W	L	Pct.
EASTERN DIVISION																			
Indiana Pacers	59	25	.702	—	36	20	.643	23	5	.821	31	10	.756	27	14	.659	1	1	.500
Kentucky Colonels	45	39	.536	14	28	29	.491	17	10	.630	30	19	.612	15	20	.429	0	0	—
Carolina Cougars	42	42	.500	17	27	29	.482	15	13	.536	28	14	.667	14	28	.333	0	0	—
New York Nets	39	45	.464	20	22	35	.386	17	10	.630	23	19	.548	16	26	.381	0	0	—
Pittsburgh Pipers	29	55	.345	30	20	47	.299	9	8	.529									
Miami Floridians	23	61	.274	36	18	49	.269	5	12	.294									
WESTERN DIVISION																			
Denver Rockets	51	33	.607	—	37	23	.617	14	10	.583	36	5	.878	13	27	.325	2	1	.667
Dallas Chaparrals	45	39	.536	6	31	29	.517	14	10	.583	27	15	.643	15	22	.405	3	2	.600
Washington Capitols	44	40	.524	7	27	33	.450	17	7	.708	21	14	.600	19	22	.463	4	4	.500
Los Angeles Stars	43	41	.512	8	25	35	.417	18	6	.750	22	16	.579	17	24	.415	4	1	.800
New Orleans Buccaneers	42	42	.500	9	33	39	.458	9	3	.750	29	13	.690	12	27	.308	1	2	.333

1969/70 A.B.A. INDIVIDUAL LEADERS

SCORING
(Minimum 70 Games Played)

Name	Team	G	FG	FT	Pts.	Avg.
Haywood	Den	84	986	547	2519	30.0
Verga	Car	82	867	458	2258	27.5
Freeman	Mia	79	766	626	2163	27.4
Dampier	KY	82	743	447	2125	25.9
Jones	Den	75	625	579	1870	24.9
Tart	NY	80	756	412	1935	24.2
Carrier	KY	77	608	454	1781	23.1
Brown	Ind	84	719	457	1935	23.0
Combs	Dal	84	640	458	1868	22.2
S. Jones	NO	84	689	412	1805	21.5

FIELD GOAL PERCENTAGE
(Minimum 560 Attempts)

Name	Team	FG	FGA	Pct.
Washington	Pit-LA	320	582	.550
Card	Was	351	666	.527
Beck	Den	440	841	.523
Becker	Ind	309	593	.521
Ligon	KY	507	1000	.507
Littles	Car	414	817	.507
J. Beasley	Dal	626	1254	.499
Barry	Was	517	1036	.499
Hammond	Den	329	660	.498
Brown	Ind	719	1444	.498

3-POINT FIELD GOAL PERCENTAGE
(Minimum 20 Made)

Name	Team	FG	FGA	Pct
Carrier	KY	105	280	.375
Dampier	KY	198	548	.361
Congdon	Den	63	178	.354
Combs	Dal	130	370	.351
Barrett	Was	62	180	.344
Brown	Ind	40	120	.333
Lehmann	LAAA	92	286	.322
Stone	LA	65	206	.316
Verga	Car	66	215	.307
Swift	NO	38	125	.304

FREE THROW PERCENTAGE
(Minimum 160 Attempts)

Name	Team	FT	FTA	Pct.
Carrier	KY	454	509	.892
C. Beasley	Dal	231	262	.882
Barry	Was	400	463	.864
Chubin	NY-Pit-Ind-KY	170	199	.854
Lehmann	LA-NY-Mia	180	211	.853
Keller	Ind	164	193	.850
Bedell	Dal	207	246	.841
Butler	NO	135	161	.839
Combs	Dal	458	548	.836
S. Jones	NO	412	495	.832

REBOUNDS PER GAME
(Minimum 70 Games Played)

Name	Team	G	Reb.	Avg.
Haywood	Den	84	1637	19.5
Daniels	Ind	83	1462	17.6
Robbins	NO	82	1332	16.2
Govan	NO	84	1217	14.5
Harge	Was	84	1177	14.0
Lewis	Pit	78	1054	13.5
Ligon	KY	84	1094	13.0
Sidle	Mia	84	1082	12.9
Leaks	Dal	84	1047	12.5
Moore	KY	83	1002	12.1

ASSISTS PER GAME
(Minimum 70 Games Played)

Name	Team	G	Ass.	Avg.
Brown	Was	80	580	7.1
Melchionni	NY	80	457	5.7
Calvin	LA	84	478	5.7
Jones	Den	75	426	5.7
Dampier	KY	82	447	5.5
Congdon	Den	83	446	5.4
Moe	Car	80	425	5.3
J. Jones	NO	70	340	4.9
Brown	Ind	84	392	4.7
Govan	NO	84	385	4.6

MINUTES PLAYED

Name	Team	Min.
Haywood	Den	3808
Govan	NO	3701
Brown	Ind	3495
Sidle	Mia	3493
Verga	Car	3411

PERSONAL FOULS

Name	Team	PF
Moore	KY	382
Ligon	KY	360
Hunter	NY	335
Harge	Was	328
Daniels	Ind	309

GAMES DISQUALIFIED

Name	Team	Disq.
Moore	KY	25
Johnson	NY	18
Hunter	NY	15
Ligon	KY	13
Beck	Den	12
Cueto	Mia	12
Dove	NY	12

TEAM STATISTICS
EASTERN DIVISION

Team		REGULAR SEASON												PLAYOFFS											
		G	FG	FGA	%	FT	FTA	%	Reb.	Ass.	PF	Points	PPG	G	FG	FGA	%	FT	FTA	%	Reb.	Ass.	PF	Points	PPG
Indiana	Off.	84	3593	7896	46	2110	2846	74	4433	1826	2125	9511	113.2	15	626	1427	44	425	562	76				1719	114.6
	Def.	84	3568	8181	44	1959	2731	72	4572	1726	2224	9220	109.8	15	636	1452	44	300	420	71				1612	107.5
	Diff.		+25	-285	+2	+151	+115	+2	-139	+100	+99	+291	+3.4		-10	-25		+125	+142	+5				+107	+7.1
Kentucky	Off.	84	3593	8378	43	2020	2733	74	4733	1765	2409	9536	113.5	12	491	1098	45	314	424	74				1338	111.5
	Def.	84	3505	7887	44	2311	3122	74	4562	1657	2276	9450	112.5	12	494	1074	46	347	467	74				1355	112.9
	Diff.		+88	+491	-1	-291	-389	—	+171	+108	-133	+86	+1.0		-3	+24	-1	-33	-43	—				-17	-1.4
Carolina	Off.	84	3470	7859	44	1942	2662	73	4309	1746	2243	8971	106.8	4	167	392	43	75	105	71				415	103.8
	Def.	84	3367	7650	44	2113	2913	73	4384	1588	2123	8990	107.0	4	167	365	46	112	158	71				451	112.8
	Diff.		+103	+209		-171	-251	—	-75	+158	-120	-19	-.2			+27	-3	-37	-53	—				-36	-9.0
New York	Off.	84	3543	7854	45	1990	2826	70	4156	1762	2381	9148	108.9	7	294	629	47	186	257	72				782	111.7
	Def.	84	3397	7363	46	2268	3034	75	4317	1781	2203	9219	109.8	7	284	612	46	203	266	76				778	111.1
	Diff.		+146	+491	-1	-278	-208	-5	-161	-19	-178	-71	-.9		+10	+17	+1	-17	-9	-4				+4	+.6
Pittsburgh	Off.	84	3721	8370	44	1875	2673	70	4720	1629	2184	9445	112.4												
	Def.	84	3741	8319	45	2192	2918	75	4870	1749	2187	9824	117.0												
	Diff.		-20	+51	-1	-317	-245	-5	-150	-120	+3	-379	-4.6												
Miami	Off.	84	3598	8345	43	2225	2991	74	4491	1281	2264	9511	113.2												
	Def.	84	3772	8093	47	2233	2940	76	4393	1719	2218	9940	118.3												
	Diff.		-174	+252	-4	-8	+51	-2	+98	-438	-46	-429	-5.1												
WESTERN DIVISION																									
Denver	Off.	84	3743	8381	45	2023	2713	75	4845	1621	2064	9697	115.4	12	574	1248	46	269	345	78				1451	120.9
	Def.	84	3619	8286	44	1927	2571	75	4442	1602	2124	9328	111.0	12	562	1174	48	264	347	76				1414	117.8
	Diff.		+124	+95	+1	+96	+142	—	+403	+19	+60	+369	+4.4		+12	+74	-2	+5	-2	+2				+37	+3.1
Dallas	Off.	84	3775	8265	46	2340	2968	79	4636	1633	2138	10079	120.0	6	303	641	47	126	170	74				748	124.7
	Def.	84	3865	8861	44	1998	2660	75	4655	1670	2319	9918	118.1	6	285	634	45	171	222	77				754	125.7
	Diff.		-90	-596	+2	+342	+308	+4	-19	-37	+181	+161	+1.9		+18	+7	+2	-45	-52	-3				-6	-1.0
Washington	Off.	84	3709	7988	46	2403	3177	76	4629	1961	2329	9929	118.2	7	336	671	50	157	201	78				845	120.7
	Def.	84	3872	8639	45	2087	2870	73	4582	1842	2321	9983	118.8	7	354	731	48	164	215	76				893	127.6
	Diff.		-163	-651	+1	+316	+307	+3	+47	+119	-8	-54	-.6		-18	-60	+2	-7	-14	+2				-48	-6.9
Los Angeles	Off.	84	3575	8120	44	2266	3022	75	4597	1772	2234	9547	113.7	17	773	1711	45	392	525	75				1980	116.5
	Def.	84	3650	8281	44	2087	2747	76	4710	1753	2390	9567	113.9	17	782	1775	44	383	494	78				2001	117.7
	Diff.		-75	-161		+179	+275	-1	-113	+19	+156	-20	-.2		-9	-64	+1	+9	+31	-3				-21	-1.2
New Orleans	Off.	84	3463	7982	43	1970	2531	78	4442	1638	2091	9064	107.9												
	Def.	84	3427	7878	44	1989	2636	75	4504	1547	2077	8999	107.1												
	Diff.		+36	+104	-1	-19	-105	+3	-62	+91	-14	+65	+.8												

1970-71 N.B.A.

Blanking the Bullets

Undaunted by a stagnant national economy and motivated to shut the rival A.B.A. out of as many markets as possible, the N.B.A. indulged in another round of expansion which brought the Buffalo Braves, Cleveland Cavaliers, and Portland Trail Blazers into the circuit. The new clubs were typically forgettable on the floor, with the Cavaliers starting their maiden campaign with 15 straight losses and ending it with a total of 15 wins in 82 contests. But their presence forced the N.B.A. into a major structural change, the creation of two divisions within both the Eastern and Western Conferences; two clubs from each of the four divisions would compete in the playoffs.

The Midwest Division was the strongest sector and had the league's strongest team, the Milwaukee Bucks. Last season center Lew Alcindor had turned the Bucks from an expansion team into a contender; this season guard Oscar Robertson turned them from a contender into a championship team. The Big 0 was unhappy under Bob Cousy in Cincinnati and was a sure bet to be traded as last season ended; the Bucks were able to pick up the all-time great guard for the relatively low price of Flynn Robinson and Charlie Paulk. Oscar furnished the ball-handing, outside shooting, and backcourt leadership that could complement and increase Alcindor's dominance in the frontcourt. With Bob Dandridge, John McGlocklin, and Greg Smith filling out the starting lineup, the Bucks won recognition as the N.B.A.'s latest superteam. The Bucks obviously were not team-oriented in the usual sense, relying most heavily on Alcindor and Robertson. Twice the Bucks strung together long winning binges, taking 16 in a row at one point and later winning a record 20 straight. The only fly in the ointment for the Bucks was their inability to beat the defending champion New York Knicks, dropping four of five contests to the New Yorkers. The Bucks easily took first place in the most competitive division in the N.B.A., with the Bucks, Chicago Bulls, Phoenix Suns, and Detroit Pistons all finishing way over the .500 level.

The Bulls blossomed into a devastatingly physical club in Dick Motta's third year as coach and they had the third best record in the league at 51-31. Phoenix enjoyed its first winning season in its three-year history, and the Pistons had their first winning season since moving to Detroit, thanks largely to veteran guard Dave Bing, a nine-game winning streak to open the season, and strong contributions from big rookie center Bob Lanier.

The Los Angeles Lakers had no rookie center in winning the Pacific Division title; they simply had Wilt Chamberlain back after missing most of last season with a knee injury. Chamberlain and Jerry West were a front-back combination to match Alcindor and Robertson in Milwaukee, but the Lakers lost their third superstar when forward Elgin Baylor had to sit out the season with bad knees. The Lakers did pick up some valuable new help by getting veteran guards Gail Goodrich and Pat Riley in deals and by signing rookie forward Jim McMillian.

The big but slow San Francisco Warriors edged out the San Diego Rockets, who relied on high-scoring Elvin Hayes, for the second playoff berth. The Rockets had one of the league's most colorful rookies in 5'9" Calvin Murphy, the slick shooter and ball-handler out of Niagara College. The fourth-place Seattle Supersonics had the most controversial rookie in forward Spencer Haywood. The star of the 1968 Olympics, Haywood had left school after his sophomore season to sign with the A.B.A. Denver Rockets last season. Midway through this season, however, he declared his contract with Denver void and signed with the Supersonics. The other league members stormed Commissioner Walter Kennedy with protests that Haywood had not gone through the college draft, and thus the Sonics had no right to sign him. The threats of penalties and lawsuits filled the air, but the Seattle team kept Haywood and thus won themselves an All-Star forward. The expansion Portland club had a fine rookie in guard Geoff Petrie but had very little else.

The New York Knicks got little help from any rookies, but they had enough returning talent to easily win the Atlantic Division with a 52-30 mark. Walt Frazier had developed into the N.B.A.'s best defensive guard and playmaker, and center Willis Reed's fine performance belied the fact that a bad knee and a bad shoulder were severely bothering him. The Philadelphia 76ers had a gaping hole at center but held on to the second playoff berth ahead of the vastly improved Boston Celtics. Given a hard dose of reality during last season's tumble into the ranks of losers, the Celtics had unloaded Larry Siegfried, Bailey Howell, and Em Bryant. They built a new starting lineup out of veteran forwards John Havlicek and Don Nelson, young guards Jo Jo White and Don Chaney, and hustling rookie center Dave Cowens. This new Celtic outfit possessed the potential to run and press as well as the departed champs. The new Buffalo team was competitive but a distant last.

None of the teams in the Central Division created much excitement, with a 42-40 record earning the Baltimore Bullets first place. The Atlanta Hawks fell under the .500 level to 36-46, hurt by Joe Caldwell's jump to the A.B.A. and by having to adjust to the fancy dribbling and passing of rookie guard Pete Maravich, the N.C.A.A. scoring champ for three seasons at Louisiana State. Minus Jerry Lucas and Oscar Robertson, the Cincinnati Royals dropped to 33-49 despite 6' Nate Archibald's emergence as a first-rate offensive threat. The new Cleveland team needed a telescope even to see a playoff berth.

As the playoffs began, fans anticipated a Milwaukee-New York final, with the star-heavy Bucks facing the smart, balanced Knicks. But while the Bucks easily handled the Warriors and Lakers in the West, Willis Reed's physical ills put the Knicks in deep trouble. They disposed of the Hawks in five games but met their match in the fast-breaking Bullets.

The New Yorkers looked safe after winning the first two games, but then Wes Unseld and Gus Johnson took control of the boards away from the Knicks. The Bullets won games three, four, and six to force a seventh game, and they walked off the court 93-91 victors as Bill Bradley missed a jump shot at the buzzer. For the Bullets, the victory over New York was the finest of the campaign, but the taste of triumph was short-lived. Unseld could not contain Alcindor, and the well-rested Bucks walked over the tired Bullets in four straight games, winning the N.B.A. championship only three seasons after joining as a weak expansion outpost.

Use Name	Pos	Hgt	Wgt	Age	TOTAL													PER GAME				
					G	Min	FG	FGA	%	FT	FTA	%	Reb	Ass	PF	DQ	Points	Min	Reb	Ass	PF	Points

1970/71 N.B.A. — ATLANTIC DIVISION

Use Name	Pos	Hgt	Wgt	Age	G	Min	FG	FGA	%	FT	FTA	%	Reb	Ass	PF	DQ	Points	Min	Reb	Ass	PF	Points
NEW YORK KNICKERBOCKERS	**52-30 .634**				**RED HOLZMAN**																	
Bill Bradley	F-G	6'5	205	27	78	2300	413	912	45	144	175	82	260	280	245	3	970	29	3.3	3.6	3.1	12.4
Dave DeBusschere	F	8'6	235	30	81	2891	523	1243	42	217	312	70	901	220	237	2	1263	36	11.1	2.7	2.9	15.6
Willis Reed	C	6'9	240	28	73	2855	614	1330	46	299	381	78	1003	148	228	1	1527	39	13.7	2.0	3.1	20.9
Dick Barnett	G	6'4	190	34	82	2843	540	1184	46	192	278	69	238	225	232	1	1273	35	2.9	2.7	2.8	15.5
Walt Frazier	G	6'4	205	25	80	3455	651	1317	49	434	557	78	544	536	240	1	1736	43	6.8	6.7	3.0	21.7
Dave Stallworth	F	6'7	210	29	81	1565	295	685	43	169	230	73	352	106	175	1	759	19	4.3	1.3	2.2	9.4
Mike Riordan	G	6'4	200	25	82	1320	162	388	42	67	108	62	169	121	151	0	391	16	2.1	1.5	1.8	4.8
Cazzie Russell (BW)	F	6'5	220	26	57	1056	216	504	43	92	119	77	192	77	74	0	524	19	3.4	1.4	1.3	9.2
Phil Jackson	C-F	6'8	220	25	71	771	118	263	45	95	133	71	238	31	169	4	331	11	3.4	0.4	2.4	4.7
Greg Fillmore	C	7'1	250	23	39	271	45	102	44	13	27	48	93	17	80	0	103	7	2.4	0.4	2.1	2.6
Mike Price	G	6'3	200	22	56	251	30	81	37	24	34	71	29	12	57	0	84	4	0.5	0.2	1.0	1.5
Eddie Mast	C-F	6'9	220	22	30	164	25	66	38	11	20	55	56	4	25	0	61	5	1.9	0.1	0.8	2.0
Milt Williams	G	6'2	185	25	5	13	1	1	100	2	3	67	0	2	3	0	4	3	0.0	0.4	0.6	0.8
PHILADELPHIA 76ers	**47-35 .573**				**JACK RAMSAY**																	
Billy Cunningham	F	6'7	220	27	81	3090	702	1519	46	455	620	73	946	395	328	5	1859	38	11.7	4.9	4.0	23.0
Jim Washington	F-C	6'7	215	27	78	2501	395	829	48	259	340	76	747	97	258	6	1049	32	9.6	1.2	3.3	13.4
Luke Jackson	C	6'9	250	29	79	1774	199	529	38	131	189	69	568	148	211	3	529	22	7.2	1.9	2.7	6.7
Hal Greer	G	6'3	176	34	81	3060	591	1371	43	326	405	80	364	369	289	4	1508	38	4.5	4.6	3.6	18.6
Archie Clark	G	6'2	175	29	82	3245	662	1334	50	422	536	79	391	440	217	2	1746	40	4.8	5.4	2.6	21.3
Bailey Howell	F	6'7	220	33	82	1589	324	686	47	230	315	73	441	115	234	2	878	19	5.4	1.4	2.9	10.7
Dennis Awtrey	C	6'10	235	22	70	1292	200	421	48	104	157	66	430	89	211	7	504	18	6.1	1.3	3.0	7.2
Wally Jones (knee injury)	G	6'2	185	28	41	962	168	418	40	79	101	78	64	128	110	1	415	23	1.6	3.1	2.7	10.1
Fred Foster(from Cin)	F-G	6'5	220	24	66	888	145	360	40	72	103	70	147	61	113	3	362	13	2.2	0.9	1.7	5.5
Connie Dierking (from Cin)	C	6'9	235	34	53	714	122	306	40	61	89	69	227	59	109	1	305	13	4.3	1.1	2.1	5.8
Freddie Crawford (from Buf)	G	6'4	200	29	36	449	74	175	42	32	72	44	69	54	59	0	180	12	1.9	1.5	1.6	5.0
Bud Ogden	F	6'6	220	24	27	133	24	66	36	18	26	69	20	17	21	0	66	5	0.7	0.6	0.8	2.4
Cliff Anderson (from Cle)	F	6 4	200	26	5	27	1	6	17	5	7	71	11	4	7	0	7	5	2.2	0.8	1.4	1.4
Al Henry	C	6'9	205	21	6	26	1	6	17	5	7	71	11	0	1	0	7	4	1.8	0.0	0.2	1.2
Matt Guokas (to Chi)	G	6'5	195	26	1	5	0	0	—	0	0	—	1	0	0	0	0	5	1.0	0.0	0.0	0.0
BOSTON CELTICS	**44-38 .537**				**TOM HEINSOHN**																	
John Havlicek	F-G	6'5	205	30	81	**3678**	892	1982	45	554	677	82	730	607	200	0	2338	**45**	9.0	7.5	2.5	28.9
Don Nelson	F	6'6	210	30	82	2254	412	881	47	317	426	74	565	153	232	2	1141	27	6.9	1.9	2.8	13.9
Dave Cowens	C-F	6'9	230	22	81	3076	550	1302	42	273	373	73	1216	228	**350**	15	1373	38	15.0	2.8	**4.3**	17.0
Don Chaney	G	6'5	210	24	81	2289	348	766	45	234	313	75	463	235	288	11	930	28	5.7	2.9	3.6	11.5
Jo Jo White	G	6'3	190	24	75	2787	693	1494	46	215	269	80	376	361	255	5	1601	37	5.0	4.8	3.4	21.3
Steve Kuberski	F	6'8	215	23	82	1867	313	745	42	133	183	73	538	78	198	1	759	23	6.6	1.0	2.4	9.3
Henry Finkel	C	7'	240	28	80	1234	214	489	44	93	127	73	343	79	196	5	521	15	4.3	1.0	2.5	6.5
Hambone Williams	G	6'2	190	31	74	1141	150	330	45	60	83	72	205	233	182	1	360	15	2.8	3.1	2.5	4.9
Bill Dinwiddie	F	6'7	220	27	61	717	123	328	38	54	74	73	209	34	90	1	300	12	3.4	0.6	1.5	4.9
Garfield Smith	C	6'9	235	25	37	281	42	116	36	22	56	39	95	9	53	0	106	8	2.6	0.2	1.4	2.9
Rex Morgan	G	6'5	190	22	34	266	41	102	40	35	54	65	61	22	58	2	117	8	1.8	0.6	1.7	3.4
Satch Sanders (knee injury)	F	6'6	210	32	17	121	16	44	36	7	8	88	17	11	25	0	39	7	1.0	0.6	1.5	2.3
Willie Williams (to Cin)	F	6'7	200	23	16	56	6	32	19	3	5	60	10	2	8	0	15	4	0.6	0.1	0.5	0.9
Rich Johnson	C	6'9	215	24	1	13	4	5	80	0	0	—	5	0	3	0	8	13	5.0	0.0	3.0	8.0
BUFFALO BRAVES	**22-60 .268**				**DOLPH SCHAYES**																	
Don May	F	6'4	220	24	76	2666	629	1336	47	277	350	79	567	150	219	4	1535	35	7.5	2.0	2.9	20.2
John Hummer	F	6'9	230	22	81	2637	339	764	44	235	405	58	717	163	284	10	913	33	8.9	2.0	3.5	11.3
Bob Kauffman	C	6'8	240	24	78	2778	616	1309	47	359	485	74	837	354	263	8	1591	36	10.7	4.5	3.4	20.4
Dick Garrett	G	6'3	185	23	75	2375	373	902	41	218	251	87	295	264	290	9	964	32	3.9	3.5	3.9	12.9
Em Bryant	G	6'1	175	32	73	2137	288	684	42	151	203	74	262	352	266	7	727	29	3.6	4.8	3.6	10.0
Herm Gilliam	G-F	6'3	190	24	80	2082	378	896	42	142	189	75	334	291	246	4	898	26	4.2	3.6	3.1	11.2
Mike Davis	G	6'3	185	24	73	1617	317	774	41	199	262	76	187	153	220	7	833	22	2.6	2.1	3.0	11.4
Cornell Warner	F	6'9	220	22	65	1293	156	376	41	79	143	55	452	53	140	2	391	20	7.0	0.8	2.2	6.0
George Wilson (broken ankle)	C	6'8	230	28	46	713	92	269	34	56	69	81	230	48	99	1	240	16	5.0	1.0	2.2	5.2
Nate Bowman	C	6'10	230	27	44	483	58	148	39	20	38	53	173	41	91	2	136	11	3.9	0.9	2.1	3.1
Mike Silliman (foot injury)	F	6'6	225	26	36	366	36	79	46	19	39	49	62	23	37	0	91	10	1.7	0.6	1.0	2.5
Bill Hosket (knee injury)	F	6'8	225	24	13	217	47	90	52	11	17	65	75	20	27	1	105	17	5.8	1.5	2.1	8.1
Paul Long	G	6'2	180	26	30	213	57	120	48	20	24	83	31	25	23	0	134	7	1.0	0.8	0.8	4.5
Freddie Crawford (to Phi)	G	6'4	200	29	15	203	36	106	34	16	26	62	35	24	18	0	88	14	2.3	1.6	1.2	5.9
Mike Lynn	F	6'7	215	25	5	25	2	7	29	3	3	100	4	1	9	0	7	5	0.8	0.2	1.8	1.4

1970/71 N.B.A. - CENTRAL DIVISION

					TOTAL													PER GAME				
Use Name	Pos	Hgt	Wgt	Age	G	Min	FG	FGA	%	FT	FTA	%	Reb	Ass	PF	DQ	Points	Min	Reb	Ass	PF	Points
BALTIMORE BULLETS	**42-40 .512**				**GENE SHUE**																	
Jack Marin	F	6'7	210	26	82	2990	626	1360	46	290	342	85	513	217	261	3	1542	36	6.3	2.6	3.2	18.8
Gus Johnson	F	6'6	235	32	66	2538	494	1090	45	214	290	74	1128	192	227	4	1202	38	17.1	2.9	3.4	18.2
Wes Unseld	C	6'7	250	24	74	2904	424	846	50	199	303	66	1253	293	235	2	1047	39	16.9	4.0	3.2	14.1
Kevin Loughery	G	6'3	190	30	82	2260	481	1193	40	275	331	83	219	301	246	2	1237	28	2.7	3.7	3.0	15.1
Earl Monroe	G	6'3	190	26	81	2843	663	1501	44	406	506	80	213	354	220	3	1732	35	2.6	4.4	2.7	21.4
Fred Carter	G	6'3	185	25	77	1707	340	815	42	119	183	65	251	165	165	0	799	22	3.3	2.1	2.1	10.4
Eddie Miles	G-F	6'4	196	30	63	1541	252	591	43	118	147	80	167	110	119	0	622	24	2.7	1.7	1.9	9.9
John Tresvant (from LA)	F-C	6'7	220	31	67	1451	184	401	46	139	195	71	359	76	185	1	507	22	5.4	1.1	2.8	7.6
Dorie Murrey (from Port)	F-C	6'8	220	27	69	696	77	172	45	66	101	65	214	31	146	4	220	10	3.1	0.4	2.1	3.2
George Johnson	C	6'11	255	23	24	337	41	100	41	11	30	37	114	10	63	1	93	14	4.8	0.4	2.6	3.9
Al Tucker (to Fla-ABA)	F	6'8	190	27	31	276	52	115	45	25	31	81	73	7	33	0	129	9	2.4	0.2	1.1	4.2
Gary Zeller	G	6'3	205	23	50	226	34	115	30	15	28	54	27	7	43	0	83	5	0.5	0.1	0.9	1.7
Jim Barnes	C	6'8	240	29	11	100	15	28	54	7	11	64	16	8	23	0	37	9	1.5	0.7	2.1	3.4
Dennis Stewart (to Fla-ABA)	F	6'6	220	23	2	6	1	4	25	2	2	100	3	1	0	0	4	3	1.5	0.5	0.0	2.0
ATLANTA HAWKS	**36-46 .439**				**RICHIE GUERIN**																	
Lou Hudson	F-G	6'5	210	26	76	3113	829	1713	48	381	502	76	386	257	186	0	2039	41	5.1	3.4	2.4	26.8
Bill Bridges	F	6'6	235	31	82	3140	382	834	46	211	330	64	1233	240	317	7	975	38	15.0	2.9	3.9	11.9
Walt Bellamy	C	6'11	245	31	82	2908	433	879	49	336	556	60	1060	230	271	4	1202	35	12.9	2.8	3.3	14.7
Pete Maravich	G	6'5	200	22	81	2926	738	1613	46	404	505	80	298	355	238	1	1880	36	3.7	4.4	2.9	23.2
Walt Hazzard	G	6'2	190	28	82	2877	517	1126	46	315	415	76	300	514	276	2	1349	35	3.7	6.3	3.4	16.5
Jim Davis	F-C	6'9	235	29	82	1864	241	503	48	195	288	68	546	108	253	5	677	23	6.7	1.3	3.1	8.3
Jerry Chambers	F	6'5	190	27	65	1168	237	526	45	106	134	79	245	61	119	0	580	18	3.8	0.9	1.8	8.9
Bob Christian	C	7'	260	26	54	524	55	127	43	40	64	63	177	30	118	0	150	10	3.3	0.6	2.2	2.8
Len Chappell (from Cle)	F	6'8	240	29	42	451	71	161	44	60	74	81	133	16	63	2	202	11	3.2	0.4	1.5	4.8
John Vallely	G	6'3	185	22	51	430	73	204	36	45	59	76	34	47	50	0	191	8	0.7	0.9	1.0	3.7
Herb White (military service)	G	6'2	195	22	38	315	34	84	40	22	39	56	48	47	62	2	90	8	1.3	1.2	1.6	2.4
Bob Riley	F	6'9	235	22	7	39	4	9	44	5	9	56	12	1	5	0	13	6	1.7	0.1	0.7	1.9
CINCINNATI ROYALS	**33-49 .402**				**BOB COUSY**																	
Tom Van Arsdale	F-G	6'5	215	28	82	3146	749	1642	46	377	523	72	499	181	294	3	1875	38	6.1	2.2	3.6	22.9
Johnny Green	F	6'5	210	37	75	2147	502	855	**59**	248	402	62	656	89	233	7	1252	29	8.7	1.2	3.1	16.7
Sam Lacey	C	6'10	235	22	81	2648	467	1117	42	156	227	69	913	117	270	8	1090	33	11.3	1.4	3.3	13.5
Norm Van Lier	G	6'1	175	23	82	3324	478	1138	42	359	440	82	583	**832**	343	12	1315	41	7.1	**10.1**	4.2	16.0
Nate Archibald	G	6'1	160	22	82	2867	486	1095	44	336	444	76	242	450	218	2	1308	35	3.0	5.5	2.7	16.0
Flynn Robinson	G	6'1	190	29	71	1368	374	817	46	195	228	86	143	138	161	0	943	19	2.0	1.9	2.3	13.3
Greg Hyder	F	6'6	215	22	77	1359	183	409	45	51	71	72	332	48	187	2	417	18	4.3	0.6	2.4	5.4
Charlie Paulk	F-C	6'8	220	26	68	1213	274	637	43	79	131	60	320	27	186	6	627	18	4.7	0.4	2.7	9.2
Darrall Imhoff	C	6'10	235	32	34	826	119	258	46	37	73	51	233	79	120	5	275	24	6.9	2.3	3.5	8.1
Bob Arnzen	F	6'6	215	23	55	594	128	277	46	45	52	87	152	24	54	0	301	11	2.8	0.4	1.0	5.5
Moe Barr	G	6'4	195	26	31	145	25	62	40	11	13	85	20	28	27	0	61	5	0.6	0.9	0.9	2.0
Tom Black (from Sea)	C	6'10	234	29	16	100	10	33	30	6	15	40	34	2	20	0	26	6	2.1	0.1	1.3	1.6
Willie Williams (from Bos)	F	6'7	200	23	9	49	4	10	40	0	0	—	13	6	6	0	8	5	1.4	0.7	0.7	0.9
Connie Dierking (to Phi)	C	6'9	235	34	1	23	3	16	19	0	0	—	7	1	5	0	6	23	7.0	1.0	5.0	6.0
Fred Foster (to Phi)	F	6'5	220	24	1	21	3	8	38	1	3	33	4	0	2	0	7	21	4.0	0.0	2.0	7.0
CLEVELAND CAVALIERS	**15-67 .183**				**BILL FITCH**																	
John Johnson	F	6'7	200	23	67	2310	435	1032	42	240	298	81	453	323	251	3	1110	34	6.8	4.8	3.7	16.6
Dave Sorenson	F	6'8	225	22	79	1940	353	794	44	184	229	80	486	163	181	3	890	25	6.2	2.1	2.3	11.3
Walt Wesley	C	6'11	220	25	82	2425	565	1241	46	325	473	69	713	83	295	5	1455	30	8.7	1.0	3.6	17.7
Bobby Smith	G-F	6'5	212	24	77	2332	495	1106	45	178	234	76	429	258	175	4	1168	30	5.6	3.4	2.3	15.2
Johnny Warren	G	6'3	180	23	82	2610	380	899	42	180	217	83	344	347	299	13	940	32	4.2	4.2	3.6	11.5
Bobby Lewis	G	6'3	185	26	79	1852	179	484	37	109	152	72	206	244	176	1	467	23	2.6	3.1	2.2	5.9
McCoy McLemore (to Mil)	F	6'7	235	28	58	1839	254	654	39	170	220	77	463	176	169	1	678	32	8.0	3.0	2.9	11.7
Luther Rackley	C	6'10	220	24	74	1434	219	470	47	121	190	64	394	66	186	3	559	19	5.3	0.9	2.5	7.6
Bobby Washington	G	6'	175	23	47	823	123	310	40	104	140	74	105	190	105	0	350	18	2.2	4.0	2.2	7.4
Joe Cooke	G	6'3	175	22	73	725	134	341	39	48	59	81	114	93	135	2	316	10	1.6	1.3	1.8	4.3
Larry Mikan	F	6'7	215	22	53	536	62	186	33	34	55	62	139	41	56	1	158	10	2.6	0.8	1.1	3.0
Johnny Egan (to SD)	G	5'11	180	31	26	410	40	98	41	25	28	89	32	58	31	0	105	16	1.2	2.2	1.2	4.0
Cliff Anderson (to Phi)	F	6'4	200	26	23	171	19	59	32	41	60	68	37	16	22	1	79	7	1.6	0.7	1.0	3.4
Gary Suiter	C-F	6'9	225	25	30	140	19	54	35	4	9	44	41	2	20	0	42	5	1.4	0.1	0.7	1.4
Len Chappell (to Atl)	F	6'8	240	29	6	86	15	38	39	11	14	79	18	1	9	0	41	14	3.0	0.2	1.5	6.8
Gary Freeman (from Mil)	F	6'9	210	22	11	47	7	12	58	1	2	50	8	4	4	0	15	4	0.7	0.4	0.4	1.4
Butch Beard-military service																						

Use Name	Pos	Hgt	Wgt	Age	TOTAL													PER GAME				
					G	Min	FG	FGA	%	FT	FTA	%	Reb	Ass	PF	DQ	Points	Min	Reb	Ass	PF	Points
1970/71 N.B.A. — MIDWEST DIVISION																						
MILWAUKEE BUCKS	**66-16 .805**				**LARRY COSTELLO**																	
Greg Smith	F	6'5	200	23	82	2428	409	799	51	141	213	66	589	227	284	5	959	30	7.2	2.8	3.5	11.7
Bob Dandridge	F	6'6	195	23	79	2862	594	1167	51	264	376	70	632	277	287	4	1452	36	8.0	3.5	3.6	18.4
Lew Alcindor	C	7'2	232	23	82	3288	**1063**	1843	58	470	681	69	1311	272	264	4	2596	40	16.0	3.3	3.2	**31.7**
Jon McGlockin	G	6'5	205	27	82	2891	574	1073	53	144	167	86	223	305	189	0	1292	35	2.7	3.7	2.3	15.8
Oscar Robertson	G	6'5	220	32	81	3194	592	1193	50	385	453	85	462	668	203	0	1569	39	5.7	8.2	2.5	19.4
Bob Boozer	F	6'8	225	33	80	1775	290	645	45	148	181	82	435	128	216	0	728	22	5.4	1.6	2.7	9.1
Lucius Allen	G	6'2	175	23	61	1162	178	398	45	77	110	70	152	161	108	0	433	19	2.5	2.6	1.8	7.1
Dick Cunningham	C	6'10	252	24	76	675	81	195	42	39	59	66	257	43	90	1	201	9	3.4	0.6	1.2	2.6
McCoy McLemore (from Cle)	F	6'7	235	28	28	415	49	133	37	34	41	83	105	30	66	1	132	15	3.8	1.1	2.4	4.7
Bill Zopf	G	6'1	170	22	53	398	49	135	36	20	36	56	46	73	34	0	118	8	0.9	1.4	0.6	2.2
Gary Freeman (to Cle)	F	6'9	210	22	41	335	62	122	51	28	38	74	98	31	63	0	152	8	2.4	0.8	1.5	3.7
Jeff Webb	G	6'4	170	22	29	300	27	78	35	11	15	73	24	19	33	0	65	10	0.8	0.7	1.1	2.2
Bob Greacen	F	6'7	205	23	2	43	1	12	8	3	7	43	6	13	7	0	5	22	3.0	6.5	3.5	2.5
Marv Winkler	G	6'1	175	22	3	14	3	10	30	2	2	100	4	2	3	0	8	5	1.3	0.7	1.0	2.7
CHICAG0 BULLS	**51-31 .622**				**DICK MOTTA**																	
Chet Walker	F	6'6	220	30	81	2927	650	1398	46	480	559	**86**	588	179	187	2	1780	36	7.3	2.2	2.3	22.0
Bob Love	F	6'8	215	28	81	3482	765	1710	45	513	619	83	690	185	259	0	2043	43	8.5	2.3	3.2	25.2
Tom Boerwinkle	C	7'	270	25	82	2370	357	736	49	168	232	72	1133	397	275	3	882	29	13.8	4.8	3.4	10.8
Jerry Sloan	G-F	6'6	200	28	80	3140	592	1342	44	278	389	71	701	281	289	5	1462	39	8.8	3.5	3.6	18.3
Bob Weiss	G	6'2	185	28	82	2237	278	659	42	226	269	84	189	387	216	1	782	27	2.3	4.7	2.6	9.5
Matt Guokas (from Phi)	G	6'5	195	26	78	2208	206	418	49	101	138	73	157	342	189	1	513	28	2.0	4.4	2.4	6.6
Jim Fox	C	6'10	230	27	82	1628	280	611	46	239	321	74	598	196	213	0	799	20	7.3	2.4	2.6	9.7
Jim King	G	6'2	175	29	55	645	100	228	44	64	79	81	68	78	55	0	264	12	1.2	1.4	1.0	4.8
Johnny Baum	F	6'5	210	24	62	543	123	293	42	40	58	69	125	31	55	0	286	9	2.0	0.5	0.9	4.6
Jimmy Collins	G	6'2	175	24	55	478	92	214	43	35	45	78	54	60	43	0	219	9	1.0	1.1	0.8	4.0
Paul Ruffner	F	6'10	225	22	10	60	15	35	43	4	8	50	16	2	10	0	34	6	1.6	0.2	1.0	3.4
Shaler Hailmon (to Port)	F	6'6	200	25	2	23	1	8	13	0	1	0	2	4	5	0	2	12	1.0	2.0	2.5	1.0
A.W. Holt	F	6'7	210	24	6	14	1	8	13	2	3	67	4	0	1	0	4	2	0.7	0.0	0.2	0.7
PHOENIX SUNS	**48-34 .585**				**COTTON FITZSIMMONS**																	
Connie Hawkins	F	6'8	220	28	71	2662	512	1181	43	457	560	82	643	322	197	2	1481	37	9.1	4.5	2.8	20.9
Paul Silas	F	6'7	225	27	81	2944	338	789	43	285	416	69	1015	247	227	3	961	36	12.5	3.0	2.8	11.9
Neal Walk	C	6'10	250	22	82	2033	426	945	45	205	268	76	674	117	282	8	1057	25	8.2	1.4	3.4	12.9
Dick Van Arsdale	G-F	6'5	210	27	81	3157	609	1346	45	553	682	81	316	329	246	1	1771	39	3.9	4.1	3.0	21.9
Clem Haskins	G	6'3	195	27	82	2764	562	1277	44	338	431	78	324	383	207	2	1462	34	4.0	4.7	2.5	17.8
Mel Counts	C	7'	235	29	80	1669	365	799	46	149	198	75	503	136	279	8	879	21	6.3	1.7	3.5	11.0
Lamar Green	F	6'7	220	23	68	1326	167	369	45	64	106	60	466	53	202	5	398	20	6.9	0.8	3.0	5.9
John Wetzel	G	6'5	192	26	70	1091	124	288	43	83	101	82	153	114	156	1	331	16	2.2	1.6	2.2	4.7
Art Harris	G	6'4	186	23	56	952	199	484	41	69	113	61	100	132	137	0	467	17	1.8	2.4	2.4	8.3
Fred Taylor	G	6'5	187	22	54	552	110	284	39	78	125	62	86	51	113	0	298	10	1.6	0.9	2.1	5.5
Greg Howard	C-F	6'9	215	22	44	426	68	173	39	37	58	64	119	26	67	0	173	10	2.7	0.6	1.5	3.9
Joe Thomas	F	6'6	205	22	39	204	23	86	27	9	20	45	43	17	19	0	55	5	1.1	0.4	0.5	1.4
DETROIT PISTONS	**45-37 .549**				**BUTCH VAN BREDA KOLFF**																	
Terry Dischinger (injury)	F	6'7	208	30	65	1855	304	568	54	161	211	76	339	113	189	2	769	29	5.2	1.7	2.9	11.8
Bill Hewitt	F	6'7	210	26	62	1725	203	435	47	69	120	58	454	124	189	5	475	28	7.3	2.0	3.0	7.7
Bob Lanier	C	6'11	265	22	82	2017	504	1108	45	273	376	73	665	146	272	4	1281	25	8.1	1.8	3.3	15.6
Jimmy Walker	G	6'3	205	26	79	2765	524	1201	44	344	414	83	207	268	173	0	1392	35	2.6	3.4	2.2	17.6
Dave Bing	G	6'3	185	27	82	3065	799	1710	47	**615**	**772**	80	364	408	228	4	2213	37	4.4	5.0	2.8	27.0
Howie Komives	G	6'1	185	29	82	1932	275	715	38	121	151	80	152	262	184	0	671	24	1.9	3.2	2.2	8.2
Dtto Moore	C	6'11	220	24	82	1926	310	696	45	121	219	55	700	88	182	0	741	23	8.5	1.1	2.2	9.0
Terry Driscoll	F	6'7	215	23	69	1255	132	318	42	108	154	70	402	54	212	2	372	18	5.8	0.8	3.1	5.4
Erwin Mueller	F	6'8	230	26	52	1224	126	309	41	60	108	56	223	113	99	0	312	24	4.3	2.2	1.9	6.0
Bob Quick	F	6'5	215	24	56	1146	155	341	45	138	176	78	230	56	142	1	448	20	4.1	1.0	2.5	8.0
Steve Mix	F	6'7	215	23	35	731	111	249	45	68	89	76	164	34	72	0	290	21	4.7	1.0	2.1	8.3
Harvey Marlatt	G	6'3	185	22	23	214	25	80	31	15	18	83	23	30	27	0	65	9	1.0	1.3	1.2	2.8

Use Name	Pos	Hgt	Wgt	Age	G	Min	FG	FGA	%	FT	FTA	%	Reb	Ass	PF	DQ	Points	Min	Reb	Ass	PF	Points
					TOTAL													PER GAME				

1970/71 N.B.A. — PACIFIC DIVISION

Use Name	Pos	Hgt	Wgt	Age	G	Min	FG	FGA	%	FT	FTA	%	Reb	Ass	PF	DQ	Points	Min	Reb	Ass	PF	Points
LOS ANGELES LAKERS	**48-34 .585**				**JOE MULUNEY**																	
Keith Erickson	F-G	6'5	200	26	73	2272	369	783	47	85	112	76	404	223	241	4	823	31	5.5	3.1	3.3	11.3
Happv Hairston	F	6'7	225	28	80	2921	574	1233	47	337	431	78	797	168	256	2	1485	37	10.0	2.1	3.2	18.6
Wilt Chamberlain	C	7'1	275	34	82	3630	668	1226	54	360	669	54	**1493**	352	174	0	1696	44	**18.2**	4.3	2.1	20.7
Jerry West (knee injury)	G	6'3	180	32	69	2845	667	1351	49	525	631	83	320	655	180	0	1859	41	4.6	9.5	2.6	26.9
Gail Goodrich	G	6'1	175	27	79	2808	558	1174	48	264	343	77	260	380	258	3	1380	36	3.3	4.8	3.3	17.5
Jim McMillian	F	6'5	225	22	81	1747	289	629	46	100	130	77	330	133	122	1	678	22	4.1	1.6	1.5	8.4
Willie McCarter	G	6'3	175	24	76	1369	247	592	42	46	77	60	122	126	152	0	540	18	1.6	1.7	2.0	7.1
Rich Roberson	F-C	6'9	230	23	65	909	125	301	42	88	143	62	304	47	125	1	338	14	4.7	0.7	1.9	5.2
Fred Hetzel	F	6'8	230	28	59	613	111	256	43	60	77	78	149	37	99	3	282	10	2.5	0.6	1.7	4.8
Pat Riley	G	6'4	208	25	54	506	105	254	41	56	87	64	54	72	84	0	266	9	1.0	1.3	1.6	4.9
John Tresvant (to Bal)	F	6'7	220	31	8	66	18	35	51	7	10	70	23	10	11	0	43	8	2.9	1.3	1.4	5.4
Elgin Baylor(knee injury)	F	6'5	225	36	2	57	8	19	42	4	6	67	11	2	6	0	20	29	5.5	1.0	3.0	10.0
Earnie Killum	G	6'3	180	22	4	12	0	4	0	1	1	100	2	0	1	0	1	3	0.5	0.0	0.3	0.3
SAN FRANCISCO WARRIORS	**41-41 .500**				**AL ATTLES**																	
Joe Ellis	F-G	6'6	175	26	80	2275	356	898	40	151	203	74	511	161	287	6	863	28	6.4	2.0	3.6	10.8
Jerry Lucas	F	6'8	230	30	80	3251	623	1250	50	289	367	79	1265	293	197	0	1535	41	15.8	3.7	2.5	19.2
Nate Thurmond	C	6'11	235	29	82	3351	623	1401	44	395	541	73	1128	257	192	1	1641	41	13.8	3.1	2.3	20.0
Jeff Mullins	G	6'4	200	28	75	2909	630	1308	48	302	358	84	341	332	246	5	1562	39	4.5	4.4	3.3	20.8
Ron Williams	G	6'3	190	26	82	2809	426	977	44	331	392	84	244	480	301	9	1183	34	3.0	5.9	3.7	14.4
Bob Portman	F	6'5	200	23	68	1395	221	483	46	77	106	73	321	67	130	0	519	21	4.7	1.0	1.9	7.6
Clyde Lee	F-C	6'10	225	26	82	1392	194	428	45	111	199	56	570	63	137	0	499	17	7.0	0.8	1.7	6.1
Nick Jones	G	6'2	190	25	81	1183	225	523	43	111	151	74	110	113	192	2	561	15	1.4	1.4	2.4	6.9
Al Attles	G	6'2	185	34	34	321	22	54	41	24	41	59	40	58	59	2	68	9	1.2	1.7	1.7	2.0
Adrian Smith	G	6'1	190	34	21	247	38	89	43	35	41	85	24	30	24	0	111	12	1.1	1.4	1.1	5.3
Levi Fontaine	G	6'4	190	22	35	210	53	145	37	28	37	76	15	22	27	0	134	6	0.4	0.6	0.8	3.8
Bill Turner	F	6'7	220	26	18	200	26	82	32	13	20	65	42	8	24	0	65	11	2.3	0.4	1.3	3.6
Ralph Ogden	F	6'5	205	22	32	162	17	71	24	8	12	67	32	9	17	0	42	5	1.0	0.3	0.5	1.3
SAN DIEGO ROCKETS	**40-42 .488**				**ALEX HANNUM**																	
John Trapp	F	6'7	215	25	82	2080	322	766	42	142	188	76	510	138	337	**16**	786	25	6.2	1.7	4.1	9.6
Don Adams	F	6'7	210	23	82	2374	391	957	41	155	212	73	581	173	344	11	937	29	7.1	2.1	4.2	11.4
Elvin Hayes	C	6'9	235	25	82	3633	948	2215	43	454	676	67	1362	186	225	1	2350	44	16.6	2.3	2.7	28.7
Stu Lantz	G	6'3	175	24	82	3102	585	1305	45	519	644	81	406	344	230	3	1689	38	5.0	4.2	2.8	20.6
Calvin Murphy	G	5'9	165	22	82	2020	471	1029	46	356	434	82	245	329	263	4	1298	25	3.0	4.0	3.2	15.8
Larry Siegtried (KJ)	G	6'3	192	31	53	1673	146	378	39	130	153	85	207	346	146	0	422	32	3.9	6.5	2.8	8.0
John Block	F-C	6'10	218	26	73	1464	245	584	42	212	270	79	442	98	193	2	702	20	6.1	1.3	2.6	9.6
Tony Kimball	F	6'8	225	28	80	1100	111	287	39	51	108	47	406	62	128	1	273	14	5.1	0.8	1.6	3.4
Rudy Tomjanovich	F	6'8	218	22	77	1062	168	439	38	73	112	65	381	73	124	0	409	14	4.9	0.9	1.6	5.3
Bernie Williams	G	6'3	175	25	56	708	112	338	33	68	81	84	85	113	76	1	292	13	1.5	2.0	1.4	5.2
Johnny Egan (from Cle)	G	5'11	180	31	36	414	27	80	34	17	23	74	31	54	40	0	71	12	0.9	1.5	1.1	2.0
Curtis Perry	F	6'7	220	22	18	100	21	48	44	11	20	55	30	5	22	0	53	6	1.7	0.3	1.2	2.9
SEATTLE SUPERSONICS	**38-44 .463**				**LENNY WILKENS**																	
Don Kojis	F	6'5	215	31	79	2143	454	1018	45	249	320	78	435	130	220	3	1157	27	5.5	1.6	2.8	14.6
Spencer Haywood (CT)	F	6'8	225	21	33	1162	260	579	45	160	218	73	396	48	84	1	680	35	12.0	1.5	2.5	20.6
Pete Cross	C-F	6'9	230	22	79	2194	245	554	44	140	203	69	949	113	212	2	630	28	12.0	1.4	2.7	8.0
Dick Snyder	G	6'5	210	26	82	2824	645	1215	53	302	361	84	257	352	249	6	1592	34	3.1	4.3	3.0	19.4
Lenny Wilkens	G	6'1	185	33	71	2641	471	1125	42	461	574	80	319	654	201	3	1403	37	4.5	9.2	2.8	19.8
Tom Meschery	F	6'6	225	32	79	1822	285	615	46	162	216	75	485	108	202	2	732	23	6.1	1.4	2.6	9.3
Lee Winfield	G	6'2	175	23	79	1605	334	716	47	162	244	66	193	225	135	1	830	20	2.4	2.8	1.7	10.5
Barry Clemens	F	6'7	220	28	78	1286	247	526	47	83	114	73	243	92	169	1	577	16	3.1	1.2	2.2	7.4
Don Smith (injury)	C	6'9	235	24	61	1276	263	597	44	139	188	74	468	42	118	0	665	21	7.7	0.7	1.9	10.9
Gar Heard	F	6'6	220	22	65	1027	152	399	38	82	125	66	328	45	126	0	386	16	5.0	0.7	1.9	5.9
Tom Black (to Cin)	C	6'10	234	29	55	773	111	268	41	51	73	70	225	42	116	1	273	14	4.1	0.8	2.1	5.0
Rod Thorn	G	6'4	200	29	63	767	141	299	47	69	102	68	103	182	60	0	351	12	1.6	2.9	1.0	5.6
Bob Rule (back injury)	C	6'9	235	26	4	142	47	98	48	25	30	83	46	7	14	0	119	36	11.5	1.8	3.5	29.8
Jake Ford	G	6'3	180	24	5	68	9	25	36	16	22	73	9	9	11	0	34	14	1.8	1.8	2.2	6.8
PORTLAND TRAIL BLAZERS	**29-53 .354**				**ROLLAND TODD**																	
Stan McKenzie	F-G	6'5	210	26	82	2290	398	902	44	331	396	84	309	235	238	2	1127	28	3.8	2.9	2.9	13.7
Shaler Halimon (from Chi)	F-G	6'6	200	25	79	1629	300	775	39	107	161	66	415	211	178	1	707	21	5.3	2.7	2.3	8.9
Leroy Ellis	C-F	6'10	225	30	74	2581	485	1095	44	209	261	80	907	235	258	5	1179	35	12.3	3.2	3.5	15.9
Geoff Petrie	G	6'4	190	22	82	3032	784	1770	44	463	600	77	280	390	196	1	2031	37	3.4	4.8	2.4	24.8
Jim Barnett	G	6'4	180	26	78	2371	559	1283	44	326	402	81	376	323	190	1	1444	30	4.8	4.1	2.4	18.5
Rick Adelman	G	6'1	185	24	81	2303	378	895	42	267	369	72	282	380	214	2	1023	28	3.5	4.7	2.6	12.6
Dale Schlueter	C	6'10	230	25	80	1823	257	527	49	143	218	66	629	192	265	4	657	23	7.9	2.4	3.3	8.2
Ed Manning	F	6'7	215	26	79	1558	243	559	43	75	93	81	411	111	198	3	561	20	5.2	1.4	2.5	7.1
Gary Gregor (leg injury)	F	6'7	235	25	44	1153	181	421	43	59	89	66	334	81	120	2	421	26	7.6	1.8	2.7	9.6
Ron Knight	F	6'7	220	23	52	662	99	230	43	19	38	50	167	50	99	1	217	13	3.2	1.0	1.9	4.2
Walt Gilmore	F	6'6	225	23	27	261	23	54	43	12	26	46	73	12	49	1	58	10	2.7	0.4	1.8	2.1
Claude English	G-F	6'4	190	24	18	70	11	42	26	5	7	71	20	6	15	0	27	4	1.1	0.3	0.8	1.5
Dorie Murrey (to Bal)	F-C	6'8	220	27	2	20	1	6	17	9	11	82	7	1	3	0	11	10	3.5	0.5	1.5	5.5
Bill Stricker	F	6'9	210	22	1	2	2	3	67	0	0	—	0	0	1	0	4	2	0.0	0.0	1.0	4.0

1970/71 N.B.A. — PLAYOFFS

MILWAUKEE BUCKS — **LARRY COSTELLO**

defeated San Francisco 4-1; 107-96, H104-90, H114-102, 104-106, H136-86
defeated Los Angeles 4-1; H106-85, H91-73, 107-118, 117-94, H116-98
defeated Baltimore 4-0; H98-88,102-83, H107-99, 118-106

Use Name	Pos	Hgt	Wgt	Age	TOTAL G	Min	FG	FGA	%	FT	FTA	%	Reb	Ass	PF	DQ	Points	PER GAME Min	Reb	Ass	PF	Points
Greg Smith	F	6'5	200	23	14	454	70	128	55	22	40	55	120	36	45	0	162	32	8.6	2.6	3.2	11.6
Bob Dandridge	F	6'6	195	23	14	535	113	244	46	43	55	78	134	48	45	1	269	38	9.6	3.4	3.2	19.2
Lew Alcindor	C	7'2	232	23	14	577	**152**	295	52	68	101	67	238	35	45	0	372	41	17.0	2.5	3.2	26.6
Oscar Robertson	G-F	6'5	220	32	14	520	102	210	49	52	69	75	70	**124**	39	0	256	37	5.0	**8.9**	2.8	18.3
Jon McGlockin	G	6'5	205	27	14	491	90	168	54	28	33	85	31	34	36	0	208	35	2.2	2.4	2.6	14.9
Lucius Allen	G	6'2	175	23	14	312	41	81	51	20	28	71	40	52	30	0	102	22	2.9	3.7	2.1	7.3
Bob Boozer	F-C	6'8	225	33	14	283	41	85	48	22	29	76	74	17	35	0	104	20	5.3	1.2	2.5	7.4
Dich Cunningham	C	6'10	252	24	14	89	9	21	43	6	9	67	24	1	10	0	24	6	1.7	0.1	0.7	1.7
McCoy McLemore	F	6'7	235	28	10	52	3	12	25	1	2	50	16	8	8	0	7	5	1.6	0.8	0.8	0.7
Jeff Webb	G	6'4	170	22	9	23	4	7	57	3	3	100	1	2	2	0	11	3	0.1	0.2	0.2	1.2
Bob Greacen	F	6'7	205	23	7	16	4	11	36	4	4	100	5	0	4	0	12	2	0.7	0.0	0.6	1.7
Marv Winkler	G	6'1	175	22	5	8	0	4	0	0	0	—	0	1	3	0	0	2	0.0	0.2	0.6	0.0

BALTIMORE BULLETS — **GENE SHUE**

defeated Philadelphia 4-3; H112-126, 119-107 H111-103, 120-105, H103-104, 94-98, H128-120
defeated New York 4-3; 111-112, 88-107, H114-88, H101-80, 84-89, H113-96, 93-91
lost to Milwaukee 0-4; 88-98, H83-102, 99-107, H106-118

Use Name	Pos	Hgt	Wgt	Age	TOTAL G	Min	FG	FGA	%	FT	FTA	%	Reb	Ass	PF	DQ	Points	PER GAME Min	Reb	Ass	PF	Points
Jack Marin	F	6'7	210	26	18	750	147	319	46	76	93	82	145	56	54	0	370	42	8.1	3.1	3.0	20.6
Gus Johnson	F	6'6	235	32	11	365	54	128	42	35	47	74	114	30	34	0	143	33	10.4	2.7	3.1	13.0
Wes Unseld	C	6'7	250	24	18	**759**	96	208	46	46	81	57	**339**	69	60	0	238	42	18.8	3.8	3.3	13.2
Kevin Loughery	G	6'3	190	30	17	500	84	212	40	64	85	75	38	52	57	2	232	29	2.2	3.1	3.4	13.6
Earl Monroe	G	6'3	190	26	18	671	145	**356**	41	**107**	**135**	79	64	74	56	0	**397**	37	3.6	4.1	3.1	22.1
Fred Carter	G-F	6'3	185	25	18	597	108	260	42	47	73	64	82	36	63	1	263	33	4.6	2.0	3.5	14.6
John Tresvant	F-C	6'7	220	31	18	484	56	137	41	38	57	67	134	19	**64**	1	150	27	7.4	1.1	3.6	8.3
Dorie Murrey	F-C	6'8	220	27	16	92	13	27	48	7	11	64	33	1	6	0	33	6	2.1	0.1	0.4	2.1
Gary Zeller	G	6'3	205	23	15	67	12	35	34	2	7	29	13	4	15	0	26	4	0.9	0.3	1.0	1.7
George Johnson	C	6'11	255	23	11	35	7	13	54	1	2	50	11	2	9	0	15	3	1.0	0.2	0.8	1.4

NEW YORK KNICKERBOCKERS — **RED HOLZMAN**

defeated Atlanta 4-1; H112-101, H104-113, 110-95, 113-107, H111-107
lost to Baltimore 3-1; H112-111, H107-88, 88-114, 80-101, H89-84, 96-113, H91-93

Use Name	Pos	Hgt	Wgt	Age	TOTAL G	Min	FG	FGA	%	FT	FTA	%	Reb	Ass	PF	DQ	Points	PER GAME Min	Reb	Ass	PF	Points
Bill Bradley	F-G	6'5	205	27	12	368	56	132	42	14	19	74	41	43	40	0	126	31	3.4	3.6	3.3	10.5
Dave DeBusschere	F	6'6	235	30	12	488	84	202	42	29	44	66	156	22	40	1	197	41	13.0	1.8	3.3	16.4
Willis Reed	C	6'9	240	28	12	504	81	196	41	26	39	67	144	27	41	0	188	42	12.0	2.3	3.4	15.7
Dich Barnett	G	6'4	190	34	12	455	95	199	48	44	63	70	38	36	33	0	234	38	3.2	3.0	2.8	19.5
Walt Frazier	G	6'4	205	25	12	501	108	204	53	55	75	73	70	54	45	0	271	42	5.8	4.5	3.8	22.6
Dave Stallworth	F	6'7	210	29	12	185	18	68	26	28	39	72	42	10	27	0	64	15	3.5	0.8	2.3	5.3
Mike Riordan	G	6'4	200	25	12	168	20	52	38	6	8	75	30	9	26	0	46	14	2.5	0.8	2.2	3.8
Cazzie Russell	F	6'5	220	26	11	120	25	64	39	12	12	100	22	8	14	0	62	11	2.0	0.7	1.3	5.6
Phil Jackson	C	6'8	220	25	5	30	4	14	29	1	1	100	10	2	8	0	9	6	2.0	0.4	1.6	1.8
Mike Price	G	6'3	200	22	8	26	4	11	36	4	6	67	5	5	11	0	12	3	0.6	0.6	1.4	1.5
Greg Fillmore	C	7'1	250	23	8	24	0	4	0	0	0	—	8	1	9	0	0	3	1.0	0.1	1.1	0.0
Eddie Mast	C	6'9	220	22	3	11	2	5	40	0	0	—	3	0	2	0	4	4	1.0	0.0	0.7	1.3

LOS ANGELES LAKERS — **JOE MULLANEY**

defeated Chicago 4-3; H100-99, H105-95, 98-106,102-112, H115-89, 99-113, H109-98
lost to Milwaukee 1-4; 85-106, 73-91, H118-107, H94-117, 98-116

Use Name	Pos	Hgt	Wgt	Age	TOTAL G	Min	FG	FGA	%	FT	FTA	%	Reb	Ass	PF	DQ	Points	PER GAME Min	Reb	Ass	PF	Points
Jim McMillian	F	6'5	225	22	12	522	79	181	44	23	34	68	65	22	27	0	181	44	5.4	1.8	2.3	15.1
Happy Hairston	F	6'7	225	28	12	471	83	164	51	38	50	76	109	34	41	1	204	39	9.1	2.8	3.4	17.0
Wilt Chamberlain	C	7'1	275	34	12	554	85	187	45	50	97	52	242	53	33	0	220	46	20.2	4.4	2.8	18.3
Keith Erickson	G-F	6'5	200	26	8	313	54	99	55	17	22	77	45	22	34	1	125	39	5.6	2.8	4.3	15.6
Gail Goodrich	G	6'1	175	27	12	518	105	247	43	95	113	84	38	91	38	0	305	43	3.2	7.6	3.2	25.4
Willie McCarter	G	6'3	175	24	12	232	27	76	36	1	6	17	26	17	30	0	55	19	2.2	1.4	2.5	4.6
Pat Riley	G	6'4	208	25	7	135	29	69	42	8	11	73	15	14	12	0	66	19	2.1	2.0	1.7	9.4
Rick Roberson	F-C	6'9	230	23	9	93	10	29	34	4	7	57	26	4	14	0	24	10	2.9	0.4	1.6	2.7
Fred Hetzel	F	6'8	230	28	7	38	5	15	33	2	2	100	7	2	5	0	12	5	1.0	0.3	0.7	1.7
Earnie Killum	G	6'3	180	22	2	4	1	1	100	2	3	67	0	0	1	0	4	2	0.0	0.0	0.5	2.0

1970/71 N.B.A. — PLAYOFFS (continued)

Use Name	Pos	Hgt	Wgt	Age	TOTAL G	Min	FG	FGA	%	FT	FTA	%	Reb	Ass	PF	DQ	Points	PER GAME Min	Reb	Ass	PF	Points
CHICAGO BULLS	**DICK MOTTA**				lost to Los Angeles 3-4; 99-100, 95-105, H106-98, H112-102, 89-115, H113-99, 98-109																	
Chet Walker	F	6'6	220	30	7	234	44	100	44	17	24	71	50	22	20	0	105	33	7.1	3.1	2.9	15.0
Bob Love	F	6'8	215	28	7	330	79	161	49	29	36	81	51	10	26	0	187	**47**	7.3	1.4	3.7	**26.7**
Tom Boerwinkle	C	7'	270	25	7	169	19	41	46	5	7	71	67	31	17	0	43	24	9.6	4.4	2.4	6.1
Jerry Sloan	G-F	6'6	200	28	7	284	51	117	44	17	23	74	63	17	25	1	119	41	9.0	2.4	3.6	17.0
Bob Weiss	G	6'2	185	28	7	250	42	92	46	26	30	87	18	57	19	0	110	36	2.6	8.1	2.7	15.7
Jim Fox	C	6'10	230	27	7	167	33	76	43	13	19	68	66	17	17	1	79	24	9.4	2.4	2.4	11.3
Jim King	G	6'2	175	29	7	147	19	45	42	8	12	67	21	27	25	0	46	21	3.0	3.9	3.6	6.6
Man Guokas	G	6'5	195	26	6	83	8	14	57	4	5	80	8	12	8	0	20	14	1.3	2.0	1.3	3.3
Jimmy Collins	G	6'2	175	24	2	8	0	1	0	3	3	100	1	0	1	0	3	4	0.5	0.0	0.5	1.5
Johnny Baum	F	6'5	210	24	2	5	0	0	—	0	0	—	1	0	2	0	0	3	0.5	0.0	1.0	0.0
Paul Ruffner	F	6'10	225	22	1	3	0	5	0	0	0	—	2	0	0	0	0	3	2.0	0.0	0.0	0.0
PHILADELPHIA 76ers	**JACK RAMSAY**				lost to Baltimore 3-4; 126-112, H107-119, 103-111, H105-120, 104-103, H98-94, 120-128																	
Billy Cunningham	F	6'7	220	27	7	301	67	142	47	47	67	70	108	40	28	0	181	43	15.4	5.7	4.0	25.9
Jim Washington	F-C	6'7	215	27	7	216	27	61	44	26	36	72	48	10	24	1	80	31	6.9	1.4	3.4	11.4
Luke Jackson	C	6'9	250	29	7	160	16	38	42	7	10	70	61	11	17	0	39	23	8.7	1.6	2.4	5.6
Hal Greer	G-F	6'3	176	34	7	265	49	112	44	27	36	75	25	33	35	**4**	125	38	3.6	4.7	**5.0**	17.9
Archie Clark	G	6'2	175	29	7	295	66	139	47	33	45	73	29	34	21	0	165	42	4.1	4.9	3.0	23.6
Dennis Awtrey	C	6'10	235	22	7	144	21	36	58	11	15	73	27	5	25	1	53	21	3.9	0.7	3.6	7.6
Bailey Howell	F	6'7	220	33	7	122	19	45	42	9	18	50	31	4	25	1	47	17	4.4	0.6	3.6	6.7
Wally Jones	G	6'2	185	28	7	115	19	52	37	10	13	77	12	11	22	0	48	16	1.7	1.6	3.1	6.9
Fred Foster	F	6'5	220	24	5	49	8	19	42	2	2	100	12	5	6	0	18	10	2.4	1.0	1.2	3.6
Freddie Crawford	G	6'4	200	29	1	9	2	4	50	3	4	75	0	1	1	0	7	9	0.0	1.0	1.0	7.0
Bud Ogden	F	6'6	220	24	1	4	0	2	0	0	0	—	2	0	1	0	0	4	2.0	0.0	1.0	0.0
ATLANTA HAWKS	**RICHIE GUERIN**				lost to New York 1-4; 101-112, 113-104, H107-113, 107-111																	
Lou Hudson	F-G	6'5	210	26	5	213	49	108	45	29	39	74	35	15	19	0	127	43	7.0	3.0	3.8	25.4
Bill Bridges	F	6'6	235	31	5	229	23	58	40	3	9	33	104	5	17	0	49	46	**20.8**	1.0	3.4	9.8
Walt Bellamy	C	6'11	245	31	5	216	41	69	**59**	22	29	76	72	10	16	0	104	43	14.4	2.0	3.2	20.8
Pete Maravich	G	6'5	200	22	5	199	46	122	38	18	26	69	26	24	14	0	110	40	5.2	4.8	2.8	22.0
Walt Hazzard	G	6'2	190	28	5	202	25	76	33	20	25	80	25	27	22	1	70	40	5.0	5.4	4.4	14.0
Jim Davis	F-C	6'9	235	29	5	119	17	36	47	22	27	81	22	4	17	1	56	24	4.4	0.8	3.4	11.2
Jerry Chambers	F	6'5	190	27	4	22	3	9	33	1	2	50	5	0	4	0	7	6	1.3	0.0	1.0	1.8
SAN FRANCISCO WARRIORS	**AL ATTLES**				lost to Milwaukee 1-4; H96-107, 90-104, 102-114, H106-104, 86-136																	
Bob Portman	F	6'5	200	23	5	110	20	39	51	6	9	67	20	2	9	0	46	22	4.0	0.4	1.8	9.2
Jerry Lucas	F	6'8	230	30	5	171	39	77	51	11	16	69	50	16	14	0	89	34	10.0	3.2	2.8	17.8
Nate Thurmond	C	6'11	235	29	5	192	36	97	37	16	20	80	51	15	20	0	88	38	10.2	3.0	4.0	17.6
Jeff Mullins	G-F	6'4	200	28	5	205	30	85	35	22	25	**88**	32	24	13	0	82	41	6.4	4.8	2.6	16.4
Ron Williams	G	6'3	190	26	5	172	24	63	38	17	19	89	17	29	19	1	65	34	3.4	5.8	3.8	13.0
Clyde Lee	F-C	6'10	225	26	5	93	10	24	42	4	8	50	37	2	13	0	24	19	7.4	0.4	2.6	4.8
Joe Ellis	F	6'6	175	26	5	91	13	42	31	2	3	67	21	0	8	0	28	18	4.2	0.0	1.6	5.6
Nick Jones	G	6'2	190	25	5	77	7	26	27	15	18	83	5	5	9	0	29	15	1.0	1.0	1.8	5.8
Al Attles	G	6'2	185	34	4	47	4	7	57	5	7	71	8	11	13	0	12	12	2.0	2.8	3.3	3.0
Bill Turner	F	6'7	220	26	2	18	1	5	20	4	6	67	3	1	2	0	6	9	1.5	0.5	1.0	3.0
Ralph Ogden	F	6'5	205	22	2	15	1	5	20	4	4	100	4	1	0	0	6	8	2.0	0.5	0.0	3.0
Levi Fontaine	G	6'4	190	22	2	9	2	3	67	1	3	33	0	0	2	0	5	5	0.0	0.0	1.0	2.5

Team	W	L	Pct.	GB	Record against playoff teams W	L	Pct.	Record against non - playoff teams W	L	Pct.	HOME W	L	Pct.	ROAD W	L	Pct.	NEUTRAL W	L	Pct.
ATLANTIC DIVISION																			
New York Knickerbockers	52	30	.634	—	20	18	.526	32	12	.762	32	9	.780	19	20	.487	1	1	.500
Philadelphia 76ers	47	35	.573	5	17	21	.447	30	14	.682	24	15	.615	21	18	.538	2	2	.500
Boston Celtics	44	38	.537	8	21	23	.477	23	15	.605	25	14	.641	18	22	.450	1	2	.333
Buffalo Braves	22	60	.268	30	7	25	.219	15	35	.429	14	23	.378	6	30	.167	2	7	.222
CENTRAL DIVISION																			
Baltimore Bullets	42	40	.512	—	15	23	.395	27	17	.614	24	13	.649	16	25	.390	2	2	.500
Atlanta Hawks	36	46	.439	6	17	21	.448	19	25	.432	21	20	.512	14	26	.350	1	0	1.000
Cincinnati Royals	33	49	.402	9	14	29	.326	19	20	.487	17	16	.515	11	28	.393	5	5	.500
Cleveland Cavaliers	15	67	.183	27	2	30	.063	13	37	.260	11	30	.268	2	37	.051	2	0	1.000
MIDWEST DIVISION																			
Milwaukee Bucks	66	16	.805	—	28	9	.757	38	7	.844	34	2	.944	28	13	.683	4	1	.800
Chicago Bulls	51	31	.622	15	20	18	.526	31	13	.705	30	11	.732	17	19	.472	4	1	.800
Phoenix Suns	48	34	.585	18	21	22	.488	27	12	.692	27	14	.659	19	20	.487	2	0	1.000
Detroit Pistons	45	37	.549	21	19	23	.452	26	14	.650	24	17	.585	20	19	.513	1	1	.500
PACIFIC DIVISION																			
Los Angeles Lakers	48	34	.585	—	20	17	.541	28	17	.622	30	11	.732	17	22	.436	1	1	.500
San Francisco Warriors	41	41	.500	7	14	24	.368	27	17	.614	20	18	.526	19	21	.475	2	2	.500
San Diego Rockets	40	42	.488	8	13	30	.302	27	12	.692	24	15	.615	15	26	.366	1	1	.500
Seattle Supersonics	38	44	.463	10	17	26	.395	21	18	.538	27	13	.675	11	30	.268	0	1	.000
Portland Trail Blazers	29	53	.354	19	8	24	.250	21	29	.420	18	21	.462	9	26	.257	2	6	.250

1970/71 N.B.A. INDIVIDUAL LEADERS

SCORING
(Minimum 70 Games Played)

Name	Team	G	FG	FT	Pts.	Avg.
Alcindor	Mil	82	1063	470	2596	31.7
Havlicek	Bos	81	892	554	2338	28.9
Hayes	SD	82	948	454	2350	28.7
Bing	Det	82	799	615	2213	27.0
Hudson	Atl	76	829	381	2039	26.8
Love	Chi	81	765	513	2043	25.2
Petrie	Port	82	784	463	2031	24.8
Maravich	Atl	81	738	404	1880	23.2
Cunningham	Phi	81	702	455	1859	23.0
Van Arsdale	Cin	82	749	377	1875	22.9

FIELD GOAL PERCENTAGE
(Minimum 700 Field Goals)

Name	Team	FG	FGA	Pct.
Green	Cin	502	855	.587
Alcindor	Mil	1063	1843	.577
Chamberlain	LA	668	1226	.545
McGlockin	Mil	574	1073	.535
Snyder	Sea	645	1215	.531
Smith	Mil	409	799	.512
Dandridge	Mil	594	1167	.509
Unseld	Bal	424	846	.501
Lucas	SF	623	1250	.498
Clark	Phi	662	1334	.496

FREE THROW PERCENTAGE
(Minimum 350 Free Throws)

Name	Team	FT	FTA	Pct.
Walker	Chi	480	559	.859
Rooertson	Mil	385	453	.850
Williams	SF	331	392	.844
Mullins	SF	302	358	.844
Snyder	Sea	302	361	.837
McKenzie	Port	331	396	.836
West	LA	525	631	.832
Walker	Det	344	414	.831
Love	Chi	513	619	.829
Murphy	SD	356	434	.820

PERSONAL FOULS

Name	Team	PF
Cowens	Bos	350
Adams	SD	344
Van Lier	Cin	343
Trapp	SD	337
Cunningham	Phi	328

GAMES DISQUALIFIED

Name	Team	Disq
Trapp	SD	16
Cowens	Bos	15
Warren	Cle	13
Van Lier	Cin	12
Adams	SD	11
Chaney	Bos	11

REBOUNDS PER GAME
(Minimum 70 Games Played)

Name	Team	G	Reb.	Avg.
Chamoerlain	LA	82	1493	18.2
Unseld	Bal	74	1253	16.9
Hayes	SD	82	1362	16.6
Alcindor	Mil	82	1311	16.0
Lucas	SF	80	1265	15.8
Bridges	Atl	82	1233	15.0
Cowens	Bos	81	1216	15.0
Boerwinkle	Chi	82	1133	13.8
Thurmond	SF	82	1128	13.8
Reed	NY	73	1003	13.7

ASSISTS PER GAME
(Minimum 70 Games Played)

Name	Team	G	Ass.	Avg.
Van Lier	Cin	82	832	10.1
Wilkens	Sea	71	654	9.2
Robertson	Mil	81	668	8.2
Havlicek	Bos	81	607	7.5
Frazier	NY	80	536	6.7
Hazzard	Atl	82	514	6.3
Williams	SF	82	480	5.9
Archibald	Cin	82	450	5.5
Clark	Phi	82	440	5.4
Bing	Det	82	408	5.0

MINUTES PLAYED

Name	Team	Min.
Havlicek	Bos	3678
Hayes	SD	3633
Chamberlain	LA	3630
Love	Chi	3482
Frazier	Nr	3455

Team		G	FG	FGA	%	FT	FTA	%	Reb.	Ass.	PF	Points	PPG	G	FG	FGA	%	FT	FTA	%	Reb.	Ass.	PF	Points	PPG
		REGULAR SEASON												PLAYOFFS											
TEAM STATISTICS																									
ATLANTIC DIVISION																									
New York	Off.	82	3633	8076	45	1760	2377	74	4075	1779	1916	9026	110.1	12	497	**1151**	43	219	306	72	569	217	296	1213	101.1
	Def.	82	3343	7752	43	1928	2565	75	4591	**1509**	1889	**8614**	**105.0**	12	479	1092	44	269	374	72	680	**204**	253	1227	102.3
	Diff.		+290	+324	+2	-168	-188	-1	-516	+270	-27	+412	+5.1		+18	+59	-1	-50	-68	—	-111	+13	-43	-14	-1.2
Philadelphia	Off.	82	3608	8026	45	2199	2967	74	4437	1976	2168	9415	114.8	7	294	650	45	**175**	**246**	71	355	154	205	763	109.0
	Def.	82	3514	7806	45	2260	3076	73	4372	1970	2089	9288	113.3	7	285	659	43	217	297	73	391	146	**183**	787	112.4
	Diff.		+94	+220	—	-61	-109	+1	+65	+6	-79	+127	+1.5		+9	-9	+2	-42	-51	-2	-36	+8	-22	-24	-3.4
Boston	Off.	82	3804	**8616**	44	2000	2648	76	**4833**	2052	2138	9608	117.2												
	Def.	82	3612	8211	44	2214	2982	74	4342	1910	1962	9438	115.1												
	Diff.		+192	**+405**	—	-214	-334	+2	**+491**	+142	-176	+170	+2.1												
Buffalo	Off.	82	3424	7860	44	1805	2504	72	4261	1962	2232	8653	105.5												
	Def.	82	3486	7666	45	2224	3018	74	4447	1998	1956	9196	112.1												
	Diff.		-62	+194	-1	-419	-514	-2	-186	-36	-276	-543	-6.6												
CENTRAL DIVISION																									
Baltimore	Off.	82	3684	8331	44	1886	2500	75	4550	1772	1966	9254	112.9	18	722	1695	43	423	591	72	973	343	418	1867	103.7
	Def.	82	3640	8164	45	1926	2584	75	4435	1862	1897	9206	112.3	18	741	1640	45	369	518	71	893	366	465	1851	102.8
	Diff.		+44	+167	-1	-40	-84	—	+115	-90	-69	+48	+0.6		-19	+55	-2	+54	+73	+1	+80	-23	**+47**	+16	+0.9
Atlantic	Off.	82	3614	7779	46	2120	2975	71	4472	1906	1958	9348	114.0	5	204	478	43	115	157	73	**289**	85	109	523	104.6
	Def.	82	3801	8525	45	1893	2515	75	4279	1996	2074	9495	115.8	5	221	500	44	108	142	76	249	98	120	550	110.0
	Diff.		-187	-746	+1	+227	+460	-4	+193	-90	+116	-147	-1.8		-17	-22	-1	+7	+15	-3	**+40**	-13	+11	-27	-5.4
Cincinnati	Off.	82	3805	8374	45	1901	2622	73	4151	2022	2126	9511	116.0												
	Def.	82	3795	8130	47	2184	2991	73	4675	2050	1979	9774	119.2												
	Diff.		+10	+244	-2	-283	-369	—	-524	-28	-147	-263	-3.2												
Cleveland	Off.	82	3299	7778	42	1775	2380	75	3982	2065	2114	8373	102.1												
	Def.	82	3476	**7480**	46	2337	3024	77	4175	2307	1899	9289	113.3												
	Diff.		-177	+298	-4	-562	-644	-2	-193	-242	-215	-916	-11.2												
MIDWEST DIVISION																									
Milwaukee	Off.	82	**3972**	7803	**51**	1766	2379	74	4344	2249	1847	9710	118.4	14	629	1266	50	269	373	72	753	358	302	1527	109.1
	Def.	82	3489	8224	**42**	1727	2322	74	4004	1923	1770	8705	106.2	14	541	1370	39	242	352	69	693	297	303	1324	94.6
	Diff.		**+483**	-421	**+9**	+39	+57	—	+340	+326	-77	+1005	+12.2		+88	-104	+11	+27	+21	+3	+60	+61	+1	+203	+14.5
Chicago	Off.	82	3460	7660	45	2150	2721	**79**	4325	2142	1797	9070	110.6	7	295	652	45	122	159	77	348	193	160	712	101.7
	Def.	82	3491	7709	45	1658	2216	75	4031	1914	2099	8640	105.4	7	286	593	48	156	208	75	319	146	145	728	104.0
	Diff.		-31	-49	—	**+492**	+505	**+4**	+294	+228	+302	+430	+5.2		+9	+59	-3	-34	-49	+2	+29	+47	-15	-16	-2.3
Phoenix	Off.	82	3503	8021	44	**2327**	**3078**	76	4442	1927	2132	9333	113.8												
	Def.	82	3506	7828	45	2165	2923	74	4173	2069	**2202**	9177	111.9												
	Diff.		-3	+193	-1	+162	+155	+2	+269	-142	+70	+156	+1.9												
Detroit	Off.	82	3468	7730	45	2093	2808	75	3923	1696	1969	9029	110.1												
	Def.	82	3525	7713	46	2040	2703	75	4292	1912	2087	9090	110.9												
	Diff.		-57	+17	-1	+53	+105	—	-369	-216	+118	-61	-0.8												
PACIFIC DIVISION																									
Los Angeles	Off.	82	3739	7857	48	1933	2717	71	4269	2205	1709	9411	114.8	12	478	1068	45	240	345	**70**	573	259	**235**	1196	99.7
	Def.	82	3796	8511	45	**1567**	**2107**	74	4552	2078	1951	9159	111.7	12	528	1106	48	**193**	**269**	72	611	330	262	1249	104.1
	Diff.		-57	-654	+3	+366	**+610**	-3	-283	+127	+242	+252	+3.1		-50	-38	-3	**+47**	**+76**	-2	-38	-71	+27	-53	-4.4
San Francisco	Off.	82	3454	7709	45	1875	2468	76	4643	1893	1833	8783	107.1	5	187	473	40	106	138	77	248	106	122	480	96.0
	Def.	82	3583	8371	43	1735	2318	75	4305	1949	1882	8901	108.5	5	225	473	48	115	155	74	272	128	116	565	113.0
	Diff.		-129	-662	+2	+140	+150	+1	+338	-56	+49	-118	-1.4		-38	—	-8	-9	-17	+3	-24	-22	-6	-85	-17.0
San Diego	Off.	82	3547	8426	42	2188	2921	75	4686	1921	2128	9282	113.2												
	Def.	82	3639	8102	45	2024	2745	74	4345	2135	2141	9302	113.4												
	Diff.		-92	+324	-3	+164	+176	+1	+341	-214	+13	-20	-0.2												
Seattle	Off.	82	3664	8034	46	2101	2790	75	4456	2049	1917	9429	115.0												
	Def.	82	3803	8117	47	1985	2679	74	4156	1994	2062	9591	117.0												
	Diff.		-139	-83	-1	+116	+111	+1	+300	+55	+145	-162	-2.0												
Portland	Off.	82	3721	8562	43	2025	2671	76	4210	2227	2024	9467	115.5												
	Def.	82	3900	8333	47	2037	2758	74	4885	2267	2035	9837	120.0												
	Diff.		-179	+229	-4	-12	-87	+2	-675	-40	+11	-370	-4.5												

1970-71 A.B.A.

Some New Blood and a Costly Defection

For the first time, the A.B.A. signed a group of first-rate rookies, All-Americans with national reputations. Dan Issel, Charlie Scott, Rick Mount, Mike Maloy, and Jim Ard all chose the A.B.A. despite overtures from the established N.B.A. Also joining this talented quintet was Ralph Simpson, a hardship case from Michigan State. However, last year's showcase rookie, Spencer Haywood, sat out the first half of the season with a broken finger, demanded renegotiation of his contract, and then signed with the N.B.A.'s Seattle Supersonics late in the season. The loss of Haywood hurt the league's appeal, but the famous newcomers offset the loss.

While the good rookie crop was novel for the A.B.A., the shifting of franchises wasn't. For once, the league champion didn't move to a new city, but the Indiana Pacers did shift from the Eastern Division to the Western. This move balanced the transfer of the Washington Capitols, who moved to Norfolk and several surrounding cities in Virginia and became known as the Virginia Squires. Other shifted clubs this season were the Utah Stars, transplanted from Los Angeles, and the Memphis Pros, who played last season as the New Orleans Buccaneers. The trend to regional teams began last season with the Carolina Cougars and continued this year with the Virginia and Utah clubs, plus the transformation of the Dallas Chaps into the Texas Chaps and the Miami Floridians into the just plain Floridians. Attendance around the A.B.A. in general, however, was still low enough to keep the teams in the red.

But one franchise was showing marked progress, and this was perhaps the most important place for the A.B.A. to make a big-league showing. The New York Nets had gone through two unnoticed seasons out on Long Island while the N.B.A. Knicks monopolized all the publicity, attention, and attendance. But respectability started to come to the new team in town with the arrival of Lou Carnesecca, the colorful coach of St. John's University who stepped up into the pros with the Nets. The biggest addition, however, was Rick Barry, the superstar needed to make the New York franchise a viable entry in the nation's media center. Barry had most reluctantly played in Washington last season after the franchise was shifted from Oakland, and he openly rebelled against the idea of playing in southern Virginia, the site of the franchise for this season. So Squire owner Earl Foreman, seeing no gate appeal in a superstar who roundly criticized the home area of the team, sent Barry and his expensive contract on to New York. Although an injured knee cost him some playing time for the third straight season, Barry put the Nets back in the game both on the court and in the publicity department.

The Virginia Squires, meanwhile, got along just fine without their reluctant star. Coach Al Bianchi had a new star in rookie Charlie Scott, a 6'5' guard with a wide variety of shots and moves. Around his young offensive star, coach Bianchi welded together a tight unit of centers Jim Eakins and Ray Scott, forwards George Carter, Doug Moe, and Neil Johnson, and guards Mike Barrett and Fatty Taylor. Although short on flashy talent outside of Scott, the Squires captured first place in the East with a strong 55-29 record.

The second-place Kentucky Colonels finished 11 games back, but came up with the league scoring champ in rookie Dan Issel, a strong center with a fine shooting touch. Issel's 29.9 scoring average marked the first time that the Colonels had any first-rate scoring punch in their forecourt. The New York team finished third, helped immeasurably by the addition of Barry, veteran forward Manny Leaks, and rookie center Billy Paultz, who accompanied coach Carnesecca from St. John's.

The Floridians had been a hopeless wreck last season, but new coach Bob Bass built a respectable outfit around guards Larrv Jones and Mack Calvin, picked up in off-season deals. Pittsburgh had two ace scorers in John Brisker and George Thompson, but just missed the final playoff berth by finishing one game behind the Floridians. The Carolina Cougars finished last, but began to move away from just local talent by signing Joe Caldwell from the N.B.A. Atlantic Hawks.

Last season's Eastern Division champ, the Indiana Pacers, won this season's Western title with a 58-29 record, only one game off last year's pace. Built around a nucleus of A.B.A. originals, the Pacers won the most games in the league for the second straight year. The starting five of Mel Daniels, Roger Brown, Freddie Lewis, Bob Netolicky, and Bill Keller had new reserve support this season: Warren Armstrong, who was obtained from Kentucky after personal difficulties led to his suspension in the preseason; rookie Rick Mount, a three-year star at Purdue; and veterans Don Sidle and Wayne Chapman, picked up in a late-season deal with Denver. But even with the Pacers' depth and consistent excellence, the Utah Stars chased them to the wire and finished a mere game short of first place The transplanted Stars had Zelmo Beaty in uniform, and the veteran N.B.A. star gave the team strength in the middle unmatched by most competitors. The forward positions were ably handled by second-year man Willie Wise and veteran Red Robbins a fortuitous pickup from the Memphis club. The backcourt positions went to Ron Boone and Glen Combs after their mid-season arrival in a trade with the Texas Chaps.

After the Pacers and Stars, the quality fell off in the West. The Memphis Pros debuted with a 41-43 performance, while Texas and Denver both finished at 30-54. Denver's fall was particularly swift, tumbling from first place last season. Spencer Haywood's defection, plus the trading of guards Larry Jones and Jeff Congdon, sent the Rockets into a downward spiral which insured an early end to the season for coach Joe Belmont, a hero only last year.

This year's playoffs went according to expectations in the opening round, with Virginia, Kentucky, Indiana, and Utah emerging victorious. But in the divisional finals, Kentucky and Utah upset their favored opponents. Thus, the two second-place finishers met for the championship, with Utah the heavy favorite to win the crown. The Colonels contested every game and forced a decisive seventh game in Salt Lake City. Before a capacity crowd of 13,260, the Stars won the championship with a 131-121 victory.

Use Name	Pos	Hgt	Wgt	Age	TOTAL G	Min	FG	FGA	%	FT	FTA	%	Reb	Ass	PF	DQ	Points	PER GAME Min	Reb	Ass	PF	Points
1970/71 A.B.A. — EASTERN DIVISION																						
VIRGINIA SQUIRES	**55-29 .655**				**AL BIANCHI**																	
George Carter	F	6'5	218	26	81	2721	594	1255	47	346	437	79	650	157	290	—	1534	34	8.0	1.9	3.6	18.9
Doug Moe	F	6'5	220	32	78	2297	397	871	46	221	259	85	473	270	284	—	1017	29	6.1	3.5	3.6	13.0
Jim Eakins	C	6'11	215	24	84	2235	332	645	51	242	319	76	778	160	282	—	906	27	9.3	1.9	3.4	10.8
Charlie Scott	G	6'5	175	22	84	3185	902	1947	46	456	611	75	438	472	298	—	2276	38	5.2	5.6	3.5	27.1
Mike Barrett	G	6'1	160	27	84	2754	458	988	46	208	274	76	272	425	202	—	1152	33	3.2	5.1	2.4	13.7
Neil Johnson	F-C	6'7	220	27	78	1838	398	758	53	194	259	75	668	179	295	—	990	24	8.6	2.3	3.8	12.7
Fatty Taylor	G	6'	175	24	84	1629	180	393	46	175	256	68	263	225	228	—	539	19	3.1	2.7	2.7	6.4
Ray Scott	C	6'9	220	32	72	1552	420	933	45	187	236	79	573	123	180	—	1028	22	8.0	1.7	2.5	14.3
Mike Maloy	F	6'7	215	21	55	725	149	334	45	98	139	71	236	43	125	—	396	13	4.3	0.8	2.3	7.2
Larry Brown (to Den)	G	5'9	160	32	29	530	42	104	40	74	89	83	47	122	49	—	159	18	1.6	4.2	1.7	5.5
Bill Bunting (from NY)	F	6'8	200	23	33	436	49	94	52	44	55	80	91	24	63	—	142	13	2.8	0.7	1.9	4.3
George Irvine	F-G	6'6	200	22	34	338	83	149	56	26	35	74	65	25	67	—	194	10	1.9	0.7	2.0	5.7
Frank Card (to Car)	F	6'7	195	26	7	70	9	17	53	2	5	40	9	2	2	—	20	10	1.3	0.3	0.3	2.9
Ron Taylor	C	7'1	275	24	1	25	1	9	11	0	1	0	0	4	6	—	2	25	0.0	4.0	6.0	2.0
KENTUCKY COLONELS	**44 -40 .524**				**GENE RHODES (10-5 .667), ALEX GROZA (2-0 1.000), FRANK RAMSEY (32-35 .478)**																	
Goose Ligon	F	6'7	215	26	84	2753	429	795	54	214	391	55	989	211	331	—	1072	33	11.8	2.5	3.9	12.8
Cincy Powell	F	6'7	227	28	81	2933	578	1173	49	302	398	76	890	255	323	—	1462	36	11.0	3.1	4.0	18.0
Dan Issel	C	6'9	235	22	83	3274	**938**	1934	49	604	748	81	1093	162	323	—	**2480**	39	13.2	2.0	3.9	**29.9**
Darel Carrier	G	6'3	185	30	84	2664	495	1140	43	327	377	87	232	244	229	—	1380	32	2.8	2.9	2.7	16.4
Louie Dampier	G	6'	180	26	84	3221	566	1353	42	320	376	85	297	460	213	—	1555	38	3.5	5.5	2.5	18.5
Les Hunter (from NY)	F-C	6'7	235	28	75	1415	274	606	45	155	215	72	472	93	242	—	713	19	6.3	1.2	3.2	9.5
Walt Simon	F-G	6'6	200	29	84	1411	274	578	47	100	156	64	315	156	253	—	649	17	3.8	1.9	3.0	7.7
Mike Pratt	G-F	6'4	195	22	78	1213	173	416	42	91	121	75	225	188	135	—	440	16	2.9	2.4	1.7	5.6
Howie Wright	G	6'3	185	22	52	612	94	245	38	40	49	82	80	63	89	—	237	12	1.5	1.2	1.7	4.6
Sam Smith (to Utah)	F	6'7	235	26	25	259	33	73	45	22	35	63	68	16	34	—	88	10	2.7	0.6	1.4	3.5
Bobby Croft (to Tex)	C	6'10	200	22	33	222	35	114	31	25	42	60	65	15	67	—	95	7	2.0	0.5	2.0	2.9
Dan Hester (from Den)	F	6'8	220	22	7	93	18	38	47	7	9	78	36	5	16	—	43	13	5.1	0.7	2.3	6.1
Al Williams	F	6'6	215	22	11	70	19	43	44	5	10	50	26	5	13	—	43	6	2.4	0.5	1.2	3.9
Tom Hagan (from Tex)	G	6'4	190	23	4	34	2	10	20	0	2	0	1	4	2	—	4	9	0.3	1.0	0.5	1.0
Dennis Hamilton	F	6'8	210	26	3	11	1	2	50	1	1	100	1	1	1	—	3	4	0.3	0.3	0.3	1.0
NEW YORK NETS	**40-44 .476**				**LOU CARNESECCA**																	
Rick Barry	F	6'7	215	26	59	2502	632	1348	47	451	507	89	401	294	205	—	1734	42	6.8	5.0	3.5	29.4
Sonny Dove	F	6'8	210	25	83	2280	467	1006	46	186	273	68	676	88	304	—	1124	27	8.1	1.1	3.7	13.5
Billy Paultz	C	6'11	235	22	83	2758	510	973	52	201	269	75	940	160	274	—	1221	33	11.3	1.9	3.3	14.7
Levern Tart (to Tex)	G	6'2	195	28	27	985	192	453	42	102	133	77	106	73	84	—	490	36	3.9	2.7	3.1	18.1
Bill Melchianni	G	6'1	165	26	81	3284	561	1244	45	301	370	81	237	**672**	273	—	1425	41	2.9	**8.3**	3.4	17.6
Joe DePre	G	6'3	190	24	72	1707	250	488	51	132	172	77	175	138	262	—	632	24	2.4	1.9	3.6	8.8
Ollie Taylor	G-F	6'2	205	23	80	1617	251	496	51	187	277	68	307	146	231	—	694	20	3.8	1.8	2.9	8.7
Manny Leaks (from Tex)	F-C	6'8	235	25	40	1427	274	553	50	130	179	73	385	49	108	—	678	36	9.6	1.2	2.7	17.0
Jim Ard	F	6'8	230	22	73	1027	174	382	46	79	132	60	337	40	119	—	427	14	4.6	0.5	1.6	5.8
Bill Bunting (to Va)	F	6'8	200	23	39	687	65	151	43	60	69	87	142	34	94	—	190	18	3.6	0.9	2.4	4.9
Ed Johnson (to Tex)	C	6'9	205	26	26	592	97	218	44	74	110	67	222	26	80	—	268	23	8.5	1.0	3.1	10.3
Jeff Congdon (from Utah)	G	6'1	180	27	42	579	62	150	41	32	37	86	54	97	50	—	160	14	1.3	2.3	1.2	3.8
Jim Hayes	G	6'3	200	22	47	494	46	109	42	52	67	78	45	47	73	—	144	11	1.0	1.0	1.6	3.1
Luther Green	F	6'7	190	24	26	164	40	88	45	18	44	41	55	3	19	—	98	6	2.1	0.1	0.7	3.8
Les Hunter (to KY)	F	6'7	235	28	5	110	14	39	36	4	8	50	21	2	11	—	32	22	4.2	0.4	2.2	6.4
Billy Deangelis	G	6'1	180	23	8	47	3	6	50	4	6	67	6	8	16	—	10	6	0.8	1.0	2.0	1.3
FLORIDIANS	**37-47 .440**				**HAL BLITMAN (18-30 .375), BOB BASS (19-17 .528)**																	
Warren Davis	F	6'6	215	28	76	1995	308	686	45	209	300	70	639	170	254	—	825	26	8.4	2.2	3.3	10.9
Trooper Washington	F-C	6'7	225	26	57	1876	216	426	51	102	167	61	606	187	184	—	534	33	10.6	3.3	3.2	9.4
Ira Harge (from Car)	C	6'9	225	29	53	2042	329	710	46	155	224	69	746	145	187	—	815	39	14.1	2.7	3.5	15.4
Larry Jones	G-F	6'2	180	29	84	3611	764	1636	47	471	587	80	453	390	269	—	2044	43	5.4	4.6	3.2	24.3
Mack Calvin	G	6'	165	22	81	3394	744	1728	43	**696**	**805**	86	283	619	263	—	2201	42	3.5	7.6	3.2	27.2
Sam Robinson	F	6'7	200	22	83	2172	405	896	45	103	134	77	410	112	182	—	917	26	4.9	1.3	2.2	11.0
Ron Franz	F	6'7	207	25	67	1596	309	637	49	188	259	73	320	97	178	—	813	24	4.8	1.4	2.7	12.1
Carl Fuller	C	6'9	225	24	70	1151	170	372	46	72	120	60	330	54	209	—	412	16	4.7	0.8	3.0	5.9
Rich Niemann	C	7'	255	24	51	642	121	241	50	43	60	72	255	29	137	—	285	13	5.0	0.6	2.7	5.6
Lonnie Wright (from Den)	G	6'2	205	26	31	629	101	230	44	40	56	71	64	55	76	—	244	20	2.1	1.8	2.5	7.9
Ron Nelson	G	6'2	180	22	59	490	72	172	42	41	54	76	53	47	95	—	186	8	0.9	0.8	1.6	3.2
Al Tucker (from Bal)	F	6'8	190	27	14	331	66	149	44	34	42	81	65	12	40	—	169	24	4.6	0.9	2.9	12.1
R.Johnson (from Bos-NBA to Car-Pit)	C	6'9	215	24	7	117	16	28	57	4	7	57	31	5	15	—	36	17	4.4	0.7	2.1	5.1
Fran O'Hanlon	G	6'1	175	22	14	101	8	22	36	6	9	67	4	13	18	—	22	7	0.3	0.9	1.3	1.6
Dennis Stewart (from Bal)	F	6'6	220	23	10	66	15	44	34	5	7	71	14	1	12	—	36	7	1.4	0.1	1.2	3.6
Clarence Brookins	F	6'4	190	24	8	59	8	26	31	5	12	42	12	1	5	—	21	7	1.5	0.1	0.6	2.6
Greg Wittman (to Tex)	F	6'8	210	23	5	40	2	12	17	4	7	57	10	0	14	—	8	8	2.0	0.0	2.8	1.6
Charlie Beasley (to Tex)	G	6'5	190	25	5	23	5	11	45	1	2	50	1	2	2	—	11	5	0.2	0.4	0.4	2.2

se Name	Pos	Hgt	Wgt	Age	G	Min	FG	FGA	%	FT	FTA	%	Reb	Ass	PF	DQ	Points	Min	Reb	Ass	PF	Points
					TOTAL													PER GAME				
1970/71 A.B.A. — EASTERN DIVISION (continued)																						
ITTSBURGH CONDORS	36-48 .429				JACK McMAHON																	
ohn Brisker	F-G	6'5	210	23	79	3089	898	1972	46	430	519	83	766	226	273	—	2315	39	9.7	2.9	3.5	29.3
tew Johnson	F-C	6'8	225	26	84	2595	593	1350	44	144	171	84	646	123	221	—	1342	31	7.7	1.5	2.6	16.0
ike Lewis	C	6'8	225	24	83	2741	420	825	51	235	306	77	1213	268	332	—	1075	33	14.6	3.2	4.0	13.0
keeter Swift (from Mem)	G	6'3	210	24	52	1627	274	582	47	136	158	86	177	225	185	—	710	31	3.4	4.3	3.6	13.7
eorge Thompson	G	6'2	200	23	82	2470	575	1220	47	347	485	72	291	207	217	—	1520	30	3.5	2.5	2.6	18.5
huck Williams	G	6'2	175	24	83	1795	268	613	44	249	317	79	185	170	161	—	786	22	2.2	2.0	1.9	9.5
oe Kennedy	F	6'6	210	23	82	1382	189	498	38	130	160	81	341	73	156	—	508	17	4.2	0.9	1.9	6.2
ave Lattin	F-C	6'7	230	27	71	1135	177	377	47	108	177	61	467	64	215	—	462	16	6.6	0.9	3.0	6.5
harle Hentz	F	6'6	235	23	57	1075	142	303	47	57	98	58	386	31	114	—	341	19	6.8	0.5	2.0	6.0
harlie Williams (to Mem)	G	6'	165	27	32	973	193	458	42	76	108	70	83	127	101	—	472	30	2.6	4.0	3.2	14.8
am Watts	G	6'3	185	22	54	650	109	287	38	49	67	73	99	45	106	—	281	12	1.8	0.8	2.0	5.2
ubie White	G	6'4	205	30	14	166	17	61	28	10	13	77	32	14	28	—	46	12	2.3	1.0	2.0	3.3
alter Banks	C	6'10	205	22	16	154	17	34	50	7	17	41	49	8	34	—	41	10	3.1	0.5	2.1	2.6
rvesta Kelly (from Car)	G	6'3	195	25	17	135	16	27	59	12	23	52	24	17	26	—	44	8	1.4	1.0	1.5	2.6
en Spain	C	6'9	235	24	11	112	8	22	36	8	17	47	40	2	17	—	24	10	3.6	0.2	1.5	2.2
arry Laurie	G	6'1	178	25	9	57	3	12	25	7	11	64	15	8	16	—	13	6	1.7	0.9	1.8	1.4
im Wilson	G	5'10	175	22	6	44	1	8	13	4	6	67	6	8	3	—	6	7	1.0	1.3	0.5	1.0
. Johnson (from Bos-NBA-Fla-Pit)	C	6'9	215	24	6	30	6	12	50	3	6	50	11	3	3	—	15	5	1.8	0.5	0.5	2.5
CAROLINA COUGARS	34-50 .405				BONES McKINNEY (17-25 .404), JERRY STEELE (17-25 .404)																	
oe Caldwell	F	6'5	210	29	72	3008	685	1528	45	302	541	56	489	301	237	—	1678	42	6.8	4.2	3.3	23.3
rank Card (from Va)	F	6'7	195	26	63	1795	293	645	45	194	298	65	448	111	210	—	781	28	7.1	1.8	3.3	12.4
eorge Peeples	C	6'8	205	27	82	2220	377	773	49	202	335	60	771	110	279	—	956	27	9.4	1.3	3.4	11.7
eorge Lehmann	G	6'3	185	28	83	2918	535	1186	45	214	256	84	203	464	221	—	1438	35	2.4	5.6	2.7	17.3
ob Verga	G	6'1	190	25	75	2009	550	1202	46	302	419	72	280	182	223	—	1412	27	3.7	2.4	3.0	18.8
andy Mahaffey	F	6'7	210	25	83	2353	385	791	49	156	239	65	618	115	304	—	926	28	7.4	1.4	3.7	11.2
arry Miller	G-F	6'4	205	24	77	2140	364	795	46	197	272	72	457	167	181	—	938	28	5.9	2.2	2.4	12.2
ene Littles	G	6'1	170	27	70	1495	223	501	45	117	168	70	205	173	175	—	567	21	2.9	2.5	2.5	8.1
ra Harge (to Fla)	C	6'9	225	29	29	892	131	289	45	42	82	51	339	57	104	—	304	31	11.7	2.0	3.6	10.5
ave Newmark	C	7'	260	24	31	457	100	209	48	34	60	57	157	28	84	—	234	15	5.1	0.9	2.7	7.5
R.Johnson(from Bos-NBA-Fla,to Pit)	C	6'9	215	24	25	395	70	151	46	29	41	71	110	11	65	—	169	16	4.4	0.4	2.6	6.8
ann Williford	F	6'6	195	22	38	295	62	141	44	21	37	57	68	15	34	—	148	8	1.8	0.4	0.9	3.9
Chuck Lloyd	C-F	6'8	220	22	14	118	23	51	45	20	30	67	25	6	25	—	66	8	1.8	0.4	1.8	4.7
Gary Bradds (to Tex)	F	6'8	225	28	7	114	17	45	38	10	18	56	41	2	15	—	44	16	5.9	0.3	2.1	6.3
Arvesta Kelly (to Pit)	G	6'3	195	25	5	45	4	8	50	6	8	75	1	0	8	—	14	9	0.2	0.0	1.6	2.8
Mack Daughtry	G	6'3	175	23	4	43	4	10	40	5	5	100	5	3	4	—	13	11	1.3	0.8	1.0	3.3
Lonnie Kluttz	F	6'7	220	25	3	8	0	4	0	0	0	—	5	0	3	—	0	3	1.7	0.0	1.0	0.0
1970/71 A.B.A. —WESTERN DIVISION																						
INDIANA PACERS	58-26 .690				BOB LEONARD																	
Roger Brown	F	6'5	207	28	82	3364	610	1266	48	407	512	79	569	395	289	—	1690	41	6.9	4.8	3.5	20.6
Bob Netolicky	F-C	6'9	225	25	82	3137	651	1305	50	237	333	71	774	104	192	—	1541	38	9.4	1.3	2.3	18.8
Mel Daniels	C	6'9	220	26	82	3170	698	1357	51	326	480	68	**1475**	178	292	—	1723	39	**18.0**	2.2	3.6	21.0
Freddie Lewis	G	6'	180	27	81	3034	547	1241	44	372	461	81	336	433	249	—	1525	37	4.1	5.3	3.1	18.8
Bill Keller	G	5'10	180	23	83	2490	417	980	43	267	308	87	240	437	170	—	1185	30	2.9	5.3	2.0	14.3
Warren Armstrong	G-F	6'2	205	24	62	1586	227	554	41	181	238	76	298	214	205	—	682	26	4.8	3.5	3.3	11.0
Art Becker (to Den)	F	6'8	210	28	51	840	187	376	50	62	69	90	217	22	153	—	440	16	4.3	0.4	3.0	8.6
Rick Mount	G	6'4	185	23	66	832	149	402	37	116	145	80	71	107	127	—	437	13	1.1	1.6	1.9	6.6
John Barnhill (to Den)	G	6'1	183	32	43	619	80	241	33	42	61	69	62	83	51	—	216	14	1.4	1.9	1.2	5.0
Don Sidle (from Den)	F-C	6'9	220	24	30	528	86	157	55	49	74	66	147	31	66	—	223	18	4.9	1.0	2.2	7.4
Earle Higgins	F	6'8	200	22	53	467	104	223	47	20	30	67	128	35	109	—	231	9	2.4	0.7	2.1	4.4
Wayne Chapman	F-G	6'6	190	25	22	192	30	78	38	24	29	83	31	21	31	—	88	9	1.4	1.0	1.4	4.0
Tom Thacker	G-F	6'2	190	31	8	92	6	17	35	1	1	100	22	7	18	—	13	12	2.8	0.9	2.3	1.6
Jay Miller	F	6'5	210	27	2	9	4	5	80	0	0	—	3	1	1	—	8	5	1.5	0.5	0.5	4.0
UTAH STARS	57-27 .679				BILL SHARMAN																	
Willie Wise	F	6'6	215	23	82	2676	491	1059	46	312	467	67	807	204	297	—	1299	33	9.8	2.5	3.6	15.8
Red Robbins	F-C	6'8	200	26	82	2995	396	908	44	227	272	83	976	178	203	—	1030	37	11.9	2.2	2.5	12.6
Zelmo Beaty	C	6'9	235	31	76	2915	661	1192	**55**	420	531	79	1190	148	299	—	1744	38	15.7	1.9	3.9	22.9
Merv Jackson	G	6'3	175	24	65	1902	351	836	42	196	244	80	262	225	207	—	905	29	4.0	3.5	3.2	13.9
Glen Combs (from Tex)	G	6'2	185	24	44	1599	310	682	45	235	274	86	160	173	162	—	886	36	3.6	3.9	3.7	20.1
George Stone	F	6'7	195	24	78	1734	372	808	46	121	156	78	363	106	173	—	915	22	4.7	1.4	2.2	11.7
Mike Butler	G	6'2	175	24	71	1414	271	646	42	153	168	**91**	131	186	142	—	727	20	1.8	2.6	2.0	10.2
Ron Boone (from Tex)	G-F	6'2	200	24	44	1163	265	640	41	139	177	79	253	114	165	—	693	26	5.8	2.6	3.8	15.8
Wayne Hightower (to Tex)	C-F	6'9	210	30	35	1135	167	427	39	134	179	75	287	104	107	—	468	32	8.2	3.0	3.1	13.4
Jeff Congdon (to NY)	G	6'1	180	27	38	983	116	337	34	47	59	80	89	155	76	—	293	26	2.3	4.1	2.0	7.7
Donnie Freeman (to Tex)	G	6'3	185	26	24	801	205	428	48	157	189	83	137	117	78	—	567	33	5.7	4.9	3.3	23.6
Dick Nemelka	G	6'	175	27	39	504	82	213	38	32	49	65	59	57	60	—	216	13	1.5	1.5	1.5	5.5
Rod McDonald	F	6'6	205	25	29	206	50	109	46	15	25	60	93	7	41	—	117	7	3.2	0.2	1.4	4.0
Tom Workman (to Den)	F	6'7	230	26	17	190	44	104	42	29	37	78	46	11	32	—	119	11	2.7	0.6	1.9	7.0
Sam Smith (from Ky)	F	6'7	235	26	10	43	6	20	30	2	4	50	13	4	8	—	15	4	1.3	0.4	0.8	1.5

Use Name	Pos	Hgt	Wgt	Age	G	Min	FG	FGA	%	FT	FTA	%	Reb	Ass	PF	DQ	Points	Min	Reb	Ass	PF	Points
					TOTAL													PER GAME				
1970/71 A.B.A — WESTERN DIVISION (continued)																						
MEMPHIS PROS	41-43 .488				**BABE McCARTHY**																	
Wendell Ladner	F	6'5	220	22	77	2504	572	1308	44	154	219	70	875	160	**334**	—	1306	33	11.4	2.1	**4.3**	17.0
Gerald Govan	F-C	6'10	220	28	84	**3698**	296	794	37	119	191	62	1138	407	284	—	712	**44**	13.5	4.8	3.4	8.5
Craig Raymond	C	6'11	235	25	56	1102	142	330	43	67	106	63	289	91	124	—	351	20	5.2	1.6	2.2	6.3
Steve Jones	G-F	6'5	205	28	83	2923	732	1556	47	332	400	83	299	182	234	—	1836	35	3.6	2.2	2.8	22.1
Jimmy Jones	G	6'4	190	25	80	3004	593	1220	49	374	481	78	386	468	240	—	1564	38	4.8	5.9	3.0	19.6
Wil Jones	F	6'8	205	23	84	2234	390	811	48	174	258	67	680	152	249	—	955	27	8.1	1.8	3.0	11.4
Charlie Williams (from Pit)	G	6'	165	27	56	1269	308	759	41	128	183	70	127	123	142	—	767	23	2.3	2.2	2.5	13.7
Al Cueto	C	6'8	230	24	71	974	134	333	40	55	77	71	279	86	166	—	323	14	3.9	1.2	2.3	4.5
Lee Davis	C-F	6'8	240	25	75	925	197	431	46	63	117	54	251	62	169	—	457	12	3.3	0.8	2.3	6.1
Bobby Warren	G	6'5	190	24	46	763	146	367	40	107	133	80	144	85	87	—	420	17	3.1	1.8	1.9	9.1
Skeeter Swift (to Pit)	G	6'3	210	24	28	507	128	313	41	70	88	80	56	44	79	—	339	18	2.0	1.6	2.8	12.1
Coby Dietrick	C	6'10	230	22	37	357	61	160	38	21	34	62	114	33	56	—	143	10	3.1	0.9	1.5	3.9
Jackie Moreland — illness																						
TEXAS CHAPARRALS	30-54 .357				**MAX WILLIAMS (5-14 .263), BILL BLAKELEY (25-40 .385)**																	
Rich Jones	F	6'8	230	24	79	2074	371	910	41	175	230	76	525	182	246	—	950	26	6.6	2.3	3.1	12.0
John Beasley	F	6'9	225	26	83	2691	532	1070	50	236	285	83	765	147	206	—	1316	32	9.2	1.8	2.5	15.9
Wayne Hightower (from Utah)	C-F	6'9	210	30	33	1220	172	421	41	134	182	74	328	90	97	—	478	37	9.9	2.7	2.9	14.5
Donnie Freeman (from Utah)	G	6'3	185	26	42	1613	391	807	48	210	270	78	187	215	114	—	992	38	4.5	5.1	2.7	23.6
Joe Hamilton	G	5'10	160	22	84	2564	500	1184	42	233	279	84	285	365	279	—	1318	31	3.4	4.3	3.3	15.7
Gene Moore	C	6'9	240	25	84	2243	467	972	48	189	280	68	850	101	303	—	1125	27	10.1	1.2	3.6	13.4
Glen Combs (to Utah)	G	6'2	185	24	42	1605	300	690	43	213	272	78	132	188	124	—	859	38	3.1	4.5	3.0	20.5
Ron Boone (to Utah)	G-F	6'2	200	24	42	1313	345	755	46	139	180	77	311	142	133	—	854	31	7.4	3.4	3.2	20.3
Manny Leaks (to NY)	F-C	6'8	235	25	40	1187	236	527	45	149	202	74	470	55	103	—	621	30	11.8	1.4	2.6	15.5
Bob Bedell	F	6'8	205	26	71	970	176	441	40	93	113	82	310	85	124	—	454	14	4.4	1.2	1.7	6.4
Levern Tart (from NY)	G-F	6'2	195	28	33	821	165	409	40	96	120	80	133	101	87	—	432	25	4.0	3.1	2.6	13.1
Tom Hagan (to KY)	G	6'4	190	23	45	656	98	236	42	43	61	70	82	102	76	—	251	15	1.8	2.3	1.7	5.6
Bobby Croft (from KY)	C	6'10	200	22	29	517	91	234	39	48	70	69	141	26	70	—	230	18	4.9	0.9	2.4	7.9
Charlie Beasley (from Fla)	G-F	6'5	190	25	43	486	52	125	42	39	47	83	45	80	67	—	150	11	1.0	1.9	1.6	3.5
Gary Bradds (from Car)	F	6'8	225	28	19	207	35	82	43	29	40	73	63	12	26	—	99	11	3.3	0.6	1.4	5.2
Ed Johnson (from NY)	C	6'9	205	26	8	159	22	47	47	8	20	40	48	8	21	—	52	20	6.0	1.0	2.6	6.5
Greg Wittman (to Fla)	F	6'8	210	23	5	30	4	13	31	0	2	0	9	0	7	—	8	6	1.8	0.0	1.4	1.6
Willie Davis	C	6'8	234	25	8	29	7	15	47	4	8	50	13	2	10	—	18	4	1.6	0.3	1.3	2.3
DENVER ROCKETS	30-54 .357				**JOE BELMONT (3-10 .231), STAN ALBECK (27-44 .380)**																	
Art Becker (from Ind.)	F	6'8	210	28	29	803	183	365	50	73	87	84	209	31	107	—	440	28	7.2	1.1	3.7	15.2
Julius Keye	F-C	6'10	225	24	83	3634	505	1177	43	212	317	67	1454	140	317	—	1222	44	17.5	1.7	3.8	14.7
Byron Beck	C	6'9	230	25	84	2849	490	1033	47	158	182	87	884	177	273	—	1142	34	10.5	2.1	3.3	13.6
Larry Cannon	G	6'5	195	23	80	3097	751	1722	44	606	763	79	333	414	237	—	2126	39	4.2	5.2	3.0	26.6
John Barnhill (from Ind)	G	6'1	183	32	24	684	101	255	40	54	73	74	54	77	55	—	274	29	2.3	3.2	2.3	11.4
Julie Hammond	F	6'5	215	27	83	2082	435	834	52	273	375	73	523	97	189	—	1143	25	6.3	1.2	2.3	13.8
Ralph Simpson	G-F	6'5	200	21	81	1820	460	1108	42	215	285	75	231	168	152	—	1152	22	2.9	2.1	1.9	14.2
Don Sidle (to Ind)	F-C	6'9	220	24	54	1623	339	694	49	192	257	75	488	66	167	—	870	30	9.0	1.2	3.1	16.1
Wayne Chapman (to Ind)	G	6'6	190	25	47	1049	184	484	38	89	129	69	143	107	127	—	468	22	3.0	2.3	2.7	10.0
Larry Brown (from Va)	G	5'9	160	30	34	813	85	236	36	112	136	82	62	208	96	—	287	24	1.8	6.1	2.8	8.4
Lonnie Wright (to Fla)	G	6'2	205	26	41	769	98	328	30	53	77	69	89	61	86	—	264	19	2.2	1.5	2.1	6.4
Tom Workman (from Utah)	F	6'7	230	26	39	489	89	199	45	57	68	84	133	37	81	—	236	13	3.4	0.9	2.1	6.1
Dan Hester (to KY)	F	6'8	220	22	35	462	79	207	38	42	51	82	198	30	66	—	205	13	5.7	0.9	1.9	5.9
Steve Wilson	G	6'5	185	22	39	261	53	132	40	22	41	54	48	29	43	—	134	7	1.2	0.7	1.1	3.4
1970/71 A.B.A. - PLAYOFFS																						
UTAH STARS	**BILL SHARMAN**				defeated Texas 4-0; H125-115, H137-107, 113-101,128-107 defeated Indiana 4-3; 120-118, 107-120, H121-107, H126-99, 109-127, H102-105, 108-101 defeated Kentucky 4-3; H136-117, H138-125, 110-116, 125-129, H137-127, 101-105, H131-121																	
Willie Wise	F	6'6	215	23	17	691	139	271	51	81	116	70	220	82	65	—	359	41	12.9	4.8	3.8	21.1
Red Robbins	F-C	6'8	200	26	18	566	94	170	55	29	41	71	183	40	44	—	222	31	10.2	2.2	2.4	12.3
Zelmo Beaty	C	6'9	235	31	18	698	157	293	54	104	123	85	**263**	43	75	—	418	39	14.6	2.4	4.2	23.2
Merv Jackson	G	6'3	175	24	18	598	114	237	48	43	54	80	79	109	47	—	274	33	4.4	6.1	2.6	15.2
Glen Combs	G	6'2	185	24	18	639	109	269	41	68	85	80	74	64	67	—	297	36	4.1	3.6	3.7	16.5
Ron Boone	G-F	6'2	200	24	18	569	113	256	44	74	86	86	110	94	71	—	309	32	6.1	5.2	3.9	17.2
George Stone	F	6'7	195	24	18	424	84	209	40	35	41	85	104	29	45	—	207	24	5.8	1.6	2.5	11.5
Mike Butler	G	6'2	175	24	10	77	19	33	58	8	9	89	11	6	8	—	48	8	1.1	0.6	0.8	4.8
Dick Nemelka	G	6'	175	27	9	51	7	21	33	4	5	80	9	9	12	—	19	6	1.0	1.0	1.3	2.1
Rod McDonald	F	6'6	205	25	5	22	8	11	73	1	2	50	13	2	3	—	18	4	2.6	0.4	0.6	3.6
Sam Smith	F	6'7	235	26	3	10	2	6	33	0	0	—	3	1	1	—	4	3	1.0	0.3	0.3	1.3
KENTUCKY COLONELS	**FRANK RAMSEY**				defeated Floridians 4-2; H116-112, H120-110, 102-120, 117-129, H118-101, 112-103 defeated Virginia 4-2; 136-132, 122-142, H137-150, H128-110, 115-107, H129-117 lost to Utah 3-4; 117-136, 125-138, H116-110, H129-125, 127-137, H105-101, 121-131																	
Goose Ligon	F	6'7	215	26	19	587	81	170	48	38	67	57	219	35	74	—	200	31	11.5	1.8	3.9	10.5
Cincy Powell	F	6'7	227	28	19	702	138	382	36	71	102	70	248	47	**83**	—	350	37	13.1	2.5	4.4	18.4
Dan Issel	C	6'9	235	22	19	670	**206**	**408**	50	**122**	**139**	88	221	28	78	—	**534**	35	11.6	1.5	4.1	28.1
Darel Carrier	G	6'3	185	30	19	675	130	280	46	88	98	90	58	69	65	—	369	36	3.1	3.6	3.4	19.4
Louie Dampier	G	6'	180	26	19	**828**	117	304	38	66	89	74	78	**179**	56	—	322	44	4.1	**9.4**	2.9	16.9
Walt Simon	F-G	6'6	200	29	19	385	70	155	45	34	49	69	97	52	67	—	174	20	5.1	2.7	3.5	9.2
Les Hunter	C-F	6'7	235	28	19	352	65	168	39	45	73	62	88	33	76	—	176	19	4.6	1.7	4.0	9.3
Mike Pratt	G-F	6'4	195	22	19	318	47	124	38	37	47	79	66	53	30	—	131	17	3.5	2.8	1.6	6.9
Dan Hester	F	6'8	220	22	7	42	4	14	29	8	9	89	13	1	9	—	16	6	1.9	0.1	1.3	2.3
Howie Wright	G	6'3	185	22	5	36	7	20	35	4	9	44	2	4	6	—	20	7	0.4	0.8	1.2	4.0

Use Name	Pos	Hgt	Wgt	Age	TOTAL G	Min	FG	FGA	%	FT	FTA	%	Reb	Ass	PF	DQ	Points	PER GAME Min	Reb	Ass	PF	Points
					1970/71 A.B.A. — PLAYOFFS (continued)																	
INDIANA PACERS	**BOB LEONARD**				defeated Memphis 4-0; H114-98, H106-104, 91-90, 102-101 lost to Utah 3-4; H118-120, H120-107,107-121, 99-126, H127-109, 105-102, H101-108																	
Roger Brown	F	6'5	207	28	11	477	88	194	45	54	69	78	84	53	42	—	240	43	7.6	4.8	3.8	21.8
Bob Netolicky	F-C	6'9	225	25	11	380	67	143	47	27	37	73	92	5	26	—	161	35	8.4	0.5	2.4	14.6
Mel Daniels	C	6'9	220	26	11	457	94	194	48	47	63	75	211	16	38	—	235	42	**19.2**	1.5	3.5	21.4
Freddie Lewis	G	6'	180	27	11	384	39	107	36	28	37	76	48	52	40	—	109	35	4.4	4.7	3.6	9.9
Bill Keller	G	5'10	180	23	11	448	82	190	43	50	58	86	42	59	23	—	237	41	3.8	5.4	2.1	21.5
Warren Armstrong	F-G	6'2	205	24	11	250	29	96	30	25	31	81	40	33	27	—	86	23	3.6	3.0	2.5	7.8
Rick Mount	G	6'4	185	23	10	129	25	73	34	5	7	71	10	9	13	—	60	13	1.0	0.9	1.3	6.0
Don Sidle	F	6'9	220	24	8	68	8	24	33	10	16	63	22	4	8	—	26	9	2.8	0.5	1.0	3.3
Earle Higgins	F	6'8	200	22	5	31	6	20	30	6	7	86	13	1	5	—	18	6	2.6	0.2	1.0	3.6
Wayne Chapman	F	6'6	190	25	5	21	6	10	60	4	6	67	7	2	3	—	17	4	1.4	0.4	0.6	3.4
VIRGINIA SQUIRES	**AL BIANCHI**				defeated New York 4-2, H113-105, H114-108, 131-135, 127-130, H127-124, 118-114 lost to Kentucky 2-4; H132-136, H142-122, 150-137, 110-128, H107-115, 117-129																	
George Carter	F	6'5	218	26	12	409	88	190	46	53	65	82	108	29	46	—	229	34	9.0	2.4	3.8	19.1
Doug Moe	F	6'5	220	32	12	421	90	177	51	31	41	76	57	37	43	—	212	35	4.8	3.1	3.6	17.7
Jim Eakins	C	6'11	215	24	12	296	50	99	51	24	32	75	120	20	44	—	124	25	10.0	1.7	3.7	10.3
Charlie Scott	G-F	6'5	175	22	12	504	115	281	41	83	110	75	79	82	45	—	321	42	6.6	6.8	3.8	26.8
Mike Barrett	G	6'1	160	27	12	456	70	177	40	49	59	83	26	55	32	—	202	38	2.2	4.6	2.7	16.8
Ray Scott	C	6'9	220	32	12	264	80	157	51	47	56	84	78	21	43	—	207	22	6.5	1.8	3.6	17.3
Neil Johnson	F-C	6'7	220	27	12	253	41	92	45	29	44	66	100	32	54	—	112	21	8.3	2.7	4.5	9.3
Fatty Taylor	G	6'	175	24	12	214	17	40	43	19	28	68	37	27	37	—	53	18	3.1	2.3	3.1	4.4
Bill Bunting	F	6'8	200	23	6	35	5	10	50	8	12	67	6	1	4	—	18	6	1.0	0.2	0.7	3.0
George Irvine	F	6'6	200	22	7	25	3	6	50	1	1	100	5	2	7	—	7	4	0.7	0.3	1.0	1.0
Mike Maloy	F	6'7	215	21	1	2	1	3	33	0	0	—	1	0	0	—	2	2	1.0	0.0	0.0	2.0
Henry Logan	G	6'	185	24	1	1	0	0	—	1	2	50	0	0	0	—	1	1	0.0	0.0	0.0	1.0
FLORIDIANS	**BOB BASS**				lost to Kentucky 2-4; 112-116, 110-120, H120-102, H129-117, 101-118, H103-112																	
Warren Davis	F	6'6	215	28	6	180	28	58	48	22	29	76	48	31	26	—	78	30	8.0	5.2	4.3	13.0
Al Tucker	F	6'8	190	27	6	165	28	65	43	19	23	83	32	12	20	—	76	28	5.3	2.0	3.3	12.7
Ira Hage	C	6'9	225	29	6	233	46	82	56	11	19	58	98	14	17	—	103	39	16.3	2.3	2.8	17.2
Larry Jones	G	6'2	180	29	6	216	34	86	40	33	36	92	25	37	20	—	103	36	4.2	6.2	3.3	17.2
Mack Calvin	G	6'	165	22	6	255	62	120	52	39	46	85	16	42	10	—	164	43	2.7	7.0	1.7	27.3
Sam Robinson	F	6'7	200	22	6	111	24	53	45	14	16	88	19	6	17	—	62	19	3.2	1.0	2.8	10.3
Lonnie Wright	G	6'2	205	26	6	105	15	45	33	6	7	86	9	3	15	—	37	18	1.5	0.5	2.5	6.2
Trooper Washington	F	6'7	225	26	6	88	7	20	35	3	8	38	29	14	10	—	17	15	4.8	2.3	1.7	2.8
Carl Fuller	C	6'9	225	24	6	43	6	22	27	4	6	67	15	4	11	—	16	7	2.5	0.7	1.8	2.7
Ron Franz	F	6'7	207	25	2	40	7	21	33	3	8	38	10	2	4	—	17	20	5.0	1.0	2.0	8.5
Ron Nelson	F	—	—	—	1	2	0	1	0	0	0	—	1	0	0	—	0	2	1.0	0.0	0.0	0.0
Rich Niemann	C	7'	255	24	1	2	1	2	50	0	0	—	0	0	0	—	2	2	0.0	0.0	0.0	2.0
NEW YORK NETS	**LOU CARNESECCA**				lost to Virginia 2-4; 105-113, 108-114, H135-131, H130-127, 124-127, H114-118																	
Rick Barry	F	6'7	215	26	6	287	70	135	52	48	59	81	70	24	23	—	202	**48**	11.7	4.0	3.8	**33.7**
Manny Leaks	F-C	6'8	235	25	6	204	35	69	51	6	12	50	47	3	16	—	76	34	7.8	0.5	2.7	12.7
Billy Paultz	C	6'11	235	22	6	239	45	76	**59**	30	40	75	90	18	29	—	121	40	15.0	3.0	4.8	20.2
Joe DePre	G	6'3	190	24	6	171	29	55	53	15	19	79	18	13	32	—	73	29	3.0	2.2	**5.3**	12.2
Bill Melchionni	G	6'1	165	26	5	205	44	82	54	24	26	**92**	7	41	16	—	112	41	1.4	8.2	3.2	22.4
Ollie Taylor	G	6'2	205	23	6	128	15	31	48	22	29	76	15	13	18	—	53	21	2.5	2.2	3.0	8.8
Jim Ard	F	6'8	230	22	6	98	16	29	55	15	22	68	29	3	15	—	47	16	4.8	0.5	2.5	7.8
Jeff Congdon	G	6'1	180	27	4	76	8	21	38	5	5	100	6	11	2	—	21	19	1.5	2.8	0.5	5.3
Sonny Dove	F	6'8	210	25	5	32	5	10	50	1	4	25	11	1	10	—	11	6	2.2	0.2	2.0	2.2
MEMPHIS PROS	**BABE McCARTHY**				lost to Indiana 0-4; 98-114, 104-106, H90-91, H101-102																	
Wendell Ladner	F	6'5	220	22	4	143	19	72	26	3	8	38	40	14	19	—	41	36	10.0	3.5	4.8	10.3
Wil Jones	F	6'8	205	23	4	158	28	56	50	4	6	67	49	13	17	—	60	40	12.3	3.3	4.3	15.0
Gerald Govan	C-F	6'10	220	28	4	182	11	32	34	9	10	90	61	22	18	—	31	46	15.3	5.5	4.5	7.8
Jimmy Jones	G	6'4	190	25	4	130	24	48	50	17	25	68	24	15	16	—	65	33	6.0	3.8	4.0	16.3
Charlie Williams	G	6'	165	27	4	129	31	74	42	13	18	72	14	8	15	—	77	32	3.5	2.0	3.8	19.3
Steve Jones	G-F	6'5	205	28	4	163	39	88	44	11	11	100	21	9	14	—	91	41	5.3	2.3	3.5	22.8
Al Cueto	C	6'8	230	24	4	51	6	14	43	2	3	67	18	3	7	—	14	13	4.5	0.8	1.8	3.5
Craig Raymond	C	6'11	235	25	2	17	3	7	43	2	2	100	4	1	1	—	8	9	2.0	0.5	0.5	4.0
Coby Dietrick	C	6'10	230	22	2	10	1	4	25	2	2	100	3	1	0	—	4	5	1.5	0.5	0.0	2.0
Lee Davis	F	6'8	240	25	1	2	0	2	0	2	2	100	1	0	1	—	2	2	1.0	0.0	1.0	2.0
TEXAS CHAPARRALS	**BILL BLAKELEY**				lost to Utah 0-4; 115-125, 107-137, H101-113, H107-128																	
Wayne Hightower	F	6'9	210	30	4	126	11	34	32	13	17	76	32	11	12	—	35	32	8.0	2.8	3.0	8.8
John Beasley	F	6'9	225	26	4	115	20	52	38	4	5	80	42	6	9	—	46	29	10.5	1.5	2.3	11.5
Gene Moore	C	6'9	240	25	4	137	26	55	47	10	13	77	47	5	14	—	62	34	11.8	1.3	3.5	15.5
Donnie Freeman	G	6'3	185	26	4	144	38	84	45	13	16	81	24	5	9	—	89	36	6.0	1.3	2.3	22.3
Levern Tart	G	6'2	195	28	4	101	32	87	37	14	20	70	23	33	12	—	80	25	5.8	8.3	3.0	20.0
Rich Jones	F	6'8	230	24	4	103	12	40	30	11	15	73	22	10	10	—	37	26	5.5	2.5	2.5	9.3
Joe Hamilton	G	5'10	160	22	4	101	17	52	33	7	7	100	20	15	10	—	44	25	5.0	3.8	2.5	11.0
Bobby Croft	C	6'10	200	22	4	55	7	23	30	5	7	71	14	3	6	—	20	14	3.5	0.8	1.5	5.0
Charlie Beasley	G	6'5	190	25	3	45	4	14	29	2	3	67	7	5	8	—	11	15	2.3	1.7	2.7	3.7
Bob Bedell	F	6'8	205	26	3	33	2	17	12	2	3	67	11	5	9	—	6	11	3.7	1.7	3.0	2.0

Team	W	L	Pct.	GB	Record against playoff teams W	L	Pct.	Record against non - playoff teams W	L	Pct.	HOME W	L	Pct.	ROAD W	L	Pct.	NEUTRAL W	L	Pct.
EASTERN DIVISION																			
Virginia Squires	55	29	.655	—	35	21	.625	20	8	.714	32	9	.780	23	20	.535	0	0	—
Kentucky Colonels	44	40	.524	11	28	29	.491	16	11	.593	26	17	.605	18	23	.439	0	0	—
New York Nets	40	44	.476	15	25	31	.446	15	13	.536	26	17	.605	14	27	.341	0	0	—
Floridians	37	47	.440	18	26	31	.456	11	16	.407									
Pittsburgh Condors	36	48	.429	19	26	41	.388	10	7	.588									
Carolina Cougars	34	50	.405	21	26	41	.388	8	9	.471	20	22	.476	14	28	.333	0	0	—
WESTERN DIVISION																			
Indiana Pacers	58	26	.690	—	39	21	.650	19	5	.792	30	10	.750	28	16	.636	0	0	—
Utah Stars	57	27	.679	1	37	23	.617	20	4	.833	35	7	.833	22	20	.524	0	0	—
Memphis Pros	41	43	.488	17	26	34	.433	15	9	.625	25	21	.543	16	22	.421	0	0	—
Texas Chaparrals	30	54	.357	28	17	43	.283	13	11	.542	17	24	.415	13	30	.302	0	0	—
Denver Rockets	30	54	.357	28	25	47	.547	5	7	.417	20	22	.475	10	32	.233	0	0	—

1970/71 — A.B.A. INDIVIDUAL LEADERS

SCORING
(Minimum 70 Games Played)

Name	Team	G	FG	FT	Pts.	Avg.
Issel	KY	83	938	604	2480	29.9
Brisker	Pit	79	898	430	2315	29.3
Calvin	Fla	81	744	696	2201	27.2
Scott	Va	84	902	456	2276	27.1
Cannon	Den	80	751	606	2126	26.6
Jones	Fla	84	764	471	2044	24.3
Caldwell	Car	72	685	302	1678	23.3
Beaty	Utah	76	661	420	1744	23.0
S. Jones	Mem	83	732	332	1836	22.1
Daniels	Ind	82	698	326	1723	21.0

FIELD GOAL PERCENTAGE
(Minimum 560 Field Goals)

Name	Team	FG	FGA	Pct.
Beaty	Utah	661	1192	.555
Ligon	KY	429	795	.540
Johnson	Va	398	758	.525
Paultz	NY	510	973	.524
Hammond	Den	435	834	.522
Eakins	Va	332	645	.515
Daniels	Ind	698	1357	.514
Lewis	Pit	420	825	.509
Sidle	Den-Ind	425	851	.499
Becker	Ind-Den	370	741	.499

3-POINT FIELD GOAL PERCENTAGE
(Minimum 20 Made)

Name	Team	FG	FTA	Pct.
Lehmann	Car	154	382	.403
Carrier	KY	63	161	.391
S. Jones	Mem	40	108	.370
Dampier	KY	103	280	.368
Combs	Tex-Utah	77	210	.367
Keller	Ind	84	230	.365
Jones	Fla	45	124	.363
Boone	Tex-Utah	49	138	.355
Jones	Tex	33	95	.347
Brisker	Pit	89	264	.337

FREE THROW PERCENTAGE
(Minimum 160 Attempts)

Name	Team	FT	FTA	Pct.
Butler	Utah	153	168	.911
Barry	NY	451	507	.890
Bech	Den	158	182	.868
Carrier	KY	327	377	.867
Keller	Ind	267	308	.867
Calvin	Fla	696	805	.865
Moe	Va	221	259	.853
Dampier	KY	320	376	.851
Johnson	Pit	144	171	.842
Swift	Mem-Pit	206	246	.837

REBOUNDS PER GAME
(Minimum 70 Games Played)

Name	Team	G	Reb.	Avg.
Daniels	Ind	82	1475	18.0
Keye	Den	83	1454	17.5
Beaty	Utah	76	1190	15.7
Govan	Mem	84	1138	13.6
Harge	Car-Fla	82	1085	13.2
Lewis	Pit	83	1213	14.6
Issel	KY	83	1093	13.2
Robbins	Utah	82	989	11.9
Ligon	KY	84	989	11.8
Ladner	Mem	77	875	11.4

ASSISTS PER GAME
(Minimum 70 Games Played)

Name	Team	G	Ass.	Avg.
Melchionni	NY	81	672	8.3
Calvin	Fla	81	619	7.6
J. Jones	Mem	80	468	5.9
Scott	Va	84	472	5.6
Lehmann	Car	83	464	5.6
Dampier	KY	84	460	5.5
Lewis	Ind	81	433	5.4
Keller	Ind	83	437	5.3
Cannon	Den	80	414	5.2
Barrett	Va	84	425	5.1

MINUTES PLAYED

Name	Team	Min.
Govan	Mem	3698
Keye	Den	3634
Jones	Fla	3611
Calvin	Fla	3394
Brown	Ind	3364

PERSONAL FOULS

Name	Team	PF
Ladner	Mem	334
Lewis	Pit	332
Ligon	KY	331
Powell	KY	323
Issel	KY	323

Team		REGULAR SEASON												PLAYOFFS											
		G	FG	FGA	%	FT	FTA	%	Reb.	Ass.	PF	Points	PPG	G	FG	FGA	%	FT	FTA	%	Reb.	Ass.	PF	Points	PPG
TEAM STATISTICS																									
EASTERN DIVISION																									
Virginia	**Off.**	84	**4014**	8497	**47**	**2273**	**2975**	76	4563	**2231**	2371	**10355**	**123.3**	12	560	1232	46	**345**	**450**	77	617	306	**355**	1488	**124.0**
	Def.	84	3786	8288	46	2318	3064	76	4314	1856	**2251**	10058	119.7	12										1483	123.6
	Diff.		+228	+209	+1	-45	-89	—	+249	**+375**	-120	+297	+3.6											**+5**	+.4
Kentucky	**Off.**	84	3929	8520	46	2213	2930	76	4790	1878	2271	10264	122.2	19	865	2027	43	513	682	75	1090	501	544	2292	120.6
	Def.	84	3948	8586	46	2205	2961	74	4530	1816	2229	10260	122.1	19										2312	121.7
	Diff.		-19	-66	—	+8	-31	+2	**+260**	+62	-42	+4	+.1											-20	-1.1
New York	**Off.**	84	3638	7704	47	2013	2653	76	4109	1877	2203	9327	111.0	6	267	508	**53**	166	216	77	293	127	161	716	119.3
	Def.	84	3552	**7727**	46	2153	2886	75	**4196**	1746	2097	9378	111.6	6										730	121.7
	Diff.		+86	-23	+1	-140	-233	+1	-87	+131	-106	-51	-.6											-14	-2.4
Floridians	**Off.**	84	3659	8026	46	2179	2852	76	4296	1939	2140	9579	114.0	6	258	575	45	154	198	78	302	**165**	150	675	112.5
	Def.	84	3737	8314	45	2103	2745	77	4409	1746	2183	9707	115.6	6										685	114.2
	Diff.		-78	-288	+1	+76	+107	-1	-113	+193	+43	-128	-1.6											-10	-1.7
Pittsburgh	**Off.**	84	3906	8661	45	2012	2659	76	4831	1619	2208	10001	119.1												
	Def.	84	3965	8428	47	2132	2794	76	4751	1959	2094	10229	121.8												
	Diff.		-59	+233	-2	-120	-135	—	+80	-340	-114	-228	-2.7												
Carolina	**Off.**	84	3823	8329	46	1851	2809	66	4222	1745	2172	9688	115.3												
	Def.	84	3916	8379	47	2078	2765	75	4732	1757	2213	10026	119.4												
	Diff.		-93	-50	-1	-227	+44	-9	-510	-12	+41	-338	-4.1												
WESTERN DIVISION																									
Indiana	**Off.**	84	3796	8202	46	2104	2741	77	4373	2068	**1953**	10002	119.1	11	444	1051	42	256	331	**77**	569	233	**225**	1189	108.1
	Def.	84	3768	8463	45	1847	2489	74	4653	1954	2138	9501	113.1	11										**1186**	107.8
	Diff.		+28	-261	+1	+257	+252	+3	-280	+114	+185	+501	+6.0											**+3**	**+.3**
Utah	**Off.**	84	3787	8409	45	2219	2831	**78**	**4866**	1789	2050	9994	119.0	18	**846**	1776	48	447	562	**80**	1069	479	428	2175	120.8
	Def.	84	3652	8478	**43**	1915	2575	74	4655	1921	2222	9400	111.9	18										2046	113.7
	Diff.		+135	-69	**+2**	+304	+256	**+4**	+211	-132	+172	**+594**	**+7**											**+129**	**+7.1**
Memphis	**Off.**	84	3700	8383	44	1664	2287	73	4638	1893	2164	9175	109.2	4	162	397	41	65	87	75	235	86	108	393	98.3
	Def.	84	**3459**	7935	44	2142	2857	75	4425	**1725**	1892	**9234**	**109.9**	4										413	**103.3**
	Diff.		**+241**	**+448**	—	-478	-570	-2	+213	+168	-272	-59	-.7											-20	-5.0
Texas	**Off.**	84	3964	**8938**	44	2038	2661	77	4697	1901	2093	10207	121.5	4	169	**458**	37	81	106	76	**242**	98	99	430	107.5
	Def.	84	4135	8962	46	2006	2633	76	4875	2213	2118	10458	124.5	4										503	125.8
	Diff.		-171	-24	-2	+32	+28	+1	-178	-312	+25	-251	-3.0											-73	-18.3
Denver	**Off.**	84	3852	8780	44	2158	2841	76	4849	1642	1996	9965	118.6												
	Def.	84	4150	8889	47	**1825**	**2470**	**74**	4694	1889	2184	10306	122.7												
	Diff.		-298	-109	-3	**+333**	**+371**	+2	+155	-247	+188	-341	-4.1												

1971-72 N.B.A.

Streaking to a Crown

As a weapon against the rival A.B.A.'s signing of undergraduate stars before their senior year, the N.B.A. now permitted the drafting of undergrads if they could be classified as hardship cases; this ruling retroactively covered the signing of Spencer Haywood by Seattle last season, and it allowed Baltimore to sign guard Phil Chenier after his junior year at California. But with the A.B.A. seriously bidding for the services of the top college talent, this year's rookies were no longer hardship cases after signing their pro contracts. Sidney Wicks, Austin Carr, Elmore Smith, Curtis Rowe, and Howard Porter all accepted lucrative pacts from N.B.A. teams, and while top collegians Artis Gilmore, George McGinnis, and Julius Erving signed with the A.B.A., the older league struck back by hiring two young A.B.A. stars, Charlie Scott and Jim McDaniels. They were signed late in the season after they had found escape clauses in their contracts.

In addition to the rich new faces around the league, the N.B.A. also had a new city, as the San Diego Rockets abandoned the West Coast to set up shop in Houston, where an A.B.A. team had failed earlier. The San Francisco Warriors changed their name to the Golden State Warriors, and Milwaukee center Lew Alcindor changed his name to Kareem Abdul-Jabbar because of his Islamic religious beliefs.

And the mantle of superteam also changed hands this season, passing from the Milwaukee Bucks to the Los Angeles Lakers. Elgin Baylor's knees had forced his retirement early in the campaign, but new Laker coach Bill Sharman, back in the N.B.A. from three years in the A.B.A., nevertheless welded together a balanced, talented outfit that put together the best record in N.B.A. history. Wilt Chamberlain's scoring average was down to 14.8, but his strength under the boards was still unmatched by any other player. Jerry West directed the team from the backcourt and scored at a 25.8 clip, while fellow guard Gail Goodrich blossomed into the Lakers' top scorer with a 25.9 average. At the forwards, Happy Hairston concentrated on rebounding and defense, while Jim McMillian inherited Baylor's spot and oiled the offense with his quick driving and shooting. Experienced subs Flynn Robinson, Leroy Ellis, and Pat Riley fit right into the Laker pattern when called upon.

The Lakers played almost mistake-free basketball from the start of the season, and a 110-106 victory over Baltimore on November 5 started the club on the longest winning streak in N.B.A. annals. The Lakers played excellent team basketball, with different men starring on different nights, and the team kept winning right through November and December. For two months, the Lakers won every game they played, with the streak reaching 33 games on January 7. Two nights later, the Milwaukee Bucks ended the string with a 120-104 decision, but the Lakers had long passed the old standard of 20 consecutive wins set by the Bucks last year. By the season's end, the Lakers had a record total of 69 wins, one better than the 1966-67 Philadelphia 76ers.

The Golden State Warriors, Los Angeles' competition in the Pacific Division, were left far behind, but still played interesting basketball. They added speed in Cazzie Russell and Jim Barnett, and finished a much-improved second. Player coach Lenny Wilkins also had his Seattle Supersonics playing good ball, but they finished out of the playoffs despite a 47-35 record. The Rockets slumped in their new Houston home, and Portland again had a horrendous record despite the addition of rookie Sidney Wicks.

In the Midwest Division, last year's superteam, the Milwaukee Bucks, were still outstanding. Illness sidelined Oscar Robertson part of the time, but Lucius Allen developed into a competent backcourt leader. Of course, the newly-named Abdul-Jabbar exhibited all of his old prowess by leading the N.B.A. in scoring with a 34.8 average. The Chicago Bulls again muscled their way into second place, with Bob Love, Chet Walker, Jerry Sloan, Tom Boerwinkle, and Bob Weiss joined this season by rookie center Cliff Ray and third-year guard Norm Van Lier, who was picked up in a trade with Cincinnati. The strong Phoenix Suns compiled a 49-33 record despite the lack of any bench strength, and the Detroit Pistons relapsed into their old losing ways after losing guard Dave Bing for the first two months of the season with a detached retina.

The Eastern Conference made a worse showing than the West, with only two of the eight clubs posting a winning record for the season. The Boston Celtics regained the excellence characteristic of the days of Bill Russell, compiling a 56-26 record to take first place in the Atlantic Division. John Havlicek and Don Nelson were the veterans on the team, and Dave Cowens, Jo Jo White, and Don Chaney were the young starters who were improving with each season.

The New York Knicks underwent some mid-season readjustments, yet finished with a strong 48-34 record in second place behind Boston. A bad knee knocked center Willis Reed out of action for most of the campaign, so the Knicks had to use 6'8" Jerry Lucas, obtained from the Warriors in a trade for Cazzie Russell, in the middle. Lucas was not the rebounder or shot-blocker that Reed was, but his outside shooting drew larger opposition centers outside and opened up the middle for the Knicks to drive. The Knicks also sent Mike Riordan and Dave Stallworth to Baltimore for guard Earl (The Pearl) Monroe, who had trouble fitting his flashy offensive skills into the New York pattern after coming over in November.

Finishing out of the playoffs in the Atlantic Division were the Philadelphia 76ers, despite an All-Star performance by Billy Cunningham, and the Buffalo Braves, despite good play from rookies Elmore Smith and Randy Smith. All the Central Division clubs finished with losing records, with Baltimore and Atlanta qualifying for playoff berths.

The Celtics, Knicks, Bucks, and Lakers emerged from the first round of the playoffs as expected, but the next matchups were harder to predict. It was the up-and-coming young Celtics against the experienced Knicks, and the New Yorkers sent the Bostonians back for more seasoning by winning their series in five games. Meanwhile, the Western finals pitted the phenomenal Lakers against the defending-champion Bucks, and Wilt Chamberlain against Kareem Abdul-Jabbar. Even with Oscar Robertson slowed by muscle pulls, the Bucks managed a split of the first four games, but the Lakers then won two straight to move on to the championship series heavily favored over New York.

The Knicks won the first game, 114-92, with superb outside shooting, but the lack of a New York center strong enough to cope with Chamberlain could not be denied any longer. The Lakers then won four straight games and made Jerry West a member of a championship team for the first time in his 12-year pro career.

se Name	Pos	Hgt	Wgt	Age	G	Min	FG	FGA	%	FT	FTA	%	Reb	Ass	PF	DQ	Points	Min	Reb	Ass	PF	Points
					TOTAL													PER GAME				
1971/72 N.B.A. — ATLANTIC DIVISION																						
OSTON CELTICS	**56-26 .683**				**TOM HEINSOHN**																	
ohn Havlicek	F-G	6'5	205	31	82	3698	897	1957	46	458	549	83	672	614	183	1	2252	45	8.2	7.5	2.2	27.5
on Nelson	F	6'6	210	31	82	2086	389	811	48	356	452	79	453	192	220	3	1134	25	5.5	2.3	2.7	13.8
ave Cowens	C	6'9	230	23	79	3186	657	1357	48	175	243	72	1203	245	314	10	1489	40	15.2	3.1	4.0	18.8
on Chaney	G	6'5	210	25	79	2275	373	786	47	197	255	77	395	202	295	7	943	29	5.0	2.6	3.7	11.9
o Jo White	G	6'3	190	25	79	3261	770	1788	43	285	343	83	446	416	227	1	1825	41	5.6	5.3	2.9	23.1
atch Sanders	F	6'6	210	33	82	1631	215	524	41	111	136	82	353	98	257	7	541	20	4.3	1.2	3.1	6.6
ambone Williams	G	6'2	190	32	81	1326	161	339	47	90	119	76	256	327	204	2	412	16	3.2	4.0	2.5	5.1
teve Kuberski	F	6'8	215	24	71	1128	185	444	42	80	102	78	320	46	130	1	450	16	4.5	0.6	1.8	6.3
enry Finkel	C	7'	240	29	78	736	103	254	41	43	74	58	251	61	118	4	249	9	3.2	0.8	1.5	3.2
ex Morgan	G	6'5	190	23	28	150	16	50	32	23	31	74	30	17	34	0	55	5	1.1	0.6	1.2	2.0
arfield Smith	F-C	6'9	235	26	26	134	28	66	42	6	31	19	37	8	22	0	62	5	1.4	0.3	0.8	2.4
larence Glover	F	6'8	210	24	25	119	25	55	45	15	32	47	46	4	26	0	65	5	1.8	0.2	1.0	2.6
EW YORK KNICKERBOCKERS	**48-34 .585**				**RED HOLZMAN**																	
ill Bradley	F	6'5	210	28	78	2780	504	1085	46	169	199	85	250	315	254	4	1177	36	3.2	4.0	3.3	15.1
ave DeBusschere	F	6'6	235	31	80	3072	520	1218	43	193	265	73	901	291	219	1	1233	38	11.3	3.6	2.7	15.4
Villis Reed (knee injury)	C	6'9	240	29	11	363	60	137	44	27	39	69	96	22	30	0	147	33	8.7	2.0	2.7	13.4
ick Barnett	G	6'4	190	35	79	2256	401	918	44	162	215	75	153	198	229	4	964	29	1.9	2.5	2.9	12.2
Valt Frazier	G	6'4	205	26	77	3126	669	1307	51	450	557	81	513	446	185	0	1788	41	6.7	5.8	2.4	23.2
erry Lucas	C-F	6'8	230	31	77	2926	543	1060	51	197	249	79	1011	318	218	1	1283	38	13.1	4.1	2.8	16.7
hil Jackson	F-C	6'8	225	26	80	1273	205	466	44	167	228	73	326	72	224	4	577	16	4.1	0.9	2.8	7.2
arl Monroe (From Bal) (KJ)	G	6'3	190	27	60	1234	261	598	44	162	206	79	92	132	130	1	684	21	1.5	2.2	2.2	11.4
ean Meminger	G	6'	175	23	78	1173	139	293	47	79	140	56	185	103	137	0	357	15	2.4	1.3	1.8	4.6
uther Rackley (from Cle)	C	6'10	225	25	62	618	92	215	43	49	84	58	187	18	104	0	233	10	3.0	0.3	1.7	3.8
ddie Mast	F	6'9	220	23	40	270	39	112	35	25	41	61	73	10	39	0	103	7	1.8	0.3	1.0	2.6
ave Stallworth (to Bal)	F	6'7	210	30	14	225	33	88	38	29	35	83	35	25	31	0	95	16	2.5	1.8	2.2	6.8
ddie Miles	G-F	6'4	196	31	42	198	23	64	36	16	18	89	16	17	46	0	62	5	0.4	0.4	1.1	1.5
harlie Paulk (from Chi)	F	6'8	220	27	28	151	16	60	27	8	12	67	49	7	24	0	40	5	1.8	0.3	0.9	1.4
reg Fillmore	C	7'1	250	24	10	67	7	27	26	1	3	33	15	3	17	0	15	7	1.5	0.3	1.7	1.5
Mike Price (to IndA)	G	6'3	200	23	6	40	5	14	36	9	11	82	6	6	10	0	19	7	1.0	1.0	1.7	3.2
Mike Riordan (to Bal)	G	6'4	200	26	4	33	4	11	36	0	1	0	1	2	2	0	8	8	0.3	0.5	0.5	2.0
PHILADELPHIA 76ers	**30-52 .366**				**JACK RAMSAY**																	
Billy Cunningham	F	6'7	220	28	75	2900	658	1428	46	428	601	71	918	443	295	12	1744	39	12.2	5.9	3.9	23.3
Bill Bridges (from Atl)	F	6'6	235	32	64	2210	328	645	51	191	272	70	861	158	219	5	847	35	13.5	2.5	3.4	13.2
Bob Rule (from Sea)	C-F	6'9	235	27	60	1987	416	934	45	203	292	70	479	110	162	4	1035	33	8.0	1.8	2.7	17.3
Fred Carter (from Bal)	G	6'3	185	26	77	2147	440	991	44	179	284	63	307	199	235	4	1059	28	4.0	2.6	3.1	13.8
Hal Greer	G	6'3	176	35	81	2410	389	866	45	181	234	77	271	316	268	10	959	30	3.3	3.9	3.3	11.8
Kevin Loughery (from Bal)	G	6'3	190	31	74	1829	337	792	43	258	312	83	178	188	208	3	932	25	2.4	2.5	2.8	12.6
Fred Foster	F	6'5	220	25	74	1699	347	837	41	185	243	76	276	90	184	3	879	23	3.7	1.2	2.5	11.9
Dave Wohl	G	6'2	185	22	79	1628	243	567	43	156	206	76	150	228	229	2	642	21	1.9	2.9	2.9	8.1
Luke Jackson	C	6'9	250	30	63	1083	137	346	40	92	133	69	309	88	141	1	366	17	4.9	1.4	2.2	5.8
Dennis Awtrey	C	6'10	240	23	58	794	98	222	44	49	76	64	248	51	141	3	245	14	4.3	0.9	2.4	4.2
Jim Washington (to Atl)	F	6'7	215	28	17	545	68	156	44	55	67	82	135	25	59	3	191	32	7.9	1.5	3.5	11.2
Al Henry	C	6'9	205	22	43	421	68	156	44	51	73	70	137	8	42	0	187	10	3.2	0.2	1.0	4.3
Barry Yates	F	6'7	215	25	24	144	31	83	37	7	11	64	40	7	14	0	69	6	1.7	0.3	0.6	2.9
Archie Clark (to Bal)	G	6'2	175	30	1	42	11	16	69	7	11	64	3	7	3	0	29	42	3.0	7.0	3.0	29.0
Jake Jones (to Cin)	G	6'3	180	22	6	41	6	18	33	7	10	70	6	2	3	0	19	7	1.0	0.3	0.5	3.2
BUFFALO BRAVES	**22-60 .268**				**DOLPH SCHAYES (0-1 .000), JOHNNY McCARTHY (22-59 .272)**																	
Randy Smith	F	6'3	180	23	76	2094	432	896	48	158	254	62	368	189	202	2	1022	28	4.8	2.5	2.7	13.4
Bob Kauffman	F-C	6'8	240	25	77	3205	558	1123	50	341	429	79	787	297	273	7	1457	42	10.2	3.9	3.5	18.9
Elmore Smith	C	7'	250	22	78	3186	579	1275	45	194	363	53	1184	111	306	10	1352	41	15.2	1.4	3.9	17.3
Dick Garrett	G	6'3	185	24	73	1905	325	735	44	136	157	87	225	165	225	5	786	26	3.1	2.3	3.1	10.8
Walt Hazzard	G	6'2	190	29	72	2389	450	998	45	237	303	78	213	406	230	2	1137	33	3.0	5.6	3.2	15.8
Fred Hilton	G	6'3	185	23	61	1349	309	795	39	90	122	74	156	116	145	0	708	22	2.6	1.9	2.4	11.6
Cornell Warner	F	6'9	220	23	62	1239	162	366	44	58	78	74	379	54	125	2	382	20	6.1	0.9	2.0	6.2
Em Bryant	G	6'1	175	33	54	1223	101	220	46	75	125	60	127	206	167	5	277	23	2.4	3.8	3.1	5.1
John Hummer	F	6'9	230	23	55	1186	113	290	39	58	124	47	229	72	178	4	284	22	4.2	1.3	3.2	5.2
Mike Davis	G	6'3	185	25	62	1068	213	501	43	138	180	77	120	82	141	5	564	17	1.9	1.3	2.3	9.1
Bill Hosket	F	6'8	228	25	44	592	89	181	49	42	52	81	123	38	79	0	220	13	2.8	0.9	1.8	5.0
Jerry Chambers	F	6'5	190	26	26	366	78	180	43	22	32	69	67	23	39	0	176	14	2.6	0.9	1.5	6.8

Use Name	Pos	Hgt	Wgt	Age	TOTAL													PER GAME				
					G	Min	FG	FGA	%	FT	FTA	%	Reb	Ass	PF	DQ	Points	Min	Reb	Ass	PF	Points
I971/72 N.B.A. — CENTRAL DIVISION																						
BALTIMORE BULLETS	**38-44 .463**				**GENE SHUE**																	
Dave Stallworth (from NY)	F	6'7	210	30	64	1815	303	690	44	123	153	80	398	133	186	3	729	28	6.2	2.1	2.9	11.4
Jack Marin	F	6'7	210	27	78	2927	690	1444	48	356	398	**89**	528	169	240	2	1736	38	6.8	2.2	3.1	22.3
Wes Unseld	C	6'7	250	25	76	3171	409	822	50	171	272	63	1336	278	218	1	989	42	17.6	3.7	2.9	13.0
Phil Chenier	G	6'3	180	21	81	2481	407	981	41	182	247	74	268	205	191	2	996	31	3.3	2.5	2.4	12.3
Archie Clark (from Phi)	G	6'2	175	30	76	3243	701	1500	47	507	656	77	265	606	191	0	1909	43	3.5	8.0	2.5	25.1
Mike Riordan (from NY)	G	6'4	200	26	54	1344	229	488	47	84	123	68	127	124	127	0	542	25	2.4	2.3	2.4	10.0
Stan Love	F	6'9	215	22	74	1327	242	536	45	103	140	74	338	52	202	0	587	18	4.6	0.7	2.7	7.9
John Tresvant	F-C	6'7	220	32	65	1227	162	360	45	121	148	82	323	83	175	6	445	19	5.0	1.3	2.7	6.8
Gus Johnson (knee injury)	C-F	6'6	235	33	39	668	103	269	38	43	63	68	226	51	91	0	249	17	5.8	1.3	2.3	6.4
Gary Zeller (to NY-A)	G	6'3	205	24	28	471	83	229	36	22	35	63	65	30	62	0	188	17	2.3	1.1	2.2	6.7
Dorie Murrey	F-C	6'8	220	28	51	421	43	113	38	24	39	62	126	17	76	2	110	8	2.5	0.3	1.5	2.2
Terry Driscoll	F	6'7	215	24	40	313	40	104	38	27	39	69	109	23	53	0	107	8	2.7	0.6	1.3	2.7
Rich Rinaldi	G	6"3	195	22	39	159	42	104	40	20	30	67	18	15	25	0	104	4	0.5	0.4	0.6	2.7
Earl Monroe (to NY) (KJ)	G	6'3	190	27	3	103	26	64	41	13	18	72	8	10	9	0	65	34	2.7	3.3	3.0	21.7
Fred Carter (to Phi)	G	6'3	185	26	2	68	6	27	22	3	9	33	19	12	7	0	15	34	9.5	6.0	3.5	7.5
Kevin Loughery (to Phi)	G	6'3	190	31	2	42	4	17	24	5	8	63	5	8	5	0	13	21	2.5	4.0	2.5	6.5
ATLANTA HAWKS	**36-46 .439**				**RICHIE GUERIN**																	
Don Adams (from Hou)	F	6'7	210	24	70	2030	307	779	39	204	273	75	494	137	259	5	818	29	7.1	2.0	3.7	11.7
Jim Washington (from Phi)	F	6'7	215	28	67	2416	325	729	45	201	256	79	601	121	217	0	851	36	9.0	1.8	3.2	12.7
Walt Bellamy	C	6'11	245	32	82	3187	593	1089	54	340	581	59	1049	262	255	2	1526	39	12.8	3.2	3.1	18.6
Lou Hudson	G-F	6'5	210	27	77	3042	775	1540	50	349	430	81	385	309	225	0	1899	40	5.0	4.0	2.9	24.7
Pete Maravich (illness)	G	6'5	190	23	66	2302	460	1077	43	355	438	81	256	393	207	0	1275	35	3.9	6.0	3.1	19.3
Herm Gilliam	G	6'3	190	25	82	2337	345	774	45	145	173	84	335	377	232	3	835	29	4.1	4.6	2.8	10.2
Don May	F	6'4	215	25	75	1285	234	476	49	126	164	77	217	55	133	0	594	17	2.9	0.7	1.8	7.9
George Trapp	F	6'8	215	23	60	890	144	388	37	105	139	76	183	51	144	2	393	15	3.1	0.9	2.4	6.6
Bill Bridges (to Phi)	F	6'6	235	32	14	546	51	134	38	31	44	70	190	40	50	1	133	39	13.6	2.9	3.6	9.5
Bob Christian	C	7'	260	27	56	485	66	142	46	44	61	72	181	28	77	0	176	9	3.2	0.5	1.4	3.1
Larry Siegfried (from Hou)	G	6'3	192	32	21	335	25	77	32	20	23	87	32	52	32	0	70	16	1.5	2.5	1.5	3.3
Jeff Halliburton	G	6'5	190	22	37	288	61	133	46	25	30	83	37	20	50	1	147	8	1.0	0.5	1.4	4.0
Tom Payne	C	7'2	240	21	29	227	45	103	44	29	46	63	69	15	40	0	119	8	2.4	0.5	1.4	4.1
Milt Williams	G	6'2	185	26	10	127	23	53	43	21	29	72	4	20	18	0	67	13	0.4	2.0	1.8	6.7
Jim Davis (to Hou-Det)	C-F	6'9	235	30	11	119	8	33	24	10	18	56	36	8	14	0	26	11	3.3	0.7	1.3	2.4
John Vallely (to Hou)	G	6'3	185	23	9	110	20	43	47	13	20	65	11	9	13	0	53	12	1.2	1.0	1.4	5.9
Shaler Halimon (to DalA)	G	6'6	200	26	1	4	0	0	—	0	0	—	0	0	1	0	0	4	0.0	0.0	1.0	0.0
CINCINNATI ROYALS	**30-52 .366**				**BOB COUSY**																	
Tom Van Arsdale	F-G	6'5	215	28	73	2598	550	1205	46	299	396	76	350	198	241	1	1399	36	4.8	2.7	3.3	19.2
Nate Williams	F	6'5	215	21	81	2173	418	968	43	127	172	74	372	174	300	11	963	27	4.6	2.1	3.7	11.9
Sam Lacey	C	6'10	235	23	81	2832	410	972	42	119	169	70	968	173	284	6	939	35	12.0	2.1	3.5	11.6
Matt Guokas	G	6'6	195	27	61	1975	191	385	50	64	83	77	142	321	150	0	446	32	2.3	5.3	2.5	7.3
Nate Archibald	G	6'1	160	23	76	3272	734	1511	49	**677**	**824**	82	222	701	198	3	2145	43	2.9	9.2	2.6	28.2
Jim Fox (from Chi)	C-F	6'10	230	28	71	2047	334	735	45	207	269	77	659	80	236	8	875	29	9.3	1.1	3.3	12.3
Johnny Green	F	6'5	210	38	82	1914	331	582	57	141	250	56	560	120	238	5	803	23	6.8	1.5	2.9	9.8
John Mengelt	G	6'2	195	22	78	1438	287	605	47	208	252	83	148	146	163	0	782	18	1.9	1.9	2.1	10.0
Gil McGregor	F	6'8	240	22	42	532	66	182	36	39	56	70	148	18	120	4	171	13	3.5	0.4	2.9	4.1
Norm Van Lier (to Chi)	G	6'1	175	24	10	275	28	90	31	17	22	77	58	51	32	1	73	28	5.8	5.1	3.2	7.3
Ken Durrett (knee injury)	F	6'7	190	23	19	233	31	79	39	21	28	75	39	14	41	0	83	12	2.1	0.7	2.2	4.4
Fred Taylor (from Phoe)	F	6'5	187	23	21	214	30	90	33	11	19	58	37	11	32	0	71	10	1.8	0.5	1.5	3.4
Jake Jones (from Phi)	G	6'3	180	22	11	161	22	54	41	13	21	62	20	10	19	0	57	15	1.8	0.9	1.7	5.2
Darrall Imhoff (to Port)	C	6'10	235	33	9	76	10	29	34	3	8	38	27	2	22	1	23	8	3.0	0.2	2.4	2.6
Sid Catlett	F	6'8	230	23	9	40	2	9	22	2	9	22	4	1	3	0	6	4	0.4	0.1	0.3	0.7
CLEVELAND CAVALIERS	**23-59 .280**				**BILL FITCH**																	
Bobby Smith	F-G	6'5	212	25	82	2734	527	1190	44	178	224	79	502	247	222	3	1232	33	6.1	3.0	2.7	15.0
John Johnson	F	6'7	200	24	82	3041	557	1286	43	277	353	78	631	415	268	2	1391	37	7.7	5.1	3.3	17.0
Walt Wesley	C	6'11	230	26	82	2185	412	1006	41	196	291	67	711	76	245	4	1020	27	8.7	0.9	3.0	12.4
Austin Carr (broken foot)	G	6'4	200	23	43	1539	381	894	43	149	196	76	150	148	99	0	911	36	3.5	3.4	2.3	21.2
Butch Beard	G	6'3	185	24	68	2434	394	849	46	260	342	76	276	456	213	2	1048	36	4.1	6.7	3.1	15.4
Rick Roberson (injury)	F-C	6'9	235	24	63	2207	304	688	44	215	366	59	801	109	251	7	823	35	12.7	1.7	**4.0**	13.1
Dave Sorenson	F	6'8	225	23	76	1162	213	475	45	106	136	78	301	81	120	1	532	15	4.0	1.1	1.6	7.0
Charlie Davis	G	6'2	160	22	61	1144	229	569	40	142	169	84	92	123	143	3	600	19	1.5	2.0	2.3	9.8
Johnny Warren	G	6'3	180	24	68	969	144	345	42	49	58	84	133	91	92	0	337	14	2.0	1.3	1.4	5.0
Bobby Washington	G	6'	175	24	69	967	123	309	40	104	128	81	129	223	135	1	350	14	1.9	3.2	2.0	5.1
Steve Patterson	C	6'9	225	23	65	775	94	263	36	23	46	50	228	54	80	0	211	12	3.5	0.8	1.2	3.2
Greg Howard	F	6'9	225	23	48	426	50	131	38	39	51	76	108	27	50	0	139	9	2.3	0.6	1.0	2.9
Jackie Ridgle	G	6'4	195	23	32	107	19	44	43	19	26	73	15	7	15	0	57	3	0.5	0.2	0.5	1.8
Luther Rackley (to NY)	C	6'10	225	25	9	65	11	25	44	1	4	25	21	3	3	0	23	7	2.3	0.3	0.3	2.6

1971/72 N.B.A. — MIDWEST DIVISION

Use Name	Pos	Hgt	Wgt	Age	G	Min	FG	FGA	%	FT	FTA	%	Reb	Ass	PF	DQ	Points	Min	Reb	Ass	PF	Points
					TOTAL													PER GAME				
MILWAUKEE BUCKS	**63-19 .768**				**LARRY COSTELLO**																	
Bob Dandridge	F	6'6	195	24	80	2957	630	1264	50	215	291	74	613	249	297	7	1475	37	7.7	3.1	3.7	18.4
Curtis Perry (from Hou)	F	6'7	220	23	50	1471	143	371	39	64	95	67	471	78	214	**13**	350	29	9.4	1.6	4.3	7.0
Kareem Abdul-Jabbar	C	7'3	232	24	81	3583	**1159**	**2019**	**57**	**504**	**732**	**69**	**1346**	**370**	**235**	**1**	**2822**	44	16.6	4.6	2.9	**34.8**
Oscar Robertson (injury)	G-F	6'5	220	33	64	2390	419	887	47	276	330	84	323	491	116	0	1114	37	5.0	7.7	1.8	17.4
Lucius Allen	G	6'2	175	24	80	2316	441	874	50	198	259	76	254	333	214	2	1080	29	3.2	4.2	2.7	13.5
Jon McGlockin	G	6'5	205	28	80	2213	374	733	51	109	126	87	181	231	146	0	857	28	2.3	2.9	1.8	10.7
John Block	F-C	6'10	220	27	79	1524	233	530	44	206	275	75	410	95	213	4	672	19	5.2	1.2	2.7	8.5
Wally Jones	G	6'2	185	29	48	1030	144	354	41	74	90	82	75	141	112	0	362	21	1.6	2.9	2.3	7.5
Toby Kimball	F	6'8	230	29	74	971	107	229	47	44	81	54	312	60	137	0	258	13	4.2	0.8	1.9	3.5
Greg Smith (to Hou)	F	6'5	200	24	28	737	97	198	49	41	58	71	161	63	92	1	235	26	5.8	2.3	3.3	8.4
Bill Dinwiddie	F	6'7	220	28	23	144	16	57	28	5	9	56	32	9	23	0	37	6	1.4	0.4	1.0	1.6
Charlie LowerY	G	6'3	185	22	20	134	17	38	45	11	18	61	19	14	16	1	45	7	1.0	0.7	0.8	2.3
Jeff Webb (to Phoe)	G	6'4	170	23	19	109	9	35	26	11	13	85	18	7	8	0	29	6	0.9	0.4	0.4	1.5
Barry Nelson	C	6'10	230	22	28	102	15	36	42	5	10	50	20	7	21	0	35	4	0.7	0.3	0.8	1.3
McCoy McLemore (to Hou)	F	6'7	235	29	10	99	9	28	32	11	12	92	34	12	18	0	29	10	3.4	1.2	1.8	2.9
CHICAGO BULLS	**57-25 .695**				**DICK MOTTA**																	
Chet Walker	F	6'6	220	31	78	2588	619	1225	51	481	568	85	473	178	171	0	1719	33	6.1	2.3	2.2	22.0
Bob Love	F	6'8	215	29	79	3108	819	1854	44	399	509	78	518	125	235	2	2037	39	6.6	1.6	3.0	25.8
Tom Boenwinkle	C	7'	270	26	80	2022	219	500	44	118	180	66	897	281	253	4	556	25	11.2	3.5	3.2	7.0
Bob Weiss	G	6'2	185	29	82	2450	358	832	43	212	254	83	170	377	212	1	928	30	2.1	4.6	2.6	11.3
Norm Van Lier (from Cin)	G	6'1	175	24	69	2140	306	671	46	220	278	79	299	491	207	4	832	31	4.3	7.1	3.0	12.1
Jerry Sloan	G-F	6'6	200	29	82	3035	535	1206	44	258	391	66	691	211	309	8	1328	37	8.4	2.6	3.8	16.2
Cliff Ray	C	6'9	235	22	82	1872	222	445	50	134	218	61	869	254	296	5	578	23	10.6	3.1	3.6	7.0
Jim King	G	6'2	175	30	73	1017	162	356	46	89	113	79	81	101	103	0	413	14	1.1	1.4	1.4	5.7
Howard Porter	F	6'8	220	23	67	730	171	403	42	59	77	77	183	24	88	0	401	11	2.7	0.4	1.3	6.0
Kenny McIntosh	F	6'7	225	22	43	405	57	168	34	21	44	48	89	18	41	0	135	9	2.1	0.4	1.0	3.1
Jimmy Collins	G	6'2	175	25	19	134	26	71	37	10	11	91	12	10	11	0	62	7	0.6	0.5	0.6	3.3
Jim Fox (to Cin)	C-F	6'10	230	28	10	133	20	53	38	20	28	71	54	6	21	0	60	13	5.4	0.6	2.1	6.0
Jackie Dinkins	F	6'5	210	21	18	89	17	41	41	11	20	55	20	7	10	0	45	5	1.1	0.4	0.6	2.5
Charlie Paulk (to NY)	F	6'8	220	27	7	60	8	28	29	7	9	78	15	4	7	0	23	9	2.1	0.6	1.0	3.3
PHOENIX SUNS	**49-33 .598**				**COTTON FITZSIMMONS**																	
Connie Hawkins	F	6'8	220	29	76	2798	571	1244	46	456	565	81	633	296	235	2	1598	37	8.3	3.9	3.1	21.0
Paul Silas	F	6'7	225	28	80	3082	485	1031	47	433	560	77	955	343	201	2	1403	39	11.9	4.3	2.5	17.5
Neal Walk	C	6'10	250	23	81	2142	506	1057	48	256	344	74	665	151	295	9	1268	26	8.2	1.9	3.6	15.7
Dick Van Arsdale	G-F	6'5	210	29	82	3096	545	1178	46	529	626	85	334	297	232	1	1619	38	4.1	3.6	2.8	19.7
Charlie Scott (from VirA)	G	6'5	175	23	6	177	48	113	42	17	21	81	23	26	19	0	113	30	3.8	4.3	3.2	18.8
Clem Haskins	G	6'3	200	28	79	2453	509	1054	48	220	258	85	270	290	194	1	1238	31	3.4	3.7	2.5	15.7
Mo Layton	G	6'1	180	23	80	1849	304	717	42	122	165	74	164	247	219	0	730	23	2.1	3.1	2.7	9.1
Otto Moore	C	6'11	230	25	81	1624	260	597	44	94	156	60	540	88	212	2	614	20	6.7	1.1	2.6	7.6
Lamar Green	F	6'7	220	24	67	991	133	298	45	66	90	73	348	45	134	1	332	15	5.2	0.7	2.0	5.0
Mel Counts	F-C	7'	235	30	76	906	147	344	43	101	140	72	257	96	159	2	395	12	3.4	1.3	2.1	5.2
John Wetzel	G	6'5	192	27	51	419	31	82	38	24	30	80	65	56	71	0	86	8	1.3	1.1	1.4	1.7
Art Harris	G	6'4	186	24	21	145	23	70	33	9	21	43	13	18	26	0	55	7	0.6	0.9	1.2	2.6
Jeff Webb (from Mil)	G	6'4	170	23	27	129	31	65	48	5	10	50	17	16	21	0	67	5	0.6	0.6	0.8	2.5
Fred Taylor (to Cin)	F	6'5	187	23	13	69	6	27	22	4	13	31	17	7	8	0	16	5	1.3	0.5	0.6	1.2
DETROIT PISTONS	**26-56 .317**				**BUTCH VAN BREDA KOLFF (6-6 .500), EARL LLOYD (20-50 .286)**																	
Terry Dischinger	F	6'7	208	31	79	2062	295	574	51	156	200	78	338	92	289	7	746	26	4.3	1.2	3.7	9.4
Curtis Rowe	F	6'7	225	22	82	2661	369	802	46	192	287	67	699	99	171	1	930	32	8.5	1.2	2.1	11.3
Bob Lanier	C	6'11	250	23	80	3092	834	1690	49	388	505	77	1132	248	297	6	2056	39	14.2	3.1	3.7	25.7
Jimmy Walker	G	6'3	205	27	78	3083	634	1386	46	397	480	83	231	315	198	2	1665	40	3.0	4.0	2.5	21.3
Dave Bing	G	6'3	185	28	45	1936	369	891	41	278	354	79	186	317	138	3	1016	43	4.1	7.0	3.1	22.6
Howie Komives	G	6'1	185	30	79	2071	262	702	37	164	203	81	172	291	196	0	688	26	2.2	3.7	2.5	8.7
Willie Norwood	F	6'7	220	24	78	1272	222	440	50	140	215	65	316	43	229	4	584	16	4.1	0.6	2.9	7.5
Bill Hewitt	F	6'7	210	27	68	1203	131	277	47	41	82	50	270	71	134	1	303	18	4.0	1.0	2.0	4.5
Jim Davis (from Atl-Hou)	C-F	6'9	235	30	52	684	121	251	48	64	98	65	196	38	106	1	306	13	3.8	0.7	2.0	5.9
Erwin Mueller	F-C	6'8	230	27	42	605	68	197	35	43	74	58	147	57	64	0	179	14	3.5	1.4	1.5	4.3
Harvey Marlatt	G	6'3	185	23	31	506	60	149	40	36	42	86	62	60	64	1	156	16	2.0	1.9	2.1	5.0
Isaiah Wilson	G	6'2	175	23	48	322	63	177	36	41	56	73	47	41	32	0	167	7	1.0	0.9	0.7	3.5
Bob Quick (to DalA)	F	6'5	215	25	18	204	39	82	48	34	45	76	51	11	29	0	112	11	2.8	0.6	1.6	6.2
Steve Mix (to DenA)	F	6'7	215	24	8	104	15	47	32	7	12	58	23	4	7	0	37	13	2.9	0.5	0.9	4.6

Use Name	Pos	Hgt	Wgt	Age	G	Min	FG	FGA	%	FT	FTA	%	Reb	Ass	PF	DQ	Points	Min	Reb	Ass	PF	Points
					TOTAL													PER GAME				
1971/72 N.B.A. — PACIFIC DIVISION																						
LOS ANGELES LAKERS	69-13 .841				BILL SHARMAN																	
Jim McMillian	F	6'5	225	23	80	3050	642	1331	48	219	277	79	522	209	209	0	1503	38	6.5	2.6	2.6	18.8
Happy Hairston	F	6'7	225	29	80	2748	368	798	46	311	399	78	1045	193	251	2	1047	34	13.1	2.4	3.1	13.1
Wilt Chamberlain	C	7'1	275	35	82	3469	496	764	**65**	221	524	42	**1572**	329	196	0	1213	42	**19.2**	4.0	2.4	14.8
Jerry West	G	6'3	185	33	77	2973	735	1540	48	515	633	81	327	747	209	0	1985	39	4.2	**9.7**	2.7	25.8
Gail Goodrich	G	6'1	175	28	82	3040	826	1695	49	475	559	85	295	365	210	0	2127	37	3.6	4.5	2.6	25.9
Leroy Ellis	F-C	6'10	225	31	74	1081	138	300	46	66	95	69	310	46	115	0	342	15	4.2	0.6	1.6	4.6
Flynn Robinson	G	6'1	190	30	64	1007	262	535	49	111	129	86	115	138	139	2	635	16	1.8	2.2	2.2	9.9
Pat Riley	G-F	6'4	208	26	67	926	197	441	45	55	74	74	127	75	110	0	449	14	1.9	1.1	1.6	6.7
John Trapp	F	6'7	215	26	58	759	139	314	44	51	73	70	180	42	130	3	329	13	3.1	0.7	2.2	5.7
Keith Erickson (injury)	G	6'5	200	27	15	262	40	83	48	6	7	86	39	35	26	0	86	17	2.6	2.3	1.7	5.7
Elgin Baylor (knee injury)	F	6'5	225	37	9	239	42	97	43	22	27	81	57	18	20	0	106	27	6.3	2.0	2.2	11.8
Jim Cleamons	G	6'3	185	22	38	201	35	100	35	28	36	78	39	35	21	0	98	5	1.0	0.9	0.6	2.6
GOLDEN STATE WARRIORS	51-31 .622				AL ATTLES																	
Cazzie Russell	F-G	6'5	220	27	79	2902	689	1514	46	315	378	83	428	248	176	0	1693	37	5.4	3.1	2.2	21.4
Clyde Lee	F-C	6'10	230	27	78	2674	256	544	47	120	222	54	1132	85	244	4	632	34	14.5	1.1	3.1	8.1
Nate Thurmond	C	6'11	235	30	78	3362	628	1454	43	417	561	74	1252	230	214	1	1673	43	16.1	2.9	2.7	21.4
Jeff Mullins	G	6'4	200	29	80	3214	685	1466	47	350	441	79	444	471	260	5	1720	40	5.6	5.9	3.3	21.5
Jim Barnett	G	6'4	180	27	80	2200	374	915	41	244	292	84	250	309	189	0	992	28	3.1	3.9	2.4	12.4
Ron Williams	G	6'3	190	27	80	1932	291	614	47	195	234	83	147	308	232	1	777	24	1.8	3.9	2.9	9.7
Joe Ellis	F	6'6	175	27	78	1462	280	681	41	95	132	72	389	97	224	4	655	19	5.0	1.2	2.9	8.4
Bill Turner	F	6'7	225	27	62	597	71	181	39	40	53	75	131	22	67	1	182	10	2.1	0.4	1.1	2.9
Bob Portman	F	6'5	200	24	61	553	89	221	40	53	60	88	133	26	69	0	231	9	2.2	0.4	1.1	3.8
Nick Jones	G	6'2	190	27	65	478	82	196	42	51	61	84	39	45	109	0	215	7	0.6	0.7	1.7	3.3
Odis Allison	F	6'6	195	22	36	166	17	78	22	33	61	54	45	10	34	0	67	5	1.3	0.3	0.9	1.9
Vic Bartolome	C	7'	230	23	38	165	15	59	25	4	5	80	60	3	22	0	34	4	1.6	0.1	0.6	0.9
SEATTLE SUPERSONICS	47-35 .573				LENNY WILKENS																	
Don Kojis	F	6'5	215	32	73	1857	322	687	47	188	237	79	335	82	168	1	832	25	4.6	1.1	2.3	11.4
Spencer Haywood	F-C	6'8	225	22	73	3167	717	1557	46	480	586	82	926	148	208	0	1914	43	12.7	2.0	2.8	26.2
Don Smith (illness)	C	6'9	235	25	58	1780	322	751	43	154	214	72	654	124	178	1	798	31	11.3	2.1	3.1	13.8
Dick Snyder	G-F	6'5	210	27	73	2534	496	937	53	218	259	84	228	283	200	3	1210	35	3.1	3.9	2.7	16.6
Lenny Wilkens	G	6'1	185	34	80	2989	479	1027	47	480	620	77	338	766	209	4	1438	37	4.2	9.6	2.6	18.0
Lee Winfield	G	6'2	175	24	81	2040	343	692	50	175	262	67	218	290	198	1	861	25	2.7	3.6	2.4	10.6
Gar Heard	F	6'6	220	23	58	1499	190	474	40	79	128	62	442	55	126	2	459	26	7.6	0.9	2.2	7.9
Barry Clemens	F	6'7	220	29	82	1447	252	484	52	76	90	84	288	64	198	4	580	18	3.5	0.8	2.4	7.1
Pete Cross	C	6'9	230	23	74	1424	152	355	43	103	140	74	509	63	135	2	407	19	6.9	0.9	1.8	5.5
Fred Brown	G	6'3	185	23	33	359	59	180	33	22	29	76	37	60	44	0	140	11	1.1	1.8	1.3	4.2
Bob Rule (to Phi)	C-F	6'9	235	27	16	243	45	124	36	23	43	53	55	6	27	0	113	15	3.4	0.4	1.7	7.1
Jim McDaniels (from CarA)	C	6'11	225	23	12	235	51	123	41	11	18	61	82	9	26	0	113	20	6.8	0.8	2.2	9.4
Jake Ford	G	6'3	180	25	26	181	33	66	50	26	33	79	11	26	21	0	92	7	0.4	1.0	0.8	3.5
HOUSTON ROCKETS	38-48 .415				TEX WINTER																	
Greg Smith (from Mil)	F	6'5	200	24	54	1519	212	473	45	70	110	64	322	159	167	3	494	28	6.0	2.9	3.1	9.1
Rudy Tomjanovich	F	6'8	220	23	78	2689	500	1010	50	172	238	72	923	117	193	2	1172	34	11.8	1.5	2.5	15.0
Elvin Hayes	C-F	6'9	235	26	82	3461	832	1918	43	399	615	65	1197	270	233	1	2063	42	14.6	3.3	2.8	25.2
Stu Lantz	G	6'13	175	25	81	3097	557	1279	44	387	462	84	345	337	211	2	1501	38	4.3	4.2	2.6	18.5
Calvin Murphy	G	5'9	165	23	82	2538	571	1255	45	349	392	89	258	393	298	6	1491	31	3.1	4.8	3.6	18.2
Cliff Meeley	F	6'8	215	24	77	1815	315	776	41	133	197	68	507	119	254	9	763	24	6.6	1.5	3.3	9.9
Mike Newlin	G-F	6'4	200	22	82	1495	256	618	41	108	144	75	228	135	233	6	620	18	2.8	1.6	2.8	7.6
Dick Gibbs	F	6'5	210	23	64	757	90	265	34	55	66	83	140	51	127	0	235	12	2.2	0.8	2.0	3.7
Dick Cunningham	C	6'10	252	25	63	720	67	174	39	37	53	70	243	57	76	0	171	11	3.9	0.9	1.2	2.7
Johnny Egan	G	5'11	180	32	38	437	42	104	40	26	32	81	26	51	55	0	110	12	0.7	1.3	1.4	2.9
Curtis Perry (to Mil)	F	6'7	220	23	25	355	38	115	33	12	24	50	122	22	47	1	88	14	4.9	0.9	1.9	3.5
John Vallely (from Atl)	G	6'3	185	23	40	256	49	128	38	17	25	68	21	28	37	0	115	6	0.5	0.7	0.9	2.9
Larry Siegfried (to Atl)	G	6'3	192	32	10	223	18	46	39	12	14	86	10	20	21	0	48	22	1.0	2.0	2.1	4.8
Jim Davis (from Atl-to Det)	C-F	6'9	235	30	12	180	18	54	33	26	38	68	44	5	18	0	62	15	3.7	0.4	1.5	5.2
McCoy McLemore (from Mil)	F	6'7	235	29	17	147	19	43	44	9	12	75	39	10	15	1	47	9	2.3	0.6	0.9	2.8
Don Adams (to Atl)	F	6'7	210	24	3	41	6	19	32	1	2	50	8	3	7	1	13	14	2.7	1.0	2.3	4.3
PORTLAND TRAIL BLAZERS	18-64 .220				ROLLAND TODD (12-44 .214), STU INMAN (6-20 .231)																	
Gary Gregor	F	6'7	225	26	82	2371	399	884	45	114	151	75	591	187	201	2	912	29	7.2	2.3	2.5	11.1
Sidney Wicks	F	6'8	225	22	82	3245	784	1837	43	441	621	71	943	350	186	1	2009	40	11.5	4.3	2.3	24.5
Dale Schlueter	C	6'10	235	26	81	2693	353	672	53	241	326	74	860	285	277	3	947	33	10.6	3.5	3.4	11.7
Geoff Petrie (knee injury)	G	6'4	200	23	60	2155	465	1115	42	202	256	79	133	248	108	0	1132	36	2.2	4.1	1.8	18.9
Rick Adelman	G	6'1	180	25	80	2445	329	753	44	151	201	75	229	413	209	2	809	31	2.9	5.2	2.6	10.1
Stan McKenzie	F-G	6'5	210	27	82	2036	410	834	49	315	379	83	272	148	240	2	1135	25	3.3	1.8	2.9	13.8
Larry Steele	G-F	6'5	180	22	72	1311	148	308	48	70	97	72	282	161	198	8	366	18	3.9	2.2	2.8	5.1
Charlie Yelverton	G-F	6'2	190	23	69	1227	206	530	39	133	188	71	201	81	145	2	545	18	2.9	1.2	2.1	7.9
Willie McCarter	G	6'3	175	25	39	612	103	257	40	37	55	67	43	85	58	0	243	16	1.1	2.2	1.5	6.2
Ron Knight	C-F	6'7	228	24	49	483	112	257	44	31	62	50	116	33	52	0	255	10	2.4	0.7	1.1	5.2
Bill Smith (knee injury)	C	7'	220	22	22	448	72	173	42	38	64	59	135	19	73	3	182	20	6.1	0.9	3.3	8.3
Darrall Imhoff (from Cin)	C	6'10	235	33	40	404	42	103	41	21	35	60	107	50	76	1	105	10	2.7	1.3	1.9	2.6
Jim Marsh	F	6'7	215	25	39	375	39	117	33	41	59	69	84	30	50	0	119	10	2.2	0.8	1.3	3.1

1971/72 NB.A. — PLAYOFFS

LOS ANGELES LAKERS — **BILL SHARMAN**

defeated Chicago 4-0; H95-80, H131-124, 108-101 108-97
defeated Milwaukee 4-2; H72-93, H135-134,108-105, 88-114, H115-90, 104-100
defeated New York 4-1; H92-114, H106-92, 107-96,116-111(OT), H114-100

Use Name	Pos	Hgt	Wgt	Age	G	Min	FG	FGA	%	FT	FTA	%	Reb	Ass	PF	DQ	Points	Min/G	Reb/G	Ass/G	PF/G	Points/G
Jim McMillian	F	6'5	225	23	15	624	113	253	45	60	70	86	85	22	43	0	286	42	5.7	1.5	2.9	19.1
Happy Hairston	F	6'7	225	29	15	577	74	168	44	54	68	79	197	31	44	1	202	38	13.1	2.1	2.9	13.5
Wilt Chamberlain	C	7'1	275	35	15	703	80	142	56	60	122	49	**315**	49	47	0	220	**47**	**21.0**	3.3	3.1	14.7
Jerry West	G	6'3	185	33	15	608	128	**340**	38	88	106	83	73	**134**	39	0	344	41	4.9	**8.9**	2.6	22.9
Gail Goodrich	G	6'1	175	28	15	575	130	292	45	**97**	108	**90**	38	50	50	0	357	38	2.5	3.3	3.3	23.8
Pat Riley	G-F	6'4	208	26	15	244	33	99	33	12	16	75	29	14	37	0	78	16	1.9	0.9	2.5	5.2
Leroy Ellis	F-C	6'10	225	31	13	134	19	41	46	1	4	25	41	10	9	0	39	10	3.2	0.8	0.7	3.0
Flynn Robinson	G	6'1	190	30	7	72	19	41	46	7	10	70	13	5	13	0	45	10	1.9	0.7	1.9	6.4
John Trapp	F	6'7	215	26	10	71	8	33	24	4	7	57	16	5	9	0	20	7	1.6	0.5	0.9	2.0
Jim Cleamons	G	6'3	185	22	6	17	4	7	57	0	0	—	4	4	3	0	8	3	0.7	0.7	0.5	1.3

NEW YORK KNICKERBOCKERS — **RED HOLZMAN**

defeated Baltimore 4-2; 105-108(OT), H110-88, 103-104, H104-98, 106-82, H107-101
defeated Boston 4-1; 116-94, H106-105, 109-115, H116-98, 111-103
lost to Los Angeles 1-4; 114-92, 92-106, H96-107, H111-116(OT), 100-114

Use Name	Pos	Hgt	Wgt	Age	G	Min	FG	FGA	%	FT	FTA	%	Reb	Ass	PF	DQ	Points	Min/G	Reb/G	Ass/G	PF/G	Points/G
Bill Bradley	F	6'5	210	28	16	594	106	227	47	47	56	84	47	54	**66**	1	259	37	2.9	3.4	4.1	16.2
Dave DeBusschere	F	6'6	235	31	16	616	109	242	45	48	64	75	193	37	51	2	266	39	12.1	2.3	3.2	16.6
Jerry Lucas	C-F	6'8	230	31	16	**737**	119	238	50	59	71	83	173	85	49	1	297	46	10.8	5.3	3.1	18.6
Walt Frazier	G	6'4	205	26	16	704	**148**	276	54	92	**125**	74	112	98	48	0	**388**	44	7.0	6.1	3.0	24.3
Earl Monroe	G	6'3	190	27	16	429	76	185	41	45	57	79	45	47	41	0	197	27	2.8	2.9	2.6	12.3
Phil Jackson	F-C	6'8	225	26	16	320	57	120	48	42	57	74	82	15	51	1	156	20	5.1	0.9	3.2	9.8
Dean Meminger	G	6'	175	23	16	277	24	57	42	17	27	63	43	20	37	0	65	17	2.7	1.3	2.3	4.1
Dick Barnett	G	6'4	190	35	12	131	23	49	47	5	12	42	8	10	19	0	51	11	0.7	0.8	1.6	4.3
Luther Rackley	C	6'10	225	25	11	29	2	14	14	4	4	100	7	1	7	0	8	3	0.6	0.1	0.6	0.7
Eddie Mast	F	6'9	220	23	9	23	4	7	57	1	5	20	7	1	4	0	9	3	0.8	0.1	0.4	1.0
Eddie Miles	G-F	6'4	196	31	9	17	0	6	0	4	5	80	8	1	2	0	4	2	0.9	0.1	0.2	0.4
Charlie Paulk	F	6'8	220	27	7	13	3	10	30	0	0	—	5	0	5	0	6	2	0.7	0.0	0.7	0.9
Willis Reed (knee injury)																						

MILWAUKEE BUCKS — **LARRY COSTELLO**

defeated Golden State 4-1; H106-117, H118-93, 122-94, 106-99, H108-100
lost to Los Angeles 2-4; 93-72,134-135, H105-108, H114-88, 90-115, H100-104

Use Name	Pos	Hgt	Wgt	Age	G	Min	FG	FGA	%	FT	FTA	%	Reb	Ass	PF	DQ	Points	Min/G	Reb/G	Ass/G	PF/G	Points/G
Bob Dandridge	F	6'6	195	24	11	441	100	202	50	37	50	74	97	21	47	1	237	40	8.8	1.9	4.3	21.5
Curtis Perry	F	6'7	220	23	11	397	43	91	47	18	23	78	141	14	45	2	104	36	12.8	1.3	4.1	9.5
Kareem Abdul-Jabbar	C	7'2	232	24	11	510	139	318	44	38	54	70	200	56	35	0	316	46	18.2	5.1	3.2	**28.7**
Oscar Robertson	G-F	6'5	220	33	11	380	57	140	41	30	36	83	64	83	29	0	144	35	5.8	7.5	2.6	13.1
Lucius Allen	G	6'2	175	24	11	386	78	166	47	41	54	76	38	42	30	0	147	35	3.5	3.8	2.7	13.4
Wally Jones	G	6'2	185	29	9	200	36	82	44	18	21	86	18	20	27	1	90	22	2.0	2.2	3.0	10.0
John Block	F-C	6'10	220	27	11	156	20	52	38	15	18	83	55	6	15	0	55	14	5.0	0.5	1.4	5.0
Jon McGlocklin	G	6'5	205	28	5	103	15	35	43	5	6	83	3	6	11	0	35	21	0.6	1.2	2.2	7.0
Toby Kimball	F	6'8	230	29	7	36	5	12	42	2	2	100	6	2	3	0	12	5	0.9	0.3	0.4	1.7
Charlie Lowery	G	6'3	185	22	7	26	2	8	25	2	3	67	3	1	4	0	6	4	0.4	0.1	0.6	0.9
Barry Nelson	C	6'10	230	22	2	5	0	0	—	0	0	—	1	1	1	0	0	3	0.5	0.5	0.5	0.0

BOSTON CELTICS — **TOM HEINSOHN**

defeated Atlanta 4-2; H126-108, 104-113, H136-113, 110-112, H124-114, 127-118
lost to New York 1-4; H94-116, 105-106, H115-109, 98-116, H103-111

Use Name	Pos	Hgt	Wgt	Age	G	Min	FG	FGA	%	FT	FTA	%	Reb	Ass	PF	DQ	Points	Min/G	Reb/G	Ass/G	PF/G	Points/G
John Havlicek	F-G	6'5	205	31	11	517	108	235	46	85	99	86	92	70	35	1	301	47	8.4	6.4	3.2	27.4
Don Nelson	F	6'6	210	31	11	308	52	99	53	41	48	85	61	21	30	0	145	28	5.5	1.9	2.7	13.2
Dave Cowens	C	6'9	230	23	11	441	71	156	46	28	47	60	152	33	50	2	170	40	13.8	3.0	**4.5**	15.5
Don Chaney	G	6'5	210	25	11	271	41	81	51	15	20	75	39	22	39	0	97	25	3.5	2.0	3.5	8.8
Jo Jo White	G	6'3	190	25	11	432	109	220	50	40	48	83	59	58	31	0	258	39	5.4	5.3	2.8	23.5
Steve Kuberski	F-C	6'8	215	24	11	218	48	87	55	32	38	84	63	3	23	0	128	20	5.7	0.3	2.1	11.6
Satch Sanders	F	6'6	210	33	11	186	17	53	32	13	21	62	26	10	36	0	47	17	2.4	0.9	3.3	4.3
Hambone Williams	G	6'2	190	32	11	173	25	64	39	15	20	75	28	33	30	0	65	16	2.5	3.0	2.7	5.9
Henry Finkel	C	7'	240	29	8	68	10	22	45	0	0	—	24	3	11	0	20	9	3.0	0.4	1.4	2.5
Clarence Glover	F	6'8	210	24	3	10	2	6	33	2	2	100	3	0	1	0	6	3	1.0	0.0	0.3	2.0
Rex Morgan	G	6'5	190	23	4	10	1	7	14	1	3	33	5	0	6	0	3	3	1.3	0.0	1.5	0.8
Garfield Smith	C	6'9	235	26	4	6	1	5	20	0	3	0	1	0	1	0	2	2	0.3	0.0	0.3	0.5

1971/72 N.B.A. — PLAYOFFS (continued)

Use Name	Pos	Hgt	Wgt	Age	TOTAL													PER GAME				
					G	Min	FG	FGA	%	FT	FTA	%	Reb	Ass	PF	DQ	Points	Min	Reb	Ass	PF	Points
ATLANTA HAWKS	**RICHIE GUERIN**				lost to Boston 2-4; 108-126, H113-104, 113-136, H112-110, 114-124, H118-127																	
Don Adams	F	6'7	210	24	6	188	20	56	36	16	23	70	38	12	25	1	56	31	6.3	2.0	4.2	9.3
Jim Washington	F-C	6'7	215	28	6	209	28	58	48	9	16	56	48	10	20	0	65	35	8.0	1.7	3.3	10.8
Walt Bellamy	C	6'11	245	32	6	247	42	86	49	27	43	63	82	11	20	0	111	41	13.7	1.8	3.3	18.5
Lou Hudson	G-F	6'5	210	27	6	266	63	139	45	24	29	83	33	21	13	0	150	44	5.5	3.5	2.2	25.0
Pete Maravich	G	6'5	190	23	6	219	54	121	45	58	71	82	32	28	24	0	166	37	5.3	4.7	4.0	27.7
Herm Gilliam	G	6'3	190	25	6	173	28	71	39	10	11	91	30	33	15	0	66	29	5.0	5.5	2.5	11.0
George Trapp	F	6'8	215	23	6	66	19	44	43	3	8	38	18	5	13	0	41	11	3.0	0.8	2.2	6.8
Bob Christian	C	7'	260	27	6	34	3	8	38	1	1	100	7	0	10	0	7	6	1.2	0.0	1.7	1.2
Don May	F	6'4	215	25	3	31	3	9	33	6	8	75	8	1	3	0	12	10	2.7	0.3	1.0	4.0
Tom Payne	C	7'2	240	21	1	5	1	1	100	2	5	40	4	0	1	0	4	5	4.0	0.0	1.0	4.0
Jeff Halliburton	G	6'5	190	22	1	2	0	1	0	0	0	—	0	0	0	0	0	2	0.0	0.0	0.0	0.0
BALTIMORE BULLETS	**GENE SHUE**				lost to New York 2-3; H108-105(OT), 88-110, H104-103, 98-104, H82-106, 101-107																	
Dave Stallworth	F	6'7	210	30	6	105	12	28	43	9	13	69	15	5	14	0	33	18	2.5	0.8	2.3	5.5
Jack Marin	F	6'7	210	27	6	229	31	78	40	41	47	87	36	12	22	1	103	38	6.0	2.0	3.7	17.2
Wes Unseld	C	6'7	250	25	6	266	32	65	49	10	19	53	75	25	22	0	74	44	12.5	4.2	3.7	12.3
Phil Chenier	G	6'3	180	21	6	153	22	59	37	10	12	83	16	5	16	0	54	26	2.7	0.8	2.7	9.0
Archie Clark	G	6'2	175	30	6	271	55	126	44	50	59	85	24	47	15	0	160	45	4.0	7.8	2.5	26.7
John Tresvant	F-C	6'7	220	32	6	180	20	48	42	7	11	64	58	6	23	1	47	30	9.7	1.0	3.8	7.8
Mike Riordan	G-F	6'4	200	26	6	161	33	57	58	17	21	81	15	11	18	0	83	27	2.5	1.8	3.0	13.8
Gus Johnson	F	6'6	235	33	5	77	9	30	30	2	2	100	25	3	17	0	20	15	5.0	0.6	3.4	4.0
Stan Love	F	6'9	215	22	4	14	1	4	25	0	0	—	6	1	3	0	2	4	1.5	0.3	0.8	0.5
Rich Rinaldi	G	6'3	195	22	3	6	1	2	50	0	0	—	0	1	3	0	2	2	0.0	0.3	1.0	0.7
Terry Driscoll	F	6'7	215	24	1	2	1	1	100	1	1	100	1	0	0	0	3	2	1.0	0.0	0.0	3.0
Dorie Murrey	F	6'8	220	28	1	1	0	0	—	0	0	—	0	0	0	0	0	1	0.0	0.0	0.0	0.0
GOLDEN STATE WARRIORS	**AL ATTLES**				lost to Milwaukee 1-4; 117-106, 93-118, H94-122, H99-106, 100-108																	
Cazzie Russell	F	6'5	220	27	5	161	31	63	49	9	12	75	22	9	13	0	71	32	4.4	1.8	2.6	14.2
Clyde Lee	F-C	6'10	230	27	5	175	8	28	29	8	12	67	64	7	14	0	24	35	12.8	1.4	2.8	4.8
Nate Thurmond	C	6'11	235	30	5	230	53	122	43	21	28	75	89	26	12	0	127	46	17.8	5.2	2.4	25.4
Jeff Mullins	G-F	6'4	200	29	5	203	31	72	43	12	13	92	24	29	11	0	74	41	4.8	5.8	2.2	14.8
Jim Barnett	G	6'4	180	27	5	197	39	91	43	30	41	73	20	26	20	0	108	39	4.0	5.2	4.0	21.6
Joe Ellis	F	6'6	175	27	5	113	21	63	33	12	17	71	21	4	9	0	54	23	4.2	0.8	1.8	10.8
Ron Williams	G	6'3	190	27	5	83	9	31	29	14	15	93	8	10	12	0	32	17	1.6	2.0	2.4	6.4
Bob Portman	F	6'5	200	24	3	22	2	12	17	1	1	100	5	0	5	0	5	7	1.7	0.0	1.7	1.7
Bill Turner	F	6'7	225	27	3	9	2	2	100	0	0	—	3	0	0	0	4	3	1.0	0.0	0.0	1.3
Nick Jones	G	6'2	190	27	2	7	1	2	50	2	2	100	0	2	0	0	4	4	0.0	1.0	0.0	2.0
CHICAGO BULLS	**DICK MOTTA**				lost to Los Angeles 0-4; 80-95,124-131, H101-108, H97-108																	
Chet Walker	F	6'6	220	31	4	97	16	38	42	13	16	81	14	4	7	0	45	24	3.5	1.0	1.8	11.3
Bob Love	F	6'8	215	29	4	173	32	89	36	11	13	85	27	7	17	0	75	43	6.8	1.8	4.3	18.8
Cliff Ray	C	6'9	235	22	4	161	27	51	53	7	9	78	66	16	15	0	61	40	16.5	4.0	3.8	15.3
Bob Weiss	G	6'2	185	29	4	119	24	49	49	7	8	88	13	12	15	1	55	30	3.3	3.0	3.8	13.8
Norm Van Lier	G	6'1	175	24	4	144	22	53	42	12	14	86	25	33	15	0	56	36	6.3	8.3	3.8	14.0
Jerry Sloan	G-F	6'6	200	29	4	170	26	64	41	11	19	58	35	10	18	1	63	43	8.8	2.5	4.5	15.8
Jim King	G	6'2	175	30	4	56	11	24	46	4	4	100	6	5	11	0	26	14	1.5	1.3	2.8	6.5
Howard Porter	F-C	6'8	220	23	4	31	9	21	43	1	1	100	11	3	3	0	19	8	2.8	0.8	0.8	4.8
Tom Boerwinkle	C	7'	270	26	1	8	0	3	0	0	0	—	6	3	0	0	0	8	6.0	3.0	0.0	0.0
Jackie Dinkins	F	6'5	210	21	1	1	1	1	100	0	0	—	0	0	0	0	2	1	0.0	0.0	0.0	2.0

Team	W	L	Pct.	GB	Record against playoff teams W	L	Pct.	Record against non - playoff teams W	L	Pct.	HOME W	L	Pct.	ROAD W	L	Pct.	NEUTRAL W	L	Pct.
ATLANTIC DIVISION																			
Boston Celtics	56	26	.683	—	17	17	.500	39	7	.848	32	9	.780	21	16	.568	3	1	.750
New York Knickerbockers	48	34	.585	8	17	19	.472	31	15	.674	27	14	.659	20	19	.513	1	1	.500
Philadelphia 76ers	30	52	.366	26	9	33	.214	21	19	.525	14	23	.378	14	26	.350	2	3	.400
Buffalo Braves	22	60	.268	34	8	32	.200	14	28	.333	13	27	.325	8	31	.205	1	2	.333
CENTRAL DIVISION																			
Baltimore Bullets	38	44	.463	—	11	25	.306	27	19	.587	18	15	.545	16	24	.400	4	5	.444
Atlanta Hawks	36	46	.439	2	10	24	.294	26	22	.542	22	19	.537	13	26	.333	1	1	.500
Cincinnati Royals	30	52	.366	8	13	28	.317	17	24	.415	20	18	.526	8	32	.200	2	2	.500
Cleveland Cavaliers	23	59	.280	15	10	30	.250	13	29	.310	13	28	.317	8	30	.211	2	1	.667
MIDWEST DIVISION																			
Milwaukee Bucks	63	19	.768	—	20	15	.571	43	4	.915	31	5	.861	27	12	.692	5	2	.714
Chicago Bulls	57	25	.695	6	20	16	.556	37	9	.804	29	12	.707	26	12	.684	2	1	.667
Phoenix Suns	49	33	.598	14	18	25	.419	31	8	.795	30	11	.732	19	20	.487	0	2	.000
Detroit Pistons	26	56	.317	37	8	34	.190	18	22	.450	16	25	.390	9	30	.231	1	1	.500
PACIFIC DIVISION																			
Los Angeles Lakers	69	13	.841	—	29	6	.829	40	7	.851	36	5	.878	31	7	.816	2	1	.667
Golden State Warriors	51	31	.622	18	17	19	.472	34	12	.739	27	8	.771	21	20	.512	3	3	.500
Seattle Supersonics	47	35	.573	22	18	25	.419	29	10	.744	28	12	.700	18	22	.450	1	1	.500
Houston Rockets	34	48	.415	35	9	34	.209	25	14	.641	15	20	.429	14	23	.378	5	5	.500
Portland Trail Blazers	18	64	.220	51	4	36	.100	14	28	.333	14	26	.350	4	35	.103	0	3	.000

1971/72 N.B.A. INDIVIDUAL LEADERS

SCORING
(Minimum 70 Games Played)

Name	Team	G	FG	FT	Pts.	Avg.
Abdul-Jabbar	Mil	81	1159	504	2822	34.8
Archibald	Cin	76	734	677	2145	28.2
Havlicek	Bos	82	897	458	2252	27.5
Haywood	Sea	73	717	480	1914	26.2
Goodrich	LA	82	826	475	2127	25.9
Love	Chi	79	819	399	2037	25.8
West	LA	77	735	515	1985	25.8
Lanier	Det	80	834	388	2056	25.7
Clark	Phi-Bal	77	712	514	1938	25.2
Hayes	Hou	82	832	399	2063	25.2

FIELD GOAL PERCENTAGE
(Minimum 700 Attempts)

Name	Team	FG	FGA	Pct.
Chamberlain	LA	496	764	.649
Abdul-Jabbar	Mil	1159	2019	.574
Bellamy	Atl	593	1089	.545
Snyder	Sea	496	937	.529
Lucas	NY	543	1060	.512
Frazier	NY	669	1307	.512
McGlockin	Mil	374	733	.510
Walker	Chi	619	1225	.505
Allen	Mil	441	874	.505
Hudson	Atl	775	1540	.503

FREE THROW PERCENTAGE
(Minimum 350 Attempts)

Name	Team	FT	FTA	Pct.
Marin	Bal	356	398	.894
Murphy	Hou	349	392	.890
Goodrich	LA	475	559	.850
Walker	Chi	481	568	.847
Van Arsdale	Phoe	529	626	.845
Lantz	Hou	387	462	.838
Havlicek	Bos	458	549	.834
Russell	GS	315	378	.833
McKenzie	Port	315	379	.831
Walker	Det	397	480	.827

PERSONAL FOULS

Name	Team	PF
Cowens	Bos	314
Sloan	Chi	309
E. Smith	Buf	306
Williams	Cin	300
Murphy	Hou	298

GAMES DISQUALIFIED

Name	Team	Disq
Perry	Hou-Mil	14
Cunningham	Phi	12
Williams	Cin	11
Cowens	Bos	10
Greer	Phi	10
E. Smith	Buf	10

REBOUNDS PER GAME
(Minimum 70 Games Played)

Name	Team	G	Reb.	Avg.
Chamberlain	LA	82	1572	19.2
Unseld	Bal	76	1336	17.6
Abdul-Jabbar	Mil	81	1346	16.6
Thurmond	GS	78	1252	16.1
Cowens	Bos	79	1203	15.2
E. Smith	Buf	78	1184	15.2
Hayes	Hou	82	1197	14.6
Lee	GS	78	1132	14.5
Lanier	Det	80	1132	14.2
Bridges	Atl-Phi	78	1051	13.5

ASSISTS PER GAME
(Minimum 70 Games Played)

Name	Team	G	Ass.	Avg.
West	LA	77	747	9.7
Wilkens	Sea	80	766	9.6
Archibald	Cin	76	701	9.2
Clark	Phi-Bal	77	613	8.0
Havlicek	Bos	82	614	7.5
Van Lier	Chi	79	542	6.9
Cunningham	Phi	75	443	5.9
Mullins	GS	80	471	5.9
Frazier	NY	77	446	5.8
Hauard	Buf	72	406	5.6

MINUTES PLAYED

Name	Team	Min.
Havlicek	Bos	3698
Abdul-Jabbar	Mil	3583
Chamberlain	LA	3469
Hayes	Hou	3461
Thurmond	GS	3362

TEAM STATISTICS

Team		REGULAR SEASON												PLAYOFFS											
		G	FG	FGA	%	FT	FTA	%	Reb	Ass	PF	Points	PPG	G	FG	FGA	%	FT	FTA	%	Reb	Ass	PF	Points	PPG
ATLANTIC DIVISION																									
Boston	Off.	82	3819	8431	45	1839	2367	78	4462	2230	2030	9477	115.6	11	485	1035	47	272	349	78	553	253	293	1242	112.9
	Def.	82	3498	7886	44	2089	2766	76	4179	1798	1842	9085	110.8	11	463	1015	46	310	413	75	531	237	268	1236	112.4
	Diff.		+321	+545	+1	-250	-399	+2	+283	+432	-188	+392	+4.8		+22	+20	+1	-38	-64	+3	+22	+16	-25	+6	+1
New York	Off.	82	3521	7673	46	1743	2303	76	3909	1985	1899	8785	107.1	16	671	1431	47	364	483	75	730	369	380	1706	106.6
	Def.	82	3332	7513	44	1920	2565	75	4169	1626	1892	8584	104.7	16	613	1444	42	405	525	77	783	315	390	1631	101.9
	Diff.		+189	+160	+2	-177	-262	+1	-260	+359	-7	+201	+2.4		+58	-13	+5	-41	-42	-2	-53	+54	+10	+75	+4.7
Philadelphia	Off.	82	3577	8057	44	2049	2825	73	4318	1920	2203	9203	112.2												
	Def.	82	3614	7882	46	2276	3063	74	4427	2005	2059	9504	115.9												
	Diff.		-37	+175	-2	-227	-238	-1	-109	-85	-144	-301	-3.7												
Buffalo	Off.	82	3409	7560	45	1549	2219	70	3978	1759	2110	8367	102.0												
	Def.	82	3479	7557	46	2167	2842	76	4187	1918	1728	9125	111.3												
	Diff.		-70	+3	-1	-618	-623	-6	-209	-159	-382	-758	-9.2												
CENTRAL DIVISION																									
Baltimore	Off.	82	3490	7748	45	1804	2378	76	4159	1816	1858	8784	107.1	6	217	498	44	147	185	79	271	116	153	581	96.8
	Def.	82	3545	7842	45	1790	2412	74	4244	1844	1869	8880	108.3	6	253	550	46	129	168	77	263	126	134	635	105.8
	Diff.		-55	-94	—	+14	-34	+2	-85	-28	+11	-96	-1.2		-36	-52	-2	+18	+17	+2	+8	-10	-19	-54	-9.0
Atlanta	Off.	82	3482	7570	46	2018	2725	74	4080	1897	1967	8982	109.5	6	261	594	44	156	215	73	300	121	144	678	113.0
	Def.	82	3601	7744	47	1925	2530	76	4004	1890	1996	9127	111.3	6	293	574	51	141	173	82	320	151	162	727	121.2
	Diff.		-119	-174	-1	+93	+195	-2	+76	+7	+29	-145	-1.8		-32	+20	-7	+15	+42	-9	-20	-30	+18	-49	-8.2
Cincinnati	Off.	82	3444	7496	46	1948	2578	76	3754	2020	2079	8836	107.8												
	Def.	82	3537	7588	47	2093	2829	74	4228	2028	1971	9167	111.8												
	Diff.		-93	-92	-1	-145	-251	+2	-474	-8	-108	-331	-4.0												
Cleveland	Off.	82	3458	8074	43	1758	2390	74	4098	2060	1936	8674	105.8												
	Def.	82	3653	7537	48	1994	2611	76	4034	2322	1937	9300	113.4												
	Diff.		-195	+537	-5	####	-221	-2	+64	-262	+1	-626	-7.6												
MIDWEST DIVISION																									
Milwaukee	Off.	82	3813	7653	50	1774	2399	74	4269	2160	1862	9400	114.6	11	495	1106	45	206	267	77	626	252	247	1196	108.7
	Def.	82	3370	8025	42	1745	2358	74	3922	1843	1788	8485	103.5	11	433	1069	41	259	360	72	589	244	204	1125	102.3
	Diff.		+443	-372	+8	+29	+41		+347	+317	-74	+915	+11.2		+62	+37	+4	-53	-93	+5	+37	+8	-43	+71	+6.5
Chicago	Off.	82	3539	7853	45	2039	2700	76	4371	2087	1964	9117	111.2	4	168	393	43	66	84	79	203	93	101	402	100.5
	Def.	82	3263	7189	45	1914	2617	73	3928	1853	2041	8440	102.9	4	168	348	48	106	128	83	199	96	80	442	110.5
	Diff.		+276	+664	—	+125	+83	+3	+443	+234	+77	+677	+8.3			+45	-5	-40	-44	-4	+4	-3	-21	-40	-10.0
Phoenix	Off.	82	3599	7877	46	2336	2999	78	4301	1976	2026	9534	116.3												
	Def.	82	3568	7896	45	1947	2658	73	4009	1929	2182	9083	110.8												
	Diff.		+31	-19	+1	+389	+341	+5	+292	+47	+156	+451	+5.5												
Detroit	Off.	82	3482	7665	45	1981	2653	75	3970	1687	1954	8945	109.1												
	Def.	82	3822	8106	47	1862	2474	75	4377	2214	1931	9506	115.9												
	Diff.		-340	-441	-2	+119	+179	—	-407	-527	-23	-561	-6.8												
PACIFIC DIVISION																									
Los Angeles	Off.	82	3920	7998	49	2080	2833	73	4628	2232	1636	9920	121.0	15	608	1416	43	383	511	75	811	324	294	1599	106.6
	Def.	82	3699	8553	43	1515	1972	77	4290	1994	1997	8913	108.7	15	652	1467	44	247	333	74	797	347	370	1551	103.4
	Diff.		+221	-555	+6	+565	+861	-4	+338	+238	+361	+1007	+12.3		-44	-51	-1	+136	+178	+1	+14	-23	+76	+48	+3.2
Golden State	Off.	82	3477	7923	44	1917	2500	77	4450	1854	1840	8871	108.2	5	197	486	41	109	141	77	256	113	96	503	100.6
	Def.	82	3560	8082	44	1688	2265	75	4381	1968	1912	8808	107.4	5	227	492	46	106	135	79	268	125	100	560	112.0
	Diff.		-83	-159		+229	+235	+2	+69	-114	+72	+63	0.8		-30	-6	-6	+3	+6	-2	-12	-12	+4	-57	-11.4
Seattle	Off.	82	3461	7457	46	2035	2659	77	4123	1976	1738	8957	109.2												
	Def.	82	3619	8029	45	1681	2248	75	4183	2037	1975	8919	108.8												
	Diff.		-158	-572	+1	+354	+411	+2	-60	-61	+237	+38	0.5												
Houston	Off.	82	3590	8277	43	1813	2424	75	4433	1777	1992	8993	109.7												
	Def.	82	3542	7817	45	2037	2737	74	4298	1945	1944	9121	111.2												
	Diff.		+48	+460	-2	-224	-313	+1	+135	-168	-48	-128	-1.6												
Portland	Off.	82	3462	7840	44	1835	2494	74	3996	2090	1873	8759	106.8												
	Def.	82	3841	7906	49	1875	2499	75	4439	2312	1903	9557	116.5												
	Diff.		-379	-66	-5	-40	-5	-1	-443	-222	+30	-798	-9.7												

1971-72 A.B.A.

Starting to Know the Players Without a Scorecard

Money problems still hounded the majority of A.B.A. team owners, but for the first time in the young league's history, the same lineup of clubs from last year returned this season. Only a few minor adjustments disturbed the returning array of teams; the Texas Chaparrals turned back into the Dallas Chaparrals after a one-year experiment with the new name, the New York Nets moved into the spanking new Nassau Coliseum on Long Island, and the Memphis Pros were sold to Charles 0. Finley, the colorful owner of the Oakland Athletics baseball team.

But if the structural changes in the circuit were minor, the impact of the rookie class was major in every respect. Artis Gilmore, Jim McDaniels, Damell Hillman, and Johnny Roche signed with the A.B.A. despite the ready availability of lucrative contracts with the established N.B.A. In addition to these graduating collegians, the A.B.A. brought in three noteworthy hardship undergrads in George McGinnis, Julius Erving, and Johnny Neumann. The biggest college reputations belonged to Gilmore, the 7'2" center from Jacksonville, and Neumann, the 6'6" guard from Mississippi who led the nation in scoring as a sophomore before turning pro.

Instant stardom came to Gilmore, Erving, and McGinnis. Gilmore was in a league by himself in the A.B.A., with no other center rivaling him either in size or shot-blocking ability; his presence in the middle made the Kentucky Colonels instant favorites for the championship. Erving, who went under the name of Dr. J, sent the entire league aglow with his dazzling array of moves and shots, putting on glittering shows reminiscent of Elgin Baylor at his peak; teamed with Charlie Scott, Erving made the Virginia Squire offense as unstoppable as an impending flood seeping through a leaky dike. McGinnis, meanwhile, started the season slowly but soon won a starting job at forward because of his overwhelming rebounding muscle. Erving, Gilmore, and McGinnis were quickly recognized as the foremost properties of the A.B.A.

Two other blue-chip young players, Charlie Scott and Jim McDaniels, made unexpected exits from the league by signing with N.B.A. clubs late in the season. Scott, a second-year guard with undeniable offensive skills, led the Virginia team through the bulk of the season with a league-pacing 34.6 scoring average, only to jump the club in March, claim a violation of his contract, and sign with the Phoenix Suns of the N.B.A. Rookie McDaniels of the Carolina Cougars ranked among the league leaders with a 26.8 scoring mark, but he also jumped his team in the spring to sign with the Seattle Supersonics. The loss of these two young stars set the league back a few steps in its struggle for national recognition.

But the development of the Kentucky Colonels into a genuinely entertaining club took some of the sting away. The Colonels had a new coach in Joe Mullaney, the ex-mentor of the Los Angeles Lakers, plus a new center in the towering Gilmore. Dan Issel, last year's rookie scoring sensation, moved over to a forward spot to make room for Gilmore and upped his scoring average to 30.6 points per game. To go with these two young frontcourt aces, Mullaney retained Cincy Powell at forward and Louie Dampier at guard, and replaced the injured Darel Carrier at guard with rookies Mike Gale and Jimmy O'Brien. With the bench containing a mixture of experience and youth, the Colonels ran away with first place in the East, accumulating a record 68 16 mark during the regular season.

Charlie Scott and Julius Erving, two dynamic one-on-one scorers, brought the Squires home in second place, but Scott's defection put the team in a doubtful condition for the playoffs. The New York Nets finished third in an enjoyable season, with their new arena boosting attendance and with Rick Barry staying healthy for the entire season for the first time in four A.B.A. campaigns. Fourth place went to the Floridians, who partially overcame a chaotic frontcourt situation with solid play by guards Mack Calvin, Larry Jones, and Warren Jabali, who changed his name from Armstrong this year. The Carolina Cougars finished fifth despite an abundance of trades, and the Pittsburgh Condors finished last with a lack of good players and paying customers.

Good players abounded on the rosters of the Utah Stars and Indiana Pacers, the cream of the Western Division. The Stars had a new coach in LaDell Anderson, who replaced Bill Sharman after his jump back to the N.B.A. The Utah starting lineup of Zelmo Beaty, Red Robbins, Willie Wise, Jimmy Jones, and Glen Combs stacked up with any in the A.B.A., and Ron Boone contributed heavily as the sixth man. Indiana coach Bob Leonard also had a full cupboard of top players to choose from. At center, he had Mel Daniels; at forward, he had veterans Bob Netolicky and Roger Brown plus rookies McGinnis and Hillman; at guard, he had veterans Freddie Lewis and Bill Keller, second-year-man Rick Mount, and Larry Cannon, whose personal troubles made him a bargain-price acquisition from Memphis. Although deep in talent, the turnover in personnel necessitated a period of adjustment, and the Pacers finished a distant second to the Stars.

The Dallas Chaps came in third, with new coach Tom Nissalke winning Coach of the Year honors for his work with the lightly-regarded Chaps. The Denver Rockets hired the respected Alex Hannum as coach, but he could urge his charges to only a 34-50 season, good enough for a playoff spot only because the Memphis Pros totally collapsed in the first year of Finley's ownership there.

The fireworks in this year's playoffs began in the opening round, as the New York Nets stunned Kentucky by winning the first two games in Louisville and going on to take the series in six games. The divisional finals produced sparks in both series, as the Nets continued their almost unbelievable surge by defeating the Squires in seven games, taking a 94-88 decision in the final match in Norfolk. In the West, the Pacers and Stars met for the second straight year, with the Pacers reversing last season's result by eliminating the Stars with a 117-113 victory in the seventh game. The sudden rise of the Nets won the A.B.A. some needed press coverage emanating from New York, but the magic couldn't continue. The talent-heavy Pacers put the Nets back in their place with a six-game series triumph which made the Pacers the first two-time champ in the A.B.A.

Use Name	Pos	Hgt	Wgt	Age	G	Min	FG	FGA	%	FT	FTA	%	Reb	Ass	PF	DQ	Points	Min	Reb	Ass	PF	Points
					TOTAL													PER GAME				
1971/72 A.B.A. — EASTERN DIVISION																						
KENTUCKY COLONELS	**68-16 .810**				**JOE MULLANEY**																	
Cincy Powell	F	6'7	227	29	65	2288	430	907	47	185	256	72	500	237	219	—	1049	35	7.7	3.6	3.4	16.1
Dan Issel	F-C	6'9	235	23	83	3570	972	2001	49	591	**753**	78	931	195	242	—	**2538**	43	11.2	2.3	2.9	30.6
Artis Gilmore	C	7'2	240	22	84	**3666**	806	1348	**60**	391	605	65	**1491**	230	280	—	2003	44	**17.8**	2.7	3.3	23.8
Darel Carrier (back injury)	G	6'3	185	31	23	629	117	288	41	76	88	86	57	44	64	—	326	27	2.5	1.9	2.8	14.2
Louis Dampier	G	6'	180	27	83	3214	477	1078	44	281	336	84	259	515	237	—	1319	39	3.1	6.2	2.9	15.9
Mike Gale	G	6'4	190	21	78	1701	201	447	45	95	140	68	271	200	206	—	497	22	3.5	2.6	2.6	6.4
Jimmy O'Brien (from Pit)	G	6'2	170	21	66	1424	139	354	39	54	66	82	174	299	152	—	336	22	2.6	4.5	2.3	5.1
Walt Simon	F-G	6'6	200	30	67	1111	243	464	52	109	156	70	233	137	157	—	596	17	3.5	2.0	2.3	8.9
Les Hunter	F	6'7	235	29	70	967	183	383	48	101	144	70	225	93	154	—	472	14	3.2	1.3	2.2	6.7
Mike Pratt	G-F	6'4	195	23	65	889	133	301	44	84	98	86	158	98	81	—	366	14	2.4	1.5	1.2	5.6
Goose Ligon (to Pit)	F	6'7	215	27	16	400	37	72	51	20	33	61	110	37	41	—	95	25	6.9	2.3	2.6	5.9
Pierre Russell	G	6'4	190	22	51	397	65	153	42	16	21	76	93	51	56	—	146	8	1.8	1.0	1.1	2.9
Howie Wright	G	6'3	185	23	1	4	0	0	—	0	1	0	0	0	0	—	0	4	0.0	0.0	0.0	0.0
VIRGINIA SQUIRES	**45-39 .536**				**AL BIANCHI**																	
Julius Erving	F	6'7	200	21	84	3513	910	1826	50	467	627	74	1319	335	264	—	2290	42	15.7	4.0	3.1	27.3
Neil Johnson	F	6'7	220	28	31	874	128	273	47	65	94	69	286	78	123	—	322	28	9.2	2.5	4.0	10.4
Jim Eakins	C	6'11	215	25	84	2718	371	764	49	288	377	76	807	181	298	—	1030	32	9.6	2.2	3.5	12.3
Charlie Scott (to Phoe-NBA)	G	6'5	175	23	73	3061	**985**	**2192**	45	525	654	80	374	347	261	—	2524	42	5.1	4.8	3.6	**34.6**
Fatty Taylor	G	6'	175	25	84	2669	306	680	45	164	258	64	416	321	302	—	777	32	5.0	3.8	3.6	9.3
Bernie Williams	G	6'3	175	26	78	1667	349	816	43	113	142	80	154	134	178	—	829	21	2.0	1.7	2.3	10.6
Doug Moe	F-G	6'5	220	33	67	1472	175	415	42	104	129	81	241	149	172	—	455	22	3.6	2.2	2.6	6.8
George Irvine	F	6'6	200	23	75	1362	200	397	50	54	75	72	217	70	202	—	457	18	2.9	0.9	2.7	6.1
Willie Sojourner	F-C	6'8	225	23	84	1313	222	448	50	124	193	64	514	56	222	—	568	16	6.1	0.7	2.6	6.8
Ray Scott	C	6'9	220	33	55	818	163	393	41	89	114	78	252	40	90	—	417	15	4.6	0.7	1.6	7.6
Adrian Smith	G	6'1	190	35	53	686	87	195	45	92	103	89	46	42	89	—	268	13	0.9	0.8	1.7	5.1
Bill Bunting	F	6'8	200	24	16	115	4	15	27	12	17	71	15	3	11	—	20	7	0.9	0.2	0.7	1.3
Mike Maloy	F	6'7	215	22	7	73	12	35	34	2	2	100	17	2	14	—	26	10	2.4	0.3	2.0	3.7
Dana Pagett	G	6'2	180	22	5	34	1	9	11	2	3	67	3	6	8	—	5	7	0.6	1.2	1.6	1.0
Mike Barrett - broken wrist																						
NEW YORK NETS	**44-40 .524**				**LOU CARNESECCA**																	
Rick Barry	F	6'7	215	27	80	3616	902	1969	46	**641**	730	88	602	327	261	—	2518	**45**	7.5	4.1	3.3	31.5
Trooper Washington	F	6'7	225	27	80	2510	387	678	57	107	166	64	750	161	291	—	881	31	9.4	2.0	3.6	11.0
Billy Paultz	C	6'11	240	23	83	2824	498	1021	49	207	299	69	1035	128	298	—	1203	34	12.5	1.5	3.6	14.5
Johnny Roche	G	6'3	170	22	82	2593	403	859	47	240	311	77	172	259	211	—	1058	32	2.1	3.2	2.6	12.9
Bill Melchionni	G	6'1	170	27	80	3326	672	1346	50	336	416	81	248	**669**	275	—	1682	42	3.1	**8.4**	3.4	21.0
Ollie Taylor	G-F	6'2	194	24	82	1891	245	542	45	218	308	71	330	153	213	—	708	23	4.0	1.9	2.6	8.6
Gene Moore (from Dal)	C	6'9	240	26	68	1149	212	445	48	77	106	73	409	40	178	—	502	17	6.0	0.6	2.6	7.4
Jim Ard	F	6'8	220	23	71	1145	159	353	45	77	127	61	368	34	150	—	397	16	5.2	0.5	2.1	5.6
Joe DePre	G	6'3	190	24	46	562	79	201	39	34	54	63	49	45	80	—	194	12	1.1	1.0	1.7	4.2
Johnny Baum	F	6'5	210	25	44	551	103	170	61	41	52	79	135	17	75	—	247	13	3.1	0.4	1.7	5.6
Manny Leaks (to Utah-Fla)	C-F	6'8	235	26	9	142	24	71	34	6	9	67	43	4	10	—	54	16	4.8	0.4	1.1	6.0
Gary Zeller (from Bal-NBA)	G	6'3	205	24	12	82	7	30	23	4	6	67	10	2	16	—	18	7	0.8	0.2	1.3	1.5
Bob Greacen	F	6'7	210	24	4	20	1	2	50	0	0	—	2	1	1	—	2	5	0.5	0.3	0.3	0.5
Elnardo Webster (to Mem)	F	6'5	195	24	8	14	3	6	50	0	2	0	1	1	2	—	6	2	0.1	0.1	0.3	0.8
Sonny Dove	F	6'8	215	26	2	9	2	5	40	2	3	67	1	1	4	—	6	5	0.5	0.5	2.0	3.0
Jarrett Durham	F	6'5	188	23	1	1	0	0	—	0	0	—	0	0	0	—	0	1	0.0	0.0	0.0	0.0
FLORIDIANS	**36-48 .429**				**BOB BASS**																	
Ron Franz	F	6'7	207	26	74	1822	342	705	49	171	243	70	342	94	209	—	857	25	4.6	1.3	2.8	11.6
Al Tucker	F	6'8	190	28	81	1799	377	810	47	157	199	79	392	100	205	—	941	22	4.8	1.2	2.5	11.6
Manny Leaks (from NY-Utah)	C-F	6'8	235	26	18	726	124	258	48	29	47	62	176	26	55	—	277	40	9.8	1.4	3.1	15.4
Warren Jabali	G-F	6'2	210	25	81	3313	569	1304	44	375	496	76	656	495	298	—	1615	41	8.1	6.1	3.7	19.9
Mack Calvin	G	6'	175	23	82	2977	552	1253	44	611	701	87	274	481	270	—	1726	36	3.3	5.9	3.3	21.0
Larry Jones	G-F	6'2	180	30	66	2255	423	797	53	300	373	80	309	210	203	—	1164	34	4.7	3.2	3.1	17.6
Willie Long	F-C	6'8	235	21	75	1925	336	761	44	206	291	71	513	66	215	—	878	26	6.8	0.9	2.9	11.7
Ira Harge (to Utah)	C	6'9	225	29	53	1809	256	561	46	84	123	68	626	99	191	—	596	34	11.8	1.9	3.6	11.2
Lonnie Wright	G	6'2	205	27	77	1638	252	599	42	95	117	81	158	133	197	—	618	21	2.1	1.7	2.6	8.0
Craig Raymond	C	6'11	235	26	64	889	104	227	46	48	76	63	284	67	108	—	256	14	4.4	1.0	1.7	4.0
Sam Robinson	F	6'7	200	23	51	686	126	300	42	54	68	79	136	48	70	—	306	13	2.7	0.9	1.4	6.0
George Tinsley	F	6'5	205	25	51	418	70	174	40	46	62	74	60	38	79	—	191	8	1.2	0.7	1.5	3.7
Carl Fuller	C	6'9	225	25	6	63	6	14	43	9	15	60	28	6	11	—	21	11	4.7	1.0	1.8	3.5
Willie Allen	F	6'6	230	22	7	30	4	13	31	5	6	83	14	4	11	—	13	4	2.0	0.6	1.6	1.9
Walt Piatkowski	F	6'8	225	26	6	28	3	16	19	0	0	—	2	2	2	—	6	5	0.3	0.3	0.3	1.0
Rick Fisher (from Utah)	F	6'9	220	23	3	7	3	5	60	0	0	—	4	2	1	—	6	2	1.3	0.7	0.3	2.0

1971/72 A.B.A. — EASTERN DIVISION (continued)

Use Name	Pos	Hgt	Wgt	Age	TOTAL													PER GAME				
					G	Min	FG	FGA	%	FT	FTA	%	Reb	Ass	PF	DQ	Points	Min	Reb	Ass	PF	Points
CAROLINA COUGARS	**35-49 .417**				**TOM MESCHERY**																	
Joe Caldwell (knee injury)	F	6'5	210	30	61	2145	434	922	47	159	318	50	343	259	208	—	1032	35	5.6	4.2	3.4	16.9
George Carter (trom Pit)	F	6'5	218	27	29	738	161	349	46	157	185	85	151	25	72	—	479	25	5.2	0.9	2.5	16.5
Jim McDaniels (to Sea-NBA)	C	6'11	225	23	58	2172	659	1276	52	234	324	72	814	97	251	—	1552	37	14.0	1.7	4.3	26.8
Larry Miller	G	6'4	210	25	83	3199	562	1228	46	393	497	79	399	235	232	—	1529	39	4.8	2.8	2.8	18.4
Gene Littles	G	6'1	170	28	69	2006	280	605	46	178	237	75	276	237	180	—	745	29	4.0	3.4	2.6	10.8
Ed Manning	F	6'7	215	27	77	1648	228	499	46	95	114	83	441	58	227	—	551	21	5.7	0.8	2.9	7.2
George Lehmann (to Mem)	G	6'3	185	29	38	1399	219	439	50	122	136	90	71	295	114	—	609	37	1.9	7.8	3.0	16.0
Warren Davis (to Mem)	F	6'6	215	29	41	1348	223	464	48	111	163	68	370	99	162	—	557	33	9.0	2.4	4.0	13.6
Wendell Ladner (from Mem)	F	6'5	220	23	43	1183	219	583	38	51	63	81	424	88	180	—	523	28	9.9	2.0	4.2	12.2
Stew Johnson (from Pit)	F-C	6'8	225	27	50	1125	283	658	43	53	73	73	272	73	116	—	632	23	5.4	1.5	2.3	12.6
Ted McClain	G	6'3	180	24	64	900	148	415	36	110	142	77	120	120	144	—	419	14	1.9	1.9	2.3	6.5
Randy Denton (to Mem)	C	6'10	245	22	39	710	147	339	43	39	55	71	260	33	67	—	333	18	6.7	0.8	1.7	8.5
Bobby Warren (from Mem)	G	6'5	190	25	37	501	73	167	44	39	49	80	54	46	59	—	188	14	1.5	1.2	1.6	5.1
Tom Owens (from Mem)	C	6'10	223	22	31	501	99	193	51	55	87	63	191	21	81	—	254	16	6.2	0.7	2.6	8.2
George Stone (from Utah)	F	6'7	195	25	16	239	28	75	37	16	17	94	39	21	23	—	72	15	2.4	1.3	1.4	4.5
Wayne Hightower	F	6'9	210	31	13	141	20	64	31	30	36	83	43	11	19	—	70	11	3.3	0.8	1.5	5.4
Franh Card (to Den)	F	6'7	195	27	9	141	10	48	21	18	25	72	28	7	16	—	38	16	3.1	0.8	1.8	4.2
Bob Verga (to Pit)	G	6'1	190	26	8	127	23	59	39	10	13	77	8	10	20	—	59	16	1.0	1.3	2.5	7.4
Ron Dorsey	G	6'4	200	23	1	12	2	8	25	0	2	0	5	0	2	—	4	12	5.0	0.0	2.0	4.0
PITSBURGH CONDORS	**25-59 .298**				**JACK McMAHON (46 .400), MARK BINSTEIN (21-43 .328)**																	
John Brisker	F-G	6'5	210	24	49	2065	563	1228	46	248	286	87	447	203	156	—	1417	42	9.1	4.1	3.2	28.9
Goose Ligon (from KY)	F	6'7	215	27	66	1941	176	356	49	121	184	66	590	126	224	—	473	29	8.9	1.9	3.4	7.2
Mike Lewis	C	6'8	225	25	82	2618	385	713	54	165	226	73	996	316	315	—	935	32	12.1	3.9	3.8	11.4
Skeeter Swift	G	6'3	210	25	79	2340	401	856	47	224	265	85	200	309	277	—	1059	30	2.5	3.9	3.5	13.4
George Thompson	G	6'2	200	24	70	2904	696	1448	48	455	584	78	353	257	201	—	1888	41	5.0	3.7	2.9	27.0
Bob Verga (from Car)	G	6'1	190	26	62	1902	436	987	44	275	385	71	229	243	178	—	1163	31	3.7	3.9	2.9	18.8
George Carter (to Car)	F	6'5	218	27	46	1885	377	878	43	231	289	80	355	103	148	—	985	41	7.7	2.2	3.2	21.4
Dave Lattin	F-C	6'7	230	28	64	1482	329	605	54	148	242	61	375	51	178	—	806	23	5.9	0.8	2.8	12.6
Paul Ruffner	C-F	6'10	225	23	79	1059	182	381	48	84	115	73	341	52	178	—	448	13	4.3	0.7	2.3	5.7
Walt Szczerbiak	F	6'6	215	22	53	598	149	237	63	35	53	66	150	41	100	—	333	11	2.8	0.8	1.9	6.3
Stew Johnson (to Car)	F-C	6'8	225	27	17	409	85	216	39	20	26	77	110	15	43	—	193	24	6.5	0.9	2.5	11.4
Jimmy O'Brien (to KY)	G	6'2	170	21	18	354	34	82	41	11	14	79	32	74	37	—	82	20	1.8	4.1	2.1	4.6
Mike Grosso	C	6'9	232	24	25	335	45	102	44	13	23	57	123	11	64	—	103	13	4.9	0.4	2.6	4.1
Nate Bowman	C	6'10	230	28	18	217	19	53	36	5	9	56	87	13	48	—	43	12	4.8	0.7	2.7	2.4
Mickey Davis	F	6'7	215	21	23	126	25	63	40	14	20	70	41	9	23	—	64	5	1.8	0.4	1.0	2.8
Arvesta Kelly (to Ind)	G	6'3	195	26	8	71	10	20	50	3	4	75	8	12	10	—	24	9	1.0	1.5	1.3	3.0
Ron Taylor	C	7'1	275	25	1	4	0	1	0	0	0	—	1	0	5	—	0	4	1.0	0.0	5.0	0.0

1971/72 A.B.A.—WESTERN DIVISION

Use Name	Pos	Hgt	Wgt	Age	TOTAL													PER GAME				
					G	Min	FG	FGA	%	FT	FTA	%	Reb	Ass	PF	DQ	Points	Min	Reb	Ass	PF	Points
UTAH STARS	**60-24 .714**				**LaDELL ANDERSEN**																	
Willie Wise	F	6'6	215	24	84	3300	743	1471	51	459	633	73	894	286	299	—	1951	39	10.6	3.4	3.6	23.2
Red Robbins	F	6'8	200	27	78	2567	379	752	50	167	201	83	711	124	171	—	954	33	9.1	1.6	2.2	12.2
Zelmo Beaty	C	6'9	235	32	84	3133	729	1353	54	522	630	83	1110	125	315	—	1980	37	13.2	1.5	3.8	23.6
Jimmy Jones	G-F	6'4	190	26	78	2903	462	903	51	282	362	78	377	485	252	—	1207	37	4.8	6.2	3.2	15.5
Glen Combs	G	6'2	185	25	84	2906	483	1109	44	319	380	84	215	306	255	—	1388	35	2.6	3.6	3.0	16.5
Ron Boone	G-F	6'2	200	25	84	2040	404	962	42	271	341	79	393	233	274	—	1092	24	4.7	2.8	3.3	13.0
Merv Jackson	G	6'3	175	25	52	1136	185	412	45	92	109	84	123	155	150	—	467	22	2.4	3.0	2.9	9.0
John Beasley (from Dal)	F	6'9	225	27	58	617	90	199	45	37	46	80	200	26	81	—	225	11	3.4	0.4	1.4	3.9
Manny Leaks (from NY, to Fla)	C-F	6'8	235	26	42	575	92	251	37	39	65	60	193	25	71	—	223	14	4.6	0.6	1.7	5.3
Ira Harge (from Fla)	C	6'9	225	29	31	455	58	118	49	20	27	74	154	31	76	—	136	15	5.0	1.0	2.5	4.4
Rod McDonald	F	6'6	205	26	33	231	34	76	45	27	37	73	74	18	40	—	95	7	2.2	0.5	1.2	2.9
George Stone (to Car)	F	6'7	195	25	8	142	21	48	44	9	11	82	23	4	17	—	52	18	2.9	0.5	2.1	6.5
Bobby Fields	G	6'3	175	22	22	124	22	48	46	8	13	62	30	20	33	—	54	6	1.4	0.9	1.5	2.5
Mike Butler	G	6'2	175	25	14	97	14	36	39	6	7	86	10	13	18	—	37	7	0.7	0.9	1.3	2.6
Rich Fisher (to Fla)	F	6'5	220	23	9	59	15	29	52	1	1	100	28	3	8	—	31	7	3.1	0.3	0.9	3.4
INDIANA PACERS	**47-37.560**				**BOB LEONARD**																	
George McGinnis	F	6'8	235	21	73	2179	465	999	47	298	462	65	711	137	260	—	1234	30	9.7	1.9	3.6	16.9
Bob Netolicky	F-C	6'9	225	29	83	2905	522	1090	48	202	279	72	764	83	185	—	1250	35	9.2	1.0	2.2	15.1
Mel Daniels	C	6'9	225	27	79	2971	598	1184	51	317	451	70	1297	176	289	—	1513	38	16.4	2.2	3.7	19.2
Rich Mount	G	6'4	185	24	78	2126	420	949	44	216	261	83	155	230	233	—	1113	27	2.0	2.9	3.0	14.3
Freddie Lewis	G	6'	180	28	77	2714	405	947	43	341	396	86	327	362	230	—	1182	35	4.2	4.7	3.0	15.4
Roger Brown	F-G	6'5	215	29	78	2987	532	1112	48	323	401	81	502	306	227	—	1444	38	6.4	3.9	2.9	18.5
Bill Keller	G	5'10	180	24	76	1729	264	619	43	153	174	88	164	264	118	—	737	23	2.2	3.5	1.6	9.7
Darnell Hillman	F	6'9	215	22	73	1386	200	410	49	114	177	64	478	49	210	—	515	19	6.5	0.7	2.9	7.1
Larry Cannon (from Mem)	G	6'5	195	24	28	478	67	175	38	51	71	72	33	72	61	—	186	17	1.2	2.6	2.2	6.6
Don Sidle (to Mem)	C	6'9	220	25	27	394	72	143	50	31	49	63	95	10	39	—	175	15	3.5	0.4	1.4	6.5
John Barnhill	G	6'1	183	33	19	194	28	87	32	8	15	53	19	16	16	—	68	10	1.0	0.8	0.8	3.6
Marv Winkler	G	6'1	175	23	20	155	15	54	28	8	14	57	16	12	16	—	40	8	0.8	0.6	0.8	2.0
Wayne Chapman	G	6'6	190	26	7	76	7	18	39	3	6	50	5	11	10	—	18	11	0.7	1.6	1.4	2.6
Arvesta Kelly (from Pit)	G	6'3	195	26	4	41	3	9	33	0	0	—	7	2	10	—	6	10	1.8	0.5	2.5	1.5
Mark Price (from NY-NBA)	G	6'3	200	23	4	25	3	9	33	0	0	—	5	1	4	—	6	6	1.3	0.3	1.0	1.5

1971/72 A.B.A. — WESTERN DIVISION (continued)

Use Name	Pos	Hgt	Wgt	Age	G (Total)	Min (Total)	FG (Total)	FGA (Total)	% (Total)	FT (Total)	FTA (Total)	% (Total)	Reb (Total)	Ass (Total)	PF (Total)	DQ (Total)	Points (Total)	Min (Per Game)	Reb (Per Game)	Ass (Per Game)	PF (Per Game)	Points (Per Game)
DALLAS CHAPARRALS	42-42 .500				TOM NISSALKE																	
Simmie Hill	F	6'7	235	25	70	1845	281	629	45	129	164	79	406	94	234	—	695	26	5.8	1.3	3.3	9.9
Rich Jones	F-C	6'8	230	25	82	2932	475	1053	45	212	279	76	696	222	298	—	1176	36	8.5	2.7	3.6	14.3
George Johnson	C	6'11	255	24	67	1477	128	282	45	61	103	59	464	59	209	—	317	22	6.9	0.9	3.1	4.7
Steve Jones	G-F	6'5	205	29	84	3091	572	1343	43	367	422	87	317	237	268	—	1537	37	3.8	2.8	3.2	18.3
Donnie Freeman	G	6'3	185	27	72	2377	628	1336	47	475	576	82	206	245	177	—	1733	33	2.9	3.4	2.5	24.1
Joe Hamilton	G	5'10	175	23	82	1959	317	791	40	201	256	79	194	240	202	—	881	24	2.4	2.9	2.5	10.7
Goo Kennedy	F	6'6	205	22	65	1453	234	406	58	88	133	66	485	65	262	—	556	22	7.5	1.0	4.0	8.6
Collis Jones	F	6'7	205	22	78	1428	163	372	44	98	154	64	334	78	200	—	425	18	4.3	1.0	2.6	5.4
Len Chappell	C	6'8	240	30	79	1403	231	511	45	144	193	75	318	69	158	—	606	18	4.0	0.9	2.0	7.7
Shaler Halimon (from Atl-NBA)	G	6'6	200	26	55	770	123	294	42	62	86	72	156	72	89	—	308	14	2.8	1.3	1.6	5.6
Rich Niemann	C	7'	255	25	33	524	48	98	49	25	34	74	155	24	87	—	121	16	4.7	0.7	2.6	3.7
John Beasley (to Utah)	F	6'9	225	27	12	268	42	85	49	24	29	83	90	13	26	—	108	22	7.5	1.1	2.2	9.0
Gene Moore (to NY)	C	6'9	240	26	9	263	41	100	41	12	14	86	74	13	43	—	94	29	8.2	1.4	4.8	10.4
Jeff Congdon	G	6'1	180	28	20	261	30	86	35	17	20	85	26	36	19	—	80	13	1.3	1.8	1.0	4.0
Gene Phillips	G	6'4	180	23	28	174	30	76	39	11	14	79	21	13	23	—	78	6	0.8	0.5	0.8	2.8
George Peeples	F	6'8	205	28	6	125	11	25	44	7	11	64	35	5	10	—	29	21	5.8	0.8	1.7	4.8
Bob Quick (from Det-NBA)	F	6'5	215	25	6	57	8	15	53	10	10	100	14	1	9	—	26	10	2.3	0.2	1.5	4.3
Ron Sanford	F	6'9	215	25	1	2	0	0	—	0	0	—	0	0	1	—	0	2	0.0	0.0	1.0	0.0
DENVER ROCKETS	34-50 .405				ALEX HANNUM																	
Art Becker	F	6'8	210	29	84	2193	435	954	46	165	195	85	471	113	271	—	1035	26	5.6	1.3	3.2	12.3
Julius Keye	F-C	6'10	225	25	84	2557	192	476	40	108	174	62	982	153	346	—	492	30	11.7	1.8	4.1	5.9
Dave Robisch	C	6'10	235	22	84	2420	505	1138	44	294	419	70	804	201	251	—	1304	29	9.6	2.4	3.0	15.5
Ralph Simpson	G-F	6'5	200	22	84	3006	920	2000	46	457	568	80	398	258	244	—	2300	36	4.7	3.1	2.9	27.4
Larry Brown	G	5'9	160	31	76	2012	243	556	44	198	244	81	166	549	207	—	689	26	2.2	7.2	2.7	9.1
Byron Beck (leg injury)	C-F	6'9	230	26	66	1816	337	669	50	140	166	84	528	136	213	—	814	28	8.0	2.1	3.2	12.3
Al Smith	G	6'1	185	24	83	1764	292	675	43	153	211	73	226	249	244	—	769	21	2.7	3.0	2.9	9.3
Chuck Williams	G	6'2	175	25	84	1580	263	583	45	205	275	75	157	160	144	—	731	19	1.9	1.9	1.7	8.7
Frank Card (from Car)	F	6'7	195	27	73	1443	225	495	45	112	172	65	330	79	204	—	562	20	4.5	1.1	2.8	7.7
Marv Roberts	F	6'8	205	21	68	1047	217	533	41	86	120	72	294	61	150	—	521	15	4.3	0.9	2.2	7.7
Julie Hammond	F	6'5	215	28	25	411	66	140	47	31	50	62	115	29	47	—	163	16	4.6	1.2	1.9	6.5
Steve Wilson	G	6'5	185	23	9	36	5	23	22	4	7	57	4	6	9	—	14	4	0.4	0.7	1.0	1.6
Dwight Waller	F	6'7	230	26	2	10	2	4	50	0	0	—	5	1	3	—	4	5	2.5	0.5	1.5	2.0
Steve Mix (from Det-NBA)	F	6'7	215	24	1	4	1	1	100	0	0	—	1	0	1	—	2	4	1.0	0.0	1.0	2.0
MEMPHIS PROS	26-58 .310				BABE McCARTHY																	
Wil Jones	F	6'8	205	24	84	3098	506	1078	47	240	320	75	876	154	322	—	1254	37	10.4	1.8	3.8	14.9
Gerald Govan	F-C	6'10	220	29	83	3414	277	719	39	162	230	70	1182	348	260	—	716	41	14.2	4.2	3.1	8.6
Randy Denton (fnom Car)	C	6'10	245	22	42	1329	283	596	47	96	113	85	480	33	113	—	662	32	11.4	0.8	2.7	15.8
George Lehmann (from Car)	G	6'3	185	29	15	522	84	224	38	47	56	84	27	116	41	—	237	35	1.8	7.7	2.7	15.8
Charlie Williams	G	6'	165	28	82	2583	480	1258	38	294	395	74	228	253	250	—	1295	32	2.8	3.1	3.0	15.8
Johnny Neumann	G-F	6'6	200	20	77	1969	545	1328	41	293	385	76	322	147	285	—	1409	26	4.2	1.9	3.7	18.3
Bobby Warren (to Car)	G	6'5	190	25	38	1300	240	540	44	174	219	79	205	136	106	—	662	34	5.4	3.6	2.8	17.4
Wendell Ladner (to Car)	F	6'5	220	23	39	1263	272	704	39	71	96	74	409	78	167	—	642	32	10.5	2.0	4.3	16.5
Loyd King	G	6'2	180	22	74	1153	185	494	37	96	119	81	113	103	76	—	487	16	1.5	1.4	1.0	6.6
Warren Davis (fnom Car)	F	6'6	215	29	45	983	114	237	48	96	136	71	323	81	117	—	324	22	7.2	1.8	2.6	7.2
Larry Cannon (to Ind)	G	6'5	195	24	26	693	161	435	37	113	150	75	74	78	63	—	437	27	2.8	3.0	2.4	16.8
Tom Owens (to Car)	C	6'10	223	22	38	617	98	209	47	54	88	61	199	30	89	—	250	16	5.2	0.8	2.3	6.6
Don Sidle (fnom Ind)	C	6'9	220	25	42	566	103	241	43	93	146	64	139	16	57	—	300	13	3.3	0.4	1.4	7.1
Lee Davis	F	6'8	240	26	58	550	101	231	44	25	43	58	178	21	90	—	228	9	3.1	0.4	1.6	3.9
Elnardo Webster (from NY)	F	6'5	195	24	16	223	47	103	46	21	27	78	43	15	37	—	116	14	2.7	0.9	2.3	7.3
Jerry Dover	G	5'8	155	22	4	13	3	9	33	0	0	—	0	1	3	—	8	3	0.0	0.3	0.8	2.0
Coby Dietrick	C	6'10	230	23	1	9	1	2	50	0	2	0	7	1	1	—	2	9	7.0	1.0	1.0	2.0

1971/72 A.B.A. — PLAYOFFS

INDIANA PACERS — **BOB LEONARD**

defeated Denver 4-3; H102-96, H105-106, 122-120(OT), 96-112, H91-79, 99-106, H91-89
defeated Utah 4-3; 100-108, 109-117, H116-111, H118-108, 130-139, H105-99, 117-113
defeated New York 4-2; H124-103, H115-117, 114-108, 105-110, H100-99, 108-105

Use Name	Pos	Hgt	Wgt	Age	G	Min	FG	FGA	%	FT	FTA	%	Reb	Ass	PF	DQ	Points	Min	Reb	Ass	PF	Points
					TOTAL													PER GAME				
Roger Brown	F-G	6'5	215	29	20	**845**	160	329	49	74	90	82	121	81	65	—	409	42	6.1	4.1	3.3	20.5
George McGinnis	F	6'8	235	21	20	633	106	261	41	94	**150**	63	227	52	75	—	310	32	11.4	2.6	3.8	15.5
Mel Daniels	C	6'9	225	27	20	744	121	252	48	64	85	75	**302**	28	**85**	—	306	37	15.1	1.4	4.3	15.3
Freddie Lewis	G	6'	180	28	20	805	142	322	44	92	108	85	81	**87**	70	—	383	40	4.1	4.4	3.5	19.2
Bill Keller	G	5'10	180	24	20	532	84	188	45	53	63	84	35	84	47	—	240	27	1.8	4.2	2.4	12.0
Bob Netolicky	F-C	6'9	225	29	20	552	91	191	48	36	61	59	118	12	36	—	218	28	5.9	0.6	1.8	10.9
Rick Mount	G	6'4	185	24	20	387	68	178	38	33	39	85	23	31	49	—	177	19	1.2	1.6	2.5	8.9
Darnell Hillman	F	6'9	215	22	20	327	53	95	56	18	33	55	110	9	52	—	124	16	5.5	0.5	2.6	6.2

NEW YORK NETS — **LOU CARNESECCA**

defeated Kentucky 4-2; 122-108, 105-90, H99-105, H100-92, 93-109, H101-96
defeated Virginia 4-3; 91-138, 106-115, H119-117, H118-107, 107-116, H146-136, 94-88
lost to Indiana 2-4; 103-124, 117-115, H108-114, H110-105, 99-100, H105-108

Use Name	Pos	Hgt	Wgt	Age	G	Min	FG	FGA	%	FT	FTA	%	Reb	Ass	PF	DQ	Points	Min	Reb	Ass	PF	Points
Rick Barry	F	6'7	215	27	18	749	**203**	**429**	47	**125**	146	86	117	69	67	—	**554**	42	6.5	3.8	3.7	30.8
Trooper Washington	F	6'7	225	27	18	548	64	107	60	14	24	58	173	43	63	—	142	30	9.6	2.4	3.5	7.9
Billy Paultz	C	6'11	240	23	19	809	140	276	51	57	90	63	288	29	74	—	337	43	15.2	1.5	3.9	17.7
Ollie Taylor	G-F	6'2	194	24	19	702	79	180	44	53	72	74	100	47	60	—	211	37	5.3	2.5	3.2	11.1
Johnny Roche	G	6'3	170	22	18	763	163	343	48	89	118	75	31	84	42	—	425	42	1.7	4.7	2.3	23.6
Bill Melchionni	G	6'1	170	27	11	376	61	152	40	37	46	80	26	69	32	—	159	34	2.4	6.3	2.9	14.5
Johnny Baum	F	6'5	210	25	17	302	59	107	55	10	16	63	72	7	34	—	128	18	4.2	0.4	2.0	7.5
Jim Ard	F	6'8	220	23	13	117	14	32	44	3	10	30	28	4	19	—	31	9	2.2	0.3	1.5	2.4
Gene Moore	C-F	6'9	240	26	18	111	16	36	44	7	8	88	29	2	21	—	39	6	1.6	0.1	1.2	2.2
Joe DePre	G	6'3	190	24	14	74	5	24	21	4	8	50	8	6	13	—	15	5	0.6	0.4	0.9	1.1
Gary Zeller	G	6'3	205	24	3	9	1	1	100	0	1	0	1	0	7	—	2	3	0.3	0.0	2.3	0.7

VIRGINIA SQUIRES — **AL BIANCHI**

defeated Floridians 4-0; H114-107(OT), H125-100, 118-113, 115-106
lost to New York 3-4; H138-91, H115-106, 117-119, 107-118, H116-107, 136-146, H88-94

Use Name	Pos	Hgt	Wgt	Age	G	Min	FG	FGA	%	FT	FTA	%	Reb	Ass	PF	DQ	Points	Min	Reb	Ass	PF	Points
Julius Erving	F	6'7	200	21	11	504	147	284	52	71	85	84	224	72	26	—	366	**46**	**20.4**	6.5	2.4	**33.3**
George Irvine	F	6'6	200	23	11	285	56	86	**65**	25	31	81	27	10	45	—	137	26	2.5	0.9	4.1	12.5
Jim Eakins	C	6'11	215	25	11	325	38	80	48	27	39	69	96	22	36	—	103	30	8.7	2.0	3.3	9.4
Bernie Williams	G	6'3	175	26	11	356	84	190	44	19	27	70	47	23	38	—	189	32	4.3	2.1	3.5	17.2
Fatty Taylor	G	6'	175	25	11	382	47	106	44	20	30	67	57	45	41	—	115	35	5.2	4.1	3.7	10.5
Adrian Smith	G	6'1	190	35	11	297	46	95	48	32	37	86	19	17	28	—	125	27	1.7	1.5	2.5	11.4
Doug Moe	F-G	6'5	220	33	11	245	37	85	44	22	25	88	43	27	40	—	96	22	3.9	2.5	3.6	8.7
Ray Scott	C-F	6'9	220	33	11	212	52	105	50	28	38	74	58	17	25	—	132	19	5.3	1.5	2.3	12.0
Willie Sojourner	F	6'8	225	23	10	58	11	21	52	4	4	100	23	6	11	—	26	6	2.3	0.6	1.1	2.6
Mike Barrett	G	6'1	160	28	1	1	0	1	0	0	0	—	0	0	1	—	0	1	0.0	0.0	1.0	0.0

UTAH STARS — **LaDELL ANDERSEN**

defeated Dallas 4-0; H106-96, H113-107, 96-89, 103-99
lost to Indiana 3-4; H108-100, H117-109, 111-116, 108-118, H139-130, 99-105, H113-117

Use Name	Pos	Hgt	Wgt	Age	G	Min	FG	FGA	%	FT	FTA	%	Reb	Ass	PF	DQ	Points	Min	Reb	Ass	PF	Points
Willie Wise	F	6'6	215	24	11	458	112	199	56	54	80	68	128	33	44	—	278	42	11.6	3.0	4.0	25.3
Red Robbins	F	6'8	200	27	9	227	20	56	36	13	16	81	61	14	12	—	53	25	6.8	1.6	1.3	5.9
Zelmo Beaty	C	6'9	235	32	11	443	74	134	55	73	88	83	154	24	43	—	221	40	14.0	2.2	3.9	20.1
Ron Boone	G	6'2	200	25	11	209	50	105	48	25	29	86	24	26	30	—	126	19	2.2	2.4	2.7	11.5
Glen Combs	G	6'2	185	25	11	317	56	116	48	26	38	68	20	27	37	—	146	29	1.8	2.5	3.4	13.3
Jimmy Jones	G-F	6'4	190	26	11	435	93	172	54	45	63	71	44	69	40	—	231	40	4.0	6.3	3.6	21.0
Merv Jackson	G	6'3	175	25	11	267	34	77	44	15	18	83	26	26	40	—	83	24	2.4	2.4	3.6	7.5
John Beasley	F	6'9	225	27	9	168	18	34	53	5	5	100	52	9	21	—	42	19	5.8	1.0	2.3	4.7
Ira Harge	C-F	6'9	225	29	10	106	11	25	44	5	7	71	40	8	23	—	27	11	4.0	0.8	2.3	2.7
Rod McDonald	F	6'6	205	26	1	10	3	4	75	0	1	0	0	0	3	—	6	10	0.0	0.0	3.0	6.0

1971/72 A.B.A. - PLAYOFFS (continued)

Use Name	Pos	Hgt	Wgt	Age	G	Min	FG	FGA	%	FT	FTA	%	Reb	Ass	PF	DQ	Points	Min	Reb	Ass	PF	Points
					TOTAL													PER GAME				
DENVER ROCKETS	**ALEX HANNUM**				lost to Indiana 3-4; 96-102, 106-105, H120-122(OT), H112-96, 79-91, H106-99, 89-91																	
Byron Beck	F-C	6'9	230	26	7	264	56	115	49	26	28	93	72	14	29	—	139	38	10.3	2.0	4.1	19.9
Julius Keye	F-C	6'10	225	25	7	302	27	59	46	3	8	38	113	20	30	—	57	43	16.1	2.9	4.3	8.1
Dave Robisch	C	6'10	235	22	7	288	50	138	36	37	52	71	99	15	25	—	137	41	14.1	2.1	3.6	19.6
Ralph Simpson	G-F	6'5	200	22	7	291	70	162	43	47	57	82	32	24	21	—	187	42	4.6	3.4	3.0	26.7
Larry Brown	G	5'9	160	31	7	211	21	50	42	23	24	96	10	36	25	—	65	30	1.4	5.1	3.6	9.3
Chuck Williams	G	6'2	175	25	7	108	18	42	43	9	12	75	19	6	14	—	45	15	2.7	0.9	2.0	6.4
Al Smith	G	6'1	185	24	7	99	12	27	44	4	5	80	18	7	14	—	30	14	2.6	1.0	2.0	4.3
Art Becker	F	6'8	210	29	7	94	14	31	45	6	9	67	12	4	18	—	34	13	1.7	0.6	2.6	4.9
Frank Card	F	6'7	195	27	4	28	4	8	50	0	1	0	7	3	10	—	8	7	1.8	0.8	2.5	2.0
Marv Roberts	F	6'8	205	21	3	20	2	7	29	2	2	100	2	0	1	—	6	7	0.7	0.0	0.3	2.0
KENTUCKY COLONELS	**JOE MULLANEY**				lost to New York 2-4; H108-122, H90-105, 105-99, 92-100, H109-93, 96-101																	
Cincy Powell	F	6'7	227	29	6	169	28	52	54	15	19	79	24	9	17	—	71	28	4.0	1.5	2.8	11.8
Dan Issel	F-C	6'9	235	23	6	269	47	114	41	38	50	76	54	5	23	—	132	45	9.0	0.8	3.8	22.0
Artis Gilmore	C	7'2	240	23	6	285	52	91	57	27	38	71	106	25	17	—	131	48	17.7	4.2	2.8	21.8
Mike Pran	G-F	6'4	195	23	6	170	33	63	52	5	5	100	17	15	23	—	72	28	2.8	2.5	3.8	12.0
Louie Dampier	G	6'	180	27	6	254	29	69	42	10	16	63	19	45	17	—	79	42	3.2	7.5	2.8	13.2
Les Hunter	F	6'7	235	29	6	123	22	41	54	9	11	82	21	8	14	—	55	21	3.5	1.3	2.3	9.2
Wart Simon	G-F	6'6	200	30	6	99	16	39	41	7	8	88	12	3	21	—	39	17	2.0	0.5	3.5	6.5
Mlke Gale	G	6'4	190	21	2	31	3	14	21	0	0	—	2	8	2	—	6	16	1.0	4.0	1.0	3.0
Jimmy O'Brien	G	6'2	170	21	5	23	3	7	43	3	3	100	3	3	0	—	9	5	0.6	0.6	0.0	1.8
Darel Carrier	G	6'3	185	31	2	17	3	8	38	0	0	—	1	1	3	—	6	9	0.5	0.5	1.5	3.0
DALLAS CHAPARRALS	**TOM NISSALKE**				lost to Utah 0-4; 96-106, 107-113, H89-96, H99-103																	
Simmie Hill	F	6'7	235	25	4	121	18	40	45	5	7	71	22	11	15	—	41	30	5.5	2.8	3.8	10.3
Rich Jones	F-C	6'8	230	25	4	145	17	43	40	3	6	50	32	14	20	—	38	36	8.0	3.5	5.0	9.5
George Johnson	C	6'11	255	24	4	96	3	9	33	0	0	—	24	9	16	—	6	24	6.0	2.3	4.0	1.5
Steve Jones	G-F	6'5	205	29	4	137	30	63	48	18	21	86	19	11	19	—	78	34	4.8	2.8	4.8	19.5
Donme Freeman	G	6'3	185	27	4	144	45	103	44	17	27	63	24	10	11	—	107	36	6.0	2.5	2.8	26.8
Len Chappell	C	6'8	240	30	4	89	12	24	50	5	8	63	18	3	13	—	29	22	4.5	0.8	3.3	7.3
Joe Hamilton	G	5'10	175	23	4	89	15	46	33	7	9	78	11	13	10	—	40	22	2.8	3.3	2.5	10.0
Shaler Halimon	G	6'6	200	26	4	55	9	17	53	4	7	57	13	7	4	—	22	14	3.3	1.8	1.0	5.5
Goo Kennedy	F	6'6	205	22	2	47	8	12	67	2	2	100	6	4	8	—	18	24	3.0	2.0	4.0	9.0
Collis Jones	F	6'7	205	22	3	35	4	10	40	4	8	50	14	1	7	—	12	12	4.7	0.3	2.3	4.0
Gene Phillips	G	6'4	180	23	1	2	0	0	—	0	0	—	0	0	0	—	0	2	0.0	0.0	0.0	0.0
FLORIDIANS	**BOB BASS**				lost to Virginia 0-4; 107-114(OT), 100-125, H113-118, H106-115																	
Sam Robinson	F	6'7	200	23	4	81	18	37	49	7	7	100	22	2	11	—	43	20	5.5	0.5	2.8	10.8
Ron Franz	F	6'7	207	26	4	88	12	36	33	3	8	38	25	4	10	—	27	22	6.3	1.0	2.5	6.8
Willie Long	C-F	6'8	235	21	4	156	24	57	42	18	25	72	40	4	16	—	66	39	10.0	1.0	4.0	16.5
Warren Jabali	G-F	6'2	210	25	4	171	22	59	37	26	33	79	52	22	17	—	75	43	13.0	5.5	4.3	18.8
Mack Calvin	G	6'	175	23	4	154	28	65	43	29	33	88	16	21	13	—	85	39	4.0	5.3	3.3	21.3
Larry Jones	G-F	6'2	180	30	4	115	13	38	34	14	17	82	13	9	12	—	40	29	3.3	2.3	3.0	10.0
Lonnie Wright	G	6'2	205	27	4	93	19	45	42	4	4	100	9	7	7	—	42	23	2.3	1.8	1.8	10.5
Craig Raymond	C	6'11	235	26	4	62	15	23	65	2	3	67	22	2	6	—	32	16	5.5	0.5	1.5	8.0
Al Tucker	F	6'8	190	28	3	51	5	20	25	0	1	0	14	4	8	—	10	17	4.7	1.3	2.7	3.3
George Tinsley	F	6'5	205	25	3	14	3	5	60	0	0	—	1	3	3	—	6	5	0.3	1.0	1.0	2.0

Team	W	L	Pct.	GB	Record against playoff teams			Record against non - playoff teams			HOME			ROAD			NEUTRAL		
					W	L	Pct.	W	L	Pct.	W	L	Pct.	W	L	Pct.	W	L	Pct.
EASTERN DIVISION																			
Kentucky Colonels	**68**	16	**.810**	—	**44**	13	**.772**	**24**	3	**.889**	**36**	6	**.857**	**28**	10	**.737**	**4**	0	**1.000**
Virginia Squires	45	39	.536	23	27	29	.482	18	10	.643	24	18	.571	21	21	.500	0	0	—
New York Nets	44	40	.524	24	24	32	.429	20	8	.714	27	15	.643	17	25	.405	0	0	—
Floridians	36	48	.429	32	18	37	.327	18	**11**	.621									
Canolina Cougars	35	49	.417	33	24	43	.358	11	6	.647	21	22	.488	14	26	.350	0	1	.000
Pittsburgh Condors	25	**59**	.298	43	17	**50**	.254	8	9	.471									
WESTERN DIVISION																			
Utah Stars	60	24	.714	—	41	19	.683	19	5	.792	33	9	.786	27	15	.643	0	0	—
Indiana Pacers	47	37	.560	13	30	32	.484	17	5	.773	29	13	.690	17	24	.415	1	0	**1.000**
Dallas Chaparrals	42	42	.500	18	28	32	.467	14	10	.583	25	15	.625	15	25	.375	2	2	.500
Denver Rockets	34	50	.405	26	21	39	.350	13	**11**	.542	25	15	.625	8	**34**	.190	1	1	.500
Memphis Pros	26	58	.310	34	22	**50**	.306	4	8	.333	18	**23**	.439	8	31	.205	0	**4**	.000

1971/72 A.B.A. INDIVIDUAL LEADERS

SCORING
(Minimum 70 Games Played)

Name	Team	G	FG	FT	Pts.	Avg.
Scott	Va	73	985	525	2524	34.6
Barry	NY	80	902	641	2518	31.5
Issel	KY	83	972	591	2538	30.6
Simpson	Den	84	920	457	2300	27.4
Erving	Va	84	910	467	2290	27.3
Thompson	Pit	70	696	455	1888	27.0
Freeman	Dal	72	628	475	1733	24.1
Gilmore	KY	84	806	391	2003	23.9
Beaty	Utah	84	729	522	1980	23.6
Wise	Utah	84	743	459	1951	23.2

FIELD GOAL PERCENTAGE
(Minimum 560 Attempts)

Name	Team	FG	FGA	Pct.
Gilmore	KY	806	1348	.598
Washington	NY	387	678	.571
Lattin	Pit	329	605	.544
Lewis	Pit	385	713	.540
Beaty	Utah	729	1353	.539
Jones	Fla	423	797	.531
McDaniels	Car	659	1276	.516
Jones	Utah	462	903	.512
Daniels	Ind	598	1184	.505
Wise	Utah	743	1471	.505

3-POINT FIELD GOAL PERCENT AGE
(Minimum 20 Made)

Name	Team	FT	FGA	Pct.
Robbins	Utah	29	71	.408
Combs	Utah	103	254	.406
Tucker	Fla	30	82	.366
Dampier	KY	84	233	.361
Jabali	Fla	102	285	.358
Lehmann	Car-Mem	71	199	.357
Hamilton	Dal	46	132	.348
S. Jones	Dal	26	78	.333
Keller	Ind	56	169	.331
Swirt	Pit	33	100	.330

FREE THROW PERCENTAGE
(Minimum 160 Attempts)

Name	Team	FT	FTA	Pct.
Lehmann	Car-Mem	169	192	.880
Keller	Ind	153	174	.879
Barry	NY	641	730	.878
Calvin	Fla	611	701	.872
S. Jones	Dal	367	422	.870
Brisker	Pit	248	286	.867
Lewis	Ind	341	395	.861
Becker	Den	165	195	.846
Swift	Pit	224	265	.845
Beck	Den	140	166	.843

REBOUNDS PER GAME
(Minimum 70 Games Played)

Name	Team	G	Reb.	Avg.
Gilmore	KY	84	1491	17.8
Daniels	Ind	79	1297	16.4
Erving	Va	84	1319	15.7
Govan	Mem	83	1182	14.2
Beaty	Utah	84	1110	13.2
Paultz	NY	83	1035	12.5
Lewis	Pit	82	996	12.2
Keye	Den	84	982	11.7
Issel	KY	83	931	11.2
Wise	Utah	84	894	10.6

ASSISTS PER GAME
(Minimum 70 Games Played)

Name	Team	G	Ass.	Avg.
Melchionni	NY	80	669	8.4
Brown	Den	76	549	7.2
Jones	Utah	78	485	6.2
Dampier	KY	83	515	6.2
Jabali	Fla	81	495	6.1
Calvin	Fla	82	481	5.9
Scott	Va	73	347	4.8
Lewis	Ind	77	362	4.7
O'Brien	Pit-KY	84	373	4.4
Govan	Mem	83	348	4.2

MINUTES PLAYED

Name	Team	Min.
Gilmore	KY	3666
Barry	NY	3616
Issel	KY	3570
Erving	Va	3513
Govan	Mem	3414

PERSONAL FOULS

Name	Team	PF
Ladner	Mem-Car	347
Keye	Den	346
Jones	Mem	322
Lewis	Pit	315
Beaty	Utah	315

TEAM STATISTICS

Team		REGULAR SEASON G	FG	FGA	%	FT	FTA	%	Reb	Ass	PF	Points	PPG	PLAYOFFS G	FG	FGA	%	FT	FTA	%	Reb	Ass	PF	Points	PPG
EASTERN DIVISION																									
Kentucky	Off.	84	3803	7796	**49**	2003	2697	74	4502	**2136**	1959	9743	116.0	6	236	498	47	114	150	76	261	122	137	600	100.0
	Def.	84	3597	8142	**44**	**1661**	**2227**	**75**	4280	1806	2094	8989	107.0	6	243	498	49	**122**	**153**	80	**270**	119	126	620	103.3
	Diff.		**+206**	-346	**+5**	+342	**+470**	-1	+222	+330	+135	**+754**	**+9.0**		-7	—	-2	-8	-3	-4	-9	+3	-11	-20	-3.3
Virginia	Off.	84	**3913**	**8458**	46	2101	2788	75	**4661**	1764	2234	9988	118.9	11	**518**	1057	49	248	316	78	594	**239**	291	1289	**117.2**
	Def.	84	3780	8333	45	2209	2923	76	4662	1830	2150	9914	118.0	11	460	1039	44	268	359	75	557	198	262	1207	109.7
	Diff.		+133	+125	+1	-108	-135	-1	-1	-66	-84	+74	+.9		**+58**	+18	+5	-20	-43	+3	+37	+41	-29	+82	**+7.5**
New York	Off.	84	3697	7698	48	1990	2589	77	4155	1842	2065	9476	112.8	19	805	1687	48	399	539	74	873	360	**432**	2043	107.5
	Def.	84	3616	7896	46	2041	2682	76	4263	1592	2068	9445	112.4	19	824	1724	48	396	526	75	952	382	461	2083	109.6
	Diff.		+81	-198	+2	-51	-93	+1	-108	+250	+3	+31	+.4		-19	-37	—	+3	+13	-1	-79	-22	+29	-40	-2.1
Floridians	Off.	84	3547	7797	45	2190	2817	78	3974	1871	2125	9471	112.8	4	159	**385**	41	103	131	79	214	78	103	426	106.5
	Def.	84	3709	7869	47	2070	2689	77	4446	1818	2229	9603	114.3	4	189	369	51	93	118	79	207	91	**107**	472	118.0
	Diff.		-162	-72	-2	+120	+128	+1	-472	+53	+104	-132	-1.5		-30	+16	-10	+10	+13	—	+7	-13	+4	-46	-11.5
Carolina	Off.	84	3818	8391	46	1870	2536	74	4309	1735	2173	9646	114.8												
	Def.	84	3883	7983	49	2039	2706	75	4462	1750	2104	9923	118.1												
	Diff.		-65	**+408**	-3	-169	-170	-1	-153	-15	-69	-277	-3.3												
Pittsburgh	Off.	84	3912	8226	48	2052	2725	75	4438	1835	2185	**10016**	**119.2**												
	Def.	84	4145	8414	49	2205	2852	77	4449	2026	2147	10617	126.4												
	Diff.		-233	-188	-1	-153	-127	-2	-11	-191	-38	-601	-7.2												
WESTERN DIVISION																									
Utah	Off.	84	3731	7767	48	**2259**	**2863**	**79**	4535	1854	2060	9892	117.8	11	471	922	**51**	261	345	76	549	236	293	1213	110.3
	Def.	84	3700	8224	45	1874	2472	76	4384	1909	**2257**	9412	112.0	11	458	1025	45	247	338	**73**	539	222	293	1186	107.8
	Diff.		+31	-457	+3	**+385**	+391	**+3**	+151	-55	+197	+480	+5.8		+13	-103	**+6**	+14	+7	+3	+10	+14	—	+27	+2.5
Indiana	Off.	84	3601	7805	46	2065	2756	75	4578	1731	**1908**	9487	112.9	20	825	1816	45	464	629	74	1017	384	479	2167	108.4
	Def.	84	3718	8183	45	1726	2298	75	4336	1918	2180	9266	110.3	20	858	1807	47	410	558	73	1002	418	532	2145	107.3
	Diff.		-117	-378	+1	+339	+458	—	**+242**	-187	**+272**	+221	+2.6		-33	+9	-2	**+54**	**+71**	+1	+15	-34	**+53**	+22	+1.1
Dallas	Off.	84	3362	7502	45	1943	2498	78	3991	1486	2315	8770	104.4	4	161	367	44	65	95	68	183	83	123	391	97.8
	Def.	84	**3267**	7255	45	2105	2781	76	**4108**	1631	2087	**8760**	**104.3**	4	**148**	**289**	51	120	143	84	190	**68**	95	418	104.5
	Diff.		+95	+247	—	-162	-283	+2	-117	-145	-228	+10	+.1		+13	**+78**	-7	-55	-48	-16	-7	**+15**	-28	-27	-6.7
Denver	Off.	84	3703	8247	45	1953	2601	75	4481	1995	2334	9400	111.9	7	274	639	43	157	198	**79**	**383**	129	187	708	101.1
	Def.	84	3557	**7840**	45	2233	2979	75	4514	1885	2122	9500	113.1	7	269	620	**43**	155	208	75	357	133	169	706	100.9
	Diff.		+146	+407	—	-280	-378	—	-33	+110	-212	-100	-1.2		+5	+19	—	+2	-10	**+4**	**+26**	-4	-18	+2	+.2
Memphis	Off.	84	3499	8408	42	1875	2525	74	4805	1611	2169	9029	107.5												
	Def.	84	3615	7956	45	2138	2786	77	4525	1695	2089	9489	113.0												
	Diff.		-116	+452	-3	-263	-261	-3	+280	-84	-80	-460	-5.5												

1972-73 N.B.A.

Defensively Sinking the Lakers

The executioner's axe stayed sharp this season as coaches went to the chopping block with some degree of regularity. At Phoenix, Butch van Breda Kolff, hired to replace Cotton Fitzsimmons, lasted just eight games before general manager Jerry Colangelo decided that he had made a mistake in hiring coaches and took over the job himself. Colangelo and star forward Connie Hawkins found each other's company quite distasteful, with the result that Hawkins' scoring average fell to 16.1 and the Suns fell to a 38-44 record. At Detroit, Earl Lloyd was on shaky ground as the season started, and a 2-5 record out of the gate did him in, with former Piston player Ray Scott assuming the task of trying to get the Pistons to work together as a team.

In Seattle, new coach Tom Nissalke started out with two strikes against him. Lenny Wilkins had decided to concentrate on playing and to give up the coaching reins, which went to Nissalke. To avoid a potentially sticky situation, the Sonics dealt the popular Wilkins to Cleveland which both alienated the fans and removed the team's backcourt leader. With Jim McDaniels and John Brisker, two expensive A.B.A. defectors, joining Spencer Haywood in the lineup, Nissalke (himself a former A.B.A. coach) was expected to win immediately. But without Wilkins, the Sonics lacked a dependable playmaker, and they stumbled to a horrible start amidst rumors that the players would not put out their best for Nissalke. With the team record standing at 13-32, Nissalke was canned and Bucky Buckwalter appointed head coach. At the season's end, the Sonics had fallen from the preseason favorite's role in the Pacific Division to a poor 26-56 record. Tex Winter's problem in Houston was that he couldn't get the Rockets to play defense, and he was fired late in the campaign in favor of Johnny Egan, who directed the club to a 16-19 mark down the stretch.

But the most abominable situation belonged to Roy Rubin, the freshman coach of the Philadelphia 76ers. Making his pro debut after many years at Long Island University, Rubin took charge of a team that had been the class of the N.B.A. six years ago but had now fallen on hard times. One bad draft after another had minimized the young talent coming to the club, and a series of bad deals had sent away the stars of the 1966-67 championship squad without bringing much in return. The courts this year ruled that star forward Billy Cunningham had signed a legal contract with the Carolina Cougars of the A.B.A. and was obligated to play there. This was the straw that broke the camel's back in Philly. Rubin fielded a miserable outfit, lacking in speed and board strength and making a multitude of mental errors. With veteran Hal Greer relegated to the bench, rookie Freddie Boyd was given the playmaker's job, a task he handled in very unsure fashion. The 76ers had expected this to be a rebuilding year, but the team lost so regularly and by such big margins that Rubin was ousted with the 76ers beaten down to a 4-47 level. Guard Kevin Loughery took over as coach and could coax only a slight improvement out of the squad, with the 76ers setting a new record for futility with a 9-73 record, much like the early New York Mets without the charm of being an expansion team.

Fifty-nine games ahead of the 76ers in the Atlantic Division were the Boston Celtics, whose sparkling 68-14 record was the class of the league. These new Celtics relied on the fast break just as earlier editions of the team had, and they often won games simply by running the opposition down. John Havlicek had won All-Star notices for several years, but the critics this year acclaimed center Dave Cowens as the league MVP. The biggest addition to the Celtics this year was rebounding forward Paul Silas, who came from Phoenix as compensation for the Suns' signing of Charlie Scott, who had been a Boston draft choice. The New York Knicks finished a strong second, with Willis Reed rounding into shape as the season progressed and with Earl (The Pearl) Monroe fitting smoothly into the New York style of play. Buffalo finished a weak third, but got a strong season out of rookie forward Bob McAdoo.

Although the Baltimore Bullets did get help from rookie guard Kevin Porter, a new pair of forwards sparked the club's improvement to a 52-30 record and first place in the Central Division. Elvin Hayes came from Houston in a trade for Jack Marin and teamed with center Wes Unseld to give the Bullets two first-rate big men, while 6'4" Mike Riordan blossomed into stardom as a small forward. Phil Chenier and Porter held down the backcourt positions while Archie Clark sat out the first half of the season in a salary dispute. The Hawks improved to 46-36 under new coach Cotton Fitzsimmons and took the second playoff berth in the Central Division.

The two playoff berths in the Midwest Division went as expected to the Milwaukee Bucks, with Kareem Abdul-Jabbar, and the Chicago Bulls, who lost center Tom Boerwinkle to a knee injury but got solid work out of subs Clifford Ray and Dennis Awtrey. Detroit improved in the later stages of the season to finish third, and the Kansas City-Omaha Kings, who were the transplanted Cincinnati Royals, finished last despite an outstanding performance by 6' Nate Archibald. With mostly mediocre talent in the lineup with him, Archibald combined speed, moves, and fine shooting to notch a league-leading 34.0 points per game and to make himself an instant gate attraction.

In the Pacific Division, the Lakers didn't put together any 33-game winning streaks this year but still managed to win first place with a 60-22 record. Behind Los Angeles in second place were the Golden State Warriors, who rejoiced over the return of star forward Rick Barry from the A.B.A. Phoenix, Seattle, and Portland brought up the rear in the division.

The West Coast produced the only upset of the first round of the playoffs, as the Warriors stunned the Bucks by eliminating them in six games. Boston and New York won handily, while the Lakers had to take a 95-92 decision in game seven to get past the Bulls. The Eastern final was a copy of last year's, as the second-place Knicks upended the first-place Celtics, with New York taking a 94-78 seventh game victory in which John Havlicek was disabled with a bad shoulder.

The Lakers disposed of the Warriors in the West and were favored to repeat as champions over the Knicks as they had last year. One factor was different this season, however, New York center Willis Reed was healthy and able to battle Chamberlain under the boards. The Lakers won the first game, 115-112, but then the Knicks pressed the Lakers and held them under 100 points for the next four games, all of which were victories for the New Yorkers, who had their second N.B.A. championship in four years.

1972/73 N.B.A. — ATLANTIC DIVISION

Use Name	Pos	Hgt	Wgt	Age	G	Min	FG	FGA	%	FT	FTA	%	Reb	Ass	PF	DQ	Points	Min	Reb	Ass	PF	Points
					TOTAL													PER GAME				
BOSTON CELTICS	68-14 .829				TOM HEINSOHN																	
John Havlicek	F-G	6'5	205	33	80	3367	766	1704	45	370	431	86	567	529	195	1	1902	42	7.1	6.6	2.4	23.8
Paul Silas	F	6'7	225	29	80	2614	400	851	47	266	380	70	1039	251	197	1	1066	33	13.0	3.1	2.5	13.3
Dave Cowens	C	6'9	230	24	82	3425	740	1637	45	204	262	78	1329	333	311	7	1684	42	16.2	4.1	3.8	20.5
Don Chaney	G	6'5	210	26	79	2488	414	859	48	210	267	79	449	221	276	6	1038	31	5.7	2.8	3.5	13.1
Jo Jo White	G	6'3	190	26	82	3250	717	1655	43	178	228	78	414	498	185	2	1612	40	5.0	6.1	2.3	19.7
Don Nelson	F	6'6	210	33	72	1425	309	649	48	159	188	85	315	102	155	1	777	20	4.4	1.4	2.2	10.8
Hambone Williams	G	6'2	190	33	81	974	110	261	42	43	56	77	182	236	136	1	263	12	2.2	2.9	1.7	3.2
Steve Kuberski	F	6'8	215	25	78	762	140	347	40	65	84	77	197	26	92	0	345	10	2.5	0.3	1.2	4.4
Henry Finkel	C	7'	240	30	76	496	78	173	45	28	52	54	151	26	83	0	184	7	2.0	0.3	1.1	2.4
Paul Westphal	G	6'4	195	22	60	482	89	212	42	67	86	78	67	69	88	0	245	8	1.1	1.2	1.5	4.1
Satch Sanders	F	6'6	210	34	59	423	47	149	32	23	35	66	88	27	82	0	117	7	1.5	0.5	1.4	2.0
Mark Mirror	F	6'6	215	22	4	20	1	4	25	3	4	75	4	2	5	0	5	5	1.0	0.5	1.3	1.3
NEW YORK KNICKERBOCKERS	57-25 .695				RED HOLZMAN																	
Bill Bradley	F	6'5	205	29	82	2998	575	1252	46	169	194	87	301	367	273	5	1319	37	3.7	4.5	3.3	16.1
Dave DeBusschere	F	6'6	235	32	77	2827	532	1224	43	194	260	75	787	259	215	1	1258	37	10.2	3.4	2.8	16.3
Willis Reed (knee injury)	C	6'9	240	30	69	1876	334	705	47	92	124	74	590	126	205	0	760	27	8.6	1.8	3.0	11.0
Walt Frazier	G	6'4	205	27	78	3181	681	1389	49	286	350	82	570	461	186	0	1648	41	7.3	5.9	2.4	21.1
Earl Monroe	G	6'3	190	28	75	2370	496	1016	49	171	208	82	245	288	195	1	1163	32	3.3	3.8	2.6	15.5
Jerry Lucas	C-F	6'8	230	32	71	2001	312	608	51	80	100	80	510	317	157	0	704	28	7.2	4.5	2.2	9.9
Dean Meminger	G	6'	175	24	80	1453	188	365	52	81	129	63	229	133	109	1	457	18	2.9	1.7	1.4	5.7
Phil Jackson	F-C	6'8	220	27	80	1393	245	553	44	154	195	79	344	94	218	2	644	17	4.3	1.2	2.7	8.1
John Gianelli	C-F	6'10	220	22	52	516	79	175	45	23	33	70	150	25	72	0	181	10	2.9	0.5	1.4	3.5
Dick Barnett	G	6'4	190	36	51	514	88	226	39	16	30	53	41	50	52	0	192	10	0.8	1.0	1.0	3.8
Henry Bibby	G	6'1	185	23	55	475	78	205	38	73	86	85	82	64	67	0	229	9	1.5	1.2	1.2	4.2
Tom Riker	F	6'10	250	22	14	65	10	24	42	15	24	63	16	2	15	0	35	5	1.1	0.1	1.1	2.5
Harthorne Wingo	F	6'8	210	24	13	59	9	22	41	2	6	33	16	1	9	0	20	5	1.2	0.1	0.7	1.5
Luther Rackley (to MemA)	C	6'10	225	26	1	2	0	0	—	0	0	—	1	0	2	0	0	2	1.0	0.0	2.0	0.0
BUFFALO BRAVES	21-61 .256				JACK RAMSAY																	
Bob McAdoo	F	6'9	210	21	80	2562	585	1293	45	271	350	77	728	139	256	6	1441	32	9.1	1.7	3.2	18.0
Bob Kauffman	F-C	6'8	240	26	77	3049	535	1059	51	280	359	78	855	396	211	1	1350	40	11.1	5.1	2.7	17.5
Elmore Smith	C	7'	250	23	76	2829	600	1244	48	188	337	56	946	192	295	16	1388	37	12.4	2.5	3.9	18.3
Randy Smith	G-F	6'3	180	24	82	2603	511	1154	44	192	264	73	391	422	247	1	1214	32	4.8	5.1	3.0	14.8
Dave Wohl (from Port)	G	6'2	185	23	56	1540	207	454	46	79	100	79	89	258	182	3	493	28	1.6	4.6	3.3	8.8
Dick Garrett	G	6'3	185	25	78	1805	341	813	42	96	110	87	209	217	217	4	778	23	2.7	2.8	2.8	10.0
John Hummer	F	6'9	230	24	66	1546	206	464	44	115	205	56	323	138	185	5	527	23	4.9	2.1	2.8	8.0
Howie Komives	G	6'1	185	31	67	1468	163	429	38	85	98	87	118	239	155	1	411	22	1.8	3.6	2.3	6.1
Bill Hewitt	F	6'7	210	28	73	1332	152	364	42	41	74	55	368	110	154	3	345	18	5.0	1.5	2.1	4.7
Fred Hilton	G-F	6'3	185	24	59	731	191	494	39	41	53	77	98	74	100	0	423	12	1.7	1.3	1.7	7.2
Mahdi Abdul-Rahman (to GS)	G	6'2	190	30	9	134	25	60	42	3	6	50	10	17	19	0	53	15	1.1	1.9	2.1	5.9
Harold Fox	G	6'2	175	23	10	84	12	32	38	7	8	88	8	10	7	0	31	8	0.8	1.0	0.7	3.1
Cornell Warner (to Cle)	F	6'9	220	24	4	47	8	17	47	1	2	50	15	6	6	0	17	12	3.8	1.5	1.5	4.3
PHILADELPHIA 76ers	9-73 .110				ROY RUBIN (4-47 .078), KEVIN LOUGHERY (5-26 .192)																	
Tom Van Arsdale (from KCO)	F	6'5	215	30	30	1029	195	496	39	140	168	83	185	62	101	1	530	34	6.2	2.1	3.4	17.7
Leroy Ellis (from LA)	F-C	6'10	225	32	69	2444	410	929	44	125	156	80	744	136	186	2	945	35	10.8	2.0	2.7	13.7
Manny Leaks	C-F	6'8	235	27	82	2530	377	933	40	144	200	72	677	95	191	5	898	31	8.3	1.2	2.3	11.0
Fred Carter	G-F	6'3	185	27	81	2993	679	1614	42	259	368	70	485	349	252	8	1617	37	6.0	4.3	3.1	20.0
Freddie Boyd	G	6'2	180	22	82	2351	362	923	39	136	200	68	210	301	184	1	860	29	2.6	3.7	2.2	10.5
John Block (to KCO)	F	6'10	220	28	48	1558	311	706	44	236	302	78	442	94	173	4	858	32	9.2	2.0	3.6	17.9
Dale Schlueter	C	6'10	235	27	78	1136	166	317	52	86	123	70	354	103	166	0	418	15	4.5	1.3	2.1	5.4
Kevin Loughery	G	6'3	190	32	32	955	169	427	40	107	130	82	113	148	104	0	445	30	3.5	4.6	3.3	13.9
John Trapp (from LA, to DenA)	F	6'7	215	27	39	854	168	408	41	83	112	74	186	47	140	4	419	22	4.8	1.2	3.6	10.7
Hal Greer	G	6'3	176	36	38	848	91	232	39	32	39	82	106	111	76	1	214	22	2.8	2.9	2.0	5.6
Mike Price	G	6'3	200	24	57	751	125	301	42	38	47	81	117	71	106	0	288	13	2.1	1.2	1.9	5.1
Dave Sorenson (from Cle)	F	6'8	225	24	48	626	113	248	46	59	79	75	173	31	91	0	285	13	3.6	0.6	1.9	5.9
Don May (from Atl)	F	6'4	215	26	26	602	128	290	44	53	62	85	143	43	80	1	309	23	5.5	1.7	3.1	11.9
Jeff Halliburton (from Atl)	G	6'5	195	23	31	549	122	280	44	50	66	76	82	68	78	1	294	18	2.6	2.2	2.5	9.5
Bill Bridges (to LA)	F	6'6	235	33	10	376	47	125	38	46	65	71	122	23	35	0	140	38	12.2	2.3	3.5	14.0
Mel Counts (to U)	C-F	7'	235	31	7	47	5	16	31	0	0	—	16	3	8	0	10	7	2.3	0.4	1.1	1.4
Dennis Awtrey (to Chi)	C	6'10	250	24	3	37	3	7	43	1	4	25	14	2	8	0	7	12	4.7	0.7	2.7	2.3
Luther Green	F	6'7	190	26	5	32	0	11	0	3	9	33	3	0	3	0	3	6	0.6	0.0	0.6	0.6
Bob Rule (to Cle) (KJ)	C	6'9	235	28	3	12	0	1	0	0	0	—	2	1	2	0	0	4	0.7	0.3	0.7	0.0

1972/73 N.B.A. - CENTRAL DIVISION

Use Name	Pos	Hgt	Wgt	Age	TOTAL													PER GAME				
					G	Min	FG	FGA	%	FT	FTA	%	Reb	Ass	PF	DQ	Points	Min	Reb	Ass	PF	Points
BALTIMORE BULLETS	52-30 .634				**GENE SHUE**																	
Mike Riordan	F-G	6'4	200	27	82	3466	652	1278	51	179	218	82	404	426	216	0	1483	42	4.9	5.2	2.6	18.1
Elvin Hayes	F-C	6'9	235	27	81	3347	713	1607	44	291	434	67	1177	127	232	3	1717	41	14.5	1.6	2.9	21.2
Wes Unseld	C	6'7	250	26	79	3085	421	854	49	149	212	70	1260	347	168	0	991	39	15.9	4.4	2.1	12.5
Phil Chenier	G	6'3	180	22	71	2776	602	1332	45	194	244	80	288	301	160	0	1398	39	4.1	4.2	2.3	19.7
Archie Clark (holdout)	G	6'2	175	31	39	1477	302	596	51	111	137	81	129	275	111	1	715	38	3.3	7.1	2.8	18.3
Kevin Porter	G	6'	175	22	71	1217	205	451	45	62	101	61	72	237	206	5	472	17	1.0	3.3	2.9	6.6
Dave Stallworth	F	6'7	220	31	73	1217	180	435	41	78	101	77	236	112	139	1	438	17	3.2	1.5	1.9	6.0
Stan Love	F	6'9	215	23	72	995	190	436	44	79	100	79	300	46	175	0	459	14	4.2	0.6	2.4	6.4
Rich Rinaldi	G	6'3	195	23	33	646	116	284	41	48	64	75	68	48	40	0	280	20	2.1	1.5	1.2	8.5
Flynn Robinson (from LA)	G	6'1	190	31	38	583	119	260	46	26	31	84	55	77	60	0	264	15	1.4	2.0	1.6	6.9
John Tresvant	F	6'7	220	33	55	541	85	182	47	41	59	69	156	33	101	0	211	10	2.8	0.6	1.8	3.8
Mike Davis (to MemA)	G	6'3	185	26	13	283	50	118	42	23	25	92	35	19	45	4	123	22	2.7	1.5	3.5	9.5
Tommy Patterson	F	6'6	220	24	23	92	21	49	43	13	16	81	22	3	18	0	55	4	1.0	0.1	0.8	2.4
Terry Driscoll (to Mil)	F	6'7	215	25	1	5	0	1	0	0	0	—	3	0	1	0	0	5	3.0	0.0	1.0	0.0
ATLANTA HAWKS	46-36 .561				**RICHIE GUERIN**																	
Lou Hudson	F-G	6'5	215	28	75	3027	816	1710	48	397	481	83	467	258	197	1	2029	40	6.2	3.4	2.6	27.1
Jim Washington	F	6'7	215	29	75	2833	308	713	43	163	224	73	801	174	252	5	779	38	10.7	2.3	3.4	10.4
Walt Bellamy	C	6'11	245	33	74	2802	455	901	50	283	526	54	964	179	244	1	1193	38	13.0	2.4	3.3	16.1
Pete Maravich	G	6'5	195	24	79	3089	789	1788	44	485	606	80	346	546	245	1	2063	39	4.4	6.9	3.1	26.1
Herm Gilliam	G	6'3	190	26	76	2741	471	1007	47	123	150	82	399	482	257	8	1065	36	5.3	6.3	3.4	14.0
George Trapp	F-C	6'8	215	24	77	1853	359	824	44	150	194	77	455	127	274	11	868	24	5.9	1.6	3.6	11.3
Steve Bracey	G	6'1	175	22	70	1050	192	395	49	73	110	66	107	125	125	0	457	15	1.5	1.8	1.8	6.5
Bob Christian	C	7'	260	28	55	759	85	155	55	60	79	76	305	47	111	2	230	14	5.5	0.9	2.0	4.2
John Wetzel	G	6'5	190	28	28	504	42	94	45	14	17	82	58	39	41	1	98	18	2.1	1.4	1.5	3.5
Eddie Mast	F	6'9	220	24	42	447	50	118	42	19	30	63	136	37	50	0	119	11	3.2	0.9	1.2	2.8
Don May(to Phi)	F	6'4	215	26	32	317	61	134	46	22	31	71	67	21	55	0	144	10	2.1	0.7	1.7	4.5
Jeff Halliburton (to Phi)	G	6'5	195	23	24	238	50	116	43	21	22	95	26	28	29	0	121	10	1.1	1.2	1.2	5.0
John Tschogl	F	6'6	210	22	10	94	14	40	35	2	4	50	21	6	25	0	30	9	2.1	0.6	2.5	3.0
Don Adams (to Det)	F	6'7	220	25	4	76	8	38	21	7	8	88	22	5	11	0	23	19	5.5	1.3	2.8	5.8
HOUSTON ROCKETS	33-49 .402				**TEX WINTER (17-30 .362), JOHNNY EGAN (16-19 .457)**																	
Jack Marin	F	6'7	210	28	81	3019	624	1334	47	248	292	85	499	291	247	4	1496	37	6.2	3.6	3.0	18.5
Rudy Tomjanovich	F	6'8	220	24	81	2972	655	1371	48	250	335	75	938	178	225	1	1560	37	11.6	2.2	2.8	19.3
Otto Moore	C	6'11	220	26	82	2712	418	859	49	127	211	60	868	167	239	4	963	33	10.6	2.0	2.9	11.7
Mike Newlin	G	6'4	200	23	82	2658	534	1206	44	327	369	89	340	409	301	5	1395	32	4.1	5.0	3.7	17.0
Jimmy Walker	G	6'3	205	28	81	3079	605	1301	47	244	276	88	268	442	207	0	1454	38	3.3	5.5	2.6	18.0
Calvin Murphy	G	5'9	165	24	77	1697	381	820	46	239	269	89	149	262	211	3	1001	22	1.9	3.4	2.7	13.0
Cliff Meely	F-C	6'8	215	25	82	1694	268	657	41	92	137	67	496	91	263	6	628	21	6.0	1.1	3.2	7.7
Don Smith	C	6'9	240	26	48	900	149	375	40	119	162	73	304	53	108	2	417	19	6.3	1.1	2.3	8.7
Paul McCracken	G	6'4	180	22	24	305	44	89	49	23	39	59	51	17	32	0	111	13	2.1	0.7	1.3	4.6
Eric McWilliams	F	6'8	200	22	44	245	34	98	35	18	37	49	60	5	46	0	86	6	1.4	0.1	1.0	2.0
Stan McKenzie (from Port)	G-F	6'5	210	28	26	187	35	83	42	16	21	76	34	15	28	0	86	7	1.3	0.6	1.1	3.3
George Johnson	C	6'11	255	25	19	169	20	39	51	3	4	75	45	3	33	0	43	9	2.4	0.2	1.7	2.3
Greg Smith (to Port)	F	6'5	200	25	4	41	5	16	31	0	0	—	8	5	8	0	10	10	2.0	1.3	2.0	2.5
Dick Gibbs (to KCO)	F	6'5	210	24	1	2	0	1	0	0	0	—	0	1	1	0	0	2	0.0	1.0	1.0	0.0
CLEVELAND CAVALIERS	32-50 .390				**BILL FITCH**																	
John Johnson	F	6'7	200	25	82	2815	492	1143	43	199	271	73	552	309	246	3	1183	34	6.7	3.8	3.0	14.4
Dwight Davis	F-C	6'8	220	23	81	2151	293	748	39	176	222	79	563	118	297	5	762	27	7.0	1.5	3.7	9.4
Rick Roberson	C	6'9	230	25	62	2127	307	709	43	167	290	58	693	134	249	5	781	34	11.2	2.2	4.0	12.6
Austin Carr	G	6'4	200	24	82	3097	702	1575	45	281	342	82	369	279	185	1	1685	38	4.5	3.4	2.3	20.5
Lenny Wilkens	G	6'1	185	35	75	2973	572	1275	45	394	476	83	346	628	221	2	1538	40	4.6	8.4	2.9	20.5
Jim Cleamons	G	6'3	185	23	80	1392	192	423	45	75	101	74	167	205	108	0	459	17	2.1	2.6	1.4	5.7
Cornell Warner(from Buf)	F	6'9	220	24	68	1323	166	404	41	58	88	66	507	66	172	3	390	19	7.5	1.0	2.5	5.7
Barry Clemens	F	6'7	220	30	72	1119	209	405	52	53	68	78	211	115	136	0	471	16	2.9	1.6	1.9	6.5
Bobby Smith	F-G	6'5	212	26	73	1068	268	603	44	64	81	79	199	108	80	0	600	15	2.7	1.5	1.1	8.2
Steve Patterson	C	6'9	225	24	62	710	71	198	36	34	65	52	228	51	79	1	176	11	3.7	0.8	1.3	2.8
Bob Rule (from Phi) (XJ)	C	6'9	235	28	49	440	60	157	38	20	31	65	106	37	66	0	140	9	2.2	0.8	1.3	2.9
Johnny Warren	G	6'3	180	25	40	290	54	111	49	18	19	95	42	34	45	0	126	7	1.1	0.9	1.1	3.2
Dave Sorenson (to Phi)	F	6'8	225	24	10	129	11	45	24	5	11	45	37	5	16	0	27	13	3.7	0.5	1.6	2.7
Walt Wesley (to Phoe)	C	6'11	230	28	12	110	14	47	30	8	12	67	38	7	21	0	36	9	3.2	0.6	1.8	3.0
Charlie Davis (to Port)	G	6'2	160	23	6	86	20	41	49	4	7	57	5	10	20	1	44	14	0.8	1.7	3.3	7.3

Use Name	Pos	Hgt	Wgt	Age	TOTAL													PER GAME				
					G	Min	FG	FGA	%	FT	FTA	%	Reb	Ass	PF	DQ	Points	Min	Reb	Ass	PF	Points

1972/73 N.B.A. — MIDWEST DIVISION

Use Name	Pos	Hgt	Wgt	Age	G	Min	FG	FGA	%	FT	FTA	%	Reb	Ass	PF	DQ	Points	Min	Reb	Ass	PF	Points
MILWAUKEE BUCKS	**60-22 .732**				**LARRY COSTELLO**																	
Bob Dandridge	F	6'6	195	25	73	2852	638	1353	47	198	251	79	600	207	279	2	1474	39	8.2	2.8	3.8	20.2
Curtis Perry	F	6'7	230	24	67	2094	265	575	46	83	126	66	644	123	246	6	613	31	9.6	1.8	3.7	9.1
Kareem Abdul-Jabbar	C	7'3	232	25	76	3254	982	1772	55	328	460	71	1224	379	208	0	2292	43	16.1	5.0	2.7	30.2
Oscar Robertson	G	6'5	220	34	73	2737	446	983	45	238	281	85	360	551	167	0	1130	37	4.9	7.5	2.3	15.5
Lucius Allen	G	6'2	175	25	80	2693	547	1130	48	143	200	72	279	426	188	1	1237	34	3.5	5.3	2.4	15.5
Jon McGlocklin	G	6'5	205	29	80	1951	351	699	50	63	73	86	158	236	119	0	765	24	2.0	3.0	1.5	9.6
Mickey Davis	F	6'7	215	22	74	1046	152	347	44	76	92	83	226	72	119	0	380	14	3.1	1.0	1.6	5.1
Terry Driscoll (from Bal)	F	6'7	215	25	59	959	140	326	43	43	62	69	297	55	143	3	323	16	5.0	0.9	2.4	5.5
Chuck Terry	F	6'6	215	22	67	693	55	162	34	17	24	71	145	40	116	1	127	10	2.2	0.6	1.7	1.9
Dick Cunningham	C	6'10	250	26	72	692	64	156	41	29	50	58	208	34	94	0	157	10	2.9	0.5	1.3	2.2
Wali Jones (ST)	G	6'2	185	30	27	419	59	145	41	16	18	89	29	56	39	0	134	16	1.1	2.1	1.4	5.0
Russ Lee	F-G	6'5	185	22	46	277	49	127	39	32	43	74	43	38	36	0	130	6	0.9	0.8	0.8	2.8
Gary Gregor (to NY-A)	F	6'7	225	27	9	88	11	33	33	5	7	71	32	9	9	0	27	10	3.6	1.0	1.0	3.0
CHICAGO BULLS	**51-31 .622**				**DICK MOTTA**																	
Chet Walker	F	6'6	220	32	79	2455	597	1248	48	376	452	83	395	179	166	1	1570	31	5.0	2.3	2.1	19.9
Bob Love	F	6'8	215	30	82	3033	774	1794	43	347	421	82	532	119	240	1	1895	37	6.5	1.5	2.9	23.1
Cliff Ray	C	6'9	235	23	73	2009	254	516	49	117	189	62	797	271	232	5	625	28	10.9	3.7	3.2	8.6
Jerry Sloan	G-F	6'6	200	30	69	2412	301	733	41	94	133	71	475	151	235	5	696	35	6.9	2.2	3.4	10.1
Norm Van Lier	G	6'1	175	25	80	2882	474	1064	45	166	211	79	438	567	269	5	1114	36	5.5	7.1	3.4	13.9
Bob Weiss	G	6'2	185	30	82	2086	279	655	43	159	189	84	148	295	151	1	717	25	1.8	3.6	1.8	8.7
Dennis Awtrey (from Phi)	C	6'10	250	24	79	1650	143	298	48	85	149	57	433	222	226	6	371	21	5.5	2.8	2.9	4.7
Gar Heard (from Sea)	F	6'6	226	24	78	1535	346	815	42	115	177	65	447	58	167	1	807	20	5.7	0.7	2.1	10.3
Jim King	G	6'2	175	31	65	785	116	263	44	44	52	85	76	81	76	0	276	12	1.2	1.2	1.2	4.2
Howard Porter	F-C	6'8	220	24	43	407	98	217	45	22	29	76	118	16	52	1	218	9	2.7	0.4	1.2	5.1
Rowland Garrett	F	6'6	212	22	35	211	52	118	44	21	31	68	61	8	29	0	125	6	1.7	0.2	0.8	3.6
Tom Boerwinkle (KJ)	C	7'	270	27	8	176	9	24	38	12	20	60	54	40	22	0	30	22	6.8	5.0	2.8	3.8
Frank Russell	G	6'3	180	23	23	131	29	77	38	16	18	89	17	15	12	0	74	6	0.7	0.7	0.5	3.2
Kenny McIntosh (to Sea)	F	6'7	225	23	3	33	8	13	62	0	2	0	9	1	4	0	16	11	3.0	0.3	1.3	5.3
DETROIT PISTONS	**40-42 .488**				**EARL LLOYD (2-5 .286), RAY SCOTT (38-37 .507)**																	
Don Adams (from Atl)	F	6'7	220	25	70	1798	257	640	40	138	176	78	419	112	220	2	652	26	6.0	1.6	3.1	9.3
Curtis Rowe	F	6'7	225	24	81	3009	547	1053	52	210	327	64	760	172	191	0	1304	37	9.4	2.1	2.4	16.1
Bob Lanier	C	6'11	260	24	81	3150	810	1654	49	307	397	77	1205	260	278	4	1927	39	14.9	3.2	3.4	23.8
Dave Bing	G	6'3	185	30	82	3361	692	1545	45	456	560	81	298	637	229	1	1840	41	3.6	7.8	2.8	22.4
Stu Lantz (broken wrist)	G	6'3	175	26	51	1603	185	455	41	120	150	80	172	138	117	0	490	31	3.4	2.7	2.3	9.6
Chris Ford	G-F	6'5	190	23	74	1537	208	434	48	60	93	65	266	194	133	1	476	21	3.6	2.6	1.8	6.4
Fred Foster	F	6'5	210	26	63	1460	243	627	39	61	87	70	183	94	150	0	547	23	2.9	1.5	2.4	8.7
John Mengelt (from KCO)	G	6'2	195	23	67	1435	294	583	50	116	141	82	159	128	124	0	704	21	2.4	1.9	1.9	10.5
Willie Norwood	F	6'7	220	25	79	1282	249	504	49	154	225	68	324	56	182	0	652	16	4.1	0.7	2.3	8.3
Jim Davis	C	6'9	235	31	73	771	131	257	51	72	114	63	261	56	126	2	334	11	3.6	0.8	1.7	4.6
Bob Nash	F	6'8	205	22	36	169	16	72	22	11	17	65	34	16	30	0	43	5	0.9	0.4	0.8	1.2
Justus Thigpen	G	6'1	170	25	18	99	23	57	40	0	0	—	9	8	18	0	46	6	0.5	0.4	1.0	2.6
Erwin Mueller	C-F	6'8	230	28	21	80	9	31	29	5	7	71	14	7	13	0	23	4	0.7	0.3	0.6	1.1
Harry Marlatt	G	6'3	185	24	7	26	2	4	50	0	0	—	1	4	1	0	4	4	0.1	0.6	0.1	0.6
KANSAS CITY — OMAHA KINGS	**36-46 .439**				**BOB COUSY**																	
Ron Riley	F	6'8	200	22	74	1634	273	634	43	79	116	68	507	76	226	3	625	22	6.9	1.0	3.1	8.4
John Bloch (from Phi)	F	6'10	220	28	25	483	80	180	44	64	76	84	120	19	69	1	224	19	4.8	0.8	2.8	9.0
Sam Lacey	C	6'10	235	24	79	2930	471	994	47	126	178	71	933	189	283	6	1068	37	11.8	2.4	3.6	13.5
Matt Guokas	G	6'5	195	28	79	2846	322	565	57	74	90	82	245	403	190	0	718	36	3.1	5.1	2.4	9.1
Nate Archibald	G	6'1	160	24	80	**3681**	**1028**	**2106**	49	**663**	**783**	85	223	**910**	207	2	**2719**	**46**	2.8	**11.4**	2.6	**34.0**
Nate Williams	G-F	6'5	215	22	80	1079	417	874	48	106	133	80	339	128	272	9	940	13	4.2	1.6	3.4	11.8
Tom Van Arsdale (to Phi)	F	6'5	215	30	49	1282	250	547	46	110	140	79	173	90	123	1	610	26	3.5	1.8	2.5	12.4
Johnny Green	F	6'5	210	39	66	1245	190	317	60	89	131	68	361	59	185	7	469	19	5.5	0.9	2.8	7.1
Don Kojis	F	6'5	215	33	77	1240	276	575	48	106	137	77	198	80	128	0	658	16	2.6	1.0	1.7	8.5
Dick Gibbs (from Hou)	F	6'5	210	24	66	733	80	221	36	47	63	75	94	61	113	1	207	11	1.4	0.9	1.7	3.1
Mike Ratliff	C	6'10	230	21	58	681	98	235	42	45	84	54	194	38	111	1	241	12	3.3	0.7	1.9	4.2
Toby Kimball	C-F	6'8	242	30	67	743	96	220	44	44	67	66	191	27	86	2	236	11	2.9	0.4	1.3	3.5
John Mengelt (to Det)	G	6'2	195	23	12	212	26	68	38	11	19	58	22	25	24	0	63	18	1.8	2.1	2.0	5.3
Frank Schade	G	6'1	170	22	9	76	2	7	29	6	6	100	6	10	12	0	10	8	0.7	1.1	1.3	1.1
Ken Durrett (knee injury)	F	6'7	190	24	8	65	8	21	38	6	8	75	14	3	16	0	22	8	1.8	0.4	2.0	2.8
Sam Sibert	F	6'7	215	23	5	26	4	13	31	4	5	80	4	0	4	0	12	5	0.8	0.0	0.8	2.4
Pete Cross (to Sea)	C	6'9	230	24	3	24	0	4	0	0	0	—	4	0	5	0	0	8	1.3	0.0	1.7	0.0

Use Name	Pos	Hgt	Wgt	Age	TOTAL G	Min	FG	FGA	%	FT	FTA	%	Reb	Ass	PF	DQ	Points	PER GAME Min	Reb	Ass	PF	Points
1972/73 N.B.A. — PACIFIC DIVISION																						
LOS ANGELES LAKERS	**60-22 .732**				**BILL SHARMAN**																	
Jim McMillian	F	6'5	225	24	81	2953	655	1431	46	223	264	84	447	221	176	0	1533	36	5.5	2.7	2.2	18.9
Happy Hairston (knee injury)	F	6'7	225	30	28	939	158	328	48	140	178	79	370	68	77	0	456	34	13.2	2.4	2.8	16.3
Wilt Chamberlain	C	7'1	275	36	82	3542	426	586	**73**	232	455	51	**1526**	365	191	0	1084	43	**18.6**	4.5	2.3	13.2
Jerry West	G	6'3	185	34	69	2460	618	1291	48	339	421	81	289	607	138	0	1575	36	4.2	8.8	2.0	22.8
Gail Goodrich	G	6'1	175	29	76	2697	750	1615	46	314	374	84	263	332	193	1	1814	35	3.5	4.4	2.5	23.9
Bill Bridges (from Phi)	F	6'6	235	33	72	2491	286	597	48	133	190	70	782	196	261	3	705	35	10.9	2.7	3.6	9.8
Keith Erickson	G-F	6'5	200	28	76	1920	299	696	43	89	110	81	337	242	190	3	687	25	4.4	3.2	2.5	9.0
Jim Price	G	6'3	195	23	59	828	158	359	44	60	73	82	115	97	119	1	376	14	1.9	1.6	2.0	6.4
Pat Riley	G	6'4	208	27	55	801	167	390	43	65	82	79	65	81	126	0	399	15	1.2	1.5	2.3	7.3
Mel Counts (from Phi)	C-F	7'	235	31	59	611	127	278	46	39	58	67	237	62	98	1	293	10	4.0	1.1	1.7	5.0
Leroy Ellis (to Phi)	F-C	6'10	225	32	10	156	11	40	28	4	5	80	33	3	13	0	26	16	3.3	0.3	1.3	2.6
Travis Grant	F	6'8	225	22	33	153	51	116	44	23	26	88	52	7	19	0	125	5	1.6	0.2	0.6	3.8
Bill Turner (from Port)	F	6'7	225	28	19	117	17	52	33	4	7	57	25	11	13	0	38	6	1.3	0.6	0.7	2.0
Flynn Robinson (to Bal)	G	6'1	190	31	6	47	14	28	50	6	8	75	7	8	11	0	34	8	1.2	1.3	1.8	5.7
John Trapp (to Phi)	F	6'7	215	27	5	35	3	12	25	7	10	70	14	2	10	0	13	7	2.8	0.4	2.0	2.6
Roger Brown (to CarA)	C	7'	225	22	1	5	0	0	—	1	3	33	0	0	1	0	1	5	0.0	0.0	1.0	1.0
GOLDEN STATE WARRIORS	**47-35 .573**				**AL ATTLES**																	
Cazzie Russell	F-G	6'5	220	28	80	2429	541	1182	46	172	199	86	350	187	171	0	1254	30	4.4	2.3	2.1	15.7
Rick Barry	F	6'7	220	28	82	3075	737	1630	45	358	397	**90**	728	399	245	2	1832	38	8.9	4.9	3.0	22.3
Nate Thurmond	C	6'11	235	31	79	3419	517	1159	45	315	439	72	1349	280	240	2	1349	43	17.1	3.5	3.0	17.1
Jeff Mullins	G	6'4	200	30	81	3005	651	1321	49	143	172	83	363	337	201	2	1445	37	4.5	4.2	2.5	17.8
Jim Barnett	G	6'4	180	28	82	2215	394	844	47	183	217	84	255	301	150	1	971	27	3.1	3.7	1.8	11.8
Clyde Lee	F-C	6'10	230	28	66	1476	170	365	47	74	131	56	598	34	183	5	414	22	9.1	0.5	2.8	6.3
Joe Ellis	F	6'6	175	28	74	1054	199	487	41	69	93	74	282	88	143	2	467	14	3.8	1.2	1.9	6.3
Ron Williams	G	6'3	190	28	73	1016	180	409	44	75	83	90	81	114	108	0	435	14	1.1	1.6	1.5	6.0
Charlie Johnson	G	6'	170	23	70	887	171	400	43	33	46	72	132	118	105	0	375	13	1.9	1.7	1.5	5.4
Mahdi Abdul-Rahman (from Buf)	G	6'2	190	30	46	629	82	196	42	44	51	86	78	112	91	1	208	14	1.7	2.4	2.0	4.5
George Johnson	C	6'11	205	24	56	349	41	100	41	7	17	41	138	8	40	0	89	6	2.5	0.1	0.7	1.6
Bob Portman	F	6'5	200	25	32	176	32	70	46	20	26	77	51	7	16	0	84	6	1.6	0.2	0.5	2.6
PHOENIX SUNS	**38-44 .463**				**BUTCH VAN BREDA KOLFF (3-5 .375), JERRY COLANGELO (35-39 .473)**																	
Lamar Green	F	6'7	220	25	80	2048	224	520	43	89	118	75	746	89	263	10	537	26	9.3	1.1	3.3	6.7
Connie Hawkins	F	6'8	220	30	75	2768	441	920	48	322	404	80	641	304	229	5	1204	37	8.5	4.1	3.1	16.1
Neal Walk	C	6'10	240	25	81	3114	678	1455	47	279	355	79	1006	287	**323**	11	1635	38	12.4	3.5	4.0	20.2
Dick Van Arsdale	G-F	6'5	210	30	81	2979	532	1118	48	426	496	86	326	268	221	2	1490	37	4.0	3.3	2.7	18.4
Charlie Scott	G	6'5	180	24	81	3062	806	1809	45	436	556	78	342	495	306	5	2048	38	4.2	6.1	3.8	25.3
Corky Calhoun	F	6'7	210	24	82	2025	211	450	47	71	96	74	338	76	214	2	493	25	4.1	0.9	2.6	6.0
Clem Haskins	G	6'3	200	29	77	1581	339	731	46	130	156	83	173	203	143	2	808	21	2.2	2.6	1.9	10.5
Mo Layton	G	6'1	180	24	65	990	187	434	43	90	119	76	77	139	127	2	464	15	1.2	2.1	2.0	7.1
Gus Johnson (to IndA)	C-F	6'6	235	34	21	417	69	181	38	25	36	69	136	31	55	0	163	20	6.5	1.5	2.6	7.8
Walt Wesley (from Cle)	C	6'11	230	28	45	364	63	155	41	18	34	53	113	24	56	1	144	8	2.5	0.5	1.2	3.2
Paul Stovall	F	6'5	225	24	25	211	26	76	34	24	38	63	61	13	37	0	76	8	2.4	0.5	1.5	3.0
Scott English	F	6'6	220	22	29	196	36	93	39	21	29	72	44	15	38	0	93	7	1.5	0.5	1.3	3.2
SEATTLE SUPERSONICS	**26-56 .317**				**TOM NISSALKE (13-32 .289), BUCKY BUCKWALTER (13-24 .351)**																	
John Brisker	F	6'5	230	25	70	1633	352	809	44	194	236	82	319	150	169	1	898	23	4.6	2.1	2.4	12.8
Spencer Haywood	F	6'8	230	23	77	3259	889	1868	48	473	564	84	995	196	213	2	2251	42	12.9	2.5	2.8	29.2
Jim Fox	C	6'10	230	29	74	2439	316	613	52	214	265	81	827	176	239	6	846	33	11.2	2.4	3.2	11.4
Dick Snyder	G	6'5	213	28	82	3060	473	1022	46	186	216	86	323	311	216	2	1132	37	3.9	3.8	2.6	13.8
Fred Brown	G	6'3	185	24	79	2320	471	1035	46	121	148	82	318	438	226	5	1063	29	4.0	5.5	2.9	13.5
Butch Beard	G	6'3	185	25	73	1403	191	435	44	100	140	71	174	247	139	0	482	19	2.4	3.4	1.9	6.6
Bud Stallworth	F	6'5	190	22	77	1225	198	522	38	86	114	75	225	58	138	0	482	16	2.9	0.8	1.8	6.3
Kenny McIntosh (from Chi))	F	6'7	225	23	56	1105	107	328	33	40	65	62	222	53	98	1	254	20	4.0	0.9	1.8	4.5
Jim McDaniels	C	6'11	230	24	68	1095	154	386	40	70	100	70	345	78	140	4	378	16	5.1	1.1	2.1	5.6
Lee Winfield	G	6'2	175	25	53	1061	143	332	43	62	108	57	126	186	92	3	348	20	2.4	3.5	1.7	6.6
Joby Wright	F-C	6'8	222	22	77	931	133	278	48	37	89	42	218	36	164	0	303	12	2.8	0.5	2.1	3.9
Pete Cross (from KCO)	C	6'9	230	24	26	133	6	21	29	8	18	44	57	11	24	0	20	5	2.2	0.4	0.9	0.8
Charles Dudley	G	6'2	186	22	12	99	10	23	43	14	16	88	6	16	15	0	34	8	0.5	1.3	1.3	2.8
Gar Heard (to Chi)	F	6'6	226	24	3	17	4	9	44	1	1	100	6	2	4	0	9	6	2.0	0.7	1.3	3.0
PORTLAND TRAIL BLAZERS	**21-61 .256**				**JACK McCLOSKEY**																	
Ollie Johnson	F	6'6	200	23	78	2138	308	620	50	156	206	76	417	200	166	0	772	27	5.3	2.6	2.1	9.9
Sidney Wicks	F-C	6'8	225	23	80	3152	761	1684	45	384	531	72	870	440	253	3	1906	39	10.9	5.5	3.2	23.8
Lloyd Neal	C	6'7	225	22	82	2723	455	921	49	187	293	64	967	146	305	6	1097	33	11.8	1.8	3.7	13.4
Geoff Petrie	G	6'4	200	24	79	3134	836	1801	46	298	383	78	273	350	163	2	1970	40	3.5	4.4	2.1	24.9
Rick Adelman	G	6'1	186	26	76	1822	214	525	41	73	102	72	157	294	155	2	501	24	2.1	3.9	2.0	6.6
Greg Smith (from Hou)	F	6'5	200	25	72	1569	229	469	49	75	128	59	375	117	210	8	533	22	5.2	1.6	2.9	7.4
Charlie Davis (from Cle)	G	6'2	160	23	69	1333	243	590	41	126	161	78	111	175	174	6	612	19	1.6	2.5	2.5	8.9
Larry Steele	G	6'5	190	23	66	1301	159	329	48	71	89	80	154	156	181	4	389	20	2.3	2.4	2.7	5.9
LaRue Martin	C	6'11	208	22	77	996	145	366	40	50	77	65	358	42	162	0	340	13	4.6	0.5	2.1	4.4
Terry Dischinger	F	6'7	205	32	63	970	161	338	48	64	96	67	190	103	125	1	386	15	3.0	1.6	2.0	6.1
Dave Wohl (to Buf)	G	6'2	185	23	22	393	47	114	41	24	33	73	20	68	45	0	118	18	0.9	3.1	2.0	5.4
Stan McKenzie (to Hou)	G-F	6'5	210	28	7	107	13	36	36	14	16	88	21	8	15	1	40	15	3.0	1.1	2.1	5.7
Bill Smith	C	7'	220	23	8	43	9	15	60	5	8	63	8	1	8	0	23	5	1.0	0.1	1.0	2.9
Bob Davis	F	6'7	215	22	9	41	6	28	21	4	6	67	5	2	5	0	16	5	0.6	0.2	0.6	1.8
Bill Turner (to LA)	F	6'7	225	28	2	8	2	6	33	0	0	—	2	0	3	0	4	4	1.0	0.0	1.5	2.0

1972/73 N.B.A. — PLAYOFFS

NEW YORK KNICKERBOCKERS — **RED HOLZMAN**

defeated Baltimore 41; H95-83, H123-103, 103-96, 89-97, H109-99
defeated Boston 4-3; 108-134, H129-96, 98-91, H117-110(2OT), 97-98, H100-110, 94-78
defeated Los Angeles 4-1; 112-115, 99-95, H87-83, H103-98, 102-93

Use Name	Pos	Hgt	Wgt	Age	G	Min	FG	FGA	%	FT	FTA	%	Reb	Ass	PF	DQ	Points	Min	Reb	Ass	PF	Points
					TOTAL													PER GAME				
Bill Bradley	F	6'5	205	29	17	587	99	221	45	40	50	80	57	45	59	1	238	35	3.4	2.6	3.5	14.0
Dave DeBusschere	F	6'6	235	32	17	632	117	265	44	31	40	78	179	58	57	0	265	37	10.5	3.4	3.4	15.6
Willis Reed	C	6'9	240	30	17	486	97	208	47	18	21	86	129	30	65	1	212	29	7.6	1.8	3.8	12.5
Walt Frazier	G	6'4	205	27	17	765	150	292	51	73	94	78	124	106	52	1	373	45	7.3	6.2	3.1	21.9
Earl Monroe	G	6'3	190	28	16	504	111	211	53	36	48	75	51	51	39	0	258	32	3.2	3.2	2.4	16.1
Jerry Lucas	C-F	6'8	230	32	17	368	54	112	48	20	23	87	85	39	47	0	128	22	5.0	2.3	2.8	7.5
Phil Jackson	F-C	6'8	220	27	17	338	60	120	50	28	38	74	72	24	59	**3**	148	20	4.2	1.4	3.5	8.7
Dean Meminger	G	6'	175	24	17	323	31	56	**55**	19	34	56	37	37	29	1	81	19	2.2	2.2	1.7	4.8
John Gianelli	C-F	6'10	220	22	7	55	11	20	55	3	7	43	13	1	6	0	25	8	1.9	0.1	0.9	3.6
Henry Bibby	G	6'1	185	23	6	43	8	18	44	4	8	50	2	3	5	0	20	7	0.3	0.5	0.8	3.3
Dick Barnett	G	6'4	190	36	4	17	3	6	50	0	0	—	0	2	5	0	6	4	0.0	0.5	1.3	1.5
Harthorne Wingo	F	6'8	210	24	3	12	5	13	38	1	2	50	7	0	1	0	11	4	2.3	0.0	0.3	3.7

LOS ANGELES LAKERS — **BILL SHARMAN**

defeated Chicago 4-3; H107-104(OT), H108-93, 86-96, 94-98, H123-102, 93-101, H95-92
defeated Golden State 4-1; H101-99, H104-93, 126-70,109-117, H128-118
lost to New York 1-4; H115-112, H95-99, 83-87 93-103, H93-102

Use Name	Pos	Hgt	Wgt	Age	G	Min	FG	FGA	%	FT	FTA	%	Reb	Ass	PF	DQ	Points	Min	Reb	Ass	PF	Points
Jim McMillian	F	6'5	225	24	17	630	143	307	47	55	75	73	82	37	41	0	341	37	4.8	2.2	2.4	20.1
Bill Bridges	F	6'6	235	33	17	582	57	136	42	38	49	78	158	29	**68**	2	152	34	9.3	1.7	4.0	8.9
Wilt Chamberlain	C	7'1	275	36	17	**801**	64	116	55	49	98	50	**383**	60	48	0	177	**47**	**22.5**	3.5	2.8	10.4
Jerry West	G	6'3	185	34	17	638	151	**336**	45	**99**	**127**	78	76	**132**	49	1	**401**	38	4.5	**7.8**	2.9	23.6
Gail Goodrich	G	6'1	175	29	17	604	139	310	45	62	79	78	61	67	53	1	340	36	3.6	3.9	3.1	20.0
Keith Erickson	G-F	6'5	200	28	17	404	66	147	45	15	22	68	59	30	52	2	147	24	3.5	1.8	3.1	8.6
Mel Counts	F-C	7'	235	31	17	327	61	133	46	32	41	78	104	28	51	1	154	19	6.1	1.6	3.0	9.1
Pat Riley	G	6'4	208	27	7	53	9	27	33	0	0	—	5	7	10	0	18	8	0.7	1.0	1.4	2.6
Happy Hairston	F	6'7	225	30	3	26	1	9	11	6	8	75	4	1	2	0	8	9	1.3	0.3	0.7	2.7
Jim Price	G	6'3	195	23	3	16	3	11	27	0	0	—	4	2	2	0	6	5	1.3	0.7	0.7	2.0
Bill Turner	F	6'7	225	28	2	13	2	5	40	2	2	100	2	0	1	0	6	7	1.0	0.0	0.5	3.0
Travis Grant	F	6'8	225	22	2	11	4	6	67	0	0	—	4	0	1	0	8	6	2.0	0.0	0.5	4.0

BOSTON CELTICS — **TOM HEINSOHN**

defeated Atlanta 4-2; H134-109, 126-113, H105-118, 94-97, H108-101, 121-103
lost to New York 3-4; H134-108, 96-129, H91-98, 110-117(2OT), H98-97, 110-100, H78-94

Use Name	Pos	Hgt	Wgt	Age	G	Min	FG	FGA	%	FT	FTA	%	Reb	Ass	PF	DQ	Points	Min	Reb	Ass	PF	Points
John Havlicek	F-G	6'5	205	33	12	479	112	235	48	61	74	82	62	65	24	0	285	40	5.2	5.4	2.0	23.8
Paul Silas	F	6'7	225	29	13	512	47	120	39	31	50	62	196	39	39	0	125	39	15.1	3.0	3.0	9.6
Dave Cowens	C	6'9	230	24	13	598	129	273	47	27	41	66	216	48	54	2	285	46	16.6	3.7	4.2	21.9
Don Chaney	G	6'5	210	26	12	288	39	82	48	12	17	71	40	25	41	1	90	24	3.3	2.1	3.4	7.5
Jo Jo White	G	6'3	190	26	13	583	135	300	45	49	54	91	54	83	44	2	319	45	4.2	6.4	3.4	24.5
Don Nelson	F	6'6	210	33	13	303	47	101	47	49	56	88	38	15	29	0	143	23	2.9	1.2	2.2	11.0
Hambone Williams	G	6'2	180	33	10	156	21	47	45	6	8	75	27	41	31	1	48	16	2.7	4.1	3.1	4.8
Paul Westphal	G	6'4	195	22	11	109	19	39	49	5	7	71	7	9	24	1	43	10	0.6	0.8	2.2	3.9
Steve Kuberski	F-C	6'8	215	25	12	95	19	46	41	7	10	70	14	3	15	0	45	8	1.2	0.3	1.3	3.8
Satch Sanders	F	6'6	210	34	5	24	5	9	56	0	2	0	5	1	7	0	10	5	1.0	0.2	1.4	2.0
Henry Finkel	C	7'	240	30	7	23	6	9	67	0	0	—	6	3	4	0	12	3	0.9	0.4	0.6	1.7

GOLDEN STATE WARRIORS — **AL ATTLES**

defeated Milwaukee 4-2, 90-110, 95-92, H93-113, H102-97, 100-97, H100-86
lost to Los Angeles 4-1; 99-101, 93-104, H70-126, H117-109, 118-128

Use Name	Pos	Hgt	Wgt	Age	G	Min	FG	FGA	%	FT	FTA	%	Reb	Ass	PF	DQ	Points	Min	Reb	Ass	PF	Points
Rick Barry	F	6'7	220	28	11	292	65	164	40	50	55	91	54	24	41	1	180	27	4.9	2.2	3.7	16.4
Clyde Lee	F-C	6'10	230	28	11	413	48	103	47	21	32	66	173	16	43	1	117	38	15.7	1.5	3.9	10.6
Nate Thurmond	C	6'11	235	31	11	460	64	161	40	32	40	80	145	40	30	1	160	42	13.2	3.6	2.7	14.5
Jeff Mullins	G	6'4	200	30	11	409	72	168	43	21	29	72	46	43	32	0	165	37	4.2	3.9	2.9	15.0
Jim Barnett	G	6'4	180	28	11	336	60	147	41	23	27	85	39	39	28	0	143	31	3.5	3.5	2.5	13.0
Cazzie Russell	F-G	6'5	220	28	11	263	72	147	49	19	22	86	36	17	24	0	163	24	3.3	1.5	2.2	14.8
Mahdi Abdul-Rahman	G	6'2	190	30	11	215	30	84	36	12	12	100	20	28	24	0	72	20	1.8	2.5	2.2	6.5
Joe Ellis	F	6'6	175	28	10	100	12	38	32	0	0	—	18	7	18	1	24	10	1.8	0.7	1.8	2.4
Charlie Johnson	G	6'	170	23	6	70	10	26	38	3	6	50	10	11	4	0	23	12	1.7	1.8	0.7	3.8
George Johnson	C	6'11	205	24	9	45	6	15	40	1	4	25	14	3	7	0	13	5	1.6	0.3	0.8	1.4
Ron Williams	G	6'3	190	28	3	20	4	6	67	1	1	100	1	5	1	0	9	7	0.3	1.7	0.3	3.0
Bob Portman	F	6'5	200	25	3	17	2	10	20	4	4	100	5	1	0	0	8	6	1.7	0.3	0.0	2.7

1972/73 N.B.A. — PLAYOFFS (continued)

Use Name	Pos	Hgt	Wgt	Age	G	Min	FG	FGA	%	FT	FTA	%	Reb	Ass	PF	DQ	Points	Min	Reb	Ass	PF	Points
					TOTAL													PER GAME				
CHICAGO BULLS	**DICK MOTTA**				lost to Los Angeles 3-4; 104-107(OT), 93-108, H96-86, H98-94, 102-123, H101-93, 92-95																	
Chet Walker	F	6'6	220	32	7	229	42	121	35	33	37	89	62	14	15	0	117	33	8.9	2.0	2.1	16.7
Bob Love	F	6'8	215	30	7	314	68	148	46	30	41	73	67	23	20	0	166	45	9.6	3.3	2.9	23.7
Dennis Awtrey	C	6'10	250	24	7	268	26	48	54	11	22	50	77	31	26	1	63	38	11.0	4.4	3.7	9.0
Jerry Sloan	G-F	6'6	200	30	7	292	45	103	44	14	19	74	59	14	31	1	104	42	8.4	2.0	4.4	14.9
Norm Van Lier	G	6'1	175	25	7	258	45	129	35	11	15	73	37	36	32	3	101	37	5.3	5.1	4.6	14.4
Bob Weiss	G	6'2	185	30	7	175	34	79	43	16	21	76	16	15	20	0	84	25	2.3	2.1	2.9	12.0
Howard Porter	F-C	6'8	220	24	6	79	12	34	35	3	4	75	18	2	5	0	27	13	3.0	0.3	0.8	4.5
Cliff Ray	C	6'9	235	23	5	36	3	8	38	0	0	—	9	1	2	0	6	7	1.8	0.2	0.4	1.2
Tom Boerwinkle	C	7'	270	27	4	30	4	6	67	1	1	100	9	11	7	0	9	8	2.3	2.8	1.8	2.3
Jim King	G	6'2	175	31	4	14	2	6	33	1	2	50	1	2	3	0	5	4	0.3	0.5	0.8	1.3
Gar Heard	F	6'6	226	24	2	9	2	4	50	0	0	—	3	0	4	0	4	5	1.5	0.0	2.0	2.0
Rowland Garrett	F	6'6	212	22	1	1	0	0	—	0	0	—	0	0	0	0	0	1	0.0	0.0	0.0	0.0
MILWAUKEE BUCKS	**LARRY COSTELLO**				lost to Golden State 2-4; H110-90, H92-95, 113-93, 97-102, H97-100, 86-100																	
Bob Dandridge	F	6'6	195	25	6	204	32	76	42	19	27	70	28	7	23	2	83	34	4.7	1.2	3.8	13.8
Curtis Perry	F	6'7	230	24	6	238	25	52	48	3	6	50	69	13	23	1	53	40	11.5	2.2	3.8	8.8
Kareem Abdul-Jabbar	C	7'2	232	25	6	276	59	138	43	19	35	54	97	17	26	0	137	46	16.2	2.8	4.3	22.8
Oscar Robertson	G-F	6'5	220	34	6	256	48	96	50	31	34	91	28	45	21	1	127	43	4.7	7.5	3.5	21.2
Lucius Allen	G	6'2	175	25	6	203	36	89	40	22	28	79	16	21	15	0	94	34	2.7	3.5	2.5	15.7
Jon McGlocklin	G	6'5	205	29	6	145	27	53	51	7	8	88	7	13	11	0	61	24	1.2	2.2	1.8	10.2
Mickey Davis	F	6'7	215	22	6	54	6	17	35	2	2	100	12	5	10	0	14	9	2.0	0.8	1.7	2.3
Chuck Terry	F	6'6	215	22	5	18	4	5	80	0	0	—	3	1	2	0	8	4	0.6	0.2	0.4	1.6
Dick Cunningham	C-F	6'10	250	26	5	17	1	1	100	0	0	—	3	2	6	0	2	3	0.6	0.4	1.2	0.4
Terry Driscoll	F	6'7	215	25	6	16	0	4	0	0	0	—	0	1	2	0	0	3	0.0	0.2	0.3	0.0
Russ Lee	F	6'5	185	22	5	13	8	14	57	0	0	—	4	2	1	0	16	3	0.8	0.4	0.2	3.2
ATLANTA HAWKS	**RICHIE GUERIN**				lost to Boston 2-4; 109-134, H113-136, 118-105, H97-94, 101-108, H103-121																	
Lou Hudson	F	6'5	215	28	6	255	76	166	46	26	29	90	47	17	16	0	178	43	7.8	2.8	2.7	29.7
Jim Washington	F	6'7	215	29	6	226	19	48	40	5	17	29	60	14	19	1	43	38	10.0	2.3	3.2	7.2
Walt Bellamy	C	6'11	245	33	6	247	34	86	40	14	31	45	73	13	17	0	82	41	12.2	2.2	2.8	13.7
Pete Maravich	G	6'5	195	24	6	234	65	155	42	27	34	79	29	40	24	1	157	39	4.8	6.7	4.0	26.2
Herm Gilliam	G	6'3	190	26	6	197	33	81	41	5	5	100	32	31	19	1	71	33	5.3	5.2	3.2	11.8
Steve Bracey	G	6'1	175	22	6	123	24	47	51	11	16	69	13	20	13	0	59	21	2.2	3.3	2.2	9.8
George Trapp	F-C	6'8	215	24	6	99	11	32	34	3	5	60	21	3	21	0	25	17	3.5	0.5	3.5	4.2
John Wetzel	G-F	6'5	190	28	3	33	3	7	43	0	0	—	2	4	6	0	6	11	0.7	1.3	2.0	2.0
Eddie Mast	F	6'9	220	24	4	15	5	5	100	0	0	—	5	1	1	0	10	4	1.3	0.3	0.3	2.5
John Tschogl	F	6'6	210	22	3	11	5	8	63	0	0	—	4	1	0	0	10	4	1.3	0.3	0.0	3.3
BALTIMORE BULLETS	**GENE SHUE**				lost to New York 1-4; 83-95, 103-123, H96-103, H97-89, 99-109																	
Mike Riordan	F-G	6'4	200	27	5	231	28	62	45	19	24	79	18	15	16	0	75	46	3.6	3.0	3.2	15.0
Elvin Hayes	F-C	6'9	235	27	5	228	53	105	50	23	33	70	57	5	16	0	129	46	11.4	1.0	3.2	25.8
Wes Unseld	C	6'7	250	26	5	201	20	48	42	9	19	47	76	17	12	0	49	40	15.2	3.4	2.4	9.8
Phil Chenier	G	6'3	180	22	5	211	43	85	51	3	4	75	21	17	13	0	89	42	4.2	3.4	2.6	17.8
Archie Clark	G	6'2	175	31	5	214	46	92	50	14	18	78	17	26	20	1	106	43	3.4	5.2	4.0	21.2
John Tresvant	F	6'7	220	33	5	50	5	15	33	2	4	50	16	3	6	0	12	10	3.2	0.6	1.2	2.4
Kevin Porter	G	6'	175	22	4	41	6	12	50	0	0	—	2	9	11	0	12	10	0.5	2.3	2.8	3.0
Dave Stallworth	F	6'7	220	31	3	14	1	1	100	0	0	—	3	1	3	0	2	5	1.0	0.3	1.0	0.7
Stan Love	F	6'9	215	23	1	7	0	3	0	0	0	—	1	0	1	0	0	7	1.0	0.0	1.0	0.0
Flynn Robinson	G	6'1	190	31	1	2	2	3	67	0	0	—	1	0	0	0	4	2	1.0	0.0	0.0	4.0
Tommy Patterson	F	6'6	220	24	1	1	0	0	—	0	0	—	0	0	0	0	0	1	0.0	0.0	0.0	0.0

					Record against playoff teams			Record against non - playoff teams			HOME			ROAD			NEUTRAL		
Team	W	L	Pct.	GB	W	L	Pct.	W	L	Pct.	W	L	Pct.	W	L	Pct.	W	L	Pct.
ATLANTIC DIVISION																			
Boston Celtics	**68**	14	**.829**	—	**26**	10	**.722**	**42**	4	**.913**	33	6	.846	**32**	8	**.800**	3	0	1.000
New York Knickerbockers	57	25	.695	11	17	19	.472	40	6	.870	**35**	6	.854	21	18	.538	1	1	.500
Buffalo Braves	21	61	.256	47	5	37	.119	16	24	.400	14	27	.341	6	31	.162	1	3	.250
Philadelphia 76ers	9	**73**	.110	59	3	**39**	.071	6	**34**	.150	5	26	.161	2	**36**	.053	2	**11**	.154
CENTRAL DIVISION																			
Banimore Bullets	52	30	.634	—	14	21	.400	38	9	.809	24	9	.727	21	17	.553	7	4	.636
Atlanta Hawks	46	36	.561	6	14	21	.400	32	15	.681	28	13	.683	17	23	.425	1	0	1.000
Houston Rockets	33	49	.402	19	11	33	.250	22	16	.579	14	14	.500	10	28	.263	**9**	7	.563
Cleveland Cavaliers	32	50	.390	20	9	34	.209	23	16	.590	20	21	.488	10	27	.270	2	2	.500
MIDWEST DIVISION																			
Milwaukee Bucks	60	22	.732	—	21	13	.618	39	9	.813	33	5	**.868**	25	15	.625	2	2	.500
Chicago Bulls	51	31	.622	9	16	18	.471	35	13	.729	29	12	.707	20	19	.513	2	0	1.000
Detroit Pistons	40	42	.488	20	15	27	.357	25	15	.625	26	15	.634	13	25	.342	1	2	.333
Kansas City-Omaha Kings	36	46	.439	24	10	32	.238	26	14	.650	24	17	.585	12	29	.293	0	0	—
PACIFIC DIVISION																			
Los Angeles Lakers	60	22	.732	—	18	17	.514	**42**	5	.894	30	11	.732	28	11	.718	2	0	1.000
Golden State Warriors	47	35	.573	13	14	21	.400	33	14	.702	27	14	.659	18	20	**.474**	2	1	.667
Phoenix Suns	38	44	.463	22	12	29	.293	26	15	.634	22	19	.537	15	25	.375	1	0	1.000
Seattle Supersonics	26	56	.317	34	6	35	.146	20	21	.488	16	25	.390	10	29	.256	0	2	.000
Portland Trail Blazers	21	61	.256	39	4	36	.100	17	25	.405	13	**28**	.317	8	32	.200	0	1	.000

1972/73 N.B.A. INDIVIDUAL LEADERS

SCORING
(Minimum 70 Games Played)

Name	Team	G	FG	FT	Pts.	Avg.
Archibald	KCO	80	1028	663	2719	34.0
Abdul-Jabbar	Mil	76	982	328	2292	30.2
Haywood	Sea	77	889	473	2251	29.2
Hudson	Atl	75	816	397	2029	27.1
Maravich	Atl	79	789	485	2063	26.1
Scott	Phoe	81	806	436	2048	25.3
Petrie	Port	79	836	298	1970	24.9
Goodrich	LA	76	750	314	1814	23.9
Wicks	Port	80	761	384	1906	23.8
Lanier	Det	81	810	307	1927	23.8

FIELD GOAL PERCENTAGE
(Minimum 560 Attempts)

Name	Team	FG	FGA	Pct.
Chamberlain	LA	426	586	.727
Guokas	KCO	322	565	.570
Abdul-Jabbar	Mil	982	1772	.554
Rowe	Det	547	1053	.519
Fox .	Sea	316	613	.515
Lucas	NY	312	608	.513
Riordan	Bal	652	1278	.510
Clark	Bal	302	596	.507
Kauffman	Buf	535	1059	.505
Bellamy	Atl	455	901	.505

FREE THROW PERCENTAGE
(Minimum 160 Attempts)

Name	Team	FT	FTA	Pct.
Barry	GS	358	397	.902
Murphy	Hou	239	269	.888
Newlin	Hou	327	369	.886
Walker	Hou	244	276	.884
Bradley	NY	169	194	.871
Russell	GS	172	199	.864
Snyder	Sea	186	216	.861
Van Arsdale	Phoe	426	496	.859
Havlicek	Bos	370	431	.858
Marin	Hou	248	292	.849

PERSONAL FOULS

Name	Team	PF
Walk	Phoe	323
Cowens	Bos	311
Scott	Phoe	306
Neal	Port	305
Newlin	Hou	301

GAMES DISQUALIFIED

Name	Team	Disq
E. Smith	Buf	16
Walk	Phoe	11
Trapp	Atl	11
Green	Phoe	10
Williams	KCO	9

REBOUNDS PER GAME
(Minimum 70 Games Played)

Name	Team	G	Reb.	Avg.
Chamberlain	LA	82	1526	18.6
Thurmond	GS	79	1349	17.1
Cowens	Bos	82	1329	16.2
Abdul-Jabbar	Mil	76	1224	16.1
Unseld	Bal	79	1260	15.9
Lanier	Det	81	1205	14.9
Hayes	Bal	81	1177	14.5
Bellamy	Atl	74	964	13.0
Silas	Bos	80	1039	13.0
Haywood	Sea	77	995	12.9

ASSISTS PER GAME
(Minimum 70 Games Played)

Name	Team	G	Ass.	Avg.
Archibald	KCO	80	910	11.4
Wilkens	Cle	75	628	8.4
Bing	Det	82	637	7.8
Robertson	Mil	73	551	7.5
Van Lier	Chi	80	567	7.1
Maravich	Atl	79	546	6.9
Havlicek	Bos	80	529	6.6
Gilliam	Atl	76	482	6.3
Scott	Phoe	81	495	6.1
White	Bos	82	498	6.1

MINUTES PLAYED

Name	Team	Min.
Archibald	KCO	3681
Chamberlain	LA	3542
Cowens	Bos	3425
Thurmond	GS	3419
Havlicek	30s	3367

TEAM STATISTICS

Team		REGULAR SEASON G	FG	FGA	%	FT	FTA	%	Reb	Ass	PF	Points	PPG	PLAYOFFS G	FG	FGA	%	FT	FTA	%	Reb	Ass	PF	Points	PPG
ATLANTIC DIVISION																									
Boston	Off.	82	3811	8511	45	1616	2073	78	4802	2320	1805	9238	112.7	13	579	1261	46	247	319	77	665	332	312	1405	108.1
	Def.	82	3513	8095	43	1540	2032	76	3958	1957	1821	8566	104.5	13	583	1271	46	218	306	71	594	312	316	1384	106.5
	Diff.		+298	+416	+2	+76	+41	+2	+844	+363	+16	+672	+8.2		-4	-10	—	+29	+13	+6	+71	+20	+4	+21	+1.6
New York	Off.	82	3627	7764	47	1356	1739	78	3882	2187	1775	8610	105.0	17	746	1542	48	273	365	75	756	396	424	1765	103.8
	Def.	82	3291	7561	44	1471	1961	75	4100	1714	1781	8053	98.2	17	680	1513	45	319	455	70	807	329	387	1679	98.8
	Diff.		+336	+203	+3	-115	-222	+3	-218	+473	+6	+557	+6.8		+66	+29	+3	-46	-90	+5	-51	+67	-37	+86	+5.0
Buffalo	Off.	82	3536	7877	45	1399	1966	71	4158	2218	2034	8471	103.3												
	Def.	82	3745	7947	47	1733	2299	75	4278	2383	1822	9223	112.5												
	Diff.		-209	-70	-2	-334	-333	-4	-120	-165	-212	-752	-9.2												
Philadelphia	Off.	82	3471	8264	42	1598	2130	75	4174	1688	1984	8540	104.1												
	Def.	82	3882	8215	47	1767	2358	75	4683	2239	1885	9531	116.2												
	Diff.		-411	+49	-5	-169	-228	—	-509	-551	-99	-991	-12.1												
CENTRAL DIVISION																									
Baltimore	Off.	82	3656	7883	46	1294	1742	74	4205	2051	1672	8606	105.0	5	204	426	48	70	102	69	212	93	98	478	95.6
	Def.	82	3531	8010	44	1269	1702	75	4226	1852	1682	8331	101.6	5	223	438	51	73	100	73	216	110	109	519	103.8
	Diff.		+125	-127	+2	+25	+40	-1	-21	+199	+10	+275	+3.4		-19	-12	-3	-3	+2	-4	-4	-17	+11	-41	-8.2
Atlanta	Off.	82	3700	8033	46	1819	2482	73	4174	2074	1916	9219	112.4	6	275	635	43	91	137	66	286	144	136	641	106.8
	Def.	82	3758	8152	46	1696	2193	77	4147	2020	2104	9212	112.3	6	290	608	48	108	136	79	334	184	138	688	114.7
	Diff.		-58	-119	—	+123	+289	-4	+27	+54	+188	+7	+.1		-15	+27	-5	-17	+1	-13	-48	-40	+2	-47	-7.9
Houston	Off.	82	3772	8249	46	1706	2152	79	4060	1939	1949	9250	112.8												
	Def.	82	3824	8119	47	1744	2290	76	4338	2104	1902	9392	114.5												
	Diff.		-52	+130	-1	-38	-138	+3	-278	-165	-47	-142	-1.7												
Cleveland	Off.	82	3431	7884	44	1556	2084	75	4063	2106	1941	8418	102.7												
	Def.	82	3465	7673	45	1707	2230	77	4115	2311	1932	8637	105.3												
	Diff.		-34	+211	-1	-151	-146	-2	-52	-205	-9	-219	-2.6												
MIDWEST DIVISION																									
Milwaukee	Off.	82	3759	7808	48	1271	1687	75	4245	2226	1763	8789	107.2	6	246	545	45	103	140	74	267	127	140	595	99.2
	Def.	82	3385	8028	42	1345	1783	75	3916	1906	1601	8115	99.0	6	239	543	44	102	130	78	287	129	125	580	96.7
	Diff.		+374	-220	+6	-74	-96	—	+329	+320	-162	+674	+8.2		+7	+2	+1	+1	+10	-4	-20	-2	-15	+15	+2.5
Chicago	Off.	82	3480	7835	44	1574	2073	76	4000	2023	1881	8534	104.1	7	283	686	41	120	162	74	358	149	165	686	98.0
	Def.	82	3343	7098	47	1562	2080	75	3915	1910	2002	8248	100.6	7	286	632	45	134	183	73	401	176	167	706	100.9
	Diff.		+137	+737	-3	+12	-7	+1	+85	+113	+121	+286	+3.5		-3	+54	-4	-14	-21	+1	-43	-27	+2	-20	-2.9
Detroit	Off.	82	3666	7916	46	1710	2294	75	4105	1882	1812	9042	110.3												
	Def.	82	3803	8064	47	1418	1862	76	4019	2263	1891	9024	110.0												
	Diff.		-137	-148	-1	+292	+432	-1	+86	-381	+79	+18	+.3												
KC-Omaha	Off.	82	3621	7581	48	1580	2036	78	3628	2118	2054	8822	107.6												
	Def.	82	3698	7640	48	1665	2174	77	3961	1885	1816	9061	110.5												
	Diff.		-77	-59	—	-85	-138	+1	-333	+233	-238	-239	-2.9												
PACIFIC DIVISION																									
Los Angeles	Off.	82	3740	7819	48	1679	2264	74	4562	2302	1636	9159	111.7	17	700	1543	45	358	501	71	942	393	378	1758	103.4
	Def.	82	3646	8409	43	1167	1583	74	4101	1963	1941	8459	103.2	17	704	1680	42	278	360	77	864	372	427	1686	99.2
	Diff.		+94	-590	+5	+512	+681	—	+461	+339	+305	+700	+8.5		-4	-137	+3	+80	+141	-6	+78	+21	+49	+72	+4.2
Golden State	Off.	82	3715	8163	46	1493	1871	80	4405	1985	1693	8923	108.8	11	445	1069	42	187	232	81	561	234	252	1077	97.9
	Def.	82	3603	8163	44	1463	1891	77	4265	2034	1766	8669	105.7	11	473	1022	46	217	288	75	544	256	236	1163	105.7
	Diff.		+112	—	+2	+30	-20	+3	+140	-49	+73	+254	+3.1		-28	+47	-4	-30	-56	+6	+17	-22	-16	-86	-7.8
Phoenix	Off.	82	3612	7942	45	1931	2437	79	4003	1944	2012	9155	111.6												
	Def.	82	3758	8005	47	1744	2318	75	4139	2166	2068	9260	112.9												
	Diff.		-146	-63	-2	+187	+119	+4	-136	-222	+56	-105	-1.3												
Seattle	Off.	82	3447	7681	45	1606	2080	77	4161	1958	1877	8500	103.7												
	Def.	82	3678	8093	45	1628	2156	76	4158	2145	1875	8984	109.6												
	Diff.		-231	-412	—	-22	-76	+1	+3	-187	-2	-484	-5.9												
Portland	Off.	82	3588	7842	46	1531	2129	72	3928	2102	1970	8707	106.2												
	Def.	82	3709	7780	48	1800	2327	77	4236	2271	1885	9218	112.4												
	Diff.		-121	+62	-2	-269	-198	-5	-308	-169	-85	-511	-6.2												

1972-73 A.B.A.

Losing One Star and Gaining Another

The A.B.A. took care of an expensive headache by folding the Pittsburgh and Florida franchises, two organizations populated by poor teams, very few paying fans, press indifference, and frustrated front offices. This paring of dead wood was one of commissioner Jack Dolph's last acts before resigning to return to the world of television.

Bob Carlson became the A.B.A.'s third chief executive, and under his direction the San Diego Conquistadors were created as the first A.B.A. expansion club. This new team brought the league back up to 10 clubs for the upcoming season, but a quick look at the cities involved showed the difficulties the A.B.A. had in obtaining a national television contract and national recognition. Only New York and Dallas were major metropolises readily recognizable to the national sporting public as "big league;" San Diego, Denver, Louisville, Indianapolis, Memphis, Salt Lake City, Norfolk, and Greensboro seemed minor league to most sports fans, and the television markets in these cities lacked the size to excite the networks into offering national coverage except on a very limited basis. To make matters worse, the Dallas and Memphis clubs were largely ignored in their hometowns.

The New York club suffered a jolt to its gate appeal when star forward Rick Barry was ordered by the courts to report back to the Golden State Warriors on the grounds that he had signed a valid contract for future services with the N.B.A. club when he had been dissatisfied with the shifting of his Oakland team to Washington and then to Virginia. Barry expressed a desire to stay in New York, where he could foster his ambitions of a career as a television commentator, but the courts upheld his contract with the Warriors. The loss of Barry hurt the entire league's drawing power, but the arrival of Billy Cunningham in Carolina somewhat softened the blow. A star forward with the Philadelphia 76ers, Cunningham had signed with the Cougars three years ago, and although he too expressed a desire to stay right where he was, the legal decision was that he had to fulfill his Carolina contract. So in the sum total of star veteran forward jumpings, the two leagues came out even.

The A.B.A. teams also made out well in terms of playing personnel, when the Pittsburgh and Florida players were dispersed to the other teams in a special draft. This draft helped the teams more than the college draft, which turned up little help this year. The two most prominent rookies were Jim Chones and Brian Taylor, both hardship cases signed by the New York Nets.

The Carolina Cougars didn't need any key rookies to suddenly rush up to the top of the league with a 57-27 record. The Cougars did have a new coach in Larry Brown, who retired from his active career to preach the gospel of the fast break in Carolina. Newcomers Cunningham and Mack Calvin, late of the Floridians, fit right in with this new style, and the rest of the team came alive with the new coach and stars leading the way. Brown shuffled guards Calvin, Steve Jones, Ted McClain, and Gene Littles in and out, constantly keeping a fresh pair in the game. Forwards Cunningham and Joe Caldwell had starred in running games during their N.B.A. days, and they kept their younger mates from making many errors. The Cougars figured to have a problem at center when Mike Lewis went out with an injury early in the campaign, but Tom Owens plugged the hole in stop-gap fashion and kept the fast break running.

But the Cougars couldn't run away from the Kentucky Colonels, who finished only one game off the pace. The addition of Rick Mount and Wendell Ladner strengthened the Colonels, but the heart of the team again was the twin towers of Artis Gilmore and Dan Issel. Third place in the East went to the Virginia Squires; Charlie Scott was lost to the N.B.A., but the Squires still had Julius Erving, whose 31.9 scoring average topped the league. Way down the ladder in fourth place were the New York Nets, who simply could not do better than 30-54 without Rick Barry. The Memphis club had a new name, the Tams. They also had a new coach, Bob Bass; a new scorer, George Thompson; and an abysmal 24-60 record.

The Western Division also had two top contenders, a strong middle club, and two weaklings trailing the rear. Utah and Indiana waged their annual battle for first place, with the Stars emerging on top this year by four games. The Stars bolstered their forward corps by picking up veterans Cincy Powell and George Govan, both A.B.A. originals from 1967, but veteran Utah stars Willie Wise, Jimmy Jones, Ron Boone, and Zelmo Beaty were the key factors in the club's 55-29 record. The Indiana Pacers dropped veterans Bob Netolicky and Rick Mount to give more playing time to youngsters like George McGinnis and rookie Don Buse; McGinnis responded by blossoming into the A.B.A.'s foremost power forward, ranking second in the league in scoring and fourth in rebounding. Veteran guard Donnie Freeman also added to the Pacers' strength, and the familiar trio of Mel Daniels, Roger Brown, and Freddie Lewis carried on as ever.

The Denver Rockets finished in the middle of the pack with a much improved 47-37 record, due greatly to Warren Jabali's steady backcourt leadership after coming over in the dispersal draft from Florida; Jabali's steady hand also helped young Ralph Simpson start cashing in on his great scoring ability. The dregs of the West were the San Diego Conquistadors and the Dallas Chaparrals, with the San Diego bunch the surprise winners of the fourth playoff spot. K.C. Jones coached the talent-thin Conquistadors to a 30-54 mark, relying heavily on the long-range shooting of Stew Johnson and Chuck Williams to offset the myriad array of weaknesses on the team. The Chaps, meanwhile, fell apart with the departure of coach Tom Nissalke to the N.B.A. Babe McCarthy replaced Nissalke and could muster little scoring power beyond Rich Jones and Bob Netolicky, and Netolicky disappointed the Chaps with his all-around play at center—a performance which cost the team a spot in the playoffs for the first time.

The Carolina, Kentucky, Utah, and Indiana clubs all got past their first round competition to set up the divisional finals between the A.B.A.'s strongest clubs. The Pacers and Stars split their first four games, but then the Pacers won game five in Salt Lake City and then wrapped it up in Indianapolis. The Cougars and Colonels, meanwhile, came down to a decisive seventh game, with the Colonels' size stopping the Cougar fast break in a 107-96 victory at Charlotte.

The championship series between the Pacers and Colonels also came down to a final seventh game, and before 16,597 fans in Louisville, the Pacers won the crown with an 88-81 triumph. This was the third A.B.A. crown for the Pacers, and the first repeat championship in the league's short history. Just as prominent, however, was the repeated failure of the Colonels, a talented club with a consistently excellent record, to win their first A.B.A. championship.

Use Name	Pos	Hgt	Wgt	Age	TOTAL G	Min	FG	FGA	%	FT	FTA	%	Reb	Ass	PF	DQ	Points	PER GAME Min	Reb	Ass	PF	Points

1972/73 A.B.A. — EASTERN DIVISION

Use Name	Pos	Hgt	Wgt	Age	G	Min	FG	FGA	%	FT	FTA	%	Reb	Ass	PF	DQ	Points	Min	Reb	Ass	PF	Points
CAROLINA COUGARS	**57-27 .679**				**LARRY BROWN**																	
Joe Caldwell	F	6'5	205	31	77	2739	555	1118	50	172	405	42	395	352	252	—	1283	36	5.1	4.6	3.3	16.7
Billy Cunningham	F-C	6'7	220	29	84	3248	771	1583	49	472	598	79	1012	530	309	—	2028	39	12.0	6.3	3.7	24.1
Tom Owens	C	6'10	223	23	83	2209	393	727	54	193	284	68	646	94	318	—	979	27	7.8	1.1	3.8	11.8
Steve Jones (from Dal)	G	6'5	205	30	67	1670	348	696	50	145	178	81	178	84	177	—	852	25	2.7	1.3	2.6	12.7
Mack Calvin	G	6'	175	24	84	2228	478	944	51	500	582	86	215	301	219	—	1467	27	2.6	3.6	2.6	17.5
Gene Littles	G	6'1	175	29	84	2060	310	622	50	179	246	73	262	245	198	—	807	25	3.1	2.9	2.4	9.6
Ted McClain	G	6'3	180	25	84	1816	325	652	50	145	204	71	263	225	256	—	803	22	3.1	2.7	3.0	9.6
Ed Manning	F	6'7	215	28	83	1631	263	554	47	64	84	76	393	64	247	—	590	20	4.7	0.8	3.0	7.1
Dennis Wuycik	F	6'6	215	22	83	973	151	329	46	75	108	69	179	79	165	—	377	12	2.2	1.0	2.0	4.5
Roger Brown (from LA-NBA)	C	7'	225	22	62	579	59	129	46	28	51	55	178	25	120	—	146	9	2.9	0.4	1.9	2.4
Mike Lewis	C	6'8	230	26	15	430	59	119	50	33	41	80	122	41	48	—	151	29	8.1	2.7	3.2	10.1
Bobby Warren (to Dal-Utah)	G-F	6'5	190	26	17	353	54	106	51	49	60	82	65	22	43	—	157	21	3.8	1.3	2.5	9.2
Steve Previs	G	6'3	183	22	30	147	23	60	38	8	15	53	14	24	26	—	55	5	0.5	0.8	0.9	1.8
Ira Harge (from Utah)	C	6'9	225	31	4	77	5	18	28	2	4	50	23	3	16	—	12	19	5.8	0.8	4.0	3.0
KENTUCKY COLONELS	**56-28 .667**				**JOE MULLANEY**																	
Walt Simon	F	6'6	200	31	83	2403	433	897	48	143	191	75	395	336	271	—	1010	29	4.8	4.0	3.3	12.2
Dan Issel	F-C	6'9	240	24	84	**3531**	**902**	1757	51	485	635	76	922	220	255	—	**2292**	42	11.0	2.6	3.0	27.3
Artis Gilmore	C	7'2	240	23	84	3502	687	1228	**56**	368	572	64	**1476**	295	302	—	1743	42	**17.6**	3.5	3.6	20.8
Rick Mount	G	6'4	185	25	61	1780	369	804	46	159	198	80	138	194	172	—	906	29	2.3	3.2	2.8	14.9
Louie Dampier	G	6'	180	28	80	3039	515	1143	45	262	334	78	213	521	216	—	1346	38	2.7	6.5	2.7	16.8
Mike Gale	G	6'4	190	22	81	1854	218	463	47	100	143	70	241	248	207	—	537	23	3.0	3.1	2.6	6.6
Jimmy O'Brien	G	6'2	180	22	68	1014	126	317	40	68	89	76	92	174	103	—	320	15	1.4	2.6	1.5	4.7
Claude Virden (injury)	F	6'6	200	25	31	825	130	327	40	46	59	78	154	74	84	—	306	27	5.0	2.4	2.7	9.9
Wendell Ladner (from Mem)	F	6'5	220	24	37	659	109	318	34	44	58	76	181	72	132	—	270	18	4.9	1.9	3.6	7.3
Pierre Russell	G-F	6'4	200	23	59	618	119	266	45	49	78	63	129	61	80	—	289	10	2.2	1.0	1.4	4.9
Bill Chamberlain (to Mem)	F	6'6	200	23	43	566	101	248	41	34	55	62	107	69	81	—	237	13	2.5	1.6	1.9	5.5
Ron Thomas	F	6'6	215	22	31	369	62	132	47	21	41	51	115	23	73	—	145	12	3.7	0.7	2.4	4.7
VIRGINIA SQUIRES	**42-42 .500**				**AL BIANCHI**																	
George Irvine	F-G	6'6	200	23	79	2075	424	805	53	169	203	83	296	149	267	—	1024	26	3.7	1.9	3.4	13.0
Julius Erving	F	6'7	210	22	71	2993	894	**1804**	50	475	612	78	867	298	197	—	2268	**42**	12.2	4.2	2.8	**31.9**
Jim Eakins	C	6'11	215	26	83	2559	430	823	52	384	479	80	733	262	287	—	1244	31	8.8	3.2	3.5	15.0
Mike Barr	G	6'3	180	22	79	2076	289	612	47	141	188	75	227	254	220	—	720	26	2.9	3.2	2.8	9.1
Fatty Taylor	G	6'	175	26	78	2553	316	679	47	150	248	60	318	374	266	—	785	33	4.1	4.8	3.4	10.1
Bernie Williams	G	6'3	175	27	71	1513	356	831	43	166	193	86	125	137	150	—	888	21	1.8	1.9	2.1	12.5
Neil Johnson	F-C	6'7	230	29	69	1442	210	429	49	103	156	66	364	158	232	—	523	21	5.3	2.3	3.4	7.6
Dave Twardzik	G	6'1	180	22	80	1357	141	306	46	178	212	84	158	184	202	—	462	17	2.0	2.3	2.5	5.8
Willie Sojourner	C	6'8	235	24	64	1065	199	410	49	84	128	66	364	75	187	—	482	17	5.7	1.2	2.9	7.5
Will Franklin	F	6'7	225	23	73	990	218	524	42	107	179	60	289	50	157	—	545	14	4.0	0.7	2.2	7.5
George Gervin	F-G	6'7	180	20	30	689	161	341	47	96	118	81	128	34	72	—	424	23	4.3	1.1	2.4	14.1
Goose Ligon	F	6'7	215	28	12	360	58	103	56	28	43	65	94	20	40	—	144	30	7.8	1.7	3.3	12.0
Erwin Mueller (from Det-NBA)	C-F	6'8	230	28	17	205	17	53	32	3	10	30	47	26	24	—	37	12	2.8	1.5	1.4	2.2
Billy Shepherd	G	5'10	260	23	16	68	7	35	20	9	10	90	5	8	12	—	27	4	0.3	0.5	0.8	1.7
Al Sanders	F	6'7	240	22	4	25	2	2	100	4	6	67	5	0	4	—	8	6	1.3	0.0	1.0	2.0
NEW YORK NETS	**30-54 .357**				**LOU CARNESECCA**																	
George Carter	F	6'5	218	27	83	2976	569	1249	46	440	529	83	515	173	308	—	1578	36	6.2	2.1	3.7	19.0
Trooper Washington	F	6'7	225	28	76	2027	229	425	54	63	101	62	553	203	242	—	521	27	7.3	2.7	3.2	6.9
Billy Paultz	C	6'11	240	24	81	2800	532	1027	52	287	405	71	1015	189	259	—	1351	35	12.5	2.3	3.2	16.7
Brian Taylor (injury)	G	6'2	185	21	63	2038	395	767	51	168	226	74	203	175	219	—	962	32	3.2	2.8	3.5	15.3
Johnny Roche	G	6'3	170	23	77	2615	404	912	44	265	347	76	146	348	170	—	1107	34	1.9	4.5	2.2	14.4
Jim Chones	C-F	6'11	220	23	82	2153	395	769	51	142	240	59	586	95	291	—	932	26	7.1	1.2	3.5	11.4
Bill Melchionni (ankle injury)	G	6'1	170	28	61	1849	291	646	45	163	194	84	127	453	155	—	751	30	2.1	7.4	2.5	12.3
Bob Lackey	G-F	6'6	210	23	68	1185	153	350	44	99	167	59	160	136	170	—	407	17	2.4	2.0	2.5	6.0
Johnny Baum	F	6'5	205	26	75	1071	221	438	50	107	143	75	201	31	99	—	549	14	2.7	0.4	1.3	7.3
Gary Gregor (from Mil-NBA)	F	6'7	235	27	40	595	99	204	49	32	39	82	150	31	84	—	231	15	3.8	0.8	2.1	5.8
Jim Ard	F	6'8	220	24	42	426	53	140	38	34	50	68	148	14	50	—	140	10	3.5	0.3	1.2	3.3
George Bruns	G	6'	160	26	13	236	31	66	47	22	27	81	8	36	26	—	86	18	0.6	2.8	2.0	6.6
Brian Mahoney	G	6'3	175	24	19	181	17	57	30	24	40	60	14	12	35	—	58	10	0.7	0.6	1.8	3.1
Art Becker (to Dal)	F	6'8	210	30	8	46	9	16	56	5	5	100	6	1	3	—	23	6	0.8	0.1	0.4	2.9
Joe DePre	G	6'3	190	25	1	12	2	4	40	0	0	—	2	2	1	—	4	12	2.0	2.0	1.0	4.0

1972/73 A.B.A. — EASTERN DIVISION (continued)

Use Name	Pos	Hgt	Wgt	Age	G (Total)	Min	FG	FGA	%	FT	FTA	%	Reb	Ass	PF	DQ	Points	Min (Per Game)	Reb	Ass	PF	Points
MEMPHIS TAMS	**24-60 .286**				**BOB BASS**																	
Warren Davis	F	6'6	220	30	73	1895	250	498	50	172	227	76	515	146	212	—	672	26	7.1	2.0	2.9	9.
Wil Jones	F	6'8	205	25	76	2316	344	722	48	146	198	74	604	117	281	—	835	30	7.9	1.5	3.7	11.
Randy Denton (broken hand)	C	6'10	245	23	66	2205	472	979	48	177	237	75	820	98	197	—	1124	33	12.4	1.5	3.0	17.
Johnny Neumann	G-F	6'6	200	21	79	2787	605	1283	47	329	423	78	310	470	304	—	1548	35	3.9	5.9	3.8	19.
George Thompson	G	6'2	200	25	80	2925	579	1269	46	**549**	700	78	265	403	246	—	1727	37	3.3	5.0	3.1	21.
Lee Davis	F-C	6'8	240	27	78	2111	453	871	52	131	209	63	608	82	266	—	1037	27	7.8	1.1	3.4	13.
Les Hunter	F	6'7	235	30	63	1333	236	474	50	95	135	70	302	95	183	—	576	21	4.8	1.5	2.9	9.
Luther Rackley (from NY-NBA)	C	6'10	225	26	57	893	170	344	49	78	120	65	287	36	130	—	418	16	5.0	0.6	2.3	7.
George Lehmann	G	6'3	190	30	28	753	95	240	40	61	74	82	34	150	74	—	277	27	1.2	5.4	2.6	9.
Mike Davis (from Bal-NBA)	G	6'3	185	26	38	553	93	222	42	62	87	71	41	47	87	—	254	15	1.1	1.2	2.3	6.
Merv Jackson	G	6'3	175	26	22	420	34	103	33	28	35	80	38	82	61	—	100	19	1.7	3.7	2.8	4.
Ron Franz (to Dal)	F	6'7	207	27	23	403	60	129	47	46	66	70	87	26	46	—	166	18	3.8	1.1	2.0	7.
Isaiah Wilson	G	6'2	175	24	30	386	68	159	43	51	64	80	39	72	46	—	190	13	1.3	2.4	1.5	6.
Dave Lattin	C	6'7	230	29	16	296	48	104	46	34	45	76	63	7	45	—	130	19	3.9	0.4	2.8	8.
Wendell Ladner (to KY)	F	6'5	220	24	15	273	37	128	29	11	15	73	96	35	54	—	89	18	6.4	2.3	3.6	5.
Charlie Williams (to Utah)	G	6'	165	29	10	219	25	75	33	19	26	73	12	42	31	—	72	22	1.2	4.2	3.1	7.
Darel Carrier	G	6'3	185	32	16	190	23	60	38	24	26	92	14	10	21	—	75	12	0.9	0.6	1.3	4.
Loyd King	G	6'2	185	23	10	102	6	29	21	7	8	88	12	14	20	—	19	10	1.2	1.4	2.0	1.
Bill Chamberlain (from KY)	F	6'6	205	23	7	99	11	34	32	2	4	50	11	7	17	—	25	14	1.6	1.0	2.4	3.
Bob Ford	F	6'7	228	22	9	74	5	17	29	4	5	80	12	4	8	—	14	8	1.3	0.4	0.9	1.
Sam Cash	F	6'8	230	22	7	52	4	18	22	12	17	71	19	0	11	—	20	7	2.7	0.0	1.6	2.

1972/73 A.B.A. — WESTERN DIVISION

Use Name	Pos	Hgt	Wgt	Age	G (Total)	Min	FG	FGA	%	FT	FTA	%	Reb	Ass	PF	DQ	Points	Min (Per Game)	Reb	Ass	PF	Points
UTAH STARS	**55-29 .655**				**LaDELL ANDERSEN**																	
Willie Wise	F	6'6	215	25	83	3131	672	1404	48	476	607	78	682	277	278	—	1823	38	8.2	3.3	3.3	22.
Gerald Govan	F-C	6'10	220	30	84	2408	229	530	43	81	135	60	795	250	279	—	539	29	9.5	3.0	3.3	6.
Zelmo Beaty	C	6'9	235	33	82	2804	521	1002	52	306	381	80	801	125	269	—	1348	34	9.8	1.5	3.3	16.
Jimmy Jones	G	6'4	190	27	80	2848	496	948	52	345	432	80	335	448	271	—	1337	36	4.2	5.6	3.4	16.
Ron Boone	G	6'2	200	26	84	2585	566	1136	50	415	479	87	425	353	308	—	1557	31	5.1	4.2	3.7	18.
Cincy Powell	F	6'7	227	30	83	1985	423	853	50	167	240	70	420	137	249	—	1016	24	5.1	1.7	3.0	12.
Glen Combs (injury)	G	6'2	185	26	50	1488	228	535	43	154	189	81	84	138	142	—	661	30	1.7	2.8	2.8	13.
Bobby Warren (from Car-Dal)	G-F	6'5	190	26	51	1046	170	345	49	158	180	88	155	109	144	—	502	21	3.0	2.1	2.8	9.
John Beasley	C	6'9	230	28	71	934	214	417	51	62	70	89	264	43	142	—	519	13	3.7	0.6	2.0	7.
Larry Jones (to Dal)	G	6'2	180	31	27	447	53	121	44	58	71	82	61	43	43	—	168	17	2.3	1.6	1.6	6.
Mike Jackson	F	6'7	230	23	30	191	36	83	43	28	46	61	62	2	46	—	100	6	2.1	0.1	1.5	3.
Charlie Williams (from Mem)	G	6'	165	29	22	151	12	40	30	22	31	71	6	17	23	—	45	7	0.3	0.8	1.0	2.
Rod McDonald	F	6'6	205	27	25	142	27	63	43	15	19	79	30	15	19	—	70	6	1.2	0.6	0.8	2.
Ira Harge (to Car)	C	6'9	225	31	13	100	9	22	41	4	6	67	36	6	27	—	22	8	2.8	0.5	2.1	1.
INDIANA PACERS	**51-33 .607**				**BOB LEONARD**																	
Darnell Hillman	F	6'9	215	23	84	2541	328	735	45	148	252	59	735	128	291	—	804	30	8.8	1.5	3.5	9.
George McGinnis	F-C	6'8	235	22	82	3347	868	1755	49	517	**778**	66	1022	205	348	—	2261	41	12.5	2.5	4.2	27.
Mel Daniels	C	6'9	225	28	81	3103	587	1217	48	322	446	72	1247	177	315	—	1497	38	15.4	2.2	3.9	18.
Donnie Freeman	G	6'3	185	28	77	2170	412	933	44	277	343	81	219	195	225	—	1103	28	2.8	2.5	2.9	14.
Freddie Lewis	G	6'	180	29	72	2217	375	860	44	287	349	82	228	288	204	—	1075	31	3.2	4.0	2.8	14.
Bill Keller	G	5'10	185	25	83	2251	421	973	43	234	269	**87**	204	361	162	—	1147	27	2.5	4.3	2.0	13.
Roger Brown	F	6'5	210	30	72	2177	332	700	47	203	247	82	348	204	181	—	909	30	4.8	2.8	2.5	12.
Don Buse	G	6'4	195	22	77	1484	163	360	45	82	109	75	210	223	143	—	413	19	2.7	2.9	1.9	5.
Gus Johnson (from Phoe-NBA)	C-F	6'6	235	34	50	753	132	299	44	31	42	74	245	62	113	—	299	15	4.9	1.2	2.3	6.
Bill Newton	C	6'9	220	22	24	117	24	56	43	9	18	50	47	9	40	—	58	5	2.0	0.4	1.7	2.
Bob Arnzen	F	6'6	215	25	23	111	20	38	53	6	8	75	23	3	12	—	46	5	1.0	0.1	0.5	2.
George Peeples	F	6'8	205	29	9	56	4	14	29	6	11	55	15	4	14	—	14	6	1.7	0.4	1.6	1.
Craig Raymond (from SD)	C	6'11	235	27	6	33	2	8	25	1	2	50	10	1	8	—	5	6	1.7	0.2	1.3	0.
DENVER ROCKETS	**-37 .560**				**ALEX HANNUM**																	
Marv Roberts	F	6'8	205	22	77	1959	374	807	46	201	255	79	398	95	194	—	950	25	5.2	1.2	2.5	12.
Julius Keye	F	6'10	225	26	83	3016	163	375	43	130	233	56	892	180	269	—	459	36	10.7	2.2	3.2	5.
Dave Robisch	C	6'10	240	23	83	2647	521	1010	52	309	409	76	744	170	271	—	1351	32	9.0	2.0	3.3	16.
Ralph Simpson	G-F	6'5	200	23	81	2589	732	1670	44	421	556	76	371	222	241	—	1890	32	4.6	2.7	3.0	23.
Warren Jabali	G	6'2	210	26	82	2738	441	974	45	480	596	81	424	539	280	—	1398	33	5.2	6.6	3.4	17.
Al Smith	G	6'1	185	25	83	2343	315	767	41	272	352	77	214	477	295	—	919	28	2.6	5.7	3.6	11.
Byron Beck	C-F	6'9	230	27	77	2303	466	879	53	158	198	80	537	107	267	—	1092	30	7.0	1.4	3.5	14.
Willie Long (broken hand)	F	6'8	235	22	56	1050	183	458	40	138	177	78	290	43	147	—	504	19	5.2	0.8	2.6	9.
Claude Terry	G	6'4	195	22	68	667	120	285	42	74	114	65	75	62	111	—	324	10	1.1	0.9	1.6	4.
Dave Bustion	F	6'8	215	23	47	355	58	133	44	42	59	71	101	21	82	—	158	8	2.1	0.4	1.7	3.
John Trapp (from LA-PhiNBA)	F	6'7	215	27	24	342	54	128	42	19	32	59	72	20	76	—	127	14	3.0	0.8	3.2	5.
Frank Card	F	6'7	195	28	4	36	6	15	40	9	13	69	7	0	4	—	21	9	1.8	0.0	1.0	5.

1972/73 A.B.A. — WESTERN DIVISION (continued)

SAN DIEGO CONQUISTADORS 30-54 .357 K. C. JONES

Use Name	Pos	Hgt	Wgt	Age	G	Min	FG	FGA	%	FT	FTA	%	Reb	Ass	PF	DQ	Points	Min	Reb	Ass	PF	Points
					TOTAL													PER GAME				
Simmie Hill (broken jaw)	F	6'7	235	26	69	1658	315	743	42	103	135	76	351	131	221	—	760	24	5.1	1.9	3.2	11.0
Stew Johnson	F	6'8	225	28	80	2952	769	1748	44	195	238	82	597	174	258	—	1770	37	7.5	2.2	3.2	22.1
Gene Moore	C	6'9	245	27	83	2481	400	804	50	180	260	69	874	152	**369**	—	984	30	10.5	1.8	**4.4**	11.9
Ollie Taylor	G	6'2	194	25	69	2121	325	757	43	286	425	67	365	275	191	—	947	31	5.3	4.0	2.8	13.7
Chuck Williams	G	6'2	175	26	83	3074	488	1020	48	493	623	79	229	**582**	275	—	1470	37	2.8	**7.0**	3.3	17.7
Larry Miller	G-F	6'4	210	26	83	2700	450	1080	42	306	422	73	355	281	174	—	1206	33	4.3	3.4	2.1	14.5
Red Robbins	F-C	6'8	200	28	58	1618	218	525	42	131	155	85	417	99	134	—	576	28	7.2	1.7	2.3	9.9
Garfield Smith	C	6'9	235	27	71	1055	116	244	48	28	93	30	306	39	197	—	260	15	4.3	0.5	2.8	3.7
Jerry Chambers	F	6'5	190	29	43	885	199	468	43	112	130	86	190	46	102	—	512	21	4.4	1.1	2.4	11.9
George Adams	F	6'6	210	23	60	865	153	312	49	65	83	78	205	64	97	—	373	14	3.4	1.1	1.6	6.2
Henry Bacon	G	6'3	205	21	47	425	60	164	37	44	73	60	82	38	72	—	166	9	1.7	0.8	1.5	3.5
Mike Barrett	G	6'2	160	29	19	284	37	101	37	18	35	51	24	46	28	—	96	15	1.3	2.4	1.5	5.1
Craig Raymond (to Ind)	C	6'11	235	27	8	135	10	31	32	9	12	75	63	6	16	—	29	17	7.9	0.8	2.0	3.6
Pete Smith	F	6'6	205	22	5	32	2	12	17	0	0	—	8	1	5	—	4	6	1.6	0.2	1.0	0.8

DALLAS CHAPARRALS 28-56 .333 BABE McCARTHY (24-48 .333), DAVE BROWN (4-8 .333)

Use Name	Pos	Hgt	Wgt	Age	G	Min	FG	FGA	%	FT	FTA	%	Reb	Ass	PF	DQ	Points	Min	Reb	Ass	PF	Points
Collis Jones	F	6'7	205	23	81	2204	357	768	46	227	318	71	522	143	230	—	941	27	6.4	1.8	2.8	11.6
Rich Jones	F	6'8	230	26	67	2691	564	1364	41	324	414	78	667	274	240	—	1495	40	10.0	4.1	3.6	22.3
Bob Netolicky	C-F	6'9	225	30	84	3409	650	1347	48	269	404	67	851	239	166	—	1569	41	10.1	2.8	2.0	18.7
James Silas	G	6'3	185	23	78	2417	341	679	50	389	467	83	336	244	262	—	1071	31	4.3	3.1	3.4	13.7
Joe Hamilton	G	5'10	175	24	83	2359	370	902	41	209	262	80	215	325	247	—	1015	28	2.6	3.9	3.0	12.2
Goo Kennedy	F	6'6	205	23	70	1809	365	664	55	148	232	64	490	75	275	—	878	26	7.0	1.1	3.9	12.5
Coby Dietrick	C	6'10	230	24	77	1347	205	489	42	96	139	69	377	136	224	—	506	17	4.9	1.8	2.9	6.6
Larry Jones (from Utah)	G	6'2	180	31	53	1254	187	400	47	144	173	83	178	163	141	—	530	24	3.4	3.1	2.7	10.0
Skeeter Swift (injury)	G	6'3	210	26	42	1123	177	374	47	128	149	86	82	150	140	—	501	27	2.0	3.6	3.3	11.9
Ron Franz (from Mem)	F	6'7	207	27	37	511	88	174	51	99	135	73	105	42	66	—	276	14	2.8	1.1	1.8	7.5
Steve Jones (to Car)	G	6'5	205	30	13	459	82	187	44	55	69	80	46	35	43	—	221	35	3.5	2.7	3.3	17.0
Shaler Halimon	G	6'6	205	27	29	355	59	149	40	23	37	62	54	49	53	—	142	12	1.9	1.7	1.8	4.9
B. Warren (from Car, to Utah)	G-F	6'5	190	26	9	172	20	53	38	29	34	85	22	16	25	—	70	19	2.4	1.8	2.8	7.8
Ansley Truitt	F	6'9	215	22	16	86	18	42	43	3	9	33	38	2	9	—	39	5	2.4	0.1	0.6	2.4
Mike Maloy	F	6'7	215	23	9	63	7	27	26	6	10	60	15	3	14	—	20	7	1.7	0.3	1.6	2.2
Art Becker (from NY)	F	6'8	210	30	6	50	7	12	58	6	6	100	12	0	3	—	20	8	2.0	0.0	0.5	3.3
Nick Jones	G	6'2	190	27	3	16	3	8	38	2	3	67	1	1	4	—	8	5	0.3	0.3	1.3	2.7
Gene Phillips	G	6'4	180	24	3	10	0	5	0	0	0	—	0	1	3	—	0	3	0.0	0.3	1.0	0.0

1972/73 A.B.A. — PLAYOFFS

INDIANA PACERS BOB LEONARD

defeated Denver 4-1; H114-91, H106-93, 94-105, 97-95, H121-107
defeated Utah 4-2; 107-124, 116-110, H118-108, H103-104, 104-102, H107-98
defeated Kentucky 4-3; 111-107,102-114, H88-92, H90-86, 86 89, H93-109, 88- 81

Use Name	Pos	Hgt	Wgt	Age	G	Min	FG	FGA	%	FT	FTA	%	Reb	Ass	PF	DQ	Points	Min	Reb	Ass	PF	Points
Roger Brown	F-G	6'5	210	30	17	584	82	160	51	37	49	76	74	41	58	—	214	34	4.4	2.4	3.4	12.6
George McGinnis	F-C	6'8	235	22	18	731	161	357	45	109	149	73	222	39	**78**	—	431	41	12.3	2.2	4.3	23.9
Mel Daniels	C	6'9	225	28	18	636	112	238	47	62	81	77	248	40	76	—	286	35	**13.8**	2.2	4.2	15.9
Donnie Freeman	G	6'3	185	28	18	557	105	237	44	71	89	80	48	50	52	—	281	31	2.7	2.8	2.9	15.6
Freddie Lewis	G	6'	180	29	18	637	102	260	39	69	80	86	66	**91**	57	—	279	35	3.7	5.1	3.2	15.5
Darnell Hillman	F	6'9	215	23	18	485	43	101	43	20	35	57	135	17	44	—	106	27	7.5	0.9	2.4	5.9
Bill Keller	G	5'10	185	25	17	348	57	149	38	31	38	82	52	63	35	—	153	20	3.1	3.7	2.1	9.0
Gus Johnson	F	6'6	235	34	17	184	15	59	25	12	16	75	69	15	27	—	42	11	4.1	0.9	1.6	2.5
Don Buse	G	6'4	195	22	14	163	16	45	36	13	21	62	25	17	30	—	45	12	1.8	1.2	2.1	3.2
Bob Arnzen	F	6'6	215	25	7	13	3	6	50	1	1	100	0	0	1	—	7	2	0.0	0.0	0.1	1.0
Bill Newton	C	6'9	220	22	4	7	2	5	40	0	0	—	5	0	3	—	4	2	1.3	0.0	0.8	1.0

KENTUCKY COLONELS JOE MULLANEY

defeated Virginia 4-1; H129-101, H94-109, 115-113, 108-90, H114-103
defeated Carolina 4-3; 113-103, 105-125, H108-94, H91-102, 107-112, H119-100, 107-96
lost to Indiana 3-4; H107-111, H114-102, 92-88, 86-90, H89-86, 109-93, H81-88

Use Name	Pos	Hgt	Wgt	Age	G	Min	FG	FGA	%	FT	FTA	%	Reb	Ass	PF	DQ	Points	Min	Reb	Ass	PF	Points
Walt Simon	F	6'6	200	31	19	639	92	207	44	27	31	87	93	79	67	—	211	34	4.9	4.2	3.5	11.1
Dan Issel	F-C	6'9	240	24	19	**825**	**198**	**398**	50	**124**	**156**	79	225	28	71	—	**521**	43	11.8	1.5	3.7	27.4
Artis Gilmore	C	7'2	240	23	19	780	142	261	54	77	123	63	**260**	75	68	—	361	41	13.7	3.9	3.6	19.0
Rich Mount	G	6'4	185	25	19	676	119	293	41	73	87	84	47	49	48	—	321	36	2.5	2.6	2.5	16.9
Louie Dampier	G	6'	180	28	12	411	65	126	52	21	30	70	25	39	35	—	161	34	2.1	3.3	2.9	13.4
Jimmy O'Brien	G	6'2	180	22	19	435	33	93	35	39	45	87	34	82	35	—	106	23	1.8	4.3	1.8	5.6
Mike Gale	G	6'4	190	22	12	291	23	58	40	20	23	87	30	40	41	—	66	24	2.5	3.3	3.4	5.5
Wendell Ladner	F	6'5	220	24	19	269	55	142	39	12	14	86	56	21	67	—	136	14	2.9	1.1	3.5	7.2
Ron Thomas	F	6'6	215	31	17	247	38	77	49	9	23	39	75	13	44	—	85	15	4.4	0.8	2.6	5.0
Pierre Russell	G-F	6'4	200	23	12	37	7	12	58	3	6	50	12	2	5	—	17	3	1.0	0.2	0.4	1.4

UTAH STARS LaDELL ANDERSEN

defeated San Diego 4-0; H107-93, H103-92, 97-96, 120-98
lost to Indiana 2-4; H124-107, H110-116, 108-118, 104-103, H102-104, 98-107

Use Name	Pos	Hgt	Wgt	Age	G	Min	FG	FGA	%	FT	FTA	%	Reb	Ass	PF	DQ	Points	Min	Reb	Ass	PF	Points
Willie Wise	F	6'6	215	25	10	414	92	181	51	65	83	78	83	38	33	—	250	41	8.3	3.8	3.3	25.0
Gerald Govan	F-C	6'10	220	30	10	330	28	78	36	12	15	80	112	36	37	—	68	33	11.2	3.6	3.7	6.8
Zelmo Beaty	C	6'9	235	33	10	387	58	105	55	43	52	83	116	14	36	—	159	39	11.6	1.4	3.6	15.9
Jimmy Jones	G	6'4	190	27	10	316	64	130	49	35	44	80	41	43	37	—	163	32	4.1	4.3	3.7	16.3
Ron Boone	G	6'2	200	26	10	360	68	135	50	33	34	**97**	43	47	41	—	169	36	4.3	4.7	4.1	16.9
Bobby Warren	G-F	6'5	190	26	10	221	32	68	47	29	32	91	39	16	33	—	95	22	3.9	1.6	3.3	9.5
Cincy Powell	F	6'7	227	30	10	192	37	89	42	18	29	62	37	6	30	—	92	19	3.7	0.6	3.0	9.2
John Beasley	C-F	6'9	230	28	8	102	22	37	59	3	4	75	23	5	14	—	49	13	2.9	0.6	1.8	6.1
Glen Combs	G	6'2	185	26	9	60	10	31	32	4	5	80	7	5	12	—	24	7	0.8	0.6	1.3	2.7
Charlie Williams	G	6'	165	29	4	12	1	5	20	0	0	—	1	1	3	—	2	3	0.3	0.3	0.8	0.5
Rod McDonald	F	6'6	205	27	3	4	1	3	33	0	0	—	1	0	0	—	2	1	0.3	0.0	0.0	0.7
Mike Jackson	F	6'7	230	23	1	2	0	0	—	0	0	—	0	0	2	—	0	2	0.0	0.0	2.0	0.0

1972/73 A.B.A. — PLAYOFFS (continued)

Use Name	Pos	Hgt	Wgt	Age	G	Min	FG	FGA	%	FT	FTA	%	Reb	Ass	PF	DQ	Points	Min	Reb	Ass	PF	Points
					TOTAL													PER GAME				
CAROLINA COUGARS	LARRY BROWN	defeated New York 4-1; H104-96, H111-114, 101-91, 112-108, H136-113 lost to Kentucky 3-4; H103-113, H125-105, 94-108, 102-91, H112-107, 100-119, H96-107																				
Joe Caldwell	F	6'5	205	31	12	467	80	163	49	24	50	48	68	40	35	—	187	39	5.7	3.3	2.9	15.6
Billy Cunningham	F-C	6'7	220	29	12	472	112	223	50	57	83	69	142	61	48	—	282	39	11.8	5.1	4.0	23.5
Tom Owens	C	6'10	223	23	12	377	65	127	51	45	60	75	137	19	49	—	175	31	11.4	1.6	4.1	14.6
Steve Jones	G-F	6'5	205	30	12	368	61	135	45	34	42	81	36	9	40	—	158	31	3.0	0.8	3.3	13.2
Mack Calvin	G	6'	175	24	12	370	72	154	47	72	88	82	34	52	35	—	218	31	2.8	4.3	2.9	18.2
Ed Manning	F	6'7	215	28	12	262	44	82	54	18	23	78	57	8	40	—	106	22	4.8	0.7	3.3	8.8
Ted McClain	G	6'3	180	25	12	234	22	74	30	11	15	73	43	22	39	—	56	20	3.6	1.8	3.3	4.7
Gene Littles	G	6'1	175	29	12	223	30	67	45	20	32	63	36	16	22	—	80	19	3.0	1.3	1.8	6.7
Dennis Wuycik	F	6'6	215	22	12	81	7	20	35	6	10	60	16	2	14	—	20	7	1.3	0.2	1.2	1.7
Roger Brown	C	7'	225	22	7	40	5	7	71	1	1	100	11	1	6	—	11	6	1.6	0.1	0.9	1.6
Steve Previs	G	6'3	183	22	2	11	1	7	14	0	0	—	3	3	2	—	3	6	1.5	1.5	1.0	1.5
DENVER ROCKETS	ALEX HANNUM	lost to Indiana 1-4; 91-114, 93-106, H105-94, H95-97, 107-121																				
Julius Keye	F	6'10	225	26	5	203	20	34	59	9	17	53	68	16	16	—	49	41	13.6	3.2	3.2	9.8
Byron Beck	F-C	6'9	230	27	4	130	28	63	44	13	17	76	39	5	16	—	69	33	9.8	1.3	4.0	17.3
Dave Robisch	C	6'10	240	23	5	184	40	85	47	21	31	68	68	8	21	—	101	37	13.6	1.6	4.2	20.2
Ralph Simpson	G-F	6'5	200	23	5	197	51	138	37	28	37	76	24	14	20	—	132	39	4.8	2.8	4.0	26.4
Al Smith	G	6'1	185	25	5	185	15	54	28	18	20	90	25	26	17	—	48	37	5.0	5.2	3.4	9.6
Warren Jabali	G	6'2	210	26	5	126	9	27	33	12	16	75	7	14	11	—	30	25	1.4	2.8	2.2	6.0
Willie Long	F	6'8	235	22	4	53	5	20	25	5	6	83	9	1	13	—	15	13	2.3	0.3	3.3	3.8
John Trapp	F	6'7	215	27	5	51	7	16	44	8	12	67	7	2	13	—	22	10	1.4	0.4	2.6	4.4
Claude Terry	G	6'5	195	22	4	36	2	9	22	1	1	100	3	2	5	—	5	9	0.8	0.5	1.3	1.3
Marv Roberts	F	6'8	205	22	2	24	4	8	50	2	2	100	3	1	5	—	10	12	1.5	0.5	2.5	5.0
Dave Bustion	F	6'8	215	23	1	11	2	7	29	6	7	86	1	1	3	—	10	11	1.0	1.0	3.0	10.0
NEW YORK NETS	LOU CARNESECCA	lost to Carolina 1-4; 96-104, 114-111, H91-101, H108-112, 113-136																				
Johnny Baum	F	6'5	205	26	5	191	41	78	53	12	17	71	21	4	20	—	94	38	4.2	0.8	4.0	18.8
George Carter	F	6'5	218	27	5	218	36	72	50	34	40	85	45	13	27	—	106	44	9.0	2.6	5.4	21.2
Billy Paultz	C	6'11	240	24	5	172	34	56	61	27	43	63	55	10	17	—	95	34	11.0	2.0	3.4	19.0
Brian Taylor	G	6'2	185	21	5	166	28	58	48	12	15	80	16	11	14	—	68	33	3.2	2.2	2.8	13.6
Bill Melchionni	G	6'1	170	28	5	174	24	43	56	17	21	81	10	31	25	—	66	35	2.0	6.2	5.0	13.2
Johnny Roche	G	6'3	170	23	4	83	16	33	48	7	12	58	1	10	7	—	41	21	0.3	2.5	1.8	10.3
Jim Chones	C	6'11	220	23	5	74	8	23	35	4	8	50	27	5	8	—	20	15	5.4	1.0	1.6	4.0
Trooper Washington	F	6'7	225	28	4	68	6	11	55	3	4	75	18	3	8	—	15	17	4.5	0.8	2.0	3.8
Bob Lackey	G	6'6	210	23	5	60	4	8	50	4	11	36	8	5	10	—	12	12	1.6	1.0	2.0	2.4
Gary Gregor	F	6'7	235	27	1	12	1	6	17	2	2	100	4	0	3	—	4	12	4.0	0.0	3.0	4.0
George Bruns	G	6'	160	26	2	7	0	1	0	1	2	50	0	1	3	—	1	4	0.0	0.5	1.5	0.5
VIRGINIA SQUIRES	AL BIANCHI	lost to Kentucky 1-4; 101-129,109-94, H113-115, H90-108, 103-114																				
Julius Erving	F	6'6	210	22	5	219	59	112	53	30	40	75	45	16	16	—	148	44	9.0	3.2	3.2	29.6
Erwin Mueller	F-C	6'8	230	28	5	112	5	18	28	6	7	86	19	15	10	—	17	22	3.8	3.0	2.0	3.4
Jim Eakins	C	6'11	215	26	5	217	48	81	59	28	34	82	57	18	22	—	124	43	11.4	3.6	4.4	24.8
George Gervin	G-F	6'7	180	20	5	200	34	77	44	24	34	71	38	8	15	—	93	40	7.6	1.6	3.0	18.6
Fatty Taylor	G	6'	175	26	5	169	13	38	34	14	15	93	21	14	19	—	41	34	4.2	2.8	3.8	8.2
Neil Johnson	F	6'7	230	29	5	98	13	26	50	6	8	75	21	5	16	—	32	20	4.2	1.0	3.2	6.4
Mike Barr	G	6'3	180	22	5	84	5	18	28	5	6	83	6	10	8	—	15	17	1.2	2.0	1.6	3.0
George Irvine	F-G	6'6	200	23	5	53	6	15	40	5	5	100	5	5	8	—	17	11	1.0	1.0	1.6	3.4
Dave Twardzik	G	6'1	180	22	2	29	3	7	43	6	6	100	1	3	3	—	12	15	0.5	1.5	1.5	6.0
Bernie Williams	G	6'3	175	27	3	24	3	8	38	1	1	100	0	1	4	—	7	8	0.0	0.3	1.3	2.3
SAN DIEGO CONQUISTADORS	K. C. JONES	lost to Utah 0-4; 93-107, 92-103, H96-97, H98-120																				
Stew Johnson	F	6'8	225	28	4	151	32	82	39	5	7	71	25	8	10	—	73	38	6.3	2.0	2.5	18.3
Red Robbins	F-C	6'8	200	28	4	147	19	55	35	24	27	89	44	5	16	—	64	37	11.0	1.3	4.0	16.0
Gene Moore	C	6'9	245	27	4	107	12	44	27	9	16	56	38	4	18	—	33	27	9.5	1.0	4.5	8.3
Ollie Taylor	G	6'2	194	25	4	139	20	52	38	7	14	50	30	12	12	—	49	35	7.5	3.0	3.0	12.3
Chuck Williams	G	6'2	175	26	4	158	27	61	44	23	30	77	10	21	12	—	77	40	2.5	5.3	3.0	19.3
Simmie Hill	F	6'7	235	26	4	85	13	36	36	3	5	60	17	3	11	—	29	21	4.3	0.8	2.8	7.3
Larry Miller	G	6'4	210	26	4	71	9	28	32	6	6	100	10	6	3	—	24	18	2.5	1.5	0.8	6.0
Garfield Smith	C	6'9	235	27	4	63	5	17	29	2	7	29	21	1	9	—	12	16	5.3	0.3	2.3	3.0
George Adams	F	6'6	210	23	3	23	4	8	50	0	0	—	6	3	1	—	8	8	2.0	1.0	0.3	2.7
Henry Bacon	G	6'3	205	21	2	16	4	9	44	0	2	0	6	1	0	—	10	8	3.0	0.5	0.0	5.0

Team	W	L	Pct.	GB	Record against playoff teams			Record against non-playoff teams			HOME			ROAD			NEUTRAL		
					W	L	Pct.	W	L	Pct.	W	L	Pct.	W	L	Pct.	W	L	Pct.
EASTERN DIVISION																			
Carolina Cougars	57	27	.679	—	41	24	.631	16	3	.842	30	12	.714	27	15	.643	0	0	—
Kentucky Colonels	56	28	.667	1	39	26	.600	17	2	.895	33	9	.786	23	19	.548	0	0	—
Virginia Squires	42	42	.500	15	30	35	.462	12	7	.632	31	11	.738	11	31	.262	0	0	—
New York Nets	30	54	.357	27	21	44	.323	9	10	.474	22	20	.524	8	33	.190	0	1	.000
Memphis Tams	24	60	.286	33	18	58	.237	6	2	.750	19	23	.452	5	35	.125	0	2	.000
WESTERN DIVISION																			
Utah Stars	55	29	.655	—	42	23	.646	13	6	.684	37	5	.881	18	24	.429	0	0	—
Indiana Pacers	51	33	.607	4	37	28	.569	14	5	.737	33	9	.786	18	24	.429	0	0	—
Denver Rockets	47	37	.560	8	32	33	.492	15	4	.789	31	9	.775	14	28	.333	2	0	1.000
San Diego Conquistadors	30	54	.357	25	18	47	.277	12	7	.632	21	21	.500	9	31	.225	0	2	.000
Dallas Chaparrals	28	56	.333	27	26	50	.342	2	6	.250	18	20	.474	7	35	.167	3	1	.750

1972/73 A.B.A. INDIVIDUAL LEADERS

SCORING
(Minimum 70 Games Played)

Name	Team	G	FG	FT	Pts.	Avg.
Erving	Va	71	892	475	2268	31.9
McGinnis	Ind	82	868	517	2261	27.6
Issel	KY	84	902	485	2292	27.3
Cunningham	Car	84	771	472	2028	24.1
Simpson	Den	81	732	421	1890	23.3
Johnson	SD	80	769	195	1770	22.1
Wise	Utah	83	672	476	1823	22.0
Thompson	Mem	80	579	549	1727	21.6
Gilmore	KY	84	687	368	1743	20.8
Neumann	Mem	79	605	329	1548	19.6

FIELD GOAL PERCENTAGE
(Minimum 560 Field Goals)

Name	Team	FG	FGA	Pct.
Gilmore	KY	687	1228	.559
Kennedy	Dal	365	664	.550
Owens	Car	393	727	.541
Irvine	Va	424	805	.527
Jones	Utah	496	948	.523
Eakins	Va	430	823	.522
Davis	Mem	453	871	.520
Beaty	Utah	521	1002	.520
Paultz	NY	532	1027	.518
Robisch	Den	521	1010	.516

3-POINT FIELD GOAL PERCENTAGE
(Minimum 20 Made)

Name	Team	FT	FTA	Pct.
Hill	SD	27	69	.391
Lehmann	Mem	26	67	.388
Combs	Utah	51	134	.381
Brown	Ind	42	118	.356
Dampier	KY	54	155	.348
Hamilton	Dal	66	191	.346
Lewis	Ind	38	110	.345
R. Jones	Dal	43	127	.339
Roche	NY	34	103	.330
Beasley	Utah	29	89	.326

FREE THROW PERCENTAGE
(Minimum 160 Attempts)

Name	Team	FT	FTA	Pct.
Keller	Ind	234	269	.870
Boone	Utah	415	479	.866
Warren	Car-Dal-Utah	236	274	.861
Williams	Va	166	193	.860
Calvin	Car	500	582	.859
Melchionni	NY	163	194	.840
Twardzik	Va	178	212	.840
Silas	Dal	389	467	.833
Irvine	Va	169	203	.833
Carter	NY	440	529	.832

REBOUNDS PER GAME
(Minimum 70 Games Played)

Name	Team	G	Reb.	Avg.
Gilmore	KY	84	1476	17.6
Daniels	Ind	81	1247	15.4
Paultz	NY	81	1015	12.5
McGinnis	Ind	82	1022	12.4
Erving	Va	71	867	12.2
Cunningham	Car	84	1012	12.0
Issel	KY	84	922	10.9
Keye	Den	83	892	10.7
Moore	SD	83	874	10.5
Netolicky	Dal	84	851	10.1

ASSISTS PER GAME
(Minimum 70 Games Played)

Name	Team	G	Ass.	Avg.
Williams	SD	83	582	7.0
Jabali	Den	82	539	6.6
Dampier	KY	80	521	6.5
Cunningham	Car	84	530	6.3
Neumann	Mem	79	470	6.0
Smith	Den	83	477	5.8
Jones	Utah	80	448	5.6
Thompson	Mem	80	403	5.0
Taylor	Va	78	374	4.8
Caldwell	Car	77	352	4.6

MINUTES PLAYED

Name	Team	Min.
Issel	KY	3531
Gilmore	KY	3502
Netolicky	Dal	3409
McGinnis	Ind	3347
Cunningham	Car	3248

PERSONAL FOULS

Name	Team	PF
Moore	SD	369
McGinnis	Ind	348
Owens	Car	318
Daniels	Ind	315
Cunningham	Car	309

Team		REGULAR SEASON												PLAYOFFS											
		G	FG	FGA	%	FT	FTA	%	Reb.	Ass.	PF	Points	PPG	G	FG	FGA	%	FT	FTA	%	Reb.	Ass.	PF	Points	PPG
TEAM STATISTICS																									
EASTERN DIVISION																									
Carolina	Off.	84	3794	7657	50	2065	2860	72	3945	2089	2394	9707	115.6	12	**499**	1059	47	288	404	71	583	233	330	1296	**108.0**
	Def.	84	3481	7325	48	2249	2983	75	3890	**1783**	2219	9296	110.7	12	480	**999**	48	291	393	74	521	230	317	1272	106.0
	Diff.		+313	+332	+2	-184	-123	-3	+55	+306	-175	+411	+4.9		+19	+60	-1	-3	+11	-3	**+62**	+3	-13	+24	+2.0
Kentucky	Off.	84	3770	7900	48	1779	2453	73	4163	**2287**	**1976**	9401	111.9	19	772	1667	46	405	538	75	857	**428**	481	1985	104.5
	Def.	84	3504	7563	46	**1768**	**2369**	75	4277	1865	2055	**8860**	**105.5**	19	**729**	1669	44	437	569	77	974	**351**	470	1909	**100.5**
	Diff.		+266	**+337**	+2	+11	+84	-2	-114	**+422**	+79	**+541**	**+6.4**		**+43**	-2	+2	-32	-31	-2	-117	**+77**	-11	+76	**+4.0**
Virginia	Off.	83	3722	7757	48	2097	2785	75	4020	2029	2317	9581	115.4	5	193	407	47	**127**	158	80	219	97	123	516	103.2
	Def.	83	3638	7727	47	2249	3031	74	4177	1932	2158	9613	115.8	5	218	440	50	118	148	80	**216**	122	131	560	112.0
	Diff.		+84	+30	+1	-152	-246	+1	-157	+97	-159	-32	-.4		-25	-33	-3	+9	+10	—	+3	-25	+8	-44	-8.8
New York	Off.	84	3400	7073	48	1851	2513	74	3834	1899	2112	8700	103.6	5	198	389	**51**	123	**175**	70	205	93	142	522	104.4
	Def.	84	3547	7611	47	2057	2738	75	4111	1894	2044	9245	110.1	5	215	422	51	129	188	**69**	225	108	**147**	564	112.8
	Diff.		-147	-538	+1	-206	-225	-1	-277	+5	-68	-545	-6.5		-17	-33	—	-6	-13	+1	-20	-15	+5	-42	-8.4
Memphis	Off.	84	3618	7758	47	2038	2721	75	4189	1943	2340	9368	111.5												
	Def.	84	3756	7743	49	2313	3070	75	4184	2047	2209	9921	118.1												
	Diff.		-138	+15	-2	-275	-349	—	+5	-104	-131	-553	-6.6												
WESTERN DIVISION																									
Utah	Off.	84	3656	7499	49	**2291**	2886	**79**	4156	1963	2240	**9708**	**115.6**	10	413	862	48	242	298	**81**	503	211	278	1073	107.3
	Def.	84	3528	7908	**45**	2085	2791	75	4106	1891	2283	9244	110.0	10	391	943	**41**	233	326	71	504	185	252	1034	103.4
	Diff.		+128	-409	**+4**	**+206**	+95	**+4**	+50	+72	+43	+464	+5.6		+22	-81	**+7**	+9	-28	**+10**	-1	+26	-26	+39	+3.9
Indiana	Off.	84	3668	7948	46	2123	2874	74	**4553**	1860	2056	9631	114.7	18	698	1617	43	425	559	76	**944**	373	461	1848	102.7
	Def.	84	3741	8207	46	1891	2547	74	4344	2033	2255	9451	112.5	18	704	1599	44	**388**	525	74	882	372	485	1812	100.7
	Diff.		-73	-259	—	**+232**	**+327**	—	+209	-173	**+199**	+180	+2.2		-6	+18	-1	**+37**	+34	+2	+62	+1	+24	+36	+2.0
Denver	Off.	83	3433	7501	46	2253	**2994**	75	4125	1936	2237	9193	110.8	5	183	461	40	123	166	74	254	90	140	491	98.2
	Def.	83	**3397**	**7234**	47	2045	2736	75	**3702**	2046	2236	8932	107.6	5	200	441	45	120	152	79	250	123	137	532	106.4
	Diff.		+36	+267	-1	+208	+258	—	**+423**	-110	-1	+261	+3.2		-17	+20	-5	+3	**+14**	-5	+4	-33	-3	-41	-8.2
San Diego	Off.	84	3542	**8009**	44	1970	2684	73	4066	1934	2139	9153	109.0	4	145	**392**	37	79	114	69	207	64	**92**	379	94.8
	Def.	84	3721	7782	48	1966	2675	**73**	4252	2150	2197	9513	113.3	4	164	341	48	96	**111**	86	200	98	108	427	106.8
	Diff.		-179	+227	-4	+4	+9	—	-186	-216	+58	-360	-4.3		-19	**+51**	-11	-17	+3	-17	+7	-34	**+16**	-48	-12.0
Dallas	Off.	84	3500	7644	46	2157	2861	75	4011	1898	2145	9302	110.7												
	Def.	84	3790	7646	50	2001	2691	74	4019	2197	**2300**	9669	115.1												
	Diff.		-290	-2	-4	+156	+170	+1	-8	-299	+155	-367	-4.4												

1973-74 N.B.A.

An Old Champion in a New Alignment

Wilt Chamberlain, the all-time N.B.A. scoring leader, made his exit from the league this season by signing as a player coach with the San Diego Conquistadors of the A.B.A. A court order, however, forbade him from playing with the A.B.A. club since he had not played out his option with the Los Angeles Lakers, so he spent the year as a bench coach in San Diego. His departure from the N.B.A. closed the books on one of the league s most colorful personalities and left Kareem Abdul-Jabbar of Milwaukee as the undisputed king of the big men on the circuit.

Chamberlain s old rival, Bill Russell, crossed Chamberlain in the other direction, quitting his post as television commentator to go to Seattle as coach of the Supersonics. Other old Celtics who had played with Russell on the great Boston clubs of the 1950's and 1960's were also on the move. Satch Sanders finally retired as an active player, leaving the Celtics to become head coach at Harvard. Bob Cousy resigned as coach of the Kansas City-Omaha Kings, tired of losing and unsuccessful in building the franchise after four and a half years. And K.C. Jones came back to the N.B.A. as coach of the Capital Bullets, who had moved from Baltimore to an arena near Washington, D.C.

The present-day Celtics did quite well for themselves, finishing comfortably in first place in the Atlantic Division for the third straight season. Veteran John Havlicek was the thread connecting this club to its illustrious ancestors, and center Dave Cowens was the key to the present, battling larger giants with mobility and hustle. The New York Knicks relied on their defense and took second place despite losing Earl Monroe with a leg injury in the early going and losing Willis Reed for most of the campaign with knee trouble.

The big news in the Atlantic Division, however, was the sudden emergence of the Buffalo Braves as a coming power. General manager Eddie Donovan and coach Jack Ramsay cleaned a lot of deadwood away and replaced it with fine young talent. Tbey signed rookie guard Ernie DiGregorio from Providence College, a superb playmaker who led the N.B.A. in assists in his rookie year. They obtained a power forward in Gar Heard through a minor trade with Chicago. And they took a big chance by trading young center Elmore Smith, a potential star, to tbe Los Angeles Lakers for Jim McMillian, one of the N.B.A.'s top small forwards. The gamble paid offwhen McMillian had a good season, and secondyear man Bob McAdoo blossomed into an immediate star when shifted to the center spot. A rangy 6'10", McAdoo used a sharp shooting eye to lead the N.B.A. in scoring with a 30.6 average. These men, along with improving holdover Randy Smith, formed a powerfill starting unit, and Donovan and Ramsay built up the bench with a late-season deal that brought Jack Marin and Matt Guokas from Houston. The Braves still had to learn to play topnotch defense, but their offensive power took them into the playoffs this year under a new rule, since their record was better than the second-place team in the central division.

Behind them this season, in fourth place, were the Philadelphia 76ers. Despite losing first draft choice Doug Collins for most of the season with a leg injury, new coach Gene Shue at least made the 76ers competitive, finding an unexpected treasure in Steve Mix, who had been playing semi-pro ball in the Midwest after flopping with the Detroit Pistons.

The Central Division was dominated by the Bullets, who built a 47-35 record despite losing Archie Clark and Wes Unseld for long stretches with injuries. Atlanta fell to a 35-47 level and failed to win a playoff spot despite edging Houston for second place. Cleveland had the rookie disappointment of the year in Jim Brewer, and as usual was not a factor in the race for the playoffs.

The hottest fight for playoff position was in the Midwest Division, where the Chicago Bulls and Detroit Pistons slugged it out for second place behind the Milwaukee Bucks. Both teams relied on muscle and ball-control offenses, with the Bulls having the edge at forward with Bob Love and Chet Walker, the Pistons having an advantage at center with Bob Lanier, and with Dave Bing, Chris Ford, Jerry Sloan, and Norm Van Lier making the backcourts an even match. Coach Ray Scott had the Pistons playing the best ball in the team's history in Detroit, and the club record of 52-30 was better than anything in the Pacific Division, thus clinching a playoff berth despite losing second place to the Bulls. In Kansas City-Omaha, Nate Archibald suffered an Achilles tendon injury and this instantly ruined the entire King offense.

The Los Angeles Lakers lost veteran star Jerry West to an injury and had to struggle for the playoffs in the Pacific Division. Chamberlain was gone, and his leaving prompted the trade of Jim McMillian to Buffalo for Elmore Smith. A mid-season trade for Connie Hawkins produced poor results, but Gail Goodrich emerged in tbe transitional surroundings as the team's scoring ace with a 25.3 average. The Golden State Warriors finished only three games behind Los Angeles despite losing big men Nate Thurmond and Clyde Lee on injuries, but their 44-38 final record wasn't good enough to earn them a playoff spot over the Pistons. Bill Russell's coaching couldn't turn Seattle into a winning club, and Phoenix and Portland did even worse.

The new playoff rule created a stronger field for the first round. The Celtics took the measure of the young Braves in six games, while the Knicks had to win a seventh game from the Bullets. In the West, the Bucks downed the weakened Lakers in five games, while the Bulls and Pistons beat on each other for seven games, with the Bulls winning a 96-94 decision in the deciding contest. After knocking heads with the tough Pistons for seven games, the Bulls simply could not stand up to the Bucks and lost four straight games to Abdul-Jabbar and Co. In the Eastern finals, Willis Reed and Dave DeBusschere were hobbled with injuries, and the Knicks bowed to the Celtics after upsetting them for the past two years .

In the championship series, the Bucks were hurting in the backcourt, with Lucius Allen out with a knee injury and with Oscar Robertson slowed down from his peak. The Celtics won the first game. The clubs then took turns winning the next five games, with the Bucks taking a 102-101 double-overtime victory in game six with their backs up against the wall. Dave Cowens hit for 28 points in the seventh game, outscoring Abdul-Jabbar by two, and the Celtics outscored the Bucks 102-87 to reclaim the title after an absence of five years.

Use Name	Pos	Hgt	Wgt	Age	TOTAL G	Min	FG	FGA	%	FT	FTA	%	Reb	Ass	PF	DQ	Points	PER GAME Min	Reb	Ass	PF	Points
1973/74 N.B.A. — ATLANTIC DIVISION																						
BOSTON CELTICS	**56-26 .683**				**TOM HEINSOHN**																	
John Havlicek	F-G	6'5	205	33	76	3091	685	1502	46	346	416	83	487	447	196	1	1716	41	6.4	5.9	2.6	22.6
Paul Silas	F	6'7	225	30	82	2599	340	772	44	264	337	78	915	186	246	3	944	32	11.2	2.3	3.0	11.5
Dave Cowens	C	6'9	230	25	80	3352	645	1475	44	228	274	83	1257	354	294	7	1518	42	15.7	4.4	3.7	19.0
Don Chaney	G	6'5	210	27	81	2258	348	750	46	149	180	83	378	176	247	7	845	28	4.7	2.2	3.0	10.4
Jo Jo White	G	6'3	190	27	82	3238	649	1445	45	190	227	84	351	448	185	1	1488	39	4.3	5.5	2.3	18.1
Don Nelson	F	6'6	210	33	82	1748	364	717	51	215	273	79	345	162	189	1	943	21	4.2	2.0	2.3	11.5
Paul Westphal	G	6'4	195	23	82	1165	238	475	50	112	153	73	143	171	173	1	588	14	1.7	2.1	2.1	7.2
Steve Kuberski	F	6'8	215	26	78	985	157	368	43	86	111	77	237	38	125	0	400	13	3.0	0.5	1.6	5.1
Hambone Williams	G	6'2	190	34	67	617	73	168	43	27	32	84	115	163	100	0	173	9	1.7	2.4	1.5	2.6
Henry Finkel	C	7'	240	31	60	427	60	130	46	28	43	65	135	27	62	1	148	7	2.3	0.5	1.0	2.5
Phil Hankinson	F	6'8	195	22	28	163	50	103	49	10	13	77	50	4	18	0	110	6	1.8	0.1	0.6	3.9
Steve Downing	C	6'8	225	23	24	137	21	64	33	22	38	58	39	11	33	0	64	6	1.6	0.5	1.4	2.7
NEW YORK KNICKERBOCKERS	**49 33 .598**				**RED HOLZMAN**																	
Bill Bradley	F	6'5	205	30	82	2813	502	1112	45	146	167	87	253	242	278	2	1150	34	3.1	3.0	3.4	14.0
Dave DeBusschere	F	6'6	235	33	71	2699	559	1212	46	164	217	76	757	253	222	2	1282	38	10.7	3.6	3.1	18.1
Willis Reed (knee injury)	C	6'9	240	31	19	500	84	184	46	42	53	79	141	30	49	0	210	26	7.4	1.6	2.6	11.1
Walt Frazier	G	6'4	205	28	80	3338	674	1429	47	295	352	84	536	551	212	2	1643	42	6.7	6.9	2.7	20.5
Earl Monroe (leg injury)	G	6'3	190	29	41	1194	240	513	47	93	113	82	121	110	97	0	573	29	3.0	2.7	2.4	14.0
Dean Meminger	G	6'	175	25	78	2079	274	539	51	103	160	64	281	162	161	0	651	27	3.6	2.1	2.1	8.3
Phil Jackson	F-C	6'8	220	28	82	2050	361	757	48	191	246	78	478	134	277	7	913	25	5.8	1.6	3.4	11.1
Jerry Lucas	C-F	6'8	230	33	73	1627	194	420	46	67	96	70	374	230	134	0	455	22	5.1	3.2	1.8	6.2
John Gianelli	C	6'10	220	23	70	1423	208	434	48	92	121	76	343	77	159	1	508	20	4.9	1.1	2.3	7.3
Henry Bibby	G	6'1	185	24	66	986	210	465	45	73	88	83	133	91	123	0	493	15	2.0	1.4	1.9	7.5
Harthorne Wingo	F	6'8	210	25	60	536	82	172	48	48	76	63	166	25	85	0	212	9	2.8	0.4	1.4	3.5
Dick Garrett (to Mil)	G	6'3	185	26	25	239	32	91	35	10	13	77	26	14	41	0	74	10	1.0	0.6	1.6	3.0
Mel Davis	F	6'7	225	23	30	167	33	95	35	12	16	75	54	8	36	0	78	6	1.8	0.3	1.2	2.6
Dick Barnett	G	6'4	190	37	5	58	10	26	38	2	3	67	4	6	2	0	22	12	0.8	1.2	0.4	4.4
Tom Riker	F	6'10	250	23	17	57	13	29	45	12	17	71	15	3	6	0	38	3	0.9	0.2	0.4	2.2
Allie McGuire	G	6'3	175	22	2	10	2	4	50	0	0	—	2	1	2	0	4	5	1.0	0.5	1.0	2.0
Dennis Bell	F	6'6	215	22	1	4	0	1	0	0	0	—	0	0	0	0	0	4	0.0	0.0	0.0	0.0
BUFFALO BRAVES	**42-40 .512**				**JACK RAMSAY**																	
Jim McMillian	F	6'5	225	25	82	3322	600	1214	49	325	379	86	610	256	186	0	1525	41	7.4	3.1	2.3	18.6
Gar Heard	F	6'6	226	25	81	2889	524	1205	43	191	294	65	947	180	300	3	1239	36	11.7	2.2	3.7	15.3
Bob McAdoo	C	6'9	210	22	74	3185	901	1647	**55**	459	579	79	1117	170	252	3	**2261**	43	15.1	2.3	3.4	**30.6**
Randy Smith	G	6'3	180	25	82	2745	531	1079	49	205	288	71	315	383	261	4	1267	33	3.8	4.7	3.2	15.5
Ernie DiGregorio	G	6'	180	22	81	2910	530	1260	42	174	193	**90**	219	**663**	242	2	1234	36	2.7	**8.2**	3.0	15.2
Bob Kauffman	F-C	6'8	240	27	74	1304	171	366	47	107	150	71	326	142	155	0	449	18	4.4	1.9	2.1	6.1
Ken Charles	G	6'3	180	22	59	693	88	185	48	53	79	67	65	54	91	0	229	12	1.1	0.9	1.5	3.9
Jack Marin	F	6'7	210	29	27	680	145	266	55	71	81	88	122	46	93	3	361	25	4.5	1.7	3.4	13.4
Dave Wohl (to Hou)	G	6'2	185	24	41	606	60	150	40	42	60	70	29	127	72	1	162	15	0.7	3.1	1.8	4.0
Matt Guokas (from KCO, Hou)	G	6'5	195	29	27	549	61	110	55	10	20	50	40	69	56	1	132	20	1.5	2.6	2.1	4.9
Lee Winfield	G	6'2	175	26	36	433	37	105	35	33	52	63	43	47	42	0	107	12	1.2	1.3	1.2	3.0
Kevin Kunnert (to Hou)	C	7'	230	22	39	340	49	101	49	11	16	69	106	25	83	0	109	9	2.7	0.6	2.1	2.8
Mike Macaluso	F	6'5	210	22	30	112	19	44	43	10	17	59	25	3	31	0	48	4	0.8	0.1	1.0	1.6
Paul Ruffner	C	6'10	225	25	20	51	11	27	41	8	13	62	11	0	10	0	30	3	0.6	0.0	0.5	1.5
Jim Garvin	F	6'7	200	23	6	11	1	4	25	0	0	—	5	0	1	0	2	2	0.8	0.0	0.2	0.3
PHILADELPHIA 76ers	**25-57 .305**				**GENE SHUE**																	
Tom Van Arsdale	F-G	6'5	215	30	78	3041	614	1433	43	298	350	85	393	202	300	6	1526	39	5.0	2.6	3.8	19.6
Steve Mix	F	6'7	215	26	82	2969	495	1042	48	228	288	79	864	152	305	9	1218	36	10.5	1.9	3.7	14.9
Leroy Ellis	C	6'10	225	33	81	2831	326	722	45	147	196	75	890	189	224	2	799	35	11.0	2.3	2.8	9.9
Fred Carter	G	6'3	185	28	78	3044	706	1641	43	254	358	71	371	443	276	4	1666	39	4.8	5.7	3.5	21.4
Larry Jones	G	6'2	180	32	72	1876	263	622	42	197	235	84	184	230	116	0	723	26	2.6	3.2	1.6	10.0
Freddie Boyd	G	6'2	180	23	75	1818	286	712	40	141	195	72	93	249	173	1	713	24	1.2	3.3	2.3	9.5
Toby Kimball	C-F	6'8	240	31	75	1592	216	456	47	127	185	69	552	73	199	1	559	21	7.4	1.0	2.7	7.5
Don May	F	6'4	215	27	56	812	152	367	41	89	102	87	136	63	137	0	393	15	2.4	1.1	2.4	7.0
Allan Bristow	F	6'7	227	22	55	643	108	270	40	42	57	74	167	92	68	1	258	12	3.0	1.7	1.2	4.7
Doug Collins (leg injury)	G	6'6	180	22	25	436	72	194	37	55	72	76	46	40	65	1	199	17	1.8	1.6	2.6	8.0
Larry Cannon (from Ind-ABA)	G	6'5	195	26	19	335	49	127	39	19	28	68	36	52	48	0	117	18	1.9	2.7	2.5	6.2
Rod Freeman	F	6'7	225	23	35	265	39	103	38	28	41	68	54	14	42	0	106	8	1.5	0.4	1.2	3.0
Luther Rackley	C	6'10	225	27	9	68	5	13	38	8	11	73	22	0	11	0	18	8	2.4	0.0	1.2	2.0

Use Name	Pos	Hgt	Wgt	Age	TOTAL													PER GAME				
					G	Min	FG	FGA	%	FT	FTA	%	Reb	Ass	PF	DQ	Points	Min	Reb	Ass	PF	Points
1973/74 N.B.A. — CENTRAL DIVISION																						
CAPITAL BULLETS	**47-35 .573**				**K. C. JONES**																	
Mike Riordan	F-G	6'4	200	28	81	3230	577	1223	47	136	174	78	380	264	237	2	1290	40	4.7	3.3	2.9	15.9
Wes Unseld (knee injury)	F-C	6'7	250	27	56	1727	146	333	44	36	55	65	517	159	121	1	328	31	9.2	2.8	2.2	5.9
Elvin Hayes	C-F	6'9	235	28	81	**3602**	689	1627	42	357	495	72	**1463**	163	252	1	1735	**44**	**18.1**	2.0	3.1	21.4
Phil Chenier	G	6'3	180	23	76	2942	697	1607	43	274	334	82	388	239	135	0	1668	39	5.1	3.1	1.8	21.9
Archie Clark (elbow injury)	G	6'2	175	32	56	1786	315	675	47	103	131	79	141	285	122	0	733	32	2.5	5.1	2.2	13.1
Kevin Porter	G	6'	175	23	81	2339	477	997	48	180	249	72	179	469	**319**	14	1134	29	2.2	5.8	**3.9**	14.0
Nick Weatherspoon (injury)	F	6'7	200	23	65	1216	199	483	41	96	139	69	397	38	179	1	494	19	6.1	0.6	2.8	7.6
Manny Leaks	F	6'8	235	28	53	845	79	232	34	58	83	70	244	25	95	1	216	16	4.6	0.5	1.8	4.1
Tom Kozelko	F	6'8	220	22	49	573	59	133	44	23	32	72	124	25	82	3	141	12	2.5	0.5	1.7	2.9
Louie Nelson	G	6'3	190	22	49	556	93	215	43	53	73	73	70	52	62	0	239	11	1.4	1.1	1.3	4.9
Dave Stallworth	F	6'7	210	32	45	458	75	187	40	47	55	85	125	25	61	0	197	10	2.8	0.6	1.4	4.4
Walt Wesley	C	6'11	230	28	39	400	71	151	47	26	43	60	136	14	74	1	168	10	3.5	0.4	1.9	4.3
Rich Rinaldi (to NY-ABA)	G	6'3	195	24	7	48	3	22	14	3	4	75	7	10	7	0	9	7	1.0	1.4	1.0	1.3
Tommy Patterson	F	6'6	220	25	2	8	0	1	0	1	2	50	2	2	0	0	1	4	1.0	1.0	0.0	0.5
ATLANTA HAWKS	**35-47 .427**				**COTTON FITZSIMMONS**																	
Lou Hudson (injury)	F	6'5	215	29	65	2588	678	1356	50	295	353	84	350	213	205	3	1651	40	5.4	3.3	3.2	25.4
Jim Washington	F	6'7	215	30	73	2519	297	612	49	134	196	68	735	156	249	5	728	35	10.1	2.1	3.4	10.0
Walt Bellamy	C	6'11	245	34	77	2440	389	801	49	233	383	61	740	189	232	2	1011	32	9.6	2.5	3.0	13.1
Pete Maravich	G	6'5	200	25	76	2903	819	**1791**	46	469	568	83	374	396	261	4	2107	38	4.9	5.2	3.4	27.7
Herm Gilliam (ankle injury)	G	6'3	190	27	62	2003	384	846	45	106	134	79	267	355	190	5	874	32	4.3	5.7	3.1	14.1
John Brown	F	6'7	220	22	77	1715	277	632	44	163	217	75	441	114	239	10	717	22	5.7	1.5	3.1	9.3
Steve Bracey	G	6'1	175	23	75	1463	241	520	46	69	96	72	146	231	157	0	551	20	1.9	3.1	2.1	7.3
Dwight Jones	C-F	6'10	210	21	74	1448	238	502	47	116	156	74	454	86	197	3	592	20	6.1	1.2	2.7	8.0
John Wetzel	G	6'5	190	29	70	1232	107	252	42	41	57	72	170	138	147	1	255	18	2.4	2.0	2.1	3.6
Dale Schlueter	C	6'10	235	28	57	547	63	135	47	38	50	76	155	45	84	0	164	10	2.7	0.8	1.5	2.9
John Tschogl	F	6'6	210	23	64	499	59	166	36	10	17	59	76	33	69	0	128	8	1.2	0.5	1.1	2.0
Tom Ingelsby	G	6'3	185	22	48	398	50	131	38	29	37	78	44	37	43	0	129	8	0.9	0.8	0.9	2.7
HOUSTON ROCKETS	**32-50 .390**				**JOHNNY EGAN**																	
Rudy Tomjanovich	F	6'8	220	25	80	3227	788	1470	54	385	454	85	717	250	230	0	1961	40	9.0	3.1	2.9	24.5
Cliff Meely	F-C	6'8	215	26	77	1754	330	773	43	90	140	64	439	124	234	5	750	23	5.7	1.6	3.0	9.7
Don Smith	C	6'9	240	27	79	2459	336	732	46	193	240	80	923	166	227	3	865	31	11.7	2.1	2.9	10.9
Mike Newlin	G-F	6'4	205	24	76	2591	510	1139	45	380	444	86	262	363	259	5	1400	34	3.4	4.8	3.4	18.4
Calvin Murphy	G	5'9	165	25	81	2922	671	1285	52	310	357	87	188	603	310	8	1652	36	2.3	7.4	3.8	20.4
Ed Ratleff	G-F	6'6	195	23	81	1773	254	585	43	103	129	80	286	181	182	2	611	22	3.5	2.2	2.2	7.5
Jack Marin (to Buf)	F	6'7	210	29	47	1102	210	443	47	82	98	84	106	121	120	2	502	23	2.3	2.6	2.6	10.7
E. C. Coleman	F	6'8	225	23	58	1075	128	250	51	47	74	64	252	76	162	4	303	19	4.3	1.3	2.8	5.2
Matt Guokas (from KCO, to Buf)	G	6'5	195	29	39	1007	93	203	46	21	28	75	60	133	73	1	207	26	1.5	3.4	1.9	5.3
Dave Wohl (from Buf)	G	6'2	185	24	26	449	61	127	48	33	42	79	17	109	64	2	155	17	0.7	4.2	2.5	6.0
Ron Riley (from KCO)	F	6'8	200	23	36	421	57	145	39	10	14	71	121	29	68	0	124	12	3.4	0.8	1.9	3.4
Kevin Kunnert (from Buf)	C	7'	230	22	25	361	56	114	49	10	17	59	111	18	68	1	122	14	4.4	0.7	2.7	4.9
Otto Moore (to KCO)	C	6'11	220	27	13	313	32	69	46	4	8	50	84	18	37	2	68	24	6.5	1.4	2.8	5.2
George Johnson	C	6'11	255	26	26	238	23	51	45	8	17	47	61	9	46	1	54	9	2.3	0.3	1.8	2.1
Stan McKenzie	F-G	6'5	210	29	11	112	7	24	29	6	8	75	16	6	17	0	20	10	1.5	0.5	1.5	1.8
Jimmy Walker (to KCO)	G	6'3	205	29	3	38	7	12	58	0	1	0	2	4	4	0	14	13	0.7	1.3	1.3	4.7
Paul McCracken	G	6'4	180	23	4	13	1	4	25	0	0	—	6	2	3	0	2	3	1.5	0.5	0.8	0.5
CLEVELAND CAVALIERS	**29-53 354**				**BILL FITCH**																	
Bobby Smith	F	6'5	212	27	82	2612	536	1179	45	139	169	82	435	198	242	4	1211	32	5.3	2.4	3.0	14.8
Dwight Davis	F	6'8	220	24	76	2477	376	862	44	197	274	72	644	186	291	6	949	33	8.5	2.4	3.8	12.5
Steve Patterson	C	6'9	225	25	76	1910	262	599	44	69	112	62	619	165	193	3	593	25	8.1	2.2	2.5	7.8
Austin Carr	G	6'4	200	25	81	3100	748	1682	44	279	326	86	289	305	189	2	1775	38	3.6	3.8	2.3	21.9
Lenny Wilkens	G	6'1	185	36	74	2483	462	994	46	289	361	80	277	522	165	2	1213	34	3.7	7.1	2.2	16.4
Jim Brewer	F-C	6'9	230	22	82	1862	210	548	38	80	123	65	524	149	192	1	500	23	6.4	1.8	2.3	6.1
Jim Cleamons	G	6'3	185	24	81	1642	236	545	43	93	133	70	230	227	152	1	565	20	2.8	2.8	1.9	7.0
Barry Clemens	F	6'7	220	31	71	913	163	346	47	62	73	85	166	80	136	2	388	13	2.3	1.1	1.9	5.5
Johnny Warren	G	6'3	180	26	69	790	132	291	45	35	41	85	128	62	117	1	299	11	1.9	0.9	1.7	4.3
Luke Witte	C	7'	240	23	57	728	105	243	43	46	62	74	227	41	91	0	256	13	4.0	0.7	1.6	4.5
Fred Foster	F	6'5	220	27	58	649	112	288	39	54	64	84	108	62	79	0	278	11	1.9	1.1	1.4	4.8
Bob Rule	C	6'9	235	29	26	540	76	192	40	34	46	74	103	47	71	0	186	21	4.0	1.8	2.7	7.2
Cornell Warner (to Mil)	F-C	6'9	220	25	5	49	2	13	15	4	4	100	17	4	7	0	8	10	3.4	0.8	1.4	1.6

Use Name	Pos	Hgt	Wgt	Age	G	Min	FG	FGA	%	FT	FTA	%	Reb	Ass	PF	DQ	Points	Min	Reb	Ass	PF	Points
					TOTAL													PER GAME				
					1973/74 N.B.A. — MIDWEST DIVISION																	
MILWAUKEE BUCKS	59-23 .720				LARRY COSTELLO																	
Bob Dandridge	F	6'6	195	26	71	2521	583	1158	50	175	214	82	479	201	271	4	1341	36	6.7	2.8	3.8	18.9
Curtis Perry	F	6'7	220	25	81	2386	325	729	45	78	134	58	703	183	301	8	728	29	8.7	2.3	3.7	9.0
Kareem Abdul-Jabbar	C	7'2	235	26	81	3548	948	1759	54	295	420	70	1178	386	238	2	2191	44	14.5	4.8	2.9	27.0
Oscar Robertson	G	6'5	220	35	70	2477	338	772	44	212	254	83	279	446	132	0	888	35	4.0	6.4	1.9	12.7
Lucius Allen (knee injury)	G	6'2	175	26	72	2388	526	1062	50	216	274	79	291	374	215	2	1268	33	4.0	5.2	3.0	17.6
Jon McGlocklin	G-F	6'5	205	30	79	1910	329	693	47	72	80	90	139	241	128	1	730	24	1.8	3.1	1.6	9.2
Cornell Warner (from Cle)	F-C	6'9	220	25	67	1356	172	336	51	81	110	74	380	67	197	8	425	20	5.7	1.0	2.9	6.3
Ron Williams	G	6'3	190	29	71	1130	192	393	49	60	68	88	69	153	114	1	444	16	1.0	2.2	1.6	6.3
Mickey Davis	F-G	6'7	215	23	73	1012	169	335	50	93	112	83	224	87	94	0	431	14	3.1	1.2	1.3	5.9
Terry Driscoll	F	6'7	215	26	64	697	88	187	47	30	46	65	199	54	121	0	206	11	3.1	0.8	1.9	3.2
Russ Lee (knee injury)	G-F	6'5	200	23	36	166	38	94	40	11	16	69	40	20	29	0	87	5	1.1	0.6	0.8	2.4
Dick Garrett (from NY)	G	6'3	185	26	15	87	11	35	31	5	6	83	14	9	15	0	27	6	0.9	0.6	1.0	1.8
Dick Cunningham (ankle injury)	C	6'10	250	27	8	45	3	6	50	0	7	0	16	0	5	0	6	6	2.0	0.0	0.6	0.8
Chuck Terry (to SA-ABA)	F	6'6	215	23	7	32	4	12	33	0	0	—	3	4	4	0	8	5	0.4	0.6	0.6	1.1
CHICAGO BULLS	54-28 .659				DICK MOTTA																	
Chet Walker	F	6'6	220	33	82	2661	572	1178	49	439	502	87	406	200	201	1	1583	32	5.0	2.4	2.5	19.3
Bob Love	F	6'8	215	31	82	3292	731	1752	42	323	395	82	492	130	221	1	1785	40	6.0	1.6	2.7	21.8
Cliff Ray	C	6'9	235	24	80	2632	313	612	51	121	199	61	977	246	281	5	747	33	12.2	3.1	3.5	9.3
Jerry Sloan	G-F	6'6	200	31	77	2860	412	921	45	194	273	71	556	149	273	3	1018	37	7.2	1.9	3.5	13.2
Norm Van Lier	G	6'1	175	26	80	2863	427	1051	41	288	370	78	377	548	282	4	1142	36	4.7	6.9	3.5	14.3
Bob Weiss	G	6'2	185	31	79	1708	263	564	47	142	170	84	103	303	156	0	668	22	1.3	3.8	2.0	8.5
Howard Porter	F	6'8	220	25	73	1229	296	658	45	92	115	80	285	32	116	0	684	17	3.9	0.4	1.6	9.4
Dennis Awtrey	C	6'10	250	25	68	756	65	123	53	54	94	57	174	86	128	3	184	11	2.6	1.3	1.9	2.7
Rick Adelman	G	6'1	186	27	55	618	64	170	38	54	76	71	69	56	63	0	182	11	1.3	1.0	1.1	3.3
Tom Boerwinkle (knee injury)	C	7'	270	28	46	602	58	119	49	42	60	70	213	94	80	0	158	13	4.6	2.0	1.7	3.4
Rowland Garrett	F	6'6	212	23	41	373	68	184	37	21	32	66	70	11	43	0	157	9	1.7	0.3	1.0	3.8
John Hummer (to Sea)	F	6'9	230	25	18	186	23	46	50	14	28	50	37	13	30	0	60	10	2.1	0.7	1.7	3.3
DETROIT PISTONS	52-30 .634				RAY SCOTT																	
Don Adams	F	6'7	220	26	74	2298	303	742	41	153	201	76	448	141	242	2	759	31	6.1	1.9	3.3	10.3
Curtis Rowe	F	6'7	225	24	82	2499	380	769	49	118	169	70	515	136	177	1	878	30	6.3	1.7	2.2	10.7
Bob Lanier	C	6'11	260	25	81	3047	748	1483	50	326	409	80	1074	343	273	7	1822	38	13.3	4.2	3.4	22.5
Chris Ford	G	6'5	190	24	82	2059	264	595	44	57	77	74	304	279	159	1	585	25	3.7	3.4	1.9	7.1
Dave Bing	G	6'3	185	30	81	3124	582	1336	44	356	438	81	281	555	216	1	1520	39	3.5	6.9	2.7	18.8
John Mengelt	G	6'2	195	24	77	1555	249	558	45	182	229	79	206	148	164	2	680	20	2.7	1.9	2.1	8.8
George Trapp	F	6'8	215	25	82	1489	333	693	48	99	134	74	313	81	226	2	765	18	3.8	1.0	2.8	9.3
Willie Norwood	F	6'7	220	26	74	1178	247	484	51	95	143	66	229	58	156	2	589	16	3.1	0.8	2.1	8.0
Stu Lantz (injury)	G	6'3	175	27	50	980	154	361	43	139	164	85	113	97	79	0	447	20	2.3	1.9	1.6	8.9
Jim Davis	C	6'9	235	32	78	947	117	283	41	90	139	65	293	86	158	1	324	12	3.8	1.1	2.0	4.2
Ben Kelso	G	6'3	195	24	46	298	35	96	36	15	22	68	31	18	45	0	85	6	0.7	0.4	1.0	1.8
Bob Nash	F	6'8	205	23	35	281	41	115	36	24	39	62	74	14	35	0	106	8	2.1	0.4	1.0	3.0
KANSAS CITY-OMAHA KINGS	33-49 .402				BOB COUSY (6-14 .300), DRAFF YOUNG (0-4 .000), PHIL JOHNSON (27-31 .466)																	
Don Kojis	F	6'5	215	34	77	2091	400	836	48	210	272	77	383	110	157	2	1010	27	5.0	1.4	2.0	13.1
Ron Behagen	F-C	6'9	235	22	80	2059	357	827	43	162	212	76	567	134	291	9	876	26	7.1	1.7	3.6	11.0
Sam Lacey	C	6'10	235	25	79	3107	467	982	48	185	247	75	1055	299	254	3	1119	39	13.4	3.8	3.2	14.2
JimmyWalker (from Hou)	G	6'3	205	29	72	2920	575	1228	47	273	332	82	202	303	166	0	1423	41	2.8	4.2	2.3	19.8
Nate Archibald (foot injury)	G	6'1	160	25	35	1272	222	492	45	173	211	82	85	266	76	0	617	36	2.4	7.6	2.2	17.6
Nate Williams	G-F	6'5	215	23	82	2513	538	1165	46	193	236	82	344	182	290	5	1269	31	4.2	2.2	3.5	15.5
John Block	F	6'10	220	29	82	1777	275	634	43	164	206	80	389	94	229	2	714	22	4.7	1.1	2.8	8.7
Mike D'Antoni	G	6'3	190	22	52	989	107	266	40	33	47	70	93	123	112	0	247	19	1.8	2.4	2.2	4.8
Howie Komives	G	6'1	185	32	44	830	78	192	41	33	38	87	43	97	83	0	189	19	1.0	2.2	1.9	4.3
Otto Moore (from Hou)	C	6'11	220	27	65	633	88	171	51	35	54	65	200	47	62	0	211	10	3.1	0.7	1.0	3.2
Larry McNeill	F	6'9	195	22	54	516	106	220	48	99	140	71	146	24	76	0	311	10	2.7	0.4	1.4	5.8
Ken Durrett (knee injury)	F	6'7	200	25	45	462	86	176	49	42	69	61	78	19	68	0	214	10	1.7	0.4	1.5	4.8
Matt Guokas (to Hou-Buf)	G	6'5	195	29	9	315	41	83	49	8	12	67	21	36	21	1	90	35	2.3	4.0	2.3	10.0
Ron Riley (to Hou)	F	6'8	200	23	12	170	24	57	42	14	24	58	56	8	27	0	62	14	4.7	0.7	2.3	5.2
Ted Manakas	G	6'2	180	22	5	45	4	10	40	4	4	100	3	2	4	0	12	9	0.6	0.4	0.8	2.4
Mike Ratliff	C	6'10	230	22	2	4	0	0	—	0	0	—	0	0	0	0	0	2	0.0	0.0	0.0	0.0
Justus Thigpen	G	6'1	170	26	1	2	1	3	33	0	0	—	1	0	0	0	2	2	1.0	0.0	0.0	2.0

e Name	Pos	Hgt	Wgt	Age	TOTAL G	Min	FG	FGA	%	FT	FTA	%	Reb	Ass	PF	DQ	Points	PER GAME Min	Reb	Ass	PF	Points
1973/74 N.B.A. — PACIFIC DIVISION																						
OS ANGELES LAKERS	**47-35 .573**				**BILL SHARMAN**																	
ppy Hairston	F	6'7	225	31	77	2634	385	759	51	343	445	77	1040	208	264	2	1113	34	13.5	2.7	3.4	14.5
nnie Hawkins (from Phoe)	F-C	6'8	220	31	71	2538	368	733	50	173	224	77	522	379	203	1	909	36	7.4	5.3	2.9	12.8
nore Smith	C	7'	250	24	81	2922	434	949	46	147	249	59	906	150	309	8	1015	36	11.2	1.9	3.8	12.5
rry West (injury)	G	6'3	185	35	31	967	232	519	45	165	198	83	116	206	80	0	629	31	3.7	6.6	2.6	20.3
il Goodrich	G	6'1	175	30	82	3061	784	1773	44	**508**	**588**	86	250	427	227	3	2076	37	3.0	5.2	2.8	25.3
n Price	G	6'3	195	24	82	2628	538	1197	45	187	234	80	378	369	229	2	1263	32	4.6	4.5	2.8	15.4
Bridges (back injury)	F	6'6	235	34	65	1812	216	513	42	116	164	71	499	148	219	3	548	28	7.7	2.3	3.4	8.4
t Riley	G-F	6'4	208	28	72	1361	287	667	43	110	144	76	128	148	173	1	684	19	1.8	2.1	2.4	9.5
an Love	F	6'9	215	24	51	698	119	278	43	49	64	77	170	48	132	3	287	14	3.3	0.9	2.6	5.6
el Counts (injury)	C	7'	235	32	45	499	61	167	37	24	33	73	146	54	85	2	146	11	3.2	1.2	1.9	3.2
rmit Washington	C	6'8	230	22	45	400	73	151	48	26	49	53	147	19	77	0	172	9	3.3	0.4	1.7	3.8
ate Hawthorne	G	6'4	190	23	33	229	38	93	41	30	48	63	32	23	33	1	106	7	1.0	0.7	1.0	3.2
avis Grant (to SD-ABA)	F	6'8	225	23	3	6	1	4	25	1	3	33	1	0	1	0	3	2	0.3	0.0	0.3	1.0
OLDEN STATE WARRIORS	**44-38 .537**				**AL ATTLES**																	
azzie Russell	F	6'5	220	29	82	2574	738	1531	48	208	249	84	353	192	194	1	1684	31	4.3	2.3	2.4	20.5
ck Barry	F	6'7	215	29	80	2918	796	1746	46	417	464	90	540	484	265	4	2009	36	6.8	6.1	3.3	25.1
ate Thurmond (injury)	C	6'11	235	32	62	2463	308	694	44	191	287	67	878	165	179	4	807	40	14.2	2.7	2.9	13.0
ff Mullins	G	6'4	200	31	77	2498	541	1144	47	168	192	88	276	305	214	2	1250	32	3.6	4.0	2.8	16.2
tch Beard	G	6'3	185	26	79	2134	316	617	51	173	234	74	389	300	241	11	805	27	4.9	3.8	3.1	10.2
n Barnett	G	6'4	180	29	77	1689	350	755	46	184	226	81	222	209	146	1	884	22	2.9	2.7	1.9	11.5
yde Lee (knee injury)	F-C	6'10	230	29	54	1642	129	284	45	62	107	58	598	68	179	3	320	30	11.1	1.3	3.3	5.9
eorge Johnson	C	6'11	215	25	66	1291	173	358	48	59	107	55	522	73	176	3	405	20	7.9	1.1	2.7	6.1
arlie Johnson	G	6'	170	24	59	1051	194	468	41	38	55	69	175	102	111	1	426	18	3.0	1.7	1.9	7.2
errek Dickey	F	6'7	218	22	66	930	115	233	49	51	66	77	339	54	112	1	281	14	5.1	0.8	1.7	4.3
e Ellis	F	6'6	175	29	50	515	61	190	32	18	31	58	122	37	76	2	140	10	2.4	0.7	1.5	2.8
EATTLE SUPERSONICS	**36-46 .439**				**BILL RUSSELL**																	
enny McIntosh	F	6'7	225	24	69	2056	223	573	39	65	107	61	361	94	178	4	511	30	5.2	1.4	2.6	7.4
pencer Haywood	F-C	6'8	230	24	75	3039	694	1520	46	373	458	81	1007	240	198	2	1761	41	13.4	3.2	2.6	23.5
n Fox	C	6'10	230	30	78	2179	322	673	48	241	293	82	714	227	247	5	885	28	9.2	2.9	3.2	11.3
ck Snyder	G	6'5	213	29	74	2670	572	1189	48	194	224	87	306	265	257	4	1338	36	4.1	3.6	3.5	18.1
ed Brown	G	6'3	185	25	82	2501	578	1226	47	195	226	86	401	414	276	6	1351	31	4.9	5.0	3.4	16.5
ck Gibbs	F-G	6'5	210	25	71	1528	302	700	43	162	201	81	223	79	195	1	766	22	3.1	1.1	2.7	10.8
ick Watts	G	6'1	175	22	62	1424	198	510	39	100	155	65	182	351	207	8	496	23	2.9	5.7	3.3	8.0
ud Stallworth	F-G	6'5	190	23	67	1019	188	479	39	48	77	62	174	33	129	0	424	15	2.6	0.5	1.9	6.3
ohn Hummer (from Chi)	F	6'9	230	25	35	933	121	259	47	45	96	47	246	94	89	0	287	27	7.0	2.7	2.5	8.2
ohn Brisker	G	6'5	220	26	35	717	178	396	45	82	100	82	146	56	70	0	438	20	4.2	1.6	2.0	12.5
ahdi Abdul Rahman	G	6'2	190	31	49	571	76	180	42	34	45	76	57	122	78	0	186	12	1.2	2.5	1.6	3.8
ilt Williams	G	6'2	185	28	53	505	62	149	42	41	63	65	47	103	82	1	165	10	0.9	1.9	1.5	3.1
m McDaniels	F	6'11	230	25	27	439	63	173	36	23	43	53	128	24	48	0	149	16	4.7	0.9	1.8	5.5
ester Marshall	F	6'7	200	25	13	174	7	29	24	3	7	43	37	4	20	0	17	13	2.8	0.3	1.5	1.3
HOENIX SUNS	**30-52 .366**				**JOHN MacLEOD**																	
eith Erickson (from LA-HO)	F-G	6'5	200	29	66	2033	393	824	48	177	221	80	414	205	193	3	963	31	6.3	3.1	2.9	14.6
orky Calhoun	F	6'7	210	23	77	2207	268	581	46	98	129	76	407	135	253	4	634	29	5.3	1.8	3.3	8.2
eal Walk	C	6'10	230	25	82	2549	573	1245	46	235	297	79	837	331	255	9	1381	31	10.2	4.0	3.1	16.8
ick Van Arsdale	G-F	6'5	210	30	78	2832	514	1028	50	361	423	85	221	324	241	2	1389	36	2.8	4.2	3.1	17.8
harlie Scon (broken arm)	G	6'5	180	25	52	2003	538	1171	46	246	315	78	222	271	194	6	1322	39	4.3	5.2	3.7	25.4
ike Bantom	F-C	6'9	220	22	76	1982	314	787	40	141	213	66	519	163	289	**15**	769	26	6.8	2.1	3.8	10.1
lem Haskins	G	6'2	195	30	81	1822	364	792	46	171	203	84	222	259	166	1	899	22	2.7	3.2	2.0	11.1
ary Melchionni	G	6'2	187	22	69	1251	202	439	46	92	107	86	142	142	85	1	496	18	2.1	2.1	1.2	7.2
ob Christian	C	7'	260	29	81	1244	140	288	49	106	151	70	339	98	191	3	386	15	4.2	1.2	2.4	4.8
amar Green	F	6'7	220	26	72	1103	129	317	41	38	68	56	350	43	150	1	296	15	4.9	0.6	2.1	4.1
ill Chamberlain	F	6'6	205	24	28	367	57	130	44	39	56	70	80	37	74	2	153	13	2.9	1.3	2.6	5.5
onnie Hawkins (to LA)	F-C	6'8	220	31	8	223	36	74	49	18	27	67	43	28	20	0	90	28	5.4	3.5	2.5	11.3
m Owens	F	6'5	200	23	17	101	21	39	54	11	14	79	9	15	6	0	53	6	0.5	0.9	0.4	3.1
oe Reaves (to Mem-ABA)	F	6'6	220	23	7	38	6	11	55	4	11	36	8	1	6	0	16	5	1.1	0.1	0.9	2.3
ORTLAND TRAIL BLAZERS	**27-55 .329**				**JACK McCLOSKEY**																	
ohn Johnson (broken elbow)	F	6'7	200	26	69	2287	459	990	46	212	261	81	515	284	221	1	1130	33	7.5	4.1	3.2	16.4
idney Wicks	F	6'8	225	24	75	2853	685	1492	46	314	412	76	684	326	214	2	1684	38	9.1	4.3	2.9	22.5
ick Roberson (injury)	C	6'9	230	26	69	2060	364	797	46	205	316	65	701	133	252	4	933	30	10.2	1.9	3.7	13.5
arry Steele	G	6'5	190	24	81	2648	325	680	48	135	171	79	310	323	295	10	785	33	3.8	4.0	3.6	9.7
eoff Petrie	G	6'4	200	25	73	2800	740	1537	48	291	341	85	208	315	199	2	1771	38	2.8	4.3	2.7	24.3
llie Johnson	F	6'6	200	24	79	1718	209	434	48	77	94	82	324	167	179	2	495	22	4.1	2.1	2.3	6.3
ernie Fryer	G	6'3	185	24	80	1674	226	491	46	107	135	79	159	279	187	1	559	21	2.0	3.5	2.3	7.0
loyd Neal	C-F	6'7	225	23	80	1517	246	502	49	117	168	70	494	89	190	0	609	19	6.2	1.1	2.4	7.6
reg Smith	F	6'5	200	26	67	878	99	228	43	48	79	61	189	78	126	1	246	13	2.8	1.2	1.9	3.7
aRue Martin	C	6'11	208	23	50	538	101	232	44	42	66	64	181	20	90	0	244	11	3.6	0.4	1.8	4.9
o Layton (to Mem-ABA)	G	6'1	180	25	22	327	55	112	49	14	26	54	33	51	45	0	124	15	1.5	2.3	2.0	5.6
ob Verga	G	6'1	190	28	21	216	42	93	45	20	32	63	18	17	22	0	104	10	0.9	0.8	1.0	5.0
ark Sibley	G	6'2	175	23	28	124	20	56	36	6	7	86	25	13	23	0	46	4	0.9	0.5	0.8	1.6
harlie Davis	G	6'2	160	24	8	90	14	40	35	3	4	75	11	11	7	0	31	11	1.4	1.4	0.9	3.9

1973/74 N.B.A. — PLAYOFFS

BOSTON CELTICS — **TOM HEINSOHN**

defeated Buffalo 4-2; H107-97, 105-115, H120-107, 102-104, H100-97, 106-104
defeated New York 4-1; H113-88, 111-99, H100-103, 98-91, H105-94
defeated Milwaukee 4-3, 98-83, 96-IO5(OT), H95-83, H89-97, 96-87, H101-102 (2 OT), 102-87

Use Name	Pos	Hgt	Wgt	Age	TOTAL G	Min	FG	FGA	%	FT	FTA	%	Reb	Ass	PF	DQ	Points	PER GAME Min	Reb	Ass	PF	Points
John Havlicek	F-G	6'5	205	33	18	**811**	199	**411**	48	**89**	**101**	88	116	108	43	0	487	45	6.4	6.0	2.4	27.
Paul Silas	F-C	6'7	225	30	18	574	50	126	40	44	53	83	191	47	51	2	144	32	10.6	2.6	2.8	8.
Don Cowens	C	6'9	230	25	18	772	161	370	44	47	59	80	240	66	**85**	2	369	43	13.3	3.7	**4.7**	20
Don Chaney	G	6'5	210	27	18	545	65	141	46	41	50	82	77	40	64	0	171	30	4.3	2.2	3.6	9.
Jo Jo White	G	6'3	190	27	18	765	132	310	43	34	46	74	75	98	56	1	298	43	4.2	5.4	3.1	16
Don Nelson	F	6'6	210	33	18	467	82	164	50	41	53	77	97	35	54	2	205	26	5.4	1.9	3.0	11.
Paul Westphal	G	6'4	195	23	18	241	46	100	46	11	15	73	21	31	37	0	103	13	1.2	1.7	2.1	5.
Hambone Williams	G	6'2	190	34	12	96	10	27	37	7	8	88	23	29	14	0	27	8	1.9	2.4	1.2	2.
Steve Kuberski	F-C	6'8	215	26	9	69	5	25	20	5	10	50	20	2	9	0	15	8	2.2	0.2	1.0	1.
Henry Finkel	C	7'	240	31	8	46	8	18	44	1	1	100	10	3	9	0	17	6	1.3	0.4	1.1	2.
Phil Hankinson	F	6'8	195	22	2	5	2	4	50	2	2	100	1	0	0	0	6	3	0.5	0.0	0.0	3.
Steve Downing	C	6'8	225	23	1	4	1	2	50	0	0	—	2	0	1	0	2	4	2.0	0.0	1.0	2.

MILWAUKEE BUCKS — **LARRY COSTELLO**

defeated Los Angeles 4-1; H99-95, H109-90, 96-98, 112-90, H114-92
defeated Chicago 4-0; H101-85, 113-111, H113-90, 115-99
lost to Boston 3-4; H83-98, H105-96(OT), 83-95, 97-89, H87-96, 102-101(2 OT), H87-102

Use Name	Pos	Hgt	Wgt	Age	TOTAL G	Min	FG	FGA	%	FT	FTA	%	Reb	Ass	PF	DQ	Points	PER GAME Min	Reb	Ass	PF	Points
Bob Dandridge	F	6'6	195	26	16	648	136	276	49	36	47	77	122	45	65	**3**	308	41	7.6	2.8	4.1	19.
Comell Warner	F-C	6'9	220	25	16	505	47	111	42	13	19	68	163	20	70	**3**	107	32	10.2	1.3	4.4	6.
Kareem Abdul-Jabbar	C	7'2	235	26	16	758	**224**	402	**56**	67	91	74	**253**	78	41	0	**515**	**47**	15.8	4.9	2.6	**32.**
Oscar Robertson	G	6'5	220	35	16	689	90	200	45	44	52	85	54	**149**	46	0	224	43	3.4	**9.3**	2.9	14.
Jon McGlocklin	G	6'5	205	30	14	333	55	111	50	8	11	73	16	44	28	0	118	24	1.1	3.1	2.0	8.
Ron Williams	G	6'3	190	29	15	354	57	122	47	16	20	80	27	47	40	1	130	24	1.8	3.1	2.7	8.
Curtis F'erry	F	6'7	220	25	16	296	46	92	50	7	12	58	81	12	43	1	99	19	5.1	0.8	2.7	6.
Mickey Davis	G-F	6'7	215	23	15	245	32	65	49	22	24	**92**	34	12	23	0	86	16	2.3	0.8	1.5	5.
Dick Garrett	G	6'3	185	26	8	46	2	7	29	2	4	50	3	7	7	0	6	6	0.4	0.9	0.9	0.
Terry Driscoll	F	6'7	215	26	9	29	5	10	50	2	2	100	14	3	12	0	12	3	1.6	0.3	1.3	1.
Russ Lee	G	6'5	185	23	6	12	5	8	63	1	4	25	3	1	0	0	11	2	0.5	0.2	0.0	1.
Lucius Allen - knee injury																						

NEW YORK KNICKERBOCKERS — **RED HOLZMAN**

defeated Capital 4-3; H102-91, 87-99, H79-88, 101-93(OT), H106-105, 92-109, H91-81
lost to Boston 1-4; 88-113, H99-111, 103-100, H91-98, 94-105

Use Name	Pos	Hgt	Wgt	Age	TOTAL G	Min	FG	FGA	%	FT	FTA	%	Reb	Ass	PF	DQ	Points	PER GAME Min	Reb	Ass	PF	Points
Bill Bradley	F	6'5	205	30	12	425	63	159	40	25	29	86	28	13	39	1	151	35	2.3	1.1	3.3	12.6
Dave DeBusschere	F	6'6	235	33	12	404	63	166	38	18	29	62	99	38	36	0	144	34	8.3	3.2	3.0	12.0
John Gianelli	C	6'10	220	23	12	338	35	86	41	18	25	72	88	23	41	0	88	28	7.3	1.9	3.4	7.3
Walt Frazier	G	6'4	205	28	12	491	113	225	50	44	49	90	95	48	41	1	270	41	7.9	4.0	3.4	22.5
Earl Monroe	G	6'3	190	29	12	407	81	165	49	47	55	85	48	25	26	0	209	34	4.0	2.1	2.2	17.4
Phil Jackson	F-C	6'8	220	28	12	297	54	116	47	27	30	90	57	15	40	0	135	25	4.8	1.3	3.3	11.3
Dean Meminger	G	6'	175	25	12	179	11	32	34	1	5	20	24	25	19	0	23	15	2.0	2.1	1.6	1.9
Willis Reed	C	6'9	240	31	11	132	17	45	38	3	5	60	22	4	26	0	37	12	2.0	0.4	2.4	3.4
Jerry Lucas	C-F	6'8	230	33	11	115	5	21	24	0	0	—	22	9	9	0	10	10	2.0	0.8	0.8	0.9
Henry Bibby	G	6'1	185	24	10	89	16	45	36	10	12	83	10	11	15	0	42	9	1.0	1.1	1.5	4.2
Harthorne Wingo	F	6'8	210	25	5	16	6	11	55	0	0	—	3	1	2	0	12	3	0.6	0.2	0.4	2.4
Mel Davis	F	6'7	225	23	4	12	6	12	50	0	0	—	5	0	1	0	12	3	1.3	0.0	0.3	3.0

CHICAGO BULLS — **DICK MOTTA**

defeated Detroit 4-3; H88-97, 108-103, H84-83, 87-102, H98-94, 88-92, H96-94
lost to Milwaukee 0-4; 85-101, H111-113, 90-113, H99-115

Use Name	Pos	Hgt	Wgt	Age	TOTAL G	Min	FG	FGA	%	FT	FTA	%	Reb	Ass	PF	DQ	Points	PER GAME Min	Reb	Ass	PF	Points
Chet Walker	F	6'6	220	33	11	403	81	159	51	68	79	86	61	18	26	0	230	37	5.5	1.6	2.4	20.9
Bob Love	F	6'8	215	31	11	489	104	257	40	45	59	76	63	24	28	0	253	44	5.7	2.2	2.5	23.0
Cliff Ray	C	6'9	235	24	11	362	51	102	50	5	15	33	122	35	45	0	107	33	11.1	3.2	4.1	9.7
Jerry Sloan	G-F	6'6	200	31	6	240	39	88	44	22	29	76	62	12	17	0	100	40	10.3	2.0	2.8	16.7
Norm Van Lier	G	6'1	175	26	11	466	61	144	42	39	47	83	47	75	41	0	161	42	4.3	6.8	3.7	14.6
Bob Weiss	G	6'2	185	31	11	251	23	74	31	6	6	100	20	32	20	0	52	23	1.8	2.9	1.8	4.7
Dennis Awtrey	C	6'10	250	25	10	158	12	28	43	6	10	60	40	13	21	0	30	16	4.0	1.3	2.1	3.0
Howard Porter	F	6'8	220	25	11	150	27	88	31	6	6	100	44	5	15	0	60	14	4.0	0.5	1.4	5.5
Rick Adelman	G	6'1	186	27	9	108	16	34	47	7	11	64	10	7	5	0	39	12	1.1	0.8	0.6	4.3
Tom Boerwinkle	C	7'	270	28	2	7	0	1	0	2	2	100	1	0	2	0	2	4	0.5	0.0	1.0	1.0
Rowland Garrett	F	6'6	212	23	2	6	0	4	0	0	0	—	1	0	1	0	0	3	0.5	0.0	0.5	0.0

1973/74 N.B.A. — PLAYOFFS (continued)

Use Name	Pos	Hgt	Wgt	Age	G	Min	FG	FGA	%	FT	FTA	%	Reb	Ass	PF	DQ	Points	Min	Reb	Ass	PF	Points
					TOTAL													PER GAME				
DETROIT PISTONS	**RAY SCOTT**				lost to Chicago 3-4; 97-88, H103-108, 83-84, H102-87, 94-98, H92-88, 94-96																	
Don Adams	F	6'7	220	26	7	256	28	73	38	8	14	57	51	20	26	0	64	37	7.3	2.9	3.7	9.1
Curtis Rowe	F	6'7	225	24	7	229	25	52	48	8	13	62	52	11	23	0	58	33	7.4	1.6	3.3	8.3
Bob Lanier	C	6'11	260	25	7	303	77	152	51	30	38	79	107	21	28	1	184	43	15.3	3.0	4.0	26.3
Dave Bing	G	6'3	185	30	7	312	55	131	42	22	30	73	26	42	20	0	132	45	3.7	6.0	2.9	18.9
Stu Lantz	G	6'3	175	27	7	227	28	59	47	28	32	88	29	14	19	0	84	32	4.1	2.0	2.7	12.0
George Trapp	F	6'8	215	25	7	119	30	51	59	2	2	100	22	2	23	1	62	17	3.1	0.3	3.3	8.9
Chris Ford	G	6'5	190	24	5	94	8	17	47	4	6	67	15	7	10	0	20	19	3.0	1.4	2.0	4.0
Jim Davis	F-C	6'9	235	32	7	69	11	19	58	4	6	67	16	5	11	0	26	10	2.3	0.7	1.6	3.7
John Mengelt	G	6'2	195	24	4	39	5	14	36	7	8	88	7	6	6	0	17	10	1.8	1.5	1.5	4.3
Willie Norwood	F	6'7	220	26	5	31	7	11	64	4	4	100	3	1	7	0	18	6	0.6	0.2	1.4	3.6
Ben Kelso	G	6'3	195	24	1	1	0	2	0	0	0	—	1	1	0	0	0	1	1.0	1.0	0.0	0.0
CAPITAL BULLETS	**K. C. JONES**				lost to New York 3-4; 91-102, H99-87, 88-79, H93-101(OT), 105-106, H109-92, 81-91																	
Mike Riordan	F-G	6'4	200	28	7	267	36	87	41	14	16	88	24	17	28	0	86	38	3.4	2.4	4.0	12.3
Wes Unseld	F-C	6'7	250	27	7	297	31	63	49	9	15	60	85	27	15	0	71	42	12.1	3.9	2.1	10.1
Elvin Hayes	C-F	6'9	235	28	7	323	76	143	53	29	41	71	111	21	23	0	181	46	15.9	3.0	3.3	25.9
Phil Chenier	G	6'3	180	23	7	310	62	137	45	33	37	89	43	12	19	0	157	44	6.1	1.7	2.7	22.4
Archie Clark	G	6'2	175	32	7	162	20	59	34	11	20	55	13	15	13	0	51	23	1.9	2.1	1.9	7.3
Kevin Porter	G	6'	175	23	7	195	33	85	39	9	14	64	17	32	30	2	75	28	2.4	4.6	4.3	10.7
Nick Weatherspoon	F	6'7	200	23	7	87	9	19	47	2	5	40	27	0	11	0	20	12	3.9	0.0	1.6	2.9
Tom Kozelko	F	6'8	220	22	7	58	10	13	77	3	4	75	8	1	10	1	23	8	1.1	0.1	1.4	3.3
Manny Leaks	F	6'8	235	28	2	5	1	2	50	0	0	—	2	0	1	0	2	3	1.0	0.0	0.5	1.0
Walt Wesley	C	6'11	230	28	1	1	0	0	—	0	0	—	0	0	0	0	0	1	0.0	0.0	0.0	0.0
BUFFALO BRAVES	**JACK RAMSAY**				lost to Boston 2-4; 97-107, H115-105, 107-120, H104-102, 97-100, H104-106																	
Jim McMillian	F	6'5	225	25	6	224	38	92	41	11	16	69	53	12	14	0	87	37	8.8	2.0	2.3	14.5
Gar Heard	F-C	6'6	226	25	6	240	42	92	46	17	24	71	88	15	20	0	101	40	14.7	2.5	3.3	16.8
Bob McAdoo	C	6'10	210	22	6	271	76	159	48	38	47	81	82	9	25	1	190	45	13.7	1.5	4.2	31.7
Randy Smith	G	6'3	180	25	6	227	36	90	40	13	20	65	26	27	21	1	85	38	4.3	4.5	3.5	14.2
Ernie DiGregorio	G	6'	180	22	6	240	37	86	43	8	9	89	16	52	14	0	82	40	2.7	8.7	2.3	13.7
Jack Marin	F	6'7	210	29	6	121	22	47	47	7	9	78	19	8	17	0	51	20	3.2	1.3	2.8	8.5
Matt Guokas	G	6'5	195	29	6	85	8	15	53	3	4	75	8	13	8	0	19	14	1.3	2.2	1.3	3.2
Lee Winfield	G	6'2	175	26	1	12	0	2	0	1	2	50	3	2	0	0	1	12	3.0	2.0	0.0	1.0
Ken Charles	G	6'3	180	22	2	10	3	4	75	0	0	—	2	0	2	0	6	5	1.0	0.0	1.0	3.0
Bob Kauffman	C	6'8	240	27	2	10	1	3	33	0	2	0	1	2	3	0	2	5	0.5	1.0	1.5	1.0
LOS ANGELES LAKERS	**BILL SHARMAN**				lost to Milwaukee 1-4; 95-99, 90-109, H98-96, H90-112, 92-114																	
Happy Hairston	F	6'7	225	31	5	172	15	36	42	16	18	89	52	19	8	0	46	34	10.4	3.8	1.6	9.2
Connie Hawkins	F-C	6'8	220	31	5	172	21	60	35	12	15	80	40	16	13	0	54	34	8.0	3.2	2.6	10.8
Elmore Smith	C	7'	250	24	5	171	42	88	48	12	17	71	53	6	20	0	96	34	10.6	1.2	4.0	19.2
Jim Price	G	6'3	195	24	5	161	25	66	38	9	13	69	19	13	21	1	59	32	3.8	2.6	4.2	11.8
Gail Goodrich	G	6'1	175	30	5	189	35	90	39	28	33	85	16	30	7	0	98	38	3.2	6.0	1.4	19.6
Bill Bridges	F	6'6	235	34	5	144	12	41	29	6	13	46	30	6	19	0	30	29	6.0	1.2	3.8	6.0
Pat Riley	G-F	6'4	208	28	5	106	18	50	36	3	4	75	6	10	11	0	39	21	1.2	2.0	2.2	7.8
Mel Counts	C	7'	235	32	4	34	6	12	50	0	0	—	6	2	3	0	12	9	1.5	0.5	0.8	3.0
Kermit Washington	C	6'8	230	22	3	14	5	11	45	5	7	71	10	1	0	0	15	5	3.3	0.3	0.0	5.0
Nate Hawthorne	G	6'4	190	23	3	14	1	7	14	4	5	80	2	2	0	0	6	5	0.7	0.7	0.0	2.0
Jerry West	G	6'3	185	35	1	14	2	9	22	0	0	—	2	1	1	0	4	14	2.0	1.0	1.0	4.0
Stan Love	F	6'9	215	24	2	9	2	3	67	2	3	67	3	1	0	0	6	5	1.5	0.5	0.0	3.0

Team	W	L	Pct.	GB	Record against playoff teams W	L	Pct.	Record against non-playoff teams W	L	Pct.	HOME W	L	Pct.	ROAD W	L	Pct.	NEUTRAL W	L	Pct.
ATLANTIC DIVISION																			
Boston Celtics	56	26	.683	—	**21**	15	.583	35	11	.761	26	6	.813	21	18	.538	**9**	2	.818
New York Knickerbockers	49	33	.598	7	18	19	.486	31	14	.689	28	13	.638	21	19	.525	0	I	.000
Buffalo Braves	42	40	.512	14	12	24	.333	30	16	.652	19	13	.594	17	21	.474	6	**6**	.500
Philadelphia 76ers	25	**57**	.305	31	10	**34**	.227	15	23	.395	14	**23**	.378	9	30	.231	2	4	.333
CENTRAL DIVISION																			
Capital Bullets	47	35	.573	—	16	18	.471	31	17	.646	31	10	.756	15	25	.375	1	0	1.000
Atlanta Hawks	35	47	.427	12	14	18	.333	21	19	.525	23	18	.561	12	25	.324	0	4	.800
Houston Rochets	32	50	.390	15	14	27	.341	18	23	.439	18	**23**	.439	13	25	.342	1	2	.333
Cleveland Cavaliers	29	53	.354	18	10	31	.244	19	22	.463	18	**23**	.439	11	28	.282	0	2	.000
MIDWEST DIVISION																			
Milwaukee Bucks	**59**	23	**.720**	—	20	16	.566	**39**	7	**.848**	31	7	**.816**	**24**	16	**.600**	4	0	1.000
Chicago Bulls	54	28	.659	5	19	16	.543	35	12	.745	**32**	9	.780	21	19	.525	1	0	1.000
Detroit Pistons	52	30	.634	7	16	20	.444	36	10	.783	29	12	.707	23	17	.575	0	1	.000
Kansas City Omaha Kings	33	49	.402	26	10	32	.238	23	17	.575	20	21	.488	13	28	.317	0	0	—
PACIFIC DIVISION																			
Los Angeles Lakers	47	35	.573	—	**21**	13	**.618**	26	22	.542	30	11	.732	17	24	.415	0	0	—
Golden State Warriors	44	38	.537	3	16	24	.400	28	14	.667	23	18	.561	20	20	.500	1	0	1.000
Seattle Supersonics	36	46	.439	11	14	27	.341	22	19	.537	22	19	.537	14	27	.341	0	0	—
Phoenix Suns	30	52	.366	17	10	30	.250	20	22	.476	24	17	.585	6	**34**	.150	0	1	.000
Portland Trail Blazers	27	55	.329	20	10	31	.244	17	**24**	.415	22	19	.537	5	**34**	.128	0	2	.000

1973/74 INDIVIDUAL LEADERS

SCORING
(Minimum 70 Games Played)

Name	Team	G	FG	FT	Pts.	Avg.
McAdoo	Buf	74	901	459	2261	30.6
Maravich	Atl	76	819	469	2107	27.7
Abdul-Jabbar	Mil	81	948	295	2191	27.0
Goodrich	LA	82	784	508	2076	25.3
Barry	GS	80	796	417	2009	25.1
Tom janovich	Hou	80	788	385	1961	24.5
Petrie	Port	73	740	291	1771	24.3
Haywood	Sea	75	694	373	1761	23.5
Havlicek	Bos	76	685	346	1716	22.6
Lanier	Det	81	748	326	1822	22.5

FIELD GOAL PERCENTAGE
(Minimum 560 Attempts)

Name	Team	FG	FGA	Pct.
McAdoo	Buf	901	1647	.547
Abdul-Jabbar	Mil	948	1759	.539
Tomjanovich	Hou	788	1470	.536
Murphy	Hou	671	1285	.522
Beard	GS	316	617	.512
Ray	Chi	313	612	.511
Nelson	Bos	364	717	.508
Hairston	LA	385	759	.507
Lanier	Det	748	1483	.504
Dandridge	Mil	583	1158	.503

FREE THROW PERCENTAGE
(Minimum 160 Attempts)

Name	Team	FT	FTA	Pct.
DiGregorio	Buf	174	193	.902
Barry	GS	417	464	.899
Mullins	GS	168	192	.875
Walker	Chi	439	502	.875
Bradley	NY	146	167	.874
Murphy	Hou	310	357	.868
Snyder	Sea	194	224	.866
Goodrich	LA	508	588	.864
Brown	Sea	195	226	.863
McMillian	Buf	325	379	.858

PERSONAL FOULS

Name	Team	PF
Porter	Cap	319
Murphy	Hou	310
Smith	LA	309
Mix	Phi	305
Perry	Mil	301

GAMES DISQUALIFIED

Name	Team	Disq.
Bantom	Phoe	15
Porter	Cap	14
Beard	GS	11
Brown	Ati	10
Steele	Port	10

TOTAL REBOUNDS PER GAME
(Minimum 70 Games Played)

Name	Team	G	Reb.	Avg.
Hayes	Cap	81	1463	18.1
Cowens	Bos	80	1257	15.7
McAdoo	Buf	74	1117	15.1
Abdul-Jabbar	Mil	81	1178	14.5
Hairston	LA	77	1040	13.5
Haywood	Sea	75	1007	13.4
Lacey	KC-O	79	1055	13.4
Lanier	Det	81	1074	13.3
Ray	Chi	80	977	12.2
Heard	Buf	81	947	11.7

ASSISTS PER GAME
(Minimum 70 Games Played)

Name	Team	G	Ass.	Avg.
DiGregorio	Buf	81	663	8.2
Murphy	Hou	81	603	7.4
Wilkens	Cle	74	522	7.1
Frazier	NY	80	551	6.9
Bing	Det	81	555	6.9
Van Lier	Chi	80	548	6.9
Robertson	Mil	70	446	6.4
Barry	GS	80	484	6.1
Havlicek	Bos	76	447	5.9
Porter	Cap	81	469	5.8

MINUTES PLAYED

Name	Team	Min.
Hayes	Cap	3602
Abdul-Jabbar	Mil	3548
Cowens	Bos	3352
Frazier	NY	3338
McMillian	Buf	3322

BLOCKED SHOTS PER GAME
(Minimum 70 Games Played)

Name	Team	G	Reb.	Avg.
Smith	LA	81	393	4.9
Addul-Jabbar	Mil	81	283	3.5
McAdoo	Buf	74	246	3.3
Lanier	Det	81	247	3.0
Hayes	Cap	81	240	3.0
Heard	Buf	81	230	2.8
Lacey	KC-O	79	184	2.3
Ray	Chi	80	173	2.2
Haywood	Sea	75	106	1.4
Smith	Hou	79	104	1.3

OFFENSIVE REBOUNDS PER GAME
(Minimum 70 Games Played)

Name	Team	G	Reb.	Avg.
Hayes	Cap	81	354	4.4
Hairston	LA	77	335	4.4
Haywood	Sea	75	318	4.2
Silas	Bos	82	334	4.1
McAdoo	Buf	74	281	3.8
Mix	Phi	82	305	3.7
Lacey	KC-O	79	293	3.7
Ellis	Phi	81	292	3.6
Ray	Chi	80	285	3.6
Abdul-Jabbar	Mil	81	287	3.5

STEALS PER GAME
(Minimum 70 Games Played)

Name	Team	G	Steals	Avg.
Steele	Port	81	217	2.7
Mix	Phi	82	212	2.6
Smith	Buf	82	203	2.5
Sloan	Chi	77	183	2.4
Barry	GS	80	169	2.1
Chenier	Cap	76	155	2.0
Van Lier	Chi	80	162	2.0
Frazier	NY	80	161	2.0
Murphy	Hou	81	157	1.9
Price	LA	82	157	1.9

TEAM STATISTICS

Team		REGULAR SEASON												PLAYOFFS											
		G	FG	FGA	%	FT	FTA	%	Reb	Ass	PF	Points	PPG	G	FG	FGA	%	FT	FTA	%	Reb	Ass	PF	Points	PPG
ATLANTIC DIVISION																									
Boston	Off.	82	3630	7969	46	1677	2097	80	**4452**	2187	1868	8937	109.0	18	761	1698	45	322	398	**81**	873	459	423	1844	102.4
	Def.	82	3561	8047	44	1494	1936	77	**3735**	1934	1858	8616	105.1	18	727	1628	45	289	381	**76**	786	388	412	1743	96.8
	Diff.		+69	-78	+2	+183	+161	+3	**+717**	+253	-10	+321	+3.9		+34	+70	—	+33	+17	**+5**	+87	**+71**	-11	+101	**+5.6**
New York	Off.	82	3478	7483	46	1350	1738	78	3684	1937	1884	8306	101.3	12	470	1083	43	193	239	81	501	212	295	1133	94.4
	Def.	82	**3292**	7377	45	1496	1974	76	3832	**1580**	1792	**8080**	**98.5**	12	482	1045	46	229	294	78	593	239	274	1193	99.4
	Diff.		+186	+106	+1	-146	-236	+2	-148	**+357**	-92	+226	+2.8		-12	+38	-3	-36	-55	+3	-92	-27	-21	-60	-5.0
Buffalo	Off.	82	**3728**	7763	48	1699	2221	76	3980	2165	1875	**9155**	**111.6**	6	**263**	**590**	45	98	133	74	**298**	140	124	624	**104.0**
	Def.	82	3786	8106	47	1592	2013	79	4004	2256	1992	9164	111.8	6	277	614	45	**86**	**105**	82	313	167	146	640	106.7
	Diff.		-58	-343	+1	+107	+208	-3	-24	-91	+117	-9	-.2		-14	-24	—	+12	+28	-8	-15	-27	+22	-16	-2.7
Philadelphia	Off.	82	3331	7702	43	1633	2118	77	3808	1799	1964	8295	101.2												
	Def.	82	3600	7685	47	1617	2066	78	4418	1930	1991	8817	107.5												
	Diff.		-269	+17	-4	+16	+52	-1	-610	-131	+27	-522	-6.3												
CENTRAL DIVISION																									
Capital	Off.	82	3480	7886	44	1393	1869	75	4173	1770	**1746**	8353	101.9	7	278	608	46	110	152	72	330	125	150	666	95.1
	Def.	82	3496	7760	45	**1239**	**1639**	76	4121	1900	1840	8231	100.4	7	278	630	44	102	128	80	319	**124**	161	658	94.0
	Diff.		-16	+126	-1	+154	+230	-1	+52	-130	+94	+122	+1.5		—	-22	+2	+8	+24	-8	+11	+1	+11	+8	+1.1
Atlanta	Off.	82	3602	7744	47	1703	2264	75	3952	1993	2073	8907	108.6												
	Def.	82	3573	7628	47	1878	2386	79	3896	2028	2128	9024	110.0												
	Diff.		+29	+116	—	-175	-122	-4	+56	-35	+55	-117	-1.4												
Houston	Off.	82	3564	7426	48	1682	2071	**81**	3651	2212	2104	8810	107.4												
	Def.	82	3551	7433	48	1719	2337	**74**	3781	2122	1994	8821	107.6												
	Diff.		+13	-7	—	-37	-266	**+7**	-130	+90	-110	-11	-.2												
Cleveland	Off.	82	3420	7782	44	1381	1788	77	3767	2048	1925	8221	100.3												
	Def.	82	3440	7342	47	1696	2163	78	3939	2120	1853	8576	104.6												
	Diff.		-20	**+440**	-3	-315	-375	-1	-172	-72	-72	-355	-4.3												
MIDWEST DIVISION																									
Milwaukee	Off.	82	3726	7571	**49**	1328	1741	76	4014	2225	1864	8780	107.1	16	699	1404	**50**	218	286	76	770	**418**	375	1616	101.0
	Def.	82	3311	7799	**42**	1499	1969	76	3756	1909	1707	8121	99.0	16	612	1474	**42**	303	394	77	**690**	366	325	1527	95.4
	Diff.		**+415**	-228	**+7**	-171	-228	—	+258	+316	-157	**+659**	**+8.1**		**+87**	-70	**+8**	-85	-108	-1	**+80**	+52	-50	+89	+5.6
Chicago	Off.	82	3292	7378	45	1784	2314	77	3759	1868	1874	8368	102.0	11	414	979	42	206	264	78	471	221	**221**	1034	94.0
	Def.	82	3336	**7246**	46	1425	1847	77	3870	1830	**2200**	8097	98.7	11	472	**934**	51	163	210	78	526	246	**273**	1107	100.6
	Diff.		-44	+132	-1	**+359**	**+467**	—	-111	+38	**+326**	+271	+3.3		-58	**+45**	**-9**	+43	+54	—	-55	-25	**+52**	-73	-6.6
Detroit	Off.	82	3453	7515	46	1654	2164	76	3881	1956	1930	8560	104.4	7	274	581	47	117	153	76	329	130	173	665	95.0
	Def.	82	3376	7499	45	1475	1932	76	3805	1980	1996	8227	100.3	7	**266**	625	43	117	149	79	317	140	152	649	**92.7**
	Diff.		+77	+16	+1	+179	+232	—	+76	-24	+66	+333	+4.1		+8	-44	+4	—	+4	-3	+12	-10	-21	+16	+2.3
KC-Omaha	Off.	82	3369	7342	46	1628	2104	77	3666	1744	1916	8366	102.0												
	Def.	82	3580	7514	48	1512	1950	78	3860	1916	1907	8672	105.8												
	Diff.		-211	-172	-2	+116	+154	-1	-194	-172	-9	-306	-3.8												
PACIFIC DIVISION																									
Los Angeles	Off.	82	3536	7803	45	**1879**	**2443**	77	4335	2179	2032	8951	109.2	5	184	473	39	**97**	**128**	76	239	107	103	465	93.0
	Def.	82	3667	8364	44	1546	2044	76	4311	2061	2135	8880	108.3	5	229	466	49	72	92	78	267	142	121	530	106.0
	Diff.		-131	-561	+1	+333	+399	+1	+24	+118	+103	+71	+.9		-45	+7	-10	**+25**	**+36**	-2	-28	-35	+18	-65	-13.0
Golden State	Off.	82	3721	8020	46	1569	2018	78	4414	1989	1893	9011	109.9												
	Def.	82	3619	7995	45	1563	2054	76	3929	2027	1826	8801	107.3												
	Diff.		+102	+25	+1	+6	-36	+2	+485	-38	-67	+210	+2.6												
Seattle	Off.	82	3584	**8056**	44	1606	2095	77	4029	2106	2074	8774	107.0												
	Def.	82	3554	7675	46	1875	2427	77	4105	2255	2012	8983	109.5												
	Diff.		+30	+381	-2	-269	-332	—	-76	-149	-62	-209	-2.5												
Phoenix	Off.	82	3555	7726	46	1737	2235	78	3813	2052	2123	8847	107.9												
	Def.	82	3648	7809	47	1843	2356	78	3993	2180	2003	9139	111.5												
	Diff.		-93	-83	-1	-106	-121	—	-180	-128	-120	-292	-3.6												
Portland	Off.	82	3585	7684	47	1591	2112	75	3852	2106	2050	8761	106.8												
	Def.	82	3664	7571	48	1825	2299	79	3875	2308	1961	9153	111.6												
	Diff.		-79	+113	-1	-234	-187	-4	-23	-202	-89	-392	-4.8												

1973-74 A.B.A.

Moving Dr. J. and His Magic Medicine Show

The A.B.A. added its biggest star ever—Wilt Chamberlain, the leading scorer in the history of professional basketball. The San Diego Conquistadors gave Wilt a massive contract to join the team as player coach, but the Los Angeles Lakers of the N.B.A. immediately cancelled half of that deal by getting a court order forcing Wilt to sit out the option year on his contract with the Los Angeles team. So the A.B.A. found itself in a similar position with Wilt as it had heen in 1967-68 with Rick Barly; his name was counted on to boost the gates around the circuit, but neither man could draw people when clad in his civies. Wilt traveled with the Conquistadors as bench coach, but few people came out to the game specifically to see a 7'1" coach urging his players on.

But other additions to the league this season turned out to be more beneficial than Wilt. The city of San Antonio enthusiastically welcomed the Dallas Chaparrals and took the rechristened Spurs to heart, turning out in respectable numbers to see the club. A group of talented rookies also came into the league; Mike Green, Larry Kenon, Svell Nater, Bo Lamar, Kevin Joyce, and Bird Averitt added some All-American glamour, but primarily improved the quality of play on the floor.

An old hand around the A.B.A. but one in a new slot was Mike Storen, the new commissioner. As general manager at Indiana and Kentucky, Storen had built those franchises into going enterprises, and as commissioner, his main concern was to shore up the growing number of sick franchises. Carolina, Virginia, Memphis, and San Diego were all decidedly on shaky footing, both financially and artistically.

But the transfer most beneficial to the A.B.A. in general was the move of star forward Julius Erving from the Virginia Squires to the New York Nets. Perhaps the foremost crowd-pleaser in professional basketball because of his dazzling array of moves, Dr. J. made contract demands which the Virginia club simply could not meet, so they sent him along to the Nets for a bundle of cash plus forward George Carter. In New York, the press made Dr. J. an instant hit, both on a local and a national basis, and the key New York franchise flourished both on the floor and at the ticket window.

Erving turned the Nets into the league's most colorful and strongest club. Although they got off to a slow start under new coach Kevin Loughery, the Nets got untracked and streaked to a 55-29 record and first place in the Eastern Division. Other players filled in the slots around Erving's all-around brilliance. Larry Kenon skipped his senior year at Memphis State to join the Nets, and showed a knack for rebounding in his rookie year at forward. At center, Billy Paultz had grown into such a competent player that young Jim Chones was sold to Carolina. The backcourt had two fine young players in Brian Taylor and rookie John Williamson, plus a steady veteran in Bill Melchionni. A mid-season deal shored up the bench by bringing in forward Wendell Ladner and guard Mike Gale from Kentucky, the Nets' chief rival for first place.

The Colonels made a slew of mid-season deals to strengthen their squad, but Dan Issel, Artis Gilmore, and Louie Dampier continued to carry the bulk of the scoring, rebounding, playmaking, and leadership duties. With Babe McCarthy the new coach this season, the Colonels ended the regular season a slim two games behind the Nets. A respectable third came the Carolina Cougars, who understandably fell off from last year's peak when Billy Cunningham went out of the lineup with severe kidney trouble. Mack Calvin continued to play up to All-Star standards for the Cougars, who were playing to more and more empty seats in Carolina.

Far down in the depths of incompetency were the Virginia Squires and Memphis Tams, with the Squires winning a playoff berth practically by default. Virginia owner Earl Foreman had large money problems and resorted to selling off his better players to get working capital. Erving had gone to New York during the summer, powerful rookie center Sven Nater went to San Antonio in November, and second-year forward George Gervin followed Nater to San Antonio in February. Coach Al Bianchi was forced to get along with cheaper, less talented players, and the team's fans practically washed their hands of the club until Foreman later sold the team to a local group. Down in Memphis, owner Charlie Finley continued to lose money, and the Tams continued losing games in regular fashion.

With this transfer of talent from Virginia to San Antonio, the Spurs grew into a strong enough club to battle with the Utah Stars and Indiana Pacers for first place in the West. The Spurs had two solid ex-Dallas players in Rich Jones and James Silas, plus an offensive-minded rookie guard in Bird Averitt. The addition of Nater, known as Bill Walton's backup during his college days at U.C.L.A., gave the Spurs a center strong enough to battle Gilmore, Beaty, Daniels, and any other A.B.A. center. The later addition of Gervin, who signed with the Squires late last season after being ruled ineligible at Eastern Michigan, provided first rate offensive firepower in the forward spot opposite Rich Jones. Tom Nissalke returned to the franchise as coach after a disastrous year with the N.B.A. in Seattle, and he orchestrated this talent into a strong third place finish with a 45-39 record.

Utah took first place for the third straight season, with Willie Wise, Jimmy Jones, and Ron Boone all winning honors on the first or second All-League teams. Indiana finished second, seemingly saving its best effort for the playoffs. In fourth and fifth, respectively, came the Denver Rockets and San Diego Conquistadors. The Denver club was a distinct disappointment, with coach Alex Hannum resigning at the conclusion of the campaign. The San Diego team had two fine rookies in guard Bo Lamar and center Caldwell Jones, but coach Wilt Chamberlain was missing his greatest asset, player Wilt Chamberlain.

At the start of the playoffs, the New York Nets were downgraded because of their lack of experience. But this youngest team in pro basketball had engineered the best record in the A.B.A. during the regular campaign, and they didn't slow down a bit in the playoffs. They disposed of the Virginia Squires in five games in the opening round, then blew the Kentucky Colonels out in four straight games, an upset which cost Kentucky coach Babe McCarthy his job.

Against Utah in the championship series, the Nets took game one, 89-85, behind Dr. J.'s 47 points, then took an easy 118-94 second-game win. When the series resumed in Salt Lake City, New York's Brian Taylor heaved in a three-pointer at the buzzer to tie the count at 94-94, with the Nets coming on to take a 103-100 overtime decision. The Stars took a rather meaningless fourth game victory by the score of 97-89, but then the Nets finished the job at home, using a balanced attack to take a 111-100 victory before 15,934 excited fans who now took the Nets to heart just as rabidly as the Knicks.

					TOTAL													PER GAME				
Use Name	Pos	Hgt	Wgt	Age	G	Min	FG	FGA	%	FT	FTA	%	Reb	Ass	PF	DQ	Points	Min	Reb	Ass	PF	Points
							1973/74 A.B.A. — EASTERN DIVISION															
NEW YORK NETS	55-29 .655				KEVIN LOUGHERY																	
Julius Erving	F	6'7	210	23	84	3398	**914**	**1785**	51	454	593	77	899	434	270	—	**2299**	40	10.7	5.2	3.2	**27.4**
Larry Kenon	F	6'9	205	22	84	2908	589	1274	46	156	222	70	962	112	251	—	1334	35	11.5	1.3	3.0	15.9
Billy Paultz	C	6'11	240	25	77	2596	519	1051	49	222	308	72	782	167	238	—	1260	34	10.2	2.2	3.1	16.4
Brian Taylor	G	6'3	185	22	75	2505	363	762	48	100	143	70	214	341	192	—	834	33	2.9	4.5	2.6	11.1
John Williamson	G	6'2	185	21	77	2264	482	982	49	150	190	79	213	243	254	—	1116	29	2.8	3.2	3.3	14.5
Willie Sojourner	C	6'8	235	25	82	1316	202	419	48	54	64	84	335	54	205	—	458	16	4.1	0.7	2.5	5.6
Johnny Roche (to KY)	G	6'3	170	24	50	1254	224	460	49	96	114	84	59	208	86	—	570	25	1.2	4.2	1.7	11.4
Bill Melchionni (anhle injury)	G	6'1	170	29	56	1146	116	276	42	59	71	83	77	207	94	—	296	20	1.4	3.7	1.7	5.3
Mike Gale (from KY)	G	6'4	190	23	32	904	114	266	43	29	36	81	152	124	84	—	257	28	4.8	3.9	2.6	8.0
Billy Schaeffer	F	6'5	200	21	59	871	171	344	50	41	54	76	141	37	140	—	385	15	2.4	0.6	2.4	6.5
Wendell Ladner (from Ky)	F	6'5	220	25	30	637	90	252	36	5	12	42	161	65	98	—	203	21	5.4	2.2	3.3	6.8
Gary Gregor	F-C	6'7	225	28	25	313	40	85	47	9	11	82	71	15	48	—	91	13	2.8	0.6	1.9	3.6
Ollie Taylor (to Car)	G	6'2	194	26	8	76	9	24	38	9	15	60	14	10	9	—	28	10	1.8	1.3	1.1	3.5
Jim O'Brien	F	6'7	200	22	11	54	15	37	41	9	15	60	17	6	5	—	39	5	1.5	0.5	0.5	3.5
Rich Rinaldi (from Bal-NBA)	G	6'3	295	24	5	28	4	14	29	4	4	100	5	1	3	—	12	6	1.0	0.2	0.6	2.4
Bob Lackey	F	6'6	210	24	3	15	3	7	43	0	0	—	4	1	2	—	6	5	1.3	0.3	0.7	2.0
Trooper Washington - holdout																						
KENTUCKY COLONELS	53-31 .631				BABE McCARTHY																	
Jim Bradley	F	6'9	215	21	35	884	130	309	42	31	44	70	214	49	106	—	291	25	6.1	1.4	3.0	8.3
Dan Issel	F-C	6'9	240	25	83	3347	829	1726	48	457	581	79	847	137	199	—	2118	40	10.2	1.7	2.4	25.5
Artis Gilmore	C	7'2	240	25	84	**3502**	621	1260	49	326	489	67	**1538**	329	302	—	1568	**42**	**18.3**	3.9	3.6	18.7
Chuck Williams (from SD)	G	6'2	175	27	33	922	109	256	43	72	97	74	76	170	67	—	291	28	2.3	5.2	2.0	8.8
Louie Dampier	G	6'	180	29	84	2942	603	1296	47	238	286	83	201	473	152	—	1492	35	2.4	5.6	1.8	17.8
Mike Gale (to NY)	G	6'4	190	23	48	1591	200	454	44	76	104	73	216	200	158	—	478	33	4.5	4.2	3.3	10.0
Walt Simon	F	6'6	200	32	80	1164	233	492	47	57	68	84	209	117	133	—	525	15	2.6	1.5	1.7	6.6
Ron Thomas	F	6'6	215	23	71	976	128	273	47	37	63	59	289	62	156	—	294	14	4.1	0.9	2.2	4.1
Wendell Ladner (to NY)	F	6'5	220	25	34	928	154	418	37	24	41	59	267	84	135	—	338	27	7.9	2.5	4.0	9.9
Johnny Roche (from NY)	G	6'3	170	24	34	926	173	369	47	52	63	83	63	155	71	—	408	27	1.9	4.6	2.1	12.0
Jimmy O'Brien	G	6'2	180	22	46	761	119	284	42	45	54	83	85	139	47	—	285	17	1.8	3.0	1.0	6.2
Collis Jones	F	6'7	205	24	58	719	102	263	39	51	78	65	184	36	91	—	255	12	3.2	0.6	1.6	4.4
Red Robbins (from SD)	F	6'8	200	29	34	615	97	201	48	41	49	84	140	31	38	—	235	18	4.1	0.9	1.1	6.9
Joe Hamilton (from SA)	G	5'10	175	25	30	546	103	250	41	25	33	76	49	80	62	—	249	18	1.6	2.7	2.1	8.3
Rich Mount (to Utah)	G	6'4	185	26	18	276	55	151	36	19	25	76	20	27	37	—	131	15	1.1	1.5	2.1	7.3
Ron King	G	6'4	195	22	9	126	24	70	34	14	17	82	19	14	14	—	64	14	2.1	1.6	1.6	7.1
Billy James	G	6'3	185	22	1	10	1	3	33	0	0	—	0	1	3	—	2	10	0.0	1.0	3.0	2.0
CAROLINA COUGARS	47-37 .560				LARRY BROWN																	
Joe Caldwell	F	6'5	205	32	79	2654	502	1027	49	128	258	50	412	350	255	—	1135	34	5.2	4.4	3.2	14.4
Billy Cunningham (illness)	F	6'7	220	30	32	1190	253	537	47	149	187	80	331	150	105	—	656	37	10.3	4.7	3.3	20.5
Jim Chones	C	6'11	220	24	83	2387	535	1017	53	155	252	62	645	118	**347**	—	1225	29	7.8	1.4	**4.2**	14.8
Ted McClain	G	6'3	180	26	84	2582	423	872	49	251	325	77	358	348	326	—	1099	31	4.3	4.1	3.9	13.1
Mack Calvin	G	6'	175	25	83	2592	498	1078	46	**490**	560	88	243	347	244	—	1496	31	2.9	4.2	2.9	18.0
Tom Owens	C-F	6'10	223	24	81	2284	444	843	53	226	294	77	717	127	308	—	1116	28	8.9	1.6	3.8	13.8
Gene Littles	G	6'1	175	30	84	2017	294	626	47	115	161	71	231	280	159	—	707	24	2.8	3.3	1.9	8.4
Ed Manning	F	6'7	215	29	82	1816	297	609	49	86	101	85	370	100	210	—	681	22	4.5	1.2	2.6	8.3
Marv Roberts (from Den)	F	6'8	205	23	39	954	160	361	44	81	102	79	240	75	81	—	401	24	6.2	1.9	2.1	10.3
Steve Jones (to Den)	G-F	6'5	205	31	44	935	161	365	44	44	59	75	95	57	96	—	366	21	2.2	1.3	2.2	8.3
Dennis Wuycik	F	6'6	215	23	49	492	88	190	46	51	77	66	106	31	88	—	228	10	2.2	0.6	1.8	4.7
Ollie Taylor (from NY)	G	6'2	194	26	23	443	56	126	44	49	71	69	74	44	54	—	162	19	3.2	1.9	2.3	7.0
Mike Lewis (foot injury)	C	6'8	230	27	3	14	3	8	38	0	0	—	5	0	2	—	6	5	1.7	0.0	0.7	2.0
VIRGINIA SQUIRES	28-56 .333				AL BIANCHI																	
George Carter	F	6'5	218	29	80	2815	561	1329	42	392	466	84	535	136	308	—	1546	35	6.7	1.7	3.9	19.3
Cincy Powell	F-C	6'7	227	31	82	2485	528	1167	45	209	296	71	519	136	270	—	1275	30	6.3	1.7	3.3	15.5
Jim Eakins	C	6'11	215	27	84	2649	445	856	52	339	432	78	806	236	265	—	1229	32	9.6	2.8	3.2	14.6
Larry Miller (from SO)	G	6'4	205	27	73	1900	276	625	44	144	218	66	200	136	133	—	696	26	2.7	1.9	1.8	9.5
Fatty Taylor	G	6'	175	27	80	2812	292	709	41	185	256	72	377	416	270	—	772	35	4.7	5.2	3.4	9.7
George Gervin (to SA)	F	6'7	180	21	49	1728	487	1031	47	262	328	80	418	97	166	—	1244	35	8.5	2.0	3.4	25.4
Dave Twardzik (injury)	G	6'1	180	23	57	1413	163	343	48	168	214	79	181	170	173	—	497	25	3.2	3.0	3.0	8.7
George Irvine	F-G	6'6	200	25	75	1140	254	516	49	120	138	87	177	76	134	—	640	15	2.4	1.0	1.8	8.5
Roger Brown (from SA)	C	7'	225	23	61	964	93	254	37	34	56	61	346	45	125	—	220	16	5.7	0.7	2.0	3.6
Barry Parkhill	G	6'4	185	22	60	869	115	310	37	50	61	82	65	96	151	—	283	14	1.1	1.6	2.5	4.7
Mike Barr	G	6'3	180	23	45	652	82	171	48	33	43	77	71	82	80	—	199	14	1.6	1.8	1.8	4.4
Swen Nater (to SA)	C	6'11	250	23	17	374	84	151	**56**	46	73	63	154	17	37	—	214	22	9.1	1.0	2.2	12.6
Goose Ligon	F	6'7	215	29	19	360	37	85	44	19	25	76	95	11	43	—	93	19	5.0	0.6	2.3	4.9
Bernie Williams	G	6'3	175	28	6	51	6	19	32	2	2	100	4	7	3	—	15	9	0.7	1.2	0.5	2.5
Scott English	F	6'6	220	23	5	48	3	15	20	4	4	100	16	4	9	—	10	10	3.2	0.8	1.8	2.0

Use Name	Pos	Hgt	Wgt	Age	TOTAL G	Min	FG	FGA	%	FT	FTA	%	Reb	Ass	PF	DQ	Points	PER GAME Min	Reb	Ass	PF	Points

1973/74 A.B.A. — EASTERN DIVISION (continued)

Use Name	Pos	Hgt	Wgt	Age	G	Min	FG	FGA	%	FT	FTA	%	Reb	Ass	PF	DQ	Points	Min	Reb	Ass	PF	Points
MEMPHIS TAMS	**21-63 .250**				**BUTCH VAN BREDA KOLFF**																	
Charlie Edge	F	6'6	210	23	78	1948	312	624	50	124	182	68	641	70	137	—	748	25	8.2	0.9	1.8	9.6
Wil Jones	F	6'8	205	26	81	2842	453	997	45	163	220	74	665	205	276	—	1072	35	8.2	2.5	3.4	13.2
Randy Denton	C	6'10	245	24	79	2218	447	902	50	156	197	79	777	152	225	—	1050	28	9.8	1.9	2.8	13.3
George Thompson	G	6'2	200	26	78	2732	539	1134	48	410	519	79	273	396	234	—	1498	35	3.5	5.1	3.0	19.2
Glen Combs (from Utah)	G	6'2	185	27	39	1369	199	448	44	99	132	75	91	233	99	—	525	35	2.3	6.0	2.5	13.5
Lee Davis	C	6'8	240	28	79	1632	266	590	45	98	152	64	419	139	237	—	631	21	5.3	1.8	3.0	8.0
Johnny Neumann (to Utah)	G	6'6	200	22	43	1300	292	665	44	113	145	78	136	178	160	—	704	30	3.2	4.1	3.7	16.4
Larry Finch	G	6'2	195	22	65	1154	164	399	41	108	136	79	74	111	162	—	443	18	1.1	1.7	2.5	6.8
Johnny Baum (to Ind)	F	6'5	205	27	47	1106	163	364	45	48	57	84	176	60	84	—	374	24	3.7	1.3	1.8	8.0
Wil Robinson (injury)	G	6'2	175	24	45	956	166	402	41	57	67	85	79	132	124	—	389	21	1.8	2.9	2.8	8.6
Ronnie Robinson (from Utah)	F	6'8	220	21	40	862	128	282	45	31	46	67	217	37	90	—	287	22	5.4	0.9	2.3	7.2
Mike Jackson (from Utah)	F	6'7	230	24	39	797	140	252	56	56	84	67	213	34	119	—	339	20	5.5	0.9	3.1	8.7
George Lehmann	G	6'3	190	31	33	554	68	177	38	18	19	95	37	117	52	—	172	17	1.1	3.5	1.6	5.2
Jim Ard	F-C	6'8	220	25	27	502	66	164	40	40	51	78	159	41	44	—	174	19	5.9	1.5	1.6	6.4
Joe Reaves (from Phoe-NBA)	F	6'6	220	23	12	172	30	70	43	4	6	67	46	6	23	—	64	14	3.8	0.5	1.9	5.3
Mo Layton (from Port-NBA)	G	6'1	180	25	3	65	8	17	47	3	3	100	4	7	4	—	19	22	1.3	2.3	1.3	6.3
Joby Wright	F	6'8	222	23	3	31	5	16	31	2	2	100	14	0	7	—	12	10	4.7	0.0	2.3	4.0
Erwin Mueller	C	6'8	230	29	3	20	0	4	0	2	5	40	3	2	5	—	2	7	1.0	0.7	1.7	0.7

1973/74 A.B.A. — WESTERN DIVISION

Use Name	Pos	Hgt	Wgt	Age	G	Min	FG	FGA	%	FT	FTA	%	Reb	Ass	PF	DQ	Points	Min	Reb	Ass	PF	Points
UTAH STARS	**51-33 .607**				**JOE MULLANEY**																	
Willie Wise	F	6'6	215	26	82	3292	714	1458	49	396	501	79	623	302	246	—	1826	40	7.6	3.7	3.0	22.3
Gerald Govan	F-C	6'10	220	31	83	2766	255	541	47	73	106	69	728	245	260	—	583	33	8.8	3.0	3.1	7.0
Zelmo Beaty	C	6'9	235	34	77	2476	417	796	52	194	244	80	615	128	229	—	1028	32	8.0	1.7	3.0	13.4
Jimmy Jones	G	6'4	188	28	83	3162	583	1060	55	229	259	88	361	429	205	—	1395	38	4.3	5.2	2.5	16.8
Ron Boone	G	6'2	200	27	84	3098	587	1188	49	300	343	87	435	417	289	—	1480	37	5.2	5.0	3.4	17.6
Bruce Seals	F	6'9	210	20	78	1358	229	605	38	68	108	63	279	54	199	—	545	17	3.6	0.7	2.6	7.0
Johnny Neumann (from Mem)	G-F	6'6	200	22	44	756	190	405	47	53	70	76	90	76	123	—	444	17	2.0	1.7	2.8	10.1
Mike Jackson (to Mem)	F	6'7	230	24	33	677	107	237	45	54	68	79	167	23	103	—	268	21	5.1	0.7	3.1	8.1
Glen Combs (to Mem)	G	6'2	185	27	37	617	105	248	42	57	80	71	53	71	55	—	291	17	1.4	1.9	1.5	7.9
Roy Ebron	C	6'9	225	21	40	529	103	211	49	43	84	51	176	19	68	—	249	13	4.4	0.5	1.7	6.2
John Beasley	C	6'9	230	29	43	481	75	181	41	10	11	91	120	19	57	—	182	11	2.8	0.4	1.3	4.2
Rick Mount (from KY)	G	6'4	185	26	34	477	124	259	48	40	46	87	40	39	40	—	298	14	1.2	1.1	1.2	8.8
Bobby Warren (to SA)	G	6'5	195	27	23	313	49	121	40	31	38	82	43	36	33	—	129	14	1.9	1.6	1.4	5.6
Ronnie Robinson (to Mem)	F	6'8	220	21	22	308	46	112	41	18	27	67	64	12	33	—	110	14	2.9	0.5	1.5	5.0
INDIANA PACERS	**46-38 .548**				**BOB LEONARD**																	
Roger Brown	F	6'5	210	31	82	2527	379	829	46	155	200	78	390	232	248	—	969	31	4.8	2.8	3.0	11.8
George McGinnis	F-C	6'8	235	23	80	3266	789	1686	47	488	715	68	1197	267	325	—	2071	41	15.0	3.3	4.1	25.9
Mel Daniels	C	6'9	225	29	78	2539	492	1117	44	217	287	76	906	122	283	—	1201	33	11.6	1.6	3.6	15.4
Donnie Freeman (injury)	G	6'3	185	29	66	1735	383	839	46	177	222	80	168	165	174	—	943	26	2.5	2.5	2.6	14.3
Freddie Lewis	G	6'	180	30	78	2164	290	728	40	182	219	83	201	322	189	—	775	28	2.6	4.1	2.4	9.9
Darnell Hillman	F-C	6'9	215	24	83	2319	328	658	50	99	191	52	676	96	295	—	758	28	8.1	1.2	3.6	9.1
Don Buse	G	6'4	195	23	77	1877	170	427	40	48	70	69	254	258	109	—	424	24	3.3	3.4	1.4	5.5
Bill Keller	G	5'10	185	26	75	1428	279	615	45	107	123	87	128	172	83	—	715	19	1.7	2.3	1.1	9.5
Bob Netolicky (from SA)	C-F	6'9	225	31	56	1157	214	449	48	77	119	65	292	50	92	—	507	21	5.2	0.9	1.6	9.1
Kevin Joyce	G	6'3	190	22	56	987	171	432	40	64	78	82	92	128	86	—	411	18	1.6	2.3	1.5	7.3
Bob Amzen	F	6'6	215	26	20	149	24	48	50	7	9	78	20	3	11	—	56	7	1.0	0.2	0.6	2.8
Johnny Baum (from Mem)	F	6'5	205	27	13	113	17	36	47	2	4	50	25	2	17	—	36	9	1.9	0.2	1.3	2.8
Bill Newton	C	6'9	220	23	11	73	7	15	47	1	2	50	18	5	12	—	15	7	1.6	0.5	1.1	1.4
Larry Cannon (to Phi-NBA)	G	6'5	195	26	3	26	3	7	43	1	3	33	3	3	2	—	7	9	1.0	1.0	0.7	2.3
SAN ANTONIO SPURS	**45-39 .536**				**TOM NISSALKE**																	
George Gervin (from Va)	F	6'7	180	21	25	783	185	395	47	116	136	85	206	45	98	—	486	31	8.2	1.8	3.9	19.4
Rick Jones	F	6'8	230	27	78	2843	510	1175	43	186	241	77	581	268	273	—	1219	36	7.4	3.4	3.5	15.6
Swen Nater (from Va)	C	6'11	250	23	62	2001	383	695	55	134	181	74	844	112	177	—	900	32	13.6	1.8	2.9	14.5
James Silas	G	6'1	185	24	84	3096	486	1017	48	349	420	83	343	319	256	—	1321	37	4.1	3.8	3.0	15.7
Bird Averitt	G	6'1	175	21	74	1639	343	912	38	156	224	70	121	132	166	—	851	22	1.6	1.8	2.2	11.5
Coby Dietrick	C-F	6'10	230	25	84	2142	251	569	44	81	114	71	532	253	285	—	583	26	6.3	3.0	3.4	6.9
Goo Kennedy	F	6'6	205	24	76	1440	194	352	55	60	87	69	387	83	240	—	448	19	5.1	1.1	3.2	5.9
Joe Hamilton (to KY)	G	5'10	175	25	43	1415	228	584	39	92	110	84	116	162	92	—	567	33	2.7	3.8	2.1	13.2
George Karl	G	6'2	185	22	74	1339	236	502	47	94	113	83	126	160	161	—	574	18	1.7	2.2	2.2	7.8
Chuck Terry (from Mil-NBA)	F	6'6	215	23	61	1093	132	294	45	36	41	88	166	72	139	—	301	18	2.7	1.2	2.3	4.9
Simmie Hill	F	6'7	225	27	60	837	112	244	46	45	62	73	172	62	145	—	269	14	2.9	1.0	2.4	4.5
Jerry Chambers	F	6'5	190	30	38	579	94	206	46	36	48	75	103	42	74	—	224	15	2.7	1.1	1.9	5.9
Bob Netolicky (to Ind)	C	6'9	225	31	19	488	100	195	51	29	46	63	101	44	21	—	229	26	5.3	2.3	1.1	12.1
Bobby Warren (from Utah)	G	6'5	195	27	36	486	61	134	46	32	35	91	61	38	40	—	154	14	1.7	1.1	1.1	4.3
Skeeter Swift	G	6'3	210	27	16	153	23	67	34	16	20	80	16	15	26	—	63	10	1.0	0.9	1.6	3.9
Roger Brown (to Va)	C	7'	225	23	2	26	5	6	83	0	0	—	6	1	4	—	10	13	3.0	0.5	2.0	5.0

Use Name	Pos	Hgt	Wgt	Age	TOTAL G	Min	FG	FGA	%	FT	FTA	%	Reb	Ass	PF	DQ	Points	PER GAME Min	Reb	Ass	PF	Points
1973/74 A.B.A. — WESTERN DIVISION (continued)																						
DENVER ROCKETS	**37-47 .440**				**ALEX HANNUM**																	
Willie Long	F	6'8	235	23	82	2058	383	925	41	270	325	83	466	100	244	—	1036	25	5.7	1.2	3.0	12.6
Julius Keye	F	6'10	225	27	79	2595	147	329	45	57	84	68	689	135	240	—	352	33	8.7	1.7	3.0	4.5
Dave Robisch	C	6'10	240	24	84	2469	449	950	47	318	411	77	708	152	225	—	1216	29	8.4	1.8	2.7	14.5
Warren Jabali	G	6'2	200	27	49	1711	257	657	39	220	274	80	246	358	167	—	779	35	5.0	7.3	3.4	15.9
Al Smith	G	6'1	185	26	76	2435	311	779	40	187	242	77	241	**619**	257	—	831	32	3.2	**8.1**	3.4	10.9
Ralph Simpson	G-F	6'5	200	24	75	2244	597	1395	43	208	276	75	326	191	190	—	1404	30	4.3	2.5	2.5	18.7
Byron Beck	C-F	6'9	230	28	82	1979	425	823	52	120	141	85	417	76	233	—	970	24	5.1	0.9	2.8	11.8
Mike Green	F-C	6'10	200	22	79	1648	367	799	46	169	226	75	584	64	191	—	904	21	7.4	0.8	2.4	11.4
Steve Jones (from Car)	G	6'5	205	31	42	1157	239	534	45	84	109	77	139	128	127	—	575	28	3.3	3.0	3.0	13.7
Pat McFarland	G-F	6'5	185	22	67	757	159	359	44	35	52	67	134	64	69	—	361	11	2.0	1.0	1.0	5.4
Marv Roberts	F	6'8	205	23	35	645	106	237	45	48	62	77	131	44	72	—	261	18	3.7	1.3	2.1	7.5
Claude Terry	G	6'4	195	23	60	587	113	255	44	60	69	87	71	73	64	—	300	10	1.2	1.2	1.1	5.0
SAN DIEGO CONQUISTADORS	**37-47 .440**				**WILT CHAMBERLAIN**																	
Travis Grant (from LA-NBA)	F	6'8	225	23	56	1324	357	681	52	141	176	80	298	63	118	—	856	24	5.3	1.1	2.1	15.3
Stew Johnson	F	6'8	225	29	84	2652	716	1668	43	199	235	85	531	127	162	—	1690	32	6.3	1.5	1.9	20.1
Caldwell Jones	C	6'11	200	23	79	2929	507	1091	46	171	230	74	1095	144	319	—	1187	37	13.9	1.8	4.0	15.0
Bo Lamar	G	6'1	180	22	84	2824	686	1726	40	272	350	78	292	288	155	—	1713	34	3.5	3.4	1.8	20.4
Billy Shepherd	G	5'10	165	24	84	1738	200	530	38	42	66	64	107	371	102	—	507	21	1.3	4.4	1.2	6.0
Chuck Williams (to KY)	G	6'2	175	27	57	1954	296	662	45	227	285	80	174	387	131	—	822	34	3.1	6.8	2.3	14.4
Tim Bassett	F-C	6'8	225	22	82	1854	233	499	47	99	167	59	595	109	185	—	565	23	7.3	1.3	2.3	6.9
George Adams	F	6'6	210	24	80	1433	253	506	50	78	103	76	341	127	111	—	585	18	4.3	1.6	1.4	7.3
Red Robbins (to KY)	F	6'8	200	29	46	1012	179	376	48	75	87	86	246	58	74	—	434	22	5.3	1.3	1.6	9.4
Gene Moore	C	6'9	240	28	49	897	154	340	45	41	85	48	292	59	133	—	350	18	6.0	1.2	2.7	7.1
Flynn Robinson	G	6'1	190	32	49	779	185	405	46	52	18	—	78	112	72	—	430	16	1.6	2.3	1.5	8.8
Jimmy O'Brien (from KY)	G	6'2	180	23	26	559	92	229	40	34	41	83	49	115	32	—	223	22	1.9	4.4	1.2	8.6
Paul Stovall	F	6'5	225	25	13	194	36	73	49	28	44	64	58	12	32	—	100	15	4.5	0.9	2.5	7.7
Jerry Pender	G	6'3	185	22	11	68	8	30	27	10	13	77	5	4	11	—	27	6	0.5	0.4	1.0	2.5
Larry Miller (to Va)	G	6'4	205	27	7	68	5	13	38	7	10	70	9	8	5	—	17	10	1.3	1.1	0.7	2.4
1973/74 A.B.A. - PLAYOFFS																						
NEW YORK NETS	**KEVIN LOUGHERY**				defeated Virginia 4-1; H108-96, H129-110, 115-116, 116-88, H108- 96 defeated Kentucky 4-0; H119-106, H99-80, 89-87, 103-90 defeated Utah 4-1; H89-85, H118-94, 103-100(OT), 89-97, H111-100																	
Julius Erving	F	6'6	210	23	14	579	161	305	53	63	85	74	135	67	40	—	390	41	9.6	4.8	2.9	**27.9**
Larry Kenon	F-C	6'9	205	22	14	470	101	204	50	19	31	61	163	25	33	—	221	34	11.6	1.8	2.4	15.8
Billy Paultz	C	6'11	240	25	14	520	81	169	48	45	57	79	132	28	49	—	207	37	9.4	2.0	3.5	14.8
Brian Taylor	G	6'3	185	22	14	507	86	166	52	23	30	77	61	62	45	—	197	36	4.4	4.4	3.2	14.1
John Williamson	G	6'2	185	21	14	425	72	160	45	22	27	81	46	40	44	—	166	30	3.3	2.9	3.1	11.9
Mike Gale	G-F	6'4	190	23	14	367	48	110	44	19	20	95	58	57	34	—	116	26	4.1	4.1	2.4	8.3
Wendell Ladner	F	6'5	220	25	14	271	52	122	43	5	11	45	70	34	49	—	115	19	5.0	2.4	3.5	8.2
Willie Sojourner	C	6'8	235	25	14	154	17	41	41	5	9	56	34	8	26	—	39	11	2.4	0.6	1.9	2.8
Bill Melchionni	G	6'1	170	29	6	60	8	16	50	2	2	100	9	16	5	—	18	10	1.5	2.7	0.8	3.0
Billy Schaeffer	F	6'5	200	21	5	23	8	16	50	3	4	75	9	3	3	—	19	5	1.8	0.6	0.6	3.8
Jim O'Brien	F	6'7	200	22	4	9	4	10	40	0	0	—	2	3	1	—	8	2	0.5	0.8	0.3	2.0
UTAH STARS	**JOE MULLANEY**				defeated San Diego 4-2; H114-99, H119-105, 96-97, 98-100, H100-93, 110-99 defeated Indiana 4-3; H105-96, H106-102, 99-90, 107-118, H101-110, 89-91, H109-87 lost to New York 1-4; 85-89, 94-118, H100-103(OT), H97-89, 100-111																	
Willie Wise	F	6'6	215	26	18	**792**	**171**	**372**	46	**77**	**101**	76	149	48	51	—	**420**	44	8.3	2.7	2.8	23.3
Gerald Govan	F-C	6'10	220	31	18	714	74	184	40	13	20	65	**246**	73	**65**	—	116	40	13.7	4.1	3.6	6.4
Zelmo Beaty	C	6'9	235	34	13	472	80	159	50	33	40	83	141	21	38	—	193	36	10.8	1.6	2.9	14.8
Jimmy Jones	G-F	6'4	188	28	18	742	154	267	**58**	66	85	78	87	98	60	—	374	41	4.8	5.4	3.3	20.8
Ron Boone	G	6'2	200	27	18	747	137	289	47	34	37	92	108	**109**	54	—	308	42	6.0	**6.1**	3.0	17.1
Rich Mount	G	6'4	185	26	16	306	78	170	46	9	10	90	24	17	18	—	170	19	1.5	1.1	1.1	10.6
Bruce Seals	F	6'9	210	20	15	260	41	98	42	7	14	50	52	14	40	—	91	17	3.5	0.9	2.7	6.1
Johnny Neumann	F-G	6'6	200	22	15	173	34	92	37	13	13	100	32	15	21	—	82	12	2.1	1.0	1.4	5.5
John Beasley	C	6'9	230	29	9	98	9	29	31	3	4	75	21	5	13	—	23	11	2.3	0.6	1.4	2.6
Roy Ebron	C	6'9	225	21	7	41	6	19	32	5	10	50	15	2	6	—	17	6	2.1	0.3	0.9	2.4
KENTUCKY COLONELS	**BABE McCARTHY**				defeated Carolina 4-0; H118-102, 99-96, 120-110, H128-119 lost to New York 0-4; 106-119, 80-99, H87-89, H90-103																	
Jim Bradley	F	6'9	215	21	8	162	27	69	39	6	11	55	39	8	21	—	60	20	4.9	1.0	2.6	7.5
Dan Issel	F-C	6'9	240	25	8	311	60	135	44	28	33	85	87	14	23	—	148	39	10.9	1.8	2.9	18.5
Artis Gilmore	C	7'2	240	25	8	344	71	127	56	38	66	58	149	28	20	—	180	43	**18.6**	3.5	2.5	22.5
Chuck Williams	G	6'2	175	27	8	213	22	54	41	23	24	**96**	20	44	12	—	67	27	2.5	5.5	1.5	8.4
Louie Dampier	G	6'	180	29	8	229	43	89	48	14	18	78	16	32	8	—	107	29	2.0	4.0	1.0	13.4
Johnny Roche	G	6'3	170	24	8	197	39	85	46	6	11	55	9	27	6	—	91	25	1.1	3.4	0.8	11.4
Joe Hamilton	G	5'10	175	25	7	129	16	47	34	13	17	76	23	21	18	—	51	18	3.3	3.0	2.6	7.3
Ron Thomas	F	6'6	215	23	8	109	15	28	54	6	10	60	37	4	14	—	36	14	4.6	0.5	1.8	4.5
Red Robbins	F	6'8	200	29	8	108	16	27	59	13	14	93	32	5	6	—	45	14	4.0	0.6	0.8	5.6
Walt Simon	F	6'6	200	32	8	90	14	35	40	2	2	100	9	7	17	—	30	11	1.1	0.9	2.1	3.8
Collis Jones	F	6'7	205	24	4	28	4	12	33	5	8	63	2	0	3	—	13	7	0.5	0.0	0.8	3.3

1973/74 A.B.A. — PLAYOFFS (continued)

Use Name	Pos	Hgt	Wgt	Age	TOTAL													PER GAME				
					G	Min	FG	FGA	%	FT	FTA	%	Reb	Ass	PF	DQ	Points	Min	Reb	Ass	PF	Points
INDIANA PACERS	**BOB LEONARD**				defeated San Antonio 4-3; H109-113, H128-101, 96-115, 91-89, H105-100, 86-102, H97-86																	
					lost to Utah 3-4; 96-105,102-106, H90-99, H118-107, 110-101, H91-89, 87-109																	
Roger Brown	F	6'5	210	31	13	452	67	151	44	40	49	82	75	48	44	—	183	35	5.8	3.7	3.4	14.1
George McGinnis	F-C	6'8	235	23	14	585	119	261	46	96	129	74	166	47	50	—	336	42	11.9	3.4	3.6	24.0
Mel Daniels	C	6'9	225	29	14	498	69	172	40	33	43	77	160	27	50	—	171	36	11.4	1.9	3.6	12.2
Don Buse	G-F	6'4	195	23	14	331	30	68	44	6	9	67	37	36	21	—	73	24	2.6	2.6	1.5	5.2
Freddie Lewis	G	6'	180	30	14	547	90	204	44	58	67	87	50	62	35	—	244	39	3.6	4.4	2.5	17.4
Darnell Hillman	F-C	6'9	215	24	14	352	47	85	55	23	46	50	100	12	44	—	117	25	7.1	0.9	3.1	8.4
Bill Keller	G	5'10	185	26	12	194	41	93	44	16	19	84	18	25	12	—	113	16	1.5	2.1	1.0	9.4
Donnie Freeman	G	6'3	185	29	6	158	30	69	43	14	20	70	10	8	14	—	74	26	1.7	1.3	2.3	12.3
Kevin Joyce	G	6'3	190	22	10	136	17	53	32	8	10	80	9	12	20	—	44	14	0.9	1.2	2.0	4.4
Johnny Baum	F	6'5	205	27	11	107	17	32	53	6	6	100	20	2	12	—	40	10	1.8	0.2	1.1	3.6
SAN ANTONIO SPURS	**TOM NISSALKE**				lost to Indiana 3-4; 113-109, 101-128, H115-96, H89-91, 100-105, H102-86, 86-97																	
George Gervin	F	6'7	180	21	7	226	57	115	50	29	31	94	52	19	28	—	144	32	7.4	2.7	4.0	20.6
Rich Jones	F	6'8	230	27	7	239	48	93	52	24	29	83	46	18	28	—	121	34	6.6	2.6	4.0	17.3
Swen Nater	C	6'11	250	23	7	211	47	85	55	10	14	71	82	15	21	—	104	30	11.7	2.1	3.0	14.9
James Silas	G	6'1	185	24	7	294	49	105	47	26	38	68	38	32	15	—	124	42	5.4	4.6	2.1	17.7
Bird Averitt	G	6'1	175	21	6	104	19	51	37	15	19	79	11	2	11	—	53	17	1.8	0.3	1.8	8.8
George Karl	G	6'2	185	22	7	141	13	28	46	2	5	40	15	23	19	—	28	20	2.1	3.3	2.7	4.0
Bobby Warren	G	6'5	195	27	7	133	14	29	48	8	8	100	21	9	21	—	36	19	3.0	1.3	3.0	5.1
Coby Dietrick	C-F	6'10	230	25	7	129	13	25	52	8	12	67	27	8	17	—	34	18	3.9	1.1	2.4	4.9
Chuck Terry	F	6'6	215	23	7	112	11	24	46	4	6	67	24	7	9	—	26	16	3.4	1.0	1.3	3.7
Goo Kennedy	F	6'6	205	24	6	71	12	28	43	3	4	75	18	1	15	—	27	12	3.0	0.2	2.5	4.5
Simmie Hill	F	6'7	225	27	4	20	1	3	33	0	0	—	0	2	2	—	2	5	0.0	0.5	0.5	0.5
SAN DIEGO CONQUISTADORS	**WILT CHAMBERLAIN**				lost to Utah 2-4; 99-114,105-119, H97-96, H100-98, 93-100, H99-100																	
Stew Johnson	F	6'8	225	29	6	213	42	114	37	4	6	67	42	13	14	—	93	36	7.0	2.2	2.3	15.5
Tim Bassett	F-C	6'8	225	22	6	244	40	77	52	8	12	67	89	20	18	—	88	41	14.8	3.3	3.0	14.7
Caldwell Jones	C	6'11	200	23	6	277	36	88	41	11	16	69	94	15	19	—	83	46	15.7	2.5	3.2	13.8
Bo Lamar	G	6'1	180	22	6	241	71	161	44	16	19	84	24	21	19	—	165	40	4.0	3.5	3.2	27.5
Billy Shepherd	G	5'10	165	24	6	152	17	56	30	3	3	100	11	21	11	—	45	25	1.8	3.5	1.8	7.5
George Adams	F-G	6'6	210	24	6	161	30	58	52	12	16	75	28	12	13	—	72	27	4.7	2.0	2.2	12.0
Jimmy O'Brien	G	6'2	180	23	6	152	21	48	44	4	7	57	9	26	6	—	47	25	1.5	4.3	1.0	7.8
VIRGINIA SQUIRES	**AL BIANCHI**				lost to New York 1-4; 96-108, 110-129, H116-115, H88-116, 96-108																	
George Carter	F	6'5	218	29	5	204	42	96	44	19	22	86	38	4	19	—	104	41	7.6	0.8	3.8	20.8
Cincy Powell	F	6'7	227	31	5	176	44	100	44	11	14	79	48	5	21	—	100	35	9.6	1.0	4.2	20.0
Jim Eakins	C	6'11	215	27	5	190	37	71	52	26	33	79	54	19	23	—	100	38	10.8	3.8	4.6	20.0
Mike Barr	G	6'3	180	23	5	186	20	44	45	7	7	100	23	18	16	—	47	37	4.6	3.6	3.2	9.4
Fatty Taylor	G	6'	175	27	5	167	16	54	30	6	11	55	25	25	11	—	39	33	5.0	5.0	2.2	7.8
George Irvine	F-G	6'6	200	25	5	109	24	55	44	10	10	100	11	10	13	—	59	22	2.2	2.0	2.6	11.8
Dave Twardzik	G	6'1	180	23	5	83	7	17	41	11	15	73	14	5	12	—	25	17	2.8	1.0	2.4	5.0
Roger Brown	C	7'	225	23	5	50	9	19	47	2	3	67	14	2	6	—	20	10	2.8	0.4	1.2	4.0
Goose Ligon	F	6'7	215	29	3	23	3	11	27	0	0	—	6	0	5	—	6	8	2.0	0.0	1.7	2.0
Barry Parkhill	G	6'4	185	22	3	9	3	7	43	0	0	—	1	2	0	—	6	3	0.3	0.7	0.0	2.0
Larry Miller	G	6'4	205	27	1	3	0	0	—	0	0	—	0	1	0	—	0	3	0.0	1.0	0.0	0.0
CAROLINA COUGARS	LARRY BROWN				lost to Kentucky 0-4; 102-118, H96-99, H110-120, 119-128																	
Joe Caldwell	F	6'5	205	32	4	105	16	34	47	6	12	50	27	13	14	—	38	26	6.8	3.3	3.5	9.5
Marv Roberts	F	6'8	205	23	4	119	20	48	42	10	12	83	25	7	10	—	50	30	6.3	1.8	2.5	12.5
Jim Chones	C	6'11	220	24	4	96	21	47	45	4	8	50	24	3	17	—	46	24	6.0	0.8	4.3	11.5
Ted McClain	G	6'3	180	26	4	133	22	53	42	7	12	58	19	11	18	—	51	33	4.8	2.8	4.5	12.8
Mack Calvin	G	6'	175	25	4	143	34	74	46	27	32	84	19	13	14	—	97	36	4.8	3.3	3.5	24.3
Gene Littles	G	6'1	175	30	4	106	15	34	44	3	8	38	11	18	7	—	37	27	2.8	4.5	1.8	9.3
Ed Manning	F	6'7	215	29	4	81	18	37	49	5	5	100	13	0	11	—	42	20	3.3	0.0	2.8	10.5
Tom Owens	C-F	6'10	223	24	4	78	15	36	42	1	3	33	15	5	18	—	31	20	3.8	1.3	4.5	7.8
Billy Cunningham	F-C	6'7	220	30	3	61	9	31	29	4	5	80	16	6	9	—	22	20	5.3	2.0	3.0	7.3
Ollie Taylor	G	6'2	194	26	2	25	4	7	57	1	1	100	3	1	2	—	9	13	1.5	0.5	1.0	4.5
Dennis Wuycik	F	6'6	215	23	3	13	1	4	25	2	2	100	3	1	0	—	4	4	1.0	0.3	0.0	1.3

Team	W	L	Pct.	GB	Record against playoff teams			Record against non-playoff teams			HOME			ROAD			NEUTRAL		
					W	L	Pct.	W	L	Pct.	W	L	Pct.	W	L	Pct.	W	L	Pct.
EASTERN DIVISION																			
New York Nets	55	29	.655	—	38	27	.585	17	2	.895	31	11	.738	24	18	.571	0	0	—
Kentucky Colonels	53	31	.631	2	36	29	.554	17	2	.895	30	12	.714	23	19	.548	0	0	—
Canolina Cougars	47	37	.560	8	33	32	.508	14	5	.737	30	12	.714	17	25	.405	0	0	—
Virginia Squires	28	56	.333	27	19	46	.292	9	10	.474	22	20	.524	6	36	.143	0	0	—
Memphis Tams	21	63	.250	34	18	58	.237	3	5	.375	14	28	.333	7	35	.167	0	0	—
WESTERN DIVISION																			
Utah Stars	51	33	.607	—	37	28	.569	14	5	.737	33	9	.786	18	24	.429	0	0	—
Indiana Pacers	46	38	.548	5	35	30	.538	11	8	.579	31	11	.738	15	27	.357	0	0	—
San Antonio Spurs	45	39	.536	6	34	31	.523	11	8	.579	27	15	.643	18	24	.429	0	0	—
Denver Rockets	37	47	.440	14	32	44	.421	5	3	.625	24	18	.571	13	29	.310	0	0	—
San Diego Conquistadors	37	47	.440	14	28	37	.431	9	10	.474	20	22	.476	17	25	.405	0	0	—

1973/74 A.B.A. INDIVIDUAL LEADERS

SCORING
(Minimum 70 Games Played)

Name	Team	G	FG	FT	Pts.	Avg.
Erving	NY	84	914	454	2299	27.4
McGinnis	Ind	80	789	488	2071	25.9
Issel	KY	83	829	457	2118	25.5
Gervin	Va-SA	74	672	378	1730	23.4
Wise	Utah	82	714	396	1826	22.3
Lamar	SD	84	686	272	1713	20.4
Johnson	SD	84	716	199	1690	20.1
Carter	Va	80	561	392	1546	19.3
Thompson	Mem	78	539	410	1498	19.2
Simpson	Den	75	597	208	1404	18.7

TOTAL FIELD GOAL PERCENTAGE
(Minimum 560 Attempts)

Name	Team	FG	FGA	Pct.
Nater	Va-SA	467	846	.552
Jones	Utah	583	1060	.550
Owens	Car	444	843	.527
Chones	Car	535	1017	.526
Grant	SD	357	681	.524
Beaty	Utah	417	796	.524
Eakins	Va	445	856	.520
Beck	Den	425	823	.516
Erving	NY	914	1785	.512
Edge	Mem	312	624	.500

3-POINT FIELD GOAL PERCENTAGE
(Minimum 190 Made)

Name	Team	FG	FGA	Pct.
Dampier	KY	48	124	.387
Keller	Ind	50	131	.382
Brown	Ind	56	155	.361
Combs	Utah-Mem	52	147	.354
Carter	Va	32	93	.344
Beasley	Utah	22	64	.344
Roche	NY-KY	36	105	.343
Buse	Ind	36	107	.336
Sheperd	SD	65	202	.322
Johnson	SD	59	190	.311

FREE THROW PERCENTAGE
(Minimum 160 Attempts)

Name	Team	FT	FTA	Pct.
Jones	Utah	229	259	.884
Calvin	Car	490	560	.875
Boone	Utah	300	343	.875
Johnson	SD	199	235	.847
Carter	Va	392	466	.841
Roche	NY-KY	148	177	.836
Dampier	KY	238	286	.832
Lewis	Ind	182	219	.831
Silas	SA	349	420	.831
Long	Den	270	325	.831

REBOUNDS PER GAME
(Minimum 70 Games Played)

Name	Team	G	Reb.	Avg.
Gilmore	KY	84	1538	18.3
McGinnis	Ind	80	1197	15.0
Jones	SD	79	1095	13.9
Nater	Va-SA	79	998	12.6
Daniels	Ind	76	885	11.6
Kenon	NY	84	962	11.5
Erving	NY	84	899	10.7
Issel	KY	83	847	10.2
Paultz	NY	77	782	10.2
Denton	Mem	79	777	9.8

ASSISTS PER GAME
(Minimum 70 Games Played)

Name	Team	G	Ass.	Avg.
Smith	Den	76	619	8.2
Williams	SD-KY	90	557	6.2
Dampier	KY	84	473	5.6
Taylor	Va	80	416	5.2
Jones	Utah	83	429	5.2
Erving	KY	84	434	5.2
Thompson	Mem	78	396	5.1
Boone	Utah	84	417	5.0
Taylor	NY	75	341	4.6
Caldwell	Car	79	350	4.4

BLOCKED SHOTS PER GAME
(Minimum 70 Games Played)

Name	Team	G	Reb.	Avg.
Jones	SD	79	316	4.0
Gilmore	KY	84	287	3.4
Erving	NY	84	204	2.4
Hillman	Ind	83	177	2.1
Paultz	NY	77	147	1.9
Keye	Den	79	149	1.9
Gervin	Va-SA	74	120	1.6
Green	Oen	79	126	1.6
Chones	Car	83	131	1.6
Eakins	Va	84	98	1.2

OFFENSIVE REBOUNDS PER GAME
(Minimum 70 Games Played)

Name	Team	G	Reb.	Avg.
Gilmore	KY	84	478	5.7
McGinnis	Ind	80	422	5.3
Kenon	NY	84	375	4.5
Issel	KY	83	346	4.2
Jones	SD	79	322	4.1
Owens	Car	81	301	3.7
Nater	Va-SA	79	286	3.6
Eakins	Va	84	296	3.5
Denton	Mem	79	255	3.2
Daniels	Ind	78	251	3.2

STEALS PER GAME
(Minimum 70 Games Played)

Name	Team	G	Steals	Avg.
McClain	Car	84	250	3.0
Taylor	Va	80	215	2.7
Erving	NY	84	190	2.3
Caldwell	Car	79	170	2.2
Gale	KY-NY	80	167	2.1
Taylor	NY	75	154	2.1
McGinnis	Ind	80	159	2.0
Buse	Ind	77	146	1.9
Jones	Utah	83	154	1.9
Calvin	Car	83	135	1.6

MINUTES PLAYED

Name	Team	Min.
Gilmore	KY	3502
Erving	NY	3398
Issel	KY	3347
Wise	Utah	3292
McGinnis	Ind	3266

PERSONAL FOULS

Name	Team	PF
Chones	Car	347
McClain	Car	326
McGinnis	Ind	325
Jones	SD	319
Carter	Va	308
Owens	Car	308

		REGULAR SEASON												PLAYOFFS											
Team		G	FG	FGA	%	FT	FTA	%	Reb	Ass	PF	Points	PPG	G	FG	FGA	%	FT	FTA	%	Reb	Ass	PF	Points	PPG
TEAM STATISTICS																									
EASTERN DIVISION																									
New York	**Off.**	84	3855	8038	48	1397	1852	75	4106	2025	1979	9188	109.4	14	**638**	1319	48	206	276	75	719	**343**	329	1496	**106.9**
	Def.	84	3476	7809	45	1677	2261	**74**	4116	1858	1839	8739	104.0	14	548	1287	**43**	233	306	76	665	**269**	275	1345	**96.1**
	Diff.		**+379**	+229	**+3**	-280	-409	+1	-10	+167	-140	**+449**	5.4		**+90**	+32	**+5**	-27	-30	-1	+54	**+74**	-54	+151	**+10.8**
Kentucky	**Off.**	84	3681	8075	46	1565	2092	75	**4417**	**2104**	1771	9024	107.4	8	327	708	46	154	214	72	**423**	190	148	828	103.5
	Def.	84	3576	8003	45	1419	1879	76	4204	**1742**	1967	8675	103.3	8	357	798	45	110	150	73	383	172	**205**	837	104.6
	Diff.		+105	+72	+1	+146	+213	-1	+213	**+362**	+196	+349	4.1		-30	-90	+1	**+44**	**+64**	-1	**+40**	+18	**+57**	-9	-1.1
Carolina	**Off.**	84	3714	7659	**48**	1825	2447	75	3827	2027	2275	9278	110.5	4	175	**405**	43	70	100	70	175	78	120	427	106.8
	Def.	84	3557	**7529**	47	1787	2338	76	3877	1811	2110	8987	107.0	4	180	347	52	95	129	74	220	107	90	465	116.3
	Diff.		+157	+130	+1	+38	+109	-1	-50	+216	-165	+291	3.5		-5	**+58**	-9	-25	-29	-4	-45	-29	-30	-38	-9.5
Virginia	**Off.**	84	3426	7581	45	**2007**	**2612**	77	3964	1665	2167	8933	106.3	5	205	474	43	92	115	**80**	234	91	126	506	101.2
	Def.	84	3724	8010	46	1804	2345	77	4122	1881	**2197**	9352	111.3	5	234	450	52	104	140	74	240	134	128	576	115.2
	Diff.		-298	-429	-1	**+203**	**+267**	-	-158	-216	+30	-419	-5.0		-29	+24	-9	-12	-25	**+6**	-6	-43	+2	-70	-14.0
Memphis	**Off.**	84	3446	7507	46	1532	2023	76	4024	1920	2082	8503	101.2												
	Def.	84	3598	7581	47	1821	2392	76	3783	1949	2000	9092	108.2												
	Diff.		-152	-74	-1	-289	-369	-	+241	-29	-82	-589	-7.0												
WESTERN DIVISION																									
Utah	**Off.**	84	3584	7422	48	1566	1985	**79**	3794	1870	1940	8828	105.1	18	784	1679	47	260	334	78	875	402	366	1839	102.2
	Def.	84	3578	7756	46	1502	1951	77	4031	1836	1918	8798	104.7	18	746	1670	45	266	363	**73**	905	377	362	1797	99.8
	Diff.		+6	-334	+2	+64	+34	+2	-237	+34	-22	+30	0.4		+38	+9	+2	-6	-29	+5	-30	+25	-4	+42	+2.4
Indiana	**Off.**	84	3546	7886	45	1625	2242	72	4370	1825	1926	8888	105.8	14	527	1179	45	**300**	**398**	75	645	279	312	1395	99.6
	Def.	84	3606	8069	45	1524	2031	75	4256	1853	2036	8816	105.0	14	590	1226	48	226	296	76	677	292	349	1415	101.1
	Diff.		-60	-183	-	+101	+211	-3	+114	-28	+110	+72	0.8		-63	-47	-3	+74	+102	-1	-32	-13	+37	-20	-1.5
San Antonio	**Off.**	84	3343	7347	46	1462	1878	78	3881	1808	2197	8199	97.6	7	284	586	**48**	129	166	78	334	138	186	699	99.9
	Def.	84	**3149**	6964	45	1721	2268	76	**3611**	1764	1970	**8126**	**96.7**	7	260	596	44	154	200	77	**308**	145	166	701	100.1
	Diff.		+194	**+383**	+1	-259	-390	+2	**+270**	+44	-227	+73	0.9		+24	-10	+4	-25	-34	+1	+26	-7	-20	-2	-.2
San Diego	**Off.**	84	**3907**	**8829**	44	1476	1960	75	4170	1984	**1642**	**9506**	**113.2**	6	257	602	43	58	79	73	297	128	**100**	593	98.8
	Def.	84	4121	8823	47	**1389**	**1803**	77	4750	2217	1949	9719	115.7	6	**282**	**587**	48	**81**	**98**	83	304	153	112	647	107.8
	Diff.		-214	+6	-3	+87	+157	-2	-580	-233	**+307**	-213	-2.5		-25	+15	-5	-23	-19	-10	-7	-25	+12	-54	-9.0
Denver	**Off.**	84	3553	8042	44	1776	2271	78	4152	2004	2079	8989	107.0												
	Def.	84	3670	7842	47	1587	2094	76	3955	2321	2072	9032	107.5												
	Diff.		-117	**+200**	**-3**	**+189**	**+177**	**+2**	**+197**	-317	-7	-43	-0.5												

1974-75 N.B.A.

Changing the Landscape to Gold

A full squad of perennial All-Stars hung up their sneakers this season while their clubs swandived into the lower levels of the N.B.A. after years at or near the top. The retirement of Jerry West triggered the collapse of the Los Angeles Lakers into the cellar in the Pacific Division with a 30-52 record, better only than the New Orleans Jazz, this year's expansion club. The defection of Wilt Chamberlain to the A.B.A. and the trade of Jim McMillian to the Buffalo Braves had broken up the championship unit of 1971-72, and West's retirement plus Cazzie Russell's knee injury finished tbe Lakers as contenders.

The Milwallkee Bucks also finished last, trailing the field in the Central Division after playing in last year's championship series. Oscar Robertson's retirement in a salary dispute left the Bucks without a backcourt leader, and when Kareem Abdul-Jabbar broke his hand aganst a backboard in a fit of anger in a preseason game, the Bucks were condemned to a slow start. The club compiled a 3 13 mark without Jabbar, but when the 7'3" center returned to the lineup, the Bucks continued their lukewarm play and ended with a 38-44 record. To add to coach Larry Costello's distress, Jabbar made a mid-season request to be traded to either Los Angeles or New York, where the cultural life was more to his taste than in Milwaukee. In New York, the Knicks lost all their forecourt muscle with the retirement of Willis Reed, Dave DeBusschere, and Jerry Lucas. Guards Walt Frazier and Earl Monroe carried more than their share of the load, but opponents regularly killed the Knicks on the boards. Only a last-day victory coupled with Cleveland's 95-94 loss to Kansas City-Omaha enabled the Knicks to sneak into the playoffs as the Eastern wildcard team in the new playoff set-up, and the New Yorkers quickly were ousted by Houston.

While tbe Lakers, Bucks, and Knicks were driven back to the drawing board to rebuild, the Portland Trail Blazers, Detroit Pistons, and Chicago Bulls failed to fully live up to their preseason expectations. The Blazers signed center Bill Walton, a three-time All-American at U.C.L.A., to a $2.5 million contract and immediately were branded title contenders in the Pacific Division. But Walton missed most of the season with a bone spur in his foot, and the Blazers finished at 38-44, an improvement over last season but not a championship showing. The Detroit Pistons also had hopes of moving into the front ranks of the N.B.A. after last season's strong record, but after an early spurt fueled by the star duo of Bob Lanier and Dave Bing, the mid-season release of forword Don Adams shot the club through with dissension and sent the team into a tailspin which lasted through a first-round playoff elimination. The Chicago Bulls captured first place in the Midwest Division, but their 47-35 record didn't measure up to the super expectations fanned by the acquisition of center Nate Thurmond from Golden State. The Bulls boasted of an All-Star starting five of Bob Love, Chet Walker, Thurmond, Norm Van Lier, and Jerry Sloan, but holdouts by Love, and Van Lier, plus a dropoff in scoring by Thurmond made the Bulls less super than expected.

So while several clubs were falling or failing to make progress, the Boston Celtics, Buffalo Braves, Washington Bullets, and Golden State Warriors rose to the top of the league this season. Team cohesion kept the Celtics together through the early going when center Dave Cowens was sidelined with a broken foot. Unlike the Bucks, the Celtics managed to stay around the .500 level without their star center, and with Cowens back in the lineup, the Celtics moved into high gear to easily capture first place in the Atlantic Division. The Buffalo Braves dropped back into second place once the Celtics started moving, but the Braves blossomed into an offensive power mainly on the strength of Bob McAdoo's phenomenal scoring. With the outside shooting touch of a forward and enough jumping ability to play center, the 6'1" McAdoo scored at a 34.5 clip to win his second straight N.B.A. scoring title and led the Braves into second place despite costly injuries to Gar Heard, Jim McMillian, and Ernie DiGregorio.

Over in the Central Division, the Washington Bullets had first place to themselves all season long. Known two years ago as the Baltimore Bullets and last year as the Capital Bullets, they tied the Celtics for the league's best record with a 60-22 season. Elvin Hayes and Phil Chenier did the heavy-duty scoring, Mike Riordan and Kevin Porter kept the floor play fluid, and Wes Unseld recovered from last year's sore knees to again dominate the boards in his accustomed manner. The deep bench featured sophomore forward Nick Weatherspoon, ex-A.B.A. All-Star guard Jimmy Jones, and rookie muscleman Len (Truck) Robinson. The Houston Rockets won a playoff berth in the division although they finished 19 games behind tbe Bullets.

The Midwest Division had a much tighter spread, with Chicago taking first place and Kansas City-Omaha and Detroit qualifying for the playoffs. The Golden State Warriors opened up a big gap in the Pacific Division, but their mid-season slump coupled with a late-season Seattle spurt made the final standings relatively close. The Warriors apparently were heading into a rebuilding season when they traded Nate Thurmond to Chicago, lost Clyde Lee to Atlanta in the completion of a past deal, and saw Cazzie Russell play out his option and sign with the Lakers. But with Rick Barry playing the best all-around ball of his career at the head of a young supporting cast, the Warriors streaked out to an early divisional lead and held on to beat out the Bill Russell-coached, rookie-laden Seattle Supersonics.

The Warriors survived some rocky play in the Western finals to beat the Chicago Bulls in their seventh game to move into the championship series. The Eastern series was a confrontation between the Celtics and Bullets, the clubs with the best records in the league. The Bullets came from behind to take the first game in Boston and went on to defeat the proud Celtics in six games. But branded as overwhelming favorites in the championship series, the Bullets suddenly fell apart. Jones was out with a knee injury, Hayes and Weatherspoon lost the shooting touches that killed Boston, and the club seemed confused on the floor. The younger Warriors, with Rick Barry leading the way, pulled a major upset by taking the N.B.A. crown with four straight victories.

As the N.B.A. ended the season witb a new champion in the Warriors, the league statistics also had taken on a new look. With defense emphasized more than in the past, the average team score per game dropped to 102.6, the lowest since the 99.6 average of 1956-57. Another changing aspect of the N.B.A. was at the top, where commissioner Walter Kennedy was resigning at the end of the season to be replaced by political figure Larry O'Brien.

Use Name	Pos	Hgt	Wgt	Age	TOTAL G	Min	FG	FGA	%	FT	FTA	%	Reb	Ass	PF	DQ	Points	PER GAME Min	Reb	Ass	PF	Points
											1974/75 N.B.A. — ATLANTIC DIVISION											
BOSTON CELTICS	**60-22 .732**				**TOM HEINSOHN**																	
John Havlicek	F-G	6'5	205	34	82	3132	642	1411	45	289	332	87	484	432	231	2	1573	39	5.9	5.3	2.8	19.2
Paul Silas	F	6'7	225	31	82	2661	312	749	42	244	344	71	1025	224	229	3	868	32	12.5	2.7	2.8	10.6
Dave Cowens (broken foot)	C	6'9	230	26	65	2632	569	1199	47	191	244	78	958	296	243	7	1329	40	14.7	4.6	3.7	20.4
Don Chaney	G	6'5	210	28	82	2208	321	750	43	133	165	81	370	181	244	5	775	27	4.5	2.2	3.0	9.5
Jo Jo White	G	6'3	190	28	82	3220	658	1440	46	186	223	83	311	458	207	1	1502	39	3.8	5.6	2.5	18.3
Don Nelson	F	6'6	210	34	79	2052	423	785	**54**	263	318	83	469	181	239	2	1109	26	5.9	2.3	3.0	14.0
Paul Westphal	G	6'4	195	24	82	1581	342	670	51	119	156	76	163	235	192	0	803	19	2.0	2.9	2.3	9.8
Jim Ard	C-F	6'8	220	26	59	719	89	266	33	48	65	74	199	40	96	2	226	12	3.4	0.7	1.6	3.8
Henry Finkel	C	7'	240	32	62	518	52	129	40	23	43	53	112	32	72	0	127	8	1.8	0.5	1.2	2.0
Kevin Stacom	G	6'3	185	23	61	447	72	159	45	29	33	88	55	49	65	0	173	7	0.9	0.8	1.1	2.8
Glenn McDonald	F-G	6'6	190	22	62	395	70	182	38	28	37	76	68	24	58	0	168	6	1.1	0.4	0.9	2.7
Ben Clyde	F	6'7	210	23	25	157	31	72	43	7	9	78	41	5	34	1	69	6	1.6	0.2	1.4	2.8
Phil Hankinson (knee injury)	F	6'8	198	23	3	24	6	11	55	0	0	—	7	2	3	0	12	8	2.3	0.7	1.0	4.0
Steve Downing	C	6'8	225	24	3	9	0	2	0	0	2	0	2	0	0	0	0	3	0.7	0.0	0.0	0.0
BUFFALO BRAVES	**49-33 .598**				**JACK RAMSAY**																	
Jim McMillian (illness)	F	6'5	225	26	62	2132	347	695	50	194	231	84	385	156	129	0	888	34	6.2	2.5	2.1	14.3
Gar Heard (ankle injury)	F	6'6	220	26	67	2148	318	819	39	106	188	56	666	190	242	2	742	32	9.9	2.8	3.6	11.1
Bob McAdoo	C-F	6'9	210	23	82	**3539**	**1095**	2138	51	641	**796**	81	**1155**	179	278	3	**2831**	**43**	14.1	2.2	3.4	**34.5**
Randy Smith	G	6'3	180	26	82	3001	610	1261	48	236	295	80	344	534	247	2	1456	37	4.2	6.5	3.0	17.8
Ernie DiGregorio (knee injury)	G	6'	180	23	31	712	103	234	44	35	45	78	45	151	62	0	241	23	1.5	4.9	2.0	7.8
Jack Marin	F	6'7	210	30	81	2147	380	836	45	193	222	87	363	133	238	7	953	27	4.5	1.6	2.9	11.8
Ken Charles	G	6'3	180	23	79	1690	240	515	47	120	146	82	164	171	165	0	600	21	2.1	2.2	2.1	7.6
Bob Weiss	G	6'2	185	32	76	1338	102	261	39	54	67	81	104	260	146	0	258	18	1.4	3.4	1.9	3.4
Lee Winfield	G	6'2	175	27	68	1259	164	312	53	49	68	72	126	134	106	1	377	19	1.9	2.0	1.6	5.5
Dale Schlueter	C	6'10	235	29	76	962	92	178	52	84	121	69	264	104	163	0	268	13	3.5	1.4	2.1	3.5
Jim Washington (fnom Atl)	F	6'7	215	31	42	674	77	162	48	21	38	55	197	43	81	3	175	16	4.7	1.0	1.9	4.2
Paul Ruffner	C	6'10	225	26	22	103	22	47	47	1	5	20	22	7	22	0	45	5	1.0	0.3	1.0	2.0
Bernie Harris	F	6'10	200	24	11	25	2	11	18	1	2	50	8	1	0	0	5	2	0.7	0.1	0.0	0.5
NEW YORK KNICKERBOCKERS	**40-42 .488**				**RED HOLZMAN**																	
Bill Bradley	F	6'5	205	31	79	2787	452	1036	44	144	165	87	251	247	283	5	1048	35	3.2	3.1	3.6	13.3
Phil Jackson	F-C	6'8	220	29	78	2285	324	712	46	193	253	76	600	136	**330**	10	841	29	7.7	1.7	**4.2**	10.8
John Gianelli	C	6'10	220	24	80	2797	343	726	47	135	195	69	689	163	263	3	821	35	8.6	2.0	3.3	10.3
Walt Frazier	G	6'4	205	29	78	3204	672	1391	48	331	400	83	465	474	205	2	1675	41	6.0	6.1	2.6	21.5
Earl Monroe	G	6'3	190	30	78	2814	668	1462	46	297	359	83	327	270	200	0	1633	36	4.2	3.5	2.6	20.9
Harthorne Wingo	F	6'8	210	26	82	1686	233	506	46	141	187	75	456	84	215	2	607	21	5.6	1.0	2.6	7.4
Mel Davis	F	6'7	225	24	62	903	154	395	39	48	70	69	321	54	105	0	356	15	5.2	0.9	1.7	5.7
Henry Bibby (to NO)	G	6'1	185	25	47	876	179	400	45	69	96	72	87	105	96	0	427	19	1.9	2.2	2.0	9.1
Jim Barnett (from NO)	G	6'4	180	30	28	538	70	172	41	43	50	86	51	39	51	0	183	19	1.8	1.4	1.8	6.5
Tom Riker	C	6'10	240	24	51	483	53	147	36	46	82	56	107	19	64	0	152	9	2.1	0.4	1.3	3.0
Dennis Bell	F	6'6	215	23	52	465	68	181	38	20	36	56	105	25	54	0	156	9	2.0	0.5	1.0	3.0
Jesse Dark	G	6'5	210	23	47	401	74	157	47	22	40	55	37	30	48	0	170	9	0.8	0.6	1.0	3.6
Neal Walk (from NO)	C	6'10	220	26	30	274	47	115	41	22	25	88	77	22	55	0	116	9	2.6	0.7	1.8	3.9
Howard Porter (to Det)	F	6'8	220	26	17	133	13	36	36	7	9	78	38	2	17	0	33	8	2.2	0.1	1.0	1.9
Dave Stallworth	F	6'7	210	33	7	57	5	18	28	0	0	—	20	2	10	0	10	8	2.9	0.3	1.4	1.4
Greg Jackson (to Phoe)	G	6'	185	22	5	27	4	10	40	0	0	—	2	3	5	0	8	5	0.4	0.6	1.0	1.6
Willis Reed - knee injury																						
PHILADELPHIA 76ers	**34-48 .415**				**GENE SHUE**																	
Billy Cunningham	F	6'7	220	31	80	2859	609	1423	43	345	444	78	726	442	270	4	1563	36	9.1	5.5	3.4	19.5
Steve Mix (brohen ankle)	F	6'7	222	27	46	1748	280	582	48	159	205	78	500	99	175	6	719	38	10.9	2.2	3.8	15.6
Leroy Ellis	C	6'10	225	34	82	2183	287	623	46	72	99	73	582	117	178	1	646	27	7.1	1.4	2.2	7.9
Doug Collins	G	6'6	180	23	81	2820	561	1150	49	331	392	84	315	213	291	6	1453	35	3.9	2.6	3.6	17.9
Fred Carter	G	6'3	185	29	77	3046	715	1598	45	256	347	74	340	336	257	5	1686	40	4.4	4.4	3.3	21.9
Clyde Lee (from Atl)	F-C	6'10	230	30	71	2279	164	391	42	87	138	63	687	97	260	9	415	32	9.7	1.4	3.7	5.8
Freddie Boyd (groin injury)	G	6'2	180	24	66	1362	205	495	41	55	115	48	89	161	134	0	465	21	1.3	2.4	2.0	7.0
Allan Bristow	F-G	6'7	227	23	72	1101	163	393	41	121	153	79	254	99	101	0	447	15	3.5	1.4	1.4	6.2
John Tschogl	F	6'6	210	24	39	623	53	148	36	13	22	59	111	30	80	2	119	16	2.8	0.8	2.1	3.1
Don Smith	G	6'	160	23	54	538	131	321	41	21	21	100	30	47	45	0	283	10	0.6	0.9	0.8	5.2
Harvey Catchings	C	6'9	218	23	37	528	41	74	55	16	25	64	153	21	82	1	98	14	4.1	0.6	2.2	2.6
Tom Van Arsdale (to Atl)	F	6'5	215	31	9	273	49	116	42	28	41	68	29	16	26	0	126	30	3.2	1.8	2.9	14.0
Ken Durrett (from KCO)	F	6'7	208	26	27	270	35	88	40	20	32	63	62	10	42	0	90	10	2.3	0.4	1.6	3.3
Connie Norman	G	6'3	176	21	12	72	23	44	52	2	3	67	12	4	9	0	48	6	1.0	0.3	0.8	4.0
Perry Warbington	G	6'2	166	22	5	70	4	21	19	2	2	100	8	16	16	0	10	14	1.6	3.2	3.2	2.0
Walt Wesley (to Mil)	C	6'11	230	29	4	33	5	9	56	2	4	50	8	1	8	0	12	8	2.0	0.3	2.0	3.0

Use Name	Pos	Hgt	Wgt	Age	TOTAL G	Min	FG	FGA	%	FT	FTA	%	Reb	Ass	PF	DQ	Points	PER GAME Min	Reb	Ass	PF	Points
1974/75 N.B.A. — CENTRAL DIVISION																						
WASHINGTON BULLETS	**60-22 .732**				**K. C. JONES**																	
Mike Riordan	F	6'4	200	29	74	2191	520	1057	49	98	117	84	284	198	238	4	1138	30	3.8	2.7	3.2	15.4
Elvin Hayes	F-C	6'9	235	29	82	3465	739	1668	44	409	534	77	1004	206	238	0	1887	42	12.2	2.5	2.9	23.0
Wes Unseld	C	6'7	250	28	73	2904	273	544	50	126	184	68	1077	297	180	1	672	40	**14.8**	4.1	2.5	9.2
Phil Chenier	G	6'3	180	24	77	2869	690	1533	45	301	365	82	292	248	158	3	1681	37	3.8	3.2	2.1	21.8
Kevin Porter	G	6'	175	24	81	2589	406	827	49	131	186	70	152	**650**	320	**12**	943	32	1.9	**8.0**	4.0	11.6
Jimmy Jones	G	6'4	188	29	73	1424	207	400	52	103	142	73	137	162	190	0	517	20	1.9	2.2	2.6	7.1
Nick Weatherspoon	F	6'7	200	24	82	1347	256	562	46	103	138	75	346	51	212	2	615	16	4.2	0.6	2.6	7.5
Truck Robinson	F	6'7	225	23	76	995	191	393	49	60	115	52	301	40	132	0	442	13	4.0	0.5	1.7	5.8
Tom Kozelko	F	6'8	220	23	73	754	60	167	36	31	36	86	140	41	125	4	151	10	1.9	0.6	1.7	2.1
Clem Haskins	G	6'3	195	31	70	702	115	290	40	53	63	84	80	79	73	0	283	10	1.1	1.1	1.0	4.0
Dick Gibbs	F-G	6'5	210	26	59	424	74	190	39	48	64	75	61	19	60	0	196	7	1.0	0.3	1.0	3.3
Dennis DuVal	G	6'3	175	22	37	137	24	65	37	12	18	67	23	14	34	0	60	4	0.6	0.4	0.9	1.6
Stan Washington	G	6'4	190	22	1	4	0	1	0	0	0	—	0	0	1	0	0	4	0.0	0.0	1.0	0.0
HOUSTON ROCKETS	**41-41 .500**				**JOHNNY EGAN**																	
Ed Ratleff	F-G	6'6	195	24	80	2563	392	851	46	157	190	83	459	259	231	5	941	32	5.7	3.2	2.9	11.8
Rudy Tomjanovich	F	6'8	220	26	81	3134	694	1323	52	289	366	79	613	236	230	1	1677	39	7.6	2.9	2.8	20.7
Kevin Kunnert	C	7'	240	23	75	1801	346	676	51	116	169	69	631	108	223	2	808	24	8.4	1.4	3.0	10.8
Mike Newlin	G	6'4	205	25	79	2709	436	905	48	265	305	87	260	403	288	4	1137	34	3.3	5.1	3.6	14.4
Cal Murphy	G	5'9	165	26	78	2513	557	1152	48	341	386	88	173	381	281	8	1455	32	2.2	4.9	3.6	18.7
Dave Wohl	G	6'2	185	25	75	1722	203	462	44	79	106	75	112	340	184	1	485	23	1.5	4.5	2.5	6.5
Ron Riley	F	6'8	200	24	77	1578	196	470	42	71	97	73	380	130	197	3	463	20	4.9	1.7	2.6	6.0
Zaid Abdul-Aziz	C	6'9	240	28	65	1450	235	538	44	159	203	78	488	84	128	1	629	22	7.5	1.3	2.0	9.7
Steve Hawes	C-F	6'9	220	24	55	987	140	279	50	45	55	82	275	88	99	1	325	18	5.0	1.6	1.8	5.9
Cliff Meely	F	6'8	220	27	48	753	156	349	45	68	94	72	164	45	117	4	380	16	3.4	0.9	2.4	7.9
Gus Bailey	G	6'5	185	23	47	446	51	126	40	20	41	49	82	59	52	0	122	9	1.7	1.3	1.1	2.6
Owen Wells	F	6'7	200	24	33	214	42	100	42	15	22	68	35	22	38	0	99	6	1.1	0.7	1.2	3.0
CLEVELAND CAVALIERS	**40-42 .488**				**BILL FITCH**																	
Bobby Smith	F-G	6'5	215	28	82	2636	585	1212	48	132	160	83	407	229	227	1	1302	32	5.0	2.8	2.8	15.9
Jim Brewer	F	6'9	230	23	82	1991	291	639	46	103	159	65	509	128	150	2	685	24	6.2	1.6	1.8	8.4
Jim Chones (broken foot)	C	6'11	220	25	72	2427	446	916	49	152	224	68	677	132	247	5	1044	34	9.4	1.8	3.4	14.5
Austin Carr (knee injury)	G	6'4	200	26	41	1081	252	538	47	89	106	84	107	154	57	0	593	26	2.6	3.8	1.4	14.5
Jim Cleamons	G	6'3	185	25	74	2691	369	768	48	144	181	80	329	381	194	0	882	36	4.4	5.1	2.6	11.9
Dick Snyder	G	6'5	213	30	82	2590	498	988	50	165	195	85	238	281	226	3	1161	32	2.9	3.4	2.8	14.2
Dwight Davis	F	6'8	220	25	78	1964	295	666	44	176	245	72	464	150	254	3	766	25	5.9	1.9	3.3	9.8
Steve Patterson	C	6'9	225	26	81	1269	161	387	42	48	73	66	329	93	128	1	370	16	4.1	1.1	1.6	4.6
Fred Foster	F	6'5	220	28	73	1136	217	521	42	69	97	71	110	103	130	1	503	16	1.5	1.4	1.8	6.9
Foots Walker	G	6'1	172	23	72	1070	111	275	40	80	117	68	146	192	126	0	302	15	2.0	2.7	1.8	4.2
Campy Russell	F	6'8	215	22	68	754	150	365	41	124	165	75	152	45	100	0	424	11	2.2	0.7	1.5	6.2
Luke Witte	C	7'	240	24	39	271	33	96	34	19	31	61	92	15	42	0	85	7	2.4	0.4	1.1	2.2
ATLANTA HAWKS	**31-51 .378**				**COTTON FITZSIMMONS**																	
Lou Hudson (elbow injury)	F	6'5	215	30	11	380	97	225	43	48	57	84	47	40	33	1	242	35	4.3	3.6	3.0	22.0
John Drew	F	6'6	205	20	78	2289	527	1230	43	388	544	71	836	138	274	4	1442	29	10.7	1.8	3.5	18.5
Dwight Jones	C	6'10	215	22	75	2086	323	752	43	132	183	72	697	152	226	1	778	28	9.3	2.0	3.0	10.4
Tom Henderson	G	6'3	190	22	79	2131	367	893	41	168	241	70	212	314	149	0	902	27	2.7	4.0	1.9	11.4
Dean Meminger	G	6'	175	26	80	2177	233	500	47	168	263	64	214	397	160	0	634	27	2.7	5.0	2.0	7.9
Tom Van Arsdale (from Phi)	G-F	6'5	215	31	73	2570	544	1269	43	294	383	77	249	207	231	5	1382	35	3.4	2.8	3.2	18.9
Mike Sojourner	C-F	6'9	225	21	73	2129	378	775	49	95	146	65	642	93	217	10	851	29	8.8	1.3	3.0	11.7
John Brown	F	6'7	220	23	73	1986	315	684	46	185	250	74	434	133	228	7	815	27	5.9	1.8	3.1	11.2
Herm Gilliam (knee injury)	G	6'3	190	28	60	1393	314	736	43	94	113	83	204	170	124	1	722	23	3.4	2.8	2.1	12.0
Jim Washington (to Buf)	F	6'7	215	31	38	905	114	259	44	41	55	75	193	68	86	2	269	24	5.1	1.8	2.3	7.1
Bob Kauffman	C-F	6'8	240	28	73	797	113	261	43	59	84	70	182	81	103	1	285	11	2.5	1.1	1.4	3.9
John Wetzel	G	6'5	190	30	63	785	87	204	43	68	77	88	114	77	108	1	242	12	1.8	1.2	1.7	3.8
Clyde Lee (to Phi)	F-C	6'10	230	30	9	177	12	36	33	32	39	82	70	8	25	0	56	20	7.8	0.9	2.8	6.2
NEW ORLEANS JAZZ	**23-59 .280**				**SCOTTY ROBERTSON (1-14 .067), ELGIN BAYLOR (0-1 .000), BUTCH VAN BREDA KOLFF (22-44 .393)**																	
Aaron James	F	6'8	210	22	76	1731	370	776	48	147	189	78	366	66	217	4	887	23	4.8	0.9	2.9	11.7
E. C. Coleman	F	6'8	225	24	77	2176	253	568	45	116	166	70	549	105	277	10	622	28	7.1	1.4	3.6	8.1
Otto Moore (from Det)	C	6'11	220	28	40	1055	117	258	45	45	67	67	328	82	146	3	279	26	8.2	2.1	3.7	7.0
Pete Maravich	G	6'5	200	26	79	2853	655	1562	42	390	481	81	422	488	227	4	1700	36	5.3	6.2	2.9	21.5
Louie Nelson	G	6'3	190	23	72	1898	307	679	45	192	250	77	196	178	186	1	806	26	2.7	2.5	2.6	11.2
Bud Stallworth	F	6'5	190	24	73	1668	298	710	42	125	182	69	246	46	208	4	721	23	3.4	0.6	2.8	9.9
Mel Counts	C	7'	235	33	75	1421	217	495	44	86	113	76	441	182	196	0	520	19	5.9	2.4	2.6	6.9
Jim Barnett (to NY)	G	6'4	180	30	45	1238	215	480	45	156	188	83	128	137	109	1	586	28	2.8	3.0	2.4	13.0
Ollie Johnson (to KCO)	F	6'6	200	25	43	1159	139	299	46	62	77	81	177	80	103	1	340	27	4.1	1.9	2.4	7.9
Neal Walk (to NY)	C	6'10	220	26	37	851	151	358	42	64	80	80	262	101	122	3	366	23	7.1	2.7	3.3	9.9
Nate Williams (from KCO)	F	6'5	220	24	35	814	209	404	52	84	102	82	158	67	99	1	502	23	4.5	1.9	2.8	14.3
Rick Adelman (from Chi, to KCO)	G	6'1	185	28	28	613	67	159	42	41	59	69	55	69	58	1	175	22	2.0	2.5	2.1	6.3
Henry Bibby (from NY)	G	6'1	185	25	28	524	91	219	42	68	93	73	50	76	61	0	250	19	1.8	2.7	2.2	8.9
Bernie Fryer (from StL-ABA)	G	6'3	185	25	31	432	47	106	44	33	43	77	46	52	54	0	127	14	1.5	1.7	1.7	4.1
Stu Lantz (to LA)	G	6'3	175	28	19	353	39	115	34	47	53	89	24	30	28	0	125	19	1.3	1.6	1.5	6.6
Rick Roberson (BN)	C	6'9	235	27	16	339	48	108	44	23	40	58	118	23	49	0	119	21	7.4	1.4	3.1	7.4
Lamar Green (to Va-ABA)	C-F	6'7	220	27	15	280	24	70	34	9	20	45	109	16	38	0	57	19	7.3	1.1	2.5	3.8
Russ Lee	F	6'5	210	24	15	139	29	76	38	7	14	50	31	7	17	1	65	9	2.1	0.5	1.1	4.3
Toby Kimball	F-C	6'8	240	32	3	90	7	23	30	6	7	86	26	4	12	0	20	30	8.7	1.3	4.0	6.7
John Block (to Chi)	F-C	6'10	220	30	4	57	9	29	31	9	10	90	18	7	11	0	27	14	4.5	1.8	2.8	6.8
Ken Boyd	F	6'5	195	22	6	25	7	13	54	5	11	45	5	2	2	0	19	4	0.8	0.3	0.3	3.2
Walt Bellamy	C	6'11	245	35	1	14	2	2	100	2	2	100	5	0	2	0	6	14	5.0	0.0	2.0	6.0

					TOTAL													PER GAME				
Use Name	Pos	Hgt	Wgt	Age	G	Min	FG	FGA	%	FT	FTA	%	Reb	Ass	PF	DQ	Points	Min	Reb	Ass	PF	Points
1974/75 N.B.A. — MIDWEST DIVISION																						
CHICAGO BULLS	**47-35 .573**				**DICK MOTTA**																	
Chet Walker	F	6'6	220	34	76	2452	524	1076	49	413	480	86	432	169	181	0	1461	32	5.7	2.2	2.4	19.2
Bob Love (holdout)	F	6'8	215	32	61	2401	539	1256	43	264	318	83	385	102	209	3	1342	39	6.3	1.7	3.4	22.0
Nate Thurmond	C	6'11	235	33	80	2756	250	686	36	132	224	59	904	328	271	6	632	34	11.3	4.1	3.4	7.9
Jerry Sloan	G	6'6	200	32	78	2577	380	865	44	193	258	75	538	161	265	5	953	33	6.9	2.1	3.4	12.2
Norm Van Lier (holdout)	G	6'1	175	27	70	2590	407	970	42	236	298	79	328	403	246	5	1050	37	4.7	5.8	3.5	15.0
Matt Guokas	G-F	6'5	195	30	82	2089	255	500	51	78	103	76	139	178	154	1	588	25	1.7	2.2	1.9	7.2
Rowland Garren	F	6'6	215	24	70	1183	228	474	48	77	97	79	247	43	124	0	533	17	3.5	0.6	1.8	7.6
Tom Boerwinkle	C	7'	270	29	80	1175	132	271	49	73	95	77	380	272	163	0	337	15	4.8	3.4	2.0	4.2
John Block (from NO)	F-C	6'10	220	30	50	882	150	317	47	105	134	78	214	44	110	0	405	18	4.3	0.9	2.2	8.1
Bill Hewitt	F	6'7	210	30	18	467	56	129	43	14	23	61	116	24	46	1	126	26	6.4	1.3	2.6	7.0
Bobby Wilson	G	6'3	180	23	48	425	115	225	51	46	58	79	52	36	54	1	276	9	1.1	0.8	1.1	5.8
Rich Adelman (to NO, KCO)	G	6'1	185	28	12	340	43	104	41	28	39	72	26	35	31	0	114	28	2.2	2.9	2.6	9.5
Michey Johnson	F	6'10	190	22	38	291	53	118	45	37	58	64	94	20	57	1	143	8	2.5	0.5	1.5	3.8
Leon Benbow	G	6'4	185	22	39	252	35	94	37	15	18	83	38	25	41	0	85	6	1.0	0.6	1.1	2.2
KANSAS CITY-OMAHA KINGS	**44-38 .537**				**PHIL JOHNSON**																	
Scott Wedman	F	6'7	215	22	80	2554	375	806	47	139	170	82	490	129	270	2	889	32	6.1	1.6	3.4	11.1
Ron Behagen	F	6'9	225	23	81	2205	333	834	40	199	264	75	592	153	301	8	865	27	7.3	1.9	3.7	10.7
Sam Lacey	C	6'10	235	26	81	3378	392	917	43	144	191	75	1149	428	274	4	928	42	14.2	5.3	3.4	11.5
Jimmy Walker	G	6'3	205	30	81	3122	553	1164	48	247	289	85	239	226	222	2	1353	39	3.0	2.8	2.7	16.7
Nate Archibald	G	6'1	165	26	82	3244	759	1664	46	652	748	87	222	557	187	0	2170	40	2.7	6.8	2.3	26.5
Larry McNeill	F-C	6'9	200	23	80	1749	296	645	46	189	241	78	497	73	229	1	781	22	6.2	0.9	2.9	9.8
Nate Williams (to NO)	G-F	6'5	220	24	50	1131	265	584	45	97	118	82	179	78	152	2	627	23	3.6	1.6	3.0	12.5
Mike D'Antoni	G	6'3	190	23	67	759	69	173	40	28	36	78	77	107	106	0	166	11	1.1	1.6	1.6	2.5
Ollie Johnson (from NO)	F	6'6	200	25	30	508	64	130	49	33	37	89	66	30	69	0	161	17	2.2	1.0	2.3	5.4
Len Kosmalshi	C	7'	245	23	67	413	33	83	40	24	29	83	119	41	64	0	90	6	1.8	0.6	1.0	1.3
Don Kojis	F	6'5	215	35	21	232	46	98	47	20	30	67	39	10	31	0	112	11	1.9	0.5	1.5	5.3
Ken Durrett (to Phi)	F	6'7	208	26	21	175	32	78	41	11	20	55	40	8	30	0	75	8	1.9	0.4	1.4	3.6
Don May	F	6'4	215	28	29	139	27	54	50	10	12	83	13	5	21	0	64	5	0.4	0.2	0.7	2.2
Rich Adelman (from Chi, NO)	G	6'1	185	28	18	121	13	28	46	4	5	80	14	8	12	0	30	7	0.8	0.4	0.7	1.7
DETROIT PISTONS	**40-42 .488**				**RAY SCOTT**																	
Curtis Rowe	F	6'7	225	25	82	2787	422	874	48	171	227	75	585	121	190	0	1015	34	7.1	1.5	2.3	12.4
Howard Porter (from NY)	F	6'8	220	26	41	1030	188	376	50	59	70	84	216	17	76	0	435	25	5.3	0.4	1.9	10.6
Bob Lanier	C	6'11	260	26	76	2987	731	1433	51	361	450	80	914	350	237	1	1823	39	12.0	4.6	3.1	24.0
Dave Bing	G	6'3	190	31	79	3222	578	1333	43	343	424	81	286	610	222	3	1499	41	3.6	7.7	2.8	19.0
John Mengelt	G	6'2	195	25	80	1995	336	701	48	211	248	85	191	201	198	2	883	25	2.4	2.5	2.5	11.0
Chris Ford	G-F	6'5	190	25	80	1962	206	435	47	63	95	66	269	230	187	0	475	25	3.4	2.9	2.3	5.9
George Trapp	F-C	6'8	215	26	78	1472	288	652	44	99	131	76	276	63	210	1	675	19	3.5	0.8	2.7	8.7
Don Adams (to StL-ABA)	F	6'7	220	27	51	1376	127	315	40	45	78	58	244	75	179	1	299	27	4.8	1.5	3.5	5.9
Jim Davis	C-F	6'9	235	33	79	1078	118	260	45	85	117	73	285	90	129	2	321	14	3.6	1.1	1.6	4.1
Eric Money	G	6'	170	19	66	889	144	319	45	31	45	69	88	101	121	3	319	13	1.3	1.5	1.8	4.8
Willie Norwood (knee injury)	F	6'7	220	27	24	347	64	123	52	31	42	74	88	16	51	0	159	14	3.7	0.7	2.1	6.6
Al Eberhard	F	6'6	225	22	34	277	31	86	36	17	21	81	47	16	33	0	79	8	1.4	0.5	1.0	2.3
Bill Ligon	G	6'4	180	22	38	272	55	143	38	16	25	64	26	25	31	0	126	7	0.7	0.7	0.8	3.3
Otto Moore (to NO)	C	6'11	220	28	2	11	1	4	25	1	2	50	2	1	2	0	3	6	1.0	0.5	1.0	1.5
MILWAUKEE BUCKS	**38-44 .463**				**LARRY COSTELLO**																	
Bob Dandridge	F-G	6'6	195	27	80	3031	691	1460	47	211	262	81	551	243	330	7	1593	38	6.9	3.0	4.1	19.9
Cornell Warner	F-C	6'9	220	26	79	2519	248	541	46	106	155	68	812	127	267	8	602	32	10.3	1.6	3.4	7.6
Kareem Abdul-Jabbar (BH)	C	7'2	245	27	65	2747	812	1584	51	325	426	76	912	264	205	2	1949	42	14.0	4.1	3.2	30.0
Jim Price (from LA) (KJ)	G	6'3	200	26	41	1531	242	550	44	128	149	86	155	223	146	0	612	37	3.8	5.4	3.6	14.9
George Thompson	G	6'2	205	27	73	1983	306	691	44	168	214	79	181	225	203	5	780	27	2.5	3.1	2.8	10.7
Jon McGlocklin	G	6'5	205	31	79	1853	323	651	50	63	72	88	119	255	142	2	709	23	1.5	3.2	1.8	9.0
Kevin Restani	F-C	6'9	240	23	76	1755	188	427	44	35	49	71	403	119	172	1	411	23	5.3	1.6	2.3	5.4
Gary Brokaw	G	6'4	180	20	73	1639	234	514	46	126	184	68	147	221	176	3	594	22	2.0	3.0	2.4	8.1
Mickey Davis	F	6'7	215	24	75	1077	174	363	48	78	88	89	237	79	103	0	426	14	3.2	1.1	1.4	5.7
Ron Williams	G	6'3	190	30	46	526	62	165	38	24	29	83	43	71	70	2	148	11	0.9	1.5	1.5	3.2
Steve Kuberski	F	6'8	215	27	59	517	62	159	39	44	56	79	123	35	59	0	168	9	2.1	0.6	1.0	2.8
Lucius Allen (to LA)	G	6'2	175	27	10	342	68	164	41	31	37	84	31	53	23	0	167	34	3.1	5.3	2.3	16.7
Walt Wesley (from Phi)	C	6'11	230	29	41	214	37	84	44	14	23	61	55	11	43	0	88	5	1.3	0.3	1.0	2.1
Terry Driscoll (to StL-ABA)	F	6'7	215	27	11	52	3	13	23	1	2	50	16	3	7	0	7	5	1.5	0.3	0.6	0.6
Bob Rule	C	6'9	235	30	1	11	0	1	0	0	0	—	0	2	2	0	0	11	0.0	2.0	2.0	0.0
Dick Cunningham (NJ)	C	6'10	257	28	2	8	0	0	—	0	0	—	2	1	1	0	0	4	1.0	0.5	0.5	0.0

Use Name	Pos	Hgt	Wgt	Age	TOTAL													PER GAME				
					G	Min	FG	FGA	%	FT	FTA	%	Reb	Ast	PF	DQ	Points	Min	Reb	Ast	PF	Points
1974/75 N.B.A. — PACIFIC DIVISION																						
GOLDEN STATE WARRIORS	**48-34 .585**				**AL ATTLES**																	
Keith Wilkes	F	6'6	190	21	82	2515	502	1135	44	160	218	73	671	183	222	0	1164	31	8.2	2.2	2.7	14.2
Rick Barry	F	6'7	220	30	80	3235	1028	**2217**	46	394	436	**90**	456	492	225	0	2450	40	5.7	6.2	2.8	30.6
Cliff Ray	C	6'9	235	25	82	2519	299	573	52	171	284	60	870	178	305	9	769	31	10.6	2.2	3.7	9.4
Butch Beard	G	6'3	185	27	82	2521	408	773	53	232	279	83	316	345	297	9	1048	31	3.9	4.2	3.6	12.8
Charlie Johnson	G	6'	170	24	79	2171	394	957	41	75	102	74	311	233	204	2	863	27	3.9	2.9	2.6	10.9
Derrek Dickey	F	6'7	218	23	80	1859	274	569	48	66	99	67	550	125	199	0	614	23	6.9	1.6	2.5	7.7
George Johnson	C	6'11	220	26	82	1439	152	319	48	60	91	66	574	67	206	1	364	18	7.0	0.8	2.5	4.4
Jeff Mullins (broken hand)	G-F	6'4	200	32	66	1141	234	514	46	71	87	82	123	153	123	0	539	17	1.9	2.3	1.9	8.2
Phil Smith	G	6'4	187	22	74	1055	221	464	48	127	158	80	140	135	141	0	569	14	1.9	1.8	1.9	7.7
Charles Dudley	G	6'2	186	24	67	756	102	217	47	70	97	72	145	103	105	1	274	11	2.2	1.5	1.6	4.1
Steve Bracey	G	6'1	175	24	42	340	54	130	42	25	38	66	38	52	41	0	133	8	0.9	1.2	1.0	3.2
Frank Kendrick	F	6'6	198	23	24	121	31	77	40	18	22	82	36	6	22	0	80	5	1.5	0.3	0.9	3.3
Bill Bridges (from LA)	F	6'6	235	35	15	108	15	36	42	1	4	25	40	4	19	0	31	7	2.7	0.3	1.3	2.1
SEATTLE SUPERSONICS	**43-39 .524**				**BILL RUSSELL**																	
Leonard Gray	F	6'8	240	23	75	2280	378	773	49	104	144	72	478	163	292	9	860	30	6.4	2.2	3.9	11.5
Spencer Haywood (illness)	F	6'8	230	25	68	2529	608	1325	46	309	381	81	630	137	173	1	1525	37	9.3	2.0	2.5	22.4
Tom Burleson	C	7'3	228	22	82	1888	322	772	42	182	265	69	572	115	221	1	826	23	7.0	1.4	2.7	10.1
Fred Brown	G	6'3	180	26	81	2669	737	1537	48	226	272	83	343	284	227	2	1700	33	4.2	3.5	2.8	21.0
Archie Clark	G	6'2	175	33	77	2481	455	919	50	161	193	83	235	433	188	4	1071	32	3.1	5.6	2.4	13.9
Slick Watts	G	6'1	175	23	82	2056	232	551	42	93	153	61	262	499	254	7	557	25	3.2	6.1	3.1	6.8
Jim Fox	C	6'10	230	31	75	1766	253	540	47	170	212	80	491	137	168	1	676	24	6.5	1.8	2.2	9.0
Tal Skinner	F-G	6'5	210	22	73	1574	142	347	41	63	97	65	344	85	161	0	347	22	4.7	1.2	2.2	4.8
Wardell Jackson	F	6'7	200	23	56	939	96	242	40	51	71	72	133	30	126	2	243	17	2.4	0.5	2.3	4.3
Rod Derline	G	6'4	175	22	58	666	142	332	43	43	56	77	59	45	47	0	327	11	1.0	0.8	0.8	5.6
John Hummer (foot injury)	C-F	6'9	230	26	43	568	41	108	38	14	51	27	104	38	63	0	96	13	2.4	0.9	1.5	2.2
John Brisker	F	6'5	220	27	21	276	60	141	43	42	49	86	33	19	33	0	162	13	1.6	0.9	1.6	7.7
Kenny McIntosh	F	6'7	225	25	6	101	6	29	21	6	9	67	15	7	12	0	18	17	2.5	1.2	2.0	3.0
Dean Tolson	F	6'8	190	23	19	87	16	37	43	11	17	65	22	5	12	0	43	5	1.2	0.3	0.6	2.3
PORTLAND TRAIL BLAZERS	**38-44 .463**				**LENNY WILKENS**																	
John Johnson	F	6'7	200	27	80	2540	527	1082	49	236	301	78	501	240	249	3	1290	32	6.3	3.0	3.1	16.1
Sidney Wicks	F	6'8	225	25	82	3162	692	1391	50	394	558	71	877	287	289	5	1778	39	10.7	3.5	3.5	21.7
Bill Walton (foot injury)	C	6'11	225	22	35	1153	177	345	51	94	137	69	441	167	115	4	448	33	12.6	4.8	3.3	12.8
Larry Steele	G	6'5	190	25	76	2389	265	484	55	122	146	84	226	287	254	6	652	31	3.0	3.8	3.3	8.6
Geoff Petrie	G	6'4	200	26	80	3109	602	1319	46	261	311	84	209	424	215	1	1465	39	2.6	5.3	2.7	18.3
Lloyd Neal	C-F	6'7	225	24	82	2278	409	869	47	189	295	64	687	139	239	2	1007	28	8.4	1.7	2.9	12.3
LaRue Martin	C	6'11	208	24	81	1372	236	522	45	99	142	70	408	69	239	5	571	17	5.0	0.9	3.0	7.0
Lenny Wilkens	G	6'1	185	37	65	1161	134	305	44	152	198	77	120	235	96	1	420	18	1.8	3.6	1.5	6.5
Barry Clemens	F	6'7	220	32	77	952	168	355	47	45	60	75	161	76	139	0	381	12	2.1	1.0	1.8	4.9
Phil Lumpkin	G	6'	167	23	48	792	86	190	45	30	39	77	59	177	80	1	202	17	1.2	3.7	1.7	4.2
Greg Smith	F	6'5	200	27	55	519	71	146	49	32	48	67	89	27	96	1	174	9	1.6	0.5	1.7	3.2
Dan Anderson	G	6'2	185	23	43	453	47	105	45	26	30	87	29	81	44	0	120	11	0.7	1.9	1.0	2.8
PHOENIX SUNS	**32-50 .390**				**JOHN MacLEOD**																	
Keith Erickson (back injury)	F-G	6'5	200	30	49	1469	237	557	43	130	156	83	243	170	150	3	604	30	5.0	3.5	3.1	12.3
Curtis Perry	F	6'7	220	26	79	2688	437	917	48	184	256	72	940	186	288	10	1058	34	11.9	2.4	3.6	13.4
Dennis Awtrey	C	6'10	250	26	82	2837	339	772	44	132	195	68	704	342	227	2	810	35	8.6	4.2	2.8	9.9
Dick Van Arsdale	G-F	6'5	210	31	70	2419	421	895	47	282	339	83	189	195	177	2	1124	35	2.7	2.8	2.5	16.1
Charlie Scott	G	6'5	180	26	69	2592	703	1594	44	274	351	78	273	311	296	11	1680	38	4.0	4.5	4.3	24.3
Mike Bantom	F-C	6'9	220	23	82	2239	418	907	46	185	259	71	553	159	273	8	1021	27	6.7	1.9	3.3	12.5
Gary Melchionni	G	6'2	187	23	68	1529	232	539	43	114	141	81	187	156	116	1	578	22	2.8	2.3	1.7	8.5
Fred Saunders	F	6'7	210	23	69	1059	176	406	43	66	95	69	253	80	151	3	418	15	3.7	1.2	2.2	6.1
Earl Williams	C-F	6'7	230	23	79	1040	163	394	41	45	103	44	456	95	146	0	371	13	5.8	1.2	1.8	4.7
Greg Jackson (from NY)	G	6'	185	22	44	775	69	166	42	36	62	58	67	93	125	5	174	18	1.5	2.1	2.8	4.0
Nate Hawthorne	G	6'4	190	24	50	618	118	287	41	61	94	65	92	39	94	0	297	12	1.8	0.8	1.9	5.9
Jim Owens	F	6'5	200	24	41	432	56	145	39	12	16	75	43	49	27	0	124	11	1.0	1.2	0.7	3.0
Corky Calhoun (to LA)	F	6'7	220	24	13	108	12	32	38	14	15	93	33	4	20	0	38	8	2.5	0.3	1.5	2.9
LOS ANGELES LAKERS	**30-52 .366**				**BILL SHARMAN**																	
Cazzie Russell (knee injury)	F	6'5	220	30	40	1055	264	580	46	101	113	89	115	109	56	0	629	26	2.9	2.7	1.4	15.7
Happy Hairston	F	6'7	225	32	74	2283	271	536	51	217	271	80	946	173	218	2	759	31	12.8	2.3	2.9	10.3
Elmore Smith	C	7'	250	25	74	2341	346	702	49	112	231	48	810	145	255	6	804	32	10.9	2.0	3.4	10.9
Lucius Allen (from Mil)	G	5'2	175	27	56	2011	443	1006	44	207	269	77	247	319	194	4	1093	36	4.4	5.7	3.5	19.5
Gail Goodrich	G	6'1	175	31	72	2668	656	1429	46	318	378	84	219	420	214	1	1630	37	3.0	5.8	3.0	22.6
Brian Winters	G-F	6'4	185	22	68	1516	359	810	44	76	92	83	138	195	168	1	794	22	2.0	2.9	2.5	11.7
Stu Lantz (from NO)	G	6'3	175	28	56	1430	189	446	42	145	176	82	170	158	134	1	523	26	3.0	2.8	2.4	9.3
Corky Calhoun (from Phoe)	F	6'7	220	24	57	1270	120	286	42	44	62	71	236	75	160	1	284	22	4.1	1.3	2.8	5.0
Zelmo Beaty	C	6'9	235	35	69	1213	136	310	44	108	135	80	327	74	130	1	380	18	4.7	1.1	1.9	5.5
Connie Hawkins	F-C	6'8	220	32	43	1026	139	324	43	68	99	69	198	120	116	1	346	24	4.6	2.8	2.7	8.0
Pat Riley	F-G	6'4	208	29	46	1016	219	523	42	69	93	74	85	121	128	0	507	22	1.8	2.6	2.8	11.0
Kermit Washington	F-C	6'8	230	23	55	949	87	207	42	72	122	59	350	66	155	2	246	17	6.4	1.2	2.8	4.5
Stan Love (to SA-A)	F	6'9	215	25	30	431	85	194	44	47	66	71	97	26	69	1	217	14	3.2	0.9	2.3	7.2
Jim Price (to Mil)	G	6'3	200	26	9	339	75	167	45	41	45	91	43	63	36	1	191	38	4.8	7.0	4.0	21.2
Bill Bridges (to GS)	F	6'6	235	35	17	307	20	57	35	16	30	53	94	27	46	1	56	18	5.5	1.6	2.7	3.3

1974/75 N.BA. — PLAYOFFS

GOLDEN STATE WARRIORS **AL ATTLES**

defeated Seattle 4-2; H123-96, H99-100, 105-96, 94-111, H124-100, 105-96
defeated Chicago 4-3; H107-89, 89-90,101-108, H111-106, H79-89, 86-72, H83-79
defeated Washington 4-0; 101-95, H92-91, H109-101, 96-95

Use Name	Pos	Hgt	Wgt	Age	TOTAL													PER GAME				
					G	Min	FG	FGA	%	FT	FTA	%	Reb	Ass	PF	DQ	Points	Min	Reb	Ass	PF	Points
Keith Wilkes	F	6'6	190	21	17	503	111	249	45	33	47	70	119	28	53	1	255	30	7.0	1.6	3.1	15.0
Rick Barry	F	6'7	220	30	17	726	**189**	**426**	44	101	110	**92**	94	103	51	1	**479**	43	5.5	6.1	3.0	28.2
Cliff Ray	C	6'9	235	25	17	495	36	69	52	32	53	60	166	38	60	0	104	29	9.8	2.2	3.5	6.1
Butch Beard	G	6'3	185	27	17	448	60	146	41	34	53	64	72	53	64	1	154	26	4.2	3.1	3.8	9.1
Charlie Johnson	G	6'	170	24	17	508	97	231	42	18	24	75	60	35	54	1	212	30	3.5	2.1	3.2	12.5
George Johnson	C	6'11	220	26	17	321	36	63	57	16	27	59	126	15	50	1	88	19	7.4	0.9	2.9	5.2
Jeff Mullins	G	6'4	200	32	17	313	60	123	49	18	31	58	35	29	43	0	138	18	2.1	1.7	2.5	8.1
Derrek Dickey	F	6'7	218	23	15	257	47	78	**60**	9	16	56	73	11	28	1	103	17	4.9	0.7	1.9	6.9
Phil Smith	G	6'4	187	22	16	235	39	104	38	25	40	63	28	30	30	0	103	15	1.8	1.9	1.9	6.4
Bill Bridges	F	6'6	235	35	14	148	10	23	43	2	7	29	49	7	23	0	22	11	3.5	0.5	1.6	1.6
Charles Dudley	G	6'2	186	24	13	112	10	24	42	16	28	57	17	17	23	0	36	9	1.3	1.3	1.8	2.8
Steve Bracey	G	6'1	175	24	4	14	3	7	43	4	4	100	1	3	1	0	10	4	0.3	0.8	0.3	2.5

WASHINGTON BULLETS **K. C. JONES**

defeated Buffalo 4-3; H102-113, 120-106, H111-96, 102-108, H97-93, 96-102, H115-96
defeated Boston 4-2; 100-95, H117-92, 90-101, H119-108, 99-103, H98-92
lost to Golden State 0-4; H95-101, 91-92, 101-109, H95-96

Use Name	Pos	Hgt	Wgt	Age	G	Min	FG	FGA	%	FT	FTA	%	Reb	Ass	PF	DQ	Points	Min	Reb	Ass	PF	Points
Nick Weatherspoon	F	6'7	200	24	17	404	70	136	51	35	43	81	81	16	56	0	175	24	4.8	0.9	3.3	10.3
Elvin Hayes	F-C	6'9	235	29	17	**751**	174	372	47	86	**127**	68	186	37	70	**3**	434	44	10.9	2.2	4.1	25.5
Wes Unseld	C	6'7	250	28	17	734	71	130	55	40	61	66	**276**	64	39	0	182	43	16.2	3.8	2.3	10.7
Phil Chenier	G	6'3	180	24	17	692	155	330	47	**102**	114	89	76	54	45	1	412	41	4.5	3.2	2.6	24.2
Kevin Porter	G	6'	175	24	17	625	99	197	50	46	69	67	41	**124**	**73**	**3**	244	37	2.4	7.3	4.3	14.4
Mike Riordan	F-G	6'4	200	29	17	378	60	151	40	14	18	78	41	27	49	1	134	22	2.4	1.6	2.9	7.9
Jimmy Jones	G	6'4	188	29	11	206	29	64	45	10	11	91	22	21	21	0	68	19	2.0	1.9	1.9	6.2
Truck Robinson	F	6'7	225	23	17	130	14	42	33	7	14	50	40	6	21	0	35	8	2.4	0.4	1.2	2.1
Clem Haskins	G	6'3	195	31	13	75	15	28	54	5	8	63	7	4	17	0	35	6	0.5	0.3	1.3	2.7
Tom Kozelko	F	6'8	220	23	13	54	5	11	45	4	5	80	7	1	8	0	14	4	0.5	0.1	0.6	1.1
Dick Gibbs	F-G	6'5	210	26	6	17	3	10	30	2	2	100	1	2	2	0	8	3	0.2	0.3	0.3	1.3
Dennis DuVal	G	6'3	175	22	5	14	3	9	33	1	2	50	3	3	1	0	7	3	0.6	0.6	0.2	1.4

BOSTON CELTICS **TOM HEINSOHN**

defeated Houston 4-1; H123-106, H112-100, 102-117, 122-117, H128-115
lost to Washington 4-2; H95-100, 92-117, H101-90, 108-119, H103-99, 92-98

Use Name	Pos	Hgt	Wgt	Age	G	Min	FG	FGA	%	FT	FTA	%	Reb	Ass	PF	DQ	Points	Min	Reb	Ass	PF	Points
John Havlicek	F-G	6'5	205	34	11	464	83	192	43	66	76	87	57	51	38	1	232	42	5.2	4.6	3.5	21.1
Paul Silas	F	6'7	225	31	11	405	42	92	46	16	25	64	130	40	45	1	100	37	11.8	3.6	4.1	9.1
Dave Cowens	C	6'9	230	26	11	479	101	236	43	23	26	88	181	46	50	2	225	44	**16.5**	4.2	4.5	20.5
Don Chaney	G	6'5	210	28	11	294	48	105	46	23	29	79	38	21	46	2	119	27	3.5	1.9	4.2	10.8
Jo Jo White	G	6'3	190	28	11	462	100	227	44	27	33	82	50	63	32	0	227	42	4.5	5.7	2.9	20.6
Don Nelson	F	6'6	210	34	11	274	66	117	56	37	41	90	45	26	36	1	169	25	4.1	2.4	3.3	15.4
Paul Westphal	G	6'4	195	24	11	183	38	81	47	12	18	67	13	32	21	0	88	17	1.2	2.9	1.9	8.0
Glenn McDonald	F-G	6'6	190	22	6	30	2	12	17	1	3	33	6	2	4	0	5	5	1.0	0.3	0.7	0.8
Henry Finkel	C	7'	240	32	7	25	3	7	43	3	5	60	6	4	2	0	9	4	0.9	0.6	0.3	1.3
Jim Ard	C	6'8	220	26	5	14	1	8	13	0	0	—	2	1	5	0	2	3	0.4	0.2	1.0	0.4
Kevin Stacom	G	6'3	185	23	4	7	0	2	0	0	0	—	0	1	0	0	0	2	0.0	0.3	0.0	0.0
Phil Hankinson	F	6'8	198	23	2	3	1	3	33	0	0	—	2	0	0	0	2	2	1.0	0.0	0.0	1,0

CHICAGO BULLS **DICK MOTTA**

defeated Kansas City-Omaha 4-2; H95-89, 95-102, H93-90, 100-104(OT), H104-77, 101-89
lost to Golden State 3-4; 89-107, H90-89, H108-101, 106-111, 89-79, H72-86, 79-83

Use Name	Pos	Hgt	Wgt	Age	G	Min	FG	FGA	%	FT	FTA	%	Reb	Ass	PF	DQ	Points	Min	Reb	Ass	PF	Points
Chet Walker	F	6'6	220	34	13	432	81	164	49	66	75	88	60	24	32	2	228	33	4.6	1.8	2.5	17.5
Bob Love	F	6'8	215	32	13	583	138	316	44	60	77	78	98	19	41	1	336	45	7.5	1.5	3.2	25.8
Tom Boerwinkle	C	7'	270	29	13	377	43	98	44	20	25	80	165	55	48	2	106	29	12.7	4.2	3.7	8.2
Jerry Sloan	G	6'6	200	32	13	470	75	163	46	20	36	56	96	26	46	0	170	36	7.4	2.0	3.5	13.1
Norm Van Lier	G	6'1	175	27	13	547	67	164	41	62	83	75	67	61	52	1	196	42	5.2	4.7	4.0	15.1
Nate Thurmond	C	6'11	235	33	13	254	14	38	37	18	37	49	87	31	36	0	46	20	6.7	2.4	2.8	3.5
Matt Guokas	G-F	6'5	195	30	13	202	12	35	34	7	8	88	14	11	20	0	31	16	1.1	0.8	1.5	2.4
Rowland Garrett	F	6'6	215	24	12	143	21	56	38	2	4	50	29	3	27	0	44	12	2.4	0.3	2.3	3.7
Bobby Wilson	G	6'3	180	23	10	93	17	41	41	10	12	83	11	4	10	0	44	9	1.1	0.4	1.0	4.4
John Block	F	6'10	220	30	4	34	6	15	40	1	3	33	6	0	5	0	13	9	1.5	0.0	1.3	3.3
Mickey Johnson	F	6'10	190	22	3	5	1	3	33	0	0	—	0	0	2	0	2	2	0.0	0.0	0.7	0.7
Leon Benbow	G	6'4	185	22	2	5	2	4	50	1	2	50	1	2	0	0	5	3	0.5	1.0	0.0	2.5

SEATTLE SUPERSONICS **BILL RUSSELL**

defeated Detroit 2-1; H90-77, 106-122, H100-93
lost to Golden State 2-4; 96-123, 100-99, H96-105, H111-94, 100-124, H96 105

Use Name	Pos	Hgt	Wgt	Age	G	Min	FG	FGA	%	FT	FTA	%	Reb	Ass	PF	DQ	Points	Min	Reb	Ass	PF	Points
Leonard Gray	F	6'8	240	23	9	263	39	80	49	11	13	85	45	20	41	0	89	29	5.0	2.2	4.6	9.9
Spencer Haywood	F	6'8	230	25	9	337	47	131	36	47	61	77	81	18	29	0	141	37	9.0	2.0	3.2	15.7
Tom Burleson	C	7'3	228	22	9	364	78	152	51	30	40	75	96	13	29	0	186	40	10.7	1.4	3.2	20.7
Fred Brown	G	6'3	180	26	8	240	69	139	50	27	32	84	36	23	19	0	165	30	4.5	2.9	2.4	20.6
Slick Watts	G	6'1	175	23	9	282	43	93	46	14	26	54	33	64	30	0	100	31	3.7	7.1	3.3	11.1
Archie Clark	G	6'2	175	33	9	269	41	94	44	18	20	90	32	31	23	0	100	30	3.6	3.4	2.6	11.1
Tal Skinner	F-G	6'5	210	22	9	211	21	45	47	14	19	74	38	12	26	0	56	23	4.2	1.3	2.9	6.2
John Hummer	F-C	6'9	230	26	6	68	0	7	0	0	0	—	9	4	7	0	0	11	1.5	0.7	1.2	0.0
Rod Derline	G	6'4	175	22	6	64	18	33	55	6	7	86	13	7	6	0	42	11	2.2	1.2	1.0	7.0
Jim Fox	C	6'10	230	31	8	40	4	14	29	4	7	57	9	2	6	0	12	5	1.1	0.3	0.8	1.5
Dean Tolson	F	6'8	190	23	4	22	1	8	13	2	2	100	7	1	3	0	4	6	1.8	0.3	0.8	1.0

Use Name	Pos	Hgt	Wgt	Age	G	Min	FG	FGA	%	FT	FTA	%	Reb	Ass	PF	DQ	Points	Min	Reb	Ass	PF	Points
					TOTAL													PER GAME				

1974/75 N.B.A. — PLAYOFFS (continued)

Use Name	Pos	Hgt	Wgt	Age	G	Min	FG	FGA	%	FT	FTA	%	Reb	Ass	PF	DQ	Points	Min	Reb	Ass	PF	Points
BUFFALO BRAVES	**JACK RAMSAY**				lost to Washington 3-4; 113-102, H106-120, 96-111 H108-102, 93-97, H102-96, 96-115																	
Jim McMillian	F	6'5	225	26	7	240	39	86	45	13	14	93	34	14	12	0	91	34	4.9	2.0	1.7	13.0
Gar Heard	F	6'6	220	26	7	250	38	96	40	6	14	43	76	18	28	0	82	36	10.9	2.6	4.0	11.7
Bob McAdoo	C-F	6'9	210	23	7	327	104	216	48	54	73	74	94	10	29	1	262	**47**	13.4	1.4	4.1	**37.4**
Randy Smith	G	6'3	180	26	7	286	50	105	48	26	30	87	30	49	23	0	126	41	4.3	7.0	3.3	18.0
Ken Charles	G	6'3	180	23	7	208	22	55	40	8	11	73	13	18	27	1	52	30	1.9	2.6	3.9	7.4
Bob Weiss	G	6'2	185	32	7	113	11	23	48	8	12	67	7	17	15	0	30	16	1.0	2.4	2.1	4.3
Jack Marin	F	6'7	210	30	7	108	12	27	44	13	15	87	17	8	12	0	37	15	2.4	1.1	1.7	5.3
Lee Winfield	G	6'2	175	27	6	65	7	16	44	3	5	60	8	9	10	1	17	11	1.3	1.5	1.7	2.8
Dale Schlueter	C	6'10	235	29	6	40	6	10	60	1	3	33	13	1	6	0	13	7	2.2	0.2	1.0	2.2
Jim Washington	F	6'7	215	31	6	39	2	5	40	0	0	—	7	3	5	0	4	7	1.2	0.5	0.8	0.7
Paul Ruffner	C	6'10	225	26	1	4	0	1	0	0	0	—	2	0	0	0	0	4	2.0	0.0	0.0	0.0
HOUSTON ROCKETS	**JONNY EGAN**				defeated New York 2-1; H99-84, 96-106, H118-86 lost to Boston 1-4; 106-123, 100-112, H117-102, H117-122, 115-128																	
Ed Ratleff	F-G	6'6	195	24	8	291	36	87	41	17	20	85	53	35	31	0	89	36	6.6	4.4	3.9	11.1
Rudy Tomjanovich	F	6'8	220	26	8	304	72	128	56	40	48	83	64	23	17	0	184	38	8.0	2.9	2.1	23.0
Kevin Kunnert	C	7'	240	23	8	244	35	81	43	17	26	65	60	12	37	1	87	31	7.5	1.5	4.6	10.9
Mike Newlin	G	6'4	205	25	8	299	52	107	49	26	29	90	33	45	25	0	130	37	4.1	5.6	3.1	16.3
Cal Murphy	G	5'9	165	26	8	305	72	156	46	51	57	89	19	45	36	2	195	38	2.4	5.6	4.5	24.4
Ron Riley	F	6'8	200	24	8	152	25	42	60	6	16	38	36	15	18	0	56	19	4.5	1.9	2.3	7.0
Steve Hawes	C-F	6'9	220	24	8	128	18	38	47	8	9	89	29	13	11	0	44	16	3.6	1.6	1.4	5.5
Gus Bailey	G	6'5	185	23	8	116	18	36	50	9	10	90	19	16	12	0	45	15	2.4	2.0	1.5	5.6
Zaid Abdul-Aziz	C	6'9	240	28	6	68	12	31	39	2	5	40	17	3	5	0	26	11	2.8	0.5	0.8	4.3
Dave Wohl	G	6'2	185	25	4	8	3	3	100	0	0	—	1	2	2	0	6	2	0.3	0.5	0.5	1.5
Owen Wells	F	6'7	200	24	4	5	3	5	60	0	0	—	1	1	1	0	6	1	0.3	0.3	0.3	1.5
KANSAS CITY-OMAHA KINGS	**PHIL JOHNSON**				lost to Chicago 2-4, 89-95, H102-95, 90-93, H104-100(OT), 77-104, H89-101																	
Ollie Johnson	F-G	6'6	200	25	6	166	26	56	46	12	12	100	23	6	16	0	64	28	3.8	1.0	2.7	10.7
Scott Wedman	F	6'7	215	22	6	230	27	68	40	12	18	67	35	16	17	0	66	38	5.8	2.7	2.8	11.0
Sam Lacey	C	6'10	235	26	6	264	23	61	38	11	18	61	94	30	19	1	57	44	15.7	5.0	3.2	9.5
Jimmy Walker	G	6'3	205	30	6	225	39	84	46	14	18	78	10	17	12	0	92	38	1.7	2.8	2.0	15.3
Nate Archibald	G	6'1	165	26	6	242	43	118	36	35	43	81	11	32	18	0	121	40	1.8	5.3	3.0	20.2
Ron Behagen	F	6'9	225	23	6	108	22	43	51	3	3	100	29	6	28	2	47	18	4.8	1.0	**4.7**	7.8
Larry McNeill	F	6'9	200	23	6	103	22	34	65	17	20	85	26	2	21	2	61	17	4.3	0.3	3.5	10.2
Mike D'Antoni	G	6'3	190	23	4	42	7	14	50	4	4	100	7	1	6	0	18	11	1.8	0.3	1.5	4.5
Rich Adelman	G	6'1	185	28	6	34	3	9	33	6	8	75	2	3	9	0	12	6	0.3	0.5	1.5	2.0
Len Kosmalshi	C	7'	245	23	6	29	2	3	67	2	3	67	10	5	4	0	6	5	1.7	0.8	0.7	1.0
Don Kojis	F	6'5	215	35	4	22	1	6	17	5	6	83	4	1	3	0	7	6	1.0	0.3	0.8	1.8
DETROIT PISTONS	**RAY SCOTT**				lost to Seattle 1-2; 77-90, H122-106, 93-100																	
Curtis Rowe	F	6'7	225	25	3	115	17	33	52	10	19	53	26	15	6	0	44	38	8.7	5.0	2.0	14.7
Howard Porter	F	6'8	220	26	3	92	23	42	55	6	7	86	20	0	5	0	52	31	6.7	0.0	1.7	17.3
Bob Lanier	C	6'11	260	26	3	128	26	51	51	9	12	75	32	19	10	0	61	43	10.7	6.3	3.3	20.3
Chris Ford	G	6'5	190	25	3	82	6	11	55	0	0	—	13	10	8	0	12	27	4.3	3.3	2.7	4.0
Dave Bing	G	6'3	190	31	3	134	20	47	43	8	13	62	11	29	12	0	48	45	3.7	**9.7**	4.0	16.0
George Trapp	F	6'8	215	26	3	81	18	33	55	5	7	71	22	4	6	0	41	27	7.3	1.3	2.0	13.7
John Mengelt	G	6'2	195	25	3	65	9	23	39	7	9	78	8	9	9	0	25	22	2.7	3.0	3.0	8.3
Jim Davis	C	6'9	235	33	2	16	2	4	50	3	5	60	4	0	1	0	7	8	2.0	0.0	0.5	3.5
Bill Ligon	G	6'6	180	22	2	7	1	1	100	0	0	—	0	0	1	0	2	4	0.0	0.0	0.5	1.0
NEW YORK KNICKERBOCKERS	**RED HOLZMAN**				lost to Houston 1-2; 84-99, H106-96, 86-118																	
Bill Bradley	F	6'5	205	31	3	88	9	24	38	2	2	100	9	6	5	0	20	29	3.0	2.0	1.7	6.7
Harthorne Wingo	F	6'8	210	26	3	76	10	23	43	7	10	70	22	7	7	0	27	25	7.3	2.3	2.3	9.0
John Gianelli	C	6'10	220	24	3	93	11	24	46	3	3	100	14	2	10	0	25	31	4.7	0.7	3.3	8.3
Walt Frazier	G	6'4	205	29	3	124	29	46	63	13	16	81	20	21	4	0	71	41	6.7	7.0	1.3	23.7
Earl Monroe	G	6'3	190	30	3	89	12	45	27	18	22	82	9	6	6	0	42	30	3.0	2.0	2.0	14.0
Phil Jackson	F-C	6'8	220	29	3	78	10	21	48	7	8	88	25	2	15	0	27	26	8.3	0.7	5.0	9.0
Jim Barnett	G	6'4	180	30	3	59	13	21	62	5	5	100	8	5	6	0	31	20	2.7	1.7	2.0	10.3
Neal Walk	C	6'10	220	26	3	39	5	10	50	0	0	—	5	2	4	0	10	13	1.7	0.7	1.3	3.3
Mel Davis	F	6'7	225	24	3	28	5	12	42	2	2	100	4	2	2	0	12	9	1.3	0.7	0.7	4.0
Dennis Bell	F	6'6	215	23	3	27	1	8	13	0	5	0	4	0	6	0	2	9	1.3	0.0	2.0	0.7
Jesse Dark	G	6'5	210	23	2	11	1	6	17	5	5	100	1	1	2	0	7	6	0.5	0.5	1.0	3.5
Tom Riker	C	6'10	240	24	1	8	1	2	50	0	0	—	2	1	1	0	2	8	2.0	1.0	1.0	2.0

Team	W	L	Pct.	GB	Record against playoff teams W	L	Pct.	Record against non-playoff teams W	L	Pct.	HOME W	L	Pct.	ROAD W	L	Pct.
ATLANTIC DIVISION																
Boston Celtics	**60**	22	**.732**	—	**29**	17	.630	31	5	**.861**	28	13	.683	**32**	9	**.780**
Buffalo Braves	49	33	.598	11	23	22	.511	26	11	.703	30	11	.732	19	22	.463
New York Knickerbockers	40	42	.488	20	17	28	.378	23	14	.622	23	18	561	17	24	415
Philadelphia 76ers	34	48	.415	26	23	31	.426	11	17	.393	20	**21**	.488	14	27	.341
CENTRAL DIVISION																
Washington Bullets	**60**	22	**.732**	—	27	12	**.692**	**33**	10	.767	**36**	5	**.878**	24	17	.585
Houston Rockets	41	41	.500	19	16	23	.410	25	18	.581	29	12	.707	12	29	.293
Cleveland Cavaliers	40	42	.488	20	20	28	.417	20	14	.588	29	12	.707	11	30	.268
Atlanta Hawks	31	51	.378	29	14	33	.378	17	18	.486	22	19	.537	9	32	.220
New Orleans Jazz	23	**59**	.280	37	10	**37**	.213	13	**22**	.371	20	**21**	.488	3	**38**	.073
MIDWEST DIVISION																
Chicago Bulls	47	35	.573	—	25	21	.543	22	14	.611	29	12	.707	18	23	.439
Kansas City-Omaha Kings	44	38	.537	3	22	23	.489	22	15	.595	29	12	.707	15	26	.366
Detroit Pistons	40	42	.488	7	18	27	.400	22	15	.595	26	15	.634	14	27	.341
Milwaukee Bucks	38	44	.463	9	23	31	.426	15	13	.536	25	16	.610	13	28	.317
PACIFIC DIVISION																
Golden State Warriors	48	34	.585	—	20	19	.513	28	15	.651	31	10	.756	17	24	.415
Seattle Supersonics	43	39	.524	5	17	22	.436	26	17	.605	24	17	.585	19	22	.463
Portland Trail Blazers	38	44	.463	10	16	32	.333	22	12	.647	28	13	.683	10	31	.244
Phoenix Suns	32	50	.390	16	18	29	.383	14	21	.400	22	19	.537	10	31	.244
Los Angeles Lakers	30	52	.366	18	10	**37**	.213	20	15	.571	21	20	.512	9	32	.220

Effective in the 1974/75 season, games won and lost at neutral sites are included in the home and road won-lost statistics.

1974/75 N.B.A. INDIVIDUAL LEADERS

SCORING
(Minimum 70 Games or 1400 Points)

Name	Team	G	FG	FT	Pts.	Avg.
McAdoo	Buf	82	1095	641	2831	34.5
Barry	GS	80	1028	394	2450	30.6
Abdul-Jabbar	Mil	65	812	325	1949	30.0
Archibald	KCO	82	759	652	2170	26.5
Scott	Phoe	69	703	274	1680	24.3
Lanier	Det	76	731	361	1823	24.0
Hayes	Was	82	739	409	1887	23.0
Goodrich	LA	72	656	318	1630	22.6
Haywood	Sea	68	608	309	1525	22.4
Carter	Phi	77	715	256	1686	21.9

FIELD GOAL PERCENTAGE
(Minimum 300 Made)

Name	Team	FG	FGA	Pct.
Nelson	Bos	423	785	.539
Beard	GS	408	773	.528
Tomjanovich	Hou	694	1323	.525
Abdul-Jabbar	Mil	812	1584	.513
McAdoo	Buf	1095	2138	.512
Kunnert	Hou	346	676	.512
Westphal	Bos	342	670	.510
Lanier	Det	731	1433	.510
Snyder	Cle	498	988	.504
McMillian	Buf	347	695	.499

FREE THROW PERCENTAGE
(Minimum 125 Made)

Name	Team	FT	FTA	Pct.
Barry	GS	394	436	.904
Murphy	Hou	341	386	.883
Bradley	NY	144	165	.873
Archibald	KCO	652	748	.872
Price	LA-Mil	169	194	.871
Havlicek	Bos	289	332	.870
Marin	Buf	193	222	.869
Newlin	Hou	265	305	.869
Walker	Chi	413	480	.860
Walker	KCO	247	289	.855

PERSONAL FOULS

Name	Team	PF
P. Jackson	NY	330
Dandridge	Mil	330
Porter	Was	320
Ray	GS	305
Behagen	KCO	301

GAMES DISQUALIFIED

Name	Team	Disq.
Porter	Was	12
Scott	Phoe	11
Sojourner	Atl	10
Coleman	NO	10
P. Jackson	NY	10
Perry	Phoe	10

MINUTES PLAYED

Name	Team	Min.
McAdoo	Buf	3539
Hayes	Was	3465
Lacey	KCO	3378
Archibald	KCO	3244
Barry	GS	3235

TOTAL REBOUNDS PER GAME
(Minimum 70 Games or 800 Rebounds)

Name	Team	G	Reb.	Avg.
Unseld	Was	73	1077	14.8
Cowens	Bos	65	958	14.7
Lacey	KCO	81	1149	14.2
McAdoo	Buf	82	1155	14.1
Abdul-Jabbar	Mil	65	912	14.0
Hairston	LA	74	946	12.8
Silas	Bos	82	1025	12.5
Hayes	Was	82	1004	12.2
Lanier	Det	76	914	12.0
Perry	Phoe	79	940	11.9

ASSISTS PER GAME
(Minimum 70 Games or 400 Assists)

Name	Team	G	Ass.	Avg.
Porter	Was	81	650	8.0
Bing	Det	79	610	7.7
Archibald	KCO	82	557	6.8
Smith	Buf	82	534	6.5
Maravich	NO	79	488	6.2
Barry	GS	80	492	6.2
Watts	Sea	82	499	6.1
Frazier	NY	78	474	6.1
Goodrich	LA	72	420	5.8
Van Lier	Chi	70	403	5.8

BLOCKED SHOTS PER GAME
(Minimum 70 Games or 100 Blocked Shots)

Name	Team	G	Reb.	Avg.
Abdul-Jabbar	Mil	65	212	3.3
Smith	LA	74	216	2.9
Thurmond	Chi	80	195	2.4
Hayes	Was	82	187	2.3
Lanier	Det	76	172	2.3
McAdoo	Buf	82	174	2.1
Lacey	KCO	71	168	2.1
Burleson	Sea	82	153	1.9
Heard	Buf	67	120	1.8
Chones	Cle	72	120	1.7

OFFENSIVE REBOUNDS PER GAME
(Minimum 70 Games Played)

Name	Team	G	Reb.	Avg.
Drew	Atl	78	357	4.6
Perry	Phoe	79	347	4.4
Unseld	Was	73	318	4.4
Silas	Bos	82	348	4.2
Hairston	LA	74	304	4.1
McAdoo	Buf	82	307	3.7
Lee	Atl-Phi	80	288	3.6
Thurmond	Chi	80	259	3.2
Ray	GS	82	259	3.2
Jones	Atl	75	236	3.1

STEALS PER GAME
(Minimum 70 Games or 125 Steals)

Name	Team	G	Steals	Avg.
Barry	GS	80	228	2.9
Frazier	NY	78	190	2.4
Steele	Port	76	183	2.4
Watts	Sea	82	190	2.3
Brown	Sea	81	187	2.3
Chenier	Was	77	176	2.3
Sloan	Chi	78	171	2.2
Allen	Mil-LA	66	136	2.1
Van Lier	Chi	70	139	2.0
Hayes	Was	82	158	1.9

TEAM STATISTICS

Team		REGULAR SEASON												PLAYOFFS											
		G	FG	FGA	%	FT	FTA	%	Reb	Ass	PF	Points	PPG	G	FG	FGA	%	FT	FTA	%	Reb	Ass	PF	Points	PPG
ATLANTIC DIVISION																									
Boston	**Off.**	82	3587	7825	46	1560	1971	79	4264	2159	1913	8734	106.5	11	**485**	**1082**	45	208	256	**81**	530	287	279	1178	107.1
	Def.	82	3432	7726	44	**1401**	1882	74	3682	1833	1869	8265	100.8	11	466	952	49	246	317	78	**468**	248	259	1178	107.1
	Diff.		+155	+99	+2	+159	+89	+5	**+582**	**+326**	-44	+469	+5.7		+19	**+130**	-4	-38	-61	+3	**+62**	+39	-20	—	—
Buffalo	**Off.**	82	3552	7469	48	1735	2224	78	3843	2063	1879	8839	107.8	7	291	640	45	132	177	75	301	147	167	714	102.0
	Def.	82	3575	7943	45	1513	1943	78	3914	2151	2030	8663	105.6	7	**303**	632	48	137	189	**72**	333	160	164	743	106.1
	Diff.		-23	-474	+3	+222	+281	—	-71	-88	+151	+176	+2.2		-12	+8	-3	-5	-12	+3	-32	-13	-3	-29	-4.1
New York	**Off.**	82	3359	7464	45	1518	1967	77	3633	1675	2001	8236	100.4	3	107	242	44	62	78	79	123	55	68	276	92.0
	Def.	82	3361	7357	46	1615	2082	78	3926	**1668**	1912	8337	101.7	3	128	271	47	57	70	81	141	77	73	313	104.3
	Diff.		-2	+107	-1	-97	-115	-1	-293	+7	-89	-101	-1.3		-21	-29	-3	+5	+8	-2	-18	-22	+5	-37	-12.3
Philadelphia	**Off.**	82	3325	7476	44	1530	2043	75	3906	1709	1974	8180	99.8												
	Def.	82	3445	7466	46	1541	1979	78	3915	1959	2036	8431	102.8												
	Diff.		-120	+10	-2	-11	+64	-3	-9	-250	+62	-251	-3.0												
CENTRAL DIVISION																									
Washington	**Off.**	82	3555	7697	46	1475	1962	75	3897	2005	1961	8585	104.7	17	698	1480	47	352	**474**	74	781	359	402	1748	102.8
	Def.	82	3249	7415	**44**	1499	1967	76	4003	1811	2004	7997	97.5	17	700	1616	**43**	303	405	75	821	363	437	1703	100.2
	Diff.		+306	+282	+2	-24	-5	-1	-106	+194	+43	**+588**	+7.2		-2	-136	+4	**+49**	+69	-1	-40	-4	+35	+45	+2.6
Houston	**Off.**	82	3448	7231	48	1625	2034	80	3672	2155	2068	8521	103.9	8	346	714	48	**176**	220	80	332	210	195	868	**108.5**
	Def.	82	3429	7127	48	1576	2127	**74**	**3416**	2024	2063	8434	102.9	8	**346**	713	49	171	208	82	348	208	193	863	107.9
	Diff.		+19	+104	—	+49	-93	**+6**	+256	+131	-5	+87	+1.0			+1	-1	+5	+12	-2	-16	+2	-2	+5	+.6
Cleveland	**Off.**	82	3408	7371	46	1301	1753	74	3560	1903	1881	8117	99.0												
	Def.	82	3263	7243	45	1621	2102	77	3929	1746	1932	8147	99.4												
	Diff.		+145	+128	+1	-320	-349	-3	-369	+157	+51	-30	-.4												
Atlanta	**Off.**	82	3424	7824	44	1772	**2435**	73	4094	1878	1964	8620	105.1												
	Def.	82	3563	7504	47	1606	2098	77	4020	1914	**2265**	8732	106.5												
	Diff.		-139	+320	-3	+166	**+337**	-4	+74	-36	+301	-112	-1.4												
New Orleans	**Off.**	82	3301	7509	44	1717	2247	76	3760	1818	2222	8319	101.5												
	Def.	82	3553	7433	48	1857	2465	75	4117	1891	2126	8963	109.3												
	Diff.		-252	+76	-4	-140	-218	+1	-357	-73	-96	-644	-7.8												
MIDWEST DIVISION																									
Chicago	**Off.**	82	3167	7085	45	1711	2203	78	3893	1840	1952	8045	98.1	13	477	1097	43	267	362	74	634	236	319	1221	93.9
	Def.	82	**3167**	**7070**	45	1457	1900	77	3655	1686	2168	**7791**	**95.0**	13	492	1107	44	223	298	75	578	252	**349**	1207	**92.8**
	Diff.		—	+15	—	+254	+303	+1	+238	+154	+216	+254	+3.1		-15	-10	-1	+44	+64	-1	+56	-16	+30	+14	+1.1
K.C.-Omaha	**Off.**	82	3257	7258	45	**1797**	2190	**82**	3736	1853	1968	8311	101.4	6	215	496	43	121	153	79	251	119	153	551	91.8
	Def.	82	3410	7400	46	1515	1972	77	3872	1840	2029	8335	101.6	6	237	531	45	114	144	79	305	**101**	155	588	98.0
	Diff.		-153	-142	-1	**+282**	+218	+5	-136	+13	+61	-24	-.2		-22	-35	-2	+7	+9	—	-54	+18	+2	-37	-6.2
Detroit	**Off.**	82	3289	7053	47	1533	1975	78	3517	1916	**1866**	8111	98.9	3	122	245	**50**	48	72	67	136	**86**	**58**	292	97.3
	Def.	82	3409	7257	47	1410	**1793**	79	3654	2012	1875	8228	100.3	3	129	285	45	**38**	**51**	75	134	67	67	296	98.7
	Diff.		-120	-204	—	+123	+182	-1	-137	**-96**	+9	-117	-1.4		-7	-40	**+5**	+10	**+21**	-8	+2	**+19**	**+9**	-4	-1.4
Milwaukee	**Off.**	82	3450	7367	47	1354	1746	78	3787	1932	1949	8254	100.7												
	Def.	82	3371	7600	44	1495	1910	78	3798	1960	1704	8237	100.5												
	Diff.		+79	-233	+3	-141	-164	—	-11	-28	-245	+17	+.2												
PACIFIC DIVISION																									
Golden State	**Off.**	82	**3714**	**7981**	47	1470	1915	77	**4270**	2076	2109	**8898**	**108.5**	17	698	1543	45	308	440	70	**840**	369	480	1704	100.2
	Def.	82	3481	7628	46	1666	2209	75	3843	2084	1855	8628	105.2	17	619	**1416**	44	376	512	73	765	347	417	1614	94.9
	Diff.		+233	**+353**	+1	-196	-294	+2	+427	-8	-254	+270	+3.3		**+79**	+127	+1	-68	-72	-3	+75	+22	-63	+90	**+5.3**
Seattle	**Off.**	82	3488	7653	46	1475	1970	75	3721	1997	1977	8451	103.1	9	361	796	45	173	227	76	399	195	219	895	99.4
	Def.	82	3490	7606	46	1560	2090	75	4040	2188	1948	8540	104.1	9	380	812	47	182	265	69	434	240	226	942	104.7
	Diff.		-2	+47	—	-85	-120	—	-319	-191	-29	-89	-1.0		-19	-16	-2	-9	-38	**+7**	-35	-45	+7	-47	-5.3
Portland	**Off.**	82	3414	7113	**48**	1680	2265	74	3807	**2209**	2055	8508	103.8												
	Def.	82	3379	7502	45	1717	2178	79	3779	2090	2085	8472	103.3												
	Diff.		+35	-389	**+3**	-37	+87	-5	+28	+119	+30	+36	+.5												
Phoenix	**Off.**	82	3381	7561	45	1535	2082	74	4033	1879	2090	8297	101.2												
	Def.	82	3356	7323	46	1780	2350	76	3676	2062	1992	8492	103.6												
	Diff.		+25	+238	-1	-245	-268	-2	+357	-183	-98	-195	-2.4												
Los Angeles	**Off.**	82	3409	7577	45	1641	2182	75	4075	2091	2079	8459	103.2												
	Def.	82	3595	7914	45	1603	2117	76	4229	2239	2015	8793	107.2												
	Diff.		-186	-337	—	+38	+65	-1	-154	-148	-64	-334	-4.0												

1974-75 A.B.A.

Surviving on a Local Level

To see the A.B.A. in action this fall was something of a surprise; summer rumors indicated the imminent collapse of the circuit. But problems were worked out, and the 1974-75 season was played. Several franchises seemed to be on the edge of folding at the end of last season, but these weak members were propped up so that the league again fielded 10 clubs. The Carolina Cougars were given up as a failure, and the franchise was shifted to St. Louis, known as the Spirits of St. Louis. Commissioner Mike Storen resigned his post to become president of the Memphis Sounds, who had suffered as the Tams under the ownership of Charles 0. Finley of baseball fame. The Utah Stars and Virginia Squires got new owners, and the Denver Rockets became the Denver Nuggets. Tedd Munchak had owned the Carolina franchise, but he found new work by replacing Storen as commissioner. Such reorganization kept the league afloat, but did not solve all its problems; the San Diego and Indiana franchises had financial problems during the season, and the lack of a national television contract hurt the entire league.

All the rumors of impending doom made it more difficult to sign graduating college stars, but the A.B.A. did gather a core of attractive rookies. Marvin Barnes of Providence signed with St. Louis for $2 million, and other star collegians joining the league were Maryland's Len Elmore, North Carolina's Bobby Jones, and Pittsburgh's Billy Knight. But the most publicized rookie was Moses Malone, a 6'11" teenager who signed a bonus contract with Utah directly out of a Virginia high school. Young Malone not only drew attention from the press but also played well at forward.

But the addition of the teenage "pheenom" could not help the Stars hold onto first place in the West. The club that went into the championship series last spring before losing to New York broke up with the defection of center Zelmo Beaty and guard Jimmy Jones to the N.B.A. and with the holdout of forward Willie Wise until his trade to Virginia late in the season. With Utah too weak to stay on top, the Denver Nuggets moved to the front in the Western Division. General manager Carl Scheer and coach Larry Brown both joined the club from the defunct Carolina franchise, and they brought along with them guard Mack Calvin, a running playmaker who could command an effective fast break. The Nuggets also added two tough rookie forwards in Bobby Jones and Jan Van Breda Kolff and a smart veteran guard in Fatty Taylor, but much of the club's improvement came from development by center Mike Green and guard Ralph Simpson. This combination of old and new faces compiled an overwhelming 40-2 record at home during the regular season and finished the year at 65-19.

The second-place San Antonio Spurs had a fine starting quintet in Swen Nater, Rich Jones, George Gervin, Donnie Freeman, and James Silas, but a thin bench kept the club from challenging the Nuggets. The Indiana Pacers sent veterans Freddie Lewis, Roger Brown, and Mel Daniels to Memphis during the summer, and coach Bob Leonard brought his club in third with a crew of mostly younger players; the focal point on the club was forward George McGinnis, who led the league with a 29.8 scoring average. Utah made the playoffs by finishing fourth, but the club had a weak bench and ended the year with three centers starting in the forecourt. The San Diego Conquistadors trailed the field with an abundance of shooters and a famine of defensive players. Wilt Chamberlain retired both as a player and coach before the season, and general manager Alex Groza filled in as coach for the first part of the schedule until Beryl Shipley could be hired.

While the Western title was sewed up early by Denver, the Eastern race was a two-team battle beteween the New York Nets and the Kentucky Colonels. The Nets had a new general manager in retired N.B.A. star Dave DeBusschere, the A.B.A.'s most exciting star in Julius Erving, an All-Star guard in Brian Taylor, and an invigorating streak of confidence left over from last year's championship. But a seemingly safe hold on first place vanished in a four-game losing streak in late March, enabling the Colonels to tie them for first place. The Colonels finished in a rush, winning their last nine games of the season. To go along with forecourt titans Artis Gilmore and Dan Issel and veteran guard Louie Dampier, the Colonels this year added a new coach in Hubie Brown, two new veteran forwards in Wilbert Jones and Marv Roberts, and three new veteran guards in Bird Averitt, Ted McClain, and Gene Littles. The new St. Louis club finished third with a bunch of talented, free-wheeling, unpolished rookies led by Marvin Barnes, who played top-notch ball after having jumped the club for several games early in the season.

At the bottom of the East came the league's two disaster franchises, Memphis and Virginia. The Sounds made the playoffs practically by default. Storen and new coach Joe Mullaney tried to build the team with deals for established players, but most of the acquired men had little left to offer. The Squires struggled through the season with a variety of castoffs and undisciplined rookies, with Willie Wise lending the club a needed professional touch after arriving in a late-season trade. When the season was over, the Squires had a 15-69 mark, the worst team record in A.B.A. history.

With only the Squires and Q's excluded, the playoffs began in early April with an Eastern Division tie-breaker between New York and Kentucky. The Colonels kept up their late-season heat by beating the Nets 108-99, then quickly defeated Memphis four games to one. The Nets, meanwhile, drew St. Louis as their first-round opponents. Having beaten the Spirits 11 straight times during the regular season, the Nets expected little trouble, but after winning the first game, they couldn't contain the young and big Spirit forwards and lost four straight contests to the rookie-laden team. With the defending champs thus upset, the Colonels did away with the Spirits in five games to move into the finals. Meanwhile, the Western Division had come down to a confrontation between Denver and Indiana, with the Pacers unexpectedly winning the seventh game on the Denver home floor. In the championship series, it was no contest; the Pacers had a big gun in George McGinnis, but the Colonels had the more balanced and deeper team. With four straight wins, the Colonels captured their first A.B.A. championship after years of knocking on the door.

At the season's end, Nets general manager Dave DeBusschece was handed the reins of league commissioner in a move to improve the A.B.A.'s image. DeBusschere's first move was to challenge the N.B.A. champion Golden State Warriors to a best three of five championship series with the Colonels. As expected, the answer was, "no".

1974/75 A.B.A. — EASTERN DIVISION

Use Name	Pos	Hgt	Wgt	Age	TOTAL G	Min	FG	FGA	%	FT	FTA	%	Reb	Ast	PF	DQ	Points	PER GAME Min	Reb	Ast	PF	Points
KENTUCKY COLONELS	**58-26 .690**				**HUBIE BROWN**				defeated New York 108-99 at home in playoff for first place.													
Wil Jones	F	6'8	205	27	84	2689	458	948	48	139	189	74	607	256	**353**	—	1055	32	7.2	3.0	4.2	12.6
Dan Issel	F-C	6'9	240	26	83	2864	614	1303	47	237	321	74	710	188	197	—	1465	35	8.6	2.3	2.4	17.7
Artis Gilmore	C	7'2	240	25	84	**3493**	784	1351	58	412	592	70	**1361**	208	318	—	1981	**42**	16.2	2.5	3.8	23.6
Ted McClain	G	6'3	180	27	72	1971	256	582	44	104	138	75	268	365	231	—	617	27	3.7	5.1	3.2	8.6
Louie Dampier	G	6'	180	30	83	2879	598	1195	50	161	199	81	211	449	140	—	1395	35	2.5	5.4	1.7	16.8
Bird Averitt	G	6'1	175	22	84	2031	422	1014	42	249	320	78	185	319	212	—	1100	24	2.2	3.8	2.5	13.1
Marv Roberts	F	6'8	205	24	83	1370	201	467	43	127	164	77	246	103	200	—	529	17	3.0	1.2	2.4	6.4
Jim Bradley (injury)	F	6'9	215	22	56	922	144	327	44	76	103	74	284	68	112	—	364	16	5.1	1.2	2.0	6.5
Gene Littles	G	6'1	175	31	61	900	85	202	42	43	58	74	86	119	81	—	215	15	1.4	2.0	1.3	3.5
Ron Thomas	F	6'6	215	24	79	830	115	256	45	57	119	48	300	46	133	—	288	11	3.8	0.6	1.7	3.6
Johnny Roche (KJ, to Utah)	G	6'3	170	25	19	258	29	79	37	15	18	83	9	34	23	—	74	14	0.5	1.8	1.2	3.9
Joe Hamilton	G	5'10	175	26	9	124	15	40	38	5	6	83	11	21	13	—	38	14	1.2	2.3	1.4	4.2
Red Robbins (to Va)	F	6'8	200	30	4	29	12	21	57	6	6	100	11	1	4	—	30	7	2.8	0.3	1.0	7.5
NEW YORK NETS	**58-26 .690**				**KEVIN LOUGHERY**				lost to Kentucky 99-108 at Kentucky in playoff for first place.													
Larry Kenon	F	6'9	205	22	84	3165	676	1327	51	217	282	77	900	122	229	—	1570	38	10.7	1.5	2.7	18.7
Julius Erving	F-C	6'7	210	24	84	3402	**914**	1806	51	486	608	80	914	462	256	—	2343	41	10.9	5.5	3.0	27.9
Billy Paultz	C	6'11	245	26	80	2826	524	1080	49	214	286	75	772	179	273	—	1262	35	9.7	2.2	3.4	15.8
Brian Taylor	G	6'2	185	23	79	2611	472	920	51	150	196	77	232	282	216	—	1104	33	2.9	3.6	2.7	14.0
John Williamson	G	6'2	185	22	75	1872	370	768	48	123	147	84	149	197	188	—	866	25	2.0	2.6	2.5	11.5
Mike Gale	G-F	6'4	190	24	72	1624	228	492	46	72	91	79	236	165	131	—	535	23	3.3	2.3	1.8	7.4
Bill Melchionni	G	6'1	170	30	77	1384	201	413	49	62	78	79	75	320	105	—	472	18	1.0	4.2	1.4	6.1
Willie Sojourner	C	6'8	235	26	79	1020	155	324	48	49	70	70	275	42	190	—	360	13	3.5	0.5	2.4	4.6
Ed Manning	F	6'7	215	30	70	992	103	243	42	35	42	83	212	58	144	—	241	14	3.0	0.8	2.1	3.4
Al Skinner	G	6'4	190	22	51	773	130	266	49	72	94	77	120	121	111	—	333	15	2.4	2.4	2.2	6.5
Wendell Ladner (knee injury)	F	6'5	220	26	25	436	45	173	26	6	10	60	68	39	68	—	103	17	2.7	1.6	2.7	4.1
Billy Schaeffer	F	6'5	200	22	27	280	61	131	47	15	25	60	37	20	36	—	139	10	1.4	0.7	1.3	5.1
SPIRITS OF ST. LOUIS	**32-52 .381**				**BOB MacKINNON**																	
Gus Gerard	F	6'8	200	21	84	2702	554	1220	45	206	279	74	655	189	274	—	1315	32	7.8	2.3	3.3	15.7
Marvin Barnes	F-C	6'9	225	22	77	3076	777	1561	50	295	440	67	1202	250	328	—	1849	40	15.6	3.2	**4.3**	24.0
Maurice Lucas	C-F	6'9	220	22	80	2464	438	937	47	180	229	79	816	287	301	—	1058	31	10.2	3.6	3.8	13.2
Steve Jones	G	6'5	210	32	69	1884	287	654	44	171	206	83	194	197	131	—	749	27	2.8	2.9	1.9	10.9
Freddie Lewis (from Mem)	G	6'	180	31	63	2563	534	1121	48	340	405	84	245	348	152	—	1425	41	3.9	5.5	2.4	22.6
Goo Kennedy	F	6'6	205	25	74	1532	281	536	52	129	178	72	373	59	190	—	692	21	5.0	0.8	2.6	9.4
Mike Barr	G	6'3	180	24	54	1341	136	269	51	28	41	68	95	176	117	—	300	25	1.8	3.3	2.2	5.6
Fly Williams	G-F	6'5	200	21	71	1239	297	643	46	69	101	68	181	142	156	—	665	17	2.5	2.0	2.2	9.4
Joe Caldwell (ST)	F	6'5	205	33	25	841	161	326	49	39	87	45	111	128	78	—	364	34	4.4	5.1	3.1	14.6
Jim Foster	G	6'1	180	22	41	806	78	209	37	27	34	79	75	143	118	—	183	20	1.8	3.5	2.9	4.5
Terry Driscoll (from Mil-NBA)	F	6'7	215	27	30	351	46	122	38	20	27	74	88	32	51	—	112	12	2.9	1.1	1.7	3.7
Tom Ingelsby	G	6'3	185	23	22	344	44	90	49	20	27	74	50	38	19	—	109	16	2.3	1.7	0.9	5.0
Don Adams (from Det-NBA)	F	6'7	220	27	16	342	42	98	43	17	22	77	68	54	38	—	101	21	4.3	3.4	2.4	6.3
Bernie Fryer (to NO-NBA)	G	6'3	185	25	9	264	24	68	35	22	28	79	22	25	28	—	70	29	2.4	2.8	3.1	7.8
Dennis Wuycik	F	6'6	215	24	25	219	34	74	46	11	19	58	38	18	40	—	79	9	1.5	0.7	1.6	3.2
Gene Moore	C	6'9	245	29	13	108	13	32	41	4	4	100	42	5	11	—	30	8	3.2	0.4	0.8	2.3
Milt Williams	G	6'2	185	29	4	95	11	19	58	0	0	—	13	12	10	—	22	24	3.3	3.0	2.5	5.5
Tom Owens (to Mem)	C	6'10	223	25	5	89	14	26	54	5	9	56	26	7	9	—	33	18	5.2	1.4	1.8	6.6
MEMPHIS SOUNDS	**27-57 .321**				**JOE MULLANEY**																	
George Carter	F-G	6'5	218	30	82	3066	690	1354	44	318	400	80	581	255	276	—	1508	37	7.1	3.1	3.4	18.4
Stew Johnson (from SD)	F	6'8	225	30	72	2559	592	1323	45	59	81	73	442	120	199	—	1280	36	6.1	1.7	2.8	17.8
Tom Owens (from StL)	C-F	6'10	223	25	77	2558	497	943	53	212	280	76	879	201	252	—	1206	33	11.4	2.6	3.3	15.7
Rick Mount (SJ)	G	6'4	185	27	26	895	181	431	42	63	73	86	51	79	44	—	445	34	2.0	3.0	1.7	17.1
Chuck Williams	G	6'2	175	28	81	3171	476	963	49	212	260	82	220	**576**	165	—	1174	39	2.7	7.1	2.0	14.5
Larry Finch	G	6'2	195	23	63	1888	264	593	45	115	133	86	143	190	164	—	663	30	2.3	3.0	2.6	10.5
Collis Jones	F	6'7	205	25	81	1880	333	702	47	134	177	76	369	81	186	—	805	23	4.6	1.0	2.3	9.9
Mel Daniels (injury)	C	6'9	225	30	71	1646	290	644	45	116	183	63	638	125	248	—	696	23	9.0	1.8	3.5	9.8
Billy Shepherd	G	5'10	165	25	69	1315	161	386	42	52	72	72	79	278	68	—	434	19	1.1	4.0	1.0	6.3
Jim O'Brien	F	6'7	200	23	47	611	88	203	43	47	60	78	121	81	56	—	229	13	2.6	1.7	1.2	4.9
Julius Keye	F-C	6'10	225	28	12	233	12	47	26	6	8	75	55	2	26	—	30	19	4.6	0.2	2.2	2.5
Freddie Lewis (to StL)	G	6'	180	31	6	227	45	111	41	15	16	94	20	19	9	—	106	38	3.3	3.2	1.5	17.7
Roger Brown (to Utah, Ind)	F	6'5	210	32	7	209	30	82	37	14	16	88	31	21	12	—	82	30	4.4	3.0	1.7	11.7
Ronnie Robinson	F	6'8	220	22	10	102	18	38	47	4	6	67	27	4	14	—	40	10	2.7	0.4	1.4	4.0

Use Name	Pos	Hgt	Wgt	Age	TOTAL G	Min	FG	FGA	%	FT	FTA	%	Reb	Ass	PF	DQ	Points	PER GAME Min	Reb	Ass	PF	Points
1974/75 A.B.A. — EASTERN DIVISION (continued)																						
VIRGINIA SQUIRES	**15-69 .169**				**AL BIANCHI**																	
Red Robbins (from Ky)	F	6'8	200	30	53	1748	295	618	48	156	181	86	404	113	102	—	749	33	7.6	2.1	1.9	14.1
Willie Wise (from Utah-HO)	F	6'6	215	27	16	574	128	296	43	77	111	69	102	54	50	—	334	36	6.4	3.4	3.1	20.9
David Vaughn	C	7'	220	22	83	2507	422	998	42	125	229	55	894	132	274	—	969	30	10.8	1.6	3.3	11.
Darrell Elston (injury)	G	6'4	190	22	72	1869	250	613	41	93	123	76	163	202	166	—	596	26	2.3	2.8	2.3	8.3
Dave Twardzik	G	6'1	180	24	76	2679	359	657	55	317	384	83	247	404	238	—	1036	35	3.3	5.3	3.1	13.
Mike Jackson	F	6'7	230	25	82	2023	382	724	53	232	295	79	457	82	308	—	997	25	5.6	1.0	3.8	12.2
Barry Parkhill	G	6'4	185	23	78	1870	266	638	42	75	100	75	133	226	228	—	607	24	1.7	2.9	2.9	7.8
George Irvine (injury)	F	6'6	200	26	59	1522	311	589	53	139	164	85	203	108	171	—	774	26	3.4	1.8	2.9	13.1
Lloyd Batts	G-F	6'4	185	23	58	1317	249	680	37	58	94	62	197	106	104	—	598	23	3.4	1.8	1.8	10.3
Cincy Powell	F	6'7	227	32	60	1224	214	530	40	119	180	66	206	94	138	—	552	20	3.4	1.6	2.3	9.2
Llonel Billingy	F-C	6'9	215	22	46	1022	150	351	43	93	143	65	280	49	112	—	393	22	6.1	1.1	2.4	8.5
Lamar Green (from NO-NBA)	C	6'7	220	27	51	856	115	270	43	40	54	74	255	47	139	—	270	17	5.0	0.9	2.7	5.3
Aulcie Perry	C	6'10	210	24	21	415	81	186	44	19	30	63	105	20	58	—	181	20	5.0	1.0	2.8	8.6
Bill Higgins	G	6'2	180	22	15	348	61	139	44	15	23	65	21	32	41	—	138	23	1.4	2.1	2.7	9.2
Glen Combs (knee injury)	G	6'2	185	28	13	190	23	67	34	24	27	89	11	23	13	—	76	15	0.8	1.8	1.0	5.8
Johnny Neumann (to Ind)	F	6'6	200	23	4	96	22	67	33	3	8	38	11	12	13	—	47	24	2.8	3.0	3.3	11.8
1974/75 A.B.A. — WESTERN DIVISION																						
DENVER NUGGETS	**65-19 .774**				**LARRY BROWN**																	
Bobby Jones	F	6'9	215	23	84	2706	529	876	**60**	187	269	70	692	303	263	—	1245	32	8.2	3.6	3.1	14.8
Byron Beck	F-C	6'9	230	29	84	1818	384	745	52	81	97	84	343	106	270	—	849	22	4.1	1.3	3.2	10.1
Mike Green	C-F	6'10	210	23	81	2557	593	1095	54	225	305	74	749	101	271	—	1411	32	9.2	1.2	3.3	17.4
Ralph Simpson	G	6'5	200	25	82	2863	694	1374	51	303	402	75	391	442	214	—	1692	35	4.8	5.4	2.6	20.6
Mack Calvin	G	6'	175	26	74	2463	483	996	48	475	530	**90**	210	570	206	—	1444	33	2.8	**7.7**	2.8	19.5
Fatty Taylor	G	6'	175	28	76	2018	251	586	43	129	172	75	221	337	238	—	637	27	2.9	4.4	3.1	8.4
Dave Robisch	C	6'10	240	25	84	1899	392	779	50	304	346	88	503	153	205	—	1088	23	6.0	1.8	2.4	13.0
Jan Van Breda Kolff	F	6'7	200	23	84	1639	155	342	45	177	211	84	358	181	164	—	487	20	4.3	2.2	2.0	5.8
Claude Terry	G-F	6'4	195	24	70	989	193	364	53	70	92	76	140	111	82	—	466	14	2.0	1.6	1.2	6.7
Pat McFarland	F-G	6'5	185	23	70	945	200	424	47	52	66	79	120	116	60	—	454	14	1.7	1.7	0.9	6.5
Don Washington	F	6'8	210	22	50	438	79	183	43	38	56	68	89	30	92	—	196	9	1.8	0.6	1.8	3.9
SAN ANTONIO SPURS	**51-33 .607**				**TOM NISSALKE (18-10 .643), BOB BASS (33-23 .589)**																	
George Gervin	F	6'7	180	22	84	3113	784	1655	47	380	458	83	697	207	295	—	1965	37	8.3	2.5	3.5	23.4
Rich Jones	F	6'8	230	28	83	3097	649	1480	44	287	374	77	645	270	297	—	1598	37	7.8	3.3	3.6	19.3
Swen Nater	C	6'11	250	24	78	2713	495	914	54	185	246	75	1279	97	240	—	1175	35	**16.4**	1.2	3.1	15.1
Donnie Freeman	G	6'3	185	30	77	2381	453	1012	45	289	352	82	184	202	169	—	1195	31	2.4	2.6	2.2	15.5
James Silas	G	6'3	185	25	82	3105	578	1136	51	430	486	88	310	398	232	—	1586	38	3.8	4.9	2.8	19.3
Coby Dietrick	C-F	6'10	230	26	82	1724	222	444	50	76	99	77	524	168	266	—	522	21	6.4	2.0	3.2	6.4
George Karl	G	6'2	185	23	82	1629	261	534	49	137	177	77	155	334	207	—	663	20	1.9	4.1	2.5	8.1
Chuck Terry	F	6'6	215	24	79	1186	148	313	47	39	53	74	217	69	146	—	338	15	2.7	0.9	1.8	4.3
Bobby Warren	G	6'5	195	28	71	992	127	265	48	77	91	85	112	91	109	—	333	14	1.6	1.3	1.5	4.7
Will Franklin	F	6'7	225	25	24	179	32	85	38	15	23	65	82	10	37	—	79	7	3.4	0.4	1.5	3.3
Collis Temple	F	6'8	225	22	24	102	17	41	41	8	10	80	31	15	29	—	42	4	1.3	0.6	1.2	1.8
Stan Love (from LA-NBA)	F	6'9	215	25	12	64	13	30	43	3	4	75	24	9	16	—	29	5	2.0	0.8	1.3	2.4
INDIANA PACERS	**45-39 .536**				**BOB LEONARD**																	
Billy Knight	F	6'6	200	22	80	2559	580	1087	53	207	259	80	632	168	194	—	1371	32	7.9	2.1	2.4	17.1
George McGinnis	F	6'8	235	24	79	3193	873	**1934**	45	**545**	**753**	72	1126	495	303	—	**2353**	40	14.3	6.3	3.8	**29.8**
Darnell Hillman	C-F	6'9	215	25	81	2603	486	923	53	152	202	75	747	131	330	—	1124	32	9.2	1.6	4.1	13.9
Don Buse	G	6'4	195	24	80	2369	216	500	43	47	59	80	272	335	149	—	517	30	3.4	4.2	1.9	6.5
Kevin Joyce	G	6'3	190	23	81	2828	530	1245	43	142	180	79	163	322	259	—	1210	35	2.0	4.0	3.2	14.9
Bill Keller	G	5'10	185	27	79	1918	397	908	44	113	128	88	211	204	101	—	987	24	2.7	2.6	1.3	12.5
Len Elmore	C	6'9	230	22	77	1414	218	523	42	72	93	77	395	35	241	—	509	18	5.1	0.5	3.1	6.6
Charlie Edge	F	6'6	210	24	77	1142	195	386	51	63	114	55	340	39	103	—	453	15	4.4	0.5	1.3	5.9
Bob Netolicky	C	6'9	225	32	59	1077	189	375	50	62	98	63	231	49	108	—	442	18	3.9	0.8	1.8	7.5
Johnny Neumann (from Va)	G-F	6'6	200	23	48	835	164	378	43	49	67	73	78	123	118	—	398	17	1.6	2.6	2.5	8.3
Wayne Pack	G	6'	165	24	21	189	23	60	38	10	12	83	20	13	21	—	61	9	1.0	0.6	1.0	2.9
Roger Brown (from Mem, Utah)	F	6'5	210	32	10	133	20	46	43	3	4	75	23	13	19	—	46	13	2.3	1.3	1.9	4.6

Use Name	Pos	Hgt	Wgt	Age	TOTAL G	Min	FG	FGA	%	FT	FTA	%	Reb	Ass	PF	DQ	Points	PER GAME Min	Reb	Ass	PF	Points
1974/75 A.B.A. — WESTERN DIVISION (continued)																						
UTAH STARS	**38-46 .452**				**BUCKY BUCKWALTER (24-32 .429), TOM NISSALKE (14-14 .500)**																	
Gerald Govan	F	6'10	220	32	84	2791	239	602	40	83	105	79	601	230	217	—	562	33	7.2	2.7	2.6	6.7
Moses Malone	F-C	6'10	215	19	83	3205	591	1035	57	375	591	63	1209	82	288	—	1557	39	14.6	1.0	3.5	18.8
Jim Eakins	C	6'11	215	28	84	2556	380	756	50	291	348	84	604	146	259	—	1051	30	7.2	1.7	3.1	12.5
Ron Boone	G-F	6'2	200	28	84	3414	872	1776	49	363	422	86	406	372	265	—	2117	41	4.8	4.4	3.2	25.2
Johnny Roche (from KY)	G	6 3	170	25	39	1129	212	430	49	70	88	80	84	157	80	—	506	29	2.2	4.0	2.1	13.0
Al Smith	G	6'1	185	27	80	2037	227	582	39	157	193	81	147	375	230	—	641	25	1.8	4.7	2.9	8.0
Randy Denton	C-F	6'10	245	25	75	1482	300	597	50	92	120	77	473	90	176	—	692	20	6.3	1.2	2.3	9.2
Wali Jones	G	6'2	185	32	71	1339	212	524	40	102	124	82	77	152	147	—	532	19	1.1	2.1	2.1	7.5
Roger Brown (from Mem, to Ind)	F	6'5	210	32	39	930	131	293	45	72	94	77	118	80	68	—	358	24	3.0	2.1	1.7	9.2
Clyde Dickey	G	6'3	185	22	58	472	71	203	35	16	21	76	61	47	46	—	160	8	1.1	0.8	0.8	2.8
Hank Williams	F	6'6	215	22	39	454	71	163	44	18	23	78	89	25	73	—	163	12	2.3	0.6	1.9	4.2
Bruce Seals	F	6'9	210	21	35	371	60	142	42	20	26	77	97	13	67	—	140	11	2.8	0.4	1.9	4.0
Roy McPipe	G	6'3	205	24	5	44	8	24	33	3	4	75	5	1	5	—	21	9	1.0	0.2	1.0	4.2
Larry Miller	G	6'4	210	28	5	26	3	9	33	3	3	100	1	4	0	—	9	5	0.2	0.8	0.0	1.8
Willie Wise (holdout, to Virginia)																						
SAN DIEGO CONQUISTADORS	**31-53 .36**				**ALEX GROZA (15-23 .395), BERYL SHIPLEY (16-30 .348)**																	
Travis Grant (knee injury)	F	6'8	225	24	53	1998	576	1058	54	182	218	83	328	98	160	—	1335	38	6.2	1.8	3.0	25.2
Tim Bassett	F-C	6'8	230	23	72	1998	244	518	47	82	146	56	526	117	159	—	573	28	7.3	1.6	2.2	8.0
Caldwell Jones	C	6'11	225	24	76	3004	606	1240	49	264	335	79	1074	162	269	—	1479	40	14.1	2.1	3.5	19.5
Warren Jabali	G	6'2	210	28	62	1861	254	648	39	179	227	79	257	358	188	—	749	30	4.1	5.8	3.0	12.1
Bo Lamar	G	6'1	180	23	77	2917	667	1571	42	247	315	78	239	427	150	—	1606	38	3.1	5.5	1.9	20.9
Jimmy O'Brien	G	6'2	180	24	79	2036	210	525	40	125	142	88	186	443	147	—	549	26	2.4	5.6	1.9	6.9
Lee Davis	C-F	6'8	240	29	75	1838	387	733	53	113	169	67	492	110	179	—	891	25	6.6	1.5	2.4	11.9
George Adams	F	6'6	210	25	75	1605	310	622	50	73	86	85	327	126	164	—	694	21	4.4	1.7	2.2	9.3
Scott English	F	6'4	190	28	71	1316	210	494	43	69	89	78	363	88	115	—	490	19	5.1	1.2	1.6	6.9
Billy Harris	G	6'2	185	23	76	1221	264	664	40	65	96	68	122	111	166	—	609	16	1.6	1.5	2.2	8.0
Stew Johnson (to Mem)	F	6'8	225	30	19	253	72	170	42	4	5	80	51	18	29	—	151	13	2.7	0.9	1.5	7.9
Bob Nash	F	6'8	205	24	17	175	27	78	35	13	18	72	55	12	30	—	67	10	3.2	0.7	1.8	3.9
Hambone Williams	G	6'2	190	35	7	89	8	12	67	0	0	—	12	20	15	—	16	13	1.7	2.9	2.1	2.3
Greg Lee	G	6'3	190	22	5	63	8	15	53	2	2	100	3	13	6	—	18	13	0.6	2.6	1.2	3.6
Reggie Royals	C	6'10	200	24	2	11	2	4	50	0	0	—	0	0	1	—	4	6	0.0	0.0	0.5	2.0
1974/75 A.B.A. — PLAYOFFS																						
KENTUCKY COLONELS	**HUBIE BROWN**				defeated Memphis 4-1; H98-91, H119-105, 101-80, 93-107, H111-99; defeated St. Louis 4-1; H112-109, H108-103, 97-103, 117-98, H123-103; defeated Indiana 4-1; H120-94, H95-93, 109-101, 86-94, H110-105																	
Wil Jones	F	6'8	205	27	15	454	62	142	44	19	24	79	100	48	60	—	143	30	6.7	3.2	4.0	9.5
Dan Issel	F-C	6'9	240	26	15	578	122	261	47	60	74	81	119	29	51	—	304	39	7.9	1.9	3.4	20.3
Artis Gilmore	C	7'2	240	25	15	679	132	245	54	98	127	77	264	38	59	—	362	45	**17.6**	2.5	3.9	24.1
Ted McClain	G	6'3	180	27	15	544	74	177	42	32	41	78	83	87	54	—	180	36	5.5	5.8	3.6	12.0
Louie Dampier	G	6'	180	30	15	604	108	212	51	33	38	87	36	113	34	—	254	40	2.4	7.5	2.3	16.9
Bird Averin	G	6'1	175	22	14	265	56	154	36	25	31	81	22	30	32	—	138	19	1.6	2.1	2.3	9.9
Marv Roberts	F	6'8	205	24	15	259	60	115	52	31	41	76	54	23	29	—	151	17	3.6	1.5	1.9	10.1
Ron Thomas	F	6'6	215	24	15	167	25	42	60	12	16	75	56	11	25	—	62	11	3.7	0.7	1.7	4.1
Gene Littles	G	6'1	175	31	8	30	2	9	22	0	0	—	5	4	0	—	4	4	0.6	0.5	0.0	0.5
Jim Bradley	F	6'9	215	22	4	20	0	7	0	1	2	50	7	3	3	—	1	5	1.8	0.8	0.8	0.3
INDIANA PACERS	**BOB LEONARD**				defeated San Antonio 4-2; 122-119, 98-93, H113-103, H109-110, 117-123, H115-100; defeated Denver 4-3; 128-131, 131-124, H118-112, H109-126, 109-90, H99-104, 104-96; lost to Kentucky 1-4; 94-120, 93-95, H101-109, H94-86, 105-110																	
Billy Knight	F-G	6'6	200	22	18	**763**	176	310	57	82	97	85	160	43	45	—	434	42	8.9	2.4	2.5	24.1
George McGinnis	F	6'8	235	24	18	731	**213**	**455**	47	**132**	**192**	69	**286**	**148**	**88**	—	**581**	41	15.9	8.2	**4.9**	32.3
Len Elmore	C	6'9	230	22	18	565	83	190	44	25	37	68	145	16	74	—	191	31	8.1	0.9	4.1	10.6
Don Buse	G	6'4	195	24	18	576	39	103	38	16	30	53	58	80	42	—	100	32	3.2	4.4	2.3	5.6
Kevin Joyce	G	6'3	190	23	18	593	88	211	42	32	41	78	31	45	55	—	213	33	1.7	2.5	3.1	11.8
Darnell Hillman	C-F	6'9	215	25	17	482	73	146	50	35	51	69	133	14	68	—	181	28	7.8	0.8	4.0	10.6
Bill Keller	G	5'10	185	27	17	405	68	162	42	30	30	**100**	24	29	24	—	183	24	1.4	1.7	1.4	10.8
Roger Brown	F	6'5	210	32	14	182	22	52	42	16	19	84	26	21	24	—	62	13	1.9	1.5	1.7	4.4
Charlie Edge	F	6'6	210	24	7	42	2	8	25	0	0	—	9	2	6	—	4	6	1.3	0.3	0.9	0.6
Bob Netolicky	C	6'9	225	32	7	31	3	8	38	4	4	100	5	1	7	—	10	4	0.7	0.1	1.0	1.4
DENVER NUGGETS	**LARRY BROWN**				defeated Utah 4-2; H122-107, H126-120, 108-122, 111-32, H130-119, 115-113; lost to Indiana 3-4, H131-128, H124-131, 112-118, 126-109, H90-109, 104-99, H96-104																	
Bobby Jones	F	6'9	215	23	13	428	69	129	53	31	40	78	111	38	49	—	169	33	8.5	2.9	3.8	13.0
Byron Beck	F	6'9	230	29	13	278	69	134	51	24	28	86	50	18	44	—	162	21	3.8	1.4	3.4	12.5
Mike Green	C-F	6'10	210	23	13	487	112	226	50	53	60	88	121	14	51	—	277	37	9.3	1.1	3.9	21.3
Ralph Simpson	G	6'5	200	25	13	471	102	214	48	53	68	78	65	74	30	—	258	36	5.0	5.7	2.3	19.8
Mack Calvin	G	6'	175	26	13	444	76	163	47	78	82	95	41	68	50	—	233	34	3.2	5.2	3.8	17.9
Dave Robisch	C-F	6'10	240	25	13	354	73	151	48	46	53	87	75	22	31	—	192	27	5.8	1.7	2.4	14.8
Fatty Taylor	G	6'	175	28	13	275	29	64	45	15	19	79	38	37	36	—	73	21	2.9	2.8	2.8	5.6
Jan Van Breda Kolff	F	6'7	200	23	12	192	17	40	43	29	31	94	40	15	27	—	63	16	3.3	1.3	2.3	5.3
Claude Terry	F-G	6'4	195	24	12	135	23	58	40	3	5	60	13	13	18	—	50	11	1.1	1.1	1.5	4.2
Pat McFarland	F-G	6'5	185	23	5	30	2	8	25	2	2	100	3	2	3	—	6	6	0.6	0.4	0.6	1.2
Don Washington	F	6'8	210	22	4	26	5	10	50	1	1	100	6	2	9	—	11	7	1.5	0.5	2.3	2.8

1974/75 A.B.A. — PLAYOFFS (continued)

Use Name	Pos	Hgt	Wgt	Age	G	Min	FG	FGA	%	FT	FTA	%	Reb	Ass	PF	DQ	Points	Min	Reb	Ass	PF	Points
					TOTAL													PER GAME				
SPIRITS OF ST. LOUIS	**BOB MacKINNON**				defeated New York 4-1; 105-111, 115-97, H113-108, H100-89, 108-107																	
					lost to Kentucky 1-4; 109-112, 103-108, H103-108, H103-97, H98-117, 103-123																	
Don Adams	F	6'7	220	27	10	301	35	82	43	20	28	71	47	46	32	—	90	30	4.7	4.6	3.2	9.
Marvin Barnes	F-C	6'9	225	22	10	444	124	249	50	60	77	78	141	16	45	—	308	44	14.1	1.6	4.5	30.
Maurice Lucas	C	6'9	220	22	10	375	68	153	44	27	41	66	147	50	44	—	163	38	14.7	5.0	4.4	16.
Mike Barr	G	6'3	180	24	10	369	33	66	50	7	11	64	36	44	38	—	74	37	3.6	4.4	3.8	7.
Freddie Lewis	G	6'	180	31	9	403	85	176	48	60	73	82	46	26	18	—	236	45	5.1	2.9	2.0	26.
Gus Gerard	F	6'8	200	21	10	268	37	87	43	9	14	64	50	16	32	—	83	27	5.0	1.6	3.2	8.
Steve Jones	G	6'5	210	32	6	128	22	45	49	11	17	65	14	14	15	—	55	21	2.3	2.3	2.5	9.
Jim Foster	G	6'1	180	22	7	52	6	16	38	4	8	50	6	6	9	—	16	7	0.9	0.9	1.3	2.
Goo Kennedy	F	6'6	205	25	8	47	9	22	41	10	14	71	18	1	8	—	28	6	2.3	0.1	1.0	3.
Fly Williams	G	6'5	200	21	2	8	1	5	20	0	0	—	1	0	2	—	2	4	0.5	0.0	1.0	1.
Gene Moore	C	6'9	245	29	2	5	1	3	33	0	0	—	1	0	2	—	2	3	0.5	0.0	1.0	1.
UTAH STARS	**TOM NISSALKE**				lost to Denver 2-4; 107-122, 120-126, H122-108, H122-110, 119-130, H113-115																	
Moses Malone	F	6'10	215	19	6	235	51	80	64	34	51	67	105	9	21	—	136	39	17.5	1.5	3.5	22.
Randy Denton	F-C	6'10	245	25	6	236	49	92	53	15	22	68	80	11	18	—	113	39	13.3	1.8	3.0	18.
Jim Eakins	C	6'11	215	28	6	194	35	55	64	11	12	92	37	7	28	—	81	32	6.2	1.2	4.7	13.
Ron Boone	G-F	6'2	200	28	6	219	54	127	43	34	38	89	24	41	22	—	142	37	4.0	6.8	3.7	23.
Johnny Roche	G	6'3	170	25	6	196	41	82	50	13	15	87	15	43	16	—	103	33	2.5	7.2	2.7	17.
Al Smith	G	6'1	185	27	6	165	32	73	44	17	20	85	12	35	24	—	84	28	2.0	5.8	4.0	14.
Gerald Govan	F	6'10	220	32	6	97	1	12	8	2	5	40	14	8	17	—	4	16	2.3	1.3	2.8	0.
Wali Jones	G	6'2	185	32	5	46	8	21	38	6	6	100	2	4	6	—	22	9	0.4	0.8	1.2	4.
Bruce Seals	F	6'9	210	21	3	41	9	14	64	6	9	67	11	0	8	—	24	14	3.7	0.0	2.7	8.
Hank Williams	F	6'6	215	22	2	7	2	6	33	0	0	—	2	0	2	—	4	4	1.0	0.0	1.0	2.
Clyde Dickey	G	6'3	185	22	1	4	0	2	0	0	0	—	1	0	0	—	0	4	1.0	0.0	0.0	0.
SAN ANTONIO SPURS	**BOB BASS**				lost to Indiana 2-4; H119-122, H93-98, 103-113, 110-109, H123-117, 100-115																	
Geone Gervin	F-G	6'7	180	22	6	276	79	171	46	43	52	83	84	8	22	—	204	**46**	14.0	1.3	3.7	**34.0**
Rich Jones	F	6'8	230	28	6	178	30	87	34	2	7	29	45	15	25	—	63	30	7.5	2.5	4.2	10.5
Swen Nater	C	6'11	250	24	6	234	40	84	48	9	21	43	99	6	18	—	89	39	16.5	1.0	3.0	14.8
Donnie Freeman	G	6'3	185	30	6	166	33	72	46	8	10	80	14	19	16	—	74	28	2.3	3.2	2.7	12.3
James Silas	G	6'3	185	25	6	271	41	87	47	31	40	78	18	60	27	—	113	45	3.0	**10.0**	4.5	18.8
Coby Dietrick	F-C	6'10	230	26	6	187	30	49	61	9	11	82	40	22	26	—	69	31	6.7	3.7	4.3	11.5
Chuck Terry	F	6'6	215	24	5	123	12	25	48	3	4	75	19	2	14	—	27	25	3.8	0.4	2.8	5.4
George Karl	G	6'2	185	23	4	40	1	8	13	3	4	75	3	5	5	—	5	10	0.8	1.3	1.3	1.3
Will Franklin	F	6'7	225	25	2	10	2	5	40	0	0	—	5	0	2	—	4	5	2.5	0.0	1.0	2.0
Bobby Warren	G	6'5	195	28	1	5	0	1	0	0	0	—	0	0	0	—	0	5	0.0	0.0	0.0	0.0
NEW YORK NETS	**KEVIN LOUGHERY**				lost to St. Louis 1-4; H111-105, H97-115, 108-113, 89-100, H107-108																	
Larry Kenon	F	6'9	205	22	5	199	47	88	53	13	17	76	64	5	17	—	107	40	12.8	1.0	3.4	21.4
Julius Erving	F	6'7	210	24	5	211	55	121	45	27	32	84	49	28	18	—	137	42	9.8	5.6	3.6	27.4
Billy Paultz	C	6'11	245	26	5	178	29	59	49	12	15	80	45	11	18	—	70	36	9.0	2.2	3.6	14.0
Brian Taylor	G	6'2	185	23	5	186	13	36	36	4	4	100	12	14	21	—	31	37	2.4	2.8	4.2	6.2
John Williamson	G	6'2	185	22	5	118	26	43	60	8	13	62	10	10	21	—	60	24	2.0	2.0	4.2	12.0
Bill Melchionni	G	6'1	170	30	5	108	14	39	36	5	7	71	12	32	10	—	34	22	2.4	6.4	2.0	6.8
Mike Gale	G	6'4	190	24	3	73	9	19	47	3	6	50	5	7	7	—	23	24	1.7	2.3	2.3	7.7
Willie Sojourner	C	6'8	235	26	5	65	12	22	55	3	5	60	13	2	13	—	27	13	2.6	0.4	2.6	5.4
Wendell Ladner	F	6'5	220	26	3	35	5	23	22	0	0	—	5	0	10	—	13	12	1.7	0.0	3.3	4.3
Ed Manning	F	6'7	215	30	3	18	2	7	29	1	1	100	1	0	2	—	5	6	0.3	0.0	0.7	1.7
Al Skinner	F	6'4	190	22	1	9	1	2	50	3	4	75	2	0	1	—	5	9	2.0	0.0	1.0	5.0
MEMPHIS SOUNDS	**JOE MULLANEY**				lost to Kentucky 1-4; 91-98, 105-119, H80-101, H107-93, 99-111																	
Collis Jones	F	6'7	205	25	5	193	20	51	39	6	10	60	33	3	18	—	46	39	6.6	0.6	3.6	9.2
Stew Johnson	F	6'8	225	30	5	205	29	68	43	11	12	92	26	12	8	—	72	41	5.2	2.4	1.6	14.4
Tom Owens	C-F	6'10	223	25	5	207	48	87	55	13	19	68	62	10	20	—	109	41	12.4	2.0	4.0	21.8
George Carter	G-F	6'5	218	30	5	223	38	82	46	28	34	82	37	12	20	—	105	45	7.4	2.4	4.0	21.0
Chuck Williams	G	6'2	175	28	5	210	33	59	56	22	24	92	8	33	13	—	88	42	1.6	6.6	2.6	17.6
Billy Shepherd	G	5'10	165	25	5	75	10	30	33	6	6	100	5	12	3	—	29	15	1.0	2.4	0.6	5.8
Mel Daniels	C	6'9	225	30	4	54	11	22	50	5	9	56	24	1	12	—	27	14	6.0	0.3	3.0	6.8
Jim O'Brien	F	6'7	200	23	3	33	2	9	22	2	2	100	6	5	2	—	6	11	2.0	1.7	0.7	2.0

Team	W	L	Pct.	GB	Record against playoff teams W	L	Pct.	Record against non-playoff teams W	L	Pct.	HOME W	L	Pct.	ROAD W	L	Pct.
EASTERN DIVISION																
*Kentucky Colonels	58	26	.690	—	42	23	.646	16	3	.842	39	3	.929	19	23	.452
New York Nets	58	26	.690	—	41	24	.631	17	2	.895	35	7	.833	23	19	.548
Spirits ot St. Louis	32	52	.381	26	18	47	.277	14	5	.737	23	19	.548	9	33	.214
Memphis Sounds	27	57	.321	31	19	46	.292	8	11	.421	17	25	.405	10	32	.238
Virginia Squires	15	69	.179	43	12	64	.158	3	5	.375	11	31	.262	4	38	.095
WESTERN DIVISION																
Denver Nuggets	65	19	.774	—	47	18	.723	18	1	.947	40	2	.952	25	17	.595
San Antonio Spurs	51	33	.607	14	33	32	.508	18	1	.947	32	10	.762	19	23	.452
Indiana Pacers	45	39	.536	20	33	32	.508	12	7	.632	31	11	.738	14	28	.333
Utah Stars	38	46	.452	27	27	38	.415	11	8	.579	29	13	.690	9	33	.214
San Diego Conquistadors	31	53	.369	34	26	50	.342	5	3	.625	22	20	.524	9	33	.214

*defeated New York in one game playoff

1974/75 A.B.A. INDIVIDUAL LEADERS

SCORING
(Minimum 1000 Points)

Name	Team	G	FG	FT	Pts.	Avg.
McGinnis	Ind	79	873	545	2353	29.8
Erving	NY	84	914	486	2343	27.9
Boone	Utah	84	872	363	2117	25.2
Grant	SD	53	576	182	1335	25.2
Barnes	StL	77	777	295	1849	24.0
Gilmore	KY	84	784	412	1981	23.6
Gervin	SA	84	784	380	1965	23.4
Lewis	Mem-StL	69	579	355	1531	22.2
Lamar	SD	77	667	247	1606	20.9
Simpson	Den	82	694	303	1692	20.6

TOTAL FIELD GOAL PERCENTAGE
(Minimum 300 Made)

Name	Team	FG	FGA	Pct.
Jones	Den	529	876	.604
Gilmore	KY	784	1351	.580
Malone	Utah	591	1035	.571
Twardzik	Va	359	657	.546
Grant	SD	576	1058	.544
Green	Den	593	1095	.542
Nater	SA	495	914	.542
Knight	Ind	580	1087	.534
Irvine	Va	311	589	.528
Davis	SD	387	733	.528

3-POINT FIELD GOAL PERCENTAGE
(Minimum 27 Made)

Name	Team	FG	FGA	Pct.
Shepherd	Mem	60	143	.420
Dampier	KY	38	96	.396
Smith	Utah	34	94	.362
McGinnis	Ind	62	175	.354
Brown	M-U-I	35	100	.350
Erving	NY	29	87	.333
Keller	Ind	80	240	.333
Jabali	SD	62	193	.321
Buse	Ind	38	123	.309
Johnson	SD-Mem	40	134	.299

FREE THROW PERCENTAGE
(Minimum 200 Made)

Name	Team	FT	FTA	Pct.
Calvin	Den	475	530	.896
Silas	SA	430	486	.885
Robisch	Den	304	346	.879
Boone	Utah	363	422	.860
Lewis	Mem-StL	355	421	.843
Eakins	Utah	291	348	.836
Gervin	SA	380	458	.830
Twardzik	Va	317	384	.826
Freeman	SA	289	352	.821
Williams	Mem	212	260	.815

REBOUNDS PER GAME
(Minimum 600 Rebounds)

Name	Team	G	Reb.	Avg.
Nater	SA	78	1279	16.4
Gilmore	KY	84	1361	16.2
Barnes	StL	77	1202	15.6
Malone	Utah	83	1209	14.6
McGinnis	Ind	79	1126	14.3
Jones	SD	75	1060	14.1
Owens	StL-Mem	82	905	11.0
Erving	NY	84	914	10.9
Vaughn	Va	83	894	10.8
Kenon	NY	84	900	10.7

ASSISTS PER GAME
(Minimum 250 Made)

Name	Team	G	Ass.	Avg.
Calvin	Den	74	570	7.7
Williams	Mem	81	576	7.1
McGinnis	Ind	79	495	6.3
Jabali	SD	62	358	5.8
Lamar	SD	77	427	5.5
O'Brien	SD	79	439	5.5
Erving	NY	84	462	5.5
Dampier	KY	83	449	5.4
Simpson	Den	82	442	5.4
Lewis	Mem-StL	69	367	5.3

BLOCKED SHOTS PER GAME
(Minimum 100)

Name	Team	G	Reb.	Avg.
Jones	SD	75	246	3.3
Gilmore	KY	84	258	3.1
Green	Den	81	174	2.1
Erving	NY	84	157	1.9
Jones	Den	84	153	1.8
Barnes	StL	77	137	1.8
Paultz	NY	80	137	1.7
Gervin	SA	84	138	1.6
Hillman	Ind	81	132	1.6
Malone	Utah	83	128	1.5

OFFENSIVE REBOUNDS PER GAME
(Minimum 70 Games Played)

Name	Team	G	Reb.	Avg.
Malone	Utah	83	455	5.5
Barnes	StL	77	419	5.4
Gilmore	KY	84	427	5.1
McGinnis	Ind	79	396	5.0
Nater	SA	78	369	4.7
Jones	SD	75	306	4.1
Hillman	Ind	81	296	3.7
Owens	StL-Mem	82	296	3.6
Knight	Ind	80	284	3.6
Lucas	StL	80	282	3.5

STEALS PER GAME
(Minimum 100)

Name	Team	G	Steals	Avg.
Taylor	NY	79	221	2.8
McGinnis	Ind	79	206	2.6
Taylor	Den	76	172	2.3
Erving	NY	84	186	2.2
Lewis	Mem-StL	69	147	2.1
Buse	Ind	80	166	2.1
Simpson	Den	82	166	2.0
Jones	Den	84	167	2.0
Calvin	Den	74	140	1.9
Jabali	SD	62	112	1.8

MINUTES PLAYED

Name	Team	Min.
Gilmore	Ky	3493
Boone	Utah	3414
Erving	NY	3402
Malone	Utah	3205
McGinnis	Ind	3193

PERSONAL FOULS

Name	Team	PF
Jones	KY	353
Hillman	Ind	330
Barnes	StL	328
Gilmore	KY	318
Jackson	Va	308

TEAM STATISTICS

EASTERN DIVISION

Team		REGULAR SEASON												PLAYOFFS											
		G	FG	FGA	%	FT	FTA	%	Reb.	Ass.	PF	Points	PPG	G	FG	FGA	%	FT	FTA	%	Reb.	Ass.	PF	Points	PPG
Kentucky	**Off.**	84	3733	7785	48	1631	2233	73	4289	2177	2017	9151	108.9	15	641	1364	47	311	394	79	746	386	347	1599	106.6
	Def.	84	**3425**	7687	**45**	1593	2012	79	3881	**1646**	2011	**8542**	**101.7**	15	**589**	**1302**	**45**	288	378	76	688	293	339	1485	**99.0**
	Diff.		+308	+98	+3	+38	+221	-6	+408	**+531**	-6	+609	+7.2		**+52**	**+62**	**+2**	+23	+16	+3	+58	+93	-8	+114	**+7.6**
New York	**Off.**	84	3879	7943	49	1501	1929	78	3990	2077	1947	9328	111.0	5	213	459	46	79	104	76	218	109	138	512	102.4
	Def.	84	3501	7726	45	1551	2022	77	4054	1813	1786	8685	103.4	5	213	444	48	110	144	76	254	113	112	541	108.2
	Diff.		**+378**	+217	+4	-50	-93	+1	-64	+264	-161	**+643**	**+7.6**		—	+15	-2	-31	-40	—	-36	-4	-26	-29	-5.8
St. Louis	**Off.**	84	3771	8005	47	1583	2136	74	**4294**	2111	2051	9156	109.0	10	421	904	47	208	283	73	507	219	245	1057	105.7
	Def.	84	3897	7952	49	1663	2166	77	3820	2276	1984	9522	113.4	10	428	913	47	204	270	76	467	239	255	1069	106.9
	Diff.		-126	+53	-2	-80	-30	-3	**+474**	-165	-67	-366	-4.4		-7	-9	—	+4	+13	-3	+40	-20	+10	-12	-1.2
Memphis	**Off.**	84	3577	7820	46	1367	1765	77	3656	2032	**1719**	8698	103.5	5	191	408	47	93	116	80	201	88	**96**	482	96.4
	Def.	84	3824	7773	49	**1429**	**1897**	75	4354	2212	1810	9149	108.9	5	218	435	50	**84**	**104**	81	222	128	106	522	104.4
	Diff.		-247	+47	-3	-62	-132	+2	-698	-180	+91	-451	-5.4		-27	-27	-3	+9	**+12**	-1	-21	-40	**+10**	-40	-8.0
Virginia	**Off.**	84	3328	7432	45	1585	2146	74	3689	1704	2160	8317	99.0												
	Def.	84	3635	**7582**	48	1864	2414	77	4070	1848	2045	9200	109.5												
	Diff.		-307	-150	-3	-279	-268	-3	-381	-144	-115	-883	-10.5												

WESTERN DIVISION

Team		G	FG	FGA	%	FT	FTA	%	Reb.	Ass.	PF	Points	PPG	G	FG	FGA	%	FT	FTA	%	Reb.	Ass.	PF	Points	PPG
Denver	**Off.**	84	**3953**	7764	**51**	**2041**	**2546**	80	3816	**2450**	2065	**9969**	**118.7**	13	577	1197	48	**335**	**389**	**86**	563	303	348	1494	114.9
	Def.	84	3809	8049	47	1629	2152	76	3803	2073	2128	9359	111.4	13	590	1201	49	297	386	77	625	325	332	1511	116.2
	Diff.		+144	-285	**+4**	**+412**	**+394**	+4	+13	+377	+63	+610	+7.3		-13	-4	-1	**+38**	+3	**+9**	-62	-22	-16	-17	-1.3
San Antonio	**Off.**	84	3779	7909	48	1926	2373	**81**	4260	1870	2043	9525	113.4	6	268	**595**	45	108	149	72	**327**	137	155	648	108.0
	Def.	84	3731	7909	47	1599	2129	**75**	3886	2082	**2157**	9173	109.2	6	269	574	47	116	170	**68**	321	**133**	153	674	112.3
	Diff.		+48	—	+1	+327	+244	**+6**	+374	-212	**+114**	+352	+4.2		-1	+21	-2	-8	-21	+4	+6	+4	-2	-26	-4.3
Indiana	**Off.**	84	3891	**8365**	47	1465	1969	74	4238	1927	1946	9471	112.8	18	767	1645	47	372	501	74	877	399	433	1959	108.8
	Def.	84	3831	7848	49	1644	2127	77	4194	2055	1906	9381	111.7	18	776	1703	46	388	475	82	919	426	455	1951	108.4
	Diff.		+60	**+517**	-2	-179	-158	-3	+44	-128	-40	+90	+1.1		-9	-58	+1	-16	+26	-8	-42	-27	+22	+8	+.4
Utah	**Off.**	84	3375	7136	47	1665	2162	77	3972	1774	1921	8509	101.3	6	**282**	564	**50**	138	178	78	303	**158**	162	713	**118.8**
	Def.	84	3503	7611	46	1549	2027	76	**3776**	1849	2029	8645	102.9	6	277	564	49	157	187	84	**246**	142	**172**	711	118.5
	Diff.		-128	-475	+1	+116	+135	+1	+196	-75	+108	-136	-1.6		+5	—	+1	-19	-9	-6	**+57**	**+16**	+10	+2	+.3
San Diego	**Off.**	84	3845	8352	46	1418	1848	77	4035	2103	1778	9231	109.9												
	Def.	84	3975	8374	47	1661	2161	77	4401	2101	1791	9699	115.5												
	Diff.		-130	-22	-1	-243	-313	-	-366	+2	+13	-468	-5.6												

1975-76 N.B.A.

Celtics Nose out Upstart Suns

The best player in the N.B.A. asked to be traded and got his wish. Kareem Abdul-Jabbar had played six seasons in Milwaukee. He had won three MVP awards, taken the Bucks to one championship, and made them perennial contenders. He decided, however, that he wanted to live either in New York, where he grew up, or in Los Angeles, where he attended college. The Bucks accommodated him in June of 1975 with a trade to the Lakers. The Bucks received center Elmore Smith, guard Brian Winters, and two rookies taken in the first round of the draft, forward David Meyers of UCLA and swingman Junior Bridgeman of Louisville. The four newcomers helped the Bucks rebound from last place to first in the Midwest Division.

Meanwhile, things did not go smoothly in Los Angeles or New York. With Kareem at center, the Lakers were expected to rise from last place to first in the Pacific Division. Kareem did post big numbers in scoring and rebounding and did win another MVP award. The Lakers, however, slumped in mid-season and were eliminated from the playoffs in the last week of the regular season.

The Knicks didn't even get that close to the playoffs. Walt Frazier and Earl Monroe still starred in the backcourt, but the Knicks were weak up front. Over the summer, they had signed star A.B.A. forward George McGinnis to a lucrative contract. N.B.A. Commissioner Larry O'Brien, who succeeded Walter Kennedy in that position last Spring, voided the contract because the Philadelphia '76ers held the draft rights to McGinnis. The Knicks did acquire forward Spencer Haywood from Seattle in October for a bundle of money, a move which bolstered the front line but did not prevent a last place finish in the Atlantic Division.

The best basketball was played up the coast from Los Angeles and New York, in mellower sites to the north. In Boston, the Celtics opened up a lead in the Atlantic Division after New Year's Day. Don Chaney had jumped to the A.B.A., but the Celtics reinforced the backcourt by trading Paul Westphal to Phoenix for Charlie Scott. Although the bench was thin, veterans John Havlicek, Dave Cowens, JoJo White, and Paul Silas kept the Celtic tradition alive for a fourteenth divisional title. The Buffalo Braves took second place on the strength of Bob McAdoo's third straight scoring title and Randy Smith's excellence at guard. Ernie DiGregorio lost playing time as the Braves adjusted poorly to his return from a knee injury. The '76ers tied Buffalo and also made the playoffs. They lost Billy Cunningham to a knee injury in December, but Doug Collins and newcomer McGinnis emerged as offensive weapons on a winning team.

A new champion reigned in the Central Division, as the Cleveland Cavaliers passed the Washington Bullets with a strong final month. Cleveland coach Bill Fitch blended a collection of role players into an effective half-court team with balanced scoring. The Bullets lost their divisional crown by losing eight of their final twelve games. The Bullets had added Dave Bing from Detroit to complement veteran stars Wes Unseld, Elvin Hayes, and Phil Chenier. Houston finished out of the playoffs despite a deep stock of scorers, as did New Orleans despite Pistol Pete Maravich's talents. The Atlanta Hawks failed to sign their two first-round draft picks and collapsed from March onwards.

None of the Midwest Division teams had a winning record. The Bucks squeezed past the Pistons by winning six of their final eight games. That hot stretch, however, raised Milwaukee's record only to 38-44. Bob Dandridge and Brian Winters took up the scoring slack left behind by Abdul-Jabbar. The Pistons were crippled by guard Kevin Porter's season-ending knee injury a month into the season. Without their newly-acquired playmaker, the Pistons could not use Bob Lanier and Curtis Rowe to best advantage. The Kansas City Kings dropped Omaha as a part-time home and disappointed high pre-season expectations despite Tiny Archibald's continued brilliance. The Chicago Bulls fell into a losing habit after Chet Walker retired and Jerry Sloan injured a knee.

In the Pacific Division, the Lakers did not blossom into instant champions with the arrival of Abdul-Jabbar. The Golden State Warriors defended last year's championship by winning the most games in the regular season. Rick Barry led the team in both scoring and assists, with Jamaal Wilkes complementing him at forward. The guard corps featured much-improved Phil Smith and rookie Gus Williams. Seattle and Phoenix finished far behind the Warriers but still earned playoff berths. Guards Slick Watts and Fred Brown were the heart of the Sonics. Phoenix improved as the season progressed, blending ex-Celtic guard Paul Westphal and rookie center Alvan Adams into a solid veteran cast. Last in the division were the Portland Trail Blazers cursed by a recurring series of injuries to Bill Walton.

In the playoffs, the Celtics beat Buffalo and Cleveland to advance to the championship series. In the west, Phoenix upset the Warriers in Oakland in game seven 94-86 to earn a shot at the Celtics and the title.

The championship series began on the parquet floor of the Boston Garden. In game one, the Suns suffered from a collective spell of bad shooting, as the Celtics won 98-87. Game two was more of the same, as the veteran Celtics beat the upstart Suns 105-90. Back in Arizona, however, the Suns beat the Celtics 105-98 in game three and 109-107 in game four.

The usual sell-out crowd of 15,320 filled the Boston Garden for the pivotal fifth game. They saw a marathon of endurance and luck. Down by five points with 55 seconds remaining, the Suns tied the game with Westphal's jumper, steal, basket, and foul shot. The Celtics and Suns played a five-minute overtime without breaking the tie. With five seconds left in the second overtime, Curtis Perry hit a long jump shot to put Phoenix ahead 110-109. The Celtics went to their clutch shooter, John Havlicek, who scored with two seconds left to put Boston ahead 111-110. When Phoenix took an illegal time-out, the Celtics converted a free throw to go ahead 112-110. The Suns then threw the ball in to Garfield Heard, who miraculously sunk a long prayer to send the game into a third overtime. Boston reserve Glenn McDonald scored six points in this final period to lead the Celtics to an exhausting 128-126 victory. When the teams reconvened in Phoenix, the Celtics ground out an 87-80 victory to reclaim their accustomed perch atop the N.B.A.

Use Name	Pos	Hgt	Wgt	Age	TOTAL													Per game				
					G	Min	FG	FGA	%	FT	FTA	%	Reb	Ass	PF	DQ	Points	Min	Reb	Ass	PF	Poin
										1975/76 N.B.A. — ATLANTIC DIVISION												
BOSTON CELTICS	**54-28 .659**				**TOM HEINSOHN**																	
John Havlicek	F-G	6'5	205	35	76	2598	504	1121	45	281	333	84	314	278	204	1	1289	34	4.1	3.7	2.7	17
Paul Silas	F	6'7	220	32	81	2662	315	740	43	236	333	71	1025	203	227	3	866	33	12.7	2.5	2.8	10
Dave Cowens	C	6'9	230	27	78	3101	611	1305	47	257	340	76	1246	325	314	10	1479	40	16.0	4.2	4.0	19
Charlie Scott	G	6'5	180	27	82	2913	588	1309	45	267	335	80	358	341	**356**	17	1443	36	4.4	4.2	**4.3**	17
Jo Jo White	G	6'3	190	29	82	3257	670	1492	45	212	253	84	313	445	183	2	1552	40	3.8	5.4	2.2	18
Kevin Stacom	G	6'3	185	24	77	1114	170	387	44	68	91	75	161	128	117	0	408	14	2.1	1.7	1.5	5
Glenn McDonald	F-G	6'6	190	23	75	1019	191	456	42	40	56	71	135	68	123	0	422	14	1.8	0.9	1.6	5
Don Nelson	F	6'6	210	35	75	943	175	379	46	127	161	79	182	77	115	0	477	13	2.4	1.0	1.5	6
Steve Kuberski (from Buf)	F	6'8	215	28	60	882	128	274	47	68	76	89	234	44	123	1	324	15	3.9	0.7	2.1	5
Jim Ard	C-F	6'8	225	27	81	853	107	294	36	71	100	71	289	48	141	2	285	11	3.6	0.6	1.7	3
Tom Boswell	F-C	6'9	230	22	35	275	41	93	44	14	24	58	71	16	70	1	96	8	2.0	0.5	2.0	2
Jerome Anderson	G	6'5	195	22	22	126	25	45	56	11	16	69	13	6	25	0	61	6	0.6	0.3	1.1	2
Ed Searcy	F	6'6	210	23	4	12	2	6	33	2	2	100	0	1	4	0	6	3	0.0	0.3	1.0	1
BUFFALO BRAVES	**46-36 .561**				**JACK RAMSAY**																	
Jim McMillan	F	6'5	220	27	74	2610	492	918	54	188	219	86	390	205	141	0	1172	35	5.3	2.8	1.9	15
John Shumate (from Phoe)	F	6'9	235	23	32	1046	146	254	57	97	143	68	314	65	83	1	389	33	9.8	2.0	2.6	12
Bob McAdoo	C	6'9	210	24	78	3328	**934**	**1918**	49	**559**	**734**	76	965	315	298	5	**2427**	**43**	12.4	4.0	3.8	**31**
Randy Smith	G	6'3	180	27	82	3167	702	1422	49	383	469	82	417	484	274	5	1784	39	5.1	5.9	3.3	21
Ken Charles	G	6'3	180	24	81	2247	328	719	46	161	205	79	219	204	257	5	817	28	2.7	2.5	3.2	10
Gar Heard (to Phoe)	F	6'6	220	27	50	1527	207	492	42	82	135	61	511	126	183	0	496	31	10.2	2.5	3.7	9
Ernie DiGregorio	G	6'	180	24	67	1364	182	474	38	86	94	91	112	265	158	1	450	20	1.7	4.0	2.4	6
Bob Weiss	G	6'2	185	33	66	995	89	183	49	35	48	73	66	150	94	0	213	15	1.0	2.3	1.4	3
Dick Gibbs	F-G	6'5	210	27	72	866	129	301	43	77	93	83	106	49	133	2	335	12	1.5	0.7	1.8	4
Dale Schlueter	C-F	6'10	235	30	71	773	61	122	50	54	81	67	224	80	141	1	176	11	3.2	1.1	2.0	2
Tom McMillen	F-C	6'11	215	23	50	708	96	222	43	41	54	76	186	69	87	1	233	14	3.7	1.4	1.7	4
Don Adams (from StL-ABA)	F	6'7	220	28	56	704	67	170	39	40	57	70	145	73	128	1	174	13	2.6	1.3	2.3	3
Jack Marin (to Chi)	F	6'7	210	31	12	278	41	94	44	27	33	82	40	23	30	0	109	23	3.3	1.9	2.5	9
Steve Kuberski (to Bos)	F	6'8	215	28	10	85	7	17	41	3	3	100	25	3	10	0	17	9	2.5	0.3	1.0	1
Jim Washington	F	6'7	215	32	1	7	0	1	0	0	0	—	1	1	0	0	0	7	1.0	1.0	0.0	0
PHILADELPHIA 76ers	**46-36 .561**				**GENE SHUE**																	
Steve Mix	F	6'7	222	28	81	3039	421	844	50	287	351	82	662	216	288	6	1129	38	8.2	2.7	3.6	13.
George McGinnis	F	6'8	235	25	77	2946	647	1552	42	475	642	74	967	367	334	13	1769	38	12.6	4.8	4.3	23
Harvey Catchings	C	6'9	218	24	75	1731	103	242	43	58	96	60	520	63	262	6	264	23	6.9	0.8	3.5	3.
Doug Collins	G-F	6'6	180	24	77	2995	614	1196	51	372	445	84	307	191	249	2	1600	39	4.0	2.5	3.2	20
Fred Carter	G	6'3	185	30	82	2992	665	1594	42	219	312	70	299	372	286	5	1579	36	3.6	4.5	3.5	19.
Clyde Lee	C-F	6'10	230	31	79	1420	123	282	44	63	95	66	453	59	188	0	309	18	5.7	0.7	2.4	3.
Joe Bryant	F-C	6'9	185	21	75	1203	233	552	42	92	147	63	278	61	165	0	558	16	3.7	0.8	2.2	7.
Lloyd Free	G	6'2	185	22	71	1121	239	533	45	112	186	60	125	104	107	0	590	16	1.8	1.5	1.5	8.
Connie Norman	G	6'3	180	22	65	818	183	422	43	20	24	83	101	66	87	1	386	13	1.6	1.0	1.3	5.
Billy Cunningham (knee injury)	F	6'7	220	32	20	640	103	251	41	68	88	77	147	107	57	1	274	32	7.4	5.4	2.9	13.
Leroy Ellis (knee injury)	C	6'10	225	35	29	489	61	132	46	17	28	61	122	21	62	0	139	17	4.2	0.7	2.1	4.
Darryl Dawkins	C	6'11	250	18	37	165	41	82	50	8	24	33	49	3	40	1	90	4	1.3	0.1	1.1	2.
Wali Jones (from Det)	G	6'2	185	33	16	157	19	38	50	9	13	69	9	31	25	0	47	10	0.6	1.9	1.6	2.
Jerry Baskerville	F	6'7	190	24	21	105	8	26	31	10	16	63	28	3	32	0	26	5	1.3	0.1	1.5	1.
Freddie Boyd (injury - to NO)	G	6'2	180	25	6	33	2	6	33	1	2	50	2	2	5	0	5	6	0.3	0.3	0.8	0.
NEW YORK KNICKERBOCKERS	**38-44 .463**				**RED HOLZMAN**																	
Bill Bradley	F	6'5	210	32	82	2709	392	906	43	130	148	88	234	247	256	2	914	33	2.9	3.0	3.1	11.
Spencer Haywood	F-C	6'8	230	26	78	2892	605	1360	44	339	448	76	878	92	255	1	1549	37	11.3	1.2	3.3	19.
John Gianelli	C-F	6'10	220	25	82	2332	325	687	47	114	160	71	552	115	194	1	764	28	6.7	1.4	2.4	9.
Walt Frazier (back injury)	G	6'4	205	30	59	2427	470	969	49	186	226	82	400	351	163	1	1126	41	6.8	5.9	2.8	19.
Earl Monroe	G	6'3	190	31	76	2889	647	1354	48	250	356	70	273	304	209	1	1574	38	3.6	4.0	2.8	20.7
Phil Jackson	F-C	6'8	220	30	80	1461	185	387	48	110	150	73	343	105	275	3	480	18	4.3	1.3	3.4	6.0
Butch Beard (from Cle)	G	6'3	185	28	60	1449	193	406	48	117	155	75	267	173	180	2	503	24	4.5	2.9	3.0	8.4
Neal Walk	C	6'10	220	27	82	1340	262	607	43	79	99	80	389	119	209	3	603	16	4.7	1.5	2.5	7.4
Jim Barnett	G	6'4	180	31	71	1026	164	371	44	90	114	79	88	90	86	0	418	14	1.2	1.3	1.2	5.9
Harthorne Wingo	F	6'8	210	27	57	533	72	163	44	40	60	67	107	18	59	0	184	9	1.9	0.3	1.0	3.2
Mel Davis	F	6'7	225	25	42	408	76	193	39	22	29	76	148	31	56	0	174	10	3.5	0.7	1.3	4.1
Gene Short (from Sea)	F	6'6	210	22	27	185	26	80	33	19	30	63	41	8	31	0	71	7	1.5	0.3	1.1	2.6
Dennis Bell	F	6'6	220	24	10	76	8	21	38	3	7	43	14	3	11	0	19	8	1.4	0.3	1.1	1.9
Kenny Mayfield	G	6'2	185	27	13	64	17	46	37	3	3	100	8	4	18	0	37	5	0.6	0.3	1.4	2.8
Larry Fogle (broken cheekbone)	G	6'5	208	22	2	14	1	5	20	0	0	—	3	0	4	0	2	7	1.5	0.0	2.0	1.0

1975/76 N.B.A — CENTRAL DIVISION

Name	Pos	Hgt	Wgt	Age	TOTAL G	Min	FG	FGA	%	FT	FTA	%	Reb	Ass	PF	DQ	Points	PER GAME Min	Reb	Ass	PF	Points
CLEVELAND CAVALIERS	**49-33 .598 BILL FITCH**																					
Bobby Smith	F	6'5	212	29	81	2338	495	1121	44	111	136	82	341	155	231	0	1101	29	4.2	1.9	2.9	13.6
Jim Brewer	F	6'9	230	24	82	2913	400	874	46	140	214	65	891	209	214	0	940	36	10.9	2.5	2.6	11.5
Jim Chones	C-F	6'11	220	26	82	2741	563	1258	45	172	260	66	739	163	241	2	1298	33	9.0	2.0	2.9	15.8
Dick Snyder	G	6'5	231	31	82	2274	441	881	50	155	188	82	198	220	215	0	1037	28	2.4	2.7	2.6	12.6
Jim Cleamons	G	6'3	185	26	82	2835	413	887	47	174	218	80	354	428	214	2	1000	35	4.3	5.2	2.6	12.2
Campy Russell	F	6'8	215	23	82	1961	483	1003	48	266	344	77	345	107	231	5	1232	24	4.2	1.3	2.8	15.0
Austin Carr (leg injury)	G	6'4	200	27	65	1282	276	625	44	106	134	79	132	122	92	0	658	20	2.0	1.9	1.4	10.1
Foots Walker	G	6'1	172	24	81	1280	143	369	39	84	108	78	182	288	136	0	370	16	2.2	3.6	1.7	4.6
Nate Thurmond (from Chi)	C	6'11	235	34	65	1133	122	292	42	54	105	51	344	68	145	1	298	17	5.3	1.0	2.2	4.6
John Lambert	C-F	6'10	225	22	54	333	49	110	45	25	37	68	102	16	54	0	123	6	1.9	0.3	1.0	2.3
Butch Beard (to NY)	G	6'3	185	28	15	255	35	90	39	27	37	73	43	45	36	0	97	17	2.9	3.0	2.4	6.5
Rowland Garrett (from Chi)	F	6'6	215	25	41	216	51	127	40	15	21	71	42	10	36	0	117	5	1.0	0.2	0.9	2.9
Steve Patterson (to Chi)	C-F	6'9	225	27	14	136	15	38	39	8	10	80	28	9	11	0	38	10	2.0	0.6	0.8	2.7
Luke Witte	C	7'	240	25	22	99	11	32	34	9	15	60	38	4	14	0	31	5	1.7	0.2	0.6	1.4
Eric Fernsten (to Chi)	F	6'10	210	22	4	9	0	2	0	0	0	—	1	0	1	0	0	2	0.3	0.0	0.3	0.0
WASHINGTON BULLETS	**48-34 .58 K.C. JONES**																					
Truck Robinson	F-C	6'7	225	24	82	2055	354	779	45	211	314	67	557	113	239	3	919	25	6.8	1.4	2.9	11.2
Elvin Hayes	F-C	6'9	235	30	80	2975	649	1381	47	287	457	63	878	121	293	5	1585	37	11.0	1.5	3.7	19.8
Wes Unseld	C	6'7	250	29	78	2922	318	567	56	114	195	58	1036	404	203	3	750	37	13.3	5.2	2.6	9.6
Phil Chenier	G	6'3	180	25	80	2952	654	1355	48	282	341	83	320	255	186	2	1590	37	4.0	3.2	2.3	19.9
Dave Bing	G	6'3	190	32	82	2945	497	1113	45	332	422	79	237	492	262	0	1326	36	2.9	6.0	3.2	16.2
Mike Riordan	F-G	6'4	200	30	78	1943	291	662	44	71	96	74	187	122	201	2	653	25	2.4	1.6	2.6	8.4
Jimmy Jones (knee injury)	G	6'4	188	30	64	1133	153	308	50	72	94	77	131	120	127	1	378	18	2.0	1.9	2.0	5.9
Nick Weatherspoon	F	6'7	205	25	64	1083	218	458	48	96	137	70	274	55	172	2	532	17	4.3	0.9	2.7	8.3
Clem Haskins	G	6'3	200	32	55	737	148	269	55	54	65	83	54	73	79	2	350	13	1.0	1.3	1.4	6.4
Tom Kozelko	F	6'8	220	24	67	584	48	99	48	19	30	63	82	33	74	0	210	9	1.2	0.5	1.1	3.1
Kevin Grevey	F	6'5	210	22	56	504	79	213	37	52	58	90	60	27	65	0	115	9	1.1	0.5	1.2	2.1
Tom Kropp (injury)	G	6'3	220	22	25	72	7	30	23	5	6	83	15	8	20	0	19	3	0.6	0.3	0.8	0.8
HOUSTON ROCKETS	**40-42 .488 JOHNNY EGAN**																					
Ed Ratleff	F-G	6'6	195	25	72	2401	314	647	49	168	206	82	379	260	234	4	796	33	5.3	3.6	3.3	11.1
Rudy Tomjanovich	F	6'8	220	27	79	2912	622	1202	52	221	288	77	666	188	206	1	1465	37	8.4	2.4	2.6	18.5
Kevin Kunnert	C	7'	232	24	80	2335	465	954	49	102	156	65	787	155	315	14	1032	29	9.8	1.9	3.9	12.9
Mike Newlin	G	6'4	205	26	82	3065	569	1123	51	385	445	87	336	457	263	5	1523	37	4.1	5.6	3.2	18.6
Cal Murphy	G	5'9	165	27	82	2995	675	1369	49	372	410	91	209	596	294	3	1722	37	2.5	7.3	3.6	21.0
Joe Meriweather	C-F	6'10	218	22	81	2042	338	684	49	154	239	64	516	82	219	4	830	25	6.4	1.0	2.7	10.2
John Johnson (from Port)	F	6'7	200	28	67	1485	275	609	45	97	128	76	292	197	163	0	647	22	4.4	2.9	2.4	9.7
Ron Riley	F	6'8	200	25	65	1049	115	280	41	38	56	68	304	75	137	1	268	16	4.7	1.2	2.1	4.1
Dave Wohl	G	6'2	185	26	50	700	66	163	40	38	49	78	56	112	112	2	170	14	1.1	2.2	2.2	3.4
Rudy White	G	6'2	195	22	32	284	42	102	41	18	25	72	38	30	32	0	102	9	1.2	0.9	1.0	3.2
Gus Bailey	G	6'5	185	24	30	262	28	77	36	14	28	50	50	41	33	1	70	9	1.7	1.4	1.1	2.3
Cliff Meely (to LA)	F	6'8	220	28	14	174	32	81	40	9	16	56	52	10	31	1	73	12	3.7	0.7	2.2	5.2
Steve Hawes (to Port)	C-F	6'9	220	25	6	51	5	13	38	0	0	—	18	10	6	0	10	9	3.0	1.7	1.0	1.7
NEW ORLEANS JAZZ	**38-44 .463 BUTCH VAN BREDA KOLFF**																					
E. C. Coleman (injury)	F	6'8	225	25	67	1850	216	479	45	59	89	66	419	87	227	3	491	28	6.3	1.3	3.4	7.3
Ron Behagen (broken cheekbone)	F	6'9	235	24	66	1733	308	691	45	144	179	80	553	139	222	6	760	26	8.4	2.1	3.4	11.5
Otto Moore	C	6'11	225	29	81	2407	293	672	44	144	226	64	793	216	250	3	730	30	9.8	2.7	3.1	9.0
Pete Maravich (shoulder separatio	G	6'5	200	27	62	2373	604	1316	46	396	488	81	300	332	197	3	1604	38	4.8	5.4	3.2	25.9
Louie Nelson	G	6'3	190	24	66	2030	327	755	43	169	230	73	202	169	147	1	823	31	3.1	2.6	2.2	12.5
Nate Williams	F-G	6'5	225	25	81	1935	421	948	44	197	239	82	360	107	253	6	1039	24	4.4	1.3	3.1	12.8
Henry Bibby	G	6'1	185	26	79	1772	266	622	43	200	251	80	179	225	165	0	732	22	2.3	2.8	2.1	9.3
Aaron James	F	6'8	210	23	75	1346	262	594	44	153	204	75	249	59	172	1	677	18	3.3	0.8	2.3	9.0
Rich Kelley	C	7'	240	22	75	1346	184	379	49	159	205	78	528	155	209	5	527	18	7.0	2.1	2.8	7.0
Jim McElroy	G	6'3	190	22	51	1134	151	296	51	81	110	74	110	107	70	0	383	22	2.2	2.1	1.4	7.5
Bud Stallworth	F	6'5	190	25	56	1051	211	483	44	85	124	69	145	53	135	1	507	19	2.6	0.9	2.4	9.1
Freddie Boyd (from Phi)	G	6'2	180	25	30	584	72	165	44	28	49	57	30	78	54	0	172	19	1.0	2.6	1.8	5.7
Mel Counts	C-F	7'	235	34	30	319	37	91	41	16	21	76	100	38	74	1	90	11	3.3	1.3	2.5	3.0
ATLANTA HAWKS	**29-53 .354 COTTON FITZSIMMONS (28-46 .378), GENE TORMOHLEN 1-7 .125)**																					
John Drew	F	6'6	205	21	77	2351	586	1168	50	488	656	74	660	150	261	11	1660	31	8.6	1.9	3.4	21.6
John Brown	F	6'7	220	24	75	1758	215	486	44	162	209	78	403	126	235	7	592	23	5.4	1.7	3.1	7.9
Mike Sojourner (knee injury)	C	6'9	225	22	67	1602	248	524	47	80	119	67	449	58	174	2	576	24	6.7	0.9	2.6	8.6
Lou Hudson	G-F	6'5	215	31	81	2558	569	1205	47	237	291	81	300	214	241	3	1375	32	3.7	2.6	3.0	17.0
Tom Henderson	G	6'3	190	23	81	2900	469	1136	41	216	305	71	265	374	195	1	1154	36	3.3	4.6	2.4	14.2
Tom Van Arsdale	F-G	6'5	215	32	75	2026	346	785	44	126	166	76	186	146	202	5	818	27	2.5	1.9	2.7	10.9
Connie Hawkins	F-C	6'8	220	33	74	1907	237	530	45	136	191	71	445	212	172	2	610	26	6.0	2.9	2.3	8.2
Dwight Jones	C	6'10	215	23	66	1762	251	542	46	163	219	74	524	83	214	8	665	27	7.9	1.3	3.2	10.1
Dean Meminger (injury)	G	6'	175	27	68	1418	155	379	41	100	152	66	151	222	116	0	410	21	2.2	3.3	1.7	6.0
Bill Willoughby	F-C	6'8	205	18	62	870	113	284	40	66	100	66	288	31	87	0	292	14	4.6	0.5	1.4	4.7
Wilbur Holland	G	6'	175	24	33	351	85	213	40	22	34	65	41	26	48	0	192	11	1.2	0.8	1.5	5.8
Jim Creighton	F	6'8	200	25	32	172	12	43	28	7	16	44	45	4	23	0	31	5	1.4	0.1	0.7	1.0
Dennis Duval	G	6'3	175	23	13	130	15	43	35	6	9	67	8	20	15	0	36	10	0.6	1.5	1.2	2.8

1975/76 N.B.A. — MIDWEST DIVISION

Use Name	Pos	Hgt	Wgt	Age	G	Min	FG	FGA	%	FT	FTA	%	Reb	Ass	PF	DQ	Points	Min	Reb	Ass	PF	Points
					TOTAL													PER GAME				
MILWAUKEE BUCKS			38-44 .463 LARRY COSTELLO																			
Bob Dandridge	F	6'6	195	28	73	2735	650	1296	50	271	329	82	540	206	263	5	1571	37	7.4	2.8	3.6	21.5
Dave Meyers	F	6'9	225	22	72	1589	198	472	42	135	210	64	445	100	145	0	531	22	6.2	1.4	2.0	7.4
Elmore Smith	C	7'	250	26	78	2809	498	962	52	222	351	63	893	97	268	7	1218	36	11.4	1.2	3.4	15.6
Jim Price	G	6'3	195	26	80	2525	398	958	42	141	166	85	261	395	264	3	937	32	3.3	4.9	3.3	11.7
Brian Winters	G	6'4	185	23	78	2795	618	1333	46	180	217	83	249	366	240	0	1416	36	3.2	4.7	3.1	18.2
Kevin Restani	F-C	6'9	225	24	82	1650	234	493	47	24	42	57	376	96	151	3	492	20	4.6	1.2	1.8	6.0
Junior Bridgeman	F-G	6'5	210	22	81	1646	286	651	44	128	161	80	294	157	235	3	700	20	3.6	1.9	2.9	8.6
Gary Brokaw	G	6'4	180	21	75	1468	237	519	46	159	227	70	125	246	138	1	633	20	1.7	3.3	1.8	8.4
Clyde Mayes	F	6'9	225	22	65	948	114	248	46	56	97	58	263	37	154	7	284	15	4.0	0.6	2.4	4.4
Jim Fox	C	6'10	230	32	70	918	105	203	52	62	79	78	235	42	129	1	272	13	3.4	0.6	1.8	3.9
Mickey Davis	F	6'7	208	25	45	411	55	152	36	50	63	79	84	37	36	0	160	9	1.9	0.8	0.8	3.6
John McGlockin (eye injury)	G	6'5	205	32	33	336	63	148	43	9	10	90	17	38	18	0	135	10	0.5	1.2	0.5	4.1
DETROIT PISTONS			36-46 .439 RAY SCOTT (17-25 .405), HERB BROWN (19-21 .475)																			
Al Eberhard	F	6'6	225	23	81	2066	283	683	41	191	229	83	390	83	250	5	757	26	4.8	1.0	3.1	9.3
Curtis Rowe	F	6'7	225	26	80	2998	514	1098	47	252	342	74	697	183	209	3	1280	37	8.7	2.3	2.6	16.0
Bob Lanier	C	6'11	255	27	64	2363	541	1017	53	284	370	77	746	217	203	2	1366	37	11.7	3.4	3.2	21.3
Chris Ford	G-F	6'5	190	26	82	2198	301	707	43	83	115	72	291	272	222	0	685	27	3.5	3.3	2.7	8.4
Kevin Porter (knee injury)	G	6'	175	25	19	687	99	235	42	42	56	75	44	193	83	3	240	36	2.3	10.2	4.4	12.6
Eric Money	G	6'	170	20	80	2267	449	947	47	145	180	81	207	338	243	4	1043	28	2.6	4.2	3.0	13.0
Archie Clark	G	6'2	175	34	79	1589	250	577	43	100	116	86	137	218	157	0	600	20	1.7	2.8	2.0	7.6
Howard Porter	F	6'8	220	27	75	1482	298	635	47	73	97	75	295	25	133	0	669	20	3.9	0.3	1.8	8.9
John Mengelt (knee injury)	G	6'2	195	26	67	1105	264	540	49	192	237	81	115	108	138	1	720	16	1.7	1.6	2.1	10.7
George Trapp	F-C	6'8	220	27	76	1091	278	602	46	63	88	72	229	50	167	3	619	14	3.0	0.7	2.2	8.1
Lindsay Hairston	F-C	6'7	185	24	47	651	104	228	46	65	112	58	179	21	84	2	273	14	3.8	0.4	1.8	5.8
Earl Williams	C	6'7	230	24	46	562	73	152	48	22	44	50	251	18	81	0	168	12	5.5	0.4	1.8	3.7
Roger Brown (from Den - ABA)	C	7'	230	25	29	454	29	72	40	14	18	78	130	12	76	1	72	16	4.5	0.4	2.6	2.5
Terry Thomas (back injury)	F	6'8	220	22	28	136	28	65	43	21	29	72	36	3	21	1	77	5	1.3	0.1	0.8	2.8
Henry Dickerson	G	6'4	190	24	17	112	9	29	31	10	16	63	3	8	17	1	28	7	0.2	0.5	1.0	1.6
Wali Jones (knee injury - to Phi)	G	6'2	185	33	1	19	4	11	36	0	0	-	0	2	2	0	8	19	0.0	2.0	2.0	8.0
KANSAS CITY KINGS			31-51 .378 PHIL JOHNSON																			
Scott Wedman	F-G	6'7	215	23	82	2968	538	1181	46	191	245	78	606	199	280	8	1267	36	7.4	2.4	3.4	15.5
Ollie Johnson	F	6'6	200	26	81	2150	348	678	51	125	149	84	357	146	217	4	821	27	4.4	1.8	2.7	10.1
Sam Lacey	C	6'10	235	27	81	3083	409	1019	40	217	286	76	1024	378	286	7	1035	38	12.6	4.7	3.5	12.8
Jimmy Walker	G	6'3	205	31	73	2490	459	950	48	231	267	87	177	176	186	2	1149	34	2.4	2.4	2.5	15.7
Nate Archibald	G	6'1	165	27	78	3184	717	1583	45	501	625	80	213	615	169	0	1935	41	2.7	7.9	2.2	24.8
Larry McNeill	F-C	6'9	200	24	82	1613	295	610	48	207	273	76	510	72	244	2	797	20	6.2	0.9	3.0	9.7
Bill Robinzine	F	6'7	230	22	75	1327	229	499	46	145	198	73	355	60	290	19	603	18	4.7	0.8	3.9	8.0
Glenn Hansen	G	6'5	205	23	66	1145	173	420	41	85	117	73	187	67	144	1	431	17	2.8	1.0	2.2	6.5
Rick Roberson	C	6'9	235	28	74	709	73	180	41	42	103	41	233	53	126	1	188	10	3.1	0.7	1.7	2.5
Matt Guokas (from Chi)	G	6'5	195	31	38	515	37	99	37	9	16	56	47	42	53	0	83	14	1.2	1.1	1.4	2.2
Lee Winfield	G	6'2	175	28	22	214	32	66	48	9	14	64	24	19	14	0	73	10	1.1	0.9	0.6	3.3
Bob Bigelow	G-F	6'7	215	22	31	163	16	47	34	24	33	73	29	9	18	0	56	5	0.9	0.3	0.6	1.8
Mike D'Antoni (to StL - ABA)	G	6'3	190	24	9	101	7	27	26	2	2	100	14	16	18	0	16	11	1.6	1.8	2.0	1.8
Len Kosmalski	C	7'	245	24	9	93	8	20	40	4	7	57	25	12	11	0	20	10	2.8	1.3	1.2	2.2
CHICAGO BULLS			24-58 .293 DICK MOTTA																			
Mickey Johnson	F	6'10	190	23	81	2390	478	1033	46	283	360	79	758	130	292	8	1239	30	9.4	1.6	3.6	15.3
Bob Love	F	6'8	215	33	76	2823	543	1391	39	362	452	80	510	145	233	3	1448	37	6.7	1.9	3.1	19.1
Tom Boerwinkle	C	7'	270	30	74	2045	265	530	50	118	177	67	792	283	263	9	648	28	10.7	3.8	3.6	8.8
Jerry Sloan (knee injury)	G	6'6	200	33	22	617	84	210	40	55	78	71	116	22	77	1	223	28	5.3	1.0	3.5	10.1
Norm Van Lier	G	6'1	175	28	76	3026	361	987	37	235	319	74	410	500	298	9	957	40	5.4	6.6	3.9	12.6
Jack Marin (from Buf)	F	6'7	210	31	67	1631	302	718	42	134	155	86	212	118	134	0	738	24	3.2	1.8	2.0	11.0
Leon Benbow	G	6'4	185	23	76	1586	219	551	40	105	140	75	176	158	186	1	543	21	2.3	2.1	2.4	7.1
John Laskowski	G	6'6	185	22	71	1570	284	690	41	87	120	73	219	55	90	0	655	22	3.1	0.8	1.3	9.2
Cliff Pondexter	C-F	6'9	235	21	75	1326	156	380	41	122	182	67	381	90	134	4	434	18	5.1	1.2	1.8	5.8
Bobby Wilson	G	6'3	180	24	58	856	197	489	40	43	58	74	94	52	96	1	437	15	1.6	0.9	1.7	7.5
Steve Patterson (from Cle)	C	6'9	225	27	52	782	69	182	38	26	44	59	200	71	82	1	164	15	3.8	1.4	1.6	3.2
Rowland Garrett (to Cle)	F	6'6	215	25	14	324	57	131	44	38	44	86	75	7	32	0	152	23	5.4	0.5	2.3	10.9
Matt Guokas (to KC)	G	6'5	195	31	18	278	36	74	49	9	11	82	16	28	23	0	81	15	0.9	1.6	1.3	4.5
Nate Thurmond (to Cle)	C	6'11	235	34	13	260	20	45	44	8	18	44	71	26	15	0	48	20	5.5	2.0	1.2	3.7
Eric Fernsten (from Cle)	F	6'10	210	22	33	259	33	84	39	26	37	70	69	19	20	0	92	8	2.1	0.6	0.6	2.8
John Block	F	6'10	220	31	2	7	2	4	50	0	2	0	2	0	2	0	4	4	1.0	0.0	1.0	2.0
GOLDEN STATE WARRIORS			59-23 .720 AL ATTLES																			
Rick Barry	F	6'7	220	31	81	3122	707	1624	44	287	311	92	496	496	215	1	1701	40	6.1	6.1	2.7	21.0
Jamaal Wilkes	F	6'6	190	22	82	2716	617	1334	46	227	294	77	720	167	222	0	1461	33	8.8	2.0	2.7	17.8
Cliff Ray	C	6'9	235	26	82	2184	212	404	52	140	230	61	776	149	247	2	564	27	9.5	1.8	3.0	6.9
Phil Smith	G	6'4	187	23	82	2793	659	1383	48	323	410	79	376	362	223	0	1641	34	4.6	4.4	2.7	20.0
Gus Williams	G	6'2	175	22	77	1728	365	853	43	173	233	74	159	240	143	2	903	22	2.1	3.1	1.9	11.7
George Johnson	C	6'11	220	27	82	1745	165	341	48	70	104	67	627	82	275	6	400	21	7.6	1.0	3.4	4.9
Charlie Johnson	G	6'	170	26	81	1549	342	732	47	60	79	76	202	122	178	1	744	19	2.5	1.5	2.2	9.2
Charles Dudley	G	6'2	186	25	82	1456	182	345	53	157	245	64	269	239	170	0	521	18	3.3	2.9	2.1	6.4
Derrek Dickey	F	6'7	218	24	79	1207	220	473	47	62	79	78	349	83	141	1	502	15	4.4	1.1	1.8	6.4
Dwight Davis	F	6'8	220	26	72	866	111	269	41	78	113	69	225	46	141	0	300	12	3.1	0.6	2.0	4.2
Jeff Mullins (eye injury)	G-F	6'4	200	33	29	311	58	120	48	23	29	79	32	39	36	0	139	11	1.1	1.3	1.2	4.8
Bubbles Hawkins	G	6'4	190	21	32	153	53	104	51	20	31	65	30	16	31	0	126	5	0.9	0.5	1.0	3.9

Use Name	Pos	Hgt	Wgt	Age	TOTAL G	Min	FG	FGA	%	FT	FTA	%	Reb	Ass	PF	DQ	Points	PER GAME Min	Reb	Ass	PF	Points

1975/76 N.B.A. — PACIFIC DIVISION (Continued)

Use Name	Pos	Hgt	Wgt	Age	G	Min	FG	FGA	%	FT	FTA	%	Reb	Ass	PF	DQ	Points	Min	Reb	Ass	PF	Points
SEATTLE SUPERSONICS	**43-39 .524**				**BILL RUSSELL**																	
Bruce Seals	F	6'9	215	22	81	2435	388	889	44	181	267	68	507	119	314	11	957	30	6.3	1.5	3.9	11.8
Leonard Gray (injury)	F-C	6'8	240	24	66	2139	394	831	47	126	163	77	398	203	260	10	914	32	6.0	3.1	3.9	13.8
Tom Burleson	C	7'3	228	23	82	2647	496	1032	48	291	388	75	742	180	273	1	1283	32	9.0	2.2	3.3	15.6
Fred Brown	G	6'3	185	27	76	2516	742	1522	49	273	314	87	317	207	186	0	1757	33	4.2	2.7	2.4	23.1
Slick Watts	G	6'1	175	24	82	2776	433	1015	43	199	344	58	365	**661**	270	3	1065	34	4.5	**8.1**	3.3	13.0
Herb Gilliam	G	6'3	190	29	81	1644	299	676	44	90	116	78	220	202	139	0	688	20	2.7	2.5	1.7	8.5
Mike Bantom (from Phoe)	F-C	6'9	220	24	66	1503	212	450	47	131	194	68	368	102	208	3	555	23	5.6	1.5	3.2	8.4
Tal Skinner	F	6'5	210	23	72	1224	132	285	46	49	80	61	264	67	116	1	313	17	3.7	0.9	1.6	4.3
Willie Norwood	F	6'7	220	28	64	1004	146	301	49	152	203	75	229	59	139	3	444	16	3.6	0.9	2.2	6.9
Frank Oleynick (injury)	G	6'2	190	20	52	650	127	316	40	53	77	69	45	53	62	0	307	13	0.9	1.0	1.2	5.9
John Hummer (ankle injury)	C-F	6'9	230	27	29	364	32	67	48	17	41	41	77	25	71	5	81	13	2.7	0.9	2.4	2.8
Rod Derline	G	6'4	175	23	49	339	73	181	40	45	56	80	27	26	22	0	191	7	0.6	0.5	0.4	3.9
Al Carlson	C	6'11	235	24	28	279	27	79	34	18	29	62	73	13	39	1	72	10	2.6	0.5	1.4	2.6
Zaid Abdul-Aziz	C	6'9	240	29	27	223	35	75	47	16	29	55	76	16	29	0	86	8	2.8	0.6	1.1	3.2
Gene Short (to NY)	F	6'6	210	22	7	37	6	11	55	1	2	50	7	2	5	0	13	5	1.0	0.3	0.7	1.9
PHOENIX SUNS	**42-40 .512**				**JOHN McLEOD**																	
Curtis Perry	F	6'7	220	27	71	2353	386	776	50	175	239	73	684	182	269	5	947	33	9.6	2.6	3.8	13.3
Gar Heard (from Buf)	F	6'6	220	27	36	1220	185	409	45	76	113	67	358	64	120	2	446	34	9.9	1.8	3.3	12.4
Alvan Adams	C-F	6'9	215	21	80	2656	629	1341	47	261	355	74	727	450	274	6	1519	33	9.1	5.6	3.4	19.0
Dick Van Arsdale (broken arm)	G-F	6'5	210	32	58	1870	276	570	48	195	235	83	137	140	113	2	747	32	2.4	2.4	1.9	12.9
Paul Westphal	G	6'4	195	25	82	2960	657	1329	49	365	440	83	259	440	218	3	1679	36	3.2	5.4	2.7	20.5
Ricky Sobers	G	6'3	195	22	78	1898	280	623	45	158	192	82	259	215	253	6	718	24	3.3	2.8	3.2	9.2
Keith Erickson	F	6'5	200	31	74	1850	305	649	47	134	157	85	332	185	196	4	744	25	4.5	2.5	2.6	10.1
Dennis Awtrey	C	6'10	250	27	74	1376	142	304	47	75	109	69	293	159	153	1	359	19	4.0	2.1	2.1	4.9
Nate Hawthorne	G	6'4	190	25	79	1144	182	423	43	115	170	68	209	46	147	0	479	14	2.6	0.6	1.9	6.1
John Shumate (to Buf)	F	6'9	235	23	43	930	186	338	55	115	183	63	240	62	76	1	487	22	5.6	1.4	1.8	11.3
Pat Riley (from LA)	F-G	6'4	208	30	60	790	112	288	39	54	74	73	47	57	107	0	278	13	0.8	1.0	1.8	4.6
Phil Lumpkin (knee injury)	G	6'	167	24	34	370	22	65	34	26	30	87	23	48	26	0	70	11	0.7	1.4	0.8	2.1
John Wetzel (injury)	G	6'5	190	31	37	249	22	46	48	20	24	83	38	19	30	0	64	7	1.0	0.5	0.8	1.7
Fred Saunders	F	6'7	210	24	17	146	28	64	44	6	11	55	37	13	23	0	62	9	2.2	0.8	1.4	3.6
Mike Bantom (to Sea)	F-C	6'9	220	24	7	68	8	26	31	5	5	100	23	3	13	1	21	10	3.3	0.4	1.9	3.0
LOS ANGELES LAKERS	**40-42 .488**				**BILL SHARMAN**																	
Don Ford	F	6'9	215	23	76	1838	311	710	44	104	139	75	333	111	186	3	726	24	4.4	1.5	2.4	9.6
Cornell Warner	F	6'9	220	27	81	2512	251	524	48	89	128	70	722	106	283	3	591	31	8.9	1.3	3.5	7.3
Kareem Abdul-Jabbar	C	7'2	240	28	82	**3379**	914	1728	53	447	636	70	**1383**	413	292	6	2275	41	**16.9**	5.0	3.6	27.7
Lucius Allen	G	6'2	175	28	76	2388	461	1004	46	197	254	78	214	357	241	2	1119	31	2.8	4.7	3.2	14.7
Gail Goodrich	G	6'1	175	32	75	2646	583	1321	44	293	346	85	214	421	238	3	1459	35	2.9	5.6	3.2	19.5
Corky Calhoun	F-G	6'7	215	25	76	1816	172	368	47	65	83	78	341	85	216	4	409	24	4.5	1.1	2.8	5.4
Cazzie Russell	F	6'5	220	31	74	1625	371	802	46	132	148	89	183	122	122	0	874	22	2.5	1.6	1.6	11.8
Donnie Freeman (knee injury)	G	6'3	185	31	64	1480	263	606	43	163	199	82	180	171	160	1	689	23	2.8	2.7	2.5	10.8
Stu Lantz	G	6'3	175	29	53	853	85	204	42	80	89	90	99	76	105	1	250	16	1.9	1.4	2.0	4.7
Kermit Washington (broken ankle)	C-F	6'8	230	24	36	492	39	90	43	45	66	68	165	20	76	0	123	14	4.6	0.6	2.1	3.4
Jim McDaniels (to KY - ABA)	C	6'11	240	27	35	242	41	102	40	9	9	100	74	15	40	1	91	7	2.1	0.4	1.1	2.6
Ron Williams	G	6'3	190	31	9	158	17	43	40	10	13	77	19	21	15	0	44	18	2.1	2.3	1.7	4.9
Cliff Meely (from Hou)	F	6'8	220	28	20	139	20	51	39	24	32	75	45	9	30	0	64	7	2.3	0.5	1.5	3.2
C J. Kupec (injury)	C-F	6'8	220	22	16	55	10	40	25	7	11	64	23	5	7	0	27	3	1.4	0.3	0.4	1.7
Johnny Roche (from Utah - ABA)	G	6'3	170	26	15	52	3	14	21	2	4	50	3	6	7	0	8	3	0.2	0.4	0.5	0.5
Pat Riley (to Phoe)	G	6'4	208	30	2	23	5	13	38	1	3	33	3	0	5	0	11	12	1.5	0.0	2.5	5.5
Walt Wesley	C	6'11	230	30	1	7	1	2	50	2	4	50	1	1	2	0	4	7	1.0	1.0	2.0	4.0
PORTLAND TRAIL BLAZERS	**37-45 .451**				**LENNY WILKENS**																	
Sidney Wicks	F	6'8	225	26	79	3044	580	1201	48	345	512	67	712	244	250	5	1505	39	9.0	3.1	3.2	19.1
Lloyd Neal	F-C	6'7	225	25	68	2320	435	904	48	186	268	69	585	118	254	4	1056	34	8.6	1.7	3.7	15.5
Bill Walton (broken ankle)	C	6'11	250	23	51	1687	345	732	47	133	228	58	681	220	144	3	823	33	13.4	4.3	2.8	16.1
Geoff Petrie	G	6'4	200	27	72	2557	543	1177	46	277	334	83	168	330	194	0	1363	36	2.3	4.6	2.7	18.9
Lionel Hollins	G	6'3	185	22	74	1891	311	738	42	178	247	72	175	306	235	5	800	26	2.4	4.1	3.2	10.8
Larry Steele	G-F	6'5	190	26	81	2382	322	651	49	154	203	76	292	324	289	8	798	29	3.6	4.0	3.6	9.9
Bob Gross	F	6'6	200	22	76	1474	209	400	52	97	142	68	307	163	186	3	515	19	4.0	2.1	2.4	6.8
Steve Hawes (from Hou)	C-F	6'9	220	25	66	1360	194	390	50	87	120	73	479	105	163	5	475	21	7.3	1.6	2.5	7.2
LaRue Martin	C	6'11	208	25	63	889	109	302	36	57	77	74	311	72	126	1	275	14	4.9	1.1	2.0	4.4
Steve Jones	G	6'5	210	33	64	819	168	380	44	78	94	83	75	63	96	0	414	13	1.2	1.0	1.5	6.5
Dan Anderson	G	6'2	185	24	52	614	88	181	49	51	61	84	62	85	58	0	227	12	1.2	1.6	1.1	4.4
Barry Clemens (illness)	F	6'7	220	33	49	443	70	143	49	31	35	89	70	33	57	0	171	9	1.4	0.7	1.2	3.5
John Johnson (to Hou)	F	6'7	200	28	9	212	41	88	47	23	27	85	40	20	31	1	105	24	4.4	2.2	3.4	11.7
Greg Lee	G	6'3	190	23	5	35	2	4	50	2	2	100	2	11	6	0	6	7	0.4	2.2	1.2	1.2
Greg Smith	F	6'5	200	28	1	3	0	1	0	0	0	-	0	0	2	0	0	3	0.0	0.0	2.0	0.0

1975/76 N.B.A.—PLAYOFFS

Name	Pos	Hgt	Wgt	Age	TOTAL G	Min	FG	FGA	%	FT	FTA	%	Reb	Ass	PF	DQ	Points	PER GAME Min	Reb	Ass	PF	Points
BOSTON CELTICS	**TOM HEINSOHN**				defeated Buffalo 4-2; H107-98, H101-98, H101-96, 93-98, 122-124, H99-88, 104-100																	
					defeated Cleveland 4-2; H111-99, H94-89, 78-83, 87-106, H99-94, 94-87																	
					defeated Phoenix 4-2; H98-97, H105-90, 98-105, 107-109, H128-126(3OT), 87-80																	
John Havlicek	F-G	6'5	205	35	15	505	80	180	44	38	47	81	56	51	32	0	198	34	3.7	3.4	2.1	13
Paul Silas	F	6'7	220	32	18	741	69	154	45	56	69	81	246	42	67	1	194	41	13.7	2.3	3.7	10
Dave Cowens	C	6'9	230	27	18	**798**	156	341	46	66	87	76	**296**	83	85	4	378	44	**16.4**	4.6	4.7	21
Charlie Scott	G	6'5	180	27	18	632	111	284	39	55	72	76	76	71	**97**	**11**	277	35	4.2	3.9	**5.4**	15
Jo Jo White	G	6'3	190	29	18	791	**165**	**371**	44	**78**	**95**	82	71	**98**	51	0	**408**	44	3.9	5.4	2.8	22
Don Nelson	F	6'6	210	35	18	315	52	108	48	60	69	87	53	17	46	1	164	18	2.9	0.9	2.6	9.
Steve Kuberski	F	6'8	215	28	18	232	38	81	47	21	26	81	51	16	38	0	97	13	2.8	0.9	2.1	5
Kevin Stacom	G	6'3	185	24	17	195	13	45	29	8	11	73	17	16	21	0	34	11	1.0	0.9	1.2	2.
Jim Ard	C-F	6'8	225	27	16	110	13	29	45	11	14	79	26	8	29	0	37	7	1.6	0.5	1.8	2
Glenn McDonald	G	6'6	190	23	13	68	8	26	31	5	6	83	8	4	12	0	21	5	0.6	0.3	0.9	1.
Jerome Anderson	G	6'5	195	22	4	5	1	3	33	0	0	—	1	1	1	0	2	1	0.3	0.3	0.3	0.
Tom Boswell	F	6'9	230	22	3	3	1	2	50	0	0	—	1	0	2	0	2	1	0.3	0.0	0.7	0.
PHOENIX SUNS	**JOHN MacLEOD**				defeated Seattle 4-2; 99-102, 116-111, H103-91, H130-114, 108-114																	
					defeated Golden State 4-3; 103-128, 108-101, H91-99, H133-129(2OT), 95-111, H105-104, 94-86																	
					lost to Boston 2-4; 87-98, 90-105, H105-98, H109-107, 126-128(3OT), H80-87																	
Curtis Perry	F	6'7	220	27	19	615	99	218	45	44	68	65	146	36	78	3	242	32	7.7	1.9	4.1	12.
Gar Heard	F	6'6	220	27	19	721	105	238	44	55	81	68	197	33	56	0	265	38	10.4	1.7	2.9	13.
Alvan Adams	C-F	6'9	215	21	19	668	137	303	45	67	82	82	191	**98**	60	1	341	35	10.1	5.2	3.2	17.
Ricky Sobers	G	6'3	195	22	19	563	96	205	47	55	66	83	63	79	77	3	247	30	3.3	4.2	4.1	13.
Paul Westphal	G	6'4	195	25	19	685	**165**	323	51	71	93	76	47	96	61	1	401	36	2.5	5.1	3.2	21.
Dick Van Arsdale	G-F	6'5	210	32	19	472	61	125	49	40	46	87	23	38	41	0	162	25	1.2	2.0	2.2	8.
Keith Erickson	F	6'5	200	31	19	426	80	173	46	55	68	81	67	35	61	1	215	22	3.5	1.8	3.2	11.
Dennis Awtry	C	6'10	250	27	19	286	21	45	47	18	33	55	63	25	38	1	60	15	3.3	1.3	2.0	3.
Phil Lumpkin	G	6'	167	24	17	136	10	30	33	11	14	79	13	21	8	0	31	8	0.8	1.2	0.5	1.
Nate Hawthorne	G	6'4	190	25	15	81	9	26	35	8	11	73	16	4	20	0	26	5	1.1	0.3	1.3	1.
Pat Riley	F	6'4	208	30	5	27	6	15	40	1	1	100	0	5	3	0	13	5	0.0	1.0	0.6	2.
John Wetzel	G	6'5	190	31	2	5	0	0	—	2	2	100	2	0	2	0	2	3	1.0	0.0	1.0	1.
GOLDEN STATE WARRIORS	**AL ATTLES**				defeated Detroit 4-2; H127-103, H111-123, 113-96, 102-106, H128-109, 118-106(OT)																	
					lost to Phoenix 3-4; H128-103, H101-108, 99-91, 129-133(2OT), H111-95, 104-105, H86-94																	
Rick Barry	F	6'7	220	31	13	532	126	289	44	60	68	88	84	84	40	1	312	41	6.5	6.5	3.1	24.0
Jamaal Wilkes	F-G	6'6	190	22	13	450	86	200	43	35	45	78	103	29	33	1	207	35	7.9	2.2	2.5	15.9
Cliff Ray	C	6'9	235	26	13	377	48	79	61	22	34	65	130	20	47	2	118	29	10.0	1.5	3.6	9.1
Phil Smith	G	6'4	187	23	13	493	127	245	52	58	79	73	61	60	33	1	312	38	4.7	4.6	2.5	24.0
Charlie Johnson	G	6'	170	26	13	284	52	127	41	16	19	84	35	20	39	0	120	22	2.7	1.5	3.0	9.2
George Johnson	C	6'11	220	27	13	261	31	54	57	14	19	74	87	17	46	0	76	20	6.7	1.3	3.5	5.8
Charles Dudley	G	6'2	186	25	13	260	33	57	58	24	33	73	36	38	29	0	90	20	2.8	2.9	2.2	6.9
Gus Williams	G	6'2	175	22	11	178	30	85	35	14	21	67	14	26	22	0	74	16	1.3	2.4	2.0	6.7
Derrek Dickey	F	6'7	218	24	12	173	31	62	50	14	17	82	42	6	27	0	76	14	3.5	0.5	2.3	6.3
Dwight Davis	F	6'8	220	26	11	142	16	37	43	18	22	82	28	10	28	1	50	13	2.5	0.9	2.5	4.5
Jeff Mullins	G	6'4	200	33	8	33	6	16	38	0	0	—	4	3	8	0	12	4	0.5	0.4	1.0	1.5
Bubbles Hawkins	G	6'4	190	21	5	12	4	5	80	2	2	100	0	2	6	0	10	2	0.0	0.4	1.2	2.0
CLEVELAND CAVALIERS	**BILL FITCH**				defeated Washington 4-3; H95-100, 80-79, H88-76, 98-109, H92-91, 98-102(OT), H87-85																	
					lost to Boston 2-4; 99-111, 89-94, H83-78, H106-87, 94-99, H87-94																	
Bobby Smith	F	6'5	212	29	13	379	71	164	43	22	25	88	43	30	41	1	164	29	3.3	2.3	3.2	12.6
Jim Brewer	F	6'9	230	24	13	489	44	101	44	26	48	54	140	37	34	0	114	38	10.8	2.8	2.6	8.8
Jim Chones	C-F	6'11	220	26	7	242	47	114	41	11	18	61	50	6	23	0	105	35	7.1	0.9	3.3	15.0
Dick Snyder	G	6'5	213	31	13	364	69	153	45	18	22	82	29	31	35	1	156	28	2.2	2.4	2.7	12.0
Jim Cleamons	G	6'3	185	26	13	503	73	184	40	33	40	83	71	61	34	0	179	39	5.5	4.7	2.6	13.8
Nate Thurmond	C	6'11	235	34	13	375	37	79	47	13	32	41	117	28	52	2	87	29	9.0	2.2	4.0	6.7
Campy Russell	F	6'8	215	23	13	328	65	161	40	47	55	85	71	14	51	0	177	25	5.5	1.1	3.9	13.6
Austin Carr	G	6'4	200	27	13	273	66	138	48	22	36	61	23	26	29	0	154	21	1.8	2.0	2.2	11.8
Foots Walker	G	6'1	172	24	13	125	11	27	41	8	10	80	16	23	17	0	30	10	1.2	1.8	1.3	2.3
John Lambert	F	6'10	225	22	6	34	5	13	38	2	2	100	11	1	7	0	12	6	1.8	0.2	1.2	2.0
Luke Witte	C	7'	240	25	7	28	6	11	55	4	4	100	9	4	4	0	16	4	1.3	0.6	0.6	2.3
Rowland Garrett	F	6'6	215	25	4	5	0	0	—	2	4	50	0	0	0	0	2	1	0.0	0.0	0.0	0.5
WASHINGTON BULLETS	**K. C. JONES**				lost to Cleveland 3-4; 100-95, H79-80, 76-88, H109-98, 91-92, H102-98(OT), 85-87																	
Nick Weatherspoon	F	6'7	205	25	7	224	36	80	45	14	25	56	42	10	28	1	86	32	6.0	1.4	4.0	12.3
Elvin Hayes	F-C	6'9	235	30	7	305	54	122	44	32	55	58	88	10	24	0	140	44	12.6	1.4	3.4	20.0
Wes Unseld	C	6'7	250	29	7	310	18	39	46	13	24	54	85	28	19	0	49	44	12.1	4.0	2.7	7.0
Phil Chenier	G	6'3	180	25	7	265	56	128	44	14	17	82	26	11	27	0	126	38	3.7	1.6	3.9	18.0
Dave Bing	G	6'3	190	32	7	209	34	76	45	28	35	80	18	28	18	0	96	30	2.6	4.0	2.6	13.7
Jimmy Jones	G	6'4	188	30	7	165	22	45	49	18	21	86	17	10	15	0	62	24	2.4	1.4	2.1	8.9
Truck Robinson	F	6'7	225	24	7	137	16	37	43	17	21	81	33	5	27	0	49	20	4.7	0.7	3.9	7.0
Clem Haskins	G	6'3	200	32	5	40	10	21	48	2	5	40	5	2	6	0	22	8	1.0	0.4	1.2	4.4
Mike Riordan	F	6'4	200	30	6	31	3	8	38	0	0	—	6	1	5	0	6	5	1.0	0.2	0.8	1.0
Tom Kozelka	F	6'8	220	24	5	14	0	1	0	2	2	100	2	0	0	0	2	3	0.4	0.0	0.0	0.4
Kevin Grevey	F	6'5	210	22	2	3	1	2	50	0	0	—	0	0	1	0	2	2	0.0	0.0	0.5	1.0
Tom Kropp	G	6'3	220	22	1	2	1	1	100	0	0	—	0	0	1	0	2	2	0.0	0.0	1.0	2.0

Use Name	Pos	Hgt	Wgt	Age	TOTAL G	Min	FG	FGA	%	FT	FTA	%	Reb	Ass	PF	DQ	Points	PER GAME Min	Reb	Ass	PF	Points

1975/76 N.B.A.— PLAYOFFS (Continued)

Use Name	Pos	Hgt	Wgt	Age	G	Min	FG	FGA	%	FT	FTA	%	Reb	Ass	PF	DQ	Points	Min	Reb	Ass	PF	Points
BUFFALO BRAVES	**JACK RAMSAY**				defeated Philadelphia 2-1; 95-89, H106-131, 124-123(OT) lost to Boston 2-4; 98-107, 96-101, H98-93, H124-122, 88-99, H100-104																	
Jim McMillian	F	6'5	220	27	9	348	61	129	47	33	38	87	37	19	29	1	155	39	4.1	2.1	3.2	17.2
John Shumate	F	6'9	235	23	9	362	54	92	59	19	38	50	77	25	29	0	127	40	8.6	2.8	3.2	14.1
Bob McAdoo	C	6'9	210	24	9	406	97	215	45	58	82	71	128	29	37	3	252	**45**	14.2	3.2	4.1	28.0
Randy Smith	G	6'3	180	27	9	386	81	161	50	41	49	84	52	77	35	0	203	43	5.8	**8.6**	3.9	22.6
Ken Charles	G	6'3	180	24	9	238	22	55	40	9	13	69	26	14	31	1	53	26	2.9	1.6	3.4	5.9
Ernie DiGregorio	G	6'	180	24	9	217	30	62	48	8	8	100	13	45	29	2	68	24	1.4	5.0	3.2	7.6
Don Adams	F	6'7	220	28	9	122	15	36	42	6	7	86	27	13	23	0	36	14	3.0	1.4	2.6	4.0
Dale Schlueter	C-F	6'10	235	30	8	44	5	7	71	5	6	83	8	2	11	0	15	6	1.0	0.3	1.4	1.9
Bob Weiss	G	6'2	185	33	7	.36	3	8	38	2	3	67	4	3	5	0	8	5	0.6	0.4	0.7	1.1
Dick Gibbs	F	6'5	210	27	5	23	4	9	44	2	2	100	1	2	8	0	10	5	0.2	0.4	1.6	2.0
Tom McMillen	F	6'11	215	23	1	3	1	2	50	0	0	—	1	0	1	0	2	3	1.0	0.0	1.0	2.0
DETROIT PISTONS	**HERB BROWN**				defeated Milwaukee 2-1; 107-110, H126-123, 107-104 lost to Golden State 2-4; 103-127, 123-111, H96-113, H106-102, 109-128, H116-118(OT)																	
Curtis Rowe	F	6'7	225	26	9	346	53	111	48	29	34	85	70	26	27	1	135	38	7.8	2.9	3.0	15.0
Howard Porter	F	6'8	220	27	9	213	51	97	53	15	17	88	42	6	24	0	117	24	4.7	0.7	2.7	13.0
Bob Lanier	C	6'11	255	27	9	359	97	152	64	45	50	**90**	114	30	34	1	235	40	12.7	3.3	3.8	26.1
Chris Ford	G	6'5	190	26	9	276	33	81	41	12	15	80	36	40	33	1	78	31	4.0	4.4	3.7	8.7
Eric Money	G	6'	170	20	9	273	48	105	46	17	21	81	22	51	36	1	113	30	2.4	5.7	4.0	12.6
Archie Clark	G	6'2	175	34	9	192	30	62	48	12	18	67	21	29	25	0	72	21	2.3	3.2	2.8	8.0
Al Eberhard	F	6'6	225	23	8	182	17	39	44	14	19	74	26	7	14	0	48	23	3.3	0.9	1.8	6.0
George Trapp	F-C	6'8	220	27	9	153	37	89	42	15	18	83	35	9	26	0	89	17	3.9	1.0	2.9	9.9
John Mengelt	G	6'2	195	26	9	113	34	56	61	19	27	70	14	10	22	0	87	13	1.6	1.1	2.4	9.7
Roger Brown	C	7'	230	25	9	51	4	9	44	2	4	50	14	2	10	0	10	6	1.6	0.2	1.1	1.1
Henry Dickerson	G	6'4	190	24	5	15	4	9	44	1	2	50	4	3	1	0	9	3	0.8	0.6	0.2	1.8
Terry Thomas	F	6'8	220	22	4	6	0	5	0	0	0	-	1	0	1	0	0	2	0.3	0.0	0.3	0.0
Kevin Porter - knee injury																						
SEATTLE SUPERSONICS	**BILL RUSSELL**				lost to Phoenix 2-4; H102-99, H111-116, 91-103, 114-130, H114-108, 112-123																	
Willie Norwood	F	6'7	220	28	6	215	24	58	41	11	18	61	38	8	25	3	59	36	6.3	1.3	4.2	9.8
Bruce Seals	F	6'9	215	22	6	181	30	68	44	18	26	69	36	3	22	0	78	30	6.0	0.5	3.7	13.0
Tom Burleson	C	7'3	228	23	6	208	45	75	60	35	46	76	57	10	25	1	125	35	9.5	1.7	4.2	20.8
Fred Brown	G	6'3	185	27	6	236	68	133	51	35	44	80	28	17	20	0	171	39	4.7	2.8	3.3	**28.5**
Slick Watts	G	6'1	175	24	6	197	30	69	43	11	23	48	18	49	28	1	71	33	3.0	8.2	4.7	11.8
Mike Bantom	F	6'9	220	24	6	114	22	38	58	14	20	70	23	8	27	1	58	19	3.8	1.3	4.5	9.7
Tal Skinner	F-G	6'5	210	23	6	86	4	14	29	11	15	73	15	7	9	0	19	14	2.5	1.2	1.5	3.2
Herm Gilliam	G	6'3	190	29	6	86	6	27	22	5	8	63	11	12	10	0	17	14	1.8	2.0	1.7	2.8
Zaid Abdul-Aziz	C	6'9	240	29	5	60	14	20	**70**	8	11	73	21	2	2	0	36	12	4.2	0.4	0.4	7.2
Rod Derline	G	6'4	175	23	4	41	2	10	20	2	2	100	4	1	4	0	6	10	1.0	0.3	1.0	1.5
John Hummer	C	6'9	230	27	3	16	2	3	67	0	0	—	1	0	3	0	4	5	0.3	0.0	1.0	1.3
Leonard Gray - injury, Frank Oleynick - injury																						
PHILADELPHIA 76ers	**GENE SHUE**				lost to Buffalo 1-2; H89-95, 131-106, H123-124(OT)																	
Steve Mix	F	6'7	222	28	3	134	18	46	39	8	10	80	18	12	13	1	44	45	6.0	4.0	4.3	14.7
George McGinnis	F	6'8	235	25	3	120	29	61	48	11	18	61	41	12	14	1	69	40	13.7	4.0	4.7	23.0
Harvey Catchings	C	6'9	218	24	3	87	8	13	62	1	3	33	28	6	11	0	17	29	9.3	2.0	3.7	5.7
Doug Collins	G-F	6'6	180	24	3	117	23	53	43	12	14	86	21	10	9	0	58	39	7.0	3.3	3.0	19.3
Fred Carter	G	6'3	185	30	3	125	29	67	43	26	30	87	10	15	12	0	84	42	3.3	5.0	4.0	28.0
Lloyd Free	G	6'2	185	22	3	62	11	28	39	10	13	77	1	5	6	0	32	21	0.3	1.7	2.0	10.7
Clyde Lee	C	6'10	230	31	3	53	4	6	67	6	7	86	16	1	15	0	14	18	5.3	0.3	5.0	4.7
Joe Bryant	F	6'9	185	21	3	43	9	12	75	5	7	71	13	1	11	1	23	14	4.3	0.3	3.7	7.7
Wali Jones	G	6'2	185	33	1	2	0	0	—	0	0	—	1	2	0	0	2	2	1.0	2.0	0.0	2.0
Connie Norman	G	6'3	180	22	1	1	0	1	100	0	0	—	1	0	0	0	0	1	1.0	0.0	0.0	0.0
Leroy Ellis	C	6'10	225	35	1	1	0	0	—	0	0	—	0	0	0	0	0	1	0.0	0.0	0.0	0.0
Billy Cunningham - knee injury																						
MILWAUKEE BUCKS	**LARRY COSTELLO**				lost to Detroit 2-1; H110-107, 123-126, H104-107																	
Bob Dandridge	F	6'6	195	28	3	122	24	49	49	18	20	90	23	8	9	0	66	41	7.7	2.7	3.0	22.0
Dave Meyers	F	6'9	225	22	3	54	5	11	45	14	17	82	14	2	8	0	24	18	4.7	0.7	2.7	8.0
Elmore Smith	C	7'	250	26	3	104	15	27	56	14	21	67	22	1	14	0	44	35	7.3	0.3	4.7	14.7
Gary Brokaw	G	6'4	180	21	3	108	23	37	62	17	18	94	11	24	10	0	63	36	3.7	8.0	3.3	21.0
Brian Winters	G	6'4	185	23	3	126	39	62	63	4	5	80	7	15	11	1	82	42	2.3	5.0	3.7	27.3
Junior Bridgeman	F-G	6'5	210	22	3	67	9	20	45	7	11	64	11	5	10	0	25	22	3.7	1.7	3.3	8.3
Clyde Mayes	F-C	6'9	225	22	3	41	1	5	20	3	4	75	6	1	6	1	5	14	2.0	0.3	2.0	1.7
Jim Fox	C	6'10	230	32	3	33	4	5	80	2	2	100	7	3	8	0	10	11	2.3	1.0	2.7	3.3
Kevin Restani	F	6'9	225	24	3	33	1	5	20	0	0	—	5	1	0	0	2	11	1.7	0.3	0.0	0.7
Jim Price	G	6'3	195	26	1	19	3	8	38	4	7	57	0	4	1	0	10	19	0.0	4.0	1.0	10.0
Jon McGlocklin	G	6'5	205	32	2	13	3	4	75	0	0	—	1	1	2	0	6	7	0.5	0.5	1.0	3.0

Team	W	L	Pct.	GB	Record against playoff teams W	L	Pct.	Record against non-playoff teams W	L	Pct.	HOME W	L	Pct.	ROAD W	L	Pct.
ATLANTIC DIVISION																
Boston Celtics	54	28	.659	—	28	16	.636	26	12	.684	31	10	.756	23	18	.561
Buffalo Braves	46	36	.561	8	21	23	.477	25	13	.658	28	13	.683	18	23	.439
Philadelphia 76ers	46	36	.561	8	22	22	.500	24	14	.632	34	7	.829	12	29	.293
New York Knickerbockers	38	44	.463	16	20	29	.408	18	15	.545	24	17	.585	14	27	.341
CENTRAL DIVISION																
Cleveland Cavaliers	49	33	.598	—	24	17	.585	25	16	.610	29	12	.707	20	21	.488
Washington Bullets	48	34	.585	1	22	19	.537	26	15	.634	31	10	.756	17	24	.414
Houston Rockets	40	42	.488	9	21	27	.438	19	15	.559	28	13	.683	12	29	.293
New Orleans Jazz	38	44	.463	11	19	30	.388	19	14	.576	22	19	.537	16	25	.390
Atlanta Hawks	29	53	.354	20	15	33	.313	14	20	.412	20	21	.488	9	32	.220
MIDWEST DIVISION																
Milwaukee Bucks	38	44	.463	—	16	26	.381	22	18	.550	22	19	.537	16	25	.390
Detroit Pistons	36	46	.439	2	15	27	.357	21	19	.525	24	17	.585	12	29	.293
Kansas City Kings	31	51	.378	7	17	32	.347	14	19	.424	25	16	.610	6	35	.146
Chicago Bulls	24	58	.293	14	14	35	.286	10	23	.303	15	26	.366	9	32	.220
PACIFIC DIVISION																
Golden State Warriors	59	23	.720	—	32	11	.744	27	12	.692	36	5	.878	23	18	.561
Seattle Supersonics	43	39	.524	16	19	25	.432	24	14	.632	31	10	.756	12	29	.293
Phoenix Suns	42	40	.512	17	15	28	.349	27	12	.692	27	14	.659	15	26	.366
Los Angeles Lakers	40	42	.488	19	20	29	.408	20	13	.606	31	10	.756	9	32	.220
Portland Trail Blazers	37	45	.451	22	19	30	.388	18	15	.545	26	15	.634	11	30	.268

1975/76 N.B.A. INDIVIDUAL LEADERS

SCORING
(Minimum 70 Games Played or 1400 Points)

Name	Team	G	FG	FT	Pts.	Avg.
McAdoo	Buf	78	934	559	2427	31.1
Abdul-Jabbar	LA	82	914	447	2275	27.7
Maravich	NO	62	604	396	1604	25.9
Brown	Sea	76	742	273	1757	23.1
McGinnis	Phi	77	647	475	1769	23.0
Smith	Buf	82	702	383	1787	21.8
Drew	Atl	77	586	488	1660	21.6
Dandridge	Mil	73	650	271	1571	21.5
Murphy	Hou	82	675	372	1722	21.0
Barry	GS	81	707	287	1701	21.0

FIELD GOAL PERCENTAGE
(Minimum 300 Made)

Name	Team	FG	FGA	Pct.
Unseld	Was	318	567	.561
Shumate	Phoe-Buf	332	592	.561
McMillian	Buf	492	918	.536
Lanier	Det	541	1017	.532
Abdul-Jabbar	LA	914	1728	.529
Smith	Mil	498	962	.518
Tomjanovich	Hou	622	1202	.517
Collins	Phi	614	1196	.513
Johnson	KC	348	678	.513
Newlin	Hou	569	1123	.505

FREE THROW PERCENTAGE
(Minimum 125 Made)

Name	Team	FT	FTA	Pct.
Barry	GS	287	311	.923
Murphy	Hou	372	410	.907
Russell	LA	132	148	.892
Bradley	NY	130	148	.878
Brown	Sea	273	314	.869
Newlin	Hou	385	445	.865
Walker	KC	231	267	.865
McMillian	Buf	188	219	.858
Marin	Buf-Chi	161	188	.856
Erickson	Phoe	134	157	.854

PERSONAL FOULS

Name	Team	PF
Scott	Bos	356
McGinnis	Phi	334
Kunnert	Hou	315
Cowens	Bos	314
Seals	Sea	314

GAMES DISQUALIFIED

Name	Team	Disq.
Robinzine	KC	19
Scott	Bos	17
Kunnert	Hou	14
McGinnis	Phi	13
Drew	Atl	11
Seals	Sea	11

TOTAL REBOUNDS PER GAME
(Minimum 70 Games or 800 Rebounds)

Name	Team	G	Reb.	Avg.
Abdul-Jabbar	LA	82	1383	16.9
Cowens	Bos	78	1246	16.0
Unseld	Was	78	1036	13.3
Silas	Bos	81	1025	12.7
McGinnis	Phi	77	967	12.6
Lacey	KC	81	1024	12.6
McAdoo	Buf	78	965	12.4
Smith	Mil	78	893	11.4
Haywood	NY	78	878	11.3
Hayes	Was	80	878	11.0

ASSISTS PER GAME
(Minimum 70 Games or 400 Assists)

Name	Team	G	Ass.	Avg.
Watts	Sea	82	661	8.1
Archibald	KS	78	615	7.9
Murphy	Hou	82	596	7.3
Van Lier	Chi	76	500	6.6
Barry	GS	81	496	6.1
Bing	Was	82	492	6.0
Smith	Buf	82	484	5.9
Adams	Phoe	80	450	5.6
Goodrich	LA	75	421	5.6
Westphal	Phoe	82	440	5.4

MINUTES PLAYED

Name	Team	Min.
Abdul-Jabbar	LA	3379
McAdoo	Buf	3328
White	Bos	3257
Archibald	KC	3184
Smith	Buf	3167

BLOCKED SHOTS PER GAME
(Minimum 70 Games or 100 Blocked Shots)

Name	Team	G	Reb.	Avg.
Abdul-Jabbar	LA	82	338	4.1
Smith	Mil	78	238	3.1
Hayes	Was	80	202	2.5
Catchings	Phi	75	164	2.2
G. Johnson	GS	82	174	2.1
McAdoo	Buf	78	160	2.1
Burleson	Sea	82	150	1.8
Moore	NO	81	136	1.7
Lacey	KC	81	134	1.7
Neal	Port	68	107	1.6

OFFENSIVE REBOUNDS PER GAME
(Minimum 70 Games Played)

Name	Team	G	Reb.	Avg.
Silas	Bos	81	365	4.5
Cowens	Bos	78	335	4.3
Drew	Atl	77	286	3.7
Brewer	Cle	82	298	3.6
Boerwinkle	Chi	74	263	3.6
Unseld	Was	78	271	3.5
Johnson	Chi	81	279	3.4
McGinnis	Phi	77	260	3.4
Kunnert	Hou	80	267	3.3
Abdul-Jabbar	LA	82	272	3.3

STEALS PER GAME
(Minimum 70 or 125 Steals)

Name	Team	G	Steals	Avg.
Watts	Sea	82	261	3.2
McGinnis	Phi	77	198	2.6
Westphal	Phoe	82	210	2.6
Barry	GS	81	202	2.5
Ford	Det	82	178	2.2
Steele	Port	81	170	2.1
Van Lier	Chi	76	150	2.0
Chenier	Was	80	158	2.0
Mix	Phi	81	158	2.0
Brown	Sea	76	143	1.9

Team		REGULAR SEASON												PLAYOFFS											
		G	FG	FGA	%	FT	FTA	%	Reb	Ass	PF	Points	PPG	G	FG	FGA	%	FT	FTA	%	Reb	Ass	PF	Points	PPG
TEAM STATISTICS																									
ATLANTIC DIVISION																									
Boston	Off.	82	3527	7901	45	1654	2120	78	4341	1980	2002	8708	106.2	18	707	1624	44	398	796	80	902	407	481	1812	100.7
	Def.	82	3489	7772	45	1538	2074	74	3696	1835	1895	8516	103.9	18	723	1569	46	313	433	72	749	412	449	1759	97.7
	Diff.		+38	+129	—	+116	+46	+4	+645	+145	-107	+192	+2.3		-16	+55	-2	+85	+363	+8	+153	-5	-32	+53	3.0
Buffalo	Off.	82	3481	7307	48	1833	2368	77	3721	2112	2017	8795	107.3	9	373	776	48	183	246	74	374	229	238	929	103.2
	Def.	82	3558	7722	46	1611	2156	75	3828	2079	2137	8727	106.4	9	392	862	45	185	239	77	438	212	253	969	107.7
	Diff.		-77	-415	+2	+222	+212	+2	-107	+33	+120	+68	+.9		-19	-86	+3	-2	+7	-3	-64	+17	+15	-40	-4.5
Philadelphia	Off.	82	3462	7752	45	1811	2469	73	4069	1658	2187	8735	106.5	3	132	287	46	79	102	77	150	64	91	343	114.3
	Def.	82	3467	7737	45	1780	2334	76	4152	1849	2151	8714	106.3	3	122	258	47	81	106	76	124	82	93	325	108.3
	Diff.		-5	+15	—	+31	+135	-3	-83	-191	-36	+21	+.2		+10	+29	-1	-2	-4	+1	+26	-18	+2	+18	6.0
New York	Off.	82	3443	7555	46	1532	1985	77	3745	1660	2006	8418	102.7												
	Def.	82	3407	7426	46	1705	2274	75	3959	1812	1954	8519	103.9												
	Diff.		+36	+129	—	-173	-289	+2	-214	-152	-52	-101	-1.2												
CENTRAL DIVISION																									
Cleveland	Off.	82	3497	7709	45	1346	1827	74	3780	1844	1871	8340	101.7	13	494	1145	43	208	296	70	580	261	327	1196	92.0
	Def.	82	3262	7188	45	1610	2152	75	3926	1728	1860	8134	99.2	13	467	1073	44	271	368	74	599	223	316	1205	92.7
	Diff.		+235	+521	—	-264	-325	-1	-146	+116	-11	+206	+2.5		+27	+72	-1	-63	-72	-4	-19	+38	-11	-9	-0.7
Washington	Off.	82	3416	7234	47	1595	2215	72	3831	1823	1921	8427	102.8	7	251	560	45	140	205	68	322	105	171	642	91.7
	Def.	82	3377	7636	44	1482	1992	74	2932	1705	1988	8236	100.4	7	257	639	40	124	170	73	335	123	184	638	91.1
	Diff.		+39	-402	+3	+113	+223	-2	+899	+118	+67	+191	+2.4		-6	-79	+5	+16	+35	-5	-13	-18	+13	+4	0.6
Houston	Off.	82	3546	7304	49	1616	2046	79	3703	2213	2045	8708	106.2												
	Def.	82	3603	7551	48	1568	2072	76	3589	2028	2050	8774	107.0												
	Diff.		-57	-247	+1	+48	-26	+3	+114	+185	+5	-66	-.8												
New Orleans	Off.	82	3352	7491	45	1831	2415	76	3968	1765	2175	8535	104.1												
	Def.	82	3396	7413	46	1816	2464	74	4028	1684	2162	8608	105.0												
	Diff.		-44	+78	-1	+15	-49	+2	-60	+81	-13	-73	-.9												
Atlanta	Off.	82	3301	7338	45	1809	2467	73	3765	1666	1983	8411	102.6												
	Def.	82	3529	7357	48	1592	2102	76	3914	1778	2177	8650	105.5												
	Diff.		-228	-19	-3	+217	+365	-3	-149	-112	+194	-239	-2.9												
MIDWEST DIVISION																									
Milwaukee	Off.	82	3456	7435	46	1437	1952	74	3782	1817	2041	8349	101.8	3	127	233	55	83	105	79	107	65	79	337	112.3
	Def.	82	3402	7624	45	1664	2182	76	3833	1897	1828	8468	103.3	3	144	300	48	52	64	81	128	67	87	340	113.3
	Diff.		+54	-189	+1	-227	-230	-2	-51	-80	-213	-119	-1.5		-17	-67	+7	+31	+41	-2	-21	-2	+8	-3	-1.0
Detroit	Off.	82	3524	7598	46	1557	2049	76	3750	1751	2086	8605	104.9	9	406	835	49	181	225	80	399	213	253	993	110.3
	Def.	82	3492	7479	47	1707	2211	77	3908	2014	1914	8691	106.0	9	410	836	49	216	272	79	403	214	236	1036	115.1
	Diff.		+32	+119	-1	-150	-162	-1	-158	-263	-172	-86	-1.1		-4	-1	—	-35	-47	+1	-4	-1	-17	-43	-4.8
Kansas City	Off.	82	3341	7379	45	1792	2335	77	3801	1864	2056	8474	103.3												
	Def.	82	3477	7454	47	1753	2310	76	3931	1825	2124	8707	106.2												
	Diff.		-136	-75	-2	+39	+25	+1	-130	+39	+68	-233	-2.9												
Chicago	Off.	82	3106	7499	41	1651	2197	75	4101	1704	1977	7863	95.9												
	Def.	82	3246	6946	47	1609	2137	75	3739	1669	2081	8101	98.8												
	Diff.		-140	+553	-6	+42	+60	—	+362	+35	+104	-238	-2.9												
PACIFIC DIVISION																									
Golden State	Off.	82	3691	7982	46	1620	2158	75	4261	2041	2022	9002	109.8	13	590	1256	47	277	359	77	624	315	358	1457	112.1
	Def.	82	3437	7742	44	1583	2150	74	4018	2006	1946	8457	103.1	13	553	1171	47	276	357	77	609	320	338	1382	106.3
	Diff.		+254	+240	+2	+37	+8	+1	+243	+35	-76	+545	+6.7		+37	+85	—	+1	+2	—	+15	-5	-20	+75	5.8
Seattle	Off.	82	3542	7730	46	1642	2309	71	3715	1935	2133	8726	106.4	6	247	515	48	150	213	70	252	117	175	644	107.3
	Def.	82	3486	7464	47	1777	2407	74	3952	2109	2111	8749	106.7	6	263	520	51	153	202	76	236	169	172	679	113.2
	Diff.		+56	+266	-1	-135	-98	-3	-237	-174	-22	-23	-.3		-16	-5	-3	-3	+11	-6	+16	-52	-3	-35	-5.9
Phoenix	Off.	82	3420	7251	47	1780	2337	76	3666	2083	2018	8620	105.1	19	789	1701	46	427	565	76	828	470	505	2005	105.5
	Def.	82	3444	7357	47	1682	2265	74	3656	1979	2163	8570	104.5	19	785	1704	46	455	601	76	917	424	550	2025	106.6
	Diff.		-24	-106	—	+98	+72	+2	+10	+104	+145	+50	+.6		+4	-3	—	-28	-36	—	-89	+46	+45	-20	-1.1
Los Angeles	Off.	82	3547	7622	47	1670	2164	77	4002	1939	2025	8764	106.9												
	Def.	82	3592	7980	45	1573	2148	73	4221	2032	1987	8757	106.8												
	Diff.		-45	-358	+2	+97	+16	+4	-219	-93	-38	+7	+.1												
Portland	Off.	82	3417	7292	47	1699	2350	72	3959	2094	2091	8533	104.1												
	Def.	82	3405	7531	45	1825	2333	78	3778	1920	2128	8635	105.3												
	Diff.		+12	-239	+2	-126	+17	-6	+181	+174	+37	-102	-1.2												

1975-76 A.B.A.

The End of the Red, White and Blue Ball

Dave Debusschere took charge of the A.B.A. just as it began to unravel. After one year as general manager of the Nets, Debusschere was the surprise choice to become commissioner of the league in the summer of 1975. The good news that summer came out of Denver. The Nuggets signed rookies David Thompson and Marvin Webster, the first and third players chosen in the N.B.A. draft. Thompson was the renowned acrobatic forward fron North Carolina State, a much needed crowd pleaser for the A.B.A. Webster was a shot-blocking center from Morgan State. The Nuggets would showcase these famous rookies in the new Sports Arena in Denver.

Negative news came out of Indiana. After years as an A.B.A. star, George McGinnis bought his way out of his Pacer contract and signed with the Philadelphia 76ers of the N.B.A. The absence of a major television contract for the A.B.A. had condemned McGinnis to play in relative obscurity. Debusschere failed to improve the A.B.A. television situation.

Without a television contract, teams had little media revenue to offset their losses. The Memphis franchise was, for all practical purposes, dead during the summer. In late August, however, Debusschere arranged for its transfer to Baltimore. The Baltimore Claws got some instant credibility by buying Dan Issel from the financially-troubled Kentucky Colonels. Ten teams thus prepared for the A.B.A.'s ninth season.

On September 24, the Denver Nuggets and the New York Nets unexpectedly applied for admission to the N.B.A. The senior league took the applications under advisement. The resulting publicity painted the A.B.A. as being on its last legs.

On October 8, the Baltimore Claws ominously traded Dan Issel to Denver for practically nothing, On October 20, three days before the season was to start, the underfinanced Claws went out of business. On that same day, the seven other A.B.A. teams joined the Nuggets and the Nets in applying for admission to the N.B.A.

Once the season started, attendance was low. The league's image was one of instability. On November 11, the San Diego Sails folded. The league continued as an eight-team circuit only until December 2, when the Utah Stars ceased operations.

Down to seven teams, the league scrapped its divisional format. Each successive team collapse had resulted in dispersal of that team's players to other teams. The dispersals, in turn, caused a series of trades and other personnel moves. The A.B.A. waited for the next shoe to drop. The Virginia Squires had an atrocious team and little money in the bank. The Spirits of St. Louis had very poor attendance at their games. These weak members hung on, however, and the A.B.A. made it through the season as a seven-team league.

On the court, the A.B.A. still offered entertaining, wide-open basketball. Its three-point shot created offensive possibilities not found in the N.B.A. The Denver Nuggets blended old and new players into a winning combination. David Thompson scored often and with flair. Marvin Webster missed most of the season with hepatitis, but Dan Issel handled the center position in style after arriving from the stillborn Baltimore team. Bobby Jones and Ralph Simpson contributed their skills to the winning mix. Although the Nuggets had sent Mack Calvin, Mike Green, and Jan van Breda Kolff to Virginia for the draft rights to Thompson, the team easily absorbed the loss of three key veterans. The high-scoring Nuggets enjoyed good attendance at their games.

The New York Nets had modest attendance at their games despite a winning team. The Nets relied most heavily on Julius Erving, the astounding offensive machine known as Dr. J. Guards Brian Taylor and John Williamson provided sharp outside shooting. A swap of big men with San Antonio turned out poorly, as center Swen Nater recovered slowly from a knee injury. San Antonio got more service from the ex-Nets Billy Paultz and Larry Kenon. Guards George Gervin and James Silas, however, were the offensive leaders of the spurs.

The defending champion Kentucky Colonels suffered from the loss of Dan Issel, who had been sold to ease financial problems. The Colonels were built around center Artis Gilmore, the league's top rebounder and fourth-best scorer. A mid-season trade brought Maurice Lucas to Kentucky. The Indiana Pacers stayed competitive despite the loss of George McGinnis. Billy Knight took up the scoring slack, while Don Buse excelled at guard.

St. Louis shuffled its lineup in front of almost-empty seats. Marvin Barnes was hounded by legal problems and played erratically. When Utah folded, the Spirits obtained Moses Malone and Ron Boone. A mid-season trade brought Caldwell Jones to St. Louis. Virginia had hopes of rising this season, but a flood of injuries decimated the team. The Squires kept changing head coaches and had a precarious grip on financial life.

In the playoffs, Kentucky beat Indiana in a three-game mini-series. The two semi-final series each went to seven games. The Nets and Spurs went the limit despite the broken ankle suffered by James Silas in the opening game. Before 15,934 fans in the Nassau Coliseum, the Nets won the seventh game 121-114. In the other semi-final series, the Nuggets and Colonels faced off in a seventh game before 18,821 fans in the Sports Arena in Denver, an A.B.A. attendance record. The Nuggets won 133-110.

The championship series began in Denver before 19,034 fans, a new record. Julius Erving scored 45 points and hit a jumper at the buzzer for a 120-118 New York victory. In game two, yet another record crowd of 19,107 saw the Nuggets even the score 127-121 despite Erving's 48 points. In game three in New York, Erving scored eight straight points in the final ninety seconds for a 117-111 Nets victory. The Nets also took game four, prohibiting the Nuggets from retaking the home court advantage. The Nuggets, however, won the fifth game at home to earn another trip to New York. In game six, David Thompson scored 42 points. The Nets, however, outscored the Nuggets 34-14 in the fourth quarter and won the game 112-106 to capture the league championship.

That championship was the A.B.A.'s last. In June, the N.B.A. announced that Denver, New York, San Antonio, and Indiana were joining the established league. Each team would pay $3.2 million for the privilege, with the Nets paying approximately an additional $4 million to the Knicks for invading their territory. Kentucky, St. Louis, and Virginia went out of business, as did the A.B.A. itself. Its red, white, and blue ball would henceforth bounce only in playgrounds.

1975/76 — A.B.A.

Use Name	Pos	Hgt	Wgt	Age	TOTAL G	Min	FG	FGA	%	FT	FTA	%	Reb	Ass	PF	DQ	Points	PER GAME Min	Reb	Ass	PF	Points
DENVER NUGGETS	**60-24 .714**				**LARRY BROWN**																	
David Thompson	F-G	6'4	195	21	83	3101	807	1567	51	541	681	79	525	308	282	—	2158	37	6.3	3.7	3.4	26.0
Bobby Jones	F	6'9	215	24	83	2845	510	898	**57**	215	308	70	791	331	253	—	1235	34	9.5	4.0	3.0	14.9
Dan Issel	C	6'9	240	27	84	2856	752	1472	51	425	521	82	923	201	266	—	1930	34	11.0	2.4	3.2	23.0
Ralph Simpson	G	6'5	200	26	84	3121	619	1211	51	273	350	78	454	597	183	—	1515	37	5.4	7.1	2.2	18.0
Chuck Williams	G	6'2	185	29	79	2529	339	660	51	188	231	81	210	375	215	—	866	32	2.7	4.7	2.7	11.0
Byron Beck	F-C	6'9	230	30	80	1586	334	646	52	97	116	84	354	116	192	—	770	20	4.4	1.5	2.4	9.6
Claude Terry	G-F	6'4	195	25	79	1349	232	500	46	80	89	90	152	146	116	—	557	17	1.9	1.8	1.5	7.1
Gus Gerard (from StL)	F	6'8	200	22	60	1185	240	553	43	111	158	70	301	122	169	—	594	20	5.0	2.0	2.8	9.9
Monte Towe	G	5'7	150	22	64	576	72	179	40	36	44	82	55	136	84	—	189	9	0.9	2.1	1.3	3.0
Marvin Webster (illness)	C	7'1	240	23	38	398	55	120	46	55	78	71	174	30	60	—	165	10	4.6	0.8	1.6	4.3
Jim Foster	G	6'1	180	23	48	352	54	145	37	39	64	61	42	47	78	—	148	7	0.9	1.0	1.6	3.1
Roger Brown (to Det-NBA)	C	7'	230	25	37	291	28	61	46	16	24	67	75	22	63	—	74	8	2.0	0.6	1.7	2.0
Jim Bradley	F	6'9	215	23	7	107	15	38	39	2	3	67	30	11	26	—	32	15	4.3	1.6	3.7	4.6
George Irvine (knee injury)	F	6'6	200	27	3	14	2	6	33	0	0	—	1	0	1	—	4	5	0.3	0.0	0.3	1.3
NEW YORK NETS	**55-29 .655**				**KEVIN LOUGHERY**																	
Julius Erving	F	6'7	210	25	84	3244	**949**	**1873**	51	530	662	80	925	423	221	—	**2462**	39	11.0	5.0	2.6	**29.3**
Rick Jones	F	6'8	230	29	83	2427	441	1153	38	199	261	76	428	131	294	—	1096	29	5.2	1.6	3.5	13.2
Kim Hughes	C	6'11	220	23	84	2162	300	566	53	92	202	46	775	18	71	—	692	26	9.2	0.2	0.8	8.2
Brian Taylor (back injury)	G	6'2	185	24	54	1733	354	722	49	164	207	79	162	204	138	—	904	32	3.0	3.8	2.6	16.7
John Williamson	G	6'2	185	23	76	2255	519	1153	45	187	232	81	190	188	224	—	1233	30	2.5	2.5	2.9	16.2
Al Skinner	G	6'4	195	23	83	2082	330	702	47	203	241	84	307	280	252	—	865	25	3.7	3.4	3.0	10.4
Tim Bassett	F-C	6'8	230	24	84	1790	173	396	44	58	98	59	531	65	247	—	405	21	6.3	0.8	2.9	4.8
Bill Melchionni	G	6'1	170	31	67	1191	149	358	42	79	93	85	88	266	66	—	386	18	1.3	4.0	1.0	5.8
Swen Nater (to Va)	C	6'11	250	25	43	1016	160	330	48	56	78	72	441	19	142	—	376	24	10.3	0.4	3.3	8.7
Chuck Terry	F	6'6	215	25	66	970	96	246	39	22	29	76	144	38	116	—	220	15	2.2	0.6	1.8	3.3
Ted McClain (from Ky)	G	6'3	180	28	30	696	128	303	42	82	101	81	73	106	112	—	340	23	2.4	3.5	3.7	11.3
Jim Eakins (NJ - from Utah & Va)	C	6'11	215	29	34	463	72	143	50	67	79	85	120	18	71	—	211	14	3.5	0.5	2.1	6.2
George Bucci	G	6'3	202	22	33	237	50	124	40	28	41	68	37	15	19	—	128	7	1.1	0.5	0.6	3.9
Billy Schaeffer (to Va)	F	6'5	200	23	20	119	31	77	40	8	9	89	22	9	15	—	72	6	1.1	0.5	0.8	3.6
SAN ANTONIO SPURS	**50-34 .595**				**BOB BASS**																	
Mark Olberding (from SD)	F	6'8	225	19	70	1621	233	463	50	161	204	79	425	124	197	—	627	23	6.1	1.8	2.8	9.0
Larry Kenon	F	6'9	205	23	81	2920	647	1344	48	221	283	78	897	151	165	—	1515	36	11.1	1.9	2.0	18.7
Billy Paultz	C	6'11	260	27	83	2958	566	1124	50	238	324	73	862	340	232	—	1370	36	10.4	4.1	2.8	16.5
George Gervin	G-F	6'7	180	23	81	2748	706	1414	50	342	399	86	546	201	288	—	1768	34	6.7	2.5	3.6	21.8
James Silas	G	6'3	185	26	84	3112	718	1384	52	**564**	647	87	335	452	263	—	2000	37	4.0	5.4	3.1	23.8
Mike Gale	G	6'4	190	25	78	1782	230	506	45	64	80	80	207	244	145	—	527	23	2.7	3.1	1.9	6.8
Coby Dietrick	C-F	6'10	230	27	81	1467	200	403	50	68	82	83	349	159	257	—	469	18	4.3	2.0	3.2	5.8
George Karl	G	6'2	185	24	75	1200	150	334	45	81	106	76	66	250	149	—	381	16	0.9	3.3	2.0	5.1
Allan Bristow (broken ankle)	F	6'7	227	24	47	882	125	271	46	78	92	85	174	121	81	—	328	19	3.7	2.6	1.7	7.0
Henry Ward	G-F	6'4	195	23	61	688	148	310	48	16	27	59	140	35	99	—	330	11	2.3	0.6	1.6	5.4
Tom Owens (from Ky & Ind)	F-C	6'10	225	26	39	538	90	182	49	46	60	77	155	41	97	—	226	14	4.0	1.1	2.5	5.8
Ken Smith	F	6'7	185	22	19	164	34	83	41	13	16	81	24	7	22	—	82	9	1.3	0.4	1.2	4.3
Stew Johnson (from SD)	F	6'8	225	31	10	123	21	78	27	2	4	50	19	15	16	—	45	12	1.9	1.5	1.6	4.5
Will Franklin	F	6'7	225	26	10	95	12	22	55	9	16	56	29	5	16	—	33	10	2.9	0.5	1.6	3.3
Skip Wise	G	6'2	170	20	2	10	2	4	50	0	0	—	3	1	4	—	4	5	1.5	0.5	2.0	2.0
Dennis Van Zant	F	6'9	210	—	1	2	0	0	—	2	2	100	1	0	1	—	2	2	1.0	0.0	1.0	2.0
KENTUCKY COLONELS	**46-38 .548**				**HUBIE BROWN**																	
Wil Jones	F	6'8	205	28	83	2635	483	1015	48	158	204	77	625	209	326	—	1127	32	7.5	2.5	3.9	13.6
Maurice Lucas (from StL)	F-C	6'9	220	23	58	1796	368	798	46	149	190	78	548	147	228	—	888	31	9.4	2.5	3.9	15.3
Artis Gilmore	C	7'2	240	26	84	3286	773	1401	55	521	**764**	68	**1303**	211	**341**	—	2067	39	**15.5**	2.5	4.1	24.6
Bird Averitt	G	6'1	175	23	78	2272	546	1274	43	266	346	77	213	297	208	—	1398	29	2.7	3.8	2.7	17.9
Louie Dampier	G	6'	180	31	82	2835	455	949	48	126	146	86	159	467	141	—	1068	35	1.9	5.7	1.7	13.0
Ted McClain (to NY)	G	6'3	180	28	43	1231	139	328	42	54	69	78	135	204	165	—	333	29	3.1	4.7	3.8	7.7
Ron Thomas	F	6'6	215	25	83	1117	134	277	48	55	94	59	371	67	168	—	324	13	4.5	0.8	2.0	3.9
Marv Roberts (to Va)	F	6'8	205	25	40	1003	170	385	44	88	113	78	159	78	96	—	428	25	4.0	2.0	2.4	10.7
Jan van Breda Kolff (from Va)	F	6'7	200	24	43	861	95	192	49	56	68	82	195	81	87	—	247	20	4.5	1.9	2.0	5.7
Johnny Neumann (from Va)	G-F	6'6	210	24	42	812	171	399	43	55	77	71	109	104	107	—	426	19	2.6	2.5	2.5	10.1
Kevin Joyce (injury - from SD)	G	6'3	190	24	34	650	78	203	38	33	42	79	42	83	75	—	190	19	1.2	2.4	2.2	5.6
Caldwell Jones (from SD - to StL)	F-C	6'11	225	25	15	457	80	171	47	26	37	70	158	13	73	—	186	30	10.5	0.9	***4.9**	12.4
Jim McDaniels (from LA - NBA)	C	6'11	240	27	29	365	78	165	47	23	28	82	124	21	64	—	179	13	4.3	0.7	2.2	6.2
Tom Owens (to Ind & SA)	F-C	6'10	225	26	19	326	46	105	44	26	44	59	93	19	50	—	118	17	4.9	1.0	2.6	6.2
Travis Grant (to Ind)	F	6'8	225	25	22	261	52	123	42	18	23	78	39	12	30	—	122	12	1.8	0.5	1.4	5.5
Allen Murphy	G	6'5	190	23	29	248	43	114	38	27	37	73	47	13	52	—	113	9	1.6	0.4	1.8	3.9
Jimmy Dan Conner	G	6'4	195	22	24	240	42	86	49	22	29	76	28	38	35	—	106	10	1.2	1.6	1.5	4.4
Jimmie Baker (injury)	F	6'9	220	22	5	40	3	15	20	0	2	0	14	4	11	—	6	8	2.8	0.8	2.2	1.2

Use Name	Pos	Hgt	Wgt	Age	TOTAL G	Min	FG	FGA	%	FT	FTA	%	Reb	Ass	PF	DQ	Points	PER GAME Min	Reb	Ass	PF	Points

1975/76 — A.B.A.

Use Name	Pos	Hgt	Wgt	Age	G	Min	FG	FGA	%	FT	FTA	%	Reb	Ass	PF	DQ	Points	Min	Reb	Ass	PF	Points
INDIANA PACERS	**39-45 .464**				**BOB LEONARD**																	
Billy Knight (broken hand)	F-G	6'6	200	23	70	2775	774	1567	49	415	501	83	708	259	206	—	1969	40	10.1	3.7	2.9	28.1
Darnell Hillman	F-G	6'9	215	26	74	2166	375	828	45	243	336	72	670	147	306	—	994	29	9.1	2.0	4.1	13.4
Len Elmore	C	6'9	230	23	76	2591	480	1193	40	152	206	74	819	122	310	—	1112	34	10.8	1.6	4.1	14.6
Don Buse	G	6'4	195	25	84	**3380**	400	887	45	179	220	81	322	**689**	194	—	1051	**40**	3.8	**8.2**	2.3	12.5
Billy Keller	G	5'10	185	28	78	2311	410	1011	41	164	183	90	228	307	116	—	1107	30	2.9	3.9	1.5	14.2
Dave Robisch (from SD)	F-C	6'10	240	26	76	2415	376	899	42	263	311	85	672	145	183	—	1015	32	8.8	1.9	2.4	13.4
Mike Flynn	G	6'2	180	22	67	1097	166	439	38	64	111	58	133	133	112	—	421	16	2.0	2.0	1.7	6.3
Bo Lamar (broken hand - from SD)	G	6'1	180	24	35	908	229	555	41	68	92	74	98	135	46	—	547	26	2.8	3.9	1.3	15.6
Charles Jordan	F	6'8	225	21	71	855	162	373	43	43	72	60	216	53	184	—	369	12	3.0	0.7	2.6	5.2
Dan Roundfield	F-C	6'8	210	22	67	767	131	309	42	77	122	63	259	35	161	—	339	11	3.9	0.5	2.4	5.1
Travis Grant (from Ky)	F	6'8	225	25	34	567	146	275	53	34	46	74	101	31	68	—	326	17	3.0	0.9	2.0	9.6
Tom Owens (from Ky, to SA)	C	6'10	225	26	16	243	42	82	51	20	25	80	69	9	53	—	104	15	4.3	0.6	3.3	6.5
Ed Manning	F	6'7	215	31	12	134	24	60	40	12	17	71	37	14	18	—	60	11	3.1	1.2	1.5	5.0
Nate Barnett	G	6'3	175	22	12	73	12	26	46	3	8	38	8	8	22	—	27	6	0.7	0.7	1.8	2.3
Bob Netolicky	C	6'9	225	33	4	53	8	21	38	3	3	100	12	0	2	—	19	13	3.0	0.0	0.5	4.8
SPIRITS OF ST. LOUIS	**35-49 .417**				**ROD THORN (20-27 .426), JOE MULLANEY (15-22 .405)**																	
M.L. Carr	F	6'6	205	24	74	2174	380	786	48	137	206	67	459	224	225	—	906	29	6.2	3.0	3.0	12.2
Marvin Barnes	F-C	6'9	225	23	67	2487	681	1355	50	251	339	74	725	149	273	—	1616	37	10.8	2.2	4.1	24.1
Caldwell Jones (from SD & Ky)	C	6'11	225	25	51	1810	274	569	48	93	116	80	559	112	206	—	641	35	11.0	2.2	**4.0**	12.6
Ron Boone (from Utah)	G	6'2	200	29	62	2325	547	1128	48	192	219	88	247	312	198	—	1300	38	4.0	5.0	3.2	21.0
Freddie Lewis	G	6'	180	32	74	2266	403	953	42	259	317	82	213	293	183	—	1096	31	2.9	4.0	2.5	14.8
Don Chaney	G-F	6'5	210	29	48	1475	191	457	42	64	82	78	234	169	170	—	447	31	4.9	3.5	3.5	9.3
Moses Malone (BF from Utah)	F-C	6'10	215	20	43	1168	251	490	51	112	183	61	413	58	113	—	614	27	9.6	1.3	2.6	14.3
Maurice Lucas (to Ky)	C	6'9	220	23	28	1065	252	548	46	68	93	73	422	77	104	—	572	38	15.1	2.8	3.7	20.4
Mike Barr	G	6'3	180	25	56	1048	124	240	52	46	55	84	109	174	76	—	300	19	1.9	3.1	1.4	5.4
Randy Denton (from Utah)	C	6'10	245	26	51	949	166	395	42	41	53	77	294	49	109	—	373	19	5.8	1.0	2.1	7.3
Mike D'Antoni (from KC - NBA)	G	6'3	190	24	50	798	77	162	48	19	26	73	76	115	134	—	173	16	1.5	2.3	2.7	3.5
Don Adams (to Buf - NBA)	F	6'7	220	28	20	725	99	251	39	63	83	76	116	88	80	—	261	36	5.8	4.4	4.0	13.1
Gus Gerard (to Den)	F	6'8	200	22	22	542	92	242	38	64	80	80	136	25	69	—	249	25	6.2	1.1	3.1	11.3
Steve Green (BW from Utah)	F	6'7	220	22	36	534	99	243	41	38	52	73	82	35	79	—	236	15	2.3	1.0	2.2	6.6
Rudy Hackett	F	6'9	215	26	22	414	55	131	42	31	49	63	78	28	48	—	141	19	3.5	1.3	2.2	6.4
Barry Parkhill	G	6'4	185	24	35	377	37	100	37	5	8	63	26	64	46	—	80	11	0.7	1.8	1.3	2.3
Harry Rogers	F	6'7	195	—	18	298	60	124	48	17	24	71	96	15	34	—	137	17	5.3	0.8	1.9	7.6
Paul Ruffner	C	6'10	225	27	2	5	2	3	67	0	0	—	3	0	0	—	4	3	1.5	0.0	0.0	2.0
VIRGINIA SQUIRES	**15-68 .181**				**AL BIANCHI (1-6 .143), MACK CALVIN (0-6 .000), BILL MUSSELMAN (FROM SD) (4-22 .154), JACK ANKERSON (1-1 .500), ZELMO BEATY (9-33 .214)**																	
Mel Bennett	F	6'7	200	20	75	2193	329	819	40	246	403	61	526	97	266	—	904	29	7.0	1.3	3.5	12.1
Mike Jackson	F	6'7	230	26	80	2230	390	781	50	199	250	80	607	113	306	—	979	28	7.6	1.4	3.8	12.2
Mike Green (knee injury)	C	6'10	210	24	54	1719	385	832	46	154	198	78	519	82	187	—	924	32	9.6	1.5	3.5	17.1
Fatty Taylor	G	6'	175	29	76	2483	243	600	41	125	173	72	341	401	212	—	622	33	4.5	5.3	2.8	8.2
Mack Calvin (knee injury)	G	6'	175	27	45	1658	306	717	43	253	285	**89**	128	271	122	—	872	37	2.8	6.0	2.7	19.4
Ticky Burden	G	6'2	185	22	71	2181	561	1247	45	283	369	77	202	131	188	—	1413	31	2.8	1.8	2.6	19.9
Willie Wise (knee injury)	F-G	6'6	215	28	46	1343	247	595	42	135	175	77	262	125	135	—	629	29	5.7	2.7	2.9	13.7
Jan van Breda Kloff (to Ky)	F	6'7	200	24	37	1117	128	296	43	109	130	84	241	101	77	—	366	30	6.5	2.7	2.1	9.9
Dave Twardzik (leg injury)	G	6'1	180	25	43	871	100	216	46	113	139	81	89	125	107	—	316	20	2.1	2.9	2.5	7.3
Johnny Neumann (to Ky)	G-F	6'6	210	24	35	777	222	550	40	96	112	86	92	67	115	—	582	22	2.6	1.9	3.3	16.6
Sven Nater (from NY)	C	6'11	250	25	33	774	160	321	50	52	77	68	325	36	96	—	372	23	9.8	1.1	2.9	11.3
Gerald Govan	C	6'10	220	33	24	658	57	131	44	23	28	82	161	54	65	—	137	27	6.7	2.3	2.7	5.7
Jim Eakins (from Utah - to NY)	C	6'11	215	29	23	636	74	177	42	66	73	90	169	37	77	—	214	28	7.3	1.6	3.3	9.3
Marv Roberts (from Ky)	F-C	6'8	205	25	32	556	89	236	38	19	24	79	77	42	55	—	197	17	2.4	1.3	1.7	6.2
Billy Schaeffer (from NY)	F	6'5	200	23	31	518	83	181	46	40	54	74	89	28	57	—	206	17	2.9	0.9	1.8	6.6
Joby Wright (from SD)	F	6'8	222	26	13	200	34	82	41	17	28	61	37	2	32	—	85	15	2.8	0.2	2.5	6.5
Rick Darnell	C-F	6'10	215	—	11	120	11	30	37	4	7	57	36	9	30	—	26	11	3.3	0.8	2.7	2.4
David Vaughn	C	7'	220	23	10	86	12	33	36	5	8	63	19	3	15	—	29	9	1.9	0.3	1.5	2.9
UTAH STARS	**4-12 .250**				**TOM NISSALKE** Stars disbanded December 2, 1975																	
Steve Green (to StL)	F	6'7	220	22	16	534	96	195	49	46	56	82	112	29	71	—	238	33	7.0	1.8	4.4	14.9
Randy Denton (to StL)	F-C	6'10	245	26	16	591	117	239	49	42	46	91	225	40	71	—	276	37	14.1	2.5	4.4	17.3
Jim Eakins (to Va & NY)	C	6'11	215	29	16	568	69	157	44	65	71	92	150	33	72	—	203	36	9.4	2.1	4.5	12.7
Ron Boone (to StL)	G-F	6'2	200	29	16	636	166	339	49	85	99	86	72	75	45	—	419	40	4.5	4.7	2.8	26.2
Johnny Roche (to LA - NBA)	G	6'3	170	26	16	484	112	212	53	31	41	76	25	79	47	—	264	30	1.6	4.9	2.9	16.5
Al Smith	G	6'1	185	28	15	392	42	105	40	48	59	81	37	73	45	—	138	26	2.5	4.9	3.0	9.2
Goo Kennedy	F	6'6	205	26	16	271	38	69	55	24	37	65	80	11	43	—	100	17	5.0	0.7	2.7	6.3
George Carter	F	6'5	218	31	10	180	25	65	38	32	41	78	31	15	27	—	82	18	3.1	1.5	2.7	8.2
Joe Hamilton	G	5'10	175	27	13	131	31	78	40	9	13	69	14	15	12	—	77	10	1.1	1.2	0.9	5.9
Don Washington	F	6'8	210	23	6	58	12	18	67	0	0	—	13	3	19	—	24	10	2.2	0.5	3.2	4.0
Kenny Gardner	F	6'5	205	—	9	51	6	18	33	2	2	100	13	3	9	—	14	6	1.4	0.3	1.0	1.6
Duane Dillard	F	—	—	—	3	19	1	3	33	2	2	100	9	2	7	—	4	6	3.0	0.7	2.3	1.3

Moses Malone broken foot (to StL) Rick Mount - leg injury

Use Name	Pos.	Hgt.	Wgt.	Age	TOTAL G	Min.	FG	FGA	%	FT	FTA	%	Reb.	Ass.	PF	Disq.	Points	PER GAME Min.	Reb.	Ass.	PF	Points
1975/76 A.B.A.																						
SAN DIEGO SAILS	**3-8 .273**		**BILL MUSSELMAN (to VA)**										Sails disbanded November 12, 1975									
Mark Olberding (to SA)	F	6'8	225	19	11	434	69	144	48	30	43	70	105	18	52	—	168	39	9.5	1.6	4.7	15.3
Dave Robisch (to Ind)	F-C	6'10	240	26	11	374	60	134	45	61	70	87	122	21	17	—	181	34	11.1	1.9	1.5	16.5
Caldwell Jones (to Ky & StL)	C	6'11	225	25	10	407	69	160	43	21	33	64	136	22	42	—	159	41	13.6	2.2	*4.2	15.9
Kelvin Joyce (to Ky)	G	6'3	190	24	9	266	36	108	33	22	32	69	7	47	21	—	95	30	0.8	5.2	2.3	10.6
Bo Lamar (broken hand-to Ind)	G	6'1	180	24	6	222	48	113	42	11	14	79	18	36	12	—	110	37	3.0	6.0	2.0	18.3
Pat McFarland	G	6'5	185	24	11	275	55	120	46	21	22	95	44	39	20	—	132	25	4.0	3.5	1.8	12.0
Bobby Warren	G	6'5	195	29	10	265	36	81	44	28	32	88	59	23	35	—	101	27	5.9	2.3	3.5	10.1
Stew Johnson (to SA)	F	6'8	225	31	10	227	40	119	34	16	18	89	29	8	19	—	96	23	2.9	0.8	1.9	9.6
Joby Wright (to Va)	F	6'8	222	26	10	105	16	27	59	4	10	40	22	0	22	—	36	11	2.2	0.0	2.2	3.6
Lee Davis	C-F	6'8	240	30	7	51	2	11	18	1	2	50	5	1	12	—	5	7	0.7	0.1	1.7	0.7
Tom Ingelsby	G	6'3	185	24	5	14	1	3	33	2	2	100	3	0	1	—	4	3	0.6	0.0	0.2	0.8

TEAM STATISTICS

Team		REGULAR SEASON G	FG	FGA	%	FT	FTA	%	Reb.	Ass.	PF	Points	PPG	PLAYOFFS G	FG	FGA	%	FT	FTA	%	Reb.	Ass.	PF	Points	PPG
Denver	Off.	84	4059	8036	51	2078	2667	78	4087	2442	1988	10237	121.9	13	584	1214	48	338	424	80	643	307	353	1509	116.1
	Def.	84	4027	8683	46	1567	2061	76	4240	2133	2287	9734	115.9	13	612	1286	48	275	357	77	617	294	382	1524	117.2
	Diff.		+32	-647	+5	+511	+606	+2	-153	+309	+299	+503	+6.0		-28	-72	—	+63	+67	+3	+26	+13	+29	-15	-1.1
New York	Off.	84	3752	8148	46	1775	2333	76	4243	1817	2209	9390	111.8	13	564	1255	45	298	393	76	618	233	384	1445	111.2
	Def.	84	3552	7837	45	1930	2515	77	4287	1986	2032	9142	108.8	13	554	1169	47	332	420	79	668	287	343	1445	111.2
	Diff.		+200	+311	+1	-155	-182	-1	-44	-169	-177	+248	+3.0		+10	+86	-2	-34	-27	-3	-50	-54	-41	—	—
San Antonio	Off.	84	3888	7945	49	1905	2342	81	4232	2146	2032	9707	115.6	7	286	627	46	178	226	79	367	153	176	753	107.6
	Def.	84	3760	8111	46	1720	2254	76	3935	2036	2141	9362	111.5	7	288	659	44	159	200	80	338	121	199	744	106.3
	Diff.		+128	-166	+3	+185	+88	+5	+297	+110	+109	+345	+4.1		-2	-32	+2	+19	+26	-1	+29	+32	+23	+9	+1.3
Kentucky	Off.	84	3756	8000	47	1703	2313	74	4362	2068	2257	9326	111.0	10	470	974	48	183	232	79	494	266	274	1138	113.8
	Def.	84	3581	8022	45	2004	2581	78	4168	1901	2132	9253	110.2	10	439	940	46	247	308	80	482	251	257	1134	113.4
	Diff.		+175	-22	+2	-301	-268	-4	+194	+167	-125	+73	+0.8		+31	+34	+2	-64	-76	-1	+12	+15	-17	+4	+0.4
Indiana	Off.	84	3735	8525	44	1740	2253	77	4352	2087	1981	9460	112.6	3	123	268	46	63	78	81	140	78	71	317	105.7
	Def.	84	3869	8132	48	1679	2156	78	4604	2139	2060	9480	112.9	3	134	284	47	47	68	69	157	84	77	315	105.0
	Diff.		-134	+393	-4	+61	+97	-1	-252	-52	+79	-20	-0.3		-11	-16	-1	+16	+10	+12	-17	-6	+6	+2	+0.7
St. Louis	Off.	84	3790	8177	46	1500	1985	76	4288	1987	2147	9146	108.9												
	Def.	84	3714	7986	47	1899	2384	80	4152	1971	1888	9416	112.1												
	Diff.		+76	+191	-1	-399	-399	-4	+136	+16	-259	-270	-3.2												
Virginia	Off.	83	3431	7844	44	1939	2533	77	3920	1724	2142	8873	106.9												
	Def.	83	3869	7905	49	1844	2437	76	4151	2014	2205	9674	116.6												
	Diff.		-438	-61	-5	+95	+96	+1	-231	-290	+63	-801	-9.7												
Utah	Off.	16	715	1498	48	386	467	83	781	378	468	1839	114.9												
	Def.	16	740	1520	49	366	478	77	742	429	461	1866	116.6												
	Diff.		-25	-22	-1	+20	-11	+6	+39	-51	-7	-27	-1.7												
San Diego	Off.	11	432	1020	42	217	278	78	550	215	253	1087	98.8												
	Def.	11	446	997	45	234	305	77	536	255	273	1138	103.5												
	Diff.		-14	+23	-3	-17	-27	+1	+14	-40	+20	-51	-4.7												

Use Name	Pos	Hgt	Wgt	Age	G	Min	FG	FGA	%	FT	FTA	%	Reb	Ass	PF	DQ	Points	Min	Reb	Ass	PF	Points
					TOTAL													PER GAME				

1975/76 A.B.A. — PLAYOFFS

Use Name	Pos	Hgt	Wgt	Age	G	Min	FG	FGA	%	FT	FTA	%	Reb	Ass	PF	DQ	Points	Min	Reb	Ass	PF	Points
NEW YORK NETS	**KEVIN LOUGHERY**				defeated San Antonio 4-3; defeated Denver 4-3;																	
Julius Erving	F	6'7	210	25	13	**551**	**160**	**300**	53	**127**	**158**	80	**164**	64	41	—	**451**	42	12.6	4.9	3.2	**34.7**
Rich Jones	F	6'8	230	29	12	421	72	193	37	18	27	67	87	27	43	—	164	35	7.3	2.3	3.6	13.7
Jim Eakins	C	6'11	215	29	13	281	30	56	54	29	36	81	78	11	52	—	89	22	6.0	0.8	4.0	6.8
Brian Taylor	G	6'2	185	24	13	475	81	213	38	34	46	74	34	46	37	—	205	37	2.6	3.5	2.8	15.8
John Williamson	G	6'2	185	23	10	360	94	189	50	32	46	70	24	26	36	—	222	36	2.4	2.6	3.6	22.2
Tim Bassett	F-C	6'8	230	24	13	312	37	81	46	8	11	73	93	9	46	—	82	24	7.2	0.7	3.5	6.3
Al Skinner	G-F	6'4	195	23	13	287	44	101	44	39	50	78	48	28	45	—	128	22	3.7	2.2	3.5	9.8
Kim Hughes	C	6'11	220	23	12	266	29	57	51	2	5	40	72	9	53	—	60	22	6.0	0.8	4.4	5.0
Ted McClain	G	6'3	180	28	8	96	10	37	27	6	10	60	11	7	19	—	26	12	1.4	0.9	2.4	3.3
Bill Melchionni	G	6'1	170	31	6	36	4	14	29	2	2	100	5	5	3	—	10	6	0.8	0.8	0.5	1.7
Chuck Terry	F	6'6	215	25	4	23	0	7	0	0	0	—	2	1	7	—	0	6	0.5	0.3	1.8	0.0
George Bucci	G	6'3	202	22	2	9	3	7	43	1	2	50	0	0	2	—	8	5	0.0	0.0	1.0	4.0
DENVER NUGGETS	**LARRY BROWN**				defeated Kentucky 4-3; lost to New York 2-4;																	
David Thompson	F-G	6'4	195	21	13	508	127	237	54	88	105	84	83	39	54	—	343	39	6.4	3.0	4.2	26.4
Bobby Jones	F	6'9	215	24	13	431	74	127	58	30	41	73	112	59	53	—	178	33	8.6	4.5	4.1	13.7
Dan Issel	C	6'9	240	27	13	470	111	227	49	44	56	79	156	32	**62**	—	266	36	12.0	2.5	4.8	20.5
Ralph Simpson	G	6'5	200	26	13	542	99	217	46	58	64	91	61	73	33	—	257	42	4.7	5.6	2.5	19.8
Chuck Williams	G	6'2	185	29	13	444	62	132	47	39	43	**91**	48	48	31	—	164	34	3.7	3.7	2.4	12.6
Byron Beck	F-C	6'9	230	30	13	276	42	95	44	28	34	82	56	11	41	—	112	21	4.3	0.8	3.2	8.6
Claude Terry	G-F	6'4	195	25	12	159	18	50	36	13	17	76	21	17	15	—	49	13	1.8	1.4	1.3	4.1
Marvin Webster	C	7'1	240	23	13	155	21	50	42	15	28	54	71	9	28	—	57	12	5.5	0.7	2.2	4.4
Gus Gerard	F	6'8	200	22	13	142	22	63	35	16	24	67	33	12	26	—	60	11	2.5	0.9	2.0	4.6
Monte Towe (injury)	G	5'7	150	22	4	30	3	8	38	4	5	80	0	6	6	—	10	8	0.0	1.5	1.5	2.5
Jim Foster	G	6'1	180	23	2	13	5	8	63	3	7	43	2	1	4	—	13	7	1.0	0.5	2.0	6.5
KENTUCKY COLONELS	**HUBIE BROWN**				defeated Indiana lost to Denver 3-4;																	
Wil Jones	F	6'8	205	28	10	324	52	108	48	16	17	94	67	20	41	—	120	32	6.7	2.0	4.1	12.0
Maurice Lucas	F	6'9	220	23	10	330	78	152	51	15	19	79	108	22	48	—	165	33	10.8	2.2	4.8	16.5
Artis Gilmore	C	7'2	240	26	10	390	93	153	**61**	56	74	76	152	19	49	—	242	39	**15.2**	1.9	**4.9**	24.2
Bird Averitt	G	6'1	175	23	10	358	80	198	40	37	42	88	22	61	31	—	199	36	2.2	6.1	3.1	19.9
Louie Dampier	G	6'	180	31	10	393	67	129	52	18	20	90	13	**77**	20	—	160	39	1.3	7.7	2.0	16.0
Jan van Breda Kolff	F	6'7	200	24	10	186	21	40	53	11	14	79	36	16	12	—	53	19	3.6	1.6	1.2	5.3
Ron Thomas	F	6'6	215	25	10	142	20	41	49	5	13	38	54	9	23	—	45	14	5.4	0.9	2.3	4.5
Kevin Joyce	G	6'3	190	24	9	117	10	36	28	10	12	83	3	30	14	—	30	13	0.3	3.3	1.6	3.3
Johnny Neumann	G	6'6	210	24	8	112	33	76	43	11	14	79	4	7	20	—	82	14	0.5	0.9	2.5	10.3
Jim McDaniels	C	6'11	240	27	10	98	19	41	46	4	7	57	35	5	16	—	42	10	3.5	0.5	1.6	4.2
SAN ANTONIO SPURS	**BOB BASS**				lost to New York 3-4;																	
Larry Kenon	F	6'9	205	23	7	277	61	131	47	27	30	90	80	16	16	—	150	40	11.4	2.3	2.3	21.4
Coby Dietrick	F-C	6'10	230	27	7	208	27	55	49	8	13	62	41	15	28	—	62	30	5.9	2.1	4.0	8.9
Billy Paultz	C	6'11	260	27	7	254	43	97	44	35	40	88	72	19	29	—	121	36	10.3	2.7	4.1	17.3
George Gervin	G-F	6'7	180	23	7	288	67	128	52	56	69	81	64	19	22	—	190	41	9.1	2.7	3.1	27.1
Mike Gale	G	6'4	190	25	7	286	45	98	46	13	17	76	40	50	16	—	103	41	5.7	7.1	2.3	14.7
Allan Bristow	F	6'7	227	24	7	97	13	35	37	19	24	79	14	12	14	—	45	14	2.0	1.7	2.0	6.4
Tom Owens	F	6'10	225	26	7	89	8	24	33	7	14	50	24	2	15	—	23	13	3.4	0.3	2.1	3.3
Mark Olberding	F	6'8	225	19	7	73	5	15	33	3	6	50	22	3	15	—	13	10	3.1	0.4	2.1	1.9
George Karl	G	6'2	185	24	6	64	10	22	45	6	9	67	4	17	12	—	26	11	0.7	2.8	3.0	4.3
James Silas (broken ankle)	G	6'3	185	26	1	26	3	10	30	4	4	100	4	0	3	—	10	26	4.0	0.0	3.0	10.0
Henry Ward	G	6'4	195	23	5	18	4	12	33	0	0	—	2	0	6	—	10	4	0.4	0.0	1.2	2.0
INDIANA PACERS	**BOB LEONARD**				lost to Kentucky																	
Billy Knight	F-G	6'6	200	23	3	143	41	74	55	19	22	86	32	12	9	—	101	**48**	10.7	4.0	3.0	33.7
Darnell Hillman	F	6'9	215	26	3	111	16	39	41	11	14	79	31	10	14	—	43	37	10.3	3.3	4.7	14.3
Len Elmore	C	6'9	230	23	3	68	9	30	30	1	1	100	15	4	10	—	19	23	5.0	1.3	3.3	6.3
Don Buse	G	6'4	195	25	3	138	15	33	45	4	4	100	14	26	7	—	37	46	4.7	**8.7**	2.3	12.3
Mike Flynn	G	6'2	180	22	3	83	15	30	50	8	11	73	10	10	6	—	41	28	3.3	3.3	2.0	13.7
Dave Robisch	C-F	6'10	240	26	3	83	11	27	41	12	16	75	20	8	8	—	34	28	6.7	2.7	2.7	11.3
Billy Keller	G	5'10	185	28	3	50	8	16	50	0	1	0	3	6	2	—	18	17	1.0	2.0	0.7	6.0
Dan Roundfield	F-C	6'8	210	22	2	25	7	12	58	8	9	89	10	0	6	—	22	13	5.0	0.0	3.0	11.0
Charles Jordan	F	6'8	225	21	2	18	1	6	17	0	0	—	5	2	9	—	2	9	2.5	1.0	4.5	1.0
Travis Grant	F	6'8	225	25	1	1	0	1	0	0	0	—	0	0	0	—	0	1	0.0	0.0	0.0	0.0
Bo Lamar - hand injury																						

Team	W	L	Pct.	GB	Record against playoff teams W	L	Pct.	Record against non-playoff teams W	L	Pct.	HOME W	L	Pct.	ROAD W	L	Pct.
Denver Nuggets	60	24	.714	—												
New York Nets	55	29	.655	5												
San Antonio Spurs	50	34	.595	10	N/A			N/A			N/A			N/A		
Kentucky Colonels	46	38	.548	14												
Indiana Pacers	39	45	.464	21												
Spirits of St. Louis	35	49	.417	25												
San Diego Sails	3	8	.273	20.5												
Utah Stars	4	12	.250	22												
Virginia Squires	15	68	.181	44.5												

1975/76 — A.B.A. INDIVIDUAL LEADERS

SCORING (Minimum 1000 Points)

Name	Team	G	FG	FT	Pts.	Avg.
Erving	NY	84	949	530	2462	29.3
Knight	Ind	70	774	415	1969	28.1
Thompson	Den	83	807	541	2158	26.0
Gilmore	Ky	84	773	521	2067	24.6
Barnes	StL	67	681	251	1616	24.1
Silas	SA	84	718	564	2000	23.8
Issel	Den	84	752	425	1930	23.0
Boone	Utah-StL	78	713	277	1719	22.0
Gervin	SA	81	706	342	1768	21.8
Burden	Va	71	561	283	1413	19.9

TOTAL FIELD GOAL PERCENTAGE (Minimum 300 Made)

Name	Team	FG	FGA	Pct.
Jones	Den	510	878	.581
Gilmore	Ky	773	1401	.552
Hughes	NY	300	566	.530
Beck	Den	334	646	.517
Thompson	Den	807	1567	.515
Williams	Den	339	660	.514
Simpson	Den	619	1211	.511
Issel	Den	752	1472	.511
Erving	NY	949	1873	.507
Barnes	StL	681	1355	.503

3-POINT FIELD GOAL PERCENTAGE (Minimum 20 Made)

Name	Team	FG	FGA	Pct.
Taylor	NY	32	76	.421
Dampier	Ky	32	87	.368
Keller	Ind	123	349	.352
Buse	Ind	72	208	.346
Neumann	Va-Ky	71	208	.341
Erving	NY	34	103	.330
Averitt	Ky	40	128	.313
Lewis	StL	31	106	.292
Lamar	SD-Ind	24	86	.279
Flynn	Ind	25	99	.253

FREE THROW PERCENTAGE (Minimum 200 Made)

Name	Team	FT	FTA	Pct.
Calvin	Va	253	285	.888
Silas	SA	564	647	.872
Boone	Utah-StL	277	318	.871
Gervin	SA	342	399	.857
Robisch	SD-Ind	324	381	.850
Skinner	NY	203	241	.842
Knight	Ind	415	501	.828
Lewis	StL	259	317	.817
Issel	Den	425	521	.816
Erving	NY	530	662	.801

REBOUNDS PER GAME (Minimum 600 Rebounds)

Name	Team	G	Reb.	Avg.
Gilmore	Ky	84	1303	15.5
Lucas	StL-Ky	86	970	11.3
Jones	SD-Ky-StL	76	853	11.2
Kenon	SA	81	897	11.1
Erving	NY	84	925	11.0
Issel	Den	84	923	11.0
Barnes	StL	67	725	10.8
Elmore	Ind	76	819	10.8
Paultz	SA	83	862	10.4
Nater	NY-Va	76	765	10.1

ASSISTS PER GAME (Minimum 250)

Name	Team	G	Ass.	Avg.
Buse	Ind	84	689	8.2
Simpson	Den	84	597	7.1
Calvin	Va	45	271	6.0
Dampier	Ky	82	467	5.7
Silas	SA	84	452	5.4
Taylor	Va	76	401	5.3
Erving	NY	84	423	5.0
Boone	Utah-StL	78	387	5.0
Williams	Den	79	375	4.7
McClain	Ky-NY	73	310	4.2

BLOCKED SHOTS PER GAME (Minimum 100)

Name	Team	G	Reb.	Avg.
Paultz	SA	83	253	3.0
Jones	SD-Ky-StL	76	218	2.9
Gilmore	Ky	84	205	2.4
Elmore	Ind	76	178	2.3
Jones	Den	83	184	2.2
Barnes	StL	67	134	2.0
Erving	NY	84	160	1.9
Gervin	SA	81	119	1.5
Hughes	NY	84	120	1.4
Thompson	Den	83	102	1.2

OFFENSIVE REBOUNDS PER GAME (Minimum 70 Games Played)

Name	Team	G	Reb.	Avg.
Gilmore	Ky	84	402	4.8
Knight	Ind	70	294	4.2
Hughes	NY	84	341	4.1
Erving	NY	84	337	4.0
Barnes	StL	67	263	3.9
Issel	Den	84	303	3.6
Kenon	SA	81	287	3.5
Hillman	Ind	74	248	3.4
Bennett	VA	75	249	3.3
Jones	SD-Ky-StL	76	246	3.2

STEALS PER GAME (Minimum 100)

Name	Team	G	Steals	Avg.
Buse	Ind	84	346	4.1
Taylor	Va	76	206	2.7
Erving	NY	84	207	2.5
Taylor	NY	54	125	2.3
Jones	Den	83	170	2.0
Boone	Utah-StL	78	154	2.0
McClain	Ky-NY	73	138	1.9
Barnes	StL	67	124	1.9
Silas	SA	84	155	1.8
Simpson	Den	84	153	1.8

MINUTES PLAYED

Name	Team	Min.
Buse	Ind	3380
Gilmore	Ky	3286
Erving	NY	3244
Simpson	Den	3121
Silas	SA	3112

PERSONAL FOULS

Name	Team	PF
Gilmore	Ky	341
Jones	Ky	326
Jones	SD-Ky-StL	321
Elmore	Ind	310
Jackson	Va	306
Hillman	Ind	306

Use Name-Nickname	Team by Year	Birth Yr	Hgt	Wgt	Pos	College	# Yr	G.	Field Goals FG	Att.	%	3 Pt. FG FG	Att	%	Free Throws FT	Att.	%	Reb.	Ass.	PF	DQ	Pts	Per Game Min	Reb	Ass	Pts
Zaid Abdul-Aziz	69Cin 69-70Mil 71-72Sea	1946	6'9	235	C-F	Iowa	10	505	1769	4138	43				1019	1400	73	4065	601	1120	12	4557	22	8.0	1.2	9.0
73-75Hou 76Sea 77Buf	70, 75, 76						3	18	37	70	53				18	26	69	64	9	12	0	92	12	3.6	0.5	5.1
78Bos 78Hou (born Don Smith-played as Smith 69-74)																										
Mahdi Abdul-Rahman	65-67LA 68Sea 69-71Atl	1942	6'2	190	G	U.C.L.A.	10	724	3597	8162	44				1893	2502	76	2146	3555	2027	18	9087	27	3.0	4.9	12.6
72 Buf 73GS74Sea	65-67, 69-71, 73						7	58	268	649	41				149	202	74	169	242	176	1	685	27	2.9	4.1	11.8
(born Walt Hazzard, played as Hazzard 65-72)																										
Bud Acton	68SD	1942	6'6	210	F	Hillsdale	1	23	29	74	39				19	29	66	47	11	35	0	77	8	2.0	0.5	3.3
Don Adams	71SD 72Hou 72-73Atl 73-75Det	1947	6'7	216	F	Northwestern	7	523	1823	4532	40	0	3	0	952	1285	74	2916	1044	1953	23	4598	26	5.6	2.0	8.8
75-76StLA 76-77Buf	72, 74-76						4	22	63	165	38				30	44	68	116	45	74	1	156	26	5.3	2.0	7.1
George Adams	73-75SD-A	1949	6'6	210	F	Gardner-Webb	3	215	716	1440	50	4	17	24	216	272	79	873	317	372		1652	18	4.1	1.5	7.7
	73-74						3	9	34	66	52	0	1	0	12	16	75	34	15	14		80	20	3.8	1.7	8.9
Rick Adelman	69-70SD 71-73Port 74-75Chi	1946	6'1	183	G	Loyola (L.A.)	7	462	1361	3330	41				817	1146	71	1129	1606	990	8	3579	23	2.4	3.5	7.7
75NO 75KCO	69, 74-75						3	21	43	96	45				35	56	63	27	39	32	0	12	16	1.3	1.9	0.6
HC89Port																										
Matt Aitch	68IndA	1944	6'7	238	F	Michigan St.	1	45	100	247	40	0	2	0	52	77	68	160	18	69	1	252	14	3.6	0.4	5.6
	68						1	2	2	4	50	0	0	—	0	0	—	0	0	0	0	4	0	0.0	0.0	2.0
Henry Akin	67NY 68Sea 69KyA	1944	6'10	232	C-F	Morehead St.	3	88	130	371	35	0	2	0	47	71	66	181	40	130	1	308	8	2.1	0.5	3.5
	67						1	2	1	7	14				1	2	50	8	0	3	0	3	8	4.0	0.0	1.5
Bill Allen	68AnaA	1945	6'8	205	C-F	N. Mexico St.	1	38	120	280	43	2	2	100	58	99	59	269	23	121	5	300	23	7.1	0.6	7.9
Bob Allen	69SF	1946	6'9	205	F	Marshall	1	27	14	43	33				20	36	56	56	10	27	0	48	9	2.1	0.4	1.8
	69						1	3	0	4	0				0	7	0	6	0	2	0	4	6	2.0	0.0	1.3
Lucius Allen	70-Sea 71-75Mil 75-77LA	1947	6'2	175	G	U.C.L.A.	10	702	3884	8385	46				1639	2157	76	2205	3174	1799	11	9407	29	3.1	4.5	13.4
78-79KC	71-73, 77, 79						5	43	202	450	45				102	135	76	133	142	100	0	506	27	3.1	3.3	11.8
Willie Allen	72FlaA	1949	6'6	230	F	Miami (Fla.)	1	7	4	13	31	0	0	—	5	6	83	14	4	11		13	4	2.0	0.6	1.9
Odis Allison	72GS	1949	6'6	195	F	Nev.-Las Vegas	1	36	17	78	22				33	61	54	45	10	34	0	67	5	1.3	0.3	1.9
Andy Anderson	68-69OakA 69-70MiaA	1945	6'2	185	G	Canisius	3	194	803	1958	41	10	61	16	465	616	75	583	369	536	3	2081	25	3.0	1.9	10.7
70LA-A	69-70						2	28	85	215	40	1	5	20	54	66	82	23	16	21	0	225	20	1.9	1.3	8.0
Cliff Anderson	68-69LA 70DenA 71Cle 71Phi	1944	6'4	200	G-F	St. Joseph's	4	84	73	206	35	0	0	—	107	183	58	107	72	108	2	253	7	1.3	0.9	3.0
	69						1	3	2	5	40				0	0	—	1	0	1	0	4	3	0.3	0.0	1.3
Dan Anderson	68NJ-A 69NY-A 69KyA	1943	6'10	230	C	Augsburg	2	140	683	1421	48	0	0	—	341	469	73	1316	158	503	19	1707	29	9.4	1.1	12.2
69MinA	69						1	5	6	13	46	0	0	—	3	4	75	10	5	8	0	15	8	2.0	1.0	3.0
Dan Andersom	75-76Port	1951	6'2	185	G	Southern Cal.	2	95	135	286	47				77	91	85	91	166	102	0	347	11	1.0	1.7	3.7
LaDell Anderson	HC72-73UtahA					Utah State																				
Wally Anderzunas	70Cin	1946	6'7	220	C-F	Creighton	1	44	65	166	39				29	46	63	82	9	47	1	159	8	1.9	0.2	3.6
Jim Ard	71-73NY-A 74MemA	1948	6'8	222	F-C	Cincinnati	8	431	748	1853	40	4	17	24	401	606	66	1832	278	384	5	1909	13	4.3	0.6	4.4
75-78Bos 78Chi	71-72, 75, 76						4	40	45	106	42	0	2	0	29	46	63	85	16	66	0	117	8	2.1	0.4	2.9
Warren Armstrong (see Warren Jabali)																										
Bob Arnzen	70NY-A 71Cin 73-74IndA	1947	6'6	215	F	Notre Dame	4	111	191	411	46	1	5	20	60	75	80	217	35	88	0	443	6	2.0	0.3	4.0
	73						1	7	3	6	50	0	2	0	1	1	100	0	0	1	0	7	2	0.0	0.0	1.0
John Arthurs	70Mil	1947	6'4	185	G	Tulane	1	11	12	35	34				11	15	73	14	17	15	0	35	8	1.3	1.5	3.2
Johnny Austin	67Bal 68NJ-A	1944	6'	175	G	Boston Coll.	2	45	113	301	38	0	11	0	114	156	73	71	62	122	0	340	17	1.6	1.4	7.6
Bird Averitt	74SA 75-76KyA 77-78Buf	1952	6'1	175	G	Pepperdine	5	366	1687	4078	41	56	225	25	892	1200	74	680	1078	769	5	4434	22	1.9	2.9	12.1
78NJ	74-76						3	30	155	403	38	1	8	13	77	92	84	55	93	74		390	24	1.8	3.1	13.0
Dennis Awtrey	71-73Phi 73-74Chi	1948	6'10	245	C	Santa Clara	12	733	1382	3009	46				752	1154	65	3342	1467	1702	24	3516	19	4.6	2.0	4.8
75-78Phoe 79Bos	71, 73-74, 76, 78-79						6	61	91	177	51				55	94	59	251	88	144	3	237	17	4.1	1.4	3.9
79Sea 80Chi 81Sea 82Port																										
Henry Bacon	73SD-A	1951	6'3	205	G	Louisville	1	47	60	164	37	2	10	20	44	73	60	82	38	72		166	9	1.7	0.8	3.5
	73						1	2	4	9	44	2	3	67	0	2	0	6	1	0		10	8	3.0	0.5	5.0
Jimmie Baker	76KyA	1953	6'9	220	F	Hawaii	1	5	3	15	20	0	0	—	0	2	0	14	4	11		6	8	2.8	0.8	1.2
Walter Banks	71PitA	1948	6'10	205	C	Western Ky.	1	16	17	34	50	0	0	—	7	17	41	49	8	34		41	10	3.1	0.5	2.6
Henry Barnes	69SD	1945	6'3	205	F	Northeastern	1	22	18	64	28				7	13	54	26	5	25	0	43	6	1.2	0.2	2.0
Jim Barnes (Bad News)	65-66NY 66Bal	1941	6'8	240	C-F	Texas-El Paso	7	454	1548	3607	43				901	1319	68	2939	377	1497	36	3997	21	6.5	0.8	8.8
67-68LA 68-69Chi	66-68						3	11	26	63	41				12	18	67	61	6	35	2	64	18	5.5	0.5	5.8
69-70Bos 71Bal																										
Jim Barnett	67Bos 68-70SD 71Port	1944	6'4	180	G-F	Oregon	9	645	3134	7207	43				1784	2231	80	2157	2119	1459	9	8052	25	3.3	3.3	12.5
72-74GS 75NO 75NY	67, 69, 72-73, 75						5	30	127	303	42				67	83	81	74	78	64	0	321	22	2.5	2.6	10.7
Mike Barr	73-74VaA 75StLA	1950	6'3	180	G	Duquesne	3	178	507	1052	48	3	11	27	202	272	74	393	512	417		1219	23	2.2	2.9	6.8
	73-75						3	20	58	128	45	1	1	100	19	24	79	65	64	56		136	32	3.3	3.2	6.8
Moe Barr	71Cin	1944	6'4	195	G	Duquesne	1	31	25	62	40				11	13	85	20	28	27	0	61	5	0.6	0.9	2.0
Mike Barrett (Bird Man)	70WasA 71VaA 72BW	1943	6'2	160	G	West Virginia	3	187	974	2215	44	94	303	31	458	614	75	592	730	473	2	2500	28	3.2	3.9	13.4
73SD-A	70-71, 72VaA						3	20	143	328	44	24	76	32	77	92	84	49	74	33		387	36	2.5	3.7	19.4
Rick Barry	66-67SF 68CT 69OakA	1944	6'7	214	F	Miami (Fla)	14	1020	9592	20911	46	##	595	30	5713	6397	89	6863	4952	3026	15	25279	37	6.7	4.9	24.8
70WasA 71-72NYA	67, 70-73, 75-77, 79-80						10	105	1040	2358	44	43	114	38	627	721	87	671	449	322	3	2870	39	6.4	4.3	27.3
73-78GS 79-80Hou																										
Vic Bartolome	72GS	1948	7'	230	C	Oregon State	1	38	15	59	25				4	5	80	60	3	22	0	34	4	1.6	0.1	0.9
Jerry Baskerville	76Phi	1951	6'7	190	F	Temple	1	21	8	26	31				10	16	63	28	3	32	0	26	6	1.3	0.1	1.2
Bob Bass	HC68-69 DenA HC71-72MaA	1929				Oklahoma Baptist																				
HC73MemA HC75-76SA-A HC80, 84SA																										
Tim Bassett	74-75SD-A 76NY-A 77NYN	1951	6'8	228	F-C	Southern Idaho	7	473	1216	2869	42	4	14	29	489	831	59	3148	576	1264	16	2933	24	6.7	1.2	6.2
78-80NJ 80SA	74, 76, 79-80					Georgia	4	24	80	165	48	0	0	—	18	35	51	185	29	75	0	178	25	7.7	1.2	7.4
Lloyd Batts	75VaA	1951	6'4	185	G-F	Cincinnati	1	58	249	680	37	42	147	29	58	94	62	197	106	104		598	23	3.4	1.8	10.3
Johnny Baum	70-71Chi 72-73NY-A	1946	6'5	206	F	Temple	5	244	630	1312	48	0	2	0	238	314	76	666	141	331	0	1498	14	2.7	0.6	6.1
74MemA 74IndA	71-74						4	35	117	217	54	0	0	—	28	39	72	114	13	66	0	262	17	3.3	0.4	7.5
Howard Bayne	68KyA	1942	6'6	235	F	Tennessee	1	69	130	361	36	1	7	14	77	143	54	456	71	199	6	338	17	6.6	1.0	4.9
	68						1	5	3	19	16	0	1	0	6	11	55	23	5	12	0	12	17	4.6	1.0	2.4

Use Name-Nickname	Team by Year	Birth Yr	Hgt.	Wgt	Pos	College	# Yr	G.	Field Goals FG	Att	%	3 pt. FG FG	Att	%	Free Throws FT	Att.	%	Reb.	Ass	PF	DQ	Pts	Per Game Min	Reb	Ass	Pts
Al Beard	68NJ-A	1944	6'9	200	C	Norfolk St.	1	12	12	23	52	0	0	—	6	11	55	46	0	39	1	30	10	3.8	0.0	2.5
Butch Beard	70Atl 71MS 72Cle	1947	6'3	185	G	Louisville	9	605	2187	4495	49				1248	1619	77	2042	2189	1581	24	5622	24	3.4	3.6	9.3
74-75GS 76-79NY	70, 75, 78						3	32	115	259	44				59	89	66	119	88	105	1	289	24	3.7	2.8	9.0
Charlie Beasley	68-70DalA 71FlaA 71TexA	1945	6'5	190	G-F	S.M.U.	4	281	943	2067	46	30	126	24	717	830	86	704	860	651	5	2633	26	2.5	3.1	9.4
	68-71						4	23	99	218	45	3	18	17	63	78	81	50	80	48	0	264	30	2.2	3.5	11.5
John Beasley	68-70DalA 71TexA 72DalA	1944	6'9	226	F-C	Texas A&M	7	506	2786	5670	49	81	256	32	1256	1512	83	3996	602	1294	12	6909	28	7.9	1.2	13.7
72-74UtahA	68-74						7	51	228	467	49	8	36	22	96	112	86	376	72	105	0	560	25	7.4	1.4	11.0
Zelmo Beatty	63-68StL 69Atl 70Ct	1939	6'9	237	C	Pr. View A&M	12	889	5724	11580	49	2	13	15	3757	4873	77	9665	1365	3344	66	15207	33	10.9	1.5	17.1
71-74UtahA	63-69, 71-74						11	115	768	1548	50	0	0	—	526	683	77	1370	200	459	7	2062	38	11.9	1.7	17.9
75LA HC76VaA																										
Bryon Beck	68-75DenA	1945	6'9	234	C-F	Denver	8	614	3240	6403	51	8	33	24	1095	1355	81	4811	829	2016	27	7583	28	7.8	1.4	12.4
	68-70, 72-73, 75						6	48	301	633	48	2	9	22	124	152	82	423	70	174	1	726	31	8.8	1.5	15.2
Art Becker	68-69HouA 70-71IndA	1942	6'8	210	F	Ariz. State	6	414	2116	4408	48	9	28	32	919	1101	83	2604	410	1411	29	5160	25	6.3	1.0	12.5
71-72DenA	68, 70, 72						3	25	68	143	48	0	1	0	42	51	82	86	14	64	0	178	17	3.4	0.6	7.1
73NY-A 73DalA																										
Bob Bedell	68AnaA 69-70DalA 71TexA	1944	6'8	205	F	Stanford	4	269	878	2075	42	11	58	19	490	633	77	1386	320	595	9	2257	17	5.2	1.2	8.4
	69-71						3	16	50	114	44	0	9	0	25	32	78	76	15	34	1	125	16	4.8	0.9	7.8
Dennis Bell	74-76NY	1951	6'6	215	F	Drake	3	63	76	203	37				23	43	53	119	28	65	0	175	9	1.9	0.4	2.8
	75						1	3	1	8	13				0	5	0	4	0	6	0	2	9	1.3	0.0	0.7
Walt Bellamy (Bells)	62-63Chi	1939	6'11	240	C	Indiana	14	1043	7914	15340	52				5113	8088	63	14241	2544	3536	58	20941	37	13.7	2.4	20.1
64-66Bal 66-69NY	65, 67-68, 70-73						7	46	323	686	47				204	318	64	680	136	160	0	850	42	14.8	3.0	18.5
69-70Det 70-74Atl 75NO																										
Joe Belmont	HC70-71DenA	1934				Duke																				
Leon Benbow	75-76Chi	1952	6'4	185	G	Jacksonville	2	115	254	645	39				120	158	76	214	183	227	1	628	16	1.9	1.6	5.5
	75						1	2	2	4	50				1	2	50	1	2	0	0	5	3	0.5	1.0	2.5
Spider Bennett	69DalA 69HouA	1943	6'3	190	G	Win-Salem	1	59	147	385	38	6	25	24	140	216	65	147	84	165	9	440	17	2.5	1.4	7.5
Larry Bergh	70PitA	1945	6'8	215	F	Weber State	1	20	49	120	41	0	1	0	23	33	70	85	18	52	2	121	13	4.3	0.9	6.1
Wes Bialosuknia	68OakA	1945	6'2	185	G	Connecticut	1	70	238	570	42	29	73	40	103	132	78	89	57	101	1	608	17	1.3	0.8	8.7
Ed Biedenbach	69Phoe	1945	6'1	175	G	N. C. State	1	7	0	6	0				4	6	67	2	3	1	0	4	3	0.3	0.4	0.6
Lionel Billingy (Big Train)	75VaA	1952	6'9	215	F-C	Duquesne	1	46	150	351	43	0	2	0	93	143	65	280	49	112		393	22	6.1	1.1	8.5
Dave Bing	67-75Det 76-77Was 78Bos	1943	6'3	184	G	Syracuse	12	901	6962	15769	44				4403	5683	77	3420	5397	2615	22	18327	36	3.8	6.0	20.3
	68, 74-77						5	31	191	452	42				95	127	75	85	133	76	0	477	31	2.7	4.3	15.4
Mark Binstein	HC72PitA					Army																				
Tom Black	71Sea 71Cin	1941	6'10	234	C	Wisconsin, South Dakota St.	1	71	121	301	40				57	88	65	259	44	136	1	299	12	3.6	0.6	4.2
Bill Blakely	HC71TexA	1934				Abilene Christian																				
Hal Blitman	HC70MiaA HC71FlaA	1933				West Chester St.																				
John Block	67LA 68-71SD 72Mil	1944	6'10	217	F-C	Southern Cal.	10	597	2592	5967	43				1922	2470	78	3965	805	1733	18	7106	24	6.6	1.3	11.9
73Phi 73KCO	67, 69, 72, 75						4	32	70	164	43				48	54	89	130	15	53	0	185	14	4.1	0.5	5.8
74Phi 75NO 75-76Chi																										
Tom Boerwinkle	69-78Chi 79KJ	1945	7'	269	C	Tennessee	10	635	1863	4109	45				870	1288	68	5745	2007	1811	31	4596	23	9.0	3.2	7.2
	70-75, 77						7	35	107	233	46				36	48	75	330	123	94	2	250	22	9.4	3.5	7.1
Butch Booker	70Mia	1945	6'10	230	C	Cheyney St.	1	12	30	61	49	0	1	0	10	18	56	91	6	23	0	70	18	7.6	0.5	5.8
Ron Boone	69-70DalA 71TexA	1946	6'2	200	G-F	Idaho State	7	584	3982	8634	46	107	372	29	2363	2861	83	2983	2182	2002	13	10434	32	5.1	3.7	17.9
71-75UtahA	69-75						7	76	506	1094	46	13	54	24	236	270	87	358	371	243	1	1261	33	4.7	4.9	16.6
Tom Bowens	68DenA 69NY-A 70NO--A	1940	6'8	220	F-C	Grambling	3	211	473	1157	41	1	5	20	185	280	66	1007	134	542	11	1132	17	4.8	0.6	5.4
	68						1	5	14	31	45	0	1	0	2	2	100	25	5	17	1	30	19	5.0	1.0	6.0
Orb Bowling	68KyA	1941	6'10	215	C	Tennessee	1	11	9	28	32	0	0	—	3	12	25	29	1	16	0	21	8	2.6	0.1	1.9
Nate Bowman	67Chi 68-70NY 71Buf	1943	6'10	230	C	Wichita St.	6	261	317	817	39	0	1	0	111	210	53	878	175	557	8	745	9	3.4	0.7	2.9
72PitA	68-70						3	29	22	66	33				10	13	77	79	9	51	0	54	0	2.7	0.3	1.9
Freddie Boyd	73-76Phi 76-78NO	1950	6'2	180	G	Oregon State	6	327	1165	2817	41				454	681	67	533	986	651	2	2784	24	1.6	3.0	8.5
Ken Boyd	75NO	1952	6'5	195	F	Boston U.	1	6	7	13	54				5	11	45	5	2	2	0	19	4	0.8	0.3	3.2
Steve Bracey	73-74Atl 75GS	1950	6'1	175	G	Tulsa	3	187	487	1045	47				167	244	68	291	408	323	0	1141	15	1.6	2.2	6.1
	73, 75						2	10	27	54	50				15	20	75	14	23	14	0	69	14	1.4	2.3	6.9
Gary Bradds (Tex)	65-66Bal	1942	6'8	216	F	Ohio State	6	254	1106	2333	47	1	18	6	889	1103	81	1398	227	634	8	3106	21	5.5	0.9	12.2
68-69OakA 70WasA	65, 69-70						3	23	148	317	47	1	1	100	94	117	80	164	15	69	1	391	26	7.1	0.7	17.0
71CarA 71TexA																										
Bill Bradley (Dollar Bill)	68-77NY	1943	6'5	206	F-G	Princeton	10	742	3927	8763	45				1363	1623	84	2354	2533	2363	27	9217	31	3.2	3.4	12.4
	68-75						8	95	510	1165	44				202	251	80	333	263	313	5	1222	33	3.5	2.8	12.9
Bill Bradley	68KyA	1941	5'11	167	G	Tenn. State	1	58	82	258	32	3	18	17	51	56	91	47	54	40	0	218	9	0.8	0.9	3.8
	68						1	2	2	2	100	0	0	—	2	2	100	1	1	3	0	6	5	0.5	0.5	3.0
Jesse Branson	68Phi 68NO-A	1942	6'7	200	F	Elon	2	83	377	883	43	2	9	22	335	477	70	550	68	252	3	1091	23	6.6	0.8	13.1
	68						1	17	61	155	39	0	3	0	71	87	82	102	20	62	0	193	24	6.0	1.2	11.4
Bill Bridges	63-68StL 69-72Atl	1939	6'6	234	F-C	Kansas	13	926	4181	9463	44				2650	3824	69	11054	2553	3375	73	11012	33	11.9	2.8	11.9
72-73Phi	63-71, 73-75						12	113	475	1135	42				235	349	67	1305	219	408	10	1185	31	11.5	1.9	10.5
73-75LA 75GS																										
John Brisker	70-72PitA 73-75Sea	1947	6'5	215	F-G	Toledo	6	331	2678	5907	45	166	517	32	1325	1588	83	2152	787	937	5	6847	30	6.5	2.4	20.7
Tyrone Britt	68SD	1944	6'4	190	G	J.C. Smith	1	11	13	34	38				2	3	67	15	12	10	0	28	8	1.4	1.1	2.5
Gary Brokaw	75-77Mil 77Cle 78Buf	1954	6'4	180	G	Notre Dame	4	241	731	1640	45				466	654	71	407	715	489	6	1928	20	1.7	3.0	8.0
	76-77						2	6	32	56	57				19	24	79	15	36	17	0	83	25	2.5	6.0	13.8
Clarence Brookins	71FlaA	1946	6'4	190	F	Temple	1	8	8	26	31	0	1	0	5	12	42	12	1	5		21	7	1.5	0.1	2.6
Dave Brown	HC73DalA	1935				Wisconsin																				
Larry Brown	69NO-A 69OakA 70Was	1940	5'9	160	G	N. Carolina	5	376	1384	3357	41	48	209	23	1413	1737	81	1005	2509	1059	11	4229	30	2.7	6.7	11.2
71VaA 71-72DenA	68-70, 72						4	47	218	508	43	5	29	17	229	270	85	121	252	132	0	670	36	2.6	5.4	14.3
HC73-74CarA HC75-76DenA HC77-79Den HC82-83NJ																										
Roger Brown	62DL 68-74IndA 75MemA	1942	6'5	209	F-G	Dayton	8	605	3660	8177	47	312	971	32	2466	3116	79	3758	2315	1929	24	10498	35	6.2	3.8	17.4
75UtahA 75IndA	68-75						8	110	765	1590	48	66	190	36	462	583	79	705	405	361	8	2060	37	6.4	3.7	18.7
Roger Brown	73LA 73CarA	1950	7'1	228	C	Kansas	6	235	233	576	40	2	2	100	111	178	62	825	117	395	5	583	11	3.5	0.5	2.5
74SA-A 74VaA	73-74, 76-77						4	23	18	36	50	0	0	—	5	8	63	39	5	22	0	41	7	1.7	0.2	1.8
76DenA 76-77Det																										

Use Name-Nickname	Team by Year	Birth Yr	Hgt	Wgt	Pos	College	# Yr	G.	Field Goals FG	Att	%	3 pt. FG FG	Att	%	Free Throws FT	Att.	%	Reb.	Ass	PF	DQ	Pts	Per Game Min	Reb	Ass	Pts
Brian Brunkhorst	69LA-A	1945	6'6	210	F	Marquette	1	3	6	11	55	0	0	—	13	17	76	13	3	8	0	25	19	4.3	1.0	8.3
George Bruns	73NY-A	1946	6'	160	G	Manhatten	1	13	31	66	47	2	4	50	22	27	81	8	36	26		86	18	0.6	2.8	6.6
	73						1	2	0	1	0	0	0	—	1	2	50	0	1	3		1	4	0.0	0.5	0.5
Em Bryant	65-68NY 69-70Bos	1938	6'1	175	G	DePaul	8	566	1501	3665	41				720	1043	69	1593	1700	1729	37	3722	20	2.8	3.0	6.6
71-72Buf	67-68						3	27	88	227	39				55	69	80	111	70	133	0	231	22	4.1	2.6	8.6
George Bucci	76NY-A	1953	6'3	202	G	Manhatten	1	33	50	120	42	0	4	0	28	41	68	37	15	19		128	7	1.1	0.5	3.9
	76						1	2	3	7	43	1			1	2	50	0	0	2		8	5	0.0	0.0	4.0
Bucky Buckwalter	HC73Sea HC75UtahA	1935				Utah																				
Larry Bunce	68AnaA 69DenA	1945	7'	245	C	Utah State	2	129	386	919	42	0	1	0	370	517	72	821	94	317	11	1142	24	6.4	0.7	8.9
69DalA 69HouA																										
Bill Bunting	70CarA 71NY-A 71-72VaA	1947	6'8	200	F-C	N. Carolina	3	145	214	508	42	0	1	0	195	247	79	417	95	274		623	13	2.9	0.7	4.3
	71						1	6	5	10	50	0	0	—	8	12	67	6	1	4		18	6	1.0	0.2	3.0
Jim Burns	68Chi 68DalA	1945	6'3	195	G	Northwestern	1	36	54	144	38	0	2	0	51	89	57	62	25	53	0	159	11	1.7	0.7	4.4
Dave Bustion	73DenA	1948	6'8	215	F	Denver	1	47	58	133	44	0	0	—	42	59	71	101	21	82		158	8	2.1	0.4	3.4
	73						1	1	2	7	29	0	0	—	6	7	86	1	1	3		10	11	1.0	1.0	10.0
Mike Butler	69-70NO-A 71-72UtahA	1946	6'2	174	G	Memphis St.	4	245	790	2010	39	172	596	29	406	469	87	375	504	483	1	2158	19	1.5	2.1	8.8
	69, 71						2	21	49	140	35	16	61	26	34	38	89	40	23	34	0	148	15	1.9	1.1	7.0
Walt Byrd	70MiaA	1942	6'7	205	F	Temple	1	22	14	43	33	0	1	0	5	17	29	25	6	22	0	33	5	1.1	0.3	1.5
Jim Caldwell	68NY 68NJ-A 68-69KyA	1943	6'10	240	C	Ga. Tech	2	137	390	917	43	2	15	13	186	295	63	1052	278	446	13	968	23	7.7	2.0	7.1
	68-69						2	12	26	66	39	0	0	—	17	27	63	80	19	36	0	69	20	6.7	1.6	5.8
Joe Caldwell (Pogo)	65-66Det 66-68StL	1941	6'5	203	F-G	Ariz. State	11	782	5295	11365	47	18	80	23	2011	3518	57	4117	2647	2328	15	12619	32	5.3	3.4	16.1
69-70Atl	66-70, 73-74						7	61	389	849	46	3	10	30	160	294	54	310	172	189	3	941	34	5.1	2.8	15.4
71-74CarA 75StLA																										
Corky Calhoun	73-75Phoe 75-76LA	1950	6'7	213	F	Pennsylvania	8	542	1200	2609	46				496	634	78	1962	601	1322	16	2896	20	3.6	1.1	5.3
77-78Port 79-80Ind	77, 78						2	18	28	54	52				6	10	60	28	7	22	0	62	11	1.6	0.4	3.4
Mack Calvin	70LA-A 71-72FlaA	1948	6'	172	G	Southern Cal.	10	734	3907	8622	45	63	256	25	4119	4786	86	1911	3596	1899	6	12120	29	2.6	4.9	16.5
73-74CarA 75DenA	70-75, 77-78						8	74	443	952	47	12	35	34	418	495	84	206	331	136	0	1316	30	2.8	4.5	17.8
76VaA 77LA 77SA 77-78Den 80Utah HC76VaA																										
Larry Cannon	70MiaA 71DenA 72MemA	1947	6'5	195	G	LaSalle	4	213	1284	3126	41	29	113	26	948	1247	76	620	777	544	2	3545	29	2.9	3.6	16.6
72IndA 73IL 74IndA 74Phi																										
Frank Card	69MinA 70WasA 71VaA	1944	6'7	195	F	S.Carolina St.	5	306	1116	2423	46	3	17	18	659	1043	63	1721	372	805	5	2894	23	5.6	1.2	9.5
71-72CarA	69-70, 72						3	17	64	110	58	0	1	0	21	41	51	84	23	27	0	149	20	4.9	1.4	8.8
72-73DenA																										
Don Carlos	69HouA	1944	6'5	210	G-F	Otterbein	1	56	207	505	41	0	3	0	214	283	76	279	159	231	10	628	27	5.0	2.8	11.2
Lou Carnesecca	HC71-73NY-A	1925				St.John's (NY)																				
Darel Carrier	68-72KyA 73MemA	1940	6'3	185	G	Western Ky.	6	350	2445	5867	42	398	1055	38	1723	2024	85	1187	896	1072	16	7011	35	3.4	2.6	20.0
	68-72						5	45	309	733	42	57	146	39	241	277	87	151	131	111	1	916	38	3.4	2.9	20.4
Fred Carter (Mad Dog)	70-72Bal 72-77Phi 77Mil	1945	6'3	185	G-F	Mt. St. Mary's	8	611	3917	9219	42				1437	2073	69	2381	2122	1740	26	9271	30	3.9	3.5	15.2
	70-71, 76						3	28	178	434	41				90	131	69	123	75	102	1	446	35	4.4	2.7	15.9
George Carter	68Det 70WasA 71VaA	1944	6'5	218	F-G	St. Bonavent.	8	480	3275	7352	45	49	163	30	2084	2564	81	3243	959	1632	1	8683	34	6.8	2.0	18.1
72PitA 72CarA	70-71, 73-75						5	30	215	461	47	2	14	14	138	166	83	246	60	112		570	37	8.2	2.0	19.0
73NY-A 74Va-A 75MemA 76UtahA																										
Jay Carty	69LA	1941	6'8	230	F	Oregon State	1	28	34	89	38				8	11	73	58	11	31	0	76	7	2.1	0.4	2.7
	69						1	3	0	2	0				1	3	33	2	1	3	0	1	3	0.7	0.3	0.3
Sam Cash	73MemA	1950	6'8	230	F	Cal-Riverside	1	7	4	18	22	0	0	—	12	17	71	19	0	11		20	7	2.7	0.0	2.9
Sid Catlett	72Cin	1948	6'8	230	F	Notre Dame	1	9	2	9	22				2	9	22	4	1	3	0	6	4	0.4	0.1	0.7
Vince Cazetta	HC68PitA	1925				Bridgeport																				
Bill Chamberlain	73KyA 73MemA 74Phoe	1949	6'6	205	F	N. Carolina	2	78	169	412	41	2	8	25	75	115	65	198	113	172	2	415	13	2.5	1.4	5.3
Jerry Chambers	67LA 68-69MS 70Phoe	1943	6'5	189	F	Utah	6	320	1115	2534	44	2	10	20	435	562	77	1032	270	565	3	2667	16	3.2	0.8	8.3
71Atl 72Buf	67, 70-71						3	14	29	69	42				13	17	76	30	8	17	0	71	10	2.1	0.6	5.1
73SD-A 74SA-A																										
Don Chaney (Duck)	69-75Bos 76StLA	1946	6'5	210	G	Houston	12	790	2703	6191	44	2	10	20	1253	1614	78	3147	1762	2248	44	6663	24	4.0	2.2	8.4
77-78LA	69, 72-75, 77						6	70	230	511	45				110	142	77	250	156	229	3	570	26	3.6	2.2	8.1
78-80Bos HC85-87LAC																										
Wayne Chapman	69-70KyA 71DenA	1945	6'6	190	G-F	Western Ky.	4	206	505	1436	35	28	109	26	304	440	69	505	316	513	7	1432	16	2.5	1.5	7.0
71-72IndA	69-71						3	20	46	93	49	2	9	22	32	44	73	33	16	16	0	126	10	1.7	0.8	6.3
Len Chappell	63Syr 64Phi 64-66NY	1941	6'8	240	F-C	Wake Forest	10	670	2443	5409	45	0	0	—	1341	1926	70	3431	503	1349	10	6227	18	5.1	0.8	9.3
67Chi 67-68Cin	63, 67-68, 70, 72						5	26	56	129	43	0	0	—	36	53	68	87	20	47	0	148	14	3.3	0.8	5.7
69-70Mil 71Cle 71Atl 72DalA																										
Ken Charles	74-76Buf 77-78Atl	1951	6'3	180	G	Fordham	5	322	1083	2458	44				581	736	79	640	806	806	9	2747	24	2.0	2.5	8.5
74Phoe	74-76						3	18	47	114	41				17	24	71	41	32	60	2	111	25	2.3	1.8	6.2
Bob Christian	70DalA 70NY-A 71-73Atl	1944	7'	260	C	Grambling	5	248	347	715	49	0	0	—	250	355	70	1005	203	500	5	944	12	4.1	0.8	3.8
	72						1	6	3	8	38				1	1	100	7	0	10	0	7	6	1.2	0.0	1.2
Steve Chubin	68AnaA 69LA-A 69MinA	1944	6'2	200	G	Rhode Island	3	226	910	2284	40	10	51	20	1074	1310	82	861	885	753	19	2904	25	3.8	3.9	12.8
69IndA 69-70NY-A	70						1	11	8	17	47	0	4	0	12	14	86					28	5			2.5
70PitA 70IndA 70KyA																										
Archie Clark	67-68LA 69-72Phi 72-73Bal	1941	6'2	175	G	Minnesota	10	725	4693	9784	48				2433	3163	77	2427	3498	1806	14	11819	33	3.3	4.8	16.3
74Cap 75Sea 76Det	67-76						10	71	444	977	45				237	307	77	229	297	197	2	1125	34	3.2	4.2	15.8
Dick Clark	68MinA 69HouA	1944	6'4	195	G	Estrn Ky.	2	56	110	372	30	1	18	6	137	203	67	140	101	148	0	358	20	2.5	1.8	6.4
	68						1	10	17	65	26	1	6	17	21	28	75	33	13	18	0	56	23	3.3	1.3	5.6
John Clark	HC70PitA	1937				Steubenville																				
John Clawson	69OakA	1944	6'4	200	F	Michigan	1	70	147	309	48	0	0	—	37	54	69	195	51	187	1	331	15	2.8	0.7	4.7
	69						1	16	42	95	44	1	3	33	15	24	63	54	14	60	2	100	20	3.4	0.9	6.3
Jim Cleamons	72LA 73-77Cle 78-80NY	1949	6'3	185	G	Ohio St.	9	652	2242	4870	46	7	31	23	921	1204	76	1981	2531	1237	5	5412	26	3.0	3.9	8.3
80Was	72, 76, 78, 80						4	27	91	230	40				39	46	85	89	89	50	0	221	25	3.3	3.3	8.2
Barry Clemens	66NY 67-69Chi 70-72Sea	1942	6'7	215	F	Ohio-	11	790	2262	4987	45				788	1043	76	2532	905	1665	14	5312	16	3.2	1.1	6.7
73-74Cle 75-76Port	67-68					Wesleyan	2	7	8	20	40				10	11	91	5	7	9	0	26	9	0.7	1.0	3.7
Ben Clyde	75Bos	1951	6'7	210	F	Florida St.	1	25	31	72	43				7	9	78	41	5	34	1	69	6	1.6	0.2	2.8
Jerry Colangelo	HC70, 73Phoe	1939				Illinois																				
E.C. Coleman	74Hou 75-77NO 78GS 79Hou	1950	6'8	225	F	Houston Bapt.	6	357	1104	2378	46				345	497	69	2151	472	1210	30	2553	26	6.0	1.3	7.2
Jimmy Collins	71-72Chi	1946	6'2	175	G	N. Mexico St.	2	74	118	285	41				45	56	80	66	70	54	0	281	8	0.9	0.9	3.8
	71						1	2	0	1	0				3	3	100	1	0	1	0	3	4	0.5	0.0	1.5

Use Name-Nickname	Team by Year	Birth Yr	Hgt	Wgt	Pos	College	# Yr	G.	Field Goals FG	Att.	%	3 pt. FG FG	Att	%	Free Throws FT	Att	%	Reb.	Ass	PF	DQ	Pts	Per Game Min	Reb	Ass	Pts
Glen Combs	69-70DalA 71TexA	1946	6'2	185	G	Va. Tech	7	465	2652	6121	43	503	1369	37	1859	2296	81	1230	1639	1333	5	7666	33	2.6	3.5	16.5
(The Kentucky Rifle)	69-73						5	51	286	678	42	34	121	28	163	207	79	141	144	134	0	769	30	2.8	2.8	15.1
71-74UtahA 74MemA 75VaA																										
John Comeaux	68NO-A	1943	6'5	193	F	Grambling	1	23	27	63	43	0	0	—	23	32	72	28	11	27	0	77	8	1.2	0.5	3.3
Jeff Congdon	68AnaA 68-70DenA 71UtahA	1943	6'1	187	G	BYU	5	306	764	2009	38	102	358	28	365	457	80	601	1002	538	5	1995	21	2.0	3.3	6.5
71NY-A 72DalA	68-71						4	26	78	202	39	18	61	30	54	66	82	59	118	69	0	228	23	2.3	4.5	8.8
Larry Conley	68KyA	1944	6'3	175	G	Kentucky	1	1	1	4	25	0	0	—	0	0	—	0	0	0	0	2	18	0.0	0.0	2.0
Jimmy Dan Connor	76KyA	1953	6'4	195	G	Kentucky	1	24	42	86	49				22	29	76	28	38	35		106	10	1.2	1.6	4.4
Joe Cooke	71Cle	1948	6'3	175	G	Indiana	1	73	134	341	39				48	59	81	114	93	135	2	316	10	1.6	1.3	4.3
Mel Counts (Goose)	65-66Bos 67Bal 67-70LA	1941	7'0	232	C-F	Oregon St.	12	789	2665	6122	44				1186	1552	76	4756	1100	2259	44	6516	17	6.0	1.4	8.3
71-72Phoe 73Phi	65-70, 73-74						8	85	255	599	43				138	178	78	519	100	263	5	648	17	6.1	1.2	7.6
73-74LA 75-76NO																										
Dave Cowens (Big Red)	71-78, PC 79,80Bos	1948	6'9	230	C-F	Florida St.	11	766	5744	12499	46	1	14	7	2027	2590	78	10444	2910	2920	90	13516	39	13.6	3.8	17.6
81-82VR 83Mil	72-77, 80						7	89	733	1627	45	0	2	0	218	293	74	1285	333	398	15	1684	42	14.4	3.7	18.9
Freddie Crawford	67-68NY 68-69LA 70Mil	1941	6'4	194	G-F	St. Bonavent.	5	297	832	1864	45				367	617	59	746	610	692	3	2031	17	2.5	2.1	6.8
71Buf 71Phi	67-71						5	35	105	252	42				48	76	63	97	73	89	2	258	17	2.8	2.1	7.4
Jim Creighton	76Atl	1950	6'8	200	F	Colorado	1	32	12	43	28				7	16	44	45	4	23	0	31	5	1.4	0.1	1.0
Rusty Critchfield	69OakA	1946	5'10	150	G	California	1	47	53	147	36	0	3	0	55	84	65	29	54	41	0	161	9	0.6	1.1	3.4
	69						1	5	1	6	17	0	0	—	2	6	33	2	7	6	0	4	4	0.4	1.4	0.8
Bobby Croft	71KyA 71TexA	1948	6'10	200	C	Tennessee	1	62	126	348	36	0	2	0	73	112	65	206	41	137		325	12	3.3	0.7	5.2
	71						1	4	7	23	30	1	1	100	5	7	71	14	3	6		20	14	3.5	0.8	5.0
Pete Cross	71-72Sea 73KCO 73Sea	1948	6'9	230	C-F	San Fransisco	3	182	403	934	43				251	361	70	1519	187	376	4	1057	21	8.3	1.0	5.8
Bill Crow	68AnaA	1941	6'1	180	G	Westminster	1	1	1	8	13	0	0	—	1	4	25	2	0	0	0	3	16	2.0	0.0	3.0
Al Cueto	70MiaA 71MemA	1946	6'8	230	C	Tulsa	2	149	316	782	40	5	21	24	157	221	71	731	144	423	12	794	15	4.9	1.0	5.3
	71						1	4	6	14	43	0	0	—	2	3	67	18	3	7		14	13	4.5	0.8	3.5
Billy Cunningham (the Kang	66-72Phi	1943	6'7	220	F-C	N. Carolina	11	770	6125	13530	45	15	57	26	4015	5502	73	7981	3305	2845	64	16310	35	10.4	4.3	21.2
73-74CarA	66-71, 73-74						8	54	410	931	44	1	6	17	240	349	69	514	192	208	3	1061	32	9.5	3.6	19.6
75-76, HC78-85Phi																										
Dick Cunningham	69-71Mil 72Hou 73-75Mil	1946	6'10	251	C	Murray St.	7	360	408	1004	41				196	308	64	1324	221	502	3	1012	11	3.7	0.6	2.8
	70-71, 73						3	27	20	40	50				7	11	64	39	5	22	0	47	6	1.4	0.2	1.7
Mike Dabich	68Oak 68DalA	1942	7'	255	C	N. Mexico St.	1	10	8	12	67	0	0	—	4	9	44	13	2	1	0	20	5	1.3	0.2	2.0
Louie Dampier	68-76KyA 77-79SA	1944	6'	177	G	Kentucky	12	960	5188	11248	46	794	2217	36	2521	3075	82	2543	4687	1852	3	15279	34	2.6	4.9	15.9
	68-75, 77-79						11	109	627	1438	44	119	317	38	278	356	78	301	649	215	0	1651	37	2.8	6.0	15.1
Bob Dandridge	70-77Mil 78-81Was 82Mil	1947	6'6	195	F-G	Norfolk St.	13	839	6445	13317	48	2	12	17	2638	3382	78	5715	2846	2940	43	15530	35	6.8	3.4	18.5
	70-74, 76, 78-79						8	98	823	1716	48				321	422	76	754	365	377	12	1967	40	7.7	3.7	20.1
Mel Daniels	68MinA 69-74IndA 75MemA	1944	6'9	223	C	New Mexico	9	637	4655	9921	47	3	34	9	2425	3692	66	9507	1138	2309	19	11734	35	14.9	1.8	18.4
77NYN HC89Ind	68-74						7	109	740	1648	45	0	5	0	421	616	68	1608	168	433	2	1901	36	14.8	1.5	17.4
Mike D'Antoni	74-75KCO	1951	6'3	190	G	Marshall	2	119	176	439	40				61	83	73	170	230	218	0	413	15	1.4	1.9	3.5
	75						1	4	7	14	50				4	4	100	7	1	6	0	18	11	1.8	0.3	4.5
Ollie Darden	68IndA 69NY-A 69-70KyA	1944	6'7	240	F-C	Michigan	3	223	815	1872	44	2	11	18	415	597	70	1381	219	693	8	2047	22	6.2	1.0	9.2
70IndA	68-70						3	18	44	83	53	1	2	50	13	20	65	62	12	35	0	102	10	3.4	0.7	5.7
Jesse Dark	75NY	1951	6'5	210	G	Va. Commonw.	1	47	74	157	47				22	40	55	37	30	48	0	170	9	0.8	0.6	3.6
	75						1	2	1	6	17				5	5	100	1	1	2	0	7	6	0.5	0.5	3.5
Mack Daughtry	71CarA	1947	6'3	175	G	Albany St.(Ga.)	1	4	4	10	40	0	0	—	5	5	100	5	3	4		13	11	1.3	0.8	3.3
Bob Davis	73Port	1950	6'7	215	F	Weber State	1	9	6	28	21				4	6	67	5	2	5	0	16	5	0.6	0.2	1.8
Charlie Davis	72-73Cle 73-74Port	1949	6'2	160	G	Wake Forest	3	144	506	1240	41				275	341	81	219	319	344	10	1287	18	1.5	2.2	8.9
Dwight Davis (Double D)	73-75Cle 76-77GS	1949	6'8	220	F	Houston	5	340	1130	2669	42				676	926	73	1991	529	1076	15	2936	24	5.9	1.6	8.6
	76						1	11	16	37	43				18	22	82	28	10	28	1	50	13	2.5	0.9	4.5
Jim Davis	68StL 69-72Atl 72Hou	1941	6'9	235	C-F	Colorado	8	597	1518	3291	46				961	1425	67	3109	739	1463	24	3997	17	5.2	1.2	6.7
72-75Det	68-71, 74-75						6	33	49	114	43				44	63	70	92	16	62	2	142	12	2.8	0.5	4.3
Lee Davis	69-70NO-A 71-74MemA	1945	6'8	240	C-F	N.C.Central	8	453	1510	3130	48	7	37	19	484	797	61	2195	435	1071	1	3511	17	4.8	1.0	7.8
75-76SD-A	69, 71						2	9	13	35	37	0	1	0	8	13	62	33	6	14	0	34	8	3.7	0.7	3.8
Mel Davis (Killer)	74-77NY 77NYN	1950	6'7	225	F	St. Johns (NY)	4	190	431	1147	38				146	206	71	816	164	327	0	1008	14	4.3	0.9	5.3
	74-75						2	7	11	24	46				2	2	100	9	2	3	0	24	6	1.3	0.3	3.4
Mickey Davis	72PitA 73-77Mil	1950	6'7	215	F-G	Duquesne	6	309	604	1326	46	0	2	0	334	400	84	841	304	386	0	1542	12	2.7	1.0	5.0
	73-74						2	21	38	82	46				24	26	92	46	17	33	0	100	14	2.2	0.8	4.8
Mike Davis	70Bal 71-72Buf 73Bal	1946	6'3	185	G	Va. Union	4	242	933	2171	43	6	23	26	571	746	77	511	412	667	17	2443	20	2.1	1.7	10.1
73MemA																										
Warren Davis	68AnaA 69-70LA-A	1942	6'6	217	F-C	N.C. A&T	6	447	2022	4215	48	2	16	13	1403	2030	69	4097	944	1507	11	5449	29	9.2	2.1	12.2
70PitA 71FlaA	71						1	6	28	58	48	0	0	—	22	29	76	48	31	26		78	30	8.0	5.2	13.0
72CarA 72-73MemA																										
Willie Davis	71TexA	1945	6'8	234	C	North Texas St.	1	8	7	15	47	0	0	—	4	8	50	13	2	10		18	4	1.6	0.3	2.3
Jimmy Dawson	68IndA	1945	6'	175	G	Illinois	1	21	46	133	35	1	7	14	25	43	58	21	32	16	0	118	14	1.0	1.5	5.6
Billy Deangelis	71NY-A	1947	6'1	180	G	St. Joseph's	1	8	3	6	50	0	0	—	4	6	67	6	8	16		10	6	0.8	1.0	1.3
Dave DeBusschere	63-64, PC65-67, 68-69Det	1940	6'6	227	F-G	Detroit	12	875	5722	13249	43				2609	3730	70	9618	2497	2801	37	14053	36	11.0	2.9	16.1
69-74NY	63, 68-74						8	96	634	1523	42				268	384	70	1155	253	327	5	1536	38	12.0	2.6	16.0
62-63 played major league baseball																										
Don Dee	69IndA	1943	6'8	210	F	St. Mary of the	1	58	138	387	36	0	1	0	56	75	75	292	33	179	9	332	17	5.0	0.5	5.7
	69					Plains, St.L.	1	12	4	13	31	0	0	—	0	0	—	10	1	10	0	8	3	0.8	1.0	0.7
Randy Denton	72CarA 72-74MemA	1949	6'10	245	C-F	Duke	6	413	2032	4289	47	3	14	21	676	868	78	3547	528	1058	1	4749	25	8.6	1.3	11.5
75-76UtahA	75						1	6	49	92	53	0	0	—	15	22	68	80	11	18	0	113	39	13.3	1.8	18.8
76StLA 77Atl																										
Joe DePre	71-73NY-A	1946	6'3	190	G	St. John's	3	117	331	694	48	2	10	20	166	226	73	226	185	343		830	19	1.9	1.6	7.1
	71-72						2	20	34	89	38	1	3	33	19	27	70	26	19	45		88	12	1.3	1.0	4.4
Rod Derline	75-76Sea	1952	6'4	175	G	Seattle	2	107	215	513	42				88	112	79	86	71	69	0	518	9	0.8	0.7	4.8
	75-76						2	10	20	43	47				8	9	89	17	8	10	0	48	11	1.7	0.8	4.8
Clyde Dickey	75UtahA	1952	6'3	185	G	Boise State	1	58	71	203	35	2	15	13	16	21	76	61	47	46	0	160	8	1.1	0.8	2.8
	75						1	1	0	2	0	0	0	—	0	0	—	1	0	0	0	0	4	1.0	0.0	0.0
Derrek Dickey	74-77GS 77-78Chi	1951	6'7	218	F	Cincinnati	5	321	854	1818	47				254	341	74	1575	346	609	3	1962	17	4.9	1.1	6.1
	75, 76						2	27	78	140	56				23	33	70	115	17	55	1	179	16	4.3	0.6	6.6
John Dickson	68NO-A	1945	6'10	240	C	Ark. State	1	21	14	39	36	0	0	—	8	13	62	33	3	11	0	36	5	1.6	0.1	1.7
	68						1	1	0	4	0	0	0	—	0	0	—	2	0	0	0	0	3	2.0	0.0	0.0

Use Name-Nickname	Team by Year	Birth Yr	Hgt	Wgt	Pos	College	# Yr	G.	Field Goals FG	Att	%	3 pt. FG FG	Att	%	Free Throws FT	Att	%	Reb.	Ass	PF	DQ	Pts	Per Game Min	Reb	Ass	Pts
Ernie DiGregorio	74-77Buf 78LA 78Bos	1951	6'	180	G	Providence	5	312	1268	3052	42				461	511	90	610	1594	656	14	2997	25	2.0	5.1	9.6
(Earnie D.)	74, 76						2	15	67	148	45				16	17	94	29	97	43	2	150	30	1.9	6.5	10.0
Craig Dill	68PitA	1944	6'11	215	C	Michigan	1	65	187	488	38	0	3	0	71	106	67	378	31	164	3	445	21	5.8	0.5	6.8
	68						1	6	3	8	38	0	0	—	1	1	100	6	2	5	0	7	3	1.0	0.3	1.2
Duane Dillard	76UtahA						1	3	1	3	33				2	2	100	9	2	7		4	6	3.0	0.7	1.3
Jackie Dinkins	72Chi	1950	6'5	210	F	Voorhees	1	18	17	41	41				11	20	55	20	7	10	0	45	5	1.1	0.4	2.5
	72						1	1	1	1	100				0	0	—	0	0	0	0	2	1	0.0	0.0	2.0
Harry Dinnel	PC68AnaA	1941	6'4	200	F	Pepperdine	1	11	6	19	32	0	0	—	7	8	88	23	5	14	0	19	8	2.1	0.5	1.7
Bill Dinwiddie	68-69Cin 70KC 71Bos 72Mil	1943	6'7	220	F	N.M.Highlands	4	220	404	1095	37				166	270	61	720	129	381	3	974	13	3.3	0.6	4.4
Terry Dischinger	63Chi 64Bal 65Det 66-67MS	1940	6'7	201	F-G	Purdue	9	652	3457	6826	51				2098	2768	76	3656	1151	2055	43	9012	27	5.6	1.8	13.8
68-72Det 73Port	68						1	6	21	56	38				14	19	74	29	9	19	0	56	26	4.8	1.5	9.3
Ron Dorsey	72CarA	1948	6'4	200	F	Tenn. State	1	1	2	8	25	0	1	0	0	2	0	5	0	2		4	12	5.0	0.0	4.0
Sonny Dove	68-69Det 70-72NY-A	1945	6'8	206	F	St. John's (NY)	5	222	994	2173	46	6	27	22	464	717	65	1334	219	679	12	2458	22	6.0	1.0	11.1
	68, 70-71						3	14	55	111	50	1	4	25	27	43	63	84	10	10	0	136	23	6.0	0.7	9.9
Jerry Dover	72MemA	1949	5'8	155	G	LeMoyne	1	4	3	9	33	2	5	40	0	0	—	0	1	3		8	3	0.0	0.3	2.0
Steve Downing	74-75Bos	1950	6'8	225	C	Indiana	2	27	21	66	32				22	40	55	41	11	33	0	64	5	1.5	0.4	2.4
	74						1	1	1	2	50				0	0	—	2	0	1	0	2	4	2.0	0.0	2.0
Terry Driscoll	71Det 72-73Bal 73-75Mil	1947	6'7	215	F	Boston Coll.	5	274	449	1071	42	0	0	—	229	330	69	1114	221	558	5	1127	13	4.1	0.8	4.1
75StLA	72-74						3	16	6	15	40				3	3	100	15	4	14	0	15	3	0.9	0.3	0.9
Rich Dumas	69HouA	1945	6'3	170	G	NE Okla. St.	1	1	1	5	20	0	0	—	0	0	—	1	0	1	0	2	5	1.0	0.0	2.0
Jarrett Durham	72NY-A	1948	6'5	188	F	Duquesne	1	1	0	0	—	0	0	—	0	0	—	0	0	0	0	0	1	0.0	0.0	0.0
Ken Durrett	72Cin 73-75KCO 75Phi	1948	6'7	197	F	LaSalle	4	120	192	442	43				100	157	64	233	54	197	0	484	10	1.9	0.5	4.0
Dennis DuVal	75Was 76Atl	1952	6'3	175	G	Syracuse	2	50	39	108	36				18	27	67	31	34	49	0	96	5	0.6	0.7	1.9
	75						1	5	3	9	33				1	2	50	3	3	1	0	7	3	0.6	0.6	1.4
Jim Eakins (Jimbo)	69OakA 70WasA 71-74VaA	1946	6'11	215	C	B.Y.U.	10	767	2900	5750	50	0	3	0	2455	3120	79	5578	1345	2395	5	8255	25	7.3	1.8	10.8
75-76UtahA 76NY-A	69-76, 78						9	78	318	592	54	0	1	0	207	272	76	559	222	209	0	843	25	7.2	2.8	10.8
77KC 78SA 78Mil																										
Al Eberhard	75-78Det	1952	6'6	225	F	Missouri	4	220	566	1308	43				358	449	80	760	175	544	9	1490	19	3.5	0.8	6.8
	76-77						2	11	18	48	38				19	27	70	35	9	20	0	55	20	3.2	0.8	5.0
Roy Ebron	74UtahA	1952	6'9	225	C	Southwestern	1	40	103	211	49	0	1	0	43	84	51	176	19	68		249	13	4.4	0.5	6.2
	74					La.	1	7	6	19	32	0	1	0	5	10	50	15	2	6		17	6	2.1	0.3	2.4
Charlie Edge	74MemA 75IndA	1950	6'6	210	F	LeMoyne-Owen	2	155	507	1010	50	0	4	0	187	296	63	981	109	250		1201	20	6.3	0.7	7.7
	75						1	7	2	8	25	0	0	—	0	0	—	9	2	6	0	4	6	1.3	0.3	0.6
Bobby Edmonds	68, 70IndA	1941	6'6	220	F	Tenn. State	2	75	214	493	43	1	6	17	151	232	65	378	29	184	4	580	18	5.0	0.4	7.7
	68						1	3	6	14	43	1	2	50	7	9	78	18	2	12	1	20	16	6.0	0.7	6.7
Joe Ellis	67-71SF 72-74GS	1944	6'6	175	F-G	San Francisco	8	524	1946	4884	40				731	1005	73	2686	716	1397	42	4623	20	5.1	1.4	8.8
	67-69, 71-73						6	38	83	270	31				36	52	69	131	23	75	1	202	15	3.4	0.6	5.3
Leroy Ellis	63-66LA 67-70Bal 71Port	1940	6'10	219	C-F	St. John's (NY)	14	1048	4143	9378	44				1890	2595	73	8709	1405	2661	26	10176	26	8.3	1.3	9.7
72-73LA 73-76Phi	63-66, 69-70, 72, 76						8	64	175	424	41				113	163	69	462	44	152	1	463	23	7.2	0.7	7.2
Darrell Elston	75VaA 77Ind	1952	6'4	190	G	N. Carolina	2	77	249	509	49	3	18	17	94	124	76	169	204	172	0	601	25	2.2	2.6	7.8
Claude English	71Port	1946	6'4	190	F	Rhode Island	1	18	11	42	26				5	7	71	20	6	15	0	27	4	1.1	0.3	1.5
Scott English	73Phoe 74Va-A 75SD-A	1950	6'6	220	F	Texas-El Paso	3	105	249	602	41	1	10	10	94	122	77	423	107	162	0	593	15	4.0	1.0	5.6
Keith Erickson	66SF 67-68Chi 69-73LA	1944	6'5	199	F-G	U.C.L.A.	12	766	3014	6926	44				1223	1591	77	3448	1991	2081	44	7251	25	4.5	2.6	9.5
74-77Phoe	67-71, 73, 76						7	87	364	806	45				144	189	76	216	386	286	7	872	28	2.5	4.4	10.0
Billy Evans	70NY-A	1947	6'	170	G	Boston Coll.	1	53	32	87	37	0	2	0	38	70	54	39	100	89	1	102	11	0.7	1.9	1.9
	70						1	6	1	2	50	0	1	0	1	3	33					3	5			0.5
John Fairchild	66LA-A 68AnaA 69DenA	1943	6'8	205	F	B.Y.U.	4	165	414	1026	40	14	38	37	243	357	68	523	115	304	1	1085	14	3.2	0.7	6.6
69-70IndA 70KyA	69						1	9	19	44	43	4	10	40	4	6	67	21	3	13	0	46	9	2.3	0.3	5.1
Bobby Fields	72UtahA	1949	6'3	175	G	LaSalle	1	22	22	48	46	2	7	29	8	13	62	30	20	33		54	6	1.4	0.9	2.5
Ron Filipek	68Phi	1944	6'5	210	F	Tenn. Tech	1	19	18	47	38				7	14	50	25	7	12	0	43	4	1.3	0.4	2.3
Greg Fillmore	71-72NY	1947	7'1	250	C	Cheyney St.	2	49	52	129	40				14	30	47	107	20	97	0	118	7	2.2	0.4	2.4
	71						1	8	0	4	0				0	0		8	1	9	0	0	3	1.0	0.1	0.0
Larry Finch	74-75MemA	1951	6'2	195	G	Memphis St.	2	128	428	992	43	27	79	34	223	269	83	217	301	326		1106	24	1.7	2.4	8.6
Harry Finkel (Hank)	67LA 68-69SD 70-75Bos	1942	7'	240	C	Dayton	9	551	1125	2508	45				540	816	66	2151	426	1090	30	2790	12	3.9	0.8	5.1
	67, 69, 72-75						6	33	27	59	46				4	6	67	53	13	29	0	58	5	1.6	0.4	1.8
Rick Fisher	72UtahA 72FlaA	1948	6'5	220	F	Colorado St.	1	12	18	34	53	0	0	—	1	1	100	32	5	9		37	6	2.7	0.4	3.1
Larry Fogle	76NY	1953	6'5	208		Canisius	1	2	1	5	20				0	0		3	0	4	0	2	7	1.5	0.0	1.0
Levi Fontaine	71SF	1948	6'4	190	G	MD. E.Shore	1	35	53	145	37				28	37	76	15	22	27	0	134	6	0.4	0.6	3.8
	71						1	2	2	3	67				1	3	33	0	0	2	0	5	5	0.0	0.0	2.5
Bob Ford	73MemA	1950	6'7	228	F	Purdue	1	9	5	17	29	0	0	—	4	5	80	12	4	8		14	8	1.3	0.4	1.6
Jake Ford	71-72Sea	1946	6'3	180	G	MD. E. Shore	2	31	42	91	46				42	55	76	20	35	32	0	126	8	0.6	1.1	4.1
Fred Foster	69-71Cin 71-72Phi 73Det	1946	6'5	217	F	Miami (Ohio)	8	523	1701	4107	41				691	950	73	1275	601	1008	9	4093	17	2.4	1.1	7.8
74-75Cle 77Buf	71						1	5	8	19	42				2	2	100	12	5	6	0	18	10	2.4	1.0	3.6
Jim Foster	75StLA 76DenA	1952	6'1	180	G	Connecticut	2	89	132	354	37	1	6	17	66	98	67	117	190	196	0	331	13	1.3	2.1	3.7
	75-76						2	9	11	24	46	0	1	0	7	15	47	8	7	13	0	20	7	0.9	0.8	2.2
Cal Fowler	70CarA	1942	6'	175	G	St. Francis(Pa.)	1	78	131	288	45	7	17	41	74	119	62	170	126	156	2	343	16	2.2	1.6	4.4
	70						1	4	6	14	43	0	1	0	7	10	70					19	19			4.8
Harold Fox	73Buf	1949	6'2	175	G	Jacksonville	1	10	12	32	38				7	8	88	8	10	7	0	31	8	0.8	1.0	3.1
Jim Fox	68Cin 68-69Det 69-70Phoe	1943	6'10	230	C-F	S. Carolina	10	743	2611	5452	48				1723	2239	77	5525	1201	2023	35	6945	23	7.4	1.6	9.3
71-72Chi 72Cin	68, 70-71, 75-76						5	30	72	183	39				51	71	72	183	33	62	2	195	17	6.1	1.1	6.5
73-75Sea 76Mil 77NYN																										
Will Franklin	73VaA 75-76Sa-A	1949	6'7	225	F	Purdue	3	107	262	631	42	2	8	25	131	218	60	400	65	210		657	12	3.7	0.6	6.1
	75						1	2	2	5	40	0	0	—	0	0	—	5	0	2	0	4	5	2.5	0.0	2.0
Ron Franz	68OakA 69-70NO-A 71-72Fla	1945	6'7	207	F	Kansas	6	403	1765	3945	45	53	190	28	1150	1635	70	2126	668	1120	19	4733	25	5.3	1.7	11.7
73MemA 73DalA	69, 71-72						3	17	57	169		1	9	11	31	53	58	82	24	42	0	146	23	4.8	1.4	8.6
Walt Frazier (Clyde)	68-77NY 78-80Cle	1945	6'4	204	G	Southern Ill.	13	825	6130	12516	49	0	1	0	3321	4226	79	4830	5040	2180	12	15581	38	5.9	6.1	18.9
	68-75						8	93	767	1500	51				393	523	75	666	599	285	2	1927	43	7.2	6.4	20.7

Use Name-Nickname	Team by Year	Birth Yr	Hgt	Wgt	Pos	College	# Yr	G.	Field Goals FG	Att	%	3 pt. FG FG	Att	%	Free Throws FT	Att	%	Reb.	Ass	PF	DQ	Pts	Per Game Min	Reb	Ass	Pts
Wilbert Frazier	65SF 68HouA 69NY-A	1942	6'7	227	C-F	Grambling	3	153	575	1386	41	1	2	50	349	572	61	1087	171	420	4	1500	23	7.1	1.1	9.8
	68						1	3	13	29	45	0	1	0	3	7	42.9	12	4	11	0	29	28	4.0	1.3	9.7
Donnie Freeman	68MinA 69-70MiaA 71UtahA	1944	6'3	185	G	Illinois	9	648	4566	9931	46	11	73	15	3090	3861	80	2292	1775	1764	18	12233	32	3.5	2.7	18.9
71TexA 72DalA	68-69, 71-74						6	60	405	913	44	0	10	0	230	300	76.7	218	198	176	4	1040	33	3.6	3.3	17.3
73-74IndA 75SA-A 76LA																										
Gary Freeman	71Mil 71Cle	1948	6'9	210	F	Oregon State	1	52	69	134	51				29	40	72.5	106	35	67	0	167	7	2.0	0.7	3.2
Rod Freeman	74Phi	1950	6'7	225	F	Vanderbilt	1	35	39	103	38				28	41	68.3	54	14	42	0	106	8	1.5	0.4	3.0
Pat Frink	69Cin	1945	6'4	195	G	Colorado	1	48	50	147	34				23	29	79.3	41	55	54	1	123	8	0.9	1.1	2.6
Bernie Fryer	74Port 75StL-A 75NO	1949	6'3	185	G	B.Y.U.	2	120	297	665	45	0	1	0	162	206	78.6	227	356	269	1	756	20	1.9	3.0	6.3
Carl Fuller	71-72FlaA	1946	6'9	225	C	Bethune-	2	76	176	386	46	0	1	0	81	135	60	358	60	220		433	16	4.7	0.8	5.7
	71					Cookman	1	6	6	22	27	0	2	0	4	6	66.7	15	4	11		16	7	2.5	0.7	2.7
Bil Gaines	69HouA	1946	6'4	185	G	E. Texas St.	1	1	1	2	50	0	0	—	0	0	—	1	0	0	0	2	5	1.0	0.0	2.0
Dave Gaines	68KyA	1941	6'1	170	G	LeMoyne	1	3	4	16	25	1	1	100	1	2	50	10	0	4	0	10	9	3.3	0.0	3.3
Chuck Gardner	68DenA	1944	6'8	205	F	Colorado	1	42	71	175	41	0	4	0	55	79	69.6	136	13	74	1	197	12	3.2	0.3	4.7
Kenny Gardner	76UtahA		6'5	205	F	Utah	1	9	6	18	33	0	0	—	2	2	100	13	3	9		14	6	1.4	0.3	1.6
Bill Garner	68AnaA	1940	6'10	220	C	Portland	1	53	28	103	27	0	1	0	25	50	50	119	24	101	4	81	10	2.2	0.5	1.5
Dick Garrett	70LA 71-73Buf 74NY 75Mil	1947	6'3	185	G	Southern Ill.	5	339	1436	3392	42				603	699	86.3	1004	849	1024	23	3475	26	3.0	2.5	10.3
	70, 74						2	26	103	205	50				30	36	83.3	55	46	75	2	236	25	2.1	1.8	9.1
Rowland Garrett	73-76Chi 76-77Cle 77Mil	1950	6'6	215	F	Florida State	5	263	562	1273	44				213	276	77.2	607	106	344	0	1337	11	2.3	0.4	5.1
	73-76						4	19	21	60	35				4	8	50	30	3	28	0	46	8	1.6	0.2	2.4
Jim Garvin	74Buf	1950	6'7	200	F	Boston U.	1	6	1	4	25				0	0	—	5	0	1	0	2	2	0.8	0.0	0.3
John Gianelli	73-77NY 77Buf 78-79Mil	1950	6'10	220	C-F	U. of the Pacif.	8	541	1798	3823	47				614	875	70.2	3186	832	1270	13	4210	25	5.9	1.5	7.8
80Utah	73-75, 78						4	31	82	189	43				44	61	72.1	173	40	81	0	208	25	5.6	1.3	6.7
Dick Gibbs	72-73Hou 73KCO 74Sea	1948	6'5	210	F-G	Texas-El Paso	5	333	675	1678	40				389	487	79.9	624	260	629	4	1739	13	1.9	0.8	5.2
75Was 76Buf	75-76						2	11	7	19	37				4	4	100	2	4	10	0	18	4	0.2	0.4	1.6
Jack Gillespie	70NY-A	1947	6'6	215	F	Montana St.	1	2	0	5	0	0	0	—	2	2	100	7	0	3	0	2	14	3.5	0.0	1.0
Herm Gilliam	70Cin 71Buf 72-75Atl 76Sea	1946	6'3	190	G-F	Purdue	8	578	2696	6120	44				860	1086	79.2	2175	2225	1519	28	6252	26	3.8	3.8	10.8
77Port	72-73, 76-77						4	36	120	302	40				29	36	80.6	93	108	73	1	269	21	2.6	3.0	7.5
Walt Gilmore	71Port	1947	6'6	225	F	Fort Valley St.	1	27	23	54	43				12	26	46.2	73	12	49	1	58	10	2.7	0.4	2.1
John Givens	HC68KyA					Western Ky.																				
Clarence Glover	72Bos	1947	6'8	210	F	Western Ky.	1	25	25	55	45				15	32	46.9	46	4	26	0	65	5	1.8	0.2	2.6
	72						1	3	2	6	33				2	2	100	3	0	1	0	6	3	1.0	0.0	2.0
Gail Goodrich	66-68LA 69-70Phoe 71-76LA	1943	6'1	174	G	U.C.L.A	14	1031	7431	####	46				4319	5354	80.7	3279	4805	2775	24	19181	33	3.2	4.7	18.6
77-79NO	66-68, 70-74						8	80	542	1227	44				366	447	81.9	250	333	219	1	1450	33	3.1	4.2	18.1
Gerald Govan	68-70NO-A 71-72MemA	1942	6'10	220	F-C	St. Mary of	9	681	2142	5286	41	5	24	21	962	1419	67.8	7119	2164	2032	11	5251	34	10.5	3.2	7.7
73-75UtahA 76VaA	68-69, 71, 73-74					the Plains	6	66	189	497	38	1	2	50	76	109	69.7	657	190	223	2	455	29	10.0	2.9	6.9
Cal Graham	68PitA	1944	6'2	195	G	Gannon	1	8	4	14	29	0	0	—	5	8	62.5	10	0	12	0	13	7	1.3	0.0	1.6
Mal Graham	68-69Bos 70IL	1945	6'1	185	G	N.Y.U.	2	100	130	327	40				67	102	65.7	118	75	150	0	327	9	1.2	0.8	3.3
	68-69						2	7	2	7	29				1	3	33.3	4	2	3	0	5	4	0.6	0.3	0.7
Travis Grant (Machine	73-74LA 74-75SD-A 76KyA	1950	6'8	225	F	Kentucky St.	4	201	1183	2257	52	2	6	33	399	492	81.1	730	540	386	0	2767	21	3.6	2.7	13.8
Gun) 76IndA	73, 76						2	3	4	7	57				0	0	—	4	0	1	0	8	4	1.3	0.0	2.7
Gary Gray	68Cin	1945	6'1	185	G	Oklahoma City	1	44	49	134	37				7	10	70	23	26	48	0	105	6	0.5	0.6	2.4
Leonard Gray	75-77Sea 77Was	1951	6'8	240	F	Long Beach St.	3	224	1030	2196	47				348	471	73.9	1169	490	825	28	2408	27	5.2	2.2	10.8
	75, 77						2	17	45	101	45				11	13	84.6	54	21	53	0	101	19	3.2	1.2	5.9
Bob Greacen	70-71Mil 72NY-A	1947	6'7	207	F	Rutgers	3	47	46	123	37	0	0	—	21	35	60	67	41	57	0	113	8	1.4	0.9	2.4
	70-71						2	8	5	15	33				4	5	80	7	3	4	0	14	3	0.9	0.4	1.8
Lamar Green	70-74Phoe 75NO 75VaA	1947	6'7	220	F-C	Morehead St.	6	411	893	2078	43	0	0	—	347	526	66	2550	310	1041	19	2133	18	6.2	0.8	5.2
	70						1	6	8	28	29				2	5	40	23	5	8	0	18	12	3.8	0.8	3.0
Luther Green	70-71NY-A 73Phi	1946	6'7	190	F	Long Island U.	3	90	154	402	38	0	7	0	76	150	50.7	321	30	139	2	384	10	3.6	0.3	4.3
	70						1	7	11	29	38	1	2	50	10	15	66.7	28	3			33	12	4.0	0.4	4.7
Gary Gregor	69Phoe 70Atl 71-72Port 73Mil	1945	6'7	230	F-C	S. Carolina	6	361	1416	3251	44	3	4	75	392	541	72.5	2286	482	870	11	3227	23	6.3	1.3	8.9
73-74NY-A	70, 73						2	8	7	27	26	0	0	—	6	8	75	21	2	17	0	20	10	2.6	0.3	2.5
Dennis Grey	69LA-A 70NY-A	1947	6'8	215	C-F	U.S.Internat'l	2	62	190	463	41	0	1	0	163	304	53.6	345	52	211	12	543	22	5.6	0.8	8.8
Mike Grosso	72PitA	1947	6'9	232	C	Louisville	1	25	45	102	44	0	0	—	13	23	56.5	123	11	64		103	13	4.9	0.4	4.1
Dick Grubar	70IndA	1947	6'4	184	G	N. Carolina	1	2	2	3	67	0	0	—	0	0	—	0	1	1	0	4	4	0.0	0.5	2.0
Matt Guokas	67-71Phi 71Chi 72Cin	1944	6'5	193	G-F	St. Joseph's	10	735	1792	3665	49				701	964	72.7	1446	2174	1485	6	4285	23	2.0	3.0	5.8
73-74KCO 74Hou	67-71, 74-75						7	60	101	242	42				52	67	77.6	118	98	121	0	254	18	2.0	1.6	4.2
74Buf 75-76Chi 76KC HC86-89Phi																										
Jim Hadnot	68OakA	1940	6'10	237	C-F	Providence	1	77	488	1045	47	0	2	0	368	551	66.8	936	135	279	9	1344	39	12.2	1.8	17.5
Tom Hagen	70DalA 71TexA 71KyA	1947	6'4	188	G	Vanderbilt	2	73	137	327	42	19	58	33	65	92	70.7	113	135	120	0	358	13	1.5	1.8	4.9
Al Hairston	69-70Sea	1945	6'1	170	G	Bowling Green	2	42	41	122	34				9	15	60	41	44	38	0	91	7	1.0	1.0	2.2
Happy Hairston	65-68Cin 68-70Det 70-75LA	1942	6'7	225	F	N.Y.U.	11	776	4240	8872	48				3025	4080	74.1	8019	1268	2334	29	11505	31	10.3	1.6	14.8
	65-68, 70-74						9	69	307	690	44				187	255	73.3	559	121	185	4	801	29	8.1	1.8	11.6
Lindsay Hairston	76Det	1951	6'7	185	F-C	Michigan St.	1	47	104	228	46				65	112	58	179	21	84	2	273	14	3.8	0.4	5.8
Hal Hale	68HouA	1943	6'1	180	G	Utah State	1	72	133	408	33	35	112	31	60	89	67.4	206	144	143	1	361	24	2.9	2.0	5.0
	68						1	3	6	16	38	3	3	100	7	7	100	8	3	10	0	22	34	2.7	1.0	7.3
Shaler Halimon	69Phi 70-71Chi 71Port 72Atl	1945	6'6	200	G-F	Utah State	5	254	667	1666	40	1	9	11	251	390	64.4	781	423	418	1	1586	14	3.1	1.7	6.2
72-73DalA	69-70, 72						3	10	31	80	39	0	0	—	6	10	60	33	25	17	0	58	16	3.3	2.5	5.8
Jeff Halliburton	72-73Atl 73Phi	1949	6'5	193	G	Drake	2	92	233	529	44				96	118	81.4	145	116	157	2	562	12	1.6	1.3	6.1
	72						1	1	0	1	0				0	0	—	0	0	0	0	0	2	0.0	0.0	0.0
Dennis Hamilton	68LA 69Atl 70PitA 71KyA	1944	6'8	210	F	Arizona St.	4	144	282	552	51	0	1	0	102	119	85.7	442	112	210	0	656	13	3.1	0.8	4.6
	68						1	2	1	3	33				0	0	—	2	1	0	0	2	6	1.0	0.5	1.0
Joe Hamilton	71TexA 72-73DalA 74SA-A	1948	5'10	172	G	N. Texas State	6	344	1564	3829	41	243	757	32	774	959	80.7	684	1208	907		4145	26	2.0	3.5	12.0
74-75KyA 76UtahA	71-72, 74						3	15	48	145	33	12	37	32	27	33	81.8	54	49	38		135	21	3.6	3.3	9.0

		Birth					#		Field Goals			3 pt. FG			Free Throws								Per Game			
Use Name-Nickname	Team by Year	Yr	Hgt	Wgt	Pos	College	Yr	G.	FG	Att	%	FG	Att	%	FT	Att	%	Reb.	Ass	PF	DQ	Pts	Min	Reb	Ass	Pts
Julie Hammond	68-72DenA	1943	6'5	210	F	Tulsa	5	329	1383	2693	51	0	1	0	781	1130	69	2036	421	744	5	3547	24	6.2	1.3	10.8
	68-70						3	24	140	272	51	0	0	—	63	93	68	157	46	92	3	343	31	6.5	1.9	14.3
Joe Hammond	68HouA	1943	6'	180	G	Houston	1	76	274	819	33	16	78	21	186	252	74	217	227	200	2	750	24	2.9	3.0	9.9
	68						1	3	3	17	18	0	3	0	1	2	50	5	2	8	0	7	14	1.7	0.7	2.3
Phil Harkinson	74-75Bos	1951	6'8	197	F	Pennsylvania	2	31	56	114	49				10	13	77	57	6	21	0	122	6	1.8	0.2	3.9
	74-75						2	4	3	7	43				2	2	100	3	0	0	0	8	2	0.8	0.0	2.0
Jim Harding	HC68MinA	1929				Iowa																				
Darrell Hardy	68HouA	1944	6'7	220	F	Baylor	1	17	32	74	43	0	1	0	25	35	71	56	8	23	0	89	10	3.3	0.5	5.2
Ira Harge	68PitA 68-69OakA 70WasA	1941	6'9	225	C	New Mexico	6	427	1783	3963	45	2	6	33	828	1253	66	4955	736	1468	16	4396	31	11.6	1.7	10.3
71CarA 71-72FlaA	69-72						4	39	132	282	47	0	3	0	51	83	61	425	61	90	1	315	27	10.9	1.6	8.1
72-73UtahA 73CarA																										
Jerry Harkness	64NY 68-69IndA	1940	6'2	175	G	Loyola (Chic)	3	86	216	491	44	1	5	20	185	278	67	233	156	140	1	618	24	2.7	1.8	7.2
	68						1	3	4	12	33	0	0	—	2	2	100	5	5	6	0	10	11	1.7	1.7	3.3
Skip Harlicka	69Atl 70MS	1946	6'1	185	G	S. Carolina	1	26	41	90	46				24	31	77	16	37	29	0	106	8	0.6	1.4	4.1
	69						1	1	0	0	—				0	0	—	0	0	1	0	0	1	0.0	0.0	0.0
Art Harris	69-70Sea 70-72Phoe	1947	6'4	186	G	Stanford	4	238	923	2331	40				325	519	63	575	639	709	14	2171	22	2.4	2.7	9.1
	70						1	7	15	42	36				0	2	0	13	12	13	0	30	13	1.9	1.7	4.3
Bernie Harris	75Buf	1950	6'10	200	F	Va. Common.	1	11	2	11	18				1	2	50	8	1	0	0	5	2	0.7	0.1	0.5
Billy Harris	75SD-A	1951	6'2	185	G	Northern Ill.	1	76	264	664	40	16	73	22	65	96	68	122	111	166		609	16	1.6	1.5	8.0
Clem Haskins	68-70Chi 71-74Phoe	1943	6'3	196	G	Western Ky.	9	681	3515	7824	45				1713	2163	79	2087	2382	1504	9	8743	26	3.1	3.5	12.8
75-76Was	68, 70, 75-76						4	28	68	145	47				28	38	74	37	38	41	0	164	12	1.3	1.4	5.9
John Havlicek (Hondo)	63-78Bos	1940	6'5	203	F-G	Ohio State	16	1270	10513	23930	44				5369	6589	81	8007	6114	3281	21	26395	37	6.3	4.8	20.8
	63-69, 72-77						13	172	1451	3329	44				874	1046	84	1186	825	517	9	3776	40	6.9	4.8	22.0
Connie Hawkins (Hawk)	62DL 68PitA 69MinA	1942	6'8	219	F-C	Iowa	9	516	4139	8616	48	5	31	16	3235	4154	78	5450	2556	1873	22	11528	43	10.6	5.0	22.3
70-74Phoe	68-70, 74						4	33	293	626	47	4	8	50	235	320	73	395	148	118	4	825	44	12.0	4.5	25.0
74-75LA 76Atl																										
Nate Hawthorne	74LA 75-76Phoe	1950	6'4	190	G	Southern Ill.	3	162	338	803	42				206	312	66	333	108	274	1	882	12	2.1	0.7	5.4
	74, 76						2	18	10	33	30				12	16	75	16	4	20	0	32	5	0.9	0.2	1.8
Jim Hayes	71NY-A	1948	6'3	200	G	Boston U.	1	47	46	109	42	0	0	—	52	67	78	45	47	73		144	11	1.0	1.0	3.1
Spencer Haywood	70DenA 71-75Sea 76-79NY	1949	6'8	228	F-C	Detroit	13	844	6776	14434	47	1	19	5	3558	4471	80	8675	2988	2388	27	17111	35	10.3	3.5	20.3
79NO 80LA 82-83Was	75, 78, 80, 82						4	33	172	384	45	0	1	0	97	123	79	188	41	98	1	441	27	5.7	1.2	13.4
Walt Hazzard (see Mahdi Abdul-Rahman)																										
Brian Heaney	70Bal	1946	6'2	180	G	Acadia	1	14	13	24	54				2	4	50	4	6	17	0	28	5	0.3	0.4	2.0
	70						1	6	0	2	0				0	0	—	1	1	0	0	0	1	0.2	0.2	0.0
Gar Heard	71-73Sea 73Chi 74-76Buf	1948	6'6	220	F	Oklahoma	11	787	2846	6877	41	0	9	0	1136	1736	65	5876	1220	2134	13	6828	25	7.5	1.6	8.7
76-80Phoe 81SD	73-76, 78-80						7	59	247	589	42				108	166	65	537	96	174	0	602	31	9.1	1.6	10.2
Al Henry	71-72Phi	1949	6'9	205	C	Wisconsin	2	49	69	162	43				56	80	70	148	8	43	0	194	9	3.0	0.2	4.0
Charlie Hentz (Helicopter)	71PitA	1947	6'6	235	F	Arkansas Tech	1	57	142	303	47	0	4	0	57	98	58	386	31	114		341	19	6.8	0.5	6.0
Dan Hester	71DenA 71KyA	1948	6'8	220	F	Louisiana St.	1	42	97	245	40	5	12	42	49	60	82	234	35	82		248	13	5.6	0.8	5.9
	71						1	7	4	14	29	0	0	—	8	9	89	13	1	9		16	6	1.9	0.1	2.3
Fred Hetzel	66-68SF 69Mil 69Cin	1942	6'8	230	F-C	Davidson	6	416	1789	4246	42				1080	1322	82	2444	462	1107	27	4658	21	5.9	1.1	11.2
70Phi 71LA	67-68, 70-71						4	35	138	323	43				83	102	81	184	44	95	3	359	21	5.3	1.3	10.3
Bill Hewitt	69-70LA 70-72Det	1944	6'7	210	F	Southern Cal.	6	361	891	2031	44				280	499	56	1996	469	792	12	2062	21	5.5	1.3	5.7
73Buf 75Chi	68						1	15	61	151	40				18	29	62	78	17	40	0	140	27	5.2	1.1	9.3
Art Heyman	64-65NY 66Cin 66Phi	1941	6'5	208	F-G	Duke	6	310	1418	3418	41	72	256	28	1122	1597	70	1361	859	763	5	4030	27	4.4	2.8	13.0
68NJ-A 69MinA	68-69						2	22	135	286	47	21	55	38	126	180	70	158	78	68	1	417	38	7.2	3.5	19.0
70PitA 70MiaA																										
Bill Higgins	75VaA	1952	6'2	180	G	Ashland	1	15	61	139	44	1	5	20	15	23	65	21	32	41		138	23	1.4	2.1	9.2
Earle Higgins	71IndA	1948	6'8	200	F	Eastern Mich.	1	53	104	223	47	3	17	18	20	30	67	128	35	109		231	9	2.4	0.7	4.4
	71						1	5	6	20	30	0	2	0	6	7	86	13	1	5		18	6	2.6	0.2	3.6
Wayne Hightower	63-65SF 65-67Bal 67Det	1940	6'9	208	F-C	Kansas	10	565	2320	6096	38	0	15	0	1928	2564	75	3966	959	1707	36	6568	27	7.0	1.7	11.6
68-69DenA 70LA-A	64-65, 68-69, 70						5	36	127	373	34	0	1	0	127	171	74	230	60	126	4	381	28	6.4	1.7	10.6
71UtahA 71TexA 72CarA																										
Simmie Hill	70LA-A 70MiaA 72DalA	1946	6'7	233	F	W. Texas St.	4	252	1005	2336	43	36	123	29	403	528	76	1330	334	801	10	2449	23	5.3	1.3	9.7
73SD-A 74SA-A	72-74						3	12	32	79	41	0	4	0	8	12	67	39	16	28		72	19	3.3	1.3	6.0
Darnell Hillman (Dr. Dunk)	72-76IndA 77Ind 78NJ 78Den	1949	6'9	215	F-C	San Jose St.	9	682	2704	5652	48	5	30	17	1243	1980	63	5187	957	2482	39	6666	26	7.6	1.4	9.8
79KC 80GS	72-76, 78-79						7	90	273	577	47	0	3	0	127	211	60	622	88	288	1	673	24	6.9	1.0	7.5
Fred Hilton	72-73Buf	1948	6'3	185	G-F	Grambling	2	120	500	1289	39				131	175	75	254	190	245	0	1131	17	2.1	1.6	9.4
Bob Hogsett	67Det 68PitA	1941	6'7	230	F	Tennessee	2	20	12	36	33	0	0	—	13	23	57	26	2	16	0	37	7	1.3	0.1	1.9
Denny Holman	68DalA	1944	6'3	175	G	S.M.U.	1	46	55	153	36	4	9	44	62	103	60	78	73	85	1	176	12	1.7	1.6	3.8
	68						1	8	9	31	29	1	2	50	12	12	100	16	15	19	0	31	16	2.0	1.9	3.9
A.W.Holt	71Chi	1946	6'7	210	F	Jackson State	1	6	1	8	13				2	3	67	4	0	1	0	4	2	0.7	0.0	0.7
Bobby Hooper	69IndA	1946	6'	180	G	Dayton	1	54	112	271	41	4	32	13	43	59	73	109	142	91	0	271	18	2.0	2.6	5.0
	69						1	16	25	74	34	4	16	25	22	26	85	38	45	41	0	76	18	2.4	2.8	4.8
Carroll Hooser	68DalA	1943	6'7	230	F	S.M.U.	1	56	128	297	43	1	1	100	59	83	71	216	29	139	6	316	13	3.9	0.5	5.6
	68						1	3	1	2	50	0	0	—	0	0	—	2	0	3	0	2	2	0.7	0.0	0.7
Bill Hosket	69-70NY 71-72Buf	1946	6'8	226	F-C	Ohio State	4	143	235	485	48				103	144	72	355	94	219	1	573	10	2.5	0.7	4.0
	69-70						2	9	7	16	44				3	5	60	12	4	9	0	17	6	1.3	0.4	1.9
Greg Howard	71Phoe 72Cle	1948	6'9	220	F-C	New Mexico	2	92	118	304	39				76	109	70	227	53	117	0	312	9	2.5	0.6	3.4
Lou Hudson (Sweet Lou)	67-68StL 69-77Atl 78-79LA	1944	6'5	216	F-G	Minnesota	13	890	7392	15129	49				3156	3960	80	3926	2432	2439	17	17940	33	4.4	2.7	20.2
	67-73, 78-79						9	61	519	1164	45				262	326	80	318	164	196	4	1300	36	5.2	2.7	21.3
John Hummer	71-73Buf 74Chi 74-76Sea	1948	6'9	230	F-C	Princeton	6	327	875	1996	44				498	950	52	1733	543	900	24	2248	23	5.3	1.7	6.9
	75-76						2	9	2	10	20				0	0	—	10	4	10	0	4	9	1.1	0.4	0.4
Les Hunter	65Bal 68MinA 69MizA	1942	6'7	232	F-C	Loyola (Chic)	7	468	2200	4968	44	32	161	20	1303	1864	70	3278	752	1549	36	5735	25	7.0	1.6	12.3
70-71NY-A	68-72						5	52	250	613	41	8	28	29	167	253	66	349	89	173	5	675	25	6.7	1.7	13.0
71-72KyA 73MemA																										
Greg Hyder	71Cin	1948	6'6	215	F	Estrn N. Mexico	1	77	183	409	45				51	71	72	332	48	187	2	417	18	4.3	0.6	5.4
Tom Ingelsby	74Atl 75StLA 76SD-A	1951	6'3	185	G	Villanova	3	75	95	224	42	1	5	20	51	66	77	97	75	63	0	242	10	1.3	1.0	3.2
Stu Inman	HC71Port					San Jose St.																				

Use Name-Nickname	Team by Year	Birth				College	#		Field Goals			3 pt FG			Free Throws								Per Game			
		Yr	Hgt	Wgt	Pos		Yr	G	FG	Att.	%	FG	Att	%	FT	Att.	%	Reb.	Ass	PF	DQ	Pts	Min	Reb	Ass	Pts
Erv Inniger	68MinA 69MiaA	1945	6'4	190	G	Indiana	2	109	418	972	43	8	48	17	120	162	74	385	156	260	2	964	23	3.5	1.4	8.8
	68						1	10	55	140	39	2	11	18	26	32	81	57	35	36	0	138	36	5.7	3.5	13.8
George Irvine	71-75VaA 76DenA	1948	6'6	200	F-G	Washington	6	325	1274	2462	52	37	134	28	508	615	83	959	428	842		3093	20	3.0	1.3	9.5
HC85-86, 89Ind	71-74						4	28	89	162	55	1	10	10	41	47	87	48	27	73		220	17	1.7	1.0	7.9
Willie Iverson	69MiaA	1945	6'	180	G	Central Mich.	1	28	50	146	34	0	2	0	36	60	60	46	80	47	0	136	19	1.6	2.9	4.9
Elvin Ivory	69LA-A	1948	6'8	215	F	Swn. La. St.	1	20	38	87	44	1	4	25	11	17	65	166	9	38	0	88	9	8.3	0.5	4.4
Warren Jabali	69OakA 70WasA 71IndA	1946	6'2	206	G-F	Wichita State	7	447	2663	6181	43	322	1010	32	2017	2669	76	2985	2389	1544	9	7665	34	6.7	5.3	17.1
72FlaA 73-74DenA	69, 71-73						4	36	221	532	42	11	66	17	198	282	70	306	115	111	1	651	34	8.5	3.2	18.1
75SD-A																										
(born and played as Warren Armstrong 69-71)																										
Al Jackson	68Cin	1943	6'1	185	G	Wilberforce	1	2	0	3	0				0	0	—	0	1	6	0	0	9	0.0	0.5	0.0
Greg Jackson	75NY 75Phoe	1952	6'	185	G	Guilford	1	49	73	176	41				36	62	58	69	96	130	5	182	16	1.4	2.0	3.7
Luke Jackson	65-72Phi	1941	6'9	244	F-C	Pan American	8	522	2004	4824	42				1162	1610	72	4619	818	1564	25	5170	26	8.8	1.6	9.9
	65-68, 70-71						6	56	216	555	39				113	152	74	508	92	186	7	545	30	9.1	1.6	9.7
Merv Jackson	69-70LA-A 71-72UtahA	1946	6'3	175	G	Utah	5	262	1162	2826	41	51	152	34	657	804	82	860	813	825	13	3032	26	3.3	3.1	11.6
73MemA	70-72						3	46	250	543	46	12	30	40	97	120	81	179	188	87		609	30	3.9	4.1	13.2
Mike Jackson	73-74UtahA 74MemA	1949	6'7	230	F	L.A. State	4	264	1055	2077	51	4	10	40	569	743	77	1506	254	882		2683	22	5.7	1.0	10.2
75-76VaA	73						1	1	0	0	—	0	0	—	0	0	—	0	0	2		0	2	0.0	0.0	0.0
Phil Jackson	68-69NY 70XJ 71-78NY	1945	6'8	221	F-C	North Dakota	12	807	2076	4583	45	0	2	0	1276	1734	74	3454	898	2366	51	5428	18	4.3	1.1	6.7
79-80NJ	68, 71-75, 78-79						8	67	437	1223	36				115	147	78	284	63	208	4	515	18	4.2	0.9	7.7
Tony Jackson	61DL 68NJ-A 69NY-A	1940	6'4	200	F-G	St. John's	2	138	659	1759	37	123	447	28	749	880	85	741	279	331	3	2190	30	5.4	2.0	15.9
69MinA 69HouA																										
Wardell Jackson	75Sea	1951	6'7	200	F	Ohio State	1	56	96	242	40				51	71	72	133	30	126	2	243	17	2.4	0.5	4.3
Billy James	74KyA	1951	6'3	185	G	Marshall	1	10	1	3	33	0	0	—	0	0	—	0	1	3		2	10	0.0	0.1	0.2
Jim Jarvis	68PitA 69MinA 69LA-A	1943	6'1	175	G	Oregon State	2	125	279	745	37	31	95	33	139	173	80	235	152	240	1	728	14	1.9	1.2	5.8
	68						1	15	39	89	44	0	2	0	16	20	80	21	15	29	0	94	14	1.4	1.0	6.3
Hal Jeter	70WasA	1943	6'4	190	G	Drake	1	5	1	4	25	0	0	—	0	0	—	1	0	8	0	2	4	0.2	0.0	0.4
Charlie Johnson (C.J.)	73-78GS 78-79Was	1949	6'	170	G	California	7	521	1935	4507	43				371	491	76	1318	973	1022	5	4241	19	2.5	1.9	8.1
	74-79						6	85	321	806	40				80	107	75	207	142	201	1	722	20	2.4	1.7	8.5
Ed Johnson	69LA-A 70-71NY-A 71TexA	1944	6'9	205	C	Tenn. State	3	166	787	1661	47	1	3	33	464	837	55	1688	180	687	36	2039	30	10.2	1.1	12.3
	70						1	7	32	69	46	0	0		30	52	58	67	5			64	31	9.6	0.7	9.1
George Johnson	71Bal 72DalA 73-74Hou	1947	6'11	255	C	S. F. Austin St.	4	136	212	472	45	0	0	—	83	154	54	684	81	351	2	507	16	5.0	0.6	3.7
	71-72						2	15	10	22	45	0	0	—	1	2	50	35	11	25	0	21	9	2.3	0.7	1.4
Gus Johnson (Honeycomb)	64-72Bal 73Phoe 73IndA	1938	6'6	235	F-C	Idaho	10	631	4258	9682	44	4	21	19	1723	2462	70	7514	1050	2150	43	10243	33	11.9	1.7	16.2
	65-66, 70-73						6	51	192	501	38	0	3	0	110	145	76	399	91	137	0	494	48	7.8	1.8	9.7
John Johnson (J.J.)	71-73Cle 74-76Port	1947	6'7	200	F	Iowa	12	869	4575	10254	45	0	1	0	2050	2633	78	4778	3285	2505	19	11200	30	5.5	3.8	12.9
76-78Hou 78-82 Sea	77-80, 82						5	73	295	656	45	0	1	0	121	173	70	359	275	195	1	711	27	4.9	3.8	9.7
Neil Johnson	67-68NY 69-70Phoe	1943	6'7	223	F-C	Tulsa,	7	380	1036	2165	48	1	6	17	560	832	67	2003	632	1067	3	2633	17	5.3	1.7	6.9
71-73VaA	67-68, 70-71, 73					Creighton	5	25	65	152	43	1	1	100	42	60	70	151	43	83	0	173	17	6.0	1.7	6.9
Rich Johnson	69-71Bos 71FlaA	1946	6'9	213	C	Grambling	3	135	292	633	46	0	0	—	93	147	63	417	58	281	3	677	12	3.1	0.4	5.0
71CarA 71PitA	69						1	2	1	1	100				0	0	—	2	0	0	0	2	2	1.0	0.0	1.0
Stew Johnson	68KyA 68NJ-A 69NY-A	1944	6'8	225	F-C	Murray State	9	638	4552	10752	42	269	862	31	1081	1377	79	4248	979	1582	5	10454	30	6.7	1.5	16.4
69HouA 70-72PitA	73-75						3	15	103	264	39	12	30	40	20	25	80	93	33	32		238	38	6.2	2.2	15.9
72CarA 73-75SD-A 75MemA 76SD-A 76SA-A																										
Collis Jones	72-73DalA 74KyA 75MemA	1949	6'7	205	F	Notre Dame	4	298	954	2101	45	6	28	21	510	727	70	1409	338	707		2426	21	4.7	1.1	8.1
	72, 74-75						3	12	28	73	38	0	0	—	15	26	58	49	4	28		71	21	4.1	0.3	5.9
Jake Jones	72Phi 72Cin	1949	6'3	180	G	Assumption	1	17	28	72	39				20	31	65	26	12	22	0	76	12	1.5	0.7	4.5
Jimmy Jones	68-70NO-A 71MemA	1945	6'4	190	G-F	Grambling	10	686	4334	8490	51	10	40	25	2668	3398	79	2930	3069	1995	16	11366	34	4.3	4.5	16.6
72-74 UtahA 75-77Was	68-69, 71-76						8	89	653	1264	52	0	7	0	364	480	76	410	371	280	2	1670	36	4.6	4.2	18.8
Johnny Jones	68Bos 69KyA	1943	6'7	210	F	L.A. State	2	80	167	466	36	0	3	0	83	139	60	231	60	113	0	417	12	2.9	0.8	5.2
	68						1	5	3	6	50				0	0	—	4	0	2	0	6	2	0.8	0.0	1.2
Larry Jones	65Phi 68-70DenA	1941	6'2	180	G-F	Toledo	8	551	3723	8153	46	152	548	28	2907	3666	79	2725	2030	1587	10	10505	34	4.9	3.7	19.1
71-72FlaA 73UtahA	65, 68-72						6	35	225	497	45	10	37	27	202	249	81	164	160	124	0	662	35	4.7	4.6	18.9
73DalA 74Phi																										
Nick Jones	68SD 69DalA 69MiaA	1945	6'2	190	G	Oregon	5	198	405	987	41	0	2	0	221	290	76	225	254	403	2	1031	12	1.1	1.3	5.2
71SF 72GS 73DalA	71-72						2	7	8	28	29				17	20	85	5	7	9	0	33	12	0.7	1.0	4.7
Rich Jones (House)	70DalA 71TexA 72-73DalA	1946	6'6	230	F-C	Memphis St.	8	508	3022	7071	43	131	432	30	1476	1931	76	3759	1394	1768	3	7922	33	7.4	2.7	15.6
74-75SA-A 76NY-A 77NYN	70-72,74-76						6	41	194	502	39	7	25	28	62	92	67	255	89	126		459	29	6.2	2.2	11.2
Steve Jones	68OakA 69-70NO-A	1942	6'5	206	G-F	Oregon	9	704	3946	8760	45	186	550	34	2222	3702	60	2467	1525	1981	14	10672	30	3.5	2.2	15.2
71MemA 72-73DalA	69, 71-73, 75						5	37	224	507	44	8	30	27	111	141	79	144	61	132	0	567	33	3.9	1.6	15.3
73-74CarA 74DenA 75StLA 76Port																										
Wali Jones	65Bal 66-71Phi 72-73Mil	1942	6'2	183	G	Villanova	11	678	2684	6553	41	6	25	24	1286	1604	80	1471	2099	1842	26	6672	23	2.2	3.1	9.8
(Wally Jones 65-72)	65-72, 75-76						10	75	341	842	40	0	0	—	173	221	78	168	206	240	5	855	24	2.2	2.7	11.4
75UtahA 76Det 76Phi																										
Wil Jones	70MiaA 71-74MemA	1947	6'8	205	F	Albany St. (GA)	9	725	3530	7637	46	12	84	14	1388	1893	73	5560	1446	2564	22	8484	30	7.7	2.0	11.7
75-76KyA 77Ind78Buf	71, 75-76						3	29	142	306	46	0	1	0	39	47	83	216	81	118		323	32	7.4	2.8	11.1
Charles Jordan	76IndA	1954	6'8	225	F		1	71	162	373	43	2			43	72	60	216	53	184		369	12	3.0	0.7	5.2
	76						1	2	1	6	17				0	0	—	5	2	9		2	9	2.5	1.0	1.0
Kevin Joyce	74-75IndA 76SD-A	1951	6'3	190	G	S. Carolina	3	180	815	1988	41	15	71	21	261	332	79	304	580	441		1906	26	1.7	3.2	10.6
76KyA 77JJ	74-76						3	37	115	300	38	7	20	35	50	62	81	43	87	65		287	23	1.2	2.4	7.8
Harry Joyner	69IndA	1946	6'5	200	F	Indiana	1	2	0	0	—	0	0	—	0	0	—	1	0	1	0	0	3	0.5	0.0	0.0
Ed Jucker	HC68-69Cin	1918				Cincinnati																				
George Karl	74-76SA-A 77-78SA	1951	6'2	185	G	N. Carolina	5	264	662	1395	47	12	54	22	343	440	78	369	795	559	0	1703	17	1.4	3.0	6.5
HC85-86Cle 87GS	74-77						4	18	24	58	41	0	2	0	11	18	61	22	45	36	0	59	8	1.2	2.5	3.3
Bob Kauffman	69Sea 70Chi 71-74Buf	1946	6'8	240	F-C	Guilford	7	525	2306	4835	48				1437	1919	75	3682	1429	1374	26	6049	26	7.0	2.7	11.5
75Atl HC78Det	70, 74						2	5	2	6	33				2	5	40	7	6	5	0	6	5	1.4	1.2	1.2
Billy Keller	70-76IndA 77KJ	1947	5'10	183	G	Purdue	7	556	2440	5740	43	506			1202	1378	87	1349	1980	903		6586	25	2.4	3.6	11.8
	70-76						7	95	415	975	43	87			222	255	87	225	234	184		1139	27	2.4	2.5	12.0
Gary Keller	68-69MiaA	1944	6'9	220	F-C	Florida	2	122	262	675	39	0	5	0	211	334	63	550	47	270	9	735	14	4.5	0.4	6.0
	68-69						2	16	37	88	42	0	0	—	19	33	58	73	11	39	0	93	12	4.6	0.7	5.8

		Birth					#		Field Goals			3 pt. FG			Free Throws								Per Game			
Use Name-Nickname	Team by Year	Yr	Hgt	Wgt	Pos	College	Yr	G	FG	Att.	%	FG	Att	%	FT	Att.	%	Reb.	Ast	PF	DQ	Pts	Min	Reb	Ast	Pts
Arvesta Kelly	68Pit 69MinA 70PitA 71CarA	1945	6'3	192	G	Lincoln (MO.)	5	188	598	1343	45	50	198	25	260	408	64	497	331	423	4	1506	21	2.6	1.8	8.0
71-72PitA 72IndA	68-69						2	13	13	36	36	7	18	39	7	8	88	16	5	22	0	40	6	1.2	0.4	3.1
Ben Kelso	74Det	1949	6'3	195	G	Central Mich.	1	46	35	96	36				15	22	68	31	18	45	0	85	6	0.7	0.4	1.8
	74						1	1	0	2	0				0	0	—	1	1	0	0	0	1	1.0	1.0	0.0
Frank Kendrick	75GS	1951	6'6	198	F	Purdue	1	24	31	77	40				18	22	82	36	6	22	0	80	5	1.5	0.3	3.3
Goo Kennedy	72-73DalA 74SA-A 75StLA	1949	6'6	205	F	T.C.U	6	333	1142	2084	55	1	1	100	452	673	67	1866	299	1055	1	2739	20	5.6	0.9	8.2
76UtahA 77Hou	72, 74-75, 77						4	22	34	72	47	0	1	0	17	22	77	54	6	37	0	85	9	2.5	0.3	3.9
Joe Kennedy	69-70Sea 71PitA	1947	6'6	210	F	Duke	3	168	366	943	39	0	2	0	230	286	80	602	140	321	2	962	16	3.6	0.8	5.7
Tom Kerwin	68PitA	1944	6'7	210	F	Centenary	1	13	7	22	32	0	0	—	0	2	0	20	1	5	0	14	5	1.5	0.1	1.1
Julius Keye	70-74DenA 75MemA	1946	6'10	225	F-C	Alcorn State	6	418	1264	3027	42	4	22	18	629	1009	62	4602	657	1407	2	3161	33	11.0	1.6	7.6
	70, 72-73						3	19	57	135	42	0	2	0	15	31	48	210	42	62	0	129	34	11.1	2.2	6.8
Earnie Killum	71LA	1948	6'3	180	G	Stetson	1	4	0	4	0				1	1	100	2	0	1	0	1	3	0.5	0.0	0.3
	71						1	2	1	1	100				2	3	67	0	0	1	0	4	2	0.0	0.0	2.0
Toby Kimball	67Bos 68-71SD 72Mil	1942	6'8	230	F-C	Connecticut	9	571	1383	3251	43				704	1229	57	3870	571	1280	14	3470	18	6.8	1.0	6.1
73KCO 74Phi 75NO	67, 69, 72						3	14	28	67	42				15	27	56	83	6	21	0	71	17	5.9	0.4	5.1
Jim King	64-66LA 67-70SF 70Cin	1941	6'2	175	G	Tulsa	10	607	1700	4067	42				977	1249	78	1500	1412	1218	10	4377	18	2.5	2.3	7.2
71-73Chi	64-69, 71-73						9	73	246	564	44				110	151	73	246	182	194	4	602	20	3.4	2.5	8.2
Loyd King	72-73MemA	1949	6'2	183	G	Va. Tech	2	84	191	523	37	21	90	23	103	127	81	125	117	188		506	15	1.5	1.4	6.0
Ron King	74KyA	1951	6'4	195	G	Florida State	1	9	24	70	34	2	6	33	14	17	82	19	14	14		64	14	2.1	1.6	7.1
Wilbur Kirkland	70PitA	1949	6'7	190	F	Cheyney St.	1	2	3	7	43	0	0	—	0	0	—	11	1	5	0	6	14	5.5	0.5	3.0
Jim Kissane	69MinA	1946	6'7	210	F	Boston Coll.	1	2	2	6	33	0	0	—	2	2	100	3	0	3	0	6	8	1.5	0.0	3.0
Lonnie Klutz	71CarA	1945	6'7	220	F	N. Car. A & T	1	3	0	4	0	0	0	—	0	0	—	5	0	3		0	3	1.7	0.0	0.0
Ron Knight	71-72Port	1947	6'7	224	F	L.A. State	2	10	211	487	43				50	100	50	283	83	151	1	472	11	2.8	0.8	4.7
Rod Knowles	69Phoe 69NY-A	1946	6'9	215	C	Davidson	1	9	4	14	29	0	0	—	1	3	33	9	0	11	0	9	5	1.0	0.0	1.0
Don Kojis	64Bal 65-66Det 67Chi	1939	6'5	215	F	Marquette	12	814	3947	8853	45				2054	3853	53	4555	1112	1937	22	9948	24	5.6	1.4	12.2
71-72Sea 73-75KCO	67, 69, 75						3	13	72	163	44				35	45	78	85	26	35	1	179	28	6.5	2.0	13.8
68-70SD																										
Howie Komives (Butch)	65-69NY 69-72Det	1941	6'1	185	G	Bowling Green	10	742	2972	7652	39				1606	1936	83	1804	2941	2046	13	7550	27	2.4	4.0	10.2
73Buf 74KCO	67-68						2	10	31	103	30				14	19	74	25	38	35	1	76	26	2.5	3.8	7.6
Tom Kondla	69MinA 69HouA	1946	6'8	225	C	Minnesota	1	42	58	145	40	0	1	0	22	46	48	125	13	56	0	138	8	3.0	0.3	3.3
Tony Koski	69NY-A	1946	6'8	215	F	Providence	1	5	2	7	29	0	0	—	2	2	100	7	4	9	0	6	6	1.4	0.8	1.2
Len Kosmalski	75KCO 76KC	1951	7'	245	C	Tennessee	2	76	41	103	40				28	36	78	144	53	75	0	110	7	1.9	0.7	1.4
	75						1	6	2	3	67				2	3	67	10	5	4	0	6	5	1.7	0.8	1.0
Tom Kozelko	74Cap 75-76Was	1951	6'8	220	F	Toledo	3	189	167	399	42				73	98	74	346	99	281	7	407	10	1.8	0.5	2.2
	74-76						3	25	15	25	60				9	11	82	17	2	18	1	39	5	0.7	0.1	1.6
Ron Kozlicki	68IndA	1943	6'7	215	F	Northwestern	1	37	41	121	34	6	29	21	21	34	62	69	14	31	0	109	10	1.9	0.4	2.9
	68						1	2	0	2	0	0	1	0	0	0	—	1	0	1	0	0	3	0.5	0.0	0.0
Steve Kramer	68AnaA 69HouA 70CarA	1944	6'5	200	G-F	B.Y.U.	3	124	380	885	43	1	8	13	287	368	78	310	236	315	7	1048	18	2.5	1.9	8.5
	70						1	2	2	5	40	0	0	—	3	3	100					7	10			3.5
Tommy Kron	67StL 68-69Sea 70KyA	1943	6'5	200	G	Kentucky	4	225	505	1305	39	7	19	37	334	435	77	672	605	525	7	1351	16	3.0	2.7	6.0
	67						1	1	0	1	0				0	0	—	0	0	1	0	0	1	0.0	0.0	0.0
Steve Kuberski	70-74Bos 75Mil	1947	6'8	215	F-C	Bradley	9	568	1254	3005	42				606	790	77	2146	338	915	3	3114	14	3.8	2.6	5.5
76Buf 76-78Bos	72-74, 76						4	50	110	239	46				65	84	77	148	24	85	0	285	12	3.0	0.5	5.7
Terry Kunze	68MinA	1943	6'4	210	G-F	Minnesota	1	46	83	245	34	5	11	45	59	102	58	75	47	77	0	230	14	1.6	1.0	5.0
Reggie Lacefield	69KyA	1945	6'5	230	F	Western Mich.	1	8	11	22	50	0	1	0	2	4	50	11	0	9	0	24	6	1.4	0.0	3.0
Bob Lakey	73-74NY-A	1949	6'6	210	G-F	Marquette	2	71	156	362	43	2	5	40	99	167	59	164	137	172		413	17	2.3	1.9	5.8
	73						1	5	4	8	50	0	2	0	4	11	36	8	5	10		12	12	1.6	1.0	2.4
Edgar Lacy	69LA-A	1944	6'6	190	F	U.C.L.A.	1	46	98	219	45	0	2	0	38	67	57	180	30	92	1	234	13	3.9	0.7	5.1
Wendall Ladner	71-72MemA 72CarA 73MemA	1948	6'5	220	F	Southern Miss.	5	300	1498	3954	38	112	444	25	366	514	71	2481	622	1168		3474	26	8.3	2.1	11.6
73-74KyA 74-75NYA	71, 73-75						4	40	131	359	36	23	87	26	20	33	61	171	69	145		305	18	4.3	1.7	7.6
Killed in plane crash June 24, 1975																										
Bo Lamar	74-76SD-A 76IndA 77LA	1951	6'1	180	G	Swn. La.	4	273	1740	4084	43	118	442	27	644	739	87	739	1063	436	0	4478	29	2.7	3.9	16.4
	74, 77						2	16	83	203	41	7	17	41	25	29	86	33	35	31	0	198	22	2.1	2.2	12.3
Stu Lantz	69-71SD 72Hou 73-74Det	1946	6'3	175	G	Nebraska	8	547	2469	5674	44				1844	2266	81	1820	1566	1320	9	6782	28	3.3	2.9	12.4
75NO 75-76LA 77JJ	69, 74						2	13	58	128	45				49	59	83	50	24	41	0	165	33	3.8	1.8	12.7
John Lasowski	76-77Chi	1953	6'6	185	G	Indiana	2	118	359	902	40				114	150	76	282	99	112	0	832	19	2.4	0.8	7.1
Dave Lattin (Big Daddy)	68SF 69Phoe 71-72PitA	1943	6'7	230	F-C	Texas-El Paso	5	263	741	1554	48	0	3	0	422	669	63	1332	184	695	9	1904	16	5.1	0.7	7.2
73MemA	68						1	5	1	5	20				5	6	83	5	1	9	0	7	5	1.0	0.2	1.4
Harry Laurie	71PitA	1945	6'1	178	G	St. Peter's	1	9	3	12	25	0	0	—	7	11	64	15	8	16		13	6	1.7	0.9	1.4
Mo Layton	72-73Phoe 74Port	1948	6'1	180	G	Southern Cal.	4	226	686	1557	44	0	0	—	287	386	74	325	598	482	2	1663	18	1.3	1.7	7.4
74MemA 77NYK																										
Manny Leaks	69KyA 69NY-A 69-70DalA	1945	6'8	235	C-F	Niagara	6	446	2141	4867	44	0	5	0	1020	1442	71	3996	471	1169	21	5302	28	9.0	1.1	11.9
71TexA 71-72NY-A	69-71, 74						4	21	112	238	47	0	0	—	46	65	71	198	20	42	0	270	31	9.4	1.0	12.9
72UtahA 72FlaA 73Phi 74Cap																										
Clyde Lee	67-71SF 72-74GS 75Atl	1944	6'10	220	F-C	Vanderbilt	10	742	2256	5223	43				1221	1988	61	7626	788	2203	42	5733	27	10.3	1.1	7.7
75-76Phi	67-69, 71-73, 76						7	51	146	368	40				68	116	59	519	61	157	3	360	27	10.2	1.2	7.1
Dave Lee	68Oak-A 69NO-A	1942	6'7	225	F	San Fransisco	2	58	126	285	44	2	6	33	120	140	86	187	20	83	2	374	13	3.2	0.3	6.4
Dick Lee	68AnaA				F		1	2	0	0		0	0	—	0	0	—	1	1	0	0	0	1	0.5	0.5	0.0
Greg Lee	75SD-A 76Port	1951	6'3	190	G	U.C.L.A.	2	10	10	19	53	0	0	—	4	4	100	5	24	12	0	24	10	0.4	0.4	2.4
Russ Lee	73-74Mil 75NO	1950	6'5	198	G-F	Marshall	3	97	116	297	39				50	73	68	114	65	82	1	282	6	1.2	0.7	2.9
	73-74						2	11	13	22	59				1	4	25	7	3	1	0	27	2	0.6	0.3	2.5
George Leemann	68StL 69Atl 69-70LA-A	1942	6'3	188	G	Campbell	7	376	1616	3863	42	409	1121	36	817	971	84	599	1677	859	1	4458	26	1.6	4.5	11.9
70NY-A 70MiaA	68						1	1	0	1	0				0	0	—	0	2	1	0	0	2	0.0	2.0	0.0
71-72CarA 72-74MemA																										
Barry Liebowitz	68PitA 68NJ-A 68OakA	1943	6'2	185	G	Long Island U.	1	82	320	873	37	6	39	15	248	306	81	170	301	208	1	894	26	2.1	3.7	10.9
Leary Lentz	68-69HouA 69NY-A	1945	6'6	200	F	Houston	2	148	478	1179	41	0	4	0	223	338	66	919	120	278	1	1179	25	6.2	0.8	8.0
	68						1	3	12	26	46	0	0	—	1	3	33	19	3	6	0	25	24	6.3	1.0	8.3

Use Name-Nickname	Team by Year	Birth Yr	Hgt	Wgt	Pos	College	# Yr	G	Field Goals FG	Att.	%	3 pt. FG FG	Att	%	Free Throws FT	Att.	%	Reb	Ass	PF	DQ	Pts	Per Game Min	Reb	Ass	Pts
Bobby Lewis	68-70SF 71Cle	1945	6'3	185	G	N. Carolina	4	255	564	1482	38				353	496	71	533	555	503	1	1481	17	2.1	2.2	5.8
	68-69						2	6	13	31	42				1	3	33	5	6	12	0	27	11	0.8	1.0	4.5
Freddie Lewis	67Cin 68-74IndA 75MemA	1943	6'	180	G	Arizona State	11	730	4027	8982	45	275	983	28	3154	3859	82	2752	2979	2172	14	12033	34	3.8	4.1	16.5
75-76StLA 77Ind	67-75						9	109	716	1688	42	43	175	25	548	643	85	441	458	349	2	2023	38	4.0	4.2	18.6
Mike Lewis	69IndA 69MinA	1946	6'8	227	C-F	Duke	6	337	1613	3237	50	0	2	0	855	1164	73	4022	2000	1249	15	4081	30	11.9	3.0	12.1
70-72PitA 73-74CarA	69						1	7	20	52	38	0	0	—	10	19	53	47	11	28	2	50	19	6.7	1.6	7.1
Bil Ligon	75DetA	1952	6'4	180	G	Vanderbilt	1	38	55	143	38				16	25	64	26	25	31	0	126	7	0.7	0.7	3.3
	75						1	2	1	1	100				0	0	—	0	0	1	0	2	9	0.0	0.0	1.0
Goose Ligon	68-72KyA 72PitA 73-74VaA	1944	6'7	215	F-C	none	7	434	2063	4232	49	3	24	13	1431	2226	64	4720	910	1658	25	5560	34	10.9	2.1	12.8
	68-71, 74						5	46	211	439	48	0	3	0	166	249	67	516	76	129	1	588	33	11.2	1.7	12.8
Sam Little	70KyA	1947	6'	180	G	Delta State	1	3	2	4	50	0	1	0	1	1	100	1	2	4	0	5	4	0.3	0.7	1.7
Gene Littles	70CarA 71-75KyA HC86Cle	1943	6'1	172	G	High Point	5	450	1606	3373	48	25	104	24	829	1124	74	1475	1336	1048	0	4066	25	3.3	3.0	9.0
	70, 73-75						4	28	65	143	45	4	9	44	29	49	59	70	52	29		163	18	2.5	1.9	5.8
Bobby Lloyd	68NJ-A 69NY-A	1946	6'2	185	G	Rutgers	2	125	362	890	41	15	39	38	388	445	87	220	229	290	2	1127	19	1.8	1.8	9.0
Chuck Lloyd	71CarA	1948	6'8	220	C-F	Yankton	1	14	23	51	45	0	0	—	20	30	67	25	6	25		66	8	1.8	0.4	4.7
Riney Lochmann	68-70DalA	1944	6'6	215	F	Kansas	3	170	296	730	41	5	16	31	134	221	61	466	143	312	6	731	13	2.7	0.8	4.3
	68-69						2	8	5	14	36	0	0	—	3	3	100	7	1	7	0	13	6	0.9	0.1	1.6
Henry Logan	69OakA 70WasA	1946	6'	183	G	Wn Carolina	2	108	449	963	47	1	7	14	359	509	71	376	244	319	7	1258	22	3.5	2.3	11.6
	69, 71VaA						2	17	75	176	43	0	0	—	68	101	67	40	34	50	3	218	22	2.4	2.0	12.8
Paul Long	68Det 69KyA 70Det 71Buf	1944	6'2	180	G	Va. Tech,	4	80	117	273	43	0	0	—	75	98	77	66	66	79	0	309	6	0.8	0.8	3.9
	68					Wake Forest	1	1	3	3	100				0	0	—	0	1	1	0	6	4	0.0	1.0	6.0
Willie Long	72FlaA 73-74DenA	1950	6'8	235	F-C	New Mexico	3	213	902	2144	42	0	5	0	614	793	77	1269	209	606		2418	24	6.0	1.0	11.4
	72-73						2	8	29	77	38	0	0	—	23	31	81	49	5	29		81	26	6.1	0.6	10.1
Plummer Lott	68-69Sea	1945	6'5	210	F-G	Seattle	2	67	63	214	29				21	36	58	123	43	74	1	147	10	1.8	0.6	2.2
Kevin Loughery	63-64Det 64-72Bal	1940	6'3	190	G	Boston Coll.,	11	755	4477	10829	41				2621	3262	80	2254	2803	2543	58	11575	29	3.0	3.7	15.3
72, PC73Phi	63, 65-66, 69-71					St. John's (NY)	6	43	196	522	38				140	186	75	107	116	140	2	532	27	2.5	2.7	12.4
HC74-76NY-A HC77NYN HC78NJ																										
HC79-83Atl HC84-85Chi HC86-87Was																										
Bob Love	67-68Cin 69Mil 69-77Chi 77NYN	1942	6'8	215	F	Southern U.	11	789	5447	12688	43				3001	3728	81	4653	1123	2130	17	13895	32	5.9	1.4	17.6
77Sea	70-75						6	47	441	1023	43				194	250	78	352	87	144	1	1076	44	7.5	1.9	22.9
Stan Love	72-73Bal 74-75LA 75SA-A	1949	6'9	215	F	Oregon	4	239	649	1474	44	0	0	—	281	374	75	929	181	594	4	1579	15	3.9	0.8	6.6
	72-74						3	7	3	10	30				2	3	67	10	2	4	0	8	4	1.4	0.3	1.1
Charlie Lowery	72Mil	1949	6'3	185	G	Puget Sound	1	20	17	38	45				11	18	61	19	14	16	1	45	7	1.0	0.7	2.3
	72						1	7	2	8	25				2	3	67	3	1	4	0	6	4	0.4	0.1	0.9
Jerry Lucas	64-70Cin 70-71SF 72-74NY	1940	6'8	231	F-C	Ohio State	11	829	5707	11441	50				2635	3365	78	12942	2730	2389	20	14053	39	15.6	3.3	17.0
	64-67, 71-74						8	72	367	786	47				162	206	79	717	214	197	2	896	33	10.0	3.0	12.4
Phil Lumpkin	75Port 76Phoe	1951	6'	167	G	Miami (Ohio)	2	82	108	255	42				56	69	81	82	225	106	1	272	14	1.0	2.7	3.3
	76						1	17	10	30	33				11	14	79	13	21	8	0	31	8	0.8	1.2	1.8
. B. Lynam	68DenA	1944	6'1	200	G	Okla. Baptist	1	7	5	17	29	0	1	0	7	8	88	5	0	10	0	17	6	0.7	0.0	2.4
Lonnie Lynn	70DenA 70PitA	1945	6'7	215	F	Wilberforce	1	52	112	275	41	0	3	0	36	74	49	258	43	120	1	260	15	5.0	0.9	5.0
Mike Lynn	70LA 71Buf	1945	6'7	215	F	U.C.L.A.	2	49	46	140	33				34	51	67	68	31	96	4	126	9	1.4	0.6	2.6
	70						1	3	2	3	67				0	0		2	1	1	0	4	2	0.7	0.3	1.3
Mike Macaluso	74Buf	1951	6'5	210	F	Canisius	1	30	19	44	43				10	17	59	25	3	31	0	48	4	0.8	0.1	1.6
Randy Mahaffey	68-69KyA 69NY-A	1945	6'7	210	F	Clemson	4	321	1476	3315	45	0	16	0	863	1262	68	2554	507	1118	30	3815	30	8.0	1.6	11.9
70-71CarA	68, 70						2	9	43	91	47	0	0	—	27	38	71	50	11	16	1	113	26	5.6	1.2	12.6
Brian Mahoney	73NY-A	1948	6'3	175	G	Manhattan	1	19	17	57	30	0	2	0	24	40	60	14	12	35		58	10	0.7	0.6	3.1
Mike Maloy	71-72VaA 73DalA	1949	6'7	215	F	Davidson	3	71	168	396	42	0	1	0	106	151	70	268	48	153		442	12	3.8	0.7	6.2
	71						1	1	1	3	33	0	0	—	0	0		1	0	0		2	1	1.0	0.0	2.0
Ted Manakas	74KCO	1951	6'2	180	G	Princeton	1	5	4	10	40				4	4	100	3	2	4	0	12	9	0.6	0.4	2.4
Ed Manning	68-70Bal 70Chi 71Port	1944	6'7	215	F	Jackson St.	9	604	1518	3392	45	1	8	13	504	660	76	2717	494	1439	7	3541	17	4.5	0.8	5.9
72-74CarA	69-70, 73-75						5	25	76	156	49	1	2	50	25	31	81	103	12	66	0	178	18	4.1	0.5	7.1
75NY-A 76IndA																										
Guy Manning	68-69HouA	1944	6'6	205	F	Pr. View A&M	2	73	233	597	39	2	8	25	136	236	58	353	39	171	4	604	17	4.8	0.5	8.3
	68						1	3	16	34	44	0	0	—	11	19	58	19	2	11	0	41	22	6.3	0.7	13.7
Pete Maravich	71-74Atl 75-79NO 80Utah	1948	6'5	197	G	L.S.U.	10	658	6187	14025	44	10	15	67	3564	4344	82	2747	3563	1985	18	15948	40	4.5	5.9	24.2
(Pistol Pete)	71-73, 80						4	26	190	449	42	2	6	33	105	134	78	95	98	74	1	487	29	3.7	3.8	18.7
80Bos																										
Jack Marin	67-72Bal 73-74Hou	1944	6'7	208	F-G	Duke	11	849	5068	10890	47				2405	2852	84	4405	1813	2416	41	12541	29	5.2	2.1	14.8
74-76Buf 76-77Chi	69-72, 74-75, 77						7	51	292	649	45				173	210	82	283	120	151	2	757	33	5.5	2.4	14.8
Harvey Marlatt	71-73Det	1948	6'3	185	G	Eastern Mich.	3	61	87	233	37				51	60	85	66	94	92	1	225	12	1.4	1.5	3.7
Jim Marsh	72Port	1946	6'7	215	F	Southern Cal.	1	39	39	117	33				41	59	69	84	30	50	0	119	10	2.2	0.8	3.1
Vester Marshall	74Sea	1948	6'7	200	F	Oklahoma	1	13	7	29	24				3	7	43	37	4	20	0	17	13	2.8	0.3	1.3
LaRue Martin	73-76Port	1950	6'11	208	C	Loyola (Chic)	4	271	591	1422	42				248	362	69	1258	203	617	6	1430	14	4.6	0.7	5.3
Eddie Mast	71NY 72-73Atl	1948	6'9	220	F-C	Temple	3	112	114	296	39				55	91	60	265	51	114	0	283	8	2.3	0.5	2.5
	71-73						3	16	11	17	65				1	5	20	15	2	7	0	23	3	0.9	0.1	1.4
Johnny Mathis	68NJ-A	1943	6'6	220	F	Savannah St.	1	51	69	186	37	0	2	0	35	55	64	194	28	102	3	173	13	3.8	0.5	3.4
Don May	69-70NY 71Buf 72-73Atl	1946	6'4	217	F	Dayton	7	379	1351	2981	45				637	798	80	1309	389	751	5	3339	17	3.5	1.0	8.8
73-74Phi 75KCO	69-70, 72						3	14	14	42	33				13	17	76	31	9	12	0	41	9	2.2	0.6	2.9
Willie McCarter	70-71LA 72Port	1946	6'3	175	G	Drake	3	155	482	1198	40				126	192	66	248	304	281	0	1090	18	1.6	2.0	7.0
	70-71						2	17	30	83	36				2	7	29	29	20	32	0	62	14	1.7	1.2	3.6
Babe McCarthy	HC67-69NO-A HC70-71MemA	1923				Miss. State																				
HC72DalA HC73KyA	1923																									
Ted McClain	72-74CarA 75-76KyA	1947	6'3	180	G	Tenn. State	8	455	1822	3991	46	27	124	22	944	1231	77	1627	1909	1499	11	4669	28	3.6	4.2	10.3
(Hound Dog)	73-79						7	64	165	431	38	1	12	8	75	102	74	182	177	166	0	406	20	2.8	2.8	6.3
76NY-A 77DenA 78Buf 78Phi 79Phoe																										
Paul McCracken	73-74Hou 77Chi	1950	6'4	180	G	Northridge St.	3	37	63	140	45				34	57	60	73	33	52	0	160	12	2.0	0.9	4.3
Jim McDaniels	72CarA 72-74Sea 76LA	1948	6'11	228	C-F	Western Ky.	5	271	1146	2459	47	0	0	—	406	464	70	1748	288	782	8	2698	19	6.5	1.1	10.0
76KyA 78Buf	76						1	10	19	41	46				4	7	57	35	5	16		42	10	3.5	0.5	4.2
Glenn McDonald	75-76Bos 77Mil	1952	6'6	190	F-G	L. Beach St.	3	146	269	672	40				71	97	73	215	99	192	0	609	10	1.5	0.7	4.2
	75-76						2	19	10	38	26				6	9	67	14	6	16	0	26	5	0.8	0.3	1.4

		Birth					#		Field Goals			3 pt. FG			Free Throws								Per Game			
Use Name-Nickname	Team by Year	Yr	Hgt	Wgt	Pos	College	Yr	G	FG	Att.	%	FG	Att	%	FT	Att.	%	Reb.	Ass	PF	DQ	Pts	Min	Reb	Ass	Pts
Rod McDonald	71-73UtahA	1945	6'6	205	F	Whitworth	3	87	111	248	45	3	8	38	57	81	70	197	40	100		282	7	2.3	0.5	3.2
	71-73						3	9	12	18	67	1	2	50	1	3	33	16	2	6		26	4	1.8	0.2	2.9
Pat McFarland	74-75DenA 76SD-A	1951	6'5	185	F-G	St. Joseph's	3	148	414	903	46	11	41	27	108	140	77	298	219	149		947	13	2.0	1.5	6.4
	75						1	5	2	8	25	0	2	0	2	2	100	3	2	3	0	6	6	0.6	0.4	1.2
Jon McGlocklin	66-67Cin 68SD 69-76Mil	1943	6'5	205	G-F	Indiana	11	792	4001	8174	49				1167	1381	85	1928	2280	1370	4	9169	26	2.4	2.9	11.6
	66, 70-74, 76						7	55	266	544	49				75	91	82	102	123	121	0	607	28	1.9	2.2	11.0
Gil McGregor	72Cin	1949	6'8	240	F	Wake Forest	1	42	66	182	36				39	56	70	148	18	120	4	171	13	3.5	0.4	4.1
Elton McGriff	68-69DalA 69NO-A 69KyA	1942	6'9	225	C	Creighton	2	56	124	260	48	0	1	0	90	152	59	258	10	150	4	338	15	4.6	0.2	6.0
	68-69						2	13	38	91	42	0	0	—	27	48	56	99	8	49	3	103	21	7.6	0.6	7.9
Allie McGuire	74NY	1951	6'3	175	G	Marquette	1	2	2	4	50				0	0	—	2	1	2	0	4	5	1.0	0.5	2.0
Maurice McHartley	68DalA 69NY-A 69-70MiaA	1942	6'3	200	G-F	N. Car. A & T	3	189	875	2175	40	15	80	19	586	785	75	599	641	625	13	2351	28	3.2	3.4	12.4
70PitA 70DalA	68-70						3	25	127	337	38	2	9	22	90	114	79	87	78	88	3	346	28	3.5	3.1	13.8
Kenny McIntosh	72-73Chi 73-75Sea	1949	6'7	225	F	Eastern Mich.	4	177	401	1111	36				132	227	58	696	173	333	5	934	21	3.9	1.0	5.3
Bob McIntyre	68NJ-A 70NY-A	1944	6'6	220	F	St. John's (NY)	2	28	82	219	37	1	4	25	34	59	58	121	16	35	0	199	19	4.3	0.6	7.1
Jerry McKee	70IndA	1946	6'3	190	G	Ohio U.	1	1	0	1	0	0	0	—	0	0	—	0	0	0	0	0	3	0.0	0.0	0.0
Stan McKenzie	68Bal 69-70Phoe 71-73Port	1944	6'5	210	F-G	N.Y.U.	7	396	1281	2885	44				1017	1268	80	1117	611	894	10	3579	19	2.8	1.5	9.0
73-74Hou	70						1	7	8	29	28				4	5	80	9	3	14	0	16	10	1.3	0.4	2.3
McCoy McLemore	65-66SF 67-68Chi 69Phoe	1942	6'7	233	F-C	Drake	8	580	1947	4943	39				1236	1603	77	3131	733	1442	26	5130	21	5.5	1.3	8.8
69-70Det 71Cle	67-68, 71						3	18	34	91	37				30	38	79	49	17	31	1	98	13	2.7	0.9	5.4
71-72Mil 72 Hou																										
John McLendon	HC69DenA	1951				Kansas																				
Jim McMillian	71-73LA 74-76Buf 77NYK	1948	6'5	225	F	Columbia	9	631	3644	7557	48				1448	1741	83	3319	1557	1200	1	8736	32	5.3	2.5	13.8
78NY 79Port	71-76, 78						7	72	497	1101	45				200	253	79	377	137	169	1	1194	38	5.2	1.9	16.6
Larry McNeill (the Hawk)	74-75KC-O 76KC 77NYN	1951	6'9	198	F-C	Marquette	6	297	915	1963	47				703	902	78	1440	225	702	5	2533	17	4.8	0.8	8.5
77-78GS 78Buf 79Det	75, 77						2	12	29	44	66				19	24	79	28	2	23	2	77	10	2.3	0.2	6.4
Roy McPipe	75UtahA	1950	6'3	205	G	Eastern Mont.	1	5	8	24	33	2	4	50	3	4	75	5	1	5		21	9	1.0	0.2	4.2
Eric McWilliams	73Hou	1950	6'8	200	F	L. Beach St.	1	44	34	98	35				18	37	49	60	5	46	0	86	6	1.4	0.1	2.0
Cliff Meely	72-76Hou 76LA	1947	6'8	216	F-C	Colorado	5	318	1121	2687	42				416	616	68	1703	398	929	25	2658	20	5.4	1.3	8.4
Bill Melchionni	67-68Phi 69HO 70-76NY-A	1944	6'1	168	G	Villanova	9	644	2753	6002	46	37	143	26	1327	1640	80	1284	3247	1398	7	6870	26	2.0	5.0	10.7
	67-68, 70-76						9	55	211	476	44	3	14	21	120	148	81	98	238	96	0	545	24	1.8	4.3	9.9
Gary Melchionni	74-75Phoe	1951	6'2	187	G	Duke	2	137	434	978	44				206	248	83	329	298	201	2	1074	20	2.4	2.2	7.8
Dean Memminger	72-74NY 75-76Atl 77NYK	1948	6'0	175	G	Marquette	6	416	1004	2112	48				544	867	63	1086	1046	700	1	2552	21	2.6	2.5	6.1
(the Dream)	72-74						3	45	66	145	46				37	66	56	104	82	85	1	169	17	2.3	1.8	3.8
John Mengelt (Crash)	72Cin 73KCO 73-76Det	1949	6'2	195	G	Auburn	10	636	2418	5047	48	0	6	0	1382	1708	81	1221	1329	1284	8	6218	20	1.9	2.1	9.8
77-80Chi 81GS	74-77						4	19	62	119	52				43	55	78	33	33	40	0	167	15	1.7	1.7	8.8
DeWitt Menyard	68HouA	1944	6'10	210	C	Utah	1	71	256	692	37	0	0	—	131	197	66	551	84	218	5	643	25	7.8	1.2	9.1
	68						1	3	7	18	39	0	1	0	1	3	33	11	0	8	0	15	21	3.7	0.0	5.0
Bill Meyer	68PitA	1943	6'3	195	G	Hiram	1	7	10	22	45	0	0	—	2	2	100	5	1	7	0	22	6	0.7	0.1	3.1
Larry Mikan	71Cle	1948	6'7	215	F	Minnesota	1	53	62	186	33				34	55	62	139	41	56	1	158	10	2.6	0.8	3.0
Eddie Miles	64-70Det 70-71Bal 72NY	1940	6'4	196	G-F	Seattle	9	605	3301	7505	44				1518	2032	75	1860	1225	1385	8	8120	26	3.1	2.0	13.4
	68, 70, 72						3	20	43	111	39				13	17	76	35	16	23	0	99	14	1.8	0.8	5.0
Jay Miller	68StL 69Mil 69LA-A	1943	6'5	210	F	Notre Dame	4	117	236	569	41	0	1	0	177	247	72	205	47	191	4	649	11	1.8	0.4	5.5
69-71IndA	69-70						2	14	16	38	42	0	0	—	4	10	40	25	2	18	0	36	5	1.8	0.1	2.6
Larry Miller	69-70LA-A 70-72CarA	1946	6'4	209	G-F	N. Carolina	7	486	2450	5670	43	82	331	25	1613	2228	72	2434	1155	1091	0	6595	31	5.0	2.4	13.6
73-74SD-A 74VaA	70, 73-74						3	9	20	61	33	2	5	40	19	43	44	20	20	3		61	17	2.2	2.2	6.8
75UtahA																										
Mark Minor	73Bos	1950	6'6	215	F	Ohio State	1	4	1	4	25				3	4	75	4	2	5	0	5	5	1.0	0.5	1.3
Leland Mitchell	68NO-A	1941	6'4	210	G	Miss. State	1	78	122	350	35	21	76	28	56	85	66	182	73	159	1	321	14	2.3	0.9	4.1
	68						1	7	1	9	11	0	4	0	1	2	50	3	3	8	0	3	8	0.4	0.4	0.4
Doug Moe	61DL 68NO-A 69OakA	1938	6'5	220	F-G	North Carolina	5	378	2301	5377	43	19	89	21	1540	1924	80	2560	1197	1286	21	6161	32	6.8	3.2	16.3
70CarA 71-72VaA	68-72						5	60	411	968	42	5	23	22	259	342	76	419	160	221	3	1086	36	7.0	2.7	18.1
HC77-80Sa HC81-87Den																										
Wayne Molis	67NY 68Oak 68HouA	1943	6'8	230	F	NEn Illinois,	2	59	115	276	42	2	3	67	48	74	65	192	41	58	1	280	10	3.3	0.7	4.7
	67					Lewis	1	1	0	2	0				0	0	—	1	1	1	0	0	10	1.0	1.0	0.0
Earl Monroe	68-72Bal 72-80NY	1944	6'3	189	G	Winston Sal. St.	13	926	6906	14898	46				3642	4513	81	2796	3594	2416	13	17454	32	3.0	3.9	18.8
(Earl the Pearl)	69-75, 78						8	82	567	1292	44				337	426	79	266	264	216	0	1471	33	3.2	3.2	17.9
Gene Moore	69-70KyA 71TexA 72DalA	1945	6'9	244	C-F	St. Louis	7	465	2334	5013	47	10	33	30	916	1350	68	4360	648	1730	43	5594	25	9.4	1.4	12.0
72NY-A 73-74SD-A	69-73, 75						6	47	196	440	45	0	1	0	87	120	73	366	52	92	2	479	20	7.8	1.1	10.2
75StL-A																										
Larry Moore	68AnaA	1943	6'7	215	F	Florida State	1	12	8	33	24	0	5	0	11	13	85	16	1	17	0	27	7	1.3	0.1	2.3
Otto Moore (Say No)	69-71Det 72Phoe 73-74Hou	1946	6'11	219	C-F	Pan American	9	682	2336	5152	45				944	1550	61	5575	1060	1775	22	5616	25	8.2	1.6	8.2
74KCO 75Det 75-77NO																										
Richie Moore	68DenA	1945	6'2	190	G	Hiram Scott,	1	18	24	71	34	0	2	0	21	28	75	19	8	16	0	69	12	1.1	0.4	3.8
						Villanova																				
Rex Morgan	71-72Bos	1948	6'5	190	G	Jacksonville	2	62	57	152	38				58	85	68	91	39	92	2	172	7	1.5	0.6	2.8
	72						1	4	1	7	14				1	3	33	5	0	6	0	2	3	1.3	0.0	0.8
John Morrison	68DenA	1944	6'2	190	G	Canisius	1	9	10	34	29	1	6	17	6	9	67	9	7	15	0	27	8	1.0	0.8	3.0
Rick Mount	71-72IndA 73-74KyA	1947	6'4	185	G	Purdue	5	283	1298	2996	43	121	382	32	613	748	82	475	676	653		3330	23	1.7	2.4	11.8
74UtahA 75MemA 76LJ	71-74						4	65	290	714	41	28	85	33	120	143	84	104	106	128		728	23	1.6	1.6	11.2
Erwin Mueller	67-68Chi 68LA 69Chi	1944	6'8	232	C-F	San Fransisco	8	445	1309	3070	43	0	0	—	669	1074	62	2100	881	927	7	3287	22	4.7	2.0	7.4
69-70Sea 70-73Det	67-68, 73						3	22	33	103	32	1	1	100	21	35	60	87	52	49	0	88	20	4.0	2.4	4.0
73VaA 74MemA																										
Jeff Mullins (Pork Chop)	65-66StL 67-71SF 72-76GS	1942	6'4	199	G-F	Duke	12	802	5383	11631	46				2251	2764	81	3427	3023	2165	30	13017	31	4.3	3.8	16.2
	65-69, 71-73, 75-76						10	83	462	1030	45				160	213	75	304	259	217	5	1084	27	3.7	3.1	13.1
Allen Murphy	76KyA 77LA	1952	6'5	190	G	Louisville	2	31	44	118	37	0	1	0	30	44	68	51	13	57	0	118	9	1.6	0.4	3.8
Willie Murrell	68DenA 69-70MiaA 70KyA	1941	6'6	225	F	Kansas State	3	228	1250	2684	47	14	46	30	474	659	72	1655	233	640	8	2988	30	7.3	1.0	13.1
	68-70						3	24	130	278	47	1	6	17	56	69	81	149	29	62	1	317	29	6.2	1.2	13.2
Dorie Murrey	67Det 68-70Sea 71Port	1943	6'8	218	F-C	Detroit	6	357	593	1394	43				497	732	68	1555	226	827	20	1683	13	4.4	0.6	4.7
71-72Bal	71-72						2	17	13	27	48				7	11	64	33	1	6	0	33	5	1.9	0.1	1.9

Use Name-Nickname	Team by Year	Birth Yr	Hgt	Wgt	Pos	College	# Yr	G	Field Goals FG	Att.	%	3 pt. FG FG	Att	%	Free Throws FT	Att.	%	Reb.	Ass.	PF	DQ	Pts	Per Game Min	Reb	Ass	Pts
Bob Nash	73-74Det 75SD-A 78-79KC	1950	6'8	205	F	Hawaii	5	29	441	1013	44				211	154	73	483	147	275	0	1036	12	2.2	6.7	4.7
	79						1	5	8	27	30				8	10	80	11	0	10	0	24	13	2.2	0.0	4.8
Cotton Nash	65LA 65SF 68KyA	1942	6'6	225	F	Kentucky	2	84	153	450	34	0	1	0	164	214	77	273	65	120	0	470	14	3.3	0.8	5.6
67, 69-70 played major league baseball																										
Lloyd Neal	73-79Port	1950	6'7	225	C-F	Tenn. State	7	431	1977	4076	49				883	1315	67	3361	631	1264	12	4837	25	7.8	1.5	11.2
	77-78						2	22	37	84	44				18	27	67	81	19	39	0	92	12	3.7	0.9	4.2
Barry Nelson	72Mil	1949	6'10	230	C	Duquesne	1	28	15	36	42				5	10	50	20	7	21	0	35	4	0.7	0.3	1.3
	72						1	2	0	0	—				0	0	—	1	1	1	0	0	3	0.5	0.5	0.0
Don Nelson	63Chi 64-65LA 66-76Bos	1940	6'6	210	F	Iowa	14	1053	4017	8373	48				2864	3744	77	5192	1526	2451	21	10898	21	4.9	1.4	10.3
HC77-87Mil HC89GS	64-69, 72-76						11	150	585	1175	50				407	498	82	719	210	399	5	1577	21	4.8	1.4	10.5
Louie Nelson	74Cap 75-76NO 77SA	1951	6'3	190	G	Washington	5	224	819	1874	44				475	644	74	527	436	437	2	2113	22	2.4	1.9	9.4
78KC 78NJ																										
Ron Nelson	71FlaA	1948	6'2	180	G	New Mexico	1	59	72	172	42	1	3	33	41	54	76	53	47	95		186	8	0.9	0.8	3.2
	71						1	1	0	1	0	0	0	—	0	0	—	1	0	0		0	2	1.0	0.0	0.0
Dick Nemelka	71UtahA	1943	6'	175	G	B.Y.U.	1	39	82	213	38	20	62	32	32	49	65	59	57	60		216	13	1.5	1.5	5.5
	71						1	9	7	21	33	1	9	11	4	5	80	9	9	12		19	6	1.0	1.0	2.1
Bob Netolicky	68-72IndA 72-74MemA 74DalA	1942	6'9	225	F-C	Drake	9	618	4058	8248	49	12	62	19	1748	2644	66	5518	848	1365	6	9876	33	8.9	1.4	16.0
74SA-A 74-76IndA	68-72, 75						6	73	475	945	50	0	4	0	193	297	65	645	61	177	2	1143	33	8.8	0.8	15.7
Johnny Neumann	72-74MemA 74UtahA 75VaA	1951	6'6	200	G-F	Mississippi	7	355	2262	5019	55	145	539	27	1063	1392	76	1234	1235	1363	2	6022	30	3.5	3.5	17.0
75IndA 76VaA 76KyA	74, 77						2	21	45	121	37	1	9	11	15	17	88	34	24	35	0	106	12	1.6	1.1	5.0
77Buf 77LA 78Ind																										
Dave Newmark	69Chi 70Atl 71CarA	1946	7'	253	C	Columbia	3	176	412	980	42	0	0	—	179	276	65	678	128	417	10	1003	13	3.9	0.7	5.7
	70						1	6	15	33	45				4	4	100	12	2	8	0	34	7	2.0	0.3	5.7
Bill Newton	73-74IndA	1950	6'9	220	C	L.S.U.	2	35	31	71	44	1	2	50	10	20	50	65	14	52		73	5	1.9	0.4	2.1
	73						1	4	2	5	40	0	1	0	0	0	—	5	0	3		4	2	1.3	0.0	1.0
Rich Neimann	69Det 69Mil 70Bos 70CarA	1946	7'	251	C	St. Louis	4	187	500	1051	48	0	0	—	230	313	73	1079	158	514	8	1230	16	5.8	0.8	6.6
71FlaA 72DalA	70-71						2	5	7	18	39	0	0	—	3	3	100	0	0	0		17	11	0.0	0.0	3.4
Connie Norman	75-76Phi	1953	6'3	176	G	Arizona	2	77	206	466	44				22	27	81	113	70	96	1	434	12	1.5	0.9	5.6
	76						1	1	1	1	100				0	0	—	1	0	0	0	2	1	1.0	0.0	2.0
Willie Norwood	72-75Det 76-77 Sea	1947	6'7	220	F	Alcorn State	7	430	1218	2494	49				773	1109	70	1597	364	1049	11	3209	17	3.7	0.8	7.5
78Det 78Port	74, 76, 78						3	14	38	81	47				16	23	70	45	13	43	4	92	21	3.2	0.9	6.6
Mel Norwell	63Chi 68NJ-A	1939	6'2	177	G	Ohio State	2	115	365	916	40	9	32	28	224	279	80	260	239	274	1	963	19	2.3	2.1	8.4
Jim O'Brien	74NY-A 75Mem A	1951	6'7	200	F	Maryland	2	58	103	240	43	6	30	20	56	65	86	138	87	61		268	11	2.4	1.5	4.6
	74-75						2	7	6	19	32	0	1	0	2	2	100	8	8	3		14	6	1.1	1.1	2.0
Jimmy O'Brien	72PitA 72-74KyA 74-75SD-A	1950	6'2	178	G	Boston Coll.	4	303	720	1791	40	18	102	18	337	406	83	618	1244	518		1795	20	2.0	4.1	5.9
	72-74						3	30	57	148	39	2	7	30	46	55	84	46	111	41		162	20	1.5	3.7	5.4
Bud Ogden	70-71Phi	1946	6'6	218	F	Santa Clara	2	74	106	238	45				45	65	69	106	48	83	2	257	7	1.4	0.6	3.5
	70-71						2	2	5	11	45				2	4	50	3	6	1	0	12	8	1.5	3.0	6.0
Ralph Ogden	71SF	1948	6'5	205	F	Santa Clara	1	32	17	71	24				8	12	67	32	9	17	0	42	5	1.0	0.3	1.3
	71						1	2	1	5	20				4	4	100	4	1	0	0	6	8	2.0	0.5	3.0
Fran O'Hanlon	71FlaA	1948	6'1	175	G	Villanova	1	14	8	22	36	0	1	0	6	9	67	4	13	18		22	7	0.3	0.9	1.6
Grady O'Malley	70Atl	1948	6'5	205	F	Manhattan	1	24	21	60	35				8	19	42	26	10	12	0	50	5	1.1	0.4	2.1
Barry Orms	69Bal 70IndA 70PitA	1946	6'3	190	G	St. Louis	2	141	348	941	37	5	26	19	181	336	54	505	181	370	6	882	21	3.6	1.3	6.3
	69						1	3	0	0	—				0	0	—	1	0	2	0	0	3	0.3	0.0	0.0
Jim Owens	74-75Phoe	1950	6'5	200	F	Arizona State	2	58	77	184	42				23	30	77	52	64	33	0	177	9	0.9	1.1	3.1
Wayne Pack	75IndA	1950	6'	165	G	Tenn. Tech	1	21	23	60	38	5	17	29	10	12	83	20	13	21		61	9	1.0	0.6	2.9
Dana Pagett	72VaA	1949	6'2	180	G	Southern Cal.	1	5	1	9	11	1	3	33	2	3	67	3	6	8		5	7	0.6	1.2	1.0
Errol Palmer	68MinA	1945	6'5	195	F	DePaul	1	63	165	453	36	0	0	—	170	253	67	471	91	169	2	500	19	7.5	1.4	7.9
	68						1	6	10	25	40	0	0	—	8	10	80	27	7	17	0	28	13	4.5	1.2	4.7
Barry Parkhill	74-75VaA 76StLA	1951	6'4	185	G	Virginia	3	173	418	1048	40	4	25	16	130	169	77	224	346	425		970	18	1.3	2.0	5.6
	74						1	3	3	7	43	0	0	—	0	0	—	1	2	0		6	3	0.3	0.7	2.0
Charlie Parks	69DenA	1946	6'5	210	F	Idaho State	1	2	0	1	0	0	0	—	0	0	—	0	0	1	0	0	3	0.0	0.0	0.0
Rich Parks	68PitA	1943	6'7	235	F	St. Louis	1	40	59	133	44	1	3	33	12	21	57	116	14	68	3	131	9	2.9	0.4	3.3
	68						1	5	0	2	0	0	1	0	1	4	25	2	0	3	0	1	1	0.4	0.0	0.2
George Patterson	68Det	1939	6'8	240	C-F	Toledo	1	59	44	133	33				32	38	84	159	51	85	0	120	9	2.7	0.9	2.0
	68						1	1	0	0					0	0	—	1	1	0	0	0	4	1.0	1.0	0.0
Steve Patterson	72-76Cle 76Chi	1948	6'9	225	C	U.C.L.A.	5	350	672	1667	40				208	350	59	1632	443	573	6	1552	16	4.6	1.2	4.4
Tommy Patterson	73Bal 74Cap	1948	6'6	220	F	Ouachita Bapt.	2	25	21	50	42				14	18	78	24	5	18	0	56	25	1.0	0.2	2.2
Charlie Paulk	69Mil 70MS 71Cin 72Chi	1944	6'8	220	F-C	NE Okla. St.	3	120	317	809	39				107	175	61	462	41	243	6	741	14	3.9	0.3	6.2
72NY	72						1	7	3	10	30				0	0	—	5	0	5	0	6	2	0.7	0.0	0.9
Tom Payne	72Atl	1950	7'2	240	C	Kenntucky	1	29	45	103	44				29	46	63	69	15	40	0	119	8	2.4	0.5	4.1
	72						1	1	1	1	100				2	5	40	4	0	1	0	4	5	4.0	0.0	4.0
Rich Peek	68DalA	1943	6'11	230	C	La. Tech	1	51	101	209	48	0	0	—	35	65	54	197	22	94	1	237	15	3.9	0.4	4.6
	68						1	8	18	37	49	0	0	—	7	15	47	42	3	17	1	43	17	5.3	0.4	5.4
George Peeples	68-69IndA 70-71CarA	1943	6'8	205	C-F	Iowa	6	309	931	2111	44	0	11	0	640	1002	64	2242	304	808	3	2502	22	7.3	1.0	8.1
72DalA 73IndA	68-70						3	24	59	144	41	0	1	0	49	73	67	201	19	50	1	167	25	8.4	0.8	7.0
Jerry Pender	74SD-A	1951	6'3	185	G	Fresno State	1	11	8	30	27	1	3	33	10	13	77	5	4	11		27	6	0.5	0.4	2.5
Aulcie Perry	75VaA	1950	6'10	210	C	Beth.-Cookmn	1	21	81	186	44	0	1	0	19	30	63	105	20	58		181	20	5.0	1.0	8.6
Curtis Perry	71SD 72Hou 72-74Mil	1948	6'7	222	F	SW Missouri	8	480	1904	4188	45				770	1101	70	4239	906	1670	48	4578	28	8.8	1.9	9.5
75-78Phoe	72-74, 76						4	52	215	453	47				72	109	66	437	75	189	7	498	30	8.4	1.4	9.6
Ron Perry	68MinA 69MiaA 69NY-A 69IndA	1943	6'3	190	G	Va. Tech	3	187	845	2210	38	139	405	34	399	568	70	517	420	484	11	2226	27	2.8	2.2	11.9
70CarA 70NO-A	69						1	17	34	114	30	11	38	29	18	27	67	21	18	33	0	97	12	1.2	1.1	5.7
Loy Petersen	69-70Chi	1945	6'5	205	G	Oregon State	2	69	77	199	39				45	66	68	67	48	61	0	199	8	1.0	0.7	2.7
Mel Peterson	64Bal 68-69OakA 70LA-A	1938	6'4	189	G-F	Wheaton	4	134	466	1055	44	9	40	23	91	111	82	635	160	228	1	1032	18	4.7	1.2	7.7
	69-70						2	18	21	36	58	1	2	50	8	14	57	28	4	11	0	51	7	1.8	0.2	2.8

Use Name-Nickname	Team by Year	Birth Yr	Hgt	Wgt	Pos	College	# Yr	G	Field Goals FG	Att.	%	3 pt. FG FG	Att	%	Free Throws FT	Att.	%	Reb.	Ass.	PF	DQ	Pts	Per Game Min	Reb	Ass	P
Geoff Petrie	71-76Port 77KJ	1948	6'4	198	G	Princeton	6	446	3970	8719	46				1792	2225	81	1271	2057	1075	6	9732	38	2.8	4.6	21
Jerry Pettway	68-69HouA	1944	6'3	185	G-F	Northwood	2	87	326	961	34	16	62	26	124	190	65	303	120	151	2	792	21	3.5	1.4	9
	68						1	3	12	29	41	1	2	50	4	5	80	14	5	5	0	29	21	4.7	1.7	9
Gene Phillips	72-73DalA	1948	6'4	180	G	S.M.U.	2	31	30	81	37	7	20	35	11	14	79	21	14	26		78	6	0.7	0.5	2
	72						1	1	0	0	—	0	0	—	0	0	—	0	0	0	0	0	2	0.0	0.0	0
Walt Piatkowski	69-70DenA 72FlaA	1945	6'8	223	F	Bowling Gn	3	157	617	1507	41	38	132	29	193	250	77	617	89	408	3	1465	20	3.9	0.6	9
	69-70						2	13	60	135	44	2	13	15	12	15	80	40	10	41	1	134	19	3.1	0.8	10
Howard Porter (Geezer)	72-74Chi 75NY 75-78Det	1948	6'8	220	F-C	Villanova	7	457	1836	3922	47				539	672	80	1872	211	818	1	4215	19	4.1	4.7	9
78NJ	72-77						6	36	151	329	46				33	39	85	152	18	59	0	335	18	4.2	0.5	9
Willie Porter	68OakA 68PitA 69MinA	1942	6'7	205	F	Tenn. State	2	69	253	598	42	0	0	—	216	325	66	504	65	213	11	722	21	7.3	0.9	10
69HouA	68						1	14	19	43	44	0	0	—	20	29	69	69	6	43	0	58	12	4.9	0.4	4
Bob Portman	70-71SF 72-73GS	1947	6'5	200	F	Creighton	4	221	519	1172	44				216	277	78	729	128	292	0	1254	13	3.3	0.6	5
	71-73						3	11	24	61	39				11	14	79	30	3	14	0	59	14	2.7	0.3	5
John Postley	68PitA	1944	6'5	220	F	Cheyney St.	1	1	1	3	33	0	0	—	0	0	—	6	1	1	0	2	6	6.0	1.0	2
Cincy Powell	68-70DalA 71-72KyA	1942	6'7	227	F-C	Portland	8	599	3823	8096	47	31	113	27	2069	2845	73	4598	1330	2016	18	9746	31	7.7	2.2	16
73UtahA 74-75VaA	68-74						7	61	412	889	46	5	18	28	242	321	75	593	123	202	0	1017	33	9.7	2.0	16
Marl Pradd	68-69NO-A	1944	6'3	170	G	Dillard	2	79	108	246	44	3	13	23	113	146	77	76	26	82	0	332	6	1.0	0.3	4
	68-69						2	13	13	31	42	4	6	67	10	18	56	9	1	10	0	40	4	0.7	0.1	3
Mike Pratt	71-72KyA	1948	6'4	195	G-F	Kentucky	2	143	306	717	43	19	51	37	175	219	80	383	286	286		806	15	2.7	2.0	5
	71-72						2	25	80	187	43	1	6	17	42	52	81	83	66	53		203	19	3.3	2.7	8
Steve Previs	73CarA	1950	6'3	183	G	North Carolina	1	30	23	60	38	1	8	13	8	15	53	14	24	26		55	5	0.5	0.8	1
	73						1	2	1	7	14	1	2	50	0	0	—	3	3	2		3	6	1.5	1.5	1
Jim Price	73-75LA 75-77Mil	1949	6'3	195	G	Louisville	7	510	2129	4798	44				830	1018	82	1566	1886	1369	10	5088	25	3.1	3.7	10
77Buf 77-78Den	73-74, 76-77, 79						5	23	50	168	35				20	32	63	55	62	61	1	138	21	2.4	2.7	6
78Det 79LA																										
Mike Price	71-72NY 72IndA 73Phi	1948	6'3	200	G	Illinois	3	123	163	405	40	0	0	—	71	92	77	157	90	177	0	397	9	1.3	0.7	3
	71						1	8	4	11	36				4	6	67	5	5	11	0	12	3	0.6	0.6	1
Bob Quick	69-70Bla 70-72Det 72DalA	1946	6'5	215	F-G	Xavier (Ohio)	4	142	295	650	45	0	0	—	258	346	75	395	94	244	1	848	14	2.8	0.7	6
	69						1	2	2	3	67				0	2	0	1	0	1	0	4	5	0.5	0.0	2
Luther Rackley	70Cin 71-72Cle 72-73NY	1946	6'10	223	C	Xavier (Ohio)	5	278	687	1490	46	0	1	0	381	604	63	1290	179	640	8	1755	16	4.6	0.6	6
73MemA 74Phi	72						1	11	2	14	14				4	4	100	7	1	7	0	8	3	0.6	0.1	0
Bobby Rascoe	68-70KyA	1940	6'4	205	G-F	Western Ky.	3	159	450	1061	42	3	21	14	325	423	77	438	208	292	3	1228	18	2.8	1.3	7
	68-69						2	12	42	90	47	0	1	0	34	36	94	25	13	32	0	118	21	2.1	1.1	9
Ed Ratleff	74-78Hou	1950	6'6	195	F-G	L. Beach St.	5	338	1160	2554	45				493	614	80	1363	896	801	11	2813	25	4.0	2.7	8
	75						1	8	36	87	41				17	20	85	53	35	31	0	89	36	6.6	10.6	11
Mike Ratliff	73-74KCO	1951	6'10	230	C	WI-Eau Claire	2	60	98	235	42				45	84	54	194	38	111	1	241	11	3.2	0.6	4
Cliff Ray	72-74Chi 75-81GS	1949	6'9	230	C	Oklahoma	10	784	2333	4450	52	0	2	0	1155	1963	59	6953	1728	2618	52	5821	25	8.9	2.2	7
	72-77						6	60	207	385	54				82	139	59	606	125	206	2	196	29	10.1	2.1	3
Jimmy Rayl	68-69IndA	1941	6'2	175	G	Indiana	2	101	389	1021	38	91	267	34	256	311	82	305	273	277	3	1125	27	3.0	2.7	11
(The Splendid	68						1	3	15	42	36	4	14	29	5	7	71	10	14	14	0	39	39	3.3	4.7	13
Splinter)																										
Craig Raymond	68Phi 70PitA 70LA-A	1945	6'11	235	C	B.Y.U.	5	241	666	1472	45	0	5	0	326	517	63	1510	327	576	10	1658	19	6.3	1.4	6
71MemA 72FlaA	70-72						3	23	131	270	49	0	0	—	74	96	77	280	44	7		336	32	12.2	1.9	14
73SD-A 73IndA																										
Joe Reaves	74Phoe 74MemA	1950	6'6	220	F	Bethel (Tenn)	1	19	36	81	44	0	0	—	8	17	47	54	7	29	0	80	11	2.8	0.4	4
Willis Reed	65-74NY 75KJ HC78-79NYK	1942	6'9	238	C-F	Grambling	10	650	4859	10202	48				2465	3298	75	8414	1186	2411	58	12183	35	12.9	1.8	18
HC88-89NJ	67-71, 73-74						7	78	570	1203	47				218	285	76	801	149	275	4	1358	34	10.3	1.9	17
Jim Reid	68Phi	1945	6'6	210	F	Winst. Sal. St.	1	6	10	20	50				1	5	20	11	3	6	0	21	9	1.8	0.5	3
George Reynolds	70Det	1947	6'4	198	G	Houston	1	10	8	19	42				5	7	71	14	12	10	0	21	4	1.4	1.2	2
Kendall Rhine	68KyA 69HouA	1943	6'10	240	C	Rice	2	125	305	787	39	0	2	0	176	321	55	1039	181	441	18	786	21	8.3	1.4	6
	68						1	5	5	17	29	0	0	—	0	7	0	15	4	16	0	10	12	3.0	0.8	2
Jackie Ridgle	72Cle	1948	6'4	195	G	California	1	32	19	44	43				19	26	73	15	7	15	0	57	3	0.5	0.2	1
Bob Riedy	68HouA	1945	6'6	215	F	Duke	1	23	45	129	35	0	0	—	41	67	61	68	5	27	0	131	14	3.0	0.2	5
Tom Riker	73-75NY	1950	6'10	247	C-F	South Carolina	3	82	76	200	38				73	123	59	138	24	85	0	225	7	1.7	0.3	2
	75						1	1	1	2	50				0	0	—	2	1	1	0	2	8	2.0	1.0	2
Bob Riley	71Atl	1948	6'9	235	F	Mt. St. Mary's	1	7	4	9	44				5	9	56	12	1	5	0	13	6	1.7	0.1	1
Pat Riley	68-70SD 71-76LA 76Phoe	1945	6'4	208	G-F	Kentucky	9	528	1619	3914	41				668	948	70	855	913	1152	3	3906	16	1.6	1.7	7
HC82-89LA	69, 71-74, 76						6	44	111	297	37				29	38	76	66	52	86	0	251	15	1.5	1.2	5
Ron Riley	73-74KCO 74-76Hou	1950	6'8	200	F	Southern Cal.	4	264	665	1586	42				307	419	69	1368	318	655	7	1542	18	5.2	1.2	5
	75						1	8	25	42	60				6	16	38	36	15	18	0	56	19	4.5	1.9	7
Rich Rinaldi	72-73Bal 74Cap 74NY-A	1949	6'3	195	G	St. Peter's	3	84	165	424	39	0	1	0	75	102	74	98	74	75	0	405	10	1.2	0.9	4
	72						1	3	1	2	50				0	0	—	0	1	3	0	2	2	0.0	0.3	0
Mike Riordan	69-72NY 72-73Bal 74Cap	1945	6'4	200	G-F	Providence	9	639	2773	5894	47				788	1059	74	1830	1524	1490	10	6334	25	2.9	2.4	9
75-77Was	69-77						9	84	253	567	45				107	138	78	199	111	203	1	613	20	2.4	1.3	7
Red Robbins	68-70NO-A 71-72UtahA	1944	6'8	200	F-C	Tennessee	8	586	3005	6954	43	69	226	31	1624	1986	82	6155	1001	1334	2	7703	32	10.5	1.7	13
73-74SD-A	68-69, 71-74						6	67	335	706	47	9	32	28	186	244	76	729	110	155	0	865	31	10.9	1.6	12
74-75KyA 75VaA																										
Rick Roberson	70-71LA 72-73Cle 74Port	1947	6'9	231	C-F	Cincinnati	7	423	1483	3369	44				860	1470	59	3522	591	1308	25	3826	24	8.3	1.4	9
75NO 76KC	70-71						2	18	18	47	38				10	17	59	42	4	27	0	46	9	2.3	0.2	2
Marv Roberts	72-74DenA 74CarA	1950	6'8	205	F	Utah State	6	402	1341	3093	43	3	9	33	654	846	73	1570	517	882	0	3345	19	3.9	1.3	8
75-76KyA 76VaA 77LA	72-75						4	15	60	115	52	0	0	—	31	41	76	54	23	29		151	17	3.6	1.5	10
Oscar Robertson	61-70Cin 71-74Mil	1938	6'5	213	G-F	Cincinnati	14	1040	9508	19620	48				7694	9185	84	7804	9887	2931	18	26710	42	7.5	9.5	25
(The Big O)	62-67, 71-74						10	86	675	1466	46				560	655	85	578	769	267	3	1910	43	6.7	8.9	22
Flynn Robinson	67-68Cin 68-69Chi 69-70Mil	1941	6'1	189	G	Wyoming	8	543	2960	6487	46	8	30	27	1649	1949	85	1372	1628	1339	18	7577	23	2.5	3.0	14
71Cin 72-73LA	67-68, 70, 72-73						5	27	129	318	41				70	88	80	54	76	57	0	328	23	2.0	2.8	12
73Bal 74SD-A																										
Ronnie Robinson	74UtahA 74-75MemA	1952	6'8	220	F	Memphis St.	2	72	192	432	44	0	1	0	53	79	67	306	53	137		437	18	4.3	0.7	6
Sam Robinson	71-72FlaA	1948	6'7	200	F	L. Beach St.	2	134	531	1196	44	4	21	19	157	202	78	546	160	252		1223	21	4.1	1.2	9
	71-72						2	10	42	90	47	0	0	—	21	23	91	41	8	28		105	19	4.1	0.8	10
Wil Robinson	74MemA	1949	6'2	175	G	West Virginia	1	45	166	402	41	0	6	0	57	67	85	79	132	124		389	21	1.8	2.9	8

se Name-Nickname	Team by Year	Birth Yr	Hgt	Wgt	Pos	College	# Yr	G	Field Goals FG	Att.	%	3 pt. FG FG	Att	%	Free Throws FT	Att.	%	Reb.	Ass.	PF	DQ	Pts	Per Game Min	Reb	Ass	Pts
ohnny Roche 75-76UtahA 76LA	72-74NY 74-75KyA	1949	6'3	170	G	S. Carolina	5	332	1456	3019	48	104	313	33	771	986	78	561	1246	695		3995	28	1.7	3.8	12.0
	72-75						4	36	259	543	48	27	65	42	115	156	74	56	164	71		660	34	1.6	4.6	18.3
larry Rogers	76StLA		6'7	195	F	St. Louis	1	18	60	124	48	0			17	24	71	96	15	34		137	17	5.3	0.8	7.6
Villie Rogers	69DenA	1945	6'3	185	G-F	Oklahoma	1	40	27	80	34	0	3	0	31	52	60	47	16	51	1	85	7	1.2	0.4	2.1
ierry Rook	70NO-A	1943	6'5	220	F	Ark. State	1	28	37	82	45	0	2	0	11	13	85	31	10	21	0	85	6	1.1	0.4	3.0
urtis Rowe	72-76Det 77-78Bos	1949	6'7	225	F	U.C.L.A.	8	590	2821	5847	48				1231	1756	70	4264	932	1352	11	6873	31	7.2	1.6	11.6
	74-77						4	28	127	264	48				69	95	73	220	62	85	2	323	33	7.9	2.2	11.5
eggie Royals	75SD-A	1950	6'10	200	C	Florida State	1	2	2	4	50	0	0	—	0	0	—	0	0	1		4	6	0.0	0.0	2.0
oy Rubin	HC73Phi	1927				Louisville, L.I.U.																				
aul Ruffner	71Chi 72PitA 74-75Buf 76StLA	1948	6'10	225	C-F	B.Y.U.	5	133	232	493	47				97	141	69	393	61	220	0	561	10	3.0	0.5	4.2
	75						1	1	0	1	0				0	0	—	0	0	0	0	0	4	0.0	0.0	0.0
ob Rule 75Mil	68-72Sea 72-73Phi 73-74Cle	1944	6'9	237	C-F	Colorado St.	8	403	2777	6029	46				1453	2119	69	3333	594	1260	28	7007	29	8.3	1.5	17.4
azzie Russell 78Chi	67-71NY 72-74GS 75-77LA	1944	6'5	219	F-G	Michigan	12	817	5172	11154	46				2033	2459	83	3068	1838	1693	7	12377	27	3.8	2.2	15.1
	67-70, 72-73, 77						7	72	359	781	46				134	154	87	222	97	151	1	852	22	3.1	1.3	11.8
rank Russell	73Chi	1949	6'3	180	G	Detroit	1	23	29	77	38				16	18	89	17	15	12	0	74	6	0.7	0.7	3.2
ierrre Russell	72-73KyA	1949	6'4	195	F-G	Kansas	2	110	184	419	44	2	2	10	65	99	66	222	112	136		435	9	2.0	1.0	4.0
	73						1	12	7	12	58	0	0	—	3	6	50	12	2	5		17	3	1.0	0.2	1.4
ubin Russell	68DalA 68KyA	1944	6'3	180	G	N. Texas St.	1	26	56	158	35	4	22	18	25	41	61	52	7	40	0	141	10	2.0	0.3	5.4
l Salvadori	68OakA	1946	6'9	220	F	S. Carolina	1	17	21	38	36	1	1	100	11	16	69	46	4	28	0	54	11	2.7	0.3	3.2
l Sanders	73VaA	1950	6'7	240	F	L.S.U.	1	4	2	2	100	0	0	—	4	6	67	5	0	4		8	6	1.3	0.0	2.0
on Sanford	72DalA	1948	6'9	215	F	New Mexico	1	1	0	0	—	0	0	—	0	0	—	0	0	1		0	2	0.0	0.0	0.0
lynn Saulters	69NO-A	1945	6'2	175	G	NE Louisiana	1	22	22	70	31	0	1	0	15	22	68	19	11	25	0	59	5	0.9	0.5	2.7
rank Schade	73KCO	1950	6'1	170	G	Wisconsin-Eau Claire	1	9	2	7	29				6	6	100	6	10	12	0	10	8	0.7	1.1	1.1
illy Schaeffer	74-76NY-A 76VaA	1952	6'5	200	F	St. John's	3	137	346	733	47	6	18	33	104	142	73	289	94	248		802	13	2.1	6.9	5.9
	74						1	5	8	16	50	0	0	—	3	4	75	9	3	3		19	5	1.8	0.6	3.8
ave Schellhase	67-68Chi	1944	6'3	205	G	Purdue	2	73	87	249	35				34	60	57	76	60	70	0	208	7	1.0	0.8	2.8
	67-68						2	3	1	5	20				1	2	50	1	0	0	0	3	3	0.3	0.0	1.0
ale Schleuter 74Atl 75-76Buf 77Phoe 78Port	69-70SF 71-72Port 73Phi	1945	6'10	232	C	Colorado St.	10	586	1176	2366	50				778	1147	68	3034	520	1367	11	3130	16	5.2	1.6	5.3
	69, 75-76						3	17	14	26	54				13	24	54	43	4	21	0	41	6	2.5	0.2	2.4
ave Shulz	70Phi	1948	6'8	220	F	Illinois	1	1	1	1	100				0	0	—	0	0	0	0	2	1	0.0	0.0	2.0
oger Schurig	68HouA	1943	6'3	195	G	Vanderbilt	1	21	35	94	37	3	8	38	27	36	75	29	18	38	0	100	12	1.4	0.9	4.8
harlie Scott 76-78Bos 78LA 79-80Den	71-72VaA 72-75Phoe	1948	6'5	178	G-F	N. Carolina	10	717	5955	13230	45	47	186	25	2790	3609	77	2846	3515	2618	63	14837	36	4.0	4.9	20.7
	71, 76-79						5	45	310	775	40	8	31	26	196	256	77	220	215	203	14	824	26	4.9	4.8	18.3
illie Scott	70DalA	1945	6'5	210	F	Alabama St.	1	8	6	15	40	0	0	—	1	6	17	4	2	16	0	13	6	0.5	0.3	1.6
aul Scranton	68AnaA	1944	6'5	230	F	Cal. Poly-(Pomona)	1	5	4	9	44	0	0	—	1	4	25	16	1	5	0	9	8	3.2	0.2	1.8
ruce Seals	74-75UtahA 76-78Sea	1953	6'9	210	F	Xavier of La.	5	338	1266	2947	43	19	93	20	518	771	67	1443	360	1052	21	3107	22	4.3	1.1	9.2
	74-76, 78						4	33	92	217	42	2	10	20	34	56	61	119	25	84	0	220	18	3.6	0.8	6.7
d Searcy	76Bos	1952	6'6	210	F	St. John's	1	4	2	6	33				2	2	100	0	1	4	0	6	3	0.0	0.3	1.5
ee Selvage	68AnaA 70LA-A	1943	6'1	175	G	NE Missouri	2	82	375	1058	35	147	465	32	206	278	74	219	252	241	3	1103	30	2.7	3.1	13.5
	70						1	1	0	0	—	0	0	—	0	0	—					0	1			0.0
ynn Shackelford	70MiaA	1947	6'5	195	F	U.C.L.A.	1	22	22	72	31	4	13	31	10	13	77	27	11	34	0	58	8	1.2	0.5	2.6
illy Shepherd	73VaA 74SD-A 75MemA	1949	5'10	163	G	Butler	3	169	368	951	39	129	361	36	103	148	70	191	657	182		968	18	1.1	3.9	5.7
	74-75						2	11	27	86	31	11	39	28	9	9	100	16	33	14		74	21	1.5	3.0	6.7
eryl Shipley	HC75SD-A	1926				Delta State																				
ene Short	76Sea 76NY	1953	6'6	200	F	Jackson St.	1	34	32	91	35				20	32	63	48	10	36	0	84	7	1.4	2.9	2.5
am Sibert	73KCO	1949	6'7	215	F	Texas Tech., Ky. State	1	5	4	13	31				4	5	80	4	0	4	0	12	5	0.8	0.0	2.4
ark Sibley	74Port	1950	6'2	175	G	Northwestern	1	28	20	56	36				6	7	86	25	13	23	0	46	4	0.9	0.5	1.6
on Sidle 72MemA	69-70MiaA 71DenA 71-72IndA	1946	6'9	218	F-C	Oklahoma	4	314	1544	3211	48	4	29	14	1155	1610	72	2502	325	813	6	4247	27	8.0	1.0	13.5
	69, 71						2	20	68	141	48	0	1	0	53	76	70	122	20	43	1	189	20	6.1	1.0	9.5
arry Siefried	64-70Bos 71SD 72Hou 72Atl	1939	6'3	192	F	Ohio State	9	550	2149	5248	41				1662	1945	85	1567	1950	1305	7	5960	25	2.8	3.5	10.8
	64-69						6	79	301	753	40				256	307	83	199	209	249	5	858	23	2.6	2.6	10.9
aul Silas 73-76Bos 77Den 78-80Sea HC81-83SD	65-68StL 69Atl 70-72Phoe	1943	6'7	230	F-C	Creighton	16	1254	4293	9949	43				3196	4748	67	####	2572	3105	32	11782	28	9.9	2.1	9.4
	65-70, 73-80						14	163	396	998	40				332	480	69	1527	335	469	7	1124	28	9.4	2.1	6.9
ike Siliman	71Buf	1944	6'6	225	F	Army	1	36	36	79	46				19	39	49	62	23	37	0	91	10	1.7	0.6	2.5
rant Simmons	68-69DenA	1943	6'3	190	G	Nebraska	2	95	314	747	42	2	24	8	228	324	70	266	197	278	5	858	26	2.8	2.1	9.0
	68-69						2	7	13	37	35	0	1	0	12	16	75	22	15	21	1	38	22	3.1	2.1	5.4
alt Simon	68NJ-A 69-70NY-A 71-74KyA	1941	6'6	200	F-G	Benedict	7	540	2639	5712	46	15	113	13	1121	1592	70	2704	1486	1671	18	6414	26	5.0	2.8	11.9
	70-74						5	59	231	514	45	0	18	0	93	118	79	264	162	172		555	24	4.5	2.7	9.4
alph Simpson 79Phi 79-80NJ	71-76DenA 77-78DetA 78Den	1949	6'5	200	G-F	Mich. State	10	704	4754	10482	45	32	168	19	2181	2857	76	2616	2357	1454	1	11785	28	3.7	3.3	16.7
	72-73, 75, 77-79						6	42	268	623	43	3	14	21	144	185	78	144	153	92	0	683	26	3.4	3.6	16.3
oug Sims	69Cin	1943	6'7	195	F	Kent State	1	4	2	5	40				0	0		4	0	4	0	4	3	1.0	0.0	1.0
al Skinner	75-76Sea	1952	6'5	210	F-G	Md. E. Shore	2	145	274	632	43				112	177	63	608	152	277	1	660	19	4.2	1.0	4.6
	75-76						2	15	25	59	42				25	34	74	53	19	35	0	75	20	3.5	1.3	5.0
erry Sloan HC89Utah	66Bal 67-76Chi HC80-82Chi	1942	6'6	199	G-F	Evansville	11	755	4116	9646	43				2339	3239	72	5615	1925	2700	61	10571	34	7.4	2.5	14.0
	66-68, 70-75						9	52	294	689	43				128	189	68	412	109	187	4	716	36	7.9	2.1	13.8
l Smith	72-74DenA 75-76UtahA	1947	6'1	185	G	Bradley	5	337	1185	2906	41	111	373	30	817	1057	77	865	1793	1071		3298	27	2.6	5.3	9.8
	72-73, 75						3	18	57	151	38	5	16	31	39	45	87	55	68	55		162	25	3.1	3.8	9.0
ill Smith	72-73Port	1949	7'	220	C	Syracuse	2	30	81	188	43				43	72	60	143	20	81	3	205	16	4.8	0.7	6.8
obby Smith (Bingo)	70SD 71-80Cle 80SD	1946	6'5	215	F-G	Tulsa	11	865	4776	10642	45	23	81	28	1307	1637	80	3630	1734	2059	22	10882	26	4.2	2.0	12.6
	76-78						3	18	88	216	41				25	28	89	54	35	48	1	201	26	3.0	1.9	11.2
Don Smith (see Zaid-Abdul-Aziz)																										

Use Name-Nickname	Team by Year	Birth Yr	Hgt	Wgt	Pos	College	# Yr	G	Field Goals FG	Att.	%	3 pt. FG FG	Att	%	Free Throws FT	Att.	%	Reb.	Ass.	PF	DQ	Pts	Per Game Min	Reb	Ass	Pts
Don Smith	75Phi	1951	6'	160	G	Dayton	1	54	131	321	41				21	21	100	30	47	45	0	283	10	0.6	0.9	5.2
Elmore Smith	72-73Buf 74-75LA 76-77Mil	1949	7'	250	C	Wiley,	8	562	3169	6578	48				1203	2079	58	5962	808	1941	55	7541	32	10.6	1.4	13.4
77-79Cle 80-81KJ	74, 76-78					Ky. State	4	13	86	172	50				34	52	65	118	8	53	0	206	30	9.1	0.6	15.8
Garfield Smith	71-72Bos 73SD-A	1945	6'9	235	C-F	Eastern Ky.	3	134	186	426	44	0	0	—	56	179	31	438	56	272	0	428	11	3.3	0.4	3.2
	72-73						2	8	6	22	27	0	0	—	2	10	20	22	1	10	0	14	9	2.8	0.1	1.8
Greg Smith	69-72Mil 72-73Hou	1947	6'5	199	F	Western Ky.	8	524	1737	3607	48				623	965	65	3249	969	1553	39	4097	23	6.2	1.8	7.8
73-76Port	70-71						2	24	117	222	53				35	62	56	205	58	79	1	269	33	8.5	2.4	11.2
John Smith	69-70DalA 70PitA 70NY-A	1944	7'	235	C	S. Colo. State	2	147	351	907	39	0	2	0	172	308	56	1213	116	513	24	874	23	8.3	0.8	5.9
	69-70						2	9	16	34	47	0	1	0	7	13	54	42	8	19	0	39	16	4.7	0.9	4.3
Ken Smith	76SA-A	1953	6'7	185	F	Tulsa	1	19	34	83	41	1			13	16	81	24	7	22		82	9	1.3	0.4	4.3
Pete Smith	73SD-A	1950	6'6	205	F	Valdosta St.	1	5	2	12	17	0	2	0	0	0	—	8	1	5		4	6	1.6	0.2	0.8
Sam Smith	68MinA 69-71KyA 71UtahA	1944	6'7	231	F	Louisville,	4	255	803	2004	40	5	25	20	486	740	66	1776	274	558	5	2097	25	7.0	1.1	8.2
	68-71					Ky. Wesleyan	4	32	131	304	43	0	4	0	70	105	67	222	34	64	0	332	28	6.9	1.1	10.4
Dick Snyder	67-68StL 69-70Phoe	1944	6'5	211	G-F	Davidson	13	964	4890	10019	49				1975	2398	82	2732	2767	2453	36	11755	27	2.8	2.9	12.2
70-74Sea 75-78Cle	67-68, 76-79						6	31	97	233	42				30	41	73	50	49	55	1	224	18	1.6	1.6	7.2
79Sea																										
Mike Sojourner	75-77Atl	1953	6'9	225	C-F	Utah	3	191	721	1502	48				216	322	67	1237	172	457	12	1658	22	6.5	0.9	8.7
Willie Sojourner (Rainbow)	72-73VaA 74-75NY-A	1948	6'8	233	C-F	Weber State	4	309	778	1601	49	1	6	17	311	455	68	1488	227	804		1868	15	4.8	0.7	6.0
	72-75						4	32	44	91	48	0	0	—	14	20	70	76	18	52		102	9	2.4	0.6	3.2
Willie Somerset	66Bal 68-69HouA 69NY-A	1942	5'10	193	G	Duquesne	3	143	1104	2595	43	69	246	28	852	1054	81	652	514	493	9	3129	39	4.6	3.6	21.9
	68						1	3	30	73	41	4	14	29	27	34	79	25	9	11	0	91	44	8.3	3.0	30.3
Dave Sorenson	71-73Cle 73Phi	1948	6'8	225	F	Ohio State	3	213	690	1562	44				354	455	78	997	260	408	4	1734	18	4.7	1.3	8.1
Ken Spain	71PitA	1946	6'9	235	C	Houston	1	11	8	22	36	0	0	—	8	17	47	40	2	17		24	10	3.6	0.2	2.2
Dan Sparks	69-70MiaA	1945	6'8	200	F	Weber State	2	67	160	414	39	0	0	—	118	171	69	303	45	178	5	438	18	4.5	0.7	6.5
	69						1	12	29	65	45	0	0	—	19	30	63	57	8	35	0	77	21	4.8	0.7	6.4
Craig Spitzer	68Chi	1945	7'	230	C	Tulane	1	10	8	21	38				2	3	67	24	0	4	0	18	4	2.4	0.0	1.8
	68						1	1	0	3	0				0	0	—	3	1	0	0	0	3	3.0	1.0	0.0
Bruce Spraggins	68NJ-A	1940	6'5	188	F	Virginia Union	1	70	306	686	45	2	5	40	238	336	71	329	66	173	2	852	23	4.7	0.9	12.2
Erv Staggs	70MiaA	1948	6'6	195	F-G	N. Car. A & T	1	53	189	474	40	2	7	29	73	114	64	122	76	155	7	453	20	2.3	1.4	8.5
Bud Stallworth	73-74Sea 75-77NO	1950	6'5	190	F-G	Kansas	5	313	1021	2466	41				361	526	69	861	213	686	6	2403	18	2.8	0.7	7.7
Dave Stallworth	66-67NY 68-69IL 70-72NY	1941	6'7	210	F-C	Witchita State	8	522	1883	4296	44				1094	1495	73	2453	872	1259	15	4860	20	4.7	1.7	9.3
(Dave the Rave)	70-73						4	40	92	230	40				52	68	76	137	36	79	0	236	14	3.4	0.9	5.9
72-73Bal 74Cap 75NY																										
Jerry Steele	HC71CarA					Wake Forest																				
Larry Steele	72-80Port	1949	6'5	188	G-F	Kentucky	9	610	2020	4180	48				969	1218	80	1761	1719	1832	45	5009	24	2.9	2.8	8.2
	77-79						3	27	67	158	42				51	62	82	64	39	60	0	185	19	2.3	1.4	6.9
Dennis Stewart	71Bal 71FlaA	1947	6'6	220	F	Michigan	1	12	16	48	33	1	3	33	7	9	78	17	2	12	0	40	6	1.4	0.2	3.3
Randy Stoll	68AnaA	1945	6'7	235	C	Wash. State	1	25	66	138	48	0	0		10	25	40	91	12	42	0	142	16	3.6	0.5	5.7
George Stone	69-70LA-A 71-72UtahA	1946	6'7	195	F	Marshall	4	259	1370	3089	44	144	446	32	646	827	78	1480	333	747	12	3530	27	5.7	1.3	13.6
72CarA	70-71						2	35	249	597	42	18	83	22	93	118	79	262	71	45		609	33	7.5	2.0	17.4
Paul Stovall	73Phoe 74SD-A	1948	6'5	225	F	Arizona State	2	38	62	149	42	0	0	—	52	82	63	119	25	69	0	176	11	3.1	0.7	4.6
Bill Stricker	71Port	1948	6'9	210	F	U. of Pacific	1	1	2	3	67				0	0	—	0	0	1	0	4	2	0.0	0.0	4.0
Red Stroud	68NO-A	1941	6'	160	G	Miss. State	1	7	5	11	45	1	1	100	9	10	90	2	1	7	0	20	5	0.3	0.1	2.9
Gary Suiter	71Cle	1945	6'9	225	C-F	Midwestern	1	30	19	54	35				4	9	44	41	2	20	0	42	5	1.4	0.1	1.4
George Sutor	68KyA 69MinA 70CarA	1943	6'8	240	C	LaSalle	3	79	151	443	34	0	3	0	78	131	60	404	30	203	8	380	13	5.1	0.4	4.8
70MiaA	69						1	1	0	1	0	0	0	—	0	1	0	0	0	2	0	0	3	0.0	0.0	0.0
Keith Swagerty	69HouA 70KyA	1945	6'7	235	F	U. of Pacific	2	80	364	892	41	0	6	0	259	424	61	828	95	242	5	987	31	10.4	1.2	12.3
Skeeter Swift	70NO-A 71MemA 71-72PitA	1946	6'3	210	G	Middle Tenn.	5	283	1218	2738	44	130	436	30	713	848	84	631	820	915	4	3279	24	2.2	2.9	11.6
73DalA 74SA-A																										
Walt Szczerbiak	72PitA	1949	6'6	215	F	G. Washington	1	53	149	237	63	0	2	0	35	53	66	150	41	100		333	11	2.8	0.8	6.3
Lavern Tart	68OakA 68NJ-A 69 NY-A	1942	6'2	195	G-F	Bradley	4	274	2020	4539	45	22	87	25	1254	1600	78	1374	830	792	6	5316	34	5.0	3.0	19.4
69HouA 69DenA	70-71						2	11	102	230	44	4	18	22	59	72	82	53	69	12		267	38	4.8	6.3	24.3
70-71NY-A 71TexA																										
Fatty Taylor	70WasA 71-74VaA 75DenA	1946	6'	175	G	LaSalle	8	640	1934	4340	45	29	141	57	1143	1692	68	2524	2563	2003	4	5098	28	3.9	4.0	8.0
76VaA 77Den	70-75, 77						7	54	127	313	41	3	14	21	74	103	72	200	167	144	0	331	25	3.7	3.1	6.1
Fred Taylor	71-72Phoe 72Cin	1948	6'5	187	G-F	Pan American	2	88	146	401	36				93	157	59	140	69	153	0	385	9	1.6	0.8	4.4
Ollie Taylor	71-72NY-A 73SD-A 74NY-A	1947	6'2	197	G-F	Houston	4	262	886	1945	46	18	77	23	749	1096	68	1090	631	696		2539	23	4.2	2.4	9.7
74CarA	71-74						4	31	118	272	43	3	8	38	80	113	71	145	73	92		319	32	4.7	2.4	10.3
Ron Taylor	70WasA 70NY-A 71VaA	1946	7'1	272	C	Southern Cal.	3	77	157	337	47	0	0	—	57	103	55	294	68	225	11	371	12	3.8	0.9	4.8
72PitA	70						1	2	0	4	0	0	0	—	0	1	0					0	3			0.0
Collis Temple	75SA-A	1952	6'8	225	F	L.S.U.	1	24	17	41	41	0	1	0	8	10	80	31	15	29		42	4	1.3	0.6	1.8
Chuck Terry	73-74Mil 74-75SA-A 76NY-A	1950	6'6	215	F	L. Beach St.	5	341	553	1314	42	10	31	32	162	209	78	818	262	641	1	1298	15	2.4	0.8	3.8
77NYN	73-76						4	21	27	61	44	0	0	—	7	10	70	48	11	32	0	61	13	2.3	0.5	2.9
Claude Terry	73-76DenA 77Buf 77-78Atl	1950	6'4	195	G-F	Stanford	6	349	732	1524	48	47	139	34	329	419	79	499	457	435	0	1934	12	1.4	1.3	5.5
	73, 75-76						3	28	43	117	37	1	12	8	17	23	74	37	32	38		104	12	1.3	1.1	3.7
Tom Thacker	64-66Cin 68Bos 69-71IndA	1939	6'2	181	G-F	Cincinatti	7	314	423	1174	36	10	44	23	164	323	51	822	466	611	4	1020	12	2.6	1.5	3.2
	64-70						6	61	73	237	31	3	16	19	43	77	56	176	124	136	1	192	13	2.9	2.0	3.1
Floyd Theard	70DenA	1944	6'1	170	G	Ky. State	1	25	39	113	35	0	1	0	18	28	64	51	44	49	1	96	16	2.0	1.8	3.8
Justus Thigpen	70PitA 73DetA 74KCO	1947	6'1	170	G	Weber State	3	22	29	79	37	0	0	—	1	3	33	18	12	32	1	59	7	0.8	0.5	2.7
Joe Thomas	71Phoe	1948	6'6	205	F	Marquette	1	39	23	86	27				9	20	45	43	17	19	0	55	5	1.1	0.4	1.4
Ron Thomas	73-76KyA	1950	6'6	215	F	Louisville	4	264	439	938	47	3	13	23	170	317	54	1075	198	530		1051	12	4.1	0.8	4.0
	73-76						4	50	98	188	52	0	1	0	32	62	52	222	37	106		228	13	4.4	0.7	4.4
Terry Thomas	76Det	1953	6'8	220	F	Detroit	1	28	28	65	43				21	29	72	36	3	21	1	77	5	1.3	0.1	2.8
	76						1	4	0	5	0				0	0	—	1	0	1	0	0	2	0.3	0.0	0.0
Willis Thomas	68DenA 68AnaA	1940	6'2	185	G	Harbor J. C.	1	62	243	550	44	0	3	0	69	93	74	114	55	107	1	555	17	1.8	0.9	9.0

Use Name-Nickname	Team by Year	Birth Yr	Hgt	Wgt	Pos	College	# Yr	G	Field Goals FG	Att.	%	3 pt. FG FG	Att	%	Free Throws FT	Att.	%	Reb.	Ass.	PF	DQ	Pts	Per Game Min	Reb	Ass	Pts
George Thompson	70-72PitA 73-74MemA 75Mil	1947	6'2	203	G	Marquette	6	441	2954	6349	47	101	381	27	2105	2762	76	1457	1561	1210	5	8114	32	3.3	3.5	18.4
Jack Thompson	69IndA	1946	6'1	185	G	S. Carolina	1	2	1	3	33	0	1	0	0	0	—	1	2	0	0	2	2	0.5	1.0	1.0
Skip Thoren	68MinA 69-70MiaA	1943	6'10	230	C	Illinois	3	170	902	1939	47	0	5	0	435	711	61	1875	329	560	16	2239	29	11.0	1.9	13.2
	68-69						2	14	75	157	48	0	0	—	42	73	58	182	21	53	3	192	32	13.0	1.5	13.7
Dallas Thornton	69-70MiaA	1946	6'4	190	G	Ky. Wesleyan	2	50	123	284	43	2	11	18	93	142	65	141	74	106	1	341	17	2.8	1.5	6.8
	69						1	7	23	59	39	0	7	0	21	34	62	23	6	9	0	67	17	3.3	0.9	9.6
Nate Thurmond	64-71SF 72-74GS 75-76Chi	1941	6'11	231	C-F	Bowling Grn	14	964	5521	13105	42				3395	5089	67	14464	2573	2624	34	14437	37	15.0	2.7	15.0
76-77Cle	64, 67, 69, 71-73, 75-77						9	81	379	912	42				208	335	62	1101	227	266	4	966	35	13.7	2.8	11.9
George Tinsley	70WasA 70KyA 72FlaA	1946	6'5	205	F	Ky. Wesleyan	2	133	245	581	42	6	30	20	208	250	74	386	114	271	3	704	14	2.9	0.9	5.3
	70, 72						2	15	44	96	46	2	7	29	32	44	73	65	19	3		122	19	4.3	1.3	8.1
Rolland Todd	HC71-72Port	1934				Fresno State																				
Rudy Tomjanovich	71SD 72-81Hou	1948	6'8	220	F	Michigan	11	768	5630	11240	50	34	130	26	2089	2666	78	6198	1573	1937	8	13383	33	8.1	2.0	17.4
	75, 77, 79-81						5	37	213	436	49	1	10	10	84	109	77	189	59	78	1	511	28	5.1	1.6	13.8
Monty Towe	76DenA 77Den	1953	5'7	150	G	N.C. State	2	115	119	275	43	9	42	21	54	69	78	89	223	145	0	319	8	0.7	1.9	2.7
	76-77						2	5	5	11	45				4	5	80	0	7	6	0	14	7	0.0	1.4	2.8
George Trapp	72-73Atl 74-77Det	1948	6'8	215	F-C	L. Beach St.	6	379	1417	3188	44				519	690	75	1466	375	1034	19	3353	18	3.9	1.0	8.8
	72-76						5	31	115	249	46				28	40	70	118	23	89	1	258	17	3.8	0.7	8.3
John Trapp	69-71SD 72-73LA 73Phi	1945	6'7	215	F	Nev.-L. Vagas	5	304	900	2142	42	0	2	0	393	548	72	1320	303	931	26	2193	17	4.3	1.0	7.2
73DenA	72-73						2	15	15	49	31	0	0	—	12	19	63	23	7	22	0	42	8	1.5	0.5	2.8
John Treevant	65-66StL 66-68Det	1939	6'7	219	F-C	Seattle	9	559	1920	4256	45				1278	1843	69	3546	806	1754	48	5118	22	6.3	1.4	9.2
68-69Cin 69-70Sea	70-73						4	40	104	251	41				66	95	69	246	44	115	3	274	22	6.2	1.1	6.9
70-71LA 71-73Bal																										
Ansley Truitt	73DalA	1950	6'9	215	C	California	1	16	18	42	43	0	0	—	3	9	33	38	2	9		39	5	2.4	0.1	2.4
John Tschogl	73-74Atl 75Phi	1950	6'6	210	F	Cal.-	3	113	126	354	36				25	43	58	208	69	174	2	277	11	1.8	0.6	2.5
	73					S. Barbara	1	3	5	8	63				0	0	—	4	1	0	0	10	4	1.3	0.3	3.3
Al Tucker	68-69Sea 69Cin 70Chi	1943	6'8	190	F	Okla. Baptist	5	352	1439	3157	46	33	89	37	630	866	73	1740	342	812	8	3541	21	4.9	1.0	10.1
70-71Bal 71-72FlaA	70-72						3	13	35	87	40	1	7	14	19	24	79	46	16	37	0	90	17	2.5	1.2	6.9
Bill Turner	68-70SF 70Cin 71SF	1944	6'7	222	F	Akron	6	294	603	1481	41				391	537	73	1039	167	605	11	1597	14	3.5	0.6	5.4
72GS 73Port 73LA	68-69, 71-73						5	22	37	87	43				22	31	71	62	18	47	2	96	13	2.8	0.9	4.4
Gary Turner	68HouA	1945	6'7	200	F	T.C.U.	1	2	2	2	100	0	0	—	2	3	67	3	0	2	0	3	11	1.5	0.0	3.0
Herschell Turner	68PitA 68AnaA	1938	6'2	195	G	Nebraska	1	41	51	159	32	6	26	23	23	47	49	74	44	72	1	131	12	1.8	1.1	3.2
Wes Unseld	69-73Bal 74Cap	1946	6'7	249	C-F	Louisville	13	984	4369	8586	51	3	6	50	1883	2976	63	13769	3822	2762	29	10624	36	14.0	3.9	10.8
75-81, HC88-89Was	69-80						12	119	513	1040	49	0	1	0	234	385	61	1777	453	371	5	1260	41	14.9	3.8	10.6
Steve Vacendak	68PitA 69MinA 70PitA	1944	6'1	185	G	Duke	3	93	316	810	39	2	10	20	190	252	75	238	194	194	1	824	20	2.6	2.1	8.9
70MiaA	68-69						2	14	41	92	45	0	0	—	37	41	90	20	14	26	0	119	16	1.4	1.0	8.5
John Vallely	71-72Atl 72Hou	1948	6'3	185	G	U.C.L.A.	2	100	142	375	38				75	104	72	66	84	100	0	359	8	0.7	0.8	3.6
Dick Van Arsdale	66-68NY 69-77Phoe	1943	6'5	211	G-F	Indiana	12	921	5415	11661	46				4253	5385	79	3807	3060	2575	25	15079	34	4.1	3.3	16.4
HC87Phoe	67-68, 70, 76						4	34	124	294	42				88	105	84	82	94	89	1	336	28	2.4	2.8	9.9
Tom Van Arsdale	66-68Det 68-72Cin 73KCO	1943	6'5	215	F-G	Indiana	12	929	5505	12763	43				3222	4226	76	3942	2085	2922	40	14232	31	4.2	2.2	15.3
73-75Phi 75-76Atl 77 Phoe																										
Norm Van Lier	70-72Cin 72-78Chi 79Mil	1947	6'1	175	G	St. Francis	10	746	3313	8003	41				2144	2749	78	3596	5217	2661	74	8770	35	4.8	7.0	11.8
	72-75, 77					(Pa.)	5	38	198	509	39				134	171	78	191	234	154	5	530	41	5.0	6.2	13.9
Dennis Van Zant	76SA-A		6'9	210	F	Azuza Pacific	1	1	0	0	—				2	2	100	1	0	1		2	2	1.0	0.0	2.0
David Vaughn	75-76VaA	1952	7'	220	C	Nev.-L. Vegas	2	93	434	1031	42	0	2	0	130	237	55	913	135	289		998	28	9.8	1.5	10.7
Bob Verga	68DalA 69DenA 69NY-A	1945	6'1	190	G	Duke	6	342	2614	5964	44	127	429	30	1583	2086	76	1336	1004	1004	5	6918	31	3.9	2.9	20.2
69Hou-A 70-72CarA	70						1	4	48	102	47	4	16	25	8	11	73	11	10			108	39	2.8	2.5	27.0
72PitA 74Port																										
CLaude Virden	73KyA	1947	6'6	200	F	Murray State	1	31	130	327	40	0	2	0	46	59	78	154	74	84		306	27	5.0	2.4	9.9
Phil Wagner	69IndA	1945	6'2	190	G	Georgia Tech	1	12	11	41	27	1	4	25	13	17	76	23	14	28	0	36	15	1.9	1.2	3.0
Neal Walk	70-74Phoe 75NO 75-77NY	1948	6'10	240	C	Florida	8	568	2928	6386	46				1301	1717	76	4392	1214	1788	44	7157	24	7.7	2.1	12.6
	70, 75						2	8	22	53	42				6	8	75	40	4	17	0	50	13	5.0	0.5	6.3
Chet Walker (Chet the Jet)	63Syr 64-69Phi 70-75Chi	1940	6'6	212	F-G	Bradley	13	1032	6876	14628	47				5079	6384	80	7314	2126	2727	23	18831	32	7.1	2.1	18.2
	63-75						13	105	687	1531	45				542	689	79	737	212	286	3	1916	35	7.0	2.0	18.2
Jimmy Walker	68-72Det 73-74Hou	1944	6'3	205	G	Providence	9	698	4624	10039	46				2407	2903	83	1860	2429	1735	12	11655	34	2.7	3.5	16.7
74-75KCO 76KC	68, 75						2	12	70	151	46				28	35	80	19	26	29	1	168	29	1.6	2.2	14.0
Dwight Waller	69Atl 70DenA 72DenA	1945	6'7	230	F	Tenn. State	3	20	14	37	38	0	1	0	12	26	46	53	6	23	0	40	6	2.7	0.3	2.0
Perry Warbington	75Phi	1952	6'2	166	G	Ga. Southern	1	5	4	21	19				2	2	100	8	16	16	0	10	14	1.6	3.2	2.0
Henry Ward	76SA-A 77SA	1952	6'4	195	G-F	Jackson State	2	87	182	400	46	6	23	26	31	44	70	173	41	129	0	413	10	2.0	0.5	4.7
	76-77						2	6	6	15	40	2			0	0	—	2	0	6	0	14	3	0.3	0.0	2.3
Jim Ware	67Cin 68SD 69DalA	1944	6'7	210	F	Okla. City	3	64	58	198	29	0	0	—	34	53	64	153	14	67	1	150	7	2.4	0.2	2.3
	67						1	3	5	13	38				0	0	—	2	0	1	0	10	4	0.7	0.0	3.3
Bob Warlick	66Det 67-68SF 69Mil 69Phoe	1941	6'5	205	G-F	Pepperdine	5	186	608	1518	40	0	1	0	257	426	60	566	387	368	1	1473	17	3.0	2.1	7.9
70LA-A	67-68						2	12	55	120	46				28	37	76	53	25	26	2	138	20	4.4	2.1	11.5
Cornell Warner	71-73Buf 73-74Cle 74-75Mil	1948	6'9	220	F-C	Jackson State	7	445	1190	2630	45				480	714	67	3353	494	1225	26	2860	24	7.5	1.1	6.4
76-77LA	74, 77						2	21	54	123	44				13	19	68	172	26	81	3	121	27	8.2	1.2	5.8
Bobby Warren	69-70LA-A 71-72MemA	1946	6'5	191	G	Vanderbilt	8	486	1526	3470	44	96	365	26	1197	1794	67	1546	898	1123	7	4347	20	3.2	1.8	8.9
72-73CarA 73DalA	70, 73-75						4	35	142	321	44	17	58	29	86	104	83	187	92	84		387	27	5.3	2.6	11.1
73-74UtahA 74-75SA-A 76SD-A																										
Johnny Warren	70NY 71-74Cle	1947	6'3	180	G-F	St. John's	5	303	754	1754	43				306	370	83	687	564	606	14	1814	16	2.3	1.9	6.0
	70					(NY)	1	10	2	5	40				0	0	—	3	2	6	0	4	2	0.3	0.2	0.4
Bobby Washington	70KyA 71-72Cle	1947	6'	175	G	Eastern Ky.	3	118	246	620	40	0	0	—	208	268	78	234	413	240	1	700	15	2.0	3.5	5.9
Don Washington	75DenA 76UtahA	1952	6'8	210	F	N. Carolina	2	56	91	201	45	0	2	0	38	56	68	102	33	111	0	220	9	1.8	0.6	3.9
	75						1	4	5	10	50	0	0	—	1	1	100	6	2	9	0	11	7	1.5	0.5	2.8
Jim Washington	66StL 67-69Chi 70-72Phi	1943	6'7	215	F-C	Villanova	11	774	3253	7238	45				1662	2358	70	6637	1105	2280	35	8168	29	8.6	1.4	10.6
72-75Atl 75-76Buf	66-68, 70-73, 75						8	42	147	334	44				65	111	59	295	64	114	2	359	27	7.0	1.5	8.5
Stan Washington	75Was	1952	6'4	190	G	San Diego	1	1	0	1	0				0	0	—	0	0	1	0	0	4	0.0	0.0	0.0

Use Name-Nickname	Team by Year	Birth Yr	Hgt	Wgt	Pos	College	# Yr	G	FG	FG Att.	FG %	3 pt. FG	3 pt. Att.	3 pt. %	FT	FT Att.	FT %	Reb.	Ass.	PF	DQ	Pts	Per Game Min	Per Game Reb	Per Game Ass	Per Game P
Tropper Washington	68PitA 69MinA 70PitA	1944	6'7	225	F-C	Cheyney St.	6	426	1885	3546	53	6	18	33	723	1176	61	4271	1021	1430	14	4499	31	10.0	2.4	10
70LA-A 71FlaA	68-73						6	66	256	472	54	0	2	0	73	137	53	748	161	158	3	585	30	11.3	2.4	8
72-73NY-A 74HO																										
Sam Watts	71PitA	1948	6'3	185	G	Great Falls	1	54	109	287	38	14	41	34	49	67	73	99	45	106		281	12	1.8	0.8	5
Slick Watts	74-78Sea 78NO 79Hou	1951	6'1	175	G	Xavier of La.	6	437	1602	3876	41				697	1166	60	1398	2678	1314	25	3901	26	3.2	6.1	8
	75-76, 79						3	17	79	177	45				27	52	52	58	120	66	1	185	31	3.4	7.1	10
Jim Weaver	HC69HouA					DePaul																				
Jeff Webb	71-72Mil 72Phoe	1948	6'4	170	G	Kansas State	2	75	67	178	38				27	38	71	59	42	62	0	161	7	0.8	0.6	2
	71						1	9	4	7	57				3	3	100	1	2	2	0	11	3	0.1	0.2	1
Elnardo Webster	72NY-A 72MemA	1947	6'5	195	F	St. Peter's	1	19	50	109	46	1	4	25	21	29	72	44	16	39		122	12	2.3	0.8	6
Bob Weiss	66-77Phi 68Sea 69Mil 69-74Chi	1942	6'2	183	G	Penn State	12	783	2288	5346	43				1413	1706	83	1398	2931	1576	4	5989	22	1.8	3.7	7
75-76Buf 77Was HC87SA	67, 70-77						9	53	167	392	43				73	91	80	89	164	111	1	407	21	1.7	3.1	7
Rick Weitzman	68Bos	1946	6'2	185	G	Northeastern	1	25	12	46	26				9	13	69	10	8	8	0	33	3	0.4	0.3	1
	68						1	3	2	3	67				0	0	—	1	1	0	0	4	2	0.3	0.3	1
Owen Wells	75Hou	1950	6'7	200	F	Detroit	1	33	42	100	42				15	22	68	35	22	38	0	99	6	1.1	0.7	3
	75						1	4	3	5	60				0	0	—	1	1	1	0	6	1	0.3	0.3	1
Walt Wesley	67-69Cin 70Chi 71-73Cle	1945	6'11	226	C	Kansas	10	590	2002	4614	43				998	1585	63	3243	385	1448	16	5002	17	5.5	0.7	8
73Phoe 74Cap 75Phi	67, 70, 74						3	8	18	41	44				6	12	50	28	2	16	0	42	10	3.5	0.3	5
75Mil 76LA																										
Jerry West	61-74, HC77-79LA	1938	6'3	179	G-F	West Virginia	14	932	9016	19032	47				7160	8801	81	5376	6238	2435	17	25192	39	5.8	6.7	27
	61-70, 72-74						13	153	1622	3460	47				1213	1507	80	855	970	451	3	4457	41	5.6	6.3	29
Roland West	68Bal	1944	6'4	178	G	Cincinnati	1	4	2	5	40				0	0	—	5	0	3	0	4	4	1.3	0.0	1
Dexter Westbrook	68NJ-A 68PitA	1943	6'8	210	F	Providence	1	12	91	39	49	0	0	—	10	14	71	23	5	30	0	48	11	1.9	0.4	4
John Wetzel	68LA 69-70MS 71-72Phoe	1944	6'5	190	G-F	Virginia Tech	7	357	465	1085	43				285	352	81	682	494	608	4	1215	13	1.9	1.4	3.
73-75Atl 76, HC88Phoe	73, 76						2	5	3	7	43				2	2	100	4	4	8	0	8	8	0.8	0.8	1
Herb White	71Atl 72KJ	1948	6'2	195	G	Georgia	1	38	34	84	40				22	39	56	48	47	62	2	90	8	1.3	1.2	2.
Hubie White	63SF 64Phi 70MiaA 71PitA	1940	6'4	205	G-F	Villanova	4	120	234	640	37	9	50	18	101	143	71	244	110	250	2	578	16	2.0	0.9	4
Jo Jo White	70-79Bos 79-80GS 81KC	1946	6'3	190	G	Kansas	12	837	6169	13884	44	1	6	17	2060	2471	83	3345	4095	2056	21	14399	36	4.0	4.9	17
	72-77						6	80	732	1629	45				256	309	83	348	452	241	3	1720	43	4.4	5.7	21
Hank Whitney	68NJ-A 69NYA 69HouA 70CarA	1939	6'7	235	F-C	Iowa State	3	145	518	1284	40	0	1	0	303	438	69	1102	168	502	8	1339	21	7.6	1.2	9
	70						1	4	17	33	52	0	0	—	4	9	44					38	15			9
Sidney Wicks	72-76Port 77-78Bos 79-81SD	1949	6'8	225	F-C	U.C.L.A.	10	760	5046	11002	46	0	2	0	2711	3955	69	6620	2437	2524	51	12803	34	8.7	3.2	16
	77						1	9	42	81	52				34	47	72	83	16	37	2	118	29	9.2	1.8	13
Ron Widby	68NO-A	1945	6'4	210	F	Tennessee	1	20	27	70	39	0	3	0	4	7	57	45	4	18	0	58	7	2.3	0.2	2
68-73 played in N.F.L.	68						1	6	8	19	42	2	3	67	0	2	0	17	1	5	0	18	5	2.8	0.2	3
Ken Wilburn	68-69Chi 69MinA	1944	6'6	205	F	Central State	2	54	84	215	39	0	0	—	40	79	51	212	29	73	1	208	9	3.9	0.5	3
69NY-A 69DenA	69					(Ohio)	1	7	16	33	48	0	0	—	4	16	25	32	5	21	0	36	13	4.6	0.7	5
Lenny Wilkens	61-68StL 69, PC 70-72Sea	1937	6'1	185	G	Providence	15	1077	6189	14327	43				5394	6973	77	5030	7211	3285	63	17772	35	4.7	6.7	16.
73-74Cle	61, 63-68						7	64	359	899	40				313	407	77	373	372	258	7	1031	38	5.8	5.8	16.
PC75, HC76Port HC78-85Sea HC87-89Cle																										
Al Williams	71KyA	1948	6'6	215	F	Drake	1	11	19	43	44	0	0	—	5	10	50	26	5	13		43	6	2.4	0.5	3
Bernie Williams	70-71SD 72-74VaA	1945	6'3	175	G	LaSalle	5	283	1074	2645	41	29	125	23	445	540	82	523	556	531	1	2622	18	1.8	2.0	9
	72-73						2	14	87	198	44	2	5	40	20	28	71	47	24	42		196	27	3.4	1.7	14
Charlie Williams	61DL 68PitA 69MinA 70-71PitA	1943	6'	165	G	Seattle	6	372	2337	5998	39	210	795	26	1136	1536	74	1157	992	1144	13	6020	31	3.1	2.7	16
71-73MemA 73UtahA	68-69, 71, 73						4	30	218	527	41	19	79	24	100	139	72	103	60	107	4	555	34	3.4	2.0	18
Chuck Williams	71PitA 72DenA 73-74SD-A	1946	6'2	175	G	Colorado	8	638	2509	5348	47	16	55	29	1828	2313	79	1489	2869	1455	0	6894	28	2.3	4.5	10.
74KyA 75MemA	72-76						5	37	161	348	46	1			116	133	87	115	152	82		441	31	3.1	4.1	11.
76DenA 77Den 77-78Buf																										
Cliff Williams	69Det	1945	6'3	180	G	Bowling Grn	1	3	2	9	22				0	0	—	3	2	7	0	4	6	1.0	0.7	1
Earl Williams (the Twirl)	75Phoe 76Det 77NYN 79Bos	1951	6'7	230	C-F	Winst.-Sal. St.	4	146	290	671	43				84	177	47	814	126	270	0	664	13	5.6	8.6	4
Fly Williams	75StLA	1953	6'5	200	G-F	Austin Peay	1	71	297	643	46	2	14	14	69	101	68	181	142	156	0	665	17	2.5	2.0	9
	75						1	2	1	5	20	0	1	0	0	0	—	1	0	2	0	2	4	0.5	0.0	1
Gene Williams	70KyA	1947	6'7	235	F	Kansas State	1	1	0	1	0	0	0	—	0	0	—	0	0	2	0	0	8	0.0	0.0	0
Hambone Williams	68-70SD 71-74Bos 75SD-A	1939	6'2		G	Cal. Poly-	8	548	1183	2884	41	0	0	—	526	722	73	1712	2397	1247	4	2892	17	3.1	4.4	5.
	69, 72-74					(Pomona)	4	39	68	163	42				31	43	72	95	135	90	1	167	14	2.4	3.5	4.
Hank Williams	75UtahA	1952	6'6	215	F	Jacksonville	1	39	71	163	44	3	22	14	18	23	78	89	25	73	0	163	12	2.3	0.6	4.
	75						1	2	2	6	33	0	0	—	0	0	—	2	0	2	0	4	4	1.0	0.0	2
Max Williams	HC70DalA HC71TexA					S.M.U.																				
Milt Williams	71NY 72Atl 74Sea 75StLA	1945	6'2	185	G	Lincoln (Mo.)	4	72	97	222	44	0	0	—	64	95	67	64	137	123	1	258	10	0.9	1.9	3.
Nate Williams	72Cin 73-75KCO 75-78NO	1950	6'5	216	F-G	Utah State	8	642	3278	7151	46				1153	1432	81	2469	963	1916	37	7709	23	3.8	1.5	12.
78-79GS																										
Ron Williams	69-71SF 72-73GS	1944	6'3	190	G	West Virginia	8	516	1858	4214	44				1081	1298	83	971	1818	1303	23	4797	22	1.9	3.5	9
74-75Mil 76LA	69, 71-74						5	32	104	248	42				52	59	88	57	94	76	2	260	21	1.8	2.9	8.
Sam Williams	69-70Mil	1945	6'3	188	G	Iowa	2	66	89	252	35				77	145	53	116	64	111	1	255	10	1.8	1.0	3.
	70						1	2	4	7	57				0	2	0	4	1	5	0	8	8	2.0	0.5	0.
Willie Williams	71Bos 71Cin	1947	6'7	200	F	Florida State	1	25	10	42	24				3	5	60	23	8	14	0	23	4	0.9	0.3	0.
Vann Williford	71CarA	1948	6'6	195	F	N.C. State	1	38	62	141	44	3	9	33	21	37	57	68	15	34		148	8	1.8	0.4	3.
Bobby Wilson	75-76Chi 77Bos 78Ind	1951	6'3	180	G	Witchita State	4	143	345	809	43				102	132	77	167	110	185	2	792	10	1.2	0.8	5.
	75						1	10	17	41	41				10	12	83	11	4	10	0	44	9	1.1	0.4	4.
Bobby Wilson	68DalA	1944	6'8	215	F	Kansas	1	69	226	581	39	1	2	50	163	265	62	450	55	209	8	616	23	6.5	0.8	8.
	68						1	6	7	25	28	1	1	100	6	13	46	26	2	12	1	21	8	4.3	0.3	3.
George Wilson	65-67Cin 67Chi 68Sea 69Phoe	1942	6'8	227	C	Cincinnati	7	410	841	2261	37				534	789	68	2144	307	901	10	2216	14	5.2	0.7	5.
69-70Phi 71Buf	65-67, 69-70						5	12	8	31	26				7	11	64	42	10	20	0	23	8	3.5	0.8	1.
Isaiah Wilson (Bunny)	72Det 73MemA	1948	6'2	175	G	Baltimore	2	78	131	336	39	3	8	38	92	120	77	86	113	78	0	357	9	1.1	1.4	4.
Jasper Wilson	69-70NO-A	1947	6'6	200	F	Southern U.	2	70	136	360	38	6	14	43	88	135	65	187	45	133	1	366	12	2.7	0.6	5.
	69						1	10	11	42	26	0	5	0	17	23	74	26	2	20	0	39	9	2.6	0.2	3.
Jim Wilson	71PitA	1948	5'10	175	G	Cheyney St.	1	6	1	8	13	0	0	—	4	6	67	6	8	3		6	7	1.0	1.3	1.

		Birth					#		Field Goals			3 pt. FG			Free Throws								Per Game			
Use Name-Nickname	Team by Year	Yr	Hgt	Wgt	Pos	College	Yr	G	FG	Att.	%	FG	Att	%	FT	Att.	%	Reb.	Ass.	PF	DQ	Pts	Min	Reb	Ass	Pts
Steve Wilson	71-72DenA	1948	6'5	185	G	Hanover	2	48	58	155	37	9	35	26	26	48	54	52	35	49		148	6	1.1	0.7	3.1
Lee Winfield	70-73Sea 74-75Buf 76KC	1947	6'2	175	G	N. Texas State	7	403	1191	2511	47				577	864	67	828	1003	682	6	2959	18	2.1	2.5	7.3
	74-75						2	7	7	18	39				4	7	57	11	11	10	1	18	11	1.6	1.6	2.6
Hawthorne Wingo (Wingy)	73-76NY	1948	6'8	210	F	Friendship J. C.	4	212	396	863	46				231	329	70	745	128	368	2	1023	13	3.5	0.6	4.8
	73-75						3	1	21	47	45				8	12	67	32	8	10	0	50	9	2.9	0.7	4.5
Mary Winkler	71Mil 72IndA	1948	6'1	175	G	Southwstn La.	2	1	18	64	28	2	4	50	10	16	63	20	14	19	0	48	7	0.9	0.6	2.1
	71						1	5	0	4	0				0	0	—	0	1	3	0	0	2	0.0	0.2	0.0
Tex Winter	HC72-73Hou	1922				Oregon State, Southern Cal.																				
Skip Wise	76SA-A	1955	6'2	170	G		1	2	2	4	50				0	0	—	3	1	4	0	4	5	1.5	0.5	2.0
Willie Wise	70LA-A 71-74,HO75UtahA	1947	6'6	215	F	Drake	9	552	3694	7717	48	21	96	22	2276	3143	72	4578	1594	1788	10	9727	33	8.3	2.9	17.6
75-76VaA 77Den 78Sea	70-74, 77						6	74	578	1158	50	2	10	20	309	336	92	672	227	209	0	1467	36	9.1	3.1	19.8
Luke Witte	74-76Cle 77JJ	1950	7'	240	C	Ohio State	3	118	149	371	40				74	108	69	357	60	147	0	372	9	3.0	0.5	3.2
	76						1	7	6	11	55				4	4	100	9	4	4	0	16	4	1.3	0.6	2.3
Greg Wittman	70DenA 71TexA 71FlaA	1947	6'8	210	F	Wstn Carolina	2	60	86	229	38	4	18	22	36	68	53	117	15	108	2	212	9	2.0	0.3	3.5
	70						1	2	1	2	50	1	1	100	1	3	33	0	0	2	0	4	2	0.0	0.0	2.0
Dave Wohl	72Phi 73Port 73-74Buf	1949	6'2	185	G	Pennsylvania	7	410	1015	2361	43				523	697	75	558	1397	1027	13	2553	20	1.4	3.4	6.2
74-77Hou 77NYN	75						1	4	3	3	100				0	0	—	1	2	2	0	6	2	0.3	0.5	1.5
78, HC86-87NJ																										
Tommy Woods	68KyA	1944	6'7	215	F	E. Tenn. State	1	18	14	43	33	0	1	0	14	16	88	55	4	25	0	42	10	3.1	0.2	2.3
Bob Woollard	70MiaA	1947	6'10	225	C	Wake Forest	1	19	32	82	39	0	1	0	20	25	80	69	6	42	1	84	12	3.6	0.3	4.4
Tom Workman	68StL 68-69Bal 70Det	1944	6'7	230	F-C	Seattle	4	127	290	649	45	4	23	17	190	241	79	325	75	216	0	774	10	2.6	0.6	6.1
70LA-A 71UtahA 71DenA	69-70						2	4	3	8	38	0	0	—	0	0	—	4	0	0	0	6	3	1.0	0.0	1.5
Willie Worsley	69NY-A	1942	5'7	175	G	Texas-El Paso	1	24	36	123	29	10	30	33	63	84	75	35	39	48	0	145	19	1.5	1.6	6.0
Howie Wright	71-72KyA	1948	6'3	185	G	Austin Peay	2	53	94	245	38	9	42	21	40	50	80	80	63	89		237	12	1.5	1.2	4.5
	71						1	5	7	20	35	2	8	25	4	9	44	2	4	6		20	7	0.4	0.8	4.0
Joby Wright	73Sea 74MemA 76SD-A	1950	6'8	222	F-C	Indiana	4	103	188	403	47	0	0	—	60	129	47	291	38	225		436	12	2.8	0.4	4.2
76VaA																										
Leroy Wright	68PitA 69MinA	1938	6'9	215	F	U. of the Pacific	2	27	28	73	38	0	0	—	9	27	33	138	15	64	1	65	16	5.1	0.6	2.4
	68-69						2	14	9	31	29	0	1	0	8	22	36	73	8	32	2	26	14	5.2	0.6	1.9
Lonnie Wright	68-71DenA 71-75FlaA	1944	6'2	205	G	Colorado State	5	335	1443	3544	41	111	435	26	593	822	72	913	641	983	9	3590	26	2.7	1.9	10.7
66-67 played in N.F.L.	68-72						5	33	110	335	33	6	34	18	57	76	75	100	78	88	0	283	27	3.0	2.4	8.6
Dennis Wuycik	73-74CArA 75StLA	1950	6'6	215	F	North Carolina	3	157	273	593	46	1	7	14	137	204	67	323	128	293	9	684	11	2.1	0.8	4.4
	73-74						2	15	8	24	33	0	1	0	8	12	67	19	3	14		24	6	1.3	0.2	1.6
Barry Yates	72Phi	1946	6'7	215	F	Maryland	1	24	31	83	37				7	11	64	40	7	10	0	69	6	1.7	0.3	2.9
Charlie Yelverton	72Port	1948	6'2	190	G-F	Fordham	1	69	206	530	39				133	188	71	201	81	145	2	545	18	2.9	1.2	7.9
Draff Young	HC74KCO					J. C. Smith																				
Gus Young	HC69MinA					Carleton																				
Gary Zeller	71-72Bal 72NY-A	1947	6'3	205	G	Drake	2	90	124	374	33	0	1	0	41	69	59	102	39	121	0	289	9	1.1	0.4	3.2
	71-72						2	18	13	36	36	0	0	—	2	8	25	14	4	22	0	28	4	0.8	0.2	1.6
Bill Zopf	71Mil	1948	6'1	170	G	Duquesne	1	53	49	135	36				20	36	56	46	73	34	0	118	8	0.9	1.4	2.2

1976-77 N.B.A.

Four More Teams in the Fold

The four surviving A.B.A. teams each paid over $3 million to enter the N.B.A. promised land. They also had to pool another $3 million to pay off John Y. Brown, the owner of the Kentucky Colonels, who were left out of the merger. Brown promptly purchased a half-interest in the Buffalo Braves. In addition, the New York Nets had to pay about $4 million to the New York Knicks to share the New York territory. Despite the high financial toll on the A.B.A. teams, A.B.A. players figured prominently in all four divisional races.

The New York Nets had won the final A.B.A. title and had high hopes in the Atlantic Division. Over the summer, they bolstered their backcourt by sending players and draft choices to Kansas City for Tiny Archibald. Star forward Julius Erving aggravated the team's financial woes, however, by demanding renegotiation of his contract and sitting out the team's pre-season schedule. Just before the season began, the Nets sold Erving's contract to the Philadelphia 76ers for approximately $3 million. While the deal eased the Nets' financial pressures, it ruined the team on the floor. When Archibald suffered a broken foot in January, the Nets' season became a fiasco.

The 76ers, meanwhile, became an elite team with the addition of Dr. J. George McGinnis and Doug Collins were also potent offensive weapons, supported by a deep cast of role players. The 76ers opened up a lead in the Atlantic Division after New Year's Day. The Celtics finished only six games back despite a series of misfortunes. Paul Silas was traded to Denver in a salary dispute, Dave Cowens left the team in November for two months for personal reasons, Charlie Scott suffered a broken arm in January and missed almost two months, and newly-acquired forwards Sidney Wicks and Curtis Rowe fit with difficulty into the Celtic system. The Knicks finished out of the playoffs despite acquiring Bob McAdoo and Jim McMillian from Buffalo. The Braves and Nets expectedly brought up the rear after dropping their star players.

In the Central Division, A.B.A. survivor Moses Malone made a difference. After spending the pre-season with Portland, Malone was traded to Buffalo. After a week with the Braves, he was then sent to the Houston Rockets. Malone developed during the season into a superb rebounder at both forward and center. Rudy Tomjanovich was Houston's offensive leader. The Rockets closed strongly, with new coach Tom Nissalke, himself an A.B.A. expatriot, taking them to the divisional title. Washington, San Antonio, and Cleveland all made the playoffs. New Orleans missed the playoffs despite Pete Maravich's scoring title, which featured 13 games of 40 points or more. Atlanta finished last again, with Ted Turner purchasing a controlling interest in the Hawks in January.

In the Midwest Division, an A.B.A. team finished first. The Denver Nuggets had stars in David Thompson, Dan Issel, and Bobby Jones, veteran strength in ex-Celtic forward Paul Silas, an exciting fast break offense, and the best attendance in the league. Chicago and Detroit also made the playoffs from the Midwest. The Bulls lost 14 of their first 17 games, then came back and won 20 of their last 24 games. Star center Artis Gilmore came to Chicago from the defunct Kentucky Colonels. The Pistons enjoyed Bob Lanier's usual excellence and were disappointed by ex-A.B.A. forward Marvin Barnes, whose season was overshadowed by a gun-related parole violation. Kansas City and Indiana were respectable also-rans while Milwaukee fell from first place to last.

In the Pacific Division, new coach Jerry West led the Los Angeles Lakers to the best record in the league. Kareem Abdul-Jabbar's dominance at center earned him another MVP award and lifted an otherwise ordinary team to a new level. Challenging the Lakers all season were the Portland Trail Blazers, beneficiaries of Bill Walton's relatively good health. New coach, Jack Ramsay traded away Sidney Wicks and Geoff Petrie, their leading scorers in recent years, and installed a running offense and tenacious defense. Maurice Lucas came from the A.B.A. to help Walton with his strong inside game. Rick Barry, Phil Smith, and Jamaal Wilkes excelled in the Warriors' unsuccessful bid to repeat as Pacific champions. Seattle hovered around the .500 mark all season in Bill Russell's finale as coach. After their cinderella trip to last year's playoff finals, the Phoenix Suns finished in last place in the division,. Paul Westphal continued his hot shooting, but injuries crippled the Suns at forward and sent them to 17 losses in their last 22 games.

In the playoffs, the four mini-series set up four interesting quarter-final series. In the west, Portland won the opener at Denver and then held home-court advantage to win six games. With Abdul-Jabbar scoring 40 points or better four times, the Lakers eliminated the Warriors in seven games. In the east, the young Houston Rockets beat the veteran Washington Bullets in six games.

In the other Eastern quarterfinal, the defending champion Celtics won the opener in Philadelphia 113-111 on a JoJo White jumper at the buzzer. The Sixers won game two and recaptured the home-court advantage by winning game three 109-100 in Boston. The Celtics evened the series by taking game four 124-119 behind Cowens' 37 points. The Sixers won game five in Philadelphia, and the Celtics captured game six in Boston. In the finale in the Spectrum, the Sixers went ahead with a 10-2 spurt in the third period and won the deciding game by an 83-77 score.

In the semi-finals, the Sixers rolled on, overwhelming Houston in six games. In the West, Kareem Abdul-Jabbar and Bill Walton both played center at a superb level. The Blazers, however, simply had better personnel around Walton. They swept the Lakers in four straight games.

In the championship series, Philadelphia's individual stars matched up against Portland's team orientation. The Sixers won the first two games at home, as the Blazers were plagued with turnovers and cold shooting. With Bill Walton excelling in scoring, rebounding, and passing, the Blazers revived and handily captured the third and fourth games in Portland. Back in Philadelphia, the Blazers staged a 26-8 spurt in the third period and won the key fifth game 110-104. The Sixers rallied in game six but could not stem the Portland tide. The Trail Blazers won game six 109-107 to take the N.B.A. championship.

1976/77 N.B.A. — EASTERN CONFERENCE
ATLANTIC CONFERENCE

Use Name	Pos	Hgt	Wgt	Age	TOTAL G	Min	FG	FGA	%	FT	FTA	%	Reb	Ass	PF	DQ	Points	PER GAME Min	Reb	Ass	PF	Points
PHILADELPHIA 76ers	50-32 .610				GENE SHUE																	
Julius Erving	F	6'7	210	26	82	2940	685	1373	50	400	515	78	695	306	251	1	1770	36	8.5	3.7	3.1	21.6
George McGinnis	F-C	6'8	235	26	79	2769	659	1439	46	372	546	68	911	302	299	4	1690	35	11.5	3.8	3.8	21.4
Caldwell Jones	C	6'11	225	26	82	2023	215	424	51	64	116	55	666	92	301	3	494	25	8.1	1.1	3.7	6.0
Doug Collins (injury)	G-F	6'6	180	25	58	2037	426	823	52	210	250	84	195	271	174	2	1062	35	3.4	4.7	3.0	18.3
Henry Bibby	G	6'1	185	27	81	2639	302	702	43	221	282	78	273	356	200	2	825	33	3.4	4.4	2.5	10.2
Lloyd Free	G	6'2	185	23	78	2253	467	1022	46	334	464	72	237	266	207	2	1268	29	3.0	3.4	2.7	16.3
Steve Mix	F	6'7	222	29	75	1958	288	551	52	215	262	82	376	152	167	0	791	26	5.0	2.0	2.2	10.5
Harvey Catchings (broken elbow)	C	6'9	223	25	53	864	62	123	50	33	47	70	234	30	130	1	157	16	4.4	0.6	2.5	3.0
Darryl Dawkins	C	6'11	265	19	59	684	135	215	63	40	79	51	230	24	129	1	310	12	3.9	0.4	2.2	5.3
Joe Bryant	F	6'9	185	22	61	612	107	240	45	53	70	76	117	48	84	1	267	10	1.9	0.8	1.4	4.4
Mike Dunleavy (leg injury)	G	6'3	180	22	32	359	60	145	41	34	45	76	34	56	64	1	154	11	1.1	1.8	2.0	4.8
Fred Carter (to Mil)	G	6'3	185	31	14	237	43	101	43	10	19	53	24	21	29	0	96	17	1.7	1.5	2.1	6.9
Jim Barnett	G	6'4	180	32	16	231	28	64	44	10	18	56	14	23	28	0	66	14	0.9	1.4	1.8	4.1
Terry Furlow	F-G	6'4	190	22	32	174	34	100	34	16	18	89	39	19	11	0	84	5	1.2	0.6	0.3	2.6
BOSTON CELTICS	44-38 .537				TOM HEINSOHN																	
Curtis Rowe	F	6'7	225	27	79	2190	315	632	50	170	240	71	563	107	215	3	800	28	7.1	1.4	2.7	10.1
Sidney Wicks	F-C	6'8	225	27	82	2642	464	1012	46	310	464	67	824	169	331	14	1238	32	10.0	2.1	4.0	15.1
Dave Cowens (leave of absence)	C	6'9	230	28	50	1888	328	756	43	162	198	82	697	248	181	7	818	38	13.9	5.0	3.6	16.4
Charlie Scott (broken arm)	G	6'5	180	28	43	1581	326	734	44	129	173	75	191	196	155	3	781	37	4.4	4.6	3.6	18.2
Jo Jo White	G	6'3	193	30	82	3333	638	1488	43	333	383	87	383	492	193	5	1609	41	4.7	6.0	2.4	19.6
John Havlicek	G-F	6'5	210	36	79	2913	580	1283	45	235	288	82	382	400	208	4	1395	37	4.8	5.1	2.6	17.7
Tom Boswell	C-F	6'9	230	23	70	1083	175	340	51	96	135	71	306	85	237	9	446	15	4.4	1.2	3.4	6.4
Fred Saunders	F	6'7	210	25	68	1051	184	395	47	35	53	66	223	85	191	3	403	15	3.3	1.3	2.8	5.9
Kevin Stacom	G	6'3	185	25	79	1051	179	438	41	46	58	79	97	117	65	0	404	13	1.2	1.5	0.8	5.1
Jim Ard	C	6'8	230	28	63	969	96	254	38	49	76	64	296	53	128	1	241	15	4.7	0.8	2.0	3.8
Steve Kuberski	F-C	6'8	215	29	76	860	131	312	42	63	83	76	209	39	89	0	325	11	2.8	0.5	1.2	4.3
Norm Cook	F	6'9	210	21	25	138	27	72	38	9	17	53	27	5	27	0	63	6	1.1	0.2	1.1	2.5
Bobby Wilson	G	6'3	180	25	25	131	19	59	32	11	13	85	9	14	19	0	49	5	0.4	0.6	0.8	2.0
NEW YORK KNICKERBOCKERS	40-42 .488				RED HOLZMAN																	
Jim McMillian (knee injury)	F	6'5	235	28	67	2158	298	642	46	67	86	78	307	139	103	0	663	32	4.6	2.1	1.5	9.9
Spencer Haywood (leg injury)	F-C	6'8	230	27	31	1021	202	449	45	109	131	83	280	50	72	0	513	33	9.0	1.6	2.3	16.5
Bob McAdoo (from Buf)	C-F	6'9	210	25	52	2031	558	1045	53	271	358	76	662	140	188	2	1387	39	12.7	2.7	3.6	26.7
Walt Frazier	G	6'4	205	31	76	2687	532	1089	49	259	336	77	293	403	194	0	1323	35	3.9	5.3	2.6	17.4
Earl Monroe	G	6'3	190	32	77	2656	613	1185	52	307	366	84	223	366	197	0	1533	34	2.9	4.8	2.6	19.9
Lonnie Shelton	C-F	6'8	245	21	82	2104	398	836	48	159	225	71	633	149	363	10	955	26	7.7	1.8	4.4	11.6
Tod McMillen (from Buf)	F-C	6'11	215	24	56	1222	221	471	47	70	87	80	317	51	134	0	528	22	5.7	0.9	2.4	9.4
Butch Beard	G	6'3	185	29	70	1082	148	293	51	75	109	69	163	144	137	0	371	15	2.3	2.1	2.0	5.3
Phil Jackson	F	6'8	220	31	76	1033	102	232	44	51	71	72	229	85	184	4	255	14	3.0	1.1	2.4	3.4
Bill Bradley	F	6'5	210	33	67	1027	127	274	46	34	42	81	103	128	122	0	288	15	1.5	1.9	1.8	4.3
Mo Layton (finger injury)	G	6'1	180	28	56	765	134	277	48	58	73	79	47	154	87	0	326	14	0.8	2.8	1.6	5.8
John Gianelli (to Buf)	C-F	6'10	225	26	19	630	86	182	47	35	48	73	178	26	54	0	207	33	9.4	1.4	2.8	10.9
Ticky Burden	G	6'2	185	23	61	608	148	352	42	51	85	60	66	62	88	0	347	10	1.1	1.0	1.4	5.7
Mel Davis (to NYN)	F	6'7	225	26	22	342	41	110	37	22	31	71	100	24	45	0	104	16	4.5	1.1	2.0	4.7
Dean Meminger	G	6'	175	28	32	254	15	36	42	13	23	57	26	29	17	0	43	8	0.8	0.9	0.5	1.3
Neal Walk	C	6'10	225	28	11	135	28	57	49	6	7	86	27	6	22	0	62	12	2.5	0.5	2.0	5.6
BUFFALO BRAVES	30-52 .366				TATES LOCKE (16-30 .348), BOB MacKINNON (3-4 .429), JOE MULLANEY (11-18 .379)																	
Adrian Dantley	F	6'5	210	20	77	2816	544	1046	52	476	582	82	587	144	215	2	1564	37	7.6	1.9	2.8	20.3
John Shumate	F-C	6'9	235	24	74	2601	407	810	50	302	450	67	701	159	197	1	1116	35	9.5	2.1	2.7	15.1
George Johnson (from GS)	C	6'11	220	28	39	1055	125	279	45	46	67	69	400	78	141	6	296	27	10.3	2.0	3.6	7.6
Randy Smith	G	6'3	180	28	82	3094	702	1504	47	294	386	76	457	441	264	2	1698	38	5.6	5.4	3.2	20.7
Ernie DeGregorio	G	6'	180	25	81	2267	365	875	42	138	146	95	184	378	150	1	868	28	2.3	4.7	1.9	10.7
Don Adams	F	6'7	220	29	77	1710	216	526	41	129	173	75	371	150	201	0	561	22	4.8	1.9	2.6	7.3
John Gianelli (from NY)	C-F	6'10	225	26	57	1283	171	394	43	55	77	71	297	57	117	0	397	23	5.2	1.0	2.1	7.0
Bird Averitt	G	6'1	175	24	75	1136	234	619	38	121	169	72	78	134	127	2	589	15	1.0	1.8	1.7	7.9
Bob McAdoo (to NY)	C-F	6'9	210	25	20	767	182	400	46	110	158	70	264	65	74	1	474	38	13.2	3.3	3.7	23.7
Fred Foster	F-G	6'5	220	30	59	689	99	247	40	30	44	68	76	48	72	0	228	12	1.3	0.8	1.2	3.9
Gus Gerard (from Den)	F-G	6'8	205	23	41	592	100	244	41	40	61	66	117	43	91	0	240	14	2.9	1.0	2.2	5.9
Chuck Williams (from Den)	G	6'2	185	30	44	556	43	117	37	38	48	79	67	88	34	0	124	13	1.5	2.0	0.8	2.8
Jim Price (from Mil - to Den)	G	6'3	195	27	20	333	44	104	42	17	20	85	34	38	52	0	105	17	1.7	1.9	2.6	5.3
Claude Terry (to Atl)	G-F	6'4	195	26	33	304	49	104	47	18	23	78	28	33	27	0	116	9	0.8	1.0	0.8	3.5
Tom McMillen (to NY)	C-F	6'11	215	24	20	270	45	92	49	26	36	72	72	16	29	0	116	14	3.6	0.8	1.5	5.8
Zaid Abdul-Aziz	C	6'9	240	30	22	195	25	74	34	33	43	77	90	7	21	0	83	9	4.1	0.3	1.0	3.8
Johnny Neumann (to LA)	G	6'6	210	25	4	49	15	34	44	5	6	83	9	4	7	0	35	12	2.3	1.0	1.8	8.8
Clyde Mayes (from Ind - to Port)	F	6'9	225	23	2	7	0	3	0	2	3	67	3	0	2	0	2	4	1.5	0.0	1.0	1.0
Moses Malone (to Hou)	F	6'10	215	21	2	6	0	0	—	0	0	—	1	0	1	0	0	3	0.5	0.0	0.5	0.0

1976/77 N.B.A. — EASTERN CONFERENCE (continued)
ATLANTIC DIVISION (continued)

Use Name	Pos	Hgt	Wgt	Age	G	Min	FG	FGA	%	FT	FTA	%	Reb	Ass	PF	DQ	Points	Min	Reb	Ass	PF	Points
					TOTAL													PER GAME				
NEW YORK NETS	**22-60 .268**				**KEVIN LOUGHERTY**																	
Jan van Breda Kolff	F-G	6'7	200	25	72	2398	271	609	44	195	228	86	460	117	205	2	737	33	6.4	1.6	2.8	10.2
Mike Bantom (from Sea)	F	6'9	220	25	33	1134	224	474	47	166	226	73	285	50	120	4	614	34	8.6	1.5	3.6	18.6
Kim Hughes	C	6'11	220	24	81	2081	151	354	43	19	69	28	564	98	308	9	321	26	7.0	1.2	3.8	4.0
John Willimason (BG to Ind)	G	6'2	185	24	42	1426	357	803	44	161	204	79	119	90	143	3	875	34	2.8	2.1	3.4	20.8
Nate Archibald (broken foot)	G	6'1	165	28	34	1277	250	560	45	197	251	78	80	254	77	1	697	38	2.4	7.5	2.3	20.5
Tim Bassett	F-C	6'8	230	25	76	2442	293	739	40	101	177	57	641	109	246	10	687	32	8.4	1.4	3.2	9.0
Al Skinner	G	6'4	195	24	79	2256	382	887	43	231	292	79	363	289	279	7	995	29	4.6	3.7	3.5	12.6
Bubbles Hawkins	G	6'4	190	22	52	1481	406	909	45	194	282	69	154	93	163	2	1006	28	3.0	1.8	3.1	19.3
Jim Fox	C	6'10	230	33	71	1165	184	398	46	95	114	83	329	49	158	1	463	16	4.6	0.7	2.2	6.5
Chuck Terry	F	6'6	215	26	61	1075	128	318	40	48	62	77	143	39	120	0	304	18	2.3	0.6	2.0	5.0
Dave Wahl (from Hou)	G	6'2	185	27	37	924	109	273	40	57	85	67	76	127	97	1	275	25	2.1	3.4	2.6	7.4
Rich Jones	F	6'8	230	30	34	877	134	348	39	92	121	76	194	46	109	2	360	26	5.7	1.4	3.2	10.6
Mel Davis (from NY)	F	6'7	225	26	34	752	127	354	36	42	60	70	193	47	85	0	296	22	5.7	1.4	2.5	8.7
Bob Love (from Chi, to Sea)	F	6'8	215	34	13	228	49	106	46	33	39	85	38	4	23	0	131	18	2.9	0.3	1.8	10.1
Mel Daniels	C	6'9	225	32	11	126	13	35	37	13	23	57	34	6	29	0	39	11	3.1	0.5	2.6	3.5
Larry McNeil (to GS)	F	6'9	200	25	8	93	18	51	35	24	30	80	26	3	13	1	60	12	3.3	0.4	1.6	7.5
Rudy Hackett (to Ind)	F	6'9	215	27	1	8	0	2	0	2	5	40	3	0	1	0	2	8	3.0	0.0	1.0	2.0
Earl Williams	C	6'7	230	25	1	7	0	2	0	3	6	50	2	1	2	0	3	7	2.0	1.0	2.0	3.0
CENTRAL DIVISION																						
HOUSTON ROCKETS	**49-33 .598**				**TOM NISSALKE**																	
John Johnson	F	6'7	200	29	79	1738	319	696	46	94	132	71	266	163	199	1	732	22	3.4	2.1	2.5	9.3
Rudy Tomjanovich	F	6'8	220	28	81	3130	733	1437	51	287	342	84	684	172	198	1	1753	39	8.4	2.1	2.4	21.6
Moses Malone (from Buf)	C-F	6'10	215	21	80	2500	389	810	48	305	440	69	1071	89	274	3	1083	31	13.4	1.1	3.4	13.5
John Lucas	G	6'3	175	23	82	2531	388	814	48	135	171	79	219	463	174	0	911	31	2.7	5.6	2.1	11.1
Cal Murphy	G	5'9	165	28	82	2764	596	1216	49	272	307	89	172	386	281	6	1464	34	2.1	4.7	3.4	17.9
Mike Newlin	G-F	6'4	205	27	82	2119	387	850	46	269	304	88	204	320	226	2	1043	26	2.5	3.9	2.8	12.7
Kevin Kunnert	C-F	7'	232	25	81	2050	333	685	49	93	126	74	669	154	361	17	759	25	8.3	1.9	4.5	9.4
Dwight Jones	F-C	6'10	220	24	74	1239	167	338	49	101	126	80	284	48	175	1	435	17	3.8	0.6	2.4	5.9
Ed Ratleff (back injury)	G-F	6'6	195	26	37	533	70	161	43	26	42	62	77	43	45	0	166	14	2.1	1.2	1.2	4.5
Tom Owens	F	6'10	225	27	46	462	68	135	50	52	76	68	142	18	96	2	188	10	3.1	0.4	2.1	4.1
Rudy White	G	6'2	195	23	46	368	47	106	44	15	25	60	41	35	39	0	109	8	0.9	0.8	0.8	2.4
Goo Kennedy	F	6'6	205	27	32	277	31	58	53	3	8	38	51	6	45	1	65	9	1.6	0.2	1.4	2.0
Dave Wohl (to NYN)	G	6'2	185	27	14	62	7	17	41	4	4	100	5	15	18	1	18	4	0.4	1.1	1.3	1.3
Phil Hicks (to Chi)	F	6'7	205	23	2	7	0	2	0	0	0	—	1	1	1	0	0	4	0.5	0.5	0.5	0.0
WASHINGTON BULLETS	**48-34 .585**				**DICK MOTTA**																	
Kevin Grevey	F	6'5	210	23	76	1306	224	530	42	79	119	66	178	68	148	1	527	17	2.3	0.9	1.9	6.9
Elvin Hayes	F-C	6'9	235	31	82	3364	760	1516	50	422	614	69	1029	158	312	1	1942	41	12.5	1.9	3.8	23.7
Wes Unseld	C	6'7	250	30	82	2860	270	551	49	100	166	60	877	363	253	5	640	35	10.7	4.4	3.1	7.8
Phl Chenier	G	6'3	180	26	78	2842	654	1472	44	270	321	84	299	294	166	0	1578	36	3.8	3.8	2.1	20.2
Tom Henderson (from Atl)	G	6'3	190	24	41	1223	175	373	47	107	145	74	115	212	74	0	457	30	2.8	5.2	1.8	11.1
Dave Bing	G	6'3	190	33	64	1516	271	597	45	136	176	77	143	275	150	1	678	24	2.2	4.3	2.3	10.6
Mitch Kupchak	C-F	6'9	230	22	82	1513	341	596	57	170	246	69	494	62	204	3	852	18	6.0	0.8	2.5	10.4
Larry Wright	G	6'1	175	22	78	1421	262	595	44	88	115	77	98	232	170	0	612	18	1.3	3.0	2.2	7.8
Truck Robinson (to Atl)	F	6'7	225	25	41	1328	264	552	48	128	189	68	366	45	123	0	656	32	8.9	1.1	3.0	16.0
Leonard Gray (from Sea)	F	6'8	250	25	58	996	144	330	44	59	80	74	186	69	189	8	347	17	3.2	1.2	3.3	6.0
Bob Weiss	G	6'2	185	34	62	768	62	133	47	29	37	78	69	130	66	0	153	12	1.1	2.1	1.1	2.5
Mike Riordan	F	6'4	200	31	49	289	34	94	36	11	15	73	27	20	33	0	79	6	0.6	0.4	0.7	1.6
Nick Weatherspoon (to Sea)	F	6'7	205	26	11	152	27	76	36	5	8	63	24	2	19	0	59	14	2.2	0.2	1.7	5.4
Joe Pace	C	6'10	220	23	30	119	24	55	44	16	29	55	34	4	29	0	64	4	1.1	0.1	1.0	2.1
Jimmy Jones (knee injury)	G	6'4	188	31	3	33	2	9	22	2	4	50	4	1	4	0	6	11	1.3	0.3	1.3	2.0
SAN ANTONIO SPURS	**44-38 .537**				**DOUG MOE**																	
Allan Bristow	F	6'7	220	25	82	2017	365	747	49	206	258	80	348	240	195	1	936	25	4.2	2.9	2.4	11.4
Larry Kenon	F	6'9	215	24	78	2936	706	1435	49	293	356	82	879	229	190	0	1705	38	11.3	2.9	2.4	21.9
Billy Paultz	C	6'11	250	28	82	2694	521	1102	47	238	320	74	687	223	262	5	1280	33	8.4	2.7	3.2	15.6
George Gervin	G-F	6'7	185	24	82	2705	726	1335	54	443	532	83	454	238	286	12	1895	33	5.5	2.9	3.5	23.1
Mike Gale	G	6'4	190	26	82	2598	353	754	47	137	167	82	273	473	224	3	843	32	3.3	5.8	2.7	10.3
Mark Olberding	F	6'8	230	20	82	1949	301	598	50	251	316	79	449	119	277	6	853	24	5.5	1.5	3.4	10.4
Coby Deitrick	C-F	6'10	230	28	82	1772	285	620	46	119	166	72	372	148	267	8	689	22	4.5	1.8	3.3	8.4
Louie Dampier	G	6'	180	32	80	1634	233	507	46	64	86	74	76	234	93	0	530	20	1.0	2.9	1.2	6.6
Mack Calvin (from LA to Den)	G	6'	175	28	35	606	93	237	39	123	146	84	31	104	58	0	309	17	0.9	3.0	1.7	8.8
James Silas (knee injury)	G	6'3	185	27	22	356	61	142	43	87	107	81	32	50	36	0	209	16	1.5	2.3	1.6	9.5
George Karl (knee injury)	G	6'2	190	25	29	251	25	73	34	29	42	69	17	46	36	0	79	9	0.6	1.6	1.2	2.7
Henry Ward	G	6'4	195	24	27	171	34	90	38	15	17	88	33	6	30	0	83	6	1.2	0.2	1.1	3.1
Louie Nelson	G	6'3	190	25	4	57	7	14	50	4	7	57	7	3	9	0	18	14	1.8	0.8	2.3	4.5
Mike D'Antoni (foot injury)	G	6'3	190	25	2	9	1	3	33	1	2	50	2	2	3	0	3	5	1.0	1.0	1.5	1.5

1976/77 N.B.A. — EASTERN CONFERNECE (continued)
CENTRAL DIVISION (continued)

Use Name	Pos	Hgt	Wgt	Age	TOTAL													PER GAME				
					G	Min	FG	FGA	%	FT	FTA	%	Reb	Ass	PF	DQ	Points	Min	Reb	Ass	PF	Points
CLEVELAND CAVALIERS	**43-39 .524**				**BILL FITCH**																	
Campy Russell (ankle injury)	F	6'8	215	24	70	2109	435	1003	43	288	370	78	419	189	196	3	1158	30	6.0	2.7	2.8	16.5
Jim Brewer	F	6'9	230	25	81	2672	296	657	45	97	178	54	762	195	214	3	689	33	9.4	2.4	2.6	8.5
Jim Chones	C-F	6'11	220	27	82	2378	450	972	46	155	212	73	688	104	258	3	1055	29	8.4	1.3	3.1	12.9
Austin Carr	G	6'4	200	28	82	2409	558	1221	46	213	268	79	240	220	221	3	1329	29	2.9	2.7	2.7	16.2
Jim Cleamons (groin injury)	G	6'3	185	27	60	2045	257	592	43	112	148	76	273	308	126	0	626	34	4.6	5.1	2.1	10.4
Bobby Smith	F-G	6'5	210	30	81	2135	513	1149	45	148	181	82	317	152	211	3	1174	26	3.9	1.9	2.6	14.5
Dick Snyder	G-F	6'5	213	32	82	1685	316	693	46	127	149	85	149	160	177	2	759	21	1.8	2.0	2.2	9.3
Foots Walker (knee injury)	G	6'1	172	25	62	1216	157	349	45	89	115	77	160	254	124	1	403	20	2.6	4.1	2.0	6.5
Nate Thurmond (knee injury)	C	6'11	235	35	49	997	100	246	41	68	106	64	374	83	128	2	268	20	7.6	1.7	2.6	5.5
Elmore Smith (from Mil)	C	7'	250	27	36	675	128	254	50	56	108	52	231	13	98	2	312	19	6.4	0.4	2.7	8.7
Gary Brokaw (from Mil)	G	6'4	180	22	39	596	112	240	47	58	82	71	59	117	79	2	282	15	1.5	3.0	2.0	7.2
John Lambert	F	6'10	225	23	63	555	67	157	43	25	36	69	154	31	75	0	159	9	2.4	0.5	1.2	2.5
Rowland Garrett (to Mil)	F	6'6	215	26	29	215	40	93	43	18	22	82	40	7	30	0	98	7	1.4	0.2	1.0	3.4
Chuckie Williams (ankle injury)	G	6'3	180	23	22	65	14	47	30	9	12	75	4	7	7	0	37	3	0.2	0.3	0.3	1.7
Mo Howard (to NO)	G	6'3	170	22	9	28	8	15	53	5	6	83	5	5	7	0	21	3	0.6	0.6	0.8	2.3
Luke Wittle - broken ankle																						
NEW ORLEANS JAZZ	**35-47 .457**				**BILL VAN BREDA KOLFF**																	
Nate Williams	F-G	6'5	225	26	79	1776	414	917	45	146	194	75	306	92	200	0	974	22	3.9	1.2	2.5	12.3
E. C. Coleman	F	6'8	225	26	77	2369	290	628	46	82	112	73	548	103	280	9	662	31	7.1	1.3	3.6	8.6
Otto Moore	C	6'11	230	30	81	2084	193	477	40	91	134	68	636	181	231	3	477	26	7.9	2.2	2.9	5.9
Pete Maravich	G	6'5	200	28	73	3041	886	**2047**	43	**501**	600	84	374	392	191	1	**2273**	**42**	5.1	5.4	2.6	**31.1**
Gail Goodrich (leg injury)	G	6'1	175	33	27	609	136	305	45	68	85	80	61	74	43	0	340	23	2.3	2.7	1.6	12.6
Jim McElroy	G	6'3	190	23	73	2029	301	640	47	169	217	78	183	260	119	3	771	28	2.5	3.6	1.6	10.6
Paul Griffin	F-C	6'9	205	22	81	1645	140	256	55	145	201	72	495	167	241	6	425	20	6.1	2.1	3.0	5.2
Rich Kelley	C	7'	240	23	76	1505	184	386	48	156	197	79	587	208	244	7	524	20	7.7	2.7	3.2	6.9
Freddie Boyd (knee injury)	G	6'2	180	26	47	1212	194	406	48	79	98	81	90	147	78	0	467	26	1.9	3.1	1.7	9.9
Ron Behagen	F-C	6'9	225	25	60	1170	213	509	42	90	126	71	431	83	166	1	516	20	7.2	1.4	2.8	8.6
Aaron James (leg injury)	F	6'8	215	24	52	1059	238	486	49	89	114	78	186	55	127	1	565	20	3.6	1.1	2.4	10.9
Bud Stallworth (ankle injury)	F	6'5	190	26	40	526	126	272	46	17	29	59	71	23	76	1	269	13	1.8	0.6	1.9	6.7
Andy Walker	G	6'4	190	21	40	438	72	156	46	36	47	77	75	32	59	0	180	11	1.9	0.8	1.5	4.5
Mo Howard (from Cle)	G	6'3	170	22	23	317	56	117	48	19	29	66	34	37	44	0	131	14	1.5	1.6	1.9	5.7
ATLANTA HAWKS	**31-51 .378**				**HUBIE BROWN**																	
John Drew (knee injury)	F	6'6	205	22	74	2688	689	1416	49	412	577	71	675	133	275	9	1790	36	9.1	1.8	3.7	24.2
Truck Robinson (from Was)	F	6'7	225	25	36	1449	310	648	48	186	241	77	462	97	130	3	806	40	12.8	2.7	3.6	22.4
Joe Merriweather	C-F	6'10	218	23	74	2068	319	607	53	182	255	71	596	82	324	**21**	820	28	8.1	1.1	4.4	11.1
Lou Hudson (back injury)	G-F	6'5	215	32	58	1745	413	905	46	142	169	84	129	155	160	2	968	30	2.2	2.7	2.8	16.7
Ken Charles	G	6'3	180	25	82	2487	354	855	41	205	256	80	168	295	240	4	913	30	2.0	3.6	2.9	11.1
Armond Hill	G	6'4	190	23	81	1825	175	439	40	139	174	80	143	403	245	8	489	23	1.8	5.0	3.0	6.0
Tom Henderson (to Was)	G	6'3	190	24	46	1568	196	453	43	126	168	75	124	386	74	0	518	34	2.7	8.4	1.6	11.3
John Brown	F	6'7	220	25	77	1405	160	350	46	121	150	81	236	103	217	7	441	18	3.1	1.3	2.8	5.7
Tom Barker	C	6'11	230	21	59	1354	182	436	42	112	164	68	401	60	223	11	476	23	6.8	1.0	3.8	8.1
Steve Hawes (leg injury)	F	6'9	220	26	44	945	147	305	48	67	88	76	261	63	141	4	361	21	5.9	1.4	3.2	8.2
Randy Denton	C	6'10	245	27	45	700	103	256	40	33	47	70	218	33	100	1	239	16	4.8	0.7	2.2	5.3
Mike Sojourner (injury)	C	6'9	225	23	51	551	95	203	47	41	57	72	146	21	66	0	231	11	2.9	0.4	1.3	4.5
Bill Willoughby	F	6'8	205	19	39	549	75	169	44	43	63	68	170	13	64	1	193	14	4.4	0.3	1.6	4.9
Claude Terry (injury - from Buf)	G	6'4	195	26	12	241	47	87	54	18	21	86	18	25	21	0	112	20	1.5	2.1	1.8	9.3
Ron Davis	G	6'6	198	22	7	67	8	35	23	4	13	31	7	2	9	0	20	10	1.0	0.3	1.3	2.9
Henry Dickerson	G	6'4	190	25	6	63	6	12	50	5	8	63	2	11	13	0	17	11	0.3	1.8	2.2	2.8
Geoff Petrie - knee injury																						

WESTERN CONFERENCE
MIDWEST DIVISION

Use Name	Pos	Hgt	Wgt	Age	G	Min	FG	FGA	%	FT	FTA	%	Reb	Ass	PF	DQ	Points	Min	Reb	Ass	PF	Points
DENVER NUGGETS	**50-32 .610**				**LARRY BROWN**																	
Bobby Jones	F	6'9	215	25	82	2419	501	879	57	236	329	72	678	264	238	3	1238	30	8.3	3.2	2.9	15.1
Paul Silas	F	6'7	225	33	81	1959	206	572	36	170	255	67	606	132	183	0	582	24	7.5	1.6	2.3	7.2
Dan Issel	C	6'9	240	28	79	2507	660	1282	51	445	558	80	696	177	246	7	1765	32	8.8	2.2	3.1	22.3
David Thompson	G-F	6'4	195	22	82	3001	824	1626	51	477	**623**	77	334	337	236	1	2125	37	4.1	4.1	2.9	25.9
Ted McClain	G	6'3	180	29	72	2002	245	551	44	99	133	74	229	324	255	9	589	28	3.2	4.5	3.5	8.2
Fatty Taylor	G	6'	175	30	79	1548	132	314	42	37	65	57	211	288	202	0	301	20	2.7	3.6	2.6	3.8
Willie Wise	F	6'6	215	29	75	1403	237	513	46	142	218	65	253	142	180	2	616	19	3.4	1.9	2.4	8.2
Jim Price (from Mil & Buf)	G	6'3	195	27	55	1384	188	422	45	59	74	80	184	208	181	3	435	25	3.3	3.8	3.3	7.9
Marvin Webster	C	7'1	225	24	80	1276	198	400	50	143	220	65	484	62	149	2	539	16	6.1	0.8	1.9	6.7
Mack Calvin (from LA & SA)	G	6'	175	28	29	625	100	225	44	123	144	85	49	115	53	0	323	22	1.7	4.0	1.8	11.1
Byron Beck (knee injury)	F-C	6'9	230	31	53	480	107	246	43	36	44	82	96	33	59	1	250	9	1.8	0.6	1.1	4.7
Gus Gerard (to Buf)	F	6'8	205	23	24	456	101	210	48	38	56	68	100	49	73	1	240	19	4.2	2.0	2.8	10.0
Monte Towe	G	5'7	150	23	51	409	56	138	41	18	25	72	34	87	61	0	130	8	0.7	1.7	1.2	2.5
Chuck Williams (to Buf)	G	6'2	185	30	21	311	35	93	38	30	39	77	34	44	26	0	100	15	1.6	2.1	1.2	4.8

Use Name	Pos	Hgt	Wgt	Age	TOTAL G	Min	FG	FGA	%	FT	FTA	%	Reb	Ass	PF	DQ	Points	PER GAME Min	Reb	Ass	PF	Points

1976/77 N.B.A. — WESTERN CONFERENCE (continued)
MIDWEST DIVISION (continued)

Use Name	Pos	Hgt	Wgt	Age	G	Min	FG	FGA	%	FT	FTA	%	Reb	Ass	PF	DQ	Points	Min	Reb	Ass	PF	Points
DETROIT PISTONS	**44-38 .537**				**HERB BROWN**																	
M. L. Carr	F	6'6	205	25	82	2643	443	931	48	205	279	73	631	181	287	8	1091	32	7.7	2.2	3.5	13.3
Howard Porter	F	6'8	220	28	78	2200	465	962	48	103	120	86	458	53	202	0	1033	28	5.9	0.7	2.6	13.2
Bob Lanier (broken hand)	C	6'11	255	28	64	2446	678	1269	53	260	318	82	745	214	174	0	1616	38	11.6	3.3	2.7	25.3
Chris Ford	G	6'5	190	27	82	2539	437	918	48	131	170	77	270	337	192	1	1005	31	3.3	4.1	2.3	12.3
Kevin Porter	G	6'	175	26	81	2117	310	605	51	97	133	73	98	592	271	8	717	26	1.2	7.3	3.3	8.9
Leon Douglas	C-F	6'10	230	22	82	1626	245	512	48	127	229	55	526	68	294	10	617	20	6.4	0.8	3.6	7.5
Ralph Simpson	G	6'5	200	27	77	1597	356	834	43	138	195	71	181	180	100	0	850	21	2.4	2.3	1.3	11.0
Eric Money	G	6'	170	21	73	1586	329	631	52	90	114	79	124	243	199	3	748	22	1.7	3.3	2.7	10.2
Al Eberhard	F	6'6	225	24	68	1219	181	380	48	109	138	79	221	50	197	4	471	18	3.3	0.7	2.9	6.9
Marvin Barnes (ankle injury)	F-C	6'9	225	24	53	989	202	452	45	106	156	68	253	45	139	1	510	19	4.8	0.8	2.6	9.6
Phil Sellers	F-G	6'5	200	23	44	329	73	190	38	52	72	72	41	25	56	0	198	7	0.9	0.6	1.3	4.5
Roger Brown	C	7'	230	26	43	322	21	56	38	18	26	69	90	12	68	4	60	7	2.1	0.3	1.6	1.4
George Trapp	F-C	6'8	220	28	6	68	15	29	52	3	4	75	10	3	13	0	33	11	1.7	0.5	2.2	5.5
Cornelius Cash	F	6'8	220	24	6	49	9	23	39	3	6	50	16	1	8	0	21	8	2.7	0.2	1.3	3.5
John Mengelt - neck injury - to Chi																						
CHICAGO BULLS	**44-38 .537**				**ED BADGER**																	
Scott May (mononucleosis)	F	6'7	220	22	72	2369	431	955	45	188	227	83	437	145	185	2	1050	33	6.1	2.0	2.6	14.6
Mickey Johnson	F	6'10	190	24	81	2847	538	1205	45	324	407	80	828	195	315	10	1400	35	10.2	2.4	3.9	17.3
Artis Gilmore	C	7'2	240	27	82	2877	570	1091	52	387	586	66	1070	199	266	4	1527	35	13.0	2.4	3.2	18.6
Wilbur Holland	G	6'	175	25	79	2453	509	1120	45	158	192	82	253	253	201	3	1176	31	3.2	3.2	2.5	14.9
Norm Van Lier	G	6'1	175	29	82	3097	300	729	41	238	306	78	370	636	268	3	838	38	4.5	7.8	3.3	10.2
John Mengelt (from Det)	G	6'2	195	27	61	1178	209	458	46	89	113	79	110	114	102	2	507	19	1.8	1.9	1.7	8.3
Tom Boerwinkle	C	7'	260	31	82	1070	134	273	49	34	63	54	312	189	147	0	302	13	3.8	2.3	1.8	3.7
Cliff Pondexter	F	6'9	230	22	78	996	107	257	42	42	65	65	236	41	82	0	256	13	3.0	0.5	1.1	3.3
Jack Marin (mononucleosis)	F	6'7	210	32	54	869	167	359	47	31	39	79	91	62	85	0	365	16	1.7	1.1	1.6	6.8
John Laskowski	G	6'6	185	23	47	562	75	212	35	27	30	90	63	44	22	0	177	12	1.3	0.9	0.5	3.8
Bob Love (to NYN & Sea)	F	6'8	215	34	14	496	68	201	34	35	46	76	73	23	47	1	171	35	5.2	1.6	3.4	12.2
Tom Kropp	G	6'3	205	23	53	480	73	152	48	28	41	68	47	39	77	1	174	9	0.9	0.7	1.5	3.3
Phil Hicks (from Hou)	F	6'7	205	23	35	255	41	87	47	11	13	85	65	23	36	0	93	7	1.9	0.7	1.0	2.7
Paul McCracken	G	6'4	180	26	9	119	18	47	38	11	18	61	16	14	17	0	47	13	1.8	1.6	1.9	5.2
Keith Starr (knee injury)	G-F	6'6	200	22	17	65	6	24	25	2	2	100	10	6	11	0	14	4	0.6	0.4	0.6	0.8
Eric Fernsten	F	6'10	210	23	5	61	3	15	20	8	11	73	16	6	9	0	14	12	3.2	1.2	1.8	2.8
Willie Smith	G	6'2	170	23	2	11	0	1	0	0	0	—	0	0	1	0	0	6	0.0	0.0	0.5	0.0
Leon Renbow - back injury																						
KANSAS CITY KINGS	**40-42 .488**				**PHIL JOHNSON**																	
Scott Wedman	F-G	6'7	215	24	81	2743	521	1133	46	206	241	85	506	227	226	3	1248	34	6.2	2.8	2.8	15.4
Richard Washington	F	6'11	225	21	82	2265	446	1034	43	177	254	70	698	85	324	13	1069	28	8.5	1.0	4.0	13.0
Sam Lacey	C	6'10	235	28	82	2595	327	774	42	215	282	76	734	386	292	9	869	32	9.0	4.7	3.6	10.6
Ron Boone	G	6'2	200	30	82	3021	747	1577	47	324	384	84	321	338	258	1	1818	37	3.9	4.1	3.1	22.2
Brian Taylor	G	6'2	185	25	72	2488	501	995	50	225	275	82	238	320	206	1	1227	35	3.3	4.4	2.9	17.0
Bill Robinzine	F	6'7	230	23	75	1594	307	677	45	159	216	74	474	95	283	7	773	21	6.3	1.3	3.8	10.3
Ollie Johnson	F	6'6	200	27	81	1386	218	446	49	101	115	88	212	105	169	1	537	17	2.6	1.3	2.1	6.6
Jim Eakins	C	6'11	215	30	82	1338	151	336	45	188	222	85	361	119	195	1	490	16	4.4	1.5	2.4	6.0
Mike Barr	G	6'3	180	26	73	1224	122	279	44	41	57	72	130	175	96	0	285	17	1.8	2.4	1.3	3.9
Andre McCarter	G	6'3	190	23	59	725	119	257	46	32	45	71	55	99	63	0	270	12	0.9	1.7	1.1	4.6
Glenn Hansen	G	6'5	205	24	41	289	67	155	43	23	32	72	59	25	44	0	157	7	1.4	0.6	1.1	3.8
Bob Bigelow	F-G	6'7	215	23	29	162	35	70	50	15	17	88	27	8	17	0	85	6	0.9	0.3	0.6	2.9
INDIANA PACERS	**36-46 .439**				**BOB LEONARD**																	
Wil Jones	F	6'8	205	29	80	2709	438	1019	43	166	223	74	604	189	305	10	1042	34	7.6	2.4	3.8	13.0
Darnell Hillman	F-C	6'8	215	27	82	2302	359	811	44	161	244	66	693	166	353	15	879	28	8.5	2.0	4.3	10.7
Dan Roundfield (back injury)	C	6'9	210	23	61	1645	342	734	47	164	239	69	518	69	243	8	848	27	8.5	1.1	4.0	13.9
Billy Knight	G-F	6'6	200	24	78	3117	831	1687	49	413	506	82	582	260	197	0	2075	40	7.5	3.3	2.5	26.6
Don Buse	G	6'4	195	26	81	2947	266	639	42	114	145	79	270	**685**	129	0	646	36	3.3	**8.5**	1.6	8.0
Dave Robisch	C	6'10	240	27	80	1966	369	811	45	213	256	83	554	158	169	1	951	25	6.9	2.0	2.1	11.9
Mike Flynn	G	6'2	190	23	73	1324	250	573	44	101	142	71	187	179	106	0	601	18	2.6	2.5	1.5	8.2
John Williamson (from NYN)	G	6'2	185	24	30	1055	261	544	48	98	125	78	74	111	103	1	620	35	2.5	3.7	3.4	20.7
Steve Green	F	6'7	220	23	70	918	183	424	43	84	113	74	177	46	157	2	450	13	2.5	0.7	2.2	6.4
Mel Bennett	F	6'7	200	21	67	911	101	294	34	112	187	60	237	70	155	0	314	14	3.5	1.0	2.3	4.7
Freddie Lewis	G	6'	180	33	32	552	81	199	41	62	77	81	47	56	58	0	224	17	1.5	1.8	1.8	7.0
Jerome Anderson	G	6'5	195	23	27	164	26	59	44	14	20	70	12	10	26	0	66	6	0.4	0.4	1.0	2.4
Len Elmore (knee injury)	C	6'9	230	24	6	46	7	17	41	4	5	80	15	2	11	0	18	8	2.5	0.3	1.8	3.0
Darrell Elston (leg injury)	G	6'4	205	24	5	40	2	14	14	1	2	50	6	2	6	0	5	8	1.2	0.4	1.2	1.0
Rudy Hackett (from NYN)	F	6'9	215	27	5	38	3	8	38	6	9	67	10	3	7	0	12	8	2.0	0.6	1.4	2.4
Clyde Mayes (to Buf & Port)	F	6'9	225	23	2	21	3	7	43	1	4	25	7	3	5	0	7	11	3.5	1.5	2.5	3.5
Kevin Joyce - cracked kneecap Billy Keller - knee injury																						

Use Name	Pos	Hgt	Wgt	Age	TOTAL G	Min	FG	FGA	%	FT	FTA	%	Reb	Ass	PF	DQ	Points	PER GAME Min	Reb	Ass	PF	Points

1976/77 N.B.A. — WESTERN CONFERENCE (Continued)
MIDWEST DIVISION (continued)

Use Name	Pos	Hgt	Wgt	Age	G	Min	FG	FGA	%	FT	FTA	%	Reb	Ass	PF	DQ	Points	Min	Reb	Ass	PF	Points
MILWAUKEE BUCKS	30-52 .366				LARRY COSTELLO (3-15 .167), DON NELSON (27-37 .422)																	
Bob Dandridge	F	6'6	195	29	70	2501	585	1253	47	283	367	77	440	268	222	1	1453	36	6.3	3.8	3.2	20.8
Dave Meyers (knee injury)	F-C	6'9	225	23	50	1262	179	383	47	127	192	66	341	86	152	4	485	25	6.8	1.7	3.0	9.7
Sven Nater	C	6'11	250	26	72	1960	383	725	53	172	228	75	865	108	214	6	938	27	12.0	1.5	3.0	13.0
Brian Winters	G	6'4	185	24	78	2717	652	1308	50	205	242	85	231	337	228	1	1509	35	3.0	4.3	2.9	19.3
Quinn Buckner	G	6'3	205	22	79	2095	299	689	43	83	154	54	264	372	291	5	681	27	3.3	4.7	3.7	8.6
Junior Bridgeman	F-G	6'5	210	23	82	2410	491	1094	45	197	228	86	416	205	221	3	1179	29	5.1	2.5	2.7	14.4
Kevin Restani (injury)	F-C	6'9	225	25	64	1116	173	334	52	12	24	50	262	88	102	0	358	17	4.1	1.4	1.6	5.6
Scott Lloyd	C-F	6'10	230	24	69	1025	153	324	47	95	126	75	210	33	158	5	401	15	3.0	0.5	2.3	5.8
Gary Brokaw (to Cle)	G	6'4	180	22	41	891	130	324	40	105	137	77	64	111	85	0	365	22	1.6	2.7	2.1	8.9
Fred Carter (from Phi)	G	6'3	185	31	47	875	166	399	42	58	77	75	93	104	96	0	390	19	2.0	2.2	2.0	8.3
Elmore Smith (to Cle)	C	7'	250	27	34	789	113	253	45	61	105	58	208	30	109	2	287	23	6.1	0.9	3.2	8.4
Lloyd Walton (bronchitis)	G	6'	160	23	53	678	88	188	47	53	65	82	51	141	52	0	229	13	1.0	2.7	1.0	4.3
Alex English	F	6'8	195	22	60	648	132	277	48	46	60	77	168	25	78	0	310	11	2.8	0.4	1.3	5.2
Rowland Garrett (from Cle)	F	6'6	215	26	33	383	66	146	45	23	29	79	72	20	50	0	155	12	2.2	0.6	1.5	4.7
Mickey Davis	F	6'7	208	26	19	165	29	68	43	23	25	92	29	20	11	0	81	9	1.5	1.1	0.6	4.3
Jim Price (to Buf & Den)	G	6'3	195	27	6	111	21	41	51	7	9	78	13	15	14	0	49	19	2.2	2.5	2.3	8.2
Glenn McDonald	F-G	6'6	190	24	9	79	8	34	24	3	4	75	12	7	11	0	19	9	1.3	0.8	1.2	2.1

PACIFIC DIVISION

Use Name	Pos	Hgt	Wgt	Age	G	Min	FG	FGA	%	FT	FTA	%	Reb	Ass	PF	DQ	Points	Min	Reb	Ass	PF	Points
LOS ANGELES LAKERS	53-29 .646				JERRY WEST																	
Cazzie Russell	F	6'5	220	32	82	2583	578	1179	49	188	219	86	294	210	163	1	1344	32	3.6	2.6	2.0	16.4
Don Ford	F	6'9	215	24	82	1782	262	570	46	73	102	72	353	133	170	1	597	22	4.3	1.6	2.1	7.3
Kareem Abdul-Jabbar	C	7'2	240	29	82	3016	**888**	1533	**58**	376	536	70	**1090**	319	262	4	2152	37	13.3	3.9	3.2	26.2
Don Chaney	G	6'5	210	30	81	2408	213	522	41	70	94	74	330	308	224	4	496	30	4.1	3.8	2.8	6.1
Lucius Allen	G	6'2	175	29	78	2482	472	1035	46	195	252	77	251	405	183	0	1139	32	3.2	5.2	2.3	14.6
Tom Abernathy	F	6'7	220	22	70	1378	169	349	48	101	134	75	291	98	118	1	439	20	4.2	1.4	1.7	6.3
Kermit Washington (knee injury)	F-C	6'8	230	25	53	1342	191	380	50	132	187	71	492	48	183	1	514	25	9.3	0.9	3.5	9.7
Earl Tatum	G-F	6'5	185	23	68	1249	283	607	47	72	100	72	236	118	168	1	638	18	3.5	1.7	2.5	9.4
Bo Lammar	G	6'1	180	25	71	1165	228	561	41	46	68	68	92	177	73	0	502	16	1.3	2.5	1.0	7.1
C. J. Kupec	C	6'8	220	23	82	908	153	342	45	78	101	77	199	53	113	0	384	11	2.4	0.6	1.4	4.7
Johnny Neumann (from Buf)	G	6'6	210	25	59	888	146	363	40	54	81	67	63	137	127	2	346	15	1.1	2.3	2.2	5.9
Marv Roberts	F	6'8	205	26	28	209	27	76	36	4	6	67	25	19	34	0	58	7	0.9	0.7	1.2	2.1
Mack Calvin (to SA &Den)	G	6'	175	28	12	207	27	82	33	41	48	85	16	21	16	0	95	17	1.3	1.8	1.3	7.9
Cornell Warner	F	6'9	220	28	14	170	25	53	47	4	6	67	69	11	28	0	54	12	4.9	0.8	2.0	3.9
Allen Murphy	G	6'5	190	24	2	18	1	5	20	3	7	43	4	0	5	0	5	9	2.0	0.0	2.5	2.5
Stu Lantz - back injury																						
PORTLAND TRAIL BLAZERS	49-33 .598				JACK RAMSAY																	
Bob Gross	F	6'6	200	23	82	2232	376	711	53	183	215	85	394	242	255	7	935	27	4.8	3.0	3.1	11.4
Maurice Lucas	F-C	6'9	225	24	79	2863	632	1357	47	335	438	76	899	229	294	6	1599	36	11.4	2.9	3.7	20.2
Bill Walton (ankle injury)	C	6'11	235	24	65	2264	491	930	53	228	327	70	934	245	174	5	1210	35	**14.4**	3.8	2.7	18.6
Lionel Hollins	G	6'3	185	23	76	2224	452	1046	43	215	287	75	210	313	265	5	1119	29	2.8	4.1	3.5	14.7
Dave Twardzik	G	6'1	180	26	74	1937	263	430	61	239	284	84	202	247	228	6	765	26	2.7	3.3	3.1	10.3
Larry Steele	F-G	6'5	190	27	81	1680	326	652	50	183	227	81	188	172	216	3	835	21	2.3	2.1	2.7	10.3
Herm Gilliam	G	6'3	190	30	80	1665	326	744	44	92	120	77	201	170	168	1	744	21	2.5	2.1	2.1	9.3
Johnny Davis	G	6'2	170	21	79	1451	234	531	44	166	209	79	126	148	128	1	634	18	1.6	1.9	1.6	8.0
Robin Jones	C	6'9	225	22	63	1065	139	299	46	66	109	61	296	80	124	3	344	17	4.7	1.3	2.0	5.5
Lloyd Neal (knee injury)	F-C	6'7	225	26	58	955	160	340	47	77	114	68	255	58	148	0	397	16	4.4	1.0	2.6	6.8
Corky Calhoun	F	6'7	215	26	70	743	85	183	46	66	85	78	144	35	123	1	236	11	2.1	0.5	1.8	3.4
Wally Walker	F	6'7	200	22	66	627	137	305	45	67	100	67	108	51	92	0	341	10	1.6	0.8	1.4	5.2
Clyde Mayers (from Ind &Buf)	F	6'9	225	23	5	24	2	9	22	0	0	—	6	0	5	0	4	5	1.2	0.0	1.0	0.8
GOLDEN STATE WARRIORS	43-36 .561				AL ATTLES																	
Rick Barry	F	6'7	220	32	79	2904	682	1551	44	359	392	92	422	475	194	2	1723	37	5.3	6.0	2.5	21.8
Jamaal Wilkes	F	6'6	190	23	76	2579	548	1147	48	247	310	80	578	211	222	1	1343	34	7.6	2.8	2.9	17.7
Cliff Ray	C-F	6'9	235	27	77	2018	263	450	58	105	199	53	615	112	242	5	631	26	8.0	1.5	3.1	8.2
Phil Smith	G	6'4	187	24	82	2880	631	1318	48	295	376	78	332	328	227	0	1557	35	4.0	4.0	2.8	19.0
Gus Williams	G	6'2	175	23	82	1930	325	701	46	112	150	75	233	292	218	4	762	24	2.8	3.6	2.7	9.3
Charles Dudley	G	6'2	186	26	79	1682	220	421	52	129	203	64	296	347	169	0	569	21	3.7	4.4	2.1	7.2
Robert Parish	C	7'	230	23	77	1384	288	573	50	121	171	71	543	74	224	7	697	18	7.1	1.0	2.9	9.1
Charlie Johnson	G	6'	170	27	79	1196	255	583	44	49	69	71	141	91	134	1	559	15	1.8	1.2	1.7	7.1
Sonny Parker	F	6'6	200	21	65	889	154	292	53	71	92	77	173	59	77	0	379	14	2.7	0.9	1.2	5.8
Derrek Dickey (broken ankle)	F	6'7	218	25	49	856	158	345	46	45	61	74	240	63	101	1	361	17	4.9	1.3	2.1	7.4
George Johnson (to Buf)	C	6'11	220	28	39	597	73	150	49	25	31	81	211	26	105	2	171	15	5.4	0.7	2.7	4.4
Dwight Davis (leg & knee injuries)	F	6'8	220	27	33	552	55	124	44	49	72	68	95	29	93	1	159	17	2.9	0.9	2.8	4.8
Marshall Rogers	G	6'1	190	23	26	176	43	116	37	14	15	93	11	10	33	0	100	7	0.4	0.4	1.3	3.8
Larry McNeil (from NYN)	F	6'9	200	25	16	137	29	61	48	28	31	90	49	3	19	0	86	9	3.1	0.2	1.2	5.4

1976/77 N.B.A. — WESTERN CONFERENCE (continued)
PACIFIC DIVISION (continued)

Use Name	Pos	Hgt	Wgt	Age	TOTAL G	Min	FG	FGA	%	FT	FTA	%	Reb	Ass	PF	DQ	Points	PER GAME Min	Reb	Ass	PF	Points
SEATTLE SUPERSONICS	**40-42 .488**				**BILL RUSSELL**																	
Nick Weatherspoon (from Was)	F	6'7	205	26	51	1505	283	614	46	86	136	63	404	51	149	1	652	30	7.9	1.0	2.9	12.8
Bruce Seals	F	6'9	215	32	81	1977	378	851	44	138	195	71	354	93	262	6	894	24	4.4	1.1	3.2	11.0
Mike Green	C	6'10	210	25	76	1928	290	658	44	166	235	71	503	120	201	1	746	25	6.6	1.6	2.6	9.8
Fred Brown	G	6'3	185	28	72	2098	534	1114	48	168	190	88	232	176	140	1	1236	29	3.2	2.4	1.9	17.2
Slick Watts	G	6'1	175	25	79	2627	428	1015	42	172	293	59	307	630	256	5	1028	33	3.9	8.0	3.2	13.0
Tom Burleson	C	7'3	235	24	82	1803	288	652	44	220	301	73	551	93	259	1	796	22	6.7	1.1	3.2	9.7
Dennis Johnson	G	6'4	185	22	81	1667	285	566	50	179	287	62	302	123	221	3	749	21	3.7	1.5	2.7	9.2
Willie Norwood	F	6'7	220	29	76	1647	216	461	47	151	206	73	292	99	191	1	583	22	3.8	1.3	2.5	7.7
Bob Wilkerson	G-F	6'7	200	22	78	1552	221	573	39	84	122	69	258	171	136	0	526	20	3.3	2.2	1.7	6.7
Mike Bantom (to NYN)	F-C	6'9	220	25	44	795	137	281	49	58	84	69	186	52	113	3	332	18	4.2	1.2	2.6	7.5
Leonard Gray (to Was)	F	6'8	250	25	25	643	114	262	44	59	78	76	107	55	84	1	287	26	4.3	2.2	3.4	11.5
Dean Tolson	F	6'8	200	25	60	587	137	242	57	85	159	53	157	27	83	0	359	10	2.6	0.5	1.4	6.0
Frank Oleynick	G	6'2	190	21	50	516	81	223	36	39	53	74	45	60	48	0	201	10	0.9	1.2	1.0	4.0
Bob Love (from Chi & NYN)	F	6'8	215	34	32	450	45	121	37	41	47	87	87	21	50	0	131	14	2.7	0.7	1.6	4.1
Norton Barnhill	G	6'4	205	23	4	10	2	6	33	0	0	—	3	1	5	0	4	3	0.8	0.3	1.3	1.0
PHOENIX SUNS	**34-48 .415**				**JOHN MACLEOD**																	
Curtis Perry (back injury)	F	6'7	220	28	44	1391	179	414	43	112	142	79	395	79	163	3	470	32	9.0	1.8	3.7	10.7
Gar Heard (leg injury)	F	6'6	220	28	46	1363	173	457	38	100	138	72	440	89	139	2	446	30	9.6	1.9	3.0	9.7
Alvan Adams (ankle injury)	C-F	6'9	215	22	72	2278	522	1102	47	252	334	75	652	322	260	4	1296	32	9.1	4.5	3.6	18.0
Paul Westphal	G	6'4	195	26	81	2600	682	1317	52	362	439	82	190	459	171	1	1726	32	2.3	5.7	2.1	21.3
Ricky Sobers	G	6'3	195	23	79	2005	414	834	50	243	289	84	234	238	258	3	1071	25	3.0	3.0	3.3	13.6
Ron Lee	G	6'4	200	24	82	1849	347	786	44	142	210	68	299	263	276	10	836	23	3.6	3.2	3.4	10.2
Dennis Awtrey	C	6'10	250	28	72	1760	160	373	43	91	126	72	356	182	170	1	411	24	4.9	2.5	2.4	5.7
Ira Terrell	F-C	6'8	195	22	78	1751	277	545	51	111	176	63	387	103	165	0	665	22	5.0	1.3	2.1	8.5
Dick Van Arsdale	G-F	6'5	210	33	78	1535	227	498	46	145	166	87	117	120	94	0	599	20	1.5	1.5	1.2	7.7
Tom Van Arsdale	F-G	6'5	210	33	77	1425	171	395	43	102	145	70	184	67	163	0	444	19	2.4	0.9	2.1	5.8
Keith Erickson (knee injury)	F-G	6'5	200	32	50	949	142	294	48	37	50	74	144	104	122	0	321	19	2.9	2.1	2.4	6.4
Butch Feher	G	6'4	185	22	48	487	86	162	53	76	99	77	74	36	46	0	248	10	1.5	0.8	1.0	5.2
Dale Schlueter	C	6'10	235	31	39	337	26	72	36	18	31	58	80	38	62	0	70	9	2.1	1.0	1.6	1.8

PLAYOFFS

PORTLAND TRAIL BLAZERS — **JACK RAMSEY**

defeated Chicago 2-1; H96-83, 104-107, H106-98
defeated Denver 4-2; 101-100, 110-121, H110-106, H105-96, 105-114 (OT), H108-92
defeated Los Angeles 4-0; 121-109, 99-97, H102-97, H105-101
defeated Philadelphia 4-2; 101-107, 89-107, H129-107, H130-98, 110-104, H109-107

Use Name	Pos	Hgt	Wgt	Age	TOTAL G	Min	FG	FGA	%	FT	FTA	%	Reb	Ass	PF	DQ	Points	PER GAME Min	Reb	Ass	PF	Points
Bob Gross	F	6'6	200	23	19	583	110	186	59	48	54	89	112	80	**84**	**5**	268	31	5.9	4.2	4.4	14.1
Maurice Lucas	F-C	6'9	225	24	19	731	164	316	52	75	101	74	188	79	79	3	403	38	9.9	4.2	4.2	21.2
Bill Walton	C	6'11	235	24	19	755	153	302	51	39	57	68	**288**	**104**	80	3	345	40	15.2	5.5	4.2	18.2
Lionel Hollins	G	6'3	185	23	19	682	134	321	42	60	88	68	52	85	74	2	328	36	2.7	4.5	3.9	17.3
Johnny Davis	G	6'2	170	21	16	436	65	133	49	38	53	72	33	52	32	0	168	27	2.1	3.3	2.0	10.5
Dave Twardzik	G	6'1	180	26	14	354	55	93	59	43	59	73	24	39	47	2	153	25	1.7	2.8	3.4	10.9
Herm Gilliam	G	6'3	190	30	18	295	53	123	43	9	12	75	20	32	29	0	115	16	1.1	1.8	1.6	6.4
Larry Steele	F-G	6'5	190	27	18	261	26	70	37	24	32	75	27	18	30	0	76	15	1.5	1.0	1.7	4.2
Lloyd Neal	F	6'7	225	26	19	206	30	63	48	17	26	65	70	17	34	0	77	11	3.7	0.9	1.8	4.1
Robin Jones	C	6'9	225	22	19	105	15	32	47	6	9	67	23	9	24	0	36	6	1.2	0.5	1.3	1.9
Corky Calhoun	F	6'7	215	26	12	94	13	25	52	2	3	67	14	4	16	0	28	8	1.2	0.3	1.3	2.3
Wally Walker	F	6'7	200	22	10	83	20	36	56	3	7	43	7	8	20	1	43	8	0.7	0.8	2.0	4.3

PHILADELPHIA 76ers — **GENE SHUE**

defeated Boston 4-3; H111-113, H113-101, 109-100, 119-124, H110-91, 108-113, H83-77
defeated Houston 4-2; H128-117, H106-97, 94-118, 107-95, H115-118, 112-109
lost to Portland 2-4; H107-101, H107-89, 107-129, 98-130, H104-110, 107-109

Use Name	Pos	Hgt	Wgt	Age	TOTAL G	Min	FG	FGA	%	FT	FTA	%	Reb	Ass	PF	DQ	Points	PER GAME Min	Reb	Ass	PF	Points
Julius Erving	F	6'7	210	26	19	758	**204**	**390**	52	**110**	**134**	82	122	85	45	0	**518**	40	6.4	4.5	2.4	27.3
George McGinnis	F	6'8	235	26	19	603	102	273	37	65	114	57	198	69	83	2	269	32	10.4	3.6	4.4	14.2
Caldwell Jones	C	6'11	225	26	19	513	37	73	51	18	30	60	150	20	81	4	92	27	7.9	1.1	4.3	4.8
Doug Collins	G	6'6	180	25	19	**759**	177	318	56	71	96	74	79	74	57	0	425	40	4.2	3.9	3.0	22.4
Henry Bibby	G	6'1	185	27	19	691	83	197	42	45	59	76	71	75	59	0	211	36	3.7	3.9	3.1	11.1
Steve Mix	F	6'7	222	29	19	412	56	107	52	37	45	82	64	44	39	0	149	22	3.4	2.3	2.1	7.8
Darryl Dawkins	C	6'11	265	19	18	331	50	95	53	31	47	66	98	17	46	1	131	18	5.4	0.9	2.6	7.3
Lloyd Free	G	6'2	185	23	15	281	63	170	37	53	77	69	32	29	33	0	179	19	2.1	1.9	2.2	11.9
Joe Bryant	F-C	6'9	185	22	10	74	12	31	39	5	8	63	15	7	13	0	29	7	1.5	0.7	1.3	2.9
Mike Dunleavy	G	6'3	180	22	11	68	9	25	36	4	5	80	4	9	14	0	22	6	0.4	0.8	1.3	2.0
Harvey Catchings	C	6'9	223	25	8	54	2	5	40	0	3	0	12	1	9	0	4	7	1.5	0.1	1.1	0.5
Terry Furlow	G	6'4	190	22	5	16	6	11	55	4	4	100	5	0	2	0	16	3	1.0	0.0	0.4	3.2

1976/77 N.B.A. — PLAYOFFS (continued)

HOUSTON ROCKETS — **TOM NISSALKE**

defeated Washington 4-2; H101-111, H124-118, 90-93, 107-103, H123-115, 108-103
lost to Philadelphia 2-4; 117-128, 97-106, H118-94, H95-107, 118-115, H109-112

Use Name	Pos	Hgt	Wgt	Age	G	Min	FG	FGA	%	FT	FTA	%	Reb	Ass	PF	DQ	Points	Min	Reb	Ass	PF	Points
					TOTAL													PER GAME				
Rudy Tomjanovich	F	6'8	220	28	12	457	107	212	50	29	37	78	65	24	36	0	243	38	5.4	2.0	3.0	20.3
Kevin Kunnert	F-C	7'	232	25	12	328	51	104	49	12	23	52	107	14	51	2	114	27	8.9	1.2	4.3	9.5
Moses Malone	C	6'10	215	21	12	518	81	162	50	63	91	69	203	7	42	0	225	43	16.9	0.6	3.5	18.8
John Lucas	G	6'3	175	23	12	430	75	139	54	26	34	76	33	83	33	1	176	36	2.8	6.9	2.8	14.7
Cal Murphy	G	5'9	165	28	12	420	102	213	48	28	30	93	19	75	47	1	232	35	1.6	6.3	3.9	19.3
Mike Newlin	G	6'4	205	27	12	316	75	143	52	21	28	75	34	53	37	0	171	26	2.8	4.4	3.1	14.3
Dwight Jones	F	6'10	220	24	12	246	28	63	44	18	23	78	51	15	32	2	74	21	4.3	1.3	2.7	6.2
John Johnson	F	6'7	200	29	12	146	24	61	39	10	15	67	29	9	20	0	58	12	2.4	0.8	1.7	4.8
Goo Kennedy	F	6'6	205	27	6	35	5	10	50	2	2	100	12	0	6	0	12	6	2.0	0.0	1.0	2.0
Tom Owens	F	6'10	225	27	3	7	0	1	0	0	0	—	2	0	1	0	0	2	0.7	0.0	0.3	0.0
Rudy White	G	6'2	195	23	1	2	1	3	33	0	0	—	1	0	0	0	2	2	1.0	0.0	0.0	2.0

Ed Ratleff - back injury

LOS ANGELES LAKERS — **JERRY WEST**

defeated Golden State 4-3; H115-106, H95-86, 105-109, 103-114, H112-105, 106-115, H97-84
lost to Portland 0-4; H109-121, H97-99, 97-102, 101-105

Use Name	Pos	Hgt	Wgt	Age	G	Min	FG	FGA	%	FT	FTA	%	Reb	Ass	PF	DQ	Points	Min	Reb	Ass	PF	Points
Cazzie Russell	F	6'5	220	32	11	382	65	157	41	44	50	88	48	25	33	0	174	35	4.4	2.3	3.0	15.8
Don Ford	F	6'9	215	24	11	333	42	98	43	27	36	75	58	37	28	0	111	30	5.3	3.4	2.5	10.1
Kareem Abdul-Jabbar	C	7'2	240	29	11	467	147	242	61	87	120	73	195	45	42	0	381	42	**17.7**	4.1	3.8	**34.6**
Don Chaney	G	6'5	210	30	11	412	36	96	38	16	22	73	52	48	32	0	88	37	4.7	4.4	2.9	8.0
Lucius Allen	G	6'2	175	29	7	186	32	82	39	13	19	68	32	24	18	0	77	27	4.6	3.4	2.6	11.0
Earl Tatum	G-F	6'5	185	23	11	356	67	134	50	16	24	67	54	27	34	2	150	32	4.9	2.5	3.1	13.6
Tom Abernathy	F	6'7	220	22	11	214	21	50	42	22	27	81	40	22	16	0	64	19	3.6	2.0	1.5	5.8
Bo Lamar	G	6'1	180	25	10	109	12	41	29	9	10	90	9	14	12	0	33	11	0.9	1.4	1.2	3.3
Johnny Neumann	G	6'6	210	25	6	68	11	29	38	2	4	50	2	9	14	0	24	11	0.3	1.5	2.3	4.0
C. J. Kupec	C	6'8	220	23	11	57	8	18	44	5	7	71	16	4	7	0	21	5	1.5	0.4	0.6	1.9
Cornell Warner	F-C	6'9	220	28	5	56	7	12	58	0	0	—	9	6	11	0	14	11	1.8	1.2	2.2	2.8

Kermit Washington - knee injury

BOSTON CELTICS — **TOM HEINSOHN**

defeated San Antonio 2-0; H104-94, 113-109
lost to Philadelphia 3-4; 113-111, 101-113, H100-109, H124-119, 91-110, H113-108, 77-83

Use Name	Pos	Hgt	Wgt	Age	G	Min	FG	FGA	%	FT	FTA	%	Reb	Ass	PF	DQ	Points	Min	Reb	Ass	PF	Points
John Havlicek	F-G	6'5	210	36	9	375	62	167	37	41	50	82	49	62	33	0	165	42	5.4	6.9	3.7	18.3
Sidney Wicks	F	6'8	225	27	9	261	42	81	52	34	47	72	83	16	37	2	118	29	9.2	1.8	4.1	13.1
Dave Cowens	C	6'9	230	28	9	379	66	148	45	17	22	77	134	36	37	3	149	42	14.9	4.0	4.1	16.6
Charlie Scott	G	6'5	180	28	9	338	52	108	48	44	52	85	38	38	41	3	148	38	4.2	4.2	4.6	16.4
Jo Jo White	G	6'3	193	30	9	395	91	201	45	28	33	85	39	52	27	0	210	44	4.3	5.8	3.0	23.3
Curtis Rowe	F	6'7	225	27	9	237	32	68	47	22	29	76	72	10	29	1	86	26	8.0	1.1	3.2	9.6
Tom Boswell	C-F	6'9	230	23	9	81	8	18	44	4	6	67	20	7	18	0	20	9	2.2	0.8	2.0	2.2
Fred Saunders	F	6'7	210	25	9	66	12	33	36	5	6	83	9	5	21	0	29	7	1.0	0.6	2.3	3.2
Kevin Stacom	G	6'3	185	25	5	25	3	6	50	1	1	100	2	4	3	0	7	5	0.4	0.8	0.6	1.4
Norm Cook	F	6'9	210	21	1	3	2	2	100	0	0	—	0	0	0	0	4	3	0.0	0.0	0.0	4.0

GOLDEN STATE WARRIORS — **AL ATTLES**

defeated Detroit 2-1; H90-95, 138-108, H109-101
lost to Los Angeles 3-4; 106-115, 86-95, H109-105, H114-103, 105-112, H115-106, 84-97

Use Name	Pos	Hgt	Wgt	Age	G	Min	FG	FGA	%	FT	FTA	%	Reb	Ass	PF	DQ	Points	Min	Reb	Ass	PF	Points
Rick Barry	F	6'7	220	32	10	415	122	262	47	40	44	91	59	47	32	0	284	42	5.9	4.7	3.2	28.4
Jamaal Wilkes	F	6'6	190	23	10	346	66	154	43	23	28	82	80	16	23	0	155	35	8.0	1.6	2.3	15.5
Cliff Ray	C-F	6'9	235	27	10	304	42	76	55	16	28	57	115	15	37	0	100	30	11.5	1.5	3.7	10.0
Phil Smith	G	6'4	187	24	10	371	53	132	40	36	45	80	50	45	24	0	142	37	5.0	4.5	2.4	14.2
Charles Dudley	G	6'2	186	26	10	236	13	37	35	15	23	65	38	69	28	0	41	24	3.8	6.9	2.8	4.1
Robert Parish	C	7'	230	23	10	239	52	108	48	17	26	65	103	11	42	1	121	24	10.3	1.1	4.2	12.1
Gus Williams	G	6'2	175	23	10	184	35	70	50	18	21	86	15	25	30	1	88	18	1.5	2.5	3.0	8.8
Charlie Johnson	G	6'	170	27	10	161	29	74	39	7	8	88	15	7	16	0	65	16	1.5	0.7	1.6	6.5
Sonny Parker	F	6'6	200	21	10	120	19	36	53	4	4	100	28	9	9	0	42	12	2.8	0.9	0.9	4.2
Larry McNeill	F	6'9	200	25	6	21	7	10	70	2	4	50	2	0	2	0	16	4	0.3	0.0	0.3	2.7
Marshall Rogers	G	6'1	190	23	1	3	0	2	0	2	2	100	1	0	0	0	2	3	1.0	0.0	0.0	2.0

Derrek Dickey - broken ankle   Dwight Davis - knee injury

DENVER NUGGETS — **LARRY BROWN**

lost to Portland 2-4; H100-101, H121-110, 106-110, 96-105, H114-105, H114-105(OT), 92-108

Use Name	Pos	Hgt	Wgt	Age	G	Min	FG	FGA	%	FT	FTA	%	Reb	Ass	PF	DQ	Points	Min	Reb	Ass	PF	Points
Bobby Jones	F	6'9	215	25	6	187	31	64	48	10	17	59	35	21	25	1	72	31	5.8	3.5	4.2	12.0
Paul Silas	F	6'7	225	33	6	141	14	33	42	13	24	54	40	16	23	1	41	24	6.7	2.7	3.8	6.8
Dan Issel	C-F	6'9	240	28	6	222	49	96	51	34	45	76	58	17	20	0	132	37	9.7	2.8	3.3	22.0
David Thompson	G-F	6'4	195	22	6	237	56	121	46	36	53	68	31	24	22	1	148	40	5.2	4.0	3.7	24.7
Ted McClain	G	6'3	180	29	6	170	19	46	41	6	8	75	14	27	12	0	44	28	2.3	4.5	2.0	7.3
Jim Price	G	6'3	195	27	6	158	19	53	36	5	8	63	24	25	18	0	43	26	4.0	4.2	3.0	7.2
Mack Calvin	G	6'	175	28	6	112	19	40	48	24	29	83	9	13	13	0	62	19	1.5	2.2	2.2	10.3
Willie Wise	F	6'6	215	29	6	106	14	41	34	17	25	68	28	3	16	0	45	18	4.7	0.5	2.7	7.5
Marvin Webster	C	7'1	225	24	6	96	13	26	50	4	6	67	40	3	12	0	30	16	6.7	0.5	2.0	5.0
Byron Beck	F	6'9	230	31	5	29	3	9	33	2	2	100	6	1	5	0	8	6	1.2	0.2	1.0	1.6
Monte Towe	G	5'7	150	23	1	6	2	3	67	0	0	—	0	1	0	0	4	6	0.0	1.0	0.0	4.0
Fatty Taylor	G	6'	175	30	1	1	0	0	—	0	0	—	0	0	0	0	0	1	0.0	0.0	0.0	0.0

1976/77 N.B.A. — PLAYOFFS (continued)

Column groups: TOTAL (G through Points), then PER GAME (Min, Reb, Ass, PF, Points).

WASHINGTON BULLETS — **DICK MOTTA** — defeated Cleveland 2-1; H109-100, 83-91, H104-98; lost to Houston 2-4; 111-101 (OT), 118-124, H93-90, H103-107, 115-123, H103-108

Use Name	Pos	Hgt	Wgt	Age	G	Min	FG	FGA	%	FT	FTA	%	Reb	Ass	PF	DQ	Points	Min	Reb	Ass	PF	Points
Kevin Grevey	F	6'5	210	23	9	225	36	88	41	15	23	65	16	8	20	0	87	25	1.8	0.9	2.2	9.7
Elvin Hayes	F-C	6'9	235	31	9	405	74	173	43	41	59	69	122	17	39	0	189	45	13.6	1.9	4.3	21.0
Wes Unseld	C	6'7	250	30	9	368	30	54	56	7	12	58	105	44	32	0	67	41	11.7	4.9	3.6	7.4
Phil Chenier	G-F	6'3	180	26	9	360	90	189	48	45	56	80	40	23	16	0	225	40	4.4	2.6	1.8	25.0
Tom Henderson	G	6'3	190	24	9	322	48	108	44	26	36	72	20	63	24	1	122	36	2.2	7.0	2.7	13.6
Mitch Kupchak	F-C	6'9	230	22	9	252	53	90	59	40	59	68	68	10	34	0	146	28	7.6	1.1	3.8	16.2
Larry Wright	G	6'1	175	22	8	104	19	39	49	15	21	71	7	16	18	1	53	13	0.9	2.0	2.3	6.6
Dave Bing	G	6'3	190	33	8	55	14	32	44	4	4	100	6	5	5	0	32	7	0.8	0.6	0.6	4.0
Leonard Gray	F	6'8	250	25	8	52	6	21	29	0	0	—	9	1	12	0	12	7	1.1	0.1	1.5	1.5
Bob Weiss	G	6'2	185	34	4	34	3	5	60	0	1	0	3	2	5	0	6	9	0.8	0.5	1.3	1.5
Mike Riordan	F	6'4	200	31	2	8	0	2	0	0	0	—	2	1	1	0	0	4	1.0	0.5	0.5	0.0

CLEVELAND CAVALIERS — **BILL FITCH** — lost to Washington 1-2; 100-109, H91-83, 98-104

Use Name	Pos	Hgt	Wgt	Age	G	Min	FG	FGA	%	FT	FTA	%	Reb	Ass	PF	DQ	Points	Min	Reb	Ass	PF	Points
Campy Russell	F	6'8	215	24	3	100	21	54	39	11	15	73	26	10	10	0	53	33	8.7	3.3	3.3	17.7
Jim Brewer	F	6'9	230	25	3	113	11	27	41	1	1	100	36	5	11	0	23	38	12.0	1.7	3.7	7.7
Jim Chones	C-F	6'11	220	27	3	99	16	27	59	7	7	100	31	3	9	0	39	33	10.3	1.0	3.0	13.0
Austin Carr	G	6'4	200	28	3	83	11	39	28	1	3	33	10	10	13	0	23	28	3.3	3.3	4.3	7.7
Foots Walker	G	6'1	172	25	3	95	18	37	49	11	15	73	12	20	12	0	47	32	4.0	6.7	4.0	15.7
Bobby Smith	F-G	6'5	210	30	3	57	9	39	23	3	3	100	8	4	5	0	21	19	2.7	1.3	1.7	7.0
Elmore Smith	C	7'	250	27	3	56	18	33	55	5	8	63	24	1	10	0	41	19	8.0	0.3	3.3	13.7
Dick Snyder	G	6'5	213	32	3	53	8	27	30	2	5	40	5	4	6	0	18	18	1.7	1.3	2.0	6.0
Gary Brokaw	G	6'4	180	22	3	44	9	19	47	2	6	33	4	12	7	0	20	15	1.3	4.0	2.3	6.7
John Lambert	F	6'10	225	23	3	19	2	4	50	0	0	—	3	0	4	0	4	6	1.0	0.0	1.3	1.3
Nate Thurmond	C	6'11	235	35	1	1	0	0	—	0	0	—	1	0	0	0	0	1	1.0	0.0	0.0	0.0

Jim Cleamons - groin injury

CHICAGO BULLS — **ED BADGER** — lost to Portland 1-2; 83-96, H107-104, 98-106

Use Name	Pos	Hgt	Wgt	Age	G	Min	FG	FGA	%	FT	FTA	%	Reb	Ass	PF	DQ	Points	Min	Reb	Ass	PF	Points
Scott May	F	6'7	220	22	3	97	10	26	38	12	15	80	14	3	10	0	32	32	4.7	1.0	3.3	10.7
Mickey Johnson	F	6'10	190	24	3	124	34	72	47	14	16	88	39	7	13	0	82	41	13.0	2.3	4.3	27.3
Artis Gilmore	C	7'2	240	27	3	126	19	40	48	18	23	78	39	6	9	0	56	42	13.0	2.0	3.0	18.7
Wilbur Holland	G	6'	175	25	3	84	17	34	50	10	10	100	9	3	8	0	44	28	3.0	1.0	2.7	14.7
Norm Van Lier	G	6'1	175	29	3	134	3	19	16	10	12	83	15	29	14	1	45	16	5.0	**9.7**	**4.7**	5.3
John Mengelt	G	6'2	195	27	3	67	14	26	54	10	11	91	4	8	3	0	38	22	1.3	2.7	1.0	12.7
Jack Marin	F	6'7	210	32	3	53	8	13	62	0	1	0	1	2	6	0	16	18	0.3	0.7	2.0	5.3
Tom Boerwinkle	C	7'	260	31	3	17	1	5	20	0	0	—	10	7	1	0	2	6	3.3	2.3	0.3	0.7
Cliff Pondexter	F	6'9	230	22	3	12	0	1	0	2	2	100	3	1	0	0	2	4	1.0	0.3	0.0	0.7
Phil Hicks	F	6'7	205	23	1	4	0	2	0	0	0	—	3	0	1	0	0	4	3.0	0.0	1.0	0.0
Tom Kropp	G	6'3	205	23	1	2	0	0	—	0	0	—	0	0	2	0	0	2	0.0	0.0	2.0	0.0

DETROIT PISTONS — **HERB BROWN** — lost to Golden State 1-2; 95-90, H108-138, 101-109

Use Name	Pos	Hgt	Wgt	Age	G	Min	FG	FGA	%	FT	FTA	%	Reb	Ass	PF	DQ	Points	Min	Reb	Ass	PF	Points
M. L. Carr	F	6'6	205	25	3	112	12	31	39	4	7	57	17	6	9	0	28	37	5.7	2.0	3.0	9.3
Howard Porter	F	6'8	220	28	3	98	29	47	62	2	4	50	17	2	7	0	60	33	5.7	0.7	2.3	20.0
Bob Lanier	C	6'11	255	28	3	118	34	54	**63**	16	19	84	50	6	10	0	84	39	16.7	2.0	3.3	28.0
Chris Ford	G	6'5	190	27	3	101	18	44	41	5	9	56	19	12	11	0	41	34	6.3	4.0	3.7	13.7
Eric Money	G	6'	170	21	3	103	22	44	50	11	13	85	9	20	9	0	55	34	3.0	6.7	3.0	18.3
Kevin Porter	G	6'	175	26	3	61	5	14	36	6	9	67	6	17	7	0	16	20	2.0	5.7	2.3	5.3
Leon Douglas	F-C	6'10	230	22	3	57	4	13	31	2	7	29	10	3	11	0	10	19	3.3	1.0	3.7	3.3
Al Eberhard	F	6'6	225	24	3	42	1	9	11	5	8	63	9	2	6	0	7	14	3.0	0.7	2.0	2.3
Ralph Simpson	G	6'5	200	27	2	17	0	9	0	0	0	—	3	1	1	0	0	9	1.5	0.5	0.5	0.0
Phil Sellers	G	6'5	200	23	1	6	1	4	25	1	4	25	2	0	2	0	3	6	2.0	0.0	2.0	3.0
Roger Brown	C	7'	230	26	2	5	0	1	0	0	0	—	0	0	0	0	0	3	0.0	0.0	0.0	0.0

Marvin Barnes - broken hand

SAN ANTONIO SPURS — **DOUG MOE** — lost to Boston 0-2; 94-104, H109-113

Use Name	Pos	Hgt	Wgt	Age	G	Min	FG	FGA	%	FT	FTA	%	Reb	Ass	PF	DQ	Points	Min	Reb	Ass	PF	Points
Mark Olberding	F	6'8	230	20	2	42	5	9	56	3	6	50	7	2	8	0	13	21	3.5	1.0	4.0	6.5
Larry Kenon	F	6'9	215	24	2	79	16	33	48	2	2	100	15	6	9	1	34	40	7.5	3.0	4.5	17.0
Billy Paultz	C	6'11	250	28	2	74	12	24	50	10	13	77	17	5	3	0	34	37	8.5	2.5	1.5	17.0
George Gervin	G	6'7	185	24	2	62	19	44	43	12	15	80	11	3	9	1	50	31	5.5	1.5	4.5	25.0
Mike Gale	G	6'4	190	26	2	67	9	23	39	4	7	57	10	10	9	1	22	34	5.0	5.0	4.5	11.0
Coby Dietrick	F-C	6'10	230	28	2	64	12	23	52	2	6	33	9	5	4	0	26	32	4.5	2.5	2.0	13.0
Louie Dampier	G	6'	180	32	2	62	4	16	25	4	4	100	3	9	4	0	12	31	31.0	4.5	2.0	6.0
Allan Bristow	F-G	6'7	220	25	2	28	3	9	33	2	9	22	4	7	6	0	8	14	2.0	3.5	3.0	4.0
Henry Ward	G	6'4	195	24	1	1	2	3	67	0	0	—	0	0	0	0	4	1	0.0	0.0	0.0	4.0
George Karl	G	6'2	190	25	1	1	0	0	—	0	0	—	0	0	0	0	0	1	0.0	0.0	0.0	0.0

James Silas - knee injury

Team		G	FG	FGA	%	FT	FTA	%	REBOUNDS			Assists	PF	Steals	Blocked Shots	Turn Overs	Points	Points per game
									Offense	Defense	Total							
TEAM STATISTICS																		
EASTERN CONFERENCE																		
ATLANTIC DIVISION																		
Philadelphia	Off.	82	3511	7322	48	2012	2732	74	1293	2752	4045	1966	2074	814	561	1915	9034	110.2
	Def.	82	3575	7920	45	1561	2074	75	1416	2448	3864	2012	2232	823	371	1769	8711	106.2
	Diff.		-64	-598	+3	+451	+658	-1	-123	+304	+181	-46	+158	-9	+190	-146	+323	+4.0
Boston	Off.	82	3462	7775	45	1648	2181	76	1241	2966	4207	2010	2039	506	263	1673	8572	104.5
	Def.	82	3559	7904	45	1616	2180	74	1110	2753	3863	1918	1954	699	349	1369	8734	106.5
	Diff.		-97	-129	—	+32	+1	+2	+131	+213	+344	+92	-85	-193	-86	-304	-162	-2.0
New York Knicks	Off.	82	3659	7530	49	1587	2078	76	974	2680	3654	1956	2007	714	304	1680	8905	108.6
	Def.	82	3577	7610	47	1752	2327	75	1163	2716	3879	1847	2008	793	412	1612	8906	108.6
	Diff.		+82	-80	+2	-165	-249	+1	-189	-36	-225	+109	+1	-79	-108	-68	-1	—
Buffalo	Off.	82	3366	7475	45	1880	2492	75	1213	2623	3836	1883	1842	683	392	1699	8612	105.0
	Def.	82	3786	7917	48	1404	1859	76	1268	2721	3989	2192	2129	729	446	1607	8976	109.5
	Diff.		-420	-442	-3	+476	+633	-1	-55	-98	-153	-309	+287	-46	-54	-92	-364	-4.5
New York Nets	Off.	82	3096	7222	43	1673	2274	74	1157	2547	3704	1422	2178	802	435	1630	7865	95.9
	Def.	82	3279	7074	46	1863	2488	75	1149	2937	4086	1910	1970	778	512	1735	8421	102.7
	Diff.		-183	+148	-3	-190	-214	-1	+8	-390	-382	-488	-208	+24	-77	+105	-556	-6.8
CENTRAL DIVISION																		
Houston	Off.	82	3535	7325	48	1656	2103	79	1254	2632	3886	1913	2132	616	411	1600	8726	106.4
	Def.	82	3424	7356	47	1746	2252	78	1121	2232	3353	1883	1978	547	350	1395	8594	104.8
	Diff.		+111	-31	+1	-90	-149	+1	+133	+400	+533	+30	-154	+69	+61	-205	+132	+1.6
Washington	Off.	82	3514	7479	47	1622	2264	72	1185	2758	3943	1935	1940	642	433	1677	8650	105.5
	Def.	82	3552	7751	46	1462	1943	75	1167	2565	3732	1893	2088	815	348	1506	8566	104.5
	Diff.		-38	-272	+1	+160	+321	-3	+18	+193	+211	+42	+148	-173	+85	-171	+84	+1.0
San Antonio	Off.	82	3711	7657	48	2010	2522	80	1110	2550	3660	2115	1966	857	499	1770	9432	115.0
	Def.	82	3935	8075	49	1512	2059	73	1329	2687	4016	2159	2189	811	420	1822	9382	114.4
	Diff.		-224	-418	-1	+498	+463	+7	-219	-137	-356	-44	+223	+46	+79	+52	+50	+.6
Cleveland	Off.	82	3451	7688	45	1468	1993	74	1312	2563	3875	1845	1951	579	472	1356	8370	102.1
	Def.	82	3265	7268	45	1748	2325	75	1202	2711	3913	1736	1908	660	389	1542	8278	101.0
	Diff.		+186	+420	—	-280	-332	-1	+110	-148	-38	+109	-43	-81	+83	+186	+92	+1.1
New Orleans	Off.	82	3443	7602	45	1688	2183	77	1249	2828	4077	1854	2099	613	357	1706	8574	104.6
	Def.	82	3486	7712	45	1833	2448	75	1318	2781	4099	1748	2125	835	361	1615	8805	107.4
	Diff.		-43	-110	—	-145	-265	+2	-69	+47	-22	+106	+26	-222	-4	-91	-231	-2.8
Atlanta	Off.	82	3279	7176	46	1836	2451	75	1244	2512	3756	1882	2302	733	330	1779	8394	102.4
	Def.	82	3409	7137	48	1909	2527	76	1121	2533	3654	2020	2174	803	442	1692	8727	106.4
	Diff.		-130	+39	-2	-73	-76	-1	+123	-21	+102	-138	-128	-70	-112	-87	-333	-4.0
WESTERN CONFERENCE																		
MIDWEST DIVISION																		
Denver	Off.	82	3590	7471	48	2053	2783	74	1288	2700	3988	2262	2142	953	471	2011	9233	112.6
	Def.	82	3585	7743	46	1635	2231	73	1269	2481	3750	2082	2285	941	470	1944	8805	107.4
	Diff.		+5	-272	+2	+418	+552	+1	+19	+219	+238	+180	+143	+12	+1	-67	+428	+5.2
Detroit	Off.	82	3764	7792	48	1442	1960	74	1169	2495	3664	2004	2200	877	459	1718	8970	109.4
	Def.	82	3561	7539	47	1933	2543	76	1317	2637	3954	1952	1827	793	381	1828	9055	110.4
	Diff.		+203	+253	+1	-491	-583	-2	-148	-142	-290	+52	-373	+84	+78	+110	-85	-1.0
Chicago	Off.	82	3249	7186	45	1613	2159	75	1292	2705	3997	1989	1871	699	364	1552	8111	98.9
	Def.	82	3306	7095	47	1425	1907	75	1055	2559	3614	1917	2166	723	460	1598	8037	98.0
	Diff.		-57	+91	-2	+188	+252	—	+237	+146	+383	+72	+295	-24	-96	+46	+74	+.9
Kansas City	Off.	82	3561	7733	46	1706	2140	80	1222	2593	3815	1982	2173	849	386	1576	8828	107.7
	Def.	82	3422	7244	47	1912	2513	76	1097	2739	3836	1744	2030	722	392	1755	8756	106.8
	Diff.		+139	+489	-1	-206	-373	+4	+125	-146	-21	+238	-143	+127	-6	+179	+72	+.9
Indiana	Off.	82	3522	7840	45	1714	2297	75	1409	2584	3993	2009	2030	924	458	1609	8758	106.8
	Def.	82	3599	7629	47	1705	2252	76	1378	2770	4148	2097	2043	715	466	1792	8903	108.6
	Diff.		-77	+211	-2	+9	+45	-1	+31	-186	-155	-88	+13	+209	-8	+183	-145	-1.8
Milwaukee	Off.	82	3668	7840	47	1553	2072	75	1220	2519	3739	1970	2094	790	342	1648	8889	108.4
	Def.	82	3712	7753	48	1721	2330	74	1265	2613	3878	2193	1940	736	410	1644	9145	111.5
	Diff.		-44	+87	-1	-168	-258	+1	-45	-94	-139	-223	-154	+54	-68	-4	-256	-3.1
PACIFIC DIVISION																		
Los Angeles	Off.	82	3663	7657	48	1437	1941	74	1177	2628	3805	2057	1867	801	445	1538	8763	106.9
	Def.	82	3515	7781	45	1510	1990	76	1348	2625	3973	1900	1816	763	362	1599	8540	104.1
	Diff.		+148	-124	+3	-73	-49	-2	-171	+3	-168	+157	-51	+38	+83	+61	+223	+2.8
Portland	Off.	82	3623	7537	48	1917	2515	76	1260	2703	3963	1990	2220	868	492	1757	9163	111.7
	Def.	82	3408	7404	46	1889	2514	75	1197	2510	3707	1817	2242	840	478	1765	8705	106.2
	Diff.		+215	+133	+2	+28	+1	+1	+63	+193	+256	+173	+22	+28	+14	+8	+458	+5.5

TEAM STATISTICS (continued)

WESTERN CONFERENCE (continued)

PACIFIC DIVISION (continued)

Team		G	FG	FGA	%	FT	FTA	%	Rebounds Offense	Rebounds Defense	Rebounds Total	Assists	PF	Steals	Blocked Shots	Turn Overs	Points	Points per game
Golden State	Off.	82	3724	7832	48	1649	2172	76	1300	2639	3939	2120	2058	904	432	1624	9097	110.9
	Def.	82	3567	7584	47	1699	2282	74	1256	2640	3896	2114	1939	757	420	1778	8833	107.7
	Diff.		+157	+248	+1	-50	-110	+2	+44	-1	+43	+6	-119	+147	+12	+154	+264	+3.2
Seattle	Off.	82	3439	7639	45	1646	2386	69	1355	2433	3788	1772	2198	932	503	1759	8524	104.0
	Def.	82	3394	7339	46	1863	2474	75	1257	2651	3908	2046	2104	726	476	1905	8651	105.5
	Diff.		+45	+300	-1	-217	-88	-6	+98	-218	-120	-274	-94	+206	+27	+146	-127	-1.5
Phoenix	Off.	82	3406	7249	47	1791	2345	76	1059	2493	3552	2100	2089	750	346	1830	8603	104.9
	Def.	82	3320	7192	46	1903	2525	75	1180	2594	3774	1856	2325	897	440	1835	8543	104.2
	Diff.		+86	+57	+1	-112	-180	+1	-121	-101	-222	+244	+236	-147	-94	+5	+60	+.7

PLAYOFFS

Team		G	FG	FGA	%	FT	FTA	%	Rebounds Offense	Rebounds Defense	Rebounds Total	Assists	PF	Steals	Blocked Shots	Turn Overs	Points	Points per game
Portland	Off.	19	838	1700	49	364	501	73	231	627	858	527	549	206	127	424	2040	107.4
	Def.	19	745	1644	45	461	625	74	260	604	864	451	500	198	107	418	1951	102.7
	Diff.		+93	+56	+4	-97	-124	-1	-29	+23	-6	+76	-49	+8	+20	-6	+89	+4.7
Philadelphia	Off.	19	801	1695	47	443	622	71	251	599	850	430	481	176	109	369	2045	107.6
	Def.	19	816	1768	46	406	545	74	309	628	937	489	525	161	77	399	2041	107.4
	Diff.		-15	-73	+1	+37	+77	-3	-58	-29	-87	-59	+44	+15	+32	+30	+4	+.2
Houston	Off.	12	549	1111	49	209	283	74	200	356	556	280	305	94	41	217	1307	108.9
	Def.	12	536	1086	49	233	338	69	161	334	495	279	281	82	59	209	1305	108.8
	Diff.		+13	+25	—	-24	-55	+5	+39	+22	+61	+1	-24	+12	-18	-8	+2	+.1
Los Angeles	Off.	11	448	959	47	241	319	76	159	356	515	261	247	116	62	220	1137	103.4
	Def.	11	475	1012	47	196	263	75	161	345	506	283	265	123	44	206	1146	104.2
	Diff.		-27	-53	—	+45	+56	+1	-2	+11	+9	-22	+18	-7	+18	-14	-9	-.8
Boston	Off.	9	370	852	43	196	246	80	135	311	446	230	246	59	26	181	936	104.0
	Def.	9	376	817	46	204	292	70	125	292	417	196	212	82	58	162	956	106.2
	Diff.		-6	+35	-3	-8	-46	+10	+10	+19	+29	+34	-34	-23	-32	-19	-20	-2.2
Golden State	Off.	10	438	961	46	180	233	77	192	314	506	244	243	87	41	180	1056	105.6
	Def.	10	411	884	46	215	300	72	158	326	484	232	227	100	60	193	1037	103.7
	Diff.		+27	+77	—	-35	-67	+5	+34	-12	+22	+12	-16	-13	-19	+13	+19	+1.9
Denver	Off.	6	239	532	45	151	217	70	92	193	285	151	166	58	41	120	629	104.8
	Def.	6	259	533	49	121	162	75	77	191	268	158	186	53	41	139	639	106.5
	Diff.		-20	-1	-4	+30	+55	-5	+15	+2	+17	-7	+20	+5	—	+19	-10	-1.7
Washington	Off.	9	373	801	47	193	271	71	114	284	398	190	206	58	44	157	939	104.3
	Def.	9	406	876	46	130	179	73	146	292	438	199	239	70	38	149	942	104.7
	Diff.		-33	-75	+1	+63	+92	-2	-32	-8	-40	-9	+33	-12	+6	-8	-3	-.4
Cleveland	Off.	3	123	306	40	43	63	68	56	104	160	69	87	26	16	48	289	96.3
	Def.	3	107	248	43	82	106	77	30	113	143	56	72	15	14	59	296	98.7
	Diff.		+16	+58	-3	-39	-43	-9	+26	-9	+17	+13	-15	+11	+2	+11	-7	-2.4
Chicago	Off.	3	106	238	45	76	90	84	48	89	137	66	67	31	14	82	288	96.0
	Def.	3	134	250	54	38	55	69	21	80	101	89	90	32	30	64	306	102.0
	Diff.		-28	-12	-9	+38	+35	+15	+27	+9	+36	-23	+23	-1	-16	-18	-18	-6.0
Detroit	Off.	3	126	270	47	52	80	65	47	95	142	69	73	22	20	57	304	101.3
	Def.	3	140	307	46	57	72	79	72	97	169	73	69	21	16	46	337	112.3
	Diff.		-14	-37	+1	-5	+8	-14	-25	-2	-27	-4	-4	+1	+4	-11	-33	-11.0
San Antonio	Off.	2	82	184	45	39	62	63	23	53	76	47	52	16	8	36	203	101.5
	Def.	2	88	184	48	41	50	82	28	79	107	59	56	12	5	47	217	108.5
	Diff.		-6	—	-3	-2	+12	-19	-5	-26	-31	-12	+4	+4	+3	+11	-14	-7.0

Team	W	L	Pct.	GB	Record against playoff teams W	L	Pct.	Record against non-playoff teams W	L	Pct.	HOME W	L	Pct.	ROAD W	L	Pct.
EASTERN CONFERENCE																
ATLANTIC DIVISION																
Philadelphia 76ers	50	32	.610	—	**25**	19	.568	25	13	.658	32	9	.780	**18**	23	**.439**
Boston Celtics	44	38	.537	6	19	24	.442	25	14	.641	28	13	.683	16	25	.390
New York Knickerbockers	40	42	.488	10	23	24	.489	17	18	.486	26	15	.634	14	27	.341
Buffalo Braves	30	52	.366	20	14	33	.298	16	19	.457	23	18	.561	7	34	.171
New York Nets	22	**60**	.268	28	11	**35**	.239	11	**25**	.306	10	**31**	.244	12	29	.293
CENTRAL DIVISION																
Houston Rockets	49	33	.598	—	22	22	.500	27	11	.711	34	7	.829	15	26	.366
Washington Bullets	48	34	.585	1	21	21	.500	27	13	.675	32	9	.780	16	25	.390
San Antonio Spurs	44	38	.537	5	19	23	.452	25	15	.625	31	10	.756	13	28	.317
Cleveland Cavaliers	43	39	.524	6	18	26	.409	25	13	.658	29	12	.707	14	27	.341
New Orleans Jazz	35	47	.427	14	16	31	.340	19	16	.543	26	15	.634	9	32	.220
Atlanta Hawks	31	51	.378	18	18	30	.375	13	21	.382	19	22	.463	12	29	.293
WESTERN CONFERENCE																
MIDWEST DIVISION																
Denver Nuggets	50	32	.610	—	22	20	.524	**28**	12	.700	36	5	.878	13	28	.317
Detroit Pistons	44	38	.537	6	20	23	.465	24	15	.615	31	10	.756	14	27	.341
Chicago Bulls	44	38	.537	6	20	23	.465	24	15	.615	31	10	.756	13	28	.317
Kansas City Kings	40	42	.488	10	17	31	.354	23	11	.676	28	13	.683	13	28	.317
Indiana Pacers	36	46	.439	14	13	33	.283	23	13	.639	25	16	.610	11	30	.268
Milwaukee Bucks	30	52	.366	20	16	31	.340	14	21	.400	24	17	.585	6	**35**	.146
PACIFIC DIVISION																
Los Angeles Lakers	**53**	29	**.646**		**25**	18	**.581**	**28**	11	**.718**	37	4	**.902**	15	26	.366
Portland Trail Blazers	49	33	.598	4	23	20	.535	26	13	.667	35	6	.854	14	27	.341
Golden State Warriors	46	36	.561	7	23	20	.535	23	16	.590	29	12	.707	17	24	.414
Seattle Supersonics	40	42	.488	13	20	28	.417	20	14	.588	27	14	.659	13	28	.317
Phoenix Suns	34	48	.415	19	15	31	.326	19	17	.528	26	15	.634	8	33	.195

1976/77 N.B.A. INDIVIDUAL LEADERS

SCORING
(Minimum 70 Games or 1400 Points)

Name	Team	G	FG	FT	Pts.	Avg.
Maravich	NO	73	886	501	2273	31.1
Knight	Ind	78	831	413	2075	26.6
Abdul-Jabbar	LA	82	888	376	2152	26.2
Thompson	Den	82	824	477	2125	25.9
McAdoo	Buf-NY	72	740	381	1861	25.8
Lanier	Det	64	678	260	1616	25.3
Drew	Atl	74	689	412	1790	24.2
Hayes	Was	82	760	422	1942	23.7
Gervin	SA	82	726	443	1895	23.1
Issel	Den	79	660	445	1765	22.3

FIELD GOAL PERCENTAGE
(Minimum 300 Made)

Name	Team	FG	FGA	Pct.
Abdul-Jabbar	LA	888	1533	.579
Kupchak	Was	341	596	.572
Jones	Den	501	879	.570
Gervin	SA	726	1335	.544
Lanier	Det	678	1269	.534
Gross	Port	376	711	.529
Nater	Mil	383	725	.528
Walton	Port	491	930	.528
Meriweather	Atl	319	607	.526
Gilmore	Chi	570	1091	.522

FREE THROW PERCENTAGE
(Minimum 125 Made)

Name	Team	FT	FTA	Pct.
DiGregorio	Buf	138	146	.945
Barry	GS	359	392	.916
Murphy	Hou	272	307	.886
Newlin	Hou	269	304	.885
Brown	Sea	168	190	.884
D.Van Arsdale	Phoe	145	166	.873
White	Bos	333	383	.869
Bridgeman	Mil	197	228	.864
Russell	LA	188	219	.858
Van Breda Kolff	NYN	195	228	.855

PERSONAL FOULS

Name	Team	PF
Shelton	Ny	363
Kunnert	Hou	361
Hillman	Ind	353
Wicks	Bos	331
Meriweather	Atl	324
Washington	KC	324

GAMES DISQUALIFIED

Name	Team	Disq.
Meriweather	Atl	21
Kunnert	Hou	17
Hillman	Ind	15
Wicks	Bos	14
Washington	KC	13

TOTAL REBOUNDS PER GAME
(Minimum 70 Games or 800 Rebounds)

Name	Team	G	Reb.	Avg.
Walton	Port	65	934	14.4
Abdul-Jabbar	LA	82	1090	13.3
Malone	Buf-Hou	82	1072	13.1
Gilmore	Chi	82	1070	13.0
McAdoo	Buf-NY	72	926	12.9
Hayes	Was	82	1029	12.5
Nater	Mil	72	865	12.0
McGinnis	Phi	79	911	11.5
Lucas	Port	79	899	11.4
Kenon	SA	78	879	11.3

ASSISTS PER GAME
(Minimum 70 Games or 400 Assists)

Name	Team	G	Ass.	Avg.
Buse	Ind	81	685	8.5
Watts	Sea	79	630	8.0
Van Lier	Chi	82	636	7.8
K. Porter	Det	81	592	7.3
Henderson	Atl-Was	87	598	6.9
Barry	GS	79	475	6.0
White	Bos	82	492	6.0
Gale	SA	82	473	5.8
Westphal	Phoe	81	459	5.7
Lucas	Hou	82	463	5.6

MINUTES PLAYED

Name	Team	Min.
Hayes	Was	3364
White	Bos	3333
Tomjanovich	Hou	3130
Knight	Ind	3117
Van Lier	Chi	3097

BLOCKED SHOTS PER GAME
(Minimum 70 Games or 100 Blocked Shots)

Name	Team	G	Blkd.	Avg.
Walton	Port	65	211	3.2
Abdul-Jabbar	LA	82	261	3.2
Hayes	Was	82	220	2.7
Gilmore	Chi	82	203	2.5
Jones	Phi	82	200	2.4
Johnson	GS-Buf	78	177	2.3
Malone	Buf-Hou	82	181	2.2
Roundfield	Ind	61	131	2.1
Paultz	SA	82	173	2.1
E. Smith	Mil-Cle	70	144	2.1

OFFENSIVE REBOUNDS PER GAME
(Minimum 70 Games Played)

Name	Team	G	Reb.	Avg.
Malone	Buf-Hou	82	435	5.3
McGinnis	Phi	79	324	4.1
Gilmore	Chi	82	313	3.8
Drew	Atl	74	280	3.8
Nater	Mil	72	266	3.7
Johnson	Chi	81	297	3.7
Kenon	SA	78	282	3.6
Hayes	Was	82	289	3.5
Lucas	Port	79	271	3.4
Brewer	Cle	81	275	3.4

STEALS PER GAME
(Minimum 70 Games Or 125 Steals)

Name	Team	G	Steals	Avg.
Buse	Ind	81	281	3.5
Taylor	KC	72	199	2.8
Watts	Sea	79	214	2.7
Buckner	Mil	79	192	2.4
Gale	SA	82	191	2.3
Jones	Den	82	186	2.3
Hollins	Port	76	166	2.2
Ford	Det	82	179	2.2
Barry	GS	79	172	2.2
Smith	Buf	82	176	2.1

1977-78 N.B.A.

The Fat Lady Finally Sings

With one post-merger season under its belt and a potentially great team poised to defend its championship, the N.B.A. had reason to expect great things in 1977-78. Instead the season was marked by injuries, bickering and one near-tragedy.

The league revealed its still-shaky economic status when it reduced rosters to 11 men, an obvious cost-cutting measure that didn't set well with the player's association. Then a turf war erupted in New York between the Knicks and the Nets. The A.B.A. expatriates expected to move to New Jersey, eventually taking up residence at a new arena in the Meadowlands complex. But the Knicks protested that the move violated the terms of the Nets' entry into the N.B.A. In the end, the financially strapped Nets were allowed to move to a temporary home at Rutgers after forking over an additional $4 million penalty.

Early in the season, the Lakers' Kareem Abdul-Jabbar broke his hand when he punched Milwaukee rookie Kent Benson, earning himself a $5,000 fine in the process. Then, on Dec 9, another altercation nearly resulted in the N.B.A.'s first on-court death. In a game with Houston, L.A.'s Kermit Washington got into a scuffle with Kevin Kunnert of the Rockets. As the fight quickly escalated, Houston's Rudy Tomjanovich ran downcourt to act as a peacemaker. Washington, seeing an enemy jersey rushing at him from behind, turned and delivered a terrifying blow that smashed Tomjanovich's face and nearly killed him. Washington was fined $10,000 and suspended for 60 days (then shipped to Boston for Charlie Scott), but the near-tragedy left a cloud over the rest of the season.

Dismal luck plagued even defending champion Portland. The Trail Blazers looked like the N.B.A.'s next dynasty in rolling to a 50-10 record. But at that point Bill Walton, the league's MVP, went down with what seemed like a minor foot injury. In time it was diagnosed as a stress fracture, and the Blazers struggled to an 8-14 finish. Walton hobbled through only two games in the playoffs as the league's best team fell to upstart Seattle.

In New Orleans, Pete Maravich seemed on his way to another scoring title when he hurt his knee after 50 games and was lost for the season, costing the Jazz a chance at the rare distinction of having the league's top scorer and rebounder. The latter honor went to Truck Robinson, signed away from Atlanta as a free agent. But with Maravich out of the way, the race for the scoring crown came to a stirring conclusion. On the season's final afternoon, David Thompson of Denver scored 73 points against Detroit--the highest single-game total by anyone other than Wilt Chamberlain--to give him the lead over San Antonio's George Gervin. Needing 61 points that night for the title, the Iceman tallied 63 against New Orleans to edge Thompson by the slimmest of margins.

Having failed in their quest for the 1976-77 title, the Philadelphia 76ers had a promise for their fans: "We owe you one." A 2-4 start brought coach Gene Shue's dismissal, but the 76ers righted themselves under Billy Cunningham, as Julius Erving, George McGinnis and Doug Collins led the way to 55 wins and another Atlantic Division title. The Knicks sent Walt Frazier to Cleveland for Jim Cleamons, but wound up treading water despite the efforts of Bob McAdoo and new coach Willis Reed. Boston collapsed to 32-50 in John Havlicek's final season, as Satch Sanders replaced Tom Heinsohn as coach in midseason. Dave Cowens led the team in points, rebounds and assists, but he didn't have much help. Buffalo had a new coach, Cotton Fitzsimmons, and two new stars, Billy Knight (acquired from Indiana for Adrian Dantley) and Nate Archibald. But Archibald tore an Achilles tendon in training camp, and Knight and Randy Smith couldn't make up for the loss. And in New Jersey, the Nets had rookie Bernard King and not much else.

With Gervin, Larry Kenon and Billy Paultz leading the way, San Antonio took the Central Division title, finishing comfortably ahead of Washington. The Bullets signed free agent Bob Dandridge but lost Phil Chenier to a back injury in midseason. The team struggled for a while, but as Kevin Grevey got comfortable in Chenier's spot and Dandridge learned to complement Elvin Hayes and Wes Unseld, the Bullets began to look formidable. Injuries hampered Frazier in Cleveland, where the Cavaliers struggled to repeat last year's 43-39 record. Coach of the year Hubie Brown brought Atlanta in at 41-41, a 10-game improvement. The Hawks featured a tough defense and Charlie Criss, a 5-foot-8 rookie who had played for years in what is now the C.B.A. But Houston fell from first to last place in the wake of the Tomjanovich incident, despite a great year from the equally undersized Calvin Murphy.

David Thompson and Dan Issel led Denver to another Midwest title, ahead of Milwaukee, which improved with the addition of rookie Marques Johnson, who replaced the departed Dandridge. Chicago and Detroit were also-rans despite the presence of two great centers in Artis Gilmore and Bob Lanier, respectively. Indiana traded off Dantley and John Williamson, its two top scorers, and Kansas City fired coach Phil Johnson in midseason en route to identical 31-51 records.

Rookie of the Year, Walter Davis, joined Paul Westphal and Alvan Adams in Phoenix, and the result was 49 wins and second place in the Pacific Division. In Seattle, new coach Bob Hopkins had lots of talent in new faces Marvin Webster, Paul Silas, Gus Williams, Jack Sikma and John Johnson, but the result was a 5-17 start. Then Lenny Wilkens took over as coach, and the Sonics went 42-18 to finish third, two games ahead of the Lakers. Rookie Norm Nixon was a bright spot for L.A., but free agent Jamaal Wilkes was slowed by injuries. Meanwhile, Rick Barry and Phil Smith led Golden State to a 43-39 record but a last-place finish in the league's toughest division.

In the Eastern playoffs, Washington stunned division champs San Antonio and Philadelphia in matching six-game series. In the West, Seattle did the same to Portland (minus Walton and Bob Gross, out with a broken ankle) and Denver, setting up a championship meeting between two teams that no one had ever expected to be there. The result was an exciting seesaw battle, with Washington rallying from a 3-2 deficit behind playoff MVP Wes Unseld and winning the decisive seventh game on Seattle's court. After being swept twice in the finals in the 1970s, the Bullets finally made the Fat Lady sing.

1977/78 N.B.A. — EASTERN CONFERENCE
ATLANTIC DIVISION

Use Name	Pos	Hgt	Wgt	Age	TOTAL													Blkd		PER GAME				
					G	Min	FG	FGA	%	FT	FTA	%	Reb	Ass	PF	DQ	Stls	Shts	Points	Min	Reb	Ass	PF	Points
PHILADELPHIA 76ers	**55-27 .671**				**GENE SHUE (2-4 .333), BILLY CUNNINGHAM (53-23 .697)**																			
Julius Erving	F	6'7	200	27	74	2429	611	1217	50	306	362	85	481	279	207	0	135	97	1528	33	6.5	3.8	2.8	20.6
George McInnis	F	6'8	235	27	78	2533	588	1270	46	411	574	72	810	294	287	6	137	27	1587	32	10.4	3.8	3.7	20.3
Darryl Dawkins	C	6'11	251	20	70	1722	332	577	58	156	220	71	555	85	268	5	34	125	820	25	7.9	1.2	3.8	11.7
Doug Collins	G	6'6	180	26	79	2770	643	1223	53	267	329	81	230	320	228	2	128	25	1553	35	2.9	4.1	2.9	19.7
Henry Bibby	G	6'1	185	28	82	2518	286	659	43	171	219	78	251	464	207	0	91	6	743	31	3.1	5.7	2.5	9.1
Lloyd Free	G	6'2	185	24	76	2050	390	857	46	411	562	73	212	306	199	0	68	41	1191	27	2.8	4.0	2.6	15.7
Steve Mix	F	6'7	222	30	82	1819	291	560	52	175	220	80	297	174	158	1	87	3	757	22	3.6	2.1	1.9	9.2
Caldwell Jones	C-F	6'11	225	27	81	1636	169	359	47	96	153	63	570	92	281	4	26	127	434	20	7.0	1.1	3.5	5.4
Joe Bryant	F-C	6'9	185	23	81	1236	190	436	44	111	144	77	280	129	185	1	56	24	491	15	3.5	1.6	2.3	6.1
Harvey Catchings	C	6'9	218	26	61	748	70	178	39	34	55	62	250	34	124	1	20	67	174	12	4.1	0.6	2.0	2.9
Ted McClain (from Buf)	G	6'2	190	30	29	293	42	96	44	7	10	70	37	34	36	0	16	4	91	10	1.3	1.2	1.2	3.1
Wilson Washington (foot injury) (to NJ)	F	6'9	227	22	14	38	8	19	42	3	6	50	14	1	3	0	1	2	19	3	1.0	0.1	0.2	1.4
Glenn Mosley	F	6'8	195	22	6	21	5	13	38	3	7	43	5	2	5	0	0	0	13	4	0.8	0.3	0.8	2.2
Mike Dunleavy (to Hou)	G	6'3	180	23	4	17	3	7	43	2	2	100	1	6	0	0	1	0	8	4	0.3	1.5	0.0	2.0
NEW YORK KNICKERBOCKERS	**43-39 .524**				**WILLIS REED**																			
Jim McMillian	F	6'5	220	29	81	1977	288	623	46	115	134	86	289	205	116	0	76	17	691	24	3.6	2.5	1.4	8.5
Lonnie Shelton	F-C	6'8	245	22	82	2319	508	988	51	203	276	74	580	195	**350**	11	109	112	1219	28	7.1	2.4	4.3	14.9
Rob McAdoo	C	6'9	210	26	79	3182	814	1564	52	469	645	73	1010	298	297	6	105	126	2097	40	12.8	3.8	3.8	26.5
Earl Monroe	G	6'3	190	33	76	2369	556	1123	50	242	291	83	182	361	189	0	60	19	1354	31	2.4	4.8	2.5	17.8
Jim Cleamons	G	6'3	185	28	79	2009	215	448	48	81	103	79	212	283	142	1	68	17	511	25	2.7	3.6	1.8	6.5
Butch Beard	G	6'3	185	30	79	1979	308	614	50	129	160	81	264	339	201	2	117	3	745	25	3.3	4.3	2.5	9.4
Spencer Haywood (knee inury)	F-C	6'9	225	28	67	1765	412	852	48	96	135	71	442	126	188	1	37	72	920	26	6.6	1.9	2.8	13.7
Ray Williams	G	6'3	190	23	81	1550	305	689	44	146	207	71	209	363	211	4	108	15	756	19	2.6	4.5	2.6	9.3
Toby Knight	F	6'9	210	22	80	1169	222	465	48	63	97	65	321	38	211	1	50	28	507	15	4.0	0.5	2.6	6.3
Glen Gondrezick	F-G	6'6	218	22	72	1017	131	339	39	83	121	69	250	83	181	0	56	18	345	14	3.5	1.2	2.5	4.8
Phil Jackson	F-C	6'8	230	32	63	654	55	115	48	43	56	77	110	46	106	0	31	15	153	10	1.7	0.7	1.7	2.4
Ticky Burden (knee injury)	G	6'2	195	24	2	15	1	2	50	0	0	—	0	1	1	0	1	0	2	8	0.0	0.5	0.5	1.0
Tom McMillen (leg injury - to Atl)																								
BOSTON CELTICS	**32-50 .390**				**TOM HEINSOHN (11-23 .324), SATCH SANDERS (21-27 .438)**																			
John Harlick	F	6'5	205	37	82	2797	546	1217	45	230	269	86	332	328	185	2	90	22	1322	34	4.0	4.0	2.3	16.1
Sidney Wicks	F	6'9	225	28	81	2413	433	927	47	217	329	66	673	171	318	9	67	46	1083	30	8.3	2.1	3.9	13.4
Dave Cowens	C	6'9	230	29	77	3215	598	1220	49	239	284	84	1078	351	297	5	102	67	1435	42	14.0	4.6	3.9	18.6
Charlie Scott (to LA)	G	6'6	175	29	31	1080	210	485	43	84	118	71	101	143	97	2	51	6	504	35	3.3	4.6	3.1	16.3
Jo Jo White (foot injury)	G	6'3	190	31	46	1641	289	690	42	103	120	86	180	209	109	2	49	7	681	36	3.9	4.5	2.4	14.8
Dave Bing	G	6'3	185	34	80	2256	422	940	45	244	296	82	212	300	247	2	79	18	1088	28	2.7	3.8	3.1	13.6
Cedrick Maxwell	F	6'8	205	22	72	1213	170	316	54	188	250	75	379	68	151	2	53	48	528	17	5.3	0.9	2.1	7.3
Tom Boswell (injury)	C-F	6'9	225	24	65	1149	185	357	52	93	123	76	288	71	204	5	25	14	463	18	4.4	1.1	3.1	7.1
Kevin Stacom	G	6'3	185	26	55	1006	206	484	43	54	71	76	106	111	60	0	28	3	466	18	1.9	2.0	1.1	8.5
Curtis Rowe (knee injury)	F	6'7	225	28	51	911	123	273	45	66	89	74	203	45	94	1	14	8	312	18	4.0	0.9	1.8	6.1
Kermit Washington (from LA)	F	6'8	230	26	32	866	137	263	52	102	136	75	335	42	114	2	28	40	376	27	10.5	1.3	3.6	11.8
Don Chaney (from LA)	G	6'5	210	31	42	702	91	233	39	33	39	85	105	49	93	0	36	10	215	17	2.5	1.2	2.2	5.1
Ernie DiGregorio (from LA)	G	6'	180	26	27	274	47	109	43	12	13	92	27	66	22	0	12	1	106	10	1.0	2.4	0.8	3.9
Fred Saunders (to NO)	F	6'7	210	26	26	243	30	91	33	14	17	82	37	11	34	0	7	4	74	9	1.4	0.4	1.3	2.8
Zaid Abdul-Aziz (to Hou)	C	6'9	235	31	2	24	3	13	23	2	3	67	15	3	4	0	1	1	8	12	7.5	1.5	2.0	4.0
Bob Bigelow(From KC)	F	6'7	215	24	4	17	3	12	25	0	0	—	4	0	1	0	0	0	6	4	1.0	0.0	0.3	1.5
Steve Kuberski (broken wrist)	F	6'8	215	30	3	14	1	4	25	0	0	—	6	0	2	0	1	0	2	5	2.0	0.0	0.7	0.7
Jim Ard (to Chi)	C	6'9	230	29	1	9	0	1	0	1	2	50	4	1	1	0	0	0	1	9	4.0	1.0	1.0	1.0
BUFFALO BRAVES	**27-55 .329**				**COTTON FITZSIMMONS**																			
Billy Knight (knee injury)	F-G	6'6	195	25	53	2155	457	926	49	301	372	81	383	161	137	0	82	13	1215	41	7.2	3.0	2.6	22.9
Marvin Barnes (from Det)	F	6'9	225	25	48	1377	226	543	42	114	153	75	348	117	198	7	57	72	566	29	7.3	2.4	4.1	11.8
Sven Nater (from Det)	C	6'11	240	27	78	2778	501	994	50	208	272	76	1029	216	274	3	40	47	1210	36	13.2	2.8	3.5	15.5
Randy Smith	G	6'3	180	29	82	3314	789	1697	46	443	554	80	310	458	224	2	172	11	2021	40	3.8	5.6	2.7	24.6
Chuck Williams	G	6'3	185	31	73	2002	208	436	48	114	138	83	137	317	137	0	48	4	530	27	1.9	4.3	1.9	7.3
Wil Jones	F	6'8	205	30	79	1711	226	514	44	84	119	71	334	116	255	7	70	43	536	22	4.2	1.5	3.2	6.8
Bill Willoughby	F	6'8	205	20	56	1079	156	363	43	64	80	80	219	38	131	2	24	47	376	19	3.9	0.7	2.3	6.7
Mike Glenn (from Chi)	G	6'3	175	22	56	947	195	370	53	51	65	78	79	78	98	0	35	5	441	17	1.4	1.4	1.8	7.9
Larry McNeil (from GS)	F-C	6'9	195	26	37	873	156	338	46	130	156	83	188	45	100	1	18	10	442	24	5.1	1.2	2.7	11.9
Ted McClain (to Phi)	G	6'2	190	30	41	727	81	184	44	50	63	79	75	123	88	2	42	2	212	18	1.8	3.0	2.1	5.2
Jim McDaniels	C-F	7'	240	29	42	694	100	234	43	36	42	86	181	44	112	3	4	37	236	17	4.3	1.0	2.7	5.6
Bird Averitt (from NJ)	G	6'2	175	25	34	676	129	296	44	64	96	67	50	128	86	2	22	8	322	20	1.5	3.8	2.5	9.5
John Shumate (to Det)	F	6'9	235	25	18	590	75	151	50	74	99	75	128	58	58	1	14	9	224	33	7.1	3.2	3.2	12.4
Scott Lloyd (from Mil)	C	6'10	230	25	56	566	68	160	43	43	58	74	119	35	83	1	11	9	179	10	2.1	0.6	1.5	3.2
Gary Brokaw	G	6'4	180	23	13	130	18	43	42	18	24	75	12	20	11	0	3	5	54	10	0.9	1.5	0.8	4.2
Gus Gerard (to Det)	F	6'8	205	24	10	85	16	40	40	11	15	73	14	9	13	0	2	3	43	9	1.4	0.9	1.3	4.3
Eddie Owens	F	6'7	210	24	8	63	9	21	43	3	6	50	5	5	9	0	1	0	21	8	0.6	0.6	1.1	2.6
Larry Johnson	G	6'3	205	23	4	38	3	13	23	0	2	0	5	7	3	0	5	2	6	10	1.3	1.8	0.8	1.5
Nate Archibald - leg injury																								

Use Name	Pos	Hgt	Wgt	Age	TOTAL G	Min	FG	FGA	%	FT	FTA	%	Reb	Ass	PF	DQ	Stls	Blkd Shts	Points	PER GAME Min	Reb	Ass	PF	Points

1977/78 N.B.A - EASTERN CONFERENCE (Continued)
ATLANTIC DIVISION

NEW JERSEY NETS 24-58 .293 KEVIN LOUGHERY

Use Name	Pos	Hgt	Wgt	Age	G	Min	FG	FGA	%	FT	FTA	%	Reb	Ass	PF	DQ	Stls	Blkd Shts	Points	Min	Reb	Ass	PF	Points
Bernard King	F	6'7	205	21	79	3092	798	1665	48	313	462	68	751	193	302	5	122	36	1909	39	9.5	2.4	3.8	24.2
Darnell Hillman (to Den)	F-C	6'9	215	28	45	1220	236	501	47	118	205	58	338	49	160	7	49	44	590	27	7.5	1.1	3.6	13.1
George Johnson	C	6'11	205	29	81	2411	285	721	40	133	185	72	779	111	339	**20**	78	**274**	703	30	9.6	1.4	4.2	8.7
John Williamson (from Ind)	G	6'2	195	25	33	1282	388	854	45	197	230	86	107	82	105	2	47	10	973	39	3.2	2.5	3.2	29.5
Kevin Porter (from Det)	G	6'	175	27	74	2686	481	1024	47	235	307	77	199	**801**	265	6	118	15	1197	36	2.7	**10.8**	3.6	16.2
Tim Bassett	F-C	6'8	225	26	65	1474	149	384	39	50	97	52	404	63	181	5	62	33	348	23	6.2	1.0	2.8	5.4
Jan van Breda Kolff	F-G	6'7	200	26	68	1419	107	292	37	87	123	71	244	105	192	7	52	46	301	21	3.6	1.5	2.8	4.4
Howard Porter (from Det)	F	6'8	220	29	55	1216	293	592	49	120	148	81	262	40	119	0	26	33	706	22	4.8	0.7	2.2	12.8
Eddie Jordan (from Cle)	G	6'1	170	22	51	1042	196	482	41	119	151	79	108	145	84	0	114	18	511	20	2.1	2.8	1.6	10.0
Bob Carrington (to Ind)	G-F	6'6	195	24	37	1032	157	392	40	72	97	74	112	55	132	5	43	12	386	28	3.0	1.5	3.6	10.4
Kim Hughes	C	6'11	220	25	56	854	57	160	36	9	29	31	240	38	163	9	49	49	123	15	4.3	0.7	2.9	2.2
Wilson Washington (from Phi)	F-C	6'9	227	22	24	523	92	187	49	26	47	55	142	9	72	2	17	35	210	22	5.9	0.4	3.0	8.8
Bird Averitt (to Buf)	G	6'2	175	25	21	409	69	188	37	36	45	80	33	68	37	1	17	1	174	19	1.6	3.2	1.8	8.3
Louie Nelson (from KC)	G	6'3	190	26	25	353	82	197	42	48	73	66	49	29	28	0	20	6	212	14	2.0	1.2	1.1	8.5
Bubbles Hawkins	G	6'4	190	23	15	343	69	150	46	25	29	86	50	37	51	1	22	13	163	23	3.3	2.5	3.4	10.9
Al Skinner (to Det)	G	6'4	195	25	8	277	41	101	41	39	44	89	52	33	34	2	13	5	121	35	6.5	4.1	4.3	15.1
Mark Crow	F	6'7	210	23	15	154	35	80	44	14	20	70	27	8	24	0	5	1	84	10	1.8	0.5	1.6	5.6
Dave Wohl	G	6'2	185	28	10	118	12	34	35	11	12	92	4	13	24	0	3	0	35	12	0.4	1.3	2.4	3.5

***Porter also with Det led league in assists with 837**

CENTRAL DIVISION

SAN ANTONIO SPURS 52-30 .634 DOUG MOE

Use Name	Pos	Hgt	Wgt	Age	G	Min	FG	FGA	%	FT	FTA	%	Reb	Ass	PF	DQ	Stls	Blkd Shts	Points	Min	Reb	Ass	PF	Points
Mark Olberding	F	6'8	230	21	79	1773	231	480	48	184	227	81	373	131	235	1	45	26	646	22	4.7	1.7	3.0	8.2
Larry Kenon	F	6'9	215	25	81	2869	698	1426	49	274	323	85	773	268	209	2	115	24	1672	35	9.5	3.3	2.6	20.6
Billy Paultz	C	6'11	250	29	80	2479	518	979	53	230	306	75	675	213	222	3	42	194	1266	31	8.4	2.7	2.8	15.8
George Gervin	G	6'7	185	25	82	2857	**864**	1611	54	507	607	84	420	302	255	3	136	110	**2232**	35	5.1	3.7	3.1	**27.2**
Mike Gale (ankle injury)	G	6'4	190	27	70	2091	275	581	47	87	100	87	223	376	170	2	159	25	637	30	3.2	5.4	2.4	9.1
Lou Dampier	G	6'	185	33	82	2037	336	660	51	76	101	75	122	285	84	0	87	13	748	25	1.5	3.5	1.0	9.1
Coby Dietrick	F-C	6'10	225	30	79	1876	250	543	46	89	114	78	358	217	231	4	81	55	589	24	4.5	2.7	2.9	7.5
Allan Bristow	F	6'7	210	26	82	1481	257	538	48	152	208	73	257	194	150	0	69	4	666	18	3.1	2.4	1.8	8.1
Mike Green (from Sea)	C-F	6'10	200	26	63	1132	195	427	46	86	111	77	304	66	167	1	24	87	476	18	4.8	1.0	2.7	7.6
Dennis Layton	G	6'1	182	29	41	498	85	168	51	12	13	92	32	108	51	0	21	4	182	12	0.8	2.6	1.2	4.4
James Silas (knee injury)	G	6'3	180	28	37	311	43	97	44	60	73	82	23	38	29	0	11	1	146	8	0.6	1.0	0.8	3.9
Jim Eakins (to Mil)	C	6'11	215	31	16	251	30	52	58	29	34	85	46	17	46	0	3	10	89	16	2.9	1.1	2.9	5.6
Scott Sims	G	6'1	170	22	12	95	10	26	38	10	15	67	13	20	16	0	3	0	30	8	1.1	1.7	1.3	2.5
George Karl (knee injury)	G	6'2	190	26	4	30	2	6	33	2	2	100	5	5	6	0	1	0	6	8	1.3	1.3	1.5	1.5

WASHINGTON BULLETS 44-38 .537 DICK MOTTA

Use Name	Pos	Hgt	Wgt	Age	G	Min	FG	FGA	%	FT	FTA	%	Reb	Ass	PF	DQ	Stls	Blkd Shts	Points	Min	Reb	Ass	PF	Points
Bob Dandridge	F	6'6	195	30	75	2777	560	1190	47	330	419	79	442	287	262	6	101	44	1450	37	5.9	3.8	3.5	19.3
Elvin Hayes	F	6'9	235	32	81	3246	636	1409	45	326	514	63	1075	149	313	7	96	159	1598	40	13.3	1.8	3.9	19.7
Wes Unseld	C	6'7	245	31	80	2644	257	491	52	93	173	54	955	326	234	2	98	45	607	33	11.9	4.1	2.9	7.6
Phil Chenier (back injury)	G	6'3	180	27	36	937	200	451	44	109	138	79	102	73	54	0	36	9	509	26	2.8	2.0	1.5	14.1
Tom Henderson	G	6'3	190	25	75	2315	339	784	43	179	240	75	193	406	131	0	93	15	857	31	2.6	5.4	1.7	11.4
Kevin Grevey	G-F	6'5	210	24	81	2121	505	1128	45	243	308	79	290	155	203	4	61	17	1253	26	3.6	1.9	2.5	15.5
Mitch Kupchak (finger injury)	C-F	6'9	230	23	67	1759	393	768	51	280	402	70	460	71	196	1	28	42	1066	26	6.9	1.1	2.9	15.9
Larry Wright	G	6'1	160	23	70	1466	283	570	50	76	107	71	102	260	195	3	68	15	642	21	1.5	3.7	2.8	9.2
Greg Ballard	F	6'7	215	22	76	936	142	334	43	88	114	77	266	62	90	1	30	13	372	12	3.5	0.8	1.2	4.9
Charles Johnson (from GS)	G	6'	170	28	39	807	141	346	41	42	51	82	93	82	76	0	31	1	324	21	2.4	2.1	1.9	8.3
Joe Pace	C	6'10	220	24	49	438	67	140	48	57	93	61	134	23	86	1	12	21	191	9	2.7	0.5	1.8	3.9
Phil Walker	G	6'3	180	21	40	384	57	161	35	64	96	67	52	54	39	0	14	5	178	10	1.3	1.4	1.0	4.5

CLEVELAND CAVALIERS 43-39 .524 BILL FITCH

Use Name	Pos	Hgt	Wgt	Age	G	Min	FG	FGA	%	FT	FTA	%	Reb	Ass	PF	DQ	Stls	Blkd Shts	Points	Min	Reb	Ass	PF	Points
Campy Russell	F	6'8	215	25	72	2520	523	1168	45	352	469	75	458	278	193	3	88	12	1398	35	6.4	3.9	2.7	19.4
Jim Chones	F-C	6'11	220	28	82	2906	525	1113	47	180	250	72	844	131	235	4	52	58	1230	35	10.3	1.6	2.9	15.0
Elmore Smith	C	7'	250	28	81	1996	402	809	50	205	309	66	678	57	241	4	502	176	1009	25	8.4	0.7	3.0	12.5
Walt Frazier (foot injury)	G	6'4	205	32	51	1664	336	714	47	153	180	85	209	209	124	1	77	13	825	33	4.1	4.1	2.4	16.2
Foots Walker	G	6'1	172	26	81	2496	287	641	45	159	221	72	294	453	218	0	176	24	733	31	3.6	5.6	2.7	9.0
Austin Carr	G	6'4	200	29	82	2186	414	945	44	183	225	81	187	225	168	1	68	19	1011	27	2.3	2.7	2.0	12.3
Jim Brewer	F	6'9	220	26	80	1798	175	390	45	46	100	46	495	98	178	1	60	48	396	22	6.2	1.2	2.2	5.0
Bobby Smith	F	6'5	212	31	82	1581	369	840	44	108	135	80	207	91	155	1	38	21	846	19	2.5	1.1	1.9	10.3
John Lambert	F-C	6'10	225	24	76	1075	142	336	42	27	48	56	324	38	169	0	27	50	311	14	4.3	0.5	2.2	4.1
Terry Furlow (illness)	G-F	6'4	190	23	53	827	192	443	43	88	99	89	107	72	67	0	21	14	472	16	2.0	1.4	1.3	8.9
Dick Snyder	G	6'5	207	33	58	660	112	252	44	56	64	88	49	56	74	0	23	19	280	11	0.8	1.0	1.3	4.8
Eddie Jordan (to NJ)	G	6'1	170	22	22	171	19	56	34	12	16	75	11	32	10	0	12	1	50	8	0.5	1.5	0.5	2.3

Use Name	Pos	Hgt	Wgt	Age	G	Min	FG	FGA	%	FT	FTA	%	Reb	Ass	PF	DQ	Stls	Blkd Shts	Points	Min	Reb	Ass	PF	Points
					TOTAL															PER GAME				
1977/78 N.B.A. EASTERN CONFERENCE (Continued)																								
CENTRAL DIVISION																								
ATLANTA HAWKS	**41-41 .500**				**HUBIE BROWN**																			
John Drew	F	6'6	205	23	70	2203	593	1236	48	437	575	76	511	141	247	8	119	27	1623	31	7.3	2.0	3.5	23.2
John Brown	F	6'7	220	26	75	1594	192	405	47	165	200	83	303	105	280	18	55	8	549	21	4.0	1.4	3.7	7.3
Steve Hawes	C-F	6'9	220	27	75	2325	387	854	45	175	214	82	690	190	230	4	78	57	949	31	9.2	2.5	3.1	12.7
Armond Hill	G	6'4	190	24	82	2530	304	732	42	189	223	85	231	427	302	15	151	15	797	31	2.8	5.2	3.7	9.7
Charlie Criss	G	5'8	165	28	77	1935	319	751	42	236	296	80	121	294	143	0	108	5	874	25	1.6	3.8	1.9	11.4
Eddie Johnson	G	6'2	190	22	79	1875	332	686	48	164	201	82	153	235	232	4	100	4	828	24	1.9	3.0	2.9	10.5
Tree Rollins	C	7'1	235	22	80	1795	253	520	49	104	148	70	552	79	326	16	57	218	610	22	6.9	1.0	4.1	7.6
Ollie Johnson	F	6'6	200	28	82	1704	292	619	47	111	130	85	260	120	180	2	80	36	695	21	3.2	1.5	2.2	8.5
Tom McMillen (from NY)	F-C	6'11	215	25	68	1683	280	568	49	116	145	80	416	84	233	8	33	16	676	25	6.1	1.2	3.4	9.9
Tony Robertson	G	6'4	195	21	63	929	168	381	44	37	53	70	70	103	133	2	74	5	373	15	1.1	1.6	2.1	5.9
R. Behagen (to Hou, Ind))	F	6'9	235	26	26	571	117	249	47	51	70	73	173	34	97	3	30	12	285	22	6.7	1.3	3.7	11.0
Ken Charles	G	6'3	180	26	21	520	73	184	40	42	50	84	24	82	53	0	25	5	188	25	1.1	3.9	2.5	9.0
Claude Terry (ankle injury)	C-F	6'5	195	27	27	166	25	68	37	9	11	82	15	7	14	0	6	0	59	6	0.6	0.3	0.5	2.2
NEW ORLEANS JAZZ	**39-43 .476**				**ELGIN BAYLOR**																			
Aaron James	F	6'8	210	25	80	2118	428	861	50	117	157	75	421	112	254	5	36	22	973	26	5.3	1.4	3.2	12.2
Truck Robinson	F	6'7	225	26	82	**3638**	748	1683	44	366	572	64	**1288**	171	265	5	73	79	1862	**44**	**15.7**	2.1	3.2	22.7
Rick Kelley	C	7'	240	24	82	2119	304	602	50	225	289	78	759	233	293	6	89	129	833	26	9.3	2.8	3.6	10.2
Pete Maravich (knee injury)	G	6'5	200	29	50	2041	556	1253	44	240	276	87	178	335	116	1	101	8	1352	41	3.6	6.7	2.3	27.0
Gail Goodrich	G	6'1	175	34	81	2553	520	1050	50	264	332	80	177	388	186	0	82	22	1304	32	2.2	4.8	2.3	16.1
Paul Griffin	F-C	6'9	205	23	82	1853	160	358	45	112	157	71	510	172	228	6	88	45	432	23	6.2	2.1	2.8	5.3
Jim McElroy	G	6'3	790	24	74	1760	287	607	47	123	167	74	148	292	110	0	58	34	697	24	2.0	3.9	1.5	9.4
Joe Meriweather	C	6'10	218	24	54	1277	194	411	47	87	133	65	372	58	188	8	18	118	475	24	6.9	1.1	3.5	8.8
Don Watts (from Sea)	G	6'1	175	26	39	775	109	286	38	62	103	60	98	161	96	0	55	17	280	20	2.5	4.1	2.5	7.2
Gus Bailey	F-G	6'5	185	26	48	449	59	139	42	37	67	55	82	40	46	0	18	15	155	9	1.7	0.8	1.0	3.2
Nate Williams (to GS)	G-F	6'5	215	27	27	434	90	214	42	31	37	84	90	34	61	1	21	12	211	16	3.3	1.3	2.3	7.8
Fred Saunders (from Bos)	F	6'7	210	26	30	400	69	143	48	12	19	63	74	35	72	3	14	10	150	13	2.5	1.2	2.4	5.0
Fred Boyd (injury)	G	6'2	180	27	21	363	44	110	40	14	22	64	19	48	23	0	9	3	102	17	0.9	2.3	1.1	4.9
HOUSTON ROCKETS	**28-54 .341**				**TOM NISSALKE**																			
Rudy Tomjanovich (BZ-CN)	F	6'8	220	29	23	849	217	447	49	61	81	75	138	32	63	0	15	5	495	37	6.0	1.4	2.7	21.5
Dwight Jones	F	6'10	210	25	82	2476	346	777	45	181	233	78	641	109	265	2	77	39	873	30	7.8	1.3	3.2	10.6
Moses Malone(FJ)	C	6'10	215	22	59	2107	413	828	50	318	443	72	886	31	179	3	48	76	1144	36	15.0	0.5	3.0	19.4
John Lucas	G	6'3	175	24	82	2933	412	947	44	193	250	77	255	768	208	1	160	9	1017	36	3.1	9.4	2.5	12.4
Cal Murphy	G	5'9	165	29	76	2900	852	**1737**	49	245	267	92	164	259	241	4	112	3	1949	38	2.2	3.4	3.2	25.6
Kevin Kunnert	C-F	7'	231	26	80	2152	368	842	44	93	135	69	693	97	315	13	44	90	829	27	8.7	1.2	3.9	10.4
Robert Reid	F	6'8	205	22	80	1849	261	574	45	63	96	66	359	121	277	8	67	51	585	23	4.5	1.5	3.5	7.3
Mike Newlin (BG-XJ)	G-F	6'4	200	28	45	1181	216	495	44	152	174	87	120	203	128	1	52	9	584	26	2.7	4.5	2.8	13.0
Ed Ratleff	G-F	6'6	195	27	68	1163	130	310	42	39	47	83	162	153	109	0	60	22	299	17	2.4	2.3	1.6	4.4
Alonzo Bradley	F	6'6	190	24	43	798	130	304	43	43	59	73	99	54	83	1	16	6	303	19	2.3	1.3	1.9	7.0
C.J. Kupec (broken leg)	F	6'8	220	24	49	626	84	197	43	27	33	82	91	50	54	0	10	3	195	13	1.9	1.0	1.1	4.0
Rudy White (broken toe)	G	6'2	195	24	21	219	31	85	36	14	18	78	21	22	24	0	8	0	76	10	1.0	1.0	1.1	3.6
Zaid Abdul-Aziz (from Bos)	C	6'9	235	31	14	134	20	47	43	15	20	75	35	7	25	0	2	2	55	10	2.5	0.5	1.8	3.9
Larry Moffett (ankle injury)	F	6'9	210	23	20	110	5	17	29	6	10	60	21	7	16	0	2	2	16	6	1.1	0.4	0.8	0.8
Mike Dunleavy (from Phi)	G	6'3	180	23	11	102	17	43	40	11	16	69	9	22	12	0	8	1	45	9	0.8	2.0	1.1	4.1
Robin Jones	F	6'9	225	23	12	66	11	20	55	4	10	40	14	2	16	0	1	1	26	6	1.2	0.2	1.3	2.2
Ron Behagen (from Atl, to Ind)	F	6'9	235	26	3	33	7	11	64	0	1	0	7	2	6	0	0	0	14	11	2.3	0.7	2.0	4.7
Phil Bond	G	6'2	175	23	7	21	2	6	33	0	0	—	4	2	1	0	1	0	4	3	0.6	0.3	0.1	0.6
John Johnson (to Sea)	F	6'7	200	30	1	11	1	4	25	2	3	67	3	1	3	0	0	0	4	11	3.0	1.0	3.0	4.0
WESTERN CONFERENCE																								
MIDWEST DIVISION																								
DENVER NUGGETS	**48-34 .585**				**LARRY BROWN**																			
Bob Wilkerson	F-G	6'6	200	23	81	2780	382	936	41	157	210	75	474	439	275	3	126	21	921	34	5.9	5.4	3.4	11.4
Bobby Jones	F	6'9	212	26	75	2440	440	761	**58**	208	277	75	636	252	221	2	137	126	1088	33	8.5	3.4	2.9	14.5
Dan Issel	C-F	6'9	240	29	82	2851	659	1287	51	428	547	78	830	304	279	5	100	41	1746	35	10.1	3.7	3.4	21.3
David Thompson	G-F	6'4	195	23	80	3025	826	1584	52	**520**	668	78	390	362	213	1	99	99	2172	38	4.9	4.5	2.7	27.2
Brian Taylor (holdout)	G	6'2	185	26	39	1222	182	403	45	88	115	77	98	132	120	1	71	9	452	31	2.5	3.4	3.1	11.6
Anthony Roberts	F	6'5	185	22	82	1598	311	736	42	153	212	72	351	105	212	1	40	7	775	19	4.3	1.3	2.6	9.5
Bo Ellis	F	6'9	190	23	78	1213	133	320	42	72	104	69	304	73	208	2	49	47	338	16	3.9	0.9	2.7	4.3
Jim Price (to Det)	G	6'3	195	28	49	1090	141	293	48	51	66	77	159	158	118	0	69	4	333	22	3.2	3.2	2.4	6.8
Mack Calvin	G	6'	175	29	77	988	147	333	44	173	206	84	84	148	87	0	46	5	467	13	1.1	1.9	1.1	6.1
Tom LaGarde	C	6'10	220	22	77	868	96	237	41	114	150	76	214	47	146	1	17	17	306	11	2.8	0.6	1.9	4.0
Darnell Hillman (from NJ)	F-C	6'9	215	28	33	746	104	209	50	49	81	60	239	53	130	4	14	37	257	23	7.2	1.6	3.9	7.8
Ralph Simpson (from Det)	G	6'5	200	28	32	584	73	230	32	31	40	78	75	72	42	0	43	4	177	18	2.3	2.3	1.3	5.5
Robert Smith	G	5'11	165	22	45	378	50	97	52	21	24	88	36	39	52	0	18	3	121	8	0.8	0.9	1.2	2.7
Jacky Dorsey (to Port)	F	6'7	230	23	7	37	3	12	25	3	5	60	20	2	9	0	2	2	9	5	2.9	0.3	1.3	1.3
Norm Cook	F	6'9	210	22	2	10	1	3	33	0	0	—	3	1	4	0	0	0	2	5	1.5	0.5	2.0	1.0

1977/78 N.B.A. - WESTERN CONFERENCE (Continued)
MIDWEST DIVISION

Use Name	Pos	Hgt	Wgt	Age	TOTAL G	Min	FG	FGA	%	FT	FTA	%	Reb	Ass	PF	DQ	Stls	Blkd Shts	Points	PER GAME Min	Reb	Ass	PF	Points
MILWAUKEE BUCKS	**44-38 .537**				**DON NELSON**																			
Marques Johnson	F	6'7	218	21	80	2765	628	1204	52	301	409	74	847	190	221	3	92	103	1557	35	10.6	2.4	2.8	19.5
David Meyers	F	6'9	225	24	80	2416	432	938	46	314	435	72	537	241	240	2	86	46	1178	30	6.7	3.0	3.0	14.7
John Gianelli	C	6'10	220	27	82	2327	307	629	49	79	123	64	509	192	189	4	54	92	693	28	6.2	2.3	2.3	8.5
Brian Winters	G	6'4	185	25	80	2751	674	1457	46	246	293	84	250	393	239	4	124	27	1594	34	3.1	4.9	3.0	19.9
Quinn Buckner	G	6'3	205	23	82	2072	314	671	47	131	203	65	247	456	287	6	188	19	759	25	3.0	5.6	3.5	9.3
Junior Bridgeman	G-F	6'5	210	24	82	1876	476	947	50	166	205	81	290	175	202	1	72	30	1118	23	3.5	2.1	2.5	13.6
Alex English	F	6'8	190	23	82	1552	343	633	54	104	143	73	395	129	178	1	41	55	790	19	4.8	1.6	2.2	9.6
Kent Benson	C	6'10	245	23	69	1288	220	473	47	92	141	65	295	99	177	1	69	54	532	19	4.3	1.4	2.6	7.7
Lloyd Walton	G	6'	160	24	76	1264	154	344	45	54	83	65	76	253	94	0	77	13	362	17	1.0	3.3	1.2	4.8
Ernie Grunfeld	F-G	6'6	215	22	73	1261	204	461	44	94	143	66	194	145	150	1	54	19	502	17	2.7	2.0	2.1	6.9
Jim Eakins (from SD)	C	6'11	215	31	17	155	14	34	41	21	26	81	29	12	25	0	4	7	49	9	1.7	0.7	1.5	2.9
Scott Lloyd (to Buf)	C	6'10	230	25	14	112	12	33	36	6	10	60	26	3	22	0	3	5	30	8	1.9	0.2	1.6	2.1
Kevin Restani (to KC)	F-C	6'9	225	26	8	84	13	28	46	0	2	0	14	9	4	0	0	1	26	11	1.8	1.1	0.5	3.3
Rich Laurel	G	6'6	190	23	10	57	10	31	32	4	4	100	10	3	10	0	3	1	24	6	1.0	0.3	1.0	2.4
CHICAGO BULLS	**40-42 .408**				**ED BADGER**																			
Scott May (knee injury)	F	6'7	220	23	55	1802	280	617	45	175	216	81	332	114	170	4	50	6	735	33	6.0	2.1	3.1	13.4
Mickey Johnson	F	6'10	190	25	81	2870	561	1215	46	362	446	81	738	267	317	8	92	68	1484	35	9.1	3.3	3.9	18.3
Artis Gilmore	C	7'2	240	28	82	3067	704	1260	26	471	**669**	70	1071	263	261	4	42	81	1879	37	13.1	3.2	3.2	22.9
Wilbur Holland	G	6'	175	56	82	2884	569	1285	44	223	279	80	294	313	258	4	164	14	1361	35	3.6	3.8	3.1	16.6
Norm Van Lier	G	6'1	173	30	78	2524	200	477	42	172	229	75	284	531	279	9	144	5	572	32	3.6	6.8	3.6	7.3
John Mengelt	G	6'2	195	28	81	1767	325	675	48	184	238	77	129	232	169	0	51	4	834	22	1.6	2.9	2.1	10.3
Mark Landsberger	F-C	6'8	215	22	62	926	127	251	51	91	157	58	301	41	78	0	21	6	345	15	4.9	0.7	1.3	5.6
Cazzy Russell	F	6'5	220	33	36	789	133	304	44	49	57	86	83	61	63	1	19	4	315	22	2.3	1.7	1.8	8.8
Tate Armstrong	G	6'3	175	22	66	716	131	280	47	22	27	81	68	74	42	0	23	0	284	11	1.0	1.1	0.6	4.3
Steve Sheppard	F	6'6	220	23	64	698	119	262	45	37	56	66	131	43	72	0	14	3	275	11	2.0	0.7	1.1	4.3
Nick Weatherspoon	F	6'7	197	27	41	611	86	194	44	37	42	88	125	32	74	0	19	10	209	15	3.0	0.8	1.8	5.1
Cliff Pondexter	F-C	6'9	235	23	44	534	37	85	44	14	20	70	130	87	66	0	19	15	88	12	3.0	2.0	1.5	2.0
Tom Boerwinkle (knee injury)	C	7'	270	32	22	227	23	50	46	10	13	77	59	44	36	0	3	4	56	10	2.7	2.0	1.6	2.5
Derreck Dickey (from GS)	F	6'7	218	26	25	220	27	68	40	14	19	74	48	10	27	0	4	2	68	9	1.9	0.4	1.1	2.7
Jim Ard (from Bos, leg injury)	C	6'9	230	29	14	116	8	16	50	2	3	67	32	7	18	0	0	0	18	8	2.3	0.5	1.3	1.3
Glenn Hansen (to KC)	G	6'5	205	25	2	4	0	2	0	0	0	—	0	0	0	0	0	0	0	2	0.0	0.0	0.0	0.0
Mike Glenn (broken neck, to Buf)																								
DETROIT PISTONS	**38-44 .463**				**HERB BROWN (9-15 .375), BOB KAUFFMAN (29-29 .500)**																			
M.L. Carr	F	6'6	205	26	79	2556	390	857	46	200	271	74	557	185	243	4	147	27	980	32	7.1	2.3	3.1	12.4
John Shumate (from Buf)	F	6'9	235	25	62	2170	316	622	51	326	409	80	554	122	142	1	76	43	958	35	8.9	2.0	2.3	15.5
Bob Lanier (knee injury)	C	6'11	250	29	63	2311	622	1159	54	298	386	77	715	216	185	2	82	93	1542	37	11.3	3.4	2.9	24.5
Chris Ford	G	6'5	190	28	82	2582	374	777	48	113	154	73	268	381	182	2	166	17	861	31	3.3	4.6	2.2	10.5
Eric Money	G	6'	170	22	76	2557	600	1200	50	214	298	72	209	356	237	5	123	12	1414	34	2.8	4.7	3.1	18.6
Leon Douglas	C-F	6'10	230	23	79	1993	321	667	48	221	345	64	582	112	295	6	57	48	863	25	7.4	1.4	3.7	10.9
Al Skinner (from NJ)	G-F	6'4	195	25	69	1274	181	387	47	123	159	77	172	113	208	4	52	15	485	18	2.5	1.6	3.0	7.0
Jim Price (from Den)	G	6'3	195	28	34	839	153	363	42	84	103	82	101	102	82	0	45	5	390	25	3.0	3.0	2.4	11.5
Gus Gerard (from Buf)	F	6'8	205	24	47	805	154	355	43	64	93	69	146	44	96	1	34	22	372	17	3.1	0.9	2.0	7.9
Ralph Simpson (to Den)	G	6'5	200	28	32	739	143	346	41	54	64	84	82	87	48	1	32	3	340	23	2.6	2.7	1.5	10.6
Ben Poquette	F-C	6'9	235	22	52	626	95	225	42	42	60	70	145	20	69	1	10	22	232	12	2.8	0.4	1.3	4.5
Al Eberhard (broken ankle)	F	6'6	225	25	37	576	71	160	44	41	61	67	102	26	64	0	13	4	183	16	2.8	0.7	1.7	4.9
Marvin Barnes (to Buf)	F	6'9	225	25	12	269	53	118	45	14	29	48	91	19	43	2	7	11	120	22	7.6	1.6	3.6	10.0
Willie Norwood (to Port)	F	6'7	215	30	16	260	34	82	41	20	29	69	54	14	45	0	13	3	88	16	3.4	0.9	2.8	5.5
Kevin Porter (to NJ)	G	6'	175	27	8	127	14	31	45	9	13	69	15	***36**	18	0	5	0	37	16	1.9	**4.5**	2.3	4.6
Howard Porter (to NJ)	F	6'8	220	29	8	107	16	43	37	4	7	57	17	2	15	0	3	5	36	13	2.1	0.3	1.9	4.5
Jim Bostic	F	6'7	225	24	4	48	12	22	55	2	5	40	16	3	5	0	0	0	26	12	4.0	0.8	1.3	6.5
Wayman Britt	G	6'2	185	23	7	16	3	10	30	3	4	75	4	2	3	0	1	0	9	2	0.6	0.3	0.4	1.3
Don Adams (leg injury)	(*also with NJ - led league in assists)																							
INDIANA PACERS	**31-51 .378**				**BOBBY LEONARD**																			
Mike Bantom	F	6'9	220	26	82	2775	502	1047	48	254	342	74	610	238	333	13	100	50	1258	34	7.4	2.9	4.1	15.3
Dan Roundfeld	F-C	6'8	205	24	79	2423	421	861	49	218	300	73	802	196	297	4	81	149	1060	31	10.2	2.5	3.8	13.4
James Edwards (from LA)	C	7'	225	22	58	1682	350	777	45	192	296	65	435	56	233	9	36	50	892	29	7.5	1.0	4.0	15.4
Earl Tatum (from LA)	G	6'5	185	24	57	1859	357	773	46	108	137	79	205	226	172	4	103	30	822	33	3.6	4.0	3.0	14.4
Ricky Sobers	G	6'3	198	24	79	3019	553	1224	45	330	400	83	327	584	308	10	170	23	1436	38	4.1	7.4	3.9	18.2
John Williamson (to NJ)	G	6'2	195	25	42	1449	335	795	42	134	161	83	120	132	131	4	47	0	804	35	2.9	3.1	3.1	19.1
Len Elmore	C	6'9	220	25	69	1327	142	386	37	88	132	67	420	80	174	4	74	71	372	19	6.1	1.2	2.5	5.4
Ron Behagen (from Atl, Hou)	F	6'9	235	26	51	1131	222	544	41	128	176	73	333	65	160	1	32	19	572	22	6.5	1.3	3.1	11.2
Mike Flynn	G	6'3	190	24	71	955	120	267	45	55	97	57	117	142	52	0	71	10	295	13	1.6	2.0	0.7	4.2
Adrian Dantley (to LA)	F	6'5	210	21	23	948	201	403	50	207	263	79	216	65	76	1	48	17	609	41	9.4	2.8	3.3	26.5
Bob Carrington (from NJ)	G-F	6'6	195	24	35	621	96	197	49	58	74	78	62	62	73	1	22	11	250	18	1.8	1.8	2.1	7.1
Dave Robisch (to LA)	C-F	6'10	240	28	23	598	73	181	40	50	64	78	173	49	59	1	20	15	196	26	7.5	2.1	2.6	8.5
Steve Green (knee injury)	F	6'7	220	24	44	449	56	128	44	39	56	70	71	30	67	0	14	2	151	10	1.6	0.7	1.5	3.4
Mel Bennett	F	6'7	200	22	31	285	23	81	28	28	45	62	93	22	54	1	11	7	74	9	3.0	0.7	1.7	2.4
John Neuman	G	6'6	200	26	20	216	35	86	41	13	18	72	14	27	24	0	6	1	83	11	0.7	1.4	1.2	4.2
Bobby Wilson	G	6'3	180	25	12	86	14	36	39	2	3	67	12	8	16	0	2	1	30	7	1.0	0.7	1.3	2.5
Willie Smith	G	6'2	170	24	1	7	0	0	—	0	0	—	0	1	1	0	0	0	0	7	0.0	1.0	1.0	0.0

Use Name	Pos	Hgt	Wgt	Age	G	Min	FG	FGA	%	FT	FTA	%	Reb	Ass	PF	DQ	Stls	Blkd Shts	Points	Min	Reb	Ass	PF	Points
					TOTAL															PER GAME				

1977/78 N.B.A. - WESTERN CONFERENCE (Continued)
MIDWEST DIVISION

Use Name	Pos	Hgt	Wgt	Age	G	Min	FG	FGA	%	FT	FTA	%	Reb	Ass	PF	DQ	Stls	Blkd Shts	Points	Min	Reb	Ass	PF	Points
KANSAS CITY KINGS	**31-51 .378**				**PHIL JOHNSON (13-34 .277), LARRY STAVERMAN (18-27 .400)**																			
Scott Wedman	F	6'7	215	25	81	2961	607	1192	51	221	254	87	463	201	242	2	99	22	1435	36.6	5.7	2.5	3.0	17.7
Richard Washington	F	6'11	225	22	78	2231	425	891	48	150	199	75	654	118	324	12	74	43	1000	28.6	8.4	1.5	4.2	12.8
Sam Lacey	C	6'10	235	29	77	2131	265	590	45	134	187	72	642	300	264	7	120	108	664	27.7	8.3	3.9	3.4	8.6
Ron Boone	G	6'2	200	31	82	2653	563	1271	44	322	377	85	269	311	233	3	105	11	1448	32.4	3.3	3.8	2.8	17.7
Lucius Allen	G	6'2	175	30	77	2147	373	846	44	174	220	79	229	360	180	0	93	28	920	27.9	3.0	4.7	2.3	11.9
Otis Birdsong	G	6'4	195	22	73	1878	470	955	49	216	310	70	175	174	179	1	74	12	1156	25.7	2.4	2.4	2.5	15.8
Bill Robinzine	F	6'7	230	24	82	1748	305	677	45	206	271	76	539	72	281	5	74	11	816	21.3	6.6	0.9	3.4	10.0
Tom Burleson	C	7'3	228	25	76	1525	228	525	43	197	248	79	482	131	259	6	62	81	653	20.1	6.3	1.7	3.4	8.6
John Kuester	G	6'2	180	22	78	1215	145	319	45	87	105	83	114	252	143	1	58	1	377	15.6	1.5	3.2	1.8	4.8
Bob Nash	F	6'8	205	27	66	800	157	304	52	50	69	72	169	46	75	0	27	18	364	12.1	2.6	0.7	1.1	5.5
Kevin Restani (from Mil)	C-F	6'9	225	26	46	463	59	139	42	9	11	82	94	21	37	0	5	4	127	10.1	2.0	0.5	0.8	2.8
Louie Nelson (to NJ)	G	6'3	190	26	8	53	3	14	21	9	11	82	3	5	5	0	2	1	15	6.6	0.4	0.6	0.6	1.9
Glen Hansen (from Chi)	G	6'5	205	25	3	9	0	5	0	0	0	-	1	1	3	0	1	0	0	3.0	0.3	0.3	1.0	0.0
Andre McCarter	G	6'3	190	24	1	9	0	2	0	0	0	-	1	0	1	0	0	0	0	9.0	1.0	0.0	1.0	0.0
Bob Bigelow (to Bos)	F	6'7	215	24	1	7	1	1	100	0	0	-	5	0	2	0	0	0	2	7.0	5.0	0.0	2.0	2.0

PACIFIC DIVISION

Use Name	Pos	Hgt	Wgt	Age	G	Min	FG	FGA	%	FT	FTA	%	Reb	Ass	PF	DQ	Stls	Blkd Shts	Points	Min	Reb	Ass	PF	Points
PORTLAND TRAILBLAZERS	**58-24 .707**				**JACK RAMSAY**																			
Bob Gross (broken ankle)	F	6'6	200	24	72	2163	381	720	53	152	190	80	400	254	234	5	100	52	914	30.0	5.6	3.5	3.3	12.7
Maurice Lucas	F-C	6'9	218	25	68	2119	453	989	46	207	270	77	621	173	221	3	61	56	1113	31.2	9.1	2.5	3.3	16.4
Bill Walton (broken foot)	C	6'11	225	25	58	1929	460	882	52	177	246	72	766	291	145	3	60	146	1097	33.3	13.2	5.0	2.5	18.9
Lionel Hollins	G	6'3	185	24	81	2741	531	1202	44	223	300	74	277	380	268	4	157	29	1285	33.8	3.4	4.7	3.3	15.9
Johnny Davis	G	6'2	170	22	82	2188	343	756	45	188	227	83	173	217	173	0	81	14	874	26.7	2.1	2.6	2.1	10.7
Dave Twardzik	G	6'1	180	27	75	1820	242	409	59	183	234	78	134	244	186	2	107	4	667	24.3	1.8	3.3	2.5	8.9
Tom Owens	C	6'10	220	28	82	1714	313	639	49	206	278	74	541	160	263	7	33	37	832	20.9	6.6	2.0	3.2	10.1
Corky Calhoun	F	6'7	210	27	79	1370	175	365	48	66	76	87	215	87	141	3	42	15	416	17.3	2.7	1.1	1.8	5.3
Lloyd Neal (knee injury)	F-C	6'7	225	27	61	1174	272	540	50	127	177	72	373	81	128	0	29	21	671	19.2	6.1	1.3	2.1	11.0
Larry Steele	F-G	6'5	180	28	65	1132	210	447	47	100	122	82	113	87	138	2	59	5	520	17.4	1.7	1.3	2.1	8.0
T.R, Dunn	G	6'4	192	22	63	768	100	240	42	37	56	66	147	45	74	0	46	8	237	12.2	2.3	0.7	1.2	3.8
Willie Norwood (from Det)	F	6'7	215	30	19	351	40	99	40	30	46	65	65	19	56	1	18	0	110	18.5	3.4	1.0	2.9	5.8
Dale Schleuter	C	6'10	235	32	10	109	8	19	42	9	18	50	21	18	20	0	3	2	25	10.9	2.1	1.8	2.0	2.5
Wally Walker (to Sea)	F	6'7	190	23	9	101	19	41	46	5	8	63	17	8	13	0	2	0	43	11.2	1.9	0.9	1.4	4.8
Jacky Dorsey (from Den)	F	6'7	230	23	4	51	9	19	47	7	11	64	10	3	8	0	0	1	25	12.8	2.5	0.8	2.0	6.3
PHOENIX SUNS	**49-33 .598**				**JOHN MacLEOD**																			
Walter Davis	F	6'6	195	23	81	2590	786	1494	53	387	466	83	484	273	242	2	113	20	1959	32.0	6.0	3.4	3.0	24.2
Gar Heard	F	6'6	219	29	80	2099	265	625	42	90	147	61	652	132	213	0	129	101	620	26.2	8.2	1.7	2.7	7.8
Alvan Adams (tonsilitis)	C-F	6'9	220	23	70	1914	434	895	48	214	293	73	565	225	242	8	86	63	1082	27.3	8.1	3.2	3.5	15.5
Paul Westphal	G	6'4	195	27	80	2481	809	1568	52	396	487	81	164	437	160	0	138	31	2014	31.0	2.1	5.5	2.0	25.2
Don Buse	G	6'4	195	27	82	2547	287	626	46	112	136	82	249	391	144	0	185	14	686	31.1	3.0	4.8	1.8	8.4
Ron Lee	G	6'4	193	25	82	1928	417	950	44	170	228	75	254	305	257	3	225	17	1004	23.5	3.1	3.7	3.1	12.2
Dennis Autrey	C	6'10	240	29	81	1623	112	264	42	69	109	63	302	163	153	0	19	25	293	20.0	3.7	2.0	1.9	3.6
Alvin Scott	F	6'7	185	22	81	1538	180	369	49	132	191	69	357	88	158	0	52	40	492	19.0	4.4	1.1	2.0	6.1
Mike Bratz	G	6'2	185	22	80	933	159	395	40	56	68	82	115	123	104	1	39	5	374	11.7	1.4	1.5	1.3	4.7
Bayard Forrest	C	6'10	235	23	64	887	111	238	47	49	103	48	250	129	105	0	23	34	271	13.9	3.9	2.0	1.6	4.2
Curtis Perry (back injury)	F	6'7	220	29	45	818	110	243	45	51	65	78	250	48	120	2	34	22	271	18.2	5.6	1.1	2.7	6.0
Greg Griffin	F	6'7	190	25	36	422	61	169	36	23	36	64	103	24	56	0	16	0	145	11.7	2.9	0.7	1.6	4.0
Ira Terrell (injured)																								
SEATTLE SUPERSONICS	**47-35 .573**				**BOB HOPKINS (5-17 .227), LENNY WILKINS (42-18 .700)**																			
John Johnson (from Hou)	F	6'7	200	30	76	1812	341	820	42	131	174	75	307	210	194	0	43	19	813	23.8	4.0	2.8	2.6	10.7
Jack Sikma	F-C	6'11	230	22	82	2238	342	752	45	192	247	78	678	134	300	6	68	40	876	27.3	8.3	1.6	3.7	10.7
Marvin Webster	C	7'1	240	25	82	2910	427	851	50	290	461	63	1035	203	262	8	48	162	1144	35.5	12.6	2.5	3.2	14.0
Dennis Johnson	G	6'4	185	23	81	2209	367	881	42	297	406	73	294	230	213	2	118	51	1031	27.3	3.6	2.8	2.6	12.7
Gus Williams	G	6'2	175	24	79	2572	602	1335	45	227	278	82	256	294	198	2	185	41	1431	32.6	3.2	3.7	2.5	18.1
Paul Silas	F	6'7	220	34	82	2172	187	464	40	109	186	59	666	145	182	0	65	16	477	26.5	8.1	1.8	2.2	5.8
Fred Brown	G	6'3	185	29	72	1965	508	1042	49	176	196	90	188	240	145	0	110	25	1192	27.3	2.6	3.3	2.0	16.6
Bruce Seals	F	6'8	215	24	73	1322	230	551	42	111	175	63	226	81	210	4	41	33	571	18.1	3.1	1.1	2.9	7.8
Wally Walker (from Port)	F	6'7	190	23	68	1083	185	420	44	70	112	63	202	69	125	1	24	10	440	14.8	3.0	1.0	1.8	6.5
Don Watts (to NO)	G	6'1	175	26	32	809	110	272	40	30	53	57	81	133	88	1	53	14	250	25.3	2.5	4.2	2.8	7.8
Joey Hassett	G	6'5	180	22	48	404	91	205	44	10	12	83	36	41	45	0	21	0	192	8.4	0.8	0.9	0.9	4.0
Mike Green (to SA)	C	6'10	200	26	9	250	43	87	49	21	31	68	55	10	26	0	6	13	107	27.8	6.1	1.1	2.9	11.9
Al Fleming	F	6'7	215	23	20	97	15	31	48	10	17	59	30	7	16	0	0	5	40	4.9	1.5	0.4	0.8	2.0
Willie Wise (knee injury)	F	6'6	210	30	2	10	0	3	0	1	4	25	3	0	2	0	0	0	1	5.0	1.5	0.0	1.0	0.5
Dean Tolson	F	6'8	200	26	1	7	0	1	0	0	0	-	0	2	2	0	0	0	0	7.0	0.0	2.0	2.0	0.0

1977/78 N.B.A. — WESTERN DIVISION (Continued)
PACIFIC DIVISION

Use Name	Pos	Hgt	Wgt	Age	TOTAL G	Min	FG	FGA	%	FT	FTA	%	Reb	Ass	PF	DQ	Stls	Blkd Shts	Points	PER GAME Min	Reb	Ass	PF	Points
LOS ANGELES LAKERS	**45-37 .549 JERRY WEST**																							
Adrian Dantley (from Ind)	F	6'5	210	21	56	1985	377	725	52	334	417	80	404	188	157	1	70	7	1088	35	7.2	3.4	2.8	19.4
Jamaal Wilkes (BG)	F	6'6	190	24	51	1490	277	630	44	106	148	72	380	182	162	1	77	22	660	29	7.5	3.6	3.2	12.9
Kareem Abdul-Jabbar (BH)	C	7'2	232	30	62	2265	633	1205	53	274	350	78	801	269	182	1	103	185	1600	37	12.9	4.3	2.9	25.8
Lou Hudson	G	6'5	210	33	82	2283	493	992	50	137	177	77	188	193	196	0	94	14	1123	28	2.3	2.4	2.4	13.7
Norm Nixon	G	6'2	175	22	81	2779	496	998	50	115	161	71	239	553	259	3	138	7	1107	34	3.0	6.8	3.2	13.7
Don Ford	F	6'9	215	25	79	1945	272	576	47	68	90	76	353	142	210	1	68	46	612	25	4.5	1.8	2.7	7.7
Charlie Scott (from Bos)	G	6'6	175	29	48	1393	225	509	44	110	142	77	148	235	155	4	59	11	560	29	3.1	4.9	3.2	11.7
Tom Abernathy	F	6'7	220	23	73	1317	201	404	50	91	111	82	265	101	122	1	55	22	493	18	3.6	1.4	1.7	6.8
Kermit Washington (ST, to Bos)	F-C	6'8	230	26	25	751	110	244	45	68	110	62	279	30	74	1	19	24	288	30	11.2	1.2	3.0	11.5
Kenny Carr	F	6'7	230	22	52	733	134	302	44	55	85	65	208	26	127	0	18	14	323	14	4.0	0.5	2.4	6.2
James Edwards (to Ind)	C	7'	225	22	25	723	145	316	46	80	125	64	180	29	89	3	16	28	370	29	7.2	1.2	3.6	14.8
Dave Robisch (from Ind)	C	6'10	240	28	55	679	104	249	42	50	65	77	179	40	71	0	19	14	258	12	3.3	0.7	1.3	4.7
Earl Tatum (to Ind)	G	6'5	185	24	25	663	153	314	49	45	59	76	90	70	85	1	37	10	351	27	3.6	2.8	3.4	14.0
Brad Davis (BH)	G	6'3	180	22	33	334	30	72	42	22	29	76	35	83	39	1	15	2	82	10	1.1	2.5	1.2	2.5
Ernie DiGregorio (to Bos)	G	6'	180	26	25	332	41	100	41	16	20	80	23	71	22	0	6	0	98	13	0.9	2.8	0.9	3.9
Don Chaney (BG, to Bos)	G	6'5	210	31	9	133	13	36	36	5	6	83	11	17	14	0	8	3	31	15	1.2	1.9	1.6	3.4
GOLDEN STATE WARRIORS	**43-39 .524 AL ATTLES**																							
Rick Barry	F	6'7	220	33	82	3024	760	1686	45	378	409	**92**	449	446	188	1	158	45	1898	37	5.5	5.4	2.3	23.1
E.C. Coleman	F	6'8	225	27	72	1801	212	446	48	40	55	73	376	100	253	4	66	23	464	25	5.2	1.4	3.5	6.4
Clifford Ray (knee injury)	C-F	6'9	235	28	79	2268	272	476	57	148	243	61	758	147	291	9	74	90	692	29	9.6	1.9	3.7	8.8
Phil Smith	G	6'4	187	25	82	2940	648	1373	47	316	389	81	300	393	219	2	108	27	1612	36	3.7	4.8	2.7	19.7
Charles Dudley	G	6'2	180	27	78	1660	127	249	51	138	195	71	287	409	181	0	68	2	392	21	3.7	5.2	2.3	5.0
Sonny Parker	F-G	6'6	200	22	82	2069	406	783	52	122	173	71	389	155	786	0	135	36	934	25	4.7	1.9	9.6	11.4
Robert Parrish	C	7'	230	24	82	1969	430	911	47	165	264	63	680	95	291	10	79	123	1025	24	8.3	1.2	3.5	12.5
Rickey Green	G	6'1	170	23	76	1098	143	375	38	54	90	60	116	149	95	0	58	1	340	14	1.5	2.0	1.3	4.5
Rickey Marsh	G	6'3	200	23	60	851	123	289	43	23	33	70	75	90	111	0	29	19	269	14	1.3	1.5	1.9	4.5
Nate Williamson	G	6'5	215	27	46	815	222	510	44	70	84	83	114	40	120	2	36	22	514	18	2.5	0.9	2.6	11.2
Charlie Johnson (to Was)	G	6'	170	28	32	492	96	235	41	7	10	70	62	48	53	0	31	4	199	15	1.9	1.5	1.7	6.2
Wesley Cox	F	6'6	215	22	43	453	69	173	40	58	100	58	143	12	82	1	21	10	196	11	3.3	0.3	1.9	4.6
Derrick Dickey (JJ, to CHI)	F	6'7	218	26	22	273	60	130	46	16	17	94	49	11	29	0	10	2	136	12	2.2	0.5	1.3	6.2
Larry McNeill (to Buf)	F	6'9	195	26	9	67	6	18	33	15	19	79	14	2	14	0	0	1	27	7	1.6	0.2	1.6	3.0

PLAYOFFS

WASHINGTON BULLETS — **DICK MOTTA**

defeated Atlanta 2-0; H103-94, 107-103(OT)
defeated San Antonio 4-2; 103-114, 121-117, H118-105, H98-95, 105-116, H103-100
defeated Philadelphia 4-2; 122-117, 104-110, H123-108, H121-105, 94-107, H101-99
defeated Seattle 4-3; 102-106, H106-98, H92-93, 120-116(OT), 94-98, H117-82, 105-99

Use Name	Pos	Hgt	Wgt	Age	G	Min	FG	FGA	%	FT	FTA	%	Reb	Ass	PF	DQ	Stls	Blkd Shts	Points	Min	Reb	Ass	PF	Points
Bob Dandridge	F	6'6	195	30	19	746	172	359	48	58	84	69	123	74	78	1	30	14	402	39	6.5	3.9	4.1	21.2
Elvin Hayes	F	6'9	235	32	21	868	**189**	**385**	49	79	133	59	279	43	86	2	32	52	**457**	**41**	**13.3**	2.0	4.1	21.8
Wes Unseld	C	6'7	245	31	18	677	71	134	53	27	46	59	216	79	62	2	17	7	169	38	12.0	4.4	3.4	9.4
Kevin Grevey	G	6'5	210	24	21	584	126	284	44	73	90	81	61	42	71	2	11	3	325	28	2.9	2.0	3.4	15.5
Tom Henderson	G	6'3	190	25	21	597	72	173	42	58	79	73	47	**106**	36	0	27	5	202	28	2.2	5.0	1.7	9.6
Mike Kupchak	C-F	6'9	230	23	21	504	84	199	42	45	69	65	127	22	58	1	4	3	213	24	6.0	1.0	2.8	10.1
Charles Johnson	G	6'	170	28	21	425	93	229	41	29	37	78	53	48	51	0	30	0	215	20	2.5	2.3	2.4	10.2
Larry Wright	G	6'1	160	23	21	402	76	163	47	19	25	76	31	67	58	1	17	2	171	19	1.5	3.2	2.8	8.1
Greg Ballard	F	6'7	215	22	19	243	21	63	33	32	41	78	79	18	29	0	9	3	74	13	4.2	0.9	1.5	3.9
Joe Pace	C	6'10	220	24	9	52	7	10	70	11	15	73	20	1	17	1	1	6	25	6	2.2	0.1	1.9	2.8
Phil Walker	G	6'3	180	21	4	17	1	8	13	4	5	80	2	2	5	0	0	0	6	4	0.5	0.5	1.3	1.5
Phil Chenier (back injury)																								

SEATTLE SUPERSONICS — **LENNY WILKINS**

defeated Los Angeles 2-1; H102-90, 99-105, H111-102
defeated Portland 4-2; 104-95, 93-96, H99-84, H100-98, 89-113, H105-94
defeated Denver 4-2; 107-116, 121-111, H105-91, H100-94, 114-123, H123-108
lost to Washington 3-4; H106-102, 98-106, 93-92, H116-120(OT), H98-94, 82-117, H99-105

Use Name	Pos	Hgt	Wgt	Age	G	Min	FG	FGA	%	FT	FTA	%	Reb	Ass	PF	DQ	Stls	Blkd Shts	Points	Min	Reb	Ass	PF	Points
John Johnson	F	6'7	200	30	22	596	95	224	42	32	46	70	99	56	64	1	8	6	222	27	4.5	2.5	2.9	10.1
Jack Sikma	F-C	6'11	230	22	22	701	115	247	47	71	91	78	178	27	**101**	**7**	18	11	301	32	8.1	1.2	4.6	13.7
Marvin Webster	C	7'1	240	25	22	**904**	137	280	49	81	120	68	**289**	**58**	76	2	6	**58**	355	41	13.1	2.6	3.5	16.1
Dennis Johnson	G	6'4	185	23	22	827	121	294	41	**112**	**159**	70	101	72	63	0	23	23	354	38	4.6	3.3	2.9	16.1
Gus Williams	G	6'2	175	24	22	701	163	342	48	77	106	73	86	88	70	2	**45**	12	403	32	3.9	4.0	3.2	18.3
Paul Silas	F	6'7	220	34	22	605	33	94	35	41	60	68	187	36	59	0	12	6	107	28	8.5	1.6	2.7	4.9
Fred Brown	G	6'3	185	29	22	575	153	341	45	75	90	83	47	53	47	0	23	2	381	26	2.1	2.4	2.1	17.3
Wally Walker	F	6'7	190	23	20	261	36	85	42	21	26	81	38	12	51	0	8	4	93	13	1.9	0.6	2.6	4.7
Bruce Seals	F	6'8	215	24	9	92	12	37	32	3	7	43	20	8	14	0	2	2	27	10	2.2	0.9	1.6	3.0
Joey Hassett	G	6'5	180	22	8	22	7	13	54	0	0	—	2	0	1	0	1	0	14	3	0.3	0.0	0.1	1.8
Al Fleming	F	6'7	215	23	5	21	2	6	33	3	4	75	4	2	5	0	1	0	7	4	0.8	0.4	1.0	1.4

1977/78 N.B.A. — PLAYOFFS (Continued)

Use Name	Pos	Hgt	Wgt	Age	TOTAL G	Min	FG	FGA	%	FT	FTA	%	Reb	Ass	PF	DQ	Stls	Blkd Shts	Points	PER GAME Min	Reb	Ass	PF	Points
PHILADELPHIA 76ers	**BILLY CUNNINGHAM**	defeated New York 4-0; H130-90, H119-100, 137-126, 112-107																						
		lost to Washington 2-4; H117-122, H110-104, 108-123, 105-121, H107-94, 99-101																						
Julius Erving	F	6'7	200	27	10	358	88	180	49	42	56	75	97	40	30	0	15	18	218	36	9.7	4.0	3.0	21.8
George McGinnis	F	6'8	235	27	10	273	53	125	42	41	49	84	78	30	40	1	15	1	147	27	7.8	3.0	4.0	14.7
Caldwell Jones	C-F	6'11	225	27	10	301	28	56	50	8	10	80	106	14	36	2	5	30	64	30	10.6	1.4	3.6	6.4
Doug Collins	G	6'6	180	26	10	342	82	165	50	40	49	82	31	27	29	0	3	0	204	34	3.1	2.7	2.9	20.4
Henry Bibby	G	6'1	185	28	10	289	33	82	40	20	22	91	30	48	25	0	12	0	86	29	3.0	4.8	2.5	8.6
Lloyd Free	G	6'2	185	24	10	268	51	124	41	59	81	73	31	37	26	0	4	6	161	27	3.1	3.7	2.6	16.1
Steve Mix	F	6'7	222	30	10	235	49	82	60	38	43	88	46	36	22	0	15	1	136	24	4.6	3.6	2.2	13.6
Darryl Dawkins	C	6'11	251	20	10	180	27	53	51	9	17	53	57	10	34	1	3	15	63	18	5.7	1.0	3.4	6.3
Joe Bryant	F-G	6'9	185	23	10	122	21	47	45	8	11	73	25	9	22	0	6	1	50	12	2.5	0.9	2.2	5.0
Ted McClain	G	6'2	190	30	5	31	3	10	30	0	0	—	6	10	4	0	5	0	6	6	1.2	2.0	0.8	1.2
Harvey Catchings	C	6'9	218	26	7	26	3	8	38	3	4	75	9	0	4	0	1	3	9	4	1.3	0.0	0.6	1.3
DENVER NUGGETS	**LARRY BROWN**	defeated Milwaukee 4-3; H119-103, H127-111, 112-143, 118-104, H112-117, 91-119, H116-110																						
		lost to Seattle 2-4; H116-107, H111-121, 91-105, 94-100, H123-114, 108-123																						
Anthony Roberts	F	6'5	185	22	13	400	86	199	43	40	50	80	108	30	57	3	11	6	212	31	8.3	2.3	4.4	16.3
Bobby Jones	F	6'9	212	26	13	390	66	116	57	34	46	74	102	35	42	1	16	9	166	30	7.8	2.7	3.2	12.8
Dan Issel	C	6'9	240	29	13	460	103	212	49	56	65	86	134	53	43	1	7	3	262	35	10.3	4.1	3.3	20.2
Bob Wilkerson	G-F	6'6	200	23	13	426	47	127	37	26	42	62	71	78	55	2	19	4	120	33	5.5	6.0	4.2	9.2
David Thompson	G-F	6'4	195	23	13	481	131	291	45	66	80	83	53	52	34	0	9	21	328	37	4.1	4.0	2.6	25.2
Darnell Hillman	F-C	6'9	215	28	13	260	31	79	39	11	15	73	80	18	49	1	6	7	73	20	6.2	1.4	3.8	5.6
Ralph Simpson	G	6'5	200	28	13	225	43	95	45	16	23	70	19	38	20	0	4	2	102	17	1.5	2.9	1.5	7.8
Bo Ellis	F	6'9	190	23	12	170	17	40	43	12	15	80	43	8	25	0	6	8	46	14	3.6	0.7	2.1	3.8
Mack Calvin	G	6'	175	29	12	135	19	42	45	27	29	93	8	21	11	0	7	0	65	11	0.7	1.8	0.9	5.4
Robert Smith	G	5'11	165	22	11	96	17	26	65	5	7	71	9	17	13	0	6	0	39	9	0.8	1.5	1.2	3.5
Tom LaGarde	C	6'10	220	22	9	77	10	19	53	5	7	71	18	7	12	0	0	2	25	9	2.0	0.8	1.3	2.8
Brian Taylor - holdout																								
MILWAUKEE BUCKS	**DON NELSON**	defeated Phoenix 2-0; 111-108, H94-90																						
		lost to Denver 3-4; 103-119, 111-127, H143-112, H104-118, 117-112, H119-91, 110-116																						
Marques Johnson	F	6'7	218	21	9	321	84	153	55	48	64	75	112	31	25	0	10	17	216	36	12.4	3.4	2.8	24.0
Dave Meyers	F-C	6'9	225	24	9	279	44	99	44	28	42	67	74	35	32	0	7	11	116	31	8.2	3.9	3.6	12.9
John Gianelli	C	6'10	220	27	9	290	25	59	42	20	26	77	58	14	24	0	8	11	70	32	6.4	1.6	2.7	7.8
Brian Winters	G	6'4	185	25	9	305	82	165	50	20	27	74	30	58	20	0	12	8	184	34	3.3	6.4	2.2	20.4
Quinn Buckner	G	6'3	205	23	9	257	43	86	50	15	23	65	27	62	30	0	18	1	101	29	3.0	6.9	3.3	11.2
Alex English	F	6'8	190	23	9	208	48	78	62	25	32	78	42	13	20	0	6	7	121	23	4.7	1.4	2.2	13.4
Junior Bridgeman	G-F	6'5	210	24	9	178	44	91	48	6	8	75	18	11	31	0	9	2	94	20	2.0	1.2	3.4	10.4
Lloyd Walton	G	6'	160	24	9	124	17	35	49	8	13	62	4	37	8	0	8	3	42	14	0.4	4.1	0.9	4.7
Kent Benson	C	6'10	245	23	9	103	11	23	48	6	11	55	15	3	20	0	5	3	28	11	1.7	0.3	2.2	3.1
Ernie Grunfeld	F	6'6	215	22	7	77	17	32	53	4	5	80	11	14	6	0	3	1	38	11	1.6	2.0	0.9	5.4
Jim Eakins	C	6'11	215	31	3	18	1	5	20	0	0	—	1	1	2	0	1	0	2	6	0.3	0.3	0.7	0.7
NEW YORK KNICKERBOCKERS	**WILLIS REED**	defeated Cleveland 2-0; 132-114, H109-107																						
		lost to Philadelphia 4-0; 90-130, 100-119, H126-137, H107-112																						
Jim McMillian	F	6'5	220	29	6	134	24	53	45	5	6	83	21	11	3	0	7	0	53	22	3.5	1.8	0.5	8.8
Spencer Haywood	F-C	6'9	225	28	6	177	43	85	51	11	11	100	42	12	24	1	2	5	97	30	7.0	2.0	4.0	16.2
BobMcAdoo	C	6'9	210	26	6	238	61	126	48	21	35	60	58	23	19	0	7	12	143	40	9.7	3.8	3.2	23.8
Earl Monroe	G	6'3	190	33	6	145	24	62	39	11	18	61	5	17	15	0	6	0	59	24	0.8	2.8	2.5	9.8
Butch Beard	G	6'3	185	30	6	160	24	48	50	6	10	60	21	27	22	0	10	2	54	27	3.5	4.5	3.7	9.0
Lonnie Shelton	F-C	6'8	245	22	6	151	30	56	54	6	8	75	44	17	29	1	2	5	66	25	7.3	2.8	4.8	11.0
Ray Williams	G	6'3	190	23	6	140	41	78	53	23	26	88	15	31	25	0	6	0	105	23	2.5	5.2	4.2	17.5
Jim Cleamons	G	6'3	185	28	6	127	14	36	39	6	6	100	13	23	13	0	3	0	34	21	2.2	3.8	2.2	5.7
Glen Gondrezick	F	6'6	218	22	6	70	10	19	53	5	8	63	17	6	12	0	5	0	25	12	2.8	1.0	2.0	4.2
Phil Jackson	F	6'8	230	32	6	50	4	8	50	4	6	67	10	3	11	0	3	0	12	8	1.7	0.5	1.8	2.0
Toby Knight	F	6'9	210	22	6	48	6	20	30	4	8	50	19	1	9	0	1	4	13	8	3.2	0.2	1.5	2.2
PORTLAND TRAIL BLAZERS	**JACK RAMSAY**	lost to Seattle 4-2; H95-104, H96-93, 84-99, 98-100, H113-89, 94-105																						
Larry Steele	F-G	6'5	180	28	6	191	25	60	42	19	21	90	26	14	22	0	7	2	69	32	4.3	2.3	3.7	11.5
Maurice Lucas	F-C	6'9	218	25	6	233	46	108	43	11	19	58	75	15	28	0	4	2	103	39	12.5	2.5	4.7	17.2
Tom Owens	C	6'10	220	28	6	200	38	69	55	15	21	71	39	26	30	1	5	7	91	33	6.5	4.3	5.0	15.2
Lionel Hollins	G	6'3	185	24	6	223	40	89	45	20	29	69	29	33	21	1	7	0	100	37	4.8	5.5	3.5	16.7
Johnny Davis	G	6'2	170	22	6	201	35	76	46	16	23	70	10	13	15	0	1	2	86	34	1.7	2.2	2.5	14.3
Corky Calhoun	F	6'7	210	27	6	109	15	29	52	4	7	57	14	3	6	0	2	1	34	18	2.3	0.5	1.0	5.7
Dave Twardzik	G	6'1	180	27	6	108	11	23	48	14	14	100	4	11	16	0	7	0	36	18	0.7	1.8	2.7	6.0
Bill Walton	C	6'11	225	25	2	49	11	18	61	5	7	71	22	4	1	0	3	3	27	25	11.0	2.0	0.5	13.5
Lloyd Neal	F-C	6'7	225	27	3	47	7	21	33	1	1	100	11	2	5	0	0	4	15	16	3.7	0.7	1.7	5.0
Willie Norwood	F	6'7	215	30	3	44	7	12	58	1	1	100	4	4	11	1	0	1	15	15	1.3	1.3	3.7	5.0
T.R. Dunn	G	6'4	192	22	4	35	2	4	50	0	0	—	5	3	3	0	1	0	4	9	1.3	0.8	0.8	1.0
Bob Gross - broken ankle																								

1977/78 N.B.A. — PLAYOFFS (continued)

Use Name	Pos	Hgt	Wgt	Age	TOTAL G	Min	FG	FGA	%	FT	FTA	%	Reb	Ass	PF	DQ	Stls	Blkd Shts	Points	PER GAME Min	Reb	Ass	PF	Points
SAN ANTONIO SPURS	**DOUG MOE**				lost to Washington 2-4; H114-103, H117-121, 105-118, 95-98, H116-105, 100-103																			
Mark Olberding	F	6'8	230	21	6	152	25	51	49	13	15	87	30	14	23	0	6	6	63	25	5.0	2.3	3.8	10.5
Larry Kenon	F	6'9	215	25	6	200	46	103	45	14	19	74	55	22	23	0	5	2	106	33	9.2	3.7	3.8	17.7
Billy Paultz	C	6'11	250	29	6	191	29	63	46	11	17	65	41	14	10	0	5	5	69	32	6.8	2.3	1.7	11.5
George Gervin	G	6'7	185	25	6	227	78	142	55	43	56	77	34	19	23	0	6	16	199	38	5.7	3.2	3.8	33.2
Mike Gale	G	6'4	190	27	6	201	25	56	45	2	4	50	25	31	15	0	7	4	52	34	4.2	5.2	2.5	8.7
Mike Green	C-F	6'10	200	26	6	174	28	58	48	9	10	90	44	11	21	0	5	16	65	29	7.3	1.8	3.5	10.8
Lou Dampier	G	6'	185	33	6	129	17	37	46	1	4	25	7	15	7	0	4	2	35	22	1.2	2.5	1.2	5.8
Coby Dietrick	F	6'10	225	30	6	96	14	27	52	1	2	50	25	4	18	1	5	5	29	16	4.2	0.7	3.0	4.8
Allan Bristow	F	6'7	210	26	5	51	9	15	60	4	6	67	11	7	10	0	2	0	22	10	2.2	1.4	2.0	4.4
James Silas	G	6'3	180	28	3	19	3	10	30	1	2	50	0	1	1	0	1	0	7	6	0.0	0.3	0.3	2.3
ATLANTA HAWKS	**HUBIE BROWN**				lost to Washington 0-2; 94-103, H103-107(OT)																			
John Drew	F	6'6	205	23	2	79	21	49	43	10	16	63	15	3	9	0	1	1	52	40	7.5	1.5	4.5	26.0
Tom McMillan	F-C	6'11	215	25	2	75	13	23	57	0	0	—	22	1	9	0	1	0	26	38	11.0	0.5	4.5	13.0
Tree Rollins	C	7'1	235	22	2	51	7	12	58	2	8	25	9	1	8	1	1	4	16	26	4.5	0.5	4.0	8.0
Eddie Johnson	G	6'2	190	22	2	64	12	19	63	7	8	88	16	6	10	1	8	1	31	32	8.0	3.0	5.0	15.5
Charlie Criss	G	5'8	165	28	2	65	10	24	42	7	9	78	4	3	5	0	4	1	27	33	2.0	1.5	2.5	13.5
Steve Hawes	C-F	6'9	220	27	2	71	7	18	39	2	3	67	17	8	5	0	1	2	16	36	8.5	4.0	2.5	8.0
Armond Hill	G	6'4	190	24	2	61	6	15	40	4	4	100	3	7	7	0	2	0	16	31	1.5	3.5	3.5	8.0
Ollie Johnson	F	6'6	200	28	2	21	4	11	36	0	0	—	3	2	4	0	1	1	8	11	1.5	1.0	2.0	4.0
Tony Robertson	G	6'4	195	21	2	12	2	6	33	1	2	50	0	0	3	0	0	0	5	6	0.0	0.0	1.5	2.5
John Brown	F	6'7	220	26	2	6	0	0	—	0	0	—	0	0	1	0	0	0	0	3	0.0	0.0	0.5	0.0
CLEVELAND CAVALIERS	**BILL FITCH**				lost to New York 0-2; H114-132, 107-109																			
Campy Russell	F	6'8	215	25	2	88	19	39	49	17	21	81	15	11	9	0	3	0	55	44	7.5	5.5	4.5	27.5
Jim Chones	F-C	6'11	220	28	2	82	13	27	48	4	8	50	15	7	7	0	2	1	30	41	7.5	3.5	3.5	15.0
Elmore Smith	C	7'	250	28	2	56	11	24	46	3	6	50	19	0	9	0	3	3	25	28	9.5	0.0	4.5	12.5
Austin Carr	G	6'4	200	29	2	69	10	27	37	15	16	94	8	5	8	0	2	1	35	35	4.0	2.5	4.0	17.5
Foots Walker	G	6'1	172	26	2	70	10	26	38	5	5	100	7	10	7	0	3	2	25	35	3.5	5.0	3.5	12.5
Terry Furlow	G	6'4	190	23	2	50	13	27	48	6	6	100	5	5	1	0	0	0	32	25	2.5	2.5	0.5	16.0
Bobby Smith	F	6'5	212	31	2	34	8	13	62	0	0	—	3	1	2	0	0	0	16	17	1.5	0.5	1.0	8.0
John Lambert	F-C	6'10	225	24	2	19	1	3	33	1	2	50	8	0	3	0	0	0	3	10	4.0	0.0	1.5	1.5
Jim Brewer	F	6'9	220	26	1	9	0	1	0	0	2	0	0	0	2	0	0	0	0	9	0.0	0.0	2.0	0.0
Dick Snyder	G	6'5	207	33	1	3	0	0	—	0	0	—	0	0	0	0	0	0	0	3	0.0	0.0	0.0	0.0
Walt Frazier (foot injury)																								
LOS ANGELES LAKERS	**JERRY WEST**				lost to Seattle 1-2; 90-102, H105-99, 111-102																			
Adrian Dantley	F	6'5	210	21	3	104	20	35	57	11	17	65	25	11	9	0	5	3	51	35	8.3	3.7	3.0	17.0
Jamaal Wilkes	F	6'6	190	24	3	108	15	32	47	6	11	55	26	8	14	1	3	1	36	36	8.7	2.7	4.7	12.0
Kareem Abdul-Jabbar	C	7'2	232	30	3	134	38	73	52	5	9	56	41	11	14	1	2	12	81	45	13.7	3.7	4.7	27.0
Charlie Scott	G	6'6	175	29	3	103	12	40	30	6	8	75	13	14	9	0	4	0	30	34	4.3	4.7	3.0	10.0
Norm Nixon	G	6'2	172	22	3	92	11	24	46	2	3	67	9	16	13	0	4	1	24	31	3.0	5.3	4.3	8.0
Lou Hudson	G	6'5	210	33	3	93	14	38	37	7	8	88	9	9	9	0	0	0	35	31	3.0	3.0	3.0	11.7
Dave Robisch	F-C	6'10	240	28	3	47	13	24	54	4	5	80	12	1	6	0	1	1	30	16	4.0	0.3	2.0	10.0
Kenny Carr	F	6'7	230	22	2	17	3	8	38	0	0	—	4	0	2	0	1	0	6	9	2.0	0.0	1.0	3.0
Tom Abernathy	F	6'7	220	23	2	12	1	4	25	2	2	100	2	1	2	0	0	0	4	6	1.0	0.5	1.0	2.0
Don Ford	F	6'9	215	25	1	10	0	3	0	0	0	—	5	0	2	0	1	0	0	10	5.0	0.0	2.0	0.0
PHOENIX SUNS	**JOHN MacLEOD**				lost to Milwaukee 2-0; H103-11, 90-94																			
Walter Davis	F	6'6	195	23	2	66	19	40	48	12	16	75	17	8	8	0	3	0	50	33	8.5	4.0	4.0	25.0
Gar Heard	F	6'6	219	29	2	62	6	17	35	1	2	50	16	5	4	0	2	4	13	31	8.0	2.5	2.0	6.5
Alvan Adams	C	6'9	225	23	2	71	15	33	45	2	2	100	16	4	8	0	2	1	32	36	8.0	2.0	4.0	16.0
Paul Westphal	G'	6'4	195	27	2	66	22	47	47	8	9	89	6	19	4	0	1	0	52	33	3.0	9.5	2.0	26.0
Don Buse	G	6'4	195	27	2	76	4	11	36	0	0	—	5	4	3	0	4	0	8	38	2.5	2.0	1.5	4.0
Ron Lee	G	6'4	193	25	2	41	5	16	31	2	2	100	6	3	7	0	4	0	12	21	3.0	1.5	3.5	6.0
Alvin Scott	F	6'7	185	22	2	37	4	8	50	5	6	83	6	3	3	0	2	0	13	19	3.0	1.5	1.5	6.5
Greg Griffin	F	6'7	190	25	2	25	3	7	43	0	0	—	4	3	5	0	1	1	6	13	2.0	1.5	2.5	3.0
Dennis Awtrey	C	6'10	240	29	2	24	1	4	25	1	1	100	2	3	0	0	1	0	3	12	1.0	1.5	0.0	1.5
Mike Bratz	G	6'2	185	22	2	9	1	5	20	0	0	—	0	1	0	0	0	0	2	5	0.0	0.5	0.0	1.0
Bayard Forrest	C	6'10	235	23	1	3	1	1	100	0	0	—	0	0	0	0	0	0	2	3	0.0	0.0	0.0	2.0
Ira Terrell (injury)																								

Team		G	FG	FGA	%	FT	FTA	%	Rebounds Offense	Rebounds Defense	Rebounds Total	Assists	PF	Steals	Blocked Shots	Turn Overs	Points	Points per game
TEAM STATISTICS EASTERN CONFERENCE ATLANTIC DIVISION																		
Philadelphia	Off.	82	3628	7471	49	**2153**	**2863**	75	1299	2694	3993	2220	2188	800	548	1752	**9409**	**114.7**
	Def.	82	3592	7788	46	1803	2435	74	1363	2473	3836	2095	2287	823	346	1709	8987	109.6
	Diff.		+36	-317	+3	+350	+428	+1	-64	+221	+157	+125	+99	-23	**+202**	-43	+422	5.1
New York	Off.	82	**3815**	7822	49	1670	2225	75	1180	2689	3869	**2338**	2193	818	442	1764	9300	113.4
	Def.	82	3658	7742	47	2029	2785	73	1254	2623	3877	2113	1989	879	357	1677	9345	114.0
	Diff.		+157	+80	+2	-359	-560	+2	-74	+66	-8	+225	-204	-61	+85	-87	-45	-0.6
Boston	Off.	82	3494	7635	46	1682	2159	78	1235	2850	4085	1969	2033	643	295	1652	8670	105.7
	Def.	82	3539	7761	46	1752	2278	77	1142	2575	3717	1981	1871	763	374	1412	8830	107.7
	Diff.		-45	-126	—	-70	-119	+1	+93	**+275**	+368	-12	-162	-120	-79	-240	-160	-2.0
Buffalo	Off	82	3413	7323	47	1808	2314	78	1083	2538	3621	1975	2017	650	327	1575	8634	105.3
	Def.	82	3623	7609	48	1695	2250	75	1178	2587	3765	2137	2003	722	375	1476	8941	109.0
	Diff.		-210	-286	—	+113	+64	+3	-95	-49	-144	-162	-14	-72	-48	-99	-307	-3.7
New Jersey	Off.	82	3547	**8004**	44	1652	2304	72	1306	2595	3901	1879	2312	857	**631**	1774	8746	106.7
	Def.	82	3544	7620	47	2135	2830	75	1312	2996	4308	2073	1999	852	560	1864	9223	112.5
	Diff.		+3	+384	-3	-483	-526	-3	-6	-401	-407	-194	-313	+5	+71	+90	-477	-5.8
CENTRAL DIVISION																		
San Antonio	Off.	82	3794	7594	**50**	1797	2234	**80**	1030	2594	3624	2240	1871	797	553	1665	9385	114.5
	Def.	82	3808	8063	47	1494	1996	75	1345	2576	3921	2145	2059	837	379	1662	9110	111.1
	Diff.		-14	-469	+3	+303	+238	**+5**	-315	+18	-297	+95	+188	-40	+174	-3	+275	3.4
Washington	Off.	82	3580	7772	46	1887	2655	71	1349	2815	4164	1948	1879	668	386	1613	9047	110.3
	Def.	82	3767	8065	47	1437	1895	76	1166	2683	3849	2144	**2312**	779	427	1437	8971	109.4
	Diff.		-187	-293	-1	**+450**	**+760**	-5	+183	+132	+315	-196	**+433**	-111	-41	-176	+76	0.9
Cleveland	Off.	82	3496	7707	45	1569	2116	74	1187	2676	3863	1740	**1832**	692	455	1382	8561	104.4
	Def.	82	3474	7620	46	1574	2113	74	1214	2779	3993	1915	1952	690	446	1475	8522	103.9
	Diff.		+22	+87	-1	-5	+3	—	-27	-103	-130	-175	+120	+2	+9	+93	+39	0.5
Atlanta	Off.	82	3335	7253	46	1836	2316	79	1160	2359	3519	1901	2470	916	408	1592	8506	103.7
	Def.	82	3162	6671	47	2193	2930	75	1160	2606	3766	1774	2122	750	484	**1980**	8517	103.9
	Diff.		+173	**+582**	-1	-357	-614	+4	—	-247	-247	+127	-348	**+166**	-76	**+388**	-11	-0.2
New Orleans	Off.	82	3568	7717	46	1690	2331	73	1309	**2907**	**4216**	2079	1938	662	514	1694	8826	107.6
	Def.	82	3659	7938	46	1661	2213	75	1273	2747	4020	2084	2062	851	476	1511	8979	109.5
	Diff.		-91	-221	—	+29	+118	-2	+36	+160	+196	-5	+124	-189	+38	-183	-153	-1.9
Houston	Off.	82	3523	7691	46	1467	1896	77	1301	2421	3722	1942	2025	683	319	**1376**	8513	103.8
	Def.	82	3571	7404	48	1699	2238	76	1195	2525	3720	1990	1752	605	360	1410	8841	107.8
	Diff.		-48	+287	-2	-232	-342	+1	+106	-104	+2	-48	-273	+78	-41	+34	-328	-4.0
WESTERN CONFERENCE MIDWEST DIVISION																		
Denver	Off.	82	3548	7441	48	2068	2705	76	1177	2736	3913	2187	2116	824	422	1748	9164	111.8
	Def.	82	3678	7799	47	1740	2365	74	1267	2546	3813	2248	2220	877	524	1620	9096	110.9
	Diff.		-130	-358	+1	+328	+340	+2	-90	+190	+100	-61	+104	-53	-102	-128	+68	0.9
Milwaukee	Off.	82	3801	7883	48	1612	2220	73	1239	2480	3719	2306	2038	867	472	1680	9214	112.4
	Def.	82	3715	7728	48	1832	2404	76	1234	2617	3851	2248	2019	790	468	1783	9262	113.0
	Diff.		+86	+155	—	-220	-184	-3	+5	-137	-132	+58	-19	+77	+4	+103	-48	-0.6
Chicago	Off.	82	3330	7041	47	1863	2471	75	1248	2577	3825	2119	1930	665	322	1667	8523	103.9
	Def.	82	3565	7273	49	1466	1980	74	**1065**	2367	3432	2076	2199	777	451	1479	8596	104.8
	Diff.		-235	-232	-2	+397	+491	+1	+183	+210	**+393**	+43	+269	-112	-129	-188	-73	-0.9
Detroit	Off.	82	3552	7424	48	1832	2490	74	1229	2601	3830	1840	1980	866	330	1858	8936	109.0
	Def.	82	3688	7706	48	1662	2177	76	1244	2494	3738	2105	2088	902	395	1719	9038	110.2
	Diff.		-136	-282	—	+170	+313	-2	-15	+107	+92	-265	+108	-36	-65	-139	-102	-1.2
Indiana	Off.	82	3500	7783	45	1904	2564	74	1386	2624	4010	1982	2230	808	456	1642	8904	108.6
	Def.	82	3634	7663	47	1841	2455	75	1350	2793	4143	2259	2135	727	466	1762	9109	111.1
	Diff.		-134	+120	-2	+63	+109	-1	+36	-169	-133	-277	-95	+81	-10	+120	-205	-2.5
Kansas City	Off.	82	3601	7731	47	1775	2262	78	1208	2632	3840	1992	2228	794	370	1690	8977	109.5
	Def.	82	3564	7521	47	2004	2635	76	1232	2684	3916	1928	2088	796	408	1694	9132	111.4
	Diff.		+37	+210	—	-229	-373	+2	-24	-52	-76	+64	-140	-2	-38	+4	-155	-1.9
PACIFIC DIVISION																		
Portland	Off.	82	3556	7367	48	1717	2259	76	1187	2686	3873	2067	2068	798	390	1625	8829	107.7
	Def.	82	3289	7318	45	1747	2282	77	1187	2523	3710	1818	2093	748	390	1624	8325	**101.5**
	Diff.		**+267**	+49	**+3**	-30	-23	-1	—	+163	+163	+249	+25	+50	—	-1	**+504**	**6.2**
Phoenix	Off.	82	3731	7836	48	1749	2329	75	1166	2579	3745	**2338**	1956	**1059**	372	1766	9211	112.3
	Def.	82	3578	7622	47	1749	2319	75	1202	2743	3945	1988	2178	937	372	1969	8905	108.6
	Diff.		+153	+214	+1	—	+10	—	-36	-164	-200	**+350**	+222	+122	—	+203	+306	3.7

TEAM STATISTICS
WESTERN CONFERENCE (Continued)
PACIFIC DIVISION (Continued)

Team		G	FG	FGA	%	FT	FTA	%	REBOUND Offense	REBOUND Defense	REBOUND Total	Assists	PF	Steals	Blocked Shots	Turn Overs	Points	Points per game
Seattle	Off.	82	3445	7715	45	1675	2352	71	1456	2601	4057	1799	2008	782	429	1636	8565	104.5
	Def.	82	3384	7377	46	1670	2203	76	1121	2600	3721	1956	2067	735	410	1646	8438	102.9
	Diff.		+61	+338	-1	+5	+149	-5	+335	+1	+336	-157	+59	+47	+19	+10	+127	+1.6
Los Angeles	Off.	82	3734	7672	49	1576	2095	75	1136	2647	3783	2229	1964	802	409	1548	9044	110.3
	Def.	82	3648	7880	46	1529	2050	75	1365	2599	3964	2073	1919	756	379	1570	8825	107.6
	Diff.		+86	-208	+3	+47	+45	—	-229	+48	-181	+156	-45	+46	+30	+22	+219	+2.7
Golden State	Off.	82	3574	7654	47	1550	2081	74	1183	2629	3812	2097	2113	873	405	1518	8698	106.1
	Def.	82	3425	7368	46	1820	2408	76	1185	2794	3979	2037	1975	728	408	1738	8670	105.7
	Diff.		+149	+286	+1	-270	-327	-2	-2	-165	-167	+60	-138	+145	-3	+220	+28	+.4

PLAYOFFS

Team		G	FG	FGA	%	FT	FTA	%	REBOUND Offense	REBOUND Defense	REBOUND Total	Assists	PF	Steals	Blocked Shots	Turn Overs	Points	Points per game
Washington	Off.	21	912	2007	45	435	624	70	361	677	1038	502	551	178	95	347	2259	107.6
	Def.	21	875	1939	45	432	583	74	318	676	994	439	585	152	159	369	2182	103.9
	Diff.		+37	+68	—	+3	+41	-4	+43	+1	+44	+65	+34	+26	-64	+22	+77	+3.7
Seattle	Off.	22	874	1963	45	516	709	73	375	676	1051	412	551	147	124	359	2264	102.9
	Def.	22	917	2044	45	422	576	73	355	676	1031	515	605	148	93	358	2256	102.5
	Diff.		-43	-81	—	+94	+133	—	+20	—	+20	-103	+54	-1	+31	-1	+8	+.4
Denver	Off.	13	570	1246	46	298	379	79	222	423	645	357	361	91	62	244	1438	110.6
	Def.	13	581	1220	48	315	439	72	205	380	585	362	330	115	98	205	1477	113.6
	Diff.		-11	+26	-2	-17	-60	+7	+17	+43	+60	-5	-31	-24	-36	-39	-39	-3.0
Philadelphia	Off.	10	438	932	47	268	342	78	148	368	516	261	272	84	75	201	1144	114.4
	Def.	10	442	1005	44	204	284	72	185	312	497	271	289	100	49	185	1088	108.8
	Diff.		-4	-73	+3	+64	+58	+6	-37	+56	+19	-10	+17	-16	+26	-16	+56	+5.6
Milwaukee	Off.	9	416	826	50	180	251	72	118	274	392	282	218	87	64	169	1012	112.4
	Def.	9	393	856	46	202	258	78	142	278	420	255	226	80	47	176	988	109.8
	Diff.		+23	-30	+4	-22	-7	-6	-24	-4	-28	+27	+8	+7	+17	+7	+24	+2.6
New York	Off.	6	281	591	48	102	142	72	96	169	265	171	182	52	28	111	664	110.7
	Def.	6	273	560	49	173	219	79	93	210	303	153	140	50	39	121	719	119.8
	Diff.		+8	+31	-1	-71	-77	-7	+3	-41	-38	+18	-42	+2	-11	+10	-55	-9.1
San Antonio	Off.	6	274	562	49	99	135	73	80	192	272	138	151	46	56	96	647	107.8
	Def.	6	275	574	48	98	151	65	90	187	277	148	146	51	25	89	648	108.0
	Diff.		-1	-12	+1	+1	-16	+8	-10	+5	-5	-10	-5	-5	+31	-7	-1	-0.2
Portland	Off.	6	237	509	47	106	143	74	64	175	239	128	158	37	22	97	580	96.7
	Def.	6	227	501	45	136	186	73	97	186	283	98	141	43	28	103	590	98.3
	Diff.		+10	+8	+2	-30	-43	+1	-33	-11	-44	+30	-17	-6	-6	+6	-10	-1.6
Los Angeles	Off.	3	127	281	45	43	63	68	61	85	146	71	80	26	18	56	297	99.0
	Def.	3	129	270	48	54	77	70	45	84	129	64	65	21	4	52	312	104.0
	Diff.		-2	+11	-3	-11	-14	-2	+16	+1	+17	+7	-15	+5	+14	-4	-15	-5.0
Atlanta	Off.	2	82	177	46	33	50	66	25	54	79	31	61	19	10	33	197	98.5
	Def.	2	80	162	49	50	70	71	31	69	100	31	50	15	6	45	210	105.0
	Diff.		+2	+15	-3	-17	-20	-5	-6	-15	-21	—	-11	+4	+4	+12	-13	-6.5
Cleveland	Off.	2	85	187	45	51	66	77	31	49	80	39	48	13	8	34	221	110.5
	Def.	2	101	182	55	39	50	78	28	58	86	62	58	10	11	34	241	120.5
	Diff.		-16	+5	-10	+12	+16	-1	+3	-9	-6	-23	+10	+3	-3	—	-20	-10.0
Phoenix	Off.	2	81	190	43	31	38	82	27	51	78	53	42	20	6	32	193	96.5
	Def.	2	84	157	54	37	49	76	19	77	96	49	40	15	9	42	205	102.5
	Diff.		-3	+33	-11	-6	-11	+6	+8	-26	-18	+4	-2	+5	-3	+10	-12	-6.0

Team	W	L	Pct.	GB	Record against playoff teams W	L	Pct.	Record against non-playoff teams W	L	Pct.	HOME W	L	Pct.	ROAD W	L	Pct.
EASTERN CONFERENCE																
ATLANTIC DIVISION																
Philadelphia 76ers	55	27	.671	—	27	15	.643	**28**	12	.700	**37**	4	**.902**	18	23	.439
New York Knickerbockers	43	39	.524	12	17	26	.395	26	13	.667	29	12	.707	14	27	.341
Boston Celtics	32	50	.390	23	14	33	.298	18	17	.514	24	17	.585	8	33	.195
Buffalo Braves	27	55	.329	28	13	35	.271	14	20	.412	20	21	.488	7	34	.171
New Jersey Nets	24	**58**	.293	31	11	**36**	.234	13	**22**	.371	18	**23**	.439	6	**35**	.146
CENTRAL DIVISION																
San Antonio Spurs	52	30	.634	—	23	20	.535	29	10	**.744**	32	9	.780	20	21	.488
Washington Bullets	44	38	.537	8	21	22	.488	23	16	.590	29	12	.707	15	26	.366
Cleveland Cavaliers	43	39	.524	9	21	23	.477	22	16	.579	27	14	.659	16	25	.390
Atlanta Hawks	41	41	.500	11	19	24	.442	22	17	.564	29	12	.707	12	29	.293
New Orleans Jazz	39	43	.476	13	17	29	.370	22	14	.611	27	14	.659	12	29	.293
Houston Rockets	28	54	.341	24	14	33	.298	14	21	.400	21	20	.512	7	34	.171
WESTERN CONFERENCE																
MIDWEST DIVISION																
Denver Nuggets	48	34	.585	—	23	20	.535	25	14	.641	33	8	.805	15	26	.366
Milwaukee Bucks	44	38	.537	4	17	26	.395	27	12	.692	28	13	.683	16	25	.390
Chicago Bulls	40	42	.488	8	24	23	.511	16	19	.457	29	12	.707	11	30	.268
Detroit Pistons	38	44	.463	10	17	29	.370	21	15	.583	24	17	.585	14	27	.341
Indiana Pacers	31	51	.378	17	15	32	.319	16	19	.457	21	20	.512	10	31	.244
Kansas City Kings	31	51	.378	17	11	**36**	.234	20	15	.571	22	19	.537	9	32	.220
PACIFIC DIVISION																
Portland Trail Blazers	**58**	24	**.707**	—	**30**	13	**.698**	**28**	11	.718	36	5	.878	**22**	19	**.537**
Phoenix Suns	49	33	.598	9	22	20	.524	27	13	.675	34	7	.829	15	26	.366
Seattle Supersonics	47	35	.573	11	19	23	.452	**28**	12	.700	31	10	.756	16	25	.390
Los Angeles Lakers	45	37	.549	13	18	26	.409	24	11	.686	29	12	.707	16	25	.390
Golden State Warriors	43	39	.524	15	22	26	.458	21	13	.618	30	11	.732	13	28	.317

1977/78 N.B.A. INDIVIDUAL LEADERS

SCORING
(Minimum 70 Games or 1400 Points)

Name	Team	G	FG	FT	Pts.	Avg.
Gervin	SA	82	864	504	2232	27.2
Thompson	Den	80	826	520	2172	27.2
McAdoo	NY	79	814	469	2097	26.5
Abdul-Jabbar	LA	62	663	274	1600	25.8
Murphy	Hou	76	852	245	1949	25.6
Westphal	Phoe	80	809	396	2014	25.2
Smith	Buf	82	789	443	2021	24.6
Lanier	Det	63	622	298	1542	24.5
Davis	Phoe	81	786	387	1959	24.2
King	NJ	79	798	313	1909	24.2

FIELD GOAL PERCENTAGE
(Minimum 300 Made)

Name	Team	FG	FGA	Pct.
Jones	Den	440	761	.578
Dawkins	Phi	332	577	.575
Gilmore	Chi	704	1260	.559
Abdul-Jabbar	LA	663	1205	.550
English	Mil	343	633	.542
Lanier	Det	622	1159	.537
Gervin	SA	864	1611	.536
Gross	Port	381	720	.529
Paultz	SA	518	979	.529
Davis	Phoe	786	1494	.526

FREE THROW PERCENTAGE
(Minimum 125 Made)

Name	Team	FT	FTA	Pct.
Barry	GS	378	409	.924
Murphy	Hou	245	267	.918
Brown	Sea	176	196	.898
Newlin	Hou	152	174	.874
Wedman	KC	221	254	.870
Maravich	NO	243	276	.880
Havlicek	Bos	230	269	.855
Kenon	SA	276	323	.854
Boone	KC	322	377	.854
Frazier	Cle	153	180	.850

PERSONAL FOULS

Name	Team	PF
Shelton	NY	350
G.Johnson	NJ	339
Bantom	Ind	333
Rollins	Atl	326
Washington	KC	324

GAMES DISQUALIFIED

Name	Team	Disq.
G.Johnson	NJ	20
Brown	Atl	18
Hill	Atl	15
Bantom	Ind	13
Kunnert	Hou	13

TOTAL REBOUNDS PER GAME
(Minimum 70 Games or 800 Rebounds)

Name	Team	G	Reb.	Avg.
Robinson	NO	82	1288	15.7
Malone	Hou	59	886	15.0
Cowens	Bos	77	1078	14.0
Hayes	Was	81	1075	13.3
Nater	Buf	78	1029	13.2
Gilmore	Chi	82	1071	13.1
Abdul-Jabbar	LA	62	801	12.9
McAdoo	NY	79	1010	12.8
Webster	Sea	82	1035	12.6
Unseld	Was	80	955	11.9

ASSISTS PER GAME
(Minimum 70 Games or 400 Assists)

Name	Team	G	Ass.	Avg.
K.Porter	Det-NJ	82	837	10.2
Lucas	Hou	82	768	9.4
Sobers	Ind	79	584	7.4
Nixon	LA	81	553	6.8
Van Lier	Chi	78	531	6.8
Bibby	Phi	82	464	5.7
Walker	Cle	81	453	5.6
Smith	Buf	82	458	5.6
Buckner	Mil	82	456	5.6
Westphal	Phoe	80	437	5.5

MINUTES PLAYED

Name	Team	Min.
Robinson	NO	3638
R.Smith	Buf	3314
Hayes	Was	3246
Cowens	Bos	3215
McAdoo	NY	3182

BLOCKED SHOTS PER GAME
(Minimum 70 Games or 100 Blocked Shots)

Name	Team	G	Reb.	Avg.
Johnson	NJ	81	274	3.4
Abdul-Jabbar	LA	62	185	3.0
Rollins	Atl	80	218	2.7
Walton	Port	58	146	2.5
Paultz	SA	80	194	2.4
Gilmore	Chi	82	181	2.2
Meriweather	NO	54	118	2.2
E.Smith	Cle	81	176	2.2
Webster	Sea	82	162	2.0
Hayes	Was	81	159	2.0

STEALS PER GAME
(Minimum 70 Games or 125 Steals)

Name	Team	G	Steals	Avg.
Lee	Phoe	82	225	2.7
Williams	Sea	79	185	2.3
Buckner	Mil	82	188	2.3
Gale	SA	70	159	2.3
Buse	Phoe	82	185	2.3
Walker	Cle	81	176	2.2
Sobers	Ind	79	170	2.2
Smith	Buf	82	172	2.1
Ford	Det	82	166	2.0
Holland	Chi	82	164	2.0

1978-79 N.B.A.

Free Agents Can Be Costly

The offseason was enlivened by controversial news involving two of the league's biggest starts and its most celebrated franchise. Bill Walton's broken foot proved much more serious that anyone had imagined; it was to sideline him for all of 1978-79. Blaming Portland officials for pressuring him to play with the injury, Walton announced that he wouldn't return to the team when his contract was up. Meanwhile, free agent Rick Barry left Golden State to sign with Houston. But the league gave the Warriers John Lucas as compensation, somewhat negating the impact of Barry's arrival.

The most unusual development came when Buffalo owner John V. Brown and Boston owner Irv Levin swapped franchises. Levin moved his new team to San Diego and renamed them the Clippers. In the process, he picked up Kermit Washington. Kevin Kunnert and rookie Freeman Williams from the Celtics for Nate Archibald, Billy Knight and Marvin Barnes. The result was another dismal season in Boston, despite the emergence of Cedric Maxwell as a top-notch player in his second year. Even player-coach Dave Cowens, who replaced Satch Sanders as head man in midseason, seemed to have lost his fire. But the Clippers lost the biggest prize of all when Red Auerbach refused to let them have Boston's top draft pick, a junior eligible named Larry Bird who had already announced that he planned to stay for his senior year at obscure Indiana State.

While Boston was falling to the Atlantic Division basement, new arrival Washington, shifted from the Central Division, took over the top spot. Led by one of the best front lines ever, with Elvin Hayes, Wes Unseld and Bob Dandridge backed up by Mitch Kupchak and Greg Ballard, the defending champs compiled the league's best record. Philadelphia disposed of Lloyd Free (to San Diego) and George McGinnis (to Denver for Bobby Jones), but slipped to second place when Doug Collins went down with a foot injury and even Julius Erving coundn't make up for the loss. Meanwhile, New Jersey jumped to 37 wins behind the high-scoring duo of Bernard King and John Williamson. In New York, the Knicks had high hopes after signing free agent Marvin Webster. But Webster was disappointing, Earl Monroe was hurt, and Red Holtzman, who replaced Willis Reed as coach early in the season, couldn't bring the team around. The Knicks dumped high-salaried Bob McAdoo and Spencer Haywood during a season brightened only by the play of second-year men Ray Williams and Toby Knight.

San Antonio again finished atop the Central Division, as James Silas returned from two injury-plagued seasons to complement George Gervin and Larry Kenon. Second place went to surprising Houston. Though the Barry-Lucas deal proved a toss-up, the Rockets got a fine year from Rudy Tomjanovich, back in form after his terrible injury a year earlier. Calvin Murphy was still at the top of his game, and Moses Malone pulled down 17 rebounds a game en route to his first MVP award. Atlanta added free agent Dan Roundfield to John Drew and improving sophomore Eddie Johnson, and the result was a third-place finish, just two games out of first. But Cleveland dropped to 31 wins despite a fine season from Campy Russell. Detroit, transplanted from the Midwest Division, lost Bob Lanier for 39 games and John Shumate for all 82. Though Kevin Porter shattered the season record for assists, the Pistons fell to 30-52 under new coach Dick Vitale. But that still left them four games ahead of New Orleans. Pete Maravich failed to bounce back from his knee injury, the Jazz shipped its other star, Truck Robinson, to Phoenix, and Haywood, picked up from the Knicks, couldn't take up the slack.

In Kansas City, Coach of the Year, Cotton Fitzsimmons and Rookie of the Year, Phil Ford, led the Kings to the Midwest title. Meanwhile, Denver struggled as McGinnis fouled out of 16 games and Dan Issel appeared to be getting old. Led by David Thompson, the Nuggets rallied after Donnie Walsh replaced Larry Brown as coach, but still fell a game short of K.C. Indiana picked up Johnny Davis (from Portland) and free agent Alex English (from Milwaukee) and improved to 38 wins. Milwaukee fell to the same total when a great year from Marques Johnson wasn't enough to overcome the loss of David Meyers to a back injury. Scotty Robinson replaced Chicago coach Larry Costello in midseason as the Bulls dropped to the cellar despite good years from old pro Artis Gilmore and sophomore Reggie Theus.

In Seattle, the loss of Webster was only a minor irritant. The Sonics still had the N.B.A.'s best backcourt in Gus Williams and Dennis Johnson, and the league awarded them Lonnie Shelton as compensation for Webster. When Tommy LaGarde, the new center, went down with a knee injury, Jack Sikma moved to the pivot and the team didn't miss a beat en route to 52 wins and the Pacific title. Phoenix finished two games back, adding Truck Robinson to its nucleus of Paul Westphal, Walter Davis and Alvan Adams. Kareem Abdul-Jabbar, the rejuvenated Jamaal Wilkes and second-year man Norm Nixon led Los Angeles to a strong third-place finish. In Portland, Tom Owens played very well at center. Maurice Lucas was still a star and the Blazers added rookies Mychal Thompson and Ron Brewer. But the loss of Walton proved debilitating, and it didn't help that Bob Gross and Lionel Hollins were slowed by knee and ankle injuries, respectively. New coach Gene Shue got fine seasons from Lloyd Free and Randy Smith as the new arrivals in San Diego finished just short of the final playoff spot. But Phil Smith was hampered by injuries and Golden State fell to last place despite good years from John Lucas and Robert Parish.

Phoenix forced Seattle to the limit in the Western playoff finals, building a 3-2 lead before the Sonics rallied to win in seven. In the East, the Bullets had an even tougher time. After outlasting Atlanta in seven games, they fell behind San Antonio 3-1 (the Spurs having survived their own seven-game showdown with Philadelphia), then staged an amazing comeback that culminated in a 107-105 win in the deciding game.

With Kupchak sidelined by a back injury, the Bullets looked tired in their championship rematch with the Sonics. After barely holding off a Seattle comeback in the series opener, they lost the next four, fading in the second half of each game. Dennis Johnson was named playoff MVP as the Sonics rolled to their first N.B.A. title.

					TOTAL													Blkd		PER GAME				
Use Name	Pos	Hgt	Wgt	Age	G	Min	FG	FGA	%	FT	FTA	%	Reb	Ass	PF	DQ	Stls	Shts	Points	Min	Reb	Ass	PF	Points
1978/79 N.B.A. — EASTERN CONFERENCE																								
ATLANTIC DIVISION																								
WASHINGTON BULLETS	**54-28 .659 DICK MOTTA**																							
Bob Dandridge	F	6'6	195	31	78	2629	629	1260	50	331	401	83	447	365	259	4	71	57	1589	34	5.7	4.7	3.3	20.4
Elvin Hayes	F-C	6'9	235	33	82	3105	720	1477	49	349	534	65	994	143	308	5	75	190	1789	38	12.1	1.7	3.8	21.8
Wes Unseld	C	6'7	245	32	77	2406	346	600	58	151	235	64	830	315	204	2	71	37	843	31	10.8	4.1	2.6	10.9
Kevin Grevey (LJ)	G	6'5	210	25	65	1856	418	922	45	173	224	77	232	153	159	1	46	14	1009	29	3.6	2.4	2.4	15.5
Tom Henderson	G	6'3	190	26	70	2081	299	641	47	156	195	80	163	419	123	0	87	10	754	30	2.3	6.0	1.8	10.8
Charles Johnson	G	6'	190	29	82	1819	342	786	44	67	79	85	202	177	161	0	95	6	751	22	2.5	2.2	2.0	9.2
Larry Wright	G	6'1	160	24	73	1658	276	589	47	125	168	74	140	298	166	3	69	13	677	23	1.9	4.1	2.3	9.3
Mitch Kupchak	F-C	6'9	230	24	66	1604	369	685	54	223	300	74	430	88	141	0	23	23	961	24	6.5	1.3	2.1	14.6
Greg Ballard	F	6'7	215	23	82	1552	260	559	47	119	172	69	450	116	167	3	58	30	639	19	5.5	1.4	2.0	7.8
Doug Corzine	C	6'11	250	22	59	532	63	118	53	49	63	78	147	49	67	0	10	14	175	9	2.5	0.8	1.1	3.0
Phil Chenier (back inury)	G	6'3	180	28	27	385	69	158	44	18	28	64	20	31	28	0	4	5	156	14	0.7	1.1	1.0	5.8
Roger Phegley (gastroenteritis)	G	6'6	205	22	29	153	28	78	36	24	29	83	22	15	21	0	5	2	80	5	0.8	0.5	0.7	2.8
PHILADELPHIA 76ers	**47-35 .573 BILLY CUNNINGHAM**																							
Julius Erving	F	6'7	200	28	78	2802	715	1455	49	373	501	74	564	357	207	0	133	100	1803	36	7.2	4.6	2.7	23.1
Bobby Jones	F	6'9	212	27	80	2304	378	704	54	209	277	75	531	201	245	2	107	96	965	29	6.6	2.5	3.1	12.1
Darryl Dawkins	C	6'11	251	21	78	2035	430	831	52	158	235	67	631	128	295	5	32	143	1018	26	8.1	1.6	3.8	13.1
Doug Collins (BF)	G	6'6	180	27	47	1595	358	717	50	201	247	81	123	191	139	1	52	20	917	34	2.6	4.1	3.0	19.5
Henry Bibby	G	6'1	185	29	82	2538	368	869	42	266	335	79	244	371	199	0	72	7	1002	31	3.0	4.5	2.4	12.2
Maurice Cheeks	G	6'1	180	22	82	2409	292	572	51	110	140	79	254	431	198	2	174	12	685	29	3.1	5.3	2.4	8.4
Caldwell Jones	C-F	6'11	225	28	78	2171	302	637	47	121	162	75	747	151	303	10	39	157	725	28	9.6	1.9	3.9	9.3
Steve Mix	F	6'7	222	31	74	1269	265	493	54	161	201	80	293	121	112	0	57	16	691	17	4.0	1.6	1.5	9.3
Joe Bryant	F	6'9	185	24	70	1064	205	478	43	123	170	72	259	103	171	1	49	9	533	15	3.7	1.5	2.4	7.6
Eric Money (from NJ)	G	6'	170	23	23	545	119	217	55	34	54	63	37	82	70	2	13	2	272	24	1.6	3.6	3.0	11.8
Ralph Simpson (to NJ)	G	6'5	200	29	37	452	87	196	44	28	40	70	35	58	27	8	25	1	202	12	0.9	1.6	0.7	5.5
Al Skinner (from NJ)	G	6'4	195	26	22	309	36	89	40	27	32	84	44	40	61	2	18	1	99	14	2.0	1.8	2.8	4.5
Harvey Catchings (to NJ)	C	6'9	218	27	25	289	28	68	41	13	17	76	98	18	42	1	8	35	69	12	3.9	0.7	1.7	2.8
Marlon Redmond (from KC)	G	6'6	188	23	4	23	1	12	8	0	0	—	1	1	3	0	0	0	2	6	0.3	0.3	0.8	0.5
NEW JERSEY NETS	**37-45 .451 KEVIN LOUGHERY**																							
Jan Van Breda Kolf	F-G	6'7	200	27	80	1998	196	423	46	146	183	80	382	180	235	4	85	74	538	25	4.8	2.3	2.9	6.7
Bernard King	F	6'7	205	22	82	2859	710	1359	52	349	619	56	669	295	326	10	118	39	1769	35	8.2	3.6	4.0	21.6
George Johnson	C	6'11	205	30	78	2058	206	483	43	105	138	76	616	88	315	8	68	253	517	26	7.9	1.1	4.0	6.6
John Williamson	G	6'2	195	26	74	2451	635	1367	46	373	437	85	196	255	215	3	89	12	1643	33	2.6	3.4	2.9	22.2
Eddie Jordan	G	6'1	170	23	82	2260	401	960	42	213	274	78	215	365	209	0	201	40	1015	28	2.6	4.5	2.5	12.4
Tim Bassett	F-C	6'8	225	27	82	1508	116	313	37	89	131	68	418	99	219	1	44	29	321	18	5.1	1.2	2.7	3.9
Eric Money (to Phi)	G	6'	170	23	47	1434	325	676	48	136	183	74	125	249	132	0	74	10	786	31	2.7	5.3	2.8	16.7
Winford Boynes	G-F	6'6	186	20	69	1176	256	595	43	133	169	79	155	75	117	1	43	7	645	17	2.2	1.1	1.7	9.3
Wilson Washington	F-C	6'9	227	23	62	1139	218	434	50	66	104	63	294	47	186	5	31	67	502	18	4.7	0.8	3.0	8.1
Phil Jackson (BC)	C-F	6'8	230	33	59	1070	144	303	48	86	105	82	178	85	168	7	45	22	374	18	3.0	1.4	2.8	6.3
Harvey Catchings (from Phi)	C	6'9	218	27	32	659	74	175	42	47	61	77	204	30	90	2	15	56	195	21	6.4	0.9	2.8	6.1
Ralph Simpson (from Phi)	G	6'5	200	29	32	527	87	237	37	48	71	68	61	68	30	0	12	4	222	16	1.9	2.1	0.9	6.9
Al Skinner (to Phi)	G	6'4	195	26	23	334	55	125	44	72	82	88	42	49	53	0	22	2	182	15	1.8	2.1	2.3	7.9
Bob Elliot (KJ)	C	6'9	225	23	14	282	41	73	56	41	56	73	56	22	34	2	6	4	123	20	4.0	1.6	2.4	8.8
NEW YORK KNICKERBOCKERS	**31-51 .378 WILLIS REED (6-8 .429), RED HOLZMAN (25-43 .368)**																							
Glen Gondrezick	F-G	6'6	218	23	75	1602	161	326	49	55	97	57	424	106	226	1	98	18	377	21	5.7	1.4	3.0	5.0
Toby Knight	F	6'9	210	23	82	2667	609	1174	52	145	206	70	548	124	309	7	61	60	1363	33	6.7	1.5	3.8	16.6
Marvin Webster (KJ)	C	7'1	240	26	60	2027	264	558	47	150	262	57	655	172	183	6	24	112	678	34	10.9	2.9	3.1	11.3
Ray Williams	G	6'3	190	24	81	2370	575	1257	46	251	313	80	291	504	274	4	128	19	1401	29	3.6	6.2	3.4	17.3
Jim Cleamons	G	6'3	185	29	79	2390	311	657	47	130	171	76	225	376	147	1	73	11	752	30	2.8	4.8	1.9	9.5
Bob McAdoo (FJ, to Bos)	F-C	6'9	210	27	40	1594	429	793	54	218	335	65	379	128	134	2	62	47	1076	40	9.5	3.2	3.4	26.9
Earl Monroe (HO)	G	6'3	190	34	64	1393	329	699	47	129	154	84	74	189	123	0	48	6	787	22	1.2	3.0	1.9	12.3
Michael Ray Richardson	F-G	6'5	190	23	72	1218	200	483	41	69	128	54	233	213	188	2	100	18	469	17	3.2	3.0	2.6	6.5
Mike Glenn	G	6'3	175	23	75	1171	263	486	54	47	63	75	82	136	113	0	37	6	583	16	1.1	1.8	1.5	7.8
Joe Meriweather (from NO)	C-F	6'10	218	25	41	1053	158	313	50	75	109	69	225	48	178	8	23	53	391	26	5.5	1.2	4.3	9.5
Spencer Hayward (to NO)	F-C	6'9	225	29	34	1023	249	509	49	107	146	73	206	56	108	2	10	29	605	30	6.1	1.6	3.2	17.8
John Rudd	F	6'7	230	23	58	723	59	133	44	66	93	71	167	35	95	1	17	8	184	12	2.9	0.6	1.6	3.2
Tom Barker (from Hou,Bos)	C-F	6'11	230	23	22	329	44	102	43	14	20	70	83	9	45	0	6	7	102	15	3.8	0.4	2.0	4.6
Greg Bunch	F	6'6	190	22	12	97	9	26	35	10	12	83	17	4	10	0	3	3	28	8	1.4	0.3	0.8	2.3
Butch Beard (RC)	G	6'3	185	31	7	85	11	26	42	0	0	—	10	19	13	0	7	0	22	12	1.4	2.7	1.9	3.1
Ron Behagen (from Det,to KC)	F	6'9	235	27	5	38	5	12	42	2	2	100	11	2	8	0	2	0	12	8	2.2	0.4	1.6	2.4
Jim McMillian (holdout, to Port)																								

Use Name	Pos	Hgt	Wgt	Age	TOTAL G	Min	FG	FGA	%	FT	FTA	%	Reb	Ass	PF	DQ	Stls	Blkd Shts	Points	PER GAME Min	Reb	Ass	PF	Points
1978/79 N.B.A. — EASTERN CONFERENCE (continued)																								
ATLANTIC DIVISION																								
BOSTON CELTICS	**29-53 .354**				**SATCH SANDERS (2-12 .143), DAVE COWENS (27-41 .397)**																			
Curtis Rowe	F	6'7	225	29	53	1222	151	346	44	52	75	69	242	69	105	2	15	13	354	23	4.6	1.3	2.0	6.7
Cedric Maxwell	F	6'8	205	23	80	2969	472	808	**58**	574	716	80	791	228	266	4	98	74	1518	37	9.9	2.9	3.3	19.0
Dave Cowens (NJ)	C	6'9	230	30	68	2517	488	1010	48	151	187	81	652	242	263	16	76	51	1127	37	9.6	3.6	3.9	16.6
Chris Ford (from Det)	G	6'5	190	29	78	2629	525	1107	47	165	219	75	256	369	200	2	114	24	1215	34	3.3	4.7	2.6	15.6
Nate Archibald	G	6'1	150	30	69	1662	259	573	45	242	307	79	103	324	132	2	55	6	760	24	1.5	4.7	1.9	11.0
Jeff Judkins	F-G	6'6	185	22	81	1521	295	587	50	119	146	82	191	145	184	1	81	12	709	19	2.4	1.8	2.3	8.8
Jo Jo White (to GS)	G	6'3	190	32	47	1455	255	596	43	79	89	89	128	214	100	1	54	4	589	31	2.7	4.6	2.1	12.5
Billy Knight (to Ind)	F-G	6'6	195	26	40	1119	219	436	50	118	146	81	173	66	86	1	31	3	556	28	4.3	1.7	2.2	13.9
Don Chaney	G	6'5	210	32	65	1074	174	414	42	36	42	86	141	75	167	3	72	11	384	17	2.2	1.2	2.6	5.9
Rick Robey (from Ind)	C-F	6'11	230	22	36	914	182	378	48	84	103	82	259	79	121	3	23	3	448	25	7.2	2.2	3.4	12.4
Marvin Barnes	F-C	6'9	225	26	38	796	133	271	49	43	66	65	177	53	144	3	38	39	309	21	4.7	1.4	3.8	8.1
Bob McAdoo (from NY)	C-F	6'9	210	27	20	637	167	334	50	77	115	67	141	40	55	1	12	20	411	32	7.1	2.0	2.8	20.6
Earl Williams (XJ)	C-F	6'7	230	27	20	273	54	123	44	14	24	58	105	12	41	0	12	9	122	14	5.3	0.6	2.1	6.1
Kevin Stacom (from Ind)	G	6'3	185	27	24	260	52	133	39	13	19	68	24	35	18	0	15	0	117	11	1.0	1.5	0.8	4.9
Dennis Awtrey (NJ, to Sea)	C	6'10	240	30	23	247	17	44	39	16	20	80	47	20	37	0	3	6	50	11	2.0	0.9	1.6	2.2
Frankie Sanders (from SA)	F-G	6'6	200	21	24	216	55	119	46	22	27	81	51	17	25	0	7	3	132	9	2.1	0.7	1.0	5.5
Tom Barker (from Hou, to NY)	C	6'11	230	23	14	131	21	48	44	11	15	73	30	6	26	0	4	4	53	9	2.1	0.4	1.9	3.8
Earl Tatum (to Det)	G-F	6'4	185	25	3	38	8	20	40	4	5	80	4	1	7	0	0	1	20	13	1.3	0.3	2.3	6.7
CENTRAL DIVISION																								
SAN ANTONIO SPURS	**48-34 .585**				**DOUG MOE**																			
Mark Olberding	F	6'8	230	22	80	1885	261	551	47	233	290	80	429	211	282	2	53	18	755	24	5.4	2.6	3.5	9.4
Larry Kenon	F	6'9	215	26	81	2947	748	1484	50	295	349	85	790	335	192	1	154	19	1791	36	9.8	4.1	2.4	22.1
Billy Paultz	C	6'11	250	30	79	2122	399	758	53	114	194	59	625	178	204	4	35	125	912	27	7.9	2.3	2.6	11.5
George Gervin	G	6'7	185	26	80	2888	**947**	**1749**	54	471	570	83	400	219	275	5	137	91	**2365**	36	5.0	2.7	3.4	**29.6**
James Silas	G	6'3	180	29	79	2171	466	922	51	334	402	83	183	273	215	1	76	20	1266	27	2.3	3.5	2.7	16.0
Mike Gale	G	6'4	190	28	82	2121	284	612	46	91	108	84	186	374	192	1	152	40	659	26	2.3	4.6	2.3	8.0
Mike Green	C-F	6'10	200	27	76	1641	235	477	49	101	144	70	354	116	230	3	37	122	571	22	4.7	1.5	3.0	7.5
Coby Dietrick	F-C	6'10	225	30	76	1487	209	400	52	79	99	80	315	198	206	7	72	38	497	20	4.1	2.6	2.7	6.5
Allan Bristow	F	6'7	210	27	74	1324	174	354	49	124	149	83	247	231	154	0	56	15	472	18	3.3	3.1	2.1	6.4
Louie Dampier	G	6'	180	34	70	760	123	251	49	29	39	74	63	124	42	0	35	8	275	11	0.9	1.8	0.6	3.9
Frankie Sanders (to Bos)	F-G	6'6	200	21	22	263	50	127	39	32	41	78	59	35	44	1	14	3	132	12	2.7	1.6	2.0	6.0
Glenn Mosley	F	6'8	195	23	26	221	31	75	41	23	38	61	64	19	35	0	8	10	85	9	2.5	0.7	1.3	3.3
HOUSTON ROCKETS	**47-35 .573**				**TOM NISSALKE**																			
Rick Barry	F	6'7	220	34	80	2566	461	1000	46	160	169	**95**	277	502	195	0	95	38	1082	32	3.5	6.3	2.4	13.5
Rudy Tomjanovich	F	6'8	220	30	74	2641	620	1200	52	168	221	76	572	137	186	0	44	18	1408	36	7.7	1.9	2.5	19.0
Moses Malone	C	6'10	215	23	82	**3390**	716	1325	54	599	811	74	**1444**	147	223	0	79	119	2031	**41**	**17.6**	1.8	2.7	24.8
Mike Newlin	G	6'4	200	29	76	1828	283	581	49	212	243	87	170	291	218	3	51	79	778	24	2.2	3.8	2.9	10.2
Calvin Murphy	G	5'9	165	30	82	2941	707	1424	50	246	265	93	173	351	288	5	117	6	1660	36	2.1	4.3	3.5	20.2
Robert Reid	F-G	6'8	205	23	82	2259	382	777	49	131	186	70	483	230	302	7	75	48	895	28	5.9	2.8	3.7	10.9
Mike Dunleavy	G	6'3	180	24	74	1486	215	425	51	159	184	86	128	324	168	2	56	5	589	20	1.7	4.4	2.3	8.0
Dwight Jones	F-C	6'10	210	26	81	1215	181	395	46	96	132	73	328	57	204	1	34	26	458	15	4.0	0.7	2.5	5.7
Slick Watts	G	6'1	175	27	61	1046	92	227	41	41	67	61	103	243	143	1	73	14	225	17	1.7	4.0	2.3	3.7
Alonzo Bradley	F	6'6	190	24	34	245	37	88	42	22	33	67	46	17	33	0	5	1	96	7	1.4	0.5	1.0	2.8
Jacky Dorsey	F	6'7	230	24	20	108	24	43	56	8	16	50	23	2	25	0	1	2	56	5	1.2	0.1	1.3	2.8
E.C. Coleman	F	6'8	225	28	6	39	5	7	71	1	1	100	7	1	11	0	2	0	11	7	1.2	0.2	1.8	1.8
Tom Barker (to Bos, NY)	C	6'11	230	23	5	16	3	6	50	2	2	100	6	0	5	0	0	0	8	3	1.2	0.0	1.0	1.6
Rudy White (broken toe)																								
ATLANTA HAWKS	**46-36 .561**				**HUBIE BROWN**																			
John Drew	F	6'6	205	24	79	2410	650	1375	47	495	677	73	522	119	332	**19**	128	16	1795	31	6.6	1.5	4.2	22.7
Dan Roundfield	F	6'8	205	25	80	2539	462	916	50	300	420	71	865	131	358	16	87	176	1224	32	10.8	1.6	4.5	15.3
Tree Rollins	C	7'1	235	23	81	1900	297	555	54	89	141	63	588	49	328	**19**	46	254	683	23	7.3	0.6	4.0	8.4
Armond Hill	G	6'4	190	25	82	2527	296	682	43	246	288	85	164	480	292	8	102	16	838	31	2.0	5.9	3.6	10.2
Eddie Johnson	G	6'2	175	23	78	2413	501	982	51	243	292	83	170	360	241	6	121	11	1245	31	2.2	4.6	3.1	16.0
Steve Hawkes	C-F	6'9	220	28	81	2205	372	756	49	108	132	82	591	184	264	1	79	47	852	27	7.3	2.3	3.3	10.5
Tom McMillen	F-C	6'11	215	26	82	1392	232	498	47	106	119	89	332	69	211	2	15	32	570	17	4.0	0.8	2.6	7.0
Jack Givens	F-G	6'5	205	22	74	1347	234	564	41	102	135	76	214	83	121	0	72	17	570	18	2.9	1.1	1.6	7.7
Butch Lee (to Cle)	G	6'	185	22	49	997	144	313	46	88	117	75	59	169	88	0	56	1	376	20	1.2	3.4	1.8	7.7
Charlie Criss (SJ)	G	5'8	165	29	54	879	109	289	38	67	86	78	60	138	70	0	41	3	285	16	1.1	2.6	1.3	5.3
Rick Wilson	G	6'5	200	22	61	589	81	197	41	24	44	55	76	72	66	1	30	8	186	10	1.2	1.2	1.1	3.0
Terry Furlow (from Cle)	G-F	6'4	190	24	29	576	113	235	48	60	70	86	71	81	42	0	18	13	286	20	2.4	2.8	1.4	9.9
Keith Herron	G	6'6	195	22	14	81	14	48	29	12	13	92	10	3	11	0	6	2	40	6	0.7	0.2	0.8	2.9

se Name	Pos	Hgt	Wgt	Age	TOTAL G	Min	FG	FGA	%	FT	FTA	%	Reb	Ass	PF	DQ	Stls	Blkd Shts	Points	PER GAME Min	Reb	Ass	PF	Points
1978/79 N.B.A.— EASTERN CONFERENCE (continued)																								
CENTRAL DIVISION																								
LEVELAND CAVALIERS	**30-52 .366**				**BILL FITCH**																			
obby Smith	F-G	6'5	212	32	72	1650	361	784	46	83	106	78	206	121	188	2	43	7	805	23	2.9	1.7	2.6	11.2
ampy Russell	F	6'8	215	26	74	2859	603	1268	48	417	523	80	503	348	222	2	98	25	1623	39	6.8	4.7	3.0	21.9
m Chones	C	6'11	220	29	82	2850	472	1073	44	158	215	73	842	181	278	4	47	102	1102	35	10.3	2.2	3.4	13.4
ustin Carr	G	6'4	200	30	82	2714	551	1161	47	292	358	86	290	217	210	1	77	14	1394	33	3.5	2.6	2.6	17.0
oots Walker (NJ)	G	6'1	172	27	55	1753	208	448	46	137	175	78	198	321	153	0	130	18	553	32	3.6	5.8	2.8	10.1
like Mitchell	F	6'7	215	22	80	1576	362	706	51	131	178	74	329	60	215	6	51	29	855	20	4.1	0.8	2.7	10.7
im Brewer (to Det)	F	6'9	220	27	55	1301	114	259	44	23	48	48	370	74	136	2	48	56	251	24	6.7	1.3	2.5	4.6
erry Furlow (to Atl)	G	6'4	190	24	49	1110	275	569	48	103	125	82	96	103	80	1	40	17	653	23	2.0	2.1	1.6	13.3
enny Higgs	G	6'	185	23	68	1050	127	279	46	85	111	77	102	141	176	2	66	11	339	15	1.5	2.1	2.6	5.0
ohn Lambert	C-F	6'10	225	25	70	1030	148	329	45	35	55	64	290	43	163	0	25	29	331	15	4.1	0.6	2.3	4.7
utch Lee (from Atl)	G	6'	185	22	33	782	146	321	45	87	113	77	67	126	58	0	30	0	379	24	2.0	3.8	1.8	11.5
arry Davis	F	6'7	220	22	40	394	66	153	43	30	43	70	66	16	66	1	13	8	162	10	1.7	0.4	1.7	4.1
lmore Smith (KJ)	C	7'	250	29	24	332	69	130	53	18	26	69	106	13	60	0	7	16	156	14	4.4	0.5	2.5	6.5
Valt Frazier (FJ)	G	6'4	205	33	12	279	54	122	44	21	27	78	20	32	22	0	13	2	129	23	1.7	2.7	1.8	10.8
ETROIT PISTONS	**30-52 .366**				**DICK VITALE**																			
I.L. Carr	F-G	6'6	205	27	80	3207	587	1143	51	323	435	74	589	262	279	2	197	46	1497	40	7.4	3.3	3.5	18.7
erry Tyler	F	6'7	215	23	82	2560	456	946	48	144	219	66	648	89	254	3	104	201	1056	31	7.9	1.1	3.1	12.9
ob Lanier (KJ)	C	6'11	250	30	53	1835	489	950	51	275	367	75	494	140	181	5	50	75	1253	35	9.3	2.6	3.4	23.6
ohn Long	G-F	6'5	210	22	82	2498	581	1240	47	157	190	83	256	121	224	1	102	19	1319	30	3.1	1.5	2.7	16.1
evin Porter	G	6'	175	28	82	3064	534	1110	48	192	266	72	209	**1099**	302	5	158	5	1260	37	2.5	**13.4**	3.7	15.4
eon Douglas	C-F	6'10	230	24	78	2215	342	698	49	208	328	63	664	74	319	13	39	55	892	28	8.5	0.9	4.1	11.4
en Poquette	F-C	6'9	235	23	76	1337	198	464	43	111	142	78	336	57	198	4	38	98	508	18	4.4	0.8	2.6	6.7
arl Tatum (to Bos)	G	6'4	185	25	76	1195	272	607	45	48	66	73	121	72	158	3	78	33	592	16	1.6	0.9	2.1	7.8
ndre Wakefield (from Chi)	G	6'3	175	23	71	578	62	176	35	48	69	70	76	69	68	0	19	2	172	8	1.1	1.0	1.0	2.4
ickey Green	G	6'1	170	24	27	431	67	177	38	45	67	67	40	63	37	0	25	1	179	16	1.5	2.3	1.4	6.6
im Brewer (from Cle)	F	6'9	220	27	25	310	27	60	45	3	15	20	105	13	38	0	13	10	57	12	4.2	0.5	1.5	2.3
ssie Hollis	F	6'6	195	23	25	154	30	75	40	9	12	75	45	6	28	0	11	1	69	6	1.8	0.2	1.1	2.8
hris Ford (to Bos)	G	6'5	190	29	3	108	13	35	37	7	8	88	18	5	9	1	1	1	33	36	6.0	1.7	3.0	11.0
tis Hayward (from Mil)	F	6'7	230	22	11	91	19	45	42	11	23	48	34	4	16	0	2	2	49	8	3.1	0.4	1.5	4.5
teve Sheppard (from Chi)	F	6'6	220	24	20	76	12	25	48	8	15	53	19	4	10	0	3	1	32	4	1.0	0.2	0.5	1.6
arry McNeill	F	6'9	195	27	11	46	9	20	45	11	12	92	10	3	7	0	0	0	29	4	0.9	0.3	0.6	2.6
ennis Boyd	G	6'1	175	24	5	40	3	12	25	0	0	—	2	7	5	0	0	0	6	8	0.4	1.4	1.0	1.2
ubbles Hawkins	G	6'4	190	24	4	28	6	16	38	6	6	100	6	4	7	0	5	0	18	7	1.5	1.0	1.8	4.5
us Gerard (to KC)	F	6'8	205	25	2	6	1	3	33	1	2	50	1	0	0	0	2	0	3	3	0.5	0.0	0.0	1.5
on Behagen (to NY, KC)	F	6'9	235	27	1	1	0	0	—	0	0	—	0	0	1	0	0	0	0	1	0.0	0.0	1.0	0.0
John Shumate (blood clot in lung)																								
EW ORLEANS JAZZ	**26-56 .317**				**ELGIN BAYLOR**																			
ames Hardy	F	6'8	220	22	68	1456	196	426	46	61	88	69	310	65	133	1	52	61	453	21	4.6	1.0	2.0	6.7
pencer Hayward (from NY)	F	6'9	225	29	34	1338	346	696	50	124	146	85	327	71	128	6	30	53	816	39	9.6	2.1	3.8	24.0
ich Kelley	C	7'	240	25	80	2705	440	870	51	373	458	81	1026	285	309	8	126	166	1253	34	12.8	3.6	3.9	15.7
ete Maravich (KJ)	G	6'5	200	30	49	1824	436	1035	42	233	277	84	121	243	104	2	60	18	1105	37	2.5	5.0	2.1	22.6
im McElroy	G	6'3	190	25	79	2698	539	1097	49	259	340	76	215	453	183	1	148	49	1337	34	2.7	5.7	2.3	16.9
ail Goodrich	G	6'1	175	35	74	2130	382	850	45	174	204	85	183	357	177	1	90	13	938	29	2.5	4.8	2.4	12.7
ruck Robinson (to Phoe)	F	6'7	225	27	43	1781	397	819	48	245	339	72	577	74	130	1	29	63	1039	41	13.4	1.7	3.0	24.2
aron James	F	6'8	210	26	73	1417	311	630	49	105	140	75	248	78	202	1	28	21	727	19	3.4	1.1	2.8	10.0
aul Griffin	F-C	6'9	205	24	77	1398	106	223	48	91	147	62	391	138	198	3	54	36	303	18	5.1	1.8	2.6	3.9
ommy Green	G	6'2	185	22	59	809	92	237	39	48	63	76	68	140	111	0	61	6	232	14	1.2	2.4	1.9	3.9
oe Meriweather (to NY)	C	6'10	218	25	36	640	84	187	45	51	78	65	184	31	105	2	17	41	219	18	5.1	0.9	2.9	6.1
a Terrall (to Port)	F	6'8	205	24	31	572	63	144	44	27	38	71	109	26	73	0	15	22	153	18	3.5	0.8	2.4	4.9
Aarty Byrnes (to Phoe)	F	6'7	215	22	36	530	78	166	47	33	54	61	94	43	42	0	12	8	189	15	2.6	1.2	1.2	5.3
on Lee (LJ, from Phoe)	G	6'4	193	26	17	398	45	124	36	24	37	65	55	73	44	1	38	2	114	23	3.2	4.3	2.6	6.7
us Bailey	G	6'5	185	25	2	9	2	7	29	0	0	—	2	2	1	0	0	0	4	5	1.0	1.0	0.5	2.0
WESTERN CONFERENCE																								
MIDWEST DIVISION																								
ANSAS CITY KINGS	**48-34 .585**				**COTTON FITZSIMMINS**																			
cott Wedman	F	6'7	215	26	73	2498	561	1050	53	216	271	80	386	144	239	4	76	30	1338	34	5.3	2.0	3.3	18.3
ill Robinzine	F	6'7	230	25	82	2179	459	837	55	180	246	73	638	104	**367**	16	105	15	1098	27	7.8	1.3	**4.5**	13.4
am Lacey	C	6'10	235	30	82	2627	350	697	50	167	226	74	702	430	309	11	106	141	867	32	8.6	5.2	3.8	10.6
tis Birdsong	G	6'4	195	23	82	2839	741	1456	51	296	408	73	354	281	255	2	125	17	1778	35	4.3	3.4	3.1	21.7
hil Ford	G	6'2	176	22	79	2723	467	1004	47	326	401	81	182	681	245	3	174	6	1260	34	2.3	8.6	3.1	15.9
arnell Hillman	F-C	6'9	215	29	78	1618	211	428	49	125	224	56	431	91	228	11	50	66	547	21	5.5	1.2	2.9	7.0
ob Nash	F	6'8	205	28	82	1307	227	522	43	69	86	80	206	71	135	0	29	15	523	16	2.5	0.9	1.6	6.4
illy McKinney	G	6'	162	23	78	1242	240	477	50	129	162	80	85	253	121	0	58	3	609	16	1.1	3.2	1.6	7.8
om Burleson (KJ)	C	7'3	228	26	56	927	157	342	46	121	169	72	281	50	183	3	26	58	435	17	5.0	0.9	3.3	7.8
Aarlon Redmond (to Phi)	G	6'6	188	23	49	736	162	375	43	31	50	62	108	57	93	2	28	16	355	15	2.2	1.2	1.9	7.2
us Gerard (from Det)	F	6'8	205	25	56	459	83	191	43	49	89	55	97	21	74	1	18	13	215	8	1.7	0.4	1.3	3.8
ucius Allen (FJ)	G	6'2	175	31	31	413	69	174	40	19	33	58	46	44	52	0	21	6	157	13	1.5	1.4	1.7	5.1
ichard Washington (BF)	F-C	6'11	225	23	18	161	14	41	34	10	16	63	48	7	31	0	7	3	38	9	2.7	0.4	1.7	2.1
on Behagen (from Det, NY)	F	6'9	235	27	9	126	23	50	46	8	11	73	31	5	27	0	2	1	54	14	3.4	0.6	3.0	6.0

Use Name	Pos	Hgt	Wgt	Age	TOTAL G	Min	FG	FGA	%	FT	FTA	%	Reb	Ass	PF	DQ	Stls	Blkd Shts	Points	PER GAME Min	Reb	Ass	PF	Points
1978/79 N.B.A — WESTERN CONFERENCE (continued) MIDWEST DIVISION																								
DENVER NUGGETS	47-35 .573				**LARRY BROWN (28-45 .528), DONNIE WALSH (19-10 .655)**																			
Bobby Wilkerson	F-G	6'6	200	24	80	2425	396	869	46	119	173	69	414	284	190	0	118	21	911	30	5.2	3.6	2.4	11.
George McGinnis	F	6'8	235	28	76	2552	603	1273	47	509	765	67	864	283	321	16	129	52	1715	34	11.4	3.7	4.2	22.
Dan Issel	C	6'9	240	30	81	2742	532	1030	52	316	419	75	738	255	233	6	61	46	1380	34	9.1	3.1	2.9	17.
David Thompson	G-F	6'4	195	24	76	2670	693	1353	51	439	583	75	274	225	180	2	70	82	1825	35	3.6	3.0	2.4	24.
Charlie Scott	G	6'6	175	30	79	2617	393	854	46	161	215	75	210	428	284	12	78	30	947	33	2.7	5.4	3.6	12.
Tom Boswell	F-C	6'9	225	25	79	2201	321	603	53	198	284	70	538	242	263	4	50	51	840	28	6.8	3.1	3.3	10.
Robert Smith	G	5'11	165	23	82	1479	184	436	42	159	180	88	146	208	165	1	58	13	527	18	1.8	2.5	2.0	6.
Anthony Roberts (IL)	F-G	6'5	185	23	63	1236	211	498	42	76	110	69	258	107	142	2	20	2	498	20	4.1	1.7	2.3	7.
Kim Hughes	C	6'11	220	26	81	1086	98	182	54	18	45	40	335	74	215	2	56	102	214	13	4.1	0.9	2.7	2.
Bo Ellis (KJ)	F	6'9	200	24	42	268	42	92	46	29	36	81	62	10	45	0	10	13	113	6	1.5	0.2	1.1	2.
John Kuester	G	6'2	180	23	33	212	16	52	31	13	14	93	13	37	29	0	18	1	45	6	0.4	1.1	0.9	1.
Phil Hicks	F	6'7	205	25	20	128	18	43	42	3	5	60	28	8	20	0	5	0	39	6	1.4	0.4	1.0	2.
Geoff Crompton (Injury)	C	6'11	268	23	20	88	10	26	38	6	12	50	23	5	19	0	0	3	26	4	1.2	0.3	1.0	1.
INDIANA PACERS	38-44 .463				**BOB LEONARD**																			
Alex English	F	6'8	190	24	81	2696	563	1102	51	173	230	75	655	271	214	3	70	78	1299	33	8.1	3.3	2.6	16.
Mike Bantom	F	6'9	220	27	81	2528	482	1036	47	227	338	67	650	223	316	8	99	62	1191	31	8.0	2.8	3.9	14.
James Edwards	C	7'	225	23	82	2546	534	1065	50	298	441	68	693	92	363	16	60	109	1366	31	8.5	1.1	4.4	16.
Ricky Sobers	G	6'3	198	25	81	2825	553	1194	46	298	338	88	301	450	315	8	138	23	1404	35	3.7	5.6	3.9	17.
Johnny Davis	G	6'2	170	23	79	2971	565	1240	46	314	396	79	191	453	177	1	95	22	1444	38	2.4	5.7	2.2	18.
Corky Calhoun	F	6'7	210	28	81	1332	153	335	46	72	86	84	238	104	199	1	37	19	378	16	2.9	1.3	2.5	4.
Len Elmore	C	6'9	220	26	80	1264	139	342	41	56	78	72	402	75	183	3	62	79	334	16	5.0	0.9	2.3	4.
Billy Knight (from Bos)	G-F	6'6	195	26	39	976	222	399	56	131	150	87	174	86	74	0	32	5	575	25	4.5	2.2	1.9	14.
Rick Robey (to Bos)	F-C	6'11	230	22	43	849	140	295	47	90	121	74	254	53	111	1	25	12	370	20	5.9	1.2	2.6	8.
Wayne Radford	G	6'3	205	22	52	649	83	175	47	36	45	80	68	57	61	0	30	1	202	12	1.3	1.1	1.2	3.
Kevin Stacom (to Bos)	G	6'3	185	27	44	571	76	209	36	31	41	76	61	77	29	0	14	1	183	13	1.4	1.8	0.7	4.
Steve Green	F	6'7	220	25	39	265	42	89	47	20	34	59	52	21	39	0	11	3	104	7	1.3	0.5	1.0	2.
Brad Davis (from LA)	G	6'3	180	23	22	233	23	44	52	13	19	68	16	43	22	0	14	2	59	11	0.7	2.0	1.0	2.
MILWAUKEE BUCKS	38-44 .463				**DON NELSON**																			
Ernie Grunfield	F-G	6'6	215	23	82	1778	326	661	49	191	251	76	360	216	220	3	58	15	843	22	4.4	2.6	2.7	10.
Marques Johnson	F	6'7	218	22	77	2779	820	1491	55	332	437	76	586	234	186	1	116	89	1972	36	7.6	3.0	2.4	25.
Kent Benson	C	6'10	245	24	82	2132	413	798	52	180	245	73	584	204	280	4	89	81	1006	26	7.1	2.5	3.4	12.
Brian Winters	G	6'4	185	26	79	2575	662	1343	49	237	277	86	177	383	243	1	83	40	1561	33	2.2	4.8	3.1	19.
Quinn Buckner	G	6'3	205	24	81	1757	251	553	45	79	125	63	210	468	224	1	156	17	581	22	2.6	5.8	2.8	7.2
John Gianelli	C-F	6'10	220	28	82	2057	256	527	49	72	102	71	408	160	196	4	44	67	584	25	5.0	2.0	2.4	7.1
Junior Bridgeman	G-F	6'5	210	25	82	1963	540	1067	51	189	228	83	297	163	184	2	88	41	1269	24	3.6	2.0	2.2	15.5
Kevin Restani	F	6'9	225	27	81	1598	262	529	50	51	73	70	385	122	155	0	30	27	575	20	4.8	1.5	1.9	7.1
Lloyd Walton	G	6'	160	25	75	1381	157	327	48	61	90	68	104	356	103	0	72	9	375	18	1.4	4.7	1.4	5.0
George Johnson	F	6'7	218	22	67	1157	165	342	48	84	117	72	360	81	187	5	75	49	414	17	5.4	1.2	2.8	6.2
Norm Van Lier	G	6'1	173	31	38	555	30	77	39	47	52	90	40	158	108	4	43	3	107	15	1.1	4.2	2.8	2.8
Sam Smith	G	6'4	200	23	16	125	19	47	40	18	24	75	9	16	12	0	8	7	56	8	0.6	1.0	0.8	3.5
Otis Howard (to Det)	F	6'7	230	22	3	22	5	11	45	0	0	—	7	1	8	0	0	0	10	7	2.3	0.3	2.7	3.3
Del Beshore	G	5'11	165	22	1	1	0	0	—	0	0	—	0	0	0	0	0	0	0	1	0.0	0.0	0.0	0.0
Dave Meyers (back injury)																								
CHICAGO BULLS	31-51 .378				**LARRY COSTELLO (20-36 .357), SCOTTY ROBERTSON (11-15 .424)**																			
Ollie Johnson	F	6'6	200	29	71	1734	281	540	52	88	110	80	227	163	182	2	54	33	650	24	3.2	2.3	2.6	9.2
Mickey Johnson	F	6'10	190	26	82	2594	496	1105	45	273	329	83	627	380	286	9	88	59	1265	32	7.6	4.6	3.5	15.4
Artis Gilmore	C	7'2	240	29	82	3265	753	1310	57	434	587	74	1043	274	280	2	50	156	1940	40	12.7	3.3	3.4	23.7
Reggie Theus	G	6'7	190	21	82	2753	537	1119	48	264	347	76	228	429	270	2	93	18	1338	34	2.8	5.2	3.3	16.3
Wilbur Holland	G	6'7	175	27	82	2483	445	940	47	141	176	80	254	330	240	9	122	10	1031	30	3.1	4.0	2.9	12.6
Mark Landsberger	F-C	6'8	230	23	80	1959	278	585	48	91	194	47	742	68	125	0	27	22	647	24	9.3	0.9	1.6	8.1
John Mengelt	G	6'2	195	29	75	1705	338	689	49	150	182	82	118	187	148	1	46	4	826	23	1.6	2.5	2.0	11.0
John Brown	F	6'7	220	27	77	1265	152	317	48	84	98	86	238	104	180	5	18	10	388	16	3.1	1.4	2.3	5.0
Charles Dudley (injury)	G	6'2	180	28	43	684	45	125	36	28	42	67	86	116	82	0	32	1	118	16	2.0	2.7	1.9	2.7
Scott Lloyd (from SD)	C	6'10	230	26	67	465	42	120	35	27	47	57	93	32	86	0	9	8	111	7	1.4	0.5	1.3	1.7
Scott May (KJ)	F	6'7	220	24	37	403	59	136	43	30	40	75	64	39	51	0	22	1	148	11	1.7	1.1	1.4	4.0
Tate Armstrong (injury)	G	6'3	175	23	26	259	28	70	40	10	13	77	20	31	22	0	10	0	66	10	0.8	1.2	0.8	2.5
Steve Sheppard (to Det)	F	6'6	220	24	22	203	24	51	47	12	19	63	28	15	16	0	5	0	60	9	1.3	0.7	0.7	2.7
Andre Wakefield (to Det)	G	6'3	175	23	2	8	0	1	0	0	0	—	0	1	2	0	0	0	0	4	0.0	0.5	1.0	0.0
Tom Boerwinkle (knee injury)																								

1978/79 N.B.A — WESTERN CONFERENCE (continued)
PACIFIC DIVISION

Use Name	Pos	Hgt	Wgt	Age	TOTAL G	Min	FG	FGA	%	FT	FTA	%	Reb	Ass	PF	DQ	Stls	Blkd Shts	Points	PER GAME Min	Reb	Ass	PF	Points
SEATTLE SUPERSONICS	**52-30 .634**				**LENNY WILKINS**																			
John Johnson	F	6'7	200	31	82	2386	356	821	43	190	250	76	412	358	245	2	59	25	902	29	5.0	4.4	3.0	11.0
Lonnie Shelton	F	6'8	245	23	76	2158	446	859	52	131	189	69	468	110	266	7	76	75	1023	28	6.2	1.4	3.5	13.5
Jack Sikma	C-F	6'11	230	23	82	2958	476	1034	46	329	404	81	1013	261	295	4	82	67	1281	36	12.4	3.2	3.6	15.6
Dennis Johnson	G	6'4	185	24	80	2717	482	1110	43	306	392	78	374	280	209	2	100	97	1270	34	4.7	3.5	2.6	15.9
Gus Williams	G	6'2	175	25	76	2266	606	1224	50	245	316	78	245	307	162	3	158	29	1457	30	3.2	4.0	2.1	19.2
Fred Brown	G	6'3	185	30	77	1961	446	951	47	183	206	89	172	260	142	0	119	23	1075	25	2.2	3.4	1.8	14.0
Paul Silas	F	6'7	220	35	82	1957	170	402	42	116	194	60	575	115	177	3	31	19	456	24	7.0	1.4	2.2	5.6
Wally Walker (BH)	F	6'7	190	24	60	969	167	343	49	58	96	60	177	69	127	0	12	26	394	16	3.0	1.2	2.1	6.6
Tom LaGarde (KJ)	C	6'10	220	23	23	575	98	181	54	57	95	60	190	32	75	2	6	18	253	25	8.3	1.4	3.3	11.0
Dick Snyder	G	6'5	207	34	56	536	81	187	43	43	51	84	48	63	52	0	14	6	205	10	0.9	1.1	0.9	3.7
Dennis Awtrey (from Bos)	C	6'10	240	30	40	499	27	63	43	25	36	69	104	49	69	0	13	7	79	12	2.6	1.2	1.7	2.0
Joey Hassett	G	6'5	180	23	55	463	100	211	47	23	23	100	45	42	58	0	14	4	223	8	0.8	0.8	1.1	4.1
Lars Hansen	C	6'10	225	24	15	205	29	57	51	18	31	58	59	14	28	0	1	1	76	14	3.9	0.9	1.9	5.1
Jackie Robinson	F	6'6	212	23	12	105	19	41	46	8	15	53	19	13	9	0	5	1	46	9	1.6	1.1	0.8	3.8
PHOENIX SUNS	**50-32 .610**				**JOHN MacLEOD**																			
Walter Davis	F	6'6	198	24	79	2437	764	1362	56	340	409	83	373	339	250	5	147	26	1868	31	4.7	4.3	3.2	23.6
Truck Robinson (IL, from NO)	F	6'7	245	27	26	756	169	333	51	79	123	64	225	39	76	1	17	12	417	29	8.7	1.5	2.9	16.0
Alvan Adams	C	6'9	220	24	77	2364	569	1073	53	231	289	80	705	360	246	4	110	63	1369	31	9.2	4.7	3.2	17.8
Paul Westphal	G	6'4	195	28	81	2641	801	1496	54	339	405	84	159	529	159	1	111	26	1941	33	2.0	6.5	2.0	24.0
Don Buse	G	6'4	195	28	82	2544	285	576	49	70	91	77	217	356	149	0	156	18	640	31	2.6	4.3	1.8	7.8
Alvin Scott	F	6'7	185	23	81	1737	212	396	54	120	168	71	360	126	139	2	80	62	544	21	4.4	1.6	1.7	6.7
Joel Kramer	F-C	6'7	203	23	82	1401	181	370	49	125	176	71	337	92	224	2	45	23	487	17	4.1	1.1	2.7	5.9
Mike Bratz	G	6'2	185	23	77	1297	242	533	45	139	170	82	141	179	151	0	64	7	623	17	1.8	2.3	2.0	8.1
Bayard Forrest	C	6'10	235	24	75	1243	118	272	43	62	115	54	315	167	151	1	29	37	298	17	4.2	2.2	2.0	4.0
Gar Heard	F	6'6	219	30	63	1213	162	367	44	71	103	69	351	60	141	1	53	57	395	19	5.6	1.0	2.2	6.3
Ron Lee (to NO)	G	6'4	193	26	43	948	173	383	45	74	104	71	113	132	138	2	69	4	420	22	2.6	3.1	3.2	9.8
Marty Byrnes (to NO)	F	6'7	215	22	43	734	109	223	49	73	100	73	97	61	69	0	15	2	291	17	2.3	1.4	1.6	6.8
Ted McClain	G	6'2	190	31	36	465	62	132	47	42	46	91	69	60	51	0	19	0	166	13	1.9	1.7	1.4	4.6
LOS ANGELES LAKERS	**47-35 .573**				**JERRY WEST**																			
Adrian Dantley (KJ)	F	6'5	210	22	60	1775	374	733	51	292	342	85	342	138	162	0	63	12	1040	30	5.7	2.3	2.7	17.3
Jamaal Wilkes	F	6'6	190	25	82	2915	626	1242	50	272	362	75	609	227	275	2	134	27	1524	36	7.4	2.8	3.4	18.6
Kareem Abdul-Jabbar	C	7'2	232	31	80	3157	777	1347	58	349	474	74	1025	431	230	3	76	**316**	1903	39	12.8	5.4	2.9	23.8
Lou Hudson	G	6'5	210	34	78	1686	329	636	52	110	124	89	140	141	133	1	58	17	768	22	1.8	1.8	1.7	9.8
Norm Nixon	G	6'2	175	23	82	3145	623	1149	54	158	204	77	231	737	250	6	**201**	17	1404	38	2.8	9.0	3.0	17.1
Ron Boone	G	6'2	200	32	82	1583	259	569	46	90	104	87	145	154	171	1	66	11	608	19	1.8	1.9	2.1	7.4
Don Ford	F	6'9	215	26	79	1540	228	450	51	72	89	81	268	101	177	2	51	25	528	19	3.4	1.3	2.2	6.7
Dave Robisch	C-F	6'10	240	29	80	1219	150	336	45	86	115	75	285	97	108	0	20	25	386	15	3.6	1.2	1.4	4.8
Jim Price	G	6'3	195	29	75	1207	171	344	50	55	79	70	123	218	128	0	66	12	397	16	1.6	2.9	1.7	5.3
Ken Carr	F	6'7	230	23	72	1149	225	450	50	83	137	61	292	60	152	0	38	31	533	16	4.1	0.8	2.1	7.4
Ron Carter	G	6'5	190	22	46	332	54	124	44	36	54	67	45	25	54	1	17	7	144	7	1.0	0.5	1.2	3.1
Brad Davis (to Ind)	G	6'3	180	23	5	65	8	11	73	3	4	75	1	9	10	0	2	0	19	13	0.2	1.8	2.0	3.8
Mike Cooper (KJ)	G	6'5	170	22	3	7	3	6	50	0	0	—	0	0	1	0	1	0	6	2	0.0	0.0	0.3	2.0
PORTLAND TRAIL BLAZERS	**45-37 .549**				**JACK RAMSEY**																			
Bob Grass (KJ)	F	6'6	200	25	53	1441	209	443	47	96	119	81	250	184	161	4	70	47	514	27	4.7	3.5	3.0	9.7
Maurice Lucas	F	6'9	218	26	69	2462	568	1208	47	270	345	78	716	215	254	3	66	81	1406	36	10.4	3.1	3.7	20.4
Tom Owens	C	6'10	220	29	82	2791	600	1095	55	320	403	79	740	301	329	15	59	58	1520	34	9.0	3.7	4.0	18.5
Ron Brewer	G	6'4	180	23	81	2454	434	878	49	210	256	82	229	165	181	3	102	79	1078	30	2.8	2.0	2.2	13.3
Lionel Hollins	G	6'3	185	25	64	1967	402	886	45	172	221	78	149	325	199	3	114	24	976	31	2.3	5.1	3.1	15.3
Mychal Thompson	F-C	6'10	226	23	73	2144	460	938	49	154	269	57	604	176	270	10	67	134	1074	29	8.3	2.4	3.7	14.7
T.R. Dunn	G-F	6'4	192	23	80	1828	246	549	45	122	158	77	344	103	166	1	86	23	614	23	4.3	1.3	2.1	7.7
Dave Twardzik	G	6'1	180	28	64	1570	203	381	53	261	299	87	119	176	185	5	84	4	667	25	1.9	2.8	2.9	10.4
Larry Steele	F-G	6'5	180	29	72	1488	203	483	42	112	136	82	171	142	208	4	74	10	518	21	2.4	2.0	2.9	7.2
Clemon Johnson	C	6'10	240	22	74	794	102	217	47	36	74	49	226	78	121	1	23	36	240	11	3.1	1.1	1.6	3.2
Jim McMillan (from NY)	F	6'5	220	30	23	278	33	74	45	17	21	81	39	33	18	0	10	3	83	12	1.7	1.4	0.8	3.6
Kim Anderson	F	6'7	200	23	21	224	24	77	31	15	28	54	45	15	42	0	4	5	63	11	2.1	0.7	2.0	3.0
Ira Terrell (from NO)	F	6'8	205	24	18	160	30	54	56	8	15	53	37	15	27	0	7	6	68	9	2.1	0.8	1.5	3.8
Willie Smith (LJ)	G	6'2	170	25	13	131	23	44	52	12	17	71	13	17	19	0	10	1	58	10	1.0	1.3	1.5	4.5
Lloyd Neal (KJ)	F	6'7	225	28	4	48	4	11	36	1	1	100	9	1	7	0	0	1	9	12	2.3	0.3	1.8	2.3
Bill Walton (foot injury)																								

1978/79 N.B.A. — WESTERN CONFERENCE (continued)
PACIFIC DIVISION

SAN DIEGO CLIPPERS 43-39 .524 **GENE SHUE**

Use Name	Pos	Hgt	Wgt	Age	G	Min	FG	FGA	%	FT	FTA	%	Reb	Ass	PF	DQ	Stls	Blkd Shts	Points	Min	Reb	Ass	PF	Points
					TOTAL															PER GAME				
Nick Weatherspoon	F	6'7	197	28	82	2642	479	998	48	176	238	74	454	135	287	6	80	37	1134	32	5.5	1.6	3.5	13.8
Kermit Washington	F	6'8	230	27	82	2764	350	623	56	227	330	69	800	125	317	11	85	121	927	34	9.8	1.5	3.9	11.3
Swen Nater	C	6'11	240	28	79	2006	357	627	57	132	165	80	701	140	244	6	38	29	846	25	8.9	1.8	3.1	10.7
Randy Smith	G	6'3	180	30	82	3111	693	1523	46	292	359	81	295	395	177	1	177	5	1678	38	3.6	4.8	2.2	20.5
Lloyd Free	G	6'2	185	25	78	2954	795	1653	48	**654**	**865**	76	301	340	253	8	111	35	2244	38	3.9	4.4	3.2	28.8
Sidney Wicks	F	6'9	225	29	79	2022	312	676	46	147	226	65	405	126	274	4	70	36	771	26	5.1	1.6	3.5	9.8
Kevin Kunnert	C	7'	231	27	81	1684	234	501	47	56	85	66	569	113	309	7	45	118	524	21	7.0	1.4	3.8	6.5
Freeman Williams	G	6'4	195	22	72	1195	335	683	49	76	98	78	98	83	88	0	42	2	746	17	1.4	1.2	1.2	10.4
Bob Bigelow(VR)	F-G	6'7	215	25	29	413	36	90	40	13	21	62	46	25	37	0	12	2	85	14	1.6	0.9	1.3	2.9
Coniel Norman	G	6'3	176	25	22	323	71	165	43	19	23	83	32	24	35	0	10	3	161	15	1.5	1.1	1.6	7.3
Brian Taylor (HO)	G	6'2	185	27	20	212	30	83	36	16	18	89	26	20	34	0	24	0	76	11	1.3	1.0	1.7	3.8
John Olive	F	6'7	210	23	34	189	13	40	33	18	23	78	19	3	32	0	4	0	44	6	0.6	0.1	0.9	1.3
Jerome Whitehead (NJ)	C	6'10	220	22	31	152	15	34	44	8	18	44	50	7	29	0	3	4	38	5	1.6	0.2	0.9	1.2
Stan Pietkiewicz	G	6'5	200	22	4	32	1	8	13	2	2	100	6	3	5	0	1	0	4	8	1.5	0.8	1.3	1.0
Scott Lloyd (to Chi)	C	6'10	230	26	5	31	0	2	0	0	0	—	3	0	6	0	1	0	0	6	0.6	0.0	1.2	0.0

GOLDEN STATE WARRIORS 38-44 .463 **AL ATTLES**

Use Name	Pos	Hgt	Wgt	Age	G	Min	FG	FGA	%	FT	FTA	%	Reb	Ass	PF	DQ	Stls	Blkd Shts	Points	Min	Reb	Ass	PF	Points
Sonny Parker	F-G	6'6	200	23	79	2893	512	1019	50	175	222	79	444	291	187	0	144	38	1199	37	5.6	3.7	2.4	15.2
Purvis Short	F	6'7	210	21	75	1703	369	771	48	57	85	67	347	97	233	6	54	12	795	23	4.6	1.3	3.1	10.6
Robert Parish	C	7'	230	25	76	2411	554	1110	50	196	281	70	916	115	303	10	100	217	1304	32	12.1	1.5	4.0	17.2
Phil Smith(LJ)	G	6'4	187	26	59	2228	489	977	50	194	255	76	212	261	159	3	101	23	1172	38	3.6	4.4	2.7	19.9
John Lucas	G	6'3	175	25	82	3095	530	1146	46	264	321	82	247	762	229	1	152	9	1324	38	3.0	9.3	2.8	16.1
Clifford Ray	C-F	6'9	235	29	82	1917	231	439	53	106	190	56	608	136	264	4	47	50	568	23	7.4	1.7	3.2	6.9
Nate Williams	F-G	6'5	215	28	81	1299	284	567	50	102	117	87	207	61	169	0	55	5	670	16	2.6	0.8	2.1	8.3
Tom Abernathy	F	6'7	220	24	70	1219	176	342	51	70	94	74	216	79	133	1	39	13	422	17	3.1	1.1	1.9	6.0
Jo Jo White (from Bos)	G	6'3	190	32	29	883	149	314	47	60	69	87	72	133	73	0	26	3	358	30	2.5	4.6	2.5	12.3
Wayne Cooper	F	6'10	220	22	65	795	128	293	44	41	61	67	280	21	118	0	7	44	297	12	4.3	0.3	1.8	4.6
Ray Townsend (NJ)	G	6'3	175	23	65	771	127	289	44	50	68	74	55	91	70	0	27	6	304	12	0.8	1.4	1.1	4.7
Wesley Cox	F	6'6	215	23	31	360	53	123	43	40	92	43	63	11	68	0	13	5	146	12	2.0	0.4	2.2	4.7
Tony Robertson	G	6'4	195	22	12	74	15	40	38	6	9	67	10	4	10	0	8	0	36	6	0.8	0.3	0.8	3.0
Ray Epps	F	6'6	195	21	13	72	10	23	43	6	8	75	5	2	7	0	1	0	26	6	0.4	0.2	0.5	2.0

PLAYOFFS

SEATTLE SUPERSONICS **LENNY WILKENS**

defeated Los Angeles 4-1; H112-101, H108-103(OT), 112-118(OT), 117-115, H106-100
defeated Phoenix 4-3; H108-93, H103-97, 103-113, 91-100, H93-99, 106-105, H114-110
defeated Washington 4-1; 97-99,92-82, H105-95,, H114-112(OT), 97-93

Use Name	Pos	Hgt	Wgt	Age	G	Min	FG	FGA	%	FT	FTA	%	Reb	Ass	PF	DQ	Stls	Blkd Shts	Points	Min	Reb	Ass	PF	Points
John Johnson	F	6'7	200	31	17	615	83	175	47	41	64	64	115	91	49	0	17	3	207	36	6.8	5.4	2.9	12.2
Lonnie Shelton	F-C	6'8	245	23	17	566	101	209	48	18	26	69	142	34	**80**	**4**	19	18	220	33	8.4	2.0	4.7	12.9
Jack Sikma	C	6'11	230	23	17	655	103	224	46	46	61	75	199	43	70	2	16	24	254	39	11.7	2.5	4.1	14.9
Dennis Johnson	G	6'4	185	24	17	691	136	302	45	84	109	77	104	69	63	0	28	26	356	41	6.1	4.1	3.7	20.9
Gus Williams	G	6'2	175	25	17	609	**181**	382	47	90	127	71	70	63	42	1	**34**	11	**452**	36	4.1	3.7	2.5	26.6
Paul Silas	F	6'7	220	35	17	418	21	54	39	31	46	67	98	19	44	1	9	5	73	25	5.8	1.1	2.6	4.3
Fred Brown	G	6'3	185	30	17	260	64	142	45	14	17	82	22	35	23	0	9	4	142	15	1.3	2.1	1.4	8.4
Dennis Awtrey	C	6'10	240	30	16	153	10	16	63	8	13	62	42	11	34	0	5	4	28	10	2.6	0.7	2.1	1.8
Dick Snyder	G	6'5	207	34	9	88	10	31	32	6	9	67	11	10	8	0	4	3	26	10	1.2	1.1	0.9	2.9
Wally Walker	F	6'7	190	24	13	85	6	16	38	2	4	50	17	2	19	0	0	6	14	7	1.3	0.2	1.5	1.1
Joey Hassett	G	6'5	180	23	8	15	3	7	43	0	0	—	1	1	0	0	0	0	6	2	0.1	0.1	0.0	0.8
Tom LaGarde (knee injury)																								

WASHINGTON BULLETS **DICK MOTTA**

defeated Atlanta4-3; H103-89, H99-107, 89-77, 120-118(OT), H103-107, 86-104, H100-94
defeated San Antonio 4-3; H97-118, H115-95, 114-116, 102-118, H107-103, 108-100, H107-105
lost to Seattle 1-4; H99-97, H82-92, 105-95, 112-114(OT), H93-97

Use Name	Pos	Hgt	Wgt	Age	G	Min	FG	FGA	%	FT	FTA	%	Reb	Ass	PF	DQ	Stls	Blkd Shts	Points	Min	Reb	Ass	PF	Points
Bob Dandridge	F-G	6'6	195	31	19	**787**	174	368	47	**91**	110	83	140	105	71	3	14	15	439	41	7.4	5.5	3.7	23.1
Elvin Hayes	F-C	6'9	235	33	19	786	170	**396**	43	87	**130**	67	**266**	38	79	3	17	**52**	427	41	**14.0**	2.0	4.2	22.5
Wes Unseld	C	6'7	245	32	19	736	78	158	49	39	64	61	253	64	66	2	17	14	195	39	13.3	3.4	3.5	10.3
Kevin Grevey	G	6'5	210	25	19	527	102	256	40	40	53	75	48	30	62	1	15	7	244	28	2.5	1.6	3.3	12.8
Tom Henderson	G	6'3	190	26	19	559	64	175	37	38	52	73	35	**107**	45	1	17	6	166	29	1.8	5.6	2.4	8.7
Larry Wright	G	6'1	160	24	18	331	62	129	48	27	30	90	25	44	49	0	10	4	151	18	1.4	2.4	2.7	8.4
Greg Ballard	F	6'7	215	23	19	312	53	101	52	31	41	76	92	17	28	0	9	6	137	16	4.8	0.9	1.5	7.2
Charles Johnson	G	6'	190	29	18	275	40	119	34	7	13	54	34	21	37	0	3	3	87	15	1.9	1.2	2.1	4.8
Mitch Kupchak	F-C	6'9	230	24	8	137	21	52	40	10	15	67	34	3	12	0	2	0	52	17	4.3	0.4	1.5	6.5
Phil Chenier	G	6'3	180	28	9	97	10	46	22	5	11	45	8	9	16	0	3	0	25	11	0.9	1.0	1.8	2.8
Dave Corzine	C	6'11	250	22	12	63	4	15	27	0	0	—	25	5	9	0	2	0	8	5	2.1	0.4	0.8	0.7
Roger Phegley (gastroenteritis)																								

1978/79 N.B.A. — PLAYOFFS (continued)

OENIX SUNS — **JOHN MacLEOD**

defeated Portland 2-1; H107-103, 92-96, H101-91
defeated Kansas City 4-1; H102-99, 91-111, H108-93, 108-94, H120-99
lost to Seattle 3-4; 93-108, 97-103, H113-103, H100-91,99-93, H105-106, 110-114

e Name	Pos	Hgt	Wgt	Age	G	Min	FG	FGA	%	FT	FTA	%	Reb	Ass	PF	DQ	Stls	Blkd Shts	Points	Min	Reb	Ass	PF	Points
alter Davis	F	6'6	198	24	15	490	127	244	52	78	96	81	69	79	41	0	26	5	332	33	4.6	5.3	2.7	22.1
uck Robinson	F	6'7	245	27	15	392	56	139	40	45	69	65	121	10	52	0	6	12	157	26	8.1	0.7	3.5	10.5
van Adams	C	6'9	220	24	12	372	66	139	47	22	31	71	90	53	41	1	11	12	154	31	7.5	4.4	3.4	12.8
ul Westphal	G	6'4	195	28	15	534	142	287	49	52	66	79	33	64	38	0	15	5	336	36	2.2	4.3	2.5	22.4
n Buse	G	6'4	195	28	15	512	47	116	41	24	33	73	55	52	31	0	23	5	118	34	3.7	3.5	2.1	7.9
ar Heard	F	6'6	219	30	15	320	32	86	37	18	30	60	106	13	39	0	12	26	82	21	7.1	0.9	2.6	5.5
ke Bratz	G	6'2	185	23	15	293	57	115	50	45	59	76	21	30	42	0	15	3	159	20	1.4	2.0	2.8	10.6
el Kramer	C-F	6'7	203	23	15	257	32	59	54	26	36	72	57	19	44	2	9	7	90	17	3.8	1.3	2.9	6.0
vin Scott	F	6'7	185	23	15	217	20	52	38	13	21	62	42	22	20	0	6	16	53	14	2.8	1.5	1.3	3.5
yard Forrest	C	6'10	235	24	14	110	10	18	56	2	10	20	29	11	21	0	0	2	22	8	2.1	0.8	1.5	1.6
d McClain	G	6'2	190	31	14	103	15	34	44	13	16	81	16	13	20	0	6	0	43	7	1.1	0.9	1.4	3.1

AN ANTONIO SPURS — **DOUG MOE**

defeated Philadelphia 4-3; H119-106, H121-120, 115-123, 115-112, H97-120, 90-92, H111-108
lost to Washington 3-4; 118-97, 95-115, H116-114, H118-102, 103-107, H100-108, 105-107

e Name	Pos	Hgt	Wgt	Age	G	Min	FG	FGA	%	FT	FTA	%	Reb	Ass	PF	DQ	Stls	Blkd Shts	Points	Min	Reb	Ass	PF	Points
ark Olberding	F	6'8	230	22	14	359	41	103	40	29	37	78	69	33	53	2	12	5	111	26	4.9	2.4	3.8	7.9
rry Kenon	F	6'9	215	26	14	557	128	292	44	39	53	74	160	42	42	0	20	1	295	40	11.4	3.0	3.0	21.1
ke Green	C	6'10	200	27	14	350	48	114	42	14	21	67	73	11	59	3	13	35	110	25	5.2	0.8	4.2	7.9
eorge Gervin	G	6'7	185	26	14	513	158	295	54	84	104	81	82	35	51	1	27	15	400	37	5.9	2.5	3.6	28.6
mes Silas	G	6'3	180	29	14	475	102	215	47	63	80	79	42	66	39	0	21	1	267	34	3.0	4.7	2.8	19.1
ke Gale	G	6'4	190	28	14	302	38	87	44	19	22	86	29	56	33	0	16	4	95	22	2.1	4.0	2.4	6.8
lly Paultz	C	6'11	250	30	13	299	30	80	38	22	33	67	98	30	33	0	4	13	82	23	7.5	2.3	2.5	6.3
oby Dietrick	F-C	6'10	225	30	14	281	39	88	44	4	8	50	65	26	41	0	12	3	82	20	4.6	1.9	2.9	5.9
lan Bristow	F	6'7	210	27	13	163	20	49	41	16	21	76	27	28	17	0	9	5	56	13	2.1	2.2	1.3	4.3
uie Dampier	G	6'	180	34	7	55	8	14	57	4	7	57	5	8	8	0	3	1	20	8	0.7	1.1	1.1	2.9
enn Mosley	F	6'8	195	23	3	6	2	3	67	1	3	33	1	1	0	0	0	1	5	2	0.3	0.3	0.0	1.7

HILADELPHIA 76ers — **BILLY CUNNINGHAM**

defeated New Jersey 2-0; H122-114,111-101
lost to San Antonio 3-4; 106-119, 120-121, H123-115, H112-115, 120-97, H92-90, 108-111

e Name	Pos	Hgt	Wgt	Age	G	Min	FG	FGA	%	FT	FTA	%	Reb	Ass	PF	DQ	Stls	Blkd Shts	Points	Min	Reb	Ass	PF	Points
lius Erving	F-G	6'7	220	28	9	372	89	172	52	51	67	76	70	53	22	0	18	17	229	41	7.8	5.9	2.4	25.4
obby Jones	F	6'9	212	27	9	260	48	87	55	22	26	85	43	19	30	0	5	4	118	29	4.8	2.1	3.3	13.1
arryl Dawkins	C	6'11	251	21	9	255	56	106	53	32	47	68	82	12	42	1	2	16	144	28	9.1	1.3	4.7	16.0
aurice Cheeks	G	6'1	180	22	9	330	66	121	55	37	56	66	35	63	29	0	37	4	169	37	3.9	7.0	3.2	18.8
enry Bibby	G	6'1	185	29	9	231	26	67	39	20	30	67	19	42	26	0	4	0	72	26	2.1	4.7	2.9	8.0
aldwell Jones	C-F	6'11	225	28	9	320	43	89	48	28	36	78	121	21	36	0	4	22	114	36	13.4	2.3	4.0	12.7
eve Mix	F	6'7	222	31	9	179	31	59	53	13	15	87	35	16	20	0	6	0	75	20	3.9	1.8	2.2	8.3
ic Money	G	6'	170	23	8	129	26	61	43	2	4	50	11	22	17	0	3	0	54	16	1.4	2.8	2.1	6.8
Skinner	G	6'4	195	26	5	47	6	17	35	6	8	75	10	11	6	0	3	1	18	9	2.0	2.2	1.2	3.6
e Bryant	F-G	6'9	185	24	7	35	10	26	38	1	2	50	1	4	8	0	1	0	21	5	0.1	0.6	1.1	3.0
arlon Redmond	G	6'6	188	23	1	2	0	2	0	0	0	—	0	0	0	0	0	0	0	2	0.0	0.0	0.0	0.0
Doug Collins (broken foot)																								

TLANTA HAWKS — **HUBIE BROWN**

defeated Houston 2-0; 109-106, H100-91
lost to Washington 3-4; 89-103, 107-99, H77-89, H118-120(OT), 107-103, H104-86, 94-100

e Name	Pos	Hgt	Wgt	Age	G	Min	FG	FGA	%	FT	FTA	%	Reb	Ass	PF	DQ	Stls	Blkd Shts	Points	Min	Reb	Ass	PF	Points
hn Drew	F	6'6	205	24	9	275	55	131	42	35	46	76	60	7	36	1	9	4	145	31	6.7	0.8	4.0	16.1
an Roundfield	F	6'8	205	25	9	338	61	133	46	36	45	80	106	25	44	3	8	23	158	38	11.8	2.8	4.9	17.6
ee Rollins	C	7'1	235	23	9	212	21	51	41	9	13	69	71	5	29	1	3	24	51	24	7.9	0.6	3.2	5.7
rmond Hill	G	6'4	190	25	9	267	29	71	41	8	12	67	17	50	33	1	12	1	66	30	1.9	5.6	3.7	7.3
ddie Johnson	G	6'2	175	23	9	262	65	128	51	18	25	72	23	45	22	0	4	2	148	29	2.6	5.0	2.4	16.4
erry Furlow	G	6'4	190	24	9	244	55	113	49	26	28	93	32	29	15	0	7	2	136	27	3.6	3.2	1.7	15.1
teve Hawes	C-F	6'9	220	28	9	243	40	81	49	9	12	75	63	29	33	2	8	3	89	27	7.0	3.2	3.7	9.9
om McMillen	F-C	6'11	215	26	9	163	20	46	43	16	19	84	34	7	21	1	2	1	56	18	3.8	0.8	2.3	6.2
harlie Criss	G	5'8	165	29	9	99	12	29	41	9	10	90	5	16	5	0	3	0	33	11	0.6	1.8	0.6	3.7
ack Givens	F	6'5	205	22	9	81	10	30	33	3	3	100	21	3	9	0	1	2	23	9	2.3	0.3	1.0	2.6
ick Wilson	G	6'5	200	22	1	1	0	0	—	0	0	—	0	0	0	0	0	0	0	1	0.0	0.0	0.0	0.0

OS ANGELES LAKERS — **JERRY WEST**

defeated Denver 2-1; 105-110, H121-109, 112-111
lost to Seattle 1-4; 101-112, 103-108(OT), H118-112(OT), H115-117, 100-106

e Name	Pos	Hgt	Wgt	Age	G	Min	FG	FGA	%	FT	FTA	%	Reb	Ass	PF	DQ	Stls	Blkd Shts	Points	Min	Reb	Ass	PF	Points
drian Dantley	F	6'5	210	22	8	236	50	89	56	41	52	79	33	11	24	0	6	1	141	30	4.1	1.4	3.0	17.6
amaal Wilkes	F	6'6	190	25	8	307	61	128	48	25	37	68	68	16	21	0	15	2	147	38	8.5	2.0	2.6	18.4
areem Abdul-Jabbar	C	7'2	232	31	8	367	88	152	58	52	62	84	101	38	26	0	8	33	228	46	12.6	4.8	3.3	28.5
on Boone	G	6'2	200	32	8	226	37	77	48	20	21	95	15	14	28	0	9	0	94	28	1.9	1.8	3.5	11.8
orm Nixon	G	6'2	175	23	8	327	56	119	47	11	15	73	28	94	37	1	11	0	123	41	3.5	11.8	4.6	15.4
an Ford	F	6'9	215	26	8	138	16	30	53	1	3	33	22	7	20	0	3	2	33	17	2.8	0.9	2.5	4.1
im Price	G	6'3	195	29	8	128	9	30	30	2	4	50	8	18	19	0	5	0	20	16	1.0	2.3	2.4	2.5
en Carr	F	6'7	230	23	8	117	19	35	54	5	8	63	17	4	18	0	4	2	43	15	2.1	0.5	2.3	5.4
ou Hudson	G	6'5	210	34	6	90	17	32	53	4	4	100	4	8	6	0	1	0	38	15	0.7	1.3	1.0	6.3
ave Robisch	C-F	6'10	240	29	5	32	3	5	60	2	2	100	10	2	4	0	0	0	8	6	2.0	0.4	0.8	1.6
on Carter	G	6'5	190	22	2	2	0	1	0	0	0	—	0	0	0	0	0	0	0	1	0.0	0.0	0.0	0.0

1978/79 N.B.A. — PLAYOFFS (continued)

Use Name	Pos	Hgt	Wgt	Age	G	Min	FG	FGA	%	FT	FTA	%	Reb	Ass	PF	DQ	Stls	Blkd Shts	Points	Min	Reb	Ass	PF	Points
					TOTAL															PER GAME				
KANSAS CITY KINGS — COTTON FITZSIMMONS — lost to Phoenix 1-4; 99-102, H111-91, 93-108, H94-108, 99-120																								
Scott Wedman	F	6'7	215	26	5	174	36	78	46	24	32	75	37	9	18	0	9	3	96	35	7.4	1.8	3.6	19.2
Bill Robinzine	F	6'7	230	25	5	118	22	51	43	6	8	75	36	3	20	1	13	0	50	24	7.2	0.6	4.0	10.0
Sam Lacey	C	6'10	235	30	5	176	16	42	38	15	19	79	51	21	20	2	9	10	47	35	10.2	4.2	4.0	9.4
Otis Birdsong	G	6'4	195	23	5	168	39	76	51	27	38	71	18	9	13	0	10	0	105	34	3.6	1.8	2.6	21.0
Phil Ford	G	6'2	176	22	5	143	15	57	26	9	16	56	12	29	14	0	12	0	39	29	2.4	5.8	2.8	7.8
Darnell Hillman	C-F	6'9	215	29	5	112	10	32	31	9	17	53	33	8	17	0	4	3	29	22	6.6	1.6	3.4	5.8
Billy McKinny	G	6'	162	23	5	96	15	40	38	6	7	86	7	24	5	0	5	0	36	19	1.4	4.8	1.0	7.2
Lucius Allen	G	6'2	175	31	5	73	15	32	47	6	6	100	7	3	7	0	2	1	36	15	1.4	0.6	1.4	7.2
Bob Nash	F	6'8	205	28	5	64	8	27	30	8	10	80	11	0	10	0	0	4	24	13	2.2	0.0	2.0	4.8
Richard Washington	F	6'11	225	23	4	52	11	20	55	2	2	100	13	0	17	1	1	1	24	13	3.3	0.0	4.3	6.0
Gus Gerard	F	6'8	205	25	5	24	4	9	44	2	4	50	8	0	6	0	1	1	10	5	1.6	0.0	1.2	2.0
Tom Burleson - knee injury																								
PORTLAND TRAIL BLAZERS — JACK RAMSEY — lost to Phoenix 1-2; 103-107, H96-92, 91-101																								
Larry Steele	F	6'5	180	29	3	73	16	28	57	8	9	89	11	7	8	0	10	0	40	24	3.7	2.3	2.7	13.3
Maurice Lucas	F	6'9	218	26	3	104	14	41	34	5	7	71	32	18	12	0	3	1	33	35	10.7	6.0	4.0	11.0
Tom Owens	C	6'10	220	29	3	80	15	31	48	5	8	63	19	5	16	1	4	1	35	27	6.3	1.7	5.3	11.7
Ron Brewer	G	6'4	180	23	3	94	22	39	56	9	13	69	11	8	7	0	1	9	53	31	3.7	2.7	2.3	17.7
Dave Twardzik	G	6'1	180	28	3	77	7	14	50	11	12	92	7	10	14	0	5	0	25	26	2.3	3.3	4.7	8.3
Mychal Thompson	F-C	6'10	226	23	3	121	27	54	50	5	10	50	31	6	11	0	2	5	59	40	10.3	2.0	3.7	19.7
Lionel Hollins	G	6'3	185	25	3	66	8	26	31	5	7	71	3	5	8	0	3	0	21	22	1.0	1.7	2.7	7.0
T.R. Dunn	G	6'4	192	23	3	52	5	11	45	0	0	—	6	4	7	0	5	0	10	17	2.0	1.3	2.3	3.3
Clemon Johnson	C	6'10	240	22	3	47	4	11	36	6	11	55	17	2	5	0	2	4	14	16	5.7	0.7	1.7	4.7
Ira Terrell	F	6'8	205	24	1	6	0	4	0	0	0	—	2	0	0	0	0	0	0	6	2.0	0.0	0.0	0.0
Bob Grass (knee injury), Willie Smith(leg injury), Bill Walton (foot injury)																								
DENVER NUGGETS — DONNIE WALSH — lost to Los Angeles 1-2; H110-105, 109-121, H111-112																								
Anthony Roberts	F	6'5	185	23	3	80	13	33	39	7	11	64	13	6	9	0	2	1	33	27	4.3	2.0	3.0	11.0
Tom Boswell	F	6'9	225	25	3	120	21	35	60	10	13	77	27	16	10	0	3	5	52	40	9.0	5.3	3.3	17.3
Dan Issel	C	6'9	240	30	3	109	24	45	53	25	31	81	28	10	15	0	0	0	73	36	9.3	3.3	5.0	24.3
David Thompson	G-F	6'4	195	24	3	122	38	69	55	8	11	73	21	12	12	0	4	1	84	41	7.0	4.0	4.0	28.0
Charlie Scott	G	6'6	175	30	3	104	20	42	48	8	14	57	14	10	11	0	2	2	48	35	4.7	3.3	3.7	16.0
Bobby Wilkerson	F-G	6'6	200	24	3	101	14	34	41	1	3	33	26	15	7	0	3	1	29	34	8.7	5.0	2.3	9.7
Kim Hughes	C	6'11	220	26	3	35	1	2	50	1	2	50	11	0	8	0	2	0	3	12	3.7	0.0	2.7	1.0
Robert Smith	G	5'11	165	23	3	25	0	7	0	2	2	100	2	4	2	0	2	0	2	8	0.7	1.3	0.7	0.7
Bo Ellis	F	6'9	200	24	3	24	2	6	33	2	2	100	4	1	2	0	2	1	6	8	1.3	0.3	0.7	2.0
George McGinnis - ankle injury																								
NEW JERSEY NETS — KEVIN LOUGHERY — lost to Philadelphia 0-2; 114-122, H101-111																								
Jan Van Breda Kolff	F-G	6'7	200	27	2	81	8	20	40	5	6	83	20	7	9	0	0	3	21	41	10.0	3.5	4.5	10.5
Bernard King	F	6'7	205	22	2	81	21	42	50	10	24	42	11	7	10	0	4	0	52	41	5.5	3.5	5.0	26.0
George Johnson	C	6'11	205	30	2	70	14	21	67	1	3	33	25	2	8	1	2	7	29	35	12.5	1.0	4.0	14.5
John Williamson	G	6'2	195	26	2	92	23	62	37	13	16	81	6	8	8	0	4	0	59	46	3.0	4.0	4.0	29.5
Eddie Jordan	G	6'1	170	23	2	83	15	38	39	8	9	89	15	17	6	0	8	3	38	42	7.5	8.5	3.0	19.0
Harvey Catchings	C	6'9	218	27	2	26	1	6	17	0	3	0	8	1	4	0	0	1	2	13	4.0	0.5	2.0	1.0
Phil Jackson	F	6'8	230	33	2	20	1	3	33	2	2	100	3	0	1	0	1	0	4	10	1.5	0.0	0.5	2.0
Tim Bassett	F	6'8	225	27	2	17	2	5	40	2	2	100	2	0	4	0	0	0	6	9	1.0	0.0	2.0	3.0
Ralph Simpson	G	6'5	200	29	2	10	2	5	40	0	0	—	2	2	0	0	0	0	4	5	1.0	1.0	0.0	2.0
HOUSTON ROCKETS — TOM NISSALKE — lost to Atlanta 0-2; H106-109, 91-100																								
Rick Barry	F	6'7	220	34	2	65	8	25	32	8	8	100	8	9	8	0	0	2	24	33	4.0	4.5	4.0	12.0
Rudy Tomjanovich	F	6'8	220	30	2	64	9	23	39	2	5	40	14	2	1	0	1	1	20	32	7.0	1.0	0.5	10.0
Moses Malone	C	6'10	215	23	2	78	18	41	44	13	18	72	41	2	5	0	1	8	49	39	20.5	1.0	2.5	24.5
Mike Newlin	G	6'4	200	29	2	67	8	20	40	8	8	100	6	5	10	1	1	1	24	34	3.0	2.5	5.0	12.0
Calvin Murphy	G	5'9	165	30	2	73	9	31	29	8	9	89	3	6	9	0	8	1	26	37	1.5	3.0	4.5	13.0
Robert Reid	F	6'8	205	23	2	45	7	17	41	6	9	67	9	2	7	0	1	2	20	23	4.5	1.0	3.5	10.0
Slick Watts	G	6'1	175	27	2	43	6	15	40	2	3	67	7	7	8	0	4	1	14	22	3.5	3.5	4.0	7.0
Dwight Jones	C-F	6'10	210	26	2	33	7	13	54	6	6	100	12	3	3	0	1	4	20	17	6.0	1.5	1.5	10.0
Mike Dunleavy	G	6'3	180	24	1	10	2	2	100	0	0	—	1	0	1	0	0	0	0	10	1.0	0.0	1.0	0.0
Alonzo Bradley	F	6'6	190	24	1	1	0	0	—	0	0	—	0	0	0	0	0	0	0	1	0.0	0.0	0.0	0.0
Jacky Dorsey	F	6'7	230	24	1	1	0	0	—	0	0	—	0	0	0	0	0	0	0	1	0.0	0.0	0.0	0.0

eam		G	FG	FGA	%	FT	FTA	%	REBOUNDS Offense	Defense	Total	Assists	PF	Steals	Blocked Shots	Turn Overs	Points	Points per game
TEAM STATISTICS EASTERN CONFERENCE ATLANTIC DIVISION																		
ashington	Off.	82	3819	7873	49	1785	2428	74	1309	**2768**	**4077**	2169	**1804**	614	401	1420	9423	114.9
	Def.	82	3804	8011	47	1406	1897	74	1178	2541	3719	2180	2144	726	434	1338	9014	109.9
	Diff.		+15	-138	+2	**+379**	+531	—	+131	+227	**+358**	-11	**+340**	-112	-33	-82	+409	+5.0
hiladelphia	Off.	82	3584	7338	49	1815	2411	75	1149	2712	3861	2253	2072	779	599	1771	8963	109.3
	Def.	82	3542	7626	46	1747	2331	75	1252	2506	3758	2094	2128	795	353	1637	8831	107.7
	Diff.		+42	-288	+3	+68	+70	—	-103	**+206**	+103	+159	+56	-16	**+246**	-134	+132	+1.6
ew Jersey	Off.	82	3464	7523	46	1904	2613	73	1241	2370	3611	1907	2329	853	**619**	1861	8832	107.7
	Def.	82	3507	7306	48	2160	2861	75	1234	2667	3901	2185	2208	861	492	**1919**	9174	111.9
	Diff.		-43	+217	-2	-256	-248	-2	+7	-297	-290	-278	-121	-8	+127	+58	-342	-4.2
ew York	Off.	82	3676	7554	49	1478	2111	70	1200	2430	3630	2121	2154	699	397	1605	8830	107.7
	Def.	82	3600	7457	48	1907	2506	76	1225	2489	3714	2114	1961	751	378	1558	9107	111.1
	Diff.		+76	+97	+1	-429	-395	-6	-25	-59	-84	+7	-193	-52	+19	-47	-277	-3.4
oston	Off.	82	3527	7347	48	1820	2321	78	1119	2396	3515	1995	1977	710	283	1713	8874	108.2
	Def.	82	3855	7593	51	1578	2079	76	1122	2453	3575	2170	2025	717	438	1603	9288	113.3
	Diff.		-328	-246	-3	+242	+242	+2	-3	-57	-60	-175	+48	-7	-155	-110	-414	-5.1
CENTRAL DIVISION																		
an Antonio	Off.	82	**3927**	7760	51	1926	2423	**79**	1096	2619	3715	2313	2071	829	509	1652	**9780**	**119.3**
	Def.	82	3798	7970	48	1759	2343	75	1297	2531	3828	2332	2168	788	405	1700	9355	114.1
	Diff.		+129	-210	+3	+167	+80	+4	-201	+88	-113	-19	+97	+41	+104	+48	**+425**	**+5.2**
ouston	Off.	82	3726	7498	50	1845	2330	79	1256	2504	3760	2302	2001	632	286	1510	9297	113.4
	Def.	82	3795	7625	50	1627	2211	74	1186	2315	3501	2278	2055	660	431	1400	9217	112.4
	Diff.		-69	-127	—	+218	+119	**+5**	+70	+189	+259	+24	+54	-28	-145	-110	+80	+1.0
tlanta	Off.	82	3505	7410	47	1940	2534	77	1381	2341	3722	1938	2424	801	596	1523	8950	109.1
	Def.	82	3367	6886	49	2045	2727	75	1176	2440	3616	1928	2135	646	559	1799	8779	107.1
	Diff.		+138	+524	-2	-105	-193	+2	**+205**	-99	+106	+10	-289	+155	+37	**+276**	+171	+2.0
leveland	Off.	82	3556	7602	47	1620	2103	77	1229	2256	3485	1796	2027	688	334	**1376**	8732	106.5
	Def.	82	3600	7150	50	1837	2423	76	1123	2587	3710	2062	2001	658	503	1557	9037	110.2
	Diff.		-44	+452	-3	-217	-320	+1	+106	-331	-225	-266	-26	+30	-169	+181	-305	-3.7
Detroit	Off.	82	3708	7802	48	1607	2242	72	1303	2380	3683	2092	2141	847	550	1599	9023	110.0
	Def.	82	3755	7623	49	1732	2295	75	1301	2628	3929	2197	1914	666	504	1744	9242	112.7
	Diff.		-47	+179	-1	-125	-53	-3	+2	-248	-246	-105	-227	**+181**	+46	+145	-219	-2.7
New Orleans	Off.	82	3517	7511	47	1868	2409	78	1234	2676	3910	2079	1940	760	559	1764	8882	108.3
	Def.	82	3864	8039	48	1666	2246	74	1486	2664	4150	2264	2061	955	566	1600	9394	114.6
	Diff.		-347	-528	-1	+202	+163	+4	-252	+12	-240	-185	+121	-195	-7	-164	-512	-6.3
WESTERN CONFERNECE MIDWEST DIVISION																		
Kansas City	Off.	82	3764	7644	49	1746	2392	73	1191	2404	3595	2239	2419	825	390	1631	9274	113.1
	Def.	82	3434	7061	49	2170	2897	75	1156	2547	3703	1776	2223	678	435	1879	9038	+110.2
	Diff.		**+330**	**+583**	—	-424	-505	-2	+35	-143	-108	**+463**	-196	+147	-45	+248	+236	+2.9
Denver	Off.	82	3517	7311	48	**2046**	**2841**	72	1307	2596	3903	2166	2106	673	416	1666	9080	110.7
	Def.	82	3631	7616	48	1713	2277	75	1218	2429	3647	2173	**2262**	738	471	1529	8975	109.5
	Diff.		-114	-305	—	+333	+564	-3	+89	+167	+256	-7	+156	-65	-55	-137	+105	+1.2
ndiana	Off.	82	3575	7525	48	1759	2317	76	1225	2530	3755	2005	2093	687	416	1536	8909	108.6
	Def.	82	3586	7499	48	1868	2416	77	1299	2605	3904	2078	2091	677	437	1618	9040	110.2
	Diff.		-11	+26	—	-109	-99	-1	-74	-75	-149	-73	-2	+10	-21	+82	-131	-1.6
Milwaukee	Off.	82	3906	7773	50	1541	2021	76	1157	2370	3527	**2562**	2106	862	435	1574	9353	114.1
	Def.	82	3676	7505	49	1819	2415	75	1229	2437	3666	2301	1928	763	462	1748	9171	111.8
	Diff.		+230	+268	+1	-278	-394	+1	-72	-67	-139	+261	-178	+99	-27	+174	+182	+2.3
Chicago	Off.	82	3478	7108	49	1632	2184	75	1224	2544	3768	2169	1970	576	324	1813	8588	104.7
	Def.	82	3682	7408	50	1549	2029	76	1095	2377	3472	2146	2093	844	503	1468	8913	108.7
	Diff.		-204	-300	-1	+83	+155	-1	+129	+167	+296	+23	+123	-268	-179	-345	-325	-4.0
PACIFIC DIVISION																		
Seattle	Off.	82	3504	7484	47	1732	2298	75	1310	2591	3901	1973	1914	690	398	1586	8740	106.6
	Def.	82	3475	7509	46	1567	2108	74	1156	2453	3609	1910	2057	755	407	1493	8517	**103.9**
	Diff.		+29	-25	+1	+165	+190	+1	+154	+138	+292	+63	+143	-65	-9	-93	+223	+2.7
Phoenix	Off.	82	3847	7516	51	1765	2299	77	1083	2379	3462	2500	1944	**915**	337	1760	9459	115.4
	Def.	82	3775	7626	50	1606	2127	76	1238	2424	3662	2091	2144	890	402	1841	9156	111.7
	Diff.		+72	-110	+1	+159	+172	+1	-155	-45	-200	+409	+200	+25	-65	+81	+303	+3.7

Team		G	FG	FGA	%	FT	FTA	%	REBOUNDS Offense	Defense	Total	Assists	PF	Steals	Blocked Shots	Turn Overs	Points	Points per gam
TEAM STATISTICS WESTERN CONFERENCE (continued) PACIFIC DIVISION																		
Los Angeles	**Off.**	82	3827	7397	**52**	1606	2088	77	949	2557	3506	2338	1851	793	500	1569	9260	112
	Def.	82	3797	7848	48	1415	1891	75	1288	2486	3774	2334	1958	737	359	1542	9009	109
	Diff.		+30	-451	**+4**	+191	**+197**	+2	-339	+71	-268	+4	+107	+56	+141	-27	+251	+3
Portland	**Off.**	82	3541	7338	48	1806	2362	76	1256	2435	3691	1946	2187	776	512	1658	8888	108
	Def.	82	3448	7059	49	1889	2501	76	1080	2350	3430	1963	2206	797	422	1650	8785	107.
	Diff.		+93	+279	-1	-83	-139	—	+176	+85	+261	-17	+19	-21	+90	-8	+103	+1.
San Diego	**Off.**	82	3721	7706	48	1836	2471	74	**1392**	2413	3805	1539	2127	703	392	1623	9278	113.
	Def.	82	3832	7801	49	1760	2295	77	1294	2322	3616	1896	2064	747	350	1517	9424	114.
	Diff.		-111	-95	-1	+76	+176	-3	+98	+91	+189	-357	-63	-44	+42	-106	-146	-1.
Golden State	**Off.**	82	3627	7453	49	1367	1872	73	1169	2513	3682	2064	2023	774	420	1500	8621	105.
	Def.	82	3493	7255	48	1604	2155	74	1147	2533	3680	2094	1854	637	362	1580	8590	104
	Diff.		+134	+198	+1	-237	-283	-1	+22	-20	+2	-30	-169	+137	+58	+80	+31	+.
PLAYOFFS																		
Seattle	**Off.**	17	718	1558	46	342	476	72	292	529	821	378	432	**141**	98	306	1778	104.
	Def.	17	696	1530	45	343	479	72	220	471	691	393	**450**	129	97	279	1735	102.
	Diff.		+22	+28	+1	-1	-3	—	**+72**	**+58**	**+130**	-15	+18	+12	+1	-27	**+43**	+2.
Washington	**Off.**	19	**778**	**1815**	43	**375**	**519**	72	**360**	**600**	**960**	**443**	474	109	**107**	301	**1931**	101.
	Def.	19	800	1770	45	356	476	75	294	599	893	439	487	144	135	269	1956	102.
	Diff.		-22	+45	-2	**+19**	**+43**	-3	+66	+1	+67	+4	+13	-35	-28	-32	-25	-1.
Phoenix	**Off.**	15	604	1289	47	338	467	72	194	445	639	366	389	133	93	297	1546	103.
	Def.	15	592	1356	44	320	441	73	266	451	717	308	420	161	85	**306**	1504	100.
	Diff.		+12	-67	+3	+18	+26	-1	-72	-6	-78	**+58**	**+31**	-28	+8	+9	+42	+2.
San Antonio	**Off.**	14	614	1340	46	295	389	76	222	429	651	366	376	137	84	221	1523	108.
	Def.	14	621	1325	47	289	417	**69**	242	459	701	393	354	96	85	254	1531	109.
	Diff.		-7	+15	-1	+6	-28	**+7**	-20	-30	-50	-27	-22	**+41**	-1	**+33**	-8	-.
Philadelphia	**Off.**	9	401	807	50	212	291	73	143	284	427	263	236	83	64	183	1014	**112.7**
	Def.	9	394	850	46	195	266	73	150	253	403	220	248	93	46	166	983	109.
	Diff.		+7	-43	**+4**	+17	+25	—	-7	+31	+24	+43	+12	-10	**+18**	-17	+31	**+3.**
Atlanta	**Off.**	9	368	813	45	169	213	**79**	154	278	432	216	247	57	62	130	905	100.6
	Def.	9	345	825	**42**	207	261	79	187	254	441	184	220	63	67	141	897	**99.7**
	Diff.		**+23**	-12	+3	-38	-48	—	-33	+24	-9	+32	-27	-6	-5	+11	+8	+.
Los Angeles	**Off.**	8	356	698	**51**	163	208	78	69	237	306	212	203	62	40	134	875	109.4
	Def.	8	360	751	48	165	226	73	140	254	394	197	203	63	28	135	885	110.6
	Diff.		-4	-53	+3	-2	-18	+5	-71	-17	-88	+15	—	-1	+12	+1	-10	-1.2
Kansas City	**Off.**	5	191	464	41	114	159	72	91	142	233	106	**147**	66	23	104	496	99.2
	Def.	5	**201**	**418**	48	**127**	**163**	78	**65**	**170**	**235**	**126**	128	**47**	**24**	128	**529**	105.8
	Diff.		-10	**+46**	-7	-13	-4	-6	+26	-28	-2	-20	-19	+19	-1	+24	-33	-6.6
Portland	**Off.**	3	118	259	46	54	77	70	42	97	139	65	88	35	20	56	290	96.7
	Def.	3	118	241	49	64	87	74	31	97	128	75	74	25	17	59	300	100.0
	Diff.		—	+18	-3	-10	-10	-4	+11	—	+11	-10	-14	+10	+3	+3	-10	-3.3
Denver	**Off.**	3	133	273	49	64	89	72	47	99	146	74	76	20	11	52	330	110.0
	Def.	3	138	267	52	62	80	78	29	95	124	87	76	23	18	45	338	112.7
	Diff.		-5	+6	-3	+2	+9	-6	+18	+4	+22	-13	—	-3	-7	-7	-8	-2.7
New Jersey	**Off.**	2	87	202	43	41	65	63	42	50	92	44	50	19	14	39	215	108
	Def.	2	92	190	48	49	64	77	43	70	113	62	52	21	16	46	233	116.5
	Diff.		-5	+12	-5	-8	+1	-14	-1	-20	-21	-18	+2	-2	-2	+7	-18	-9.0
Houston	**Off.**	2	72	187	39	53	66	80	51	50	101	36	52	17	20	37	197	98.5
	Def.	2	83	182	46	43	59	73	40	67	107	55	58	14	15	32	209	104.5
	Diff.		-11	+5	-7	+10	+7	+7	+11	-17	-6	-19	+6	+3	+5	-5	-12	-6.0

Team	W	L	Pct.	GB	Record against playoff teams W	L	Pct.	Record against non - playoff teams W	L	Pct.	HOME W	L	Pct.	ROAD W	L	Pct.
EASTERN CONFERENCE																
ATLANTIC DIVISION																
Washington Bullets	**54**	28	**.659**	—	22	21	.512	**32**	7	**.821**	31	10	.756	**23**	18	**.561**
Philadelphia 76ers	47	35	.573	7	25	17	.595	22	18	.550	31	10	.756	16	25	.390
New Jersey Nets	37	45	.451	17	14	29	.326	23	16	.590	25	16	.610	12	29	.293
New York Knickerbockers	31	51	.378	23	14	32	.304	17	19	.472	23	18	.561	8	33	.195
Boston Celtics	29	53	.354	25	12	**36**	.250	17	17	.500	21	20	.512	8	33	.195
CENTRAL DIVISION																
San Antonio Spurs	48	34	.585	—	18	25	.419	30	9	.769	29	12	.707	19	22	.463
Houston Rockets	47	35	.573	1	24	19	.558	23	16	.590	30	11	.732	17	24	.415
Atlanta Hawks	46	36	.561	2	23	20	.535	23	16	.590	**34**	7	**.829**	12	29	.293
Cleveland Cavaliers	30	52	.366	18	14	33	.298	16	19	.457	20	21	.488	10	31	.244
Detroit Pistons	30	52	.366	18	13	34	.277	17	18	.486	22	19	.537	8	33	.195
New Orleans Jazz	26	**56**	.317	22	13	34	.277	13	**22**	.371	22	19	.537	4	**37**	.098
WESTERN CONFERENCE																
MIDWEST DIVISION																
Kansas City Kings	48	34	.585	—	22	21	.512	26	13	.667	32	9	.780	16	25	.390
Denver Nuggets	47	35	.573	1	21	22	.488	26	13	.667	29	12	.707	18	23	.439
Indiana Pacers	38	44	.463	10	21	26	.447	17	18	.486	25	16	.610	13	28	.317
Milwaukee Bucks	38	44	.463	10	19	28	.404	19	16	.543	28	13	.683	10	31	.244
Chicago Bulls	31	51	.378	17	15	32	.319	16	19	.457	19	**22**	.463	12	29	.293
PACIFIC DIVISION																
Seattle Supersonics	52	30	.634	—	**27**	17	**.614**	25	13	.658	31	10	.756	21	20	.512
Phoenix Suns	50	32	.610	2	19	23	.452	31	9	.775	32	9	.780	18	23	.439
Los Angeles Lakers	47	35	.573	5	20	23	.465	27	12	.692	31	10	.756	16	25	.390
Portland Trail Blazers	45	37	.549	7	22	20	.524	23	17	.575	33	8	.805	12	29	.293
San Diego Clippers	43	39	.524	9	17	29	.370	26	10	.722	29	12	.707	14	27	.341
Golden State Warriors	38	44	.463	14	21	27	.438	17	17	.500	23	18	.561	15	26	.366

1978/79 N.B.A. INDIVIDUAL LEADERS

SCORING
(Minimum 70 Games or 1400 Points)

Name	Team	G	FG	FT	Pts.	Avg.
Gervin	SA	80	947	471	2365	29.6
Free	SD	78	795	654	2244	28.8
W. Johnson	Mil	77	820	332	1972	25.6
McAdoo	NY-Bos	60	596	295	1487	24.8
Malone	Hou	82	716	599	2031	24.8
Thompson	Den	76	693	439	1835	24.1
Westphal	Phoe	81	801	339	1941	24.0
Abdul-Jabbar	LA	80	777	349	1903	23.8
Gilmore	Chi	82	753	434	1940	23.7
Davis	Phoe	79	764	340	1868	23.6

FIELD GOAL PERCENTAGE
(Minimum 300 Made)

Name	Team	FG	FGA	Pct.
Maxwell	Bos	472	808	.584
Abdul-Jabbar	LA	777	1347	.577
Unseld	Was	346	600	.577
Gilmore	Chi	753	1310	.575
Nater	SD	357	627	.569
Washington	SD	350	623	.562
Davis	Phoe	764	1362	.561
M.Johnson	Mil	820	1491	.550
Robinzine	KC	459	837	.548
Owens	Port	600	1095	.548

FREE THROW PERCENTAGE
(Minimum 125 Made)

Name	Team	FT	FTA	Pct.
Barry	Hou	160	169	.947
Murphy	Hou	246	265	.928
Brown	Sea	183	206	.888
Smith	Den	159	180	.883
Sobers	Ind	298	338	.882
White	Bos-GS	139	158	.880
Twardzik	Port	261	299	.873
Newlin	Hou	212	243	.872
Dunleavy	Hou	159	184	.864
Winters	Mil	237	277	.856

PERSONAL FOULS

Name	Team	PF
Robinzine	KC	367
Edwards	Ind	363
Roundfield	Atl	358
Drew	Atl	332
Owens	Port	329

GAMES DISQUALIFIED

Name	Team	Disq.
Drew	Atl	19
Rollins	Atl	19
Cowens	Bos	16
Edwards	Ind	16
McGinnis	Den	16
Robinzine	KC	16
Roundfield	Atl	16

TOTAL REBOUNDS PER GAME
(Minimum 70 Games or 800 Rebounds)

Name	Team	G	Reb.	Avg.
Malone	Hou	82	1444	17.6
Kelly	NO	80	1026	12.8
Abdul-Jabbar	LA	80	1025	12.8
Gilmore	Chi	82	1043	12.7
Sikma	Sea	82	1013	12.4
Hayes	Was	82	994	12.1
Parish	GS	76	916	12.1
Robinson	Phoe	69	802	11.6
McGinnis	Den	76	864	11.4
Roundfield	Atl	80	865	10.8

ASSISTS PER GAME
(Minimum 70 Games or 400 Assists)

Name	Team	G	Ass.	Avg.
Porter	Det	82	1099	13.4
Lucas	GS	82	762	9.3
Nixon	LA	82	737	9.0
Ford	KC	79	681	8.6
Westphal	Phoe	81	529	6.5
Barry	Hou	80	502	6.3
Williams	NY	81	504	6.2
Henderson	Was	70	419	6.0
Hill	Atl	82	480	5.9
Buckner	Mil	81	468	5.8

MINUTES PLAYED

Name	Team	Min.
Malone	Hou	3390
Gilmore	Chi	3265
M.L. Carr	Det	3207
Abdul-Jabbar	LA	3157
Nixon	LA	3145

BLOCKED SHOTS PER GAME
(Minimum 70 Games or 100 Blocked Shots)

Name	Team	G	Reb.	Avg.
Abdul-Jabbar	LA	80	316	4.0
Johnson	NJ	78	253	3.2
Rollins	Atl	81	254	3.1
Parish	GS	76	217	2.9
Tyler	Det	82	201	2.5
Hayes	Was	82	190	2.3
Roundfield	Atl	80	176	2.2
Kelley	NO	80	166	2.1
C.Jones	Phi	78	157	2.0
Gilmore	Chi	82	156	1.9

STEALS PER GAME
(Minimum 70 Games or 125 Steals)

Name	Team	G	Steals	Avg.
Carr	Det	80	197	2.5
Jordan	NJ	82	201	2.5
Nixon	LA	82	201	2.5
Walker	Cle	55	130	2.4
Ford	KC	79	174	2.2
Smith	SD	82	177	2.2
Cheeks	Phi	82	174	2.1
Williams	Sea	76	158	2.1
Porter	Det	82	158	1.9
Buckner	Mil	81	156	1.9

1979-80 N.B.A.

A New Era Begins: Bird and Johnson

Plagued by declining TV ratings and a lack of charismatic teams, the N.B.A. got a tremendous boost from the return to power of the league's proudest franchises, Boston and Los Angeles, behind the two most heralded rookies since Bill Walton.

The Celtic's improvement was more dramatic, coming on the heels of consecutive 32- and 29- win seasons. The catalyst was Rookie of the Year Larry Bird, who amassed all-pro statistics and made his teammates better as well. Nate Archibald bounced back from three injury-plagued years, Dave Cowens and Cedric Maxwell continued their strong play, and the result was 61 wins and a Coach of the Year award for Bill Fitch, who came over from Cleveland. Despite Red Auerbach's opposition to the rule, Boston also benefited from the newly instituted 3-point shot, with Bird and Chris Ford among the top long-range marksmen.

The Lakers, under flamboyant new owner Jerry Buss, shipped Adrian Dantley to Utah for Spencer Haywood and picked up Jim Chones from Cleveland. New coach Jack McKinney suffered a near-fatal bicycle accident after 14 games and was replaced temporarily by assistant Paul Westhead, but the Lakers kept rolling and finished with 60 wins. Leading the charge was Kareen Abdul-Jabbar, who won his sixth MVP award, but he had plenty of help from versatile rookie Magic Johnson, plus old standbys Jamaal Wilkes and Norm Nixon. By midseason McKinney had recovered, but Buss chose to stay the course with Westhead, who was ultimately rewarded with a multi-year contract.

The league's other power was in Philadelphia, where Julius Erving, Maurice Cheeks and Bobby Jones again led the 76ers, along with Caldwell Jones and the improving Darryl Dawkins. Oft-injured Doug Collins failed to return to top form, but Lionel Hollins, from Portland, helped fill that gap, and the 76ers improved to 59-23, second in the Atlantic Division.

The previous Atlantic titlist, Washington, signed free agent playmaker Kevin Porter, but lost Thomas Henderson to Houston, and when Porter struggled, the team lacked direction. Bob Dandridge and Mitch Kupchak played in only 85 games between them, negating another great season from Elvin Hayes and the improvement of Greg Ballard, as the Bullets sank to 39-43. That tied them with the rising New York Knicks, who added rookie star Bill Cartwright to an exciting young backcourt of Ray Williams and Michael Ray Richardson. New Jersey's top rookie, Calvin Natt, went to Portland in midseason for Maurice Lucas. Lucas and Mike Newlin, picked up from Houston, played well, but offered little hope for the future.

In the Central Division, John Drew, Dan Roundfield and Eddie Johnson led Atlanta to 50 wins, while Houston and San Antonio each slipped to 41-41. Under new coach Del Harris, the Rockets again relied on Moses Malone and Calvin Murphy, but Rudy Tomjanovich and Rick Barry had sub-par seasons. For Barry, it would be his last. Meanwhile, the Spur's failure to repeat as division champs despite good years from George Gervin, Larry Kenon and James Silas cost coach Doug Moe his job. Indiana, transplanted from the Midwest Division, lost Ricky Sobers through free agency, but got Mickey Johnson as compensation and didn't lose any ground. What did cost the Pacers in the long run was the midseason trade of Alex English to Denver for fading George McGinnis. Cleveland improved under new coach Stan Albeck as sophomore Mike Mitchell became a star, but Campy Russell missed half the season with injuries. Detroit gave up M.L. Carr and a No. 1 draft pick to get Bob McAdoo from Boston, rookie Greg Kelser was disappointing, and in a final gesture of futility, the Pistons traded Bob Lanier to Milwaukee for Kent Benson before finishing 16-66.

Marques Johnson, Junior Bridgeman and Brian Winters led the way as Milwaukee rebounded from a poor 1978-79 to win the Midwest Division. Besides picking up Lanier, the Bucks also got David Meyers back from a year's absence with a back injury. Kansas City finished two games back, led again by Otis Birdsong, Scott Wedman and Phil Ford. Denver collapsed to 30-52, with the loss of David Thompson for 43 games negating a big year from Dan Issel, but the McGinnis-for-English trade would pay dividends for the next decade. Chicago had a new coach, Jerry Sloan, a top rookie, David Greenwood, and a much-improved second-year man, Reggie Theus, but injuries plagued Artis Gilmore and kept the Bulls from going anywhere. The New Orleans Jazz went all the way to Salt Lake City, whereas the Utah Jazz finished last again, though in a different division. Pete Maravich was released in January, replaced by Dantley as the team's scoring star. The Jazz also sent Rich Kelley to New Jersey for Bernard King, but King, plagued by problems with alcohol, played only 19 games.

In the Pacific Division the Laker's faced strong challenges from Seattle and Phoenix. The Sonics had Gus Williams and Dennis Johnson in the backcourt, plus Jack Sikma and the league's top 3-point shooter in Fred Brown, while the Suns were led again by Paul Westphal, Walter Davis, Truck Robinson and Alvan Adams. Portland lost Mychal Thompson for the season with a broken leg, and four members of the 1977 champs--Lucas, Hollins, Dave Twardzik and Larry Steele--played their last in Portland. Free agent Bill Walton signed with San Diego, but the league's awarding of Kermit Washington, Randy Smith and Kevin Kunnert to Portland as compensation decimated the Clippers, and Walton reinjured his foot and played only 14 games. Lloyd Free averaged 30 points and Swen Nater, Walton's backup at UCLA, led the league in rebounding, but it was a long season in San Diego. It was even longer in Golden State, where injuries hampered Phil Smith and the Warriers dropped to 24 wins.

The best playoff series matched Seattle and Wilwaukee in the Western semifinals, with the Sonics squeaking by in seven games before falling to the Lakers in five. Meanwhile, Philadelphia spoiled the possibility of a Magic vs. Bird matchup in the finals by blowing out Boston in five games. In the championship series, Abdul-Jabbar led the Lakers to a 3-2 lead but severely sprained an ankle while scoring 40 points in the fifth game. In his absence L.A. went to a small lineup featuring Johnson at center, and the rookie responded with 42 points and 15 rebounds as the Lakers won the sixth game and their first title since 1972. That performance earned Johnson the playoff MVP award in a close vote over Abdul-Jabbar.

1979/80 N.B.A. — EASTERN CONFERENCE
ATLANTIC DIVISION

Use Name	Pos	Hgt	Wgt	Age	G	Min	FG	FGA	%	FT	FTA	%	Reb	Ass	PF	DQ	Stls	Blkd Shts	Points	Min	Reb	Ass	PF	Points
BOSTON CELTICS	61-21 .744				BILL FITCH																			
Cedric Maxwell	F	6'8	205	24	80	2744	457	750	61	436	554	79	704	199	266	6	76	61	1350	34	8.8	2.5	3.3	16.9
Larry Bird	F	6'9	220	23	82	2955	693	1463	47	301	360	84	852	370	279	4	143	53	1745	36	10.4	4.5	3.4	21.3
Dave Cowens (FJ)	C	6'9	230	31	66	2159	422	932	45	95	122	78	534	206	216	2	69	61	940	33	8.1	3.1	3.3	14.2
Chris Ford	G	6'1	190	30	73	2115	330	709	47	86	114	75	181	215	178	0	111	27	816	29	2.5	2.9	2.4	11.2
Nate Archibald	G	6'1	150	31	80	2864	383	794	48	361	435	83	197	671	218	2	106	10	1131	36	2.5	8.4	2.7	14.1
M.L. Carr	F-G	6'6	205	28	82	1994	362	763	47	178	241	74	330	156	214	1	120	36	914	24	4.0	1.9	2.6	11.1
Rick Robey	C-F	6'11	230	23	82	1918	379	727	52	184	269	68	530	92	244	2	53	15	942	23	6.5	1.1	3.0	11.5
Gerald Henderson	G	6'2	175	23	76	1061	191	382	50	89	129	69	83	147	96	0	45	15	473	14	1.1	1.9	1.3	6.2
Jeff Judkins	G	6'6	185	23	65	674	139	276	50	62	76	82	66	47	91	0	29	5	351	10	1.0	0.7	1.4	5.4
Don Chaney (LJ)	G	6'5	210	33	60	523	67	189	35	32	42	76	73	38	80	1	31	11	167	9	1.2	0.6	1.3	2.8
Pete Maravich (from Utah)	G	6'5	200	31	26	442	123	249	49	50	55	91	38	29	49	1	9	2	299	17	1.5	1.1	1.9	11.5
Eric Fernsten	C	6'10	205	26	56	431	71	153	46	33	52	63	96	28	43	0	17	12	175	8	1.7	0.5	0.8	3.1

3 PT FG Bird 58-143, Cowens 1-12, Ford 70-164, Archibald 4-18, Carr 12-41, Robey 0-1, Henderson 2-6, Judkins 11-27, Chaney 1-6, Maravich 3-4

Use Name	Pos	Hgt	Wgt	Age	G	Min	FG	FGA	%	FT	FTA	%	Reb	Ass	PF	DQ	Stls	Blkd Shts	Points	Min	Reb	Ass	PF	Points
PHILADELPHIA 76ers	59-23 .720				BILLY CUNNINGHAM																			
Julius Erving	F	6'7	200	29	78	2812	838	1614	52	420	534	79	576	355	208	0	170	140	2100	36	7.4	4.6	2.7	26.9
Bobby Jones	F	6'9	212	28	81	2125	398	748	53	257	329	78	450	146	223	3	102	118	1053	26	5.6	1.8	2.8	13.0
Darryl Dawkins	C	6'11	251	22	80	2541	494	946	52	190	291	65	693	149	**328**	8	49	142	1178	32	8.7	1.9	**4.1**	14.7
Doug Collins (BF,KJ)	G	6'6	180	28	36	963	191	410	47	113	124	91	94	100	76	0	30	7	495	27	2.6	2.8	2.1	13.8
Maurice Cheeks	G	6'1	180	23	79	2623	357	661	54	180	231	78	274	556	197	1	183	32	898	33	3.5	7.0	2.5	11.4
Caldwell Jones	C-F	6'11	225	29	80	2771	232	532	43	124	178	70	950	164	298	5	43	162	588	35	11.9	2.1	3.7	7.4
Henry Bibby	G	6'1	185	30	82	2035	251	626	40	226	286	79	208	307	161	0	62	6	739	25	2.5	3.7	2.0	9.0
Steve Mix	F	6'7	222	32	81	1543	363	703	52	207	249	83	290	149	114	0	67	9	937	19	3.6	1.8	1.4	11.6
Clint Richardson	G	6'3	195	23	52	988	159	348	46	28	45	62	123	107	97	0	24	15	347	19	2.4	2.1	1.9	6.7
Lionel Hollis (from Port)	G	6'3	185	26	27	796	130	313	42	67	87	77	69	112	68	0	46	9	329	29	2.6	4.1	2.5	12.2
Jim Spanarke	G	6'5	190	22	40	442	72	153	47	54	65	83	54	51	58	0	12	6	198	11	1.4	1.3	1.5	5.0
Bernard Toone	F	6'9	210	23	23	124	23	64	26	8	10	80	34	12	20	0	4	5	55	5	1.5	0.5	0.9	2.4
Eric Money (to Det)	G	6'	170	24	6	82	14	36	39	2	2	100	7	16	11	0	0	1	30	14	1.2	2.7	1.8	5.0
Al Skinner (KJ)	G	6'4	195	27	2	10	1	2	50	0	0	—	0	2	1	0	0	0	2	5	0.0	1.0	0.5	1.0

3 PT FG Erving 4-20, B. Jones 0-3, Dawkins 0-6, Collins 0-1, Cheeks 4-9, C. Jones 0-2, Bibby 11-52, Mix 4-10, Richardson 1-3, Spanarkel 0-2, Toone 1-7

Use Name	Pos	Hgt	Wgt	Age	G	Min	FG	FGA	%	FT	FTA	%	Reb	Ass	PF	DQ	Stls	Blkd Shts	Points	Min	Reb	Ass	PF	Points
WASHINGTON BULLETS	39-43 .476				DICK MOTTA																			
Bob Dandridge (KJ)	F	6'6	195	32	45	1457	329	729	45	123	152	81	246	178	112	1	29	36	783	32	5.5	4.0	2.5	17.4
Elvin Hayes	F	6'9	235	34	81	3183	761	1677	45	334	478	70	896	129	309	9	62	189	1859	39	11.1	1.6	3.8	23.0
Wes Unseld	C	6'7	245	33	82	2973	327	637	51	139	209	67	1094	366	249	5	65	61	794	36	13.3	4.5	3.0	9.7
Kevin Grevey (LJ)	G	6'5	210	26	65	1818	331	804	41	216	249	87	187	177	158	0	56	16	912	28	2.9	2.7	2.4	14.0
Jim Cleamons (from NY)	G	6'3	185	30	57	1535	184	381	48	72	98	73	133	248	120	0	44	9	444	27	2.3	4.4	2.1	7.8
Greg Ballard	F	6'7	215	24	82	2438	545	1101	50	171	227	75	638	159	197	2	90	36	1277	30	7.8	1.9	2.4	15.6
Kevin Porter	G	6'	175	29	70	1494	201	438	46	110	137	80	82	457	180	1	59	11	512	21	1.2	6.5	2.6	7.3
Larry Wright	G	6'1	160	25	76	1286	229	500	46	96	108	89	122	222	144	3	49	18	558	17	1.6	2.9	1.9	7.3
Roger Phegley (to NJ)	G-F	6'6	205	23	50	971	224	473	47	104	120	87	115	70	106	1	19	3	554	19	2.3	1.4	2.1	11.1
Dave Corzine	C-F	6'11	250	23	78	826	90	216	42	45	68	66	270	63	120	1	9	31	225	11	3.5	0.8	1.5	2.9
John Williamson (from NJ)	G	6'2	195	27	30	603	153	356	43	40	50	80	45	39	66	0	10	10	349	20	1.5	1.3	2.2	11.6
Phil Chenier (to Ind)	G	6'3	180	29	20	470	84	214	39	31	41	76	43	42	26	0	18	5	202	24	2.2	2.1	1.3	10.1
Mitch Kupchak (KJ)	C-F	6'9	230	25	40	451	67	160	42	52	75	69	105	16	49	1	8	8	186	11	2.6	0.4	1.2	4.7
Gus Bailey	G	6'5	185	28	20	180	16	35	46	5	13	38	28	26	18	0	7	4	38	9	1.4	1.3	0.9	1.9
Lawrence Boston	F	6'8	225	23	13	125	24	52	46	8	13	62	39	2	25	0	4	2	56	10	3.0	0.2	1.9	4.3
Ron Behajen	F	6'9	235	28	6	64	9	23	39	5	6	83	14	7	14	0	0	4	23	11	2.3	1.2	2.3	3.8
Steve Malovic (to SD,Det)	F	6'10	230	23	1	6	0	0	—	1	4	25	0	0	0	0	1	0	1	6	0.0	0.0	0.0	1.0

3 PT FG Dandridge 2-11, Hayes 3-13, Unseld 1-2, Grevey 34-92, Cleamons 4-23, Ballard 16-47, Porter 0-4, Wright 4-16, Phegley 2-5, Williamson 3-16, Chenier 3-6, Kupchak 0-2, Bailey 1-1

Use Name	Pos	Hgt	Wgt	Age	G	Min	FG	FGA	%	FT	FTA	%	Reb	Ass	PF	DQ	Stls	Blkd Shts	Points	Min	Reb	Ass	PF	Points
NEW YORK KNICKERBOCKERS	39-43 .476				RED HOLZMAN																			
Toby Knight	F	6'9	210	24	81	2945	669	1265	53	211	261	81	493	150	302	4	117	86	1549	36	6.1	1.9	3.7	19.1
Larry Demic	F-C	6'9	225	22	82	1872	230	528	44	110	183	60	483	64	306	10	56	30	570	23	5.9	0.8	3.7	7.0
Bill Cartwright	C	7'1	255	22	82	3150	665	1215	55	451	566	80	726	165	279	2	48	101	1781	38	8.9	2.0	3.4	21.7
Michael Ray Richardson	G-F	6'5	190	24	82	3060	502	1063	47	223	338	66	539	**832**	260	3	**265**	35	1254	37	6.6	**10.1**	3.2	15.3
Ray Williams	G	6'3	190	25	82	2582	687	1384	50	333	423	79	412	512	295	5	167	24	1714	31	5.0	6.2	3.6	20.9
Joe Meriweather	F-C	6'10	218	26	65	1565	252	477	53	78	121	64	350	66	239	8	37	120	582	24	5.4	1.0	3.7	9.0
Hollis Copeland	F	6'6	180	24	75	1142	182	368	49	63	86	73	156	80	154	0	61	25	427	15	2.1	1.1	2.1	5.7
Geoff Huston	G	6'2	175	22	71	923	94	241	39	28	38	74	58	159	83	0	39	5	219	13	0.8	2.2	1.2	3.1
Mike Glenn	G	6'3	175	24	75	800	188	364	52	63	73	86	66	85	79	0	35	7	441	11	0.9	1.1	1.1	5.9
Earl Monroe (FJ)	G	6'3	190	35	51	633	161	352	46	56	64	88	36	67	46	0	21	3	378	12	0.7	1.3	0.9	7.4
Sly Williams	F	6'7	210	21	57	556	104	267	39	58	90	64	121	36	73	0	19	8	266	10	2.1	0.6	1.3	4.7
Marvin Webster (KJ)	C	7'1	240	27	20	298	38	79	48	12	16	75	80	9	39	1	3	11	88	15	4.0	0.5	2.0	4.4
Jim Cleamons (to Was)	G	6'3	185	30	22	254	30	69	43	12	15	80	19	40	13	0	13	2	75	12	0.9	1.8	0.6	3.4

3 PT FG Knight 0-2, Richardson 27-110, R. Williams 7-37, Meriweather 0-1, Copeland 0-2, Huston 3-17, Glenn 2-10, S. Williams 0-4, Cleamons 3-8

1979/80 N.B.A — EASTERN CONFERENCE
ATLANTIC CONFERENCE (continued)

Use Name	Pos	Hgt	Wgt	Age	G	Min	FG	FGA	%	FT	FTA	%	Reb	Ass	PF	DQ	Stls	Blkd Shts	Points	Min	Reb	Ass	PF	Points
NEW JERSEY NETS	34-48 .415				KEVIN LOUGHERY																			
Jan Van Breda Kolff	F	6'7	200	28	82	2399	212	458	46	130	155	84	429	247	307	11	100	76	564	29	5.2	3.0	3.7	6.9
Maurice Lucas (from Port)	F	6'9	218	27	22	708	128	261	49	79	102	77	212	83	82	1	19	27	335	32	9.6	3.8	3.7	15.2
George Johnson	C	6'11	205	31	81	2119	248	543	46	89	126	71	602	173	312	7	53	258	585	26	7.4	2.1	3.9	7.2
Mike Newlin	G	6'4	200	30	78	2510	611	1329	46	367	415	88	264	314	195	1	115	4	1634	32	3.4	4.0	2.5	20.9
Eddie Jordon	G	6'1	170	24	82	2657	437	1017	43	201	258	78	270	557	238	7	223	27	1087	32	3.3	6.8	2.9	13.3
Calvin Natt (to Port)	F	6'6	220	22	53	2046	421	879	48	199	280	71	513	112	148	1	78	22	1042	39	9.7	2.1	2.8	19.7
Cliff Robinson	F	6'9	220	19	70	1661	391	833	47	168	242	69	506	98	178	1	61	34	951	24	7.2	1.4	2.5	13.6
Rich Kelley (to Phoe)	C	7'	240	26	57	1466	186	399	47	197	250	79	397	128	215	5	50	79	569	26	7.0	2.2	3.8	10.0
Winford Boynes	G-F	6'6	186	21	64	1102	221	467	47	104	136	76	133	95	132	1	59	19	546	17	2.1	1.5	2.1	8.5
John Williamson (to Was)	G	6'2	195	27	28	771	206	461	45	76	88	86	54	87	71	1	26	9	496	28	1.9	3.1	2.5	17.7
Robert Smith (from Utah)	G	5'11	165	24	59	736	113	254	44	75	87	86	76	85	102	1	22	4	309	12	1.3	1.4	1.7	5.2
Bob Elliott	C-F	6'9	225	24	54	722	101	228	44	104	152	68	185	53	97	0	29	14	307	13	3.4	1.0	1.8	5.7
Roger Phegley (from Was)	G	6'6	205	23	28	541	126	260	48	73	83	88	70	32	52	0	15	4	327	19	2.5	1.1	1.9	11.7
Phil Jackson	F-C	6'8	230	34	16	194	29	46	63	7	10	70	24	12	35	1	5	4	65	12	1.5	0.8	2.2	4.1
Tim Bassett (to SA)	F	6'8	225	28	7	92	8	22	36	8	12	67	18	4	14	0	5	0	24	13	2.6	0.6	2.0	3.4
Ralph Simpson	G	6'5	200	30	8	81	18	47	38	5	10	50	11	14	3	0	9	0	41	10	1.4	1.8	0.4	5.1

3-PT FG — Van Breda Kolff 7-20, Lucas 0-4, Johnson 0-1, Newlin 45-152, Jordon 12-48, Natt 1-5, Robinson 1-4, Kelley 0-3, Boynes 0-4, Williamson 8-19, Smith 8-26, Elliot 1-4, Phegley 2-4, Jackson 0-2, Simpson 0-2

CENTRAL DIVISION

Use Name	Pos	Hgt	Wgt	Age	G	Min	FG	FGA	%	FT	FTA	%	Reb	Ass	PF	DQ	Stls	Blkd Shts	Points	Min	Reb	Ass	PF	Points
ATLANTA HAWKS	50-32 .610				HUBIE BROWN																			
John Drew	F	6'6	205	25	80	2306	535	1182	45	489	646	76	471	101	313	10	91	23	1559	29	5.9	1.3	3.9	19.5
Dan Roundfield	F	6'8	205	26	81	2588	502	1007	50	330	465	71	837	184	317	6	101	139	1334	32	10.3	2.3	3.9	16.5
Tree Rollins	C	7'1	235	24	82	2123	287	514	56	157	220	71	774	76	322	12	54	244	731	26	9.4	0.9	3.9	8.9
Armond Hill	G	6'4	190	26	79	2092	177	431	41	124	146	85	138	424	261	7	107	8	479	26	1.7	5.4	3.3	6.1
Eddie Johnson	G	6'2	190	24	79	2622	590	1212	49	280	338	83	200	370	216	2	120	24	1465	33	2.5	4.7	2.7	18.5
Steve Hawes	C	6'9	220	29	82	1853	304	605	50	150	182	82	496	144	205	4	74	29	761	23	6.0	1.8	2.5	9.3
Charlie Criss	G	5'8	165	30	81	1794	249	578	43	172	212	81	116	246	133	0	74	4	671	22	1.4	3.0	1.6	8.3
Jack Givens	F-G	6'5	205	23	82	1254	182	473	38	106	128	83	242	59	132	1	51	19	470	15	3.0	0.7	1.6	5.7
Tom McMillen (KJ)	F-C	6'11	215	27	53	1071	191	382	50	81	107	76	220	62	126	2	36	14	463	20	4.2	1.2	2.4	8.7
Jim McElroy (from Det)	G	6'3	190	26	31	516	66	171	39	17	53	32	49	65	45	1	21	5	171	17	1.6	2.1	1.5	5.5
Terry Furlow (to Utah)	G	6'4	190	25	21	404	66	161	41	44	51	86	42	72	19	0	19	9	177	19	2.0	3.4	0.9	8.4
Sam Pellom	C-F	6'9	225	28	44	373	44	108	41	21	30	70	92	18	70	0	12	12	109	8	2.1	0.4	1.6	2.5
Ron Lee (BG, to Det)	G	6'4	195	27	30	364	29	91	32	9	17	53	33	67	65	1	15	4	67	12	1.1	2.2	2.2	2.2
John Brown (from Utah)	F	6'7	220	28	28	361	37	98	38	34	44	77	62	14	66	0	3	4	108	13	2.2	0.5	2.4	3.9
Rick Wilson	G	6'5	200	23	5	59	2	14	14	4	6	67	3	11	3	0	4	1	8	12	0.6	2.2	0.6	1.6

3-PT FG — Drew 0-7, Roundfield 0-4, Hill 1-4, Johnson 5-13, Hawes 3-8, Criss 1-17, Givens 0-2, McMillen 0-1, McElroy 2-7, Furlow 1-9, Lee 0-3

Use Name	Pos	Hgt	Wgt	Age	G	Min	FG	FGA	%	FT	FTA	%	Reb	Ass	PF	DQ	Stls	Blkd Shts	Points	Min	Reb	Ass	PF	Points
HOUSTON ROCKETS	41-41 .500				DEL HARRIS																			
Rick Barry	F	6'7	220	35	72	1816	325	771	42	143	153	**93**	236	268	182	0	80	28	866	25	3.3	3.7	2.5	12.0
Rudy Tomjanovich	F	6'8	220	31	62	1834	370	778	48	118	147	80	358	109	161	2	32	10	880	30	5.8	1.8	2.6	14.2
Moses Malone	C	6'10	215	24	82	3140	778	1549	50	563	**783**	72	1190	147	210	0	80	107	2119	38	14.5	1.8	2.6	25.8
Allen Leavell	G	6'1	170	22	77	2123	330	656	50	180	221	81	184	417	197	1	127	28	843	28	2.4	5.4	2.6	10.9
Calvin Murphy	G	5'9	165	31	76	2676	624	1267	49	271	302	90	150	299	269	3	143	9	1520	35	2.0	3.9	3.5	20.0
Robert Reid	F-G	6'8	205	24	76	2304	419	861	49	153	208	74	441	244	281	2	132	57	991	30	5.8	3.2	3.7	13.0
Tom Henderson	G	6'3	190	27	66	1551	154	323	48	56	77	73	111	274	107	1	55	4	364	24	1.7	4.2	1.6	5.5
Major Jones	F	6'9	225	26	82	1545	188	392	48	61	108	56	381	67	186	0	50	67	438	19	4.6	0.8	2.3	5.3
Mike Dunleavy (RJ)	G	6'3	180	25	51	1036	148	319	46	111	134	83	100	210	120	2	40	4	410	20	2.0	4.1	2.4	8.0
Billy Paultz (from SA)	C-F	6'11	250	31	37	980	138	292	47	43	82	52	265	70	86	0	22	39	319	26	7.2	1.9	2.3	8.6
John Shumate (from Det to SA)	F-C	6'9	235	27	29	332	34	64	53	33	44	75	79	23	39	0	8	9	101	11	2.7	0.8	1.3	3.5
Dwight Jones (to Chi)	F-C	6'10	210	27	21	278	50	119	42	27	36	75	72	11	48	0	4	5	127	13	3.4	0.5	2.3	6.0
Paul Mokeski (XJ)	C	7'	250	22	12	113	11	33	33	7	9	78	29	2	24	0	1	6	29	9	2.4	0.2	2.0	2.4
Rudy White	G	6'2	195	26	9	106	13	24	54	10	13	77	9	5	8	0	5	0	36	12	1.0	0.6	0.9	4.0
Alonzo Bradley	F	6'6	190	26	22	96	17	48	35	6	9	67	6	3	9	0	3	0	41	4	0.3	0.1	0.4	1.9
Jacky Dorsey (knee injury)																								

3-PT FG — Barry 73-221, Tomjanovich 22-79, Malone 0-6, Leavell 3-19, Murphy 1-25 Reid 0-3, Henderson 0-2, M. Jones 1-3, Dunleavy 3-20, Bradley 1-1

Use Name	Pos	Hgt	Wgt	Age	G	Min	FG	FGA	%	FT	FTA	%	Reb	Ass	PF	DQ	Stls	Blkd Shts	Points	Min	Reb	Ass	PF	Points
SAN ANTONIO SPURS	41-41 .500				DOUG MOE 33-33 (.500), BOB BASS 8-8 (.500)																			
Mark Olberding	F	6'8	230	23	75	2111	291	609	48	210	264	80	418	327	274	7	67	22	792	28	5.6	4.4	3.7	10.6
Larry Kenon	F	6'9	215	27	78	2798	647	1333	49	270	345	78	775	231	192	0	111	18	1565	36	9.9	3.0	2.5	20.1
John Shumate (from Det, Hou)	C	6'9	235	27	27	777	138	263	52	115	147	78	214	52	71	1	23	31	391	29	7.9	1.9	2.6	14.5
George Gervin	G	6'7	185	27	78	2934	**1024**	**1940**	53	505	593	85	403	202	208	0	110	79	**2585**	38	5.2	2.6	2.7	**33.1**
James Silas	G	6'3	180	30	77	2293	513	999	51	339	382	89	167	347	206	2	61	14	1365	30	2.2	4.5	2.7	17.7
Kevin Restani	F-C	6'9	225	28	82	1966	369	727	51	131	161	81	386	189	186	0	54	12	874	24	4.7	2.3	2.3	10.7
Paul Griffin	C-F	6'9	205	25	82	1812	173	313	55	174	240	73	438	250	306	9	81	53	520	22	5.3	3.0	3.7	6.3
Mike Gale (FJ)	G	6'4	190	29	67	1474	171	377	45	97	120	81	152	312	134	2	123	13	441	22	2.3	4.7	2.0	6.6
Mike Evans	G	6'1	170	24	79	1246	208	464	45	58	85	68	107	230	194	2	60	9	486	16	1.4	2.9	2.5	6.2
Billy Paultz (to Hou	C	6'11	250	31	47	1213	189	381	50	66	100	66	321	118	127	3	47	45	444	26	6.8	2.5	2.7	9.4
Wiley Peck	G	6'7	220	22	52	628	73	169	43	34	55	62	183	33	100	2	17	23	180	12	3.5	0.6	1.9	3.5
Irv Kiffin	F	6'9	225	28	26	212	32	96	33	18	25	72	40	19	43	0	10	2	82	8	1.5	0.7	1.7	3.2
Sylvester Norris	C	6'11	220	22	17	189	18	43	42	4	6	67	43	6	41	1	3	12	40	11	2.5	0.4	2.4	2.4
Tim Bassett (from NJ)	F	6'8	225	28	5	72	4	12	33	2	3	67	15	10	13	0	3	0	10	14	3.0	2.0	2.6	2.0
Harry Davis	F	6'7	220	23	4	30	6	12	50	1	2	50	6	0	8	0	1	0	13	8	1.5	0.0	2.0	3.3

3-PT FG — Olberding 0-3, Kenon 1-9, Shumate 0-1, Gervin 32-102, Silas 0-4, Restani 5-29 Gale 2-13, Evans 12-42, Paultz 0-1, Peck 0-2

1979/80 N.B.A. — EASTERN CONFERENCE
CENTRAL DIVISION (Continued)

INDIANA PACERS 37-45 .451 **BOB LEONARD**

Use Name	Pos	Hgt	Wgt	Age	G	Min	FG	FGA	%	FT	FTA	%	Reb	Ass	PF	DQ	Stls	Blkd Shts	Points	Min	Reb	Ass	PF	Points
Mickey Johnson	F	6'10	190	27	82	2647	588	1271	46	385	482	80	681	344	291	11	153	112	1566	32	8.3	4.2	3.5	19.1
Mike Bantom	F-C	6'9	220	28	77	2330	384	760	51	139	209	67	456	279	268	7	85	49	908	30	5.9	3.6	3.5	11.8
James Edwards	C	7'	225	24	82	2314	528	1032	51	231	339	68	578	127	324	**12**	55	104	1287	28	7.0	1.5	**4.0**	15.7
Billy Knight	G-F	6'6	195	27	75	1910	385	722	53	212	262	81	361	155	96	0	82	9	986	25	4.8	2.1	1.3	13.1
Johnny Davis	G	6'2	170	24	82	2912	496	1159	43	304	352	86	226	440	178	0	110	23	1300	36	2.8	5.4	2.2	15.9
Dudley Bradley	G-F	6'6	195	22	82	2027	275	609	45	136	174	78	223	252	194	1	211	48	688	25	2.7	3.1	2.4	8.4
Clemon Johnson	C	6'10	240	23	79	1541	199	396	50	74	117	63	394	115	211	2	48	121	472	20	5.0	1.5	2.7	6.0
Alex English (to Den)	F	6'8	190	25	54	1526	346	686	50	114	140	81	380	142	128	0	45	33	806	28	7.0	2.6	2.4	14.9
Joey Hassett	G	6'5	180	24	74	1135	215	509	42	24	29	83	94	104	85	0	46	8	523	15	1.3	1.4	1.1	7.1
George McGinnis (from Den)	F	6'8	235	29	28	784	132	302	44	104	181	57	237	112	116	*4	32	6	369	28	8.5	4.0	4.1	13.2
Paul Chenier (from Was)	G	6'3	180	29	23	380	52	135	39	18	26	69	35	47	29	0	15	10	124	17	1.5	2.0	1.3	5.4
Ron Carter	G	6'5	190	23	13	117	15	37	41	2	7	29	19	9	19	0	2	3	32	9	1.5	0.7	1.5	2.5
John Kuester	G	6'2	180	24	24	100	12	34	35	5	7	71	14	16	8	0	7	1	29	4	0.6	0.7	0.3	1.2
Tony Zeno	F	6'8	210	22	8	59	6	21	29	2	2	100	14	1	13	0	4	3	14	7	1.8	0.1	1.6	1.8
Brad Davis (to Utah)	G	6'3	180	24	5	43	2	7	29	3	4	75	2	5	7	0	3	0	7	9	0.4	1.0	1.4	1.4
Corky Calhoun	F	6'7	210	29	7	30	4	9	44	0	2	0	10	0	6	0	2	0	8	4	1.4	0.0	0.9	1.1

Len Elmore - finger injury

3-PT FG — M. Johnson 5-32, Bantom 1-3, Edwards 0-1, Knight 4-15, Davis 4-42, Bradley 2-5, English 0-3, Hassett 69-198, McGinnis 1-8, Chenier 5-12, Kuester 0-1

CLEVELAND CAVALIERS 37-45 .451 **STAN ALBECK**

Use Name	Pos	Hgt	Wgt	Age	G	Min	FG	FGA	%	FT	FTA	%	Reb	Ass	PF	DQ	Stls	Blkd Shts	Points	Min	Reb	Ass	PF	Points
Mike Mitchell	F	6'7	215	23	82	2802	755	1482	51	270	343	79	591	93	259	4	70	77	1820	34	7.2	1.1	3.2	22.2
Campy Russell (GJ)	F	6'8	215	27	41	1331	284	630	45	178	239	74	225	173	113	1	72	20	747	32	5.5	4.2	2.8	18.2
Dave Robisch	C	6'10	240	30	82	2670	489	940	52	277	329	84	658	192	211	2	53	53	1255	33	8.0	2.3	2.6	15.3
Randy Smith	G	6'3	180	31	82	2677	599	1326	45	233	283	82	256	363	190	1	125	7	1441	33	3.1	4.4	2.3	17.6
Foots Walker	G	6'1	172	28	76	2422	258	568	45	195	243	80	287	607	202	2	155	12	712	32	3.8	8.0	2.7	9.4
Kenny Carr (from LA)	F	6'7	230	24	74	1781	371	752	49	171	261	66	571	76	240	3	64	51	913	24	7.7	1.0	3.2	12.3
Austin Carr	F	6'4	200	31	77	1595	390	839	46	127	172	74	165	150	120	0	39	3	909	21	2.1	1.9	1.6	11.8
Bill Willoughby	F	6'8	205	22	78	1447	219	457	48	96	127	76	329	72	189	0	32	62	535	19	4.2	0.9	2.4	6.9
John Lambert	C	6'10	225	26	74	1324	165	400	41	73	101	72	352	56	203	4	47	42	403	18	4.8	0.8	2.7	5.4
Willie Smith	G	6'2	170	26	62	1051	121	315	38	40	52	77	121	259	110	1	75	1	299	17	2.0	4.2	1.8	4.8
Don Ford (from LA)	F	6'9	215	27	21	419	65	144	45	22	25	88	87	29	45	0	11	6	153	20	4.1	1.4	2.1	7.3
Earl Tatum (KJ)	G-F	6'4	185	26	33	225	36	94	38	11	19	58	26	20	29	0	16	5	85	7	0.8	0.6	0.9	2.6
Bingo Smith (to SD)	F	6'5	212	33	8	135	33	72	46	7	8	88	14	7	21	0	3	2	74	17	1.8	0.9	2.6	9.3
Walt Frazier	G	6'4	205	34	3	27	4	11	36	2	2	100	3	8	2	0	2	1	10	9	1.0	2.7	0.7	3.3
Butch Lee (KJ, to LA)	G	6'	185	23	3	24	2	11	18	0	1	0	3	3	0	0	0	0	4	8	1.0	1.0	0.0	1.3

Elmore Smith - knee injury

3-PT FG — Mitchell 0-6, Russell 1-9, Robisch 0-3, R. Smith 10-53, Walker 1-9, K. Carr 0-4, A. Carr 2-6 Willoughby 1-9, Lambert 0-3, W. Smith 17-71, Ford 1-2, B. Smith 1-5, Frazier 0-1

DETROIT PISTONS 16-66 .195 **DICK VITALE**

Use Name	Pos	Hgt	Wgt	Age	G	Min	FG	FGA	%	FT	FTA	%	Reb	Ass	PF	DQ	Stls	Blkd Shts	Points	Min	Reb	Ass	PF	Points
Terry Tyler	F	6'7	215	23	82	2670	430	925	46	143	187	76	627	129	237	3	107	220	1005	33	7.6	1.6	2.9	12.3
Bob McAdoo (GJ)	F-C	6'9	210	28	58	2097	492	1025	48	235	322	73	467	200	178	3	73	65	1222	36	8.1	3.4	3.1	21.1
Kent Benson (from Mil)	C	6'10	245	25	17	502	86	187	46	33	44	75	120	51	68	3	19	18	206	30	7.1	3.0	4.0	12.1
John Long	G-F	6'5	210	23	69	2364	588	1164	51	160	194	82	337	206	221	4	129	26	1337	34	4.9	3.0	3.2	19.4
Eric Money (from Phi)	G	6'	170	24	55	1467	259	510	51	81	104	78	97	238	135	3	53	10	599	27	1.8	4.3	2.5	10.9
Leon Douglas	C-F	6'10	230	25	70	1782	221	455	49	125	185	68	501	121	249	10	30	62	567	25	7.2	1.7	3.6	8.1
Bob Lanier (BH, to Mil)	C	6'11	250	31	37	1392	319	584	55	164	210	78	373	122	130	2	38	60	802	38	10.1	3.3	3.5	21.7
Terry Duerod (LJ)	G	6'2	180	23	67	1331	282	598	47	45	66	68	98	117	102	0	41	11	624	20	1.5	1.7	1.5	9.3
Greg Kelser (KJ)	F	6'7	190	22	50	1233	280	593	47	146	203	72	276	108	176	5	60	34	709	25	5.5	2.2	3.5	14.2
Phil Hubbard	F-C	6'8	215	23	64	1189	210	451	47	165	220	75	320	70	202	9	48	10	585	19	5.0	1.1	3.2	9.1
Roy Lee Hamilton	G	6'2	180	22	72	1116	115	287	40	103	150	69	107	192	82	0	48	5	333	16	1.5	2.7	1.1	4.6
Jim McElroy (NJ, to Atl)	G	6'3	190	26	36	1012	162	356	46	95	119	80	50	162	78	1	25	14	422	28	1.4	4.5	2.2	11.7
Ron Lee (from Atl)	G	6'4	195	27	31	803	84	214	39	35	53	66	90	174	107	4	84	13	225	26	2.9	5.6	3.5	7.3
Earl Evans	F	6'8	202	24	36	381	63	140	45	24	42	57	75	37	64	0	14	1	157	11	2.1	1.0	1.8	4.4
John Shumate (to Hou, SA)	F	6'9	235	27	9	228	35	65	54	17	25	68	70	9	16	0	9	5	87	25	7.8	1.0	1.8	9.7
Steve Malovic (from Was, SD)	F	6'10	230	23	10	162	8	25	32	10	14	71	28	14	16	0	2	5	26	16	2.8	1.4	1.6	2.6
Jackie Robinson	F	6'6	212	24	7	51	9	17	53	9	11	82	5	0	8	0	3	3	27	7	0.7	0.0	1.1	3.9

3-PT FG — Tyler 2-12, McAdoo 3-24, Benson 1-4, Long 1-12, Douglas 0-1, Lanier 0-5, Duerod 15-53 Kelser 3-15, Hubbard 0-2, Hamilton 0-2, McElroy 3-14, Lee 22-56, Evans 7-18, Robinson 0-1

WESTERN CONFERENCE
MIDWEST DIVISION

MILWAUKEE BUCKS 49-33 .598 **DON NELSON**

Use Name	Pos	Hgt	Wgt	Age	G	Min	FG	FGA	%	FT	FTA	%	Reb	Ass	PF	DQ	Stls	Blkd Shts	Points	Min	Reb	Ass	PF	Points
Marques Johnson	F	6'7	218	23	77	2686	689	1267	54	291	368	79	566	273	173	0	100	70	1671	35	7.4	3.5	2.2	21.7
David Meyers	F	6'9	225	26	79	2204	399	830	48	156	246	63	448	225	218	3	72	40	955	28	5.7	2.8	2.8	12.1
Bob Lanier (from Det)	C	6'11	250	31	26	739	147	283	52	113	144	78	179	62	70	1	36	29	408	28	6.9	2.4	2.7	15.7
Brian Winters	G	6'4	185	27	80	2623	535	1116	48	184	214	86	223	362	208	0	101	28	1292	33	2.8	4.5	2.6	16.2
Quinn Buckner	G	6'3	205	25	67	1690	306	655	47	105	143	73	238	383	202	1	135	4	719	25	3.6	5.7	3.0	10.7
Junior Bridgeman	F-G	6'5	210	26	81	2316	594	1243	48	230	266	86	301	237	216	3	94	20	1423	29	3.7	2.9	2.7	17.6
Sidney Moncrief	G	6'4	190	22	77	1557	211	451	47	232	292	79	338	133	106	0	72	16	654	20	4.4	1.7	1.4	8.5
Kent Benson (to Det)	C	6'10	245	25	56	1389	213	431	49	66	97	68	333	127	178	1	54	74	492	25	5.9	2.3	3.2	8.8
Harvey Catchings	C	6'9	218	28	72	1366	97	244	40	39	62	63	410	82	191	1	23	162	233	19	5.7	1.1	2.7	3.2
Lloyd Walton	G	6'	160	26	76	1243	110	242	45	49	71	69	91	285	68	0	43	2	270	16	1.2	3.8	0.9	3.6
Richard Lee Washington	F-C	6'11	225	24	75	1092	197	421	47	46	76	61	276	55	166	2	26	48	440	15	3.7	0.7	2.2	5.9
Pat Cummings	F-C	6'9	235	23	71	900	187	370	51	94	123	76	238	53	141	0	22	17	468	13	3.4	0.7	2.0	6.6

3-PT FG — Johnson 2-9, Meyers 1-5, Lanier 1-1, Winters 38-102, Buckner 2-5, Bridgeman 5-27, Moncrief 0-1, Benson 0-1, Catchings 0-1, Walton 1-3

Use Name	Pos	Hgt	Wgt	Age	TOTAL G	Min	FG	FGA	%	FT	FTA	%	Reb	Ass	PF	DQ	Stls	Blkd Shts	Points	PER GAME Min	Reb	Ass	PF	Points
1979/80 N.B.A. — WESTERN CONFERENCE																								
MIDWEST DIVISION																								
KANSAS CITY KINGS	47-35 .573				COTTON FITZSIMMONS																			
Scott Wedman (BC)	F	6'7	215	27	68	2347	569	1112	51	145	181	80	386	145	230	1	84	45	1290	35	5.7	2.1	3.4	19.0
Reggie King	F	6'6	225	22	82	2052	257	499	52	159	219	73	566	106	230	2	69	31	673	25	6.9	1.3	2.8	8.2
Sam Lacey	C	6'10	235	31	81	2412	303	677	45	137	185	74	645	460	307	8	111	109	743	30	8.0	5.7	3.8	9.2
Otis Birdsong	G	6'4	195	24	82	2885	781	1546	51	286	412	69	331	202	226	2	136	22	1858	35	4.0	2.5	2.8	22.7
Phil Ford	G	6'2	176	23	82	2621	489	1058	46	346	423	82	172	610	208	0	136	4	1328	32	2.1	7.4	2.5	16.2
Bill Robinzine	F	6'7	230	26	81	1917	362	723	50	200	274	73	526	62	311	5	106	23	925	24	6.5	0.8	3.8	11.4
Ernie Grunfeld	G-F	6'6	215	24	80	1397	186	420	44	101	131	77	232	109	151	1	56	9	474	17	2.9	1.4	1.9	5.9
Billy McKinney	G	6'	162	24	76	1333	206	459	45	107	133	80	86	248	87	0	58	5	520	18	1.1	3.3	1.1	6.8
Len Elmore (from Ind)	C	6'9	220	27	58	915	104	242	43	51	74	69	257	64	154	0	41	39	259	16	4.4	1.1	2.7	4.5
Gus Gerard	F	6'8	205	26	73	869	159	348	46	66	100	66	177	43	96	1	41	26	385	12	2.4	0.6	1.3	5.3
Mike Green (BA)	C-F	6'10	200	28	21	459	69	159	43	24	42	57	113	28	55	0	13	21	162	22	5.4	1.3	2.6	7.7
Marlon Redmon	G	6'6	188	24	24	298	59	138	43	24	34	71	52	19	27	0	4	9	142	12	2.2	0.8	1.1	5.9
Tom Burleson (BT)	C	7'3	228	27	37	272	36	104	35	23	40	58	72	20	49	0	8	13	95	7	1.9	0.5	1.3	2.6
Terry Crosby	G	6'4	195	22	4	28	2	4	50	2	2	100	1	7	4	0	0	0	6	7	0.3	1.8	1.0	1.5
3-PT FG — Wedman 7-22, King 0-1, Lacey 0-1, Birdsong 10-36, Ford 4-23, Robinzine 1-2, Grunfeld 1-2, McKinney 1-10, Gerard 1-3, Green 0-2, Redmond 0-9, Burleson 0-3																								
DENVER NUGGETS	30-52 .366				DONNIE WALSH																			
Alex English (from Ind)	F	6'8	190	25	24	875	207	427	48	96	126	76	225	82	78	0	28	29	512	36	9.4	3.4	3.3	21.3
George Johnson	F	6'7	218	23	75	1938	309	649	48	148	189	78	584	157	260	4	84	67	768	26	7.8	2.1	3.5	10.2
Dan Issel	C-F	6'9	240	31	82	2938	715	1416	50	517	667	78	719	198	190	1	88	54	1951	36	8.8	2.4	2.3	23.8
David Thompson (FJ)	G-F	6'4	195	25	39	1239	289	617	47	254	335	76	174	124	106	0	39	38	839	32	4.5	3.2	2.7	21.5
Bob Wilkerson	G-F	6'6	200	25	75	2381	430	1030	42	166	222	75	316	243	194	1	93	27	1033	32	4.2	3.2	2.6	13.8
John Roche	G	6'3	170	30	82	2286	354	741	48	175	202	87	115	405	139	0	82	12	932	28	1.4	4.9	1.7	11.4
Charlie Scott	G	6'6	175	31	69	1860	276	688	40	85	118	72	166	250	197	3	47	23	639	27	2.4	3.6	2.9	9.3
George McGinnis (to Ind)	F	6'8	235	29	45	1424	268	584	46	166	307	54	462	221	187	*8	69	17	703	32	10.3	4.9	4.2	15.6
Kim Hughes	C	6'11	220	27	70	1208	102	202	50	15	41	37	326	74	184	3	66	77	219	17	4.7	1.1	2.6	3.1
Gary Garland	G	6'4	180	22	78	1106	155	356	44	18	26	69	138	145	80	1	54	4	334	14	1.8	1.9	1.0	4.3
Glen Gondrezick	F-G	6'6	218	24	59	1020	148	286	52	92	121	76	259	81	119	0	68	16	390	17	4.4	1.4	2.0	6.6
Tom Boswell (to Utah)	F	6'9	225	26	18	522	72	135	53	58	70	83	114	46	56	1	5	8	203	29	6.3	2.6	3.1	11.3
Bo Ellis	F	6'9	200	25	48	502	61	136	45	40	53	75	116	30	67	1	10	24	162	10	2.4	0.6	1.4	3.4
Anthony Roberts	F	6'5	185	24	23	486	69	181	38	39	60	65	109	20	52	1	13	3	177	21	4.7	0.9	2.3	7.7
David Kramer	C	6'9	200	23	8	45	7	22	32	2	2	100	12	3	8	0	0	5	16	6	1.5	0.4	1.0	2.0
3-PT FG — English 2-3, Johnson 2-9, Issel 4-12, Thompson 7-19, Wilkerson 7-34, Roche 49-129, Scott 2-11, McGinnis 1-7, Garland 6-19, Gondrezick 2-6, Boswell 1-2, Ellis 0-3, Roberts 0-1																								
CHICAGO BULLS	30-52 .366				JERRY SLOAN																			
Scott May (BW)	F	6'7	220	25	54	1298	264	587	45	144	172	84	218	104	126	2	45	5	672	24	4.0	1.9	2.3	12.4
Dave Greenwood	F	6'9	222	22	82	2791	498	1051	47	337	416	81	773	182	313	8	60	129	1334	34	9.4	2.2	3.8	16.3
Artis Gilmore (KJ)	C	7'2	240	30	48	1568	305	513	59	245	344	71	432	133	167	5	29	59	855	33	9.0	2.8	3.5	17.8
Reggie Theus	G	6'7	190	22	82	3029	566	1172	48	500	597	84	329	515	262	4	114	20	1660	37	4.0	6.3	3.2	20.2
Rickey Sobers	G	6'3	198	26	82	2673	470	1002	47	200	239	84	242	426	294	4	136	17	1161	33	3.0	5.2	3.6	14.2
Coby Dietrick	C-F	6'10	225	31	79	1830	227	500	45	90	118	76	363	216	230	2	89	51	545	23	4.6	2.7	2.9	6.9
Ollie Johnson	F	6'6	200	30	79	1535	262	527	50	82	93	88	163	161	165	0	59	24	607	19	2.1	2.0	2.1	7.7
Dwight Jones (from Hou)	C-F	6'10	210	27	53	1170	207	387	53	119	165	72	296	90	159	0	24	37	533	22	5.6	1.7	3.0	10.1
Mark Landsberger (to LA)	F	6'8	230	24	54	1136	183	346	53	87	166	52	450	32	113	1	23	17	453	21	8.3	0.6	2.1	8.4
Del Beshore	G	5'11	165	23	68	869	88	250	35	58	87	67	63	139	105	0	58	5	244	13	0.9	2.0	1.5	3.6
Dennis Awtrey (KJ)	C	6'10	240	31	26	560	27	60	45	32	50	64	115	40	66	0	12	15	86	22	4.4	1.5	2.5	3.3
Ollie Mack (from LA)	G	6'3	195	22	23	526	77	149	52	29	33	88	49	33	34	0	20	3	183	23	2.1	1.4	1.5	8.0
Sam Smith	G	6'4	200	24	30	496	97	230	42	57	63	90	54	42	54	0	25	7	259	17	1.8	1.4	1.8	8.6
John Mengelt (XJ, cyst)	G	6'2	195	30	36	387	80	166	48	39	49	80	23	38	54	0	10	0	219	11	0.6	1.1	1.5	6.1
Roger Brown	C	6'11	225	29	4	37	1	3	33	0	0	—	10	1	4	0	0	3	2	9	2.5	0.3	1.0	0.5
3-PT FG — May 0-4, Greenwood 1-7, Theus 28-105, Sobers 21-68, Dietrick 1-9, Johnson 1-11, Beshore 10-26, Mack 0-4, Smith 8-35, Mengelt 0-6																								
UTAH JAZZ	24-58 .293				TOM NISSALKE																			
Adrian Dantley	F	6'5	210	23	68	2674	730	1267	58	443	526	84	516	191	211	2	96	14	1903	39	7.6	2.8	3.1	28.0
Allan Bristow	F	6'7	210	28	82	2304	377	785	48	197	243	81	512	341	211	2	88	6	953	28	6.2	4.2	2.6	11.6
Ben Poquette	C-F	6'9	235	24	82	2349	296	566	52	139	167	83	560	131	283	8	45	162	731	29	6.8	1.6	3.5	8.9
Terry Furlow (from Atl)	G	6'4	195	25	55	1718	364	765	48	127	145	88	152	221	79	0	54	14	878	31	2.8	4.0	1.4	16.0
Ron Boone (from LA)	G	6'2	200	33	75	2286	391	875	45	169	189	89	216	302	219	3	92	3	970	30	2.9	4.0	2.9	12.9
Duck Williams	G	6'2	180	23	77	1794	232	519	45	42	60	70	106	183	166	0	100	11	506	23	1.4	2.4	2.2	6.6
James Hardy	C-F	6'8	220	23	76	1600	184	363	51	51	66	77	399	107	207	4	47	87	420	21	5.3	1.4	2.7	5.5
Tom Boswell (from Den)	F	6'9	225	26	61	1555	274	478	57	148	203	73	328	115	214	8	24	29	700	25	5.4	1.9	3.5	11.5
Paul Dawkins	F	6'5	190	22	57	776	141	300	47	33	48	69	125	77	112	0	33	9	316	14	2.2	1.4	2.0	5.5
Mack Calvin	G	6'	175	31	48	772	100	227	44	105	117	90	84	134	72	0	27	0	306	16	1.8	2.8	1.5	6.4
Pete Maravich (to Bos)	G	6'5	200	31	17	522	121	294	41	41	50	82	40	54	30	0	15	4	290	31	2.4	3.2	1.8	17.1
Bernard King (FJ, ST)	F	6'7	205	23	19	419	71	137	52	34	63	54	88	52	66	3	7	4	176	22	4.6	2.7	3.5	9.3
Jerome Whitehead (from SD)	C	6'10	220	23	32	328	31	69	45	5	17	29	97	18	65	3	7	11	67	10	3.0	0.6	2.0	2.1
John Gianelli	C	6'10	220	29	17	285	23	66	35	9	16	56	62	17	26	0	6	7	55	17	3.6	1.0	1.5	3.2
Brad Davis (from Ind)	G	6'3	180	24	13	225	33	56	59	10	12	83	15	45	21	0	10	1	76	17	1.2	3.5	1.6	5.8
Robert Smith (to NJ)	G	5'11	165	24	6	73	5	15	33	5	5	100	3	7	3	0	4	0	15	12	0.5	1.2	0.5	2.5
Greg Deane	G	6'4	190	22	7	48	2	11	18	5	7	71	6	6	3	0	0	0	11	7	0.9	0.9	0.4	1.6
Andre Wakefield	G	6'3	175	24	8	47	6	15	40	3	3	100	4	3	13	0	1	0	15	6	0.5	0.4	1.6	1.9
John Brown (to Atl)	F	6'7	220	28	4	24	0	7	0	4	4	100	9	4	4	0	0	0	4	6	2.3	1.0	1.0	1.0
Carl Kilpatrick	C	6'10	230	23	2	6	1	2	50	1	2	50	4	0	1	0	0	0	3	3	2.0	0.0	0.5	1.5
3-PT FG — Dantley 0-2, Bristow 2-7, Poquette 0-2, Furlow 23-73, Boone 19-50, Williams 0-12, Hardy 1-2, Boswell 4-8, Dawkins 1-5, Calvin 1-11, Maravich 7-11, Davis 0-1, Deane 1-1																								

1979/80 N.B.A. — WESTERN CONFERENCE
PACIFIC DIVISION

Use Name	Pos	Hgt	Wgt	Age	G	Min	FG	FGA	%	FT	FTA	%	Reb	Ass	PF	DQ	Stls	Blkd Shts	Points	Min	Reb	Ass	PF	Points
					TOTAL															PER GAME				
LOS ANGELES LAKERS	60-22 .732				JACK MCKINNEY 9-4 (.692), PAUL WHITHEAD 51-18(.739)																			
Jamaal Wilkes	F	6'6	190	26	82	3111	726	1358	53	189	234	81	525	250	220	1	129	28	1644	38	6.4	3.0	2.7	20.0
Jim Chones	F-C	6'11	220	30	82	2394	372	760	49	125	169	74	564	151	271	5	56	65	869	29	6.9	1.8	3.3	10.6
Kareem Abdul-Jabbar	C	7'2	232	32	82	3143	835	1383	60	364	476	76	886	371	216	2	81	280	2034	38	10.8	4.5	2.6	24.8
Magic Johnson	G-F	6'9	215	20	77	2795	503	949	53	374	462	81	596	563	218	1	187	41	1387	36	7.7	7.3	2.8	18.0
Norm Nixon	G	6'2	175	24	82	3226	624	1209	52	197	253	78	229	642	241	1	147	14	1446	39	2.8	7.8	2.9	17.6
Michael Cooper	G-F	6'5	170	23	82	1973	303	578	52	111	143	78	229	221	215	3	86	38	722	24	2.8	2.7	2.6	8.8
Spencer Hayward	F	6'9	225	30	76	1544	208	591	35	159	206	77	346	93	197	2	35	57	736	20	4.6	1.2	2.6	9.7
Don Ford (to Cle)	F	6'9	215	27	52	580	66	130	51	23	28	82	98	36	86	0	11	15	155	11	1.9	0.7	1.7	3.0
Mark Landsberger (from Chi)	F	6'8	230	24	23	374	66	137	48	29	56	52	163	14	27	0	10	5	161	16	7.1	0.6	1.2	7.0
Brad Holland	G	6'3	185	23	38	197	44	104	42	15	16	94	17	22	24	0	15	1	106	5	0.4	0.6	0.6	2.8
Marty Byrnes	F	6'7	215	23	32	194	25	50	50	13	15	87	27	13	32	0	5	1	63	6	0.8	0.4	1.0	2.0
Ollie Mack (to Chi)	G	6'3	195	22	27	155	21	50	42	9	18	50	22	20	16	0	4	0	51	6	0.8	0.7	0.6	1.9
Ron Boone (to Utah)	G	6'2	200	33	6	106	14	40	35	6	7	86	11	7	13	0	5	0	34	18	1.8	1.2	2.2	5.7
Kenny Carr (to Cle)	F	6'7	230	24	5	57	7	16	44	2	2	100	17	1	6	0	2	1	16	11	3.4	0.2	1.2	3.2
Butch Lee (from Cle)	G	6'	185	23	11	31	4	13	31	6	7	86	8	9	2	0	1	0	14	3	0.7	0.8	0.2	1.3

3-PT FG — Wilkes 3-17, Chones 0-2, Abdul-Jabbar 0-1, Johnson 7-31, Nixon 1-8, Cooper 5-20, Hayward 1-4, Ford 0-1, Holland 3-15, Mack 0-1

Use Name	Pos	Hgt	Wgt	Age	G	Min	FG	FGA	%	FT	FTA	%	Reb	Ass	PF	DQ	Stls	Blkd Shts	Points	Min	Reb	Ass	PF	Points
SEATTLE SUPERSONICS	56 -26 .683				LENNY WILKENS																			
John Johnson	F	6'7	200	32	81	2533	377	772	49	161	201	80	426	424	213	1	76	35	915	31	5.3	5.2	2.6	11.3
Lonnie Shelton	F-C	6'8	245	24	76	2243	425	802	53	184	241	76	582	145	292	11	92	79	1035	30	7.7	1.9	3.8	13.6
Jack Sikma	C-F	6'11	230	24	82	2793	470	989	48	235	292	80	908	279	232	5	68	77	1175	34	11.1	3.4	2.8	14.3
Dennis Johnson	G	6'4	185	25	81	2937	574	1361	42	380	487	78	414	332	267	6	144	82	1540	36	5.1	4.1	3.3	19.0
Gus Willaims	G	6'2	175	26	82	2969	739	1533	48	331	420	79	275	397	160	1	200	37	1816	36	3.4	4.8	2.0	22.1
Fred Brown	G	6'3	185	31	80	1701	404	843	48	113	135	84	155	174	117	0	65	17	960	21	1.9	2.2	1.5	12.0
Paul Silas	F	6'7	220	36	82	1595	113	299	38	89	136	65	436	66	120	0	25	5	315	19	5.3	0.8	1.5	3.8
Tom LaGarde	C	6'10	220	24	82	1164	146	306	48	90	137	66	312	91	206	2	19	34	382	14	3.8	1.1	2.5	4.7
Wally Walker	F	6'7	190	25	70	844	139	274	51	48	64	75	170	53	102	0	21	4	326	12	2.4	0.8	1.5	4.7
James Bailey	F-C	6'9	220	22	67	726	122	271	45	68	101	67	197	28	116	1	21	64	312	11	2.9	0.4	1.7	4.7
Vinnie Johnson	G	6'2	200	23	38	325	45	115	39	31	39	79	55	54	40	0	19	4	121	9	1.4	1.4	1.1	3.2

3-PT FG — Shelton 1-5, Sikma 0-1, D.Johnson 12-58, Williams 7-36, Brown 39-88, V.Johnson 0-1

Use Name	Pos	Hgt	Wgt	Age	G	Min	FG	FGA	%	FT	FTA	%	Reb	Ass	PF	DQ	Stls	Blkd Shts	Points	Min	Reb	Ass	PF	Points
PHOENIX SUNS	55-27 .671				JOHN Mac CLEOD																			
Walter Davis	F	6'6	195	25	75	2309	657	1166	56	299	365	82	272	337	202	2	114	19	1613	31	3.6	4.5	2.7	21.5
Truck Robinson	F	6'7	225	28	82	2710	545	1064	51	325	487	67	770	142	262	2	58	59	1415	33	9.4	1.7	3.2	17.3
Alvan Adams	C	6'9	220	25	75	2168	468	875	53	188	236	80	609	322	237	4	108	55	1118	29	8.1	4.3	3.2	14.9
Paul Westphal	G	6'4	195	29	82	2565	692	1317	53	382	443	86	187	416	162	0	119	35	1792	31	2.3	5.1	2.0	21.9
Don Buse	G	6'4	195	29	81	2499	261	589	44	85	128	66	233	320	111	0	132	10	626	31	2.9	4.0	1.4	7.7
Mike Bratz	G	6'2	185	24	82	1589	269	687	39	141	162	87	167	223	165	0	93	9	700	19	2.0	2.7	2.0	8.5
Gar Heard	F	6'6	219	31	82	1403	171	410	42	64	86	74	380	97	177	0	84	49	406	17	4.6	1.2	2.2	5.0
Alvin Scott	F	6'7	185	24	79	1303	127	301	42	95	122	78	228	98	101	0	47	53	350	16	2.9	1.2	1.3	4.4
Johnny High	G	6'3	185	22	82	1121	144	323	45	120	178	67	173	119	172	1	71	15	409	14	2.1	1.5	2.1	5.0
Jeff Cook	C	6'10	215	23	66	904	129	275	47	104	129	81	241	84	102	0	28	18	362	14	3.7	1.3	1.5	5.5
Joel Kramer	C-F	6'7	203	24	54	711	67	143	47	56	70	80	151	75	104	0	26	5	190	13	2.8	1.4	1.9	3.5
Rich Kelley (fron NJ)	C	7'1	240	26	23	373	43	85	51	47	60	78	118	50	58	0	28	17	133	16	5.1	2.2	2.5	5.8

Bayard Forrest - back injury

3-PT FG — Davis 0-4, Adams 0-2, Westphal 26-93, Buse 19-79, Bratz 21-86, Heard 0-2, Scott 1-3, High 1-7, Kramer 0-1

Use Name	Pos	Hgt	Wgt	Age	G	Min	FG	FGA	%	FT	FTA	%	Reb	Ass	PF	DQ	Stls	Blkd Shts	Points	Min	Reb	Ass	PF	Points
PORTALAND TRAIL BLAZERS	38-44 .463				JACK RAMSAY																			
Calvin Natt (from NJ)	F	6'6	220	22	25	811	201	419	48	107	139	77	178	57	57	0	24	12	511	32	7.1	2.3	2.3	20.4
Kermit Washington	F	6'8	230	28	80	2657	421	761	55	231	360	64	842	167	307	8	73	131	1073	33	10.5	2.1	3.8	13.4
Tom Owens	C	6'10	220	30	76	2337	518	1008	51	213	283	75	573	194	270	5	45	53	1250	31	7.5	2.6	3.6	16.4
Ron Brewer	G	6'4	180	24	82	2815	548	1182	46	184	219	84	214	216	154	0	98	48	1286	34	2.6	2.6	1.9	15.7
Dave Twardzik	G	6'1	180	29	67	1594	183	394	46	197	252	78	156	273	149	2	77	1	567	24	2.3	4.1	2.2	8.5
T.R. Dunn	G	6'4	192	24	82	1841	240	551	44	84	111	76	324	147	145	1	102	31	564	22	4.0	1.8	1.8	6.9
Bob Gross	F	6'6	200	26	62	1581	221	472	47	95	114	83	249	228	179	3	60	47	538	26	4.0	3.7	2.9	8.7
Abdul Jeelani	F-C	6'8	210	25	77	1286	288	565	51	161	204	79	270	95	155	0	40	40	737	17	3.5	1.2	2.0	9.6
Jim Paxson	G-F	6'6	200	22	72	1270	189	460	41	64	90	71	109	144	97	0	48	5	443	18	1.5	2.0	1.3	6.2
Maurice Lucas (to NJ)	F-C	6'9	218	27	41	1176	243	552	44	100	137	73	325	125	141	1	23	35	588	29	7.9	3.0	3.4	14.3
Jim Brewer	F	6'9	220	28	67	1016	90	184	49	14	29	48	257	75	129	2	42	43	194	15	3.8	1.1	1.9	2.9
Larry Steele (KJ)	F-G	6'5	180	30	16	446	62	146	42	22	27	81	45	67	53	0	25	1	146	28	2.8	4.2	3.3	9.1
Lionel Hollins (KJ,to Phi)	G	6'3	185	26	20	413	82	213	38	34	53	64	20	50	35	0	30	1	199	21	1.0	2.5	1.8	10.0
Kevin Kunnert (KJ)	C	7'1	231	28	18	302	50	114	44	26	43	60	112	29	59	1	7	22	126	17	6.2	1.6	3.3	7.0
Billy Ray Bates	G	6'4	210	23	16	235	72	146	49	28	39	72	29	31	26	0	14	2	180	15	1.8	1.9	1.6	11.3

Mychal Thompson - broken leg

3-PT FG — Natt 2-4, Washington 0-3, Owens 1-2, R.Brewer 6-32, Twardzik 4-7, Dunn 0-3, Gross 1-10, Jeelani 0-6, Paxson 1-22, Lucas 2-5, J.Brewer 0-5, Steele 0-4, Hollins 1-10, Bates 8-19

1979/80 N.B.A. — WESTERN CONFERENCE
PACIFIC DIVISION (continued)

SAN DIEGO CLIPPERS 35-47 .427 **GENE SHUE**

Use Name	Pos	Hgt	Wgt	Age	G	Min	FG	FGA	%	FT	FTA	%	Reb	Ass	PF	DQ	Stls	Blkd Shts	Points	Min	Reb	Ass	PF	Points
Bingo Smith (from Cle)	F	6'5	212	33	70	1988	352	819	43	93	107	87	245	93	188	4	59	15	819	28	3.5	1.3	2.7	11.7
Sidney Wicks	F	6'9	225	30	71	2146	219	496	44	83	152	55	409	213	241	5	76	52	503	30	5.8	3.0	3.4	7.1
Sven Nater	C	6'11	240	29	81	2860	443	799	55	196	273	72	**1216**	233	259	3	45	37	1082	35	**15.0**	2.9	3.2	13.4
Lloyd Free	G	6'2	185	26	68	2585	737	1556	47	**572**	760	75	235	283	195	0	81	32	2055	38	3.5	4.2	2.9	30.2
Brian Taylor	G	6'2	185	28	78	2754	418	895	47	130	162	80	188	335	246	6	147	25	1056	35	2.4	4.3	3.2	13.5
Joe Bryant	F	6'9	185	25	81	2328	294	682	43	161	217	74	516	144	258	4	102	39	754	29	6.4	1.8	3.2	9.3
Freeman Williams	G	6'4	195	23	82	2118	645	1343	48	194	238	82	192	166	145	0	72	9	1526	26	2.3	2.0	1.8	18.6
Nick Weatherspoon	F	6'7	197	29	57	1124	164	378	43	63	91	69	208	54	136	1	34	17	391	20	3.6	0.9	2.4	6.9
Stan Pietkiewick	G-F	6'5	200	23	50	577	91	179	51	37	46	80	45	94	52	1	25	4	228	12	0.9	1.9	1.0	4.6
Bill Walton (FJ)	C	6'11	225	27	14	337	81	161	50	32	54	59	126	34	37	0	8	38	194	24	9.0	2.4	2.6	13.9
Marvin Barnes	F	6'9	225	27	20	287	24	60	40	16	32	50	77	18	52	0	5	12	64	14	3.9	0.9	2.6	3.2
Steve Malovie (from Was to Det)	F	6'10	230	23	28	277	23	42	55	7	9	78	58	12	35	0	5	1	53	10	2.1	0.4	1.3	1.9
Jerome Whitehead (to Utah)	C	6'10	220	23	18	225	27	45	60	5	18	28	70	6	32	0	1	6	59	13	3.9	0.3	1.8	3.3
Bob Carrington	F-G	6'6	195	26	10	134	15	37	41	6	8	75	13	3	18	0	4	1	36	13	1.3	0.3	1.8	3.6
John Olive (XJ)	F	6'7	210	24	1	15	0	2	0	0	0	—	1	0	2	0	0	0	0	15	1.0	0.0	2.0	0.0

3-PT FG — Smith 22-76, Wicks 0-1, Nater 0-2, Free 9-25, Taylor 90-239, Bryant 5-34, Willaims 42-128, Pietkiewicz 9-36, Carrington 0-2

GOLDEN STATE WARRIORS 24-58 .293 **AL ATTLES**

Use Name	Pos	Hgt	Wgt	Age	G	Min	FG	FGA	%	FT	FTA	%	Reb	Ass	PF	DQ	Stls	Blkd Shts	Points	Min	Reb	Ass	PF	Points
Sonny Parker	F-G	6'6	200	24	82	2849	483	988	49	237	302	78	464	254	195	2	173	32	1203	35	5.7	3.1	2.4	14.7
Purvis Short (SJ)	F	6'7	210	22	62	1636	461	916	50	134	165	81	316	123	186	4	63	9	1056	26	5.1	2.0	3.0	17.0
Robert Parish	C	7'	230	26	72	2119	510	1006	51	203	284	71	783	122	248	6	58	115	1223	29	10.9	1.7	3.4	17.0
Phil Smith (LJ)	G	6'4	187	27	51	1552	325	685	47	135	171	79	146	187	154	1	62	15	792	30	2.9	3.7	3.0	15.5
John Lucas	G	6'3	175	26	80	2763	388	830	47	222	289	77	220	602	196	2	138	3	1010	35	2.8	7.5	2.5	12.6
Jo Jo White	G	6'3	190	33	78	2052	336	706	48	97	114	85	181	239	186	0	88	13	770	26	2.3	3.1	2.4	9.9
Wayne Cooper	F-C	6'10	220	23	79	1781	367	750	49	136	181	75	507	42	246	5	20	79	871	23	6.4	0.5	3.1	11.0
Clifford Ray	C	6'9	235	30	81	1683	203	383	53	84	149	56	466	183	266	6	51	32	490	21	5.8	2.3	3.3	6.0
Tom Abernathy (NJ)	F	6'7	220	25	67	1222	153	318	48	56	82	68	191	87	118	0	35	12	362	18	2.9	1.3	1.8	5.4
Raymond Townsend	G	6'3	175	24	75	1159	171	421	41	60	84	71	89	116	113	0	60	4	406	15	1.2	1.5	1.5	5.4
Darnell Hillman	F	6'9	215	30	49	708	82	179	46	34	68	50	180	47	128	2	21	24	198	14	3.7	1.0	2.6	4.0
John Coughran	F	6'8	230	28	24	160	29	81	36	8	14	57	19	12	24	0	7	1	68	7	0.8	0.5	1.0	2.8
Bubba Wilson	G	6'3	175	24	16	143	7	25	28	3	6	50	16	12	11	0	2	0	17	9	1.0	0.8	0.7	1.1
Cheese Johnson	F-G	6'6	195	22	9	53	12	30	40	3	5	60	14	2	11	0	1	0	27	6	1.6	0.2	1.2	3.0

3-PT FG — Parker 0-2, Short 0-6, Parish 0-1, Smith 7-22, Lucas 12-42, White 1-6, Cooper 1-4, Ray 0-2, Abernathy 0-1, Townsend 4-26, Coughran 2-9

PLAYOFFS

LOS ANGELES LAKERS **PAUL WHITEHEAD**

defeated Phoenix 4-1; H119-110, H131-128, 108-105, 101-127, H126-101
defeated Seattle 4-1; H107-108, H108-99, 104-100, 98-93, H111-105
defeated Philadelphia 4-2; H109-102, H104-107, 111-101, 102-105, H108-103, 123-107

Use Name	Pos	Hgt	Wgt	Age	G	Min	FG	FGA	%	FT	FTA	%	Reb	Ass	PF	DQ	Stls	Blkd Shts	Points	Min	Reb	Ass	PF	Points
Michael Cooper	F-G	6'5	170	23	16	464	57	140	41	31	36	86	59	58	54	0	24	11	145	29	3.7	3.6	3.4	9.1
Jamaal Wilkes	F	6'6	190	26	16	652	140	294	48	44	54	81	128	48	51	0	24	5	324	41	8.0	3.0	3.2	20.3
Kareem Abdul-Jabbar	C	7'2	232	32	15	618	**198**	**346**	57	83	105	79	181	46	51	0	17	**58**	**479**	41	12.1	3.1	3.4	**31.9**
Magic Johnson	G-F-C	6'8	215	20	16	658	103	199	52	85	106	80	168	**151**	47	1	**49**	6	293	41	10.5	**9.4**	2.9	18.3
Norm Nixon	G	6'2	175	24	16	648	114	239	48	41	51	80	56	125	59	0	32	3	270	41	3.5	7.8	3.7	16.9
Jim Chones	F-C	6'11	220	30	16	439	48	118	41	23	34	68	104	28	60	0	8	6	119	27	6.5	1.8	3.8	7.4
Mark Landsberger	F	6'8	230	24	16	195	25	69	36	5	6	83	69	2	35	0	3	2	55	12	4.3	0.1	2.2	3.4
Spencer Haywood	F	6'9	225	30	11	145	25	53	47	13	16	81	26	4	17	0	0	6	63	13	2.4	0.4	1.5	5.7
Brad Holland	G	6'3	185	23	9	32	5	10	50	4	4	100	5	3	8	0	5	0	14	4	0.6	0.3	0.9	1.6
Marty Byrnes	F	6'7	215	23	4	8	1	3	33	4	6	67	1	1	0	0	0	0	6	2	0.3	0.3	0.0	1.5
Butch Lee	G	6'	185	23	3	6	0	0	—	2	2	100	1	0	2	0	0	0	2	2	0.3	0.0	0.7	0.7

3-PT FG — Cooper 0-2, Wilkes 0-1, Johnson 2-8, Nixon 1-5, Landsberger 0-1, Haywood 0-1

PHILADELPHIA 76ers **BILLY CUNNINGHAM**

defeated Washington 2-0; H 111-96, 112-104
defeated Atlanta 4-1; H107-104, H99-92, 93-105, 107-83, H105-100
defeated Boston 4-1; 96-93, 90-96, H99-97, H102-90, 105-94
lost to Los Angeles 2-4; 102-109, 107-104, H101-111, H105-102, 103-108, H107-123

Use Name	Pos	Hgt	Wgt	Age	G	Min	FG	FGA	%	FT	FTA	%	Reb	Ass	PF	DQ	Stls	Blkd Shts	Points	Min	Reb	Ass	PF	Points
Julius Erving	F	6'7	200	29	18	**694**	165	338	49	**108**	**136**	79	136	79	56	0	36	37	440	39	7.6	4.4	3.1	24.4
Bobby Jones	F	6'9	212	28	18	470	90	172	52	53	62	85	86	31	56	1	21	32	233	26	4.8	1.7	3.1	12.9
Darryl Dawkins	C	6'11	251	22	18	607	126	238	53	60	93	65	137	33	**75**	2	13	42	312	34	7.6	1.8	**4.2**	17.3
Lionel Hollins	G	6'3	185	26	18	618	97	233	42	54	68	79	71	113	49	0	27	3	248	34	3.9	6.3	2.7	13.8
Maurice Cheeks	G	6'1	180	23	18	675	89	174	51	29	41	71	74	111	43	0	45	4	208	38	4.1	6.2	2.4	11.6
Caldwell Jones	F-C	6'11	225	29	18	639	58	129	45	42	52	81	**185**	34	**75**	1	13	37	158	36	10.3	1.9	4.2	8.8
Henry Bibby	G	6'1	185	30	18	400	45	124	36	40	50	80	44	52	35	0	7	0	135	22	2.4	2.9	1.9	7.5
Steve Mix	F	6'7	222	32	17	200	44	96	46	25	28	89	31	13	22	0	8	5	113	12	1.8	0.8	1.3	6.6
Jim Spanarkel	G	6'5	190	22	5	8	0	2	0	2	2	100	1	1	1	0	0	0	2	2	0.2	0.2	0.2	0.4
Bernard Toone	F	6'9	210	23	4	6	0	4	0	0	0	—	1	1	1	0	0	0	0	2	0.3	0.3	0.3	0.0
Clint Richardson	G	6'3	195	23	3	3	1	3	33	0	0	—	0	0	0	0	1	0	2	1	0.0	0.0	0.0	0.7

Doug Collins - knee injury

3-PT FG — Erving 2-9, B.Jones 0-1, Dawkins 0-3, Hollins 0-10, Cheeks 1-5, C.Jones 0-3, Bibby 5-13, Toone 0-1, Richardson 0-2

1979/80 N.B.A. — PLAYOFFS (continued)

SEATTLE SUPERSONICS — **LENNY WILKINS**

defeated Portland 2-1; H120-110, 95-105, H103-86
defeated Milwaukee 4-3; H114-113, H112-114, 91-95, 112-107, H97-108, 86-85, H98-94
lost to Los Angeles 1-4; 108-107, 99-108, H100-104, H93-98, 105-111

Use Name	Pos	Hgt	Wgt	Age	G	Min	FG	FGA	%	FT	FTA	%	Reb	Ass	PF	DQ	Stls	Blkd Shts	Points	Min	Reb	Ass	PF	Points
					TOTAL															PER GAME				
John Johnson	F	6'7	200	32	15	486	78	158	49	30	37	81	102	85	45	0	8	3	186	32	6.8	5.7	3.0	12.4
Lonnie Shelton	F	6'8	245	24	15	469	74	146	51	32	51	63	125	25	54	0	23	12	180	31	8.3	1.7	3.6	12.0
Jack Sikma	C	6'11	230	24	15	534	65	163	40	46	54	85	126	55	55	1	17	5	176	36	8.4	3.7	3.7	11.7
Dennis Johnson	G	6'4	185	25	15	582	100	244	41	52	62	84	64	57	48	2	27	10	257	39	4.3	3.8	3.2	17.1
Gus Williams	G	6'2	175	26	15	564	146	284	51	62	86	72	60	84	38	0	34	7	355	38	4.0	5.6	2.5	23.7
Fred Brown	G	6'3	185	31	15	313	80	182	44	18	21	86	38	32	23	0	2	1	188	21	2.5	2.1	1.5	12.5
Paul Silas	F	6'7	220	36	15	257	13	43	30	11	15	73	75	15	29	0	9	2	37	17	5.0	1.0	1.9	2.5
Tom LaGarde	C-F	6'10	220	24	14	163	17	46	37	9	11	82	40	12	25	0	2	0	43	12	2.9	0.9	1.8	3.1
Wally Walker	F	6'7	190	25	13	157	18	35	51	18	24	75	29	7	20	0	1	3	54	12	2.2	0.5	1.5	4.2
James Bailey	C-F	6'9	220	22	12	138	21	44	48	13	20	65	25	5	22	0	9	9	55	12	2.1	0.4	1.8	4.6
Vinnie Johnson	G	6'2	200	23	5	12	1	3	33	0	0	—	2	2	1	0	1	0	2	2	0.4	0.4	0.2	0.4

3-PT FG — J.Johnson 0-1, Shelton 0-1, Sikma 0-2 D.Johnson 5-15, Williams 1-5, Brown 10-34

BOSTON CELTICS — **BILL FITCH**

defeated Houston 4-0; H119-101, H95-75, 100-81,138-121
lost to Philadelphia 1-4; H93-96, H96-90, 97-99, 90-102, H94-105

Use Name	Pos	Hgt	Wgt	Age	G	Min	FG	FGA	%	FT	FTA	%	Reb	Ass	PF	DQ	Stls	Blkd Shts	Points	Min	Reb	Ass	PF	Points
Cedric Maxwell	F	6'8	205	24	9	320	59	93	63	46	61	75	90	19	25	0	5	10	164	36	10.0	2.1	2.8	18.2
Larry Bird	F	6'10	220	23	9	372	83	177	47	22	25	88	101	42	30	0	14	8	192	41	11.2	4.7	3.3	21.3
Dave Cowens	C	6'9	230	31	9	301	49	103	48	10	11	91	66	21	37	0	9	7	108	33	7.3	2.3	4.1	12.0
Chris Ford	G	6'5	190	30	9	279	34	79	43	12	15	80	25	21	35	1	14	6	82	31	2.8	2.3	3.9	9.1
Nate Archibald	G	6'1	150	31	9	332	45	89	51	37	42	88	11	71	28	1	10	0	128	37	1.2	7.9	3.1	14.2
M.L. Carr	F-G	6'6	205	28	9	172	32	80	40	16	24	67	33	11	20	0	6	1	82	19	3.7	1.2	2.2	9.1
Rick Robey	C-F	6'11	230	23	9	151	24	53	45	7	14	50	32	10	27	0	7	3	55	17	3.6	1.1	3.0	6.1
Pete Maravich	G	6'5	200	31	9	104	24	51	47	2	3	67	8	6	12	0	3	0	54	12	0.9	0.7	1.3	6.0
Gerald Henderson	G	6'2	175	23	9	101	15	37	41	12	20	60	10	12	8	0	4	0	42	11	1.1	1.3	0.9	4.7
Eric Fernsten	F	6'10	205	26	5	18	2	6	33	2	3	67	5	0	1	0	0	3	6	4	1.0	0.0	0.2	1.2
Jeff Judkins	G	6'6	185	23	7	10	4	8	50	0	0	—	4	0	0	0	1	0	9	1	0.6	0.0	0.0	1.3

3-PT FG — Bird 4-15, Cowens 0-2, Ford 2-13, Archibald 1-2, Carr 2-5, Robey 0-1 Maravich 2-6, Henderson 0-2, Judkins

PHOENIX SUNS — **JOHN MACLEOD**

defeated Kansas City 2-1; H96-93, 96-106, H114-99
lost to Los Angeles 4-1; 110-119, 128-131, H105-108,H127-101, 101-126

Use Name	Pos	Hgt	Wgt	Age	G	Min	FG	FGA	%	FT	FTA	%	Reb	Ass	PF	DQ	Stls	Blkd Shts	Points	Min	Reb	Ass	PF	Points
Walter Davis	F	6'6	195	25	8	245	69	137	50	28	38	74	23	35	20	0	4	1	166	31	2.9	4.4	2.5	20.8
Gar Heard	F	6'6	219	31	8	223	22	56	39	11	15	73	51	12	23	0	9	11	55	28	6.4	1.5	2.9	6.9
Alvan Adams	C-F	6'9	220	25	8	251	56	99	57	17	19	89	77	46	24	1	7	10	129	31	9.6	5.8	3.0	16.1
Paul Westphal	G	6'4	195	29	8	253	69	142	49	28	32	88	10	31	20	0	11	3	167	32	1.3	3.9	2.5	20.9
Don Buse	G	6'4	195	29	8	236	28	64	44	7	11	64	21	44	15	0	6	0	68	30	2.6	5.5	1.9	8.5
Mike Bratz	G	6'2	185	24	8	169	43	84	51	9	10	90	20	16	20	0	9	0	104	21	2.5	2.0	2.5	13.0
Rich Kelley	C	7'	240	26	8	146	19	44	43	9	10	90	36	22	17	0	9	7	47	18	4.5	2.8	2.1	5.9
Alvin Scott	F	6'1	185	24	8	140	17	33	52	4	8	50	22	10	8	0	4	5	38	18	2.8	1.3	1.0	4.8
Johnny High	G	6'3	185	22	8	120	12	31	39	8	16	50	25	20	20	0	6	2	32	15	3.1	2.5	2.5	4.0
Jeff Cook	F-C	6'10	215	23	7	98	16	24	67	22	26	85	21	7	10	0	4	2	54	14	3.0	1.0	1.4	7.7
Truck Robinson	F	6'7	225	28	3	64	6	16	38	5	7	71	20	4	6	0	3	2	17	21	6.7	1.3	2.0	5.7

Bayard Forrest - back injury

3-PT FG — Davis 0-3, Westphal 1-12, Buse 5-13, Bratz 9-23, Kelley 0-1, Scott 0-2, High 0-2

HOUSTON ROCKETS — **DEL HARRIS**

defeated San Antonio 2-1; H95-85, 101-106, H141-120
lost to Boston 0-4; 101-119, 75-95, H81-100, H121-138

Use Name	Pos	Hgt	Wgt	Age	G	Min	FG	FGA	%	FT	FTA	%	Reb	Ass	PF	DQ	Stls	Blkd Shts	Points	Min	Reb	Ass	PF	Points
Robert Reid	F	6'8	205	24	7	266	52	102	51	22	26	85	55	26	28	0	6	7	126	38	7.9	3.7	4.0	18.0
Rudy Tomjanovich	F	6'8	220	31	7	185	24	64	38	9	13	69	40	10	21	1	2	0	58	26	5.7	1.4	3.0	8.3
Moses Malone	C	6'10	215	24	7	275	74	138	54	33	43	77	97	7	18	0	4	16	181	39	13.9	1.0	2.6	25.9
Tom Henderson	G	6'3	190	27	7	203	22	46	48	12	15	80	16	42	19	0	7	4	56	29	2.3	6.0	2.7	8.0
Calvin Murphy	G	5'9	165	31	7	265	58	108	54	13	13	100	10	26	29	1	11	0	131	38	1.4	3.7	4.1	18.7
Allen Leavell	G	6'1	170	22	7	149	10	38	26	19	21	90	12	24	12	0	6	0	39	21	1.7	3.4	1.7	5.6
Billy Paultz	F-C	6'11	250	31	7	128	13	40	33	4	7	57	33	8	13	0	1	3	30	18	4.7	1.1	1.9	4.3
Rick Barry	F	6'7	220	35	6	79	12	33	36	6	6	100	6	15	11	0	1	1	33	13	1.0	2.5	1.8	5.5
Major Jones	F	6'9	225	26	6	70	11	18	61	6	9	67	22	4	8	0	0	2	28	12	3.7	0.7	1.3	4.7
Mike Dunleavy	G	6'3	180	25	6	45	6	12	50	5	6	83	5	13	11	0	5	0	17	8	0.8	2.2	1.8	2.8
Alonzo Bradley	F	6'6	190	26	4	15	6	9	67	3	5	60	3	1	2	0	1	0	16	4	0.8	0.3	0.5	4.0

3-PT FG — Reid 0-1, Tomjanovich 1-7, Malone 0-1, Henderson 0-1, Murphy 2-4, Leavell 0-4, Barry 3-12, Dunleavy 0-2, Bradley 1-1

MILWAUKEE BUCKS — **DON NELSON**

lost to Seattle 4-3; 113-114, 114-112, H95-91, H107-112, 108-97, H85-86, 94-98

Use Name	Pos	Hgt	Wgt	Age	G	Min	FG	FGA	%	FT	FTA	%	Reb	Ass	PF	DQ	Stls	Blkd Shts	Points	Min	Reb	Ass	PF	Points
Marques Johnson	F	6'7	218	23	7	303	54	128	42	30	40	75	48	20	20	0	5	6	139	43	6.9	2.9	2.9	19.9
David Meyers	F	6'9	225	26	7	195	26	62	42	14	30	47	35	14	25	1	9	6	66	28	5.0	2.0	3.6	9.4
Bob Lanier	C	6'11	250	31	7	256	52	101	51	31	42	74	65	31	23	0	7	8	135	37	9.3	4.4	3.3	19.3
Brian Winters	G	6'4	185	27	7	268	46	100	46	10	10	100	21	37	25	1	11	0	111	38	3.0	5.3	3.6	15.9
Sidney Moncrief	G	6'4	190	22	7	182	30	51	59	27	31	87	31	11	14	0	5	1	87	26	4.4	1.6	2.0	12.4
Quinn Buckner	G	6'3	205	25	7	165	18	53	34	7	11	64	16	31	20	0	15	0	43	24	2.3	4.4	2.9	6.1
Junior Bridgeman	F-G	6'5	210	26	5	124	20	56	36	11	15	73	19	17	17	0	5	2	51	25	3.8	3.4	3.4	10.2
Richard Lee Washington	F	6'11	225	24	7	112	25	47	53	1	4	25	20	3	22	0	4	8	51	16	2.9	0.4	3.1	7.3
Harvey Catchings	C	6'9	218	28	6	64	2	6	33	2	4	50	21	2	13	0	8	6	6	11	3.5	0.3	2.2	1.0
Pat Cummings	F-C	6'9	235	23	6	57	11	17	65	5	6	83	16	2	9	0	1	0	27	10	2.7	0.3	1.5	4.5
Lloyd Walton	G	6'	160	26	1	4	0	1	0	0	0	—	1	1	0	0	0	0	0	4	1.0	1.0	0.0	0.0

3-PT FG — Johnson 1-3, Meyers 0-3, Winters 9-21, Buckner 0-1, Bridgeman 0-1

1979/80 N.B.A. — PLAYOFFS (continued)

Use Name	Pos	Hgt	Wgt	Age	G	Min	FG	FGA	%	FT	FTA	%	Reb	Ass	PF	DQ	Stls	Blkd Shts	Points	Min	Reb	Ass	PF	Points
					TOTAL															PER GAME				
ATLANTA HAWKS	**HUBIE BROWN**				lost to Philadelphia 1-4; 104-107, 92-99, H105-93, H83-107, 100-105																			
John Drew	F	6'6	205	25	5	150	24	63	38	25	35	71	30	4	21	1	7	0	73	30	6.0	0.8	4.2	14.6
Dan Roundfield	F	6'8	205	26	5	174	32	69	46	22	35	63	58	11	22	1	4	8	86	35	11.6	2.2	4.4	17.2
Tree Rollins	C	7'1	235	24	5	134	18	31	58	6	10	60	38	3	25	3	2	14	42	27	7.6	0.6	5.0	8.4
Eddie Johnson	G	6'2	190	24	5	188	38	74	51	21	28	75	18	21	12	0	8	2	97	38	3.6	4.2	2.4	19.4
Charlie Criss	G	5'8	165	30	5	152	29	59	49	11	12	92	5	22	12	0	6	0	70	30	1.0	4.4	2.4	14.0
Steve Hawes	C-F	6'9	220	29	5	149	18	41	44	16	18	89	35	12	22	1	9	1	52	30	7.0	2.4	4.4	10.4
Avmond Hill	G	6'4	190	26	5	109	12	30	40	11	12	92	6	15	14	0	4	1	35	22	1.2	3.0	2.8	7.0
John Brown	F	6'7	220	28	5	58	4	13	31	2	2	100	10	1	9	0	1	1	10	12	2.0	0.2	1.8	2.0
Jack Givens	F	6'5	205	23	4	36	3	14	21	0	0	—	5	3	7	0	2	0	6	9	1.3	0.8	1.8	1.5
Jim McElroy	G	6'3	190	26	5	32	4	9	44	4	5	80	2	4	1	0	0	0	12	6	0.4	0.8	0.2	2.4
Sam Pellom	C	6'9	225	28	4	18	0	3	0	1	3	33	0	1	3	0	0	1	1	5	0.0	0.3	0.8	0.3
Ron Lee - broken finger, Tom McMillen - knee injury																								
3-PT FG —	Roundfield 0-1, Criss 1-3, Hill 0-1, Brown 0-1, McElroy 0-1																							
KANSAS CITY KINGS	**COTTON FITZSIMMONS**				lost to Phoenix 1-2; 93-96, H106-96, 99-114																			
Scott Wedman	F	6'7	215	27	3	116	29	64	45	8	11	73	21	9	9	0	1	3	68	39	7.0	3.0	3.0	22.7
Reggie King	F	6'6	225	22	3	77	10	21	48	5	9	56	25	4	10	0	1	0	25	26	8.3	1.3	3.3	8.3
Sam Lacey	C	6'10	235	31	3	101	8	21	38	1	4	25	22	13	11	0	7	2	20	34	7.3	4.3	3.7	6.7
Otis Birdsong	G	6'4	195	24	3	112	30	62	48	6	14	43	23	7	5	0	4	0	66	37	7.7	2.3	1.7	22.0
Phil Ford	G	6'2	176	23	3	110	20	43	47	9	11	82	6	26	6	0	5	0	52	37	2.0	8.7	2.0	17.3
Bill Robinzine	F	6'7	230	26	3	69	13	24	54	7	10	70	18	0	6	0	3	0	33	23	6.0	0.0	2.0	11.0
Len Elmore	C	6'9	220	27	3	43	4	13	31	1	2	50	11	1	4	0	3	1	9	14	3.7	0.3	1.3	3.0
Billy McKinney	G	6'	162	24	3	34	2	5	40	0	0	—	3	8	2	0	0	0	4	11	1.0	2.7	0.7	1.3
Ernie Grunfield	G	6'6	215	24	3	32	5	9	56	1	3	33	1	0	3	0	1	0	11	11	0.3	0.0	1.0	3.7
Gus Gerard	F	6'8	205	26	3	26	4	10	40	2	4	50	8	2	2	0	0	0	10	9	2.7	0.7	0.7	3.3
Tom Burleson - broken toe, Mike Green - broken arm																								
3-PT FG —	Wedman 2-3, Lacey 1-1, Birdsong 0-3, Ford 3-4, McKinney 0-1																							
PORTLAND TRAIL BLAZERS	**JACK RAMSAY**				lost to Seattle 2-1; 110-120, H105-95, 86-103																			
Calvin Natt	F	6'6	220	22	3	125	21	48	44	6	10	60	24	2	7	0	2	1	48	42	8.0	0.7	2.3	16.0
Kermit Washington	F-C	6'8	230	28	3	121	13	26	50	5	8	63	31	6	9	0	1	4	31	40	10.3	2.0	3.0	10.3
Tom Owens	C	6'10	220	30	3	83	14	26	54	5	8	63	21	2	14	1	1	2	33	28	7.0	0.7	4.7	11.0
Ron Brewer	G	6'4	180	24	3	106	26	61	43	5	9	56	3	6	10	0	3	1	57	35	1.0	2.0	3.3	19.0
Billy Ray Bates	G	6'4	210	23	3	104	31	59	53	11	14	79	10	12	13	0	5	1	75	35	3.3	4.0	4.3	25.0
Jim Brewer	F-C	6'9	220	28	3	67	10	10	100	1	3	33	16	3	6	0	5	2	21	22	5.3	1.0	2.0	7.0
Bob Gross	F	6'6	200	26	3	51	3	9	33	6	6	100	4	4	8	0	1	0	12	17	1.3	1.3	2.7	4.0
Jim Paxson	G-F	6'6	200	22	3	44	5	16	31	6	6	100	4	3	2	0	2	1	16	15	1.3	1.0	0.7	5.3
T.R. Dunn	G	6'4	192	24	3	24	2	8	25	2	2	100	4	4	3	0	1	0	6	8	1.3	1.3	1.0	2.0
Dave Twardzik	G	6'1	180	29	2	20	1	4	25	0	0	—	4	2	2	0	2	0	2	10	2.0	1.0	1.0	1.0
Michael Thompson - broken leg, Kevin Kunnert - knee injury, Larry Steele- knee injury																								
3-PT FG —	Natt 0-2, Washington 0-1, R.Brewer 0-3, Bates 2-7																							
SAN ANTONIO SPURS	**BOB BASS**				lost to Houston 2-1; 85-95, H106-101, 120-141																			
Mark Olberding	F	6'8	230	23	3	97	13	23	57	3	4	75	22	11	14	1	2	1	29	32	7.3	3.7	4.7	9.7
Larry Kenon	F	6'9	215	27	3	81	10	34	29	6	11	55	13	4	6	0	0	0	26	27	4.3	1.3	2.0	8.7
John Shumate	C	6'9	235	27	3	78	9	20	45	3	3	100	13	5	9	0	4	4	21	26	4.3	1.7	3.0	7.0
George Gervin	G	6'7	185	27	3	122	37	74	50	26	30	87	20	12	8	0	5	3	100	41	6.7	4.0	2.7	33.3
James Silas	G	6'3	180	30	3	90	16	36	44	11	11	100	7	9	8	0	6	1	43	30	2.3	3.0	2.7	14.3
Kevin Restani	F-C	6'9	225	28	3	74	17	28	61	4	9	44	16	3	8	0	0	1	38	25	5.3	1.0	2.7	12.7
Mike Gale	G	6'4	190	29	3	69	8	20	40	4	7	57	6	16	6	0	5	0	21	23	2.0	5.3	2.0	7.0
Paul Griffin	C-F	6'9	205	25	3	69	7	14	50	6	6	100	15	6	9	0	0	1	20	23	5.0	2.0	3.0	6.7
Tim Bassett	F-C	6'8	225	28	3	19	1	2	50	0	0	—	1	0	7	0	0	0	2	6	0.3	0.0	2.3	0.7
Mike Evans	G	6'1	170	24	2	12	3	8	38	3	4	75	2	2	2	0	0	0	11	6	1.0	1.0	1.0	5.5
Wiley Peck	F	6'7	220	22	2	9	0	3	0	0	0	—	3	0	1	0	0	1	0	5	1.5	0.0	0.5	0.0
3-PT FG —	Gervin 0-2, Restani 0-1, Gale 1-4, Evans 2-4																							
WASHINGTON BULLETS	**DICK MOTTA**				lost to Philadelphia 2-0; 96-111, H104-112																			
Greg Ballard	F	6'7	215	24	2	73	9	28	32	4	7	57	14	7	8	0	1	1	22	37	7.0	3.5	4.0	11.0
Elvin Hayes	F	6'9	235	34	2	92	16	41	39	8	10	80	22	6	8	0	0	4	40	46	11.0	3.0	4.0	20.0
Wes Unseld	C	6'7	245	33	2	87	7	14	50	4	6	67	28	7	5	0	0	3	18	44	14.0	3.5	2.5	9.0
Kevin Grevey	G-F	6'5	210	26	2	72	16	30	53	4	4	100	6	8	9	1	5	2	41	36	3.0	4.0	4.5	20.5
Kevin Porter	G	6'	175	29	2	49	7	16	44	2	5	40	2	9	7	0	3	0	16	25	1.0	4.5	3.5	8.0
Larry Wright	G	6'1	160	25	2	33	9	17	53	4	5	80	2	6	6	0	3	0	22	17	1.0	3.0	3.0	11.0
John Williamson	G	6'2	195	27	2	31	11	19	58	3	3	100	2	1	7	0	0	0	27	16	1.0	0.5	3.5	13.5
Jim Cleamons	G	6'3	185	30	2	20	0	3	0	0	0	—	1	1	0	0	1	0	0	10	0.5	0.5	0.0	0.0
Ron Behagen	F	6'9	235	28	2	14	2	7	29	0	0	—	2	3	4	0	0	0	4	7	1.0	1.5	2.0	2.0
Dave Corzine	C	6'11	250	23	2	9	4	5	80	2	2	100	3	0	2	0	0	0	10	5	1.5	0.0	1.0	5.0
Bob Dandridge - knee injury, Mitch Kupchak - knee injury																								
3-PT FG —	Unseld 0-1, Grevey 5-10, Porter 0-1, Wright 0-1, Williamson 2-6																							

Team		G	FG	FGA	%	FT	FTA	%	REBOUNDS Offense	Defense	Total	Assists	PF	Steals	Blocked Shots	Turn Overs	Points	Points per game
									TEAM STATISTICS EASTERN CONFERENCE ATLANTIC DIVISION									
Boston	**Off.**	82	3617	7389	49	1907	2449	78	1227	2457	3684	2198	1974	809	308	1539	9303	113.5
	Def.	82	3439	7313	47	1712	2222	77	1168	2294	3462	1867	2059	686	419	1635	8664	105.7
	Diff.		+178	+76	+2	+195	+227	+1	+59	+163	+222	+331	+85	+123	-111	+96	**+639**	**+7.8**
Philadelphia	**Off.**	82	3523	7156	49	1876	2431	77	1187	2635	3822	2226	1860	792	**652**	1708	8949	109.1
	Def.	82	3444	7561	46	1640	2145	76	1318	2352	3670	2089	2100	876	388	1561	8603	104.9
	Diff.		+79	-405	+3	+236	+286	+1	-131	+283	+152	+137	**+240**	-84	**+264**	-147	+346	+4.2
Washington	**Off.**	82	3574	7796	46	1552	2048	76	1334	**2723**	**4057**	2201	1893	530	443	1380	8773	107.0
	Def.	82	3615	7771	47	1696	2184	78	1197	2672	3869	2120	1901	734	519	1222	8982	109.5
	Diff.		-41	+25	-1	-144	-136	-2	+137	+51	+188	+81	+8	-204	-76	-158	-209	-2.5
New York	**Off.**	82	3802	7672	50	1698	2274	75	1236	2303	3539	2265	2168	881	457	1613	9344	114.0
	Def.	82	3707	7492	49	1969	2556	77	1293	2432	3725	2143	2042	813	390	1694	9439	115.1
	Diff.		+95	+180	+1	-271	-282	-2	-57	-129	-186	+122	-126	+68	+67	+81	-95	-1.1
New Jersey	**Off.**	82	3456	7504	46	1882	2406	78	1229	2535	3764	2094	2181	869	581	1702	8879	108.3
	Def.	82	3480	7427	47	1957	2572	76	1285	2596	3881	2189	2042	849	514	1692	8975	109.5
	Diff.		-24	+77	-1	-75	-166	+2	-56	-61	-117	-95	-139	+20	+67	-10	-96	-1.2
									CENTRAL DIVISION									
Atlanta	**Off.**	82	3261	7027	46	**2038**	**2645**	77	1369	2406	3775	1913	2293	782	539	1495	8573	104.5
	Def	82	3144	6872	46	2000	2616	76	1261	2339	3600	1758	2171	682	554	1650	8334	**101.6**
	Diff.		+117	+155	—	+38	+29	+1	+108	+67	+175	+155	-122	+100	-15	+155	+239	+2.9
Houston	**Off.**	82	3599	7496	48	1782	2326	77	1394	2217	3611	2149	1927	782	373	1565	9084	110.8
	Def.	82	3658	7382	50	1696	2153	79	1290	2317	3607	2223	2049	778	428	1597	9070	110.6
	Diff.		-59	+114	-2	+86	+173	-2	+104	-100	+4	-74	+122	+4	-55	+32	+14	+.2
San Antonio	**Off.**	82	3856	7738	50	2024	2528	80	1153	2515	3668	2326	2103	771	333	1589	**9788**	**119.4**
	Def.	82	4000	7997	50	1731	2283	76	1248	2472	3720	2537	2192	828	457	1513	9819	119.7
	Diff.		-144	-259	—	+293	+245	**+4**	-95	+43	-52	-211	+89	-57	-124	-76	-31	-.3
Indiana	**Off.**	82	3639	7689	47	1753	2333	75	**1398**	2326	3724	2148	1973	900	530	1517	9119	111.2
	Def.	82	3693	7545	49	1734	2295	76	1394	2552	3946	2323	2028	738	470	1758	9176	111.9
	Diff.		-54	+144	-2	+19	+38	-1	+4	-226	-222	-175	+55	+162	+60	+241	-57	-.7
Cleveland	**Off.**	82	3811	**8041**	47	1702	2205	77	1307	2381	3688	2108	1934	764	342	**1370**	9360	114.1
	Def.	82	3811	7610	50	1645	2150	77	1230	2638	3868	2208	2033	708	490	1667	9332	113.8
	Diff.		—	+431	-3	+57	+55	—	+77	-257	-180	-100	+99	+56	-148	+297	+28	+.3
Detroit	**Off.**	82	3643	7596	48	1590	2149	74	1226	2415	3641	1950	2069	783	562	1742	8933	108.9
	Def.	82	3847	7761	50	1858	2405	77	1319	2572	3891	2306	1871	874	470	1583	9609	117.2
	Diff.		-204	-165	-2	-268	-256	-3	-93	-157	-250	-356	-198	-91	+92	-159	-676	-8.3
									WESTERN CONFERENCE MIDWEST DIVISION									
Milwaukee	**Off.**	82	3685	7553	49	1605	2102	76	1245	2396	3641	2277	1937	778	510	1496	9025	110.1
	Def.	82	3456	7487	46	1714	2275	75	1360	2293	3653	2154	1912	717	358	1638	8702	106.1
	Diff.		+229	+66	+3	-109	-173	+1	-115	+103	-12	+123	-25	+61	+152	+142	+323	+4.0
Kansas City	**Off.**	82	3582	7849	46	1671	2250	74	1187	2429	3616	2123	2135	863	356	1439	8860	108.0
	Def.	82	3328	6992	48	1906	2497	76	1140	2644	3784	1778	2072	695	425	**1762**	8603	104.9
	Diff.		**+254**	**+857**	-2	-235	-247	-2	+47	-215	-168	**+345**	-63	**+168**	-69	**+323**	+257	+3.1
Denver	**Off.**	82	3462	7470	46	1871	2539	74	1311	2524	3835	2079	1917	746	404	1533	8878	108.3
	Def.	82	3736	7591	49	1698	2235	76	1197	2587	3784	2289	2033	812	455	1438	9240	112.7
	Diff.		-274	-121	-3	+173	+304	-2	+114	-63	+51	-210	+116	-66	-51	-95	-362	-4.4
Chicago	**Off.**	82	3362	6943	48	2019	2572	78	1115	2465	3580	2152	2146	704	392	1684	8813	107.5
	Def.	82	3585	7222	50	1811	2358	77	1159	2345	3504	2109	**2203**	846	498	1543	9035	110.2
	Diff.		-223	-279	-2	+208	+214	+1	-44	+120	+76	+43	+57	-142	-106	-141	-222	-2.7
Utah	**Off.**	82	3382	6817	50	1571	1943	**81**	967	2359	3326	2005	2006	656	362	1543	8394	102.4
	Def.	82	3559	7182	50	1702	2205	77	1159	2288	3447	1997	1782	710	398	1274	8887	108.4
	Diff.		-177	-365	—	-131	-262	**+4**	-192	+71	-121	+8	-224	-54	-36	-269	-493	-6.0

Team		G	FG	FGA	%	FT	FTA	%	Rebounds Offense	Rebounds Defense	Rebounds Total	Assists	PF	Steals	Blocked Shots	Turn Overs	Points	Points per game
TEAM STATISTICS WESTERN CONFERENCE (continued) PACIFIC DIVISION																		
Los Angeles	Off.	82	**3898**	7368	**53**	1622	2092	78	1085	2653	3738	**2413**	**1784**	774	546	1639	9438	115.1
	Def.	82	3723	7921	47	1430	1884	76	1312	2242	3554	2324	1860	797	382	1420	8954	109.2
	Diff.		+175	-553	**+6**	+192	+208	+2	-227	**+411**	+184	+89	+76	-23	+164	-219	+484	**+5.9**
Seattle	Off.	82	3554	7565	47	1730	2253	77	1380	2550	3930	2043	1865	750	428	1496	8897	108.5
	Def.	82	3408	7424	46	1640	2147	76	1203	2409	3612	2016	1997	728	393	1519	8515	103.8
	Diff.		+146	+141	+1	+90	+106	+1	**+177**	+141	**+318**	+27	+132	+22	+35	+23	+382	+4.7
Phoenix	Off.	82	3570	7235	49	1906	2466	77	1071	2458	3529	2283	1853	**908**	344	1629	9114	111.1
	Def.	82	3563	7480	48	1593	2119	75	1216	2447	3663	2026	2051	882	389	1663	8819	107.5
	Diff.		+7	-245	+1	**+313**	**+347**	+2	-145	+11	-134	+257	+198	+26	-45	+34	+295	+3.6
Portland	Off.	82	3408	7167	48	1560	2100	74	1295	2408	3703	1898	1956	708	472	1552	8402	102.5
	Def.	82	3349	7008	48	1716	2281	75	1138	2358	3496	2008	1880	756	395	1450	8469	103.3
	Diff.		+59	+159	—	-156	-181	-1	+157	+50	+207	-110	-76	-48	+77	-102	-67	-.8
San Diego	Off.	82	3524	7494	47	1595	2167	74	1294	2308	3602	1688	1896	664	288	1443	8820	107.6
	Def.	82	3752	7508	50	1613	2086	77	1222	2487	3709	2012	1889	764	408	1391	9160	111.7
	Diff.		-228	-14	-3	-18	+81	-3	+72	-179	-107	-324	-7	-100	-120	-52	-340	-4.1
Golden State	Off.	82	3527	7318	48	1412	1914	74	1155	2437	3592	2028	2082	779	339	1492	8493	103.6
	Def.	82	3438	6975	49	1905	2544	75	1056	2564	3620	2091	1785	720	361	1486	8853	108.0
	Diff.		+89	+343	-1	-493	-630	-1	+99	-127	-28	-63	-297	+59	-22	-6	-360	-4.4
PLAYOFFS																		
Los Angeles	Off.	16	**716**	1471	49	335	420	80	**271**	527	**798**	466	384	162	97	306	1770	**110.6**
	Def.	16	692	1461	47	293	386	76	204	438	642	484	366	150	105	269	1701	106.3
	Diff.		+24	+10	+2	+42	+34	+4	**+67**	**+89**	**+156**	-18	-18	+12	-8	-37	+69	+4.3
Philadelphia	Off.	18	715	**1513**	47	**413**	**532**	78	218	**548**	766	**468**	413	**171**	**160**	300	1851	102.8
	Def.	18	721	1563	46	354	471	75	272	544	816	403	**483**	146	97	**333**	1811	100.6
	Diff.		-6	-50	+1	**+59**	**+61**	+3	-54	+4	-50	**+65**	**+70**	+25	**+63**	**+33**	+40	+2.2
Seattle	Off.	15	613	1348	45	291	379	77	249	437	686	379	360	133	52	273	1533	102.2
	Def.	15	631	1353	47	270	377	72	224	432	656	364	378	136	88	256	1545	103.0
	Diff.		-18	-5	-2	+21	+2	+5	+25	+5	+30	+15	+18	-3	-36	-17	-12	-.8
Boston	Off.	9	372	776	48	166	218	76	120	265	385	213	223	73	38	148	922	102.4
	Def.	9	343	753	46	174	225	77	110	263	373	212	210	74	53	164	870	**96.7**
	Diff.		**+29**	**+23**	**+2**	-8	-7	-1	+10	+2	+12	+1	-13	-1	-15	+16	+52	**+5.7**
Phoenix	Off.	8	357	730	**49**	148	192	77	104	222	326	247	183	72	43	130	877	109.6
	Def.	8	350	727	48	175	226	77	137	249	386	225	179	81	30	145	883	110.4
	Diff.		+7	+3	+1	-27	-34	—	-33	-27	-60	+22	-4	-9	+13	+15	-6	-.8
Houston	Off.	7	288	608	47	132	164	**80**	102	197	299	176	172	44	33	121	715	102.1
	Def.	7	305	613	50	145	178	81	94	190	284	183	169	60	28	96	763	109.0
	Diff.		-17	-5	-3	-13	-14	-1	+8	+7	+15	-7	-3	-16	+5	-25	-48	-6.9
Milwaukee	Off.	7	284	622	46	138	193	72	97	196	293	169	188	62	40	119	716	102.3
	Def.	7	279	624	**45**	146	189	77	117	205	322	163	183	25	57	132	710	101.4
	Diff.		+5	-2	+1	-8	+4	-5	-20	-9	-29	+6	-5	**+37**	-17	+13	+6	+.9
Atlanta	Off.	5	182	406	45	119	160	74	75	132	207	97	**148**	43	28	**82**	484	96.8
	Def.	5	182	386	47	145	175	83	71	154	225	114	121	39	46	97	511	102.2
	Diff.		—	+20	-2	-26	-15	-9	+4	-22	-18	-17	-27	+4	-18	+15	-27	-5.4
Kansas City	Off.	3	125	272	46	42	68	62	50	88	138	70	58	25	6	47	298	99.3
	Def.	3	131	257	51	42	60	**70**	37	93	130	89	64	22	15	41	306	102.0
	Diff.		-6	+15	-5	—	+8	-8	+13	-5	+8	-19	+6	+3	-9	-6	-8	-2.7
Portland	Off.	3	126	267	47	47	66	71	46	75	121	44	74	23	12	51	301	100.3
	Def.	3	126	266	47	66	80	83	52	89	141	76	65	32	10	53	318	106.0
	Diff.		—	+1	—	-19	-14	-12	-6	-14	-20	-32	-9	-9	+2	+2	-17	-5.7
San Antonio	Off.	3	121	262	46	66	85	78	41	77	118	68	78	22	12	41	311	103.7
	Def.	3	139	275	51	57	79	72	50	97	147	86	78	23	19	41	337	112.3
	Diff.		-18	-13	-5	+9	+6	**+6**	-9	-20	-29	-18	—	-1	-7	—	-26	-8.6
Washington	Off.	2	81	180	45	31	42	74	27	55	82	48	56	13	10	36	200	100.0
	Def.	2	81	177	46	61	73	84	32	65	97	46	41	23	15	27	223	111.5
	Diff.		—	+3	-1	-30	-31	-10	-5	-10	-15	+2	-15	-10	-5	-9	-23	-11.5

Team	W	L	Pct.	GB	Record against playoff teams			Record against non - playoff teams			HOME			ROAD		
					W	L	Pct.	W	L	Pct.	W	L	Pct.	W	L	Pct.
EASTERN CONFERENCE																
ATLANTIC DIVISION																
Boston Celtics	**61**	21	**.744**	—	**27**	15	**.642**	34	6	.850	35	6	.854	**26**	15	**.634**
Philadelphia 76ers	59	23	.720	2	26	16	.619	33	7	.825	36	5	.878	23	18	.561
Washington Bullets	39	43	.476	22	16	26	.381	23	17	.575	24	17	.585	15	26	.366
New York Knickerbockers	39	43	.476	22	19	29	.396	20	14	.588	25	16	.610	14	27	.341
New Jersey Nets	34	48	.415	27	17	31	.370	17	17	.500	22	19	.537	12	29	.293
CENTRAL DIVISION																
Atlanta Hawks	50	32	.610	—	21	21	.500	29	11	.725	32	9	.780	18	23	.439
Houston Rockets	41	41	.500	9	15	27	.357	26	14	.650	29	12	.707	12	29	.293
San Antonio Spurs	41	41	.500	9	18	24	.429	23	17	.575	27	14	.659	14	27	.341
Indiana Pacers	37	45	.451	13	16	32	.333	21	13	.618	26	15	.634	11	30	.268
Cleveland Cavaliers	37	45	.451	13	18	30	.375	19	15	.559	28	13	.683	9	32	.220
Detroit Pistons	16	**66**	.195	34	7	41	.146	9	25	.265	13	**28**	.317	3	**38**	.073
WESTERN CONFERENCE																
MIDWEST DIVISION																
Milwaukee Bucks	49	33	.598	—	20	22	.476	29	11	.725	28	13	.683	21	20	.512
Kansas City Kings	47	35	.573	2	19	23	.452	28	12	.700	30	11	.732	17	24	.415
Denver Nuggets	30	52	.366	19	12	36	.250	18	16	.529	24	17	.585	6	35	.146
Chicago Bulls	30	52	.366	19	14	34	.292	16	18	.471	21	20	.512	9	32	.220
Utah Jazz	24	58	.293	25	8	40	.167	16	18	.471	17	24	.414	7	34	.171
PACIFIC DIVISION																
Los Angeles Lakers	60	22	.732	—	25	17	.595	**35**	5	**.875**	**37**	4	**.902**	23	18	.561
Seattle Supersonics	56	26	.683	4	24	18	.571	32	8	.800	33	8	.804	23	18	.561
Phoenix Suns	55	27	.671	5	**27**	15	**.642**	28	12	.700	36	5	.878	19	22	.463
Portland Trail Blazers	38	44	.463	22	14	28	.333	24	16	.600	26	15	.634	12	29	.293
San Diego Clippers	35	47	.427	25	16	32	.333	19	15	.559	24	17	.585	11	30	.268
Golden State Warriors	24	58	.293	36	11	39	.220	13	19	.406	15	26	.366	9	32	.220

1979/80 N.B.A. INDIVIDUAL LEADERS

SCORING
(Minimum 70 Games or 1400 Points)

Name	Team	G	FG	FT	Pts.	Avg.
Gervin	SA	78	1024	505	2585	33.1
Free	SD	68	737	572	2055	30.2
Dantley	Utah	68	730	443	1903	28.0
Erving	Phi	78	838	420	2100	26.9
Malone	Hou	82	778	563	2119	25.8
Abdul-Jabbar	LA	82	835	364	2034	24.8
Issel	Den	82	715	517	1951	23.8
Hayes	Was	81	761	334	1859	23.0
Birdsong	KC	82	781	286	1858	22.7
Mitchell	Cle	82	775	270	1820	22.2

FIELD GOAL PERCENTAGE
(Minimum 300 Made)

Name	Team	FG	FGA	Pct.
Maxwell	Bos	457	750	.609
Abdul-Jabbar	LA	835	1383	.604
Gilmore	Chi	305	513	.595
Dantley	Utah	730	1267	.576
Boswell	Utah	346	613	.564
Davis	Phoe	657	1166	.563
Nater	SD	443	799	.554
Washington	Port	421	761	.553
Cartwright	NY	665	1215	.547
Johnson	Mil	689	1267	.544

FREE THROW PERCENTAGE
(Minimum 125 Made)

Name	Team	FT	FTA	Pct.
Barry	Hou	143	153	.935
Murphy	Hou	271	302	.897
Boone	Utah	175	196	.893
Silas	SA	339	382	.887
Newlin	NJ	367	415	.884
Furlow	Atl-Utah	171	196	.872
Phegley	NJ	177	203	.872
Bratz	Phoe	141	162	.870
Greavey	Was	216	249	.867
Roche	Den	175	202	.866

PERSONAL FOULS

Name	Team	PF
Dawkins	Phi	328
Edwards	Ind	324
Rollins	Atl	322
Roundfield	Atl	317
Drew	Atl	313
Greenwood	Chi	313

GAMES DISQUALIFIED

Name	Team	Disq.
Edwards	Ind	12
McGinnis	Den-Ind	12
Rollins	Atl	12
van Breda Kolff	NJ	11
Demic	NY	10
Drew	Atl	10

MINUTES PLAYED

Name	Team	Min.
Nixon	LA	3226
Hayes	Was	3183
Cartwright	NY	3150
Abdul-Jabbar	LA	3143
Malone	Hou	3140

TOTAL REBOUNDS PER GAME
(Minimum 70 Games or 800 Rebounds)

Name	Team	G	Reb.	Avg.
Nater	SD	81	1216	15.0
Malone	Hou	82	1190	14.5
Unseld	Was	82	1094	13.3
C.Jones	Phi	80	950	11.9
Sikma	Sea	82	908	11.1
Hayes	Was	81	896	11.1
Parish	GS	72	783	10.9
Abdul-Jabbar	LA	82	886	10.8
Washington	Port	80	842	10.5
Bird	Bos	82	852	10.4

ASSISTS PER GAME
(Minimum 70 Games or 400 Assists)

Name	Team	G	Ass.	Avg.
Richardson	NY	82	832	10.1
Archibald	Bos	80	671	8.4
Walker	Cle	76	607	8.0
Nixon	LA	82	642	7.8
Lucas	GS	80	602	7.5
Ford	KC	82	610	7.4
Johnson	LA	77	553	7.2
Cheeks	Phi	79	556	7.0
Jordan	NJ	82	557	6.8
Porter	Was	70	457	6.5

BLOCKED SHOTS PER GAME
(Minimum 70 Games or 100 Blocked Shots)

Name	Team	G	Reb.	Avg.
Abdul-Jabbar	LA	82	280	3.4
Johnson	NJ	81	258	3.2
Rollins	Atl	82	244	3.0
Tyler	Det	82	220	2.7
Hayes	Was	81	189	2.3
Catchings	Mil	72	162	2.3
C.Jones	Phi	80	162	2.0
Poquette	Utah	82	162	2.0
Meriweather	NY	65	120	1.8
Erving	Phi	78	140	1.8

3 POINT FIELD GOALS PER GAME
(Minimum 25 Made)

Name	Team	FG	FGA	Avg.
Brown	Sea	39	88	.443
Ford	Bos	70	164	.427
Bird	Bos	58	143	.406
Roche	Den	49	129	.380
Taylor	SD	90	239	.377
Winters	Mil	38	102	.373
Grevey	Was	34	92	.370
Hassett	Ind	69	198	.348
Barry	Hou	73	221	.330
Williams	SD	42	128	.328

STEALS PER GAME
(Minimum 70 Games or 125 Steals)

Name	Team	G	Steals	Avg.
Richardson	NY	82	265	3.2
Johnson	NJ	82	223	2.7
Bradley	Ind	82	211	2.6
Williams	Sea	82	200	2.4
Johnson	LA	77	187	2.4
Cheeks	Phi	79	183	2.3
Erving	Phi	78	170	2.2
Parker	GS	82	173	2.1
Walker	Cle	76	155	2.0
R.Williams	NY	82	167	2.0

1980-81 N.B.A.
A 25 Year Contract

The N.B.A. expanded for the first time in six years, adding a third Texas team, this one in Dallas. The fledgling Mavericks hired Dick Motta as coach, but got little help from the other clubs in the expansion draft. Still, Jim Spanarkel (from Philadelphia) and Tom LaGarde (from Seattle) played well, as did Bill Robinzine, acquired from Cleveland early in the season. And in December the Mavs picked up well-traveled (and often-released) Brad Davis from the C.B.A. He alone from this 15-67 team would still be around when Dallas became an N.B.A. power.

Among current N.B.A. powers, the champs in Los Angeles had a tough year, losing Magic Johnson to an early-season knee injury and finishing behind Phoenix in the Pacific Devision, despite fine seasons from Kareem Abdul-Jabbar, Jamaal Wilkes and Norm Nixon. Worse yet, when Johnson returned some of the Lakers thought he didn't fit in with the team. That assessment looked prophetic when Magic played poorly in the miniseries against Houston and L.A. went down in a major ujpset. Still, owner Jerry Buss made it clear where his sympathies lay when he signed Johnson to a 25-year, $25 million contract in June.

An eventful year in Boston began on draft day, when the Celtics sent the No.1 pick (acquired from Detroit for Bob McAdoo) to Golden State so the Warriers could take Joe Barry Carroll. In exchange Boston got Robert Parish and Kevin McHale, the No.3 pick. The addition of two stellar big men proved crucial after Dave Cowens retired in training camp. The shaken Celtics started slowly, but Larry Bird led them in a season-long pursuit of Philadelphia that ended with a win over the 76ers on the final day. Both teams finished 62-20, but a better conference record gave Boston the Atlantic Division title.

Despite the disappointing finish, it was a good year in Philadelphia. Julius Erving won the MVP award, and rookie Andrew Toney stepped in for Doug Collins, who played only 12 games before giving up his comeback attempt. New York improved to 50 wins as Bill Cartwright, Ray Williams and Michael Ray Richardson gave coach Red Holtzman his last winning season. But in Washington, new coach Gene Shue found that even Elvin Hayes was showing his age. Mitch Kupchak recovered from a back injury and played well, but Bob Dandridge played even less than a year ago, and Wes Unseld ended his final season on the sidelines. New Jersey coach Kevin Loughery didn't survive the season, but the Nets had hopes for rookies Mike Gminski, Mike O'Koren and Darwin Cook, plus second-year man Cliff Robinson.

The addition of Dallas brought realignment in the Midwest and Central Divisions, with Milwaukee and Chicago swapping places with San Antonio and Houston—and all four had successful seasons. Milwaukee lost David Meyers, who quit because of religious beliefs, but Marques Johnson, Junior Bridgeman, Bob Lanier and second-year man Sidney Moncrief led the Bucks to 60 wins and the Central title. A healthy Artis Gilmore and new arrival Larry Kenon joined Reggie Theus and David Greenwood as the Bulls improved to 45-37. That put them a game ahead of Indiana, where Billy Knight, Mike Bantom, Johnny Davis and James Edwards helped earn Jack McKinney the Coach of the Year award with his new team. Atlanta coach Hubie Brown wasn't so lucky, losing his job as his team plummeted to 31 wins. New Cleveland coach Bill Musselman was also fired, despite a fine year from Mike Mitchell and a promising rookie in Bill Laimbeer. Detroit's new coach, Scotty Robertson, did finish the season, but his team won just 21 games.

New San Antonio coach Stan Albeck made an effective center tandem of Dave Corzine (from Washington) and George Johnson (from New Jersey). With George Gervin and James Silas still going strong in the backcourt, the Spurs won the Midwest title easily. In Houston, Calvin Murphy was fading and Rudy Tomjanovich looked finished, but Moses Malone was better than ever, and he kept the Rockets at 40-42, tied with Kansas City. A 26-25 finish awakened hopes for the future in Denver, where Alex English, Dan Issel and a healthy David Thompson gave the Nuggets a trip of 20-point-per-game scorers. Two key moves came in December, when the Nuggets acquired Dallas's top draft pick, Kiki Vandeweghe, who had been a holdout, and Doug Moe replaced Donnie Walsh as coach. In Utah, Adrien Dantley and Darrell Griffith were all that kept the Jazz ahead of Dallas.

Phoenix replaced the Lakers at the top of the Pacific Division after a big trade that brought Dennie Johnson from Seattle for Paul Westphal. Johnson had been in Lenny Wilken's doghouse, but he fit right in with Truck Robinson, Walter Davis and Alvan Adams. Meanwhile, in Seattle, Westphal broke his foot, Lonnie Shelton hurt his wrist, Gus Williams sat out the season in a contract dispute, and the Sonics fell to last place. Only a fine year from Jack Sikma kept them competitive. Portland got Mychal Thompson back, and he combined with rookie Kelvin Ransey and sophomore Jim Paxson to lead the Blazers to 45 wins. Rookie Joe Barry Carroll and new arrival Bernard King, recovered from his alcohol problem, helped Golden State, as did World Free, acquired from San Diego for Phil Smith. But the Clippers fell to last place under new coach Phil Silas after Bill Walton went down in the preseason.

The Western playoffs were up for grabs after Houston's shocking elimination of the Lakers, and the result was two seven-game struggles in the semifinals. Injury-plagued Kansas City built a 3-1 lead and held on to upset Phoenix while Houston was outlasting favored San Antonio. Then the Rockets disposed of the Kings in five games to earn an unexpected trip to the championship series.

In the East, Milwaukee extended Philadelphia to seven games before the 76ers eked out a 99-98 win in the finale. Then, in a rematch with Boston, the 76ers jumped out to a 3-1 lead and held a commanding advantage in the final minutes of the fifth game. But the Celtics beat the odds and rallied for a 111-109 win. Another two-point win evened the series, and Bird's last-minute jumper decided the seventh game, a 91-90 thriller.

The championship series was somewhat anticlimactic, but Houston put up a good fight before losing in six games. With Bird slowed for much of the series by the defense of Robert Reid, Boston's Cedric Maxwell was voted playoff MVP as the Celtics won their 14th N.B.A. title.

					TOTAL													Blkd		PER GAME				
Use Name	Pos	Hgt	Wgt	Age	G	Min	FG	FGA	%	FT	FTA	%	Reb	Ass	PF	DQ	Stls	Shts	Points	Min	Reb	Ass	PF	Points
1980/81 N.B.A. — EASTERN CONFERENCE																								
ATLANTIC DIVISION																								
BOSTON CELTICS	**62-20 .756**				**BILL FITCH**																			
Cedric Maxwell	F	6'8	205	25	81	2730	441	750	59	352	450	78	525	219	256	5	79	68	1234	34	6.5	2.7	3.2	15.2
Larry Bird	F	6'9	220	24	82	3239	719	1503	48	283	328	86	895	451	239	2	161	63	1741	40	10.9	5.5	2.9	21.2
Robert Parish	C	7'	230	27	82	2298	635	1166	54	282	397	71	777	144	310	9	81	214	1552	28	9.5	1.8	3.8	18.9
Chris Ford	G	6'5	190	31	82	2723	314	707	44	64	87	74	163	295	212	2	100	23	728	33	2.0	3.6	2.6	8.9
Nate Archibald	G	6'1	150	32	80	2820	382	766	50	342	419	82	176	618	201	1	75	18	1106	35	2.2	7.7	2.5	13.8
Kevin McHale	F-C	6'10	235	23	82	1645	355	666	53	108	159	68	359	55	260	3	27	151	818	20	4.4	0.7	3.2	10.0
Gerald Henderson	G	6'2	175	24	82	1608	261	579	45	113	157	72	132	213	177	0	79	12	636	20	1.6	2.6	2.2	7.8
Rick Robey	C-F	6'11	235	24	82	1569	298	547	54	144	251	57	390	126	204	0	38	19	740	19	4.8	1.5	2.5	9.0
M.L. Carr	G-F	6'6	205	29	41	655	97	216	45	53	67	79	83	56	74	0	30	18	248	16	2.0	1.4	1.8	6.0
Eric Fernsten	C	6'10	205	27	45	279	38	79	48	20	30	67	62	10	29	0	6	7	96	6	1.4	0.2	0.6	2.1
Terry Duerod (from Dal)	G	6'2	180	24	32	114	30	73	41	13	14	93	5	6	8	0	5	0	79	4	0.2	0.2	0.3	2.5
Wayne Kreklow	G	6'4	175	23	25	100	11	47	23	7	10	70	12	9	20	0	2	1	30	4	0.5	0.4	0.8	1.2

Dave Cowens - voluntarily retired

3-PT FG — Maxwell 0-1, Bird 20-74, Parish 0-1, Ford 36-109, Archibald 0-9, McHale 0-2, Henderson 1-16, Robey 0-1, Carr 1-14, Duerod 6-10, Kreklow 1-4

1980/81 N.B.A. — EASTERN CONFERENCE
ATLANTIC DIVISION (continued)

Use Name	Pos	Hgt	Wgt	Age	TOTAL G	Min	FG	FGA	%	FT	FTA	%	Reb	Ass	PF	DQ	Stls	Blkd Shts	Points	PER GAME Min	Reb	Ass	PF	Points
PHILADELPHIA 76ers	62-20 .756				**BILLY CUNNINGHAM**																			
Julius Erving	F	6'7	210	30	82	2874	794	1524	52	422	536	79	657	364	233	0	173	147	2014	35	8.0	4.4	2.8	24.6
Bobby Jones	F	6'9	205	29	81	2046	407	755	54	282	347	81	435	226	226	2	95	74	1096	25	5.4	2.8	2.8	13.5
Caldwell Jones	C-F	6'11	225	30	81	2639	218	485	45	148	193	77	813	122	271	2	53	134	584	33	10.0	1.5	3.3	7.2
Lionel Hollins	G	6'3	185	27	82	2154	327	696	47	125	171	73	191	352	205	2	104	18	781	26	2.3	4.3	2.5	9.5
Maurice Cheeks	G	6'1	181	24	81	2415	310	581	53	140	178	79	245	560	231	1	193	39	763	30	3.0	6.9	2.9	9.4
Darryl Dawkins	C	6'11	252	23	76	2088	423	697	61	219	304	72	545	109	316	9	38	112	1065	27	7.2	1.4	4.2	14.0
Andrew Toney	G	6'3	190	23	75	1768	399	806	50	161	226	71	143	273	234	5	59	10	968	24	1.9	3.6	3.1	12.9
Steve Mix	F	6'7	219	33	72	1327	288	575	50	200	240	83	264	114	107	0	59	18	776	18	3.7	1.6	1.5	10.8
Clint Richardson	G	6'3	195	24	77	1313	227	464	49	84	108	78	176	152	102	0	36	10	538	17	2.3	2.0	1.3	7.0
Earl Curreton	F	6'9	215	23	52	528	93	205	45	33	64	52	155	25	68	0	20	23	219	10	3.0	0.5	1.3	4.2
Ollie Johnson	F	6'6	200	31	40	372	87	158	55	27	31	87	55	30	45	0	20	2	202	9	1.4	0.8	1.1	5.1
Doug Collins (FJ)	G	6'6	180	29	12	329	62	126	49	24	29	83	29	42	23	0	7	4	148	27	2.4	3.5	1.9	12.3
Monti Davis (to Dal)	F	6'7	205	22	1	2	1	1	100	0	0	—	1	0	0	0	0	0	2	2	1.0	0.0	0.0	2.0
	3-PT FG —				Erving 4-18, B.Jones 0-3, Hollins 2-15, Cheeks 3-8, Toney 9-29, Mix 0-3, Richardson 0-1, Cureton 0-1, Johnson 1-6																			
NEW YORK KNICKERBOCKERS	50-32 .610				**RED HOLZMAN**																			
Campy Russell	F	6'8	215	28	79	2865	508	1095	46	268	343	78	353	257	248	2	99	8	1292	36	4.5	3.3	3.1	16.4
Sly Williams (ankle injury)	F	6'7	210	22	67	1976	349	708	49	185	268	69	416	180	199	0	116	18	885	29	6.2	2.7	3.0	13.2
Bill Cartwright	C-F	7'1	255	23	82	2925	619	1118	55	408	518	79	613	111	259	2	48	83	1646	36	7.5	1.4	3.2	20.1
Ray Williams	G	6'3	190	26	79	2742	616	1335	46	312	382	82	321	432	270	4	185	37	1560	35	4.1	5.5	3.4	19.7
Michael Ray Richardson	G	6'5	190	25	79	3175	523	1116	47	224	338	66	545	627	258	2	**232**	35	1293	40	6.9	7.9	3.3	16.4
Marvin Webster	C	7'1	240	28	82	1708	159	341	47	104	163	64	465	72	187	2	27	97	423	21	5.7	0.9	2.3	5.2
Mike Glenn	G	6'3	175	25	82	1506	285	511	56	98	110	89	88	108	126	0	72	5	672	18	1.1	1.3	1.5	8.2
Larry Demic	F	6'9	225	23	76	964	128	254	50	58	92	63	243	28	153	0	12	13	314	13	3.2	0.4	2.0	4.1
Mike Woodson	F	6'5	195	22	81	949	165	373	44	49	64	77	97	75	95	0	36	12	380	12	1.2	0.9	1.2	4.7
Reagie Carter	G	6'3	175	23	60	536	59	179	33	51	69	74	69	76	68	0	22	2	169	9	1.2	1.3	1.1	2.8
DeWayne Scales	F	6'8	208	22	44	484	94	225	42	26	39	67	132	10	54	0	12	4	215	11	3.0	0.2	1.2	4.9
Toby Knight - knee injury	3-PT FG —				Russell 8-26, S.Williams 2-8, Cartwright 0-1, R.Williams 16-68, Richardson 23-102, Webster 1-4, Glenn 4-11, Demic 0-2, Woodson 1-5, Carter 0-3, Scales 1-6																			
WASHINGTON BULLETS	39-43 .476				**GENE SHUE**																			
Greg Ballard	F	6'7	215	25	82	2610	549	1186	46	166	196	85	580	195	194	1	118	39	1271	32	7.1	2.4	2.4	15.5
Elvin Hayes	F	6'9	235	35	81	2931	584	1296	45	271	439	62	789	98	300	6	68	171	1439	36	9.7	1.2	3.7	17.8
Wes Unseld	C	6'7	245	34	63	2032	225	429	52	55	86	64	673	170	171	1	52	36	507	32	10.7	2.7	2.7	8.0
Kevin Grevey	G	6'5	210	27	75	2616	500	1103	45	244	290	84	219	300	161	1	58	17	1289	35	2.9	4.0	2.1	17.2
Kevin Porter	G	6'	175	30	81	2577	446	859	52	191	247	77	124	**734**	257	4	110	10	1086	32	1.5	9.1	3.2	13.4
Mitch Kupchak	C-F	6'9	230	26	82	1934	392	747	52	240	340	71	569	62	195	1	36	26	1024	24	6.9	0.8	2.4	12.5
Wes Matthews (to Atl)	G	6'1	170	21	45	1161	224	449	50	99	129	77	67	199	120	1	46	10	552	26	1.5	4.4	2.7	12.3
Rick Mahorn	C	6'10	240	22	52	696	111	219	51	27	40	68	215	25	134	3	21	44	249	13	4.1	0.5	2.6	4.8
Don Collins (from Atl)	F-G	6'6	190	22	34	661	130	281	46	74	110	67	81	75	93	1	35	14	334	19	2.4	2.2	2.7	9.8
Austin Carr (from Dal, KJ))	G	6'4	200	32	39	580	80	206	39	32	50	64	52	49	43	0	14	2	192	15	1.3	1.3	1.1	4.9
Bob Dandridge (KJ)	F	6'6	195	33	23	545	101	237	43	28	39	72	83	60	54	1	16	9	230	24	3.6	2.6	2.3	10.0
Carlos Terry (KJ)	G-F	6'5	210	24	26	504	80	160	50	28	42	67	116	70	68	1	27	13	188	19	4.5	2.7	2.6	7.2
Andre McCarter	G	6'3	190	27	43	448	51	135	38	18	24	75	39	73	36	0	14	0	122	10	0.9	1.7	0.8	2.8
Anthony Roberts	F	6'5	185	25	26	350	54	144	38	19	29	66	68	20	52	0	11	0	127	13	2.6	0.8	2.0	4.9
John Williamson	G	6'2	195	28	9	112	18	56	32	5	6	83	7	17	13	0	4	1	42	12	0.8	1.9	1.4	4.7
Dave Britton	G	6'4	180	22	2	9	2	3	67	0	0	—	2	3	2	0	0	0	4	5	1.0	1.5	1.0	2.0
Keith McCord	G	6'7	210	23	2	9	2	4	50	0	0	—	2	1	0	0	0	0	4	5	1.0	0.5	0.0	2.0
Lewis Brown	C	6'11	225	25	2	5	0	3	0	2	5	40	2	0	2	0	0	0	2	3	1.0	0.0	1.0	1.0
	3-PT FG —				Ballard 7-32, Hayes 0-10, Unseld 2-4, Grevey 45-136, Porter 3-12, Kupchak 0-1, Matthews 5-15, Collins 0-3, Dandridge 0-1, Terry 0-6, McCarter 2-8, Carr 0-7, Williamson 1-6																			
NEW JERSEY NETS	24-58 .293				**KEVIN LOUGHERY 11-23 (.343), BOB MCKINNON 13-35 (.271)**																			
Mike O'Koren	F	6'7	207	22	79	2473	365	751	49	135	212	64	478	252	243	8	86	27	870	31	6.1	3.2	3.1	11.0
Cliff Robinson (NJ)	F	6'9	220	20	63	1822	525	1070	49	178	248	72	481	105	216	6	58	52	1229	29	7.6	1.7	3.4	19.5
Mike Gminski (EJ)	C	6'11	250	21	56	1579	291	688	42	155	202	77	419	72	127	1	54	100	737	28	7.5	1.3	2.3	13.2
Mike Newlin	G	6'4	200	31	79	2911	632	1272	50	414	466	89	219	299	237	2	87	9	1688	37	2.8	3.8	3.0	21.4
Foots Walker (GJ)	G	6'1	172	29	41	1172	72	169	43	88	111	79	102	253	105	0	52	1	234	29	2.5	6.2	2.6	5.7
Maurice Lucas (NJ)	C-F	6'9	218	28	68	2162	404	835	48	191	254	75	575	173	260	3	57	59	999	32	8.5	2.5	3.8	14.7
Darwin Cook	G	6'3	190	22	81	1980	383	819	47	132	180	73	236	297	197	4	141	36	904	24	2.9	3.7	2.4	11.2
Jan Van Breda Kolff	F	6'7	200	29	78	1426	100	245	41	98	117	84	202	129	214	3	38	50	300	18	2.6	1.7	2.7	3.8
Lowes Moore	G	6'1	170	23	71	1406	212	478	44	69	92	75	168	228	179	1	61	17	497	20	2.4	3.2	2.5	7.0
Bob Elliott	F	6'9	225	25	73	1320	214	419	51	121	202	60	261	129	175	3	34	16	550	18	3.6	1.8	2.4	7.5
Edgar Jones (KJ)	C	6'10	225	24	60	950	189	357	53	146	218	67	263	43	185	4	36	81	524	16	4.4	0.7	3.1	8.7
Eddie Jordan (to LA)	G	6'1	170	25	14	239	30	73	41	24	32	75	18	46	29	0	24	1	87	17	1.3	3.3	2.1	6.2
Rory Sparrow	G	6'2	175	22	15	212	22	63	35	12	16	75	18	32	15	0	13	3	56	14	1.2	2.1	1.0	3.7
Bob McAdoo (from Det)	C	6'9	210	29	10	153	38	75	51	17	21	81	26	10	22	0	9	6	93	15	2.6	1.0	2.2	9.3
	3-PT FG —				O'Koren 5-18, Robinson 1-1, Gminski 0-1, Newlin 10-30, Walker 2-9, Lucas 0-2, Cook 6-25, Van Breda Kolff 2-8, Moore 4-27, Elliot 1-2, Jones 0-4, Jordan 3-10, McAdoo 0-1																			

1980/81 N.B.A. — EASTERN CONFERENCE (Continued)
CENTRAL DIVISION

Use Name	Pos	Hgt	Wgt	Age	G	Min	FG	FGA	%	FT	FTA	%	Reb	Ass	PF	DQ	Stls	Blkd Shts	Points	Min	Reb	Ass	PF	Points
					TOTALS															PER GAME				
MILWAUKEE BUCKS	60-22 .732				**DON NELSON**																			
Marques Johnson	F	6'7	218	24	76	2542	636	1153	55	269	381	71	518	346	196	1	115	41	1541	33	6.8	4.6	2.6	20.3
Mickey Johnson	F	6'10	190	28	82	2118	379	846	45	262	332	79	545	286	256	4	94	71	1023	26	6.6	3.5	3.1	12.5
Bob Lanier	C	6'11	250	32	67	1753	376	716	53	207	277	75	413	179	184	0	73	81	961	26	6.2	2.7	2.7	14.3
Sidney Moncrief	G	6'4	190	23	80	2417	400	739	54	320	398	80	406	264	156	1	90	37	1122	30	5.1	3.3	2.0	14.0
Quinn Buckner	G	6'3	205	26	82	2384	471	956	49	149	203	73	298	384	271	3	197	3	1092	29	3.6	4.7	3.3	13.3
Junior Bridgeman	F-G	6'5	210	27	77	2215	537	1102	49	213	241	88	289	234	182	2	88	28	1290	29	3.8	3.0	2.4	16.8
Brian Winters	G	6'4	185	28	69	1771	331	697	47	119	137	87	140	229	185	2	70	10	799	26	2.0	3.3	2.7	11.6
Harvey Catchings	C-F	6'9	218	29	77	1635	134	300	45	59	92	64	473	99	284	7	33	184	327	21	6.1	1.3	3.7	4.2
Pat Cummings	F	6'9	235	24	74	1084	248	460	54	99	140	71	292	62	192	4	31	19	595	15	3.9	0.8	2.6	8.0
Len Elmore	C-F	6'9	220	28	72	925	76	212	36	54	75	72	208	69	178	3	37	52	206	13	2.9	1.0	2.5	2.9
Mike Evans	G	6'1	170	25	71	911	134	291	46	50	64	78	87	167	114	0	34	4	320	13	1.2	2.4	1.6	4.5
3-PT FG — Ma. Johnson 0-9, Mi. Johnson 3-19, Lanier 1-1, Moncrief 2-9, Buckner 1-6, Bridgeman 3-21, Winters 18-51, Cummings 0-2, Evans 2-14																								
CHICAGO BULLS	45-37 .549				**JERRY SLOAN**																			
Larry Kenon	F	6'9	215	28	77	2161	454	946	48	180	245	73	398	120	160	2	75	18	1088	28	5.2	1.6	2.1	14.1
Dave Greenwood	F	6'9	222	23	82	2710	481	969	50	217	290	75	724	218	282	5	77	124	1179	33	8.8	2.7	3.4	14.4
Artis Gilmore	C	7'2	240	31	82	2832	547	816	**67**	375	532	70	828	172	295	2	47	198	1469	35	10.1	2.1	3.6	17.9
Reggie Theus	G	6'7	190	23	82	2820	543	1097	49	445	550	81	287	426	258	1	122	20	1549	34	3.5	5.2	3.1	18.9
Rickey Sobers	G	6'3	198	27	71	1803	355	769	46	231	247	94	144	284	225	3	98	17	958	25	2.0	4.0	3.2	13.5
Bob Wilkerson	G	6'6	200	26	80	2238	330	715	46	137	163	84	282	272	170	0	102	23	798	28	3.5	3.4	2.1	10.0
Dwight Jones	F	6'10	210	28	81	1574	245	507	48	125	161	78	401	99	200	1	40	36	615	19	5.0	1.2	2.5	7.6
Coby Dietrick	C-F	6'10	225	32	82	1243	146	320	46	77	111	69	265	118	176	1	48	53	371	15	3.2	1.4	2.1	4.5
Sam Worthen	G	6'5	195	22	64	945	95	192	49	45	60	75	115	115	115	0	57	6	235	15	1.8	1.8	1.8	3.7
Scott May (HJ)	F	6'7	220	26	63	815	165	338	49	113	149	76	155	63	83	0	35	7	443	13	2.5	1.0	1.3	7.0
James Wilkes	F	6'7	195	22	48	540	85	184	46	29	46	63	96	30	86	0	25	12	199	11	2.0	0.6	1.8	4.1
Ronnie Lester (KJ)	G	6'2	175	21	8	83	10	24	42	10	11	91	6	7	5	0	2	0	30	10	0.8	0.9	0.6	3.8
Ollie Mack (to Dall)	G	6'3	195	23	3	16	1	6	17	1	2	50	1	1	3	0	1	0	3	5	0.3	0.3	1.0	1.0
3-PT FG — Greenwood 0-2, Theus 18-90, Sobers 17-66, Wilkerson 1-10, Dietrick 2-6, Worthen 0-4, Wilkes 0-1																								
INDIANA PACERS	44-38 .537				**JACK McKINNEY**																			
Mike Bantom	F	6'9	220	29	76	2375	431	882	49	199	281	71	427	240	284	9	80	85	1061	31	5.6	3.2	3.7	14.0
George McGinnis	F	6'8	235	30	69	1845	348	768	45	207	385	54	528	210	242	3	99	28	903	27	7.7	3.0	3.5	13.1
James Edwards	C	7'	225	25	81	2375	511	1004	51	244	347	70	571	212	304	7	32	128	1266	29	7.0	2.6	3.8	15.6
Billy Knight	G-F	6'6	195	28	82	2385	546	1025	53	341	410	83	410	157	155	1	84	12	1436	29	5.0	1.9	1.9	17.5
Johnny Davis	G	6'2	170	25	76	2536	426	917	46	238	299	80	170	480	179	2	95	14	1094	33	2.2	6.3	2.4	14.4
Dudley Bradley	G	6'6	195	23	82	1867	265	559	47	125	178	70	193	188	236	2	186	37	657	23	2.4	2.3	2.9	8.0
Louis Orr	F	6'8	175	22	82	1787	348	709	49	163	202	81	361	132	153	0	55	22	859	22	4.4	1.6	1.9	10.5
Clemon Johnson	C-F	6'10	240	24	81	1643	235	466	50	112	189	59	468	144	185	1	44	119	582	20	5.8	1.8	2.3	7.2
Don Buse (from Phoe)	G	6'4	195	30	58	1095	114	287	40	50	65	77	84	140	61	0	74	8	297	19	1.4	2.4	1.1	5.1
George Johnson (KJ)	C-F	6'7	218	24	43	930	182	394	46	93	122	76	278	86	120	1	47	23	457	22	6.5	2.0	2.8	10.6
Jerry Sichting	G	6'1	168	24	47	450	34	95	36	25	32	78	43	70	38	0	23	1	93	10	0.9	1.5	0.8	2.0
Tom Abernathy (from GS)	F	6'7	220	26	29	259	24	56	43	11	19	58	40	18	29	0	6	3	59	9	1.4	0.6	1.0	2.0
Kenny Natt	G	6'3	185	22	19	149	25	77	32	7	11	64	15	10	18	0	5	1	59	8	0.8	0.5	0.9	3.1
Dick Miller (to Utah)	F	6'6	215	22	5	34	2	6	33	0	0	—	4	4	2	0	3	0	4	7	0.8	0.8	0.4	0.8
3-PT FG — Bantom 0-6, McGinnis 0-7, Edwards 0-3, Knight 3-19, Davis 4-33, Bradley 2-16, Orr 0-6, C. Johnson 0-1, Buse 19-58, G. Johnson 0-5, Sichting 0-5, Abernathy 0-1, Natt 2-8, Miller 0-1																								
ATLANTA HAWKS	31-51 .378				**HUBIE BROWN (31-48 .392), MIKE FRATELLO (0-3 .000)**																			
John Drew (KJ)	F	6'6	205	26	67	2075	500	1096	46	454	577	79	383	79	264	9	98	15	1454	31	5.7	1.2	3.9	21.7
Dan Roundfield	F	6'8	205	27	63	2128	426	808	53	256	355	72	634	161	258	8	76	119	1108	34	10.1	2.6	4.1	17.6
Steve Hawes	C-F	6'9	220	30	74	2309	333	637	52	222	278	80	561	168	289	13	73	32	889	31	7.6	2.3	3.9	12.0
Eddie Johnson	G	6'2	190	25	75	2693	573	1136	50	279	356	78	179	407	188	2	126	11	1431	36	2.4	5.4	2.5	19.1
Wes Matthews (from Wash)	G	6'1	170	21	34	1105	161	330	49	103	123	84	72	212	122	1	61	7	425	33	2.1	6.2	3.6	12.5
Charlie Criss	G	5'8	165	31	66	1708	220	485	45	185	214	86	100	283	87	0	61	3	626	26	1.5	4.3	1.3	9.5
Tom McMillen	C-F	6'11	215	28	79	1564	253	519	49	80	108	74	295	72	165	0	23	25	587	20	3.7	0.9	2.1	7.4
Sam Pellom	F	6'9	225	29	77	1472	186	380	49	81	116	70	356	48	228	6	50	92	453	19	4.6	0.6	3.0	5.9
Don Collins (to Wash)	G-F	6'6	190	22	47	1184	230	530	43	137	162	85	187	115	166	5	69	11	597	25	4.0	2.4	3.5	12.7
Tree Rollins (KJ)	C	7'1	235	25	40	1044	116	210	55	46	57	81	286	35	151	7	29	117	278	26	7.2	0.9	3.8	7.0
Jim McElroy (XJ)	G	6'3	190	27	54	680	78	202	39	48	59	81	48	84	62	0	20	9	205	13	0.9	1.6	1.1	3.8
Armond Hill (to Sea)	G	6'4	190	27	24	624	39	116	34	42	50	84	51	118	60	0	26	3	120	26	2.1	4.9	2.5	5.0
Craig Shelton	F	6'7	210	23	55	586	100	219	46	35	58	60	138	27	128	1	18	5	235	11	2.5	0.5	2.3	4.3
Art Collins	G	6'4	200	26	29	395	35	99	35	24	36	67	41	25	35	0	11	1	94	14	1.4	0.9	1.2	3.2
Tom Burleson (BW)	C	7'3	228	28	31	363	41	99	41	20	41	49	94	12	73	2	8	19	102	12	3.0	0.4	2.4	3.3
3-PT FG — Drew 0-7, Roundfield 0-1, Hawes 1-4, Johnson 6-20, Matthews 0-6, Criss 1-21, McMillen 1-6, Pellom 0-1, D. Collins 0-3, Rollins 0-1, McElroy 1-8, Hill 0-1, Shelton 0-1, A. Collins 0-2																								

Use Name	Pos	Hgt	Wgt	Age	G	Min	FG	FGA	%	FT	FTA	%	Reb	Ass	PF	DQ	Stls	Blkd Shts	Points	Min	Reb	Ass	PF	Points
					TOTAL															PER GAME				
1980/81 N.B.A. — EASTERN CONFERENCE (continued)																								
CENTRAL DIVISION (continued)																								
CLEVELAND CAVALIERS	28-54 .341				DON DELANEY 3-8 (.273), BILL MUSSELMAN 25-46 (.352)																			
Mike Mitchell	F	6'7	215	24	82	3194	853	**1791**	48	302	385	78	502	139	199	0	63	52	2012	39	6.1	1.7	2.4	24.5
Kenny Carr	F	6'7	230	25	81	2615	469	918	51	292	409	71	835	192	296	3	76	42	1230	32	10.3	2.4	3.7	15.2
Bill Laimbeer	C	6'11	245	23	81	2460	337	670	50	117	153	76	693	216	332	14	56	78	791	30	8.6	2.7	4.1	9.8
Randy Smith	G	6'3	180	32	82	2199	486	1043	47	221	271	82	193	357	132	0	113	14	1194	27	2.4	4.4	1.6	14.6
Mike Bratz	G	6'2	185	25	80	2595	319	817	39	107	132	81	198	452	194	1	136	17	802	32	2.5	5.7	2.4	10.0
Roger Phegley	G-F	6'6	205	24	82	2269	474	965	49	224	267	84	246	184	262	7	65	15	1180	28	3.0	2.2	3.2	14.4
Richard Washington (from Dall)	C-F	6'11	225	25	69	1505	289	630	46	102	136	75	369	113	246	3	41	54	681	22	5.3	1.6	3.6	9.9
Don Ford (IL)	F	6'9	215	28	64	996	100	224	45	22	24	92	164	84	100	1	15	12	222	16	2.6	1.3	1.6	3.5
Geoff Huston (from Dall)	G	6'2	175	23	25	542	76	153	50	22	27	81	39	117	35	0	13	1	174	22	1.6	4.7	1.4	7.0
Dave Robisch (to Den)	C	6'10	240	31	11	372	37	98	38	29	36	81	85	44	21	0	7	6	103	34	7.7	4.0	1.9	9.4
Kim Hughes (from Den)	C	6'11	220	28	45	331	16	45	36	0	0	—	77	24	73	0	17	21	32	7	1.7	0.5	1.6	0.7
Chad Kinch (to Dall)	G	6'4	190	22	29	247	38	96	40	4	5	80	24	35	24	0	9	5	80	9	0.8	1.2	0.8	2.8
Walter Jordon (NJ)	F	6'7	198	24	30	207	29	75	39	10	17	59	42	11	35	0	11	5	68	7	1.4	0.4	1.2	2.3
Mack Calvin	G	6'	175	32	21	128	13	39	33	25	35	71	12	28	13	0	5	0	52	6	0.6	1.3	0.6	2.5
Bill Robinzine (to Dall)	F	6'7	230	27	8	84	14	32	44	5	8	63	13	5	19	1	4	0	33	11	1.6	0.6	2.4	4.1
Robert Smith	G	5'11	165	25	1	20	2	5	40	4	4	100	3	3	6	1	0	0	8	20	3.0	3.0	6.0	8.0
Jerome Whitehead (from Dall to SD)	C	6'10	220	24	3	8	1	3	33	0	0	—	3	0	6	0	1	0	2	3	1.0	0.0	2.0	0.7
John Lambert (XJ, to KC)	C	6'10	225	27	3	8	3	5	60	0	0	—	3	3	2	0	0	0	6	3	1.0	1.0	0.7	2.0
Elmore Smith - knee injury, Bill Willoughby - hold out, to Hou					3-PT FG — Mitchell 4-9, Carr 0-4, Ra. Smith 1-28, Bratz 57-169, Phegley 8-28, Washington 1-2, Ford 0-3, Huston 0-1, Calvin 1-5																			
DETROIT PISTONS	21-61 .256				SCOTTY ROBERTSON																			
Phil Hubbard	F	6'8	215	24	80	2289	433	880	49	294	426	69	586	150	317	14	80	20	1161	29	7.3	1.9	4.0	14.5
Terry Tyler	F	6'7	215	24	82	2549	476	895	53	148	250	59	567	136	215	2	112	180	1100	31	6.9	1.7	2.6	13.4
Kent Benson (BT)	C	6'10	245	26	59	1956	364	770	47	196	254	77	400	172	184	1	72	67	924	33	6.8	2.9	3.1	15.7
John Long (KJ)	G	6'5	210	24	59	1750	441	957	46	160	184	87	197	106	164	3	95	22	1044	30	3.3	1.8	2.8	17.7
Ron Lee	G	6'4	193	28	82	1829	113	323	35	113	156	72	220	362	260	4	166	29	341	22	2.7	4.4	3.2	4.2
Keith Herron	G-F	6'6	195	24	80	2270	432	954	45	228	267	85	211	148	154	1	91	26	1094	28	2.6	1.9	1.9	13.7
Paul Mokeski	C	7'	250	23	80	1815	224	458	49	120	200	60	418	135	267	7	38	73	568	23	5.2	1.7	3.3	7.1
Wayne Robinson	F	6'8	217	22	81	1592	234	509	46	175	240	73	294	112	186	2	46	24	643	20	3.6	1.4	2.3	7.9
Larry Drew	G	6'1	170	22	76	1581	197	484	41	106	133	80	120	249	125	0	88	7	504	21	1.6	3.3	1.6	6.6
Larry Wright	G	6'1	160	26	45	997	140	303	46	53	66	80	88	153	114	1	42	7	335	22	2.0	3.4	2.5	7.4
Greg Kelser (KJ)	F	6'7	190	23	25	654	120	285	42	68	106	64	120	45	89	0	34	29	308	26	4.8	1.8	3.6	12.3
Tony Fuller	G	6'4	185	22	15	248	24	66	36	12	16	75	42	28	25	0	10	1	60	17	2.8	1.9	1.7	4.0
Bob McAdoo (GJ, FJ, to NJ)	C	6'9	210	29	6	168	30	82	37	12	20	60	41	20	16	0	8	7	72	28	6.8	3.3	2.7	12.0
Norman Black	G	6'6	185	23	3	28	3	10	30	2	8	25	2	2	2	0	1	0	8	9	0.7	0.7	0.7	2.7
Edmund Lawrence	C	7'	228	28	3	19	5	8	63	2	4	50	4	1	6	0	1	0	12	6	1.3	0.3	2.0	4.0
3-PT FG —					Hubbard 1-3, Tyler 0-8, Benson 0-4, Long 2-11, Lee 2-13, Herron 2-11, Mokeski 0-1, Robinson 0-6, Drew 4-17, Wright 2-7, Kelser 0-2, Fuller 0-1																			
WESTERN CONFERENCE																								
MIDWEST DIVISION																								
SAN ANTONIO SPURS	52-30 .634				STAN ALBECK																			
Paul Griffin	F	6'9	205	26	82	1930	166	325	51	170	253	67	505	249	207	3	77	38	502	24	6.2	3.0	2.5	6.1
Mark Olberding	F	6'8	230	24	82	2408	348	685	51	315	380	83	471	277	307	6	75	31	1012	29	5.7	3.4	3.7	12.3
Dave Corzine	C	6'11	250	24	82	1960	366	747	49	125	175	71	636	117	212	0	42	99	857	24	7.8	1.4	2.6	10.5
George Gervin	G	6'7	185	28	82	2765	850	1729	49	512	620	83	419	260	212	4	94	56	2221	34	5.1	3.2	2.6	27.1
James Silas	G	6'3	180	31	75	2055	476	997	48	374	440	85	231	285	129	0	51	12	1326	27	3.1	3.8	1.7	17.7
George Johnson	C	6'11	205	32	82	1935	164	347	47	80	109	73	602	92	273	3	47	**278**	408	24	7.3	1.1	3.3	5.0
Reggie Johnson	F	6'9	205	23	79	1716	340	682	50	128	193	66	358	78	283	8	45	48	808	22	4.5	1.0	3.6	10.2
Johnny Moore	G	6'2	175	22	82	1578	249	520	48	105	172	61	196	373	178	0	120	22	604	19	2.4	4.5	2.2	7.4
Kevin Restani (BR)	F	6'9	225	29	64	999	192	369	52	62	88	70	174	81	103	0	16	14	449	16	2.7	1.3	1.6	7.0
Ron Brewer (from Port)	G	6'4	180	25	46	904	180	385	47	65	80	81	53	93	53	0	27	25	425	20	1.2	2.0	1.2	9.2
Mike Gale (to Port)	G	6'4	190	30	35	636	86	164	52	19	26	73	52	99	56	0	55	2	192	18	1.5	2.8	1.6	5.5
John Shumate (to Sea)	F	6'9	235	28	22	519	56	128	44	53	73	73	87	24	46	0	21	9	165	24	4.0	1.1	2.1	7.5
Michael Wiley (KJ)	F	6'9	200	23	33	271	76	138	55	36	48	75	64	11	38	1	8	6	188	8	1.9	0.3	1.2	5.7
Gus Gerard (from KC)	F	6'8	205	27	11	129	22	60	37	8	11	73	38	9	17	0	7	3	52	12	3.5	0.8	1.5	4.7
3-PT FG —					Olberding 1-7, Corzine 0-3, Gervin 9-35, Silas 0-2, R. Johnson 0-1, Moore 1-19, Restani 3-8, Brewer 0-4, Gale 1-3, Wiley 0-2, Gerard 0-1																			
KANSAS CITY KINGS	40-42 .488				COTTON FITZSIMMONS																			
Scott Wedman	F	6'7	215	28	81	2902	685	1437	48	140	204	69	433	226	294	4	97	46	1535	36	5.3	2.8	3.6	19.0
Reggie King	F	6'6	225	23	81	2743	472	867	54	264	386	68	786	122	227	2	102	41	1208	34	9.7	1.5	2.8	14.9
Sam Lacey	C	6'10	235	32	82	2228	237	536	44	92	117	79	584	399	302	5	95	120	567	27	7.1	4.9	3.7	6.9
Otis Birdsong	G	6'4	195	25	71	2593	710	1306	54	317	455	70	258	233	172	2	93	18	1747	37	3.6	3.3	2.4	24.6
Phil Ford (KJ)	G	6'2	176	24	66	2287	424	887	48	294	354	83	128	580	190	3	99	6	1153	35	1.9	8.8	2.9	17.5
Ernie Grunfeld	G	6'6	215	25	79	1584	260	486	53	75	101	74	206	205	155	1	60	15	595	20	2.6	2.6	2.0	7.5
Joe Meriweather	C-F	6'10	218	27	74	1514	206	415	50	148	213	69	393	77	219	4	27	80	560	20	5.3	1.0	3.0	7.6
Leon Douglas	C-F	6'10	230	26	79	1356	185	323	57	102	186	55	384	69	251	2	25	38	472	17	4.9	0.9	3.2	6.0
Lloyd Walton	G	6'	160	27	61	821	90	218	41	26	33	79	48	208	45	0	32	2	206	13	0.8	3.4	0.7	3.4
Hawkeye Whitney (KJ)	G-F	6'5	235	23	47	782	149	306	49	50	65	77	106	68	98	0	47	6	350	17	2.3	1.4	2.1	7.4
John Lambert (from Cle)	F	6'10	225	27	43	475	65	160	41	18	23	78	90	24	74	0	12	5	148	11	2.1	0.6	1.7	3.4
JoJo White	G	6'3	190	34	13	236	36	82	44	11	18	61	21	37	21	0	11	1	83	18	1.6	2.8	1.6	6.4
Frankie Sanders	F	6'6	200	23	23	186	34	77	44	20	22	91	21	17	20	0	16	1	88	8	0.9	0.7	0.9	3.8
Gus Gerard (to SA)	F	6'8	205	27	16	123	19	51	37	19	29	66	29	6	24	0	3	6	57	8	1.8	0.4	1.5	3.6
3-PT FG —					Wedman 25-77, Lacey 1-5, Birdsong 10-35, Ford 11-36, Douglas 0-3, Walton 0-1, Whitney 2-6, Lambert 0-2, Gerard 0-3																			

					TOTAL													Blkd		PER GAME				
Use Name	Pos	Hgt	Wgt	Age	G	Min	FG	FGA	%	FT	FTA	%	Reb	Ass	PF	DQ	Stls	Shts	Points	Min	Reb	Ass	PF	Points
					1980/81 N.B.A. — WESTERN CONFERENCE (continued) MIDWEST DIVISION (continued)																			
HOUSTON ROCKETS	40-42 .488				DEL HARRIS																			
Pobert Reid	F-G	6'8	205	25	82	2963	536	1113	48	229	303	76	583	344	325	4	163	66	1301	36	7.1	4.2	4.0	15.9
Rudy Tomjanovich	F	6'8	220	32	52	1264	263	563	47	65	82	79	208	81	121	0	19	6	603	24	4.0	1.6	2.3	11.6
Moses Malone	C	6'10	215	25	80	3245	806	1545	52	609	**804**	76	**1180**	141	223	0	83	150	2222	41	**14.8**	1.8	2.8	27.8
Calvin Murphy	G	5'9	165	32	76	2014	528	1074	49	206	215	**96**	87	222	209	0	111	6	1266	27	1.1	2.9	2.8	16.7
Mike Dunleavy	G	6'3	180	26	74	1609	310	632	49	156	186	84	118	268	165	1	64	2	777	22	1.6	3.6	2.2	10.5
Allen Leavell	G	6'1	170	23	79	1686	258	548	47	124	149	83	134	384	160	1	97	15	642	21	1.7	4.9	2.0	8.1
Billy Paultz	F-C	6'11	250	32	81	1659	262	517	51	75	153	49	391	105	182	1	28	72	599	20	4.8	1.3	2.2	7.4
Calvin Garrett	F	6'7	190	24	70	1638	188	415	45	50	62	81	264	132	167	0	50	10	427	23	3.8	1.9	2.4	6.1
Tom Henderson	G	6'3	190	28	66	1411	137	332	41	78	95	82	104	307	111	1	53	4	352	21	1.6	4.7	1.7	5.3
Bill Willoughby	F	6'8	205	23	55	1145	150	287	52	49	64	77	227	64	102	0	18	31	349	21	4.1	1.2	1.9	6.3
Major Jones	F	6'9	225	27	68	1003	117	252	46	64	101	63	234	41	112	0	18	23	298	15	3.4	0.6	1.6	4.4
John Stroud (IL)	F	6'7	215	23	9	88	11	34	32	3	4	75	13	9	7	0	1	0	25	10	1.4	1.0	0.8	2.8
Lee Johnson (to Det)	F	6'11	210	23	10	80	7	23	30	3	5	60	20	1	17	0	0	5	17	8	2.0	0.1	1.7	1.7
	3-PT FG —	Reid 0-4, Tomjanovich 12-51, Malone 1-3, Murphy 4-17, Dunleavy 1-16, Leavell 2-17, Paultz 0-3, Garrett 1-3, Henderson 0-3, Jones 0-1																						
DENVER NUGGETS	37-45 .451				DONNIE WALSH 11-20 (.355), DOUG MOE 26-25 (.510)																			
Alex English	F	6'8	190	26	81	3093	768	1555	49	390	459	85	646	290	255	2	106	100	1929	38	8.0	3.6	3.1	23.8
Kiki Vanderweghe (from Dall)	F	6'8	220	22	51	1376	229	537	43	130	159	82	270	94	116	0	29	24	588	27	5.3	1.8	2.3	11.5
Dan Issel	C	6'9	240	32	80	2641	614	1220	50	519	684	76	676	158	249	6	83	53	1749	33	8.5	2.0	3.1	21.9
David Thompson	G	6'4	195	26	77	2620	734	1451	51	489	615	80	287	231	231	3	53	60	1967	34	3.7	3.0	3.0	25.5
Kenny Higgs	G	6'	185	25	72	1689	209	474	44	140	172	81	145	408	243	5	101	6	562	23	2.0	5.7	3.4	7.8
Dave Robisch (from Cle)	C-F	6'10	240	31	73	1744	293	642	46	171	211	81	414	129	152	0	30	28	757	24	5.7	1.8	2.1	10.4
Cedric Hordges (KJ)	F	6'8	220	23	68	1599	221	480	46	130	186	70	458	104	226	4	33	19	572	24	6.7	1.5	3.3	8.4
T.R. Dunn	G	6'4	192	25	82	1427	146	354	41	79	121	65	301	81	141	0	66	29	371	17	3.7	1.0	1.7	4.5
Bill McKinney (from Utah)	G	6'	162	25	49	1134	203	412	49	118	140	84	110	203	124	0	61	7	525	23	2.2	4.1	2.5	10.7
Glen Gondrezick	F	6'6	218	25	73	1077	155	329	47	112	137	82	307	83	185	2	91	20	422	15	4.2	1.1	2.5	5.8
John Roche (NJ)	G	6'3	170	31	26	611	82	179	46	58	77	75	37	140	44	0	17	8	231	24	1.4	5.4	1.7	8.9
Carl Nicks (to Utah)	G	6'3	185	22	27	493	65	149	44	35	59	59	49	80	52	0	28	2	165	18	1.8	3.0	1.9	6.1
Kim Hughes (to Cle)	C	6'11	220	28	8	159	11	25	44	1	2	50	50	11	33	2	11	14	23	20	6.3	1.4	4.1	2.9
James Ray (KJ)	F	6'8	215	23	18	148	15	49	31	7	10	70	37	11	31	0	4	4	37	8	2.1	0.6	1.7	2.1
Ron Valentine	F	6'7	210	23	24	123	37	98	38	9	19	47	30	7	23	0	7	4	84	5	1.3	0.3	1.0	3.5
Jawann Oldham	C	7'	215	23	4	21	2	6	33	0	0	—	5	0	3	0	0	2	4	5	1.3	0.0	0.8	1.0
	3-PT FG —	English 3-5, Vanderweghe 0-7, Thompson 10-39, Higgs 4-34, Hordges 0-3, Dunn 0-2, McKinney 1-10, Gondrezick 0-2, Roche 9-27, Nicks 0-1, Ray 0-1, Valentine 1-2																						
UTAH JAZZ	28-54 .341				TOM NISSALKE																			
Adrian Dantley	F	6'5	210	24	80	**3417**	**909**	1627	56	**632**	784	81	509	322	245	1	109	18	**2452**	43	6.4	4.0	3.1	**30.7**
Ben Poquette	F-C	6'9	235	23	82	2808	324	614	53	126	162	78	629	161	342	18	67	174	777	34	7.7	2.0	4.2	9.5
Wayne Cooper	C	6'10	220	24	71	1420	213	471	45	62	90	69	440	52	219	8	18	51	489	20	6.2	0.7	3.1	6.9
Darrell Griffith	G	6'4	190	22	81	2867	716	1544	46	229	320	72	288	194	219	0	106	50	1671	35	3.6	2.4	2.7	20.6
Rickey Green	G	6'1	170	26	47	1307	176	366	48	70	97	72	116	235	123	2	75	1	422	28	2.5	5.0	2.6	9.0
Allan Bristow	F	6'7	210	29	82	2001	271	611	44	166	198	84	430	383	190	1	63	3	713	24	5.2	4.7	2.3	8.7
Ron Boone	G	6'2	200	34	52	1146	160	371	43	75	94	80	84	161	126	0	33	8	406	22	1.6	3.1	2.4	7.8
Jeff Wilkins	C	6'11	240	25	56	1058	117	260	45	27	40	68	274	40	169	3	32	46	261	19	4.9	0.7	3.0	4.7
Billy McKinney (to Den)	G	6'	162	25	35	1032	124	233	53	44	48	92	74	157	107	3	38	4	293	29	2.1	4.5	3.1	8.4
Jeff Judkins	G-F	6'6	185	24	62	666	92	216	43	45	51	88	93	59	84	0	16	2	238	11	1.5	1.0	1.4	3.8
Carl Nicks (from Den)	G	6'3	185	22	40	616	107	210	51	36	67	54	61	69	89	0	32	1	250	15	1.5	1.7	2.2	6.3
James Hardy	F	6'8	220	24	23	509	52	111	47	11	20	55	133	36	58	2	21	20	115	22	5.8	1.6	2.5	5.0
John Duren (KJ)	G	6'3	195	22	40	458	33	101	33	5	9	56	35	54	54	0	18	2	71	11	0.9	1.4	1.4	1.8
Mel Bennett	F	6'7	200	25	28	313	26	60	43	53	81	65	93	15	56	0	3	11	105	11	3.3	0.5	2.0	3.8
Brett Vroman	C	7'	220	25	11	93	10	27	37	14	19	74	25	9	26	1	5	5	34	8	2.3	0.8	2.4	3.1
Dick Miller (from Ind)	F	6'6	215	22	3	19	2	3	67	0	0	—	3	1	3	0	1	0	4	6	1.0	0.3	1.0	1.3
	3-PT FG —	Dantley 2-7, Poquette 3-6, Cooper 1-3, Griffith 10-52, Green 0-1, Bristow 5-18, Boone 11-39, McKinney 1-2, Judkins 9-28, Nicks 0-3, Duren 0-1, Bennett 0-2, Vroman 0-1																						
DALLAS MAVERICKS	15-67 .183				DICK MOTTA																			
Jim Spanarkel	F-G	6'5	190	23	82	2317	404	866	47	375	423	89	297	232	230	3	117	20	1184	28	3.6	2.8	2.8	14.4
Bill Robizine (from Cle)	F	6'7	230	27	70	1932	378	794	48	213	273	78	520	113	256	5	71	9	970	28	7.4	1.6	3.7	13.9
Tom LaGarde	C-F	6'10	230	25	82	2670	417	888	47	288	444	65	665	237	293	6	35	45	1122	33	8.1	2.9	3.6	13.7
Brad Davis	G	6'3	180	25	56	1686	230	410	56	163	204	80	151	385	156	2	52	11	626	30	2.7	6.9	2.8	11.2
Geoff Huston (to Cle)	G	6'2	175	23	56	1892	385	789	49	128	185	69	99	277	113	1	45	6	899	34	1.8	4.9	2.0	16.1
Scott Lloyd	C	6'10	230	28	72	2186	245	547	45	147	205	72	454	159	269	8	34	25	637	30	6.3	2.2	3.7	8.8
Oliver Mack (from Chi)	G	6'3	195	23	62	1666	278	600	46	79	123	64	229	162	114	0	55	7	635	27	3.7	2.6	1.8	10.2
Marty Byrnes	F	6'7	215	24	72	1360	216	451	48	120	157	76	177	113	126	0	29	17	561	19	2.5	1.6	1.8	7.8
Abdul Jeelani	F	6'8	210	26	66	1108	187	440	43	179	220	81	230	65	123	2	44	31	553	17	3.5	1.0	1.9	8.4
Winford Boynes	G-F	6'6	186	22	44	757	121	313	39	45	55	82	75	37	79	1	23	16	287	17	1.7	0.8	1.8	6.5
Stan Pietkiewicz (from SD)	G	6'5	200	24	36	431	55	133	41	11	14	79	41	75	26	0	15	2	140	12	1.1	2.1	0.7	3.9
Terry Duerod (to Bos)	G	6'2	180	24	18	337	74	161	46	18	27	67	39	30	19	0	12	4	168	19	2.2	1.7	1.1	9.3
Richard Washington (to Cle)	F-C	6'11	225	25	11	307	51	117	44	17	23	74	84	16	37	0	5	7	119	28	7.6	1.5	3.4	10.8
Joey Hassett (to GS)	G	6'5	180	25	17	280	59	142	42	10	13	77	25	18	21	0	5	0	138	16	1.5	1.1	1.2	8.1
Darrell Allums	F	6'9	220	22	22	276	23	67	34	13	22	59	65	25	51	2	5	8	59	13	3.0	1.1	2.3	2.7
Clarence Kea	F	6'6	218	21	16	199	37	81	46	43	62	69	67	5	44	2	6	1	117	12	4.2	0.3	2.8	7.3
Jerome Whitehead (to Cle, SD)	C	6'10	220	24	7	118	16	38	42	5	11	45	28	2	16	0	4	1	37	17	4.0	0.3	2.3	5.3
Chad Kinch (from Cle)	G	6'4	190	22	12	106	14	45	31	10	13	77	9	10	9	0	2	1	38	9	0.8	0.8	0.8	3.2
Austin Carr (to Wash)	G	6'4	200	32	8	77	7	28	25	2	4	50	9	9	10	0	1	0	16	10	1.1	1.1	1.3	2.0
Ralph Drollinger (KJ)	C	7'2	250	26	6	67	7	14	50	1	4	25	19	14	16	0	1	2	15	11	3.2	2.3	2.7	2.5
Monti Davis (from Phi)	F	6'7	205	22	1	8	0	4	0	1	5	20	3	0	0	0	0	1	1	8	3.0	0.0	0.0	1.0
Kiki Vandeweghe - holdout, to Den	3-PT FG —	Spanarkel 1-10, Robinzine 1-6, B. Davis 3-17, Huston 1-4, Lloyd 0-2, Mack 0-9, Byrnes 9-20, Jeelani 0-1, Pietkiewicz 19-48, Duerod 2-6, Hassett 10-14, Allums 0-1, Kea 0-1																						

Use Name	Pos	Hgt	Wgt	Age	G	Min	FG	FGA	%	FT	FTA	%	Reb	Ass	PF	DQ	Stls	Blkd Shts	Points	Min	Reb	Ass	PF	Points
					TOTAL															PER GAME				

1980/81 N.B.A. — WESTERN CONFERENCE
PACIFIC DIVISION

Use Name	Pos	Hgt	Wgt	Age	G	Min	FG	FGA	%	FT	FTA	%	Reb	Ass	PF	DQ	Stls	Blkd Shts	Points	Min	Reb	Ass	PF	Points
PHOENIX SUNS	**57-25 .695**				**JOHN McCLEOD**																			
Truck Robinson	F	6'7	225	29	82	3088	647	1280	51	249	396	63	789	206	220	1	68	38	1543	38	9.6	2.5	2.7	18.8
Jeff Cook	F-C	6'10	215	24	79	2192	286	616	46	100	155	65	467	201	236	3	82	54	672	28	5.9	2.5	3.0	8.5
Alvan Adams	C	6'9	220	26	75	2054	458	870	53	199	259	77	546	344	226	2	106	69	1115	27	7.3	4.6	3.0	14.9
Walter Davis	G-F	6'6	195	26	78	2182	593	1101	54	209	250	84	200	302	192	3	97	12	1402	28	2.6	3.9	2.5	18.0
Dennis Johnson	G	6'4	195	26	79	2615	532	1220	44	411	501	82	363	291	244	2	136	61	1486	33	4.6	3.7	3.1	18.8
Johnny High	G	6'3	185	23	81	1750	246	576	43	183	264	69	228	202	251	2	129	26	677	22	2.8	2.5	3.1	8.4
Rich Kelley	C	7'	240	27	81	1686	196	387	51	175	231	76	441	282	210	0	79	63	567	21	5.4	3.5	2.6	7.0
Kyle Macy	G	6'3	175	23	82	1469	272	532	51	107	119	90	132	160	120	0	76	5	663	18	1.6	2.0	1.5	8.1
Alvin Scott	F	6'7	185	25	82	1423	173	348	50	97	127	76	268	114	124	0	60	70	444	17	3.3	1.4	1.5	5.4
Joel Kramer	F	6'7	203	25	82	1065	136	258	53	63	91	69	232	88	132	0	35	17	335	13	2.8	1.1	1.6	4.1
Mike Niles	F	6'6	225	25	44	231	48	138	35	17	37	46	58	15	41	0	8	1	115	5	1.3	0.3	0.9	2.6
Don Buse - holdout, (to Ind),																								
Bayard Forrest - cancer																								
3-PT FG —	Cook 0-5, Davis 7-17, Johnson 11-51, High 2-24, Kelley 0-2, Macy 12-51, Scott 1-6, Kramer 0-1, Niles 2-4																							
LOS ANGELES LAKERS	**54-28 .659**				**PAUL WESTHEAD**																			
Jamaal Wilkes	F	6'6	190	27	81	3028	786	1495	53	254	335	76	435	235	223	1	121	29	1827	37	5.4	2.9	2.8	22.6
Jim Chones	F-C	6'11	220	31	82	2562	378	751	50	126	193	65	657	153	324	4	39	96	882	31	8.0	1.9	4.0	10.8
Kareem Abdul-Jabbar	C	7'2	232	33	80	2976	836	1457	57	423	552	77	821	272	244	4	59	228	2095	37	10.3	3.4	3.1	26.2
Magic Johnson (KJ)	G	6'8	215	21	37	1371	312	587	53	171	225	76	320	317	100	0	127	27	798	37	8.6	8.6	2.7	21.6
Norm Nixon	G	6'2	175	25	79	2962	576	1210	48	196	252	78	232	696	226	2	146	11	1350	37	2.9	8.8	2.9	17.1
Michael Cooper	G-F	6'5	170	24	81	2625	321	654	49	117	149	79	336	332	249	4	133	78	763	32	4.1	4.1	3.1	9.4
Jim Brewer	F	6'9	220	29	78	1107	107	197	54	15	40	38	281	55	158	2	43	58	217	14	3.6	0.7	2.0	2.8
Mark Landsberger (NJ)	F	6'8	230	25	69	1086	164	327	50	62	116	53	377	27	135	0	19	6	390	16	5.5	0.4	2.0	5.7
Eddie Jordan (from NJ)	G	6'1	170	25	60	987	120	279	43	63	95	66	80	195	136	0	74	7	306	16	1.3	3.3	2.3	5.1
Butch Carter (IL)	G	6'5	180	22	54	672	114	247	46	70	95	74	65	52	99	0	23	1	301	12	1.2	1.0	1.8	5.6
Brad Holland	G	6'3	185	24	41	295	47	111	42	35	49	71	29	23	44	0	21	1	130	7	0.7	0.6	1.1	3.2
Alan Hardy (VJ)	F	6'7	195	23	22	111	22	59	37	7	10	70	19	3	13	0	1	9	51	5	0.9	0.1	0.6	2.3
Tony Jackson	G	6'	170	22	2	14	1	3	33	0	0	—	2	2	1	0	2	0	2	7	1.0	1.0	0.5	1.0
Myles Patrick (BJ)	F	6'8	220	26	3	9	2	5	40	1	2	50	2	1	3	0	0	0	5	3	0.7	0.3	1.0	1.7
3-PT FG —	Wilkes 1-13, Chones 0-4, Abdul-Jabbar 0-1, Johnson 3-17, Nixon 2-12, Cooper 4-19, Brewer 0-2, Landsberger 0-1, Jordan 3-12, Carter 3-10, Holland 1-3																							
PORTLAND TRAIL BLAZERS	**45-37 .549**				**JACK RAMSAY**																			
Calvin Natt	F	6'6	220	23	74	2111	395	794	50	200	283	71	431	159	188	2	73	18	994	29	5.8	2.1	2.5	13.4
Kermit Washington	F	6'8	230	29	73	2120	325	571	57	181	288	63	686	149	258	5	85	86	831	29	9.4	2.0	3.5	11.4
Mychal Thompson	C-F	6'10	226	25	79	2790	569	1151	49	207	323	64	686	284	260	5	62	170	1345	35	8.7	3.6	3.3	17.0
Jim Paxson	G	6'6	200	23	79	2701	585	1092	54	182	248	73	211	299	172	1	140	9	1354	34	2.7	3.8	2.2	17.1
Kelvin Ransey	G	6'1	170	22	80	2431	525	1162	45	164	219	75	195	555	201	1	88	9	1217	30	2.4	6.9	2.5	15.2
Bob Gross	F-G	6'6	200	27	82	1934	253	479	53	135	159	85	328	251	238	5	90	67	641	24	4.0	3.1	2.9	7.8
Tom Owens	C-F	6'10	220	31	79	1843	322	630	51	191	250	76	456	140	273	10	36	47	835	23	5.8	1.8	3.5	10.6
Billy Ray Bates	G	6'4	210	24	77	1560	439	902	49	170	199	85	157	196	120	0	82	6	1062	20	2.0	2.5	1.6	13.8
Kelvin Kunnert (KJ)	C	7'	231	29	55	842	101	216	47	42	54	78	287	67	143	1	17	32	244	15	5.2	1.2	2.6	4.4
Ron Brewer (to SA)	G	6'4	180	25	29	548	95	246	39	26	36	72	33	55	42	0	34	9	217	19	1.1	1.9	1.4	7.5
Mike Gale (from SA)	G	6'4	190	30	42	476	71	145	49	36	42	86	47	70	61	0	39	5	179	11	1.1	1.7	1.5	4.3
Mike Harper	F-C	6'10	195	23	55	461	56	136	41	37	85	44	93	17	73	0	23	20	149	8	1.7	0.3	1.3	2.7
Geoff Crompton (KJ)	C	6'11	288	25	6	33	4	8	50	1	5	20	18	2	4	0	0	2	9	6	3.0	0.3	0.7	1.5
Roy Lee Hamilton	G	6'2	180	23	1	5	1	3	33	1	2	50	3	0	1	0	0	0	3	5	3.0	0.0	1.0	3.0
3-PT FG —	Natt 4-8, Washington 0-1, Thompson 0-1, Paxson 2-30, Ransey 3-31, Gross 0-9, Owens 0-4, Bates 14-54, Brewer 1-3, Gale 1-4, Harper 0-3																							
GOLDEN STATE WARRIORS	**39-43 .476**				**AL ATTLES**																			
Bernard King	F	6'7	205	24	81	2914	731	1244	59	307	439	70	551	287	304	5	72	34	1771	36	6.8	3.5	3.8	21.9
Larry Smith	F	6'8	215	22	82	2578	304	594	51	177	301	59	994	93	316	10	70	63	785	31	12.1	1.1	3.9	9.6
Joe Barry Carroll	C	7'	225	22	82	2919	616	1254	49	315	440	72	759	117	313	10	50	121	1547	36	9.3	1.4	3.8	18.9
World Free (RJ)	G	6'2	185	27	65	2370	516	1157	45	528	649	81	159	361	183	1	85	11	1565	36	2.4	5.6	2.8	24.1
John Lucas	G	6'3	175	27	66	1919	222	506	44	107	145	74	154	464	140	1	83	2	555	29	2.3	7.0	2.1	8.4
Purvis Short	F-G	6'7	210	23	79	2309	549	1157	47	168	205	82	391	249	244	3	78	19	1269	29	4.9	3.2	3.1	16.1
Sonny Parker	G-F	6'6	200	25	73	1317	191	388	49	94	128	73	194	106	112	0	67	13	476	18	2.7	1.5	1.5	6.5
Clifford Ray	C	6'9	235	31	66	838	64	152	42	29	62	47	217	52	194	2	24	13	157	13	3.3	0.8	2.9	2.4
Lorenzo Romar (XJ)	G	6'1	175	22	53	726	87	211	41	43	63	68	56	136	64	0	27	3	219	14	1.1	2.6	1.2	4.1
Billy Reid	G	6'5	195	23	59	597	84	185	45	22	39	56	60	71	111	0	33	5	190	10	1.0	1.2	1.9	3.2
Rickey Brown (KJ)	F-C	6'10	215	22	45	580	83	162	51	16	21	76	166	21	103	4	9	14	182	13	3.7	0.5	2.3	4.0
Joe Hassett (from Dall)	G	6'5	180	25	24	434	84	198	42	7	8	88	43	56	44	0	8	2	218	18	1.8	2.3	1.8	9.1
Phil Chenier	G	6'3	180	30	9	82	11	33	33	6	6	100	8	7	10	0	0	0	29	9	0.9	0.8	1.1	3.2
William Mayfield	F	6'7	205	23	7	54	8	18	44	1	2	50	9	1	8	0	0	1	17	8	1.3	0.1	1.1	2.4
Rudy White (to Sea)	G	6'2	195	27	4	43	9	18	50	4	4	100	0	2	7	0	4	0	22	11	0.0	0.5	1.8	5.5
Tom Abernathy (to Ind)	F	6'7	220	26	10	39	1	3	33	2	3	67	8	1	5	0	1	0	4	4	0.8	0.1	0.5	0.4
John Mengelt	F	6'2	195	31	2	11	0	4	0	0	0	-	0	2	0	0	0	0	0	6	0.0	1.0	0.0	0.0
3-PT FG —	King 2-6, Carrol 0-2, Free 5-31, Lucas 4-24, Short 3-17, Romar 2-6, Reid 0-5, Hassett 43-116, Chenier 1-3																							

1980/81 N.B.A. — WESTERN CONFERENCE
PACIFIC DIVISION (Continued)

SAN DIEGO CLIPPERS 36-46 .439 **PAUL SILAS**

Use Name	Pos	Hgt	Wgt	Age	G	Min	FG	FGA	%	FT	FTA	%	Reb	Ass	PF	DQ	Stls	Blkd Shts	Points	Min	Reb	Ass	PF	Points
					TOTAL															PER GAME				
Joe Bryant	F	6'9	185	26	82	2359	379	791	48	193	244	79	440	189	264	4	72	34	953	29	5.4	2.3	3.2	11.6
Michael Brooks	F	6'7	220	22	82	2479	488	1018	48	226	320	71	442	208	234	2	99	31	1202	30	5.4	2.5	2.9	14.7
Sven Nater	C	6'11	240	30	82	2809	517	935	55	244	307	79	1017	199	295	8	49	46	1278	34	12.4	2.4	3.6	15.6
Freeman Williams	G	6'4	195	24	82	1976	642	1381	46	253	297	85	129	164	157	0	91	5	1585	24	1.6	2.0	1.9	19.3
Brian Taylor	G	6'2	185	29	80	2312	310	591	52	146	185	79	151	440	212	0	118	23	810	29	1.9	5.5	2.7	10.1
Phil Smith	G	6'4	187	28	76	2378	519	1057	49	237	313	76	156	372	231	1	84	18	1279	31	2.1	4.9	3.0	16.8
Garfield Heard	F	6'6	219	32	78	1631	149	396	38	79	101	78	348	122	196	0	104	72	377	21	4.5	1.6	2.5	4.8
Henry Bibby	G	6'1	185	31	73	1112	118	306	39	67	98	68	74	200	85	0	47	2	335	15	1.0	2.7	1.2	4.6
Sidney Wicks	F-C	6'9	225	31	49	1083	125	286	44	76	150	51	223	111	168	3	40	40	326	22	4.6	2.3	3.4	6.7
Ron Davis	F-G	6'6	198	26	64	817	139	314	44	94	158	59	119	47	98	0	36	11	374	13	1.9	0.7	1.5	5.8
Jerome Whitehead (from Dall, Cle)	C	6'10	220	24	38	562	66	139	47	23	45	51	183	24	100	2	15	8	155	15	4.8	0.6	2.6	4.1
Wally Rank	F-G	6'6	220	22	25	153	21	57	37	13	28	46	30	17	33	1	7	1	55	6	1.2	0.7	1.3	2.2
Tony Price	G	6'6	190	23	5	29	2	7	29	0	0	—	0	3	3	0	2	1	4	6	0.0	0.6	0.6	0.8
Stan Pietkewicz (to Dall)	G	6'5	200	24	6	30	2	5	40	0	0	—	1	2	2	0	0	0	4	5	0.2	0.3	0.3	0.7

Bill Walton - foot injury

3-PT FG — Bryant 2-15, Brooks 0-6, Williams 48-141, Taylor 44-115, Smith 4-18, Heard 0-7, Bibby 32-95, Wicks 0-1, Davis 2-8, Whitehead 0-1

SEATTLE SUPER SONICS 34-48 .415 **LENNY WILKENS**

Use Name	Pos	Hgt	Wgt	Age	G	Min	FG	FGA	%	FT	FTA	%	Reb	Ass	PF	DQ	Stls	Blkd Shts	Points	Min	Reb	Ass	PF	Points
John Johnson	F	6'7	200	33	80	2324	373	866	43	173	214	81	362	312	202	2	57	25	919	29	4.5	3.9	2.5	11.5
James Bailey	F	6'9	220	23	82	2539	444	889	50	256	361	71	607	98	332	11	74	143	1145	31	7.4	1.2	4.0	14.0
Jack Sikma	C-F	6'11	230	25	82	2920	595	1311	45	340	413	82	852	248	282	5	78	93	1530	36	10.4	3.0	3.4	18.7
Paul Westphal (BF)	G	6'4	195	30	36	1078	221	500	44	153	184	83	68	148	70	0	46	14	601	30	1.9	4.1	1.9	16.7
Vinnie Johnson	G	6'2	200	24	81	2311	419	785	53	214	270	79	366	341	198	0	78	20	1053	29	4.5	4.2	2.4	13.0
Fred Brown	G	6'3	185	32	78	1986	505	1035	49	173	208	83	175	233	141	0	88	13	1206	25	2.2	3.0	1.8	15.5
Wally Walker	F	6'7	190	26	82	1796	290	626	46	109	169	64	315	122	168	1	53	15	689	22	3.8	1.5	2.0	8.4
Bill Hanzlik	G	6'7	185	23	74	1259	138	289	48	119	150	79	153	111	168	1	58	20	369	17	2.1	1.5	2.3	5.0
Armond Hill (from Atl)	G	6'4	190	27	51	1114	78	219	36	99	122	81	108	174	147	3	40	8	255	22	2.1	3.4	2.9	5.0
James Donaldson	C	7'2	278	23	68	980	129	238	54	101	170	59	309	42	79	0	8	74	359	14	4.5	0.6	1.2	5.3
Dennis Awtrey (XJ)	C	6'10	240	32	47	607	44	93	47	14	20	70	108	54	85	0	12	8	102	13	2.3	1.1	1.8	2.2
Lonnie Shelton (BW)	F	6'8	245	25	14	440	73	174	42	36	55	65	78	35	48	0	22	3	182	31	5.6	2.5	3.4	13.0
Jacky Dorsey	F	6'7	230	26	29	253	20	70	29	13	25	52	88	9	47	0	9	1	53	9	3.0	0.3	1.6	1.8
Rudy White (from GS)	G	6'2	195	27	12	165	14	47	30	11	12	92	11	18	16	0	5	1	39	14	0.9	1.5	1.3	3.3
John Shumate (from SA)	F	6'9	235	28	2	8	0	3	0	2	3	67	1	0	3	0	0	0	2	4	0.5	0.0	1.5	1.0

Gus Williams - holdout

3-PT FG — J. Johnson 0-1, Bailey 1-2, Sikma 0-5, Westphal 6-25, V. Johnson 1-5, Brown 23-64, Walker 0-3, Hanzlik 1-5, Hill 0-6, White 0-1

PLAYOFFS

BOSTON CELTICS **BILL FITCH**

defeated Chicago 4-0; H121-109, H106-97, 113-107, 109-103
defeated Philadelphia 4-3; H104-105, H118-99, 100-110, 105-107, H111-109, 100-98, H91-90
defeated Houston 4-2; H98-95, H90-92, 94-71, 86-91, H80-109, 102-91

Use Name	Pos	Hgt	Wgt	Age	G	Min	FG	FGA	%	FT	FTA	%	Reb	Ass	PF	DQ	Stls	Blkd Shts	Points	Min	Reb	Ass	PF	Points
Cedric Maxwell	F	6'8	205	25	17	598	101	174	58	72	88	82	125	46	53	0	12	16	274	35	7.4	2.7	3.1	16.1
Larry Bird	F	6'9	220	24	17	750	147	313	47	76	85	89	218	103	53	0	39	17	373	44	12.8	6.1	3.1	21.9
Robert Parish	C	7'	230	27	17	492	108	219	49	39	58	67	146	19	74	2	21	39	255	29	8.6	1.1	4.4	15.0
Chris Ford	G	6'5	190	31	17	507	66	146	45	15	25	60	45	46	47	0	14	1	154	30	2.6	2.7	2.8	9.1
Nate Archibald	G	6'1	150	32	17	630	95	211	45	76	94	81	28	107	39	0	13	0	266	37	1.6	6.3	2.3	15.6
Kevin McHale	F-C	6'10	235	23	17	296	61	113	54	23	36	64	59	14	51	1	4	25	145	17	3.5	0.8	3.0	8.5
M.L. Carr	G-F	6'6	205	29	17	288	42	101	42	18	24	75	25	14	32	0	10	6	102	17	1.5	0.8	1.9	6.0
Rick Robey	C	6'11	235	24	17	265	35	81	43	16	35	46	60	12	44	0	2	5	86	16	3.5	0.7	2.6	5.1
Gerald Henderson	G	6'2	175	24	16	228	41	86	48	10	12	83	25	26	24	0	10	3	92	14	1.6	1.6	1.5	5.8
Eric Fernsten	F	6'10	205	27	8	14	0	3	0	2	3	67	4	1	3	0	1	0	2	2	0.5	0.1	0.4	0.3
Terry Duerod	G	6'2	180	24	10	12	4	10	40	0	0	—	0	0	0	0	1	0	8	1	0.0	0.0	0.0	0.8

3-PT FG — Bird 3-8, Ford 7-25, Archibald 0-5, Carr 0-4, Henderson 0-1, Duerod 0-2

HOUSTON ROCKETS **DEL HARRIS**

defeated Los Angeles 2-1; 111-107, H106-111, 89-86
defeated San Antonio 4-3; 107-98, 113-125, H112-99, H112-114, 123-117, H96-101, 105-100
defeated Kansas City 4-1; 97-78, 79-88, H92-88, H100-89, 97-88
lost to Boston 2-4; 95-98, 92-90, H71-94, H91-86, 80-109, H91-102

Use Name	Pos	Hgt	Wgt	Age	G	Min	FG	FGA	%	FT	FTA	%	Reb	Ass	PF	DQ	Stls	Blkd Shts	Points	Min	Reb	Ass	PF	Points
Robert Reid	F-G	6'8	205	25	21	868	139	303	46	61	92	66	142	98	**80**	**2**	**50**	24	339	41	6.8	4.7	3.8	16.1
Billy Paultz	F-C	6'11	250	32	21	720	111	246	45	32	48	67	147	35	69	1	13	27	254	34	7.0	1.7	3.3	12.1
Moses Malone	C	6'10	215	25	21	**955**	**207**	**432**	48	**148**	**208**	71	**305**	35	54	0	13	34	**562**	**45**	**14.5**	1.7	2.6	26.8
Calvin Murphy	G	5'9	165	32	19	540	142	287	49	58	60	97	24	57	69	0	26	0	344	28	1.3	3.0	3.6	18.1
Tom Henderson	G	6'3	190	28	21	615	59	132	45	23	28	82	55	104	39	0	17	1	141	29	2.6	5.0	1.9	6.7
Mike Dunleavy	G	6'3	180	26	20	472	69	152	45	33	38	87	42	68	59	1	15	1	177	24	2.1	3.4	3.0	8.9
Bill Willoughby	F	6'8	205	23	19	417	42	116	36	30	40	75	85	22	42	0	14	19	114	22	4.5	1.2	2.2	6.0
Allen Leavell	G	6'1	170	23	17	217	30	77	39	15	17	88	17	44	26	0	18	4	75	13	1.0	2.6	1.5	4.4
Calvin Garrett	F	6'7	190	24	13	117	9	21	43	7	8	88	15	6	10	0	5	1	25	9	1.2	0.5	0.8	1.9
Major Jones	F	6'9	225	27	12	88	10	21	48	2	5	40	18	5	15	0	3	2	22	7	1.5	0.4	1.3	1.8
Rudy Tomjanovich	F	6'8	220	32	8	31	1	9	11	4	6	67	6	0	3	0	0	0	6	4	0.8	0.0	0.4	0.8

3-PT FG — Reid 0-2, Paultz 0-1, Malone 0-2, Murphy 2-7, Henderson 0-1, Dunleavy 6-15, Willoughby 0-1, Tomjanovich 0-3

Use Name	Pos	Hgt	Wgt	Age	G	Min	FG	FGA	%	FT	FTA	%	Reb	Ass	PF	DQ	Stls	Blkd Shts	Points	Min	Reb	Ass	PF	Points
					TOTAL															PER GAME				

1980/81 N.B.A. — PLAYOFFS

PHILADELPHIA 76ers — **BILLY CUNNINGHAM**

defeated Indiana 2-0; H124-108, 96-85
defeated Milwaukee 4-3; H125-122, H99-109, 108-103, 98-109, H116-99, 86-109, H99-98
lost to Boston 3-4; 105-104, 99-118, H110-100, H107-105, 109-111, H98-100, 91-90

Use Name	Pos	Hgt	Wgt	Age	G	Min	FG	FGA	%	FT	FTA	%	Reb	Ass	PF	DQ	Stls	Blkd Shts	Points	Min	Reb	Ass	PF	Points
Julius Erving	F	6'7	210	30	16	592	143	301	48	81	107	76	114	54	54	0	22	**41**	367	37	7.1	3.4	3.4	22.9
Bobby Jones	F	6'9	205	29	16	443	81	160	51	73	88	83	88	33	60	1	18	21	235	28	5.5	2.1	3.8	14.7
Caldwell Jones	C-F	6'11	225	30	16	580	54	95	57	31	42	74	155	27	53	0	7	31	139	36	9.7	1.7	3.3	8.7
Lionel Hollins	G	6'3	185	27	16	490	67	152	44	29	37	78	34	65	42	0	17	1	163	31	2.1	4.1	2.6	10.2
Maurice Cheeks	G	6'1	187	24	16	513	68	125	54	32	42	76	51	116	55	1	40	12	168	32	3.2	**7.3**	3.4	10.5
Darryl Dawkins	C	6'11	252	23	16	421	86	153	56	49	68	72	98	14	71	**2**	3	16	221	26	6.1	0.9	4.4	13.8
Andrew Toney	G	6'3	190	23	16	356	77	180	43	66	81	81	37	54	50	0	11	7	221	22	2.3	3.4	3.1	13.8
Steve Mix	F	6'7	219	33	16	206	32	77	42	24	26	92	42	10	16	0	4	2	88	13	2.6	0.6	1.0	5.5
Clint Richardson	G	6'3	195	24	13	181	20	38	53	9	17	53	21	12	15	0	6	3	49	14	1.6	0.9	1.2	3.8
Earl Cureton	F	6'9	215	23	9	36	6	18	33	0	2	0	9	2	3	0	1	2	12	4	1.0	0.2	0.3	1.3
Ollie Johnson	F	6'6	200	31	8	22	3	10	30	0	0	—	5	2	1	0	2	1	6	3	0.6	0.3	0.1	0.8

3-PT FG — Erving 0-1, Hollins 0-1, Cheeks 0-3, Toney 1-9, Mix 0-1, Johnson 0-1

KANSAS CITY KINGS — **COTTON FITZSIMMONS**

defeated Portland 2-1; 98-97(OT), H119-124(OT), 104-95
defeated Phoenix 4-3; 80-102, 88-83, H93-92, H102-95, 89-101, H76-81, 95-88
lost to Houston 1-4; H78-97, H88-79, 88-92, 89-100, H88-97

Use Name	Pos	Hgt	Wgt	Age	G	Min	FG	FGA	%	FT	FTA	%	Reb	Ass	PF	DQ	Stls	Blkd Shts	Points	Min	Reb	Ass	PF	Points
Scott Wedman	F-G	6'7	215	28	15	657	129	297	43	40	56	71	87	58	51	0	18	8	307	44	5.8	3.9	3.4	20.5
Reggie King	F	6'6	225	23	15	620	122	248	49	75	102	74	149	25	49	0	18	10	319	41	9.9	1.7	3.3	21.3
Sam Lacey	C	6'10	235	32	15	533	60	143	42	30	35	86	120	80	63	**2**	28	23	150	36	8.0	5.3	4.2	10.0
Ernie Grunfeld	G	6'6	215	25	15	633	98	201	49	54	67	81	63	88	51	1	30	9	252	42	4.2	5.9	3.4	16.8
Phil Ford (KJ)	G	6'2	176	24	5	158	15	35	43	9	13	69	8	29	9	0	5	0	39	32	1.6	5.8	1.8	7.8
Leon Douglas	F-C	6'10	230	26	15	318	15	32	47	15	35	43	65	11	47	1	4	3	45	21	4.3	0.7	3.1	3.0
Otis Birdsong	G	6'4	195	25	8	234	56	98	57	11	18	61	21	27	13	1	12	0	124	29	2.6	3.4	1.6	15.5
Joe Meriweather	C-F	6'10	218	27	10	199	24	49	49	8	14	57	31	5	31	1	5	7	56	20	3.1	0.5	3.1	5.6
John Lambert	F	6'10	225	27	15	175	22	54	41	5	6	83	37	9	21	0	5	4	49	12	2.5	0.6	1.4	3.3
Lloyd Walton	G	6'	160	27	8	73	4	15	27	3	4	75	7	19	6	0	4	0	11	9	0.9	2.4	0.8	1.4
Frankie Sanders	F	6'6	200	23	9	50	9	18	50	4	4	100	5	2	8	0	3	0	23	6	0.6	0.2	0.9	2.6

3-PT FG — Wedman 9-32, King 0-1, Lacey 0-3, Grunfeld 2-4, Ford 0-1, Birdsong 1-1, Lambert 0-3, Walton 0-1, Sanders 1-2

SAN ANTONIO SPURS — **STAN ALBECK**

lost to Houston 3-4; H98-107, H125-113, 99-112, 114-112, H117-123, 101-96, H100-105

Use Name	Pos	Hgt	Wgt	Age	G	Min	FG	FGA	%	FT	FTA	%	Reb	Ass	PF	DQ	Stls	Blkd Shts	Points	Min	Reb	Ass	PF	Points
Reggie Johnson	F	6'9	205	23	7	224	35	73	48	17	25	68	34	16	27	**2**	4	5	89	32	4.9	2.3	3.9	12.7
Mark Olberding	F	6'8	230	24	7	254	58	105	55	21	25	84	41	30	31	1	4	0	138	36	5.9	4.3	**4.4**	19.7
George Johnson	C	6'11	205	32	7	165	12	26	46	7	10	70	63	6	20	0	3	16	31	24	9.0	0.9	2.9	4.4
George Gervin	G	6'7	185	28	7	274	77	154	50	36	45	80	35	24	19	1	5	5	190	39	5.0	3.4	2.7	**27.1**
James Silas	G	6'3	180	31	7	161	27	69	39	26	32	81	15	19	9	0	4	0	80	23	2.1	2.7	1.3	11.4
Paul Griffin	F	6'9	205	26	7	183	14	24	58	9	20	45	40	29	28	**2**	6	5	37	26	5.7	4.1	4.0	5.3
Dave Corzine	C	6'11	250	24	7	161	27	55	49	9	13	69	48	16	15	0	4	8	63	23	6.9	2.3	2.1	9.0
Johnny Moore	G	6'2	175	22	7	124	18	37	49	6	8	75	13	27	14	0	10	1	42	18	1.9	3.9	2.0	6.0
Ron Brewer	G	6'4	180	25	7	118	29	61	48	21	29	72	5	13	6	0	1	6	80	17	0.7	1.9	0.9	11.4
Kevin Restani	C-F	6'9	225	29	3	11	1	3	33	0	0	—	2	0	2	0	0	1	2	4	0.7	0.0	0.7	0.7
Michael Wiley	F	6'9	200	23	3	5	0	1	0	2	2	100	0	0	2	0	0	0	2	2	0.0	0.0	0.7	0.7

3-PT FG — Olberding 1-3, Gervin 0-3, Moore 0-3, Brewer 1-3

MILWAUKEE BUCKS — **DON NELSON**

lost to Philadelphia 3-4; 122-125, 109-99, H103-108, H109-98, 99-116, H109-86, 98-99

Use Name	Pos	Hgt	Wgt	Age	G	Min	FG	FGA	%	FT	FTA	%	Reb	Ass	PF	DQ	Stls	Blkd Shts	Points	Min	Reb	Ass	PF	Points
Marques Johnson	F	6'7	218	24	7	266	75	135	56	23	32	72	66	34	14	0	10	7	173	38	9.4	4.9	2.0	24.7
Mickey Johnson	F	6'10	190	28	7	170	26	65	40	30	35	86	47	13	25	0	9	6	82	24	6.7	1.9	3.6	11.7
Bob Lanier	C	6'11	250	32	7	236	50	85	**59**	23	32	72	52	28	18	0	12	8	123	34	7.4	4.0	2.6	17.6
Sidney Moncrief	G-F	6'4	190	23	7	277	30	69	43	38	51	75	47	20	24	0	12	3	98	40	6.7	2.9	3.4	14.0
Quinn Buckner	G	6'3	205	26	7	183	26	60	43	11	16	69	20	35	26	1	11	0	63	26	2.9	5.0	3.7	9.0
Junior Bridgeman	F-G	6'4	210	27	7	183	42	91	46	13	16	81	15	23	27	0	6	0	98	26	2.1	3.3	3.9	14.0
Brian Winters	G	6'4	185	28	7	181	28	61	46	12	16	75	23	22	22	1	10	1	70	26	3.3	3.1	3.1	10.0
Harvey Catchings	C-F	6'9	218	29	7	109	3	16	19	2	2	100	26	8	24	0	0	11	8	16	3.7	1.1	3.4	1.1
Mike Evans	G	6'1	170	25	4	38	9	17	53	7	8	88	1	6	9	0	0	1	25	10	0.3	1.5	2.3	6.3
Pat Cummings	F	6'9	235	24	5	25	3	11	27	3	4	75	6	0	2	0	1	0	9	5	1.2	0.0	0.4	1.8
Len Elmore	C	6'9	220	28	4	12	0	1	0	0	0	—	0	0	4	0	0	0	0	3	0.0	0.0	1.0	0.0

3-PT FG — Ma. Johnson 0-1, Mi. Johnson 0-1, Bridgeman 1-1, Winters 2-6, Evans 0-2

PHOENIX SUNS — **JOHN McLEOD**

lost to Kansas City 3-4; H102-80, H83-88, 92-93, 95-102, H101-89, 81-76, H88-95

Use Name	Pos	Hgt	Wgt	Age	G	Min	FG	FGA	%	FT	FTA	%	Reb	Ass	PF	DQ	Stls	Blkd Shts	Points	Min	Reb	Ass	PF	Points
Truck Robinson	F	6'7	205	29	7	233	27	77	35	20	34	59	75	13	15	0	5	2	74	33	10.7	1.9	2.1	10.6
Jeff Cook	F	6'10	215	24	7	206	25	54	46	14	19	74	47	11	29	1	1	0	65	29	6.7	1.6	4.1	9.3
Alvan Adams	C	6'9	220	26	7	218	27	60	45	20	28	71	41	26	20	0	4	1	74	31	5.9	3.7	2.9	10.6
Walter Davis	G	6'6	195	26	7	199	51	106	48	10	17	59	19	22	17	0	7	1	112	28	2.7	3.1	2.4	16.0
Dennis Johnson	G	6'4	185	26	7	267	52	110	47	32	42	76	33	20	18	1	9	9	137	38	4.7	2.9	2.6	19.6
Alvin Scott	F	6'7	185	25	7	120	14	30	47	10	15	67	19	7	6	0	4	6	38	17	2.7	1.0	0.9	5.4
Johnny High	G	6'3	185	23	7	117	14	33	42	9	14	64	19	6	24	0	6	2	37	17	2.7	0.9	3.4	5.3
Rich Kelley	C	7'	240	27	7	113	10	25	40	9	14	64	35	13	12	0	6	3	29	16	5.0	1.9	1.7	4.1
Kyle Macy	G	6'3	175	23	7	102	19	36	53	7	7	**100**	13	11	8	0	5	0	49	15	1.9	1.6	1.1	7.0
Joel Kramer	F	6'7	203	25	7	101	13	25	52	1	2	50	16	4	18	0	2	2	27	14	2.3	0.6	2.6	3.9
Mike Niles	F	6'6	225	25	2	4	0	5	0	0	0	—	0	0	0	0	1	0	0	2	0.0	0.0	0.0	0.0

3-PT FG — Cook 1-1, Davis 0-1, Johnson 1-5, Kelley 0-1, Macy 4-8

1980/81 N.B.A. — PLAYOFFS

CHICAGO BULLS — **JERRY SLOAN** — defeated New York 2-0; 90-80, H115-114(OT); lost to Boston 0-4; 109-121, 97-106, H117-113, H103-109

Use Name	Pos	Hgt	Wgt	Age	G	Min	FG	FGA	%	FT	FTA	%	Reb	Ass	PF	DQ	Stls	Blkd Shts	Points	Min	Reb	Ass	PF	Points
Dave Greenwood	F	6'9	222	23	6	212	51	87	59	5	12	42	44	11	26	0	9	5	107	35	7.3	1.8	4.3	17.
Dwight Jones	F	6'10	210	28	6	217	29	61	48	17	17	100	59	11	21	0	5	3	75	36	9.8	1.8	3.5	12.
Artis Gilmore	C	7'2	240	31	6	247	35	60	58	38	55	69	67	12	15	0	6	17	108	41	11.2	2.0	2.5	18.
Reggie Theus	G	6'7	190	23	6	232	40	90	44	37	43	86	21	38	22	0	15	0	119	39	3.5	6.3	3.7	19.
Rickey Sobers	G	6'3	198	27	6	162	35	81	43	8	9	89	11	22	26	1	4	0	79	27	1.8	3.7	4.3	13.
Bob Wilkerson	G	6'6	200	26	6	152	25	59	42	5	5	100	16	14	13	0	5	1	55	25	2.7	2.3	2.2	9.
Larry Kenon	F	6'9	215	28	6	114	18	46	39	4	8	50	27	8	4	0	4	1	40	19	4.5	1.3	0.7	6.
Coby Dietrick	C-F	6'10	225	32	6	81	8	26	31	3	4	75	15	4	19	0	2	3	19	14	2.5	0.7	3.2	3.
Ronnie Lester	G	6'2	175	21	5	42	7	18	39	5	7	71	6	4	4	0	2	0	19	8	1.2	0.8	0.8	3.
James Wilkes	F	6'7	195	22	2	5	0	1	0	0	0	—	1	1	0	0	1	0	0	3	0.5	0.5	0.0	0.
Sam Worthen	G	6'5	195	22	1	1	0	0	—	0	0	—	0	0	0	0	0	0	0	1	0.0	0.0	0.0	0.

3-PT FG — Greenwood 0-2, Theus 2-9, Sobers 1-6, Wilkerson 0-1, Kenon 0-1, Dietrick 0-3, Lester 0-1

PORTLAND TRAIL BLAZERS — **JACK RAMSAY** — lost to Kansas City 1-2; H97-98(OT), 124-109(OT), H95-104

Use Name	Pos	Hgt	Wgt	Age	G	Min	FG	FGA	%	FT	FTA	%	Reb	Ass	PF	DQ	Stls	Blkd Shts	Points	Min	Reb	Ass	PF	Points
Calvin Natt	F	6'6	220	23	3	95	14	31	45	4	8	50	20	1	4	0	1	1	32	32	6.7	0.3	1.3	10.
Kermit Washington	F	6'8	230	29	3	128	12	23	52	2	2	100	52	7	9	0	8	2	26	43	17.3	2.3	3.0	8.
Mychal Thompson	C-F	6'10	226	25	3	132	31	51	61	13	18	72	23	4	10	0	3	9	75	44	7.7	1.3	3.3	25.
Billy Ray Bates	G	6'4	210	24	3	115	35	62	56	14	17	82	7	13	11	0	5	1	85	38	2.3	4.3	3.7	28.
Kelvin Ransey	G	6'1	170	22	3	131	23	65	35	3	6	50	12	25	8	0	6	1	49	44	4.0	8.3	2.7	16.
Bob Gross	F-G	6'6	200	27	3	60	9	14	64	9	14	64	8	5	9	0	2	2	27	20	2.7	1.7	3.0	9.
Mike Gale	G	6'4	190	30	3	51	4	16	25	0	0	—	5	9	2	0	5	0	8	17	1.7	3.0	0.7	2.
Kevin Kunnert	C	7'	231	29	3	43	5	10	50	1	4	25	9	1	7	0	1	0	11	14	3.0	0.3	2.3	3.
Mike Harper	C	6'10	195	23	1	6	1	1	100	1	1	100	1	0	0	0	0	0	3	6	1.0	0.0	0.0	3.
Tom Owens	C	6'10	220	31	1	5	0	0	—	0	0	—	1	0	1	0	0	0	0	5	1.0	0.0	1.0	0.
Jim Paxson	G	6'6	200	23	1	4	0	3	0	0	0	—	0	0	0	0	0	0	0	4	0.0	0.0	0.0	0.

3-PT FG — Washington 0-1, Bates 1-1, Ransey 0-1, Kunnert 0-1

LOS ANGELES LAKERS — **PAUL WESTHEAD** — lost to Houston 1-2; H107-111, 111-106, H86-89

Use Name	Pos	Hgt	Wgt	Age	G	Min	FG	FGA	%	FT	FTA	%	Reb	Ass	PF	DQ	Stls	Blkd Shts	Points	Min	Reb	Ass	PF	Points
Jamaal Wilkes	F	6'6	190	27	3	113	21	48	44	12	18	67	8	4	10	0	1	1	54	38	2.7	1.3	3.3	18.
Magic Johnson	F-G	6'8	215	21	3	127	19	49	39	13	20	65	41	21	14	1	8	3	51	42	13.7	7.0	4.7	17.
Kareem Abdul-Jabbar	C	7'2	232	33	3	134	30	65	46	20	28	71	50	12	14	0	3	8	80	45	16.7	4.0	4.7	26.
Michael Cooper	G-F	6'5	170	24	3	102	11	20	55	4	8	50	17	1	9	0	1	4	24	34	5.7	0.3	3.0	8.
Norm Nixon	G	6'2	175	25	3	133	25	49	51	8	10	80	11	26	9	0	1	1	58	44	3.7	8.7	3.0	19.
Jim Chones	F-C	6'11	220	31	3	67	10	17	59	4	8	50	17	1	9	0	1	4	24	22	5.7	0.3	3.0	8.
Mark Landsberger	F	6'8	230	25	3	32	2	7	29	1	1	100	15	0	5	0	1	0	5	11	5.0	0.0	1.7	1.
Jim Brewer	F	6'9	220	29	3	7	0	0	—	0	0	—	1	0	1	0	0	0	0	2	0.3	0.0	0.3	0.
Eddie Jordan	G	6'1	170	25	2	4	0	0	—	0	0	—	0	1	0	0	0	0	0	2	0.0	0.5	0.0	0.
Brad Holland	G	6'3	185	24	1	1	0	0	—	0	0	—	0	0	0	0	0	0	0	1	0.0	0.0	0.0	0

3-PT FG — Wilkes 0-1, Cooper 0-3

INDIANA PACERS — **JACK McKINNEY** — lost to Philadelphia 0-2; 108-124, H85-96

Use Name	Pos	Hgt	Wgt	Age	G	Min	FG	FGA	%	FT	FTA	%	Reb	Ass	PF	DQ	Stls	Blkd Shts	Points	Min	Reb	Ass	PF	Points
Louis Orr	F	6'8	175	22	2	56	9	25	36	6	7	86	10	4	4	0	5	1	24	28	5.0	2.0	2.0	12.
Mike Bantom	F	6'9	220	29	2	51	12	16	75	5	7	71	8	1	10	0	1	1	29	26	4.0	0.5	5.0	14
James Edwards	C	7'	225	25	2	56	7	24	29	0	0	—	14	5	8	0	1	1	14	28	7.0	2.5	4.0	7.
Billy Knight	G-F	6'6	195	28	2	71	16	30	53	5	8	63	12	5	5	0	1	0	37	36	6.0	2.5	2.5	18.
Johnny Davis	G	6'2	170	25	2	74	14	35	40	12	13	92	8	11	6	0	2	0	40	37	4.0	5.5	3.0	20.
Clemon Johnson	C-F	6'10	240	24	5	55	5	12	42	5	10	50	20	3	3	0	4	2	15	11	4.0	0.6	0.6	3.
George McGinnis	F	6'8	235	30	2	39	3	15	20	4	8	50	10	7	6	0	2	0	10	20	5.0	3.5	3.0	5.
Don Buse	G	6'4	195	30	2	35	1	8	13	2	2	100	5	7	4	0	3	0	5	18	2.5	3.5	2.0	2.
George Johnson	F	6'7	218	24	2	23	5	8	63	0	0	—	4	1	1	0	0	0	10	12	2.0	0.5	0.5	5.
Dudley Bradley	G	6'6	195	23	2	19	3	9	33	2	2	100	2	2	4	0	2	0	9	10	1.0	1.0	2.0	4.
Jerry Sichting	G	6'1	168	24	1	1	0	0	—	0	0	—	0	0	0	0	1	0	0	1	0.0	0.0	0.0	0.

3-PT FG — Davis 0-1, Buse 1-4, Bradley 1-1

NEW YORK KNICKERBOCKERS — **RED HOLZMAN** — lost to Chicago 0-2; H80-90, 114-115(OT)

Use Name	Pos	Hgt	Wgt	Age	G	Min	FG	FGA	%	FT	FTA	%	Reb	Ass	PF	DQ	Stls	Blkd Shts	Points	Min	Reb	Ass	PF	Points
Campy Russell	F	6'8	215	28	2	89	15	34	44	16	17	94	9	9	9	0	4	1	46	45	4.5	4.5	4.5	23.
Sly Williams	F	6'7	210	22	2	56	13	18	72	0	0	—	9	5	7	0	3	0	26	28	4.5	2.5	3.5	13.
Marvin Webster	C	7'1	240	28	2	63	6	12	50	0	4	0	10	1	6	0	0	1	12	32	5.0	0.5	3.0	6.
Ray Williams	G	6'3	190	26	2	84	18	41	44	6	11	55	8	9	10	1	4	0	43	42	4.0	4.5	5.0	21.
Michael Ray Richardson	G	6'5	190	25	2	86	8	33	24	7	12	58	19	11	8	0	7	0	23	43	9.5	5.5	4.0	11.
Bill Cartwright	C-F	7'1	255	23	2	49	6	17	35	8	12	67	13	1	7	0	1	1	20	25	6.5	0.5	3.5	10.
Larry Demic	F	6'9	225	23	2	37	4	5	80	1	2	50	7	0	3	0	0	1	9	19	3.5	0.0	1.5	4.
Mike Glenn	G	6'3	175	25	2	26	4	7	57	3	3	100	4	1	0	0	1	0	11	13	2.0	0.5	0.0	5.
Mike Woodson	F	6'5	195	22	2	8	1	3	33	2	2	100	2	0	3	0	0	0	4	4	1.0	0.0	1.5	2.
Reggie Carter	G	6'3	175	23	1	7	0	1	0	0	0	—	2	0	4	0	0	0	0	7	2.0	0.0	4.0	0.

3-PT FG — Russell 0-2, R. Williams 1-3, Richardson 0-4, Glenn 0-1

TEAM STATISTICS
EASTERN CONFERENCE
ATLANTIC DIVISION

Team		G	FG	FGA	%	FT	FTA	%	Rebounds Offense	Rebounds Defense	Rebounds Total	Assists	PF	Steals	Blocked Shots	Turn Overs	Points	Points per game
Boston	Off.	82	3581	7099	50	1781	2369	75	1155	2424	3579	2202	1990	683	594	1577	9008	109.9
	Def.	82	3372	7296	46	1752	2277	77	1192	2174	3366	1890	2059	736	351	1473	8526	104.0
	Diff.		+209	-197	+4	+29	+92	-2	-37	+250	+213	+312	+69	-53	**+243**	-104	+482	+5.9
Philadelphia	Off.	82	3636	7073	**51**	1865	2427	77	1091	**2618**	3709	**2369**	2061	857	591	1702	9156	111.7
	Def.	82	3307	7337	45	1850	2487	74	1286	2287	3573	2033	2044	818	379	1642	8512	**103.8**
	Diff.		+329	-264	**+6**	+15	-60	+3	-195	+331	+136	+336	-17	+39	+212	-60	**+644**	**+7.9**
New York	Off.	82	3505	7255	48	1783	2386	75	1137	2205	3342	1976	1917	861	314	1461	8849	107.9
	Def.	82	3555	7092	50	1563	2082	75	1147	2457	3604	2088	1994	689	452	1660	8716	106.3
	Diff.		-50	+163	-2	+220	+304	—	-10	-252	-262	-112	+77	**+172**	-138	**+199**	+133	+1.6
Washington	Off.	82	3549	7517	47	1499	2072	72	1155	2533	3688	2151	**1895**	641	392	1422	8662	105.6
	Def.	82	3518	7491	47	1588	2161	73	1204	2638	3842	2060	1888	739	469	1410	8661	105.6
	Diff.		+31	+26	—	-89	-89	-1	-49	-105	-154	+91	-7	-98	-77	-12	+1	—
New Jersey	Off.	82	3477	7314	48	1780	2371	75	1092	2374	3466	2068	2204	750	458	1664	8768	106.9
	Def.	82	3612	7159	50	2010	2663	75	1059	2499	3558	2144	2092	815	502	1637	9262	113.0
	Diff.		-135	+155	-2	-230	-292	—	+33	-125	-92	-76	-112	-65	-44	-27	-494	-6.1
CENTRAL DIVISION																		
Milwaukee	Off.	82	3722	7472	50	1802	2340	77	1261	2408	3669	2319	2198	862	530	1581	9276	113.1
	Def.	82	3311	7220	46	2023	2701	75	1265	2209	3474	2033	2050	735	400	1670	8680	105.9
	Diff.		**+411**	+252	+4	-221	-361	+2	-4	+199	+195	+286	-148	+127	+130	+89	+596	+7.2
Chicago	Off.	82	3457	6903	50	1985	2563	77	1227	2475	3702	1925	2058	729	514	1672	8937	109.0
	Def.	82	3527	7209	49	1669	2211	75	1145	2096	3241	1950	2135	784	441	1502	8775	107.0
	Diff.		-70	-306	+1	+316	+352	+2	+82	+379	+461	-25	+77	-55	+73	-170	+162	+2.0
Indiana	Off.	82	3491	7245	48	1815	2540	71	1325	2267	3592	2091	2006	833	484	1491	8827	107.6
	Def.	82	3457	7071	49	1757	2290	77	1246	2407	3653	2113	2064	695	439	1655	8712	106.2
	Diff.		+34	+174	-1	+58	+250	-6	+79	-140	-61	-22	+58	+138	+45	+164	+115	+1.4
Atlanta	Off.	82	3291	6866	48	2012	2590	78	1201	2224	3425	1846	2276	749	469	1605	8604	104.9
	Def.	82	3401	6867	50	2024	2641	77	1207	2318	3525	1935	2209	748	555	1685	8858	108.0
	Diff.		-110	-1	-2	-12	-51	+1	-6	-94	-100	-89	-67	+1	-86	+80	-254	-3.1
Cleveland	Off.	82	3556	7609	47	1486	1909	78	1258	2243	3501	2007	1995	632	322	**1396**	8670	105.7
	Def.	82	3608	7174	50	1800	2395	75	1158	2499	3657	2166	1956	681	454	1474	9068	110.6
	Diff.		-52	**+435**	-3	-314	-486	+3	+100	-256	-156	-159	-39	-49	-132	+78	-398	-4.9
Detroit	Off.	82	3236	6986	46	1689	2330	72	1201	2111	3312	1819	2125	**884**	492	1759	8174	99.7
	Def.	82	3499	6869	51	1663	2217	75	1090	2396	3486	2033	2095	793	585	**1797**	8692	106.0
	Diff.		-263	+117	-5	+26	+113	-3	+111	-285	-174	-214	-30	+91	-93	+38	-518	-6.3
WESTERN CONFERENCE																		
MIDWEST DIVISION																		
San Antonio	Off.	82	3571	7276	49	2052	2668	77	1304	2582	**3886**	2048	2114	685	**643**	1533	9209	112.3
	Def.	82	3581	7582	47	1766	2387	74	1214	2177	3391	2206	2198	700	481	1422	8973	109.4
	Diff.		-10	-306	+2	+286	+281	+3	+90	**+405**	**+495**	-158	+84	-15	+162	-111	+236	+2.9
Kansas City	Off.	82	3572	7151	50	1576	2206	71	1037	2450	3487	2271	2092	719	385	1448	8769	106.9
	Def.	82	3424	7117	48	1889	2500	76	1138	2510	3648	1857	2015	717	383	1520	8768	106.9
	Diff.		+148	+34	+2	-313	-294	-5	-101	-60	-161	**+414**	-77	+2	+2	+72	+1	—
Houston	Off.	82	3573	7335	49	1711	2223	77	1216	2347	3563	2099	1901	705	390	1451	8878	108.3
	Def.	82	3617	7341	49	1568	2108	74	1177	2367	3544	2191	1977	689	367	1430	8851	107.9
	Diff.		-44	-6	—	+143	+115	+3	+39	-20	+19	-92	+76	+16	+23	-21	+27	+.4
Denver	Off.	82	**3784**	**7960**	48	**2388**	**3051**	**78**	1325	2497	3822	2030	2108	720	380	1444	**9986**	**121.8**
	Def.	82	4059	8017	51	1863	2507	74	1320	2680	4000	2529	**2387**	704	547	1555	10025	122.3
	Diff.		-275	-57	-3	**+525**	**+544**	**+4**	+5	-183	-178	-499	**+279**	+16	-167	+111	-39	-.5
Utah	Off.	82	3332	6825	49	1595	2080	77	962	2325	3287	1948	2110	637	386	1423	8301	101.2
	Def.	82	3430	7018	49	1879	2472	76	1154	2440	3594	1985	1855	596	406	1303	8784	107.1
	Diff.		-98	-193	—	-284	-392	+1	-192	-115	-307	-37	-255	+41	-20	-120	-483	-5.9
Dallas	Off.	82	3204	6928	46	1868	2487	75	1109	2177	3286	1984	2008	561	214	1439	8322	101.5
	Def.	82	3622	7060	51	1731	2297	75	1173	2498	3671	2098	2187	713	480	1433	9011	109.9
	Diff.		-418	-132	-5	+137	+190	—	-64	-321	-385	-114	+179	-152	-266	-6	-689	-8.4

Team		G	FG	FGA	%	FT	FTA	%	Rebounds Offense	Rebounds Defense	Rebounds Total	Assists	PF	Steals	Blocked Shots	Turn Overs	Points	Points per game
TEAM STATISTICS WESTERN CONFERENCE PACIFIC DIVISION																		
Phoenix	Off.	82	3587	7326	49	1810	2430	74	1234	2490	3724	2205	1996	876	416	1733	9019	110.
	Def.	82	3368	7221	47	1762	2383	74	1160	2284	3444	1970	2116	912	401	1752	8567	104.
	Diff.		+219	+105	+2	+48	+47	—	+74	+206	+280	+235	+120	-36	+15	+19	+452	+5.
Los Angeles	Off.	82	3780	7382	51	1540	2113	73	1165	2491	3656	2363	1955	808	551	1557	9117	111.
	Def.	82	3581	7701	47	1598	2158	74	1378	2274	3652	2280	1869	754	357	1473	8802	107.
	Diff.		+199	-319	+4	-58	-45	-1	-213	+217	+4	+83	-86	+54	+194	-84	+315	+3.
Portland	Off.	82	3741	7635	49	1573	2191	72	1243	2388	3631	2244	2034	769	480	1518	9080	110.
	Def.	82	3584	7351	49	1805	2377	76	1249	2419	3668	2109	1932	802	422	1575	9007	109.
	Diff.		+157	+284	—	-232	-186	-4	-6	-31	-37	+135	-102	-33	+58	+57	+73	+0.
Golden State	Off.	82	3560	7284	49	1826	2513	73	**1403**	2366	3769	2026	2158	611	301	1547	9006	109.
	Def.	82	3631	7204	50	1804	2411	75	1137	2210	3347	2223	2093	714	386	1385	9103	111.
	Diff.		-71	+80	-1	+22	+102	-2	**+266**	+156	+422	-197	-65	-103	-85	-162	-97	-1.
San Diego	Off.	82	3477	7283	48	1561	2246	74	1169	2144	3313	2098	2078	764	292	1407	8737	106.
	Def.	82	3508	6951	50	1818	2433	75	1091	2377	3468	2097	2006	683	392	1553	8867	108.
	Diff.		-31	+332	-2	-257	-187	-1	+78	-233	-155	+1	-72	+81	-100	+146	-130	-1.
Seattle	Off.	82	3343	7145	47	1813	2376	76	1167	2434	3601	1945	1986	628	438	1524	8531	104.
	Def.	82	3453	7421	47	1718	2323	74	1247	2357	3604	2044	2044	747	387	1348	8666	105.
	Diff.		-110	-276	—	+95	+53	+2	-80	+77	-3	-99	+58	-119	+51	-176	-135	-1.
PLAYOFFS																		
Boston	Off.	17	700	1457	48	347	460	75	246	509	755	388	420	127	112	277	1757	103.
	Def.	17	645	1471	44	357	473	75	261	457	718	356	412	122	103	261	1654	97.
	Diff.		**+55**	-14	**+4**	-10	-13	—	-15	**+52**	+37	**+32**	-8	+5	+9	-16	**+103**	**+6.**
Houston	Off.	21	**819**	**1796**	46	**413**	**550**	75	**309**	**547**	**856**	**474**	466	**174**	113	296	**2059**	98.
	Def.	21	835	1743	48	389	534	73	293	616	909	508	**490**	148	117	**341**	2068	98.
	Diff.		-16	**+53**	-2	**+24**	+16	+2	+16	-69	-53	-34	**+24**	**+26**	-4	**+45**	-9	-0.
Philadelphia	Off.	16	637	1309	49	394	510	**77**	205	449	654	389	420	131	137	293	1669	104.
	Def.	16	646	1413	46	373	497	75	265	440	705	388	434	147	93	263	1671	104.
	Diff.		-9	-104	+3	+21	+13	+2	-60	+9	-51	+1	+14	-16	**+44**	-30	-2	-0.
Kansas City	Off.	15	554	1190	47	254	354	72	178	415	593	353	349	132	64	252	1375	91.
	Def.	15	580	1226	47	255	366	70	204	453	657	307	326	133	65	248	1423	94.
	Diff.		-26	-36	—	-1	-12	+2	-26	-38	-64	+46	-23	-1	-1	-4	-48	-3.
San Antonio	Off.	7	298	608	**49**	156	209	75	100	196	296	180	173	41	47	**107**	754	**107.**
	Def.	7	300	586	51	165	214	77	79	171	250	178	174	54	37	98	768	109.
	Diff.		-2	+22	-2	-9	-5	-2	+21	+25	**+46**	+2	+1	-13	+10	-9	-14	-2.
Milwaukee	Off.	7	292	611	48	162	212	76	124	179	303	189	195	71	37	119	749	107.
	Def.	7	272	564	48	187	239	78	100	169	269	171	175	62	62	133	731	104.
	Diff.		+20	+47	—	-25	-27	-2	+24	+10	+34	+18	-20	+9	-25	+14	+18	+2.
Phoenix	Off.	7	252	561	45	132	192	69	99	218	317	133	**167**	50	26	115	642	91.
	Def.	7	236	554	43	146	206	71	95	192	287	146	172	62	34	**112**	**623**	**89.**
	Diff.		+16	+7	+2	-14	-14	-2	+4	+26	+30	-13	+5	-12	-8	-3	+19	+2.
Chicago	Off.	6	248	529	47	122	160	76	99	168	267	125	150	47	30	99	621	103.
	Def.	6	255	496	51	126	166	76	73	172	245	135	150	53	33	112	643	107.
	Diff.		-7	+33	-4	-4	-6	—	**+26**	-4	+22	-10	—	-6	-3	+13	-22	-3.
Portland	Off.	3	134	276	49	47	70	67	42	96	138	65	61	31	16	53	316	105.
	Def.	3	140	268	52	37	51	73	33	97	130	88	68	24	9	51	321	107.
	Diff.		-6	+8	-3	+10	+19	-6	+9	-1	+8	-23	+7	+7	+7	-2	-5	-1.
Los Angeles	Off.	3	118	255	46	68	99	69	43	110	153	72	69	21	17	43	304	101.
	Def.	3	122	285	43	61	77	79	55	93	148	79	73	21	19	36	306	102.
	Diff.		-4	-30	+3	+7	**+22**	-10	-12	+17	+5	-7	+4	—	-2	-7	-2	-0.
Indiana	Off.	2	75	182	41	41	57	72	37	56	93	46	51	22	5	39	193	96.
	Def.	2	92	173	53	36	57	63	24	69	93	56	52	22	19	40	220	110.
	Diff.		-17	+9	-12	+5	—	**+9**	+13	-13	—	-10	+1	—	-14	+1	-27	-13.
New York	Off.	2	75	171	44	43	63	68	31	52	83	37	57	20	4	42	194	97.
	Def.	2	79	166	48	47	56	84	31	66	97	39	52	19	17	40	205	102.
	Diff.		-4	+5	-4	-4	+7	-16	—	-14	-14	-2	-5	+1	-13	-2	-11	-5.

Team	W	L	Pct.	GB	Record against playoff teams W	L	Pct.	Record against non-playoff teams W	L	Pct.	HOME W	L	Pct.	ROAD W	L	Pct.
EASTERN CONFERENCE																
ATLANTIC DIVISION																
Boston Celtics	**62**	20	**.756**	—	**30**	12	**.714**	32	8	.800	35	6	.854	**27**	14	**.659**
Philadelphia 76ers	**62**	20	**.756**	—	27	14	.659	**35**	6	**.854**	**37**	4	**.902**	25	16	.610
New York Knickerbockers	50	32	.610	12	17	24	.415	33	8	.805	28	13	.683	22	19	.537
Washington Bullets	39	43	.476	23	15	32	.319	24	11	.686	26	15	.634	13	28	.317
New Jersey Nets	24	58	.293	38	8	39	.170	16	14	.457	16	25	.390	8	33	.195
CENTRAL DIVISION																
Milwaukee Bucks	60	22	.732	—	25	16	.610	35	6	**.854**	34	7	.829	26	15	.634
Chicago Bulls	45	37	.549	15	16	25	.390	29	12	.707	26	15	.634	19	22	.463
Indiana Pacers	44	38	.537	16	16	24	.400	28	14	.667	27	14	.659	17	24	.415
Atlanta Hawks	31	51	.378	29	13	35	.452	18	16	.529	20	21	.488	11	30	.268
Cleveland Cavaliers	28	54	.341	32	7	39	.152	21	15	.583	20	21	.488	8	33	.195
Detroit Pistons	21	61	.256	39	9	37	.196	12	24	.333	14	27	.341	7	34	.171
WESTERN CONFERENCE																
MIDWEST DIVISION																
San Antonio Spurs	52	30	.634	—	20	19	.513	32	11	.744	34	7	.829	18	23	.439
Kansas City Kings	40	42	.488	12	15	24	.385	25	18	.581	24	17	.585	16	25	.390
Houston Rockets	40	42	.488	12	13	26	.333	27	16	.628	25	16	.610	15	26	.366
Denver Nuggets	37	45	.451	15	18	27	.400	19	18	.514	23	18	.561	14	27	.341
Utah Jazz	28	54	.341	24	11	34	.029	17	20	.459	20	21	.488	8	33	.195
Dallas Mavericks	15	**67**	.183	37	5	**40**	.111	10	**27**	.270	11	30	.268	4	**37**	.098
PACIFIC DIVISION																
Phoenix Suns	57	25	.695	—	22	17	.564	**35**	8	.814	36	5	.878	21	20	.512
Los Angeles Lakers	54	28	.659	3	21	18	.538	33	10	.767	30	11	.732	24	17	.585
Portland Trail Blazers	45	37	.549	12	20	21	.488	25	16	.610	30	11	.732	15	26	.366
Golden State Warriors	39	43	.476	18	20	25	.444	19	18	.514	26	15	.634	13	28	.317
San Diego Clippers	36	46	.439	21	14	31	.311	22	15	.595	22	19	.537	14	27	.341
Seattle Supersonics	34	48	.415	23	13	32	.289	21	16	.568	22	19	.537	12	29	.293

1980/81 N.B.A. INDIVIDUAL LEADERS

SCORING
(Minimum 70 Games or 1400 Points)

Name	Team	G	FG	FT	Pts.	Avg.
Dantley	Utah	80	909	632	2452	30.7
Malone	Hou	80	806	609	2222	27.8
Gervin	SA	82	850	512	2221	27.1
Abdul-Jabbar	LA	80	836	423	2095	26.2
Thompson	Den	77	734	489	1967	25.5
Birdsong	KC	71	710	317	1747	24.6
Erving	Phi	82	794	422	2014	24.6
Mitchell	Cle	82	853	302	2012	24.5
Free	GS	65	516	528	1565	24.1
English	Den	81	768	390	1929	23.8

FIELD GOAL PERCENTAGE
(Minimum 300 Made)

Name	Team	FG	FGA	Pct.
Gilmore	Chi	547	816	.670
Dawkins	Phi	423	697	.607
Maxwell	Bos	441	750	.588
King	GS	731	1244	.588
Abdul-Jabbar	LA	836	1457	.574
Washington	Port	325	571	.569
Dantley	Utah	909	1627	.559
Cartwright	NY	619	1118	.554
Nater	SD	517	935	.553
Mar. Johnson	Mil	636	1153	.552

FREE THROW PERCENTAGE
(Minimum 125 Made)

Name	Team	FT	FTA	Pct.
Murphy	Hou	206	215	.958
Sobers	Chi	231	241	.959
Newlin	NJ	414	466	.888
Spanarkel	Dall	375	423	.887
Bridgeman	Mil	213	241	.884
Long	Det	160	184	.870
Criss	Atl	185	214	.864
Bird	Bos	283	328	.863
McKinney	Den	162	188	.862
Bates	Port	170	199	.854

PERSONAL FOULS

Name	Team	PF
Poquette	Utah	342
Bailey	Sea	332
Laimbeer	Cle	332
Reid	Hou	325
Chones	LA	324

GAMES DISQUALIFIED

Name	Team	Disq.
Poquette	Utah	18
Hubbard	Det	14
Laimbeer	Cle	14
Hawes	Atl	13
Bailey	Sea	11

TOTAL REBOUNDS PER GAME
(Minimum 70 Games or 800 Rebounds)

Name	Team	G	Reb.	Avg.
Malone	Hou	80	1180	14.8
Nater	SD	82	1017	12.4
Smith	GS	82	994	12.1
Bird	Bos	82	895	10.9
Sikma	Sea	82	852	10.4
Carr	Cle	81	835	10.3
Abdul-Jabbar	LA	80	821	10.3
Gilmore	Chi	82	828	10.1
C. Jones	Phi	81	813	10.0
Hayes	Was	81	789	9.7

ASSISTS PER GAME
(Minimum 70 Games or 400 Assists)

Name	Team	G	Ass.	Avg.
Porter	Was	81	734	9.1
Nixon	LA	79	696	8.8
Ford	KC	66	580	8.8
Richardson	NY	79	627	7.9
Archibald	Bos	80	618	7.7
Lucas	GS	66	464	7.0
Ransey	Port	80	555	6.9
Cheeks	Phi	81	560	6.9
Davis	Ind	76	480	6.3
Higgs	Den	72	408	5.7

MINUTES PLAYED

Name	Team	Min.
Dantley	Utah	3417
Malone	Hou	3245
Bird	Bos	3239
Mitchell	Cle	3194
Richardson	NY	3175

BLOCKED SHOTS PER GAME
(Minimum 70 Games or 100 Blocked Shots)

Name	Team	G	Reb.	Avg.
G. Johnson	SA	82	278	3.4
Rollins	Atl	40	117	2.9
Abdul-Jabbar	LA	80	228	2.9
Parish	Bos	82	214	2.6
Gilmore	Chi	82	198	2.4
Catchings	Mil	77	184	2.4
Tyler	Det	82	180	2.2
Thompson	Port	79	170	2.2
Poquette	Utah	82	174	2.1
Hayes	Wash	81	171	2.1

3 POINT FIELD GOALS PER GAME
(Minimum 25 Made)

Name	Team	FG	FGA	Avg.
Taylor	SD	44	115	.383
Williams	SD	48	141	.340
Hassett	Dall-GS	53	156	.340
Bratz	Cle	57	169	.337
Bibby	SD	32	95	.337
Grevey	Was	45	136	.331
Ford	Bos	36	109	.330
Wedman	KC	25	77	.325

STEALS PER GAME
(Minimum 70 Games or 125 Steals)

Name	Team	G	Steals	Avg.
Johnson	LA	37	127	3.4
Richardson	NY	79	232	2.9
Buckner	Mil	82	197	2.4
Cheeks	Phi	81	193	2.4
R. Williams	NY	79	185	2.3
Bradley	Ind	82	186	2.3
Erving	Phi	82	173	2.1
Lee	Det	82	166	2.0
Reid	Hou	82	163	2.0
Bird	Bos	82	161	2.0

1981-82 N.B.A.

Good Rookies Help Parity

In a season that featured the deepest rookie crop in the league's history, Dallas and Detroit were the biggest beneficiaries. The Mavericks picked up forwards Jay Vincent and Mark Aquirre, plus guard Rolando Blackman, en route to a 28-54 record that represented a 13-game improvement over their inaugural season. The Pistons, coming off a dismal 21-61 season, got forward Kelly Tripucka and guard Isiah Thomas in the draft, then added second-year center Bill Laimbeer in a midseason trade with Cleveland, and wound up with 39 wins. But despite these gains, both teams failed to make the playoffs.

In New Jersey, the Nets had a new coach, Larry Brown; a new high-scoring guard, Ray Williams, lured away from the Knicks as a free agent; and two productive rookies, Albert King and Rookie of the Year Buck Williams. They parlayed these changes into a 44-win season and a berth in the playoffs. There they fell to the Washington Bullets, who relied heavily on rookies Jeff Ruland and Frank Johnson and second-year man Rick Mahorn in a rebuilding season that earned Gene Shue his second Coach of the Year award.

The league's other top rookie, forward Tom Chambers, wasn't enough to keep San Diego from slipping into the Pacific Division cellar. And Indiana fell apart despite a good year from promising freshman Herb Williams. The arrival of Orlando Woolridge wasn't enough to keep the Chicago Bulls from losing 48 games, or coach Jerry Sloan from losing his job. Likewise, future all-star Larry Nance couldn't contribute enough as a rookie with Phoenix to offset the loss of Walter Davis for 37 games with a broken arm. As a result,the Suns slipped from first to third in the Pacific Division, though still posting 46 wins.

Of all the year's notable freshman, probably the least impressive was Boston's Danny Ainge, who was persuaded to give up his foundering baseball career for a shot at basketball. But the Celtics didn't appear to need him very much anyway. For the third consecutive year since the arrival of Larry Bird they posted the league's best record, highlighted by an 18-game winning streak. Even so, they were hard pressed to beat out Philadelphia, whose 58 wins were more than any other team in the league. Julius Erving again led the 76ers, but he had help from high-scoring guard Andrew Toney, emerging as a star in his second year. Meanwhile, the Knicks plunged to the bottom of the Atlantic Division in Red Holzman's final year as coach.

In the Central Division, Milwaukee suffered a lengthly holdout by Marques Johnson and injuries to Brian Winters and Junior Bridgeman but coach Don Nelson and versatile guard Sidney Moncrief led the Bucks to 55 wins and another title. Atlanta used a league-leading defense to gain the final playoff berth in the East. Cleveland went through four coaches ending up with Bill Musselman (the first of their three coaches in 1980-81), but the net result was the league's worst record.

San Antonio added high-scoring forward Mike Mitchell to scoring leader George Gervin and squeaked by Denver for the Mideast Division title. The Nuggets' frontcourt of Alex English, Dan Issel and Kiki Vandeweghe each averaged more than 20 points per game as the team set N.B.A. records for points scored and points allowed. Houston, the surprise team of last year's playoffs, matched Denver with 46 wins. The Rockets got a good year from newly acquired Elvin Hayes, but their main man was still Moses Malone, who averaged 31.1 points, led the league in rebounding and won the MVP award. Among the also-rans, Kansas City couldn't overcome the loss of Otis Birdsong and Scott Wedman, while Utah wasted another outstanding season from Adrian Dantley.

In Los Angeles, a near-rebellion led by Magic Johnson resulted in the ousting of Coach Paul Westhead after 11 games. Free-agent forward Mitch Kupchak went down shortly thereafter with a severe knee injury, but the Lakers regrouped under new coach Pat Riley and drove to the title in the strong Pacific Division. Seattle, with Gus Williams back after his year-long holdout, jumped from last place to second. Though failing to make the playoffs, Golden State won 45 games behind high scorers Bernard King and World Free. And Portland had an emerging star in second-year center Mychal Thompson.

The playoffs promised a matchup of Magic vs. Bird for the championship, but Boston ran into trouble against Philadelphia. Down 3-1, the Celtics rallied to force a seventh game, as they had a year earlier; but this ime the 76ers refused to fold, winning in Boston Garden to earn the right to face Los Angeles. But balanced scoring and the all-around brilliance of playoff MVP Magic Johnson proved desisive for the Lakers, who emerged with a 4-2 series victory and their second title in three years.

					TOTAL													Blkd		PER GAME				
Use Name	Pos	Hgt	Wgt	Age	G	Min	FG	FGA	%	FT	FTA	%	Reb	Ass	PF	DQ	Stls	Shts	Points	Min	Reb	Ass	PF	Points
1981/82 N.B.A. — EASTERN CONFERENCE																								
ATLANTIC DIVISION																								
BOSTON CELTICS	63-19 .768	BILL FITCH																						
Cedric Maxwell	F	6'8	205	26	78	2590	397	724	55	357	478	75	499	183	263	6	79	49	1151	33	6.4	2.3	3.4	14.8
Larry Bird	F	6'9	220	25	77	2923	711	1414	50	328	380	86	837	447	244	0	143	66	1761	38	10.9	5.8	3.2	22.9
Robert Parish	C	7'	230	28	80	2534	669	1235	54	252	355	71	866	140	267	5	68	192	1590	32	10.8	1.8	3.3	19.9
Gerald Henderson	G	6'2	175	25	82	1844	353	705	50	125	172	73	152	252	199	3	82	11	833	22	1.9	3.1	2.4	10.2
Nate Archibald (WJ)	G	6'1	150	33	68	2167	308	652	47	236	316	75	116	541	131	1	52	3	858	32	1.7	8.0	1.9	12.6
Kevin McHale	F-C	6'10	235	24	82	2332	465	875	53	187	248	75	556	91	264	1	30	185	1117	28	6.8	1.1	3.2	13.6
Chris Ford	G	6'5	190	32	76	1591	188	450	42	39	56	70	108	142	143	0	42	10	435	21	1.4	1.9	1.9	5.7
M.L. Carr	G-F	6'6	205	30	56	1296	184	409	45	82	116	71	150	128	136	2	67	21	455	23	2.7	2.3	2.4	8.1
Rick Robey	C-F	6'11	235	25	80	1186	185	375	49	84	157	54	295	68	183	2	27	14	454	15	3.7	0.9	2.3	5.7
Danny Ainge	G	6'4	175	22	53	564	79	221	36	56	65	86	56	87	86	1	37	3	219	11	1.1	1.6	1.6	4.1
Charles Bradley	G	6'5	215	22	51	339	55	122	45	42	62	68	38	22	61	0	14	6	152	7	0.7	0.4	1.2	3.0
Eric Fernsten	F	6'10	205	28	43	202	19	49	39	19	30	63	42	8	23	0	5	7	57	5	1.0	0.2	0.5	1.3
Terry Duerod	G	6'2	180	25	21	146	34	77	44	4	12	33	15	12	9	0	3	1	72	7	0.7	0.6	0.4	3.4
Tracy Jackson (to Chi)	G	6'6	205	22	11	66	10	26	38	6	10	60	12	5	5	0	3	0	26	6	1.1	0.5	0.5	2.4

Dave Cowens - voluntarily retired

3-PT FG — Maxwell 0-3, Bird 49-184, Henderson 2-12, Archibald 6-16, Ford 20-63, Carr 5-17, Robey 0-2, Ainge 5-17, Bradley 0-1, Duerod 0-1

1981/82 N.B.A. — EASTERN CONFERENCE (continued)
ATLANTIC DIVISION

Use Name	Pos	Hgt	Wgt	Age	G	Min	FG	FGA	%	FT	FTA	%	Reb	Ass	PF	Disq	Stls	Blkd Shts	Points	Per Game Min	Per Game Reb	Per Game Ass	Per Game PF	Per Game Points
PHILADELPHIA 76ers	**58-24 .707 BILLY CUNNINGHAM**																							
Julius Erving	F	6'7	200	31	81	2789	780	1428	55	411	539	76	557	319	229	1	161	141	1974	34	6.9	3.9	2.8	24.4
Bobby Jones	F	6'9	212	30	76	2181	416	737	56	263	333	79	393	189	211	3	99	112	1095	29	5.2	2.5	2.8	14.4
Caldwell Jones	C	6'11	225	31	81	2446	231	465	50	179	219	82	708	100	301	3	38	146	641	30	8.7	1.2	3.7	7.9
Andrew Toney	G	6'3	178	24	77	1909	511	979	52	227	306	74	134	283	269	5	64	17	1274	25	1.7	3.7	3.5	16.5
Maurice Cheeks	G	6'1	180	25	79	2498	352	676	52	171	220	78	248	667	247	0	209	33	881	32	3.1	8.4	3.1	11.2
Lionel Hollins	G	6'3	185	28	81	2257	380	797	48	132	188	70	187	316	198	1	103	20	894	28	2.3	3.9	2.4	11.0
Steve Mix	F	6'7	222	34	75	1235	202	399	51	136	172	79	225	93	86	0	42	17	541	16	3.0	1.2	1.1	7.2
Darryl Dawkins	C	6'11	251	24	48	1124	207	367	56	114	164	70	305	55	193	5	19	55	528	23	6.4	1.1	4.0	11.0
Clint Richardson	G	6'3	195	25	77	1040	140	310	45	69	88	78	118	109	109	0	36	9	351	14	1.5	1.4	1.4	4.6
Mike Bantom (from Ind)	F	6'9	220	30	43	979	156	306	51	67	114	59	226	46	133	0	25	37	380	23	5.3	1.1	3.1	8.8
Earl Cureton	F-C	6'9	210	24	66	956	149	306	49	51	94	54	270	32	142	0	31	27	349	14	4.1	0.5	2.2	5.3
Franklin Edwards	G	6'1	170	22	42	291	65	150	43	20	27	74	27	45	37	0	16	5	150	7	0.6	1.1	0.9	3.6
Ollie Johnson	F	6'6	200	32	26	150	27	54	50	6	7	86	22	10	28	0	13	3	61	6	0.8	0.4	1.1	2.3
	3-PT FG —	Erving 3-11, B. Jones 0-3, C. Jones 0-3, Toney 25-59, Cheeks 6-22, Hollins 2-15, Mix 1-4, Dawkins 0-2, Richardson 2-2, Bantom 1-3, Cureton 0-2, Edwards 0-9, Johnson 1-3																						
NEW JERSEY NETS	**44-38 .537 LARRY BROWN**																							
Mike O'Koren	F	6'7	207	23	80	2018	383	778	49	135	189	71	305	192	175	0	83	13	909	25	3.8	2.4	2.2	11.4
Buck Williams	F	6'8	215	21	82	2825	513	881	58	242	388	62	1005	107	285	5	84	84	1268	34	12.3	1.3	3.5	15.5
Len Elmore	C	6'9	220	29	81	2100	300	652	46	135	170	79	441	100	280	6	92	92	735	26	5.4	1.2	3.5	9.1
Otis Birdsong	G	6'4	195	26	37	1025	225	480	47	74	127	58	97	124	74	0	30	5	524	28	2.6	3.4	2.0	14.2
Ray Williams	G	6'3	190	27	82	2732	639	1383	46	387	465	83	325	488	302	9	199	43	1674	33	4.0	6.0	3.7	20.4
Darwin Cook	G	6'3	190	23	82	2090	387	803	48	118	162	73	155	319	196	2	146	24	899	25	1.9	3.9	2.4	11.0
Foots Walker	G	6'1	172	30	77	1861	156	378	41	141	194	73	150	398	179	1	120	6	456	24	1.9	5.2	2.3	5.9
Albert King	F	6'6	190	22	76	1694	391	812	48	133	171	78	312	142	261	4	64	36	918	22	4.1	1.9	3.4	12.1
James Bailey (from Sea)	F-C	6'9	220	24	67	1288	230	440	52	133	213	62	343	52	228	3	39	76	593	19	5.1	0.8	3.4	8.9
Mike Gminski	C	6'11	250	22	64	740	119	270	44	97	118	82	186	41	69	0	17	48	335	12	2.9	0.6	1.1	5.2
Sam Lacey (from KC)	C	6'10	235	33	54	650	64	149	43	27	35	77	103	73	137	1	20	37	155	12	1.9	1.4	2.5	2.9
Jan van Breda Kolff	F	6'7	200	30	41	452	41	82	50	62	76	82	48	32	63	1	12	13	144	11	1.2	0.8	1.5	3.5
Mike Woodson (to KC)	G	6'5	195	23	7	145	30	68	44	23	32	72	13	16	21	1	7	2	83	21	1.9	2.3	3.0	11.9
Ray Tolbert (to Sea)	F	6'9	225	23	12	115	20	44	45	4	8	50	27	8	19	0	4	2	44	10	2.3	0.7	1.6	3.7
David Burns (to Den)	F	6'2	180	23	3	34	2	5	40	3	6	50	2	4	4	0	1	0	7	11	0.7	1.3	1.3	2.3
Joe Cooper	C	6'10	230	24	1	11	1	2	50	0	0	—	2	0	2	0	0	0	2	11	2.0	0.0	2.0	2.0
	3-PT FG —	O'Koren 8-23, B. Williams 0-1, Birdsong 0-10, R. Williams 9-54, Cook 7-31, Walker 3-9, King 3-13, Lacey 0-1, van Breda Kolff 0-2, Woodson 0-1, Tolbert 0-1																						
WASHINGTON BULLETS	**43-39 .524 GENE SHUE**																							
Greg Ballard	F	6'7	215	26	79	2946	621	1307	48	235	283	83	633	250	204	0	137	22	1486	37	8.0	3.2	2.6	18.8
Spencer Hayward	F	6'9	225	32	76	2086	395	829	48	219	260	84	422	64	249	6	45	68	1009	27	5.6	0.8	3.3	13.3
Rick Mahorn	C	6'10	240	23	80	2664	414	816	51	148	234	63	704	150	349	12	57	138	976	33	8.8	1.9	4.4	12.2
Kevin Grevey	G	6'5	210	28	71	2164	376	857	44	165	193	85	195	149	151	1	44	23	945	30	2.7	2.1	2.1	13.3
John Lucas	G	6'3	175	28	79	1940	263	618	43	138	176	78	166	551	105	0	95	6	666	25	2.1	7.0	1.3	8.4
Jeff Ruland	C-F	6'10	240	23	82	2214	420	749	56	342	455	75	762	134	319	7	44	58	1183	27	9.3	1.6	3.9	14.4
Frank Johnson	G	6'2	185	23	79	2027	336	812	41	153	204	75	147	380	196	1	76	7	842	26	1.9	4.8	2.5	10.7
Don Collins	G-F	6'6	190	23	79	1609	334	653	51	121	169	72	196	148	195	3	89	24	790	20	2.5	1.9	2.5	10.0
Jim Chones	F-C	6'11	220	32	59	867	74	171	43	36	46	78	185	64	114	1	15	32	184	15	3.1	1.1	1.9	3.1
Charlie Davis	F	6'7	215	23	54	575	88	184	48	30	37	81	133	31	89	0	10	13	206	11	2.5	0.6	1.6	3.8
Garry Witts	G-F	6'7	190	22	46	493	49	84	58	33	40	83	62	38	74	1	17	4	132	11	1.3	0.8	1.6	2.9
Brad Holland (to Mil)	G	6'3	185	25	13	185	27	73	37	3	4	75	13	16	12	0	11	1	57	14	1.0	1.2	0.9	4.4
Carlos Terry	G-F	6'5	210	25	13	60	3	15	20	3	4	75	12	8	15	0	3	1	9	5	0.9	0.6	1.2	0.7
Kevin Porter - leg injury	**3-PT FG —**	Ballard 9-22, Haywood 0-3, Mahorn 0-3, Grevey 28-82, Lucas 2-22, Ruland 1-3, Johnson 17-79, Collins 1-12, Davis 0-2, Witts 1-2, Holland 0-3, Terry 0-3																						
NEW YORK KNICKERBOCKERS	**33-49 .402 RED HOLZMAN**																							
Campy Russell	F	6'8	215	29	77	2358	410	858	48	228	294	78	263	284	221	1	77	12	1073	31	3.4	3.7	2.9	13.9
Maurice Lucas	F	6'9	218	29	80	2671	505	1001	50	253	349	72	903	179	309	4	68	70	1263	33	11.3	2.2	3.9	15.8
Bill Cartwright	C	7'1	255	24	72	2060	390	694	56	257	337	76	421	87	208	2	48	65	1037	29	5.8	1.2	2.9	14.4
Randy Smith	G	6'3	180	33	82	2033	348	748	47	122	151	81	155	255	199	1	91	1	821	25	1.9	3.1	2.4	10.0
Michael Ray Richardson	G	6'5	190	26	82	3044	619	1343	46	212	303	70	565	572	317	3	**213**	41	1469	37	6.9	7.0	3.9	17.9
Marvin Webster	C	7'1	240	29	82	1883	199	405	49	108	170	64	490	99	211	2	22	91	506	23	6.0	1.2	2.6	6.2
Sly Williams	F	6'7	210	23	60	1521	349	628	56	131	173	76	227	142	153	0	77	16	831	25	3.8	2.4	2.6	13.9
Mike Newlin	G	6'4	200	32	76	1507	286	615	47	126	147	86	91	170	194	2	33	3	705	20	1.2	2.2	2.6	9.3
Reggie Carter	G	6'3	175	24	75	923	119	280	43	64	80	80	95	130	124	1	36	6	302	12	1.3	1.7	1.7	4.0
Toby Knight (KJ)	F	6'9	210	26	40	550	102	183	56	17	25	68	82	23	74	0	14	11	221	14	2.1	0.6	1.9	5.5
Paul Westphal (BF)	G	6'4	195	31	18	451	194	451	43	36	47	77	22	100	61	1	19	8	210	25	1.2	5.6	3.4	11.7
Larry Demic	F	6'9	225	24	48	356	39	83	47	14	39	36	79	14	65	1	4	6	92	7	1.6	0.3	1.4	1.9
Alex Bradley	F	6'6	215	22	39	331	54	103	52	29	48	60	65	11	37	0	12	5	137	8	1.7	0.3	0.9	3.5
Hollis Copeland	F	6'6	180	26	18	118	16	38	42	5	6	83	5	9	19	0	4	2	37	7	0.3	0.5	1.1	2.1
DeWayne Scales	F	6'8	208	23	3	24	1	5	20	1	2	50	5	0	3	0	1	1	3	8	1.7	0.0	1.0	1.0
	3-PT FG —	Russell 25-57, Lucas 0-3, Smith 3-11, Richardson 19-101, Williams 2-9, Newlin 7-23, Westphal 2-8, Demic 0-1, Bradley 0-1																						

1981/82 N.B.A — EASTERN CONFERENCE
CENTRAL DIVISION

Use Name	Pos	Hgt	Wgt	Age	G	Min	FG	FGA	%	FT	FTA	%	Reb	Ass	PF	DQ	Stls	Blkd Shts	Points	Min	Reb	Ass	PF	Points
					TOTAL															PER GAME				
MILWAUKEE BUCKS	55-27 .671				DON NELSON																			
Marques Johnson (HO)	F	6'7	218	25	60	1900	404	760	53	182	260	70	364	213	142	1	59	35	990	32	6.1	3.6	2.4	16.5
Mickey Johnson	F	6'10	190	29	76	1934	372	757	49	233	291	80	454	215	240	4	72	45	978	25	6.0	2.8	3.2	12.9
Bob Lanier	C	6'11	250	33	74	1986	407	729	56	182	242	75	388	219	211	3	72	56	996	27	5.2	3.0	2.9	13.5
Sidney Moncrief	G	6'4	190	24	80	2980	556	1063	52	468	573	82	534	382	206	3	138	22	1581	37	6.7	4.8	2.6	19.8
Quinn Buckner	G	6'3	205	27	70	2156	396	822	48	110	168	65	250	328	218	2	174	3	906	31	3.6	4.7	3.1	12.9
Brian Winters	G	6'4	185	29	61	1829	404	806	50	123	156	79	170	253	187	1	57	9	967	30	2.8	4.1	3.1	15.9
Harvey Catchings	F-C	6'9	218	30	80	1603	94	224	42	41	69	59	356	97	237	3	42	135	229	20	4.5	1.2	3.0	2.9
Scott May	F	6'7	220	27	65	1187	212	417	51	159	193	82	218	133	151	2	50	6	583	18	3.4	2.0	2.3	9.0
Alton Lister	C	7'	240	23	80	1186	149	287	52	64	123	52	387	84	239	4	18	118	362	15	4.8	1.1	3.0	4.5
Pat Cummings	F	6'9	235	25	78	1132	219	430	51	67	91	74	245	99	227	6	22	8	505	15	3.1	1.3	2.9	6.5
Junior Bridgeman (FJ)	F-G	6'5	210	28	41	924	209	433	48	89	103	86	125	109	91	0	28	3	511	23	3.0	2.7	2.2	12.5
Robert Smith	G	5'11	165	26	17	316	52	110	47	10	12	83	14	44	35	0	10	1	116	19	0.8	2.6	2.1	6.8
Geff Crompton	C	6'11	288	26	35	203	11	32	34	6	15	40	41	13	39	0	6	12	28	6	1.2	0.4	1.1	0.8
Mike Evans (to Cle)	G	6'1	170	26	14	196	24	51	47	8	12	67	12	22	26	1	9	0	56	14	0.9	1.6	1.9	4.0
Bobby Dandridge	F	6'6	195	34	11	174	21	55	38	10	17	59	17	13	25	0	5	2	52	16	1.5	1.2	2.3	4.7
Kevin Stacom	G	6'3	185	30	7	90	14	34	41	1	2	50	7	7	6	0	1	0	30	13	1.0	1.0	0.9	4.3
Brad Holland (from Was)	G	6'3	185	25	1	9	0	5	0	0	2	0	0	2	1	0	0	0	0	9	0.0	2.0	1.0	0.0

3-PT FG — Ma. Johnson 0-4, Mi. Johnson 1-7, Lanier 0-2, Moncrief 1-14, Buckner 4-15, Winters 36-93, May 0-4, Cummings 0-2, Bridgeman 4-9, Smith 2-10, Evans 0-2, Stacom 1-2

Use Name	Pos	Hgt	Wgt	Age	G	Min	FG	FGA	%	FT	FTA	%	Reb	Ass	PF	DQ	Stls	Blkd Shts	Points	Min	Reb	Ass	PF	Points
ATLANTA HAWKS	42-40 .512				KEVIN LOUGHERY																			
John Drew	F	6'6	205	27	70	2040	465	957	49	364	491	74	375	96	250	6	64	3	1298	29	5.4	1.4	3.6	18.5
Dan Roundfield (LJ)	F	6'8	205	28	61	2217	424	910	47	285	375	76	721	162	210	3	64	93	1134	36	11.8	2.7	3.4	18.6
Tree Rollins	C	7'1	235	26	79	2018	202	346	58	79	129	61	611	59	285	4	35	224	483	26	7.7	0.7	3.6	6.1
Eddie Johnson	G	6'2	190	26	68	2314	455	1011	45	294	385	76	191	358	188	1	102	16	1211	34	2.8	5.3	2.8	17.8
Rory Sparrow	G	6'2	175	23	82	2610	366	730	50	124	148	84	224	424	240	2	87	13	857	32	2.7	5.2	2.9	10.5
Tom McMillen	C-F	6'11	215	29	73	1792	291	572	51	140	170	82	336	129	202	1	25	24	723	25	4.6	1.8	2.8	9.9
Rudy Macklin	F	6'7	205	23	79	1516	210	484	43	134	173	77	263	47	225	5	40	20	554	19	3.3	0.6	2.8	7.0
Steve Hawes	:-F 6'	6'9	220	31	49	1317	178	370	48	96	126	76	320	142	156	4	36	34	456	27	6.5	2.9	3.2	9.3
Sam Pellom	F	6'9	225	30	69	1037	114	251	45	61	79	77	229	28	164	0	29	47	289	15	3.3	0.4	2.4	4.2
Wes Matthews	G	6'1	170	22	47	837	131	298	44	60	79	76	58	139	129	3	53	2	324	18	1.2	3.0	2.7	6.9
Mike Glenn	G	6'3	175	26	49	833	158	291	54	59	67	88	61	87	80	0	26	3	376	17	1.2	1.8	1.6	7.7
Charlie Criss (to SD)	G	5'8	165	32	27	552	84	210	40	65	73	89	38	75	40	0	23	2	235	20	1.4	2.8	1.5	8.7
Jim McElroy	G	6'3	190	28	20	349	52	125	42	29	36	81	17	39	44	0	8	3	134	17	0.9	2.0	2.2	6.7
Al Wood (to SD)	G	6'6	193	23	19	238	36	105	34	20	28	71	44	11	34	0	9	1	92	13	2.3	0.6	1.8	4.8
Freeman Williams (from SD)	G	6'4	195	25	23	189	42	110	38	22	26	85	12	19	18	0	6	0	110	8	0.5	0.8	0.8	4.8
Craig Shelton	F	6'7	210	24	4	21	2	6	33	1	2	50	3	0	3	0	1	0	5	5	0.8	0.0	0.8	1.3

3-PT FG — Drew 4-12, Roundfield 1-5, Johnson 7-30, Sparrow 1-15, McMillen 1-3, Macklin 0-3, Hawes 4-10, Pellom 0-1, Matthews 2-8, Glenn 1-2, Criss 2-8, McElroy 1-5, Wood 0-6, Williams 4-20

Use Name	Pos	Hgt	Wgt	Age	G	Min	FG	FGA	%	FT	FTA	%	Reb	Ass	PF	DQ	Stls	Blkd Shts	Points	Min	Reb	Ass	PF	Points
DETROIT PISTONS	39-43 .476				SCOTTY ROBERTSON																			
Kelly Tripucka	F	6'6	230	22	82	3077	636	1281	50	495	621	80	443	270	241	0	89	16	1772	38	5.4	3.3	2.9	21.6
Terry Tyler	F	6'7	215	25	82	1989	336	643	52	142	192	74	493	126	182	1	77	160	815	24	6.0	1.5	2.2	9.9
Kent Benson	C-F	6'10	245	27	75	2467	405	802	50	127	158	80	653	159	214	2	66	98	940	33	8.7	2.1	2.9	12.5
John Long	G	6'5	210	25	69	2211	637	1294	49	238	275	87	257	148	173	0	65	25	1514	32	3.7	2.1	2.5	21.9
Isiah Thomas	G	6'1	180	20	72	2433	453	1068	42	302	429	70	209	565	253	2	150	17	1225	34	2.9	7.8	3.5	17.0
Ron Lee	G	6'4	193	29	81	1467	88	246	36	84	119	71	155	312	221	3	116	20	278	18	1.9	3.9	2.7	3.4
Vinnie Johnson (from Sea)	G	6'2	200	25	67	1191	208	422	49	98	130	75	144	160	93	0	50	23	517	18	2.1	2.4	1.4	7.7
Phil Hubbard (to Cle)	F	6'8	215	25	52	1104	207	410	50	106	163	65	272	67	176	1	38	16	520	21	5.2	1.3	3.4	10.0
Bill Laimbeer (from Cle)	C	6'11	245	24	30	935	146	283	52	91	112	81	340	55	126	2	17	34	384	31	11.3	1.8	4.2	12.8
Edgar Jones	F-C	6'10	225	25	48	802	142	259	55	90	129	70	207	40	149	3	28	92	375	17	4.3	0.8	3.1	7.8
Paul Mokeski (to Cle)	C	7'	250	24	39	523	49	111	44	25	33	76	122	24	103	2	13	23	123	13	3.1	0.6	2.6	3.2
Kenny Carr (from Cle)	F	6'7	230	26	28	444	77	168	46	53	82	65	137	23	69	0	6	6	207	16	4.9	0.8	2.5	7.4
Steve Hayes (from SA)	C	7'	225	26	26	412	46	93	49	25	41	61	100	24	54	0	3	18	117	16	3.8	0.9	2.1	4.5
Alan Hardy	G	6'7	195	24	38	310	62	136	46	18	29	62	34	20	32	0	9	4	142	8	0.9	0.5	0.8	3.7
Jeff Judkins	G	6'6	185	25	30	251	31	81	38	16	26	62	34	14	33	0	6	5	79	8	1.1	0.5	1.1	2.6
Greg Kelser (to Sea)	F	6'7	190	24	11	183	35	86	41	27	41	66	39	12	32	0	5	7	97	17	3.5	1.1	2.9	8.8
Glenn Hagan	G	6'	170	26	4	25	3	7	43	1	1	100	4	8	7	0	3	0	7	6	1.0	2.0	1.8	1.8
Larry Wright	G	6'1	160	27	1	6	0	1	0	0	0	—	0	0	2	0	0	0	0	6	0.0	0.0	2.0	0.0

3-PT FG — Tripucka 5-22, Tyler 1-4, Benson 3-11, Long 2-15, Thomas 17-59, Lee 18-59, Johnson 3-11, Hubbard 0-3, Laimbeer 1-7, Jones 1-2, Mokeski 0-1, Carr 0-2, Hardy 0-5, Judkins 1-10, Kelser 0-3

Use Name	Pos	Hgt	Wgt	Age	G	Min	FG	FGA	%	FT	FTA	%	Reb	Ass	PF	DQ	Stls	Blkd Shts	Points	Min	Reb	Ass	PF	Points
INDIANA PACERS	35-47 .427				JACK McKINNEY																			
Louis Orr	F	6'8	175	23	80	1051	357	717	50	203	254	80	331	134	182	1	56	26	918	24	4.1	1.7	2.3	11.5
Herb Williams	F-C	6'11	242	23	82	2277	407	854	48	126	188	67	605	139	200	0	53	178	942	28	7.4	1.7	2.4	11.5
Clemon Johnson	C-F	6'10	240	25	79	1979	312	641	49	123	189	65	571	127	241	3	60	112	747	25	7.2	1.6	3.1	9.5
Johnny Davis	G	6'2	170	26	82	2664	538	1153	47	315	394	80	178	346	176	1	76	11	1396	32	2.2	4.2	2.1	17.0
Don Buse	G	6'4	195	31	82	2529	312	685	46	100	123	81	223	407	176	0	164	27	797	31	2.7	5.0	2.1	9.7
Billy Knight	F-G	6'6	195	29	81	1803	378	764	49	233	282	83	257	118	132	0	63	14	998	22	3.2	1.5	1.6	12.3
Tom Owens	C	6'10	220	32	74	1599	299	636	47	181	226	80	372	127	259	7	41	37	780	22	5.0	1.7	3.5	10.5
George McGinnis	F	6'8	235	31	76	1341	141	378	37	72	159	45	398	204	198	4	96	28	354	18	5.2	2.7	2.6	4.7
Mike Bantom (to Phi)	F	6'9	220	30	39	1037	178	406	44	101	153	66	214	68	139	5	38	24	458	27	5.5	1.7	3.6	11.7
Butch Carter	G	6'5	180	23	75	1035	188	402	47	58	70	83	79	60	110	0	34	11	442	14	1.1	0.8	1.5	5.9
Jerry Sichting	G	6'1	168	25	51	800	91	194	47	29	38	76	55	117	63	0	33	1	212	16	1.1	2.3	1.2	4.2
George Johnson	F	6'7	218	25	59	720	120	291	41	60	80	75	217	40	147	2	36	25	300	12	3.7	0.7	2.5	5.1
Raymond Townsend	G	6'3	175	26	14	95	11	41	27	11	20	55	13	10	18	0	3	0	35	7	0.9	0.7	1.3	2.5

3-PT FG — Orr 1-8, Williams 2-7, Davis 5-27, Buse 73-189, Knight 9-32, Owens 1-2, McGinnis 0-3, Bantom 1-3, Carter 8-25, Sichting 1-9, G. Johnson 0-2, Townsend 2-9

Use Name	Pos	Hgt	Wgt	Age	TOTAL G	Min	FG	FGA	%	FT	FTA	%	Reb	Ass	PF	DQ	Stls	Blkd Shts	Points	PER GAME Min	Reb	Ass	PF	Points
1981/82 N.B.A. — EASTERN CONFERENCE — CENTRAL DIVISION (continued)																								
CHICAGO BULLS	34-48 .415				JERRY SLOAN (19-32 .373), PHIL JOHNSON (0-1 .000), ROD THORN (15-15 .500)																			
Dave Greenwood	F	6'9	222	24	82	2914	480	1014	47	240	291	82	786	262	292	1	70	92	1200	36	9.6	3.2	3.6	14.6
Dwight Jones	F-C	6'10	210	29	78	2040	303	572	53	172	238	72	507	114	217	0	49	36	779	26	6.5	1.5	2.8	10.0
Artis Gilmore	C	7'2	240	32	82	2796	546	837	65	424	552	77	835	136	287	4	49	221	1517	34	10.2	1.7	3.5	18.5
Reggie Theus	G	6'7	190	24	82	2838	560	1194	47	363	449	81	312	476	243	1	87	16	1508	35	3.8	5.8	3.0	18.4
Ronnie Lester	G	6'2	175	22	75	2252	329	657	50	208	256	81	213	362	158	2	80	14	870	30	2.8	4.8	2.1	11.6
Ricky Sobers	G	6'3	198	28	80	1938	363	801	45	195	254	77	142	301	238	6	73	18	940	24	1.8	3.8	3.0	11.8
Orlando Woolridge	F	6'9	215	22	75	1188	202	394	51	144	206	70	227	81	152	1	23	24	548	16	3.0	1.1	2.0	7.3
Larry Kenon	F	6'9	215	29	60	1036	192	412	47	50	88	57	180	65	71	0	30	7	434	17	3.0	1.1	1.2	7.2
Coby Dietrick	C	6'10	225	33	74	999	92	200	46	38	54	70	188	87	131	1	49	30	222	14	2.5	1.2	1.8	3.0
James Wilkes	F	6'7	195	23	57	862	128	266	48	58	80	73	159	64	112	0	30	18	314	15	2.8	1.1	2.0	5.5
Ray Blume	G	6'4	186	23	49	546	102	222	46	18	28	64	41	68	57	0	23	2	226	11	0.8	1.4	1.2	4.6
Tracy Jackson (from Bos)	G-F	6'6	205	22	38	412	69	146	47	32	39	82	51	22	43	0	11	3	170	11	1.3	0.6	1.1	4.5
Roger Burkman	G	6'5	175	23	6	30	0	4	0	5	6	83	6	5	6	0	6	2	5	5	1.0	0.8	1.0	0.8
Jackie Robinson	F	6'6	212	26	3	29	3	9	33	4	4	100	3	0	1	0	0	0	10	10	1.0	0.0	0.3	3.3
3-PT FG —	Greenwood 0-3, Jones 1-1, Gilmore 1-1, Theus 25-100, Lester 4-8, Sobers 19-76, Woolridge 0-3, Dietrick 0-1, Wilkes 0-1, Blume 4-18, Burkman 0-1																							
CLEVELAND CAVALIERS	15-67 .183				DON DE LANY (4-11 .267), BOB KOPPENBERG (0-3 .000), CHUCK DALEY (9-32 .220), BILL MUSSELMAN (2-21 .087)																			
Scott Wedman (FJ)	F	6'7	215	29	54	1638	260	589	44	66	90	73	304	133	189	4	73	14	591	30	5.6	2.5	3.5	10.9
Kenny Carr (to Det)	F	6'7	230	26	46	1482	271	524	52	145	220	66	394	63	180	0	58	16	688	32	8.6	1.4	3.9	15.0
James Edwards	C	7'	225	26	77	2539	528	1033	51	232	339	68	581	123	347	17	24	117	1288	33	7.5	1.6	4.5	16.7
Ron Breuer (to Sea)	G	6'4	180	26	47	1724	387	833	46	134	172	78	111	121	114	0	59	23	913	37	2.4	2.6	2.4	19.4
Geoff Huston	G	6'2	175	24	78	2409	325	627	52	153	200	77	150	590	169	1	70	11	806	31	1.9	7.6	2.2	10.3
Bob Wilkerson	G-F	6'6	200	27	65	1805	284	679	42	145	185	78	250	237	188	3	92	25	716	28	3.8	3.6	2.9	11.0
James Silas	G	6'3	180	32	67	1447	251	573	44	246	286	86	109	222	109	0	40	6	748	22	1.6	3.3	1.6	11.2
Mike Mitchell (to SA)	F	6'7	215	25	27	973	229	504	45	72	100	72	141	39	77	0	27	15	530	36	5.2	1.4	2.9	19.6
Cliff Robinson (from KC)	F	6'9	220	21	30	946	196	435	45	97	133	73	287	49	102	3	42	43	489	32	9.6	1.6	3.4	16.3
Bill Laimbeer (to Det)	C	6'11	245	24	50	894	119	253	47	93	120	78	277	45	170	3	22	30	334	18	5.5	0.9	3.4	6.7
Phil Hubbard (from Det)	F	6'8	215	25	31	735	119	255	47	85	117	73	201	24	116	2	27	3	323	24	6.5	0.8	3.7	10.4
R. Johnson (from SA to KC)	F	6'9	205	24	23	617	94	175	54	35	44	80	125	22	73	1	6	17	223	27	5.4	1.0	3.2	9.7
Roger Phegley (to SA)	G	6'6	205	25	27	566	104	214	49	36	45	80	71	53	61	0	16	2	248	21	2.6	2.0	2.3	9.2
Paul Mokeski (from Det)	C	7'	250	24	28	345	35	82	43	23	30	77	86	11	61	0	20	17	93	12	3.1	0.4	2.4	3.3
Kevin Restani (from SA)	F	6'9	225	30	34	338	23	60	38	7	12	58	77	15	40	0	10	7	53	10	2.3	0.4	1.2	1.6
Richard Washington (KJ)	F	6'11	225	26	18	313	50	115	43	9	15	60	75	15	51	0	8	2	109	17	4.2	0.8	2.8	6.1
Keith Herron	F-G	6'6	195	25	30	269	39	106	37	7	8	88	21	23	25	0	8	2	85	9	0.7	0.8	0.8	2.8
Mickey Dillard	G	6'3	170	23	33	221	29	79	37	15	23	65	15	34	40	0	8	2	73	7	0.5	1.0	1.2	2.2
Don Ford	F	6'9	215	29	21	201	9	24	38	5	6	83	35	11	30	0	8	0	23	10	1.7	0.5	1.4	1.1
Brad Branson	C	6'10	220	23	10	176	21	52	40	11	12	92	33	6	17	0	5	4	53	18	3.3	0.6	1.7	5.3
Mike Evans (from MIL)	G	6'1	170	26	8	74	11	35	31	5	8	63	10	20	10	0	4	0	27	9	1.3	2.5	1.3	3.4
Lowes Moore	G	6'1	170	24	4	70	19	38	50	6	8	75	4	15	15	1	6	1	45	18	1.0	3.8	3.8	11.3
Mel Bennett	F	6'7	200	26	3	23	2	4	50	1	6	17	3	0	2	0	1	0	5	8	1.0	0.0	0.7	1.7
3-PT FG —	Wedman 5-23, Carr 1-9, Edwards 0-4, Brewer 5-21, Huston 3-10, Wilkerson 3-18, Silas 0-5, Mitchell 0-6, Robinson 0-1, Laimbeer 3-6, Hubbard 0-1, Phegley 4-13, Mokeski 0-2, Restani 0-1, Washington 0-2, Herron 0-1, Dillard 0-4, Ford 0-1, Evans 0-4, Moore 1-5																							
1981/82 N.B.A. - WESTERN CONFERENCE - MIDWEST DIVISION																								
SAN ANTONIO SPURS	48-34. 585				STAN ALBECK																			
Mike Mitchell (from Cle)	F	6'7	215	25	57	2090	524	973	54	148	202	73	449	43	200	4	33	28	1196	37	7.9	0.8	3.5	21.0
Mark Olberding	F	6'8	230	25	68	2098	333	705	47	273	338	81	439	202	253	5	57	29	941	31	6.5	3.0	3.7	13.8
Dave Corzine	C	6'11	250	25	82	2189	336	648	52	159	213	75	629	130	235	3	33	126	832	27	7.7	1.6	2.9	10.1
George Gervin	G	6'7	185	29	79	2817	993	1987	50	555	642	86	392	187	215	2	77	45	2551	36	5.0	2.4	2.7	32.3
Johnny Moore	G	6'2	175	23	79	2294	309	667	46	122	182	67	275	762	254	6	163	12	741	29	3.5	9.6	3.2	9.4
Gene Banks	F	6'7	215	22	80	1700	311	652	48	145	212	68	411	147	199	2	55	17	767	21	5.1	1.8	2.5	9.6
Mike Bratz	G	6'2	185	26	81	1616	230	565	41	119	152	78	166	438	183	0	65	11	625	20	2.0	5.4	2.3	7.7
George Johnson	C	6'11	205	33	75	1578	91	195	47	43	64	67	454	79	259	6	20	234	225	21	6.1	1.1	3.5	3.0
Ed Rains	F	6'7	190	25	49	637	77	177	44	38	64	59	80	40	74	0	18	2	192	13	1.6	0.8	1.5	3.9
Roger Phegley (from Cle)	G	6'6	205	25	54	617	129	293	44	49	64	77	83	61	91	0	20	6	308	11	1.5	1.1	1.7	5.7
Ron Brewer (to Cle)	G	6'4	180	26	25	595	182	361	50	77	88	88	50	67	37	0	23	7	444	24	2.0	2.7	1.5	17.8
R. Johnson (to Cle, KC)	F	6'9	205	24	21	504	94	194	48	32	40	80	137	20	67	0	7	16	220	24	6.5	1.0	3.2	10.5
Paul Griffin	F	6'9	205	27	23	459	32	66	48	24	37	65	95	54	67	0	20	8	88	20	4.1	2.3	2.9	3.8
John Lambert (from KC)	F-C	6'10	225	28	21	271	26	58	45	13	14	93	51	13	43	0	6	6	65	13	2.4	0.6	2.0	3.1
Kevin Restani (to Cle)	F	6'9	225	30	13	145	9	28	32	3	4	75	35	7	16	0	1	4	21	11	2.7	0.5	1.2	1.6
Steve Hayes (to Det)	C	7'	225	26	9	75	8	18	44	7	12	58	17	4	17	0	1	2	23	8	1.9	0.4	1.9	2.6
Rich Yonakor	F	6'9	220	23	10	70	14	26	54	5	7	71	27	3	7	0	1	2	33	7	2.7	0.3	0.7	3.3
3-PT FG —	Mitchell 0-1, Olberding 2-12, Corzine 1-4, Gervin 10-36, Moore 1-21, Banks 0-8, Bratz 46-138, Rains 0-2, Phegley 1-18, Brewer 3-10, Lambert 0-1, Restani 0-1																							
DENVER NUGGETS	46-36 .561				DOUG MOE																			
Alex English	F	6'8	190	27	82	3015	855	1553	55	372	443	84	558	433	261	2	87	120	2082	37	6.8	5.3	3.2	25.4
Kiki Vanderweghe	F	6'8	220	23	82	2775	706	1260	56	347	405	86	461	247	217	1	52	29	1760	34	5.6	3.0	2.6	21.5
Dan Issel	C	6'9	240	33	81	2472	651	1236	53	546	655	83	608	179	245	4	67	55	1852	31	7.5	2.2	3.0	22.9
T.R. Dunn	G	6'4	192	26	82	2519	258	504	51	153	215	71	559	188	210	1	135	36	669	31	6.8	2.3	2.6	8.2
Billy McKinney	G	6'	162	26	81	1963	369	699	53	137	170	81	142	338	186	0	69	16	875	24	1.8	4.2	2.3	10.8
Kenny Higgs	G	6'	185	26	76	1696	202	468	43	161	197	82	144	395	263	8	72	6	569	22	1.9	5.2	3.5	7.5
Glen Gondrezick	F	6'6	218	26	80	1699	250	495	51	160	217	74	423	152	229	0	92	36	660	21	5.3	1.9	2.9	8.3
Cedric Hordges	C-F	6'8	220	24	77	1372	204	414	49	116	199	58	395	65	230	1	76	19	527	18	5.1	0.8	3.0	6.8
David Thompson	G	6'4	195	27	61	1246	313	644	49	276	339	81	148	117	149	1	34	29	906	20	2.4	1.9	2.4	14.9
John Roche	G	6'3	170	32	39	501	68	150	45	28	38	74	23	89	40	0	15	2	187	13	0.6	2.3	1.0	4.8
James Ray	F	6'8	215	24	40	262	51	116	44	21	36	58	65	26	59	0	10	16	124	7	1.6	0.7	1.5	3.1
Dave Robisch	C	6'10	240	32	12	257	48	106	45	48	55	87	63	32	29	0	3	4	144	21	5.3	2.7	2.4	12.0
David Burns (from NJ)	G	6'2	180	23	6	53	5	11	45	6	9	67	3	11	13	0	2	0	16	9	0.5	1.8	2.2	2.7
3-PT FG —	English 0-8, Vanderweghe 1-13, Issel 4-6, Dunn 0-1, McKinney 0-17, Higgs 4-21, Gondrezick 0-3, Hordges 3-13, Thompson 4-14, Roche 23-52, Ray 1-1																							

1981/82 N.B.A. — WESTERN CONFERENCE
MIDWEST DIVISION (Continued)

HOUSTON ROCKETS 46-36 .561 DEL HARRIS

Use Name	Pos	Hgt	Wgt	Age	G	Min	FG	FGA	%	FT	FTA	%	Reb	Ass	PF	DQ	Stls	Blkd Shts	Points	Min	Reb	Ass	PF	Points
Bill Willoughby	F	6'8	205	24	69	1475	240	464	52	56	77	73	264	75	146	1	31	59	539	21	3.8	1.1	2.1	7.8
Elvin Hayes	F	6'9	235	36	82	3032	519	1100	47	280	422	66	747	144	287	4	62	104	1318	37	9.1	1.8	3.5	16.1
Moses Malone	C	6'10	235	26	81	3398	945	1822	52	630	827	76	1188	142	208	0	76	125	2520	42	14.7	1.8	2.6	31.1
Robert Reid	G-F	6'8	205	26	77	2913	437	958	46	160	214	75	511	314	297	2	115	48	1035	38	6.6	4.1	3.9	13.4
Allen Leavell	G	6'1	170	24	79	2150	370	793	47	115	135	85	168	457	182	2	150	15	864	27	2.1	5.8	2.3	10.9
Tom Henderson	G	6'3	190	29	75	1721	183	403	45	105	150	70	138	306	120	0	55	7	471	23	1.8	4.1	1.6	6.3
Mike Dunleavy	G	6'3	180	27	70	1315	206	450	46	75	106	71	104	227	161	0	45	3	520	19	1.5	3.2	2.3	7.4
Calvin Murphy	G	5'9	165	33	64	1204	277	648	43	100	110	91	61	163	142	0	43	1	655	19	1.0	2.5	2.2	10.2
Calvin Garrett	F	6'7	190	25	51	858	183	403	45	105	150	70	94	76	94	0	32	6	230	17	1.8	1.5	1.8	4.5
Billy Paultz	C-F	6'11	250	33	65	807	89	226	39	34	65	52	180	41	99	0	15	22	212	12	2.8	0.6	1.5	3.3
Major Jones	F	6'9	225	28	60	746	113	213	53	42	77	55	202	25	100	0	20	29	268	12	3.4	0.4	1.7	4.5
Jawann Oldham	C	7'	215	24	22	124	13	36	36	8	14	57	24	3	28	0	2	10	34	6	1.1	0.1	1.3	1.5
Larry Spriggs	F	6'7	230	22	4	37	7	11	64	0	2	0	6	4	7	0	2	0	14	9	1.5	1.0	1.8	3.5

3-PT FG — Willoughby 3-7, Hayes 0-5, Malone 0-6, Reid 11-10, Leavell 9-31, Henderson 0-2, Dunleavy 33-86, Murphy 1-16, Garrett 3-10, Jones 0-3

KANSAS CITY KINGS 30-52 .366 COTTON FITZSIMMONS

Use Name	Pos	Hgt	Wgt	Age	G	Min	FG	FGA	%	FT	FTA	%	Reb	Ass	PF	DQ	Stls	Blkd Shts	Points	Min	Reb	Ass	PF	Points
Reggie King	F	6'6	225	24	80	2609	383	752	51	201	285	71	523	173	221	6	84	29	967	33	6.5	2.2	2.8	12.1
Cliff Robinson (to Cle)	F	6'9	220	21	38	1229	322	708	45	125	180	69	322	71	120	1	46	60	769	32	8.5	1.9	3.2	20.2
Steve Johnson	C	6'10	235	24	78	1741	395	644	61	212	330	64	459	91	372	25	39	89	1002	22	5.9	1.2	4.8	12.8
Mike Woodson (from NJ)	G	6'5	195	23	76	2186	508	1001	51	198	254	78	234	206	199	2	135	33	1221	29	3.1	2.7	2.6	16.1
Phil Ford	G	6'2	176	25	72	1952	285	649	44	136	166	82	105	451	160	0	63	1	713	27	1.5	6.3	2.2	9.9
Larry Drew	G	6'1	170	23	81	1973	358	757	47	150	189	79	149	419	150	0	110	1	874	24	1.8	5.2	1.9	10.8
Ernie Grunfeld	G-F	6'6	215	26	81	1892	420	822	51	188	229	82	182	276	191	0	72	39	1030	23	2.2	3.4	2.4	12.7
Eddie Johnson	F	6'8	215	22	74	1517	295	643	46	99	149	66	322	109	210	6	50	14	690	21	4.4	1.5	2.8	9.3
Kevin Loder	F	6'6	205	22	71	1139	208	448	46	77	107	72	195	88	147	0	35	30	493	16	2.7	1.2	2.1	6.9
Leon Douglas	C	6'10	230	27	63	1093	70	140	50	32	80	40	290	35	210	5	15	38	172	17	4.6	0.6	3.3	2.7
R. Johnson (from SA,Cle)	F-C	6'9	205	24	31	783	163	293	56	51	72	71	189	31	117	4	20	27	377	25	6.1	1.0	3.8	12.2
Kenny Dennard	F	6'8	220	23	30	607	62	121	51	26	40	65	133	42	81	0	35	8	150	20	4.4	1.4	2.7	5.0
John Lambert (to SA)	C	6'10	225	28	42	493	60	139	43	21	28	75	127	24	80	0	12	10	142	12	3.0	0.6	1.9	3.4
Joe C. Meriweather	C	6'10	218	28	18	380	47	91	52	31	40	78	88	17	68	1	13	21	125	21	4.9	0.9	3.8	6.9
Hawkeye Whitney	F-G	6'5	235	24	23	266	25	71	35	4	7	57	40	19	31	0	12	1	54	12	1.7	0.8	1.3	2.3
Sam Lacey (to NJ)	C	6'10	235	33	2	20	3	5	60	0	2	0	4	4	2	0	2	1	6	10	2.0	2.0	1.0	3.0

3-PT FG — Robinson 0-3, Woodson 7-24, Ford 7-32, Drew 8-27, Grunfeld 2-14, E. Johnson 1-1, Loder 0-11, R. Johnson 0-1, Lambert 1-6, Whitney 0-1

DALLAS MAVERICKS 28-54 .341 DICK MOTTA

Use Name	Pos	Hgt	Wgt	Age	G	Min	FG	FGA	%	FT	FTA	%	Reb	Ass	PF	DQ	Stls	Blkd Shts	Points	Min	Reb	Ass	PF	Points
Mark Aquirre (BJ)	F	6'6	235	22	51	1468	381	820	46	168	247	68	249	164	152	0	37	22	955	29	4.9	3.2	3.0	18.7
Jay Vincent	F	6'7	225	22	81	2626	719	1448	50	293	409	72	565	176	308	8	89	22	1732	32	7.0	2.2	3.8	21.4
Wayne Cooper	C	6'10	220	25	76	1818	281	669	42	119	160	74	550	115	285	10	37	106	682	24	7.2	1.5	3.8	9.0
Rolando Blackman	G	6'6	190	22	82	1979	439	855	51	212	276	77	254	105	122	0	46	30	1091	24	3.1	1.3	1.5	13.3
Brad Davis	G	6'3	180	26	82	2614	397	771	51	185	230	80	226	509	218	5	73	6	993	32	2.8	6.2	2.7	12.1
Allan Bristow	F	6'7	210	30	82	2035	218	499	44	134	164	82	339	448	222	2	65	6	573	25	4.1	5.5	2.7	7.0
Elston Turner	G-F	6'5	190	22	80	1996	282	639	44	97	138	70	301	189	182	1	75	2	661	25	3.8	2.4	2.3	8.3
Jim Spanarkel	G-F	6'5	190	24	82	1755	270	564	48	279	327	85	210	206	140	0	86	9	827	21	2.6	2.5	1.7	10.1
Kurt Nimphius	C	6'10	218	23	63	1085	137	297	46	63	108	58	295	61	190	5	17	82	337	17	4.7	1.0	3.0	5.3
Scott Lloyd	C	6'10	230	29	74	1047	108	285	38	69	91	76	163	67	175	6	15	7	287	14	2.2	0.9	2.4	3.9
Tom LaGarde	F-C	6'10	220	26	47	909	113	269	42	86	166	52	210	49	138	3	17	17	312	19	4.5	1.0	2.9	6.6
Clarence Kea	F	6'6	218	22	35	248	26	49	53	29	42	69	61	14	55	0	4	3	81	7	1.7	0.4	1.6	2.3
Oliver Mack	G	6'3	195	24	13	150	19	59	32	6	8	75	18	14	6	0	5	1	44	12	1.4	1.1	0.5	3.4

3-PT FG — Aguirre 25-71, Vincent 1-4, Cooper 1-8, Blackman 1-4, Davis 14-49, Bristow 3-18, Turner 0-4, Spanarkel 8-24, Lloyd 2-4, LaGarde 0-2, Mack 0-2

UTAH JAZZ 25-57 .305 TOM NISSALKE (8-12 .400), FRANK LAYDEN (17-45 .274)

Use Name	Pos	Hgt	Wgt	Age	G	Min	FG	FGA	%	FT	FTA	%	Reb	Ass	PF	DQ	Stls	Blkd Shts	Points	Min	Reb	Ass	PF	Points
Adrian Dantley	F-G	6'5	210	25	81	3222	904	1586	57	648	818	79	514	324	252	1	95	14	2457	40	6.3	4.0	3.1	30.3
James Hardy	F	6'8	220	25	82	1814	179	369	49	64	93	69	470	110	192	2	58	67	422	22	5.7	1.3	2.3	5.1
Jeff Wilkins	C	6'11	240	26	82	2274	314	718	44	137	176	78	611	90	248	4	32	77	765	28	7.5	1.1	3.0	9.3
Darrell Griffith	G	6'4	190	23	80	2597	689	1429	48	189	271	70	305	187	213	0	95	34	1582	32	3.8	2.3	2.7	19.8
Rickey Green	G	6'1	170	27	81	2822	500	1015	49	202	264	77	243	630	183	0	185	9	1202	35	3.0	7.8	2.3	14.8
Ben Poquette	F-C	6'9	235	26	82	1698	220	428	51	97	120	81	411	94	235	4	51	65	540	21	5.0	1.1	2.9	6.6
Dan Schayes	C	6'11	235	22	82	1623	252	524	48	140	185	76	427	146	292	4	46	72	644	20	5.2	1.8	3.6	7.9
Carl Nicks	G	6'3	185	23	80	1322	252	555	45	85	150	57	161	89	184	0	66	4	589	17	2.0	1.1	2.3	7.4
John Duren	G	6'3	195	23	79	1056	121	268	45	27	37	73	84	157	143	0	20	4	272	13	1.1	2.0	1.8	3.4
Bill Robinzine	F	6'7	230	28	56	651	131	294	45	61	75	81	144	49	156	5	37	5	323	12	2.6	0.9	2.8	5.8
Howard Wood	F	6'7	235	22	42	342	55	120	46	34	52	65	65	9	37	0	8	6	144	8	1.5	0.2	0.9	3.4
Bobby Cattage	F	6'9	250	23	49	337	60	135	44	30	41	73	73	7	58	0	7	0	150	7	1.5	0.1	1.2	3.1
Sam Worthen	G	6'5	195	23	5	22	2	5	40	0	0	—	1	3	3	0	0	0	4	4	0.2	0.6	0.6	0.8

3-PT FG — Dantley 1-3, Hardy 0-1, Wilkins 0-3, Griffith 15-52, Green 0-8, Poquette 3-10, Schayes 0-1, Nicks 0-5, Duren 3-11, Wood 0-1, Cattage 0-2

1981/82 N.B.A. - WESTERN CONFERENCE
PACIFIC DIVISION

LOS ANGELES LAKERS 57-25 .695 PAUL WESTHEAD (7-4 .636), PAT RILEY (50-21 .704)

Use Name	Pos	Hgt	Wgt	Age	G	Min	FG	FGA	%	FT	FTA	%	Reb	Ass	PF	DQ	Stls	Blkd Shts	Points	Min	Reb	Ass	PF	Points
					TOTAL															PER GAME				
Jamaal Wilkes	F	6'6	190	28	82	2906	744	1417	53	246	336	73	393	143	240	1	89	24	1734	35	4.8	1.7	2.9	21.1
Mitch Kupchak (KJ)	F-C	6'9	230	27	26	821	153	267	57	65	98	66	210	33	80	1	12	10	371	32	8.1	1.3	3.1	14.3
Kareem Abdul-Jabbar	C	7'2	232	34	76	2677	753	1301	58	312	442	71	659	225	224	0	63	207	1818	35	8.7	3.0	2.9	23.9
Magic Johnson	G	6'8	215	22	78	2991	556	1036	54	329	433	76	751	743	223	1	208	34	1447	38	9.6	9.5	2.9	18.6
Norm Nixon	G	6'2	175	26	82	3024	628	1274	49	181	224	81	176	652	264	3	132	7	1440	37	2.1	8.0	3.2	17.6
Michael Cooper	G-F	6'5	170	25	76	2197	383	741	52	139	171	81	269	230	216	1	120	61	907	29	3.5	3.0	2.8	11.9
Mark Landsberger	F-C	6'8	230	26	75	1134	144	329	44	33	65	51	401	32	134	0	10	7	321	15	5.3	0.4	1.8	4.3
Kurt Rambis	F	6'8	215	23	64	1131	118	228	52	59	117	50	348	56	167	2	60	76	295	18	5.4	0.9	2.6	4.6
Jim Brewer	F	6'9	220	30	71	966	81	175	46	7	19	37	264	42	127	1	39	46	170	14	3.7	0.6	1.8	2.4
Bob McAdoo	C	6'9	210	30	41	746	151	330	46	90	126	71	159	32	109	1	22	36	392	18	3.9	0.8	2.7	9.6
Eddie Jordan	G	6'1	170	26	58	608	89	208	43	43	56	77	43	131	98	0	62	1	222	10	0.7	2.3	1.7	3.8
Mike McGee	F-G	6'5	190	22	39	352	80	172	47	31	53	58	49	16	59	0	18	3	191	9	1.3	0.4	1.5	4.9
Kevin McKenna	F-G	6'5	205	22	36	237	28	87	32	11	17	65	29	14	45	0	10	2	67	7	0.8	0.4	1.3	1.9
Clay Johnson	G	6'4	175	25	7	65	11	20	55	3	6	50	12	7	13	0	3	3	25	9	1.7	1.0	1.9	3.6

3-PT FG — Wilkes 0-4, Abdul-Jabbar 0-3, Johnson 6-29, Nixon 3-12, Cooper 2-17, Landsberger 0-2, Rambis 0-1, Brewer 1-6, MacAdoo 0-4, Jordan 1-9, McGee 0-5, McKenna 0-2

SEATTLE SUPERSONICS 52-30 .634 LENNY WILKENS

Use Name	Pos	Hgt	Wgt	Age	G	Min	FG	FGA	%	FT	FTA	%	Reb	Ass	PF	DQ	Stls	Blkd Shts	Points	Min	Reb	Ass	PF	Points
Wally Walker	F	6'7	190	27	70	1965	302	629	48	90	134	67	305	218	215	2	36	28	694	28	4.4	3.1	3.1	9.9
Lonnie Shelton	F	6'8	245	26	81	2667	508	1046	49	188	240	78	509	252	317	12	99	43	1204	33	6.3	3.1	3.9	14.9
Jack Sikma	C-F	6'11	230	26	82	3049	581	1212	48	447	523	85	1038	277	268	5	102	107	1611	37	12.7	3.4	3.3	19.6
Bill Hanzlik	G	6'7	185	24	81	1974	167	357	47	138	176	78	266	183	250	3	81	30	472	24	3.3	2.3	3.1	5.8
Gus Williams	G	6'2	175	28	80	2876	773	1592	49	320	436	73	244	549	163	0	172	36	1875	36	3.1	6.9	2.0	23.4
Fred Brown	G	6'3	185	33	82	1785	393	863	49	111	129	86	140	238	111	0	69	4	922	22	1.7	2.9	1.4	11.2
James Donaldson	C	7'2	278	24	82	1710	255	419	61	151	240	63	490	51	186	2	27	139	661	21	6.0	0.6	2.3	8.1
Danny Vranes	F	6'7	210	23	77	1075	143	262	55	89	148	60	198	56	150	0	28	21	375	14	2.6	0.7	1.9	4.9
Phil Smith (from SD)	G	6'4	187	29	26	596	87	186	47	40	55	73	69	74	62	0	22	8	214	23	2.7	2.8	2.4	8.2
Greg Kelser (from SD)	F	6'7	190	24	49	558	81	185	44	78	119	66	154	45	99	0	13	14	240	11	3.1	0.9	2.0	4.9
Ray Tolbert (from NJ)	F	6'9	225	23	52	492	80	158	51	15	27	56	99	25	64	0	8	14	175	9	1.9	0.5	1.2	3.4
Mark Radford	G	6'4	190	22	43	369	54	100	54	35	69	51	29	57	65	0	16	2	145	9	0.7	1.3	1.5	3.4
Armond Hill (to SD)	G	6'4	190	28	21	243	19	37	51	17	23	74	25	25	37	0	5	2	55	12	1.2	1.2	1.8	2.6
John Johnson	F	6'7	200	34	14	187	22	45	49	15	20	75	18	29	20	0	4	3	59	13	1.3	2.1	1.4	4.2
James Bailey (to NJ)	F	6'9	220	24	10	180	31	65	48	4	11	36	48	13	42	2	3	7	66	18	4.8	1.3	4.2	6.6
Vinnie Johnson (to Det)	G	6'2	200	25	7	104	9	22	41	9	12	75	15	11	8	0	6	2	27	15	2.1	1.6	1.1	3.9
Paul Westphal - holdout, to NY																								

3-PT FG — Walker 0-2, Shelton 0-8, Sikma 2-13, Hanzlik 0-4, Williams 9-40, Brown 25-77, Vranes 0-1, Smith 0-3, Tolbert 0-1, Radford 2-3, V. Johnson 0-1

PHOENIX SUNS 46.36 .561 JOHN MCCLEOD

Use Name	Pos	Hgt	Wgt	Age	G	Min	FG	FGA	%	FT	FTA	%	Reb	Ass	PF	DQ	Stls	Blkd Shts	Points	Min	Reb	Ass	PF	Points
Alvin Scott	F	6'7	185	26	81	1740	189	380	50	108	148	73	294	149	169	0	59	70	486	21	3.6	1.8	2.1	6.0
Truck Robinson	F	6'7	225	30	74	2745	529	1128	47	255	371	69	721	179	215	2	42	28	1414	37	9.7	2.4	2.9	19.1
Alvan Adams	C-F	6'9	220	27	79	2393	507	1027	49	182	233	78	586	356	269	7	114	78	1196	30	7.4	4.5	3.4	15.1
Dennis Johnson	G	6'4	185	27	80	2937	577	1228	47	399	495	81	410	369	253	6	105	55	1561	37	5.1	4.6	3.2	19.5
Kyle Macy	G	6'3	175	24	82	2845	486	945	51	152	169	90	261	384	185	1	143	9	1163	35	3.2	4.7	2.3	14.2
Rich Kelly	C	7'	240	28	81	1892	236	505	47	167	223	75	497	293	292	14	64	71	639	23	6.1	3.6	3.6	7.9
Jeff Cook	F	6'10	215	25	76	1298	151	358	42	89	134	66	301	100	174	1	37	23	391	17	4.0	1.3	2.3	5.1
Larry Nance	F	6'10	205	22	80	1186	227	436	52	75	117	64	256	82	169	2	42	71	529	15	3.2	1.0	2.1	6.6
Walter Davis (BA)	G	6'6	195	27	55	1182	350	669	52	91	111	82	103	162	104	1	46	3	794	21	1.9	2.9	1.9	14.4
Dudley Bradley	G	6'6	195	24	64	937	125	281	44	74	100	74	87	80	115	0	78	10	325	15	1.4	1.3	1.8	5.1
Joel Kramer	F	6'7	203	26	56	549	55	133	41	33	42	79	108	51	62	0	19	11	143	10	1.9	0.9	1.1	2.6
Craig Dykema	F	6'8	190	22	32	103	17	37	46	7	9	78	12	15	19	0	2	0	43	3	0.4	0.5	0.6	1.3
John McCullough	G	6'4	190	25	8	23	9	13	69	3	5	60	4	3	3	0	2	0	21	3	0.5	0.4	0.4	2.6

3-PT FG — Scott 0-2, Robinson 1-1, Adams 0-1, Johnson 8-42, Macy 39-100, Kelly 0-1, Cook 0-2, Nance 0-1, Davis 3-16, Bradley 1-4, Dykema 2-4

GOLDEN STATE WARRIORS 45-37 .549 AL ATTLES

Use Name	Pos	Hgt	Wgt	Age	G	Min	FG	FGA	%	FT	FTA	%	Reb	Ass	PF	DQ	Stls	Blkd Shts	Points	Min	Reb	Ass	PF	Points
Bernard King	F	6'7	205	25	79	2861	740	1307	57	352	499	71	469	282	285	6	78	23	1833	36	5.9	3.6	3.6	23.2
Larry Smith	F	6'8	215	23	74	2213	220	412	53	88	159	55	813	83	291	7	65	54	528	30	11.0	1.1	3.9	7.1
Joe Barry Carroll	C	7'	225	23	76	2627	527	1016	52	235	323	73	633	64	265	8	64	127	1289	35	8.3	0.8	3.5	17.0
Purvis Short	G-F	6'7	210	24	76	1782	456	935	49	177	221	80	266	209	220	3	65	10	1095	23	3.5	2.8	2.9	14.4
World Free	G	6'2	185	28	78	2796	650	1452	45	479	647	74	248	419	222	1	71	8	1789	36	3.2	5.4	2.8	22.9
Mike Gale	G	6'4	190	31	75	1793	185	373	50	51	65	78	189	261	173	1	121	28	421	24	2.5	3.5	2.3	5.6
Rickey Brown	C	6'10	215	23	82	1260	192	418	46	86	122	70	364	19	243	4	36	29	470	15	4.4	0.2	3.0	5.7
Lorenzo Romar	G	6'1	175	23	79	1259	203	403	50	79	96	82	98	226	103	0	60	13	488	16	1.2	2.9	1.3	6.2
Sam Williams	F	6'8	210	22	59	1073	154	277	56	49	89	55	308	38	156	0	45	76	357	18	5.2	0.6	2.6	6.1
Sonny Parker	G-F	6'6	200	26	71	899	116	245	47	48	72	67	177	89	101	0	39	11	280	13	2.5	1.3	1.4	3.9
Joe Hassett	G	6'5	180	26	68	787	144	382	38	31	37	84	53	104	94	1	30	3	390	12	0.8	1.5	1.4	5.7
Hank McDowell	F-C	6'9	215	22	30	335	34	84	40	27	41	66	100	20	52	1	6	8	95	11	3.3	0.7	1.7	3.2
Lewis Lloyd	F	6'6	215	22	16	95	25	45	56	7	11	64	16	6	20	0	5	1	57	6	1.0	0.4	1.3	3.6

3-PT FG — King 1-5, Smith 0-1, Carroll 0-1, Short 6-28, Free 10-56, Gale 0-5, Romar 3-15, Hassett 71-214

1981/82 N.B.A. — WESTERN CONFERENCE
PACIFIC DIVISION (Continued)

PORTLAND TRAILBLAZERS 42-40 .512 **JACK RAMSEY**

Use Name	Pos	Hgt	Wgt	Age	TOTAL G	Min	FG	FGA	%	FT	FTA	%	Reb	Ass	PF	DQ	Stls	Blkd Shts	Points	PER GAME Min	Reb	Ass	PF	Points
Bob Gross	F-G	6'6	200	28	59	1377	173	322	54	78	104	75	259	125	162	2	75	41	427	23	4.4	2.1	2.7	7.
Calvin Natt	F	6'6	220	24	75	2599	515	894	58	294	392	75	613	150	175	1	62	36	1326	35	8.2	2.0	2.3	17.
Mychal Thompson	C-F	6'10	226	26	79	3129	681	1303	52	280	446	63	921	319	233	2	69	107	1642	40	11.7	4.0	2.9	20.
Jim Paxon	G	6'6	200	24	82	2756	662	1258	53	220	287	77	221	276	159	0	129	12	1552	34	2.7	3.4	1.9	18.
Kelvin Rahsey	G	6'1	170	23	78	2418	504	1095	46	242	318	76	186	555	169	1	97	4	1253	31	2.4	7.1	2.2	16.
Mike Harper	C-F	6'10	195	24	68	1433	184	370	50	96	153	63	339	54	229	7	55	82	464	21	5.0	0.8	3.4	6.
Darnell Valentine	G	6'2	185	22	82	1387	187	453	41	152	200	76	149	270	187	1	94	3	526	17	1.8	3.3	2.3	6.
Billy Ray Bates	G	6'4	210	25	75	1229	327	692	47	166	211	79	108	111	100	0	41	5	832	16	1.4	1.5	1.3	11.
Peter Verhoeven	F	6'9	215	22	71	1207	149	296	50	51	72	71	254	52	215	4	42	22	349	17	3.6	0.7	3.0	4.9
Petur Gudmundsson	C	7'2	260	23	68	845	83	166	50	52	76	68	186	59	163	2	13	30	219	12	2.7	0.9	2.4	3.2
Jeff Lamp	F	6'6	195	22	54	617	100	196	51	50	61	82	64	28	83	0	16	1	250	11	1.2	0.5	1.5	4.6
Kermit Washington	F	6'8	230	30	20	418	38	78	49	24	41	59	117	29	56	0	9	16	100	21	5.9	1.5	2.8	5.
Kevin Kunnert	C	7'	231	30	21	237	20	48	42	7	19	37	66	18	51	1	3	6	49	11	3.1	0.9	2.4	2.3
Dennis Awtrey	C	6'10	240	33	10	121	5	15	33	5	9	56	14	8	28	1	1	2	15	12	1.4	0.8	2.8	1.5
Carl Bailey	C	7'	210	23	1	7	1	1	100	0	0	—	0	0	2	0	0	0	2	7	0.0	0.0	2.0	2.0

3-PT FG — Gross 3-6, Natt 2-8, Paxson 8-35, Ransey 3-38, Harper 0-1, Valentine 0-9, Bates 12-41, Gudmundsson 1-1, Lamp 0-1

SAN DIEGO CLIPPERS 17-65 .207 **PAUL SILAS**

Use Name	Pos	Hgt	Wgt	Age	TOTAL G	Min	FG	FGA	%	FT	FTA	%	Reb	Ass	PF	DQ	Stls	Blkd Shts	Points	PER GAME Min	Reb	Ass	PF	Points
Michael Brooks	F	6'7	220	23	82	2750	537	1066	50	202	267	76	624	236	285	7	113	39	1276	34	7.6	2.9	3.5	15.6
Tom Chambers	F-C	6'10	220	22	81	2682	554	1056	52	284	458	62	561	146	341	17	58	46	1392	33	6.9	1.8	4.2	17.2
Jerome Whitehead	C	6'10	220	25	72	2214	406	726	56	184	241	76	664	102	290	16	48	44	996	31	9.2	1.4	4.0	13.8
Phil Smith (to Sea)	G	6'4	187	29	48	1446	253	575	44	123	168	73	117	233	151	0	45	19	634	30	2.4	4.9	3.1	13.2
Brian Taylor (LJ)	G	6'2	185	30	41	1274	165	328	50	90	110	82	96	229	113	1	47	9	443	31	2.3	5.6	2.8	10.8
Joe Bryant	F-G	6'9	215	27	75	1988	341	701	49	194	247	79	274	189	250	1	78	29	884	27	3.7	2.5	3.3	11.8
John Douglas	G	6'2	170	25	64	1031	181	389	47	67	102	66	90	146	147	2	48	9	447	16	1.4	2.3	2.3	7.0
Jim Brogan	G	6'5	185	23	63	1027	165	364	45	61	84	73	120	156	123	2	49	13	400	16	1.9	2.5	2.0	6.3
Michael Wiley	F	6'9	200	24	61	1013	203	359	57	98	141	70	182	52	127	1	40	16	504	17	3.0	0.9	2.1	8.3
Charlie Criss (from Atl)	G	5'8	165	22	28	840	138	288	48	76	86	88	44	112	56	0	21	4	360	30	1.6	4.0	2.0	12.9
Freeman Williams (to Atl)	G	6'4	195	25	37	808	234	513	46	118	140	84	50	67	85	1	23	0	610	22	1.4	1.8	2.3	16.5
Al Wood (from Atl)	G	6'6	193	23	29	692	143	276	52	73	91	80	90	47	74	4	22	8	362	24	3.1	1.6	2.6	12.5
Swen Nater (KJ)	C	6'11	240	31	21	575	101	175	58	59	79	75	192	30	64	1	6	9	262	27	9.1	1.4	3.0	12.5
Armond Hill (from Sea)	G	6'4	190	28	19	480	34	89	38	22	32	69	27	81	51	0	16	3	90	25	1.4	4.3	2.7	4.7
Ron Davis	G	6'6	198	27	7	67	10	25	40	3	6	50	13	4	8	0	0	0	23	10	1.9	0.6	1.1	3.3
Rock Lee	C	6'10	220	26	2	10	1	2	50	0	4	0	1	2	3	0	0	0	2	5	0.5	1.0	1.5	1.0
Jim Smith	F	6'9	225	23	72	858	86	169	51	39	85	46	182	46	185	5	22	51	211	12	2.5	0.6	2.6	2.9
Bill Walton - foot injury																								

3-PT FG — Brooks 0-7, Chambers 0-2, P. Smith 5-24, Taylor 23-63, Bryant 8-30, Douglas 18-59, Brogan 9-32, Wiley 0-5, Criss 8-21, Williams 24-74, Wood 3-18, Nater 1-1, Hill 0-2

PLAYOFFS

LOS ANGELES LAKERS **PAT RILEY**

defeated Phoenix 4-0; H115-96, H117-98, 114-106, 112-107
defeated San Antonio 4-0; H128-117, H110-101, 118-108, 128-123
defeated Philadelphia 4-2; 124-117, 94-110, H129-108, H 101-101, 102-135, H114-104

Use Name	Pos	Hgt	Wgt	Age	TOTAL G	Min	FG	FGA	%	FT	FTA	%	Reb	Ass	PF	DQ	Stls	Blkd Shts	Points	PER GAME Min	Reb	Ass	PF	Points
Jamaal Wilkes	F	6'6	190	28	14	535	121	241	50	38	49	78	70	37	43	0	16	3	280	38	5.0	2.6	3.1	20.0
Bob McAdoo	F-C	6'9	210	30	14	388	101	179	56	32	47	68	95	22	43	2	10	21	234	28	6.8	1.6	3.1	16.7
Kareem Abdul-Jabbar	C	7'2	232	34	14	493	115	221	52	55	87	63	119	51	45	0	14	45	285	35	8.5	3.6	3.2	20.4
Magic Johnson	G	6'8	215	22	14	562	83	157	53	77	93	83	158	130	50	0	40	3	243	40	11.3	9.3	3.6	17.4
Norm Nixon	G	6'2	175	26	14	549	121	253	48	43	57	75	43	114	43	0	23	2	286	39	3.1	8.1	3.1	20.4
Michael Cooper	G-F	6'5	170	25	14	383	70	124	56	25	34	74	61	62	47	0	24	11	166	27	4.4	4.4	3.4	11.9
Kurt Rambis	F	6'8	215	23	14	279	33	64	52	16	26	62	86	11	47	0	8	12	82	20	6.1	0.8	3.4	5.9
Mark Landsberger	F-C	6'8	230	26	9	60	3	9	33	4	9	44	22	2	12	0	0	0	10	7	2.4	0.2	1.3	1.1
Jim Brewer	F	6'9	220	30	8	57	3	6	50	0	0	—	11	4	5	0	2	6	6	7	1.4	0.5	0.6	0.8
Clay Johnson	G	6'4	175	25	7	38	5	9	56	2	2	100	3	1	6	0	1	0	12	5	0.4	0.1	0.9	1.7
Mike McGee	F	6'5	190	22	4	10	6	13	46	0	0	—	3	0	1	0	0	0	12	3	0.0	0.0	0.3	3.0
Eddie Jordon	G	6'1	170	26	3	6	0	2	0	0	0	—	0	5	0	0	2	0	0	2	0.0	1.7	0.0	0.0
Mitch Kupchak-knee injury																								

3-PT FG — Wilkes 0-1, M. Johnson 0-4, Nixon 1-3, Cooper 1-2, McGee 0-1, Jordon 0-1

PHILADELPHIA 76ers **BILLY CUNNINGHAM**

defeated Atlanta 2-0; H111-76, 98-95
defeated Milwaukee 4-2; H125-122, H120-108, 91-92, 100-93, H98-110, 102-90
defeated Boston 4-3; 81-121, 121-113, H99-97, H119-94, 85-114, H75-88, 120-106
lost to Los Angeles 2-4; H117-124, H110-94, 108-129,101-111, H135-102, 104-114

Use Name	Pos	Hgt	Wgt	Age	TOTAL G	Min	FG	FGA	%	FT	FTA	%	Reb	Ass	PF	DQ	Stls	Blkd Shts	Points	PER GAME Min	Reb	Ass	PF	Points
Julius Erving	F	6'7	200	31	21	**780**	168	324	52	**124**	**165**	75	156	99	55	0	37	37	**461**	37	7.4	4.7	2.6	22.0
Bobby Jones	F	6'9	212	30	21	589	94	174	54	68	81	84	99	52	69	0	15	22	256	28	4.7	2.5	3.3	12.2
Caldwell Jones	C-F	6'11	225	31	21	679	74	160	46	35	41	85	**189**	19	77	1	11	40	183	32	9.0	0.9	3.7	8.7
Andrew Toney	G	6'3	178	24	21	707	**185**	**365**	51	82	103	80	51	102	86	1	18	2	457	34	2.4	4.9	4.1	21.8
Maurice Cheeks	G	6'1	180	25	21	765	125	265	47	50	65	77	62	**172**	58	0	**48**	6	301	36	3.0	8.2	2.8	14.3
Darryl Dawkins	C	6'11	251	24	21	460	99	178	56	33	50	66	98	11	**94**	**4**	7	35	231	22	4.7	0.5	4.5	11.0
Clint Richardson	G	6'3	195	25	21	415	47	104	45	17	30	57	69	40	48	0	13	5	111	20	3.3	1.9	2.3	5.3
Mike Bantom	F	6'9	220	30	21	399	36	91	40	19	42	45	77	24	60	1	15	9	91	19	3.7	1.1	2.9	4.3
Lionel Hollins	G	6'3	185	28	8	114	15	49	31	4	6	67	9	25	11	0	9	1	34	14	1.1	3.1	1.4	4.3
Earl Cureton		6'9	210	24	12	75	13	41	32	6	9	67	26	2	12	0	1	0	32	6	2.2	0.2	1.0	2.7
Steve Mix	F	6'7	222	34	7	50	12	22	55	5	7	71	11	6	5	0	0	0	30	7	1.6	0.9	0.7	4.3
Franklin Edwards	G	6'1	170	22	9	32	12	20	60	8	9	89	5	5	0	0	3	0	33	4	0.6	0.6	0.0	3.7

3-PT FG — Erving 1-6, Toney 5-15, Cheeks 1-9, Hollins 0-1, Cureton 0-1, Mix 1-1, Edwards 1-1

1981/82 N.B.A. — PLAYOFFS

Use Name	Pos	Hgt	Wgt	Age	G	Min	FG	FGA	%	FT	FTA	%	Reb	Ass	PF	DQ	Stls	Blkd Shts	Points	Min (Per Game)	Reb (Per Game)	Ass (Per Game)	PF (Per Game)	Points (Per Game)
BOSTON CELTICS	**BILL FITCH**				defeated Washington 4-1; H109-91, H102-102, 92-83, 103-99, H131-126(OT)																			
					lost to Philadelphia 4-3; H121-81, H113-121, 97099, 94-119, H114-85, 88-75, H106-120																			
Cedric Maxwell	F	6'8	205	26	12	385	62	120	52	50	70	71	87	26	40	0	18	11	174	32	7.3	2.2	3.3	14.5
Larry Bird	F	6'9	220	25	12	490	88	206	43	37	45	82	150	67	43	0	23	17	214	41	12.5	5.6	3.6	17.8
Robert Parish	C	7'	230	28	12	426	102	209	49	51	75	68	135	18	47	1	5	48	255	36	11.3	1.5	3.9	21.3
M.L. Carr	G	6'6	205	30	12	305	37	105	35	15	23	65	43	28	30	0	11	0	89	25	3.6	2.3	2.5	7.4
Nate Archibald (SJ)	G	6'1	150	33	8	277	30	70	43	25	28	89	17	52	21	0	5	2	85	35	2.1	6.5	2.6	10.6
Kevin McHale	F-C	6'10	235	24	12	344	77	134	57	40	53	75	85	11	44	0	5	27	194	29	7.1	0.9	3.7	16.2
Gerald Henderson	G	6'2	175	25	12	310	38	93	41	24	35	69	25	48	30	0	14	2	100	26	2.1	4.0	2.5	8.3
Chris Ford	G	6'5	190	32	12	138	20	42	48	5	7	71	15	15	15	0	3	1	47	12	1.3	1.3	1.3	3.9
Danny Ainge	G	6'4	175	22	10	129	19	45	42	10	13	77	13	11	21	0	2	1	50	13	1.3	1.1	2.1	5.0
Rick Robey	C-F	6'11	235	25	12	122	21	40	53	13	17	76	29	4	27	0	2	3	55	10	2.4	0.3	2.3	4.6
Charles Bradley	G	6'5	215	22	7	18	2	8	25	0	2	0	5	1	6	0	1	0	4	3	0.7	0.1	0.9	0.6
Eric Fernsten	F	6'10	205	28	5	11	1	2	50	1	2	50	2	0	0	0	0	1	3	2	0.4	0.0	0.0	0.6
	3-PT FG —				Bird 1-6, Carr 0-4, Archibald 0-4, Henderson 0-2, Ford 2-7, Ainge 2-4																			
SAN ANTONIO SPURS	**STAN ALBECK**				defeated Seattle 4-1; 95-93, 99-114, H99-97, H115-113, 109-103																			
					lost to Los Angeles 4-0; 117-128, 101-110, H108-118, H123-128																			
Mike Mitchell	F	6'7	215	25	9	365	90	169	53	43	57	75	73	7	22	0	5	1	223	41	8.1	0.8	2.4	24.8
Mark Olberding	F	6'8	230	25	9	328	53	120	44	26	31	84	58	32	39	1	9	6	132	36	6.4	3.6	4.3	14.7
Dave Corzine	C	6'11	250	25	9	258	49	106	46	24	34	71	85	17	30	0	6	9	122	29	9.4	1.9	3.3	13.6
George Gervin	G	6'7	185	29	9	373	103	228	45	59	71	83	66	41	36	1	10	4	265	41	7.3	4.6	4.0	29.4
Johnny Moore	G	6'2	175	23	9	292	39	82	48	16	27	59	31	93	38	0	15	6	94	32	3.4	10.3	4.2	10.4
Mike Bratz	G	6'2	185	26	9	180	15	52	29	8	10	80	14	48	20	0	9	0	43	20	1.6	5.3	2.2	4.8
George Johnson	C	6'11	205	33	9	175	4	8	50	3	5	60	46	12	34	0	6	15	11	19	5.1	1.3	3.8	1.2
Gene Banks	F	6'7	215	22	9	146	30	65	46	4	10	40	43	9	12	0	4	3	64	16	4.8	1.0	1.3	7.1
Ed Rains	F	6'7	190	25	5	30	3	6	50	4	9	44	8	1	5	0	1	0	10	6	1.6	0.2	1.0	2.0
Roger Phegley	G	6'6	205	25	5	6	0	2	0	0	0	—	0	0	0	1	0	0	0	1	0.0	0.0	0.0	0.0
Rich Yonaker	F	6'9	220	23	2	4	1	2	50	0	0	—	1	1	1	0	1	0	2	2	0.5	0.5	0.5	1.0
John Lambert	F	6'10	225	28	2	3	0	1	0	0	0	—	1	1	0	0	0	0	0	2	0.5	0.5	0.0	0.0
	3-PT FG —				Olberding 0-1, Gervin 0-3, Moore 0-3, Bratz 5-18, Banks 0-1, Phegley 0-1, Lambert 0-1																			
SEATTLE SUPERSONICS	**LENNY WILKENS**				defeated Houston 2-1; H102-87, 70-91, H104-83																			
					lost to Seattle 4-1; H93-95, H114-99, 97-99, 113-115, H103-109																			
Bill Hanzlik	F-G	6'7	185	24	8	203	16	34	47	10	22	45	32	20	26	1	6	5	52	25	4.0	2.5	3.3	6.5
Lonnie Shelton	F	6'8	245	26	8	266	40	85	47	22	32	69	59	16	38	3	5	7	102	33	7.4	2.0	4.8	12.8
Jack Sikma	C-F	6'11	230	26	8	315	57	128	45	50	58	86	97	24	34	1	9	8	164	39	12.1	3.0	4.3	20.5
John Johnson	G	6'7	200	34	7	159	15	38	39	8	11	73	14	34	17	0	6	0	38	23	2.0	4.9	2.4	5.4
Gus Williams	G	6'2	175	28	8	315	82	186	44	44	56	79	26	65	13	0	13	5	210	39	3.3	8.1	1.6	26.3
James Donaldson	C	7'2	278	24	8	189	18	43	42	18	24	75	74	7	16	0	2	5	54	24	9.3	0.9	2.0	6.8
Fred Brown	G	6'3	185	33	8	158	43	89	48	7	10	70	15	18	5	0	5	0	95	20	1.9	2.3	0.6	11.9
Wally Walker	F	6'7	190	27	8	157	19	45	42	1	4	25	32	15	26	0	4	4	39	20	4.0	1.9	3.3	4.9
Phil Smith	G	6'4	187	29	8	92	12	30	40	1	3	33	8	7	11	0	5	1	25	12	1.0	0.9	1.4	3.1
Ray Tolbert	F	6'9	225	23	4	31	3	5	60	4	8	50	5	1	7	0	4	0	10	8	1.3	0.3	1.8	2.5
Danny Vranes	F	6'7	210	23	6	29	1	5	20	1	2	50	2	0	2	0	1	0	3	5	0.3	0.0	0.3	0.5
Greg Kelser	F	6'7	190	24	3	6	0	2	0	4	4	100	3	1	2	0	0	0	4	2	1.0	0.3	0.7	1.3
	3-PT FG —				Hanzlik 0-1, Williams 2-6, Brown 2-5, Smith 0-1																			
PHOENIX SUNS	**JOHN McCLOUD**				defeated Denver 2-1; 113-129, H126-110, 124-119																			
					lost to Los Angeles 4-0; 96-115, 98-117, H106-114, H107-112																			
Alvin Scott	F	6'7	185	26	7	127	14	32	44	4	8	50	16	14	12	0	8	13	32	18	2.3	2.0	1.7	4.6
Truck Robinson	F	6'7	225	30	7	213	45	80	56	3	10	30	53	19	17	0	5	1	93	30	7.6	2.7	2.4	13.3
Alvan Adams	C-F	6'9	220	27	7	233	48	92	52	22	28	79	51	26	22	0	14	10	118	33	7.3	3.7	3.1	16.9
Dennis Johnson	G	6'4	185	27	7	271	63	132	48	30	39	77	31	32	28	2	15	4	156	39	4.4	4.6	4.0	22.3
Kyle Macy	G	6'3	175	24	7	243	38	89	43	15	16	94	22	28	21	0	7	1	95	35	3.1	4.0	3.0	13.6
Rich Kelley	C	7'	240	28	7	191	27	54	50	14	20	70	48	30	25	0	6	3	68	27	6.9	4.3	3.6	9.7
Walter Davis	G-F	6'6	195	27	7	173	52	116	45	22	24	92	22	30	19	0	5	1	127	25	3.1	4.3	2.7	18.1
Larry Nance	F	6'10	205	22	7	128	25	41	61	4	8	50	32	7	15	1	10	11	54	18	4.6	1.0	2.1	7.7
Jeff Cook	F	6'10	215	25	7	45	4	8	50	0	0	—	9	7	5	0	2	2	8	6	1.3	1.0	0.7	1.1
Dudley Bradley	G	6'6	195	24	7	24	2	8	25	1	1	100	1	5	3	0	1	1	5	3	0.1	0.7	0.4	0.7
Joel Kramer	F	6'7	203	26	4	20	5	7	71	2	3	67	5	1	2	0	1	0	12	5	1.3	0.3	0.5	3.0
Craig Dykema	F	6'8	190	22	6	12	1	6	17	0	0	—	4	1	2	0	0	0	2	2	0.7	0.2	0.3	0.3
	3-PT FG —				Scott 0-4, Johnson 0-3, Macy 4-11, Davis 1-3																			
WASHINGTON BULLETS	**GENE SHUE**				defeated New Jersey 2-0; 96-83, H103-92																			
					lost to Boston 4-1; 91-109, 103-102, H92-83, H99-103, 126-131(OT)																			
Greg Ballard	F	6'7	215	26	7	268	36	100	36	21	25	84	63	22	20	1	14	3	93	38	9.0	3.1	2.9	13.3
Spencer Hayward	F	6'9	225	32	7	231	57	115	50	26	35	74	39	7	28	0	4	14	140	33	5.6	1.0	4.0	20.0
Rick Mahorn	C	6'10	240	23	7	242	32	73	44	10	14	71	61	13	30	1	10	5	74	35	8.7	1.9	4.3	10.6
Kevin Grevey	G	6'5	210	28	7	159	23	56	41	16	19	84	10	11	12	0	3	1	66	23	1.4	1.6	1.7	9.4
Frank Johnson	G	6'2	185	23	7	280	40	104	38	24	28	86	22	59	24	0	10	0	109	40	3.1	8.4	3.4	15.6
Jeff Ruland	F-C	6'10	240	23	7	237	38	79	48	43	56	77	66	5	24	1	3	4	119	34	9.4	0.7	3.4	17.0
Don Collins	G	6'6	190	23	7	149	19	44	43	5	7	71	22	6	25	1	4	1	43	21	3.1	0.9	3.6	6.1
John Lucas	G	6'3	175	28	7	74	14	26	54	2	3	67	8	20	6	0	3	1	31	11	1.1	2.9	0.9	4.4
Charlie Davis	F	6'7	215	23	6	52	7	17	41	2	2	100	5	3	6	0	1	1	16	9	0.8	0.5	1.0	2.7
Jim Chones	F-C	6'11	220	32	5	30	2	9	22	1	3	33	6	2	8	0	1	2	5	6	1.2	0.4	1.6	1.0
Garry Witts	G	6'7	190	22	4	28	2	2	100	1	2	50	3	2	6	0	1	0	5	7	0.8	0.5	1.5	1.3
Carlos Terry	G	6'5	210	25	3	5	0	0	—	0	0	—	1	0	0	0	0	0	0	2	0.3	0.0	0.0	0.0
	3-PT FG —				Grevey 4-8, Johnson 5-12, Ruland 0-1, Lucas 1-3, Davis 0-1																			

1981/82 N.B.A. — PLAYOFFS

Use Name	Pos	Hgt	Wgt	Age	G	Min	FG	FGA	%	FT	FTA	%	Reb	Ass	PF	DQ	Stls	Blkd Shts	Points	Min	Reb	Ass	PF	Points
					TOTAL															PER GAME				
MILWAUKEE BUCKS	**DON NELSON**	lost to Philadelphia 4-2; 122-125, 108-120, H92-91, H93-100, 100-98, H90-102																						
Marques Johnson	F	6'7	218	25	6	235	44	100	44	24	42	57	44	20	25	0	6	2	113	39	7.3	3.3	4.2	18.8
Mickey Johnson	F	6'10	190	29	6	206	43	75	57	33	39	85	32	18	27	1	8	4	119	34	5.3	3.0	4.5	19.8
Bob Lanier	C	6'11	250	33	6	212	41	80	51	14	25	56	45	22	21	2	8	5	96	35	7.5	3.7	3.5	16.0
Sidney Moncrief	G	6'4	190	24	6	252	31	74	42	30	38	79	30	24	22	1	9	2	92	42	5.0	4.0	3.7	15.3
Brian Winters	G	6'4	185	29	6	232	38	77	49	20	24	83	15	28	23	0	8	1	101	39	2.5	4.7	3.8	16.8
Alton Lister	C-F	7'	240	23	6	112	14	24	58	5	7	71	27	5	23	0	2	15	33	19	4.5	0.8	3.8	5.5
Robert Smith	G	5'11	165	26	6	68	10	26	38	7	8	88	7	8	12	0	1	0	29	11	1.2	1.3	2.0	4.8
Scott May	F	6'7	220	27	4	50	4	20	20	9	14	64	11	10	6	0	2	0	17	13	2.8	2.5	1.5	4.3
Pat Cummings	F	6'9	235	25	6	44	4	11	36	1	2	50	11	2	7	0	0	2	9	7	1.8	0.3	1.2	1.5
Harvey Catchings	F	6'9	218	30	6	26	2	3	67	0	0	—	7	0	9	0	0	3	4	4	1.2	0.0	1.5	0.7
Brad Holland	G	6'3	185	25	1	3	1	1	100	0	0	—	0	1	0	0	0	0	2	3	0.0	1.0	0.0	2.0
Junior Bridgeman (foot injury)	**3-PT FG —**	Ma. Johnson 1-4, Mi. Johnson 0-1, Lanier 0-1, Moncrief 0-1, Winters 5-10, Smith 2-7																						
DENVER NUGGETS	**DOUG MOE**	lost to Phoenix 2-1; H129-113, 110-126, H119-124																						
Alex English	F	6'8	190	27	3	118	26	55	47	6	7	86	23	17	6	0	3	3	58	39	7.7	5.7	2.0	19.3
Kiki Vanderweghe	F	6'8	220	23	3	109	25	43	58	18	18	100	18	9	7	0	2	4	68	36	6.0	3.0	2.3	22.7
Dan Issel	C	6'9	240	33	3	103	32	60	53	12	12	100	21	5	10	0	3	1	76	34	7.0	1.7	3.3	25.3
T.R. Dunn	G	6'4	192	26	3	81	6	13	46	7	8	88	18	10	11	0	8	1	19	27	6.0	3.3	3.7	6.3
Billy McKinney	G	6'	162	26	3	91	16	27	59	10	12	83	6	10	9	0	3	0	42	30	2.0	3.3	3.0	14.0
David Thompson	G	6'4	195	27	3	66	15	33	45	4	7	57	10	6	8	0	1	0	35	22	3.3	2.0	2.7	11.7
Kenny Higgs	G	6'	185	26	3	54	8	21	38	7	12	58	3	6	12	0	3	0	23	18	1.0	2.0	4.0	7.7
Glen Gondrezick	F	6'6	218	26	3	51	8	20	40	2	3	67	8	9	8	0	2	1	18	17	2.7	3.0	2.7	6.0
Cedric Hordges	C	6'8	220	24	3	45	8	19	42	3	4	75	13	2	4	0	1	0	19	15	4.3	0.7	1.3	6.3
James Ray	F	6'8	215	24	1	2	0	0	—	0	0	—	0	0	1	0	0	1	0	2	0.0	0.0	1.0	0.0
	3-PT FG —	McKinney 0-1, Thompson 1-3, Higgs 0-2, Gondrezick 0-1, Hordges 0-1																						
HOUSTON ROCKETS	**DEL HARRIS**	lost to Seattle 2-1; 87-102, H91-70, 83-104																						
Robert Reid	F	6'8	205	26	3	115	15	31	48	4	5	80	26	9	10	0	5	2	34	38	8.7	3.0	3.3	11.3
Elvin Hayes	F	6'9	235	36	3	124	17	50	34	8	15	53	30	3	12	0	2	10	42	41	10.0	1.0	4.0	14.0
Moses Malone	C	6'10	235	26	3	136	29	67	43	14	15	93	51	10	8	0	2	2	72	45	17.0	3.3	2.7	24.0
Tom Henderson	G	6'3	190	29	3	68	5	16	31	4	4	100	8	9	5	0	0	0	14	23	2.7	3.0	1.7	4.7
Allen Leavell	G	6'1	170	24	3	93	20	47	43	2	2	100	5	10	9	0	3	1	42	31	1.7	3.3	3.0	14.0
Mike Dunleavy	G	6'3	180	27	3	66	9	22	41	5	6	83	3	9	7	0	2	0	23	22	1.0	3.0	2.3	7.7
Calvin Murphy	G	5'9	165	33	3	57	5	22	23	7	8	88	3	4	7	0	1	0	17	19	1.0	1.3	2.3	5.7
Billy Paultz	F-C	6'11	250	33	3	34	3	9	33	1	3	33	4	1	4	0	0	2	7	11	1.3	0.3	1.3	2.3
Bill Willoughby	F	6'8	205	24	2	17	1	2	50	2	2	100	6	1	1	0	0	0	4	9	3.0	0.5	0.5	2.0
Larry Sprigs	F	6'7	230	22	2	9	3	4	75	0	1	0	1	2	3	0	0	0	6	5	0.5	1.0	1.5	3.0
Calvin Garrett	F	6'7	190	25	1	1	0	1	0	0	0	—	0	0	0	0	0	0	0	1	0.0	0.0	0.0	0.0
	3-PT FG —	Leavell 0-1, Dunleavy 0-4, Murphy 0-3, Garrett 0-1																						
ATLANTIC HAWKS	**KEVIN LOUGHERY**	lost to Philadelphia 2-0; 76-111, H95-98																						
John Drew	F	6'6	205	27	2	59	8	22	36	7	12	58	10	1	11	1	0	0	23	30	5.0	0.5	5.5	11.5
Dan Roundfield	F	6'8	205	28	2	85	17	36	47	8	14	57	22	2	8	0	2	4	42	43	11.0	1.0	4.0	21.0
Tree Rollins	C	7'1	235	26	2	65	2	6	33	3	4	75	8	2	8	1	0	6	7	33	4.0	1.0	4.0	3.5
Eddie Johnson	G	6'2	190	26	2	67	9	26	35	4	4	100	6	9	8	0	0	1	22	34	3.0	4.5	4.0	11.0
Rory Sparrow	G	6'2	175	23	2	69	5	12	42	6	6	100	3	1	6	1	0	0	14	35	1.5	0.5	3.0	7.0
Tom McMillen	C-F	6'11	215	29	2	47	8	13	62	4	6	67	7	1	5	0	3	0	20	24	3.5	0.5	2.5	10.0
Mike Glenn	G	6'3	175	26	2	35	5	7	71	2	2	100	1	2	3	0	3	0	12	18	0.5	1.0	1.5	6.0
Rudy Macklin	F	6'7	205	23	2	30	4	8	50	6	6	100	3	1	6	1	0	0	14	15	1.5	0.5	3.0	7.0
Wes Matthews	G	6'1	170	22	2	28	2	10	20	4	4	100	0	4	4	0	0	1	8	14	0.0	2.0	2.0	4.0
Steve Hawes	C-F	6'9	220	31	1	12	2	5	40	3	4	75	5	0	1	0	0	0	7	12	5.0	0.0	1.0	7.0
Sam Pellom	F	6'9	225	30	1	4	1	3	33	0	0	—	1	0	0	0	0	0	2	4	1.0	0.0	0.0	2.0
Freeman Williams	G	6'4	195	25	1	4	0	2	0	0	0	—	0	0	0	0	0	0	0	4	0.0	0.0	0.0	0.0
	3-PT FG —	Sparrow 0-1, Macklin 0-1, Williams 0-1																						
NEW JERSEY NETS	**LARRY BROWN**	lost to Washington 2-0; H83-96, 92-103																						
Albert King	F	6'6	190	22	2	58	18	33	55	4	5	80	8	6	8	0	5	1	40	29	4.0	3.0	4.0	20.0
Buck Williams	F	6'8	215	21	2	79	14	26	54	7	15	47	21	3	7	0	1	2	35	40	10.5	1.5	3.5	17.5
Len Elmore	C	6'9	220	29	2	76	9	16	56	4	4	100	16	2	4	0	1	2	22	38	8.0	1.0	2.0	11.0
Darwin Cook	G	6'3	190	23	2	86	13	33	39	2	6	33	3	9	7	0	2	2	28	43	1.5	4.5	3.5	14.0
Ray Williams	G	6'3	190	27	2	77	14	47	30	4	5	80	12	14	10	0	4	0	34	39	6.0	7.0	5.0	17.0
Mike O'Koren	F-G	6'7	207	23	2	44	3	11	27	1	2	50	8	3	8	1	1	0	7	22	4.0	1.5	4.0	3.5
James Bailey	F-C	6'9	220	24	2	26	1	3	33	2	2	100	6	1	5	0	2	1	4	13	3.0	0.5	2.5	2.0
Jan van Breda Kolff	F	6'7	200	30	2	16	0	1	0	0	0	—	3	0	0	0	2	1	0	8	1.5	0.0	0.0	0.0
Mike Gminski	C	6'11	250	22	1	10	2	3	67	1	2	50	2	0	2	0	0	0	5	10	2.0	0.0	2.0	5.0
Ed Sherod	G	6'2	170	22	2	8	0	1	0	0	0	—	1	1	1	0	1	0	0	4	0.5	0.5	0.5	0.0
	3-PT FG —	Cook 0-3, R. Williams 2-5, O'Koren 0-1																						

Team		G	FG	FGA	%	FT	FTA	%	REBOUNDS Offense	Defense	Total	Assists	PF	Steals	Blocked Shots	Turn Overs	Points	Points per game
TEAM STATISTICS																		
EASTERN CONFERENCE ATLANTIC DIVISION																		
Boston	Off.	82	3657	7334	50	1847	2457	75	1253	2489	3742	2126	2014	652	568	1452	9180	112.0
	Def.	82	3490	7429	47	1638	2172	75	1193	2247	3440	1972	2240	681	367	1432	8657	105.6
	Diff.		+167	-95	+3	+209	+285	—	+60	+242	**+302**	+154	+226	-29	**+201**	-20	**+523**	**+6.4**
Philadelphia	Off.	82	3616	6974	52	1846	2471	75	1031	2389	3420	2264	2183	856	**622**	1474	9119	111.2
	Def.	82	3371	7083	48	1852	2496	74	1289	2344	3633	1965	2216	702	470	1615	8649	105.5
	Diff.		+245	-109	**+4**	-6	-25	+1	-258	+45	-213	**+299**	+33	**+154**	+152	+141	+470	+5.7
New Jersey	Off.	82	3501	7227	48	1714	2354	73	1194	2320	3514	2096	2295	**918**	481	1650	8746	106.7
	Def.	82	3343	6934	48	1946	2597	75	1142	2346	3488	1931	2164	832	539	**1809**	8690	106.0
	Diff.		+158	**+293**	—	-232	-243	-2	+52	-26	+26	+165	-131	+86	-58	**+159**	+56	+.7
Washington	Off.	82	3400	7168	47	1626	2105	77	1047	**2583**	3630	1983	2072	643	397	1390	8485	103.5
	Def.	82	3362	7229	47	1645	2237	74	1110	2516	3626	1889	1907	624	543	1325	8413	102.6
	Diff.		+38	-61	—	-19	-132	+3	-63	+67	+4	+94	-165	+19	-146	-65	+72	+.9
New York	Off.	82	3523	7178	49	1603	2171	74	1168	2273	3441	2075	2195	719	338	1486	8707	106.2
	Def.	82	3541	7018	50	1793	2369	76	1125	2366	3491	2089	2017	703	358	1462	8926	108.9
	Diff.		-18	+160	-1	-190	-198	-2	+43	-93	-50	-14	-178	+16	-20	-24	-219	-2.7
CENTRAL DIVISION																		
Milwaukee	Off.	82	3544	7015	51	1753	2329	75	1167	2415	3582	2233	2281	763	455	1589	8890	108.4
	Def.	82	3297	7066	47	1790	2470	72	1172	2155	3327	2016	2189	720	350	1538	8441	102.9
	Diff.		**+247**	-51	**+4**	-37	-141	+3	-5	+260	+255	+217	-92	+43	+105	-51	+449	+5.5
Atlanta	Off.	82	3210	6776	47	1833	2387	77	1135	2368	3503	1815	2268	608	485	1343	8281	101.0
	Def.	82	3150	6709	47	1891	2482	76	1135	2388	3523	1871	2179	578	434	1444	8237	**100.5**
	Diff.		+60	+67	—	-58	-95	+1	—	-20	-20	-56	-89	+30	+51	+101	+44	+.5
Detroit	Off.	82	3561	7391	48	1938	2581	75	1298	2345	3643	2027	2160	741	564	1629	9112	111.1
	Def.	82	3749	7362	51	1648	2211	75	1159	2434	3593	2191	2383	782	581	1637	9187	112.0
	Diff.		-188	+29	-3	+290	+370	—	+139	-89	+50	-164	+223	-41	-17	+8	-75	-.9
Indiana	Off.	82	3332	7164	47	1612	2176	74	1141	2372	3513	1897	2041	753	494	1393	8379	102.2
	Def.	82	3470	7062	49	1558	2133	73	1204	2598	3802	2053	2016	678	397	1517	8532	104.0
	Diff.		-138	+102	-2	+54	+43	+1	-63	-226	-289	-156	-25	+75	+97	+124	-153	-1.8
Chicago	Off.	82	3369	6728	50	1951	2545	77	1125	2525	3650	2043	2008	580	483	1636	8743	106.6
	Def.	82	3659	7388	50	1533	2053	75	1134	2225	3359	2043	2220	807	469	1257	8909	108.6
	Diff.		-290	-660	—	+418	+492	+2	-9	**+300**	+291	—	+212	-227	+14	-379	-166	-2.0
Cleveland	Off.	82	3405	7334	46	1628	2179	75	1190	2170	3360	1871	2193	634	357	1319	8463	103.2
	Def.	82	3608	7044	51	1906	2529	75	1125	2529	3654	2169	2071	655	480	1405	9161	111.7
	Diff.		-203	+290	-5	-278	-350	—	+65	-359	-294	-298	-122	-21	-123	+86	-698	-8.5
WESTERN CONFERENCE																		
MIDWEST DIVISION																		
San Antonio	Off.	82	3698	7613	49	1812	2335	78	1253	2537	**3790**	2257	2217	600	555	**1293**	9272	113.1
	Def.	82	3566	7385	48	1893	2497	76	1151	2434	3585	2036	2179	611	429	1352	9083	110.8
	Diff.		+132	+228	+1	-81	-162	+2	+102	+103	+205	+221	-38	-11	+126	+59	+189	+2.3
Denver	Off.	82	**3980**	**7656**	**52**	**2371**	**2978**	**80**	1149	2443	3592	2272	2131	664	368	1470	**10371**	**126.5**
	Def.	82	4265	8142	52	1734	2354	74	1358	2459	3817	2516	**2453**	749	569	1476	10328	126.0
	Diff.		-285	-486	—	**+637**	**+624**	**+6**	-209	-16	-225	-244	**+322**	-85	-201	+6	+43	+.5
Houston	Off.	82	3504	7366	48	1622	2225	73	**1403**	2284	3687	1977	**1871**	648	429	1321	8680	105.9
	Def.	82	3566	7180	50	1503	2011	75	1170	2304	3474	2128	2047	678	353	1341	8683	105.9
	Diff.		-62	+186	-2	+119	+214	-2	**+233**	-20	+213	-151	+176	-30	+76	+20	-3	—
Kansas City	Off.	82	3604	7284	49	1551	2158	72	1086	2276	3362	2056	2359	743	402	1507	8785	107.1
	Def.	82	3493	6984	50	2005	2653	76	1171	2552	3723	1853	2136	707	450	1609	9039	110.2
	Diff.		+111	+300	-1	-454	-495	-4	-85	-276	-361	+203	-223	+36	-48	+102	-254	-3.1
Dallas	Off.	82	3390	7224	47	1740	2366	74	1213	2228	3441	2117	2193	566	313	1317	8575	104.6
	Def.	82	3530	6953	51	1847	2491	74	1108	2361	3469	1984	2243	643	509	1370	8938	109.0
	Diff.		-140	+271	-4	-107	-125	—	+105	-133	-28	+133	+50	-77	-196	+53	-363	-4.4
Utah	Off.	82	3679	7446	49	1714	2282	75	1147	2362	3509	1895	2196	700	357	1435	9094	110.9
	Def.	82	3835	7530	51	1837	2466	74	1253	2599	3852	2148	2052	663	420	1413	9558	116.6
	Diff.		-156	-84	-2	-123	-184	+1	-106	-237	-343	-253	-144	+37	-63	-22	-464	-5.7

Team		G	FG	FGA	%	FT	FTA	%	REBOUNDS Offense	Defense	Total	Assists	PF	Steals	Blocked Shots	Turn Overs	Points	Points per game

TEAM STATISTICS
WESTERN CONFERENCE — PACIFIC DIVISION

Team		G	FG	FGA	%	FT	FTA	%	Reb. Offense	Reb. Defense	Reb. Total	Assists	PF	Steals	Blocked Shots	Turn Overs	Points	Points per game
Los Angeles	Off.	82	3919	7585	52	1549	2161	72	1258	2505	3763	2356	1999	848	517	1468	9400	114.6
	Def.	82	3745	7679	49	1433	2008	71	1275	2255	3530	2319	2004	718	435	1483	9001	109.8
	Diff.		+174	-94	+3	+116	+153	+1	-17	+250	+233	+37	+5	+130	+82	+15	+399	4.8
Seattle	Off.	82	3505	7178	49	1747	2362	74	1103	2544	3647	2103	2057	691	460	1351	8795	107.3
	Def.	82	3411	7407	46	1586	2183	73	1241	2420	3661	1994	2150	660	311	1405	8456	103.1
	Diff.		+94	-229	+3	+161	+179	+1	-138	+124	-14	+109	+93	+31	+149	+54	+339	4.2
Phoenix	Off.	82	3508	7140	49	1635	2157	76	1123	2517	3640	2223	2029	753	429	1528	8705	106.2
	Def.	82	3350	7186	47	1671	2215	75	1158	2366	3524	1949	2064	775	360	1391	8422	102.7
	Diff.		+158	-46	+2	-36	-58	+1	-35	+151	+116	+274	+35	-22	+69	-137	+283	3.5
Golden State	Off.	82	3646	7349	50	1709	2382	72	1282	2452	3734	1820	2225	685	391	1424	9092	110.9
	Def.	82	3555	7250	49	1857	2466	75	1112	2407	3519	2079	2156	661	393	1368	9007	109.8
	Diff.		+91	+99	+1	-148	-84	-3	+170	+45	+215	-259	-69	+24	-2	-56	+85	1.1
Portland	Off.	82	3629	7187	50	1719	2387	72	1142	2355	3497	2054	2012	706	367	1390	9006	109.8
	Def.	82	3637	7293	50	1629	2149	76	1221	2367	3588	2114	2142	708	427	1452	8957	109.2
	Diff.		-8	-106	—	+90	+238	-4	-79	-12	-91	-60	+130	-2	-60	+62	+49	0.6
San Diego	Off.	82	3552	7101	50	1693	2341	72	1131	2196	3327	1878	2353	636	299	1570	8896	108.5
	Def.	82	3739	7105	53	1988	2647	75	1033	2276	3309	2129	2124	772	487	1334	9502	115.9
	Diff.		-187	-4	-3	-295	-306	-3	+98	-80	+18	-251	-229	-136	-188	-236	-606	-7.4

PLAYOFFS

Team		G	FG	FGA	%	FT	FTA	%	Reb. Offense	Reb. Defense	Reb. Total	Assists	PF	Steals	Blocked Shots	Turn Overs	Points	Points per game
Los Angeles	Off.	14	661	1278	52	292	404	72	231	440	671	439	342	140	103	254	1616	115.4
	Def.	14	632	1335	47	258	360	72	227	369	596	405	347	124	83	225	1531	109.4
	Diff.		+29	-57	+5	+34	+44	—	+4	+71	+75	+34	+5	+16	+20	-29	+85	6.0
Philadelphia	Off.	21	880	1793	49	451	608	74	291	561	852	557	575	177	158	359	2220	105.7
	Def.	21	857	1827	47	465	657	71	372	579	951	539	578	174	148	393	2193	104.4
	Diff.		+23	-34	+2	-14	-49	+3	-81	-18	-99	+18	+3	+3	+10	+34	+27	1.3
Boston	Off.	12	497	1074	46	271	370	73	216	390	606	281	324	89	113	217	1270	105.8
	Def.	12	462	1072	43	270	354	76	187	334	521	273	341	93	69	211	1202	100.2
	Diff.		+35	+2	+3	+1	+16	-3	+29	+56	+85	+8	+17	-4	+44	-6	+68	5.6
San Antonio	Off.	9	387	841	46	187	254	74	152	274	426	262	238	66	44	145	966	107.3
	Def.	9	390	801	49	220	278	79	120	281	401	257	236	80	62	138	1004	111.6
	Diff.		-3	+40	-3	-33	-24	-5	+32	-7	+25	+5	-2	-14	-18	-7	-38	-4.3
Seattle	Off.	8	306	690	44	180	234	77	123	244	367	208	197	60	35	115	796	99.5
	Def.	8	310	711	44	155	202	77	132	238	370	198	207	59	48	115	778	97.3
	Diff.		-4	-21	—	+25	+32	—	-9	+6	-3	+10	+10	+1	-13	—	+18	2.2
Phoenix	Off.	7	324	665	49	117	157	75	109	185	294	200	171	74	47	121	770	110.0
	Def.	7	335	644	52	145	186	78	111	211	322	196	160	65	40	125	816	116.6
	Diff.		-11	+21	-3	-28	-29	-3	-2	-26	-28	+4	-11	+9	+7	+4	-46	-6.6
Washington	Off.	7	270	625	43	151	194	78	103	203	306	150	189	54	32	128	701	100.1
	Def.	7	282	613	46	146	202	72	101	218	319	144	183	52	62	114	712	101.7
	Diff.		-12	+12	-3	+5	-8	+6	+2	-15	-13	+6	-6	+2	-30	-14	-11	-1.6
Milwaukee	Off.	6	232	491	47	143	199	72	95	134	229	142	171	44	34	101	615	102.5
	Def.	6	250	474	53	133	171	78	69	153	222	165	166	46	34	99	636	106.0
	Diff.		-18	+17	-6	+10	+28	-6	+26	-19	+7	-23	-5	-2		-2	-21	-3.5
Denver	Off.	3	144	291	49	69	83	83	42	78	120	74	76	26	11	44	358	119.3
	Def.	3	153	286	53	55	77	71	48	93	141	89	80	26	28	54	363	121.0
	Diff.		-9	+5	-4	+14	+6	+12	-6	-15	-21	-15	+4		-17	+10	-5	-1.7
Houston	Off.	3	107	271	39	47	61	77	56	81	137	58	66	16	17	28	261	87.0
	Def.	3	113	263	43	49	68	72	55	96	151	80	66	17	5	32	276	92.0
	Diff.		-6	+8	-4	-2	-7	+5	+1	-15	-14	-22		-1	+12	+4	-15	-5.0
Atlanta	Off.	2	63	150	42	45	60	75	26	45	71	33	61	10	12	39	171	85.5
	Def.	2	85	157	54	39	66	70	24	59	83	51	55	18	22	35	209	104.5
	Diff.		-22	-7	-12	+6	-6	+5	+2	-14	-12	-18	-6	-8	-10	-4	-32	19.0
New Jersey	Off.	2	74	174	43	25	41	61	26	54	80	39	52	19	9	32	175	87.5
	Def.	2	85	157	54	39	56	70	24	59	83	51	55	18	22	35	209	104.5
	Diff.		-11	+17	-11	-14	-15	-9	+2	-5	-3	-12	+3	+1	-13	+3	-34	-17.0

Team	W	L	Pct.	GB	Record against playoff teams W	L	Pct.	Record against non-playoff teams W	L	Pct.	HOME W	L	Pct.	ROAD W	L	Pct.
EASTERN CONFERENCE																
ATLANTIC DIVISION																
Boston Celtics	63	19	.768	—	29	13	.690	34	6	.850	35	6	.854	28	13	.683
Philadelphia 76ers	58	24	.707	5	22	20	.523	36	4	.900	32	9	.780	26	15	.634
New Jersey Nets	44	38	.537	19	17	23	.425	27	15	.643	25	16	.610	19	22	.463
Washington Bullets	43	39	.524	20	11	30	.268	32	9	.780	22	19	.537	21	20	.512
New York Knickerbockers	33	49	.402	30	13	35	.271	20	14	.588	19	22	.463	14	27	.341
CENTRAL DIVISION																
Milwaukee Bucks	55	27	.671	—	23	17	.575	32	10	.762	31	10	.756	24	17	.585
Atlanta Hawks	42	40	.512	13	18	23	.436	24	17	.585	24	17	.585	18	23	.439
Detroit Pistons	39	43	.476	16	15	31	.326	24	12	.667	23	18	.561	16	25	.390
Indiana Pacers	35	47	.427	20	14	33	.298	21	14	.600	25	16	.610	10	31	.243
Chicago Bulls	34	48	.415	21	17	30	.362	17	18	.486	22	19	.537	12	29	.293
Cleveland Cavaliers	15	67	.183	40	4	42	.087	11	25	.306	9	32	.220	6	35	.146
WESTERN CONFERENCE																
MIDWEST DIVISION																
San Antonio Spurs	48	34	.585	—	21	18	.538	27	16	.628	29	12	.707	19	22	.463
Denver Nuggets	46	36	.561	2	19	20	.487	27	16	.628	29	12	.707	17	24	.415
Houston Rockets	46	36	.561	2	16	23	.410	30	13	.698	25	16	.610	21	20	.512
Kansas City Kings	30	52	.366	18	14	31	.311	16	21	.432	23	18	.561	7	34	.171
Dallas Mavericks	28	54	.341	20	13	32	.289	15	22	.405	16	25	.390	12	29	.293
Utah Jazz	25	57	.305	23	9	36	.200	16	21	.432	18	23	.439	7	34	.171
PACIFIC DIVISION																
Los Angeles Lakers	57	25	.695	—	25	14	.641	32	11	.744	30	11	.732	27	14	.659
Seattle Supersonics	52	30	.634	5	20	19	.513	32	11	.744	31	10	.756	21	20	.512
Phoenix Suns	46	36	.561	11	19	20	.487	27	16	.628	31	10	.756	15	26	.366
Golden State Warriors	45	37	.549	12	21	24	.467	24	13	.649	28	13	.683	17	24	.415
Portland Trail Blazers	42	40	.512	15	16	29	.356	26	11	.703	27	14	.659	15	26	.366
San Diego Clippers	17	65	.207	40	8	37	.178	9	28	.243	11	30	.268	6	35	.146

1981/82 N.B.A. INDIVIDUAL LEADERS

SCORING
(Minimum 70 Games or 1400 Points)

Name	Team	G	FG	FT	Pts.	Avg.
Gervin	SA	79	993	555	2551	32.3
Malone	Hou	81	945	630	2520	31.1
Dantley	Utah	81	904	648	2457	30.3
English	Den	82	855	372	2082	25.4
Erving	Phi	81	780	411	1974	24.4
Abdul-Jabbar	LA	76	753	312	1818	23.9
Williams	Sea	80	773	320	1875	23.4
King	GS	79	740	352	1833	23.2
Free	GS	78	650	479	1789	22.9
Bird	Bos	77	711	328	1761	22.9

FIELD GOAL PERCENTAGE
(Minimum 300 Made)

Name	Team	FG	FGA	Pct.
Gilmore	Chi	546	837	.652
S.Johnson	KC	395	644	.613
B.Williams	NJ	513	881	.582
Abdul-Jabbar	LA	753	1301	.579
Natt	Port	515	894	.576
Dantley	Utah	904	1586	.570
King	GS	740	1307	.566
B.Jones	Phi	416	737	.564
Cartwright	NY	390	694	.562
Ruland	Was	420	749	.561

FREE THROW PERCENTAGE
(Minimum 125 Made)

Name	Team	FT	FTA	Pct.
Macy	Phoe	152	169	.899
Criss	Atl+SD	141	159	.887
Long	Det	238	275	.865
Gervin	SA	555	642	.864
Bird	Bos	328	380	.863
Silas	Cle	246	286	.860
Newlin	NY	126	147	.857
Vandeweghe	Det	347	405	.857
Grevey	Was	165	193	.855
Sikma	Sea	447	523	.855

PERSONAL FOULS

Name	Team	PF
S.Johnson	KC	372
Mahorn	Was	349
Edwards	Cle	347
Chambers	SD	341
Ruland	Was	319

GAMES DISQUALIFIED

Name	Team	Disq.
S.Johnson	KC	25
Chambers	SD	17
Edwards	Cle	17
Whitehead	SD	16
Kelley	Phoe	14

TOTAL REBOUNDS PER GAME
(Minimum 70 Games or 800 Rebounds)

Name	Team	G	Reb.	Avg.
Malone	Hou	81	1188	14.7
Sikma	Sea	82	1038	12.7
B.Williams	NJ	82	1005	12.3
Thompson	Port	79	921	11.7
Lucas	NY	80	903	11.3
Smith	GS	74	813	11.0
Bird	Bos	77	837	10.9
Parish	Bos	80	866	10.8
Gilmore	Chi	82	835	10.2
Robinson	Phoe	74	721	9.7

ASSISTS PER GAME
(Minimum 70 Games or 400 Assists)

Name	Team	G	Ass.	Avg.
Moore	SA	79	762	9.6
M.Johnson	LA	78	743	9.5
Cheeks	Phi	79	667	8.4
Archibald	Bos	68	541	8.0
Nixon	LA	82	652	8.0
Thomas	Det	72	565	7.8
Green	Utah	81	630	7.8
Huston	Cle	78	590	7.6
Ransey	Port	78	555	7.1
Richardson	NY	82	572	7.0

MINUTES PLAYED

Name	Team	Min.
Malone	Hou	3398
Dantley	Utah	3222
Thompson	Port	3129
Tripucka	Det	3077
Mitchell	Cle+SA	3063

BLOCKED SHOTS PER GAME
(Minimum 70 Games or 100 Blocked Shots)

Name	Team	G	Reb.	Avg.
G.Johnson	SA	75	234	3.1
Rollins	Atl	79	224	2.8
Abdul-Jabbar	LA	76	207	2.7
Gilmore	Chi	82	221	2.7
Parish	Bos	80	192	2.4
McHale	Bos	82	185	2.3
Williams	Ind	82	178	2.2
Tyler	Det	82	160	2.0
C.Jones	Phi	81	146	1.8
Erving	Phi	81	141	1.7

3 POINT FIELD GOALS PER GAME
(Minimum 25 Made)

Name	Team	FG	FGA	Avg.
Russell	NY	25	57	.439
Toney	Phi	25	59	.424
Macy	Phoe	39	100	.390
Winters	Mil	36	93	.387
Buse	Ind	73	189	.386
Dunleavy	Hou	33	86	.384
Aguirre	Dall	25	71	.352
Greavy	Was	28	82	.341
Bratz	SA	46	138	.333
Hassett	GS	71	214	.332

STEALS PER GAME
(Minimum 70 Games or 125 Steals)

Name	Team	G	Steals	Avg.
M.Johnson	LA	78	208	2.7
Cheeks	Phi	79	209	2.6
Richardson	NY	82	213	2.5
Buckner	Mil	70	174	2.5
R.Williams	NJ	82	199	2.4
Green	Utah	81	185	2.3
Willimas	Sea	80	172	2.2
Thomas	Det	72	150	2.1
Moore	SA	79	163	2.1
Buse	Ind	82	164	2.0

1982-83 N.B.A.

Free Agents and TV Deals

The league signed a new cable television deal in 1982. With weekly games on ESPN supplementing the usual coverage on CBS (USA was added to the cable team a year later). Fittingly enough, the season that followed was about as predictable as a made-for-TV movie.

The script was written in the offseason when Philadelphia signed Houston's Moses Malone as a free agent. The addition of the two-time MVP to a cast including Julius Erving, Andrew Toney, Maurice Cheeks and Bobby Jones made the 76ers prohibitive favorites for the championship, and coach Billy Cunningham's crew lived up to that assessment during the regular season, rolling to a 65-17 record and finishing nine games ahead of Boston in the Atlantic Division. Though Larry Bird and Robert Parish again turned in outstanding seasons, an unsettled backcourt and dissatisfaction with coach Bill Fitch plagued the Celtics. Buck Williams led New Jersey to 49 wins, but coach Larry Brown was ousted just before the the season's end after applying for a college post. The demoralized Nets staggered into the playoffs and lost in the first round to the Knicks, who had improved to 44-38 behind free agent acquisition Bernard King. Though out of the playoff picture, Washington posted the best record ever for a last-place team, winning 42 games with a rugged frontcourt of Jeff Ruland, Greg Ballard and Rick Mahorn.

Not much was new in the Central Division, where Sidney Moncrief and Marques Johnson led Milwaukee to another title, earning Don Nelson the Coach of the Year award. Second-place Atlanta improved by only a game despite the presence of veteran Dan Roundfield and rookie Dominique Wilkens. In Detroit, the Pistons slipped to 37-45, failing to put together an adequate supporting cast for Isiah Thomas, Bill Laimbeer and Kelly Tripucka. Chicago sent Artis Gilmore to San Antonio for Dave Corzine and Mark Olberding, but fell to 28 wins and wasted a fine season from Reggie Theus. Cleveland picked up World Free from Golden State and "improved" to 23-59, while Indiana fell to the basement despite the arrival of the league's second-best rookie in Clark Kellogg.

The addition of Gilmore, plus solid performances from George Gervin and Mike Mitchell, brought 53 wins and another Midwest Division title to San Antonio. Alex English and Kiki Vandeweghe, the league's two top scorers, led Denver to a second-place tie with surprising Kansas City. The Kings improved by 15 games, with Larry Drew emerging as a star under coach Cotton Fitzsimmons. Though missing the playoffs, Dallas gained 10 games in the standings through the development of its young players—particularly Mark Aquirre, who averaged 24 points a game as a sophomore. In Utah, the financially troubled Jazz were unable to sign Dominique Wilkins, their No. 1 draft choice, and shipped him off to Atlanta for John Drew and Freeman Williams. Drew, however, spent two months in drug rehabilitation and Williams was released in December. On top of that, Adrain Dantley missed 60 games with an injured wrist, and a fine season from Darrell Griffith couldn't compensate for the loss. Still, the Jazz finished comfortably ahead of 14-68 Houston.

In the Pacific Division, Kareem Abdul-Jabbar, Magic Johnson, Jamaal Wilkes and Norm Nixon led Los Angeles to another title, while rookie James Worthy showed star potential. Phoenix won 53 games with a balanced team featuring Walter Davis, Dennis Johnson, new acquisition Maurice Lucas and much-improved sophomore Larry Nance. Gus Williams and Jack Sikma led Seattle to third place, two games ahead of Portland, where Jim Paxson and Calvin Natt were the scoring stars. Golden State lost its top scorers when Bernard King signed with New York and Free was traded to Cleveland, and slipped to 30 wins despite the emergence of two new 20-point men in Joe Barry Carroll and Purvis Short. The return of Bill Walton was big news in San Diego, but Walton played only 33 games, and the Clippers finished last again despite adding Rookie of the Year Terry Cummings to second-year man Tom Chambers

The big surprise of the playoffs was Milwaukee's four-game sweep of Boston in the Eastern semifinals. But in the finals the Bucks were no match for the 76ers, who won in five games to advance to the championship series. Meanwhile, the Lakers rolled over Portland and San Antonio to win the West despite the absence of James Worthy, who missed the playoffs with a broken leg. With Worthy out, and Bob McAdoo and Nixon slowed by injuries, Los Angeles was no match for the 76ers, who swept to the title in four games, completing a 12-1 postseason. Malone averaged 26 points and 18 rebounds for the series, winning the playoff MVP trophy to go along with his second straight regular-season MVP award.

					TOTAL														Blkd		PER GAME				
Use Name	Pos	Hgt	Wgt	Age	G	Min	FG	FGA	%	FT	FTA	%	Reb	Ass	PF	DQ	Stls	Shts	Points	Min	Reb	Ass	PF	Points

1982/83 N.B.A. — EASTERN CONFERENCE

ATLANTIC DIVISION

Use Name	Pos	Hgt	Wgt	Age	G	Min	FG	FGA	%	FT	FTA	%	Reb	Ass	PF	DQ	Stls	Blkd Shts	Points	Min	Reb	Ass	PF	Points
PHILADELPHIA 76ers	**65-17 .793 BILLY CUNNINGHAM**																							
Julius Erving	F	6'7	205	32	72	2421	605	1170	52	330	435	76	491	263	202	1	112	131	1542	34	6.8	3.7	2.8	21.4
Bobby Jones	F	6'9	212	31	74	1749	250	460	54	165	208	79	344	142	199	4	85	91	665	24	4.6	1.9	2.7	9.0
Moses Malone	C	6'10	255	27	78	2922	654	1305	50	**600**	**788**	76	**1194**	101	206	0	89	157	1908	37	**15.3**	1.3	2.6	24.5
Andrew Toney	G	6'3	188	25	81	2474	626	1250	50	324	411	79	225	365	255	0	80	17	1598	31	2.8	4.5	3.1	19.7
Maruice Cheeks	G	6'1	180	26	79	2465	404	745	54	181	240	75	209	543	182	0	184	31	990	31	2.6	6.9	2.3	12.5
Clint Richardson	G	6'3	195	26	77	1755	259	559	46	71	111	64	247	168	164	0	71	18	589	23	3.2	2.1	2.1	7.6
Marc Iavaroni	F	6'9	225	26	80	1612	163	353	46	78	113	69	329	83	238	0	32	44	404	20	4.1	1.0	3.0	5.1
Franklin Edwards	G	6'1	170	23	81	1266	228	483	47	86	113	76	85	221	119	0	81	6	542	16	1.0	2.7	1.5	6.7
Earl Cureton	F-C	6'9	215	25	73	987	108	258	42	33	67	49	269	43	144	1	37	24	249	14	3.7	0.6	2.0	3.4
Russ Schoene (to Ind)	F	6'10	210	22	46	702	106	207	51	21	28	75	154	32	118	2	13	9	233	15	3.3	0.7	2.6	5.1
Clemon Johnson (from Ind)	C	6'10	240	26	32	698	91	182	50	34	58	59	205	24	84	1	16	29	216	22	6.4	0.8	2.6	6.8
Reggie Johnson (from KC)	F	6'9	205	25	29	549	69	154	45	22	30	73	90	23	82	1	8	17	160	19	3.1	0.8	2.8	5.5
Mark McNamara	C	6'11	235	23	36	182	29	64	45	20	45	44	76	7	42	1	3	3	78	5	2.1	0.2	1.2	2.2
J.J. Anderson (to Utah)	F	6'8	195	22	13	48	8	22	36	1	3	33	12	1	6	0	1	0	17	4	0.9	0.1	0.5	1.3

3-PT FG — Erving 2-7, Jones 0-1, Malone 0-1, Toney 22-76, Cheeks 1-6, Richardson 0-6, Iavaroni 0-2, Edwards 1-8, Schoene 0-1, Anderson 0-1

1982/83 N.B.A. — EASTERN CONFERENCE
ATLANTIC DIVISION

BOSTON CELTICS 56-26 .683 BILL FITCH

Use Name	Pos	Hgt	Wgt	Age	G	Min	FG	FGA	%	FT	FTA	%	Reb	Ass	PF	DQ	Stls	Blkd Shts	Points	Min (per game)	Reb (per game)	Ass (per game)	PF (per game)	Points (per game)
Cedric Maxwell	F	6'8	215	27	79	2252	331	663	50	280	345	81	422	186	202	3	65	39	942	29	5.3	2.4	2.6	11.9
Larry Bird	F	6'9	220	26	79	2982	747	1481	50	351	418	84	870	458	197	0	148	71	1867	38	11.0	5.8	2.5	23.6
Robert Parish	C	7'	230	29	78	2459	619	1125	55	271	388	70	827	141	222	4	79	148	1509	32	10.6	1.8	2.8	19.3
Danny Ainge	G	6'4	175	23	80	2048	357	720	50	72	97	74	214	251	259	2	109	6	791	26	2.7	3.1	3.2	9.9
Nate Archibald	G	6'1	160	34	66	1811	235	553	42	220	296	74	91	409	110	1	38	4	695	27	1.4	6.2	1.7	10.5
Kevin McHale	F-C	6'10	225	25	82	2345	483	893	54	193	269	72	553	104	241	3	34	192	1159	29	6.7	1.3	2.9	14.1
Quinn Buckner	G	6'3	205	28	72	1565	248	561	44	74	117	63	187	275	195	2	108	5	570	22	2.6	3.8	2.7	7.9
Gerald Henderson	G	6'2	175	26	82	1551	286	618	46	96	133	72	124	195	190	6	95	3	671	19	1.5	2.4	2.3	8.2
M. L. Carr	F-G	6'6	205	31	77	883	135	315	43	60	81	74	137	70	140	0	48	10	333	11	1.8	0.9	1.8	4.3
Rick Robey	C	6'11	230	26	59	855	100	214	47	45	78	58	219	65	131	1	13	8	245	14	3.7	1.1	2.2	4.2
Charles Bradley	G	6'5	215	23	51	532	69	176	39	46	90	51	78	28	84	0	32	27	184	10	1.5	0.5	1.6	3.6
Scott Wedman (from Cle)	F	6'7	235	30	40	503	94	205	46	20	30	67	74	31	83	1	20	6	209	13	1.9	0.8	2.1	5.2
Darrren Tillis (to Cle)	C	6'11	215	22	15	44	7	23	30	2	6	33	9	2	8	0	0	2	16	3	0.6	0.1	0.5	1.1

3 PT FG - Maxwell 0-1, Bird 22-77, Parish 0-1, Ainge 5-29, Archibald 5-24, McHale 0-1, Buckner 0-4, Henderson 3-16, Carr 3-19, Bradley 0-3, Wedman 1-10, Tillis 0-1

NEW JERSEY NETS 49-33 .598 LARRY BROWN (47-29 .618), BILL BLAIR (2-4 .333)

Use Name	Pos	Hgt	Wgt	Age	G	Min	FG	FGA	%	FT	FTA	%	Reb	Ass	PF	DQ	Stls	Blkd Shts	Points	Min (per game)	Reb (per game)	Ass (per game)	PF (per game)	Points (per game)
Albert King	F	6'6	190	23	79	2447	582	1226	47	176	227	78	456	291	278	5	95	41	1346	31	5.8	3.7	3.5	17.0
Buck Williams	F	6'8	215	22	82	2961	536	912	59	324	523	62	1027	125	270	4	91	110	1396	36	12.5	1.5	3.3	17.0
Darrell Dawkins	C	6'11	251	25	81	2093	401	669	60	166	257	65	420	114	**379**	**23**	67	152	968	26	5.2	1.4	4.7	12.0
Otis Birdsong	G	6'4	195	27	62	1885	426	834	51	82	145	57	150	239	155	0	85	16	936	30	2.4	3.9	2.5	15.1
Darwin Cook	G	6'3	190	24	82	2625	443	986	45	186	242	77	240	448	213	2	194	48	1080	32	2.9	5.5	2.6	13.2
Foots Walker	G	6'1	172	31	79	1388	114	250	46	116	149	78	136	264	134	1	78	3	346	18	1.7	3.3	1.7	4.4
Mike Gminski	C	6'11	250	23	80	1255	213	426	50	175	225	78	382	61	118	0	35	116	601	16	4.8	0.8	1.5	7.5
M. R. Richardson (from GS)	G	6'5	195	27	31	1002	170	338	50	51	76	67	150	187	116	2	81	15	395	32	4.8	6.0	3.7	12.7
Mi. Johnson (from Mil, to GS)	F	6'10	190	30	42	1001	199	496	40	164	201	82	224	144	135	4	56	21	564	24	5.3	3.4	3.2	13.4
Len Elmore	C-F	6'9	220	30	74	975	97	244	40	54	84	64	238	39	125	2	44	38	248	13	3.2	0.5	1.7	3.4
Mike O'Koren (BW)	F-G	6'7	217	24	46	803	136	259	53	34	48	71	114	82	67	0	42	11	308	17	2.5	1.8	1.5	6.7
Eric Floyd (to GS)	G	6'3	175	22	43	494	92	216	43	38	45	84	42	67	56	1	19	9	226	11	1.0	1.6	1.3	5.3
Eddie Phillips	F	6'7	225	21	48	416	56	138	41	40	59	68	77	29	58	0	14	8	152	9	1.6	0.6	1.2	3.2
Phil Ford (to Mil)	G	6'2	186	26	7	163	20	35	57	7	10	70	7	38	22	0	6	0	47	23	1.0	5.4	3.1	6.7
Bill Willoughby (from SA)	F	6'8	205	25	10	84	11	29	38	2	2	100	11	8	16	0	1	1	24	8	1.1	0.8	1.6	2.4
Jan Van Breda Kolff	F	6'7	200	31	13	63	5	14	36	5	6	83	13	5	9	0	2	2	15	5	1.0	0.4	0.7	1.2
James Bailey (to Hou)	F	6'9	220	25	6	50	9	18	50	2	2	100	6	2	15	0	1	1	20	8	1.0	0.3	2.5	3.3

3 PT FG — King 6-23, Williams 0-4, Birdsong 2-6, Cook 8-38, Walker 2-12, Gminski 0-1, Richardson 4-20, Johnson 2-17 Elmore 0-1, O'Koren, Floyd 4-14, Phillips 0-2, Ford 0-1, Willoughby 0-1

NEW YORK KNICKERBOCKERS 44-38 .537 HUBIE BROWN

Use Name	Pos	Hgt	Wgt	Age	G	Min	FG	FGA	%	FT	FTA	%	Reb	Ass	PF	DQ	Stls	Blkd Shts	Points	Min (per game)	Reb (per game)	Ass (per game)	PF (per game)	Points (per game)
Bernard King (KJ)	F	6'7	205	26	68	2207	603	1142	53	280	388	72	326	195	233	5	90	13	1486	32	4.8	2.9	3.4	21.9
Truck Robinson	F	6'7	225	31	81	2426	326	706	46	118	201	59	657	145	241	4	57	24	770	30	8.1	1.8	3.0	9.5
Bill Cartwright	C	7'1	245	25	82	2468	455	804	57	380	511	74	590	136	315	7	41	127	1290	30	7.2	1.7	3.8	15.7
Sly Williams	G	6'7	215	24	68	1385	314	647	49	176	259	68	290	133	166	3	73	3	806	20	4.3	2.0	2.4	11.9
Rory Sparrow (from Atl)	G	6'2	195	24	32	880	128	298	43	63	86	73	89	159	93	2	37	4	321	28	2.8	5.0	2.9	10.0
Paul Westphal	G	6'4	195	32	80	1978	318	693	46	148	184	80	115	439	180	1	87	16	798	25	1.4	5.5	2.3	10.0
Trent Tucker	G	6'5	193	23	78	1830	299	647	46	43	64	67	216	195	235	1	56	6	655	23	2.8	2.5	3.0	8.4
Louis Orr	F	6'8	195	24	82	1666	274	593	46	140	175	80	228	94	134	0	64	24	688	20	2.8	1.1	1.6	8.4
Ed Sherod	G	6'2	170	23	64	1624	171	421	41	52	80	65	149	311	112	2	96	14	395	25	2.3	4.9	1.8	6.2
Marvin Webster	C	7'1	240	30	82	1472	168	331	51	106	180	59	443	49	210	3	35	131	442	18	5.4	0.6	2.6	5.4
Ernie Grunfield	F	6'6	215	27	77	1422	167	377	44	81	98	83	163	136	172	1	40	10	415	18	2.1	1.8	2.2	5.4
Vince Taylor	G-F	6'5	180	22	31	321	37	102	36	21	32	66	36	41	54	1	20	2	95	10	1.2	1.3	1.7	3.1
Scott Hatings (to Atl)	F-C	6'10	235	22	21	98	8	22	36	7	14	50	31	1	31	0	5	0	23	5	1.5	0.0	1.5	1.1
Mike Davis	F	6'10	230	26	8	28	4	10	40	6	10	60	10	0	4	0	0	4	14	4	1.3	0.0	0.5	1.8

Campy Russell - knee injury

3 PT FG — King 0-6, Williams 2-19, Sparrow 2-7, Westphal 14-48, Tucker 14-30, Orr 0-2, Sherod 1-13, Webster 0-1, Grunfield 0-4, Hastings 0-1

WASHINGTON BULLETS 42-40 .512 GENE SHUE

Use Name	Pos	Hgt	Wgt	Age	G	Min	FG	FGA	%	FT	FTA	%	Reb	Ass	PF	DQ	Stls	Blkd Shts	Points	Min (per game)	Reb (per game)	Ass (per game)	PF (per game)	Points (per game)
Greg Ballard	F	6'7	215	27	78	2840	603	1274	47	182	233	78	508	262	176	2	135	25	1401	36	6.5	3.4	2.3	18.0
Jeff Ruland	F-C	6'10	240	24	79	2862	580	1051	55	375	544	69	871	234	312	12	74	77	1536	36	11.0	3.0	3.9	19.4
Rick Mahorn	C	6'10	240	24	82	3023	376	768	49	146	254	57	779	115	335	13	86	148	898	37	9.5	1.4	4.1	11.0
Ricky Sobers (injury)	G	6'3	198	29	41	1438	234	534	44	154	185	83	102	218	158	3	61	14	645	35	2.5	5.3	3.9	15.7
Frank Johnson	G	6'2	185	24	68	2324	321	786	41	196	261	75	178	549	170	1	110	6	852	34	2.6	8.1	2.5	12.5
Don Collins	G-F	6'6	190	24	65	1575	332	635	52	101	136	74	210	132	166	1	87	30	765	24	3.2	2.0	2.6	11.8
Charlie Davis	F	6'7	215	24	74	1161	251	534	47	56	89	63	213	73	122	0	32	22	560	16	2.9	1.0	1.6	7.6
Spencer Haywood (injury)	F	6'9	225	33	38	775	125	312	40	63	87	72	183	30	94	2	12	27	313	20	4.8	0.8	2.5	8.2
Kevin Grevey (IL)	G	6'5	210	29	41	756	114	294	39	54	69	78	49	49	61	0	18	7	297	18	1.2	1.2	1.5	7.2
Bryan Warrick	G	6'5	195	23	43	727	65	171	38	42	57	74	69	126	103	5	21	8	172	17	1.6	2.9	2.4	4.0
Dave Batton	C	6'10	240	26	54	558	85	191	45	8	17	47	119	29	56	0	15	13	178	10	2.2	0.5	1.0	3.3
Carlos Terry	G-F	6'5	220	26	55	514	39	106	37	10	15	67	99	46	79	1	24	13	88	9	1.8	0.8	1.4	1.6
John Lucas	G	6'3	185	29	35	386	62	131	47	21	42	50	29	102	18	0	25	1	145	11	0.8	2.9	0.5	4.1
Billy Ray Bates (to LA)	G	6'4	210	26	15	277	53	129	41	10	20	50	18	14	18	0	13	3	118	18	1.2	0.9	1.2	7.9
Kevin Porter	G	6'	170	32	11	210	21	40	53	5	6	83	5	46	30	0	10	0	47	19	0.5	4.2	2.7	4.3
Joe Kopicki	F	6'9	240	22	17	201	23	51	45	21	25	84	62	9	21	0	9	2	67	12	3.6	0.5	1.2	3.9
Chubby Cox	G	6'2	180	27	7	78	13	37	35	3	6	50	10	6	16	0	0	1	29	11	1.4	0.9	2.3	4.1
Steve Lingenfelter	F	6'9	225	24	7	53	4	6	67	0	4	0	12	4	16	1	1	3	8	8	1.7	0.6	2.3	1.1
Joe Cooper (from LA, to SD)	C	6'10	230	25	5	47	5	9	56	5	9	56	13	2	7	0	0	0	15	9	2.6	0.4	1.4	3.0

3 PT FG — Ballard 13-37, Ruland 1-3, Mahorn 0-3, Sobers 23-55, Johnson 14-61, Collins 0-6, Davis 2-10, Haywood 0-1, Grevey 15-38, Warrick 0-5, Batton 0-3, Terry 0-2, Lucas 0-5, Bates 2-5, Kopicki 0-1, Cox 0-2

Use Name	Pos	Hgt	Wgt	Age	TOTAL G	Min	FG	FGA	%	FT	FTA	%	Reb	Ass	PF	DQ	Stls	Blkd Shts	Points	PER GAME Min	Reb	Ass	PF	Points
1982/83 N.B.A. — EASTERN CONFERENCE CENTRAL DIVISION																								
MILWAUKEE BUCKS	51-31 .622				**DON NELSON**																			
Junior Bridgeman	F-G	6'5	210	29	70	1855	421	856	49	164	196	84	246	207	155	0	40	9	1007	27	3.5	3.0	2.2	14.4
Marques Johnson	F	6'7	218	26	80	2853	723	1420	51	264	359	74	562	363	211	0	100	56	1714	36	7.0	4.5	2.6	21.4
Bob Lanier (KJ)	C	6'11	265	34	39	918	163	332	49	91	133	68	200	105	125	2	34	24	417	24	5.1	2.7	3.2	10.7
Sidney Mancrief	G	6'4	190	25	76	2710	606	1156	52	499	604	83	437	300	180	1	113	23	1712	36	5.8	3.9	2.4	22.5
Brian Winters	G	6'4	185	30	57	1361	255	587	43	73	85	86	110	156	132	2	45	4	605	24	1.9	2.7	2.3	10.6
Alton Lister	G-F	7'	240	24	80	1885	272	514	53	130	242	54	568	111	328	18	50	117	674	24	7.1	1.4	4.1	8.4
Harvey Catchings	F-C	6'9	218	31	74	1554	90	197	46	62	92	67	408	77	224	4	26	148	242	21	5.5	1.0	3.0	3.3
Paul Pressey	G-F	6'5	185	24	79	1528	213	466	46	105	176	60	281	207	174	2	99	47	532	19	3.6	2.6	2.2	6.7
Phil Ford (from NJ)	G	6'2	186	26	70	1447	193	410	47	90	113	80	96	252	168	2	46	3	477	21	1.4	3.6	2.4	6.8
Dave Cowens	C-F	6'9	230	34	40	1014	136	306	44	52	63	83	274	82	137	4	30	15	324	25	6.9	2.1	3.4	8.1
Charlie Criss	G	5'8	165	33	66	922	169	375	45	68	76	89	79	127	44	0	27	0	412	14	1.2	1.9	0.7	6.2
Steve Mix (to LA)	F	6'7	222	35	57	792	133	273	49	74	87	85	136	68	70	0	33	3	341	14	2.4	1.2	1.2	6.0
Paul Mokeski (from Cle)	C	7'	250	25	50	589	64	139	46	34	42	81	122	23	138	3	9	21	162	12	2.4	0.5	2.8	3.2
Armond Hill	G	6'4	190	29	14	169	14	26	54	18	22	82	20	27	20	0	9	0	46	12	1.4	1.9	1.4	3.3
Mickey Johnson (to NJ, GS)	F	6'10	190	30	6	153	30	66	45	7	9	78	25	11	22	0	1	2	67	26	4.2	1.8	3.7	11.2
Sam Pellom (from Atl)	F	6'9	225	31	4	20	4	10	40	0	0	—	8	0	3	0	0	0	8	5	2.0	0.0	0.8	2.0
3-PT FG — Bridgeman 1-13, Ma. Johnson 4-20, Lanier 0-1, Moncrief 1-10, Winters 22-68, Pressey 1-9, Ford 1-8, Cowens 0-2, Criss 6-31, Mix 1-4, Mokeski 0-1, Mi. Johnson 0-2																								
ATLANTA HAWKS	43-39 .529				**KEVIN LOUGHERY**																			
Dominique Wilkins	F	6'8	200	22	82	2697	601	1220	49	230	337	68	478	129	210	1	84	63	1434	33	5.8	1.6	2.6	17.5
Dan Roundfield	F	6'8	215	29	77	2811	561	1193	47	337	450	75	880	225	239	1	60	115	1464	37	11.4	2.9	3.1	19.0
Tree Rollins	C	7'1	235	27	80	2472	261	512	51	98	135	73	743	75	294	7	49	**343**	620	31	9.3	0.9	3.7	7.8
Eddie Johnson (KJ)	G	6'2	190	27	61	1813	389	858	45	186	237	78	124	318	138	2	61	6	978	30	2.0	5.2	2.3	16.0
Rory Sparrow (to NYN)	G	6'2	195	24	49	1548	264	512	52	84	113	74	141	238	162	2	70	1	615	32	2.9	4.9	3.3	12.6
Johnny Davis	G	6'2	180	27	53	1465	258	567	46	164	206	80	128	315	100	0	43	7	685	28	2.4	5.9	1.9	12.9
Tom McMillen	C-F	6'11	235	30	61	1364	198	424	47	108	133	81	217	76	143	2	17	24	504	22	3.6	1.2	2.3	8.3
Wes Matthews	G	6'1	170	23	64	1187	171	424	40	86	112	77	91	249	129	0	60	8	442	19	1.4	3.9	2.0	6.9
Rudy Macklin	F-G	6'7	215	24	73	1171	170	360	47	101	131	77	190	71	189	4	41	10	441	16	2.6	1.0	2.6	6.0
Mike Glenn	G	6'3	185	27	73	1124	230	444	52	74	89	83	90	125	132	0	30	9	534	15	1.2	1.7	1.8	7.3
Steve Hawes (to Sea)	F-C	6'9	220	32	46	860	91	244	37	46	62	74	228	59	110	2	29	8	230	19	5.0	1.3	2.4	5.0
George Johnson	C	6'11	205	34	37	461	25	57	44	14	19	74	117	17	69	0	10	59	64	12	3.2	0.5	1.9	1.7
Keith Edmonson	G	6'5	205	22	32	309	48	139	35	16	27	59	39	22	41	0	11	6	112	10	1.2	0.7	1.3	3.5
Rickey Brown (from GS)	F-C	6'10	235	24	26	305	49	104	47	25	40	63	88	9	46	1	5	5	123	12	3.4	0.3	1.8	4.7
Randy Smith (from SD)	G	6'3	185	34	15	142	29	66	44	13	14	93	8	14	17	0	2	0	71	9	0.5	0.9	1.1	4.7
Scott Hastings (from NY)	F-C	6'10	235	22	10	42	5	16	31	4	6	67	10	2	3	0	1	1	14	4	1.0	0.2	0.3	1.4
Sam Pellom (to Mil)	F	6'9	225	31	2	9	2	6	33	0	0	—	0	0	1	0	0	0	4	5	0.0	0.0	0.5	2.0
3-PT FG — Wilkins 2-11, Roundfield 5-27, Rollins 0-1, E. Johson 14-41, Sparrow 3-15, Davis 5-18, McMillen 0-1, Matthews 14-48, Macklin 0-4, Glenn 0-1, Hawes 2-14, Edmonson 0-2, Brown 0-1, Smith 0-2, Hastings 0-2																								
DETROIT PISTONS	37-45 .451				**SCOTTY ROBERTSON**																			
Kelly Tripucka	F	6'6	220	23	58	2252	565	1156	49	392	464	84	264	237	157	0	67	20	1536	39	4.6	4.1	2.7	26.5
Terry Tyler	F	6'7	220	26	82	2543	421	880	48	146	196	74	540	157	221	3	103	160	990	31	6.6	1.9	2.7	12.1
Bill Laimbeer	C	6'11	245	25	82	2871	436	877	50	245	310	79	993	263	320	9	51	118	1119	35	12.1	3.2	3.9	13.6
Vinnie Johnson	G	6'2	200	26	82	2511	520	1013	51	245	315	78	353	301	263	2	93	49	1296	31	4.3	3.7	3.2	15.8
Isiah Thomas	G	6'1	185	21	81	3093	725	1537	47	368	518	71	328	634	318	8	199	29	1854	38	4.0	7.8	3.9	22.9
John Long	G	6'5	200	26	70	1485	312	692	45	111	146	76	180	105	130	1	44	12	737	21	2.6	1.5	1.9	10.5
Edgar Jones (to SA)	F	6'10	225	26	49	1036	145	294	49	117	172	68	271	69	160	5	28	77	409	21	5.5	1.4	3.3	8.3
Cliff Levingston	F	6'8	210	21	62	879	131	270	49	84	147	57	232	52	125	2	23	36	346	14	3.7	0.8	2.0	5.6
Walker Russell	G	6'5	195	22	68	757	67	184	36	47	58	81	73	131	71	0	16	1	183	11	1.1	1.9	1.0	2.7
Tom Owens	C	6'10	220	33	49	725	81	192	42	45	66	68	186	44	115	0	12	14	207	15	3.8	0.9	2.3	4.2
Kent Benson (KJ, FJ)	F-C	6'10	245	28	21	599	85	182	47	38	50	76	155	49	61	0	14	17	208	29	7.4	2.3	2.9	9.9
Ray Tolbert (from Sea)	F	6'9	225	24	28	395	57	124	46	28	59	47	91	19	56	0	10	23	142	14	3.3	0.7	2.0	5.1
Ricky Pierce	F-G	6'5	205	23	39	265	33	88	38	18	32	56	35	14	42	0	8	4	85	7	0.9	0.4	1.1	2.2
Scott May	F	6'7	220	28	9	155	21	50	42	17	21	81	26	12	24	1	5	2	59	17	2.9	1.3	2.7	6.6
Jim Johnstone (from SA)	C-F	6'11	245	22	16	137	9	20	45	6	15	40	30	10	24	0	2	6	24	9	1.9	0.6	1.5	1.5
James Wilkes	F	6'7	195	24	9	129	11	34	32	12	15	80	19	10	22	0	3	1	34	14	2.1	1.1	2.4	3.8
Jim Zoet	C	7'1	240	29	7	30	1	5	20	0	0	—	8	1	9	0	1	3	2	4	1.1	0.1	1.3	0.3
Jim Smith	F	6'9	225	24	4	18	3	4	75	2	4	50	5	0	4	0	0	0	8	5	1.3	0.0	1.0	2.0
3-PT FG — Tripucka 14-37, Tyler 2-15, Laimbeer 2-13, Johnson 11-40, Thomas 36-125, Long 2-7, Jones 2-6, Levingston 0-1, Russell 2-18, Tolbert 0-1, Pierce 1-7, Wilkes 0-1, Benson 0-1																								
CHICAGO BULLS	28-54 .341				**PAUL WESTHEAD**																			
Orlando Woolridge (KJ)	F	6'9	215	23	57	1627	361	622	58	217	340	64	298	97	177	1	38	44	939	29	5.2	1.7	3.1	16.5
Dave Greenwood	F-C	6'9	232	25	79	2355	312	686	45	165	233	71	765	151	261	5	54	90	789	30	9.7	1.9	3.3	10.0
Dave Corzine	C	6'11	260	26	82	2496	457	920	50	232	322	72	717	154	242	4	47	109	1146	30	8.7	1.9	3.0	14.0
Quinton Dailey	G	6'3	180	21	76	2081	470	1008	47	206	282	73	260	280	248	7	72	10	1151	27	3.4	3.7	3.3	15.1
Reggie Theus	G	6'7	205	25	82	2856	749	1567	48	434	542	80	300	484	281	6	143	17	1953	35	3.7	5.9	3.4	23.8
Rod Higgins	F	6'7	250	22	82	2196	313	698	45	209	264	79	366	175	248	3	66	65	848	27	4.5	2.1	3.0	10.3
Mark Olberding	F	6'8	230	26	80	1817	251	522	48	194	248	78	358	131	246	3	50	9	698	23	4.5	1.6	3.1	8.7
Ronnie Lester (KJ)	G	6'2	175	23	65	1437	202	446	45	124	171	73	172	332	121	2	51	6	528	22	2.6	5.1	1.9	8.1
Tracy Jackson	G-F	6'6	215	23	78	1309	199	426	47	92	126	73	179	105	132	0	64	11	492	17	2.3	1.3	1.7	6.3
Dudley Bradley	G	6'6	195	25	58	683	82	159	52	36	45	80	105	106	91	0	49	10	201	12	1.8	1.8	1.6	3.5
Dwight Jones (to LA)	C	6'10	210	30	49	673	86	193	45	47	75	63	195	40	90	0	18	14	219	14	4.0	0.8	1.8	4.5
Jawann Oldham	C	7'	215	25	16	171	31	58	53	12	22	55	47	5	30	1	5	13	74	11	2.9	0.3	1.9	4.6
Mike Brate	G	6'2	185	27	15	140	14	42	33	10	13	77	19	23	20	0	7	0	39	9	1.3	1.5	1.3	2.6
Larry Spriggs	F	6'7	230	23	9	39	8	20	40	5	7	71	9	3	3	0	1	2	21	4	1.0	0.3	0.3	2.3
Larry Kenon (to GS, Cle)	F	6'9	215	30	5	25	2	6	33	0	0	—	4	0	2	0	1	0	4	5	0.8	0.0	0.4	0.8
3-PT FG — Woolridge 0-3, Greenwood 0-4, Corzine 0-2, Dailey 5-25, Theus 21-91, Higgins 13-41, Olberding 2-12, Lester 0-5, Jackson 2-13, Bradley 1-5, Bratz 1-8																								

1982/83 N.B.A. — EASTERN CONFERENCE
CENTRAL DIVISION

Use Name	Pos	Hgt	Wgt	Age	G	Min	FG	FGA	%	FT	FTA	%	Reb	Ass	PF	DQ	Stls	Blkd Shts	Points	Min	Reb	Ass	PF	Points
					TOTAL															PER GAME				
CLEVELAND CAVALIERS	23-59 .290				TOM NISSALKE																			
Phil Hubbard	F	6'8	215	26	82	1953	288	597	48	204	296	69	471	89	271	11	87	8	780	24	5.7	1.1	3.3	9.5
Cliff Robinson	F	6'9	230	22	77	2601	587	1230	48	213	301	71	856	145	272	7	61	58	1387	34	11.1	1.9	3.5	18.0
Sam Lacey	C	6'10	235	34	60	1232	111	264	42	29	37	78	231	118	209	3	29	25	253	21	3.9	2.0	3.5	4.2
World Free (from GS)	G	6'2	185	29	54	1938	485	1059	46	324	434	75	157	201	175	3	82	12	1309	36	2.9	3.7	3.2	24.2
Geoff Huston	G	6'2	175	25	80	2716	401	832	48	168	245	69	159	487	215	1	74	4	974	34	2.0	6.1	2.7	12.2
Bob Wilkerson	G-F	6'6	200	28	77	1702	213	511	42	93	124	75	242	189	157	0	68	16	519	22	3.1	2.5	2.0	6.7
Scott Wedman (to Bos)	F	6'7	235	30	35	1290	280	583	48	65	77	84	208	86	145	5	23	11	634	37	5.9	2.5	4.1	18.1
Steve Hayes	C	7'	235	27	65	1058	104	217	48	29	51	57	236	36	215	9	17	41	237	16	3.6	0.6	3.3	3.6
John Bagley	G	6'0	190	22	68	990	161	373	43	64	84	76	96	167	74	0	54	5	386	15	1.4	2.5	1.1	5.7
Jeff Cook (from Phoe)	F-C	6'10	215	26	30	782	87	162	54	38	50	76	206	44	92	3	27	18	212	26	6.9	1.5	3.1	7.1
Bruce Flowers	F	6'8	225	25	53	699	110	206	53	41	53	77	180	47	99	2	19	12	261	13	3.4	0.9	1.9	4.9
Larry Kenon (from Chi, GS)	F	6'9	215	30	32	624	100	212	47	35	46	76	117	34	49	0	21	9	235	20	3.7	1.1	1.5	7.3
Ron Brewer (to GS)	G	6'4	185	27	21	563	98	245	40	44	51	86	37	27	27	0	20	6	240	27	1.8	1.3	1.3	11.4
Paul Makeski (to Mil)	C	7'	250	25	23	539	55	121	45	16	26	62	138	26	85	6	12	23	126	23	6.0	1.1	3.7	5.5
Darren Tillis (from Bos)	C	6'11	215	22	37	482	69	158	44	14	22	64	121	16	86	3	8	28	152	13	3.3	0.4	2.3	4.1
James Edwards (to Phoe)	C	7'	225	27	15	382	73	150	49	38	61	62	96	13	61	3	7	14	184	25	6.4	0.9	4.1	12.3
Carl Nicks	G	6'3	185	24	9	148	26	59	44	11	17	65	26	11	17	0	6	0	63	16	2.9	1.2	1.9	7.0
Dave Magley	F	6'8	212	23	14	56	4	16	25	4	8	50	10	2	5	0	2	0	12	4	0.7	0.1	0.4	0.9

James Silas - injured, Richard Washington - injured

3-PT FG — Hubbard 0-2, Robinson 0-5, Lacey 2-9, Free 15-42, Huston 4-12, Wilkerson 0-4, Wedman 9-22, Hayes 0-1, Bagley 0-14, Cook 0-1, FLowers 0-2, Kenon 0-1, Brewer 0-3, Tillis 0-0 Nicks 0-1, Magley 0-1

Use Name	Pos	Hgt	Wgt	Age	G	Min	FG	FGA	%	FT	FTA	%	Reb	Ass	PF	DQ	Stls	Blkd Shts	Points	Min	Reb	Ass	PF	Points
INDIANA PACERS	20-62 .244				JACK McKINNEY																			
George Johnson	F	6'7	218	26	82	2297	409	858	48	126	172	73	545	220	279	6	77	53	951	28	6.6	2.7	3.4	11.6
Clark Kellogg	F	6'7	227	21	81	2761	680	1420	48	261	352	74	860	223	298	6	141	43	1625	34	10.6	2.8	3.7	20.1
Herb Williams	C	6'11	242	24	78	2513	580	1163	50	155	220	70	583	262	230	4	54	171	1315	32	7.5	3.4	2.9	16.9
Billy Knight	G-F	6'6	195	30	80	2262	512	984	52	343	408	84	324	192	143	0	66	8	1370	28	4.1	2.4	1.8	17.1
Jerry Sichting	G	6'1	178	26	78	2435	316	661	48	92	107	86	155	433	185	0	104	2	727	31	2.0	5.6	2.4	9.3
Butch Carter	G	6'5	185	24	81	1716	354	706	50	124	154	81	150	194	207	5	78	13	849	21	1.9	2.4	2.6	10.5
Marty Byrnes	F	6'7	220	26	80	1436	157	374	42	71	95	75	191	179	149	1	41	6	391	18	2.4	2.2	1.9	4.9
John Duren	G	6'3	195	24	82	1433	163	360	45	43	54	80	107	200	203	2	66	5	369	17	1.3	2.4	2.5	4.5
Clemon Johnson (to Phi)	C	6'10	240	26	51	1216	208	399	52	77	122	63	319	115	137	2	51	63	493	24	6.3	2.3	2.7	9.7
Brad Branson	F	6'10	220	24	62	680	131	308	43	76	108	70	173	46	81	0	27	26	338	11	2.8	0.7	1.3	5.5
Russ Schoene (from Phi)	F-C	6'10	210	22	31	520	101	228	44	40	55	73	101	27	74	1	12	14	243	17	3.3	0.9	2.4	7.8
Jose Slaughter	G	6'5	215	22	63	515	89	238	37	38	59	64	68	52	93	0	36	7	225	8	1.1	0.8	1.5	3.6
Guy Morgan	G	6'8	215	22	8	46	7	24	29	1	4	25	17	7	7	0	2	0	15	6	2.1	0.9	0.9	1.9

Johnny Davis — holdout (to Atl)

3-PT FG — G. Johnson 7-38, Kellogg 4-8, Williams 0-7, Knight 3-17, Sichting 3-18, Carter 17-51, Byrnes 6-26, Duren 0-13, C. Johnson 0-1, Branson 0-1, Schoene 1-3, Slaughter 9-41

MIDWEST DIVISION

Use Name	Pos	Hgt	Wgt	Age	G	Min	FG	FGA	%	FT	FTA	%	Reb	Ass	PF	DQ	Stls	Blkd Shts	Points	Min	Reb	Ass	PF	Points
SAN ANTONIO SPURS	53-29 .646				STAN ALBECK																			
Mike Mitchell	F	6'7	215	26	80	2803	686	1342	51	219	289	76	537	98	248	6	57	52	1591	35	6.7	1.2	3.1	19.9
Gene Banks	F	6'7	215	23	81	2722	505	919	55	196	278	71	612	279	229	3	78	21	1206	34	7.6	3.4	2.8	14.9
Artis Gilmore	C	7'2	255	33	82	2797	556	888	**63**	367	496	74	984	126	273	4	40	192	1479	34	12.0	1.5	3.3	18.0
George Gervin	G	6'7	185	30	78	2830	757	1553	49	517	606	85	357	264	243	5	88	67	2043	36	4.6	3.4	3.1	26.2
Johnny Moore	G	6'2	185	24	77	2552	394	841	47	148	199	74	277	753	247	2	194	32	941	33	3.6	9.8	3.2	12.2
Mike Dunleavy	G	6'3	180	28	79	1619	213	510	42	120	154	78	134	437	210	1	74	4	613	20	1.7	5.5	2.7	7.8
Bill Willoughby (to NJ)	F	6'8	205	25	52	1062	136	295	46	41	53	77	190	56	123	0	24	16	319	20	3.7	1.1	2.4	6.1
Paul Griffin	F-C	6'9	225	28	53	956	60	116	52	53	76	70	216	86	153	0	33	25	173	18	4.1	1.6	2.9	3.3
Edgar Jones (from Det)	C	6'10	225	26	28	622	92	185	50	84	114	74	177	20	107	5	14	31	268	22	6.3	0.7	3.8	9.6
Roger Phegley	G	6'6	215	26	62	599	120	267	45	43	56	77	84	60	92	0	30	8	286	10	1.4	1.0	1.5	4.6
Mike Sanders	F-G	6'6	210	22	26	393	76	157	48	31	43	72	94	19	57	0	18	6	183	15	3.6	0.7	2.2	7.0
Ed Rains	F	6'7	195	26	34	292	33	83	40	29	43	67	44	22	35	0	10	1	95	9	1.3	0.6	1.0	2.8
Geff Crompton	C	6'11	288	27	14	148	14	34	41	3	5	60	48	7	25	0	3	5	31	11	3.4	0.5	1.8	2.2
Oliver Robinson	G	6'4	185	22	35	147	35	97	36	30	45	67	17	21	18	0	4	2	101	4	0.5	0.6	0.5	2.9
Billy Paultz (from Hou)	C	6'11	255	34	7	125	12	27	44	1	2	50	33	4	14	0	5	6	25	18	4.7	0.6	2.0	3.6
Jim Johnstone (to Det)	C	6'11	245	22	7	54	2	10	20	3	5	60	16	1	9	0	1	1	7	8	2.3	0.1	1.3	1.0
Coby Dietrick	C	6'10	225	34	8	34	1	5	20	0	2	0	8	6	6	0	1	0	2	4	1.0	0.8	0.8	0.3
Robert Smith (from SD)	G	5'11	170	27	7	25	5	11	45	2	2	100	3	2	6	0	1	0	12	4	0.4	0.3	0.9	1.7

3-PT FG — Mitchell 0-3, Banks 0-5, Gilmore 0-6, Grevin 12-33, Moore 5-22, Dunleavy 67-194, Willoughby 6-13, Jones 0-3, Phegley 3-14, Sanders 0-2, Rains 0-1, Robinson 1-11, Smith 0-1

Use Name	Pos	Hgt	Wgt	Age	G	Min	FG	FGA	%	FT	FTA	%	Reb	Ass	PF	DQ	Stls	Blkd Shts	Points	Min	Reb	Ass	PF	Points
DENVER NUGGETS	45-37 .543				DOUG MOE																			
Alex English	F	6'8	190	28	82	2988	**959**	**1857**	52	406	490	83	601	397	235	1	116	126	**2326**	36	7.3	4.8	2.9	**28.4**
Kiki Vandeweghe	F	6'8	220	24	82	2909	841	1537	55	489	559	87	437	203	198	0	66	38	2186	35	5.3	2.5	2.4	26.7
Dan Issel	C	6'9	240	34	80	2431	661	1296	51	400	479	84	596	223	227	0	83	43	1726	30	7.5	2.8	2.8	21.6
T. R. Dunn	G	6'4	192	27	82	2640	254	527	48	119	163	73	615	189	218	2	147	25	627	32	7.5	2.3	2.7	7.6
Billy McKinney	G	6'	172	27	68	1559	266	546	49	136	167	81	121	288	142	0	39	5	668	23	1.8	4.2	2.1	9.8
Bill Hanzlik	G	6'7	185	25	82	1547	187	437	43	125	160	78	236	268	220	0	75	15	500	19	2.9	3.3	2.7	6.1
Rob Williams	G	6'2	175	21	74	1443	191	468	41	131	174	75	136	361	221	4	89	12	515	20	1.8	4.9	3.0	7.0
Glenn Gondrezick	F	6'6	218	27	76	1130	134	294	46	82	114	72	301	100	161	0	80	9	350	15	4.0	1.3	2.1	4.6
Dave Robisch	F-C	6'10	240	33	61	711	96	251	38	92	118	78	151	53	61	0	10	9	284	12	2.5	0.9	1.0	4.7
Mike Evans	G	6'1	170	27	42	695	115	243	47	33	41	80	58	113	94	3	23	3	263	17	1.4	2.7	2.2	6.3
Dan Schayes (from Utah)	C	6'11	245	23	32	646	111	235	47	71	100	71	186	40	109	1	15	30	293	20	5.8	1.3	3.4	9.2
Rick Kelley (to Utah)	C	7'	240	29	38	565	59	141	42	55	70	79	172	59	115	3	21	18	173	15	4.5	1.6	3.0	4.6
James Ray	F	6'8	215	25	45	433	70	153	46	33	51	65	126	39	83	2	24	19	173	10	2.8	0.9	1.8	3.8
Dwight Anderson	G	1'3	185	22	5	33	7	14	50	7	10	70	2	3	7	0	1	0	21	7	0.4	0.6	1.4	4.2

3-PT FG — English 2-12, Vandweghe 15-51, Issel 4-19, Dunn 0-1, McKinney 0-7, Hanzlik 1-7, Williams 2-15, Gondrezick 0-3, Robisch 0-1, Evans 0-9, Ray 0-1

1982/83 N.B.A. — WESTERN CONFERENCE
MIDWEST DIVISION

Use Name	Pos	Hgt	Wgt	Age	G	Min	FG	FGA	%	FT	FTA	%	Reb	Ass	PF	DQ	Stls	Blkd Shts	Points	Min	Reb	Ass	PF	Points
					TOTAL															PER GAME				
KANSAS CITY KINGS	45-37 .543				COTTON FITZSIMMONS																			
Eddie Johnson	F	6'8	215	23	82	2933	677	1370	49	247	317	78	501	216	259	3	70	20	1621	36	6.1	2.6	3.2	19.8
Ed Nealy	F	6'7	238	22	82	1643	147	247	60	70	114	61	485	62	247	4	68	12	364	20	5.9	0.8	3.0	4.4
Joe C. Meriweather	C	6'10	218	29	78	1706	258	453	57	102	163	63	424	64	285	4	47	86	618	22	5.4	0.8	3.7	7.9
Mike Woodson	G-F	6'5	198	24	81	2426	584	1154	51	298	377	79	248	254	203	0	137	59	1473	30	3.1	3.1	2.5	18.2
Larry Drew	G	6'1	180	24	75	2690	599	1218	49	310	378	82	207	610	207	1	126	10	1510	36	2.8	8.1	2.8	20.1
Ray Williams	G	6'3	195	28	72	2170	419	1068	39	256	333	77	327	569	248	3	120	26	1109	30	4.5	7.9	3.4	15.4
Steve Johnson	C-F	6'10	245	25	79	1544	371	595	62	186	324	57	398	95	323	9	40	83	928	20	5.0	1.2	4.1	11.7
Reggie Kng	F	6'6	230	25	58	995	104	225	46	73	96	76	240	58	94	1	28	11	281	17	4.1	1.0	1.6	4.8
Reggie Johnson (to Phi)	F	6'9	205	25	50	992	178	355	50	73	100	73	201	48	150	2	18	26	430	20	4.0	1.0	3.0	8.6
LaSalle Thompson	C	6'10	248	21	71	987	147	287	51	89	137	65	375	33	186	1	40	61	383	14	5.3	0.5	2.6	5.4
Kevin Loder	G-F	6'6	205	23	66	818	138	300	46	53	80	66	125	72	98	0	29	8	334	12	1.9	1.1	1.5	5.1
Brook Steppe	G	6'5	195	23	62	606	84	176	48	76	100	76	73	68	92	0	26	3	245	10	1.2	1.1	1.5	4.0
Kenny Dennard	F	6'8	220	24	22	224	11	34	32	6	9	67	52	6	27	0	16	1	28	10	2.4	0.3	1.2	1.3
Leon Douglas	F	6'10	230	28	5	46	2	3	67	0	2	0	7	0	13	0	0	3	4	9	1.4	0.0	2.6	0.8

3-PT FG — E.Johnson 20-71, Woodson 7-33, Drewe 2-16, Williams 15-74, R. Johnson 1-4, Thompson 0-1, Loder 5-9, Steppe 1-7

Use Name	Pos	Hgt	Wgt	Age	G	Min	FG	FGA	%	FT	FTA	%	Reb	Ass	PF	DQ	Stls	Blkd Shts	Points	Min	Reb	Ass	PF	Points
DALLAS MAVERICKS	33-44 .463				DICK MOTTA																			
Mark Aguirre	F	6'6	235	23	81	2784	767	1589	48	429	589	73	508	332	247	5	80	26	1979	34	6.3	4.1	3.0	24.4
Jay Vincent	F	6'8	225	23	81	2726	622	1272	49	269	343	78	592	212	295	4	70	45	1513	34	7.3	2.6	3.6	18.7
Pat Cummings	C-F	6'9	235	26	81	2317	433	878	49	148	196	76	668	144	296	9	57	35	1014	29	8.2	1.8	3.7	12.5
Rolando Blackman	G	6'6	190	23	75	2349	513	1042	49	297	381	78	293	185	116	0	37	29	1326	31	3.9	2.5	1.5	17.7
Brad Davis	G	6'3	180	27	79	2323	359	628	57	186	220	85	198	565	176	2	80	11	915	29	2.5	7.2	2.2	11.6
Kelvin Ransey	G	6'1	180	24	76	1607	343	746	46	152	199	76	147	280	109	1	58	4	840	21	1.9	3.7	1.4	11.1
Kurt Nimphius	C	6'10	218	24	81	1515	174	355	49	77	140	55	404	115	287	11	24	111	426	19	5.0	1.4	3.5	5.3
Bill Garnett	F	6'9	225	22	75	1411	170	319	53	129	174	74	406	103	245	3	48	70	469	19	5.4	1.4	3.3	6.3
Elston Turner	G	6'5	220	23	59	879	96	238	40	20	30	67	152	88	75	0	47	0	214	15	2.6	1.5	1.3	3.6
Jim Spanarkel	G	6'5	195	25	48	722	91	197	46	88	113	78	84	78	59	0	27	3	272	15	1.8	1.6	1.2	5.7
Corny Thompson (EJ)	F	6'8	225	22	44	520	43	137	31	36	46	78	120	34	92	0	12	7	122	12	2.7	0.8	2.1	2.8
Allan Bristow	F	6'7	210	31	37	371	44	99	44	10	14	71	59	70	46	0	6	1	104	10	1.6	1.9	1.2	2.8
Scott Lloyd	C	6'10	235	30	15	206	19	50	38	11	17	65	46	21	24	0	6	6	49	14	3.1	1.4	1.6	3.3

3-PT FG — Aguirre 16-76, Vincent 0-3, Cummings 0-1, Blackman 3-15, Davis 11-43, Ransey 2-16 Nimphius 1-1, Garnett 0-3, Turner 2-3, Spanarkel 2-10, Bristow 6-13, Lloyd 0-1

Use Name	Pos	Hgt	Wgt	Age	G	Min	FG	FGA	%	FT	FTA	%	Reb	Ass	PF	DQ	Stls	Blkd Shts	Points	Min	Reb	Ass	PF	Points
UTAH JAZZ	30-52 .366				FRANK LAYDEN																			
Adrian Dantley (WS)	F	6'5	210	26	22	887	233	402	58	210	248	85	140	105	62	2	20	0	676	40	6.4	4.8	2.8	30.7
Ben Poquette	F	6'9	235	27	75	2331	329	697	47	166	221	75	521	168	264	5	64	116	825	31	6.9	2.2	3.5	11.0
Dan Schayes (to Den)	C	6'11	245	23	50	1638	231	514	45	157	195	81	449	165	216	7	39	68	619	33	9.0	3.3	4.3	12.4
Darrell Griffith	G	6'4	190	24	77	2787	752	1554	48	167	246	68	304	270	184	0	138	33	1709	36	3.9	3.5	2.4	22.2
Rickey Green	G	6'1	170	28	78	2783	464	942	49	185	232	80	223	697	154	0	**220**	4	1115	36	2.9	8.9	2.0	14.3
Jeff Wilkins	F	6'11	240	27	81	2307	389	816	48	156	200	78	596	132	251	4	41	42	934	28	7.4	1.6	3.1	11.5
Jerry Eaves	G	6'4	185	23	82	1588	280	575	49	200	247	81	122	210	116	0	51	3	761	19	1.5	2.6	1.4	9.3
Mark Eaton	C	7'4	280	25	81	1528	146	353	41	59	90	66	462	112	257	6	24	275	351	19	5.7	1.4	3.2	4.3
John Drew (DR)	F	6'6	205	28	44	1206	318	671	47	296	392	76	235	97	152	8	35	7	932	27	5.3	2.2	3.5	21.2
J.J. Anderson (from Phi)	F	6'8	195	22	52	1154	182	357	51	99	172	58	282	66	147	1	62	21	463	22	5.4	1.3	2.8	8.9
Rich Kelley (from Den)	C	7'	240	29	32	780	71	152	47	87	105	83	232	79	106	1	33	21	229	24	7.3	2.5	3.3	7.2
Rickey Williams	G	6'2	175	25	44	346	56	135	41	35	53	66	38	37	42	0	20	4	147	8	0.9	0.8	1.0	3.3
Freeman Williams	G	6'4	195	26	18	210	36	101	36	18	25	72	17	10	30	0	6	1	92	12	0.9	0.6	1.7	5.1
Kenny Natt	G	6'3	185	24	22	210	38	73	52	9	14	64	22	28	36	0	5	0	85	10	1.0	1.3	1.6	3.9

3-PT FG — Poquette 1-5, Schayes 0-1, Griffith 38-132, Green 2-13, Wilkins 0-3, Eaves 1-8, Eaton 0-1, Drew 0-5, Anderson 0-3, R.Williams 0-3, F.Williams 2-7, Natt 0-2

Use Name	Pos	Hgt	Wgt	Age	G	Min	FG	FGA	%	FT	FTA	%	Reb	Ass	PF	DQ	Stls	Blkd Shts	Points	Min	Reb	Ass	PF	Points
HOUSTON ROCKETS	14-68 .171				DEL HARRIS																			
Wally Walker	F	6'7	210	28	82	2251	362	806	45	72	116	62	373	199	202	3	37	22	797	27	4.5	2.4	2.5	9.7
Elvin Hayes	F	6'9	235	37	81	2302	424	890	48	196	287	68	616	158	232	2	50	81	1046	28	7.6	2.0	2.9	12.9
Caldwell Jones	C	6'11	225	32	82	2440	307	677	45	162	206	79	668	138	278	2	46	131	776	30	8.1	1.7	3.4	9.5
Terry Teagle	G	6'5	195	22	73	1708	332	776	43	87	125	70	194	150	171	0	53	18	761	23	2.7	2.1	2.3	10.4
Allen Leavell	G	6'1	190	25	79	2602	439	1059	41	247	297	83	195	530	215	0	165	14	1167	33	2.5	6.7	2.7	14.8
Joe Bryant	F	6'9	225	28	81	2055	344	768	45	116	165	70	277	186	258	4	82	30	812	25	3.4	2.3	3.2	10.0
James Bailey (from NJ)	F-C	6'9	220	25	69	1715	376	756	50	224	320	70	468	65	256	7	42	59	976	25	6.8	0.9	3.7	14.1
Calvin Murphy	G	5'9	165	34	64	1423	337	754	45	138	150	92	74	158	163	3	59	4	816	22	1.2	2.5	2.5	12.8
Major Jones	F	6'9	225	29	60	878	142	311	46	56	102	55	263	39	104	0	22	22	340	15	4.4	0.7	1.7	5.7
Tom Henderson	G	6'3	190	30	51	789	107	263	41	45	57	79	69	138	57	0	37	2	259	15	1.4	2.7	1.1	5.1
Jeff Taylor	G	6'4	175	22	44	774	64	160	40	30	46	65	78	110	82	1	40	15	158	18	1.8	2.5	1.9	3.6
Billy Paultz (to SA)	C	6'11	255	34	57	695	89	200	45	26	57	46	167	57	95	0	12	12	204	12	2.9	1.0	1.7	3.6
Chuck Nevitt	C	7'5	237	23	6	64	11	15	73	1	4	25	17	0	14	0	1	12	23	11	2.8	0.0	2.3	3.8
Calvin Garrett	F	6'7	195	26	4	34	4	11	36	2	2	100	7	3	4	0	0	0	10	9	1.8	0.8	1.0	2.5

Robert Reid — sat out season for religious reasons

3-PT FG — Walker 1-4, Hayes 2-4, C.Jones 0-2, Teggle 10-29, Leavell 42-175, Bryant 8-36, Bailey 0-1, Murphy 4-14, M.Jones 0-2, Henderson 0-2, Taylor 0-1, Garrett 0-1

1982/83 N.B.A. — WESTERN CONFERENCE
PACIFIC DIVISION

58-24 .707 PAT RILEY

Use Name	Pos	Hgt	Wgt	Age	G	Min	FG	FGA	%	FT	FTA	%	Reb	Ass	PF	DQ	Stls	Blkd Shts	Points	Min	Reb	Ass	PF	Points
LOS ANGELELES LAKERS																								
Jamaal Wilkes	F	6'6	190	29	80	2552	684	1290	53	203	268	76	343	182	221	0	65	17	1571	32	4.3	2.3	2.8	19.6
James Worthy	F	6'9	225	21	77	1970	447	772	58	138	221	62	399	132	221	2	91	64	1033	26	5.2	1.7	2.9	13.4
Kareem Abdul-Jabbar	C	7'2	232	35	79	2554	722	1228	59	278	371	75	592	200	220	1	61	170	1722	32	7.5	2.5	2.8	21.8
Magic Johnson	G	6'8	215	23	79	2907	511	933	55	304	380	80	683	829	200	1	176	47	1326	37	8.6	10.5	2.5	16.8
Norm Nixon	G	6'2	175	27	79	2711	533	1123	47	125	168	74	205	566	176	1	104	4	1191	34	2.6	7.2	2.2	15.1
Michael Cooper	G-F	6'5	170	26	82	2148	266	497	54	102	130	78	274	315	208	0	115	50	639	26	3.3	3.8	2.5	7.8
Kurt Rambis	F	6'8	220	24	78	1806	235	413	57	114	166	69	531	90	233	2	105	63	584	23	6.8	1.2	3.0	7.5
Bob McAdoo	C	6'9	225	31	47	1019	292	562	52	119	163	73	247	39	153	2	40	40	703	22	5.3	0.8	3.3	15.0
Dwight Jones (from Chi)	C-F	6'10	210	30	32	491	62	132	47	32	48	67	114	22	82	0	13	9	156	15	3.6	0.7	2.6	4.9
Clay Johnson	G	6'4	185	26	48	447	53	135	39	38	48	79	69	24	62	0	22	4	144	9	1.4	0.5	1.3	3.0
Mike McGee	G-F	6'5	190	23	39	381	69	163	42	17	23	74	53	26	50	1	11	5	156	10	1.4	0.7	1.3	4.0
Mark Landsberger	F	6'8	230	27	39	356	43	102	42	12	25	48	128	12	48	0	8	4	98	9	3.3	0.3	1.2	2.5
Eddie Jordan	G	6'1	170	27	35	333	40	132	30	11	17	65	26	80	52	0	31	1	94	10	0.7	2.3	1.5	2.7
Billy Ray Bates (from Was)	G	6'4	210	26	4	27	2	16	13	1	2	50	1	0	1	0	1	0	5	7	0.3	0.0	0.3	1.3
Steve Mix (from Mil)	F	6'7	222	35	1	17	4	10	40	1	1	100	1	2	1	0	0	0	9	17	1.0	2.0	1.0	9.0
Joe Cooper (to Was, SD)	C	6'10	230	25	2	11	1	4	25	0	0	—	2	0	3	0	1	1	2	6	1.0	0.0	1.5	1.0
Mitch Kupchak - knee injury																								

3-PT FG — Wilkes 0-6, Worthy 1-4, Jabbar 0-2, Johnson 0-21, Nixon 0-13, M.Cooper 5-21, Rambis 0-2, McAdoo 0-1, Jones 0-1, McGee 1-7, C.Johnson 0-2, Jordan 3-16

53-29 .646 JOHN MacLEOD

Use Name	Pos	Hgt	Wgt	Age	G	Min	FG	FGA	%	FT	FTA	%	Reb	Ass	PF	DQ	Stls	Blkd Shts	Points	Min	Reb	Ass	PF	Points
PHOENIX SUNS	F	6'10	215	23	82	2914	588	1069	55	193	287	67	710	197	254	4	99	217	1370	36	8.7	2.4	3.1	16.7
Larry Nance	F-C	6'9	238	30	77	2586	495	1045	47	278	356	78	799	219	274	5	56	43	1269	34	10.3	2.8	3.6	16.5
Maurice Lucas	C	6'9	220	28	80	2447	477	981	49	180	217	83	548	376	287	7	114	74	1135	31	6.9	4.7	3.6	14.2
Alvan Adams	G-F	6'6	200	28	80	2491	665	1289	52	184	225	82	197	397	186	2	117	12	1521	31	2.5	5.0	2.3	19.0
Walter Davis	G	6'4	200	28	77	2551	398	861	46	292	369	79	335	388	204	1	97	39	1093	33	4.4	5.0	2.6	14.2
Dennis Johnson																								
	G	6'3	190	25	82	1836	328	634	52	129	148	87	165	278	130	0	64	8	808	22	2.0	3.4	1.6	9.9
Kyle Macy	G	6'3	185	25	82	1155	100	217	46	63	136	46	150	153	205	0	85	34	264	14	1.8	1.9	2.5	3.2
Johnny High	F	6'7	215	27	81	1139	124	259	48	81	110	74	224	97	133	0	48	31	329	14	2.8	1.2	1.6	4.1
Alvin Scott	F	6'8	210	23	65	626	127	234	54	70	109	64	105	30	54	0	16	2	324	10	1.6	0.5	0.8	5.0
Rory White	C	6'10	215	26	45	551	61	142	43	41	54	76	129	58	89	0	12	13	163	12	2.9	1.3	2.0	3.6
Jeff Cook (to Cle)	F	6'7	215	22	49	521	74	170	44	45	78	58	72	36	93	1	19	4	194	11	1.5	0.7	1.9	4.0
David Thirdkill	F	6'7	203	27	54	458	44	104	42	14	16	88	88	37	63	0	15	6	102	8	1.6	0.7	1.2	1.9
Joel Kramer	C	7'	225	27	16	285	55	113	49	31	47	66	59	27	49	2	5	5	141	18	3.7	1.7	3.1	8.8
James Edwards (from Cle)	F	6'8	220	24	28	170	19	40	48	25	37	68	31	7	41	0	2	7	63	6	1.1	0.3	1.5	2.3
Charles Pittman																								

3-PT FG — Nance 1-3, Lucas 1-3, Adams 1-3, Davis 7-23, Johnson 5-31, Macy 23-76, High 1-5, Scott 0-2, White 0-1, Cook 0-2, Thirdkill 1-7, Kramer 0-1, Pittman 0-1

48-34 .585 LENNY WILKINS

Use Name	Pos	Hgt	Wgt	Age	G	Min	FG	FGA	%	FT	FTA	%	Reb	Ass	PF	DQ	Stls	Blkd Shts	Points	Min	Reb	Ass	PF	Points
SEATTLE SUPERSONICS	F	6'7	210	24	82	2054	226	429	53	115	209	55	425	120	254	2	53	49	567	25	5.2	1.5	3.1	6.9
Danny Vranes	F	6'8	255	27	82	2572	437	915	48	141	187	75	495	237	310	8	75	72	1016	31	6.0	2.9	3.8	12.4
Lonnie Shelton	C-F	6'11	250	27	75	2564	484	1043	46	400	478	84	858	233	263	4	87	65	1368	34	11.4	3.1	3.5	18.2
Jack Sikma	G-F	6'4	195	28	75	2155	445	925	48	298	380	78	270	222	142	0	47	33	1190	29	3.6	3.0	1.9	15.9
David Thompson	G	6'2	175	29	80	2761	660	1384	48	278	370	75	205	643	117	0	182	26	1600	35	2.6	8.0	1.5	20.0
Gus Williams																								
	C	7'2	278	25	82	1789	289	496	58	150	218	69	501	97	171	1	19	101	728	22	6.1	1.2	2.1	8.9
James Donaldson	F	6'7	205	25	80	1507	247	450	55	173	257	67	403	97	243	5	52	35	667	19	5.0	1.2	3.0	8.3
Greg Kelser	G	6'3	185	34	80	1432	371	714	52	58	72	81	97	242	98	0	59	13	814	18	1.2	3.0	1.2	10.2
Fred Brown	G	6'4	197	30	79	1238	175	400	44	101	133	76	130	216	113	0	44	8	454	16	1.6	2.7	1.4	5.7
Phil Smith	F	6'9	225	24	45	712	100	190	53	24	44	55	151	31	97	1	16	24	224	16	3.4	0.7	2.2	5.0
Ray Tolbert (to Det)	F-C	6'9	220	32	31	556	72	146	49	23	32	72	133	36	79	0	9	6	170	18	4.3	1.2	2.5	5.5
Steve Hawes (from Atl)	G	6'4	190	23	54	439	84	172	49	30	73	41	47	104	78	0	34	4	202	8	0.9	1.9	1.4	3.7
Mark Rudford	F	6'7	215	21	9	26	7	13	54	5	6	83	6	0	4	0	0	1	19	3	0.7	0.0	0.4	2.1
John Grieg																								

3-PT FG — Vranes 0-1, Shelton 1-6, Sikma 0-8, Thompson 2-10, Williams 2-43, Kelser 0-3, Brown 14-32, Smith 3-8, Tolbert 0-2, Hawes 3-7, Radford 4-18

46-36 .561 JACK RAMSAY

Use Name	Pos	Hgt	Wgt	Age	G	Min	FG	FGA	%	FT	FTA	%	Reb	Ass	PF	DQ	Stls	Blkd Shts	Points	Min	Reb	Ass	PF	Points
PORTLAND TRAIL BLAZERS	F	6'6	220	25	80	2879	644	1187	54	339	428	79	599	171	184	2	63	29	1630	36	7.5	2.1	2.3	20.4
Calvin Natt	F	6'7	230	27	82	2331	362	717	50	255	366	70	589	116	306	10	62	42	981	28	7.2	1.4	3.7	12.0
Kenny Carr	C-F	6'10	226	27	80	3017	505	1033	49	249	401	62	753	380	213	1	68	110	1259	38	9.4	4.8	2.7	15.7
Mychal Thompson	G	6'6	200	25	81	2740	682	1323	52	388	478	81	174	231	160	0	140	17	1756	34	2.1	2.9	2.0	21.7
Jim Paxon	G	6'2	185	23	47	1298	209	460	45	169	213	79	117	293	139	1	101	5	587	28	2.5	6.2	3.0	12.5
Darnell Valentine (BF)																								
	C	6'10	220	26	80	2099	320	723	44	135	197	69	611	116	318	5	27	136	775	26	7.6	1.5	4.0	9.7
Wayne Cooper	G	6'3	175	22	81	2020	256	594	43	116	159	73	225	426	179	2	153	15	633	25	2.8	5.3	2.2	7.8
LaFayette Lever	G	6'6	195	23	59	690	107	252	42	42	52	81	76	58	67	0	20	3	257	12	1.3	1.0	1.1	4.4
Jeff Lamp	G	6'4	195	32	41	643	72	182	40	41	46	89	54	115	60	0	44	2	194	16	1.3	2.8	1.5	4.7
Don Buse	F	6'9	215	23	48	527	87	171	51	21	31	68	96	32	95	2	18	9	195	11	2.0	0.7	2.0	4.1
Pete Verhoeven	F-G	6'7	195	23	55	516	105	234	45	28	38	74	65	31	81	0	19	5	247	9	1.2	0.6	1.5	4.5
Linton Townes	F	6'9	215	23	42	375	45	97	46	33	43	77	89	20	58	0	6	7	123	9	2.1	0.5	1.4	2.9
Hank McDowell (from GS)	C	6'9	250	22	30	311	26	63	41	14	30	47	69	24	61	0	13	2	66	10	2.3	0.8	2.0	2.2
Audie Norris	G	6'6	185	26	34	309	39	88	44	25	30	83	43	17	39	0	15	2	105	9	1.3	0.5	1.1	3.1
Jeff Judkins																								

3-PT FG — Natt 3-20, Carr 2-6, Thompson 0-1, Paxson 4-25, Valentine 0-1, Cooper 0-5, Lever 5-15, Lamp 1-6, Buse 9-35, Verhoeven 0-1, Townes 9-25, McDowell 0-2, Judkins 0-2

Use Name	Pos	Hgt	Wgt	Age	G	Min	FG	FGA	%	FT	FTA	%	Reb	Ass	PF	DQ	Stls	Blkd Shts	Points	Min	Reb	Ass	PF	Points
					TOTAL															PER GAME				
1982/83 N.B.A. — WESTERN CONFERENCE PACIFIC DIVISION																								
GOLDEN STATE WARRIORS	**30-52 .366**				**AL ATTLES**																			
Purvis Short	F-G	6'7	220	25	67	2397	589	1209	49	255	308	83	354	228	242	3	94	14	1437	36	5.3	3.4	3.6	21.4
Larry Smith (EJ)	F	6'8	225	24	49	1433	180	306	59	53	99	54	485	46	186	5	36	20	413	29	9.9	0.9	3.8	8.4
Joe Barry Carroll	C	7'	250	24	79	2988	785	1529	51	337	469	72	688	169	260	7	108	155	1907	38	8.7	2.1	3.3	24.1
Ron Brewer (from Cle)	G	6'4	185	27	53	1401	246	562	44	98	119	82	107	69	96	0	70	19	597	26	2.0	1.3	1.8	11.3
Lorenzo Romar	G	6'1	180	24	82	2130	266	572	47	78	105	74	138	455	142	0	98	5	620	26	1.7	5.5	1.7	7.6
Sam Williams	F	6'8	215	23	75	1533	252	479	53	123	171	72	393	45	244	4	71	89	627	20	5.2	0.6	3.3	8.4
Lester Connor	G	6'4	185	23	75	1416	145	303	48	79	113	70	221	253	141	1	116	7	369	19	2.9	3.4	1.9	4.9
Lewis Lloyd	F	6'6	215	23	73	1350	293	566	52	100	139	72	260	130	109	0	61	31	687	18	3.6	1.8	1.5	9.4
M.R. Richardson (to NJ)	G	6'5	195	27	33	1074	176	427	41	55	87	63	145	245	124	2	101	9	411	33	4.4	7.4	3.8	12.5
Mickey Johnson (from Mil, NJ)	F	6'10	190	30	30	899	162	359	45	141	170	83	245	100	131	6	25	23	466	30	8.2	3.3	4.4	15.5
Eric Floyd (from NJ)	G	6'3	175	22	33	754	134	311	43	112	135	83	95	71	78	2	39	8	386	23	2.9	2.2	2.4	11.7
Rickey Brown (to Atl)	C-F	6'10	235	24	50	743	118	245	48	40	65	62	178	16	126	0	8	21	276	15	3.6	0.3	2.5	5.5
World Free (to Cle)	G	6'2	185	29	19	700	164	364	45	106	149	71	44	89	66	1	15	3	434	37	2.3	4.7	3.5	22.8
Chris Engler	C	6'11	248	23	54	369	38	94	40	5	16	31	104	11	95	1	7	17	81	7	1.9	0.2	1.8	1.5
Derek Smith	F	6'6	215	21	27	154	21	51	41	17	25	68	38	2	40	0	0	4	59	6	1.4	0.1	1.5	2.2
Joe Hassett	G	6'5	185	27	6	139	19	44	43	0	0	—	11	21	14	0	2	0	39	23	1.8	3.5	2.3	6.5
Hank McDowell (to Port)	F	6'9	215	23	14	130	13	29	45	14	18	78	30	4	26	0	2	4	40	9	2.1	0.3	1.9	2.9
L. Kenon (from Chi, to Cle)	F	6'9	215	30	11	121	17	39	44	7	11	64	26	5	13	0	1	0	41	11	2.4	0.5	1.2	3.7
Terry Duerod	G	6'2	180	26	5	49	9	19	47	0	0	—	3	5	5	0	2	1	18	10	0.6	1.0	1.0	3.6
	3-PT FG —				Short 4-15, Carroll 0-3, Brewer 7-15, Romar 10-33, Williams 0-1, Connor 0-4, Lloyd 1-4, Richardson 4-31, Johnson 1-17, Floyd 6-11, Brown 0-2, Free 0-3, D.Smith 0-2, Hassett 1-9																			
SAN DIEGO CLIPPERS	**25-57 .305**				**PAUL SILAS**																			
Terry Cummings	F	6'9	220	21	70	2531	684	1309	52	292	412	71	744	177	294	10	129	62	1660	36	10.6	2.5	4.2	23.7
Tom Chambers	F-C	6'10	225	23	79	2665	519	1099	47	353	488	72	519	192	333	15	79	57	1391	34	6.6	2.4	4.2	17.6
Bill Walton (FJ)	C	6'11	225	30	33	1099	200	379	53	65	117	56	323	120	113	0	34	119	465	33	9.8	3.6	3.4	14.1
Craig Hodges	G	6'3	190	22	76	2022	318	704	45	94	130	72	122	275	192	3	82	4	750	27	1.6	3.6	2.5	9.9
Lionel Hollins	G	6'3	185	29	56	1844	313	717	44	129	179	72	128	373	155	2	111	14	758	33	2.3	6.7	2.8	13.5
Michael Brooks	F	6'7	220	24	82	2457	402	830	48	193	277	70	521	262	297	6	112	39	1002	30	6.4	3.2	3.6	12.2
Al Wood	G-F	6'6	193	24	76	1822	343	740	46	124	161	77	236	134	188	5	55	36	825	24	3.1	1.8	2.5	10.9
Richard Anderson	C-F	6'10	240	22	78	1274	174	431	40	48	69	70	272	120	170	2	57	26	403	16	3.5	1.5	2.2	5.2
Randy Smith (to Atl)	G	6'3	185	34	65	1264	244	499	49	101	117	86	88	192	122	1	54	0	592	19	1.4	3.0	1.9	9.1
Jerome Whitehead	C	6'10	225	26	46	905	164	306	54	72	87	83	261	42	139	2	21	15	400	20	5.7	0.9	3.0	8.7
Lowes Moore	G	6'1	170	25	37	642	81	190	43	42	56	75	55	73	72	1	22	1	210	17	1.5	2.0	1.9	5.7
Jim Brogan	G	6'5	185	24	58	466	91	213	43	34	43	79	62	66	79	0	26	9	219	8	1.1	1.1	1.4	3.8
Bob Gross	F	6'6	200	30	27	373	35	82	43	12	19	63	66	34	69	1	22	7	83	14	2.4	1.3	2.6	3.1
Joe Cooper (from LA, Was)	C	6'10	230	25	13	275	31	59	53	11	20	55	71	15	39	0	8	19	73	21	5.5	1.2	3.0	5.6
Hutch Jones	F	6'8	195	23	9	85	17	37	46	6	6	100	17	4	14	0	3	0	40	9	1.9	0.4	1.6	4.4
Swen Nater	C	6'11	250	32	7	51	6	20	30	4	4	100	13	1	1	0	1	0	16	7	1.9	0.1	0.1	2.3
Robert Smith (to SA)	G	5'11	170	27	5	43	2	13	15	7	8	88	3	6	7	0	4	0	11	9	0.6	1.2	1.4	2.2
John Douglas	G	6'2	180	26	3	12	1	6	17	2	2	100	1	1	0	0	0	0	5	4	0.3	0.3	0.0	1.7
	3-PT FG —				Cummings 0-1, Chambers 0-8, Hodges 20-90, Hollins 3-21, Brooks 5-15, Wood 15-50, Anderson 7-19, Ra. Smith 3-16, Moore 6-23, Brogan 3-13, Gross 1-3, Ro. Smith 0-1, Douglas 1-2																			
PLAYOFFS																								
PHILADELPHIA 76ers	**BILLY CUNNINGHAM**				defeated New York 4-0, H112 -102, H98 -91, 107-105, 105-102; deafeated Milwaukee 4-1; H111-109, H87-81, 104-96, 94-100, H115-103; defeated Los Angeles 4-0; H113-107, H103-93, 111-94, 115 -108																			
Julius Erving	F	6'7	205	32	13	493	95	211	45	49	68	72	99	44	42	1	15	27	239	38	7.6	3.4	3.2	18.4
Bobby Jones	F	6'9	212	31	12	324	43	78	55	17	20	85	58	34	29	0	15	18	103	27	4.8	2.8	2.4	8.6
Moses Malone	C	6'10	255	27	13	524	126	235	54	**86**	**120**	72	**206**	20	40	0	19	25	338	40	15.8	1.5	3.1	26.0
Andrew Toney	G	6'3	188	25	12	357	87	185	47	52	69	75	28	55	43	1	11	1	226	30	2.3	4.6	3.6	18.8
Maurice Cheeks	G	6'1	180	26	13	483	83	165	50	45	64	70	39	91	23	0	26	2	212	37	3.0	7.0	1.8	16.3
Clint Richardson	G	6'3	195	26	13	319	37	83	45	14	17	82	39	23	37	0	15	3	88	25	3.0	1.8	2.8	6.8
Marc Iavaroni	F	6'9	225	26	13	283	29	52	56	9	18	50	57	19	42	1	8	7	67	22	4.4	1.5	3.2	5.2
Clemon Johnson	C-F	6'10	240	26	12	202	25	49	51	0	4	0	43	7	28	0	4	5	50	17	3.6	0.6	2.3	4.2
Franklin Edwards	G	6'1	170	23	12	101	13	32	41	14	17	82	9	17	7	0	5	0	40	8	0.8	1.4	0.6	3.3
Reggie Johnson	F	6'9	205	25	5	32	2	4	50	2	2	100	0	3	5	0	1	0	6	6	0.0	0.6	1.0	1.2
Earl Cureton	F	6'9	215	25	5	25	1	4	25	0	0	—	5	1	5	0	2	0	2	5	1.0	0.2	1.0	0.4
Mark McNamara	C	6'11	235	23	2	2	2	2	100	0	0	—	1	0	0	0	0	0	4	1	0.5	0.0	0.0	2.0
	3-PT FG —				Erving 0-1, Jones 0-1, Malone 0-1, Toney 0-5, Cheeks 1-2																			
LOS ANGELES LAKERS	**PAT RILEY**				defeated Portland 4-1; H118-97, H112-106, 115-109(OT), 95-108, H116-108; defeated San Antonio 4-2; H119-107, H113-122, 113-100, 129-121, H112-117, 101-100; lost to Philadelphia 0-4; 107-113, 93-103, H94-111, H108-115																			
Jamaal Wilkes	F	6'6	190	29	15	589	136	273	50	27	44	61	90	51	51	0	20	11	299	39	6.0	3.4	3.4	19.9
Kurt Rambis	F	6'8	220	24	15	377	45	79	57	23	35	66	90	19	51	0	13	16	113	25	6.0	1.3	3.4	7.5
Kareem Abdul-Jabbar	C	7'2	232	35	15	588	**163**	**287**	57	80	106	75	115	42	**61**	1	17	**55**	406	39	7.7	2.8	4.1	**27.1**
Magic Johnson	G	6'8	215	23	15	**643**	100	206	49	68	81	84	128	**192**	49	0	**34**	12	268	43	8.5	12.8	3.3	17.9
Norm Nixon	G	6'2	175	27	14	538	113	237	48	37	50	74	48	90	40	0	18	1	266	38	3.4	6.4	2.9	19.0
Michael Cooper	G-F	6'5	170	26	15	453	53	114	46	34	41	83	59	44	54	1	26	6	141	30	3.9	2.9	3.6	9.4
Bob McAdoo	C-F	6'9	225	31	8	166	37	84	44	11	14	79	46	5	23	0	11	10	87	21	5.8	0.6	2.9	10.9
Mark Landsberger	F	6'8	230	27	11	141	12	28	43	2	4	50	44	3	24	0	0	2	26	13	4.0	0.3	2.2	2.4
Dwight Jones	F	6'10	210	30	7	59	5	16	31	2	5	40	12	0	11	0	1	0	12	8	1.7	0.0	1.6	1.7
Steve Mix	F	6'7	222	35	8	26	2	5	40	3	3	100	1	0	6	0	0	0	7	3	0.1	0.0	0.8	0.9
Mike McGee	F	6'5	190	23	6	25	4	11	36	3	4	75	7	1	5	0	0	0	12	4	1.2	0.2	0.8	2.0
Clay Johnson	G	6'4	185	26	7	20	4	7	57	0	0	—	4	1	3	0	1	0	8	3	0.6	0.1	0.4	1.1
James Worthy — broken leg	**3 PT FG -**				Wilkes 0-2, Jabbar 0-1, Johnson 0-11, Nixon 3-7, Cooper 1-7, McAdoo 2-6, Landsberger 0-1, McGee 1-1, C.Johnson 0-1																			

Use Name	Pos	Hgt	Wgt	Age	G	Min	FG	FGA	%	FT	FTA	%	Reb	Ass	PF	DQ	Stls	Blkd Shts	Points	Min	Reb	Ass	PF	Points
					TOTAL															PER GAME				
1982/83 N.B.A. — PLAYOFFS																								
SAN ANTONIO SPURS	**STAN ALBECK**	defeated Denver 4-1; H152-133, H126-109, 127-126(ot), 114-124, H145-105; lost to Los Angeles 2-4; 107-119, 122-113, H100-113, H121-129, 117-112, H100-101																						
Mike Mitchell	F	6'7	215	26	11	422	102	200	51	25	33	76	105	12	34	0	7	19	230	38	9.5	1.1	3.1	20.9
Gene Banks	F	6'7	215	23	11	398	76	150	51	23	35	66	76	50	25	1	11	1	175	36	6.9	4.5	2.3	15.9
Artis Gilmore	C	7'2	255	33	11	401	76	132	58	32	46	70	142	18	46	1	9	34	184	36	12.9	1.6	4.2	16.7
George Gervin	G	6'7	185	30	11	437	108	208	52	61	69	88	74	37	39	1	12	4	277	40	6.7	3.4	3.5	25.2
Johnny Moore	G	6'2	185	24	11	414	105	197	53	28	35	80	47	161	41	0	28	3	247	38	4.3	14.6	3.7	22.5
Edgar Jones	F	6'10	225	26	11	193	28	62	45	19	33	58	53	17	44	1	6	14	75	18	4.8	1.5	4.0	6.8
Mike Dunleavy	G	6'3	180	28	11	174	22	65	34	9	13	69	13	49	22	0	9	1	61	16	1.2	4.5	2.0	5.5
Billy Paultz	C	6'11	255	34	11	133	13	32	41	4	4	100	32	11	18	0	4	2	30	12	2.9	1.0	1.6	2.7
Roger Phegley	G-F	6'6	215	26	8	38	9	17	53	3	4	75	8	1	6	0	0	0	24	5	1.0	0.1	0.8	3.0
Mike Sanders	F	6'6	210	22	6	25	7	13	54	0	0	—	9	4	3	0	0	0	14	4	1.5	0.7	0.5	2.3
Robert Smith	G	5'11	170	27	6	19	4	9	44	2	2	100	5	6	2	0	1	0	10	3	0.8	1.0	0.3	1.7
Ed Rains	F	6'7	195	26	3	11	2	5	40	0	0	—	1	1	0	0	0	0	4	4	0.3	0.3	0.0	1.3
3-PT FG —	Mitchell 1-2, Gervin 0-2, Moore 9-17, Jones 0-2, Dunleavy 8-30, Smith 0-1, Rains 0-1																							
MILWAUKEE BUCKS	**DON NELSON**	defeated Boston 4-0; 116-95, 95-91, H107-99, H107-93; lost to Philadelphia 1-4; 109-111, 81-87, H96-104, H100-94, 103-115																						
Junior Bridgeman	F-G	6'5	210	29	9	308	61	130	47	28	30	93	45	28	26	1	10	2	152	34	5.0	3.1	2.9	16.9
Marques Johnson	F	6'7	218	26	9	382	85	175	49	28	43	65	72	38	22	0	8	7	198	42	8.0	4.2	2.4	22.0
Bob Lanier	C	6'11	265	34	9	250	51	89	57	21	35	60	63	23	32	2	5	14	123	28	7.0	2.6	3.6	13.7
Sidney Moncrief	G	6'4	190	25	9	377	62	142	44	46	61	75	60	23	25	1	18	3	170	42	6.7	2.6	2.8	18.9
Brian Winters	G	6'4	185	30	9	240	36	84	43	14	17	82	22	32	22	0	6	4	89	27	2.4	3.6	2.4	9.9
Alton Lister	C-F	7'	240	24	9	206	27	63	43	4	5	80	61	11	30	1	9	15	58	23	6.8	1.2	3.3	6.4
Paul Pressey	G-F	6'5	185	24	9	150	19	47	40	8	20	40	33	14	23	0	9	6	46	17	3.7	1.6	2.6	5.1
Harvey Catchings	F-C	6'9	218	31	9	139	9	19	47	3	3	100	38	4	18	0	2	10	21	15	4.2	0.4	2.0	2.3
Charlie Criss	G	5'8	165	33	9	116	15	34	44	17	18	94	14	12	12	0	9	0	47	13	1.6	1.3	1.3	5.2
Paul Mokeski	C	7'	250	25	4	12	2	4	50	0	0	—	2	1	1	0	1	0	4	3	0.5	0.3	0.3	1.0
Phil Ford	G	6'2	186	26	2	5	0	2	0	6	6	100	0	1	1	0	0	0	6	3	0.0	0.5	0.5	3.0
3-PT FG —	Birdgeman 2-5, Johnson 0-1, Moncrief 0-1, Winters 3-11, Lister 0-1, Pressey 0-1, Criss 0-1																							
DENVER NUGGETS	**DOUG MOE**	defeated Phoenix 2-1; 108-121, H113-99, 117-112(ot); lost to San Antonio 1-4; 133-152, 109-126, H126-127(ot) H124-114, 105-145																						
Alex English	F	6'8	190	28	7	270	67	150	45	47	53	89	44	42	21	0	4	7	181	39	6.3	6.0	3.0	25.9
Kiki Vandeweghe	F	6'8	220	24	8	317	87	160	54	40	50	80	52	32	16	0	4	7	214	40	6.5	4.0	2.0	26.8
Dan Issel	C	6'9	240	34	8	227	69	136	51	25	29	86	58	25	18	0	9	5	163	28	7.3	3.1	2.3	20.4
T.R. Dunn	G	6'4	192	27	8	300	18	41	44	5	8	63	78	20	21	0	12	3	41	38	9.8	2.5	2.6	5.1
Mike Evans	G	6'1	170	27	8	183	36	74	49	11	17	65	19	38	20	0	5	0	86	23	2.4	4.8	2.5	10.8
Dan Schayes	C	6'11	245	23	8	163	21	43	49	15	15	100	40	14	25	0	2	5	57	20	5.0	1.8	3.1	7.1
Bill Hanalik	F-G	6'7	185	25	8	157	20	50	40	14	17	82	25	21	26	0	6	5	54	20	3.1	2.6	3.3	6.8
Rob Williams	G	6'2	175	21	7	134	24	54	44	7	7	100	13	37	27	1	8	1	57	19	1.9	5.3	3.9	8.1
Billy McKinney	G	6'	172	27	8	113	26	46	57	10	18	56	13	18	15	0	2	0	62	14	1.6	2.3	1.9	7.8
Glenn Gondrezick	F	6'6	218	27	6	66	7	19	37	1	2	50	20	4	7	0	0	1	15	11	3.3	0.7	1.2	2.5
Dave Robisch	F-C	6'10	240	33	3	22	1	7	14	0	2	0	9	1	2	0	0	1	2	7	3.0	0.3	0.7	0.7
James Ray	F	6'8	215	25	3	18	1	6	17	1	4	25	3	0	3	0	0	1	3	6	1.0	0.0	1.0	1.0
3-PT FG —	English 0-2, Vandeweghe 0-4, Issel 0-1, Evans 3-10, Hanzlik 0-2, Williams 2-3																							
PORTLAND TRAIL BLAZERS	**JACK RAMSAY**	defeated Seattle 2-0; 108-97, H105-96; lost to Los Angeles 1-4; 97-118, 106-112, H109-115(ot), H108-116																						
Calvin Natt	F	6'6	220	25	7	274	50	102	49	25	33	76	15	18	11	0	9	1	163	39	2.1	2.6	1.6	23.3
Mychal Thompson	F-C	6'10	226	27	7	284	40	85	47	25	38	66	56	39	24	0	6	8	105	41	8.0	5.6	3.4	15.0
Wayne Cooper	C	6'10	220	26	7	228	36	74	49	15	17	88	56	9	33	3	2	8	87	33	8.0	1.3	4.7	12.4
Jim Paxson	G	6'6	200	25	7	260	68	116	59	25	33	76	15	18	11	0	9	1	163	37	2.1	2.6	1.6	23.3
Darnell Valentine	G	6'2	185	23	7	205	34	80	43	16	21	76	15	61	21	0	10	3	85	29	2.1	8.7	3.0	12.1
Kenny Carr	F	6'7	230	27	7	171	26	60	43	18	23	78	51	10	26	0	3	5	70	24	7.3	1.4	3.7	10.0
Lafayette Lever	G	6'3	175	22	7	134	19	42	45	4	5	80	14	31	13	0	7	0	42	19	2.0	4.4	1.9	6.0
Linton Townes	G-F	6'7	195	23	6	60	13	27	48	6	7	86	3	5	11	0	0	0	33	10	0.5	0.8	1.8	5.5
Audie Norris	C	6'9	250	22	7	53	7	13	54	1	2	50	12	5	5	0	2	2	15	8	1:7	0.7	0.7	2.1
Don Buse	G	6'4	195	32	5	31	2	8	25	3	4	75	2	7	2	0	0	0	7	6	0.4	1.4	0.4	1.4
Hank McDowell	F	6'9	215	23	2	4	0	1	0	0	0	—	2	2	2	0	0	0	0	2	1.0	1.0	1.0	0.0
Jeff Lamp	G	6'6	195	23	1	1	1	2	50	0	0	—	0	0	0	0	0	0	2	1	0.0	0.0	0.0	2.0
3-PT FG —	Natt 1-2, Paxson 2-4, Valentine 1-2, Townes 1-3																							
BOSTON CELTICS	**BILL FITCH**	defeated Atlanta 2-1; H103-95, 93-95, H98-79; lost to Milwaukee 4-0; H95-116, H91-95, 99-107, 93-107																						
Cedric Maxwell	F	6'8	215	27	7	246	29	55	53	32	38	84	51	23	18	0	4	4	90	35	7.3	3.3	2.6	12.9
Larry Bird	F	6'9	220	26	6	240	49	116	42	24	29	83	75	41	15	0	13	3	123	40	12.5	6.8	2.5	20.5
Robert Parish	C	7'	230	29	7	249	43	89	48	17	20	85	74	9	18	0	5	9	103	36	10.6	1.3	2.6	14.7
Danny Ainge	G	6'4	175	23	7	201	28	72	39	8	11	73	14	25	24	0	5	1	66	29	2.0	3.6	3.4	9.4
Gerald Henderson	G	6'2	175	26	7	187	35	85	41	6	7	86	14	31	25	1	11	1	76	27	2.0	4.4	3.6	10.9
Kevin McHale	F-C	6'10	225	25	7	177	34	62	55	10	18	56	42	5	16	0	3	7	78	25	6.0	0.7	2.3	11.1
Nate Archibald	G	6'1	160	34	7	161	22	68	32	22	29	76	10	44	12	0	2	0	67	23	1.4	6.3	1.7	9.6
Quinn Buckner	G	6'3	205	28	7	98	16	37	43	0	2	0	10	2	18	1	1	0	32	14	1.4	0.3	2.6	4.6
Scott Wedman	F	6'7	235	30	6	66	14	24	58	1	2	50	14	0	11	0	1	0	29	11	2.3	0.0	1.8	4.8
Rick Robey	C	6'11	230	26	5	29	0	4	0	2	4	50	8	1	4	0	0	0	2	6	1.6	0.2	0.8	0.4
M.L. Carr	G	6'6	205	31	3	22	2	8	25	2	2	100	1	0	3	0	2	0	6	7	0.3	0.0	1.0	2.0
Charles Bradley	G	6'5	215	23	2	4	0	0	—	0	0	—	0	0	0	0	0	0	0	2	0.0	0.0	0.0	0.0
3-PT FG —	Bird 1-4, Ainge 2-5, Henderson 0-3, McHale 0-1, Archibald 1-6, Buckner 0-2, Wedman 0-2, Robey 0-1, Carr 0-1																							

1982/83 N.B.A. — PLAYOFFS

NEW YORK KNICKERBOCKERS — **HUBIE BROWN** — defeated New Jersey 2-0; 118-107, H105-99
lost to Philadelphia 0-4; 102-112, 91-98, H105-107, H102-105

Use Name	Pos	Hgt	Wgt	Age	G	Min	FG	FGA	%	FT	FTA	%	Reb	Ass	PF	DQ	Stls	Blkd Shts	Points	Min (per game)	Reb (per game)	Ass (per game)	PF (per game)	Points (per game)
Bernard King	F	6'7	205	26	6	184	56	97	58	28	35	80	24	13	16	0	2	0	141	31	4.0	2.2	2.7	23.5
Truck Robinson	F	6'7	225	31	6	205	39	73	53	16	28	57	66	13	25	1	10	2	94	34	11.0	2.2	4.2	15.7
Bill Cartwright	C	7'1	245	25	6	172	25	43	58	17	22	77	34	4	25	0	3	7	67	29	5.7	0.7	4.2	11.2
Paul Westphal	G	6'4	195	32	6	156	22	50	44	10	13	77	8	34	13	0	2	2	57	26	1.3	5.7	2.2	9.5
Rory Sparrow	G	6'2	195	24	6	202	30	71	42	17	21	81	13	2	18	1	7	0	78	34	2.2	0.3	3.0	13.0
Ernie Grunfeld	F-G	6'6	215	27	6	118	15	34	44	18	19	95	8	10	17	0	7	2	48	20	1.3	1.7	2.8	8.0
Marvin Webster	C	7'1	240	30	6	115	7	18	39	14	22	64	28	3	18	0	0	7	28	19	4.7	0.5	3.0	4.7
Louis Orr	F	6'8	195	24	6	105	18	47	38	10	10	100	21	3	10	0	5	4	46	18	3.5	0.5	1.7	7.7
Trent Tucker	G	6'5	193	23	6	85	9	15	60	7	10	70	9	5	7	0	2	0	26	14	1.5	0.8	1.2	4.3
Sly Williams	G	6'7	215	24	5	82	16	41	39	3	3	100	21	6	4	0	3	1	36	16	4.2	1.2	0.8	7.2
Ed Sherod	G	6'2	170	23	4	15	1	4	25	0	0	—	1	3	2	0	3	0	2	4	0.3	0.8	0.5	0.5
Mike Davis	F	6'10	230	26	1	1	0	0	—	0	0	—	0	0	0	0	0	0	0	1	0.0	0.0	0.0	0.0

3-PT FG — King 1-3, Westphal 3-8, Sparrow 1-5, Tucker 1-2, Williams 1-1

ATLANTA HAWKS — **KEVIN LOUGHERY** — lost to Boston 1-2; 95-103, H95-93, 79-98

Use Name	Pos	Hgt	Wgt	Age	G	Min	FG	FGA	%	FT	FTA	%	Reb	Ass	PF	DQ	Stls	Blkd Shts	Points	Min (per game)	Reb (per game)	Ass (per game)	PF (per game)	Points (per game)
Dominique Wilkins	F	6'8	200	22	3	109	17	42	40	12	14	86	15	1	9	0	2	1	47	36	5.0	0.3	3.0	15.7
Dan Roundfield	F	6'8	215	29	3	124	24	50	48	5	11	45	42	10	5	0	4	4	35	41	14.0	3.3	1.7	11.7
Tree Rollins	C	7'1	235	27	3	118	13	27	48	3	9	33	30	3	12	1	1	10	29	39	10.0	1.0	4.0	9.7
Mike Glenn	G	6'3	185	27	3	67	12	22	55	4	4	100	5	3	10	0	2	0	28	22	1.7	1.0	3.3	9.3
Johnny Davis	G	6'2	180	27	3	113	21	52	40	9	10	90	5	27	6	0	0	0	51	38	1.7	9.0	2.0	17.0
Rudy Macklin	G-F	6'7	215	24	3	78	11	24	46	8	10	80	15	2	12	0	2	2	30	26	5.0	0.7	4.0	10.0
Tom McMillen	C-F	6'11	235	30	3	39	4	12	33	2	2	100	7	2	5	0	1	2	10	13	2.3	0.7	1.7	3.3
Wes Matthews	G	6'1	170	23	3	38	3	9	33	4	5	80	0	11	5	0	0	1	10	13	0.0	3.7	1.7	3.3
Randy Smith	G	6'3	185	34	2	15	1	5	20	4	4	100	1	4	1	0	1	0	6	8	0.5	2.0	0.5	3.0
Rickey Brown	F	6'10	235	24	2	15	1	3	33	1	2	50	3	0	3	0	0	0	3	8	1.5	0.0	1.5	1.5
Keith Edmonson	G	6'5	205	22	1	2	1	1	100	0	0	—	1	1	0	0	0	0	2	2	1.0	1.0	0.0	2.0
George Johnson	C	6'11	205	34	1	2	0	0	—	0	0	—	0	0	0	0	0	0	0	2	0.0	0.0	0.0	0.0

Eddie Johnson-knee injury

3-PT FG — Wilkins 1-1, Roundfield 0-1, Davis 0-1, Matthews 0-1

PHOENIX SUNS — **JOHN MACLEOD** — lost to Dnever 1-2; H121-108, 99-113, H112-117(OT)

Use Name	Pos	Hgt	Wgt	Age	G	Min	FG	FGA	%	FT	FTA	%	Reb	Ass	PF	DQ	Stls	Blkd Shts	Points	Min (per game)	Reb (per game)	Ass (per game)	PF (per game)	Points (per game)
Alvin Scott	F	6'7	215	27	3	62	6	13	46	2	2	100	12	5	6	0	2	5	14	21	4.0	1.7	2.0	4.7
Larry Nance	F	6'10	215	23	3	103	14	35	40	8	10	80	25	3	12	1	3	6	36	34	8.3	1.0	4.0	12.0
Alvan Adams	C	6'9	220	28	3	84	15	32	47	5	7	71	18	14	15	0	2	5	35	28	6.0	4.7	5.0	11.7
Walter Davis	G	6'6	200	28	3	113	30	69	43	17	21	81	15	13	6	0	6	5	78	38	5.0	4.3	2.0	26.0
Dennis Johnson	G	6'4	200	28	3	108	22	48	46	10	12	83	23	17	9	0	5	2	54	36	7.7	5.7	3.0	18.0
Kyle Macy	G	6'3	190	25	3	72	15	35	43	5	7	71	8	9	6	0	1	0	35	24	2.7	3.0	2.0	11.7
Maurice Lucas	F-C	6'9	238	30	2	57	12	21	57	2	4	50	12	8	5	0	3	0	26	29	6.0	4.0	2.5	13.0
James Edwards	C	7'	225	27	3	54	11	26	42	6	6	100	18	4	7	0	1	1	28	18	6.0	1.3	2.3	9.3
Johnny High	G	6'3	185	25	3	45	5	11	45	0	2	0	10	6	7	0	3	1	10	15	3.3	2.0	2.3	3.3
Rory White	F	6'8	210	23	3	40	7	14	50	2	4	50	10	0	4	0	0	0	16	13	3.3	0.0	1.3	5.3
Joel Kramer	F	6'7	203	27	2	6	0	2	0	0	0	—	0	0	0	0	0	0	0	3	0.0	0.0	0.0	0.0
Charles Pittman	F	6'8	220	24	1	1	0	0	—	0	0	—	0	0	0	0	0	0	0	1	0.0	0.0	0.0	0.0

3-PT FG — Davis 1-2, Johnson 0-1, Macy 0-3, High 0-1, White 0-1

NEW JERSEY NETS — **BILL BLAIR** — lost to New York 0-2; H107-118, 99-105

Use Name	Pos	Hgt	Wgt	Age	G	Min	FG	FGA	%	FT	FTA	%	Reb	Ass	PF	DQ	Stls	Blkd Shts	Points	Min (per game)	Reb (per game)	Ass (per game)	PF (per game)	Points (per game)
Albert King	F	6'6	190	23	2	68	18	38	47	5	6	83	8	3	12	2	2	0	42	34	4.0	1.5	6.0	21.0
Buck Williams	F	6'8	215	22	2	85	11	22	50	16	20	80	23	4	12	2	2	2	38	43	11.5	2.0	6.0	19.0
Darrell Dawkins	C	6'11	251	25	2	59	17	22	77	2	2	100	10	2	7	0	4	5	36	30	5.0	1.0	3.5	18.0
Darwin Cook	G	6'3	190	24	2	63	9	27	33	2	2	100	6	10	8	0	1	0	20	32	3.0	5.0	4.0	10.0
Michael Ray Richardson	G	6'5	195	27	2	58	8	21	38	3	5	60	8	5	3	0	5	0	19	29	4.0	2.5	1.5	9.5
Otis Birdsong	G	6'4	195	27	2	37	6	16	38	1	2	50	2	9	3	0	3	0	13	19	1.0	4.5	1.5	6.5
Foots Walker	G	6'1	172	31	2	36	2	6	33	3	3	100	0	11	1	0	0	0	7	18	0.0	5.5	0.5	3.5
Mike Gminski	C	6'11	250	23	2	29	6	9	67	3	4	75	9	1	2	0	0	4	15	15	4.5	0.5	1.0	7.5
Mike O'Koren	F	6'7	217	24	2	18	2	8	25	0	0	—	6	3	3	0	0	0	4	9	3.0	1.5	1.5	2.0
Len Elmore	C-F	6'9	220	30	2	15	2	5	40	1	2	50	9	1	4	0	1	0	5	8	4.5	0.5	2.0	2.5
Eddie Phillips	F	6'7	225	21	2	12	3	6	50	1	4	25	5	3	2	0	0	0	7	6	2.5	1.5	1.0	3.5

3-PT FG — King 1-2, Dawkins 0-1, Cook 0-1, Richardson 0-1, Birdsong 0-1, Phillips 0-2

SEATTLE SUPERSONICS — **LENNY WILKINS** — lost to Portland 0-2; H97-108, 96-105

Use Name	Pos	Hgt	Wgt	Age	G	Min	FG	FGA	%	FT	FTA	%	Reb	Ass	PF	DQ	Stls	Blkd Shts	Points	Min (per game)	Reb (per game)	Ass (per game)	PF (per game)	Points (per game)
Danny Vranes	F	6'7	210	24	2	56	6	17	35	0	0	—	19	1	7	0	0	1	12	28	9.5	0.5	3.5	6.0
Lonnie Shelton	F	6'8	255	27	2	53	4	23	17	2	5	40	21	5	7	0	1	0	10	27	10.5	2.5	3.5	5.0
Jack Sikma	C-F	6'11	250	27	2	75	11	31	35	9	12	75	26	11	7	0	2	2	30	38	13.0	5.5	3.5	15.0
David Thompson	G	6'4	195	28	2	65	9	25	36	6	10	60	0	7	7	0	1	1	24	33	0.0	3.5	3.5	12.0
Gus Williams	G	6'2	175	29	2	81	26	47	55	13	15	87	7	8	5	0	5	0	65	41	3.5	4.0	2.5	32.5
James Donaldson	C	7'2	278	25	2	47	11	22	50	2	3	67	17	2	4	0	0	3	24	24	8.5	1.0	2.0	12.0
Steve Hawes	F	6'9	220	32	2	35	5	10	50	2	3	67	6	2	8	0	0	0	12	18	3.0	1.0	4.0	6.0
Fred Brown	G	6'3	185	34	2	30	2	9	22	2	2	100	3	5	3	0	1	0	6	15	1.5	2.5	1.5	3.0
Phil Smith	G	6'4	197	30	2	19	3	6	50	0	0	—	3	1	1	0	0	0	6	10	1.5	0.5	0.5	3.0
Greg Kelser	F	6'7	205	25	2	19	2	5	40	0	0	—	6	1	4	0	1	0	4	10	3.0	0.5	2.0	2.0

3-PT FG — Shelton 0-3, Sikma 0-1, Williams 0-2

TEAM STATISTICS

EASTERN CONFERENCE

ATLANTIC DIVISION

Team		G	FG	FGA	%	FT	FTA	%	Rebounds Offense	Rebounds Defense	Rebounds Total	Assists	PF	Steals	Blocked Shots	Turn Overs	Points	Points per game
Philadelphia	Off.	82	3600	7212	50	1966	2650	74	1334	2596	**3930**	2016	2041	812	577	1627	9191	112.1
	Def.	82	3442	7470	46	1624	2253	72	1325	2263	3588	2089	2246	755	511	1590	8562	104.4
	Diff.		+158	-258	+4	+342	+397	+2	+9	+333	+342	-73	+205	+57	+66	-37	**+629**	**7.7**
Boston	Off.	82	3711	7547	49	1730	2348	74	1273	2532	3805	2216	2062	789	521	1541	9191	112.1
	Def.	82	3477	7401	47	1750	2307	76	1186	2393	3579	2027	2137	699	340	1607	8752	106.7
	Diff.		+234	+146	+2	-20	+41	-2	+87	+139	+226	+189	+75	+90	+181	+66	+439	5.4
New Jersey	Off.	82	3510	7140	49	1622	2301	70	1266	2427	3693	2143	2166	**911**	592	1873	8672	105.8
	Def.	82	3327	6962	48	1746	2370	74	1102	2176	3278	1978	2129	860	495	**1871**	8445	103.0
	Diff.		+183	+178	+1	-124	-69	-4	+164	+251	**+415**	+165	-37	+51	+97	-2	+227	2.8
New York	Off.	82	3272	6793	48	1621	2282	71	1080	2263	3343	2034	2180	701	378	1509	8198	100.0
	Def.	82	3132	6592	48	1695	2260	75	1073	2337	3410	1873	2116	694	399	1682	**7997**	**97.5**
	Diff.		+140	+201	—	-74	+22	-4	+7	-74	-67	+161	-64	+7	-21	**+173**	+201	2.5
Washington	Off.	82	3306	7059	47	1452	2059	71	1099	2430	3529	2046	1958	733	400	1588	8134	99.2
	Def.	82	3299	7044	47	1510	2084	72	1114	2514	3628	1871	1975	698	555	1543	8145	99.3
	Diff.		+7	+15	—	-58	-25	-1	-15	-84	-99	+175	+17	+35	-155	-45	-11	-0.1

CENTRAL DIVISION

Team		G	FG	FGA	%	FT	FTA	%	Rebounds Offense	Rebounds Defense	Rebounds Total	Assists	PF	Steals	Blocked Shots	Turn Overs	Points	Points per game
Milwaukee	Off.	82	3486	7133	49	1731	2299	75	1095	2477	3572	2116	2131	662	532	1447	8740	106.6
	Def.	82	3338	7318	46	1665	2243	74	1303	2343	3646	2043	2145	623	300	1523	8379	102.2
	Diff.		+148	-185	+3	+66	+56	+1	-208	+134	-74	+73	+14	+39	+232	+76	+361	4.4
Atlanta	Off.	82	3352	7146	47	1586	2111	75	1139	2433	3572	1945	2022	573	**665**	1424	8335	101.6
	Def.	82	3383	7201	47	1608	2235	72	1303	2571	3874	1927	1981	656	388	1468	8413	102.6
	Diff.		-31	-55	—	-22	-124	+3	-164	-138	-302	+18	-41	-83	**+277**	+44	-78	-1.0
Detroit	Off.	82	3623	7602	48	1921	2588	74	1312	2477	3789	2108	2122	679	572	1557	9239	112.7
	Def.	82	3802	7679	50	1647	2287	72	1266	2594	3860	2252	2326	761	561	1580	9272	113.1
	Diff.		-179	-77	-2	+274	+301	+2	+46	-117	-71	-144	+204	-82	+11	+23	-33	-0.4
Chicago	Off.	82	3537	7373	48	1983	2690	74	1267	2527	3794	2086	2192	666	400	1743	9102	111.0
	Def.	82	3816	7712	49	1825	2438	75	1197	2456	3653	2230	2266	845	633	1462	9503	115.9
	Diff.		-279	-339	-1	+158	+252	-1	+70	+71	+141	-144	+74	-179	-233	-281	-401	-4.9
Cleveland	Off.	82	3252	6995	46	1430	1983	72	1173	2414	3587	1738	2236	617	290	1538	7964	97.1
	Def.	82	3381	6911	49	1780	2396	74	974	2382	3356	2005	1830	621	431	1275	8574	104.6
	Diff.		-129	+84	-3	-350	-413	-2	+199	+32	+231	-267	-406	-4	-141	-263	-610	-7.5
Indiana	Off.	82	3707	7723	48	1447	1910	76	1299	2294	3593	2150	2086	755	411	1535	8911	108.7
	Def.	82	3768	7284	52	1815	2413	75	1206	2564	3770	2237	1886	761	439	1643	9391	114.5
	Diff.		-61	+439	-4	-368	-503	+1	+93	-270	-177	-87	-200	-6	-28	+108	-480	-5.8

WESTERN CONFERENCE

MIDWEST DIVISION

Team		G	FG	FGA	%	FT	FTA	%	Rebounds Offense	Rebounds Defense	Rebounds Total	Assists	PF	Steals	Blocked Shots	Turn Overs	Points	Points per game
San Antonio	Off.	82	3697	7340	50	1887	2468	76	1232	**2599**	3831	2261	2095	675	469	1504	9375	114.3
	Def.	82	3654	7531	49	1716	2239	77	1160	2263	3423	2329	2199	654	457	1430	9075	110.7
	Diff.		+43	-191	+1	+171	+229	-1	+72	**+336**	+408	-68	+104	+21	+12	-74	+300	3.6
Denver	Off.	82	**3951**	**7999**	49	**2179**	**2696**	**81**	1214	2524	3738	2336	2091	789	352	1496	**10105**	**123.2**
	Def.	82	4098	8120	50	1787	2393	75	1369	2697	4066	2389	**2356**	728	611	1636	10054	122.6
	Diff.		-147	-121	-1	**+392**	+303	**+6**	-155	-173	-328	-53	+265	+61	-259	+140	+51	0.6
Kansas City	Off.	82	3719	7485	50	1839	2530	73	1256	2407	3663	2155	2432	765	409	1691	9328	113.8
	Def.	82	3531	7250	49	2107	2885	73	1250	2403	3653	1997	2245	809	439	1716	9209	112.3
	Diff.		+188	+235	+1	-268	-355	—	+6	+4	+10	+158	-187	-44	-30	+25	+119	1.5
Dallas	Off.	82	3674	7550	49	1852	2462	75	1296	2381	3677	2227	2067	552	348	**1348**	9243	112.7
	Def.	82	3758	7481	50	1708	2347	73	1217	2433	3650	2291	2227	607	562	1383	9277	113.1
	Diff.		-84	+69	-1	+144	+115	+2	+79	-52	+27	-64	+160	-55	-214	+35	-34	-0.4
Utah	Off.	82	3525	7342	48	1844	2440	76	1093	2550	3643	2176	2107	758	595	1683	8938	109.0
	Def.	82	3794	7932	48	1646	2288	72	1439	2671	4110	2202	2102	826	448	1601	9282	113.2
	Diff.		-269	-590		+198	+152	+4	-346	-121	-467	-26	-5	-68	+147	-82	-344	-4.2
Houston	Off.	82	3338	7446	45	1402	1934	72	1206	2260	3466	1931	2131	646	422	1571	8145	99.3
	Def.	82	3641	7244	50	1781	2375	75	1198	2710	3908	2252	1933	772	406	1504	9096	110.9
	Diff.		-303	+202	-5	-379	-441	-3	+8	-450	-442	-321	-198	-126	+16	-67	-951	-11.6

Team		G	FG	FGA	%	FT	FTA	%	REBOUNDS			Assists	PF	Steals	Blocked Shots	Turn Overs	Points	Points per game
									Offense	Defense	Total							
TEAM STATISTICS																		
WESTERN CONFERENCE																		
PACIFIC DIVISION																		
Los Angeles	Off.	82	3964	7512	53	1495	2031	74	1235	2433	3668	2519	1931	844	479	1584	9433	115.0
	Def.	82	3734	7619	49	1455	2008	72	1294	2166	3460	2389	1863	766	380	1562	8978	109.5
	Diff.		+230	-107	+4	+40	+23	+2	-59	+267	+208	+130	-68	+78	+99	-22	+455	+5.5
Phoenix	Off.	82	3555	7158	50	1626	2189	74	1094	2518	3612	2300	2062	749	495	1545	8776	107.0
	Def.	82	3305	7265	45	1707	2268	75	1210	2326	3536	1988	2039	712	343	1560	8361	102.0
	Diff.		+250	-107	+5	-81	-79	-1	-116	+192	+76	+312	-23	+37	+152	+15	+415	+5.0
Seattle	Off.	82	3597	7277	49	1796	2459	73	1152	2569	3721	2278	1969	677	437	1533	9019	110.0
	Def.	82	3541	7703	46	1615	2184	74	1314	2397	3711	2146	2152	726	360	1443	8756	106.8
	Diff.		+56	-426	+3	+181	+275	-1	-162	+172	+10	+132	+183	-49	+77	-90	+263	+3.2
Portland	Off.	82	3459	7124	49	1855	2512	74	1180	2380	3560	2030	1960	749	384	1495	8808	107.4
	Def.	82	3503	7211	49	1572	2046	77	1126	2364	3490	2072	2232	658	500	1546	8633	105.3
	Diff.		-44	-87	—	+283	+466	-3	+54	+16	+70	-42	+272	+91	-116	+51	+175	+2.1
Golden State	Off.	82	3627	7508	48	1620	2199	74	1281	2284	3565	1964	2138	856	430	1606	8908	108.6
	Def.	82	3706	7260	51	1751	2391	73	1249	2495	3744	2170	2026	758	489	1690	9205	112.3
	Diff.		-79	+248	-3	-131	-192	+1	+32	-211	-179	-206	-112	+98	-59	+84	-297	-3.7
San Diego	Off.	82	3625	7634	47	1589	2195	72	1394	2108	3502	2087	2284	820	408	1600	8903	108.6
	Def.	82	3652	6910	53	1963	2626	75	1095	2365	3460	2105	1962	789	519	1723	9299	113.4
	Diff.		-27	+724	-6	-374	-431	-3	+299	-257	+42	-18	-322	+31	-111	+123	-396	-4.8
PLAYOFFS																		
Philadelphia	Off.	13	543	1100	49	288	399	72	202	382	584	314	301	121	88	235	1375	105.8
	Def.	13	513	1131	45	253	333	76	197	347	544	304	351	114	80	232	1291	99.3
	Diff.		+30	-31	+4	+35	+66	-4	+5	+35	+40	+10	+50	+7	+8	-3	+84	+6.5
Los Angeles	Off.	15	674	1347	50	290	387	75	215	429	644	448	378	141	113	260	1645	109.7
	Def.	15	668	1361	49	284	397	72	242	431	673	441	343	117	88	270	1637	109.1
	Diff.		+6	-14	+1	+6	-10	+3	-27	-2	-29	+7	-35	+24	+25	+10	+8	+.6
San Antonio	Off.	11	552	1090	51	206	274	75	170	395	565	367	280	87	78	190	1331	121.0
	Def.	11	519	1060	49	241	317	76	161	334	495	358	260	97	68	187	1284	116.7
	Diff.		+33	+30	+2	-35	-43	-1	+9	+61	+70	+9	-20	-10	+10	-3	+47	+4.3
Milwaukee	Off.	9	367	789	47	175	238	74	153	257	410	197	212	77	61	147	914	101.6
	Def.	9	359	764	47	170	230	74	121	254	375	212	213	74	42	150	889	98.8
	Diff.		+8	+25	—	+5	+8	—	+32	+3	+35	-15	+1	+3	+19	+3	+25	+2.8
Denver	Off.	8	377	786	48	176	222	79	105	269	374	252	201	52	36	134	935	116.9
	Def.	8	411	837	49	164	214	77	121	310	431	260	217	76	67	121	996	124.5
	Diff.		-34	-51	-1	+12	+8	+2	-16	-41	-57	-8	+16	-24	-31	-13	-61	-7.6
Portland	Off.	7	296	610	49	144	198	73	94	196	290	198	162	47	28	113	741	105.9
	Def.	7	309	627	49	130	181	72	104	218	322	197	176	59	44	105	749	107.0
	Diff.		-13	-17	—	+14	+17	+1	-10	-22	-32	+1	+14	-12	-16	-8	-8	-1.1
Boston	Off.	7	272	620	44	124	162	77	100	213	313	181	164	47	25	110	672	96.0
	Def.	7	277	597	46	137	184	74	99	215	314	147	153	40	43	109	694	99.1
	Diff.		-5	+23	-2	-13	-22	+3	+1	-2	-1	+34	-11	+7	-18	-1	-22	-3.1
New York	Off.	6	238	493	48	140	183	77	76	157	233	136	155	44	25	102	623	103.8
	Def.	6	250	508	49	126	173	73	91	170	261	152	154	49	33	105	628	104.7
	Diff.		-12	-15	-1	+14	+10	+4	-15	-13	-28	-16	-1	-5	-8	+3	-5	-.9
Atlanta	Off.	3	108	247	44	52	71	73	33	91	124	64	68	13	20	48	269	89.7
	Def.	3	118	274	43	55	70	79	52	103	155	79	66	19	17	51	294	98.0
	Diff.		-10	-27	+1	-3	+1	-6	-19	-12	-31	-15	-2	-6	+3	+3	-25	-8.3
Phoenix	Off.	3	137	306	45	57	75	76	49	102	151	79	77	26	25	40	332	110.7
	Def.	3	139	280	50	57	68	84	35	103	138	90	76	12	15	45	338	112.7
	Diff.		-2	+26	-5	—	+7	-8	+14	-1	+13	-11	-1	+14	+10	+5	-6	-2.0
New Jersey	Off.	2	84	180	47	37	50	74	34	52	86	52	57	18	11	33	206	103.0
	Def.	2	86	162	53	50	68	74	27	53	80	44	51	16	12	36	223	111.5
	Diff.		-2	+18	-6	-13	-18	—	+7	-1	+6	+8	-6	+2	-1	+3	-17	-8.5
Seattle	Off.	2	79	195	41	35	50	70	41	67	108	43	53	11	7	23	193	96.5
	Def.	2	78	162	48	57	74	77	22	72	94	47	48	11	8	24	213	106.5
	Diff.		+1	+33	-7	-22	-24	-7	+19	-5	+14	-4	-5	—	-1	+1	-20	-10.0

Team	W	L	Pct.	GB	Record against playoff teams W	L	Pct.	Record against non-playoff teams W	L	Pct.	HOME W	L	Pct.	ROAD W	L	Pct.
EASTERN CONFERENCE																
ATLANTIC DIVISION																
Philadelphia 76ers	**65**	17	**.793**	—	**29**	13	**.690**	**36**	4	**.900**	**35**	6	**.854**	**30**	11	**.732**
Boston Celtics	56	26	.683	9	**29**	13	**.690**	27	13	.675	26	15	.634	**30**	11	**.732**
New Jersey Nets	49	33	.598	16	20	21	.488	29	12	.707	30	11	.732	19	22	.463
New York Knickerbockers	44	38	.537	21	16	25	.390	28	13	.683	26	15	.634	18	23	.439
Washington Bullets	42	40	.512	23	21	27	.438	21	13	.618	22	19	.537	20	21	.488
CENTRAL DIVISION																
Milwaukee Bucks	51	31	.622	—	20	20	.500	31	11	.738	31	10	.756	20	21	.488
Atlanta Hawks	43	39	.524	8	13	27	.325	30	12	.714	26	15	.634	17	24	.415
Detroit Pistons	37	45	.451	14	16	31	.340	21	14	.600	23	18	.561	14	27	.341
Chicago Bulls	28	54	.341	23	10	36	.217	18	18	.500	18	23	.439	10	31	.243
Cleveland Cavaliers	23	59	.280	28	5	**42**	.106	18	17	.514	15	26	.366	8	33	.195
Indiana Pacers	20	62	.244	31	9	37	.196	11	25	.306	14	27	.341	6	35	.146
WESTERN CONFERENCE																
MIDWEST DIVISION																
San Antonio Spurs	53	29	.646	—	19	19	.500	34	10	.773	31	10	.756	22	19	.537
Denver Nuggets	45	37	.549	8	16	22	.421	29	15	.659	29	12	.707	16	25	.390
Kansas City Kings	45	37	.549	8	17	27	.386	28	10	.737	30	11	.732	15	26	.366
Dallas Mavericks	38	44	.463	15	15	29	.341	23	15	.605	23	18	.561	15	26	.366
Utah Jazz	30	52	.366	23	8	36	.182	22	16	.579	21	20	.512	9	32	.220
Houston Rockets	14	**68**	.171	39	4	40	.091	10	**28**	.263	9	**32**	.220	5	**36**	.122
PACIFIC DIVISION																
Los Angeles Lakers	58	24	.707	—	23	17	.575	35	7	.833	33	8	.804	25	16	.610
Phoenix Suns	53	29	.646	5	22	18	.550	31	11	.738	32	9	.780	21	20	.512
Seattle Supersonics	48	34	.585	10	16	24	.400	32	10	.762						
Portland Trail Blazers	46	36	.561	12	18	22	.450	28	14	.667	31	10	.756	15	26	.366
Golden State Warriors	30	52	.366	28	15	31	.326	15	21	.417	21	20	.512	9	32	.220
San Diego Clippers	25	57	.305	33	12	24	.333	13	23	.361	18	23	.439	7	34	.171

1982/83 N.B.A. INDIVIDUAL LEADERS

SCORING
(Minimum 70 Games or 1400 Points)

Name	Team	G	FG	FT	Pts.	Avg.
English	Den	82	959	406	2326	28.4
Vandeweghe	Den	82	841	489	2186	26.7
Tripucka	Det	58	565	392	1536	26.5
Gervin	SA	78	757	517	2043	26.2
Malone	Phi	78	654	600	1908	24.5
Aguirre	Dall	81	767	429	1979	24.4
Carroll	GS	79	785	337	1907	24.1
Free	Cle	73	649	430	1743	23.9
Theus	Chi	82	749	434	1953	23.8
Cummings	SD	70	684	292	1660	23.7

FIELD GOAL PERCENTAGE
(Minimum 300 Made)

Name	Team	FG	FGA	Pct.
Gilmore	SA	556	888	.626
S. Johnson	KC	371	595	.624
Dawkins	NJ	401	669	.599
Abdul-Jabbar	LA	722	1228	.588
B. Williams	NJ	536	912	.588
Woolridge	Chi	361	622	.580
Worthy	LA	447	772	.579
B. Davis	Dall	359	628	.572
Cartwright	NY	455	804	.566
Ruland	Was	580	1051	.552

FREE THROW PERCENTAGE
(Minimum 125 Made)

Name	Team	FT	FTA	Pct.
Murphy	Hou	138	150	.920
Vandeweghe	Den	489	559	.875
Macy	Phoe	129	148	.872
Gervin	SA	517	606	.853
Dantley	Utah	210	248	.847
B. Davis	Dall	186	220	.845
Tripucka	Det	392	464	.845
Knight	Ind	343	408	.841
Bird	Bos	351	418	.840
Sikma	Sea	400	478	.837

PERSONAL FOULS

Name	Team	PF
Dawkins	NJ	379
Mahorn	Was	335
Chambers	SD	333
Lister	Mil	328
Schayes	Utah-Den	325

GAMES DISQUALIFIED

Name	Team	Disq.
Dawkins	NJ	23
Lister	Mil	18
Chambers	SD	15
Mahorn	Was	13
Ruland	Was	12

TOTAL REBOUNDS PER GAME
(Minimum 70 Games or 800 Rebounds)

Name	Team	G	Reb.	Avg.
Malone	Phi	78	1194	15.3
B. Williams	NJ	82	1027	12.5
Laimbeer	Det	82	993	12.1
Gilmore	SA	82	984	12.0
Sikma	Sea	75	858	11.4
Roundfield	Atl	77	880	11.4
C. Robinson	Cle	77	856	11.1
Ruland	Was	79	871	11.0
Bird	Bos	79	870	11.0
Cummings	SD	70	744	10.6

ASSISTS PER GAME
(Minimum 70 Games or 400 Assists)

Name	Team	G	Ass.	Avg.
M. Johnson	LA	79	829	10.5
Moore	SA	77	753	9.8
Green	Utah	78	697	8.9
Drew	KC	75	610	8.1
F. Johnson	Was	68	549	8.1
G. Williams	Sea	80	642	8.0
R. Williams	KC	72	569	7.9
Thomas	Det	81	634	7.8
Nixon	LA	79	566	7.2
B. Davis	Dall	79	565	7.2

MINUTES PLAYED

Name	Team	Min.
Thomas	Det	3093
Mahorn	Was	3023
Thompson	Port	3017
English	Den	2988
Carroll	GS	2988

BLOCKED SHOTS PER GAME
(Minimum 70 Games or 100 Blocked Shots)

Name	Team	G	Reb.	Avg.
Rollins	Atl	80	343	4.3
Walton	SD	33	119	3.6
Eaton	Utah	81	275	3.4
Nance	Phoe	82	217	2.6
Gilmore	SA	82	192	2.3
McHale	Bos	82	192	2.3
Lister	Mil	80	177	2.2
H. Williams	Ind	78	171	2.2
Abdul-Jabbar	LA	79	170	2.2
Malone	Phi	78	157	2.0

3 POINT FIELD GOALS PER GAME
(Minimum 25 Made)

Name	Team	FG	FGA	Avg.
Dunleavy	SA	67	194	.345
Thomas	Det	36	125	.288
Griffith	Utah	38	132	.288
Leavell	Hou	42	175	.240

STEALS PER GAME
(Minimum 70 Games or 125 Steals)

Name	Team	G	Steals	Avg.
Richardson	NJ	64	182	2.8
Green	Utah	78	220	2.8
Moore	SA	77	194	2.5
Thomas	Det	81	199	2.5
Cook	NJ	82	194	2.4
Cheeks	Phi	79	184	2.3
G. Williams	Sea	80	182	2.3
M. Johnson	LA	79	176	2.2
Leavell	Hou	79	165	2.1
Lever	Port	81	153	1.9

1983-84 N.B.A.
16 of 23 Teams into the Playoffs

Two legends of the N.B.A. passed important milestones and a potential legend began his pro career. In the end, however, the 1983-84 season belonged to another legend-in-the making in Boston.

Elvin Hayes, winding up his 16-year career in Houston as Ralph Sampson's backup, passed John Havlicek as the all-time leader in games played. He finished as the third-leading scorer and rebounder in N.B.A. history. Meanwhile, under the tutelage of Hayes and new coach Bill Fitch, the 7-foot-4 Sampson captured the Rookie of the Year award. The Rockets improved by 15 games, but couldn't escape the Midwest Division cellar.

In Los Angeles, Kareem Abdul-Jabbar was still going strong in his 15th season. On April 5 he passed Wilt Chamberlain's career scoring mark of 31,419 points; in addition he replaced Moses Malone as center on the all-pro team while leading the Lakers to their third straight Pacific Division title.

Though he led the league's rebounders for the fourth time in a row, Malone had a disappointing season in Philadelphia. Picked by most to repeat as champs, the 76ers fell to 52 wins, then suffered a shocking first-round playoff loss to New Jersey. Replacing them atop the Atlantic Division were the revitalized Celtics. New coach K.C. Jones eliminated the dissension that had developed under Fitch; Dennis Johnson, acquired from Phoenix, added stability in the backcourt; Robert Parish and Kevin McHale provided power up front; and when all else failed, Boston called on Larry Bird, who was named MVP after finishing second in the balloting three times in a row.

Many thought the award should have gone to New York's Bernard King, who led the Knicks to a 47-35 record. In fact, King edged Bird by two votes for Player of the Year in a Sporting News poll of the league's players. New Jersey had no MVP candidates, but Buck Williams and Otis Birdsong led the Nets to 45 wins under new coach Stan Abeck, Washington's Jeff Ruland emerged as a major force at center, but the Bullets fell to 35-47. Still, they qualified for the last playoff spot under the league's new expanded format.

In the Central Division, Sidney Moncrief and Marques Johnson led Milwaukee to its fourth straight title, a game ahead of Detroit. The Pistons, under new coach Chuck Daly, won 49 games, relying as usual on their "class of 1981-82"—Isiah Thomas, Kelly Tripucka and Bill Laimbeer. Atlanta also slipped into the playoffs, but Cleveland, Chicago and Indiana managed only 81 wins among them.

Scoring champion Adrian Dantley and Coach of the Year Frank Layden led Utah, the league's surprise team, to the Midwest Division title. The Jazz backed up Dantley with scorers Darrell Griffith and John Drew and shot-blocker Mark Eaton. Dallas, two games back, continued to improve with the nucleus they picked up in the 1981 draft—Mark Aquirre and Rolando Blackman in particular. Despite the scoring of Kiki Vandewenghe and Alex English, Denver fell to 38-44. A 186-184 triple-overtime loss to Detroit, the highest-scoring game in league history, epitomized their frustrating season. Kansas City and San Antonio also fell off, with the Kings edging out the Spurs for the final playoff berth in the West.

All that earned them the right to be demolished in three games by the Lakers, who lost their usual first-round bye with the playoff field increased from 12 to 16 teams. Rookie Byron Scott, obtained from San Diego for Norm Nixon, was erratic, and a stomach infection hampered Jamaal Wilkes late in the season, but the Lakers moved in Michael Cooper and James Worthy as starters and scarcely missed a beat. Portland finished second with a balanced offense orchestrated by coach Jack Ramsey; Seattle and Phoenix made the playoffs though falling to 42 and 41 wins, respectively. Golden State missed out by a game despite the scoring of Purvis Short and Joe Barry Carroll, and San Diego again brought up the rear despite the presence of Nixon, Terry Cummings and Bill Walton.

Phoenix upset Portland and Utah in the playoffs before falling to Los Angeles in the Western finals. In the East, Boston survived a seven-game series with New York, then disposed of Milwaukee in five games. Then the Lakers and Celtics squared off for the first time since the days of Bill Russell. In addition, it was the first confrontation between Magic Johnson and Larry Bird since the 1979 NCAA championship game. The Lakers won the first and third games easily, but lost the second and fourth, both in overtime. Boston took the next one, but the Lakers came back to force a seventh game. The largest TV audience in N.B.A. history watched as the Celtics scratched out a 111-102 win. Bird, the playoff MVP, led everyone with 27 points and 11 rebounds per game, providing a taste of what was to come in the next few years.

					TOTAL													Blkd		PER GAME				
Use Name	Pos	Hgt	Wgt	Age	G	Min	FG	FGA	%	FT	FTA	%	Reb	Ass	PF	DQ	Stls	Shts	Points	Min	Reb	Ass	PF	Points
1983/84 N.B.A. — EASTERN CONFERENCE																								
ATLANTIC DIVISION																								
BOSTON CELTICS	**62-20 .756**	**K. C. JONES**																						
Cedric Maxwell	F	6'8	215	28	80	2502	317	596	53	320	425	75	461	205	224	4	63	24	955	31	5.8	2.6	2.8	11.9
Larry Bird	F	6'9	220	27	79	3028	758	1542	49	374	421	89	796	520	197	0	144	69	1908	38	10.1	6.6	2.5	24.2
Robert Parish	C	7'	230	30	80	2867	623	1140	55	274	368	74	857	139	266	7	55	116	1520	36	10.7	1.7	3.3	19.0
Dennis Johnson	G	6'4	200	29	80	2665	384	878	44	281	330	85	280	338	251	6	93	57	1053	33	3.5	4.2	3.1	13.2
Gerald Henderson	G	6'2	175	27	78	2088	376	718	52	136	177	77	147	300	209	1	117	14	908	27	1.9	3.8	2.7	11.6
Kevin McHale	F-C	6'10	225	26	82	2577	587	1055	56	336	439	77	610	104	243	5	23	126	1511	31	7.4	1.3	3.0	18.4
Quinn Buckner	G	6'3	205	29	79	1249	138	323	43	48	74	65	137	214	187	0	84	3	324	16	1.7	2.7	2.4	4.1
Danny Ainge	G	6'4	175	24	71	1154	166	361	46	46	56	82	116	162	143	2	41	4	384	16	1.6	2.3	2.0	5.4
Scott Wedman	F-G	6'7	235	31	68	916	148	333	44	29	35	83	139	67	107	0	27	7	327	13	2.0	1.0	1.6	4.8
M.L.Carr	G	6'6	205	32	60	585	70	171	41	42	48	88	75	49	67	0	17	4	185	10	1.3	0.8	1.1	3.1
Greg Kite	C	6'11	250	22	35	197	30	66	45	5	16	31	62	7	42	0	1	5	65	6	1.8	0.2	1.2	1.9
Carlos Clark	G	6'4	210	23	31	127	19	52	37	16	18	89	17	17	13	0	8	1	54	4	0.5	0.5	0.4	1.7

3-PT FG — Maxwell 1-6, Bird 18-73, Johnson 4-32, Henderson 20-57, McHale 1-3, Buckner 0-6, Ainge 6-22, Wedman 2-13, Carr 3-15, Clark 0-2

1983/84 N.B.A. — EASTERN CONFERENCE
ATLANTIC DIVISION

Use Name	Pos	Hgt	Wgt	Age	G	Min	FG	FGA	%	FT	FTA	%	Reb	Ass	PF	DQ	Stls	Blkd Shts	Points	PER GAME Min	Reb	Ass	PF	Points
PHILADELPHIA 76ers	52-30 .654				**BILLY CUNNINGHAM**																			
Julius Erving	F	6'7	205	33	77	2683	678	1324	51	364	483	75	532	309	217	3	141	139	1727	35	6.9	4.0	2.8	22.4
Bobby Jones	F	6'9	212	32	75	1761	226	432	52	167	213	78	323	187	199	1	107	103	619	23	4.3	2.5	2.7	8.3
Moses Malone	C	6'10	255	28	71	2613	532	1101	48	545	727	75	950	96	188	0	71	110	1609	37	13.4	1.4	2.6	22.7
Andrew Toney	G	6'3	188	26	78	2556	593	1125	53	390	465	84	193	373	251	1	70	23	1588	33	2.5	4.8	3.2	20.4
Maurice Cheeks	G	6'1	180	27	75	2494	386	702	55	170	232	73	205	478	196	1	171	20	950	33	2.7	6.4	2.6	12.7
Clemon Johnson	C-F	6'10	240	27	80	1721	193	412	47	69	113	61	398	55	205	1	35	65	455	22	5.0	0.7	2.6	5.7
Clint Richardson	G	6'3	195	27	69	1571	221	473	47	79	103	77	165	155	145	0	49	23	521	23	2.4	2.2	2.1	7.6
Marc la Varoni	F	6'9	225	27	78	1532	149	322	46	97	131	74	310	95	222	1	36	55	395	20	4.0	1.2	2.8	5.1
Sam Williams (from GS)	F	6'8	215	24	70	1375	193	405	48	86	133	65	326	60	203	3	62	103	472	20	4.7	0.9	2.9	6.7
Franklin Edwards	G	6'1	170	24	60	654	84	221	38	34	48	71	59	90	78	1	31	5	202	11	1.0	1.5	1.3	3.4
Sedale Threatt	G	6'2	175	22	45	464	62	148	42	23	28	82	40	41	65	1	13	2	148	10	0.9	0.9	1.4	3.3
Wes Matthews (from Atl)	F	6'1	170	24	14	292	45	101	45	9	14	64	23	62	32	0	11	2	100	21	1.6	4.4	2.3	7.1
Leo Rautins	F	6'8	215	23	28	196	21	58	36	6	10	60	33	29	31	0	9	2	48	7	1.2	1.0	1.1	1.7
B. Kuczenski (from NJ, to Ind)	F	6'10	230	22	3	40	1	8	13	1	2	50	6	2	7	0	1	1	3	13	2.0	0.7	2.3	1.0
Charles Jones	F	6'9	215	26	1	3	0	1	0	1	4	25	0	0	1	0	0	0	1	3	0.0	0.0	1.0	1.0

3-PT FG — Erving 7-21, B.Jones 0-1, Malone 0-4, Toney 12-38, Cheeks 8-12, Richardson 0-4
Iavaroni 0-2, Williams 0-1, Threatt 1-8, Matthews 1-7

Use Name	Pos	Hgt	Wgt	Age	G	Min	FG	FGA	%	FT	FTA	%	Reb	Ass	PF	DQ	Stls	Blkd Shts	Points	PER GAME Min	Reb	Ass	PF	Points
NEW YORK KNICKERBOCKERS	47-35 .573				**HUBIE BROWN**																			
Bernard King	F	6'7	205	27	77	2667	795	1391	57	437	561	78	394	164	273	2	75	17	2027	35	5.1	2.1	3.5	26.3
Truck Robinson (WJ, NJ)	F	6'7	225	32	65	2135	284	581	49	133	206	65	545	94	217	6	43	27	701	33	8.4	1.4	3.3	10.8
Bill Cartwright	C	7'1	245	26	77	2487	453	808	56	404	502	80	649	107	262	4	44	97	1310	32	8.4	1.4	3.4	17.0
Ray Williams	G	6'3	195	29	76	2230	418	939	45	263	318	83	267	449	274	5	162	26	1124	29	3.5	5.9	3.6	14.8
Rory Sparrow	G	6'2	195	25	79	2436	350	738	47	108	131	82	189	539	230	4	100	8	818	31	2.4	6.8	2.9	10.4
Louis Orr	F	6'8	195	25	78	1640	262	572	46	173	211	82	228	61	142	0	66	17	697	21	2.9	0.8	1.8	8.9
Darrell Walker	G	6'4	180	22	82	1324	216	518	42	208	263	79	167	284	202	1	127	15	644	16	2.0	3.5	2.5	7.9
Marvin Webster	C	7'1	240	31	76	1290	112	239	47	66	117	56	366	53	187	2	34	100	290	17	4.8	0.7	2.5	3.8
Trent Trucker	G	6'5	193	24	63	1228	225	450	50	25	33	76	130	138	124	0	63	8	481	19	2.1	2.2	2.0	7.6
Ernie Grunfield	G-F	6'6	215	28	76	1119	166	362	46	64	83	77	121	108	151	0	43	7	398	15	1.6	1.4	2.0	5.2
Len Elmore	F-C	6'9	220	31	65	832	64	157	41	27	38	71	165	30	153	3	29	30	155	13	2.5	0.5	2.4	2.4
Eric Fernsten	F	6'10	205	30	32	402	29	52	56	25	34	74	86	11	49	0	16	8	83	13	2.7	0.3	1.5	2.6
Rudy Macklin	F	6'7	215	25	8	65	12	30	40	11	13	85	11	3	17	0	1	0	35	8	1.4	0.4	2.1	4.4

3-PT FG — King 0-4, Cartwright 0-1, Williams 25-81, Sparrow 10-39, Walker 4-15,
Tucker 6-16, Grunfield 2-9

Use Name	Pos	Hgt	Wgt	Age	G	Min	FG	FGA	%	FT	FTA	%	Reb	Ass	PF	DQ	Stls	Blkd Shts	Points	PER GAME Min	Reb	Ass	PF	Points
NEW JERSEY NETS	45-37 .549				**STAN ALBECK**																			
Albert King	F	6'6	190	24	79	2103	465	946	49	232	295	79	388	203	258	6	91	33	1165	27	4.9	2.6	3.3	14.7
Buck Williams	F	6'8	215	23	81	3003	495	926	53	284	498	57	1000	130	298	3	81	125	1274	37	12.3	1.6	3.7	15.7
Darryl Dawkins	C	6'11	251	26	81	2417	507	855	59	341	464	73	541	123	**386**	**22**	60	136	1357	30	6.7	1.5	4.8	16.8
Otis Birdsong	G	6'4	195	28	69	2168	583	1147	51	194	319	61	170	266	180	2	86	17	1365	31	2.5	3.9	2.6	19.8
Michael Ray Richardson (DR)	G	6'5	195	28	48	1285	243	528	46	76	108	70	172	214	156	4	103	20	576	27	3.6	4.5	3.3	12.0
Kelvin Ransey	G	6'1	180	25	80	1937	304	700	43	145	183	79	127	483	182	2	91	6	760	24	1.6	6.0	2.3	9.5
Darwin Cook	G	6'3	190	25	82	1870	304	687	44	95	126	75	156	356	184	3	164	36	714	23	1.9	4.3	2.2	8.7
Mike Gminski	C-F	6'11	250	24	82	1655	237	462	51	147	184	80	433	92	162	0	37	70	621	20	5.3	1.1	2.0	7.6
Mike O'Koren	F-G	6'7	217	25	73	1191	186	385	48	53	87	61	175	95	148	3	34	11	430	16	2.4	1.3	2.0	5.9
Bill Willoughby	F	6'8	205	26	67	936	124	258	48	55	63	87	193	56	106	0	23	24	303	14	2.9	0.8	1.6	4.5
Reggie Johnson	F	6'9	205	26	72	818	127	256	50	92	126	73	138	40	141	1	24	18	346	11	1.9	0.6	2.0	4.8
Foots Walker	G	6'	172	32	34	378	32	90	36	24	27	89	31	81	37	0	20	3	90	11	0.9	2.4	1.1	2.6
B. Kuczenski (to Phi, Ind)	F	6'10	230	22	7	28	4	12	33	3	6	50	8	4	3	0	0	0	11	4	1.1	0.6	0.4	1.6
Mark Jones	G	6'2	175	22	6	16	3	6	50	1	2	50	2	5	2	0	0	0	7	3	0.3	0.8	0.3	1.2

3-PT FG — King 3-22, Williams 0-4, Dawkins 2-5, Birdsong 5-20, Richardson 14-58, Ransey 7-32,
Cook 11-46, Gminski 0-3, O'Koren 5-28, Willoughby 0-7, Johnson 0-1, Walker 2-5, Jones 0-1

Use Name	Pos	Hgt	Wgt	Age	G	Min	FG	FGA	%	FT	FTA	%	Reb	Ass	PF	DQ	Stls	Blkd Shts	Points	PER GAME Min	Reb	Ass	PF	Points
WASHINGTON BULLETS	35-47 .427				**GENE SHUE**																			
Greg Ballard	F	6'7	215	28	82	2701	510	1061	48	166	208	80	488	290	214	1	94	35	1188	33	6.0	3.5	2.6	14.5
Jeff Ruland	F-C	6'10	240	25	75	3082	599	1035	58	466	636	73	922	296	285	8	68	72	1665	41	12.3	3.9	3.8	22.2
Rick Mahorn	C	6'10	240	25	82	2701	307	605	51	125	192	65	738	131	358	14	62	123	739	33	9.0	1.6	4.4	9.0
Ricky Sobers	G	6'3	198	30	81	2624	508	1115	46	221	264	84	179	377	278	10	117	17	1266	32	2.2	4.7	3.4	15.6
Frank Johnson	G	6'2	185	25	82	2686	392	840	47	187	252	74	184	567	174	1	96	6	982	33	2.2	6.9	2.1	12.0
Jeff Malone	G	6'4	205	22	81	1976	408	918	44	142	172	83	155	151	162	1	23	13	982	24	1.9	1.9	2.0	12.1
Tom McMillen	F	6'11	235	31	62	1294	222	447	50	127	156	81	199	73	162	0	14	17	572	21	3.2	1.2	2.6	9.2
Darren Daye	F	6'8	220	23	75	1174	180	408	44	95	133	71	188	176	154	0	38	12	455	16	2.5	2.3	2.1	6.1
Joe Kopicki	F	6'9	240	23	59	678	64	132	48	91	112	81	166	46	71	0	15	0	220	11	2.8	0.8	1.2	3.7
Charlie Davis	F	6'7	215	25	46	467	103	218	47	24	39	62	103	30	58	1	14	10	231	10	2.2	0.7	1.3	5.0
Bryan Warrick	G	6'5	195	24	32	254	27	66	41	8	16	50	22	43	37	0	9	3	63	8	0.7	1.3	1.2	2.0
Mike Gibson	F	6'10	205	23	32	229	21	55	38	11	17	65	66	9	30	1	5	7	53	7	2.1	0.3	0.9	1.7
Michael Wilson	G	6'4	180	24	6	26	0	2	0	1	2	50	1	3	5	0	0	0	1	4	0.2	0.5	0.8	0.2
DeWayne Scales	F	6'8	208	25	2	13	3	5	60	0	2	0	3	0	1	0	1	0	6	7	1.5	0.0	0.5	3.0

3-PT FG — Ballard 2-15, Ruland 1-7, Sobers 29-111, Johnson 11-43, Malone 24-74, McMillen 1-6,
Daye 0-6, Kopicki 1-7, Davis 1-9, Warrick 1-3, Wilson 0-1

1983/84 N.B.A. — EASTERN CONFERENCE
CENTRAL DIVISION

MILWAUKEE BUCKS 50-32 .610 DON NELSON

Use Name	Pos	Hgt	Wgt	Age	TOTAL G	Min	FG	FGA	%	FT	FTA	%	Reb	Ass	PF	DQ	Stls	Blkd Shts	Points	PER GAME Min	Reb	Ass	PF	Points
Marques Johnson	F	6'7	218	27	74	2715	646	1288	50	241	340	71	480	315	194	1	115	45	1535	37	6.5	4.3	2.6	20.7
Alton Lister	F-C	7'	240	25	82	1955	256	512	50	114	182	63	603	110	327	11	41	140	626	24	7.4	1.3	4.0	7.6
Bob Lanier	C	6'11	265	35	72	2007	392	685	57	194	274	71	455	186	228	8	58	51	978	28	6.3	2.6	3.2	13.6
Sidney Moncrief	G	6'4	190	26	79	3075	560	1125	50	529	624	85	528	358	204	2	108	27	1654	39	6.7	4.5	2.6	20.9
Nate Archibald	G	6'1	160	35	46	1038	136	279	49	64	101	63	76	160	78	0	33	0	340	23	1.7	3.5	1.7	7.4
Junior Bridgeman	F-G	6'5	210	30	81	2431	509	1094	47	196	243	81	332	265	224	2	53	14	1220	30	4.1	3.3	2.8	15.1
Paul Pressey	G-F	6'5	185	25	81	1730	276	528	52	120	200	60	282	252	241	6	86	50	674	21	3.5	3.1	3.0	8.3
Harvey Catchings	F-C	6'9	218	32	69	1156	61	153	40	22	42	52	271	43	172	3	25	81	144	17	3.9	0.6	2.5	2.1
Lorenzo Romar (from GS)	G	6'1	180	25	65	1007	159	346	46	65	90	72	92	192	76	0	55	8	387	15	1.4	3.0	1.2	6.0
Kevin Grevey	G	6'5	210	30	64	923	178	395	45	75	84	89	81	75	95	0	27	4	446	14	1.3	1.2	1.5	7.0
Paul Mokelski	F-C	7'	250	26	68	838	102	213	48	50	72	69	166	44	168	1	11	29	255	12	2.4	0.6	2.5	3.8
Randy Breuer	C	7'3	230	23	57	472	68	177	38	32	46	70	109	17	98	1	11	38	168	8	1.9	0.3	1.7	2.9
Mike Dunleavy	G	6'3	180	29	17	404	70	127	55	32	40	80	28	78	51	0	12	1	191	24	1.6	4.6	3.0	11.2
Charlie Criss (to Atl)	G	5'8	165	34	6	107	11	30	37	7	11	64	9	17	7	0	5	0	30	18	1.5	2.8	1.2	5.0
Rory White (from Phoe, to SD)	F	6'8	210	24	8	45	7	17	41	2	5	40	8	1	3	0	2	1	16	6	1.0	0.1	0.4	2.0
Linton Townes (to SD)	F	6'7	195	24	2	2	1	1	100	0	0	—	0	0	1	0	0	0	2	1	0.0	0.0	0.5	1.0

3-PT FG — Johnson 2-13, Lanier 0-3, Moncrief 5-18, Archibald 4-18, Bridgeman 6-31, Pressey 2-9, Catchings 0-1, Romar 4-32, Grevey 15-53, Mokelski 1-3, Dunleavy 19-45, Criss 1-6

DETROIT PISTONS 49-33 .598 CHUCK DALY

Use Name	Pos	Hgt	Wgt	Age	TOTAL G	Min	FG	FGA	%	FT	FTA	%	Reb	Ass	PF	DQ	Stls	Blkd Shts	Points	PER GAME Min	Reb	Ass	PF	Points
Kelly Tripucka	F	6'6	230	24	76	2493	595	1296	46	426	523	81	306	228	190	0	65	17	1618	33	4.0	3.0	2.5	21.3
Cliff Levingston	F	6'8	220	22	80	1746	229	436	53	125	186	67	545	109	281	7	44	78	583	22	6.8	1.4	3.5	7.3
Bill Laimbeer	C	6'11	245	26	82	2064	553	1044	53	316	365	87	**1003**	149	273	4	49	84	1422	25	12.2	1.8	3.3	17.3
John Long	G	6'5	200	27	82	2514	545	1155	47	243	275	88	289	205	199	1	93	18	1334	31	3.5	2.5	2.4	16.3
Isiah Thomas	G	6'1	185	22	82	3007	669	1448	46	388	529	73	327	**914**	324	8	204	33	1748	37	4.0	11.1	4.0	21.3
Vinnie Johnson	G	6'2	200	27	82	1909	426	901	47	207	275	75	237	271	196	1	44	19	1063	23	2.9	3.3	2.4	13.0
Kent Benson	C-F	6'10	245	29	82	1734	248	451	55	83	101	82	409	130	230	4	71	53	579	21	5.0	1.6	2.8	7.1
Terry Tyler	F	6'7	220	27	82	1602	113	691	16	94	132	71	285	76	151	1	63	59	722	20	3.5	0.9	1.8	8.8
Earl Cureton	F-C	6'9	215	26	73	907	81	177	46	31	59	53	287	36	143	3	24	31	193	12	3.9	0.5	2.0	2.6
Ray Tolbert	F	6'9	225	25	49	475	64	121	53	23	45	51	98	26	88	1	12	20	151	10	2.0	0.5	1.8	3.1
David Thirdkill	F-G	6'7	215	23	46	291	31	72	43	15	31	48	31	27	44	0	10	3	77	6	0.7	0.6	1.0	1.7
Lionel Hollins	G	6'3	185	30	32	216	24	63	38	11	13	85	22	62	26	0	13	1	59	7	0.7	1.9	0.8	1.8
Walker Russell	G	6'5	195	23	16	119	14	42	33	12	13	92	19	22	25	0	4	0	41	7	1.2	1.4	1.6	2.6
Ken Austin	F	6'9	205	22	7	28	6	13	46	0	0	—	3	1	7	0	1	1	12	4	0.4	0.1	1.0	1.7

3-PT FG — Tripucka 2-17, Levingston 0-3, Laimbeer 0-11, Long 1-5, Thomas 22-65, Johnson 4-19, Benson 0-1, Tyler 2-13, Cureton 0-1, Tolbert 0-1, Thirdkill 0-1, Hollins 0-2, Russell 1-2

ATLANTA HAWKS 40-42 .488 MIKE FRATELLO

Use Name	Pos	Hgt	Wgt	Age	TOTAL G	Min	FG	FGA	%	FT	FTA	%	Reb	Ass	PF	DQ	Stls	Blkd Shts	Points	PER GAME Min	Reb	Ass	PF	Points
Dominique Wilkins	F	6'7	200	23	81	2961	684	1429	48	382	496	77	582	126	197	1	117	87	1750	37	7.2	1.6	2.4	21.6
Dan Roundfield	F	6'8	215	30	73	2610	503	1038	48	374	486	77	721	184	221	2	61	74	1380	36	9.9	2.5	3.0	18.9
Tree Rollins	C	7'1	235	28	77	2351	274	529	52	118	190	62	593	62	297	9	35	277	666	31	7,7	0.8	3.9	8.6
Eddie Johnson	G	6'2	190	28	67	1893	353	798	44	164	213	77	146	374	155	2	58	7	886	28	2.2	5.6	2.3	13.2
Johnny Davis	G	6'2	180	28	75	2079	354	800	44	217	256	85	139	326	146	0	62	6	925	28	1.9	4.3	1.9	12.3
Glenn Rivers	G	6'4	185	22	81	1938	250	541	46	255	325	78	220	314	286	8	127	30	757	24	2.7	3.9	3.5	9.3
Mike Glenn	G	6'3	185	28	81	1503	312	554	56	56	70	80	104	171	146	1	46	5	681	19	1.3	2.1	1.8	8.4
Scott Hastings	F-C	6'10	235	23	68	1135	111	237	47	82	104	79	270	46	220	7	40	36	305	17	4.0	0.7	3.2	4.5
Randy Wittman	F-G	6'6	210	24	78	1071	160	318	50	28	46	61	71	71	82	0	17	0	350	14	0.9	0.9	1.1	4.5
Rickey Brown	C-F	6'10	235	25	68	785	94	201	47	48	65	74	181	29	161	4	18	23	236	12	2.7	0.4	2.4	3.5
Billy Paultz	C	6'11	255	35	40	486	36	88	41	17	33	52	113	18	57	0	8	7	89	12	2.8	0.5	1.4	2.2
Mark Landsberger	F-C	6'8	230	28	35	335	19	51	37	15	26	58	119	10	32	0	6	3	53	10	3.4	0.3	0.9	1.5
Sly Williams	F	6'7	215	25	13	258	34	114	30	36	46	78	50	16	33	0	14	1	105	20	3.8	1.2	2.5	8.1
Armand Hill	G	6'4	190	30	15	181	14	46	30	17	21	81	10	35	30	1	7	0	45	12	0.7	2.3	2.0	3.0
Charlie Criss (from Mil)	G	5'8	165	34	9	108	9	22	41	5	5	100	11	21	4	0	3	0	23	12	1.2	2.3	0.4	2.6
Wes Matthews (to Phi)	G	6'7	190	23	6	96	6	13	46	18	22	82	4	21	13	0	5	1	50	16	0.7	3.5	2.2	8.3
John Pinone	F	6'8	230	22	7	65	7	13	54	6	10	60	10	3	11	0	2	1	20	9	1.4	0.4	1.6	2.9

3-PT FG — Wilkins 0-11, Roundfield 0-11, Johnson 16-43, Davis 0-8, Rivers 2-12, Glenn 1-2, Hastings 1-4, Wittman 2-5, Williams 1-9, Matthews 0-1

CLEVELAND CAVALIERS 28-54 .341 TOM NISSALKE

Use Name	Pos	Hgt	Wgt	Age	TOTAL G	Min	FG	FGA	%	FT	FTA	%	Reb	Ass	PF	DQ	Stls	Blkd Shts	Points	PER GAME Min	Reb	Ass	PF	Points
Cliff Robinson	F	6'9	230	23	73	2402	533	1185	45	234	334	70	753	185	195	2	51	32	1301	33	10.3	2.5	2.7	17.8
Lonnie Shelton	F	6'8	255	28	79	2101	371	779	48	107	140	76	381	179	279	9	76	55	850	27	4.8	2.3	3.5	10.8
Jeff Cook	C-F	6'10	215	27	81	1950	188	387	49	94	130	72	484	123	282	7	68	47	471	24	6.0	1.5	3.5	5.8
World Free	G	6'2	185	30	75	2375	626	1407	44	395	504	78	217	226	214	2	94	8	1669	32	2.9	3.0	2.9	22.3
Geoff Huston	G	6'2	175	26	77	2041	348	699	50	110	154	71	96	413	126	0	38	1	808	27	1.2	5.4	1.6	10.5
Roy Hinson	C-F	6'9	210	22	80	1858	184	371	50	69	117	59	499	69	306	11	31	145	437	23	6.2	0.9	3.8	5.5
Phil Hubbard	F	6'8	215	27	80	1799	321	628	51	221	299	74	380	86	244	3	71	6	863	22	4.8	1.1	3.1	10.8
Paul Thompson	G-F	6'6	210	22	82	1731	309	662	47	115	149	77	312	122	192	2	70	37	742	21	3.8	1.5	2.3	9.0
John Bagley	G	6'	190	23	76	1712	257	607	42	157	198	79	156	333	113	1	78	4	673	23	2.1	4.4	1.5	8.9
Ben Poquette	C	6'9	235	28	51	858	75	171	44	34	43	79	182	49	114	1	20	33	185	17	3.6	1.0	2.2	3.6
Stewart Granger	G	6'3	190	22	56	738	97	226	43	53	70	76	55	134	97	0	24	0	251	13	1.0	2.4	1.7	4.5
John Garris	F	6'8	205	24	33	267	52	102	51	27	34	79	77	10	40	0	8	6	131	8	2.3	0.3	1.2	4.0
Geff Crompton	C	6'11	288	28	7	23	1	8	13	3	6	50	9	1	4	0	1	1	5	3	1.3	0.1	0.6	0.7

3-PT FG — Robinson 1-2, Shelton 1-5, Cook 1-2, Free 22-69, Huston 2-11, Hubbard 0-1, Thompson 9-39, Bagley 2-17, Poquette 1-5, Granger 4-13

Name	Pos	Hgt	Wgt	Age	G	Min	FG	FGA	%	FT	FTA	%	Reb	Ass	PF	DQ	Stls	Blkd Shts	Points	Min	Reb	Ass	PF	Points
					TOTAL															**PER GAME**				
1983/84 N.B.A. — EASTERN CONFERENCE																								
CENTRAL DIVISION																								
CHICAGO BULLS	**27-55 .329 KEVIN LOUGHERY**																							
Orlando Woolridge	F	6'9	215	24	75	2544	570	1086	52	303	424	71	369	136	253	6	71	60	1444	34	4.9	1.8	3.4	19.3
Dave Greenwood	F	6'9	232	26	78	2718	369	753	49	213	289	74	786	139	265	9	67	72	951	35	10.1	1.8	3.4	12.2
Dave Corzine	C	6'11	260	27	82	2674	385	824	47	231	275	84	575	202	227	3	58	120	1004	33	7.0	2.5	2.8	12.2
Quinton Dailey	G	6'3	180	22	82	2449	583	1229	47	321	396	81	235	254	218	4	109	11	1491	30	2.9	3.1	2.7	18.2
Ennis Whatley	G	6'3	177	21	80	2159	261	556	47	146	200	73	197	662	223	4	119	17	668	27	2.5	8.3	2.8	8.4
Mitchell Wiggins	G	6'4	185	24	82	2123	399	890	45	213	287	74	328	187	278	8	106	11	1018	26	4.0	2.3	3.4	12.4
Rod Higgins	F	6'7	205	23	78	1577	193	432	45	113	156	72	206	116	161	0	49	29	500	20	2.6	1.5	2.1	6.4
Jawaan Oldham	C	7'	215	26	64	870	110	218	50	39	66	59	233	33	139	2	15	76	259	14	3.6	0.5	2.2	4.0
Ronnie Lester	G	6'2	175	24	43	687	78	188	41	75	87	86	46	168	59	1	30	6	232	16	1.1	3.9	1.4	5.4
Sidney Green	F	6'9	220	22	49	667	100	228	44	55	77	71	174	25	128	1	18	17	255	14	3.6	0.5	2.6	5.2
Reggie Theus (to KC)	G	6'7	205	26	31	601	92	237	39	84	108	78	46	142	78	2	21	3	271	19	1.5	4.6	2.5	8.7
Steve Johnson (from KC)	F-C	6'10	245	26	31	594	113	198	57	64	110	58	116	18	119	8	15	21	290	19	3.7	0.6	3.8	9.4
Wallace Bryant	C	7'	245	24	29	317	52	133	39	14	33	42	80	13	48	0	9	11	118	11	2.8	0.4	1.7	4.1
	3-PT FG —	Woolridge 0-1, Greenwood 0-1, Corzine 3-9, Dailey 4-32, Whatley 0-2, Wiggins 7-29, Higgins 1-22, Lester 1-5, Theus 3-15																						
INDIANA PACERS	**26-56 .317 JACK McKINNEY**																							
Clark Kellogg	F	6'7	227	22	79	2676	619	1193	52	261	340	77	719	234	242	2	121	28	1506	34	9.1	3.0	3.1	19.1
Herb Williams	F-C	6'11	242	25	69	2279	411	860	48	207	295	70	554	215	193	4	60	108	1029	33	8.0	3.1	2.8	14.9
Steve Stipanovich	C	6'11	245	23	81	2426	392	816	48	183	243	75	562	170	303	4	73	67	970	30	6.9	2.1	3.7	12.0
Butch Carter	G	6'5	195	25	73	2045	413	862	48	136	178	76	153	206	211	1	128	13	977	28	2.1	2.8	2.9	13.4
Jerry Sichting	G	6'1	178	27	80	2497	397	746	53	117	135	87	171	457	179	0	90	8	917	31	2.1	5.7	2.2	11.5
George Johnson	F	6'7	218	27	81	2073	411	884	46	223	270	83	460	195	256	3	82	49	1056	26	5.7	2.4	3.2	13.0
Sidney Lowe	G	6'	195	23	78	1238	107	259	41	108	139	78	122	269	112	0	93	5	324	16	1.6	3.4	1.4	4.2
Jim Thomas	G	6'3	190	23	72	1219	187	403	46	80	110	73	149	130	115	1	60	6	455	17	2.1	1.8	1.6	6.3
Granville Waiters	C	6'11	225	22	78	1040	123	238	52	31	51	61	227	60	164	2	24	85	277	13	2.9	0.8	2.1	3.6
Kevin McKenna	G-F	6'5	195	24	61	923	152	371	41	80	98	82	95	114	133	3	46	5	387	15	1.6	1.9	2.2	6.3
Brook Steppe	G-F	6'5	195	24	61	857	148	314	47	134	161	83	122	79	93	0	34	6	430	14	2.0	1.3	1.5	7.0
Leroy Combs	F	6'8	210	22	48	446	81	163	50	56	91	62	56	38	49	0	23	18	218	9	1.2	0.8	1.0	4.5
B. Kuczenski (from NJ, Phi)	F	6'10	230	22	5	51	5	17	29	4	4	100	9	2	8	0	0	0	14	10	1.8	0.4	1.6	2.8
Tracy Jackson	G	6'6	215	24	2	10	1	4	25	4	4	100	1	0	3	0	0	0	6	5	0.5	0.0	1.5	3.0
	3-PT FG —	Kellogg 7-21, Williams 0-4, Stipanovich 3-16, Carter 15-46, Sichting 6-20, Johnson 11-47, Lowe 2-18, Thomas 1-11, Waiters 0-1, McKenna 3-17, Steppe 0-3, Combs 0-3																						
WESTERN CONFERENCE																								
MIDWEST DIVISION																								
UTAH JAZZ	**43-37 .549 FRANK LAYDEN**																							
Adrian Dantley	F	6'5	210	27	79	2984	802	1438	56	**813**	**946**	86	448	310	201	0	61	4	**2418**	38	5.7	3.9	2.5	**30.6**
Thurl Bailey	F	6'11	215	22	81	2009	302	590	51	88	117	75	464	129	193	1	38	122	692	25	5.7	1.6	2.4	8.5
Mark Eaton	C	7'4	280	26	82	2139	194	416	47	73	123	59	595	113	303	4	25	**351**	461	26	7.3	1.4	3.7	5.6
Darrell Griffith	G	6'4	190	25	82	2650	697	1423	49	151	217	70	338	283	202	1	114	23	1636	32	4.1	3.5	2.5	20.0
Rickey Green	G	6'1	170	29	81	2768	439	904	49	192	234	82	230	748	155	1	**215**	13	1072	34	2.8	9.2	1.9	13.2
John Drew	G-F	6'6	205	29	81	1797	511	1067	48	402	517	78	338	135	208	1	88	2	1430	22	4.2	1.7	2.6	17.7
Jeff Wilkins	F-C	6'11	240	28	81	1734	249	520	48	134	182	74	455	73	205	1	27	42	632	21	5.6	0.9	2.5	7.8
Rich Kelley	C-F	7'	240	30	75	1674	132	264	50	124	162	77	490	157	273	6	55	29	388	22	6.5	2.1	3.6	5.2
Jerry Eaves	G	6'4	185	24	80	1034	132	293	45	92	132	70	85	200	90	0	33	5	356	13	1.1	2.5	1.1	4.5
Bob Hansen	G	6'6	190	22	55	419	65	145	45	18	28	64	48	44	62	0	15	4	148	8	0.9	0.8	1.1	2.7
J.J. Anderson	F	6'8	195	23	48	311	55	130	42	12	29	41	63	22	38	0	15	9	122	6	1.3	0.5	0.8	2.5
Tom Boswell	F	6'9	225	30	38	261	28	52	54	16	21	76	64	16	58	1	9	0	73	7	1.7	0.4	1.5	1.9
	3-PT FG —	Dantley 1-4, Eaton 0-1, Griffith 91-252, Green 2-17, Drew 6-22, Wilkins 0-3, Eaves 0-6, Hansen 0-8, Anderson 0-8, Boswell 1-1																						
DALLAS MAVERICKS	**43-39 .524 DICK MOTTA**																							
Mark Aguirre	F	6'6	235	24	79	2900	**925**	**1765**	52	465	621	75	469	358	246	5	80	22	2330	37	5.9	4.5	3.1	29.5
Jay Vincent	F	6'7	225	24	61	1421	252	579	44	168	215	78	247	114	159	1	30	10	672	23	4.0	1.9	2.6	11.0
Kurt Nimphius	C	6'10	218	25	82	2284	272	523	52	101	162	62	513	176	283	5	41	144	646	28	6.3	2.1	3.5	7.9
Rolando Blackman	G	6'6	190	24	81	3025	721	1320	55	372	458	81	373	288	127	0	56	37	1815	37	4.6	3.6	1.6	22.4
Brad Davis	G	6'3	180	28	81	2665	345	651	53	199	238	84	187	561	218	4	94	13	896	33	2.3	6.9	2.7	11.1
Pat Cummings	C-F	6'9	235	27	80	2492	452	915	49	141	190	74	658	158	282	2	64	23	1045	31	8.2	2.0	3.5	13.1
Derek Harper	G	6'4	185	22	82	1712	200	451	44	66	98	67	172	239	143	0	95	21	469	21	2.1	2.9	1.7	5.7
Bill Garnett	F	6'9	225	23	80	1529	141	299	47	129	176	73	331	128	217	4	44	66	411	19	4.1	1.6	2.7	5.1
Dale Ellis	F	6'7	205	23	67	1059	225	493	46	87	121	72	250	56	118	0	41	9	549	16	3.7	0.8	1.8	8.2
Elston Turner	G	6'5	220	24	47	536	54	150	36	28	34	82	93	59	40	0	26	0	137	11	2.0	1.3	0.9	2.9
Mark West	C	6'10	230	23	34	202	15	42	36	7	22	32	46	13	55	0	1	15	37	6	1.4	0.4	1.6	1.1
Roger Phegley (from SA)	G	6'6	215	27	10	76	9	31	29	2	2	100	9	9	10	0	1	0	21	8	0.9	0.9	1.0	2.1
Jim Spanarkel	G	6'5	195	26	7	54	7	16	44	9	13	69	7	5	8	0	6	0	24	8	1.0	0.7	1.1	3.4
	3-PT FG —	Aguirre 15-56, Vincent 0-1, Nimphius 1-4, Blackman 1-11, Davis 7-38, Cummings 0-2, Harper 3-26, Garnett 0-2, Ellis 12-29, Turner 1-9, Phegley 1-4, Spanarkel 1-2																						

Use Name	Pos	Hgt	Wgt	Age	TOTAL G	Min	FG	FGA	%	FT	FTA	%	Reb	Ass	PF	DQ	Stls	Blkd Shts	Points	PER GAME Min	Reb	Ass	PF	Points
1983/84 N.B.A. — WESTERN CONFERENCE MIDWEST DIVISION																								
DENVER NUGGETS	**38-44 .463 DOUG MOE**																							
Alex English	F	6'8	190	29	82	2870	907	1714	53	352	427	82	474	406	252	3	83	95	2167	35	5.8	5.0	3.1	26.
Kiki Vandeweghe	F	6'8	220	25	78	2734	895	1603	56	494	580	85	373	238	187	1	53	50	2295	35	4.8	3.1	2.4	29.
Dan Issel	C	6'9	240	35	76	2076	569	1153	49	364	428	85	513	173	182	2	60	44	1506	27	6.8	2.3	2.4	19.
T. R. Dunn	G	6'4	192	28	80	2705	174	370	47	106	145	73	574	228	233	5	173	32	454	34	7.2	2.9	2.9	5.
Rob Williams	G	6'2	175	22	79	1924	309	671	46	171	209	82	194	464	268	4	84	5	804	24	2.5	5.9	3.4	10.
Mike Evans	G	6'1	170	28	78	1687	243	564	43	111	131	85	138	288	175	2	61	4	629	22	1.8	3.7	2.2	8.
Bill Hanzlik	G-F	6'7	185	26	80	1469	132	306	43	167	207	81	205	252	255	6	68	19	434	18	2.6	3.2	3.2	5.
Dan Schayes	C	6'11	245	24	82	1420	183	371	49	215	272	79	433	91	308	5	32	60	581	17	5.3	1.1	3.8	7.
Richard Anderson	F-C	6'10	240	23	78	1380	272	638	43	116	150	77	406	193	183	0	46	28	663	18	5.2	2.5	2.3	8.
Howard Carter	G	6'5	215	22	55	688	145	316	46	47	61	77	86	71	81	0	19	4	342	13	1.6	1.3	1.5	6.
Kenny Dennard	F	6'8	220	25	43	413	36	99	36	15	24	63	101	45	83	0	23	8	90	10	2.3	1.0	1.9	2.
Anthony Roberts	F	6'5	185	28	19	197	34	91	37	13	18	72	51	13	43	1	5	1	81	10	2.7	0.7	2.3	4.
Dave Robisch (to SA, KC)	C	6'10	240	34	19	141	13	40	33	11	13	85	21	13	13	0	0	1	37	7	1.1	0.7	0.7	1.
Keith Edmondson (from SA)	G	6'5	205	23	15	101	23	47	49	18	25	72	18	7	16	0	4	1	64	7	1.2	0.5	1.1	4.
3-PT FG — English 1-7, Vandeweghe 11-30, Issel 4-19, Dunn 0-1, Williams 15-47, Evans 32-89, Hanzlik 3-12, Schayes 0-2, Anderson 3-19, Carter 5-19, Dennard 3-10,																								
KANSAS CITY KINGS	**38-44 .463 COTTON FITZSIMMONS**																							
Eddie Johnson	F	6'8	215	24	82	2920	753	1552	49	268	331	81	455	296	266	4	76	21	1794	36	5.5	3.6	3.2	21.
Mark Olberding	F	6'8	230	27	81	2160	249	504	49	261	318	82	445	192	291	2	50	28	759	27	5.5	2.4	3.6	9.
LaSalle Thompson	C	6'10	248	22	80	1915	333	637	52	160	223	72	709	86	327	8	71	145	826	24	8.9	1.1	4.1	10.
Mike Woodson	G	6'5	198	25	71	1838	389	816	48	247	302	82	175	175	174	2	83	28	1027	26	2.5	2.5	2.5	14.
Larry Drew	G	6'1	180	25	73	2363	474	1026	46	243	313	78	146	558	170	0	121	10	1194	32	2.0	7.6	2.3	16.
Billy Knight	G-F	6'6	195	31	75	1885	358	729	49	243	283	86	255	160	122	0	54	6	963	25	3.4	2.1	1.6	12.
Joe C. Meriweather	C	6'10	218	30	73	1501	193	363	53	94	123	76	353	51	247	8	35	61	480	21	4.8	0.7	3.4	6.
Don Buse	G	6'4	195	33	76	1327	150	352	43	63	80	79	116	303	62	0	86	1	381	17	1.5	4.0	0.8	5.
Ed Nealy	F	6'7	238	23	71	960	63	126	50	48	60	80	222	50	138	1	41	9	174	14	3.1	0.7	1.9	2.
Reggie Theus (from Chi)	G	6'7	205	26	30	897	170	388	44	130	173	75	83	210	93	1	29	9	474	30	2.8	7.0	3.1	15.
Steve Johnson (to Chi)	C-F	6'10	245	26	50	893	189	342	55	101	177	57	252	63	188	7	22	48	479	18	5.0	1.3	3.8	9.
Dane Suttle	G	6'3	190	22	40	469	109	214	51	40	47	85	46	46	46	0	20	0	258	12	1.2	1.2	1.2	6.
Larry Micheaux	F	6'9	220	23	39	332	49	90	54	21	39	54	113	19	46	0	21	11	119	9	2.9	0.5	1.2	3.
Dave Robisch (fromDen, SA)	C-F	6'10	240	34	8	162	18	48	38	11	13	85	29	6	15	0	3	1	47	20	3.6	0.8	1.9	5.
Kevin Loder (to SD)	F	6'6	205	24	10	133	19	43	44	9	13	69	18	14	15	0	3	5	48	13	1.8	1.4	1.5	4.
3-PT FG — E. Johnson 20-64, Olberding 0-1, Woodson 2-8, Drew 3-10, Knight 4-14, Buse 18-59,Thues 4-27, Suttle 0-3, Loder 1-3																								
SAN ANTONIO SPURS	**37-45 .451 MORRIS MCHONE 11-20 (.354), BOB BASS 26-25 (.510)**																							
Mike Mitchell	F	6'7	215	27	79	2853	779	1597	49	275	353	78	570	93	251	6	62	73	1839	36	7.2	1.2	3.2	23.
Gene Banks	F	6'7	215	24	80	2600	424	747	57	200	270	74	582	254	256	5	105	23	1049	33	7.3	3.2	3.2	13.
Artis Gilmore (BY)	C	7'2	255	34	64	2034	351	556	63	280	390	72	662	70	229	4	36	132	982	32	10.3	1.1	3.6	15.
George Gervin	G	6'7	185	31	76	2584	765	1561	49	427	507	84	313	220	219	3	79	47	1967	34	4.1	2.9	2.9	25.
John Lucas	G	6'3	185	30	63	1807	275	595	46	120	157	76	180	673	123	1	92	5	689	29	2.9	10.7	2.0	10.
Edgar Jones	F-C	6'10	225	27	81	1770	322	644	50	176	242	73	449	85	298	7	64	107	826	22	5.5	1.0	3.7	10.
Johnny Moore	G	6'2	185	25	59	1650	231	518	45	105	139	76	178	566	168	2	123	20	595	28	3.0	9.6	2.8	10.
Fred Roberts	F	6'10	220	23	79	1531	214	399	54	144	172	84	304	98	219	4	52	38	573	19	3.8	1.2	2.8	7.
Mark McNamara	C	6'11	235	24	70	1037	157	253	62	74	157	47	317	31	138	2	14	12	388	15	4.5	0.4	2.0	5.
Ron Brewer (from GS)	G	6'4	185	28	40	782	152	345	44	41	50	82	50	44	54	0	18	16	348	20	1.3	1.1	1.4	8.
Keith Edmondson (to Dew)	G-F	6'5	205	23	40	521	135	274	49	76	101	75	70	27	67	1	22	6	346	13	1.8	0.7	1.7	8.
John Paxson	G	6'2	185	23	49	458	61	137	45	16	26	62	33	149	47	0	10	2	142	9	0.7	3.0	1.0	2.
Kevin Williams	G	6'3	175	22	19	200	25	58	43	25	32	78	13	43	42	1	8	4	75	11	0.7	2.3	2.2	3.
Brant Weidner	F	6'9	230	23	8	38	2	9	22	4	4	100	11	0	5	0	0	2	8	5	1.4	0.0	0.6	1.
D. Robisch (from Den, to KC)	C	6'10	240	34	4	37	4	8	50	0	0	—	8	1	8	1	0	0	8	9	2.0	0.3	2.0	2.
Dave Batton	C	6'10	240	27	4	31	5	10	50	0	0	—	4	3	5	0	0	3	10	8	1.0	0.8	1.3	2.
Darrell Lockhart	C	6'9	245	23	2	14	2	2	100	0	0	—	3	0	5	0	0	0	4	7	1.5	0.0	2.5	2.
Steve Lingenfeller	F	6'9	225	25	3	14	1	1	100	0	2	0	4	1	6	0	0	0	2	5	1.3	0.3	2.0	0.
Roger Phegley (to Dal)	G-F	6'6	215	27	3	11	2	4	50	2	2	100	2	2	1	0	0	0	7	4	0.7	0.7	0.3	2.
Bob Miller	F	6'10	3-PT	27	2	8	2	3	67	0	0	—	5	1	5	0	0	1	4	4	2.5	0.5	2.5	2.
3 PT FG — Mitchell 6-14, Banks 1-6, Gillmore 0-3, Gervin 10-24, Lucas 19-69, Jones 6-19, Moore 28-87, Roberts 1-4, Brewer 3-13, Paxson 4-22, Williams 0-1, Phegley 1-1																								
HOUSTON ROCKETS	**29-53 .354 BILL FITCH**																							
Robert Reid	F-G	6'8	205	28	64	1936	406	857	47	81	123	66	341	217	243	5	88	30	895	30	5.3	3.4	3.8	14.
Caldwell Jones	F-C	6'11	225	33	81	2506	318	633	50	164	196	84	582	156	335	7	46	80	801	31	7.2	1.9	4.1	9.
Ralph Sampson	C	7'4	228	23	82	2693	716	1369	52	287	434	66	913	163	339	16	70	197	1720	33	11.1	2.0	4.1	21.
Lewis Lloyd	G-F	6'6	215	24	82	2578	610	1182	52	235	298	79	295	321	211	4	102	44	1458	31	3.6	3.9	2.6	17.
Allen Leavell	G	6'1	190	26	82	2009	349	731	48	238	286	83	117	459	199	2	107	12	947	25	1.4	5.6	2.4	11.
Rodney McCray	F-G	6'8	220	22	79	2081	335	672	50	182	249	73	450	176	205	1	53	54	853	26	5.7	2.2	2.6	10.
Phil Ford	G	6'2	186	27	81	2020	236	470	50	98	117	84	137	410	243	7	59	8	572	25	1.7	5.1	3.0	7.
James Bailey	F-C	6'9	220	26	73	1174	254	517	49	138	192	72	294	79	197	8	33	40	646	16	4.0	1.1	2.7	8.
Elvin Hayes	F	6'9	235	38	81	994	158	389	41	86	132	65	260	71	123	1	16	23	402	12	3.2	0.9	1.5	5.
Terry Teagle	G	6'5	195	23	68	616	148	315	47	37	44	84	78	63	81	1	13	4	340	9	1.1	0.9	1.2	5.
Wally Walker	F	6'7	210	29	58	612	118	241	49	6	18	33	92	55	65	0	17	4	244	11	1.6	0.9	1.1	4.
Major Jones	F	6'9	225	30	57	473	70	130	54	30	49	61	115	28	63	0	14	14	170	8	2.0	0.5	1.1	3.
Craig Ehlo	G	6'7	180	22	7	63	11	27	41	1	1	100	9	6	13	0	3	0	23	9	1.3	0.9	1.9	3.
3-PT FG — Reid 2-8, C. Jones 1-3, Sampson 1-4, Lloyd 3-13, Leavell 11-71, McCray 1-4, Ford 2-15, Bailey 0-1, Hayes 0-2, Teagle 7-27, Walker 2-6																								

1983/84 N.B.A. — WESTERN CONFERENCE
PACIFIC DIVISION

LOS ANGELES LAKERS — 54-28 .659 PAT RILEY

Use Name	Pos	Hgt	Wgt	Age	G	Min	FG	FGA	%	FT	FTA	%	Reb	Ass	PF	DQ	Stls	Blkd Shts	Points	Min (per game)	Reb (per game)	Ass (per game)	PF (per game)	Points (per game)
Jamaal Wilkes	F	6'6	190	30	75	2507	542	1055	51	208	280	74	340	214	205	0	72	41	1294	33	4.5	2.9	2.7	17.3
James Worthy	F	6'9	225	22	82	2415	495	.890	56	195	257	76	515	207	244	5	77	70	1185	29	6.3	2.5	3.0	14.5
Kareem Abdul-Jabbar	C	7'2	232	36	80	2622	716	1238	58	285	394	72	587	211	211	1	55	143	1717	33	7.3	2.6	2.6	21.5
Michael Cooper	G	6'5	170	27	82	2387	273	549	50	155	185	84	262	482	267	3	113	67	739	29	3.2	5.9	3.3	9.0
Magic Johnson	G	6'8	215	24	67	2567	441	780	57	290	358	81	491	875	169	1	150	49	1178	38	7.3	13.1	2.5	17.6
Byron Scott	G	6'3	195	22	74	1637	334	690	48	112	139	81	164	177	174	0	81	19	788	22	2.2	2.4	2.4	10.6
Bob McAdoo	F-C	6'9	225	32	70	1456	352	748	47	212	264	80	289	74	182	0	42	50	916	21	4.1	1.1	2.6	13.1
Mike McGee	G-F	6'5	190	24	77	1425	347	584	59	61	113	54	193	81	176	0	49	6	757	19	2.5	1.1	2.3	9.8
Swen Nater	C	6'11	250	33	69	829	124	253	49	63	91	69	264	27	150	0	25	7	311	12	3.8	0.4	2.2	4.5
Kurt Rambis	F	6'8	220	25	47	743	63	113	56	42	66	64	266	34	108	0	30	14	168	16	5.7	0.7	2.3	3.6
Calvin Garrett	F	6'7	195	27	41	478	78	152	51	30	39	77	71	31	62	2	12	2	188	12	1.7	0.8	1.5	4.6
Larry Spriggs	F	6'7	230	24	38	363	44	82	54	36	50	72	61	30	55	0	12	4	124	10	1.6	0.8	1.4	3.3
Mitch Kupchak(KJ)	F	6'9	230	29	34	324	41	108	38	22	34	65	87	7	46	0	4	6	104	10	2.6	0.2	1.4	3.1
Eddie Jordan (from Port)	G	6'1	170	28	3	27	4	8	50	1	2	50	4	5	5	0	4	0	9	9	1.3	1.7	1.7	3.0

3-PT FG — Wilkes 2-8, Worthy 0-6, Abdul-Jabbar 0-1, Cooper 38-121, Johnson 6-29, Scott 8-34, McAdoo 0-5, McGee 2-12, Nater 0-1, Garrett 2-6, Spriggs 0-2, Kupchak 0-1

PORTLAND TRAIL BLAZERS — 48-34 .585 JACK RAMSAY

Use Name	Pos	Hgt	Wgt	Age	G	Min	FG	FGA	%	FT	FTA	%	Reb	Ass	PF	DQ	Stls	Blkd Shts	Points	Min (per game)	Reb (per game)	Ass (per game)	PF (per game)	Points (per game)
Calvin Natt	F	6'6	220	26	79	2638	500	857	58	275	345	80	476	179	218	3	69	22	1277	33	6.0	2.3	2.8	16.2
Kenny Carr	F	6'7	230	28	82	2455	518	923	56	247	367	67	642	157	274	3	68	33	1283	30	7.8	1.9	3.3	15.6
Wayne Cooper	C	6'10	220	27	81	1662	304	663	46	185	230	80	476	76	247	2	26	106	793	21	5.9	0.9	3.0	9.8
Jim Paxon	G-F	6'6	200	26	81	2686	680	1322	51	345	410	84	173	251	165	0	122	10	1722	33	2.1	3.1	2.0	21.3
Darnell Valentine	G	6'2	185	24	68	1893	251	561	45	194	246	79	127	395	179	1	107	6	696	28	1.9	5.8	2.6	10.2
Mychal Thompson	F-C	6'10	226	28	79	2648	487	929	52	266	399	67	688	308	237	2	84	108	1240	34	8.7	3.9	3.0	15.7
Lafayette Lever	G	6'3	175	23	81	2010	313	701	45	159	214	74	218	372	178	1	135	31	788	25	2.7	4.6	2.2	9.7
Clyde Drexler	G-F	6'7	210	21	82	1408	252	559	45	123	169	73	235	153	209	2	107	29	628	17	2.9	1.9	2.5	7.7
Audie Norris	C	6'9	250	23	79	1157	124	246	50	104	149	70	257	76	231	2	30	34	352	15	3.3	1.0	2.9	4.5
Jeff Lamp	G	6'6	195	24	64	660	128	261	49	60	67	90	63	51	67	0	22	4	318	10	1.0	0.8	1.0	5.0
Peter Verhoeven	F	6'9	215	24	43	327	50	100	50	17	25	68	61	20	75	0	22	11	117	8	1.4	0.5	1.7	2.7
Eddie Jordan (to LA)	G	6'1	170	28	13	183	13	41	32	7	10	70	13	39	32	0	21	0	33	14	1.0	3.0	2.5	2.5
Tom Piotrowski	C	7'1	240	23	18	78	12	26	46	6	6	100	16	5	22	0	1	3	30	4	0.9	0.3	1.2	1.7

3-PT FG — Natt 2-17, Carr 0-5, Cooper 0-7, Paxon 17-59, Valentine 0-3, Thompson 0-2, Lever 3-15, Drexler 1-4, Lamp 2-13, Verhoeven 0-1, Jordan 0-3

SEATTLE SUPERSONICS — 42-40 .512 LENNY WILKENS

Use Name	Pos	Hgt	Wgt	Age	G	Min	FG	FGA	%	FT	FTA	%	Reb	Ass	PF	DQ	Stls	Blkd Shts	Points	Min (per game)	Reb (per game)	Ass (per game)	PF (per game)	Points (per game)
Danny Vranes	F	6'7	210	25	80	2174	258	495	52	153	236	65	395	132	263	4	51	54	669	27	4.9	1.7	3.3	8.4
Tom Chambers	F	6'10	225	24	82	2570	554	1110	50	375	469	80	532	133	309	8	47	51	1483	31	6.5	1.6	3.8	18.1
Jack Sikma	C	6'11	250	28	82	2993	576	1155	50	411	480	86	911	327	301	6	95	92	1563	37	11.1	4.0	3.7	19.1
Al Wood	G-F	6'6	193	25	81	2236	467	945	49	223	271	82	275	166	207	1	64	32	1160	28	3.4	2.0	2.6	14.3
Gus Williams	G	6'2	175	30	80	2818	598	1306	46	297	396	75	204	675	151	0	189	25	1497	35	2.6	8.4	1.9	18.7
Reggie King	F	6'6	230	26	77	2086	233	448	52	136	206	66	470	179	159	2	54	24	602	27	6.1	2.3	2.1	7.8
Jon Sundvold	G	6'2	170	22	73	1284	217	488	44	64	72	89	91	239	81	0	29	1	507	18	1.2	3.3	1.1	6.9
Steve Hawes	C-F	6'9	220	33	79	1153	114	237	48	61	78	78	220	99	144	2	24	16	290	15	2.8	1.3	1.8	3.7
Fred Brown	G	6'3	185	35	71	1129	258	506	51	77	86	90	62	194	84	0	49	2	602	16	0.9	2.7	1.2	8.5
Scotter McCray	F-G	6'9	215	23	47	520	47	121	39	35	50	70	115	44	73	1	11	19	129	11	2.4	0.9	1.6	2.7
David Thompson	G	6'4	195	29	19	349	89	165	54	62	73	85	44	13	30	0	10	13	240	18	2.3	0.7	1.6	12.6
Steve Hayes	C	7'	235	28	43	253	26	50	52	5	14	36	62	13	52	0	5	18	57	6	1.4	0.3	1.2	1.3
Clay Johnson	G	6'4	185	27	25	176	20	50	40	14	22	64	12	14	24	0	8	2	55	7	0.5	0.6	1.0	2.2
Charles Bradley	G	6'5	215	24	8	39	3	7	43	5	7	71	3	5	6	0	0	1	11	5	0.4	0.6	0.8	1.4

3-PT FG — Vranes 0-1, Chanbers 0-12, Sikma 0-2, Wood 3-21, Williams 4-25, King 0-2, Sundvold 9-37, Hawes 1-4, Brown 9-34, Thompson 0-1, Johnson 1-1

PHOENIX SUNS — 41-41 .500 JOHN MAC LEOD

Use Name	Pos	Hgt	Wgt	Age	G	Min	FG	FGA	%	FT	FTA	%	Reb	Ass	PF	DQ	Stls	Blkd Shts	Points	Min (per game)	Reb (per game)	Ass (per game)	PF (per game)	Points (per game)
Larry Nance	F	6'10	215	24	82	2899	601	1044	58	249	352	71	678	214	274	5	86	173	1451	35	8.3	2.6	3.3	17.7
Maurice Lucas	F	6'9	238	31	75	2309	451	908	50	293	383	77	725	203	235	2	55	39	1195	31	9.7	2.7	3.1	15.9
James Edwards	C	7'	225	28	72	1897	438	817	54	183	254	72	348	184	254	3	23	30	1059	26	4.8	2.6	3.5	14.7
Walter Davis	G-F	6'6	200	29	78	2546	652	1274	51	233	270	86	202	429	202	0	10	12	1557	33	2.6	5.5	2.6	20.0
Kyle Macy	G	6'3	190	26	82	2402	357	713	50	95	114	83	186	353	181	0	123	6	832	29	2.3	4.3	2.2	10.1
Alvan Adams	C	6'9	220	29	70	1452	269	582	46	132	160	83	319	219	195	1	73	32	670	21	4.6	3.1	2.8	9.6
Rod Foster	G	6'1	160	23	80	1424	260	580	45	122	155	79	120	172	193	0	54	9	664	18	1.5	2.2	2.4	8.3
Charles Pittman	F	6'8	220	25	69	989	126	209	60	69	101	68	214	70	129	1	16	22	321	14	3.1	1.0	1.9	4.7
Paul Westphal	G	6'4	195	33	59	865	144	313	46	117	142	82	43	148	69	0	41	6	412	15	0.7	2.5	1.2	7.0
Rick Robey	C-F	6'11	230	27	61	856	140	257	54	61	88	69	198	65	120	0	20	14	342	14	3.2	1.1	2.0	5.6
Alvin Scott	F	6'7	215	28	65	735	55	124	44	56	72	78	100	48	85	0	19	20	167	11	1.5	0.7	1.3	2.6
Mike Sanders	F	6'6	210	23	50	586	97	203	48	29	42	69	103	44	101	0	23	12	223	12	2.1	0.9	2.0	4.5
Johnny High	G	6'3	185	26	29	512	18	52	35	10	29	34	66	51	84	1	40	11	46	18	2.3	1.8	2.9	1.6
Rory White (to Mil, SD)	F	6'8	210	24	22	308	69	144	48	24	42	57	62	14	25	0	13	2	162	14	2.8	0.6	1.1	7.4

3-PT FG — Nance 0-7, Lucas 0-5, Edwards 0-1, Davis 20-87, Macy 23-70, Adams 0-4, Foster22-84, Pittman 0-2, Westphal 7-26, Robey 1-1, Scott 1-2, High 0-2

1983/84 N.B.A. — WESTERN CONFERENCE
PACIFIC DIVISION

GOLDEN STATE WARRIORS 37-45 .451 JOHN BACH

Use Name	Pos	Hgt	Wgt	Age	TOTAL G	Min	FG	FGA	%	FT	FTA	%	Reb	Ass	PF	DQ	Stls	Blkd Shts	Points	PER GAME Min	Reb	Ass	PF	Points
Purvis Short	F-G	6'7	220	26	79	2945	714	1509	47	353	445	79	438	246	252	2	103	11	1803	37	5.5	3.1	3.2	22.8
Larry Smith	F	6'8	225	25	75	2091	244	436	56	94	168	56	672	72	274	6	61	22	582	28	9.0	1.0	3.7	7.8
Joe Barry Carroll	C	7'	250	25	80	2962	663	1390	48	313	433	72	636	198	244	9	103	142	1639	37	8.0	2.5	3.1	20.5
Eric Floyd	G	6'3	175	23	77	2555	484	1045	46	315	386	82	271	269	216	0	103	31	1291	33	3.5	3.5	2.8	16.8
Lester Conner	G	6'4	185	24	82	2573	360	730	49	186	259	72	305	401	176	1	162	12	907	31	3.7	4.9	2.1	11.1
Mickey Johnson	F	6'10	190	31	78	2122	359	852	42	339	432	78	518	219	290	3	101	30	1062	27	6.6	2.8	3.7	13.6
Mike Bratz	G	6'2	185	28	82	1428	213	521	41	120	137	88	143	252	155	0	84	6	561	17	1.7	3.1	1.9	6.8
Don Collins	F-G	6'6	190	25	61	957	187	387	48	65	89	73	129	67	119	1	43	14	440	16	2.1	1.1	2.0	7.2
Darren Tillis	F-C	6'11	215	23	72	730	108	254	43	41	63	65	184	24	176	1	12	60	257	10	2.6	0.3	2.4	3.6
Pace Mannion	F	6'7	190	23	57	469	50	126	40	18	23	78	59	47	63	0	25	2	121	8	1.0	0.8	1.1	2.1
Chris Engler	C	6'11	248	24	46	360	33	83	40	14	23	61	97	11	68	0	9	3	80	8	2.1	0.2	1.5	1.7
Russell Cross	C	6'10	215	22	45	354	64	112	57	38	91	42	82	22	58	0	12	7	166	8	1.8	0.5	1.3	3.7
Ron Brewer (to SA)	G	6'4	185	28	13	210	27	58	47	11	17	65	13	6	10	0	6	5	65	16	1.0	0.5	0.8	5.0
Sam Williams (to Phi)	F	6'8	215	24	7	59	11	26	42	6	7	86	13	2	6	0	6	3	28	8	1.9	0.3	0.9	4.0
Lorenzo Romar (to Mil)	G	6'1	180	25	3	15	2	5	40	2	4	50	1	1	1	0	0	0	6	5	0.3	0.3	0.3	2.0

3-PT FG — Short 22-72, Carroll 0-1, Floyd 8-45, Conner 1-6, Johnson 5-29, Bratz 15-51, Collins 1-5, Tillis 0-2, Manion 3-13, Brewer 0-1, Romar 0-1

SAN DIEGO CLIPPERS 30-52 .366 JIM LYNAM

Use Name	Pos	Hgt	Wgt	Age	TOTAL G	Min	FG	FGA	%	FT	FTA	%	Reb	Ass	PF	DQ	Stls	Blkd Shts	Points	PER GAME Min	Reb	Ass	PF	Points
Michael Brooks	F	6'7	220	25	47	1405	213	445	48	104	151	69	342	88	125	1	50	14	530	30	7.3	1.9	2.7	11.3
Terry Cummings	F	6'9	220	22	81	2907	737	1491	49	380	528	72	777	139	298	6	92	57	1854	36	9.6	1.7	3.7	22.9
James Donaldson	C	7'2	278	26	82	2525	360	604	60	249	327	76	649	90	214	1	40	139	969	31	7.9	1.1	2.6	11.8
Craig Hodges	G	6'3	190	23	76	1571	258	573	45	66	88	75	86	116	166	2	58	1	592	21	1.1	1.5	2.2	7.8
Norm Nixon	G	6'2	175	28	82	3053	587	1270	46	206	271	76	203	**914**	180	1	94	4	1391	37	2.5	11.1	2.2	17.0
Greg Kelser	F	6'7	205	26	80	1783	313	603	52	250	356	70	391	91	249	3	68	31	878	22	4.9	1.1	3.1	11.0
Bill Walton	C	6'11	225	31	55	1476	288	518	56	92	154	60	477	183	153	1	45	88	668	27	8.7	3.3	2.8	12.1
Derek Smith	G-F	6'6	215	22	61	1297	238	436	55	123	163	75	170	82	165	2	33	22	600	21	2.8	1.3	2.7	9.8
Ricky Pierce	G	6'5	205	24	69	1280	268	570	47	149	173	86	135	60	143	1	27	13	685	19	2.0	0.9	2.1	9.9
Jerome Whitehead	F	6'10	225	27	70	921	144	294	49	88	107	82	245	19	159	2	17	12	376	13	3.5	0.3	2.3	5.4
Billy McKinney	G	6'	172	28	80	843	136	305	45	39	46	85	54	161	84	0	27	0	311	11	0.7	2.0	1.1	3.9
Hank McDowell	F	6'9	215	24	57	611	85	197	43	38	56	68	155	37	77	0	14	2	208	11	2.7	0.6	1.4	3.6
Rory White (from Phoe, Mil)	F	6'8	210	24	6	19	4	9	44	0	0	—	4	0	3	0	0	0	8	3	0.7	0.0	0.5	1.3
Hutch Jones	F	6'8	195	24	4	18	0	3	0	1	4	25	0	0	0	0	1	0	1	5	0.0	0.0	0.0	0.3
Linton Townes (from Mil)	F	6'7	195	24	2	17	3	7	43	0	0	—	1	1	3	0	1	2	6	9	0.5	0.5	1.5	3.0
Kevin Loder (from KC)	F	6'6	205	24	1	4	0	0	—	0	0	—	0	0	1	0	0	0	0	4	0.0	0.0	1.0	0.0

3-PT FG — Brooks 0-5, Cummings 0-3, Hodges 10-46, Nixon 11-46, Kelser 2-6, Walton 0-2, Smith 1-6, Pierce 0-9, McKinney 0-2, McDowell 0-3

PLAYOFFS

BOSTON CELTICS K. C. JONES

defeated Washington 3-1; H91-83, H88-85, 108-111(ot), 99-96
defeated New York 4-3; H110-92, H116-102, 92-100, 113-118, H121-99, 104-106, H121-104
defeated Milwaukee 4-1; H119-96, H125-100, 109-100, 113-122, H115-108
defeated Los Angeles 4-3; H109-115, H124-121(ot), 104-137, 129-125(ot), H121-103, 108-119, H111-102

Use Name	Pos	Hgt	Wgt	Age	TOTAL G	Min	FG	FGA	%	FT	FTA	%	Reb	Ass	PF	DQ	Stls	Blkd Shts	Points	PER GAME Min	Reb	Ass	PF	Points
Cedric Maxwell	F	6'8	215	28	23	752	84	167	50	106	136	78	119	55	77	1	22	7	274	33	5.2	2.4	3.3	11.9
Larry Bird	F	6'9	220	27	23	**961**	**229**	**437**	52	**167**	**190**	88	**252**	136	71	0	**54**	27	**632**	42	11.0	5.9	3.1	27.5
Robert Parish	C	7'	230	30	23	869	139	291	48	64	99	65	248	27	100	6	23	41	342	38	10.8	1.2	4.3	14.9
Dennis Johnson	G	6'4	200	29	22	808	129	319	40	104	120	87	79	97	75	1	25	7	365	37	3.6	4.4	3.4	16.6
Gerald Henderson	G	6'2	175	27	23	616	115	237	49	54	75	72	52	97	78	0	34	1	287	27	2.3	4.2	3.4	12.5
Kevin McHale	F-C	6'10	225	26	23	702	123	244	50	94	121	78	143	27	75	1	3	35	340	31	6.2	1.2	3.3	14.8
Quinn Buckner	G	6'3	205	29	23	268	32	79	41	12	22	55	35	28	52	0	13	0	76	12	1.5	1.2	2.3	3.3
Danny Ainge	G	6'4	175	24	19	253	41	90	46	7	10	70	16	38	36	0	9	2	91	13	0.8	2.0	1.9	4.8
Scott Wedman	F-G	6'7	235	31	17	226	40	96	42	5	10	50	47	17	19	0	6	0	89	13	2.8	1.0	1.1	5.2
M. L. Carr	G	6'6	205	32	16	82	13	32	41	10	11	91	8	4	13	0	7	0	38	5	0.5	0.3	0.8	2.4
Greg Kite	C	6'11	250	22	11	38	1	8	13	5	6	83	9	3	9	0	0	1	7	3	0.8	0.3	0.8	0.6
Carlos Clark	G	6'4	210	23	8	20	4	10	40	1	2	50	1	1	3	0	1	2	9	3	0.1	0.1	0.4	1.1

3-PT FG — Maxwell 0-1, Bird 7-17, Johnson 3-7, Henderson 3-11, McHale 0-3, Buckner 0-1, Ainge 2-9, Wedman 4-7, C

LOS ANGELES LAKERS PAT RILEY

defeated Kansas City 3-0; H116-105, H109-102, 108-102
defeated Dallas 4-1; H134-91, H117-101, 115-125(ot), H119-99
defeated Phoenix 4-2; H110-94, H118-102, 127-135(ot), 126-115, H121-126, 99-97
lost to Boston 3-4; 115-109, 121-124(ot), H137-104, H125-129(ot), 103-121, H119-108, 102-111

Use Name	Pos	Hgt	Wgt	Age	TOTAL G	Min	FG	FGA	%	FT	FTA	%	Reb	Ass	PF	DQ	Stls	Blkd Shts	Points	PER GAME Min	Reb	Ass	PF	Points
James Worthy	F	6'9	225	22	21	708	164	274	**60**	42	69	61	105	56	57	0	27	11	371	34	5.0	2.7	2.7	17.7
Kurt Rambis	F	6'8	220	25	21	428	60	92	65	21	33	64	121	14	57	0	10	10	141	20	5.8	0.7	2.7	6.7
Abdul-Jabbar	C	7'2	232	36	21	767	206	371	56	90	120	75	173	79	71	2	23	**45**	502	37	8.2	3.8	3.4	23.9
Michael Cooper	G	6'5	170	27	21	723	88	191	46	50	62	81	82	119	80	1	24	20	238	34	3.9	5.7	3.8	11.3
Magic Johnson	G	6'8	215	24	21	837	151	274	55	80	100	80	139	**284**	71	0	42	20	382	40	6.6	**13.5**	3.4	18.2
Bob McAdoo	F-C	6'9	225	32	20	447	111	215	52	57	81	70	108	12	63	0	12	27	279	22	5.4	0.6	3.2	14.0
Bryan Scott	G	6'3	195	22	20	404	74	161	46	21	35	60	37	34	39	1	18	2	171	20	1.9	1.7	2.0	8.6
Mike McGee	F-G	6'5	190	24	17	370	90	157	57	25	39	64	34	23	52	0	11	1	211	22	2.0	1.4	3.1	12.4
Jamaal Wilkes	F	6'6	190	30	14	196	28	70	40	7	11	64	26	9	27	0	4	2	63	14	1.9	0.6	1.9	4.5
Swen Nater	C	6'11	250	33	17	146	19	38	50	20	26	77	40	1	27	0	1	2	58	9	2.4	0.1	1.6	3.4
Mitch Kupchak (KJ)	F	6'9	230	29	9	69	5	17	29	8	14	57	29	2	12	0	1	2	18	8	3.2	0.2	1.3	2.0
Larry Spriggs	F	6'7	230	24	9	45	7	19	37	11	11	**100**	9	3	11	0	0	1	25	5	1.0	0.3	1.2	2.8

3-PT FG — Worthy 1-2, Cooper 12-36, Johnson 0-7, McAdoo 0-1, Scott 2-10, McGee 6-17, Wilkes 0-1

1983/84 N.B.A. — PLAYOFFS

ILWAUKEE BUCKS — DON NELSON

defeated Atlanta 3-2; H105-89, H101-87, 94-103, 97-100, H118-89
defeated New Jersey 4-2; H100-106, H98-94, 100-93, 99-106, H94-82, 98-97
lost to Boston 1-4; 96-119, 110-125, H100-109, H122-113, 108-115

se Name	Pos	Hgt	Wgt	Age	G	Min	FG	FGA	%	FT	FTA	%	Reb	Ass	PF	DQ	Stls	Blkd Shts	Points	Min	Reb	Ass	PF	Points
larques Johnson	F	6'7	218	27	16	605	129	273	47	65	90	72	85	55	50	0	17	6	324	38	5.3	3.4	3.1	20.3
lton Lister	F-C	7'	240	25	16	368	39	78	50	30	48	63	96	10	63	2	5	24	108	23	6.0	0.6	3.9	6.8
ob Lanier	C	6'11	265	35	16	499	82	171	48	39	44	89	117	55	57	1	11	10	203	31	7.3	3.4	3.6	12.7
idney Moncrief	G	6'4	190	26	16	618	99	191	52	106	134	79	111	68	54	1	28	9	305	39	6.9	4.3	3.4	19.1
like Dunleavy	G	6'3	180	29	15	393	59	129	46	33	36	92	35	46	59	2	17	0	169	26	2.3	3.1	3.9	11.3
unior Bridgeman	F-G	6'5	210	30	16	499	88	193	46	53	65	82	64	44	37	1	6	5	230	31	4.0	2.8	2.3	14.4
'aul Pressey	G-F	6'5	185	25	16	351	52	100	52	38	56	68	59	50	53	1	22	9	142	22	3.7	3.1	3.3	8.9
'aul Mokeski	F-C	7'	250	26	16	322	34	63	54	30	45	67	88	6	62	0	9	11	98	20	5.5	0.4	3.9	6.1
orenzo Romar	G	6'1	180	25	13	67	9	20	45	7	11	64	3	15	9	0	0	0	25	5	0.2	1.2	0.7	1.9
landy Breuer	C	7'3	230	23	12	66	11	26	42	3	5	60	17	4	18	0	0	6	25	6	1.4	0.3	1.5	2.1
evin Grevey	G	6'5	210	36	5	27	2	9	22	4	6	67	2	1	1	0	0	0	8	5	0.4	0.2	0.2	1.6
larvey Catchings	F-C	6'9	218	32	5	25	1	2	50	1	2	50	5	1	7	0	0	0	3	5	1.0	0.2	1.4	0.6
Nate Archibald (foot injury)																								

3-PT FG — Johnson 1-4, Moncrief 1-4, Dunleavy 18-50, Bridgeman 1-9, Pressey 0-3, Mokeski 0-2, Romar 0-3

HOENIX SUNS — JOHN MAC LEOD

defeated Portland 3-2; 113-106, 116-122, H106-103, H110-113, 117-105
defeated Utah 4-2; 95-105, 102-97, H106-94, H111-110(OT), 106-118, H102-82
lost to Los Angeles 2-4; 94-110, 102-118, H135-127(OT), H115-126, 126-121, H97-99

se Name	Pos	Hgt	Wgt	Age	G	Min	FG	FGA	%	FT	FTA	%	Reb	Ass	PF	DQ	Stls	Blkd Shts	Points	Min	Reb	Ass	PF	Points
arry Nance	F	6'10	215	24	17	633	118	200	59	51	76	67	148	40	59	1	16	34	287	37	8.7	2.4	3.5	16.9
laurice Lucas	F	6'9	238	31	17	570	116	227	51	63	78	81	169	61	66	2	12	8	295	34	9.9	3.6	3.9	17.4
ames Edwards	C	7'	225	28	17	463	93	189	49	48	68	71	91	27	62	3	4	11	234	27	5.4	1.6	3.6	13.8
Valter Davis	G	6'6	200	29	17	623	175	327	54	70	78	90	46	109	55	0	29	3	423	37	2.7	6.4	3.2	24.9
yle Macy	G	6'3	190	26	17	620	77	157	49	12	16	75	54	98	43	0	22	2	176	36	3.2	5.8	2.5	10.4
lvan Adams	C	6'9	220	29	17	312	53	126	42	36	53	68	87	42	53	0	17	11	142	18	5.1	2.5	3.1	8.4
harles Pittman	F	6'8	220	25	17	253	28	51	55	18	29	62	64	12	31	0	5	5	74	15	3.8	0.7	1.8	4.4
'aul Westphal	G	6'4	195	33	17	222	30	80	38	28	32	88	8	37	23	0	12	0	90	13	0.5	2.2	1.4	5.3
like Sanders	F-G	6'6	210	23	15	152	22	46	48	16	17	94	20	7	31	0	6	4	60	10	1.3	0.5	2.1	4.0
lod Foster	G	6'1	160	23	16	128	10	39	26	9	9	100	13	18	21	0	5	1	29	8	0.8	1.1	1.3	1.8
lvin Scott	F	6'7	215	28	16	111	10	26	38	4	6	67	24	7	14	0	2	2	25	7	1.5	0.4	0.9	1.6
lick Robey	C	6'11	230	27	10	43	7	16	44	4	8	50	10	2	5	0	2	0	18	4	1.0	0.2	0.5	1.8

3-PT FG — Davis 3-11, Macy 10-22, Pittman 0-1, Westphal 2-9, Foster 0-5, Scott 1-1, Robey 0-1

ALLAS MAVERICKS — DICK MOTTA

defeated Seattle 3-2; H88-86, H92-95, 94-104, 107-96, H105-104(OT)
lost to Los Angeles 1-4; 91-134, 101-117, H125-115, H115-122 (OT), 99-115

se Name	Pos	Hgt	Wgt	Age	G	Min	FG	FGA	%	FT	FTA	%	Reb	Ass	PF	DQ	Stls	Blkd Shts	Points	Min	Reb	Ass	PF	Points
lark Aguirre	F	6'6	235	24	10	350	88	184	48	44	57	77	76	32	34	2	5	5	220	35	7.6	3.2	3.4	22.0
ay Vincent	F	6'7	225	24	10	353	48	124	39	56	62	90	70	19	36	1	7	1	152	35	7.0	1.9	3.6	15.2
'at Cummings	C-F	6'9	235	27	10	300	47	115	41	14	15	93	72	15	30	0	4	2	108	30	7.2	1.5	3.0	10.8
lolando Blackman	G	6'6	190	24	10	397	93	175	53	53	63	84	41	40	15	0	6	4	239	40	4.1	4.0	1.5	23.9
rad Davis	G	6'3	180	28	10	304	33	73	45	15	19	79	19	50	18	0	6	0	81	30	1.9	5.0	1.8	8.1
erek Harper	G	6'4	185	22	10	226	24	51	47	5	7	71	20	28	16	0	11	2	50	23	2.0	2.8	1.6	5.0
ale Ellis	F	6'7	205	23	8	178	26	80	33	6	8	75	42	4	17	0	10	2	59	22	5.3	0.5	2.1	7.4
urt Nimphius	C	6'10	218	25	10	178	14	33	42	14	17	82	53	13	24	0	0	14	42	18	5.3	1.3	2.4	4.2
ill Garnett	F	6'9	225	23	8	74	15	30	50	7	8	88	22	4	10	0	0	2	38	9	2.8	0.5	1.3	4.8
lston Turner	G	6'5	220	24	8	53	7	20	35	0	0	—	10	8	4	0	6	1	14	7	1.3	1.0	0.5	1.8
lark West	C	6'10	230	23	4	32	5	9	56	2	3	67	7	3	11	1	0	3	12	8	1.8	0.8	2.8	3.0
loger Phegley	G	6'6	215	27	1	5	0	4	0	2	2	100	0	1	0	0	2	0	2	5	0.0	1.0	0.0	2.0

3-PT FG — Aguirre 0-5, Vincent 0-1, Davis 0-2, Harper 3-8, Ellis 1-12, Garnett 1-1, Phegley 0-1

IEW JERSEY NETS — STAN ALBECK

defeated Philadelphia 3-2; 101-116, 102-116, H100-108, H102-110, 101-98
lost to Milwaukee 2-4; 106-100, 94-98, H93-100, H106-99, 82-94, H97-98

se Name	Pos	Hgt	Wgt	Age	G	Min	FG	FGA	%	FT	FTA	%	Reb	Ass	PF	DQ	Stls	Blkd Shts	Points	Min	Reb	Ass	PF	Points
lbert King	F	6'6	190	24	11	295	53	128	41	32	46	70	58	25	32	0	10	4	138	27	5.3	2.3	2.9	12.5
uck Williams	F	6'8	215	23	11	473	63	130	48	45	81	56	155	16	44	2	15	17	171	43	14.1	1.5	4.0	15.5
arryl Dawkins	C	6'11	251	26	11	340	66	118	56	70	83	84	68	13	52	4	5	10	202	31	6.2	1.2	4.7	18.4
tis Birdsong	G	6'4	195	28	11	387	71	171	42	25	48	52	26	41	38	0	20	1	167	35	2.4	3.7	3.5	15.2
lichael Ray Richardson	G	6'5	195	28	11	443	69	169	41	41	56	73	54	79	40	1	34	4	185	40	4.9	7.2	3.6	16.8
like Gminski	C-F	6'11	250	24	11	223	29	50	58	36	52	69	55	6	17	0	7	15	94	20	5.0	0.5	1.5	8.5
like O'Koren	F	6'7	217	27	11	216	25	59	42	5	6	83	35	21	37	1	3	4	55	20	3.2	1.9	3.4	5.0
arwin Cook	G	6'3	190	25	11	185	30	82	37	17	24	71	18	31	26	0	15	0	81	17	1.6	2.8	2.4	7.4
elvin Ransey	G	6'1	180	25	5	44	6	14	43	0	0	—	1	10	6	0	1	1	13	9	0.2	2.0	1.2	2.6
eggie Johnson	F	6'9	205	26	7	17	0	4	0	5	6	83	5	0	2	0	0	1	5	2	0.7	0.0	0.3	0.7
ill Willoughby	F	6'8	205	26	3	13	1	3	33	0	0	—	3	0	2	0	0	0	2	4	1.0	0.0	0.7	0.7
oots Walker	G	6'	172	32	2	4	0	1	0	0	0	—	0	0	0	0	0	0	0	2	0.0	0.0	0.0	0.0

3-PT FG — King 0-2, Dawkins 0-3, Birdsong 0-1, Richardson 6-22, O'Koren 0-1, Cook 4-13, Ransey 1-1

1983/84 N.B.A. — PLAYOFFS

NEW YORK KNICKERBOCKERS — **HUBIE BROWN** — defeated Detroit 3-2; 94-93, 105-113, H120-113, H112-119, 127-123(OT)
lost to Boston 3-4; 92-110, 102-116, H100-92, H118-113, 99-121, H106-104, 104-121

Use Name	Pos	Hgt	Wgt	Age	G	Min	FG	FGA	%	FT	FTA	%	Reb	Ass	PF	DQ	Stls	Blkd Shts	Points	Min	Reb	Ass	PF	Points
Bernard King	F	6'7	205	27	12	477	162	282	57	93	123	76	74	36	48	0	14	6	417	40	6.2	3.0	4.0	34.
Truck Robinson	F	6'7	225	32	12	362	38	74	51	9	15	60	97	7	41	2	7	9	85	30	8.1	0.6	3.4	7.
Bill Cartwright	C	7'1	245	26	12	398	70	126	56	69	80	86	99	5	44	0	2	14	209	33	8.3	0.4	3.7	17.
Ray Williams	G	6'3	195	29	11	310	46	130	35	29	39	74	39	88	39	1	17	1	123	28	3.5	8.0	3.5	11.
Rory Sparrow	G	6'2	195	25	12	389	54	121	45	24	30	80	26	86	41	2	12	1	134	32	2.2	7.2	3.4	11.
Trent Tucker	G	6'5	193	24	12	254	42	84	50	6	10	60	18	27	32	0	11	3	91	21	1.5	2.3	2.7	7
Louis Orr	F	6'8	195	25	12	229	29	70	41	15	19	79	50	6	32	1	4	1	73	19	4.2	0.5	2.7	6.
Marvin Webster	C	7'1	240	31	12	204	14	29	48	9	15	60	56	3	32	0	4	17	37	17	4.7	0.3	2.7	3.
Darrell Walker	G	6'4	180	22	12	195	27	73	37	28	46	61	35	20	29	0	24	2	82	16	2.9	1.7	2.4	6
Ernie Grunfield	F-G	6'6	215	28	11	84	11	23	48	4	4	100	9	6	12	0	2	0	26	8	0.8	0.5	1.1	2.
Eric Frensten	F	6'10	205	30	2	3	1	2	50	0	0	—	0	0	0	0	0	0	2	2	0.0	0.0	0.0	1.

3-PT FG — King 0-1, Williams 2-12, Sparrow 2-6, Tucker 1-5

UTAH JAZZ — **FRANK LAYDEN** — defeated Denver 3-2; H123-121, H116-132, 117-121, 129-124, H127-111
lost to Phoenix 2-4; H105-95, H97-102, 94-106, 110-111(OT), H118-106, 82-102

Use Name	Pos	Hgt	Wgt	Age	G	Min	FG	FGA	%	FT	FTA	%	Reb	Ass	PF	DQ	Stls	Blkd Shts	Points	Min	Reb	Ass	PF	Points
Adrian Dantley	F	6'5	210	27	11	454	117	232	50	120	139	86	83	46	30	0	10	1	354	41	7.5	4.2	2.7	32
Thurl Bailey	F	6'11	215	22	11	340	50	97	52	17	21	81	61	10	33	0	2	11	117	31	5.5	0.9	3.0	10.
Mark Eaton	C	7'4	280	26	11	254	21	41	51	8	17	47	76	9	33	1	5	34	50	23	6.9	0.8	3.0	4.
Darrell Griffith	G	6'4	190	25	11	417	81	183	44	33	48	69	65	41	24	0	19	2	211	38	5.9	3.7	2.2	19.
Rickey Green	G	6'1	170	29	11	404	64	151	42	32	43	74	34	104	17	0	19	4	161	37	3.1	9.5	1.5	14.
Jeff Wilkins	F-C	6'11	240	29	11	205	30	57	53	17	22	77	49	5	32	0	0	5	77	19	4.5	0.5	2.9	7.
Rich Kelley	C	7'	240	30	11	201	15	27	56	25	29	86	58	22	42	1	9	6	55	18	5.3	2.0	3.8	5.
John Drew	F-G	6'6	205	29	11	172	43	85	51	26	33	79	25	9	26	0	4	0	112	16	2.3	0.8	2.4	10.
Jerry Eaves	G	6'4	185	24	11	132	22	46	48	10	13	77	10	13	10	0	5	2	55	12	0.9	1.2	0.9	5.
Tom Boswell	F	6'9	225	30	5	55	3	4	75	2	5	40	6	2	12	0	0	1	8	11	1.2	0.4	2.4	1.
Bob Hansen	G	6'6	190	22	4	18	2	7	29	1	2	50	7	2	4	0	0	0	7	5	1.8	0.5	1.0	1.
J.J. Anderson	F	6'8	195	23	5	13	5	8	63	0	0	—	4	0	2	0	0	1	11	3	0.8	0.0	0.4	2.

3 PT-FG — Bailey 0-2, Griffith 16-45, Green 1-4, Eaves 1-3, Hansen 2-3, Anderson 1-1

ATLANTA HAWKS — **MIKE FRATELLO** — lost to Milwaukee 2-3; 89-105, 87-101, H103-94, H100-97, 89-118

Use Name	Pos	Hgt	Wgt	Age	G	Min	FG	FGA	%	FT	FTA	%	Reb	Ass	PF	DQ	Stls	Blkd Shts	Points	Min	Reb	Ass	PF	Points
Dominique Wilkins	F	6'8	200	23	5	197	35	84	42	26	31	84	41	11	13	0	12	1	96	39	8.2	2.2	2.6	19.
Dan Roundfield	F	6'8	215	30	5	191	30	69	43	25	35	71	44	8	16	1	2	7	86	38	8.8	1.6	3.2	17.
Tree Rollins	C	7'1	235	28	5	152	10	25	40	5	8	63	34	1	23	1	2	10	25	30	6.8	0.2	4.6	5.
Glenn Rivers	G	6'4	185	22	5	130	16	32	50	36	41	88	10	16	16	0	12	4	68	26	2.0	3.2	3.2	13.
Johnny Davis	G	6'2	180	28	5	131	22	55	40	6	6	100	10	24	10	0	1	0	50	26	2.0	4.8	2.0	10.
Eddie Johnson	G	6'2	190	28	5	123	19	54	35	15	22	68	9	24	11	0	6	0	54	25	1.8	4.8	2.2	10.
Randy Wittman	F-G	6'6	210	24	5	96	20	37	54	0	0	—	9	11	5	0	1	0	40	19	1.8	2.2	1.0	8.
Rickey Brown	C-F	6'10	235	25	5	83	10	21	48	10	12	83	19	2	19	0	0	1	30	17	3.8	0.4	3.8	6.
Mike Glenn	G	6'3	185	28	5	53	5	14	36	0	0	—	5	5	9	0	2	0	10	11	1.0	1.0	1.8	2.
Scott Hastings	F-C	6'10	235	23	5	32	2	9	22	3	4	75	8	1	4	0	1	0	7	6	1.6	0.2	0.8	1.
Billy Paultz	C	6'11	255	35	2	7	1	3	33	0	0	—	0	0	0	0	0	0	2	4	0.0	0.0	0.0	1.
Mark Landsberger	F	6'8	230	28	2	5	0	1	0	0	0	—	1	0	1	0	0	0	0	3	0.5	0.0	0.5	0.

3-PT FG — Wilkins 0-1, Roundfield 1-1, Rivers 0-3, Johnson 1-6

DENVER NUGGETS — **DOUG MOE** — lost to Utah 2-3; 121-123, 132-116, H121-117, H124-129, 111-127

Use Name	Pos	Hgt	Wgt	Age	G	Min	FG	FGA	%	FT	FTA	%	Reb	Ass	PF	DQ	Stls	Blkd Shts	Points	Min	Reb	Ass	PF	Points
Alex English	F	6'8	190	29	5	203	60	102	59	25	28	89	40	28	17	0	3	2	145	41	8.0	5.6	3.4	29.
Kiki Vandeweghe	F	6'8	220	25	5	180	49	96	51	27	28	96	23	20	14	1	9	5	127	36	4.6	4.0	2.8	25.
Dan Issel	C	6'9	240	35	5	153	52	102	51	32	39	82	40	8	15	0	6	6	137	31	8.0	1.6	3.0	27.
T. R. Dunn	G	6'4	192	28	5	178	14	25	56	5	7	71	39	8	19	0	10	4	33	36	7.8	1.6	3.8	6.
Rob Williams	G	6'2	175	22	5	149	21	47	45	10	12	83	19	24	19	1	3	1	57	30	3.8	4.8	3.8	11.
Bill Hanzlik	F-G	6'7	185	26	5	82	11	19	58	6	6	100	8	21	16	0	3	0	28	16	1.6	4.2	3.2	5.
Dan Schayes	C	6'11	245	24	5	81	11	18	61	6	8	75	24	4	20	0	4	3	28	16	4.8	0.8	4.0	5.
Mike Evans	G	6'1	170	28	5	77	9	28	32	4	4	100	3	12	13	0	0	0	23	15	0.6	2.4	2.6	4.
Howard Carter	G	6'5	215	22	5	60	7	22	32	0	0	—	5	5	3	0	4	1	15	12	1.0	1.0	0.6	3.
Richard Anderson	F	6'10	240	23	4	37	6	15	40	4	6	67	9	5	6	0	0	1	16	9	2.3	1.3	1.5	4.

3-PT FG — English 0-1, Vandeweghe 2-5, Issel 1-2, Williams 5-13, Hanzlik 0-2, Evans 1-8, Carter 1-5, Anderson 0-1

DETROIT PISTONS — **CHUCK DALY** — lost to New York 2-3; H93-94, H113-105, 113-120, 119-112, H123-127(OT)

Use Name	Pos	Hgt	Wgt	Age	G	Min	FG	FGA	%	FT	FTA	%	Reb	Ass	PF	DQ	Stls	Blkd Shts	Points	Min	Reb	Ass	PF	Points
Kelly Tripucka	F	6'6	230	24	5	208	48	102	47	41	51	80	23	15	22	1	11	0	137	42	4.6	3.0	4.4	27.
Kent Benson	F-C	6'10	245	29	5	129	16	37	43	6	10	60	30	7	14	0	5	7	38	26	6.0	1.4	2.8	7.
Bill Laimbeer	C	6'11	245	26	5	165	29	51	57	18	20	90	62	12	23	2	4	3	76	33	12.4	2.4	4.6	15.
John Long	G	6'5	200	27	5	149	20	55	36	15	15	100	11	2	15	0	7	0	55	30	2.2	0.4	3.0	11.
Isiah Thomas	G	6'1	185	22	5	198	39	83	47	27	35	77	19	55	22	1	13	6	107	40	3.8	11.0	4.4	21.
Vinnie Johnson	G	6'2	200	27	5	132	17	46	37	17	19	89	14	12	9	0	1	1	51	26	2.8	2.4	1.8	10.
Cliff Levingston	F	6'8	220	22	5	101	15	19	79	10	16	63	24	1	15	0	1	2	40	20	4.8	0.2	3.0	8.
Earl Cureton	F-C	6'9	215	26	5	93	15	31	48	2	6	33	33	2	9	0	2	1	32	19	6.6	0.4	1.8	6.
Terry Tyler	F	6'7	220	27	5	42	10	24	42	5	9	56	7	1	4	0	0	3	25	8	1.4	0.2	0.8	5.
Lionell Hollins	G	6'3	185	30	2	6	0	1	0	0	0	—	0	0	0	0	0	1	0	3	0.0	0.0	0.0	0.
Ray Tolbert	F	6'9	225	25	1	2	0	0	—	0	0	—	0	0	0	0	0	0	0	2	0.0	0.0	0.0	0.

3-PT FG — Tripucka 0-1, Long 0-1, Thomas 2-6, Johnson 0-1

se Name	Pos	Hgt	Wgt	Age	TOTAL G	Min	FG	FGA	%	FT	FTA	%	Reb	Ass	PF	DQ	Stls	Blkd Shts	Points	PER GAME Min	Reb	Ass	PF	Points

1983/84 N.B.A. — PLAYOFFS

se Name	Pos	Hgt	Wgt	Age	G	Min	FG	FGA	%	FT	FTA	%	Reb	Ass	PF	DQ	Stls	Blkd Shts	Points	Min	Reb	Ass	PF	Points
ANSAS CITY KINGS	**COTTON FITZSIMMONS** lost to Los Angeles 0-3; 105-116, 102-109, H102-108																							
ddie Johnson	F	6'8	215	24	3	107	21	48	44	7	7	100	10	12	8	0	3	1	51	36	3.3	4.0	2.7	17.0
arry Micheaux	F	6'9	220	23	3	65	12	18	67	6	10	60	21	3	10	0	0	5	30	22	7.0	1.0	3.3	10.0
aSalle Thompson	C	6'10	248	22	3	93	18	40	45	9	11	82	30	4	14	0	3	4	45	31	10.0	1.3	4.7	15.0
like Woodson	G	6'5	198	25	3	87	18	44	41	13	15	87	8	9	11	0	2	0	49	29	2.7	3.0	3.7	16.3
arry Drew	G	6'1	180	25	3	70	7	19	37	3	5	60	4	11	5	0	3	0	17	23	1.3	3.7	1.7	5.7
leggie Theus	G	6'7	205	26	3	81	17	43	40	9	10	90	11	16	9	0	5	0	43	27	3.7	5.3	3.0	14.3
lark Olberding	F	6'8	230	27	3	60	6	15	40	8	14	57	15	6	6	0	0	0	20	20	5.0	2.0	2.0	6.7
ave Robinson	C	6'10	240	24	3	51	4	12	33	1	2	50	15	2	6	0	1	0	9	17	5.0	0.7	2.0	3.0
on Buse	G	6'4	195	33	3	50	7	16	44	4	6	67	3	11	5	0	1	1	21	17	1.0	3.7	1.7	7.0
illy Knight	F	6'6	195	31	3	37	8	24	33	2	2	100	3	2	2	0	0	0	18	12	1.0	0.7	0.7	6.0
d Nealy	F	6'7	238	23	2	19	2	2	100	2	2	100	6	2	1	0	0	0	6	10	3.0	1.0	0.5	3.0
	3-PT FG — Johnson 2-5, Woodson 0-1, Theus 0-3, Buse 3-6																							
HILADELPHIA 76ers	**BILLY CUNNINGHAM** lost to New Jersey 2-3; H101-116, H102-116, 108-100, 110-102, H98-101																							
ulius Erving	F	6'7	205	33	5	194	36	76	47	19	22	86	32	25	14	0	8	6	91	39	6.4	5.0	2.8	18.2
obby Jones	F	6'9	212	32	5	130	15	31	48	18	19	95	23	9	12	0	3	7	48	26	4.6	1.8	2.4	9.6
loses Malone	C	6'10	255	28	5	212	38	83	46	31	32	97	69	7	15	0	3	11	107	42	13.8	1.4	3.0	21.4
ndrew Toney	G	6'3	188	26	5	180	40	77	52	23	30	77	11	19	24	0	4	1	103	36	2.2	3.8	4.8	20.6
laurice Cheeks	G	6'1	180	27	5	171	35	67	52	13	15	87	12	19	18	0	13	0	83	34	2.4	3.8	3.6	16.6
lint Richardson	G	6'3	195	27	5	115	13	23	57	11	12	92	16	10	17	0	3	1	37	23	3.2	2.0	3.4	7.4
larc Iavaroni	F	6'9	225	27	4	64	7	15	47	7	8	88	8	3	18	1	1	1	22	16	2.0	0.8	4.5	5.5
am Williams	F	6'8	215	24	4	55	2	8	25	1	2	50	6	3	7	0	2	6	8	14	1.5	0.8	1.8	2.0
lemon Johnson	C-F	6'10	240	27	5	45	4	12	33	0	0	—	6	0	8	0	1	4	5	9	1.2	0.0	1.6	1.0
Ves Matthews	G	6'1	170	24	4	23	4	8	50	1	2	50	0	4	4	0	1	0	10	6	0.0	1.0	1.0	2.5
edale Threatt	G	6'2	175	22	3	6	1	3	33	0	0	—	2	1	0	0	1	0	3	2	0.7	0.3	0.0	1.0
eo Rautins	F	6'8	215	23	3	5	1	3	33	0	0	—	2	1	2	0	1	0	2	2	0.7	0.3	0.7	0.7
	3-PT FG — Erving 0-2, Toney 0-5, Cheeks 0-1, Iavaroni 1-2, Matthews 1-2, Threatt 0-2, Rautins 1-2																							
ORTLAND TRAIL BLAZERS	**JACK RAMSAY** lost to Phoenix 2-3; H106-113, H112-116, 103-106, 113-110, H105-117																							
alvin Natt	F	6'6	220	26	5	195	37	72	51	25	36	69	38	9	10	0	6	1	99	39	7.6	1.8	2.0	19.8
enny Carr	F	6'7	230	28	5	180	31	59	53	12	19	63	35	6	22	1	2	2	74	36	7.0	1.2	4.4	14.8
lychal Thompson	C-F	6'10	226	28	4	121	22	44	50	17	22	77	29	15	11	0	5	3	61	30	7.3	3.8	2.8	15.3
im Paxon	G-F	6'6	200	26	5	172	40	78	51	363	40	908	19	12	13	0	2	0	114	34	3.8	2.4	2.6	22.8
arnell Valentine	G	6'2	185	24	5	178	30	60	50	32	35	91	11	42	23	2	9	1	92	36	2.2	8.4	4.6	18.4
Vayne Cooper	C	6'10	220	27	5	104	10	27	37	4	8	50	20	4	14	0	1	4	24	21	4.0	0.8	2.8	4.8
lyde Drexler	G-F	6'7	210	21	5	85	15	35	43	6	7	86	17	8	11	0	5	1	36	17	3.4	1.6	2.2	7.2
afayette Lever	G	6'3	175	23	5	75	8	30	27	8	10	80	15	9	6	0	4	0	26	15	3.0	1.8	1.2	5.2
udie Norris	C	6'9	250	23	5	52	6	10	60	5	8	63	15	4	13	1	1	1	17	10	3.0	0.8	2.6	3.4
eff Lamp	G	6'6	195	24	3	19	2	6	33	0	0	—	0	0	1	0	0	0	4	6	0.0	0.0	0.3	1.3
ete Verhoeven	F	6'9	215	24	3	19	0	0	—	2	2	100	0	0	10	0	1	0	2	6	0.0	0.0	3.3	0.7
	3-PT FG — Natt 0-3, Paxson 1-5, Drexler 0-1, Lever 2-3																							
EATTLE SUPERSONICS	**LENNY WILKINS** lost to Dallas 2-3; 86-88, 95-92, H104-94, H96-107, 104-105(ot)																							
Danny Vranes	F	6'7	210	25	5	147	16	39	41	4	7	57	38	11	24	1	3	6	36	29	7.6	2.2	4.8	7.2
Tom Chambers	F	6'10	225	24	5	191	28	59	47	12	18	67	33	8	23	0	5	3	68	38	6.6	1.6	4.6	13.6
Jack Sikma	C	6'11	250	28	5	193	49	98	50	12	14	86	51	5	22	1	3	7	110	39	10.2	1.0	4.4	22.0
Al Wood	G-F	6'6	193	25	5	157	26	56	46	8	12	67	34	10	16	0	1	1	60	31	6.8	2.0	3.2	12.0
Gus Williams	G	6'2	175	30	5	215	50	98	51	15	21	71	12	57	7	0	8	3	117	43	2.4	11.4	1.4	23.4
Reggie King	F	6'6	230	26	5	91	5	12	42	0	0	—	17	6	14	0	2	3	10	18	3.4	1.2	2.8	2.0
Fred Brown	G	6'3	185	35	5	88	20	47	43	8	11	73	7	10	4	0	4	0	49	18	1.4	2.0	0.8	9.8
Steve Hawes	C-F	6'9	220	33	5	74	6	14	43	2	2	100	20	7	6	0	2	0	15	15	4.0	1.4	1.2	3.0
Scooter McCray	F	6'9	215	23	4	38	4	6	67	0	1	0	6	3	8	0	1	0	8	10	1.5	0.8	2.0	2.0
Jon Sundvold	G	6'2	170	22	3	22	3	8	38	2	2	100	2	5	1	0	0	0	8	7	0.7	1.7	0.3	2.7
Clay Johnson	G	6'4	185	27	3	9	2	4	50	0	0	—	1	1	3	0	1	0	4	3	0.3	0.3	1.0	1.3
	3-PT FG — Vranes 0-1, Chambers 0-1, Sikma 0-1, Wood 0-1, Williams 2-6, Brown 1-3, Hawes 1-2, McCray 0-1, Sundvold 0-3, Johnson 0-1																							
WASHINGTON BULLETS	**GENE SHUE** lost to Boston 1-3; 83-91, 85-88, H111-108(OT), H96-99																							
Greg Ballard	F-G	6'7	215	28	4	168	27	59	46	12	13	92	24	14	12	0	7	3	66	42	6.0	3.5	3.0	16.5
Jeff Ruland	F-C	6'10	240	25	4	187	37	71	52	22	27	81	51	31	15	0	2	3	96	47	12.8	7.8	3.8	24.0
Rick Mahorn	C	6'10	240	25	4	154	15	25	60	8	10	80	43	6	19	0	1	6	38	39	10.8	1.5	4.8	9.5
Ricky Sobers	G	6'3	198	30	4	150	25	57	44	8	10	80	5	6	19	1	5	2	61	38	1.3	1.5	4.8	15.3
Frank Johnson	G	6'2	185	25	4	156	24	42	57	8	8	100	13	25	16	0	5	0	57	39	3.3	6.3	4.0	14.3
Jeff Malone	G	6'4	205	22	4	71	12	26	46	0	0	—	5	2	6	0	1	2	24	18	1.3	0.5	1.5	6.0
Tom McMillen	F	6'11	235	31	4	42	4	16	25	1	2	50	2	5	6	0	0	0	9	11	0.5	1.3	1.5	2.3
Joe Kopicki	F	6'9	240	23	3	25	3	6	50	0	0	—	5	1	6	0	0	0	6	8	1.7	0.3	2.0	2.0
Charlie Davis	F	6'7	215	25	3	17	7	12	58	0	0	—	3	0	0	0	0	0	14	6	1.0	0.0	0.0	4.7
Darren Daye	G	6'8	220	23	3	15	1	5	20	2	2	100	0	1	2	0	0	1	4	5	0.0	0.3	0.7	1.3
	3-PT FG — Ballard 0-1, Ruland 0-1, Mahorn 0-1, Sobers 3-10, Johnson 1-3, Malone 0-1																							

Team		G	FG	FGA	%	FT	FTA	%	REBOUNDS			Assists	PF	Steals	Blocked Shots	Turn Overs	Points	Points per game
									Offense	Defense	Total							
TEAM STATISTICS EASTERN CONFERENCE ATLANTIC DIVISION																		
Boston	Off.	82	3616	7235	50	1907	2407	79	1159	**2538**	3697	2122	1949	673	430	1420	9194	112.1
	Def.	82	3463	7372	47	1659	2143	77	1101	2227	3328	1957	2090	703	328	1329	8656	105.6
	Diff.		+153	-137	+3	+248	+264	+2	+58	+311	**+369**	+165	+141	-30	+102	-91	**+538**	**+6.5**
Philadelphia	Off.	82	3384	6833	50	2041	2706	75	1181	2382	3563	2032	2040	807	**653**	1628	8838	107.8
	Def.	82	3427	7136	48	1757	2367	74	1235	2237	3472	2062	2237	805	483	1559	8658	105.6
	Diff.		-43	-303	+2	+284	**+339**	+1	-54	+145	+91	-30	+197	+2	**+170**	-69	+180	+2.2
New York	Off.	82	3386	6837	50	1944	2510	77	1088	2230	3318	2041	2281	803	360	1587	8763	106.9
	Def.	82	3260	6687	49	1876	2474	76	1045	2171	3216	2049	2197	721	397	1683	8448	103.0
	Diff.		+126	+150	+1	+68	+36	+1	+43	+59	+102	-8	-84	+82	-37	+96	+315	+3.9
New Jersey	Off.	82	3614	7258	50	1742	2488	70	1221	2313	3534	2148	2243	814	499	1608	9019	110.0
	Def.	82	3422	6974	49	2037	2675	76	1097	2307	3404	1913	2161	781	416	1674	8929	108.9
	Diff.		+192	+284	+1	-295	-187	-6	+124	+6	+130	**+235**	-82	+33	+83	+66	+90	+1.1
Washington	Off.	82	3344	6907	48	1664	2201	76	1027	2387	3414	2192	1989	556	320	1448	8423	102.7
	Def.	82	3465	7086	49	1693	2218	76	1037	2381	3418	2038	2021	706	492	1277	8660	105.6
	Diff.		-121	-179	-1	-29	-17	—	-10	+6	-4	+154	+32	-150	-172	-171	-237	-2.9
CENTRAL DIVISION																		
Milwaukee	Off.	82	3432	6970	49	1743	2354	74	1135	2385	3520	2113	2167	642	489	1415	8666	105.7
	Def.	82	3207	7033	46	1869	2489	75	1252	2235	3487	1959	2093	653	319	1404	**8325**	**101.5**
	Diff.		**+225**	-63	+3	-126	-135	-1	-117	+150	+33	+154	-74	-11	**+170**	-11	+341	+4.2
Detroit	Off.	82	3798	7910	48	1974	2547	78	**1427**	2434	**3861**	2256	2177	697	417	1310	9602	117.1
	Def.	82	3657	7369	50	1941	2577	75	1163	2457	3620	2193	2187	621	527	1480	9308	113.5
	Diff.		+141	**+541**	-2	+33	-30	+3	**+264**	-23	+241	+63	+10	+76	-110	+170	+294	+3.6
Atlanta	Off.	82	3230	6809	47	1838	2414	76	1112	2232	3344	1827	2091	626	558	1329	8321	101.5
	Def.	82	3277	6845	48	1834	2380	77	1191	2410	3601	2026	2087	579	424	1409	8427	102.8
	Diff.		-47	-36	-1	+4	+34	-1	-79	-178	-257	-199	-4	+47	+134	+80	-106	-1.3
Cleveland	Off.	82	3362	7232	46	1619	2178	74	1213	2388	3601	1930	2206	630	375	1332	8386	102.3
	Def.	82	3373	6930	49	1939	2541	76	963	2405	3368	2141	1906	579	395	1224	8735	106.5
	Diff.		-11	+302	-3	-320	-363	-2	+250	-17	+233	-211	-300	+51	-20	-108	-349	-4.2
Chicago	Off.	82	3305	6972	47	1871	2508	75	1141	2300	3441	2095	2196	687	454	1578	8501	103.7
	Def.	82	3502	7092	49	1885	2471	76	1125	2388	3513	2235	2110	786	514	1513	8926	108.9
	Diff.		-197	-120	-2	-14	+37	-1	+16	-88	-72	-140	-86	-99	-60	-65	-425	-5.2
Indiana	Off.	82	3447	7130	48	1624	2119	77	1002	2398	3400	2169	2061	**834**	398	1525	8566	104.5
	Def.	82	3552	7175	50	1828	2415	76	1194	2564	3758	2117	1930	761	444	1587	8961	109.3
	Diff.		-105	-45	-2	-204	-296	+1	-192	-166	-358	+52	-131	+73	-46	+62	-395	-4.8
WESTERN CONFERENCE MIDWEST DIVISION																		
Utah	Off.	82	3606	7242	50	2115	2708	78	1096	2522	3618	2230	1978	695	604	1510	9428	115.0
	Def.	82	3745	7872	48	1799	2414	75	1458	2461	3919	2237	2194	747	466	1438	9335	113.8
	Diff.		-139	-630	+2	**+316**	+294	+3	-362	+61	-301	-7	+216	-52	+138	-72	+93	+1.2
Dallas	Off.	82	3618	7235	50	1774	2350	75	1090	2265	3355	2164	1906	579	360	**1303**	9052	110.4
	Def.	82	3633	7282	50	1688	2198	77	1180	2346	3526	2131	2213	632	417	1386	9017	110.0
	Diff.		-15	-47	—	+86	+152	-2	-90	-81	-171	+33	**+307**	-53	-57	+83	+35	+.4
Denver	Off.	82	**3935**	**7983**	49	**2200**	2690	**82**	1133	2444	3577	**2482**	2279	711	352	1344	**10147**	**123.7**
	Def.	82	4016	7747	52	2143	2860	75	1228	2737	3965	2453	**2272**	671	545	1538	10237	124.8
	Diff.		-81	+236	-3	+57	-170	**+7**	-95	-293	-388	+29	-7	+40	-193	**+194**	-90	-1.1
Kansas City	Off.	82	3516	7230	49	1939	2495	78	1144	2273	3417	2229	2200	715	383	1504	9023	110.0
	Def.	82	3601	7169	50	1909	2510	76	1126	2387	3513	2108	2191	660	493	1584	9144	111.5
	Diff.		-85	+61	-1	+30	-15	+2	+18	-114	-96	+121	-9	+55	-110	+80	-121	-1.5
San Antonio	Off.	82	3909	7721	51	1965	2604	75	1230	2528	3758	2361	2146	685	491	1447	9862	120.3
	Def.	82	3996	7910	51	1840	2427	76	1293	2455	3748	2518	2187	652	464	1427	9884	120.5
	Diff.		-87	-189	—	+125	+177	-1	-63	+73	+10	-157	+41	+33	+27	-20	-22	-.2
Houston	Off.	82	3729	7533	50	1583	2139	74	1200	2483	3683	2204	2317	621	515	1562	9071	110.6
	Def.	82	3583	7412	48	2116	2803	75	1197	2458	3655	2023	1916	782	426	1421	9324	113.7
	Diff.		+146	+121	+2	-533	-664	-1	+3	+25	+28	+181	-401	-161	+89	-141	-253	-3.1
PACIFIC DIVISION																		
Los Angeles	Off.	82	3854	7250	**53**	1712	2272	75	1095	2499	3594	2455	2054	726	478	1578	9478	115.6
	Def.	82	3672	7600	48	1763	2346	75	1253	2154	3407	2261	1973	797	376	1443	9170	111.8
	Diff.		+182	-350	**+5**	-51	-74		-158	**+345**	+187	+194	-81	-71	+102	-135	+308	+3.8
Portland	Off.	82	3632	7189	51	1988	2637	75	1251	2194	3445	2082	2134	814	397	1483	9277	113.1
	Def.	82	3566	6943	51	1797	2366	76	1059	2185	3244	2119	2184	649	440	1633	8986	109.6
	Diff.		+66	+246	—	+191	+271	-1	+192	**+9**	+201	-37	+50	**+165**	-43	+150	+291	+3.5

Team		G	FG	FGA	%	FT	FTA	%	REBOUNDS Offense	Defense	Total	Assists	PF	Steals	Blocked Shots	Turn Overs	Points	Points per game
TEAM STATISTICS																		
WESTERN CONFERENCE PACIFIC DIVISION																		
Seattle	**Off.**	82	3460	7083	49	1918	2460	78	1064	2332	3396	2233	1884	636	350	1360	8865	108.1
	Def.	82	3585	7337	49	1655	2168	76	1167	2404	3571	2278	2097	663	388	1330	8879	108.3
	Diff.		-125	-254	—	+263	+292	+2	-103	-72	-175	-45	+213	-27	-38	-30	-14	-.2
Phoenix	**Off.**	82	3677	7220	51	1673	2204	76	1066	2298	3364	2214	2147	693	388	1451	9101	111.0
	Def.	82	3509	7061	50	1956	2540	77	1180	2346	3526	2131	2213	660	493	1584	9144	111.5
	Diff.		+168	+159	+1	-283	-336	-1	-114	-48	-162	+83	+66	+33	-105	+133	-43	-.5
Gloden State	**Off.**	82	3519	7534	47	1915	2577	74	1390	2171	3561	1837	2108	830	348	1518	9008	109.9
	Def.	82	3725	7210	52	1801	2377	76	1211	2513	3724	2150	2246	691	494	1694	9287	113.3
	Diff.		-206	+324	-5	+114	+200	-2	+179	-342	-163	-313	+138	+139	-146	+176	-279	-3.4
San Diego	**Off.**	82	3634	7325	50	1785	2424	74	1307	2382	3689	1981	2020	567	385	1515	9077	110.7
	Def.	82	3771	7406	51	1749	2233	78	1112	2163	3275	2370	2043	727	458	1242	9344	114.0
	Diff.		-137	-81	-1	+36	+191	-4	+195	+219	+414	-389	+23	-160	-73	-273	-267	-3.3
PLAYOFFS																		
Boston	**Off.**	23	950	2110	45	629	802	78	356	653	1009	530	608	197	123	368	2550	110.9
	Def.	23	956	1956	49	523	696	75	305	641	946	553	646	173	104	383	2454	106.7
	Diff.		-6	+154	-4	+106	+106	+3	+51	+12	+63	-23	+38	+24	+19	+15	+96	+4.2
Los Angeles	**Off.**	21	1003	1879	53	432	601	72	276	627	903	636	567	173	143	336	2459	117.1
	Def.	21	891	1934	46	510	654	78	349	576	925	524	534	161	85	340	2315	110.2
	Diff.		+112	-55	+7	-78	-53	-6	-73	+51	-22	+112	-33	+12	+58	+4	+144	+6.9
Milwaukee	**Off.**	16	605	1255	48	409	542	75	198	484	682	355	470	115	80	291	1640	102.5
	Def.	16	580	1327	44	456	598	76	245	424	669	324	435	127	74	257	1627	101.7
	Diff.		+25	-72	+4	-47	-56	-1	-47	+60	+13	+31	-35	-12	+6	-34	+13	+.8
Phoenix	**Off.**	17	739	1484	50	359	470	76	232	502	734	460	463	132	81	274	1853	109.0
	Def.	17	714	1452	49	406	541	75	239	466	705	447	432	135	75	272	1856	109.2
	Diff.		+25	+32	+1	-47	-71	+1	-7	+36	+29	+13	-31	-3	+6	-2	-3	-.2
Dallas	**Off.**	10	397	901	44	218	261	84	159	273	432	217	215	57	36	131	1017	101.7
	Def.	10	461	891	52	153	212	72	132	315	447	277	255	64	69	133	1088	108.8
	Diff.		-64	+10	-8	+65	+49	+8	+27	-42	-15	-60	+40	-7	-33	+2	-71	-7.1
New Jersey	**Off.**	11	413	929	44	276	402	69	183	295	478	242	296	109	47	193	113	10.3
	Def.	11	404	854	47	291	363	80	132	321	453	237	336	83	69	237	1108	100.7
	Diff.		+9	+75	-3	-15	+39	-11	+51	-26	+25	+5	+40	+26	-22	+44	-995	-90.4
New York	**Off.**	12	494	1014	49	286	381	75	177	326	503	284	350	97	54	219	1279	106.6
	Def.	12	508	1055	48	314	411	76	193	334	527	280	327	112	66	201	1338	111.5
	Diff.		-14	-41	+1	-28	-30	-1	-16	-8	-24	+4	-23	-15	-12	-18	-59	-4.9
Utah	**Off.**	11	453	938	48	291	372	78	145	333	478	263	265	73	67	188	1218	110.7
	Def.	11	487	1013	48	243	293	83	160	321	481	286	311	101	57	166	1231	111.9
	Diff.		-34	-75	—	+48	+79	-5	-15	+12	-3	-23	+46	-28	+10	-22	-13	-1.2
Atlanta	**Off.**	5	170	404	42	126	159	79	68	122	190	103	127	39	23	87	468	93.6
	Def.	5	199	375	53	111	150	74	58	147	205	114	133	31	24	89	515	103.0
	Diff.		-29	+29	-11	+15	+9	+5	+10	-25	-15	-11	+6	+8	-1	+2	-47	-9.4
Denver	**Off.**	5	240	474	51	119	138	86	66	144	210	135	142	42	23	76	609	121.8
	Def.	5	230	448	51	144	178	81	60	151	211	122	126	37	29	81	612	122.4
	Diff.		+10	+26		-25	-40	+5	+6	-7	-1	+13	-16	+5	-6	+5	-3	-.6
Detroit	**Off.**	5	209	449	47	141	181	78	82	141	223	107	133	44	24	83	561	112.2
	Def.	5	218	444	49	117	158	74	73	150	223	133	151	46	30	89	558	111.6
	Diff.		-9	+5	-2	+24	+23	+4	+9	-9	—	-26	+18	-2	-6	+6	+3	+.6
Kansas City	**Off.**	3	120	281	43	64	82	78	49	77	126	78	77	18	11	42	309	103.0
	Def.	3	134	253	53	65	87	75	34	99	133	87	75	17	32	50	333	111.0
	Diff.		-14	+28	-10	-1	-5	+3	+15	-22	-7	-9	-2	+1	-21	+8	-24	-8.0
Philadelphia	**Off.**	5	196	406	48	124	142	87	59	128	187	101	139	41	37	110	519	103.8
	Def.	5	212	426	50	105	152	69	77	140	217	126	123	57	29	106	535	107.0
	Diff.		-16	-20	-2	+19	-10	+18	-18	-12	-30	-25	-16	-16	+8	-4	-16	-3.2
Portland	**Off.**	5	201	421	48	144	187	77	79	121	200	109	154	36	13	70	549	109.8
	Def.	5	223	419	53	110	153	72	53	149	202	136	146	35	22	74	562	112.4
	Diff.		-22	+2	-5	+34	+34	+5	+26	-28	-2	-27	-8	+1	-9	+4	-13	-2.6
Seattle	**Off.**	5	209	441	47	63	88	72	61	160	221	123	128	30	23	59	485	97.0
	Def.	5	187	435	43	110	123	89	75	156	231	103	100	17	20	59	486	97.2
	Diff.		+22	+6	+4	-47	-35	-17	-14	+4	-10	+20	-28	+13	+3	—	-1	-.2
Washington	**Off.**	4	155	319	49	61	72	85	40	111	151	99	101	21	15	61	375	93.8
	Def.	4	150	323	46	84	111	76	43	107	150	93	85	28	25	45	386	96.5
	Diff.		+5	-4	+3	-23	-39	+9	-3	+4	+1	+6	-16	-7	-10	-16	-11	-2.7

Team	W	L	Pct.	GB	Record against playoff teams			Record against non-playoff teams			HOME			ROAD		
					W	L	Pct.	W	L	Pct.	W	L	Pct.	W	L	Pct.
EASTERN CONFERENCE																
ATLANTIC DIVISION																
Boston Celtics	**62**	20	**.756**	—	**40**	17	**.702**	**22**	3	**.880**	**33**	8	**.804**	**29**	12	**.707**
Philadelphia 76ers	52	30	.634	10	33	25	.569	19	5	.792	32	9	.780	20	21	.488
New York Knickerbockers	47	35	.573	15	27	29	.482	20	6	.769	29	12	.707	18	23	.439
New Jersey Nets	45	37	.549	17	28	29	.491	17	8	.680	29	12	.707	16	25	.390
Washington Bullets	35	47	.427	27	22	36	.379	13	11	.542	25	16	.610	10	31	.244
CENTRAL DIVISION																
Milwaukee Bucks	50	32	.610	—	31	25	.554	19	7	.731	30	11	.732	20	21	.488
Detroit Pistons	49	33	.598	1	30	26	.536	19	7	.731	30	11	.732	19	22	.463
Atlanta Hawks	40	42	.488	10	25	31	.446	15	11	.577	31	10	.756	9	32	.220
Cleveland Cavaliers	28	54	.341	22	18	44	.290	10	10	.500	23	18	.561	5	**36**	.122
Chicago Bulls	27	55	.329	23	19	43	.306	8	12	.400	18	**23**	.439	9	32	.220
Indiana Pacers	26	**56**	.317	24	17	**45**	.274	9	11	.450	20	21	.488	6	35	.146
WESTERN CONFERENCE																
MIDWEST DIVISION																
Utah Jazz	45	37	.549	—	27	27	.500	18	10	.643	31	10	.756	14	27	.341
Dallas Mavericks	43	39	.524	2	23	31	.426	20	8	.714	31	10	.756	12	29	.293
Denver Nuggets	38	44	.463	7	22	32	.407	16	12	.571	27	14	.659	11	30	.268
Kansas City Kings	38	44	.463	7	20	34	.37	18	10	.643	26	15	.634	12	29	.293
San Antonio Spurs	37	45	.451	8	22	35	.386	15	7	.682	28	13	.683	9	32	.220
Houston Rockets	29	53	.354	16	18	42	.300	11	11	.500	21	20	.512	8	33	.195
PACIFIC DIVISION																
Los Angeles Lakers	54	28	.659	—	36	18	.667	18	10	.643	28	13	.683	26	15	.634
Portland Trail Blazers	48	34	.585	6	30	24	.556	18	10	.643	**33**	8	**.804**	15	26	.366
Seattle Supersonics	42	40	.512	12	26	26	.500	16	**14**	.533	32	9	.780	10	31	.244
Phoenix Suns	41	41	.500	13	21	33	.389	20	8	.714	31	10	.756	10	31	.244
Golden State Warriors	37	45	.451	17	26	34	.433	11	11	.500	27	14	.659	10	31	.244
San Diego Clippers	30	52	.366	24	20	40	.333	10	12	.455	25	16	.610	5	**36**	.122

1983/84 N.B.A. INDIVIDUAL LEADERS

SCORING
(Minimum 70 Games or 1400 Points)

Name	Team	G	FG	FT	Pts.	Avg.
Dantley	Utah	79	802	813	2418	30.6
Aguirre	Dal	79	925	456	2330	29.5
Vandeweghe	Den	78	895	494	2295	29.4
English	Den	82	907	352	2167	26.4
Gervin	SA	76	765	427	1967	25.9
Bird	Bos	79	758	374	1908	24.2
Mitchell	SA	79	779	275	1839	23.3
Cummings	SD	81	737	380	1854	29.9
Short	GS	79	714	353	1803	22.8

FIELD GOAL PERCENTAGE
(Minimum 300 Made)

Name	Team	FG	FGA	Pct.
Gilmore	SA	351	556	.631
Donaldson	SD	360	604	.596
McGee	LA	347	584	.594
Dawkins	NJ	507	855	.583
Ruland	Was	599	1035	.579
Abdul-Jabbar	LA	716	1238	.578
Nance	Phoe	601	1044	.576
Lanier	Mil	392	685	.572
King	NY	795	1391	.572

FREE THROW PERCENTAGE
(Minimum 125 Made)

Name	Team	FT	FTA	Pct.
Bird	Bos	374	421	.888
Long	Det	243	275	.883
Laimbeer	Det	316	365	.865
Pierce	SD	149	173	.861
Dantley	Utah	813	946	.859
Knight	KC	243	283	.858
Sikma	Sea	411	480	.856
Vandeweghe	Den	494	580	.851
Johnson	Bos	281	330	.851

PERSONAL FOULS

Name	Team	PF
Dawkins	NJ	386
Mahorn	Was	358
Sampson	Hou	339
C. Jones	Hou	335
Lister	Mil	327
Thompson	KC	327

GAMES DISQUALIFIED

Name	Team	Disq.
Dawkins	NJ	22
Sampson	Hou	16
Johnson	KC-Chi	15
Mahorn	Was	14
Hinson	Cle	11
Lister	Mil	11

MINUTES PLAYED

Name	Team	Min.
Ruland	Was	3082
Moncrief	Mil	3075
Nixon	SD	3053
Gilmore	SA	3034
Bird	Bos	3028

TOTAL REBOUNDS PER GAME
(Minimum 70 Games or 800 Rebounds)

Name	Team	G	Reb.	Avg.
Malone	Phi	71	950	13.4
Williams	NJ	81	1000	12.3
Ruland	Was	75	922	12.3
Laimbeer	Det	82	1003	12.2
Sampson	Hou	82	913	11.1
Sikma	Sea	82	911	11.1
Parish	Bos	80	857	10.7
Robinson	Cle	73	753	10.3
Greenwood	Chi	78	786	10.1
Bird	Bos	79	796	10.1

ASSISTS PER GAME
(Minimum 70 Games or 400 Assists)

Name	Team	G	Ass.	Avg.
Johnson	LA	67	875	13.1
Nixon	SD	82	914	11.1
Thomas	Det	82	914	11.1
Lucas	SA	63	673	10.7
Moore	SA	59	566	9.6
Green	Utah	81	748	9.2
Williams	Sea	80	675	8.4
Whatley	Chi	80	662	8.3
Drew	KC	73	558	7.6
Davis	Dal	81	561	6.9

BLOCKED SHOTS PER GAME
(Minimum 70 Games or 100 Blocked Shots)

Name	Team	G	Reb.	Avg.
Eaton	Utah	82	351	4.3
Rollins	Atl	77	277	3.6
Sampson	Hou	82	197	2.4
Nance	Phoe	82	173	2.1
Gilmore	SA	64	132	2.1
Hinson	Cle	80	145	1.8
Thompson	KC	80	145	1.8
Erving	Phi	77	139	1.8
Abdul-Jabbar	LA	80	143	1.8
Carroll	GS	80	142	1.8

3 POINT FIELD GOALS PER GAME
(Minimum 25 Made)

Name	Team	FG	FGA	Avg.
Griffith	Utah	91	252	.361
Evans	Den	32	89	.360
Moore	SA	28	87	.322
Cooper	LA	38	121	.314
Williams	NY	25	81	.309
Sobers	Was	29	111	.261

STEALS PER GAME
(Minimum 70 Games or 125 Steals)

Name	Team	G	Steals	Avg.
Green	Utah	81	215	2.7
Thomas	Det	82	204	2.5
Williams	Sea	80	189	2.4
Cheeks	Phi	75	171	2.3
Johnson	LA	67	150	2.2
Dunn	Den	80	173	2.2
Williams	NY	76	162	2.1
Cook	NJ	82	164	2.0
Conner	GS	82	162	2.0
Erving	Phi	77	141	1.8

1984-85 N.B.A.

Bird—MVP Again; But Kareem Leads the Lakers

The exceptional rookies grabbed headlines, but another important newcomer was Ted Turner's WTBS, which replaced ESPN and USA as the cable portion of the league's TV package. The expanded coverage on the "superstation" contributed to the N.B.A.'s unprecedented growth for the rest of the decade. So did Rookie of the Year Michael Jordan, who joined the Chicago Bulls and immediately evoked comparisons to Julius Erving with his electrifying style of play. The other top rookie, Akeem Olajuwon, teamed with Ralph Sampson in Houston to give the Rockets the most dominating pair of big men in N.B.A. history.

Still, the new favorites had to take a back seat to two N.B.A. standbys, the Boston Celtics and the Los Angeles Lakers, who staged a season-long battle for the league's best record, with Boston finishing on top, 63 wins to 62. The Celtics sent Gerald Henderson to Seattle and installed Danny Ainge as a starter, but their most improved player may have been Larry Bird, who averaged nearly 29 points and became the most feared 3-point shooter in the league en route to his second straight MVP award. Jamaal Wilkes had reached the end of the line in Los Angeles, but the development of James Worthy and Byron Scott, plus the continued excellence of Kareem Abdul-Jabbar and Magic Johnson, made the Lakers better than ever.

The league's other top teams were both in the East. Milwaukee got Terry Cummings in a blockbuster deal with San Diego, and he teamed with Sidney Moncrief to lead the Bucks to 59 wins and help Don Nelson win another Coach of the Year award. Meanwhile, with powerful rookie Charles Barkley joining veterans Moses Malone, Julius Erving and Andrew Toney in Philadelphia, the 76ers regained some of the ground they'd lost a year earlier, and finished with 58 wins.

After Boston and Philadelphia, the big story in the Atlantic Division was injuries. New Jersey lost three of its starters for long stretches and relied on Michael Ray Richardson and Buck Williams in a 42-40 season. Washington lost center Jeff Ruland for half the season and finished 40-42 despite good play from a backcourt of Gus Williams, acquired from Seattle, and second-year man Jeff Malone. Hardest-hit were the Knicks, who lost their whole frontcourt and fell to 24 wins. The worst blow was a career-threatening knee injury to league scoring champion Bernard King.

In Detroit, the Pistons hoped to move up with the addition of Dan Roundfield from Atlanta, but he was hampered all year by injuries. Jordan and Orlando Woolridge gave Chicago more than 50 points per game, but the Bulls had little else. Cleveland squeezed into the playoffs for the first time in seven years as new coach George Karl got good seasons from Roy Hinson and Phil Hubbard up front to go with the outside scoring of World Free. With Roundfield gone, Dominique Wilkens averaged 27 points for Atlanta, and Doc Rivers made strides as a point guard, but the Hawkes still sank to 34 wins. Likewise, promising youngsters Clark Kellogg, Herb Williams, Vern Fleming and Steve Stipanovich couldn't lift Indiana out of last place.

The revitalized Denver Nuggets took the Mideast Division crown, winning 52 games. Alex English had another fine season, and he had help from Calvin Natt and Lafayette Lever, both acquired from Portland for Kiki Vandeweghe. Meanwhile, Houston's "Twin Towers", Sampson and Olajuwon, led the Rockets to 48 wins. Dallas added rookie Sam Perkins but dropped a notch to third, behind Houston. Adrian Dantley's holdout and John Drew's suspension hurt Utah, but the Jazz won 41 wins, but new coach Cotton Fitzsimmons could take comfort in the fact that he finished 10 games ahead of his old team, Kansas City.

In Portland, Vandewenge had trouble adjusting to Jack Ramsay's patterned offense; still other than the Lakers, the Trail Blazers were the only Pacific Division team over .500. Injuries to Walter Davis crippled Phoenix, while Seattle collapsed in the wake of the Gus Williams trade. The Clippers moved to Los Angeles in search of big crowds but found that losing teams don't draw anywhere. And Golden State lost Joe Barry Carroll to Italy and dropped to last place despite the play of Purvis Short and Sleepy Floyd.

As expected, Boston and Los Angeles met again in the championship series after easy victories in the conference playoffs. The Celtics looked unbeatable in a 148-114 opening-game win, but the Lakers asserted themselves thereafter and won the series in six games, clinching the title in Boston Garden. Elbow and finger injuries hampered Bird's shooting in the series, but the deciding factor was the play of Abdul-Jabbar, who averaged 26 points and won the playoff MVP award.

					TOTAL													Blkd		PER GAME				
Use Name	Pos	Hgt	Wgt	Age	G	Min	FG	FGA	%	FT	FTA	%	Reb	Ass	PF	DQ	Stls	Shts	Points	Min	Reb	Ass	PF	Points
1984/85 N.B.A. — EASTERN CONFERENCE																								
ATLANTIC DIVISION																								
Boston Celtics	63-19 .768 K. C. Jones																							
Larry Bird	F	6'9	220	28	80	3161	918	1760	52	403	457	88	842	531	208	0	129	98	2295	40	10.5	6.6	2.6	28.7
Kevin McHale	F-C	6'10	225	27	79	2653	605	1062	57	355	467	76	712	141	234	3	28	120	1565	34	9.0	1.8	3.0	19.8
Robert Parish	C	7'0	230	31	79	2850	551	1016	54	292	393	74	840	125	223	2	56	101	1394	36	10.6	1.6	2.8	17.6
Danny Ainge	G	6'4	175	25	75	2564	419	792	53	118	136	87	268	399	228	4	96	6	971	34	3.6	5.3	3.0	12.9
Dennis Johnson	G	6'4	200	30	80	2976	493	1066	46	261	306	85	317	543	224	2	122	39	1254	37	4.0	6.8	2.8	15.7
Cedric Maxwell (KJ)	F	6'8	215	29	57	1495	201	377	53	231	278	83	242	102	140	2	36	15	633	26	4.2	1.8	2.5	11.1
Scott Wedman	F-G	6'7	235	32	78	1127	220	460	48	42	55	76	159	94	111	0	23	10	499	14	2.0	1.2	1.4	6.4
Quinn Buckner	G	6'3	205	30	75	858	74	193	38	32	50	64	87	148	142	0	63	2	180	11	1.2	2.0	1.9	2.4
Carlos Clark	G	6'4	210	24	62	562	64	152	42	41	53	77	69	48	66	0	35	2	169	9	1.1	0.8	1.1	2.7
Ray Williams	G	6'3	195	30	23	459	55	143	38	31	46	67	57	90	56	1	30	5	147	20	2.5	3.9	2.4	6.4
Greg Kite	C	6'11	250	23	55	424	33	88	38	22	32	69	89	17	84	3	3	10	88	8	1.6	0.3	1.5	1.6
M. L. Carr	F	6'6	205	33	47	397	62	149	42	17	17	100	43	24	44	0	21	6	150	8	0.9	0.5	0.9	3.2
Rick Carlisle	G	6'5	210	25	38	179	26	67	39	15	17	88	21	25	21	0	3	0	67	5	0.6	0.7	0.6	1.8

3-PT FG — Bird 56-131, McHale 0-6, Ainge 15-56, Johnson 7-26, Maxwell 0-2, Wedman 17-34, Buckner 0-1, Clark 0-5, Williams 6-23, Carr 9-23, Carlisle 0-2

1984/85 N.B.A. — EASTERN CONFERENCE
ATLANTIC DIVISION

PHILADELPHIA 76ers 58-24 .707 **BILLY CUNNINGHAM**

Use Name	Pos	Hgt	Wgt	Age	G	Min	FG	FGA	%	FT	FTA	%	Reb	Ass	PF	DQ	Stls	Blkd Shts	Points	Min	Reb	Ass	PF	Points
Julius Erving	F	6'7	205	34	78	2535	610	1236	49	338	442	76	414	233	199	0	135	109	1561	33	5.3	3.0	2.6	20
Charles Barkley	F	6'6	260	21	82	2347	427	783	55	293	400	73	703	155	301	5	95	80	1148	29	8.6	1.9	3.7	14
Moses Malone	C	6'10	255	29	79	2957	602	1284	47	**737**	**904**	82	**1031**	130	216	0	67	123	1941	37	**13.1**	1.6	2.7	24.
Andrew Toney (BF)	G	6'3	188	27	70	2237	450	914	49	306	355	86	177	363	211	1	65	24	1245	32	2.5	5.2	3.0	17
Maurice Cheeks	G	6'1	180	28	78	2616	422	741	57	175	199	88	217	497	184	0	169	24	1025	34	2.8	6.4	2.4	13.
Bobby Jones	F	6'9	212	33	80	1633	207	385	54	186	216	86	297	155	183	2	84	50	600	20	3.7	1.9	2.3	7.
Clint Richardson	G	6'3	195	28	74	1531	183	404	45	76	89	85	155	157	143	0	37	15	443	21	2.1	2.1	1.9	6.
Sedule Threatt	G	6'2	175	23	82	1304	188	416	45	66	90	73	99	175	171	2	80	16	446	16	1.2	2.1	2.1	5.
Clemon Johnson	C	6'10	240	28	58	875	117	235	50	36	49	73	221	33	112	0	15	44	270	15	3.8	0.6	1.9	4.
George Johnson	F	6'7	218	28	55	756	107	263	41	49	56	88	164	38	99	0	31	16	264	14	3.0	0.7	1.8	4.
Sam Williams	F	6'8	215	25	46	488	58	148	39	28	47	60	106	11	92	1	26	26	144	11	2.3	0.2	2.0	3.
Leon Wood	G	6'3	185	22	38	269	50	134	37	18	26	69	18	45	17	0	8	0	122	7	0.5	1.2	0.4	3.
Marc Iavaroni (to SA)	F	6'9	225	28	12	156	12	31	39	6	6	100	29	6	24	0	4	3	30	13	2.4	0.5	2.0	2
Steve Hayes	C	7'	235	29	11	101	10	18	56	2	4	50	34	1	19	0	1	4	22	9	3.1	0.1	1.7	2.

3-PT FG — Erving 3-14, Barkley 1-6, Malone 0-2, Toney 39-105, Cheeks 6-26, Jones 0-4
Richardson 1-3, Threatt 4-22, C. Johnson 0-1, G. Johnson 1-10, Williams 0-1, Wood 4-30

NEW JERSEY NETS 42-40 .521 **STAN ALBECK**

Use Name	Pos	Hgt	Wgt	Age	G	Min	FG	FGA	%	FT	FTA	%	Reb	Ass	PF	DQ	Stls	Blkd Shts	Points	Min	Reb	Ass	PF	Points
Mike O'Koren	F	6'7	217	26	43	1119	194	393	49	42	67	63	166	102	115	1	32	16	438	26	3.9	2.4	2.7	10.
Buck Williams	F	6'8	215	24	82	**3182**	577	1089	53	336	538	63	1005	167	293	7	63	110	1491	39	12.3	2.0	3.6	18.
Mike Gminski	C	6'11	250	25	81	2418	380	818	46	276	328	84	633	158	135	0	38	92	1036	30	7.8	2.0	1.7	12.
Otis Birdsong	G	6'4	195	29	56	1842	495	968	51	161	259	62	148	232	145	1	84	7	1155	33	2.6	4.1	2.6	20.
M. Ray Richardson	G	6'5	195	29	82	3127	690	1470	47	240	313	77	457	669	277	3	243	22	1649	38	5.6	8.2	3.4	20.
Kelvin Ransey	G	6'1	180	26	81	1689	300	654	46	122	142	86	130	355	134	0	87	7	724	21	1.6	4.4	1.7	8.
Jeff Turner	F-C	6'9	230	22	72	1429	171	377	45	79	92	86	218	108	243	8	29	7	421	20	3.0	1.5	3.4	5.
Darwin Cook	G	6'3	190	26	58	1063	212	453	47	47	54	87	92	160	96	0	74	10	473	18	1.6	2.8	1.7	8.
Darryl Dawkins (XJ)	C	6'11	251	27	39	972	192	339	57	143	201	71	181	45	171	11	14	35	527	25	4.6	1.2	4.4	13.
Albert King	F	6'6	190	25	42	860	226	460	49	85	104	82	159	58	110	0	41	9	537	20	3.8	1.4	2.6	12.
George Johnson	F	6'11	205	36	65	800	42	79	53	22	27	81	185	22	151	2	19	78	107	12	2.8	0.3	2.3	1.
Kevin McKenna	F-G	6'5	195	25	29	535	61	134	46	38	43	88	49	58	63	0	30	7	165	18	1.7	2.0	2.2	5.
Wayne Sappleton	F	6'9	230	24	33	298	41	87	47	14	34	41	75	7	50	0	7	4	96	9	2.3	0.2	1.5	2.
Ron Brewer (from SA)	F-G	6'4	185	29	11	245	49	84	58	16	18	89	18	11	15	0	5	5	114	22	1.6	1.0	1.4	10.
Michael Wilson (from Cle)	G	6'4	180	25	8	92	9	23	39	4	6	67	13	11	7	0	4	2	22	12	1.6	1.4	0.9	2.
Chris Engler (to Chi, Mil)	C	6'11	248	25	7	76	7	16	44	5	9	56	27	0	4	0	2	4	19	11	3.9	0.0	0.6	2.7
Tom LaGarde	F	6'10	220	29	1	8	0	1	0	1	2	50	2	0	2	0	0	0	1	8	2.0	0.0	2.0	1.0

3-PT FG — O'Koren 8-21, Williams 1-4, Gminski 0-1, Birdsong 4-21, Richardson 29-115, Ransey 2-11,
Turner 0-3, Cook 2-23, Dawkins 0-1, King 0-8, Johnson 1-1, McKenna 5-13, Brewer 0-2

WASHINGTON BULLETS 40-42 .488 **GENE SHUE**

Use Name	Pos	Hgt	Wgt	Age	G	Min	FG	FGA	%	FT	FTA	%	Reb	Ass	PF	DQ	Stls	Blkd Shts	Points	Min	Reb	Ass	PF	Points
Greg Ballard	F	6'7	215	29	82	2664	469	978	48	120	151	79	531	208	221	0	100	33	1072	32	6.5	2.5	2.7	13.1
Cliff Robinson	F	6'9	230	24	60	1870	422	896	47	158	213	74	546	149	187	4	51	47	1003	31	9.1	2.5	3.1	16.7
Jeff Ruland (SJ)	C	6'10	240	26	37	1436	250	439	57	200	292	68	410	162	128	2	31	27	700	39	11.1	4.4	3.5	18.9
Jeff Malone	G	6'4	205	23	76	2613	605	1213	50	211	250	84	206	184	176	1	52	9	1436	34	2.7	2.4	2.3	18.9
Gus Williams	G	6'2	175	31	79	2960	638	1483	43	251	346	73	195	608	159	1	178	32	1578	37	2.5	7.7	2.0	20.0
Rick Mahorn	C	6'10	240	26	77	2072	206	413	50	71	104	68	608	121	308	11	59	104	483	27	7.9	1.6	4.0	6.3
Darren Daye	F-G	6'8	220	24	80	1573	258	504	51	178	249	71	272	240	164	1	53	19	695	20	3.4	3.0	2.1	8.7
Tom McMillen	F-C	6'11	235	32	69	1547	252	534	47	112	135	83	210	52	163	3	8	17	616	22	3.0	0.8	2.4	8.9
Dudley Bradley	G	6'6	195	27	73	1232	142	299	47	54	79	68	134	173	152	0	96	21	358	17	1.8	2.4	2.1	4.9
Frank Johnson (BF)	G	6'2	185	26	46	925	175	358	49	72	96	75	63	143	72	0	43	3	428	20	1.4	3.1	1.6	9.3
Charles Jones (from Chi)	F	6'9	215	27	28	638	65	123	53	36	52	69	178	25	101	3	22	74	166	23	6.4	0.9	3.6	5.9
Guy Williams	F	6'9	200	24	21	119	29	63	46	2	5	40	27	9	17	0	5	2	61	6	1.3	0.4	0.8	2.9
Don Collins	F	6'6	190	26	11	91	12	34	35	8	9	89	19	7	5	0	7	4	32	8	1.7	0.6	0.5	2.9
Tom Sewell	G	6'5	185	22	21	87	9	36	25	2	4	50	4	6	13	0	3	1	20	4	0.2	0.3	0.6	1.0
Charlie Davis (to Mil)	F	6'7	215	26	4	28	2	10	20	3	4	75	4	1	3	0	1	0	7	7	1.0	0.3	0.8	1.8

3-PT FG — Ballard 14-46, Robinson 1-3, Ruland 0-2, Malone 15-72, Gus Williams 51-176
Daye 1-7, McMillen 0-5, Bradley 20-64, Johnson 6-17, Guy Williams 1-4, Sewell 0-2

NEW YORK KNICKERBOCKERS 24-58 .293 **HUBIE BROWN**

Use Name	Pos	Hgt	Wgt	Age	G	Min	FG	FGA	%	FT	FTA	%	Reb	Ass	PF	DQ	Stls	Blkd Shts	Points	Min	Reb	Ass	PF	Points
Louis Orr	F	6'8	195	26	79	2452	372	766	49	262	334	78	391	134	195	1	100	27	1007	31	4.9	1.7	2.5	12.7
Bernard King (KJ)	F	6'7	205	28	55	2063	691	1303	53	426	552	77	317	204	191	3	71	15	1809	38	5.8	3.7	3.5	**32.9**
Pat Cummings	C-F	6'9	235	28	63	2069	410	797	51	177	227	78	518	109	247	6	50	17	997	33	8.2	1.7	3.9	15.8
Darrell Walker	G	6'4	180	23	82	2489	430	989	43	243	347	70	278	408	244	2	167	21	1103	30	3.4	5.0	3.0	13.5
Rory Sparrow	G	6'2	195	26	79	2292	326	662	49	122	141	87	169	557	200	2	81	9	781	29	2.1	7.1	2.5	9.9
Trent Tucker	G	6'5	193	25	77	1819	293	606	48	38	48	79	188	199	195	0	75	15	653	24	2.4	2.6	2.5	8.5
Ken Bannister	C-F	6'9	235	24	75	1404	209	445	47	91	192	47	330	39	279	16	38	40	509	19	4.4	0.5	3.7	6.8
James Bailey	C	6'9	220	27	74	1297	156	349	45	73	108	68	344	39	286	10	30	50	385	18	4.6	0.5	3.9	5.2
Butch Carter	G	6'5	195	26	69	1279	214	476	45	109	134	81	95	167	151	1	57	5	548	19	1.4	2.4	2.2	7.9
Ernie Grunfield	F	6'6	215	29	69	1061	188	384	49	77	104	74	151	105	129	2	50	7	455	15	2.2	1.5	1.9	6.6
Eddie Wilkins	F-G	6'10	220	22	54	917	116	233	50	66	122	54	262	16	155	3	21	16	298	17	4.9	0.3	2.9	5.5
Ron Cavenall	C	7'1	230	25	53	653	28	86	33	22	39	56	166	19	123	2	12	42	78	12	3.1	0.4	2.3	1.5
Truck Robinson (FJ)	F	6'7	225	33	2	35	2	5	40	0	2	0	9	3	3	0	2	3	4	18	4.5	1.5	1.5	2.0

Bill Cartwright (FJ), Marvin Webster (IL)

3-PT FG — Orr 1-10, King 1-10, Cummings 0-4, Walker 0-17, Sparrow 7-31,
Tucker 29-72, Bailey 0-1, Carter 11-43, Grunfield 2-8, Wilkins 0-2

1984/85 N.B.A. — EASTERN CONFERENCE
CENTRAL DIVISION

Use Name	Pos	Hgt	Wgt	Age	G	Min	FG	FGA	%	FT	FTA	%	Reb	Ass	PF	DQ	Stls	Blkd Shts	Points	Min	Reb	Ass	PF	Points
							TOTAL													PER GAME				
MILWAUKEE BUCKS	59-23 .720					DON NELSON																		
Ricky Pierce	F	6'5	205	25	44	882	165	307	54	102	124	82	117	94	117	0	34	5	433	20	2.7	2.1	2.7	9.8
Terry Cummings	F	6'9	220	23	79	2722	759	1532	50	343	463	74	716	228	264	4	117	67	1861	34	9.1	2.9	3.3	23.6
Alton Lister	C	7'	240	26	81	2091	322	598	54	154	262	59	647	127	287	5	49	167	798	26	8.0	1.6	3.5	9.9
Sidney Moncrief	G	6'4	190	27	73	2734	561	1162	48	454	548	83	391	382	197	1	117	39	1585	37	5.4	5.2	2.7	21.7
Craig Hodges	G	6'3	190	24	82	2496	359	732	49	106	130	82	186	349	262	8	96	1	871	30	2.3	4.3	3.2	10.6
Paul Pressey	G-F	6'5	185	26	80	2876	480	928	52	317	418	76	429	543	258	4	129	56	1284	36	5.4	6.8	3.2	16.1
Paul Mokeski	F-C	7'	250	27	79	1586	205	429	48	81	116	70	410	99	266	6	28	35	491	20	5.2	1.3	3.4	6.2
Kevin Grevey	G	6'5	210	31	78	1182	190	424	45	88	107	82	103	94	85	1	30	2	476	15	1.3	1.2	1.1	6.1
Randy Brever	C	7'3	230	24	78	1083	162	317	51	89	127	70	256	40	179	4	21	82	413	14	3.3	0.5	2.3	5.3
Kenny Fields	G	6'5	220	22	51	535	84	191	44	27	36	75	84	38	84	2	9	10	195	10	1.6	0.7	1.6	3.8
Mike Dunleavy	G	6'3	180	30	19	433	64	135	47	25	29	86	31	85	55	1	15	3	169	23	1.6	4.5	2.9	8.9
Charlie Davis (from Was)	F	6'7	215	26	57	746	151	346	44	48	58	83	149	50	110	1	21	5	351	13	2.6	0.9	1.9	6.2
Paul Thompson (from Cle)	F	6'6	210	23	16	227	41	105	39	24	34	71	42	20	42	0	15	5	106	14	2.6	1.3	2.6	6.6
Larry Micheaux (to Hou)	F	6'9	220	24	18	171	17	35	49	12	17	71	44	13	26	0	8	7	46	10	2.4	0.7	1.4	2.6
Lorenzo Romar (to Det)	G	6'1	180	26	4	16	1	8	13	0	0	—	0	2	2	0	0	0	2	4	0.0	0.5	0.5	0.5
D. Thirdkill (from Det, to SA)	F	6'7	215	24	6	16	3	4	75	1	2	50	2	0	1	0	0	0	7	3	0.3	0.0	0.2	1.2
Mark West (to Cle)	F	6'10	230	24	1	6	0	1	0	2	2	100	1	0	4	0	0	1	2	6	1.0	0.0	4.0	2.0
Chris Engler (From NJ, Chi)	C	6'11	248	25	1	3	0	2	0	0	0	—	1	0	0	0	0	1	0	3	1.0	0.0	0.0	0.0

3-PT FG — Pierce 1-4, Cummings 0-1, Lister 0-1, Moncrief 9-33, Hodges 47-135, Pressey 7-20, Mokeski 0-2, Grevey 8-33, Dunleavy 16-47, Davis 1-10, Thompson 0-7, Romar 0-1

Use Name	Pos	Hgt	Wgt	Age	G	Min	FG	FGA	%	FT	FTA	%	Reb	Ass	PF	DQ	Stls	Blkd Shts	Points	Min	Reb	Ass	PF	Points
DETROIT PISTONS	46-36 .561					CHUCK DALY																		
Kelly Tripucka (NJ)	F-G	6'6	220	25	55	1675	396	831	48	255	288	89	218	135	118	1	49	14	1049	30	4.0	2.5	2.1	19.1
Dan Roundfield (KJ)	F	6'8	215	31	56	1492	236	505	47	139	178	78	453	102	147	0	26	54	611	27	8.1	1.8	2.6	10.9
Bill Laimbeer	C	6'11	245	27	82	2892	595	1177	51	244	306	80	1013	154	308	4	69	71	1438	35	12.4	1.9	3.8	17.5
John Long (HO)	G	6'5	200	28	66	1820	431	885	49	106	123	86	190	130	139	0	71	14	973	28	2.9	2.0	2.1	14.7
Isiah Thomas	G	6'1	185	23	81	3089	646	1410	46	399	493	81	361	**1123**	288	8	187	25	1720	38	4.5	**13.9**	3.6	21.2
Vinnie Johnson	G	6'2	200	28	82	2093	428	942	45	190	247	77	252	325	205	2	71	20	1051	26	3.1	4.0	2.5	12.8
Terry Tyler	F	6'7	220	28	82	2004	422	855	49	106	148	72	423	63	192	0	49	90	950	24	5.2	0.8	2.3	11.6
Earl Cureton	F-C	6'9	215	27	81	1642	207	428	48	82	144	57	419	83	216	1	56	42	496	20	5.2	1.0	2.7	6.1
Kent Benson	C-F	6'10	245	30	72	1401	201	397	51	76	94	81	324	93	207	4	53	44	478	19	4.5	1.3	2.9	6.6
Tony Campbell	F	6'7	215	22	56	625	130	262	50	56	70	80	89	24	107	1	28	3	316	11	1.6	0.4	1.9	5.6
Brooke Steppe	G	6'5	195	25	54	486	83	178	47	87	104	84	57	36	61	0	16	4	253	9	1.1	0.7	1.1	4.7
Major Jones	F	6'9	225	31	47	418	48	87	55	33	51	65	128	15	58	0	9	14	129	9	2.7	0.3	1.2	2.7
David Thirdkill (to Mil, SA)	F	6'7	215	24	10	115	12	23	52	5	11	45	8	1	16	0	3	2	29	12	0.8	0.1	1.6	2.9
Lorenzo Romar (from Mil)	G	6'1	180	26	5	35	2	8	25	5	5	100	0	10	5	0	4	0	9	7	0.0	2.0	1.0	1.8
Sidney Lowe (to Atl)	G	6'	195	24	6	31	2	7	29	0	0	—	1	8	5	0	0	0	4	5	0.2	1.3	0.8	0.7
Dale Wilkinson (to LAC)	F	6'10	220	24	2	7	0	2	0	0	0	—	1	0	2	0	0	0	0	4	0.5	0.0	1.0	0.0
Terry Teagle (to GS)	G	6'5	195	24	2	5	1	2	50	0	0	—	0	0	2	0	0	0	2	3	0.0	0.0	1.0	1.0

3-PT FG — Tripucka 2-5, Roundfield 0-2, Laimbeer 4-18, Long 5-15, Thomas 29-113, Johnson 5-27, Tyler 0-8, Cureton 0-3, Benson 0-3, Campbell 0-1, Steppe 0-1, Thirdkill 0-1,Romar 0-2

Use Name	Pos	Hgt	Wgt	Age	G	Min	FG	FGA	%	FT	FTA	%	Reb	Ass	PF	DQ	Stls	Blkd Shts	Points	Min	Reb	Ass	PF	Points
CHICAGO BULLS	38-44 .463					KEVIN LOUGHERY																		
Orlando Woolridge	F	6'9	215	25	77	2816	679	1225	55	409	521	79	435	135	185	0	58	38	1767	37	5.6	1.8	2.4	22.9
Dave Greenewood (FJ)	F	6'9	232	27	61	1523	152	332	46	67	94	71	388	78	190	1	34	18	371	25	6.4	1.3	3.1	6.1
Dave Corzine	C	6'11	260	28	82	2062	276	568	49	149	200	75	422	140	189	2	32	64	701	25	5.1	1.7	2.3	8.5
Michael Jordan	G-F	6'6	195	21	82	3144	837	1625	52	630	746	84	534	481	285	4	196	69	2313	38	6.5	5.9	3.5	28.2
Wes Matthews	G	6'1	170	25	78	1523	191	386	49	59	85	69	67	354	133	0	73	12	443	20	0.9	4.5	1.7	5.7
Quintin Dailey	G	6'3	180	23	79	2101	525	1111	47	205	251	82	208	191	192	0	71	5	1262	27	2.6	2.4	2.4	16.0
Steve Johnson	F	6'10	245	27	74	1659	281	516	54	181	252	72	437	64	265	7	37	62	743	22	5.9	0.9	3.6	10.0
Ennis Whatley	G	6'3	177	22	70	1385	140	313	45	68	86	79	101	381	141	1	66	10	349	20	1.4	5.4	2.0	5.0
Jawaan Oldham	C	7'	215	27	63	993	89	192	46	34	50	68	236	31	166	3	11	127	212	16	3.7	0.5	2.6	3.4
Rod Higgins	F	6'7	205	24	68	942	119	270	44	60	90	67	147	73	91	0	21	13	308	14	2.2	1.1	1.3	4.5
Caldwell Jones	C	6'11	225	34	42	885	53	115	46	36	47	77	211	34	125	3	12	31	142	21	5.0	0.8	3.0	3.4
Sidney Green	F	6'9	220	23	48	740	108	250	43	79	98	81	246	29	102	0	11	14	295	15	5.1	0.6	2.1	6.1
Charles Jones (to Was)	F	6'9	215	27	3	29	2	4	50	4	6	67	6	1	6	0	0	5	8	10	2.0	0.3	2.0	2.7
Chris Engler (from NJ, to Mil)	C	6'11	248	25	3	3	1	2	50	0	0	—	2	0	1	0	0	0	2	1	0.7	0.0	0.3	0.7

3 PT-FG — Woolridge 0-5, Greenwood 0-1, Corzine 0-1, Jordan 9-52, Matthews 2-16, Dailey 7-30, Johnson 0-3, Whatley 1-9, Oldham 0-1, Higgins 10-37, Cald. Jones 0-2, Green 0-4

Use Name	Pos	Hgt	Wgt	Age	G	Min	FG	FGA	%	FT	FTA	%	Reb	Ass	PF	DQ	Stls	Blkd Shts	Points	Min	Reb	Ass	PF	Points
CLEVELAND CAVALIERS	36-46 .439					GEORGE KARL																		
Phil Hubbard	F	6'8	215	28	76	2249	415	822	50	371	494	75	479	114	258	8	81	9	1201	30	6.3	1.5	3.4	15.8
Roy Hinson	F-C	6'9	210	23	76	2344	465	925	50	271	376	72	596	68	311	13	51	173	1201	31	7.8	0.9	4.1	15.8
Melvin Turpin	C	6'11	240	24	79	1949	363	711	51	109	139	78	452	36	211	3	38	87	835	25	5.7	0.5	2.7	10.6
World Free	G	6'2	185	30	71	2249	609	1328	46	308	411	75	211	320	163	0	75	16	1597	32	3.0	4.5	2.3	22.5
John Bagley	G	6'	190	24	81	2401	338	693	49	125	167	75	291	697	132	0	129	5	804	30	3.6	8.6	1.6	9.9
Johnny Davis	G	6'2	180	29	76	1920	337	791	43	255	300	85	119	426	136	1	43	4	941	25	1.6	5.6	1.8	12.4
Ben Poquette	C-F	6'9	235	29	79	1656	210	457	46	109	137	80	473	79	220	3	47	58	532	21	6.0	1.0	2.8	6.7
Lonnie Shelton	F	6'8	255	29	57	1244	158	363	44	51	77	66	267	96	187	3	44	18	367	22	4.7	1.7	3.3	6.4
Mark West (from Mil)	F-C	6'10	230	24	65	882	106	193	55	41	85	48	250	15	193	7	13	48	253	14	3.8	0.2	3.0	3.9
Paul Thompson (to Mil)	G-F	6'6	210	23	33	715	148	354	42	45	53	85	116	58	77	1	41	20	347	22	3.5	1.8	2.3	10.5
Ron Anderson	F	6'7	215	26	36	520	84	195	43	41	50	82	88	34	40	0	9	7	210	14	2.4	0.9	1.1	5.8
Edgar Jones (from SA)	F-C	6'10	225	28	26	447	86	184	47	41	60	68	109	11	71	1	11	11	213	17	4.2	0.4	2.7	8.2
Jeff Cook (to SA)	F-C	6'10	215	28	18	440	46	105	44	17	27	63	104	23	53	0	5	9	109	24	5.8	1.3	2.9	6.1
Kevin Williams	G	6'3	175	23	46	413	58	134	43	47	64	73	63	61	86	1	22	4	163	9	1.4	1.3	1.9	3.5
Michael Wilson (to NJ)	G	6'4	180	25	11	175	27	54	50	23	30	77	18	24	14	0	10	3	77	16	1.6	2.2	1.3	7.0

(continued next page)

1984/85 N.B.A. — EASTERN CONFERENCE
CENTRAL DIVISION

CLEVELAND (continued)

Use Name	Pos	Hgt	Wgt	Age	G	Min	FG	FGA	%	FT	FTA	%	Reb	Ast	PF	DQ	Stls	Blkd Shts	Points	Min	Reb	Ast	PF	Points
Geoff Huston	G	6'2	175	27	8	93	12	25	48	2	3	67	1	23	8	0	0	0	26	12	0.1	2.9	1.0	3.3
Robert Smith	G	5'11	170	29	7	48	4	17	24	8	10	80	4	7	6	0	2	0	16	7	0.6	1.0	0.9	2.3
Campy Russell	F	6'8	215	32	3	24	2	7	29	2	3	67	5	3	3	0	0	0	6	8	1.7	1.0	1.0	2.0
Butch Graves	G	6'3	200	22	4	11	2	6	33	1	5	20	2	1	4	0	1	0	5	3	0.5	0.3	1.0	1.3

3-PT FG — Hubbard 0-4, Hinson 0-3, Free 71-193, Bagley 3-26, Davis 12-46, Poquette 3-17, Shelton 0-5, West 0-1 Thompson 6-23, Anderson 1-2, Jones 0-3, Cook 0-1, Williams 0-5, Smith 0-4, Russell 0-1, Graves 0-1

ATLANTA HAWKS 34-48 .415 **MIKE FRATELLO**

Use Name	Pos	Hgt	Wgt	Age	G	Min	FG	FGA	%	FT	FTA	%	Reb	Ast	PF	DQ	Stls	Blkd Shts	Points	Min	Reb	Ast	PF	Points
Dominique Wilkins	F	6'8	200	24	81	3023	853	**1891**	45	486	603	81	557	200	170	0	135	54	2217	37	6.9	2.5	2.1	27.4
Cliff Levingston	F	6'8	220	23	74	2017	291	552	53	145	222	65	566	104	231	3	70	69	727	27	7.6	1.4	3.1	9.8
Tree Rollins	C	7'1	235	29	70	1750	186	339	55	67	93	72	442	52	213	6	35	167	439	25	6.3	0.7	3.0	6.3
Eddie Johnson	G	6'2	190	29	73	2367	453	946	48	265	332	80	192	566	184	1	43	7	1193	32	2.6	7.8	2.5	16.3
Glenn Rivers	G	6'4	185	23	69	2126	334	701	48	291	378	77	214	410	250	7	163	53	974	31	3.1	5.9	3.6	14.1
Kevin Willis	G	7'	220	22	82	1785	322	690	47	119	181	66	522	36	226	4	31	49	765	22	6.4	0.4	2.8	9.3
Antoine Carr	F	6'9	225	23	62	1195	198	375	53	101	128	79	232	80	219	4	29	78	499	19	3.7	1.3	3.5	8.0
Randy Wittman	G	6'6	210	25	41	1168	187	352	53	30	41	73	73	125	58	0	28	7	406	28	1.8	3.0	1.4	9.9
Mike Glenn	G	6'3	185	29	60	1126	228	388	59	62	76	82	81	122	74	0	27	0	518	19	1.4	2.0	1.2	8.6
Sly Williams	F-G	6'7	215	26	34	867	167	380	44	79	123	64	168	94	83	1	28	8	417	26	4.9	2.8	2.4	12.3
Scott Hastings	F-C	6'10	235	24	64	825	89	188	47	63	81	78	159	46	135	1	24	23	241	13	2.5	0.7	2.1	3.8
Rickey Brown	F-C	6'10	235	26	69	814	78	192	41	39	68	57	223	25	117	0	19	22	195	12	3.2	0.4	1.7	2.8
Walker Russell	G	6'5	195	24	21	377	34	63	54	14	17	82	40	66	37	1	17	4	83	18	1.9	3.1	1.8	4.0
Sidney Lowe (from Det)	G	6'	195	24	15	159	8	20	40	8	8	100	15	42	23	0	11	0	24	11	1.0	2.8	1.5	1.6
Charlie Criss	G	5'8	165	35	4	115	7	17	41	4	6	67	14	22	5	0	3	0	18	29	3.5	5.5	1.3	4.5
Stewart Granger	G	6'3	190	23	9	92	6	17	35	4	8	50	6	12	13	0	2	0	16	10	0.7	1.3	1.4	1.8
Jerry Eaves	G	6'4	185	25	3	37	3	6	50	5	6	83	0	4	6	0	0	0	11	12	0.0	1.3	2.0	3.7
Leo Rautins	F	6'8	215	24	4	12	0	2	0	0	0	—	2	3	3	0	0	0	0	3	0.5	0.8	0.8	0.0

3-PT FG — Wilkins 25-81, Levingston 0-2, Johnson 22-72, Rivers 15-36, Willis 2-9, Carr 2-6, Wittman 2-7, Glenn 0-2, Williams 4-15, Russell 1-1, Lowe 0-1, Criss 0-2, Granger 0-1

INDIANA PACERS 22-60 .268 **GEORGE IRVINE**

Use Name	Pos	Hgt	Wgt	Age	G	Min	FG	FGA	%	FT	FTA	%	Reb	Ast	PF	DQ	Stls	Blkd Shts	Points	Min	Reb	Ast	PF	Points
Clark Kellogg	F	6'7	227	23	77	2449	562	1112	51	301	396	76	724	244	247	2	86	26	1432	32	9.4	3.2	3.2	18.6
Herb Williams	F-C	6'11	242	26	75	2557	575	1211	47	224	341	66	634	252	218	1	54	134	1375	34	8.5	3.4	2.9	18.3
Steve Stipanovich	C	6'11	245	24	82	2315	414	871	48	297	372	80	614	199	265	4	71	78	1126	28	7.5	2.4	3.2	13.7
Vern Fleming	G	6'5	195	23	80	2486	433	922	47	260	339	77	323	247	232	4	99	8	1126	31	4.0	3.1	2.9	14.1
Jerry Sichting	G	6'1	178	28	70	1808	325	624	52	112	128	88	114	264	116	0	47	4	771	26	1.6	3.8	1.7	11.0
Jim Thomas	G	6'3	190	24	80	2059	347	726	48	183	234	78	261	234	195	2	76	5	885	26	3.3	2.9	2.4	11.1
Tony Brown	F-G	6'6	185	24	82	1586	214	465	46	116	171	68	288	159	212	3	59	12	544	19	3.5	1.9	2.6	6.6
Terence Stansbury	G	6'5	170	23	74	1278	210	458	46	102	126	81	114	127	205	2	47	12	526	17	1.5	1.7	2.8	7.1
Bill Garnett	F	6'9	225	24	65	1123	149	310	48	120	174	69	286	67	196	3	28	15	418	17	4.4	1.0	3.0	6.4
Devin Durrant	F	6'7	200	24	59	756	114	274	42	72	102	71	124	80	106	0	19	10	300	13	2.1	1.4	1.8	5.1
Granville Waiters	C	6'11	225	23	62	703	85	190	45	29	50	58	170	30	107	2	16	44	199	11	2.7	0.5	1.7	3.2
Stuart Gray	C	7'0	235	21	52	391	35	92	38	32	47	68	123	15	82	1	9	14	102	8	2.4	0.3	1.6	2.0
Kenton Edelin	F	6'8	205	22	10	143	4	13	31	3	8	38	26	10	39	1	5	4	11	14	2.6	1.0	3.9	1.1
Greg Kelser	F	6'7	205	27	10	114	21	53	40	20	28	71	19	13	16	0	7	0	62	11	1.9	1.3	1.6	6.2
Ralph Jackson	G	6'2	190	22	1	12	1	3	33	0	0	—	1	4	1	0	2	0	2	12	1.0	4.0	1.0	2.0

3 PT-FG — Kellogg 7-14, Williams 1-9, Stipanovich 1-11, Fleming 0-4, Sichting 9-37, Thomas 8-42, Brown 0-6, Stansbury 4-25, Garnett 0-2, Durrant 0-3, Waiters 0-1, Kelser 0-1

1984/85 N.B.A. — WESTERN CONFERENCE
MIDWEST DIVISION

DENVER NUGGETS 52-30 .634 **DOUG MOE**

Use Name	Pos	Hgt	Wgt	Age	G	Min	FG	FGA	%	FT	FTA	%	Reb	Ast	PF	DQ	Stls	Blkd Shts	Points	Min	Reb	Ast	PF	Points
Alex English	F	6'8	190	30	81	2924	**939**	1812	52	383	462	83	458	344	259	1	101	46	2262	36	5.7	4.2	3.2	27.9
Calvin Natt	F	6'6	220	27	78	2657	685	1255	55	447	564	79	610	238	182	1	75	33	1817	34	7.8	3.1	2.3	23.3
Wayne Cooper	C	6'10	220	28	80	2031	404	856	47	161	235	69	631	86	304	2	28	197	969	25	7.9	1.1	3.8	12.1
T.R. Dunn	G	6'4	192	29	81	2290	175	358	49	84	116	72	385	153	213	3	140	14	434	28	4.8	1.9	2.6	5.4
Lafayette Lever	G	6'3	175	24	82	2559	424	985	43	197	256	77	411	613	226	1	202	30	1051	31	5.0	7.5	2.8	12.8
Dan Issel	C	6'9	240	36	77	1684	363	791	46	257	319	81	331	137	171	1	65	31	984	22	4.3	1.8	2.2	12.8
Bill Hanzlik	F-G	6'7	185	27	80	1673	220	522	42	180	238	76	207	210	291	5	84	26	621	21	2.6	2.6	3.6	7.8
Elston Turner	G-F	6'5	220	25	81	1491	181	388	47	51	65	78	216	158	152	0	96	7	414	18	2.7	2.0	1.9	5.1
Mike Evans	G	6'1	170	29	81	1437	323	661	49	113	131	86	119	231	174	2	65	12	816	18	1.5	2.9	2.1	10.1
Danny Schayes	C	6'11	245	25	56	542	60	129	47	79	97	81	144	38	98	2	20	25	199	10	2.6	0.7	1.8	3.6
Joe Kopicki	F	6'9	240	24	42	308	50	95	53	43	54	80	86	29	58	0	13	1	145	7	2.0	0.7	1.4	3.5
Willie White	G	6'3	195	22	39	234	52	124	42	21	31	68	36	29	24	0	5	2	129	6	0.9	0.7	0.6	3.3

3 PT-FG — English 1-5, Natt 0-3, Cooper 0-2, Dunn 0-2, Lever 6-24, Issel 1-7, Hanzlik 1-15, Turner 1-6, Evans 57-157, Kopicki 0-2, White 4-11

HOUSTON ROCKETS 48-34 .585 **BILL FITCH**

Use Name	Pos	Hgt	Wgt	Age	G	Min	FG	FGA	%	FT	FTA	%	Reb	Ast	PF	DQ	Stls	Blkd Shts	Points	Min	Reb	Ast	PF	Points
Rodney McCray	F	6'7	220	23	82	3001	476	890	53	231	313	74	539	355	215	2	90	75	1183	37	6.6	4.3	2.6	14.4
Ralph Sampson	F-C	7'4	228	24	82	3086	753	1499	50	303	448	68	853	224	306	10	81	168	1809	38	10.4	2.7	3.7	22.1
Akeem Olajawon	C	7'0	250	21	82	2914	677	1258	54	338	551	61	974	111	**344**	10	99	220	1692	36	11.9	1.4	4.2	20.6
Lewis Lloyd	G-F	6'6	215	25	82	2128	457	869	53	161	220	73	231	280	196	1	73	28	1077	26	2.8	3.4	2.4	13.1
Lionel Hollins	G	6'3	185	31	80	1950	249	540	46	108	136	79	173	417	187	1	78	10	609	24	2.2	5.2	2.3	7.6
Robert Reid	F-G	6'8	205	29	82	1763	312	648	48	88	126	70	273	171	196	1	48	22	713	22	3.3	2.1	2.4	8.7
Mitchell Wiggins	G	6'4	185	25	82	1575	318	657	48	96	131	73	235	119	195	1	83	13	738	19	2.9	1.5	2.4	9.0
John Lucas (DR)	G	6'3	185	31	47	1158	206	446	46	103	129	80	85	318	78	0	62	2	536	25	1.8	6.8	1.7	11.4
Jim Peterson	F	6'10	235	22	60	714	70	144	49	50	66	76	147	29	125	1	14	32	190	12	2.5	0.5	2.1	3.2
Allen Leavell	G	6'1	190	27	42	536	88	209	42	44	57	77	37	102	61	0	23	4	228	13	0.9	2.4	1.5	5.4
Larry Micheaux (from Mil)	F	6'9	220	24	39	394	74	122	61	17	26	65	99	17	49	0	12	14	165	10	2.5	0.4	1.3	4.2

(continued next page)

1984/85 N.B.A. — WESTERN CONERENCE
MIDWEST DIVISION

Name	Pos	Hgt	Wgt	Age	G	Min	FG	FGA	%	FT	FTA	%	Reb	Ass	PF	DQ	Stls	Blkd Shts	Points	Min	Reb	Ass	PF	Points
					TOTAL															PER GAME				
HOUSTON (continued)																								
Phil Ford	G	6'2	186	28	25	290	14	47	30	16	18	89	27	61	33	0	6	1	44	12	1.1	2.4	1.3	1.8
Craig Ehlo	G	6'6	180	23	45	189	34	69	49	19	30	63	25	26	26	0	11	3	87	4	0.6	0.6	0.6	1.9
Hank McDowell	F	6'9	215	25	34	132	20	42	48	7	10	70	22	9	22	0	3	5	47	4	0.6	0.3	0.6	1.4
3-PT FG — McCray 0-6, Sampson 0-6, Lloyd 2-8, Hollins 3-13, Reid 1-16, Wiggins 6-23, Lucas 21-66, Leavell 8-37, Micheaux 0-3, Ford 0-4, Ehlo 0-3, McDowell 0-1																								
DALLAS MAVERICKS	44-38 .537				DICK MOTTA																			
Mark Aguirre	F	6'6	235	25	80	2699	794	1569	51	440	580	76	477	249	250	3	60	24	2055	34	6.0	3.1	3.1	25.7
Sam Perkins	F-C	6'9	235	23	82	2317	347	736	47	200	244	82	605	135	236	1	63	63	903	28	7.4	1.6	2.9	11.0
Kurt Nimphius	C	6'10	218	26	82	2010	196	434	45	108	140	77	408	183	262	4	30	126	500	25	5.0	2.2	3.2	6.1
Rolando Blackman	G	6'6	190	25	81	2834	625	1230	51	342	413	83	300	289	96	0	61	16	1598	35	3.7	3.6	1.2	19.7
Brad Davis	G	6'3	180	29	82	2539	310	614	50	158	178	89	193	581	219	1	91	10	825	31	2.4	7.1	2.7	10.1
Jay Vincent	F	6'8	225	25	79	2943	545	1138	48	351	420	84	704	169	226	0	48	22	1441	37	8.9	2.1	2.9	18.2
Derek Harper	G	6'4	185	23	82	2218	329	633	52	111	154	72	199	360	194	1	144	37	790	27	2.4	4.4	2.4	9.6
Dale Ellis	F	6'7	205	24	72	1314	274	603	45	77	104	74	238	56	131	1	46	7	667	18	3.3	0.8	1.8	9.3
Wallace Bryant	C	7'	245	25	56	860	67	148	45	30	44	68	241	84	110	1	21	24	164	15	4.3	1.5	2.0	2.9
Charlie Sitton	F	6'8	210	22	43	304	39	94	41	13	25	52	60	26	50	0	7	6	91	7	1.4	0.6	1.2	2.1
Tom Sluby	G	6'4	200	22	31	151	30	58	52	13	21	62	12	16	18	0	3	0	73	5	0.4	0.5	0.6	2.4
Howard Carter	G	6'5	215	23	11	66	4	23	17	1	1	100	3	4	4	0	1	0	9	6	0.3	0.4	0.4	0.8
3-PT FG — Aguirre 27-85, Perkins 9-36, Nimphius 0-6, Blackman 6-20, Davis 47-115, Vincent 0-4, Harper 21-61, Ellis 42-109, Sitton 0-2, Sluby 0-2, Carter 0-3																								
SAN ANTONIO SPURS	41-41 .500				COTTON FITZSIMMONS																			
Mike Mitchell	F	6'7	215	28	82	2853	775	1558	50	269	346	78	417	151	219	1	61	27	1824	35	5.1	1.8	2.7	22.2
Gene Banks	F	6'7	215	25	82	2091	289	493	59	199	257	77	445	234	220	3	65	13	778	26	5.4	2.9	2.7	9.5
Artis Gilmore	C	7'2	255	35	81	2756	532	854	62	484	646	75	846	131	306	4	40	173	1548	34	10.4	1.6	3.8	19.1
George Gervin	G-F	6'7	185	32	72	2091	600	1182	51	324	384	84	234	178	208	2	66	48	1524	29	3.3	2.5	2.9	21.2
Johnny Moore	G	6'2	185	26	82	2689	416	910	46	189	248	76	378	816	247	3	229	18	1046	33	4.6	10.0	3.0	12.8
Alvin Robertson	G	6'3	185	22	79	1685	299	600	50	124	169	73	265	275	217	1	127	24	726	21	3.4	3.5	2.7	9.2
John Paxson	G	6'2	185	24	78	1259	196	385	51	84	100	84	68	215	117	0	45	3	486	16	0.9	2.8	1.5	6.2
Marc Iavaroni (from Phi)	F	6'9	225	28	57	1178	150	323	46	81	122	66	275	113	193	5	31	32	381	21	4.8	2.0	3.4	6.7
Ozell Jones	C	6'11	235	24	67	888	106	180	59	33	83	40	238	56	139	1	30	57	245	13	3.6	0.8	2.1	3.7
Jeff Cook (from Cle)	F-C	6'10	215	28	54	848	92	174	53	30	37	81	210	39	150	2	25	14	214	16	3.9	0.7	2.8	4.0
Billy Knight (from KC)	G-F	6'6	195	32	52	611	125	285	44	51	57	89	96	59	48	0	14	1	311	12	1.8	1.1	0.9	6.0
Edgar Jones (to Cle)	F-C	6'10	225	28	18	322	44	91	48	41	51	80	62	18	52	1	9	18	129	18	3.4	1.0	2.9	7.2
Fred Roberts (to Utah)	F	6'10	220	24	22	305	44	98	45	29	38	76	35	22	45	0	10	12	117	14	1.6	1.0	2.0	5.3
Ron Brewer (to NJ)	G	6'4	185	29	9	81	13	34	38	7	7	100	3	6	8	0	1	1	33	9	0.3	0.7	0.9	3.7
Mark McNamara (to KC)	C-F	6'11	235	25	12	63	12	18	67	9	18	50	17	0	5	0	2	1	33	5	1.4	0.0	0.4	2.8
D. Thirdkill (from Det, Mil)	F	6'7	215	24	2	52	5	11	45	5	6	83	7	3	5	0	2	1	15	26	3.5	1.5	2.5	7.5
Linton Townes	F	6'7	195	25	1	8	0	6	0	2	2	100	1	0	1	0	0	0	2	8	1.0	0.0	1.0	2.0
3-PT FG — Mitchell 5-23, Banks 1-3, Gilmore 0-2, Gervin 0-10, Moore 25-89, Robertson 4-11, Paxson 10-34, Iavaroni 0-4, O. Jones 0-1, Knight 10-24, E. Jones 0-1																								
UTAH JAZZ	41-41 .500				FRANK LAYDEN																			
Adrian Dantley (HO)	F	6'5	210	28	55	1971	512	964	53	438	545	80	323	186	133	0	57	8	1462	36	5.9	3.4	2.4	26.6
Thurl Bailey	F	6'11	215	23	80	2481	507	1034	49	197	234	84	525	138	215	2	51	105	1212	31	6.6	1.7	2.7	15.2
Mark Eaton	C	7'4	280	27	82	2813	302	673	45	190	267	71	927	124	312	5	36	**456**	794	34	11.3	1.5	3.8	9.7
Darrell Griffith	G	6'4	190	26	78	2776	728	1593	46	216	298	72	344	243	178	1	133	30	1764	36	4.4	3.1	2.3	22.6
Rickey Green	G	6'1	170	30	77	2431	381	798	48	232	267	87	189	597	131	0	132	3	1000	32	2.5	7.8	1.7	13.0
Jeff Wilkins	C-F	6'11	240	29	79	1505	285	582	49	61	80	76	366	81	173	0	35	18	631	19	4.6	1.0	2.2	8.0
John Stockton	G	6'1	170	22	82	1490	157	333	47	142	193	74	105	415	203	3	109	11	458	18	1.3	5.1	2.5	5.6
Rich Kelley	F	7'	240	31	77	1276	103	216	48	84	112	75	350	120	227	5	42	30	290	17	4.5	1.6	2.9	3.8
Fred Roberts (from SA)	F	6'10	220	24	52	873	164	320	51	121	144	84	151	65	96	0	18	10	450	17	2.9	1.3	1.8	8.7
Bob Hansen	G	6'6	190	23	54	646	110	225	49	40	72	56	70	75	88	0	25	1	261	12	1.3	1.4	1.6	4.8
John Drew (DR)	G-F	6'6	205	30	19	463	107	260	41	94	122	77	82	35	65	0	22	2	308	24	4.3	1.8	3.4	16.2
J.J. Anderson	F	6'8	195	24	44	457	61	149	41	27	45	60	82	21	70	0	29	9	149	10	1.9	0.5	1.6	3.4
Billy Paultz	C	6'11	255	36	62	370	32	87	37	18	28	64	96	16	51	0	6	11	82	6	1.5	0.3	0.8	1.3
Pace Mannion	G	6'7	190	24	34	190	27	63	43	16	23	70	23	27	17	0	16	3	70	6	0.7	0.8	0.5	2.1
Kenny Natt (to KC)	G	6'3	185	26	4	13	2	5	40	2	4	50	2	0	2	0	1	0	6	3	0.5	0.0	0.5	1.5
3-PT FG — Bailey 1-1, Griffith 92-257, Green 6-20, Wilkins 0-1, Stockton 2-11, Kelley 0-2, Roberts 1-1, Hansen 1-7, Drew 0-4, Anderson 0-2, Mannion 0-1																								
KANSAS CITY KINGS	31-51 .378				JACK McKINNEY 1-8(.111) PHIL JACKSON 30-43(.411)																			
Eddie Johnson	F	6'8	215	25	82	3029	769	1565	49	325	373	87	407	273	237	2	83	22	1876	37	5.0	3.3	2.9	22.9
Mark Olberding	F	6'8	230	28	81	2277	265	528	50	293	352	83	513	243	298	8	56	11	823	28	6.3	3.0	3.7	10.2
LaSalle Thompson	C	6'10	248	23	82	2458	369	695	53	227	315	72	854	130	328	4	98	128	965	30	10.4	1.6	4.0	11.8
Reggie Theus	G	6'7	205	27	82	2543	501	1029	49	334	387	86	270	656	250	0	95	18	1341	31	3.3	8.0	3.0	16.4
Larry Drew	G	6'1	180	26	72	2373	457	913	50	154	194	79	164	484	147	0	93	8	1075	33	2.3	6.7	2.0	14.9
Mike Woodson	G-F	6'5	198	26	78	1998	530	1068	50	264	330	80	198	143	216	1	117	28	1329	26	2.5	1.8	2.8	17.0
Otis Thorpe	F-C	6'11	225	22	82	1918	411	685	60	230	371	62	556	111	256	2	34	37	1052	23	6.8	1.4	3.1	12.8
Joe C. Meriweather	C	6'10	218	31	76	1061	121	243	50	96	124	77	263	27	181	1	17	28	339	14	3.5	0.4	2.4	4.5
Don Buse	G	6'4	195	34	65	939	82	203	40	23	30	77	61	203	75	0	38	1	218	14	0.9	3.1	1.2	3.4
Pete Verhoeven	F	6'9	215	25	54	366	51	108	47	21	25	84	63	17	85	1	15	7	123	7	1.2	0.3	1.6	2.3
Ed Nealy	F	6'7	238	24	22	225	26	44	59	10	19	53	44	18	26	0	3	1	62	10	2.0	0.8	1.2	2.8
Mark McNamara (from SA)	C	6'11	235	25	33	210	28	58	48	23	44	52	57	6	22	0	5	7	79	6	1.7	0.2	0.7	2.4
Billy Knight (to SA)	G	6'6	195	32	16	189	31	69	45	13	16	81	22	21	14	0	2	1	76	12	1.4	1.3	0.9	4.8

(continued next page)

1984/85 N.B.A. — WESTERN CONFERENCE
MIDWEST DIVISION

Use Name	Pos	Hgt	Wgt	Age	G	Min	FG	FGA	%	FT	FTA	%	Reb	Ass	PF	DQ	Stls	Blkd Shts	Points	Min	Reb	Ass	PF	Points
					TOTAL															PER GAME				
David Pope	F	6'7	220	22	22	129	17	53	32	7	13	54	18	5	30	0	3	3	41	6	0.8	0.2	1.4	1.9
Dane Suttle	G	6'3	190	23	6	24	6	13	46	2	2	100	3	2	3	0	1	0	14	4	0.5	0.3	0.5	2.3
Kenny Natt (from Utah)	G	6'3	185	26	4	16	0	1	0	0	0	—	1	3	1	0	1	0	0	4	0.3	0.8	0.3	0.0

3 PT-FG — Johnson 13-54, Olberding 0-3, Theus 5-38, Drew 7-28, Woodson 5-21, Thorpe 0-2, Meriweather 1-2, Buse 37-87, Knight 1-1, Pope 0-1, Suttle 0-1

PACIFIC DIVISION

LOS ANGELES LAKERS 62-20 .756 **PAT RILEY**

Use Name	Pos	Hgt	Wgt	Age	G	Min	FG	FGA	%	FT	FTA	%	Reb	Ass	PF	DQ	Stls	Blkd Shts	Points	Min	Reb	Ass	PF	Points
James Worthy	F	6'9	225	23	80	2696	610	1066	57	190	245	78	511	201	196	0	87	67	1410	34	6.4	2.5	2.5	17.6
Kurt Rambis	F	6'8	220	26	82	1617	181	327	55	68	103	66	528	69	211	0	82	47	430	20	6.4	0.8	2.6	5.2
Kareem Abdul-Jabbar	C	7'2	232	37	79	2630	723	1207	60	289	395	73	622	249	238	3	63	162	1735	33	7.9	3.2	3.0	22.0
Byron Scott	G	6'3	195	23	81	2305	541	1003	54	187	228	82	210	244	197	1	100	17	1295	28	2.6	3.0	2.4	16.0
Magic Johnson	G	6'8	215	25	77	2781	504	899	56	391	464	84	476	968	155	0	133	25	1406	36	6.2	12.6	2.0	18.3
Michael Cooper	G	6'5	170	28	82	2189	276	593	47	115	133	86	255	429	208	0	93	49	702	27	3.1	5.2	2.5	8.6
Larry Spriggs	F	6'7	230	25	75	1292	194	354	55	112	146	77	227	132	195	2	47	13	500	17	3.0	1.8	2.6	6.7
Bob McAdoo	C-F	6'9	225	33	66	1254	284	546	52	122	162	75	295	67	170	0	18	53	690	19	4.5	1.0	2.6	10.5
Mike McGee	F-G	6'5	190	25	76	1170	329	612	54	94	160	59	165	71	147	1	39	7	774	15	2.2	0.9	1.9	10.2
Jamaal Wilkes	F	6'6	190	31	42	761	148	303	49	51	66	77	94	41	65	0	19	3	347	18	2.2	1.0	1.5	8.3
Mitch Kupchak (KJ)	F-C	6'9	230	30	58	716	123	244	50	60	91	66	184	21	104	0	19	20	306	12	3.2	0.4	1.8	5.3
Ronnie Lester	G	6'2	175	25	32	278	34	82	41	21	31	68	26	80	25	0	15	3	89	9	0.8	2.5	0.8	2.8
Chuck Nevitt	C	7'5	237	25	11	59	5	17	29	2	8	25	20	3	20	0	0	15	12	5	1.8	0.3	1.8	1.1
Earl Jones	C	7'	230	23	2	7	0	1	0	0	0	—	0	0	0	0	0	0	0	4	0.0	0.0	0.0	0.0

3 PT-FG — Worthy 0-7, Abdul-Jabbar 0-1, Scott 26-60, Johnson 7-37, Cooper 35-123, Spriggs 0-3, McAdoo 0-1, McGee 22-61, Wilkes 0-1, Lester 0-1

PORTLAND TRAIL BLAZERS 42-40 .512 **JACK RAMSEY**

Use Name	Pos	Hgt	Wgt	Age	G	Min	FG	FGA	%	FT	FTA	%	Reb	Ass	PF	DQ	Stls	Blkd Shts	Points	Min	Reb	Ass	PF	Points
Kiki Vandeweghe	F	6'8	220	26	72	2502	618	1158	53	369	412	90	228	106	116	0	37	22	1616	35	3.2	1.5	1.6	22.4
Mychal Thompson	F-C	6'10	226	29	79	2616	572	1111	51	307	449	68	618	205	216	0	78	104	1451	33	7.8	2.6	2.7	18.4
Sam Bowie	C	7'1	235	23	76	2216	299	557	54	160	225	71	656	215	278	9	55	203	758	29	8.6	2.8	3.7	10.0
Jim Paxon	G-F	6'6	200	27	68	2253	508	988	51	196	248	79	222	264	115	0	101	5	1218	33	3.3	3.9	1.7	17.9
Darnell Valentine	G	6'2	185	25	75	2278	321	679	47	230	290	79	219	522	189	1	143	5	872	30	2.9	7.0	2.5	11.6
Clyde Drexler	G-F	6'7	210	22	80	2555	573	1161	49	223	294	76	476	441	265	3	177	68	1377	32	6.0	5.5	3.3	17.2
Steve Colter	G	6'3	165	22	78	1462	216	477	45	98	130	75	150	243	142	0	75	9	556	19	1.9	3.1	1.8	7.1
Kenny Carr (KJ)	F	6'7	230	29	48	1120	190	363	52	118	164	72	323	56	141	0	25	17	496	23	6.7	1.2	2.9	10.3
Audie Norris	C	6'9	250	24	78	1117	133	245	54	135	203	67	250	47	221	7	42	33	401	14	3.2	0.6	2.8	5.1
Jerome Kersey	F	6'7	215	22	77	958	178	372	48	117	181	65	206	63	147	1	49	29	473	12	2.7	0.8	1.9	6.1
Bernard Thompson	F	6'6	215	22	59	535	79	212	37	39	51	76	76	52	79	0	31	10	197	9	1.3	0.9	1.3	3.3
Tom Scheffler	C	6'11	240	30	39	268	21	51	41	10	20	50	76	11	48	0	8	11	52	7	1.9	0.3	1.2	1.3

3 PT-FG — Vandeweghe 11-33, Paxon 6-39, Valentine 0-2, Drexler 8-37, Colter 26-74, Carr 0-3, Norris 0-3, Kersey 0-3, B.Thompson 0-8

PHOENIX SUNS 36-46 .439 **JOHN MAC LEOD**

Use Name	Pos	Hgt	Wgt	Age	G	Min	FG	FGA	%	FT	FTA	%	Reb	Ass	PF	DQ	Stls	Blkd Shts	Points	Min	Reb	Ass	PF	Points
Larry Nance	F	6'10	215	25	61	2202	515	877	59	180	254	71	536	159	185	2	88	104	1211	36	8.8	2.6	3.0	19.9
Maurice Lucas	F	6'9	238	32	63	1670	346	727	48	150	200	75	557	145	183	0	39	17	842	27	8.8	2.3	2.9	13.4
Alvan Adams	C	6'9	220	30	82	2136	476	915	52	250	283	88	500	308	254	2	115	48	1202	26	6.1	3.8	3.1	14.7
Walter Davis (NJ, KJ)	G	6'6	200	30	23	570	139	309	45	64	73	88	35	98	42	0	18	0	345	25	1.5	4.3	1.8	15.0
Kyle Macy	G	6'3	190	27	65	2018	282	582	48	127	140	91	179	380	128	0	85	3	714	31	2.8	5.8	2.0	11.0
Jay Humphries	G	6'3	185	22	80	2062	279	626	45	141	170	83	164	350	209	2	107	8	703	26	2.1	4.4	2.6	8.8
James Edwards	C	7'	225	29	70	1787	384	766	50	276	370	75	387	153	237	5	26	52	1044	26	5.5	2.2	3.4	14.9
Michael Holton	G	6'4	185	23	74	1761	257	576	45	96	118	81	132	198	141	0	59	6	624	24	1.8	2.7	1.9	8.4
Charles Jones	F	6'8	215	22	78	1565	236	454	52	182	281	65	394	128	149	0	45	61	654	20	5.1	1.6	1.9	8.4
Rod Foster	G	6'1	160	24	79	1318	286	636	45	83	110	75	80	166	171	1	61	0	696	17	1.0	2.1	2.2	8.8
Alvin Scott	F-G	6'7	215	29	77	1238	111	259	43	53	74	72	161	127	125	0	39	25	276	16	2.1	1.6	1.6	3.6
Charles Pittman	F	6'8	220	26	68	1001	107	227	47	109	146	75	227	69	144	1	20	21	323	15	3.3	1.0	2.1	4.8
Mike Sanders	F	6'6	210	24	21	418	85	175	49	45	59	76	89	29	59	0	23	4	215	20	4.2	1.4	2.8	10.2
Rick Robey	C-F	6'11	230	28	4	48	2	9	22	1	2	50	8	5	7	0	2	0	5	12	2.0	1.3	1.8	1.3
Michael Young	F	6'7	220	23	2	11	2	6	33	0	0	—	2	0	0	0	0	0	4	6	1.0	0.0	0.0	2.0

3 PT-FG — Nance 1-2, Lucas 0-4, Davis 3-10, Macy 23-85, Humphries 4-20, Edwards 0-3, Holton 14-45, Jones 0-4, Foster 41-126, Scott 1-5, Pittman 0-2, Young 0-1

LOS ANGELES CLIPPERS 31-51 .378 **JIM LYNAM 22-39 (.361), DON CHANEY 9-12 (.429)**

Use Name	Pos	Hgt	Wgt	Age	G	Min	FG	FGA	%	FT	FTA	%	Reb	Ass	PF	DQ	Stls	Blkd Shts	Points	Min	Reb	Ass	PF	Points
Marques Johnson	F	6'7	218	28	72	2448	494	1094	45	190	260	73	428	248	193	2	72	30	1181	34	5.9	3.4	2.7	16.4
Michael Cage	F	6'9	225	22	75	1610	216	398	54	101	137	74	392	51	164	1	41	32	533	21	5.2	0.7	2.2	7.1
James Donaldson	C	7'2	278	27	82	2392	351	551	64	227	303	75	668	48	217	1	28	130	929	29	8.1	0.6	2.6	11.3
Derek Smith	G-F	6'7	215	23	80	2762	682	1271	54	400	504	79	427	216	317	8	77	52	1767	35	5.3	2.7	4.0	22.1
Norm Nixon	G	6'2	175	29	81	2894	596	1281	47	170	218	78	218	711	175	2	95	4	1395	36	2.7	8.8	2.2	17.2
Junior Bridgeman	G-F	6'5	210	31	80	2042	460	990	46	181	206	88	230	171	128	0	47	18	1115	26	2.9	2.1	1.6	13.9
Bill Walton	C-F	6'11	225	32	67	1647	269	516	52	138	203	68	600	156	184	0	50	140	676	25	9.0	2.3	2.7	10.1
Rory White	F	6'8	210	25	80	1106	144	279	52	90	130	69	195	34	115	0	35	20	378	14	2.4	0.4	1.4	4.7
Harvey Catchings	F-C	6'9	218	33	70	1049	72	149	48	59	89	66	262	14	162	0	15	57	203	15	3.7	0.2	2.3	2.9
Bryan Warrick	G	6'5	195	25	58	713	85	173	49	44	57	77	58	153	85	0	23	6	215	12	1.0	2.6	1.5	3.7
Lancaster Gordon	G	6'3	185	22	63	682	110	287	38	37	49	76	61	88	61	0	33	6	259	11	1.0	1.4	1.0	4.1
Franklin Edwards	G	6'1	170	25	16	198	36	66	55	19	24	79	14	38	10	0	17	0	91	12	0.9	2.4	0.6	5.7
Jay Murphy	F	6'9	220	22	23	149	8	50	16	12	21	57	41	4	21	0	1	2	28	6	1.8	0.2	0.9	1.2
Dale Wilkinson (from Det)	F	6'10	220	24	10	38	4	14	29	6	7	86	3	2	8	0	0	0	14	4	0.3	0.2	0.8	1.4

Michael Brooks - knee injury

3 PT-FG — Johnson 3-13, Smith 3-19, Nixon 33-99, Bridgeman 14-39, Walton 0-2, Cathcings 0-1, Warrick 1-4, Gordon 2-9, Murphy 0-1, Wilkinson 0-1

1984/85 N.B.A. — WESTERN CONFERENCE
PACIFIC DIVISION

Use Name	Pos	Hgt	Wgt	Age	G	Min	FG	FGA	%	FT	FTA	%	Reb	Ass	PF	DQ	Stls	Blkd Shts	Points	Min	Reb	Ass	PF	Points
SEATTLE SUPERSONICS	31-51 .378				LEN WILKINS																			
Danny Vranes	F	6'7	210	26	76	2163	186	402	46	67	127	53	436	152	256	4	76	57	440	28	5.7	2.0	3.4	5.8
Tom Chambers	F	6'10	225	25	81	2923	629	1302	48	475	571	83	579	209	312	4	70	57	1739	36	7.1	2.6	3.9	21.5
Jack Sikma	C-F	6'11	250	29	68	2402	461	943	49	335	393	85	723	285	239	1	83	91	1259	35	10.6	4.2	3.5	18.5
Al Wood	G-F	6'6	193	26	80	2545	515	1061	49	166	214	78	279	236	187	3	84	42	1203	32	3.5	3.0	2.3	15.0
Gerald Henderson	G	6'2	175	28	79	2648	427	891	48	199	255	78	190	559	196	1	140	9	1062	34	2.4	7.1	2.5	13.4
Tim McCormick	C	7'	240	22	78	1584	269	483	56	188	263	71	398	78	207	2	18	33	726	20	5.1	1.0	2.7	9.3
Ricky Sobers	G	6'3	198	31	71	1490	280	628	45	132	162	81	103	252	156	0	49	9	700	21	1.5	3.5	2.2	9.9
Jon Sundvold	G	6'2	170	23	73	1150	170	400	43	48	59	81	70	206	87	0	36	1	400	16	1.0	2.8	1.2	5.5
Frank Brickowski	F	6'10	240	25	78	1115	150	305	49	85	127	67	260	100	171	1	34	15	385	14	3.3	1.3	2.2	4.9
Reggie King	F	6'6	230	27	60	860	63	149	42	41	59	69	122	53	74	1	28	11	167	14	2.0	0.9	1.2	2.8
Cory Blackwell	F	6'6	210	21	60	551	87	237	37	28	55	51	96	26	55	0	25	3	202	9	1.6	0.4	0.9	3.4
John Schweitz	G	6'6	210	24	19	110	25	74	34	7	10	70	21	18	12	0	0	1	57	6	1.1	0.9	0.6	3.0
Scotter McCray	F	6'9	215	24	6	93	6	10	60	3	4	75	17	7	13	0	1	3	15	16	2.8	1.2	2.2	2.5
Joe Cooper	F	6'10	230	27	3	45	7	15	47	3	6	50	9	2	7	1	2	1	17	15	3.0	0.7	2.3	5.7
Danny Young	G	6'4	175	22	3	26	2	10	20	0	0	—	3	2	2	0	3	0	4	9	1.0	0.7	0.7	1.3

3 PT-FG — Vranes 1-4, Chambers 6-22, Sikma 2-10, Wood 7-33, Henderson 9-38, McCormick 0-1, Sobers 8-28, Sundvold 12-38, Brikowski 0-4, Blackwell 0-2, Schweitz 0-4, Young 0-1

Use Name	Pos	Hgt	Wgt	Age	G	Min	FG	FGA	%	FT	FTA	%	Reb	Ass	PF	DQ	Stls	Blkd Shts	Points	Min	Reb	Ass	PF	Points
GOLDEN STATE WARRIORS	22-60 .268				JOHN BACH																			
Purvis Short	F	6'7	220	27	78	3081	819	1780	46	501	613	82	398	234	255	4	116	27	2186	40	5.1	3.0	3.3	28.0
Larry Smith	F	6'8	225	26	80	2497	366	690	53	155	256	61	869	96	285	5	78	54	887	31	10.9	1.2	3.6	11.1
Jerome Whitehead	C	6'10	225	28	79	2536	421	825	51	184	235	78	622	53	322	8	45	43	1026	32	7.9	0.7	4.1	13.0
Lester Conner	G	6'4	185	25	79	2258	246	546	45	144	192	75	246	369	136	1	161	13	640	29	3.1	4.7	1.7	8.1
Eric Floyd	G	6'3	175	24	82	2873	610	1372	44	336	415	81	202	406	226	1	134	41	1598	35	2.5	5.0	2.8	19.5
Mickey Johnson	F	6'10	190	32	66	1565	304	714	43	260	316	82	396	149	221	5	70	35	875	24	6.0	2.3	3.3	13.3
Othell Wilson	G	6'	190	23	74	1260	134	291	46	54	76	71	131	217	122	0	77	12	325	17	1.8	2.9	1.6	4.4
Chuck Aleksinas	C	6'11	260	25	74	1114	161	337	48	55	75	73	270	36	171	1	15	15	377	15	3.6	0.5	2.3	5.1
Mike Bratz	G	6'2	185	29	56	746	106	250	42	69	82	84	58	122	76	1	47	4	287	13	1.0	2.2	1.4	5.1
Gary Plummer	F-C	6'9	215	22	66	702	92	232	40	65	92	71	134	26	127	1	15	14	250	11	2.0	0.4	1.9	3.8
Peter Thibeaux	F	6'7	210	23	51	461	94	195	48	43	67	64	69	17	85	1	11	17	231	9	1.4	0.3	1.7	4.5
Steve Burtt	G	6'2	185	22	47	418	72	188	38	53	77	69	28	20	76	0	21	4	197	9	0.6	0.4	1.6	4.2
Terry Teagle (from Det)	G	6'5	195	24	19	344	73	135	54	25	35	71	43	13	34	0	13	5	173	18	2.3	0.7	1.8	9.1
Joe Barry Carroll - holdout																								

3 PT-FG — Short 47-150, Connor 4-20, Floyd 42-143, Johnson 7-30, Alexsinas 0-1, Bratz 6-26, Plummer 1-4, Thibeaux 0-2, Burtt 0-1, Teagle 2-4

PLAYOFFS

LOS ANGELES LAKERS — PAT RILEY

defeated Phoenix 3-0; H142-114, H147-130, 119-103
defeated Portland 4-1; H125-101, H134-118, 130-126, 107-115, H139-120
defeated Denver 4-1; H139-122, H114-136, 136-118, 120-116, H153-109
defeated Boston 4-2; 114-148, 109-102, H136-111, H105-107, H120-111, 111-100

Use Name	Pos	Hgt	Wgt	Age	G	Min	FG	FGA	%	FT	FTA	%	Reb	Ass	PF	DQ	Stls	Blkd Shts	Points	Min	Reb	Ass	PF	Points
James Worthy	F	6'9	225	23	19	626	166	267	**62**	75	111	68	96	41	53	1	17	13	408	33	5.1	2.2	2.8	21.5
Kurt Rambis	F	6'8	220	26	19	375	48	81	59	19	28	68	129	17	52	0	18	9	115	20	6.8	0.9	2.7	6.1
Kareem Abdul-Jabbar	C	7'2	232	37	19	610	168	300	56	80	103	78	154	76	67	1	23	36	416	32	8.1	4.0	3.5	21.9
Byron Scott	G	6'3	195	23	19	585	138	267	52	35	44	80	52	50	47	0	**41**	4	321	31	2.7	2.6	2.5	16.9
Magic Johnson	G	6'8	215	25	19	687	116	226	51	100	118	85	134	**289**	48	0	32	4	333	36	7.1	15.2	2.5	17.5
Michael Cooper	G-F	6'5	170	28	19	501	71	126	56	48	52	92	76	93	46	0	21	9	198	26	4.0	4.9	2.4	10.4
Bob McAdoo	C-F	6'9	225	33	19	398	91	193	47	35	47	74	86	15	66	2	9	26	217	21	4.5	0.8	3.5	11.4
Mike McGee	F-G	6'5	190	25	17	260	76	142	54	29	42	69	36	12	26	0	7	1	190	15	2.1	0.7	1.5	11.2
Larry Spriggs	F	6'7	230	25	16	230	40	77	52	18	29	62	51	33	36	0	4	5	98	14	3.2	2.1	2.3	6.1
Mitch Kupchak	F	6'9	230	30	16	197	31	53	58	13	22	59	48	5	42	0	2	7	75	12	3.0	0.3	2.6	4.7
Ronnie Lester	G	6'2	175	25	9	54	6	15	40	7	9	78	8	9	7	0	0	0	19	6	0.9	1.0	0.8	2.1
Chuck Nevitt	C	7'5	237	25	7	37	3	9	33	4	8	50	6	1	11	0	4	6	10	5	0.9	0.1	1.6	1.4

3 PT-FG — Worthy 1-2, Scott 10-21, Johnson 1-7, Cooper 8-26, McAdoo 0-1, McGee 9-18, Spriggs 0-2, Kupchak 0-1

BOSTON CELTICS — K.C. JONES

defeated Cleveland 3-1; H126-123, H108-106, 98-105, 117-115
defeated Detroit 4-2; H133-99, H121-114, 117-125, 99-102, H130-123, 123-113
defeated Philadelphia 4-1; H108-93, H106-98, 105-94, 104-115, H102-100
lost to Los Angeles 2-4; H148-114, H102-109, 111-136, 107-105, 111-120, H100-111

Use Name	Pos	Hgt	Wgt	Age	G	Min	FG	FGA	%	FT	FTA	%	Reb	Ass	PF	DQ	Stls	Blkd Shts	Points	Min	Reb	Ass	PF	Points
Larry Bird	F	6'9	220	28	20	815	**196**	**425**	46	**121**	136	89	182	115	54	0	34	19	**520**	41	9.1	5.8	2.7	26.0
Kevin McHale	F-C	6'10	225	27	21	837	172	303	57	**121**	**150**	81	208	32	73	**3**	13	**46**	465	40	9.9	1.5	3.5	22.1
Robert Parish	C	7'	230	31	21	803	136	276	49	87	111	78	**219**	31	68	0	21	34	359	38	10.4	1.5	3.2	17.1
Danny Ainge	G	6'4	175	25	21	687	97	208	47	30	39	77	58	121	**76**	1	32	1	231	33	2.8	5.8	3.6	11.0
Dennis Johnson	G	6'4	200	30	21	**848**	142	319	45	80	93	86	84	154	66	0	31	9	364	40	4.0	7.3	3.1	17.3
Scott Wedman	F-G	6'7	235	32	21	350	73	134	54	26	38	68	59	33	50	1	13	0	182	17	2.8	1.6	2.4	8.7
Ray Williams	G	6'3	195	30	19	278	47	116	41	24	25	96	36	60	44	0	12	1	120	15	1.9	3.2	2.3	6.3
Cedric Maxwell	F	6'8	215	29	20	238	21	43	49	34	43	79	47	7	29	0	9	2	76	12	2.4	0.4	1.5	3.8
Quinn Buckner	G	6'3	203	30	15	86	13	22	59	5	8	63	7	12	24	0	6	0	31	6	0.5	0.8	1.6	2.1
Greg Kite	C	6'11	250	23	9	63	5	12	42	1	2	50	16	3	13	0	1	0	11	7	1.8	0.3	1.4	1.2
M.L. Carr	G	6'6	205	33	7	24	4	15	27	0	0	—	2	1	4	0	1	0	9	3	0.3	0.1	0.6	1.3
Carlos Clark	G	6'4	210	24	3	11	3	5	60	2	2	100	2	3	2	0	1	0	8	4	0.7	1.0	0.7	2.7

3 PT-FG — Bird 7-25, Ainge 7-16, Johnson 0-14, Wedman 10-22, Williams 2-15, Carr 1-2

1984/85 N.B.A. — PLAYOFFS

DENVER NUGGETS — **DOUG MOE**

defeated San Antonio 3-2; H141-111, H111-113, 115-112, 111-116, H126-99
defeated Utah 4-1; H130-113, H131-123(OT), 123-131, 125-118, H116-104
lost to Los Angeles 1-4; 122-139, 136-114, H118-136, H116-120, 109-153

Use Name	Pos	Hgt	Wgt	Age	G	Min	FG	FGA	%	FT	FTA	%	Reb	Ass	PF	DQ	Stls	Blkd Shts	Points	Min	Reb	Ass	PF	Points
					TOTAL															PER GAME				
Alex English	F	6'8	190	30	14	536	163	304	54	97	109	89	92	63	40	1	17	5	423	38	6.6	4.5	2.9	30.2
Calvin Natt	F	6'6	220	27	15	508	131	238	55	72	89	81	99	57	25	0	8	5	334	34	6.6	3.8	2.3	22.3
Dan Issel	C	6'9	240	36	15	325	73	159	46	39	48	81	54	27	36	0	12	5	186	22	3.6	1.8	2.4	12.4
T.R. Dunn	G	6'4	192	29	15	371	27	65	42	14	19	74	60	34	45	0	24	3	68	25	4.0	2.3	3.0	4.5
Lafayette Lever	G	6'3	175	24	11	342	49	122	40	48	63	76	71	93	33	0	26	2	146	31	6.5	8.5	3.0	13.3
Elston Turner	G-F	6'5	220	25	15	358	50	102	49	12	19	63	73	46	42	0	17	1	114	24	4.9	3.1	2.8	7.6
Bill Hanzlik	F-G	6'7	185	27	15	310	45	92	49	30	41	73	46	33	57	2	14	6	120	21	3.1	2.2	3.8	8.0
Wayne Cooper	C-F	6'10	220	28	15	321	67	143	47	30	40	75	93	20	52	0	8	36	164	21	6.2	1.3	3.5	10.9
Mike Evans	G	6'1	170	29	15	281	62	143	43	14	17	82	32	46	39	0	13	3	155	19	2.1	3.1	2.6	10.3
Willie White	G	6'3	195	22	10	123	27	57	47	7	12	58	17	17	6	0	5	0	63	12	1.7	1.7	0.6	6.3
Danny Schayes	C	6'11	245	25	9	118	11	26	42	14	20	70	30	12	22	0	3	4	36	13	3.3	1.3	2.4	4.0
Joe Kopicki	F	6'9	240	24	7	32	6	16	38	9	17	53	13	3	5	0	1	1	21	5	1.9	0.4	0.7	3.0

3 PT-FG — English 0-1, Issel 1-1, Lever 0-2, Turner 2-2, Hanzlik 0-1, Evans 17-51, White 2-3

PHILADELPHIA 76ers — **BILLY CUNNINGHAM**

defeated Washington 3-1; H104-97, H113-94, 100-118, 106-98
defeated Milwaukee 4-0; 127-105, 112-108, H109-104, H121-112
lost to Boston 1-4; 93-108, 98-106, H94-105, H115-104, 100-102

Use Name	Pos	Hgt	Wgt	Age	G	Min	FG	FGA	%	FT	FTA	%	Reb	Ass	PF	DQ	Stls	Blkd Shts	Points	Min	Reb	Ass	PF	Points
Julius Erving	F	6'7	205	34	13	434	84	187	45	54	63	86	73	48	34	0	25	11	222	33	5.6	3.7	2.6	17.1
Charles Barkley	F	6'6	260	21	13	408	75	139	54	40	63	63	144	26	49	0	23	15	194	31	11.1	2.0	3.8	14.9
Moses Malone	C	6'10	255	29	13	505	90	212	42	82	103	80	138	24	39	0	17	22	262	39	10.6	1.8	3.0	20.2
Andrew Toney	G	6'3	188	27	13	442	83	174	48	47	61	77	32	66	46	0	12	5	219	34	2.5	5.1	3.5	16.8
Maurice Cheeks	G	6'1	180	28	13	483	81	153	53	36	42	86	46	67	29	0	31	5	198	37	3.5	5.2	2.2	15.2
Bobby Jones	F	6'9	220	33	13	309	46	78	59	14	20	70	48	16	38	0	12	15	106	24	3.7	1.2	2.9	8.2
Clint Richardson	G	6'3	195	28	13	281	53	94	56	9	10	90	38	27	23	0	10	2	115	22	2.9	2.1	1.8	8.8
Clemon Johnson	C-F	6'10	240	28	13	165	13	33	39	16	21	76	36	2	32	0	3	6	42	13	2.8	0.2	2.5	3.2
Sedale Threatt	G	6'2	175	23	4	28	2	7	29	0	0	—	1	5	2	0	1	0	4	7	0.3	1.3	0.5	1.0
Sam Williams	F	6'8	215	25	5	26	1	6	17	3	10	30	12	0	2	0	0	0	5	5	2.4	0.0	0.4	1.0
George Johnson	F	6'7	218	28	5	24	5	8	63	0	0	—	7	0	2	0	0	0	11	5	1.4	0.0	0.4	2.2
Leon Wood	G	6'3	185	22	5	15	4	9	44	6	8	75	1	2	0	0	0	0	14	3	0.2	0.4	0.0	2.8

3 PT-FG — Erving 0-1, Barkley 4-6, Malone 0-1, Toney 6-14, Cheeks 0-5, C.Johnson 0-1, G.Johnson 1-1, Wood 0-1

UTAH JAZZ — **FRANK LAYDEN**

defeated Houston 3-2; 115-101, 96-122, H112-104, H94-96, 104-97
lost to Denver 1-4; 113-130, 123-131(OT), H131-123, H118-125, 104-116

Use Name	Pos	Hgt	Wgt	Age	G	Min	FG	FGA	%	FT	FTA	%	Reb	Ass	PF	DQ	Stls	Blkd Shts	Points	Min	Reb	Ass	PF	Points
Adrian Dantley	F-G	6'5	210	28	10	398	79	151	52	95	122	78	75	20	39	1	16	0	253	40	7.5	2.0	3.9	25.3
Thurl Bailey	F	6'11	215	23	10	375	62	152	41	45	55	82	92	27	30	0	5	18	169	38	9.2	2.7	3.0	16.9
Mark Eaton	C	7'3	280	27	5	158	12	34	35	5	7	71	45	5	19	0	4	29	29	32	9.0	1.0	3.8	5.8
Darrell Griffith	G	6'4	190	26	10	340	72	158	46	18	25	72	29	25	21	0	12	5	175	34	2.9	2.5	2.1	17.5
Rickey Green	G	6'1	170	30	10	302	57	106	54	35	38	92	30	75	23	0	12	0	150	30	3.0	7.5	2.3	15.0
Jeff Wilkins	C-F	6'11	240	29	10	257	51	118	43	27	35	77	63	13	27	0	4	5	129	26	6.3	1.3	2.7	12.9
John Stockton	G	6'1	170	22	10	186	21	45	47	26	35	74	28	43	30	0	11	2	68	19	2.8	4.3	3.0	6.8
Rich Kelley	C-F	7'	240	31	9	174	18	38	47	13	15	87	57	14	32	1	7	5	49	19	6.3	1.6	3.6	5.4
Fred Roberts	F	6'10	220	24	10	130	19	43	44	16	20	80	17	9	16	0	7	3	54	13	1.7	0.9	1.6	5.4
Pace Mannion	G	6'7	190	24	8	41	4	12	33	10	12	83	7	4	5	0	1	2	18	5	0.9	0.5	0.6	2.3
Bob Hansen	G	6'6	190	23	8	34	2	8	25	5	8	63	4	6	6	0	3	0	9	4	0.5	0.8	0.8	1.1
Billy Paultz	C	6'11	255	36	5	30	3	8	38	1	4	25	8	2	7	0	1	1	7	6	1.6	0.4	1.4	1.4

3 PT-FG — Dantley 0-1, Griffith 13-36, Green 1-7, Wilkins 0-1, Stockton 0-2, Mannion 0-1

PORTLAND TRAIL BLAZERS — **JACK RAMSEY**

defeated Dallas 3-1; 131 139(2OT), 124-121(OT) H122-108, H115-113
lost to Los Angeles 1-4; 101-125, 118-134, H126-130, H115-107, 120-139

Use Name	Pos	Hgt	Wgt	Age	G	Min	FG	FGA	%	FT	FTA	%	Reb	Ass	PF	DQ	Stls	Blkd Shts	Points	Min	Reb	Ass	PF	Points
Kiki Vandeweghe	F	6'8	220	26	9	311	85	158	54	31	33	94	27	17	23	0	8	3	202	35	3.0	1.9	2.6	22.4
Kenny Carr	F	6'7	230	29	9	265	50	95	53	16	20	80	70	10	40	2	3	2	116	29	7.8	1.1	4.4	12.9
Sam Bowie	C	7'1	235	23	9	259	26	59	44	14	25	56	76	21	36	2	4	21	66	29	8.4	2.3	4.0	7.3
Clyde Drexler	G	6'7	210	22	9	339	55	134	41	38	45	84	55	83	37	0	23	9	150	38	6.1	9.2	4.1	16.7
Darnell Valentine	G	6'2	185	25	9	244	43	88	49	29	31	94	17	58	28	1	16	0	115	27	1.9	6.4	3.1	12.8
Mychal Thompson	F-C	6'10	226	29	9	250	50	102	49	33	49	67	72	14	32	7	7	12	133	28	8.0	1.6	3.6	14.8
Jim Paxson	G-F	6'6	200	27	9	212	47	101	47	19	24	79	20	21	16	0	6	0	116	24	2.2	2.3	1.8	12.9
Steve Colter	G	6'3	165	22	9	166	36	75	48	5	8	63	16	37	24	1	5	0	80	18	1.8	4.1	2.7	8.9
Audie Norris	C	6'9	250	24	8	109	19	32	59	9	22	41	43	3	25	0	4	5	47	14	5.4	0.4	3.2	5.9
Jerome Kersey	F	6'7	215	22	8	60	16	31	52	6	8	75	9	6	11	0	7	2	38	8	1.1	0.8	1.4	4.8
Tom Scheffler	C	6'11	240	30	3	10	2	3	67	3	4	75	5	0	0	0	1	0	7	3	1.7	0.0	0.0	2.3
Bernard Thompson	F	6'6	215	22	2	10	0	5	0	2	2	100	3	2	1	0	0	1	2	5	1.5	1.0	0.5	1.0

3 PT- FG— Vandeweghe 1-7, Carr 0-1, Drexler 2-7, Paxson 3-10, Colter 3-11

1984/85 N.B.A. — PLAYOFFS

Use Name	Pos	Hgt	Wgt	Age	G	Min	FG	FGA	%	FT	FTA	%	Reb	Ass	PF	DQ	Stls	Blkd Shts	Points	Min	Reb	Ass	PF	Points
					TOTAL															PER GAME				
DETROIT PISTONS	**CHUCK DALY**	defeated New Jersey 3-0; H125-105, H121-111, 116-115; lost to Boston 2-4; 99-133, 114-121, H125-117, H102-99, 123-130, H113-123																						
Kelly Tripucka	F	6'6	220	25	9	288	49	118	42	35	40	88	39	29	22	0	4	3	133	32	4.3	3.2	2.4	14.8
Dan Roundfield	F	6'8	215	31	9	215	33	68	49	16	17	94	60	15	21	0	4	6	82	24	6.7	1.7	2.3	9.1
Bill Laimbeer	C	6'11	245	27	9	325	48	107	45	36	51	71	96	15	32	1	7	7	132	36	10.7	1.7	3.6	14.7
John Long	G	6'5	200	28	9	255	48	105	46	15	15	100	17	13	22	0	14	2	112	28	1.9	1.4	2.4	12.4
Isiah Thomas	G	6'1	185	23	9	355	83	166	50	47	62	76	47	101	39	2	19	4	219	39	5.2	11.2	4.3	24.3
Vinnie Johnson	G	6'2	200	28	9	235	53	103	51	22	28	79	27	29	24	0	6	1	128	26	3.0	3.2	2.7	14.2
Terry Tyler	F	6'7	220	28	9	179	49	100	49	22	27	81	40	3	17	0	6	4	120	20	4.4	0.3	1.9	13.3
Kent Benson	F-C	6'10	245	30	9	142	25	46	54	13	15	87	36	4	27	0	8	2	63	16	4.0	0.4	3.0	7.0
Earl Cureton	F-C	6'9	215	27	9	133	16	34	47	5	9	56	41	4	20	0	9	2	37	15	4.6	0.4	2.2	4.1
Brooke Steppe	G	6'5	195	25	4	20	2	7	29	4	6	67	3	2	3	0	0	0	8	5	0.8	0.5	0.8	2.0
Tony Campbell	F	6'7	215	22	2	9	1	3	33	0	0	—	2	1	1	0	0	0	2	5	1.0	0.5	0.5	1.0
Major Jones	F	6'9	225	31	1	4	1	1	100	0	0	—	0	0	0	0	0	0	2	4	0.0	0.0	0.0	2.0
3 PT-FG —	Tripucka 0-1, Laimbeer 0-2, Long 1-4, Thomas 6-15, Johnson 0-3, Tyler 0-1, Cureton 0-1, Steppe 0-1																							
MILWAUKEE BUCKS	**DON NELSON**	defeated Chicago 3-1; H109-100, H122-115, 107-109, 105-97; lost to Philadelphia 0-4; H105-127, H108-112, H104-109, 112-121																						
Paul Pressey	F-G	6'5	185	26	8	296	45	88	51	31	38	82	48	61	27	1	18	5	122	37	6.0	7.6	3.4	15.3
Terry Cummings	F	6'9	220	23	8	311	86	149	58	48	58	83	70	20	33	1	12	7	220	39	8.8	2.5	4.1	27.5
Alton Lister	C	7'	240	26	8	203	27	60	45	15	32	47	62	15	36	1	6	15	69	25	7.8	1.9	4.5	8.6
Sidney Moncrief	G	6'4	190	27	8	319	55	99	56	70	75	93	34	40	26	0	5	4	184	40	4.3	5.0	3.3	23.0
Craig Hodges	G	6'3	190	24	8	216	28	77	36	4	5	80	13	26	29	2	12	1	64	27	1.6	3.3	3.6	8.0
Ricky Pierce	G-F	6'5	205	25	8	198	36	73	49	7	9	78	18	15	26	0	3	1	79	25	2.3	1.9	3.3	9.9
Paul Mokeski	C-F	7'	250	27	8	154	16	36	44	12	12	100	34	12	28	1	2	4	44	19	4.3	1.5	3.5	5.5
Randy Breuer	C	7'3	230	24	8	104	15	26	58	14	21	67	24	0	15	0	2	2	44	13	3.0	0.0	1.9	5.5
Charlie Davis	F	6'7	215	26	5	51	8	20	40	3	4	75	10	4	2	0	0	0	19	10	2.0	0.8	0.4	3.8
Paul Thompson	F	6'6	210	23	3	34	5	12	42	3	5	60	5	2	3	0	4	1	13	11	1.7	0.7	1.0	4.3
Kevin Grevey	G	6'5	210	31	5	28	4	13	31	4	4	100	2	2	5	0	2	0	12	6	0.4	0.4	1.0	2.4
Chris Engler	C	6'11	248	25	1	6	1	1	100	0	0	—	2	0	2	0	0	0	2	6	2.0	0.0	2.0	2.0
3 PT-FG —	Pressey 1-3, Cummings 0-1, Moncrief 4-10, Hodges 4-23, Pierce 0-2, Davis 0-2, Thompson 0-2																							
CHICAGO BULLS	**KEVIN LOUGHERY**	lost to Milwaukee 1-3; 100-109, 115-122, H109-107, H97-105																						
Orlando Woolridge	F	6'9	215	25	4	167	34	68	50	14	18	78	13	8	19	1	6	1	82	42	3.3	2.0	4.8	20.5
Dave Greenwood	F	6'9	232	27	4	139	15	28	54	8	10	80	31	5	14	0	6	4	38	35	7.8	1.3	3.5	9.5
Jawaan Oldham	C	7'	215	27	4	91	7	15	47	0	0	—	22	3	19	1	6	7	14	23	5.5	0.8	4.8	3.5
Quintin Dailey	G	6'3	180	23	4	129	26	62	42	8	11	73	13	11	9	0	4	0	61	32	3.3	2.8	2.3	15.3
Michael Jordan	G	6'6	195	21	4	171	34	78	44	48	58	83	23	34	15	0	11	4	117	43	5.8	8.5	3.8	29.3
Wes Matthews	G	6'1	170	25	4	91	11	32	34	7	9	78	6	12	10	0	3	0	29	23	1.5	3.0	2.5	7.3
Dave Corzine	C	6'11	260	28	4	77	14	21	67	5	6	83	22	3	14	0	2	1	33	19	5.5	0.8	3.5	8.3
Sidney Green	F	6'9	220	23	3	54	12	24	50	7	11	64	15	2	8	0	0	1	31	18	5.0	0.7	2.7	10.3
Steve Johnson	F	6'10	245	27	3	22	2	7	29	2	2	100	5	2	4	0	0	0	6	7	1.7	0.7	1.3	2.0
Caldwell Jones	C	6'11	225	34	2	18	5	6	83	0	0	—	5	0	7	1	0	1	10	9	2.5	0.0	3.5	5.0
Rod Higgins	F	6'7	205	24	1	1	0	0	—	0	0	—	0	0	0	0	0	0	0	1	0.0	0.0	0.0	0.0
3 PT-FG —	Dailey 1-7, Jordan 1-8, Matthews 0-3, Jones 0-1																							
CLEVELAND CAVALIERS	**GEORGE KARL**	lost to Boston 1-3; 123-126, 106-108, H105-98, H115-117																						
Phil Hubbard	F	6'8	215	28	4	101	24	45	53	13	17	76	20	3	16	0	3	0	62	25	5.0	0.8	4.0	15.5
Lonnie Shelton	F	6'8	255	29	4	106	19	34	56	8	10	80	22	4	20	2	2	1	46	27	5.5	1.0	5.0	11.5
Roy Hinson	C-F	6'9	210	23	4	120	26	48	54	15	23	65	30	3	18	1	3	9	67	30	7.5	0.8	4.5	16.8
World Free	G	6'2	185	30	4	150	41	93	44	23	25	92	10	31	12	0	6	0	105	38	2.5	7.8	3.0	26.3
John Bagley	G	6'	190	24	4	168	22	56	39	7	10	70	16	40	7	0	10	0	51	42	4.0	10.0	1.8	12.8
Ben Poquette	F-C	6'9	235	29	4	91	13	21	62	4	5	80	14	1	16	2	2	6	30	23	3.5	0.3	4.0	7.5
Mark West	F-C	6'10	230	24	4	68	3	5	60	2	5	40	18	4	19	0	2	0	8	17	4.5	1.0	4.8	2.0
Johhny Davis	G	6'2	189	29	3	50	12	16	75	4	5	80	6	15	5	0	5	0	28	17	2.0	5.0	1.7	9.3
Edgar Jones	F-C	6'10	225	28	4	45	9	18	50	7	8	88	8	3	6	0	2	0	25	11	2.0	0.8	1.5	6.3
Melvin Turpin	C	6'11	240	24	4	45	12	19	63	1	2	50	8	0	3	0	4	1	25	11	2.0	0.0	0.8	6.3
Ron Anderson	F	6'7	215	26	2	9	0	3	0	0	0	—	3	0	0	0	0	0	0	5	1.5	0.0	0.0	0.0
Kevin Williams	G	6'3	175	23	2	7	1	2	50	0	0	—	0	1	1	0	0	0	2	4	0.0	0.5	0.5	1.0
3 PT-FG —	Hubbard 1-1, Free 0-4, Bagley 0-3, Davis 0-1, Jones 0-1																							
DALLAS MAVERICKS	**DICK MOTTA**	lost to Portland 1-3; H139-131(2ot), H121-124(ot), 109-122, 113-115																						
Mark Aguirre	F	6'6	235	25	4	164	44	89	49	27	32	84	30	16	16	1	3	0	116	41	7.5	4.0	4.0	29.0
Jay Vincent	F	6'7	225	25	4	134	20	56	36	22	29	76	22	3	16	0	6	3	62	34	5.5	0.8	4.0	15.5
Sam Perkins	C-F	6'9	235	23	4	169	24	49	49	26	34	76	51	11	13	1	2	1	75	42	12.8	2.8	3.3	18.8
Rolando Blackman	G	6'6	190	25	4	169	47	92	51	36	38	95	26	19	8	0	2	2	131	42	6.5	4.8	2.0	32.8
Derek Harper	G	6'4	185	23	4	132	10	21	48	5	7	71	12	20	12	0	6	1	26	33	3.0	5.0	3.0	6.5
Brad Davis	G	6'3	180	29	4	113	13	26	50	12	13	92	8	22	11	0	4	1	41	28	2.0	5.5	2.8	10.3
Dale Ellis	F	6'7	205	24	4	68	10	23	43	1	2	50	7	3	3	0	4	0	23	17	1.8	0.8	0.8	5.8
Kurt Nimphius	C	6'10	218	26	4	50	3	6	50	0	0	-	6	3	10	0	1	1	6	13	1.5	0.8	2.5	1.5
Wallace Bryant	C	7'	245	25	2	36	0	1	0	2	2	100	7	1	5	0	1	1	2	18	3.5	0.5	2.5	1.0
3 PT-FG —	Aguirre 1-2, Perkins 1-4, Blackman 1-2, Harper 1-3, Davis 3-8, Ellis 2-5																							

1984/85 N.B.A. — PLAYOFFS

HOUSTON ROCKETS — **BILL FITCH** — lost to Utah 2-3; H101-115, H122-96, 104-112, 96-94, H97-104

Use Name	Pos	Hgt	Wgt	Age	G	Min	FG	FGA	%	FT	FTA	%	Reb	Ass	PF	DQ	Stls	Blkd Shts	Points	Min	Reb	Ass	PF	Points
					TOTAL															PER GAME				
Rodney McCray	F	6'8	220	23	5	181	19	34	56	15	23	65	30	11	17	0	6	1	53	36	6.0	2.2	3.4	10.6
Ralph Sampson	F-C	7'4	228	24	5	193	43	100	43	19	37	51	83	7	23	2	2	8	106	39	16.6	1.4	4.6	21.2
Akeem Olajuwan	C	7'	250	21	5	187	42	88	48	22	46	48	65	7	22	0	7	13	106	37	13.0	1.4	4.4	21.2
Lewis Lloyd	G-F	6'6	215	25	5	174	38	77	49	10	14	71	29	25	12	0	7	8	86	35	5.8	5.0	2.4	17.2
John Lucas	G	6'3	185	31	5	152	26	80	33	14	22	64	21	27	14	0	6	0	68	30	4.2	5.4	2.8	13.6
Lionel Hollins	G	6'3	185	31	5	94	8	26	31	1	1	100	9	18	16	1	4	0	17	19	1.8	3.6	3.2	3.4
Robert Reid	F-G	6'8	205	29	5	87	19	45	42	0	0	—	17	5	22	0	4	2	38	17	3.4	1.0	4.4	7.6
Larry Micheaux	F	6'9	220	24	5	57	6	19	32	4	10	40	21	0	8	0	0	2	16	11	4.2	0.0	1.6	3.2
Mitchell Wiggins	G	6'4	185	25	5	45	9	18	50	0	0	—	4	1	6	0	4	0	18	9	0.8	0.2	1.2	3.6
Allen Leavell	G	6'1	190	27	5	16	2	6	33	2	2	100	3	3	2	0	0	0	6	3	0.6	0.6	0.4	1.2
Jim Peterson	F	6'10	235	22	3	8	1	1	100	0	0	—	2	1	2	0	0	0	2	3	0.7	0.3	0.7	0.7
Craig Ehlo	G	6'7	180	23	3	6	1	1	100	2	2	100	0	0	3	0	4	0	4	2	0.0	0.0	1.0	1.3

3 PT-FG — Sampson 1-1, Lucas 2-14, Reid 0-4, Micheaux 0-1, Leavell 0-2

NEW JERSEY NETS — **STAN ALBECK** — lost to Detroit 0-3; 105-125, 111-121, H115-116

Use Name	Pos	Hgt	Wgt	Age	G	Min	FG	FGA	%	FT	FTA	%	Reb	Ass	PF	DQ	Stls	Blkd Shts	Points	Min	Reb	Ass	PF	Points
Albert King	F	6'6	190	25	3	105	28	57	49	9	13	69	23	5	14	0	7	2	66	35	7.7	1.7	4.7	22.0
Buck Williams	F	6'8	215	24	3	123	26	40	65	22	30	73	32	1	12	0	3	5	74	41	10.7	0.3	4.0	24.7
Mike Gminski	C	6'11	250	25	3	81	18	33	55	6	6	100	19	4	5	0	3	5	42	27	6.3	1.3	1.7	14.0
Ron Brewer	G	6'4	185	29	3	93	15	30	50	6	8	75	5	5	7	0	3	0	36	31	1.7	1.7	2.3	12.0
M. Ray Richardson	G	6'5	195	29	3	125	23	57	40	9	14	64	18	34	12	0	4	0	55	42	6.0	11.3	4.0	18.3
Darryl Dawkins	C	6'11	251	27	3	64	11	23	48	3	4	75	14	4	13	1	2	6	25	21	4.7	1.3	4.3	8.3
Kelvin Ransey	G	6'1	180	26	3	63	6	16	38	5	5	100	5	17	10	0	2	1	17	21	1.7	5.7	3.3	5.7
Mike O'Koren	F	6'7	217	26	3	34	3	7	43	0	2	0	10	4	6	0	0	0	6	11	3.3	1.3	2.0	2.0
Jeff Turner	F	6'9	230	22	3	21	2	5	40	0	0	—	4	2	6	0	0	0	4	7	1.3	0.7	2.0	1.3
Darwin Cook	G	6'3	190	26	1	7	3	4	75	0	0	—	0	1	2	0	0	0	6	7	0.0	1.0	2.0	6.0
George Johnson	F	6'11	205	36	1	4	0	0	-	0	0	—	0	0	0	0	0	0	0	4	0.0	0.0	0.0	0.0

3 PT-FG — King 1-1, Brewer 0-1, Richardson 0-2

PHOENIX SUNS — **JOHN MAC LEOD** — lost to Los Angeles 0-3; 114-142, 130-147, H103-119

Use Name	Pos	Hgt	Wgt	Age	G	Min	FG	FGA	%	FT	FTA	%	Reb	Ass	PF	DQ	Stls	Blkd Shts	Points	Min	Reb	Ass	PF	Points
Mike Sanders	F	6'6	210	24	3	91	22	37	59	8	10	80	15	10	8	0	5	0	52	30	5.0	3.3	2.7	17.3
Charles Pittman	F	6'8	220	26	3	82	14	63	22	12	17	71	19	9	10	0	0	3	40	27	6.3	3.0	3.3	13.3
Alvan Adams	C	6'9	220	30	3	79	23	46	50	5	6	83	17	11	8	0	7	1	51	26	5.7	3.7	2.7	17.0
Kyle Macy	G	6'3	190	27	3	85	13	26	50	4	5	80	8	9	5	0	6	0	31	28	2.7	3.0	1.7	10.3
Jay Humphries	G	6'3	185	22	3	90	20	31	65	9	12	75	5	16	12	0	2	0	49	30	1.7	5.3	4.0	16.3
Maurice Lucas	C-F	6'9	238	32	3	84	22	47	47	15	19	79	33	10	12	0	2	2	59	28	11.0	3.3	4.0	19.7
Alvin Scott	F	6'7	215	29	3	64	3	12	25	5	6	83	8	10	8	0	1	4	11	21	2.7	3.3	2.7	3.7
Rod Foster	G	6'1	160	24	3	56	7	25	28	6	8	75	3	7	4	0	5	0	20	19	1.0	2.3	1.3	6.7
Michael Holton	G	6'4	185	23	3	55	9	19	47	4	4	100	2	9	8	0	0	0	22	18	0.7	3.0	2.7	7.3
Charles Jones	F	6'8	215	22	2	34	3	5	60	6	6	100	3	3	4	0	0	3	12	17	1.5	1.5	2.0	6.0

3 PT-FG — Macy 1-4, Scott 0-1, Foster 0-4, Holton 0-4

SAN ANTONIO SPURS — **COTTON FITZSIMMONS** — lost to Denver 2-3; 111-141, 113-111, H112-115, H116-111, 99-126

Use Name	Pos	Hgt	Wgt	Age	G	Min	FG	FGA	%	FT	FTA	%	Reb	Ass	PF	DQ	Stls	Blkd Shts	Points	Min	Reb	Ass	PF	Points
Mike Mitchell	F	6'7	215	28	5	180	44	78	56	21	24	88	19	12	19	1	3	4	109	36	3.8	2.4	3.8	21.8
Marc Iavaroni	F	6'9	225	28	5	116	15	28	54	15	20	75	26	13	23	1	5	2	45	23	5.2	2.6	4.6	9.0
Artis Gilmore	C	7'2	255	35	5	185	29	52	56	31	45	69	50	7	18	0	2	7	89	37	10.0	1.4	3.6	17.8
George Gervin	G-F	6'7	185	32	5	183	42	79	53	27	34	79	18	14	19	0	3	3	111	37	3.6	2.8	3.8	22.2
Johnny Moore	G	6'2	185	26	5	168	25	54	46	15	23	65	30	42	17	0	10	2	66	34	6.0	8.4	3.4	13.2
John Paxson	G	6'2	185	24	5	114	21	42	50	7	9	78	5	21	9	0	5	0	51	23	1.0	4.2	1.8	10.2
Jeff Cook	G	6'10	215	28	5	98	9	18	50	17	25	68	29	4	23	0	5	6	35	20	5.8	0.8	4.6	7.0
Ozell Jones	C-F	6'11	235	24	5	73	8	11	73	1	6	17	17	4	18	1	1	4	17	15	3.4	0.8	3.6	3.4
Billy Knight	G-F	6'6	195	32	5	45	8	15	53	0	0	—	6	3	2	0	2	0	16	9	1.2	0.6	0.4	3.2
David Thirdkill	F	6'7	215	24	5	22	1	4	25	2	4	50	2	2	4	0	0	0	4	4	0.4	0.4	0.8	0.8
Gene Banks	F	6'7	215	25	1	10	0	1	0	0	0	—	0	1	3	0	0	0	0	10	0.0	1.0	3.0	0.0
Linton Townes	F	6'7	195	25	2	6	4	8	50	0	0	—	3	0	1	0	0	0	8	3	1.5	0.0	0.5	4.0

3 PT-FG — Mitchell 0-1, Iavaroni 0-1, Gervin 0-3, Moore 1-3, Paxson 2-9, Cook 0-1, Knight 0-4, Thirdkill 0-2, Townes 0-1

WAHINGTON BULLETS — **GENE SHUE** — lost to Philadelphia 1-3; 97-104, 94-113, H118-100, H98-106

Use Name	Pos	Hgt	Wgt	Age	G	Min	FG	FGA	%	FT	FTA	%	Reb	Ass	PF	DQ	Stls	Blkd Shts	Points	Min	Reb	Ass	PF	Points
Darren Daye	F	6'8	220	24	4	85	17	30	57	7	16	44	12	14	8	0	3	0	41	21	3.0	3.5	2.0	10.3
Cliff Robinson	F	6'9	230	24	4	123	25	56	45	9	12	75	30	4	14	0	4	2	59	31	7.5	1.0	3.5	14.8
Jeff Ruland	C-F	6'10	240	26	4	162	28	47	60	14	20	70	34	21	15	0	9	4	70	41	8.5	5.3	3.8	17.5
Jeff Malone	G	6'4	205	23	4	126	27	56	48	10	13	77	6	8	14	1	5	0	65	32	1.5	2.0	3.5	16.3
Gus Williams	G	6'2	175	31	4	159	30	71	42	9	12	75	8	20	5	0	5	1	72	40	2.0	5.0	1.3	18.0
Chrales Jones	F-C	6'9	215	27	4	110	10	19	53	9	16	56	26	3	16	0	3	10	29	28	6.5	0.8	4.0	7.3
Greg Ballard	F	6'7	215	29	4	65	11	24	46	8	9	89	14	6	7	0	3	0	30	16	3.5	1.5	1.8	7.5
Dudley Bradley	G	6'6	195	27	4	41	5	9	56	3	4	75	6	6	5	0	2	0	14	10	1.5	1.5	1.3	3.5
Rick Mahorn	C	6'10	240	26	4	41	4	8	50	4	4	100	7	0	9	0	0	3	12	10	1.8	0.0	2.3	3.0
Frank Johnson	G	6'2	185	26	2	39	4	14	29	6	6	100	4	7	5	0	2	0	15	20	2.0	3.5	2.5	7.5
Tom McMillen	F	6'11	235	32	1	7	0	4	0	0	0	—	5	1	1	0	0	0	0	7	5.0	1.0	1.0	0.0
Don Collins	G	6'6	190	26	1	2	0	0	—	0	0	—	0	0	0	0	0	0	0	2	0.0	0.0	0.0	0.0

3 PT-FG — Ruland 0-2, Malone 1-3, Williams 3-10, Ballard 0-2, Bradley 1-5, Johnson 1-6, McMillen 0-1

Team		G	FG	FGA	%	FT	FTA	%	REBOUNDS Offense	Defense	Total	Assists	PF	Steals	Blocked Shots	Turn Overs	Points	Points per game
TEAM STATISTICS																		
EASTERN CONFERENCE ATLANTIC DIVISION																		
Boston	Off.	82	3721	7325	51	1860	2307	81	1116	2630	3746	2287	1781	645	414	1332	9412	114.8
	Def.	82	3642	7642	48	1512	1922	79	1105	2287	3392	2041	1964	641	315	1222	8867	108.1
	Diff.		+79	-317	+3	+348	+385	+2	+11	+343	+354	+246	+183	+4	+99	-110	+545	+6.7
Philadelphia	Off.	82	3443	6992	49	2316	2883	80	1301	2364	3665	1999	1971	817	534	1575	9261	112.9
	Def.	82	3494	7157	49	1857	2397	77	1183	2173	3356	2139	2209	753	391	1534	8925	108.8
	Diff.		-51	-165	—	+459	+486	+3	+118	+191	+309	-140	+238	+64	+143	-41	+336	+4.1
New Jersey	Off.	82	3646	7445	49	1631	2237	73	1233	2325	3558	2163	2011	772	415	1355	8975	109.5
	Def.	82	3514	7040	50	1849	2454	75	1084	2405	3489	1975	1933	680	352	1496	8956	109.2
	Diff.		+132	+405	-1	-218	-217	-2	+149	-80	+69	+188	-78	+92	+63	+141	+19	+.3
Washington	Off.	82	3534	7383	48	1478	1989	74	1012	2395	3407	2088	1869	709	393	1282	8655	105.5
	Def.	82	3494	7179	49	1623	2172	75	1119	2673	3792	1988	1833	630	397	1467	8677	105.8
	Diff.		+40	+204	-1	-145	-183	-1	-107	-278	-385	+100	-36	+79	-4	+185	-22	-.3
New York	Off.	82	3435	7101	48	1706	2350	73	1116	2102	3218	1999	2398	754	267	1458	8627	105.2
	Def.	82	3329	6732	49	2282	3006	76	1219	2401	3620	2143	2038	667	446	1589	9007	109.8
	Diff.		+106	+369	-1	-576	-656	-3	-103	-299	-402	-144	-360	+87	-179	+131	-380	-4.6
CENTRAL DIVISION																		
Milwaukee	Off.	82	3564	7256	49	1873	2473	76	1256	2353	3609	2164	2239	689	486	1382	9090	110.9
	Def.	82	3214	6972	46	2020	2700	75	1236	2293	3529	1904	2104	642	389	1562	8528	104.0
	Diff.		+350	+284	+3	-147	-227	+1	+20	+60	+80	+260	-135	+47	+97	+180	+562	+6.9
Detroit	Off.	82	3840	7999	48	1783	2262	79	1403	2534	3937	2302	2076	691	397	1341	9508	116.0
	Def.	82	3700	7457	50	1826	2404	76	1109	2563	3672	2107	2017	642	508	1486	9304	113.5
	Diff.		+140	+542	-2	-43	-142	+3	+294	-29	+265	+195	-59	+49	-111	+145	+204	+2.5
Chicago	Off.	82	3453	6909	50	1981	2526	78	1074	2366	3440	1992	2071	622	468	1463	8916	108.7
	Def.	82	3521	7210	49	1852	2394	77	1137	2260	3397	2045	2040	668	447	1323	8985	109.6
	Diff.		-68	-301	+1	+129	+132	+1	-63	+106	+43	-53	-31	-46	+21	-140	-69	-.9
Cleveland	Off.	82	3470	7364	47	1867	2491	75	1203	2445	3648	2096	2173	622	472	1387	8903	108.6
	Def.	82	3547	7415	48	1965	2554	77	1210	2451	3661	2215	2101	610	429	1357	9129	111.3
	Diff.		-77	-51	-1	-98	-63	-2	-7	-6	-13	-119	-72	+12	+43	-30	-226	-2.7
Atlanta	Off.	82	3444	7119	48	1782	2371	75	1161	2345	3506	2009	2047	665	541	1475	8743	106.6
	Def.	82	3504	7267	48	1808	2384	76	1332	2411	3743	2087	1972	674	373	1488	8862	108.1
	Diff.		-60	-148	—	-26	-13	-1	-171	-66	-237	-78	-75	-9	+168	+13	-119	-1.5
Indiana	Off.	82	3489	7324	48	1871	2516	74	1198	2623	3821	1945	2237	625	366	1622	8879	108.3
	Def.	82	3628	7332	49	2068	2707	76	1098	2583	3681	2242	2072	777	523	1424	9388	114.5
	Diff.		-139	-8	-1	-197	-191	-2	+100	+40	+140	-297	-165	-152	-157	-198	-509	-6.2
WESTERN CONFERENCE MIDWEST DIVISION																		
Denver	Off.	82	3876	7976	49	2016	2568	79	1331	2303	3634	2266	2152	894	424	1382	9841	120.0
	Def.	82	3775	7379	51	2027	2648	77	1181	2628	3809	2154	2178	670	589	1744	9641	117.6
	Diff.		+101	+597	-2	-11	-80	+2	+150	-325	-175	+112	+26	+224	-165	+362	+200	+2.4
Houston	Off.	82	3748	7440	50	1581	2261	70	1325	2395	3720	2239	2033	683	597	1605	9118	111.2
	Def.	82	3500	7274	48	1887	2425	78	1159	2222	3381	2117	1903	773	415	1495	8977	109.5
	Diff.		+248	+166	+2	-306	-164	-8	+166	+173	+339	+122	-130	-90	+182	-110	+141	+1.7
Dallas	Off.	82	3560	7280	49	1844	2324	79	1095	2345	3440	2152	1796	575	335	1184	9116	111.2
	Def.	82	3626	7200	50	1588	2080	76	1062	2470	3532	2113	2066	572	430	1340	8938	109.0
	Diff.		-66	+80	-1	+256	+244	+3	+33	-125	-92	+39	+270	+3	-95	+156	+178	+2.2
San Antonio	Off.	82	3698	7202	51	1961	2571	76	1127	2470	3597	2316	2180	757	443	1542	9412	114.8
	Def.	82	3649	7348	50	1977	2548	78	1136	2265	3401	2283	2154	749	472	1489	9337	113.9
	Diff.		+49	-146	+1	-16	+23	-2	-9	+205	+196	+33	-26	+8	-29	-53	+75	+.9
Utah	Off.	82	3478	7302	48	1878	2434	77	1081	2554	3635	2143	1961	712	697	1575	8937	109.0
	Def.	82	3532	7604	46	1810	2375	76	1360	2645	4005	2069	2076	806	443	1606	8946	109.1
	Diff.		-54	-302	+2	+68	+59	+1	-279	-91	-370	+74	+115	-94	+254	+31	-9	-.1
Kansas City	Off.	82	3664	7275	50	2022	2595	78	1167	2327	3494	2342	2169	661	300	1593	9413	114.8
	Def.	82	3805	7461	51	1957	2546	77	1166	2267	3433	2344	2205	761	512	1424	9632	117.5
	Diff.		-141	-186	-1	+65	+49	+1	+1	+60	+61	-2	+36	-100	-212	-169	-219	-2.7
PACIFIC DIVISION																		
L.A. Lakers	Off.	82	3952	7254	54	1702	2232	76	1063	2550	3613	2575	1931	695	481	1537	9696	118.2
	Def.	82	3665	7639	48	1679	2244	75	1248	2078	3326	2313	1905	756	370	1365	9093	110.9
	Diff.		+287	-385	+6	+23	-12	+1	-185	+472	+287	+262	-26	-61	+111	-172	+603	+7.3
Portland	Off.	82	3708	7374	50	2002	2667	75	1202	2298	3500	2225	1957	821	516	1481	9469	115.5
	Def.	82	3697	7494	49	1737	2269	77	1268	2336	3604	2235	2160	726	459	1607	9190	112.1
	Diff.		+11	-120	+1	+265	+398	-2	-66	-38	-104	-10	+203	+95	+57	+126	+279	+3.4

TEAM STATISTICS

WESTERN CONFERENCE
PACIFIC DIVISION

Team		G	FG	FGA	%	FT	FTA	%	Rebounds Off.	Rebounds Def.	Rebounds Total	Assists	PF	Steals	Blocked Shots	Turn Overs	Points	Points per game
Phoenix	Off.	82	3507	7144	49	1757	2280	77	1026	2425	3451	2335	2034	727	349	1583	8858	108.0
	Def.	82	3605	7309	49	1756	2295	77	1125	2416	3541	2181	2019	771	410	1468	9031	110.1
	Diff.		-98	-165	—	+1	-15	—	-99	+9	-90	+154	+15	-44	-61	+115	-173	-2.1
Los Angeles Cli	Off.	82	3527	7119	50	1674	2208	76	1163	2434	3597	1934	1840	534	497	1587	8784	107.1
	Def.	82	3737	7630	49	1604	2115	76	1248	2282	3530	2264	1887	770	422	1242	9152	111.6
	Diff.		-210	-511	+1	+70	+93	—	-85	+152	+67	-330	+47	-236	+75	-345	-368	-4.5
Seattle	Off.	82	3277	6910	47	1777	2305	77	1019	2287	3306	2185	1974	649	343	1493	8376	102.1
	Def.	82	3520	7142	49	1703	2212	77	1113	2379	3492	2220	2020	732	458	1383	8822	107.6
	Diff.		-243	-232	-2	+74	+93	—	-94	-92	-186	-35	+46	-83	-115	-110	-446	-5.5
Golden State	Off.	82	3498	7555	46	1944	2531	77	1327	2139	3466	1759	2136	803	284	1460	9052	110.4
	Def.	82	3839	7165	54	1919	2530	76	1101	2521	3622	2336	2180	650	469	1583	9654	117.7
	Diff.		-341	+390	-8	+25	+1	+1	+226	-382	-156	-577	+44	+153	-185	+123	-602	-7.3

PLAYOFFS

Team		G	FG	FGA	%	FT	FTA	%	Rebounds Off.	Rebounds Def.	Rebounds Total	Assists	PF	Steals	Blocked Shots	Turn Overs	Points	Points per game
Los Angeles	Off.	19	**954**	1756	**54**	463	613	76	251	625	876	**641**	501	**178**	**120**	327	**2400**	**126.3**
	Def.	19	857	1822	47	466	612	76	284	509	793	587	487	185	101	**314**	2207	116.2
	Diff.		+97	-66	+7	-3	+1	—	-33	+116	+83	+54	-14	-7	+19	-13	**+193**	**+10.1**
Boston	Off.	21	909	**1878**	48	**531**	**647**	**82**	**291**	**629**	**920**	572	503	174	112	338	2376	113.1
	Def.	21	930	1909	49	441	581	76	285	609	894	543	**546**	196	98	**314**	2320	110.5
	Diff.		-21	-31	-1	+90	+66	+6	+6	+20	+26	+29	+43	-22	+14	-24	+56	+2.6
Denver	Off.	15	711	1467	48	386	494	78	241	439	680	451	412	148	71	246	1830	122.0
	Def.	15	700	1330	53	383	513	75	187	486	673	429	418	131	98	304	1802	120.1
	Diff.		+11	+137	-5	+3	-19	+3	+54	-47	+7	+22	+6	+17	-27	+58	+28	+1.9
Philadelphia	Off.	13	537	1100	49	307	401	77	198	378	576	283	296	134	81	243	1392	107.1
	Def.	13	533	1117	48	280	362	77	185	353	538	319	342	123	82	239	1361	104.7
	Diff.		+4	-17	+1	+27	+39	—	+13	+25	+38	-36	+46	+11	-1	-4	+31	+2.4
Utah	Off.	10	400	873	46	296	376	79	131	324	455	243	255	83	70	185	1110	111.0
	Def.	10	460	992	46	213	314	68	198	351	549	252	292	90	57	171	1145	114.5
	Diff.		-60	-119	—	+83	+62	+11	-67	-27	-94	-9	+37	-7	+13	-14	-35	-3.5
Portland	Off.	9	429	883	49	205	271	76	159	254	413	272	273	84	55	146	1072	119.1
	Def.	9	408	816	50	286	356	80	142	274	416	264	224	73	48	157	1117	124.1
	Diff.		+21	+67	-1	-81	-85	-4	+17	-20	-3	+8	-49	+11	+7	+11	-45	-5.0
Detroit	Off.	9	408	858	48	215	270	80	145	263	408	216	228	77	31	129	1038	115.3
	Def.	9	411	812	51	223	274	81	129	280	409	239	235	72	43	147	1054	117.1
	Diff.		-3	+46	-3	-8	-4	-1	+16	-17	-1	-23	+7	+5	-12	+18	-16	-1.8
Milwaukee	Off.	8	326	654	50	211	263	80	108	214	322	197	232	66	40	159	872	109.0
	Def.	8	342	693	49	201	257	78	122	202	324	187	208	85	42	137	890	111.3
	Diff.		-16	-39	+1	+10	+6	+2	-14	+12	-2	+10	-24	-19	-2	-22	-18	-2.3
Chicago	Off.	4	160	341	47	99	125	79	61	94	155	80	119	40	19	67	421	105.3
	Def.	4	159	312	51	122	151	81	49	105	154	96	113	28	21	75	443	110.8
	Diff.		+1	+29	-4	-23	-26	-2	+12	-11	+1	-16	-6	+12	-2	+8	-22	-5.5
Cleveland	Off.	4	182	360	51	84	110	76	48	107	155	105	123	39	17	62	449	112.3
	Def.	4	165	349	47	116	135	86	56	108	164	97	98	25	70	15	449	112.3
	Diff.		+17	+11	+4	-32	-25	-10	-8	-1	-9	+8	-25	+14	-53	-47	—	—
Dallas	Off.	4	171	363	47	131	157	83	62	107	169	98	94	29	10	61	482	120.5
	Def.	4	206	394	52	75	97	77	70	130	200	123	120	31	20	61	492	123.0
	Diff.		-35	-31	-5	+56	+60	+6	-8	-23	-31	-25	+26	-2	-10	—	-10	-2.5
Houston	Off.	5	214	495	43	89	157	57	110	174	284	105	147	44	34	80	520	104.0
	Def.	5	180	418	43	153	188	81	66	169	235	116	126	36	43	96	521	104.2
	Diff.		+34	+77	—	-64	-31	-24	+44	+5	+49	-11	-21	+8	-9	+16	-1	-.2
New Jersey	Off.	3	135	272	50	60	82	73	34	96	130	77	87	24	19	49	331	110.3
	Def.	3	130	271	48	100	118	85	43	102	145	76	72	23	10	44	362	120.7
	Diff.		+5	+1	+2	-40	-36	-12	-9	-6	-15	+1	-15	+1	+9	-5	-31	-10.4
Phoenix	Off.	3	136	271	50	74	93	80	38	75	113	94	79	28	13	63	347	115.7
	Def.	3	165	275	60	73	101	72	38	87	125	104	86	31	15	53	408	136.0
	Diff.		-29	-4	-10	+1	-8	+8	—	-12	-12	-10	+7	-3	-2	-10	-61	-20.3
San Antonio	Off.	5	206	390	53	136	190	72	55	150	205	123	156	36	28	113	551	110.2
	Def.	5	230	460	50	140	174	80	70	137	207	145	145	50	25	73	604	120.8
	Diff.		-24	-70	+3	-4	+16	-8	-15	+13	-2	-22	-11	-14	+3	-40	-53	-10.6
Washington	Off.	4	161	338	48	79	112	71	60	92	152	90	99	36	20	69	407	101.8
	Def.	4	163	329	50	94	128	73	68	119	187	70	92	41	22	82	423	105.8
	Diff.		-2	+9	-2	-15	-16	-2	-8	-27	-35	+20	-7	-5	-2	+13	-16	-4.0

Team	W	L	Pct.	GB	Record against playoff teams W	L	Pct.	Record against non - playoff teams W	L	Pct.	HOME W	L	Pct.	ROAD W	L	Pct.
EASTERN CONFERENCE																
ATLANTIC DIVISION																
Boston Celtics	63	19	.768	—	41	16	.719	22	3	.880	35	6	.854	28	13	.682
Philadelphia 76ers	58	24	.707	5	37	20	.649	21	4	.840	34	7	.829	24	17	.585
New Jersey Nets	42	40	.512	21	25	32	.439	17	8	.680	27	14	.659	15	26	.366
Wahington Bullets	40	42	.488	23	24	33	.421	16	9	.640	28	13	.683	12	29	.293
New York Knickerbockers	24	58	.293	39	12	50	.194	12	8	.600	19	22	.463	5	36	.122
CENTRAL DIVISION																
Milwaukee Bucks	59	23	.720	—	37	20	.649	22	3	.880	36	5	.878	23	18	.561
Detroit Pistons	46	36	.561	13	27	30	.474	19	6	.760	26	15	.634	20	21	.488
Chicago Bulls	38	44	.463	21	22	34	.393	16	10	.615	26	15	.634	12	29	.293
Cleveland Cavaliers	36	46	.439	23	20	36	.357	16	10	.615	20	21	.488	16	25	.390
Atlanta Hawks	34	48	.415	25	20	42	.323	14	6	.700	19	22	.463	15	26	.366
Indiana Pacers	22	60	.268	37	17	45	.274	5	15	.250	16	25	.390	6	35	.146
WESTERN CONFERENCE																
MIDWEST DIVISION																
Denver Nuggets	52	30	.634	—	33	22	.600	19	8	.704	34	7	.829	18	23	.439
Houston Rockets	48	34	.585	4	30	25	.545	18	9	.667	29	12	.707	19	22	.463
Dallas Mavericks	44	38	.537	8	21	34	.382	23	4	.852	24	17	.585	20	21	.488
San Antonio Spurs	41	41	.500	11	22	33	.400	19	8	.704	30	11	.732	11	30	.268
Utah Jazz	41	41	.500	11	28	27	.509	13	14	.481	26	15	.634	15	26	.366
Kansas City Kings	31	51	.378	21	18	41	.305	13	10	.565	23	18	.561	8	33	.195
PACIFIC DIVISION																
Los Angeles Lakers	62	20	.756	—	38	15	.717	24	5	.828	36	5	.878	26	15	.634
Portland Trail Blazers	42	40	.512	20	21	32	.396	21	8	.724	30	11	.732	12	29	.293
Phoenix Suns	36	46	.439	26	18	35	.340	18	11	.621	26	15	.634	10	31	.244
Los Angeles Clippers	31	51	.378	31	20	39	.339	11	12	.478	20	21	.488	11	30	.268
Seattle Supersonics	31	51	.378	31	19	40	.322	12	11	.522	20	21	.488	11	30	.268
Golden State Warriors	22	60	.268	40	14	45	.237	8	15	.348	17	24	.415	5	36	.122

1984/85 N.B.A. INDIVIDUAL LEADERS

SCORING
(Minimum 70 Games or 1400 Points)

Name	Team	G	FG	FT	Pts.	Avg.
King	NY	55	691	426	1809	32.9
Bird	Bos	80	918	403	2295	28.7
Jordan	Chi	82	837	630	2313	28.2
Short	GS	78	819	501	2186	28.0
English	Den	81	939	383	2262	27.9
Wilkins	Atl	81	853	486	2217	27.4
Dantley	Utah	55	512	438	1462	26.6
Aguirre	Dal	80	794	440	2055	25.7
Malone	Phi	79	602	737	1941	24.6
Cummings	Mil	79	759	343	1861	23.6

FIELD GOAL PERCENTAGE
(Minimum 300 Made)

Name	Team	FG	FGA	Pct.
Donaldson	LAC	351	551	.637
Gilmore	SA	532	854	.623
Thorpe	KC	411	685	.600
Abdul-Jabbar	LAL	723	1207	.599
Nance	Phoe	515	877	.587
Worthy	LAL	610	1066	.572
McHale	Bos	605	1062	.570
Cheeks	Phi	422	741	.570
Johnson	LAL	504	899	.561
Woolridge	Chi	679	1225	.554

FREE THROW PERCENTAGE
(Minimum 125 Made)

Name	Team	FT	FTA	Pct.
Macy	Phoe	127	140	.907
Vandeweghe	Port	369	412	.896
Davis	Dal	158	178	.888
Tripucka	Det	255	288	.885
Adams	Phoe	250	283	.883
Bird	Bos	403	457	.882
Cheeks	Phi	175	199	.879
Bridgeman	LAC	181	206	.879
Johnson	KC	325	373	.871
Green	Utah	232	267	.869

PERSONAL FOULS

Name	Team	PF
Olajuwon	Hou	344
Thompson	KC	328
Whitehead	GS	322
Smith	LAC	317
Chambers	Sea	312
Eaton	Utah	312

GAMES DISQUALIFIED

Name	Team	Disq.
Bannister	NY	16
Hinson	Cle	13
Dawkins	NJ	11
Mahorn	Was	11
Bailey	NJ	10
Olajuwon	Hou	10
Sampson	Hou	10

MINUTES PLAYED

Name	Team	Min.
Williams	NJ	3182
Bird	Bos	3161
Jordan	Chi	3144
Richardson	NJ	3127
Thomas	Det	3089

TOTAL REBOUNDS PER GAME
(Minimum 70 Games or 800 Rebounds)

Name	Team	G	Reb.	Avg.
Malone	Phi	79	1031	13.1
Laimbeer	Det	82	1013	12.4
Williams	NJ	82	1005	12.3
Olajuwon	Hou	82	974	11.9
Eaton	Utah	82	927	11.3
Smith	GS	80	869	10.9
Parish	Bos	79	840	10.6
Bird	Bos	80	842	10.5
Gilmore	SA	81	846	10.4
Thompson	KC	82	854	10.4

ASSISTS PER GAME
(Minimum 70 Games or 400 Assists)

Name	Team	G	Ass.	Avg.
Thomas	Det	81	1123	13.9
Johnson	LAL	77	968	12.6
Moore	SA	82	816	10.0
Nixon	LAC	81	711	8.8
Bagley	Cle	81	697	8.6
Richardson	NJ	82	669	8.2
Theus	KC	82	656	8.0
Johnson	Atl	73	566	7.8
Green	Utah	77	597	7.8
Gus Williams	Was	79	608	7.7

BLOCKED SHOTS PER GAME
(Minimum 70 Games or 100 Blocked Shots)

Name	Team	G	Reb.	Avg.
Eaton	Utah	82	476	5.8
Olajuwon	Hou	82	220	2.7
Bowie	Port	76	203	2.7
Cooper	Den	80	197	2.5
Rollins	Atl	70	167	2.4
Hinson	Cle	76	173	2.3
Gilmore	SA	81	173	2.1
Walton	LAC	67	140	2.1
Lister	Mil	81	167	2.1
Abdul-Jabbar	LAL	79	162	2.1

3 POINT FIELD GOALS PER GAME
(Minimum 25 Made)

Name	Team	FG	FGA	Avg.
Scott	LAL	26	60	.433
Bird	Bos	56	131	.427
Davis	Dal	47	115	.409
Tucker	NY	29	72	.403
Ellis	Dal	42	109	.385
Toney	Phi	39	105	.371
Free	Cle	71	193	.368
Evans	Den	57	157	.363
Griffith	Utah	92	257	.358
Buse	KC	31	87	.356

STEALS PER GAME
(Minimum 70 Games or 125 Steals)

Name	Team	G	Steals	Avg.
Richardson	NJ	82	243	3.0
Moore	SA	82	229	2.8
Lever	Den	82	202	2.5
Jordan	Chi	82	196	2.4
Rivers	Atl	69	163	2.4
Thomas	Det	81	187	2.3
Gus Williams	Was	79	178	2.3
Drexler	Port	80	177	2.2
Cheeks	Phi	78	169	2.2
Conner	GS	79	161	2.0

1985-86 N.B.A.
Rockets Nearly Blast the Celtic Dynasty

In a season of highs and lows, no one stood higher than 7' 6" Manute Bol, drafted by Washington, and no one was "lower" than 5-foot-7 Spud Webb, who joined Atlanta. Despite criticism that the N.B.A. was becoming a freak show, both proved they belonged: Bol led the league in shot-blocking, and Webb's speed fueled a running game that turned the Hawks around.

Also in the "high" category were New Jersey's Michael Ray Richardson, kicked out of the league after failing his third drug test; John Lucas, released by Houston after a similar failure; and Walter Davis of Phoenix, who missed a month getting treatment for his drug problem.

The "lows" included 11 major players who missed more than half the season with injuries. Once again New York had the worst of it; Rookie of the Year Patrick Ewing, who missed 32 games was the healthiest member of the Knick's projected front line. In Philadelphia, a stress fracture sidelined Andrew Toney. The emergence of Charles Barkley as a major star, however, kept the 76ers in the running for the title under new coach Matt Guokas until Moses Malone went out with an eye injury just before the playoffs. Chicago lost only one player, but it was Michael Jordan, who broke a bone in his foot and missed 64 games. The Bullets' Jeff Ruland missed 52, and Bol and Jeff Malone weren't enough to save coach Gene Shue's job. Likewise, Indiana added Wayman Tisdale to its promising young front line, but a knee injury to Clark Kellogg negated the gain.

It was the same story in the West. San Antonio got off to a good start, then collapsed after losing Johnny Moore to meningitis. The 44-game absence of Sam Bowie and a 12-game losing streak in midseason dropped Portland under .500. Utah picked up a gem in rookie Karl Malone, but Darrell Griffith was out all year with a stress fracture. And the Clippers' leading scorer, Derek Smith, missed 71 games for knee surgery.

Even Boston's Larry Bid was dragged down by a back injury that reduced him to a mere all-star for the first half of the season. But treatment by a chiropractor finally corrected the problem, and Bird soared back to his accustomed heights, winning his third straight MVP award. Another change in Boston was the presence of former MVP Bill Walton, acquired from San Diego. Though a series of foot injuries had made it impossible for Walton to play full-time, he proved as effective as ever when limited to 20 minutes a game. And with Walton, veteran Scott Wedman and new acquisition Jerry Sichting coming off the bench, the Celtics climbed to a 67-15 record. Meanwhile, the Lakers picked up Walton's former teammate Maurice Lucas from Phoenix. Though he led them in rebounding, Lucas had trouble fitting in with the Lakers' high-speed offense. Still, Los Angeles rolled to 62 wins and another Pacific Division title.

In Milwaukee, the blue-collar Bucks topped 50 wins and topped the Central Division for the sixth straight time. Right behind them was the season's surprise team, the Atlanta Hawks. Coach of the year Mike Fratello's young team improved by 16 games, led by Dominique Wilkins, "The Human Highlight Film". Houston also reached the 50-win level as Akeem Olajuwon and Ralph Sampson improved with experience. Two other rising teams, Detroit and Dallas, made key additions to their talented nucleus: Detroit, with rookie guard Joe Dumars, and Dallas, with center James Donaldson, acquired from the Clippers.

It was the season of disappointment in Cleveland, where the Cavaliers' high hopes dissolved and coach George Karl was dismissed during a 29-win season. Golden State was only a game better despite the return of Joe Barry Carroll and the addition of rookie Chris Mullin. Seattle had a new coach, Bernie Bickerstaff, and rookie star Xavier McDaniel, but couldn't improve on last year's 31-51 record. Also disappointing were the Nets, who collapsed after a strong start despite fine seasons from big men Buck Williams and Mike Gminski. But the Kings found a way to make mediocrity pay; they moved to Sacramento and sold out every home game while going 37-45.

The Celtics' toughest playoff challenge may have come in the opening round against Chicago. The high-flying Jordan had returned just in time to lead the Bulls into the playoffs, and he scored 49 and 63 points in the first two games. But the Celtics' overall superiority was just too much, and the Bulls fell in three games. Meanwhile, the Lakers' season ended with a shocking 4-1 loss to Houston in the Western finals. The championship series featured a fifth-game-free-for-all started by Sampson, but in the end Boston had too much talent, too much depth, and too much Larry Bird. The Celtics' 4-2 victory gave them 82 playoff and regular-season wins, the highest total in N.B.A. history, and Bird added another playoff MVP trophy to his collection.

					TOTAL														Blkd		PER GAME				
Use Name	Pos	Hgt	Wgt	Age	G	Min	FG	FGA	%	FT	FTA	%	Reb	Ass	PF	DQ	Stls	Shts	Points	Min	Reb	Ass	PF	Points
1985/86 N.B.A. - EASTERN CONFERENCE																								
ATLANTIC CONFERENCE																								
BOSTON CELTICS	67-15 .817				**K.C. JONES**																			
Larry Bird	F	6'9	220	29	82	3113	796	1606	50	441	492	.90	805	557	182	0	166	51	2115	38	9.8	6.8	2.2	25.8
Kevin McHale	F	6'10	225	28	68	2397	561	978	57	326	420	78	551	181	192	2	29	134	1448	35	8.1	2.7	2.8	21.3
Robert Parish	C	7'	230	32	81	2567	530	966	55	245	335	73	770	145	215	3	65	116	1305	32	9.5	1.8	2.7	16.1
Danny Ainge	G	6'4	175	26	80	2407	353	701	50	123	136	90	235	405	204	4	94	7	855	30	2.9	5.1	2.6	10.7
Dennis Johnson	G	6'4	200	31	78	2732	482	1060	45	243	297	82	268	456	206	3	110	35	1213	35	3.4	5.8	2.6	15.6
Jerry Sichting	G	6'1	178	29	82	1596	235	412	57	61	66	92	104	188	118	0	50	0	537	19	1.3	2.3	1.4	6.5
Bill Walton	C-F	6'11	225	33	80	1546	231	411	56	144	202	71	544	165	210	1	38	106	606	19	6.8	2.1	2.6	7.6
Scott Wedman	F	6'7	235	33	79	1402	286	605	47	45	68	66	192	83	127	0	38	22	634	18	2.4	1.1	1.6	8.0
Rick Carlisle	G	6'5	210	26	77	760	92	189	49	15	23	65	77	104	92	1	19	4	199	10	1.0	1.4	1.2	2.6
Greg Kite	C	6'11	250	24	64	464	34	91	37	15	39	38	128	17	81	1	3	28	83	7	2.0	0.3	1.3	1.3
Sam Vincent	G	6'2	185	22	57	432	59	162	36	65	70	93	48	69	59	0	17	4	184	8	0.8	1.2	1.0	3.2
David Thirdkill	F	6'7	215	25	49	385	54	110	49	55	88	63	70	15	55	0	11	3	163	8	1.4	0.3	1.1	3.3
Sly Williams	F	6'7	215	27	6	54	5	21	24	7	12	58	15	2	15	0	1	1	17	9	2.5	0.3	2.5	2.8

3-PT FG — Bird 82-194, Ainge 26-73, Johnson 6-42, Sichting 6-16, Wedman 17-48, Carlisle 0-10, Kite 0-1, Vincent 1-4, Thirdkill 0-1, Williams 0-4

1985/86 N.B.A. — EASTERN CONFERENCE
ATLANTIC DIVISION

Use Name	Pos	Hgt	Wgt	Age	TOTAL G	Min	FG	FGA	%	FT	FTA	%	Reb	Ass	PF	DQ	Stls	Blkd Shts	Points	PER GAME Min	Reb	Ass	PF	Points
PHILADELPHIA 76ers	**54-28 .659**				**MATT GUOKAS**																			
Julius Erving	F-G	6'7	205	35	74	2474	521	1085	48	289	368	79	370	248	196	3	113	82	1340	33	5.0	3.4	2.6	18.1
Charles Barkley	F	6'6	260	22	80	2952	595	1041	57	396	578	69	1026	312	**333**	8	173	125	1603	37	12.8	3.9	**4.2**	20.0
Moses Malone	C	6'10	255	30	74	2706	571	1246	46	**617**	**784**	79	872	90	194	0	67	71	1759	37	11.8	1.2	2.6	23.8
Sedale Threatt	G	6'2	175	24	70	1754	310	684	45	75	90	83	121	193	157	1	93	5	696	25	1.7	2.8	2.2	9.9
Maurice Cheeks	G	6'1	180	29	82	3270	490	913	54	282	335	84	235	753	160	0	207	68	1266	**40**	2.9	9.2	2.0	15.4
Bobby Jones	F	6'9	212	34	70	1519	189	338	56	114	145	79	169	126	159	0	48	49	492	22	2.4	1.8	2.3	7.0
Terry Catledge	F	6'8	220	22	64	1092	202	431	47	90	139	65	272	21	127	0	31	8	494	17	4.3	0.3	2.0	7.7
Clemon Johnson	C	6'10	240	29	75	1069	105	223	47	51	81	63	255	15	129	0	23	62	261	14	3.4	0.2	1.7	3.5
Perry Moss (from Was)	G	6'2	190	27	60	852	95	239	40	54	74	73	90	89	106	0	50	12	249	14	1.5	1.5	1.8	4.2
Bob McAdoo	F-C	6'9	225	34	29	609	116	251	46	62	81	77	103	35	64	0	10	18	294	21	3.6	1.2	2.2	10.1
Leon Wood (to Was)	G	6'3	185	23	29	455	57	136	42	27	34	79	27	75	24	0	14	0	154	16	0.9	2.6	0.8	5.3
Paul Thompson	G	6'6	210	24	23	432	70	194	36	37	43	86	63	24	49	1	15	17	179	19	2.7	1.0	2.1	7.8
Greg Stokes	F-C	6'10	220	22	31	350	56	119	47	14	21	67	57	17	56	0	14	11	126	11	1.8	0.5	1.8	4.1
Kenny Green (from Was)	G	6'7	210	21	21	232	39	91	43	14	23	61	35	6	27	0	1	2	92	11	1.7	0.3	1.3	4.4
Andrew Toney (FJ)	G	6'3	188	28	6	84	11	36	31	3	8	38	5	12	8	0	2	0	25	14	0.8	2.0	1.3	4.2
Butch Carter (from NY)	G	6'5	195	27	4	36	5	16	31	5	6	83	1	1	8	0	0	0	15	9	0.3	0.3	2.0	3.8
Voise Winters	F	6'8	200	23	4	17	3	13	23	0	0	—	3	0	1	0	1	0	6	4	0.8	0.0	0.3	1.5
Michael Young	F	6'7	220	24	2	2	0	2	0	0	0	—	0	0	0	0	0	0	0	1	0.0	0.0	0.0	0.0
	3 PT-FG —				Erving 9-32, Barkley 17-75, Malone 0-1, Threatt 1-24, Cheeks 4-17, Jones 0-1. Catledge 0-4, Moss 5-25, Wood 13-39, Thommpson 2-12, Stokes 0-1, Joney 0-2, Winters 0-1																			
WASHINGTON BULLETS	**39-43 .476**				**GENE SHUE 32-37 (.464), KEVIN LOUGHERY 7-6 (.538)**																			
Cliff Robinson	F	6'9	230	25	78	2563	595	1255	47	269	353	76	680	186	217	2	98	44	1460	33	8.7	2.4	2.8	18.7
Dan Roundfield	F	6'8	215	32	79	2321	322	660	49	273	362	75	642	167	194	1	36	51	917	29	8.1	2.1	2.5	11.6
Jeff Ruland (KJ)	C	6'10	240	27	30	1114	212	383	55	145	200	73	320	159	100	1	23	25	569	37	10.7	5.3	3.3	19.0
Jeff Malone	G	6'4	205	24	80	2992	735	1522	48	322	371	87	288	191	180	2	70	12	1795	37	3.6	2.4	2.3	22.4
Gus Williams	G	6'2	175	32	77	2284	434	1013	43	138	188	73	166	435	113	0	96	15	1036	30	2.2	5.6	1.5	13.5
Manute Bol	C	7'6	200	23	80	2090	128	278	46	42	89	47	477	23	255	5	28	**397**	298	26	6.0	0.3	3.2	3.7
Charles Jones	F-C	6'9	215	28	81	1609	129	254	51	54	86	63	321	76	235	2	57	133	312	20	4.0	0.9	2.9	3.9
Darren Daye	F	6'8	220	25	64	1075	198	399	50	159	237	67	183	109	121	0	46	11	556	17	2.9	1.7	1.9	8.7
Tom McMillen (FJ)	C-F	6'11	235	33	56	863	131	285	46	64	79	81	113	35	85	0	9	10	326	15	2.0	0.6	1.5	5.8
Dudley Bradley	G	6'6	195	28	70	842	73	209	35	32	56	57	95	107	101	0	85	3	195	12	1.4	1.5	1.4	2.8
Leon Wood (from Phi)	G	6'3	185	23	39	743	127	330	38	96	121	79	63	107	46	0	20	0	378	19	1.6	2.7	1.2	9.7
Kevin McKenna	G	6'5	195	26	30	430	61	166	37	25	30	83	36	23	54	1	29	2	174	14	1.2	0.8	1.8	5.8
Frank Johnson (BF)	G	6'2	185	27	14	402	69	154	45	38	54	70	28	76	30	0	11	1	176	29	2.0	5.4	2.1	12.6
Kenny Green (to Phi)	G	6'7	210	21	20	221	44	101	44	21	26	81	38	3	26	0	4	7	109	11	1.9	0.2	1.3	5.5
Perry Moss (to Phi)	G	6'2	190	27	12	160	21	53	40	11	15	73	25	19	26	1	6	3	55	13	2.1	1.6	2.2	4.6
Freeman Williams	G	6'4	195	29	9	110	25	67	37	12	17	71	12	7	10	0	7	1	69	12	1.3	0.8	1.1	7.7
Ennis Whatley (from Cle)	G	6'3	177	23	4	27	5	14	36	1	3	33	7	7	1	0	0	1	11	7	2	1.8	0.3	2.8
George Johnson	F	6'7	218	29	2	7	1	3	33	2	2	100	2	0	1	0	0	0	4	4	1.0	0.0	0.5	2.0
Claude Gregory (to SA)	F	6'9	235	27	2	2	1	2	50	0	0	—	2	0	1	0	1	0	2	1	1.0	0.0	0.5	1.0
	3 PT-FG —				Robinson 1-4, Roundfield 0-6, Ruland 0-4, Malone 3-17, G.Williams 30-116, Bol 0-1, Jones 0-1, Daye 1-3,McMillen 0-3, Bradley 17-68, Wood 28-85, McKenna 27-75, F. Johnson 0-3, Green 0-1, Moss 2-7, F.Williams 7-14																			
NEW JERSEY NETS	**39-43 .476**				**DAVE WOHL**																			
Albert King	F	6'6	190	26	73	1998	438	961	44	167	203	82	366	181	205	4	58	24	1047	27	5.0	2.5	2.8	14.3
Buck Williams	F	6'8	215	25	82	3070	500	956	52	301	445	68	986	131	294	9	73	9.6	1301	37	12.0	1.6	3.6	15.9
Mike Gminski	C	6'11	250	26	81	2525	491	949	52	351	393	89	668	133	163	0	56	71	1333	31	8.2	1.6	2.0	16.5
Otis Birdsong	G	6'4	195	30	77	2395	542	1056	51	122	210	58	202	261	228	8	85	17	1214	31	2.6	3.4	3.0	15.8
M.R. Richardson (DR)	G	6'5	195	30	47	1604	296	661	45	141	179	79	250	340	163	2	125	11	737	34	5.3	7.2	3.5	15.7
Darwin Cook	G	6'3	190	27	79	1965	267	627	43	84	111	76	177	390	172	0	156	22	629	25	2.2	4.9	2.2	8.0
Mickey Johnson	F	6'10	190	33	79	1574	214	507	42	183	233	79	332	217	248	1	67	25	616	20	4.2	2.7	3.1	7.8
Kelvin Ransey	G	6'1	180	27	79	1504	231	505	46	121	148	82	116	252	128	0	51	4	586	19	1.5	3.2	1.6	7.4
Darryl Dawkins (XJ)	C	6'11	251	28	51	1207	284	441	64	210	297	71	251	77	227	10	16	59	778	24	4.9	1.5	4.5	15.3
Mike O'Koven	F-G	6'7	217	27	67	1031	160	336	48	23	39	59	135	118	134	3	29	9	350	15	2.0	1.8	2.0	5.2
Jeff Turner	F-C	6'9	230	23	53	650	84	171	49	58	78	74	137	14	125	4	21	3	226	15	2.6	0.3	2.4	4.3
Bobby Cattage	F	6'9	250	27	29	185	28	83	34	35	44	80	34	4	23	0	6	0	92	·6	1.2	0.1	0.8	3.2
Ray Williams (from Atl, SA)	G	6'3	195	31	5	63	10	32	31	12	14	86	4	9	12	0	5	0	32	13	0.8	1.8	2.4	6.4
Rod Higgins (from Sea, SA, to Chi)	F	6'7	205	25	2	29	3	16	19	0	0	—	8	1	6	0	1	4	6	15	4.0	0.5	3.0	3.0
Yvon Joseph	C	6'11	245	28	1	5	0	0	—	2	2	100	0	0	1	0	0	0	2	5	0.0	0.0	1.0	2.0
	3 PT-FG —				King 4-23,B.Williams 0-2, Gminski 0-1, Birdsong 8-22, Richardson 4-27, Cook 11-53, Johnson 5-24, Ransey 3-24, Dawkins 0-1, O'Koven 7-27, Turner 0-1, Cattage 1-5, R.Williams 0-2, Higgins 0-2																			
NEW YORK KNICKERBOCKERS	**23-59 .280**				**HUBIE BROWN**																			
Louis Orr	F	6'8	195	27	74	2237	330	741	45	218	278	78	312	179	177	4	61	26	878	30	4.2	2.4	2.4	11.9
Pat Cummings (NJ)	F-C	6'9	235	29	31	1007	195	408	48	97	139	70	280	47	136	7	27	12	487	32	9.0	1.5	4.4	15.7
Patrick Ewing (KJ)	C	7'	240	23	50	1771	386	814	47	226	306	74	451	102	191	7	54	103	998	35	9.0	2.0	3.8	20.0
Darrell Walker	G	6'4	180	24	81	2023	324	753	43	190	277	69	220	337	216	1	146	36	838	25	2.7	4.2	2.7	10.3
Rory Sparrow	G	6'2	195	27	74	2344	345	723	48	101	127	80	170	472	182	1	85	14	796	32	2.3	6.4	2.5	10.8
Gerald Wilkins	F-G	6'6	185	22	81	2025	437	934	47	132	237	56	208	161	155	0	68	9	1013	25	2.6	2.0	1.9	12.5
Trent Tucker	G	6'5	193	26	77	1788	349	740	47	79	100	79	169	192	167	0	65	8	818	23	2.2	2.5	2.2	10.6
Ken Bannister	F	6'9	235	25	70	1405	235	479	49	131	249	53	322	42	208	5	42	24	601	20	4.6	0.6	3.0	8.6
Ernie Grunfeld	G-F	6'6	215	30	76	1402	148	355	42	90	108	83	206	119	192	2	39	13	412	18	2.7	1.6	2.5	5.4
Bob Thornton	F-C	6'10	225	23	71	1323	125	274	46	86	162	53	290	43	209	5	30	7	336	19	4.1	0.6	2.9	4.7
James Bailey (KJ)	C	6'9	220	28	48	1245	202	443	46	129	167	77	334	50	207	12	33	40	533	26	7.0	1.0	4.3	11.1
Chris McNealy	F	6'7	215	24	30	627	70	144	49	31	47	66	203	41	88	2	38	12	171	21	6.8	1.4	2.9	5.7
Fred Cofield	G	6'3	190	23	45	469	75	184	41	12	20	60	46	82	65	1	20	3	165	10	1.0	1.8	1.4	3.7

(continued on next page)

Use Name	Pos	Hgt	Wgt	Age	TOTAL G	Min	FG	FGA	%	FT	FTA	%	Reb	Ass	PF	DQ	Stls	Blkd Shts	Points	PER GAME Min	Reb	Ass	PF	Points
					1985/86 N.B.A. — EASTERN CONFERENCE																			
NEW YORK (continued)					ATLANTIC DIVISION																			
Ken Green	F	6'8	215	26	7	72	13	27	48	5	9	56	27	2	8	0	4	0	31	10	3.9	0.3	1.1	4.4
Bill Cartwright (BF)	C	7'1	245	28	2	36	3	7	43	6	10	60	10	5	6	0	1	1	12	18	5.0	2.5	3.0	6.0
Butch Carter (to Phi)	G	6'5	195	27	5	31	2	8	25	1	1	100	3	3	6	0	1	0	5	6	0.6	0.6	1.2	1.0
Bernard King - knee injury, Marvin Webster - illness, Eddie Wilkins - knee injury																								
3 PT-FG — Orr 0-4, Cummings 0-2, Ewing 0-5, Walker 0-10, Sparrow 5-20, Wilkins 7-25, Tucker 41-91, Bannister 0-1, Grunfeld 26-61, Bailey 0-4, Cofield 3-15, Carter 0-1																								
					CENTRAL DIVISION																			
MILWAUKEE BUCKS	57-25 .695				DON NELSON																			
Ricky Pierce	F-G	6'5	205	26	81	2147	429	798	54	266	310	86	231	177	252	6	83	6	1127	27	2.9	2.2	3.1	13.9
Terry Cummings	F	6'9	225	24	82	2669	681	1438	47	265	404	66	694	193	283	4	121	51	1627	33	8.5	2.4	3.5	19.8
Alton Lister	C	7'	240	27	81	1812	318	577	55	160	266	60	592	101	300	8	49	142	796	22	7.3	1.2	3.7	9.8
Sidney Moncrief	G	6'4	190	28	73	2567	470	962	49	498	580	86	334	357	178	1	103	18	1471	35	4.6	4.9	2.4	20.2
Paul Pressey	G	6'5	185	27	80	2704	411	843	49	316	392	81	399	623	247	4	168	71	1146	34	5.0	7.8	3.1	14.3
Randy Brewer	C	7'3	230	25	82	1792	272	570	48	141	198	71	458	114	214	2	50	116	685	22	5.6	1.4	2.6	8.4
Craig Hodges	G	6'3	190	25	66	1739	284	568	50	75	86	87	117	229	157	3	74	2	716	26	1.8	3.5	2.4	10.8
Kenny Fields	F	6'5	220	23	78	1120	204	398	51	91	132	69	203	79	170	3	51	15	499	14	2.6	1.0	2.2	6.4
Charlie Davis	F	6'7	215	27	57	873	188	397	47	61	75	81	170	55	113	1	26	7	440	15	3.0	1.0	2.0	7.7
Jeff Lamp (to SA)	F-G	6'6	195	26	44	701	109	243	45	55	64	86	121	64	88	1	20	3	276	16	2.8	1.5	2.0	6.3
Mike Glenn	G	6'3	185	30	38	573	94	190	49	47	49	96	57	39	42	0	9	3	235	15	1.5	1.0	1.1	6.2
Paul Mokeski	C-F	7'	250	28	45	521	59	139	42	25	34	74	139	30	92	1	6	6	143	12	3.1	0.7	2.0	3.2
Jerry Reynolds	F	6'8	200	23	55	508	72	162	44	58	104	56	80	86	57	0	43	19	203	9	1.5	1.6	1.0	3.7
Earl Jones	C	7'	230	24	12	43	5	12	42	3	4	75	10	4	13	0	0	1	13	4	0.8	0.3	1.1	1.1
Bryan Warrick (to Ind)	G	6.5	195	26	5	27	4	10	40	1	1	100	3	6	3	0	2	0	10	5	0.6	1.2	0.6	2.0
Derrick Rowland	G	6'5	195	26	2	9	1	3	33	1	2	50	1	1	1	0	0	0	3	5	0.5	0.5	0.5	1.5
3 PT-FG — Pierce 3-23, Cummings 0-2, Lister 0-2, Moncrief 33-103, Pressey 8-44, Brewer 0-1, Hodges 73-162, Fields 0-4, Davis 3-24, Lamp 3-13, Reynolds 1-2, Warrick 1-2																								
ATLANTIC HAWKS	50-32 .610				MIKE FRATELLO																			
Dominique Wilkins	F	6'8	200	25	78	3049	888	**1897**	47	577	705	82	618	206	170	0	138	49	2366	39	7.9	2.6	2.2	**30.3**
Kevin Willis	F-C	7'	220	23	82	2300	419	511	82	172	263	65	704	45	294	6	66	44	1010	28	8.6	0.5	3.6	12.3
Tree Rollins	C	7'1	235	30	74	1781	173	347	50	69	90	77	458	41	239	5	38	167	415	24	6.2	0.6	3.2	5.6
Randy Wittman	G	6'6	210	26	81	2760	467	881	53	104	135	77	170	306	118	0	81	14	1043	34	2.1	3.8	1.5	12.9
Glenn Rivers	G	6'4	185	24	53	1571	220	464	47	172	283	61	162	443	185	2	120	13	612	30	3.1	8.4	3.5	11.5
Cliff Levingston	F	6'8	220	24	81	1945	294	551	53	164	242	68	534	72	260	5	76	39	752	24	6.6	0.9	3.2	9.3
Jon Koncak	C	7'	250	22	82	1695	263	519	51	156	257	61	467	55	296	10	37	69	682	21	5.7	0.7	3.6	8.3
Spud Webb	G	5'7	135	22	79	1229	199	412	48	216	275	79	123	337	164	1	82	5	616	16	1.6	4.3	2.1	7.8
Eddie Johnson (to Cle)	G	6'2	190	30	39	862	155	328	47	79	110	72	75	219	72	1	10	1	394	22	1.9	5.6	1.8	10.1
Scott Hastings	F	6'10	235	25	62	650	65	159	41	60	70	86	124	26	118	2	14	8	193	10	2.0	0.4	1.9	3.1
John Battle	G	6'2	175	23	64	639	101	222	45	75	103	73	62	74	80	0	23	3	277	10	1.0	1.2	1.3	4.3
Johnny Davis (from Cle)	G	6'2	180	30	27	402	46	107	43	51	59	86	19	112	32	0	13	0	144	15	0.7	4.1	1.2	5.3
Ray Williams (to SA, NJ)	G	6'3	195	31	19	367	57	143	40	41	48	85	45	67	48	1	28	1	159	19	2.4	3.5	2.5	8.4
Lorenzo Charles	F	6'7	225	22	36	273	49	88	56	24	36	67	39	8	37	0	2	6	122	8	1.1	0.2	1.0	3.4
Antoine Carr	F	6'9	225	24	17	258	49	93	53	18	27	67	52	14	51	1	7	15	116	15	3.1	0.8	3.0	6.8
Sedric Toney (to Phoe)	G	6'2	178	23	3	24	2	7	29	1	1	100	2	0	6	0	1	0	5	8	0.7	0.0	2.0	1.7
3 PT-FG — Wilkins 13-70, Willis 0-6, Rollins 0-1, Wittman 5-16, Rivers 0-16, Levingston 0-1, Koncak 0-1, Webb 2-11, Johnson 5-20, Hastings 3-4, Battle 0-7, Davis 1-2, Williams 4-11																								
DETROIT PISTONS	46-36 .561				CHUCK DALY																			
Kelly Tripucka	F	6'6	220	26	81	2626	615	1236	50	380	444	86	348	265	167	0	93	10	1622	32	4.3	3.3	2.1	20.0
Earl Cureton	F.	6'9	215	28	80	2017	285	564	51	117	211	55	504	137	239	3	58	58	687	25	6.3	1.7	3.0	8.6
Bill Laimbeer	C	6'11	245	28	82	2891	545	1107	49	266	319	83	**1075**	146	291	4	59	65	1360	35	**13.1**	1.8	3.5	16.6
Vinnie Johnson	G	6'2	200	29	79	1978	465	996	47	165	214	77	226	269	180	2	80	23	1097	25	2.9	3.4	2.3	13.9
Isiah Thomas	G	6'1	185	24	77	2790	609	1248	49	365	462	79	277	830	245	9	171	20	1609	36	3.6	10.8	3.2	20.9
Joe Dumars	G	6'3	190	22	82	1957	297	597	50	190	238	80	119	390	200	1	66	11	769	24	1.5	4.8	2.4	9.4
Rick Mahorn	C-F	6'10	240	27	80	1442	157	345	46	81	119	68	412	64	261	4	40	61	395	18	5.2	0.8	3.3	4.9
Kent Benson	F	6'10	245	31	72	1344	201	415	48	66	83	80	376	80	196	3	58	51	469	19	5.2	1.1	2.7	6.5
Tony Campbell	F	6'7	215	23	82	1292	294	608	48	58	73	79	236	45	164	0	62	7	648	16	2.9	0.5	2.0	7.9
John Long	G	6'5	200	29	62	1176	264	548	48	89	104	86	98	82	92	0	41	13	620	19	1.6	1.3	1.5	10.0
Mike Gibson	F	6'10	205	25	32	161	20	51	39	8	11	73	40	5	35	0	8	4	48	5	1.3	0.2	1.1	1.5
Chuck Nevitt (from LA)	C	7'5	237	26	25	101	12	32	38	15	20	75	25	5	29	0	2	17	39	4	1.0	0.2	1.2	1.6
Ron Crevier (from GS)	C	7	235	27	2	3	0	2	0	0	2	0	1	0	2	0	0	0	0	2	0.5	0.0	1.0	0.0
Walker Russell	G	6'5	195	25	1	2	0	1	0	0	0	—	0	1	0	0	0	0	0	2	0.0	1.0	0.0	0.0
3 PT-FG — Tripucka 12-25, Cureton 0-2, Laimbeer 4-14, Johnson 2-13, Thomas 26-84, Dumars 5-16, Mahorn 0-1, Benson 1-2, Campbell 2-9, Long 3-16																								
CHICAGO BULLS	30-52 .366				STAN ALBECK																			
Orlando Woolridge	F	6'9	215	26	70	2248	540	1090	50	364	462	79	350	213	186	2	49	47	1448	32	5.0	3.0	2.7	20.7
Sidney Green	F-C	6'9	220	24	80	2307	407	875	47	262	335	78	658	139	292	5	70	37	1076	29	8.2	1.7	3.7	13.5
Dave Corzine	C	6'11	260	29	67	1709	255	519	49	127	171	74	433	150	133	0	28	53	640	26	6.5	2.2	2.0	9.6
Michael Jordan (BF)	G	6'6	195	22	18	451	150	328	46	105	125	84	64	53	46	0	37	21	408	25	3.6	2.9	2.6	22.7
Kyle Macy	G	6'3	190	28	82	2426	286	592	48	73	90	81	178	446	201	1	81	11	703	30	2.2	5.4	2.5	8.6
Gene Banks	F-G	6'7	215	26	82	2139	356	688	52	183	255	72	360	251	212	4	81	10	895	26	4.4	3.1	2.6	10.9
George Gervin	G	6'7	185	33	82	2065	519	1100	47	283	322	88	215	144	210	4	49	23	1326	25	2.6	1.8	2.6	16.2
Charles Oakley	F	6'8	225	22	77	1772	281	541	52	178	269	66	664	133	250	9	68	30	740	23	8.6	1.7	3.2	9.6
John Paxson	G	6'2	185	25	75	1570	153	328	47	74	92	80	94	274	172	2	55	2	395	21	1.3	3.7	2.3	5.3
Jawaan Oldham	C	7'	215	28	52	1276	167	323	52	53	91	58	306	37	206	6	28	134	387	25	5.9	0.7	4.0	7.4
Quntin Dailey	G	6'3	180	24	35	723	203	470	43	163	198	82	68	67	86	0	22	5	569	21	1.9	1.9	2.5	16.3
Michael Holton (from Phoe)	G	6'4	185	24	24	447	73	155	47	24	38	63	30	48	40	1	23	0	171	19	1.3	2.0	1.7	7.1

(continued on next page)

1985/86 N.B.A. — EASTERN CONFERENCE
CENTRAL DIVISION

CHICAGO (continued)

Use Name	Pos	Hgt	Wgt	Age	G	Min	FG	FGA	%	FT	FTA	%	Reb	Ass	PF	DQ	Stls	Blkd Shts	Points	Min	Reb	Ass	PF	Points
					TOTAL															PER GAME				
Mike Smrek	C	7'	250	23	38	408	46	142	38	16	29	55	110	19	95	0	6	23	108	11	2.9	0.5	2.5	2.8
Tony Brown	F	6'6	195	25	10	132	18	41	44	9	13	69	16	14	16	0	5	1	45	13	1.6	1.4	1.6	4.5
Billy McKinney	G	6'	172	30	9	83	10	23	43	2	2	100	5	13	9	0	3	0	22	9	0.6	1.4	1.0	2.4
Rod Higgins (from SEA, SA, NJ)	F	6'7	205	25	5	81	9	23	39	5	6	83	7	5	11	0	4	3	23	16	1.4	1.0	2.2	4.6
Ron Brewer (to CLE)	G	6'4	185	30	4	18	3	9	33	1	1	100	0	0	1	0	0	0	7	5	0.0	0.0	0.3	1.8

3-PT FG — Woolridge 4-23, Green 0-8, Corzine 3-12, Jordan 3-18, Macy 58-141, Banks 0-19, Gervin 4-19, Oakley 0-3, Paxon 15-50, Oldham 0-1, Dailey 0-8, Holton 1-10, Smrek 0-2, Brown 0-2, Higgins 0-1

CLEVELAND CAVALIERS 29-53 .354 **GEORGE KARL 25-42 (.373), GENE LITTLES 4-11 (.267)**

Use Name	Pos	Hgt	Wgt	Age	G	Min	FG	FGA	%	FT	FTA	%	Reb	Ass	PF	DQ	Stls	Blkd Shts	Points	Min	Reb	Ass	PF	Points
Phil Hubbard	F	6'8	215	29	23	640	93	198	47	76	112	68	120	29	78	2	20	3	262	28	5.2	1.3	3.4	11.4
Roy Hinson	F	6'9	210	24	82	2834	621	1167	53	364	506	72	639	102	316	7	62	112	1606	35	7.8	1.2	3.9	19.6
Melvin Turpin	C	6'11	240	25	80	2292	456	838	54	185	228	81	556	55	260	6	65	106	1097	29	7.0	0.7	3.3	13.7
World Free	G	6'2	185	32	75	2535	652	1433	45	379	486	78	218	314	186	1	91	19	1754	34	2.9	4.2	2.5	23.4
John Bagley	G	6'	190	25	78	2472	366	865	42	170	215	79	275	735	165	1	122	10	911	32	2.9	9.4	2.1	11.7
Ben Poquette	F-C	6'9	235	30	81	1496	166	348	48	72	100	72	373	78	187	2	33	32	406	18	4.6	1.0	2.3	5.0
Keith Lee	F	6'10	215	23	58	1197	177	380	47	75	96	78	351	67	204	9	29	37	431	21	6.1	1.2	3.5	7.4
Mark West	F-C	6'10	230	25	67	1172	113	209	54	54	103	52	322	20	235	6	27	62	280	17	4.8	0.3	3.5	4.2
Dirk Minnifield	G	6'3	190	24	76	1131	167	347	48	73	93	78	131	269	165	1	65	1	417	15	1.7	3.5	2.2	5.5
Edgar Jones	F-C	6'10	225	29	53	1011	187	370	51	132	178	74	207	45	142	0	30	38	513	19	3.9	0.8	2.7	9.7
Lonnie Shelton	F	6'8	255	30	44	682	92	188	49	14	16	88	143	61	128	2	21	4	198	16	3.3	1.4	2.9	4.5
Eddie Johnson (from Atl)	G	6'2	190	30	32	615	129	293	44	33	45	73	46	114	56	0	8	1	315	19	1.4	3.6	1.8	9.8
Johnny Davis (from Atl)	G	6'2	180	30	39	612	102	237	43	67	79	85	36	105	44	0	24	4	273	16	0.9	2.7	1.1	7.0
Ron Brewer (from Chi)	G	6'4	185	30	40	552	83	215	39	33	37	89	53	40	43	0	17	6	204	14	1.3	1.0	1.1	5.1
Ben McDonald	F	6'8	210	23	21	266	28	58	48	5	8	63	38	9	30	0	7	1	61	13	1.8	0.4	1.4	2.9
Ron Anderson (to Ind)	F	6'7	215	27	17	207	37	74	50	12	16	75	26	8	20	0	1	0	86	12	1.5	0.5	1.2	5.1
Ennis Whatley (to Was, SA)	G	6'3	177	23	8	66	9	19	47	4	7	57	7	13	8	0	5	0	22	8	0.9	1.6	1.0	2.8

3-PT FG — Hubbard 0-1, Hinson 0-4, Turpin 0-4, Free 71-169, Bagley 9-37, Poquette 2-10, Lee 2-9, Minniefield 10-37, Jones 7-23, Shelton 0-2, Johnson 24-65, Davis 2-71, Brewer 5-17, McDonald 0-1, Anderson 0-1

INDIANA PACERS 26-56 .317 **GEORGE IRVINE**

Use Name	Pos	Hgt	Wgt	Age	G	Min	FG	FGA	%	FT	FTA	%	Reb	Ass	PF	DQ	Stls	Blkd Shts	Points	Min	Reb	Ass	PF	Points
Clark Kellogg (KJ)	F	6'7	227	24	19	568	139	294	47	53	69	77	168	57	59	2	28	8	335	30	8.8	3.0	3.1	17.6
Herb Williams	F-C	6'11	242	27	78	2770	627	1275	49	294	403	73	710	174	244	2	50	184	1549	36	9.1	2.2	3.1	19.9
Steve Stipanovich	C	6'11	245	25	79	2397	416	885	47	242	315	77	623	206	261	1	75	69	1076	30	7.9	2.6	3.3	13.6
Clint Richardson	G	6'3	195	29	82	2224	335	736	46	123	147	84	251	372	153	1	58	8	794	27	3.1	4.5	1.9	9.7
Vern Fleming	G	6'5	195	24	80	2870	436	862	51	263	353	75	386	505	230	3	131	5	1136	36	4.8	6.3	2.9	14.2
Wayman Tisdale	F	6'9	250	21	81	2277	516	1002	51	160	234	68	584	79	290	3	32	44	1192	28	7.2	1.0	3.6	14.7
Ron Anderson (from Cle)	F	6'7	215	27	60	1469	273	554	49	73	111	66	248	136	105	0	55	6	621	24	4.1	2.3	1.8	10.4
Terence Stansbury	G	6'5	170	24	74	1331	191	441	43	107	132	81	139	209	200	2	59	8	498	18	1.9	2.8	2.7	6.7
Bill Garrett	F	6'9	225	25	80	1197	112	239	47	116	162	72	275	95	174	0	39	22	340	15	3.4	1.2	2.2	4.3
Bill Martin	F	6'7	215	23	66	691	143	298	48	46	54	85	102	52	108	1	21	7	332	10	1.5	0.8	1.6	5.0
Bryan Warrick (from Mil)	G	6'5	195	26	31	658	81	172	47	53	67	79	66	109	76	0	25	2	217	21	2.1	3.5	2.5	7.0
Dwayne McClain	G	6'6	185	22	45	461	69	180	38	18	35	51	30	67	61	0	38	4	157	10	0.7	1.5	1.4	3.5
Stuart Gray	C	7'	235	22	67	423	54	108	50	47	74	64	118	15	94	0	8	11	155	6	1.8	0.2	1.4	2.3
Quinn Buckner	G	6'3	205	31	32	419	49	104	47	19	27	70	51	86	80	0	40	3	117	13	1.6	2.7	2.5	3.7

3-PT FG— Kellog 4-13, Williams 1-12, Stipanovich 2-10, Richardson 1-9, Fleming 1-6, Tisdale 0-2, Anderson 2-8, Stansbury 9-53, Garrett 0-2, Martin 0-8, Warrick 2-10, McClain 1-9, Buckner 0-1

1985/86 N.B.A. — WESTERN CONFERENCE — MIDWEST DIVISION

HOUSTON ROCKETS 51-31 .622 **BILL FITCH**

Use Name	Pos	Hgt	Wgt	Age	G	Min	FG	FGA	%	FT	FTA	%	Reb	Ass	PF	DQ	Stls	Blkd Shts	Points	Min	Reb	Ass	PF	Points
Rodney McCray	F-G	6'8	220	24	82	2610	338	629	54	171	222	77	520	292	197	2	50	58	847	32	6.3	3.6	2.4	10.3
Ralph Sampson	F-C	7'4	228	25	79	2864	624	1280	49	241	376	64	879	283	308	12	99	129	1491	36	11.1	3.6	3.9	18.9
Akeem Olajuwon	C	7'	250	22	68	2467	625	1188	53	347	538	64	781	137	271	9	134	231	1597	36	11.5	2.0	4.0	23.5
Lewis Lloyd	G-F	6'6	215	26	82	2444	592	1119	53	199	236	84	324	300	216	0	102	24	1386	30	4.0	3.7	2.6	16.9
John Lucas (DR)	G	6'3	185	32	65	2120	365	818	45	231	298	78	143	571	124	0	77	5	1006	33	2.2	8.8	1.9	15.5
Robert Reid	F-G	6'8	205	30	82	2157	409	881	46	162	214	76	301	222	231	3	91	16	986	26	3.7	2.7	2.8	12.0
Jim Petersen	F-C	6'10	235	23	82	1664	196	411	48	113	160	71	396	85	231	2	38	54	505	20	4.8	1.0	2.8	6.2
Mitchell Wiggins	G	6'4	185	26	78	1198	222	489	45	86	118	73	159	101	155	1	59	5	531	15	2.0	1.3	2.0	6.8
Allen Leavell	G	6'1	190	28	74	1190	212	458	46	135	158	85	67	234	126	1	58	8	583	16	0.9	3.2	1.7	7.9
Steve Harris	G	6'5	195	22	57	482	103	233	44	50	54	93	57	50	55	0	21	4	257	8	1.0	0.9	1.0	4.5
Hank McDowell	F	6'9	215	26	22	204	24	42	57	17	25	68	49	6	25	0	1	3	65	9	2.2	0.3	1.1	3.0
Craig Ehlo	G	6'7	180	24	36	199	36	84	43	23	29	79	46	29	22	0	11	4	98	6	1.3	0.8	0.6	2.7
Granville Waiters	C	6'11	225	24	43	156	13	39	33	1	6	17	28	8	30	0	4	10	27	4	0.7	0.2	0.7	0.6

3-PT FG— McCray 0-3, Sampson 2-15, Lloyd 3-15, Lucas 45-146, Reid 6-33, Peterson 0-3, Wiggins 1-12, Leavell 24-67, Harris 1-5, McDowell 0-1, Ehlo 3-9, Waiters 0-1

DENVER NUGGETS 47-35 .573 **DOUG MOE**

Use Name	Pos	Hgt	Wgt	Age	G	Min	FG	FGA	%	FT	FTA	%	Reb	Ass	PF	DQ	Stls	Blkd Shts	Points	Min	Reb	Ass	PF	Points
Alex English	F	6'8	190	31	81	3024	**951**	1888	50	511	593	86	405	320	235	1	73	29	**2414**	37	5.0	4.0	2.9	29.8
Calvin Natt	F	6'6	220	28	69	2007	469	930	50	278	347	80	436	164	143	1	58	13	1218	29	6.3	2.4	2.1	17.7
Wayne Cooper	C	6'10	220	29	78	2112	422	906	47	174	219	79	610	81	315	6	42	227	1021	27	7.8	1.0	4.0	13.1
T.R. Dunn	G	6'4	192	30	82	2401	172	379	45	68	88	77	377	171	228	1	155	16	412	29	4.6	2.1	2.8	5.0
Lafayette Lever	G	6'3	175	25	78	2616	468	1061	44	132	182	73	420	584	204	3	178	15	1080	34	5.4	7.5	2.6	13.8
Bill Hanzlik	F-G	6'7	185	28	79	1982	331	741	45	318	405	79	264	316	277	2	107	16	988	25	3.3	4.0	3.5	12.5
Danny Schayes	C-F	6'11	245	26	80	1654	221	440	50	216	278	78	439	79	298	7	42	63	658	21	5.5	1.0	3.7	8.2
Mike Evans	G	6'1	170	30	81	1389	304	715	43	126	149	85	101	177	159	1	61	1	773	17	1.2	2.2	2.0	9.5
Elston Turner	G-F	6'5	220	22	73	1324	165	379	44	39	53	74	201	165	150	1	70	6	369	18	2.8	2.3	2.1	5.1
Pete Williams	F	6'7	190	20	53	573	67	111	60	17	40	43	146	14	68	1	19	23	151	11	2.8	0.3	1.3	2.8
Willie White	G	6'3	195	23	43	343	74	168	44	19	23	83	44	53	24	0	18	2	173	8	1.0	1.2	0.6	4.0
Blair Rasmussen	C	7'	250	23	48	330	61	150	41	31	39	79	97	16	63	0	3	10	153	7	2.0	0.3	1.3	3.2

3-PT FG— English 1-5, Natt 2-6, Cooper 3-7, Dunn 0-1, Lever 12-38, Hanzlik 8-41, Schayes 0-1, Evans 39-176, Turner 0-9, White 6-21

1985/86 N.B.A. — WESTERN CONFERENCE
MIDWEST DIVISION

Use Name	Pos	Hgt	Wgt	Age	G	Min	FG	FGA	%	FT	FTA	%	Reb	Ass	PF	DQ	Stls	Blkd Shts	Points	Min	Reb	Ass	PF	Points
					TOTAL															PER GAME				
DALLAS MAVERICKS	47-35 .573				**DICK MOTTA**																			
Mark Aguirre	F	6'6	235	26	74	2501	668	1327	50	318	451	71	445	339	229	6	62	14	1670	34	6.0	4.6	3.1	22.6
Sam Perkins	F-C	6'9	235	24	80	2626	458	910	50	307	377	81	685	153	212	2	75	94	1234	33	8.6	1.9	2.7	15.4
James Donaldson (from LAC)	C	7'2	278	28	69	2241	213	375	57	147	184	80	664	84	156	0	23	110	573	32	9.6	1.2	2.3	8.3
Rolando Blackman	G	6'6	190	26	82	2787	677	1318	51	404	483	84	291	271	138	0	79	25	1762	34	3.5	3.3	1.7	21.5
Derek Harper	G	6'4	185	24	79	2150	390	730	53	171	229	75	226	416	166	1	153	23	963	27	2.9	5.3	2.1	12.2
Jay Vincent	F	6'7	225	26	80	1994	442	919	48	222	274	81	368	180	193	2	66	21	1106	25	4.6	2.3	2.4	13.8
Brad Davis	G	6'3	180	30	82	1971	267	502	53	198	228	87	146	467	174	2	57	15	764	24	1.8	5.7	2.1	9.3
Dale Ellis	F	6'7	205	25	72	1086	193	470	41	59	82	72	168	37	78	0	40	9	508	15	2.3	0.5	1.1	7.1
Detlef Schrempf	F	6'9	220	22	64	969	142	315	45	110	152	72	198	88	166	1	23	10	397	15	3.1	1.4	2.6	6.2
Bill Wennington	C	7'	245	21	56	562	72	153	47	45	62	73	132	21	83	0	11	22	189	10	2.4	0.4	1.5	3.4
Uwe Blab	C	7'1	255	23	48	409	44	94	47	36	67	54	91	17	65	0	3	12	124	9	1.9	0.4	1.4	2.6
Kurt Nimphius (to LAC)	C	6'10	218	27	13	280	37	72	51	17	29	59	60	14	38	1	3	12	91	22	4.6	1.1	2.9	7.0
Wallace Bryant (to LAC)	C	7'	245	26	9	154	11	30	37	6	11	55	33	11	26	2	3	2	28	17	3.7	1.2	2.9	3.1
Harold Keeling	G	6'4	185	22	20	75	17	39	44	10	14	71	6	10	9	0	7	0	44	4	0.3	0.5	0.5	2.2
	3-PT FG —				Aguirre 16-56, Perkins 11-33, Blackman 4-29, Harper 12-51, Vincent 0-3, Davis 32-89, Ellis 63-173, Schrempf 3-7, Wennington 0-4, Nimphius 0-1																			
UTAH JAZZ	42-40 .512				**FRANK LAYDEN**																			
Adrian Dantley	F-G	6'5	210	29	76	2744	818	1453	56	630	796	79	395	264	206	2	64	4	2267	36	5.2	3.5	2.7	29.8
Karl Malone	F	6'9	250	22	81	2475	504	1016	50	195	405	48	718	236	295	2	105	44	1203	31	8.9	2.9	3.6	14.9
Mark Eaton	C	7'4	280	28	80	2551	277	589	47	122	202	60	675	101	282	5	33	369	676	32	8.4	1.3	3.5	8.5
Bob Hansen	G	6'6	190	24	82	2032	299	626	48	95	132	72	244	193	205	1	74	9	710	25	3.0	2.4	2.5	8.7
John Stockton	G	6'1	170	23	82	1935	228	466	49	172	205	84	179	610	227	2	157	10	630	24	2.2	7.4	2.8	7.7
Thurl Bailey	F-C	6'11	215	24	82	2358	483	1077	45	230	277	83	493	153	160	0	42	114	1196	29	6.0	1.9	2.0	14.6
Rickey Green	G	6'1	170	31	80	2012	357	758	47	213	250	85	135	411	130	0	106	6	932	25	1.7	5.1	1.6	11.7
Carey Scurry	F	6'7	190	23	78	1168	142	301	47	78	126	62	242	85	171	2	78	66	363	15	3.1	1.1	2.2	4.7
Pace Mannion	G	6'7	190	25	57	673	97	214	45	53	82	65	82	55	68	0	32	5	255	12	1.4	1.0	1.2	4.5
Jeff Wilkins (to SA)	C	6'11	240	30	48	604	96	240	40	30	47	64	145	28	86	0	3	11	222	13	3.0	0.6	1.8	4.6
Fred Roberts	F	6'10	220	25	58	469	74	167	44	67	87	77	80	27	72	0	8	6	216	8	1.4	0.5	1.2	3.7
Steve Hayes	C	7'	235	30	58	397	39	87	45	11	36	31	77	7	81	0	5	19	89	7	1.3	0.1	1.4	1.5
Marc Iavaroni (from SA)	F	6'9	225	29	26	345	36	81	44	33	48	69	77	29	54	0	10	3	105	13	3.0	1.1	2.1	4.0
Jeff Cook (from SA)	C	6'10	215	29	2	17	3	6	50	1	1	100	5	0	1	0	0	0	7	9	2.5	0.0	0.5	3.5
Darrell Griffith- broken foot	**3-PT FG —**				Dantley 1-11, Malone 1-2, Hansen 17-50, Stockton 2-15, Bailey 0-7, Green 5-29, Scurry 1-11, Mannion 8-42, Roberts 1-2																			
SACRAMENTO KINGS	37-45 .451				**PHIL JOHNSON**																			
Eddie Johnson	F	6'8	215	26	82	2514	623	1311	48	280	343	82	419	214	237	0	54	17	1530	31	5.1	2.6	2.9	18.7
Mark Olberding	F	6'8	230	29	81	2157	225	403	56	162	210	77	423	266	276	3	43	23	612	27	5.2	3.3	3.4	7.6
LaSalle Thompson	C	6'10	248	24	80	2377	411	794	52	202	276	73	770	168	295	8	71	109	1024	30	9.6	2.1	3.7	12.8
Mike Woodson	G	6'5	198	27	81	2417	510	1073	48	242	289	84	226	197	215	1	92	37	1264	30	2.8	2.4	2.7	15.6
Reggie Theus	G	6'7	205	28	82	2919	546	1137	48	405	490	83	304	788	231	3	112	20	1503	36	3.7	9.6	2.8	18.3
Larry Drew	G	6'1	180	27	75	1971	376	776	48	128	161	80	125	338	134	0	66	2	890	26	1.7	4.5	1.8	11.9
Otis Thorpe	F-C	6'11	225	23	75	1675	289	492	59	164	248	66	420	84	233	3	35	34	742	22	5.6	1.1	3.1	9.9
Terry Tyler	F	6'7	220	29	71	1651	295	649	45	84	112	75	313	94	159	0	64	108	674	23	4.4	1.3	2.2	9.5
Joe Kleine	C	7'	255	23	80	1180	160	344	47	94	130	72	373	46	224	1	24	34	414	15	4.7	0.6	2.8	5.2
Rich Kelley	C	7'	240	32	37	324	28	49	57	18	22	82	81	43	62	0	10	3	74	9	2.2	1.2	1.7	2.0
Mike Bratz	G	6'2	185	30	33	269	26	70	37	14	18	78	23	39	43	0	13	0	70	8	0.7	1.2	1.3	2.1
Carl Henry	G	6'6	205	25	28	149	31	67	46	12	17	71	19	4	11	0	5	0	78	5	0.7	0.1	0.4	2.8
Michael Adams	G	5'11	165	22	18	139	16	44	36	8	12	67	6	22	9	0	9	1	40	8	0.3	1.2	0.5	2.2
David Cooke	F	6'8	230	22	6	38	2	11	18	5	10	50	10	1	5	0	4	0	9	6	1.7	0.2	0.8	1.5
	3-PT FG —				Johnson 4-20, Olberding 0-2, Thompson 0-1, Woodson 2-13, Theus 6-35, Drew 10-31, Tyler 0-3, Kelley 0-2, Bratz 4-14, Henry 4-10, Adams 0-3																			
SAN ANTONIO SPURS	35-47 .427				**COTTON FITZSIMMONS**																			
Mike Mitchell	F	6'7	215	29	82	2970	802	1697	47	317	392	81	409	188	175	0	56	25	1921	36	5.0	2.3	2.1	23.4
Dave Greenwood	F	6'9	232	28	68	1910	198	388	51	142	184	77	531	90	207	3	37	52	538	28	7.8	1.3	3.0	7.9
Artis Gilmore	C	7'2	255	36	71	2395	423	684	62	338	482	70	600	102	239	3	39	108	1184	34	8.5	1.4	3.4	16.7
Alvin Robertson	G	6'3	185	23	82	2878	562	1093	51	260	327	80	516	448	296	4	301	40	1392	35	6.3	5.5	3.6	17.0
Johnny Moore (IL)	G	6'2	185	27	28	856	150	303	50	59	86	69	86	252	78	0	70	6	363	31	3.1	9.0	2.8	13.0
Wes Matthews	G	6'1	170	26	75	1853	320	603	53	173	211	82	131	476	168	1	87	32	817	25	1.7	6.3	2.2	10.9
Steve Johnson	C-F	6'10	245	28	71	1828	362	573	63	259	373	69	462	95	291	13	44	66	983	26	6.5	1.3	4.1	13.8
Jon Sundvold	G	6'2	170	24	70	1150	220	476	46	39	48	81	80	261	110	0	34	0	500	16	1.1	3.7	1.6	7.1
Alfred Hughes	F-G	6'5	215	23	68	866	152	372	41	49	84	58	113	61	79	0	26	5	356	13	1.7	0.9	1.2	5.2
Marc Iavaroni (to Utah)	F	6'9	225	29	42	669	74	163	45	43	67	64	132	53	109	0	22	14	191	16	3.1	1.3	2.6	4.5
Jeff Lamp (from Mil)	G	6'6	195	26	30	620	136	271	50	56	69	81	79	53	67	0	19	1	332	21	2.6	1.8	2.2	11.1
Jeff Wilkins (from Utah)	C-F	6'11	240	30	27	522	51	134	38	28	46	61	127	18	71	1	8	10	130	19	4.7	0.7	2.6	4.8
Ray Williams (from Atl, to NJ)	G	6'3	195	31	23	397	50	131	38	62	64	97	37	111	64	1	28	3	164	17	1.6	4.8	2.8	7.1
Jeff Cook (to Utah)	F-C	6'10	215	29	34	356	28	67	42	26	41	63	81	21	64	0	13	11	82	10	2.4	0.6	1.9	2.4
Mike Brittain	C	7'	235	22	32	219	22	43	51	10	19	53	49	5	54	1	3	12	54	7	1.5	0.2	1.7	1.7
Tyrone Corbin	F	6'6	210	23	16	174	27	64	42	10	14	71	25	11	21	0	11	2	64	11	1.6	0.7	1.3	4.0
Rod Higgins (from Sea, to Cle, Was)	F	6'7	205	25	11	128	18	40	45	11	16	69	24	12	21	0	2	3	47	12	2.2	1.1	1.9	4.3
Ennis Whatley (from Cle, Was)	G	6'3	177	23	2	14	1	2	50	0	0	—	0	3	1	0	0	0	2	7	0.0	1.5	0.5	1.0
	3-PT FG —				Mitchell 0-12, Greenwood 0-1, Gilmore 0-1, Robertson 8-29, Moore 4-22, Matthews 4-25, Sundvold 21-60, Hughes 3-17, Iavaroni 0-2, Lamp 4-17, Williams 2-6, Cook 0-1, Corbin 0-1, Higgins 0-2																			

1985/86 N.B.A. — WESTERN CONFERENCE
PACIFIC DIVISION

Use Name	Pos	Hgt	Wgt	Age	TOTAL G	Min	FG	FGA	%	FT	FTA	%	Reb	Ass	PF	DQ	Stls	Blkd Shts	Points	PER GAME Min	Reb	Ass	PF	Points
LOS ANGELES LAKERS	**62-20 .756**				**PAT RILEY**																			
James Worthy	F	6'9	225	24	75	2454	629	1086	58	242	314	77	387	201	195	0	82	77	1500	33	5.2	2.7	2.6	20.0
Kurt Rambis	F	6'8	220	27	74	1573	160	269	59	88	122	72	517	69	198	0	66	33	408	21	7.0	0.9	2.7	5.5
Kareem Abdul-Jabbar	C	7'2	232	38	79	2629	755	1338	56	336	439	77	478	280	248	2	67	130	1846	33	6.1	3.5	3.1	23.4
Byron Scott	G	6'3	195	24	76	2190	507	989	51	138	176	78	189	164	167	0	85	15	1174	29	2.5	2.2	2.2	15.4
Magic Johnson	G	6'8	215	26	72	2578	483	918	53	378	434	87	426	**907**	133	0	113	16	1354	36	5.9	12.6	1.8	18.8
Michael Cooper	G-F	6'5	170	29	82	2269	274	606	45	147	170	86	244	466	238	2	89	43	758	28	3.0	5.7	2.9	9.2
Maurice Lucas	C-F	6'9	238	33	77	1750	302	653	46	180	230	78	566	84	253	1	45	24	785	23	7.4	1.1	3.3	10.2
A.C. Green	F	6'9	220	22	82	1542	209	388	54	102	167	61	381	54	229	2	49	49	521	19	4.6	0.7	2.8	6.4
Mike McGee	G-F	6'5	190	26	71	1213	252	544	46	42	64	66	140	83	131	0	53	7	587	17	2.0	1.2	1.8	8.3
Mitch Kupchak (KJ)	F	6'9	230	31	55	783	124	257	48	84	112	75	191	17	102	0	12	7	332	14	3.5	0.3	1.9	6.0
Larry Spriggs	F	6'7	230	26	43	471	88	192	46	38	49	78	81	49	78	0	18	9	214	11	1.9	1.1	1.8	5.0
Ronnie Lester	G	6'2	175	26	27	222	26	52	50	15	19	79	10	54	27	0	9	3	67	8	0.4	2.0	1.0	2.5
Petur Gudmundsson	C	7'2	260	27	8	128	20	37	54	18	27	67	38	3	25	1	3	4	58	16	4.8	0.4	3.1	7.3
Chuck Nevitt (to Det)	C	7'5	237	26	4	25	3	11	27	4	6	67	7	2	6	0	2	2	10	6	1.8	0.5	1.5	2.5
Jerome Henderson	C	6'11	230	26	1	3	2	3	67	0	0	—	1	0	1	0	0	0	4	3	1.0	0.0	1.0	4.0
3-PT FG -	Worthy 0-13, Abdul-Jabbar 0-2, Scott 22-61, Johnson 10-43, Cooper 63-163, Lucas 1-2, Green 1-6, McGee 41-114, Kupchak 0-1, Spriggs 0-1, Lester 0-3																							
PORTLAND TRAIL BLAZERS	**40-42 .488**				**JACK RAMSAY**																			
Kiki Vandeweghe	F	6'8	220	27	79	2791	719	1332	54	523	602	87	216	187	161	0	54	17	1962	35	2.7	2.4	2.0	24.8
Mychal Thompson	F-C	6'10	226	30	82	2569	503	1011	50	198	309	64	608	176	267	5	76	35	1204	31	7.4	2.1	3.3	14.7
Sam Bowie (BL)	C	7'1	235	24	38	1132	167	345	48	114	161	71	327	99	142	4	21	96	448	30	8.6	2.6	3.7	11.8
Jim Paxon	G-F	6'6	200	28	75	1931	372	792	47	217	244	89	148	278	156	3	94	5	981	26	2.0	3.7	2.1	13.1
Clyde Drexler	G	6'7	210	23	75	2576	542	1142	47	293	381	77	421	600	270	8	197	46	1389	34	5.6	8.0	3.6	18.5
Steve Colter	G	6'3	165	23	81	1868	272	597	46	135	164	82	177	257	188	0	113	10	706	23	2.2	3.2	2.3	8.7
Kenny Carr (KJ)	F	6'7	230	30	55	1557	232	466	50	149	217	69	492	70	203	5	38	30	613	28	8.9	1.3	3.7	11.1
Caldwell Jones	C	6'11	225	35	80	1437	126	254	50	124	150	83	355	74	244	2	38	61	376	18	4.4	0.9	3.1	4.7
Jerome Kersey	F	6'7	215	23	79	1217	258	470	55	156	229	68	293	83	208	2	85	32	672	15	3.7	1.1	2.6	8.5
Terry Porter	G	6'3	195	22	79	1214	212	447	47	125	155	81	117	198	136	0	81	1	562	15	1.5	2.5	1.7	7.1
Ken Johnson	F	6'8	240	23	64	815	113	214	53	37	85	44	243	19	147	1	13	22	263	13	3.8	0.3	2.3	4.1
Darnell Valentine (to LAC)	G	6'2	185	26	28	734	92	206	45	71	100	71	72	139	78	0	49	1	256	26	2.6	5.0	2.8	9.1
Brian Martin (from Sea)	F	6'9	212	23	5	14	2	5	40	0	2	0	0	0	5	0	0	0	4	3	0.0	0.0	1.0	0.8
3-PT FG -	Vandeweghe 1-8, Paxon 20-62, Drexler 12-60, Colton 27-83, Carr 0-4, Jones 0-7, Kersey 0-6, Porter 13-42, Valentine 1-3																							
LOS ANGELES CLIPPERS	**32-50 .390**				**DON CHANEY**																			
Marqes Johnson	F-G	6'7	218	29	75	2605	613	1201	51	298	392	76	416	283	214	2	107	50	1525	35	5.5	3.8	2.9	20.3
Cedric Maxwell	F	6'8	215	30	76	2458	314	661	48	447	562	80	624	215	252	2	61	29	1075	32	8.2	2.8	3.3	14.1
Benoit Benjamin	C	7'	250	21	79	2088	324	661	49	229	307	75	600	79	286	5	64	206	878	26	7.6	1.0	3.6	11.1
Derek Smith (KJ)	G	6'7	215	24	11	339	100	181	55	58	84	69	41	31	35	2	9	13	259	31	3.7	2.8	3.2	23.5
Norm Nixon	G	6'2	175	30	67	2138	403	921	44	131	162	81	180	576	143	0	84	3	979	32	2.7	8.6	2.1	14.6
Kurt Nimphius (from Dal)	C-F	6'10	218	27	67	1946	314	622	50	177	233	76	393	48	229	7	30	93	805	29	5.9	0.7	3.4	12.0
Rory White	F	6'8	210	26	75	1761	355	684	52	164	222	74	181	74	161	2	74	8	875	23	2.4	1.0	2.1	11.7
Michael Cage	F	6'9	225	23	78	1566	204	426	48	113	174	65	417	81	176	1	62	34	521	20	5.3	1.0	2.3	6.7
Franklin Edwards	G	6'1	170	26	73	1491	262	577	45	132	151	87	86	259	87	0	89	4	657	20	1.2	3.5	1.2	9.0
Junior Bridgeman (thumb injury)	G	6'5	210	32	58	1161	199	451	44	106	119	89	123	108	81	1	31	8	510	20	2.1	1.9	1.4	8.8
Lancaster Gordon	G	6'3	185	23	60	704	130	345	38	45	56	80	68	60	91	1	33	10	312	12	1.1	1.0	1.5	5.2
Darnell Valentine (from Port)	G	6'2	185	26	34	483	69	182	38	59	75	79	53	107	45	0	23	1	200	14	1.6	3.1	1.3	5.9
James Donaldson (to Dal)	C	7'2	278	28	14	441	43	84	51	57	70	81	131	12	33	0	5	29	143	32	9.4	0.9	2.4	10.2
Jamaal Wilkes	G	6'6	190	32	13	195	26	65	40	22	27	81	29	15	19	0	7	2	75	15	2.2	1.2	1.5	5.8
Jeff Cross	F	6'10	242	24	21	128	6	24	25	14	25	56	30	1	38	0	2	3	26	6	1.4	0.0	1.8	1.2
Jay Murphy	F	6'9	220	23	14	100	16	45	36	9	14	64	15	3	12	0	4	3	41	7	1.1	0.2	0.9	2.9
Jim Thomas	G	6'3	190	25	6	69	6	15	40	1	2	50	8	12	12	0	5	1	13	12	1.3	2.0	2.0	2.2
Wallace Bryant (from Dal)	C	7'	245	26	8	64	4	18	22	5	8	63	20	4	12	0	2	3	13	8	2.5	0.5	1.5	1.6
Ozell Jones	F	6'11	235	25	3	18	0	2	0	0	0	—	2	0	5	0	2	1	0	6	0.7	0.0	1.7	0.0
3-PT FG -	Johnson 1-15, Maxwell 0-3, Benjamin 1-3, Smith 1-2, Nixon 42-121, Nimphius 0-2, White 1-9, Cage 0-3, Edwards 1-9, Bridgeman 6-18, Gordon 7-28, Valentine 3-11, Wilkes 1-3, Murphy 0-2																							
PHOENIX SUNS	**32-50 .390**				**JOHN MACLEOD**																			
Larry Nance	F	6'10	215	26	73	2484	582	1001	58	310	444	70	618	240	247	6	70	130	1474	34	8.5	3.3	3.4	20.2
Ed Pinckney	F	6'9	195	22	80	1602	255	457	56	171	254	67	308	90	190	3	71	37	681	20	3.9	1.1	2.4	8.5
Alvan Adams	C	6'9	220	31	78	2005	341	649	53	159	203	78	477	324	272	7	103	46	841	26	6.1	4.2	3.5	10.8
Walter Davis (DR)	G	6'6	200	31	70	2239	624	1287	48	257	305	84	203	361	153	1	99	3	1523	32	2.9	5.2	2.2	21.8
Jay Humphries	G	6'3	185	23	82	2733	352	735	48	197	257	77	260	526	222	1	132	9	905	33	3.2	6.4	2.7	11.0
Mike Sanders	F-G	6'6	210	25	82	1644	347	676	51	208	257	81	273	150	236	3	76	31	905	20	3.3	1.8	2.9	11.0
James Edwards	C	7'	225	30	52	1314	318	587	54	212	302	70	301	74	200	5	23	29	848	25	5.8	1.4	3.8	16.3
Bernard Thompson	G	6'6	215	23	61	1281	195	399	49	127	157	81	141	132	151	0	51	10	517	21	2.3	2.2	2.5	8.5
Charles Pittman	F	6'8	220	27	69	1132	127	218	58	99	141	70	246	58	140	2	37	23	353	16	3.6	0.8	2.0	5.1
Georgi Glouchkov	F	6'8	235	25	49	772	84	209	40	70	122	57	163	32	124	0	26	25	239	16	3.3	0.7	2.5	4.9
Charles Jones	F	6'8	215	23	43	742	75	164	46	50	98	51	193	52	87	0	32	25	200	17	4.5	1.2	2.0	4.7
Rod Foster	G	6'1	160	25	48	704	85	218	39	23	32	72	58	121	77	0	22	1	202	15	1.2	2.5	1.6	4.2
Rick Robey	C-F	6'11	230	29	46	629	72	191	38	33	48	69	148	58	92	1	19	5	177	14	3.2	1.3	2.0	3.8
Sedric Toney (from Atl)	G	6'2	178	23	10	206	26	59	44	20	30	67	23	26	18	0	5	0	75	21	2.3	2.6	1.8	7.5
Nick Vanos	C	7'1	255	22	11	202	23	72	32	8	23	35	60	16	34	0	2	5	54	18	5.5	1.5	3.1	4.9
Michael Holton (to Chi)	F	6'4	185	24	4	65	4	20	20	4	6	67	3	7	7	0	2	0	12	16	0.8	1.8	1.8	3.0
Devin Durrant	F	6'7	200	25	4	51	8	21	38	1	4	25	8	5	10	0	3	0	17	13	2.0	1.3	2.5	4.3
3-PT FG -	Nance 0-8, Pinckney 0-2, Adams 0-2, Davis 18-76, Humphries 4-29, Sanders 3-15, Thompson 0-2, Glauchkov 1-1, Jones 0-1, Foster 9-32, Robey 0-3, Toney 3-10, Holton 0-2																							

1985/86 N.B.A. — WESTERN CONFERENCE
PACIFIC DIVISION

SEATTLE SUPERSONICS 31-51 .378 BERNIE BICKERSTAFF

Use Name	Pos	Hgt	Wgt	Age	G	Min	FG	FGA	%	FT	FTA	%	Reb	Ass	PF	DQ	Stls	Blkd Shts	Points	Min	Reb	Ass	PF	Points
					TOTAL															PER GAME				
Xavier McDaniel	F	6'7	205	22	82	2706	576	1176	49	250	364	69	655	193	305	8	101	37	1404	33	8.0	2.4	3.7	17.1
Tom Chambers	F	6'10	225	26	66	2019	432	928	47	346	414	84	431	132	248	6	55	37	1223	31	6.5	2.0	3.8	18.5
Jack Sikma	C-F	6'11	250	30	80	2790	508	1100	46	355	411	86	748	301	293	4	92	73	1371	35	9.4	3.8	3.7	17.1
Danny Young	G	6'4	175	23	82	1901	227	449	51	90	106	85	120	303	113	0	110	9	568	23	1.5	3.7	1.4	6.9
Gerald Henderson	G	6'2	175	29	82	2568	434	900	48	185	223	83	187	487	230	2	138	11	1071	31	2.3	5.9	2.8	13.1
Al Wood	G-F	6'6	193	27	78	1749	355	817	43	187	239	78	244	114	171	2	57	19	902	22	3.1	1.5	2.2	11.6
Tim McCormick	C	7'	240	23	77	1705	253	444	57	174	244	71	403	83	219	4	19	28	681	22	5.2	1.1	2.8	8.8
Danny Vranes	F	6'7	210	27	80	1569	131	284	46	39	75	52	281	68	218	3	63	31	301	20	3.5	0.9	2.7	3.8
Ricky Sobers	G	6'3	198	32	78	1279	240	541	44	110	125	88	99	180	139	1	44	2	603	16	1.3	2.3	1.8	7.7
Michael Phelps	G	6'4	180	24	70	880	117	286	41	44	74	59	89	71	86	0	45	1	279	13	1.3	1.0	1.2	4.0
Frank Brickowski	F	6'10	240	26	40	311	30	58	52	18	27	67	54	21	74	2	11	7	78	8	1.4	0.5	1.9	2.0
George Johnson	C	6'11	205	37	41	264	12	23	52	11	16	69	60	13	46	0	6	37	35	6	1.5	0.3	1.1	0.9
Rod Higgens (to SA, NJ, Chi)	F	6'7	205	25	12	94	9	27	33	3	5	60	12	6	11	0	2	1	22	8	1.0	0.5	0.9	1.8
David Pope	F	6'7	220	23	11	74	9	20	45	2	4	50	11	4	11	0	2	1	21	7	1.0	0.4	1.0	1.9
Alex Stivrins	F	6'8	220	23	3	14	1	4	25	1	4	25	3	1	2	0	0	0	3	5	1.0	0.3	0.7	1.0
Brian Martin (tp Port)	F	6'9	212	23	3	7	1	2	50	0	0	—	4	0	2	0	0	1	2	2	1.3	0.0	0.7	0.7

3-PT FG — McDaniel 2-10, Chambers 13-48, Sikma 0-13, Young 24-74, Henderson 18-52, Wood 5-37, McCormick 1-2, Vranes 0-4, Sobers 13-43, Phelps 1-12, Higgins 1-4, Pope 1-1

GOLDENSTATE WARRIORS 30-52 .366 JOHN BACH

Use Name	Pos	Hgt	Wgt	Age	G	Min	FG	FGA	%	FT	FTA	%	Reb	Ass	PF	DQ	Stls	Blkd Shts	Points	Min	Reb	Ass	PF	Points
Purvis Short	F	6'7	220	28	64	2427	633	1313	48	351	406	86	329	237	229	5	92	22	1632	38	5.1	3.7	3.6	25.5
Larry Smith	F	6'8	225	27	77	2441	314	586	54	112	227	49	856	95	286	7	62	50	740	32	11.1	1.2	3.7	9.6
Joe Barry Carroll	C	7'	250	27	79	2801	650	1404	46	377	501	75	670	176	277	13	101	143	1677	35	8.5	2.2	3.5	21.2
Terry Teagle	G	6'5	195	25	82	2158	475	958	50	211	265	80	235	115	241	2	71	34	1165	26	2.9	1.4	2.9	14.2
Eric Floyd	G	6'3	175	25	82	2764	510	1007	51	351	441	80	297	746	199	2	157	16	1410	34	3.6	9.1	2.4	17.2
Greg Ballard	F	6'7	215	30	75	1794	272	570	48	101	126	80	417	83	174	0	65	8	662	24	5.6	1.1	2.3	8.8
Chris Mullin	G	6'6	200	22	55	1391	287	620	46	189	211	90	115	105	130	1	70	23	768	25	2.1	1.9	2.4	14.0
Geoff Huston	G	6'2	175	28	82	1208	140	273	51	63	92	68	65	342	67	0	38	4	345	15	0.8	4.2	0.8	4.2
Jerome Whitehead	C	6'10	225	29	81	1079	126	294	43	60	97	62	328	19	176	2	18	19	312	13	4.0	0.2	2.2	3.9
Pete Verhoeven	F	6'9	215	26	61	749	90	167	54	25	43	58	160	29	141	3	29	17	206	12	2.6	0.5	2.3	3.4
Peter Thibeaux	F	6'7	210	24	42	531	100	233	43	29	48	60	75	28	82	1	23	15	231	13	1.8	0.7	2.0	5.5
Lester Conner	G	6'4	185	26	36	413	51	136	38	40	54	74	62	43	23	0	24	1	144	11	1.7	1.2	0.6	4.0
Guy Williams	F	6'9	200	25	5	25	2	5	40	3	6	50	6	0	7	1	1	2	7	5	1.2	0.0	1.4	1.4
Ron Crevier (to Det)	C	7'	235	27	1	1	0	1	0	0	0	—	0	0	0	0	0	0	0	1	0.0	0.0	0.0	0.0

3-PT FG — Short 15-49, Smith 0-1, Carroll 0-2, Teagle 4-25, 4-25, Floyd 39-119, Ballard 17-35, Mullin 5-27, Huston 2-6, Verhoeven 1-2, Thibeaux 2-5, Conner 2-7

PLAYOFFS

BOSTON CELTICS K.C. JONES

defeated Chicago 3-0; H123-104, H135-131 (2 OT), 122-104
defeated Atlanta 4-1; H103-91, H119-108, 111-107, 94-106, H132-99
defeated Milwaukee 4-0; H128-96, H122-111, 111-107, 111-98
defeated Houston 4-2; H112-100, H117-95, 104-106, 106-103, 96-111, H114-97

Use Name	Pos	Hgt	Wgt	Age	G	Min	FG	FGA	%	FT	FTA	%	Reb	Ass	PF	DQ	Stls	Blkd Shts	Points	Min	Reb	Ass	PF	Points
Larry Bird	F	6'9	220	29	18	770	171	331	52	101	109	93	168	148	55	0	37	11	466	43	9.3	8.2	3.1	25.9
Kevin McHale	F	6'10	225	28	18	715	168	290	58	112	141	79	155	48	64	0	8	43	448	40	8.6	2.7	3.6	24.9
Robert Parish	C	7'1	230	32	18	591	106	225	47	58	89	65	158	25	47	1	9	30	270	33	8.8	1.4	2.6	15.0
Danny Ainge	G	6'4	175	26	18	652	107	193	55	52	60	87	76	93	57	0	41	1	280	36	4.2	5.2	3.2	15.6
Dennis Johnson	G	6'4	200	31	18	715	109	245	44	67	84	80	76	107	58	2	39	5	291	40	4.2	5.9	3.2	16.2
Bill Walton	C-F	6'11	225	33	16	291	54	93	58	19	23	83	103	27	45	1	6	12	127	18	6.4	1.7	2.8	7.9
Jerry Sichting	G	6'1	178	29	18	274	27	61	44	3	7	43	16	40	18	0	5	0	57	15	0.9	2.2	1.0	3.2
Scott Wedman	F	6'7	235	33	12	142	20	51	39	3	4	75	22	8	14	0	9	3	45	12	1.8	0.7	1.2	3.8
Greg Kite	C	6'11	250	24	13	78	7	10	70	4	7	57	19	3	20	0	2	4	18	6	1.5	0.2	1.5	1.4
Rick Carlisle	G	6'5	210	26	10	54	8	15	53	3	4	75	5	8	9	0	2	0	19	5	0.5	0.8	0.9	1.9
David Thirdkill	F	6'7	215	25	13	47	6	18	33	5	11	45	8	3	5	0	2	0	17	4	0.6	0.2	0.4	1.3
Sam Vincent	G	6'2	185	22	9	41	8	28	29	6	6	100	7	5	9	0	2	0	22	5	0.8	0.6	1.0	2.4

3-PT FG — Bird 23-56, McHale 0-1, Ainge 14-34, Johnson 6-16, Walton 0-1, Sichting 0-1, Weldman 2-4, Thirdkill 0-1, Vincent 0-1

HOUSTON ROCKETS BILL FITCH

defeated Sacramento 3-0; H107-87, H111-103, 113-98
defeated Denver 4-2; H126-119, H119-101, 115-116, 111-114 (OT), H131-103, 126-122 (2OT)
defeated Los Angeles Lakers 4-1; 107-119, 112-102, H117-109, H105-95, 114-112
lost to Boston 2-4; 100-112, 95-117, H106-104, H103-106, H111-96, 97-114

Use Name	Pos	Hgt	Wgt	Age	G	Min	FG	FGA	%	FT	FTA	%	Reb	Ass	PF	DQ	Stls	Blkd Shts	Points	Min	Reb	Ass	PF	Points
Rodney McCray	F	6'8	220	24	20	**835**	108	202	53	43	58	74	118	125	45	0	18	19	259	42	5.9	6.3	2.3	13.0
Ralph Sampson	F-C	7'4	228	25	20	741	156	301	52	86	118	73	215	80	79	1	30	35	399	37	10.8	4.0	4.0	20.0
Akeem Olajuwon	C	7'	250	22	20	766	**205**	**387**	53	**127**	**199**	64	**236**	39	**87**	**3**	40	**69**	**537**	38	11.8	2.0	4.4	26.9
Lewis Lloyd	G-F	6'6	215	26	20	589	116	241	48	47	58	81	66	86	47	0	16	6	281	29	3.3	4.3	2.4	14.1
Robert Reid	G-F	6'8	205	30	20	773	124	288	43	47	59	80	83	137	74	1	27	1	298	39	4.2	6.9	3.7	14.9
Mitchell Wiggins	G	6'4	185	26	20	443	89	179	50	21	28	75	76	31	44	0	14	3	199	22	3.8	1.6	2.2	10.0
Jim Petersen	F-C	6'10	235	23	20	378	44	108	41	23	33	70	111	21	58	1	9	9	111	19	5.6	1.1	2.9	5.6
Allen Leavwll	G	6'1	190	28	15	170	24	80	30	20	23	87	15	40	12	0	9	0	75	11	1.0	2.7	0.8	5.0
Steve Harris	G	6'5	195	22	15	83	14	29	48	2	5	40	10	2	3	0	4	3	30	6	0.7	0.1	0.2	2.0
Craig Ehlo	G	6'7	180	24	10	38	8	16	50	4	5	80	3	6	4	0	4	1	20	4	0.3	0.6	0.4	2.0
Hank McDowell	F	6'9	215	26	13	33	2	7	29	5	8	63	8	2	6	0	0	0	9	3	0.6	0.2	0.5	0.7
Granville Waiters	C	6'11	225	24	11	26	4	7	57	0	0	—	5	0	3	0	1	3	8	2	0.5	0.0	0.3	0.7

3-PT FG — McCray 0-3, Sampson 1-1, Olajuwan 0-1, Lloyd 2-5, Reid 3-21, Wiggins 0-3, Leavell 7-15, Ehlo 0-1

1985/86 N.B.A. — PLAYOFFS (continued)

LOS ANGELES LAKERS — **PAT RILEY**

defeated San Antonio 3-0; H135-88, H122-94, 114-94
defeated Dallas 4-2; H130-116, H113-113, 108-110, 118-120, H116-113, 120-107
lost to Houston 1-4; H119-107, H102-112, 109-117, 95-105, H112-114

Use Name	Pos	Hgt	Wgt	Age	G	Min	FG	FGA	%	FT	FTA	%	Reb	Ass	PF	DQ	Stls	Blkd Shts	Points	Min/G	Reb/G	Ass/G	PF/G	Points/G
James Worthy	F	6'9	225	24	14	539	121	217	56	32	47	68	65	45	43	0	16	10	274	39	4.6	3.2	3.1	19.6
Maurice Lucas	F-C	6'9	238	33	14	319	59	112	53	14	19	74	91	10	53	0	6	5	132	23	6.5	0.7	3.8	9.4
Kareem Abdul-Jabbar	C	7'2	232	38	14	489	157	282	56	48	61	79	83	49	54	0	15	24	362	35	5.9	3.5	3.9	25.9
Byron Scott	G	6'3	195	24	14	470	90	181	50	38	42	90	55	42	38	0	19	2	224	34	3.9	3.0	2.7	16.0
Magic Johnson	G	6'8	215	26	14	541	110	205	54	82	107	77	100	**211**	43	0	27	1	302	39	7.1	15.1	3.1	21.6
Michael Cooper	G-F	6'5	170	29	14	421	54	115	47	9	11	82	46	68	24	0	18	4	136	30	3.3	4.9	1.7	9.7
Kurt Rambis	F	6'8	220	27	14	267	27	45	60	13	18	72	83	14	39	0	10	7	67	19	5.9	1.0	2.8	4.8
Petur Gudmundson	C	7'2	260	27	12	111	16	27	59	10	15	67	26	3	23	1	3	4	42	9	2.2	0.3	1.9	3.5
A.C. Green	F	6'9	220	22	9	106	9	17	53	4	9	44	16	0	13	0	1	3	22	12	1.8	0.0	1.4	2.4
Mitch Kupchak	F	6'9	230	31	5	56	8	15	53	4	6	67	15	2	6	0	2	0	20	11	3.0	0.4	1.2	4.0
Mike McGee	G-F	6'5	190	26	6	28	8	18	44	0	4	0	5	2	3	0	1	0	16	5	0.8	0.3	0.5	2.7
Larry Spriggs	F	6'7	230	26	3	13	5	6	83	10	10	100	7	2	0	0	1	0	20	4	2.3	0.7	0.0	6.7

3-PT FG — Worthy 0-4, Scott 6-17, Johnson 0-11, Cooper 19-41,Gudmundsson 0-2, McGee 0-3

MILWAUKEE BUCKS — **DON NELSON**

defeated New Jersey 3-0; H119-107, H111-97, 118-113
defeated Philadelphia 4-3; H112-118, H119-107, 103-107, 109-104, H113-108, 108-126, H113-112
lost to Boston 0-4; 96-128, 111-122, H107-111; H98-11

Use Name	Pos	Hgt	Wgt	Age	G	Min	FG	FGA	%	FT	FTA	%	Reb	Ass	PF	DQ	Stls	Blkd Shts	Points	Min/G	Reb/G	Ass/G	PF/G	Points/G
Ricky Pierce	F	6'5	205	26	13	322	52	113	46	40	45	89	36	20	42	0	8	3	144	25	2.8	1.5	3.2	11.1
Terry Cummings	F	6'9	225	24	14	510	130	253	51	43	62	69	138	42	52	0	20	16	303	36	9.9	3.0	3.7	21.6
Alton Lister	C	7'	240	27	14	335	66	103	64	35	58	60	96	12	56	3	7	22	167	24	6.9	0.9	4.0	11.9
Sidney Moncrief	G	6'4	190	28	9	327	52	122	43	44	63	70	41	44	30	0	5	5	152	36	4.6	4.9	3.3	16.9
Paul Pressey	G	6'5	185	27	14	530	76	157	48	67	88	76	60	110	48	0	18	13	225	38	4.3	7.9	3.4	16.1
Craig Hodges	G	6'3	190	25	14	460	74	145	51	27	34	79	25	63	44	1	32	2	189	33	1.8	4.5	3.1	13.5
Randy Breuer	C	7'3	230	25	14	318	46	86	53	26	38	68	60	11	38	1	11	18	118	23	4.3	0.8	2.7	8.4
Kenny Fields	F	6'5	220	23	12	158	38	69	55	12	23	52	28	10	23	0	8	0	89	13	2.3	0.8	1.9	7.4
Charlie Davis	F	6'7	215	27	12	145	21	58	36	18	20	90	25	6	28	1	4	0	60	12	2.1	0.5	2.3	5.0
Mike Glenn	G	6'3	185	30	10	114	13	36	36	10	12	83	11	8	6	0	1	0	36	11	1.1	0.8	0.6	3.6
Paul Mokeski	F-C	7'	250	28	14	101	14	27	52	6	9	67	24	8	27	1	6	3	34	7	1.7	0.6	1.9	2.4
Jerry Reynolds	F	6'8	200	23	7	40	7	17	41	6	11	55	9	4	5	0	4	3	20	6	1.3	0.6	0.7	2.9

3-PT FG — Pierce 0-2, Lester 0-1, Moncrief 4-14, Pressey 6-18, Hodges 14-31, Fields 1-3, Davis 0-1, Glenn 0-1, Reynolds 0-1

PHILADELPHIA 76ERS — **MATT GUOKAS**

defeated Washington 3-2; H94-95, H102-97, 91-86, 111-116, H134-109
lost to Milwaukee 3-4; 118-112, 107-119, H107-103, H104-109, 118-113, H126-108, 112-113

Use Name	Pos	Hgt	Wgt	Age	G	Min	FG	FGA	%	FT	FTA	%	Reb	Ass	PF	DQ	Stls	Blkd Shts	Points	Min/G	Reb/G	Ass/G	PF/G	Points/G
Bobby Jones	F	6'9	212	34	12	329	39	74	53	38	50	76	32	34	39	0	10	14	116	27	2.7	2.8	3.3	9.7
Charles Barkley	F	6'6	260	22	12	497	104	180	58	91	131	69	189	67	52	2	27	15	300	41	15.8	5.6	4.3	25.0
Clemon Johnson	C	6'10	240	29	12	303	29	53	55	16	25	64	60	8	35	0	11	15	74	25	5.0	0.7	2.9	6.2
Maurice Cheeks	G	6'1	180	29	12	519	94	182	52	62	75	83	56	85	18	0	13	3	250	43	4.7	7.1	1.5	20.8
Julius Erving	G-F	6'7	205	35	12	433	81	180	45	48	65	74	70	50	32	0	11	16	212	36	5.8	4.2	2.7	17.7
Sedale Threatt	G	6'2	175	24	12	312	67	143	47	26	33	79	25	42	35	0	23	2	160	26	2.1	3.5	2.9	13.3
Terry Catledge	F-C	6'8	220	22	11	293	46	117	39	22	38	58	75	5	34	0	6	8	114	27	6.8	0.5	3.1	10.4
Greg Stokes	C	6'10	220	22	7	90	8	28	29	11	13	85	13	4	12	0	2	6	27	13	1.9	0.6	1.7	3.9
Bob McAdoo	C	6'9	225	34	5	73	20	36	56	14	16	88	14	2	13	0	4	5	54	15	2.8	0.4	2.6	10.8
Perry Moss	G	6'2	190	27	7	28	2	8	25	1	1	100	3	2	6	0	0	1	5	4	0.4	0.3	0.9	0.7
Michael Young	F	6'7	220	24	3	3	1	4	25	0	0	—	1	0	0	0	0	0	2	1	0.3	0.0	0.0	0.7

Moses Malone - eye injury
Andrew Toney - foot injury

3-PT FG — Jones 0-1, Barkley 1-15, Cheeks 0-7, Erving 2-11, Threatt 0-2, Jones 0-1

DALLAS MAVERICKS — **DICK MOTTA**

defeated Utah 3-1; H101-93, H113-106, 98-100, 117-113
lost to L.A. Lakers 2-4; 116-130, 113-117, H110-108, H120-118, 113-116, H107-120

Use Name	Pos	Hgt	Wgt	Age	G	Min	FG	FGA	%	FT	FTA	%	Reb	Ass	PF	DQ	Stls	Blkd Shts	Points	Min/G	Reb/G	Ass/G	PF/G	Points/G
Mark Aguirre	F-G	6'6	235	26	10	345	105	214	49	35	55	64	71	54	28	1	9	0	247	35	7.1	5.4	2.8	24.7
Sam Perkins	F-C	6'9	235	24	10	347	57	133	43	33	43	77	83	24	32	0	9	14	149	35	8.3	2.4	3.2	14.9
James Donaldson	C	7'2	278	28	10	410	36	48	**75**	37	40	93	117	10	26	0	6	12	109	41	11.7	1.0	2.6	10.9
Rolando Blackman	G	6'6	190	26	10	371	83	167	50	42	53	79	35	32	26	1	8	1	208	37	3.5	3.2	2.6	20.8
Derek Harper	G	6'4	185	24	10	348	57	107	53	12	16	75	19	76	27	0	23	0	134	35	1.9	7.6	2.7	13.4
Jay Vincent	F	6'7	225	26	10	204	38	99	38	30	34	88	39	15	19	0	4	1	106	20	3.9	1.5	1.9	10.6
Brad Davis	G	6'3	180	30	10	163	24	44	55	19	24	79	19	23	22	0	3	0	77	16	1.9	2.3	2.2	7.7
Detlef Schrempf	F	6'9	220	22	10	120	13	28	46	11	17	65	23	14	24	0	2	1	37	12	2.3	1.4	2.4	3.7
Dale Ellis	F	6'7	205	25	7	67	9	22	41	5	5	100	7	2	6	0	2	2	30	10	1.0	0.3	0.9	4.3
Bill Wennington	C	7'	245	21	6	18	2	6	33	2	2	100	5	0	4	0	0	0	7	3	0.8	0.0	0.7	1.2
Uwe Blab	C	7'1	255	23	1	6	2	3	67	0	0	—	1	0	1	0	0	0	4	6	1.0	0.0	1.0	4.0
Harold Keeling	G	6'4	185	22	1	1	0	0	—	0	0	—	0	0	0	0	0	0	0	1	0.0	0.0	0.0	0.0

3-PT FG — Aguirre 2-6, Perkins 2-8, Blackman 0-1, Harper 8-14, Davis 10-15, Schrempff 0-1, Ellis 7-12, Wennington 1-1

1985/86 N.B.A. — PLAYOFFS (continued)

DENVER NUGGETS — **DOUG MOE** — defeated Portland 3-1; H133-126, H106-108, 115-104, 116-112
lost to Houston 2-4; 119-126, 101-119, H116-115, H114-111(OT), 103-131, H122-126(2OT)

Use Name	Pos	Hgt	Wgt	Age	G	Min	FG	FGA	%	FT	FTA	%	Reb	Ass	PF	DQ	Stls	Blkd Shts	Points	Per Game Min	Reb	Ass	PF	Points
Alex English	F	6'8	190	31	10	394	106	229	46	61	71	86	35	52	29	0	4	4	273	39	3.5	5.2	2.9	27.3
Calvin Natt	F	6'6	220	28	10	293	66	142	46	46	59	78	79	28	25	0	2	3	179	29	7.9	2.8	2.5	17.9
Danny Schayes	C-F	6'11	245	26	10	295	46	86	53	24	30	80	82	9	37	1	4	17	116	30	8.2	0.9	3.7	11.6
T.R. Dunn	G	6'4	192	30	10	276	20	46	43	9	14	64	53	13	34	1	16	0	49	28	5.3	1.3	3.4	4.9
Lafayette Lever	G	6'3	175	25	10	347	59	131	45	17	24	71	48	53	33	0	20	2	143	35	4.8	5.3	3.3	14.3
Mike Evans	G	6'1	170	30	10	204	30	82	37	25	30	83	20	25	19	0	10	3	92	20	2.0	2.5	1.9	9.2
Elston Turner	G-F	6'5	220	26	10	196	29	54	54	7	8	88	29	22	19	1	7	0	66	20	2.9	2.2	1.9	6.6
Blair Rasmussen	C	7'	250	23	10	175	39	96	41	33	41	80	60	10	28	1	5	9	111	18	6.0	1.0	2.8	11.1
Wayne Cooper	C	6'10	220	29	8	154	24	56	43	15	22	68	40	7	31	2	2	5	63	19	5.0	0.9	3.9	7.9
Bill Hanzlik	F-G	6'7	185	28	6	102	15	28	54	13	16	81	6	19	12	0	1	1	44	17	1.0	3.2	2.0	7.3
Willie White	G	6'3	195	23	4	21	2	7	29	0	0	—	3	6	4	0	1	0	5	5	0.8	1.5	1.0	1.3
Pete Williams	F	6'7	190	22	4	18	2	4	50	0	0	—	4	3	2	0	0	0	4	5	1.0	0.8	0.5	1.0

3-PT FG — English 0-1, Natt 1-2, Lever 8-14, Evans 7-29, Turner 1-1, Cooper 0-1, Hanzlik 1-1, White 1-4, Williams 0-1

ATLANTA HAWKS — **MIKE FRATELLO** — defeated Detroit 3-1; H144-122, H137-125, 97-106, 114-113(2OT)
lost to Boston 1-4; 91-103, 108-119, H107-111, H106-94, 99-132

Use Name	Pos	Hgt	Wgt	Age	G	Min	FG	FGA	%	FT	FTA	%	Reb	Ass	PF	DQ	Stls	Blkd Shts	Points	Per Game Min	Reb	Ass	PF	Points
Dominique Wilkins	F	6'8	200	25	9	360	94	217	43	68	79	86	54	25	24	0	9	2	257	40	6.0	2.8	2.7	**28.6**
Kevin Willis	F	7'	220	23	9	280	55	98	56	15	23	65	65	5	38	2	7	8	125	31	7.2	0.6	4.2	13.9
Tree Rollins	C	7'1	235	30	9	248	26	47	55	7	11	64	78	3	32	2	2	15	59	28	8.7	0.3	3.6	6.6
Randy Wittman	G	6'6	210	26	9	348	71	135	53	18	26	69	24	30	16	0	10	1	160	39	2.7	3.3	1.8	17.8
Glenn Rivers	G	6'4	185	24	9	262	40	92	43	31	42	74	42	78	38	2	18	0	114	29	4.7	8.7	4.2	12.7
Jon Koncak	C	7'	250	22	9	193	14	29	48	26	46	57	34	5	27	2	6	10	54	21	3.8	0.6	3.0	6.0
Spud Webb	G	5'7	135	22	9	183	42	81	52	26	33	79	31	65	13	0	4	1	110	20	3.4	7.2	1.4	12.2
Cliff Levingston	F	6'8	220	24	9	180	22	37	59	7	9	78	41	3	23	0	4	9	52	20	4.6	0.3	2.6	5.8
Johnny Davis	G	6'2	180	30	8	65	9	25	36	4	4	100	6	15	6	0	2	0	22	8	0.8	1.9	0.8	2.8
Scott Hastings	F	6'10	235	25	9	49	11	14	79	5	11	45	10	2	11	0	2	0	28	5	1.1	0.2	1.2	3.1
John Battle	G	6'2	175	23	6	27	4	11	36	3	4	75	4	2	5	0	2	0	11	5	0.7	0.3	0.8	1.8
Lorenzo Charles	F	6'7	225	22	4	15	3	4	75	1	1	100	2	2	1	0	0	0	7	4	0.5	0.5	0.3	1.8

3-PT FG — Wilkins 1-5, Wittman 0-2, Rivers 3-6, Webb 0-2, Levingston 1-1, Hastings 1-4, Battle 0-1

WASHINGTON BULLETS — **KEVIN LOUGHERY** — lost to Philadelphia 2-3; 95-94, 97-102, H86-91, H116-111, 109-134

Use Name	Pos	Hgt	Wgt	Age	G	Min	FG	FGA	%	FT	FTA	%	Reb	Ass	PF	DQ	Stls	Blkd Shts	Points	Per Game Min	Reb	Ass	PF	Points
Cliff Robinson	F	6'9	230	25	5	177	46	93	49	15	31	48	43	17	19	1	10	3	107	35	8.6	3.4	3.8	21.4
Dan Roundfield	F	6'8	215	32	5	177	28	53	53	14	17	82	46	10	17	0	2	4	70	35	9.2	2.0	3.4	14.0
Manute Bol	C	7'6	200	23	5	152	10	17	59	3	8	38	38	1	15	0	3	29	23	30	7.6	0.2	3.0	4.6
Jeff Malone	G	6'4	205	24	5	197	42	103	41	26	29	90	16	17	13	0	7	3	110	39	3.2	3.4	2.6	22.0
Gus Williams	G	6'2	175	32	5	199	38	79	48	14	18	78	10	33	11	0	11	0	91	40	2.0	6.6	2.2	18.2
Dudley Bradley	G	6'6	195	28	5	82	12	29	41	6	9	67	5	7	14	0	5	0	33	16	1.0	1.4	2.8	6.6
Charles Jones	F	6'9	215	28	5	72	4	11	36	4	4	100	9	3	13	0	2	2	12	14	1.8	0.6	2.6	2.4
Jeff Ruland	C	6'10	240	27	2	54	7	14	50	14	17	82	12	10	6	0	0	2	28	27	6.0	5.0	3.0	14.0
Tom McMillan	C-F	6'11	235	33	4	54	8	16	50	0	0	—	5	7	2	0	3	0	16	14	1.3	1.8	0.5	4.0
Darren Dave	F	6'8	220	25	4	32	4	12	33	0	2	0	8	0	3	0	0	0	8	8	2.0	0.0	0.8	2.0
Leon Wood	G	6'3	185	23	1	2	1	5	20	2	2	100	0	0	0	0	0	0	5	2	0.0	0.0	0.0	5.0
Kevin McKenna	G	6'5	195	26	1	2	0	0	—	0	0	—	0	0	0	0	0	0	0	2	0.0	0.0	0.0	0.0

3-PT FG — Roundfield 0-1, Malone 0-2, Williams 1-10, Bradley 3-10, Wood 1-1

UTAH JAZZ — **FRANK LAYDEN** — lost to Dallas 1-3; 93-101, 106-113, H100-98, H113-117

Use Name	Pos	Hgt	Wgt	Age	G	Min	FG	FGA	%	FT	FTA	%	Reb	Ass	PF	DQ	Stls	Blkd Shts	Points	Per Game Min	Reb	Ass	PF	Points
Marc Iavaroni	F	6'9	225	29	4	73	5	16	31	3	4	75	9	6	9	0	1	0	13	18	2.3	1.5	2.3	3.3
Karl Malone	F	6'9	250	22	4	144	38	72	53	11	26	42	30	4	18	1	8	0	87	36	7.5	1.0	4.5	21.8
Mark Eaton	C	7'4	280	28	4	157	28	57	49	2	3	67	36	10	12	0	1	18	58	39	9.0	2.5	3.0	14.5
Bob Hansen	G	6'6	190	24	4	140	27	37	73	8	9	89	18	11	16	0	3	1	64	35	4.5	2.8	4.0	16.0
Rickey Green	G	6'1	170	31	4	119	21	43	49	10	11	91	9	38	1	0	2	0	53	30	2.3	9.5	0.3	13.3
Thurl Bailey	F-G-C	6'11	215	24	4	147	28	77	36	8	11	73	32	13	13	0	2	2	64	37	8.0	3.3	3.3	16.0
John Stockton	G	6'1	170	23	4	73	9	17	53	8	9	89	6	14	10	0	5	0	27	18	1.5	3.5	2.5	6.8
Carey Scurry	F	6'7	190	23	4	54	8	20	40	1	2	50	16	3	12	0	1	4	17	14	4.0	0.8	3.0	4.3
Fred Roberts	F	6'10	220	25	4	31	7	15	47	8	9	89	7	3	5	0	0	0	22	8	1.8	0.8	1.3	5.5
Jeff Cook	C	6'10	215	29	4	21	1	4	25	3	4	75	5	2	4	0	0	0	5	5	1.3	0.5	1.0	1.3
Steve Hayes	C	7'	235	30	1	1	1	1	100	0	0	—	1	0	0	0	0	0	2	1	1.0	0.0	0.0	2.0

3-PT FG — Hansen 2-3, Green 1-2, Bailey 0-1, Stockton 1-1, Scurry 0-2

PORTLAND TRAIL BLAZERS — **JACK RAMSAY** — lost to Denver 3-1; 126-133, 108-106, H104-115, H112-116

Use Name	Pos	Hgt	Wgt	Age	G	Min	FG	FGA	%	FT	FTA	%	Reb	Ass	PF	DQ	Stls	Blkd Shts	Points	Per Game Min	Reb	Ass	PF	Points
Kiki Vandeweghe	F	6'8	220	27	4	149	40	69	58	32	32	**100**	5	8	12	0	2	2	112	37	1.3	2.0	3.0	28.0
Kenny Carr	F	6'7	230	30	4	143	24	42	57	11	15	73	53	7	18	1	5	1	59	36	13.3	1.8	4.5	14.8
Mychal Thompson	C-F	6'10	226	30	4	140	31	54	57	14	26	54	33	14	13	0	1	3	76	35	8.3	3.5	3.3	19.0
Clyde Drexler	G	6'7	210	23	4	145	26	57	46	18	23	78	25	26	19	1	6	3	72	36	6.3	6.5	4.8	18.0
Steve Colter	G	6'3	165	23	4	104	12	26	46	2	2	100	15	23	13	0	5	1	26	26	3.8	5.8	3.3	6.5
Caldwell Jones	C	6'11	225	35	4	73	6	17	35	2	4	50	19	3	13	0	0	2	14	18	4.8	0.8	3.3	3.5
Jim Paxon	G-F	6'6	200	28	4	71	14	37	38	12	15	80	4	15	12	1	3	0	42	18	1.0	3.8	3.0	10.5
Terry Porter	G	6'3	195	22	4	68	12	27	44	2	4	50	5	12	10	0	3	2	27	17	1.3	3.0	2.5	6.8
Jerome Kersey	F	6'7	215	23	4	56	9	22	41	4	4	100	15	4	13	0	1	4	22	14	3.8	1.0	3.3	5.5
Ken Johnson	F	6'8	240	23	2	11	0	0	—	0	0	—	2	0	1	0	2	0	0	6	1.0	0.0	0.5	0.0

3-PT FG — Vandeweghe 0-2, Carr 0-1, Drexler 2-5, Colter 0-1, Paxon 2-6, Porter 1-6, Kersey 0-1

1985/86 N.B.A. — PLAYOFFS

Use Name	Pos	Hgt	Wgt	Age	G	Min	FG	FGA	%	FT	FTA	%	Reb	Ass	PF	Disq	Stls	Blkd Shts	Points	Min	Reb	Ass	PF	Points
					TOTAL															PER GAME				
DETROIT PISTONS	**CHUCK DALY**				lost to Atlanta 1-3; 122-140, 125-137, H106-97, 114-113 (2OT)																			
Kelly Tripucka	F	6'6	220	26	4	175	33	71	46	21	23	91	23	4	14	1	3	2	87	44	5.8	1.0	3.5	21.8
Earl Cureton	F	6'9	215	28	4	126	17	31	55	2	8	25	30	9	14	0	5	0	36	32	7.5	2.3	3.5	9.0
Bill Laimbeer	C	6'11	245	28	4	168	34	68	50	21	23	91	56	1	19	1	2	3	90	42	14.0	0.3	4.8	22.5
Joe Dumars	G	6'3	190	22	4	147	25	41	61	10	15	67	13	25	16	0	4	0	60	37	3.3	6.3	4.0	15.0
Isiah Thomas	G	6'1	185	24	4	163	41	91	45	24	36	67	22	48	17	0	9	3	106	41	5.5	12.0	4.3	26.5
Vinnie Johnson	G	6'2	200	29	4	85	22	49	45	7	13	54	17	11	9	0	3	0	51	21	4.3	2.8	2.3	12.8
Rick Mahorn	C-F	6'10	240	27	4	61	5	13	38	2	2	100	12	0	14	0	1	0	12	15	3.0	0.0	3.5	3.0
Kent Benson	F	6'10	245	31	4	55	4	10	40	0	0	—	13	0	11	0	0	2	8	14	3.3	0.0	2.8	2.0
Tony Campbell	F	6'7	215	23	2	16	4	10	40	1	2	50	2	0	5	0	0	0	9	8	1.0	0.0	2.5	4.5
John Long	G	6'5	200	29	1	13	2	5	40	3	3	100	1	0	1	0	1	0	7	13	1.0	0.0	1.0	7.0
Chuck Nevitt	C	7'5	237	26	1	1	0	0	—	0	0	—	0	0	0	0	0	0	0	1	0.0	0.0	0.0	0.0
3-PT FG —	Cureton 0-1, Laimbeer 1-1, Thomas 0-5, Johnson 0-1																							
CHICAGO BULLS	**STAN ALBECK**				lost to Boston 0-3; 104-123, 131-135 (2OT), H104-122																			
Orlando Woolridge	F	6'9	215	26	3	135	25	62	40	13	15	87	14	4	12	0	3	1	63	45	4.7	1.3	4.0	21.0
Charles Oakey	F	6'8	225	22	3	88	11	21	52	8	13	62	30	3	13	0	6	2	30	29	10.0	1.0	4.3	10.0
Dave Corzine	C	6'11	260	29	3	103	16	29	55	4	4	100	27	6	12	0	1	2	36	34	9.0	2.0	4.0	12.0
Michael Jordan	G	6'6	195	22	3	135	48	95	51	34	39	87	19	17	13	1	7	4	131	45	6.3	5.7	4.3	43.7
Kyle Macy	G	6'3	190	28	3	87	5	14	36	1	1	100	4	10	9	0	2	0	12	29	1.3	3.3	3.0	4.0
John Paxon	G	6'2	185	25	3	80	7	15	47	13	17	76	0	5	9	0	3	0	27	27	0.0	1.7	3.0	9.0
Gene Banks	F	6'7	215	26	3	69	10	18	56	2	4	50	10	5	10	0	1	0	22	23	3.3	1.7	3.3	7.3
Sidney Green	C-F	6'9	220	24	3	53	6	20	30	6	12	50	12	0	9	0	1	1	18	18	4.0	0.0	3.0	6.0
George Gervin	G	6'7	185	33	2	11	0	1	0	0	0	—	1	1	3	0	0	0	0	6	0.5	0.5	1.5	0.0
Mike Smrek	C	7'	250	23	3	5	0	1	0	0	0	—	0	0	2	0	0	0	0	2	0.0	0.0	0.7	0.0
Jawaan Oldham	C	7'	215	28	1	4	0	1	0	0	0	—	2	0	0	0	0	0	0	4	2.0	0.0	0.0	0.0
3-PT FG —	Woolridge 0-1, Jordan 1-1, Macy 1-4, Banks 0-2																							
NEW JERSEY NETS	**DAVE WOHL**				lost to Milwaukee 0-3; 107-119, 97-111, H113-118																			
Albert King	F	6'6	190	26	3	98	18	42	43	4	4	100	13	10	15	1	2	1	41	33	4.3	3.3	5.0	13.7
Buck Williams	F	6'8	215	25	3	126	21	29	72	20	26	77	31	2	15	1	6	1	62	42	10.3	0.7	5.0	20.7
Mike Gminski	C	6'11	250	26	3	109	16	43	37	26	27	96	30	5	11	0	4	2	58	36	10.0	1.7	3.7	19.3
Otis Birdsong	G	6'4	195	30	3	132	29	55	53	11	19	58	12	10	14	0	6	3	69	44	4.0	3.3	4.7	23.0
Darwin Cook	G	6'3	190	27	3	77	13	29	45	2	6	33	7	17	11	1	5	2	28	26	2.3	5.7	3.7	9.3
Kelvin Ransey	G	6'1	180	27	3	68	10	22	45	6	8	75	7	12	9	0	1	0	27	23	2.3	4.0	3.0	9.0
Mickey Johnson	F	6'10	190	33	3	54	5	19	26	7	11	64	11	2	7	0	2	0	17	18	3.7	0.7	2.3	5.7
Mike O'Koren	F-G	6'7	217	27	2	21	1	6	17	0	0	—	2	2	5	0	2	1	2	11	1.0	1.0	2.5	1.0
Jeff Turner	C	6'9	230	23	3	18	1	3	33	1	1	100	3	3	7	0	0	0	3	6	1.0	1.0	2.3	1.0
Darryl Dawkins	C	6'11	251	28	1	17	4	6	67	2	3	67	3	3	4	0	0	2	10	17	3.0	3.0	4.0	10.0
3-PT FG —	King 1-4, Birdsong 0-3, Cook 0-4, Ransey 1-3, Johnson 0-2, O'Koren 0-1																							
SACRAMENTO KINGS	**PHIL JOHNSON**				lost to Houston 0-3; 87-107, 130-111, H98-113																			
Eddie Johnson	F	6'8	215	26	3	96	24	55	44	8	9	89	21	4	7	0	3	1	56	32	7.0	1.3	2.3	18.7
Mark Olberding	F	6'8	230	29	3	74	3	9	33	9	12	75	13	3	9	0	2	1	15	25	4.3	1.0	3.0	5.0
LaSalle Thompson	C	6'10	248	24	3	99	11	32	34	7	12	58	35	2	8	0	2	6	29	33	11.7	0.7	2.7	9.7
Mike Woodson	G	6'5	198	27	3	110	22	49	45	12	12	100	11	5	13	0	4	2	56	37	3.7	1.7	4.3	18.7
Reggie Theus	G	6'7	205	28	3	102	18	46	39	9	12	75	8	19	9	0	3	2	45	34	2.7	6.3	3.0	15.0
Larry Drew	G	6'1	180	27	3	56	14	25	56	2	2	100	1	14	2	0	5	0	31	19	0.3	4.7	0.7	10.3
Terry Tyler	F	6'7	220	29	3	51	2	10	20	4	4	100	8	4	5	0	2	3	8	17	2.7	1.3	1.7	2.7
Joe Kleine	C	7'	255	23	3	45	5	13	38	5	6	83	14	1	8	0	1	1	15	15	4.7	0.3	2.7	5.0
Otis Thorpe	F	6'11	225	23	3	35	3	13	23	6	13	46	12	0	4	0	0	1	12	12	4.0	0.0	1.3	4.0
Rich Kelley	F	7'	240	32	3	35	3	9	33	5	6	83	12	4	5	0	2	0	11	12	4.0	1.3	1.7	3.7
Mike Bratz	G	6'2	185	30	3	15	3	6	50	1	1	100	4	1	0	0	0	0	7	5	1.3	0.3	0.0	2.3
Carl Henry	G	6'6	205	25	1	2	1	1	100	0	0	—	0	0	0	0	0	0	3	2	0.0	0.0	0.0	3.0
3-PT FG —	Johnson 0-3, Woodson 0-2, Theus 0-1, Drew 1-3, Henry 1-1																							
SAN ANTONIO SPURS	**COTTON FITZSIMMONS**				lost to LA Lakers 3-0; 88-135, 94-122, H94-114																			
Mike Mitchell	F	6'7	215	29	3	107	21	52	40	5	10	50	9	10	8	1	3	3	47	36	3.0	3.3	2.7	15.7
Dave Greenwood	F	6'9	232	28	3	101	12	23	52	6	8	75	18	3	12	0	3	1	30	34	6.0	1.0	4.0	10.0
Artis Gilmore	C	7'2	255	36	3	107	16	24	67	8	14	57	18	3	11	0	7	1	40	36	6.0	1.0	3.7	13.3
Alvin Robertson	G	6'3	185	23	3	98	8	29	28	11	13	85	14	19	10	0	7	1	27	33	4.7	6.3	3.3	9.0
Wes Matthews	G	6'1	170	26	3	116	35	54	65	6	8	75	7	24	7	0	6	0	76	39	2.3	8.0	2.3	25.3
Steve Johnson	F-C	6'10	245	28	3	53	5	15	33	5	11	45	6	2	14	1	0	1	15	18	2.0	0.7	4.7	5.0
Jeff Lamp	G-F	6'6	195	26	3	45	7	18	39	0	0	—	1	7	6	0	1	0	15	15	0.3	2.3	2.0	5.0
Jon Sundvold	G	6'2	170	24	3	43	7	18	39	1	1	100	1	5	1	0	0	0	16	14	0.3	1.7	0.3	5.3
Alfred Hughes	F	6'5	215	23	3	18	4	9	44	0	0	—	0	1	3	0	1	0	8	6	0.0	0.3	1.0	2.7
Jeff Wilkins	C	6'11	240	30	3	16	0	1	0	0	0	—	3	0	6	0	0	2	0	5	1.0	0.0	2.0	0.0
Tyrone Corbin	F	6'6	210	23	1	14	0	4	0	0	0	—	1	1	0	0	0	0	0	14	1.0	1.0	0.0	0.0
Mike Brittain	C	7'	235	22	1	2	1	2	50	0	0	—	1	0	0	0	0	1	2	2	1.0	0.0	0.0	2.0
3-PT FG —	Matthews 0-1, Lamp 1-3, Sunvold 1-6																							

Team		G	FG	FGA	%	FT	FTA	%	REBOUNDS Offense	Defense	Total	Assists	PF	Steals	Blocked Shots	Turn Overs	Points	Points per game
TEAM STATISTICS																		
EASTERN CONFERENCE ATLANTIC DIVISION																		
Boston	Off.	82	3718	7312	51	1785	2248	79	1054	**2753**	**3807**	2387	1756	641	511	1360	9359	114.1
	Def.	82	3444	7476	46	1617	2162	75	1089	2317	3406	1924	1966	725	341	1258	8587	104.7
	Diff.		+274	-164	**+5**	+168	+86	+4	-35	**+436**	**+401**	**+463**	+210	-84	+170	-102	**+772**	**+9.4**
Philadelphia	Off.	82	3435	7058	49	2130	**2810**	76	**1326**	2378	3704	2017	1798	**862**	490	1595	9051	110.4
	Def.	82	3615	7328	49	1546	2041	76	1189	2228	3417	2255	2187	802	469	1520	8858	108.0
	Diff.		-180	-270	—	**+584**	**+769**	—	+137	+150	+287	-238	+389	+60	+21	-75	+193	+2.4
Washington	Off.	82	3311	7148	46	1704	2286	75	1066	2432	3498	1784	1796	626	**716**	1346	8442	103.0
	Def.	82	3435	7360	47	1649	2181	76	1249	2591	3840	2014	1907	712	454	1373	8590	104.8
	Diff.		-124	-212	-1	+55	+105	-1	-183	-159	-342	-230	+111	-86	**+262**	+27	-148	-1.8
New Jersey	Off.	82	3548	7301	49	1810	2396	76	1183	2483	3666	2128	2129	749	345	1575	8949	109.1
	Def.	82	3504	7124	49	2008	2622	77	1036	2369	3405	2019	2002	783	390	1523	9112	111.1
	Diff.		+44	+177	—	-198	-226	-1	+147	+114	+261	+109	-127	-34	-45	-52	-163	-2.0
New York	Off.	82	3239	7034	46	1534	2237	69	1081	2170	3251	1877	2213	714	308	1438	8094	98.7
	Def.	82	3192	6672	48	2102	2744	77	1166	2587	3753	2007	2018	701	444	1629	**8554**	**104.3**
	Diff.		+47	+362	-2	-568	-507	-8	-85	-417	-502	-130	-195	+13	-136	+191	-460	-5.6
CENTRAL DIVISION																		
Milwaukee	Off.	82	3601	7310	49	2063	2701	76	1189	2420	3609	2158	2210	805	460	1369	9390	114.5
	Def.	82	3286	7043	47	1980	2674	74	1169	2325	3494	1952	2139	633	397	1631	8649	105.5
	Diff.		+315	+267	+2	+83	+27	+2	+20	+95	+115	+206	-71	+172	+63	+262	+741	+9.0
Atlanta	Off.	82	3447	7029	49	1979	2704	73	1249	2405	3654	2025	2170	736	434	1483	8906	108.6
	Def.	82	3360	7074	47	1905	2508	76	1202	2329	3531	1945	2129	697	371	1494	8712	106.2
	Diff.		+87	-45	+2	+74	+196	-3	+47	+76	+123	+80	-41	+39	+63	+11	+194	+2.4
Detroit	Off.	82	3754	7750	48	1800	2300	78	1276	2461	3737	2319	2101	738	340	1343	9363	114.2
	Def.	82	3620	7365	49	1956	2589	76	1180	2538	3718	2083	1977	662	500	1490	9267	113.0
	Diff.		+134	+385	-1	-156	-289	+2	+96	-77	+19	+236	-124	+76	-160	+147	+96	+1.2
Chicago	Off.	82	3476	7227	48	1922	2499	77	1280	2278	3558	2006	2166	609	400	1436	8962	109.3
	Def.	82	3601	7138	50	2002	2627	76	1104	2362	3466	2170	2002	664	491	1298	9274	113.1
	Diff.		-125	+89	-2	-80	-128	+1	**+176**	-84	+92	-164	-164	-55	-91	-138	-312	-3.8
Cleveland	Off.	82	3478	7239	48	1748	2325	75	1086	2455	3541	2064	2267	627	436	1411	8836	107.8
	Def.	82	3435	7239	47	2115	2758	77	1131	2494	3625	2122	1945	711	364	1331	9071	110.6
	Diff.		+43	—	+1	-367	-433	-2	-45	-39	-84	-58	-322	-84	+72	-80	-235	-2.8
Indiana	Off.	82	3441	7150	48	1614	2183	74	1138	2613	3751	2159	2135	659	381	1515	8519	103.9
	Def.	82	3372	7123	47	1975	2571	77	1050	2479	3529	2057	1909	745	445	1315	8792	107.2
	Diff.		+69	+27	+1	-361	-388	-3	+88	+134	+222	+102	-226	-86	-64	-200	-273	-3.3
WESTERN CONFERENCE MIDWEST DIVISION																		
Houston	Off.	82	**3759**	7671	49	1776	2434	73	1316	2434	3750	2318	1991	745	551	1374	9379	114.4
	Def.	82	3638	7402	49	1802	2406	75	1190	2389	3579	2196	1977	683	386	1464	9165	111.8
	Diff.		+121	+269	—	-26	+28	-2	+126	+45	+171	+122	-14	+62	+165	+90	+214	+2.6
Denver	Off.	82	3705	**7868**	47	1929	2416	**80**	1223	2317	3540	2140	2164	826	421	1336	9410	114.8
	Def.	82	3638	7404	49	1967	2693	73	1295	2732	4027	2106	2117	639	484	**1741**	9303	113.5
	Diff.		+67	**+464**	-2	-38	-277	**+7**	-72	-415	-487	+34	-47	**+187**	-63	**+405**	+107	+1.3
Dallas	Off.	82	3631	7254	50	2050	2643	78	1059	2454	3513	2108	**1733**	605	369	**1289**	9453	115.3
	Def.	82	3864	7689	50	1545	2049	75	1219	2469	3688	2381	2196	617	423	1279	9363	114.2
	Diff.		-233	-435	—	+505	+594	+3	-160	-15	-175	-273	**+463**	-12	-54	-10	+90	+1.1
Utah	Off.	82	3453	7083	49	1930	2694	72	1068	2479	3547	2199	2038	717	666	1518	8871	108.2
	Def.	82	3470	7339	47	1896	2483	76	1208	2510	3718	1977	2221	752	464	1531	8901	108.5
	Diff.		-17	-256	+2	+34	+211	-4	-140	-31	-171	+222	+183	-35	+202	+13	-30	-.3
Sacramento	Off.	82	3538	7220	49	1818	2338	78	1135	2377	3512	2304	2134	602	388	1533	8924	108.8
	Def.	82	3566	7225	49	1971	2609	76	1142	2339	3481	2118	2083	751	478	1409	9176	111.9
	Diff.		-28	-5	—	-153	-271	+2	-7	+38	+31	+186	-51	-149	-90	-124	-252	-3.1
San Antonio	Off.	82	3596	7104	51	1882	2523	75	1069	2413	3482	2260	2115	800	390	1624	9120	111.2
	Def.	82	3629	7365	49	1916	2491	77	1157	2304	3461	2269	2108	800	453	1519	9272	113.1
	Diff.		-33	-261	+2	-34	+32	-2	-88	+109	+21	-9	-7	—	-63	-105	-152	-1.9
PACIFIC DIVISION																		
L.A. Lakers	Off.	82	3834	7343	**52**	1812	2329	78	1101	2555	3656	**2433**	2031	693	419	1467	**9618**	**117.3**
	Def.	82	3577	7450	48	1778	2369	75	1104	2226	3330	2235	1992	792	359	1330	8983	109.5
	Diff.		+257	-107	+4	+34	-40	+3	-3	+329	+326	+198	-39	-99	+60	-137	+635	+7.8
Portland	Off.	82	3610	7281	50	**2142**	2799	77	1153	2316	3469	2180	2205	859	356	1529	**9436**	**115.1**
	Def.	82	3637	7249	50	1992	2638	76	1179	2362	3541	2254	**2262**	760	426	1645	9349	114.0
	Diff.		-27	+32	—	+150	+161	+1	-26	-46	-72	-74	+57	+99	-70	+116	+87	+1.1

Team		G	FG	FGA	%	FT	FTA	%	REBOUNDS			Assists	PF	Steals	Blocked Shots	Turn Overs	Points	Points per game
									Offense	Defense	Total							
TEAM STATISTICS WESTERN CONFERENCE PACIFIC DIVISION																		
L.A. Clippers	Off.	82	3388	7165	47	2067	2683	77	1159	2258	3417	1968	1931	694	501	1506	8907	108.6
	Def.	82	3849	7888	49	1704	2280	75	1268	2458	3726	2649	2113	760	457	1396	9475	115.5
	Diff.		-461	-723	-2	+363	+403	+2	-109	-200	-309	-681	+182	-66	+44	-110	-568	-6.9
Phoenix	Off.	82	3518	6993	50	1949	2683	73	1034	2449	3483	2272	2260	773	379	1763	9023	110.0
	Def.	82	3569	7307	49	2041	2692	76	1137	2265	3402	2149	2216	841	466	1515	9268	113.0
	Diff.		-51	-314	+1	-92	-9	-3	-103	+184	+81	+123	-44	-68	-87	-248	-245	-3.0
Seattle	Off.	82	3335	7059	47	1815	2331	78	1145	2256	3401	1977	2168	745	295	1435	8564	104.4
	Def.	82	3301	6774	49	1913	2491	77	1027	2308	3335	2038	2008	654	406	1467	8572	104.5
	Diff.		+34	+285	-2	-98	-160	+1	+118	-52	+66	-61	-160	+91	-111	+32	-8	-0.1
Golden State	Off.	82	3650	7567	48	1912	2517	76	1271	2344	3615	2018	2032	751	354	1400	9299	113.4
	Def.	82	3863	7432	52	1791	2401	75	1170	2519	3689	2325	2069	692	442	1487	9582	116.9
	Diff.		-213	+135	-4	+121	+116	+1	+101	-175	-74	-307	+37	+59	-88	+87	-283	-3.5
PLAYOFFS																		
Boston	Off.	18	791	1560	51	433	545	79	233	580	813	515	401	162	109	274	2060	114.4
	Def.	18	746	1629	46	360	491	73	267	492	759	426	450	151	92	268	1874	104.1
	Diff.		+45	-69	+5	+73	+54	+6	-34	+88	+54	+89	+49	+11	+17	-6	+186	+10.3
Houston	Off.	20	894	1845	48	425	594	72	337	609	946	569	462	172	149	303	2226	111.3
	Def.	20	842	1808	47	427	545	78	301	571	872	534	480	175	101	329	2149	107.5
	Diff.		+52	+37	+1	-2	+49	-6	+36	+38	+74	+35	+18	-3	+48	+26	+77	+3.8
L.A. Lakers	Off.	14	664	1240	54	264	349	76	175	417	592	448	339	118	60	226	1617	115.5
	Def.	14	603	1236	49	278	383	73	176	353	529	391	317	118	60	209	1510	107.9
	Diff.		+61	+4	+5	-14	-34	+3	-1	+64	+63	+57	-22	—	—	-17	+107	+7.6
Milwaukee	Off.	14	589	1186	50	334	463	72	180	373	553	338	399	124	85	231	1537	109.8
	Def.	14	581	1170	50	391	515	76	193	397	590	354	353	131	77	235	1571	112.2
	Diff.		+8	+16		-57	-52	-4	-13	-24	-37	-16	-46	-7	+8	+4	-34	-2.4
Philadelphia	Off.	12	491	1005	49	329	445	74	189	349	538	299	276	107	85	201	1314	109.5
	Def.	12	503	1018	49	259	364	71	166	300	466	278	327	111	88	201	1280	106.7
	Diff.		-12	-13		+70	+81	+3	+23	+49	+72	+21	+51	-4	-3	—	+34	+2.8
Dallas	Off.	10	426	871	49	226	289	78	139	280	419	250	215	66	31	142	1108	110.8
	Def.	10	462	900	51	179	240	75	133	284	417	288	248	65	49	120	1121	112.1
	Diff.		-36	-29	-2	+47	+49	+3	+6	-4	+2	-38	+33	+1	-18	-22	-13	-1.3
Denver	Off.	10	438	961	46	250	315	79	166	293	459	247	273	72	44	144	1145	114.5
	Def.	10	466	943	49	239	325	74	158	345	503	292	269	67	68	174	1178	117.8
	Diff.		-28	+18	-3	+11	-10	+5	+8	-52	-44	-45	-4	+5	-24	+30	-33	-3.3
Atlanta	Off.	9	391	790	49	211	289	73	120	271	391	235	234	66	46	138	999	111.0
	Def.	9	406	819	50	199	269	74	131	280	411	243	222	73	32	134	1025	113.9
	Diff.		-15	-29	-1	+12	+20	-1	-11	-9	-20	-8	-12	-7	+14	-4	-26	-2.9
Washington	Off.	5	200	432	46	98	137	72	72	120	192	105	113	43	43	76	503	100.6
	Def.	5	210	441	48	111	151	74	93	162	255	131	115	37	44	80	532	106.4
	Diff.		-10	-9	-2	-13	-14	-2	-21	-42	-63	-26	+2	+6	-1	+4	-29	-5.8
Utah	Off.	4	173	359	48	62	88	70	62	107	169	104	100	23	25	44	412	103.0
	Def.	4	156	331	47	107	127	84	59	127	186	81	85	22	17	60	429	107.3
	Diff.		+17	+28	+1	-45	-39	-14	+3	-20	-17	+23	-15	+1	+8	+16	-17	-4.3
Portland	Off.	4	174	351	50	97	125	78	52	124	176	112	124	28	18	76	450	112.5
	Def.	4	179	375	48	109	139	78	73	113	186	96	109	26	19	58	470	117.5
	Diff.		-5	-24	+2	-12	-14	—	-21	+11	-10	+16	-15	+2	-1	-18	-20	-5.0
Detroit	Off.	4	187	389	48	91	125	73	70	119	189	103	120	26	10	65	466	116.5
	Def.	4	182	354	51	121	164	74	53	128	181	115	110	26	25	60	488	122.0
	Diff.		+5	+35	-3	-30	-39	-1	+17	-9	+8	-12	-10	—	-15	-5	-22	-5.5
Chicago	Off.	3	128	277	46	81	105	77	41	78	119	51	92	24	11	44	339	113.0
	Def.	3	136	263	52	102	121	84	39	100	139	91	81	23	25	45	380	126.7
	Diff.		-8	+14	-6	-21	-16	-7	+2	-22	-20	-40	-11	+1	-14	+1	-41	-13.7
New Jersey	Off.	3	118	254	46	79	105	75	46	73	119	66	98	28	52	12	288	96.0
	Def.	3	128	241	53	89	123	72	38	84	122	73	84	23	20	47	348	116.0
	Diff.		-10	+13	-7	-10	-18	+3	+8	-11	-3	-7	-14	+5	+32	+35	-60	-20.0
Sacramento	Off.	3	109	268	41	68	89	76	65	74	139	57	70	24	17	52	288	96.0
	Def.	3	134	249	54	61	90	68	74	84	158	79	75	33	23	45	331	110.3
	Diff.		-25	+19	-13	+7	-1	+8	-9	-10	-19	-22	+5	-9	-6	-7	-43	-14.3
San Antonio	Off.	3	116	249	47	42	65	65	21	58	79	75	78	28	10	54	276	92.0
	Def.	3	155	260	60	58	81	72	43	105	148	102	69	30	15	57	371	123.7
	Diff.		-39	-11	-13	-16	-16	-7	-22	-47	-69	-27	-9	-2	-5	+3	-95	-31.7

Team	W	L	Pct.	GB	Record against playoff teams W	L	Pct.	Record against non-playoff teams W	L	Pct.	HOME W	L	Pct.	ROAD W	L	Pct.
EASTERN CONFERENCE																
ATLANTIC DIVISION																
Boston Celtics	67	15	.817	—	45	11	.804	22	4	.846	40	1	.976	27	14	.659
Philadelphia 76ers	54	28	.659	13	30	26	.536	24	2	.923	31	10	.756	23	18	.561
Washington Bullets	39	43	.476	28	25	31	.446	14	12	.538	26	15	.634	13	28	.317
New Jersey Nets	39	43	.476	28	25	32	.439	14	11	.560	26	15	.634	13	28	.317
New York Knickerbockers	23	59	.280	44	14	49	.222	9	10	.474	15	26	.366	8	33	.195
CENTRAL DIVISION																
Milwaukee Bucks	57	25	.695	—	36	20	.643	21	5	.808	33	8	.805	24	17	.585
Atlanta Hawks	50	32	.610	7	30	26	.536	20	6	.769	34	7	.829	16	25	.390
Detroit Pistons	46	36	.561	11	27	30	.474	19	6	.760	31	10	.756	15	26	.366
Chicago Bulls	30	52	.366	27	15	41	.268	15	11	.577	22	19	.537	8	33	.195
Cleveland Cavaliers	29	53	.354	28	18	46	.281	11	7	.611	16	25	.390	13	28	.317
Indiana Pacers	26	56	.317	31	16	47	.254	10	9	.526	19	22	.463	7	34	.170
WESTERN CONFERENCE																
MIDWEST DIVISION																
Houston Rockets	51	31	.622	—	31	25	.554	20	6	.769	36	5	.878	15	26	.366
Denver Nuggets	47	35	.573	4	30	26	.536	17	9	.654	34	7	.829	13	28	.317
Dallas Mavericks	44	38	.537	7	26	30	.464	18	8	.692	26	15	.634	18	23	.439
Utah Jazz	42	40	.512	9	24	32	.429	18	8	.692	27	14	.659	15	26	.366
Sacramento Kings	37	45	.451	14	23	33	.411	14	12	.538	25	16	.610	12	29	.293
San Antonio Spurs	35	47	.427	16	20	35	.364	15	12	.556	21	20	.512	14	27	.341
PACIFIC DIVISION																
Los Angeles Lakers	62	20	.756	—	41	11	.788	21	9	.700	35	6	.854	27	14	.659
Portland Trail-Blazers	40	42	.488	22	16	36	.308	24	6	.800	27	14	.659	13	28	.317
Los Angeles Clippers	32	50	.390	30	23	35	.397	9	15	.375	22	19	.537	10	31	.244
Phoenix Suns	32	50	.390	30	18	40	.310	14	10	.583	23	18	.561	9	32	.220
Seattle Supersonics	31	51	.378	31	21	37	.362	10	14	.417	24	17	.585	7	34	.171
Golden State Warriors	30	52	.366	32	17	41	.293	13	11	.542	24	17	.585	6	35	.146

1985/86 N.B.A. INDIVDIUAL LEADERS

SCORING
(Minimum 70 Games or 1400 Points)

Name	Team	G	FG	FT	Pts.	Avg.
Wilkins	Atl	78	888	577	2366	30.3
Dantley	Utah	76	818	630	2267	29.8
English	Den	81	951	511	2414	29.8
Bird	Bos	82	796	541	2115	25.8
Short	GS	64	633	351	1632	25.5
Vandeweghe	Port	79	719	523	1962	24.8
Malone	Phi	74	571	617	1759	23.8
Olajuwon	Hou	68	625	347	1597	23.5
Mitchell	SA	82	802	317	1921	23.4
Free	Cle	75	652	379	1754	23.4

FIELD GOAL PERCENTAGE
(Minimum 300 Made)

Name	Team	FG	FGA	Pct.
Johnson	SA	362	573	.632
Gilmore	SA	423	684	.618
Nance	Phoe	582	1001	.581
Worthy	LAL	629	1086	.579
McHale	Bos	561	978	.574
Barkley	Phi	595	1041	.572
Abdul-Jabbar	LAL	755	1338	.564
Dantley	Utah	818	1453	.563
Lister	Mil	318	577	.551
Parish	Bos	530	966	.549

FREE THROW PERCENTAGE
(Minimum 125 Made)

Name	Team	FT	FTA	Pct.
Bird	Bos	441	492	.896
Mullin	GS	189	211	.896
Gminski	NJ	351	393	.893
Paxson	Port	217	244	.889
Gervin	Chi	283	322	.879
Edwards	LAC	132	151	.874
Johnson	LAL	378	434	.871
Vandeweghe	Port	523	602	.869
Davis	Dal	198	228	.868
Malone	Was	322	371	.868

PERSONAL FOULS

Name	Team	PF
Barkley	Phi	333
Hinson	Cle	316
Cooper	Den	315
Sampson	Hou	308
McDaniel	Sea	305

GAMES DISQUALIFIED

Name	Team	Disq.
Carroll	GS	13
Johnson	SA	13
Sampson	Hou	12
Bailey	NY	12
Koncak	Atl	10
Dawkins	NJ	10

MINUTES PLAYED

Name	Team	Min.
Cheeks	Phi	3270
Bird	Bos	3113
B. Williams	NJ	3070
Wilkins	Atl	3049
English	Den	3024

TOTAL REBOUNDS PER GAME
(Minimum 70 Games or 800 Rebounds)

Name	Team	G	Reb.	Avg.
Laimbeer	Det	82	1075	13.1
Barkley	Phi	80	1026	12.8
B. Williams	NJ	82	986	12.0
Malone	Phi	74	872	11.8
Sampson	Hou	79	879	11.1
Smith	GS	77	856	11.1
Bird	Bos	82	805	9.8
Thompson	Sac	80	770	9.6
Donaldson	Dal	83	795	9.6
Parish	Bos	81	770	9.5

ASSISTS PER GAME
(Minimum 70 Games or 400 Assists)

Name	Team	G	Ass.	Avg.
Johnson	LAL	72	907	12.6
Thomas	Det	77	830	10.8
Theus	Sac	82	788	9.6
Bagley	Cle	78	735	9.4
Cheeks	Phi	82	753	9.2
Floyd	GS	82	746	9.1
Lucas	Hou	65	571	8.8
Nixon	LAC	67	576	8.6
Rivers	Atl	53	443	8.4
Drexler	Port	75	600	8.0

BLOCKED SHOTS PER GAME
(Minimum 70 Games of 100 Blocked Shots)

Name	Team	G	Reb.	Avg.
Bol	Was	80	397	5.0
Eaton	Utah	80	369	4.6
Olajawon	Hou	68	231	3.4
Cooper	Den	78	227	2.9
Benjamin	LAC	79	206	2.6
Oldham	Chi	52	132	2.5
Williams	Ind	78	184	2.4
Rollins	Atl	74	167	2.3
Ewing	NY	50	103	2.1
McHale	Bos	68	134	2.0

3 POINT FIELD GOALS PER GAME
(Minimum 25 Made)

Name	Team	FG	FGA	Avg.
Hodges	Mil	73	162	.451
Tucker	NY	41	91	.451
Grunfeld	NY	26	61	.426
Bird	Bos	82	194	.423
Free	Cle	71	169	.420
Macy	Chi	58	141	.411
Cooper	LAL	63	163	.387
Ellis	Dal	63	173	.364
McKenna	Was	27	75	.360

STEALS PER GAME
(Minimum 70 Games or 125 Steals)

Name	Team	G	Steals	Avg.
Robertson	SA	82	301	3.7
Richardson	NJ	47	125	2.7
Drexler	Port	75	197	2.6
Cheeks	Phi	82	207	2.5
Lever	Den	78	178	2.3
Thomas	Det	77	171	2.2
Barkley	Phi	80	173	2.2
Pressey	Mil	80	168	2.1
Bird	Bos	82	166	2.0
Cook	NJ	79	156	2.0

1986-87 N.B.A.
Dr. J's Finale

Draft-day deals resulted in the creation of a potential new dynasty and the death of an old one. The big winners were the Cleveland Cavaliers. General manager Wayne Embry sent Roy Hinson to Philadelphia for the No. 1 pick and took center Brad Dougerty, who made the all-rookie team, where he joined fellow Cavs Ron Harper and John (Hot Rod) Williams. It wasn't enough to lift Cleveland out of the Central Division cellar, but new coach Lenny Wilkens had a contender in the making.

Not so successful were the 76ers, who also sent Moses Malone to Washington for Jeff Ruland. A knee injury limited Ruland to five games and forced his premature retirement. Andrew Toney's comeback got mixed reviews, and Hinson proved disappointing. Only the inspired play of Charles Barkley kept them above .500. It was fitting that Julius Erving, whose arrival in 1976 had begun a new era in Philadelphia, ended his 16-year pro career at the end of the season.

The Celtics looked like winners in the draft, using the second pick (acquired from Seattle for Gerald Henderson) to grab forward Len Bias. But Bias's death two days later of cocaine intoxication was a serious blow. With Bill Walton and Scott Wedman sidelined most of the season, the Celtics were forced to rely almost exclusively on their starters, who were showing the effects of overwork by playoff time.

The Lakers had also appeared to be slowing down in their playoff loss to Houston last spring. So they let Maurice Lucas go in favor of the younger and faster A.C. Green at power forward. Coach Pat Riley also moved the focus of the offense away from Kareem Abdul-Jabbar and relied more on Magic Johnson, who averaged 24 points and ended Larry Bird's three-year reign as MVP.

As for Bird, he again led the Celtics to the best record in the East, with help fom Kevin McHale, having the best season of his career. Boston was chased to the wire by the Hawks, who won 57 games en route to the Central Division title. Many thought Atlanta could dethrone the Celtics in the playoffs, but Detroit stopped the Hawks cold in five games. The Pistons, still in need of inside scoring, sent Kelly Tripucks to Utah for Adrian Dantley, and jumped to 52 wins. Milwaukee won its usual 50 games, but coach Don Nelson resigned after the season, citing differences with owner Herb Kohl.

Jack Ramsey left Portland to coach Indiana and moved the Pacers to the .500 mark, with help from Rookie of the Year Chuck Person. New Chicago coach Doug Collins gave Michael Jordan free reign, and Jordan led the league with 37 points a game as the Bulls improved to 40 wins. But in Washington the acquisition of Moses Malone lifted the Bullets to only 42 wins.

There was trouble in Phoenix, where five players were implicated in a drug scandal and coach John Macleod was fired as the Suns fell short of the playoffs again. Still, they won three times as many games as the L.A. Clippers, who lost Marques Johnson and Norm Nixon to injuries and challenged the N.B.A. record for futility before finishing at 12-70.

Things were better in Portland, where Mike Schuler replaced Ramsey and became Coach of the Year as the Trail Blazers improved to 49 wins behind Kiki Vandweghe and Clyde Drexler. In Dallas, the talented Mavericks finally put it all together, winning 55 games, while second-year man Karl Malone made Utah fans forget the departed Dantley. But in Houston, drugs brought the expulsion of guards Mitchell Wiggins and Lewis Lloyd, and Ralph Sampson missed 39 games with injuries—problems that even the play of Akeem Olajuwon couldn't overcome. Golden State, under new coach George Karl, made the playoffs for the first time in 10 years; and Seattle improved to 39 wins as three players—Dale Ellis (acquired from Dallas), Tom Chambers and Xavier McDaniel—averaged 23 points or better.

The Sonics took off in the playoffs, upsetting Dallas and Houston before falling to the Lakers in the Western finals. In the East, the Celtics looked tired in a seven-game victory over Milwaukee, then looked beaten in the next series when Detroit had a one-point lead and the ball with five seconds left in the pivotal fifth game. But Bird stole Isiah Thomas's pass and passed to Dennis Johnson for the winning basket; then, after Detroit won the sixth game, Boston prevailed, 117-114, setting up another meeting with Los Angeles.

McHale was playing on a broken foot, Robert Parish on a sprained ankle, and the Celtics looked sad as the Lakers won the first two games easily. Boston rallied at home, winning two of the three—but the fourth game proved decisive. Bird's 3-pointer put the Celtics up by two with seconds remaining; but after a free throw by Abdul-Jabbar, Johnson sank a "junior sky hook" to sink Boston. The Lakers went on to win in six games, and Johnson was an easy choice as playoff MVP.

					TOTAL													Blkd		PER GAME				
Use Name	Pos	Hgt	Wgt	Age	G	Min	FG	FGA	%	FT	FTA	%	Reb	Ass	PF	DQ	Stls	Shts	Points	Min	Reb	Ass	PF	Points
1986/87 N.B.A. — EASTERN CONFERENCE																								
ATLANTIC DIVISION																								
OSTON CELTICS	59-23 .720				K.C. JONES																			
rry Bird	F	6'9	220	30	74	3005	786	1497	53	414	455	91	682	566	185	3	135	70	2076	41	9.2	7.6	2.5	28.1
evin McHale	F-C	6'10	225	29	77	3060	790	1307	60	428	512	84	763	198	240	1	38	172	2008	40	9.9	2.6	3.1	26.1
obert Parish	C	7'	230	33	80	2995	588	1057	56	227	309	73	851	173	266	5	64	144	1403	37	10.6	2.2	3.3	17.5
anny Ainge	G	6'4	185	27	71	2499	410	844	49	148	165	90	242	400	189	3	101	14	1053	35	3.4	5.6	2.7	14.8
ennis Jonhson	G	6'4	200	32	79	2933	423	953	44	209	251	83	261	594	201	0	87	38	1062	37	3.3	7.5	2.5	13.4
rry Sichting	G	6'1	180	30	78	1566	202	398	51	37	42	88	91	187	124	0	40	1	448	20	1.2	2.4	1.6	5.7
ed Roberts	F	6'10	220	26	73	1079	139	270	51	124	153	81	190	62	129	1	22	20	402	15	2.6	0.8	1.8	5.5
reg Kite	C	6'11	250	25	74	745	47	110	43	29	76	38	169	27	148	2	17	46	123	10	2.3	0.4	2.0	1.7
arren Daye (from Chi)	F	6'8	220	26	61	724	101	202	50	34	65	52	124	75	98	0	25	7	236	12	2.0	1.2	1.6	3.9
am Vincent	G	6'2	185	23	46	374	60	136	44	51	55	93	27	59	33	0	13	1	171	8	0.6	1.3	0.7	3.7
ck Carlisle	G	6'5	210	26	42	297	30	92	33	15	20	75	30	35	28	0	8	0	80	7	0.7	0.8	0.7	1.9
onnor Henry (from Hou)	G	6'7	195	23	36	231	38	103	37	10	17	59	27	27	27	0	6	1	98	6	0.8	0.8	0.8	2.7
ll Walton (FJ-NJ)	C	6'11	235	34	10	112	10	26	38	8	15	53	31	9	23	0	1	10	28	11	3.1	0.9	2.3	2.8
avid Thirdkill	F	6'7	215	26	17	89	10	24	42	5	16	31	19	2	12	0	2	0	25	5	1.1	0.1	0.7	1.5
cott Wedman (LJ)	F	6'7	220	34	6	78	9	27	33	1	2	50	9	6	6	0	2	2	20	13	1.5	1.0	1.0	3.3
ndre Turner	G	5'11	160	22	3	18	2	5	40	0	0	—	2	1	1	0	0	0	4	6	0.7	0.3	0.3	1.3

3-PT FG — Bird 90-225, McHale 0-4, Parish 0-1, Ainge 85-192, Johnson 7-62, Sichting 7-26, Roberts 0-3
Kite 0-1, Carlisle 5-16, Henry 12-31, Thirdkill 0-1, Wedman 1-2, Turner 0-1

1986/87 N.B.A. — EASTERN CONFERENCE
ATLANTIC DIVISION

Use Name	Pos	Hgt	Wgt	Age	G	Min	FG	FGA	%	FT	FTA	%	Reb	Ass	PF	DQ	Stls	Blkd Shts	Points	Min	Reb	Ass	PF	Points
					TOTAL															PER GAME				
PHILADELPHIA 76ers	45-37 .541				MATT GUOKAS																			
Julius Erving	F-G	6'7	210	36	60	1918	400	850	47	191	235	81	264	191	137	0	76	94	1005	32	4.4	3.2	2.3	16.8
Charles Barkley	F	6'6	263	23	68	2740	557	937	59	429	564	76	994	331	252	5	119	104	1564	40	14.6	4.9	3.7	23.0
Tim McCormick	C	7'	240	24	81	2817	391	718	54	251	349	72	611	114	270	4	36	64	1033	35	7.5	1.4	3.3	12.8
Andrew Toney	G	6'3	190	29	52	1058	197	437	45	133	167	80	85	188	78	0	18	8	549	20	1.6	3.6	1.5	10.6
Maurice Cheeks	G	6'1	180	30	68	2624	415	788	53	227	292	78	215	538	109	0	180	15	1061	39	3.2	7.9	1.6	15.6
Roy Hinson	F-C	6'9	220	25	76	2489	393	823	48	273	360	76	488	60	281	4	45	161	1059	33	6.4	0.8	3.7	13.9
Dave Wingate	G	6'5	185	23	77	1612	259	602	43	149	201	74	156	155	169	1	93	19	680	21	2.0	2.0	2.2	8.8
Cliff Robinson	F	6'9	240	26	55	1586	338	729	46	139	184	76	307	89	150	1	86	30	815	29	5.6	1.6	2.7	14.8
Steve Colter (fromChi)	G	6'3	175	24	43	849	120	255	47	49	68	72	66	116	61	0	37	6	293	20	1.5	2.7	1.4	6.8
Danny Vranes	F	6'8	220	28	58	817	59	138	43	21	45	47	146	30	127	0	35	25	140	14	2.5	0.5	2.2	2.4
Sedale Threatt (to Chi)	G	6'2	177	25	28	668	108	261	41	42	53	79	57	82	76	0	32	4	265	24	2.0	2.9	2.7	9.5
World Free	G	6'3	190	33	20	285	39	123	32	36	47	77	19	30	26	0	5	4	116	14	1.0	1.5	1.3	5.8
Kenny Green	G	6'7	215	22	19	172	25	70	36	14	19	74	28	7	8	0	4	2	64	9	1.5	0.4	0.4	3.4
Jeff Ruland	C	6"11	275	28	5	116	19	28	68	9	12	75	28	10	13	0	0	4	47	23	5.6	2.0	2.6	9.4
Mark McNamara	C	6'11	235	27	11	113	14	30	47	7	19	37	36	2	17	0	1	0	35	10	3.3	0.2	1.5	3.2
Jim Lampley	C	6'10	230	26	1	16	1	3	33	1	2	50	5	0	0	0	1	0	3	16	5.0	0.0	0.0	3.0

3-PT FG — Erving 14-53, Barkley 21-104, McCormick 0-4, Toney 22-67, Cheeks 4-17, Hinson 0-1
Wingate 13-52, Robinson 0-4, Colter 4-8, Vranes 1-5, Threatt 7-16, Free 2-9

Use Name	Pos	Hgt	Wgt	Age	G	Min	FG	FGA	%	FT	FTA	%	Reb	Ass	PF	DQ	Stls	Blkd Shts	Points	Min	Reb	Ass	PF	Points
WASHINGTON BULLETS	42-40 .512				KEVIN LOUGHERY																			
Jay Vincent (RJ)	F	6'7	220	27	51	1386	274	613	45	130	169	77	210	85	127	0	40	17	678	27	4.1	1.7	2.5	13.3
Terry Catledge	F	6'8	230	23	78	2149	413	835	49	199	335	59	560	56	195	1	43	14	1025	28	7.2	0.7	2.5	13.1
Moses Malone	C-F	6'10	255	31	73	2488	595	1311	45	570	692	82	824	120	139	0	59	92	1760	34	11.3	1.6	1.9	24.1
Jeff Malone	G	6'4	205	25	80	2763	689	1509	46	376	425	88	218	298	154	0	75	13	1758	35	2.7	3.7	1.9	22.0
Ennis Whatley	G	6'3	177	24	73	1816	246	515	48	126	165	76	194	392	172	0	92	10	618	25	2.7	5.4	2.4	8.5
John Williams	F	6'9	235	20	78	1773	283	624	45	144	223	65	366	191	173	1	128	30	718	23	4.7	2.4	2.2	9.2
Charles Jones	F	6'9	215	29	79	1609	118	249	47	48	76	63	356	80	252	2	67	165	284	20	4.5	1.0	3.2	3.6
Manute Bol	C	7'6	225	24	82	1552	103	231	45	45	67	67	362	11	189	1	20	302	251	19	4.4	0.1	2.3	3.1
Darwin Cook	G	6'3	195	28	82	1420	265	622	43	82	103	80	145	151	136	0	98	17	614	17	1.8	1.8	1.7	7.5
Michael Adams	G	5'11	165	23	63	1303	160	393	41	105	124	85	123	244	88	0	86	6	453	21	2.0	3.9	1.4	7.2
Dan Roundfield	F	6'8	215	33	36	669	90	220	41	57	72	79	170	39	77	0	11	16	238	19	4.7	1.1	2.1	6.6
Frank Johnson	G	6'3	185	26	18	399	59	128	46	35	49	71	30	58	31	0	21	0	153	22	1.7	3.2	1.7	8.5
Jay Murphy	F	6'9	220	24	21	141	31	72	43	9	16	56	39	5	21	0	3	2	71	7	1.9	0.2	1.0	3.4
Mike O'Koren	G-F	6'7	225	28	15	123	16	42	38	0	2	0	14	13	10	0	2	0	32	8	0.9	0.9	0.7	2.1
Anthony Jones (to SA)	G	6'6	195	24	16	114	14	33	42	9	13	69	9	7	11	0	10	1	37	7	0.6	0.4	0.7	2.3

3-PT FG — Vincent 0-3, Catledge 0-4, M.Malone 0-11, J.Malone 4-26,Whatley 0-2, Williams 8-36, C. Jones 0-1,
Bol 0-1, Cook 2-23, Adams 28-102, Roundfield 1-5, Johnson 0-l, O'Koren 0-2, A.Jones 0-1

Use Name	Pos	Hgt	Wgt	Age	G	Min	FG	FGA	%	FT	FTA	%	Reb	Ass	PF	DQ	Stls	Blkd Shts	Points	Min	Reb	Ass	PF	Points
NEW JERSEY NETS	24-58 .293				DAVE WOHL																			
Orlando Woolridge	F	6'9	215	27	75	2638	556	1067	52	438	564	78	367	261	243	4	54	86	1551	35	4.9	3.5	3.2	20.7
Buck Williams	F	6'8	225	26	82	2976	521	936	56	430	588	73	1023	129	315	8	78	91	1472	36	12.5	1.6	3.8	18.0
Mike Gminski	C	6'11	260	27	72	2272	433	947	46	313	370	85	630	99	159	0	52	69	1179	32	8.8	1.4	2.2	16.4
Tony Brown	G	6'6	185	26	77	2339	358	810	44	152	206	74	219	259	273	12	89	14	873	30	2.8	3.4	3.5	11.3
Leon Wood	G	6'3	185	24	76	1733	187	501	37	123	154	80	120	370	126	0	48	3	557	23	1.6	4.9	1.7	7.3
Pearl Washington	G	6'2	195	22	72	1600	257	538	48	98	125	78	129	301	184	5	92	7	616	22	1.8	4.2	2.6	8.6
Albert King	F-G	6'6	215	27	61	1291	244	573	43	81	100	81	214	103	177	5	34	28	582	21	3.5	1.7	2.9	9.5
Ben Coleman	F	6'9	235	25	68	1029	182	313	58	88	121	73	288	37	200	7	32	31	452	15	4.2	0.5	2.9	6.6
Jeff Turner	C-F	6"9	240	24	76	1003	151	325	46	76	104	73	197	60	200	6	33	13	378	13	2.6	0.8	2.6	5.0
Kevin McKenna	G	6'5	195	26	56	942	153	337	45	43	57	75	77	93	141	0	54	7	401	17	1.4	1.7	2.5	7.2
Ray Williams	G	6'3	200	32	32	800	131	290	45	49	60	82	75	185	111	4	38	9	318	25	2.3	5.8	3.5	9.9
James Bailey	C	6'9	220	29	34	542	112	239	47	58	80	73	137	20	119	5	12	23	282	16	4.0	0.6	3.5	8.3
Pace Mannion	G	6'7	190	26	23	284	31	94	33	18	31	58	39	45	32	0	18	4	83	12	1.7	2.0	1.4	3.6
C.Engler (from Port, Mil)	C	6'11	250	27	18	130	16	31	52	8	12	67	33	4	23	0	3	9	40	7	1.8	0.2	1.3	2.2
Otis Birdsong	G	6'4	195	31	7	127	19	42	45	6	9	67	7	17	16	0	3	0	44	18	1.0	2.4	2.3	6.3
Darryl Dawkins	C	6'11	270	29	6	106	20	32	63	17	24	71	19	2	25	0	2	3	57	18	3.2	0.3	4.2	9.5
Michael Wilson (to Atl)	G	6'4	180	27	5	43	3	8	38	2	2	100	4	6	9	0	1	0	8	9	0.8	1.2	1.8	1.6

Michael Ray Richardson - drug problems

3-PT FG — Woolridge 1-8, B.Williams 0-1, Brown 5-20, Wood 60-200, Washington 4-24, King 13-32,
Coleman 0-1, Turner 0-l, McKenna 52-124, R.Williams 7-28, Mannion 3-9, Birdsong 0-1

Use Name	Pos	Hgt	Wgt	Age	G	Min	FG	FGA	%	FT	FTA	%	Reb	Ass	PF	DQ	Stls	Blkd Shts	Points	Min	Reb	Ass	PF	Points
NEW YORK KNICKERBOCKERS	24-58 .293				HUBIE BROWN (4-12 .250), BOB HILL (20-46 .303)																			
Gerald Wilkins	F-G	6'6	190	23	80	2758	633	1302	49	235	335	70	294	354	165	0	88	18	1527	34	3.7	4.4	2.1	19.1
Patrick Ewing	F-C	7'	240	24	63	2206	530	1053	50	296	415	71	555	104	248	5	89	147	1356	35	8.8	1.7	3.9	21.5
Bill Cartwright (FJ)	C	7'1	245	29	58	1989	335	631	53	346	438	79	445	96	188	2	40	26	1016	34	7.7	1.7	3.2	17.5
Kenny Walker	G-F	6'8	210	22	68	1719	285	581	49	140	185	76	338	75	236	7	49	49	710	25	5.0	1.1	3.5	10.4
Gerald Henderson (from SEA)	G	6'2	180	30	68	1890	273	624	44	173	212	82	166	439	191	1	95	11	738	28	2.4	6.5	2.8	10.9
Rory Sparrow	G	6'2	175	28	80	1951	263	590	45	71	89	80	115	432	160	0	67	6	608	24	1.4	5.4	2.0	7.6
Trent Tucker	G	6'5	193	27	70	1691	325	691	47	77	101	76	135	166	169	1	116	13	795	24	1.9	2.4	2.4	11.4
Louis Orr	F	6'8	200	28	65	1440	166	389	43	125	172	73	232	110	123	0	47	18	458	22	3.6	1.7	1.9	7.0
Pat Cummings	F-C	6'9	235	30	49	1056	172	382	45	79	110	72	312	38	145	2	26	7	423	22	6.4	0.8	3.0	8.6
Chris McNealy	F	6'7	215	25	59	972	88	179	49	52	80	65	227	46	136	1	36	16	228	16	3.8	0.8	2.3	3.9
Jawaan Oldham	C	7'	215	29	44	776	71	174	41	31	57	54	179	19	95	1	22	71	173	18	4.1	0.4	2.2	3.9
Eddie Wilkins	F	6'10	220	24	24	454	56	127	44	27	58	47	107	6	67	1	9	2	139	19	4.5	0.3	2.8	5.8
Bob Thornton	F	6'10	225	24	33	282	29	67	43	13	20	65	56	8	48	0	4	3	71	9	1.7	0.2	1.5	2.2
Bernard King (KJ)	F	6'7	205	30	6	214	52	105	50	32	43	74	32	19	14	0	2	0	136	36	5.3	3.2	2.3	22.7
Stewart Granger	G	6'3	190	25	15	166	20	54	37	9	11	82	17	27	17	0	7	1	49	11	1.1	1.8	1.1	3.3
Brad Wright	F	6'11	225	24	14	138	20	46	43	12	28	43	53	1	20	0	3	6	52	10	3.8	0.1	1.4	3.7
Bill Martin	F	6'7	205	24	8	68	9	25	36	7	8	88	7	0	5	0	4	2	25	9	0.9	0.0	0.6	3.1
McKinley Singleton	G	6'5	175	25	2	10	2	3	67	0	0	—	0	1	1	0	0	0	4	5	0.0	0.5	0.5	2.0

3-PT FG — G.Wilkins 26-74, Ewing 0-7, Walker 0-4, Henderson I9-74, Sparrow II-42, Tucker 68-161, Orr I-5,
Oldham 0-l, E.Wilkins 0-1, Thornton 0-1, Granger 0-3,Wright 0-1, Singleton 0-1

Use Name	Pos	Hgt	Wgt	Age	G	Min	FG	FGA	%	FT	FTA	%	Reb	Ass	PF	DQ	Stls	Blkd Shts	Points	Min	Reb	Ass	PF	Points
					TOTAL															PER GAME				

l986/87 N.B.A. — EASTERN CONFERENCE
CENTRAL DIVISION

Use Name	Pos	Hgt	Wgt	Age	G	Min	FG	FGA	%	FT	FTA	%	Reb	Ass	PF	DQ	Stls	Blkd Shts	Points	Min	Reb	Ass	PF	Points
ATLANTA HAWKS	57-25 .695				**MIKE FRATELLO**																			
Dominique Wilkins	F	6'8	200	26	79	2969	828	1787	46	607	742	82	494	261	149	0	117	51	2294	38	6.3	3.3	1.9	29.0
Kevin Willis	F-C	7'	235	24	81	2626	538	1003	54	227	320	71	849	62	313	4	65	61	1304	32	10.5	0.8	3.9	16.1
Tree Rollins	C	7'1	240	31	75	1764	171	313	55	63	87	72	488	22	240	1	43	140	405	24	6.5	0.3	3.2	5.4
Glenn Rivers	G	6'4	185	25	82	2590	342	758	45	365	441	83	299	823	287	5	171	30	1053	32	3.6	10.0	3.5	12.8
Randy Wittman	G	6'6	210	27	71	2049	398	792	50	100	127	79	124	211	107	0	39	16	900	29	1.7	3.0	1.5	12.7
Cliff Levingston	F	6'8	220	25	82	1848	251	496	51	155	212	73	533	40	261	4	48	68	657	23	6.5	0.5	3.2	8.0
Jon Koncak	C	7'	260	23	82	1684	169	352	48	125	191	65	493	31	262	2	52	76	463	21	6.0	0.4	3.2	5.6
Mike McGee	G	6'5	207	27	76	1420	311	677	46	80	137	58	159	149	156	1	61	2	788	19	2.1	2.0	2.1	10.4
John Battle	G	6'2	175	24	64	804	144	315	46	93	126	74	60	124	76	0	29	5	381	13	0.9	1.9	1.2	6.0
Antoine Carr	F	6'9	235	25	65	695	134	265	51	73	103	71	156	34	146	1	14	48	342	11	2.4	0.5	2.2	5.3
Spud Webb	G	5'7	135	23	33	532	71	162	44	80	105	76	60	167	65	1	34	2	223	16	1.8	5.1	2.0	6.8
Gus Williams	G	6'2	175	33	33	481	53	146	36	27	40	68	40	139	53	0	17	5	138	15	1.2	4.2	1.6	4.2
Scott Hastings	F	6'10	235	26	40	256	23	68	34	23	29	79	70	13	35	0	10	7	71	6	1.8	0.3	0.9	1.8
Cedric Henderson (to Mil)	F	6'8	210	21	6	10	2	5	40	1	1	100	3	0	1	0	0	0	5	2	0.5	0.0	0.2	0.8
Michael Wilson (from NJ)	G	6'4	180	27	2	2	0	2	0	0	0	—	0	1	1	0	0	0	0	1	0.0	0.5	0.5	0.0
3-PT FG —	Wilkins 31-106, Willis 1-4, Rivers 4-2,Wittman 4-12, Levingston 0-3, Koncak 0-1 McGee 86-229, Battle 0-10, Carr 1-3, Webb 1-6, Williams5-18, Hastibngs 2-12																							
DETROIT PISTONS	52-30 .634				**CHUCK DALY**																			
Adrian Dantley	F-G	6'5	210	30	81	2736	601	1126	53	539	664	81	332	162	193	1	63	7	1742	34	4.1	2.0	2.4	21.5
Sidney Green	F	6'9	220	25	80	1792	256	542	47	119	177	67	653	62	197	0	41	50	631	22	8.2	0.8	2.5	7.9
Bill Laimbeer	C	6'11	260	29	82	2854	506	1010	50	245	274	89	955	151	283	4	72	69	1263	35	11.6	1.8	3.5	15.4
Joe Dumars	G	6'3	190	23	79	2439	369	749	49	184	246	75	167	352	194	1	83	5	931	31	2.1	4.5	2.5	11.8
Isiah Thomas	G	6'1	185	25	81	3013	626	1353	46	400	521	77	319	813	251	5	153	20	1671	37	3.9	10.0	3.1	20.6
Vinnie Johnson	G	6'2	200	30	78	2166	533	1154	46	158	201	79	257	300	159	0	92	16	1228	28	3.3	3.8	2.0	15.7
John Salley	F-C	7'	230	22	82	1463	163	290	56	105	171	61	296	54	256	5	44	125	431	18	3.6	0.7	3.1	5.3
Rick Mahorn	F-C	6'10	255	28	63	1278	144	322	45	96	117	82	375	38	221	4	32	50	384	20	6.0	0.6	3.5	6.1
Dennis Rodman	F	6'8	210	25	77	1155	213	391	54	74	126	59	332	56	166	1	38	48	500	15	4.3	0.7	2.2	6.5
Tony Campbell	F	6'7	215	24	40	332	57	145	39	24	39	62	58	19	40	0	12	1	138	8	1.5	0.5	1.0	3.5
Kurt Nimphius (from LAC)	C	6'11	225	28	28	277	36	78	46	24	32	75	54	7	38	0	4	13	96	10	1.9	0.3	1.4	3.4
Chuck Nevitt	C	7'5	237	27	41	267	31	63	49	14	24	58	83	4	73	0	7	30	76	7	2.0	0.1	1.8	1.9
Jeff Taylor	G	6'4	175	26	12	44	6	10	60	9	10	90	4	3	4	0	2	1	21	4	0.3	0.3	0.3	1.8
Cozell McQueen	F	6'11	235	24	3	7	3	3	100	0	0	—	8	0	1	0	0	1	6	2	2.7	0.0	0.3	2.0
John Schweitz	G	6'6	210	26	3	7	0	1	0	0	0	—	1	0	2	0	0	0	0	2	0.3	0.0	0.7	0.0
3-PT FG —	Dantley 1-6, Green 0-2, Laimbeer 6-21, Dumars 9-22, Thomas 9-98, Johnson 4-14, Salley 0-1, Rodman 0-1, Campbell 0-3, Nimphius 0-1																							
MILWAUKEE BUCKS	50-32 .610				**DON NELSON**																			
Rickey Pierce	F-G	6'4	222	27	79	2505	575	1077	53	387	440	88	266	144	222	0	64	24	1540	32	3.4	1.8	2.8	19.5
Terry Cummings	F	6'9	235	25	82	2770	729	1426	51	249	376	66	700	229	296	3	129	81	1707	34	8.5	2.8	3.6	20.8
Jack Sikma	C-F	7'	260	31	82	2536	390	842	46	265	313	85	822	203	328	14	88	90	1045	31	10.0	2.5	4.0	12.7
Paul Pressey (RJ)	G	6'5	205	28	61	2057	294	616	48	242	328	74	296	441	213	4	110	47	846	34	4.9	7.2	3.5	13.9
John Lucas	G	6'3	185	33	43	1358	285	624	46	137	174	79	125	290	82	0	71	6	753	32	2.9	6.7	1.9	17.5
Craig Hodges	G	6'3	195	26	78	2147	315	682	46	131	147	89	140	240	189	3	76	7	846	28	1.8	3.1	2.4	10.8
Randy Breuer	C	7'3	263	26	76	1467	241	497	48	118	202	58	350	47	229	9	56	61	600	19	4.6	0.6	3.0	7.9
Sidney Moncrief (KJ)	G	6'4	180	29	39	992	158	324	49	136	162	84	127	121	73	0	27	10	460	25	3.3	3.1	1.9	11.8
Jerry Reunolds	F	6'8	206	24	58	963	140	356	39	118	184	64	173	106	91	0	50	30	404	17	3.0	1.8	1.6	7.0
Dudley Bradley	G-F	6'6	195	29	68	900	76	213	36	47	58	81	102	66	118	2	105	8	212	13	1.5	1.0	1.7	3.1
Paul Mokeski	F	7'	255	29	62	626	52	129	40	46	64	72	138	22	126	0	18	13	150	10	2.2	0.4	2.0	2.4
Keith Smith	G	6'3	193	22	42	461	57	150	38	21	28	75	32	43	74	0	25	3	138	11	0.8	1.0	1.8	3.3
Junior Bridgeman	F	6'5	215	33	34	418	79	171	46	16	20	80	52	35	50	0	10	2	175	12	1.5	1.0	1.5	5.1
Scott Skiles	G	6'1	200	22	13	205	18	62	29	10	12	83	26	45	18	0	5	1	49	16	2.0	3.5	1.4	3.8
Marvin Webster	C	7'1	240	34	15	102	10	19	53	6	8	75	26	3	17	0	3	7	27	7	1.7	0.2	1.1	1.8
Hank McDowell	F	6'9	215	27	7	70	8	17	47	6	7	86	19	2	14	0	2	0	22	10	2.7	0.3	2.0	3.1
Don Collins	F	6'6	190	28	6	57	10	28	36	5	7	71	15	2	11	0	2	1	25	10	2.5	0.3	1.8	4.2
C.Engler (from Port, to NJ)	C	6'11	250	27	5	48	3	12	25	1	1	100	16	3	10	0	1	1	7	10	3.2	0.6	2.0	1.4
Jerome Henderson	F	6'11	230	27	6	36	4	13	31	4	4	100	7	0	12	0	1	1	12	6	1.2	0.0	2.0	2.0
Mike Glenn	G	6'2	189	31	4	34	5	13	38	5	7	71	2	1	3	0	1	0	15	9	0.5	0.3	0.8	3.8
Kenny Fields (to LAC)	F	6'5	240	24	4	22	6	8	75	1	5	20	2	1	3	0	1	0	13	6	0.5	0.3	0.8	3.3
Cedric Henderson (from Atl)	F	6'8	210	21	2	6	2	3	67	2	2	100	5	0	1	0	0	0	6	3	2.5	0.0	0.5	3.0
3-PT FG —	Pierce 3-28, Cummings 0-23, Sikma 0-2, Pressey 16-55, Lucas 46-126, Hodges 85-228, Moncrief 8-31, Reynolds 6-18, Bradley 13-50, Mokeski 0-1, Smith 3-9, Bridgeman 1-6, Skiles 3-14, Webster 1-1																							
INDIANA PACERS	41-41 .500				**JACK RAMSAY**																			
Chuck Person	F	6'9	225	22	82	2956	635	1358	47	222	297	75	677	295	310	4	90	16	1541	36	8.3	3.6	3.8	18.8
Herb Williams	F-C	6'11	242	28	74	2526	451	939	48	199	269	74	543	174	255	9	59	93	1101	34	7.3	2.4	3.4	14.9
Steve Stipanovich	C	7'	250	26	81	2761	382	760	50	307	367	84	670	180	304	9	106	97	1072	34	8.3	2.2	3.8	13.2
John Long	G	6'5	200	31	80	2265	490	1170	42	219	246	89	217	258	167	1	96	8	1218	28	2.7	3.2	2.1	15.2
Vern Fleming	G	6'5	195	25	82	2549	370	727	51	238	302	79	334	473	222	3	109	18	980	31	4.1	5.8	2.7	12.0
Wayman Tisdale	F	6'9	240	22	81	2159	458	892	51	258	364	71	475	117	293	9	50	26	1174	27	5.9	1.4	3.6	14.5
Clint Richardson	G	6'3	195	30	78	1396	218	467	47	59	74	80	143	241	106	0	49	7	501	18	1.8	3.1	1.4	6.4
Kyle Macy	G	6'3	195	29	76	1250	164	341	48	34	41	83	113	197	136	0	59	7	376	16	1.5	2.6	1.8	4.9
Ron Anderson	F	6'4	215	28	63	721	139	294	47	85	108	79	151	54	65	0	31	3	363	11	2.4	0.9	1.0	5.8
Walker Russell	G	6'5	195	26	48	511	64	165	39	27	37	73	55	129	62	0	20	5	157	11	1.1	2.7	1.3	3.3
Stuart Gray	C	7'	245	23	55	456	41	101	41	28	39	72	129	26	93	0	10	28	110	8	2.3	0.5	1.7	2.0
Michael Brooks	F	6'7	220	28	10	148	13	37	35	7	10	70	28	11	19	0	9	0	33	15	2.8	1.1	1.9	3.3
Greg Dreiling	C	7'1	250	23	24	128	16	37	43	10	12	83	43	7	42	0	2	2	42	5	1.8	0.3	1.8	1.8

(continued next page)

1986/87 N.B.A. — EASTERN CONFERENCE — CENTRAL DIVISION

Use Name	Pos	Hgt	Wgt	Age	G	Min	FG	FGA	%	FT	FTA	%	Reb	Ass	PF	DQ	Stls	Blkd Shts	Points	Min	Reb	Ass	PF	Points
					TOTAL															PER GAME				
INDIANA (continued)																								
Clark Kellogg	F	6'7	227	25	4	60	8	22	36	3	4	75	11	6	12	0	5	0	20	15	2.8	1.5	3.0	5.0
Pete Verhoeven	F	6'9	220	27	5	44	5	14	36	0	0	—	7	2	11	1	2	1	10	9	1.4	0.4	2.2	2.0

3 PT FG - Person 49-138, Williams 0-9, Stipanovich 1-4, Long 19-67, Fleming 2-l0, Tisdale 0-2, Richardson 6-17, Macy 14-46, Anderson 0-5, Russell 2-16, Kellogg l-2

Use Name	Pos	Hgt	Wgt	Age	G	Min	FG	FGA	%	FT	FTA	%	Reb	Ass	PF	DQ	Stls	Blkd Shts	Points	Min	Reb	Ass	PF	Points
CHICAGO BULLS	40-42 .488				DOUG COLLINS																			
Gene Banks	F	6'7	215	27	63	1822	249	462	54	112	146	77	308	170	173	3	52	17	610	29	4.9	2.7	2.7	9.7
Charles Oakley	F	6'8	225	23	82	2980	468	1052	44	245	357	69	**1074**	296	315	4	85	36	1192	36	13.1	3.6	3.8	14.5
Dave Corzine	C	6'11	260	30	82	2287	294	619	47	95	129	74	540	209	202	1	38	87	683	28	6.6	2.5	2.5	8.3
Michael Jordan	G	6'6	195	23	82	**3281**	**1069**	**2279**	47	**833**	**972**	86	430	377	237	0	236	125	**3041**	40	5.2	4.6	2.9	**37.1**
John Paxson	G	6'2	185	26	82	2689	386	793	49	106	131	81	139	467	207	1	66	8	930	33	1.7	5.7	2.5	11.3
Brad Sellers	C-F	7'	210	24	80	1751	276	606	46	126	173	73	373	102	194	1	44	68	680	22	4.7	1.3	2.4	8.5
Earl Cureton (to LAC)	F	6'9	215	29	43	1105	129	276	47	39	73	53	227	70	102	2	15	26	297	26	5.3	1.6	2.4	6.9
Elston Turner	G	6'5	200	27	70	936	112	252	44	23	31	74	115	102	97	1	30	4	248	13	1.6	1.5	1.4	3.5
Mike Brown	F	6'10	260	23	62	818	106	201	53	46	72	64	214	24	129	2	20	7	258	13	3.5	0.4	2.1	4.2
Sedale Threatt (from Phi)	G	6'2	177	25	40	778	131	273	48	53	66	80	51	177	88	0	42	9	315	19	1.3	4.4	2.2	7.9
Granville Waiters	C	6'11	225	25	44	534	40	93	43	5	9	56	87	22	83	1	10	31	85	12	2.0	0.5	1.9	1.9
Steve Colter (to Phi)	G	6'3	175	24	27	473	49	142	35	33	39	85	42	94	38	0	19	6	131	18	1.6	3.5	1.4	4.9
Ben Poquette (from Cle)	C	6'9	235	31	21	167	21	40	53	9	11	82	24	7	26	0	3	12	51	8	1.1	0.3	1.2	2.4
Pete Myers	G	6'6	180	23	29	155	19	52	37	28	43	65	17	21	25	0	14	2	66	5	0.6	0.7	0.9	2.3
Fred Cofield	G	6'3	190	24	5	27	2	11	18	0	0	—	5	4	1	0	2	0	4	5	1.0	0.8	0.2	0.8
Perry Young (to Port)	G	6'5	210	23	5	20	2	4	50	1	2	50	1	0	3	0	1	0	5	4	0.2	0.0	0.6	1.0
Darren Daye (to Bos)	F	6'8	220	26	1	7	0	0	—	0	0	—	1	1	2	0	0	0	0	7	1.0	1.0	2.0	0.0

3-PT FG — Banks 0-5, Oakley 11-30, Paxson 52-140, Jordan 12-66, Paxson 52-140, Sellers 2-10, Cureton 0-l, Turner 1-8, Threatt 0-16, Waiters 0-1, Colter 0-9, Poquette 0-1, Myers 0-6, Cofield 0-1

Use Name	Pos	Hgt	Wgt	Age	G	Min	FG	FGA	%	FT	FTA	%	Reb	Ass	PF	DQ	Stls	Blkd Shts	Points	Min	Reb	Ass	PF	Points
CLEVELAND CAVALIERS	31-5l .378				LENNY WILKENS																			
Phil Hubbard	F	6'8	215	30	68	2083	321	605	53	162	272	60	388	136	224	6	66	7	804	31	5.7	2.0	3.3	11.8
John Williams	F	6'11	230	25	80	2714	435	897	48	298	400	75	629	154	197	0	58	167	1168	34	7.9	1.9	2.5	14.6
Brad Daugherty	C	7'	245	21	80	2695	487	905	54	279	401	70	647	304	248	3	49	63	1253	34	8.1	3.8	3.1	15.7
Ron Harper	G	6'6	205	22	82	3064	734	1614	45	386	564	68	392	394	247	3	209	84	1874	37	4.8	4.8	3.0	22.9
John Bagley	G	6'	192	26	72	2182	312	732	43	113	136	83	252	379	114	0	91	7	768	30	3.5	5.3	1.6	10.7
Mark West	F-C	6'10	230	26	78	1333	209	385	54	89	173	51	339	41	229	5	22	81	507	17	4.3	0.5	2.9	6.5
Mark Price	G	6'1	175	22	67	1217	173	424	41	95	114	83	117	202	75	1	43	4	464	18	1.7	3.0	1.1	6.9
Craig Ehlo	G	6'7	185	25	44	890	99	239	41	70	99	71	161	92	80	0	40	30	273	20	3.7	2.1	1.8	6.2
Keith Lee (KJ)	F	6'10	220	24	67	870	170	374	45	72	101	71	251	69	147	0	25	40	412	13	3.7	1.0	2.2	6.1
Mel Turpin	C	6'11	240	26	64	801	169	366	46	55	77	71	190	33	90	1	11	40	393	13	3.0	0.5	1.4	6.1
Johnny Newman	F-G	6'7	190	23	59	630	113	275	41	66	76	87	70	27	67	0	20	7	293	11	1.2	0.5	1.1	5.0
Tyrone Corbin (from SA)	G-F	6'6	220	24	32	438	43	117	37	42	57	74	96	17	48	0	17	2	129	14	3.0	0.5	1.5	4.0
Ben Poquette (to Chi)	C-F	6'9	235	31	37	437	41	82	50	31	39	79	77	28	51	1	6	22	113	12	2.1	0.8	1.4	3.1
Scooter McCray	F	6'9	215	26	24	279	30	65	46	20	41	49	58	23	28	0	9	4	80	12	2.4	1.0	1.2	3.3
Dirk Minniefield (to Hou)	G	6'3	180	25	11	122	13	42	31	1	4	25	10	13	8	0	6	1	27	11	0.9	1.2	0.7	2.5

3-PT FG — Hubbard 0-4, Williams 0-l, Harper 20-94, Bagley 31-l03, West 0-2, Price 23-70, Ehlo 5-29, Lee 0-1, Newman 1-22, Corbin 1-4, Poquette 0-3, Minniefield 0-5

1986/1987 N.B.A. — WESTERN CONFERENCE
MIDWEST DIVISION

Use Name	Pos	Hgt	Wgt	Age	G	Min	FG	FGA	%	FT	FTA	%	Reb	Ass	PF	DQ	Stls	Blkd Shts	Points	Min	Reb	Ass	PF	Points
DALLAS MAVERICKS	55-27 .671				DICK MOTTA																			
Mark Aguirre	F-G	6'6	235	27	80	2663	787	1590	49	429	557	77	427	254	243	4	84	30	2056	33	5.3	3.2	3.0	25.7
Sam Perkins	F	6'9	235	25	80	2687	461	957	48	245	296	83	616	146	269	6	109	77	1186	34	7.7	1.8	3.4	14.8
James Donaldson	C	7'2	278	29	82	3028	311	531	59	267	329	81	973	63	191	0	51	136	889	37	11.9	0.8	2.3	10.8
Rolando Blackman	G	6'6	194	27	80	2758	626	1264	50	419	474	88	278	266	142	0	64	21	1676	34	3.5	3.3	1.8	21.0
Derek Harper	G	6'4	203	25	77	2556	497	993	50	160	234	68	199	609	195	0	167	25	1230	33	2.6	7.9	2.5	16.0
Detlef Schrempf	F	6'10	214	23	81	1711	265	561	47	193	260	74	303	161	224	2	50	16	756	21	3.7	2.0	2.8	9.3
Brad Davis	G	6'3	180	31	82	1582	199	436	46	147	171	86	114	373	159	0	63	10	577	19	1.4	4.5	1.9	7.0
Roy Tarpley	F-C	6'11	240	22	75	1405	233	499	47	94	139	68	533	52	232	3	56	79	561	19	7.1	0.7	3.1	7.5
Al Wood	G	6'6	210	28	54	657	121	310	39	109	139	78	94	34	83	0	19	11	358	12	1.7	0.6	1.5	6.6
Bill Wennington	C	7'	245	22	58	560	56	132	42	45	60	75	129	24	95	0	13	10	157	10	2.2	0.4	1.6	2.7
Uwe Blab	C	7'1	255	24	30	160	20	51	39	13	28	46	36	13	33	0	4	9	53	5	1.2	0.4	1.1	1.8
Dennis Nutt	G	6'2	170	23	25	91	16	40	40	20	22	91	8	16	6	0	7	0	57	4	0.3	0.6	0.2	2.3
Myron Jackson	G	6'3	185	22	8	22	2	9	22	7	8	88	3	6	1	0	1	0	11	3	0.4	0.8	0.1	1.4

3-PT FG — Aguirre 53-150, Perkins l9-54, Blackman 5-15, Harper 76-212, Schrempf 33-69, Davis 32-106, Tarpley 1-3, Wood 7-25, Wennington 0-2,Nutt 5-17

Use Name	Pos	Hgt	Wgt	Age	G	Min	FG	FGA	%	FT	FTA	%	Reb	Ass	PF	DQ	Stls	Blkd Shts	Points	Min	Reb	Ass	PF	Points
UTAH JAZZ	44-38 .537				FRANK LAYDEN																			
Kelly Tripucka	F	6'6	225	27	79	1865	291	621	47	197	226	87	242	243	147	0	85	11	798	24	3.1	3.1	1.9	10.1
Karl Malone	F	6'9	254	23	82	2857	728	1422	51	323	540	60	855	158	323	6	104	60	1779	35	10.4	1.9	3.9	21.7
Mark Eaton	C	7'4	290	29	79	2505	234	585	40	140	213	66	697	105	273	5	43	**321**	608	32	8.8	1.3	3.5	7.7
Darrell Griffith	G	6'4	190	28	76	1843	463	1038	45	149	212	70	227	129	167	0	97	29	1142	24	3.0	1.7	2.2	15.0
Rickey Green	G	6'	172	32	81	2090	301	644	47	172	208	83	163	541	108	0	110	2	781	26	2.0	6.7	1.3	9.6
Thurl Bailey	F-C	6'11	222	25	81	2155	463	1036	45	190	236	81	432	102	150	0	38	88	1116	27	5.3	1.3	1.9	13.8
John Stockton	G	6'1	175	24	82	1858	231	463	50	179	229	78	151	670	224	1	177	14	648	23	1.8	8.2	2.7	7.9
Bob Hansen	G	6'6	195	25	72	1453	272	601	45	136	179	76	203	102	146	0	44	6	696	20	2.8	1.4	2.0	9.7
Kent Benson	C	6'10	240	32	73	895	140	316	44	47	58	81	231	39	138	0	39	28	329	12	3.2	0.5	1.9	4.5
Marc Iavaroni	F	6'10	225	30	78	845	100	215	47	78	116	67	173	36	154	0	16	11	278	11	2.2	0.5	2.0	3.6
Carey Scurry	F	6'7	190	24	69	753	123	247	50	94	134	70	198	57	124	1	55	54	344	11	2.9	0.8	1.8	5.0
Dell Curry	G	6'5	195	22	67	636	139	326	43	30	38	79	78	58	86	0	27	4	325	9	1.2	0.9	1.3	4.9

3-PT FG — Tripucka 19-52, Malone 0-7, Griffith 67-200, Green 7-19, Bailey 0-2, Stockton 7-39, Hansen 16-45, Benson 2-7, Iavaroni 0-4, Scurry 4-13, Curry 17-60

Use Name	Pos	Hgt	Wgt	Age	G	Min	FG	FGA	%	FT	FTA	%	Reb	Ass	PF	DQ	Stls	Blkd Shts	Points	Min	Reb	Ass	PF	Points
					TOTAL															PER GAME				

1986/87 N.B.A. — WESTERN CONFERENCE
MIDWEST DIVISION

Use Name	Pos	Hgt	Wgt	Age	G	Min	FG	FGA	%	FT	FTA	%	Reb	Ass	PF	DQ	Stls	Blkd Shts	Points	Min	Reb	Ass	PF	Points
HOUSTON ROCKETS	42-40 .512				BILL FITCH																			
Rodney McCray	F-G	6'8	235	25	81	3136	432	783	55	306	393	78	578	434	172	2	88	53	1170	39	7.1	5.4	2.1	14.4
Ralph Sampson (KJ)	F-C	7'4	230	26	43	1326	277	566	49	118	189	62	372	120	169	6	40	58	672	31	8.7	2.8	3.9	15.6
Akeem Olajuwon	C	7'	250	23	75	2760	677	1332	51	400	570	70	858	220	294	8	140	254	1755	37	11.4	2.9	3.9	23.4
Robert Reid	G-F	6'8	215	31	75	2594	420	1006	42	136	177	77	289	323	232	2	75	21	1029	35	3.9	4.3	3.1	13.7
Dirk Minnifield (from Cle)	G	6'3	180	25	63	1478	205	440	47	61	86	71	130	335	166	2	66	6	482	23	2.1	5.3	2.6	7.7
Jim Peterson	F-C	6'10	235	24	82	2403	386	755	51	152	209	73	557	127	268	5	43	102	924	29	6.8	1.5	3.3	11.3
Allen Leavell	G	6'2	190	29	53	1175	147	358	41	100	119	84	61	224	126	1	53	10	412	22	1.2	4.2	2.4	7.8
Steve Harris	G	6'5	195	23	74	1174	251	599	42	111	130	85	170	100	111	1	37	16	613	16	2.3	1.4	1.5	8.3
Cedric Maxwell (from LAC)	F	6'8	225	31	46	836	103	188	55	126	163	77	184	75	76	0	13	5	332	18	4.0	1.6	1.7	7.2
Mitchell Wiggins (DR)	G	6'4	185	27	32	788	153	350	44	49	65	75	133	76	82	1	44	3	355	25	4.2	2.4	2.6	11.1
Lewis Lloyd (DR)	G	6'6	205	27	32	688	165	310	53	65	86	76	48	90	69	0	19	5	396	22	1.5	2.8	2.2	12.4
Buck Johnson	F	6'7	190	22	60	520	94	201	47	40	58	69	88	40	81	0	17	15	228	9	1.5	0.7	1.4	3.8
Dave Feitl	C	7'	240	24	62	498	88	202	44	53	71	75	117	22	83	0	9	4	229	8	1.9	0.4	1.3	3.7
Richard Anderson	F-C	6'10	240	26	51	312	59	139	42	22	29	76	79	33	37	0	7	3	144	6	1.5	0.6	0.7	2.8
Conner Henry (to Bos)	G	6'7	195	23	18	92	8	33	24	7	10	70	7	8	7	0	3	0	24	5	0.4	0.4	0.4	1.3

3-PT FG — McCray 0-9, Sampson 0-3, Olajuwon 1-5, Reid 53-162, Minnifield 11-34, Peterson 0-4, Leavell 18-57, Harris 0-8, Maxwell 0-l, Wiggins 0-5, Lloyd 1-7, Johnson 0-l, Feitl 0-l, Anderson 4-16, Henry l-11

Use Name	Pos	Hgt	Wgt	Age	G	Min	FG	FGA	%	FT	FTA	%	Reb	Ass	PF	DQ	Stls	Blkd Shts	Points	Min	Reb	Ass	PF	Points
DENVER NUGGETS	37-45 .451				DOUG MOE																			
Alex English	F	6'7	190	32	82	3085	965	1920	50	411	487	84	344	422	216	0	73	21	2345	38	4.2	5.1	2.6	28.6
Bill Hanzlik	F	6'7	200	29	73	1990	307	746	41	316	402	79	256	280	245	3	87	28	952	27	3.5	3.8	3.4	13.0
Wayne Cooper	C	6'10	220	30	69	1561	235	524	45	79	109	72	473	68	257	5	13	101	549	23	6.9	1.0	3.7	8.0
Darrell Walker	G	6'4	180	25	81	2020	358	742	48	272	365	75	327	282	229	0	120	37	988	25	4.0	3.5	2.8	12.2
Lafayette Lever	G	6'3	175	26	82	3054	643	1370	47	244	312	78	729	654	219	1	201	34	1552	37	8.9	8.0	2.7	18.9
T.R. Dunn	G-F	6'4	192	31	81	1932	118	276	43	36	55	65	265	147	160	0	100	21	272	24	3.3	1.8	2.0	3.4
Mike Evans	G	6'1	170	31	81	1567	334	729	46	96	123	78	128	185	149	1	79	12	817	19	1.6	2.3	1.8	10.1
Danny Schayes	C-F	6'11	245	27	76	1556	210	405	52	229	294	78	380	85	266	5	20	74	649	20	5.0	1.1	3.5	8.5
Blair Rasmussen	C	7'	250	24	74	1421	268	570	47	169	231	73	465	60	224	6	24	58	705	19	6.3	0.8	3.0	9.5
Mark Alarie	F	6'8	217	23	64	1110	217	443	49	67	101	66	214	74	138	1	22	28	503	17	3.3	1.2	2.2	7.9
Maurice Martin	F	6'6	200	22	43	286	51	135	38	42	66	64	41	35	48	0	13	6	147	7	1.0	0.8	1.1	3.4
Otis Smith	F-G	6'5	210	22	28	168	33	79	42	12	21	57	34	22	30	0	1	1	78	6	1.2	0.8	1.1	2.8
Calvin Natt (LJ)	F	6'6	220	29	1	20	4	10	40	2	2	100	5	2	2	0	1	0	10	20	5.0	2.0	2.0	10.0
Pete Williams	F	6'7	190	23	5	10	1	2	50	0	0	---	1	1	1	0	0	0	2	2	0.2	0.2	0.2	0.4

3-PT FG — English 4-15, Hanzlik 22-80, Cooper 0-3, Walker 0-4, Lever 22-92, Dunn 0-2, Evans 53-169, Alarie 2-9, Martin 3-5, Smith 0-2

Use Name	Pos	Hgt	Wgt	Age	G	Min	FG	FGA	%	FT	FTA	%	Reb	Ass	PF	DQ	Stls	Blkd Shts	Points	Min	Reb	Ass	PF	Points
SACRAMENTO KINGS	29-53 .354				(PHIL JOHNSON (14-32 .304), JERRY REYNOLDS 15-21 .417)																			
Eddie Johnson	F	6'9	218	27	81	2457	606	1309	46	267	322	83	353	251	218	4	42	19	1516	30	4.4	3.1	2.7	18.7
Otis Thorpe	F	6'11	236	24	82	2956	567	1050	54	413	543	76	819	201	292	11	46	60	1547	36	10.0	2.5	3.6	18.9
LaSalle Thompson	C	6'10	253	25	82	2166	362	752	48	188	255	74	687	122	290	6	69	126	912	26	8.4	1.5	3.5	11.1
Derek Smith	G	6'6	218	25	52	1658	338	757	45	178	228	78	182	204	184	3	46	23	863	32	3.5	3.9	3.5	16.6
Reggie Theus	G	6'7	213	29	79	2872	577	1223	47	429	495	87	266	692	208	3	78	16	1600	36	3.4	8.8	2.6	20.3
Terry Tyler	F-G	6'7	228	30	82	1930	329	664	50	101	140	72	328	73	151	1	55	78	760	24	4.0	0.9	1.8	9.3
Joe Kleine	C	7'	271	24	79	1658	256	543	47	110	140	79	483	71	213	2	35	30	622	21	6.1	0.9	2.7	7.9
Mark Olberding	F	6'9	247	30	76	1002	69	165	42	116	131	89	185	91	144	0	18	9	254	13	2.4	1.2	1.9	3.3
Harold Pressley	G-F	6'8	210	23	67	913	134	317	42	35	48	73	176	120	96	1	40	21	310	14	2.6	1.8	1.4	4.6
Othell Wilson	G	6'	190	25	53	789	82	185	44	43	54	80	81	207	67	0	42	4	210	15	1.5	3.9	1.3	4.0
Brooke Steppe	G	6'5	195	27	34	665	95	199	48	73	88	83	61	81	56	0	18	3	266	20	1.8	2.4	1.6	7.8
Johnny Rogers	F-C	6'11	231	23	45	468	90	185	49	9	15	60	77	26	66	0	9	8	189	10	1.7	0.6	1.5	4.2
Franklin Edwards	G	6'1	190	27	8	122	9	32	28	10	14	71	10	29	7	0	5	0	28	15	1.3	3.6	0.9	3.5
Bruce Douglas	G	6'3	195	22	8	98	7	24	29	0	4	0	14	17	9	0	9	0	14	12	1.8	2.1	1.1	1.8
Jerry Eaves	G	6'4	185	27	3	26	1	8	13	2	2	100	1	0	6	0	1	0	4	9	0.3	0.0	2.0	1.3

3-PT FG — Johnson 37-118, Thorpe 0-3, Thompson 0-5, Smith 9-33, Theus 17-78, Tyler l-3, Kleine 0-1, Olberding 0-1, Pressley 7-28, Wilson 3-18, Steppe 3-9,Rogers 0-5, Edwards 0-4, Douglas 0-1

Use Name	Pos	Hgt	Wgt	Age	G	Min	FG	FGA	%	FT	FTA	%	Reb	Ass	PF	DQ	Stls	Blkd Shts	Points	Min	Reb	Ass	PF	Points
SAN ANTONIO SPURS	28-54 .341				BOB WEISS																			
Walter Berry (from Port)	F	6'8	215	22	56	1567	401	758	53	186	287	65	302	104	188	2	36	40	988	28	5.4	1.9	3.4	17.6
Dave Greenwood	F	6'9	225	29	79	2587	336	655	51	241	307	79	783	237	248	3	71	50	916	33	9.9	3.0	3.1	11.6
Artis Gilmore	C	7'2	265	37	82	2405	346	580	60	242	356	68	579	150	235	2	39	95	934	29	7.1	1.8	2.9	11.4
Alvin Robertson	G	6'4	190	24	81	2697	589	1264	47	244	324	75	424	421	264	2	260	35	1435	33	5.2	5.2	3.3	17.7
Johnny Moore (IL)	G	6'3	185	28	55	1234	198	448	44	56	70	80	100	250	97	0	83	3	474	22	1.8	4.5	1.8	8.6
Jon Sundvold	G	6'2	170	25	76	1765	365	751	49	70	84	83	98	315	109	1	35	0	850	23	1.3	4.1	1.4	11.2
Johnny Dawkins	G	6'2	165	23	81	1682	334	764	44	153	191	80	169	290	118	0	67	3	835	21	2.1	3.6	1.5	10.3
Mychal Thompson (to LAL)	C	6'10	235	31	49	1210	230	528	44	144	196	73	276	87	117	0	31	41	605	25	5.6	1.8	2.4	12.3
Larry Krystkowiak	F-C	6'9	220	22	68	1004	170	373	46	110	148	74	239	85	141	1	22	12	451	15	3.5	1.3	2.1	6.6
Ed Nealy	F	6'7	238	26	60	980	84	192	44	51	69	74	284	83	144	1	40	11	223	16	4.7	1.4	2.4	3.7
Mike Mitchell (DR)	F	6'7	215	30	40	922	208	478	44	92	112	82	103	38	68	0	19	9	509	23	2.6	1.0	1.7	12.7
Anthony Jones (from Was)	G-F	6'6	195	24	49	744	119	289	41	41	52	79	95	66	68	0	32	18	286	15	1.9	1.3	1.4	5.8
Tyrone Corbin (to Cle)	F-G	6'6	222	24	31	732	113	264	43	49	67	73	119	80	81	0	38	3	275	24	3.8	2.6	2.6	8.9
Kevin Duckworth (to Port)	C	7'	280	22	14	122	18	45	40	9	14	64	31	6	27	0	5	3	45	9	2.2	0.4	1.9	3.2
Frank Brickowski (from LAL)	C	6'10	240	27	7	83	10	30	33	10	11	91	19	5	13	0	6	2	30	12	2.7	0.7	1.9	4.3
Forrest McKenzie	F	6'7	200	23	6	42	7	28	25	2	2	100	7	1	9	0	1	0	17	7	1.2	0.2	1.5	2.8
Mike Brittain	C	7'1	235	23	6	29	4	9	44	1	2	50	4	2	3	0	1	0	9	5	0.7	0.3	0.5	1.5

3-PT FG — Berry 0-3, Greenwood 3-6, Robertson 13-48,Moore 22-79, Sundvold 50-149, Dawkins 14-47, Thompson 1-1, Krystkowiak 1-12, Nealy 4-31, Mitchell 1-2, Jones 7-19, Brickowski 0-4, McKenzie 1-2

Use Name	Pos	Hgt	Wgt	Age	G	Min	FG	FGA	%	FT	FTA	%	Reb	Ass	PF	DQ	Stls	Blkd Shts	Points	Min	Reb	Ass	PF	Points
					TOTAL															PER GAME				

1986/87 N.B.A. — WESTERN CONFERENCE
PACIFIC DIVISION

Use Name	Pos	Hgt	Wgt	Age	G	Min	FG	FGA	%	FT	FTA	%	Reb	Ass	PF	DQ	Stls	Blkd Shts	Points	Min	Reb	Ass	PF	Points
LOS ANGELES LAKERS	**65-17 .793**				**PAT RILEY**																			
James Worthy	F	6'9	235	25	82	2819	651	1207	54	292	389	75	466	226	206	0	108	83	1594	34	5.7	2.8	2.5	19.4
A.C. Green	F-C	6'9	230	23	79	2240	316	587	54	220	282	78	615	84	171	0	70	80	852	28	7.8	1.1	2.2	10.8
Kareem Abdul-Jabbar	C	7'2	267	39	78	2441	560	993	56	245	343	71	523	203	245	2	49	97	1366	31	6.7	2.6	3.1	17.5
Byron Scott	G	6'4	195	25	82	2729	554	1134	49	224	251	89	286	281	163	0	125	18	1397	33	3.5	3.4	2.0	17.0
Magic Johnson	G	6'9	222	27	80	2904	683	1308	52	535	631	85	504	**977**	168	0	138	36	1909	36	6.3	**12.2**	2.1	23.9
Michael Cooper	G-F	6'5	176	30	82	2253	322	736	44	126	148	85	254	373	199	1	78	43	859	27	3.1	4.5	2.4	10.5
Kurt Rambis	F	6'8	220	28	78	1514	163	313	52	120	157	76	453	63	201	1	74	41	446	19	5.8	0.8	2.6	5.7
Billy Thompson	F	6'7	220	23	59	762	142	261	54	48	74	65	171	60	148	1	15	30	332	13	2.9	1.0	2.5	5.6
Mychal Thompson (from SA)	C	6'10	235	31	33	680	129	269	48	75	101	74	136	28	85	1	14	30	333	21	4.1	0.8	2.6	10.1
Wes Matthews	G	6'1	170	27	50	532	89	187	48	29	36	81	47	100	53	0	23	4	208	11	0.9	2.0	1.1	4.2
Frank Brickowski (to SA)	C	6'10	240	27	37	404	53	94	56	40	59	68	97	12	105	4	14	4	146	11	2.6	0.3	2.8	3.9
Mike Smrek	C	7'	260	24	35	233	30	60	50	16	25	64	37	5	70	1	4	13	76	7	1.1	0.1	2.0	2.2
Adrian Branch	G	6'8	185	23	32	219	48	96	50	42	54	78	53	16	39	0	16	3	138	7	1.7	0.5	1.2	4.3
3-PT FG —	Worthy 0-13, Green 0-5, Abdul-Jabbar 1-3, Scott 65-149, Johnson 8-39, Cooper 89-231, B. Thompson 0-l, M.Thopmpson 0-1, Matthews 1-3, Branch 0-2																							
PORTLAND TRAILBLAZERS	**49-33 .598**				**MIKE SCHULER**																			
Kiki Vanderweghe	C-F	6'8	220	28	79	3029	808	1545	52	467	527	89	251	220	137	0	52	17	2122	38	3.2	2.8	1.7	26.9
Kenny Carr	F	6'7	230	31	49	1443	201	399	50	126	169	75	499	83	159	1	29	13	528	29	10.2	1.7	3.2	10.8
Sam Bowie (LJ)	C	7'1	235	25	5	163	30	66	45	20	30	67	33	9	19	0	1	10	80	33	6.6	1.8	3.8	16.0
Clyde Drexler	G	6'7	215	24	82	3114	707	1408	50	357	470	76	518	566	281	7	204	71	1782	38	6.3	6.9	3.4	21.7
Terry Porter	G	6'3	195	23	80	2714	376	770	49	280	334	84	337	715	192	0	159	9	1045	34	4.2	8.9	2.4	13.1
Steve Johnson	C-F	6'10	235	29	79	2345	494	889	56	342	490	70	566	155	**340**	**16**	49	76	1330	30	7.2	2.0	4.3	16.8
Jerome Kersey	F	6'7	220	24	82	2088	373	733	51	262	364	72	496	194	328	5	122	77	1009	25	6.0	2.4	4.0	12.3
Jim Paxson	G-F	6'6	210	29	72	1798	337	733	46	174	216	81	139	237	134	0	76	12	874	25	1.9	3.3	1.9	12.1
Caldwell Jones	C	7'	·225	36	78	1578	111	224	50	97	124	78	455	64	227	5	23	77	319	20	5.8	0.8	2.9	4.1
Kevin Duckworth (from SA)	C	7'	280	22	51	753	112	228	49	83	120	69	192	23	165	3	16	18	307	15	3.8	0.5	3.2	6.0
Michael Holton	G	6'4	195	25	58	479	70	171	41	44	55	80	38	73	51	0	16	2	191	8	0.7	1.3	0.9	3.3
Fernando Martin	C	6'10	238	24	24	146	9	31	29	4	11	36	28	9	24	0	7	1	22	6	1.2	0.4	1.0	0.9
Perry Young (from Chi)	G	6'5	210	23	4	52	4	17	24	0	0	—	7	7	11	0	4	1	8	13	1.8	1.8	2.8	2.0
Joe Binion	F	6'8	215	22	11	51	4	10	40	6	10	60	18	1	5	0	2	2	14	5	1.6	0.1	0.5	1.3
Walter Berry (to SA)	F	6'8	215	22	7	19	6	8	75	1	1	100	7	1	8	0	2	0	13	3	1.0	0.1	1.1	1.9
Chris Engler (to Mil, NJ)	C	6'11	250	27	7	17	4	8	50	3	3	100	8	1	0	0	1	1	11	2	1.1	0.1	0.0	1.6
Ron Rowan	G	6'5	200	23	7	16	4	9	44	3	4	75	1	1	1	0	4	0	12	2	0.1	0.1	0.1	1.7
3-PT FG —	Vanderweghe 39-8l, Carr 0-2, Drexler 11-47, Porter 13-60, Kersey 1-23, Paxson 26-98, Jones 0-2, Duckworth 0-1, Holton 7-23, Martin 0-1, Rowan 1-1																							
GOLDEN STATE WARRIORS	**42-40 .512**				**GEORGE KARL**																			
Purvis Short	F	6'7	220	29	34	950	240	501	48	137	160	86	137	86	103	1	45	7	621	28	4.0	2.5	3.0	18.3
Larry Smith	F	6'8	235	28	80	2374	297	544	55	113	197	57	917	95	295	7	71	56	707	30	11.5	1.2	3.7	8.8
Joe Barry Carroll	C	7'	255	28	81	2724	690	1461	47	340	432	79	589	214	255	2	92	123	1720	34	7.3	2.6	3.1	21.2
Chris Mullin	G	6'7	220	23	82	2377	477	928	51	269	326	83	181	261	217	1	98	36	1242	29	2.2	3.2	2.6	15.1
Eric Floyd	G	6'3	175	26	82	3064	503	1030	49	462	537	86	268	848	199	1	146	18	1541	37	3.3	10.3	2.4	18.8
Terry Teagle	G	6'5	195	26	82	1650	370	808	46	182	234	78	175	105	190	0	68	13	922	20	2.1	1.3	2.3	11.2
Greg Ballard	F	6'7	215	31	82	1579	248	564	44	68	91	75	340	108	167	0	50	15	579	19	4.1	1.3	2.0	7.1
Rod Higgins	F	6'7	205	26	73	1497	214	412	52	200	240	83	237	96	145	0	40	21	631	21	3.2	1.3	2.0	8.6
Ben Mcdonald	F	6'8	225	24	63	1284	164	360	46	24	38	63	183	84	200	5	27	8	353	20	2.9	1.3	3.2	5.6
Jerome Whitehead	C	6'10	240	30	73	937	147	327	45	79	113	70	262	24	175	1	16	12	373	13	3.6	0.3	2.4	5.1
Perry Moss	G	6'2	185	28	64	698	91	207	44	49	69	71	95	90	96	0	42	3	232	11	1.5	1.4	1.5	3.6
Chris Washburn	C-F	6'11	255	21	35	385	57	145	39	18	51	35	101	16	51	0	6	8	132	11	2.9	0.5	1.5	3.8
Clinton Smith	G-F	6'6	210	22	41	341	50	117	43	27	36	75	56	45	36	0	13	1	127	8	1.4	1.1	0.9	3.1
Kevin Henderson	G	6'4	195	22	5	45	3	8	38	2	2	100	3	11	9	0	1	0	8	9	0.6	2.2	1.8	1.6
3-PT FG —	Short 4-17, L.Smith o-1, Mullin l9-63, Floyd 73-190, Teagle 0-10, Ballard 15-40, Higgens 3-17, McDonald l-8, Whitehead 0-1, Moss 1-14, Washburn 0-1, C.Smith 0-2																							
SEATTLE SUPERSONICS	**39-43 .476**				**BERNIE BICKERSTAFF**																			
Xavier McDaniel	F	6'8	205	23	82	3031	806	1583	51	275	395	70	705	207	300	4	115	52	1890	37	8.6	2.5	3.7	23.0
Tom Chambers	F	6'10	230	27	82	3018	660	1446	46	535	630	85	545	245	307	9	81	50	1909	37	6.6	3.0	3.7	23.3
Alton Lister	C	7'	240	28	75	2288	346	687	50	179	265	68	705	110	289	11	32	180	871	31	9.4	1.5	3.9	11.6
Dale Ellis	G-F	6'7	215	26	82	3073	785	1520	52	385	489	79	447	238	267	2	104	32	2041	37	5.5	2.9	3.3	24.9
Nate McMillan	G	6'5	195	22	71	1972	143	301	48	87	141	62	331	583	238	4	125	45	373	28	4.7	8.2	3.4	5.3
Danny Young	G	6'3	175	24	73	1482	132	288	46	59	71	83	113	353	72	0	74	3	352	20	1.5	4.8	1.0	4.8
Clemon Johnson	C	6'10	240	30	78	1051	88	178	49	70	110	64	277	21	137	0	21	42	246	13	3.6	0.3	1.8	3.2
Maurice Lucas	F-C	6'9	238	34	63	1120	175	388	45	150	187	80	307	65	171	1	34	21	500	18	4.9	1.0	2.7	7.9
Kevin Williams	G	6'2	180	25	65	703	132	296	45	55	66	83	83	66	154	1	45	8	319	11	1.3	1.0	2.4	4.9
Russ Schoene	C-F	6'10	215	26	63	579	71	190	37	29	46	63	117	27	94	1	20	11	173	9	1.9	0.4	1.5	2.7
Eddie Johnson	G	6'2	190	31	24	508	85	186	46	42	55	76	46	115	36	0	12	1	217	21	1.9	4.8	1.5	9.0
Michael Phelps	G	6'4	180	26	60	469	75	176	43	31	44	70	50	64	60	0	21	2	182	8	0.8	1.1	1.0	3.0
Terence Stansbury	G	6'5	178	25	44	375	67	156	43	31	50	62	24	57	78	0	13	0	176	9	0.5	1.3	1.8	4.0
Gerald Henderson (to NY)	G	6'2	280	30	6	155	25	50	50	17	18	94	9	32	17	0	6	0	67	26	1.5	5.3	2.8	11.2
Curtis Kitchen	F	6'9	235	22	6	31	3	6	50	3	4	75	9	1	4	0	2	3	9	5	1.5	0.2	0.7	1.5
3-PT FG —	McDaniel 3-14, Chambers 54-145, Lister 0-l, Ellis 86-240, McMillan 0-7, Young 29-79, C.Johnson 0-2, Lucas 0-5, Williams 0-7, Schoene 2-13, E.Johnson 5-15, Phelps 1-10, Stansbury 11-29, Henderson 0-3, Kitchen 0-1																							

1986/87 N.B.A. — WESTERN CONFERENCE
PACIFIC DIVISION

PHOENIX SUNS 36-46 .439 JOHN MacLEOD (22-34 .393), DICK VAN ARSDALE (14-12 .538)

Use Name	Pos	Hgt	Wgt	Age	G	Min	FG	FGA	%	FT	FTA	%	Reb	Ass	PF	DQ	Stls	Blkd Shts	Points	Min	Reb	Ass	PF	Points
Larry Nance	F	6'10	217	27	69	2569	585	1062	55	381	493	77	599	233	223	4	86	148	1552	37	8.7	3.4	3.2	22.5
Ed Pinckney	F	6'10	215	23	80	2250	290	497	58	257	348	74	580	116	196	1	86	54	837	28	7.3	1.5	2.5	10.5
Alvan Adams	C	6'9	220	32	68	1690	311	618	50	134	170	79	338	223	207	3	62	37	756	25	5.0	3.3	3.0	11.1
Walter Davis	G	6'6	200	32	79	2646	779	1515	51	288	334	86	244	364	184	1	96	5	1867	33	3.1	4.6	2.3	23.6
Jay Humphries	G	6'3	185	24	82	2579	359	753	48	200	260	77	260	632	239	1	112	9	923	31	3.2	7.7	2.9	11.3
Mike Sanders	F	6'6	210	26	82	1655	357	722	49	143	183	78	271	126	210	1	61	23	859	20	3.3	1.5	2.6	10.5
Jeff Hornacek	G	6'3	195	23	80	1561	159	350	45	94	121	78	184	361	130	0	70	5	424	20	2.3	4.5	1.6	5.3
Kenny Gattison	F-C	6'8	225	22	77	1104	148	311	48	108	171	63	270	36	178	1	24	33	404	14	3.5	0.5	2.3	5.2
William Bedford	C	7'	225	23	50	979	142	358	40	50	86	58	246	57	125	1	18	37	334	20	4.9	1.1	2.5	6.7
Grant Gondrezick	G	6'5	205	23	64	836	135	300	45	75	107	70	110	81	91	0	25	4	349	13	1.7	1.3	1.4	5.5
Rafael Addison	F	6'7	215	22	62	711	146	331	44	51	64	80	106	45	75	1	27	7	359	11	1.7	0.7	1.2	5.8
Nick Vanos	C	7'1	255	23	57	640	65	158	41	38	59	64	180	43	94	0	19	23	168	11	3.2	0.8	1.6	2.9
Bernard Thompson	G	6'7	215	24	24	331	42	105	40	27	33	82	31	18	53	0	11	5	111	14	1.3	0.8	2.2	4.6
James Edwards	C	7'	235	31	14	304	57	110	52	54	70	77	60	19	42	1	6	7	168	22	4.3	1.4	3.0	12.0

3-PT FG — Nance 1-5, Pinckney 0-2, Adams 0-1, Davis 21-81, Humphries 5-27, Sanders 2-17, Hornacek 12-43, Gattison 0-3, Bedford 0-1, Gondrezick 4-17, Addison 16-50, Vanos 0-2, Thompson 0-3

LOS ANGELES CLIPPERS 12-70 .146 DON CHANEY

Use Name	Pos	Hgt	Wgt	Age	G	Min	FG	FGA	%	FT	FTA	%	Reb	Ass	PF	DQ	Stls	Blkd Shts	Points	Min	Reb	Ass	PF	Points
Marques Johnson (ZJ)	F	6'7	233	30	10	302	68	155	44	30	42	71	33	28	24	0	12	5	166	30	3.3	2.8	2.4	16.6
Michael Cage	F	6'9	225	24	80	2922	457	878	52	341	467	73	922	131	221	1	99	67	1255	37	11.5	1.6	2.8	15.7
Benoit Benjamin	C	7'	250	22	72	2230	320	713	45	188	263	71	586	135	251	7	60	187	828	31	8.1	1.9	3.5	11.5
Mike Woodson	G	6'5	198	28	74	2126	494	1130	44	240	290	83	162	196	201	1	100	16	1262	29	2.2	2.6	2.7	17.1
Darnell Valentine	G	6'2	185	27	65	1759	275	671	41	163	200	82	150	447	148	3	116	10	726	27	2.3	6.9	2.3	11.2
Larry Drew	G	6'2	190	28	60	1566	295	683	43	139	166	84	103	326	107	0	60	2	741	26	1.7	5.4	1.8	12.4
Rory White	F	6'8	210	27	68	1545	265	552	48	94	144	65	194	79	159	1	47	19	624	23	2.9	1.2	2.3	9.2
Cedric Maxwell (to Hou)	F	6'8	225	31	35	1132	150	289	52	177	228	78	251	122	102	1	26	9	477	32	7.2	3.5	2.9	13.6
Lancaster Gordon	G	6'3	185	24	70	1130	221	545	41	70	95	74	126	139	106	1	61	13	526	16	1.8	2.0	1.5	7.5
Tim Kempton	C	6'10	245	22	66	936	97	206	47	95	137	69	194	53	162	6	38	12	289	14	2.9	0.8	2.5	4.4
Quintin Dailey	G	6'3	180	25	49	924	200	491	41	119	155	77	83	79	113	4	43	8	520	19	1.7	1.6	2.3	10.6
Earl Cureton (from Chi)	F	6'9	215	29	35	868	114	234	49	43	79	54	225	52	86	0	18	30	271	25	6.4	1.5	2.5	7.7
Kenny Fields (from Mil)	F	6'5	240	24	44	861	153	344	44	72	89	81	146	60	120	2	31	11	381	20	3.3	1.4	2.7	8.7
Kurt Nimphius (to Det)	C	6'10	220	28	38	811	119	252	47	57	88	65	133	18	118	1	16	41	295	21	3.5	0.5	3.1	7.8
Geoff Huston	G	6'2	175	29	19	428	55	121	45	18	34	53	17	101	28	0	14	0	129	23	0.9	5.3	1.5	6.8
Steffond Johnson	F	6'8	240	24	29	234	27	64	42	20	38	53	43	5	55	2	9	2	74	8	1.5	0.2	1.9	2.6
Dwayne Polee	G	6'5	180	24	1	6	1	4	25	0	0	--	0	0	3	0	1	0	2	6	0.0	0.0	3.0	2.0

Norm Nixon - knee injury

3-PT FG — M.Johnson 0-6, Cage 0-3, Benjamin 0-2, Woodson 34-123, Valentine 13-56, Drew 12-72, White 0-3, Gordon 14-48, Kempton 0-1, Dailey 1-10, Cureton 0-1, Fields 3-12, Nimphius 0-3, Huston 1-2, S. Johnson 0-3, Polee 0-3

PLAYOFFS

LOS ANGELES LAKERS PAT RILEY

defeated Denver 3-0; H128-95, H139-127, 140-103
defeated Golden State 4-1; H125-116, H116-101, 133-108, 121-129, H118-106
defeated Seattle 4-0; H92-87, H112-104, 122-121, 133-102
defeated Boston 4-2; H126-113, H141-122, 103-109, 107-106, 108-123, H106-93

Use Name	Pos	Hgt	Wgt	Age	G	Min	FG	FGA	%	FT	FTA	%	Reb	Ass	PF	DQ	Stls	Blkd Shts	Points	Min	Reb	Ass	PF	Points
James Worthy	F	6'9	235	25	18	681	176	298	59	73	97	75	101	63	42	1	28	22	425	38	5.6	3.5	2.3	23.6
A.C. Green	F	6'9	230	23	18	505	71	130	55	65	87	75	142	11	47	0	9	8	207	28	7.9	0.6	2.6	11.5
Kareem Abdul-Jabbar	C	7'2	267	39	18	559	124	234	53	97	122	80	123	36	56	0	8	35	345	31	6.8	2.0	3.1	19.2
Byron Scott	G	6'4	195	25	18	608	103	210	49	53	67	79	62	57	52	0	19	4	266	34	3.4	3.2	2.9	14.8
Magic Johnson	G	6'9	222	27	18	666	146	271	54	98	118	83	139	**219**	37	0	31	7	392	37	7.7	12.2	2.1	21.8
Michael Cooper	G-F	6'5	176	30	18	522	77	159	48	46	54	85	59	90	46	0	25	14	234	29	3.3	5.0	2.6	13.0
Mychal Thompson	C-F	6'10	235	31	18	401	62	137	45	34	50	68	88	9	50	0	7	17	158	22	4.9	0.5	2.8	8.8
Kurt Rambis	F	6'8	220	28	17	215	24	41	59	31	34	91	67	9	42	0	8	3	79	13	3.9	0.5	2.5	4.6
Wes Matthews	G	6'1	170	27	12	61	11	23	48	6	7	86	4	9	9	0	1	0	28	5	0.3	0.8	0.8	2.3
Adrian Branch	G	6'8	185	23	11	42	4	21	19	6	12	50	10	5	10	0	2	0	14	4	0.9	0.5	0.9	1.3
Mike Smrek	C	7'	260	24	10	33	2	10	20	4	6	67	7	0	15	0	0	6	8	3	0.7	0.0	1.5	0.8
Billy Thompson	F	6'7	220	23	3	27	6	11	55	2	2	100	6	2	2	0	4	0	14	9	2.0	0.7	0.7	4.7

3-PT FG — Worthy 0-2, Abdul-Jabbar 0-1, Scott 7-34 ,Johnson 2-l0, Cooper 34-70, Matthews 0-1, Branch 0-1

BOSTON CELTICS K. C. JONES

defeated Chicago 3-0; H108-104, H105-96,105-94
defeated Milwaukee 4-3; H111-98, H1216-124, 121-126(OT), 138-137(OT), H124-129, 111-121, H119-113
defeated Detroit 4-3; H104-91, H110-101,104-122, 119-145, H108-107, 105-113, H117-114
lost to Los Angeles 2-4; 113-126, 122-141, H109-103, H106-107, H123-108, 93-106

Use Name	Pos	Hgt	Wgt	Age	G	Min	FG	FGA	%	FT	FTA	%	Reb	Ass	PF	DQ	Stls	Blkd Shts	Points	Min	Reb	Ass	PF	Points
Larry Bird	F	6'9	220	30	23	**1015**	**216**	**454**	48	**176**	**193**	91	**231**	165	55	1	27	19	622	44	10.0	7.2	2.4	27.0
Kevin McHale	F-C	6'10	225	29	21	827	174	298	58	96	126	76	194	39	71	2	7	30	444	39	9.2	1.9	3.4	21.1
Robert Parish	C	7'	230	33	21	734	149	263	57	79	103	77	198	28	**79**	**4**	18	35	377	35	9.4	1.3	3.8	18.0
Danny Ainge	G	6'4	185	27	20	762	116	238	49	31	36	86	52	92	62	0	24	4	295	38	2.6	4.6	3.1	14.8
Dennis Johnson	G	6'4	200	32	23	964	168	361	47	96	113	85	91	205	71	0	16	8	435	42	4.0	8.9	3.1	18.9
Jerry Sichting	G	6'1	180	30	23	338	35	82	43	8	10	80	20	33	36	0	9	0	79	15	0.9	1.4	1.6	3.4
Fred Roberts	F	6'10	220	26	20	265	30	59	51	31	44	70	33	12	47	0	6	3	91	13	1.7	0.6	2.4	4.6
Darren Daye	F	6'8	220	26	23	240	42	72	58	32	37	86	32	13	33	1	9	3	116	10	1.4	0.6	1.4	5.0
Greg Kite	C	6'11	250	25	20	172	7	20	35	3	7	43	46	8	43	1	2	8	17	9	2.3	0.4	2.2	0.9
Sam Vincent	G	6'2	185	23	17	141	23	56	41	27	35	77	12	19	13	0	3	2	74	8	0.7	1.1	0.8	4.4
Bill Walton	C	6'11	235	34	12	102	12	25	48	5	14	36	31	10	23	0	3	4	29	9	2.6	0.8	1.9	2.4
Conner Henry	G	6'7	195	23	11	35	8	16	50	5	10	50	6	0	3	2	2	2	22	3	0.5	0.0	0.3	2.0

3-PT FG — Bird 52-154, Parish 0-1, Ainge 32-73, Johnson 3-26, Sichting 1-6, Vincent 1-2, Henry 1-5

1986/87 N.B.A. — PLAYOFFS

DETROIT PISTONS — **CHUCK DALY**

defeated Washington 3-0; H106-92, H128-85, 97-96
defeated Atlanta 4-1; 112-111, 102-115, H108-99, H89-88,104-96
lost to Boston 3-4; 91-104, 101-110, H122-104, H145-119,107-108, H113-105, 114-117

Use Name	Pos	Hgt	Wgt	Age	G	Min	FG	FGA	%	FT	FTA	%	Reb	Ass	PF	DQ	Stls	Blkd Shts	Points	Min (per game)	Reb (per game)	Ass (per game)	PF (per game)	Points (per game)
Adrian Dantley	F-G	6'5	210	30	15	500	111	206	54	86	111	77	68	35	36	0	13	0	308	33	4.5	2.3	2.4	20.5
Rick Mahorn	F-C	6'10	255	28	15	483	59	109	54	28	35	80	142	5	60	1	6	11	146	32	9.5	0.3	4.0	9.7
Bill Laimbeer	C	6'11	260	29	15	543	84	163	52	15	24	63	156	37	53	2	15	12	184	36	10.4	2.5	3.5	12.3
Joe Dumars	G	6'3	190	23	15	473	78	145	54	32	41	78	19	72	26	0	12	1	190	32	1.3	4.8	1.7	12.7
Isiah Thomas	G	6'1	185	25	15	562	134	297	45	83	110	75	67	130	51	1	**39**	4	361	37	4.5	8.7	3.4	24.1
Vinnie Johnson	G	6'2	200	30	15	388	95	207	46	31	36	86	44	62	33	0	9	4	221	26	2.9	4.1	2.2	14.7
John Salley	F	7'	230	22	15	311	33	66	50	27	42	64	72	11	60	1	3	17	93	21	4.8	0.7	4.0	6.2
Dennis Rodman	F	6'8	210	25	15	245	40	74	54	18	32	56	71	3	48	0	6	17	98	16	4.7	0.2	3.2	6.5
Sidney Green	F	6'9	220	25	9	42	6	10	60	5	6	83	9	1	2	0	1	2	17	5	1.0	0.1	0.2	1.9
Kurt Nimphius	C	6'10	225	28	4	30	3	9	33	2	4	50	10	0	10	0	0	2	8	8	2.5	0.0	2.5	2.0
Tony Campbell	F	6'7	215	24	4	13	3	6	50	2	2	100	5	0	1	0	0	0	9	3	1.3	0.0	0.3	2.3
Chuck Nevitt	C	7'5	237	27	3	10	1	5	20	2	2	100	6	0	1	0	0	3	4	3	2.0	0.0	0.3	1.3

3-PT FG — Mahorn 0-1, Laimbeer 1-5, Dumars 2-3, Thomas 10-33, Johnson 0-2, Campbell 1-1

SEATTLE SUPERSONICS — **BERNIE BICKERSTAFF**

defeated Dallas 3-1; 129-151, 112-110, H117-107, H124-98
defeated Houston 4-2; 111-106(OT), 99-97, H84-102, H117-102, 107-112, H128-125(2OT)
lost to L.A.Lakers 0-4; 87-92, 104-112, H121-122, H102-133

Use Name	Pos	Hgt	Wgt	Age	G	Min	FG	FGA	%	FT	FTA	%	Reb	Ass	PF	DQ	Stls	Blkd Shts	Points	Min (per game)	Reb (per game)	Ass (per game)	PF (per game)	Points (per game)
Xavier McDaniel	F	6'8	205	23	14	528	124	254	49	34	56	61	117	42	63	2	21	9	284	38	8.4	3.0	4.5	20.3
Tom Chambers	F	6'10	230	27	14	498	118	263	45	80	99	81	90	32	51	0	12	13	322	36	6.4	2.3	3.6	23.0
Alton Lister	C	7'	240	28	9	206	20	50	40	14	20	70	56	7	37	3	7	13	54	23	6.2	0.8	4.1	6.0
Dale Ellis	G-F	6'7	215	26	14	530	148	304	49	44	54	81	90	37	54	1	10	6	353	38	6.4	2.6	3.9	25.2
Nate McMillan	G	6'5	195	22	14	356	27	62	44	17	24	71	54	112	42	1	14	10	71	25	3.9	8.0	3.0	5.1
Maurice Lucas	F-C	6'9	238	34	14	265	35	90	39	28	38	74	65	19	43	1	12	5	98	19	4.6	1.4	3.1	7.0
Clemon Johnson	C	6'10	240	30	14	262	24	53	45	12	19	63	49	4	18	0	7	15	60	19	3.5	0.3	1.3	4.3
Kevin Williams	G	6'2	180	25	14	255	45	94	48	30	40	75	34	30	44	0	16	1	120	18	2.4	2.1	3.1	8.6
Danny Young	G	6'3	175	24	14	208	21	52	40	10	10	100	16	48	21	1	15	0	57	15	1.1	3.4	1.5	4.1
Eddie Johnson	G	6'2	190	31	14	181	31	58	53	26	30	87	14	45	16	0	5	0	90	13	1.0	3.2	1.1	6.4
Russ Schoene	C	6'10	215	26	14	123	10	28	36	9	12	75	26	3	16	1	1	4	31	9	1.9	0.2	1.1	2.2
Curtis Kitchen	F	6'9	235	22	8	23	1	2	50	0	4	0	6	0	7	0	0	2	2	3	0.8	0.0	0.9	0.3

3-PT FG — McDaniel 2-10,Chambers 6-17,Ellis 13-36, Lucas 0-1,C.Johnson 0-1,
Williams 0-2, Young 5-16, E.Johnson 2-5, Schoene 2-6

MILWAUKEE BUCKS — **DON NELSON**

defeated Philadelphia 3-2; H107-104, H122-125(OT), 121-120, 118-124, H102-89
lost to Boston 4-3; 98-111, 124-126, H126-121(OT), H137-138(2OT),129-124, H121-111, 113-119

Use Name	Pos	Hgt	Wgt	Age	G	Min	FG	FGA	%	FT	FTA	%	Reb	Ass	PF	DQ	Stls	Blkd Shts	Points	Min (per game)	Reb (per game)	Ass (per game)	PF (per game)	Points (per game)
Sidney Moncrief	F-G	6'4	180	29	12	426	78	165	47	73	90	81	54	36	43	0	13	6	233	36	4.5	3.0	3.6	19.4
Terry Cummings	F	6'9	235	25	12	443	105	215	49	57	83	69	95	28	51	1	12	13	267	37	7.9	2.3	4.3	22.3
Jack Sikma	C	6'11	260	31	12	426	73	150	49	48	49	98	130	23	56	3	15	10	194	36	10.8	1.9	4.7	16.2
Paul Pressey	G	6'5	205	28	12	465	68	146	47	34	46	74	62	103	51	3	28	8	171	39	5.2	8.6	4.3	14.3
Jihn Lucas	G	6'3	185	33	12	362	68	150	45	39	48	81	25	62	17	0	14	1	187	30	2.1	5.2	1.4	15.6
Rickey Pierce	F	6'5	222	27	12	317	68	142	48	55	67	82	28	16	39	0	10	5	191	26	2.3	1.3	3.3	15.9
Craig Hodges	G	6'3	195	26	12	226	40	77	52	10	11	91	22	20	16	0	9	2	95	19	1.8	1.7	1.3	7.9
Randy Breuer	C	7'3	263	26	12	156	16	33	48	8	12	67	31	4	32	1	7	9	40	13	2.6	0.3	2.7	3.3
Paul Mokeski	F-C	6'11	255	29	12	107	8	22	36	12	15	80	29	2	22	1	3	2	28	9	2.4	0.2	1.8	2.3
Dudley Bradley	G-F	6'6	195	29	12	46	4	11	36	1	2	50	0	2	9	0	3	0	9	4	0.0	0.2	0.8	0.8
Jerry Reynolds	F	6'8	206	24	4	5	1	3	33	1	2	50	1	2	0	0	3	0	3	1	0.3	0.5	0.0	0.8
Jerome Henderson	F	6'11	230	27	1	1	0	0	—	0	0	—	0	0	1	0	0	0	0	1	0.0	0.0	1.0	0.0

3-PT FG — Moncrief 4-14, Sikma 0-1, Pressey 1-8, Lucas 12-36,
Hodges 5-17, Mokeski 0-1, Bradley 0-6, Reynolds 0-1

GOLDEN STATE WARRIORS — **GEORGE KARL**

defeated Utah 3-2; 85-99, 100-103, H110-95, H98-94, 118-113
lost to L.A. Lakers 1-4; 116-125, 101-116, H108-133, H129-121, 106-118

Use Name	Pos	Hgt	Wgt	Age	G	Min	FG	FGA	%	FT	FTA	%	Reb	Ass	PF	DQ	Stls	Blkd Shts	Points	Min (per game)	Reb (per game)	Ass (per game)	PF (per game)	Points (per game)
Purvis Short	F	6'7	220	29	10	253	57	123	46	32	36	89	33	27	34	0	12	2	146	25	3.3	2.7	3.4	14.6
Larry Smith	F	6'8	235	28	10	329	43	81	53	17	24	71	137	17	39	0	12	6	103	33	13.7	1.7	3.9	10.3
Joe Barry Carroll	C	7'	255	28	10	334	74	163	45	41	51	80	65	19	42	2	14	25	189	33	6.5	1.9	4.2	18.9
Chris Mullin	G	6'7	220	23	10	262	49	98	50	12	16	75	15	23	31	0	9	2	113	26	1.5	2.3	3.1	11.3
Eric Floyd	G	6'3	175	26	10	414	77	152	51	47	51	92	30	102	24	0	18	2	214	41	3.0	10.2	2.4	21.4
Terry Teagle	G	6'5	195	26	10	233	57	124	46	30	38	79	20	13	27	0	8	1	144	23	2.0	1.3	2.7	14.4
Greg Ballard	F	6'7	215	31	10	179	26	48	54	3	4	75	40	19	16	0	8	0	59	18	4.0	1.9	1.6	5.9
Rod Higgins	F	6'7	205	26	10	177	18	46	.39	6	9	67	21	12	20	0	11	6	43	18	2.1	1.2	2.0	4.3
Jerome Whitehead	C	6'10	240	30	10	100	9	27	33	4	10	40	14	3	22	1	2	2	22	10	1.4	0.3	2.2	2.2
Perry Moss	G	6'2	185	28	8	45	8	14	57	8	9	89	5	5	5	0	6	0	25	6	0.6	0.6	0.6	3.1
Ben McDonald	F	6'8	225	24	5	45	1	11	9	0	0	—	6	9	7	0	2	0	2	9	1.2	1.8	1.4	0.4
Chris Washburn	C	6'11	255	21	5	29	3	7	43	5	6	83	1	2	2	0	0	0	11	6	0.2	0.4	0.4	2.2

3-PT FG — Short 0-2, Carroll 0-1, Mullin 3-4, Floyd 13-28, Teagle 0-2,
Ballard 4-10, Higgins 1-1, Moss 1-1, McDonald 0-2

1986/87 — N.B.A. — PLAYOFFS

HOUSTON ROCKETS — **BILL FITCH**

defeated Portland 3-1; 125-115, 98-111, H117-108, H113-101
lost to Seattle 2-4; H106-111(OT), H07-99, 102-84, 102-117, H112-107, 125-128(2OT)

Use Name	Pos	Hgt	Wgt	Age	G	Min	FG	FGA	%	FT	FTA	%	Reb	Ass	PF	DQ	Stls	Blkd Shts	Points	Min (per game)	Reb (per game)	Ass (per game)	PF (per game)	Points (per game)
Rodney McCray	F-G	6'8	235	25	10	436	57	101	56	43	54	80	83	56	21	0	5	9	157	44	8.3	5.6	2.1	15.7
Ralph Sampson	F-C	7'4	230	26	10	330	75	146	51	35	43	81	88	21	47	1	2	12	186	33	8.8	2.1	4.7	18.6
Akeem Olajuwon	C	7'	250	23	10	389	110	179	61	72	97	74	113	25	44	1	13	**43**	292	39	11.3	2.5	4.4	**29.2**
Robert Reid	G	6'8	215	31	10	431	56	155	36	15	23	65	36	48	36	0	10	3	129	43	3.6	4.8	3.6	12.9
Allen Leavell	G	6'1	190	29	10	384	44	107	41	49	60	82	25	72	42	2	19	3	141	38	2.5	7.2	4.2	14.1
Jim Peterson	F-C	6'10	235	24	10	187	28	51	55	12	18	67	46	6	26	1	5	2	68	19	4.6	0.6	2.6	6.8
Cedric Maxwell	F	6'8	225	31	10	177	18	34	53	26	35	74	33	17	17	1	4	0	62	18	3.3	1.7	1.7	6.2
Steve Harris	G	6'5	195	23	9	91	16	43	37	5	6	83	7	5	15	0	3	0	37	10	0.8	0.6	1.7	4.1
Dirk Minniefield	G	6'3	180	25	8	27	4	8	50	6	6	100	2	2	8	0	1	0	14	3	0.3	0.3	1.0	1.8
Buck Johnson	F	6'7	190	22	5	10	2	6	33	0	0	—	0	0	1	0	0	0	4	2	0.0	0.0	0.2	0.8
Dave Feitl	C	7'	240	24	6	8	0	0	—	2	2	100	1	0	0	0	0	0	2	1	0.2	0.0	0.0	0.3
Richard Anderson	F	6'10	240	26	5	5	1	3	33	2	2	100	1	0	1	0	0	0	5	1	0.2	0.0	0.2	1.0

3 PT FG — McCray 0-2, Sampson 1-2, Olajuwon 0-1, Reid 2-17, Leavell 4-16, Maxwell 0-l, Harris 0-1, Minniefield 0-1, Anderson 1-2

ATLANTA HAWKS — **MIKE FRATELLO**

defeated Indiana 3-1; H110-94, H94-93, 87-96, 101-97
lost to Detroit 1-4; H111-112, H115-102, 99-108, 88-89, H96-104

Use Name	Pos	Hgt	Wgt	Age	G	Min	FG	FGA	%	FT	FTA	%	Reb	Ass	PF	DQ	Stls	Blkd Shts	Points	Min (per game)	Reb (per game)	Ass (per game)	PF (per game)	Points (per game)
Dominique Wilkins	F	6'8	200	26	9	360	86	210	41	66	74	70	70	25	25	0	16	8	241	40	7.8	2.8	2.8	26.8
Kevin Willis	F-C	7'	235	24	9	356	60	115	52	21	31	68	83	6	33	0	9	7	141	40	9.2	0.7	3.7	15.7
Tree Rollins	C	7'1	240	31	9	221	15	28	54	10	14	71	53	3	33	0	3	16	40	25	5.9	0.3	3.7	4.4
Randy Wittman	G	6'6	210	27	9	300	67	121	55	14	17	82	18	30	22	0	4	4	148	33	2.0	3.3	2.4	16.4
Glenn Rivers	G	6'4	185	25	8	245	18	47	38	26	52	50	27	90	32	0	9	3	60	31	3.4	11.3	4.0	7.5
Aintoine Carr	F	6'9	235	25	9	162	39	56	**70**	26	32	81	27	13	36	1	3	8	104	18	3.0	1.4	4.0	11.6
Spud Webb	G	5'7	135	23	8	122	9	19	47	13	17	76	8	38	10	6	6	0	31	15	1.0	4.8	1.3	3.9
Cliff Levingston	F	6'8	220	25	9	108	7	18	39	14	18	78	34	3	21	0	0	3	28	12	3.8	0.3	2.3	3.1
Mike McGee	G	6'5	207	27	8	101	10	39	26	5	10	50	20	15	7	0	4	0	27	13	2.5	1.9	0.9	3.4
Jon Koncak	C	7'	260	23	8	86	7	13	54	6	8	75	25	3	24	0	3	4	20	11	3.1	0.4	3.0	2.5
John Battle	G	6'2	175	24	8	78	15	34	44	21	23	91	10	8	13	0	1	0	53	10	1.3	1.0	1.6	6.6
Scott Hastings	F	6'10	235	26	4	21	2	3	67	2	2	100	6	0	5	0	1	1	6	5	1.5	0.0	1.3	1.5

3 PT FG — Wilkins 3-10, Webb 0-1, Levingston 0-l, McGee 2-14, Battle 2-5

PHILADELPHIA 76ers — **MATT GUOKAS**

lost to Milwaukee 2-3; 104-107, 125-122(ot), H120-121, H124-118, 89-102

Use Name	Pos	Hgt	Wgt	Age	G	Min	FG	FGA	%	FT	FTA	%	Reb	Ass	PF	DQ	Stls	Blkd Shts	Points	Min (per game)	Reb (per game)	Ass (per game)	PF (per game)	Points (per game)
Julius Erving	F-G	6'7	210	36	5	180	34	82	41	21	25	84	25	17	19	0	7	6	91	36	5.0	3.4	3.8	18.2
Charles Barkley	F	6'6	263	23	5	210	43	75	57	36	45	80	63	12	21	0	4	8	123	42	12.6	2.4	4.2	24.6
Roy Hinson	C-F	6'9	220	25	5	159	31	52	60	24	38	63	23	3	18	0	4	10	86	32	4.6	0.6	3.6	17.2
Andrew Toney	G	6'3	190	29	5	104	13	34	38	2	2	100	9	27	16	1	2	2	28	21	1.8	5.4	3.2	5.6
Maurice Cheeks	G	6'1	180	30	5	210	35	66	53	18	21	86	13	44	14	0	9	4	88	42	2.6	8.8	2.8	17.6
Cliff Robinson	F	6'9	240	26	5	138	30	61	49	13	15	87	43	6	15	0	3	7	73	28	8.6	1.2	3.0	14.6
Tim McCormick	C	7'	240	24	5	121	12	24	50	4	4	100	31	6	19	0	1	2	28	24	6.2	1.2	3.8	5.6
Dave Wingate	G	6'5	185	23	5	90	15	37	41	9	14	64	12	9	11	1	5	1	41	18	2.4	1.8	2.2	8.2
Steve Colter	G	6'3	175	24	2	8	1	2	50	0	0	—	0	2	1	0	0	0	2	4	0.0	1.0	0.5	1.0
Danny Vranes	F	6'7	220	28	2	3	0	0	—	0	0	—	3	0	1	0	0	0	0	2	1.5	0.0	0.5	0.0
Mark McNamara	C	6'11	235	27	1	2	1	1	100	0	0	—	1	0	0	0	0	0	2	2	1.0	0.0	0.0	2.0

3 PT FG — Erving 2-6, Barkley 1-8, Toney 0-3, Cheeks 0-1, Wingate 2-2

UTAH JAZZ — **FRANK LAYDEN**

lost to Golden State 2-3; H99-85, H103-100, 95-110, 94-98, H113-118

Use Name	Pos	Hgt	Wgt	Age	G	Min	FG	FGA	%	FT	FTA	%	Reb	Ass	PF	DQ	Stls	Blkd Shts	Points	Min (per game)	Reb (per game)	Ass (per game)	PF (per game)	Points (per game)
Kelly Tripucka	F	6'6	225	27	5	70	14	20	70	4	4	100	7	3	6	0	4	0	32	14	1.4	0.6	1.2	6.4
Karl Malone	F	6'9	254	23	5	200	37	88	42	26	36	72	48	6	20	1	11	4	100	40	9.6	1.2	4.0	20.0
Mark Eaton	C	7'4	290	29	5	193	19	41	46	16	25	64	55	3	18	0	1	21	54	39	11.0	0.6	3.6	10.8
Bob Hansen	G	6'6	195	25	5	142	21	49	43	17	20	85	15	11	14	0	1	1	61	28	3.0	2.2	2.8	12.2
John Stockton	G	6'1	175	24	5	157	18	29	62	10	13	77	11	40	18	0	15	1	50	31	2.2	8.0	3.6	10.0
Thurl Bailey	F-C	6'11	222	25	5	151	30	63	48	18	18	**100**	30	9	12	1	3	6	78	30	6.0	1.8	2.4	15.6
Darrell Griffith	G	6'4	190	28	5	104	24	65	37	14	19	74	12	8	5	0	6	2	68	21	2.4	1.6	1.0	13.6
Rickey Green	G	6'	172	32	4	72	11	23	48	5	6	83	8	25	5	0	2	0	27	18	2.0	6.3	1.3	6.8
Carey Scurry	F	6'7	190	24	4	57	10	22	45	3	7	43	14	0	10	0	4	5	24	14	3.5	0.0	2.5	6.0
Marc Iavaroni	F	6'9	225	30	5	47	4	10	40	2	3	67	13	4	7	0	0	3	10	9	2.6	0.8	1.4	2.0
Dell Curry	G	6'5	195	22	2	4	0	3	0	0	0	—	0	0	1	0	0	0	0	2	0.0	0.0	0.5	0.0
Kent Benson	C	6'10	240	32	2	3	0	0	—	0	0	—	0	0	0	0	0	0	0	2	0.0	0.0	0.0	0.0

3 PT FG — Tripucka 0-3, Hansen 2-5, Stockton 4-5, Griffith 6-15, Green 0-1, Scurry 1-2, Curry 0-1

DALLAS MAVERICKS — **DICK MOTTA**

lost to Seattle 1-3; H151-129, H110-112, 107-117, 98-124

Use Name	Pos	Hgt	Wgt	Age	G	Min	FG	FGA	%	FT	FTA	%	Reb	Ass	PF	DQ	Stls	Blkd Shts	Points	Min (per game)	Reb (per game)	Ass (per game)	PF (per game)	Points (per game)
Mark Aguirre	F-G	6'6	235	27	4	130	31	62	50	23	30	77	24	8	15	1	8	0	85	33	6.0	2.0	3.8	21.3
Sam Perkins	F	6'9	235	25	4	133	26	52	50	16	23	70	34	5	16	0	4	1	68	33	8.5	1.3	4.0	17.0
Roy Tarpley	C-F	7'	240	22	4	114	24	48	50	5	7	71	42	1	18	1	1	7	53	29	10.5	0.3	4.5	13.3
Rolando Blackman	G	6'6	194	27	4	153	36	73	49	22	24	92	14	17	7	0	2	0	94	38	3.5	4.3	1.8	23.5
Derek Harper	G	6'4	203	25	4	123	20	40	50	24	30	80	12	27	7	0	7	0	66	31	3.0	6.8	1.8	16.5
Detlef Schrempf	F	6'10	214	23	4	97	13	35	37	5	11	45	12	6	13	0	3	2	31	24	3.0	1.5	3.3	7.8
Brad Davis	G	6'3	180	31	4	75	13	23	57	7	9	78	9	17	4	0	0	0	33	19	2.3	4.3	1.0	8.3
James Donaldson	C	7'2	278	29	3	68	4	5	80	8	9	89	17	2	6	0	1	3	16	23	5.7	0.7	2.0	5.3
Bill Wennington	C	7'	245	22	4	47	6	12	50	3	5	60	10	4	9	0	0	3	15	12	2.5	1.0	2.3	3.8
Uwe Blab	C	7'1	255	24	1	10	1	1	100	1	4	25	3	0	4	0	1	1	3	10	3.0	0.0	4.0	3.0
Dennis Nutt	G	6'2	170	23	1	10	1	5	20	0	0	—	2	1	0	0	0	0	2	10	2.0	1.0	0.0	2.0

3 PT FG — Aguirre 0-4, Perkins 0-4, Blackman 0-1, Harper 2-9, Schrempf 0-3, Davis 0-2, Nutt 0-2

Use Name	Pos	Hgt	Wgt	Age	G	Min	FG	FGA	%	FT	FTA	%	Reb	Ass	PF	DQ	Stls	Blkd Shts	Points	Min	Reb	Ass	PF	Points
					TOTAL															PER GAME				
1986/87 N.B.A. — PLAYOFFS																								
INDIANA PACERS	**JACK RAMSEY**				lost to Atlanta 1-3; 94-110, 93-94, H96-87, H97-101																			
Chuck Person	F	6'8	225	22	4	159	38	74	51	30	39	77	33	20	14	0	5	2	108	40	8.3	5.0	3.5	27.0
Wayman Tisdale	F	6'9	240	22	4	108	19	31	61	13	23	57	16	9	17	1	1	0	51	27	4.0	2.3	4.3	12.8
Steve Stipanovich	C	6'11	250	26	4	149	21	38	55	13	19	68	30	3	14	0	3	2	55	37	7.5	0.8	3.5	13.8
John Long	F	6'5	200	30	4	109	16	52	31	11	13	85	6	9	16	0	6	0	44	27	1.5	2.3	4.0	11.0
Vern Fleming	G	6'5	195	25	4	141	13	36	36	23	30	77	26	24	15	1	4	1	49	35	6.5	6.0	3.8	12.3
Herb Williams	F-C	6'11	242	28	4	134	20	34	59	7	13	54	20	7	12	0	0	1	47	34	5.0	1.8	3.0	11.8
Clint Richardson	G	6'3	195	30	4	73	7	12	58	2	4	50	10	8	12	0	0	0	16	18	2.5	2.0	3.0	4.0
Kyle Macy	G	6'3	195	29	4	49	2	6	33	0	1	0	3	5	7	0	1	0	4	12	0.8	1.3	1.8	1.0
Ron Anderson	F	6'7	215	28	4	24	2	4	50	0	0	—	3	0	2	0	0	0	4	6	0.8	0.0	0.5	1.0
Stuart Gray	C	7'	245	23	3	14	0	1	0	2	4	50	7	0	3	0	0	0	2	5	2.3	0.0	1.0	0.7
3-PT FG —	Person 2-8, Stipanovich 0-1, Long 1-6, Fleming 0-1, Richardson 0-1, Macy 0-1																							
PORTLAND TRAIL BLAZERS	**MIKE SCHULER**				lost to Houston 1-3; H115-125, H111-98, 108-117, 101-113																			
Kiki Vanderweghe	F	6'8	220	28	4	174	38	71	54	22	26	85	13	11	10	0	1	1	99	44	3.3	2.8	2.5	24.8
Steve Johnson	F-C	6'10	235	29	4	137	28	61	46	27	43	63	40	2	15	0	2	1	83	34	10.0	0.5	3.8	20.8
Caldwell Jones	C	7'	225	36	4	129	5	12	42	5	6	83	31	6	15	0	0	6	15	32	7.8	1.5	3.8	3.8
Clyde Drexler	G	6'7	215	24	4	153	36	79	46	23	29	79	30	15	16	1	7	3	96	38	7.5	3.8	4.0	24.0
Terry Porter	G	6'3	195	23	4	150	24	50	48	18	20	90	19	40	14	0	10	2	68	38	4.8	10.0	3.5	17.0
Jim Paxson	G-F	6'6	210	29	4	94	13	32	41	8	9	89	9	13	8	0	5	0	34	24	2.3	3.3	2.0	8.5
Jerome Kersey	F	6'7	220	24	4	60	10	25	40	4	4	100	19	3	13	0	5	1	24	15	4.8	0.8	3.3	6.0
Kevin Duckworth	C	7'	280	22	4	53	6	12	50	2	5	40	8	1	14	0	4	1	14	13	2.0	0.3	3.5	3.5
Michael Holton	G	6'4	195	25	2	9	1	2	50	0	0	—	1	0	1	0	0	0	2	5	0.5	0.0	0.5	1.0
Fernando Martin	C	6'10	238	24	1	1	0	1	0	0	0	—	0	0	0	0	0	0	0	1	0.0	0.0	0.0	0.0
3-PT FG —	Vanderweghe 1-4, Drexler 1-4, Porter 2-3, Paxson 0-2																							
CHICAGO BULLS	**DOUG COLLINS**				lost to Boston 0-3; 104-108, 96-105, H94-105																			
Gene Banks	F	6'7	215	27	3	79	13	22	59	5	8	63	8	2	13	1	0	0	31	26	2.7	0.7	4.3	10.3
Charles Oakley	F	6'8	225	23	3	129	19	50	38	20	24	83	46	6	13	0	4	1	60	43	15.3	2.0	4.3	20.0
Dave Corzine	C	6'11	260	30	3	122	10	22	45	7	9	78	21	7	6	0	1	3	27	41	7.0	2.3	2.0	9.0
Michael Jordan	G-F	6'6	195	23	3	128	35	84	42	35	39	90	21	18	11	0	6	7	107	43	7.0	6.0	3.7	35.7
John Paxson	G	6'2	185	26	3	87	11	22	50	1	1	100	3	11	9	0	2	0	26	29	1.0	3.7	3.0	8.7
Sedale Threatt	G	6'2	177	25	3	70	8	17	47	4	4	100	5	16	11	0	1	0	20	23	1.7	5.3	3.7	6.7
Brad Sellers	F-C	7'	210	24	3	68	6	19	32	3	3	100	7	3	8	0	0	1	15	23	2.3	1.0	2.7	5.0
Elston Turner	G	6'5	200	27	3	25	4	5	80	0	0	—	2	1	3	0	2	0	8	8	0.7	0.3	1.0	2.7
Granville Waiters	C	6'11	225	25	2	8	0	0	—	0	0	—	1	0	1	0	0	1	0	4	0.5	0.0	0.5	0.0
Mike Brown	F	6'9	260	23	1	3	0	1	0	0	0	—	0	0	1	0	1	0	0	3	0.0	0.0	1.0	0.0
Pete Myers	G	6'6	180	23	1	1	0	1	0	0	0	—	0	0	0	0	0	0	0	1	0.0	0.0	0.0	0.0
3-PT FG —	Oakley 2-4, Jordan 2-5, Paxson 3-7																							
DENVER NUGGETS	**DOUG MOE**				lost to L.A.Lakers 0-3; 95-128, 127-139, H103-140																			
Alex English	F	6'8	190	32	3	76	25	49	51	6	7	86	14	10	9	1	0	0	56	25	4.7	3.3	3.0	18.7
Danny Schayes	F-C	6'11	245	27	3	75	12	17	71	6	9	67	17	2	10	0	1	2	30	25	5.7	0.7	3.3	10.0
Blair Rasmussen	C	7'	250	24	3	92	22	45	49	5	10	50	23	7	12	0	2	2	49	31	7.7	2.3	4.0	16.3
Darrell Walker	G	6'4	180	25	3	68	11	34	32	4	7	57	10	5	4	0	2	0	26	23	3.3	1.7	1.3	8.7
Lafeyette Lever	G	6'3	175	26	3	99	19	50	38	6	9	67	18	22	7	0	7	0	46	33	6.0	7.3	2.3	15.3
Bill Hanzlik	F-G	6'7	200	29	3	76	8	25	32	9	15	60	6	7	6	0	4	0	25	25	2.0	2.3	2.0	8.3
Mike Evans	G	6'1	170	31	3	57	7	19	37	2	2	100	7	8	6	0	3	0	18	19	2.3	2.7	2.0	6.0
Maurice Martin	F	6'6	200	22	3	54	12	29	41	7	12	58	9	10	12	0	0	1	31	18	3.0	3.3	4.0	10.3
Mark Alarie	F	6'8	217	23	3	41	9	15	60	2	2	100	5	1	9	0	2	2	20	14	1.7	0.3	3.0	6.7
Wayne Cooper	C	6'10	220	30	3	41	5	12	42	2	2	100	17	2	9	0	0	1	12	14	5.7	0.7	3.0	4.0
T.R. Dunn	G	6'4	192	31	3	22	1	4	25	0	0	—	3	2	3	0	1	1	2	7	1.0	0.7	1.0	0.7
Otis Smith	G	6'5	210	22	3	19	2	6	33	6	9	67	5	4	1	0	0	2	10	6	1.7	1.3	0.3	3.3
3-PT FG —	Lever 2-8, Hanzlik 0-2, Evans 2-7, Martin 0-1																							
WASHINGTON BULLETS	**KEVIN LOUGHERY**				lost to Detroit 0-3; 92-106, 85-128, H96-97																			
Jay Vincent	F	6'7	220	27	3	72	11	30	37	8	9	89	9	3	10	0	2	0	30	24	3.0	1.0	3.3	10.0
Terry Catledge	F	6'8	230	23	3	98	23	41	56	9	17	53	25	0	5	0	3	1	55	33	8.3	0.0	1.7	18.3
Moses Malone	C-F	6'10	255	31	3	114	21	47	45	20	21	95	38	5	5	0	0	3	62	38	12.7	1.7	1.7	20.7
Jeff Malone	G	6'4	205	25	3	105	17	46	37	11	11	100	7	9	8	0	1	0	45	35	2.3	3.0	2.7	15.0
Michael Adams	G	5'11	165	23	3	82	8	25	32	1	3	33	7	10	6	0	7	0	19	27	2.3	3.3	2.0	6.3
Charles Jones	F	6'9	215	29	3	56	3	5	60	0	0	—	8	3	9	0	2	5	6	19	2.7	1.0	3.0	2.0
John Williams	F	6'9	235	20	3	49	8	14	57	4	7	57	11	2	3	0	2	0	20	16	3.7	0.7	1.0	6.7
Manute Bol	C	7'6	225	24	3	43	4	10	40	0	2	0	9	0	6	0	0	5	8	14	3.0	0.0	2.0	2.7
Darwin Cook	G	6'3	195	28	3	41	6	24	25	1	2	50	7	3	4	0	4	0	14	14	2.3	1.0	1.3	4.7
Ennis Whatley	G	6'3	177	24	2	32	3	12	25	0	0	—	3	6	2	0	2	0	6	16	1.5	3.0	1.0	3.0
Frank Johnson	G	6'2	185	26	3	28	2	7	29	4	4	100	2	5	3	0	1	0	8	9	0.7	1.7	1.0	2.7
3-PT FG —	Adams 2-9, Williams 0-1, Bol 0-1, Cook 1-2																							

eam		G	FG	FGA	%	FT	FTA	%	Rebounds			Assists	PF	Steals	Blocked Shots	Turn Overs	Points	Points per game
									Offense	Defense	Total							
TEAM STATISTICS EASTERN CONFERENCE ATLANTIC DIVISION																		
oston	Off.	82	3645	7051	**52**	1740	2153	**81**	933	2585	3518	2421	**1710**	561	526	1300	9237	112.6
	Def.	82	3470	7500	46	1628	2148	76	1237	2287	3524	2060	1911	722	338	1156	8692	106.0
	Diff.		+175	-449	**+6**	+112	+5	**+5**	-304	+298	-6	**+361**	+201	-161	+188	-144	+545	+6.6
hiladelphia	Off.	82	3335	6792	49	1971	2617	75	1178	2327	3505	1943	1774	768	540	1519	8729	106.5
	Def.	82	3537	7204	49	1552	2049	76	1214	2202	3416	2202	1982	813	446	1372	8745	106.6
	Diff.		-202	-412		+219	**+568**	-1	-36	+125	+89	-259	+208	-45	+94	-147	-16	-.1
ashimgton	Off.	82	3356	7397	45	1935	2531	76	1305	2315	3620	1750	1775	755	**685**	1301	8690	106.0
	Def.	82	3522	7453	47	1654	2183	76	1334	2483	3817	2144	1938	699	548	1439	8802	107.3
	Diff.		-166	-56	-2	+281	+348		-29	-168	-197	-394	+163	+56	+137	+138	-112	-1.3
ew Jersey	Off.	82	3374	7083	48	2000	2607	77	1169	2409	3578	1991	2353	643	397	1617	8893	108.5
	Def.	82	3418	7125	48	2353	3018	78	1129	2352	3481	1958	2126	814	566	1357	9307	113.5
	Diff.		-44	-42		-353	-411	-1	+40	+57	+97	+33	-227	-171	-169	-260	-414	-5.0
ew York	Off.	82	3329	7023	47	1725	2362	73	1108	2162	3270	1941	2028	704	396	1420	8508	103.8
	Def.	82	3500	7142	49	1928	2534	76	1331	2448	3779	2152	1950	761	400	1417	9022	110.0
	Diff.		-171	-119	-2	-203	-172	-3	-223	-286	-509	-211	-78	-57	-4	-3	-514	-6.2
CENTRAL DIVISION																		
tlanta	Off.	82	3435	7141	48	2019	2661	76	1350	2478	3828	2077	2152	700	511	1279	9024	110.0
	Def.	82	3158	6998	45	1987	2598	76	1196	2277	3473	1917	2034	619	385	1314	8431	102.8
	Diff.		**+277**	+143	+3	+32	+63		+154	+201	+355	+160	-118	+81	+126	+35	**+593**	**+7.2**
etroit	Off.	82	3544	7237	49	1991	2602	77	1245	**2649**	**3894**	2021	2078	643	436	1417	9118	111.2
	Def.	82	3376	7307	46	1951	2608	75	1143	2339	3482	2029	2067	670	472	1294	8836	107.8
	Diff.		+168	-70	+3	+40	-6	+2	+102	**+310**	**+412**	-8	-11	-27	-36	-123	+282	+3.4
ilwaukee	Off.	82	3457	7282	47	1953	2549	77	1119	2322	3441	2044	2180	**845**	393	1260	9052	110.4
	Def.	82	3247	6906	47	2117	2796	76	1191	2477	3668	2014	2024	659	460	1551	8731	106.5
	Diff.		+210	+376		-164	-247	+1	-72	-155	-227	+30	-156	+186	-67	+291	+321	+3.9
ndiana	Off.	82	3454	7324	47	1696	2170	78	1132	2464	3596	2170	2097	697	311	1276	8698	106.1
	Def.	82	3344	6969	48	1960	2584	76	1117	2584	3701	2019	1852	660	472	1416	8751	106.7
	Diff.		+110	+355	-1	-264	-414	+2	+15	-120	-105	+151	-245	+37	-161	+140	-53	-.6
hicago	Off.	82	3382	7155	47	1754	2234	79	1248	2400	3648	2143	1922	677	438	1257	8596	104.8
	Def.	82	3337	6910	48	1734	2255	77	1027	2317	3344	2028	1844	583	492	1269	8523	103.9
	Diff.		+45	+245	-1	+20	-21	+2	**+221**	+83	+304	+115	-78	+94	-54	+12	+73	+.9
leveland	Off.	82	3349	7122	47	1779	2554	70	1257	2420	3677	1912	2853	672	559	1619	8558	104.4
	Def.	82	3556	7441	48	1664	2209	75	1254	2396	3650	2056	2076	810	479	1398	8871	108.2
	Diff.		-207	-319	-1	+115	+345	-5	+3	+24	+27	-144	-777	-138	+80	-221	-313	-3.8
WESTERN CONFERENCE MIDWEST DIVISION																		
allas	Off.	82	3594	7373	49	2148	2717	79	1219	2494	3713	2017	1873	688	424	**1205**	9567	116.7
	Def.	82	3586	7503	48	1750	2293	76	1254	2386	3640	2304	2136	571	421	1332	9050	110.4
	Diff.		+8	-130	+1	**+398**	+424	+3	-35	+108	+73	-287	**+263**	+117	+3	+127	+517	**+6.3**
tah	Off.	82	3485	7514	46	1735	2389	73	1194	2456	3650	2240	2040	835	628	1403	8844	107.9
	Def.	82	3347	7338	46	1974	2564	77	1310	2637	3947	2011	1942	718	457	**1579**	8811	107.5
	Diff.		+138	+176	—	-239	-175	-4	-116	-181	-297	+229	-98	+117	+171	+176	+33	+.4
ouston	Off.	82	3465	7262	48	1746	2355	74	1190	2481	3671	2227	1973	654	555	1384	8765	106.9
	Def.	82	3348	7225	46	1887	2422	78	1167	2364	3531	2126	1922	721	368	1366	8683	105.9
	Diff.		+117	+37	+2	-141	-67	-4	+23	+117	+140	+101	-51	-67	+187	-18	+82	+1.0
enver	Off.	82	**3744**	**7951**	47	1975	2568	77	1294	2368	3662	2317	2184	754	421	1216	9569	116.7
	Def.	82	3636	7343	50	2255	2901	78	1166	2720	3886	2189	2145	558	452	1564	9640	117.6
	Diff.		+108	**+608**	-3	-280	-333	-1	+128	-352	-224	+128	-39	+196	-31	**+348**	-71	-.9
acramento	Off.	82	3522	7413	48	1974	2479	80	1282	2441	3723	2185	2007	513	397	1403	9095	110.9
	Def.	82	3656	7469	49	1922	2500	77	1160	2355	3515	2154	2068	707	487	1210	9359	114.1
	Diff.		-134	-56	-1	+52	-21	+3	+122	+86	+208	+31	+61	-194	-90	-193	-264	-3.2
San Antonio	Off.	82	3532	7456	47	1701	2292	74	1285	2347	3632	2220	1930	786	325	1406	8882	108.3
	Def.	82	3704	7310	51	1786	2364	76	1100	2461	3561	2375	1844	463	699	1417	9300	113.4
	Diff.		-172	+146	-4	-85	-72	-2	+185	-114	+71	-155	-86	**+323**	-374	+9	-418	-5.1
PACIFIC DIVISION																		
L.A. Lakers	Off.	82	3740	7245	52	2012	2550	79	1127	2515	3642	**2428**	1853	728	482	1358	9656	117.8
	Def.	82	3520	7531	47	1731	2265	76	1280	2174	3454	2212	2004	721	404	1370	8893	108.5
	Diff.		+220	-286	-5	+281	+285	+3	-153	+341	+188	+216	+151	+7	+78	+12	+763	**+9.3**
Portland	Off.	82	3650	7249	50	**2269**	**2928**	77	1180	2413	3593	2359	2082	767	387	1546	**9667**	**117.9**
	Def.	82	3649	7523	49	1996	2589	77	1208	2279	3487	2189	**2228**	735	473	1504	9410	114.8
	Diff.		+1	-274	+1	+273	+339		-28	+134	+106	+170	+146	+32	-86	-42	+257	+3.1

TEAM STATISTICS
WESTERN CONFERENCE
PACIFIC DIVISION

Team		G	FG	FGA	%	FT	FTA	%	Rebounds Offense	Rebounds Defense	Rebounds Total	Assists	PF	Steals	Blocked Shots	Turn Overs	Points	Points per game
Golden State	Off.	82	3551	7412	48	1970	2526	78	1193	2351	3544	2083	2138	715	321	1354	9188	112.0
	Def.	82	3615	7339	49	1995	2665	75	1249	2481	3730	2174	2052	688	450	1412	9380	114.4
	Diff.		-64	+73	-1	-25	-139	+3	-56	-130	-186	-91	-86	+27	-129	+58	-192	-2.4
Seattle	Off.	82	3593	7451	48	1948	2571	76	1373	2395	3768	2184	2224	705	450	1509	9325	113.7
	Def.	82	3514	7329	48	2166	2819	77	1236	2278	3514	2023	2027	731	409	1342	9287	113.3
	Diff.		+79	+122	—	-218	-248	-1	+137	+117	+254	+161	-197	-26	+41	-167	+38	+.5
Phoenix	Off.	82	3575	7190	50	1900	2499	76	1113	2366	3479	2354	2047	703	397	1498	9111	111.1
	Def.	82	3623	7336	49	1942	2570	76	1235	2355	3590	2246	2034	799	435	1428	9311	113.5
	Diff.		-48	-146	+1	-42	-71	—	-122	+11	-111	+108	-13	-96	-38	-70	-200	-2.4
L.A. Clippers	Off.	82	3311	7332	45	1866	2515	74	1231	2137	3368	1971	2004	751	432	1493	8566	104.5
	Def.	82	3759	7254	52	1875	2515	75	1187	2643	3830	2416	2021	806	534	1533	9503	115.9
	Diff.		-448	+78	-7	-9	—	-1	+44	-506	-462	-445	+17	-55	-102	+40	-937	-11.4

PLAYOFFS

Team		G	FG	FGA	%	FT	FTA	%	Rebounds Offense	Rebounds Defense	Rebounds Total	Assists	PF	Steals	Blocked Shots	Turn Overs	Points	Points per game
L.A.Lakers	Off.	18	806	1545	**52**	515	656	79	234	574	808	510	408	**142**	**116**	262	2170	**120.6**
	Def.	18	785	1668	47	360	479	75	275	461	736	492	477	145	80	263	1965	109.2
	Diff.		+21	-123	+5	+155	+177	+4	-41	+113	+72	+18	+69	-3	+36	+1	+205	**+11.4**
Boston	Off.	23	**980**	**1944**	50	**589**	**728**	**81**	**264**	**682**	**946**	**624**	536	124	**116**	327	**2601**	113.1
	Def.	23	1022	2059	50	536	700	77	290	636	926	579	**617**	174	102	**266**	2626	114.2
	Diff.		-42	-115	—	+53	+28	+4	-26	+46	+20	+45	+81	-50	+14	-61	-25	-1.1
Detroit	Off.	15	647	1297	50	331	445	74	221	448	669	356	381	104	73	204	1639	109.3
	Def.	15	581	1237	47	368	464	79	199	418	617	351	369	93	76	232	1549	103.3
	Diff.		+66	+60	+3	-37	-19	-5	+22	+30	+52	+5	-12	+11	-3	+28	+90	+6.0
Seattle	Off.	14	604	1310	46	304	406	75	243	374	617	379	412	120	78	198	1542	110.1
	Def.	14	569	1153	49	423	545	78	182	428	610	323	351	96	75	232	1569	112.1
	Diff.		+35	+157	-3	-119	-139	-3	+61	-54	+7	+56	-61	+24	+3	+34	-27	-2.0
Milwaukee	Off.	12	529	1114	47	338	425	80	160	317	477	298	337	117	56	144	1418	118.2
	Def.	12	528	1052	50	330	413	80	164	371	535	327	319	77	81	195	1412	117.7
	Diff.		+1	+62	-3	+8	+12	—	-4	-54	-58	-29	-18	+40	-25	+51	+6	+.5
Golden State	Off.	10	422	894	47	205	254	81	145	242	387	251	269	102	46	156	1071	107.1
	Def.	10	415	831	50	261	342	76	150	305	455	251	215	80	73	187	1117	111.7
	Diff.		+7	+63	-3	-56	-88	+5	-5	-63	-68	—	-54	+22	-27	+31	-46	-4.6
Houston	Off.	10	411	833	49	267	346	77	141	294	435	252	**258**	62	72	181	1097	109.7
	Def.	10	414	915	45	233	307	76	161	274	435	252	278	92	44	141	1081	108.1
	Diff.		-3	-82	+4	+34	+39	+1	-20	+20	—	—	+20	-30	+28	-40	+16	+1.6
Atlanta	Off.	9	335	703	48	224	298	75	129	252	381	234	261	59	54	**137**	901	100.1
	Def.	9	320	690	46	247	326	76	125	246	371	187	239	59	32	134	895	99.4
	Diff.		+15	+13	+2	-23	-28	-1	+4	+6	+10	+47	-22	—	+22	-3	+6	+.7
Philadelphia	Off.	5	215	434	50	127	164	77	72	151	223	126	135	35	40	86	562	112.4
	Def.	5	218	460	47	129	170	76	77	131	208	117	131	52	26	64	570	114.0
	Diff.		-3	-26	+3	-2	-6	+1	-5	+20	+15	+9	-4	-17	+14	-22	-8	-1.6
Utah	Off.	5	188	413	46	115	151	76	72	141	213	109	116	47	43	88	504	100.8
	Def.	5	195	415	47	111	136	82	64	134	198	107	129	43	27	86	511	102.2
	Diff.		-7	-2	-1	+4	+15	-6	+8	+7	+15	+2	+13	+4	+16	-2	-7	-1.4
Dallas	Off.	4	175	356	49	114	152	75	61	118	179	88	99	27	17	59	466	116.5
	Def.	4	188	373	50	97	126	77	67	120	187	117	119	28	32	53	482	120.5
	Diff.		-13	-17	-1	+17	+26	-2	-6	-2	-8	-29	+20	-1	-15	-6	-16	-4.0
Indiana	Off.	4	138	288	48	101	146	69	39	115	154	85	112	20	6	59	380	95.0
	Def.	4	143	294	49	102	144	71	42	117	159	103	112	25	19	58	392	98.0
	Diff.		-5	-6	-1	-1	+2	-2	-3	-2	-5	-18	—	-5	-13	-1	-12	-3.0
Portland	Off.	4	161	345	47	109	142	77	61	109	170	91	106	34	15	61	435	108.8
	Def.	4	173	339	51	102	128	80	59	110	169	118	107	32	31	71	453	113.3
	Diff.		-12	+6	-4	+7	+14	-3	+2	-1	+1	-27	+1	+2	-16	+10	-18	-4.5
Chicago	Off.	3	106	243	44	75	88	85	39	75	114	64	76	17	13	35	294	98.0
	Def.	3	122	242	50	70	83	84	30	87	117	82	65	17	15	31	318	106.0
	Diff.		-16	+1	-6	+5	+5	+1	+9	-12	-3	-18	-11	—	-2	-4	-24	-8.0
Denver	Off.	3	133	305	44	55	84	65	46	88	134	80	88	22	11	44	325	108.3
	Def.	3	143	280	51	110	135	81	40	119	159	107	65	22	34	32	407	135.7
	Diff.		-10	+25	-7	-55	-51	-16	+6	-31	-25	-27	-23	—	-23	-12	-82	-27.4
Washington	Off.	3	106	261	41	58	76	76	42	84	126	46	61	24	14	50	273	91.0
	Def.	3	140	277	51	48	63	76	44	107	151	80	62	21	23	46	331	110.3
	Diff.		-34	-16	-10	+10	+13	—	-2	-23	-25	-34	+1	+3	-9	-4	-58	-19.3

Team	W	L	Pct.	GB	Record against playoff teams W	L	Pct.	Record against non - playoff teams W	L	Pct.	HOME W	L	Pct.	ROAD W	L	Pct.
EASTERN CONFERENCE																
ATLANTIC DIVISION																
Boston Celtics	59	23	.720	—	40	17	.702	19	6	.760	39	2	.951	20	21	.488
Philadelphia 76ers	45	37	.549	14	29	27	.518	16	10	.615	28	13	.683	17	24	.415
Washington Bullets	42	40	.512	17	23	33	.411	19	7	.731	27	14	.659	15	26	.366
New Jersey Nets	24	58	.293	35	15	47	.242	9	11	.450	19	22	.463	5	36	.122
New York Knickerbockers	24	58	.293	35	16	47	.254	8	11	.421	18	23	.439	6	35	.146
CENTRAL DIVISION																
Atlanta Hawks	57	25	.695	—	36	21	.632	21	4	.840	35	6	.854	22	19	.537
Detroit Pistons	52	30	.634	5	31	25	.554	21	5	.808	32	9	.780	20	21	.488
Milwaukee Bucks	50	32	.610	7	30	26	.536	20	6	.769	32	9	.780	18	23	.439
Indiana Pacers	41	41	.500	16	24	33	.421	17	8	.680	28	13	.683	13	28	.317
Chicago Bulls	40	42	.488	17	23	34	.404	17	8	.680	29	12	.707	11	30	.268
Cleveland Cavaliers	31	51	.378	26	18	45	.286	13	6	.684	25	16	.610	6	35	.146
WESTERN CONFERENCE																
MIDWEST DIVISION																
Dallas Mavericks	55	27	.671	—	32	21	.604	23	6	.793	35	6	.854	20	21	.488
Utah Jazz	44	38	.537	11	27	27	.500	17	11	.607	31	10	.756	13	28	.317
Houston Rockets	42	40	.512	13	21	33	.389	21	7	.750	25	16	.610	17	24	.415
Denver Nuggets	37	45	.451	18	20	34	.370	17	11	.607	27	14	.659	10	31	.244
Sacramento Kings	29	53	.354	26	16	44	.267	13	9	.591	20	21	.488	9	32	.220
San Antonio Spurs	28	54	.341	27	14	46	.233	14	8	.636	21	20	.512	7	34	.171
PACIFIC DIVISION																
Los Angeles Lakers	65	17	.793	—	39	15	.722	26	2	.929	37	4	.902	28	13	.683
Portland Trail Blazers	49	33	.598	16	27	27	.500	22	6	.786	34	7	.829	15	26	.366
Golden State Warriors	42	40	.512	23	22	32	.407	20	8	.714	25	16	.610	17	24	.415
Seattle Supersonics	39	43	.476	26	18	36	.333	21	7	.750	25	16	.610	24	27	.471
Phoenix Suns	36	46	.439	29	24	36	.400	12	10	.545	26	15	.634	10	31	.244
Los Angeles Clippers	12	70	.146	53	8	52	.133	4	18	.182	9	32	.220	3	38	.073

1986/87 N.B.A. INDIVIDUAL LEADERS

SCORING
(Minimum 70 Games or 1400 Points)

Name	Team	G	FG	FT	Pts.	Avg.
Jordan	Chi	82	1098	833	3041	37.1
Wilkins	Atl	79	828	607	2294	29.0
English	Den	82	965	411	2345	28.6
Bird	Bos	74	786	414	2076	28.1
Vandeweghe	Port	79	808	467	2122	26.9
McHale	Bos	77	790	428	2008	26.1
Aguirre	Dall	80	787	429	2056	25.7
Ellis	Sea	82	785	385	2041	24.9
M.Malone	Was	73	595	570	1760	24.1
Johnson	LAL	80	683	535	1909	23.9

FIELD GOAL PERCENTAGE
(Minimum 300 Made)

Name	Team	FG	FGA	Pct.
McHale	Bos	790	1307	.604
Gilmore	SA	346	580	.597
Barkley	Phi	557	937	.594
Donaldson	Dall	311	531	.586
Abdul-Jabbar	LAL	560	993	.564
B.Williams	NJ	521	936	.557
Parish	Bos	588	1057	.556
Johnson	Port	494	889	.556
McCray	Hou	432	783	.552
Nance	Phoe	585	1062	.551

FREE THROW PERCENTAGE
(Minimum 125 Made)

Name	Team	FT	FTA	Pct.
Bird	Bos	414	455	.910
Ainge	Bos	148	165	.897
Laimbeer	Det	245	274	.894
Scott	LAL	224	251	.892
Hodges	Mil	131	147	.891
Long	Ind	219	246	.890
Vandeweghe	Port	467	527	.886
J.Malone	Was	376	425	.885
Blackman	Dall	419	474	.884
Pierce	Mil	387	440	.880

PERSONAL FOULS

Name	Team	PF
Johnson	Port	340
Kersey	Port	328
Sikma	Mil	328
Malone	Utah	323
Oakley	Chi	315
Williams	NJ	315

GAMES DISQUALIFIED

Name	Team	Disq.
Johnson	Port	16
Sikma	Mil	14
Brown	NJ	12
Thorpe	Sac	11
Lister	Sea	11

TOTAL REBOUNDS PER GAME
(Minimum 70 Games or 800 Rebounds)

Name	Team	G	Reb.	Avg.
Barkley	Phi	68	994	14.6
Oakley	Chi	82	1074	13.1
B.Williams	NJ	82	1023	12.5
Donaldson	Dall	82	973	11.9
Laimbeer	Det	82	955	11.6
Cage	LAC	80	922	11.5
L.Smith	GS	80	917	11.5
Olajuwon	Hou	75	858	11.4
M.Malone	Was	73	824	11.3
Parish	Bos	80	851	10.6

ASSISTS PER GAME
(Minimum 70 Games or 400 Assists)

Name	Team	G	Ass.	Avg.
Johnson	LAL	80	977	12.2
Floyd	GS	82	848	10.3
Thomas	Det	81	813	10.0
Rivers	Atl	82	823	10.0
Porter	Port	80	715	8.9
Theus	Sac	79	692	8.8
McMillan	Sea	71	583	8.2
Stockton	Utah	82	670	8.2
Lever	Den	82	654	8.0
Cheeks	Phi	68	538	7.9

MINUTES PLAYED

Name	Team	Min.
Jordan	Chi	3281
McCray	Hou	3136
Drexler	Port	3114
English	Den	3085
Ellis	Sea	3073

BLOCKED SHOTS PER GAME
(Minimum 70 Games of 100 Blocked Shots)

Name	Team	G	Reb.	Avg.
Eaton	Utah	79	321	4.1
Bol	Was	82	302	3.7
Olajuwon	Hou	75	254	3.4
Benjamin	LAC	72	187	2.6
Lister	Sea	75	180	2.4
Ewing	NY	63	147	2.3
McHale	Bos	77	172	2.2
Nance	Phoe	69	148	2.1
Hinson	Phi	76	161	2.1
C.Jones	Was	79	165	2.1

3 POINT FIELD GOALS PER GAME
(Minimum 25 Made)

Name	Team	FG	FGA	Avg.
Vandeweghe	Port	39	81	.481
Schrempf	Dall	33	69	.478
Ainge	Bos	85	192	.443
Scott	LAL	65	149	.436
Tucker	NY	68	161	.422
McKenna	NJ	52	124	.419
Bird	Bos	90	225	.400
Cooper	LAL	89	231	.385
Floyd	GS	73	190	.384
Megee	Atl	86	229	.376

STEALS PER GAME
(Minimum 70 Games or 125 Steals)

Name	Team	G	Steals	Avg.
Robertson	SA	81	260	3.2
Jordan	Chi	82	236	2.9
Cheeks	Phi	68	180	2.6
Harper	Cle	82	209	2.5
Drexler	Port	82	204	2.5
Lever	Den	82	201	2.5
Harper	Dall	77	167	2.2
Stockton	Utah	82	177	2.2
Rivers	Atl	82	171	2.1
Porter	Port	80	159	2.0

1987-88 N.B.A.
Lakers—Team of the Eighties

Just as many were wondering when the N.B.A. would produce a team capable of challenging the Lakers and Celtics, the league produced four legitimate contenders, with another on the horizon. But somebody forgot to tell the Lakers.

For most of the season the spotlight was on the Central Division. In Detroit, Dennis Rodman, John Salley and the rest of the league's strongest bench backed up an already powerful first team, a combination that added up to 54 wins and a first-place finish and becoming the first team to draw more than a million fans. Atlanta won 50 for the third straight time as Dominique Wilkins continued to shine despite poor seasons from Kevin Willis and Randy Wittman. And Michael Jordan led Chicago to the 50-win level while earning his second scoring title and first MVP award. The emergence of Mark Price as a star brought visions of a title in Cleveland's future, and the Cavs reacted by sending No. 1 draft pick Kevin Johnson to Phoenix for all-star Larry Nance. For once, "Wait till next year" was a legitimate slogan in Cleveland. Meanwhile, the aging Milwaukee Bucks slipped to 42 wins under new coach Del Harris, and the young Indiana Pacers collapsed in midseason to finish 38-44.

The Celtics, with Larry Bird still in near-MVP form, had no competition in the Atlantic Division, where no one else could manage a winning record but everyone had a new coach: Wes Unseld in Washington, Rick Pitino in New York, Jim Lyman in Philadelphia and Willis Reed in New Jersey. The Bullets' Moses and Jeff Malone, the Knicks' Patrick Ewing and Rookie of the Year Mark Jackson, the 76ers' Charles Barkley and the Nets' Buck Williams were stars for the also-rans. Also noteworthy was Washington rookie Tyone Bogues, the smallest player in N.B.A. history at 5-foot-3.

Meanwhile, Denver reclaimed the Midwest Division title and earned Doug Moe the Coach of the Year award with strong seasons from Alex English and pesky guards Lafayette Lever and Michael Adams. Dallas finished a game back with John Macleod replacing Dick Motta as coach and Roy Tarpley blossoming as an outstanding sixth man. John Stockton emerged as a star in Utah, setting a record for assists and blending with Karl Malone to give the Jazz their strongest team yet. Houston took a big gamble, sending Ralph Sampson to Golden State for Joe Barry Carroll and Sleepy Floyd. Floyd, however, failed to solve the Rockets' problems at guard. Still Akeem Olajuwon led them to 46 wins. Meanwhile, San Antonio was waiting for No. 1 draft pick David Robinson to get out of the Navy (target date: 1989), and Sacramento was waiting for a miracle in the form of a winning season. The smart money was on San Antonio.

Out West the smart money was on the Lakers, as a 38-4 streak beginning in December made coach Pat Riley's guarentee of a repeat championship look almost reasonable. Kareem Abdul-Jabbar, who turned 41 in April, was fading, but Mychal Thompson was a solid backup, A.C. Green was improving, and Byron Scott was emerging as a star. A late-season injury to Magic Johnson slowed the Lakers a bit, but they still finished with 62 wins, comfortably ahead of Portland. Clyde Drexler led the Trail Blazers to 53 wins with help from Jerome Kersey and Terry Porter, and Seattle improved by five games as Dale Ellis, Xavier McDaniel and Tom Chambers all repeated as 20-point-per-game scorers. Phoenix cleaned house during a 28-win season; Golden State sank to 20-62 with Sampson injured and Chris Mullin missing time for alcohol rehabilitation; and the Clippers played like—well, like the Clippers.

The playoffs brought severe tests for the Lakers and the Celtics, and only the Lakers passed. Atlanta extended Boston to seven games, losing only when Bird exploded for 20 points in the fourth quarter of the finale; then Detroit wore down the Celtics, and only the Lakers passed. Atlanta extended Boston to seven games, losing only when Bird exploded for 20 points in the fourth quarter of the finals; then Detroit wore down the Celtics' overworked starters in an extremely physical six-game series to earn a shot at the title. Meanwhile, the Lakers ran up against a stout Utah defense built around Mark Eaton. With sixth man Thurl Bailey complementing Stockton and Malone on offense, the Jazz scared Los Angeles before falling in seven games. Next came Dallas, and again the Lakers were forced to the brink of elimination; but again the champs came through, earning a return to the finals with another seven-game win.

Detroit split two games in Los Angeles, then took two of three at home, and returned to L.A. with a 3-2 lead. The Lakers won the sixth game despite 43 points from Isiah Thomas, playing on a badly sprained ankle, then hung on for a 108-105 win in the climactic game behind 36 points and 16 rebounds from James Worthy—a performance that earned him the playoff MVP award. No team had ever won three straight seven-game series, and no team had repeated since 1969—but then, Riley had guarenteed it.

Use Name	Pos	Hgt	Wgt	Age	TOTAL G	Min	FG	FGA	%	FT	FTA	%	Reb	Ass	PF	DQ	Stls	Blkd Shts	Points	PER GAME Min	Reb	Ass	PF	Points
1987/88 N.B.A — EASTERN CONFERENCE																								
ATLANTIC DIVISION																								
BOSTON CELTICS	57-25 .695				K.C. JONES																			
Larry Bird	F-G	6'9	220	31	76	2965	881	1672	53	415	453	92	703	467	157	0	125	97	2275	39	9.3	6.1	2.1	29.9
Kevin McHale	F-C	6'10	225	30	64	2390	550	911	60	346	434	80	536	171	179	1	27	92	1446	37	8.4	2.7	2.8	22.6
Robert Parish	C	7'	230	34	74	2312	442	750	59	177	241	73	628	115	198	5	55	84	1061	31	8.5	1.6	2.7	14.3
Danny Ainge	G	6'4	185	28	81	3018	482	982	49	158	180	88	249	503	203	1	115	17	1270	37	3.1	6.2	2.5	15.7
Dennis Johnson	G	6'4	202	33	77	2670	352	803	44	255	298	86	240	598	204	0	93	29	971	35	3.1	7.8	2.6	12.6
Mark Acres	F	6'11	225	25	79	1151	108	203	53	71	111	64	270	42	198	2	29	27	287	15	3.4	0.5	2.5	3.6
Fred Roberts	F	6'10	220	27	74	1032	161	330	49	128	165	78	162	81	118	0	16	15	450	14	2.2	1.1	1.6	6.1
Dirk Minniefield (from GS)	G	6'3	180	26	61	868	83	173	48	27	32	84	75	190	107	0	44	3	196	14	1.2	3.1	1.8	3.2
Brad Lohaus	C	7'	230	23	70	718	122	246	50	50	62	81	138	49	123	1	20	41	297	10	2.0	0.7	1.8	4.2
Darren Daye	F	6'8	220	27	47	655	112	217	52	59	87	68	76	71	68	0	29	4	283	14	1.6	1.5	1.4	6.0
Jim Paxson (from Port)	G	6'6	210	30	28	538	94	191	49	54	61	89	27	49	44	0	23	4	244	19	1.0	1.8	1.6	8.7
Artis Gilmore (from Chi)	C	7'2	265	38	47	521	58	101	57	48	91	53	148	12	94	0	10	18	164	11	3.1	0.3	2.0	3.5
Reggie Lewis	F-G	6'7	195	22	49	405	90	193	47	40	57	70	63	26	54	0	16	15	220	8	1.3	0.5	1.1	4.5
Jerry Sichting (to Port)	G	6'1	180	31	24	370	44	82	54	8	12	67	21	60	30	0	14	0	98	15	0.9	2.5	1.3	4.1
Greg Kite (to LAC)	C	6'11	250	26	13	86	9	23	39	1	6	17	24	2	16	0	3	8	19	7	1.8	0.2	1.2	1.5
Connor Henry (to Mil, Sac)	G	6'7	195	24	10	81	11	28	39	9	10	90	10	12	11	0	1	1	34	8	1.0	1.2	1.1	3.4

3-PT FG — Bird 92-237, Parish 0-1, Ainge 148-357, Johnson 12-47, Roberts 0-6, Minniefield 3-11, Lohaus 3-13, Daye 0-1, Paxson 2-13, Lewis 0-4, Sichting 2-8, Henry 3-8

1987/88 N.B.A. — EASTERN CONFERENCE
ATLANTIC DIVISION

Use Name	Pos	Hgt	Wgt	Age	G	Min	FG	FGA	%	FT	FTA	%	Reb	Ass	PF	DQ	Stls	Blkd Shts	Points	Min	Reb	Ass	PF	Points
					TOTAL															PER GAME				
WASHINGTON BULLETS	38-44 .463				KEVIN LOUGHERY (8-19 .296), WES UNSELD (30-25 .575)																			
Bernard King	F	6'7	215	31	69	2044	470	938	50	247	324	76	280	192	202	3	49	10	1188	30	4.1	2.8	2.9	17.2
John Williams	F	6'9	235	21	82	2428	427	910	47	188	256	73	444	232	217	3	117	34	1047	30	5.4	2.8	2.6	12.8
Moses Malone	C	6'10	255	32	79	2692	531	1090	49	543	689	79	884	112	160	0	59	72	1607	34	11.2	1.4	2.0	20.3
Jeff Malone	G	6'4	205	26	80	2655	648	1360	48	335	380	88	206	237	198	1	51	13	1641	33	2.6	3.0	2.5	20.5
Steve Colter (from Phi)	G	6'3	175	25	56	1361	188	401	47	68	86	79	155	235	112	0	56	14	447	24	2.8	4.2	2.0	8.0
Muggsy Bogues	G	5'3	140	22	79	1628	166	426	39	58	74	78	136	404	138	1	127	5	393	21	1.7	5.1	1.7	5.0
Terry Catledge	F	6'8	230	24	70	1610	296	585	51	154	235	66	397	63	172	0	33	9	746	23	5.7	0.9	2.5	10.7
Charles Jones	F	6'9	215	30	69	1313	72	177	41	53	75	71	325	59	226	5	53	113	197	19	4.7	0.9	3.3	2.9
Frank Johnson	G	6'2	185	29	75	1258	216	498	43	121	149	81	121	188	120	0	70	4	554	17	1.6	2.5	1.6	7.4
Manute Bol	C	7'6	225	25	77	1136	75	165	45	26	49	53	275	13	160	0	11	208	197	15	3.6	0.2	2.1	2.6
Darrell Walker (ankle injury)	G	6'4	180	26	52	940	114	291	39	82	105	78	127	100	105	2	62	10	310	18	2.4	1.9	2.0	6.0
Mark Alarie	F	6'8	217	24	63	769	144	300	48	35	49	71	160	39	107	1	10	12	327	12	2.5	0.6	1.7	5.2
Jay Murphy	F	6'9	220	25	9	46	8	23	35	4	5	80	16	1	5	0	0	0	20	5	1.8	0.1	0.6	2.2

3-PT FG — King 1-6, Williams 5-38, M. Malone 2-7, J. Malone 10-24, Colter 3-10, Bogues 3-16
Catledge 0-2, Jones 0-1, Johnson 1-9, Bol 0-1, Walker 0-6, Alarie 4-18

Use Name	Pos	Hgt	Wgt	Age	G	Min	FG	FGA	%	FT	FTA	%	Reb	Ass	PF	DQ	Stls	Blkd Shts	Points	Min	Reb	Ass	PF	Points
NEW YORK KNICKERBOCKERS	38-44 .463				RICK PITINO																			
Johnny Newman	F	6'7	190	24	77	1589	270	620	44	207	246	84	159	62	204	5	72	11	773	21	2.1	0.8	2.6	10.0
Sidney Green	F	6'9	220	26	82	2049	258	585	44	126	190	66	642	93	318	9	65	32	642	25	7.8	1.1	3.9	7.8
Patrick Ewing	C	7'	240	25	82	2546	656	1183	55	341	476	72	676	125	332	5	104	245	1653	31	8.2	1.5	4.0	20.2
Gerald Wilkins	G-F	6'6	195	24	81	2703	591	1324	45	191	243	79	270	326	183	1	90	22	1412	33	3.3	4.0	2.3	17.4
Mark Jackson	G	6'3	205	22	82	3249	438	1013	43	206	266	77	396	868	244	2	205	6	1114	40	4.8	10.6	3.0	13.6
Kenny Walker	F	6'8	210	23	82	2139	344	728	47	138	178	78	389	86	290	5	63	59	826	26	4.7	1.0	3.5	10.1
Bill Cartwright	C-F	7'1	245	30	82	1676	287	528	54	340	426	80	384	85	234	4	43	43	914	20	4.7	1.0	2.9	11.1
Trent Tucker	G	6'5	193	28	71	1248	193	455	42	51	71	72	119	117	158	3	53	6	506	18	1.7	1.6	2.2	7.1
Pat Cummings	F	6'9	235	31	62	946	140	307	46	59	80	74	235	37	143	0	20	10	339	15	3.8	0.6	2.3	5.5
Billy Donovan	G	5'11	171	22	44	364	44	109	40	17	21	81	25	87	35	0	16	1	105	8	0.6	2.0	0.8	2.4
Chris McNealy	F	6'7	215	26	19	265	23	74	31	21	31	68	64	23	50	1	16	2	67	14	3.4	1.2	2.6	3.5
Louis Orr	F	6'8	200	29	29	180	16	50	32	8	16	50	34	9	27	0	6	0	40	6	1.2	0.3	0.9	1.4
Ray Tolbert (to LAL)	F	6'9	225	29	11	177	19	41	46	9	17	53	35	5	25	0	5	2	47	16	3.2	0.5	2.3	4.3
Sedric Toney	G	6'2	178	25	21	139	21	48	44	10	11	91	8	24	20	0	9	1	57	7	0.4	1.1	1.0	2.7
Tony White (from Chi, to GS)	G	6'2	170	22	12	117	17	46	37	9	13	69	3	10	14	0	1	0	43	10	0.3	0.8	1.2	3.6
Bob Thornton (to Phi)	F	6'10	225	25	7	85	6	19	32	5	8	63	13	4	23	0	2	0	17	12	1.9	0.6	3.3	2.4
Gerald Henderson (to Phi)	G	6'2	180	31	6	69	5	14	36	2	2	100	10	13	14	0	2	0	14	12	1.7	2.2	2.3	2.3
Rory Sparrow (to Chi)	G	6'2	175	29	3	52	5	19	26	0	0	—	2	5	7	0	4	0	10	17	0.7	1.7	2.3	3.3
Carey Scurry (from Utah)	F	6'7	190	25	4	8	1	2	50	0	0	—	3	1	3	0	2	1	2	2	0.8	0.3	0.8	0.5
Rick Carlisle	G	6'5	210	28	26	204	29	67	43	10	11	91	13	32	39	1	11	4	74	8	0.5	1.2	1.5	2.8

3-PT FG — Newman 26-93, Green 0-2, Ewing 0-3, Wilkins 39-129,Jackson 32-126, Walker 0-1, Tucker 69-167,
Cummings 0-1, Donovan 0-7, Carlisle 6-17, Orr0-1, Toney 5-14, White 0-1, Henderson 2-4, Sparrow 0-1

Use Name	Pos	Hgt	Wgt	Age	G	Min	FG	FGA	%	FT	FTA	%	Reb	Ass	PF	DQ	Stls	Blkd Shts	Points	Min	Reb	Ass	PF	Points
PHILADELPHIA 76ERS	36-46 .439				MATT GUOKAS (20-23 .465), JIM LYNAM (16-23 .410)																			
Cliff Robinson (XJ)	F	6'9	240	27	62	2110	483	1041	46	210	293	72	405	131	192	4	79	39	1178	34	6.5	2.1	3.1	19.0
Charles Barkley	F	6'6	263	24	80	3170	753	1283	59	714	951	75	951	254	278	6	100	103	2264	40	11.9	3.2	3.5	28.3
Mike Gminski (from NJ)	C	6'11	260	28	47	1767	290	652	44	212	226	94	494	84	98	0	36	85	792	38	10.5	1.8	2.1	16.9
David Wingate (KJ)	G	6'5	185	24	61	1419	218	545	40	99	132	75	101	119	125	0	47	22	545	23	1.7	2.0	2.0	8.9
Maurice Cheeks	G	6'1	181	31	79	2871	428	865	49	227	275	83	253	635	116	0	167	22	1086	36	3.2	8.0	1.5	13.7
Albert King	G-F	6'6	215	28	72	1593	211	540	39	78	103	76	216	109	219	4	39	18	517	22	3.0	1.5	3.0	7.2
Gerald Henderson (from NY)	G	6'2	180	31	69	1436	189	439	43	136	168	81	97	218	173	0	67	5	581	21	1.4	3.2	2.5	8.4
Roy Hinson (to NJ)	C	6'9	220	26	29	845	123	272	45	89	124	72	169	27	90	3	24	68	335	29	5.8	0.9	3.1	11.6
Ben Coleman (from NJ)	F	6'9	235	26	43	841	110	213	52	76	101	75	177	23	120	1	15	25	296	20	4.1	0.5	2.8	6.9
Danny Vranes	F	6'7	220	29	57	772	53	121	44	15	35	43	117	36	100	0	27	33	121	14	2.1	0.6	1.8	2.1
Tim McCormick (to NJ)	C	7'	240	25	23	601	71	138	51	37	53	70	144	26	75	1	14	8	179	26	6.3	1.1	3.3	7.8
Mark McNamara	C	6'11	238	28	42	581	52	133	39	48	66	73	157	18	67	0	4	12	152	14	3.7	0.4	1.6	3.6
Andrew Toney	G	6'3	190	30	29	522	72	171	42	58	72	81	47	108	35	0	11	6	211	18	1.6	3.7	1.2	7.3
Bob Thornton (from NY)	F-C	6'10	225	25	41	508	59	111	53	29	47	62	99	11	80	1	9	3	147	12	2.4	0.3	2.0	3.6
Dave Henderson	G	6'5	195	23	22	351	47	116	41	32	47	68	35	34	41	0	12	5	126	16	1.6	1.5	1.9	5.7
Vincent Askew	G	6'6	210	21	14	234	22	74	30	8	11	73	22	33	12	0	10	6	52	17	1.6	2.4	0.9	3.7
Steve Colter (to Was)	G	6'3	175	25	12	152	15	40	38	7	9	78	18	26	20	0	6	0	37	13	1.5	2.2	1.7	3.1
Chris Welp (KJ)	C	7'	245	23	10	132	18	31	58	12	18	67	24	5	25	0	5	5	48	13	2.4	0.5	2.5	4.8

3-PT FG — Robinson 2-9, Barkley 44-157, Wingate 10-40, Cheeks 3-22, King 17-49, G. Henderson 67-159,
Hinson 0-1, Coleman 0-1, Vranes 0-3, Toney 9-27, Thornton 0-2, D.Henderson 0-1,

Use Name	Pos	Hgt	Wgt	Age	G	Min	FG	FGA	%	FT	FTA	%	Reb	Ass	PF	DQ	Stls	Blkd Shts	Points	Min	Reb	Ass	PF	Points
NEW JERSEY NETS	19-23 .232				DAVE WOHL (2-13 .133), BOB MacKINNON (10-29 .256), WILLIS REED (7-21 .250)																			
Roy Hinson (from Phi)	F-C	6'9	220	26	48	1747	330	658	50	183	227	81	348	72	185	3	45	72	843	36	7.3	1.5	3.9	17.6
Buck Williams	F	6'8	230	27	70	2637	466	832	56	346	518	67	834	109	266	5	68	44	1279	38	11.9	1.6	3.8	18.3
Tim McCormick (from Phi)	C	7'	240	25	47	1513	277	510	54	108	162	67	323	92	159	2	18	15	662	32	6.9	2.0	3.4	14.1
Otis Birdsong	G	6'4	195	32	67	1882	337	736	46	47	92	51	167	222	143	2	54	11	730	28	2.5	3.3	2.1	10.9
John Bagley	G	6'	192	27	82	2774	393	896	44	148	180	82	257	479	162	0	110	10	981	34	3.1	5.8	2.0	12.0
Dudley Bradley (from Mil)	G-F	6'6	195	30	63	1432	156	364	43	74	97	76	126	150	170	1	114	43	423	23	2.0	2.4	2.7	6.7
Pearl Washington	G	6'2	190	23	68	1379	245	547	45	132	189	70	118	206	163	2	91	4	633	20	1.7	3.0	2.4	9.3
Dennis Hopson	F-G	6'5	205	22	61	1365	222	549	40	131	177	74	143	118	145	0	57	25	587	22	2.3	1.9	2.4	9.6
Mike Gminski (to Phi)	C	6'11	260	28	34	1194	215	474	45	143	166	86	320	55	78	0	28	33	573	35	9.4	1.6	2.3	16.9
Dallas Comegys	F	6'9	205	23	75	1122	156	363	43	106	150	71	218	65	175	3	36	70	418	15	2.9	0.9	2.3	5.6
Ben Coleman (to Phi)	F	6'9	235	26	29	657	116	240	48	65	84	77	173	39	110	4	28	16	297	23	6.0	1.3	3.8	10.2
Orlando Woolridge (DR)	F	6'9	215	28	19	622	110	247	45	92	130	71	91	71	73	2	13	20	312	33	4.8	3.7	3.8	16.4
Chris Engler	C	7'	250	28	54	399	36	88	41	31	35	89	98	15	73	1	9	6	103	7	1.8	0.3	1.4	1.9
Kevin McKenna	G	6'5	195	28	31	393	43	109	39	24	25	96	31	40	55	1	15	2	126	13	1.0	1.3	1.8	4.1
Adrian Branch	F	6'7	190	25	20	308	56	134	42	20	23	87	48	16	41	1	16	11	133	15	2.4	0.8	2.1	6.7
Duane Washington	F	6'4	195	23	15	156	18	42	43	16	20	80	22	34	23	0	12	0	54	10	1.5	2.3	1.5	3.6

(continued next page)

Use Name	Pos	Hgt	Wgt	Age	G	Min	FG	FGA	%	FT	FTA	%	Reb	Ass	PF	DQ	Stls	Blkd Shts	Points	Min	Reb	Ass	PF	Points
					TOTAL															PER GAME				

1987/88 — N.B.A. EASTERN CONFERENCE
ATLANTIC DIVISION (continued)

Use Name	Pos	Hgt	Wgt	Age	G	Min	FG	FGA	%	FT	FTA	%	Reb	Ass	PF	DQ	Stls	Blkd Shts	Points	Min	Reb	Ass	PF	Points
NEW JERSEY NETS (continued)																								
Jamie Waller	G	6'4	215	23	9	91	16	40	40	10	18	56	13	3	13	0	4	1	42	10	1.4	0.3	1.4	4.7
Mike O'Koren	F	6'7	225	29	4	52	9	16	56	0	4	0	4	2	2	0	3	2	18	13	1.0	0.5	0.5	4.5
Ricky Wilson (to SA)	G	6'3	185	23	6	47	7	11	64	6	11	55	1	6	6	0	6	0	21	8	0.2	1.0	1.0	3.5
Johnny Moore (from SA)	G	6'2	185	29	1	10	0	1	0	0	0	—	2	1	0	0	0	0	0	10	2.0	1.0	0.0	0.0

3-PT FG — Hinson 0-1, Williams 1-1, McCormick 0-2, Birdsong 9-25, Bagley 47-161, Bradley 37-101, P.Washington 11-49, Hopson 12-45, Gminski 0-2, Comegys 0-1, Coleman 0-2, Woolridge 0-2, McKenna 16-50, Branch 1-5, D. Washington 2-4, Waller 0-2, Wilson 1-1, O'Koren 0-1

CENTRAL DIVISION

Use Name	Pos	Hgt	Wgt	Age	G	Min	FG	FGA	%	FT	FTA	%	Reb	Ass	PF	DQ	Stls	Blkd Shts	Points	Min	Reb	Ass	PF	Points
DETROIT PISTONS	**54-28 .659**				**CHUCK DALY**																			
Adrian Dantley	F	6'5	210	31	69	2144	444	863	51	492	572	86	227	171	144	0	39	10	1380	31	3.3	2.5	2.1	20.0
Rick Mahorn (XJ)	F-C	6'10	255	29	67	1963	276	481	57	164	217	76	565	60	262	4	43	42	717	29	8.4	0.9	3.9	10.7
Bill Laimbeer	C	6'11	260	30	82	2897	455	923	49	187	214	87	832	199	284	6	66	78	1110	35	10.1	2.4	3.5	13.5
Joe Dumars	G	6'3	190	24	82	2732	453	960	47	251	308	81	200	387	155	1	87	15	1161	33	2.4	4.7	1.9	14.2
Isiah Thomas	G	6'1	185	26	81	2927	621	1341	46	305	394	77	278	678	217	0	141	17	1577	36	3.4	8.4	2.7	19.5
Dennis Rodman	F	6'8	210	26	82	2147	398	709	56	152	284	54	715	110	273	5	75	45	953	26	8.7	1.3	3.3	11.6
John Salley	F	7'	231	23	82	2003	258	456	57	185	261	71	402	113	294	4	53	137	701	24	4.9	1.4	3.6	8.5
Vinnie Johnson	G	6'2	200	31	82	1935	425	959	44	147	217	68	231	267	164	0	58	18	1002	24	2.8	3.3	2.0	12.2
James Edwards (from Phoe)	C	7'	252	32	26	328	48	101	48	45	61	74	77	5	57	0	2	5	141	13	3.0	0.2	2.2	5.4
Ralph Lewis	G	6'6	200	24	50	310	27	87	31	29	48	60	51	14	36	0	13	4	83	6	1.0	0.3	0.7	1.7
William Bedford	C	7'1	235	24	38	298	44	101	44	13	23	57	65	4	47	0	8	17	101	8	1.7	0.1	1.2	2.7
Chuck Nevitt	C	7'5	237	28	17	63	7	21	33	3	6	50	18	0	12	0	1	5	17	4	1.1	0.0	0.7	1.0
Ron Moore (to Phoe)	C	7'	260	25	9	25	4	13	31	2	4	50	2	1	8	0	2	0	10	3	0.2	0.1	0.9	1.1
Darryl Dawkins (from Utah)	C	6'11	270	30	2	7	1	2	50	2	3	67	0	1	4	0	0	1	4	4	0.0	0.5	2.0	2.0
Walker Russell	G	6'5	195	27	1	1	0	1	0	0	0	—	0	1	0	0	0	0	0	1	0.0	1.0	0.0	0.0

3-PT FG — Dantley 0-2, Mahorn 1-2, Laimbeer 13-39, Dumars 4-19, Thomas 30-97, Rodman 5-17, Johnson 5-24, Lewis 0-1, Russell 0-1

Use Name	Pos	Hgt	Wgt	Age	G	Min	FG	FGA	%	FT	FTA	%	Reb	Ass	PF	DQ	Stls	Blkd Shts	Points	Min	Reb	Ass	PF	Points
ATLANTA HAWKS	**50-32 .6**				**MIKE FRATELLO**																			
Dominique Wilkins	F-G	6'8	200	27	78	2948	909	1957	46	541	655	83	502	224	162	0	103	47	2397	38	6.4	2.9	2.1	30.7
Cliff Levingston	F	6'8	210	26	82	2135	314	564	56	190	246	77	504	71	287	5	52	84	819	26	6.1	0.9	3.5	10.0
Tree Rollins	C	7'1	240	32	76	1765	133	260	51	70	80	88	459	20	229	2	31	132	336	23	6.0	0.3	3.0	4.4
Randy Wittman	G	6'6	210	28	82	2412	376	787	48	71	89	80	170	302	117	0	50	18	823	29	2.1	3.7	1.4	10.0
Glenn Rivers	G	6'4	185	26	80	2502	403	890	45	319	421	76	366	747	272	3	140	41	1134	31	4.6	9.3	3.4	14.2
Kevin Willis	F-C	7'	235	25	75	2091	356	687	52	159	245	65	547	28	240	2	68	41	871	28	7.3	0.4	3.2	11.6
Aintoine Carr	F	6'9	235	26	80	1483	281	517	54	142	182	78	289	103	272	7	38	83	705	19	3.6	1.3	3.4	8.8
Spud Webb	G	5'7	135	24	82	1347	191	402	48	107	131	82	146	337	125	0	63	12	490	16	1.8	4.1	1.5	6.0
John Battle	G	6'2	175	25	67	1227	278	613	45	141	188	75	113	158	84	0	31	5	713	18	1.7	2.4	1.3	10.6
Jon Koncak	C	7'	260	24	49	1073	98	203	48	83	136	61	333	19	161	1	36	56	279	22	6.8	0.4	3.3	5.7
Scott Hastings	C-F	6'10	235	27	55	403	40	82	49	25	27	93	97	16	67	1	8	10	110	7	1.8	0.3	1.2	2.0
Chris Washburn (from GS)	C	6'11	255	22	29	174				13	23	57	55	3	19	0	4	8	57	6	1.9	0.1	0.7	2.0
Mike McGee (to Sac)	G	6'5	207	28	11	117	22	52	42	2	6	33	16	13	6	0	5	0	51	11	1.5	1.2	0.5	4.6
Leon Wood (from SA)	G	6'3	185	25	14	79	16	30	53	7	8	88	6	19	6	0	4	0	48	6	0.4	1.4	0.4	3.4
Ennis Whatley	G	6'3	177	25	5	24	4	9	44	3	4	75	4	2	3	0	2	0	11	5	0.8	0.4	0.6	2.2

3-PT FG — Wilkins 38-129, Levbingston 1-2, Rivers 9-33, Willis 0-2, Carr 1-4, Webb 9-19, Battle 16-41, Koncak 0-2, Hastings 5-12, McGee 5-19, Wood 9-19

Use Name	Pos	Hgt	Wgt	Age	G	Min	FG	FGA	%	FT	FTA	%	Reb	Ass	PF	DQ	Stls	Blkd Shts	Points	Min	Reb	Ass	PF	Points
CHICAGO BULLS	**50-32 .610**				**DOUG COLLINS**																			
Scottie Pippin	F	6'7	210	22	79	1650	261	564	46	99	172	58	298	169	214	3	91	52	625	21	3.8	2.1	2.7	7.9
Charles Oakley	F	6'8	225	24	82	2816	375	776	48	261	359	73	**1066**	248	272	2	68	28	1014	34	13.0	3.0	3.3	12.4
Dave Corzine	C	6'11	265	31	80	2328	344	715	48	115	153	75	527	154	149	1	36	95	804	29	6.6	1.9	1.9	10.1
Michael Jordan	G	6'6	198	24	82	**3311**	**1069**	**1998**	54	**723**	860	84	449	485	270	2	**259**	131	**2868**	40	5.5	5.9	3.3	**35.0**
Sam Vincent (from Sea)	G	6'2	185	24	29	953	138	309	45	99	107	93	103	244	82	0	34	12	378	33	3.6	8.4	2.8	13.0
Brad Sellers	F-C	7'	210	25	82	2212	326	714	46	124	157	79	250	141	174	0	34	66	777	27	3.0	1.7	2.1	9.5
John Paxson	G	6'2	185	27	81	1888	287	582	49	33	45	73	104	303	154	2	49	1	640	23	1.3	3.7	1.9	7.9
Horace Grant	F	6'10	220	22	81	1827	254	507	50	114	182	63	447	89	221	3	51	53	622	23	5.5	1.1	2.7	7.7
Rory Sparrow (from NY)	G	6'2	175	29	55	992	112	274	41	24	33	73	70	162	72	1	37	3	250	18	1.3	2.9	1.3	4.5
Sedale Threatt (to Sea)	G	6'2	177	26	45	701	132	263	50	32	41	78	55	107	71	0	27	3	298	16	1.2	2.4	1.6	6.6
Mike Brown	C	6'9	250	24	46	591	78	174	45	41	71	58	159	28	85	0	11	4	197	13	3.5	0.6	1.8	4.3
Artis Gilmore (to Bos)	C	7'2	255	38	24	372	41	80	51	19	37	51	63	9	54	0	5	12	101	16	2.6	0.4	2.3	4.2
Granville Waiters	C	6'11	225	26	22	114	9	29	31	0	2	0	28	1	26	0	2	15	18	5	1.3	0.0	1.2	0.8
Elston Turner	G	6'5	200	28	17	98	8	30	27	1	2	50	10	9	5	0	8	0	17	6	0.6	0.5	0.3	1.0
Tony White (to NY, GS)	G	6'2	170	22	2	2	0	0	—	0	0	—	0	0	0	0	0	0	0	1	0.0	0.0	0.0	0.0

3-PT FG — Pippen 4-23, Oakley 3-12, Corzine 1-9, Jordan 7-53, Vincent 3-8, Sellers 1-7, Paxson 33-95, Grant 0-2, Sparrow 2-12, Threatt 2-20, Brown 0-1, Waiters 0-1

Use Name	Pos	Hgt	Wgt	Age	G	Min	FG	FGA	%	FT	FTA	%	Reb	Ass	PF	DQ	Stls	Blkd Shts	Points	Min	Reb	Ass	PF	Points
CLEVELAND CAVALIERS	**44-40 .512**				**LENNY WILKINS**																			
Phil Hubbard	F	6'8	215	31	78	1631	237	485	49	182	243	75	281	81	167	1	50	7	656	21	3.6	1.0	2.1	8.4
Larry Nance (from Phoe)	F	6'10	217	28	27	906	160	304	53	117	141	83	213	84	90	3	18	63	437	34	7.9	3.1	3.3	16.2
Brad Daugherty	C	7'	255	22	79	2957	551	1081	51	378	528	72	665	333	235	2	48	56	1480	37	8.4	4.2	3.0	18.7
Ron Harper (ankle injury)	G	6'6	205	23	57	1830	340	732	46	196	278	71	223	281	157	3	122	52	879	32	3.9	4.9	2.8	15.4
Mark Price	G	6'1	175	23	80	2626	493	974	51	221	252	88	180	480	119	1	99	12	1279	33	2.3	6.0	1.5	16.0
John Williams	F-C	6'11	230	26	71	2106	316	663	48	211	279	76	506	103	203	2	61	145	843	30	7.1	1.5	2.9	11.9
Craig Ehlo	G-F	6'7	195	26	79	1709	226	485	47	89	132	67	274	206	182	0	82	30	563	22	3.5	2.6	2.3	7.1
Dell Curry	G	6'5	195	23	79	1709	340	742	46	79	101	78	166	149	128	0	94	22	787	22	2.1	1.9	1.6	10.0
Mark West (to Phoe)	F-C	6'10	230	27	54	1183	182	316	58	95	153	62	281	50	158	2	25	79	459	22	5.2	0.9	2.9	8.5
Tyrone Corbin (to Phoe)	F	6'6	222	25	54	1148	158	322	49	77	98	79	220	56	128	2	42	15	393	21	4.1	1.0	2.4	7.3
Kevin Johnson (to Phoe)	G	6'2	180	21	52	1043	143	311	46	92	112	82	72	193	96	1	60	17	380	20	1.4	3.7	1.8	7.3

(continued next page)

Use Name	Pos	Hgt	Wgt	Age	G	Min	TOTAL FG	FGA	%	FT	FTA	%	Reb	Ass	PF	DQ	Stls	Blkd Shts	Points	PER GAME Min	Reb	Ass	PF	Points

1987/88 N.B.A.—EASTERN CONFERENCE
CENTRAL DIVISION

Use Name	Pos	Hgt	Wgt	Age	G	Min	FG	FGA	%	FT	FTA	%	Reb	Ass	PF	DQ	Stls	Blkd Shts	Points	Min	Reb	Ass	PF	Points
Chris Dudley	C-F	6'11	235	22	55	513	65	137	47	40	71	56	144	23	87	2	13	19	170	9	2.6	0.4	1.6	3.1
Mike Sanders (from Phoe)	F	6'6	215	27	22	417	71	132	54	20	23	87	47	26	58	1	13	5	162	19	2.1	1.2	2.6	7.4
Johnny Rogers	C	6'11	231	24	24	168	26	61	43	10	13	77	27	3	23	0	4	3	62	7	1.1	0.1	1.0	2.6
Kevin Henderson (from GS)	G	6'4	195	23	5	20	2	5	40	5	12	42	4	2	2	0	0	0	9	4	0.8	0.4	0.4	1.8
Kent Benson	F	6'10	240	33	2	12	2	2	100	1	2	50	1	0	2	0	1	1	5	6	0.5	0.0	1.0	2.5
Kannard Johnson	F	6'9	220	22	4	12	1	3	33	0	0	—	0	0	1	0	1	0	2	3	0.0	0.0	0.3	0.5

3-PT FG — Hubbard 0-5, Nance 0-1, Daugherty 0-2, Harper 3-20, Price 72-148, Williams 0-1, Ehlo 22-64, Curry 28-81,Corbin 0-3, Kev.Johnson 2-9, Rogers 0-2

Use Name	Pos	Hgt	Wgt	Age	G	Min	FG	FGA	%	FT	FTA	%	Reb	Ass	PF	DQ	Stls	Blkd Shts	Points	Min	Reb	Ass	PF	Points
MILWAUKEE BUCKS	**42-40 .512**				**DEL HARRIS**																			
Terry Cummings	F	6'9	235	36	76	2629	675	1392	48	270	406	67	553	181	274	6	78	46	1621	35	7.3	2.4	3.6	21.3
Jack Sikma	F-C	6'11	260	32	82	2923	514	1058	49	321	348	92	709	279	316	11	93	80	1352	36	8.6	3.4	3.9	16.5
Randy Breuer	C	7'3	258	27	81	2258	390	788	50	188	286	66	551	103	198	3	46	107	968	28	6.8	1.3	2.4	12.0
Sidney Moncrief (KJ)	G	6'4	185	30	56	1428	217	444	49	164	196	84	180	204	109	0	41	14	603	26	3.2	3.6	1.9	10.8
Paul Pressey	G	6'5	200	29	75	2484	345	702	49	285	357	80	375	523	233	6	112	34	983	33	5.0	7.0	3.1	13.1
John Lucas	G	6'3	185	34	81	1766	281	631	45	130	162	80	159	392	102	1	88	3	743	22	2.0	4.8	1.3	9.2
Jerry Reynolds	F	6'8	200	25	62	1161	188	419	45	119	154	77	160	104	97	0	74	32	498	19	2.6	1.7	1.6	8.0
Larry Krystkowiak	F	6'9	240	23	50	1050	128	266	48	103	127	81	231	50	137	0	18	8	359	21	4.6	1.0	2.7	7.2
Craig Hodges (to Phoe)	G	6'3	190	27	43	983	155	345	45	32	39	82	46	109	80	1	30	0	397	23	1.1	2.5	1.9	9.2
Ricky Pierce (HO)	F-G	6'5	205	28	37	965	248	486	51	107	122	88	83	73	94	0	21	7	606	26	2.2	2.0	2.5	16.4
Paul Mokeski	C	7'	255	30	60	848	100	210	48	51	72	71	221	22	194	5	27	27	251	14	3.7	0.4	3.2	4.2
Pace Mannion	G	6'7	190	27	35	477	48	118	41	25	37	68	51	55	53	0	13	7	123	14	1.5	1.6	1.5	3.5
John Stroeder	F	6'10	260	29	41	271	29	79	37	20	30	67	71	20	48	0	3	12	78	7	1.7	0.5	1.2	1.9
Jay Humphries (from Phoe)	G	6'3	185	25	18	252	20	54	37	9	14	64	23	41	23	0	20	1	49	14	1.3	2.3	1.3	2.7
Connor Henry (from Bos, to Sac)	G	6'7	195	24	14	145	13	41	32	4	7	57	19	29	11	0	4	1	32	10	1.4	2.1	0.8	2.3
Richie Winslow	F	6'8	225	23	7	45	3	13	23	1	2	50	7	2	9	0	1	0	7	6	1.0	0.3	1.3	1.0
Charlie Davis (to SA)	F	6'7	215	29	5	39	6	18	33	0	0	—	3	3	4	0	2	1	12	8	0.6	0.6	0.8	2.4
Dave Hoppen (to GS)	F	6'11	235	23	3	35	4	11	36	3	3	100	7	2	3	0	0	0	11	12	2.3	0.7	1.0	3.7
Andre Moore (fron Den)	F	6'9	215	23	3	16	2	3	67	0	2	0	2	1	2	0	0	0	4	5	0.7	0.3	0.7	1.3
Dudley Bradley (to NJ)	G	6'6	195	30	2	5	0	1	0	0	0	—	1	1	2	0	0	0	0	3	0.5	0.5	1.0	0.0

3-PT FG — Cummings 1-3, Sikma 3-14, Moncrief 5-31, Pressey 8-39, Lucas 51-131, Reynolds 3-7, Krystkowiak 0-3, Hodges 55-118, Pierce 3-14,Mokeski 0-4, Mannion 2-12, Stroeder 0-2, Humphries 0-2, Henry 2-6, Winslow 0-1, Davis 0-2, Bradley 0-1

Use Name	Pos	Hgt	Wgt	Age	G	Min	FG	FGA	%	FT	FTA	%	Reb	Ass	PF	DQ	Stls	Blkd Shts	Points	Min	Reb	Ass	PF	Points
INDIANA PACERS	**38-44 .463**				**JACK RAMSAY**																			
Chuck Person	F	6'8	225	23	79	2807	575	1252	46	132	197	67	536	309	266	4	73	9	1341	36	6.8	3.9	3.4	17.0
Wayman Tisdale	F	6'9	250	23	79	2378	511	998	51	246	314	78	491	103	274	5	54	34	1268	30	6.2	1.3	3.5	16.1
Steve Stipanovich	C	6'11	250	27	80	2692	411	828	50	254	314	81	662	183	302	8	90	69	1079	34	8.3	2.3	3.8	13.5
John Long	G	6'5	195	31	81	2022	417	879	47	166	183	91	229	173	164	1	84	11	1034		2.8	2.1	2.0	12.8
Vern Fleming	G	6'5	195	26	80	2733	442	845	52	227	283	80	364	568	225	0	115	11	1111	34	4.6	7.1	2.8	13.9
Herb Williams	F-C	6'11	240	29	75	1966	311	732	42	126	171	74	469	98	244	1	37	146	748	26	6.3	1.3	3.3	10.0
Reggie Miller	G	6'7	190	22	82	1840	306	627	49	149	186	80	190	132	157	0	53	19	822	22	2.3	1.6	1.9	10.0
Ron Anderson	F	6'7	215	29	74	1097	217	436	50	108	141	77	216	78	98	0	41	6	542	15	2.9	1.1	1.3	7.3
Stuart Gray	C-F	7'	245	24	74	807	90	193	47	44	73	60	250	44	152	1	11	32	224	11	3.4	0.6	2.1	3.0
Scott Skiles	G	6'1	200	23	51	760	86	209	41	45	54	83	66	180	97	0	22	3	223	15	1.3	3.5	1.9	4.4
Clinton Wheeler	G	6'1	185	28	59	513	62	132	47	25	34	74	40	103	37	0	36	2	149	9	0.7	1.7	0.6	2.5
Greg Dreiling	C	7'1	250	24	20	74	8	17	47	18	26	69	17	5	19	0	2	4	34	4	0.9	0.3	1.0	1.7
Brian Rowsom	F	6'9	220	22	4	16	0	6	0	6	6	100	5	1	3	0	1	0	6	4	1.3	0.3	0.8	1.5

3-PT FG — Person 59-177, Tisdale 0-2, Stipanovich 3-15, Long 34-77, Fleming 0-13, Williams 0-6, Miller 61-172, Anderson 0-2, Gray 0-1, Skiles 6-20

WESTERN CONFERENCE
MIDWEST DIVISION

Use Name	Pos	Hgt	Wgt	Age	G	Min	FG	FGA	%	FT	FTA	%	Reb	Ass	PF	DQ	Stls	Blkd Shts	Points	Min	Reb	Ass	PF	Points
DENVER NUGGETS	**54-28 .659**				**DOUG MOE**																			
Alex English	F	6'8	190	33	80	2818	843	1704	49	314	379	83	373	377	193	1	70	23	2000	35	4.7	4.7	2.4	25.0
Jay Vincent	F	6'7	220	28	73	1755	446	958	47	231	287	80	309	143	198	1	46	26	1124	24	4.2	2.0	2.7	15.4
Dan Schayes	C-F	6'11	260	28	81	2166	361	668	54	407	487	84	662	106	323	9	62	92	1129	27	8.2	1.3	4.0	13.9
Lafayette Lever	G	6'3	175	27	82	3061	643	1360	47	248	316	78	665	639	214	0	223	21	1546	37	8.1	7.8	2.6	18.9
Michael Adams	G	5'11	165	24	82	2778	416	927	45	166	199	83	223	503	138	0	168	16	1137	34	2.7	6.1	1.7	13.9
Blair Rasmussen	C	7'	260	25	79	1779	435	884	49	132	170	78	437	78	241	2	22	81	1002	23	5.5	1.0	3.1	12.7
T.R. Dunn	G	6'4	192	32	82	1534	70	156	45	40	52	77	240	87	152	0	101	11	180	19	2.9	1.1	1.9	2.2
Bill Hanzlik	F-G	6'7	200	30	77	1334	109	287	38	129	163	79	171	166	185	1	64	17	350	17	2.2	2.2	2.4	4.5
Wayne Cooper (back injury)	C-F	6'10	220	31	45	865	118	270	44	50	67	75	270	30	145	3	12	94	286	19	6.0	0.7	3.2	6.4
Mike Evans	G	6'1	170	32	56	656	139	307	45	30	37	81	48	81	78	0	34	6	344	12	0.9	1.4	1.4	6.1
Calvin Natt	F	6'6	220	30	27	533	102	208	49	54	73	74	96	47	43	0	13	3	258	20	3.6	1.7	1.6	9.6
Otis Smith (to GS)	F	6'5	210	23	15	191	37	93	40	21	28	75	30	11	23	0	5	6	95	13	2.0	0.7	1.5	6.3
Maurice Martin	G	6'6	200	23	26	136	23	61	38	10	21	48	24	14	21	0	6	3	57	5	0.9	0.5	0.8	2.2
Michael Brooks	F	6'7	220	29	16	133	20	49	41	3	4	75	44	13	21	1	4	1	43	8	2.8	0.8	1.3	2.7
Andre Moore (to Mil)	F	6'9	215	23	7	34	7	24	29	6	6	100	12	5	4	0	2	1	20	5	1.7	0.7	0.6	2.9
Brad Wright	F	6'11	225	25	2	7	1	5	20	0	0	—	1	0	3	0	0	0	2	4	0.5	0.0	1.5	1.0

3-PT FG — English 0-6, Vincent 1-4, Schayes 0-2, Lafayette Lever 12-57, Adams 139-379, Dunn 0-1, Hanzlik 3-16, Cooper 0-1, Evans 36-91, Natt 0-1, Martin 1-4

Use Name	Pos	Hgt	Wgt	Age	G	Min	FG	FGA	%	FT	FTA	%	Reb	Ass	PF	DQ	Stls	Blkd Shts	Points	Min	Reb	Ass	PF	Points
DALLAS MAVERICKS	**53-29 .646**				**JOHN MacLEOD**																			
Mark Aguirre	F-G	6'6	221	28	77	2610	746	1571	47	388	504	77	434	278	223	1	70	57	1932	34	5.6	3.6	2.9	25.1
Sam Perkins	F	6'9	235	26	75	2499	294	876	34	273	332	82	601	118	227	2	74	54	1066	33	8.0	1.6	3.0	14.2
James Donaldson	C	7'2	278	30	81	2523	212	380	56	147	189	78	755	66	175	2	40	104	571	31	9.3	0.8	2.2	7.0
Rolando Blackman	G	6'6	200	28	71	2580	497	1050	47	331	379	87	246	262	112	0	64	18	1325	36	3.5	3.7	1.6	18.7
Derek Harper	G	6'4	206	26	82	3032	536	1167	46	261	344	76	246	634	164	0	168	35	1393	37	3.0	7.7	2.0	17.0

(continued next page)

I987/88 N.B.A. — WESTERN CONFERENCE
MIDWEST DIVISION

Use Name	Pos	Hgt	Wgt	Age	G	Min	FG	FGA	%	FT	FTA	%	Reb	Ass	PF	DQ	Stls	Blkd Shts	Points	Min	Reb	Ass	PF	Points
					TOTAL															PER GAME				
DALLAS MAVERICKS (continued)																								
Roy Tarpley	F-C	7'	256	23	81	2307	444	888	50	205	277	74	959	86	313	8	103	86	1093	28	11.8	1.1	3.9	13.5
Detlef Schrempf	F	6'10	222	24	82	1587	246	539	46	201	266	76	279	159	189	0	42	32	698	19	3.4	1.9	2.3	8.5
Brad Davis	G	6'3	180	32	75	1480	208	415	50	91	108	84	102	303	149	0	51	18	537	20	1.4	4.0	2.0	7.2
Uwe Blab	C	7'1	225	25	73	658	58	132	44	46	65	71	134	35	108	1	8	29	162	9	1.8	0.5	1.5	2.2
Steve Alford	G	6'2	185	23	28	197	21	55	38	16	17	94	23	23	23	0	17	3	59	7	0.8	0.8	0.8	2.1
Jim Farmer	G	6'4	190	23	30	157	26	69	38	9	10	90	18	16	18	0	3	1	61	5	0.6	0.5	0.6	2.0
Bill Wennington	C	7'	247	23	30	125	25	49	51	12	19	63	39	4	33	0	5	9	63	4	1.3	0.1	1.1	2.1

3-PT FG — Aguirre 52-172, Perkins 5-30, Blackman 0-5, Harper 60-192, Tarpley 0-5, Schrempf 5-32, Davis 30-74, Alford 1-8, Farmer 0-6, Wennington 1-2

Use Name	Pos	Hgt	Wgt	Age	G	Min	FG	FGA	%	FT	FTA	%	Reb	Ass	PF	DQ	Stls	Blkd Shts	Points	Min	Reb	Ass	PF	Points
UTAH JAZZ	**47-35 .573**				**FRANK LAYDEN**																			
Thurl Bailey	F	6'11	232	26	82	2804	633	1286	49	337	408	83	531	158	186	1	49	125	1604	34	6.5	1.9	2.3	19.6
Karl Malone	F-C	6'9	254	24	82	3198	858	1650	52	552	789	70	986	199	296	2	117	50	2868	39	12.0	2.4	3.6	35.0
Mark Eaton	C	7'4	290	30	82	2731	226	541	42	119	191	62	717	55	320	8	41	**304**	571	33	8.7	0.7	3.9	7.0
Bob Hansen	G	6'6	195	26	81	1796	316	611	52	113	152	74	187	175	193	2	65	5	777	22	2.3	2.2	2.4	9.6
John Stockton	G	6'1	175	25	82	2842	454	791	57	272	324	84	237	**1128**	247	5	242	16	1204	35	2.9	13.8	3.0	14.7
Marc Iavaroni	F	6'9	225	31	81	1238	143	308	46	78	99	79	268	67	162	1	23	25	364	15	3.3	0.8	2.0	4.5
Rickey Green	G	6'1	172	33	81	1116	157	370	42	75	83	90	80	300	83	0	57	1	393	14	1.0	3.7	1.0	4.9
Darrell Griffith	G	6'4	190	29	52	1052	251	585	43	59	92	64	127	91	102	0	52	5	589	20	2.4	1.8	2.0	11.3
Melvin Turpin	C	6'11	240	27	79	1011	199	389	51	71	98	72	236	32	157	2	26	68	470	13	3.0	0.4	2.0	5.9
Kelly Tripucka	G-F	6'6	225	28	49	976	139	303	46	59	68	87	117	105	68	1	34	4	368	20	2.4	2.1	1.4	7.5
Carey Scurry (to NY)	F	6'7	190	25	29	447	54	116	47	27	39	69	81	49	78	0	47	22	138	15	2.8	1.7	2.7	4.8
Bart Kofoed	G	6'4	210	23	36	225	18	48	38	8	13	62	15	23	42	0	6	1	46	6	0.4	0.6	1.2	1.3
Scott Roth	F	6'8	212	23	26	201	30	74	41	22	30	73	28	16	37	0	12	0	84	8	1.1	0.6	1.4	3.2
Ed Hughes	G	5'10	165	27	11	42	5	13	38	6	6	##	4	8	5	0	0	0	17	4	0.4	0.7	0.5	1.5
Darryl Hawkins (to Det)	C	6'11	270	30	4	26	1	7	14	4	12	33	5	1	10	0	0	1	6	7	1.3	0.3	2.5	1.5

3-PT FG — Bailey 1-3, Malone 0-5, Hansen 32-97, John Stockton 24-67, Marc Iavaroni 0-2, Rickey Green 14-19, Griffith 28-102, Turpin 1-3, Tripucka 31-74, Scurrey 3-8, Kofoed 2-7, Roth 2-11, Hughes 1-6

Use Name	Pos	Hgt	Wgt	Age	G	Min	FG	FGA	%	FT	FTA	%	Reb	Ass	PF	DQ	Stls	Blkd Shts	Points	Min	Reb	Ass	PF	Points
HOUSTON ROCKETS	**46-36 .561**				**BILL FITCH**																			
Rodney McCray	F-G	6'8	235	26	81	2689	359	746	48	288	367	78	631	264	166	2	57	51	1006	33	7.8	3.3	2.0	12.4
Jim Peterson	F-C	6'10	235	25	69	1793	249	488	51	114	153	75	436	106	203	3	36	40	613	26	6.3	1.5	2.9	8.9
Akeem Olajuwon	C	7'	250	24	79	2825	712	1385	51	381	548	70	959	163	324	7	162	214	1805	36	12.1	2.1	4.1	22.8
Eric Floyd (from GS)	G	6'3	175	27	59	1834	288	668	43	185	215	86	205	366	144	1	68	0	774	31	3.5	6.2	2.4	13.1
Allen Leavell	G	6'1	190	30	80	2150	291	666	44	218	251	87	148	405	162	1	124	9	819	27	1.9	5.1	2.0	10.2
Purvis Short	G-F	6'7	220	30	81	1949	474	986	48	206	240	86	222	162	197	0	58	14	1159	24	2.7	2.0	2.4	14.3
Joe Barry Carroll (from GS)	F-C	7'	255	29	63	1596	323	715	45	113	151	75	396	94	149	0	37	81	759	25	6.3	1.5	2.4	12.0
Robert Reid	G	6'8	215	32	62	980	165	356	46	50	63	79	125	67	118	0	27	5	393	16	2.0	1.1	1.9	6.3
Buck Johnson	F	6'7	190	23	70	879	155	298	52	67	91	74	168	49	127	0	30	26	378	13	2.4	0.7	1.8	5.4
Cedric Maxwell	F	6'8	225	32	71	848	80	171	47	110	143	77	179	60	75	0	22	12	270	12	2.5	0.8	1.1	3.8
Ralph Sampson (to GS)	F-C	7'4	230	27	19	705	119	271	44	63	85	74	172	37	63	1	17	33	303	37	9.1	1.9	3.3	15.9
World Free	G	6'2	190	34	58	682	143	350	41	80	100	80	44	60	74	2	20	3	374	12	0.8	1.0	1.3	6.4
Lester Conner	G	6'4	185	28	52	399	50	108	46	32	41	78	38	59	31	0	38	1	132	8	0.7	1.1	0.6	2.5
Steve Harris (to GS)	G	6'5	195	24	14	199	34	86	40	15	16	94	21	17	15	0	8	2	83	14	1.5	1.2	1.1	5.9
Andre Turner	G	5'11	160	23	12	99	12	34	35	10	14	71	8	23	13	0	7	1	35	8	0.7	1.9	1.1	2.9
Richard Anderson (to Port)	F	6'10	240	27	12	53	11	26	42	4	5	80	17	4	4	0	1	0	32	4	1.4	0.3	0.3	2.7

3-PT FG — McCray 0-4, Peterson 1-6, Olajuwon 0-4, Floyd 13-52, Leavell 19-88, Short 5-21, Carroll 0-1, Reid 13-34, Johnson 1-8, Maxwell 0-2, Sampson 2-6, Free 8-35, Conner 0-7, Harris 0-1, Turner 1-7, Anderson 6-15

Use Name	Pos	Hgt	Wgt	Age	G	Min	FG	FGA	%	FT	FTA	%	Reb	Ass	PF	DQ	Stls	Blkd Shts	Points	Min	Reb	Ass	PF	Points
SAN ANTONIO SPURS	**31-51 .378**				**BOB WEISS**																			
Walter Berry	F	6'8	215	23	73	1922	540	960	56	192	320	60	395	110	207	2	55	63	1272	26	5.4	1.5	2.8	17.4
Greg Anderson	F	6'10	230	23	82	1984	379	756	50	198	328	60	513	79	228	1	54	122	957	24	6.3	1.0	2.8	11.7
Frank Brickowski	C-F	6'10	240	28	70	2227	425	805	53	268	349	77	483	266	275	11	74	36	1119	32	6.9	3.8	3.9	16.0
Johnny Dawkins	G	6'2	165	24	65	2179	405	835	49	198	221	90	204	480	95	0	88	2	1027	34	3.1	7.4	1.5	15.8
Alvin Robertson	G	6'4	190	25	82	2978	655	1408	47	273	365	75	498	557	300	4	243	69	1610	36	6.1	6.8	3.7	19.6
Mike Mitchell	F-G	6'7	215	31	68	1501	378	784	48	160	194	82	198	68	101	0	31	13	919	22	2.9	1.0	1.5	13.5
Dave Greenwood	F	6'9	225	30	45	1236	151	328	46	83	111	75	300	97	134	2	33	22	385	27	6.7	2.2	3.0	8.6
Jon Sundvold	G	6'2	170	26	52	1024	176	379	46	43	48	90	48	183	54	0	27	2	421	20	0.9	3.5	1.0	8.1
Petur Gudmundsson	C	7'2	260	29	69	1017	139	280	50	117	145	81	323	86	197	5	18	61	395	15	4.7	1.2	2.9	5.7
Kurt Nimphius	C	6'10	225	29	72	919	128	257	50	60	83	72	153	53	141	2	22	56	316	13	2.1	0.7	2.0	4.4
Ed Nealy	F	6'7	238	27	68	837	50	109	46	41	63	65	222	49	94	0	29	5	142	12	3.3	0.7	1.4	2.1
Leon Wood (to Atl)	G	6'3	185	25	38	830	120	282	43	69	91	76	51	155	44	0	22	1	352	22	1.3	4.1	1.2	9.3
Ricky Wilson (from NJ)	G	6'3	195	23	18	373	36	99	36	23	29	79	26	63	34	0	17	3	104	21	1.4	3.5	1.9	5.8
Pete Myers	G	6'6	180	24	22	328	43	95	45	26	39	67	37	48	30	0	17	6	112	15	1.7	2.2	1.4	5.1
Charlie Davis (from Mil)	F	6'7	215	29	16	187	42	97	43	7	10	70	38	17	25	0	0	3	92	12	2.4	1.1	1.6	5.8
Nate Blackwell	G	6'4	170	22	10	112	15	41	37	5	6	83	6	18	16	0	3	0	37	11	0.6	1.8	1.6	3.7
Phil Zevenbergen	C	6'10	230	23	8	58	15	27	56	0	2	0	13	3	12	0	3	1	30	7	1.6	0.4	1.5	3.8
Johnny Moore (to NJ)	G	6'2	185	24	4	51	4	9	44	0	0	—	4	11	1	0	3	0	8	13	1.0	2.8	0.3	2.0
Richard Rellford	F	6'6	230	23	4	42	5	8	63	6	8	75	7	1	3	0	0	3	16	11	1.8	0.3	0.8	4.0

3-PT FG — Anderson 1-5, Brickowski 1-5, Dawkins 19-61, Robertson 27-95, Mitchell 3-12, Greenwood 0-2, Sundvold 26-64, Gudmundsson 0-1, Nimphius 0-1, Nealy 1-2, Wood 43-108, Wilson 9-25, Myers 0-4, Davis 1-15, Blackwell 2-11, Moore 0-1

Use Name	Pos	Hgt	Wgt	Age	G	Min	FG	FGA	%	FT	FTA	%	Reb	Ass	PF	DQ	Stls	Blkd Shts	Points	Min	Reb	Ass	PF	Points
SACRAMENTO KINGS	**24-58 .293**				**BILL RUSSELL 17-41 (.293), JERRY REYNOLDS 7-17 (.292)**																			
Harold Pressley	F-G	6'8	210	24	80	2029	318	702	45	103	130	79	369	185	211	4	84	55	775	25	4.6	2.3	2.6	9.7
Otis Thorpe	F	6'11	236	25	82	3072	622	1226	51	460	609	76	837	266	264	3	62	56	1704	37	10.2	3.2	3.2	20.8
Joe Kleine	C-F	7'	271	25	82	1999	324	686	47	153	188	81	579	93	228	1	28	59	801	24	7.1	1.1	2.8	9.8
Reggie Theus	G	6'7	213	30	73	2653	619	1318	47	320	385	83	232	463	173	0	59	16	1574	36	3.2	6.3	2.4	21.6
Kenny Smith (HJ)	G	6'3	170	22	61	2170	331	694	48	167	204	82	138	434	140	1	92	8	841	36	2.3	7.1	2.3	13.8

continued next page

1987/88 N.B.A. — WESTERN CONFEERNCE
MIDWEST DIVISION

Use Name	Pos	Hgt	Wgt	Age	G	Min	FG	FGA	%	FT	FTA	%	Reb	Ass	PF	DQ	Stls	Blkd Shts	Points	Min	Reb	Ass	PF	Points
					TOTAL															PER GAME				
SACRAMENTO (continued)																								
LaSalle Thompson (KJ)	C	6'10	253	26	69	1257	215	456	47	118	164	72	427	68	217	1	54	73	550	18	6.2	1.0	3.1	8.0
Ed Pinckney	F	6'9	215	24	79	1177	179	343	52	133	178	75	230	66	118	0	39	32	491	15	2.9	0.8	1.5	6.2
Terry Tyler	F-G	6'7	228	31	74	1185	184	407	45	41	64	64	242	56	85	0	43	47	410	16	3.3	0.8	1.1	5.5
Jawann Oldham (KJ)	C	7'	215	30	54	946	119	250	48	59	87	68	304	33	143	2	12	110	297	18	5.6	0.6	2.6	5.5
Derek Smith	G-F	6'6	218	26	35	899	174	364	48	87	113	77	103	89	108	2	21	17	443	26	2.9	2.5	3.1	12.7
Mike McGee(from Atl)	G	6'5	207	28	37	886	201	478	42	74	96	77	112	58	75	0	47	6	524	24	3.0	1.6	2.0	14.2
Michael Jackson	G	6'2	185	23	58	760	64	171	37	23	32	72	59	179	81	0	20	5	157	13	1.0	3.1	1.4	2.7
Franklin Edwards	G	6'1	190	28	16	414	54	115	47	24	32	75	19	92	10	0	10	1	132	26	1.2	5.8	0.6	8.3
Connor Henry (from Bos, Mil)	G	6'7	195	24	15	207	38	81	47	26	30	87	20	26	15	0	7	3	117	14	1.3	1.7	1.0	7.8
Joe Arlauckas	F	6'9	230	22	9	85	14	43	33	6	8	75	13	8	16	0	3	4	34	9	1.4	0.9	1.8	3.8
Martin Nessley (from LAC)	C	7'2	260	22	9	41	2	3	67	1	4	25	9	0	11	0	1	1	5	5	1.0	0.0	1.2	0.6

3-PT FG — Pressley 36-110, Thorpe 0-6, Theus 16-59, K.Smith 12-39, Thompson 2-5, Pinckney 0-2
Tyler 1-7, D.Smith 8-23, McGee 48-141, Jackson 6-25, Edwards 0-2, Henry 15-31

PACIFIC DIVISION

Use Name	Pos	Hgt	Wgt	Age	G	Min	FG	FGA	%	FT	FTA	%	Reb	Ass	PF	DQ	Stls	Blkd Shts	Points	Min	Reb	Ass	PF	Points
LOS ANGELES LAKERS	62-20 .656				**PAT RILEY**																			
James Worthy	F	6'9	235	26	75	2655	617	1161	53	242	304	80	374	289	175	1	72	55	1478	35	5.0	3.9	2.3	19.7
A.C. Green	F	6'9	230	24	82	2636	322	640	50	293	379	77	710	93	204	0	87	45	937	32	8.7	1.1	2.5	11.4
Kareem Abdul-Jabbar	C	7'2	267	40	80	2308	480	903	53	205	269	76	478	135	216	1	48	92	1165	29	6.0	1.7	2.7	14.6
Byron Scott	G	6'3	195	26	81	3048	710	1348	53	272	317	86	333	335	204	2	155	27	1754	38	4.1	4.1	2.5	21.7
Magic Johnson	G	6'8	226	28	72	2637	490	996	49	417	489	85	449	858	147	0	114	13	1408	37	6.2	11.9	2.0	19.6
Mychal Thompson	C-F	6'10	235	32	80	2007	370	722	51	185	292	63	489	66	251	1	38	79	925	25	6.1	0.8	3.1	11.6
Michael Cooper	G-F	6'5	176	31	61	1793	189	482	39	97	113	86	228	289	136	1	66	26	532	29	3.7	4.7	2.2	8.7
Kurt Rambis	F	6'8	213	29	70	845	102	186	55	73	93	78	268	54	103	0	39	13	277	12	3.8	0.8	1.5	4.0
Wes Matthews	G	6'1	170	27	51	706	114	248	46	54	65	83	66	138	65	0	25	3	289	14	1.3	2.7	1.3	5.7
Mike Smrek	C	7'	260	25	48	421	44	103	43	44	66	67	85	8	105	3	7	42	132	9	1.8	0.2	2.2	2.8
Milt Wagner	G	6'5	185	24	40	380	62	147	42	26	29	90	28	61	42	0	6	4	152	10	0.7	1.5	1.1	3.8
Tony Campbell	F	6'7	215	25	13	242	57	101	56	28	39	72	27	15	41	0	11	2	143	19	2.1	1.2	3.2	11.0
Ray Tolbert (from NY)	F	6'9	225	29	14	82	16	28	57	10	13	77	20	5	14	0	3	3	42	6	1.4	0.4	1.0	3.0
Billy Thompson (KJ)	F	6'7	220	24	9	38	3	13	23	8	10	80	9	1	11	0	1	0	14	4	1.0	0.1	1.2	1.6
Jeff Lamp (SJ)	G	6'6	195	28	3	7	0	0	—	2	2	—	0	0	1	0	0	0	2	2	0.0	0.0	0.3	0.7

3-PT FG — Worthy 2-16, Green 0-2, Abdul-Jabbar 0-1, Scott 62-179, Johnson 11-56,
M.Thompson 0-3, Cooper 57-178, Matthews 7-30, Wagner 2-10, Campbell 1-3

Use Name	Pos	Hgt	Wgt	Age	G	Min	FG	FGA	%	FT	FTA	%	Reb	Ass	PF	DQ	Stls	Blkd Shts	Points	Min	Reb	Ass	PF	Points
PORTLAND TRAIL BLAZERS	53-29 .646				**MIKE SCHULER**																			
Kiki Vandeweghe (XJ)	F	6'8	220	29	37	1038	283	557	51	159	181	88	109	71	68	0	21	7	747	28	2.9	1.9	1.8	20.2
Jerome Kersey	F	6'7	222	25	79	2888	611	1225	50	291	396	73	657	243	302	8	127	65	1516	37	8.3	3.1	3.8	19.2
Kevin Duckworth	C	7'	280	23	78	2223	450	907	50	331	430	77	576	66	280	5	31	32	1231	29	7.4	0.8	3.6	15.8
Clyde Drexler	G	6'7	215	25	81	3060	849	1679	51	476	587	81	533	467	250	2	203	52	2185	38	6.6	5.8	3.1	27.0
Terry Porter	G	6'3	195	24	82	2991	462	890	52	274	324	85	378	831	204	1	150	16	1222	36	4.6	10.1	2.5	14.9
Caldwell Jones	C-F	6'11	225	27	79	1778	128	263	49	78	106	74	408	81	251	0	29	99	334	23	5.2	1.0	3.2	4.2
Richard Anderson (from Hou)	F	6'10	240	27	62	1297	160	413	39	54	72	75	286	108	133	1	50	16	416	21	4.6	1.7	2.1	6.7
Michael Holton	G	6'4	185	26	82	1279	163	353	46	107	129	83	149	211	154	0	41	10	436	16	1.8	2.6	1.9	5.3
Maurice Lucas	F	6'9	238	35	73	1181	168	373	45	109	148	74	315	94	188	0	33	10	445	16	4.3	1.3	2.6	6.1
Steve Johnson (FJ)	F-C	6'10	235	30	43	1050	258	488	53	149	249	60	242	57	151	4	17	32	662	24	5.6	1.3	3.5	15.4
Jerry Sichting (from Bos)	G	6'1	180	31	28	324	49	90	54	9	11	82	15	33	30	0	7	0	115	12	0.5	1.2	1.1	4.1
Jim Paxson (FJ, to Bos)	G	6'6	210	30	17	263	43	107	40	14	18	78	18	27	29	0	7	1	103	15	1.1	1.6	1.7	6.1
Charles Jones	F	6'8	215	25	37	186	16	40	40	19	33	58	31	8	28	0	3	6	51	5	0.8	0.2	0.8	1.4
Ronnie Murphy (BL,KJ)	F	6'5	225	23	18	89	14	49	29	7	11	64	11	6	14	0	5	1	36	5	0.6	0.3	0.8	2.0
Nikita Wilson	F	6'8	200	23	15	54	7	23	30	5	6	83	11	3	7	0	0	0	19	4	0.7	0.2	0.5	1.3
Kevin Gamble	G	6'5	215	22	9	19	0	3	0	0	0	—	3	1	2	0	2	0	0	2	0.3	0.1	0.2	0.0
Sam Bowie - leg injury																								

3-PT FG — Vandeweghe 22-58, Kersey 3-15, Drexler 11-52, Porter 24-69, Ca. Jones 0-4, Anderson 42-135, Holton 3-15
Lucas 0-3, Johnson 0-1, Sichting 8-14, Paxson 3-8, Ch. Jones 0-1, Murphy 1-4, Gamble 0-1

Use Name	Pos	Hgt	Wgt	Age	G	Min	FG	FGA	%	FT	FTA	%	Reb	Ass	PF	DQ	Stls	Blkd Shts	Points	Min	Reb	Ass	PF	Points
SEATTLE SUPERSONICS	44-38 .537				**BERNIE BICKERSTAFF**																			
Xavier McDaniel	F	6'7	205	24	78	2703	687	1407	49	281	393	72	518	263	230	2	96	52	1669	35	6.6	3.4	2.9	21.4
Tom Chambers	F	6'10	230	28	82	2680	611	1364	45	419	519	81	490	212	297	4	87	53	1674	33	6.0	2.6	3.6	20.4
Alton Lister	C	7'	240	29	82	1812	173	343	50	114	188	61	627	58	319	8	27	140	461	22	7.6	0.7	3.9	5.6
Dale Ellis	G-F	6'7	215	27	75	2790	764	1519	50	303	395	77	340	197	221	1	74	11	1938	37	4.5	2.6	2.9	25.8
Nate McMillan	G	6'5	195	23	82	2453	235	496	47	145	205	71	338	702	238	1	169	47	624	30	4.1	8.6	2.9	7.6
Derrick McKey	F	6'9	205	21	82	1706	255	519	49	173	224	77	328	107	237	3	70	63	694	21	4.0	1.3	2.9	8.5
Kevin Williams	G	6'3	180	26	80	1084	199	450	44	103	122	84	127	96	207	1	62	7	502	14	1.6	1.2	2.6	6.3
Olden Polynice	C	6'11	220	23	82	1080	118	254	46	101	158	64	330	33	215	1	32	26	337	13	4.0	0.4	2.6	4.1
Russ Schoene	F-C	6'10	210	27	81	973	208	454	46	51	63	81	198	53	151	0	39	13	484	12	2.4	0.7	1.9	6.0
Danny Young	G	6'4	175	25	77	949	89	218	41	43	53	81	75	218	69	0	52	2	243	12	1.0	2.8	0.9	3.2
Clemon Johnson	C	6'10	240	31	74	723	49	105	47	22	32	69	174	17	104	0	13	24	120	10	2.4	0.2	1.4	1.6
Sam Vincent (to Chi)	G	6'2	185	24	43	548	72	152	47	46	60	77	49	137	63	0	21	4	195	13	1.1	3.2	1.5	4.5
Sedale Threatt (from Chi)	G	6'2	177	26	26	354	84	162	52	25	30	83	33	53	29	0	33	5	194	14	1.3	2.0	1.1	7.5

3-PT FG — McDaniel 14-50, Chambers 33-109, Lister 1-2, Ellis 107-259, McMillan 9-24, McKey 11-30,
Williams 1-7, Polynice 0-2, Schoene 17-58, Young 22-77, Vincent 5-13, Threatt 1-7

Use Name	Pos	Hgt	Wgt	Age	G	Min	FG	FGA	%	FT	FTA	%	Reb	Ass	PF	DQ	Stls	Blkd Shts	Points	Min	Reb	Ass	PF	Points
PHOENIX SUNS	28-54 .341				**JOHN WETZEL**																			
Eddie Johnson	F	6'8	218	28	73	2177	533	2177	24	204	240	85	318	180	190	0	33	9	1294	30	4.4	2.5	2.6	17.7
Armon Gilliam (BT)	F	6'9	230	23	55	1807	342	1720	47	131	193	68	434	72	143	1	58	29	813	33	7.9	1.3	2.6	14.8
James Edwards (to Det)	C	7'1	252	32	43	1377	254	542	47	165	260	63	335	73	159	2	14	32	673	32	7.8	1.7	3.7	15.7
Walter Davis	G	6'6	200	33	68	1951	488	1031	47	205	231	89	159	278	131	0	86	3	1217	29	2.3	4.1	1.9	17.9
Kevin Johnson (from Cle)	G	6'2	180	21	28	874	132	285	46	85	99	86	119	244	59	0	43	7	352	31	4.3	8.7	2.1	12.6

(continued next page)

I987/88 N.B.A. — WESTERN CONFERENCE
PACIFIC DIVISION

Use Name	Pos	Hgt	Wgt	Age	G	Min	FG	FGA	%	FT	FTA	%	Reb	Ass	PF	DQ	Stls	Blkd Shts	Points	Min	Reb	Ass	PF	Points
					TOTAL															PER GAME				
PHOENIX (continued)																								
Jeff Hornacek	G	6'4	190	24	82	2243	306	605	51	152	185	82	262	540	151	0	107	10	781	27	3.2	6.6	1.8	9.5
Alvan Adams	C	6'9	220	33	82	1646	251	506	50	108	128	84	365	183	245	3	82	41	611	20	4.5	2.2	3.0	7.5
Jay Humphries (to Mil)	G	6'3	185	25	50	1557	264	484	55	103	139	74	151	354	154	1	61	4	634	31	3.0	7.1	3.1	12.7
Larry Nance (to Cle)	F	6'10	215	28	40	1477	327	616	53	187	249	75	394	123	152	7	45	96	843	37	9.9	3.1	3.8	21.1
Mark West (from Cle)	F-C	6'10	230	27	29	915	134	257	52	75	132	57	242	24	107	2	22	68	343	32	8.3	0.8	3.7	11.8
James Bailey	C-F	6'9	220	30	65	869	109	241	45	70	89	79	210	42	180	1	17	28	288	13	3.2	0.6	2.8	4.4
Tyrone Corbin (from Cle)	G-F	6'6	222	25	30	591	99	203	49	33	40	83	130	59	53	0	30	3	232	20	4.3	2.0	1.8	7.7
Bernard Thompson (XJ)	G-F	6'6	210	25	37	566	74	159	47	43	60	72	76	51	75	1	21	1	191	15	2.1	1.4	2.0	5.2
Mike Sanders (to Cle)	F	6'6	215	27	35	466	82	171	48	39	53	74	62	30	73	0	18	4	203	13	1.8	0.9	2.1	5.8
Craig Hodges (from Mil)	G	6'3	190	27	23	462	87	178	49	27	32	84	32	44	38	0	16	2	232	20	1.4	1.9	1.7	10.1
Jeff Cook	F-C	6'10	215	31	33	359	14	59	24	23	28	82	106	14	64	1	9	8	51	11	3.2	0.4	1.9	1.5
Winston Crite (NJ)	F	6'7	233	22	29	258	34	68	50	19	25	76	64	15	42	0	5	8	87	9	2.2	0.5	1.4	3.0
Bill Martin	F	6'7	205	25	10	101	16	51	31	8	13	62	27	6	16	0	5	0	40	10	2.7	0.6	1.6	4.0
Ron Moore (from Det)	C	7'	260	25	5	34	5	16	31	4	4	100	6	0	13	0	3	0	14	7	1.2	0.0	2.6	2.8

3-PT FG— E. Johnson 24-94, Edwards 0-1, Davis 36-96, K.Johnson 3-15, Hornacek 17-58, Adams 1-2, Humphries 3-16, Nance 2-5, West 0-1, Bailey 0-4, Corbin 1-3, Thompson 0-2, Sanders 0-1, Hodges 31-57, Cook 0-1, Martin 0-1

GOLDEN STATE WARRIORS 20-62 .244 **GEORGE KARL 16-48 (.250), ED GREGORY 4-14 (.222)**

Use Name	Pos	Hgt	Wgt	Age	G	Min	FG	FGA	%	FT	FTA	%	Reb	Ass	PF	DQ	Stls	Blkd Shts	Points	Min	Reb	Ass	PF	Points
Chris Mullin (AL)	F	6'7	220	24	60	2033	470	926	51	239	270	89	205	290	136	3	113	32	1213	34	3.4	4.8	2.3	20.2
Larry Smith (LJ)	F	6'8	235	29	20	499	58	123	47	11	27	41	182	25	63	1	12	11	127	25	9.1	1.3	3.2	6.4
Ralph Sampson (from Hou, LJ)	C	7'4	230	27	29	958	180	411	44	86	111	77	290	85	101	2	24	55	446	33	10.0	2.9	3.5	15.4
Rod Higgins	G-F	6'7	205	27	68	2188	381	725	53	273	322	85	293	188	188	2	70	31	1054	32	4.3	2.8	2.8	15.5
Winston Garland	G	6'2	170	23	67	2122	340	775	44	138	157	88	227	429	188	2	116	7	831	32	3.4	6.4	2.8	12.4
Ben McDonald	F	6'8	225	25	81	2039	258	552	47	87	111	78	335	138	246	4	39	8	612	25	4.1	1.7	3.0	7.6
Tellis Frank	F	6'10	225	22	78	1597	242	565	43	150	207	72	330	111	267	5	53	23	634	20	4.2	1.4	3.4	8.1
Otis Smith (from Den)	G-F	6'5	210	23	57	1358	288	569	51	157	201	78	217	144	137	0	86	36	746	24	3.8	2.5	2.4	13.1
Jerome Whitehead	C	6'10	225	31	72	1221	174	360	48	59	82	72	321	39	209	3	32	21	407	17	4.5	0.5	2.9	5.7
Dave Feitl	C	7'	240	25	70	1182	182	404	45	94	134	70	335	53	146	1	15	9	458	17	4.8	0.8	2.1	6.5
Terry Teagle	G	6'5	195	27	47	958	248	546	45	97	121	80	81	61	95	0	32	4	594	20	1.7	1.3	2.0	12.6
Steve Harris (from Hou)	G	6'5	195	24	44	885	189	401	47	74	97	76	105	70	74	0	42	6	452	20	2.4	1.6	1.7	10.3
Eric Floyd (to Hou)	G	6'3	175	27	18	680	132	301	44	116	139	83	91	178	46	0	27	2	381	38	5.1	9.9	2.6	21.2
Dave Hoppen (from Mil)	F-C	6'11	235	23	36	607	80	172	47	51	59	86	167	30	84	1	13	6	211	17	4.6	0.8	2.3	5.9
Tony White (from Chi,NY,KJ)	G	6'2	170	22	35	462	94	203	46	30	41	73	28	49	43	0	19	2	218	13	0.8	1.4	1.2	6.2
Joe Barry Carroll (to Hou)	C	7'	255	29	14	408	79	209	38	59	74	80	93	19	46	1	13	25	217	29	6.6	1.4	3.3	15.5
Dirk Minniefield (to Bos)	G	6'3	180	26	11	202	25	48	52	14	23	61	21	38	26	0	15	0	65	18	1.9	3.5	2.4	5.9
Kevin Henderson (to Cle)	G	6'4	195	23	12	170	19	48	40	10	14	71	17	21	24	0	8	0	48	14	1.4	1.8	2.0	4.0
Mark Wade	G	5'11	160	22	11	123	3	20	15	2	4	50	15	34	13	0	7	1	8	11	1.4	3.1	1.2	0.7
Chris Washburn (to Atl)	C	6'11	255	22	8	86	14	32	44	5	8	63	20	3	10	0	1	0	33	11	2.5	0.4	1.3	4.1
Kermit Washington	F	6'8	230	36	6	56	7	14	50	2	2	100	19	0	13	0	4	4	16	9	3.2	0.0	2.2	2.7

3-PT FG — Mullin 34-97, L.Smith 0-2l, Sampson 0-5, Higgins 19-39, Garland 13-39, McDonald 9-35, Frank 0-1, O. Smith 13-41, Feitl 0-4, Teagle 1-9, Harris 0-6, Floyd 1-20, Hoppen 0-1, White 0-5, Carroll 0-1, Minniefield 1-5, Henderson 0-1, Wade 0-2

LOS ANGELES CLIPPERS 17-65.207 **GENE SHUE**

Use Name	Pos	Hgt	Wgt	Age	G	Min	FG	FGA	%	FT	FTA	%	Reb	Ass	PF	DQ	Stls	Blkd Shts	Points	Min	Reb	Ass	PF	Points
Reggie Williams (KJ)	F	6'7	190	23	35	857	152	427	36	48	66	73	118	58	108	1	29	21	365	24	3.4	1.7	3.1	10.4
Michael Cage	F	6'9	235	25	72	2660	360	766	47	326	474	69	938	110	194	1	91	58	1046	37	13.0	1.5	2.7	14.5
Benoit Benjamin	C	7'	250	23	66	2171	340	693	49	180	255	71	530	172	203	2	50	225	860	33	8.0	2.6	3.1	13.0
Mike Woodson	G	6'5	198	29	80	2534	562	1263	44	296	341	87	190	273	210	1	109	26	1438	32	2.4	3.4	2.6	18.0
Larry Drew	G	6'1	190	29	74	2024	328	720	46	83	108	77	119	383	114	0	65	0	765	27	1.6	5.2	1.5	10.3
Darnell Valentine	G	6'2	183	28	79	1636	223	533	42	101	136	74	156	382	135	0	122	8	562	21	2.0	4.8	1.7	7.1
Snake Norman	F	6'8	215	23	66	1435	241	500	48	87	170	51	263	78	123	0	44	34	569	22	4.0	1.2	1.9	8.6
Quinton Dailey	G	6'3	180	26	67	1282	328	755	43	243	313	78	154	109	128	1	69	4	901	19	2.3	1.6	1.9	13.4
Joe Wolf (KJ)	F-C	6'11	230	23	42	1137	136	334	41	45	54	83	187	98	139	8	38	16	320	27	4.5	2.3	3.3	7.6
Earl Cureton	F-c	6'9	215	30	69	1128	133	310	43	33	63	52	271	63	135	1	32	36	299	16	3.9	0.9	2.0	4.3
Greg Kite (from Bos)	C	6'11	250	26	40	977	83	182	46	39	73	53	240	45	137	1	16	50	205	24	6.0	1.1	3.4	5.1
Norris Coleman	F	6'8	210	26	29	431	66	191	35	20	36	56	81	13	51	1	11	6	153	15	2.8	0.4	1.8	5.3
Eric White	F	6'8	200	22	17	352	66	124	53	45	57	79	62	9	32	0	7	3	178	21	3.6	0.5	1.9	10.5
Claude Gregory	F	6'9	235	29	23	313	61	134	46	12	36	33	95	16	37	0	9	13	134	14	4.1	0.7	1.6	5.8
Steve Burtt	G	6'2	185	25	19	312	62	138	45	47	69	68	27	38	56	0	10	5	171	16	1.4	2.0	2.9	9.0
Martin Nessley (to Sac)	C	7'2	260	22	35	295	18	49	37	7	14	50	73	16	78	1	7	11	43	8	2.1	0.5	2.2	1.2
Kenny Fields	F	6'5	240	25	7	154	16	36	44	20	26	77	29	10	17	0	5	2	52	22	4.1	1.4	2.4	7.4
Lancaster Gordon (KJ)	G	6'3	195	25	8	65	11	31	35	6	6	100	4	7	8	0	1	2	28	8	0.5	0.9	1.0	3.5
Michael Phelps	G	6'4	185	26	2	23	3	7	43	3	4	75	2	3	1	0	5	0	9	12	1.0	1.5	0.5	4.5
Tod Murphy	F	6'9	220	24	1	19	1	1	100	3	4	75	2	2	2	0	1	0	5	19	2.0	2.0	2.0	5.0

Norm Nixon - knee and achilles injuries

3-PT FG— Williams 13-58, Cage 0-1, Banjamin 0-8, Woodson 18-78, Drew 26-90, Valentine 15-33, Norman 0-10, Dailey Wolf 3-15, Cureton 0-3, Kite 0-1, Coleman 1-2, White 1-1, Gregory 0-1, burtt 0-4

PLAYOFFS

LOS ANGELES LAKERS **PAT RILEY**

defeated San Antonio 3-0; H122-110, H130-112, 109-107
defeated Utah 4-3; H110-91, H97-101, 86-96, 113-100, H111-109, 80-108, HI09-98
defeated Dallas 4-3; H113-98, H123-101, 94-106, 104-118, H119-102, 103-105, H117-102
defeated Detroit 4-3; H93-105, H108-96, 99-86, 86-111, 94-104, H103-102, H108-105

Use Name	Pos	Hgt	Wgt	Age	G	Min	FG	FGA	%	FT	FTA	%	Reb	Ass	PF	DQ	Stls	Blkd Shts	Points	Min	Reb	Ass	PF	Points
James Worthy	F	6'9	235	26	24	896	**204**	390	52	97	128	76	139	106	58	0	33	19	**506**	37	5.8	4.4	2.4	21.1
A. C. Green	F	6'9	230	24	24	726	92	169	54	55	73	75	175	20	61	0	11	12	239	30	7.3	0.8	2.5	10.0
Kareem Abdul-Jabbar	C	7'2	167	40	24	718	141	304	46	56	71	79	131	36	81	1	15	**37**	338	30	5.5	1.5	3.4	14.1
Byron Scott	G	6'3	195	26	24	879	178	357	50	90	104	87	100	60	65	0	34	5	470	37	4.2	2.5	2.7	19.6
Magic Johnson	G	6'8	226	28	24	**965**	169	329	51	132	155	85	130	**303**	61	0	34	4	477	40	5.4	12.6	2.5	19.9

(continued next page)

1987/88 N.B.A. — PLAYOFFS

Use Name	Pos	Hgt	Wgt	Age	G	Min	FG	FGA	%	FT	FTA	%	Reb	Ass	PF	DQ	Stls	Blkd Shts	Points	Min	Reb	Ass	PF	Points
					TOTAL															PER GAME				
LOS ANGELES LAKERS (continued)																								
Mychal Thompson	C-F	6'11	225	27	24	615	98	191	51	36	62	58	170	12	70	1	17	21	232	26	7.1	0.5	2.9	9.7
Michael Coper	G-F	6'5	176	31	24	588	54	131	41	20	27	74	58	66	57	0	19	9	153	25	2.4	2.8	2.4	6.4
Kurt Rambis	F	6'8	213	29	19	186	21	34	62	9	13	69	51	9	28	0	5	2	51	10	2.7	0.5	1.5	2.7
Tony Campbell	F	6'7	215	25	15	94	18	42	43	11	16	69	10	5	16	0	3	0	47	6	0.7	0.3	1.1	3.1
Mike Smrek	C	7'	260	25	8	34	1	5	20	1	3	33	6	0	4	0	1	3	3	4	0.8	0.0	0.5	0.4
Wes Matthews	G	6'1	170	27	10	27	2	5	40	8	10	80	1	2	4	0	1	0	12	3	0.1	0.2	0.4	1.2
Milt Wagner	G	6'5	185	24	5	14	2	5	40	2	2	100	2	3	3	0	0	1	6	3	0.4	0.6	0.6	1.2

3-PT FG— Worthy 1-9, Abdul-Jabbar0-2, Scott 24-55, Johnson 7-14, Cooper 25-62, Campbell 0-1, Matthews 0-1, Wagner 0-1

DETROIT PISTONS — **CHUCK DALY**

defeated Washington 3-2; H96-87, H102-101, 106-114(OT), 103-106, H99-78
defeated Chicago 4-1; H93-82, H95-105, 101-79, 96-77, H102-95
defeated Boston 4-2; 104-96, 115-119(2OT), H98-94, H78-79, 102-96(OT), H95-90
lost to L.A. Lakers 3-4; 105-93, 96-108, H86-99, H111-86, H104-94, 102-103, 105-108

Use Name	Pos	Hgt	Wgt	Age	G	Min	FG	FGA	%	FT	FTA	%	Reb	Ass	PF	DQ	Stls	Blkd Shts	Points	Min	Reb	Ass	PF	Points
Adrian Dantley	F	6'5	210	31	23	804	153	292	52	**140**	**178**	79	107	46	15	0	19	1	446	35	4.7	2.0	0.7	19.4
John Salley	F	7'	231	23	23	623	56	104	54	49	69	71	155	21	**88**	2	15	**37**	161	27	6.7	0.9	3.8	7.0
Bill Laimbeer	C	6'11	260	30	23	779	114	250	46	40	45	89	**221**	44	77	2	18	19	273	34	9.6	1.9	3.3	11.9
Joe Dumars	G	6'3	190	24	23	804	113	247	46	56	63	89	50	112	50	1	13	2	284	35	2.2	4.9	2.2	12.3
Isiah Thomas	G	6'1	185	26	23	911	183	**419**	44	125	151	83	107	201	71	2	**66**	8	504	40	4.7	8.7	3.1	21.9
Vinnie Johnson	G	6'2	200	31	23	477	101	239	42	33	50	66	75	43	48	0	17	4	236	21	3.3	1.9	2.1	10.3
Dennis Rodman	F	6'8	210	26	23	474	71	136	52	22	54	41	136	21	87	1	14	14	164	21	5.9	0.9	3.8	7.1
Rick Mahorn	F-C	6'10	255	29	23	409	31	90	34	13	19	68	89	13	64	2	5	10	75	18	3.9	0.6	2.8	3.3
James Edwards	C	7'	252	32	22	308	56	110	51	27	41	66	68	11	55	0	2	10	139	14	3.1	0.5	2.5	6.3
Ralph Lewis	G	6'6	200	24	10	17	2	6	33	0	0	—	8	1	2	0	0	0	4	2	0.8	0.1	0.2	0.4
Walker Russell	G	6'5	195	27	7	10	2	5	40	2	2	100	0	1	1	0	1	0	2	1	0.0	0.1	0.1	0.3
Chuck Nevitt	C	7'5	237	28	3	4	1	2	50	0	0	—	3	0	1	0	0	0	2	1	1.0	0.0	0.3	0.7

3-PT FG— Dantley 0-2, Salley 0-1, Laimbeer 5-17, Dumars 2-6, Thomas 13-44, Johnson 1-7, Rodman 0-2, Edwards 0-1, Lewis 0-1

DALLAS MAVERICKS — **JOHN MacLEOD**

defeated Houston 3-l; H120-110, H108-119, 93-92, 107-97
defeated Denver 4-2; 115-126, 112-108, H105-107, H124-103, 110-106, H108-95
lost to L.A. Lakers 3-4; 98-113, 101-123, H106-94, H118-104, 102-119, H105-103, 102-117

Use Name	Pos	Hgt	Wgt	Age	G	Min	FG	FGA	%	FT	FTA	%	Reb	Ass	PF	DQ	Stls	Blkd Shts	Points	Min	Reb	Ass	PF	Points
Mark Aguirre	F	6'6	221	28	17	558	147	294	50	60	86	70	100	56	49	0	14	9	367	33	5.9	3.3	2.9	21.6
Sam Perkins	F	6'9	235	26	17	572	88	195	45	53	66	80	112	31	51	1	25	17	230	34	6.6	1.8	3.0	13.5
James Donaldson	C	7'2	278	30	17	499	68	104	65	22	37	59	146	12	41	0	7	15	158	29	8.6	0.7	2.4	9.3
Rolando Blackman	G	6'6	200	28	17	672	126	261	48	55	62	89	55	77	28	0	15	3	307	40	3.2	4.5	1.6	18.1
Derek Harper	G	6'4	206	26	17	602	89	202	44	43	59	73	43	121	44	0	32	5	230	35	2.5	7.1	2.6	13.5
Roy Tarpley	C-F	7'	256	23	17	563	125	241	52	54	73	74	219	30	69	3	21	26	304	33	12.9	1.8	4.1	17.9
Brad Davis	G	6'3	180	32	17	295	42	70	60	24	26	92	20	55	34	0	3	5	109	17	1.2	3.2	2.0	6.4
Detlef Schrempf	F	6'10	222	24	15	274	40	86	47	36	51	71	55	24	29	0	8	7	117	18	3.7	1.6	1.9	7.8
Bill Wennington	C	7'	247	23	6	14	0	4	0	0	0	—	4	1	5	0	1	0	0	2	0.7	0.2	0.8	0.0
Steve Alford	G	6'2	185	23	4	12	3	8	38	0	0	—	2	2	0	0	0	0	6	3	0.5	0.5	0.0	1.5
Jim Farmer	G	6'4	190	23	3	11	2	6	33	0	0	—	4	1	2	0	0	0	4	4	1.3	0.3	0.7	1.3
Uwe Blab	C	7'1	225	25	3	8	0	2	0	2	2	100	1	1	1	0	0	0	2	3	0.3	0.3	0.3	0.7

3-PT FG— Aguirre 13-34, Perkins 1-7, Blackman 0-3, Harper 9-36, Tarpley 0-3, Schrempf 1-3, Davis 1-5, Alfgord 0-2

BOSTON CELTICS — **K.C. JONES**

defeated New York 3-1; H112-92, H128-102, 100-109, H102-94
defeated Atlanta 4-3; H110-101, H108-97, 92-110, 109-118, H1904-112, 102-100, H118-116
lost to Detroit 2-4; H96-104, H119-115(2OT), 94-98, 79-78, H96-102(OT), 90-95

Use Name	Pos	Hgt	Wgt	Age	G	Min	FG	FGA	%	FT	FTA	%	Reb	Ass	PF	DQ	Stls	Blkd Shts	Points	Min	Reb	Ass	PF	Points
Larry Bird	F	6'9	220	31	17	763	152	338	45	101	113	89	150	115	45	0	36	14	417	45	8.8	6.8	2.6	24.5
Kevin mcHale	F-C	6'10	225	30	17	716	158	262	**60**	115	137	84	136	40	65	1	7	30	432	42	8.0	2.4	3.8	25.4
Robert Parish	C	7'	230	34	17	626	100	188	53	50	61	82	168	21	42	0	11	19	250	37	9.9	1.2	2.5	14.7
Danny Ainge	G	6'4	185	28	17	670	71	184	39	37	42	88	53	109	64	2	9	1	198	39	3.1	6.4	3.8	11.6
Dennis Johnson	G	6'4	202	33	17	702	91	210	43	82	103	80	77	139	51	0	24	8	270	41	4.5	8.2	3.0	15.9
Jim Paxson	G	6'6	210	30	15	188	17	59	29	16	20	80	9	11	18	0	6	2	50	13	0.6	0.7	1.2	3.3
Mark Acres	F	6'11	225	25	17	158	14	26	54	9	18	50	36	2	33	0	1	1	37	9	2.1	0.1	1.9	2.2
Fred Roberts	F	6'10	220	27	15	100	11	21	52	7	11	64	16	3	20	1	3	0	29	7	1.1	0.2	1.3	1.9
Artis Gilmore	C	7'2	265	38	14	86	4	8	50	7	14	50	20	1	14	0	0	4	15	6	1.4	0.1	1.0	1.1
Reggie Lewis	F-G	6'7	195	22	12	70	13	34	38	3	5	60	16	4	13	0	3	2	29	6	1.3	0.3	1.1	2.4
Dirk Minniefield	G	6'3	180	26	11	50	6	14	43	2	2	100	2	11	13	0	2	0	16	5	0.2	1.0	1.2	1.5
Brad Lohaus	C	7'	230	23	9	26	8	11	73	0	0	—	4	0	4	0	0	1	16	3	0.4	0.0	0.4	1.8

3-PT FG— Bird 12-32, McHale 1-1,Ainge 19-57, Johnson 6-16, Paxson 0-2, Acres 0-1, Lewis 0-1, Minniefield 2-4, Lohaus 0-2

ATLANTA HAWKS — **MIKE FRATELLO**

defeated Milwaukee 3-2; H110-107, H104-97, 115-123, 99-105, H121-111
lost to Boston 3-4; 101-110, 97-108, H110-92, H118-109, 112-104, H100-102, 116-118

Use Name	Pos	Hgt	Wgt	Age	G	Min	FG	FGA	%	FT	FTA	%	Reb	Ass	PF	DQ	Stls	Blkd Shts	Points	Min	Reb	Ass	PF	Points
Dominique Wilkins	F	6'8	200	27	12	473	137	300	46	96	125	77	77	34	24	0	16	6	374	39	6.4	2.8	2.0	31.2
Kevin Willis	F-C	7'	235	25	12	462	80	138	58	34	50	68	108	11	51	1	10	10	194	39	9.0	0.9	4.3	16.2
Tree Rollins	C	7'1	240	32	12	133	20	36	56	13	15	87	71	6	46	0	10	19	53	11	5.9	0.5	3.8	4.4
Randy Wittman	G-F	6'6	210	28	12	344	66	122	54	5	7	71	26	43	24	0	7	1	137	29	2.2	3.6	2.0	11.4
Glenn Rivers	G	6'4	185	26	12	509	71	137	52	39	43	91	59	115	40	1	25	2	188	42	4.9	9.6	3.3	15.7
Spud Webb	G	5'7	135	24	12	211	35	81	43	34	37	92	20	56	22	0	9	0	106	18	1.7	4.7	1.8	8.8
Antoine Carr	F	6'9	235	26	12	210	36	68	53	9	14	64	41	15	47	2	4	17	81	18	3.4	1.3	3.9	6.8
John Battle	G	6'2	175	25	12	166	32	67	48	17	25	68	20	26	14	0	2	0	81	14	1.7	2.2	1.2	6.8
Cliff Levingston	F	6'8	210	26	12	163	24	50	48	12	16	75	26	7	25	0	5	5	60	14	2.2	0.6	2.1	5.0
Scott Hastings	C-F	6'10	235	27	11	103	9	14	64	8	8	100	17	3	21	1	3	1	26	9	1.5	0.3	1.9	2.4
Leon Wood	G	6'3	185	25	4	4	1	1	100	0	0	—	0	1	0	0	0	0	3	1	0.0	0.3	0.0	0.8
Chris Washburn	C	6'11	255	22	1	2	0	0	—	0	0	—	0	0	0	0	0	0	0	2	0.0	0.0	0.0	0.0

John Koncak - knee injury

3-PT FG— Wilkins 4-18, Willis 0-1, Rivers 7-22, Webb 2-8, Carr 0-1, Battle 0-2, Hastings 0-1, Wood 1-1

Use Name	Pos	Hgt	Wgt	Age	G	Min	FG	FGA	%	FT	FTA	%	Reb	Ass	PF	DQ	Stls	Blkd Shts	Points	Min	Reb	Ass	PF	Points
					TOTAL															PER GAME				
1987/88 N.B.A — PLAYOFFS																								
DENVER NUGGETS	**DOUG MOE**	defeated Seattle 3-2; H126-123, H91-111, 125-114, 117-127, H115-96 lost to Dallas 4-2; H126-115, H108-112, 107-105, 103-124, H106-110, 95-108																						
Alex English	F	6'8	190	33	11	438	116	255	45	35	43	81	59	48	34	0	7	3	267	40	5.4	4.4	3.1	24.3
Jay Vincent	F	6'7	220	28	8	200	53	104	51	34	50	68	37	6	25	0	5	4	140	25	4.6	0.8	3.1	17.5
Dan Schayes	C-F	6'11	260	28	11	314	55	88	63	70	83	84	79	18	46	1	3	10	180	29	7.2	1.6	4.2	16.4
Lafayette Lever	G	6'3	175	27	7	273	45	98	46	26	33	79	65	49	15	0	13	4	119	39	9.3	7.0	2.1	17.0
Michael Adams	G	5'11	165	24	11	406		47	0	36	41	88	36	64	19	0	18	2	147	37	3.3	5.8	1.7	13.4
Blair Rasmussen	C	7'	260	25	11	277	60	127	47	18	20	90	71	7	33	0	1	12	138	25	6.5	0.6	3.0	12.5
Mike Evans	F	6'1	170	32	11	219	45	114	39	14	15	93	22	23	19	0	12	0	116	20	2.0	2.1	1.7	10.5
Bill Hanzlik	F-G	6'7	200	30	11	212	20	56	36	18	26	69	29	26	40	1	5	9	58	19	2.6	2.4	3.6	5.3
T.R. Dunn	G	6'4	192	32	11	185	11	20	55	4	8	50	29	3	20	0	8	0	26	17	2.6	0.3	1.8	2.4
Wayne Cooper	F-C	6'10	220	31	9	96	8	23	35	2	2	100	33	6	19	0	3	8	18	11	3.7	0.7	2.1	2.0
Michael Brooks	F	6'7	220	29	4	11	1	3	33	0	0	—	4	2	1	0	0	0	3	3	1.0	0.5	0.3	0.8
Maurice Martin	G	6'6	200	23	3	9	1	5	20	5	6	83	1	0	1	0	0	1	7	3	0.3	0.0	0.3	2.3
3-PT FG—	English 0-3, Vincent 0-1, Lever 3-7, Adams 17-54, Evans 12-44, Hanzlik 0-8, Brooks 1-2, Martin 0-1																							
UTAH JAZZ	**FRANK LAYDEN**	defeated Portland 3-1; 96-108, 114-105, H113-108, H111-96 lost to L. A. Lakers 4-3; 91-110, 101-97, H96-89, H100-113, 109-111, H108-80, 98-109																						
Thurl Bailey	F	6'11	232	26	11	449	99	203	49	57	68	84	63	18	32	0	6	23	255	41	5.7	1.6	2.9	23.2
Karl Malone	F-C	6'9	254	24	11	494	123	255	48	81	112	72	130	17	35	0	13	7	327	45	11.8	1.5	3.2	29.7
Mark Eaton	C	7'4	290	30	11	461	31	65	48	23	36	64	103	13	48	3	12	34	85	42	9.4	1.2	4.4	7.7
Bob Hansen	G	6'6	195	26	11	408	67	135	50	16	22	73	39	32	42	1	7	0	169	37	3.5	2.9	3.8	15.4
John Stockton	G	6'1	175	25	11	478	68	134	51	75	91	82	45	163	36	0	37	3	215	43	4.1	14.8	3.3	19.5
Mark Iavaroni	F	6'9	225	31	11	137	16	29	55	12	14	86	19	14	26	0	2	2	44	12	1.7	1.3	2.4	4.0
Bart Kofoed	G	6'4	210	23	10	109	9	23	39	2	2	100	14	11	18	0	1	0	21	11	1.4	1.1	1.8	2.1
Rickey Green	G	6'1	172	33	7	38	2	8	25	0	0	—	1	9	2	0	2	0	4	5	0.1	1.3	0.3	0.6
Melvin Turpin	C	6'11	240	27	7	31	3	9	33	2	2	100	6	2	5	0	1	4	8	4	0.9	0.3	0.7	1.1
Ed Hughes	G	5'10	165	27	7	16	2	7	29	0	0	—	0	1	1	0	1	0	5	2	0.0	0.1	0.1	0.7
Scott Roth	F	6'8	212	24	6	10	1	3	33	0	0	—	0	0	0	0	2	0	2	2	0.0	0.0	0.0	0.3
Kelly Tripucka	G-F	6'6	225	28	2	9	1	3	33	0	0	—	1	1	1	0	0	0	2	5	0.5	0.5	0.5	1.0
3-PT FG—	Bailey 0-1, Malone 0-1, Hansen 19-36, Stockton 4-14, Kofoed 1-5, Hughes1-3																							
CHICAGO BULLS	**DOUG COLLINS**	defeated Cleveland 3-2; H104-93, H106-101, 102-110, 91-97, H107-101 lost to Detroit 4-1; 82-93, 95-105, H79-101, H77-96, 95-102																						
Scottie Pippen	F	6'7	210	22	10	294	46	99	46	5	7	71	52	24	33	1	8	8	100	29	5.2	2.4	3.3	10.0
Charles Oakley	F	6'8	225	24	10	373	40	91	44	21	24	88	128	32	33	0	6	4	101	37	12.8	3.2	3.3	10.1
Dave Corzine	C	6'11	265	31	10	308	27	76	36	7	13	54	57	8	21	0	3	8	61	31	5.7	0.8	2.1	6.1
Michael Jordan	G	6'6	198	24	10	427	138	260	53	86	99	87	71	47	38	1	24	11	363	43	7.1	4.7	3.8	36.3
Sam Vincent	G	6'2	185	24	10	251	41	110	37	20	25	80	19	44	23	0	8	1	102	25	1.9	4.4	2.3	10.2
Horace Grant	F-C	6'10	220	22	10	299	46	81	57	9	15	60	70	16	35	2	14	2	101	30	7.0	1.6	3.5	10.1
John Paxson	G	6'2	185	27	10	165	20	53	38	4	4	100	4	30	24	1	1	1	46	17	0.4	3.0	2.4	4.6
Brad Sellers	C	7'	210	25	10	144	15	43	35	15	17	88	21	8	18	0	2	5	45	14	2.1	0.8	1.8	4.5
Rory Sparrow	G	6'2	125	29	7	106	10	32	31	4	6	67	3	18	11	0	4	0	26	15	0.4	2.6	1.6	3.7
Elston Turner	G	6'5	200	28	4	29	1	6	17	0	0	—	5	6	2	0	0	0	2	7	1.3	1.5	0.5	0.5
Mike Brown	C	6'9	250	24	1	4	0	0	—	1	2	50	0	1	0	0	1	0	1	4	0.0	1.0	0.0	1.0
3-PT FG—	Pippen 3-6, Oakley 0-2, Jordan 1-3, Vincent 0-3, Grant 0-1, Paxson 2-12, Sparrow 2-4																							
MILWAUKEE BUCKS	**DEL HARRIS**	lost to Atlanta 3-2; 107-110, 97-104, H123-115, H105-99, 111-121																						
Terry Cummings	F	6'9	235	36	5	193	50	89	56	29	44	66	39	13	16	0	9	3	129	39	7.8	2.6	3.2	25.8
Larry Krystkowiak	F	6'9	240	23	5	163	13	29	45	16	18	89	34	7	17	0	4	0	42	33	6.8	1.4	3.4	8.4
Jack Sikma	C-F	6'11	260	32	5	190	35	76	46	25	30	83	62	13	23	0	2	4	95	38	12.4	2.6	4.6	19.0
Sidney Moncrief	G	6'4	185	30	5	173	24	50	48	26	27	96	19	26	14	0	3	1	75	35	3.8	5.2	2.8	15.0
Paul Pressey	G	6'5	200	29	5	178	23	50	46	23	30	77	19	33	21	0	4	3	70	36	3.8	6.6	4.2	14.0
Ricky Pierce	F-G	6'5	205	28	5	105	25	53	47	8	9	89	14	9	9	0	1	2	59	21	2.8	1.8	1.8	11.8
John Lucas	G	6'3	185	34	5	80	10	27	37	6	9	67	8	19	5	0	5	0	29	16	1.6	3.8	1.0	5.8
Randy Breuer	C	7'3	258	27	4	47	9	16	56	6	6	100	12	1	7	0	1	2	19	12	3.0	0.3	1.8	4.8
Paul Mokeski	C	7'	255	30	4	40	5	14	36	4	6	67	9	0	4	0	3	2	14	10	2.3	0.0	1.0	3.5
Jay Humphries	G	6'3	185	25	2	18	0	5	0	0	0	—	3	1	6	0	1	0	0	9	1.5	0.5	3.0	0.0
Jerry Reynolds	F	6'8	200	25	3	12	4	6	67	0	0	—	1	1	1	0	0	0	8	4	0.3	0.3	0.3	2.7
John Stroeder	F	6'10	260	29	1	1	1	1	100	0	0	—	0	0	0	0	0	0	3	1	0.0	0.0	0.0	3.0
3-PT FG —	Sikma 0-3, Moncrief 1-1, Pressey 1-3, Lucas 3-13, Stroeder 1-1																							
CLEVELAND CAVALIERS	**LENNY WILKINS**	lost to Chicago 3-2; 93-104, 101-106, H110-102, H97-91, 101-107																						
Mike Sanders	F	6'6	215	27	5	134	28	52	54	8	10	80	25	7	21	0	3	2	64	27	5.0	1.4	4.2	12.8
Larry Nance	F	6'10	217	28	5	200	34	64	53	16	18	89	36	18	13	0	2	11	84	40	7.2	3.6	2.6	16.8
Brad Daugherty	C	7'	255	22	5	204	29	63	46	21	31	68	46	16	11	0	2	7	79	41	9.2	3.2	2.2	15.8
Ron Harper	G	6'6	205	23	4	134	30	63	48	11	16	69	20	15	9	0	11	4	71	34	5.0	3.8	2.3	17.8
Mark Price	G	6'1	175	23	5	205	38	67	57	24	25	96	18	38	11	1	3	0	105	41	3.6	7.6	2.2	21.0
John Williams	F-C	6'11	230	26	5	133	20	40	50	6	13	46	29	4	13	0	3	7	46	27	5.8	0.8	2.6	9.2
Craig Ehlo	G	6'7	195	26	5	128	17	40	43	10	16	63	18	17	14	0	5	0	44	26	3.6	3.4	2.8	8.8
Chris Dudley	C	6'11	235	22	4	24	2	4	50	1	2	50	6	2	3	0	0	0	5	6	1.5	0.5	0.8	1.3
Phil Hubbard	F	6'8	215	31	3	21	1	6	17	0	1	0	3	0	1	0	0	0	2	7	1.0	0.0	0.3	0.7
Dell Curry	G	6'5	195	23	2	17	1	4	25	0	0	—	1	2	1	0	0	1	2	9	0.5	1.0	0.5	1.0
3-PT FG—	Sanders 0-1; Harper 0-2, Price 5-12, Ehlo 0-8, Curry 0-l																							
SEATTLE SUPERSONICS	**BERNIE SICKERSTAFI**	lost to Denver 3-2; 123-126, 111-91, H114-125, H127-117, 96-115																						
Xavier McDaniel	F	6'7	205	24	5	180	45	81	56	12	24	50	48	25	15	0	3	1	106	36	9.6	5.0	3.0	21.2
Tom Chambers	F-C	6'10	230	28	5	168	50	91	55	29	35	83	31	11	24	1	3	1	129	34	6.2	2.2	4.8	25.8
Alton Lister	C	7'	240	29	5	77	12	17	71	4	5	80	29	5	17	0	1	5	28	15	5.8	1.0	3.4	5.6
Dale Ellis	G-F	6'7	215	27	5	172	40	83	48	21	29	72	23	15	17	0	3	2	104	34	4.6	3.0	3.4	20.8
Nate McMillan	G	6'5	195	23	5	127	12	35	34	9	14	64	21	33	11	0	2	3	33	25	4.2	6.6	2.2	6.6

(continued next page)

Use Name	Pos	Hgt	Wgt	Age	G	Min	FG	FGA	%	FT	FTA	%	Reb	Ass	PF	DQ	Stls	Blkd Shts	Points	Min	Reb	Ass	PF	Points
					TOTAL															PER GAME				
					1987/88 N.B.A. — PLAYOFFS																			
SEATTLE SUPERSONICS (continued)																								
Derrick McKey	F	6'9	205	21	5	109	24	38	63	10	17	59	20	8	12	0	3	5	60	22	4.0	1.6	2.4	12.0
Danny Young	G	6'4	175	25	5	95	11	21	52	10	10	100	10	19	7	0	2	2	32	19	2.0	3.8	1.4	6.4
Sedale Threatt	G	6'2	177	26	5	80	13	34	38	4	4	100	11	11	7	0	1	0	32	16	2.2	2.2	1.4	6.4
Kevin Williams	G	6'3	180	26	5	70	7	16	44	0	0	—	8	9	15	0	3	0	14	14	1.6	1.8	3.0	2.8
Olden Polynice	C	6'11	220	23	5	44	5	11	45	0	2	0	8	0	6	0	3	0	10	9	1.6	0.0	1.2	2.0
Clemon Johnson	C	6'10	240	31	5	39	3	7	43	1	2	50	7	0	10	0	1	1	7	8	1.4	0.0	2.0	1.4
Russ Schoene	F-C	6'10	210	27	5	39	7	12	58	0	0	—	7	2	8	0	1	0	16	8	1.4	0.4	1.6	3.2
	3-PT FG—				McDaniel 4-8, Chambers 0-2, Ellis 3-12, McMillan 0-1, McKey 2-6, Young 0-3, Threatt 0-1, Williams 0-2, Schoene 2-4																			
WASHINGTON BULLETS	**KEVIN LOUGHERY**				lost to Detroit 2-3; 87-96, 101-102, H114-106(OT), H106-103, 78-99																			
Bernard King	F	6'7	215	31	5	168	26	53	49	17	21	81	11	9	17	0	3	0	69	34	2.2	1.8	3.4	13.8
John Williams	F	6'9	235	21	5	185	23	48	48	19	32	59	29	21	18	1	8	4	65	37	5.8	4.2	3.6	13.0
Mose Malone	C	6'10	255	32	5	198	30	65	46	33	40	83	56	7	9	0	3	4	93	40	11.2	1.4	1.8	18.6
Jeff Malone	G	6'4	205	26	5	199	50	97	52	28	37	76	17	11	16	0	5	5	128	40	3.4	2.2	3.2	25.6
Darrell Walker	G	6'4	180	26	5	155	22	54	41	11	16	69	24	14	18	0	7	4	55	31	4.8	2.8	3.6	11.0
Charles Jones	F	6'9	215	30	5	95	1	5	20	1	2	50	17	2	18	0	2	4	3	19	3.4	0.4	3.6	0.6
Steve Colter	G	6'3	175	25	5	86	14	31	45	4	7	57	15	13	9	0	3	3	32	17	3.0	2.6	1.8	6.4
Terry Catledge	F	6'8	230	24	5	45	4	11	36	3	4	75	6	2	9	0	0	0	11	9	1.2	0.4	1.8	2.2
Frank Johnson	G	6'2	185	29	5	44	7	22	32	4	4	100	2	1	2	0	4	0	18	9	0.4	0.2	0.4	3.6
Manute Bol	C	7'6	225	25	5	44	4	7	57	1	1	100	12	0	5	0	0	2	9	9	2.4	0.0	1.0	1.8
Mark Alarie	F	6'8	217	24	1	4	1	2	50	0	0	—	1	0	0	0	0	0	3	4	1.0	0.0	0.0	3.0
Muggsy Bogues	G	5'3	140	22	1	2	0	0	—	0	0	—	0	2	0	0	0	0	0	2	0.0	2.0	0.0	0.0
	3-PT FG—				Williams 0-1, M.Malone 0-1, J. Malone 0-1, Walker 0-1, Catledge 0-1, Johnson 0-2, Alarie 1-2																			
HOUSTON ROCKETS	**BILL FITCH**				lost to Dallas 1-3; 120-110, 119-108, H92-93, H97-107																			
Rodney McCray	F	6'8	235	26	4	159	12	31	39	9	12	75	27	9	12	0	4	3	32	40	6.8	2.3	3.0	8.0
Joe Barry Carroll	F-C	7'	255	29	4	116	18	47	38	8	10	80	19	2	12	0	3	1	44	29	4.8	0.5	3.0	11.0
Akeem Olajuwon	C	7'	250	24	4	162	56	98	57	38	43	88	67	7	14	0	9	11	150	41	16.8	1.8	3.5	37.5
Robert Reid	G-F	6'8	215	32	4	114	15	33	45	2	3	67	15	8	13	0	2	0	35	29	3.8	2.0	3.3	8.8
Eric Floyd	G	6'3	175	27	4	154	26	61	43	19	22	86	7	34	10	0	8	0	75	39	1.8	8.5	2.5	18.8
Jim Peterson	F	6'10	235	25	4	98	12	23	52	7	12	58	21	6	11	1	1	2	31	25	5.3	1.5	2.8	7.8
Purvis Short	F-G	6'7	220	30	4	71	7	26	27	8	8	100	9	1	8	0	1	0	22	18	2.3	0.3	2.0	5.5
Allen Leavell	G	6'1	190	30	4	38	7	19	37	4	4	100	3	9	6	0	2	0	20	10	0.8	2.3	1.5	5.0
Buck Johnson	F	6'7	190	23	4	20	2	3	67	1	2	50	4	0	1	0	1	0	5	5	1.0	0.0	0.3	1.3
Cedric Maxwell	F	6'8	225	32	4	15	1	2	50	0	0	—	1	1	1	0	0	0	2	4	0.3	0.3	0.3	0.5
World Free	G	6'2	190	34	2	12	0	2	0	0	0	—	2	1	2	0	0	0	0	6	1.0	0.5	1.0	0.0
Lester Conner	G	6'4	185	28	1	1	0	0	—	2	2	100	1	1	0	0	1	0	2	1	1.0	1.0	0.0	2.0
	3-PT FG—				McCray 0-1, Olajuwon 0-1, Reid 3-7, Floyd 4-8, Short 0-1, Leavell 2-6, Free 0-1																			
NEW YORK KNICKERBOCKERS	**RICK PITINO**				lost to Boston 1-3; 92-112, 102-128, H109-100, H94-102																			
Johnny Newman	F	6'7	190	24	4	113	31	68	46	14	16	88	11	7	16	0	6	1	76	28	2.8	1.8	4.0	19.0
Sidney Green	F	6'9	220	26	4	93	8	17	47	0	0	—	33	7	14	0	0	1	16	23	8.3	1.8	3.5	4.0
Patrick Ewing	C	7'	240	25	4	153	28	57	49	19	22	86	51	10	17	0	6	13	75	38	12.8	2.5	4.3	18.8
Gerald Wilkins	G-F	6'6	195	24	4	149	33	69	48	12	14	86	8	19	12	0	4	0	80	37	2.0	4.8	3.0	20.0
Mark Jackson	G	6'3	205	22	4	171	22	60	37	8	11	73	19	39	13	0	10	0	57	43	4.8	9.8	3.3	14.3
Kenny Walker	F	6'8	210	23	4	80	8	24	33	2	2	100	9	5	11	0	2	3	18	20	2.3	1.3	2.8	4.5
Bill Carwright	C-F	7'1	245	30	4	76	9	18	50	11	15	73	19	6	12	0	0	3	29	19	4.8	1.5	3.0	7.3
Trent Tucker	G	6'5	193	28	4	71	8	19	42	3	4	75	2	4	4	0	3	0	25	18	0.5	1.0	1.0	6.3
Pat Cummings	F	6'9	235	31	3	28	2	5	40	3	4	75	3	4	11	0	0	0	7	9	1.0	1.3	3.7	2.3
Sedric Toney	G	6'2	178	25	3	15	3	6	50	2	2	100	0	2	4	0	1	0	11	5	0.0	0.7	1.3	3.7
Rick Carlisle	G	6'5	210	28	2	8	1	4	25	0	0	—	2	0	1	0	1	0	2	4	1.0	0.0	0.5	1.0
Louis Orr	F	6'8	200	29	2	3	0	1	0	1	2	50	2	0	0	0	0	0	1	2	1.0	0.0	0.0	0.5
	3-PT FG—				Newman 0-9, Ewing 0-1, Wilkins 2-4, Jackson 5-12, Tucker 6-13, Toney 3-6, Carlisle 0-2																			
PORTLAND TRAIL BLAZERS	**MIKE SCHULER**				lost to Utah 1-3; H108-96, H105-114, 108-113, 96-111																			
Jerome Kersey	F	6'7	222	25	4	127	32	65	49	15	21	71	30	9	17	1	7	4	79	32	7.5	2.3	4.3	19.8
Caldwell Jones	F-C	6'11	225	27	4	98	6	16	38	1	2	50	17	1	17	0	2	8	13	25	4.3	0.3	4.3	3.3
Kevin Duckworth	C	7'	280	23	4	151	34	70	49	18	23	78	44	7	14	0	1	2	86	38	11.0	1.8	3.5	21.5
Clyde Drexler	G	6'7	215	25	4	170	32	83	39	21	29	72	28	21	14	0	12	2	88	43	7.0	5.3	3.5	22.0
Terry Porter	G	6'3	195	24	4	149	29	52	56	9	13	69	14	28	13	0	10	0	68	37	3.5	7.0	3.3	17.0
Kiki Vandeweghe	F	6'8	220	29	4	72	11	40	28	9	9	100	13	7	8	0	1	0	31	18	3.3	1.8	2.0	7.8
Richard Anderson	F	6'10	240	27	3	63	11	24	46	4	4	100	13	1	11	0	2	1	32	21	4.3	0.3	3.7	10.7
Maurice Lucas	F	6'9	238	35	4	63	4	13	31	2	4	50	25	5	12	0	1	0	10	16	6.3	1.3	3.0	2.5
Michael Holton	G	6'4	185	26	4	34	3	13	23	0	0	—	5	6	6	0	2	0	6	9	1.3	1.5	1.5	1.5
Jerry Sichting	G	6'1	180	31	4	31	2	7	29	0	0	—	2	5	4	0	1	0	4	8	0.5	1.3	1.0	1.0
Charles Jones	F	6'8	215	25	2	2	0	1	0	0	0	—	1	0	0	0	0	0	0	1	0.5	0.0	0.0	0.0
	3-PT FG—				Kersey 0-1, Duckworth 0-1, Drexler 3-6, Porter 1-3, Vandeweghe 0-5, Anderson 6-14, Holton 0-1																			
SAN ANTONIO SPURS	**BOB WEISS**				lost to L.A.Lakers 0-3; 110-122, 112-130, H107-109																			
Walter Berry	F	6'8	215	23	3	94	27	50	54	12	15	80	21	6	10	0	5	2	66	31	7.0	2.0	3.3	22.0
Greg Anderson	F	6'10	230	23	3	95	17	36	47	4	9	44	21	3	10	1	2	4	38	32	7.0	1.0	3.3	12.7
Frank Brickowski	C-F	6'10	240	28	3	113	22	44	50	13	19	68	22	14	12	0	6	2	58	38	7.3	4.7	4.0	19.3
Jon Sundvold	G	6'2	170	26	3	90	15	30	50	3	2	150	4	15	3	0	4	0	35	30	1.3	5.0	1.0	11.7
Alvin Robertson	G	6'4	190	25	3	119	30	53	57	7	9	78	14	28	15	1	12	1	70	40	4.7	9.3	5.0	23.3
Mike Mitchell	F-G	6'7	215	31	3	74	13	37	35	5	6	83	15	4	5	0	1	1	31	25	5.0	1.3	1.7	10.3
Johnny Dawkins	G	6'2	165	24	3	53	6	23	26	3	4	75	3	5	2	0	2	0	15	18	1.0	1.7	0.7	5.0
Ed Nealy	F	6'7	238	27	2	36	2	4	50	0	0	—	7	4	6	0	1	0	4	18	3.5	2.0	3.0	2.0
Kurt Nimphius	C	6'10	225	29	3	30	5	10	50	2	2	100	8	2	7	0	0	1	12	10	2.7	0.7	2.3	4.0
Ricky Wilson	G	6'3	195	23	2	9	0	2	0	0	0	—	0	1	2	0	0	0	0	5	0.0	0.5	1.0	0.0
Petur Gudmundsson	C	7'2	260	29	2	6	0	2	0	0	0	—	0	1	0	0	0	0	0	3	0.0	0.5	0.0	0.0
Phil Zevenbergen	C	6'10	230	23	1	1	0	0	—	0	0	—	0	0	0	0	0	0	0	1	0.0	0.0	0.0	0.0
	3-PT FG—				Berry 0-1, Brickowski 1-1, Sundvold 3-9, Robertson 3-7, Dawkins 0-2																			

Team		G	FG	FGA	%	FT	FTA	%	Rebounds Offense	Rebounds Defense	Rebounds Total	Assists	PF	Steals	Blocked Shots	Turn Overs	Points	Points per game
TEAM STATISTICS EASTERN CONFERENCE ATLANTIC DIVISON																		
Boston	Off.	82	3599	6905	**52**	1846	2300	80	930	2440	3370	**2448**	1804	620	415	1304	9315	113.6
	Def.	82	3497	7260	48	1724	2249	77	1122	2194	3316	2061	1989	734	346	1176	8828	107.7
	Diff.		+102	-355	+4	+122	+51	+3	-192	+246	+54	+387	+185	-114	+69	-128	+487	**+5.9**
Washington	Off.	82	3355	7164	47	1914	2476	77	1229	2297	3526	1875	1922	698	502	1384	8653	105.5
	Def.	82	3459	7235	48	1670	2246	74	1228	2364	3592	2134	1966	690	527	1384	8716	106.3
	Diff.		-104	-71	-1	+244	+230	+3	+1	-67	-66	-259	+44	+8	-25	—	-63	-.8
New York	Off.	82	3363	7232	47	1750	2306	76	1286	2194	3480	2012	2361	789	445	1518	8655	105.5
	Def.	82	3202	6710	48	2177	2806	78	1155	2284	3439	2005	1969	705	447	**1631**	8695	106.0
	Diff.		+161	+522	-1	-427	-500	-2	+131	-90	+41	+7	-392	+84	-2	+113	-40	-.5
Philadelphia	Off.	82	3214	6785	47	**2087**	**2731**	76	1219	2307	3526	1897	1866	672	465	1433	8667	105.7
	Def.	82	3501	7063	50	1640	2163	76	1109	2225	3334	2217	2118	718	441	1280	8785	107.1
	Diff.		-287	-278	-3	+447	+568	—	+110	+82	+192	-320	+252	-46	+24	-153	-118	-1.4
New Jersey	Off.	82	3208	6857	47	1682	2308	73	1075	2262	3337	1795	2042	727	385	1503	8235	100.4
	Def.	82	3437	6918	50	1895	2419	78	1034	2461	3495	1993	1942	809	522	1433	8900	108.5
	Diff.		-229	-61	-3	-213	-111	-5	+41	-199	-158	-198	-100	-82	-137	-70	-665	-8.1
CENTRAL DIVISION																		
Detroit	Off.	82	3461	7018	49	1977	2612	76	1181	2482	3663	2011	1957	558	394	1348	8957	109.2
	Def.	82	3334	7134	47	1751	2298	76	1144	2276	3420	1964	**2164**	649	406	1328	8533	104.1
	Diff.		+127	-116	+2	+226	+314	—	+37	+206	+243	+47	+207	-91	-12	-20	+424	+5.1
Atlanta	Off.	82	3443	7102	48	1873	2441	77	1228	2379	3607	2062	2050	635	537	1225	8844	107.9
	Def.	82	3243	6885	47	1927	2480	78	1156	2353	3509	1976	2008	640	353	1322	8549	104.3
	Diff.		+200	+217	+1	-54	-39	-1	+72	+26	+98	+86	-42	-5	+184	+97	+295	+3.6
Chicago	Off.	82	3434	7015	49	1685	2221	76	1170	2459	3629	2149	1849	712	475	1263	8609	105.0
	Def.	82	3276	6967	47	1670	2205	76	1023	2268	3291	2079	1880	597	415	1244	8330	**101.6**
	Diff.		+158	+48	+2	+15	+16	—	+147	+191	+338	+70	+31	+115	+60	-19	+279	+3.4
Cleveland	Off.	82	3313	6755	49	1813	2438	74	1015	2289	3304	2070	1836	733	526	1439	8566	104.5
	Def.	82	3383	7101	48	1611	2044	79	1159	2255	3414	1989	2021	692	449	1439	8504	103.7
	Diff.		-70	-346	+1	+202	+394	-5	-144	+34	-110	+81	+185	+41	+77	—	+62	+.8
Milwaukee	Off.	82	3366	7079	48	1832	2364	77	1117	2335	3452	2194	1989	671	380	1275	8697	106.1
	Def.	82	3344	7063	47	1832	2410	76	1172	2400	3572	2135	1952	621	449	1346	8653	105.5
	Diff.		+22	+16	+1	—	-46	+1	-55	-65	-120	+59	-37	+50	-69	+71	+44	+.6
Indiana	Off.	82	3436	7154	48	1546	1982	78	1078	2457	3535	1977	2038	619	345	1318	8581	104.6
	Def.	82	3335	7060	47	1858	2446	76	1160	2500	3660	1933	1859	700	407	1269	8646	105.4
	Diff.		+101	+94	+1	-312	-464	+2	-82	-43	-125	+44	-179	-81	-62	-49	-65	-.8
WESTERN CONFERENCE — MIDWEST DIVISION																		
Denver	Off.	82	**3770**	**7961**	47	1841	2289	**80**	1163	2442	3605	2300	1982	**832**	401	**1186**	**9573**	**116.7**
	Def.	82	3608	7356	49	1910	2508	76	1179	2748	3927	2171	1989	621	510	1606	9239	112.7
	Diff.		+162	+605	-2	-69	-219	+4	-16	-306	-322	+129	+7	+211	-109	+420	+334	+4.0
Dallas	Off.	82	3413	7191	47	1980	2510	79	**1341**	2495	**3836**	1984	1734	645	446	1257	8960	109.3
	Def.	82	3468	7385	47	1499	1957	77	1200	2233	3433	2240	1997	612	436	1228	8602	104.9
	Diff.		-55	-194	—	+481	+553	+2	+141	+262	+403	-256	+263	+33	+10	-29	+358	+4.4
Utah	Off.	82	3484	7092	49	1802	2404	75	1066	**2553**	3619	2407	1986	771	**627**	1481	8899	108.5
	Def.	82	3273	7283	45	1905	2475	77	1277	2444	3721	1991	2013	771	472	1467	8597	104.8
	Diff.		+211	-191	+4	-103	-71	-2	-211	+109	-102	+416	+27	—	+155	-14	+302	+3.7
Houston	Off.	82	3465	7354	47	1936	2483	78	1239	2530	3769	1936	1865	712	502	1367	8935	109.0
	Def.	82	3454	7420	47	1805	2352	77	1261	2506	3767	1951	2012	737	365	1405	8821	107.6
	Diff.		+11	-66		+131	+131	+1	-22	+24	+2	-15	+147	-25	+137	+38	+114	+1.4
San Antonio	Off.	82	3706	7559	49	1769	2412	73	1184	2335	3519	2344	1991	739	468	1418	9314	113.6
	Def.	82	3851	7678	50	1855	2390	78	1292	2513	3805	2470	1969	690	537	1427	9714	118.5
	Diff.		-145	-119	-1	-86	+22	-5	-108	-178	-286	-126	-22	+49	-69	+9	-400	-4.9
Sacramento	Off.	82	3458	7337	47	1795	2324	77	1232	2461	3693	2116	1895	582	493	1457	8855	108.0
	Def.	82	3718	7465	50	1771	2326	76	1153	2424	3577	2176	1951	784	533	1195	9327	113.7
	Diff.		-260	-128	-3	+24	-2	+1	+79	+37	+116	-60	+56	-202	-40	-262	-472	-5.7
PACIFIC DIVISION																		
L.A. Lakers	Off.	82	3576	7078	51	1956	2480	79	1073	2491	3564	2347	**1715**	672	404	1318	9250	112.8
	Def.	82	3551	7467	48	1538	2020	76	1175	2249	3424	2200	1940	732	390	1246	8771	107.0
	Diff.		+25	-389	+3	+418	+460	+3	-102	+242	+140	+147	+225	-60	+14	-72	+479	+5.8
Portland	Off.	82	3661	7460	49	2079	2701	77	1251	2491	3742	2307	2091	726	347	1351	9518	116.1
	Def.	82	3492	7341	48	2022	2632	77	1153	2400	3553	2154	2135	648	376	1443	9147	111.5
	Diff.		+169	+119	+1	+57	+69	—	+98	+91	+189	+153	+44	+78	-29	+92	+371	+4.6
Seattle	Off.	82	3544	7443	48	1826	2442	75	1313	2314	3627	2146	2380	775	447	1376	9135	111.4
	Def.	82	3298	6798	49	2240	2992	75	1128	2306	3434	1964	1963	606	423	1533	8966	109.3
	Diff.		+246	+645	-1	-414	-550	—	+185	+8	+193	+182	-417	+169	+24	+157	+169	+2.1

TEAM STATISTICS
WESTERN CONFERENCE
PACIFIC DIVISION

Team		G	FG	FGA	%	FT	FTA	%	Rebounds Offense	Rebounds Defense	Rebounds Total	Assists	PF	Steals	Blocked Shots	Turn Overs	Points	Points per game
Phoenix	Off.	82	3551	7302	49	1681	2200	76	1113	2379	3492	2332	2045	675	373	1413	8901	108.5
	Def.	82	3609	7248	50	1922	2506	77	1104	2416	3520	2225	1901	710	441	1296	9268	113.0
	Diff.		-58	+54	-1	-241	-306	-1	+9	-37	-28	+107	-144	-35	-68	-117	-367	-4.5
Golden State	Off.	82	3463	7404	47	1754	2204	80	1140	2252	3392	2005	2155	741	283	1395	8771	107.0
	Def.	82	3627	7244	50	2047	2700	76	1209	2509	3718	2271	1811	747	432	1413	9453	115.3
	Diff.		-164	+160	-3	-293	-496	+4	-69	-257	-326	-266	-344	-6	-149	+18	-682	-8.3
L.A. Clippers	Off.	82	3190	7194	44	1644	2305	71	1191	2350	3541	1885	1908	721	520	1534	8103	98.8
	Def.	82	3513	7360	48	1799	2309	78	1241	2666	3907	2300	1912	842	483	1452	8949	109.1
	Diff.		-323	-166	-4	-155	-4	-7	-50	-316	-366	-415	+4	-121	+37	-82	-846	-10.3

PLAYOFFS

Team		G	FG	FGA	%	FT	FTA	%	Rebounds Offense	Rebounds Defense	Rebounds Total	Assists	PF	Steals	Blocked Shots	Turn Overs	Points	Points per game
L.A. Lakers	Off.	24	**980**	**1962**	50	**517**	664	78	313	660	973	**622**	508	**173**	**113**	336	**2534**	105.6
	Def.	24	979	2055	48	471	618	76	356	622	978	595	**547**	195	119	330	2473	103.0
	Diff.		+1	-93	+2	+46	+46	+2	-43	+38	-5	+27	+39	-22	-6	-6	+61	+2.6
Detroit	Off.	23	883	1900	46	507	**672**	75	**321**	**698**	**1019**	514	594	170	105	318	2294	99.7
	Def.	23	812	1830	44	530	695	76	271	640	911	502	542	143	97	**338**	2189	**95.2**
	Diff.		+71	+70	+2	-23	-23	-1	+50	+58	+108	+12	-52	+27	+8	+20	+105	+4.5
Dallas	Off.	17	730	1473	50	349	462	76	279	482	761	411	353	126	87	253	1834	107.9
	Def.	17	726	1503	48	335	411	82	253	451	704	442	381	128	78	210	1836	108.0
	Diff.		+4	-30	+2	+14	+51	-6	+26	+31	+57	-31	+28	-2	+9	-43	-2	-.1
Boston	Off.	17	645	1355	48	429	526	82	203	484	687	456	382	102	82	253	1759	103.5
	Def.	17	681	1440	47	350	450	78	209	473	682	427	460	123	76	229	1743	102.5
	Diff.		-36	-85	+1	+79	+76	+4	-6	+11	+5	+29	+78	-21	+6	-24	+16	+1.0
Atlanta	Off.	12	511	1016	50	267	340	79	152	313	465	317	314	91	61	145	1303	108.6
	Def.	12	476	949	50	313	393	80	157	336	493	316	276	61	44	187	1286	107.2
	Diff.		+35	+67	—	-46	-53	-1	-5	-23	-28	+1	-38	+30	+17	+42	+17	+1.4
Denver	Off.	11	462	1023	45	262	317	83	166	299	465	252	272	75	53	**124**	1219	110.8
	Def.	11	490	958	51	250	342	73	159	359	518	280	272	62	53	178	1245	113.2
	Diff.		-28	+65	-6	+12	-25	+10	+7	-60	-53	-28	—	+13	—	+54	-26	-2.4
Utah	Off.	11	422	874	48	268	347	77	116	305	421	281	246	84	73	179	1137	103.4
	Def.	11	444	977	45	206	267	77	186	311	497	242	271	90	56	164	1126	102.4
	Diff.		-22	-103	+3	+62	+80	—	-70	-6	-76	+39	+25	-6	+17	-15	+11	+1.0
Chicago	Off.	10	384	851	45	172	212	81	143	287	430	234	**238**	71	40	149	948	94.8
	Def.	10	391	837	47	199	264	75	137	303	440	228	205	69	51	144	989	98.9
	Diff.		-7	+14	-2	-27	-52	+6	+6	-16	-10	+6	-33	+2	-11	-5	-41	-4.1
Cleveland	Off.	5	200	403	50	97	132	73	60	142	202	119	97	29	32	78	502	100.4
	Def.	5	210	453	46	90	104	87	84	139	223	125	122	40	21	63	510	102.0
	Diff.		-10	-50	+4	+7	+28	-14	-24	+3	-21	-6	+25	-11	+11	-15	-8	-1.6
Milwaukee	Off.	5	199	416	48	138	179	77	80	140	220	123	123	33	17	76	543	108.6
	Def.	5	211	407	52	123	163	75	62	137	199	125	136	41	30	69	549	109.8
	Diff.		-12	+9	-4	+15	+16	+2	+18	+3	+21	-2	+13	-8	-13	-7	-6	-1.2
Seattle	Off.	5	230	446	52	100	242	41	69	154	223	138	149	26	20	77	571	114.2
	Def.	5	200	442	45	160	189	85	69	132	201	97	116	35	25	56	574	114.8
	Diff.		+30	+4	+7	-60	+53	-44	—	+22	+22	+41	-33	-9	-5	-21	-3	-.6
Washington	Off.	5	182	395	46	164	221	74	67	123	190	82	123	35	26	76	486	97.2
	Def.	5	194	416	47	114	151	75	84	139	223	109	131	42	28	75	506	101.2
	Diff.		-12	-21	-1	+50	+70	-1	-17	-16	-33	-27	+8	-7	-2	-1	-20	-4.0
Houston	Off.	4	156	345	45	97	118	82	64	112	176	79	90	32	17	59	418	104.5
	Def.	4	168	337	50	86	112	77	56	115	171	99	92	36	24	62	428	107.0
	Diff.		-12	+8	-5	+11	+6	+5	+8	-3	+5	-20	+2	-4	-7	+3	-10	-2.5
New York	Off.	4	153	348	44	75	92	82	54	109	163	102	115	33	21	63	397	99.3
	Def.	4	160	316	51	112	136	82	53	110	163	118	80	38	24	60	442	110.5
	Diff.		-7	+32	-7	-37	-44	—	+1	-1	—	-16	-35	-5	-3	-3	-45	-11.2
Portland	Off.	4	164	384	43	79	105	75	76	116	192	90	116	39	17	65	417	104.3
	Def.	4	152	301	50	118	154	77	33	125	158	102	97	24	29	80	434	108.5
	Diff.		+12	+83	-7	-39	-49	-2	+43	-9	+34	-12	-19	+15	-12	+15	-17	-4.2
San Antonio	Off.	3	137	291	47	48	67	72	45	70	115	83	72	33	11	54	329	109.7
	Def.	3	144	261	55	69	90	77	39	102	141	96	64	25	20	60	361	120.3
	Diff.		-7	+30	-8	-21	-23	-5	+6	-32	-26	-13	-8	+8	-9	+6	-32	-10.6

Team	W	L	Pct.	GB	Record against playoff teams W	L	Pct.	Record against non-playoff teams W	L	Pct.	HOME W	L	Pct.	ROAD W	L	Pct.
EASTERN CONFERENCE																
ATLANTIC DIVISION																
Boston Celtics	57	25	.695		35	22	.614	22	3	.880	**36**	5	**.878**	21	20	.512
Washington Bullets	38	44	.463	19	17	39	.304	21	5	.808	25	16	.610	13	28	.317
New York Knickerbockers	38	44	.463	19	24	33	.421	14	11	.560	29	12	.707	9	32	.220
Philadelphia 76ers	36	46	.439	21	24	38	.387	12	8	.600	27	14	.659	9	32	.220
New Jersey Nets	19	63	.232	38	13	49	.210	6	**14**	.300	16	25	.390	3	**38**	.073
CENTRAL DIVISION																
Detroit Pistons	54	28	.659		35	22	.614	19	6	.760	34	7	.829	20	21	.488
Atlanta Hawks	50	32	.610	4	29	28	.509	21	4	.840	30	11	.732	20	21	.488
Chicago Bulls	50	32	.610	4	31	25	.554	19	7	.731	30	11	.732	20	21	.488
Cleveland Cavaliers	42	40	.512	12	26	31	.456	16	9	.640	31	10	.756	11	30	.268
Milwaukee Bucks	42	40	.512	12	27	30	.474	15	10	.600	30	11	.732	12	29	.293
Indianna Pacers	38	44	.463	16	23	39	.371	15	5	.750	25	16	.610	13	28	.317
WESTERN CONFERENCE																
MIDWEST DIVISION																
Denver Nuggets	54	28	.659		33	22	.600	21	6	.778	35	6	.854	19	22	.463
Dallas Mavericks	53	29	.646	1	30	25	.545	23	4	.852	33	8	.805	20	21	.488
Utah Jazz	47	35	.573	7	29	26	.527	18	9	.667	33	8	.805	14	27	.341
Houston Rockets	46	36	.561	8	26	29	.473	20	7	.741	31	10	.756	15	26	.366
San Antonio Spurs	31	51	.378	23	16	39	.291	15	12	.556	23	18	.561	8	33	.195
Sacramento Kings	24	58	.293	30	15	46	.246	9	12	.429	19	22	.463	5	36	.122
PACIFIC DIVISION																
Los Angeles Lakers	**62**	20	**.756**		**37**	16	**.698**	25	4	.862	**36**	5	**.878**	**26**	15	**.634**
Portland Trail Blazers	53	29	.646	9	27	26	.509	**26**	3	**.897**	33	8	.805	20	21	.488
Seattle Supersonics	44	38	.537	18	22	31	.415	22	7	.759	32	9	.780	12	29	.293
Phoenix Suns	28	54	.341	34	15	44	.254	13	10	.565	22	19	.537	6	35	.146
Golden State Warriors	20	62	.244	42	10	49	.169	10	13	.435	16	25	.390	4	37	.098
Los Angeles Clippers	17	**65**	.207	45	7	**52**	.119	10	13	.435	14	**27**	.341	3	**38**	.073

1987/88 N.B.A. IINDIVIDUAL LEADERS

SCORING
(Minimum 70 Games or 1400 Points)

Name	Team	G	FG	FT	Pts.	Avg.
Jordan	Chi	82	1069	723	2868	35.0
Wilkins	Atl	78	909	541	2397	30.7
Bird	Bos	76	881	415	2275	29.9
Barkley	Phi	80	753	714	2264	28.3
Malone	Utah	82	858	552	2268	27.7
Drexler	Port	81	849	476	2185	27.0
Ellis	Sea	75	764	303	1938	25.8
Aguirre	Dal	77	746	308	1932	25.1
English	Den	80	843	314	2000	25.0
Olajuwon	Hou	79	712	381	1805	22.8

FIELD GOAL PERCENTAGE
(Minimum 300 Made)

Name	Team	FG	FGA	Pct.
McHale	Bos	550	911	.604
Parish	Bos	442	750	.589
Barkley	Phi	753	1283	.587
Stockton	Utah	454	791	.574
Berry	SA	540	960	.563
Rodman	Det	398	709	.561
Williams	NJ	466	832	.560
Levingston	Atl	314	564	.557
Ewing	NY	656	1183	.555
West	Cle + Phoe	316	573	.551

FREE THROW PERCENTAGE
(Minimum 125 Made)

Name	Team	FT	FTA	Pct.
Sikma	Mil	321	348	.922
Bird	Bos	415	453	.916
Long	Ind	166	183	.907
Gminski	NJ+Phi	355	392	.906
Dawkins	SA	198	221	.896
Davis	Phoe	205	231	.887
Mullin	GS	239	270	.885
J.Malone	Was	335	380	.882
Garland	GS	138	157	.879
Vandeweghe	Port	159	181	.878

PERSONAL FOULS

Name	Team	PF
Ewing	NY	332
Olajuwon	Hou	324
Schayes	Den	323
Eaton	Utah	320
Lister	Sea	319

GAMES DISQUALIFIED

Name	Team	Disq.
Brickowski	SA	11
Sikma	Mil	11
Nance	Phoe+Cle	10
Green	NY	9
Schayes	Den	9

TOTAL REBOUNDS PER GAME
(Minimum 70 Games or 800 Rebounds)

Name	Team	G	Reb.	Avg.
Cage	LAC	72	938	13.0
Oakley	Chi	82	1066	13.0
Olajuwon	Hou	79	959	12.1
Malone	Utah	82	986	12.0
Williams	NJ	70	834	11.9
Barkley	Phi	80	951	11.9
Tarpley	Dall	81	959	11.8
M.Malone	Was	79	884	11.2
Thorpe	Sac	82	837	10.2
Laimbeer	Det	82	832	10.1

ASSISTS PER GAME
(Minimum 70 Games or 400 Assists)

Name	Team	G	Ass.	Avg.
Stockton	Utah	82	1128	13.8
Johnson	LAL	72	858	11.9
Jackson	NY	82	868	10.6
Porter	Port	82	831	10.1
Rivers	Atl	80	747	9.3
McMillan	Sea	82	702	8.6
Thomas	Det	81	678	8.4
Cheeks	Phi	79	635	8.0
Lever	Den	82	639	7.8
Johnson	Bos	77	598	7.8

MINUTES PLAYED

Name	Team	Min.
Jordan	Chi	3311
Malone	Utah	3198
Lever	Den	3061
Scott	LAL	3048
Harper	Dal	3032

BLOCKED SHOTS PER GAME
(Minimum 70 Games of 100 Blocked Shots)

Name	Team	G	Reb.	Avg.
Eaton	Utah	82	304	3.7
Banjamin	LAC	66	225	3.4
Ewing	NY	82	245	3.0
Olajuwon	Hou	79	214	2.7
Bol	Was	77	208	2.7
Nance	Phoe+Cle	67	159	2.4
Oldham	Sac	54	110	2.0
Williams	Ind	75	146	1.9
Williams	Cle	77	145	1.9
Hinson	Phi+NJ	77	140	1.8

3 POINT FIELD GOALS PER GAME
(Minimum 25 Made)

Name	Team	FG	FGA	Avg.
Hodges	Mil+Phoe	86	175	.491
Price	Cle	72	148	.486
Long	Ind	34	77	.442
G.Henderson	NY+Phi	69	163	.423
Tripucka	Utah	31	74	.419
Ainge	Bos	148	357	.415
Bird	Bos	98	237	.414
Tucker	NY	69	167	.413
Ellis	Sea	107	259	.413
Wood	SA+Atl	52	127	.409

STEALS PER GAME
(Minimum 70 Games or 125 Steals)

Name	Team	G	Steals	Avg.
Jordan	Chi	82	259	3.2
Robertson	SA	82	243	3.0
Stockton	Utah	82	242	3.0
Lever	Den	82	223	2.7
Drexler	Port	81	203	2.5
Jackson	NY	82	205	2.5
Cheeks	Phi	79	167	2.1
McMillan	Sea	82	169	2.1

1988-89 N.B.A.

Goodbye Kareem: Hello Charlotte, Miami, The Pistons and Unrestricted Free Agents

In a season of transition, the N.B.A. welcomed two new teams and said goodbye to a legend. The standings also indicated a league in flux, with 12 teams moving up or down by nine games or more. It was only fitting that the championship went to a franchise that had never won a title in its long history.

The legend, of course, was Kareem Abdul-Jabbar, who became only a part-time player for the Lakers while making a grand farewell tour of the league. The pomp and circumstance didn't seem to distract his teammates, though, as they won 57 games and their eighth straight Pacific Division title, led by MVP Magic Johnson, plus James Worthy, Byron Scott and A.C. Green.

The two expansion teams took different approaches in stocking their rosters. The Charlotte Hornets blended veterans Kelly Tripucka, Robert Reid and Kurt Rambis with rookie Rex Chapman, but the Miami Heat went almost entirely for youth, with top draft pick Rony Seikaly the most recognizable name. Charlotte got better results, winning 20 to Miami's 15, but both finished last in their respective divisions, as expected. And with the talent pool further diminished, the prospects looked bleak for two more expansion teams, in Minnesota and Orlando, Fla., slated to begin play in the 1989-90 season.

Among the teams in transition, the biggest gains came in Phoenix and Golden State, where veteran coaches Cotton Fitzsimmons and Don Nelson returned to the sidelines and worked miracles. Fitzsimmons won Coach of the Year honors by leading the Suns to 55 wins, a 27-game improvement, behind free agent acquisition Tom Chambers, second-year man Kevin Johnson and sixth man Eddie Johnson. With Ralph Sampson slowed all year by injuries, Nelson started a lineup of four guards and a forward, installed a motion offense, and watched the Warriors improve by 23 games. Leading the way were Chris Mullin, back from a bout with alcoholism, and Rookie of the Year Mitch Richmond.

Another success story was written in Cleveland, where the Cavaliers got off to a 30-8 start behind Larry Nance and young stars Brad Daugherty, Ron Harper, Mark Price and John (Hot Rod) Williams. Unfortunately for the Cavs, they were in the same division with Detroit. The Pistons started slowly, but took off after sending moody Adrian Dantley to Dallas for Mark Aquirre. Aided by a Cleveland slump, they overtook the Cavs and finished with 63 wins, best in the league. The Pistons' strengths were a suffocating defense and the deepest frontcourt ever.

Atlanta picked up Moses Malone and Reggie Theus, but failed to move up when Kevin Willis missed the whole season. Milwaukee improved to 49 wins as Larry Krystowiak showed signs of becoming a star (before a serious knee injury in the playoffs) and Terry Cummings remained one. Second-year men Scottie Pippen and Horace Grant made progress in Chicago, but again the main man was Michael Jordan, who shifted to point guard but still won another scoring title. Though losing the official MVP award to Johnson by an eyelash, Jordan won the player's vote in The Sporting News by a lopsided 84-37 margin.

In the Atlantic Division, New York coach Rick Pitino saw his young team win the title behind Patrick Ewing, Mark Jackson and Charles Oakley, picked up from Chicago for Bill Cartwright. Meanwhile, Philadelphia added Ron Anderson (from Indiana) and rookie Hersey Hawkins to Charles Barkley and Mike Gminski, and the result was 46 wins and second place. That put them ahead of Boston, one of the year's big losers. The Celtics' season went up in smoke when bone spurs finished Larry Bird after only six games. Still, new coach Jimmy Rodgers had rookie Brian Shaw, sophomore Reggie Lewis and veterans Robert Parish and Kevin McHale. A late-season trade that sent Danny Ainge to Sacramento for Ed Pinckney and Joe Kleine gave Boston high hopes once Bird returned next fall. Just behind the Celtics came the Washington Bullets, minus Moses Malone. Coach Wes Unseld went without a center for most of the season, but a new motion offense brought out the best in Jeff Malone, John Williams and Bernard King, now all the way back from his 1985 knee injury. In New Jersey even Buck Williams was beginning to slip as the Nets finished only six games ahead of Charlotte.

The Midwest Division saw three of the year's biggest declines in Dallas, Denver and San Antonio. The Mavericks lost Roy Tarpley to knee surgery and drug rehabilitation and went downhill from there. Alex English scored 2,000 points for a record eighth season in Denver, and Lafayette Lever was better than ever, but sub-par play from the big men brought the Nuggets down. And new coach Larry Brown's Spurs sank even lower despite the play of rookie Willie Anderson.

The Midwest title went to the Utah Jazz, who won 51 games despite the midseason resignation of coach Frank Layden, who moved to the front office and handed the reins to Jerry Sloan. Karl Malone and John Stockton again led the offense, and Mark Eaton anchored an outstanding defense. But the Jazz fell apart in the playoffs, losing three straight to Golden State. In Houston, another great season from Akeem Olajuwon and the acquisition of Otis Thorpe didn't boost the Rockets to the top.

In the Pacific Division, coach Mike Schuler lost his job as Portland fell to 39 wins despite the presence of Clyde Drexler, Kevin Duckworth, Terry Porter and Jerome Kersey, and new coach Rick Adelman couldn't stop the slide. Seattle moved up again as Michael Cage replaced Chambers, sophomore Derrick McKey made great strides, and Dale Ellis and Xavier McDaniel continued their fine play. Sacramento, transplanted from the Midwest Division, added Ainge and Wayman Tisdale to improving sophomore Kenny Smith, but it had little immediate effect. And the Clippers fired coach Gene Shue after No. 1 draft pick Danny Manning went out with a knee injury.

With Jordan playing brilliantly, the Bulls were the surprise team of the playoffs, upsetting Cleveland and New York and throwing a scare into Detroit before falling to the Pistons in six games. Meanwhile, the Lakers romped through the Western playoffs, winning 11 straight games and setting up a rematch with the Pistons for the championship. Many fans had visions of Abdul-Jabbar bowing out with a third consecutive title, but when hamstring injuries sidelined Byron Scott and Magic Johnson, the Lakers were unable to handle Detroit's backcourt. With playoff MVP Joe Dumars averaging 27 points, the Pistons won four straight to complete their long climb to the top.

1988/89 N.B.A. — EASTERN CONFERENCE
ATLANTIC DIVISION

Use Name	Pos	Hgt	Wgt	Age	G	Min	FG	FGA	%	FT	FTA	%	Reb	Ass	PF	DQ	Stls	Blkd Shts	Points	Min	Reb	Ass	PF	Points
					TOTAL															PER GAME				
NEW YORK KNICKERBOCKERS	**52-30 .634**				**RICH PITINO**																			
Johnny Newman	F	6'7	190	25	81	2336	455	957	48	286	351	81	206	162	259	4	111	23	1293	29	2.5	2.0	3.2	16.0
Charles Oakley	F	6'8	225	25	82	2604	426	835	51	197	255	77	861	187	270	1	104	14	1061	32	10.5	2.3	3.3	12.9
Patrick Ewing	C	7'	240	26	80	2896	727	1282	57	361	484	75	740	188	311	5	117	281	1815	36	9.3	2.4	3.9	22.7
Gerald Wilkins	G-F	6'6	190	25	81	2414	462	1025	45	186	246	76	244	274	166	1	115	22	1161	30	3.0	3.4	2.0	14.3
Mark Jackson	G	6'3	205	23	72	2477	479	1025	47	180	258	70	341	619	163	1	139	7	1219	34	4.7	8.6	2.3	16.9
Trent Tucker	G	6'5	193	29	81	1824	263	579	45	43	55	78	176	132	163	0	88	6	687	23	2.2	1.6	2.0	8.5
Rod Strickland	G	6'3	180	22	81	1358	265	567	47	172	231	74	160	319	142	2	98	3	721	17	2.0	3.9	1.8	8.9
Sidney Green	F	6'9	220	27	82	1277	194	422	46	129	170	76	394	76	172	0	47	18	517	16	4.8	0.9	2.1	6.3
Kenny Walker	F	6'8	210	24	79	1163	174	356	49	66	85	78	230	36	190	1	41	45	419	15	2.9	0.5	2.4	5.3
Eddie Lee Wilkins	F-C	6'10	220	26	71	584	114	245	47	61	111	55	148	7	110	1	10	16	289	8	2.1	0.1	1.5	4.1
Kiki Vandeweghe (from Port)	F	6'8	220	30	27	502	97	209	46	51	56	91	36	35	38	0	12	7	248	19	1.3	1.3	1.4	9.2
Pete Myers (from Phi)	F-G	6'6	180	25	29	230	25	61	41	31	44	70	23	46	41	0	17	19	81	8	0.8	1.6	1.4	2.8
Greg Butler (LJ)	C	6'11	240	22	33	140	20	48	42	16	20	80	28	2	28	0	1	17	56	4	0.8	0.1	0.8	1.7

3-PT FG — Newmann 97-287, Oakley 12-48, Ewing 0-6, G.Wilkins 51-172, Jackson 81-240, Tucker 112-296, Strickland 19-59, Green 0-3, Walker 5-20, E.Wilkins 0-1, Vandeweghe 3-10, Myers 0-2, Butler 0-3

Use Name	Pos	Hgt	Wgt	Age	G	Min	FG	FGA	%	FT	FTA	%	Reb	Ass	PF	DQ	Stls	Blkd Shts	Points	Min	Reb	Ass	PF	Points
PHILADELPHIA 76ers	**46-36 .561**				**JIM LYNAM**																			
Shelton Jones (from SA, GS)	F	6'9	210	22	42	577	81	179	45	50	67	75	95	33	50	0	16	13	212	14	2.3	0.8	1.2	5.0
Charles Barkley	F	6'6	263	25	79	3088	700	1208	58	602	799	75	986	325	262	3	126	67	2037	39	12.5	4.1	3.3	25.8
Mike Gminski	C	6'11	260	29	82	2618	566	1152	49	196	229	86	406	139	166	1	71	23	1330	32	5.0	1.7	2.0	16.2
Hersey Hawkins	G	6'3	190	23	79	2577	442	971	46	241	290	83	225	239	184	0	120	37	1196	33	2.8	3.0	2.3	15.1
Maurice Cheeks	G	6'1	180	32	71	2298	336	696	48	151	195	77	183	554	114	0	105	17	824	32	2.6	7.8	1.6	11.6
Ron Anderson	F	6'7	215	30	82	2618	566	1152	49	196	229	86	406	139	166	1	71	23	1330	32	5.0	1.7	2.0	16.2
Scott Brooks	G	5'11	165	23	82	1372	156	371	42	61	69	88	94	306	116	0	69	3	428	17	1.1	3.7	1.4	5.2
Gerald Henderson	G	6'2	180	32	65	986	144	348	41	104	127	82	68	140	121	1	42	3	425	15	1.0	2.2	1.9	6.5
Chris Welp	C	7'	245	24	72	843	99	222	45	48	73	66	193	29	176	0	23	41	246	12	2.7	0.4	2.4	3.4
Ben Coleman (EJ)	F	6'9	235	27	58	703	117	241	49	61	77	79	177	17	120	0	10	18	295	12	3.1	0.3	2.1	5.1
Derek Smith (from Sac)	F	6'6	218	27	36	695	105	220	48	65	93	70	86	68	100	3	24	15	279	19	2.4	1.9	2.8	7.8
Bob Thornston	F-C	6'10	225	26	54	449	47	111	42	32	60	53	92	15	87	0	8	7	127	8	1.7	0.3	1.6	2.4
David Wingate (KJ)	G	6'5	185	25	33	372	54	115	47	27	34	79	37	73	43	0	9	2	137	11	1.1	2.2	1.3	4.2
Pete Meyers (to NY)	F-G	6'6	180	25	4	40	6	12	50	3	4	75	10	2	3	0	3	0	14	10	2.5	0.5	0.8	3.5
Jim Rowinski (from Det)	F	6'9	250	28	3	7	1	2	50	1	2	50	3	0	0	0	0	0	3	2	1.0	0.0	0.0	1.0
Cliff Robinson - knee injury																								

3-PT FG — Jones 0-1, Barkley 35-162, Gminski 0-6, Hawkins 71-166, Cheeks 1-13, Anderson 2-11 Brooks 55-153, Henderson 33-107, Welp 0-1, Smith 4-16, Thornton 1-3, Wingate 2-6

Use Name	Pos	Hgt	Wgt	Age	G	Min	FG	FGA	%	FT	FTA	%	Reb	Ass	PF	DQ	Stls	Blkd Shts	Points	Min	Reb	Ass	PF	Points
BOSTON CELTICS	**42-40 .512**				**JIMMY RODGERS**																			
Reggie Lewis	F-G	6'7	195	23	81	2657	604	1242	49	284	361	79	377	218	258	5	124	72	1495	33	4.7	2.7	3.2	18.5
Kevin McHale	F-C	6'10	225	31	78	2876	661	1211	55	436	533	82	637	172	223	2	26	97	1758	37	8.2	2.2	2.9	22.5
Robert Parish	C	7'	230	35	80	2840	596	1045	57	294	409	72	996	175	209	2	79	116	1486	36	12.5	2.2	2.6	18.6
Brian Shaw	G	6'6	190	22	82	2301	297	686	43	109	132	83	376	472	211	1	78	27	703	28	4.6	5.8	2.6	8.6
Dennis Johnson	G	6'4	200	34	72	2309	277	638	43	160	195	82	190	472	211	3	94	21	721	32	2.6	6.6	2.9	10.0
Danny Ainge (to Sac)	G	6'4	185	29	45	1349	271	589	46	114	128	89	154	215	108	0	52	1	714	30	3.4	4.8	2.4	15.9
Jim Paxson (WJ)	G	6'6	210	31	57	1138	202	445	45	84	103	82	74	107	96	0	38	8	492	20	1.3	1.9	1.7	8.6
Brad Lohaus (to Sac)	C-F	7'	235	24	48	738	117	270	43	35	46	76	142	49	101	1	21	26	269	15	3.0	1.0	2.1	5.6
Ed Pinckney (from Sac)	F-G	6'9	215	25	29	678	95	176	54	103	129	80	148	44	77	1	29	23	293	23	5.1	1.5	2.7	10.1
Mark Acres	F	6'11	220	26	62	632	55	114	48	26	48	54	146	19	94	0	19	6	137	10	2.4	0.3	1.5	2.2
Ron Grandison	F	6'8	217	25	72	528	59	142	42	59	80	74	92	42	71	0	18	3	177	7	1.3	0.6	1.0	2.5
Joe Kleine (from Sac)	C	7'	271	26	28	498	59	129	46	53	64	83	137	32	66	0	15	5	171	18	4.9	1.1	2.4	6.1
Kelvin Upshaw (from Mia)	G	6'2	180	26	23	473	73	149	49	14	20	70	36	97	62	1	19	3	162	21	1.6	4.2	2.7	7.0
Kevin Gamble	G	6'5	215	23	44	375	75	136	55	35	55	64	42	34	40	0	14	3	187	9	1.0	0.8	0.9	4.3
Larry Bird (heel spurs)	F	6'9	220	32	6	189	49	104	47	18	19	95	37	29	18	0	6	5	116	32	6.2	4.8	3.0	19.3
Otis Birdsong	G	6'4	195	33	13	108	18	36	50	0	2	0	13	9	10	0	3	1	37	8	1.0	0.7	0.8	2.8
Ramon Rivas (XJ)	F-C	6'10	260	23	28	91	12	31	39	16	25	64	24	3	21	0	4	1	40	3	0.9	0.1	0.8	1.4

3-PT FG — Lewis 3-22, McHale 0-4, Shaw 0-13, Johnson 7-50, Ainge 58-155, Paxson 4-24, Lohaus 0-4, Acres 1-1, Grandison 0-10, Kleine 0-1, Upshaw 2-10, Gamble 2-11, Birdsong 1-3, Rivas 0-1

Use Name	Pos	Hgt	Wgt	Age	G	Min	FG	FGA	%	FT	FTA	%	Reb	Ass	PF	DQ	Stls	Blkd Shts	Points	Min	Reb	Ass	PF	Points
WASHINGTON BULLETS	**40-42 .488**				**WES UNSELD**																			
Bernard King	F	6'7	205	32	81	2559	654	1351	48	361	441	82	384	294	219	1	64	13	1674	32	4.7	3.6	2.7	20.7
Terry Catledge	F	6'8	213	25	79	2077	334	681	49	153	254	60	572	75	250	5	46	120	822	26	7.2	0.9	3.2	10.4
Charles Jones (KJ)	C-F	6'9	215	31	53	1154	60	125	48	16	25	64	257	42	187	4	39	76	136	22	4.8	0.8	3.5	2.6
Jeff Malone	G	6'4	205	27	76	2418	677	1410	48	296	340	87	179	219	155	0	39	14	1651	32	2.4	2.9	2.0	21.7
Darrell Walker	G	6'4	180	27	79	2565	296	681	43	142	184	77	507	496	215	2	155	23	714	32	6.4	6.3	2.7	9.0
John Williams	F	6'9	235	22	82	2413	438	940	47	225	290	78	573	356	213	1	142	70	1120	29	7.0	4.3	2.6	13.7
Ledell Eackles	G-F	6'5	220	22	80	1459	318	732	43	272	346	79	180	123	156	1	41	5	917	18	2.3	1.5	2.0	11.5
Steve Colter	G	6'3	175	26	80	1425	203	457	44	125	167	75	182	225	158	0	69	14	534	18	2.3	2.8	2.0	6.7
Harvey Grant (BF)	F	6'8	200	23	71	1193	181	390	46	34	57	60	163	79	147	2	35	29	396	17	2.3	1.1	2.1	5.6
Mark Alarie	F	6'8	217	25	74	1141	206	431	48	73	87	84	255	63	160	1	25	22	498	15	3.4	0.9	2.2	6.7
Dave Feitl	C	7'	240	26	57	828	116	266	44	54	65	83	202	36	136	0	17	18	286	15	3.5	0.6	2.4	5.0
Charles A. Jones	F	6'8	215	26	43	516	38	62	61	33	53	62	140	18	49	0	18	16	110	12	3.3	0.4	1.1	2.6
Dominic Pressley (to Chi)	G	6'3	170	25	10	107	8	25	32	5	9	56	14	22	9	0	4	0	21	11	1.4	2.2	0.9	2.1

3-PT FG — King 5-30, Catledge 1-5, C. Jones 0-1, Malone 1-19, Walker 0-9, Williams 19-71, Eackles 9-40, Colter 3-25, Grant 0-1, Alarie13-38, Feitl 0-1, C.A. Jones1-3

1988/89 N.B.A. — EASTERN CONFERENCE
ATLANTIC DIVISION (continued)

Use Name	Pos	Hgt	Wgt	Age	G	Min	FG	FGA	%	FT	FTA	%	Reb	Ass	PF	DQ	Stls	Blkd Shts	Points	Min	Reb	Ass	PF	Points
					TOTAL															PER GAME				
NEW JERSEY NETS	26-56 .317				**WILLIS REED**																			
Buck Williams	F	6'8	225	28	74	2446	373	702	53	213	320	67	896	78	223	0	61	36	959	33	12.1	1.1	3.0	13.0
Roy Hinson	F	6'9	220	27	82	2542	495	1027	48	318	420	76	522	71	298	3	34	121	1308	31	6.4	0.9	3.6	16.0
Joe Barry Carroll	C	7'	255	30	64	1996	363	810	45	176	220	80	473	105	193	2	71	81	902	31	7.4	1.6	3.0	14.1
Mike McGee	G	6'5	207	29	80	2027	434	917	47	77	144	53	189	116	184	1	80	12	1038	25	2.4	1.5	2.3	13.0
Lester Conner	G	6'4	185	29	82	2532	309	676	46	212	269	79	355	604	132	1	181	5	843	31	4.3	7.4	1.6	10.3
Chris Morris	F	6'8	210	22	76	2096	414	505	82	182	254	72	397	119	250	4	102	60	1074	28	5.2	1.6	3.3	14.1
John Bagley	G	6'	192	28	68	1642	200	481	42	89	123	72	144	391	117	0	72	5	500	24	2.1	5.8	1.7	7.4
Dennis Hopson	G	6'5	200	23	62	1551	299	714	42	186	219	85	202	103	150	0	70	30	788	25	3.3	1.7	2.4	12.7
Keith Lee (turf toe)	F	6'10	220	26	57	840	109	258	42	53	71	75	259	42	138	1	20	33	271	15	4.5	0.7	2.4	4.8
Walter Berry (to Hou)	F	6'8	215	24	29	556	108	231	47	43	63	68	115	20	69	0	10	13	259	19	4.0	0.7	2.4	8.9
Charles Shackleford	F-C	6'10	225	22	60	484	83	168	49	21	42	50	153	21	71	0	15	18	187	8	2.6	0.4	1.2	3.1
Kevin Williams (to LAC)	G	6'3	180	27	41	433	67	168	40	40	51	78	50	36	74	0	25	8	175	11	1.2	0.9	1.8	4.3
Corey Gaines	G	6'3	195	23	32	337	27	64	42	12	16	75	19	67	27	0	15	1	67	11	0.6	2.1	0.8	2.1
Bill Jones	F	6'7	175	23	37	307	50	102	49	29	43	67	47	20	38	0	17	6	129	8	1.3	0.5	1.0	3.5
Ron Cavenall	C	7'1	240	29	5	16	2	3	67	2	5	40	2	0	2	0	0	2	6	3	0.4	0.0	0.4	1.2

Duane Washington - banned by NBA for drug abuse

3-PT FG — B.Williamson 0-3, Hinson 0-2, McGee 93-255, Conner 13-37, Morris 64-175, Bagley 11-54, Hopson 4-27, Lee 0-2, Shackleford 0-1, K.Williams 1-6, Gaines 1-5, Jones 0-1

Use Name	Pos	Hgt	Wgt	Age	G	Min	FG	FGA	%	FT	FTA	%	Reb	Ass	PF	DQ	Stls	Blkd Shts	Points	Min	Reb	Ass	PF	Points
CHARLOTTE HORNETS	20-62 .244				**DICK HARTER**																			
Kelly Tripucka	F	6'6	225	29	71	2302	568	1215	47	440	508	87	267	224	196	0	88	16	1606	32	3.8	3.2	2.8	22.6
Kurt Rambis	F	6'8	213	30	75	2233	325	627	52	182	248	73	703	159	208	4	100	57	832	30	9.4	2.1	2.8	11.1
Dave Hoppen	C-F	6'11	235	24	77	1419	199	353	56	101	139	73	384	57	239	4	25	21	500	18	5.0	0.7	3.1	6.5
Rex Chapman	G	6'4	185	21	75	2219	526	1271	41	155	195	79	187	176	167	1	70	25	1267	30	2.5	2.3	2.2	16.9
Mike Holton (BL)	G	6'4	185	27	67	1696	215	504	43	120	143	84	105	424	165	0	66	12	553	25	1.6	6.3	2.5	8.3
Robert Reid	F-G	6'8	215	33	82	2152	519	1214	43	152	196	78	302	153	235	2	53	20	1207	26	3.7	1.9	2.9	14.7
Earl Cureton	F-C	6'9	215	31	82	2047	233	465	50	66	123	54	488	130	230	3	50	61	532	25	6.0	1.6	2.8	6.5
Muggsy Bogues	G	5'3	140	23	79	1755	178	418	43	66	88	75	165	620	141	1	111	7	423	22	2.1	7.8	1.8	5.4
Tom Kempton	F-C	6'10	245	24	79	1341	171	335	51	142	207	69	304	102	215	3	41	14	484	17	3.8	1.3	2.7	6.1
Dell Curry (BW)	G	6'5	195	24	48	813	256	521	49	40	46	87	104	50	68	0	42	4	571	17	2.2	1.0	1.4	11.9
Brian Rowsom (FJ)	F	6'9	220	23	34	517	80	162	49	65	81	80	137	24	69	1	10	12	226	15	4.0	0.7	2.0	6.6
Rickey Green (to Mil)	G	6'1	172	34	33	370	57	132	43	13	14	93	23	82	16	0	18	0	128	11	0.7	2.5	0.5	3.9
Ralph Lewis	G	6'6	200	25	48	336	58	121	48	19	39	49	61	15	28	0	11	3	136	7	1.3	0.3	0.6	2.8
Sidney Lowe	G	6'	195	28	14	250	8	25	32	7	11	64	34	93	28	0	14	0	23	18	2.4	6.6	2.0	1.6
Greg Kite (from LAC)	C	6'11	250	27	12	213	16	30	53	6	10	60	53	7	43	1	4	8	38	18	4.4	0.6	3.6	3.2
Tom Tolbert	F	6'7	240	23	14	117	17	37	46	6	12	50	21	7	20	0	2	4	40	8	1.5	0.5	1.4	2.9

3-PT FG — Tripucka 30-84, Rambis 0-3, Hoppen 1-2, Chapman 60-191, Holton 3-14, Reid 17-52, Cureton 0-1, Bogues 1-13, Kempton 0-1, Curry 19-55, Rowsom 1-1, Green 1-5, Lewis 1-3, Lowe 0-2, Tolbert 0-3

CENTRAL DIVISION

Use Name	Pos	Hgt	Wgt	Age	G	Min	FG	FGA	%	FT	FTA	%	Reb	Ass	PF	DQ	Stls	Blkd Shts	Points	Min	Reb	Ass	PF	Points
DETROIT PISTONS	63-19 .768				**CHUCK DALY**																			
Adrian Dantley (to Dal)	F	6'5	210	32	42	1341	248	495	50	256	305	84	164	93	99	1	23	6	772	32	3.9	2.2	2.4	18.4
Rick Mahorn (XJ)	F-C	6'10	255	30	72	1795	293	393	75	116	155	75	496	59	206	1	40	66	522	25	6.9	0.8	2.9	7.3
Bill Laimbeer	C	6'11	260	31	81	2640	449	900	50	178	212	84	776	177	259	2	51	100	1106	33	9.6	2.2	3.2	13.7
Joe Dumars (BH)	G	6'3	190	25	69	2408	456	903	50	260	306	85	172	390	103	1	63	5	1186	35	2.5	5.7	1.5	17.2
Isiah Thomas	G	6'1	185	27	80	2924	569	1227	46	287	351	82	273	663	209	0	133	20	1458	37	3.4	8.3	2.6	18.2
Dennis Rodman	F-G	6'8	210	27	82	2208	316	531	60	97	155	63	772	99	292	4	55	76	735	27	9.4	1.2	3.6	9.0
Vinnie Johnson	G	6'2	200	32	82	2073	462	996	46	193	263	73	255	242	155	0	74	17	1130	25	3.1	3.0	1.9	13.8
John Salley	F	7'	230	24	67	1458	166	333	50	135	195	69	335	75	197	3	40	72	467	22	5.0	1.1	2.9	7.0
James Edwards	C	7'	252	33	76	1254	211	422	50	133	194	69	231	49	226	1	11	31	555	17	3.0	0.6	3.0	7.3
Mark Aguirre (from Dal)	F	6'6	232	29	36	1068	213	441	48	110	149	74	151	89	101	2	16	7	558	30	4.2	2.5	2.8	15.5
Michael Williams	G	6'2	175	22	49	358	47	129	36	31	47	66	27	70	44	0	13	3	127	7	0.6	1.4	0.9	2.6
John Long (from Ind)	G	6'5	200	32	24	152	13	40	33	11	13	85	11	15	16	0	0	2	49	6	0.5	0.6	0.7	2.0
Fennis Dembo	F	6'5	215	22	31	74	14	42	33	8	10	80	23	5	15	0	1	0	36	2	0.7	0.2	0.5	1.2
Darryl Dawkins (SJ)	C	6'11	270	31	14	48	9	19	47	9	18	50	7	1	13	0	0	1	27	3	0.5	0.1	0.9	1.9
Pace Mannion (to Atl)	G	6'7	190	27	5	14	2	2	100	0	0	—	3	0	3	0	1	0	4	3	0.6	0.0	0.6	0.8
Jim Rowinski (to Phi)	F	6'9	250	28	6	8	0	2	0	0	0	—	4	4	2	0	0	0	4	1	0.7	0.7	0.3	0.7
Steve Harris	G	6'5	195	25	3	7	1	4	25	2	2	100	2	0	1	0	1	0	4	2	0.7	0.0	0.3	1.3

3-PT FG — Mahorn 0-2, Laimbeer 30-86, Dumars 14-29, Thomas 33-121, Rodman 6-26, Johnson 13-44, Salley 0-2, Edwards 0-2, Aguirre 22-75, Williams 2-9, Dembo 0-4

Use Name	Pos	Hgt	Wgt	Age	G	Min	FG	FGA	%	FT	FTA	%	Reb	Ass	PF	DQ	Stls	Blkd Shts	Points	Min	Reb	Ass	PF	Points
CLEVELAND CAVALIERS	57-25 .695				**LENNY WILKENS**																			
Mike Sanders	F	6'6	210	28	82	2102	332	733	45	97	135	72	307	133	230	2	89	32	764	26	3.7	1.6	2.8	9.3
Larry Nance	F	6'10	215	29	73	2526	496	920	54	267	334	80	581	159	186	0	57	206	1259	35	8.0	2.2	2.5	17.2
Brad Daugherty	C	7'	245	23	78	2821	544	1012	54	386	524	74	718	285	175	1	63	40	1475	36	9.2	3.7	2.2	18.9
Ron Harper	G	6'6	205	24	82	2851	587	1149	51	323	430	75	409	434	224	1	185	74	1526	35	5.0	5.3	2.7	18.6
Mark Price	G	6'1	175	24	75	2728	529	1006	53	263	292	90	226	631	98	0	115	7	1414	36	3.0	8.4	1.3	18.9
John Williams	F-C	6'11	230	27	82	2125	356	700	51	235	314	75	477	108	188	1	77	134	948	26	5.8	1.3	2.3	11.6
Craig Ehlo	G-F	6'7	185	27	82	1867	249	524	48	71	117	61	295	266	161	0	110	19	608	23	3.6	3.2	2.0	7.4
Darnell Valentine	G	6'2	183	29	77	1086	136	319	43	91	112	81	103	174	88	0	57	7	366	14	1.3	2.3	1.1	4.8
Tree Rollins	C	7'1	240	33	60	583	62	138	45	12	19	63	139	19	89	0	11	38	136	10	2.3	0.3	1.5	2.3
Chris Dudley	C	6'11	235	23	61	544	73	168	43	39	107	36	157	21	82	0	9	23	185	9	2.6	0.3	1.3	3.0
Randolph Keys	F	6'9	195	22	42	331	74	172	43	20	29	69	56	19	51	0	12	6	169	8	1.3	0.5	1.2	4.0
Phil Hubbard	F	6'8	215	32	31	191	28	63	44	17	25	68	40	11	20	0	6	0	73	6	1.3	0.4	0.6	2.4

Gary Voce - back injury

3-PT FG — Sanders 3-10, Nance 0-4, Daugherty 1-3, Harper 29-116, Price 93-211, Williams 1-4, Ehlo 39-100, Valentine 3-14, Rollins 0-1, Dudley 0-1, Keys 1-10

Use Name	Pos	Hgt	Wgt	Age	TOTAL G	Min	FG	FGA	%	FT	FTA	%	Reb	Ass	PF	DQ	Stls	Blkd Shts	Points	PER GAME Min	Reb	Ass	PF	Points
1988/89 N.B.A. — EASTERN CONFERENCE CENTRAL DIVISION																								
ATLANTA HAWKS	**20-30 .634**				**MIKE FRATELLO**																			
Dominique Wilkins	F-G	6'8	200	28	80	2997	814	1756	46	442	524	84	553	211	138	0	117	52	2099	37	6.9	2.6	1.7	26.2
Cliff Levingston	F	6'8	220	27	80	2184	300	568	53	133	191	70	498	75	270	4	97	70	734	27	6.2	0.9	3.4	9.2
Moses Malone	C	6'10	255	33	81	2878	538	1096	49	561	711	79	956	112	154	0	79	100	1637	36	11.8	1.4	1.9	20.2
Reggie Theus	G	6'7	213	31	82	2517	497	1067	47	285	335	85	242	387	236	0	108	16	1296	31	3.0	4.7	2.9	15.8
Glenn Rivers	G	6'4	185	27	76	2462	371	816	45	247	287	86	286	525	263	6	181	40	1032	32	3.8	6.9	3.5	13.6
John Battle	G	6'2	175	26	82	1672	287	628	46	194	238	82	140	197	125	0	42	9	779	20	1.7	2.4	1.5	9.5
Jon Koncak	C-F	7'	260	25	74	1531	141	269	52	63	114	55	453	56	238	4	54	98	345	21	6.1	0.8	3.2	4.7
Aintoine Carr	F	6'9	235	27	78	1488	226	471	48	130	152	86	274	91	221	0	31	62	582	19	3.5	1.2	2.8	7.5
Spud Webb	G	5'7	135	25	81	1219	133	290	46	52	60	87	123	284	104	0	70	6	319	15	1.5	3.5	1.3	3.9
Ray Tolbert	F	6'9	240	30	50	341	40	94	43	23	37	62	88	16	55	0	13	13	103	7	1.8	0.3	1.1	2.1
Dudley Bradley	G	6'6	195	31	38	267	28	86	33	8	16	50	32	24	41	0	16	2	72	7	0.8	0.6	1.1	1.9
Duane Ferrell	F	6'7	209	24	41	231	35	83	42	30	44	68	41	10	33	0	7	6	100	6	1.0	0.2	0.8	2.4
Pace Mannion (from Det)	G	6'7	190	27	5	18	2	6	33	0	0	—	2	2	2	0	2	0	4	4	0.4	0.4	0.4	0.8
Kevin Willis (KJ)	**3-PT FG —**				Wilkins 29-105, Levingston 1-5, Malone 0-12, Theus 17-58, Rivers 43-124, Batle 11-34																			
Chris Washburn (DR)					Koncak 0-3, Carr 0-1, Webb 1-22, Bradley 8-31, Mannion 0-2																			
MILWAUKEE BUCKS	**49-33 .598**				**DEL HARRIS**																			
Terry Cummings	F	6'9	235	27	80	2824	730	1563	47	362	460	79	650	198	265	5	106	72	1829	35	8.1	2.5	3.3	22.9
Larry Krystkowiak	F	6'9	220	24	80	2472	362	766	47	289	351	82	610	107	219	0	93	9	1017	31	7.6	1.3	2.7	12.7
Jack Sikma	C	6'11	260	33	80	2587	360	835	43	266	294	90	623	289	300	6	85	61	1068	32	7.8	3.6	3.8	13.4
Jay Humphries	G	6'3	185	26	73	2220	345	714	48	129	158	82	189	405	187	1	142	5	844	30	2.6	5.5	2.6	11.6
Paul Pressey	G	6'5	205	30	67	2170	307	648	47	187	241	78	262	439	221	2	119	44	813	32	3.9	6.6	3.3	12.1
Ricky Pierce	F-G	6'5	222	29	75	2078	527	1018	52	255	297	86	197	156	193	1	77	19	1217	28	2.6	2.1	2.6	16.2
Sidney Moncrief (LJ)	G	6'4	180	31	62	1594	261	532	49	205	237	86	172	188	114	1	65	13	751	26	2.8	3.0	1.8	12.1
Fred Roberts (BJ)	F-C	6'10	220	28	71	1251	155	319	49	104	129	81	209	66	126	0	36	33	417	18	2.9	0.9	1.8	5.9
Paul Mokeski	C	7'	255	31	74	690	59	164	36	40	51	78	187	36	153	0	29	21	165	9	2.5	0.5	2.1	2.2
Randy Breuer	C	7'3	263	28	48	513	86	179	48	28	51	55	135	22	59	0	9	37	200	11	2.8	0.5	1.2	4.2
Rickey Green (from Char)	G	6'1	172	34	30	501	72	132	55	17	19	89	46	105	19	0	22	2	163	17	1.5	3.5	0.6	5.4
Tony Brown (from Hou)	F	6'6	195	28	29	274	36	73	49	18	23	78	29	21	28	1	12	4	92	9	1.0	0.7	1.0	3.2
Mark Davis (to Phoe)	F-G	6'5	195	25	31	251	48	97	49	26	32	81	36	14	38	0	13	5	123	8	1.2	0.5	1.2	4.0
Jeff Grayer (IL, KJ)	G	6'5	200	23	11	200	32	73	44	17	20	85	35	22	15	0	10	1	81	18	3.2	2.0	1.4	7.4
Tito Horford (toe injury)	C	7'1	245	22	25	112	15	46	33	12	19	63	22	3	14	0	1	7	42	4	0.9	0.1	0.6	1.7
Andre Turner	G	5'11	160	24	4	13	3	6	50	0	0	—	3	0	2	0	2	0	6	3	0.8	0.0	0.5	1.5
Mike Dunleavy	G	6'3	180	34	2	5	1	2	50	0	0	—	0	0	0	0	0	0	3	3	0.0	0.0	0.0	1.5
	3-PT FG —				Cummings 7-15, Krystkowiak 4-12, Sikma 82-216, Humphries 25-94, Pressey 12-55, Pierce 8-36,																			
					Moncrief 25-73, Roberts 3-14, Mokeski 7-26, Green 2-6, Brown 2-7, Davis 1-9, Grayer 0-2, Dunleavy 1-2																			
CHICAGO BULLS	**47-35 .573**				**DOUG COLLINS**																			
Scottie Pippen	F	6'7	210	23	73	2413	413	867	48	201	301	67	445	256	261	8	139	61	1048	33	6.1	3.5	3.6	14.4
Horace Grant	F-C	6'10	215	23	79	2809	405	781	52	140	199	70	681	168	251	1	86	62	950	36	8.6	2.1	3.2	12.0
Bill Cartwright	C	7'1	245	31	78	2333	365	768	48	236	308	77	521	90	234	2	21	41	966	30	6.7	1.2	3.0	12.4
Sam Vincent (XJ)	G	6'2	185	25	70	1703	274	566	48	106	129	82	190	335	124	0	53	10	656	24	2.7	4.8	1.8	9.4
Michael Jordan	G-F	6'6	185	25	81	**3255**	**966**	**1795**	54	674	793	85	652	650	247	2	234	65	**2633**	40	8.0	8.0	3.0	**32.5**
John Paxson	G	6'2	185	28	78	1738	246	513	48	31	36	86	94	308	162	1	53	6	567	22	1.2	3.9	2.1	7.3
Brad Sellers	C	7'	210	26	80	1732	231	476	49	86	101	85	227	99	176	2	35	69	551	22	2.8	1.2	2.2	6.9
Dave Corzine	C	6'11	260	32	81	1483	203	440	46	71	96	74	315	103	134	0	29	45	479	18	3.9	1.3	1.7	5.9
Craig Hodges (from Phoe)	G	6'3	190	28	49	1112	187	394	47	45	53	85	84	138	82	0	41	4	490	23	1.7	2.8	1.7	10.0
Charlie Davis (LJ)	F	6'7	215	30	49	545	81	190	43	19	26	73	114	31	58	1	11	5	185	11	2.3	0.6	1.2	3.8
Jack Haley	C-F	6'10	240	24	51	289	37	78	47	36	46	78	71	10	56	0	11	0	110	6	1.4	0.2	1.1	2.2
Will Perdue	C	7'	240	23	30	190	29	72	40	8	14	57	45	11	28	0	4	6	66	6	1.5	0.4	0.9	2.2
Ed Nealy (to Phoe)	F	6'7	240	28	13	94	5	7	71	1	2	50	23	6	23	0	3	1	11	7	1.8	0.5	1.8	0.8
Anthony Jones (to Dall)	G	6'6	195	26	8	65	5	15	33	2	2	100	8	4	7	0	2	1	12	8	1.0	0.5	0.9	1.5
Dominic Pressley (from Was)	G	6'3	170	24	3	17	1	6	17	0	0	—	1	4	2	0	0	0	2	6	0.3	1.3	0.7	0.7
David Wood	F	6'9	225	24	2	2	0	0	—	0	0	—	0	0	0	0	0	0	0	1	0.0	0.0	0.0	0.0
	3-PT FG —				Pippen 21-77, Grant 0-5, Vincent 2-17, Jordan 27-98, Paxson 44-133, Sellers 3-6,																			
					Corzine 2-8, Hodges 71-168, Davis 4-5, Jones 0-1, Pressley 0-2																			
INDIANA PACERS	**28-54 .341**				**JACK RAMSAY (0-6 .000), MEL DANIELS & DANNY TWRADZIK (0-2 .000),**																			
					GEORGE IRVINE (6-14 .240), DICK VERSACE (22-32 .407)																			
Chuck Person	F	6'8	225	24	80	3012	711	1453	49	243	307	79	516	289	280	12	83	18	1728	38	6.5	3.6	3.5	21.6
Herb Williams (to Dal)	F-C	6'11	240	30	46	1567	244	542	45	90	126	71	396	88	156	3	31	80	578	34	8.6	1.9	3.4	12.6
Rik Smits	C	7'4	250	22	82	2041	386	746	52	184	255	72	500	70	310	**14**	37	151	956	25	6.1	0.9	3.8	11.7
Reggie Miller	G-F	6'7	190	23	74	2536	398	831	48	287	340	84	292	224	170	2	93	29	1181	34	3.9	3.0	2.3	16.0
Vern Fleming	G	6'5	195	27	76	2552	419	814	51	243	304	80	310	494	212	4	77	12	1064					
Scott Skiles	G	6'1	200	24	80	1571	198	442	45	130	144	90	149	390	151	1	64	2	546	20	1.9	4.9	1.9	6.8
Waymon Tisdale (to Sac)	F	6'9	240	24	48	1326	285	564	51	198	250	79	310	75	181	5	35	32	768	28	6.5	1.6	3.8	16.0
LaSalle Thompson (to Sac)	C	6'10	253	27	33	1053	169	314	54	75	93	81	326	37	132	6	33	39	413	32	9.9	1.1	4.0	12.5
Detlef Schrempf (from Dal)	F-C	6'10	226	25	32	1005	162	315	51	146	189	77	229	93	102	0	29	10	**475**	31	7.2	2.9	3.2	14.8
Stuart Gray	C-F	7'	245	25	72	783	72	153	47	44	64	69	245	29	128	0	11	21	188	11	3.4	0.4	1.8	2.6
John Long (to Det)	G	6'5	200	32	44	767	128	319	40	59	63	94	66	65	68	1	29	1	323	17	1.5	1.5	1.5	7.3
Randy Wittman (fromSac)	G-F	6'6	210	29	33	704	80	169	47	12	19	63	54	79	31	0	13	2	173	21	1.6	2.4	0.9	5.2
Greg Dreiling	C	7'1	250	25	53	396	43	77	56	43	64	67	92	18	100	0	5	11	129	7	1.7	0.3	1.9	2.4
Anthony Frederick	F	6'7	205	24	46	313	63	125	50	24	34	71	52	20	59	0	14	6	152	7	1.1	0.4	1.3	3.3
Everette Stephens	G	6'2	175	22	35	209	23	72	32	17	22	77	23	37	22	0	9	4	65	6	0.7	1.1	0.6	1.9
Richard Morton	G	6'3	195	23	2	11	3	4	75	0	0	—	0	1	2	0	0	0	6	6	0.0	0.5	1.0	3.0
Sedric Toney	G	6'2	178	26	2	9	1	5	20	0	1	0	2	0	1	0	0	0	2	5	1.0	0.0	0.5	1.0
Steve Stepanovich - knee injury	**3-PT FG —**				Person 63-205, Williams 0-3, Smits 0-1, Miller 98-244, Fleming 3-23, Skiles 20-75, Tisdale 0-4,																			
					Schrempf 5-19, Gray 0-1, Long 8-20, Wittman 1-2, Frederick 2-5, Stephens 2-10, Toney 0-3																			

Use Name	Pos	Hgt	Wgt	Age	TOTAL G	Min	FG	FGA	%	FT	FTA	%	Reb	Ass	PF	DQ	Stls	Blkd Shts	Points	PER GAME Min	Reb	Ass	PF	Points

1988/89 N.B.A. — WESTERN CONFERENCE
MIDWEST DIVISION

Use Name	Pos	Hgt	Wgt	Age	G	Min	FG	FGA	%	FT	FTA	%	Reb	Ass	PF	DQ	Stls	Blkd Shts	Points	Min	Reb	Ass	PF	Points
UTAH JAZZ	51-31 .622				FRANK LAYDEN (11-6 . 647), JERRY SLOAN (40-25 . 615)																			
Thurl Bailey	F	6'11	232	27	82	2777	615	1272	48	363	440	83	447	138	185	0	48	91	1595	34	5.5	1.7	2.3	19.5
Karl Malone	F-C	6'9	254	25	80	3126	809	1559	52	**703**	**910**	77	853	219	286	3	144	70	2326	39	10.7	2.7	3.6	29.1
Mark Eaton	C	7'4	290	31	82	2914	188	407	46	132	200	66	843	83	290	6	40	315	508	36	10.3	1.0	3.5	6.2
Darrell Griffith	G	6'4	190	30	82	2382	466	1045	45	142	182	78	330	130	175	0	86	141	1135	29	4.0	1.6	2.1	13.8
John Stockton	G	6'1	175	26	82	3171	497	923	54	390	452	86	248	**1118**	241	3	**263**	14	1400	39	3.0	13.6	2.9	17.1
Mike Brown	F-C	6'9	240	25	66	1051	104	248	42	92	130	71	258	41	133	0	25	17	300	16	3.9	0.6	2.0	4.5
Bob Hansen (BH, BY)	G	6'6	195	27	46	964	140	300	47	42	75	56	128	50	105	0	37	6	341	21	2.8	1.1	2.3	7.4
Marc Iavaroni	F	6'9	225	32	77	796	72	163	44	36	44	82	132	32	99	0	11	13	180	10	1.7	0.4	1.3	2.3
Jim Les	G	5'11	175	26	82	781	40	133	30	57	73	78	87	215	88	0	27	5	138	10	1.1	2.6	1.1	1.7
Eric Leckner	F-C	6'11	265	22	75	779	120	220	55	79	113	70	199	16	174	1	8	22	319	10	2.7	0.2	2.3	4.3
Jim Farmer	G	6'4	190	24	37	412	57	142	40	29	41	71	55	28	41	0	9	0	152	11	1.5	0.8	1.1	4.1
Jose Ortiz	F	6'10	225	25	51	327	55	125	44	31	52	60	58	11	40	0	8	7	141	6	1.1	0.2	0.8	2.8
Bart Kofoed	G	6'4	210	24	19	176	12	33	36	6	11	55	11	20	22	0	9	0	30	9	0.6	1.1	1.2	1.6
Scott Roth (to SA)	F	6'8	212	25	16	72	7	24	29	8	11	73	8	7	14	0	5	1	23	5	0.5	0.4	0.9	1.4
Eric White (to LAC)	F	6'8	200	23	1	2	0	1	0	0	0	—	0	0	1	0	0	0	0	2	0.0	0.0	1.0	0.0

3-PT FG — Bailey 2-5, Malone 5-16, Griffith 61-196, Stockton 16-66, Hansen 19-54, Lavaroni 0-1, Les 1-14, Farmer 9-20, Ortiz 0-1, Kofoed 0-1, Roth 1-6

Use Name	Pos	Hgt	Wgt	Age	G	Min	FG	FGA	%	FT	FTA	%	Reb	Ass	PF	DQ	Stls	Blkd Shts	Points	Min	Reb	Ass	PF	Points
HOUSTON ROCKETS	45-37 .549				DON CHANEY																			
Buck Johnson	F	6'7	190	24	67	1850	270	515	52	101	134	75	286	126	213	4	64	35	642	28	4.3	1.9	3.2	9.6
Otis Thorpe	F	6'11	236	26	82	3135	521	621	84	328	450	73	787	202	259	6	82	37	1370	38	9.6	2.5	3.2	16.7
Akeem Olajuwaon	C	7'	250	25	82	3024	790	1556	51	454	652	70	**1105**	149	329	10	213	282	2034	37	13.5	1.8	4.0	24.8
Eric Floyd	G	6'3	175	28	82	2788	396	893	44	261	309	84	306	709	196	1	124	11	1162	34	3.7	8.6	2.4	14.2
Mike Woodson	G	6'5	198	30	81	2259	410	936	44	195	137	142	194	206	195	1	89	18	1046	28	2.4	2.5	2.4	12.9
Derrick Chievous	F	6'7	195	21	81	1539	277	634	44	191	244	78	256	77	161	1	48	11	750	19	3.2	1.0	2.0	9.3
Tim McCormick	C	7'	240	26	81	1257	169	351	48	87	129	67	261	54	193	0	18	24	425	16	3.2	0.7	2.4	5.2
Purvis Short (LJ)	F-G	6'7	215	31	65	1157	198	480	41	77	89	87	179	107	116	1	44	13	482	18	2.8	1.6	1.8	7.4
Frank Johnson	G	6'2	185	30	67	879	109	246	44	75	93	81	79	181	91	0	42	0	294	13	1.2	2.7	1.4	4.4
Walter Berry (from NJ)	F	6'8	215	24	40	799	146	270	54	57	80	71	152	57	114	1	19	35	350	20	3.8	1.4	2.9	8.8
Allen Leavell	G	6'1	190	31	55	627	65	188	35	44	60	73	53	127	61	0	25	5	179	11	1.0	2.3	1.1	3.3
Chuck Nevitt	C	7'5	237	29	43	228	27	62	44	11	16	69	64	3	51	1	5	29	65	5	1.5	0.1	1.2	1.5
Bernard Thompson	F-G	6'6	210	26	23	222	20	59	34	22	26	85	28	13	33	0	13	1	62	10	1.2	0.6	1.4	2.7
Tony Brown (XJ, to Mil)	F	6'6	195	28	14	91	14	45	31	6	8	75	15	5	14	0	3	0	36	7	1.1	0.4	1.0	2.6

3-PT FG — B.Johnson 1-9, Thorpe 0-2, Olajuwon 0-10, Floyd 109-292, Woodson 31-89, Cheivous 5-24, McCormick 0-4, Short 9-33, F. Johnson 1-6, Berry 1-2, Leavell 5-41, Thompson 0-2, Brown 2-9

Use Name	Pos	Hgt	Wgt	Age	G	Min	FG	FGA	%	FT	FTA	%	Reb	Ass	PF	DQ	Stls	Blkd Shts	Points	Min	Reb	Ass	PF	Points
DENVER NUGGETS	44-38 .537				DOUG MOE																			
Alex English	F	6'8	190	34	82	2990	924	1881	49	325	379	86	326	383	174	0	66	12	2175	36	4.0	4.7	2.1	26.5
Wayne Cooper	F-C	6'10	220	32	79	1864	220	444	50	79	106	75	619	78	302	7	36	211	520	24	7.8	1.0	3.8	6.6
Dan Schayes	C	6'11	260	29	76	1918	317	607	52	332	402	83	500	105	320	8	42	81	969	25	6.6	1.4	4.2	12.8
Lafayette Lever	G	6'3	175	28	71	2745	558	1221	46	270	344	78	662	559	178	1	195	20	1409	39	9.3	7.9	2.5	19.8
Michael Adams	G	5'11	165	25	77	2787	468	1082	43	322	393	82	283	490	149	0	166	11	1424	36	3.7	6.4	1.9	18.5
Walter Davis	G	6'6	200	34	81	1857	536	1076	50	175	199	88	151	190	187	1	72	5	1267	23	1.9	2.3	2.3	15.6
Elston Turner	G	6'5	200	29	78	1746	151	353	43	33	56	59	287	144	209	2	90	8	337	22	3.7	1.8	2.7	4.3
Blair Rasmussen	C	7'	260	26	77	1308	257	577	45	69	81	85	287	49	194	2	29	41	583	17	3.7	0.6	2.5	7.6
Bill Hanzlik (XJ)	G	6'7	200	31	41	701	66	151	44	68	87	78	93	86	82	1	25	5	201	17	2.3	2.1	2.0	4.9
Jerome Lane (NJ)	F	6'8	230	22	54	550	109	256	43	43	112	38	200	60	105	1	20	4	261	10	3.7	1.1	1.9	4.8
Dave Greenwood (from SA)	F	6'9	225	31	29	491	62	148	42	48	71	68	164	41	78	3	17	28	172	17	5.7	1.4	2.7	5.9
Darwin Cook (from SA)	G	6'3	195	30	30	386	71	163	44	17	22	77	48	43	44	0	28	6	161	13	1.6	1.4	1.5	5.4
Eddie Hughes	G	5'10	165	28	26	224	28	64	44	7	12	58	19	35	30	0	17	2	70	9	0.7	1.3	1.2	2.7
Calvin Natt (KG, to SA)	F	6'6	220	31	14	168	22	50	44	22	31	71	46	7	13	0	6	1	66	12	3.3	0.5	0.9	4.7
Jay Vincent (FJ, to SA)	F	6'7	220	29	5	95	13	38	34	5	9	56	18	5	11	0	1	1	32	19	3.6	1.0	2.2	6.4
Wayne Englestad	F	6'8	245	25	11	50	11	29	38	6	10	60	16	7	12	0	1	0	28	5	1.5	0.6	1.1	2.5

Maurice Martin - knee injury

3-PT FG — English 2-8, Cooper 1-4, Schayes 3-9, Lever 23-66, Adams 166-466, Davis 20-69, Turner 2-7, Hanzlik 1-5, Lane 0-7, Cook 2-10, Hughes 7-22, Natt 0-1, Vincent 1-2

Use Name	Pos	Hgt	Wgt	Age	G	Min	FG	FGA	%	FT	FTA	%	Reb	Ass	PF	DQ	Stls	Blkd Shts	Points	Min	Reb	Ass	PF	Points
DALLAS MAVERICKS	38-44 .463				JOHN MACLEOD																			
Mark Aguirre (to Det)	F-G	6'6	232	29	44	1529	373	829	45	178	244	73	235	189	128	0	29	29	953	35	5.3	4.3	2.9	21.7
Sam Perkins	F	6'9	237	27	78	2860	445	959	46	274	329	83	668	127	224	1	76	92	1171	37	8.6	1.6	2.9	15.0
James Donaldson (KJ)	C	7'2	275	31	53	1746	193	337	57	95	124	77	570	38	111	0	24	81	481	33	10.8	0.7	2.1	9.1
Rolando Blackman	G	6'6	201	29	78	2946	594	1249	48	316	370	85	273	288	137	0	65	20	1534	38	3.5	3.7	1.8	19.7
Derek Harper	G	6'4	202	27	81	2968	538	1127	48	229	284	81	228	570	219	3	172	41	1404	37	2.8	7.0	2.7	17.3
Brad Davis	G	6'3	180	33	78	1395	183	379	48	99	123	80	108	242	151	0	48	18	497	18	1.4	3.1	1.9	6.4
Adrian Dantley (from Det)	F	6'5	210	32	31	1081	212	459	46	204	263	78	153	78	87	0	20	7	628	35	4.9	2.5	2.8	20.3
Bill Wennington	C	7'	245	24	65	1074	119	275	43	61	82	74	286	46	211	3	16	35	300	17	4.4	0.7	3.2	4.6
Terry Tyler	F	6'7	228	32	70	1057	169	360	47	47	62	76	209	40	90	0	24	39	386	15	3.0	0.6	1.3	5.5
Herb Williams (from Ind)	F-C	6'11	240	30	30	903	78	197	40	43	68	63	197	36	80	2	15	54	199	30	6.6	1.2	2.7	6.6
Detlef Schrempf (LJ, to Ind)	F	6'10	226	25	37	845	112	263	43	127	161	79	166	86	188	3	24	9	353	23	4.5	2.3	5.1	9.5
Roy Tarpley (KJ, DR)	C-F	7'	244	24	19	591	131	242	54	66	96	69	218	17	70	2	28	30	328	31	11.5	0.9	3.7	17.3
Morlon Wiley	G	6'4	190	22	51	408	46	114	40	13	16	81	47	76	61	0	25	6	111	8	0.9	1.5	1.2	2.2
Uwe Blab	C	7'1	251	26	37	208	24	52	46	20	25	80	44	12	36	0	3	13	68	6	1.2	0.3	1.0	1.8
Anthony Jones (from Chi)	G	6'6	195	26	25	131	24	64	38	12	14	86	20	13	13	0	9	2	64	5	0.8	0.5	0.5	2.6
Steve Alford (to GS)	G	6'2	179	24	9	38	3	11	27	1	2	50	3	9	3	0	1	0	7	4	0.3	1.0	0.3	0.8

3-PT FG — Aguirre 29-99, Perkins 7-38, Blackman 30-85, Harper 99-278, Davis 32-102, Dantley 0-1, Wennington 1-9, Tyler 1-9, Williams 0-2, Schrempf 2-16, Tarpley 0-1, Wiley 6-24, Jones 4-15, Alford 0-2

1988/89 N.B.A. — WESTERN CONFERENCE

Use Name	Pos	Hgt	Wgt	Age	G	Min	FG	FGA	%	FT	FTA	%	Reb	Ass	PF	DQ	Stls	Blkd Shts	Points	Min	Reb	Ass	PF	Points
SAN ANTONIO SPURS	21-61 .256				**LARRY BROWN**																			
Willie Anderson	F-G	6'7	190	21	79	2738	640	1285	50	224	289	78	417	372	295	8	150	62	1508	35	5.3	4.7	3.7	19.1
Greg Anderson	F-C	6'10	230	24	82	2401	460	914	50	207	403	51	676	61	221	2	102	103	1127	29	8.2	0.7	2.7	13.7
Frank Brickowski	C-F	6'10	240	29	64	1822	337	634	53	201	281	72	406	131	252	10	102	35	875	28	6.3	2.0	3.9	13.7
Vernon Maxwell	G	6'5	188	23	79	2065	357	827	43	181	243	74	202	301	136	0	86	8	927	26	2.6	3.8	1.7	11.7
Alvin Robertson (KJ)	G	6'4	190	26	65	2287	465	962	48	183	253	72	384	393	259	6	197	36	1122	35	5.9	6.0	4.0	17.3
Dallas Comegys	F	6'9	210	24	67	1119	116	341	34	106	161	66	234	30	160	2	42	63	438	17	3.5	0.4	2.4	6.5
Johnny Dawkins (LJ)	G	6'2	165	25	32	1083	177	400	44	100	112	89	101	224	64	0	55	0	454	34	3.2	7.0	2.0	14.2
Dave Greenwood (to Den)	F	6'9	225	31	38	912	105	247	43	84	105	80	238	55	123	2	30	24	294	24	6.3	1.4	3.2	7.7
Albert King	F	6'6	210	29	46	791	141	327	43	37	48	77	140	79	97	2	27	7	327	17	3.0	1.7	2.1	7.1
Darwin Cook (to Den)	G	6'3	195	30	36	757	147	315	47	46	56	82	59	84	77	0	43	4	346	21	1.6	2.3	2.1	9.6
Michael Anderson	G	5'11	184	23	36	730	73	175	42	57	82	70	89	153	64	0	44	3	204	20	2.5	4.3	1.8	5.7
Mike Smrek (LJ)	C	7'	263	26	43	623	72	153	47	49	76	64	129	12	102	2	13	58	193	14	3.0	0.3	2.4	4.5
Jerome Whitehead (from GS)	C-F	6'10	240	32	52	580	69	176	39	30	45	67	129	17	107	1	22	4	168	11	2.5	0.3	2.1	3.2
Jay Vincent (from Den)	F	6'7	220	29	24	551	91	219	42	35	51	69	92	22	52	0	5	3	217	23	3.8	0.9	2.2	9.0
Scott Roth (from Utah)	F	6'8	212	25	47	464	52	143	36	52	76	68	56	48	55	0	19	4	158	10	1.2	1.0	1.2	3.4
Anthony Bowie	F	6'6	190	26	18	438	72	144	50	10	15	67	56	29	43	1	18	4	155	24	3.1	1.6	2.4	8.6
Calvin Natt (from Den)	F	6'6	220	31	10	185	25	66	38	35	48	73	32	11	19	0	2	2	85	19	3.2	1.1	1.9	8.5
Shelton Jones (to GS, Phi)	F	6'9	210	22	7	92	9	25	36	8	13	62	16	7	8	0	2	2	26	13	2.3	1.0	1.1	3.7
Petur Gudmundsson (KJ)	C	7'2	265	30	5	70	9	25	36	3	4	75	16	5	15	0	1	1	21	14	3.2	1.0	3.0	4.2
Todd Mitchell (from Mia)	F	6'7	205	22	2	33	2	9	22	1	4	25	3	1	2	0	1	0	5	17	1.5	0.5	1.0	2.5
Keith Smart	G	6'1	175	24	2	12	0	2	0	2	2	100	1	2	0	0	0	0	2	6	0.5	1.0	0.0	1.0
John Stroeder (to GS)	F	6'10	260	30	1	2	0	0	—	0	0	—	0	0	0	0	0	0	0	2	0.0	0.0	0.0	0.0

3-PT FG — W. Anderson 4-21, G.Anderson 0-3, Brickowski 0-2, Maxwell 32-129, Robertson 9-45, Comegys 0-2, Dawkins 0-4, King 8-32, Cook 6-31, M.Anderson 1-7, Vincent 0-1, Roth 2-10, Bowie 1-5, Smart 0-1

Use Name	Pos	Hgt	Wgt	Age	G	Min	FG	FGA	%	FT	FTA	%	Reb	Ass	PF	DQ	Stls	Blkd Shts	Points	Min	Reb	Ass	PF	Points
MIAMI HEAT	15-67 .183				**RON ROTHSTEIN**																			
Billy Thompson	F	6'7	215	25	79	2273	349	716	49	156	214	73	572	176	260	8	56	105	854	29	7.2	2.2	3.3	10.8
Grant Long	F	6'8	230	22	82	2435	336	692	49	304	406	75	546	149	**337**	13	122	48	976	30	6.7	1.8	4.1	11.9
Rony Seikaly	C	6'11	240	23	78	1962	333	744	45	181	354	51	549	55	258	8	46	96	848	25	7.0	0.7	3.3	10.9
Kevin Edwards	G	6'3	190	23	79	2349	470	1105	43	144	193	75	262	349	154	0	139	27	1094	30	3.3	4.4	1.9	13.8
Rory Sparrow	G	6'2	175	30	80	2613	444	982	45	94	107	88	216	429	168	0	103	17	1000	33	2.7	5.4	2.1	12.5
Jon Sundvold	G	6'2	170	27	68	1338	307	675	45	47	57	82	87	137	78	0	27	1	709	20	1.3	2.0	1.1	10.4
Sylvester Gray (RJ)	F	6'6	240	21	55	1220	167	398	42	105	156	67	286	117	144	1	36	25	440	22	5.2	2.1	2.6	8.0
Scott Hastings (JJ)	F-C	6'10	245	28	75	1206	143	328	44	91	107	85	231	59	203	5	32	42	386	16	3.1	0.8	2.7	5.1
Pat Cummings	F	6'9	245	32	53	1096	197	394	50	72	97	74	281	47	160	3	29	18	466	21	5.3	0.9	3.0	8.8
Pearl Washington (GJ)	G	6'2	200	24	54	1065	164	387	42	82	104	79	123	226	101	0	73	4	411	20	2.3	4.2	1.9	7.6
John Shasky	C	6'11	240	24	65	944	121	248	49	115	167	69	232	22	94	0	14	13	357	15	3.6	0.3	1.4	5.5
Anthony Taylor	G	6'4	175	23	21	368	60	151	40	24	32	75	34	43	37	0	22	5	144	18	1.6	2.0	1.8	6.9
Craig Neal (from Port)	G	6'5	180	24	32	341	34	88	39	13	21	62	18	86	46	0	15	4	89	11	0.6	2.7	1.4	2.8
Todd Mitchell (to SA)	F	6'7	205	22	22	320	41	88	47	36	60	60	47	20	49	0	15	2	118	15	2.1	0.9	2.2	5.4
Kelvin Upshaw (to Bos)	G	6'2	180	25	9	144	26	63	41	4	6	67	13	20	18	0	7	0	57	16	1.4	2.2	2.0	6.3
Clinton Wheeler (to Port)	G	6'1	185	29	8	143	24	42	57	8	10	80	12	21	9	0	8	0	56	18	1.5	2.6	1.1	7.0
David Popson (from LAC)	F-C	6'10	220	24	7	38	5	15	33	1	2	50	11	2	8	0	0	1	11	5	1.6	0.3	1.1	1.6
Hansi Gnad - suspended (returned to play in West Germany)																								

3-PT FG — Thompson 0-4, Long 0-5, Seikaly 1-4, Edwards 10-37, Sparrow 18-74, Sundvold 48-92, Gray 1-4, Hastings 9-28, Cummings 0-2, Washington 1-14, Shasky 0-2, Taylor 0-2, Neal 8-25, Upshaw 1-5

PACIFIC DIVISION

Use Name	Pos	Hgt	Wgt	Age	G	Min	FG	FGA	%	FT	FTA	%	Reb	Ass	PF	DQ	Stls	Blkd Shts	Points	Min	Reb	Ass	PF	Points
LOS ANGELES LAKERS	57-25 .695				**PAT RILEY**																			
James Worthy	F	6'9	225	27	81	2960	702	1282	55	251	321	78	489	288	175	0	108	56	1657	37	6.0	3.6	2.2	20.5
A. C. Green	F	6'9	224	25	82	2510	401	758	53	282	359	79	739	103	172	0	94	117	1088	31	9.0	1.3	2.1	13.3
Kareem Abdul-Jabbar	C	7'2	267	41	74	1695	313	659	47	122	165	74	334	74	196	1	38	95	748	23	4.5	1.0	2.6	10.1
Byron Scott	G	6'3	193	27	74	2605	588	1198	49	195	226	86	302	231	181	1	114	27	1448	35	4.1	3.1	2.4	19.6
Magic Johnson	G	6'8	220	29	77	2886	579	1137	51	513	563	**91**	607	988	172	0	138	22	1730	37	7.9	12.8	2.2	22.5
Mychal Thompson	F-C	6'10	235	33	80	1994	291	521	56	156	230	68	467	48	224	0	58	59	738	25	5.8	0.6	2.8	9.2
Michael Cooper	G-F	6'5	176	32	80	1943	213	494	43	81	93	87	191	314	186	0	72	32	587	24	2.4	3.9	2.3	7.3
Orlando Woolridge	F	6'9	215	29	74	1491	231	494	47	253	343	74	270	58	130	0	30	65	715	20	3.6	0.8	1.8	9.7
Tony Campbell	F	6'7	215	26	63	787	158	345	46	70	83	84	130	47	108	0	37	6	388	12	2.1	0.7	1.7	6.2
David Rivers	G	6'	180	23	47	440	49	122	40	35	42	83	43	106	50	0	23	9	134	9	0.9	2.3	1.1	2.9
Mark McNamara	C	6'11	235	29	39	318	32	64	50	49	78	63	100	10	51	0	4	3	113	8	2.6	0.3	1.3	2.9
Jeff Lamp	G-F	6'6	205	29	37	176	27	69	39	4	5	80	34	15	27	0	8	2	60	5	0.9	0.4	0.7	1.6

3-PT FG — Worthy 2-23, Green 4-17, Abdul-Jabbar 0-3, Scott 77-193, Johnson 59-188, Thompson 0-1, Cooper 80-210, Woolridge 0-1, Campbell 2-21, Rivers 1-6, Lamp 2-4

Use Name	Pos	Hgt	Wgt	Age	G	Min	FG	FGA	%	FT	FTA	%	Reb	Ass	PF	DQ	Stls	Blkd Shts	Points	Min	Reb	Ass	PF	Points
PHOENIX SUNS	55-27 .671				**COTTON FITZSIMMONS**																			
Mark West	F-C	6'10	246	28	82	2019	243	372	65	108	202	53	551	39	273	4	35	187	594	25	6.7	0.5	3.3	7.2
Armon Gilliam	F	6'9	245	24	74	2120	468	930	50	240	323	74	541	52	176	2	54	27	1176	29	7.3	0.7	2.4	15.9
Tom Chambers	C-F	6'10	230	29	81	3002	774	1643	47	509	598	85	684	231	271	2	87	55	2085	37	8.4	2.9	3.3	25.7
Jeff Hornacek	G	6'4	190	25	78	2487	440	889	49	147	178	83	266	465	188	0	129	8	1054	32	3.4	6.0	2.4	13.5
Kevin Johnson	G	6'2	188	22	81	3179	570	1128	51	508	576	88	340	991	226	1	135	24	1650	39	4.2	12.2	2.8	20.4
Eddie Johnson	F	6'8	215	29	70	2043	608	1224	50	217	250	87	306	162	198	0	47	7	1504	29	4.4	2.3	2.8	21.5
Tyron Corbin	G-F	6'6	222	26	77	1655	245	454	54	141	179	79	398	118	222	2	82	13	631	21	5.2	1.5	2.9	8.2
Dan Majerle	F	6'6	220	23	54	1354	181	432	42	78	127	61	209	130	139	1	63	14	467	25	3.9	2.4	2.6	8.6
Tim Perry	F-C	6'9	219	23	62	614	108	201	54	40	65	62	132	18	47	0	19	32	257	10	2.1	0.3	0.8	4.1
Andrew Lang	F-C	6'11	245	22	62	526	60	117	51	39	60	65	147	9	112	1	17	48	159	8	2.4	0.1	1.8	2.6
T. R. Dunn	G	6'4	195	33	34	321	12	35	34	9	12	75	60	25	35	0	12	1	33	9	1.8	0.7	1.0	1.0
Ed Nealy (from Chi)	F	6'7	240	28	30	164	8	29	28	2	7	29	55	8	22	0	4	0	19	5	1.8	0.3	0.7	0.6
Steve Kerr (NJ)	G	6'3	175	23	26	157	20	46	43	6	9	67	17	24	12	0	7	0	54	6	0.7	0.9	0.5	2.1
Craig Hodges (to Chi)	G	6'3	190	28	10	92	16	36	44	3	4	75	5	8	8	0	2	0	39	9	0.5	0.8	0.8	3.9
Kenny Gattison	F	6'8	252	24	2	9	0	1	0	1	2	50	1	0	2	0	0	0	1	5	0.5	0.0	1.0	0.5
Mark Davis (to Mil)	F-G	6'5	195	25	2	7	1	5	20	2	2	100	1	0	1	0	0	0	4	4	0.5	0.0	0.5	2.0
Winston Crite (NJ)	F	6'7	233	23	2	6	0	3	0	0	0	—	1	0	1	0	0	0	0	3	0.5	0.0	0.5	0.0

3-PT FG — Chambers 28-86, Hornacek 27-81, K.Johnson 2-22, E.Johnson 71-172, Corbin 0-2, Majerle 27-82, Perry 1-4, Nealy 0-2, Kerr 8-17, Hodges 4-12, Davis 0-1

e Name	Pos	Hgt	Wgt	Age	TOTAL G	Min	FG	FGA	%	FT	FTA	%	Reb	Ass	PF	DQ	Stls	Blkd Shts	Points	PER GAME Min	Reb	Ass	PF	Points
								1988/89 N.B.A. — WESTERN CONFERENCE PACIFIC DIVISION (continued)																
EATTLE SUPERSONICS	**47-35 .573**				**BERNIE BICKERSTAFF**																			
errick McKey	F-C	6'9	210	22	82	2804	487	970	50	301	375	80	464	219	264	4	105	70	1305	34	5.7	2.7	3.2	15.9
chael Cage	F	6'9	230	26	80	2536	314	630	50	197	265	74	765	126	184	1	92	52	825	32	9.6	1.6	2.3	10.3
on Lister	C	7'	240	30	82	1806	271	543	50	115	178	65	545	54	310	3	28	180	657	22	6.6	0.7	3.8	8.0
le Ellis	G-F	6'7	215	28	82	3190	857	1710	50	377	462	82	342	164	197	0	108	22	2253	39	4.2	2.0	2.4	27.5
ate McMillan	G	6'5	197	24	75	2341	199	485	41	119	189	63	388	696	236	3	156	42	532	31	5.2	9.3	3.1	7.1
vier McDaniel	F	6'7	205	25	82	2385	677	1385	49	312	426	73	433	134	231	0	84	40	1677	29	5.3	1.6	2.8	20.5
dale Threatt	G	6'2	177	27	63	1220	235	476	49	63	77	82	117	238	155	0	83	4	544	19	1.9	3.8	2.5	8.6
hn Lucas	G	6'3	185	35	74	842	119	299	40	54	77	70	79	260	53	0	60	1	310	11	1.1	3.5	0.7	4.2
den Polynice	C-F	6'11	242	24	80	835	91	180	51	51	86	59	206	21	164	0	37	30	233	10	2.6	0.3	2.1	2.9
ss Schoene	F-C	6'10	215	28	69	774	135	349	39	46	57	81	165	36	136	1	37	24	358	11	2.4	0.5	2.0	5.2
rry Reynolds	F	6'8	198	26	56	737	149	357	42	127	167	76	100	62	58	0	53	26	428	13	1.8	1.1	1.0	7.6
ery Johnson	G	5'10	175	23	43	291	29	83	35	9	16	56	24	73	34	0	21	3	68	7	0.6	1.7	0.8	1.6
eg Ballard	F	6'7	230	33	2	15	1	8	13	4	4	100	7	0	3	0	0	0	6	8	3.5	0.0	1.5	3.0
ke Champion	F	6'10	230	24	2	4	0	3	0	0	0	—	0	0	2	0	0	0	0	2	0.0	0.0	1.0	0.0
				3-PT FG —	McKey 30-89, Cage 0-4, Ellis 162-339, McMillan 15-70, McDaniel 11-36, Threatt 11-30, Lucas 18-68, Polynice 0-2, Schoene 42-110, Reynolds 3-15, Johnson 1-9, Ballard 0-1, Champion 0-1																			
OLDEN STATE WARRIORS	**43-39 .524**				**DON NELSON**																			
aris Mullin	F-G	6'7	215	25	82	3093	830	1630	51	493	553	89	483	415	178	1	176	39	2176	38	5.9	5.1	2.2	26.5
rry Smith	F-C	6'8	235	30	80	1897	219	397	55	18	58	31	652	118	248	2	61	54	456	24	8.2	1.5	3.1	5.7
alph Sampson (KJ)	C	7'4	230	28	61	1086	164	365	45	62	95	65	307	77	170	3	31	65	393	18	5.0	1.3	2.8	6.4
tch Richmond	G	6'5	215	23	79	2717	649	1386	47	410	506	81	468	334	223	5	82	13	1741	34	5.9	4.2	2.8	22.0
inston Garland	G	6'2	170	24	79	2661	466	1074	43	203	251	81	328	505	216	2	175	14	1145	34	4.2	6.4	2.7	14.5
od Higgins	G-F-C	6'7	205	26	81	1887	301	633	48	188	229	82	376	160	172	2	39	42	856	23	4.6	2.0	2.1	10.6
anute Bol	C	7'6	225	26	80	1769	127	344	37	40	66	61	462	27	226	2	11	**345**	314	22	5.8	0.3	2.8	3.9
is Smith	G	6'5	210	24	80	1597	311	715	43	174	218	80	330	140	165	1	88	40	803	20	4.1	1.8	2.1	10.0
rry Teagle	G	6'5	195	28	66	1569	409	859	48	182	225	81	263	96	173	2	79	17	1002	24	4.0	1.5	2.6	15.2
eve Alford (from Dal)	G	6'2	179	24	57	868	145	313	46	49	59	83	69	83	54	0	44	3	359	15	1.2	1.5	0.9	6.3
hn Starks	G	6'3	180	23	36	316	51	125	41	34	52	65	41	27	36	0	23	3	146	9	1.1	0.8	1.0	4.1
llis Frank (SJ)	F-C	6'10	240	23	32	245	34	91	37	39	51	76	61	15	59	1	14	6	107	8	1.9	0.5	1.8	3.3
en McDonald	F	6'8	225	26	11	103	13	19	68	9	15	60	12	5	11	0	4	0	35	9	1.1	0.5	1.0	3.2
rome Whitehead (to SA)	C-F	6'10	240	32	5	42	3	6	50	1	2	50	5	2	8	0	1	0	7	8	1.0	0.4	1.6	1.4
rlando Graham	F	6'8	240	23	7	22	3	10	30	2	4	50	11	0	6	0	0	0	8	3	1.6	0.0	0.9	1.1
hn Stroeder (from SA)	F	6'10	260	30	4	20	2	5	40	0	0	—	14	3	1	0	0	2	4	5	3.5	0.8	0.3	1.0
elton Jones (from SA, to Phi)	F	6'9	210	22	2	13	3	5	60	0	0	—	2	2	0	0	3	0	6	7	1.0	1.0	0.0	3.0
				3-PT FG —	Mullin 23-100, Sampson 3-8, Richmond 33-90, Garland 10-43, Higgins 66-168, Bol 20-91, O.Smith 7-37, Teagle 2-12, Alford 20-53, Starks 10-26, Frank 0-1																			
ORTLAND TRAIL BLAZERS	**39-43 .476**				**MIKE SCHULER (25-22 .532), RICK ADELMAN (14-21.400.)**																			
rome Kersay	F	6'7	222	26	76	2716	533	1137	47	258	372	69	629	243	277	6	137	84	1330	36	8.3	3.2	3.6	17.5
aldwell Jones	F-C	6'11	225	38	72	1279	77	183	42	48	61	79	300	59	166	0	24	85	202	18	4.2	0.8	2.3	2.8
evin Duckworth	C	7'	270	24	79	2662	554	1161	48	324	428	76	635	60	300	6	56	49	1432	34	8.0	0.8	3.8	18.1
yde Drexler	G-F	6'7	215	26	78	3064	829	1672	50	438	548	80	615	450	269	2	213	54	2123	39	7.9	5.8	3.4	27.2
erry Porter	G	6'3	195	25	81	3102	540	1146	47	272	324	84	367	770	187	1	146	8	1431	38	4.5	9.5	2.3	17.7
teve Johnson	C-F	6'10	240	31	72	1477	296	565	52	129	245	53	358	105	254	3	20	44	721	21	5.0	1.5	3.5	10.0
chard Anderson	F-C	6'10	240	28	72	1082	145	348	42	32	38	84	231	98	100	1	44	12	371	15	3.2	1.4	1.4	5.2
anny Young (BW)	G	6'4	175	26	48	952	115	252	46	50	64	78	74	123	50	0	55	3	297	20	1.5	2.6	1.0	6.2
drian Branch	F	6'7	190	26	67	811	202	436	46	87	120	73	132	60	99	0	45	3	498	12	2.0	0.9	1.5	7.4
ark Bryant	F	6'9	245	23	56	803	120	247	49	40	69	58	179	33	144	3	20	7	280	14	3.2	0.6	2.6	5.0
ki Vandeweghe (XJ, to NY)	F	6'8	220	30	18	432	103	217	47	29	33	88	35	34	40	0	7	4	251	24	1.9	1.9	2.2	13.9
am Bowie (FJ)	C	7'1	240	27	20	412	69	153	45	28	49	57	106	36	43	0	7	33	171	21	5.3	1.8	2.2	8.6
rry Sichting (FJ)	G	6'1	180	32	25	390	46	104	44	7	8	88	29	59	17	0	15	0	102	16	1.2	2.4	0.7	4.1
rook Steppe	G-F	6'5	195	28	27	244	33	78	42	32	37	86	32	16	32	0	11	1	103	9	1.2	0.6	1.2	3.8
linton Wheeler (from Mia)	G	6'1	185	29	20	211	21	45	47	7	10	70	19	33	17	0	19	0	49	11	1.0	1.7	0.9	2.5
raig Neal (to Mia)	G	6'5	180	24	21	159	11	25	44	1	2	50	11	32	24	0	9	0	25	8	0.5	1.5	1.1	1.2
olando Ferreira (KJ)	C	7'1	240	24	12	34	1	18	6	7	8	88	13	1	7	0	0	1	9	3	1.1	0.1	0.6	0.8
				3-PT FG —	Kersey 6-21, Jones 0-1, Duckworth 0-2, Drexler 27-104, Porter 79-219, Anderson 49-141, Young 17-50, Branch 7-31, Vandeweghe 16-38, Bowie 5-7, Sichting 3-12, Steppe 5-9, Wheeler 0-1, Neal 2-9																			
ACRAMENTO KINGS	**27-55 .329**		**235**		**JERRY REYNOLDS**																			
odney McCray	F	6'8	210	27	68	2435	340	729	47	169	234	72	514	293	121	0	57	36	854	36	7.6	4.3	1.8	12.6
arold Presley	F-G	6'8	253	25	80	2257	383	873	44	93	123	76	485	174	215	1	93	76	981	28	6.1	2.2	2.7	12.3
aSalle Thompson (to Ind)	C	6'10	185	27	43	1276	247	536	46	152	188	81	392	44	153	6	46	55	646	30	9.1	1.0	3.6	15.0
anny Ainge (from Bos)	G	6'4	170	29	28	1028	209	462	45	91	112	81	101	187	8	1	41	7	567	37	3.6	6.7	0.3	20.3
enny Smith	G	6'3		23	81	3145	547	1183	46	263	357	74	226	621	173	0	102	7	1403	39	2.8	7.7	2.1	17.3
m Peterson	F-C	6'10	235	26	66	1633	278	606	46	115	154	75	413	81	236	8	47	68	671	25	6.3	1.2	3.6	10.2
nny Del Negro	G	6'4	185	22	80	1556	239	503	48	85	100	85	171	206	160	2	65	14	569	19	2.1	2.6	2.0	7.1
cky Berry	F	6'8	207	24	64	1406	255	567	45	131	166	79	197	80	197	4	37	22	706	22	3.1	1.3	3.1	11.0
d Pinckney (to Bos)	F	6'9	215	25	51	1334	224	446	50	177	221	80	301	74	125	1	54	43	625	26	5.9	1.5	2.5	12.3
ayman Tisdale (from Ind)	F	6'9	240	24	31	1108	247	472	52	119	160	74	299	53	109	2	20	20	613	36	9.6	1.7	3.5	19.8
e Kleine (to Bos)	C	7'	271	26	47	913	116	303	38	81	88	92	241	35	126	2	18	18	313	19	5.1	0.7	2.7	6.7
erek Smith (to Phi)	F-G	6'6	218	27	29	600	111	276	40	64	95	67	81	60	64	1	19	8	289	21	2.8	2.1	2.2	10.0
rad Lohaus (from Bos)	C-F	7'	235	24	29	476	93	216	43	46	57	81	114	17	60	0	9	30	233	16	3.9	0.6	2.1	8.0
andy Wittman (to Ind)	G-F	6'6	210	29	31	416	50	117	43	16	22	73	26	32	12	0	10	0	118	13	0.8	1.0	0.4	3.8
en Gillery	C	7'	235	23	24	84	6	19	32	13	23	57	23	2	29	0	2	4	25	4	1.0	0.1	1.2	1.0
ichael Jackson (NJ)	G	6'2	180	24	14	70	9	24	38	1	2	50	4	11	12	0	3	0	21	5	0.3	0.8	0.9	1.5
andy Allen	F	6'8	220	23	7	43	8	19	42	1	2	50	7	0	7	0	1	1	17	6	1.0	0.0	1.0	2.4
Jawaan Oldham - injured				**3-PT FG —**	McCray 5-22, Pressley 119-295, Thompson 0-1, Ainge 58-150, K.Smith 46-128, Peterson 0-8, Del Negro 6-20, Berry 65-160, Pickney 0-6, Kleine 0-1, D.Smith 3-15, Lohaus 1-7, Wittman 2-4, Jackson 2-6, Allen 0-1																			

1988/89 N.B.A. — WESTERN CONFERENCE
PACIFIC DIVISION (continued)

LOS ANGELES CLIPPERS 21-61 .256 GENE SHUE (10-28 .263), DON CASEY (11-33 .250

Use Name	Pos	Hgt	Wgt	Age	G	Min	FG	FGA	%	FT	FTA	%	Reb	Ass	PF	DQ	Stls	Blkd Shts	Points	Min	Reb	Ass	PF	Points
					TOTAL															PER GAME				
Snake Norman	F	6'8	225	24	80	3020	638	1271	50	70	270	26	667	277	223	2	106	66	1450	38	8.3	3.5	2.8	18.
Charles Smith	F	6'10	230	23	71	2161	435	878	50	285	393	73	465	103	273	6	68	89	1155	30	6.5	1.5	3.8	16.
Benoit Benjamin	C	7'	255	24	79	2585	491	907	54	317	426	74	696	157	221	4	57	221	1299	33	8.8	2.0	2.8	16.
Quintin Dailey	G	6'3	200	27	69	1722	448	964	46	217	286	76	204	154	154	0	90	6	1114	25	3.0	2.2	2.2	16.
Gary Grant	G	6'3	195	23	71	1924	361	830	43	119	162	73	238	506	170	1	144	9	846	27	3.4	7.1	2.4	11.
Tom Garrick	G	6'2	195	22	71	1499	176	359	49	102	127	80	156	243	141	1	78	9	454	21	2.2	3.4	2.0	6.
Joe Wolf	F-C	6'11	230	24	66	1450	170	402	42	44	64	69	271	113	152	1	32	16	386	22	4.1	1.7	2.3	5.
Norm Nixon	G	6'2	175	33	53	1318	153	370	41	48	65	74	78	339	69	0	46	0	362	25	1.5	6.4	1.3	6.
Reggie Williams	F	6'7	195	24	63	1303	260	594	44	92	122	75	179	103	181	1	81	29	642	21	2.8	1.6	2.9	10.
Danny Manning (KJ)	F	6'10	230	22	26	950	177	358	49	79	103	77	171	81	89	1	44	25	434	37	6.6	3.1	3.4	16.
Greg Kite (to Char)	C	6'11	250	27	58	729	49	121	40	14	31	45	190	29	118	0	23	46	112	13	3.3	0.5	2.0	1.
Eric White (from Utah)	F	6'8	200	23	37	434	62	119	52	34	42	81	70	17	39	0	10	1	158	12	1.9	0.5	1.1	4.
Grant Gondrezick	G	6'5	205	25	27	244	38	95	40	26	40	65	36	34	36	0	13	1	105	9	1.3	1.3	1.3	3.
Kenny Bannister	F-C	6'9	235	28	9	130	22	36	61	30	53	57	33	3	17	0	7	2	74	14	3.7	0.3	1.9	8.
Kevin Williams (from NJ)	G	6'3	180	27	9	114	13	22	59	6	8	75	20	17	17	0	5	3	34	13	2.2	1.9	1.9	3.
Rob Lock	F	6'9	235	27	20	110	9	32	28	12	15	80	32	4	15	0	3	4	30	6	1.6	0.2	0.8	1.
Ennis Whatley	G	6'3	177	26	8	90	12	33	36	10	11	91	16	22	15	0	7	1	34	11	2.0	2.8	1.9	4.
David Popson (to Mia)	F-C	6'10	220	24	10	68	11	25	44	1	2	50	16	6	9	0	1	2	23	7	1.6	0.6	0.9	2.
Rob Rose	G	6'5	185	24	2	3	0	1	0	0	0	—	2	0	0	0	0	0	0	2	1.0	0.0	0.0	0.
Barry Sumpter	F-C	6'11	245	23	1	1	0	1	0	0	0	—	0	0	0	0	0	0	0	1	0.0	0.0	0.0	0.

3-PT FG — Norman 4-21, Smith 0-3, Benjamin 0-2, Dailey 1-9, Grant 5-22, Garrick 0-13, Wolf 2-14, Nixon 8-29, Williams 30-104, Manning 1-5, Gondrezick 3-11, Bannister 0-1

1988/89 N.B.A. — PLAYOFFS

DETROIT PISTONS CHUCK DALY

defeated Boston 3-0; H101-91, H102-95, 100-85
defeated Milwaukee 4-0; H85-80, H112-92, 110-90, 96-94
defeated Chicago 4-0; H88-94, H100-91, 97-99, 86-80, H94-85, 103-94
defeated L.A. Lakers 4-0; H109-97, H108-105, 114-110, 105-97

Use Name	Pos	Hgt	Wgt	Age	G	Min	FG	FGA	%	FT	FTA	%	Reb	Ass	PF	DQ	Stls	Blkd Shts	Points	Min	Reb	Ass	PF	Points
Mark Aguirre	F	6'6	232	29	17	462	89	182	49	28	38	74	75	28	38	0	8	3	214	27	4.4	1.6	2.2	12.
Rick Mahorn	F-C	6'10	255	30	17	360	40	69	58	17	26	65	87	7	59	1	9	13	97	21	5.1	0.4	3.5	5.
Bill Laimbeer	C	6'11	260	31	17	497	66	142	46	25	31	81	140	31	55	1	6	8	172	29	8.2	1.8	3.2	10.
Joe Dumars	G	6'3	190	25	17	620	106	233	45	87	101	86	44	96	31	0	12	1	300	36	2.6	5.6	1.8	17.
Isiah Thomas	G	6'1	185	27	17	633	115	279	41	71	96	74	73	141	39	0	27	4	309	37	4.3	8.3	2.3	18.
Dennis Rodman	F	6'8	210	27	17	409	37	70	53	24	35	69	**170**	16	58	0	6	12	98	24	10.0	0.9	3.4	5.
John Salley	F	7'	230	24	17	392	58	99	59	36	54	67	79	9	58	0	9	25	152	23	4.6	0.5	3.4	8.
Vinnie Johnson	G	6'2	200	32	17	372	91	200	46	47	62	76	45	43	32	0	4	3	239	22	2.6	2.5	1.9	14.
James Edwards	C	7'1	252	33	17	317	40	85	47	40	51	78	36	12	53	0	1	8	120	19	2.1	0.7	3.1	7.
John Long	G	6'5	200	32	4	8	1	1	100	3	3	100	0	0	0	0	0	0	5	2	0.0	0.0	0.0	1.
Michael Williams	G	6'2	175	22	4	6	0	0	—	2	2	100	2	2	1	0	1	0	2	2	0.5	0.5	0.3	0.
Fennis Dembo	F	6'5	215	22	2	4	1	1	100	0	0	—	0	0	1	0	0	0	2	2	0.0	0.0	0.5	1.

3-PT FG — Aguirre 8-29, Laimbeer 15-42, Dumars 1-12, Thomas 8-30, Rodman 0-4, Johnson 10-24, Edwards 0-1

LOS ANGELES LAKERS PAT RILEY

defeated Portland 3-0; H128-108, H113-105, 116-108
defeated Seattle 4-0; H113-102, H130-108, 91-86, 97-95
defeated Phoenix 4-0; H127-119, H101-95, 110-107, 122-117
lost to Detroit 0-4; 97-109, 105-108, H110-114, H97-105

Use Name	Pos	Hgt	Wgt	Age	G	Min	FG	FGA	%	FT	FTA	%	Reb	Ass	PF	DQ	Stls	Blkd Shts	Points	Min	Reb	Ass	PF	Points
James Worthy	F-G	6'9	225	27	15	600	153	270	57	63	80	79	101	42	36	0	18	16	372	40	6.7	2.8	2.4	24.
A.C. Green	F	6'9	224	25	15	502	47	114	41	58	76	76	137	18	37	1	16	6	152	33	9.1	1.2	2.5	10.
Kareem Abdul Jabbarr	C	7'2	267	41	15	351	68	147	46	31	43	72	59	19	43	0	5	11	167	23	3.9	1.3	2.9	11.
Byron Scott	G	6'3	193	27	11	402	79	160	49	46	55	84	45	25	31	0	18	2	219	37	4.1	2.3	2.8	19.
Magic Johnson	G	6'8	220	29	14	518	85	174	49	78	86	91	83	**165**	30	1	27	3	258	37	5.9	11.8	2.1	18.
Michael Cooper	G	6'5	176	32	15	414	37	89	42	20	24	83	40	71	38	0	9	8	115	28	2.7	4.7	2.5	7.
Mychal Thompson	F-C	6'10	235	33	15	377	65	128	51	41	60	68	77	11	52	1	6	12	171	25	5.1	0.7	3.5	11.
Olando Woolridge	F	6'9	215	29	15	276	39	75	52	44	62	71	70	17	35	0	2	15	122	18	4.7	1.1	2.3	8.
Tony Campbell	F	6'7	215	26	9	106	19	31	61	16	22	73	12	6	26	1	3	0	65	12	1.3	0.7	2.9	7.
David Rivers	G	6'	180	23	6	33	4	12	33	7	8	88	4	6	6	0	0	0	15	6	0.7	1.0	1.0	2.
Jeff Lamp	G	6'6	205	29	5	14	3	6	50	1	2	50	3	1	3	0	0	0	7	3	0.6	0.2	0.6	1.
Mark McNamara	C	6'11	235	29	3	7	1	2	50	1	2	50	1	0	0	0	0	0	3	2	0.3	0.0	0.0	1.

3-PT FG — Worthy 3-8, Green 0-3, Scott 15-39, Johnson 10-35, Cooper 21-55, Campbell 2-4, Rivers 0-2

CHICAGO BULLS DOUG COLLINS

defeated Cleveland 3-2; 95-88, 88-96, H101-94, H105-108(OT), 101-100
defeated New York 4-2; 120-109(OT), 97-114, H111-88, H106-93, 114-121, H113-111
lost to Detroit 2-4; 94-88, 91-100, H99-97, H80-86, 85-94, H94-103

Use Name	Pos	Hgt	Wgt	Age	G	Min	FG	FGA	%	FT	FTA	%	Reb	Ass	PF	DQ	Stls	Blkd Shts	Points	Min	Reb	Ass	PF	Points
Scottie Pippen	F	6'7	210	23	17	619	84	182	46	32	50	64	129	67	63	**2**	23	16	222	36	7.6	3.9	3.7	13.1
Horace Grant	F	6'10	215	23	17	625	72	139	52	40	50	80	167	35	68	**2**	11	16	184	37	9.8	2.1	4.0	10.8
Bill Cartwright	C	7'1	245	31	17	583	72	148	49	56	80	70	121	20	**70**	1	9	12	200	34	7.1	1.2	4.1	11.8
Craig Hodges	G	6'3	190	28	17	554	73	177	41	10	14	71	25	62	55	1	22	3	191	33	1.5	3.6	3.2	11.2
Michael Jordan	G-F	6'6	185	25	17	**718**	**199**	**390**	**51**	**183**	**229**	80	119	130	65	1	**42**	3	**591**	42	7.0	7.6	3.8	**34.8**
John Paxson	G	6'2	185	28	16	302	37	78	47	14	16	88	10	34	35	1	12	0	93	19	0.6	2.1	2.2	5.8
Dave Corzine	C	6'11	260	32	16	219	27	64	42	11	17	65	41	9	27	0	4	6	65	14	2.6	0.6	1.7	4.1
Charlie Davis	F	6'7	215	30	17	191	19	47	40	7	9	78	43	5	29	0	4	1	46	11	2.5	0.3	1.7	2.7
Brad Sellers	C	7'	210	26	13	177	22	58	38	10	12	83	31	15	21	0	3	4	54	14	2.4	1.2	1.6	4.2
Sam Vincent	G	6'2	185	25	16	113	10	33	30	9	12	75	8	19	9	0	3	1	29	7	0.5	1.2	0.6	1.8
Will Perdue	C	7'	240	23	3	22	6	9	67	2	3	67	6	2	4	0	0	0	14	7	2.0	0.7	1.3	4.7
Jack Haley	C-F	6'10	240	24	5	7	2	3	67	1	2	50	1	1	2	0	0	0	5	1	0.2	0.2	0.4	1.0

3-PT FG — Pippen 22-56, Hodges 35-88, Jordan 10-35, Paxson 5-19, Davis 1-6, Vincent 0-2, Perdue 0-1

1988/89 N.B.A. — PLAYOFFS

PHOENIX SUNS — **COTTON FITZSIMMONS**

defeated Denver 3-0; H104-103, H132-114, 130-121
defeated Golden State 4-1; H130-103, H122-127, 113-104, 135-99, H116-104
lost to L.A. Lakers 0-4; 119-127, 95-101, H107-110, H117-122

Use Name	Pos	Hgt	Wgt	Age	TOTAL G	Min	FG	FGA	%	FT	FTA	%	Reb	Ass	PF	DQ	Stls	Blkd Shts	Points	PER GAME Min	Reb	Ass	PF	Points
Mark West	F-C	6'10	246	28	12	227	32	50	64	10	14	71	53	6	36	1	7	19	74	19	4.4	0.5	3.0	6.2
Tyrone Corbin	F-G	6'6	222	26	12	310	45	86	52	19	25	76	85	26	37	0	24	4	109	26	7.1	2.2	3.1	9.1
Tom Chambers	C-F	6'10	230	29	12	495	118	257	46	67	78	86	131	46	44	0	13	15	312	41	10.9	3.8	3.7	26.0
Jeff Hornacek	G	6'4	190	25	12	374	74	149	50	21	25	84	69	62	34	0	16	3	169	31	5.8	5.2	2.8	14.1
Kevin Johnson	G	6'2	188	22	12	494	90	182	49	102	110	93	51	147	28	0	19	5	285	41	4.3	12.3	2.3	23.8
Eddie Johnson	F	6'8	215	29	12	392	85	206	41	30	39	77	87	25	41	1	12	2	213	33	7.3	2.1	3.4	17.8
Dan Majerle	F	6'6	220	23	12	352	63	144	44	38	48	79	57	14	28	0	13	4	172	29	4.8	1.2	2.3	14.3
Armon Gilliam	F	6'9	245	24	9	126	27	51	53	19	22	86	45	2	11	0	1	2	73	14	5.0	0.2	1.2	8.1
T.R. Dunn	G	6'4	195	33	8	79	3	7	43	1	2	50	15	1	11	0	5	0	7	10	1.9	0.1	1.4	0.9
Tim Perry	F	6'9	219	23	4	17	2	4	50	0	2	0	2	0	1	0	2	1	4	4	0.5	0.0	0.3	1.0
Andrew Lang	F-C	6'11	245	22	4	8	0	2	0	0	0	—	6	1	3	0	0	0	0	2	1.5	0.3	0.8	0.0
Ed Nealy	F	6'7	240	28	4	6	1	3	33	0	0	—	3	0	0	0	0	0	2	2	0.8	0.0	0.0	0.5

3-PT FG — Chambers 9-22, Hornacek 8-28, K.Johnson 3-10, E.Johnson 13-38, Majerle 8-28

NEW YORK KNICKERBOCKERS — **RICK PITINO**

defeated Phildelphia 3-0; H102-96, H107-106, 116-115(OT)
lost to Chicago 2-4; H109-120(OT), H114-97, 88-111, 93-106, H121-114, 111-113

Use Name	Pos	Hgt	Wgt	Age	TOTAL G	Min	FG	FGA	%	FT	FTA	%	Reb	Ass	PF	DQ	Stls	Blkd Shts	Points	PER GAME Min	Reb	Ass	PF	Points
Johnny Newman	F	6'7	190	25	9	258	50	107	47	38	49	78	25	17	27	1	8	1	145	29	2.8	1.9	3.0	16.1
Charles Oakley	F	6'8	225	25	9	299	35	73	48	16	24	67	101	11	31	1	12	1	87	33	11.2	1.2	3.4	9.7
Patrick Ewing	C	7'	240	26	9	340	70	144	49	39	52	75	90	20	35	0	9	18	179	38	10.0	2.2	3.9	19.9
Gerald Wilkins	G	6'6	190	25	9	290	63	131	48	18	23	78	33	42	27	1	12	3	145	32	3.7	4.7	3.0	16.1
Mark Jackson	G	6'3	205	23	9	336	51	100	51	19	28	68	31	91	9	0	10	3	132	37	3.4	10.1	1.0	14.7
Trent Tucker	G	6'5	193	29	9	159	27	58	47	2	4	50	19	4	20	0	10	2	71	18	2.1	0.4	2.2	7.9
Kiki Vandeweghe	F	6'8	220	30	9	159	25	49	51	20	21	95	11	7	10	0	3	2	73	18	1.2	0.8	1.1	8.1
Sidney Green	F	6'9	220	27	9	128	13	30	43	10	14	71	36	5	23	0	2	1	36	14	4.0	0.6	2.6	4.0
Rod Strickland	G	6'3	180	22	9	111	22	49	45	9	17	53	13	25	21	0	4	1	54	12	1.4	2.8	2.3	6.0
Kenny Walker	F	6'8	210	24	9	90	3	13	23	14	19	74	16	2	22	0	1	3	20	10	1.8	0.2	2.4	2.2
Eddie Lee Wilkins	F-C	6'10	220	26	7	26	5	11	45	5	10	50	11	0	3	0	0	0	15	4	1.6	0.0	0.4	2.1
Pete Meyers	F	6'6	180	25	4	14	0	0	—	4	6	67	3	1	2	0	0	1	4	4	0.8	0.3	0.5	1.0

3-PT FG — Newman 7-28, Oakley 1-2, G.Wilkins 1-10, Jackson 11-28, Tucker 15-32, Vandeweghe 3-8, Strickland 1-1

MILWAUKEE BUCKS — **DEL HARRIS**

defeated Atlanta 3-2; 92-100, 98-108, H117-113(OT), H106-113(OT), 96-92
lost to Detroit 0-4; 80-85, 92-112, H90-110, H94-96

Use Name	Pos	Hgt	Wgt	Age	TOTAL G	Min	FG	FGA	%	FT	FTA	%	Reb	Ass	PF	DQ	Stls	Blkd Shts	Points	PER GAME Min	Reb	Ass	PF	Points
Fred Roberts	F-C	6'10	220	28	9	345	49	100	49	34	40	85	29	20	29	1	5	4	132	38	3.2	2.2	3.2	14.7
Larry Krystkowiak	F	6'9	220	24	8	239	29	68	43	27	31	87	45	12	22	0	2	1	85	30	5.6	1.5	2.8	10.6
Jack Sikma	C	6'11	260	33	9	301	37	94	39	23	28	82	50	30	41	2	8	4	105	33	5.6	3.3	4.6	11.7
Jay Humphries	G	6'3	185	26	9	323	49	99	49	30	34	88	27	70	29	0	8	0	131	36	3.0	7.8	3.2	14.6
Sidney Moncrief	G	6'4	180	31	9	184	19	48	40	15	16	94	26	13	17	0	5	2	55	20	2.9	1.4	1.9	6.1
Ricky Pierce	F-G	6'5	222	29	9	292	77	141	55	41	47	87	25	25	31	1	11	2	201	32	2.8	2.8	3.4	22.3
Randy Breuer	C	7'3	263	28	9	162	17	32	53	5	13	38	40	5	17	0	2	6	39	18	4.4	0.6	1.9	4.3
Terry Cummings	F	6'9	235	27	5	124	25	69	36	14	16	88	33	7	16	0	3	0	64	25	6.6	1.4	3.2	12.8
Rickey Green	G	6'	172	34	8	110	12	29	41	4	4	100	13	18	9	0	5	0	29	14	1.6	2.3	1.1	3.6
Tony Brown	F	6'6	195	28	6	69	4	11	36	3	4	75	7	6	9	1	2	0	11	12	1.2	1.0	1.5	1.8
Paul Mokeski	C	7'	255	31	5	61	8	14	57	6	8	75	17	3	16	0	0	0	23	12	3.4	0.6	3.2	4.6

3-PT FG — Roberts 0-3, Krystkowiak 0-2, Sikma 8-28, Humphries 3-18, Moncrief 2-7,
Pierce 6-8, Cummings 0-1, Green 1-2, Brown 0-1, Mokeski 1-1

GOLDEN STATE WARRIORS — **DON NELSON**

defeated Utah 3-0; 123-119, 99-91, H120-106
lost to Phoenix 1-4; 103-130, 127-122, H104-113, H99-135, 104-116

Use Name	Pos	Hgt	Wgt	Age	TOTAL G	Min	FG	FGA	%	FT	FTA	%	Reb	Ass	PF	DQ	Stls	Blkd Shts	Points	PER GAME Min	Reb	Ass	PF	Points
Chris Muulin	F	6'7	215	25	8	341	88	163	54	58	67	87	47	36	19	0	14	11	235	43	5.9	4.5	2.4	29.4
Larry Smith	F-C	6'8	235	30	8	148	4	16	25	0	0	—	40	16	24	0	6	11	8	19	5.0	2.0	3.0	1.0
Rod Higgins	C-F	6'7	205	28	8	267	40	82	49	29	34	85	59	20	19	0	13	7	119	33	7.4	2.5	2.4	14.9
Mitch Richmond	G	6'5	215	23	8	314	62	135	46	34	38	89	58	35	25	0	14	1	161	39	7.3	4.4	3.1	20.1
Winston Garland	G	6'2	170	24	8	270	41	98	42	24	28	86	33	29	31	1	13	2	107	34	4.1	3.6	3.9	13.4
Terry Teagle	G	6'5	195	28	8	240	70	141	50	18	22	82	37	10	27	0	8	3	158	30	4.6	1.3	3.4	19.8
Manute Bol	C	7'6	225	26	8	148	7	36	19	2	7	29	31	1	21	0	2	**29**	18	19	3.9	0.1	2.6	2.3
Steve Alford	G	6'2	179	24	6	52	9	22	41	3	4	75	4	5	7	0	2	0	25	9	0.7	0.8	1.2	4.2
Otis Smith	G	6'5	210	24	4	49	9	24	38	1	2	50	13	6	5	0	2	1	19	12	3.3	1.5	1.3	4.8
Ralph Sampson	C	7'4	230	28	3	43	9	22	41	2	4	50	14	1	8	0	1	2	20	14	4.7	0.3	2.7	6.7
Ben McDonald	F	6'8	225	26	5	40	2	10	20	2	4	50	8	1	8	0	3	1	6	8	1.6	0.2	1.6	1.2
Orlando Graham	F	6'8	240	23	2	8	1	2	50	1	2	50	1	0	0	0	0	0	3	4	0.5	0.0	0.0	1.5

3-PT FG — Mullin 1-8, Higgins 10-35, Richmond 3-16, Garland 1-3, Teagle 0-2,
Bol 2-22, Alford 4-9, Sampson 0-4, McDonald 0-3

1988/89 N.B.A. — PLAYOFFS

SEATTLE SUPERSONICS — **BERNIE BICKERSTAFF** — defeated Houston 3-1; 111-107, H109-97, 107-126, 98-96; lost to L.A. Lakers 0-4; 102-113, 108-130, H86-91, H95-97

Use Name	Pos	Hgt	Wgt	Age	G	Min	FG	FGA	%	FT	FTA	%	Reb	Ass	PF	DQ	Stls	Blkd Shts	Points	Min	Reb	Ass	PF	Points
Derrick McKey	F	6'9	210	22	8	286	44	89	49	17	21	81	52	18	33	1	6	15	106	36	6.5	2.3	4.1	13.
Xavier McDaniel	F	6'7	205	25	8	281	58	144	40	31	41	76	67	22	30	0	2	5	150	35	8.4	2.8	3.8	18.
Alton Lister	C	7'	240	30	8	160	17	39	44	22	26	85	38	2	28	0	2	21	56	20	4.8	0.3	3.5	7.
Dale Ellis	G-F	6'7	215	28	8	304	72	160	45	24	33	73	32	10	19	1	11	1	183	38	4.0	1.3	2.4	22.
Nate McMillan	G	6'5	197	24	8	200	19	40	48	16	25	64	25	63	21	0	10	5	54	25	3.1	7.9	2.6	6.
Sedale Threatt	G	6'2	177	27	8	201	39	82	48	17	20	85	13	49	22	0	17	0	96	25	1.6	6.1	2.8	12.
Michael Cage	F	6'9	230	26	8	175	24	40	60	9	22	41	46	5	14	0	7	3	57	22	5.8	0.6	1.8	7.
Olden Polynice	C-F	6'11	242	24	8	162	25	41	61	7	13	54	62	1	32	1	6	4	57	20	7.8	0.1	4.0	7.
Russ Schoene	F-C	6'10	215	28	3	43	4	17	24	5	6	83	5	2	7	0	2	0	13	14	1.7	0.7	2.3	4.
Jerry Reynolds	F	6'8	198	26	4	40	7	22	32	7	10	70	5	1	6	0	2	6	22	10	1.3	0.3	1.5	5.
John Lucas	G	6'3	185	35	4	37	5	17	29	1	2	50	1	8	5	0	0	0	11	9	0.3	2.0	1.3	2.
Avery Johnson	G	5'10	175	23	6	31	5	12	42	1	2	50	4	5	1	0	4	0	11	5	0.7	0.8	0.2	1.

3-PT FG — McKey 1-9, McDaniel 3-9, Ellis 15-37, McMillan 0-2, Threatt 1-4, Cage 0-1, Schoene 0-7, Reynolds 1-4, Lucas 0-3, Johnson 0-4

ATLANTA HAWKS — **MIKE FRATELLO** — lost to Milwaukee 2-3; H100-92, H98-108, 113-117(OT), 113-106(OT), H92-96

Use Name	Pos	Hgt	Wgt	Age	G	Min	FG	FGA	%	FT	FTA	%	Reb	Ass	PF	DQ	Stls	Blkd Shts	Points	Min	Reb	Ass	PF	Points
Dominique Wilkins	F-G	6'8	200	28	5	212	52	116	45	27	38	71	27	17	5	0	4	8	136	42	5.4	3.4	1.0	27.
Jon Koncak	F-C	7'	260	25	5	192	18	29	62	28	33	85	48	4	23	1	2	8	64	38	9.6	0.8	4.6	12.8
Moses Malone	C	6'10	255	33	5	197	32	64	50	40	51	78	60	9	5	0	7	4	105	39	12.0	1.8	1.0	21.
Reggie Theus	G	6'7	213	31	5	127	14	38	37	9	12	75	7	24	18	1	1	0	37	25	1.4	4.8	3.6	7.4
Glenn Rivers	G	6'4	185	27	5	191	22	57	39	17	24	71	24	34	22	2	7	2	67	38	4.8	6.8	4.4	13.4
John Battle	G	6'2	175	26	5	118	20	46	43	9	12	75	13	16	13	0	2	0	49	24	2.6	3.2	2.6	9.8
Antoine Carr	F	6'9	235	27	5	81	13	21	62	8	11	73	8	7	13	0	0	4	34	16	1.6	1.4	2.6	6.8
Cliff Levingston	F	6'8	220	27	5	77	3	11	27	9	10	90	17	2	15	0	0	3	16	15	3.4	0.4	3.0	3.2
Spud Webb	G	5'7	135	25	5	55	3	11	27	2	2	100	4	15	6	0	4	0	8	11	0.8	3.0	1.2	1.6

3-PT FG — Wilkins 5-17, Malone 1-1, Theus 9-12, Rivers 6-19, Battle 0-6, Levingston 1-1

CLEVELAND CAVALIERS — **LENNY WILKENS** — lost to Chicago 2-3; H88-95, H96-88, 94-101, 108-105(OT), H100-101

Use Name	Pos	Hgt	Wgt	Age	G	Min	FG	FGA	%	FT	FTA	%	Reb	Ass	PF	DQ	Stls	Blkd Shts	Points	Min	Reb	Ass	PF	Points
Mike Sanders	F	6'6	210	28	5	87	15	30	50	3	5	60	16	4	11	0	2	1	33	17	3.2	0.8	2.2	6.6
Larry Nance	F	6'10	215	29	5	195	38	69	55	21	32	66	39	16	12	0	3	12	97	39	7.8	3.2	2.4	19.4
Brad Daugherty	C	7'	245	23	5	167	17	47	36	21	35	60	46	12	18	0	6	5	55	33	9.2	2.4	3.6	11.0
Ron Harper	G	6'6	205	24	5	189	39	69	57	20	26	77	21	20	20	1	11	4	98	38	4.2	4.0	4.0	19.6
Mark Price	G	6'1	175	24	4	158	22	57	39	14	15	93	13	22	3	0	3	1	48	40	3.3	5.5	0.8	12.0
John Williams	F-C	6'11	230	27	5	161	21	45	47	13	18	72	34	10	12	0	2	7	55	32	6.8	2.0	2.4	11.0
Craig Ehlo	G-F	6'7	185	27	4	97	17	39	44	9	11	82	6	13	10	0	3	1	48	24	1.5	3.3	2.5	12.0
Darnell Valentine	G	6'2	183	29	5	80	7	20	35	7	8	88	7	16	7	0	5	0	21	16	1.4	3.2	1.4	4.2
Tree Rollins	C	7'1	240	33	5	74	6	8	75	3	5	60	16	1	10	0	3	7	15	15	3.2	0.2	2.0	3.0
Randolph Keys	F	6'9	195	22	1	12	0	3	0	0	0	—	3	1	1	0	0	0	0	12	3.0	1.0	1.0	0.0
Chris Dudley	C	6'11	235	23	1	4	0	1	0	0	0	—	0	0	1	0	0	0	0	4	0.0	0.0	1.0	0.0
Phil Hubbard	F	6'8	215	32	1	1	0	0	—	0	0	—	0	0	0	0	0	0	0	1	0.0	0.0	0.0	0.0

3-PT FG — Daugherty 0-1, Harper 0-2, Price 6-16, Ehlo 5-13, Keys 0-1

HOUSTON ROCKETS — **DON CHANEY** — lost to Seattle 1-3; 107-111, 97-109, H126-107, H96-98

Use Name	Pos	Hgt	Wgt	Age	G	Min	FG	FGA	%	FT	FTA	%	Reb	Ass	PF	DQ	Stls	Blkd Shts	Points	Min	Reb	Ass	PF	Points
Buck Johnson	F	6'7	190	24	4	118	19	40	48	8	14	57	15	13	15	0	3	2	46	30	3.8	3.3	3.8	11.5
Otis Thorpe	F	6'11	236	26	4	152	24	37	65	16	21	76	20	12	17	1	5	1	64	38	5.0	3.0	4.3	16.0
Akeem Olajuwon	C	7'	250	25	4	162	42	81	52	17	25	68	52	12	17	0	10	11	101	41	13.0	3.0	4.3	25.3
Eric Floyd	G	6'3	175	28	4	160	22	46	48	10	14	71	18	26	10	0	8	1	62	40	4.5	6.5	2.5	15.5
Mike Woodson	G	6'5	198	30	4	137	17	49	35	10	12	83	9	18	7	0	4	2	47	34	2.3	4.5	1.8	11.8
Walter Berry	F	6'8	215	24	4	57	13	26	50	7	8	88	9	5	8	0	2	1	33	14	2.3	1.3	2.0	8.3
Tim McCormick	C	7'	240	26	4	53	7	13	54	8	9	89	13	0	9	0	3	2	22	13	3.3	0.0	2.3	5.5
Derrick Chievous	F	6'7	195	21	4	40	5	17	29	8	10	80	6	2	7	0	1	1	18	10	1.5	0.5	1.8	4.5
Purvis Short	F-G	6'7	215	31	4	37	8	21	38	3	5	60	9	1	7	0	0	0	19	9	2.3	0.3	1.8	4.8
Frank Johnson	G	6'2	185	30	4	36	2	6	33	6	10	60	5	7	3	0	1	0	10	9	1.3	1.8	0.8	2.5
Allen Leavell	G	6'1	190	31	2	5	1	3	33	2	2	100	0	1	0	0	0	0	4	3	0.0	0.5	0.0	2.0
Chuck Nevitt	C	7'5	237	29	2	3	0	0	—	0	0	—	1	0	0	0	0	0	0	2	0.5	0.0	0.0	0.0

3-PT FG — B.Johnson 0-1, Floyd 8-15, Woodson 3-19, McCormick 0-1, Short 0-2, F.Johnson 0-1

Use Name	Pos	Hgt	Wgt	Age	G	Min	FG	FGA	%	FT	FTA	%	Reb	Ass	PF	DQ	Stls	Blkd Shts	Points	Min	Reb	Ass	PF	Points
					TOTAL															PER GAME				

1988/89 N.B.A. — PLAYOFFS

Use Name	Pos	Hgt	Wgt	Age	G	Min	FG	FGA	%	FT	FTA	%	Reb	Ass	PF	DQ	Stls	Blkd Shts	Points	Min	Reb	Ass	PF	Points
BOSTON CELTICS	**JIMMY RODGERS**				lost to Detroit 0-3; 91-101, 95-102, H85-100																			
Reggie Lewis	F	6'7	195	23	3	125	26	55	47	9	13	69	21	11	11	0	5	0	61	42	7.0	3.7	3.7	20.3
Kevin McHale	F	6'10	225	31	3	115	20	41	49	17	23	74	24	9	13	0	1	2	57	38	8.0	3.0	4.3	19.0
Robert Parish	C	7'	230	35	3	112	20	44	45	7	9	78	26	6	5	0	4	2	47	37	8.7	2.0	1.7	15.7
Brian Shaw	G	6'6	190	22	3	124	22	43	51	7	9	78	17	19	11	0	3	0	51	41	5.7	6.3	3.7	17.0
Dennis Johnson	G	6'4	200	34	3	59	4	15	27	0	0	—	4	9	8	0	3	0	8	20	1.3	3.0	2.7	2.7
Joe Kleine	C	7'	271	26	3	65	6	11	55	7	9	78	17	2	9	0	0	1	19	22	5.7	0.7	3.0	6.3
Ed Pinckney	F	6'9	215	25	3	45	3	12	25	2	2	100	5	1	7	0	1	1	8	15	1.7	0.3	2.3	2.7
Kevin Gamble	G	6'5	215	23	1	29	4	11	36	0	2	0	1	2	1	0	1	0	8	29	1.0	2.0	1.0	8.0
Kelvin Upshaw	G	6'2	180	26	3	24	5	12	42	0	0	—	2	5	4	0	1	0	10	8	0.7	1.7	1.3	3.3
Otis Birdsong	G	6'4	195	33	3	20	1	5	20	0	0	—	2	1	3	0	1	1	2	7	0.7	0.3	1.0	0.7
Mark Acres	F	6'11	220	26	2	2	0	1	0	0	0	—	1	0	0	0	0	0	0	1	0.5	0.0	0.0	0.0
	3-PT FG —				Lewis 0-2, Shaw 0-1, Kleine 0-1, Gamble 0-1, Birdsong 0-2, Acres 0-1																			
DENVER NUGGETS	**DOUG MOE**				lost to Phoenix 0-3; 103-104, 114-132, H121-130																			
Alex English	F	6'8	190	34	3	108	32	62	52	14	16	88	13	11	6	0	1	0	78	36	4.3	3.7	2.0	26.0
Bill Hanzlik	F-G	6'7	200	31	3	106	14	33	42	7	12	58	20	9	13	0	5	1	38	35	6.7	3.0	4.3	12.7
Wayne Cooper	C-F	6'10	220	32	3	44	6	12	50	0	0	—	13	2	10	0	1	2	12	15	4.3	0.7	3.3	4.0
Darwin Cook	G	6'3	195	30	3	66	12	24	50	6	6	100	13	11	12	0	3	0	31	22	4.3	3.7	4.0	10.3
Michael Adams	G	5'11	165	25	2	75	15	36	42	7	8	88	17	9	6	0	3	0	47	38	8.5	4.5	3.0	23.5
Walter Davis	G	6'6	200	34	3	94	31	60	52	15	15	100	5	4	11	0	3	0	77	31	1.7	1.3	3.7	25.7
Elston Turner	G	6'5	200	29	3	74	6	13	46	2	6	33	11	3	9	0	1	0	14	25	3.7	1.0	3.0	4.7
Fat Lever	G	6'3	175	28	2	58	9	24	38	2	2	100	13	19	4	0	4	0	22	29	6.5	9.5	2.0	11.0
Dan Schayes	C	6'11	260	29	2	36	1	7	14	6	8	75	11	1	4	0	1	1	8	18	5.5	0.5	2.0	4.0
Dave Greenwoo	F	6'9	225	31	3	34	2	6	33	1	2	50	11	1	7	0	1	1	5	11	3.7	0.3	2.3	1.7
Jerome Lane	F	6'8	230	22	2	21	2	7	29	2	2	100	6	2	4	0	0	0	6	11	3.0	1.0	2.0	3.0
Blair Rasmussen	C	7'	260	26	2	4	0	0	—	0	0	—	0	0	1	0	0	0	0	2	0.0	0.0	0.5	0.0
	3-PT FG —				Hanzlik 3-5, Cook 1-2, Adams 10-22, Davis 0-4, Turner 0-1, Lever 2-3, Lane 0-1																			
PHILADELPHIA 76ers	**JIM LYNAM**				lost to New York 0-3; 96-102, 106-107, H115-116(OT)																			
Charles Barkley	F	6'6	263	25	3	135	29	45	64	22	31	71	35	16	9	0	5	2	81	45	11.7	5.3	3.0	27.0
Ron Anderson	F	6'7	215	30	3	109	29	51	57	4	5	80	16	13	10	0	1	2	62	36	5.3	4.3	3.3	20.7
Mike Gminski	C	6'11	260	29	3	118	19	48	40	11	16	69	23	2	8	0	0	8	49	39	7.7	0.7	2.7	16.3
Hersey Hawkins	G	6'3	190	23	3	72	3	24	13	2	2	100	5	4	6	0	3	1	8	24	1.7	1.3	2.0	2.7
Maurice Cheeks	G	6'1	180	32	3	128	21	41	51	11	13	85	11	39	4	0	7	1	53	43	3.7	13.0	1.3	17.7
Gerald Henderson	G	6'2	180	32	3	69	10	25	40	2	6	33	7	5	10	0	2	0	24	23	2.3	1.7	3.3	8.0
Derek Smith	F	6'6	218	27	3	48	9	14	64	1	2	50	7	3	9	0	1	0	19	16	2.3	1.0	3.0	6.3
Ben Coleman	F	6'9	235	27	3	23	6	8	75	2	2	100	5	0	8	0	1	0	14	8	1.7	0.0	2.7	4.7
Chris Welp	C	7'	245	24	3	22	1	3	33	0	2	0	7	0	7	0	0	0	2	7	2.3	0.0	2.3	0.7
Scott Brooks	G	5'11	165	23	3	21	1	6	17	2	2	100	4	5	4	0	0	0	5	7	1.3	1.7	1.3	1.7
	3-PT FG —				Barkley 1-5, Anderson 0-1, Hawkins 0-5, Cheeks 0-1, Henderson 2-7, Brooks 1-2																			
PORTLAND TRAIL BLAZERS	**RICK ADELMAN**				lost to L.A. Lakers 0-3; 108-128, 105-113, H108-116																			
Jerome Kersey	F	6'7	222	26	3	117	23	47	49	15	19	79	24	7	12	0	10	1	61	39	8.0	2.3	4.0	20.3
Sam Bowie	F-C	7'1	240	27	3	67	12	28	43	6	8	75	20	3	8	0	0	7	31	22	6.7	1.0	2.7	10.3
Kevin Duckworth	C-F	7'	270	24	3	83	14	35	40	6	11	55	17	2	17	2	1	1	34	28	5.7	0.7	5.7	11.3
Clyde Drexler	G-F	6'7	215	26	3	128	35	71	49	13	17	76	20	25	11	0	6	2	83	43	6.7	8.3	3.7	27.7
Terry Porter	G	6'3	195	25	3	124	26	52	50	10	12	83	16	25	8	0	1	1	66	41	5.3	8.3	2.7	22.0
Danny Young	G	6'4	175	26	3	66	12	26	46	1	2	50	8	12	2	0	1	0	28	22	2.7	4.0	0.7	9.3
Caldwell Jones	F	6'11	225	38	3	50	2	3	67	0	0	—	8	0	6	0	0	3	4	17	2.7	0.0	2.0	1.3
Richard Anderson	F	6'10	240	28	3	35	2	6	33	0	0	—	3	4	2	0	0	1	5	12	1.0	1.3	0.7	1.7
Steve Johnson	C	6'10	240	31	3	34	2	8	25	3	3	100	6	0	7	0	2	0	7	11	2.0	0.0	2.3	2.3
Jerry Sichting	G	6'1	180	22	1	11	0	3	0	0	0	—	1	1	1	0	0	0	0	11	1.0	1.0	1.0	0.0
Adrian Branch	F	6'7	190	26	1	5	0	3	0	2	2	100	1	2	0	0	0	0	2	5	1.0	2.0	0.0	2.0
	3-PT FG —				Kersey 0-2, Bowie 1-2, Drexler 0-2, Porter 4-11, Young 3-8, Anderson 1-4																			
UTAH JAZZ	**JERRY SLOAN**				lost to Golden State 0-3; H119-123, H91-99, 106-120																			
Thurl Bailey	F	6'11	232	27	3	122	12	34	35	12	15	80	25	3	11	0	1	4	36	41	8.3	1.0	3.7	12.0
Karl Malone	F	6'9	254	25	3	136	33	66	50	26	32	81	49	4	16	1	3	1	92	45	16.3	1.3	5.3	30.7
Mark Eaton	C	7'4	290	31	3	99	8	17	47	9	11	82	33	1	6	0	1	2	25	33	11.0	0.3	2.0	8.3
Bob Hansen	G	6'6	195	27	3	123	11	35	31	8	10	80	17	4	15	0	1	2	33	41	5.7	1.3	5.0	11.0
John Stockton	G	6'1	175	26	3	139	30	95	32	19	21	90	10	41	15	0	11	5	82	46	3.3	13.7	5.0	27.3
Darrell Griffith	G	6'4	190	30	3	71	20	49	41	0	0	—	12	0	7	0	4	1	46	24	4.0	0.0	2.3	15.3
Mike Brown	F	6'9	240	25	2	11	0	2	0	0	0	—	2	0	3	0	0	0	0	6	1.0	0.0	1.5	0.0
Eric Leckner	F-C	6'11	265	22	3	10	1	4	25	0	0	—	2	0	2	0	0	0	2	3	0.7	0.0	0.7	0.7
Jim Les	G	5'11	175	26	3	5	0	0	—	0	0	—	0	1	2	0	0	0	0	2	0.0	0.3	0.7	0.0
Jim Farmer	G	6'4	190	24	2	3	0	2	0	0	0	—	0	0	0	0	0	0	0	2	0.0	0.0	0.0	0.0
Mark Iavaroni	F	6'10	225	32	1	1	0	0	—	0	0	—	0	0	1	0	0	0	0	1	0.0	0.0	1.0	0.0
	3-PT FG —				Hansen 3-9, Stockton 3-4, Griffith 6-19, Farmer 0-1, Iavaroni 0-1																			

Team		G	FG	FGA	%	FT	FTA	%	REBOUNDS Offense	Defense	Total	Assists	PF	Steals	Blocked Shots	Turn Overs	Points	Points per ga
TEAM STATISTICS EASTERN CONFERENCE — ATLANTIC DIVISION																		
New York	Off.	82	3701	7611	49	1779	2366	75	1322	2265	3587	2083	2053	900	446	1572	9567	11
	Def.	82	3636	7358	49	1834	2390	77	1213	2326	3539	2292	1898	915	545	**1728**	9249	11
	Diff.		+65	+253	—	-55	-24	-2	+109	-61	+48	-209	-155	-15	-99	+156	+318	+
Philadelphia	Off.	82	3500	7201	49	1970	2504	79	1143	2356	3499	2110	1721	689	354	**1214**	9174	11
	Def.	82	3658	7296	50	1565	2023	77	1149	2412	3561	2281	1984	640	445	1269	9051	11
	Diff.		-158	-95	-1	+405	+481	+2	-6	-56	-62	-171	+263	+49	-91	+55	+123	+
Boston	Off.	82	3520	7143	49	1840	2349	78	1179	2442	3621	2189	1876	639	418	1336	8958	10
	Def.	82	3475	7183	48	1780	2294	78	1048	2222	3270	2124	1950	752	387	1191	8863	10
	Diff.		+45	-40	+1	+60	+55	—	+131	+220	+351	+65	+74	-113	+31	-145	+95	+1
Washington	Off.	82	3519	7591	46	1789	2318	77	1254	2354	3608	2048	2054	694	325	1291	8879	108
	Def.	82	3486	7235	48	1929	2510	77	1132	2538	3670	2082	1921	655	523	1381	9056	110
	Diff.		+33	+356	-2	-140	-192	—	+122	-184	-62	-34	-133	+39	-198	+90	-177	-2
New Jersey	Off.	82	3333	7226	46	1653	2260	73	1204	2419	3623	1793	1966	773	431	1449	8506	103
	Def.	82	3560	7162	50	1749	2286	77	1030	2476	3506	2134	1834	744	485	1376	9027	110
	Diff.		-227	+64	-4	-96	-26	-4	+174	-57	+117	-341	-132	+29	-54	-73	-521	-6
Charlotte	Off.	82	3426	7430	46	1580	2060	77	1138	2200	3338	**2323**	2068	705	264	1318	8566	104
	Def.	82	3555	7113	50	2040	2629	78	1191	2621	3812	2061	1791	710	441	1425	9265	113
	Diff.		-129	+317	-4	-460	-569	-1	-53	-421	-474	+262	-277	-5	-177	+107	-699	-8
CENTRAL DIVISION																		
Detroit	Off.	82	3395	6879	49	1830	2379	77	1154	2546	3700	2027	1939	522	406	1336	8740	106
	Def.	82	3140	7022	45	1826	2325	79	1131	2188	3319	1855	2088	646	341	1225	8264	100
	Diff.		+255	-143	+4	+4	+54	-2	+23	+358	+381	+172	+149	-124	+65	-111	+476	+5
Cleveland	Off.	82	3466	6904	50	1821	2438	75	1033	2475	3508	2260	**1592**	791	586	1323	8923	108
	Def.	82	3385	7346	46	1358	1748	78	1214	2283	3497	2043	1970	685	363	1429	8300	101
	Diff.		+81	-442	+4	+463	+690	-3	-181	+192	+11	+217	+378	+106	+223	+106	+623	+7
Atlanta	Off.	82	3412	7230	47	**2168**	2709	80	1372	2316	3688	1990	1860	817	474	1310	9102	111
	Def.	82	3363	7124	47	1826	2329	78	1261	2325	3586	2037	**2109**	687	348	1487	8699	106
	Diff.		+49	+106		+342	+380	+2	+111	-9	+102	-47	+249	+130	+126	+177	+403	+4
Milwuakee	Off.	82	3399	7167	47	1955	2382	**82**	1133	2272	3405	2071	1953	821	323	1305	8932	108
	Def.	82	3301	6901	48	1838	2369	78	1094	2335	3429	2109	1935	707	425	1522	8636	105
	Diff.		+98	+266	-1	+117	+13	+4	+39	-63	-24	-38	-18	+114	-102	+217	+296	+3
Chicago	Off.	82	3448	6968	49	1656	2106	79	1018	2453	3471	2213	1855	722	376	1327	8726	106
	Def.	82	3361	7098	47	1693	2190	77	1078	2300	3378	2099	1781	686	348	1255	8608	105
	Diff.		+87	-130	+2	-37	-84	+2	-60	+153	+93	+114	-74	+36	+28	-72	+118	+1
Indiana	Off.	82	3385	6945	49	1795	2275	79	1065	2497	3562	2012	2105	563	418	1547	8767	106
	Def.	82	3453	7400	47	2036	2606	78	1288	2312	3600	2034	2029	836	389	1206	9109	111
	Diff.		-68	-455	+2	-241	-331	+1	-223	+185	-38	-22	-76	-273	+29	-341	-342	-4
WESTERN CONFERENCE - - MIDWEST DIVISION																		
Utah	Off.	82	3182	6595	48	2110	2742	77	1050	2607	3657	2108	1894	720	583	1532	8588	104
	Def.	82	3113	7170	43	1765	2342	75	1220	2233	3453	1812	2086	779	505	1329	8179	**99**
	Diff.		+69	-575	+5	+345	+400	+2	-170	+374	+204	+296	+192	-59	+78	-203	+409	+5
Houston	Off.	82	3412	7196	47	1909	2527	76	1211	2554	3765	2016	2026	789	501	1569	8897	108.
	Def.	82	3413	7290	47	1806	2372	76	1145	2428	3573	2015	2013	800	439	1455	8819	107
	Diff.		-1	-94		+103	+155	—	+66	+126	+192	+1	-13	-11	+62	-114	+78	+1
Denver	Off.	82	**3813**	**8140**	47	1821	2314	79	1206	2513	3719	2282	2088	811	436	1225	9675	118
	Def.	82	3701	7484	49	1977	2683	74	1136	2864	4000	2136	2001	665	485	1597	9536	116
	Diff.		+112	+656	-2	-156	-369	+5	+70	-351	-281	+146	-87	+146	-49	+372	+139	+1.
Dallas	Off.	82	3244	6917	47	1785	2263	79	1048	2397	3445	1867	1739	579	476	1233	8484	103.
	Def.	82	3422	7304	47	1573	2090	75	1231	2500	3731	2133	1869	660	386	1175	8583	104.
	Diff.		-178	-387	—	+212	+173	+4	-183	-103	-286	-266	+130	-81	+90	-58	-99	-1.
San Antonio	Off.	82	3469	7409	47	1651	2367	70	1295	2181	3476	2037	2153	**961**	423	1712	8652	105.
	Def.	82	3486	7148	49	2105	2714	78	1256	2462	3718	2062	1938	915	545	**1728**	9249	112
	Diff.		-17	+261	-2	-454	-347	-8	+39	-281	-242	-25	-215	+46	-122	+16	-597	-7.
Miami	Off.	82	3221	7116	45	1477	2103	70	1309	2211	3520	1958	2124	744	408	1728	8016	97
	Def.	82	3384	6928	49	2021	2613	77	1188	2366	3554	2062	1830	926	553	1543	8937	109.
	Diff.		-163	+188	-4	-544	-510	-7	+121	-155	-34	-104	-294	-182	-145	-185	-921	-11.
PACIFIC DIVISION																		
L. A. Lakers	Off.	82	3584	7143	50	2011	2508	80	1094	2612	3706	2282	1672	724	421	1344	9406	114.
	Def.	82	3541	7540	47	1542	2051	75	1178	2222	3400	2157	1941	752	432	1263	8818	107.
	Diff.		+43	-397	+3	+469	+457	+5	-84	+390	+306	+125	+269	-28	-11	-81	+588	+7.
Phoenix	Off.	82	3754	7545	50	2051	2594	79	1095	**2619**	3714	2280	1933	693	416	1279	**9727**	**118.**
	Def.	82	3589	7736	46	1737	2308	75	1252	2458	3710	2166	2057	625	427	1368	9096	110.
	Diff.		+165	-191	+4	+314	+286	+4	-157	+161	+4	+114	+124	+68	-11	+89	+631	+7.

TEAM STATISTICS
WESTERN CONFERENCE - PACIFIC DIVISION (continued)

eam		G	FG	FGA	%	FT	FTA	%	REBOUNDS Offense	Defense	Total	Assists	PF	Steals	Blocked Shots	Turn Overs	Points	Points per game
eattle	Off.	82	3564	7478	48	1775	2379	75	1397	2238	3635	2083	2027	864	494	1403	9196	112.1
	Def.	82	3437	7067	49	1915	2489	77	1188	2252	3440	1958	1881	670	413	1553	8958	109.2
	Diff.		+127	+411	-1	-140	-110	-2	+209	-14	+195	+125	-146	+194	+81	+150	+238	+2.9
olden State	Off.	82	3730	7977	47	1904	2384	80	1323	2561	3884	2009	1946	831	643	1488	9558	116.6
	Def.	82	3693	8000	46	1916	2501	77	1437	2639	4076	2215	1935	861	485	1554	9583	116.9
	Diff.		+37	-23	+1	-12	-117	+3	-114	-78	-192	-206	-11	-30	+158	+66	-25	-.3
ortland	Off.	82	3695	7795	47	1789	2416	74	1384	2381	3765	2212	2026	828	388	1435	9395	114.6
	Def.	82	3572	7322	49	1933	2504	77	1151	2391	3542	2073	1960	738	358	1569	9275	113.1
	Diff.		+123	+473	-2	-144	-88	-3	+233	-10	+223	+139	-66	+90	+30	+134	+120	+1.5
acramento	Off.	82	3362	7351	46	1620	2104	77	1141	2454	3595	1970	1877	624	409	1370	8651	105.5
	Def.	82	3589	7420	48	1747	2301	76	1171	2604	3775	2107	1821	759	442	1284	9106	111.0
	Diff.		-227	-69	-2	-127	-197	+1	-30	-150	-180	-137	-56	-135	-33	-86	-455	-5.5
. A. Clippers	Off.	82	3526	7428	47	1606	2220	72	1156	2384	3540	2208	1937	815	530	1666	8712	106.2
	Def.	82	3747	7738	48	1834	2400	76	1342	2550	3892	2384	1882	933	551	1440	9525	116.2
	Diff.		-221	-310	-1	-228	-180	-4	-186	-166	-352	-176	-55	-118	-21	-226	-813	-10.0

PLAYOFFS

eam		G	FG	FGA	%	FT	FTA	%	REBOUNDS Offense	Defense	Total	Assists	PF	Steals	Blocked Shots	Turn Overs	Points	Points per game
etroit	Off.	17	644	1361	47	380	499	76	235	516	751	385	425	83	77	205	1710	100.6
	Def.	17	583	1300	45	368	491	75	178	462	640	357	431	97	60	215	1579	92.9
	Diff.		+61	+61	+2	+12	+8	+1	+57	+54	+111	+28	+6	-14	+17	+10	+131	+7.7
.A. Lakers	Off.	15	600	1208	50	406	520	78	188	444	632	381	337	104	73	220	1657	110.5
	Def.	15	627	1333	47	298	393	76	227	392	619	379	396	103	79	201	1586	105.7
	Diff.		-27	-125	+3	+108	+127	+2	-39	+52	+13	+2	+59	+1	-6	-19	+71	+4.8
hicago	Off.	17	623	1328	47	375	494	76	208	493	701	399	448	133	72	271	1694	99.6
	Def.	17	625	1376	45	385	531	73	252	467	719	402	411	129	75	255	1690	99.4
	Diff.		-2	-48	+2	-10	-37	+3	-44	+26	-18	-3	-37	+4	-3	-16	+4	+.2
hoenix	Off.	12	540	1141	47	307	365	84	203	401	604	330	274	112	55	190	1420	118.3
	Def.	12	517	1108	47	259	317	82	151	377	528	281	298	102	68	191	1335	111.3
	Diff.		+23	+33	—	+48	+48	+2	+52	+24	+76	+49	+24	+10	-13	+1	+85	+7.0
ew York	Off.	9	364	765	48	194	267	73	137	252	389	235	230	71	36	145	961	106.8
	Def.	9	369	742	50	209	273	77	110	259	369	247	226	73	39	143	978	108.7
	Diff.		-5	+23	-2	-15	-6	-4	+27	-7	+20	-12	-4	-2	-3	-2	-17	-1.9
ilwaukee	Off.	9	326	705	46	202	241	84	96	226	322	209	236	51	19	101	875	97.2
	Def.	9	328	702	47	235	305	77	132	262	394	227	210	37	49	113	919	102.1
	Diff.		-2	+3	-1	-33	-64	+7	-36	-36	-72	-18	-26	+14	-30	+12	-44	-4.9
olden State	Off.	8	342	751	46	174	212	82	113	232	345	160	194	78	68	116	879	109.9
	Def.	8	353	770	46	198	236	84	165	268	433	195	189	68	43	143	932	116.5
	Diff.		-11	-19	—	-24	-24	-2	-52	-36	-88	-35	-5	+10	+25	+27	-53	-6.6
eattle	Off.	8	319	703	45	157	221	71	139	211	350	186	218	69	60	126	816	102.0
	Def.	8	310	648	48	221	285	78	108	220	328	195	176	65	38	126	857	107.1
	Diff.		+9	+55	-3	-64	-64	-7	+31	-9	+22	-9	-42	+4	+22	—	-41	-5.1
tlanta	Off.	5	177	393	45	149	193	77	76	132	208	128	120	27	29	66	516	103.2
	Def.	5	192	402	48	122	139	88	57	126	183	127	145	30	11	65	519	103.8
	Diff.		-15	-9	-3	+27	+54	-11	+19	+6	+25	+1	+25	-3	+18	-1	-3	-.6
leveland	Off.	5	182	388	47	111	155	72	63	139	202	115	105	38	37	78	486	97.2
	Def.	5	188	414	45	92	124	74	67	149	216	121	133	46	18	75	490	98.0
	Diff.		-6	-26	+2	+19	+31	-2	-4	-10	-14	-6	+28	-8	+19	-3	-4	-.8
ouston	Off.	4	160	339	47	95	130	73	51	106	157	97	100	37	21	66	426	106.5
	Def.	4	163	345	47	90	119	76	62	116	178	98	105	35	35	66	425	106.3
	Diff.		-3	-6	—	+5	+11	-3	-11	-10	-21	-1	+5	+2	-14	—	+1	+.2
oston	Off.	3	111	250	44	49	67	73	29	91	120	65	72	20	7	42	271	90.3
	Def.	3	121	251	48	53	67	79	34	94	128	68	71	20	21	33	303	101.0
	Diff.		-10	-1	-4	-4	—	-6	-5	-3	-8	-3	-1	—	-14	-9	-32	-10.7
enver	Off.	3	130	284	46	62	77	81	36	97	133	72	87	23	5	50	338	112.7
	Def.	3	126	264	48	105	126	83	40	118	158	76	69	33	10	48	366	122.0
	Diff.		+4	+20	-2	-43	-49	-2	-4	-21	-25	-4	-18	-10	-5	-2	-28	-9.3
Philadelphia	Off.	3	128	265	48	57	81	70	32	88	120	87	75	20	14	37	317	105.7
	Def.	3	126	261	48	64	86	74	47	101	148	69	73	17	13	47	325	108.3
	Diff.		+2	+4	—	-7	-5	-4	-15	-13	-28	+18	-2	+3	+1	+10	-8	-2.6
Portland	Off.	3	128	282	45	56	74	76	53	71	124	81	74	21	16	40	321	107.0
	Def.	3	129	248	52	81	110	74	43	93	136	71	69	22	11	49	357	119.0
	Diff.		-1	+34	-7	-25	-36	+2	+10	-22	-12	+10	-5	-1	+5	+9	-36	-12.0
Utah	Off.	3	115	269	43	74	89	83	54	96	150	54	78	21	15	56	316	105.3
	Def.	3	132	268	49	68	83	82	39	91	130	71	71	31	34	39	342	114.0
	Diff.		-17	+1	-6	+6	+6	+1	+15	+5	+20	-17	-7	-10	-19	-17	-26	-8.7

Team	W	L	Pct.	GB	Record against playoff teams W	L	Pct.	Record against non-playoff teams W	L	Pct.	HOME W	L	Pct.	ROAD W	L	Pct.
EASTERN CONFERENCE																
ATLANTIC DIVISION																
New York Knickerbockers	52	30	.634	—	27	22	.551	25	8	.758	25	6	.806	17	24	.415
Philadelphia 76ers	46	36	.561	6	22	28	.440	24	8	.750	30	11	.732	16	25	.390
Boston Celtics	42	40	.512	10	18	31	.367	24	9	.727	32	9	.780	10	31	.244
Washington Bullets	40	42	.488	12	19	37	.339	21	5	.808	30	11	.732	10	31	.244
New Jersey Nets	26	56	.317	26	13	43	.232	13	13	.500	17	24	.415	9	32	.220
Charlotte Hornets	20	62	.244	32	11	47	.190	9	15	.375	12	**29**	.293	8	33	.195
CENTRAL DIVISION																
Detroit Pistons	**63**	19	**.768**	—	**36**	17	**.679**	**27**	2	**.931**	**37**	4	**.902**	**26**	15	.634
Cleveland Cavaliers	57	25	.695	6	33	21	.611	24	4	.857	**37**	4	**.902**	20	21	.488
Atlanta Hawks	52	30	.634	11	29	23	.558	23	7	.767	33	8	.805	19	22	.463
Milwaukee Bucks	49	33	.598	14	24	28	.462	25	5	.833	31	10	.756	18	23	.439
Chicago Bulls	47	35	.573	16	25	28	.472	22	7	.759	30	11	.732	17	24	.415
Indiana Pacers	28	54	.341	35	18	42	.300	10	12	.455	20	21	.488	8	33	.195
WESTERN CONFERENCE																
MIDWEST DIVISION																
Utah Jazz	51	31	.622	—	27	21	.563	24	10	.706	34	7	.829	17	24	.415
Houston Rockets	45	37	.549	6	20	28	.417	25	9	.735	31	10	.756	14	27	.341
Denver Nuggets	44	38	.537	7	23	25	.479	21	13	.618	35	6	.854	9	32	.220
Dallas Mavericks	38	44	.463	13	17	37	.315	21	7	.750	24	17	.585	14	27	.341
San Antonio Spurs	21	61	.256	30	11	43	.204	10	18	.357	18	23	.439	3	**38**	.073
Miami Heat	15	**67**	.183	36	6	**48**	.111	9	**19**	.321	12	29	.293	3	**38**	.073
PACIFIC DIVISION																
Los Angeles Lakers	57	25	.695	—	30	20	.600	**27**	5	.844	35	6	.854	22	19	.537
Phoenix Suns	55	27	.671	2	29	21	.580	26	6	.813	35	6	.854	20	21	.488
Seattle Supersonics	47	35	.573	10	25	26	.490	22	9	.710	31	10	.756	16	25	.390
Golden State Warriors	43	39	.524	14	20	31	.392	23	8	.742	29	12	.707	14	27	.341
Portland Trail Blazers	39	43	.476	18	16	34	.320	23	9	.719	25	13	.658	11	30	.268
Sacramento Kings	27	55	.329	30	14	43	.246	13	12	.520	21	20	.512	6	35	.146
Los Angeles Clippers	21	61	.256	36	12	45	.211	9	16	.360	17	24	.415	4	37	.098

1988/89 N.B.A. INDIVIDUAL LEADERS

SCORING
(Minimum 70 Games or 1400 Points)

Name	Team	G	FG	FT	Pts.	Avg.
Jordan	Chi	81	966	674	2633	32.5
Malone	Utah	80	809	703	2326	29.1
Ellis	Sea	82	857	377	2253	27.5
Drexler	Port	78	829	438	2123	27.2
Mullin	G.S.	82	830	493	2176	26.5
English	Den	82	924	325	2175	26.5
Wilkins	Atl	80	814	442	2099	26.2
Barkley	Phi	79	700	602	2037	25.8
Chambers	Phoe	81	774	509	2087	25.8
Olajuwon	Hou	82	790	454	2034	24.8

FIELD GOAL PERCENTAGE
(Minimum 300 Made)

Name	Team	FG	FGA	Pct.
Rodman	Det	316	531	.595
Barkley	Phi	700	1208	.579
Parish	Bos	596	1045	.570
Ewing	NY	727	1282	.567
Worthy	LAL	702	1282	.548
McHale	Bos	661	1211	.546
Thorpe	Hou	521	961	.542
Benjamin	LAC	491	907	.541
Nance	Cle	496	920	.539
Stockton	Utah	497	923	.538

FREE THROW PERCENTAGE
(Minimum 125 Made)

Name	Team	FT	FTA	Pct.
Johnson	LAL	513	563	.911
Sikma	Mil	266	294	.905
Skiles	Ind	130	144	.903
Price	Cle	263	292	.901
Mullin	GS	493	553	.892
K. Johnson	Phoe	508	576	.882
Kleine	Sac-Bos	134	152	.882
Davis	Den	175	199	.879
Gminski	Phi	297	341	.871
Malone	Was	296	340	.871

PERSONAL FOULS

Name	Team	PF
Long	Mia	337
Olajuwon	Hou	329
Schayes	Den	320
Ewing	NY	311
Lister	Sea	310
Smits	Ind	310

GAMES DISQUALIFIED

Name	Team	Disq.
Smits	Ind	14
Long	Mia	12
Person	Ind	12
Thompson	Sac-Ind	12
Brickowski	SA	10
Olajuwon	Hou	10

TOTAL REBOUNDS PER GAME
(Minimum 70 Games or 800 Rebounds)

Name	Team	G	Reb.	Avg.
Olajuwon	Hou	82	1105	13.5
Barkley	Phi	79	986	12.5
Parish	Bos	80	996	12.5
Malone	Atl	81	956	11.8
Malone	Utah	80	853	10.7
Oakley	NY	82	861	10.5
Eaton	Utah	82	843	10.3
Thorpe	Hou	82	787	9.6
Laimbeer	Det	81	776	9.6
Cage	Sea	80	765	9.6

ASSISTS PER GAME
(Minimum 70 Games or 400 Assists)

Name	Team	G	Ass.	Avg.
Stockton	Utah	82	1118	13.6
Johnson	LAL	77	988	12.8
K.Johnson	Phoe	81	991	12.2
Porter	Port	81	770	9.5
McMillan	Sea	75	696	9.3
Floyd	Hou	82	709	8.6
Jackson	NY	72	619	8.6
Price	Cle	75	631	8.4
Thomas	Det	80	663	8.3
Jordan	Chi	81	650	8.0

MINUTES PLAYED

Name	Team	Min.
Jordan	Chi	3255
Ellis	Sea	3190
Johnson	Phoe	3179
Stockton	Utah	3171
K.Smith	LAC	3145

BLOCKED SHOTS PER GAME
(Minimum 70 Games of 100 Blocked Shots)

Name	Team	G	Reb.	Avg.
Bol	GS	80	345	4.3
Eaton	Utah	82	315	3.8
Ewing	NY	80	281	3.5
Olajuwon	Hou	82	282	3.4
Nance	Cle	73	206	2.8
Benjamin	LAC	79	221	2.8
Cooper	Den	79	211	2.7
West	Phoe	82	187	2.3
Lister	Sea	82	180	2.2
Smits	Ind	82	151	1.8

3 POINT FIELD GOALS PER GAME
(Minimum 25 Made)

Name	Team	FG	FGA	Avg.
Sundvold	Mia	48	92	.522
Ellis	Sea	162	339	.478
Price	Cle	93	211	.441
Hawkins	Phi	71	166	.428
Hodges	Chi	75	180	.417
E.Johnson	Phoe	71	172	.413
Berry	Sac	65	160	.406
Pressley	Sac	119	295	.403
Miller	Ind	98	244	.402
Scott	LAL	77	193	.399

STEALS PER GAME
(Minimum 70 Games or 125 Steals)

Name	Team	G	Steals	Avg.
Stockton	Utah	82	263	3.2
Robertson	SA	65	197	3.0
Jordan	Chi	81	234	2.9
Lever	Den	71	195	2.7
Drexler	Port	78	213	2.7
Olajuwon	Hou	82	213	2.6
Rivers	Atl	76	181	2.4
Harper	Cle	82	185	2.3
Garland	GS	79	175	2.2
Conner	NJ	82	181	2.2

1989-90 N.B.A.
IMPORTS AND EXPORTS

Brian Shaw and Danny Ferry (Cleveland's number one draft choice) opted to play this season in Italy rather than the N.B.A. However, the N.B.A. picked up five foreigners from Europe and most did quite well:

Vlade Divac - Yugoslavia - L.A. Lakers
Sarunas Marciulionis - USSR - Golden State
Zarko Paspalj - Yugoslavia - San Antonio
Drazen Petrovic - Yugoslavia - Portland
Alexander Volkov - USSR - Atlanta

More than seventy ex-N.B.A. or C.B.A. players were on rosters in the Italian League with another thirty on rosters in the Spanish League.

For the second year in a row expansion became a part of the N.B.A. with the addition of the Minnesota Timberwolves and the Orlando Magic teams bringing the N.B.A. up to 27 teams. The Timberwolves outdid the Magic with 22 wins to 18 wins.

Record-setting attendance was attained by the N.B.A. with 17,368,659 fans going through the turnstyles. The top club was the Timberwolves with over a million and averaging 26,160 for their home games. Last year's expansion team, the Charlotte Hornets were second averaging 23,901 fans per game. The Hornets have now sold out their last 71 games.

On the court the biggest gain was by the San Antonio Spurs, who enjoyed a 35-game improvement in the win column, the best turn-around in N.B.A. history. The big additions to the Spurs were starting rookies David Robinson and Sean Elliott. Also new to the Spurs were Terry Cummings, Caldwell Jones, David Wingate and the return of Johnny Moore.

In the Atlantic Division, Charles Barkley led the Philadelphia 76ers to the crown just edging out the Celtics by one game. The addition of Rick Mahorn and Hersey Hawkins helped to offset the loss of guard Maurice Cheeks.

Boston, with a healthy Larry Bird, felt the loss of Brian Shaw. Reggie Lewis and the arrival of John Bagley took up the slack. Kevin McHale had an excellent year as the sixth man, but at times the Celtics showed their age.

The Knicks had a new young coach in Stu Jackson and a great year from Patrick Ewing, who broke the team scoring record. Injuries shelved Kiki Vandeweghe again and took their toll on Charles Oakley who had one of his best years. The Knicks were on top or second in the division until March when they lost 12 of 16. The late addition of Maurice Cheeks, from San Antonio, helped pull the team together.

Washington, Miami and New Jersey were also-rans in the Atlantic Division. The Bullets missed the playoff for only the fourth time in 21 seasons. The Heat in their second year overtook the Nets, who had the worst record in the N.B.A. Miami only gained three wins in their second season. The Nets used 19 players during the season and had an eleven game losing steak in March.

There was no question of who would lead the Central Division, as the Pistons ran off a 13-game winning streak in the middle of the season. The loss of Mahorn was eased with the play of James Edwards and Dennis Rodman. The Pistons are on the verge of a dynasty with strong play at every position with a still fairly young team.

The Bulls tried to make it a close race but just couldn't stay with the Pistons. For the fourth successive year Michael Jordan led the league in scoring average—his fourth year in-a-row with over a 30 ppg average. On March 28th Jordan scored 69 points and had a career high 18 rebounds vs the Cavaliers. The Bulls came up with a couple of good rookies in Stacey King and B.J. Armstrong.

The rest of the Central Divison, except for Orlando, was challenging for third place with the Bucks, the Cavs and the Pacers all making the playoffs and the Hawks just missing. The Bucks were led by the best sixth man in the league, Ricky Pierce but were hurt by a bad knee injury to starting forward Larry Krystkowiak. The Bucks again activated assistant coach Dave Dunleavy, who after the season was named head coach of the L.A. Lakers. Jack Sikma reached a milestone going over 10,000 in rebounds. The Cavaliers fell 15 games in the win column, while the Pacers increased by 14 games from the previous season. Orlando played to 99.9 percent of capacity in their maiden season.

The Spurs increased unbelievably and were able to just eke out a division lead of one game over the Jazz in the Midwest Division, led by Rookie of the Year David Robinson. Utah was again led by Karl Malone, second to Jordan with a 31.0 ppg average and John Stockton who set an all-time N.B.A. record with 1,134 assists. The Jazz' 55 wins was only the second time in the franchise history they've won over 50 games. Stockton became the first ever N.B.A. player to record three successive 1,000 assist seasons.

The Midwest Division was deep as the next three teams all made the playoffs playing over .500 ball. Dallas, under new coach Richie Adubato, was led by guards Rolando, Blackman and Derek Harper and were hurt by a lengthy suspension to Roy Tarpley. Denver was again led by Fat Lever and Alex English as the team averaged 114.6 points per game but the defense was certainly questionable allowing 113.2 points per game. Akeem Olajuwon led the league in rebounds and blocked shots, the first player since 1977, and averaged 24.3 points per game. Olajuwon became only the third player in N.B.A. history to record a quadruple double against the Bucks on March 29. He scored 18 points, had 16 rebounds, 11 blocked shots and 10 assists. The Rockets seem a couple of players away from being a top team. The expansion Timberwolves edged out the Hornets.

If the Lakers missed Kareem Abdul-Jabbar it certainly didn't show in the standings as they had the best record in the N.B.A. They won their ninth straight division crown and qualified for the playoffs for the fourteenth consecutive year. The Lakers played an overtime game in December against Detroit and became only the second team in N.B.A. history to go scoreless in the overtime. Pat Riley became the fastest coach to reach the 500 win level.

The Portland Trailblazers increased 20 games in the win column. The big acquisition was Buck Williams who came in an off-season trade for Sam Bowie. He led the six new players on the club. The other four starters all had good years.

Phoenix, coached by Cotton Fitzsimmons, was led by Tom Chambers who on March 24 set a club record with 60 points in a win over Seattle. The Suns broke a league record on April 9 vs the Jazz when they made 61 of 80 free throws. The Suns were hit hard by the injury bug but Kurt Rambis, picked up in a trade from Charlotte, helped as an experienced starter.

The rest of the division teams finished out of the money. The Supersonics played with injury after injury, especially to top scorer Dale Ellis. The Warriors were led by Chris Mullin who became the first player in team history to play in two consecutive All-Star Games. Coach Don Nelson reached a milestone with 600 wins. The Warriors became the first team since the 1973-74 Buffalo Braves to lead the league in scoring with a rookie point guard. The Clippers and the Kings were both again mired in the basement. The Clippers won 30 games for the first time since the 1985/86 season. Purvis Ellison, the number one draft pick by Sacramento, missed 2 1/2 months to a foot injury.

The All-N.B.A. team:

F Barkley, Malone
C Ewing
G M. Johnson, Jordan

When the playoffs began it was predicted by most of the experts to be a Lakers vs Piston final. Unfortunately, the Lakers lost in the second round to the Phoenix Suns, who had defeated the Lakers only once during the season. In the first round Indiana, Denver, Dallas, Milwaukee, Houston, Utah, Cleveland and Boston were eliminated. The Celtics set a playoff record defeating the Knicks in game 2, 157-128 to take a 2 games to 0 lead but lost the next three. Cleveland and Houston also went five games before going down.

In the second round Detroit defeated New York, 4 games to 1, holding the Knicks under 92 points per game. The Trailblazers needed seven games to just beat out the Spurs in an overtime game as the home team won each game. The Bulls took the 76ers in five games.

The Conference finals pitted Detroit against Chicago and Portland against Phoenix. The Pistons needed seven games to gain their third consecutive trip to the Championship finals. A low scoring series resulted with the Pistons averaging 96 points and the Bulls only 93 points. The home team won each game with Jordan scoring 47 and 42 points respectively in games 3 and 4. The Portland-Phoenix series went six games with the home team winning the first five games but Portland won game 6 in Phoenix 112-109.

Detroit became only the sixth team to repeat as N.B.A. champions: Minneapolis 1949-50, Minneapolis 1952-54, Boston 1959-66, Boston 1968-1969, and Los Angeles 1987-88. The Series lasted only five games with Detroit only losing a game 2 overtime contest. When the series resumed in Portland, Detroit won all three road games to gain their second consecutive championship.

After the season, a federal judge ordered Brian Shaw to play only for the Celtics to honor a contract he signed. But Shaw who was refused permission to play in Italy stated, he would not play for the Celtics. Michael Cooper also signed to play in Italy after being released by the Lakers. N.B.A. players will be allowed to play in the 1992 Olympics. Will more moves be forthcoming?

1989-90 N.B.A. -- EASTERN CONFERENCE
ATLANTIC DIVISION

PHILADELPHIA 76ERS 53-29 .646 JIM LYMAN

	Pos	Hgt	Wgt	Age	G	Min	FG	FGA	%	FT	FTA	%	Reb	Ass	PF	DQ	Stls	Blkd Shts	Points	Min	Reb	Ass	PF	Points
					TOTAL															PER GAME				
Charles Barkley	F	6'6	253	26	79	3085	706	1177	60	557	744	75	909	307	250	2	148	50	1989	39	11.5	3.9	3.2	25.2
Rick Mahorn	F-C	6'10	255	31	75	2271	313	630	50	183	256	71	568	98	251	2	44	103	811	30	7.6	1.3	3.3	10.8
Mike Gminski	C	6'11	260	30	81	2659	458	1002	46	193	235	82	687	128	136	0	43	102	1112	33	8.5	1.6	1.7	13.7
Hersey Hawkins	G	6'3	190	24	82	2856	522	1136	46	387	436	89	304	261	217	2	130	28	1515	35	3.7	3.2	2.6	18.5
Johnny Dawkins	G	6'2	170	26	81	2865	465	950	49	210	244	86	247	601	159	1	121	9	1162	35	3.0	7.4	2.0	14.3
Ron Anderson	F	6'7	215	31	78	2089	379	841	45	165	197	84	295	143	143	0	72	13	926	27	3.8	1.8	1.8	11.9
Derek Smith	G-F	6'6	216	28	75	1405	261	514	51	130	186	70	172	109	198	2	35	20	668	19	2.3	1.5	2.6	8.9
Scott Brooks	G	5'11	165	24	72	975	119	276	43	50	57	88	64	207	105	0	47	0	319	14	0.9	2.9	1.5	4.4
Bob Thornton (BF)	F-C	6'10	225	27	56	592	48	112	43	26	51	51	133	17	105	1	20	12	123	11	2.4	0.3	1.9	2.2
Kurt Nimphius	C	6'10	225	31	38	314	38	91	42	14	30	47	61	6	45	0	4	18	90	8	1.6	0.2	1.2	2.4
Jay Vincent (to LAL)	F	6'7	220	30	17	259	45	105	43	33	37	89	36	8	23	0	10	2	124	15	2.1	0.5	1.4	7.3
Kenny Payne	F	6'8	215	23	35	216	47	108	44	16	18	89	26	10	37	0	7	6	114	6	0.7	0.3	1.1	3.3
Lanard Copeland	G	6'6	185	24	23	110	31	68	46	11	14	79	10	9	12	0	1	1	74	5	0.4	0.4	0.5	3.2
Corey Gaines	G	6'3	195	24	9	81	4	12	33	1	4	25	5	26	11	0	4	0	10	9	0.6	2.9	1.2	1.1
Dexter Shouse	G	6'2	200	26	3	18	1	2	50	0	0	—	0	2	2	0	1	1	0	6	0.0	0.7	0.7	0.0
Lewis Lloyd (to Hou)	G-F	6'6	225	30	2	10	0	4	0	0	0	—	0	0	3	0	0	0	2	5	0.0	0.0	1.5	1.0

3-PT FG - Barkley 20-92, Mahorn 2-9, Gminski 3-17, Hawkins 84-200, Dawkins 22-66, Anderson 3-21, Smith 16-36, Brooks 31-79, Thornton 1-3, Nimphius 0-1, Vincent 1-1, Payne 4-10, Copeland 1-5, Gaines 1-2, Shouse 0-1

BOSTON CELTICS 52-30 .634 JIMMY RODGERS

	Pos	Hgt	Wgt	Age	G	Min	FG	FGA	%	FT	FTA	%	Reb	Ass	PF	DQ	Stls	Blkd Shts	Points	Min	Reb	Ass	PF	Points
Larry Bird	F	6'9	220	33	75	2944	718	1517	47	319	343	93	712	562	173	2	106	61	1820	39	9.5	7.5	2.3	24.3
Ed Pinckney	F	6'9	215	26	77	1082	135	249	54	92	119	77	225	68	126	1	34	42	362	14	2.9	0.9	1.6	4.7
Robert Parish	C	7'	230	36	79	2396	505	871	58	233	312	75	796	103	189	2	38	69	1243	30	10.1	1.3	2.4	15.7
Reggie Lewis	G-F	6'7	195	24	79	2522	540	1089	50	256	317	81	347	225	216	2	88	63	1340	32	4.4	2.8	2.7	17.0
Dennis Johnson	G	6'4	200	35	75	2036	206	475	43	118	140	84	201	485	179	2	81	14	531	27	2.7	6.5	2.4	7.1
Kevin McHale	F-C	6'10	225	32	82	2722	648	1181	55	393	440	89	677	172	250	3	30	157	1720	33	8.3	2.1	3.0	20.9
Joe Kleine	C	7'	271	27	81	1365	176	367	48	83	100	83	355	46	170	0	15	27	435	17	4.4	0.6	2.1	5.4
Jim Paxson	G	6'6	210	32	72	1283	191	422	45	73	90	81	77	137	115	0	33	5	460	18	1.1	1.9	1.6	6.4
John Bagley (SJ)	G	6'	192	29	54	1095	100	218	46	29	39	74	89	296	77	0	40	4	230	20	1.6	5.5	1.4	4.3
Kevin Gamble	G-F	6'5	215	24	71	990	137	301	46	85	107	79	112	119	77	1	28	8	362	14	1.6	1.7	1.1	5.1
Michael Smith	F	6'10	225	24	65	620	136	286	48	53	64	83	100	79	51	0	9	54	327	10	1.5	1.2	0.8	5.0
Charles Smith	G	6'1	160	22	60	519	59	133	44	53	76	70	69	103	75	0	35	36	171	9	1.2	1.7	1.3	2.9
Kelvin Upshaw (To Dal, GS)	G	6'2	180	26	14	131	12	39	31	4	6	67	13	28	19	0	2	12	30	9	0.9	2.0	1.4	2.1

Brian Shaw - played in Italy

3-PT FG - Bird 60-195, Pinckney 0-1, Lewis 4-15, Johnson 1-24, McHale 23-69, Kleine 0-4, Paxson 5-20, Bagley 1-18, Gamble 3-18, M.Smith 2-28, C.Smith 0-7, Upshaw 2-5

NEW YORK KNICKERBOCKERS 45-37 .549 STU JACKSON

	Pos	Hgt	Wgt	Age	G	Min	FG	FGA	%	FT	FTA	%	Reb	Ass	PF	DQ	Stls	Blkd Shts	Points	Min	Reb	Ass	PF	Points
Johnny Newman	F-G	6'7	190	26	80	2277	374	786	48	239	399	60	191	180	254	3	95	22	1032	28	2.4	2.3	3.2	12.9
Charles Oakley (BH)	F	6'8	225	26	61	2196	336	641	52	217	285	76	727	146	220	3	64	16	889	36	11.9	2.4	3.6	14.6
Patrick Ewing	C	7'	240	27	82	3165	922	1673	55	502	648	77	893	182	325	7	78	327	2347	39	10.9	2.2	4.0	28.6
Gerald Wilkins	G-F	6'6	195	26	82	2609	472	1032	46	208	259	80	371	330	188	0	95	194	1191	32	4.5	4.0	2.3	14.5
Mark Jackson	G	6'3	206	24	82	2428	327	749	44	120	165	73	318	604	121	0	109	4	809	30	3.9	7.4	1.5	9.9
Trent Tucker	G	6'5	190	30	81	1725	253	606	42	66	86	77	174	173	159	0	74	8	667	21	2.1	2.1	2.0	8.2
Kenny Walker	F	6'8	210	25	68	1595	204	384	53	125	173	72	343	49	178	1	33	52	535	23	5.0	0.7	2.6	7.9
Rod Strickland (to SA)	G	6'3	175	23	51	1019	170	386	44	83	130	64	126	219	71	0	70	8	429	20	2.5	4.3	1.4	8.4
Eddie Lee Wilkins	C-F	6'10	220	27	71	972	141	310	45	89	147	61	265	16	152	1	18	18	371	14	3.7	0.2	2.1	5.2
Maurice Cheeks (from SA)	G	6'1	180	33	31	753	92	159	58	57	65	88	73	151	32	0	42	5	244	24	2.4	4.9	1.0	7.9
Kiki Vandeweghe (XJ)	F	6'8	220	31	22	563	102	231	44	44	48	92	53	41	28	0	15	3	258	26	2.4	1.9	1.3	11.7
Pete Myers (to NJ)	G-F	6'6	180	26	24	208	15	45	33	16	31	52	28	35	39	0	15	2	46	9	1.2	1.5	1.6	1.9
Brian Quinnett	F	6'8	235	28	31	193	19	58	33	2	3	67	28	11	27	0	3	4	40	6	0.9	0.4	0.9	1.3
Stuart Gray (from Char)	C	7'	245	26	19	94	4	17	24	7	8	88	14	2	26	0	3	2	15	5	0.7	0.1	1.4	0.8
Greg Butler (JJ)	C	6'11	240	23	13	33	3	12	25	0	2	0	9	1	8	0	0	0	6	3	0.7	0.1	0.6	0.5

3-PT FG - Newman 45-142, Oakley 0-3, Ewing 1-4, G.Wilkins 39-125, Jackson 35-131, Walker 2-5, Tucker 95-245, Strickland 6-21, E.Wilkins 0-2, Cheeks 3-7, Vandeweghe 10-19, Myers 0-1, Quinnett 0-2, Gray 0-3

WASHINGTON BULLETS 31-51 .378 WES UNSELD

	Pos	Hgt	Wgt	Age	G	Min	FG	FGA	%	FT	FTA	%	Reb	Ass	PF	DQ	Stls	Blkd Shts	Points	Min	Reb	Ass	PF	Points
Bernard King	F	6'7	205	33	82	2687	711	1459	49	412	513	80	404	376	230	1	51	7	1837	33	4.9	4.6	2.8	22.4
Harvey Grant	F	6'8	215	24	81	1846	284	601	47	93	137	68	342	131	194	1	52	43	664	23	4.2	1.6	2.4	8.2
John Williams (KJ)	C	6'9	235	23	18	632	130	274	47	65	84	77	136	84	33	0	21	9	327	35	7.6	4.7	1.8	18.2
Jeff Malone	G	6'4	205	28	75	2567	781	1592	49	257	293	88	206	243	116	1	48	6	1820	34	2.7	3.2	1.5	24.3
Darrell Walker	G	6'4	180	28	81	2883	316	696	45	138	201	69	714	652	220	1	139	30	772	36	8.8	8.0	2.7	9.5
Charles Jones	C	6'9	215	32	81	2240	94	185	51	68	105	65	504	139	296	10	50	197	256	28	6.2	1.7	3.7	3.2
Mark Alarie	F	6'8	225	26	82	1893	371	785	47	108	133	81	374	142	219	2	60	39	860	23	4.6	1.7	2.7	10.5
Ledell Eackles	G-F	6'5	220	23	78	1696	413	940	44	210	280	75	175	182	157	0	50	4	1055	22	2.2	2.3	2.0	13.5
Steve Colter	G	6'3	175	27	73	977	142	297	48	77	95	81	176	148	98	0	47	10	361	13	2.4	2.0	1.3	4.9
Melvin Turpin	C	6'11	265	29	59	818	110	209	53	56	71	79	221	27	135	0	15	47	276	14	3.7	0.5	2.3	4.7
Tom Hammonds	F	6'9	220	22	61	805	129	295	44	63	98	64	168	51	98	0	11	14	321	13	2.8	0.8	1.6	5.3
Doug Roth (JJ)	C	6'11	255	22	42	412	37	86	43	7	14	50	120	20	70	1	8	13	81	10	2.9	0.5	1.7	1.9
Ed Horton	F	6'8	230	22	45	374	80	162	49	42	69	61	108	19	63	1	9	5	202	8	2.4	0.4	1.4	4.5

3-PT FG - King 3-23, Grant 0-8, Malone 1-6, Walker 2-21, Alarie 10-49, Eakles 19-59, Colter 0-5, Turpin 0-2, Hammonds 0-1, Williams 2-18, Roth 0-1, Horton 0-4

					TOTAL													Blkd		PER GAME				
	Pos	Hgt	Wgt	Age	G	Min	FG	FGA	%	FT	FTA	%	Reb	Ass	PF	DQ	Stls	Shts	Points	Min	Reb	Ass	PF	Points

1989/90 N.B.A. - EASTERN CONFERENCE
ATLANTIC DIVISION (Continued)

	Pos	Hgt	Wgt	Age	G	Min	FG	FGA	%	FT	FTA	%	Reb	Ass	PF	DQ	Stls	Blkd Shts	Points	Min	Reb	Ass	PF	Points
MIAMI HEAT	18-64 .220	RON ROTHSTEIN																						
Glen Rice	F	6'7	215	22	77	2311	470	1071	44	91	124	73	352	138	198	1	67	27	1048	30	4.6	1.8	2.6	13.6
Billy Thompson	F	6'7	220	26	79	2142	375	727	52	115	185	62	551	166	237	1	54	89	867	27	7.0	2.1	3.0	11.0
Rony Seikaly	C	6'11	252	24	74	2409	486	968	50	256	431	59	766	78	258	8	78	124	1228	33	10.4	1.1	3.5	16.6
Kevin Edwards	G	6'3	195	24	78	2211	395	959	41	139	183	76	282	252	149	1	125	33	938	28	3.6	3.2	1.9	12.0
Sherman Douglas	G	6'	180	23	81	2470	463	938	49	224	326	69	206	619	187	0	145	10	1155	30	2.5	7.6	2.3	14.3
Grant Long	F	6'6	235	23	81	1856	257	532	48	172	241	71	402	96	300	11	91	38	686	23	5.0	1.2	3.7	8.5
Tellis Frank	C-F	6'10	240	24	77	1762	278	607	46	179	234	76	385	85	282	6	51	27	735	23	5.0	1.1	3.7	9.5
Rory Sparrow	G	6'2	175	31	82	1756	210	510	41	59	77	77	138	298	140	0	49	4	487	21	1.7	3.6	1.7	5.9
Terry Davis	F	6'9	225	22	63	884	122	262	47	54	87	62	229	25	171	2	25	28	298	14	3.6	0.4	2.7	4.7
Jan Sundvold	G	6'2	170	28	63	867	148	363	41	44	52	85	71	102	69	0	25	0	384	14	1.1	1.6	1.1	6.1
Scott Haffner (JJ)	G	6'3	190	23	43	559	88	217	41	17	25	68	51	80	53	0	13	2	196	13	1.2	1.9	1.2	4.6
Pat Cummings (JJ)	F-C	6'9	245	33	37	391	77	159	48	21	37	57	93	13	60	1	12	4	175	11	2.5	0.4	1.6	4.7
Jim Rowinski	F	6'9	250	28	14	112	14	32	44	22	26	85	29	5	19	0	1	2	50	8	2.1	0.4	1.4	3.6

3-PT FG - Thompson 2-4, Rice 17-69, Seikaly 0-1, Edwards 9-30, Douglas 5-31, Long 0-3, Sparrow 8-40, Davis 0-1, Sundvold 44-100, Haffner 3-21

	Pos	Hgt	Wgt	Age	G	Min	FG	FGA	%	FT	FTA	%	Reb	Ass	PF	DQ	Stls	Blkd Shts	Points	Min	Reb	Ass	PF	Points
NEW JERSEY NETS	17-65 .207	BILL FITCH																						
Chris Morris	F	6'8	210	23	80	2449	449	1065	42	228	316	72	422	143	219	1	130	79	1187	31	5.3	1.8	2.7	14.8
Roy Hinson (KJ)	F	6'9	215	28	25	793	145	286	51	86	99	87	172	22	87	0	14	27	376	32	6.9	0.9	3.5	15.0
Sam Bowie	C	7'1	240	28	68	2207	347	834	42	294	379	78	690	91	211	5	38	121	998	32	10.1	1.3	3.1	14.7
Dennis Hopson	G	6'5	205	24	79	2551	474	1093	43	271	342	79	279	151	183	1	100	51	1251	32	3.5	1.9	2.3	15.8
Lester Conner	G	6'4	185	30	82	2355	237	573	41	172	214	80	265	385	182	0	172	8	648	29	3.2	4.7	2.2	7.9
Purvis Short	F-G	6'7	220	30	82	2213	432	950	45	198	237	84	248	145	202	2	66	20	1072	27	3.0	1.8	2.5	13.1
Charles Shackelford	F	6'10	225	24	70	1557	247	535	46	79	115	69	479	56	183	1	40	35	573	22	6.8	0.8	2.6	8.2
Mookie Blaylock (BG)	G	6'	185	22	50	1267	212	571	37	63	81	78	140	210	110	0	82	14	505	25	2.8	4.2	2.2	10.1
Jack Haley (from Chi)	F-C	6'10	240	25	56	1026	129	327	39	78	118	66	282	22	163	1	18	11	336	18	5.0	0.4	2.9	6.0
Joe Barry Carroll (to Den)	C	7'	255	31	46	1002	159	405	39	85	107	79	250	43	122	4	19	56	403	22	5.4	0.9	2.7	8.8
Chris Dudley (from Cle)	C	6'11	240	24	27	672	67	152	44	32	105	30	220	19	81	1	22	31	166	25	8.1	0.7	3.0	6.1
Pete Myers (from NY)	G-F	6'6	180	26	28	543	74	180	41	50	69	72	68	100	70	0	20	9	198	19	2.4	3.6	2.5	7.1
Derrick Gervin	F	6'8	215	26	21	339	93	197	47	65	89	73	65	8	47	0	20	7	251	16	3.1	0.4	2.2	12.0
Leon Wood	G	6'3	185	27	28	200	16	49	33	14	16	88	12	47	16	0	6	0	50	7	0.4	1.7	0.6	1.8
Jaren Jackson	G	6'4	190	22	28	160	25	69	36	17	21	81	24	13	16	0	13	1	67	6	0.9	0.5	0.6	2.4
Stanley Brundy (DR)	F	6'7	215	22	16	128	15	30	50	7	18	39	26	3	24	0	6	5	37	8	1.6	0.2	1.5	2.3
Jay Taylor	G	6'3	190	22	17	114	21	52	40	6	9	67	11	5	9	0	5	3	51	7	0.6	0.3	0.5	3.0
Anthony Mason	F	6'7	250	23	21	108	14	40	35	9	15	60	34	7	20	0	2	2	37	5	1.6	0.3	1.0	1.8
Rick Carlisle	G	6'5	210	30	5	21	1	7	14	0	0	—	0	5	7	0	1	1	2	4	0.0	1.0	1.4	0.4

3-PT FG - Morris 61-193, Bowie 10-31, Hopson 32-101, Connor 2-13, Short 10-35, Schackelford 0-1, Blaylock 18-80, Haley 0-1, Carroll 0-2, Meyers 0-6, Gervin 0-3, Wood 4-21, Jackson 0-3, Taylor 3-13, Carlisle 0-3

CENTRAL DIVISION

	Pos	Hgt	Wgt	Age	G	Min	FG	FGA	%	FT	FTA	%	Reb	Ass	PF	DQ	Stls	Blkd Shts	Points	Min	Reb	Ass	PF	Points
DETROIT PISTONS	57-23 .700	CHUCK DALY																						
Dennis Rodman	F-G	6'8	210	28	82	2377	288	496	58	142	217	65	792	72	276	2	52	60	719	29	9.7	0.9	3.4	8.8
James Edwards	F-C	7'	250	34	82	2283	462	928	50	265	354	75	345	63	295	4	23	37	1189	28	4.2	0.8	3.6	14.5
Bill Laimbeer	F	6'11	260	32	81	2675	380	785	48	164	192	85	780	171	278	4	57	84	981	33	9.6	2.1	3.4	12.1
Joe Dumars	G	6'3	190	26	75	2578	508	1058	48	297	330	90	212	368	129	1	63	2	1335	34	2.8	4.9	1.7	17.8
Isiah Thomas	G	6'1	185	28	81	2993	579	1322	44	292	377	77	308	765	206	0	139	19	1492	37	3.8	9.4	2.5	18.4
Mark Aguirre	F	6'6	232	30	78	2005	438	898	49	192	254	76	305	145	201	2	34	19	1099	26	3.9	1.9	2.6	14.1
Vinnie Johnson	G	6'2	200	33	82	1972	334	775	43	131	196	67	256	255	143	0	71	13	804	24	3.1	3.1	1.7	9.8
John Salley	F-C	7'	230	25	82	1914	209	408	51	174	244	71	439	67	282	7	51	153	593	23	5.4	0.8	3.4	7.2
Gerald Henderson (from Mil)	G	6'2	180	33	46	335	42	83	51	10	13	77	31	61	36	0	8	2	108	7	0.7	1.3	0.8	2.3
William Bedford	C	7'1	235	26	42	246	54	125	43	9	22	41	58	4	39	0	3	17	118	6	1.4	0.1	0.9	2.8
David Greenwood	F	6'9	225	32	37	205	22	52	42	16	29	55	78	12	40	0	4	9	60	6	2.1	0.3	1.1	1.6
Scott Hastings (JJ)	F-C	6'11	245	29	40	166	10	33	30	19	22	86	32	8	31	0	3	3	42	4	0.8	0.2	0.8	1.1
Stan Kimbrough	G	5'11	150	23	10	50	7	16	44	2	2	100	7	5	4	0	4	0	16	5	0.7	0.5	0.4	1.6
Ralph Lewis (to Char)	G	6'6	200	26	4	6	0	1	0	0	0	—	0	0	1	0	0	0	0	2	0.0	0.0	0.3	0.0

3-PT FG - Rodman 1-9, Edwards 0-3, Laimbeer 57-168, Dumars 22-55, Thomas 42-136, Aguirre 31-93, Johnson 5-34, Salley 1-4, Henderson 14-31, Bedford 1-6, Hastings 3-12

	Pos	Hgt	Wgt	Age	G	Min	FG	FGA	%	FT	FTA	%	Reb	Ass	PF	DQ	Stls	Blkd Shts	Points	Min	Reb	Ass	PF	Points
CHICAGO BULLS	55-27 .671	PHIL JACKSON																						
Scottie Pippen	F	6'8	210	24	82	3148	562	1150	49	199	295	67	547	444	298	6	211	101	1351	38	6.7	5.4	3.6	16.5
Horace Grant	F-C	6'10	215	24	80	2753	446	853	52	179	256	70	629	227	230	1	92	84	1071	34	7.9	2.8	2.9	13.4
Bill Cartwright	C	7'1	245	32	71	2160	292	598	49	227	280	81	465	145	243	6	38	34	811	30	6.5	2.0	3.4	11.4
John Paxson	G	6'2	185	29	82	2365	365	708	52	56	68	82	119	335	176	1	83	6	819	29	1.5	4.1	2.1	10.0
Michael Jordon	G	6'6	195	26	82	3197	1034	1964	53	593	699	85	565	519	241	0	227	54	2753	39	6.9	6.3	2.9	33.6
Stacey King	F-C	6'11	230	22	82	1777	267	530	50	194	267	73	384	87	215	0	38	58	728	22	4.7	1.1	2.6	8.9
B.J. Armstrong	G	6'3	190	22	81	1291	190	392	48	69	78	88	102	199	105	0	46	6	452	16	1.3	2.5	1.3	5.6
Craig Hodges (XJ)	G	6'3	195	29	63	1055	145	331	44	30	33	91	53	110	87	1	30	2	407	17	0.8	1.7	1.4	6.5
Will Perdue	C	7'	240	24	77	884	111	268	41	72	104	69	214	46	150	0	19	26	294	11	2.8	0.6	1.9	3.8
Ed Nealy	F	6'7	240	29	46	503	37	70	53	30	41	73	138	28	67	0	16	4	104	11	3.0	0.6	1.5	2.3
Charlie Davis	F	6'7	215	31	53	429	58	158	37	7	8	88	81	18	52	0	10	8	130	8	1.5	0.3	1.0	2.5
Jeff Sanders (BF)	F	6'8	230	23	31	182	13	40	33	2	4	50	39	9	27	0	4	4	28	6	1.3	0.3	0.9	0.9
Jack Haley (to NJ)	C	6'10	240	25	11	58	9	20	45	7	7	100	18	4	7	0	0	1	25	5	1.6	0.4	0.6	2.3
Clifford Lett	G	6'3	170	24	4	28	2	8	25	0	0	—	0	1	8	0	0	0	4	7	0.0	0.3	2.0	1.0

3-PT FG - Pippen 28-112, Paxson 33-92, Jordan 92-245, King 0-1, Armstrong 3-6, Hodges 87-181, Perdue 0-5, Nealy 0-2, Davis 7-25

1989/90 N.B.A. - EASTERN CONFERENCE
CENTRAL DIVISION (continued)

MILWAUKEE BUCKS 44-38 .537 **DEL HARRIS**

	Pos	Hgt	Wgt	Age	G	Min	FG	FGA	%	FT	FTA	%	Reb	Ass	PF	DQ	Stls	Blkd Shts	Points	Min	Reb	Ass	PF	Points
					TOTAL															PER GAME				
Jeff Grayer	F-G	6'5	200	24	71	1427	224	487	46	99	152	65	217	107	125	0	48	10	548	20	3.1	1.5	1.8	7.7
Fred Roberts	F	6'10	220	29	82	2235	330	666	50	195	249	78	311	147	210	5	56	25	857	27	3.8	1.8	2.6	10.5
Jack Sikma	C	6'11	250	34	71	2250	344	827	42	230	260	88	492	229	244	5	76	48	986	32	6.9	3.2	3.4	13.9
Jay Humphries	G	6'3	185	27	81	2818	496	1005	49	224	285	79	269	472	253	2	156	11	1237	35	3.3	5.8	3.1	15.3
Alvin Robertson	G	6'4	190	27	81	2599	476	946	50	197	266	74	559	445	280	2	207	17	1153	32	6.9	5.5	3.5	14.2
Ricky Pierce	G-F	6'5	220	30	59	1709	503	987	51	307	366	84	167	133	158	2	50	7	1359	29	2.8	2.3	2.7	23.0
Paul Pressey (JJ)	G-F	6'5	201	31	57	1400	239	506	47	144	190	76	172	244	149	3	71	23	628	25	3.0	4.3	2.6	11.0
Brad Lohaus (from Min)	C	7'	235	25	52	1353	211	461	46	54	77	70	288	106	145	2	44	66	522	26	5.5	2.0	2.8	10.0
Greg Anderson (KJ)	F	6'10	230	25	60	1291	219	432	51	91	170	54	373	24	176	3	32	54	529	22	6.2	0.4	2.9	8.8
Tony Brown	G-F	6'6	195	29	61	635	88	206	43	38	56	68	72	41	79	0	32	4	219	10	1.2	0.7	1.3	3.6
Randy Breuer (to Min)	C	7'3	258	29	30	554	86	186	46	32	51	63	127	13	63	0	9	33	204	18	4.2	0.4	2.1	6.8
Frank Kornet	F	6'9	225	22	57	438	42	114	37	24	39	62	71	21	54	0	14	3	113	8	1.2	0.4	0.9	2.0
Larry Krystkowiak (KJ)	F	6'9	240	25	16	381	43	118	36	26	33	79	76	25	41	0	10	2	112	24	4.8	1.6	2.6	7.0
Ben Coleman (AJ, XJ)	F	6'9	225	28	22	305	46	97	47	34	41	83	87	12	54	0	7	7	126	14	4.0	0.5	2.5	5.7
Tito Horford (JJ)	C	7'1	245	23	35	236	18	62	29	15	24	63	59	2	33	0	5	16	51	7	1.7	0.1	0.9	1.5
Gerald Henderson (to Det)	G	6'2	180	33	11	129	11	26	42	2	2	100	12	13	14	0	8	0	27	12	1.1	1.2	1.3	2.5
Mike Dunleavy	G	6'3	180	35	5	43	4	14	29	7	8	88	2	10	7	0	1	0	17	9	0.4	2.0	1.4	3.4
Jerry Sichting (from Char)	G	6'1	180	33	1	27	0	6	0	3	4	75	0	2	1	0	0	0	3	27	0.0	2.0	1.0	3.0

3-PT FG - Grayer 1-8, Roberts 2-11 , Sikma 68-199, Humpries 21-70, Robertson 4-26, Pierce 46-133,Pressey 6-43, Lohaus 46-121, Brown 5-20, Kornet 5-20, Krystkowiak 0-2, Coleman 0-1, Henderson 3-7, Dunleavy 2-9

CLEVELAND CAVALIERS 42-40 .512 **LENNY WILKENS**

	Pos	Hgt	Wgt	Age	G	Min	FG	FGA	%	FT	FTA	%	Reb	Ass	PF	DQ	Stls	Blkd Shts	Points	Min	Reb	Ass	PF	Points
Chucky Brown	F	6'7	230	21	75	1339	210	447	47	125	164	76	231	50	148	0	33	26	545	18	3.1	0.7	2.0	7.3
Larry Nance (NJ)	F	6'10	235	30	62	2065	412	807	51	186	239	78	516	161	185	3	54	122	1011	33	8.3	2.6	3.0	16.3
Brad Daughterty (FJ)	C	7'	263	24	41	1438	244	509	48	202	287	70	373	130	108	1	29	22	690	35	9.1	3.2	2.6	16.8
Craig Ehlo	G-F	6'7	205	28	81	2894	436	940	46	126	185	68	439	371	226	2	126	23	1102	36	5.4	4.6	2.8	13.6
Mark Price	G	6'1	178	25	73	2706	489	1066	46	300	338	89	251	666	89	0	114	5	1430	37	3.4	9.1	1.2	19.6
John Williams	F-C	6'11	238	28	82	2776	528	1070	49	325	440	74	663	168	214	2	86	167	1381	34	8.1	2.0	2.6	16.8
Steve Kerr	G	6'3	180	24	78	1664	192	432	44	63	73	86	98	248	59	0	45	7	520	21	1.3	3.2	0.8	6.7
Winston Bennett	F	6'7	210	24	55	990	137	286	48	64	96	67	188	54	133	1	23	10	338	18	3.4	1.0	2.4	6.1
Randolph Keys (to Char)	F-G	6'9	212	23	48	892	131	359	36	61	82	74	137	39	117	0	38	2	365	19	2.9	0.8	2.4	7.6
Chris Dudley (BW, to NJ)	C	6'11	240	24	37	684	79	203	39	26	77	34	203	20	83	1	19	41	184	18	5.5	0.5	2.2	5.0
Tree Rollins	C	7'1	250	34	48	674	57	125	46	11	16	69	153	24	83	3	13	53	125	14	3.2	0.5	1.7	2.6
Reggie Williams (from LAC, to SA)	G	6'7	188	25	32	542	91	239	38	30	41	73	60	38	79	2	22	10	218	17	1.9	1.2	2.5	6.8
Paul Mokeski	C	7'	270	32	38	449	63	150	42	25	36	69	99	17	76	0	8	10	151	12	2.6	0.4	2.0	4.0
John Morton (LJ)	G	6'3	195	23	37	402	48	161	30	43	62	69	32	67	30	0	18	4	146	11	0.9	1.8	0.8	3.9
Ron Harper (to LAC)	G	6'6	198	25	7	262	61	138	44	31	41	76	48	49	25	1	14	9	154	37	6.9	7.0	3.6	22.0
Derrick Chievous (from Hou)	F-G	6'7	200	22	14	99	15	42	36	19	24	79	15	4	11	0	3	1	49	7	1.1	0.3	0.8	3.5
Gary Voce	F	6'9	225	24	1	4	1	3	33	0	0	—	2	0	0	0	0	0	2	4	2.0	0.0	0.0	2.0

3-PT FG - Brown 0-7, Nance 1-1, Daugherty 0-2, Ehlo 104-248, Price 152-374, Kerr 73-144, Keys 2-10, Rollins 0-1, R. Williams 6-27, Mokeski 0-1, Morton 7-30, Harper 1-5, Chievous 0-1

INDIANA PACERS 42-40 .512 **DICK VERSACE**

	Pos	Hgt	Wgt	Age	G	Min	FG	FGA	%	FT	FTA	%	Reb	Ass	PF	DQ	Stls	Blkd Shts	Points	Min	Reb	Ass	PF	Points
Chuck Person	F	6'8	220	25	77	2714	605	1242	49	**211**	**270**	**78**	**445**	**230**	**217**	**1**	**53**	**20**	**1515**	**35**	**5.8**	**3.0**	**2.8**	**19.7**
LaSalle Thompson	F	6'10	245	28	82	2126	223	471	47	107	134	80	630	106	313	11	65	71	554	26	7.7	1.3	3.8	6.8
Rik Smits	C	7'4	250	23	82	2404	515	967	53	241	297	81	512	142	328	11	45	169	1271	29	6.2	1.7	4.0	15.5
Reggie Miller	G	6'7	185	24	82	3192	661	1287	51	544	627	87	295	311	175	1	110	18	2016	39	3.6	3.8	2.1	24.6
Vern Fleming	G	6'5	180	28	82	2876	467	919	51	230	294	78	322	610	213	1	92	10	1176	35	3.9	7.4	2.6	14.3
Detlef Schrempf	F-C	6'10	215	26	78	2573	424	822	52	402	490	82	620	247	271	6	59	16	1267	33	7.9	3.2	3.5	16.2
Mike Sanders	F	6'6	210	29	82	1531	225	479	47	55	75	73	230	89	220	1	43	23	510	19	2.8	1.1	2.7	6.2
Rickey Green	G	6'1	172	35	69	927	100	231	43	43	51	84	54	182	60	0	51	1	244	13	0.8	2.6	0.9	3.5
Randy Wittman	G	6'6	210	30	61	544	62	122	51	5	6	83	30	39	21	0	7	4	130	9	0.5	0.6	0.3	2.1
George McCloud	G	6'6	205	22	44	413	45	144	31	15	19	79	42	45	56	0	19	3	118	9	1.0	1.0	1.3	2.7
Greg Dreiling	C	7'1	250	26	49	307	20	53	38	25	34	74	87	8	69	0	4	14	65	6	1.8	0.2	1.4	1.3
Calvin Natt (KJ)	F	6'6	220	32	14	164	20	31	65	17	22	77	35	9	14	0	1	0	57	12	2.5	0.6	1.0	4.1
Dyron Nix (FJ)	F	6'7	210	22	20	109	14	39	36	11	16	69	26	5	15	0	3	1	39	5	1.3	0.3	0.8	2.0

3-PT FG - Person 94-253, Thompson 1-5, Smits 0-1, Miller 150-362, Fleming 12-40,Schrempf 17-48, Sanders 5-14, Green 1-11, Wittman 1-2, McCloud 13-40

ATLANTA HAWKS 41-41 .500 **MIKE FRATELLO**

	Pos	Hgt	Wgt	Age	G	Min	FG	FGA	%	FT	FTA	%	Reb	Ass	PF	DQ	Stls	Blkd Shts	Points	Min	Reb	Ass	PF	Points
Dominique Wilkins	F	6'8	200	29	80	2888	810	1672	48	459	569	81	521	200	141	0	126	47	2138	36	6.5	2.5	1.8	26.7
Kevin Willis	F-C	7'	235	27	81	2273	418	805	52	168	246	68	645	57	259	4	63	47	1006	28	8.0	0.7	3.2	12.4
Moses Malone	C	6'10	255	34	81	2735	517	1077	48	493	631	78	812	130	158	0	47	84	1528	34	10.0	1.6	2.0	18.9
John Battle	G	6'2	175	27	60	1477	275	544	51	102	135	76	99	154	115	0	28	3	654	25	1.7	2.6	1.9	10.9
Glenn Rivers (XJ)	G	6'4	185	28	48	1526	218	480	45	138	170	81	200	264	151	2	116	22	598	32	4.2	5.5	3.1	12.5
Spud Webb	G	5'7	135	26	82	2184	294	616	48	162	186	87	201	477	185	0	105	12	751	27	2.5	5.8	2.3	9.2
Cliff Levingston	F	6'8	210	28	75	1706	216	424	51	83	122	68	319	80	216	2	55	41	516	23	4.3	1.1	2.9	6.9
John Long	G	6'5	203	33	48	1030	174	384	45	46	55	84	83	85	66	0	45	5	404	21	1.7	1.8	1.4	8.4
Jon Koncak (KJ)	C-F	7'	260	26	54	977	78	127	61	42	79	53	226	23	182	4	38	34	198	18	4.2	0.4	3.4	3.7
Alexander Volkov	F	6'10	278	25	72	937	137	284	48	70	120	58	119	83	166	3	36	22	357	13	1.7	1.2	2.3	5.0
Aintoine Carr (to SAC)	F	6'9	235	28	44	803	128	248	52	83	122	68	319	80	216	2	55	41	516	18	7.3	1.8	4.9	11.7
Kenny Smith (from SAC)	G	6'3	170	24	33	674	98	204	48	55	65	85	37	142	45	0	22	1	255	20	1.1	4.3	1.4	7.7
Sedric Toney (to SAC)	G	6'2	178	27	32	286	30	72	42	21	25	84	14	52	35	0	10	0	88	9	0.4	1.6	1.1	2.8
Roy Marble (DR)	G	6'6	190	23	24	162	16	58	28	19	29	66	24	11	16	0	7	1	51	7	1.0	0.5	0.7	2.1
Duane Ferrell	F	6'7	209	24	14	29	5	14	36	2	6	33	7	2	3	0	1	0	12	2	0.5	0.1	0.2	0.9
Haywoode Workman	G	6'2	180	23	6	16	2	3	67	2	2	100	3	2	3	0	3	0	6	3	0.5	0.3	0.5	1.0
Mike Williams (from SAC)	F	6'8	225	26	5	14	0	4	0	0	0	—	1	0	2	0	0	0	0	3	0.2	0.0	0.4	0.0
Wes Matthews	G	6'1	170	30	1	13	1	3	33	2	2	100	0	5	0	0	0	0	4	13	0.0	5.0	0.0	4.0

3-PT FG - Wilkens59-183, Willis 2-7, Malone 1-9, Battle 2-13, Rivers 24-66, Webb 1-19, Levingston 1-5, Long 10-29, Koncak 0-1, Volkov 13-34, Carr 0-4, Smith 4-24, Toney 7-13, Marble 0-2, Ferrell 0-1, Matthews 0-1

1989/90 N.B.A. - EASTERN CONFERENCE
CENTRAL DIVISION (continued)

	Pos	Hgt	Wgt	Age	G	Min	FG	FGA	%	FT	FTA	%	Reb	Ass	PF	DQ	Stls	Blkd Shts	Points	Min	Reb	Ass	PF	Points
					TOTAL															PER GAME				
ORLANDO MAGIC	18-64 .220				MATT GOUKAS																			
Terry Catledge	F	6'8	220	26	74	2462	546	1152	47	341	486	70	563	72	201	0	36	19	1435	33	7.6	1.0	2.7	19.4
Sidney Green	F	6'9	220	28	73	1860	312	667	47	136	209	65	588	99	231	4	50	26	761	25	8.1	1.4	3.2	10.4
Mark Acres	C-F	6'11	225	27	80	1691	138	285	48	83	120	69	431	67	248	4	36	25	362	21	5.4	0.8	3.1	4.5
Reggie Theus	G	6'7	213	32	76	2350	517	1178	44	378	443	85	221	407	194	1	60	12	1438	31	2.9	5.4	2.6	18.9
Sam Vincent	G	6'2	185	26	63	1657	258	564	46	188	214	88	194	354	108	1	65	20	705	26	3.1	5.6	1.7	11.2
Jerry Reynolds	F-G	6'8	208	27	67	1817	309	741	42	239	322	74	323	180	162	1	93	64	858	27	4.8	2.7	2.4	12.8
Nick Anderson	F	6'6	215	21	81	1785	372	753	49	186	264	70	316	124	140	0	69	34	931	22	3.9	1.5	1.7	11.5
Otis Smith	G-F	6'5	210	25	65	1644	348	708	49	169	222	76	300	147	174	0	76	57	875	25	4.6	2.3	2.7	13.5
Scott Skiles	G	6'1	188	25	70	1460	190	464	41	104	119	87	159	334	126	0	36	4	536	21	2.3	4.8	1.8	7.7
Michael Ansley	F	6'7	225	22	72	1221	231	465	50	164	227	72	362	40	152	0	24	17	626	17	5.0	0.6	2.1	8.7
Jeff Turner	F	6'9	240	27	60	1105	132	308	43	42	54	78	227	53	161	4	23	12	308	18	3.8	0.9	2.7	5.1
Morlon Wiley (NJ)	G	6'4	192	24	40	638	92	208	44	28	38	74	52	114	65	0	45	3	229	16	1.3	2.9	1.6	5.7
Dave Corzine (KJ)	C	6'11	260	33	6	79	11	29	38	0	2	0	18	2	7	0	2	0	22	13	3.0	0.3	1.2	3.7
Jawaan Oldham (to LAC)	C	7'	215	32	3	36	1	3	33	2	5	40	15	0	6	0	2	3	4	12	5.0	0.0	2.0	1.3

3-PT FG - Catledge 2-8, Green 1-3, Acres 3-4, Theus 26-105, Vincent 1-14, Reynolds 1-14, Anderson 1-17, Smith 10-40, Skiles 52-132, Turner 2-10, Wiley 17-46

1989/90 N.B.A. - WESTERN CONFERENCE
MIDWEST DIVISION

	Pos	Hgt	Wgt	Age	G	Min	FG	FGA	%	FT	FTA	%	Reb	Ass	PF	DQ	Stls	Blkd Shts	Points	Min	Reb	Ass	PF	Points
SAN ANTONIO SPURS	56-26 .683				LARRY BROWN																			
Sean Elliott	F	6'8	205	21	81	2032	311	647	48	187	216	87	297	154	172	0	45	14	810	25	3.7	1.9	2.1	10.0
Terry Cummings	F	6'9	240	28	81	2821	728	1532	48	343	440	78	677	219	286	1	110	52	1818	35	8.4	2.7	3.5	22.4
David Robinson	C	7'1	235	24	82	3002	690	1300	53	613	837	73	983	164	259	3	138	319	1993	37	12.0	2.0	3.2	24.3
Willie Anderson	G-F	6'7	185	22	82	2788	532	1082	49	217	290	75	372	364	252	3	111	58	1288	34	4.5	4.4	3.1	15.7
Maurice Cheeks (to NY)	G	6'1	180	33	50	1766	215	450	48	114	137	83	167	302	46	0	82	5	545	35	3.3	6.0	0.9	10.9
David Wingate	G	6'5	185	26	78	1856	220	491	45	87	112	78	195	208	154	2	89	18	527	24	2.5	2.7	2.0	6.8
Frank Brickowski	F-C	6'10	240	30	78	1438	211	387	55	95	141	67	327	105	226	4	66	37	517	18	4.2	1.3	2.9	6.6
Rod Strickland (from NY)	G	6'3	175	23	31	1121	173	370	47	91	148	61	133	249	89	3	57	6	439	36	4.3	8.0	2.9	14.2
Vernon Maxwell (to Hou)	G	6'5	185	24	49	1118	133	306	43	59	95	62	141	146	79	0	42	5	340	23	2.9	3.0	1.6	6.9
Caldwell Jones	C-F	6'11	225	39	72	885	67	144	47	38	54	70	230	20	146	2	20	27	173	12	3.2	0.3	2.0	2.4
Johnny Moore	G	6'2	185	31	53	516	47	126	37	16	27	59	52	82	55	0	32	3	118	10	1.0	1.5	1.0	2.2
Zarko Paspalj	F	6'9	220	23	28	181	27	79	34	18	22	82	30	10	37	0	3	7	72	6	1.1	0.4	1.3	2.6
Reggie Williams (from Cle)	F	6'7	195	25	10	68	19	42	45	4	6	67	8	5	16	0	1	3	42	7	0.8	0.5	1.6	4.2
Chris Welp (to GS)	C	7'	250	25	13	56	7	23	30	1	2	50	12	5	21	0	1	0	15	4	0.9	0.4	1.6	1.2
Uwe Blab (from GS)	C	7'1	250	27	7	50	6	11	55	3	6	50	9	1	9	0	0	0	15	7	1.3	0.1	1.3	2.1
Jeff Lebo	G	6'4	190	23	4	32	2	7	29	2	2	100	4	3	7	0	2	0	6	8	1.0	0.8	1.8	1.5

3-PT FG - Elliott 1-9, Cummings 19-59, Robinson 0-2, Anderson 7-26, Cheeks 1-9, Wingate 0-13, Brickowski 0-2, Strickland 2-9, Maxwell 15-52, Jones 1-5, Moore 8-34, Paspalj 0-1, Williams 0-5

	Pos	Hgt	Wgt	Age	G	Min	FG	FGA	%	FT	FTA	%	Reb	Ass	PF	DQ	Stls	Blkd Shts	Points	Min	Reb	Ass	PF	Points
UTAH JAZZ	55-27 .671				JERRY SLOAN																			
Blue Edwards	F-G	6'5	200	24	82	1889	286	564	51	146	203	72	251	145	280	2	76	36	727	23	3.1	1.8	3.4	8.9
Karl Malone	F-C	6'9	256	26	82	3122	914	1627	56	696	913	76	911	226	259	1	121	50	2540	38	11.1	2.8	3.2	31.0
Mark Eaton	C	7'4	290	32	82	2281	158	300	53	79	118	67	601	39	238	3	33	201	395	28	7.3	0.5	2.9	4.8
Bob Hansen	G	6'6	200	28	81	2174	265	568	47	33	64	52	229	149	194	2	52	11	617	27	2.8	1.8	2.4	7.6
John Stockton	G	6'1	175	27	78	2915	472	918	51	354	432	82	206	1134	233	3	207	18	1345	37	2.6	14.5	3.0	17.2
Thurl Bailey	F	6'11	232	28	82	2583	470	977	48	222	285	78	410	137	175	2	32	100	1162	32	5.0	1.7	2.1	14.2
Darrell Griffith	G	6'4	195	31	82	1444	301	649	46	51	78	65	166	63	149	0	68	19	733	18	2.0	0.8	1.8	8.9
Mike Brown	F-C	6'9	260	26	82	1397	177	344	51	157	199	79	373	47	187	0	32	28	512	17	4.5	0.6	2.3	6.2
Delaney Rudd	G	6'2	195	27	77	850	111	259	43	35	53	66	55	177	81	0	22	1	273	11	0.7	2.3	1.1	3.5
Eric Leckner	C	6'11	265	23	77	764	125	222	56	81	109	74	192	19	157	0	15	23	331	10	2.5	0.2	2.0	4.3
Eric Johnson	G	6'2	205	23	48	272	20	84	24	13	17	76	28	64	49	1	17	2	54	6	0.6	1.3	1.0	1.1
Jose Ortiz	F	6'10	225	26	13	64	19	42	45	3	5	60	15	7	15	0	2	1	42	5	1.2	0.5	1.2	3.2
Raymond Brown	F	6'8	225	24	16	56	8	28	29	0	2	0	15	4	11	0	0	0	16	4	0.9	0.3	0.7	1.0
Nate Johnston (to Por)	F	6'8	210	23	6	13	4	11	36	2	2	100	0	0	0	0	0	1	11	2	0.0	0.0	0.0	1.8
Jim Les (to LAC)	G	5'11	175	26	1	6	0	0	—	2	4	50	0	0	1	3	0	0	0	2	6	0.0	1.0	3.0
																								2.0

3-PT FG - Edwards 9-30, Malone 16-43, Hansen 54-154, Srockton 47-113, Bailey 0-8, Griffith 80-215, M. Brown 1-2, Rudd 16-56, Johnson 1-6, Ortiz 1-2, Johnston 1-1

	Pos	Hgt	Wgt	Age	G	Min	FG	FGA	%	FT	FTA	%	Reb	Ass	PF	DQ	Stls	Blkd Shts	Points	Min	Reb	Ass	PF	Points
DALLAS MAVERICKS	47-35 .573				JOHN MACCLEOD (6-6				RICHIE ABUDATO (41-29 .586)															
Adrian Dantley (JJ)	F	6'5	217	33	45	1300	231	484	48	200	254	79	172	80	99	0	20	7	662	29	3.8	1.8	2.2	14.7
Sam Perkins	F-C	6'9	260	28	76	2668	435	883	49	330	424	78	572	175	225	4	88	64	1206	35	7.5	2.3	3.0	15.9
James Donaldson	C	7'2	280	32	73	2265	258	479	54	149	213	70	630	57	129	0	22	47	665	31	8.6	0.8	1.8	9.1
Rolando Blackman	G	6'6	206	30	82	2934	626	1256	50	287	340	84	280	289	128	0	77	21	1552	36	3.4	3.5	1.6	18.9
Derek Harper	G	6'4	208	28	82	3007	567	1161	49	250	315	79	244	609	224	1	187	26	1473	37	3.0	7.4	2.7	18.0
Herb Williams	F-C	6'11	242	31	81	2199	295	665	44	108	159	68	391	119	243	4	51	106	700	27	4.8	1.5	3.0	8.6
Roy Tarpley (DR)	F-C	7'	250	25	45	1648	314	696	45	130	172	76	589	67	160	0	79	70	758	37	13.1	1.5	3.6	16.8
Brad Davis	G	6'3	183	34	73	1292	179	365	49	77	100	77	93	242	151	2	47	9	470	18	1.3	3.3	2.1	6.4
Bill Wennington	C	7'	258	25	60	814	105	234	45	60	75	80	198	41	144	2	20	21	270	14	3.3	0.7	2.4	4.5
Randy White	F	6'8	250	22	55	707	93	252	37	50	89	56	173	21	124	0	24	6	237	13	3.1	0.4	2.3	4.3
Anthony Jones	G-F	6'6	201	27	66	650	72	194	37	47	69	68	82	29	77	0	32	16	195	10	1.2	0.4	1.2	3.0
Steve Alford	G	6'2	182	25	41	302	63	138	46	35	37	95	25	39	22	0	15	3	168	7	0.6	1.0	0.5	4.1
Bob McCann	F	6'6	240	25	10	62	7	21	33	12	14	86	12	6	7	0	2	2	26	6	1.2	0.6	0.7	2.6
Kelvin Upshaw (from Bos, to GS)	G	6'2	180	26	3	4	1	3	33	0	0	—	0	0	0	0	0	0	2	1	0.0	0.0	0.0	0.7
Mark Wade	G	5'11	180	24	1	3	0	0	—	0	0	—	0	2	0	0	0	0	0	3	0.0	2.0	0.0	0.0

3-PT FG - Dantley 0-2, Perkins 6-28, Blackman 13-43, Harper 89-240, Williams 2-9, Tarpley 0-6, Davis 35-104, Wennington 0-4, White 1-14, Jones 4-13, Alford 7-22, Upshaw 0-1

1989/90 N.B.A. - WESTERN CONFERENCE
MIDWEST DIVISION (continued)

	Pos	Hgt	Wgt	Age	TOTAL G	Min	FG	FGA	%	FT	FTA	%	Reb	Ass	PF	DQ	Stls	Blkd Shts	Points	PER GAME Min	Reb	Ass	PF	Points
DENVER NUGGETS	43-39 .534	DOUG MOE																						
Alex English	F	6'8	190	35	80	2211	635	1293	49	161	183	88	286	225	130	0	51	23	1433	28	3.6	2.8	1.6	17.9
Dan Schayes (JJ)	F-C	6'11	260	30	53	1194	163	330	49	225	264	85	342	61	200	7	41	45	551	23	6.5	1.2	3.8	10.4
Blair Rasmussen	C	7'	260	27	81	1995	445	895	50	111	134	83	594	82	300	10	40	104	1001	25	7.3	1.0	3.7	12.4
Lafayette Lever	G	6'3	175	29	79	2932	568	1283	44	271	337	80	734	517	172	1	168	13	1443	37	9.3	6.5	2.2	18.3
Michael Adams	G	5'11	165	26	79	2690	398	989	40	267	314	85	225	495	133	0	121	3	1221	34	2.8	6.3	1.7	15.5
Walter Davis	F-G	6'6	200	35	69	1635	497	1033	48	207	227	91	179	155	160	1	59	9	1207	24	2.6	2.2	2.3	17.5
Bill Hanzlik	F-G	6'7	200	32	81	1605	179	396	45	136	183	74	207	186	249	7	78	29	500	20	2.6	2.3	3.1	6.2
Todd Lichti	G	6'4	205	22	79	1326	250	514	49	130	174	75	151	116	145	1	55	13	630	17	1.9	1.5	1.8	8.0
Tim Kempton	C-F	6'10	245	25	71	1061	153	312	49	77	114	68	218	118	144	2	30	9	383	15	3.1	1.7	2.0	5.4
Jerome Lane	F	6'6	232	23	67	956	145	309	47	44	120	37	361	105	189	1	53	17	334	14	5.4	1.6	2.8	5.0
Eddie Hughes	G	5'10	164	29	60	892	83	202	41	23	34	68	70	116	87	0	48	1	209	15	1.2	1.9	1.5	3.5
Joe Barry Carroll (from NJ)	C	7'	255	31	30	719	153	354	43	52	70	74	193	54	70	0	28	59	358	24	6.4	1.8	2.3	11.9
T.R. Dunn	G	6'4	192	34	65	657	44	97	45	26	39	67	138	43	67	1	41	4	114	10	2.1	0.7	1.0	1.8
Mike Higgins	F	6'9	220	22	5	32	3	8	38	7	8	88	3	2	1	0	1	2	13	6	0.6	0.4	0.2	2.6
3-PT FG - English 2-5, Schayes 0-4, Rasmussen 0-1, Lever 36-87, Adams 158-432, Davis 6-46, Hanzlik 6-31, Lichti 0-14, Kempton 0-1, Lane 0-5, Hughes 20-49, Dunn 0-2																								
HOUSTON ROCKETS	41.41 .500	DON CHANEY																						
Buck Johnson	F	6'7	206	25	82	2832	504	1019	49	205	270	76	381	252	321	8	104	62	1215	35	4.6	3.1	3.9	14.8
Otis Thorpe	F	6'11	246	27	82	2947	547	998	55	307	446	69	734	261	270	5	66	24	1401	36	9.0	3.2	3.3	17.1
Akeem Olajuwon	C	7'	258	26	82	3124	806	1609	50	382	536	71	1149	234	314	6	174	376	1995	38	14.0	2.9	3.8	24.3
Mitchell Wiggins	G	6'4	199	30	66	1852	416	853	49	192	237	81	286	104	165	0	85	1	1024	28	4.3	1.6	2.5	15.5
Eric Floyd	G	6'3	183	29	82	2630	362	803	45	185	232	80	198	600	159	0	94	11	1000	32	2.4	7.3	1.9	12.2
Larry Smith	F	6'8	251	31	74	1300	101	213	47	20	55	36	452	69	203	3	56	28	222	18	6.1	0.9	2.7	3.0
Mike Woodson (JJ)	G	6'5	200	31	61	982	160	405	40	62	86	72	88	66	100	1	42	11	394	16	1.4	1.1	1.6	6.5
John Lucas	G	6'3	180	36	49	938	109	291	37	42	55	76	90	238	59	0	45	2	286	19	1.8	4.9	1.2	5.8
Anthony Bowie	G	6'6	190	26	66	918	119	293	41	40	54	74	118	96	80	0	42	5	284	14	1.8	1.5	1.2	4.3
Vernon Maxwell (from SA)	G	6'5	185	24	30	869	142	321	44	77	116	66	87	150	69	0	42	5	374	29	2.9	5.0	2.3	12.5
Derrick Chievous (to Cle)	G-F	6'7	200	22	41	492	90	178	51	61	87	70	75	27	59	0	23	4	244	12	1.8	0.7	1.4	6.0
Bryon Dinkins (JJ)	G	6'1	170	22	33	362	44	109	40	26	30	87	40	75	30	0	19	2	115	11	1.2	2.3	0.9	3.5
Adrian Caldwell	F-C	6'8	265	23	51	331	42	76	55	13	28	46	109	7	69	0	11	18	97	6	2.1	0.1	1.4	1.9
Tim McCormick (KJ)	C	7'	237	27	18	116	10	29	34	10	19	53	27	3	24	0	3	1	30	6	1.5	0.2	1.3	1.7
Lewis Lloyd (from Phi)	G-F	6'6	225	30	19	113	29	51	57	9	16	56	18	11	9	0	3	0	67	6	0.9	0.6	0.5	3.5
Chuck Nevitt	C	7'5	240	30	3	9	2	2	100	0	0	—	3	1	3	0	0	1	4	3	1.0	0.3	1.0	1.3
3-PT FG - Johnson 2-17, Thorpe 0-10, Olajuwon 1-6, Wiggins 0-3, Floyd 89-234, Smith 0-2, Woodson 12-41, Lucas 26-87, Bowie 6-21, Maxwell 13-53, Chievous 3-8, Dinkins 1-9																								
MINNESOTA TIMBERWOLVES	22-60 .268	BILL MUSSELMAN																						
Tyrone Corbin	F	6'6	222	27	82	3011	521	1083	48	161	209	77	604	216	288	5	175	41	1203	37	7.4	2.6	3.5	14.7
Tod Murphy	F-C	6'9	220	26	82	2493	260	552	47	144	203	71	564	106	229	2	76	60	680	30	6.9	1.3	2.8	8.3
Randy Brewer (from Mil)	C	7'3	258	29	51	1325	212	510	42	94	142	66	290	84	133	2	33	75	518	26	5.7	1.6	2.6	10.2
Tony Campbell	G-F	6'7	215	27	82	3164	723	1581	46	448	569	79	451	213	260	7	111	31	1903	39	5.5	2.6	3.2	23.2
Pooh Richardson	G	6'1	180	23	82	2581	426	925	46	63	107	59	217	554	143	0	133	25	938	31	2.6	6.8	1.7	11.4
Sam Mitchell	F-C	6'7	210	26	80	2414	372	834	45	268	349	77	462	89	301	7	66	54	1012	30	5.8	1.1	3.8	12.7
Sidney Lowe	G	6'	190	29	80	1744	73	229	32	39	54	72	163	337	114	0	73	4	187	22	2.0	4.2	1.4	2.3
Scott Roth	F	6'8	212	26	71	1061	159	420	38	150	201	75	112	115	144	1	51	6	486	15	1.6	1.6	2.0	6.8
Donald Royal	F	6'8	210	23	66	746	117	255	46	153	197	78	137	43	107	0	32	8	387	11	2.1	0.7	1.6	5.9
Brad Lohaus (to Mil)	C	7'	235	25	28	596	94	202	47	21	26	81	110	62	66	1	14	22	210	21	3.9	2.2	2.4	7.5
Doug West	G	6'6	205	22	52	378	53	135	39	26	32	81	70	18	61	0	10	6	135	7	1.3	0.3	1.2	2.6
Gary Leonard	C	7'1	250	22	22	127	13	31	42	6	14	43	27	1	26	0	3	9	32	6	1.2	0.0	1.2	1.5
Brad Sellers (from Sea)	F	7'	227	27	14	113	19	56	34	9	12	75	19	1	11	0	6	3	47	8	1.4	0.1	0.8	3.4
Adrian Branch	G-F	6'7	215	26	11	91	25	61	41	14	22	64	20	4	14	0	6	0	65	8	1.8	0.4	1.3	5.9
Steve Johnson (from Sea, HO)	C	6'10	235	32	7	17	0	2	0	0	0	—	3	1	4	0	0	0	0	2	0.4	0.1	0.6	0.0
3-PT FG - Corbin 0-11, Murphy 16-43, Brewer 0-1, Campbell 9-54, Richardson 23-83, Mitchell 0-9, Lowe 2-9, Roth 18-52, Royal 0-1, Lohaus 1-16, West 3-11, Leonard 0-1, Sellers 0-2, Branch 1-1																								
CHARLOTTE HORNETS	19-63 .232	DICK HARTER (8-22 .200), GENE LITTLES (11-31 .262)																						
Kelly Tripucka	F-G	6'6	225	30	79	2404	442	1029	43	310	351	88	322	224	220	1	75	16	1232	30	4.1	2.8	2.8	15.6
Armon Gilliam (from Pho)	F	6'9	245	25	60	2159	432	819	53	264	363	73	529	91	184	4	63	46	1128	36	8.8	1.5	3.1	18.8
J.R. Reid	C	6'9	255	21	82	2757	358	814	44	192	289	66	691	101	292	7	92	54	908	34	8.4	1.2	3.6	11.1
Rex Chapman (BF)	G	6'4	185	22	54	1762	377	924	41	144	192	75	179	132	113	0	46	6	945	33	3.3	2.4	2.1	17.5
Mugsey Bogues	G	5'3	140	24	81	2743	326	664	49	106	134	79	207	867	168	1	166	3	763	34	2.6	10.7	2.1	9.4
Dell Curry	G	6'5	200	25	67	1860	461	990	47	96	104	92	168	159	148	0	98	26	1070	28	2.5	2.4	2.2	16.0
Robert Reid (from Por)	F-G	6'8	215	34	60	1117	164	414	40	50	78	64	143	82	136	0	36	14	383	19	2.4	1.4	2.3	6.4
Kenny Gattison	F	6'8	252	25	63	941	148	269	55	75	110	68	197	39	150	1	35	31	372	15	3.1	0.6	2.4	5.9
Randolph Keys (from Cle)	F	6'9	212	23	32	723	142	319	45	40	58	69	116	49	107	1	30	6	336	23	3.6	1.5	3.3	10.5
Richard Anderson	C-F	6'10	240	29	54	604	88	211	42	18	23	78	127	55	64	0	20	9	231	11	2.4	1.0	1.2	4.3
Brian Rowsom	F	6'9	230	24	44	559	78	179	44	68	83	82	131	22	58	0	18	11	225	13	3.0	0.5	1.3	5.1
Jerry Sichting (to Mil)	G	6'1	180	33	34	469	50	119	42	15	18	83	19	92	39	0	16	2	118	14	0.6	2.7	1.1	3.5
Stuart Gray (to NY)	C	7'	245	26	39	466	38	82	46	25	39	64	131	17	64	0	12	24	101	12	3.4	0.4	1.6	2.6
Kurt Rambis (to Pho)	F	6'8	218	31	16	448	58	116	50	30	55	55	120	28	45	0	32	10	146	28	7.5	1.8	2.8	9.1
Michael Williams (from Pho)	G	6'2	175	23	22	303	58	109	53	35	44	80	31	77	39	0	22	1	151	14	1.4	3.5	1.8	6.9
Dave Hoppen	C	6'11	240	25	10	135	16	41	39	8	10	80	36	6	26	0	2	1	40	14	3.6	0.6	2.6	4.0
Mike Holton (JJ)	G	6'4	185	28	16	109	14	26	54	1	2	50	2	16	19	0	1	0	29	7	0.1	1.0	1.2	1.8
Terry Dozier	F	6'9	210	23	9	92	9	27	33	4	8	50	15	3	10	0	6	2	22	10	1.7	0.3	1.1	2.4
Andre Turner (from LAC)	G	5'11	160	25	8	84	9	25	36	4	4	100	3	20	5	0	7	0	22	11	0.4	2.5	0.6	2.8
Ralph Lewis (from Det)	G	6'6	200	26	3	20	4	6	67	2	2	100	6	0	2	0	1	0	10	7	2.0	0.0	0.7	3.3
3-PT FG - Tripucka 38-104, Gilliam 0-2, Reid 0-5, Chapman 47-142, Bogues 5-26, Curry 52-147, R. Reid 9-29, Gattison 1-1, Keys 12-33, Anderson 37-100, Rowsom 1-2, Sichting 3-12, Gray 0-2, Rambis 0-1, Williams 0-3, Dozier 0-1, Turner 0-1																								

1989/90 N.B.A. - WESTERN CONFERENCE
PACIFIC DIVISION

LOS ANGELES LAKERS 63-19 .768 **PAT RILEY**

Player	Pos	Hgt	Wgt	Age	G	Min	FG	FGA	%	FT	FTA	%	Reb	Ass	PF	DQ	Stls	Blkd Shts	Points	Min (per game)	Reb (per game)	Ass (per game)	PF (per game)	Points (per game)
James Worthy	F	6'9	225	28	80	2960	711	1298	55	248	317	78	478	288	190	0	99	49	1685	37	6.0	3.6	2.4	21.1
A.C. Green	F-C	6'9	224	26	82	2709	385	806	48	278	370	75	712	90	207	0	66	50	1061	33	8.7	1.1	2.5	12.9
Mychal Thompson	C	6'10	235	34	70	1883	281	562	50	144	204	71	477	43	207	0	33	73	706	27	6.8	0.6	3.0	10.1
Byron Scott	G	6'3	193	28	77	2593	472	1005	47	160	209	77	242	274	180	2	77	31	1197	34	3.1	3.6	2.3	15.5
Magic Johnson	G-F	6'8	220	30	79	2937	546	1138	48	567	637	89	522	907	167	1	132	34	1765	37	6.6	11.5	2.1	22.3
Michael Cooper	G-F	6'5	176	33	80	1831	191	493	39	83	94	88	227	215	206	1	67	36	515	23	2.8	2.7	2.6	6.4
Vlader Divac	C	6'11	245	21	82	1611	274	549	50	153	216	71	512	75	240	2	79	114	701	20	6.2	0.9	2.9	8.5
Orlando Woolridge	F	6'9	215	30	62	1421	306	550	56	176	240	73	185	96	160	2	39	46	788	23	3.0	1.5	2.6	12.7
Larry Drew	G	6'1	190	31	80	1333	170	383	44	46	60	77	98	217	92	0	47	4	418	17	1.2	2.7	1.2	5.2
Jay Vincent (from Phi)	F	6'7	220	30	24	200	41	78	53	8	12	67	26	10	29	0	8	3	90	8	1.1	0.4	1.2	3.8
Mark McNamara	C	6'11	233	30	33	190	38	86	44	26	40	65	63	3	31	1	2	1	102	6	1.9	0.1	0.9	3.1
Steve Bucknall	G	6'6	215	23	18	75	9	33	27	5	6	83	7	10	10	0	2	1	23	4	0.4	0.6	0.6	1.3
Melvin McCants	F	6'8	250	22	13	65	8	26	31	6	8	75	6	2	11	0	3	1	22	5	0.5	0.2	0.8	1.7
Mike Higgins	F	6'9	220	22	6	18	0	0	—	1	2	50	1	1	4	0	1	2	1	3	0.2	0.2	0.7	0.2
Jawaan Oldham (from Orl)	C	7'	215	32	3	9	2	3	67	1	2	50	1	1	3	0	0	0	5	3	0.3	0.3	1.0	1.7

3-PT FG - Worthy 15-49, Green 13-46, Scott 93-220, Johnson 106-276, Cooper 50-157, Divac 0-5, Woolridge 0-5, Drew 32-81, Vincent 0-1, Bucknall 0-1

PORTLAND TRAILBLAZERS 59-23 .720 **RICK ADELMAN**

Player	Pos	Hgt	Wgt	Age	G	Min	FG	FGA	%	FT	FTA	%	Reb	Ass	PF	DQ	Stls	Blkd Shts	Points	Min (per game)	Reb (per game)	Ass (per game)	PF (per game)	Points (per game)
Jerome Kersey	F	6'7	225	27	82	2843	519	1085	48	269	390	69	690	188	304	7	121	63	1310	35	8.4	2.3	3.7	16.0
Buck Williams	F	6'8	225	29	82	2801	413	754	55	288	408	71	800	116	285	4	69	39	1114	34	9.8	1.4	3.5	13.6
Kevin Duckworth	C	7'	270	25	82	2462	548	1146	48	231	312	74	509	91	271	2	36	34	1327	30	6.2	1.1	3.3	16.2
Clyde Drexler	G-F	6'7	222	27	73	2683	670	1357	49	333	430	77	507	432	222	1	145	51	1703	37	6.9	5.9	3.0	23.3
Terry Porter	G	6'3	195	26	80	2781	448	969	46	421	472	89	272	726	150	0	151	4	1406	35	3.4	9.1	1.9	17.6
Cliff Robinson	F	6'11	225	23	82	1565	298	751	40	138	251	55	308	72	226	4	53	53	746	19	3.8	0.9	2.8	9.1
Danny Young	G	6'4	175	27	82	1393	138	328	42	91	112	81	122	231	84	0	82	4	383	17	1.5	2.8	1.0	4.7
Wayne Cooper	C	6'10	220	33	79	1176	138	304	45	25	39	64	339	44	211	2	18	95	301	15	4.3	0.6	2.7	3.8
Drazen Petrovic	G	6'5	195	25	77	967	207	427	48	135	160	84	111	116	134	0	23	2	583	13	1.4	1.5	1.7	7.6
Mark Bryant	C-F	6'9	245	24	58	562	70	153	46	28	50	56	146	13	93	0	18	9	168	10	2.5	0.2	1.6	2.9
Byron Irvin	G	6'5	190	23	50	488	96	203	47	61	91	67	74	47	40	0	28	1	258	10	1.5	0.9	0.8	5.2
Robert Reid (to Char)	G-F	6'8	215	34	12	85	13	33	39	4	8	50	8	8	17	0	2	2	31	7	0.7	0.7	1.4	2.6
Nate Johnson (from Utah)	F	6'8	210	23	15	74	14	37	38	7	11	64	21	1	11	1	3	7	35	5	1.4	0.1	0.7	2.3

3-PT FG - Kersey 3-20, Williams 0-1, Drexler 30-106, Porter 89-238, Robinson 12-44, Young 16-59, Cooper 0-3, Petrovic 34-74, Irvin 5-14, Reid 1-3, Johnston 0-3

PHOENIX SUNS 54-28 .659 **COTTON FITZSIMMONS**

Player	Pos	Hgt	Wgt	Age	G	Min	FG	FGA	%	FT	FTA	%	Reb	Ass	PF	DQ	Stls	Blkd Shts	Points	Min (per game)	Reb (per game)	Ass (per game)	PF (per game)	Points (per game)
Kurt Rambis (from Cha)	F	6'8	213	31	58	1456	132	257	51	52	72	72	405	107	163	0	68	27	316	25	7.0	1.8	2.8	5.4
Tom Chambers	F-C	6'10	230	30	81	3046	810	1617	50	557	647	86	571	190	260	1	88	47	2201	38	7.0	2.3	3.2	27.2
Mark West	C	6'10	234	29	82	2399	331	530	63	199	288	69	728	45	277	5	36	184	861	29	8.9	0.5	3.4	10.5
Jeff Hornacek(KJ)	G	6'4	190	26	67	2278	483	901	54	173	202	86	313	337	144	2	117	14	1179	34	4.7	5.0	2.1	17.6
Kevin Johnson	G	6'2	190	23	74	2782	578	1159	50	501	598	84	270	846	143	0	95	14	1665	38	3.6	11.4	1.9	22.5
Dan Majerle(SJ)	G-F	6'6	220	24	73	2244	296	698	42	198	260	76	430	188	177	5	100	32	809	31	5.9	2.6	2.4	11.1
Eddie Johnson(SJ)	F	6'8	215	30	64	1811	411	907	45	188	205	92	246	107	174	4	32	10	1080	28	3.8	1.7	2.7	16.9
Andrew Lang	C	6'11	250	23	74	1011	97	174	56	64	98	65	271	21	171	1	22	133	258	14	3.7	0.3	2.3	3.5
Kenry Battle	F	6'6	210	25	59	729	93	170	55	55	82	67	124	38	94	2	35	11	242	12	2.1	0.6	1.6	4.1
Greg Grant	G	5'7	145	23	67	678	83	216	38	39	59	66	59	168	58	0	36	1	208	10	0.9	2.5	0.9	3.1
Tim Perry	F	6'9	220	24	60	612	100	195	51	53	90	59	152	17	76	0	21	22	254	10	2.5	0.3	1.3	4.2
Mike McGee	G	6'5	207	30	14	280	42	87	48	10	21	48	36	16	28	0	8	1	102	20	2.6	1.1	2.0	7.3
Mike Morrison	G	6'4	195	22	36	153	23	68	34	24	30	80	20	11	20	0	2	0	72	4	0.6	0.3	0.6	2.0
Armon Gilliam (to Cha)	F	6'9	245	25	16	267	52	121	43	39	56	70	70	8	28	0	6	5	143	17	4.4	0.5	1.8	8.9
Tim Legler	G	6'4	210	23	11	83	11	29	38	6	6	100	8	6	12	0	2	0	28	8	0.7	0.5	1.1	2.5
	G	6'2	175	23	6	26	2	10	20	1	2	50	1	4	0	0	0	0	5	4	0.2	0.7	0.0	0.8

3-PT FG - Rambis 0-2, Chambers 24-86, Hornacek 40-98, K. Johnson 8-41, Majerle 19-80, E. Johnson 70-184, Battle 1-4, Grant 3-16, Perry 1-1, McGee 8-23, Morrison 2-7, Legler 0-1

SEATTLE SUPERSONICS 41-41 .500 **BERNIE BICKERSTAFF**

Player	Pos	Hgt	Wgt	Age	G	Min	FG	FGA	%	FT	FTA	%	Reb	Ass	PF	DQ	Stls	Blkd Shts	Points	Min (per game)	Reb (per game)	Ass (per game)	PF (per game)	Points (per game)
Xavier McDaniel (KJ)	F	6'7	205	26	69	2432	611	1233	50	244	333	73	447	171	231	2	73	36	1471	35	6.5	2.5	3.3	21.3
Derrick McKey	F-C	6'9	215	23	80	2748	468	949	49	315	403	78	489	187	247	2	87	81	1254	34	6.1	2.3	3.1	15.7
Michael Cage	C-F	6'9	245	27	82	2595	325	645	50	148	212	70	821	70	232	1	79	45	798	32	10.0	0.9	2.8	9.7
Dale Ellis (AA)	G-F	6'7	215	29	55	2033	502	1011	50	193	236	82	238	110	124	3	59	7	1293	37	4.3	2.0	2.3	23.5
Nate McMillian	G	6'5	197	25	82	2338	207	438	47	98	153	64	403	598	289	7	140	37	523	29	4.9	7.3	3.5	6.4
Dana Barros	G	5'11	170	22	81	1630	299	738	41	89	110	81	132	205	97	0	53	1	782	20	1.6	2.5	1.2	9.7
Sedale Threatt (BH)	G	6'2	177	28	65	1481	303	599	51	130	157	83	115	216	164	0	65	8	744	23	1.8	3.3	2.5	11.4
Shawn Kemp	F-C	6'10	240	20	81	1120	203	424	48	117	159	74	346	26	204	5	47	70	525	14	4.3	0.3	2.5	6.5
Olden Polynice	C	6'11	244	25	79	1085	156	289	54	47	99	47	300	15	187	0	25	21	360	14	3.8	0.2	2.4	4.6
Brad Sellers (to Min)	F	7'	227	27	45	587	84	198	42	49	61	80	70	32	63	1	11	19	217	13	1.6	0.7	1.4	4.8
Avery Johnson	G	5'10	175	25	53	575	55	142	39	29	40	73	43	162	55	0	26	1	140	11	0.8	3.1	1.0	2.6
Quintin Dailey	G	6'3	200	28	30	491	97	240	40	52	66	79	51	34	63	0	12	0	247	16	1.7	1.1	2.1	8.2
Jim Farmer	G	6'4	190	25	38	400	89	203	44	57	80	71	43	25	44	0	17	1	243	11	1.1	0.7	1.2	6.4
Steve Johnson (from Min)	C	6'10	235	32	21	242	48	90	53	21	35	60	50	16	52	0	3	5	117	12	2.4	0.8	2.5	5.6
Scott Meents	F	6'10	235	25	26	148	19	44	43	17	23	74	30	7	12	0	4	3	55	6	1.2	0.3	0.5	2.1

3-PT FG - McDaniel 5-17, McKey 3-23, Ellis 96-256, McMillian 11-31, Barros 95-238, Threatt 8-32, Kemp 2-12, Polynice 1-2, Sellers 0-3, A. Johnson 1-4, Dailey 1-5, Farmer 8-27

1989/90 N.B.A. - WESTERN CONFERENCE
PACIFIC DIVISION (continued)

GOLDEN STATE WARRIORS 37-45 .451 DON NELSON

	Pos	Hgt	Wgt	Age	G	Min	FG	FGA	%	FT	FTA	%	Reb	Ast	PF	DQ	Stls	Blkd Shts	Points	Per Game Min	Reb	Ast	PF	Points
Chris Mullin	F	6'7	215	26	78	2830	682	1272	54	505	568	89	463	319	142	1	123	45	1956	36	5.9	4.1	1.8	25.1
Terry Teagle	F	6'5	195	29	82	2376	538	1122	48	244	294	83	367	155	231	3	91	15	1323	29	4.5	1.9	2.8	16.1
Rod Higgins	C-F-G	6'7	205	29	82	1993	304	632	48	234	285	82	422	129	184	0	47	53	909	24	5.1	1.6	2.2	11.1
Mitch Richmond	G	6'5	215	24	78	2799	640	1287	50	406	469	87	360	223	210	3	98	24	1720	36	4.6	2.9	2.7	22.1
Tim Hardaway	G	6'	175	23	79	2663	464	985	47	211	276	76	310	689	232	6	165	12	1162	34	3.9	8.7	2.9	14.7
Sarunas Marciulionis	G	6'5	200	25	75	1695	289	557	52	317	403	79	221	121	230	5	94	7	905	23	2.9	1.6	3.1	12.1
Tom Tolbert	F	6'7	240	24	70	1347	218	442	49	175	241	73	363	58	191	0	23	25	616	19	5.2	0.8	2.7	8.8
Manute Bol	C	7'7	225	27	75	1310	56	169	33	25	49	51	276	36	194	3	13	238	146	17	3.7	0.5	2.6	1.9
Winston Garland (to LAC)	G	6'2	170	25	51	891	108	288	38	53	63	84	111	157	77	1	48	5	270	17	2.2	3.1	1.5	5.3
Jim Peterson (KJ)	C	6'10	235	27	43	592	60	141	43	52	73	71	160	23	103	0	17	20	172	14	3.7	0.5	2.4	4.0
Uwe Blab (to SA)	C	7'1	250	27	40	481	33	87	38	17	31	55	99	24	93	0	1	22	83	12	2.5	0.6	2.3	2.1
Kelvin Upshaw (from Bos, Dal)	G	6'2	180	26	23	252	51	104	49	24	31	77	28	26	34	0	25	0	128	11	1.2	1.1	1.5	5.6
Chris Welp (from SA)	C	7'	250	25	14	142	16	38	42	18	23	78	36	4	37	0	5	8	50	10	2.6	0.3	2.6	3.6
Mike Smrek	C	7'	265	27	13	107	10	24	42	1	6	17	34	1	18	0	4	11	21	8	2.6	0.1	1.4	1.6
Marques Johnson	F	6'7	235	33	10	99	12	32	38	14	17	82	17	9	12	0	0	1	40	10	1.7	0.9	1.2	4.0
John Shasky	C	6'11	240	25	14	51	4	14	29	2	6	33	13	1	10	0	1	2	10	4	0.9	0.1	0.7	0.7
Alton Lister	C	7'	240	31	3	40	4	8	50	4	7	57	8	2	8	0	1	0	12	13	2.7	0.7	2.7	4.0
Leonard Taylor	F	6'8	225	23	10	37	0	6	0	11	16	69	12	1	4	0	0	0	11	4	1.2	0.1	0.4	1.1

3-PT FG - Mullin 87-234, Teagle 3-14, Higgins 67-193, Richmond 34-95, Hardaway 23-84, Marciulionis 10-39, Tolbert 5-18, Bol 9-48, Garland 1-10, Petersen 0-1, Upshaw 2-9, Johnson 2-3, Lister 0-1, Taylor 0-1

LOS ANGELES CLIPPERS 30-52 DON CASEY

	Pos	Hgt	Wgt	Age	G	Min	FG	FGA	%	FT	FTA	%	Reb	Ast	PF	DQ	Stls	Blkd Shts	Points	Per Game Min	Reb	Ast	PF	Points
Snake Norman	F	6'8	219	25	70	2334	484	969	50	153	242	63	470	160	196	0	78	59	1128	33	6.7	2.3	2.8	16.1
Charles Smith	F-C	6'10	238	24	78	2732	595	1145	52	454	572	79	524	114	294	6	86	119	1645	35	6.7	1.5	3.8	21.1
Benoit Benjamin	C	7'	255	25	71	2313	362	688	53	235	321	73	657	159	217	3	59	187	959	33	9.3	2.2	3.1	13.5
Ron Harper (from Cle)	G	6'6	196	25	28	1105	240	499	48	151	190	79	158	133	80	0	67	32	644	39	5.6	4.8	2.9	23.0
Gary Grant (NJ)	G	6'3	196	24	44	1529	241	517	47	88	113	78	195	442	120	1	108	5	575	35	4.4	10.0	2.7	13.1
Danny Manning (KJ)	F	6'10	230	23	71	2269	440	826	53	274	370	74	422	187	261	4	91	39	1154	32	5.9	2.6	3.7	16.3
Tom Garrick	G	6'2	195	23	73	1721	208	421	49	88	114	77	162	289	151	4	90	7	508	24	2.2	4.0	2.1	7.0
Jeff Martin	G	6'5	195	22	69	1351	170	414	41	91	129	71	159	44	97	0	41	16	433	20	2.3	0.6	1.4	6.3
Joe Wolf	C	6'11	230	25	77	1325	155	392	40	55	71	77	232	62	129	0	30	24	370	17	3.0	0.8	1.7	4.8
Winston Garland (from GS)	G	6'2	170	25	28	871	122	285	43	49	59	83	103	146	75	0	30	5	304	31	3.7	5.2	2.7	10.9
David Rivers	G	6'1	180	24	52	724	80	197	41	59	78	76	85	155	53	0	31	0	219	14	1.6	3.0	1.0	4.2
Ken Bannister	F-C	6'9	260	29	52	589	77	161	48	52	110	47	112	18	92	1	17	7	206	11	2.2	0.3	1.8	4.0
Michael Young	F-G	6'6	225	28	45	459	92	194	47	27	38	71	86	24	47	0	25	3	219	10	1.9	0.5	1.0	4.9
Reggie Williams (to Cle)	G-F	6'7	188	25	5	133	21	57	37	18	21	86	15	10	7	0	9	1	60	27	3.0	2.0	1.4	12.0
Carlton McKinney	G	6'4	188	25	7	104	8	32	25	2	4	50	12	7	15	1	6	1	18	15	1.7	1.0	2.1	2.6
Steve Harris	G	6'5	195	26	15	93	14	40	35	3	4	75	10	1	9	0	7	1	31	6	0.7	0.1	0.6	2.1
Jim Les (from Utah)	G	5'11	175	26	6	86	5	14	36	11	13	85	7	20	6	0	3	0	21	14	1.2	3.3	1.0	3.5
Andre Turner (to Cha)	G	5'11	160	25	3	31	2	13	15	0	0	—	5	3	1	0	1	0	4	10	1.7	1.0	0.3	1.3
Jay Edwards	G	6'4	200	20	4	26	3	7	43	1	3	33	2	4	4	0	1	0	7	7	0.5	0.5	1.0	1.8
Torgeir Bryn	C	6'10	250	25	3	10	0	2	0	4	6	67	2	0	5	0	2	1	4	3	0.7	0.0	1.7	1.3

3-PT FG - Norman 7-16, Smith 1-12, Benjamin 0-1, Harper 13-46, Grant 5-21, Manning 0-5, Garrick 4-21, Martin 2-15, Wolf 5-25, Garland 11-26, Rivers 0-5, Bannister 0-1, Young 8-26, Williams 0-5, MacKinney 0-1, Les 0-1, Turner 0-1, Edwards 0-2

SACRAMENTO KINGS 23-59 .280 JERRY REYNOLDS (7-21 .250), DICK MOTTA (16-38 .296)

	Pos	Hgt	Wgt	Age	G	Min	FG	FGA	%	FT	FTA	%	Reb	Ast	PF	DQ	Stls	Blkd Shts	Points	Per Game Min	Reb	Ast	PF	Points
Rodney McCray	F	6'8	235	28	82	3238	537	1043	51	273	348	78	669	377	176	0	60	70	1358	39	8.2	4.6	2.1	16.6
Wayman Tisdale	F-C	6'9	240	25	79	2937	726	1383	52	306	391	78	595	108	251	3	54	54	1758	37	7.5	1.4	3.2	22.3
Greg Kite	C	6'11	250	28	71	1515	101	234	43	27	54	50	377	76	201	2	31	51	230	21	5.3	1.1	2.8	3.2
Danny Ainge	G	6'4	185	30	75	2727	506	1154	44	222	267	83	326	453	238	2	113	18	1342	36	4.3	6.0	3.2	17.9
Kenny Smith (to Atl)	G	6'3	170	24	46	1747	280	607	46	106	131	81	120	303	98	0	57	7	688	38	2.6	6.6	2.1	15.0
Vinny Del Negro	G	6'5	185	23	76	1858	297	643	46	135	155	87	198	250	182	2	64	10	739	24	2.6	3.3	2.4	9.7
Harold Pressley	G-F	6'8	210	26	72	1603	240	566	42	110	141	78	309	149	148	0	58	36	636	22	4.3	2.1	2.1	8.8
Antoine Carr (from Atl)	F	6'9	235	28	33	924	228	473	48	158	196	81	173	66	119	2	15	34	614	28	5.2	2.0	3.6	18.6
Purvis Ellison (NJ)	C	6'9	225	22	34	866	111	251	44	49	78	63	196	65	132	4	19	57	271	25	5.8	1.9	3.9	8.0
Randy Allen	F	6'8	220	24	63	746	106	239	44	23	43	53	138	23	102	0	16	19	235	12	2.2	0.4	1.6	3.7
Sedric Toney (from Atl)	G	6'2	178	27	32	682	57	178	32	46	58	79	46	122	71	1	23	0	176	21	1.4	3.8	2.2	5.5
Ralph Sampson (KJ)	C	7'4	235	29	26	417	48	129	37	12	23	52	84	28	66	1	14	22	109	16	3.2	1.1	2.5	4.2
Henry Turner	F	6'7	195	23	36	315	58	122	48	40	65	62	50	22	40	0	17	7	156	9	1.4	0.6	1.1	4.3
Mike Williams (to Atl)	F	6'8	225	26	16	88	6	14	43	3	6	50	22	2	28	0	3	7	15	6	1.4	0.1	1.8	0.9
Michael Jackson	G	6'2	180	25	17	58	3	11	27	3	6	50	7	8	3	0	5	0	10	3	0.4	0.5	0.2	0.6
Greg Stokes	C	6'10	220	26	11	34	1	9	11	2	2	100	5	0	8	0	0	0	4	3	0.5	0.0	0.7	0.4

3-PT FG - Mcray 11-42, Tisdale 0-6, Kite 1-1, Ainge 108-289, Smith 22-59, Del Negro 10-32, Pressley 46-148, Carr 0-3, Ellison 0-2, Allen 0-7, Toney 16-50, Sampson 1-4, Turner 0-3, Williams 0-1, Jackson 1-2

1989/90 N.B.A. PLAYOFFS

DETROIT PISTONS — CHUCK DALY

defeated Indiana 3-0; H104-92, H100-87, 108-96
defeated New York 4-1; H112-77, H104-97, 103-111, 102-90, H95-84
defeated Chicago 4-3; H86-77, H102-93, 102-107, 101-108, H97-83, 91-109, H93-74
defeated Portland 4-1; H105-99, H105-106(OT), 121-106, 112-109, 92-90

					TOTAL													Blkd		PER GAME				
	Pos	Hgt	Wgt	Age	G	Min	FG	FGA	%	FT	FTA	%	Reb	Ass	PF	DQ	Stls	Shts	Points	Min	Reb	Ass	PF	Points
Dennis Rodman	F	6'8	210	28	19	560	54	95	57	18	35	51	161	17	62	1	9	13	126	29	8.5	0.9	3.3	6.6
James Edwards	F-C	7'	230	34	20	536	114	231	49	58	96	60	71	13	74	0	5	11	286	36	3.6	0.7	3.7	14.3
Bill Laimbeer	C	6'11	250	32	20	667	91	199	46	25	29	86	211	28	77	3	23	18	222	33	10.6	1.4	3.9	11.1
Joe Dumars	G	6'3	190	26	20	754	130	284	46	99	113	88	44	95	37	0	22	0	364	38	2.2	4.8	1.9	18.2
Isiah Thomas	G	6'1	185	28	20	758	148	320	46	81	102	79	109	163	65	1	43	7	409	38	5.5	8.2	3.3	20.5
John Salley	F-C	7'	230	25	20	547	58	122	48	74	98	76	117	20	76	2	9	33	190	27	5.9	1.0	3.8	9.5
Vinnie Johnson	G	6'2	200	33	20	463	85	184	46	34	43	79	56	54	38	0	8	4	206	23	2.8	2.7	1.9	10.3
Mark Aguirre	F	6'6	233	30	20	439	86	184	47	39	52	75	91	27	51	0	10	3	219	22	4.6	1.4	2.6	11.0
David Greenwood	F	6'9	225	32	5	47	2	4	50	1	4	25	9	0	11	0	2	0	5	9	1.8	0.0	2.2	1.0
William Bedford	C	7'1	235	26	5	19	1	6	17	2	2	100	2	0	4	0	0	1	4	4	0.4	0.0	0.8	0.8
Gerald Henderson	G	6'2	180	33	8	19	1	5	20	0	0	—	3	4	3	0	2	0	2	2	0.4	0.5	0.4	0.3
Scott Hastings	F	6'10	245	29	5	16	1	4	25	0	0	—	0	0	4	0	1	0	2	3	0.0	0.0	0.8	0.4

3-PT FG - Edwards 0-1, Laimbeer 15-43, Dumars 5-19, Thomas 32-68, Johnson 2-7, Aquirre 8-24, Henderson 0-3, Hastings 0-3

PORTLAND TRAILBLAZERS — RICK ADELMAN

defeated Dallas 3-0; H109-102, H114-107, 106-92
defeated San Antonio 4-3; H107-94, H122-112, 98-121, 105-115, H138-132(2OT), 97-112, H108-105(OT)
defeated Phoenix 4-2; H100-98, H108-107, 89-123, 107-119, H120-114, 112-109
lost to Detroit 1-4; 99-105, 106-105(OT), H106-121, H109-112, H90-92

	Pos	Hgt	Wgt	Age	G	Min	FG	FGA	%	FT	FTA	%	Reb	Ass	PF	DQ	Stls	Blkd Shts	Points	Min	Reb	Ass	PF	Points
Jerome Kersey	F	6'7	225	27	21	831	166	361	46	103	144	72	174	45	87	2	34	20	435	40	8.3	2.1	4.1	20.7
Buck Williams	F	6'8	225	29	21	776	101	199	51	71	105	68	193	39	74	1	13	6	273	37	9.2	1.9	3.5	13.0
Kevin Duckworth	C	7'	270	25	15	453	82	187	44	33	46	72	87	16	60	2	5	9	197	30	5.8	1.1	4.0	13.1
Clyde Drexler	G-F	6'7	215	27	21	**853**	**172**	**390**	44	96	124	77	151	150	72	2	53	18	449	41	7.2	7.1	3.4	21.4
Terry Porter	G	6'3	195	26	21	815	127	274	46	**139**	**165**	84	61	155	51	1	28	3	433	39	2.9	7.4	2.4	20.6
Cliff Robinson	C-F	6'11	225	23	21	391	54	151	36	29	52	56	87	23	71	1	19	24	137	19	4.1	1.1	3.4	6.5
Danny Young	G	6'4	175	27	21	294	28	72	39	19	27	70	30	32	29	0	14	2	86	14	1.4	1.5	1.4	4.1
Drazen Petrovic	G	6'5	195	25	20	253	48	109	44	21	36	58	32	20	37	0	6	0	122	13	1.5	1.0	1.8	6.1
Wayne Cooper	C	6'10	220	33	18	248	19	47	40	10	19	53	71	5	40	0	5	29	48	14	3.9	0.3	2.2	2.7
Mark Bryant	C-F	6'9	245	24	13	160	18	33	55	6	8	75	29	3	27	1	3	2	42	14	2.2	0.2	2.1	3.2
Byron Irvin	G	6'5	190	23	4	47	5	22	23	5	6	83	8	52	7	0	2	0	15	12	2.0	13.0	1.8	3.8
Nate Johnson	F	6'8	210	23	3	19	6	11	55	1	1	100	6	1	5	0	1	1	13	6	2.0	0.3	1.7	4.3

3-PT FG -Kersey 0-3, Drexler 9-41, Porter 40-102, Robinson 0-4, Young 11-29, Petrovic 5-16

CHICAGO BULLS — PHIL JACKSON

defeated Milwaukee 3-1; H111-97, H109-102, 112-119, 110-86
defeated Philadelphia 4-1; H96-85, H101-96, 112-118, 111-101, H117-99
lost to Detroit 3-4; 77-86, 93-102, H107-102, H108-101, 83-97, H109-91, 74-93

	Pos	Hgt	Wgt	Age	G	Min	FG	FGA	%	FT	FTA	%	Reb	Ass	PF	DQ	Stls	Blkd Shts	Points	Min	Reb	Ass	PF	Points
Scotty Pippen	F	6'8	210	24	15	612	104	210	50	71	100	71	108	83	62	0	31	19	289	41	7.2	5.3	1.3	19.3
Horace Grant	F	6'10	215	24	16	616	81	159	51	33	53	62	159	40	51	1	18	18	195	39	9.9	2.5	3.2	12.2
Bill Cartwright	C	7'1	245	32	16	462	50	121	41	29	43	67	75	16	52	0	5	4	129	29	4.7	1.0	3.3	8.1
John Paxson	G	6'2	185	29	15	395	37	87	43	14	14	100	22	54	42	3	9	0	92	26	1.5	3.6	2.8	6.1
Michael Jordan	G	6'6	195	26	16	674	**219**	**426**	51	133	159	84	115	109	54	0	45	14	**587**	42	7.2	6.8	3.4	**36.7**
Stacey King	C-F	6'11	230	22	16	281	37	91	41	36	47	77	51	9	32	0	6	8	110	18	3.2	0.6	2.0	6.9
Craig Hodges	G	6'3	195	29	16	254	28	74	38	3	4	75	18	17	31	1	4	0	71	16	1.1	1.1	1.9	4.4
Ed Nealy	F	6'7	240	29	15	228	17	36	47	13	21	62	52	5	45	1	10	1	47	15	3.5	0.3	3.0	3.1
B.J. Armstrong	G	6'2	175	22	16	217	21	62	34	22	24	92	20	29	22	0	10	0	64	14	1.2	0.2	1.0	4.0
Will Purdue	C	7'	240	24	13	78	13	28	46	13	18	72	19	2	13	0	0	5	40	6	1.5	0.2	1.0	3.1
Charlie Davis	F	6'7	215	31	6	20	2	7	29	0	0	—	3	1	5	0	0	0	4	3	0.5	0.2	0.8	0.7
Jeff Sanders	F	6'8	225	23	3	3	1	1	100	0	0	—	0	0	0	0	0	0	2	1	0.0	0.0	0.0	0.7

3-PT FG - Pippen 10-31, Grant 0-2, Paxson 4-9, Jordan 16-50, King 0-1, Hodges 12-41, Nealy 0-1, Armstrong 0-4, Perdue 1-2, Davis 0-1

PHOENIX SUNS — COTTON FITZSIMMONS

defeated Utah 3-2; 96-113, 105-87, H120-105, H94-105, 104-102
defeated Lakers 4-1; 104-102, 100-124, H117-103, H114-101, 106-103
lost to Portland 2-4; 98-100, 107-108, H119-107, H129-107, 114-120, H109-112

	Pos	Hgt	Wgt	Age	G	Min	FG	FGA	%	FT	FTA	%	Reb	Ass	PF	DQ	Stls	Blkd Shts	Points	Min	Reb	Ass	PF	Points
Kurt Rambis	F	6'8	213	31	16	385	24	54	44	19	28	68	123	22	51	0	8	8	67	24	7.7	1.4	3.2	4.2
Tom Chambers	F-C	6'10	230	30	16	612	117	275	43	116	132	88	107	31	54	0	7	7	355	38	6.7	1.9	3.4	22.2
Mark West	C	6'10	234	29	16	544	75	130	58	27	50	54	164	5	73	3	4	41	177	34	10.3	0.3	4.6	11.1
Jeff Hornacek	G	6'4	190	26	16	583	112	219	51	68	73	93	62	73	43	1	24	0	298	36	3.9	4.6	2.7	18.6
Kevin Johnson	G	6'2	190	23	16	582	123	257	48	92	112	82	53	170	28	0	25	0	340	36	3.3	10.6	1.8	21.3
Dan Majerle	G-F	6'6	220	24	16	479	73	150	49	51	65	78	81	34	34	0	20	2	201	30	2.1	2.1	2.1	12.6
Eddie Johnson	F	6'8	215	30	16	337	72	160	45	37	47	79	57	17	40	0	10	4	196	21	1.1	1.1	2.5	12.3
Tim Perry	F	6'9	220	24	11	100	13	25	52	8	18	44	21	2	19	0	3	6	34	9	1.9	0.2	1.7	3.1
Andrew Lang	C	6'11	250	23	12	93	6	9	67	4	7	57	20	2	17	0	5	10	16	8	1.7	0.2	1.4	1.3
Greg Grant	G	5'7	145	23	7	47	9	20	45	0	0	—	6	10	2	0	2	0	19	7	0.9	1.4	0.3	2.7
Mike McGee	G	6'5	207	30	10	44	7	20	35	1	4	25	4	2	6	0	1	1	18	4	0.4	0.2	0.6	1.8
Kenny Battle	F	6'6	210	25	8	34	4	13	31	1	1	100	5	0	5	0	0	0	9	4	0.6	0.0	0.6	1.1

3-PT FG - Rambis 0-1, Chambers 5-19, Hornacek 6-24, K. Johnson 2-11, Majerle 4-12, E. Johnson 15-38, Grant 1-3, McGee 3-7

1989/90 N.B.A. PLAYOFFS

NEW YORK KNICKERBOCKERS — **STU JACKSON**

defeated Boston 3-2; 105-116, 128-157, H102-99, H135-108, 121-114
lost to Detroit 1-4; 77-112, 97-104, H111-103, H90-102, 84-95

	Pos	Hgt	Wgt	Age	TOTAL G	Min	FG	FGA	%	FT	FTA	%	Reb	Ass	PF	DQ	Stls	Blkd Shts	Points	PER GAME Min	Reb	Ass	PF	Points
Kiki Vandeweghe	F	6'8	220	31	10	236	31	74	42	8	10	80	12	14	14	0	5	2	76	24	1.2	1.4	1.4	7.6
Charles Oakley	F	6'8	225	26	10	336	43	84	51	34	52	65	110	27	33	1	11	2	121	34	11.0	2.7	3.3	12.1
Patrick Ewing	C	7'	240	27	10	395	114	219	52	65	79	82	105	31	41	0	13	20	294	40	10.5	3.1	4.1	29.4
Gerald Wilkins	G-F	6'6	195	26	10	319	63	137	46	18	22	82	36	52	23	0	14	1	146	32	3.6	5.2	2.3	14.6
Maurice Cheeks	G	6'1	180	33	10	388	50	104	48	28	31	90	39	85	21	0	17	2	128	37	3.9	8.5	2.1	12.8
Johnny Newman	F	6'7	190	26	10	231	38	85	45	37	49	76	21	10	41	1	9	3	117	23	2.1	1.0	4.1	11.7
Trent Tucker	G	6'5	190	30	10	178	22	55	40	6	6	100	14	20	19	0	10	0	60	18	1.4	2.0	1.9	6.0
Kenny Walker	F	6'8	210	25	10	154	16	29	55	9	14	64	25	6	22	0	0	4	41	15	2.5	0.6	2.2	4.1
Mark Jackson	G	6'3	206	24	9	81	13	31	42	8	11	73	5	21	5	0	2	0	34	9	0.6	2.3	0.6	3.8
Eddie Lee Wilkins	C	6'10	220	27	7	54	9	18	50	6	11	55	11	0	7	0	2	0	24	8	1.6	0.0	1.0	3.4
Brian Quinnett	F	6'8	235	23	3	16	2	4	50	0	0	—	8	2	2	0	0	0	5	5	2.7	0.7	0.7	1.7
Stuart Gray	C	7'	245	26	4	12	2	5	40	0	0	—	8	0	3	0	1	0	4	3	2.0	0.0	0.8	1.0

3-PT FG - Vandeweghe 6-13, Oakley 1-1, Ewing 1-2, G. Wilkins 2-8, Cheeks 0-4, Newman 4-10, Tucker 10-27, Walker 0-1, Jackson 0-2, Quinnett 1-1

PHILADELPHIA 76ers — **JIM LYMAN**

defeated Cleveland 3-2; H111-106, H107-101, 95-122, 96-108, H113-97
lost to Chicago 1-4; 85-96, 96-101, H118-112, H101-111, 99-117

	Pos	Hgt	Wgt	Age	TOTAL G	Min	FG	FGA	%	FT	FTA	%	Reb	Ass	PF	DQ	Stls	Blkd Shts	Points	PER GAME Min	Reb	Ass	PF	Points
Charles Barkley	F	6'6	253	26	10	419	88	162	54	65	108	60	155	43	36	0	8	7	247	42	15.5	4.3	3.6	24.7
Rick Mahorn	F-C	6'10	255	31	10	342	37	86	43	20	26	77	70	10	41	1	7	8	94	34	7.0	1.0	4.1	9.4
Mike Gminski	C	6'11	260	30	10	342	57	117	49	14	15	93	54	11	27	0	8	23	128	34	5.4	1.1	2.7	12.8
Hersey Hawkins	G	6'3	190	24	10	415	81	163	50	59	63	94	31	36	25	0	12	7	235	42	3.1	3.6	2.5	23.5
Johnny Dawkins	G	6'2	170	26	10	386	53	115	46	36	43	84	22	99	22	0	17	2	142	39	2.2	9.9	2.2	14.2
Ron Anderson	F	6'7	215	31	10	256	40	93	43	29	30	97	37	14	22	0	4	0	112	26	3.7	1.4	2.2	11.2
Scott Brooks	G	5'11	165	24	9	99	6	19	32	6	9	67	8	16	13	0	3	0	21	11	0.9	1.8	1.4	2.3
Bob Thornton	F-C	6'10	225	27	9	89	7	18	39	5	10	50	15	4	22	0	2	1	19	10	1.7	0.4	2.4	2.1
Kurt Nimphius	C	6'10	225	31	4	18	1	7	14	0	0	—	4	0	1	0	1	1	2	5	1.0	0.0	0.3	0.5
Derek Smith	G	6'6	218	28	1	15	5	8	63	1	2	50	0	1	3	0	1	0	11	15	0.0	1.0	3.0	11.0
Kenny Payne	F	6'8	215	23	3	10	2	5	40	2	2	100	2	0	3	0	0	0	6	3	0.7	0.0	1.0	2.0
Lanard Copeland	G	6'6	185	24	4	9	2	6	33	0	0	—	1	0	1	0	0	0	4	2	0.3	0.0	0.3	1.0

3-PT FG - Barkley 6-18, Mahorn 0-1, Gminski 0-5, Hawkins 14-36, Dawkins 0-7, Anderson 3-5, Brooks 3-7, Smith 0-1, Payne 0-2

SAN ANTONIO SPURS — **LARRY BROWN**

defeated Denver 3-0; H119-103, H129-120, 131-120
lost to Portland 3-4; 94-107, 112-122, H121-98, H115-105, 132-138(2OT), H112-97, 105-108(OT)

	Pos	Hgt	Wgt	Age	TOTAL G	Min	FG	FGA	%	FT	FTA	%	Reb	Ass	PF	DQ	Stls	Blkd Shts	Points	PER GAME Min	Reb	Ass	PF	Points
Sean Elliott	F	6'8	205	21	10	291	53	96	55	21	29	72	41	18	37	0	9	6	127	29	4.1	1.8	3.7	12.7
Terry Cummings	F	6'9	240	28	10	374	103	195	53	42	52	81	94	22	39	0	7	4	249	37	9.4	2.2	3.9	24.9
David Robinson	C	7'1	235	24	10	375	89	167	53	65	96	68	120	23	35	1	11	40	243	38	12.0	2.3	3.5	24.3
Willie Anderson	G-F	6'7	185	22	10	375	87	168	52	29	36	81	54	52	40	2	9	4	205	38	5.4	5.2	4.0	20.5
Rod Strickland	G	6'3	175	23	10	384	54	127	43	15	27	56	53	112	30	2	14	0	123	38	5.3	11.2	3.0	12.3
David Wingate	G	6'5	185	26	10	298	40	77	52	9	12	75	37	38	34	1	18	3	91	30	3.7	3.8	3.4	9.1
Frank Brickowski	F-C	6'10	240	30	10	161	31	54	57	17	26	65	44	11	31	0	8	1	79	16	4.4	1.1	3.1	7.9
Johnny Moore	G	6'2	185	31	9	86	6	24	25	4	8	50	11	21	11	0	7	1	16	10	1.2	2.3	1.2	1.8
Caldwell Jones	C	6'11	225	39	9	66	4	9	44	0	1	0	13	2	10	0	0	3	8	7	1.4	0.2	1.1	0.9
Reggie Williams	F	6'7	195	25	9	49	9	27	33	2	2	100	11	3	8	0	2	0	20	5	1.2	0.3	0.9	2.2
Michael Mitchell	F	6'7	215	33	4	15	3	8	38	0	0	—	3	2	2	0	0	0	6	4	0.8	0.5	0.5	1.5
Uwe Blab	C	7'1	250	27	2	5	0	1	0	3	6	50	2	0	0	0	0	0	3	3	1.0	0.0	0.0	1.5

3-PT FG - Elliott 0-1, Cummings 1-5, Anderson 2-5, Strickland 0-7, Wingate 2-3, Moore 0-6, Williams 0-2

LOS ANGELES LAKERS — **PAT RILEY**

defeated Houston 3-1, H101-89, H104-100, 108-114, 109-88
lost to Phoenix 4-1; H102-104, H124-100, 103-117, 101-114, H103-106

	Pos	Hgt	Wgt	Age	TOTAL G	Min	FG	FGA	%	FT	FTA	%	Reb	Ass	PF	DQ	Stls	Blkd Shts	Points	PER GAME Min	Reb	Ass	PF	Points
James Worthy	F	6'9	225	28	9	366	90	181	50	36	43	84	50	27	18	0	14	3	218	41	5.6	3.0	2.0	24.2
A.C. Green	F-C	6'9	224	26	9	252	41	79	52	24	32	75	81	9	22	0	5	4	106	28	9.0	1.0	2.4	11.8
Mychal Thompson	C	6'10	235	34	9	225	21	44	48	16	26	62	39	2	26	0	2	13	58	25	4.3	0.2	2.9	6.4
Byron Scott	G	6'3	193	28	9	325	49	106	46	10	13	77	37	23	32	1	20	3	121	36	4.1	2.6	3.6	13.4
Magic Johnson	G	6'8	220	30	9	376	76	155	49	70	79	89	57	115	28	0	11	1	227	42	6.3	12.8	3.1	25.2
Orlando Woolridge	F	6'9	215	30	9	199	40	70	57	26	37	70	23	10	25	1	8	8	106	22	2.6	1.1	2.8	11.8
Vlade Divac	C	6'11	248	21	9	175	32	44	73	17	19	89	48	10	27	1	8	15	82	19	5.3	1.1	3.0	9.1
Michael Cooper	F-G	6'5	176	33	9	173	10	35	29	0	0	—	24	25	21	0	7	4	23	19	2.7	2.8	2.3	2.6
Larry Drew	G	6'1	190	31	9	51	3	8	38	5	6	83	2	4	9	0	3	0	12	6	0.2	0.4	1.0	1.7
Jay Vincent	F	6'7	220	30	3	8	0	2	0	0	0	—	0	0	1	0	0	0	0	3	0.0	0.0	0.3	0.0
Melvin McCants	F	6'8	250	22	2	5	0	0	—	0	0	—	0	0	1	0	0	0	0	3	0.0	0.0	0.5	0.0
Mark McNamara	C	6'11	233	30	2	5	1	4	25	0	0	—	1	0	1	0	0	0	2	3	0.5	0.0	0.5	1.0

3-PT FG - Worthy 2-8, Scott 13-34, Johnson 5-25, Woolridge 0-1, Divac 1-2, Cooper 3-12, Drew 1-4

1989/90 N.B.A. PLAYOFFS

BOSTON CELTICS — **JIMMY RODGERS** — lost to New York 2-3; H116-105, H157-128, 99-102, 108-135,H114-121

	Pos	Hgt	Wgt	Age	G	Min	FG	FGA	%	FT	FTA	%	Reb	Ass	PF	DQ	Stls	Blkd Shts	Points	Min	Reb	Ass	PF	Points
Larry Bird	F	6'9	220	33	5	207	44	99	44	29	32	91	46	44	10	0	5	5	122	41	9.2	8.8	2.0	24.4
Kevin McHale	F	6'10	225	32	5	192	42	69	61	25	29	86	39	13	17	0	2	10	110	38	7.8	2.6	3.4	22.0
Robert Parish	C	7'	230	36	5	170	31	54	57	17	18	94	50	13	21	0	5	7	79	34	10.0	2.6	5.2	15.8
Reggie Lewis	G-F	6'7	195	24	5	200	37	62	60	27	35	77	25	22	14	0	7	2	101	40	5.0	4.4	2.8	20.2
Dennis Johnson	G	6'4	200	35	5	162	30	62	48	7	7	100	14	28	17	1	2	2	69	32	2.8	5.6	3.4	13.8
Joe Kleine	C	7'	271	27	5	79	13	17	76	5	6	83	14	2	12	0	2	3	31	16	2.8	0.4	2.4	6.2
John Bagley	G	6'1	192	29	5	70	8	15	53	3	4	75	4	17	9	0	4	1	19	14	0.8	3.4	1.8	3.8
Jim Paxson	G	6'6	210	32	5	62	8	16	50	3	4	75	0	7	1	0	5	0	19	12	0.0	1.4	0.2	3.8
Ed Pinckney	F	6'9	215	26	4	25	6	7	86	7	9	78	6	0	3	0	0	0	19	6	1.5	0.0	0.8	4.8
Michael Smith	F	6'10	225	24	4	16	5	8	63	7	7	100	0	0	1	0	1	0	17	4	0.0	0.0	0.3	4.3
Charles Smith	G	6'1	160	22	3	9	1	2	50	0	0	—	1	3	0	0	1	0	2	3	0.3	1.0	0.0	0.7
Kevin Gamble	G	6'5	215	24	3	8	3	5	60	0	0	—	1	2	1	0	0	0	6	3	0.3	0.7	0.3	2.0

3-PT FG - Bird 5-19, McHale 1-3, Lewis 0-1, Johnson 2-6, Kleine 0-1, Bagley 0-1, Paxson 0-1, M. Smith 0-2

CLEVELAND CAVALIERS — **LENNY WILKENS** — lost to Philadelphia 2-3; 106-111, 101-107, H122-95, H108-96, 97-113

	Pos	Hgt	Wgt	Age	G	Min	FG	FGA	%	FT	FTA	%	Reb	Ass	PF	DQ	Stls	Blkd Shts	Points	Min	Reb	Ass	PF	Points
Benoit Bennett	F	6'7	210	24	5	135	23	47	49	4	6	67	21	5	11	0	3	1	50	27	4.2	1.0	2.2	10.0
Larry Nance	F	6'10	235	30	5	159	26	45	58	9	12	75	24	12	20	0	3	10	61	32	4.8	2.4	4.0	12.2
Brad Daugherty	C	7'	263	24	5	186	41	70	59	32	46	70	48	20	12	0	2	4	114	37	9.6	4.0	2.4	22.8
Craig Ehlo	G	6'7	205	28	5	196	26	62	42	12	19	63	32	32	18	0	6	0	69	39	6.4	6.4	3.6	13.8
Mark Price	G	6'1	178	25	5	192	32	61	52	30	30	100	14	44	9	0	9	1	100	38	2.8	8.8	1.8	20.0
John Williams	F-C	6'11	238	28	5	174	39	70	56	17	22	77	46	11	23	1	2	5	95	35	9.2	2.2	4.6	19.0
Steve Kerr	G	6'3	180	24	5	73	4	14	29	0	0	—	6	10	6	0	4	0	8	15	1.2	2.0	1.2	1.6
Tree Rollins	C	7'1	250	34	3	38	1	3	33	6	8	75	8	1	7	0	2	1	8	13	2.7	0.3	2.3	2.7
Derrick Chievous	F-G	6'7	200	22	3	28	6	10	60	7	9	78	3	2	2	0	1	0	19	9	1.0	0.7	0.7	6.3
Paul Mokeski	C	7'	270	32	3	10	1	2	50	2	2	100	2	0	2	0	1	1	4	3	0.7	0.0	0.7	1.3
John Morton	G	6'3	195	23	2	9	2	5	40	2	2	100	0	0	1	0	0	0	6	5	0.0	0.0	0.5	3.0

3-PT FG - Ehlo 5-15, Price 6-17, Kerr 0-3

UTAH JAZZ — **JERRY SLOAN** — lost to Phoenix 2-3; H113-96, H87-105, 105-120, 105-94, H102-104

	Pos	Hgt	Wgt	Age	G	Min	FG	FGA	%	FT	FTA	%	Reb	Ass	PF	DQ	Stls	Blkd Shts	Points	Min	Reb	Ass	PF	Points
Thurl Bailey	F	6'11	232	28	5	190	43	88	49	19	24	79	32	7	19	1	5	6	105	38	6.4	1.4	3.8	21.0
Karl Malone	F-C	6'9	256	26	5	203	46	105	44	34	45	76	51	11	22	1	11	5	126	41	10.2	2.2	4.4	25.2
Mark Eaton	C	7'4	290	32	5	128	9	17	53	1	5	20	30	0	17	0	3	14	19	26	6.0	0.0	3.4	3.8
Bob Hansen	G	6'6	200	28	5	145	21	43	49	1	4	25	14	5	14	0	3	0	50	29	2.8	1.0	2.8	10.0
John Stockton	G	6'1	175	27	5	194	29	69	42	16	20	80	16	75	20	0	6	0	75	39	3.2	15.0	4.0	15.0
Darrell Griffith	G	6'4	195	31	5	97	19	42	45	4	5	80	21	3	3	0	6	1	47	19	4.2	0.6	0.6	9.4
Blue Edwards	F	6'5	200	24	5	94	14	26	54	7	8	88	18	8	16	0	7	2	36	19	3.6	1.6	3.2	7.2
Mike Brown	F-C	6'9	260	26	5	67	7	15	47	4	5	80	10	3	11	0	1	1	18	13	2.0	0.3	2.2	3.6
Delaney Rudd	G	6'2	195	27	5	45	8	23	35	1	2	50	3	13	10	0	1	0	18	9	0.6	2.6	2.0	3.6
Eric Leckner	C	6'11	265	23	3	28	6	10	60	5	9	56	8	2	8	0	0	0	18	9	2.7	0.7	2.7	6.0
Raymond Brown	F	6'8	225	24	3	6	0	0	—	0	0	—	0	0	2	0	0	0	0	2	0.0	0.0	0.7	0.0
Eric Johnson	G	6'2	205	23	1	3	0	0	—	0	0	—	0	0	0	0	0	0	0	3	0.0	0.0	0.0	0.0

3-PT FG - Malone 0-1, Hansen 7-14, Stockton 1-13, Griffith 5-9, Edwards 1-3, Rudd 1-7, Leckner 1-1

HOUSTON ROCKETS — **DON CHANEY** — lost to L.A. Lakers 1-3; 89-101, 100-104, H114-108, H88-109

	Pos	Hgt	Wgt	Age	G	Min	FG	FGA	%	FT	FTA	%	Reb	Ass	PF	DQ	Stls	Blkd Shts	Points	Min	Reb	Ass	PF	Points
Buck Johnson	F	6'7	206	25	4	148	20	48	42	11	13	85	16	9	16	0	6	2	51	37	4.0	2.3	4.0	12.8
Otis Thorpe	F	6'11	246	27	4	164	27	45	60	26	30	67	33	7	2	0	5	0	80	41	8.3	1.8	0.5	20.0
Akeem Olajuwon	C	7'	258	26	4	161	31	70	44	12	17	71	46	8	19	0	10	23	74	40	11.5	2.0	4.8	18.5
Vernon Maxwell	G	6'5	185	24	4	159	30	81	37	11	21	52	12	17	12	0	5	0	79	40	3.0	4.3	3.0	19.8
Eric Floyd	G	6'3	183	29	4	172	30	64	47	11	17	65	15	41	5	0	5	1	74	43	3.8	10.3	1.3	18.5
Larry Smith	F-C	6'8	251	31	4	73	6	8	75	0	0	—	13	5	11	0	4	0	12	18	3.3	1.3	2.8	3.0
Mitchell Wiggins	G	6'4	199	30	4	51	7	15	47	2	3	67	13	2	5	0	1	0	16	13	3.3	0.5	1.3	4.0
Tim McCormick	C	7'	237	27	3	21	1	3	33	1	2	50	8	0	5	0	0	0	3	7	2.7	0.0	1.7	1.0
Mike Woodson	G	6'5	200	31	1	6	1	3	33	0	0	—	0	2	1	0	0	0	2	6	0.0	2.0	1.0	2.0
Anthony Bowie	F	6'6	190	26	2	4	0	1	0	0	0	—	0	0	1	0	0	0	0	2	0.0	0.0	0.5	0.0
Adrian Caldwell	F	6'8	265	23	1	1	0	0	—	0	0	—	0	0	0	0	0	0	0	1	0.0	0.0	0.0	0.0

3-PT FG - Johnson 0-1, Maxwell 8-26, Floyd 3-12, Woodson 0-1

1989/90 N.B.A. PLAYOFFS

MILWAUKEE BUCKS — **DEL HARRIS** — lost to Chicago 1-3; 97-111, 102-109, H119-112, H86-110

	Pos	Hgt	Wgt	Age		TOTAL Min	FG	FGA	%	FT	FTA	%	Reb	Ass	PF	DQ	Stls	Blkd Shts	Points	PER GAME Min	Reb	Ass	PF	Points
Fred Roberts	F	6'10	220	29	4	79	13	20	65	13	16	81	8	3	9	0	0	1	39	20	2.0	0.8	2.3	9.5
Jack Sikma	F-C	6'11	250	34	4	117	6	23	26	6	8	75	14	7	19	0	2	4	20	29	3.5	1.8	4.8	5.0
Brad Lohaus	C	7'	235	25	4	147	16	40	40	0	0	—	27	5	17	1	8	9	38	37	6.8	1.3	4.3	9.5
Paul Pressey	G-F	6'5	201	31	4	129	19	44	43	21	26	81	21	30	14	0	6	1	59	32	5.3	7.5	3.5	14.8
Alvin Robertson	G	6'4	190	27	4	155	35	67	52	24	34	71	23	19	16	0	9	0	94	39	5.8	4.8	4.0	23.5
Ricky Pierce	F-G	6'5	220	30	4	122	28	60	47	28	31	90	9	6	14	0	5	0	89	31	2.3	1.5	3.5	22.3
Greg Anderson	F	6'10	230	25	4	101	13	19	68	7	14	50	24	0	19	2	1	4	33	25	6.0	0.0	4.8	8.3
Jay Humphries	G	6'3	185	27	3	79	8	15	53	10	13	77	5	19	6	0	3	0	27	26	1.7	6.3	2.0	9.0
Tony Brown	G-F	6'6	195	29	2	13	1	3	33	0	0	—	0	0	3	0	2	0	3	7	0.0	0.0	1.5	1.5
Jeff Grayer	F-G	6'5	200	24	4	12	0	0	—	0	0	—	2	1	1	0	0	0	0	3	0.5	0.3	0.3	0.0
Frank Kornet	F	6'9	225	22	2	4	0	1	0	0	0	—	1	0	1	0	0	0	0	2	0.5	0.0	0.5	0.0
Tito Harford	C	7'1	245	23	2	2	1	1	100	0	0	—	0	0	0	0	0	0	2	1	0.0	0.0	0.0	1.0

3-PT FG - Roberts 0-1, Sikma 2-7, Lohaus 6-16, Pressey 0-3, Robertson 0-1, Pierce 5-10, Humphries 1-3, Brown 1-1, Kornet 0-1

DALLAS MAVERICKS — **RICHIE ABUDATO** — lost to Portland 0-3; 102-109, 107-114, H92-106

	Pos	Hgt	Wgt	Age		TOTAL Min	FG	FGA	%	FT	FTA	%	Reb	Ass	PF	DQ	Stls	Blkd Shts	Points	PER GAME Min	Reb	Ass	PF	Points
Sam Perkins	F	6'9	260	28	3	118	16	36	44	13	17	76	22	8	17	2	3	2	45	39	7.3	2.7	5.7	16.7
Roy Tarpley	F-C	7'	250	25	3	129	22	46	48	6	12	50	46	1	12	0	7	10	50	43	15.3	0.3	4.0	15.0
James Donaldson	C	7'2	280	32	3	74	9	13	69	4	5	80	16	2	8	0	2	0	22	25	5.3	0.7	2.7	7.3
Rolando Blackman	G	6'6	206	30	3	127	24	54	44	10	10	100	9	13	7	0	6	2	60	42	3.0	4.3	2.3	20.0
Derek Harper	G	6'4	208	28	3	119	21	48	44	11	16	69	8	23	13	0	4	0	58	40	2.7	7.7	4.3	19.3
Herb Williams	F-C	6'11	242	31	3	81	14	23	61	13	16	81	13	5	16	1	1	2	41	27	4.3	1.7	5.3	13.7
Steve Alford	G	6'2	182	25	3	42	8	18	44	5	5	100	3	8	4	0	1	0	23	14	1.0	2.7	1.3	7.7
Bill Wennington	C	7'	258	25	3	25	1	25	4	0	0	—	3	1	5	0	0	1	2	8	1.0	0.3	1.7	0.7
Anthony Jones	F	6'6	201	27	1	3	0	0	—	0	0	—	0	0	0	0	0	0	0	3	0.0	0.0	0.0	0.0
Randy White	F	6'8	250	22	1	2	0	0	—	0	0	—	0	0	0	0	0	0	0	2	0.0	0.0	0.0	0.0

3-PT FG - Perkins 0-1, Tarpley 0-1, Blackman 2-5, Harper 5-16, Alford 2-6

DENVER NUGGETS — **DOUG MOE** — lost to San Antonio 0-3; 103-119, 120-129, H120-131

	Pos	Hgt	Wgt	Age		TOTAL Min	FG	FGA	%	FT	FTA	%	Reb	Ass	PF	DQ	Stls	Blkd Shts	Points	PER GAME Min	Reb	Ass	PF	Points
Alex English	F	6'8	190	35	3	76	25	44	57	9	11	82	9	9	6	0	2	1	59	25	3.0	3.0	2.0	19.7
Bill Hanzlik	F	6'7	200	32	3	79	5	17	29	10	10	100	10	11	13	1	5	2	21	26	3.3	3.7	4.3	7.0
Blair Rosmussen	C	7'	260	27	3	84	19	48	40	9	10	90	26	1	10	0	2	4	47	28	8.7	0.3	3.3	18.7
Lafayette Lever	G	6'3	175	29	3	113	19	51	37	13	14	93	32	21	7	0	8	1	52	38	10.7	7.0	2.3	17.3
Michael Adams	G	5'11	165	26	3	105	13	34	38	7	8	88	6	18	10	0	4	0	39	35	2.0	6.0	3.3	13.0
Walter Davis	F	6'6	200	35	3	70	18	45	40	6	6	100	9	6	4	0	1	0	42	23	3.0	2.0	1.3	14.0
Todd Lichti	G	6'4	205	22	3	70	15	29	52	14	19	74	18	9	6	0	1	0	44	23	6.0	3.0	2.0	14.7
Tim Kempton	F-C	6'10	245	25	3	32	7	9	78	4	4	100	5	4	8	0	0	0	18	11	1.7	1.3	2.7	6.0
Joe Barry Carroll	C	7'	255	31	3	46	9	16	56	2	2	100	9	3	6	0	1	5	20	15	3.0	1.0	2.0	6.7
T.R. Dunn	G-F	6'4	192	34	3	31	0	0	—	0	0	—	7	2	3	0	4	1	0	15	2.3	0.7	1.0	0.0
Jerome Lane	F	6'8	232	23	2	14	0	3	0	1	2	50	1	2	4	0	0	0	1	7	0.5	1.0	2.0	0.5
Dan Schayes (JJ)																								

3-PT FG - Hanzlik 1-3, Lever 1-7, Adams 6-20, Davis 0-1, Lichti 0-1

INDIANA PACERS — **DICK VERSACE** — lost to Detroit 0-3; 92-104, 87-100, H96-108

	Pos	Hgt	Wgt	Age		TOTAL Min	FG	FGA	%	FT	FTA	%	Reb	Ass	PF	DQ	Stls	Blkd Shts	Points	PER GAME Min	Reb	Ass	PF	Points
Chuck Person	F	6'8	220	25	3	123	17	45	38	5	12	42	20	12	11	0	1	0	40	41	6.7	4.0	3.7	13.3
Detlef Schrempf	F-C	6'10	215	26	3	125	23	47	49	15	16	94	22	5	13	0	2	1	61	42	7.3	1.7	4.3	20.3
Rik Smits	C	7'4	250	23	3	96	14	28	50	9	11	82	16	3	12	0	2	4	37	32	5.3	1.0	4.0	12.3
Reggie Miller	G	6'7	185	24	3	125	20	35	57	19	21	90	12	6	6	0	3	0	62	42	4.0	2.0	2.0	20.7
Vern Fleming	G	6'5	180	28	3	113	16	34	47	8	9	89	13	18	6	0	2	1	40	38	4.3	6.0	2.0	13.3
LaSalle Thompson	F-C	6'10	245	28	3	54	7	15	47	4	4	100	15	2	13	0	0	1	18	18	5.0	0.7	4.3	6.0
Rickey Green	G	6'1	172	35	3	31	1	7	14	0	0	—	1	3	5	0	1	0	2	10	0.3	1.0	1.7	0.7
Mike Sanders	F	6'6	210	29	3	24	5	11	45	0	0	—	6	2	4	0	0	0	11	8	2.0	0.7	1.3	3.7
Calvin Natt	F	6'6	220	32	2	14	1	3	33	0	0	—	2	1	5	0	0	0	2	7	1.0	0.5	2.5	0.7
Randy Wittman	G	6'6	210	30	2	11	0	1	0	0	0	—	1	0	0	0	0	0	0	6	0.5	0.0	0.0	0.0
George McCloud	G	6'6	205	22	1	4	1	2	50	0	0	—	1	0	2	0	0	0	2	4	1.0	0.0	2.0	0.7

3-PT FG - Person 1-10, Schrempf 0-3, Miller 3-7, Fleming 0-2, Sanders 1-1

TEAM STATISTICS

EASTERN CONFERENCE - ATLANTIC DIVISION

Team		G	FG	FGA	%	FT	FTA	%	REBOUNDS			Assists	PF	Steals	Blocked	Turn	Points	Points
									Offense	Defense	Total				Shots	Overs		per game
Philadelphia	Off.	82	3437	7028	49	1976	2509	79	1111	2406	3517	1932	1697	539	455	1209	9039	110.2
	Def.	82	3417	7117	48	1584	2054	77	1113	2356	3469	2155	1945	380	380	1234	8630	105.2
	Diff.		+20	-89	+1	+392	+455	+2	-2	+50	+48	-223	+248	+159	+75	+25	+409	+5.0
Boston	Off.	82	3563	7148	50	1791	2153	83	1066	2707	3773	2423	1717	539	455	1256	9023	110.0
	Def.	82	3438	7383	47	1648	2133	77	1046	2318	3364	2078	1845	736	356	1003	8696	106.0
	Diff.		+125	-235	+3	+143	+20	+6	+20	+389	+409	+345	+128	-197	+99	-253	+327	+4.0
New York	Off.	82	3434	7089	48	1775	2349	76	1187	2426	3613	2140	1028	714	492	1412	8879	108.3
	Def.	82	3497	7430	47	1598	2100	76	1249	2285	3534	2126	1869	719	418	1287	8763	106.9
	Diff.		-63	-341	+1	+177	+249	—	-62	+141	+79	+14	+841	-5	+74	-125	+116	+1.4
Washington	Off.	82	3598	7581	47	1599	2093	76	1198	2450	3648	2214	1929	561	424	1201	8832	107.7
	Def.	82	3511	7403	47	1845	2376	78	1198	2503	3701	1952	1780	644	430	1200	9009	109.9
	Diff.		+87	+178	—	-246	-283	-2	—	-53	-53	+262	-149	-83	-6	-1	-177	-2.2
Miami	Off.	82	3383	7345	46	1393	2028	69	1242	2313	3555	1957	2123	736	388	1557	8247	100.6
	Def.	82	3418	7010	49	2050	2716	75	1125	2467	3592	2076	1781	860	477	1473	9044	110.3
	Diff.		-35	+335	-3	-657	-688	-6	+117	-154	-37	-119	-342	-124	-89	-84	-797	-9.7
New Jersey	Off.	82	3157	7415	43	1754	2350	75	1363	2324	3687	1475	1952	774	481	1360	8208	100.1
	Def.	82	3403	7020	48	1906	2491	77	1144	2590	3734	1871	1886	768	478	1419	8853	108.0
	Diff.		-246	+395	-5	-152	-141	-2	+219	-266	-47	-396	-66	+6	+3	+59	-645	-7.9

CENTRAL DIVISION

Team		G	FG	FGA	%	FT	FTA	%	Offense	Defense	Total	Assists	PF	Steals	Blocked Shots	Turn Overs	Points	Points per game
Detroit	Off.	82	3333	6980	48	1713	2252	76	1185	2458	3643	1996	1961	512	418	1233	8556	104.3
	Def.	82	3043	6809	45	1785	2342	76	1040	2281	3321	1764	2072	606	304	1248	8057	98.3
	Diff.		+290	+171	+3	-72	-90	—	+145	+177	+322	+232	+111	-94	+114	+15	+499	+6.0
Chicago	Off.	82	3531	7090	50	1665	2140	78	1075	2279	3354	2172	1906	814	388	1247	8977	109.5
	Def.	82	3361	6819	49	1784	2392	75	1068	2296	3364	2110	1742	665	383	1411	8710	106.2
	Diff.		+170	+271	+1	-119	-252	+3	+7	-17	-10	+62	-164	+149	+5	+164	+267	+3.3
Milwaukee	Off.	82	3380	7146	47	1722	2273	76	1108	2246	3354	2046	2086	826	326	1315	8691	106.0
	Def.	82	3292	6871	48	1990	2570	77	1158	2405	3563	2023	1879	685	444	1506	8755	106.8
	Diff.		+88	+275	-1	-268	-297	-1	-50	-159	-209	+23	-207	+141	-118	+191	-64	-0.8
Cleveland	Off.	82	3214	6977	46	1637	2201	74	1128	2380	3508	2106	1666	645	512	1243	8411	102.6
	Def.	82	3418	7135	48	1444	1898	76	1134	2451	3585	2137	1893	680	379	1294	8436	102.9
	Diff.		-204	-158	-2	+193	+303	-2	-6	-71	-77	-31	+227	-35	+133	+51	-25	-0.3
Indiana	Off.	82	3381	6807	50	1906	2335	82	940	2388	3328	2023	1972	552	350	1342	8962	109.3
	Def.	82	3486	7225	48	1804	2395	75	1173	2297	3470	1945	2021	716	321	1189	8949	109.1
	Diff.		-105	-418	+2	+102	-60	+7	-233	+91	-142	+78	+49	-164	+29	-153	+13	+0.2
Atlanta	Off.	82	3417	7019	49	1943	2544	76	1273	2187	3460	1820	1871	717	353	1270	8901	108.5
	Def.	82	3438	6935	50	1760	2279	77	1151	2236	3387	2144	1961	672	389	1294	8817	107.5
	Diff.		-21	+84	-1	+183	+265	-1	+122	-49	+73	-324	+90	+45	-36	+24	+84	+1.0
Orlando	Off.	82	3457	7525	46	2060	2725	76	1304	2465	3769	1993	1975	617	294	1407	9090	110.9
	Def.	82	3864	7757	50	1897	2502	76	1173	2569	3742	2333	2060	734	556	1216	9821	119.8
	Diff.		-407	-232	-4	+163	+223	—	+131	-104	+27	-340	+85	-117	-262	-191	-731	-8.9

Team		G	FG	FGA	%	FT	FTA	%	REBOUNDS Offense	Defense	Total	Assists	PF	Steals	Blocked Shots	Turn Overs	Points	Points per game
TEAM STATISTICS WESTERN CONFERENCE - MIDWEST DIVISION																		
San Antonio	Off.	82	3388	6997	48	1888	2535	74	1163	2474	3637	2037	1854	799	554	1399	8718	106.3
	Def.	82	3269	7090	46	1663	2169	77	1125	2241	3366	1916	1919	760	416	1420	8432	102.8
	Diff.		+119	-93	+2	+225	+366	-3	+38	+233	+271	+121	+65	+39	+138	+21	+286	+3.5
Utah	Off.	82	3330	6593	51	1874	2484	75	953	2501	3454	2212	2031	677	491	1410	8760	106.8
	Def.	82	3164	6949	46	1865	2452	76	1100	2210	3310	1885	1910	736	452	1241	8367	102.0
	Diff.		+166	-356	+5	+9	+32	-1	-147	+291	+144	+327	-121	-59	+39	-169	+393	+4.8
Dallas	Off.	82	3246	6831	48	1735	2261	77	1042	2419	3461	1776	1733	664	398	1228	8384	102.2
	Def.	82	3288	7013	47	1627	2161	75	1142	2398	3540	1961	1832	649	388	1236	8378	102.2
	Diff.		-42	-182	+1	+108	+100	+2	-100	+21	-79	-185	+99	+15	+10	+8	+6	-
Denver	Off.	82	3716	8015	46	1737	2201	79	1169	2532	3701	2275	2047	814	329	1136	9397	114.6
	Def.	82	3589	7334	49	1939	2517	77	1021	2846	3867	2073	1911	613	462	1514	9281	113.2
	Diff.		+127	+681	-3	-202	-316	+2	+148	-314	-166	+202	-136	+201	-133	+378	+116	+1.4
Houston	Off.	82	3483	7250	48	1633	2267	72	1217	2638	3855	2194	1934	809	551	1513	8752	106.7
	Def.	82	3399	7322	46	1671	2256	74	1175	2460	3635	2010	1819	790	392	1428	8632	105.3
	Diff.		+84	-72	+2	-38	+11	-2	+42	+178	+220	+184	-115	+19	+159	-85	+120	+1.4
Minnesota	Off.	82	3067	6876	45	1596	2137	75	1196	2053	3249	1844	1901	789	344	1197	7803	95.2
	Def.	82	3081	6391	48	1859	2420	77	1050	2322	3372	1880	1748	578	489	1366	8150	99.4
	Diff.		-14	+485	-3	-263	-283	-2	+146	-269	-123	-36	-153	+211	-145	+169	-347	-4.2
Charlotte	Off.	82	3270	7183	46	1487	1967	76	962	2211	3173	2080	1889	778	262	1226	8232	100.4
	Def.	82	3438	6922	50	1865	2380	78	1063	2723	3786	2066	1754	638	384	1376	8873	108.2
	Diff.		-168	+261	-4	-378	-413	-2	-101	-512	-613	+14	-135	+140	-122	+150	-641	-7.8
PACIFIC DIVISION																		
L.A. Lakers	Off.	82	3434	7010	49	1902	2417	79	1097	2460	3557	2232	1737	655	445	1226	9079	110.7
	Def.	82	3382	7247	47	1584	2111	75	1131	2243	3374	2009	1909	669	426	1200	8523	103.9
	Diff.		+52	-237	+2	+318	+306	+4	-34	+217	+183	+223	+172	-14	+19	-26	+556	+6.8
Portland	Off.	82	3572	7547	47	2031	2734	74	1355	2552	3907	2085	2048	749	364	1356	9365	114.2
	Def.	82	3351	7227	46	1917	2500	77	1055	2357	3412	2026	2086	667	432	1489	8847	107.9
	Diff.		+221	+320	+1	+114	+234	-3	+300	+195	+495	+59	+38	+82	-68	+133	+518	+6.3
Phoenix	Off.	82	3544	7139	50	2159	2716	79	1053	2651	3704	2109	1825	668	501	1275	9423	114.9
	Def.	82	3528	7588	46	1585	2163	73	1202	2335	3537	2125	2151	677	395	1254	8841	107.8
	Diff.		+16	-449	+4	+574	+553	+6	-149	+316	+167	-16	+326	-9	+106	-21	+582	+7.1
Seattle	Off.	82	3466	7243	48	1606	2167	74	1323	2255	3578	1874	2064	701	335	1336	8769	106.9
	Def.	82	3257	6704	49	1992	2533	79	1007	2204	3211	1862	1796	634	406	1303	8684	105.9
	Diff.		+209	+539	-1	-386	-366	-5	+316	+51	+367	+12	-268	+67	-71	-33	+85	+1.0
Golden State	Off.	82	3489	7208	48	2313	2858	81	915	2385	3300	1978	2010	756	488	1415	9534	116.3
	Def.	82	3766	7885	48	1998	2633	76	1495	2594	4089	2331	2219	817	430	1422	9791	119.4
	Diff.		-277	-677	—	+315	+225	+5	-580	-209	-789	-353	+209	-61	+58	+7	-257	-3.1
L.A. Clippers	Off.	82	3319	6853	48	1815	2458	74	1056	2362	3418	1978	1859	782	507	1547	8509	103.8
	Def.	82	3432	7207	48	1737	2251	77	1149	2367	3516	2092	1950	828	429	1364	8787	107.2
	Diff.		-113	-354	—	+78	+207	-3	-93	-5	-98	-114	+91	-46	+78	-183	-278	-3.4
Sacramento	Off.	82	3305	7056	47	1515	1964	77	952	2363	3315	2052	1863	546	292	1239	8341	101.7
	Def.	82	3384	7158	47	1828	2324	79	1146	2531	3677	2022	1740	704	391	1168	8756	106.8
	Diff.		-79	-102	—	-313	-360	-2	-194	-168	-362	+30	-123	-158	-99	-71	-415	-5.1

Team		G	FG	FGA	%	FT	FTA	%	REBOUNDS Offense	REBOUNDS Defense	REBOUNDS Total	Assists	PF	Steals	Blocked Shots	Turn Overs	Points	Points per game
PLAYOFFS																		
Detroit	Off.	20	771	1638	47	431	574	75	279	595	874	421	502	134	90	302	2035	101.8
	Def.	20	698	1604	44	449	570	79	245	543	788	410	521	132	75	305	1895	94.8
	Diff.		+73	+34	+3	-18	+4	-4	+34	+52	+86	+11	+19	+2	+15	+3	+140	+7.0
Portland	Off.	21	826	1856	45	533	733	73	326	603	929	494	560	183	114	337	2250	107.1
	Def.	21	888	1857	48	472	641	74	288	646	934	507	571	144	115	357	2297	109.4
	Diff.		-62	-1	-3	+61	+92	-1	+38	-43	-5	-13	+11	+39	-1	+20	-47	-2.3
Chicago	Off.	16	610	1302	47	367	483	76	209	433	642	365	409	138	69	230	1630	101.9
	Def.	16	566	1202	47	401	523	77	192	448	640	356	405	118	72	275	1575	98.4
	Diff.		+44	+100	—	-34	-40	-1	+17	-15	+2	+9	-4	+20	-3	+45	+55	+3.5
Phoenix	Off.	16	635	1332	48	424	537	79	197	506	703	368	372	107	79	248	1730	108.1
	Def.	16	651	1440	45	329	439	75	243	446	689	395	426	141	89	224	1681	105.1
	Diff.		-16	-108	+3	+95	+98	+4	-46	+60	+14	-27	+54	-34	-10	-24	+49	+3.0
New York	Off.	10	403	845	48	219	285	77	130	264	394	268	231	84	34	133	1050	105.0
	Def.	10	439	837	52	208	262	79	129	292	421	268	214	67	52	153	1110	111.0
	Diff.		-36	+8	-4	+11	+23	-2	+1	-28	-27	—	-17	+17	-18	+20	-60	-6.0
Philadelphia	Off.	10	379	799	47	237	308	77	128	271	399	228	216	63	49	150	1021	102.1
	Def.	10	417	809	52	213	280	76	109	293	402	268	228	86	44	127	1071	107.1
	Diff.		-38	-10	-5	+24	+28	+1	+19	-22	-3	-40	+12	-23	+5	-23	-50	-5.0
San Antonio	Off.	10	479	953	50	207	295	70	156	327	483	304	277	85	65	168	1170	117.0
	Def.	10	398	904	44	288	382	75	152	289	441	255	259	95	57	166	1118	111.8
	Diff.		+81	+49	+6	-81	-87	-5	+4	+38	+42	+49	-18	-10	+8	-2	+52	+5.2
L. A. Lakers	Off.	9	363	728	50	204	255	80	112	250	362	225	211	78	51	142	955	106.1
	Def.	9	355	755	47	202	277	73	128	237	365	205	199	77	49	127	932	103.6
	Diff.		+8	-27	+3	+2	-22	+7	-16	+13	-3	+20	-12	+1	+2	-15	+23	+2.5
Boston	Off.	5	228	416	55	130	151	86	59	141	200	151	106	34	30	87	594	118.8
	Def.	5	229	449	51	118	158	75	67	126	193	150	124	46	14	63	591	118.2
	Diff.		-1	-33	+4	+12	-7	+11	-8	+15	+7	+1	+18	-12	+16	-24	+3	+0.6
Cleveland	Off.	5	201	389	52	121	156	78	46	158	204	137	111	33	23	65	534	106.8
	Def.	5	194	420	46	119	154	77	69	137	206	108	111	38	28	64	522	104.4
	Diff.		+7	-31	+6	+2	+2	+1	-23	+21	-2	+29	—	-5	-5	-1	+12	+2.4
Utah	Off.	5	202	438	46	92	127	72	65	138	203	127	142	43	29	64	512	102.4
	Def.	5	180	393	46	142	170	84	59	158	217	103	116	31	25	76	519	103.8
	Diff.		+22	+45	—	-50	-43	-12	+6	-20	-14	+24	-26	+12	+4	+12	-7	-1.4
Houston	Off.	4	153	338	45	74	111	67	61	95	156	91	87	36	26	58	391	97.8
	Def.	4	165	303	54	80	105	76	38	115	153	105	80	33	27	66	422	105.5
	Diff.		-12	+35	-9	-6	+6	-9	+23	-20	+3	-14	-7	+3	-1	+8	-31	-7.7
Milwaukee	Off.	4	140	293	48	109	142	77	40	94	134	90	119	36	19	68	404	101.0
	Def.	4	162	312	52	112	158	71	54	114	168	97	104	38	17	61	442	110.5
	Diff.		-22	-19	-4	-3	-16	+6	-14	-20	-34	-7	-15	-2	+2	-7	-38	-9.5
Dallas	Off.	3	115	243	47	62	81	77	34	86	120	61	82	24	17	54	301	100.3
	Def.	3	120	261	46	82	116	71	52	89	141	74	76	27	18	41	329	109.7
	Diff.		-5	-18	+1	-20	-35	+6	-18	-3	-21	-13	-6	-3	-1	-13	-28	-9.4
Denver	Off.	3	130	296	44	75	86	87	39	93	132	86	77	28	14	38	343	114.3
	Def.	3	156	295	53	67	93	72	45	118	163	103	70	28	20	45	379	126.3
	Diff.		-26	+1	-9	+8	-7	+15	-6	-25	-31	-17	-7	—	-6	+7	-36	-12.0
Indiana	Off.	3	105	228	46	60	73	82	33	76	109	52	77	11	7	44	275	91.7
	Def.	3	122	253	48	63	79	80	44	79	123	64	75	16	11	36	312	104.0
	Diff.		-17	-25	-2	-3	-6	+2	-11	-3	-14	-12	-2	-5	-4	-8	-37	-12.3

Team	W	L	Pct.	GB	Record against playoff teams			Record against non-playoff teams			HOME			ROAD		
					W	L	Pct.	W	L	Pct.	W	L	Pct.	W	L	Pct.
EASTERN CONFERENCE																
ATLANTIC DIVISION																
Philadelphia 76ers	53	29	.646	—	27	19	.587	26	10	.722	34	7	.829	19	22	.463
Boston Celtics	52	30	.634	1	24	22	.522	28	8	.778	30	11	.732	22	19	.537
New York Knickerbockers	45	37	.549	8	17	29	.370	28	8	.778	29	12	.707	16	25	.390
Washington Bullets	31	51	.378	22	13	39	.250	18	12	.600	20	21	.488	11	30	.268
Miami Heat	18	64	.220	35	7	45	.135	11	19	.367	11	30	.268	7	34	.171
New Jersey Nets	17	65	.207	36	5	47	.096	12	18	.400	13	28	.317	4	37	.098
CENTRAL DIVISON																
Detroit Pistons	59	23	.720	—	32	16	.667	27	7	.794	35	6	.854	24	17	.585
Chicago Bulls	55	27	.671	4	28	20	.583	27	7	.794	36	5	.878	19	22	.463
Milwaukee Bucks	44	38	.537	15	19	29	.396	25	9	.735	27	14	.659	17	24	.415
Cleveland Cavaliers	42	40	.512	17	17	31	.354	25	9	.735	27	14	.659	15	26	.366
Indiana Pacers	42	40	.512	17	20	28	.417	22	12	.647	28	13	.683	14	27	.341
Atlanta Hawks	41	41	.500	18	20	33	.377	21	8	.724	25	16	.610	16	25	.390
Orlando Magic	18	64	.220	41	11	42	.208	7	22	.241	12	29	.293	6	35	.146
WESTERN CONFERENCE																
MIDWEST DIVISION																
San Antonio Spurs	56	26	.683	—	25	21	.543	31	5	.861	34	7	.829	22	19	.537
Utah Jazz	55	27	.671	1	26	20	.565	29	7	.806	36	5	.878	19	22	.463
Dallas Mavericks	47	35	.573	9	20	27	.426	27	8	.771	30	11	.732	17	24	.415
Denver Nuggets	43	39	.524	13	18	28	.391	25	11	.694	28	13	.683	15	26	.366
Houston Rockets	41	41	.500	15	20	27	.426	21	14	.600	31	10	.756	10	31	.244
Minnesota Timberwolves	22	60	.268	34	10	42	.192	12	18	.400	17	24	.415	5	36	.122
Charlotte Hornets	19	63	.232	37	9	43	.173	10	20	.333	13	28	.317	6	35	.146
PACIFIC DIVISION																
Los Angeles Lakers	63	19	.768	—	30	15	.667	33	4	.892	37	4	.902	26	15	.634
Portland Trailblazers	59	23	.720	4	30	16	.652	29	7	.806	35	6	.854	24	17	.585
Phoenix Suns	54	28	.659	9	20	25	.444	34	3	.919	32	9	.780	22	19	.537
Seattle Supersonics	41	41	.500	22	18	32	.360	23	9	.719	30	11	.732	11	30	.268
Golden State Warriors	37	45	.451	26	17	33	.340	20	12	.625	27	14	.659	10	31	.244
Los Angeles Clippers	30	52	.366	33	13	37	.260	17	15	.531	20	21	.488	10	31	.244
Sacramento Kings	23	59	.280	40	6	44	.120	17	15	.531	16	25	.390	7	34	.171

SCORING
(Minimum 70 Games or 1400 Points)

Name	Team	G	FG	FT	Pts.	Avg.
Jordan	Chi	82	1034	593	2753	33.6
Malone	Utah	82	914	696	2540	31.0
Ewing	NY	82	992	502	2347	28.6
Chambers	Phoe	81	810	557	2201	27.2
Wilkins	Atl	80	810	459	2138	26.7
Barkley	Phi	79	706	557	1989	25.2
Mullin	GS	78	682	505	1956	25.1
Miller	Ind	82	661	544	2016	24.6
Olajuwon	Hou	82	806	382	1995	24.3
Robinson	SA	82	690	613	1993	24.3

FIELD GOAL PERCENTGE
(Minimum 300 Made)

Name	Team	FG	FGA	Pct.
West	Phoe	331	530	.625
Barkley	Phi	706	1177	.600
Parish	Bos	505	871	.580
Malone	Utah	914	1627	.562
Woolridge	LAL	306	550	.556
Ewing	NY	922	1673	.551
McHale	Bos	648	1181	.549
Thorpe	Hou	547	998	.548
Worthy	LAL	711	1298	.548
Williams	Port	413	754	.548

FREE THROW PERCENTAGE
(Minimum 125 Made)

Name	Team	FT	FTA	Pct
Bird	Bos	319	343	.930
E. Johnson	Phoe	188	205	.917
Davis	Den	207	227	.912
Dumars	Det	297	330	.900
McHale	Bos	393	440	.893
Porter	Port	421	472	.892
Johnson	LAL	567	637	.890
Mullin	GS	505	568	.889
Hawkins	Phi	387	436	.888
Price	Cle	300	338	.888

PERSONAL FOULS

Name	Team	PF
Smits	Ind	328
Ewing	NY	325
Johnson	Hou	321
Olajuwon	Hou	314
Thompson	Ind	313

GAMES DISQUALIFIED

Name	Team	Disq.
Long	Mia	11
Smits	Ind	11
Thompson	Ind	11
Rasmussen	Den	10
Johnson	Hou	8

MINUTES PLAYED

Name	Team	PF
McCray	Sac	3238
Jordan	Chi	3197
Miller	Ind	3192
Ewing	NY	3165
Campbell	Min	3164

TOTAL REBOUNDS PER GAME
(Minimum 70 Games or 800 Rebounds)

Name	Team	G	Reb.	Avg.
Olajuwon	Hou	82	1149	14.0
Robinson	SA	82	983	12.0
Barkley	Phi	79	909	11.5
Malone	Utah	82	911	11.1
Ewing	NY	82	893	10.9
Seikaly	Mia	74	766	10.4
Parish	Bos	79	796	10.1
Malone	Atl	81	812	10.0
Cage	Sea	82	821	10.0
Williams	Port	82	800	9.8

ASSISTS PER GAME
(Minimum 70 Games or 400 Assists)

Name	Team	G	Ass.	Avg.
Stockton	Utah	78	1134	14.5
Johnson	LAL	79	907	11.5
K. Johnson	Phoe	74	846	11.4
Bogues	Char	81	867	10.7
Grant	LAC	44	442	10.0
Thomas	Det	81	765	9.4
Price	Cle	73	666	9.1
Porter	Port	80	726	9.1
Hardaway	GS	79	689	8.7
Walker	Was	82	652	8.0

BLOCKED SHOTS PER GAME
(Minimum 70 Games or 100 Blocked Shots)

Name	Team	G	Reb.	Avg.
Olajuwon	Hou	82	376	4.6
Ewing	NY	82	327	4.0
Robinson	SA	82	319	3.9
Bol	GS	75	238	3.2
Benjamin	LAC	71	187	2.6
Eaton	Utah	82	201	2.5
Jones	Was	81	197	2.4
West	Phoe	82	184	2.2
Smits	Ind	82	169	2.1
J. Williams	Cle	82	167	2.0

3 POINT FIELD GOALS PERCENTAGE
(Minimum 25 Made)

Name	Team	FG	FGA	Avg.
Kerr	Cle	73	144	.507
Hodges	Chi	87	181	.481
Petrovic	Port	34	74	.459
Sundvold	Mia	44	100	.440
Scott	LAL	93	220	.423
Hawkins	Phi	84	200	.420
Ehlo	Cle	104	248	.419
Stockton	Utah	47	113	.416
Miller	Ind	150	362	.414
Lever	Den	36	87	.414

STEALS PER GAME
(Minimum 70 Games or 125 Steals)

Name	Team	G	Steals	Avg
Jordan	Chi	82	227	2.8
Stockton	Utah	78	207	2.7
Pippen	Chi	82	211	2.6
Robertson	Mil	81	207	2.6
Harper	Dal	82	187	2.3
Corbin	Min	82	175	2.1
Lever	Den	79	168	2.1
Olajuwon	Hou	82	174	2.1
Conner	NJ	82	172	2.1
Hardaway	GS	79	165	2.1

Use Name-Nickname	Team by Name	Birth Yr.	Hgt	Wgt	Pos	College	# Yr	G	Field Goals FG	Att.	%	3 pt. FG FG	Att.	%	Free Throws FT	Att.	%	Reb	Ass	PF	DQ	Pts	Per Game Min	Reb	Ass.	Pts
Kareem Abdul-Jabbar	70-75Mil 76-84LA	1947	7'2	232	C	U.C.L.A.	20	1560	15837	28307	56	1	18	6	6712	9304	72	17440	5660	4657	48	38387	37	11.2	3.6	24.6
85-89LAL (born Lew Alcindor	70-74, 77-89						18	237	2356	4422	53	0	4	0	1050	1419	74	2481	767	797	7	5762	37	10.5	3.2	24.3
played as Alcindor-1970,71)																										
Tom Abernathy	77-78LA 79-81GS 81Ind	1954	6'7	220	F	Indiana	5	319	724	1472	49	0	2	0	331	443	75	1011	384	525	3	1779	17	3.2	1.2	5.6
	77-78						2	13	22	54	41	0	0	—	24	29	83	42	23	18	0	68	17	3.2	1.8	5.2
Mark Acres	88-89Bos 90Orl	1962	6'11	220	F-C	Oral Roberts	3	221	301	602	50	4	5	80	180	279	65	847	128	540	6	786	16	3.8	0.6	3.6
	88-89						2	19	14	27	52	0	2	0	9	18	50	37	2	33	0	37	8	1.9	0.1	1.9
Alvan Adams	76-88Phoe	1954	6'9	221	C-F	Oklahoma	13	988	5709	11464	50	2	15	13	2490	3160	79	6937	4012	3214	58	13910	28	7.0	4.1	14.1
	76, 78-85						9	78	440	930	47	0	0	—	196	256	77	588	320	251	3	1076	29	7.5	4.1	13.8
Michael Adams	86Sac 87Was 88-90Den	1963	5'11	165	G	Boston College	5	319	1458	3435	42	493	1382	36	868	1042	83	860	1754	517	1	4275	30	2.7	5.5	13.4
	87-90						4	19	83	225	37	35	105	33	51	60	85	66	101	41	0	252	35	3.5	5.3	13.3
Rafael Addison	87Phoe	1964	6'7	225		Syracuse	1	62	146	331	44	16	50	32	51	64	80	106	45	75	1	359	11	1.7	0.7	5.8
Richie Adubato	HC80Det HC90Dal	1939				Will. Patterson																				
Mark Aguirre	82-89Dal 89-90Det	1959	6'6	233	F-G	DePaul	9	680	6092	12399	49	286	933	31	3117	4196	74	3700	2397	2020	28	15587	33	5.4	3.5	22.9
	84-90						7	80	590	1209	49	32	104	31	256	348	74	467	221	231	5	1468	31	5.8	2.8	18.4
Danny Ainge	82-89Bos 89-90Sac	1959	6'4	178	G	Brigham Young	9	659	3252	6826	48	514	1340	38	1148	1342	86	1961	3062	1734	20	7966	29	3.0	4.6	12.1
(played major league baseball 1979-81)	82-88						7	112	479	1030	47	78	198	39	175	211	83	282	489	340	3	1211	30	2.5	4.4	10.8
Mark Alarie	87Den 88-90Was	1963	6'8	217	F	Duke	4	283	938	1959	48	29	114	25	283	370	76	1003	318	624	5	2188	17	3.5	1.1	7.7
	87-88						2	4	10	17	59	1	2	50	2	2	100	6	1	9	0	23	11	1.5	0.3	5.8
Stan Albeck	HC71DenA HC80Cle	1931				Bradley																				
HC81-83SA HC84-85NJ HC86Chi																										
Chuck Aleksinas	85GS	1959	6'11	260	C	Kentucky, Connecticut	1	74	161	337	48	0	1	0	55	75	73	270	36	171	1	377	15	3.6	0.5	5.1
Steve Alford	88-89Dal 89GS 90Dal	1964	6'2	183	G	Indiana	3	135	232	517	45	28	85	33	101	115	88	120	154	102	0	593	10	0.9	1.1	4.4
	88-90						3	13	20	48	42	6	17	35	8	9	89	9	15	11	0	54	8	0.7	1.2	4.2
Randy Allen	89-90Sac	1965	6'8	220	F	Florida State	2	70	114	258	44	0	8	0	24	46	52	145	23	109	0	252	11	2.1	0.3	3.6
Darrell Allums	81Dal	1958	6'9	220	F	U.C.L.A.	1	22	23	67	34	0	1	0	13	22	59	65	25	51	2	59	13	3.0	1.1	2.7
Dwight Anderson	83Den	1960	6'3	185	G	Kentucky, Southern Calif.	1	5	135	286	47				7	10	70	2	3	7	0	21	7	0.4	0.6	4.2
Greg Anderson (Cadillac)	88-89SA 90Mil	1964	6'10	230	F-C	Houston	3	224	1058	2102	50	1	8	13	496	901	55	1532	164	625	6	2613	25	7.0	0.7	11.7
	88,90						2	7	30	55	55	0	0	—	11	23	48	45	3	29	3	71	28	6.4	0.4	10.1
J. J. Anderson	83Phi 83-85Utah	1960	6'8	195	F	Bradley	3	157	306	658	47	0	9	0	139	249	56	439	110	251	1	751	13	2.8	0.7	4.8
	84						1	5	5	8	63	1	1	100	0	0	-	4	0	2	0	11	3	0.8	0.0	2.2
Jerome Anderson	76Bos 77Ind	1953	6'5	195	G	West Virginia	2	49	51	104	49				25	36	69	25	16	51	0	127	6	0.5	0.3	2.6
	76						1	4	1	3	33				0	0		1	1	1	0	2	1	0.3	0.3	0.5
Kim Anderson	79Port	1955	6'7	200	F	Missouri	1	21	24	77	31				15	28	54	45	15	42	0	63	11	2.1	0.7	3.0
Michael Anderson	89SA	1966	5'11	184	G	Drexel	1	36	73	175	42	1	7	14	57	82	70	89	153	64	0	204	20	2.5	4.3	5.7
Nick Anderson	90Orl	1968	6'6	215	F	Illinois	1	81	372	753	49	1	17	6	186	264	70	316	124	140	0	431	22	3.9	1.5	11.5
Richard Anderson	83SD 84Den 87-88Hou	1960	6'10	240	F-C	Cal - Santa Barbara	6	407	909	2206	41	148	445	33	294	386	76	1418	611	691	4	2260	15	3.5	1.5	5.6
88-89Port 90Char	83, 87-89 89-90						4	15	20	48	42	8	21	38	10	12	83	26	10	20	0	58	9	1.7	0.7	3.9
Ron Anderson	85-86Cle 86-88Ind 89-90Phi	1958	6'7	215	F	Fresno State	5	410	1695	3546	48	8	50	16	680	852	80	1430	592	637	1	4078	21	3.5	1.4	9.9
	85, 87, 89-90						4	19	71	151	47	3	6	50	33	35	94	59	27	34	0	178	21	3.1	1.4	9.4
Willie Anderson	89-90SA	1967	6'7	190	G-F	Georgia	2	163	1172	2367	50	11	47	23	441	579	76	789	736	547	11	2796	34	4.8	4.5	17.2
	90						1	10	87	168	52	2	5	40	29	36	81	54	52	40	2	205	38	5.4	5.2	20.5
Michael Ansley	90Orl	1967	6'7	225	F	Alabama	1	72	231	465	50	0	0	—	164	227	72	362	40	152	0	626	17	5.0	0.6	8.7
Nate Archibald (Tiny)	71-72Cin 73-75KC-O 76KC	1948	6'1	158	G	Arizona Wstrn, Texas - El Paso	13	876	5899	12628	47	19	85	22	4664	5760	81	2046	6476	2002	15	16481	36	2.3	7.4	18.8
77NYN 78FJ 79-83Bos 84Mil	75, 80-83						5	47	235	556	42	2	17	12	195	236	83	77	306	118	1	667	35	1.6	6.5	14.2
Joe Arlauckas	88Sac	1965	6'9	230	F	Niagara	1	9	14	43	33	0	0	—	6	8	75	13	8	16	0	34	9	1.4	0.9	3.8
B.J. Armstrong	90Chi	1967	6'2	175	G	Iowa	1	81	190	392	48	3	6	50	69	78	88	102	199	105	0	452	16	1.3	2.5	5.6
	90						1	16	21	62	34	0	4	0	22	24	92	20	29	22	0	64	14	1.3	1.8	4.0
Tate Armstrong	78-79Chi	1955	6'3	175	G	Duke	2	92	159	350	45				32	40	80	88	105	64	0	350	11	1.0	1.1	3.8
Vincent Askew	88Phi	1966	6'6	210	G	Memphis State	1	14	22	74	30	0	0	—	8	11	73	22	33	12	0	52	17	1.6	2.4	3.7
Ken Austin	84Det	1961	6'9	205	F	Rice	1	7	6	13	46	0	0	—	0	0	—	3	1	7	0	12	4	0.4	0.1	1.7
Ed Badger	HC77-78Chi	1933				Iowa																				
John Bagley	83-87Cle 88-89NJ 90Bos	1960	6'	192	G	Boston College	8	579	2127	4865	44	104	430	24	895	1142	78	1560	3477	954	2	5253	26	2.7	6.0	9.1
	85,90						2	9	30	71	42	0	4	0	10	14	71	20	57	16	0	70	26	2.2	6.3	7.8
Carl Bailey	82Port	1958	7'	210	C	Tuskegee	1	1	1	1	100	0	0	—	0	0	—	0	0	2	0	2	7	0.0	0.0	2.0
Gus Bailey	75-76Hou 78-79NO 80Was	1951	6'5	185	G-F	Texas - El Paso	5	147	156	384	41	1	1	100	76	149	51	244	168	150	1	389	9	1.7	1.1	2.6
	75						1	8	18	36	50				9	10	90	19	16	12	0	45	15	2.4	2.0	5.6
James Bailey	80-82Sea 82-83NJ 83-84Hou	1957	6'9	220	F-C	Rutgers	9	595	2045	4228	48	1	13	8	1155	1644	70	2988	488	1978	60	5246	20	5.0	0.8	8.8
85-86NY 87NJ 88Phoe	80, 82						2	14	22	47	47	0	0	—	15	22	68	31	6	27	0	59	12	2.2	0.4	4.2
Thurl Bailey	84-90Utah	1961	6'11	222	F-C	N Carolina State	7	570	3473	7272	48	4	26	15	1627	1997	81	3302	955	1244	6	8577	30	5.8	1.7	15.0
	84-90						7	49	324	714	45	0	4	0	176	212	83	325	87	150	2	824	36	6.6	1.8	16.8
Greg Ballard	78-85Was 86-87GS 89Sea	1955	6'7	217	F	Oregon	11	802	4220	8942	47	93	275	34	1420	1805	79	4458	1733	1807	10	9953	28	5.6	2.2	12.4
	78-80, 82, 84-85, 87						7	65	183	423	43	4	13	31	111	140	79	326	103	120	1	481	20	5.0	1.6	7.4
Gene Banks	82-85SA 86-87Chi 88JJ	1959	6'7	215	F-G	Duke	6	468	2134	3961	54	2	46	4	1035	1418	73	2718	1335	1289	20	5305	28	5.8	2.9	11.3
	82-83, 85-87						5	27	129	256	50	0	3	0	34	57	60	137	67	63	2	292	26	5.1	2.5	10.8
Ken Bannister	85-86NY 89-90LAC	1960	6'9	235	F-C	Indiana State, St. Augustine's	4	206	543	1121	48	0	3	0	304	604	50	797	102	596	22	1390	17	3.9	0.5	6.7
Mike Bantom	74-76Phoe 76-77Sea	1951	6'9	220	F-C	St. Joseph's - Pa.	9	706	3446	7362	47	3	15	20	1673	2418	69	4517	1623	2489	76	8568	28	6.4	2.3	12.1
77NYN 78-82Ind 82Phi	76, 81-82						3	29	70	145	48	0	0	—	38	69	55	108	33	97	2	178	19	3.7	1.1	6.1
Tom Barker	77Atl 79Hou 79Bos 79NY	1955	6'11	230	C-F	Hawaii	2	98	250	592	42				139	201	69	520	75	299	11	639	19	5.3	0.8	6.5
Charles Barkley	85-90Phi	1963	6'6	262	F	Auburn	6	468	3738	6429	58	138	596	23	2991	4036	74	5569	1684	1676	29	10605	37	11.9	3.6	22.7
	85-87, 89-90						5	43	339	601	56	13	52	25	254	378	67	586	164	167	2	936	39	13.6	3.8	21.8
Marvin Barnes	75-76StLA 77-78Det 78Buf	1952	6'9	225	F-C	Providence	6	315	2096	4360	48	3	14	21	839	1215	69	2873	651	1177	13	5034	29	9.1	2.1	16.0
79Bos 80SD	75						1	10	124	249	50	0	1	0	60	77	78	141	16	45	0	308	44	14.1	1.6	30.8
Norton Barnhill	77Sea	1953	6'4	205	G	Washington State	1	4	2	6	33				0	0	—	3	1	5	0	4	3	0.8	0.3	1.0
Dana Barros	90Sea	1967	5'11	170	G	Boston College	1	81	299	738	41	95	238	40	89	110	81	132	205	97	0	782	20	1.6	2.5	9.7
Tim Bassett	74-75SD-A 76NY-A 77NYN	1951	6'8	227	F-C	Georgia	7	473	1220	2883	42	4	14	29	489	831	59	3148	576	1264	16	2933	24	6.7	1.2	6.2
78-80NJ 80SA	74,76 79-80						4	24	80	165	48	0	1	0	18	25	72	185	29	75	0	178	25	7.7	1.2	7.4

Use Name-Nickname	Team by Name	Birth Yr.	Hgt	Wgt	Pos	College	# Yr	G	Field Goals FG	Att.	%	3 pt. FG FG	Att.	%	Free Throws FT	Att.	%	Reb	Ass	PF	DQ	Pts	Per Game Min	Reb	Ass.	Pts
Billy Ray Bates	80-82Port 83Was 83LA 80-81	1956	6'4	210	G	Kentucky State	4 2	187 6	893 66	1885 121	47 55	36 3	119 8	30 38	375 25	471 31	80 81	313 17	352 25	265 24	0 0	2197 160	18 37	1.7 2.8	1.9 4.2	11.7 26.7
John Battle	86-90Atl 86-89	1962	6'2	175	G	Rutgers	5 4	337 31	1085 71	2322 158	47 45	29 2	105 14	28 14	605 50	790 64	77 78	474 47	707 52	480 45	0 0	2804 194	17 13	1.4 1.5	2.1 1.7	8.3 6.3
Kenny Battle	90Phoe 90	1964	6'6	210	F	Northern Illinois, Illinois	1 1	59 8	93 4	170 13	55 31	1 0	4 0	25 —	55 1	82 1	67 100	124 5	38 0	94 5	2 0	242 9	12 4	2.1 0.6	0.6 0.0	4.1 1.1
Dave Batton	83Was 84SA	1956	6'10	240	C	Notre Dame	2	58	90	201	45	0	3	0	8	17	47	123	32	61	0	188	10	2.1	0.6	3.2
William Bedford	87Phoe 88,90Det 90	1963	7'1	235	C	Memphis State	3 1	130 5	240 1	584 6	41 17	1 0	7 0	14 —	72 2	127 2	57 100	369 2	66 0	211 4	1 0	553 4	12 4	2.8 0.4	0.5 0.0	4.3 0.8
Ron Behagen	74-75KC-O 76-77NO 78Atl 78Hou 78Ind 79Det 79NY 79KC 80Was 75, 80	1951	6'9	232	F-C	Minnesota	7 2	388 8	1594 24	3750 50	43 48	0 0	0 0	—	789 3	1047 3	75 100	2712 31	624 9	1293 32	28 2	3977 51	24 15	7.0 3.9	1.6 1.1	10.3 6.4
Benoit Benjamin	86-90LAC	1964	7'	250	C	Creighton	5	367	1837	3662	50	1	16	6	1149	1572	73	3069	702	1178	21	4824	31	8.4	1.9	13.1
Mel Bennett	76Va-A 77-78Ind 81Utah 82Cle	1955	6'7	200	F	Pittsburgh	5	204	481	1256	38	0	2	0	440	722	61	952	204	533	1	1402	4	4.7	1.0	6.9
Winston Bennett	90Cle 90	1965	6'7	210	F	Kentucky	1 1	55 5	137 23	286 47	48 49	0 0	0 0	— —	64 4	96 6	67 67	188 21	54 5	133 11	1 0	338 50	18 27	3.4 4.2	1.0 1.0	6.1 10.0
Kent Benson	78-80Mil 80-86Det 87Utah 88Cle 78, 84-87	1954	6'10	245	G-F	Indiana	11 5	680 29	2578 56	5224 116	49 48	7 0	34 0	21 —	1005 25	1327 36	76 69	3881 94	1203 14	1935 72	23 0	6168 137	23 15	5.7 3.2	1.8 0.5	9.1 4.7
Ricky Berry died Aug. 14, 1989	89Sac	1964	6'8	207	F	Oregon State, San Jose State	1	64	255	567	45	65	160	41	131	166	79	197	80	197	4	706	22	3.1	1.3	11.0
Walter Berry	87Port 87-88SA 89NJ 89Hou 88-89	1964	6'8	215	F	St. John's (NY)	3 2	205 7	1201 40	2227 76	54 53	1 0	5 1	20 0	479 19	751 23	64 83	971 30	292 11	586 18	5 0	2882 99	24 22	4.7 4.3	1.4 1.6	14.1 14.1
Del Beshore	79Mil 80Chi	1956	5'11	165	G	California (Pa.)	2	69	88	250	35	10	26	38	58	87	67	63	139	105	0	244	13	0.9	2.0	3.5
Henry Bibby	73-75NY 75-76NO 77-80Phi 81SD 73-74, 77-80	1949	6'1	185	G	U.C.L.A.	9 6	675 72	2149 211	5073 533	42 40	43 5	147 13	29 38	1434 139	1834 181	78 77	1581 176	2259 231	1364 165	2 0	5775 566	23 24	2.3 2.4	3.3 3.2	8.6 7.9
Bernie Bickerstaff	HC86-90Sea	1944				Cal.-San Diego																				
Bob Bigelow	76-78KC 78Bos 79SD	1953	6'7	215	F-G	Pennsylvania	4	94	91	220	41				52	71	73	111	42	75	0	234	8	1.2	0.4	2.5
Joe Binion	87Port	1961	6'8	235	F	N. Carolina A&T	1	11	4	10	40	0	0	—	6	10	60	18	1	5	0	14	5	1.6	0.1	1.3
Larry Bird	80-90Bos 80-88, 90	1956	6'9	220	F-G	Indiana, Indiana State	11 10	772 150	7776 1375	15559 2896	50 47	520 77	1401 223	37 35	3647 854	4126 957	88 89	8031 1593	4958 976	2079 431	11 1	19719 3681	40 43	10.4 10.6	6.4 6.5	25.5 24.5
Otis Birdsong	78-81KC 82-88NJ 89Bos 79-81, 83-84, 86, 89	1955	6'4	195	G	Houston	12 7	696 35	5347 232	10562 483	51 48	49 1	179 11	27 9	1801 81	2748 139	66 58	2072 104	2260 104	1783 89	20 1	12544 546	31 31	3.0 3.0	3.2 3.0	18.0 15.6
Uwe Blab	86-89Dal 90GS 90SA 86-88, 90	1962	7'1	244	C	Indiana	5 4	235 7	185 3	427 7	43 43	0 0	0 0	— —	135 6	222 12	61 50	413 7	102 1	344 6	1 0	505 12	8 4	1.8 1.0	0.4 0.1	2.1 1.7
Norman Black	81Det	1957	6'6	185	G	St. Joseph's-Pa.	1	3	3	10	30	0	0	—	2	8	25	2	2	2	0	8	9	0.7	0.7	2.7
Rolando Blackman	82-90Dal 84-88, 90	1959	6'6	193	G	Kansas State	9 6	710 48	5318 409	10584 822	50 50	63 3	227 12	28 25	2980 218	3574 250	83 87	2588 180	2243 198	1118 91	0 1	13679 1039	34 39	3.6 3.8	3.2 4.1	19.3 21.6
Cory Blackwell	85Sea	1963	6'6	210	F	Wisconsin	1	60	87	237	37	0	2	0	28	55	51	96	26	55	0	202	9	1.6	0.4	3.4
Nate Blackwell	88SA	1965	6'4	170	G	Temple	1	10	15	41	37	2	11	18	5	6	83	6	18	16	0	37	11	0.6	1.8	3.7
Bill Blair	HC83NJ	1942				V.M.I.																				
Mookie Blaylock	90NJ	1967	6'	180	G	Oklahoma	1	50	212	571	37	18	80	23	63	81	78	140	210	110	0	505	25	2.8	4.2	10.1
Ray Blume	82Chi	1958	6'4	186	G	Oregon State	1	49	102	222	46	4	18	22	18	28	64	41	68	57	0	226	11	0.8	1.4	4.6
Tyrone Bogues (Muggsy)	88Was 89-90Char 88	1965	5'3	140	G	Wake Forest	3 1	239 1	670 0	1508 0	44 —	9 0	55 0	16 —	230 0	296 0	78 —	508 0	1891 2	447 0	3 0	1579 0	26 2	2.1 0.0	7.9 2.0	6.6 0.0
Manute Bol	86-88Was 89-90GS 86-89	1962	7'6	219	C	Bridgeport	5 4	394 21	489 25	1187 70	41 36	29 2	142 23	20 9	178 6	317 18	56 33	1852 90	110 2	1024 47	11 0	1185 58	20 18	4.7 4.3	0.3 0.1	3.0 2.8
Phil Bond	78Hou	1954	6'2	175	G	Louisville	1	7	2	6	33				0	0	—	4	2	1	0	4	3	0.6	0.3	0.6
Jim Bostic	78Det	1953	6'7	225	F	New Mexico State	1	4	12	22	55				2	5	40	16	3	5	0	26	12	4.0	0.8	6.5
Lawrence Boston	80Was	1956	6'8	225	F	Maryland	1	13	24	52	46	0	0	—	8	13	62	39	2	25	0	56	10	3.0	0.2	4.3
Tom Boswell	76-78Bos 79-80Den 80Utah 76-77, 79	1953	6'9	227	F-C	S. Carolina State, South Carolina	5 3	328 15	1068 30	2006 55	53 55	5 0	10 0	50 —	607 14	839 19	72 74	1645 48	575 23	1044 30	28 0	2748 74	21 14	5.0 3.2	1.8 1.5	8.4 4.9
Anthony Bowie	89SA 90Hou 90	1963	6'6	190	F-G	Oklahoma	2 1	84 2	191 0	437 1	44 0	7 0	26 0	27 —	50 0	69 0	72 —	174 0	125 0	123 1	1 0	439 0	16 2	2.1 0.0	1.5 0.0	5.2 0.0
Sam Bowie	85-87Port 88FJ 89Port 90NJ 85, 89	1961	7'1	237	C	Kentucky	5 2	207 12	912 38	1955 87	47 44	15 1	38 2	39 50	616 20	844 33	73 61	1812 96	450 24	693 44	18 2	2455 97	30 27	8.8 8.0	2.2 2.0	11.9 8.1
Dennis Boyd	79Det	1954	6'1	175	G	Detroit	1	5	3	12	25				0	0	—	2	7	5	0	6	8	0.4	1.4	1.2
Winford Boynes	79-80NJ 81Dall	1958	6'6	186	G-F	San Fransisco	3	177	598	1375	43	0	4	0	282	360	78	363	207	328	3	1478	17	2.1	1.2	8.4
Alex Bradley	82NY	1959	6'6	215	F	Villanova	1	39	54	103	52	0	1	0	29	48	60	65	11	37	0	137	8	1.7	0.3	3.5
Alonzo Bradley	78-80Hou 79-80	1953	6'6	190	F	Texas Southern	3 2	99 5	184 6	440 9	42 67	1 1	1 1	100 100	71 3	101 5	70 60	151 3	74 1	125 2	1 0	440 16	12 3	1.5 0.6	0.7 0.2	4.4 3.2
Charles Bradley	82-83Bos 84Sea 82-83	1959	6'5	215	G	Wyoming	3 2	110 9	127 2	305 8	42 25	0 0	4 0	0 —	93 0	159 2	58 0	119 5	55 1	151 6	0 0	347 4	8 24	1.1 0.6	0.5 0.1	3.2 0.4
Dudley Bradley	80-81Ind 82Phoe 83Chi 85-86Was 87-88Mil 88NJ 89Atl 81-82, 85-87	1957	6'6	195	G-F	North Carolina	9 5	600 30	1222 26	2780 66	44 39	101 5	346 22	29 23	586 13	803 18	73 72	1098 14	1147 22	1220 35	6 0	3131 70	17 7	1.3 0.5	1.9 0.7	5.2 2.3
Adrian Branch	87LAL 88NJ 89Port 90Min 87, 89	1963	6'7	190	F-G	Maryland	4 2	130 12	331 4	727 25	46 16	9 0	39 1	23 0	163 8	219 14	74 57	253 11	96 7	193 10	1 0	834 16	11 4	1.9 0.9	0.7 0.6	6.4 1.3
Brad Branson	82Cle 83Ind	1958	6'10	220	C-F	S.M.U.	2	72	152	360	42	0	1	0	87	120	73	206	52	96	0	391	12	2.9	0.7	5.4
Mike Bratz	78-80Phoe 81Cle 82SA 83Chi 84-85GS 86Sac 78-80, 82, 86	1955	6'2	185	G	Stanford	9 5	586 37	1578 119	3880 262	41 45	150 14	492 41	30 34	775 63	934 80	83 79	1030 59	1851 96	1091 82	3 0	4061 315	18 18	1.8 1.6	3.2 2.6	7.0 8.5
Randy Breuer	84-90Mil 90Min 84-89	1960	7'3	246	C	Minnesota	7 6	503 59	1517 114	3224 219	47 52	0 0	2 0	0 —	722 57	1103 95	65 60	2276 184	440 25	1173 127	21 2	3756 285	19 14	4.5 3.1	0.9 0.4	7.5 4.8
Jim Brewer	74-79Cle 79Det 80Port 81-82LA 76-78, 80-82	1951	6'9	224	F-C	Minnesota	9 6	703 31	1785 68	3983 145	45 47	1 0	13 0	8 —	528 28	925 54	57 52	4458 204	1038 49	1536 59	14 0	4099 164	23 24	6.3 6.6	1.5 1.6	5.8 5.3
Ron Brewer	79-81Port 81-82SA 82-83Cle 83-84GS 84-85SA 85NJ 86Chi 86Cle 79-81, 85	1955	6'4	183	G	Arkansas	8 4	501 16	2497 92	5437 191	46 48	30 1	121 7	25 14	947 41	1149 59	82 69	971 24	920 32	835 30	3 0	5971 226	26 26	1.9 1.5	1.8 2.0	11.9 14.1
Frank Brickowski	85-86Sea 87LAL 87-90SA 88,90	1959	6'10	240	F-C	Penn State	6 2	374 13	1216 53	2333 98	52 54	1 1	17 1	6 100	717 30	995 45	72 67	1646 66	640 25	1116 43	32 0	3150 137	20 21	4.4 5.1	1.7 1.9	8.4 10.5
Junior Bridgeman	76-84Mil 85-86LAC 87Mil 76, 78, 80-81, 83-84	1953	6'5	210	F-G	Louisville	12 6	849 49	4801 264	10099 581	48 45	40 4	164 16	24 25	1875 118	2216 145	85 81	2995 172	2066 128	1969 148	17 2	11517 650	25 28	3.5 3.5	2.4 2.6	13.6 13.3

Use Name-Nickname	Team by Name	Birth Yr.	Hgt	Wgt	Pos	College	# Yr	G	Field Goals FG	Att.	%	3 pt. FG FG	Att.	%	Free Throws FT	Att.	%	Reb	Ass	PF	DQ	Pts	Per Game Min	Reb	Ass.	Pts
Allan Bristow	74-75Phi 76SA-A 77-79SA 80-81Utah 82-83Dall	1951	6'7	216	F-G	Virginia Tech	10	695	2102	4567	46	16	57	28	1230	1536	80	2787	2219	1418	7	5450	20	4.0	3.2	7.8
	76-79						4	27	45	108	42	0	1	0	41	60	68	56	54	47	0	131	13	2.1	2.0	4.9
Wayman Britt	78Det	1954	6'2	185	G	Michigan	1	7	3	10	30				3	4	75	4	2	3	0	9	2	0.6	0.3	1.3
Mike Brittain	86-87SA	1963	7'1	235	C	South Carolina	2	38	26	52	50	0	0	—	11	21	52	53	7	57	1	63	7	1.4	0.2	1.7
	86						1	1	1	2	50	0	0	—	0	0	—	1	0	0	0	2	2	1.0	0.0	2.0
Dave Britton	81Was	1958	6'4	180	G	Texas A&M	1	2	2	3	67	0	0	—	0	0	—	2	3	3	0	4	5	1.0	1.5	2.0
Jim Brogan	82-83SD	1958	6'5	185	G	West Va. Wesleyan	2	121	256	577	44	12	45	27	95	127	75	182	222	202	2	619	12	1.5	1.8	5.1
Mike Brooks	81-84SD 85-86JJ 87Ind 88Den	1958	6'7	220	F	LaSalle	6	319	1673	3445	49	5	33	15	735	1029	71	2001	818	981	17	4086	29	6.3	2.6	12.8
	88						1	4	1	3	33	1	2	50	0	0	—	4	2	1	0	3	3	1.0	0.5	0.8
Scott Brooks	89-90Phi	1965	5'11	165	G	Cal. - Irvine	2	154	275	647	43	86	232	37	111	126	88	158	513	221	0	747	15	1.0	3.3	4.9
	89-90						2	12	7	25	28	4	9	44	8	11	73	12	21	17	0	26	10	1.0	1.8	2.2
Chucky Brown	90Cle	1968	6'7	230	F	N. Carolina State	1	75	210	447	47	0	7	0	125	164	76	231	50	148	0	545	18	3.1	0.7	7.3
Fred Brown (Downtown)	72-84Sea	1948	6'3	185	G	Iowa	13	963	6006	12568	48	110	295	37	1896	2211	86	2637	3160	1937	14	14018	25	2.7	3.3	14.6
	75, 78-80, 82-84						7	83	499	1082	46	13	42	31	186	227	82	196	193	144	0	1197	23	2.4	2.3	14.4
Herb Brown	HC76-78Det	1936				Vermont																				
Hubie Brown	HC75-76KyA HC77-81Atl HC85-87NY	1933				Niagara																				
John Brown	74-78Atl 79Chi 80Utah 80Atl	1951	6'7	220	F	Missouri	7	486	1348	2979	45	0	0	—	918	1172	78	2126	703	1449	54	3614	21	4.4	1.4	7.4
	78, 80						2	7	4	13	31	0	1	0	2	2	100	10	1	10	0	10	9	1.4	0.1	1.4
Lewis Brown	81Was	1955	6'11	225	C	Nev.-Las Vegas	1	2	0	3	0	0	0	—	2	5	40	2	0	2	0	2	3	1.0	0.0	1.0
Mike Brown	87-88Chi 89-90Utah	1963	6'9	245	C-F	Geo. Washington	4	256	465	967	48	1	3	33	336	472	71	1004	140	534	2	1267	15	3.9	0.5	4.9
	87-90						4	9	7	18	39	0	0	—	5	7	71	12	4	15	0	19	9	1.3	0.4	2.1
Raymond Brown	90Utah	1965	6'8	225	F	Idaho	1	16	8	28	29	0	0	—	0	2	0	15	4	11	0	16	4	0.9	0.3	1.0
	90						1	3	0	0		0	0	—	0	0	—	0	0	2	0	0	2	0.0	0.0	0.0
Rickey Brown	81-83GS 83-85Atl	1958	6'10	227	C-F	Mississippi St.	5	340	614	1322	46	0	3	0	254	381	67	1200	119	796	13	1482	13	3.5	0.4	4.4
	83-84						2	7	11	24	46	0	0	—	11	14	79	22	2	22	0	33	14	3.1	0.3	4.7
Tony Brown	85Ind 86Chi 87NJ 88JJ 89Hou 89-90Mil	1960	6'6	195	F-G	Arkansas	5	273	728	1640	44	14	64	22	339	477	71	639	499	622	15	1807	19	2.3	1.8	6.6
	89-90						2	8	5	14	36	1	2	50	3	4	75	7	6	12	1	14	10	0.9	0.8	1.8
Stanley Brundy	90NJ	1967	6'6	210	F	DePaul	1	16	15	30	50	0	0	—	7	18	39	26	3	24	0	37	8	1.6	0.2	2.3
Joe Bryant (Jellybean)	76-79Phi 80-82SD 83Hou	1954	6'9	194	F-C-G	LaSalle	8	606	2093	4648	45	23	115	20	1043	1404	74	2441	1049	1635	16	5252	21	4.0	1.7	8.7
	76-79						4	30	52	116	45				19	28	68	54	21	54	1	123	9	1.8	0.7	4.1
Mark Bryant	89-90Port	1965	6'9	245	F-C	Seton Hall	2	114	190	400	48	0	0	—	68	119	57	325	46	237	3	448	12	2.9	0.4	3.9
	90						1	13	18	33	55	0	0	—	6	8	75	29	3	27	1	42	12	2.2	0.2	3.2
Wallace Bryant	84Chi 85-86Dal 86LAC	1959	7'	245	C	San Francisco	3	102	134	329	41	0	0	—	55	96	57	374	112	196	3	323	14	3.7	1.1	3.2
	85						1	2	0	1	0	0	0	—	2	2	100	7	1	5	0	2	18	3.5	0.5	1.0
Torgeir Bryn	90LAC	1964	6'10	250	C	SW Texas State	1	3	0	2	0	0	0	—	4	6	67	2	0	5	0	4	3	0.7	0.0	1.3
Steve Bucknall	90LAL	1966	6'6	215	G	North Carolina	1	18	9	33	27	0	0	—	5	6	83	7	10	10	0	23	4	0.4	0.6	1.3
Quinn Buckner	77-82Mil 83-85Bos 86Ind	1954	6'3	205	G	Indiana	10	719	2546	5527	46	7	38	18	830	1264	66	1969	3114	2097	20	5929	2	2.7	4.3	8.2
	78, 80-81, 83-85						6	68	148	337	44	0	4	0	50	82	61	115	170	170	2	346	16	1.7	2.5	5.1
Greg Bunch	79NY	1956	6'6	190	F	Fullerton State	1	12	9	26	35				10	12	83	17	4	10	0	28	8	1.4	0.3	2.3
Rickey Burden	76VaV 77NYK 78NY	1953	6'2	188	G	Utah	3	134	710	1601	44	8	36	22	334	454	74	268	194	277	0	1762	21	2.0	1.4	13.1
Roger Burkman	82Chi	1958	6'5	175	G	Louisville	1	6	0	4	0	0	1	0	5	6	83	6	5	6	0	5	5	1.0	0.8	0.8
Tom Burleson	75-77Sea 78-80KC 81Atl 82KJ	1952	7'3	226	C	N. Carolina State	7	446	1568	3526	44	0	3	0	1054	1452	73	2794	601	1317	14	4190	21	6.3	1.3	9.4
	75-76						2	15	123	227	54				65	86	76	153	23	54	1	311	38	10.2	1.5	20.7
David Burns	82NJ 82Den	1958	6'2	180	G	St. Louis	1	9	7	16	44	0	0	—	9	15	60	5	15	17	0	23	10	0.6	1.7	2.6
Steve Burtt	85GS 88LAC	1962	6'2	185	G	Iona	2	66	134	326	41	0	5	0	100	146	68	55	58	132	0	368	11	0.8	0.9	5.6
Don Buse (Boo)	73-76IndA 77Ind 78-80Phoe 81-82Ind 83Port 84-85KC	1950	6'4	195	G	Evansville	13	966	2778	6313	44	320	969	33	1014	1302	78	2565	4425	1562	0	6890	27	2.7	4.6	7.1
	73-76, 78-81, 83-84						10	84	189	472	40	25	87	29	79	120	66	225	284	160	0	482	26	2.7	3.4	5.7
Greg Butler	89-90NY	1966	6'11	240	C	Stanford	2	46	23	60	38	0	3	0	16	22	73	37	3	36	0	62	4	0.8	0.1	1.3
Marty Byrnes	79Phoe 79NO 80LA 81Dal 83Ind	1956	6'7	215	F	Syracuse	4	263	585	1264	46	15	46	33	310	421	74	586	409	418	1	1495	16	2.2	1.6	5.7
	80						1	4	1	3	33				4	6	67	1	1	0	0	6	2	0.3	0.3	1.5
Michael Cage	85-88LAC 89-90Sea	1962	6'9	229	F	San Diego State	6	467	1876	3741	50	0	11	0	1226	1739	71	4255	569	1171	6	4978	30	9.1	1.2	10.7
	89						1	8	24	40	60	0	1	0	9	22	41	46	5	14	0	57	22	5.8	0.6	7.1
Adrian Caldwell	90Hou	1966	6'8	265	F	Lamar	1	51	42	76	55	0	0	—	13	28	46	109	7	69	0	97	6	2.1	0.1	1.9
	90						1	1	0	0	—	0	0	—	0	0	—	0	0	0	0	0	1	0.0	0.0	0.0
Tony Campbell	85-87Det 88-89LAL 90Min	1962	6'7	215	F-G	Ohio State	6	336	1419	3042	47	14	91	15	684	873	78	991	363	720	8	3536	19	2.9	1.1	10.5
	85-89						5	32	45	92	49	3	6	50	30	42	71	31	12	49	1	123	7	1.0	0.4	3.8
Rick Carlisle	85-87Bos 88NY 90NJ	1959	6'5	210	G	Maine, Virginia	5	188	178	422	42	11	48	23	55	71	77	141	201	187	2	422	8	0.8	1.1	2.2
	86, 88						2	12	9	19	47	0	2	0	3	4	75	7	8	10	0	21	5	0.6	0.7	1.8
Antoine Carr	85-90Atl 90Sac	1961	6'9	225	F	Wichita State	6	379	1244	2442	51	4	21	19	701	890	79	1325	441	1156	19	3193	18	3.5	1.2	8.4
	87-89						3	26	88	145	61	0	1	0	43	57	75	76	35	96	3	219	17	2.9	1.3	8.4
Austin Carr	72-80Cle 81Dal 81Was	1948	6'4	200	G	Notre Dame	10	682	4359	9714	45	2	13	15	1753	2181	80	1990	1878	1394	8	10473	29	2.9	2.8	15.4
	76-78						3	18	87	204	43				38	55	69	41	41	50	0	212	24	2.3	2.3	11.8
Kenny Carr	78-80LA 80-82Cle 82Det 83-87Port	1955	6'7	230	F	N. Carolina State	10	674	3057	5998	51	3	38	8	1696	2479	68	4999	923	2153	25	7813	25	7.4	1.4	11.6
	78-79, 83-86						6	35	153	299	51	0	2	0	62	85	73	230	37	126	4	368	26	6.6	1.1	10.5
M. L. Carr	76StL-A 77-79Det 80-85Bos	1951	6'6	205	F-G	Guilford	10	676	2710	5740	47	42	153	27	1297	1761	74	3054	1336	1709	17	6759	24	4.5	2.0	10.0
	77, 80-85						7	67	142	372	38	5	22	23	65	91	71	129	64	111	0	354	15	1.9	1.0	5.3
Bob Carrington	78NJ 78Ind 80SD	1953	6'6	195	G-F	Boston College	2	82	268	626	43	0	2	0	136	179	76	187	120	223	6	672	22	2.3	1.5	8.2
Joe Barry Carroll	81-84GS 85HO 86-88GS 88Hou 89-90NJ 90Den	1958	7'	244	C-F	Purdue	10	694	5008	10547	47	0	13	0	2402	3220	75	5380	1253	2194	56	12418	33	7.8	1.8	17.9
	87-88, 90						3	17	101	226	45	0	1	0	51	63	81	93	24	60	2	253	29	5.5	1.4	14.9
Butch Carter	81LA 82-84Ind 85-86NY 86Phi	1958	6'5	188	G	Indiana	6	361	1290	2717	47	54	176	31	503	638	79	546	683	792	7	3137	19	1.5	1.9	8.7
Howard Carter	84Den 85Dal	1961	6'5	215	G	Louisiana State	2	66	149	339	44	5	22	23	48	62	77	89	75	85	0	351	11	1.3	1.1	5.3
	84						1	5	7	22	32	1	5	20	0	0	—	5	5	3	0	15	12	1.0	1.0	3.0
Reggie Carter	81-82NY	1957	6'3	175	G	Hawaii, St. John's (NY)	2	135	178	459	39	0	3	0	115	149	77	164	206	192	1	471	11	1.2	1.5	3.5
	81						1	1	0	1	0	0	0	—	0	0	—	2	0	4	0	0	7	2.0	0.0	0.0
Ron Carter	79LA 80Ind	1956	6'5	190	G	V.M.I.	2	59	69	161	43	0	0	—	38	61	62	64	34	73	1	176	8	1.1	0.6	3.0
	79						1	2	0	1	0				0	0	—	0	0	0	0	0	1	0.0	0.0	0.0

Use Name-Nickname	Team by Name	Birth Yr.	Hgt	Wgt	Pos	College	# Yr	G	Field Goals FG	Att.	%	3 pt. FG FG	Att.	%	Free Throws FT	Att.	%	Reb	Ass	PF	DQ	Pts	Per Game Min	Reb	Ass.	Pts
Bill Cartwright	80-84NY 85FJ 86-88NY 89-90Chi	1957	7'1	249	C	San Francisco	10	686	3864	7171	54	0	2	0	3055	3896	78	4824	1027	2228	31	10783	31	7.0	1.5	15.7
	81, 83-84, 86-90						6	57	232	473	49	0	0	—	190	252	75	361	52	210	1	654	31	6.3	0.9	11.5
Don Casey	HC89-90SAC	1937				Temple																				
Cornelius Cash	77Det	1952	6'8	220	F	Bowling Green	1	6	9	23	39				3	6	50	16	1	8	0	21	8	2.7	0.2	3.5
Harvey Catchings	75-79Phi 79NJ 80-84Mil 85LAC	1951	6'9	218	C-F	Hardin-Simmons	11	724	926	2127	44	0	3	0	483	747	65	3639	608	2000	30	2335	18	5.0	0.8	3.2
	76-84						9	50	31	78	40	0	0	—	12	24	50	154	23	99	0	74	11	3.1	0.5	1.5
Terry Catledge	86Phi 87-89Was 90Orl	1963	6'8	226	F	South Alabama	5	365	1791	3684	49	3	23	13	937	1449	65	2364	287	945	6	4522	26	6.5	0.8	12.4
	86-88						3	19	73	169	43	0	1	0	34	59	58	106	7	48	0	180	23	5.6	0.4	9.5
Bobby Cattage	82Utah 86NJ	1958	6'9	250	F	Auburn	2	78	88	218	40	1	7	14	65	85	76	107	11	81	0	242	7	1.4	0.1	3.1
Ron Cavenall	85NY 89NJ	1959	7'1	235	C	Texas Southern	2	58	30	89	34	0	0	—	24	44	55	168	19	125	2	84	12	2.9	0.3	1.4
Tom Chambers	82-83SD 84-88Sea 89-90Phoe	1959	6'10	226	F-C	Utah	9	715	5543	11565	48	158	518	31	3853	4790	80	4911	1690	2678	66	15097	34	6.9	2.4	21.1
	84, 87-90						5	52	431	945	46	20	61	33	304	362	84	392	128	196	1	1186	38	7.5	2.5	22.8
Mike Champion	89Sea	1964	6'10	230	F	Gonzaga	1	2	0	3	0	0	1	0	0	0	—	0	0	2	0	0	2	0.0	0.0	0.0
Rex Chapman	89-90Char	1967	6'4	185	G	Kentucky	2	129	903	2195	41	107	333	32	299	387	77	366	308	280	1	2212	31	2.8	2.4	17.1
Lorenzo Charles	86Atl	1963	6'7	225	F	N. Carolina State	1	36	49	88	56	0	0	—	24	36	67	39	8	37	0	122	8	1.1	0.2	3.4
	86						1	4	3	4	75	0	0	—	1	1	100	2	2	1	0	7	4	0.5	0.5	1.8
Maurice Cheeks	79-89Phi 90SA 90NY	1956	6'1	180	G	West Texas State	12	934	4499	8549	53	44	176	25	2176	2739	79	2778	6665	2012	5	11218	33	3.0	7.1	12.0
	79-87, 89-90						11	125	747	1463	51	3	38	8	361	463	78	438	892	312	1	1858	37	3.5	7.1	14.9
Phil Chenier	72-73Bal 74Cap	1950	6'3	180	G	California	10	578	4120	9271	44	6	15	40	1685	2091	81	2063	1742	1143	7	9931	33	3.6	3.0	17.2
75-80Was 80Ind 81GS	72-77, 79						7	60	438	974	45				212	251	84	230	131	152	1	1088	35	3.8	2.2	18.1
Derrick Chievous	89-90Hou 90Cle	1967	6'7	195	F	Missouri	2	136	382	854	45	8	33	24	271	355	76	346	108	231	1	1043	16	2.5	0.8	7.7
	89-90						2	7	11	27	41	0	0	—	15	19	79	9	4	9	0	37	10	1.3	0.6	5.3
Jim Chones	73NY-A 74CarA 75-79Cle	1949	6'11	220	C-F	Marquette	10	788	4210	8797	48	0	9	0	1401	2061	68	6427	1292	2606	28	9821	30	8.2	1.6	12.5
80-81LA 82Was	73-74, 76-78, 80-82						8	45	165	382	43	0	0	—	58	94	62	274	55	141	0	388	25	6.1	1.2	8.6
Carlos Clark	84-85Bos	1960	6'4	210	G	Mississippi	2	93	83	204	41	0	7	0	57	71	80	86	65	79	0	223	7	0.9	0.7	2.4
	84-85						2	11	7	15	47	0	0	—	3	4	75	3	4	5	0	17	3	0.3	0.4	1.5
Fred Cofield	86NY 87Chi	1962	6'3	190	G	Oregon, Eastern Michigan	2	50	77	195	39	3	16	19	12	20	60	51	86	66	1	169	10	1.0	1.7	3.4
Ben Coleman	87-88NJ 88-89Phi 90Mil	1961	6'9	235	F	Minnesota, Maryland	4	218	571	1104	52	0	5	0	324	424	76	902	128	604	12	1466	16	4.1	0.6	6.7
	89						1	3	6	8	75	0	0	—	2	2	100	5	0	8	0	14	8	1.7	0.0	4.7
Norris Coleman	88LAC	1961	6'8	210	F	Kansas State	1	29	66	191	35	1	2	50	20	36	56	81	13	51	1	153	15	2.8	0.4	5.3
Art Collins	81Atl	1954	6'4	200	G	Biscayne Coll.	1	29	35	99	35	0	2	0	24	36	67	41	25	35	0	94	14	1.4	0.9	3.2
Don Collins	81Atl 81-83Was 84GS 85Was 87Mil	1958	6'6	190	F-G	Washington State	6	303	1235	2548	48	2	29	7	511	682	75	837	546	755	11	2983	20	2.8	1.8	9.8
	82, 85						2	8	19	44	43	0	0	—	5	7	71	22	6	25	1	43	19	2.8	0.8	5.4
Doug Collins	74-81Phi HC86-89Chi	1951	6'6	180	G-F	Illinois State	8	415	2927	5839	50	0	1	0	1573	1888	83	1339	1368	1245	14	7427	34	3.2	3.3	17.9
	76-78						3	32	282	536	53				123	159	77	131	111	95	0	687	38	4.1	3.5	21.5
Steve Colter	85-86Port 87Chi 87-88Phi 88-90Was	1962	6'3	175	G	New Mexico State	6	450	1205	2666	45	63	214	29	592	758	78	966	1344	817	0	3065	19	2.1	3.0	6.8
	85-86						4	20	63	134	47	3	12	25	11	17	65	46	75	47	1	140	18	2.3	3.8	7.0
Leroy Combs	84Ind	1961	6'8	210	F	Oklahoma State	1	48	81	163	50	0	3	0	56	91	62	56	38	49	0	218	9	1.2	0.8	4.5
Dallas Comegys	88NJ 89SA	1964	6'9	208	F	DePaul	2	142	322	704	46	0	3	0	212	311	68	452	95	335	5	856	16	3.2	0.7	6.0
Lester Conner	83-86GS 88Hou 89-90NJ	1959	6'4	185	G	Oregon State	7	488	1398	3072	46	22	94	23	865	1142	76	1492	2114	821	4	3683	24	3.1	4.3	7.5
	88						1	1	0	0	—	0	0	—	2	2	100	1	1	0	0	2	1	1.0	1.0	2.0
Darwin Cook	81-86NJ 87Was 89SA 89Den	1958	6'3	191	G	Portland	8	612	2479	5475	45	55	280	20	807	1056	76	1308	2348	1315	11	5820	23	2.1	3.8	9.5
	82-87, 89						7	25	86	223	39	6	25	24	30	46	65	54	82	70	1	208	21	2.2	3.3	8.3
Jeff Cook	80-83Phoe 83-85Cle	1956	6'10	215	F-C	Idaho State	8	518	1085	2351	46	1	18	6	563	786	72	2334	707	1307	17	2734	19	4.5	1.4	5.3
85-86SA 86Utah 88Phoe	80-82, 85-86						5	30	55	108	51	1	2	50	56	74	76	111	31	71	1	167	16	3.7	1.0	5.6
Norm Cook	77Bos 78Den	1955	6'9	210	F	Kansas	2	27	28	75	37				7	19	37	30	6	31	0	65	5	1.1	0.2	2.4
	77						1	1	2	2	100.				0	0	—	0	0	0	0	4	3	0.0	0.0	4.0
David Cook	86Sac	1963	6'8	230	F	St. Mary's	1	6	2	11	18	0	0	—	5	10	50	10	1	5	0	9	6	1.7	0.2	1.5
Joe Cooper	82NJ 83LA 83Was 83SD 85Sea	1957	6'10	230	C-F	Tulsa, Colorado	3	24	45	89	51	0	0	—	19	35	54	97	19	58	1	109	16	4.0	0.8	4.5
Michael Cooper	79-84LA 85-90LAL	1956	6'5	171	G-F	New Mexico	12	873	3014	6429	47	428	1260	34	1273	1529	83	2769	3666	2329	16	7729	27	3.2	4.2	8.9
	80-90						11	168	582	1244	47	124	316	39	293	355	83	574	703	474	2	1581	28	3.4	4.2	9.4
Wayne Cooper	79-80GS 81Utah 82Dal	1956	6'10	220	C-F	New Orleans	12	882	3150	6873	46	7	47	15	1246	1694	74	5806	809	2967	55	7553	22	6.6	0.9	8.6
83-84Port 85-89Den 90Port	83-86, 90						7	68	175	394	44	0	0	—	78	110	71	343	55	208	5	428	18	5.0	0.8	6.3
Hollis Copeland	80, 82NY	1955	6'6	180	F	Rutgers	2	93	196	406	49	0	2	0	68	92	74	161	89	173	0	464	14	1.7	1.0	5.0
Lanard Copeland	90Phi	1965	6'6	185	G	Georgia State	1	23	31	68	46	1	5	20	11	14	79	10	9	12	0	74	5	0.4	0.4	3.2
	90						1	4	2	6	33	0	0	—	0	0	—	1	0	1	0	4	2	0.3	0.0	1.0
Tyrone Corbin	86-87SA 87-88Cle	1962	6'6	218	G-F	DePaul	5	322	1206	2507	48	2	24	8	513	664	77	1592	557	841	9	2927	24	4.9	1.7	9.1
88-89Phoe 90Min	86, 89						2	13	45	90	50	0	0	—	19	25	76	86	27	37	0	109	25	6.6	2.1	8.4
Dave Corzine	79-80Was 81-82SA	1956	6'11	257	C	DePaul	12	863	3080	6363	48	10	53	19	1398	1867	75	5229	1473	1917	15	7568	24	6.1	1.7	8.8
83-89Chi 90Orl	79-82, 85-89						9	66	178	393	45	0	0	—	69	98	70	329	71	136	0	425	20	5.0	1.1	6.4
John Coughran	80GS	1951	6'8	230	F	California	1	24	29	81	36	2	9	22	8	14	57	19	12	24	0	68	7	0.8	0.5	2.8
Chubby Cox	83Was	1955	6'2	180	G	Villanova, San Francisco	1	7	13	37	35	0	2	0	3	6	50	10	6	16	0	29	11	1.4	0.9	4.1
Wesley Cox	78-79GS	1955	6'6	215	F	Louisville	2	74	122	296	41				98	192	51	206	23	150	1	342	11	2.8	0.3	4.6
Ron Crevier	86GS 86Det	1958	7'	235	C	Boston College	1	3	0	3	0	0	0	—	0	2	0	1	0	2	0	0	1	0.3	0.0	0.0
Charlie Criss	78-82Atl 82SD 83-84Mil 84-85Atl	1949	5'8	165	G	New Mexico State	8	418	1315	3045	43	19	106	18	885	1065	83	592	1335	589	0	3534	21	1.4	3.2	8.5
	78-80, 83						4	25	66	146	45	1	4	25	44	49	90	28	53	34	0	177	17	1.1	2.1	7.1
Winston Crite	88-89Phoe	1965	6'7	233	F	Texas A&M	2	31	34	71	48	0	0	—	19	25	76	65	15	43	0	87	9	2.1	0.5	2.8
Geoff Crompton	79Den 81Port 82Mil 83SA 84Cle	1955	6'11	283	C	North Carolina	5	82	40	108	37	0	0	—	19	43	44	139	28	91	0	99	6	1.7	0.3	1.2
Terry Crosby	80KC	1957	6'4	195	G	Tennessee	1	4	2	4	50	0	0	—	2	2	100	1	7	4	0	6	7	0.3	1.8	1.5
Jeff Cross	86LAC	1961	6'10	242	F	Maine	1	21	6	24	25	0	0	—	14	25	56	30	1	38	0	26	6	1.4	0.0	1.2
Russell Cross	84GS	1961	6'10	215	C	Purdue	1	45	64	112	57	0	0	—	38	91	42	82	22	58	0	166	8	1.8	0.5	3.7
Mark Crow	78NJ	1954	6'7	210	F	Duke	1	15	35	80	44				14	20	70	27	8	24	0	84	10	1.8	0.5	5.6
Pat Cummings	80-82Mil 83-84Dal	1956	6'9	236	F-C	Cincinnati	11	679	2730	5500	50	0	16	0	1054	1430	74	3820	807	2029	40	6514	21	5.6	1.2	9.6
85-88NY 89-90Mia	80-82, 84, 86						5	30	67	159	42	0	0	—	26	31	84	112	22	59	0	160	15	3.7	0.7	5.3
Terry Cummings	83-84SD 85-89Mil 90SA	1961	6'9	226	F	DePaul	8	631	5723	11683	49	27	87	31	2504	3489	72	5511	1564	2260	39	13977	35	8.7	2.5	22.2
	85-90								499	970	51	1	7	14	233	315	74	469	132	207	2	1232	36	8.7	2.4	22.8

Use Name-Nickname	Team by Name	Birth Yr.	Hgt	Wgt	Pos	College	# Yr	G	Field Goals FG	Att.	%	3 pt. FG FG	Att.	%	Free Throws FT	Att.	%	Reb	Ass	PF	DQ	Pts	Per Game Min	Reb	Ass.	Pts
Earl Cureton	81-83Phi 84-86Det 87Chi	1957	6'9	215	F-C	Robert Morris, Detroit	9	654	1532	3223	48	0	15	0	528	977	54	3115	671	1505	14	3592	19	4.8	1.0	5.5
87-88LAC 89Char	81-86						6	44	68	159	43	0	3	0	15	34	44	144	20	63	0	151	11	3.3	0.5	3.4
Dell Curry	87Utah 88Cle 89-90Char	1964	6'5	195	G	Virginia Tech	4	261	1196	2579	46	116	343	34	245	289	85	516	416	430	0	2753	18	2.0	1.6	10.5
	87-88						2	4	1	7	14	0	2	0	0	0	—	1	2	2	0	2	5	0.3	0.5	0.5
Quintin Dailey	83-86Chi 87-89LAC 90Sea	1961	6'3	180	G	San Francisco	8	487	2854	6268	46	21	131	16	1526	1947	78	1263	1168	1200	16	7255	24	2.6	2.4	14.9
	85						1	4	26	62	42	1	7	14	8	11	73	13	11	9	0	61	32	3.3	2.8	15.3
Chuck Daly	HC82cle HC84-90Det	1930				St. Bonaventure, Bloomsburg																				
Adrain Dantley	77Buf 78Ind 78-79LA 80-86Utah	1956	6'5	210	F-G	Notre Dame	14	945	8150	15071	54	6	36	16	6814	8325	82	5442	2821	2542	14	23120	36	5.8	3.0	24.5
87-89Det 89-90Dal	78-79, 84-85, 87-88						6	70	530	1005	53	0	3	0	493	619	80	391	169	186	1	1553	36	5.6	2.4	22.2
Brad Daugherty	87-90Cle	1965	7'	248	C	North Carolina	4	278	1826	3507	52	1	7	14	1245	1740	72	2403	1052	766	7	4898	35	8.6	3.8	17.6
	88-90						3	15	87	180	48	0	1	0	74	112	66	140	48	41	0	248	37	9.3	3.2	16.5
Brad Davis	78-79LA 79-80Ind 80Utah 81-90Dal	1955	6'3	180	G	Maryland	13	848	2773	5361	52	243	738	33	1554	1868	83	1587	4415	1870	19	7343	24	1.9	5.2	8.7
	84-88						5	45	125	236	53	14	32	44	77	91	85	75	167	89	0	341	21	1.7	3.7	7.6
Charlie Davis	82-85Was 85-86, 88Mil	1958	6'7	215	F	Vanderbilt	8	415	970	2152	45	19	112	17	255	346	74	1008	309	594	4	2214	12	2.4	0.7	5.3
88SA 89-90Chi	82, 84-86, 89-90						6	49	64	161	40	1	11	9	30	35	86	89	19	70	1	159	10	1.8	0.4	3.2
Harry Davis	79Cle 80SA	1956	6'7	220	F	Florida State	2	44	72	165	44	0	0	—	31	45	69	72	16	74	1	175	10	1.6	0.4	4.0
Johnny Davis	77-78Port 79-82Ind 83-84Atl	1955	6'2	180	G	Dayton	10	750	3699	8258	45	33	187	18	2279	2777	82	1505	3368	1469	6	9710	28	2.0	4.5	12.9
85-86Cle 86Atl	77-78, 81, 83-86						7	43	178	392	45	0	3	0	89	114	78	78	157	80	0	445	25	1.8	3.7	10.3
Mark Davis	89Mil 89Phoe	1963	6'5	195		Old Dominion	1	33	49	102	48	1	10	10	28	34	82	37	14	39	0	127	8	1.1	0.4	3.8
Mike Davis	83NY	1956	6'10	230	F	Maryland	1	8	4	10	40	0	0	—	6	10	60	10	0	4	0	14	4	1.3	0.0	1.8
	83						1	1	0	0	—	0	0	—	0	0	—	0	0	0	0	0	1	0.0	0.0	0.0
Monti Davis	81Phi 81Dal	1958	6'7	205	F	Tennessee State	1	2	1	5	20	0	0	—	1	5	20	4	0	0	0	3	5	2.0	0.0	1.5
Ron Davis	77Atl 81-82SD	1954	6'6	198	G-F	Washington State	3	78	157	374	42	2	8	25	111	177	63	139	53	115	0	417	5	1.8	0.7	5.3
Terry Davis	90Mia	1967	6'9	225	F	Virginia Union	1	63	122	262	47	0	1	0	54	87	62	229	25	171	2	298	14	3.6	0.4	4.7
Walter Davis	78-88Phoe 89-90Den	1954	6'6	198	G-F	North Carolina	13	916	7530	14606	52	141	525	27	2939	3465	82	2802	3685	2235	19	18140	29	3.1	4.0	19.8
	78-84, 89-90						9	65	572	1144	50	5	25	20	258	311	83	225	306	181	0	1407	32	3.5	4.7	21.6
Darryl Dawkins	76-82Phi 83-87NJ 88Utah	1957	6'11	255	C	none	14	726	3477	6079	57	2	15	13	1777	2593	69	4432	917	2784	100	8733	24	6.1	1.3	12.0
88-89Det	77-86						10	109	542	992	55	0	7	0	291	414	70	665	119	438	16	1375	25	6.1	1.1	12.6
Johnny Dawkins	87-89SA 90Phi	1963	6'2	165	G	Duke	4	259	1381	2949	47	55	178	31	661	768	86	721	1595	436	1	3478	30	2.8	6.2	13.4
	86, 90						2	13	59	138	43	0	9	0	39	47	83	25	98	24	0	157	34	1.9	7.5	12.1
Paul Dawkins	80Utah	1957	6'5	190	F	Northern Illinois	1	57	141	300	47	1	5	20	33	48	69	125	77	112	0	316	14	2.2	1.4	5.5
Darren Daye	84-86Was 87Chi 87-88Bos	1960	6'8	220	F-G	U.C.L.A.	5	328	849	1730	49	2	17	12	525	771	68	844	672	607	1	2225	16	2.6	2.0	6.8
	84-87						4	34	64	119	54	0	0	—	41	57	72	52	28	46	1	169	11	1.5	0.8	5.0
Greg Deane	80Utah	1957	6'4	190	G	Utah	1	7	2	11	18	1	1	100	5	7	71	6	6	3	0	10	7	0.9	0.9	1.4
Don Delaney	HC81-82Cle	1936				Kent State																				
Vinny Del Negro	89-90Sac	1966	6'5	185	G	N. Carolina State	2	156	536	1146	47	16	52	31	220	255	86	369	456	342	4	1308	22	2.4	2.9	8.4
Fennis Dembo	89Det	1966	6'5	215	F	Wyoming	1	31	14	42	33	0	4	0	8	10	80	23	5	15	0	36	2	0.7	0.2	1.2
	89						1	2	1	1	100	0	0	—	0	0	—	0	0	1	0	2	2	0.0	0.0	1.0
Larry Demic	80-82NY	1957	6'9	225	F-C	Arizona	3	206	397	865	46	0	3	0	182	314	58	805	106	524	11	976	15	3.9	0.5	4.7
	81						1	2	4	5	80	0	0	—	1	2	50	7	0	3	0	9	19	3.5	0.0	4.5
Kenny Dennard	82-83KC 84Den	1958	6'8	220	F	Duke	3	95	109	254	43	3	10	30	47	73	64	286	93	191	0	268	13	3.0	1.0	2.8
Henry Dickerson	76Det 77Atl	1951	6'4	190	G	Charleston	2	23	15	41	37				15	24	63	5	19	30	1	45	8	0.2	0.8	2.0
	76						1	5	4	9	44				1	2	50	4	3	1	0	9	3	0.8	0.6	1.8
Coby Dietrick	71-72MemA 73DalA 74-76SA-A	1948	6'10	228	C-F	San Jose State	13	842	2150	4645	46	6	31	19	834	1134	74	3772	1740	2336	23	5140	19	4.5	2.1	6.1
77-79SA 80-82Chi 83SA	71, 74-76, 77-83						10	50	144	297	48	0	7	0	37	58	64	225	86	153	1	325	21	4.5	1.7	6.5
Mickey Dillard	82Cle	1958	6'3	170	G	Florida State	1	33	29	79	37	0	4	0	15	23	65	15	34	40	0	73	7	0.5	1.0	2.2
Byron Dinkins	90Hou	1967	6'1	170	G	N.C.-Charlotte	1	33	44	109	40	1	9	11	26	30	87	40	75	30	0	115	11	1.2	2.3	3.5
Vlade Divac	90LAL	1968	6'11	245	C	none	1	82	274	549	50	0	5	0	153	216	71	512	75	240	2	701	20	6.2	0.9	8.5
	90						1	9	32	44	73	1	2	50	17	19	89	48	10	27	1	82	19	5.3	1.1	9.1
James Donaldson	81-83Sea 84SD 85-86LAC	1957	7'2	278	C	Washington State	10	768	2614	4494	58	0	0	—	1740	2367	74	6340	648	1662	7	6968	28	8.3	0.8	9.1
86-89Dall	82-83, 86-88, 90						6	43	146	235	62	0	0	—	91	118	77	387	35	101	0	383	30	9.0	0.8	8.9
Billy Donovan	88NY	1965	5'11	171	G	Providence	1	44	44	109	40	0	7	0	17	21	81	25	87	33	0	105	8	0.6	2.0	2.4
Jacky Dorsey	78Den 78Port 79Hou 81Sea	1954	6'7	230	F	Georgia	3	60	56	144	39	0	0	—	31	57	54	141	16	89	0	143	7	2.4	0.3	2.4
	79						1	1	0	0	—	0	0	—	0	0	—	0	0	0	0	0	1	0.0	0.0	0.0
Bruce Douglas	87Sac	1964	6'3	195	G	Illinois	1	8	7	24	29	0	1	0	0	4	0	14	17	9	0	14	12	1.8	2.1	1.8
John Douglas	82-83SD	1956	6'2	175	G	Kansas	2	67	182	395	46	19	61	31	69	104	66	91	147	147	2	452	16	1.4	2.2	6.7
Leon Douglas	77-78Det 81-83KC	1954	6'10	230	C-F	Alabama	7	456	1386	2796	50	0	1	0	815	1355	60	2954	479	1631	46	3587	22	6.5	1.1	7.9
	77, 81						2	18	19	45	.42	0	0	—	17	42	40	75	14	58	1	55	21	4.2	0.8	3.1
Sherman Douglas	90Mia	1966	6'	180	G	Syracuse	1	81	463	938	49	5	31	16	224	326	69	206	619	187	0	1155	30	2.5	7.6	14.3
Terry Dozier	90Char	1966	6'9	210	F	South Carolina	1	9	9	27	33	0	1	0	4	8	50	15	3	10	0	22	10	1.7	0.3	2.4
Greg Dreiling	87-90Ind	1963	7'1	250	C	Wichita State, Kansas	4	116	87	184	47	0	0	—	96	136	71	239	38	230	0	270	8	2.1	0.3	2.3
John Drew	75-82Atl 83-85Utah	1954	6'6	205	F-G	Gardner-Webb	11	739	5481	11658	47	10	57	18	4319	5774	75	5088	1224	2641	85	15291	30	6.9	1.7	20.7
	78-80, 82, 84						5	29	151	350	43	0	0	—	103	142	73	140	24	103	3	405	25	4.8	0.8	14.0
Larry Drew	81Det 82-85KC 86Sac	1958	6'1	179	G	Missouri	9	666	3254	6960	47	104	372	28	1359	1702	80	1231	3584	1246	1	7971	27	1.8	5.4	12.0
87-88LAC 90LAL	84, 86, 90						3	13	24	52	46	2	7	29	10	11	91	7	29	16	0	60	14	0.5	2.2	4.6
Clyde Drexler	84-90Port	1962	6'7	213	G-F	Houston	7	551	4422	8978	49	100	410	24	2243	2879	78	3305	3109	1766	25	11187	34	6.0	5.6	20.3
	84-90						7	50	371	849	44	17	66	26	215	274	78	326	328	180	4	974	37	6.5	6.6	19.5
Ralph Drollinger	81Dal	1954	7'2	250	C	U.C.L.A.	1	6	7	14	50	0	0	—	1	4	25	19	14	16	0	15	11	3.2	2.3	2.5
Kevin Duckworth	87SA 87-90Port	1964	7'	275	C	Eastern Illinois	4	304	1682	3487	48	0	3	0	978	1304	75	1943	246	1043	16	4342	27	6.4	0.8	14.3
	87-90						4	26	136	304	45	0	1	0	59	85	69	156	26	105	4	331	28	6.0	1.0	12.7
Charles Dudley (Grasshopper)	73Sea 75-78GS	1950	6'2	184	G	Washington	6	361	686	1380	50				536	796	67	1089	1230	722	1	1908	18	3.0	3.4	5.3
79Chi	75-77						3	36	56	118	47				55	84	65	91	124	80	0	167	17	2.5	3.4	4.6
Chris Dudley	88-89Cle 90NJ	1965	6'11	235	C	Yale	3	180	284	660	43	0	1	0	137	360	38	724	83	333	4	705	13	4.0	0.5	3.9
	88-89						2	5	2	5	40	0	0	—	1	2	50	6	2	4	0	5	6	1.2	0.4	1.0
Terry Duerod	80Det 81Dal 81-82Bos 83GS	1956	6'2	180	G	Detroit	4	143	429	928	46	23	70	33	80	119	67	160	170	143	0	961	14	1.1	1.2	6.7
	81						1	10	4	10	40	0	2	0	0	0	—	0	0	0	0	8	1	0.0	0.0	0.8

Use Name-Nickname	Team by Name	Birth Yr.	Hgt	Wgt	Pos	College	# Yr	G	Field Goals FG	Att.	%	3 pt. FG FG	Att.	%	Free Throws FT	Att.	%	Reb	Ass	PF	DQ	Pts	Per Game Min	Reb	Ass.	Pts
Joe Dumars	86-90Det	1963	6'3	190	G	McNeese State	5	387	2073	4267	49	54	141	38	1182	1428	83	870	1887	781	5	5382	31	2.2	4.9	13.9
	86-90						5	79	452	950	48	10	40	25	284	333	85	170	400	160	1	1198	35	2.2	5.1	15.2
Mike Dunleavy	77-78Phi 78-82Hou 83SA	1954	6'3	180	G	South Carolina	11	438	1311	2809	47	142	419	34	732	904	81	689	1723	1013	8	3496	19	1.6	3.9	8.0
84-85, 89-90Mil	77, 79-84						7	67	174	407	43	32	101	32	89	104	86	103	194	173	3	469	18	1.5	2.9	7.0
T. R. Dunn	78-80Port 81-88Den 89Phoe 90Den	1955	6'4	192	G-F	Alabama	13	976	2009	4396	46	0	16	0	963	1331	72	4329	1607	2042	15	4981	23	4.4	1.6	5.1
	78-80, 82-90						12	76	109	244	45	0	0	—	47	68	69	317	104	180	1	265	22	4.2	1.4	3.5
John Duren	81-82Utah 83Ind	1958	6'3	195	G	Georgetown	3	201	317	729	43	3	25	12	75	100	75	226	411	400	2	712	15	1.1	2.0	3.5
Devin Durrant	85Ind 86Phoe	1960	6'7	200	F	Brigham Young	2	63	122	295	41	0	3	0	73	106	69	132	85	116	0	317	13	2.1	1.3	5.0
Craig Dykema	82Phoe	1959	6'8	190	F	Long Beach State	1	32	17	37	46	2	4	50	7	9	78	12	15	19	0	43	3	0.4	0.5	1.3
	82						1	6	1	6	17	0	0	—	0	0	—	4	1	2	0	2	2	0.7	0.2	0.3
Ledell Eackles	89-90Was	1966	6'5	220	G-F	New Orleans	2	158	731	1672	44	28	99	28	482	626	77	3351	305	313	1	1972	20	21.2	1.9	12.5
Mark Eaton	83-90Utah	1957	7'4	284	C	U.C.L.A.	8	650	1725	3864	45	0	2	0	914	1404	65	5517	732	2275	42	4364	30	8.5	1.1	6.7
	84-90						7	44	128	272	47	0	0	—	64	104	62	378	41	153	4	320	33	8.6	0.9	7.3
Jerry Eaves	83-84Utah 85Atl 87Sac	1959	6'4	185	G	Louisville	4	168	416	882	47	1	14	7	299	387	77	208	414	218	0	1132	16	1.2	2.5	6.7
	84						1	11	22	46	48	1	3	33	10	13	77	10	13	10	0	55	12	0.9	1.2	5.0
Kenton Edelin	85Ind	1962	6'8	205	F	Virginia	1	10	4	13	31	0	0	—	3	8	38	26	10	39	1	11	14	2.6	1.0	1.1
Keith Edmonson	83Atl 84SA 84Den	1960	6'5	205	G	Purdue	2	87	206	460	45	0	2	0	110	153	72	127	56	124	1	522	11	1.5	0.6	6.0
	83						1	1	1	1	100	0	0	—	0	0	—	1	1	0	0	2	2	1.0	1.0	2.0
Blue Edwards	90Utah	1965	6'5	200	F-G	East Carolina	1	82	286	564	51	9	30	30	146	203	72	251	145	280	2	727	23	3.1	1.8	8.9
	90						1	5	14	26	54	1	3	33	7	8	88	18	8	16	0	36	19	3.6	1.6	7.2
Franklin Edwards	82-84Phi 85-86LAC 87-88Sac	1959	6'1	173	G	Cleveland State	7	296	738	1644	45	1	33	3	325	409	79	300	774	348	1	1802	15	1.0	2.6	6.1
	82-83						2	21	25	52	48	1	1	100	22	26	85	14	22	7	0	73	6	0.7	1.0	3.5
James Edwards	78LA 78-81Ind 82-83Cle	1955	7'	230	C-F	Washington	13	871	4896	9763	50	0	18	0	2679	3860	69	5277	1299	3240	90	12471	27	6.1	1.5	14.3
83-88Phoe 88-90Det	81, 83-84, 88-90						6	81	321	665	48	0	3	0	179	262	68	298	72	259	3	821	21	3.7	0.9	10.1
Jay Edwards	90LAC	1969	6'4	200	G	Indiana	1	4	3	7	43	0	2	0	1	3	33	2	4	4	0	7	7	0.5	1.0	1.8
Kevin Edwards	89-90Mia	1965	6'3	190	G	DePaul	2	157	865	2064	42	19	67	28	283	376	75	544	601	303	1	2032	29	3.5	3.8	12.9
Craig Ehlo	84-86Hou 87-90Cle	1961	6'7	184	G-F	Washington State	7	374	1091	2368	46	173	453	38	399	593	67	1249	996	710	2	2754	21	3.3	2.7	7.4
	85-86, 88-90						5	27	69	158	44	10	37	27	37	53	70	59	68	49	0	185	17	2.2	2.5	6.9
Bob Elliott	79-81NJ	1955	6'9	225	C-F	Arizona	3	141	356	720	49	2	6	33	266	410	65	502	204	306	5	980	16	3.6	1.4	7.0
Sean Elliott	90SA	1968	6'8	205	F	Arizona	1	81	311	647	48	1	9	11	187	216	87	297	154	172	0	810	25	3.7	1.9	10.0
	90						1	10	53	96	55	0	1	0	21	29	72	41	18	37	0	127	29	4.1	1.8	12.7
Bo Ellis	78-80Den	1954	6'9	197	F	Marquette	3	168	236	548	43	0	3	0	141	193	73	482	113	320	3	613	12	2.9	0.7	3.6
	78-79						2	15	19	46	41	0	0	—	14	17	82	47	9	27	0	52	13	3.1	0.6	3.5
Dale Ellis	84-86Dal 87-90Sea	1960	6'7	205	G-F	Tennessee	7	505	3600	7326	49	568	1405	40	1479	1889	78	2023	858	1136	7	9249	29	4.0	1.7	18.3
	84-89						6	46	305	672	45	41	114	36	101	131	77	201	71	116	2	752	29	4.4	1.5	16.3
Purvis Ellison	90Sac	1967	6'9	220	C	Louisville	1	34	111	251	44	0	2	0	49	78	63	196	65	132	4	271	25	5.8	1.9	8.0
Len Elmore	75-76IndA 77-80Ind 80KC	1952	6'9	223	C-F	Maryland	9	658	1627	3968	41	1	5	20	693	955	73	3360	616	1815	21	3948	19	5.1	0.9	6.0
81Mil 82-83NJ 84NY	75-76, 80-83						6	32	107	255	42	0	0	—	32	46	70	196	24	100	0	246	24	6.1	0.8	7.7
Chris Engler	83-84GS 85NJ 85Chi 85Mil	1959	7'	250	C	Minnesota,	5	195	138	336	41	0	0	—	67	99	68	386	45	274	2	343	7	2.0	0.2	1.8
87Port 87Mil 87-88NJ	85					Wyoming	1	1	1	1	100	0	0	—	0	0	—	2	0	2	0	2	6	2.0	0.0	2.0
Wayne Englestad	89Den	1963	6'8	245	F	Cal-Irvine	1	11	11	29	38	0	0	—	6	10	60	16	7	12	0	28	5	1.5	0.6	2.5
Alex English	77-78Mil 79-80Ind 80-90Den	1954	6'8	190	F	South Carolina	14	1114	10337	20302	51	18	82	22	4158	5001	83	6282	4246	2886	15	24850	33	5.6	3.8	22.3
	78, 82-90						10	68	668	1328	50	0	8	0	325	377	86	371	293	188	2	1661	36	5.5	4.3	24.4
Ray Epps	79GS	1957	6'6	195	F	Norfolk State	1	13	10	23	43				6	8	75	5	2	7	0	26	6	0.4	0.2	2.0
Julius Erving (Dr. J)	72-73Va-A 74-76NY-A	1950	6'7	206	F-C	Massachusetts	16	1243	11818	23370	51	134	449	30	6256	8052	78	10525	5176	3494	9	30026	36	8.5	1.8	24.2
77-87Phi	72-87						16	189	1769	3563	50	17	76	22	1025	1308	78	1611	841	544	1	4580	39	8.5	4.4	24.2
Earl Evans	80Det	1955	6'8	202	F	Southern Calif., Nevada-LasVegas	1	36	63	140	45	7	18	39	24	42	57	75	37	64	0	157	11	2.1	1.0	4.4
Mike Evans	80SA 81-82Mil 82Cle 83-88Den	1955	6'1	170	G	Kansas State	9	591	1835	4060	45	231	753	31	630	781	81	808	1514	1173	12	4531	17	1.4	2.6	7.7
	80-81, 83-88						8	58	201	485	41	44	155	28	80	97	82	106	160	127	0	526	18	1.8	2.8	9.1
Patrick Ewing	86-90NY	1962	7'	240	C-F	Georgetown	5	357	3221	6005	54	1	25	4	1726	2329	74	3315	701	1387	29	8169	35	9.3	2.0	22.9
	88-90						3	23	212	420	50	1	3	33	123	153	80	246	61	93	0	548	39	10.7	2.7	23.8
Jim Farmer	88Dal 89Utah 90Sea	1964	6'4	190	G	Alabama	3	105	172	414	42	17	53	32	95	131	73	118	69	103	0	456	9	1.1	0.7	4.3
	88-89						2	5	2	8	25	0	1	0	0	0	—	4	1	2	0	4	3	0.8	0.2	0.8
Butch Feher	77Phoe	1954	6'4	185	G	Vanderbilt	1	48	86	162	53				76	99	77	74	36	46	0	248	10	1.5	0.8	5.2
Dave Feitl	87Hou 88GS 89Was	1962	7'	240	C	Texas - El Paso	3	189	386	872	44	0	6	0	201	270	74	654	111	365	1	973	13	3.5	0.6	5.1
	87						1	6	0	0		0	0	—	2	2	100	1	0	0	0	2	1	0.2	0.0	0.3
Eric Fernsten	76Cle 76-77Chi 80-82Bos 84NY	1953	6'10	207	C-F	San Francisco	6	218	193	434	44	0	0	—	131	194	68	372	82	174	0	517	8	1.7	0.4	2.4
	80-82, 84						4	20	4	13	31	0	0	—	5	8	63	11	1	4	0	13	2	0.6	0.1	0.7
Rolando Ferreira	89Port	1964	7'1	240	C	Houston	1	12	1	18	6	0	0	—	7	8	88	13	1	7	0	9	3	1.1	0.1	0.8
Duane Ferrell	89-90Atl	1965	6'7	209	F	Georgia Tech	2	55	40	97	41	0	1	0	32	50	64	48	12	36	0	112	5	0.9	0.2	2.0
Kenny Fields	85-87Mil 87-88LAC	1962	6'5	230	F-G	U.C.L.A.	4	184	463	977	47	3	16	19	211	288	73	464	188	394	7	1140	15	2.5	1.0	6.2
	86						1	12	38	69	55	1	3	33	12	23	52	28	10	23	0	89	13	2.3	0.8	7.4
Bill Fitch	HC71-79Cle HC80-83Bos	1934				Coe																				
HC84-88Hou HC90NJ																										
Cotton Fitzsimmons	HC71-72Phoe HC73-76Atl	1931				Midwestern																				
HC78Buf HC79-84KC HC85-86SA HC89-90Phoe																										
Al Fleming	78Sea	1954	6'7	215	F	Arizona	1	20	15	31	48				10	17	59	30	7	16	0	40	5	1.5	0.4	2.0
	78						1	5	2	6	33				3	4	75	4	2	5	0	7	4	0.8	0.4	1.4
Vern Fleming	85-90Ind	1961	6'5	195	G	Georgia	5	480	2567	5089	50	18	90	20	1461	1875	78	2039	2897	1334	15	6613	33	4.2	6.0	13.8
	87, 90						2	7	29	70	41	0	3	0	31	39	79	39	42	21	1	89	36	5.6	6.0	12.7
Bruce Flowers	83Cle	1957	6'8	225	F	Notre Dame	1	53	110	206	53	0	2	0	41	53	77	180	47	99	2	261	13	3.4	0.9	4.9
Eric Floyd (Sleepy)	83NJ 83-88GS 88-90Hou	1960	6'3	175	G	Georgetown	8	640	3511	7646	46	384	1120	34	2363	2845	83	1975	4260	1519	9	9769	32	3.1	6.7	15.3
	87-90						4	23	155	323	48	28	63	44	87	104	84	70	203	49	0	425	41	3.2	9.2	19.3
Mike Flynn	76IndA 77-78Ind	1953	6'2	187	G	Kentucky	3	211	536	1279	42	25	99	25	220	350	63	437	454	270	0	1317	16	2.1	2.2	6.2
	76						1	3	15	30	50	3	8	38	8	11	73	10	10	6	0	41	28	3.3	3.3	13.7
Chris Ford	73-79Det 79-82Bos	1949	6'5	190	G-F	Villanova	10	794	3160	6874	46	126	336	38	868	1188	73	2394	2719	1817	10	7314	28	3.0	3.4	9.2
	74-77, 80-82						7	58	185	420	44	11	45	24	53	77	69	168	151	159	2	434	25	2.9	2.6	7.5
Don Ford	76-80LA 80-82Cle	1952	6'9	215	F	New Mexico,	7	474	1313	2828	46	1	7	14	389	503	77	1691	647	1004	7	3016	20	3.6	1.4	6.4
	77-79					Cal.-Santa Barbara	3	20	58	131	44	0	0	—	28	39	72	85	44	50	0	144	24	4.3	2.2	7.2

Use Name-Nickname	Team by Name	Birth Yr.	Hgt	Wgt	Pos	College	# Yr	G	Field Goals FG	Att.	%	3 pt. FG FG	Att.	%	Free Throws FT	Att.	%	Reb	Ass	PF	DQ	Pts	Per Game Min	Reb	Ass.	Pts
Phil Ford	79-82KC 83NJ 83Mil 84-85Hou	1956	6'2	180	G	North Carolina	7	482	2128	4560	47	25	119	21	1313	1602	82	854	3083	1269	15	5594	28	1.8	6.4	11.6
	79-81, 83						4	15	50	137	36	0	0	—	33	46	72	26	85	30	0	136	28	1.7	5.7	9.1
Bayard Forrest	78-79Phoe 80XJ	1954	6'10	235	C	Grand Canyon	2	139	229	510	45				111	218	51	565	296	256	1	569	15	4.1	2.1	4.1
	78-79						2	15	11	19	58				2	10	20	29	11	21	0	24	8	1.9	0.7	1.6
Rod Foster	84-86Phoe	1960	6'1	160	G	U.C.L.A.	3	207	631	1434	44	72	242	30	228	297	77	258	479	441	1	1562	17	1.2	2.3	7.5
	84-85						2	19	17	64	27	0	9	0	15	17	88	16	25	25	0	49	10	0.8	1.3	2.6
Tellis Frank	88-89GS 90Mia	1965	6'10	233	F-C	Western Kentucky	3	187	554	1263	44	0	2	0	368	492	75	776	211	608	12	1476	19	4.1	1.1	7.9
Mike Fratello	HC84-90Atl	1947				Montclair State																				
Anthony Frederick	89Ind	1964	6'7	205	F	Pepperdine	1	46	63	125	50	2	5	40	24	34	71	52	20	59	0	152	7	1.1	0.4	3.3
World Free	76-78Phi 79-80SD	1953	6'2	185	G	Guilford	13	886	6512	14294	46	213	632	34	4718	6264	75	2430	3319	2270	21	17955	30	2.7	3.7	20.3
(known as Lloyd to 1980)	76-78, 85, 88						5	34	166	417	40	0	5	0	145	196	74	76	103	79	0	477	23	2.2	3.0	14.0
81-83GS 83-86Cle 87Phi 88Hou																										
Tony Fuller	81Det	1958	6'4	185	G	Pepperdine	1	15	24	66	36	0	1	0	12	16	75	42	28	25	0	60	17	2.8	1.9	4.0
Terry Furlow	77Phi 78-79Cle 79-80Atl 80Utah	1954	6'4	190	G-F	Michigan State	4	239	1044	2273	46	24	82	29	438	508	86	507	568	298	1	2550	20	2.1	2.4	10.7
killed in auto accident 5/23/80	77-79						3	16	74	151	49	0	0	—	36	38	95	42	34	18	0	184	19	2.6	2.1	11.5
Corey Gaines	89NJ 90Phi	1965	6'3	195	G	Loyola Marymount	2	41	31	76	41	2	7	29	13	20	65	24	93	38	0	77	10	0.6	2.3	1.9
Mike Gale	72-73KyA 74-75NY-A 76SA-A 77-81SA	1950	6'4	190	G	Elizabeth City St.	11	842	2616	5634	46	17	91	19	954	1222	78	2445	3146	1941	9	6203	25	2.9	3.7	7.4
81Port 82GS 83JJ	72-81						10	66	212	501	42	4	15	27	84	106	79	212	284	165	1	512	26	3.2	4.3	7.8
Kevin Gamble	88Port 89-90Bos	1965	6'5	215	G	Iowa	3	124	212	440	48	5	30	17	120	162	74	157	154	119	1	549	11	1.3	1.2	4.4
	89-90						2	4	7	16	44	0	1	0	0	2	0	2	4	2	0	14	9	0.5	1.0	3.5
Gary Garland	80Den	1957	6'4	180	G	DePaul	1	78	155	356	44	6	19	32	18	26	69	138	145	80	1	334	14	1.8	1.9	4.3
Winston Garland	88-89GS 90LAC	1964	6'2	170	G	SW Missouri St.	3	225	1036	2422	43	35	118	30	443	530	84	769	1237	556	5	2550	29	3.4	5.5	11.3
	89						1	8	41	98	42	1	3	33	24	28	86	33	29	31	1	107	34	4.1	3.6	13.4
Bill Garnett	83-84Dal 85-86Ind	1960	6'9	225	F	Wyoming	4	300	572	1167	49	0	9	0	494	686	72	1298	393	832	10	1638	18	4.3	1.3	5.5
	84						1	8	15	30	50	1	1	100	7	8	88	22	4	10	0	38	9	2.8	0.5	4.8
Calvin Garrett	81-83Hou 84LA	1956	6'7	193	F	Austin Peay,	4	166	375	820	46	6	20	30	99	129	77	436	242	327	2	855	18	2.6	1.5	5.2
	81-82					Oral Roberts	2	14	9	22	41	0	1	0	7	8	88	15	6	10	0	25	8	1.1	0.4	1.8
Tom Garrick	89-90LAC	1956	6'2	185	G	Rhode Island	2	144	384	780	49	4	34	12	190	241	79	318	532	292	5	962	22	2.2	3.7	6.7
John Garris	84Cle	1959	6'8	205	F	Michigan,	1	33	52	102	51	0	0	—	27	34	79	77	10	40	0	131	8	2.3	0.3	4.0
						Boston College																				
Kenny Gattison	87, 89Phoe 90Char	1964	6'8	225	F	Old Dominion	3	142	296	581	51	1	1	100	184	283	65	468	75	330	2	777	14	3.3	0.5	5.5
Gus Gerard	75-76StL-A 76DenA 77Den	1953	6'8	205	F-G	Virginia	7	446	1541	3517	44	6	22	27	677	973	70	1811	560	996	4	3765	18	4.1	1.3	8.4
77-78Buf 78-79Det 79-81KC	75-76, 79-80						4	31	67	169	40	0	1	0	29	46	63	99	30	66	0	163	15	3.2	1.0	5.3
Derrick Gervin	90NJ	1963	6'8	215	F	Texas-San Antonio	1	21	93	197	47	0	3	0	65	89	73	65	8	47	0	251	16	3.1	0.4	12.0
George Gervin (Ice)	73-74VaA 74-76SA-A	1952	6'7	184	G-F	Eastern Michigan	14	1060	10368	20583	50	122	451	27	5737	6822	84	5602	2798	3250	40	26595	34	5.3	2.6	25.1
77-85SA 86Chi	73-86						14	84	859	1716	50	5	34	15	499	610	82	579	240	294	5	2223	38	6.9	2.9	26.5
Mike Gibson	84Was 86Det	1960	6'10	205	F	South Carolina-	2	64	41	106	39	0	0	—	19	28	68	106	14	65	1	101	6	1.7	0.2	1.6
						Spartanburg																				
Ben Gillery	89Sac	1965	7'	235	C	Georgetown	1	24	6	19	32	0	0	—	13	23	57	23	2	29	0	25	4	1.0	0.1	1.0
Armon Gilliam	88-90Phoe 90Char	1964	6'9	237	F	Nevada - Las Vegas	3	205	1294	2590	50	0	2	0	674	935	72	1574	223	531	7	3262	31	7.7	1.1	15.9
	89						1	9	27	51	53	0	0	—	19	22	86	45	2	11	0	73	14	5.0	0.2	8.1
Artis Gilmore	72-76KyA 77-82Chi	1949	7'2	246	C	Jacksonville	17	1329	9403	16158	58	3	20	15	6132	8790	70	16330	3050	4529	38	24941	35	12.3	2.3	18.8
83-87SA 88Chi 88Bos	72-77, 81, 83, 85-86, 88						11	100	669	1192	56	0	0	—	430	626	69	1267	232	279	1	1768	36	12.7	2.3	17.7
Jack Givens (Goose)	79-80Atl	1956	'65	205	F-G	Kentucky	2	156	416	1037	40	0	2	0	208	263	79	456	142	253	1	1040	17	2.9	0.9	6.7
	79-80						2	13	13	44	30	0	0	—	3	3	100	26	6	16	0	29	9	2.0	0.5	2.2
Mike Glenn	78Chi 78Buf 79-81NY	1955	6'3	178	G	Southern Illinois	10	593	1958	3611	54	8	28	29	572	669	86	710	952	893	1	4496	16	1.2	1.6	7.6
82-85Atl 86-87Mil	81-84, 86						5	22	39	86	45	0	2	0	19	21	90	26	19	28	0	97	13	1.2	0.9	4.4
Georgie Glouchkov	86Phoe	1960	6'8	235	F	Akademik Varna -	1	49	84	209	40	1	1	100	70	122	57	163	32	124	0	239	16	3.3	0.7	4.9
						Bulgaria																				
Mike Gminski	81-88NJ 88-90Phi	1959	6'11	254	C-F	Duke	10	760	3683	7854	47	3	32	9	2359	2788	85	5621	1061	1387	1	9728	27	7.4	1.4	12.8
	82-86, 89-90						7	33	147	303	49	0	5	0	98	122	80	192	29	32	0	391	28	5.8	0.9	11.8
Glen Gondrezick	78-79NY 80-83Den	1955	6'6	218	F-G	Nevada-Las Vegas	6	435	979	2069	47	2	14	14	584	807	72	1964	605	1101	3	2544	17	4.5	1.4	5.8
	78, 82-83						3	15	25	58	43	0	1	0	8	13	62	45	19	27	0	58	12	3.0	1.3	3.9
Grant Gondrezick	87Phoe 89LAC	1963	6'5	205	G	Pepperdine	2	91	173	395	44	7	28	25	101	147	69	146	115	127	0	454	12	1.6	1.3	5.0
Lancaster Gordon	85-88LAC	1962	6'3	188	G	Louisville	4	201	472	1208	39	23	85	27	158	206	77	259	294	266	2	1125	13	1.3	1.5	5.6
Orlando Graham	89GS	1965	6'8	240	F	Auburn	1	7	3	10	30	0	0	—	2	4	50	11	0	6	0	8	3	1.6	0.0	1.1
	89						1	2	1	2	50	0	0	—	1	2	50	1	0	0	0	3	4	0.5	0.0	1.5
Ron Grandison	89Bos	1964	6'8	217	F	New Orleans	1	72	59	142	42	0	10	0	59	80	74	92	42	71	0	177	7	1.3	0.6	2.5
Stewart Granger	84Cle 85Atl 87NY	1961	6'3	190	G	Villanova	3	80	123	297	41	4	17	24	66	89	74	78	173	127	0	316	12	1.0	2.2	4.0
Gary Grant	89-90LAC	1965	6'3	195	G	Michigan	2	115	602	1347	45	10	43	23	207	275	75	433	948	290	2	1421	30	3.8	8.2	12.4
Greg Grant	90Phoe	1966	5'7	145	G	Morris Brown,	1	67	83	216	38	3	16	19	39	59	66	59	168	58	0	208	10	0.9	2.5	3.1
	90					Trenton State	1	7	9	20	45	1	3	33	0	0	—	6	10	2	0	19	7	0.9	1.4	2.7
Harvey Grant	89-90Was	1965	6'8	200	F	Clemson,	2	152	465	991	47	0	9	0	130	194	67	505	210	341	3	1060	20	3.3	1.4	7.0
						Oklahoma																				
Horace Grant	88-90Chi	1969	6'10	218	F-C	Clemson	3	240	1105	2141	52	0	7	0	433	637	68	1757	484	702	5	2643	31	7.3	2.0	11.0
	88-90						3	43	199	379	53	0	3	0	82	118	69	396	91	154	5	480	36	9.2	2.1	11.2
Butch Graves	85Cle	1962	6'3	200	G	Yale	1	4	2	6	33	0	1	0	1	5	20	2	1	4	0	5	3	0.5	0.3	1.3
Stuart Gray	85-89Ind 90Char 90NY	1963	7'	243	C-F	U.C.L.A.	5	378	334	746	45	0	7	0	227	344	66	1010	144	639	2	895	9	2.7	0.4	2.4
	87, 90						2	7	2	6	33	0	0	—	2	4	50	15	0	6	0	6	4	2.1	0.0	0.9
Sylvester Gray	89Mia	1967	6'6	240	F	Memphis State	1	55	167	398	42	1	4	25	105	156	67	286	117	144	1	440	22	5.2	2.1	8.0
Jeff Grayer	89-90Mil	1965	6'5	200	F-G	Iowa State	2	82	256	560	46	1	10	10	116	172	67	252	129	140	0	629	20	3.1	1.6	7.7
	90						1	4	0	0		0	0	—	0	0	—	2	1	1	0	0	3	0.5	0.3	0.0
A. C. Green	86-90LAL	1963	6'9	225	F-C	Oregon State	5	407	1633	3179	51	18	76	24	1175	1557	75	3157	424	983	2	4459	29	7.8	1.0	11.0
	86-90						5	75	260	509	51	0	3	0	206	277	74	551	58	180	1	726	28	7.3	0.8	9.7
Ken Green	86NY	1959	6'8	215	F	Pan American	1	7	13	27	48	0	0	—	5	9	56	27	2	8	0	31	10	3.9	0.3	4.4
Kenny Green	86Was 86-87Phi	1964	6'7	213	G	Wake Forest	2	60	108	262	41	0	1	0	49	68	72	101	16	61	0	265	10	1.7	0.3	4.4
Mike Green	74-75DenA 76VAA 77-78Sea	1951	6'10	204	C-F	Louisiana Tech	7	459	2177	4534	48	1	12	8	946	1292	73	3181	587	1228	5	5301	25	6.9	1.3	11.5
78-79SA 80KC	75, 78-79						3	33	188	398	47	0	1	0	76	91	84	238	36	131	3	452	31	7.2	1.1	13.7
Rickey Green	78GS 79Det 81-88Utah	1954	6'1	170	G	Michigan	12	841	3214	7134	45	30	148	20	1513	1876	81	1658	4740	1294	3	7971	25	2.0	5.6	9.5
89Char 89Mil 90Ind	84-90						7	47	168	367	46	4	16	25	86	102	84	96	272	62	0	426	23	2.0	5.8	9.1

		Birth					#		Field Goals			3 pt. FG			Free Throws								Per Game			
Use Name-Nickname	Team by Name	Yr.	Hgt	Wgt	Pos	College	Yr	G	FG	Att.	%	FG	Att.	%	FT	Att.	%	Reb	Ass	PF	DQ	Pts	Min	Reb	Ass.	Pts
Sidney Green	84-86Chi 87Det 88-89NY 90Orl	1961	6'9	220	F-C	Nevada - Las Vegas	7	494	1635	3569	46	1	22	5	906	1256	72	3355	523	1440	19	4177	22	6.8	1.1	8.5
	85-89						5	28	45	101	45	0	0	—	28	43	65	105	15	56	0	118	13	3.8	0.5	4.2
Steve Green	76UtahA 76StLA 77-79Ind	1953	6'7	220	F	Indiana	4	205	476	1079	44	0	5	0	227	311	73	494	161	413	2	1179	13	2.4	0.8	5.8
Tommy Green	79NO	1956	6'2	185	G	Southern U.	1	59	92	237	39				48	63	76	68	140	111	0	232	14	1.2	2.4	3.9
Dave Greenwood	80-85Chi 86-89SA 89Den 90Det	1957	6'9	227	F-C	U.C.L.A.	11	760	3166	6643	48	4	27	15	1853	2420	77	6314	1562	2433	42	8189	29	8.3	2.1	10.8
	81, 85-86, 89-90						5	21	82	148	55	0	2	0	21	36	58	113	20	70	0	185	25	5.4	1.0	8.8
Claude Gregory	86Was 88LAC	1958	6'9	235	F	Wisconsin	2	25	62	136	46	0	1	0	12	36	33	97	16	38	0	136	21	3.9	0.6	5.4
Ed Gregory	HC88GS	1932				Pepperdine																				
John Greig	83Sea	1961	6'7	215	F	Oregon	1	9	7	13	54	0	0	—	5	6	83	6	0	4	0	19	3	0.7	0.0	2.1
Kevin Grevey	76-83Was 84-85Mil	1953	6'5	210	G-F	Kentucky	10	672	2915	6670	44	145	434	33	1389	1701	82	1594	1247	1286	9	7364	23	2.4	1.9	11.0
	76-80, 82, 84-85						8	70	310	736	42	9	18	50	156	199	78	145	102	181	4	785	23	2.1	1.5	11.2
Greg Griffin	78Phoe	1952	6'7	190	F	Idaho State	1	36	61	169	36				23	36	64	103	24	56	0	145	12	2.9	0.7	4.0
	78						1	2	3	7	43				0	0	—	4	3	5	0	6	13	2.0	1.5	3.0
Paul Griffin	77-79NO 80-83SA	1954	6'9	208	F-C	Western Michigan	7	480	837	1657	51	0	0	—	769	1111	69	2650	1116	1400	27	2443	21	5.5	2.3	5.1
	80-81						2	10	21	38	55	0	0	—	15	26	58	55	35	37	2	57	25	5.5	3.5	5.7
Darrell Griffith	81-85Utah 86JJ 87-90Utah	1958	6'4	190	G	Louisville	9	690	5063	10860	47	482	1458	33	1353	1916	71	2429	1590	1589	2	11961	30	3.5	2.3	17.3
	84-85, 87, 89-90						5	36	216	497	43	46	124	37	69	97	71	139	77	60	0	547	29	3.9	2.1	15.2
Bob Gross	76-82Port 83SD	1953	6'6	200	F-G	Seattle,	8	513	1857	3629	51	5	28	18	848	1062	80	2253	1481	1484	30	4567	25	4.4	2.9	8.9
	77, 80-81					Long Beach State	3	25	122	209	58	0	0	—	63	74	85	124	89	101	5	307	28	5.0	3.6	12.3
Ernie Grunfeld	78-79Mil 80-82KC 83-86NY	1955	6'6	215	G-F	Tennessee	9	693	2065	4328	48	33	98	34	961	1248	77	1815	1419	1511	11	5124	19	2.6	2.0	7.4
	78, 80-81, 83-84						5	42	146	299	49	2	4	50	81	98	83	92	121	89	0	375	22	2.2	2.9	8.9
Petur Gudmundsson	82Port 86LAL 87JJ 88-89SA	1958	7'2	261	C	Washington	4	150	251	508	49	1	2	50	190	252	75	563	153	400	8	693	14	3.8	1.0	4.6
	86,88						2	14	16	29	55	0	2	0	10	15	67	26	4	23	1	42	8	1.9	0.3	3.0
Scott Haffner	90Mia	1966	6'3	190	G	Illinois, Evansville	1	43	88	217	41	3	21	14	17	25	68	51	80	53	0	196	13	1.2	1.9	4.6
Glenn Hagen	82Det	1955	6'	170	G	St. Bonaventure	1	4	3	7	43	0	0	—	1	1	100	4	8	7	0	7	6	1.0	2.0	1.8
Jack Haley	89-90Chi 90NJ	1964	6'10	240	C-F	U.C.L.A.	2	118	175	425	41	0	1	0	121	171	71	371	36	226	1	471	12	3.1	0.3	4.0
	89						1	5	2	3	67	0	0	—	1	2	50	1	1	2	0	5	1	0.2	0.2	1.0
Roy Lee Hamilton	80Det 81Port	1957	6'2	180	G	U.C.L.A.	2	73	116	290	40	0	2	0	104	152	68	110	192	83	0	336	15	1.5	2.6	4.6
Tom Hammonds	90Was	1967	6'9	220	F	Georgia Tech	1	61	129	295	44	0	1	0	63	98	64	168	51	98	0	321	13	2.8	0.8	5.3
Bob Hansen	84-90Utah	1961	6'6	192	G	Iowa	7	471	1467	3078	48	139	415	33	477	702	68	1109	788	993	5	3550	20	2.4	1.7	7.5
	84-90						7	40	151	314	48	35	70	50	56	75	75	114	71	111	1	393	25	2.9	1.8	9.8
Glenn Hansen	76-77KC 78Chi 78KC	1952	6'5	205	G	Louisiana State	3	112	240	582	41				108	149	72	247	93	191	1	588	13	2.2	0.8	5.3
Lars Hansen	79Sea	1954	6'10	225	C	Washington	1	15	29	57	51				18	31	58	59	14	28	0	76	14	3.9	0.9	5.1
Bill Hanzlik	81-82Sea 83-90Den	1957	6'7	195	G-F	Notre Dame	10	748	1836	4232	43	46	216	21	1696	2171	78	2058	2058	2222	29	5414	21	2.8	2.8	7.2
	82-90						9	62	154	354	44	5	26	19	127	165	77	182	167	209	5	440	21	2.9	2.7	7.1
Tim Hardaway	90GS	1966	6'	175	G	Texas-El Paso	1	79	464	985	47	23	84	27	211	276	76	310	689	232	6	1162	34	3.9	8.7	14.7
Alan Hardy	81LA 82Det	1957	6'7	195	F	Michigan	2	60	84	195	43	0	5	0	25	39	64	53	23	45	0	193	7	0.9	0.4	3.2
James Hardy	79NO 80-82Utah	1956	6'8	220	F-C	San Francisco	4	249	611	1269	48	1	3	33	187	267	70	1312	315	590	9	1410	22	5.3	1.3	5.7
Derek Harper	84-90Dal	1961	6'4	194	G	Illinois	7	565	3057	6262	49	360	1060	34	1248	1658	75	1514	3437	1305	6	7722	31	2.7	6.1	13.7
	84-88, 90						6	48	218	472	46	28	86	33	89	119	75	114	295	119	0	564	33	2.4	6.1	11.8
Mike Harper	81-82Port	1957	6'10	195	C-F	North Park	2	123	240	506	47	0	4	0	133	238	56	432	71	302	7	613	15	3.5	0.6	5.0
	81						1	1	1	1	100	0	0	—	1	1	100	1	0	0	0	3	6	1.0	0.0	3.0
Ron Harper	87-90Cle 90LAC	1964	6'6	205	G	Miami - Ohio	4	256	1962	4132	47	66	281	23	1087	1503	72	1230	1291	733	8	5077	36	4.8	5.0	19.8
	88-89						2	9	69	132	52	0	4	0	31	42	74	41	35	29	1	169	36	4.6	3.9	18.8
Del Harris	HC80-83Hou HC88-90Mil	1937				Milligan																				
Steve Harris	86-88Hou 88GS 89Det 90LAC	1963	6'5	195	G	Tulsa	5	207	592	1363	43	1	20	5	255	303	84	365	238	265	1	1440	14	1.8	1.1	7.0
	86-87						2	24	30	72	42	0	1	0	7	11	64	17	7	18	0	67	7	0.7	0.3	2.8
Dick Harter	HC89-90Char	1930				Pennsylvania																				
Joey Hassett	78-79Sea 80Ind 81Dal 81-83GS	1955	6'5	181	G	Providence	6	292	712	1691	42	194	577	34	105	122	86	307	386	361	1	1723	12	1.1	1.3	5.9
	78-79						2	16	10	20	50	0	0	—	0	0	—	3	1	1	0	20	2	0.2	0.1	1.3
Scott Hastings	83NY 83-88Atl 89Mia 90Det	1960	6'10	236	F-C	Arkansas	8	435	494	1133	44	23	75	31	374	460	81	1024	217	843	16	1385	11	2.4	0.5	3.2
	84, 86-88, 90						5	34	25	44	57	1	8	13	18	25	72	41	6	45	1	69	7	1.2	0.2	2.0
Steve Hawes	75-76Hou 76Port 77-83Atl 83-84Sea	1950	6'9	220	C-F	Washington	10	688	2337	4836	48	14	47	30	1080	1367	79	4272	1288	1886	40	5768	23	6.2	1.9	8.4
	75, 78-80, 82-84						7	32	96	207	46	1	2	50	42	51	82	175	71	86	3	235	22	5.5	2.2	7.3
Robert Hawkins (Bubbles)	76GS 77NYN 78NJ 79Det	1954	6'4	190	G	Illinois State	4	103	534	1179	45				245	348	70	240	150	252	3	1313	19	2.3	1.5	12.7
	76						1	5	4	5	80				2	2	100	0	2	6	0	10	2	0.0	0.4	2.0
Hersey Hawkins	89-90Phi	1965	6'3	190	G	Bradley	2	161	964	2107	46	155	366	42	628	726	87	529	500	401	2	2711	34	3.3	3.1	16.8
	89-90						2	13	84	187	45	14	41	34	61	65	94	36	40	31	0	243	37	2.8	3.1	18.7
Elvin Hayes	69-71SD 72Hou 73Bal 74Cap 75-81Was 82-84Hou	1945	6'9	235	F-C	Houston	16	1303	10976	24272	45	5	34	15	5356	7999	67	16279	2398	4193	53	27313	38	12.5	1.8	21.0
	69, 73-80, 82						10	96	883	1901	46	0	0	—	428	656	65	1244	185	378	8	2194	43	13.0	1.9	22.9
Steve Hayes	82SA 82Det 83Cle 84Sea 85Phi 86Utah	1955	7'	233	C	Idaho State	5	212	233	483	48	0	1	0	79	158	50	526	85	438	9	545	11	2.5	0.4	2.6
	86						1	1	1	1	100	0	0	—	0	0	—	1	0	0	0	2	1	1.0	0.0	2.0
Cedric Henderson	87Atl 87Mil	1965	6'8	210	F	Georgia	1	8	4	8	50	0	0	—	3	3	100	8	0	2	0	11	2	1.0	0.0	1.4
Dave Henderson	88Phi	1964	6'5	195	G	Duke	1	22	47	116	41	0	1	0	32	47	68	35	34	41	0	126	16	1.6	1.5	5.7
Gerald Henderson	80-84Bos 85-87Sea 87-88NY 88-89Phi 90Mil 90Det	1956	6'2	177	G	Va. Commonw.	11	832	3017	6377	47	194	582	33	1387	1788	78	1408	3069	1863	15	7614	22	1.7	3.7	9.2
	80-84, 89-90						7	78	255	568	45	5	29	17	108	155	70	136	223	178	1	623	20	1.7	2.9	8.0
Jerome Henderson	86LAL 87Mil	1959	6'11	230	C-F	New Mexico	2	7	6	16	38	0	0	—	4	4	100	8	0	13	0	16	6	1.1	0.0	2.3
	87						1	1	0	0	—	0	0	—	0	0	—	0	0	1	0	0	1	0.0	0.0	0.0
Kevin Henderson	87-88GS 88Cle	1964	6'4	195	G	Fullerton State	2	22	24	61	39	0	1	0	17	28	61	24	34	35	0	65	11	1.1	1.5	3.0
Tom Henderson	75-77Atl 77-79Was 80-83Hou	1952	6'3	190	G	Hawaii	9	650	2426	5601	43	0	9	0	1236	1673	74	1494	3136	1141	3	6088	27	2.3	4.8	9.4
	77-82						6	80	270	650	42	0	2	0	161	214	75	181	431	168	2	701	30	2.3	5.4	8.8
Carl Henry	86Sac	1960	6'6	205	G	Oklahoma City,	1	28	31	67	46	4	10	40	12	17	71	19	4	11	0	78	5	0.7	0.1	2.8
	86					Kansas	1	1	1	1	100	1	1	100	0	0	—	0	0	0	0	3	2	0.0	0.0	3.0
Connor Henry	87Hou 87-88Bos 83Mil 88Sac	1963	6'7	195	G	Cal.-Santa Barbara	2	93	108	286	38	33	87	38	56	74	76	83	102	71	0	305	8	0.9	1.1	3.3
	87						1	11	8	16	50	1	5	20	5	10	50	6	0	3	0	22	3	0.5	0.0	2.0
Keith Herron	79Atl 81Det 82Cle	1956	6'6	195	G-F	Villanova	3	124	485	1108	44	2	11	18	247	288	86	242	174	190	1	1219	21	2.0	1.4	9.8
Phil Hicks	77Hou 77Chi 79Den	1953	6'7	205	F	Tulane	2	57	59	132	45				14	18	78	94	32	57	0	132	7	1.6	0.6	2.3
	77						1	1	0	2	0				0	0	—	3	0	1	0	0	4	3.0	0.0	0.0

se Name-Nickname	Team by Name	Birth Yr.	Hgt	Wgt	Pos	College	# Yr	G	Field Goals FG	Att.	%	3 pt. FG FG	Att.	%	Free Throws FT	Att.	%	Reb	Ass	PF	DQ	Pts	Per Game Min	Reb	Ass.	Pts
ike Higgins	90LAL 90Den	1967	6'9	220	F	Northern Colorado	1	11	3	8	38	0	0	—	8	10	80	4	3	5	0	14	5	0.4	0.3	1.3
od Higgins	83-85Chi 86Sea 86SA	1960	6'7	205	F-C-G	Fresno State	8	562	1864	3908	48	180	526	34	1296	1611	80	2098	961	1238	7	5204	22	3.7	1.7	9.3
86NJ 86Chi 87-90GS	85, 87, 89						3	19	58	126	45	11	36	31	35	43	81	80	32	39	0	162	23	4.2	1.7	8.5
enny Higgs	79Cle 81-82Den	1955	6'	185	G	Louisiana State	3	216	538	1221	44	8	55	15	386	480	80	391	944	682	15	1470	21	1.8	4.4	6.8
	82						1	3	8	21	38	0	2	0	7	12	58	3	6	12	0	23	18	1.0	2.0	7.7
ohnny High	80-81, 83-84Phoe	1957	6'8	185	G	Nevada-Reno	4	274	508	1168	43	4	38	11	376	607	62	617	525	712	4	1396	17	2.3	1.9	5.1
	80-81, 83						3	18	31	75	41	0	3	0	17	32	53	54	32	51	0	79	16	3.0	1.8	4.4
rmond Hill	77-81Atl 81-82Sea 82SD 83Mil 84Atl	1953	6'4	190	G	Princeton	8	468	1150	2817	41	1	13	8	913	1101	83	917	2194	1445	42	3214	25	2.0	4.7	6.9
	78-80						3	16	47	116	41	0	1	0	23	28	82	26	72	54	1	117	27	1.6	4.5	7.3
ob Hill	HC87NY	1946				Bowling Green																				
oy Hinson	84-86Cle 87-88Phi 88-90NJ	1961	6'9	215	F-C	Rutgers	7	498	2756	5529	50	0	12	0	1653	2229	74	3433	491	1874	44	7165	31	6.9	1.0	14.4
	85, 87						2	9	57	100	57	0	0	—	39	61	64	53	6	36	1	153	31	5.9	0.7	17.0
raig Hodges	83-84SD 85-88Mil	1960	6'3	190	G	Long Beach State	8	566	2124	4544	47	483	1197	40	609	742	82	871	1616	1261	21	5340	24	1.5	2.9	9.4
88-89Phoe 89-90Chi	85-87, 89-90						5	67	243	550	44	70	200	35	54	69	78	103	188	175	5	610	26	1.5	2.8	9.1
rad Holland	80-81LA 82Was 82Mil	1956	6'3	185	G	U.C.L.A.	3	93	118	293	40	4	21	19	53	71	75	59	63	81	0	293	7	0.6	0.7	3.2
	80-82						3	11	6	11	55	0	0	—	4	4	100	5	4	8	0	16	3	0.5	0.4	1.5
Vilbur Holland	76Atl 77-79Chi	1951	6'	175	G	New Orleans	4	276	1608	3558	45				544	681	80	842	922	747	16	3760	30	3.1	3.3	13.6
	77						1	3	17	34	50				10	10	100	9	3	8	0	44	28	3.0	1.0	14.7
ionel Hollins	76-80Port 80-82Phi 83SD	1953	6'3	185	G	Arizona State	10	673	3201	7211	44	13	87	15	1394	1882	74	1601	3006	1841	23	7809	27	2.4	4.5	11.6
84Det 85Hou	77-82, 84-85						8	77	369	897	41	0	12	0	173	236	73	207	344	221	4	911	30	2.7	4.5	11.8
ssie Hollis	79Det	1955	6'6	195	F	St. Bonaventure	1	25	30	75	40				9	12	75	45	6	28	0	69	6	1.8	0.2	2.8
ike Holton	85-86Phoe 86Chi	1961	6'4	185	G	U.C.L.A.	6	325	796	1805	44	28	109	26	396	491	81	459	977	577	1	2016	18	1.4	3.0	6.2
87-88Port 89-90Char	85, 87-88						3	9	13	34	38	0	5	0	4	4	100	8	15	15	0	30	11	0.9	1.7	3.3
ave Hoppen	88Mil 88GS 89-90Char	1964	6'11	235	C-F	Nebraska	3	126	299	577	52	1	3	33	163	211	77	594	95	352	5	762	17	4.7	0.8	6.0
ennis Hopson	88-90NJ	1965	6'5	203	G-F	Ohio State	3	202	995	2356	42	48	173	28	588	738	80	624	372	478	10	2626	27	3.1	1.8	13.0
edrick Hordges	81-82Den	1957	6'8	220	F-C	Auburn,	2	145	425	894	48	3	16	19	246	385	64	853	169	456	5	1099	20	5.9	1.2	7.6
	82					South Carolina	1	3	8	19	42	0	1	0	3	4	75	13	2	4	0	19	15	4.3	0.7	6.3
ito Horford	89-90Mil	1966	7'1	245	C	Louisiana State	2	60	33	108	31	0	0	—	27	43	63	81	5	47	0	93	6	1.4	0.1	1.6
	90					Miami (Fla.)	1	2	1	1	100	0	0	—	0	0	—	0	0	0	0	2	1	0.0	0.0	1.0
eff Hornacek	87-90Phoe	1963	6'4	190	G	Iowa State	4	307	1388	2745	51	96	280	34	566	686	83	1025	1703	613	2	3438	28	3.3	5.5	11.2
	89-90						2	28	186	368	51	6	31	19	89	98	91	131	135	77	1	467	34	4.7	4.8	16.7
d Horton	90Was	1967	6'8	230	F	Iowa	1	45	80	162	49	0	4	0	42	69	61	108	19	63	1	202	8	2.4	0.4	4.5
Mo Howard	77Cle 77NO	1954	6'3	170	G	Maryland	1	32	64	132	48				24	35	69	39	42	51	0	152	11	1.2	1.3	4.8
tis Howard	79Mil 79Det	1956	6'7	230	F	Austin Peay	1	14	24	56	43				11	23	48	41	5	24	0	59	8	2.9	0.4	4.2
Phil Hubbard	80-82Det 82-89Cle	1956	6'8	215	F-C	Michigan	10	665	2672	5394	50	1	26	4	1883	2667	71	3538	857	2073	51	7228	24	5.3	1.3	10.9
	85, 88-89						3	8	25	51	49	1	1	100	13	18	72	23	3	17	0	64	15	2.9	0.4	8.0
lfred Hughes	86SA	1962	6'5	215	F-G	Loyola (Chic.)	1	68	152	372	41	3	17	18	49	84	58	113	61	79	0	356	13	1.7	0.9	5.2
	86						1	3	4	9	44	0	0	—	0	0	—	0	1	3	0	8	6	0.0	0.3	2.7
Eddie Hughes	88Utah 89-90Den	1960	5'10	165	G	Colorado State	3	90	116	279	42	28	77	36	36	52	69	93	159	122	0	296	13	1.0	1.8	3.3
	88						1	7	2	7	29	1	3	33	0	0	—	0	1	1	0	5	2	0.0	0.1	0.7
im Hughes	76NY-A 77NYN 78NJ 79-81Cle	1952	6'11	220	C	Wisconsin	6	425	735	1534	48	0	0	—	154	388	40	2367	374	1268	25	1624	19	5.6	0.9	3.8
	76, 79						2	15	30	59	51	0	0	—	3	7	43	83	9	61	0	63	20	5.5	0.6	4.2
ay Humphries	85-88Phoe 88-90Mil	1962	6'3	185	G	Colorado	6	466	2115	4371	48	62	258	24	1003	1283	78	1316	2780	1287	8	5295	31	2.8	6.0	11.4
	85, 88-90						4	17	77	150	51	4	21	19	49	59	83	40	106	53	0	207	30	2.4	6.2	12.2
Geoff Huston	80NY 81Dal 81-85Cle 86GS 87LAC	1957	6'2	175	G	Texas Tech	8	496	1836	3805	48	16	63	25	692	978	71	684	2509	844	3	4380	25	1.4	5.1	8.8
Marc Iavaroni	83-85Phi 85-86SA 86-89Utah	1956	6'10	225	F	Virginia	7	531	899	1959	46	0	17	0	530	746	71	1725	514	1255	7	2328	16	3.2	1.0	4.4
	83-89						7	43	76	151	50	1	4	25	48	67	72	132	59	126	3	201	17	3.1	1.4	4.7
Byron Irvin	90Port	1966	6'5	190	G	Arkansas, Missouri	1	50	96	203	47	5	14	36	61	91	67	74	47	40	0	258	10	1.5	0.9	5.2
	90						1	4	5	22	23	0	0	—	5	6	83	8	5	7	0	15	12	2.0	1.3	3.8
Dan Issel	71-75KyA 76DenA 77-85Den	1948	6'9	240	C-F	Kentucky	15	1218	10431	20964	50	29	132	22	6591	8315	79	11133	2907	3504	32	27482	34	9.1	2.4	22.6
	71-79, 82-85						13	133	1146	2345	49	3	12	25	639	777	82	1255	281	465	1	2934	35	9.4	2.1	22.1
Jaren Jackson	90NJ	1967	6'4	190	G	Georgetown	1	28	25	69	36	0	3	0	17	21	81	24	13	16	0	67	6	0.9	0.5	2.4
Mark Jackson	88-90NY	1965	6'3	205	G	St. John's (NY)	3	236	1244	2787	45	148	497	30	506	689	73	1055	2091	528	3	3142	35	4.5	8.9	13.3
	88-90						3	22	84	187	45	16	42	38	35	50	70	55	151	27	0	223	27	2.5	6.9	10.1
Michael Jackson	88-90Sac	1964	6'2	183	G	Georgetown	3	89	78	210	37	9	33	27	27	40	68	70	198	96	0	188	10	0.8	2.2	2.1
Myron Jackson	87Dal	1964	6'3	185	G	Arkansas	1	8	2	9	22	0	0	—	7	8	88	3	6	1	0	11	3	0.4	0.8	1.4
Ralph Jackson	85Ind	1962	6'2	190	G	U.C.L.A.	1	1	1	3	33	0	0	—	0	0	—	1	4	1	0	2	14	1.0	4.0	2.0
Stu Jackson	HC90NY	1955				Oregon, Seattle																				
Tony Jackson	81LA	1958	6'	170	G	Florida State	1	2	1	3	33	0	0	—	0	0	—	2	2	1	0	2	7	1.0	1.0	1.0
Tracy Jackson	82Bos 82-83Chi 84Ind	1959	6'6	215	G-F	Notre Dame	3	129	279	602	46	2	13	15	134	179	75	243	132	183	0	694	14	1.9	1.0	5.4
Aaron James	75-79NO	1952	6'8	211	F	Grambling	5	356	1609	3347	48				611	804	76	1470	370	972	12	3829	22	4.1	1.0	10.8
Abdul Jeelani	80Port 81Dal	1954	6'8	210	F-C	Wis.-Parkside	2	143	475	1005	47	0	7	0	340	424	80	500	160	278	2	1290	17	3.5	1.1	9.0
Avery Johnson	89-90Sea	1964	5'10	175	G	Southern U.	2	96	84	225	37	2	13	15	38	56	68	67	235	89	0	208	9	0.7	2.4	2.2
	89						1	6	5	12	42	0	4	0	1	2	50	4	5	1	0	11	5	0.7	0.8	1.8
Buck Johnson	87-90Hou	1964	6'7	190	F	Alabama	4	279	1023	2033	50	4	35	11	411	553	74	923	467	742	12	2463	22	3.3	1.7	8.8
	87-90						4	17	43	97	44	0	2	0	20	29	69	35	22	33	0	106	17	2.1	1.3	6.2
Cheese Johnson	80GS	1957	6'6	195	F-G	Wichita State	1	9	12	30	40	0	0	—	3	5	60	14	2	11	0	27	6	1.6	0.2	3.0
Clay Johnson	82-83LA 84Sea	1956	6'4	182	G	Missouri	3	80	84	205	41	1	3	33	55	76	72	93	45	99	0	224	9	1.2	0.6	2.8
	82-84						3	17	11	20	55	0	2	0	2	2	100	8	3	12	0	24	4	0.5	0.2	1.4
Clemon Johnson	79Port 80-83Ind 83-86Phi	1956	6'10	240	C-F	Florida A & M	10	761	1699	3454	49	0	5	0	704	1134	62	3508	744	1666	11	4102	17	4.6	1.0	5.4
87-88Sea	79, 81, 83-88						8	66	107	230	47	0	2	0	56	92	61	238	26	139	0	270	17	3.6	0.4	4.1
Dennis Johnson (D.J.)	77-80Sea 81-83Phoe	1954	6'4	191	G	Pepperdine	14	100	5832	13100	45	80	464	17	3791	4754	80	4249	5499	3087	38	15535	33	3.9	5.0	14.1
84-90Bos	78-90						13	180	1167	2661	44	26	109	24	756	943	80	781	1006	575	8	3116	39	4.3	5.8	17.3
Eddie Johnson (Fast Eddie)	78-86Atl 86Cle 87Sea	1955	6'2	190	G	Auburn	10	675	4015	8436	48	104	319	33	2029	2564	79	1522	3436	1706	21	10163	30	2.3	5.1	15.1
	78-80, 82-84, 87						6	37	174	359	48	3	11	27	91	117	78	76	150	79	1	442	24	2.1	4.1	11.9
Eddie Johnson	82-85KC 86-87Sac 88-90Phoe	1959	6'8	218	F	Illinois	9	690	5275	10991	48	260	788	33	2095	2530	83	3327	1808	1989	23	12905	31	4.8	2.6	18.7
	84, 86, 89-90						4	34	202	469	43	30	84	36	82	102	80	175	58	96	1	516	27	5.1	1.7	15.2
Eric Johnson	90Utah	1966	6'2	205	G	Nebraska	1	48	20	84	24	1	6	17	13	17	76	28	64	49	1	54	6	0.6	1.3	1.1
	90						1	1	0	0	—	0	0	—	0	0	—	0	0	0	0	0	3	0.0	0.0	0.0

		Birth					#		Field Goals			3 pt. FG			Free Throws								Per Game			
Use Name-Nickname	Team by Name	Yr.	Hgt	Wgt	Pos	College	Yr	G	FG	Att.	%	FG	Att.	%	FT	Att.	%	Reb	Ass	PF	DQ	Pts	Min	Reb	Ass.	Pts
Frank Johnson	82-88Was 89Hou	1958	6'2	185	G	Wake Forest	8	449	1677	3822	44	50	219	23	877	1158	76	830	2142	884	3	4281	24	1.8	4.8	9.5
	82, 84-85, 87-89						6	25	79	195	41	7	24	29	52	60	87	48	104	55	0	217	23	1.9	4.2	8.7
George Johnson 81-82SA 83Atl 85NJ 86Sea	72-77GS 77Buf 78-80NJ	1948	6'11	209	C	Dillard	14	904	1802	3995	45	1	2	50	764	1101	69	5887	929	2707	64	4369	20	6.5	1.0	4.8
	73, 75-76, 79, 81-83, 85						8	59	103	187	55	0	0	—	42	68	62	361	55	165	2	248	18	6.1	0.9	4.2
George Johnson 86Was	79Mil 80Den 81-84Ind 85Phi	1956	6'7	218	F-C	St. John's (NY)	8	464	1704	3684	46	21	111	19	785	1008	78	2610	817	1349	21	4214	21	5.6	1.8	9.1
	81, 85						2	7	10	16	63	1	1	100	0	0	—	11	1	3	0	21	7	1.6	0.1	3.0
Kennard Johnson	88Cle	1965	6'9	220	F	Western Kentucky	1	4	1	3	33	0	0	—	0	0	—	0	0	1	0	2	3	0.0	0.0	0.5
Ken Johnson	86Port	1962	6'8	240	F	Southern Calif.,	1	64	113	214	53	0	0	—	37	85	44	243	19	147	1	263	13	3.8	0.3	4.1
	86					Michigan State	1	2	0	0		0	0	—	0	0	—	2	0	1	0	0	6	1.0	0.0	0.0
Kevin Johnson	88Cle 88-90Phoe	1966	6'2	184	G	California	3	235	1423	2883	49	15	87	17	1186	1385	86	801	2274	524	2	4047	34	3.4	9.7	17.2
	89-90						2	28	213	439	49	5	21	24	194	222	87	104	317	56	0	625	38	3.7	11.3	22.3
Larry Johnson	78Buf	1954	6'3	205	G	Kentucky	1	4	3	13	23				0	2	0	5	7	3	0	6	10	1.3	1.8	1.5
Lee Johnson	81Hou 81Det	1957	6'11	210	F	Montana, East Texas State	1	12	7	25	28	0	0	—	3	5	60	22	1	18	0	17	8	1.8	0.1	1.4
Magic Johnson	80-84LA 85-90LAL	1959	6'8	217	G-F	Michigan State	11	795	5608	10681	53	233	766	30	4269	5076	84	5825	8932	1852	5	15708	37	7.3	11.2	19.8
	80-90						11	167	1158	2245	52	27	132	20	883	1063	83	1277	2080	478	3	3225	39	7.6	12.5	19.3
Marques Johnson	78-84Mil 85-87LAC 88JJ 90GS	1956	6'7	218	F-G	U.C.L.A.	11	691	5733	11065	52	14	92	15	2410	3265	74	4817	2502	1766	11	13892	34	7.0	3.6	20.1
	78, 80-84						6	54	471	964	49	3	13	23	218	311	70	427	198	156	0	1163	39	7.9	3.7	21.5
Mickey Johnson 83NJ 83-85GS 86NJ	75-79Chi 80Ind 81-83Mil	1952	6'10	190	F	Aurora	12	904	4733	10544	45	29	176	16	3253	4066	80	6465	2677	3101	74	12748	28	7.2	3.0	14.1
	75, 77, 81-82, 86						5	22	109	234	47	0	4	0	84	101	83	129	40	74	1	302	25	5.9	1.8	13.7
Ollie Johnson 79-80Chi 81-82Phi	73-74Port 75NO 75-77KC 78Atl	1949	6'6	200	F	Temple	10	690	2235	4505	50	3	20	15	868	1049	83	2280	1212	1503	12	5341	21	3.3	1.8	7.7
	75, 78, 81						3	16	33	77	43	0	1	0	12	12	100	31	10	21	0	78	13	1.9	0.6	4.9
Phil Johnson HC82Chi HC85KC HC86-87Sac	HC74-75KC-O HC76-78KC	1941				Utah State																				
Reggie Johnson	81-82SA 82-83KC 83Phi 84NJ	1957	6'9	205	F-C	Tennessee	4	305	1065	2109	50	1	7	14	433	605	72	1238	262	913	17	2564	20	4.1	0.9	8.4
	81, 83-84						3	19	37	81	46	0	0	—	26	33	79	39	19	34	2	100	14	2.1	1.0	5.3
Steffond Johnson	87LAC	1962	6'8	240	F	Louisiana State, San Diego State	1	29	27	64	42	0	3	0	20	38	53	43	5	55	2	74	8	1.5	0.2	2.6
Steve Johnson 87-89Port 90Min 90Sea	82-84KC 84-85Chi 86SA	1957	6'10	241	C-F	Oregon State	9	602	2807	4902	57	0	4	0	1641	2585	63	3393	760	2359	92	7255	22	5.6	1.3	12.1
	85-87, 89						4	13	37	91	41	0	0	—	37	59	63	57	6	40	1	111	19	4.4	0.5	8.5
Vinnie Johnson	80-82Sea 82-90Det	1956	6'2	200	G	Baylor	11	842	4274	9080	47	53	233	23	1788	2379	75	2647	2796	1804	7	10389	24	3.1	3.3	12.3
	80, 84-90						8	98	465	1021	46	13	45	29	191	251	76	280	256	194	0	1134	22	2.9	2.6	11.6
Nate Johnston	90Utah 90Port	1966	6'8	210	F	Tampa	1	21	18	48	38	1	4	25	9	13	69	23	1	11	1	46	4	1.1	0.0	2.2
	90						1	3	6	11	55	0	0	—	1	1	100	6	1	5	0	13	6	2.0	0.3	4.3
Jim Johnstone	83SA 83Det	1960	6'11	245	C-F	Wake Forest	1	23	11	30	37	0	0	—	9	20	45	46	11	33	0	31	8	2.0	0.5	1.3
Anthony Jones	87Was 87SA 89Chi 89-90Dal	1962	6'6	195	G-F	Georgetown,	3	164	234	595	39	15	49	31	111	150	74	214	119	176	0	594	10	1.3	0.7	3.6
	90					Nevada - Las Vegas	1	1	0	0	—	0	0	—	0	0	—	0	0	0	0	0	3	0.0	0.0	0.0
Bill Jones	89NJ	1966	6'7	175	F	Iowa	1	37	50	102	49	0	1	0	29	43	67	47	20	38	0	129	8	1.3	0.5	3.5
Bobby Jones	75-76DenA 77-78Den 79-86Phi	1951	6'9	212	F	North Carolina	12	941	4451	7953	56	0	17	0	2489	3251	77	5739	2522	2620	22	11391	27	6.1	2.7	12.1
	75-86						12	151	696	1290	54	0	4	0	408	510	80	837	381	502	4	1800	28	5.5	2.5	11.9
Caldwell Jones 77-82Phi 83-84Hou 85Chi 86-89Port 90SA	74-76SD-A 76KyA 76StLA	1950	6'11	225	C-F	Albany State (Ga.)	17	1299	4090	8482	48	7	57	12	2054	2716	76	10685	1800	4436	48	10241	27	8.2	1.4	7.9
	74, 77-82, 85-90						13	125	358	753	48	0	4	0	181	240	75	1093	162	445	9	897	30	8.7	1.3	7.2
Charles Jones	84Phi 85Chi 85-90Was	1957	6'9	215	F-C	Albany State (Ga.)	7	395	540	1118	48	0	5	0	280	429	65	1947	422	1302	26	1360	22	4.9	1.1	3.4
	85-88						4	17	18	40	45	0	0	—	14	22	64	60	11	56	0	50	20	3.5	0.6	2.9
Charles A. Jones	85-86Phoe 88Port 89Was	1962	6'8	215	F	Louisville	4	201	365	740	49	1	9	11	284	465	61	758	206	313	0	1015	15	3.8	1.0	5.0
	85, 88						2	4	3	6	50	0	0	—	6	6	100	4	3	4	0	12	9	1.0	0.8	3.0
Dwight Jones	74-76Atl 77-80Hou 80-83Chi 83LA	1952	6'10	212	F-C	Houston	10	766	2459	5216	47	1	2	50	1311	1772	74	4513	911	2077	17	6230	21	5.9	1.2	8.1
	78-79, 81, 83						4	27	69	153	45	0	0	—	43	51	84	134	29	67	2	181	21	5.0	1.1	6.7
Earl Jones	85LA 86Mil	1961	7'	230	C	U. of D.C.	2	14	5	13	38	0	0	—	3	4	75	10	4	13	0	13	4	0.7	0.3	0.9
Edgar Jones	81NJ 82-83Det 83-85SA 85-86Cle	1956	6'10	225	F-C	Nevada-Reno	6	363	1207	2384	51	16	61	26	827	1164	71	1745	331	1164	26	3257	19	4.8	0.9	9.0
	83, 85						2	15	37	80	46	0	3	0	26	41	63	61	20	50	1	100	16	4.1	1.3	6.7
Hutch Jones	83-84SD	1959	6'8	195	F	Buffalo State, Vanderbilt	2	13	17	40	43	0	0	—	7	10	70	17	4	14	0	41	8	1.3	0.3	3.2
Major Jones	80-84Hou 85Det	1953	6'9	225	F	Albany State (Ga.)	6	374	678	1385	49	1	9	11	286	488	59	1323	215	623	0	1643	14	3.5	0.6	4.4
	80-81, 85						3	19	22	40	55	0	0	—	8	14	57	40	9	23	0	52	9	2.1	0.5	2.7
Mark Jones	84NJ	1961	6'2	175	G	St. Bonaventure	1	6	3	6	50	0	1	0	1	2	50	2	5	2	0	7	3	0.3	0.8	1.2
Ozell Jones	85SA 86LAC	1960	6'11	235	C-F	Wichita State,	2	70	106	182	58	0	1	0	33	83	40	240	56	144	1	245	13	3.4	0.8	3.5
	85					Fullerton State	1	5	8	11	73	0	0	—	1	6	17	17	4	18	1	17	15	3.4	0.8	3.4
Robin Jones	77Port 78Hou	1954	6'9	225	F-C	St. Louis	2	75	150	319	47				70	119	59	310	82	140	3	370	15	4.1	1.1	4.9
	77						1	19	15	32	47				6	9	67	23	9	24	0	36	6	1.2	0.5	1.9
Eddie Jordan (Fast Eddie) 81-83LA 84Port 84LA	78Cle 78-81NJ	1955	6'1	170	G	Rutgers	7	420	1349	3256	41	22	98	22	694	909	76	788	1595	893	7	3414	20	1.9	3.8	8.1
	79, 81-82						3	7	15	40	38	0	1	0	8	9	89	15	23	6	0	38	13	2.1	3.3	5.4
Michael Jordan	85-90Chi	1963	6'6	194	G-F	North Carolina	6	427	5154	9989	52	150	532	28	3558	4195	85	2694	2565	1326	8	14016	39	6.3	6.0	32.8
	85-90						6	53	673	1333	50	31	102	30	519	623	83	368	355	196	3	1896	42	6.9	6.7	35.8
Walter Jordan	81Cle	1956	6'7	198	F	Purdue	1	30	29	75	39	0	0	—	10	17	59	42	11	35	0	68	7	1.4	0.4	2.3
Yvon Joseph	86NJ	1957	6'11	245	C	Georgia Tech	1	1	0	0		0	0	—	2	2	100	0	0	1	0	2	5	0.0	0.0	2.0
Jeff Judkins	79-80Bos 81Utah 82Det 83Port	1956	6'6	185	G-F	Utah	5	272	596	1248	48	23	73	32	267	329	81	427	282	431	1	1482	13	1.6	1.0	5.4
	80						1	7	4	8	50	1	3	33	0	0	—	4	0	0	0	9	1	0.6	0.0	1.3
Clarence Kea	81-82Dal	1959	6'6	218	F	Lamar	2	51	63	130	48	0	1	0	72	104	69	128	19	99	2	198	9	2.5	0.4	3.9
Harold Keeling	86Dal	1963	6'4	185	G	Santa Clara	1	20	17	39	44	0	0	—	10	14	71	6	10	9	0	44	4	0.3	0.5	2.2
	86						1	1	0	0	—	0	0	—	0	0	—	0	0	0	0	0	1	0.0	0.0	0.0
Rich Kelley 83Den 83-85Utah 86Sac	76-79NO 80NJ 80-82Phoe	1953	7'	240	C-F	Stanford	11	814	2166	4435	49	0	10	0	1867	2384	78	5678	2092	2613	60	6199	22	7.0	2.6	7.6
	80-82, 84-86						6	45	92	197	47	0	2	0	75	94	80	246	105	133	2	259	19	5.5	2.3	5.8
Clark Kellogg	83-87Ind	1961	6'7	227	F	Ohio State	5	260	2008	4041	50	23	68	34	879	1161	76	2482	764	858	12	4918	33	9.5	2.9	18.9
Greg Kelser	80-82Det 82-83Sea 84SD 85Ind	1957	6'7	198	F	Michigan State	6	305	1097	2255	49	5	30	17	762	1110	69	1402	411	904	13	2961	20	4.6	1.3	9.7
	82-83						2	5	2	7	29	0	0	—	4	4	100	9	2	6	0	8	5	1.8	0.4	1.6
Shawn Kemp	90Sea	1969	6'10	240	F-C	Kentucky	1	81	203	424	48	2	12	17	117	159	74	346	26	204	5	525	14	4.3	0.3	6.5
Tim Kempton	87LAC 89Char 90Den	1964	6'10	245	F-C	Notre Dame	3	216	421	853	49	0	3	0	314	458	69	716	273	521	11	1156	15	3.3	1.3	5.4
	90						1	3	7	9	78	0	0	—	4	4	100	5	4	8	0	18	11	1.7	1.3	6.0
Larry Kenon (Special K) 77-80SA 80-83Chi 83GS 83Cle	74-75NY-A 76SA-A	1952	6'9	212	F	Memphis State	10	752	5476	11238	49	2	14	14	2000	2550	78	6701	1672	1723	5	12954	33	8.9	2.2	17.2
	74-81						8	57	427	931	46	1	4	25	121	171	71	577	128	150	1	979	35	10.1	2.2	17.2

		Birth					#		Field Goals			3 pt. FG			Free Throws								Per Game			
Use Name-Nickname	Team by Name	Yr.	Hgt	Wgt	Pos	College	Yr	G	FG	Att.	%	FG	Att.	%	FT	Att.	%	Reb	Ass	PF	DQ	Pts	Min	Reb	Ass.	Pts
Steve Kerr	89Phoe 90Cle	1965	6'3	175	G	Arizona	2	104	212	478	44	81	161	50	69	82	84	115	272	71	0	574	18	1.1	2.6	5.5
	90						1	5	4	14	29	0	3	0	0	0	—	6	10	6	0	8	15	1.2	2.0	1.6
Jerome Kersey	85-90Port	1962	6'7	232	F	Longwood	6	475	2472	5022	49	13	88	15	1353	1932	70	2971	1014	1566	29	6310	27	6.3	2.1	13.3
	85-90						6	44	256	551	46	0	7	0	147	200	74	271	74	153	3	659	28	6.2	1.7	15.0
Randolph Keys	89-90Cle 90Char	1966	6'9	195	F-G	Southern Miss.	2	122	367	850	43	15	53	28	121	169	72	309	107	275	1	870	16	2.5	0.9	7.1
	89						1	1	0	3	0	0	1	0	0	0	—	3	1	1	0	0	12	3.0	1.0	0.0
Irv Kiffin	80SA	1951	6'9	225	F	Virginia Union, Oklahoma Baptist	1	26	32	96	33				18	25	72	40	19	43	0	82	8	1.5	0.7	3.2
Carl Kilpatrick	80Utah	1956	6'10	230	C	Northeast La.	1	2	1	2	50				1	2	50	4	0	1	0	3	3	2.0	0.0	1.5
Stan Kimbrough	90Det	1966	5'11	185	G	Xavier	1	10	7	16	44	0	0	—	2	2	100	7	5	4	0	16	5	0.7	0.5	1.6
Chad Kinch	81Cle 81Dal	1958	6'4	190	G	North Carolina	1	41	52	141	37	0	0	—	14	18	78	33	45	33	0	118	9	0.8	1.1	2.9
Albert King	82-87NJ 88Phi 89SA	1959	6'6	198	F-G	Maryland	8	528	2698	5845	46	54	202	27	989	1251	79	2251	1166	1605	30	6439	24	4.3	2.2	12.2
	82-86						5	21	135	298	45	3	9	33	54	74	73	110	49	81	3	327	30	5.2	2.3	15.6
Bernard King	78-79NJ 80Utah 81-82GS 83-85NY 86KJ 87NY 88-90Was	1956	6'7	205	F	Tennessee	12	778	7026	13421	52	13	90	14	3550	4902	72	4665	2553	2645	44	17615	34	6.0	3.3	22.6
	79, 83-84, 88						4	25	265	474	56	1	4	25	148	203	73	120	65	91	0	679	36	4.8	2.6	27.2
Reggie King	80-83KC 84-85Sea	1957	6'6	228	F	Alabama	6	438	1512	2940	51	0	3	0	874	1251	70	2707	691	1005	14	4545	26	6.2	1.6	10.4
	80-81, 84						3	23	137	281	49	0	1	0	80	111	72	191	35	73	0	354	34	8.3	1.5	15.4
Stacey King	90Chi	1967	6'11	230	C-F	Oklahoma	1	82	267	530	50	0	1	0	194	267	73	384	87	215	0	728	22	4.7	1.1	8.9
	90						1	16	37	91	41	0	1	0	36	47	77	51	9	32	0	110	18	3.2	0.6	6.9
Curtis Kitchen	87Sea	1964	6'9	235	F	South Florida	1	6	3	6	50	0	1	0	3	4	75	9	1	4	0	9	5	1.5	0.2	1.5
	87						1	8	1	2	50	0	0	—	0	4	0	6	0	7	0	2	3	0.8	0.0	0.3
Greg Kite	84-88Bos 88-89LAC 89Char 90Sac	1961	6'11	250	C	Brigham Young	7	422	402	945	43	1	4	25	158	337	47	1332	227	870	10	963	13	3.2	0.5	2.3
	84-87						4	53	20	50	40	0	0	—	13	22	59	90	17	85	1	53	7	1.7	0.3	1.0
Joe Kleine	86-89Sac 89-90Bos	1962	7'	267	C-F	Notre Dame, Arkansas	5	397	1091	2372	46	0	7	0	574	710	81	2168	323	1027	6	2756	19	5.5	0.8	6.9
	86, 89-90						3	11	24	41	59	0	2	0	17	21	81	45	5	29	0	65	17	4.1	0.5	5.9
Bob Kloppenberg	HC82Cle	1928																								
Billy Knight	75-76IndA 77Ind 78Buf 79Bos 79-83Ind 84-85KC 85SA	1952	6'6	195	G-F	Pittsburgh	11	821	5418	10680	51	44	155	28	3021	3652	83	4377	1862	1604	2	13901	29	5.3	2.3	16.9
	75-76, 81, 84-85						5	31	249	453	55	0	7	0	108	129	84	213	65	63	0	606	34	6.9	2.1	19.5
Toby Knight	78-80, 82NY 81KJ	1955	6'9	210	F	Notre Dame	4	283	1602	3087	52	0	2	0	436	589	74	1444	335	896	12	3640	26	5.1	1.2	12.9
	78						1	6	6	20	30	0	0	—	4	8	50	19	1	9	0	16	8	3.2	0.2	2.7
Bart Kofoed	88-89Utah	1964	6'4	210	G	Hastings, Kearney State	2	55	30	81	37	2	8	25	14	24	58	26	43	64	0	76	7	0.5	0.8	1.4
	88						1	10	9	23	39	1	5	20	2	2	100	14	11	18	0	21	11	1.4	1.1	2.1
Jon Koncak	86-90Atl	1963	7'	260	C-F	S.M.U.	5	341	749	1470	51	0	8	0	469	777	60	1972	184	1139	21	1967	20	5.8	0.5	5.8
	86-87, 89						3	22	39	71	55	0	0	—	60	87	69	107	12	74	3	138	21	4.9	0.5	6.3
Joe Kopicki	83-84Was 85Den	1960	6'9	240	F	Detroit	3	118	137	278	49	3	11	27	155	191	81	314	84	150	0	432	10	2.7	0.7	3.7
	84-85						2	10	9	22	41	0	0	—	7	19	37	18	4	11	0	27	6	1.8	0.4	2.7
Frank Kornet	90Mil	1967	6'9	225	F	Vanderbilt	1	57	42	114	37	5	20	25	24	39	62	71	21	54	0	113	8	1.2	0.4	2.0
	90						1	2	0	1	0	0	1	0	0	0	—	1	0	1	0	0	2	0.5	0.0	0.0
Arvid Kramer	80Den	1956	6'9	220	C	Augustana	1	8	7	22	32				2	2	100	12	3	8	0	16	6	1.5	0.4	2.0
Joel Kramer	79-83Phoe	1955	6'7	203	F-C	San Diego State	5	328	483	1008	48	0	3	0	291	395	74	916	343	585	2	1257	13	2.8	1.0	3.8
	79, 81-83						4	28	50	93	54	0	0	—	29	41	71	78	24	64	2	129	12	2.8	0.9	4.6
Wayne Kreklow	81Bos	1957	6'4	175	G	Drake	1	25	11	47	23	1	4	25	7	10	70	12	9	20	0	30	4	0.5	0.4	1.2
Tom Kropp	76Was 77Chi	1953	6'3	213	G	Kearney State	2	78	80	182	44				33	47	70	62	47	97	1	193	7	0.8	0.6	2.5
	76-77						2	2	1	1	100				0	0	—	0	0	3	0	2	2	0.0	0.0	1.0
Larry Krystkowiak	87SA 88-90Mil	1964	6'9	227	F-C	Montana	4	214	703	1523	46	5	29	17	528	659	80	1156	267	538	1	1939	23	5.4	1.2	9.1
	88-89						2	13	42	97	43	0	2	0	43	49	88	79	19	39	0	127	31	6.1	1.5	9.8
Bruce Kuczenski	84NJ 84Phi 84Ind	1961	6'10	230	F	Connecticut	1	15	10	37	27	0	0	—	8	12	67	23	8	18	0	28	8	1.5	0.5	1.9
John Kuester	78KC 79Den 80Ind	1955	6'2	180	G	North Carolina	3	135	173	405	43	0	1	0	105	126	83	141	305	180	1	451	11	1.0	2.3	3.3
Kevin Kunnert	74Buf 74-78Hou 79SD 80-82Port	1951	7'	232	C-F	Iowa	9	555	2022	4251	48	0	0	—	558	818	68	4031	784	1927	57	4602	22	7.3	1.4	8.3
	75, 77, 81						3	23	91	195	47	0	1	0	30	53	57	176	27	95	3	212	27	7.7	1.2	9.2
Mitch Kupchak	77-81Was 82LA 83JJ 84-86LA	1954	6'9	230	F-C	North Carolina	9	510	2003	3832	52	0	4	0	1196	1698	70	2730	377	1117	7	5202	19	5.4	0.7	10.2
	77-79, 84-86						6	68	202	426	47	0	1	0	120	185	65	321	44	164	1	524	18	4.7	0.6	7.7
C.J. Kupec	76-77LA 78Hou	1953	6'8	220	F-C	Michigan	3	147	247	579	43				112	145	77	313	108	174	0	606	11	2.1	0.7	4.1
	77						1	11	8	18	44				5	7	71	16	4	7	0	21	5	1.5	0.4	1.9
Sam Lacey	71-72Cin 73-75KC-O 76-82KC 82NJ 83Cle	1948	6'10	235	C	New Mexico State	13	1002	4276	9693	44	3	16	19	1748	2369	74	9687	3754	3473	78	10303	32	9.7	3.7	10.3
	75, 79-81						4	29	107	267	40	1	4	25	59	76	78	287	144	113	5	274	37	9.9	5.0	9.4
Tom LaGarde	78Den 79-80Sea 81-82Dal 85NJ	1955	6'10	223	C-F	North Carolina	6	312	870	1882	46	0	2	0	636	994	64	1593	456	860	14	2376	20	5.1	1.5	7.6
	78, 80						2	23	27	65	42	0	0	—	14	18	78	58	19	37	0	68	10	2.5	0.8	3.0
Bill Laimbeer	81-82Cle 82-90Det	1957	6'11	250	C	Notre Dame	10	815	4521	9029	50	120	373	32	2146	2577	83	8737	1726	2924	56	11308	33	10.7	2.1	13.9
	84-90						7	93	466	980	48	37	110	34	180	223	81	942	168	336	12	1149	34	10.1	1.8	12.4
John Lambert	76-81Cle 81-82KC 82SA	1953	6'10	225	C-F	Southern Calif.	7	446	725	1694	43	1	12	8	237	342	69	1493	248	863	4	1688	12	3.3	0.6	3.8
	76-78, 81-82						5	28	30	75	40	0	4	0	8	10	80	60	11	35	0	68	9	2.1	0.4	2.4
Jeff Lamp	82-84Port 86Mil 86SA 88-89LAL	1959	6'6	195	F-G	Virginia	6	291	607	1292	47	12	54	22	269	320	84	437	269	400	1	1495	12	1.5	0.9	5.1
	83-84, 86, 89						4	12	13	32	41	1	3	33	1	2	50	4	8	10	0	28	7	0.3	0.7	2.3
Jim Lampley	87Phi	1960	6'10	230	C	Vanderbilt, Arkansas	1	1	1	3	33	0	0	—	1	2	50	5	0	0	0	3	16	5.0	0.0	3.0
Mark Landsberger	78-80Chi 80-83LA 84Atl	1955	6'8	228	F-C	Minnesota, Arizona State	7	437	1024	2128	48	0	3	0	420	805	52	2681	236	692	1	2468	17	6.1	0.5	5.6
	80-84						5	41	42	114	37	0	2	0	12	20	60	151	7	77	0	96	11	3.7	0.2	2.3
Jerome Lane	89-90Den	1966	6'8	230	F	Pittsburgh	2	121	254	565	45	0	12	0	87	232	38	561	165	294	2	595	12	4.6	1.4	4.9
	89-90						2	4	2	10	20	0	1	0	3	4	75	7	4	8	0	7	9	1.8	1.0	1.8
Andrew Lang	89-90Phoe	1966	6'11	245	C-F	Arkansas	2	136	157	291	54	0	0	—	103	158	65	418	30	283	2	417	11	3.1	0.2	3.1
	89-90						2	16	6	11	55	0	0	—	4	7	57	26	3	20	0	16	6	1.6	0.2	1.0
Bob Lanier	71-80Det 80-84Mil	1948	6'11	256	C	St. Bonaventure	14	959	7761	15092	51	2	13	15	3724	4858	77	9698	3007	3048	47	19248	33	10.1	3.1	20.1
	74-77, 80-84						9	67	508	955	53	0	1	0	228	297	77	645	235	233	7	1244	35	9.6	3.5	18.6
Rich Laurel	78Mil	1954	6'6	190	G	Hofstra	1	10	10	31	32				4	4	100	10	3	10	0	24	6	1.0	0.3	2.4
Edmund Lawrence	81Det	1952	7'	228	C	McNeese State	1	3	5	8	63	0	0	—	2	4	50	4	1	6	0	12	6	1.3	0.3	4.0
Frank Layden	HC82-89Utah	1932				Niagara																				
Allen Leavell	80-89Hou	1957	6'1	190	G	Oklahoma City	10	700	2549	5666	45	141	603	23	1445	1733	83	1164	3339	1489	9	1684	23	1.7	4.8	2.4
	80-82, 85-89						8	63	138	377	37	13	44	30	113	131	86	80	203	109	2	402	17	1.3	3.2	6.4
Jeff Lebo	90SA	1966	6'4	190	G	North Carolina	1	4	2	7	29	0	0	—	2	2	100	4	3	7	0	6	8	1.0	0.8	1.5

Use Name-Nickname	Team by Name	Birth Yr.	Hgt	Wgt	Pos	College	# Yr	G	Field Goals FG	Att.	%	3 pt. FG FG	Att.	%	Free Throws FT	Att.	%	Reb	Ass	PF	DQ	Pts	Per Game Min	Reb	Ass.	Pts
Eric Leckner	89-90Utah	1966	6'11	265	C-F	Wyoming	2	152	245	442	55	0	0	—	160	222	72	391	35	331	1	650	10	2.6	0.2	4.3
	89-90						2	6	7	14	50	1	1	100	5	9	56	10	2	10	0	20	6	1.7	0.3	3.3
Butch Lee	79Atl 79-80Cle 80LA	1956	6'	185	G	Marquette	2	96	296	658	45				181	238	76	137	307	148	0	773	19	1.4	3.2	8.1
	80						1	3	0	0	-				2	2	100	1	0	2	0	2	2	0.3	0.0	0.7
Keith Lee	86-87Cle 88JJ 89NJ	1962	6'10	220	F	Memphis State	3	182	456	1012	45	2	12	17	200	268	75	861	178	489	10	1114	16	4.7	1.0	6.1
Rock Lee	82SD	1955	6'10	220	C	California, San Diego State	1	2	1	2	50	0	0	—	0	4	0	1	2	3	0	2	5	0.5	1.0	1.0
Ron Lee	77-79Phoe 79NO 80Atl 80-82Det	1952	6'4	195	G	Oregon	6	448	1296	3117	42	42	131	32	651	924	70	1219	1688	1368	28	3285	21	2.7	3.8	7.3
	78						1	2	5	16	31				2	2	100	6	3	7	0	12	21	3.0	1.5	6.0
Tim Legler	90Phoe	1966	6'4	210	G	LaSalle	1	11	11	29	38	0	1	0	6	6	100	8	6	12	0	28	8	0.7	0.5	2.5
Gary Leonard	90Min	1967	7'1	250	C	Missouri	1	22	13	31	42	0	1	0	6	14	43	27	1	26	0	32	6	1.2	0.0	1.5
Jim Les	89-90Utah 90LAC	1963	5'11	175	G	Bradley	2	89	45	147	31	1	15	7	70	90	78	94	236	97	0	161	10	1.1	2.7	1.8
	89						1	3	0	0	—	0	0	—	0	0	—	0	1	2	0	0	2	0.0	0.3	0.0
Ronnie Lester	81-84Chi 85-86LAL	1959	6'2	175	G	Iowa	6	250	679	1449	47	5	22	23	453	575	79	473	1003	395	5	1816	20	1.9	4.0	7.3
	81, 85						2	14	13	33	39	0	1	0	12	16	75	14	13	11	0	38	7	1.0	0.9	2.7
Clifford Lett	90Chi	1965	6'3	170	G	Florida	1	4	2	8	25	0	0	—	0	0	—	0	1	8	0	4	7	0.0	0.3	1.0
Lafayette Lever (Fat)	83-84Port 85-90Den	1960	6'3	175	G	Arizona State	8	636	3873	8575	45	119	394	30	1637	2120	77	4064	4364	1568	10	9502	33	6.4	6.9	14.9
	83-90						8	48	227	548	41	18	44	41	124	160	78	276	297	118	0	596	30	5.8	6.2	12.4
Cliff Levingston	83-84Det 85-90Atl	1961	6'8	220	F	Wichita State	8	616	2026	3861	52	3	22	14	1079	1568	69	3731	603	1931	32	5134	23	6.1	1.0	8.3
	84, 86-89						5	40	71	135	53	2	3	67	52	69	75	142	16	99	0	196	16	3.6	0.4	4.9
Ralph Lewis	88Det 89Char 90Det 90Char	1963	6'6	200	G	La Salle	2	99	99	215	46	1	4	25	50	89	56	128	29	67	0	229	7	1.3	0.3	2.3
	88						1	10	2	6	33	0	1	0	0	0	—	8	1	2	0	4	2	0.8	0.1	0.4
Reggie Lewis	88-90Bos	1965	6'7	195	F-G	Northeastern	3	209	1234	2524	49	7	41	17	580	735	79	787	469	528	7	3055	27	3.8	2.2	14.6
	88-90						3	20	76	151	50	0	4	0	39	53	74	62	37	38	0	191	20	3.1	1.9	9.6
Todd Lichti	90Den	1967	6'4	205	G-F	Stanford	1	79	250	514	49	0	14	0	130	174	75	151	116	145	1	630	17	1.9	1.5	8.0
	90						1	3	15	29	52	0	1	0	14	19	74	18	9	6	0	44	23	6.0	3.0	14.7
Steve Lingenfelter	83Was 84SA	1958	6'9	225	F	Minnesota, S. Dakota State	2	10	5	7	71	0	0	—	0	6	0	16	5	22	1	10	7	1.6	0.5	1.0
Alton Lister	82-86Mil 87-89Sea 90GS	1958	7'	240	C-F	Arizona State	9	646	2111	4069	52	1	7	14	1034	1713	60	4682	757	2407	68	5257	23	7.2	1.2	8.1
	82-89						8	75	222	434	51	0	2	0	129	201	64	465	67	290	10	573	22	6.2	0.9	7.6
Lewis Lloyd 90Phi 90Hou	82-83GS 84-87Hou 88-89DR	1959	6'6	215	G-F	Drake	7	388	2172	4144	52	10	46	22	776	1006	77	1192	1138	833	5	5130	24	3.1	2.9	13.2
	85-86						2	25	154	318	48	2	5	40	57	72	79	95	111	59	0	367	31	3.8	4.4	14.7
Scott Lloyd	77-78Mil 78Buf 79SD 79Chi 81-83Dal	1952	6'10	231	C-F	Arizona State	6	372	647	1521	43	2	7	29	398	554	72	1114	356	723	20	1694	15	3.0	1.0	4.6
Rob Lock	89LAC	1961	6'9	235	F	Kentucky	1	20	9	32	28	0	0	—	12	15	80	32	4	15	0	30	6	1.6	0.2	1.5
Tates Locke	HC77Buf	1937				Ohio Wesleyan																				
Darrell Lockhart	84SA	1960	6'9	245	C	Auburn	1	2	2	2	100	0	0	—	0	0	—	3	0	5	0	4	7	1.5	0.0	2.0
Kevin Loder	82-84KC 84SD	1959	6'6	205	F-G	Kentucky State, Alabama State	3	148	365	791	46	6	23	26	139	200	70	338	174	261	0	875	14	2.3	1.2	5.9
Brad Lohaus	88-89Bos 89Sac 90Min 90Mil	1964	7'	233	C-F	Iowa	3	227	637	1395	46	51	161	32	206	268	77	792	283	495	5	1731	17	3.5	1.2	7.6
	88, 90						2	13	24	51	47	6	18	33	0	0	—	31	5	21	1	54	13	2.4	0.4	4.2
John Long	79-86Det 87-89Ind 89Det 90Atl	1956	6'5	203	G-F	Detroit	12	836	5027	10627	47	87	274	32	1765	2051	86	2420	1699	1823	13	11906	26	2.9	2.0	14.2
	84-87, 89						5	23	87	218	40	2	11	18	47	49	96	35	24	54	0	223	23	1.5	1.0	9.7
Grant Long	89-90Mia	1966	6'8	230	F	Eastern Michigan	2	163	593	1224	48	0	8	0	476	647	74	948	245	637	24	1662	26	5.8	1.5	10.2
Sidney Lowe	84Ind 85Det 85Atl 89Char 90Min	1960	6'	195	G	N. Carolina State	4	193	198	540	37	4	30	13	162	212	76	335	749	282	0	562	18	1.7	3.9	2.9
John Lucas 85-86Hou 87-88Mil 89Sea 90Hou	77-78Hou 79-81GS 82-83Was 84SA	1953	6'3	180	G	Maryland	14	928	3905	8696	45	244	806	30	1897	2446	78	2151	6454	1691	7	9951	28	2.3	7.0	10.7
	77, 82, 85, 87-89						6	45	198	439	45	18	69	26	88	118	75	96	218	80	1	502	25	2.1	4.9	11.2
Maurice Lucas 80-81NJ 82NY 83-85Phoe 86LAL 87Sea 88Port	75-76StLA 76KyA 77-80Port	1952	6'9	227	F-C	Marquette	14	1021	5928	12580	47	9	63	14	2992	3911	77	9306	2498	3498	30	14857	29	9.1	2.4	14.6
	75-79, 83-88						11	102	615	1280	48	0	2	0	257	349	74	945	297	354	6	1487	31	9.3	2.9	14.6
Jim Lynam	HC84SD HC85LAC HC88-90Phi	1941				St. Joseph's - Pa.																				
Ollie Mack	80LA 80-81Chi 81-82Dal	1957	6'3	185	G	East Carolina	3	128	396	864	46	0	16	0	124	184	67	319	230	173	0	916	20	2.5	1.8	7.2
Bob MacKinnon	HC77Buf HC81, HC88NJ					Canisius																				
Rudy Macklin	82-83Atl 84NY	1958	6'7	212	F-G	Louisiana State	3	160	392	874	45	0	7	0	246	317	78	464	121	431	9	1030	17	2.9	0.8	6.4
	82-83						2	5	15	32	47	0	1	0	14	16	88	18	3	18	1	44	22	3.6	0.6	8.8
John MacLeod	HC74-87Phoe HC88-90Dal	1937				Bellarmine																				
Kyle Macy	81-85Phoe 86Chi 87Ind	1957	6'3	186	G	Purdue, Kentucky	7	551	2175	4339	50	192	568	34	717	821	87	1214	2198	1089	2	5259	26	2.2	4.0	9.5
	81-87						7	44	169	363	47	20	53	38	44	53	83	112	170	99	0	402	29	2.5	3.9	9.1
Dave Magley	83Cle	1959	6'8	212	F	Kansas	1	14	4	16	25	0	1	0	4	8	50	10	2	5	0	12	4	0.7	0.1	0.9
Rick Mahorn	81-85Was 86-89Det 90Phi	1958	6'10	245	C-F	Hampton U.	10	721	2507	4992	50	3	20	15	1157	1688	69	5460	861	2685	68	6174	28	7.6	1.2	8.6
	82, 84-90						8	84	223	473	47	0	3	0	102	136	75	511	54	296	6	548	25	6.1	0.6	6.5
Dan Majerle	89-90Phoe	1965	6'6	220	F-G	Central Michigan	2	127	477	1130	42	46	162	28	276	387	71	639	318	316	6	1276	28	5.0	2.5	10.0
	89-90						2	28	136	294	46	12	40	30	89	113	79	138	48	62	0	373	30	4.9	1.7	13.3
Jeff Malone	84-90Was	1961	6'4	205	G	Mississippi State	7	548	4543	9524	48	58	238	24	1939	2229	87	1458	1523	1141	6	11083	33	2.7	2.8	20.2
	84-88						5	21	148	326	45	1	7	14	75	90	83	51	47	57	1	372	33	2.4	2.2	17.7
Karl Malone	86-90Utah	1963	6'9	253	F-C	Louisiana Tech	5	407	3813	7274	52	21	73	29	2469	3565	69	4323	1038	1459	14	10116	36	10.6	2.6	24.9
	86-90						5	28	277	586	47	0	2	0	178	251	71	308	42	111	4	732	42	11.0	1.5	26.1
Moses Malone 77-82Hou 83-86Phi 87-88Was 89-90Atl	75-76UtahA 76StLA 77Buf	1955	6'10	240	C-F	none	16	1208	9429	18914	50	4	65	6	8177	10808	76	16105	1726	3134	5	27039	37	13.3	1.4	22.4
	75, 77, 79-85, 87-89						12	95	797	1626	49	1	7	14	597	793	75	1369	142	261	0	2192	42	14.4	1.5	23.1
Steve Malovic	80Was 80SD 80Det	1956	6'10	230	F	Southern Calif., San Diego State	1	39	31	67	46	0	0	—	18	27	67	86	26	51	0	80	11	2.2	0.7	2.1
Danny Manning	89-90LAC	1966	6'10	230	F	Kansas	2	97	617	1184	52	1	10	10	353	473	75	593	268	350	5	1588	33	6.1	2.8	16.4
Pace Mannion 88Chi 89Det 89Atl	84GS 85-88Utah 87NJ 88Mil	1960	6'7	190	G	Utah	6	216	257	623	41	16	79	20	130	196	66	259	231	238	0	660	10	1.2	1.1	3.1
	85						1	8	4	12	33	0	1	0	10	12	83	7	4	5	0	18	5	0.9	0.5	2.3
Roy Marble	90Atl	1966	6'6	190	G	Iowa	1	24	16	58	28	0	2	0	19	29	66	24	11	16	0	51	7	1.0	0.5	2.1
Sarunas Marciulonis	90GS	1964	6'5	200	G	State U. of Vilnius	1	75	289	557	52	10	39	26	317	403	79	221	121	230	5	905	23	2.9	1.6	12.1
Ricky Marsh	78GS	1954	6'3	200	G	Manhattan	1	60	123	289	43				23	33	70	75	90	111	0	269	14	1.3	1.5	4.5
Bill Martin	86Ind 87NY 88Phoe	1962	6'7	208	F	Georgetown	3	84	168	374	45	0	9	0	61	75	81	136	58	129	1	397	10	1.6	0.7	4.7
Brian Martin	86Sea 86Port	1962	6'9	212	F	Kansas	1	8	3	7	43	0	0	—	0	2	0	4	0	7	0	6	3	0.5	0.0	0.8
Fernando Martin	87Port	1962	6'10	238	C	none	1	24	9	31	29	0	1	0	4	11	36	26	9	24	0	22	6	1.2	0.4	0.9
	87						1	1	0	1	0	0	0	—	0	0	—	0	0	0	0	0	1	0.0	0.0	0.0

		Birth					#		Field Goals			3 pt. FG			Free Throws								Per Game			
Use Name-Nickname	Team by Name	Yr.	Hgt	Wgt	Pos	College	Yr	G	FG	Att.	%	FG	Att.	%	FT	Att.	%	Reb	Ass	PF	DQ	Pts	Min	Reb	Ass.	Pts
Jeff Martin	90LAC	1967	6'5	195	G	Murray State	1	69	170	414	41	2	15	13	91	129	71	159	44	97	0	433	20	2.3	0.6	6.3
Maurice Martin (Mo)	87-88Den 89KJ 87-88	1964	6'6	200	F-G	St. Joseph's -Pa.	2 2	69 6	74 13	196 34	38 38	4 0	19 2	21 0	52 12	87 18	60 67	65 10	49 10	69 13	0 0	204 38	6 11	0.9 1.7	0.7 1.7	3.0 6.3
Anthony Mason	90NJ	1966	6'7	250	F	Tennessee State	1	21	14	40	35	0	0	—	9	15	60	34	7	20	0	37	5	1.6	0.3	1.8
Wes Matthews	81Was 81-84Atl 84Phi 85Chi 86SA 87-88LAL 90Atl 82-88	1959	6'1	170	G	Wisconsin	9 7	465 38	1463 68	3059 141	48 48	36 1	160 9	23 11	692 36	878 45	79 80	626 18	1955 66	964 43	6 0	3654 173	20 10	1.3 0.5	4.2 1.7	7.9 4.6
Cedric Maxwell (Cornbread)	78-85Bos 86-87LAC 87-88Hou 80-85, 87-88	1955	6'8	212	F	N.C.-Charlotte	11 8	835 102	3433 375	6293 688	55 55	1 0	19 2	5 0	3598 366	4592 471	78 78	5261 553	1862 194	2273 260	35 2	10465 1116	28 27	6.3 5.4	2.2 1.9	12.5 10.9
Vernon Maxwell	89-90SA 90Hou 90	1965	6'5	188	G	Florida	2 1	158 4	632 30	1454 81	43 37	60 8	234 26	26 31	317 11	454 21	70 52	430 12	597 17	284 12	0 0	1641 79	26 40	2.7 3.0	3.8 4.3	10.4 19.8
Scott May	77-81Chi 82Mil 83Det 71, 82	1954	6'7	220	F	Indiana	7 2	355 7	1432 14	3100 46	46 30	0 0	8 0	0 —	826 21	1018 29	81 72	1450 25	610 13	790 16	11 0	3690 49	23 21	4.1 3.6	1.7 1.9	10.4 7.0
Clyde Mayes	76Mil 77Ind 77Buf 77Port 76	1953	6'9	225	F	Furman	2 1	74 3	119 1	267 5	45 20				59 3	104 4	57 75	279 6	40 1	166 6	7 1	297 5	14 32	3.8 2.0	0.5 0.3	4.0 1.7
Bill Mayfield	81GS	1957	6'7	205	F	Iowa	1	7	8	18	44	0	0	—	1	2	50	9	1	8	0	17	8	1.3	0.1	2.4
Bob McAdoo	73-77Buf 77-79NY 79Bos 80-81Det 81NJ 82-84LAL 86Phi 74-76, 78, 82-86	1951	6'9	214	C-F	North Carolina	14 9	852 94	7420 698	14751 1423	50 49	3 2	37 8	8 25	3944 320	5229 442	75 72	8048 711	1951 127	2726 318	35 9	18787 1718	33 29	9.4 7.6	2.3 1.4	22.1 18.3
Bob McCann	90Dal	1964	6'6	240	F	Morehead State	1	10	7	21	33	0	0	—	12	14	86	12	6	7	0	26	6	1.2	0.6	2.6
Melvin McCants	90LAL 90	1967	6'8	250	F	Purdue	1 1	13 2	8 0	26 0	31 —	0 0	0 0	— —	6 0	8 0	75 —	6 0	2 0	11 1	0 0	22 0	5 3	0.5 0.0	0.2 0.0	1.7 0.0
Andre McCarter	77-78KC 81Was	1953	6'3	190	G	U.C.L.A.	3	103	170	394	43	2	8	25	50	69	72	95	172	100	0	392	11	0.9	1.7	3.8
Dwayne McClain	86Ind	1963	6'6	185	G	Villanova	11	45	69	180	38	1	9	11	18	35	51	30	67	61	0	157	3	0.7	1.5	3.5
George McCloud	90Ind 90	1967	6'6	205	G	Florida State	1 1	44 1	45 1	144 2	31 50	13 0	40 0	33 —	15 0	19 0	79 —	42 1	45 0	56 2	0 0	118 2	9 4	1.0 1.0	1.0 0.0	2.7 2.0
Keith McCord	81Was	1957	6'7	210	G	Alabama, Ala.-Birmingham	1	2	2	4	50	0	0	—	0	0	—	2	1	0	0	4	5	1.0	0.5	2.0
Tim McCormick	85-86Sea 87-88Phi 88NJ 89-90Hou 87, 89-90	1962	7'	240	C	Michigan	6 3	405 12	1440 20	2673 40	54 50	1 0	13 1	8 0	855 13	1219 15	70 87	2157 52	450 6	1147 33	10 0	3736 53	24 16	5.3 4.3	1.1 0.5	9.2 4.4
Rodney McCray	84-88Hou 89-90Sac 85-88	1961	6'8	228	F-G	Louisville	7 4	555 39	2817 196	5492 368	51 53	17 0	90 6	19 0	1620 109	2126 147	76 74	3901 258	2191 201	1252 95	9 0	7271 501	35 41	7.0 6.6	3.9 5.2	13.1 12.8
Scooter McCray	84-85Sea 87Cle 84	1960	6'9	215	F-G	Louisville	3 1	77 4	83 4	196 6	42 67	0 0	0 1	— 0	58 0	95 1	61 0	190 6	74 3	114 8	1 0	224 8	12 10	2.5 1.5	1.0 0.8	2.9 2.0
John McCullough	82 Phoe	1956	6'4	190	G	Oklahoma	1	8	9	13	69	0	0	—	3	5	60	4	3	3	0	21	3	0.5	0.4	2.6
Xavier McDaniel	86-90Sea 87, 89	1963	6'7	205	F	Wichita State	5 3	393 27	3357 227	6784 479	49 47	35 9	127 27	28 33	1362 77	1911 121	71 64	2758 232	968 89	1297 108	16 2	8111 540	34 37	7.0 8.6	2.5 3.3	20.6 20.0
Ben McDonald	86Cle 87-89GS 87,86	1962	6'8	220	F	Cal.-Irvine	4 2	176 10	463 3	989 21	47 14	10 0	44 5	23 0	125 2	172 4	73 50	568 14	236 10	487 15	9 0	1061 8	21 9	3.2 1.4	1.3 1.0	6.0 0.8
Hank McDowell	82-83GS 83Port 84SD 85-86Hou 87Mil 83, 86	1959	6'9	215	F-C	Memphis State	6 2	206 15	229 2	508 8	45 25	0 0	8 0	0 —	142 5	200 8	71 63	464 10	98 4	274 8	1 0	600 9	9 2	2.3 0.7	0.5 0.3	2.9 0.6
Jim McElroy	76-79NO 80Det 80-82Atl 80	1953	6'3	190	G	Central Michigan	7 1	418 5	1636 4	3494 9	47 44	7 0	34 1	21 0	841 4	1101 5	76 80	820 2	1462 4	711 1	6 0	4120 12	24 6	2.0 0.4	3.5 0.8	9.9 2.4
Mike McGee	82-84LA 85-86LAL 87-88Atl 88Sac 89NJ 90Phoe 82-87, 90	1959	6'5	196	G-F	Michigan	9 7	520 68	2087 201	4286 400	49 50	306 21	866 61	35 34	488 63	817 101	60 62	1112 109	629 55	1012 100	4 0	4968 516	18 12	2.1 1.6	1.2 0.8	9.6 7.6
George McGinnis	72-75IndA 76-78Phi 79-80Den 80-82Ind 72-78, 81	1950	6'8	235	F-C	Indiana	11 8	847 104	6381 786	13940 1808	46 43	83 29	304 100	27 29	4164 552	6267 809	66 68	9233 1228	3089 404	3220 434	58 4	17009 2153	33 36	10.9 11.8	3.6 3.9	20.1 20.7
Kevin McHale	81-90Bos 81-90	1957	6'10	227	F-C	Minnesota	10 10	776 144	5705 1029	10139 1816	56 57	24 2	89 9	27 22	3108 653	3921 834	79 78	5954 1085	1389 238	2326 489	24 8	14542 2713	32 34	7.7 7.5	1.8 1.7	18.7 18.8
Morris McHone	HC84SA	1943																								
Kevin McKenna	82LA 84Ind 85NJ 86Was 87-88NJ 86	1959	6'5	195	G-F	Creighton	6 1	243 1	498 0	1204 0	41 —	103 0	283 0	36 —	221 0	270 0	82 —	317 0	342 0	491 0	5 0	1320 0	14 2	1.3 0.0	1.4 0.0	5.4 0.0
Forrest McKenzie	87SA	1963	6'7	200	F	Loyola Marymount	1	6	7	28	25	1	2	50	2	2	100	7	1	9	0	17	7	1.2	0.2	2.8
Derrick McKey	88-90Sea 88-89	1966	6'9	208	F-C	Alabama	3 2	244 13	1210 68	2438 127	50 54	44 3	142 15	31 20	789 27	1002 38	79 71	1281 72	513 26	748 45	9 1	3253 166	30 30	5.3 5.5	2.1 2.0	13.3 12.8
Billy McKinney	79-80KC 81Utah 81-83Den 84SD 86Chi 79-80, 82-83	1955	6'	169	G	Northwestern	7 4	476 19	1554 59	3154 118	49 50	3 0	48 2	6 0	712 26	868 37	82 70	677 29	1661 60	860 31	3 0	3823 144	19 18	1.4 1.5	3.5 3.2	8.0 7.6
Carlton McKinney	90LAC	1964	6'4	205	G	S.M.U.	1	7	8	32	25	0	1	0	2	4	50	12	7	15	1	18	15	1.7	1.0	2.6
Jack McKinney	HC80-81LA HC82-84Ind HC85KC	1935				St. Joseph's - Pa.																				
Nate McMillan	87-90Sea 87-89	1964	6'5	195	G	N. Carolina State	4 3	310 27	784 58	1720 137	46 42	35 0	132 3	27 0	449 42	688 63	65 67	1460 100	2559 208	1001 74	15 1	2052 158	29 25	4.7 3.7	8.3 7.7	6.6 5.9
Tom McMillen	76-77Buf 77NYK 78-83Atl 84-86Was 76, 78-79, 82-86	1952	6'11	222	F-C	Maryland	11 8	729 26	2420 58	5014 132	48 44	3 0	23 1	13 0	1071 23	1329 29	81 79	2913 83	788 22	1740 50	19 1	5914 139	20 17	4.0 3.2	1.1 0.8	8.1 5.3
Mark McNamara	83Phi 84-85SA 85KC 87-88Phi 89-90LAL 83, 87, 89-90	1959	6'11	235	C-F	Santa Clara, California	7 4	276 8	362 5	706 9	51 56	0 0	0 0	— —	256 1	467 2	55 50	823 4	77 0	373 1	4 0	980 11	10 2	3.0 0.5	0.3 0.0	3.6 1.4
Chris McNealy	86-88NY	1961	6'7	215	F	Cal.-Santa Barbara, San Jose State	3	108	181	397	46	0	0	—	104	158	66	494	110	274	4	466	17	4.6	1.0	4.3
Cozell McQueen	87Det	1962	6'11	235	F	N. Carolina State	1	3	3	3	100	0	0	—	0	0	—	8	0	1	0	6	2	2.7	0.0	2.0
Scott Meents	90Sea	1964	6'10	235	F	Illinois	1	26	19	44	43	0	0	—	17	23	74	30	7	12	0	55	6	1.2	0.3	2.1
Joe Meriweather	76Hou 77Atl 78-79NO 79-80NY 81-85KC 81	1953	6'10	218	C	Southern Illinois	10 1	669 10	2170 24	4244 49	51 49	1 0	3 0	33 —	1098 8	1598 14	69 57	3764 31	603 5	2253 31	69 1	5439 56	22 20	5.6 3.1	0.9 0.5	8.1 5.6
Dave Meyers	76-78Mil 79XJ 80Mil 76, 78, 80	1953	6'9	225	F-C	U.C.L.A.	4 3	281 19	1208 75	2623 172	46 44	1 0	5 3	20 0	732 56	1083 89	68 63	1771 123	652 51	755 65	9 1	3149 206	27 28	6.3 6.5	2.3 2.7	11.2 10.8
Larry Micheaux	84KC 85Mil 85Hou 84-85	1960	6'9	220	F	Houston	2 2	96 8	140 18	247 37	57 49	0 0	0 1	— 0	50 10	82 20	61 50	256 42	49 3	121 18	0 0	330 46	9 15	2.7 5.3	0.5 0.4	3.4 5.8
Bob Miller	84SA	1956	6'10	230	F	Cincinnati	1	2	2	3	67	0	0	—	0	0	—	5	1	5	0	4	4	2.5	0.5	2.0
Dick Miller	81Ind 81Utah	1958	6'6	215	F	Toledo	1	8	4	9	44	0	1	0	0	0	—	7	5	5	0	8	7	0.9	0.6	1.0
Reggie Miller	88-90Ind 90	1965	6'7	190	G-F	U.C.L.A.	3 1	238 3	1365 20	2745 35	50 57	309 3	778 7	40 43	980 19	1153 21	85 90	777 12	670 6	502 6	3 0	4019 62	32 42	3.3 4.0	2.8 2.0	16.9 20.7
Dirk Minnifield	86-87Cle 87Hou 88GS 88Bos 87-88	1961	6'3	183	G	Kentucky	3 2	222 19	493 10	1050 22	47 45	25 2	92 5	27 40	176 8	238 8	74 100	367 4	845 13	472 21	3 0	1187 30	17 4	1.7 0.2	3.8 0.7	5.3 1.6
Mike Mitchell	79-82Cle 82-88SA 82-83, 85-86, 88,90SA	1956	6'7	215	F	Auburn	10 6	759 35	6371 273	12912 544	49 50	19 1	88 3	22 33	2255 99	2894 130	78 76	4246 224	1010 47	2012 90	27 2	15016 646	32 33	5.6 6.4	1.3 1.3	19.8 18.5

Use Name-Nickname	Team by Name	Birth Yr.	Hgt	Wgt	Pos	College	# Yr	G	Field Goals FG	Att.	%	3 pt. FG FG	Att.	%	Free Throws FT	Att.	%	Reb	Ass	PF	DQ	Pts	Per Game Min	Reb	Ass.	Pts
Sam Mitchell	90Min	1963	6'7	210	F	Mercer	1	80	372	834	45	0	9	0	268	349	77	462	89	301	7	1012	30	5.8	1.1	12.7
Todd Mitchell	89Mia 89SA	1966	6'7	205	F	Purdue	1	24	43	97	44	0	0	—	37	64	58	50	21	51	0	123	15	2.1	0.9	5.1
Steve Mix	70-72Det 72DenA 74-82Phi 83Mil 83LA	1947	6'7	217	F	Toledo	13	788	3205	6429	50	6	21	29	1941	2417	80	4159	1393	1694	22	8357	24	5.3	1.8	10.6
	76-83						8	89	244	494	49	1	2	50	153	177	86	248	137	143	1	642	16	2.8	1.5	7.2
Larry Moffett	78Hou	1954	6'9	210	F	Nevada-Las Vegas	1	20	5	17	29				6	10	60	21	7	16	0	16	6	1.1	0.4	0.8
Paul Mokeski 83-89Mil 90Cle	80Hou 81-82Det 82-83Cle	1957	7'	252	C-F	Kansas	11	658	1078	2378	45	8	42	19	543	785	69	2275	491	1760	31	2707	14	3.5	0.7	4.1
	83-90						8	66	88	182	48	1	4	25	72	97	74	205	32	162	3	249	12	3.1	0.5	3.8
Sidney Moncrief (the Squid)	80-89Mil	1957	6'4	187	G	Arkansas	10	695	4000	7958	50	89	323	28	3505	4214	83	3447	2689	1523	10	11594	32	5.0	3.9	16.7
	83-89						10	88	480	1011	47	16	52	31	475	586	81	453	315	269	3	1451	36	5.1	3.6	16.5
Eric Money	75-78Det 79NJ 79-80Phi 80Det	1955	6'	170	G	Arizona	6	425	2239	4536	49	0	0	—	733	980	75	894	1623	1148	20	5211	25	2.1	3.8	12.3
	76-77, 79						3	20	96	210	46				30	38	79	42	93	62	1	222	25	2.1	4.7	11.1
Andre Moore	88Den 88Mil	1964	6'9	215	F	Illinois, Loyola (Chic)	1	10	9	27	33	0	0	—	6	8	75	14	6	6	0	24	5	1.4	0.6	2.4
Johnny Moore	81-88SA 88NJ 89IL 90SA	1958	6'2	182	G	Texas	10	520	1998	4343	46	94	374	25	800	1123	71	1548	3869	1325	13	4890	26	3.0	7.4	9.4
	81-83, 85, 90						5	41	193	394	49	10	32	31	69	101	68	132	344	121	0	465	26	3.2	8.4	11.3
Lowes Moore	81NJ 82Cle 83SD	1957	6'1	170	G	West Virginia	3	112	312	706	44	11	55	20	117	156	75	227	316	266	3	752	19	2.0	2.8	6.7
Ron Moore	88Det 88Phoe	1962	7'	260	C	Salem, W. Virginia St.	1	14	9	29	31	0	0	—	6	8	75	8	1	21	0	24	4	0.6	0.1	1.7
Guy Morgen	83Ind	1960	6'8	215	G	Wake Forest	1	8	7	24	29	0	0	—	1	4	25	17	7	7	0	15	6	2.1	0.9	1.9
Chris Morris	89-90NJ	1966	6'8	210	F	Auburn	2	156	863	1970	44	125	368	34	410	570	72	819	262	469	5	2261	29	5.3	1.7	14.5
Mike Morrison	90Phoe	1967	6'4	195	G	Loyola (Balt.)	1	36	23	68	34	2	7	29	24	30	80	20	11	20	0	72	4	0.6	0.3	2.0
John Morton	90Cle	1966	6'3	195	G	Seton Hall	1	37	48	161	30	7	30	23	43	62	69	32	67	30	0	146	11	0.9	1.8	3.9
	90						1	2	2	5	40	0	0	—	2	2	100	0	0	1	0	6	5	0.0	0.0	3.0
Richard Morton	89Ind	1966	6'3	195	G	Fullerton State	1	2	3	4	75	0	0	—	0	0	—	0	1	2	0	6	6	0.0	0.5	3.0
Glenn Mosley	78Phi 79SA	1955	6'8	195	F	Seton Hall	2	32	36	88	41				26	45	58	69	21	40	0	98	8	2.2	0.7	3.1
	79						1	3	2	3	67				1	3	33	1	1	0	0	5	2	0.3	0.3	1.7
Perry Moss	86Was 86Phi 87GS	1958	6'2	185	G	Northestern	2	136	207	499	41	8	46	17	114	158	72	210	198	228	1	536	13	1.5	1.5	3.9
	86-87						2	15	10	22	45	1	2	50	9	10	90	8	7	11	0	30	5	0.5	0.5	2.0
Dick Motta HC81-87Dal HC90SAC	HC69-76Chi HC77-80Was	1931				Utah State																				
Joe Mullaney	HC76StLA HC77Buf	1925				Holy Cross																				
Chris Mullin	86-90GS	1963	6'7	212	F-G	St. John's (NY)	5	357	2746	5376	51	168	521	32	1695	1928	88	1447	1390	803	7	7355	33	4.1	3.9	20.6
	87, 89						2	18	137	261	52	4	12	33	70	83	84	62	59	50	0	348	34	3.4	3.3	19.3
Calvin Murphy (Cal)	71SD 72-83Hou	1948	5'9	165	G	Niagara	13	1002	7247	15030	48	10	72	14	3445	3864	89	2103	4402	3250	53	17949	31	2.1	4.4	17.9
	75, 77, 79-82						6	51	388	817	47	4	14	29	165	177	93	78	213	197	4	945	33	1.5	4.2	18.5
Jay Murphy	85-86LAC 87-88Was	1962	6'9	220	F	Boston College	4	67	63	190	33	0	3	0	34	56	61	111	13	59	0	160	7	1.7	0.2	2.4
Ronnie Murphy	88Port	1964	6'5	225	F	Jacksonville	1	18	14	49	29	1	4	25	7	11	64	11	6	14	0	36	5	0.6	0.3	2.0
Tod Murphy	88LAC 90Min	1963	6'9	220	C-F	Cal.-Irvine	2	83	261	553	47	16	43	37	147	207	71	566	108	231	2	685	30	6.8	1.3	8.3
Bill Musselman HC82Cle HC90Min	HC76StLA HC76VaA	1940				Wittenberg																				
Pete Myers	87Chi 88SA 89Phi 89-90NY 90NJ	1963	6'6	180	G-F	Ark.-Little Rock	4	136	182	445	41	0	19	0	153	230	67	183	252	208	0	517	11	1.3	1.9	3.8
	87, 89						2	5	0	1	0	0	0	—	4	6	67	3	1	2	0	4	3	0.6	0.2	0.8
Larry Nance	82-88Phoe 88-90Cle	1959	6'10	215	F	Clemson	9	649	4493	8136	55	6	37	16	2145	2910	74	5101	1652	1965	36	11137	33	7.9	2.5	17.2
	82-84, 88-90						6	42	255	454	56	0	0	—	109	156	70	304	96	131	3	619	34	7.2	2.3	14.7
Swen Nater 77Mil 78Buf 79-83SD 84LA	74VaA 74-75SA-A 76NY-A 76VaA	1950	6'11	245	C	U.C.L.A.	11	722	3714	6933	54	1	10	10	1551	2074	75	8340	1235	2193	27	8980	29	11.6	1.7	12.4
	74-76, 84						3	30	106	207	51	0	0	—	39	61	64	221	22	66	0	251	20	7.4	0.7	8.4
Calvin Natt 89SA 90Ind	80NJ 80-84Port 85-89Den	1957	6'6	220	F	Northeast La.	11	599	4003	7580	53	16	73	22	2269	2954	77	4070	1306	1386	10	10291	31	6.8	2.2	17.2
	80-81, 83-86, 90						7	45	320	636	50	2	9	22	184	250	74	326	109	100	0	826	33	7.2	2.4	18.4
Kenny Natt	81Ind 83,85 Utah 85KC	1958	6'3	185	G	Northeast La.	3	49	65	156	42	2	10	20	18	29	62	40	41	57	0	150	8	0.8	0.8	3.1
Craig Neal	89Port 89Mia	1964	6'5	180	G	Georgia Tech	1	53	45	123	37	10	34	29	14	23	61	29	118	70	0	114	9	0.5	2.2	2.2
Ed Nealy 89Phoe 90Chi	83-85KC 87-88SA 89Chi	1960	6'7	238	F	Kansas State	7	392	420	824	51	5	37	14	254	375	68	1473	304	761	6	1099	14	3.8	0.8	2.8
	84, 88-90						4	23	22	45	49	0	1	0	15	23	65	68	11	52	1	59	13	3.0	0.5	2.6
Martin Nessley	88LAC 88Sac	1965	7'2	260	C	Duke	1	44	20	52	38	0	0	—	8	18	44	82	16	89	1	48	8	1.9	0.4	1.1
Chuck Nevitt 86-88Det 89-90Hou	83Hou 85-86LAL	1959	7'5	237	C	N.Carolina State	7	150	98	223	44	0	0	—	50	84	60	237	18	208	1	246	5	1.6	0.1	1.6
	85-89						5	16	5	16	31	0	0	—	6	10	60	16	1	13	0	16	3	1.0	0.1	1.0
Mike Newlin	72-79Hou 80-81NJ 82NY	1949	6'4	202	G-F	Utah	11	837	4720	10133	47	62	205	30	3005	3456	87	2494	3364	2542	36	12507	29	3.0	4.0	14.9
	75, 77, 79						3	22	135	270	50				55	65	85	73	103	72	1	325	31	3.3	4.7	14.8
Johnny Newman	87 Cle 88-90NY	1963	6'7	190	F-G	Richmond	4	297	1212	2638	46	169	544	31	798	972	82	626	431	784	12	3391	23	2.1	1.5	11.4
	88-90						3	23	119	260	46	11	47	23	89	114	78	57	34	84	2	338	26	2.5	1.5	14.7
Carl Nicks	81Den 81-82Utah 83Cle	1958	6'3	185	G	Indiana State	3	156	450	973	46	0	10	0	167	293	57	297	249	342	0	1067	17	1.9	1.6	6.8
Mike Niles	81Phoe	1955	6'6	225	F	Fullerton State	1	44	48	138	35	2	4	50	17	37	46	58	15	41	0	115	5	1.3	0.3	2.6
	81						1	2	0	5	0	0	0	—	0	0	—	0	0	0	0	0	2	0.0	0.0	0.0
Kurt Nimphius 88SA 90Phi	82-86Dal 86-87LAC 87Det	1958	6'10	220	C-F	Arizona State	8	564	1451	2981	49	2	20	10	698	1045	67	2474	681	1631	36	3602	20	4.4	1.2	6.4
	84-85,87-88, 90						5	25	26	65	40	0	0	—	18	23	78	81	18	52	0	70	12	3.2	0.7	2.8
Tom Nissalke HC80-82Utah HC83-84Cle	HC76UtahA HC77-79Hou	1934				Wisconsin Florida State																				
Dyron Nix	90Ind	1967	6'7	210	F	Tennessee	1	20	14	39	36	0	0	—	11	16	69	26	5	15	0	39	5	1.3	0.3	2.0
Norm Nixon 87-88KJ 89LAC	78-83LA 84SD 85-86LAC	1955	6'2	175	G	Duquesne	9	768	5219	10805	48	100	340	29	1527	1978	77	1991	6386	1983	19	12065	35	2.6	8.3	15.7
	78-83						6	58	440	921	48	5	15	33	142	186	76	195	464	201	1	1027	39	3.4	8.0	17.7
Snake Norman	88-90LAC	1964	6'8	220	F	Illinois	3	216	1363	2720	50	11	47	23	410	682	60	1400	515	542	2	3147	31	6.5	2.4	14.6
Audie Norris	83-85Port	1960	6'9	250	C	Jackson State	3	187	283	554	51	0	3	0	253	382	66	576	147	513	9	819	14	3.1	0.8	4.4
	83-85						3	20	32	55	58	0	0	—	15	32	47	71	12	43	1	79	11	3.6	0.6	4.0
Sylvester Norris	80SA	1957	6'11	220	C	Jackson State	1	17	18	43	42	0	0	—	4	6	67	43	6	41	1	40	11	2.5	0.4	2.4
Dennis Nutt	87Dal	1963	6'2	170	G	Texas Christian	1	25	16	40	40	5	17	29	20	22	91	8	16	6	0	57	4	0.3	0.6	2.3
	87						1	1	1	5	20	0	2	0	0	0	—	2	1	0	0	2	10	2.0	1.0	2.0
Charles Oakley	86-88Chi 89-90NY	1963	6'8	225	F	Virginia Union	5	384	1886	3845	49	26	96	27	1098	1525	72	4392	1010	1327	19	4896	32	11.4	2.6	12.8
	86-90						5	35	148	319	46	4	9	44	99	137	72	415	79	123	2	399	35	11.9	2.3	11.4
Mike O'Koren	81-86NJ 87Was 88 NJ	1958	6'7	217	F-G	North Carolina	8	407	1449	2960	49	35	129	27	422	648	65	1391	856	894	15	3355	22	3.4	2.1	8.2
	82-86						5	20	34	91	37	0	3	0	6	10	60	61	33	59	2	74	17	3.1	1.7	3.7

Use Name-Nickname	Team by Name	Birth Yr.	Hgt	Wgt	Pos	College	# Yr	G	Field Goals FG	Att.	%	3 pt. FG FG	Att.	%	Free Throws FT	Att.	%	Reb	Ass	PF	DQ	Pts	Per Game Min	Reb	Ass.	Pts
Akeem Olajuwan	85-90Hou	1963	7'	250	C	Houston	6	468	4287	8328	51	2	25	8	2302	3395	68	5826	1014	1876	50	10878	37	12.4	2.2	23.2
	85-90						6	47	486	903	54	0	3	0	288	427	67	579	98	203	4	1260	39	12.3	2.1	26.8
Mark Olberding	76SA-A 77-82SA 83 Chi 84-88SKC 86-87Sac	1956	6'8	230	F	Minnesota	12	946	3126	6357	49	5	41	12	2683	3321	81	5033	2332	3132	43	8940	25	5.3	2.5	9.5
	76-82,84,86						9	54	209	450	46	1	4	25	115	150	77	277	134	198	5	534	27	5.1	2.5	9.9
Jawann Oldham	81Den 82Hou 83-86Chi 87NY 88Sac 89JJ 90Orl 90LAL	1957	7'	215	C	Seattle	9	325	605	1263	48	0	3	0	239	394	61	1350	162	799	15	1449	16	4.2	0.5	4.5
	85-86						2	5	7	16	44	0	0	—	0	0	—	24	3	19	1	14	19	4.8	0.6	2.8
John Olive	79-80SD	1955	6'7	210	F	Villanova	2	35	13	42	31	0	0	—	18	23	78	20	3	34	0	44	6	0.6	0.1	1.3
Louis Orr	81-82Ind 83-88NY	1958	6'8	191	F	Syracuse	8	569	2125	4539	47	3	36	8	1292	1642	79	2117	853	1133	6	5545	23	3.7	1.5	9.7
	81,83-84,88						4	22	56	143	39	0	0	—	32	38	84	83	13	46	1	144	18	3.8	0.6	6.5
Jose Ortiz	89-90Utah	1963	6'10	225	F	Oregon State	2	64	74	167	44	1	3	33	34	57	60	73	18	55	0	183	6	1.1	0.3	2.9
Eddie Owens	78Buf	1953	6'7	210	F	Nevada-Las Vegas	1	8	9	21	43				3	6	50	10	5	9	0	21	8	1.3	0.6	2.6
Tom Owens	72MemA 72-74CarA 75StL-A 75MemA 76KyA 76IndA 76SA-A 77Hou 78-81Port 82Ind 83Det	1949	6'10	222	C-F	South Carolina	12	877	3924	7645	51	5	23	22	2045	2753	74	5985	1533	2862	46	9898	24	6.8	1.7	11.3
	73-81						9	44	203	401	51	0	1	0	91	133	68	320	69	164	3	497	26	7.3	1.6	11.3
Joe Pace	77-78Was	1953	6'10	220	C	Coppin State, Md. Eastern Shore	2	79	91	195	47				73	122	60	168	27	115	1	255	7	2.1	0.3	3.2
	78						1	9	7	10	70				11	15	73	20	1	17	1	25	6	2.2	0.1	2.8
Robert Parish (the Chief)	77-80GS 81-90Bos	1953	7'	230	C	Centenary	14	1100	7540	13971	54	0	5	0	3232	4507	72	11130	1806	3431	77	18312	31	10.1	1.6	16.6
	77, 81-90						11	154	986	1966	50	0	1	0	476	669	71	1525	208	543	15	2458	34	9.9	1.4	16.0
Sonny Parker	77-82GS	1955	6'6	200	F-G	Texas A&M	6	452	1862	3715	50	0	2	0	747	989	76	1841	954	852	2	4471	24	4.1	2.1	9.9
	77						1	10	19	36	53				4	4	100	28	9	9	0	42	12	2.8	0.9	4.2
Zarka Paspalj	90SA	1966	6'9	220	F	none	1	28	27	79	34	0	1	0	18	22	82	30	10	37	0	72	6	1.1	0.4	2.6
Myles Patrick	81LA	1954	6'8	220	F	Auburn	1	3	2	5	40	0	0	—	1	2	50	2	1	3	0	5	3	0.7	0.3	1.7
Billy Paultz (Whopper)	71-75NY-A 76SA-A 77-80SA 80-83Hou 83SA 84Atl 85Utah	1948	6'11	248	C-F	Cameron, St. John's (NY)	15	1124	5434	10933	50	0	13	0	2231	3231	69	8959	2206	2973	16	13099	27	8.0	2.0	11.7
	71-75						15	127	597	1238	48	1	4	25	291	414	70	1062	221	373	1	1466	30	8.4	1.7	11.5
Jim Paxson	80-88Port 88-90Bos	1957	6'6	202	G-F	Dayton	11	784	4545	9133	50	98	435	23	2011	2493	81	1593	2300	1442	4	11199	27	2.0	2.9	14.3
	80-81, 83-88, 90						9	53	212	458	46	8	30	27	122	151	81	80	100	81	1	554	21	1.5	1.9	10.5
John Paxson	84-85SA 86-90Chi	1960	6'2	185	G	Notre Dame	7	525	1694	3446	49	191	567	34	400	498	80	651	2051	1035	7	3979	23	1.2	3.9	7.6
	85-90						6	52	133	297	45	16	56	29	53	61	87	44	155	128	5	335	22	0.8	3.0	6.4
Kenny Payne	90Phi	1966	6'8	215	F	Louisville	1	35	47	108	44	4	10	40	16	18	89	26	10	37	0	114	6	0.7	0.3	3.3
	90						1	3	2	5	40	0	2	0	2	2	100	2	0	3	0	6	3	0.7	0.0	2.0
Wiley Peck	80SA	1957	6'7	220	G	Mississippi State	1	52	73	169	43	0	2	0	34	55	62	183	33	100	2	180	12	3.5	0.6	3.5
	80						1	2	0	3	0	0	0	—	0	0	—	3	0	1	0	0	5	1.5	0.0	0.0
Sam Pellom	80-83Atl 83Mil	1951	6'9	225	F-C	Buffalo State	4	196	350	755	46	0	2	0	163	225	72	685	95	465	6	863	15	3.5	0.5	4.4
	80, 82						2	5	1	6	17	0	0	—	1	3	33	1	1	3	0	3	4	0.2	0.2	0.6
Will Perdue	89-90Chi	1965	7'	240	C	Vanderbilt	2	107	140	340	41	0	5	0	80	118	68	259	57	188	0	360	10	2.4	0.5	3.4
	89-90						2	16	19	37	51	1	3	33	15	21	71	25	4	17	0	54	6	1.6	0.3	3.4
Sam Perkins	85-90Dal	1961	6'9	235	F	North Carolina	6	471	2540	5321	48	57	219	26	1629	2002	81	3767	854	1391	16	6766	33	8.0	1.8	14.4
	85-88, 90						5	38	211	465	45	4	24	17	141	183	77	302	79	129	4	567	35	7.9	2.1	14.9
Tim Perry	89-90Phoe	1965	6'9	219	F-C	Temple	2	122	208	396	53	2	5	40	93	155	60	284	35	123	0	511	10	2.3	0.3	4.2
	89-90						2	15	15	29	52	0	0	—	8	20	40	23	2	20	0	38	8	1.5	0.1	2.5
Chuck Person	87-90Ind	1964	6'8	225	F	Auburn	4	318	2526	5305	48	265	773	34	808	1071	75	2174	1123	1073	21	6125	36	6.8	3.5	19.3
	87, 90						2	7	55	119	46	3	18	17	35	51	69	53	32	25	0	148	40	7.6	4.6	21.1
Jim Petersen	85-88Hou 89Sac 90GS	1962	6'10	235	F-C	Minnesota	6	402	1239	2545	49	1	22	5	596	815	73	2109	451	1166	19	3075	22	5.2	1.1	7.6
	85-88						4	37	85	183	46	0	0	—	42	63	67	180	34	97	3	212	18	4.9	0.9	5.7
Drazen Petrovic	90Port	1964	6'5	195	G	none	1	77	207	427	48	34	74	46	135	160	84	111	116	134	0	583	13	1.4	1.5	7.6
	90						1	20	48	109	44	5	16	31	21	36	58	32	20	37	0	122	13	1.6	1.0	6.1
Roger Phegley	79-80Was 80NJ 81-82Cle 82-84SA 84Dal	1956	6'6	215	G-F	Bradley	6	345	1216	2585	47	22	87	25	557	668	83	702	486	696	8	3011	17	2.0	1.4	8.7
	82-84						3	14	9	23	39	3	6	50	5	6	83	8	2	7	0	26	4	0.6	0.1	1.9
Michael Phelps	86-87Sea 88LAC	1961	6'4	185	G	Alcorn State	3	132	195	469	42	2	22	9	78	122	64	141	138	147	0	470	10	1.1	1.0	3.6
Eddie Phillips	83NJ	1961	6'7	225	F	Alabama	1	48	56	136	41	0	2	0	40	59	68	77	29	58	0	152	9	1.6	0.6	3.2
	83						1	2	3	6	50	0	2	0	1	4	25	5	3	2	0	7	6	2.5	1.5	3.5
Ricky Pierce	83Det 84SD 85-90Mil	1959	6'5	210	F-G	Rice	8	483	2748	5331	52	65	254	26	1591	1862	85	1231	851	1221	10	7152	24	2.5	1.8	14.8
	85-90						6	51	286	582	49	12	27	44	179	208	86	130	91	161	1	763	27	2.5	1.8	15.0
Stan Pietkiewicz	79-81SD 81Dal	1956	6'5	200	G-F	Auburn	3	96	149	325	46	28	84	33	50	62	81	93	174	85	1	376	11	1.0	1.8	3.9
Ed Pinckney	86-87Phoe 88-89Sac 89-90Bos	1963	6'9	215	F	Villanova	5	396	1178	2168	54	0	13	0	933	1249	75	1792	458	832	7	3289	21	4.5	1.2	8.3
	89-90						2	7	9	19	47	0	0	—	9	11	82	11	1	10	0	27	10	1.6	0.1	3.9
John Pinone	84Atl	1961	6'8	230	F	Villanova	4	7	7	13	54	0	0	—	6	10	60	10	3	11	0	20	9	1.4	0.4	2.9
Tom Piotrowski	84Port	1960	7'1	240	C	La Salle	1	18	12	26	46	0	0	—	6	6	100	16	5	22	0	30	4	0.9	0.3	1.7
Scottie Pippen	88-90Chi	1965	6'8	210	F	Central Arkansas	3	234	1236	2581	48	53	212	25	499	768	65	1290	869	773	17	3024	31	5.5	3.7	12.9
	88-90						3	42	234	491	48	35	93	38	108	157	69	289	174	158	3	611	36	6.9	4.1	14.5
Rick Pitino	HC88-89NY	1952				Massachusetts																				
Charles Pittman	83-86Phoe	1958	6'8	220	F	Maryland	4	234	379	694	55	0	5	0	302	425	71	718	204	454	4	1060	14	3.1	0.9	4.5
	83-85						3	21	42	74	57	0	1	0	30	46	65	83	21	41	0	114	16	4.0	1.0	5.4
Gary Plummer	85GS	1962	6'9	215	F-C	Boston U.	1	66	92	232	40	1	4	25	65	92	71	134	26	127	1	250	11	2.0	0.4	3.8
Dwayne Polee	87LAC	1963	6'5	180	G	Nevada-LasVegas, Pepperdine	1	1	1	4	25	0	3	0	0	0	—	0	0	0	3	2	6	0.0	0.0	2.0
Olden Polynice	88-90Sea	1964	6'11	231	C-F	Virginia	3	241	365	723	50	1	6	17	199	343	58	836	69	566	1	930	12	3.5	0.3	3.9
	88-89						2	13	30	52	58	0	0	—	7	15	47	70	1	38	1	67	16	5.4	0.1	5.2
Cliff Pondexter	76-78Chi	1954	6'9	233	F-C	Long Beach State	3	197	300	722	42				178	267	67	747	218	282	4	778	14	3.8	1.1	3.9
	77						1	3	0	1	0				2	2	100	3	1	0	0	2	4	1.0	0.3	0.7
David Pope	85KC 86Sea	1962	6'7	220	F	Norfolk State	2	33	26	73	36	1	2	50	9	17	53	29	9	41	0	62	6	0.9	0.3	1.9
David Popson	89LAC 89Mia	1964	6'10	220	F-C	North Carolina	1	17	16	40	40	0	0	—	2	4	50	27	8	17	0	34	6	1.6	0.5	2.0
Ben Poquette	78-79Det 80-83Utah 84-87Cle 87Chi	1955	6'9	235	F-C	Central Michigan	10	718	1975	4092	48	13	59	22	936	1202	78	3731	872	1989	47	4899	22	5.2	1.2	6.8
	85						1	4	13	21	62	0	0	—	4	5	80	14	1	16	2	30	23	3.5	0.3	7.5
Kevin Porter	73Bal 74Cap 75Was 76-78Det 78NJ 79Det 80-81Was 82FJ 83Was	·1950	6'	175	G	St. Francis - Pa.	10	659	3194	6617	48	3	19	16	1254	1701	74	1179	5314	2251	58	7645	29	1.8	8.1	11.6
	73-75, 77, 80						5	33	150	324	46	0	1	0	63	97	65	68	191	128	5	363	29	2.1	5.8	11.0
Terry Porter	86-90Port	1963	6'3	195	G	Wis. - Stevens Pt.	5	402	2038	4222	48	218	628	35	1372	1609	85	1471	3240	869	2	5686	32	3.7	8.1	14.1
	86-90						5	36	218	455	48	48	127	38	178	214	83	115	260	96	1	662	36	3.2	7.2	18.4
Paul Pressey	83-90Mil	1958	6'5	193	G-F	Tulsa	8	580	2565	5237	49	60	274	22	1716	2302	75	2496	3272	1736	31	6906	29	4.3	5.6	11.9
	83-88, 90						7	68	302	632	48	9	39	23	222	304	73	302	401	237	5	835	31	4.4	5.9	12.3

Use Name-Nickname	Team by Name	Birth Yr.	Hgt	Wgt	Pos	College	# Yr	G	Field Goals FG	Field Goals Att.	Field Goals %	3 pt. FG FG	3 pt. FG Att.	3 pt. FG %	Free Throws FT	Free Throws Att.	Free Throws %	Reb	Ass	PF	DQ	Pts	Per Game Min	Per Game Reb	Per Game Ass.	Per Game Pts
Dominic Pressley	89Was 89Chi	1964	6'3	170	G	Boston College	1	13	9	31	29	0	2	0	5	9	56	15	26	11	0	23	10	1.2	2.0	1.8
Harold Pressley	87-90Sac	1963	6'8	210	F-G	Villanova	4	299	1075	2458	44	208	581	36	344	442	78	1339	628	670	6	2702	23	4.5	2.1	9.0
Mark Price	87-90Cle	1964	6'1	175	G	Georgia Tech	4	295	1684	3470	49	340	803	42	879	996	88	774	1979	331	2	4587	31	2.6	6.7	15.5
	88-90						3	14	92	185	50	17	45	38	68	70	97	45	104	23	1	269	40	3.2	7.4	19.2
Tony Price	81SD	1957	6'6	190	G	Pennsylvania	1	5	2	7	29	0	0	—	0	0	—	0	3	3	0	4	6	0.0	0.6	0.8
Brian Quinnett	90NY	1966	6'8	235	F	Washington State	1	31	19	58	33	0	2	0	2	3	67	28	11	27	0	40	6	0.9	0.4	1.3
	90						1	3	2	4	50	1	1	100	0	0	—	8	2	2	0	5	5	2.7	0.7	1.7
Mark Radford	82-83Sea	1959	6'4	190	G	Oregon State	2	97	138	272	51	6	24	25	65	142	46	76	161	143	0	347	8	0.8	1.7	3.6
Wayne Radford	79Ind	1956	6'3	205	G	Indiana	1	52	83	175	47				36	42	86	68	57	61	0	202	12	1.3	1.1	3.9
Ed Rains	82-83SA	1956	6'7	193	F	South Alabama	2	83	110	260	42	0	3	0	67	107	63	124	62	109	0	287	11	1.5	0.7	3.5
	82-83						2	8	5	11	45	0	1	0	4	9	44	9	2	5	0	14	5	1.1	0.3	1.8
Kurt Rambis	82-84LA 85-88LAL 89-90Char 90Phoe	1958	6'8	218	F	Santa Clara	9	642	1537	2849	54	0	9	0	826	1199	69	4139	729	1637	9	3902	21	6.4	1.1	6.1
	82-88, 90						8	135	282	490	58	0	1	0	151	215	70	750	115	367	0	715	19	5.6	0.9	5.3
Jack Ramsay	HC69-72Phi HC73-76Buf HC77-86Port HC87-89Ind	1925				St. Joseph's - Pa.																				
Wally Rank	81SD	1958	6'6	220	F-G	San Jose State	1	25	21	57	37	0	0	—	13	28	46	30	17	33	1	55	6	1.2	0.7	2.2
Kelvin Ransey	81-82Port 83Dal 84-86NJ	1958	6'1	177	G	Ohio State	6	474	2207	4862	45	20	152	13	946	1209	78	901	2480	923	5	5380	24	1.9	5.2	11.4
	81, 84-86						4	14	45	117	38	2	5	40	14	19	74	25	64	33	0	106	22	1.8	4.6	7.6
Blair Rasmussen	86-90Den	1962	7'	255	C	Oregon	5	359	1466	3076	48	0	1	0	512	655	78	1880	285	1022	20	3444	19	5.2	0.8	9.6
	86-90						5	29	140	316	44	0	0	—	65	81	80	180	25	84	1	345	22	6.2	0.9	11.9
Leo Rautins	84Phi 85Atl	1960	6'8	215	F	Minnesota, Syracuse	2	32	21	60	35	0	0	—	6	10	60	35	32	34	0	48	7	1.1	1.0	1.5
	84						1	3	1	3	33	1	2	50	0	0	—	2	1	2	0	3	2	0.7	0.3	1.0
James Earl Ray	81-83Den	1957	6'8	215	F	Jacksonville	3	103	136	318	43	1	3	33	61	97	63	228	76	173	2	334	8	2.2	0.7	3.2
	82-83						2	4	1	6	17	0	0	—	1	4	25	3	0	4	0	3	5	0.8	0.0	0.8
Marlon Redmon	79KC 79Phi 80KC	1955	6'6	188	G	San Francisco	2	77	222	525	42	0	9	0	55	84	65	161	77	123	2	499	14	2.1	1.0	6.5
	79						1	1	0	2	0			—	0	0	—	0	0	0	0	0	2	0.0	0.0	0.0
Billy Reid	81GS	1957	6'5	195	G	New Mexico, San Francisco	1	59	84	185	45	0	5	0	22	39	56	60	71	111	0	190	10	1.0	1.2	3.2
J.R. Reid	90Char	1968	6'9	255	C	North Carolina	1	82	358	814	44	0	5	0	192	289	66	691	101	292	7	908	34	8.4	1.2	11.1
Robert Reid	78-82Hou 83SR 84-88Hou 89Char 90Port 90Char	1955	6'8	208	F-G	St. Mary's (Tex.)	12	916	4441	9692	46	103	354	29	1459	1992	73	4159	2496	2890	36	10444	27	4.5	2.7	11.4
	79-82, 85-88						8	72	427	974	44	8	52	15	157	217	72	383	333	270	3	1019	37	5.3	4.6	14.2
Richard Rellford	88SA	1964	6'6	230	F	Michigan	1	4	5	8	63	0	0	—	6	8	75	7	1	3	0	16	11	1.8	0.3	4.0
Kevin Restani	75-78Mil 78KC 79Mil 80-82SA 82Cle	1951	6'9	225	F-C	San Francisco	8	550	1522	3134	49	8	39	21	334	466	72	2206	747	996	4	3386	18	4.0	1.4	6.2
	76, 80-81						3	9	19	36	53	0	1	0	4	9	44	23	4	10	0	42	13	2.6	0.4	4.7
Jerry Reynolds	HC87-90Sac	1944				Oakland City Coll.																				
Jerry Reynolds	86-88Mil 89Sea 90Orl	1962	6'8	201	F-G	Louisiana State	5	298	858	2035	42	14	56	25	661	931	71	836	538	465	1	2391	17	2.8	1.8	8.0
	86-89						4	18	19	48	40	1	6	17	14	23	61	16	8	12	0	53	5	0.9	0.4	2.9
Glen Rice	90Mia	1967	6'7	215	F	Michigan	1	77	470	1071	44	17	69	25	91	124	73	352	138	198	1	1048	30	4.6	1.8	13.6
Clint Richardson	80-85Phi 86-87Ind	1956	6'3	195	G	Seattle	8	586	1742	3761	46	11	45	24	589	765	77	1378	1461	1019	1	4084	20	2.4	2.5	7.0
	80-85, 87						7	72	178	357	50	0	3	0	62	90	69	193	120	152	0	418	19	2.7	1.7	5.8
Micheal Ray Richardson	79-82NY 83GS 83-86NJ 87-88DR	1955	6'5	193	G-F	Montana	8	556	3419	7479	46	124	564	22	1291	1870	69	3056	3899	1859	23	8253	33	5.5	7.0	14.8
	81, 83-85						4	18	108	260	39	6	29	21	60	87	69	99	129	63	1	282	40	5.5	7.2	15.7
Pooh Richardson	90Min	1966	6'1	180	G	U.C.L.A.	1	82	426	925	46	23	83	28	63	107	59	217	554	143	0	938	31	2.6	6.8	11.4
Mitch Richmond	89-90GS	1965	6'5	215	G	Kansas State	2	157	1289	2673	48	67	185	36	816	975	84	828	557	433	8	3461	35	5.3	3.5	22.0
	89						1	8	62	135	46	3	16	19	34	38	89	58	35	25	0	161	39	7.3	4.4	20.1
Ramon Rivas	89Bos	1966	6'10	260	F-C	Temple	1	28	12	31	39	0	1	0	16	25	64	24	3	21	0	40	3	0.9	0.1	1.4
David Rivers	89LAL 90LAC	1965	6'	180	G	Notre Dame	2	99	129	319	40	1	11	9	94	120	78	128	261	103	0	353	12	1.3	2.6	3.6
	89						1	6	4	12	33	0	2	0	7	8	88	4	6	6	0	15	6	0.7	1.0	2.5
Glenn Rivers (Doc)	84-90Atl	1961	6'4	185	G	Marquette	7	489	2138	4650	46	97	308	31	1787	2305	78	1747	3526	1694	33	6160	30	3.6	7.2	12.6
	84, 86-89						5	39	167	367	46	16	50	32	149	202	74	162	333	148	5	499	32	4.2	8.5	12.8
Anthony Roberts	78-80Den 81Was 84Den	1955	6'5	185	F-G	Oral Roberts	5	213	679	1650	41	0	1	0	300	429	70	837	265	501	5	1658	18	3.9	1.2	7.8
	78-79						2	16	99	232	43				47	61	77	121	36	66	3	245	30	7.6	2.3	15.3
Fred Roberts	84-85SA 85-86Utah 87-88Bos 89-90Mil	1960	6'10	220	F-C	Brigham Young	7	511	1281	2569	50	8	41	20	912	1137	80	1442	588	1015	10	3482	17	2.8	1.1	6.8
	85-90						6	62	129	258	50	0	4	0	109	140	78	120	50	126	2	367	15	1.9	0.8	5.9
Alvin Robertson	85-89SA, 90Mil	1962	6'4	190	G	Arkansas	6	470	3046	6273	49	65	254	26	1281	1704	75	2646	2539	1618	19	7438	32	5.6	5.4	15.8
	86, 88, 90						3	10	73	149	49	3	8	38	42	56	75	51	66	41	1	191	37	5.1	6.6	19.1
Scotty Robertson	HC79Chi HC80Hou HC81-83Det	1930				Texas, Louisiana Tech																				
Tony Robertson	78Atl 79GS	1956	6'4	195	G	West Virginia	2	75	183	421	43				43	62	69	80	107	143	2	409	13	1.1	1.4	5.5
	78						1	2	2	6	33				1	2	50	0	0	3	0	5	6	0.0	0.0	2.5
Rick Robey	79Ind 79-83Bos 84-86Phoe	1956	6'11	231	C-F	Kentucky	8	493	1498	2993	50	1	8	13	726	1117	65	2301	611	1213	10	3723	18	4.7	1.2	7.6
	80-84						5	53	87	194	45	0	3	0	42	78	54	139	29	107	0	216	23	2.6	0.5	4.1
Cliff Robinson	90Port	1966	6'11	225	F-C	Connecticut	1	82	298	751	40	12	44	27	138	251	55	308	72	226	4	746	19	3.8	0.9	9.1
	90						1	21	54	151	36	0	4	0	29	52	56	87	23	71	1	137	19	4.1	1.1	6.5
Cliff Robinson	80-81NJ 82KC 82-84Cle 85-86Was 87-88Phi 89KJ	1960	6'9	229	F	Southern Calif.	10	620	4482	9569	47	7	35	20	1823	2525	72	5218	1240	1866	31	12794	31	8.4	2.0	20.6
	85-87						3	14	101	210	48				37	58	64	116	27	48	1	239	31	8.3	1.9	17.1
David Robinson	90SA	1965	7'1	235	C	Navy	1	82	690	1300	53	0	2	0	613	837	73	983	164	259	3	1993	37	12.0	2.0	24.3
	90						1	10	89	167	53	0	0	—	65	96	68	120	23	35	1	243	38	12.0	2.3	24.3
Jackie Robinson	79Sea 80Det 82Chi	1955	6'6	212	F	Nevada-Las Vegas	3	22	31	67	46	0	1	0	21	30	70	27	13	18	0	83	8	1.2	0.6	3.8
Oliver Robinson	83SA	1960	6'4	185	G	Ala.-Birmingham	1	35	35	97	36	1	11	9	30	45	67	17	21	18	0	101	4	0.5	0.6	2.9
Truck Robinson	75-77Was 77Atl 78-79NO 79-82Phoe 83-85NY	1951	6'7	225	F-C	Tennessee State	11	772	4816	9971	48	1	1	100	2355	3556	66	7267	1348	2253	28	11988	33	9.4	1.7	15.5
	75-76, 79-84						8	74	241	538	45	0	0	—	122	198	62	505	77	204	3	604	23	6.8	1.0	8.2
Wayne Robinson	81Det	1958	6'8	217	F	Virginia Tech	1	81	234	509	46	0	6	0	175	240	73	294	112	186	2	643	20	3.6	1.4	7.9
Bill Robinzine	76-80KC 81Cle 81Dal 82Utah	1953	6'7	230	F	DePaul	7	529	2185	4533	48	2	8	25	1169	1561	75	3209	560	1963	63	5541	22	6.1	1.1	10.5
	79-80						2	8	35	75	47	0	0	—	13	18	72	54	3	26	1	83	23	6.8	0.4	10.4
Dave Robisch	72-75DenA 76SDA 76IndA 77-78Ind 78-79LA 80-81Cle 81-84Den 84SA 84KC	1949	6'10	240	C-F	Kansas	13	930	3997	8620	46	0	14	0	2587	3241	80	6173	1655	2069	5	10581	24	6.6	1.8	11.4
	72-73, 75-76, 78-79, 83-84						8	42	195	458	43	0	0	—	123	163	75	308	59	103	0	513	25	7.3	1.4	12.2
Dennis Rodman (Worm)	87-90Det	1961	6'8	210	F	Southeastern Okla.	4	323	1215	2127	57	12	53	23	465	782	59	2611	337	1007	12	2907	24	8.1	1.0	9.0
	87-90						4	74	202	375	54	0	6	0	82	156	53	538	57	255	2	486	23	7.3	0.8	6.6

Use Name-Nickname	Team by Name	Birth Yr.	Hgt	Wgt	Pos	College	# Yr	G	Field Goals FG	Att.	%	3 pt. FG FG	Att.	%	Free Throws FT	Att.	%	Reb	Ass	PF	DQ	Pts	Per Game Min	Reb	Ass.	Pts
Jimmy Rodgers	HC89-90Bos	1943				Iowa																				
Johnny Rogers	87Sac 88Cle	1963	6'11	231	F-C	Stanford, Cal.-Irvine	2	69	116	246	47	0	7	0	19	28	68	104	29	89	0	251	9	1.5	0.4	3.6
Marshall Rogers	77GS	1953	6'1	190	G	Pan American	1	28	43	116	37				14	15	93	11	10	33	0	100	6	0.4	0.4	3.6
	77						1	1	0	2	0				2	2	100	1	0	0	0	2	3	1.0	0.0	2.0
Tree Rollins	78-88Atl 89-90Cle	1955	7'1	237	C	Clemson	13	925	2472	4708	53	0	5	0	983	1405	70	6286	613	3096	91	5927	24	6.8	0.7	6.4
	78-80, 82-90						12	64	139	274	51	0	0	—	67	105	64	416	29	233	10	345	26	6.5	0.5	5.4
Lorenzo Romar	81-84GS 84-85Mil 85Det	1958	6'1	178	G	Washington	5	291	720	1553	46	19	90	21	272	363	75	385	1022	393	0	1731	18	1.3	3.5	5.9
	84						1	13	9	20	45	0	3	0	7	11	64	3	15	9	0	25	5	0.2	1.2	1.9
Rob Rose	89LAC	1964	6'5	185	G	George Mason	1	2	0	1	0	0	0	—	0	0	—	2	0	0	0	0	2	1.0	0.0	0.0
Doug Roth	90Was	1967	6'11	255	C	Tennessee	1	42	37	86	43	0	1	0	7	14	50	120	20	70	1	81	10	2.9	0.5	1.9
Scott Roth	88-89Utah 89SA 90Min	1963	6'8	212	F	Wisconsin	3	162	248	661	38	23	79	29	232	318	73	204	186	250	1	751	11	1.3	1.1	4.6
	88						1	6	1	3	33	0	0	—	0	0	—	0	0	0	1	2	2	0.0	0.0	0.3
Ron Rothstein	HC89-90Mia	1942				Rhode Island																				
Dan Roundfield (Danny)	76IndA 77-78Ind 79-84Atl 85Det 86-87Was	1953	6'8	210	F-C	Central Michigan	12	813	4420	9161	48	7	63	11	2810	3824	73	7502	1655	2722	49	11657	30	9.2	2.0	14.3
	76, 78-80, 82-86						8	40	232	490	47	1	4	25	134	183	73	388	8	139	5	599	33	9.7	0.2	15.0
Ron Rowan	87Port	1963	6'5	200	G	Notre Dame, St. John's (NY)	1	7	4	9	44	1	1	100	3	4	75	1	1	1	0	12	2	0.1	0.1	1.7
Jim Rowinski	89Det 89Phi 90Mia	1961	6'9	250	F	Purdue	2	23	15	36	42	0	0	—	27	32	84	34	5	19	0	57	6	1.5	0.2	2.5
Derrick Rowland	86Mil	1959	6'5	195	G	Potsdam State	1	2	1	3	33	0	0	—	1	2	50	1	1	1	0	3	5	0.5	0.5	1.5
Brian Rowsom	88Ind 89-90Char	1965	6'9	220	F	N.C.-Wilmington	3	82	158	347	46	2	3	67	139	170	82	273	47	130	1	457	13	3.3	0.6	5.6
Donald Royal	90Min	1966	6'8	210	F	Notre Dame	1	66	117	255	46	0	1	0	153	197	78	137	43	107	0	387	11	2.1	0.7	5.9
Delaney Rudd	90Utah	1962	6'2	195	G	Wake Forest	1	77	111	259	43	16	56	29	35	53	66	55	177	81	0	273	11	0.7	2.3	3.5
	90						1	5	8	23	35	1	7	14	1	2	50	3	13	10	0	18	9	0.6	2.6	3.6
John Rudd	79NY	1955	6'7	230	F	McNeese State	1	58	59	133	44				66	93	71	167	35	95	1	184	12	2.9	0.6	3.2
Jeff Ruland	82-86Was 87Phi	1958	6'10	240	C-F	Iona	6	308	2080	3685	56	3	19	16	1537	2139	72	3313	995	1157	30	5700	35	10.8	3.2	18.5
	82, 84-86						4	17	110	211	52	0	4	0	93	120	78	163	67	60	1	313	38	9.6	3.9	18.4
Campy Russell (Mr. Moves)	75-80Cle 81-82NY 83JJ 85Cle	1952	6'8	215	F	Michigan	8	566	3398	7397	46	34	93	37	2123	2750	77	2696	1684	1527	17	8953	30	4.8	3.0	15.8
	76-78,81						4	20	120	288	42	0	2	0	91	108	84	121	44	79	0	331	30	6.1	2.2	16.6
Walker Russell	83-84Det 85Atl 86Det 87Ind 88Det	1960	6'5	195	G	Houston, Western Michigan	6	155	179	456	39	6	38	16	100	125	80	187	350	195	1	464	11	1.2	2.3	3.0
	88						1	7	2	5	40	0	0	—	2	2	100	0	1	1	0	6	1	0.0	0.1	0.9
John Salley	87-90Det	1964	7'	230	F-C	Georgia Tech	4	313	796	1487	54	1	7	14	599	871	69	1472	309	1029	19	2192	22	4.7	1.0	7.0
	87-90						4	75	205	391	52	0	1	0	186	263	71	423	61	282	5	596	25	5.6	0.8	7.9
Ralph Sampson	84-88Hou 88-89GS 90Sac	1960	7'4	230	C-F	Virginia	7	421	2881	5890	49	9	51	18	1172	1761	67	3870	1017	1522	49	6943	31	9.2	2.4	16.5
	85-87,89						4	38	283	569	50	3	8	38	142	202	70	400	109	157	4	711	34	10.5	2.9	18.7
Frankie Sanders	79SA 79Bos 81KC	1957	6'6	200	F-G	Southern U.	2	69	139	323	43	0	3	0	74	90	82	131	69	89	1	352	10	1.9	1.0	5.1
	81						1	9	9	18	50	1	2	50	4	4	100	5	2	8	0	23	6	0.6	0.2	2.6
Jeff Sanders	90Chi	1966	6'8	225	F	Ga. Southern	1	31	13	40	33	0	0	—	2	4	50	39	9	27	0	28	6	1.3	0.3	0.9
	90						1	3	1	1	100	0	0	—	0	0	—	0	0	0	0	2	1	0.0	0.0	0.7
Mike Sanders	83SA 84-88Phoe 88-89Cle 90Ind	1960	6'6	210	F-G	U.C.L.A.	8	484	1672	3448	48	13	59	22	667	870	77	1476	646	1244	8	4024	19	3.0	1.3	8.3
	83-85, 88-90						6	37	99	189	52	1	2	50	35	42	83	91	34	78	0	234	14	2.5	0.9	6.3
Wayne Sappleton	85NJ	1960	6'9	230	F	Loyola (Chic.)	1	33	41	87	47	0	0	—	14	34	41	75	7	50	0	96	9	2.3	0.2	2.9
Fred Saunders	75-76Phoe 77-78Bos 78NO	1951	6'7	210	F	Syracuse	4	210	487	1099	44				133	195	68	624	29	471	9	1107	14	3.0	0.1	5.3
	77						1	9	12	33	36				5	6	83	9	5	21	0	29	7	1.0	0.6	3.2
DeWayne Scales (Hot Man)	81-82NY 84Was	1958	6'8	208	F	Louisiana State	3	49	98	235	42	1	6	17	27	43	63	140	10	58	0	224	11	2.9	0.2	4.6
Dan Schayes (Danny)	82-83Utah 83-90Den	1959	6'11	248	C-F	Syracuse	9	668	2109	4223	50	3	20	15	2071	2574	80	3962	916	2430	55	6292	21	5.9	1.4	9.4
	83-89						7	48	157	285	55	0	0	—	141	173	82	283	60	164	2	455	23	5.9	1.3	9.5
Tom Scheffler	85 Port	1954	6'11	240	C	Purdue	1	39	21	51	41	0	0	—	10	20	50	76	11	48	0	224	7	1.9	0.3	5.7
	85						1	3	2	3	67	0	0	—	3	4	75	5	0	0	0	7	3	1.7	0.0	2.3
Russ Schoene	83Phi 83Ind 87-89Sea	1960	6'10	211	F-C	Tenn.-Chattanooga	7	290	621	1428	43	62	185	34	187	249	75	735	167	573	5	1591	12	2.5	0.6	5.5
	87-89						3	22	21	57	37	4	17	24	14	18	78	38	7	31	1	60	9	1.7	0.3	2.7
Detlef Schrempf	86-89Dal 89-90Ind	1963	6'10	220	F-C	Washington	5	374	1351	2815	48	65	191	34	1179	1518	78	1798	834	1070	12	3946	23	4.8	2.2	10.6
	86-88, 90						4	32	89	196	45	1	10	10	67	95	71	112	49	79	0	246	19	3.5	1.5	7.7
Mike Schuler	HC87-89Port	1940				Ohio U.																				
John Schweitz	85Sea 87Det	1960	6'6	210	G	Richmond	2	22	25	75	33	0	4	0	7	10	70	22	18	14	0	57	5	1.0	0.8	2.6
Alvin Scott	78-85Phoe	1955	6'7	215	F-G	Oral Roberts	8	627	1171	2436	48	4	20	20	742	1012	73	1992	847	1034	2	3088	17	3.2	1.4	4.9
	78-85						8	61	88	206	43	1	8	13	47	72	65	149	78	77	0	224	14	2.4	1.3	3.7
Byron Scott	84-90LAL	1961	6'3	195	G	Arizona State	7	545	3706	7367	50	353	896	39	1288	1546	83	1726	1706	1268	6	9053	31	3.2	3.1	16.6
	84-90						7	115	711	1442	49	77	208	37	293	360	81	388	291	304	2	1792	32	3.4	2.5	15.6
Carey Scurry	86-88Utah 88NY	1962	6'7	190	F	Northeastern Okla., Long Island U.	3	180	320	666	48	8	33	24	199	299	67	524	192	376	3	847	13	2.9	1.1	4.7
	86-87						2	8	18	42	43	1	4	25	4	9	44	30	3	22	0	41	14	3.8	0.4	5.1
Rony Seikaly	89-90Ma	1965	6'11	240	C	Syracuse	2	152	819	1712	48	1	5	20	437	785	56	1315	133	516	16	2076	29	8.7	0.9	13.7
Brad Sellers	87-89Chi 90Sea 90Min	1962	7'	210	C-F	Wisconsin, Ohio State	4	301	936	2050	46	6	28	21	394	504	78	939	375	618	4	2272	21	3.1	1.2	7.5
	87-89						3	26	43	120	36	0	0	—	28	32	88	59	26	47	0	114	15	2.3	1.0	4.4
Phil Sellers	77Det	1953	6'5	200	F-G	Rutgers	1	44	73	190	38				52	72	72	41	25	56	0	198	7	0.9	0.6	4.5
	77						1	1	1	4	25				1	4	25	2	0	2	0	3	6	2.0	0.0	3.0
Tom Sewell	85Was	1962	6'5	185	G	Lamar	1	21	9	36	25	0	2	0	2	4	50	4	6	13	0	20	4	0.2	0.3	1.0
Charles Shackleford	89-90NJ	1966	6'10	225	F-C	N.Carolina State	2	130	330	701	47	0	2	0	100	157	64	632	77	254	1	760	16	4.9	0.6	5.8
John Shasky	89Mia 90GS	1964	6'11	240	C	Minnesota	2	79	125	262	48	0	2	0	117	173	68	245	23	104	0	367	13	3.1	0.3	4.6
Brian Shaw	89Bos 90EU	1966	6'6	190	G	St. Mary's, Cal.- Santa Barbara	1	82	297	686	43	0	13	0	109	132	83	376	472	211	1	703	26	4.6	5.8	8.6
	89						1	3	22	43	51	0	1	0	7	9	78	17	19	11	0	51	41	5.7	6.3	17.0
Craig Shelton	81-82Atl	1957	6'7	210	F	Georgetown	2	59	102	225	45	0	1	0	36	60	60	141	27	131	1	240	10	2.4	0.5	4.1
Lonnie Shelton	77NYK 78NY 79-83Sea 84-86Cle	1955	6'8	249	F-C	Oregon State	10	673	3416	6950	49	3	31	10	1214	1646	74	4136	1459	2540	73	8049	28	6.1	2.2	12.0
	78-80, 82-83, 85						6	52	268	553	48	0	1	0	88	132	67	413	101	228	10	624	31	7.9	1.9	12.0
Steve Sheppard	78-79Chi 79Det	1954	6'6	220	F	Maryland	2	106	155	338	46				57	90	63	178	62	98	0	367	9	1.7	0.6	3.5
Ed Sherod	82NJ(DNP) 83NY	1959	6'2	170	G	Va. Commonw.	1	64	171	421	41	1	13	8	52	80	65	149	311	112	2	395	25	2.3	4.9	6.2
	82-83						2	6	1	5	20	0	0	—	0	0	—	2	4	3	0	2	4	0.3	0.7	0.3
Purvis Short	79-87 GS 88-89Hou 90NJ	1959	6'7	215	F-G	Jackson State	12	842	5934	12507	47	125	443	28	2614	3174	82	3625	2123	2479	34	14607	29	4.3	2.5	17.3
	87-89						3	18	72	170	42	0	5	0	43	49	88	51	29	49	0	187	20	2.8	1.6	10.4
Dexter Shouse	90Phi	1963	6'2	200	G	South Alabama	1	3	0	4	0	0	1	0	0	0	—	0	2	2	0	0	6	0.0	0.7	0.0

Use Name-Nickname	Team by Name	Birth Yr.	Hgt	Wgt	Pos	College	# Yr	G	Field Goals FG	Att.	%	3 pt. FG FG	Att.	%	Free Throws FT	Att.	%	Reb	Ass	PF	DQ	Pts	Per Game Min	Reb	Ass.	Pts
John Shumate	76Phoe 76-78Buf 78Det 79IL 80Det 80Hou 80-81SA 81Sea	1952	6'9	235	F-C	Notre Dame	5	318	1393	2698	52	0	1	0	1134	1576	72	2388	574	731	6	3920	29	7.5	1.8	12.3
	76, 80						2	12	63	112	56	0	0	—	22	41	54	90	30	38	0	148	37	7.5	2.5	12.3
Jerry Sichting	81-85Ind 86-88Bos 88-89Port 90Char 90Mil	1956	6'1	176	G	Purdue	10	598	1789	3531	51	48	177	27	515	601	86	817	1960	940	0	4141	21	1.4	3.3	6.9
	81, 86-89						5	47	64	153	42	1	7	14	11	17	65	39	79	59	0	140	14	0.8	1.7	3.0
Jack Sikma	78-86Sea 87-90Mil	1955	6'11	244	C-F	Illinois Wesleyan	13	1030	6101	13101	47	157	483	33	4126	4856	85	10375	3345	3661	76	16485	34	10.1	3.2	16.0
	78-80, 82-84, 87-88, 90						9	99	551	1234	45	10	43	23	337	405	83	933	238	428	17	1449	35	9.4	2.4	14.6
James Silas (Captain Late)	73DalA 74-76SA-A 77-81SA 82Cle 83JJ	1949	6'3	183	G	S.F. Austin State	10	685	3933	7946	49	0	16	0	3172	3710	85	2069	2628	1737	3	11038	30	3.0	3.8	16.1
	74-76, 78-81						7	41	241	532	45	0	1	0	162	207	78	124	187	102	0	644	33	3.0	4.6	15.7
Scott Sims	78SA	1955	6'1	170	G	Missouri	1	12	10	26	38				10	15	67	13	20	16	0	30	8	1.1	1.7	2.5
McKinley Singleton	87NY	1961	6'5	175	G	Ala.-Birmingham	1	2	2	3	67	0	1	0	0	0	—	0	1	1	0	4	5	0.0	0.5	2.0
Charlie Sitton	85Dal 86JJ	1962	6'8	210	F	Oregon State	1	43	39	94	41	0	2	0	13	25	52	60	26	50	0	91	7	1.4	0.6	2.1
Scott Skiles	87Mil 88-89Ind 90Orl	1964	6'1	200	G	Michigan State	4	214	492	1177	42	81	241	34	289	329	88	400	949	292	1	1354	19	1.9	4.4	6.3
Al Skinner	75-76NY-A 77NYN 78NJ 78Det 79NJ 79-80Phi	1952	6'4	195	G	Massachusetts	6	337	1156	2559	45	3	11	27	767	944	81	1100	927	999	15	3082	22	3.3	2.8	9.1
	75-76, 79						3	19	51	120	43	1	1	100	48	62	77	60	39	52	0	151	18	3.2	2.1	7.9
Jose Slaughter	83Ind	1960	6'5	215	G	Portland	1	63	89	238	37	9	41	22	38	59	64	68	52	93	0	225	8	1.1	0.8	3.6
Tom Sluby	85Dal	1962	6'4	200	G	Notre Dame	1	31	30	58	52	0	2	0	13	21	62	12	16	18	0	73	5	0.4	0.5	2.4
Keith Smart	89SA	1964	6'1	175	G	Indiana	1	2	0	2	0	0	1	0	2	2	100	1	2	0	0	2	6	0.5	1.0	1.0
Charles Smith	89-90LAC	1965	6'10	230	F-C	Pittsburgh	2	149	1030	2023	51	1	15	7	737	965	76	989	217	567	12	2800	33	6.6	1.5	18.8
Charles Smith	90Bos	1967	6'1	160	G	Georgetown	1	60	59	133	44	0	7	0	53	76	70	69	103	75	0	171	9	1.2	1.7	2.9
	90						1	3	1	2	50	0	0	—	0	0	—	1	3	0	0	2	3	0.3	1.0	0.7
Clinton Smith	87GS	1964	6'6	210	F	Ohio State, Cleveland State	1	41	50	117	43	0	2	0	27	36	75	56	45	36	0	127	8	1.4	1.1	3.1
Derek Smith	83GS 84SD 85-86LAC 87-89Sac 89-90Phi	1961	6'6	216	G-F	Louisville	8	406	2030	4070	50	45	152	30	1122	1491	75	1300	861	1211	23	5227	24	3.2	2.1	12.9
	89-90						2	4	14	22	64	0	1	0	2	4	50	7	4	12	0	30	16	1.8	1.0	7.5
Jim Smith	82SD 83Det	1958	6'9	225	F	Ohio State	2	76	89	173	51	0	0	—	41	89	46	187	46	189	5	219	12	2.5	0.6	2.9
Keith Smith	87Mil	1964	6'3	193	G	Loyola Marymount	1	42	57	150	38	3	9	33	21	28	75	32	43	74	0	138	11	0.8	1.0	3.3
Kenny Smith	88-90Sac 90Atl	1965	6'3	170	G	North Carolina	3	221	1256	2688	47	84	250	34	591	757	78	521	1500	456	1	3187	35	2.4	6.8	14.4
Larry Smith (Mr. Mean)	81-89GS 90Hou	1958	6'8	225	F-C	Alcorn State	10	691	2303	4301	54	0	6	0	841	1547	54	6892	792	2447	53	5447	28	10.0	1.1	7.9
	87, 89-90						3	22	53	105	50	0	0	—	17	24	71	190	38	74	0	123	25	8.6	1.7	5.6
Michael Smith	90Bos	1965	6'10	225	F	Brigham Young	1	65	136	286	48	2	28	7	53	64	83	100	79	51	0	327	10	1.5	1.2	5.0
	90						1	4	5	8	63	0	2	0	7	7	100	0	0	1	0	17	4	0.0	0.0	4.3
Otis Smith	87-88Den 88-89GS 90Orl	1964	6'5	210	G-F	Jacksonville	4	245	1017	2164	47	30	120	25	533	690	77	911	464	529	1	2597	20	3.7	1.9	10.6
	87, 89						2	7	11	30	37	0	0	—	7	11	64	18	10	6	0	29	10	2.6	1.4	4.1
Phil Smith	75-80GS 81-82SD 82-83Sea	1952	6'4	188	G	San Francisco	9	659	4007	8418	48	19	75	25	1891	2428	78	1978	2561	1680	7	9924	29	3.0	3.9	15.1
	75-77, 82-83						5	49	234	517	45	0	1	0	120	167	72	150	143	99	1	588	25	3.1	2.9	12.0
Randy Smith	72-78Buf 79SD 80-81Cle 82NY 83SD 83Atl	1948	6'3	180	G-F	Buffalo State	12	976	6676	14218	47	17	110	15	2893	3705	78	3597	4487	2556	22	16262	32	3.7	4.6	16.7
	74-76, 83						4	24	168	361	47	0	0	—	84	103	82	109	157	80	1	420	38	4.5	6.5	17.5
Robert Smith	78-79Den 80Utah 80NJ 81Cle 82Mil 83SD 83SA 85Cle	1955	5'11	165	G	Arizona Western., Nevada-Las Vegas	7	229	417	958	44	10	42	24	291	332	88	288	401	382	3	1135	14	1.3	1.8	5.0
	78-79, 82-83						4	26	31	68	46	2	8	25	16	19	84	23	39	25	0	80	8	0.9	1.5	3.1
Sam Smith	79Mil 80Chi	1955	6'4	200	G	Nevada-Las Vegas	2	46	116	277	42	8	35	23	75	87	86	63	58	66	0	315	14	1.4	1.3	6.8
Willie Smith	77Chi 78Ind 79Port 80Cle	1953	6'2	170	G	Missouri	4	78	144	360	40	17	71	24	52	69	75	134	277	131	1	357	15	1.7	3.6	4.6
Rik Smits	89-90Ind	1966	7'4	250	C	Marist	2	164	901	1711	53	0	1	0	425	552	77	1012	212	638	25	2227	27	6.2	1.3	13.6
	90						1	3	14	28	50	0	0	—	9	11	82	16	3	12	0	37	32	5.3	1.0	12.3
Mike Smrek	86Chi 87-88LAL 89SA 90GS	1962	7'	258	C	Canisius	5	177	202	462	44	0	2	0	126	202	62	395	45	390	6	530	10	2.2	0.3	3.0
	86-88						3	21	3	16	19	0	0	—	5	9	56	13	0	21	0	11	3	0.6	0.0	0.5
Rickey Sobers	76-77Phoe 78-79Ind 80-82Chi 83-84Was 85-86Sea	1953	6'3	198	G	Nevada-Las Vegas	11	821	4250	9262	46	130	447	29	2272	2695	84	2132	3525	2622	54	10902	28	2.6	4.3	13.3
	76, 81, 84						3	29	156	343	45	4	16	25	71	85	84	79	117	122	5	387	30	2.7	4.0	13.3
Jim Spanarkel	80Phi 81-84Dal	1957	6'5	192	G-F	Duke	5	259	844	1796	47	12	48	25	805	941	86	652	572	495	3	2505	20	2.5	2.2	9.7
	80						1	5	0	2	0	0	0	—	2	2	100	1	1	1	0	2	2	0.2	0.2	0.4
Rory Sparrow	81NJ 82-83Atl 83-88NY 88Chi 89-90Mia	1958	6'2	184	G	Villanova	10	710	2835	6101	46	67	296	23	862	1068	81	1541	3747	1669	14	6599	28	2.2	5.3	9.3
	82-84, 88						4	27	99	236	42	5	16	31	49	61	80	50	157	77	3	252	28	1.9	5.8	9.3
Larry Spriggs	82Hou 83Chi 84LA 85-86LAL	1959	6'7	230	F	Howard	5	169	341	659	52	0	6	0	191	254	75	384	218	338	2	873	13	2.3	1.3	5.2
	82, 84-86						4	30	55	106	52	0	2	0	39	51	76	68	40	50	0	149	10	2.3	1.3	5.0
Kevin Stacom	75-78Bos 79Ind 79Bos 82Mil	1951	6'3	185	G	Providence	6	347	769	1844	42	1	2	50	242	315	77	511	524	360	0	1781	0	1.5	1.5	5.1
	75-77						3	26	16	53	30				9	12	75	19	21	24	0	41	9	0.7	0.8	1.6
Terence Stansbury	85-86Ind 87Sea	1961	6'5	170	G	Temple	3	192	468	1055	44	24	107	22	240	308	78	277	390	483	4	1200	16	1.4	2.0	6.3
John Starks	89GS	1965	6'3	180	G	Oklahoma State	1	36	51	125	41	10	26	38	34	52	65	41	27	36	0	146	9	1.1	0.8	4.1
Keith Starr	77Chi	1954	6'6	200	G-F	Pittsburgh	1	17	6	24	25				2	2	100	10	6	11	0	14	4	0.6	0.4	0.8
Everette Stephens	89Ind	1966	6'2	175	G	Purdue	1	35	23	72	32	2	10	20	17	22	77	23	37	22	0	65	6	0.7	1.1	1.9
Brooke Steppe	83KC 84Ind 85Det 87Sac 89Port	1959	6'5	195	G-F	Georgia Tech	5	238	443	945	47	9	29	31	402	490	82	345	280	334	0	1297	12	1.4	1.2	5.4
	85						1	4	2	7	29	0	1	0	4	6	67	3	2	3	0	8	5	0.8	0.5	2.0
Steve Stipanovich	84-88Ind	1960	6'11	247	C	Missouri	5	403	2015	4160	48	10	56	18	1283	1611	80	3131	938	1435	26	5323	31	7.8	2.3	13.2
	87						1	4	21	38	55	0	1	0	13	19	68	30	3	14	0	55	37	7.5	0.8	13.8
Alex Stivrins	86Sea	1962	6'8	220	F	Creighton, Colorado	1	3	1	4	25	0	0	—	1	4	25	3	1	2	0	3	5	1.0	0.3	1.0
John Stockton	85-90Utah	1962	6'1	174	G	Gonzaga	6	488	2039	3894	52	98	310	32	1509	1835	82	1126	5075	1375	17	5685	29	2.3	10.4	11.6
	85-90						6	38	175	353	50	13	49	27	154	189	81	116	376	129	0	517	32	3.1	9.9	13.6
Greg Stokes	86Phi 90Sac	1963	6'10	220	F-C	Iowa	2	42	57	128	45	0	1	0	16	23	70	62	17	64	0	130	9	1.5	0.4	3.1
	86						1	7	8	28	29	0	0	—	11	13	85	13	4	12	0	27	13	1.9	0.6	3.9
Rod Strickland	89-90NY 90SA	1966	6'3	180	G	DePaul	3	163	608	1323	46	27	89	30	346	509	68	419	787	302	5	1589	21	2.6	4.8	9.7
	89-90						2	19	76	176	43	1	8	13	24	44	55	66	137	51	2	177	26	3.5	7.2	9.3
John Stroeder	88Mil 89SA 89GS	1958	6'10	260	F	Montana	2	46	31	84	37	0	2	0	20	30	67	85	23	51	0	82	6	1.8	0.5	1.8
	88						1	1	1	1	100	1	1	100	0	0	—	0	0	0	0	3	1	0.0	0.0	3.0
John Stroud	81Hou	1957	6'7	215	F	Mississippi	1	9	11	34	32	0	0	—	3	4	75	13	9	7	0	25	10	1.4	1.0	2.8
Barry Sumpter	89LAC	1965	6'11	245	F-C	Austin Peay	1	1	0	1	0	0	0	—	0	0	—	0	0	0	0	0	1	0.0	0.0	0.0
Jon Sundvold	84-85Sea 86-88SA 89-90Mia	1961	6'2	170	G	Missouri	7	475	1603	3532	45	210	540	39	355	420	85	545	1443	588	1	3771	18	1.1	3.0	7.9
	84, 86, 88						3	9	25	56	45	4	18	22	5	6	83	7	25	5	0	59	17	0.8	2.8	6.6
Dane Suttle	84-85KC	1961	6'3	190	G	Pepperdine	2	46	115	227	51	0	4	0	42	49	86	49	48	49	0	272	11	1.1	1.0	5.9

Use Name-Nickname	Team by Name	Birth Yr.	Hgt	Wgt	Pos	College	# Yr	G	Field Goals FG	Att.	%	3 pt. FG FG	Att.	%	Free Throws FT	Att.	%	Reb	Ass	PF	DQ	Pts	Per Game Min	Reb	Ass.	Pts
Roy Tarpley	87-90Dal	1964	7'	247	C-F	Michigan	4	220	1122	2325	48	1	15	7	495	684	72	2299	222	775	13	2740	27	10.5	1.0	12.5
	87-88, 90						3	24	171	335	51	0	4	0	65	92	71	307	32	99	4	407	34	12.8	1.3	17.0
Anthony Taylor	89Mia	1965	6'4	175	G	Oregon	1	21	60	151	40	0	2	0	24	32	75	34	43	37	0	144	18	1.6	2.0	6.9
Brian Taylor	73-76NY-A 77KC 78Den 79-82SD	1951	6'2	185	G	Princeton	10	601	3190	6468	49	211	593	36	1277	1637	78	1608	2478	1696	15	7868	32	2.7	4.1	13.1
	73-76						4	37	208	473	44	12	37	32	73	95	77	123	133	117	0	501	36	3.3	3.6	13.5
Jay Taylor	90NJ	1967	6'3	190	G	Eastern Illinois	1	17	21	52	40	3	13	23	6	9	67	11	5	9	0	51	7	0.6	0.3	3.0
Jeff Taylor	83Hou 87Det	1960	6'4	175	G	Texas Tech	2	56	70	170	41	0	1	0	39	56	70	82	113	86	1	179	15	1.5	2.0	3.2
Leonard Taylor	90GS	1966	6'8	225	F	California	1	10	0	6	0	0	1	0	11	16	69	12	1	4	0	11	4	1.2	0.1	1.1
Vince Taylor	83NY	1960	6'5	180	G-F	Duke	1	31	37	102	36	0	0	—	21	32	66	36	41	54	1	95	10	1.2	1.3	3.1
Terry Teagle	83-84Hou 85Det 85-90GS	1960	6'5	195	G-F	Baylor	8	521	2594	5521	47	29	130	22	1065	1343	79	1436	759	1118	8	6282	22	2.8	1.5	12.1
	87, 89						2	18	127	265	48	0	4	0	48	60	80	57	23	54	0	302	26	3.2	1.3	16.8
Ira Terrell	77Phoe 78JJ 79NO 79Port	1954	6'8	200	F-C	S.M.U.	2	127	370	743	50				146	229	64	533	144	265	0	886	20	4.2	1.1	7.0
	79						1	1	0	4	0				0	0	—	2	2	0	0	0	6	2.0	2.0	0.0
Carlos Terry	81-83Was	1956	6'5	217	G-F	Winston-Salem St.	3	94	122	281	43	0	11	0	41	61	67	227	124	162	2	285	11	2.4	1.3	3.0
	83						1	3	0	0	—	0	0	—	0	0	—	1	0	0	0	0	2	0.3	0.0	0.0
Reggie Theus	79-84Chi 84-85KC 86-88Sac 89Atl 90Orl	1957	6'7	204	G	Nevada-Las Vegas	12	945	6474	13726	47	186	801	23	4371	5301	82	3120	6075	2777	24	17505	33	3.3	6.4	18.5
	81, 84, 86, 89						4	17	89	217	41	2	15	13	64	77	83	47	97	58	1	244	32	2.8	5.7	14.4
Peter Thibeaux	85-86GS	1961	6'7	210	F	St. Mary's	2	93	194	428	45	2	7	29	72	115	63	144	45	167	2	462	11	1.5	0.5	5.0
David Thirdkill	83Phoe 84-85Det 85Mil 85SA 86-87Bos	1960	6'7	215	F-G	Bradley	5	179	189	414	46	1	11	9	131	232	56	209	84	226	1	510	8	1.2	0.5	2.8
	85-86						2	18	7	22	32	0	3	0	7	15	47	10	5	9	0	21	4	0.6	0.3	1.2
Isiah Thomas	82-90Det	1961	6'1	185	G	Indiana	9	716	5497	11954	46	254	898	28	3106	4074	76	2680	6985	2311	40	14354	37	3.7	9.8	20.0
	84-90						7	93	743	1555	48	71	201	35	458	592	77	444	839	304	7	2015	38	4.8	9.0	21.7
Jim Thomas	84-85Ind 86LAC	1960	6'3	190	G	Indiana	3	158	540	1144	47	9	53	17	264	346	76	418	376	322	3	1353	21	2.6	2.4	8.6
Bernard Thompson	85Port 86-88Pho 89Hou	1962	6'6	213	F-G	Fresno State	5	204	410	934	44	0	17	0	258	327	79	352	266	391	1	1078	14	1.7	1.3	5.3
	85						1	2	0	5	0	0	0	—	2	2	100	3	2	1	0	2	5	1.5	1.0	1.0
Billy Thompson	87-88LAL 89-90Mia	1963	6'7	220	F	Louisville	4	226	869	1717	51	2	9	22	327	493	66	1303	403	656	10	2067	23	5.8	1.8	9.1
	87						1	3	6	11	55	0	0	—	2	2	100	6	2	2	0	14	9	2.0	0.7	4.7
Corny Thompson	83Dal	1960	6'8	225	F	Connecticut	1	44	43	137	31	0	0	—	36	46	78	120	34	92	0	122	12	2.7	0.8	2.8
David Thompson	76DenA 77-82Den 83-84Sea	1954	6'4	195	G-F	N.Carolina State	9	592	5020	9932	51	26	102	25	3356	4297	78	2446	1939	1569	8	13422	33	4.1	3.3	22.7
	76-79, 82-83						6	40	376	779	48	2	7	29	208	266	78	198	140	137	1	962	37	5.0	3.5	24.1
LaSalle Thompson	83-85KC 86-89Sac 89-90Ind	1961	6'10	250	C-F	Texas	8	622	2476	4942	50	3	18	17	1318	1785	74	5170	794	2241	51	6273	25	8.3	1.3	10.1
	84, 86, 90						3	9	36	87	41	0	0	—	20	27	74	80	8	35	0	92	27	8.9	0.9	10.2
Mychal Thompson	79Port 80BL 81-86Port 87SA 87-90LAL	1955	6'10	229	C-F	Minnesota	11	863	5078	10078	50	1	10	10	2365	3619	65	6723	2120	2580	27	12522	31	7.8	2.5	14.5
	79, 81, 83-90						10	96	447	890	50	0	0	—	234	361	65	618	126	299	4	1128	28	6.4	1.3	11.8
Paul Thompson	84-85Cle 85Mil 86Phi	1961	6'6	210	G-F	Tulane	3	154	568	1315	43	17	81	21	221	279	79	533	224	360	4	1374	20	3.5	1.5	8.9
	85						1	3	5	12	42	0	2	0	3	5	60	5	2	3	0	13	11	1.7	0.7	4.3
Bob Thornton	86-88NY 88-90Phi	1962	6'10	225	F-C	Cal.-Irvine	4	262	314	694	45	2	9	22	191	348	55	683	98	552	7	819	12	2.6	0.4	3.1
	90						1	9	7	18	39	0	0	—	5	10	50	15	4	22	0	19	10	1.7	0.4	2.1
Otis Thorpe	85KC 86-88Sac 89-90Hou	1962	6'11	232	F-C	Providence	6	485	2957	5412	55	0	23	0	1902	2667	71	4153	1125	1574	30	7816	32	8.6	2.3	16.1
	86, 89-90						3	11	54	95	57	0	0	—	48	72	67	65	19	33	1	156	32	5.9	1.7	14.2
Sedale Threatt	84-87Phi 87-88Chi 88-90Sea	1961	6'2	176	G	West Virginia Tech	7	464	1553	3282	47	35	175	20	509	632	81	688	1282	976	4	3650	19	1.5	2.8	7.9
	84-89						6	35	131	286	46	1	9	11	51	61	84	57	124	77	0	314	20	1.6	3.5	9.0
Darren Tillis	83Bos 83Cle 84GS	1960	6'11	215	C-F	Cleveland State	2	124	184	435	42	0	3	0	57	91	63	314	42	252	4	425	10	2.5	0.3	3.4
Wayman Tisdale	86-89Ind 89-90Sac	1964	6'9	245	F-C	Oklahoma	5	399	2743	5311	52	0	16	0	1287	1713	75	2754	535	1398	27	6773	31	6.9	1.3	17.0
	87						1	4	19	31	61	0	0	—	13	23	57	16	9	17	1	51	27	4.0	2.3	12.8
Tom Tolbert	89Char 90GS	1965	6'7	240	F	Cal.-Irvine, Arizona	2	84	235	479	49	5	21	24	181	253	72	384	65	211	0	656	17	4.6	0.8	7.8
Ray Tolbert	82NJ 82-83Sea 83-84Det 88NY 88LAL 89Atl	1958	6'9	228	F	Indiana	5	261	396	800	50	0	6	0	136	250	54	609	135	418	2	928	11	2.3	0.5	3.6
	82						1	4	3	5	60	0	0	—	4	8	50	5	1	7	0	10	8	1.3	0.3	2.5
Dean Tolson	75, 77-78Sea	1951	6'8	197	F	Arkansas	3	80	153	280	55				96	176	55	179	34	97	0	402	9	2.2	0.4	5.0
	75						1	4	1	8	13				2	2	100	7	1	3	0	4	6	1.8	0.3	1.0
Andrew Toney	81-88Phi	1957	6'3	188	G	Southwestern La.	8	468	2859	5718	50	138	403	34	1602	2010	80	1009	1965	1341	12	7458	27	2.2	4.2	15.9
	81-85, 87						6	72	485	1015	48	12	51	24	272	346	79	168	323	265	3	1254	30	2.3	4.5	17.4
Sedric Toney	86Atl 86Phoe 88NY 89Ind 90Atl 90Sac	1962	6'2	178	G	Dayton	4	100	137	369	37	31	90	34	98	126	78	95	224	151	1	403	13	1.0	2.2	4.0
	88						1	3	3	6	50	3	6	50	2	2	100	0	2	4	0	11	5	0.0	0.7	3.7
Bernard Toone	80Phi	1956	6'9	210	F	Marquette	1	23	23	64	36	1	7	14	8	10	80	34	12	20	0	55	5	1.5	0.5	2.4
	80						1	4	0	4	0	0	1	0	0	0	—	1	1	1	0	0	2	0.3	0.3	0.0
Linton Townes	83Port 84Mil 84SD 85SA	1959	6'7	195	F-G	James Madison	3	60	109	248	44	9	25	36	30	40	75	67	32	86	0	257	9	1.1	0.5	4.3
	83, 85						2	8	17	35	49	1	4	25	6	7	86	6	5	12	0	41	8	0.8	0.6	5.1
Raymond Townsend	79-80GS 82Ind	1955	6'3	175	G	U.C.L.A.	3	154	309	751	41	6	35	17	121	172	70	157	217	201	0	745	13	1.0	1.4	4.8
Kelly Tripucka	82-86Det 87-88Utah 89-90Char	1959	6'6	224	F-G	Notre Dame	9	630	4247	8968	47	153	420	36	2954	3493	85	2527	1931	1504	3	11601	31	4.0	3.1	18.4
	84-86						5	25	145	314	46	0	5	0	101	118	86	93	57	65	2	391	30	3.7	2.3	15.6
Trent Tucker	83-90NY	1959	6'5	193	G	Minnesota	8	598	2200	4772	46	440	1078	41	422	558	76	1307	1312	1370	5	5262	22	2.2	2.2	8.8
	83-84, 88-90						5	41	108	231	47	33	79	42	24	34	71	62	70	82	0	273	18	1.5	1.7	6.7
Andre Turner	87Bos 88Hou 89 Mil 90LAC 90Char	1964	5'11	160	G	Memphis State	4	30	28	83	34	1	10	10	14	18	78	21	47	22	0	71	7	0.7	1.6	2.4
Elston Turner	82-84Dal 85-86Den 87-88Chi 89Den	1959	6'5	209	G-F	Mississippi	8	505	1049	2429	43	7	46	15	292	409	71	1375	914	910	5	2397	18	2.7	1.8	4.7
	84-89						5	43	97	200	49	1	2	50	21	33	64	130	86	79	1	218	17	3.0	2.0	5.1
Henry Turner	90Sac	1966	6'7	195	F	Fullerton State	1	36	58	122	48	0	3	0	40	65	62	50	22	40	0	156	9	1.4	0.6	4.3
Jeff Turner	85-87NJ 90Orl	1962	6'9	233	F-C	Vanderbilt	4	261	538	1181	46	2	15	13	255	328	78	779	235	729	22	1333	16	3.0	0.9	5.1
	85-86						2	6	3	8	38	0	0	—	1	1	100	7	5	13	0	7	7	1.2	0.8	1.2
Melvin Turpin	85-87Cle 88Utah 90Was	1960	6'11	240	C	Kentucky	5	361	1297	2513	52	1	9	11	476	613	78	1655	183	853	12	3071	19	4.6	0.5	8.5
	85, 88						2	11	15	28	54	0	0	—	3	4	75	14	2	8	0	33	7	1.3	0.2	3.0
Dave Twardzik (Pinball)	73-76VaA 77-80Port 81XJ HC89Ind	1950	6'1	180	G	Old Dominion	8	536	1654	3136	53	13	53	25	1656	2018	82	1286	1823	1468	15	4977	25	2.4	3.4	9.3
	73-74, 77-80						6	32	84	158	53	0	1	0	85	106	80	54	70	94	2	253	20	1.7	2.2	7.9
Terry Tyler	79-85Det 86-88Sac 89Dal	1956	6'7	215	F-G	Detroit	11	871	3831	7915	48	10	82	12	1196	1702	70	4675	1039	1937	14	8868	25	5.4	1.2	10.2
	84-86						3	17	61	134	46	0	1	0	31	40	78	55	8	26	0	153	16	3.2	0.5	9.0
Kelvin Upshaw	89Mia 89-90Bos 90Dal 90GS	1963	6'2	180	G	Utah	2	72	163	358	46	7	30	23	46	63	73	90	171	133	1	379	14	1.3	2.4	5.3
	89						1	3	5	12	42	0	0	—	0	0	—	2	5	4	0	10	8	0.7	1.7	3.3
Darnell Valentine	82-86Port 86-88LAC 89Cle	1959	6'2	184	G	Kansas	8	555	1763	4064	43	35	132	27	1230	1572	78	1146	2729	1188	7	4791	23	2.1	4.9	8.6
	83-85, 89						4	26	114	248	46	1	2	50	84	95	88	50	177	79	3	313	27	1.9	6.8	12.0
Ronnie Valentine	81Den	1957	6'7	210	F	Old Dominion	1	24	37	98	38	1	2	50	9	19	47	30	7	23	0	84	5	1.3	0.3	3.5

Use Name-Nickname	Team by Name	Birth Yr.	Hgt	Wgt	Pos	College	# Yr	G	Field Goals FG	Att.	%	3 pt. FG FG	Att.	%	Free Throws FT	Att.	%	Reb	Ass	PF	DQ	Pts	Per Game Min	Reb	Ass.	Pts
Jan Van Breda Kolff 77NYN 78-83NJ	75DenA 76VaA 76KY-A 75-76, 79, 82	1951	6'7	200	F-G	Vanderbilt	9 4	598 26	1310 46	2953 101	44 46	11 0	39 0	28 —	1065 45	1297 51	82 88	2572 99	1178 48	1553 36	28 0	3696 137	23 18	4.3 3.8	2.0 1.8	6.2 5.3
Kiki Vandeweghe	81-84Den 85-89Port 89-90NY 82-90	1958	6'8	220	F	U.C.L.A.	10 9	627 56	5401 391	10186 760	53 51	129 13	348 48	37 27	3102 207	3562 227	87 91	2469 174	1476 125	1306 114	2 1	14033 1002	33 30	3.9 3.1	2.4 2.2	22.4 17.9
Nick Vanos	86-87Phoe	1963	7'2	260	C	Santa Clara	2	68	88	230	38	0	2	0	46	82	56	240	59	128	0	222	12	3.5	0.9	3.3
Dick Versace	HC89-90Ind					Wisconsin																				
Pete Verhoeven	82-84Port 85KC 86GS 87Ind 84	1959	6'9	215	F	Fresno State	6 1	282 3	432 0	856 0	50 —	1 0	4 0	25 —	135 2	196 2	69 100	641 0	152 0	622 10	11 0	1000 2	11 6	2.3 0.0	0.5 0.0	3.5 0.7
Jay Vincent 89SA 90Phi 90LAL	82-86Dal 87Was 88-89Den 84-88, 90	1959	6'7	223	F	Michigan State	9 6	576 38	3190 170	7367 415	43 41	4 0	27 2	15 0	1745 150	2226 174	78 86	3167 177	1124 46	1621 107	16 1	8729 490	27 26	5.5 4.7	2.0 1.2	15.2 12.9
Sam Vincent	86-87Bos 88Sea 88-89Chi 90Orl 86-89	1963	6'2	185	G	Michigan State	5 4	308 52	861 82	1889 227	46 36	12 1	56 8	21 13	555 62	635 76	87 82	611 46	1198 87	469 54	1 0	2289 227	18 11	2.0 0.9	3.9 1.7	7.4 4.4
Dick Vitale	HC79-80Det	1939				Seton Hall																				
Gary Voce	90Cle	1965	6'9	225	F	Notre Dame	1	1	1	3	33	0	0	—	0	0	—	2	0	0	0	2	4	2.0	0.0	2.0
Alexander Volkov (Sasha)	90Atl	1964	6'10	218	F	Kiev I.P.C.	1	72	137	284	48	13	34	38	70	120	58	119	83	166	3	357	13	1.7	1.2	5.0
Danny Vranes	82-86Sea 87-88Phi 82-84, 87	1958	6'7	213	F	Utah	7 4	510 15	1056 23	2131 61	50 38	2 0	19 1	11 0	499 5	875 9	57 56	1998 62	594 12	1368 34	13 1	2613 51	21 16	3.9 4.1	1.2 0.8	5.1 3.4
Brett Vroman	81Utah	1955	7'	220	C	U.C.L.A., Nevada - Las Vegas	1	11	10	27	37	0	1	0	14	19	74	25	9	26	1	34	8	2.3	0.8	3.1
Mark Wade	88GS 90Dal	1965	5'11	160	G	Oklahoma, Nevada - Las Vegas	2	12	3	20	15	0	2	0	2	4	50	15	36	13	0	8	11	1.3	3.0	0.7
Milt Wagner	88LAL 88	1963	6'5	185	G	Louisville	1 1	40 5	62 2	147 5	42 40	2 0	10 1	20 0	26 2	29 2	90 100	28 2	61 3	42 3	0 0	152 6	10 3	0.7 0.4	1.5 0.6	3.8 1.2
Granville Waiters	84-85Ind 86Hou 87-88Chi 86-87	1961	6'11	225	C	Ohio State	5 2	249 13	270 4	589 7	46 57	0 0	5 0	0 —	66 0	118 0	56 —	540 6	121 0	410 4	5 0	606 8	10 3	2.2 0.5	0.5 0.0	2.4 0.6
Andre Wakefield	79Chi 79Det 80Utah	1955	6'3	175	G	Loyola (Chic.)	2	81	68	192	35	0	0	—	51	72	71	80	73	83	0	187	8	1.0	0.9	2.3
Andy Walker	77NO	1955	6'4	190	G	Niagara	1	40	72	156	46				36	47	77	75	32	59	0	180	11	1.9	0.8	4.5
Darrell Walker	84-86NY 87Den 88-90Was 84, 87-88	1961	6'4	180	G	Arkansas	7 3	538 20	2044 60	4670 161	44 37	6 0	82 1	7 0	1275 43	1742 69	73 62	2340 69	2559 39	1431 51	9 0	5369 163	25 21	4.3 3.5	4.8 2.0	10.0 8.2
Foots Walker	75-80Cle 81-84NJ 76-78, 83-84	1951	6'1	172	G	West Georgia	10 5	658 22	1538 41	3537 97	43 42	10 0	44 0	23 —	1113 27	1460 33	76 82	1686 35	3111 64	1414 37	5 0	4199 109	23 15	2.6 1.6	4.7 2.9	6.4 5.0
Kenny Walker	87-90NY 88-90	1964	6'8	210	F-G	Kentucky	4 3	297 23	1007 27	2049 65	49 42	7 0	30 1	23 0	469 25	621 35	76 71	1300 50	246 13	894 55	14 0	2490 79	22 14	4.4 2.2	0.8 0.6	8.4 3.4
Phil Walker	78Was 78	1956	6'3	180	G	Millersville	1 1	40 4	57 1	161 8	35 13				64 4	96 5	67 80	52 2	54 2	39 5	0 0	178 6	10 4	1.3 0.5	1.4 0.5	4.5 1.5
Wally Walker	77-78Port 78-82Sea 83-84Hou 77-80, 82	1954	6'7	196	F	Virginia	8 5	565 64	1720 99	3685 217	47 46	3 0	15 0	20 —	525 45	817 65	64 69	1759 123	844 44	1109 136	7 1	3968 243	18 12	3.1 1.9	1.5 0.7	7.0 3.8
Jamie Waller	88NJ	1964	6'4	215	G	Virginia Union	1	9	16	40	40	0	2	0	10	18	56	13	3	13	0	42	10	1.4	0.3	4.7
Bill Walton 83-84SD 85LAC 86-87Bos 88-89FJ	75-78Port 79FJ 80SD 81-82FJ 77-78, 86-87	1952	6'11	230	C-F	U.C.L.A.	10 4	468 49	2552 230	4900 438	52 53	0 0	4 1	0 0	1111 68	1683 101	66 67	4923 444	1590 145	1298 149	17 4	6215 528	28 24	10.5 9.1	3.4 3.0	13.3 10.8
Lloyd Walton	77-80Mil 81KC 78, 80-81	1953	6'	160	G	Marquette	5 3	341 18	599 21	1319 51	45 41	1 0	4 1	25 0	243 11	342 17	71 65	370 12	1243 57	362 14	0 0	1442 53	16 11	1.1 0.7	3.6 3.2	4.2 2.9
Donnie Walsh	HC79-81Den	1941				North Carolina																				
Bryan Warrick	83-84Was 85LAC 86Mil 86Ind	1959	6'5	195	G	St. Joseph's - Pa.	4	169	262	592	44	5	24	21	148	198	75	218	437	304	5	677	14	1.3	2.6	4.0
Chris Washburn	87-88GS 88Atl 89DR 87-88	1965	6'11	225	C	N. Carolina State	2 2	72 6	93 3	226 7	41 43	0 0	1 0	0 —	36 5	82 6	44 83	176 1	22 2	80 2	0 0	222 11	9 5	2.4 0.2	0.3 0.3	3.1 1.8
Duane Washington	88NJ	1964	6'4	195	G	Middle Tenn. St.	1	15	18	42	43	2	4	50	16	20	80	22	34	23	0	54	10	1.5	2.3	3.6
Kermit Washington (Special K) 79SD 80-82Port 88GS	74-78LA 78Bos 74, 80-81	1951	6'8	230	F-C	American	10 3	507 9	1778 30	3382 60	53 50	0 0	4 2	0 0	1110 12	1691 17	66 71	4232 93	695 14	1630 18	30 0	4666 72	25 29	8.3 10.3	1.4 1.6	9.2 8.0
Pearl Washington	87-88NJ 89Mia	1964	6'2	195	G	Syracuse	3	194	666	1472	45	16	87	18	312	418	75	370	733	448	7	1660	21	1.9	3.8	8.6
Richard Washington 81Dal 81-82Cle 83KJ	77-79KC 80Mil 79-80	1955	6'11	225	F-C	U.C.L.A.	6 2	351 11	1472 36	3249 67	45 54	1 0	4 0	25 —	511 3	719 6	71 50	2204 33	409 3	1169 39	30 1	3456 75	22 15	6.3 3.0	1.2 0.3	9.8 6.8
Wilson Washington	78Phi 78-79NJ	1955	6'9	227	F-C	Old Dominion	2	100	318	640	50				95	157	61	450	57	261	7	731	17	4.5	0.6	7.3
Nick Weatherspoon 78Chi 79-80SD	74Cap 75-77Was 77Sea 74-76	1950	6'7	200	F	Illinois	7 3	453 31	1712 115	3763 235	45 49	0	0	—	662 51	929 73	71 70	2232 150	418 26	1228 95	13 1	4086 281	21 23	4.9 4.8	0.9 0.8	9.0 9.1
Spud Webb	86-90Atl 86-89	1963	5'7	135	G	N.Carolina State	5 4	357 34	888 89	1882 192	47 46	6 2	77 11	8 18	617 75	757 89	82 84	653 63	1602 174	643 51	2 0	2399 255	18 17	1.8 1.9	4.5 5.1	6.7 7.5
Marvin Webster (The Human Eraser) 77Den 78Sea 79-84NY 85IL 86VR 87Mil	76DenA 76-78, 81, 83-84	1952	7'1	240	C	Morgan State	10 6	617 61	1630 198	3343 415	49 48	2 0	7 0	29 —	1040 123	1675 195	62 63	4218 494	752 77	1505 172	26 2	4302 519	22 25	6.8 8.1	1.2 1.3	7.0 8.5
Scott Wedman 82-83Cle 83-87Bos	75KC-O 76-81KC 75, 79-81, 83-86	1952	6'7	222	F-G	Colorado	13 8	906 85	5153 368	10713 812	48 45	84 27	251 70	33 39	1526 119	1923 171	79 70	4355 322	1771 150	2549 189	34 1	11916 882	29 23	4.8 3.8	2.0 1.8	13.2 10.4
Brant Weidner	84SA	1960	6'9	230	F	William & Mary	1	8	2	9	22	0	0	—	4	4	100	11	0	5	0	8	5	1.4	0.0	1.0
Chris Welp	88-89Phi 90SA 90GS 89	1964	7'	245	C	Washington	3 1	109 3	140 1	314 3	45 33	0 0	1 0	0 —	79 0	116 2	68 0	265 7	43 0	259 7	0 0	359 2	11 7	2.4 2.3	0.4 0.0	3.3 0.7
Bill Wennington	86-90Dal 86-88, 90	1964	7'	245	C	St. John's (NY)	5 4	269 19	377 9	843 27	45 33	2 1	21 1	10 100	223 5	298 7	75 71	784 22	136 6	566 23	5 0	979 24	12 5	2.9 1.2	0.5 0.3	3.6 1.3
Doug West	90Min	1967	6'6	205	G	Villanova	1	52	53	135	39	3	11	27	26	32	81	70	18	61	0	135	7	1.3	0.3	2.6
Mark West	84Dal 85Mil 85-88Cle 88-90Phoe 84-85, 89-90	1960	6'10	234	C-F	Old Dominion	7 4	492 36	1333 115	2305 194	58 59	0 0	4 0	0 —	670 41	1160 72	58 57	2760 242	247 18	1531 139	31 5	3336 271	21 24	5.6 6.7	0.5 0.5	6.8 7.5
Paul Westhead	HC80-82LA HC83Chi	1939				St. Joseph's - Pa.																				
Paul Westphal 81Sea 82-83NY 84Phoe	73-75Bos 76-80Phoe 73-76, 78-80, 83-84	1950	6'4	195	G	Southern Calif.	12 9	823 107	5079 553	10084 1149	50 48	55 6	200 29	28 21	2596 225	3166 285	82 79	1580 153	3591 353	1705 241	8 2	12809 1337	25 23	1.9 1.4	4.4 3.3	15.6 12.5
Ennis Whatley 86SA 87Was 88Atl 89LAC	84-85Chi 86Cle 86Was 87	1962	6'3	177	G	Alabama	6 1	250 2	678 3	1461 12	46 25	1 0	13 0	8 —	358 0	476 0	75 —	526 3	1482 6	564 2	5 0	1715 6	22 16	2.1 1.5	5.9 3.0	6.9 3.0
Clinton Wheeler	88Ind 89Mia 89Port	1959	6'1	185	G	Will. Paterson	2	87	107	219	49	0	1	0	40	54	74	71	157	63	0	254	10	0.8	1.8	2.9
Eric White	88LAC 89Utah 89LAC	1965	6'8	200	F	Pepperdine	2	55	128	244	52	1	1	100	79	99	80	132	26	72	0	336	14	2.4	0.5	6.1
Randy White	90Dal 90	1967	6'8	250	F	Louisiana Tech	1 1	55 1	93 0	252 0	37	1 0	14 0	7 —	50 0	89 0	56 —	173 0	21 0	124 0	0 0	237 0	13 2	3.1 0.0	0.4 0.0	4.3 0.0
Rory White	83-84Phoe 84Mil 84SD 85-87LAC 83	1959	6'8	210	F	South Alabama	5 1	324 3	971 7	1919 14	51 50	1 0	13 1	8 0	444 2	652 4	68 50	749 10	232 0	520 4	3 0	2387 16	17 13	2.3 3.3	0.7 0.0	7.4 5.3

		Birth					#		Field Goals			3 pt. FG			Free Throws								Per Game			
Use Name-Nickname	Team by Name	Yr.	Hgt	Wgt	Pos	College	Yr	G	FG	Att.	%	FG	Att.	%	FT	Att.	%	Reb	Ass	PF	DQ	Pts	Min	Reb	Ass.	Pts
Rudy White	76-78Hou 79JJ 80Hou 81GS 81Sea	1953	6'2	195	G	Arizona State	5	124	156	382	41	0	1	0	72	97	74	120	112	126	0	384	10	1.0	0.9	3.1
	77						1	1	1	3	33	0	0	—	0	0	—	1	0	0	0	2	2	1.0	0.0	2.0
Tony White	88Chi 88NY 88GS	1965	6'2	170	G	Tennessee	1	49	111	249	45	0	6	0	39	54	72	31	59	57	0	261	12	0.6	1.2	5.3
Willie White	85-86Den	1962	6'3	195	G	Tenn.-Chattanooga	2	82	126	292	43	10	32	31	40	54	74	80	82	48	0	302	7	1.0	1.0	3.7
	85-86						2	14	29	64	45	3	7	43	7	12	58	20	23	10	0	68	10	1.4	1.6	4.9
erome Whitehead	79-80SD 80Utah 81Dal 81Cle 81-84SD 85-89GS 89SA	1956	6'10	222	C-F	Marquette	11	679	1810	3642	50	0	2	0	803	1118	72	3268	374	1833	40	4423	17	4.8	0.6	6.5
	87						1	10	9	27	33	0	0	—	4	10	40	14	3	22	1	22	10	1.4	0.3	1.2
awkeye Whitney	81-82KC	1957	6'5	235	G-F	N. Carolina State	2	70	174	377	46	2	7	29	54	72	75	146	87	129	0	404	15	2.1	1.2	5.8
itchell Wiggins	84Chi 85-87Hou 88-89DR 90Hou	1959	6'4	185	G	Clemson, Florida State	5	340	1508	3271	46	14	72	19	636	838	76	1141	587	875	11	3666	22	3.4	1.7	10.8
	85-86, 90						3	29	105	212	50	0	3	0	23	31	74	93	34	55	0	233	19	3.2	1.3	8.0
ichael Wiley	81SA 82SD	1957	6'9	200	F	Long Beach State	2	94	279	497	56	0	7	0	134	189	71	246	63	165	2	692	14	2.6	0.7	7.4
	81						1	3	0	1	0	0	0	—	2	2	100	0	0	2	0	2	2	0.0	0.0	0.7
orlon Wiley	89Dal 90Orl	1966	6'4	190	G	Long Beach State	2	91	138	322	43	23	70	33	41	54	76	99	190	126	0	340	11	1.1	2.1	3.7
ob Wilkerson	77Sea 78-80Den 81Chi 82-83Cle	1954	6'6	200	G-F	Indiana	7	535	2250	5298	42	11	66	17	900	1197	75	2231	1834	1309	7	5411	28	4.2	3.4	10.1
	78-79, 81						3	22	86	220	39	0	1	0	32	50	64	113	107	75	2	204	31	5.1	4.9	9.3
amaal Wilkes	75-77GS 78-84LA 85LAL 86LAC	1953	6'6	190	F-G	U.C.L.A.	12	828	6226	12471	50	7	52	13	2185	2878	76	5117	2050	2296	7	14644	33	6.2	2.5	17.7
(known as Keith - 1975)	75-84						10	113	785	1689	46	0	6	0	250	344	73	718	246	326	3	1820	34	6.4	2.2	16.1
ames Wilkes	81-82Chi 83Det	1958	6'7	195	F	U.C.L.A.	3	114	224	484	46	0	3	0	99	137	72	274	104	220	2	547	13	2.4	0.9	4.8
	81						1	2	0	1	0	0	0	—	0	0	—	1	1	0	0	0	3	0.5	0.5	0.0
ominique Wilkins	83-90Atl	1960	6'8	200	F-G	Georgia	8	639	6387	13609	47	197	696	28	3724	4631	80	4305	1557	1337	2	16695	37	6.7	2.4	26.1
	83-89						7	43	421	969	43	14	52	27	295	361	82	284	113	100	0	1151	40	6.6	2.6	26.8
ddie Lee Wilkins	85NY 86KJ 87,89-90NY	1962	6'10	220	F-C	Gardner-Webb	4	226	427	915	47	0	6	0	243	438	55	782	45	484	6	1097	13	3.4	0.2	4.8
	89-90						2	14	14	29	48	0	0	—	11	21	52	22	0	10	0	39	6	1.6	0.0	2.8
erald Wilkins	86-90NY	1963	6'6	190	G-F	Tenn.-Chattanooga	5	405	2595	5617	46	162	525	31	952	1320	72	1387	1445	857	2	6304	31	3.4	3.6	15.6
	88-90						3	23	159	337	47	5	22	23	48	59	81	77	113	62	1	371	33	3.3	4.9	16.1
eff Wilkins	81-86Utah 86SA	1955	6'11	240	C-F	Illinois State	6	454	1501	3270	46	0	10	0	573	771	74	2574	462	1203	13	3575	22	5.7	1.0	7.9
	84-86						3	24	81	176	46	0	1	0	44	57	77	115	18	65	0	206	20	4.8	0.8	8.6
ale Wilkinson	85Det 85LAC	1960	6'10	220	F	Idaho State	1	12	4	16	25	0	1	0	6	7	86	4	2	10	0	14	4	0.3	0.2	1.2
uck Williams	82-89NJ 90Port	1960	6'8	219	F	Maryland	9	717	4394	7988	55	2	21	10	2764	4222	65	8376	1092	2529	45	11554	36	11.7	1.5	16.1
	82-86, 90						6	42	236	446	53	0	0	—	181	277	65	455	65	164	6	653	40	10.8	1.5	15.5
huckie Williams	77Cle	1953	6'3	180	G	Kansas State	1	22	14	47	30				9	12	75	4	7	7	0	37	3	0.2	0.3	1.7
uck Williams	80Utah	1956	6'2	180	G	Notre Dame	1	77	232	519	45	0	12	0	42	60	70	106	183	166	0	506	23	1.4	2.4	6.6
reeman Williams	79-82SD 82Atl 83Utah 86Was	1956	6'4	195	G-F	Portland State	6	323	1959	4198	47	127	384	33	693	841	82	510	516	533	1	4738	20	1.6	1.6	14.7
	82						1	1	0	2	0	0	1	0	0	0	—	0	0	0	0	0	4	0.0	0.0	0.0
us Williams (The Wizard)	76-77GS 78-80Sea 81HO 82-84Sea 85-86Was 87Atl	1953	6'2	175	G	Southern Calif.	11	825	5793	12570	46	108	454	24	2399	3173	76	2222	4597	1637	13	14093	31	2.7	5.6	17.1
	76-80, 82-86						10	99	781	1644	48	9	39	23	356	483	74	308	469	243	4	1927	32	3.1	4.7	19.5
uy Williams	85Was 86GS	1960	6'9	200	F	San Francisco, Washington State	2	26	31	68	46	1	4	25	5	11	45	33	9	24	1	68	6	1.3	0.3	2.6
erb Williams	82-89Ind 89-90Dal	1958	6'11	242	F-C	Ohio State	9	688	3979	8438	47	6	68	9	1572	2240	70	5082	1557	2063	30	9536	31	7.4	2.3	13.9
	87, 90						2	7	34	57	60	0	0	—	20	29	69	33	12	28	1	88	31	4.7	1.7	12.6
ohn Williams (Hot Rod)	87-90Cle	1961	6'11	230	F-C	Tulane	4	321	1635	3330	49	1	6	17	1069	1433	75	2275	533	802	5	4340	30	7.1	1.7	13.5
	88-90						3	15	80	155	52	0	0	—	36	53	68	109	25	48	0	196	31	7.3	1.7	13.1
ohn Williams	87-90Was	1966	6'9	235	F-C	Louisiana State	4	260	1278	2748	47	34	163	21	622	853	73	1519	863	636	5	3212	28	5.8	3.3	12.4
	87-88						2	8	31	62	50	0	2	0	23	39	59	40	23	21	1	85	29	5.0	2.9	10.6
evin Williams	84SA 85Cle 87-88Sea 89NJ 89LAC	1961	6'3	180	G	St. John's (NY)	5	260	495	1138	43	2	26	8	276	343	80	356	319	580	4	1268	11	1.4	1.2	4.9
	85, 87-88						3	21	53	112	47	0	4	0	30	40	75	42	40	60	0	136	16	2.0	1.9	6.5
ichael Williams	89Det 90Phoe 90Char	1966	6'2	175	G	Baylor	2	77	107	248	43	2	12	17	67	93	72	59	151	83	0	283	9	0.8	2.0	3.7
	89						1	4	0	0	—	0	0	—	2	2	100	2	2	1	0	2	2	0.5	0.5	0.5
ike Williams	90Sac 90Atl	1963	6'8	225	F	Bradley	1	21	6	18	33	0	1	0	3	6	50	23	2	30	0	15	5	1.1	0.1	0.7
ete Williams	86-87Den	1963	6'7	190	F	Arizona	2	58	68	113	60	0	0	—	17	40	43	147	15	69	1	153	10	2.5	0.3	2.6
	86						1	4	2	4	50	0	1	0	0	0	—	4	3	2	0	4	5	1.0	0.8	1.0
ay Williams	78-81NY 82NJ 83KC 84NY 85Bos 86Atl 86SA 86-87NJ	1954	6'3	193	G	Minnesota	10	655	3962	8794	45	91	384	24	2143	2673	80	2370	3779	2165	41	10158	28	3.6	5.8	15.5
	78, 81-82, 84-85						5	40	166	412	40	7	35	20	86	106	81	110	202	128	2	425	22	2.8	5.1	10.6
eggie Williams	88-90LAC 90Cle 90SA	1964	6'7	193	F-G	Georgetown	3	145	543	1359	40	49	199	25	192	256	75	380	214	391	4	1327	20	2.6	1.5	9.2
	90						1	9	9	27	33	0	2	0	2	2	100	11	3	8	0	20	5	1.2	0.3	2.2
ickey Williams	83Utah	1957	6'2	175	G	New Mexico, Long Beach State	1	44	56	135	41	0	3	0	35	53	66	38	37	42	0	147	8	0.9	0.8	3.3
ob Williams	83-84Den	1961	6'2	175	G	Houston	2	153	500	1139	44	17	62	27	302	383	79	330	825	489	8	1319	22	2.2	5.4	8.6
	83-84						2	12	45	101	45	7	16	44	17	19	89	32	61	46	2	114	24	2.7	5.1	9.5
am Williams	82-84GS 84-85Phi	1959	6'8	214	F	Arizona State	4	257	668	1335	50	0	3	0	292	447	65	1146	156	701	8	1628	18	4.5	0.6	6.3
	84-85						2	9	3	14	21	0	0	—	4	12	33	18	3	9	0	10	9	2.0	0.3	1.1
y Williams (The Garbage Man)	80-83NY 84-85Atl 86Bos	1958	6'7	231	F-G	Rhode Island	7	305	1322	2765	48	11	68	16	672	971	69	1287	603	722	4	3327	22	4.2	2.0	10.9
	81, 83						2	7	29	59	49	1	1	100	3	3	100	30	11	11	0	62	20	4.3	1.6	8.9
ohn Williamson (Super John)	74-76NY-A 77NYN 77-78Ind 78-80NJ 80-81Was	1952	6'2	188	G	New Mexico State	8	516	3724	8139	46	25	107	23	1544	1870	83	1274	1441	1513	14	9017	30	2.5	2.8	17.5
	74-76, 79-80						5	33	224	463	48	4	15	27	78	105	74	88	85	116	0	534	31	2.7	2.6	16.2
evin Willis	85-88Atl 89KJ 90Atl	1962	7'	228	F-C	Michigan State	5	401	2053	3996	51	5	28	18	845	1255	67	3267	228	1332	20	4956	28	8.1	0.6	12.4
	86-88						3	30	195	351	56	0	1	0	70	104	67	256	22	122	3	460	37	8.5	0.7	15.3
ll Willoughby	76-77Atl 78Buf 80Cle 81-82Hou 83SA 83-84NJ	1957	6'8	205	F-C	none	9	488	1224	2606	47	10	40	25	472	629	75	1891	413	964	4	2930	18	3.9	0.8	6.0
	81-82, 84						3	24	44	121	36	0	1	0	32	42	76	94	23	45	0	120	19	3.9	1.0	5.0
ubba Wilson	80GS	1955	6'3	175	G	Western Carolina	1	16	7	25	28	0	0	—	3	6	50	16	12	11	0	17	9	1.0	0.8	1.1
ichael Wilson	84Was 85Cle 85, 87NJ 87Atl	1959	6'4	180	G	Marquette	3	32	39	89	44	0	1	0	30	40	75	36	45	36	0	108	11	1.1	1.4	3.4
kita Wilson	88Port	1964	6'8	200	F	Louisiana State	1	15	7	23	30	0	0	—	5	6	83	11	3	7	0	19	4	0.7	0.2	1.3
thell Wilson	85GS 87Sac	1961	6'	190	G	Virginia	2	127	216	476	45	6	34	18	97	130	75	212	424	189	0	535	16	1.7	3.3	4.2
ck Wilson	79-80Atl	1956	6'5	200	G	Louisville	2	66	83	211	39	0	0	—	28	50	56	79	83	69	1	194	10	1.2	1.3	2.9
	79						1	1	0	0	—				0	0	—	0	0	0	0	0	1	0.0	0.0	0.0
cky Wilson	88NJ 88SA	1964	6'3	195	G	George Mason	1	24	43	110	39	10	26	38	29	40	73	27	69	40	0	125	18	1.1	2.9	5.2
	88						1	2	0	2	0	0	0	—	0	0	—	0	1	2	0	0	5	0.0	0.5	0.0
avid Wingate	87-89Phi 90SA	1963	6'5	185	G	Georgetown	4	249	751	1753	43	25	111	23	362	479	76	489	555	491	3	1889	21	2.0	2.2	7.6
	87, 90						2	13	55	114	48	4	5	80	18	26	69	47	47	45	2	132	29	3.6	3.6	10.2
ckie Winslow	88Mil	1964	6'8	225	F	Houston	1	7	3	13	23	0	1	0	1	2	50	7	2	9	0	7	6	1.0	0.3	1.0
ian Winters	75LA 76-83Mil	1952	6'4	185	G-F	South Carolina	9	650	4490	9457	47	114	314	36	1443	1713	84	1688	2674	1830	12	10537	31	2.6	4.1	16.2
	76, 78, 80-83						6	41	269	549	49	19	48	40	80	99	81	118	192	123	3	637	33	2.9	4.7	15.5

Use Name-Nickname	Team by Name	Birth Yr.	Hgt	Wgt	Pos	College	# Yr	G	Field Goals FG	Att.	%	3 pt. FG FG	Att.	%	Free Throws FT	Att.	%	Reb	Ass	PF	DQ	Pts	Per Game Min	Reb	Ass.	Pts
Voise Winters	86Phi	1962	6'8	200	F	Bradley	1	4	3	13	23	0	1	0	0	0	—	3	0	1	0	6	4	0.8	0.0	1.5
Randy Wittman	84-88Atl 89Sac 89-90Ind	1959	6'6	210	G-F	Indiana	7	478	1780	3538	50	17	48	35	366	485	75	718	1165	546	0	3943	23	1.5	2.4	8.2
	84, 86-88, 90						5	37	224	416	54	0	2	0	37	50	74	78	114	67	0	485	30	2.1	3.1	13.1
Garry Witts	82Was	1959	6'7	190	G-F	Holy Cross	1	46	49	84	58	1	2	50	33	40	83	62	38	74	1	132	11	1.3	0.8	2.9
	82						1	4	2	2	100	0	0	—	1	2	50	3	2	6	0	5	7	0.8	0.5	1.3
Joe Wolf	88-90LAC	1964	6'11	230	F-C	North Carolina	3	185	461	1128	41	10	54	19	144	189	76	690	273	420	9	1076	21	3.7	1.5	5.8
Al Wood	82Atl 82-83SD 84-86Sea 87Dal	1958	6'6	196	G-F	North Carolina	6	417	1980	4254	47	40	190	21	902	1143	79	1262	742	944	15	4902	24	3.0	1.8	11.8
	84						1	5	26	56	46	0	1	0	8	12	67	34	10	16	0	60	31	6.8	2.0	12.0
David Wood	89Chi	1964	6'9	225	F	Nevada - Reno	1	2	0	0	—	0	0	—	0	0	—	0	0	0	0	0	1	0.0	0.0	0.0
Howard Wood	82Utah	1959	6'7	235	F	Tennessee	1	42	55	120	46	0	1	0	34	52	65	65	9	37	0	144	8	1.5	0.2	3.4
Leon Wood	85-86Phi 86Was 87NJ 88SA 88Atl 90NJ	1962	6'3	185	G	Arizona, Fullerton State	5	262	573	1462	39	161	492	33	354	450	79	297	818	279	0	1661	16	1.1	3.1	6.3
	85-86, 88						3	10	6	15	40	2	3	67	8	10	80	1	3	0	0	22	2	0.1	0.3	2.2
Mike Woodson	81NY 82NJ 82-85KC 86Sac 87-88LAC 89-90Hou	1958	6'5	198	G-F	Indiana	10	771	4342	9287	47	119	436	27	2114	2602	81	1825	1807	1829	11	10917	26	2.4	2.3	14.2
	81, 84, 86, 89-90						5	13	59	148	40	3	13	23	37	41	90	30	34	35	0	158	27	2.3	2.6	12.2
Orlando Woolridge	82-86Chi 87-88NJ 89-90LAL	1959	6'9	215	F	Notre Dame	9	584	3555	6775	52	6	52	12	2396	3230	74	2592	1148	1559	18	9512	28	4.4	2.0	16.3
	85-86, 89-90						4	31	138	275	50	0	2	0	97	132	73	120	39	91	2	373	23	3.9	1.3	12.0
Haywoode Workman	90Atl	1966	6'2	180	G	Winston-Salem St., Oral Roberts	1	6	2	3	67	0	0	—	2	2	100	3	2	3	0	6	3	0.5	0.3	1.0
Sam Worthen	81Chi 82Utah	1958	6'5	195	G	Marquette	2	69	97	197	49	0	4	0	45	60	75	116	118	118	0	239	14	1.7	1.7	3.5
	81						1	1	0	0	—	0	0	—	0	0	—	0	0	0	0	0	1	0.0	0.0	0.0
James Worthy	83-84LA 85-90LAL	1961	6'9	228	F	North Carolina	8	632	4862	8762	55	20	131	15	1798	2368	76	3619	1832	1602	8	11542	33	5.7	2.9	18.3
	84-90						7	120	1074	1897	57	8	35	23	418	575	73	657	380	307	2	2574	37	5.5	3.2	21.5
Brad Wright	87NY 88Den	1962	6'11	225	F	U.C.L.A.	2	16	21	51	41	0	1	0	12	28	43	54	1	23	0	54	9	3.4	0.1	3.4
Larry Wright	77-80Was 81-82Det	1954	6'1	163	G	Grambling	6	343	1190	2558	47	6	23	26	438	564	78	550	1165	791	10	2824	20	1.6	3.4	8.2
	77-80						4	49	166	348	48	0	1	0	65	81	80	65	133	131	2	397	18	1.3	2.7	8.1
Rich Yonakor	82SA	1958	6'9	220	F	North Carolina	1	10	14	26	54	0	0	—	5	7	71	27	3	7	0	33	7	2.7	0.3	3.3
	82						1	2	1	2	50	0	0	—	0	0	—	1	1	1	0	2	2	0.5	0.5	1.0
Danny Young	85-88Sea 89-90Port	1962	6'4	175	G	Wake Forest	6	365	703	1543	46	108	340	32	333	406	82	507	1230	390	0	1847	18	1.4	3.4	5.1
	87-90						4	43	72	171	42	19	56	34	40	49	82	64	111	59	1	203	15	1.5	2.6	4.7
Michael Young	85Phoe 86Phi 90LAC	1961	6'7	220	F-G	Houston	3	49	94	202	47	8	27	30	27	38	71	88	24	47	0	223	10	1.8	0.5	4.6
	86						1	3	1	4	25	0	0	—	0	0	—	1	0	0	0	2	1	0.3	0.0	0.7
Perry Young	87Chi 87Port	1963	6'5	210	G	Virginia Tech	1	9	6	21	29	0	0	—	1	2	50	8	7	14	0	13	8	0.9	0.8	1.4
Tony Zeno	80Ind	1957	6'8	210	F	Arizona State	1	8	6	21	29	0	0	—	2	2	100	14	1	13	0	14	7	1.8	0.1	1.8
Phil Zevenbergen	88SA	1964	6'10	230	C	Seattle Pacific, Washington	1	8	15	27	56	0	0	—	0	2	0	13	3	12	0	30	7	1.6	0.4	3.8
	88						1	1	0	0	—	0	0	—	0	0	—	0	0	0	0	0	1	0.0	0.0	0.0
Jim Zoet	83Det	1953	7'1	240	C	Kent State	1	7	1	5	20	0	0	—	0	0	—	8	1	9	0	2	4	1.1	0.1	0.3

Leaders

YEARLY INDIVIDUAL LEADERS - REGULAR SEASON

Year	League	POINTS PER GAME			FIELD GOAL PERCENTAGE			FREE THROW PERCENTAGE			Year	League
		Name	Team	PPG	Name	Team	FG%	Name	Team	FT%		
1937/38	N.B.A.	Leroy Edwards	Osh	16.2								
1938/39	N.B.L.	Leroy Edwards	Osh	11.9								
1939/40	N.B.L	Leroy Edwards	Osh	12.9								
1940/41	N.B.L.	Ben Stephens	AG	11.0								
1941/42	N.B.L.	Chuck Chuchovits	Tol	18.5								
1942/43	N.B.L.	Bobby McDermott	FtW	13.7								
1943/44	N.B.L	Mel Riebe	Cle	17.9								
1944/45	N.B.L.	Mel Riebe	Cle	20.2								
1945/46	N.B.L.	Bob Carpenter	Osh	13.9				Herm Feutsch	Cle	.813	1945/46	N.B.L.
1946/47	N.B.L.	George Mikan	Chi	16.5				Bruce Hale	Chi	.823	1946/47	N.B.L.
1946/47	B.A.A.	Joe Fulks	Phi	23.2	Bob Feerick	Was	.401	Freddie Scolari	Was	.811	1946/47	B.A.A.
1947/48	N.B.L.	George Mikan	Min	21.3				Hal Tidrick	Tol	.778	1947/48	N.B.L.
1947/48	B.A.A.	Joe Fulks	Phi	22.1	Buddy Jeannene	Bal	.349	Stan Stutz	NY	.837	1947/48	B.A.A.
1948/49	N.B.L.	Don Otten	TC	14.0				Frankie Brian	And	.785	1948/49	N.B.L.
1948 49	B.A.A.	George Mikan	Min	28.3	Arnie Risen	Roch	.423	Bob Feerick	Was	.859	1948/49	B.A.A.
1949/50	N.B.A.	George Mikan	Min	27.4	Alex Groza	Ind	.478	Max Zaslofsky	Chi	.843	1949/50	N.B.A.
1950/51	N.B.A.	George Mikan	Min	28.4	Alex Groza	Ind	.470	Joe Fulks	Phi	.855	1950/51	N.BA.
1951/52	N.B.A.	Paul Arizin	Phi	25.4	Paul Arizin	Phi	.448	Bobby Wanzer	Roch	.904	1951/52	N.B.A.
1952/53	N.B.A.	Neil Johnston	Phi	22.3	Neil Johnston	Phi	.452	Bill Sharman	Bos	.850	1952/53	N.BA.
1953/54	N.B.A.	Neil Johnston	Phi	24.4	Ed Macauley	Bos	.486	Bill Sharman	Bos	.844	1953/54	N.B.A.
1954/55	N.B.A.	Neil Johnston	Phi	22.7	Larry Foust	FtW	.487	Bill Sharman	Bos	.897	1954/55	N.B.A.
1955/56	N.B.A.	Bob Pettit	StL	25.7	Neil Johnston	Phi	.457	Bill Sharman	Bos	.867	1955/56	N.B.A.
1956/57	N.B.A.	Paul Arizin	Phi	25.6	Neil Johnston	Phi	.447	Bill Sharman	Bos	.905	1956/57	N.B.A.
1957/58	N.B.A.	George Yardley	Det	27.8	Jack Twyman	Cin	.452	Dolph Schayes	Syr	.904	1957/58	N.B.A.
1958/59	N.B.A.	Bob Pettit	StL	29.2	Kenny Sears	NY	.490	Bill Sharman	Bos	.932	1958/59	N.B.A.
1959/60	N.B.A.	Wilt Chamberlain	Phi	37.6	Kenny Sears	NY	.477	Dolph Schayes	Syr	.893	1959/60	N.B.A.
1960/61	N.B.A.	Wilt Chamberlain	Phi	38.4	Wilt Chamberlain	Phi	.509	Bill Sharman	Bos	.921	1960/61	N.B.A.
1961/62	N.B.A.	Wilt Chamberlain	Phi	50.4	Walt Bellamy	Chi	.519	Dolph Schayes	Syr	.896	1961/62	N.B.A.
1962/63	N.B.A.	Wilt Chamberlain	SF	44.8	Wilt Chamberlain	SF	.528	Larry Costello	Syr	.881	1962/63	N.BA.
1963/64	N.B.A.	Wilt Chamberlain	SF	36.9	Jerry Lucas	Cin	.527	Oscar Robertson	Cin	.853	1963/64	N.BA.
1964/65	N.B.A.	Wilt Chamberlain	SF-Phi	34.7	Wilt Chamberlain	SF-Phi	.510	Larry Costello	Phi	.877	1964/65	N.B.A.
1965/66	N.B.A.	Wilt Chamberlain	Phi	33.5	Wilt Chamberlain	Phi	.540	Larry Siegfried	Bos	.881	1965/66	N.B.A.
1966/67	N.B.A.	Rick Barry	SF	35.6	Wilt Chamberlain	Phi	.683	Adrian Smith	Cin	.903	1966/67	N.B.A.
1967/68	N.B.A.	Dave Bing	Det	27.1	Wilt Chamberlain	Phi	.595	Oscar Robertson	Cin	.873	1967/68	N.B.A.
1967/68	A.B.A.	Connie Hawkins	Pit	26.8	Trooper Washington	Pit	.523	Charlie Beasley	Dal	.872	1968/68	A.B.A.
1968/69	N.B.A.	Elvin Hayes	SD	28.4	Wilt Chamberlain	LA	.583	Larry Siegfried	Bos	.864	1968/69	N.B.A.
1968/69	A.B.A.	Larry Jones	Den	28.4	Bill McGill	Den	.552	Rick Barry	Oak	.888	1968/69	A.B.A.
1969/70	N.B.A.	Jerry West	LA	31.2	Johnny Green	Cin	.559	Flynn Robinson	Mil	.898	1969/70	N.B.A.
1969/70	A.B.A.	Spencer Haywood	Den	30.0	Frank Card	Den	.527	Darel Carrier	Ky	.892	1969/70	A.B.A.
1970/71	N.B.A.	Lew Alcindor (Jabbar)	Mil	31.7	Johnny Green	Cin	.587	Chet Walker	Chi	.859	1970/71	N.B.A.
1970/71	A.B.A.	Dan Issel	Ky	29.9	Zelmo Beaty	Utah	.555	Rick Barry	NY	.890	1970/71	A.B.A.
1971/72	N.B.A.	Kareem Abdul-Jabbar	Mil	34.8	Wilt Chamberlain	LA	.649	Jack Marin	Bal	.894	1971/72	N.B.A.
1971/72	A.B.A.	Charlie Scott	Va	34.6	Artis Gilmore	Ky	.598	Rick Barry	NY	.878	1971/72	A.B.A.
1972/73	N.B.A.	Nate Archibald	KCO	34.9	Wilt Chamberlain	LA	.727	Rick Barry	GS	.902	1972/73	N.B.A.
1972/73	A.B.A.	Julius Erving	Va	31.9	Artis Gilmore	Ky	.550	Bill Keller	Ind	.870	1972/73	A.B.A.
1973/74	N.B.A.	Bob McAdoo	But	30.6	Bob McAdoo	Buf	.547	Ernie DiGregorio	Buf	.902	1973/74	N.B.A.
1973/74	A.B.A.	Julius Erving	NY	27.4	Swen Nater	Va-SA	.552	Jimmy Jones	Utah	.884	1973/74	A.B.A.
1974/75	N.B.A.	Bob McAdoo	Buf	34.5	Don Nelson	Bos	.539	Rick Barry	GS	.904	1974/75	N.B.A.
1974/75	A.B.A.	George McGinnis	Ind	29.8	Bobby Jones	Den	.604	Mack Calvin	Den	.896	1974/75	A.B.A.
1975/76	N.B.A.	Bob McAdoo	Buf	31.1	Wes Unseld	Was	.561	Rick Barry	GS	.923	1975/76	N.B.A.
1975/76	A.B.A.	Julius Erving	NY	29.3	Bobby Jones	Den	.581	Mack Calvin	Va	.888	1975/76	A.B.A.
1976/77	N.B.A.	Pete Maravich	NO	31.1	Kareem Abdul-Jabbar	LA	.579	Ernie DiGregorio	Buf	.945	1976/77	N.B.A.
1977/78	N.B.A.	George Gervin	SA	27.2	Bobby Jones	Den	.578	Rick Barry	GS	.924	1977/78	N.B.A.
1978/79	N.B.A.	George Gervin	SA	29.6	Cedric Maxwell	Bos	.584	Rick Barry	Hou	.947	1978/79	N.B.A.
1979/80	N.B.A.	George Gervin	SA	33.1	Cedric Maxwell	Bos	.609	Rick Barry	Hou	.935	1979/80	N.B.A.
1980/81	N.B.A.	Adrian Dantley	Utah	30.7	Artis Gilmore	Chi	.670	Calvin Murphy	Hou	.958	1980/81	N.B.A.
1981/82	N.B.A.	George Gervin	SA	32.3	Artis Gilmore	Chi	.652	Kyle Macy	Phoe	.899	1981/82	N.B.A.
1982/83	N.B.A.	Alex English	Den	28.4	Artis Gilmore	SA	.626	Calvin Murphy	Hou	.920	1982/83	N.B.A.
1983/84	N.B.A.	Adrian Dantley	Utah	30.6	Artis Gilmore	SA	.631	Larry Bird	Bos	.888	1983/84	N.B.A.
1984/85	N.B.A.	Bernard King	NY	32.9	James Donaldson	LAC	.637	Kyle Macy	Phoe	.907	1984/85	N.B.A.
1985/86	N.B.A.	Dominique Wilkins	Atl	30.3	Steve Johnson	SA	.632	Larry Bird	Bos	.896	1985/86	N.B.A.
1986/87	N.B.A.	Michael Jordan	Chi	37.1	Kevin McHale	Bos	.604	Larry Bird	Bos	.910	1986/87	N.B.A.
1987/88	N.B.A.	Michael Jordan	Chi	35.0	Kevin McHale	Bos	.604	Jack Sikma	Mil	.922	1987/88	N.B.A.
1988/89	N.B.A.	Michael Jordan	Chi	32.5	Dennis Rodman	Det	.595	Magic Johnson	LAL	.911	1988/89	N.B.A.
1989/90	N.B.A.	Michael Jordan	Chi	33.6	Mark West	Phoe	.625	Larry Bird	Bos	.930	1989/90	N.B.A.

YEARLY INDIVIDUAL LEADERS - REGULAR SEASON

Year	League	FIELD GOALS			FREE THROWS			POINTS			Year	League
		Name	Team	FG	Name	Team	FT	Name	Team	Pts.		
1937/38	N.B.L.	Leroy Edwards	Osh	83	Soup Cable	AF	45	Leroy Edwards	Osh	210	1937/38	N.B.L.
1938/39	N.B.L.	Leroy Edwards	Osh	124	Leroy Edwards	Osh	86	Leroy Edwards	Osh	334	1938/39	N.B.L.
1939/40	N.B.L.	Ernie Andres	Ind	130	Leroy Edwards	Osh	139	Leroy Edwards	Osh	361	1939/40	N.B.L.
1940/41	N.B.L.	Ben Stephens	AG	98	Leroy Edwards	Osh	76	Ben Stephens	AG	265	1940/41	N.B.L.
1941/42	N.B.L.	Chuck Chuckovits	Tol	143	Chuck Chuckovits	Tol	120	Chuck Chuckovits	Tol	406	1941/42	N.B.L.
1942/43	N.B.L.	Bobby McDermott	FtW	132	Bernie Price	Chi	77	Bobby McDermott	FtW	316	1942/43	N.B.L.
1943/44	N.B.L.	Bobby McDermott	FtW	123	Mel Riebe	Cle	97	Mel Riebe	Cle	323	1943/44	N.B.L.
1944/45	N.B.L.	Bobby McDermott	FtW	258	Mel Riebe	Cle	161	Mel Riebe	Cle	607	1944/45	N.B.L.
1945/46	N.B.L.	Bob Carpenter	Osh	186	Leroy Edwards	Osh	119	Bob Carpenter	Osh	473	1945/46	N.B.L.
1946/47	N.B.L.	Hal Tidrick	Tol	232	George Sobek	Tol	179	Al Cervi	Roch	632	1946/47	N.B.L.
1946/47	B.A.A.	Joe Fulks	Phi	475	Joe Fulks	Phi	439	Joe Fulks	Phi	1389	1946/47	B.A.A.
1947/48	N.B.L.	George Mikan	Min	406	George Mikan	Min	383	George Mikan	Min	1195	1947/48	N.B.L.
1947/48	B.A.A.	Max Zaslofsky	Chi	373	Joe Fulks	Phi	297	Max Zaslofsky	Chi	1007	1947/48	B.A.A.
1948/49	N.B.L.	Don Otten	TC	301	Don Otten	TC	297	Don Otten	TC	899	1948/49	N.B.L.
1948/49	B.AA	George Mikan	Min	583	George Mikan	Min	532	George Mikan	Min	1698	1948/49	B.A.A
1949/50	N.B.A.	George Mikan	Min	649	George Mikan	Min	567	George Mikan	Min	1865	1949/50	N.B.A
1950/51	N.B.A.	George Mikan	Min	678	George Mikan	Min	576	George Mikan	Min	1932	1950/51	N.B.A.
1951/52	N.B.A.	Paul Arizin	Phi	548	Paul Arizin	Phi	178	Paul Arizin	Phi	1674	1951/52	N.B.A.
1952/53	N.B.A.	Neil Johnston	Phi	504	Neil Johnston	Phi	556	Neil Johnston	Phi	1564	1952 53	N.B.A.
1953/54	N.B.A.	Neil Johnston	Phi	591	Neil Johnston	Phi	577	Neil Johnston	Phi	1759	1953/54	N.B.A.
1954/55	N.B.A.	Paul Arizin	Phi	529	Neil Johnston	Phi	589	Neil Johnston	Phi	1631	1954/55	N.B.A.
1955/56	N.B.A.	Bob Pettit	StL	646	Bob Pettit	StL	557	Bob Pettit	StL	1849	1955/56	N.B.A.
1956/57	N.B.A.	Paul Arizin	Phi	613	Dolph Schayes	Syr	625	Paul Arizin	Phi	1817	1956/57	N.B.A.
		Bob Pettit	StL	613								
1957/58	N.B.A.	Clyde Lovellette	Cin	679	George Yardley	Det	655	George Yardley	Det	2001	1957/58	N.B.A.
1958/59	N.B.A.	Bob Pettit	StL	719	Bob Pettit	StL	667	Bob Pettit	StL	2105	1958/59	N.B.A.
1959/60	N.B.A.	Wilt Chamberlain	Phi	1065	Jack Twyman	Cin	598	Wilt Chamberlain	Phi	2707	1959/60	N.B.A.
1960/61	N.B.A.	Wilt Chamberlain	Phi	1251	Dolph Schayes	Syr	680	Wilt Chamberlain	Phi	3033	1960/61	N.B.A.
1961/62	N.B.A.	Wilt Chamberlain	Phi	1597	Wilt Chamberlain	Phi	835	Wilt Chamberlain	Phi	4029	1961/62	N.B.A.
1962/63	N.B.A.	Wilt Chamberlain	SF	1463	Bob Pettit	StL	685	Wilt Chamberlain	SF	3586	1962/63	N.B.A.
1963/64	N.B.A.	Wilt Chamberlain	SF	1204	Oscar Robertson	Cin	800	Wilt Chamberlain	SF	2948	1963/64	N.B.A.
1964/65	N.B.A.	Wilt Chamberlain	SF-Phi	1063	Oscar Robertson	Cin	665	Wilt Chamberlain	SF-Phi	2534	1964/65	N.B.A.
1965/66	N.B.A.	Wilt Chamberlain	Phi	1074	Jerry West	LA	840	Wilt Chamberlain	Phi	2649	1965/66	N.B.A.
1966/67	N.B.A.	Rick Barry	SF	1011	Rick Barry	SF	753	Rick Barry	SF	2775	1966/67	N.B.A.
1967/68	N.B.A.	Dave Bing	Det	835	Oscar Robertson	Cin	576	Dave Bing	Det	2142	1967/68	N.B.A.
1967/68	A.B.A.	Mel Daniels	Min	669	Connie Hawkins	Pit	603	Doug Moe	NO	1884	1967/68	A.B.A.
1968/69	N.B.A.	Elvin Hayes	SD	930	Oscar Robertson	Cin	643	Elvin Hayes	SD	2327	1968/69	N.B.A.
1968/69	A.B.A.	Jimmy Jones	NO	763	Larry Jones	Den	591	Larry Jones	Den	2133	1968 69	A.B.A.
1969/70	N.B.A.	Lew Alcindor (Jabbar)	Mil	938	Jerry West	LA	647	Lew Alcindor (Jabbar)	Mil	2361	1969/70	N.B.A.
1969/70	A.B.A.	Spencer Haywood	Den	986	Donnie Freeman	Mia	626	Spencer Haywood	Den	2519	1969/70	A.B.A.
1970/71	N.B.A.	Lew Alcindor (Jabbar)	Mil	1063	Dave Bing	Det	615	Lew Alcindor (Jabbar)	Mil	2596	1970/71	N.B.A.
1970/71	A.B.A.	Dan Issel	Ky	938	Mack Calvin	Fla	696	Dan Issel	Ky	2480	1970/71	A.B.A.
1971/72	N.B.A.	Kareem Abdul-Jabbar	Mil	1159	Nate Archibald	Cin	677	Kareem Abdul-Jabbar	Mil	2822	1971/72	N.B.A.
1971/72	A.B.A.	Charlie Scott	Va	985	Rick Barry	NY	641	Dan Issel	Ky	2538	1971/72	A.B.A.
1972/73	N.BA.	Nate Archibald	KCO	1028	Nate Archibald	KCO	663	Nate Archibald	KCO	2719	1972/73	N.B.A.
1972/73	A.B.A.	Dan Issel	Ky	902	George Thompson	Mem	549	Dan Issel	Ky	2292	1972/73	A.B.A.
1973/74	N.B.A.	Kareem Abdul-Jabbar	Mil	948	Gail Goodrich	LA	508	Bob McAdoo	Buf	2261	1973/74	N.B.A.
1973/74	A.B.A.	Julius Erving	NY	914	Mack Calvin	Car	490	Julius Erving	NY	2299	1973/74	A.B.A.
1974/75	N.B.A.	Bob McAdoo	Buf	1095	Nate Archibald	KCO	652	Bob McAdoo	Buf	2831	1974/75	N.B.A.
1974/75	A.B.A.	Julius Erving	NY	885	George McGinnis	Ind	545	George McGinnis	Ind	2353	1974/75	A.B.A.
1975/76	N.B.A.	Bob McAdoo	Buf	934	Bob McAdoo	Buf	559	Bob McAdoo	Buf	2427	1975/76	N.B.A.
1975/76	A.B.A.	Julius Erving	NY	949	James Silas	NY	564	Julius Erving	NY	2462	1975/76	A.B.A
1976/77	N.B.A.	Kareem Abdul-Jabbar	LA	888	Pete Maravich	NO	501	Pete Maravich	NO	2273	1976/77	N.B.A.
1977/78	N.B.A.	George Gervin	NY	864	David Thompson	Den	520	George Gervin	SA	2232	1977/78	N.B.A.
1978/79	N.B.A.	Marques Johnson	Mil	820	Moses Malone	Hou	599	George Gervin	SA	2365	1978/79	N.B.A.
1979/80	N.B.A.	George Gervin	SA	1024	World Free	SD	572	George Gervin	SA	2585	1979/80	N.B.A.
1080/81	N.B.A.	Adrian Dantley	Utah	909	Adrian Dantley	Utah	632	Adrian Dantley	Utah	2452	1980/81	N.B.A.
1981/82	N.B.A.	George Gervin	SA	993	George Gervin	SA	555	George Gervin	SA	2551	1981/82	N.B.A.
1982/83	N.B.A.	Alex English	Den	959	Moses Malone	Phi	600	Alex English	Den	2326	1982/83	N.B.A.
1983/84	N.B.A.	Mark Aguirre	Dal	925	Adrian Dantley	Utah	813	Adrian Dantley	Utah	2418	1983/84	N.B.A.
1984/85	N.B.A.	Alex English	Den	939	Moses Malone	Phi	737	Michael Jordan	Chi	2313	1984/85	N.B.A.
1985/86	N.B.A.	Alex English	Den	951	Adrian Dantley	Utah	630	Alex English	Den	2414	1985/86	N.B.A.
1986/87	N.B.A.	Michael Jordan	Chi	1098	Michael Jordan	Chi	833	Michael Jordan	Chi	3041	1986/87	N.B.A.
1987/88	N.B.A.	Michael Jordan	Chi	1069	Michael Jordan	Chi	723	Michael Jordan	Chi	2868	1987/88	N.B.A.
1988/89	N.B.A.	Michael Jordan	Chi	966	Karl Malone	Utah	703	Michael Jordan	Chi	2633	1988/89	N.B.A.
1989/90	N.B.A.	Michael Jordan	Chi	1034	Karl Malone	Utah	696	Michael Jordan	Chi	2753	1989/90	N.B.A.

YEARLY INDIVIDUAL LEADERS - REGULAR SEASON

		ASSISTS			ASSISTS PER GAME			PERSONAL FOULS				
Year	League	Name	Team	Ass.	Name	Team	Ass./G	Name	Team	PF	Year	League
1946/47	B.A.A.	Ernie Calverly	Prov	202	Ernie Calverly	Prov	3.4	Stan Miasek	Det	208	1946/47	B.A.A.
1947/48	B.A.A.	Howie Dallmar	Phi	120	Ernie Calverly	Prov	2.5	Chuck Gilmur	Chi	231	1947/48	B.A.A.
1948/49	B.A.A.	Bob Davies	Roch	321	Bob Davies	Roch	5.4	Ed Sadowshi	Phi	273	1948/49	B.A.A.
1949/50	N.B.A.	Dick McGuire	NY	386	Andy Phillip	Chi	5.8	George Mikan	Min	297	1949/50	N.B.A.
1950/51	N.B.A.	Andy Phillip	Phi	414	Andy Phillip	Phi	6.3	George Mikan	Min	308	1950/51	N.B.A.
1951/52	N.B.A.	Andy Phillip	Phi	539	Andy Phillip	Phi	8.2	George Mikan	Min	286	1951/52	N.B.A.
1952/53	N.B.A.	Bob Cousy	Bos	547	Bob Cousy	Bos	7.7	Monk Meineke	FtW	334	1952/53	N.B.A.
1953/54	N.B.A.	Bob Cousy	Bos	518	Bob Cousy	Bos	7.2	Earl Lloyd	Syr	303	1953/54	N.B.A.
1954/55	N.B.A.	Bob Cousy	Bos	557	Bob Cousy	Bos	7.8	Vern Mikkelsen	Min	319	1954/55	N.B.A.
1955/56	N.B.A.	Bob Cousy	Bos	642	Bob Cousy	Bos	8.9	Vern Mikkelsen	Min	319	1955/56	N.B.A.
1956/57	N.B.A.	Bob Cousy	Bos	478	Bob Cousy	Bos	7.5	Vern Mikkelsen	Min	312	1956/57	N.B.A.
1957/58	N.B.A.	Bob Cousy	Bos	463	Bob Cousy	Bos	7.1	Walter Dukes	Det	311	1957/58	N.B.A.
1958/59	N.B.A.	Bob Cousy	Bos	557	Bob Cousy	Bos	8.6	Walter Dukes	Det	332	1958/59	N.B.A.
1959/60	N.B.A.	Bob Cousy	Bos	715	Bob Cousy	Bos	9.5	Tom Gola	Phi	311	1959/60	N.B.A.
1960/61	N.B.A.	Oscar Robertson	Cin	690	Oscar Robertson	Cin	9.7	Paul Arizin	Phi	335	1960/61	N.B.A.
1961/62	N.B.A.	Oscar Rooertson	Cin	899	Oscar Robertson	Cin	11.4	Tom Meschery	Phi	330	1961/62	N.B.A.
1962/63	N.B.A.	Guy Rodgers	SF	825	Guy Rodgers	SF	10.4	Zelmo Beaty	StL	312	1962 63	N.B.A.
1963/64	N.B.A.	Oscar Robertson	Cin	868	Oscar Rooenson	Cin	11.0	Wayne Embry	Cin	325	1963/64	N.B.A.
1964/65	N.B.A.	Oscar Robertson	Cin	861	Oscar Robertson	Cin	11.5	Bailey Howell	Bal	345	1964/65	N.B.A.
1965/66	N.B.A.	Oscar Robertson	Cin	847	Oscar Robertson	Cin	11.1	Zelmo Beaty	StL	344	1965/66	N.B.A.
1966/67	N.B.A.	Guy Rodgers	Chi	908	Guy Rodgers	Chi	11.2	Joe Strawder	Det	344	1966/67	N.B.A.
1967/68	N.B.A.	Wilt Chamberlain	Phi	702	Wilt Chamberlain	Phi	8.6	Bill Bridges	StL	366	1967/68	N.B.A.
1967/68	A.B.A.	Larry Brown	NO	506	Larry Brown	NO	6.5	Dan Anderson	NJ	329	1967/68	A.B.A.
1968/69	N.B.A.	Oscar Robertson	Cin	772	Oscar Robertson	Cin	9.8	Billy Cunningham	Phi	329	1968/69	N.B.A.
1968/69	A.B.A.	Larry Brown	Oak	544	Larry Brown	Oak	7.1	John Smith	Dal	328	1968/69	A.B.A.
1969/70	N.B.A.	Lenny Wilkens	Sea	683	Lenny Wilkens	Sea	9.1	Jim Davis	Atl	335	1969/70	N.B.A.
1969/70	A.B.A.	Larry Brown	Was	580	Larry Brown	Was	7.1	Gene Moore	Ky	382	1969/70	A.B.A.
1970/71	N.B.A.	Norm Van Lier	Cin	832	Norm Van Lier	Cin	10.1	Dave Cowens	Bos	350	1970/71	N.B.A.
1970/71	A.B.A.	Bill Melchionni	NY	672	Bill Melchionni	NY	8.3	Wendell Ladner	Mem	334	1970/71	A.B.A.
1971/72	N.B.A.	Lenny Wilkens	Sea	766	Jerry West	LA	9.7	Dave Cowens	Bos	314	1971/72	N.B.A.
1971/72	A.B.A.	Bill Melchionni	NY	669	Bill Melchionni	NY	8.4	Wendell Ladner	Mem-Car	347	1971/72	A.B.A.
1972/73	N.B.A.	Nate Archibald	KCO	910	Nate Archibald	KCO	11.4	Neal Walk	Phoe	323	1972/73	N.B.A.
1972/73	A.B.A.	Chuck Williams	SD	582	Bill Melchionni	NY	7.5	Gene Moore	SD	369	1972/73	A.B.A.
1973/74	N.B.A.	Ernie DiGregorio	Buf	663	Ernie DiGregorio	Buf	8.2	Kevin Porter	Cap	319	1973/74	N.B.A.
1973/74	A.B.A.	Al Smith	Den	619	Al Smith	Den	8.2	Jim Chones	Car	347	1973/74	A.B.A.
1974/75	N.B.A.	Kevin Porter	Was	650	Kevin Porter	Was	8.0	Bob Dandridge	Mil	330	1974/75	N.B.A.
								Phil Jackson	NY	330		
1974/75	A.B.A.	Chuck Williams	Mem	576	Mack Calvin	Den	7.7	Darnell Hillman	Ind	330	1974/75	A.B.A.
1975/76	N.B.A.	Slick Watts	Sea	661	Slick Watts	Sea	8.1	Charlie Scott	Bos	356	1975/76	N.B.A.
1975/76	A.B.A.	Don Buse	Ind	689	Don Buse	Ind	8.2	Artis Gilmore	Ky	341	1975/76	A.B.A.
1976/77	N.B.A.	Don Buse	Ind	685	Don Buse	Ind	8.5	Lonnie Shelton	NY	363	1976/77	N.B.A.
1977/78	N.B.A.	Kevin Porter	Det-NJ	837	Kevin Porter	Det-NJ	10.2	Lonnie Shelton	NY	350	1977/78	N.B.A.
1978/79	N.B.A.	Kevin Porter	Det	1099	Kevin Porter	Det	13.4	Bill Robinzine	KC	367	1978/79	N.B.A.
1979/80	N.B.A.	Micheal Ray Richardson	NY	832	Micheal Ray Richardson	NY	10.1	Darryl Dawkins	Phi	328	1979/80	N.B.A.
1980/81	N.B.A.	Kevin Porter	Det	734	Kevin Porter	Det	9.1	Ben Poquette	Utah	342	1980/81	N.B.A.
1981/82	N.B.A.	Johnny Moore	SA	762	Johnny Moore	SA	9.6	Steve Johnson	KC	372	1981/82	N.B.A.
1982/83	N.B.A.	Magic Johnson	LA	829	Magic Johnson	LA	10.5	Darryl Dawkins	NJ	379	1982/83	N.B.A.
1983/84	N.B.A.	Norm Nixon	SD	914	Magic Johnson	LA	13.1	Darryl Dawkins	NJ	386	1983/84	N.B.A.
		Isiah Thomas	Det	914								
1984/85	N.B.A.	Isiah Thomas	Det	1123	Isiah Thomas	Det	13.9	Akeem Olajuwon	Hou	344	1984/85	N.B.A.
1985/86	N.B.A.	Magic Johnson	LAL	907	Magic Johnson	LAL	12.6	Charles Barkley	Phi	333	1985/86	N.B.A.
1986/87	N.B.A.	Magic Johnson	LAL	977	Magic Johnson	LAL	12.2	Steve Johnson	Port	340	1986/87	N.B.A.
1987/88	N.B.A.	John Stockton	Utah	1128	John Stockton	Utah	13.8	Patrick Ewing	NY	332	1987/88	N.B.A.
1988/89	N.B.A.	John Stockton	Utah	1118	John Stockton	Utah	13.6	Grant Long	Mia	337	1988/89	N.B.A.
1989/90	N.B.A.	John Stockton	Utah	1134	John Stockton	Utah	14.5	Rik Smits	Ind	328	1989/90	N.B.A.

YEARLY INDIVIDUAL LEADERS - REGULAR SEASON

Year	League	MINUTES PER GAME			REBOUNDS			REBOUNDS PER GAME			Year	League
		Name	Team	Min./G	Name	Team	Reb.	Name	Team	Reb./G		
1950/51	N.B.A.				Dolph Schayes	Syr	1080	Dolph Schayes	Syr	16.4	1950/51	N.B.A.
1951/52	N.B.A.	Paul Arizin	Phi	44.5	Larry Foust	FtW	880	George Mikan	Min	13.5	1951/52	N.B.A.
					Mel Hutchins	Mil	880					
1952/53	N.B.A.	Neil Johnston	Phi	45.2	George Mikan	Min	1007	George Mikan	Min	14.4	1952/53	N.B.A.
1953/54	N.B.A.	Neil Johnston	Phi	45.8	Harry Gallatin	NY	1098	Harry Gallatin	NY	15.3	1953/54	N.B.A.
1954/55	N.B.A.	Paul Arizin	Phi	41.0	Neil Johnston	Phi	1085	Neil Johnston	Phi	15.1	1954/55	N.B.A.
1955/56	N.B.A.	Jack George	Phi	39.4	Bob Pettit	StL	1164	Maurice Stokes	Roch	16.3	1955/56	N.B.A.
1956/57	N.B.A.	Dolph Schayes	Syr	39.6	Maurice Stokes	Roch	1256	Bill Russell	Bos	19.6	1956/57	N.B.A.
1957/58	N.B.A.	Dolph Schayes	Syr	40.5	Bill Russell	Bos	1564	Bill Russell	Bos	22.7	1957/58	N.B.A.
1958/59	N.B.A.	Bill Russell	Bos	42.6	Bill Russell	Bos	1612	Bill Russell	Bos	23.0	1958/59	N.B.A.
1959/60	N.B.A.	Wilt Chamberlain	Phi	46.4	Wilt Chamberlain	Phi	1941	Wilt Chamberlain	Phi	27.0	1959/60	N.B.A.
1960/61	N.B.A.	Wilt Chamberlain	Phi	47.8	Wilt Chamberlain	Phi	2149	Wilt Chamberlain	Phi	27.2	1960/61	N.B.A.
1961/62	N.B.A.	Wilt Chamberlain	Phi	48.5	Wilt Chamberlain	Phi	2052	Wilt Chamberlain	Phi	25.7	1961/62	N.B.A.
1962/63	N.B.A.	Wilt Chamberlain	SF	47.6	Wilt Chamberlain	SF	1946	Wilt Chamberlain	SF	24.3	1962/63	N.B.A.
1963/64	N.B.A.	Wilt Chamberlain	SF	46.1	Bill Russell	Bos	1930	Bill Russell	Bos	24.7	1963/64	N.B.A.
1964/65	N.B.A.	Oscar Robertson	Cin	45.6	Bill Russell	Bos	1878	Bill Russell	Bos	24.1	1964/65	N.B.A.
1965/66	N.B.A.	Wilt Chamberlain	Phi	47.3	Wilt Chamberlain	Phi	1943	Wilt Chamberlain	Phi	24.6	1965/66	N.B.A.
1966/67	N.B.A.	Wilt Chamberlain	Phi	45.5	Wilt Chamberlain	Phi	1957	Wilt Chamberlain	Phi	24.2	1966/67	N.B.A.
1967/68	N.B.A.	Wilt Chamberlain	Phi	46.8	Wilt Chamberlain	Phi	1952	Wilt Chamberlain	Phi	23.8	1967/68	N.B.A.
1967/68	A.B.A.	Connie Hawkins	Pit	44.9	Mel Daniels	Min	1213	Mel Daniels	Min	15.6	1967/68	A.B.A.
1968/69	N.B.A.	Wilt Chamberlain	LA	45.3	Wilt Chamberlain	LA	1712	Wilt Chamberlain	LA	21.1	1968/69	N.B.A.
1968/69	A.B.A.	Louie Dampier	Ky	42.6	Mel Daniels	Ind	1256	Mel Daniels	Ind	16.5	1968/69	A.B.A.
1969/70	N.B.A.	Elvin Hayes	SD	44.7	Elvin Hayes	SD	1386	Elvin Hayes	SD	16.9	1969/70	N.B.A.
1969/70	A.B.A.	Spencer Haywood	Den	45.3	Spencer Haywood	Den	1637	Spencer Haywood	Den	19.5	1969/70	A.B.A.
1970/71	N.B.A.	John Havlicek	Bos	45.4	Wilt Chamberlain	LA	1493	Wilt Chamberlain	LA	18.2	1970/71	N.B.A.
1970/71	A.B.A.	Gerald Govan	Mem	44.0	Mel Daniels	Ind	1475	Mel Daniels	Ind	18.0	1970/71	A.B.A.
1971/72	N.B.A.	John Havlicek	Bos	45.1	Wilt Chamberlain	LA	1572	Wilt Chamberlain	LA	19.2	1971/72	N.B.A.
1971/72	A.B.A.	Rick Barry	NY	45.2	Artis Gilmore	Ky	1491	Artis Gilmore	Ky	17.8	1971/72	A.B.A.
1972/73	N.B.A.	Nate Archibald	KCO	46.0	Wilt Chamberlain	LA	1526	Wilt Chamberlain	LA	18.6	1972/73	N.B.A
1972/73	A.B.A.	Julius Erving	Va	42.2	Artis Gilmore	Ky	1476	Artis Gilmore	Ky	17.5	1972/73	A.B.A.
1973/74	N.B.A.	Elvin Hayes	Cap	44.5	Elvin Hayes	Cap	146	Elvin Hayes	Cap	18.1	1973/74	N.B.A.
1973/74	A.B.A.	Arbs Gilmore	Ky	41.7	Antis Gilmore	Ky	1538	Artis Gilmore	Ky	18.3	1973/74	A.B.A.
1974/75	N.B.A.	Bob McAdoo	Buf	43.2	Bob McAdoo	Buf	1155	Wes Unseld	Was	14.8	1974/75	N.B.A.
1974/75	A.B.A.	Artis Gilmore	Ky	41.6	Artis Gilmore	Ky	1361	Swen Nater	SA	16.4	1974/75	A.B.A.
1975/76	N.B.A.	Bob McAdoo	Buf	42.7	Kareem Abdul-Jabbar	LA	1383	Kareem Abdul-Jabbar	LA	16.9	1975/76	N.B.A.
1975/76	A.B.A.	Don Buse	Ind	40.2	Artis Gilmore	Ky	1303	Artis Gilmore	Ky	15.5	1975/76	A.B.A.
1976/77	N.B.A.	Pete Maravich	NO	41.7	Kareem Abdul-Jabbar	LA	1090	Bill Walton	Port	14.4	1976/77	N.B.A.
1977/78	N.B.A.	Truck Robinson	NO	44.4	Truck Robinson	NO	1288	Truck Robinson	NO	15.7	1977/78	N.B.A.
1978/79	N.B.A.	Moses Malone	Hou	41.3	Moses Malone	Hou	1444	Moses Malone	Hou	17.6	1978/79	N.B.A.
1979/80	N.B.A.	Norm Nixon	LA	39.3	Swen Nater	SD	1216	Swen Nater	SD	15.0	1979/80	N.B.A.
1980/81	N.B.A.	Adrian Dantley	Utah	42.7	Moses Malone	Hou	1180	Moses Malone	Hou	14.8	1980/81	N.B.A.
1981/82	N.B.A.	Moses Malone	Hou	42.0	Moses Malone	Hou	1188	Moses Malone	Hou	14.7	1981/82	N.B.A.
1982/83	N.B.A.	Adrian Dantley	Utah	40.3	Moses Malone	Phi	1194	Moses Malone	Phi	15.3	1982/83	N.B.A.
1983/84	N.B.A.	Jeff Ruland	Wash	41.1	Bill Luimbeer	Det	1003	Moses Malone	Phi	13.4	1983/84	N.B.A.
1984/85	N.B.A.	Larry Bird	Bos	39.5	Moses Malone	Phi	1031	Moses Malone	Phi	13.1	1984/85	N.B.A.
1985/86	N.B.A.	Maurice Cheeks	Phi	39.9	Bill Laimbeer	Det	1075	Bill Laimbeer	Det	13.1	1985/86	N.B.A.
1986/87	N.B.A.	Michael Jordan	Chi	40.0	Charles Oakley	Chi	1074	Charles Barkley	Phi	14.6	1986/87	N.B.A.
1987/88	N.B.A.	Michael Jordan	Chi	40.4	Charles Oakley	Chi	1066	Michael Cage	LAC	13.0	1987/88	N.B.A.
1988/89	N.B.A.	Michael Jordan	Chi	40.2	Akeem Olajuwon	Hou	1105	Akeem Olajuwon	Hou	13.5	1988/89	N.B.A.
1989/90	N.B.A.	Rodney McCray	Sac	39.5	Akeem Olajuwon	Hou	1134	Akeem Olajuwon	Hou	14.0	1989/90	N.B.A.

YEARLY INDIVIDUAL LEADERS - REGULAR SEASON

Year	League	3-POINT FIELD GOALS			3-POINT FIELD GOAL PERCENTAGE			Year	League
		Name	Team	3-Pt. FG	Name	Team	%		
1967/68	A.B.A.	Les Selvage	Ana	147	Darel Carrier	Ky	.357	1967/68	A.B.A.
1968/69	A.B.A.	Louie Dampier	Ky	199	Darel Carrier	Ky	.379	1968/69	A.B.A.
1969/70	A.B.A.	Louie Dampier	Ky	198	Darel Carrier	Ky	.375	1969/70	A.B.A.
1970/71	A.B.A.	George Lehmann	Car	154	George Lehmann	Car	.403	1970/71	A.B.A.
1971/72	A.B.A.	Glen Combs	Utah	103	Glen Combs	Utah	.406	1971/72	A.B.A.
1972/73	A.B.A.	Bill Keller	Ind	71	Glen Combs	Utah	.381	1972/73	A.B.A.
1973/74	A.B.A.	Bo Lamar	SD	69	Louie Dampier	Ky	.387	1973/74	A.B.A.
1974/75	A.B.A.	Bill Keller	Ind	80	Billy Shepherd	Mem	.420	1974/75	A.B.A.
1975/76	A.B.A.	Bill Keller	Ind	123	Brian Taylor	NY	.421	1975/76	A.B.A.
1979/80	N.B.A.	Brian Taylor	SD	90	Fred Brown	Sea	.443	1979/80	N.B.A.
1980/81	N.B.A.	Mike Bratz	Cle	57	Brian Taylor	SD	.383	1980/81	N.B.A.
1981/82	N.B.A.	Don Buse	Ind	73	Campy Russell	NY	.439	1981/82	N.B.A.
1982/83	N.B.A.	Mike Dunleavy	SA	67	Mike Dunleavy	SA	.345	1982/83	N.B.A.
1983/84	N.B.A.	Darrell Griffith	Utah	91	Darrell Griffith	Utah	.361	1983/84	N.B.A.
1984/85	N.B.A.	Darrell Griffith	Utah	92	Byron Scott	LAL	.433	1984/85	N.B.A.
1985/86	N.B.A.	Larry Bird	Bos	82	Craig Hodges	Mil	.451	1985/86	N.B.A.
1986/87	N.B.A.	Larry Bird	Bos	90	Kiki Vandeweghe	Port	.481	1986/87	N.B.A.
1987/88	N.B.A.	Danny Ainge	Bos	148	Craig Hodges	Mil-Phoe	.491	1987/88	N.B.A.
1988/89	N.B.A.	Mike Adams	Den	166	Jon Sundvold	Mia	.522	1988/89	N.B.A.
1989/90	N.B.A.	Mike Adams	Den	158	Steve Kerr	Cle	.507	1989/90	N.B.A.

YEARLY INDIVIDUAL LEADERS - REGULAR SEASON

Year	League	BLOCKED SHOTS			STEALS			Year	League
		Name	Team	3-Pt. FG	Name	Team	%		
1972/73	A.B.A.	Artis Gilmore	Ky	259	Billy Cunningham	Car	216	1972/73	A.B.A.
1973/74	N.B.A.	Elmore Smith	LA	393	Larry Steele	Port	217	1973/74	N.B.A.
1973/74	A.B.A.	Caldwell Jones	SD	316	Ted McClain	Car	250	1973/74	A.B.A.
1974/75	N.B.A.	Elmore Smith	LA	216	Rick Barry	GS	228	1974/75	N.B.A.
1974/75	A.B.A.	Artis Gilmore	Ky	258	Brian Taylor	NY	221	1974/75	A.B.A.
1975/76	N.B.A.	Kareem Abdul-Jabbar	LA	338	Slick Watts	Sea	261	1975/76	N.B.A.
1975/76	A.B.A.	Bill Paultz	SA	253	Don Buse	Ind	346	1975/76	A.B.A.
1976/77	N.B.A.	Kareem Abdul-Jabbar	LA	261	Don Buse	Ind	281	1976/77	N.B.A.
1977/78	N.B.A.	George Johnson	NJ	274	Ron Lee	Phoe	225	1977/78	N.B.A.
1978/79	N.B.A.	Kareem Abdul-Jabbar	LA	316	Eddie Jordan	NJ	201	1978/79	N.B.A.
					Norm Nixon	LA	201		
1979/80	N.B.A.	Kareem Abdul-Jabbar	LA	280	Micheal Ray Richardson	NY	265	1979/80	N.B.A.
1980/81	N.B.A.	George Johnson	SA	278	Micheal Ray Richardson	NY	232	1980/81	N.B.A.
1981/82	N.B.A.	George Johnson	SA	234	Micheal Ray Richardson	NY	213	1981/82	N.B.A.
1982/83	N.B.A.	Tree Rollins	Atl	343	Rickey Green	Utah	220	1982/83	N.B.A.
1983/84	N.B.A.	Mark Eaton	Utah	351	Rickey Green	Utah	215	1983/84	N.B.A.
1984/85	N.B.A.	Mark Eaton	Utah	456	Micheal Ray Richardson	NJ	243	1984/85	N.B.A.
1985/86	N.B.A.	Manute Bol	Was	397	Alvin Robertson	SA	301	1985/86	N.B.A.
1986/87	N.B.A.	Mark Eaton	GS	321	Alvin Robertson	SA	260	1986/87	N.B.A.
1987/88	N.B.A.	Mark Eaton	Utah	304	Michael Jordon	Chi	259	1987/88	N.B.A.
1988/89	N.B.A.	Manute Bol	GS	345	John Stockton	Utah	263	1988/89	N.B.A.
1989/90	N.B.A.	Akeem Olajuwon	Hou	376	Michael Jordon	Chi	227	1989/90	N.B.A.

YEARLY INDIVIDUAL LEADERS - PLAYOFFS

Year	League	POINTS PER GAME Name	Team	G	PPG	FIELD GOAL PERCENTAGE (Minimum 20 Attempts) Name	Team	G	FG%	FREE THROW PERCENTAGE (Minimum 20 Attempts) Name	Team	G	FT%	Year	League
1937/38	N.B.L.	Johnny Wooden	Whi	2	16.5										
1938/39	N.B.L.	Leroy Edwards	Osh	5	14.0										
1939/40	N.B.L.	Leroy Edwards	Osh	8	11.6										
1940/41	N.B.L.	Leroy Edwards	Osh	5	14.2										
1941/42	N.B.L.	Jewell Young	Ind	2	17.5										
1942/43	N.B.L.	Bobby McDermott	FtW	6	12.3										
1943/44	N.B.L.	Bobby McDermott	FtW	5	13.4										
1944/45	N.B.L.	Mel Riebe	Cle	2	20.5										
1945/46	N.B.L.	Ed Sadowski	FtW	4	14.3					Bob Carpenter	Osh	5	.810	1945/46	N.B.L.
1946/47	N.B.L.	George Mikan	Chi	11	19.7					Bobby McDermott	Chi	9	.917	1946/47	N.B.L.
1946/47	B.A.A.	Ed Sadowski	Cle	3	23.7	George Munroe	StL	3	.484	Stan Stutz	NY	5	.875	1946/47	B.A.A.
1947/48	N.B.L.	George Mikan	Min	10	24.4					Bobby Wanzer	Roch	11	.857	1947/48	N.B.L.
1947/48	B.A.A.	Joe Fulks	Phi	13	21.7	Buddy Jeannette	Bal	11	.492	Buddy Jeannette	Bal	11	.881	1947/48	B.A.A.
1948/49	N.B.L.	Don Otten	TC	6	15.2					Frankie Brian	And	7	.844	1948/49	N.B.L.
1948/49	B.A.A.	George Mikan	Min	10	30.3	Herm Schaefer	Min	10	.462	Chick Reiser	Bal	3	.900	1948/49	B.A.A.
1949/50	N.B.A.	George Mikan	Min	12	31.3	Alex Groza	Ind	6	.595	Connie Simmons	NY	5	.952	1949/50	N.B.A.
1950/51	N.B.A.	Alex Groza	Ind	3	32.3	Paul Arizin	Phi	2	.519	Vince Boryla	NY	14	.911	1950/51	N.B.A.
1951/52	N.B.A.	Bob Cousy	Bos	3	31.0	Ed Macauley	Bos	3	.551	Bobby Wanzer	Roch	6	.959	1951/52	N.B.A.
1952/53	N.B.A.	Bob Cousy	Bos	6	25.5	Jim Baechtold	Bal	2	.533	Bill Sharman	Bos	6	.938	1952/53	N.B.A.
1953/54	N.B.A.	Bob Cousy	Bos	6	21.0	Bob Harris	Bos	6	.640	Carl Braun	NY	4	.875	1953/54	N.B.A
1954/55	N.B.A.	Bob Cousy	Bos	7	21.7	Frank Ramsey	Bos	7	.519	Bob Cousy	Bos	7	.958	1954/55	N.B.A
1955/56	N.B.A.	Paul Arizin	Phi	10	28.9	Dich Schnittker	Min	3	.565	Bob Cousy	Bos	3	.920	1955/56	N.B.A.
1956/57	N.B.A.	Bob Pettit	StL	10	29.8	Ed Kalafat	Min	5	.583	Bill Sharman	Bos	10	.953	1956/57	N.B.A.
1957/58	N.B.A.	Cliff Hagan	StL	11	27.7	Cliff Hagan	StL	11	.502	Gene Shue	Det	7	.930	1957/58	N.B.A.
1958 59	N.B.A.	Clin Hagan	StL	6	28.5	Dich McGuire	Det	3	.625	Bill Sharman	Bos	11	.966	1958/59	N.B.A
1959/60	N.B.A.	Elgin Baylor	Min	9	33.4	Walter Dukes	Det	2	.516	Dolph Schayes	Syr	3	.933	1959/60	N.B.A.
1960/61	N.B.A.	Elgin Baylor	LA	12	38.1	Bill Sharman	Bos	10	.511	Dolph Schayes	Syr	8	.900	1960/61	N.B.A.
1961/62	N.B.A.	Elgin Baylor	LA	13	38.6	Bob Boozer	Cin	4	.561	Frank Ramsey	Bos	13	.911	1961/62	N.B.A.
1962/63	N.B.A.	Elgin Baylor	LA	13	32.6	Chet Walker	Syr	5	.509	Oscar Robertson	Cin	12	.864	1962/63	N.B.A.
						Leroy Ellis	LA	13	.509	Don Ohl	Det	4	.864		
1963/64	N.B.A.	Wilt Chamberlain	SF	12	34.7	Wilt Chamberlain	SF	12	.543	Rudy LaRusso	LA	5	.864	1963/64	N.B.A.
1964/65	N.B.A.	Jerry West	LA	11	40.6	Darrall Imhoff	LA	11	.542	Adrian Smith	Cin	4	.955	1964/65	N.B.A.
1965/66	N.B.A.	Jerry West	LA	14	34.2	Johnny Green	Bal	3	.588	Adrian Smith	Cin	5	.955	1965/66	N.B.A.
1966/67	N.B.A.	Rich Barry	SF	15	34.7	Bob Boozer	Chi	3	.632	Willis Reed	NY	4	.960	1966/67	N.B.A.
1967/68	N.B.A.	Jerry West	LA	15	30.8	Cazzie Russell	NY	6	.561	Larry Siegfried	Bos	19	.906	1967/68	N.B.A.
1967/68	A.B.A.	Willie Somerset	Hou	3	30.3	Connie Hawkins	Pit	14	.594	Freddie Lewis	Ind	3	.966	1967/68	A.B.A.
1968/69	N.B.A.	Jerry West	LA	18	30.9	Wilt Chamberlain	LA	18	.545	John Havlicek	Bos	18	.855	1968/69	N.B.A
1968/69	A.B.A.	Jimmy Jones	NO	11	30.2	Jimmy Jones	NO	11	.552	Jeff Congdon	Den	7	1.000	1968/69	A.B.A.
1969/70	N.B.A.	Lew Alcindor (Jabbar)	Mil	10	35.2	Lew Alcindor (Jabbar)	Mil	10	.567	Flynn Robinson	Mil	10	.880	1969/70	N.B.A.
1969/70	A.B.A.	Rich Barry	Was	7	40.1	Trooper Washington	LA	17	.624	Bill Keller	Ind	15	.913	1969/70	A.B.A.
1970/71	N.B.A.	Bob Love	Chi	7	26.7	Walt Bellamy	Atl	5	.594	Jeff Mullins	SF	5	.880	1970/71	N.B.A.
1970/71	A.B.A.	Rich Barry	NY	6	33.7	Billy Paultz	NY	6	.592	Bill Melchionni	NY	5	.923	1970/71	A.B.A.
1971/72	N.B.A.	Kareem Abdul-Jabbar	Mil	11	28.7	Mike Riordan	Bal	6	.579	Gail Goodrich	LA	15	.898	1971/72	N.B.A.
1971/72	A.B.A.	Julius Erving	Va	11	33.3	George Irvine	Va	11	.651	Larry Brown	Den	7	.958	1971/72	A.B.A.
1972/73	N.B.A.	Lou Hudson	Atl	6	29.7	Wilt Chamberlain	LA	17	.552	Oscar Robertson	Mil	6	.912	1972/73	N.B.A.
1972/73	A.B.A.	Julius Erving	Va	5	29.6	Billy Paultz	NY	5	.607	Ron Boone	Utah	10	.971	1972/73	A.B.A.
1973/74	N.B.A.	Kareem Abdul-Jabbar	Mil	16	32.2	George Trapp	Det	7	.588	Phil Jackson	NY	12	.900	1973/74	N.B.A.
1973/74	A.B.A.	Julius Erving	NY	14	27.9	Jimmy Jones	Utah	18	.577	Chuck Williams	Ky	8	.958	1973/74	A.B.A.
1974/75	N.B.A.	Bob McAdoo	Buf	7	37.4	Larry McNeill	KCO	6	.647	Rick Barry	GS	17	.918	1974/75	N.B.A.
1974/75	A.B.A.	George Gervin	SA	6	34.0	Moses Malone	Utah	6	.637	Bill Keller	Ind	17	1.000	1974/75	A.B.A.
1975/76	N.B.A.	Fred Brown	Sea	6	28.5	Zaid Abdul-Aziz	Sea	5	.700	Bob Lanier	Det	9	.900	1975/76	N.B.A.
1975/76	A.B.A.	Julius Erving	NY	13	34.7	Artis Gilmore	Ky	10	.608	Chuck Williams	Den	13	.907	1975/76	A.B.A.
1976/77	N.B.A.	Kareem Abdul-Jabbar	LA	11	34.6	Bob Lanier	Det	3	.630	Cal Murphy	Hou	12	.923	1976/77	N.B.A.
1977/78	N.B.A.	George Gervin	SA	6	33.2	Alex English	Mil	9	.615	Henry Bibby	Phi	10	.909	1977/78	N.B.A.
1978/79	N.B.A.	George Gervin	SA	14	28.6	Tom Boswell	Den	3	.600	Ron Boone	LA	8	.952	1978/79	N.B.A.
1979/80	N.B.A.	Kareem Abdul-Jabbar	LA	15	31.9	Jeff Cook	Phoe	7	.667	Calvin Murphy	Hou	7	1.000	1979/80	N.B.A.
										Brian Winters	Mil	7	1.000		
1980/81	N.B.A.	George Gervin	SA	7	27.1	Bob Lanier	Mil	7	.588	Kyle Macy	Phoe	7	1.000	1980/81	N.B.A.
										Dwight Jones	Chi	6	1.000		
1981/82	N.B.A.	George Gervin	SA	9	29.4	Larry Nance	Phoe	7	.610	Kyle Macy	Phoe	7	.938	1981/82	N.B.A.
1982/83	N.B.A.	Kareem Abdul-Jabbar	LA	15	27.1	Jim Paxson	Port	7	.586	Dan Schayes	Den	8	1.000	1982/83	N.B.A.
1983/84	N.B.A.	Adrian Dantley	Utah	11	32.2	Cliff Levingston	Det	5	.789	Larry Spriggs	LA	9	1.000	1983/84	N.B.A.
1984/85	N.B.A.	Alex English	Den	14	30.2	James Worthy	LAL	19	.622	Paul Mokeski	Mil	8	1.000	1984/85	N.B.A.
										John Long	Det	9	1.000		
1985/86	N.B.A.	Dominique Wilkins	Atl	9	28.6	James Donaldson	Dal	10	.750	Larry Bird	Bos	18	.927	1985/86	N.B.A.
1986/87	N.B.A.	Akeem Olajuwon	Hou	10	29.2	Aintoine Carr	Atl	9	.696	Danny Young	Sea	14	1.000	1986/87	N.B.A.
										Thurl Bailey	Utah	5	1.000		
										Jeff Malone	Was	3	1.000		
1987/88	N.B.A.	Michael Jordan	Chi	10	36.3	Kevin McHale	Bos	17	.603	Danny Young	Sea	5	1.000	1987/88	N.B.A.
1988/89	N.B.A.	Michael Jordan	Chi	17	34.8	Tree Rollins	Cle	5	.750	Walter Davis	Den	3	1.000	1988/89	N.B.A.
1089/90	N.B.A.	Michael Jordan	Chi	16	36.7	Kevin McHale	Bos	5	.609	Mark Price	Cle	5	1.000	1989/90	N.B.A.

YEARLY INDIVIDUAL LEADERS - PLAYOFFS

Year	League	FIELD GOALS Name	Team	G	FG	FREE THROWS Name	Team	G	FT	POINTS Name	Team	G	Pts.	Year	League
1937/38	N.B.L.	Leroy Edwards	Osh	5	24	Leroy Edwards	Osh	5	21	Leroy Edwards	Osh	5	69	1937/38	N.B.L.
1938/39	N.B.L.	Leroy Edwards	Osh	5	23	Leroy Edwards	Osh	5	24	Leroy Edwards	Osh	5	70	1938/39	N.B.L.
1939/40	N.B.L.	Leroy Edwards	Osh	8	33	Leroy Edwards	Osh	8	27	Leroy Edwards	Osh	8	93	1939/40	N.B.L.
1940/41	N.B.L.	Leroy Edwards	Osh	5	23	Leroy Edwards	Osh	5	25	Leroy Edwards	Osh	5	71	1940/41	N.B.L.
						Bob Carpenter	Osh	5	25						
1941/42	N.B.L.	Leroy Edwards	Osh	5	30	Leroy Edwards	Osh	5	23	Leroy Edwards	Osh	5	83	1941/42	N.B.L.
1942/43	N.B.L.	Bobby McDermott	FtW	6	29	Curly Armstrong	FtW	6	19	Bobby McDermott	FtW	6	74	1942/43	N.B.L.
1943/44	N.B.L.	Bobby McDermott	FtW	5	27	Ed Dancker	Sheb	6	15	Bobby McDermott	FtW	5	67	1943/44	N.B.L.
1944/45	N.B.L.	Bobby McDermott	FtW	7	45	Dick Schulz	Sheb	8	32	Ed Dancker	Sheb	8	109	1944/45	N.B.L.
1945/46	N.B.L.	George Glamach	Roch	7	34	Bob Davies	Roch	7	30	George Glamach	Roch	7	88	1945/46	N.B.L.
1946/47	N.B.L.	George Mikan	Chi	7	72	George Mikan	Chi	11	73	George Mikan	Chi	11	217	1946/47	N.B.L.
1946/47	B.A.A.	Joe Fulks	Phi	10	74	Joe Fulks	Phi	10	74	Joe Fulks	Phi	10	222	1946/47	B.A.A.
1947/48	N.B.L.	George Mikan	Min	10	88	George Mikan	Min	10	68	George Mikan	Min	10	244	1947/48	N.B.L.
1947/48	B.A.A.	Joe Fulks	Phi	13	92	Joe Fulks	Phi	13	98	Joe Fulks	Phi	13	282	1947/48	B.A.A.
1948/49	N.B.L.	Boag Johnson	And	7	34	Don Otten	TC	6	43	Gene Englund	Osh	7	95	1948/49	N.B.L.
1948/49	B.A.A.	George Mikan	Min	10	103	George Mikan	Min	10	97	George Mikan	Min	10	303	1948/49	B.A.A.
1949/50	N.B.A.	George Mikan	Min	12	121	George Mikan	Min	12	134	George Mikan	Min	12	376	1949/50	N.B.A.
1950/51	N.B.A.	Arnie Risen	Roch	14	93	Arnie Risen	Roch	14	87	Arnie Risen	Roch	14	273	1950/51	N.B.A.
1951/52	N.B.A.	George Mikan	Min	13	99	George Mikan	Min	13	109	George Mikan	Min	13	307	1951/52	N.B.A.
1952/53	N.B.A.	George Mikan	Min	12	78	George Mikan	Min	12	82	George Mikan	Min	12	238	1952/53	N.B.A.
1953/54	N.B.A.	George Mikan	Min	13	87	Dolph Schayes	Syr	13	80	George Mikan	Min	13	252	1953/54	N.B.A.
1954/55	N.B.A.	Dolph Schayes	Syr	11	60	Dolph Schayes	Syr	11	89	Dolph Schayes	Syr	11	209	1954/55	N.B.A.
1955/56	N.B.A.	Paul Arizin	Phi	10	103	Paul Arizin	Phi	10	83	Paul Arizin	Phi	10	289	1955/56	N.B.A.
1956/57	N.B.A.	Bob Pettit	StL	10	98	Bob Pettit	StL	10	102	Bob Petit	StL	10	298	1956/57	N.B.A.
1957/58	N.B.A.	Cliff Hagan	StL	11	111	Bob Pettit	StL	11	86	Cliff Hagan	StL	11	305	1957/58	N.B.A.
1958/59	N.B.A.	Elgin Baylor	Min	13	122	Dolph Schayes	Syr	9	98	Elgin Baylor	Min	13	331	1958/59	N.B.A.
1959/60	N.B.A.	Bob Pettit	StL	14	129	Bob Pettit	StL	14	107	Bob Pettit	StL	14	365	1959/60	N.B.A.
1960/61	N.B.A.	Elgin Baylor	LA	12	170	Elgin Baylor	LA	12	117	Elgin Baylor	LA	12	457	1960/61	N.B.A.
1961/62	N.B.A.	Elgin Baylor	LA	13	186	Elgin Baylor	LA	13	130	Elgin Baylor	LA	13	502	1961/62	N.B.A.
1962/63	N.B.A.	Elgin Baylor	LA	13	160	Oscar Robertson	Cin	12	133	Elgin Baylor	LA	13	424	1962/63	N.B.A.
1963/64	N.B.A.	Wilt Chamberlain	SF	12	175	Oscar Robertson	Cin	10	109	Wilt Chamberlain	SF	12	416	1963/64	N.B.A.
1964/65	N.B.A.	Jerry West	LA	11	155	Jerry West	LA	11	137	Jerry West	LA	11	447	1964/65	N.B.A.
1965/66	N.B.A.	Jerry West	LA	14	185	Sam Jones	Bos	17	114	Jerry West	LA	14	479	1965/66	N.B.A.
1966/67	N.B.A.	Rick Barry	SF	15	197	Rick Barry	SF	15	127	Rick Barry	SF	15	521	1966/67	N.B.A.
1967/68	N.B.A.	John Havlicek	Bos	19	184	Jerry West	LA	15	132	John Havlicek	Bos	19	493	1967/68	N.B.A.
1967/68	A.B.A.	Connie Hawkins	Pit	14	145	Connie Hawkins	Pit	14	129	Connie Hawkins	Pit	14	419	1967/68	A.B.A.
1968/69	N.B.A.	Jerry West	LA	18	196	Jerry West	LA	18	164	Jerry West	LA	18	556	1968/69	N.B.A.
1968/69	A.B.A.	Roger Brown	Ind	17	169	Warren Armstrong	Oak	16	135	Warren Armstrong	Oak	16	460	1968/69	A.B.A.
1969/70	N.B.A.	Jerry West	LA	18	196	Jerry West	LA	18	170	Jerry West	LA	18	562	1969/70	N.B.A.
1969/70	A.B.A.	Spencer Haywood	Den	12	185	Mack Calvin	LA	17	122	Spencer Haywood	Den	12	440	1969/70	A.B.A.
1970/71	N.B.A.	Lew Alcindor (Jabbar)	Mil	14	152	Earl Monroe	Bal	18	107	Earl Monroe	Bal	18	397	1970/71	N.B.A.
1970/71	A.B.A.	Dan Issel	Ky	19	206	Dan Issel	Ky	19	122	Dan Issel	Ky	19	534	1970/71	A.B.A.
1971/72	N.B.A.	Walt Frazier	NY	16	148	Gail Goodrich	LA	15	97	Walt Frazier	NY	16	388	1971/72	N.B.A.
1971/72	A.B.A.	Rick Barry	NY	18	203	Rick Barry	NY	18	125	Rick Barry	NY	18	554	1971/72	A.B.A.
1972/73	N.B.A.	Jerry West	LA	17	151	Jerry West	LA	17	99	Jerry West	LA	17	401	1972/73	N.B.A.
1972/73	A.B.A.	Dan Issel	Ky	19	198	Dan Issel	Ky	19	124	Dan Issel	Ky	19	521	1972/73	A.B.A.
1973/74	N.B.A.	Kareem Abdul-Jabbar	Mil	16	224	John Havlicek	Bos	18	89	Kareem Abdul-Jabbar	Mil	16	516	1973/74	N.B.A.
1973/74	A.B.A.	Willie Wise	Utah	18	171	George McGinnis	Ind	14	96	Willie Wise	Utah	18	420	1973/74	A.B.A.
1974/75	N.B.A.	Rick Barry	GS	17	189	Phil Chenier	Was	17	102	Rick Barry	GS	17	479	1974/75	N.B.A.
1974/75	A.B.A.	George McGinnis	Ind	18	213	George McGinnis	Ind	18	132	George McGinnis	Ind	18	581	1974/75	A.B.A.
1975/76	N.B.A.	Jo-Jo White	Bos	18	165	Jo-Jo White	Bos	18	78	Jo-Jo White	Bos	18	408	1975/76	N.B.A.
1975/76	A.B.A.	Julius Erving	NY	18	160	Julius Erving	NY	18	127	Julius Erving	NY	13	451	1975/76	A.B.A.
1976/77	N.B.A.	Julius Erving	Phi	19	204	Julius Erving	Phi	19	110	Julius Erving	NY	19	518	1976/77	N.B.A.
1977/78	N.B.A.	Elvin Hayes	Was	21	189	Dennis Johnson	Sea	22	112	Elvin Hayes	Was	21	457	1977/78	N.B.A.
1978/79	N.B.A.	Gus Williams	Sea	17	181	Bob Dandrige	Was	19	91	Gus Williams	Sea	17	452	1978/79	N.B.A.
1979/80	N.B.A.	Kareem Abdul-Jabbar	LA	15	198	Julius Erving	Phi	18	108	Kareem Abdul-Jabbar	LA	15	479	1979/80	N.B.A.
1980/81	N.B.A.	Moses Malone	Hou	21	207	Moses Malone	Hou	21	148	Moses Malone	Hou	21	562	1980/81	N.B.A.
1981/82	N.B.A.	Andrew Toney	Phi	21	185	Julius Erving	Phi	21	124	Julius Erving	NY	21	461	1981/82	N.B.A.
1982/83	N.B.A.	Kareem Abdul-Jabbar	LA	15	163	Moses Malone	Phi	13	86	Kareem Abdul-Jabbar	LA	15	406	1982/83	N.B.A.
1983/84	N.B.A.	Larry Bird	Bos	23	229	Larry Bird	Bos	23	167	Larry Bird	Bos	23	632	1983/84	N.B.A.
1984/85	N.B.A.	Larry Bird	Bos	20	196	Larry Bird	Bos	20	121	Larry Bird	Bos	20	520	1984/85	N.B.A.
						Kevin McHale	Bos	21	121						
1985/86	N.B.A.	Akeem Olajuwon	Hou	20	205	Akeem Olajuwon	Hou	20	127	Akeem Olajuwon	Hou	20	537	1985/86	N.B.A.
1986/87	N.B.A.	Larry Bird	Bos	23	216	Larry Bird	Bos	23	176	Larry Bird	Bos	23	622	1986/87	N.B.A.
1987/88	N.B.A.	James Worthy	LAL	24	204	Adrian Dantley	Det	23	140	James Worthy	LAL	24	506	1987/88	N.B.A.
1988/89	N.B.A.	Michael Jordan	Chi	17	199	Michael Jordan	Chi	17	183	Michael Jordan	Chi	17	591	1988/89	N.B.A.
1989/90	N.B.A.	Clyde Drexler	Port	21	172	Terry Porter	Port	21	139	Michael Jordan	Chi	16	587	1989/90	N.B.A.

YEARLY INDIVIDUAL LEADERS - PLAYOFFS

Years	League	ASSISTS Name	Team	G	Ass.	ASSISTS PER GAME Name	Team	G	Ass./G
1946/47	B.A.A.	Howie Dallmar	Phi	10	16	Ray Wertis	Cle	3	2.0
1947/48	B.A.A.	Howie Dallmar	Phi	13	37	Howie Dallmar	Phi	13	2.8
1948/49	B.A.A.	Jim Pollard	Min	10	39	Andy Phillip	Chi	2	6.0
1949/50	N.B.A.	Jim Pollard	Min	12	56	Andy Phillip	Chi	2	6.0
1950/51	N.B.A.	Dick McGuire	NY	14	78	George Senesky	Phi	2	7.5
1951/52	N.B.A.	Dick McGuire	NY	14	90	Andy Phillip	Phi	3	7.3
1952/53	N.B.A.	Dick McGuire	NY	11	70	Dick McGuire	NY	11	6.4
1953/54	N.B.A.	Slater Martin	Min	13	60	Bob Cousy	Bos	6	6.3
		Paul Seymour	Syr	13	60				
1954/55	N.B.A.	Andy Phillip	FtW	11	78	Bob Cousy	Bos	7	9.3
1955/56	N.B.A.	George King	Syr	8	60	Bob Cousy	Bos	3	8.7
1956/57	N.B.A.	Bob Cousy	Bos	10	93	Bob Cousy	Bos	10	9.3
1957/58	N.B.A.	Bob Cousy	Bos	11	82	Bob Cousy	Bos	11	7.5
1958 59	N.B.A.	Bob Cousy	Bos	11	119	Bob Cousy	Bos	11	10.8
1959/60	N.B.A.	Bob Cousy	Bos	13	116	Bob Cousy	Bos	13	8.9
1960/61	N.B.A.	Bob Cousy	Bos	10	91	Bob Cousy	Bos	10	9.1
1961/62	N.B.A.	Bob Cousy	Bos	14	123	Oscar Robertson	Cin	4	11.0
1962/63	N.B.A.	Bob Cousy	Bos	13	116	Oscar Robertson	Cin	12	9.0
1963/64	N.B.A.	Guy Rodgers	SF	12	90	Oscar Robertson	Cin	10	8.4
1964/65	N.B.A.	Bill Russell	Bos	12	76	Oscar Robertson	Cin	4	12.0
1965/66	N.B.A.	Bill Russell	Bos	17	85	Richie Guerin	StL	10	7.9
1966/67	N.B.A.	Wilt Chamberlain	Phi	15	135	Oscar Robertson	Cin	4	11.3
1967/68	N.B.A.	John Havlicek	Bos	19	142	Lenny Wilkens	StL	6	7.8
1967/68	A.B.A.	Larry Brown	NO	17	129	Larry Brown	NO	17	7.6
1968/69	N.B.A.	Jerry West	LA	18	135	Walt Frazier	NY	10	9.1
1968/69	A.B.A.	Larry Brown	Oak	16	87	Larry Brown	Oak	16	5.4
1969/70	N.B.A.	Walt Frazier	NY	19	156	Jerry West	LA	18	8.4
1969/70	A.B.A.	Mack Calvin	LA	17	101	Larry Brown	Was	7	9.7
1970/71	N.B.A.	Oscar Robertson	Mil	14	124	Oscar Robertson	Mil	14	8.9
1970/71	A.B.A.	Louie Dampier	Ky	19	179	Louie Dampier	Ky	19	9.4
1971/72	N.B.A.	Jerry West	LA	15	134	Jerry West	LA	15	8.9
1971/72	A.B.A.	Freddie Lewis	Ind	20	87	Louie Dampier	Ky	6	7.5
1972 73	N.B.A.	Jerry West	LA	17	132	Jerry West	LA	17	7.8
1972 73	A.B.A.	Freddie Lewis	Ind	18	91	Bill Melchionni	NY	5	6.2
1973/74	N.B.A.	Oscar Robertson	Mil	16	149	Oscar Robertson	Mil	16	9.3
1973/74	A.B.A.	Ron Boone	Utah	18	109	Ron Boone	Utah	18	6.1
1974/75	N.B.A.	Kevin Porter	Was	17	124	Dave Bing	Det	3	9.7
1974/75	A.B.A.	George McGinnis	Ind	18	148	James Silas	SA	6	10.0
1975/76	N.B.A.	Jo-Jo White	Bos	18	98	Randy Smith	Buf	9	8.6
1975/76	A.B.A.	Louie Dampier	Ky	10	77	Don Buse	Ind	3	8.7
1976/77	N.B.A.	Bill Walton	Port	19	104	Norm VanLier	Chi	3	9.7
1977/78	N.B.A.	Tom Henderson	Was	21	106	Quinn Buckner	Mil	9	6.9
1978/79	N.B.A.	Tom Henderson	Was	19	107	Norm Nixon	LA	8	11.8
1979/80	N.B.A.	Magic Johnson	LA	16	151	Magic Johnson	LA	16	9.4
1980/81	N.B.A.	Maurice Cheeks	Phi	16	116	Maurice Cheeks	Phi	16	7.3
1981/82	N.B.A.	Maurice Cheeks	Phi	21	172	Johnny Moore	SA	9	10.3
1982/83	N.B.A.	Magic Johnson	LA	15	192	Johnny Moore	SA	11	14.6
1983/84	N.B.A.	Magic Johnson	LA	21	284	Magic Johnson	LA	21	13.5
1984/85	N.B.A.	Magic Johnson	LAL	19	289	Magic Johnson	LAL	19	15.2
1985/86	N.B.A.	Magic Johnson	LAL	14	211	Magic Johnson	LAL	14	15.1
1986/87	N.B.A.	Magic Johnson	LAL	18	219	Magic Johnson	LAL	18	12.2
1987/88	N.B.A.	Magic Johnson	LAL	24	303	John Stockton	Utah	11	14.8
1988/89	N.B.A.	Magic Johnson	LAL	14	165	John Stockton	Utah	3	13.7
1989/90	N.B.A.	Kevin Johnson	Phoe	16	176	John Stockton	Utah	5	15.0

PERSONAL FOULS Name	Team	G	PF	Year	League
Chuck Gilmur	Chi	11	45	1946/47	B.A.A.
Joe Fulks	Phi	13	55	1947/48	B.A.A.
Howie Dallmar	Phi	13	55		
Kleggie Hermsen	Was	11	53	1948/49	B.A.A.
Arnie Ferrin	Min	12	51	1949/50	N.B.A.
Arnie Johnson	Roch	14	68	1950/51	N.B.A.
Sweetwater Clifton	NY	14	67	1951/52	N.B.A.
Vern Mikkelsen	Min	12	59	1952/53	N.B.A.
Whitey Skoog	Min	13	60	1953/54	N.B.A.
Dolph Schayes	Syr	11	48	1954/55	N.B.A.
Tom Gola	Phi	10	47	1955/56	N.B.A.
Arnie Risen	Bos	10	48	1956/57	N.B.A.
Jack McMahon	StL	10	48		
Tom Heinsohn	Bos	11	52	1957/58	N.B.A.
Vern Mikkelsen	Min	13	54	1958/59	N.B.A.
Gene Conley	Bos	13	59	1959/60	N.B.A.
Ray Felix	LA	12	52	1960/61	N.B.A.
Satch Sanders	Bos	14	65	1961/62	N.B.A.
Satch Sanders	Bos	13	61	1962/63	N.B.A.
Zelmo Beaty	StL	12	56	1963/64	N.B.A.
Satch Sanders	Bos	12	58	1964/65	N.B.A.
Satch Sanders	Bos	17	70	1965/66	N.B.A.
Tom Meschery	SF	15	68	1966/67	N.B.A.
Larry Siegfried	Bos	19	75	1967/68	N.B.A.
Jackie Moreland	NO	17	74	1967/68	A.B.A.
Em Bryant	Bos	18	75	1968/69	N.B.A.
Roger Brown	Ind	17	86	1968/69	A.B.A.
Dick Garrett	LA	18	68	1969/70	N.B.A.
				1969/70	A.B.A.
John Tresvant	Bal	18	64	1970/71	N.B.A.
Cincy Powell	Ky	19	83	1970/71	A.B.A.
Bill Bradley	NY	16	66	1971/72	N.B.A.
Mel Daniels	Ind	20	85	1971/72	A.B.A.
Bill Bridges	LA	17	68	1972/73	N.B.A.
George McGinnis	Ind	18	78	1972/73	A.B.A.
Dave Cowens	Bos	18	85	1973/74	N.B.A.
Gerald Govan	Utah	18	65	1973/74	A.B.A.
Kevin Porter	Was	17	73	1974/75	N.B.A.
George McGinnis	Ind	18	88	1974/75	A.B.A.
Charlie Scott	Bos	18	97	1975/76	N.B.A.
Dan Issel	Den	13	62	1975/76	A.B.A.
Bob Gross	Port	19	84	1976/77	N.B.A.
Jack Sikma	Sea	22	101	1977/78	N.B.A.
Lonnie Shelton	Sea	17	80	1978/79	N.B.A.
Darryl Dawkins	Phi	18	75	1979/80	N.B.A.
Caldwell Jones	Phi	18	75		
Robert Reid	Hou	21	80	1980/81	N.B.A.
Darryl Dawkins	Phi	21	94	1981/82	N.B.A.
Kareem Abdul-Jabbar	LA	15	61	1982/83	N.B.A.
Robert Parish	Bos	23	100	1983/84	N.B.A.
Danny Ainge	Bos	21	76	1984/85	N.B.A.
Akeem Olajuwon	Hou	20	87	1985/86	N.B.A.
Robert Parish	Bos	21	79	1986/87	N.B.A.
John Salley	Det	23	88	1987/88	N.B.A.
Bill Cartwright	Chi	17	70	1988/89	N.B.A.
Jerome Kersey	Port	21	87	1989/90	N.B.A.

YEARLY INDIVIDUAL LEADERS - PLAYOFFS

		MINUTES PER GAME				REBOUNDS				REBOUNDS PER GAME					
Years	League	Name	Team	G	Min/G	Name	Team	G	Reb.	Name	Team	G	Reb/G	Year	League
1950/51	N.B.A.					Arnie Risen	Roch	14	196	Dolph Schayes	Syr	7	14.6	1950/51	N.B.A.
1951/52	N.B.A.	Joe Graboski	Ind	2	48.0	George Mikan	Min	13	207	George Mikan	Min	13	15.9	1951/52	N.B.A.
1952/53	N.B.A.	Paul Seymour	Syr	2	56.0	George Mikan	Min	12	185	Eddie Miller	Bal	2	18.0	1952/53	N.B.A.
1953/54	N.B.A.	Bob Cousy	Bos	6	43.3	George Mikan	Min	13	171	Harry Gallatin	NY	4	15.3	1953/54	N.B.A.
1954/55	N.B.A.	Slater Martin	Min	7	45.0	Dolph Schayes	Syr	11	141	Harry Gallatin	NY	3	14.7	1954/55	N.B.A.
1955/56	N.B.A.	Jack Coleman	StL	8	41.4	Neil Johnston	Phi	10	143	Arnie Risen	Bos	3	14.7	1955/56	N.B.A.
1956/57	N.B.A.	Joe Graboski	Phi	2	45.5	Bill Russell	Bos	10	244	Bill Russell	Bos	10	24.4	1956/57	N.B.A.
1957/58	N.B.A.	Larry Costello	Syr	3	44.7	Bill Russell	Bos	9	221	Bill Russell	Bos	9	24.6	1957/58	N.B.A.
1958 59	N.B.A.	Bill Russell	Bos	11	45.1	Bill Russell	Bos	11	305	Bill Russell	Bos	11	27.7	1958/59	N.B.A.
1959/60	N.B.A.	Wilt Chamberlain	Phi	9	46.1	Bill Russell	Bos	13	336	Bill Russell	Bos	13	25.8	1959/60	N.B.A.
1960/61	N.B.A.	Wilt Chamberlain	Phi	3	48.0	Bill Russell	Bos	10	299	Bill Russell	Bos	10	29.9	1960/61	N.B.A.
1961/62	N.B.A.	Wilt Chamberlain	Phi	12	48.0	Bill Russell	Bos	14	370	Wilt Chamberlain	Phi	12	26.6	1961/62	N.B.A.
1962/63	N.B.A.	Oscar Robertson	Cin	12	47.5	Bill Russell	Bos	13	326	Bill Russell	Bos	13	25.1	1962/63	N.B.A.
1963/64	N.B.A.	Oscar Robertson	Cin	10	47.1	Wilt Chamberlain	SF	12	302	Bill Russell	Bos	10	27.2	1963/64	N.B.A.
1964/65	N.B.A.	Oscar Robertson	Cin	4	48.8	Bill Russell	Bos	12	302	Wilt Chamberlain	Phi	11	27.2	1964/65	N.B.A.
		Jerry Lucas	Cin	4	48.8										
1965/66	N.B.A.	Bill Russell	Bos	17	47.9	Bill Russell	Bos	17	428	Wilt Chamberlain	Phi	5	30.2	1965/66	N.B.A.
1966/67	N.B.A.	Wilt Chamberlain	Phi	15	47.9	Wilt Chamberlain	Phi	15	437	Wilt Chamberlain	Phi	15	29.1	1966/67	N.B.A.
1967/68	N.B.A.	Wilt Chamberlain	Phi	13	48.5	Bill Russell	Bos	19	434	Wilt Chamberlain	Phi	13	24.7	1967/68	N.B.A.
1967/68	A.B.A.	Jimmy Jones	NO	17	46.2	Trooper Washington	Pit	15	261	Trooper Washington	Pit	15	17.4	1967/68	A.B.A.
1968/69	N.B.A.	John Havlicek	Bos	18	47.2	Wilt Chamberlain	LA	18	444	Wilt Chamberlain	LA	18	24.7	1968/69	N.B.A.
1968/69	A.B.A.	Louie Dampier	Ky	7	46.1	Mel Daniels	Ind	17	237	Red Robbins	NO	11	15.9	1968/69	A.B.A.
1969/70	N.B.A.	Wilt Chamberlain	LA	18	47.3	Wilt Chamberlain	LA	18	399	Wes Unseld	Bal	7	23.6	1969/70	N.B.A.
1969/70	A.B.A.	Spencer Haywood	Den	12	47.3	Mel Daniels	Ind	15	265	Spencer Haywood	Den	12	19.8	1969/70	A.B.A.
1970/71	N.B.A.	Bob Love	Chi	7	47.1	Wes Unseld	Bal	18	339	Bill Bridges	Atl	5	20.8	1970/71	N.B.A.
1970/71	A.B.A.	Rick Barry	NY	6	47.8	Zelmo Beaty	Utah	18	263	Mel Daniels	Ind	11	19.2	1970/71	A.B.A.
1971/72	N.B.A.	John Havlicek	Bos	11	47.0	Wilt Chamberlain	LA	15	315	Wilt Chamberlain	LA	15	21.0	1971/72	N.B.A.
1971/72	A.B.A.	Artis Gilmore	Ky	6	47.5	Mel Daniels	Ind	20	302	Julius Erving	Va	11	20.4	1971/72	A.B.A.
1972/73	N.B.A.	Wilt Chamberlain	LA	17	47.1	Wilt Chamberlain	LA	17	383	Wilt Chamberlain	LA	17	22.5	1972/73	N.B.A.
1972/73	A.B.A.	Julius Erving	Va	5	43.8	Artis Gilmore	Ky	19	260	Mel Daniels	Ind	18	13.8	1972/73	A.B.A.
1973/74	N.B.A.	Kareem Abdul-Jabbar	Mil	16	47.4	Kareem Abdul-Jabbar	Mil	16	253	Elvin Hayes	Cap	7	15.9	1973/74	N.B.A.
1973/74	A.B.A.	Caldwell Jones	SD	6	46.2	Gerald Govan	Utah	18	246	Artis Gilmore	Ky	8	18.6	1973/74	A.B.A.
1974/75	N.B.A.	Bob McAdoo	Buf	7	46.7	Wes Unseld	Was	17	276	Dave Cowens	Bos	11	16.5	1974/75	N.B.A.
1974/75	A.B.A.	George Gervin	SA	6	46.0	George McGinnis	Ind	18	286	Artis Gilmore	Ky	15	17.6	1974/75	A.B.A.
1975/76	N.B.A.	Bob McAdoo	Buf	9	45.1	Dave Cowens	Bos	18	296	Dave Cowens	Bos	18	16.4	1975/76	N.B.A.
1975/76	A.B.A.	Billy Knight	Ind	3	47.7	Julius Erving	NY	13	164	Artis Gilmore	Ky	10	15.2	1975/76	A.B.A.
1976/77	N.B.A.	Elvin Hayes	Was	9	45.0	Bill Walton	Port	19	288	Kareem Abdul-Jabbar	LA	11	17.7	1976/77	N.B.A.
1977/78	N.B.A.	Kareem Abdul-Jabbar	LA	3	44.7	Marvin Webster	Sea	22	289	Elvin Hayes	Was	21	13.3	1977/78	N.B.A.
1978/79	N.B.A.	Kareem Abdul-Jabbar	LA	8	45.9	Elvin Hayes	Was	19	266	Elvin Hayes	Was	19	14.0	1978/79	N.B.A.
1979/80	N.B.A.	Marques Johnson	Mil	7	43.3	Caldwell Jones	Phi	28	185	Moses Malone	Hou	7	13.9	1979/80	N.B.A.
1980/81	N.B.A.	Moses Malone	Hou	21	45.5	Moses Malone	Hou	21	305	Moses Malone	Hou	21	14.5	1980/81	N.B.A.
1981/82	N.B.A.	Moses Malone	Hou	3	45.3	Caldwell Jones	Phi	21	189	Larry Bird	Bos	12	12.5	1981/82	N.B.A.
1982/83	N.B.A.	Magic Johnson	LA	15	42.9	Moses Malone	Phi	13	206	Moses Malone	Phi	13	15.8	1982/83	N.B.A.
1983/84	N.B.A.	Buck Williams	NJ	11	43.0	Larry Bird	Bos	23	252	Buck Williams	NJ	11	14.1	1983/84	N.B.A.
1984/85	N.B.A.	Michael Jordan	Chi	4	42.8	Robert Parish	Bos	21	219	Charles Barkley	Phi	13	11.1	1984/85	N.B.A.
1985/86	N.B.A.	Orlando Woolridge	Chi	3	45.0	Akeem Olajuwon	Hou	20	236	Charles Barkley	Phi	12	15.8	1985/86	N.B.A.
		Michael Jordan	Chi	3	45.0										
1986/87	N.B.A.	Larry Bird	Bos	23	44.1	Larry Bird	Bos	23	231	Charles Oakley	Chi	3	15.3	1986/87	N.B.A.
1987/88	N.B.A.	Karl Malone	Utah	11	44.9	Bill Laimbeer	Det	23	221	Akeem Olajuwon	Hou	4	16.8	1987/88	N.B.A.
1988/89	N.B.A.	John Stockton	Utah	3	46.3	Dennis Rodman	Det	17	170	Akeem Olajuwon	Hou	4	13.0	1988/89	N.B.A.
1989/90	N.B.A.	Eric Floyd	Hou	4	43.0	Bill Laimbeer	Det	20	211	Charles Barkley	Phi	10	15.5	1989/90	N.B.A.
		Roy Tarpley	Dal	3	43.0										

YEARLY INDIVIDUAL LEADERS - PLAYOFFS

3-POINT FIELD GOALS

Years	League	Name	Team	G	3-Pt. FG
1967/68	A.B.A.	Chico Vaughn	Pit	15	24
1968/69	A.B.A.	Louie Dampier	Ky	7	16
1969/70	A.B.A.	Louie Dampier	Ky	12	25
1970/71	A.B.A.	Bill Keller	Ind	11	23
1971/72	A.B.A.	Rick Barry	NY	18	23
1972/73	A.B.A.	Wendell Ladner	Ky	19	14
1973/74	A.B.A.	Bill Keller	Ind	12	15
1974/75	A.B.A.	George McGinnis	Ind	18	23
1975/76	A.B.A.	Brian Taylor	NY	13	9
1979/80	N.B.A.	Fred Brown	Sea	15	10
1980/81	N.B.A.	Scott Wedman	KC	15	9
1981/82	N.B.A.	Mike Bratz	SA	9	5
		Frank Johnson	Was	7	5
		Andrew Toney	Phi	21	5
		Brian Winters	Mil	6	5
1982/83	N.B.A.	Johnny Moore	SA	11	9
1983/84	N.B.A.	Mike Dunleavey	Mil	15	18
1984/85	N.B.A.	Mike Evans	Den	15	17
1985/86	N.B.A.	Larry Bird	Bos	18	23
1986/87	N.B.A.	Michael Cooper	LAL	18	34
1987/88	N.B.A.	Michael Cooper	LAL	24	25
1988/89	N.B.A.	Craig Hodges	Chi	17	35
1989/90	N.B.A.	Terry Porter	Port	21	40

3-POINT FIELD GOAL PERCENTAGE

Name	Team	G	%	Year	League
Louie Dampier	Ky	5	.405	1967/68	A.B.A.
Darel Carrier	Ky	7	.500	1968/69	A.B.A.
Ben Warley	Den	10	.438	1969/70	A.B.A.
Rick Barry	NY	6	.519	1970/71	A.B.A.
Louie Dampier	Ky	6	.478	1971/72	A.B.A.
Louie Dampier	Ky	12	.455	1972/73	A.B.A.
Rick Mount	Ky	19	.455		
Gene Littles	Car	4	.571	1973/74	A.B.A.
Johnny Roche	Utah	6	.533	1974/75	A.B.A.
Louie Dampier	Ky	10	.500	1975/76	A.B.A.
Brian Winters	Mil	7	.429	1979/80	N.B.A.
Scott Wedman	KC	15	.281	1980/81	N.B.A.
Brian Winters	Mil	6	.500	1981/82	N.B.A.
Johnny Moore	SA	11	.529	1982/83	N.B.A.
Kyle Macy	Phoe	17	.455	1983/84	N.B.A.
Mike McGee	LAL	17	.500	1984/85	N.B.A.
Brad Davis	Dal	10	.667	1985/86	N.B.A.
Michael Cooper	LAL	18	.486	1986/87	N.B.A.
Bob Hansen	Utah	11	.528	1987/88	N.B.A.
Eric Floyd	Hou	4	.533	1988/89	N.B.A.
Darrell Griffith	Utah	5	.556	1989/90	N.B.A.

YEARLY TEAM LEADERS - REGULAR SEASON

Year	League	WINNING PCT. Team	Pct.	HOME-WINNING PCT. Team	Pct.	ROAD-WINNING PCT. Team	Pct.
1937/38	N.B.L.	Oshkosh	.857	Whiting	1.000	Oshkosh	.667
1938/39	N.B.L.	Akron Firestone	.889	Akron Firestone	.846	Akron Firestone	.929
1939/40	N.B.L.	Akron Firestone	.667	Detroit	.857	Akron Firestone	.571
				Oshkosh	.857		
1940/41	N.B.L.	Oshkosh	.750	Oshkosh	.917	Oshkosh	.583
1941/42	N.B.L.	Oshkosh	.833	Oshkosh	.929	Oshkosh	.700
1942/43	N.B.L.	Fort Wayne	.739	Fort Wayne	.833	Fort Wayne	.636
1943/44	N.B.L.	Fort Wayne	.818	Fort Wayne	.818	Fort Wayne	.818
1944/45	N.B.L.	Fort Wayne	.833	Fort Wayne	.933	Fort Wayne	.733
1945/46	N.B.L.	Fort Wayne	.765	Fort Wayne	.824	Fort Wayne	.706
				Rochester	.824		
1946/47	N.B.L.	Rochester	.705	Sheboygan	.909	Rochester	.545
1946/47	B.A.A.	Washington	.817	Washington	.967	Washington	.667
1947/48	N.B.L.	Rochester	.733	Anderson	.931	Rochester	.607
1947/48	B.A.A.	St.Louis	.604	Washington	.792	Chicago	.583
						New York	.583
1948/49	N.B.L.	Anderson	.766	Anderson	.941	anderson	.567
1948/49	B.A.A.	Rochester	.750	Minneapolis	.897	Rochester	.667
1949/50	N.B.A.	Syracuse	.797	Rochester	.971	Syracuse	.556
1950/51	N.B.A.	Minneapolis	.647	Minneapolis	.906	Minneapolis	.364
				Philadelphia	.906		
1951/52	N.B.A.	Rochester	.621	Rochester	.848	Minneapolis	.406
1952/53	N.B.A.	Minneapolis	.686	Syracuse	.941	New York	.517
1953/54	N.B.A.	Minneapolis	.639	Syracuse	.844	New York	.536
1954/55	N.B.A.	Syracuse	.597	Boston	.800	Minneapolis	.417
		Fort Wayne	.597				
1955/56	N.B.A.	Philadelphia	.625	Philadelphia	.750	Syracuse	.517
1956/57	N.B.A.	Boston	.611	Boston	.871	Boston	.387
						Syracuse	.387
1957/58	N.B.A.	Boston	.681	Boston	.862	Boston	.567
1958/59	N.B.A.	Boston	.722	St. Louis	.903	New York	.500
1959/60	N.B.A.	Boston	.787	Boston	.926	Boston	.719
1960/61	N.B.A.	Boston	.722	St. Louis	.853	Boston	.686
1961/62	N.B.A.	Boston	.750	Los Angeles	.839	Boston	.684
1962/63	N.B.A.	Boston	.725	Boston	.833	Boston	.568
1963/64	N.B.A.	Boston	.738	Boston	.867	San Francisco	.583
1964/65	N.B.A.	Boston	.775	Boston	.900	Boston	.711
1965/66	N.B.A.	Philadelphia	.688	Philadelphia	.880	Philadelphia	.541
1966/67	N.B.A.	Philadelphia	.840	Philadelphia	.933	Philadelphia	.765
1967/68	N.B.A.	Philadelphia	.756	St. Louis	.781	Philadelphia	.676
1967/68	A.B.A.	Pittsburgh	.692	Pittsburgh	.838	Pittsburgh	.556
1968/69	N.B.A.	Baltimore	.695	New York	.811	Baltimore	.615
1968/69	A.B.A.	Oakland	.769	Denver	.821	Oakland	.737
1969/70	N.B.A.	New York	.732	New York	.732	New York	.730
1969/70	A.B.A.	Indiana	.702	Denver	.878	Indiana	.659
1970/71	N.B.A.	Milwaukee	.805	Milwaukee	.944	Milwaukee	.683
1970/71	A.B.A.	Indiana	.690	Utah	.833	Indiana	.636
1971/72	N.B.A.	Los Angeles	.841	Los Angeles	.878	Los Angeles	.816
1971/72	A.B.A.	Kentucky	.810	Kentucky	.857	Kentucky	.737
1972/73	N.B.A.	Boston	.829	Milwaukee	.868	Boston	.800
1972/73	A.B.A.	Carolina	.679	Utah	.881	Carolina	.643
1973/74	N.B.A.	Milwaukee	.720	Milwaukee	.816	Milwaukee	.600
1973/74	A.B.A.	New York	.655	Utah	.786	New York	.571
1974/75	N.B.A.	Washington	.732	Washington	.878	Boston	.780
		Boston	.732				
1974/75	A.B.A.	Denver	.774	Denver	.952	Denver	.595
1975/76	N.B.A.	Golden State	.720	Golden State	.878	Golden State	.561
						Boston	.561
1975/76	A.B.A.	Denver	.714	N/A		N/A	
1976/77	N.B.A.	Los Angeles	.646	Los Angeles	.902	Philadelphia	.439
1977/78	N.B.A.	Portland	.707	Philadelphia	.902	Portland	.537
1978/79	N.B.A.	Washington	.659	Atlanta	.829	Washington	.561
1979/80	N.B.A.	Boston	.744	Los Angeles	.902	Boston	.634
1980/81	N.B.A.	Boston	.756	Philadelphia	.902	Boston	.659
		Philadelphia	.756				
1981/82	N.B.A.	Boston	.762	Boston	.854	Boston	.683
1982/83	N.B.A.	Philadelphia	.793	Philadelphia	.854	Philadelphia	.732
						Boston	.732
1983/84	N.B.A.	Boston	.756	Boston	.804	Boston	.707
1984/85	N.B.A.	Boston	.768	Los Angeles	.878	Boston	.682
				Milwaukee	.878		
1985/86	N.B.A.	Boston	.817	Boston	.976	Boston	.658
						L.A. Lakers	.658
1986/87	N.B.A.	L.A. Lakers	.793	Boston	.951	L.A. Lakers	.682
1987/88	N.B.A.	L.A. Lakers	.756	Boston	.878	L.A. Lakers	.634
				L.A. Lakers	.878		
1988/89	N.B.A.	Detroit	.768	Detroit	.902	Detroit	.634
				Cleveland	.902		
1989/90	N.B.A.	L.A. Lakers	.768	L.A. Lakers	.902	L.A. Lakers	.634

FIELD GOAL PCT. Team	FG%	FREE THROW PCT. Team	FT%	Year	League
				1937/38	N.B.L.
				1938/39	N.B.L.
				1939/40	N.B.L.
				1940/41	N.B.L.
				1941/42	N.B.L.
				1942/43	N.B.L.
				1943/44	N.B.L.
				1944/45	N.B.L.
		Fort Wayne	.703	1945/46	N.B.L.
		Oshkosh	.687	1946/47	N.B.L.
Chicago	.298	Washington	.706	1946/47	B.A.A.
		Toledo	.703	1947/48	N.B.L.
Baltimore	.301	Washington	.719	1947/48	B.A.A.
		Syracuse	.694	1948/49	N.B.L.
Rochester	.372	Baltimore	.753	1948/49	B.A.A.
Indianapolis	.375	Washington	.746	1949/50	N.B.A.
New York	.379	Philadelphia	.763	1950/51	N.B.A.
Rochester	.399	Rochester	.773	1951/52	N.B.A.
Boston	.392	Syracuse	.745	1952/53	N.B.A.
Boston	.400	Minneapolis	.731	1953/54	N.B.A.
Boston	.399	Boston	.776	1954/55	N.B.A.
Philadelphia	.410	Minneapolis	.786	1955/56	N.B.A.
Philadelphia	.396	Syracuse	.794	1956/57	N.B.A.
New York	.395	Syracuse	.793	1957/58	N.B.A.
St. Louis	.410	New York	.791	1958/59	N.B.A.
St. Louis	.419	Syracuse	.791	1959/60	N.B.A.
Cincinnati	.438	Syracuse	.773	1960/61	N.B.A.
Cincinnati	.452	Syracuse	.780	1961/62	N.B.A.
Cincinnati	.459	Syracuse	.782	1962/63	N.B.A.
Cincinnati	.453	Los Angeles	.766	1963/64	N.B.A.
Cincinnati	.447	Los Angeles	.763	1964/65	N.B.A.
New York	.450	Los Angeles	.773	1965/66	N.B.A.
Philadelphia	.483	Cincinnati	.777	1966/67	N.B.A.
Los Angeles	.477	Cincinnati	.762	1967/68	N.B.A.
Dallas	.455	New Orleans	.748	1967/68	A.B.A.
Los Angeles	.469	Cincinnati	.751	1968/69	N.B.A.
Oakland	.462	Oakland	.759	1968/69	A.B.A.
Milwaukee	.488	Boston	.786	1969/70	N.B.A.
Washington	.464	Dallas	.788	1969/70	A.B.A.
Milwaukee	.509	Chicago	.790	1970/71	N.B.A.
Virginia	.472	Utah	.784	1970/71	A.B.A.
Milwaukee	.498	Phoenix	.779	1971/72	N.B.A.
Kentucky	.488	Utah	.789	1971/72	A.B.A.
Milwaukee	.481	Golden State	.798	1972/73	N.B.A.
Carolina	.495	Utah	.794	1972/73	A.B.A.
Milwaukee	.492	Houston	.812	1973/74	N.B.A.
Carolina	.485	Utah	.789	1973/74	A.B.A.
Portland	.480	K.C.-Omaha	.821	1974/75	N.B.A.
Denver	.509	San Antonio	.812	1974/75	A.B.A.
Houston	.485	Houston	.790	1975/76	N.B.A.
Denver	.505	Utah	.827	1975/76	A.B.A.
San Antonio	.485	Kansas City	.797	1976/77	N.B.A.
San Antonio	.500	San Antonio	.804	1977/78	N.B.A.
Los Angeles	.517	San Antonio	.795	1978/79	N.B.A.
Los Angeles	.529	Utah	.809	1979/80	N.B.A.
Philadelphia	.514	Denver	.783	1980/81	N.B.A.
Denver	.520	Denver	.796	1981/82	N.B.A.
Los Angeles	.528	Denver	.808	1982/83	N.B.A.
Los Angeles	.532	Denver	.818	1983/84	N.B.A.
L.A. Lakers	.545	Boston	.806	1984/85	N.B.A.
L.A. Lakers	.522	Denver	.798	1985/86	N.B.A.
Boston	.517	Boston	.818	1986/87	N.B.A.
Boston	.521	Denver	.804	1987/88	N.B.A.
Cleveland	.502	Milwaukee	.821	1988/89	N.B.A.
Utah	.505	Boston	.832	1989/90	N.B.A.

YEARLY TEAM LEADERS - REGULAR SEASON

Year	League	POINTS PER GAME		OPPONENTS PPG		PPG DIFFERENCE		REBOUNDS PER GAME		ASSISTS PER GAME		Year	League
		Team	PPG	Team	PPG	Team	Diff.	Team	Reb/G	Team	Ass/G		
1937/38	N.B.L.	Oshkosh	49.1	Akron Goodyear	27.7	Oshkosh	+13.9					1937/38	N.B.L.
1938/39	N.B.L.	Akron Firestone	44.6	Akron Goodyear	35.5	Akron Firestone	+8.7					1938/39	N.B.L.
1939/40	N.B.L.	Akron Firestone	44.2	Chicago	36.4	Akron Firestone	+3.4					1939/40	N.B.L.
1940/41	N.B.L.	Akron Firestone	42.3	Sheboygan	34.7	Oshkosh	+5.1					1940/41	N.B.L.
1941/42	N.B.L.	Oshkosh	49.3	Oshkosh	40.7	Oshkosh	+8.6					1941/42	N.B.L.
1942/43	N.B.L.	Fort Wayne	51.1	Sheboygan	43.7	Fort Wayne	+4.5					1942/43	N.B.L.
1943/44	N.B.L.	Fort Wayne	49.0	Sheboygan	40.9	Fort Wayne	+6.0					1943/44	N.B.L.
1944/45	N.B.L.	Fort Wayne	56.9	Sheboygan	46.0	Fort Wayne	+6.7					1944/45	N.B.L.
1945/46	N.B.L.	Fort Wayne	58.7	Sheboygan	48.2	Fort Wayne	+7.7					1945/46	N.B.L.
1946/47	N.B.L.	Rochester	62.9	Tri-Cities	51.8	Rochester	+6.4					1946 47	N B.L.
1946/47	B.A.A.	Chicago	77.0	Washington	63.9	Washington	+9.9			Cleveland	8.2	1946/47	B A.A.
1947/48	N.B.L.	Anderson	65.0	Minneapolis	56.6	Minneapolis	+7.5					1947/48	N.B.L.
1947/48	B.A.A.	Chicago	75.8	St. Louis	69.5	Baltimore	+3.9			Chicago	9.0	1947/48	B.A.A.
1948/49	N.B.L.	Anderson	72.1	Oshkosh	59.0	Anderson	+9.0					1948/49	N.B.L.
1948/49	B.A.A.	Minnespolis	84.0	Minneapolis	76.7	Minneapolis	+7.3			St. Louis	21.2	1948/49	B.A.A.
		Rochester	84.0										
1949/50	N.B.A.	Anderson	87.3	Rochester	74.6	Minneapolis	+8.4			Syracuse	23.0	1949/50	N.B.A.
1950/51	N.B.A.	Syracuse	86.1	Minneapolis	77.4	Minneapolis	+5.4	Fort Wayne	54.8	New York	23.5	1950/51	N.B.A.
1951/52	N.B.A.	Boston	91.3	Minneapolis	79.5	Minneapolis	+6.1	New York	58.1	Boston	24.3	1951/52	N.B.A.
1952/53	N.B.A.	Boston	88.1	Indianapolis	77.4	Minneapolis	+6.1	New York	57.2	Boston	23.5	1952 53	N.B.A.
1953/54	N.B.A.	Boston	87.7	Milwaukee	75.3	Syracuse	+4.9	Boston	53.7	Boston	24.6	1953/54	N.B.A.
1954/55	N.B.A.	Boston	101.4	Syracuse	89.7	Fort Wayne	+2.4	New York	60.8	Boston	26.5	1954/55	N.B.A.
1955/56	N.B.A.	Boston	106.0	Fort Wayne	93.7	Philadelphia	+4.3	Boston	63.7	Philadelphia	26.2	1955/56	N.B.A.
1956/57	N.B.A.	Boston	105.5	Rochester	95.6	Boston	+5.3	Boston	68.9	Philadelphia	20.4	1956/57	N.B.A.
1957/58	N.B.A.	New York	112.1	Cincinnati	103.1	Boston	+5.5	St. Louis	75.6	Cincinnati	21.9	1957/58	N.B.A.
1958/59	N.B.A.	Boston	116.4	St. Louis	105.1	Boston	+6.5	Boston	77.8	Boston	21.8	1958 59	N.B.A.
1959/60	N.B.A.	Boston	124.5	St. Louis	110.7	Boston	+8.3	Boston	80.2	St. Louis	25.1	1959/60	N.B.A.
1960/61	N.B.A.	Syracuse	121.3	Los Angeles	114.1	Boston	+5.6	Boston	77.6	St. Louis	27.0	1960/61	N.B.A.
1961/62	N.B.A.	Philadelphia	125.4	Boston	111.9	Boston	+9.2	Boston	76.0	Cincinnati	26.9	1961/62	N.B.A.
1962/63	N.B.A.	Syracuse	121.6	St. Louis	107.8	Boston	+7.2	Boston	72.7	Boston	24.5	1962/63	N.B.A.
1963/64	N.B.A.	Cincinnati	114.7	San Francisco	102.6	Boston	+7.9	Boston	71.7	Cincinnati	24.0	1963/64	N.B.A.
1964/65	N.B.A.	Cincinnati	114.2	Boston	104.5	Boston	+8.3	Boston	71.9	Cincinnati	23.0	1964/65	N.B.A.
1965/66	N.B.A.	Los Angeles	119.5	Boston	107.8	Boston	+4.9	San Francisco	71.6	Los Angeles	24.2	1965/66	N.B.A.
1966/67	N.B.A.	Philadelphia	125.2	Boston	111.3	Philadelphia	+9.4	San Francisco	73.8	Philadelphia	26.4	1966/67	N.B.A.
1967/68	N.B.A.	Philadelphia	122.6	St. Louis	110.3	Philadelphia	+8.6	San Francisco	73.5	Philadelphia	26.8	1967/68	N.B.A.
1967/68	A.B.A.	Pittsburgh	111.9	Denver	101.5	New Orleans	+4.7	Minnesota	61.9	New Orleans	17.4	1967/68	A.B.A.
1968/69	N.B.A.	Philadelphia	118.9	New York	105.2	New York	+5.6	San Francisco	62.3	New York	25.3	1968/69	N.B.A.
1968/69	A.B.A.	Oakland	126.5	Kentucky	111.0	Oakland	+8.4	Oakland	57.8	Oakland	21.4	1968/69	A.B.A.
1969/70	N.B.A.	Philadelphia	121.9	New York	105.9	New York	+9.1	San Diego	58.4	Seattle	27.0	1969/70	N.B.A.
1969/70	A.B.A.	Dallas	120.0	Carolina	107.0	Denver	+4.4	Denver	57.7	Washington	23.3	1969/70	A.B.A.
1970/71	N.B.A.	Milwaukee	118.4	New York	105.0	Milwaukee	+12.2	Boston	58.9	Milwaukee	27.4	1970/71	N.B.A.
1970/71	A.B.A.	Virginia	123.3	Memphis	109.9	Utah	+7.1	Utah	57.9	Virginia	26.6	1970/71	A.B.A.
1971/72	N.B.A.	Los Angeles	121.0	Chicago	102.9	Los Angeles	+12.3	Los Angeles	56.4	Los Angeles	27.2	1971/72	N.B.A.
1971/72	A.B.A.	Pittsburgh	119.2	Dallas	104.3	Kentucky	+9.0	Memphis	57.2	Kentucky	25.4	1971/72	A.B.A.
1972/73	N.B.A.	Houston	112.8	New York	98.2	Los Angeles	+8.5	Boston	58.6	Boston	28.3	1972/73	N.BA.
1972/73	A.B.A.	Utah	115.6	Kentucky	105.5	Kentucky	+6.4	Indiana	54.2	Kentucky	27.2	1972/73	A.B.A.
1973/74	N.B.A.	Buffalo	111.6	New York	98.5	Milwaukee	+8.1	Boston	54.3	Milwaukee	27.1	1973/74	N.B.A.
1973/74	A.B.A.	San Diego	113.2	San Antonio	96.7	New York	+5.4	Kentucky	52.6	Kentucky	25.0	1973/74	A.B.A.
1974/75	N.B.A.	Golden State	108.5	Chicago	95.0	Washington	+7.2	Golden State	52.1	Portland	26.9	1974/75	N.B.A.
1974/75	A.B.A.	San Antonio	118.7	Kentucky	101.7	New York	+7.7	St. Louis	51.1	Denver	29.2	1974/75	A.B.A.
1975/76	N.B.A.	Golden State	109.8	Chicago	98.8	Golden State	+6.7	Boston	52.9	Houston	27.0	1975/76	N.B.A.
1975/76	A.B.A.	Denver	121.9	San Diego	103.5	Denver	+6.0	Kentucky	51.9	Denver	29.1	1975/76	A.B.A.
1976/77	N.B.A.	San Antonio	115.0	Chicago	98.0	Portland	+5.5	Boston	51.3	Denver	27.6	1976/77	N.B.A.
1977/78	N.B.A.	Philadelphia	114.7	Portland	101.5	Portland	+6.2	New Orleans	51.4	New York	28.5	1977/78	N.B.A.
										Phoenix	28.5		
1978/79	N.B.A.	San Antonio	119.3	Seattle	103.9	San Antonio	+5.2	Washington	49.7	Milwaukee	31.2	1978/79	N.B.A.
1979/80	N.B.A.	San Antonio	119.4	Atlanta	101.6	Boston	+7.8	Washington	49.5	Los Angeles	29.4	1979/80	N.B.A.
1980/81	N.B.A.	Denver	121.8	Philadelphia	103.8	Philadelphia	+7.9	San Antonio	47.4	Philadelphia	28.9	1980/81	N.B.A.
1981/82	N.B.A.	Denver	126.5	Atlanta	100.5	Boston	+6.4	San Antonio	46.2	Los Angeles	28.7	1981/82	N.B.A.
1982/83	N.B.A.	Denver	123.2	New York	97.5	Philadelphia	+7.7	Philadelphia	47.9	Los Angeles	30.7	1982/83	N.B.A.
1983/84	N.B.A.	Denver	123.7	Milwaukee	101.5	Boston	+6.6	Detroit	47.1	Denver	30.3	1983/84	N.B.A.
1984/85	N.B.A.	Denver	120.0	Milwaukee	104.0	L.A. Lakers	+7.4	Detroit	48.0	L.A. Lakers	31.4	1984/85	N.B.A.
1985/86	N.B.A.	L.A. Lakers	117.3	New York	104.3	Milwaukee	+9.0	Boston	46.4	L.A. Lakers	29.6	1985/86	N.B.A.
1986/87	N.B.A.	Portland	117.9	Atlanta	102.8	L.A. Lakers	+9.3	Detroit	47.5	L.A. Lakers	29.6	1986/87	N.B.A.
1987/88	N.B.A.	Denver	116.7	Chicago	101.6	Boston	+5.9	Dallas	46.8	Boston	29.9	1987/88	N.B.A.
1988/89	N.B.A.	Phoenix	118.6	Utah	99.7	Phoenix	+7.7	Golden State	47.4	Charlotte	28.3	1988/89	N.B.A.
1989/90	N.B.A.	Golden State	116.3	Detroit	98.3	Phoenix	+7.1	Portland	47.6	Boston	29.5	1989/90	N.B.A.

YEARLY TEAM LEADERS - REGULAR SEASON

		3-POINT FIELD GOALS		3-POINT FG PERCENTAGE		REB. DIFF. PER GAME		ASSIISTS DIFF. PER GAME		STEALS DIFF. PER GAME			
Year	League	Team	3-Pt. FG	Team	%	Team	Diff.	Team	Diff.	Team	Diff.	Year	League
1967/68	A.B.A.	Pittsburgh	243	Pittsburgh	.308	Minnesota	+11.8	New Orleans	+3.5			1967/68	A.B.A.
1968/69	A.B.A.	Kentucky	335	Kentucky	.353	Oakland	+6.3	Oakland	+3.4			1968/69	A.B.A.
1969/70	A.B.A.	Kentucky	330	Kentucky	.358	Denver	+4.8	Carolina	+1.9			1969/70	A.B.A.
1970/71	N.B.A.					Boston	+6.0	Milwaukee	+4.0			1970/71	N.B.A.
1970/71	A.B.A.	Indiana	306	Carolina	.344	Kentucky	+3.1	Virginia	+4.5			1970/71	A.B.A.
1971/72	N.B.A.					Chicago	+5.4	Boston	+5.3			1971/72	N.B.A.
1971/72	A.B.A.	Indiana	220	Utah	.356	Memphis	+3.3	Memphis	+5.3			1971/72	A.B.A.
1972/73	N.B.A.					Boston	+10.3	New York	+5.8			1972/73	N.B.A.
1972/73	A.B.A.	Indiana	172	Dallas	.330	Kentucky	+6.4	Kentucky	+5.0			1972/73	A.B.A.
1973/74	N.B.A.					Boston	+8.7	Milwaukee	+6.3	Chicago	+1.8	1973/74	N.B.A.
1973/74	A.B.A.	San Diego	216	Denver	.329	New York	+5.3	Kentucky	+4.3	Carolina	+4.1	1973/74	A.B.A.
1974/75	N.B.A.					Boston	+7.1	Boston	+4.0	Washington	+2.7	1974/75	N.B.A.
1974/75	A.B.A.	Indiana	224	Memphis	.356	Kentucky	+4.9	Denver	+4.5	Indiana	+2.5	1974/75	A.B.A.
1975/76	N.B.A.					Boston	+7.9	Houston	+2.3	Golden State	+2.3	1975/76	N.B.A.
1975/76	A.B.A.	Indiana	250	Kentucky	.335	San Antonio	+3.5	Denver	+3.7	Indiana	+2.3	1975/76	A.B.A.
1976/77	N.B.A.					Houston	+6.5	Phoenix	+3.0	Indiana	+2.5	1976/77	N.B.A.
1977/78	N.B.A.					Boston	+4.5	Phoenix	+4.3	Atlanta	+2.0	1977/78	N.B.A.
1978/79	N.B.A.					Washington	+4.4	Kansas City	+5.6	New Orleans	+2.4	1978/79	N.B.A.
1979/80	N.B.A.	San Diego	117	Boston	.384	Seattle	+3.9	Kansas City	+4.2	Kansas City	+2.0	1979/80	N.B.A.
1980/81	N.B.A.	San Diego	132	San Diego	.324	San Antonio	+6.0	Kansas City	+5.0	New York	+2.1	1980/81	N.B.A.
1981/82	N.B.A.	Indiana	103	Indiana	.326	Boston	+4.9	Philadelphia	+3.6	Philadelphia	+1.9	1981/82	N.B.A.
1982/83	N.B.A.	San Antonio	94	San Antonio	.305	New Jersey	+5.1	Phoenix	+3.8	Golden State	+1.2	1982/83	N.B.A.
1983/84	N.B.A.	Utah	101	Utah	.310	Boston	+4.5	New Jersey	+2.9	Portland	+2.0	1983/84	N.B.A.
1984/85	N.B.A.	Dallas	152	Boston	.356	Boston	+4.3	L.A. Lakers	+3.2	Denver	+2.7	1984/85	N.B.A.
1985/86	N.B.A.	Dallas	141	Boston	.351	Boston	+4.9	Boston	+5.6	Denver	+2.3	1985/86	N.B.A.
1986/87	N.B.A.	Dallas	231	L.A. Lakers	.367	Detroit	+5.0	Boston	+4.4	San Antonio	+3.9	1986/87	N.B.A.
1987/88	N.B.A.	Boston	271	Boston	.384	Dallas	+4.9	Utah	+5.1	Denver	+2.6	1987/88	N.B.A.
1988/89	N.B.A.	New York	386	Seattle	.379	Detroit	+4.6	Utah	+3.6	Seattle	+2.4	1988/89	N.B.A.
1989/90	N.B.A.	Cleveland	346	Cleveland	.407	Portland	+6.0	Boston	+4.2	Minnesota	+2.6	1989/90	N.B.A.

YEARLY TEAM LEADERS - PLAYOFFS

Year	League	CHAMPION		POINTS PER GAME		OPPONENTS PPG		PPG DIFFERENCE		Year	League
		Team	W-L	Team	PPG	Team	PPG	Team	Diff.		
1937/38	N.B.L.	Akron Goodyear	4-1	Whiting	35.5	Akron Goodyear	29.2	Akron Goodyear	+2.4	1937/38	N.B.L.
1938/39	N.B.L.	Akron Firestone	3-2	Akron Firestone	40.0	Akron Firestone	36.8	Akron Firestone	+3.2	1938/39	N.B.L.
1939/40	N.B.L.	Akron Firestone	5-3	Oshkosh	44.1	Sheboygan	38.0	Oshkosh	+4.6	1939/40	N.B.L.
1940/41	N.B.L.	Oshkosh	5-0	Oshkosh	45.6	Detroit	36.0	Oshkosh	+9.4	1940/41	N.B.L.
1941/42	N.B.L.	Oshkosh	4-1	Oshkosh	53.4	Akron Goodyear	43.3	Oshkosh	+3.8	1941/42	N.B.L.
1942/43	N.B.L.	Sheboygan	4-1	Sheboygan	47.2	Fort Wayne	40.7	Sheboygan	+4.4	1942/43	N.B.L.
1943/44	N.B.L.	Fort Wayne	5-0	Fort Wayne	49.0	Oshkosh	34.7	Fort Wayne	+12.0	1943/44	N.B.L.
1944/45	N.B.L.	Fort Wayne	5-2	Fort Wayne	58.7	Sheboygan	48.5	Fort Wayne	+8.3	1944/45	N.B.L.
1945/46	N.B.L.	Rochester	6-1	Rochester	59.6	Oshkosh	50.4	Rochester	+7.6	1945/46	N.B.L.
1946/47	N.B.L.	Chicago	8-3	Chicago	68.2	Oshkosh	50.1	Chicago	+4.2	1946/47	N.B.L.
1946/47	B.A.A.	Philadelphia	8-2	Philadelphia	75.3	St. Louis	66.3	Philadelphia	+5.9	1946/47	B.A.A.
1947/48	N.B.L.	Minneapolis	8-2	Minneapolis	75.8	Anderson	65.3	Minneapolis	+8.5	1947/48	N.B.L.
1947/48	B.A.A.	Baltimore	8-3	New York	79.0	Philadelphia	66.0	Philadelphia	+5.7	1947/48	B.A A.
1948/49	N.B.L.	Anderson	6-1	Anderson	78.6	Tri-Cities	64.3	Anderson	+7.0	1948/49	N.B.L.
1948/49	B.A.A.	Minneapolis	8-2	Baltimore	85.0	Minneapolis	72.9	Minneapolis	+7.4	1948/49	B.A.A.
1949/50	N.B.A.	Minneapolis	10-2	Sheboygan	88.0	Minneapolis	75.4	Minneapolis	+9.1	1949/50	N.B.A.
1950/51	N.B.A.	Rochester	9-5	Indianapolis	89.7	Rochester	76.8	Rochester	+7.1	1950/51	N.B.A.
1951/52	N.B A.	Minneapolis	9-4	Boston	96.3	Minneapolis	78.9	Minneapolis	+3.4	1951/52	N.B.A.
1952/53	N.B.A.	Minneapolis	9-3	Syracuse	93.0	Minneapolis	77.8	Minneapolis	+5.1	1952 53	N.B.A.
1953/54	N.B.A.	Minneapolis	9-4	Boston	87.0	Minneapolis	74.1	Minneapolis	+6.2	1953/54	N.B.A.
1954/55	N.B.A.	Syracuse	7-4	Boston	105.3	Fort Wayne	91.5	Syracuse	+2.3	1954/55	N.B.A.
1955/56	N.B.A.	Philadelphia	7-3	Minneapolis	121.0	Fort Wayne	92.2	Minneapolis	+18.7	1955/56	N.B.A.
1956/57	N.B.A.	Boston	7-3	St. Louis	109.5	Syracuse	92.7	Boston	+5.6	1957/58	N.B.A.
1958/59	N.B.A.	Boston	8-3	Boston	123.3	St. Louis	100.8	Boston	+7.8	1958/59	N.B.A.
1959/60	N.B.A.	Boston	8-5	Philadelphia	113.9	Minneapolis	106.0	Boston	+4.7	1959/60	N.B.A.
1960/61	N.B A.	Boston	8-2	Boston	120.7	Boston	109.1	Boston	+11.6	1960/61	N.B.A.
1961/62	N.B.A.	Boston	8-6	Los Angeles	117.7	Syracuse	105.4	Boston	+4.8	1961/62	N.B.A.
1962/63	N.B.A.	Boston	8-5	Cincinnati	121.2	St. Louis	109.5	Los Angeles	+2.5	1962/63	N.B.A.
1963/64	N.B.A.	Boston	8-2	Philadelphia	113.2	Boston	97.2	Boston	+6.2	1963/64	N.B.A.
1964/65	N.B.A.	Boston	8-4	Boston	116.8	Boston	109.8	Boston	+7.0	1964/65	N.B A.
1965/66	N.B.A.	Boston	11-6	Los Angeles	116.6	Boston	110.2	Boston	+5.6	1965/66	N.B.A.
1966/67	N.B.A.	Philadelphia	11-4	Philadelphia	121.7	Philadelphia	112.3	Philadelphia	+9.4	1966/67	N.B.A.
1967/68	N.B.A.	Boston	12-7	Boston	114.6	Chicago	106.6	Los Angeles	+4.6	1967/68	N.B.A.
1967/68	A.B.A.	Pittsburgh	11-4	Pittsburgh	117.4	Kentucky	105.2	Pittsburgh	+5.0	1967/68	A.B.A.
1968/69	N.B.A.	Boston	12-6	Boston	107.8	Los Angeles	99.1	Los Angeles	+4.6	1968/69	N.B.A.
1968/69	A.B A.	Oakland	12-4	Oakland	124.8	Minnesota	112.3	Oakland	+7.5	1968/69	A.B A.
1969/70	N.B.A.	New York	12-7	Atlanta	114.3	Baltimore	106.6	Los Angeles	+3.9	1969/70	N.B.A.
1969/70	A.B.A.	Indiana	12-3	Dallas	124.7	Indiana	107.5	Indiana	+7.1	1969/70	A.B.A.
1970/71	N.B.A.	Milwaukee	12-2	Milwaukee	109.1	Milwaukee	94.6	Milwaukee	+14.5	1970/71	N.B A.
1970/71	A.B.A.	Utah	12-6	Virginia	124.0	Mem phis	103.3	Utah	+7.1	1970/71	A.B.A.
1971/72	N.B.A.	Los Angeles	12-3	Atlanta	113.0	New York	101.9	Milwaukee	+6.4	1971/72	N.B.A.
1971/72	A.B.A.	Indiana	12-8	Virginia	117.2	Denver	100.9	Virginia	+7.5	1971/72	A.B.A.
1972/73	N.B A.	New York	12-5	Boston	108.1	Milwaukee	96.7	New York	+5.0	1972/73	N.B.A.
1972/73	A.B A.	Indiana	12-6	Carolina	108.0	Kentucky	100.5	Kentucky	+4.0	1972/73	A.B.A.
1973/74	N.B.A.	Boston	12-6	Buffalo	104.0	Detroit	92.7	Boston	+5.6	1973/74	N.B.A.
1973/74	A.B.A.	New York	12-2	New York	106.9	New York	96.1	New York	+10.8	1973/74	A.B.A.
1974/75	N.B.A.	Golden State	12-5	Houston	108.5	Chicago	92.8	Golden State	+5.3	1974/75	N.B.A.
1974/75	A.B.A.	Kentucky	12-3	Utah	118.8	Kentucky	99.0	Kentucky	+9.0	1974/75	A.B A.
1975/76	N.B.A.	Boston	12-6	Philadelphia	114.3	Washington	91.1	Philadelphia	+6.0	1975/76	N.B.A.
1975/76	A.B.A.	New York	8-5	Denver	116.1	Indiana	105.0	San Antonio	+1.3	1975/76	A.B.A.
1976/77	N.B.A.	Portland	14-5	Houston	108.9	Cleveland	98.7	Portland	+4.7	1976/77	N.B.A.
1977/78	N.B.A.	Washington	14-7	Philadelphia	114.4	Portland	98.3	Philadelphia	+5.6	1977/78	N.B.A.
1978/79	N.B.A.	Seattle	12-5	Philadelphia	112.7	Atlanta	99.7	Philadelphia	+3.4	1978/79	N.B.A.
1979/80	N.B.A.	Los Angeles	12-4	Los Angeles	110.6	Boston	96.7	Boston	+5.7	1979/80	N.B.A.
1980/81	N.B.A.	Boston	12-5	San Antonio	107.7	Phoenix	89.0	Boston	+6.1	1980/81	N.B.A.
1981/82	N.B.A.	Los Angeles	12-2	Denver	119.3	Houston	92.0	Los Angeles	+6.1	1981/82	N.B.A.
1982/83	N.B.A.	Philadelphia	12-1	San Antonio	121.0	Atlanta	98.0	Philadelphia	+6.5	1982/83	N.B.A.
1983/84	N.B.A.	Boston	15-8	Denver	121.8	Washington	96.5	Los Angeles	+6.9	1983/84	N.B.A.
1984/85	N.B.A.	L.A. Lakers	15-4	L.A. Lakers	126.3	Houston	104.2	L.A. Lakers	+10.2	1984/85	N.B.A.
1985/86	N.B.A.	Boston	15-3	Detroit	116.5	Boston	104.1	Boston	+10.3	1985/86	N.B.A.
1986/87	N.B.A.	L.A. Lakers	15-3	L.A. Lakers	120.6	Indiana	98.0	L.A. Lakers	+11.4	1986/87	N.B.A.
1987/88	N.B.A.	L.A. Lakers	15-9	Seattle	114.2	Detroit	95.2	Detroit	+4.6	1987/88	N.B.A.
1988/89	N.B.A.	Detroit	15-2	Phoenix	118.3	Detroit	92.9	Detroit	+7.7	1988/89	N.B.A.
1989/90	N.B.A.	Detroit	15-5	Boston	118.8	Detroit	94.8	Detroit	+7.0	1989/90	N.B.A.

YEARLY TEAM LEADERS - PLAYOFFS

Year	League	FIELD GOAL PCT.		FREE THROW PCT.		REBOUNDS PER GAME		ASSISTS PER GAME		Year	League
		Team	FG%	Team	FT%	Team	Reb/G	Team	Ass/G		
1945/46	N.B.L.			Oshkosh	.722					1945/46	N.B.L.
1946/47	N.B.L.			Chicago	.722					1946/47	N.B.L.
1946/47	B.A.A.	Cleveland	.313	Philadelphia	.772			Cleveland	7.7	1946/47	B.A.A.
1947/48	N.B.L.			Oshkosh	.764					1947/48	N.B.L.
1947/48	B.A.A.	New York	.336	Baltimore	.731			Boston	7.3	1947/48	B A.A.
1948/49	N.B.L.			Sheboygan	.761					1948/49	N.B.L.
1948/49	B.A.A.	Minneapolis	.360	Minneapolis	.736			Rochester	20.3	1948/49	B.A.A.
1949/50	N.B.A.	Sheboygan	.385	New York	.826			Indianapolis	20.8	1949/50	N.B.A.
1950/51	N.B.A.	Tri-Cities	.402	Philadelphia	.766	Syracuse	58.6	Syracuse	24.0	1950/51	N.B.A.
1951/52	N.B.A.	Boston	.419	Boston	.792	Fort Wayne	55.0	Fort Wayne	28.5	1951/52	N.B.A.
1952/53	N.B.A.	New York	.386	Boston	.767	New York	58.2	Boston	22.8	1952/53	N.B.A.
1953/54	N.B.A.	Minneapolis	.400	Fort Wayne	.748	Boston	52.0	Boston	22.3	1953/54	N.B.A.
1954/55	N.B.A.	Boston	.435	Boston	.804	Minneapolis	58.7	Boston	28.9	1954/55	N.B.A.
1955/56	N.B.A.	Minneapolis	.441	Boston	.770	Boston	68.3	Philadelphia	25.9	1955/56	N.B.A.
1956/57	N.B.A.	Fort Wayne	.435	Syracuse	.773	Boston	72.9	Fort Wayne	26.0	1956/57	N.B.A.
1957/58	N.B.A.	St. Louis	.404	Boston	.781	Boston	77.7	St. Louis	21.5	1957/58	N.B.A.
1958/59	N.B.A.	St. Louis	.430	Syracuse	.847	Boston	82.6	Boston	26.1	1958/59	N.B.A.
1959/60	N.B.A.	St. Louis	.418	Syracuse	.842	Philadelphia	77.8	St. Louis	27.6	1959/60	N.B.A.
1960/61	N.B.A.	Los Angeles	.430	Syracuse	.799	Boston	82.1	Detroit	26.2	1960/61	N.B.A.
1961/62	N.B.A.	Cincinnati	.468	Cincinnati	.815	Philadelphia	73.6	Boston	25.7	1961/62	N.B.A.
1962/63	N.B.A.	Los Angeles	.450	Syracuse	.792	Boston	68.7	Boston	24.3	1962/63	N.B.A.
1963/64	N.B.A.	St. Louis	.437	Philadelphia	.778	Boston	73.6	St. Louis	23.4	1963/64	N.B.A.
1964/65	N.B.A.	Baltimore	.442	Cincinnati	.869	Boston	72.3	Cincinnati	24.8	1964/65	N.B.A.
1965/66	N.B.A.	Baltimore	.465	Cincinnati	.799	Philadelphia	72.2	St. Louis	25.1	1965/66	N.B.A.
1966/67	N.B.A.	Philadelphia	.450	Cincinnati	.775	San Francisco	75.6	Philadelphia	26.7	1966/67	N.B.A.
1967/68	N.B.A.	Los Angeles	.474	Chicago	.753	Philadelphia	68.5	St. Louis	26.3	1967/68	N.B.A.
1967/68	A.B.A.	Pittsburgh	.461	Indiana	.755	Minnesota	59.6	Indiana	21.7	1967/68	A.B.A.
1968/69	N.B.A.	San Diego	.463	Boston	.756	San Francisco	68.0	Los Angeles	23.3	1968/69	N.B.A.
1968/69	A.B.A.	Oakland	.449	Dallas	.819	Oakland	60.2	Indiana	19.1	1968/69	A.B.A.
1969/70	N.B.A.	Los Angeles	.483	Baltimore	.769	Phoenix	60.4	Los Angeles	28.1	1969/70	N.B.A.
1969/70	A.B.A.	Washington	.501	Washington	.781	Indiana	57.7	Dallas	26.8	1969/70	A.B.A.
1970/71	N.B.A.	Milwaukee	.497	San Francisco	.768	Atlanta	57.8	Chicago	27.6	1970/71	N.B.A.
1970/71	A.B.A.	New York	.526	Utah	.795	Texas	60.5	Floridians	27.5	1970/71	A.B.A.
1971/72	N.B.A.	New York	.469	Baltimore	.795	Milwaukee	56.9	New York	23.1	1971/72	N.B.A.
1971/72	A.B.A.	Utah	.511	Denver	.793	Denver	54.7	Virginia	21.7	1971/72	A.B.A.
1972/73	N.B.A.	New York	.484	Golden State	.806	Los Angeles	55.4	Boston	25.5	1972/73	N.B.A.
1972/73	A.B.A.	New York	.509	Utah	.812	Indiana	52.4	Kentucky	22.5	1972/73	A.B.A.
1973/74	N.B.A.	Milwaukee	.498	Boston	.809	Buffalo	49.7	Milwaukee	26.1	1973/74	N.B.A.
1973/74	A.BA.	San Antonio	.485	Virginia	.800	Kentucky	52.9	New York	24.5	1973/74	A.B.A.
1974/75	N.B.A.	Detroit	.498	Boston	.813	Golden State	49.4	Detroit	28.7	1974/75	N.B.A.
1974/75	A.B.A.	Utah	.500	Denver	.881	St. Louis	50.7	Utah	26.3	1974/75	A.B.A.
1975/76	N.B.A.	Milwaukee	.545	Golden State	.804	Boston	50.1	Buffalo	25.4	1975/76	N.B.A.
1975/76	A.B.A.	Kentucky	.483	Indiana	.808	San Antonio	52.4	Kentucky	26.6	1975/76	A.B.A.
1976/77	N.B.A.	Houston	.494	Boston	.797	Cleveland	53.3	Portland	27.7	1976/77	N.B.A.
1977/78	N.B.A.	Milwaukee	.504	Phoenix	.816	Philadelphia	51.6	Milwaukee	31.3	1977/78	N.B.A.
1978/79	N.B.A.	Philadelphia	.497	Atlanta	.793	Washington	50.5	Philadelphia	29.2	1978/79	N.B.A.
1979/80	N.B.A.	Phoenix	.489	Houston	.805	Los Angeles	49.9	Phoenix	30.9	1979/80	N.B.A.
1980/81	N.B.A.	San Antonio	.490	Philadelphia	.773	Los Angeles	51.0	Milwaukee	27.0	1980/81	N.B.A.
1981/82	N.B.A.	Los Angeles	.517	Denver	.831	Boston	50.5	Los Angeles	31.4	1981/82	N.B.A.
1982/83	N.B.A.	San Antonio	.506	Denver	.793	Seattle	54.0	San Antonio	33.4	1982/83	N.B.A.
1983/84	N.B.A.	Los Angeles	.534	Denver	.862	Seattle	44.2	Los Angeles	30.3	1983/84	N.B.A.
1984/85	N.B.A.	L.A. Lakers	.543	Boston	.821	Houston	56.8	L.A. Lakers	33.8	1984/85	N.B.A.
1985/86	N.B.A.	L.A. Lakers	.535	Boston	.794	Houston	47.3	L.A. Lakers	32.0	1985/86	N.B.A.
1986/87	N.B.A.	L.A. Lakers	.522	Boston	.809	L.A. Lakers	44.9	L.A. Lakers	28.3	1986/87	N.B.A.
1987/88	N.B.A.	Seattle	.516	Denver	.826	Portland	48.0	Seattle	27.6	1987/88	N.B.A.
1988/89	N.B.A.	L.A. Lakers	.497	Phoenix	.841	Phoenix	50.3	Philadelphia	29.0	1988/89	N.B.A.
1989/90	N.B.A.	Boston	.548	Denver	.872	San Antonio	48.3	San Antonio	30.4	1989/90	N.B.A.

YEARLY TEAM LEADERS - PLAYOFFS

Year	League	3-POINT FIELD GOAL PCT.		REBOUND DIFF. PER GAME		ASSIST DIFF. PER GAME		STEALS DIFF. PER GAME		Year	League
		Team	%	Team	Diff.	Team	Diff.	Team	Diff.		
1967/68	A.B.A.	Kentucky	.383	Minnesota	+8.8	New Orleans	+4.5			1967/68	A.B.A.
1968/69	A.B.A.	Kentucky	.352	Oakland	+5.9	Indiana	+2.1			1968/69	A.B.A.
1969/70	A.B.A.	Washington	.327	Kentucky	+4.3	Kentucky	+2.6			1969/70	A.B.A.
1970/71	N.B.A.			Atlanta	+8.0	Chicago	+6.7			1970/71	N.B.A.
1970/71	A.B.A.	New York	.500	-						1970/71	A.B.A.
1971/72	N.B.A.			Milwaukee	+3.4	New York	+3.4			1971/72	N.B.A.
1971/72	A.B.A.	Kentucky	.350	Denver	+3.7	Dallas	+3.8			1971/72	A.B.A.
1972/73	N.B.A.			Boston	+5.5	New York	+3.9			1972/73	N.B.A.
1972/73	A.B.A.	San Diego	.333	Carolina	+5.2	Kentucky	+4.1			1972/73	A.B.A.
1973/74	N.B.A.			Milwaukee	+5.0	Boston	+3.9	Chicago	+3.5	1973/74	N.B.A.
1973/74	A.B.A.	Kentucky	.444	Kentucky	+5.0	New York	+5.3	Carolina	+4.0	1973/74	A.B.A.
1974/75	N.B.A.			Boston	+5.6	Detroit	+7.3	Golden State	+2.2	1974/75	N.B.A.
1974/75	A.B.A.	Utah	.423	Utah	+9.5	Kentucky	+6.2	Indiana	+1.3	1974/75	A.B.A.
1975/76	N.B.A.			Philadelphia	+8.7	Cleveland	+2.9	Golden State	+4.8	1975/76	N.B.A.
1975/76	A.B.A.	Kentucky	.349	San Antonio	+4.1	San Antonio	+4.6	Indiana	+2.7	1975/76	A.B.A.
1976/77	N.B.A.			Chicago	+12.0	Cleveland	+4.3	Cleveland	+3.7	1976/77	N.B.A.
1977/78	N.B.A.			Denver	+4.6	Washington	+3.1	Washington	+1.2	1977/78	N.B.A.
1978/79	N.B.A.			Seattle	+7.6	Phoenix	+3.9	San Antonio	+2.9	1978/79	N.B.A.
1979/80	N.B.A.	Kansas City	.500	Los Angeles	+9.8	Philadelphia	+3.6	Milwaukee	+5.3	1979/80	N.B.A.
1980/81	N.B.A.			San Antonio	+6.6	Boston	+1.9	Houston	+1.3	1980/81	N.B.A.
1981/82	N.B.A.	Milwaukee	.333	Boston	+7.1	Los Angeles	+2.4	Los Angeles	+1.1	1981/82	N.B.A.
1982/83	N.B.A.	Portland	.455	San Antonio	+6.4	Boston	+4.9	Los Angeles	+1.6	1982/83	N.B.A.
1983/84	N.B.A.	Utah	.362	Boston	+2.7	Los Angeles	+5.3	New Jersey	+2.4	1983/84	N.B.A.
1984/85	N.B.A.	Dallas	.375	L.A. Lakers	+4.4	L.A. Lakers	+2.8	Denver	+1.1	1984/85	N.B.A.
1985/86	N.B.A.	Dallas	.517	Houston	+3.7	Boston	+4.9	Boston	+0.6	1985/86	N.B.A.
1986/87	N.B.A.	Chicago	.438	L.A. Lakers	+4.0	Seattle	+4.0	Milwaukee	+3.3	1986/87	N.B.A.
1987/88	N.B.A.	Utah	.417	Detroit	+4.7	Seattle	+8.2	Portland	+3.8	1987/88	N.B.A.
1988/89	N.B.A.	Houston	.379	Detroit	+6.5	Philadelphia	+6.0	Milwaukee	+1.6	1988/89	N.B.A.
1989/90	N.B.A.	Detroit	.369	Detroit	+4.3	Cleveland	+5.8	Portland	+1.8	1989/90	N.B.A.

LIFETIME LEADERS - REGULAR SEASON

FIELD GOALS

		Years	FG
1	Kareem Abdul-Jabbar	70-89	15837
2	Wilt Chamberlain	60-73	12681
3	Julius Erving	72-87	11313
4	Elvin Hayes	69-84	10976
5	John Havlicek	63-78	10513
6	Dan Issel	71-85	10431
7	George Gervin	73-86	10368
8	Alex English	77-	10337
9	Rick Barry	66-80	9592
10	Oscar Robertson	61-74	9508
11	Moses Malone	75-	9429
12	Artis Gilmore	72-88	9401
13	Jerry West	61-74	9016
14	Elgin Baylor	59-72	8693
15	Hal Greer	59-73	8504
16	Adrian Dantley	77-	8150
17	Walt Bellamy	62-75	7914
18	Larry Bird	80-	7776
19	Bob Lanier	71-84	7761
20	Robert Parish	77-	7540
21	Walter Davis	78-	7530
22	Gail Goodrich	66-79	7431
23	Bob McAdoo	73-86	7420
24	Lou Hudson	67-79	7392
25	Bob Pettit	55-65	7349

FREE THROWS

		Years	FT
1	Moses Malone	75-	8177
2	Oscar Robertson	61-74	7694
3	Jerry West	61-74	7160
4	Dolph Schayes	49-64	6979
5	Adrian Dantley	77-	6814
6	Kareem Abdul-Jabbar	70-89	6712
7	Dan Issel	71-85	6591
8	Julius Erving	72-87	6256
9	Bob Pettit	55-65	6182
10	Artis Gilmore	72-88	6132
11	Wilt Chamberlain	60-73	6057
12	Elgin Baylor	59-72	5763
13	George Gervin	73-86	5737
14	Rick Barry	66-80	5713
15	Lenny Wilkens	61-75	5394
16	John Havlicek	63-78	5369
17	Elvin Hayes	69-84	5356
18	Walt Bellamy	62-75	5113
19	Chet Walker	63-75	5079
20	Paul Arizin	51-52, 55-62	5010
21	Bailey Howell	60-71	4740
22	World Free	76-88	4718
23	Nate Archibald	71-77, 79-84	4664
24	Bob Cousy	51-63, 70	4624
25	Hal Greer	59-73	4578

POINTS

		Years	Points
1	Kareem Abdul-Jabbar	70-89	38387
2	Wilt Chamberlain	60-73	31419
3	Julius Erving	72-87	30026
4	Dan Issel	71-85	27482
5	Elvin Hayes	69-84	27313
6	Moses Malone	75-	27039
7	Oscar Robertson	61-74	26710
8	George Gervin	73-86	26595
9	John Havlicek	63-78	26395
10	Rick Barry	66-80	25279
11	Jerry West	61-74	25192
12	Artis Gilmore	72-88	24941
13	Alex English	77-	24850
14	Elgin Baylor	59-72	23149
15	Adrian Dantley	77-	23120
16	Hal Greer	59-73	21586
17	Walt Bellamy	62-75	20941
18	Bob Pettit	55-65	20880
19	Larry Bird	80-	19719
20	Bob Lanier	71-84	19248
21	Dolph Schayes	49-64	19247
22	Gail Goodrich	66-79	19181
23	Chet Walker	63-75	18831
24	Bob McAdoo	73-86	18757
25	Dave Bing	67-78	18327

FIELD GOAL PERCENTAGE
(Minimum 2000 Field Goal Attempts)

		Years	Pct.
1	James Donaldson	81-	.582
2	Charles Barkley	85-	.581
3	Mark West	84-	.578
4	Steve Johnson	82-	.573
5	Darryl Dawkins	76-89	.572
6	Dennis Rodman	87-	.571
7	Jeff Ruland	82-87	.564
8	Kevin McHale	81-	.563
9	Bobby Jones	75-86	.560
10	Tim McCormick	85-	.560
11	Kareem Abdul-Jabbar	70-89	.559
12	Artis Gilmore	72-88	.559
13	James Worthy	83-	.555
14	Larry Nance	82-	.552
15	Goo Kennedy	72-76	.548
16	Otis Thorpe	85-	.546
17	Cedric Maxwell	78-88	.546
18	Ed Pinckney	86-	.542
19	Mike Glenn	78-87	.542
20	Adrian Dantley	77-	.541
21	Robert Parish	77-	.540
22	Wilt Chamberlain	60-73	.540
23	Kurt Rambis	82-	.540
24	Walter Berry	87-89	.539
25	Bill Cartwright	80-	.539

FREE THROW PERCENAGE
(Minimum 2000 free throw attempts)

		Years	Pct.
1	Rick Barry	66-80	.893
2	Calvin Murphy	71-83	.892
3	Larry Bird	80-	.884
4	Bill Sharman	51-61	.883
5	Kiki Vandeweghe	81-	.871
6	Mike Newlin	72-82	.870
7	Jeff Malone	84-	.870
8	Mack Calvin	70-78,80	.864
9	John Long	79-	.861
10	Fred Brown	72-84	.858
11	James Silas	73-82	.855
12	Darel Carrier	68-73	.851
13	Jack Sikma	78-	.850
14	Michael Jordan	85-	.848
15	Mike Gminski	81-	.846
16	Junior Bridgeman	76-87	.846
17	Kelly Tripucka	82-	.846
18	Rickey Sobers	76-86	.844
19	Dolph Schayes	49-64	.843
20	Larry Costello	55,57-68	.841
21	Magic Johnson	80-	.841
22	George Gervin	73-86	.841
23	Adrian Smith	62-74	.838
24	Oscar Robertson	61-74	.838
25	Doug Collins	74-81	.833

POINTS PER GAME
(Minimum 350 Games Played)

		Years	PPG
1	Michael Jordan	85-	32.8
2	Wilt Chamberlain	60-73	30.1
3	Elgin Baylor	59-72	27.4
4	Jerry West	61-74	27.0
5	Bob Pettit	55-65	26.4
6	Dominique Wilkins	83-	26.1
7	Oscar Robertson	61-74	25.7
8	Larry Bird	80-	25.5
9	George Gervin	73-86	25.1
10	Karl Malone	86-	24.9
11	Rick Barry	66-80	24.8
12	Kareem Abdul-Jabbar	70-	24.6
13	Adrian Dantley	77-	24.5
14	Pete Maravich	71-80	24.2
15	Julius Erving	72-87	24.2
16	Akeem Olajuwon	85-	23.2
17	Mark Aguirre	82-	22.9
18	Patrick Ewing	86-	22.9
19	Paul Arizin	51-52, 55-62	22.8
20	David Thompson	76-84	22.7
21	Charles Barkley	85-	22.7
22	Bernard King	78-85, 87-	22.6
23	George Mikan	47-54, 56	22.6
24	Dan Issel	71-85	22.6
25	Moses Malone	75-	22.4

3-POINT FIELD GOALS

		Years	FG
1	Louie Dampier	68-79	794
2	Dale Ellis	84-	568
3	Larry Bird	80-	520
4	Danny Ainge	82-	514
5	Bill Keller	70-76	506
6	Glen Combs	69-75	503
7	Michael Adams	86-	493
8	Craig Hodges	83-	483
9	Darrell Griffith	81-85, 87-	482
10	Trent Tucker	83-	440

3-POINT FIELD GOAL PERCENTAGE (ABA only)
(Minimum 10 Attempts)

		Years	Pct.
1	Steve Kerr	89-	.503
2	Hersey Hawkins	89-	.424
3	Mark Price	87-	.423
4	Trent Tucker	83-	.408
5	Ricky Berry	89	.408
6	Dale Ellis	84-	.404
7	Craig Hodges	83-	.404
8	Reggie Miller	88-	.397
9	Byron Scott	84-	.394
10	Jon Sundvold	84-	.389

REBOUNDS

		Years	Reb.
1	Wilt Chamberlain	60-73	23924
2	Bill Russell	57-69	21620
3	Kareem Abdul-Jabbar	70-89	17440
4	Artis Gilmore	72-88	16330
5	Elvin Hayes	69-84	16279
6	Moses Malone	75-	16105
7	Nate Thurman	64-77	14464
8	Walt Bellamy	62-75	14241
9	Wes Unseld	69-81	13769
10	Jerry Lucas	64-74	12942
11	Bob Pettit	55-65	12849
12	Paul Silas	65-80	12357
13	Elgin Baylor	59-72	11463
14	Dolph Schayes	51-64*	11256
15	Dan Issel	71-85	11133
16	Robert Parish	77-	11130
17	Caldwell Jones	74-	10685
18	Bill Bridges	63-75	11054
19	Julius Erving	72-87	10525
20	Dave Cowens	71-80, 83	10444
21	Jack Sikma	78-	10375
22	Johnny Kerr	55-66	10092
23	Bob Lanier	71-84	9698
24	Sam Lacey	71-83	9687
25	Zelmo Beaty	63-75	9665

ASSISTS

		Years	Ass.
1	Oscar Robertson	61-74	9887
2	Magic Johnson	80-	8025
3	Lenny Wilkens	61-75	7211
4	Bob Cousy	51-63, 70	6955
5	Isiah Thomas	82-	6985
6	Guy Rodgers	59-70	6917
7	Maurice Cheeks	79-	6665
8	Nate Archibald	71-77, 79-84	6386
9	John Lucas	77-	6454
10	Norm Nixon	78-86, 89	6238
11	Jerry West	61-74	6216
12	John Havlicek	63-78	6114
13	Reggie Theus	79-	6075
14	Kareem Abdul-Jabbar	70-89	5660
15	Dennis Johnson	77-	5499
16	Dave Bing	67-78	5397
17	Kevin Porter	73-81, 83	5314
18	Julius Erving	72-87	5276
19	Norm VanLier	70-79	5217
20	John Stockton	85-	5075
21	Walter Frazier	68-80	5040
22	Rick Barry	66-80	4952
23	Gail Goodrich	66-79	4805
24	Rickey Green	78-	4740
25	Louie Dampier	68-79	4687

GAMES PLAYED

		Years	Games
1	Kareem Abdul-Jabbar	70-89	1560
2	Artis Gilmore	72-88	1329
3	Elvin Hayes	69-84	1303
4	Caldwell Jones	74-	1299
5	John Havlicek	63-78	1270
6	Paul Silas	65-80	1254
7	Julius Erving	72-87	1243
8	Dan Issel	71-85	1218
9	Moses Malone	75-	1203
10	Billy Paultz	71-85	1124
11	Hal Greer	59-73	1122
12	Alex English	77-	1114
13	Dennis Johnson	77-	1100
	Robert Parish	77-	1100
15	Lenny Wilkins	61-75	1067
16	George Gervin	73-86	1060
17	Dolph Schayes	49-64	1059
18	Johnny Green	60-73	1057
19	Leroy Ellis	63-76	1048
20	Wilt Chamberlain	60-73	1045
21	Walt Bellamy	62-75	1043
22	Oscar Robertson	61-74	1040
23	Chet Walker	63-75	1032
24	Gail Goodrich	66-79	1031
25	Jack Sikma	78-	1030

REBOUNDS PER GAME
(Minimum 350 Games Played)

		Years	Reb/G
1	Wilt Chamberlain	60-73	22.9
2	Bill Russell	57-69	22.5
3	Bob Pettit	55-65	16.2
4	Jerry Lucas	64-74	15.6
5	Nate Thurmond	64-77	15.0
6	Mel Daniels	68-75, 77	14.9
7	Wes Unseld	69-81	14.0
8	Walt Bellamy	62-75	13.7
9	Dave Cowens	71-80, 83	13.6
10	Elgin Baylor	59-72	13.5
11	George Mikan	51-54, 56*	13.4
12	Moses Malone	75-	13.3
13	Willis Reed	65-74	12.9
14	Elvin Hayes	69-84	12.5
15	Akeem Olajuwon	85-	12.4
16	Artis Gilmore	72-88	12.3
17	Dolph Schayes	51-64*	12.1
18	Charles Barkley	85-	11.9
19	Gus Johnson	64-73	11.9
20	Harry Gallatin	51-58*	11.9
21	Buck Williams	82-	11.7
22	Ira Harge	68-73	11.6
23	Swen Nater	74-84	11.6
24	Charles Oakley	86-	11.4
25	Neil Johnston	52-79	11.3

ASSISTS PER GAME
(Minimum 350 Games Played)

		Years	Ass/G
1	Magic Johnson	80-	11.21
2	John Stockton	85-	10.40
3	Isiah Thomas	82-	9.76
4	Oscar Robertson	61-74	9.51
5	Norm Nixon	78-86, 89	8.32
6	Terry Porter	86-	8.07
7	Kevin Porter	73-81, 83	8.06
8	Guy Rodgers	59-70	7.75
9	Bob Cousy	61-63, 70	7.53
10	Johnny Moore	81-88, 90	7.40
11	Nate Archibald	71-77, 79-84	7.40
12	Glenn Rivers	84-	7.21
13	Maurice Cheeks	79-	7.14
14	Micheal Ray Richardson	79-86	7.01
15	Norm Van Lier	70-79	6.99
16	John Lucas	77-	6.96
17	Lafayette Lever	83-	6.86
18	Jerry West	61-74	6.69
19	Larry Brown	68-72	6.67
20	Eric Floyd	80-	6.66
21	Reggie Theuss	79-	6.43
22	Larry Bird	80-	6.42
23	Phil Ford	74-85	6.40
24	Slick Watts	74-79	6.13
25	Walter Frazier	68-80	6.11

MINUTES PLAYED

		Years	Min.
1	Kareem Abdul-Jabbar	70-89	57446
2	Elvin Hayes	69-84	50000
3	Wilt Chamberlain	60-73	47859
4	Artis Gilmore	72-88	47134
5	John Havlicek	63-78	46471
6	Julius Erving	72-87	45227
7	Moses Malone	75-	44152
8	Oscar Robertson	61-74	43866
9	Dan Issel	71-85	41786
10	Bill Russell	57-69	40726
11	Hal Greer	59-73	39759
12	Walt Bellamy	62-75	38940
13	Rick Barry	66-80	38153
14	Lenny Wilkens	61-75	38064
15	Jerry West	61-74	36571
16	Alex English	77-	36315
17	Dennis Johnson	77-	35954
18	Nate Thurmond	64-77	35875
19	Wes Unseld	69-81	35832
20	George Gervin	73-86	35597
21	Caldwell Jones	74-	35081
22	Jack Sikma	78-	35003
23	Paul Silas	65-80	34989
24	Adrian Dantley	77-	34025
25	Robert Parish	77-	34001

PERSONAL FOULS

		Years	PF
1	Kareem Abdul-Jabbar	70-89	4657
2	Artis Gilmore	72-88	4529
3	Caldwell Jones	74-	4436
4	Elvin Hayes	69-84	4193
5	Hal Greer	59-73	3855
6	George McGinnis	72-82	3720
7	Jack Sikma	78-	3661
8	Walt Bellamy	62-75	3534
9	Dan Issel	71-85	3504
10	Bailey Howell	60-71	3498

GAMES DISQUALIFIED

		Years	Disq.
1	Vern Mikkelsen	51-59*	127
2	Walter Dukes	56-63	121
3	Paul Arizin	51-52, 55-62	101
4	Darryl Dawkins	76-89	100
5	Tom Gola	56, 58-66	94
6	Satch Sanders	61-73	94
7	Steve Johnson	82-	92
8	Tree Rollins	78-	91
9	Dolph Schayes	51-64*	90
	Bailey Howell	60-71	90
	Dave Cowens	71-80, 83	90

MINUTES PLAYED PER GAME
(Minimum 350 Games Played)

		Years	Min./G
1	Wilt Chamberlain	60-73	45.8
2	Connie Hawkins	68-76	43.1
3	Bill Russell	57-69	42.3
4	Oscar Robertson	61-74	42.2
5	Elgin Baylor	59-72	40.0
6	Jerry Lucas	64-74	39.0
7	Dave Cowens	71-80, 83	38.6
8	Larry Bird	80-	38.4
9	Elvin Hayes	69-84	38.4
10	Walt Frazier	68-80	37.5

* Incomplete career

GAMES PLAYED		G
1	Kareem Abdul-Jabbar	237
2	Julius Erving	189
3	Dennis Johnson	180
4	John Havlicek	172
5	Michael Cooper	168
6	Magic Johnson	167
7	Bill Russell	165
8	Wilt Chamberlain	160
9	Sam Jones	154
	Robert Parish	154

FIELD GOALS		FG
1	Kareem Abdul-Jabbar	2376
2	Julius Erving	1769
3	Jerry West	1622
4	John Havlicek	1451
5	Wilt Chamberlain	1425
6	Elgin Baylor	1388
7	Larry Bird	1375
8	Dennis Johnson	1167
9	Magic Johnson	1158
10	Sam Jones	1149

FREE THROWS		FT
1	Jerry West	1213
2	Kareem Abdul-Jabbar	1050
3	Julius Erving	1025
4	Elvin Hayes	883
5	Magic Johnson	883
6	John Havlicek	874
7	Larry Bird	854
8	Elgin Baylor	847
9	Dennis Johnson	781
10	Wilt Chamberlain	757

POINTS		Points
1	Kareem Abdul-Jabbar	5762
2	Julius Erving	4580
3	Jerry West	4457
4	John Havlicek	3776
5	Larry Bird	3681
6	Elgin Baylor	3623
7	Wilt Chamberlain	3607
8	Magic Johnson	3225
9	Dennis Johnson	3116
10	Dan Issel	2936

MINUTES PLAYED		Min.
1	Kareem Abdul-Jabbar	8851
2	Wilt Chamberlain	7559
3	Bill Russell	7497
4	Julius Erving	7352
5	Dennis Johnson	7004
6	John Havlicek	6860
7	Magic Johnson	6580
8	Larry Bird	6383
9	Jerry West	6321
10	Elgin Baylor	5510

FIELD GOAL PERCENTAGE (Minimum 150 Attempts)		FG%
1	James Donaldson	.621
2	Charles Barkley	.597
3	Mark West	.593
4	Bob Gross	.584
5	Kurt Rambis	.576
6	Artis Gilmore	.570
7	Kevin McHale	.567
8	James Worthy	.566
9	Larry Nance	.566
10	Bernard King	.559

FREE THROW PERCENTAGE (Minimum 100 Attempts)		FT%
1	Calvin Murphy	.932
2	Willie Wise	.920
3	Kiki Vandeweghe	.912
4	Bill Sharman	.911
5	Larry Bird	.892
6	Vince Boryla	.889
7	Bobby Wanzer	.877
8	Kevin Johnson	.874
9	Chuck Williams	.872
10	Cazzie Russell	.870

POINTS PER GAME (Minimum 25 Games)		PPG
1	Michael Jordan	35.8
2	Jerry West	29.1
3	Rick Barry	27.3
4	Bernard King	27.2
5	Elgin Baylor	27.0
6	Akeem Olajuwon	26.8
7	Dominique Wilkins	26.8
8	George Gervin	26.5
9	Bob Pettit	25.5
10	Connie Hawkins	25.0

MINUTES PER GAME (Minimum 25 Games)		Min/G
1	Wilt Chamberlain	47.2
2	Bill Russell	45.4
3	Connie Hawkins	44.0
4	Bob Love	43.9
5	Elvin Hayes	43.3
6	Jo-Jo White	42.9
7	Oscar Robertson	42.7
8	Larry Bird	42.6
9	Walter Frazier	42.5

REBOUNDS		Reb.
1	Bill Russell	4104
2	Wilt Chamberlain	3913
3	Kareem Abdul-Jabbar	2481
4	Wes Unseld	1777
5	Elgin Baylor	1725
6	Julius Erving	1611
7	Mel Daniels	1608
8	Larry Bird	1593
9	Robert Parish	1525
10	Zelmo Beatty	1370

ASSISTS		Ass.
1	Magic Johnson	2080
2	Dennis Johnson	1006
3	Larry Bird	976
4	Jerry West	970
5	Bob Cousy	937
6	Maurice Cheeks	892
7	Julius Erving	841
8	Isiah Thomas	839
9	John Havlicek	825
10	Bill Russell	770

3-POINT FIELD GOALS		FG
1	Michael Cooper	124
2	Louie Dampier	119
3	Bill Keller	87
4	Danny Ainge	78
5	Larry Bird	77
	Byron Scott	77
7	Isiah Thomas	71
8	Craig Hodges	70
9	Roger Brown	68
10	Darel Carrier	57

PERSONAL FOULS		PF
1	Kareem Abdul-Jabbar	797
2	Dennis Johnson	575
3	Julius Erving	544
4	Robert Parish	543
5	Bill Russell	536
6	John Havlicek	517
7	Satch Sanders	508
8	Bobby Jones	502
9	Kevin McHale	489
10	Magic Johnson	478

REBOUNDS PER GAME (Minimum 25 Games)		Reb/G
1	Bill Russell	24.9
2	Wilt Chamberlain	24.5
3	Wes Unseld	14.9
4	Bob Pettit	14.8
5	Walt Bellamy	14.8
6	Mel Daniels	14.8
7	Moses Malone	14.4
8	Dave Cowens	14.4
9	Nate Thurmond	13.6
10	Charles Barkley	13.1

ASSISTS PER GAME (Minimum 25 Games)		Ass/G
1	Magic Johnson	12.5
2	Kevin Johnson	11.3
3	John Stockton	9.9
4	Isiah Thomas	9.0
5	Oscar Robertson	8.9
6	Bob Cousy	8.6
7	Glenn Rivers	8.5
8	Johnny Moore	8.4
9	Norm Nixon	8.0
10	Nate McMillan	7.7

3-POINT FIELD GOAL PERCENTAGE (Minimum 15 Attempts)		%
1	Bob Hansen	.500
2	Eric Floyd	.490
3	Lafayette Lever	.459
4	Trent Tucker	.442
5	Scotty Pippin	.403
6	Mark Jackson	.400
7	Michael Cooper	.398
8	Brian Winters	.396
9	Danny Ainge	.394
10	Mark Price	.393

GAMES DISQUALIFIED		Disq.
1	Satch Sanders	26
2	Vern Mikkelsen*	24
3	Bailey Howell	22
4	Chuck Share	17
	Jack Sikma	17
6	Darryl Dawkins	16
7	Alex Hannum	15
	Dave Cowens	15
	Robert Parish	15
10	Tom Heinsohn	14

* Incomplete data

FIELD GOALS

		Year	Team	FG
1	Wilt Chamberlain	61-62	Phi	1597
2	Wilt Chamberlain	62-63	SF	1463
3	Wilt Chamberlain	60-61	Phi	1251
4	Wilt Chamberlain	63-64	SF	1207
5	Kareem Abdul-Jabbar	71-72	Mil	1159
6	Michael Jordan	85-86	Chi	1098
7	Bob McAdoo	74-75	Buf	1095
8	Wilt Chamberlain	65-66	Phi	1074
9	Michael Jordan	87-88	Chi	1069
10	Wilt Chamberlain	59-60	Phi	1065
11	Wilt Chamberlain	64-65	SF-Phi	1063
	Lew Alcindor (Jabbar)	70-71	Mil	1063
13	Michael Jordan	89-90	Chi	1034
14	Elgin Baylor	62-63	LA	1029
	Rick Barry	72-73	KCO	1028
16	Nate Archibald	74-75	GS	1028
17	George Gervin	79-80	SA	1024
18	Rick Barry	66-67	SF	1011
19	Spencer Haywood	69-70	DenA	986
20	Charile Scott	71-72	VaA	985
21	Kareem Abdul-Jabbar	72-73	Mil	982
22	Walt Bellamy	61-62	Chi	973
23	Dan Issel	71-72	KyA	972
24	Alex English	85-86	Den	965
25	Julius Erving	75-76	NYA	949

FREE THROWS

		Year	Team	FT
1	Jerry West	65-66	LA	840
2	Wilt Chamberlain	61-62	Phi	835
3	Michael Jordan	86-87	Chi	833
4	Adrian Dantley	83-84	Utah	813
5	Oscar Robertson	63-64	Cin	800
6	Rick Barry	66-67	SF	753
7	Oscar Robertson	65-66	Cin	742
8	Moses Malone	82-83	Phi	737
9	Oscar Robertson	66-67	Cin	736
10	Michael Jordan	87-88	Chi	723
11	Charles Barkley	87-88	Phi	714
12	Jerry West	61-62	LA	712
13	Karl Malone	88-89	Utah	703
14	Oscar Robertson	61-62	Cin	700
15	Mack Calvin	70-71	FlaA	696
	Karl Malone	89-90	Utah	696
17	Bob Pettit	61-62	StL	695
18	Bob Pettit	62-63	StL	685
19	Dolph Schayes	60-61	Syr	680
20	Nate Archibald	71-72	Cin	677
21	Elgin Baylor	60-61	LA	676
22	Michael Jordan	88-89	Chi	674
23	Bob Pettit	58-59	StL	667
24	Oscar Robertson	64-65	Cin	665
25	Nate Archibald	72-73	KCO	663

POINTS

		Year	Team	Points
1	Wilt Chamberlain	61-62	Phi	4029
2	Wilt Chamberlain	62-63	SF	3586
3	Michael Jordan	86-87	Chi	3041
4	Wilt Chamberlain	60-61	Phi	3033
5	Wilt Chamberlain	63-64	SF	2948
6	Michael Jordan	87-88	Chi	2868
7	Bob McAdoo	74-75	Buf	2831
8	Kareem Abdul-Jabbar	71-72	Mil	2822
9	Rich Barry	66-67	SF	2775
10	Michael Jordan	89-90	Chi	2753
11	Nate Archibald	72-73	KCO	2719
	Jerry West	62-63	LA	2719
13	Wilt Chamberlain	59-60	Phi	2707
14	Wilt Chamberlain	65-66	Phi	2649
15	Michael Jordan	88-89	Chi	2633
16	Lew Alcindor (Jabbar)	70-71	Mil	2596
17	George Gervin	79-80	SA	2585
18	George Gervin	81-82	SA	2551
19	Karl Malone	89-90	Utah	2540
20	Elgin Baylor	60-61	LA	2538
	Dan Issel	71-72	KyA	2538
22	Wilt Chamberlain	64-65	SF-Phi	2534
23	Charlie Scott	71-72	VaA	2524
24	Moses Malone	81-82	Hou	2520
25	Spencer Haywood	69-70	DenA	2519

FIELD GOAL PERCENTAGE

		Year	Team	Pct.
1	Wilt Chamberlain	72-73	LA	.727
2	Wilt Chamberlain	66-67	Phi	.683
3	Artis Gilmore	80-81	Chi	.670
4	Artis Gilmore	81-82	Chi	.652
5	Wilt Chamberlain	71-72	LA	.649
6	James Donaldson	84-85	LAC	.637
7	Steve Johnson	85-86	SA	.632
8	Artis Gilmore	82-83	SA	.626
9	Mark West	89-90	Phoe	.625
10	Artis Gilmore	84-85	SA	.623
11	Artis Gilmore	85-86	SA	.618
12	Steve Johnson	81-82	KC	.613
13	Cedric Maxwell	79-80	Bos	.609
14	Darryl Dawkins	80-81	Phi	.607
15	Bobby Jones	74-75	DenA	.604
	Kevin McHale	87-88	Bos	.604
	Kevin McHale	86-87	Bos	.604
18	Otis Thorpe	84-85	KC	.600
	Charles Barkley	89-90	Phi	.600
20	Kareem Abdul-Jabbar	84-85	LAL	.599
21	Artis Gilmore	71-72	KyA	.598
22	Wilt Chamberlain	67-68	Phi	.595
	Dennis Rodman	88-89	Det	.595
24	Robert Parish	88-89	Bos	.589
25	Cedric Maxwell	80-81	Bos	.588
	Rick Barry	80-81	GS	.588

FREE THROW PERCENTAGE

		Year	Team	Pct.
1	Calvin Murphy	80-81	Hou	.958
2	Rick Barry	78-79	Hou	.947
3	Ernie DiGregorio	76-77	Buf	.945
4	Ricky Sobers	80-81	Chi	.935
5	Rick Barry	79-80	Hou	.935
6	Bill Sharman	58-59	Bos	.932
7	Larry Bird	89-90	Bos	.930
8	Calvin Murphy	78-79	Hou	.928
9	Rick Barry	77-78	GS	.924
10	Rick Barry	75-76	GS	.923
11	Jack Sikma	87-88	Mil	.922
12	Bill Sharman	60-61	Bos	.921
13	Calvin Murphy	82-83	Hou	.920
14	Calvin Murphy	77-78	Hou	.918
15	Eddie Johnson	89-90	Phoe	.917
16	Rick Barry	76-77	GS	.916
17	Larry Bird	87-88	Bos	.916
18	Walter Davis	89-90	Den	.912
19	Magic Johnson	88-89	LAL	.911
20	Larry Bird	86-87	Bos	.910
21	Calvin Murphy	75-76	Hou	.907
22	Kyle Macy	84-85	Phoe	.907
23	John Long	87-88	Ind	.907
24	Mike Gminski	87-88	NJ-Phil	.906
25	Jack Sikma	88-89	Mil	.905

POINTS PER GAME

		Year	Team	PPG
1	Wilt Chamberlain	61-62	Phi	50.4
2	Wilt Chamberlain	62-63	SF	44.8
3	Wilt Chamberlain	60-61	Phi	38.4
4	Wilt Chamberlain	59-60	Phi	37.6
5	Michael Jordan	86-87	Chi	37.1
6	Wilt Chamberlain	63-64	SF	36.9
7	Rick Barry	66-67	SF	35.6
8	Michael Jordan	87-88	Chi	35.0
9	Nate Archibald	72-73	KCO	34.9
10	Kareem Abdul-Jabbar	71-72	Mil	34.8
11	Elgin Baylor	60-61	LA	34.8
12	Wilt Chamberlain	64-65	SF-Phi	34.7
13	Charlie Scott	71-72	VaA	34.6
14	Bob McAdoo	74-75	Buf	34.5
15	Elgin Baylor	62-63	LA	34.0
16	Michael Jordan	89-90	Chi	33.6
17	Wilt Chamberlain	65-66	Phi	33.5
18	George Gervin	79-80	SA	33.1
19	Bernard King	84-85	NY	32.9
20	Michael Jordan	88-89	Chi	32.5
21	George Gervin	81-82	SA	32.3
22	Julius Erving	72-73	VaA	31.9
23	Lew Alcindor (Jabbar)	70-71	Mil	31.7
24	Walt Bellamy	61-62	Chi	31.6
25	Rick Barry	71-72	NY-A	31.5
26	Oscar Robertson	63-64	Cin	31.4
27	Jerry West	65-66	LA	31.3
28	Oscar Robertson	65-66	Cin	31.3
29	Jerry West	69-70	LA	31.2
30	JackTwyman	59-60	Cin	31.2
31	Bob Pettit	61-62	StL	31.1
32	Pete Maravich	76-77	NO	31.1
33	Bob McAdoo	75-76	Buf	31.1

3-POINT FIELD GOAL

		Year	Team	FG
1	Louie Dampier	68-69	KyA	199
2	Louie Dampier	69-70	KyA	198
3	Mike Adams	88-89	Den	166
4	Dale Ellis	88-89	Sea	162
5	Mike Adams	89-90	Den	158
6	George Lehmann	70-71	CarA	154
7	Mark Price	89-90	Cle	152
8	Reggie Miller	89-90	Ind	150
9	Danny Ainge	87-88	Bos	148
10	Lee Selvage	67-68	AnaA	147

3-POINT FIELD GOAL PERCENTAGE

		Year	Team	Pct.
1	Jon Sundvold	88-89	Mia	.522
2	Steve Kerr	89-90	Cle	.507
3	Craig Hodges	87-88	Mil-Phoe	.491
4	Craig Hodges	89-90	Chi	.491
5	Mark Price	87-88	Cle	.486
6	Kiki Vandeweghe	86-87	Port	.481
7	Detlef Schrempf	86-87	Dal	.478
8	Dale Ellis	88-89	Sea	.478
9	Drazen Petrovic	89-90	Port	.459
10	Craig Hodges	85-86	Mil	.451

REBOUNDS

		Year	Team	Reb.
1	Wilt Chamberlain	60-61	Phi	2149
2	Wilt Chamberlain	61-62	Phi	2052
3	Wilt Chamberlain	66-67	Phi	1957
4	Wilt Chamberlain	67-68	Phi	1952
5	Wilt Chamberlain	62-63	SF	1946
6	Wilt Chamberlain	65-66	Phi	1943
7	Wilt Chamberlain	59-60	Phi	1941
8	Bill Russell	63-64	Bos	1930
9	Bill Russell	64-65	Bos	1878
10	Bill Russell	60-61	Bos	1868
11	Bill Russell	62-63	Bos	1843
12	Bill Russell	61-62	Bos	1790
13	Wilt Chamberlain	63-64	SF	1787
14	Bill Russell	65-66	Bos	1779
15	Bill Russell	59-60	Bos	1778
16	Wilt Chamberlain	68-69	LA	1712
17	Bill Russell	66-67	Bos	1700
18	Wilt Chamberlain	64-65	SF-Phi	1673
19	Jerry Lucas	65-66	Cin	1668
20	Spencer Haywood	69-70	DenA	1637
21	Bill Russell	58-59	Bos	1612
22	Wilt Chamberlain	71-72	LA	1572
23	Bill Russell	57-58	Bos	1564
24	Jerry Lucas	67-68	Cin	1560
25	Jerry Lucas	66-67	Cin	1547

ASSISTS

		Year	Team	Ass.
1	John Stockton	89-90	Utah	1134
2	John Stockton	87-88	Utah	1128
3	Isiah Thomas	84-85	Det	1123
4	John Stockton	88-89	Utah	1118
5	Kevin Porter	78-79	Det	1099
6	Kevin Johnson	88-89	Phoe	991
7	Magic Johnson	88-89	LAL	988
8	Magic Johnson	86-87	LAL	977
9	Magic Johnson	84-85	LAL	968
10	Norm Nixon	83-84	SD	914
	Isiah Thomas	83-84	Det	914
12	Nate Archibald	72-73	KCO	910
13	Guy Rodgers	66-67	Chi	908
14	Magic Johnson	85-86	LAL	907
	Magic Johnson	89-90	LAL	907
16	Oscar Robertson	61-62	Cin	889
	Magic Johnson	83-84	LA	875
18	Oscar Robertson	63-64	Cin	868
19	Magic Johnson	87-88	LAL	868
20	Oscar Robertson	64-65	Cin	861
21	Mark Jackson	87-88	NY	858
22	Eric Floyd	86-87	GS	848
23	Oscar Robertson	65-66	Cin	847
24	Guy Rodgers	65-66	SF	846
	Kevin Johnson	89-90	Phoe	846

PERSONAL FOULS

		Year	Team	PF
1	Darryl Dawkins	83-84	NJ	386
2	Gene Moore	69-70	KyA	382
3	Darryl Dawkins	82-83	NJ	379
4	Steve Johnson	81-82	KC	372
5	Gene Moore	72-73	SD-A	369
6	Bill Robinzine	78-79	KC	367
7	Bill Bridges	67-68	StL	366
8	Lonnie Shelton	76-77	NY	363
	James Edwards	78-79	Ind	363
10	Kevin Kunnert	76-77	Hou	361
11	Goose Ligon	69-70	KyA	360
12	Dan Roundfield	78-79	Atl	358
	Rick Mahorn	83-84	Was	358
14	Charlie Scott	75-76	Bos	356
15	Darnell Hillman	76-77	Ind	353
16	Dave Cowens	70-71	Bos	350
	Lonnie Shelton	77-78	Bos	350
18	Rick Mahorn	81-82	Was	349
19	George McGinnis	72-73	IndA	348
20	Wendell Ladner	71-72	MemA-CarA	347
	Jim Chones	73-74	CarA	347
	James Edwards	81-82	Cle	347
23	Julius Keye	71-72	DenA	346
24	Bailey Howel	64-65	Bal	345
25	Zelmo Beaty	65-66	StL	344
	Joe Strawder	66-67	Det	344
	John Tresvant	67-68	Det-Cin	344
	Don Adams	70-71	SD	344

REBOUNDS PER GAME

		Year	Team	Reb/G
1	Wilt Chamberlain	60-61	Phi	27.2
2	Wilt Chamberlain	59-60	Phi	27.0
3	Wilt Chamberlain	61-62	Phi	25.7
4	Bill Russell	63-64	Bos	24.7
5	Wilt Chamberlain	65-66	Phi	24.6
6	Wilt Chamberlain	62-63	SF	24.3
7	Wilt Chamberlain	66-67	Phi	24.2
8	Bill Russell	64-65	Bos	24.1
9	Bill Russell	59-60	Bos	24.0
10	Bill Russell	60-61	Bos	23.9
11	Wilt Chamberlain	67-68	Phi	23.8
12	Bill Russell	62-63	Bos	23.6
13	Bill Russell	61-62	Bos	23.6
14	Bill Russell	58-59	Bos	23.0
15	Wilt Chamberlain	64-65	SF-Phi	22.9
16	Bill Russell	65-66	Bos	22.8
17	Bill Russell	57-58	Bos	22.7
18	Wilt Chamberlain	63-64	SF	22.3
19	Nate Thurmond	66-67	SF	21.3
20	Wilt Chamberlain	68-69	LA	21.1
21	Jerry Lucas	65-66	Cin	21.1
22	Bill Russell	66-67	Bos	21.0
23	Bob Pettit	60-61	StL	20.3
24	Jerry Lucas	64-65	Cin	20.0
25	Elgin Baylor	60-61	LA	19.8

ASSISTS PER GAME

		Year	Team	Ass/G
1	John Stockton	89-90	Utah	14.5
2	Isiah Thomas	84-85	Det	13.9
3	John Stockton	87-88	Utah	13.8
4	John Stockton	88-89	Utah	13.6
5	Kevin Porter	78-79	Det	13.4
6	Magic Johnson	83-84	LA	13.1
7	Magic Johnson	88-89	LAL	12.8
8	Magic Johnson	85-86	LAL	12.6
9	Magic Johnson	84-85	LAL	12.6
10	Kevin Johnson	88-89	Phoe	12.2
11	Magic Johnson	86-87	LAL	12.2
12	Magic Johnson	87-88	LAL	11.9
13	Oscar Robertson	64-65	Cin	11.5
14	Magic Johnson	89-90	LAL	11.5
15	Kevin Johnson	89-90	Phoe	11.4
16	Oscar Robertson	61-62	Cin	11.4
	Nate Archibald	72-73	KCO	11.4
18	Guy Rodgers	66-67	Chi	11.2
19	Norm Nixon	83-84	SD	11.1
20	Isiah Thomas	83-84	Det	11.1
21	Oscar Robertson	65-66	Cin	11.1
22	Oscar Robertson	63-64	Cin	11.0
23	Isiah Thomas	85-86	Det	10.8
24	Guy Rodgers	65-66	SF	10.7
25	Oscar Robertson	66-67	Cin	10.7

GAMES DISQUALIFIED

		Year	Team	Disq.
1	Monk Meineke	52-53	Ftw	26
2	Gene Moore	69-70	KyA	25
	Steve Johnson	81-82	KC	25
4	Darryl Dawkins	82-83	NJ	23
5	Walter Dukes	58-59	Det	22
	Darryl Dawkins	83-84	NJ	22
7	Joe Meriweather	76-77	Atl	21
8	Joe Fulks	52-53	Phi	20
	Vern Mikkelsen	57-58	Min	20
	Walter Dukes	59-60	Det	20
	Walter Dukes	61-62	Det	20
	George Johnson	77-78	NJ	20
13	Cal Christensen	50-51	TC	19
	Satch Sanders	65-66	Bos	19
	Joe Strawder	66-67	Det	19
	John Smith	68-69	DalA	19
	Bill Robinzine	75-76	KC	19
	John Drew	78-79	Atl	19
	Tree Rollins	78-79	Atl	19
20	16 players tied with			18

MINUTES PLAYED PER GAME

		Year*	Team	Min/G
1	Wilt Chamberlain	61-62	Phi	48.5
2	Wilt Chamberlain	60-61	Phi	47.8
3	Wilt Chamberlain	62-63	SF	47.6
4	Wilt Chamberlain	65-66	Phi	47.3
5	Wilt Chamberlain	67-68	Phi	46.8
6	Wilt Chamberlain	59-60	Phi	46.4
7	Wilt Chamberlain	63-64	SF	46.1
8	Nate Archibald	72-73	KCO	46.0
9	Neil Johnston	53-54	Phi	45.8
10	Oscar Robertson	64-65	Cin	45.6

* statistics begin with 50-51 season

SINGLE SEASON LEADERS - PLAYOFFS

FIELD GOALS

		Year	Team	FG
1	Larry Bird	1984	Bos	229
2	Kareem Abdul-Jabbar	1974	Mil	224
3	Larry Bird	1987	Bos	216
4	George McGinnis	1975	IndA	213
5	Moses Malone	1981	Hou	207
6	Dan Issel	1971	KyA	206
	Kareem Abdul-Jabbar	1984	LA	206
8	Akeem Olajuwon	1986	Hou	205
9	Julius Erving	1977	Phi	204
	James Worthy	1988	LAL	204

FREE THROWS

		Year	Team	FT
1	Michael Jordan	1989	Chi	183
2	Larry Bird	1987	Bos	176
3	Jerry West	1970	LA	170
4	Larry Bird	1984	Bos	167
5	Jerry West	1969	LA	164
6	Moses Malone	1981	Hou	148
7	Adrian Dantley	1988	Det	140
8	Clyde Drexler	1990	Port	139
9	Jerry West	1965	LA	137
10	Warren Armstrong	1969	OakA	135

POINTS

		Year	Team	Points
1	Larry Bird	1984	Bos	632
2	Larry Bird	1987	Bos	622
3	Michael Jordan	1989	Chi	591
4	Michael Jordan	1990	Chi	587
5	George McGinnis	1975	IndA	581
	Jerry West	1970	LA	562
7	Moses Malone	1981	Hou	562
8	Jerry West	1969	LA	556
9	Rick Barry	1972	NY-A	554
10	Akeem Olajuwon	1986	Hou	537

FIELD GOAL PERCENTAGE
(NBA, BAA, ABA Only)

		Year	Team	Pct.
1	Cliff Levingston	1984	Det	.789
2	James Donaldson	1986	Dal	.750
	Tree Rollins	1989	Cle	.750
4	Zaid Abdul-Aziz	1975	Sea	.700
5	Aintoine Carr	1987	Atl	.696
6	Jeff Cook	1980	Phoe	.667
7	George Irvine	1972	VaA	.651
8	Larry McNeill	1975	KCO	.647
9	Bob Harris	1954	Bos	.640
10	Moses Malone	1975	UtahA	.637

FREE THROW PERCENTAGE
(Starting 1946)

		Year	Team	Pct.
1	Bill Keller (30FT)	1975	IndA	1.000
	Mark Price (30FT)	1990	Cle	1.000
3	Jeff Congdon (22FT)	1969	DenA	1.000
4	Thurl Bailey (18FT)	1988	Utah	1.000
5	Dwight Jones (17FT)	1981	Chi	1.000
6	Dan Schayes (15FT)	1983	Den	1.000
	John Long (15FT)	1985	Det	1.000
	Walter Davis (15FT)	1989	Den	1.000
9	Calvin Murphy (13FT)	1980	Hou	1.000
10	Paul Mokeski (12FT)	1985	Mil	1.000

POINTS PER GAME

		Year	Team	PPG
1	Jerry West	1965	LA	40.6
2	Rick Barry	1970	WasA	40.1
3	Elgin Baylor	1962	LA	38.6
4	Elgin Baylor	1961	LA	38.1
5	Bob McAdoo	1975	Buf	37.4
6	Wilt Chamberlain	1961	Phi	37.0
7	Spencer Haywood	1970	DenA	36.7
8	Michael Jordan	1990	Chi	36.7
9	Michael Jordan	1988	Chi	36.3
10	Lew Alcindor (Jabbar)	1970	Mil	35.2

REBOUNDS

		Year	Teams	Reb.
1	Wilt Chamberlain	1969	LA	444
2	Wilt Chamberlain	1967	Phi	437
3	Bill Russell	1968	Bos	434
4	Bill Russell	1966	Bos	428
5	Wilt Chamberlain	1970	LA	399
6	Wilt Chamberlain	1973	LA	383
7	Bill Russell	1962	Bos	370
8	Bill Russell	1969	Bos	369
9	Nate Thurmond	1967	SF	346
10	Wes Unseld	1971	Bal	339

ASSISTS

		Year	Teams	Ass.
1	Magic Johnson	1988	LAL	303
2	Magic Johnson	1985	LAL	289
3	Magic Johnson	1984	LA	284
4	Magic Johnson	1987	LAL	219
5	Magic Johnson	1986	LAL	211
6	Dennis Johnson	1987	Bos	205
7	Isiah Thomas	1988	Det	201
8	Magic Johnson	1983	LA	192
9	Louie Dampier	1971	KyA	179
10	Maurice Cheeks	1982	Phi	172

3-POINT FIELD GOALS

		Year	Teams	FG
1	Terry Porter	1990	Port	40
2	Craig Hodges	1989	Chi	35
3	Michael Cooper	1987	LAL	34
4	Danny Ainge	1987	Bos	32
	Isiah Thomas	1990	Det	32
6	Louie Dampier	1970	LAL	25
7	Michael Cooper	1988	KyA	25
8	Chico Vaughn	1968	PitA	24
9	Bill Keller	1971	IndA	23
	Rick Barry	1972	NY-A	23
	George Mcginnis	1975	IndA	23
	Larry Bird	1986	Bos	23

REBOUNDS PER GAME
(Starting 1951)

		Year	Teams	Reb/G
1	Wilt Chamberlain	1966	Phi	30.2
2	Bill Russell	1961	Bos	29.9
3	Wilt Chamberlain	1967	Phi	29.1
4	Bill Russell	1959	Bos	27.7
5	Bill Russell	1964	Bos	27.2
6	Wilt Chamberlain	1965	Phi	27.2
7	Wilt Chamberlain	1962	Phi	26.6
8	Bill Russell	1962	Bos	26.4
9	Bill Russell	1960	Bos	25.8
10	Wilt Chamberlain	1960	Phi	25.8

ASSISTS PER GAME
(NBA, BAA, ABA only)

		Year	Teams	Ass/G
1	Magic Johnson	1985	LAL	15.2
2	Magic Johnson	1986	LAL	15.1
3	John Stockton	1990	Utah	15.0
4	John Stockton	1988	Utah	14.8
5	Johnny Moore	1983	SA	14.6
6	John Stockton	1989	Utah	13.7
7	Magic Johnson	1984	LAL	13.5
8	Magic Johnson	1983	LAL	12.8
9	Magic Johnson	1990	LAL	12.8
10	Magic Johnson	1988	LAL	12.6

3-POINT FIELD GOAL PERCENTAGE
(Minimum 4 3-point Field Goals)

		Year	Teams	%
1	Gene Littles	1974	CarA	.571
2	Darrell Griffith	1990	Utah	.556
3	Johnny Roche	1975	UtahA	.533
	Eric Floyd	1989	Hou	.533
5	Johhny Moore	1983	SA	.529
6	Bob Hansen	1988	Utah	.528
7	Rick Barry	1971	NY-A	.519
8	Darel Carrier	1969	KyA	.500
	Louie Dampier	1974	KyA	.500
	Johnny Roche	1974	KyA	.500
	Louie Dampier	1976	KyA	.500
	Brian Winters	1982	Mil	.500
	Mike McGee	1985	LAL	.500
	Ricky Pierce	1990	Mil	.500
	Bob Hansen	1990	Utah	.500

PERSONAL FOULS

		Year	Teams	PF
1	Jack Sikma	1978	Sea	101
2	Robert Parish	1984	Bos	100
3	Charlie Scott	1976	Bos	97
4	Darryl Dawkins	1982	Phi	94
5	George McGinnis	1975	IndA	88
	John Salley	1988	Det	88
7	Akeem Olajuwon	1986	Hou	87
	Dennis Rodman	1988	Det	87
	Jerome Kersey	1990	Port	87
10	Roger Brown	1969	IndA	86
	Elvin Hayes	1979	Was	86
	Andrew Toney	1982	Phi	86

SINGLE SEASON TEAM LEADERS - REGULAR SEASON

WINNING PERCENTAGE

			Year	%
1	Akron Firestone	NBL	38-39	.889
2	Oshkosh	NBL	37-38	.857
3	Los Angeles	NBA	71-72	.841
4	Philadelphia	NBA	66-67	.840
5	Fort Wayne	NBL	44-45	.833
	Oshkosh	NBL	41-42	.833
7	Boston	NBA	72-73	.829
8	Fort Wayne	NBL	43-44	.818
9	Washington	BAA	46-47	.817
10	Boston	NBA	85-86	.817

HOME WINNING PERCENTAGE

			Year	%
1	Whiting	NBL	37-38	1.000
2	Boston	NBA	85-86	.926
3	Rochester	NBA	49-50	.969
4	Syracuse	NBA	49-50	.968
5	Minneapolis	NBA	49-50	.967
6	Washington	BAA	46-47	.952
7	Denver	ABA	74-75	.944
8	Boston	NBA	86-87	.951
9	Milwaukee	NBA	70-71	.944
10	Syracuse	NBA	52-53	.941
	Anderson	NBL	48-49	.941

ROAD WINNING PERCENTAGE

			Year	%
1	Akron Firestone	NBL	38-39	.929
2	Fort Wayne	NBL	43-44	.818
3	Los Angeles	NBA	71-72	.816
4	Boston	NBA	72-73	.800
5	Boston	NBA	74-75	.780
6	Philadelphia	NBA	66-67	.765
7	Oakland	ABA	68-69	.737
	Kentucky	ABA	71-72	.737
9	Fort Wayne	NBL	44-45	.733
10	Boston	NBA	82-83	.732
	Philadelphia	NBA	82-83	.732

WINS

			Year	Wins
1	Los Angeles	NBA	71-72	69
2	Philadelphia	NBA	66-67	68
	Kentucky	ABA	71-72	68
	Boston	NBA	72-73	68
5	Milwaukee	NBA	70-71	66
6	Denver	ABA	74-75	65
	Philadelphia	NBA	82-83	65
	L.A. Lakers	NBA	86-87	65
9	Milwaukee	NBA	71-72	63
	Boston	NBA	81-82	63
	Boston	NBA	84-85	63
	Detroit	NBA	88-89	63
	L.A. Lakers	NBA	89-90	63

POINTS PER GAME

			Year	PPG
1	Oakland	ABA	68-68	126.5
2	Denver	NBA	81-82	126.5
3	Philadelphia	NBA	61-62	125.4
4	Philadelphia	NBA	66-67	125.2
5	Boston	NBA	59-60	124.5
6	Denver	NBA	83-84	123.7
7	Virginia	ABA	70-71	123.3
8	Denver	NBA	82-83	123.2
9	Cincinnati	NBA	61-62	123.1
10	Philadelphia	NBA	67-68	122.6

POINTS PER GAME DIFFERENCE
(PPG Minus Opponents PPG)

			Year	Diff.
1	Oshkosh	NBL	37-38	13.9
2	Los Angeles	NBA	71-72	12.3
3	Milwaukee	NBA	70-71	12.3
4	Milwaukee	NBA	71-72	11.1
5	Washington	BAA	46-47	9.9
6	Philadelphia	NBA	66-67	9.4
7	L.A. Lakers	NBA	86-87	9.3
8	Boston	NBA	61-62	9.2
9	New York	NBA	69-70	9.1
10	Anderson	NBL	48-49	9.0

FIELD GOAL PERCENTAGE
(NBA, BAA, ABA Only)

			Year	%
1	L.A. Lakers	NBA	'84-85	.545
2	Los Angeles	NBA	83-84	.532
3	Los Angeles	NBA	79-80	.529
4	Los Angeles	NBA	82-83	.528
5	L.A. Lakers	NBA	85-86	.522
6	Boston	NBA	87-88	.521
7	Denver	NBA	81-82	.520
8	Los Angeles	NBA	78-79	.517
9	Boston	NBA	86-87	.517
10	L.A. Lakers	NBA	86-87	.516

FREE THROW PERCENTAGE
(Starting 1945-46)

			Year	%
1	Boston	NBA	89-90	.832
2	Utah	ABA	75-76	.827
3	Milwaukee	NBA	88-89	.821
4	KC-Omaha	NBA	74-75	.821
5	Denver	NBA	83-84	.818
6	Houston	NBA	73-74	.812
7	San Antonio	ABA	74-75	.812
8	Utah	NBA	79-80	.809
9	Denver	NBA	82-83	.808
10	Boston	NBA	86-87	.808

REBOUNDS PER GAME
(Starting 1950-51)

			Year	Reb/G
1	Boston	NBA	59-60	80.2
2	Philadelphia	NBA	59-60	78.9
3	Boston	NBA	58-59	77.8
4	Boston	NBA	60-61	77.6
5	Boston	NBA	61-62	76.0
6	St. Louis	NBA	60-61	75.9
7	St. Louis	NBA	57-58	75.6
8	Philadelphia	NBA	60-61	75.2
9	Boston	NBA	57-58	75.0
10	Philadelphia	NBA	61-62	74.2

ASSISTS PER GAME
(NBA, BAA, ABA Only)

			Year	Ass/G
1	L.A. Lakers	NBA	84-85	31.4
2	Milwaukee	NBA	78-79	31.2
3	Los Angeles	NBA	82-83	30.7
4	Phoenix	NBA	78-79	30.5
5	Denver	NBA	83-84	30.3
6	Los Angeles	NBA	83-84	29.9
7	Boston	NBA	87-88	29.9
8	L.A. Lakers	NBA	85-86	29.6
9	L.A. Lakers	NBA	86-87	29.6
10	Boston	NBA	89-90	29.5

PERSONAL FOULS PER GAME
(NBA, BAA, ABA Only)

			Year	PF/G
1	Tri-Cities	NBA	49-50	32.1
2	Rochester	NBA	52-53	31.6
3	Tri-Cities	NBA	50-51	30.8
4	Fort Wayne	NBA	52-53	30.7
5	Baltimore	NBA	52-53	30.6
6	Fort Wayne	NBA	49-50	30.4
7	Syracuse	NBA	50-51	30.4
8	Atlanta	NBA	77-78	30.1
9	Syracuse	NBA	52-53	30.0
10	Washington	NBA	50-51	30.0

3-POINT FIELD GOAL PERCENTAGE

			Year	%
1	Cleveland	NBA	89-90	.407
2	Boston	NBA	87-88	.384
3	Boston	NBA	79-80	.384
4	Indiana	NBA	89-90	.382
5	Seattle	NBA	88-89	.379
6	Cleveland	NBA	87-88	.378
7	Chicago	NBA	89-90	.374
8	Sacramento	NBA	88-89	.373
9	L.A. Lakers	NBA	86-87	.367
10	Boston	NBA	86-87	.366

SINGLE SEASON TEAM LEADERS - PLAYOFFS

POINTS PER GAME				
			Year	PPG
1	L.A. Lakers	NBA	1985	126.3
2	Oakland	ABA	1969	124.8
3	Dallas	ABA	1970	124.7
4	Virginia	ABA	1971	124.0
5	Boston	NBA	1959	123.3
6	Denver	NBA	1984	121.8
7	Philadelphia	NBA	1967	121.7
8	Cincinnati	NBA	1963	121.2
9	Minneapolis	NBA	1956	121.0
10	San Antonio	NBA	1983	121.0

POINTS PER GAME DIFFERENCE (PPG Minus Opponents PPG)				
			Year	Diff.
1	Minneapolis	NBA	1956	18.7
2	Milwaukee	NBA	1971	14.5
3	Fort Wayne	NBL	1944	12.0
4	Boston	NBA	1961	11.6
5	L.A. Lakers	NBA	1987	11.4
6	New York	ABA	1974	10.8
7	Boston	NBA	1986	10.3
8	L.A. Lakers	NBA	1985	10.2
9	Oshkosh	NBL	1941	9.4
10	Philadelphia	NBA	1967	9.4

FIELD GOAL PERCENTAGE				
			Year	%
1	Boston	NBA	1990	.548
2	Milwaukee	NBA	1976	.545
3	L.A. Lakers	NBA	1985	.543
4	L.A. Lakers	NBA	1986	.535
5	Los Angeles	NBA	1984	.534
6	New York	ABA	1971	.526
7	L.A. Lakers	NBA	1987	.522
8	Los Angeles	NBA	1982	.517
9	Cleveland	NBA	1990	.517
10	Seattle	NBA	1988	.516

FREE THROW PERCENTAGE				
			Year	%
1	Philadelphia	NBA	1984	.873
2	Denver	NBA	1990	.872
3	Cincinnati	NBA	1965	.869
4	Denver	NBA	1984	.862
5	Denver	ABA	1975	.861
6	Boston	NBA	1990	.861
7	Chicago	NBA	1987	.852
8	Washington	NBA	1984	.847
9	Syracuse	NBA	1959	.847
10	Syracuse	NBA	1960	.842

REBOUNDS PER GAME (Starting 1950-51)				
			Year	Reb/G
1	Boston	NBA	1959	82.6
2	Boston	NBA	1961	82.1
3	Philadelphia	NBA	1960	77.8
4	Boston	NBA	1958	77.7
5	New York	NBA	1959	77.5
6	Boston	NBA	1960	77.2
7	San Francisco	NBA	1967	75.6
8	Cincinnati	NBA	1958	75.5
	Syracuse	NBA	1961	75.5
10	Detroit	NBA	1960	74.5

ASSISTS PER GAME (NBA, BAA, ABA Only)				
			Year	Ass/G
1	L.A. Lakers	NBA	1985	33.8
2	San Antonio	NBA	1983	33.4
3	L.A. Lakers	NBA	1986	32.0
4	Denver	NBA	1983	31.5
5	Los Angeles	NBA	1982	31.4
6	Milwaukee	NBA	1978	31.3
	Phoenix	NBA	1985	31.3
8	Phoenix	NBA	1980	30.9
9	San Antonio	NBA	1990	30.4
10	Los Angeles	NBA	1984	30.3

PERSONAL FOULS PER GAME (NBA, BAA, ABA Only)				
			Year	PF/G
1	Syracuse	NBA	1953	54.5
2	Boston	NBA	1952	42.7
3	Rochester	NBA	1953	39.7
4	Baltimore	BAA	1949	38.7
5	Boston	NBA	1954	38.5
6	Tri-Cities	NBA	1950	37.7
	Philadelphia	NBA	1972	37.7
8	New York	NBA	1954	37.3
9	Syracuse	NBA	1952	36.4
10	Boston	NBA	1953	36.0